New International Version

The
devotional
BIBLE
for
Dads

Notes by

Robert Wolgemuth

Zondervan Publishing House
Grand Rapids, Michigan, 49530, U.S.A.

You will be pleased to know that a portion of the purchase price
of your new NIV Bible has been provided to International Bible
Society to help spread the gospel of Jesus Christ around the world!

The Devotional Bible for Dads

The sharp pain in my right shoulder was getting worse with every outing. What had started as a twinge in the spring of 1990 had turned into full-blown torture. I knew I couldn't go on.

My wife, Jamie, and I were sitting across the desk from Dr. Frank Jobe. His medical staff had taken me through a rigorous series of MRI's and tests, and we were meeting with Dr. Jobe to hear his diagnosis.

Over the years, as our team doctor, this friend of mine had helped me through the usual minor aches and pains every professional athlete experiences. But there was nothing minor about this meeting. My career depended on his wisdom, skill and experience. And I knew that bad news from Dr. Jobe would change my life.

"I'm sorry, Orel," Dr. Jobe began, "I'm afraid this is very serious." Jamie and I sat there in silence while his words sunk in.

On May 29, 1991, just over one year later, I walked to the mound in Dodger Stadium, the first major-league pitcher to recover from radical shoulder reconstruction. Even street-wise sports reporters were calling it "a miracle." The crowd knew of the long and difficult road I'd taken to get back to this moment and they were on their feet. I wound up and threw my first pitch. Above their cheering I could hear the pop of my fastball making contact with Mike Scoscia's mitt. It was loud and wonderfully familiar. I rotated the baseball in my hand and threw again. The snapping break of my curveball was back. I glanced into the stands and saw Jamie and my family. My eyes welled up with tears. Words were impossible, but they were not necessary.

And because I had said, "Please Lord, heal my shoulder," a thousand times, I breathed a prayer of gratitude to my heavenly Father. I was filled with indescribable emotion.

I recalled the hours that Pat Screnar, the knowledgeable Dodgers' physical therapist, had spent with me. I owed this moment to him, too. And in my mind I could see the face of my friend, Dr. Frank Jobe. Trusting my shoulder to this wise surgeon was a very good choice.

I have known Robert Wolgemuth for many years. Jamie and I know and love his wife, Bobbie. We have watched his children grow to adulthood. My sons respect Robert. And I have watched him both in public and private—when he thought no one was looking. He's an "all-star, veteran dad," so over the years, I have prayed with him, I have asked for his advice, and I have listened carefully . . . because I trust him.

You and I face many tough challenges as dads. Knowing how to introduce our children to a God who loves them is at the top of our to-do list. Leading them with fairness and consistency and teaching them with godly wisdom are our most significant responsibilities. And because these things are so important, going it alone is not a good idea. Getting expert counsel is the right thing to do.

The Devotional Bible for Dads was a good choice for you, dad. Robert's "Daily Insights" are clearly written, completely reliable and extremely helpful. You are going to be encouraged by reading them. You're also going to enjoy the other features, especially "Quiet Times with Dad." My sons and I have had the fun of doing many of them together.

I enthusiastically recommend *The Devotional Bible for Dads* to you.

Every major league baseball player faces the challenge of dealing with hungry autograph seekers—people who hand them baseballs, gloves, pennants, programs and baseball cards wherever they go. Throughout my career, I have signed my share of memorabilia. But during my twenty years of professional baseball, I don't remember many times when I have taken the initiative and asked someone if they would let me sign something for them.

This is one of those exceptions.

Not long ago, I asked Robert if I could "sign" *The Devotional Bible for Dads* so you would know how important this book is to me.

He smiled and said I could.

Orel Hershiser

Table of Contents

Books in Alphabetical Order

The books of the New Testament are *italic*.

Introduction

The Devotional Bible for Dads

I have no idea what you just read," my friend reported, a blank stare on his face. "It made absolutely no sense to me."

"Whew," I responded with a sigh, "I don't have any idea what it means, either!"

We both laughed, although in retrospect, it really wasn't that funny.

Orel Hershiser, the father of two sons, and I, the father of two daughters, were eating breakfast at a Denny's, just west of Cleveland, early one morning during the summer of 1996. As we had done for many years and in many different baseball cities, we were having our morning quiet time together. I had just finished reading from a devotional book, and we were going to discuss what I had just read. But instead of discussing how the devotional reading had inspired or challenged us, we were joking over the convoluted obscurity of the words I had just finished reading. "Why," I said after our omelets had arrived, "can't a devotional be written in plain English so we don't have to get our Ph.D.'s to figure it out?"

One year later, my twenty-two-year-old daughter and I were standing in the hallway at Zondervan Publishing House in Grand Rapids, Michigan. Tom Mockabee, the Publisher for the Bible Division, and I were discussing a number of issues when he asked me, "Do you know of anyone who would be willing to help us write a dad's Bible?"

Julie glanced at me with that winsome grin I have loved since she was in a highchair. "Dad," she whispered, "Why don't you do it?"

Another year later, the notes were complete. And what has happened to me as a result of having composed this manuscript has been absolutely incredible.

In my imagination, I have returned to that Denny's two hundred and sixty times. I have opened my Bible, read a few verses to Orel, then he and I have had imaginary discussions as to what these verses might mean to us.

It's been an unspeakable honor to have had a chance to spend many hours soaking in God's Word and asking him how this might make a difference in my life and in the lives of you and your children.

If you have a few minutes every morning, Orel and I would love to have you join us for breakfast. We think it will be a great adventure.

Here's what The Devotional Bible for Dads includes:

The New International Version of the Bible

This book contains the entire text of the Bible in the New International Version (NIV). Acclaimed by many of the world's leading Bible scholars and millions of satisfied Bible readers, the NIV is now the most widely read modern English translation in the world.

DAILY INSIGHT

These two hundred and sixty daily readings are each linked to a particular Biblical text, and they have been written with one purpose: To bring God's Word to life for men. In my years as an advertising copywriter, my greatest challenge was to answer the "so what" question. The Insights are meant to help you understand what the truths of God's Word really mean in the day-to-day challenges of being a man, a husband and a dad. They're meant to help you understand the "so what."

The Daily Insights can be read in sequence, Monday through Friday. At the bottom of each Insight, you will be directed to the next one. Then on Saturday or Sunday, you can turn to a special interactive weekend reading with one of your children.

QUIET TIMES with Dad

These are fifty-two "experiences" you can have with one of your kids. They are meant to be done on weekends, although you're certainly welcome to do them at any time. Like the Daily Insights, these Quiet Times with Dad are linked to a Bible text. They will help you and your child understand and discuss something special for the two of you as you grow together in God's Word.

QUESTIONS KIDS ASK

Children are famous for asking their dads difficult questions. Questions about God can be the toughest to answer. From "What language did Jesus speak?" to "What is grace?," you will find answers to these tough questions scattered throughout this Bible. This feature is meant to help you and your child become more knowledgeable about God, the Scripture, the times in which the Bible was written, and some basic doctrinal and theological issues. You'll find a complete index of this feature on page 1435.

DADS IN THE BIBLE

Believe it or not, there are lots of dads in the Bible. Some were exemplary models of fatherhood and some were . . . well, they were scoundrels. You'll find Dads in the Bible commentaries near the Biblical texts that introduce us to these men. Today's dads can learn some profound lessons from the lives of these men. Some model godly fatherhood for us, and some warn us about what *not* to do. You'll find a complete index of this feature on page 1434.

BUILDING YOUR CHILDREN

Seven special articles are placed throughout the text of this Bible to help you in your role as a father. These articles reflect the main points of my book, *She Calls Me Daddy*. In these articles I outline seven key things that a dad needs to exhibit and foster to build his child's character: Protection, Conversation, Affection, Discipline, Laughter, Faith and Conduct. These subjects are discussed from a Biblical perspective, and are linked to specific Bible texts. You can locate them by looking at this Bible's table of contents on page v.

Indexes

Starting on page 1434 you'll find a series of indexes that will help you locate and use the many features of this Bible. The Dads in the Bible (p. 1434) and Questions Kids Ask (p. 1435) indexes are defined above. The Fruit of the Spirit Topical Index (p. 1438) links each of the Daily Insights and the Quiet Times with Dad to one of the fruits of the Spirit, listed in the book of Galatians (5:22).

Welcome to *The Devotional Bible for Dads*. It is my sincere prayer that you will find inspiration, encouragement, challenge and even some laughter within its pages. May God's remarkable grace be yours to enjoy.

Jon and Missy Schrader with Abby and Luke
Bobbie, Robert and Julie Wolgemuth —and Bear!

No one was more surprised than Robert Wolgemuth himself when representatives from Zondervan Publishing House asked him to write the notes in *The Devotional Bible for Dads*. Even though he had an undergraduate degree in Biblical literature, had spent several years in professional youth ministry, and had taught church school classes as a layman for over thirty years, he didn't know if he would actually be able to tackle the daunting task.

"But," Robert says, "soaking in God's Word like this has been one of the most fantastic experiences of my life. I never realized all the wonderful 'dad things' there are in the Bible."

Robert Wolgemuth has spent most of his career on the business side of the publishing industry. His credits include executive marketing and management positions in the magazine and book industry in Illinois and Texas, the presidency of a large Nashville book publisher, and the co-founding of a publishing company.

Following the sale of his publishing business in 1992, he and his partner, Mike Hyatt, founded a talent management agency, of which he served as chairman. In 1998, Wolgemuth acquired the agency from his partner. Wolgemuth & Associates, Inc. represents the literary work of approximately twenty-five authors.

In August of 1996, Robert released his first book, *She Calls Me Daddy: Seven Things* *Every Man Needs to Know About Building a Complete Daughter* (Focus on the Family Publishing). The book became a bestseller ninety days later. He has also written *Daddy, Pray With Me: Prayers for Dads and Daughters; Just Daddy and Me: 75 Things to Do With Your Daughter; Postcards From Daddy;* and *The Portable She Calls Me Daddy* (Honor Books).

His speaking assignments have taken him across America and through several foreign countries.

Robert Wolgemuth has served two terms as the president of the Evangelical Christian Publishers Association. A consultant for DreamWorks, SKG, Wolgemuth is co-founder of Hershiser, Wolgemuth & Friends, a company that partners with producers and publishers to create animated products for kids. Every Sunday morning he teaches "The Adventure Class" at the First Presbyterian Church in Nashville. With five hundred on the rolls of the class, the students range in age from teenagers to several people in their eighties.

Robert is also the executive director of The Foundation Conferences, Inc., a national ministry that encourages people to move from success to significance.

A 1969 graduate of Taylor University, Robert is the father of two adult daughters. He and his wife, Bobbie, live in Tennessee.

Acknowledgments

For six solid months I crawled out of bed during the pre-dawn hours to work on the material in *The Devotional Bible for Dads*. Each morning I was filled with an overwhelming sense of God's presence and grace. The strange combination of fear—knowing my own inadequacy, and confidence—knowing God's sufficiency—was indescribable. When I was finished, I knew, without any doubt whatsoever, that my heavenly Father deserved the credit, so I first thank him.

I have never met a self-made man. Who he is, what he can do, and what he owns are all gifts from those who love and nurture him. I am not a self-made man either. My parents, Samuel and Grace Wolgemuth, poured their affection and instruction into this youngster with generous abandon. My five siblings and their spouses continue to be sources of encouragement, friendship and wise counsel. And my own family—Bobbie, my exquisite wife and friend; Missy, our precious firstborn who lives tenderness and compassion; Jon, God's gift to me by way of marriage and, because of Abby and Luke, the other dad in our family; and Julie, our second-born, my business colleague, and the one who brings nonstop joy to my life—how could I ever adequately express my gratitude to them for their love and encouragement?

In my writing of the notes in *The Devotional Bible for Dads*, my Managing Editor and friend, Jennifer Case Cortez, has been the rock. Her intense attention to details—deadlines, accuracy and readability—has given me the freedom to be creative without encumbrances. Her enthusiasm has been contagious when the task seemed insurmountable. I am so thankful to Jennifer.

I have been in publishing for almost twenty-five years. I know the business pretty well. The Zondervan team is first class. Michael Vander Klipp has, from the first day, been a consummate professional . . . and cheerleader. Becoming the father of a precious little girl—Sabrina—right before the project began, inextricably linked Mike's heart to our work. Bruce Ryskamp, Tom Mockabee, Jean Syswerda, Dirk Buursma, John Sawyer and Helen Schmitt have put their feet on the floor, their shoulders to the wheel, and their noses to the grindstone. Amazingly, they have been able to do very well in these awkward positions.

Since 1984, I have had the privilege of teaching "The Adventure Sunday School Class" at the First Presbyterian Church in Nashville. God has given me this class and this setting as a laboratory. The members of this class are the finest, most gracious and honest people you'd ever want to know. I thank them.

And then there are other friends whose lives will forever be intertwined with mine. These are men and women who take time to visit over lunch; call with an encouraging word; play golf with me (patiently waiting while I try to find my ball in the tall grass); ask me to fix their sprinkler systems or their leaking roofs; laugh with me; loan me their get-a-ways for writing; ask my professional advice; trust me with the technicalities of their literary pursuits; convict and inspire me with their writing; and pray with me. They know who they are and they know how deeply grateful I am for them.

Finally, I thank you . . . a dad who wants to do his best and is looking for companionship in this adventure called fatherhood. Welcome friend. My hope is that my words will encourage you to bask in the light of God's holy Word—and be challenged to faithfulness and obedience as his representative to your family. God bless you.

NASHVILLE, TENNESSEE

Preface

THE NEW INTERNATIONAL VERSION is a completely new translation of the Holy Bible made by over a hundred scholars working directly from the best available Hebrew, Aramaic and Greek texts. It had its beginning in 1965 when, after several years of exploratory study by committees from the Christian Reformed Church and the National Association of Evangelicals, a group of scholars met at Palos Heights, Illinois, and concurred in the need for a new translation of the Bible in contemporary English. This group, though not made up of official church representatives, was transdenominational. Its conclusion was endorsed by a large number of leaders from many denominations who met in Chicago in 1966.

Responsibility for the new version was delegated by the Palos Heights group to a self-governing body of fifteen, the Committee on Bible Translation, composed for the most part of biblical scholars from colleges, universities and seminaries. In 1967 the New York Bible Society (now the International Bible Society) generously undertook the financial sponsorship of the project—a sponsorship that made it possible to enlist the help of many distinguished scholars. The fact that participants from the United States, Great Britain, Canada, Australia and New Zealand worked together gave the project its international scope. That they were from many denominations—including Anglican, Assemblies of God, Baptist, Brethren, Christian Reformed, Church of Christ, Evangelical Free, Lutheran, Mennonite, Methodist, Nazarene, Presbyterian, Wesleyan and other churches—helped to safeguard the translation from sectarian bias.

How it was made helps to give the New International Version its distinctiveness. The translation of each book was assigned to a team of scholars. Next, one of the Intermediate Editorial Committees revised the initial translation, with constant reference to the Hebrew, Aramaic or Greek. Their work then went to one of the General Editorial Committees, which checked it in detail and made another thorough revision. This revision in turn was carefully reviewed by the Committee on Bible Translation, which made further changes and then released the final version for publication. In this way the entire Bible underwent three revisions, during each of which the translation was examined for its faithfulness to the original languages and for its English style.

All this involved many thousands of hours of research and discussion regarding the meaning of the texts and the precise way of putting them into English. It may well be that no other translation has been made by a more thorough process of review and revision from committee to committee than this one.

From the beginning of the project, the Committee on Bible Translation held to certain goals for the New International Version: that it would be an accurate translation and one that would have clarity and literary quality and so prove suitable for public and private reading, teaching, preaching, memorizing and liturgical use. The Committee also sought to preserve some measure of continuity with the long tradition of translating the Scriptures into English.

In working toward these goals, the translators were united in their commitment to the authority and infallibility of the Bible as God's Word in written form. They believe that it contains the divine answer to the deepest needs of humanity, that it sheds unique light on our path in a dark world, and that it sets forth the way to our eternal well-being.

The first concern of the translators has been the accuracy of the translation and its fidelity to the thought of the biblical writers. They have weighed the significance of the lexical and grammatical details of the Hebrew, Aramaic and Greek texts. At the same time, they have striven for more than a word-for-word translation. Because thought patterns and syntax differ from language to language, faithful communication of the meaning of the writers of the Bible demands frequent modifications in sentence structure and constant regard for the contextual meanings of words.

A sensitive feeling for style does not always accompany scholarship. Accordingly the Committee on Bible Translation submitted the developing version to a number of stylistic consultants. Two of them read every book of both Old and New Testaments twice—once before and once after the last major revision—and made invaluable suggestions. Samples of the translation were tested for clarity and ease of reading by various kinds of people—young and old, highly educated and less well educated, ministers and laymen.

Concern for clear and natural English—that the New International Version should be idiomatic but not idiosyncratic, contemporary but not dated—motivated the translators and consultants. At the same time, they tried to reflect the differing styles of the biblical writers. In view of the international use of English, the translators sought to avoid obvious Americanisms on the one hand and obvious Anglicisms on the other. A British edition reflects the comparatively few differences of significant idiom and of spelling.

As for the traditional pronouns "thou," "thee" and "thine" in reference to the Deity, the translators judged that to use these archaisms (along with the old verb forms such as "doest," "wouldest" and "hadst") would violate accuracy in translation. Neither Hebrew, Aramaic nor Greek uses special pronouns for the persons of the Godhead. A present-day translation is not enhanced by forms that in the time of the King James Version were used in everyday speech, whether referring to God or man.

For the Old Testament the standard Hebrew text, the Masoretic Text as published in the latest editions of Biblia Hebraica, was used throughout. The Dead Sea Scrolls contain material bearing on an earlier stage of the Hebrew text. They were consulted, as were the Samaritan Pentateuch and the ancient scribal traditions relating to textual changes. Sometimes a variant Hebrew reading in the margin of the Masoretic Text was followed instead of the text itself. Such instances, being variants within the Masoretic tradition, are not specified by footnotes. In rare cases, words in the consonantal text were divided differently from the way they appear in the Masoretic Text. Footnotes indicate this. The translators also consulted the more important early versions—the Septuagint; Aquila, Symmachus and Theodotion; the Vulgate; the Syriac Peshitta; the Targums; and for the Psalms the Juxta Hebraica of Jerome. Readings from these versions were occasionally followed where the Masoretic Text seemed doubtful and where accepted principles of textual criticism showed that one or more of these textual witnesses appeared to provide the correct reading. Such instances are footnoted. Sometimes vowel letters and vowel signs did not, in the judgment of the translators, represent the correct vowels for the original consonantal text. Accordingly some words were read with a different set of vowels. These instances are usually not indicated by footnotes.

The Greek text used in translating the New Testament was an eclectic one. No other piece of ancient literature has such an abundance of manuscript witnesses as does the New Testament. Where existing manuscripts differ, the translators made their choice of readings according to accepted principles of New Testament textual criticism. Footnotes call attention to places where there was uncertainty about what the original text was. The best current printed texts of the Greek New Testament were used.

There is a sense in which the work of translation is never wholly finished. This applies to all great literature and uniquely so to the Bible. In 1973 the New Testament in the New International Version was published. Since then, suggestions for corrections and revisions have been received from various sources. The Committee on Bible Translation carefully considered the suggestions and adopted a number of them. These were incorporated in the first printing of the entire Bible in 1978. Additional revisions were made by the Committee on Bible Translation in 1983 and appear in printings after that date.

As in other ancient documents, the precise meaning of the biblical texts is sometimes uncertain. This is more often the case with the Hebrew and Aramaic texts than with the Greek text. Although archaeological and linguistic discoveries in this century aid in understanding difficult passages, some uncertainties remain. The more significant of these have been called to the reader's attention in the footnotes.

In regard to the divine name YHWH, commonly referred to as the Tetragrammaton, the translators adopted the device used in most English versions of rendering that name as "Lord" in capital letters to distinguish it from Adonai, another Hebrew word rendered "Lord," for which small letters are used. Wherever the two names stand together in the Old Testament as a compound name of God, they are rendered "Sovereign Lord."

Because for most readers today the phrases "the Lord of hosts" and "God of hosts" have little meaning, this version renders them "the Lord Almighty" and "God Almighty." These renderings convey the sense of the Hebrew, namely, "he who is sovereign over all the 'hosts' (powers) in heaven and on earth, especially over the 'hosts' (armies) of Israel." For readers unacquainted with Hebrew this does not make clear the distinction between Sabaoth ("hosts" or "Almighty") and Shaddai (which can also be translated "Almighty"), but the latter occurs infrequently and is always footnoted. When Adonai and YHWH Sabaoth occur together, they are rendered "the Lord, the Lord Almighty."

As for other proper nouns, the familiar spellings of the King James Version are generally retained. Names traditionally spelled with "ch," except where it is final, are usually spelled in this translation with "k" or "c," since the biblical languages do not have the sound that "ch" frequently indicates in English—for example, in chant. For well-known names such as Zechariah, however, the traditional spelling has been retained. Variation in the spelling of names in the original languages has usually not been indicated. Where a person or place has two or more different names in the Hebrew, Aramaic or Greek texts, the more familiar one has generally been used, with footnotes where needed.

To achieve clarity the translators sometimes supplied words not in the original texts but required by the context. If there was uncertainty about such material, it is enclosed in brackets. Also for the sake of clarity or style, nouns, including some proper nouns, are sometimes substituted for pronouns, and vice versa. And though the Hebrew writers often shifted back and forth between first, second and third personal pronouns without change of antecedent, this translation often makes them uniform, in accordance with English style and without the use of footnotes.

Poetical passages are printed as poetry, that is, with indentation of lines and with separate stanzas. These are generally designed to reflect the structure of Hebrew poetry. This poetry is normally characterized by parallelism in balanced lines. Most of the poetry in the Bible is in the Old Testament, and scholars differ regarding the scansion of Hebrew lines. The translators determined the stanza divisions for the most part by analysis of the subject matter. The stanzas therefore serve as poetic paragraphs.

As an aid to the reader, italicized sectional headings are inserted in most of the books. They are not to be regarded as part of the NIV text, are not for oral reading, and are not intended to dictate the interpretation of the sections they head.

The footnotes in this version are of several kinds, most of which need no explanation. Those giving alternative translations begin with "Or" and generally introduce the alternative with the last word preceding it in the text, except when it is a single-word alternative; in poetry quoted in a footnote a slant mark indicates a line division. Footnotes introduced by "Or" do not have uniform significance. In some cases two possible translations were considered to have about equal validity. In other cases, though the translators were convinced that the translation in the text was correct, they judged that another interpretation was possible and of sufficient importance to be represented in a footnote.

In the New Testament, footnotes that refer to uncertainty regarding the original text are introduced by "Some manuscripts" or similar expressions. In the Old Testament, evidence for the reading chosen is given first and evidence for the alternative is added after a semicolon (for example: Septuagint; Hebrew father). In such notes the term "Hebrew" refers to the Masoretic Text.

It should be noted that minerals, flora and fauna, architectural details, articles of clothing and jewelry, musical instruments and other articles cannot always be identified with precision. Also measures of capacity in the biblical period are particularly uncertain (see the table of weights and measures following the text).

Like all translations of the Bible, made as they are by imperfect man, this one undoubtedly falls short of its goals. Yet we are grateful to God for the extent to which he has enabled us to realize these goals and for the strength he has given us and our colleagues to complete our task. We offer this version of the Bible to him in whose name and for whose glory it has been made. We pray that it will lead many into a better understanding of the Holy Scriptures and a fuller knowledge of Jesus Christ the incarnate Word, of whom the Scriptures so faithfully testify.

The Committee on Bible Translation

June 1978
(Revised Aug 1983)

Names of the translators and editors may be secured
from the International Bible Society
translation sponsors of the New International Version,
1820 Jet Stream Drive, Colorado Springs, Colorado
80921-3696 U.S.A.

Old
TESTAMENT

Welcome to the world of the patriarchs—men whose names are indelibly chiseled on the marbled walls of history: Adam, Noah, Abraham, Isaac, Jacob and Joseph. Two things can be said about these men. First, they were ordinary. Read on; you'll see. Second, they had no idea that people would be talking about them three millennia after their deaths.

These common men did what dads have been doing since time began. They got married, had careers and had children. And although this may be hard to comprehend, you are a patriarch, too. Thousands of years from now, your name will be familiar to a myriad of offspring. They'll remember your gifts and your flaws, your successes and your failures. This is amazing . . . and it's true. Genesis provides some clues about how to prepare for this kind of notoriety.

Genesis

The Beginning

1 In the beginning God created the heavens and the earth. ²Now the earth was[a] formless and empty, darkness was over the surface of the deep, and the Spirit of God was hovering over the waters.

³And God said, "Let there be light," and there was light. ⁴God saw that the light was good, and he separated the light from the darkness. ⁵God called the light "day," and the darkness he called "night." And there was evening, and there was morning—the first day.

⁶And God said, "Let there be an expanse between the waters to separate water from water." ⁷So God made the expanse and separated the water under the expanse from the water above it. And it was so. ⁸God called the expanse "sky." And there was evening, and there was morning—the second day.

⁹And God said, "Let the water under the sky be gathered to one place, and let dry ground appear." And it was so. ¹⁰God called the dry ground "land," and the gathered waters he called "seas." And God saw that it was good.

¹¹Then God said, "Let the land produce vegetation: seed-bearing plants and trees on the land that bear fruit with seed in it, according to their various kinds." And it was so. ¹²The land produced vegetation: plants bearing seed according to their kinds and trees bearing fruit with seed in it according to their kinds. And God saw that it was good. ¹³And there was evening, and there was morning—the third day.

a2 Or possibly *became*

¹⁴And God said, "Let there be lights in the expanse of the sky to separate the day from the night, and let them serve as signs to mark seasons and days and years, ¹⁵and let them be lights in the expanse of the sky to give light on the earth." And it was so. ¹⁶God made two great lights—the greater light to govern the day and the lesser light to govern the night. He also made the stars. ¹⁷God set them in the expanse of the sky to give light on the earth, ¹⁸to govern the day and the night, and to separate light from darkness. And God saw that it was good. ¹⁹And there was evening, and there was morning—the fourth day.

²⁰And God said, "Let the water teem with living creatures, and let birds fly above the earth across the expanse of the sky." ²¹So God created the great creatures of the sea and every living and moving thing with which the water teems, according to their kinds, and every winged bird according to its kind. And God saw that it was good. ²²God blessed them and said, "Be fruitful and increase in number and fill the water in the seas, and let the birds increase on the earth." ²³And there was evening, and there was morning—the fifth day.

²⁴And God said, "Let the land produce living creatures according to their kinds: livestock, creatures that move along the ground, and wild animals, each according to its kind." And it was so. ²⁵God made the wild animals according to their kinds, the livestock according to their kinds, and all the creatures that move along the ground according to their kinds. And God saw that it was good.

²⁶Then God said, "Let us make man

Don't Hold Back
God, the Generous Father

"In the beginning God created the heavens and the earth" (1:1).

Text: Genesis 1

In this amazing chapter we read about how our heavenly Father tackled the building project of a lifetime—he made everything that exists. He created light and separated the earth from the sky, dry land from the seas, and night from the day. Then God created plants, fish, birds and animals. Finally, he created a man and a woman. I get tired just thinking about it!

Then God did an incredible thing: He *gave* everything to the man and the woman to rule over (v. 26) and to enjoy (vv. 28-30).

Throughout the Bible, God demonstrates abundant generosity to his children. And his giving does not stop at tangible things. He does not withhold his presence (Psalm 21:6), his mercies (Psalm 40:11), or any good thing (Psalm 84:11). In fact, God loves his children so much that he cares enough to discipline and correct them (Revelation 3:19). As you read through Genesis chapter two you will discover that, because of his love, God also told Adam and Eve that there was something they could *not* do—eat of the tree (2:17).

As a Father who loves his children with a perfect love, isn't it wonderful to consider that God's unselfishness included good things and tough things? God, in his divine benevolence, lavished his offspring with those things they wanted and a measure of discipline that would give them a framework in which to enjoy them. God knew that the difference between a river and a swamp is that the flowing, productive river has boundaries, and the mucky, stagnant swamp does not.

The first picture of a father in the Bible is one of the Sovereign Lord of the universe. He provides every good thing for his family, then he dares to hold them accountable to be obedient stewards of these good things.

Since you truly love your children, don't withhold anything from them . . . yourself, your mercy, your provisions, or your discipline.

For a complete listing of Dads in the Bible, turn to page 1434.

in our image, in our likeness, and let them rule over the fish of the sea and the birds of the air, over the livestock, over all the earth,[a] and over all the creatures that move along the ground."

27 So God created man in his own image,
    in the image of God he created him;
    male and female he created them.

28 God blessed them and said to them, "Be fruitful and increase in number; fill the earth and subdue it. Rule over the fish of the sea and the birds of the air and over every living creature that moves on the ground."

29 Then God said, "I give you every seed-bearing plant on the face of the whole earth and every tree that has fruit with seed in it. They will be yours for food. 30 And to all the beasts of the earth and all the birds of the air and all the creatures that move on the ground—everything that has the breath of life in it—I give every green plant for food." And it was so. 31 God saw all that he had made, and

a26 Hebrew; Syriac all the wild animals

Paying Attention

DAILY INSIGHT

"Daddy, watch this." "Honey, are you listening to me?"

Almost every dad on earth has heard these words. They come from the members of his family who see him in the room but suspect he's somewhere else: "The lights are on, but no one's home."

The first chapter of Genesis contains the story of creation. It's the written account of an Almighty God who literally took nothingness and made something of it with the sound of his voice. God spoke and the worlds appeared—how utterly, unspeakably amazing!

As you read this account, you'll notice that after each day of creation, God stepped back and took a look at what he had done. And when he had taken it all in, he declared it "good."

You're a dad, and of all the things you're about, what follows is one of the most important.

It may be a stretch to say that you created this family, but it's for sure that you had a lot to do with putting it together. You and your wife found each other, celebrated your rights, and you had babies together. None of this would have happened without you. (Don't let your wife read this part.)

But the way life is, new things happen every day. There are new challenges at work; there is new information to deal with, and new aches and pains to face as your body gets older. It's only natural to get distracted and forget to keep noticing this thing you've built—your family.

The story of God's creation is really the story of God paying close attention to what he had done. He did what he did, he took a good look, and he was pleased. And interestingly enough, the rest of the Bible confirms that God kept looking, day after day. He paid attention.

Most dads will readily admit that they have a lot to learn. This is a whole new experience for us—something our formal education didn't include. So we learn as we go. Through some trial and error, we discover what works and what doesn't. But given God's example, we should rarely catch ourselves saying, "You know, I never saw it coming," "When did she start doing that?" or "I guess I just wasn't paying attention."

Our challenge is not just to live with our families, but to really be there. To understand our job as the dad is to see what's going on—to not succumb to the temptation of having our families, then getting on to the next thing without continuing to watch.

God's pattern was to create, to see, and to celebrate. That's a pretty good model to follow, don't you think?

MONDAY

Passage:
Genesis 1

Verse:
Genesis 1:31a

For your next devotional reading, go to page 5.

it was very good. And there was evening, and there was morning—the sixth day.

2 Thus the heavens and the earth were completed in all their vast array.

[2]By the seventh day God had finished the work he had been doing; so on the seventh day he rested[a] from all his work. [3]And God blessed the seventh day and made it holy, because on it he rested from all the work of creating that he had done.

Adam and Eve

[4]This is the account of the heavens and the earth when they were created.

When the LORD God made the earth and the heavens— [5]and no shrub of the field had yet appeared on the earth[b] and no plant of the field had yet sprung up, for the LORD God had not sent rain on the earth[b] and there was no man to work the ground, [6]but streams[c] came up from the earth and watered the whole surface of the ground— [7]the LORD God formed the man[d] from the dust of the ground and breathed into his nostrils the breath of life, and the man became a living being. [8]Now the LORD God had planted a garden in the east, in Eden; and there he put the man he had formed. [9]And the LORD God made all kinds of trees grow out of the ground—trees that were pleasing to the eye and good for food. In the middle of the garden were the tree of life and the tree of the knowledge of good and evil.

[10]A river watering the garden flowed from Eden; from there it was separated into four headwaters. [11]The name of the first is the Pishon; it winds through the entire land of Havilah, where there is gold. [12](The gold of that land is good; aromatic resin[e] and onyx are also there.) [13]The name of the second river is the Gihon; it winds through the entire land of Cush.[f] [14]The name of the third river is the Tigris; it runs along the east side of Asshur. And the fourth river is the Euphrates.

[15]The LORD God took the man and put him in the Garden of Eden to work it and take care of it. [16]And the LORD God commanded the man, "You are free to eat from any tree in the garden; [17]but you must not eat from the tree of the knowledge of good and evil, for when you eat of it you will surely die."

[a]2 Or *ceased*; also in verse 3   [b]5 Or *land*; also in verse 6   [c]6 Or *mist*   [d]7 The Hebrew for *man (adam)* sounds like and may be related to the Hebrew for *ground (adamah)*; it is also the name *Adam* (see Gen. 2:20).   [e]12 Or *good; pearls*   [f]13 Possibly southeast Mesopotamia

HEY DAD
Can scientists prove that creation isn't true?

Text: Genesis 1

Science doesn't prove evolution or creation; it simply points out evidence for one theory or the other. Many schools teach evolution as if it were scientific fact. But the scientific method is based on observation, and since no human alive today witnessed the beginnings of the world, that method won't work for this discussion.

What we know from Genesis is that God created the heavens and the earth. And scientists have discovered that fossils favor the idea of special creation rather than evolution. How do fossils point toward creation? The answer is simple but very significant. Scientists have never found "in-between life forms."

In order for the fossil evidence to support the theory of evolution, fossils should show life forms in the process of changing. Charles Darwin, the man who popularized the theory of evolution, actually said that fossils were "perhaps the most obvious and serious objection" to his theory (Parker, 60).

Much has been written about creation and evolution. And while we don't have room to discuss all the evidence here, this question provides you with a wonderful opportunity to investigate the issue with your son or daughter—and uncover the facts yourself.

Parker, G. (1979). Dry Bones and Other Fossils. *El Cajon, CA: Creation Life Publishers.*

For a complete listing of Questions Kids Ask, turn to page 1435.

[18]The LORD God said, "It is not good for the man to be alone. I will make a helper suitable for him."

[19]Now the LORD God had formed out of the ground all the beasts of the field and all the birds of the air. He brought them to the man to see what he would name them; and whatever the man called each living creature, that was its name. [20]So the man gave names to all the livestock, the birds of the air and all the beasts of the field.

But for Adam[a] no suitable helper was found. [21]So the LORD God caused the man to fall into a deep sleep; and while he was sleeping, he took one of the man's ribs[b] and closed up the place with flesh. [22]Then the LORD God made a woman from the rib[c] he had taken out of the man, and he brought her to the man.

[23]The man said,

[a]20 Or the man   [b]21 Or took part of the man's side
[c]22 Or part

Perfect Fathering Includes Some "No's"

DAILY INSIGHT

TUESDAY

Passage:
Genesis 2:4–8, 15–17

Verse:
Genesis 2:17

At this very moment I'm looking out on a mid-October Tennessee morning. The sky is crystal clear, the bluest blue you could ever imagine. Because we have had lots of rain over the past few weeks, our yard is a spectacular shade of green. The leaves of the trees in the woods behind our house are just beginning to give us a hint of the vibrant fall colors we're in for. The geraniums look electric.

Still, as hard as it may be for me to imagine, the Garden of Eden makes the scene outside my window look like a smoldering city dump.

Not only was Eden pretty to look at, it was perfect in every other way, too. Man's relationship to woman was tenderly flawless. Woman's relationship to man was filled with respect. It was without dissension or fear. And both of their relationships with their Creator were literally impeccable. Adam and Eve were delighted by all of this.

But, amazingly, right in the middle of this pristine flawlessness was a "no." A centrally-located, exquisite tree, the fruit of which could not be eaten. Isn't that incredible? The Garden of Eden included a "no."

Most of the time, I think of enjoyment as no boundaries. No inhibitions. No "no's," if you will. All "yes's." I want it, I get it, and no one stops me. Sounds great, doesn't it?

But God, knowing us better than we know ourselves, has created us to need discipline—to actually be *happier* when certain restrictions and guidelines are placed before us.

Now that I think about it, the view of my back yard has been enhanced by some nasty stuff that I have to do. Every month or so I spread smelly fertilizer on the grass. Every spring I prowl around the woods, pruning dead branches (and touching every sprig of poison oak available). And every few days I have to pinch off ugly, drooping geranium blossoms.

Similarly, sometimes being a dad can be a drag. You feel like the house policeman, prosecuting attorney and judge. It seems like you're saying "no" all the time, you're charging your children with "crimes" you didn't witness, and you're trying to determine a fair punishment. Not exactly the stuff to make you your county's Dad of the Year.

Take heart. Even Eden, as perfect as it was, included some discipline—a "no tree." And, even though they may never celebrate this, your family is happier—and more pleasant—with the discipline you're imposing than they would be without it.

Let me quickly say that the Garden of Eden was a perfect home that God, the Creator of the universe, built himself. Yes, it included the discipline of forbidden fruit, but it also included a heavenly Father's tender love for his children that was unshakable and everlasting. What a great example of balance this is for us to follow today.

For your next devotional reading, go to page 7.

"This is now bone of my bones
  and flesh of my flesh;
she shall be called 'woman,'[a]
  for she was taken out of man."

²⁴For this reason a man will leave his father and mother and be united to his wife, and they will become one flesh.

²⁵The man and his wife were both naked, and they felt no shame.

The Fall of Man

3 Now the serpent was more crafty than any of the wild animals the LORD God had made. He said to the woman, "Did God really say, 'You must not eat from any tree in the garden'?"

²The woman said to the serpent, "We may eat fruit from the trees in the garden, ³but God did say, 'You must not eat fruit from the tree that is in the middle of the garden, and you must not touch it, or you will die.'"

⁴"You will not surely die," the serpent said to the woman. ⁵"For God knows that when you eat of it your eyes will be opened, and you will be like God, knowing good and evil."

⁶When the woman saw that the fruit of the tree was good for food and pleasing to the eye, and also desirable for gaining wisdom, she took some and ate it. She also gave some to her husband, who was with her, and he ate it. ⁷Then the eyes of both of them were opened, and they realized they were naked; so they sewed fig leaves together and made coverings for themselves.

⁸Then the man and his wife heard the sound of the LORD God as he was walking in the garden in the cool of the day, and they hid from the LORD God among the trees of the garden. ⁹But the LORD God called to the man, "Where are you?"

¹⁰He answered, "I heard you in the garden, and I was afraid because I was naked; so I hid."

¹¹And he said, "Who told you that you were naked? Have you eaten from the tree that I commanded you not to eat from?"

¹²The man said, "The woman you put here with me—she gave me some fruit from the tree, and I ate it."

¹³Then the LORD God said to the woman, "What is this you have done?"

The woman said, "The serpent deceived me, and I ate."

¹⁴So the LORD God said to the serpent, "Because you have done this,

"Cursed are you above all the livestock
  and all the wild animals!
You will crawl on your belly
  and you will eat dust
  all the days of your life.
¹⁵And I will put enmity

---

[a]23 The Hebrew for *woman* sounds like the Hebrew for *man*.

HEY DAD

Why did God rest on the seventh day?

Text: Genesis 2:2–3

God didn't have to rest on the seventh day, but he rested to set an example for us. He knew that we would need rest for many reasons. God doesn't need to rest to stay healthy, but we do. If we work all the time and never rest, our bodies will get sick. We also need rest so we can spend time with our family and friends.

The Jews in the Bible observed this day with great care. They called it the Sabbath, and they had very specific rules regarding how much activity could be done on this day. One such rule regulated how far they could walk on the Sabbath. A "Sabbath day's journey" was about a thousand yards. This law kept the people from moving too far away from the center of the city, so the community stayed closely knit. And, in a symbolic sense, the rule kept them close to God because they couldn't move far from the temple, their place of worship. (You can read more about sabbath observance in Exodus 31:14–17.)

God sent us a message on the seventh day of creation: "Work hard, then rest. Take a break. Spend time with your family. Worship me, and give me your full attention. Enjoy the blessings I've given you. Rest is one of them."

QUESTIONS KIDS ASK

For a complete listing of Questions Kids Ask, turn to page 1435.

between you and the woman,
and between your offspring[a] and
hers;
he will crush[b] your head,
and you will strike his heel."

16To the woman he said,

"I will greatly increase your pains in
childbearing;
with pain you will give birth to
children.
Your desire will be for your husband,
and he will rule over you."

17To Adam he said, "Because you listened to your wife and ate from the tree

about which I commanded you, 'You
must not eat of it,'

"Cursed is the ground because of you;
through painful toil you will eat of it
all the days of your life.
18It will produce thorns and thistles for
you,
and you will eat the plants of the
field.
19By the sweat of your brow
you will eat your food
until you return to the ground,
since from it you were taken;

a15 Or seed b15 Or strike

There's No Hiding Place Down Here

The meeting was heating up. We had intended to clear the air of some unfortunate misunderstandings, but things were deteriorating. People were standing to express their anger. Voices were being raised to hurtful decibels.

"You lied," one individual finally charged, his eyes bearing down on me.

My heart raced. I'm sure my faced flushed with embarrassment as I recalled the incident in question. *Had I lied?* I didn't think so. *Had I been deceptive?* Yes. My accuser wasn't satisfied. He wanted a full confession. Then, in a moment of sympathy, he softened his tone. "You deceived me," he said, "but I'm not calling you a liar."

For the next hour, I sat there stunned. Even though the meeting continued with pointed exchanges, I hardly spoke a word. In retrospect, I know God was speaking to me. And what I heard him whisper to me was incredibly helpful.

I had sincerely held my ground over the difference between a "lie" and a "deception," but the concession that "I wasn't a liar" had pierced my conscience. The truth is, I am a sinful man—a liar, a thief, a selfish and lustful man. I can rightly justify certain actions, clarifying my position, but the Bible makes it abundantly clear about me: "There is no one righteous, not even one" (Romans 3:10).

The passage for today shows Adam in a

**DAILY
INSIGHT**

WEDNESDAY

Passage:
Genesis 3:1–19

Verse:
Genesis 3:10

similar situation. He got caught. He blamed Eve, which, at the moment, was about all he thought he could have done. In this case, Adam *did* have the misfortune of having a wife who disobeyed first, encouraging him to come along. But what should have dawned on Adam was that this action was a symptom of a much bigger problem—Adam's disobedience should have revealed that he was a sinful man with a dark heart. And, like many, many others in the Bible, he did a very foolish thing. He tried to escape, to hide from God.

When the meeting was finished, I asked my challenger to step into an empty office. And through tears of confession and remorse, I acknowledged that, even though we disagreed on what to call this particular deed, I was a sinful man, capable of lying, deceiving, cheating and more. Through deep sobs, I asked his forgiveness. My former adversary accepted my confession, forgave me, then embraced me with a few tears of his own.

God's grace is the only chance we have to be fit as the dads in our homes. Our family must hear words of confession coming from our lips. Their forgiveness must be sought when we fail—that's *when*, not *if*. When we confess, they'll forgive. If we try to hide, we'll lose.

For your next devotional reading, go to page 13.

for dust you are
and to dust you will return."

²⁰Adam*a* named his wife Eve,*b* because she would become the mother of all the living. ²¹The LORD God made garments of skin for Adam and his wife and clothed them. ²²And the LORD God said, "The man has now become like one of us, knowing good and evil. He must not be allowed to reach out his hand and take also from the tree of life and eat, and live forever." ²³So the LORD God banished him from the Garden of Eden to work the ground from which he had been taken. ²⁴After he drove the man out, he placed on the east side*c* of the Garden of Eden cherubim and a flaming sword flashing back and forth to guard the way to the tree of life.

Cain and Abel

4 Adam*a* lay with his wife Eve, and she became pregnant and gave birth to Cain.*d* She said, "With the help of the LORD

I have brought forth*e* a man." ²Later she gave birth to his brother Abel.

Now Abel kept flocks, and Cain worked the soil. ³In the course of time Cain brought some of the fruits of the soil as an offering to the LORD. ⁴But Abel brought fat portions from some of the firstborn of his flock. The LORD looked with favor on Abel and his offering, ⁵but on Cain and his offering he did not look with favor. So Cain was very angry, and his face was downcast.

⁶Then the LORD said to Cain, "Why are you angry? Why is your face downcast? ⁷If you do what is right, will you not be accepted? But if you do not do what is right, sin is crouching at your door; it desires to have you, but you must master it."

⁸Now Cain said to his brother Abel, "Let's go out to the field."*f* And while they

a20,1 Or The man   *b20 Eve probably means living.*
c24 Or placed in front   *d1 Cain sounds like the Hebrew for brought forth or acquired.*   *e1 Or have acquired*   *f8 Samaritan Pentateuch, Septuagint, Vulgate and Syriac; Masoretic Text does not have "Let's go out to the field."*

"I'm in charge here . . . if that's okay with everyone."
Adam, the Wimpy Father

"The man said, 'The woman you put here with me—she gave me some fruit from the tree, and I ate it' " (3:12).

DADS
IN THE
BIBLE

Text: Genesis 3

Adam was no dummy. In case you forgot high school biology, Adam came up with all those names (let's see . . . was it genus *then* species, or the other way around?). This was one smart man.

Adam was no sissy. His virility is legendary . . . where do you think you and I came from? That's right, our great grandfather Adam.

But Adam was a wimp. When faced with temptation, Adam's knees buckled. His unwillingness to step up and do the right thing is a historical fact. Somehow, in the face of indescribable prosperity, a happy marriage and a career he enjoyed, Adam didn't have the fortitude to say "no." He didn't have the courage to go face-to-face with the serpent and call his bluff. Adam wasn't even able to warn his wife that she was making the mistake of a lifetime.

Adam's tombstone, if he'd had one, might have read, "I Acquiesced." This is not how you and I want to be remembered, I'm sure of it.

God has given us the incredible privilege of leadership. He has given us the tools to direct and to serve, the wherewithal to set the goals and the experience to set the example. We have the chance to take charge in our families, to lovingly correct and direct them as we've seen God directing us. What we do with this opportunity will not only make an impact on our own family; it will also have an effect on generations to follow. Ask Adam about that.

You've been given a role that is going to take some work, some heart and a lot of wisdom. Take a tip from Adam. Don't wimp out.

For a complete listing of Dads in the Bible, turn to page 1434.

were in the field, Cain attacked his brother Abel and killed him.

[9]Then the LORD said to Cain, "Where is your brother Abel?"

"I don't know," he replied. "Am I my brother's keeper?"

[10]The LORD said, "What have you done? Listen! Your brother's blood cries out to me from the ground. [11]Now you are under a curse and driven from the ground, which opened its mouth to receive your brother's blood from your hand. [12]When you work the ground, it will no longer yield its crops for you. You will be a restless wanderer on the earth."

[13]Cain said to the LORD, "My punishment is more than I can bear. [14]Today you are driving me from the land, and I will be hidden from your presence; I will be a restless wanderer on the earth, and whoever finds me will kill me."

[15]But the LORD said to him, "Not so[a]; if anyone kills Cain, he will suffer vengeance seven times over." Then the LORD put a mark on Cain so that no one who found him would kill him. [16]So Cain went out from the LORD's presence and lived in the land of Nod,[b] east of Eden.

[17]Cain lay with his wife, and she became pregnant and gave birth to Enoch. Cain was then building a city, and he named it after his son Enoch. [18]To Enoch was born Irad, and Irad was the father of Mehujael, and Mehujael was the father of Methushael, and Methushael was the father of Lamech.

[19]Lamech married two women, one named Adah and the other Zillah. [20]Adah gave birth to Jabal; he was the father of those who live in tents and raise livestock. [21]His brother's name was Jubal; he was the father of all who play the harp and flute. [22]Zillah also had a son, Tubal-Cain, who forged all kinds of tools out of[c] bronze and iron. Tubal-Cain's sister was Naamah.

[23]Lamech said to his wives,

"Adah and Zillah, listen to me;
    wives of Lamech, hear my words.
I have killed[d] a man for wounding me,
    a young man for injuring me.
[24]If Cain is avenged seven times,
    then Lamech seventy-seven times."

[25]Adam lay with his wife again, and she gave birth to a son and named him Seth,[e] saying, "God has granted me another child in place of Abel, since Cain killed him." [26]Seth also had a son, and he named him Enosh.

At that time men began to call on[f] the name of the LORD.

From Adam to Noah

5 This is the written account of Adam's line.

When God created man, he made him in the likeness of God. [2]He created them male and female and blessed them. And when they were created, he called them "man."[g]

[3]When Adam had lived 130 years, he had a son in his own likeness, in his own image; and he named him Seth. [4]After Seth was born, Adam lived 800 years and had other sons and daughters. [5]Altogether, Adam lived 930 years, and then he died.

[6]When Seth had lived 105 years, he became the father[h] of Enosh. [7]And after he became the father of Enosh, Seth lived 807 years and had other sons and daughters. [8]Altogether, Seth lived 912 years, and then he died.

[9]When Enosh had lived 90 years, he became the father of Kenan. [10]And after he became the father of Kenan, Enosh lived 815 years and had other sons and daughters. [11]Altogether, Enosh lived 905 years, and then he died.

[12]When Kenan had lived 70 years, he became the father of Mahalalel. [13]And after he became the father of Mahalalel, Kenan lived 840 years and had other sons and daughters. [14]Altogether, Kenan lived 910 years, and then he died.

[15]When Mahalalel had lived 65 years, he became the father of Jared. [16]And after he became the father of Jared, Mahalalel lived 830 years and had other sons and daughters. [17]Altogether, Mahalalel lived 895 years, and then he died.

[18]When Jared had lived 162 years, he became the father of Enoch. [19]And after he became the father of Enoch, Jared lived 800 years and had other sons and daughters. [20]Altogether, Jared lived 962 years, and then he died.

[21]When Enoch had lived 65 years, he became the father of Methuselah. [22]And after he became the father of Methuselah, Enoch walked with God 300 years and had other sons and daughters. [23]Altogether,

---

[a]15 Septuagint, Vulgate and Syriac; Hebrew Very well   [b]16 Nod means wandering (see verses 12 and 14).   [c]22 Or who instructed all who work in   [d]23 Or I will kill   [e]25 Seth probably means granted.   [f]26 Or to proclaim   [g]2 Hebrew adam   [h]6 Father may mean ancestor; also in verses 7-26.

Enoch lived 365 years. ²⁴Enoch walked with God; then he was no more, because God took him away.

²⁵When Methuselah had lived 187 years, he became the father of Lamech. ²⁶And after he became the father of Lamech, Methuselah lived 782 years and had other sons and daughters. ²⁷Altogether, Methuselah lived 969 years, and then he died.

²⁸When Lamech had lived 182 years, he had a son. ²⁹He named him Noah*a* and said, "He will comfort us in the labor and painful toil of our hands caused by the ground the LORD has cursed." ³⁰After Noah was born, Lamech lived 595 years and had other sons and daughters. ³¹Altogether, Lamech lived 777 years, and then he died.

³²After Noah was 500 years old, he became the father of Shem, Ham and Japheth.

The Flood

6 When men began to increase in number on the earth and daughters were born to them, ²the sons of God saw that the daughters of men were beautiful, and they married any of them they chose. ³Then the LORD said, "My Spirit will not contend with*b* man forever, for he is mortal*c*; his days will be a hundred and twenty years."

⁴The Nephilim were on the earth in those days—and also afterward—when the sons of God went to the daughters of

a29 Noah sounds like the Hebrew for *comfort.*
b3 Or *My spirit will not remain in*   *c3* Or *corrupt*

Hand Me That Board Over There
Noah, the Dutiful Father

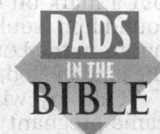

DADS
IN THE
BIBLE

"Noah was a righteous man, blameless among the people of his time, and he walked with God" (6:9).

Text: Genesis 6

The story of Noah is one of the most amazing in the Bible. It may also be the most frequently used story in church school classes for small children. But don't be misled—this guy wasn't just some sticker-book hero for little kids. Noah was a rugged man of God, and he was a dad we can learn from.

Picture the culture Noah and his family dealt with. The word that seems to summarize Noah's surroundings best is "wicked" (6:5). So God pronounces judgment on the earth and decides to completely destroy it. In fact, God is so upset that he regrets even having come to work on the fifth and sixth days of creation (6:7b)!

"But Noah found favor in the eyes of the LORD" (6:8). What an incredible statement. Here was a man who, because of the way he conducted himself, "found favor" in God's eyes. Noah was a man who "walked with God" (6:9).

You know the rest of the story. Not only was Noah commanded to jump into the biggest building project of his life, he had to endure years of painful and embarrassing ridicule from his friends and neighbors as he worked. Imagine how your local deed-restriction committee would react to the construction of a boat that was as long as a football field and a half!

The take-away for Christian dads everywhere is found in Genesis 7:1. God says, "Go into the ark, you and your whole family, because I have found you righteous in this generation." God called Noah to do two things for him, regardless of his surroundings. They are the same things he has called you and me to do: first, walk with him; second, take your family along.

The reason we first heard about Noah in church school was not primarily because of his ability to drive a nail, although he was certainly good at it. It was not because of the intensity of his work, although he must have been the most single-minded man in his town. No, we heard about Noah because he obeyed God, and he took his job as a dad very, very seriously.

And because Noah did these things, God used him to change the world.

For a complete listing of Dads in the Bible, turn to page 1434.

men and had children by them. They were the heroes of old, men of renown.

⁵The LORD saw how great man's wickedness on the earth had become, and that every inclination of the thoughts of his heart was only evil all the time. ⁶The LORD was grieved that he had made man on the earth, and his heart was filled with pain. ⁷So the LORD said, "I will wipe mankind, whom I have created, from the face of the earth—men and animals, and creatures that move along the ground, and birds of the air—for I am grieved that I have made them." ⁸But Noah found favor in the eyes of the LORD.

⁹This is the account of Noah.

Noah was a righteous man, blameless among the people of his time, and he walked with God. ¹⁰Noah had three sons: Shem, Ham and Japheth.

¹¹Now the earth was corrupt in God's sight and was full of violence. ¹²God saw how corrupt the earth had become, for all the people on earth had corrupted their ways. ¹³So God said to Noah, "I am going to put an end to all people, for the earth is filled with violence because of them. I am surely going to destroy both them and the earth. ¹⁴So make yourself an ark of cypress*a* wood; make rooms in it and coat it with pitch inside and out. ¹⁵This is how you are to build it: The ark is to be 450 feet long, 75 feet wide and 45 feet high.*b* ¹⁶Make a roof for it and finish*c* the ark to within 18 inches*d* of the top. Put a door in the side of the ark and make lower, middle and upper decks. ¹⁷I am going to bring floodwaters on the earth to destroy all life under the heavens, every creature that has the breath of life in it. Everything on earth will perish. ¹⁸But I will establish my covenant with you, and you will enter the ark—you and your sons and your wife and your sons' wives with you. ¹⁹You are to bring into the ark two of all living creatures, male and female, to keep them alive with you. ²⁰Two of every kind of bird, of every kind of animal and of every kind of creature that moves along the ground will come to you to be kept alive. ²¹You are to take every kind of food that is to be eaten and store it away as food for you and for them."

²²Noah did everything just as God commanded him.

7 The LORD then said to Noah, "Go into the ark, you and your whole family, because I have found you righteous in this generation. ²Take with you seven*e* of every kind of clean animal, a male and its mate, and two of every kind of unclean animal, a male and its mate, ³and also seven of every kind of bird, male and female, to keep their various kinds alive throughout the earth. ⁴Seven days from now I will send rain on the earth for forty days and forty nights, and I will wipe from the face of the earth every living creature I have made."

⁵And Noah did all that the LORD commanded him.

⁶Noah was six hundred years old when the floodwaters came on the earth. ⁷And Noah and his sons and his wife and his sons' wives entered the ark to escape the waters of the flood. ⁸Pairs of clean and unclean animals, of birds and of all creatures that move along the ground, ⁹male and female, came to Noah and entered the ark, as God had commanded Noah. ¹⁰And after the seven days the floodwaters came on the earth.

¹¹In the six hundredth year of Noah's life, on the seventeenth day of the second month—on that day all the springs of the great deep burst forth, and the floodgates of the heavens were opened. ¹²And rain fell on the earth forty days and forty nights.

¹³On that very day Noah and his sons, Shem, Ham and Japheth, together with his wife and the wives of his three sons, entered the ark. ¹⁴They had with them every wild animal according to its kind, all livestock according to their kinds, every creature that moves along the ground according to its kind and every bird according to its kind, everything with wings. ¹⁵Pairs of all creatures that have the breath of life in them came to Noah and entered the ark. ¹⁶The animals going in were male and female of every living thing, as God had commanded Noah. Then the LORD shut him in.

¹⁷For forty days the flood kept coming on the earth, and as the waters increased they lifted the ark high above the earth. ¹⁸The waters rose and increased greatly on the earth, and the ark floated on the surface of the water. ¹⁹They rose greatly on the earth, and all the high mountains under the entire heavens were covered.

a14 The meaning of the Hebrew for this word is uncertain. *b15* Hebrew *300 cubits long, 50 cubits wide and 30 cubits high* (about 140 meters long, 23 meters wide and 13.5 meters high) *c16* Or *Make an opening for light by finishing* *d16* Hebrew *a cubit* (about 0.5 meter) *e2* Or *seven pairs*; also in verse 3

[20]The waters rose and covered the mountains to a depth of more than twenty feet.[a,b] [21]Every living thing that moved on the earth perished—birds, livestock, wild animals, all the creatures that swarm over the earth, and all mankind. [22]Everything on dry land that had the breath of life in its nostrils died. [23]Every living thing on the face of the earth was wiped out; men and animals and the creatures that move along the ground and the birds of the air were wiped from the earth. Only Noah was left, and those with him in the ark.

[24]The waters flooded the earth for a hundred and fifty days.

8 But God remembered Noah and all the wild animals and the livestock that were with him in the ark, and he sent a wind over the earth, and the waters receded. [2]Now the springs of the deep and the floodgates of the heavens had been closed, and the rain had stopped falling from the sky. [3]The water receded steadily from the earth. At the end of the hundred and fifty days the water had gone down,

[4]and on the seventeenth day of the seventh month the ark came to rest on the mountains of Ararat. [5]The waters continued to recede until the tenth month, and on the first day of the tenth month the tops of the mountains became visible.

[6]After forty days Noah opened the window he had made in the ark [7]and sent out a raven, and it kept flying back and forth until the water had dried up from the earth. [8]Then he sent out a dove to see if the water had receded from the surface of the ground. [9]But the dove could find no place to set its feet because there was water over all the surface of the earth; so it returned to Noah in the ark. He reached out his hand and took the dove and brought it back to himself in the ark. [10]He waited seven more days and again sent out the dove from the ark. [11]When the dove returned to him in the evening, there

[a]20 Hebrew *fifteen cubits* (about 6.9 meters)
[b]20 Or *rose more than twenty feet, and the mountains were covered*

HEY DAD
Where's Noah's ark now?

Text: Genesis 6–8

Genesis 8:4 tells us that Noah's ark came to rest on the mountains of Ararat. Most "arkeologists" have directed their searches to one specific mountain called Ararat, a 16,946-foot-high peak in eastern Turkey.

The Kurds (the local villagers who live near Mount Ararat) consider this mountain's peak sacred territory. Often refusing to guide expeditions all the way to the summit, the Kurds say, "It is Holy ground. To proceed further would provoke heavenly wrath" (Kite, 67).

Countless numbers of explorers would argue that the Kurds' beliefs are well founded. Many have ventured up Mount Ararat's slopes only to be beaten down by violent storms, blizzards, avalanches, wild animals, razor-sharp rocks and slippery cliffs. But a French explorer named Fernand Navarra is one of the few adventurers to have actually reached the top of the mysterious mountain.

In the mid-1950's, Navarra and his group found beneath them a well-defined black patch in the ice of Mount Ararat. He reported, "The shape was unmistakably that of a ship's hull!" Later, in that same spot, Navarra actually uncovered hand-tooled and evenly cut wooden beams. He brought a large piece of the wood home with him, but scientists still disagree about the wood's age and authenticity.

Most researchers believe that the ancient ark lies somewhere beneath the ice of Mount Ararat, and the evidence does seem to favor their claim. The Kurds, however, may be wise in their respect for the unknown.

Kite, L. Patricia (1989). Noah's Ark. Great Mysteries: Opposing Viewpoints. Saint Paul: Greenhaven Press, Inc.

For a complete listing of Questions Kids Ask, turn to page 1435.

QUESTIONS KIDS ASK

in its beak was a freshly plucked olive leaf! Then Noah knew that the water had receded from the earth. ¹²He waited seven more days and sent the dove out again, but this time it did not return to him. ¹³By the first day of the first month of Noah's six hundred and first year, the water had dried up from the earth. Noah then removed the covering from the ark and saw that the surface of the ground was dry. ¹⁴By the twenty-seventh day of the second month the earth was completely dry.

¹⁵Then God said to Noah, ¹⁶"Come out of the ark, you and your wife and your sons and their wives. ¹⁷Bring out every kind of living creature that is with you— the birds, the animals, and all the creatures that move along the ground—so they can multiply on the earth and be fruitful and increase in number upon it." ¹⁸So Noah came out, together with his sons and his wife and his sons' wives. ¹⁹All the animals and all the creatures that move along the ground and all the birds— everything that moves on the earth—

God's Waiting Room

DAILY INSIGHT

THURSDAY

Passage:
Genesis 8

Verses:
Genesis 8:18–19

My wife was fascinated by the unusual intensity with which I was watching the final game of the 1984 National League Championships. I groaned with every strike and hollered with every ground ball that snaked its way through the infield. This was the most important baseball game I had ever watched.

I have always been a Cubs fan. Having grown up in the "Windy City," it was almost inevitable—little boys in Chicago followed the Cubs. We made believe we were playing in Wrigley Field, we wore Cubs baseball caps, and we were Ron Santo, Don Kessinger, Glenn Beckert and Ernie Banks, third to first. One day, we were going to the World Series. Every season we waited for the fulfillment of that hope.

The Bible is full of two-part stories. The first part is the account of God's spoken promise. The second part is the fulfillment of that promise. The problem is that between the first part and the second part, there is usually a gap—a length of time endured by those who received the verbal promise before it actually came to pass. Kind of like being a Cubs fan.

From a purely practical standpoint, Noah had to wait it out in the middle of some pretty miserable circumstances. He, his family, and all those animals had been cooped up for over two-hundred days. We can only imagine what the place must have looked and smelled like.

Wouldn't it be great if we could read from Noah's nautical journal? Day 1 might have read, "God, you really *did* keep your word. Thank you for giving me the strength to obey. Thank you for being so faithful." But day 173 may have read a bit differently: "Okay, God, I've had enough. This is the most miserable experience of my life. Are you there? Are you listening to me?"

Have you been there? Have you done something radical— moved your family to a new town or changed jobs—sincerely believing it was what God wanted you to do, only to find yourself completely miserable? I've been there, too.

Well we're in good company—Noah, Abraham, Jacob, David, Job. These were men who heard God's voice, believed the promise, then had to wait. And wait. And wait some more.

Are you waiting for something you thought God would have delivered by now ... satisfaction at work, healing from an illness, reconciliation with a friend? Well, the assurance we have from the Bible is that, in every case, in his own way, God's promise was good. Those who had to wait did not wait in vain. Take that promise with you today.

By the way, the Cubs, after taking an early lead, lost that championship game to the Padres 6 to 4. Oh, but wait 'til next year.

For your next devotional reading, go to page 16.

came out of the ark, one kind after another.

20Then Noah built an altar to the LORD and, taking some of all the clean animals and clean birds, he sacrificed burnt offerings on it. **21**The LORD smelled the pleasing aroma and said in his heart: "Never again will I curse the ground because of man, even though*a* every inclination of his heart is evil from childhood. And never again will I destroy all living creatures, as I have done.

22"As long as the earth endures,
  seedtime and harvest,
  cold and heat,
  summer and winter,
  day and night
  will never cease."

God's Covenant With Noah

9 Then God blessed Noah and his sons, saying to them, "Be fruitful and increase in number and fill the earth. **2**The fear and dread of you will fall upon all the beasts of the earth and all the birds of the air, upon every creature that moves along the ground, and upon all the fish of the sea; they are given into your hands. **3**Everything that lives and moves will be food for you. Just as I gave you the green plants, I now give you everything.

4"But you must not eat meat that has its lifeblood still in it. **5**And for your lifeblood I will surely demand an accounting. I will demand an accounting from every animal. And from each man, too, I will demand an accounting for the life of his fellow man.

6 "Whoever sheds the blood of man,
  by man shall his blood be shed;
 for in the image of God
  has God made man.

7As for you, be fruitful and increase in number; multiply on the earth and increase upon it."

8Then God said to Noah and to his sons with him: **9**"I now establish my covenant with you and with your descendants after you **10**and with every living creature that was with you—the birds, the livestock and all the wild animals, all those that came out of the ark with you—every living creature on earth. **11**I establish my covenant with you: Never again will all life be cut off by the waters of a flood; never again will there be a flood to destroy the earth."

12And God said, "This is the sign of the covenant I am making between me and you and every living creature with you, a covenant for all generations to come: **13**I have set my rainbow in the clouds, and it will be the sign of the covenant between me and the earth. **14**Whenever I bring clouds over the earth and the rainbow appears in the clouds, **15**I will remember my covenant between me and you and all living creatures of every kind. Never again will the waters become a flood to destroy all life. **16**Whenever the rainbow appears in the clouds, I will see it and remember the everlasting covenant between God and all living creatures of every kind on the earth."

17So God said to Noah, "This is the sign of the covenant I have established between me and all life on the earth."

The Sons of Noah

18The sons of Noah who came out of the ark were Shem, Ham and Japheth. (Ham was the father of Canaan.) **19**These were the three sons of Noah, and from them came the people who were scattered over the earth.

20Noah, a man of the soil, proceeded*b* to plant a vineyard. **21**When he drank some of its wine, he became drunk and lay uncovered inside his tent. **22**Ham, the father of Canaan, saw his father's nakedness and told his two brothers outside. **23**But Shem and Japheth took a garment and laid it across their shoulders; then they walked in backward and covered their father's nakedness. Their faces were turned the other way so that they would not see their father's nakedness.

24When Noah awoke from his wine and found out what his youngest son had done to him, **25**he said,

"Cursed be Canaan!
  The lowest of slaves
  will he be to his brothers."

26He also said,

"Blessed be the LORD, the God of Shem!
  May Canaan be the slave of Shem.*c*
27May God extend the territory of
   Japheth*d*;
  may Japheth live in the tents of
   Shem,
  and may Canaan be his*e* slave."

---

a21 Or man, for   b20 Or soil, was the first   c26 Or be his slave   d27 Japheth sounds like the Hebrew for extend.   e27 Or their

²⁸After the flood Noah lived 350 years. ²⁹Altogether, Noah lived 950 years, and then he died.

The Table of Nations

10 This is the account of Shem, Ham and Japheth, Noah's sons, who themselves had sons after the flood.

The Japhethites

² The sons^a of Japheth:
   Gomer, Magog, Madai, Javan, Tubal, Meshech and Tiras.
³ The sons of Gomer:
   Ashkenaz, Riphath and Togarmah.
⁴ The sons of Javan:
   Elishah, Tarshish, the Kittim and the Rodanim.^b ⁵(From these the maritime peoples spread out into their territories by their clans within their nations, each with its own language.)

The Hamites

⁶ The sons of Ham:
   Cush, Mizraim,^c Put and Canaan.
⁷ The sons of Cush:
   Seba, Havilah, Sabtah, Raamah and Sabteca.
   The sons of Raamah:
   Sheba and Dedan.

⁸Cush was the father^d of Nimrod, who grew to be a mighty warrior on the earth. ⁹He was a mighty hunter before the LORD; that is why it is said, "Like Nimrod, a mighty hunter before the LORD." ¹⁰The first centers of his kingdom were Babylon, Erech, Akkad and Calneh, in^e Shinar.^f ¹¹From that land he went to Assyria, where he built Nineveh, Rehoboth Ir,^g Calah ¹²and Resen, which is between Nineveh and Calah; that is the great city.

¹³Mizraim was the father of
   the Ludites, Anamites, Lehabites, Naphtuhites, ¹⁴Pathrusites, Casluhites (from whom the Philistines came) and Caphtorites.
¹⁵Canaan was the father of
   Sidon his firstborn,^h and of the Hittites, ¹⁶Jebusites, Amorites, Girgashites, ¹⁷Hivites, Arkites, Sinites, ¹⁸Arvadites, Zemarites and Hamathites.

Later the Canaanite clans scattered ¹⁹and the borders of Canaan reached from Sidon toward Gerar as far as Gaza, and then toward Sodom, Gomorrah, Admah and Zeboiim, as far as Lasha.

²⁰These are the sons of Ham by their clans and languages, in their territories and nations.

The Semites

²¹Sons were also born to Shem, whose older brother wasⁱ Japheth; Shem was the ancestor of all the sons of Eber.

²² The sons of Shem:
   Elam, Asshur, Arphaxad, Lud and Aram.
²³ The sons of Aram:
   Uz, Hul, Gether and Meshech.^j
²⁴Arphaxad was the father of^k Shelah, and Shelah the father of Eber.
²⁵Two sons were born to Eber:
   One was named Peleg,^l because in his time the earth was divided; his brother was named Joktan.
²⁶Joktan was the father of
   Almodad, Sheleph, Hazarmaveth, Jerah, ²⁷Hadoram, Uzal, Diklah, ²⁸Obal, Abimael, Sheba, ²⁹Ophir, Havilah and Jobab. All these were sons of Joktan.

³⁰The region where they lived stretched from Mesha toward Sephar, in the eastern hill country.
³¹These are the sons of Shem by their clans and languages, in their territories and nations.

³²These are the clans of Noah's sons, according to their lines of descent, within their nations. From these the nations spread out over the earth after the flood.

The Tower of Babel

11 Now the whole world had one language and a common speech. ²As men moved eastward,^m they found a plain in Shinar^f and settled there.

³They said to each other, "Come, let's make bricks and bake them thoroughly." They used brick instead of stone, and tar

^a2 Sons may mean descendants or successors or nations; also in verses 3, 4, 6, 7, 20-23, 29 and 31. ^b4 Some manuscripts of the Masoretic Text and Samaritan Pentateuch (see also Septuagint and 1 Chron. 1:7); most manuscripts of the Masoretic Text Dodanim ^c6 That is, Egypt; also in verse 13 ^d8 Father may mean ancestor or predecessor or founder; also in verses 13, 15, 24 and 26. ^e10 Or Erech and Akkad—all of them in ^f10,2 That is, Babylonia ^g11 Or Nineveh with its city squares ^h15 Or of the Sidonians, the foremost ⁱ21 Or Shem, the older brother of ^j23 See Septuagint and 1 Chron. 1:17; Hebrew Mash ^k24 Hebrew; Septuagint father of Cainan, and Cainan was the father of ^l25 Peleg means division. ^m2 Or from the east; or in the east

for mortar. [4]Then they said, "Come, let us build ourselves a city, with a tower that reaches to the heavens, so that we may make a name for ourselves and not be scattered over the face of the whole earth."

[5]But the LORD came down to see the city and the tower that the men were building. [6]The LORD said, "If as one people speaking the same language they have begun to do this, then nothing they plan to do will be impossible for them. [7]Come, let us go down and confuse their language so they will not understand each other."

[8]So the LORD scattered them from there over all the earth, and they stopped building the city. [9]That is why it was called Babel[a]—because there the LORD confused the language of the whole world. From

there the LORD scattered them over the face of the whole earth.

From Shem to Abram

[10]This is the account of Shem.

Two years after the flood, when Shem was 100 years old, he became the father[b] of Arphaxad. [11]And after he became the father of Arphaxad, Shem lived 500 years and had other sons and daughters.

[12]When Arphaxad had lived 35 years, he became the father of Shelah. [13]And after he became the father of Shelah, Arphaxad

[a]9 That is, Babylon; *Babel* sounds like the Hebrew for *confused*.   [b]10 *Father* may mean *ancestor*; also in verses 11-25.

Making a Name for Yourself

DAILY INSIGHT

FRIDAY
Passage:
Genesis 11:1–9
Verse:
Genesis 11:4

Life was getting a little mundane and ordinary for Noah's descendants—up every morning, off to the fields, home for lunch, off to the fields again, back for dinner, a few hours with the family, a good night's rest, and back at it again. Not a lot of glamour here. No bright lights. No pizzazz.

So a group of men got together and decided that it was time to make a name for themselves. "Enough of the straight life," they must have grumbled. "Forget this faithful employee, husband, and father stuff. Let's go do something fantastic so everyone knows who we are. Then we'll really be something." They started work on a tower.

Think about what it may have been like the first day of construction. All the blueprints had been approved, the materials were in place, the workers ready to go. But no one suggested that, before they began to build, perhaps they ought to ask for God's blessing. It's probably safe to say that when the plans were being drawn up, God wasn't included there, either. "God will understand," they may have said to each other in their strategic planning meetings. "After all, this project isn't about him, it's about us. We'll get back to him when

we're ready to build something religious."

But God stopped the project. He created incredible confusion by giving these arrogant men different languages to speak. No longer could they work together. Cooperation became confusion. What had begun as a project to make these men famous, turned into an everlasting monument to conflict, failure, and shame—Babel.

In Genesis 28, we have the account of Jacob on an overnight trip to meet his wife. He spent the night under the stars, and God visited him in a profound and life-changing way. The next morning, Jacob carefully took the rock he had been using as his pillow and stood it on end as a memorial to God's awesomeness. And this simple tower—Bethel—became an everlasting monument to God's presence and leadership in the life of men who are willing to humble themselves in his presence. Bethel became a project to honor God. A place, if you will, to make *him* famous.

What are we building today, Babel or Bethel? Who will be honored? And what should we expect the outcome to be?

For your next devotional reading, go to page 18.

lived 403 years and had other sons and daughters.^a

¹⁴When Shelah had lived 30 years, he became the father of Eber. ¹⁵And after he became the father of Eber, Shelah lived 403 years and had other sons and daughters.

¹⁶When Eber had lived 34 years, he became the father of Peleg. ¹⁷And after he became the father of Peleg, Eber lived 430 years and had other sons and daughters.

¹⁸When Peleg had lived 30 years, he became the father of Reu. ¹⁹And after he became the father of Reu, Peleg lived 209 years and had other sons and daughters.

²⁰When Reu had lived 32 years, he became the father of Serug. ²¹And after he became the father of Serug, Reu lived 207 years and had other sons and daughters.

²²When Serug had lived 30 years, he became the father of Nahor. ²³And after he became the father of Nahor, Serug lived 200 years and had other sons and daughters.

²⁴When Nahor had lived 29 years, he became the father of Terah. ²⁵And after he became the father of Terah, Nahor lived 119 years and had other sons and daughters.

²⁶After Terah had lived 70 years, he became the father of Abram, Nahor and Haran.

²⁷This is the account of Terah.

Terah became the father of Abram, Nahor and Haran. And Haran became the father of Lot. ²⁸While his father Terah was still alive, Haran died in Ur of the Chaldeans, in the land of his birth. ²⁹Abram and Nahor both married. The name of Abram's wife was Sarai, and the name of Nahor's wife was Milcah; she was the daughter of Haran, the father of both Milcah and Iscah. ³⁰Now Sarai was barren; she had no children.

³¹Terah took his son Abram, his grandson Lot son of Haran, and his daughter-in-law Sarai, the wife of his son Abram, and together they set out from Ur of the Chaldeans to go to Canaan. But when they came to Haran, they settled there.

³²Terah lived 205 years, and he died in Haran.

The Call of Abram

12 The LORD had said to Abram, "Leave your country, your people and your father's household and go to the land I will show you.

²"I will make you into a great nation
  and I will bless you;
I will make your name great,
  and you will be a blessing.
³I will bless those who bless you,
  and whoever curses you I will curse;
and all peoples on earth
  will be blessed through you."

⁴So Abram left, as the LORD had told him; and Lot went with him. Abram was seventy-five years old when he set out from Haran. ⁵He took his wife Sarai, his nephew Lot, all the possessions they had accumulated and the people they had acquired in Haran, and they set out for the land of Canaan, and they arrived there.

⁶Abram traveled through the land as far as the site of the great tree of Moreh at Shechem. At that time the Canaanites were in the land. ⁷The LORD appeared to Abram and said, "To your offspring^b I will give this land." So he built an altar there to the LORD, who had appeared to him.

⁸From there he went on toward the hills east of Bethel and pitched his tent, with Bethel on the west and Ai on the east. There he built an altar to the LORD and called on the name of the LORD. ⁹Then Abram set out and continued toward the Negev.

Abram in Egypt

¹⁰Now there was a famine in the land, and Abram went down to Egypt to live there for a while because the famine was severe. ¹¹As he was about to enter Egypt, he said to his wife Sarai, "I know what a beautiful woman you are. ¹²When the Egyptians see you, they will say, 'This is his wife.' Then they will kill me but will let you live. ¹³Say you are my sister, so that I will be treated well for your sake and my life will be spared because of you."

¹⁴When Abram came to Egypt, the Egyptians saw that she was a very beautiful woman. ¹⁵And when Pharaoh's officials saw her, they praised her to Pharaoh, and she was taken into his palace. ¹⁶He treated Abram well for her sake, and Abram acquired sheep and cattle, male

---

^a12,13 Hebrew; Septuagint (see also Luke 3:35, 36 and note at Gen. 10:24) *35 years, he became the father of Cainan.* ¹³*And after he became the father of Cainan, Arphaxad lived 430 years and had other sons and daughters, and then he died. When Cainan had lived 130 years, he became the father of Shelah. And after he became the father of Shelah, Cainan lived 330 years and had other sons and daughters* ^b7 Or *seed*

The New Kids on the Block

Key Verse: *"The LORD had said to Abram, 'Leave your country, your people and your father's household and go to the land I will show you.'"* Genesis 12:1

Text: Genesis 12:1–8 *(Dad or child reads the text.)*

QUIET
TIMES
WITH **Dad**

DAD READS: Did you know that every day over seventy-five thousand American families move? They pack up all their furniture, clothing, tools, kitchen things and toys in a big truck and leave all their friends behind. This can be a very hard thing to do, especially if these families have lived in one place for a long time.

Child reads: But moving to a new city can be exciting—a new job for dad or mom, a new house, a new neighborhood to explore, new friends to meet. Even though moving can be hard, sometimes it can also be an adventure.

DAD READS: In the verses we read today, God told Abram to move. Abram had lived in the same town all his life. He knew lots of people, and he had many friends. And to make it more difficult, God didn't tell him very much about where he was going or what he was supposed to do when he got there. What God said to Abram was, "Go and I'll be with you. In the meantime, trust me."

Child reads: If you would tell me that God had told you to move our family but he didn't tell you much more than that, I would wonder if it was the right thing to do. I may even try to see if I could change your mind. Moving is hard enough, but packing up everything and going to a place we have never heard of would be a scary thing to do.

DAD READS: You're right. But this is exactly what God asked Abram and Sarai, his wife, to do. And even though he didn't have any idea what his new home was going to be like, he went because he trusted God. Because Abram trusted God and obeyed him, a whole nation was formed—a nation God called "his very own." Can you believe it?

Child reads: As I grow up, there will be times when you will make decisions that affect our whole family. You may ask me to tell you what I think you should do. I may ask if you have asked God what you should do. But I will trust you because you're my dad.

DAD READS: Being a dad is a very important thing. I want you to know that, like Abram, I never want to make big or small decisions on my own. I always want to be sure that I have asked God to help your mom and me to make right decisions. You can count on me to do this. Now, let me pray this prayer with you:

Our Father in heaven, thank you for giving me the job of being a dad. Please help me to understand how very important my decisions are to our whole family. I promise to always ask for your wisdom when I'm trying to make good choices. Thank you for caring for our family. We love you. In Jesus' name, **Amen.**

For your next devotional reading, go to page 23.

and female donkeys, menservants and maidservants, and camels. [17]But the LORD inflicted serious diseases on Pharaoh and his household because of Abram's wife Sarai. [18]So Pharaoh summoned Abram. "What have you done to me?" he said. "Why didn't you tell me she was your wife? [19]Why did you say, 'She is my sister,' so that I took her to be my wife? Now then, here is your wife. Take her and go!" [20]Then Pharaoh gave orders about Abram to his men, and they sent him on his way, with his wife and everything he had.

Abram and Lot Separate

13 So Abram went up from Egypt to the Negev, with his wife and everything he had, and Lot went with him. [2]Abram had become very wealthy in livestock and in silver and gold.

[3]From the Negev he went from place to place until he came to Bethel, to the place between Bethel and Ai where his tent had been earlier [4]and where he had first built an altar. There Abram called on the name of the LORD.

[5]Now Lot, who was moving about with Abram, also had flocks and herds and tents. [6]But the land could not support them while they stayed together, for their possessions were so great that they were not able to stay together. [7]And quarreling arose between Abram's herdsmen and the herdsmen of Lot. The Canaanites and Perizzites were also living in the land at that time.

[8]So Abram said to Lot, "Let's not have any quarreling between you and me, or between your herdsmen and mine, for we are brothers. [9]Is not the whole land before you? Let's part company. If you go to the

Transfer from Ur
Abram, the Daring Father

"Leave your country, your people and your father's household and go to the land I will show you" (12:1).

Text: Genesis 12

These are the words that Abram, a wealthy landowner who was quietly minding his own business in the land of Ur, heard from heaven. We don't know if the words were actually audible, but we're sure that Abram heard them clearly.

Can you imagine his first conversation with his wife after receiving the call? "Sarai, my dear, you're not going to believe this," Abram must have blurted out. "I don't know where we're going; I don't know how we're going to get there, and I don't know how long we're going to stay. But we're going anyway."

Sarai's only logical response? "You've been in the sun too long, Abram."

However, as amazing as it seems to us, Abram pulled up the stakes and moved. He had no doubt that he had been called to do something else, and even though he wasn't quite sure who had told him to go, Abram dared to obey.

Have you ever heard—or sensed—a call from God? Perhaps it was a change in location or an opportunity for a new career. What did you do with this message?

Several years ago, a good friend of mine was enjoying a short cruise around the Florida Keys. The huge yacht was privately owned by one of the men on board. Midway through the voyage, my friend found himself deep in conversation with his millionaire host. "I'm surrounded by more luxury than I could have ever comprehended," the affluent man finally said. "But if the truth were known, I have been miserable since I was a sophomore in college. A missionary came to our school and challenged us to consider serving God on the mission field. I felt God's call, but I opted for this instead. I'm unthinkably wealthy, but I feel worthless."

Abram knew God had called him. He didn't know what it meant or what it would cost him, but he knew that not following the call would destine him for misery. So Abram dared to move—straight into God's blessing.

For a complete listing of Dads in the Bible, turn to page 1434.

left, I'll go to the right; if you go to the right, I'll go to the left."

¹⁰Lot looked up and saw that the whole plain of the Jordan was well watered, like the garden of the LORD, like the land of Egypt, toward Zoar. (This was before the LORD destroyed Sodom and Gomorrah.) ¹¹So Lot chose for himself the whole plain of the Jordan and set out toward the east. The two men parted company: ¹²Abram lived in the land of Canaan, while Lot lived among the cities of the plain and pitched his tents near Sodom. ¹³Now the men of Sodom were wicked and were sinning greatly against the LORD.

¹⁴The LORD said to Abram after Lot had parted from him, "Lift up your eyes from where you are and look north and south, east and west. ¹⁵All the land that you see I will give to you and your offspringᵃ forever. ¹⁶I will make your offspring like the dust of the earth, so that if anyone could count the dust, then your offspring could be counted. ¹⁷Go, walk through the length and breadth of the land, for I am giving it to you."

¹⁸So Abram moved his tents and went to live near the great trees of Mamre at Hebron, where he built an altar to the LORD.

Abram Rescues Lot

14 At this time Amraphel king of Shinar,ᵇ Arioch king of Ellasar, Kedorlaomer king of Elam and Tidal king of Goiim ²went to war against Bera king of Sodom, Birsha king of Gomorrah, Shinab king of Admah, Shemeber king of Zeboiim, and the king of Bela (that is, Zoar). ³All these latter kings joined forces in the Valley of Siddim (the Salt Seaᶜ). ⁴For twelve years they had been subject to Kedorlaomer, but in the thirteenth year they rebelled. ⁵In the fourteenth year, Kedorlaomer and the kings allied with him went out and defeated the Rephaites in Ashteroth Karnaim, the Zuzites in Ham, the Emites in Shaveh Kiriathaim ⁶and the Horites in the hill country of Seir, as far as El Paran near the desert. ⁷Then they turned back and went to En Mishpat (that is, Kadesh), and they conquered the whole territory of the Amalekites, as well as the Amorites who were living in Hazazon Tamar.

⁸Then the king of Sodom, the king of Gomorrah, the king of Admah, the king of Zeboiim and the king of Bela (that is, Zoar) marched out and drew up their battle lines in the Valley of Siddim ⁹against

Kedorlaomer king of Elam, Tidal king of Goiim, Amraphel king of Shinar and Arioch king of Ellasar—four kings against five. ¹⁰Now the Valley of Siddim was full of tar pits, and when the kings of Sodom and Gomorrah fled, some of the men fell into them and the rest fled to the hills. ¹¹The four kings seized all the goods of Sodom and Gomorrah and all their food; then they went away. ¹²They also carried off Abram's nephew Lot and his possessions, since he was living in Sodom.

¹³One who had escaped came and reported this to Abram the Hebrew. Now Abram was living near the great trees of Mamre the Amorite, a brotherᵈ of Eshcol and Aner, all of whom were allied with Abram. ¹⁴When Abram heard that his relative had been taken captive, he called out the 318 trained men born in his household and went in pursuit as far as Dan. ¹⁵During the night Abram divided his men to attack them and he routed them, pursuing them as far as Hobah, north of Damascus. ¹⁶He recovered all the goods and brought back his relative Lot and his possessions, together with the women and the other people.

¹⁷After Abram returned from defeating Kedorlaomer and the kings allied with him, the king of Sodom came out to meet him in the Valley of Shaveh (that is, the King's Valley).

¹⁸Then Melchizedek king of Salemᵉ brought out bread and wine. He was priest of God Most High, ¹⁹and he blessed Abram, saying,

"Blessed be Abram by God Most High,
    Creatorᶠ of heaven and earth.
²⁰And blessed beᵍ God Most High,
    who delivered your enemies into
        your hand."

Then Abram gave him a tenth of everything.

²¹The king of Sodom said to Abram, "Give me the people and keep the goods for yourself."

²²But Abram said to the king of Sodom, "I have raised my hand to the LORD, God Most High, Creator of heaven and earth, and have taken an oath ²³that I will accept nothing belonging to you, not even a thread or the thong of a sandal, so that you will never be able to say, 'I made

---

ᵃ15 Or seed; also in verse 16   ᵇ1 That is, Babylonia; also in verse 9   ᶜ3 That is, the Dead Sea   ᵈ13 Or a relative; or an ally   ᵉ18 That is, Jerusalem ᶠ19 Or Possessor; also in verse 22   ᵍ20 Or And praise be to

Abram rich.' ²⁴I will accept nothing but what my men have eaten and the share that belongs to the men who went with me—to Aner, Eshcol and Mamre. Let them have their share."

God's Covenant With Abram

15 After this, the word of the LORD came to Abram in a vision:

"Do not be afraid, Abram.
    I am your shield,ᵃ
    your very great reward.ᵇ"

²But Abram said, "O Sovereign LORD, what can you give me since I remain childless and the one who will inheritᶜ my estate is Eliezer of Damascus?" ³And Abram said, "You have given me no children; so a servant in my household will be my heir." ⁴Then the word of the LORD came to him: "This man will not be your heir, but a son coming from your own body will be your heir." ⁵He took him outside and said, "Look up at the heavens and count the stars—if indeed you can count them." Then he said to him, "So shall your offspring be." ⁶Abram believed the LORD, and he credited it to him as righteousness.

⁷He also said to him, "I am the LORD, who brought you out of Ur of the Chaldeans to give you this land to take possession of it."

⁸But Abram said, "O Sovereign LORD, how can I know that I will gain possession of it?"

⁹So the LORD said to him, "Bring me a heifer, a goat and a ram, each three years old, along with a dove and a young pigeon."

¹⁰Abram brought all these to him, cut them in two and arranged the halves opposite each other; the birds, however, he did not cut in half. ¹¹Then birds of prey came down on the carcasses, but Abram drove them away.

¹²As the sun was setting, Abram fell into a deep sleep, and a thick and dreadful darkness came over him. ¹³Then the LORD said to him, "Know for certain that your descendants will be strangers in a country not their own, and they will be enslaved and mistreated four hundred years. ¹⁴But I will punish the nation they serve as slaves, and afterward they will come out with great possessions. ¹⁵You, however, will go to your fathers in peace and be buried at a good old age. ¹⁶In the fourth generation your descendants will come back here, for the sin of the Amorites has not yet reached its full measure."

¹⁷When the sun had set and darkness had fallen, a smoking firepot with a blazing torch appeared and passed between the pieces. ¹⁸On that day the LORD made a covenant with Abram and said, "To your descendants I give this land, from the riverᵈ of Egypt to the great river, the Euphrates— ¹⁹the land of the Kenites, Kenizzites, Kadmonites, ²⁰Hittites, Perizzites, Rephaites, ²¹Amorites, Canaanites, Girgashites and Jebusites."

Hagar and Ishmael

16 Now Sarai, Abram's wife, had borne him no children. But she had an Egyptian maidservant named Hagar; ²so she said to Abram, "The LORD has kept me from having children. Go, sleep with my maidservant; perhaps I can build a family through her."

Abram agreed to what Sarai said. ³So after Abram had been living in Canaan ten years, Sarai his wife took her Egyptian maidservant Hagar and gave her to her husband to be his wife. ⁴He slept with Hagar, and she conceived.

When she knew she was pregnant, she began to despise her mistress. ⁵Then Sarai said to Abram, "You are responsible for the wrong I am suffering. I put my servant in your arms, and now that she knows she is pregnant, she despises me. May the LORD judge between you and me."

⁶"Your servant is in your hands," Abram said. "Do with her whatever you think best." Then Sarai mistreated Hagar; so she fled from her.

⁷The angel of the LORD found Hagar near a spring in the desert; it was the spring that is beside the road to Shur. ⁸And he said, "Hagar, servant of Sarai, where have you come from, and where are you going?"

"I'm running away from my mistress Sarai," she answered.

⁹Then the angel of the LORD told her, "Go back to your mistress and submit to her." ¹⁰The angel added, "I will so increase your descendants that they will be too numerous to count."

¹¹The angel of the LORD also said to her:

"You are now with child
    and you will have a son.

ᵃ1 Or *sovereign*   ᵇ1 Or *shield; / your reward will be very great*   ᶜ2 The meaning of the Hebrew for this phrase is uncertain.   ᵈ18 Or *Wadi*

You shall name him Ishmael,[a]
  for the LORD has heard of your
    misery.
[12]He will be a wild donkey of a man;
  his hand will be against everyone
  and everyone's hand against him,
  and he will live in hostility
    toward[b] all his brothers."

[13]She gave this name to the LORD who spoke to her: "You are the God who sees me," for she said, "I have now seen[c] the One who sees me." [14]That is why the well was called Beer Lahai Roi[d]; it is still there, between Kadesh and Bered.

[15]So Hagar bore Abram a son, and Abram gave the name Ishmael to the son she had borne. [16]Abram was eighty-six years old when Hagar bore him Ishmael.

The Covenant of Circumcision

17 When Abram was ninety-nine years old, the LORD appeared to him and said, "I am God Almighty[e]; walk before me and be blameless. [2]I will confirm my covenant between me and you and will greatly increase your numbers."

[3]Abram fell facedown, and God said to him, [4]"As for me, this is my covenant with you: You will be the father of many nations. [5]No longer will you be called Abram[f]; your name will be Abraham,[g] for I have made you a father of many nations. [6]I will make you very fruitful; I will make nations of you, and kings will come from you. [7]I will establish my covenant as an everlasting covenant between me and you and your descendants after you for the generations to come, to be your God and the God of your descendants after you. [8]The whole land of Canaan, where you are now an alien, I will give as an everlasting possession to you and your descendants after you; and I will be their God."

[9]Then God said to Abraham, "As for you, you must keep my covenant, you and your descendants after you for the generations to come. [10]This is my covenant with you and your descendants after you, the covenant you are to keep: Every male among you shall be circumcised. [11]You are to undergo circumcision, and it will be the sign of the covenant between me and you. [12]For the generations to come every male among you who is eight days old must be circumcised, including those born in your household or bought with money from a foreigner—those who are not your offspring. [13]Whether born in your household or bought with your money, they must be circumcised. My covenant in your flesh is to be an everlasting covenant. [14]Any uncircumcised male, who has not been circumcised in the flesh, will be cut off from his people; he has broken my covenant."

[15]God also said to Abraham, "As for Sarai your wife, you are no longer to call her Sarai; her name will be Sarah. [16]I will bless her and will surely give you a son by her. I will bless her so that she will be the mother of nations; kings of peoples will come from her."

[17]Abraham fell facedown; he laughed and said to himself, "Will a son be born to a man a hundred years old? Will Sarah bear a child at the age of ninety?" [18]And Abraham said to God, "If only Ishmael might live under your blessing!"

[19]Then God said, "Yes, but your wife Sarah will bear you a son, and you will call him Isaac.[h] I will establish my covenant with him as an everlasting covenant for his descendants after him. [20]And as for Ishmael, I have heard you: I will surely bless him; I will make him fruitful and will greatly increase his numbers. He will be the father of twelve rulers, and I will make him into a great nation. [21]But my covenant I will establish with Isaac, whom Sarah will bear to you by this time next year." [22]When he had finished speaking with Abraham, God went up from him.

[23]On that very day Abraham took his son Ishmael and all those born in his household or bought with his money, every male in his household, and circumcised them, as God told him. [24]Abraham was ninety-nine years old when he was circumcised, [25]and his son Ishmael was thirteen; [26]Abraham and his son Ishmael were both circumcised on that same day. [27]And every male in Abraham's household, including those born in his household or bought from a foreigner, was circumcised with him.

The Three Visitors

18 The LORD appeared to Abraham near the great trees of Mamre while he was sitting at the entrance to his tent in the heat of the day. [2]Abraham looked up and

---

[a]11 *Ishmael* means *God hears.*   [b]12 Or *live to the east / of*   [c]13 Or *seen the back of*   [d]14 *Beer Lahai Roi* means *well of the Living One who sees me.*   [e]1 Hebrew *El-Shaddai*   [f]5 *Abram* means *exalted father.*   [g]5 *Abraham* means *father of many.*   [h]19 *Isaac* means *he laughs.*

saw three men standing nearby. When he saw them, he hurried from the entrance of his tent to meet them and bowed low to the ground.

3He said, "If I have found favor in your eyes, my lord,*a* do not pass your servant by. **4**Let a little water be brought, and then you may all wash your feet and rest under this tree. **5**Let me get you something to eat, so you can be refreshed and then go on your way—now that you have come to your servant."

"Very well," they answered, "do as you say."

6So Abraham hurried into the tent to Sarah. "Quick," he said, "get three seahs*b* of fine flour and knead it and bake some bread."

a3 Or *O Lord*   *b6* That is, probably about 20 quarts (about 22 liters)

Abraham, Isaac, Jacob, and You

DAILY INSIGHT

MONDAY

Passage:
Genesis 17:1–8

Verse:
Genesis 17:7

For many years, there were two large portraits that hung in my parents' home: one was of my paternal grandfather and one was of my maternal grand-father. Both of these were godly men—full-time farmers, in order to keep bread on the table, and full-time parish ministers.

No two men could have been more dissimilar. Grandpa Wolgemuth was an immaculate, focused, intense man. One of the most prominent rooms in his home was his study. The walls in this familiar room were lined with biblical commentaries and reference books, biographies of great missionaries, and other inspirational volumes. His car was never dirty. I can still see him headed toward the barn with a single bucket of water to wash it. Thick, black eyebrows and furrowed crevasses across his forehead let us know that he was on a mission. He embodied hard work and the serious business of life.

Grandpa Dourte was in love with life. His laughter filled every room of their home. Music from his harmonica cheered us for part of the day; his humming and silly rhymes took care of the rest. The two most memorable places in his home were the parlor with the player piano—he loved music—and his workshop in the shed—he loved building things.

And, like Grandpa Wolgemuth, this man loved God. His blue eyes would fill with tears as he quoted something from the Psalms by heart.

How well I remember these two men. As a young boy, I studied their every move,

I listened to their voices, and I believed what they believed. And why shouldn't I have? They were for me what the Bible calls "patriarchs." These were men who started a whole generation of offspring, men who set the pace for dozens of others who would follow—including me.

In today's passage, we read that God promised Abram that some day his descendants would be greatly multiplied. Then God sealed his promise by changing Abram's name (meaning "exalted father") to Abraham (meaning "father of nations"). Imagine how this news, coupled with God's promise, must have affected Abraham.

You and I are dads. Someday our children will have children. Then they will have children who will have children. And every one of these people will know us, either because they remember us or because they hear stories about us from others. In a word, we're patriarchs to a whole generation.

Who we are, the words we speak, how we treat others, and what is truly important to us will become common knowledge to many, many people. Some of those people will even say that they inherited certain character traits from us. What an awesome thing this is!

This might be a good day for us to begin to see ourselves in the light of those who are to follow in our footsteps. Who we are today will become a legacy for others to follow tomorrow.

For your next devotional reading, go to page 27.

[7]Then he ran to the herd and selected a choice, tender calf and gave it to a servant, who hurried to prepare it. [8]He then brought some curds and milk and the calf that had been prepared, and set these before them. While they ate, he stood near them under a tree.

[9]"Where is your wife Sarah?" they asked him.

"There, in the tent," he said.

[10]Then the LORD[a] said, "I will surely return to you about this time next year, and Sarah your wife will have a son."

Now Sarah was listening at the entrance to the tent, which was behind him. [11]Abraham and Sarah were already old and well advanced in years, and Sarah was past the age of childbearing. [12]So Sarah laughed to herself as she thought, "After I am worn out and my master[b] is old, will I now have this pleasure?"

[13]Then the LORD said to Abraham, "Why did Sarah laugh and say, 'Will I really have a child, now that I am old?' [14]Is anything too hard for the LORD? I will return to you at the appointed time next year and Sarah will have a son."

[15]Sarah was afraid, so she lied and said, "I did not laugh."

But he said, "Yes, you did laugh."

Abraham Pleads for Sodom

[16]When the men got up to leave, they looked down toward Sodom, and Abraham walked along with them to see them on their way. [17]Then the LORD said, "Shall I hide from Abraham what I am about to do? [18]Abraham will surely become a great and powerful nation, and all nations on earth will be blessed through him. [19]For I have chosen him, so that he will direct his children and his household after him to keep the way of the LORD by doing what is right and just, so that the LORD will bring about for Abraham what he has promised him."

[20]Then the LORD said, "The outcry against Sodom and Gomorrah is so great and their sin so grievous [21]that I will go down and see if what they have done is as bad as the outcry that has reached me. If not, I will know."

[22]The men turned away and went toward Sodom, but Abraham remained standing before the LORD.[c] [23]Then Abraham approached him and said: "Will you sweep away the righteous with the wicked? [24]What if there are fifty righteous people in the city? Will you really sweep it away and not spare[d] the place for the sake of the fifty righteous people in it? [25]Far be it from you to do such a thing—to kill the righteous with the wicked, treating the righteous and the wicked alike. Far be it from you! Will not the Judge[e] of all the earth do right?"

[26]The LORD said, "If I find fifty righteous people in the city of Sodom, I will spare the whole place for their sake."

[27]Then Abraham spoke up again: "Now that I have been so bold as to speak to the Lord, though I am nothing but dust and ashes, [28]what if the number of the righteous is five less than fifty? Will you destroy the whole city because of five people?"

"If I find forty-five there," he said, "I will not destroy it."

[29]Once again he spoke to him, "What if only forty are found there?"

He said, "For the sake of forty, I will not do it."

[30]Then he said, "May the Lord not be angry, but let me speak. What if only thirty can be found there?"

He answered, "I will not do it if I find thirty there."

[31]Abraham said, "Now that I have been so bold as to speak to the Lord, what if only twenty can be found there?"

He said, "For the sake of twenty, I will not destroy it."

[32]Then he said, "May the Lord not be angry, but let me speak just once more. What if only ten can be found there?"

He answered, "For the sake of ten, I will not destroy it."

[33]When the LORD had finished speaking with Abraham, he left, and Abraham returned home.

Sodom and Gomorrah Destroyed

19 The two angels arrived at Sodom in the evening, and Lot was sitting in the gateway of the city. When he saw them, he got up to meet them and bowed down with his face to the ground. [2]"My lords," he said, "please turn aside to your servant's house. You can wash your feet and spend the night and then go on your way early in the morning."

"No," they answered, "we will spend the night in the square."

---

[a]10 Hebrew Then he   [b]12 Or husband
[c]22 Masoretic Text; an ancient Hebrew scribal tradition but the LORD remained standing before Abraham   [d]24 Or forgive; also in verse 26
[e]25 Or Ruler

³But he insisted so strongly that they did go with him and entered his house. He prepared a meal for them, baking bread without yeast, and they ate. ⁴Before they had gone to bed, all the men from every part of the city of Sodom—both young and old—surrounded the house. ⁵They called to Lot, "Where are the men who came to you tonight? Bring them out to us so that we can have sex with them."

⁶Lot went outside to meet them and shut the door behind him ⁷and said, "No, my friends. Don't do this wicked thing. ⁸Look, I have two daughters who have never slept with a man. Let me bring them out to you, and you can do what you like with them. But don't do anything to these men, for they have come under the protection of my roof."

⁹"Get out of our way," they replied. And they said, "This fellow came here as an alien, and now he wants to play the judge! We'll treat you worse than them." They kept bringing pressure on Lot and moved forward to break down the door.

¹⁰But the men inside reached out and pulled Lot back into the house and shut the door. ¹¹Then they struck the men who were at the door of the house, young and old, with blindness so that they could not find the door.

¹²The two men said to Lot, "Do you have anyone else here—sons-in-law, sons or daughters, or anyone else in the city who belongs to you? Get them out of here, ¹³because we are going to destroy this place. The outcry to the LORD against its people is so great that he has sent us to destroy it."

¹⁴So Lot went out and spoke to his sons-in-law, who were pledged to marry*a* his daughters. He said, "Hurry and get out of this place, because the LORD is about to destroy the city!" But his sons-in-law thought he was joking.

¹⁵With the coming of dawn, the angels urged Lot, saying, "Hurry! Take your wife and your two daughters who are here, or you will be swept away when the city is punished."

¹⁶When he hesitated, the men grasped his hand and the hands of his wife and of his two daughters and led them safely out of the city, for the LORD was merciful to them. ¹⁷As soon as they had brought them out, one of them said, "Flee for your lives! Don't look back, and don't stop anywhere in the plain! Flee to the mountains or you will be swept away!"

¹⁸But Lot said to them, "No, my lords,*b*

please! ¹⁹Your*c* servant has found favor in your*c* eyes, and you*c* have shown great kindness to me in sparing my life. But I can't flee to the mountains; this disaster will overtake me, and I'll die. ²⁰Look, here is a town near enough to run to, and it is small. Let me flee to it—it is very small, isn't it? Then my life will be spared."

²¹He said to him, "Very well, I will grant this request too; I will not overthrow the town you speak of. ²²But flee there quickly, because I cannot do anything until you reach it." (That is why the town was called Zoar.*d*)

²³By the time Lot reached Zoar, the sun had risen over the land. ²⁴Then the LORD rained down burning sulfur on Sodom and Gomorrah—from the LORD out of the heavens. ²⁵Thus he overthrew those cities and the entire plain, including all those living in the cities—and also the vegetation in the land. ²⁶But Lot's wife looked back, and she became a pillar of salt.

²⁷Early the next morning Abraham got up and returned to the place where he had stood before the LORD. ²⁸He looked down toward Sodom and Gomorrah, toward all the land of the plain, and he saw dense smoke rising from the land, like smoke from a furnace.

²⁹So when God destroyed the cities of the plain, he remembered Abraham, and he brought Lot out of the catastrophe that overthrew the cities where Lot had lived.

Lot and His Daughters

³⁰Lot and his two daughters left Zoar and settled in the mountains, for he was afraid to stay in Zoar. He and his two daughters lived in a cave. ³¹One day the older daughter said to the younger, "Our father is old, and there is no man around here to lie with us, as is the custom all over the earth. ³²Let's get our father to drink wine and then lie with him and preserve our family line through our father."

³³That night they got their father to drink wine, and the older daughter went in and lay with him. He was not aware of it when she lay down or when she got up.

³⁴The next day the older daughter said to the younger, "Last night I lay with my father. Let's get him to drink wine again tonight, and you go in and lie with him so we can preserve our family line through

---

a14 Or *were married to*   *b18* Or *No, Lord*; or *No, my lord*   *c19* The Hebrew is singular.   *d22 Zoar* means *small.*

our father." ³⁵So they got their father to drink wine that night also, and the younger daughter went and lay with him. Again he was not aware of it when she lay down or when she got up.

³⁶So both of Lot's daughters became pregnant by their father. ³⁷The older daughter had a son, and she named him Moabᵃ; he is the father of the Moabites of today. ³⁸The younger daughter also had a son, and she named him Ben-Ammiᵇ; he is the father of the Ammonites of today.

Abraham and Abimelech

20 Now Abraham moved on from there into the region of the Negev and lived between Kadesh and Shur. For a while he stayed in Gerar, ²and there Abraham said of his wife Sarah, "She is my sister." Then Abimelech king of Gerar sent for Sarah and took her.

³But God came to Abimelech in a dream one night and said to him, "You are as good as dead because of the woman you have taken; she is a married woman."

⁴Now Abimelech had not gone near her, so he said, "Lord, will you destroy an innocent nation? ⁵Did he not say to me, 'She is my sister,' and didn't she also say, 'He is my brother'? I have done this with a clear conscience and clean hands."

⁶Then God said to him in the dream, "Yes, I know you did this with a clear conscience, and so I have kept you from sinning against me. That is why I did not let you touch her. ⁷Now return the man's wife, for he is a prophet, and he will pray for you and you will live. But if you do not return her, you may be sure that you and all yours will die."

⁸Early the next morning Abimelech summoned all his officials, and when he told them all that had happened, they were very much afraid. ⁹Then Abimelech called Abraham in and said, "What have you done to us? How have I wronged you that you have brought such great guilt upon me and my kingdom? You have done things to me that should not be done." ¹⁰And Abimelech asked Abraham, "What was your reason for doing this?"

¹¹Abraham replied, "I said to myself, 'There is surely no fear of God in this place, and they will kill me because of my wife.' ¹²Besides, she really is my sister, the daughter of my father though not of my mother; and she became my wife. ¹³And when God had me wander from my father's household, I said to her, 'This is how you can show your love to me: Everywhere we go, say of me, "He is my brother." ' "

¹⁴Then Abimelech brought sheep and cattle and male and female slaves and gave them to Abraham, and he returned Sarah his wife to him. ¹⁵And Abimelech said, "My land is before you; live wherever you like."

¹⁶To Sarah he said, "I am giving your brother a thousand shekelsᶜ of silver. This is to cover the offense against you before all who are with you; you are completely vindicated."

¹⁷Then Abraham prayed to God, and God healed Abimelech, his wife and his slave girls so they could have children again, ¹⁸for the LORD had closed up every womb in Abimelech's household because of Abraham's wife Sarah.

The Birth of Isaac

21 Now the LORD was gracious to Sarah as he had said, and the LORD did for Sarah what he had promised. ²Sarah became pregnant and bore a son to Abraham in his old age, at the very time God had promised him. ³Abraham gave the name Isaacᵈ to the son Sarah bore him. ⁴When his son Isaac was eight days old, Abraham circumcised him, as God commanded him. ⁵Abraham was a hundred years old when his son Isaac was born to him.

⁶Sarah said, "God has brought me laughter, and everyone who hears about this will laugh with me." ⁷And she added, "Who would have said to Abraham that Sarah would nurse children? Yet I have borne him a son in his old age."

Hagar and Ishmael Sent Away

⁸The child grew and was weaned, and on the day Isaac was weaned Abraham held a great feast. ⁹But Sarah saw that the son whom Hagar the Egyptian had borne to Abraham was mocking, ¹⁰and she said to Abraham, "Get rid of that slave woman and her son, for that slave woman's son will never share in the inheritance with my son Isaac."

¹¹The matter distressed Abraham greatly because it concerned his son.

ᵃ37 *Moab* sounds like the Hebrew for *from father*. ᵇ38 *Ben-Ammi* means *son of my people*.   ᶜ16 That is, about 25 pounds (about 11.5 kilograms) ᵈ3 *Isaac* means *he laughs*.

¹²But God said to him, "Do not be so distressed about the boy and your maidservant. Listen to whatever Sarah tells you, because it is through Isaac that your offspring[a] will be reckoned. ¹³I will make the son of the maidservant into a nation also, because he is your offspring."

¹⁴Early the next morning Abraham took some food and a skin of water and gave them to Hagar. He set them on her shoulders and then sent her off with the boy. She went on her way and wandered in the desert of Beersheba.

¹⁵When the water in the skin was gone, she put the boy under one of the bushes. ¹⁶Then she went off and sat down nearby, about a bowshot away, for she thought, "I cannot watch the boy die." And as she sat there nearby, she[b] began to sob.

¹⁷God heard the boy crying, and the angel of God called to Hagar from heaven and said to her, "What is the matter, Hagar? Do not be afraid; God has heard the boy crying as he lies there. ¹⁸Lift the boy up and take him by the hand, for I will make him into a great nation."

¹⁹Then God opened her eyes and she saw a well of water. So she went and filled the skin with water and gave the boy a drink.

²⁰God was with the boy as he grew up. He lived in the desert and became an

a12 Or seed   b16 Hebrew; Septuagint the child

The Day that Changed Your Life Forever

DAILY INSIGHT

Our basement was full of high school kids. My wife, Bobbie, and I were in full-time youth ministry, and I was conducting a Bible study with about forty-five fired-up young people. It was great.

Then, right in the middle of my saying something quite profound, my wife's college-age sister interrupted. She walked down the stairs, stepped toward me through the kids crowded on the floor, and whispered something in my ear. Noticeably perturbed by this thoughtless interruption, I remember thinking to myself, *This had better be good*. And "good" it was. Becky's hushed words gripped me. She could have shouted them and they wouldn't have had any more impact. "Bobbie's in labor upstairs. You've got to get her to the hospital. The baby's on its way."

I announced the message to the teenagers who cheered the news, then scurried to move their cars from my driveway.

My life, from that moment until today, has not been the same. Several weeks after we brought our baby daughter home, I remember thinking to myself, *This is incredible. I can't believe it. I'm a dad. I'll be a dad for the rest of my life!*

You know that feeling, don't you? It's pretty overwhelming, isn't it?

TUESDAY

Passage:
Genesis 21:1–7

Verse:
Genesis 21:6

Today's text tells of the moment Abraham and Sarah became parents. And although they were much older than you and I when we became dads, the excitement level has a familiar ring to it. We know this for sure because they named their brand new son "Isaac," which means "he laughs." What a great name. Sarah celebrates with a wonderful statement in 21:6, giving God personal credit for bringing such joy to their home.

You and I know all about this. Our lives have been indescribably blessed with a little one (or more than one!) who has proven his or her ability to transform our adult sophistication and poise into a face-making, baby-talking embarrassment—a grown-up who tumbles on the living room floor or holds a tiny tea cup, pretending to lavish its delicious contents. It's laughable to realize what we've become. And we don't care what others might say. We are dads, and it's time to celebrate.

Today would be a good day to thank God for bringing such laughter into your life. Praise him for the miracle and the blessing of a baby; and not just *any* baby, but one of your very own.

For your next devotional reading, go to page 29.

archer. ²¹While he was living in the Desert of Paran, his mother got a wife for him from Egypt.

The Treaty at Beersheba

²²At that time Abimelech and Phicol the commander of his forces said to Abraham, "God is with you in everything you do. ²³Now swear to me here before God that you will not deal falsely with me or my children or my descendants. Show to me and the country where you are living as an alien the same kindness I have shown to you."

²⁴Abraham said, "I swear it."

²⁵Then Abraham complained to Abimelech about a well of water that Abimelech's servants had seized. ²⁶But Abimelech said, "I don't know who has done this. You did not tell me, and I heard about it only today."

²⁷So Abraham brought sheep and cattle and gave them to Abimelech, and the two men made a treaty. ²⁸Abraham set apart seven ewe lambs from the flock, ²⁹and Abimelech asked Abraham, "What is the meaning of these seven ewe lambs you have set apart by themselves?"

³⁰He replied, "Accept these seven lambs from my hand as a witness that I dug this well."

³¹So that place was called Beersheba,ᵃ because the two men swore an oath there.

³²After the treaty had been made at Beersheba, Abimelech and Phicol the commander of his forces returned to the land of the Philistines. ³³Abraham planted a tamarisk tree in Beersheba, and there he called upon the name of the LORD, the Eternal God. ³⁴And Abraham stayed in the land of the Philistines for a long time.

Abraham Tested

22 Some time later God tested Abraham. He said to him, "Abraham!"

ᵃ31 *Beersheba* can mean *well of seven* or *well of the oath.*

Listen. Obey. Period.
Abraham, the Obedient Father

DADS
IN THE
BIBLE

"Take your son, your only son, Isaac, whom you love, and . . . sacrifice him there as a burnt offering" (22:2).

Text: Genesis 22

In one way, Abraham was exactly like you and me: There wasn't anything in the world he wouldn't have done for his precious son. He and Sarah had waited a long, long time for this boy to be born. In fact, when he arrived, the child had brought such delight to his parents that they had named him Isaac ("he laughs"). As Abraham and Sarah's only child, Isaac was the sole heir, the apple of his daddy's eye.

That's when God stepped up with what seemed like a cruel assignment for this elderly father. "Kill your boy," God told an astonished Abraham. "Sacrifice him to me." What an incomprehensible request! But Isaac's dad was willing to obey his heavenly Father, regardless of the message. He had acted in faith before, and he would do it again this time.

The story of Abraham's willingness to sacrifice his son is not only about the incredible tug of a dad's heart toward his child. It's also about a man who knew that obedience was more important than the potential losses incurred in the sacrifice.

The story of the Bible is filled with this principle: If you want to come into God's presence, everything else—even your most precious possession—has to be offered up to him. When the Israelites brought an offering from the flock to lay on the altar, it had to be a perfect one. A second-stringer wasn't good enough. If this sacrifice wasn't painful, it wasn't a sacrifice at all. God was so adamant about this principle that he was willing to lay his own unblemished Son on the altar.

Abraham is a great example for us. He knew these things and would have wanted us to learn them, too: *God must be first; when I hear his voice, I must obey. Nothing else really matters. Period.*

For a complete listing of Dads in the Bible, turn to page 1434.

"Here I am," he replied. ²Then God said, "Take your son, your only son, Isaac, whom you love, and go to the region of Moriah. Sacrifice him there as a burnt offering on one of the mountains I will tell you about."

³Early the next morning Abraham got up and saddled his donkey. He took with him two of his servants and his son Isaac. When he had cut enough wood for the burnt offering, he set out for the place God had told him about. ⁴On the third day Abraham looked up and saw the place in the distance. ⁵He said to his servants, "Stay here with the donkey while I and the boy go over there. We will worship and then we will come back to you."

⁶Abraham took the wood for the burnt offering and placed it on his son Isaac, and he himself carried the fire and the knife. As the two of them went on together, ⁷Isaac spoke up and said to his father Abraham, "Father?"

"Yes, my son?" Abraham replied.

God's Wake-Up Call

DAILY INSIGHT

WEDNESDAY

Passage:
Genesis 22:1–18

Verse:
Genesis 22:12

Have you ever wondered what it would be like to be the person at the hotel who makes the early morning telephone calls to wake people up? Ordinarily, we are embarrassed when we call someone, rudely disrupting their peaceful sleep.

"Did I wake you up?" you ask your friend who's desperately trying to mask the fact that only moments before, he was completely comatose.

"No, that's okay," your friend diplomatically answers. "I had to get up to answer the phone anyway."

Yesterday we celebrated the miracle of the birth of your child. But today, like the lucky person who's assigned to stir everyone's luxurious slumber, it's time for God to get our attention.

Abraham had literally waited a lifetime for the birth of Isaac. He must have been thrilled beyond description. Can you imagine how he spontaneously told everyone—whether they wanted to hear it or not—how this boy was born to such an old man? How Abraham must have proudly pointed out young Isaac to anyone who would listen, "See that boy over there? That's my boy."

Then came the contemptuous "ringing phone" from the heavens. Go back and read verse two … "Take your son … whom you love … sacrifice him … as a burnt offering." What kinds of thoughts must have crashed through Abraham's conscious mind? *Kill my son? Why? How?* This must have dazed him—gripped his heart like nothing ever had before.

The text doesn't give us any clues to what was actually going on in Abraham's mind, but as dads, we can only imagine the trauma and the protests: "I've spent my life protecting this child, and you want me to kill him?" "I'd give my life for him, and you want me to snuff his out?"

Why did God put Abraham through this horrific experience? Was this some sort of cruel celestial prank? No, actually it wasn't.

There's a principle that runs throughout this Bible that cannot be overlooked: Everything we have—our homes, our families, even our own lives—is a miraculous gift to us from our heavenly Father. "Children [are] a reward from him" (Psalm 127:3b). "You are not your own; you were bought at a price" (1 Corinthians 6:19b, 20a). These two passages make this fact abundantly clear.

We have in this story a gripping sequence that gives us three snapshots of Abraham as a dad: proud—Have you seen my son's latest trophy?; bewildered—What does this mean?; and grateful—Thank you, God, for your miraculous gift of this boy.

Today's wake-up call lets us know that our children are on loan to us from the Creator of the universe. Our charge as dads is to take excellent care of his treasured property.

For your next devotional reading, go to page 38.

"The fire and wood are here," Isaac said, "but where is the lamb for the burnt offering?"

[8]Abraham answered, "God himself will provide the lamb for the burnt offering, my son." And the two of them went on together.

[9]When they reached the place God had told him about, Abraham built an altar there and arranged the wood on it. He bound his son Isaac and laid him on the altar, on top of the wood. [10]Then he reached out his hand and took the knife to slay his son. [11]But the angel of the LORD called out to him from heaven, "Abraham! Abraham!"

"Here I am," he replied.

[12]"Do not lay a hand on the boy," he said. "Do not do anything to him. Now I know that you fear God, because you have not withheld from me your son, your only son."

[13]Abraham looked up and there in a thicket he saw a ram[a] caught by its horns. He went over and took the ram and sacrificed it as a burnt offering instead of his son. [14]So Abraham called that place The LORD Will Provide. And to this day it is said, "On the mountain of the LORD it will be provided."

[15]The angel of the LORD called to Abraham from heaven a second time [16]and said, "I swear by myself, declares the LORD, that because you have done this and have not withheld your son, your only son, [17]I will surely bless you and make your descendants as numerous as the stars in the sky and as the sand on the seashore. Your descendants will take possession of the cities of their enemies, [18]and through your offspring[b] all nations on earth will be blessed, because you have obeyed me."

[19]Then Abraham returned to his servants, and they set off together for Beersheba. And Abraham stayed in Beersheba.

Nahor's Sons

[20]Some time later Abraham was told, "Milcah is also a mother; she has borne sons to your brother Nahor: [21]Uz the firstborn, Buz his brother, Kemuel (the father of Aram), [22]Kesed, Hazo, Pildash, Jidlaph and Bethuel." [23]Bethuel became the father of Rebekah. Milcah bore these eight sons to Abraham's brother Nahor. [24]His concubine, whose name was Reumah, also had sons: Tebah, Gaham, Tahash and Maacah.

The Death of Sarah

23 Sarah lived to be a hundred and twenty-seven years old. [2]She died at Kiriath Arba (that is, Hebron) in the land of Canaan, and Abraham went to mourn for Sarah and to weep over her.

[3]Then Abraham rose from beside his dead wife and spoke to the Hittites.[c] He said, [4]"I am an alien and a stranger among you. Sell me some property for a burial site here so I can bury my dead."

[5]The Hittites replied to Abraham, [6]"Sir, listen to us. You are a mighty prince among us. Bury your dead in the choicest of our tombs. None of us will refuse you his tomb for burying your dead."

[7]Then Abraham rose and bowed down before the people of the land, the Hittites. [8]He said to them, "If you are willing to let me bury my dead, then listen to me and intercede with Ephron son of Zohar on my behalf [9]so he will sell me the cave of Machpelah, which belongs to him and is at the end of his field. Ask him to sell it to me for the full price as a burial site among you."

[10]Ephron the Hittite was sitting among his people and he replied to Abraham in the hearing of all the Hittites who had come to the gate of his city. [11]"No, my lord," he said. "Listen to me; I give[d] you the field, and I give[d] you the cave that is in it. I give[d] it to you in the presence of my people. Bury your dead."

[12]Again Abraham bowed down before the people of the land [13]and he said to Ephron in their hearing, "Listen to me, if you will. I will pay the price of the field. Accept it from me so I can bury my dead there."

[14]Ephron answered Abraham, [15]"Listen to me, my lord; the land is worth four hundred shekels[e] of silver, but what is that between me and you? Bury your dead."

[16]Abraham agreed to Ephron's terms and weighed out for him the price he had named in the hearing of the Hittites: four hundred shekels of silver, according to the weight current among the merchants. [17]So Ephron's field in Machpelah near Mamre—both the field and the cave in it, and all the trees within the borders of the field—was deeded [18]to Abraham as his

---

[a]13 Many manuscripts of the Masoretic Text, Samaritan Pentateuch, Septuagint and Syriac; most manuscripts of the Masoretic Text *a ram behind him*   [b]18 Or *seed*   [c]3 Or *the sons of Heth*; also in verses 5, 7, 10, 16, 18 and 20   [d]11 Or *sell*   [e]15 That is, about 10 pounds (about 4.5 kilograms)

property in the presence of all the Hittites who had come to the gate of the city. ¹⁹Afterward Abraham buried his wife Sarah in the cave in the field of Machpelah near Mamre (which is at Hebron) in the land of Canaan. ²⁰So the field and the cave in it were deeded to Abraham by the Hittites as a burial site.

Isaac and Rebekah

24 Abraham was now old and well advanced in years, and the LORD had blessed him in every way. ²He said to the chief[a] servant in his household, the one in charge of all that he had, "Put your hand under my thigh. ³I want you to swear by the LORD, the God of heaven and the God of earth, that you will not get a wife for my son from the daughters of the Canaanites, among whom I am living, ⁴but will go to my country and my own relatives and get a wife for my son Isaac."

⁵The servant asked him, "What if the woman is unwilling to come back with me to this land? Shall I then take your son back to the country you came from?"

⁶"Make sure that you do not take my son back there," Abraham said. ⁷"The LORD, the God of heaven, who brought me out of my father's household and my native land and who spoke to me and promised me on oath, saying, 'To your offspring[b] I will give this land'—he will send his angel before you so that you can get a wife for my son from there. ⁸If the woman is unwilling to come back with you, then you will be released from this oath of mine. Only do not take my son back there." ⁹So the servant put his hand under the thigh of his master Abraham and swore an oath to him concerning this matter.

¹⁰Then the servant took ten of his master's camels and left, taking with him all kinds of good things from his master. He set out for Aram Naharaim[c] and made his way to the town of Nahor. ¹¹He had the camels kneel down near the well outside the town; it was toward evening, the time the women go out to draw water.

¹²Then he prayed, "O LORD, God of my master Abraham, give me success today, and show kindness to my master Abraham. ¹³See, I am standing beside this spring, and the daughters of the townspeople are coming out to draw water. ¹⁴May it be that when I say to a girl, 'Please let down your jar that I may have a drink,' and she says, 'Drink, and I'll water your camels too'—let her be the one you have chosen for your servant Isaac. By this I will know that you have shown kindness to my master."

¹⁵Before he had finished praying, Rebekah came out with her jar on her shoulder. She was the daughter of Bethuel son of Milcah, who was the wife of Abraham's brother Nahor. ¹⁶The girl was very beautiful, a virgin; no man had ever lain with her. She went down to the spring, filled her jar and came up again.

¹⁷The servant hurried to meet her and said, "Please give me a little water from your jar."

¹⁸"Drink, my lord," she said, and quickly lowered the jar to her hands and gave him a drink.

¹⁹After she had given him a drink, she said, "I'll draw water for your camels too, until they have finished drinking." ²⁰So she quickly emptied her jar into the trough, ran back to the well to draw more water, and drew enough for all his camels. ²¹Without saying a word, the man watched her closely to learn whether or not the LORD had made his journey successful.

²²When the camels had finished drinking, the man took out a gold nose ring weighing a beka[d] and two gold bracelets weighing ten shekels.[e] ²³Then he asked, "Whose daughter are you? Please tell me, is there room in your father's house for us to spend the night?"

²⁴She answered him, "I am the daughter of Bethuel, the son that Milcah bore to Nahor." ²⁵And she added, "We have plenty of straw and fodder, as well as room for you to spend the night."

²⁶Then the man bowed down and worshiped the LORD, ²⁷saying, "Praise be to the LORD, the God of my master Abraham, who has not abandoned his kindness and faithfulness to my master. As for me, the LORD has led me on the journey to the house of my master's relatives."

²⁸The girl ran and told her mother's household about these things. ²⁹Now Rebekah had a brother named Laban, and he hurried out to the man at the spring. ³⁰As soon as he had seen the nose ring, and the bracelets on his sister's arms, and had heard Rebekah tell what the man said to her, he went out to the man and

---

[a]2 Or *oldest*   [b]7 Or *seed*   [c]10 That is, Northwest Mesopotamia   [d]22 That is, about 1/5 ounce (about 5.5 grams)   [e]22 That is, about 4 ounces (about 110 grams)

found him standing by the camels near the spring. **31**"Come, you who are blessed by the LORD," he said. "Why are you standing out here? I have prepared the house and a place for the camels."

32So the man went to the house, and the camels were unloaded. Straw and fodder were brought for the camels, and water for him and his men to wash their feet. **33**Then food was set before him, but he said, "I will not eat until I have told you what I have to say."

"Then tell us," Laban said.

34So he said, "I am Abraham's servant. **35**The LORD has blessed my master abundantly, and he has become wealthy. He has given him sheep and cattle, silver and gold, menservants and maidservants, and camels and donkeys. **36**My master's wife Sarah has borne him a son in her*a* old age, and he has given him everything he owns. **37**And my master made me swear an oath, and said, 'You must not get a wife for my son from the daughters of the Canaanites, in whose land I live, **38**but go to my father's family and to my own clan, and get a wife for my son.'

39"Then I asked my master, 'What if the woman will not come back with me?'

40"He replied, 'The LORD, before whom I have walked, will send his angel with you and make your journey a success, so that you can get a wife for my son from my own clan and from my father's family. **41**Then, when you go to my clan, you will be released from my oath even if they refuse to give her to you—you will be released from my oath.'

42"When I came to the spring today, I said, 'O LORD, God of my master Abraham, if you will, please grant success to the journey on which I have come. **43**See, I am standing beside this spring; if a maiden comes out to draw water and I say to her, "Please let me drink a little water from your jar," **44**and if she says to me, "Drink, and I'll draw water for your camels too," let her be the one the LORD has chosen for my master's son.'

45"Before I finished praying in my heart, Rebekah came out, with her jar on her shoulder. She went down to the spring and drew water, and I said to her, 'Please give me a drink.'

46"She quickly lowered her jar from her shoulder and said, 'Drink, and I'll water your camels too.' So I drank, and she watered the camels also.

47"I asked her, 'Whose daughter are you?'

"She said, 'The daughter of Bethuel son of Nahor, whom Milcah bore to him.'

"Then I put the ring in her nose and the bracelets on her arms, **48**and I bowed down and worshiped the LORD. I praised the LORD, the God of my master Abraham, who had led me on the right road to get the granddaughter of my master's brother for his son. **49**Now if you will show kindness and faithfulness to my master, tell me; and if not, tell me, so I may know which way to turn."

50Laban and Bethuel answered, "This is from the LORD; we can say nothing to you one way or the other. **51**Here is Rebekah; take her and go, and let her become the wife of your master's son, as the LORD has directed."

52When Abraham's servant heard what they said, he bowed down to the ground before the LORD. **53**Then the servant brought out gold and silver jewelry and articles of clothing and gave them to Rebekah; he also gave costly gifts to her brother and to her mother. **54**Then he and the men who were with him ate and drank and spent the night there.

When they got up the next morning, he said, "Send me on my way to my master."

55But her brother and her mother replied, "Let the girl remain with us ten days or so; then you*b* may go."

56But he said to them, "Do not detain me, now that the LORD has granted success to my journey. Send me on my way so I may go to my master."

57Then they said, "Let's call the girl and ask her about it." **58**So they called Rebekah and asked her, "Will you go with this man?"

"I will go," she said.

59So they sent their sister Rebekah on her way, along with her nurse and Abraham's servant and his men. **60**And they blessed Rebekah and said to her,

"Our sister, may you increase
    to thousands upon thousands;
may your offspring possess
    the gates of their enemies."

61Then Rebekah and her maids got ready and mounted their camels and went back with the man. So the servant took Rebekah and left.

62Now Isaac had come from Beer Lahai Roi, for he was living in the Negev. **63**He went out to the field one evening to

a36 Or *his*   *b55* Or *she*

meditate,[a] and as he looked up, he saw camels approaching. [64]Rebekah also looked up and saw Isaac. She got down from her camel [65]and asked the servant, "Who is that man in the field coming to meet us?"

"He is my master," the servant answered. So she took her veil and covered herself.

[66]Then the servant told Isaac all he had done. [67]Isaac brought her into the tent of his mother Sarah, and he married Rebekah. So she became his wife, and he loved her; and Isaac was comforted after his mother's death.

The Death of Abraham

25 Abraham took[b] another wife, whose name was Keturah. [2]She bore him Zimran, Jokshan, Medan, Midian, Ishbak and Shuah. [3]Jokshan was the father of Sheba and Dedan; the descendants of Dedan were the Asshurites, the Letushites and the Leummites. [4]The sons of Midian were Ephah, Epher, Hanoch, Abida and Eldaah. All these were descendants of Keturah.

[5]Abraham left everything he owned to Isaac. [6]But while he was still living, he gave gifts to the sons of his concubines and sent them away from his son Isaac to the land of the east.

[7]Altogether, Abraham lived a hundred and seventy-five years. [8]Then Abraham breathed his last and died at a good old age, an old man and full of years; and he was gathered to his people. [9]His sons Isaac and Ishmael buried him in the cave of Machpelah near Mamre, in the field of Ephron son of Zohar the Hittite, [10]the field Abraham had bought from the Hittites.[c] There Abraham was buried with his wife Sarah. [11]After Abraham's death, God blessed his son Isaac, who then lived near Beer Lahai Roi.

Ishmael's Sons

[12]This is the account of Abraham's son Ishmael, whom Sarah's maidservant, Hagar the Egyptian, bore to Abraham.

[13]These are the names of the sons of Ishmael, listed in the order of their birth: Nebaioth the firstborn of Ishmael, Kedar, Adbeel, Mibsam, [14]Mishma, Dumah, Massa, [15]Hadad, Tema, Jetur, Naphish and Kedemah. [16]These were the sons of Ishmael, and these are the names of the twelve tribal rulers according to their settlements

and camps. [17]Altogether, Ishmael lived a hundred and thirty-seven years. He breathed his last and died, and he was gathered to his people. [18]His descendants settled in the area from Havilah to Shur, near the border of Egypt, as you go toward Asshur. And they lived in hostility toward[d] all their brothers.

Jacob and Esau

[19]This is the account of Abraham's son Isaac.

Abraham became the father of Isaac, [20]and Isaac was forty years old when he married Rebekah daughter of Bethuel the Aramean from Paddan Aram[e] and sister of Laban the Aramean.

[21]Isaac prayed to the LORD on behalf of his wife, because she was barren. The LORD answered his prayer, and his wife Rebekah became pregnant. [22]The babies jostled each other within her, and she said, "Why is this happening to me?" So she went to inquire of the LORD.

[23]The LORD said to her,

"Two nations are in your womb,
    and two peoples from within you will
    be separated;
one people will be stronger than the
    other,
    and the older will serve the younger."

[24]When the time came for her to give birth, there were twin boys in her womb. [25]The first to come out was red, and his whole body was like a hairy garment; so they named him Esau.[f] [26]After this, his brother came out, with his hand grasping Esau's heel; so he was named Jacob.[g] Isaac was sixty years old when Rebekah gave birth to them.

[27]The boys grew up, and Esau became a skillful hunter, a man of the open country, while Jacob was a quiet man, staying among the tents. [28]Isaac, who had a taste for wild game, loved Esau, but Rebekah loved Jacob.

[29]Once when Jacob was cooking some stew, Esau came in from the open country, famished. [30]He said to Jacob, "Quick, let me have some of that red stew! I'm

---

[a]63 The meaning of the Hebrew for this word is uncertain.   [b]1 Or *had taken*   [c]10 Or *the sons of Heth*   [d]18 Or *lived to the east of*   [e]20 That is, Northwest Mesopotamia   [f]25 *Esau* may mean *hairy*; he was also called Edom, which means *red*.   [g]26 *Jacob* means *he grasps the heel* (figuratively, *he deceives*).

famished!" (That is why he was also called Edom.[a])

[31]Jacob replied, "First sell me your birthright."

[32]"Look, I am about to die," Esau said. "What good is the birthright to me?"

[33]But Jacob said, "Swear to me first." So he swore an oath to him, selling his birthright to Jacob.

[34]Then Jacob gave Esau some bread and some lentil stew. He ate and drank, and then got up and left.

So Esau despised his birthright.

Isaac and Abimelech

26 Now there was a famine in the land— besides the earlier famine of Abraham's time—and Isaac went to Abimelech king of the Philistines in Gerar. [2]The LORD appeared to Isaac and said, "Do not go down to Egypt; live in the land where I tell you to live. [3]Stay in this land for a while, and I will be with you and will bless you. For to you and your descendants I will give all these lands and will confirm the oath I swore to your father Abraham. [4]I will make your descendants as numerous as the stars in the sky and will give them all these lands, and through your offspring[b] all nations on earth will be blessed, [5]because Abraham obeyed me and kept my requirements, my commands, my decrees and my laws." [6]So Isaac stayed in Gerar.

[7]When the men of that place asked him about his wife, he said, "She is my sister," because he was afraid to say, "She is my wife." He thought, "The men of this place might kill me on account of Rebekah, because she is beautiful."

[8]When Isaac had been there a long time, Abimelech king of the Philistines looked down from a window and saw Isaac caressing his wife Rebekah. [9]So Abimelech summoned Isaac and said, "She is really your wife! Why did you say, 'She is my sister'?"

Isaac answered him, "Because I thought I might lose my life on account of her."

[10]Then Abimelech said, "What is this you have done to us? One of the men might well have slept with your wife, and you would have brought guilt upon us."

[11]So Abimelech gave orders to all the people: "Anyone who molests this man or his wife shall surely be put to death."

[12]Isaac planted crops in that land and the same year reaped a hundredfold, because the LORD blessed him. [13]The man became rich, and his wealth continued to grow until he became very wealthy. [14]He had so many flocks and herds and servants that the Philistines envied him. [15]So all the wells that his father's servants had dug in the time of his father Abraham, the Philistines stopped up, filling them with earth.

[16]Then Abimelech said to Isaac, "Move away from us; you have become too powerful for us."

[17]So Isaac moved away from there and encamped in the Valley of Gerar and settled there. [18]Isaac reopened the wells that had been dug in the time of his father Abraham, which the Philistines had stopped up after Abraham died, and he gave them the same names his father had given them.

[19]Isaac's servants dug in the valley and discovered a well of fresh water there. [20]But the herdsmen of Gerar quarreled with Isaac's herdsmen and said, "The water is ours!" So he named the well Esek,[c] because they disputed with him. [21]Then they dug another well, but they quarreled over that one also; so he named it Sitnah.[d] [22]He moved on from there and dug another well, and no one quarreled over it. He named it Rehoboth,[e] saying, "Now the LORD has given us room and we will flourish in the land."

[23]From there he went up to Beersheba. [24]That night the LORD appeared to him and said, "I am the God of your father Abraham. Do not be afraid, for I am with you; I will bless you and will increase the number of your descendants for the sake of my servant Abraham."

[25]Isaac built an altar there and called on the name of the LORD. There he pitched his tent, and there his servants dug a well. [26]Meanwhile, Abimelech had come to him from Gerar, with Ahuzzath his personal adviser and Phicol the commander of his forces. [27]Isaac asked them, "Why have you come to me, since you were hostile to me and sent me away?"

[28]They answered, "We saw clearly that the LORD was with you; so we said, 'There ought to be a sworn agreement between us'—between us and you. Let us make a treaty with you [29]that you will do us no harm, just as we did not molest you but always treated you well and sent you away

---

[a]30 *Edom* means *red.*   [b]4 Or *seed*   [c]20 *Esek* means *dispute.*   [d]21 *Sitnah* means *opposition.*   [e]22 *Rehoboth* means *room.*

in peace. And now you are blessed by the LORD."

[30]Isaac then made a feast for them, and they ate and drank. [31]Early the next morning the men swore an oath to each other. Then Isaac sent them on their way, and they left him in peace.

[32]That day Isaac's servants came and told him about the well they had dug. They said, "We've found water!" [33]He called it Shibah,[a] and to this day the name of the town has been Beersheba.[b]

[34]When Esau was forty years old, he married Judith daughter of Beeri the Hittite, and also Basemath daughter of Elon the Hittite. [35]They were a source of grief to Isaac and Rebekah.

Jacob Gets Isaac's Blessing

27 When Isaac was old and his eyes were so weak that he could no longer see, he called for Esau his older son and said to him, "My son."

"Here I am," he answered.

[2]Isaac said, "I am now an old man and don't know the day of my death. [3]Now then, get your weapons—your quiver and bow—and go out to the open country to hunt some wild game for me. [4]Prepare me the kind of tasty food I like and bring it to me to eat, so that I may give you my blessing before I die."

[5]Now Rebekah was listening as Isaac spoke to his son Esau. When Esau left for the open country to hunt game and bring it back, [6]Rebekah said to her son Jacob, "Look, I overheard your father say to your brother Esau, [7]'Bring me some game and prepare me some tasty food to eat, so that I may give you my blessing in the presence of the LORD before I die.' [8]Now, my son, listen carefully and do what I tell you: [9]Go out to the flock and bring me two choice young goats, so I can prepare some

[a]33 *Shibah* can mean *oath* or *seven*.   [b]33 *Beersheba* can mean *well of the oath* or *well of seven*.

Duped by the Soup
Isaac, a Man of His Word

"Isaac trembled violently and said,
'Who was it, then, that hunted game and
brought it to me? . . . I blessed him—
and indeed he will be blessed!' " (27:33).

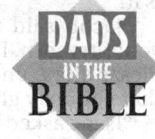

Text: Genesis 27

What do your words stand for? When you make a promise to someone, do you mean it? Or do you just move on to the next thing, hoping that if you fail to keep your promise that no one will notice? One of the powerful lessons to be learned from father Isaac is that when a man gives his word, it amounts to an unbreakable contract.

Isaac had two sons. Esau was the oldest, the first in line for his father's blessing . . . and for the inheritance. Jacob, the second son, was a conniver. With his mother's help, Jacob managed to wrest the blessing and the full inheritance from his older brother.

Esau, knowing nothing of this treachery, approached his elderly father to receive his due. At that moment, Isaac realized he had been deceived and "trembled violently" at the news. He had already given his blessing, a once-in-a-lifetime event, to Jacob. Esau wept out loud, something that tough, firstborn sons rarely do. But despite Esau's pleading, Isaac did not recant his promise to Jacob. He had given his word.

Was Isaac angry at Jacob for "pulling the wool" over his eyes? Absolutely. Did Isaac wish he could have taken his words back and given the blessing to Esau instead? Of course. But he refused to compromise.

Isaac was a man of his word. Jesus spoke to the same issue hundreds of years later to a large gathering that must have included many, many fathers. "Let your 'Yes' be 'Yes,' and your 'No,' 'No' " (Matthew 5:37).

On his deathbed, W.C. Fields' friends caught him reading a Bible. Knowing that Fields had lived his entire life as an agnostic, their queries were inevitable. "I'm looking for a loophole," was his reply. Sorry, W.C., God is a God of his word. You'll not find any loopholes here.

For a complete listing of Dads in the Bible, turn to page 1434.

tasty food for your father, just the way he likes it. ¹⁰Then take it to your father to eat, so that he may give you his blessing before he dies."

¹¹Jacob said to Rebekah his mother, "But my brother Esau is a hairy man, and I'm a man with smooth skin. ¹²What if my father touches me? I would appear to be tricking him and would bring down a curse on myself rather than a blessing."

¹³His mother said to him, "My son, let the curse fall on me. Just do what I say; go and get them for me."

¹⁴So he went and got them and brought them to his mother, and she prepared some tasty food, just the way his father liked it. ¹⁵Then Rebekah took the best clothes of Esau her older son, which she had in the house, and put them on her younger son Jacob. ¹⁶She also covered his hands and the smooth part of his neck with the goatskins. ¹⁷Then she handed to her son Jacob the tasty food and the bread she had made.

¹⁸He went to his father and said, "My father."

"Yes, my son," he answered. "Who is it?"

¹⁹Jacob said to his father, "I am Esau your firstborn. I have done as you told me. Please sit up and eat some of my game so that you may give me your blessing."

²⁰Isaac asked his son, "How did you find it so quickly, my son?"

"The LORD your God gave me success," he replied.

²¹Then Isaac said to Jacob, "Come near so I can touch you, my son, to know whether you really are my son Esau or not."

²²Jacob went close to his father Isaac, who touched him and said, "The voice is the voice of Jacob, but the hands are the hands of Esau." ²³He did not recognize him, for his hands were hairy like those of his brother Esau; so he blessed him. ²⁴"Are you really my son Esau?" he asked.

"I am," he replied.

²⁵Then he said, "My son, bring me some of your game to eat, so that I may give you my blessing."

Jacob brought it to him and he ate; and he brought some wine and he drank. ²⁶Then his father Isaac said to him, "Come here, my son, and kiss me."

²⁷So he went to him and kissed him. When Isaac caught the smell of his clothes, he blessed him and said,

"Ah, the smell of my son
    is like the smell of a field

that the LORD has blessed.
²⁸May God give you of heaven's dew
    and of earth's richness—
    an abundance of grain and new
        wine.
²⁹May nations serve you
    and peoples bow down to you.
Be lord over your brothers,
    and may the sons of your mother
        bow down to you.
May those who curse you be cursed
    and those who bless you be
        blessed."

³⁰After Isaac finished blessing him and Jacob had scarcely left his father's presence, his brother Esau came in from hunting. ³¹He too prepared some tasty food and brought it to his father. Then he said to him, "My father, sit up and eat some of my game, so that you may give me your blessing."

³²His father Isaac asked him, "Who are you?"

"I am your son," he answered, "your firstborn, Esau."

³³Isaac trembled violently and said, "Who was it, then, that hunted game and brought it to me? I ate it just before you came and I blessed him—and indeed he will be blessed!"

³⁴When Esau heard his father's words, he burst out with a loud and bitter cry and said to his father, "Bless me—me too, my father!"

³⁵But he said, "Your brother came deceitfully and took your blessing."

³⁶Esau said, "Isn't he rightly named Jacob^a? He has deceived me these two times: He took my birthright, and now he's taken my blessing!" Then he asked, "Haven't you reserved any blessing for me?"

³⁷Isaac answered Esau, "I have made him lord over you and have made all his relatives his servants, and I have sustained him with grain and new wine. So what can I possibly do for you, my son?"

³⁸Esau said to his father, "Do you have only one blessing, my father? Bless me too, my father!" Then Esau wept aloud.

³⁹His father Isaac answered him,

"Your dwelling will be
    away from the earth's richness,
    away from the dew of heaven above.
⁴⁰You will live by the sword
    and you will serve your brother.

---

^a36 Jacob means *he grasps the heel* (figuratively, *he deceives*).

But when you grow restless,
  you will throw his yoke
  from off your neck."

Jacob Flees to Laban

41Esau held a grudge against Jacob because of the blessing his father had given him. He said to himself, "The days of mourning for my father are near; then I will kill my brother Jacob."

42When Rebekah was told what her older son Esau had said, she sent for her younger son Jacob and said to him, "Your brother Esau is consoling himself with the thought of killing you. **43**Now then, my son, do what I say: Flee at once to my brother Laban in Haran. **44**Stay with him for a while until your brother's fury subsides. **45**When your brother is no longer angry with you and forgets what you did to him, I'll send word for you to come back from there. Why should I lose both of you in one day?"

46Then Rebekah said to Isaac, "I'm disgusted with living because of these Hittite women. If Jacob takes a wife from among the women of this land, from Hittite women like these, my life will not be worth living."

28 So Isaac called for Jacob and blessed[a] him and commanded him: "Do not marry a Canaanite woman. **2**Go at once to Paddan Aram,[b] to the house of your mother's father Bethuel. Take a wife for yourself there, from among the daughters of Laban, your mother's brother. **3**May God Almighty[c] bless you and make you fruitful and increase your numbers until you become a community of peoples. **4**May he give you and your descendants the blessing given to Abraham, so that you may take possession of the land where you now live as an alien, the land God gave to Abraham." **5**Then Isaac sent Jacob on his way, and he went to Paddan Aram, to Laban son of Bethuel the Aramean, the brother of Rebekah, who was the mother of Jacob and Esau.

6Now Esau learned that Isaac had blessed Jacob and had sent him to Paddan Aram to take a wife from there, and that when he blessed him he commanded him, "Do not marry a Canaanite woman," **7**and that Jacob had obeyed his father and mother and had gone to Paddan Aram. **8**Esau then realized how displeasing the Canaanite women were to his father Isaac; **9**so he went to Ishmael and married Mahalath, the sister of Nebaioth and daughter of Ishmael son of Abraham, in addition to the wives he already had.

Jacob's Dream at Bethel

10Jacob left Beersheba and set out for Haran. **11**When he reached a certain place, he stopped for the night because the sun had set. Taking one of the stones there, he put it under his head and lay down to sleep. **12**He had a dream in which he saw a stairway[d] resting on the earth, with its top reaching to heaven, and the angels of God were ascending and descending on it. **13**There above it[e] stood the LORD, and he said: "I am the LORD, the God of your father Abraham and the God of Isaac. I will give you and your descendants the land on which you are lying. **14**Your descendants will be like the dust of the earth, and you will spread out to the west and to the east, to the north and to the south. All peoples on earth will be blessed through you and your offspring. **15**I am with you and will watch over you wherever you go, and I will bring you back to this land. I will not leave you until I have done what I have promised you."

16When Jacob awoke from his sleep, he thought, "Surely the LORD is in this place, and I was not aware of it." **17**He was afraid and said, "How awesome is this place! This is none other than the house of God; this is the gate of heaven."

18Early the next morning Jacob took the stone he had placed under his head and set it up as a pillar and poured oil on top of it. **19**He called that place Bethel,[f] though the city used to be called Luz.

20Then Jacob made a vow, saying, "If God will be with me and will watch over me on this journey I am taking and will give me food to eat and clothes to wear **21**so that I return safely to my father's house, then the LORD[g] will be my God **22**and[h] this stone that I have set up as a pillar will be God's house, and of all that you give me I will give you a tenth."

Jacob Arrives in Paddan Aram

29 Then Jacob continued on his journey and came to the land of the eastern peoples. **2**There he saw a well in the field,

---

[a]1 Or *greeted*   [b]2 That is, Northwest Mesopotamia; also in verses 5, 6 and 7   [c]3 Hebrew *El-Shaddai*   [d]12 Or *ladder*   [e]13 Or *There beside him*   [f]19 *Bethel* means *house of God.*   [g]20,21 Or *Since God . . . father's house, the LORD*   [h]21,22 Or *house, and the LORD will be my God,* [h]*then*

with three flocks of sheep lying near it because the flocks were watered from that well. The stone over the mouth of the well was large. ³When all the flocks were gathered there, the shepherds would roll the stone away from the well's mouth and water the sheep. Then they would return the stone to its place over the mouth of the well.

⁴Jacob asked the shepherds, "My brothers, where are you from?"

"We're from Haran," they replied.

⁵He said to them, "Do you know Laban, Nahor's grandson?"

"Yes, we know him," they answered.

⁶Then Jacob asked them, "Is he well?"

"Yes, he is," they said, "and here comes his daughter Rachel with the sheep."

Your Child's Marriage Partner

DAILY INSIGHT

THURSDAY

Passage:
Genesis 28:1, 10–17

Verse:
Genesis 28:15

How are you at making decisions?

Over the years, you and I have seen two extremes. First there are those who make decisions like sports photographers snap their automatic shutters. They click away, figuring that when they get back to their darkrooms they'll be able to sort the good ones from the bad ones, throwing out the trash and holding onto the winners.

Then there are those who can never make up their minds. Because of their fear of making bad decisions, they live their lives in the middle of tire-kicking, door-slamming, and "No thanks, I'm just looking."

Jacob was on his way to find a wife. This decision would change his life. His dad had asked him to look for "Miss Right" in a country that was familiar to the family. Because the trip was more than a day's journey, Jacob had to spend the night along the way. And during that night, God spoke to an awestruck Jacob, promising him children and a blessing. Amazingly, Jacob's father had prepared him for this experience. (28:3–4)

Your children may be a long way from marriage, or they may be right around the corner from making this incredible decision. In either case, believe it or not, you have the opportunity to play a critical role in helping your child to avoid foolish carelessness or frozen indecision. Today's text gives us a few clues.

As Jacob was preparing for this wife-locating excursion (today we call this "going to college"), his father did two

wonderful things. First, he blessed him. In Old Testament times, a blessing had two implications. Coming from a dad, it was both a prayer and a tender word of encouragement. Because of what Isaac had done for his son, Jacob was assured of God's involvement in this huge decision, and he knew that he had his father's support.

Then Jacob's dad gave him instructions. The word "command" or "charge" has strategic implications, just like a coach would give to his quarterback right before the kid jogs onto the field for an important play. Isaac wasn't afraid to give his son some advice right after he had given him a blessing.

Can you picture this young man, looking over his shoulder at his slowly disappearing homestead? Can you see him a bit frightened by the ominous assignment? But can you also imagine him feeling optimistic? His dad had reminded him of God's presence, provided his own encouragement, then had given Jacob some helpful and direct advice.

As dads, you and I have one hope for our children—that they walk with God when they're on their own. And because of what his dad had done for him as he prepared to make the decision of a lifetime, Jacob had his own experience with God. And God promised Jacob his blessing.

Don't be afraid to be involved in helping your children make this extraordinary decision. Bless them. Then direct them.

For your next devotional reading, go to page 44.

7"Look," he said, "the sun is still high; it is not time for the flocks to be gathered. Water the sheep and take them back to pasture."

8"We can't," they replied, "until all the flocks are gathered and the stone has been rolled away from the mouth of the well. Then we will water the sheep."

9While he was still talking with them, Rachel came with her father's sheep, for she was a shepherdess. 10When Jacob saw Rachel daughter of Laban, his mother's brother, and Laban's sheep, he went over and rolled the stone away from the mouth of the well and watered his uncle's sheep. 11Then Jacob kissed Rachel and began to weep aloud. 12He had told Rachel that he was a relative of her father and a son of Rebekah. So she ran and told her father.

13As soon as Laban heard the news about Jacob, his sister's son, he hurried to meet him. He embraced him and kissed him and brought him to his home, and there Jacob told him all these things. 14Then Laban said to him, "You are my own flesh and blood."

Jacob Marries Leah and Rachel

After Jacob had stayed with him for a whole month, 15Laban said to him, "Just because you are a relative of mine, should you work for me for nothing? Tell me what your wages should be."

16Now Laban had two daughters; the name of the older was Leah, and the name of the younger was Rachel. 17Leah had weak*a* eyes, but Rachel was lovely in form, and beautiful. 18Jacob was in love with Rachel and said, "I'll work for you seven years in return for your younger daughter Rachel."

19Laban said, "It's better that I give her to you than to some other man. Stay here with me." 20So Jacob served seven years to get Rachel, but they seemed like only a few days to him because of his love for her.

21Then Jacob said to Laban, "Give me my wife. My time is completed, and I want to lie with her."

22So Laban brought together all the people of the place and gave a feast. 23But when evening came, he took his daughter Leah and gave her to Jacob, and Jacob lay with her. 24And Laban gave his servant girl Zilpah to his daughter as her maidservant.

25When morning came, there was Leah! So Jacob said to Laban, "What is this you have done to me? I served you for Rachel, didn't I? Why have you deceived me?"

26Laban replied, "It is not our custom here to give the younger daughter in marriage before the older one. 27Finish this daughter's bridal week; then we will give you the younger one also, in return for another seven years of work."

28And Jacob did so. He finished the week with Leah, and then Laban gave him his daughter Rachel to be his wife. 29Laban gave his servant girl Bilhah to his daughter Rachel as her maidservant. 30Jacob lay with Rachel also, and he loved Rachel more than Leah. And he worked for Laban another seven years.

Jacob's Children

31When the LORD saw that Leah was not loved, he opened her womb, but Rachel was barren. 32Leah became pregnant and gave birth to a son. She named him Reuben,*b* for she said, "It is because the LORD has seen my misery. Surely my husband will love me now."

33She conceived again, and when she gave birth to a son she said, "Because the LORD heard that I am not loved, he gave me this one too." So she named him Simeon.*c*

34Again she conceived, and when she gave birth to a son she said, "Now at last my husband will become attached to me, because I have borne him three sons." So he was named Levi.*d*

35She conceived again, and when she gave birth to a son she said, "This time I will praise the LORD." So she named him Judah.*e* Then she stopped having children.

30 When Rachel saw that she was not bearing Jacob any children, she became jealous of her sister. So she said to Jacob, "Give me children, or I'll die!"

2Jacob became angry with her and said, "Am I in the place of God, who has kept you from having children?"

3Then she said, "Here is Bilhah, my maidservant. Sleep with her so that she can bear children for me and that through her I too can build a family."

4So she gave him her servant Bilhah as a

a17 Or delicate   b32 Reuben sounds like the Hebrew for he has seen my misery; the name means see, a son.   c33 Simeon probably means one who hears.   d34 Levi sounds like and may be derived from the Hebrew for attached.   e35 Judah sounds like and may be derived from the Hebrew for praise.

wife. Jacob slept with her, [5]and she became pregnant and bore him a son. [6]Then Rachel said, "God has vindicated me; he has listened to my plea and given me a son." Because of this she named him Dan.[a]

[7]Rachel's servant Bilhah conceived again and bore Jacob a second son. [8]Then Rachel said, "I have had a great struggle with my sister, and I have won." So she named him Naphtali.[b]

[9]When Leah saw that she had stopped having children, she took her maidservant Zilpah and gave her to Jacob as a wife. [10]Leah's servant Zilpah bore Jacob a son. [11]Then Leah said, "What good fortune!"[c] So she named him Gad.[d]

[12]Leah's servant Zilpah bore Jacob a second son. [13]Then Leah said, "How happy I am! The women will call me happy." So she named him Asher.[e]

[14]During wheat harvest, Reuben went out into the fields and found some mandrake plants, which he brought to his mother Leah. Rachel said to Leah, "Please give me some of your son's mandrakes."

[15]But she said to her, "Wasn't it enough that you took away my husband? Will you take my son's mandrakes too?"

"Very well," Rachel said, "he can sleep with you tonight in return for your son's mandrakes."

[16]So when Jacob came in from the fields that evening, Leah went out to meet him. "You must sleep with me," she said. "I have hired you with my son's mandrakes." So he slept with her that night.

[17]God listened to Leah, and she became pregnant and bore Jacob a fifth son. [18]Then Leah said, "God has rewarded me for giving my maidservant to my husband." So she named him Issachar.[f]

[19]Leah conceived again and bore Jacob a sixth son. [20]Then Leah said, "God has presented me with a precious gift. This time my husband will treat me with honor, because I have borne him six sons." So she named him Zebulun.[g]

[21]Some time later she gave birth to a daughter and named her Dinah.

[22]Then God remembered Rachel; he listened to her and opened her womb. [23]She became pregnant and gave birth to a son and said, "God has taken away my disgrace." [24]She named him Joseph,[h] and said, "May the LORD add to me another son."

Jacob's Flocks Increase

[25]After Rachel gave birth to Joseph, Jacob said to Laban, "Send me on my way so I can go back to my own homeland. [26]Give me my wives and children, for whom I have served you, and I will be on my way. You know how much work I've done for you."

[27]But Laban said to him, "If I have found favor in your eyes, please stay. I have learned by divination that[i] the LORD has blessed me because of you." [28]He added, "Name your wages, and I will pay them."

[29]Jacob said to him, "You know how I have worked for you and how your livestock has fared under my care. [30]The little you had before I came has increased greatly, and the LORD has blessed you wherever I have been. But now, when may I do something for my own household?"

[31]"What shall I give you?" he asked.

"Don't give me anything," Jacob replied. "But if you will do this one thing for me, I will go on tending your flocks and watching over them: [32]Let me go through all your flocks today and remove from them every speckled or spotted sheep, every dark-colored lamb and every spotted or speckled goat. They will be my wages. [33]And my honesty will testify for me in the future, whenever you check on the wages you have paid me. Any goat in my possession that is not speckled or spotted, or any lamb that is not dark-colored, will be considered stolen."

[34]"Agreed," said Laban. "Let it be as you have said." [35]That same day he removed all the male goats that were streaked or spotted, and all the speckled or spotted female goats (all that had white on them) and all the dark-colored lambs, and he placed them in the care of his sons. [36]Then he put a three-day journey between himself and Jacob, while Jacob continued to tend the rest of Laban's flocks.

[37]Jacob, however, took fresh-cut branches from poplar, almond and plane trees and made white stripes on them by peeling the bark and exposing the white inner wood of the branches. [38]Then he placed the peeled branches in all the watering troughs, so that they would be directly in front of the flocks when they came to drink. When the flocks were in

---

[a]6 *Dan* here means *he has vindicated.*   [b]8 *Naphtali* means *my struggle.*   [c]11 Or *"A troop is coming!"*   [d]11 *Gad* can mean *good fortune* or *a troop.*   [e]13 *Asher* means *happy.*   [f]18 *Issachar* sounds like the Hebrew for *reward.*   [g]20 *Zebulun* probably means *honor.*   [h]24 *Joseph* means *may he add.*   [i]27 Or possibly *have become rich and*

heat and came to drink, [39]they mated in front of the branches. And they bore young that were streaked or speckled or spotted. [40]Jacob set apart the young of the flock by themselves, but made the rest face the streaked and dark-colored animals that belonged to Laban. Thus he made separate flocks for himself and did not put them with Laban's animals. [41]Whenever the stronger females were in heat, Jacob would place the branches in the troughs in front of the animals so they would mate near the branches, [42]but if the animals were weak, he would not place them there. So the weak animals went to Laban and the strong ones to Jacob. [43]In this way the man grew exceedingly prosperous and came to own large flocks, and maidservants and menservants, and camels and donkeys.

Jacob Flees From Laban

31 Jacob heard that Laban's sons were saying, "Jacob has taken everything our father owned and has gained all this wealth from what belonged to our father." [2]And Jacob noticed that Laban's attitude toward him was not what it had been.

[3]Then the LORD said to Jacob, "Go back to the land of your fathers and to your relatives, and I will be with you."

[4]So Jacob sent word to Rachel and Leah to come out to the fields where his flocks were. [5]He said to them, "I see that your father's attitude toward me is not what it was before, but the God of my father has been with me. [6]You know that I've worked for your father with all my strength, [7]yet your father has cheated me by changing my wages ten times. However, God has not allowed him to harm me. [8]If he said, 'The speckled ones will be your wages,' then all the flocks gave birth to speckled young; and if he said, 'The streaked ones will be your wages,' then all the flocks bore streaked young. [9]So God has taken away your father's livestock and has given them to me.

[10]"In breeding season I once had a dream in which I looked up and saw that the male goats mating with the flock were streaked, speckled or spotted. [11]The angel of God said to me in the dream, 'Jacob.' I answered, 'Here I am.' [12]And he said, 'Look up and see that all the male goats mating with the flock are streaked, speckled or spotted, for I have seen all that Laban has been doing to you. [13]I am the God of Bethel, where you anointed a pillar and

where you made a vow to me. Now leave this land at once and go back to your native land.' "

[14]Then Rachel and Leah replied, "Do we still have any share in the inheritance of our father's estate? [15]Does he not regard us as foreigners? Not only has he sold us, but he has used up what was paid for us. [16]Surely all the wealth that God took away from our father belongs to us and our children. So do whatever God has told you."

[17]Then Jacob put his children and his wives on camels, [18]and he drove all his livestock ahead of him, along with all the goods he had accumulated in Paddan Aram,[a] to go to his father Isaac in the land of Canaan.

[19]When Laban had gone to shear his sheep, Rachel stole her father's household gods. [20]Moreover, Jacob deceived Laban the Aramean by not telling him he was running away. [21]So he fled with all he had, and crossing the River,[b] he headed for the hill country of Gilead.

Laban Pursues Jacob

[22]On the third day Laban was told that Jacob had fled. [23]Taking his relatives with him, he pursued Jacob for seven days and caught up with him in the hill country of Gilead. [24]Then God came to Laban the Aramean in a dream at night and said to him, "Be careful not to say anything to Jacob, either good or bad."

[25]Jacob had pitched his tent in the hill country of Gilead when Laban overtook him, and Laban and his relatives camped there too. [26]Then Laban said to Jacob, "What have you done? You've deceived me, and you've carried off my daughters like captives in war. [27]Why did you run off secretly and deceive me? Why didn't you tell me, so I could send you away with joy and singing to the music of tambourines and harps? [28]You didn't even let me kiss my grandchildren and my daughters good-by. You have done a foolish thing. [29]I have the power to harm you; but last night the God of your father said to me, 'Be careful not to say anything to Jacob, either good or bad.' [30]Now you have gone off because you longed to return to your father's house. But why did you steal my gods?"

[31]Jacob answered Laban, "I was afraid, because I thought you would take your

---

[a]18 That is, Northwest Mesopotamia   [b]21 That is, the Euphrates

daughters away from me by force. ³²But if you find anyone who has your gods, he shall not live. In the presence of our relatives, see for yourself whether there is anything of yours here with me; and if so, take it." Now Jacob did not know that Rachel had stolen the gods.

³³So Laban went into Jacob's tent and into Leah's tent and into the tent of the two maidservants, but he found nothing. After he came out of Leah's tent, he entered Rachel's tent. ³⁴Now Rachel had taken the household gods and put them inside her camel's saddle and was sitting on them. Laban searched through everything in the tent but found nothing.

³⁵Rachel said to her father, "Don't be angry, my lord, that I cannot stand up in your presence; I'm having my period." So he searched but could not find the household gods.

³⁶Jacob was angry and took Laban to task. "What is my crime?" he asked Laban. "What sin have I committed that you hunt me down? ³⁷Now that you have searched through all my goods, what have you found that belongs to your household? Put it here in front of your relatives and mine, and let them judge between the two of us.

³⁸"I have been with you for twenty years now. Your sheep and goats have not miscarried, nor have I eaten rams from your flocks. ³⁹I did not bring you animals torn by wild beasts; I bore the loss myself. And you demanded payment from me for whatever was stolen by day or night. ⁴⁰This was my situation: The heat consumed me in the daytime and the cold at night, and sleep fled from my eyes. ⁴¹It was like this for the twenty years I was in your household. I worked for you fourteen years for your two daughters and six years for your flocks, and you changed my wages ten times. ⁴²If the God of my father, the God of Abraham and the Fear of Isaac, had not been with me, you would surely have sent me away empty-handed. But God has seen my hardship and the toil of my hands, and last night he rebuked you."

⁴³Laban answered Jacob, "The women are my daughters, the children are my children, and the flocks are my flocks. All you see is mine. Yet what can I do today about these daughters of mine, or about the children they have borne? ⁴⁴Come now, let's make a covenant, you and I, and let it serve as a witness between us."

⁴⁵So Jacob took a stone and set it up as a pillar. ⁴⁶He said to his relatives, "Gather some stones." So they took stones and piled them in a heap, and they ate there by the heap. ⁴⁷Laban called it Jegar Sahadutha,^a and Jacob called it Galeed.^b

⁴⁸Laban said, "This heap is a witness between you and me today." That is why it was called Galeed. ⁴⁹It was also called Mizpah,^c because he said, "May the LORD keep watch between you and me when we are away from each other. ⁵⁰If you mistreat my daughters or if you take any wives besides my daughters, even though no one is with us, remember that God is a witness between you and me."

⁵¹Laban also said to Jacob, "Here is this heap, and here is this pillar I have set up between you and me. ⁵²This heap is a witness, and this pillar is a witness, that I will not go past this heap to your side to harm you and that you will not go past this heap and pillar to my side to harm me. ⁵³May the God of Abraham and the God of Nahor, the God of their father, judge between us."

So Jacob took an oath in the name of the Fear of his father Isaac. ⁵⁴He offered a sacrifice there in the hill country and invited his relatives to a meal. After they had eaten, they spent the night there.

⁵⁵Early the next morning Laban kissed his grandchildren and his daughters and blessed them. Then he left and returned home.

Jacob Prepares to Meet Esau

32 Jacob also went on his way, and the angels of God met him. ²When Jacob saw them, he said, "This is the camp of God!" So he named that place Mahanaim.^d

³Jacob sent messengers ahead of him to his brother Esau in the land of Seir, the country of Edom. ⁴He instructed them: "This is what you are to say to my master Esau: 'Your servant Jacob says, I have been staying with Laban and have remained there till now. ⁵I have cattle and donkeys, sheep and goats, menservants and maidservants. Now I am sending this message to my lord, that I may find favor in your eyes.' "

⁶When the messengers returned to Jacob, they said, "We went to your brother Esau, and now he is coming to meet you, and four hundred men are with him."

^a47 The Aramaic *Jegar Sahadutha* means *witness heap.*   ^b47 The Hebrew *Galeed* means *witness heap.*   ^c49 *Mizpah* means *watchtower.*
^d2 *Mahanaim* means *two camps.*

[7]In great fear and distress Jacob divided the people who were with him into two groups,[a] and the flocks and herds and camels as well. [8]He thought, "If Esau comes and attacks one group,[b] the group[b] that is left may escape."

[9]Then Jacob prayed, "O God of my father Abraham, God of my father Isaac, O LORD, who said to me, 'Go back to your country and your relatives, and I will make you prosper,' [10]I am unworthy of all the kindness and faithfulness you have shown your servant. I had only my staff when I crossed this Jordan, but now I have become two groups. [11]Save me, I pray, from the hand of my brother Esau, for I am afraid he will come and attack me, and also the mothers with their children. [12]But you have said, 'I will surely make you prosper and will make your descendants like the sand of the sea, which cannot be counted.' "

[13]He spent the night there, and from what he had with him he selected a gift for his brother Esau: [14]two hundred female goats and twenty male goats, two hundred ewes and twenty rams, [15]thirty female camels with their young, forty cows and ten bulls, and twenty female donkeys and ten male donkeys. [16]He put them in the care of his servants, each herd by itself, and said to his servants, "Go ahead of me, and keep some space between the herds."

[17]He instructed the one in the lead: "When my brother Esau meets you and asks, 'To whom do you belong, and where are you going, and who owns all these animals in front of you?' [18]then you are to say, 'They belong to your servant Jacob. They are a gift sent to my lord Esau, and he is coming behind us.' "

[19]He also instructed the second, the third and all the others who followed the herds: "You are to say the same thing to Esau when you meet him. [20]And be sure to say, 'Your servant Jacob is coming behind us.' " For he thought, "I will pacify him with these gifts I am sending on ahead; later, when I see him, perhaps he will receive me." [21]So Jacob's gifts went on ahead of him, but he himself spent the night in the camp.

Jacob Wrestles With God

[22]That night Jacob got up and took his two wives, his two maidservants and his eleven sons and crossed the ford of the Jabbok. [23]After he had sent them across the stream, he sent over all his possessions. [24]So Jacob was left alone, and a man wrestled with him till daybreak. [25]When the man saw that he could not overpower him, he touched the socket of Jacob's hip so that his hip was wrenched as he wrestled with the man. [26]Then the man said, "Let me go, for it is daybreak."

But Jacob replied, "I will not let you go unless you bless me."

[27]The man asked him, "What is your name?"

"Jacob," he answered.

[28]Then the man said, "Your name will no longer be Jacob, but Israel,[c] because you have struggled with God and with men and have overcome."

[29]Jacob said, "Please tell me your name."

But he replied, "Why do you ask my name?" Then he blessed him there.

[30]So Jacob called the place Peniel,[d] saying, "It is because I saw God face to face, and yet my life was spared."

[31]The sun rose above him as he passed Peniel,[e] and he was limping because of his hip. [32]Therefore to this day the Israelites do not eat the tendon attached to the socket of the hip, because the socket of Jacob's hip was touched near the tendon.

Jacob Meets Esau

33 Jacob looked up and there was Esau, coming with his four hundred men; so he divided the children among Leah, Rachel and the two maidservants. [2]He put the maidservants and their children in front, Leah and her children next, and Rachel and Joseph in the rear. [3]He himself went on ahead and bowed down to the ground seven times as he approached his brother.

[4]But Esau ran to meet Jacob and embraced him; he threw his arms around his neck and kissed him. And they wept. [5]Then Esau looked up and saw the women and children. "Who are these with you?" he asked.

Jacob answered, "They are the children God has graciously given your servant."

[6]Then the maidservants and their children approached and bowed down. [7]Next, Leah and her children came and bowed down. Last of all came Joseph and Rachel, and they too bowed down.

---

[a]7 Or *camps*; also in verse 10   [b]8 Or *camp*
[c]28 *Israel* means *he struggles with God.*   [d]30 *Peniel* means *face of God.*   [e]31 Hebrew *Penuel*, a variant of *Peniel*

⁸Esau asked, "What do you mean by all these droves I met?"

"To find favor in your eyes, my lord," he said.

⁹But Esau said, "I already have plenty, my brother. Keep what you have for yourself."

¹⁰"No, please!" said Jacob. "If I have found favor in your eyes, accept this gift from me. For to see your face is like seeing the face of God, now that you have received me favorably. ¹¹Please accept the present that was brought to you, for God has been gracious to me and I have all I need." And because Jacob insisted, Esau accepted it.

¹²Then Esau said, "Let us be on our way; I'll accompany you."

¹³But Jacob said to him, "My lord knows that the children are tender and that I must care for the ewes and cows that are nursing their young. If they are driven hard just one day, all the animals will die. ¹⁴So let my lord go on ahead of his servant, while I move along slowly at the pace of the droves before me and that of the children, until I come to my lord in Seir."

He's My Brother

DAILY
INSIGHT

FRIDAY
Passage:
Genesis 33:1 –12

Verse:
Genesis 33:4

Ray Dourte has always been my favorite cousin. Our birth dates are only a few months apart, and when we were small, our parents gave us the chance to spend time together. He played the ukulele, told funny stories, and, for several years, lived in California. Ray was very cool.

As a kid, I can remember how my parents used to beg me to write letters to grownups who had done particularly nice things for me—grandparents, mostly. But no one needed to prompt me to write to Ray. I wrote lots of letters to Ray. I *wanted* to write to him, because I wanted him to think I was cool, too.

On one occasion when I was about ten years old, I left one of those letters out, sitting face-up in my room. Unfortunately, my mother, who would never have done such a thing unless God had specifically directed her to do so, picked it up and read my letter to Ray. One particular sentence caught my mother's discerning eye. It was a thoughtless and unkind comment I had made about my older brother, Ken—something I'm sure that I had done to impress Ray.

The moment I walked into our house from school that afternoon, I could tell I was in trouble. It was clearly written across my mother's face (she would have made a terrible poker player). She asked if we could talk, and we sat down on two kitchen chairs.

"I read your letter to Ray," she began. "And I read what you said about your brother."

My heart stopped. I knew that I had written something cruel just to show off. "Robert," she continued, "Ken is your *brother*."

She stopped talking, but the look on her face finished the thought completely. In fact, she never said another thing about my letter. She didn't even ask me to rewrite it (which I did, of course). I had gotten the message. In fact, I've never forgotten the message.

Jacob and Esau were brothers. Jacob was, in a word, a scoundrel. As a young man he had lied, deceived and stolen from his brother. Now that these two men were about to see each other face to face, Jacob feared for his life. Given this backlog of conflict, shame and regret, isn't verse four incredible? Can you see these grown men crying like broken-hearted children, regretting the years of alienation?

There are two messages for us today. First, as a dad, one of your family's core values must be the lesson I learned that day from my mother as we sat on those chrome and vinyl kitchen chairs. Teach your children how to treat each other. The second message is for us. How is it with our brother? Maybe it's time for that meeting.

For your next devotional reading, go to page 49.

¹⁵Esau said, "Then let me leave some of my men with you."

"But why do that?" Jacob asked. "Just let me find favor in the eyes of my lord."

¹⁶So that day Esau started on his way back to Seir. ¹⁷Jacob, however, went to Succoth, where he built a place for himself and made shelters for his livestock. That is why the place is called Succoth.ᵃ

¹⁸After Jacob came from Paddan Aram,ᵇ he arrived safely at theᶜ city of Shechem in Canaan and camped within sight of the city. ¹⁹For a hundred pieces of silver,ᵈ he bought from the sons of Hamor, the father of Shechem, the plot of ground where he pitched his tent. ²⁰There he set up an altar and called it El Elohe Israel.ᵉ

Dinah and the Shechemites

34 Now Dinah, the daughter Leah had borne to Jacob, went out to visit the women of the land. ²When Shechem son of Hamor the Hivite, the ruler of that area,

saw her, he took her and violated her. ³His heart was drawn to Dinah daughter of Jacob, and he loved the girl and spoke tenderly to her. ⁴And Shechem said to his father Hamor, "Get me this girl as my wife."

⁵When Jacob heard that his daughter Dinah had been defiled, his sons were in the fields with his livestock; so he kept quiet about it until they came home.

⁶Then Shechem's father Hamor went out to talk with Jacob. ⁷Now Jacob's sons had come in from the fields as soon as they heard what had happened. They were filled with grief and fury, because Shechem had done a disgraceful thing inᶠ Israel by lying with Jacob's daughter—a thing that should not be done.

⁸But Hamor said to them, "My son

ᵃ17 *Succoth* means *shelters.*   ᵇ18 That is, Northwest Mesopotamia   ᶜ18 Or *arrived at Shalem, a*   ᵈ19 Hebrew *hundred kesitahs;* a kesitah was a unit of money of unknown weight and value.   ᵉ20 *El Elohe Israel* can mean *God, the God of Israel* or *mighty is the God of Israel.*   ᶠ7 Or *against*

Is That Our Daddy on His Knees?
Jacob, the Penitent Father

"Jacob . . bowed down to the ground seven times as he approached his brother. But Esau ran to meet Jacob and embraced him . . . And they wept" (33:3–4).

DADS IN THE BIBLE

Text: Genesis 33

Jacob deserved what he was about to get: a major-league whipping from his big brother, Esau. Years before, Jacob had deceived his father, Isaac, and had stolen the blessing Esau had deserved. He'd not seen his brother since, and was now traveling to meet him, face to face.

We can only imagine how Jacob's children must have reacted to their dad's anxiety. They had never seen him act this way. As Esau approached, Jacob hurriedly divided his family into strategic ranks.

Can't you hear his children asking him why he was so frantic? They watched this painful encounter as Jacob approached Uncle Esau. And then, to the amazement of his whole family, Jacob "bowed down to the ground seven times as he approached his brother" (33:3). Can't you see the children, their mouths wide open and their eyes as big as saucers, aghast at their dad's humble contrition? Don't you wonder what they must have felt like, seeing their proud father bowing once, twice . . . seven times?

On our journey through life, it's nearly impossible to avoid thoughtlessly hurting others. Jacob was no exception to this rule. But Jacob's indiscretion had been intentional and directed against his brother—someone he was inevitably going to have to see again.

The image of Jacob's public humility before his older brother must have burned itself into the memories of his children. No doubt they reminisced about this moment long after their dad was gone. They probably also recalled their Uncle Esau's gracious forgiveness in the face of their dad's humility.

Now *there's* a picture that's worth a thousand words.

For a complete listing of Dads in the Bible, turn to page 1434.

Shechem has his heart set on your daughter. Please give her to him as his wife. [9]Intermarry with us; give us your daughters and take our daughters for yourselves. [10]You can settle among us; the land is open to you. Live in it, trade[a] in it, and acquire property in it."

[11]Then Shechem said to Dinah's father and brothers, "Let me find favor in your eyes, and I will give you whatever you ask. [12]Make the price for the bride and the gift I am to bring as great as you like, and I'll pay whatever you ask me. Only give me the girl as my wife."

[13]Because their sister Dinah had been defiled, Jacob's sons replied deceitfully as they spoke to Shechem and his father Hamor. [14]They said to them, "We can't do such a thing; we can't give our sister to a man who is not circumcised. That would be a disgrace to us. [15]We will give our consent to you on one condition only: that you become like us by circumcising all your males. [16]Then we will give you our daughters and take your daughters for ourselves. We'll settle among you and become one people with you. [17]But if you will not agree to be circumcised, we'll take our sister[b] and go."

[18]Their proposal seemed good to Hamor and his son Shechem. [19]The young man, who was the most honored of all his father's household, lost no time in doing what they said, because he was delighted with Jacob's daughter. [20]So Hamor and his son Shechem went to the gate of their city to speak to their fellow townsmen. [21]"These men are friendly toward us," they said. "Let them live in our land and trade in it; the land has plenty of room for them. We can marry their daughters and they can marry ours. [22]But the men will consent to live with us as one people only on the condition that our males be circumcised, as they themselves are. [23]Won't their livestock, their property and all their other animals become ours? So let us give our consent to them, and they will settle among us."

[24]All the men who went out of the city gate agreed with Hamor and his son Shechem, and every male in the city was circumcised.

[25]Three days later, while all of them were still in pain, two of Jacob's sons, Simeon and Levi, Dinah's brothers, took their swords and attacked the unsuspecting city, killing every male. [26]They put Hamor and his son Shechem to the sword and took Dinah from Shechem's house and left. [27]The sons of Jacob came upon the dead bodies and looted the city where[c] their sister had been defiled. [28]They seized their flocks and herds and donkeys and everything else of theirs in the city and out in the fields. [29]They carried off all their wealth and all their women and children, taking as plunder everything in the houses.

[30]Then Jacob said to Simeon and Levi, "You have brought trouble on me by making me a stench to the Canaanites and Perizzites, the people living in this land. We are few in number, and if they join forces against me and attack me, I and my household will be destroyed."

[31]But they replied, "Should he have treated our sister like a prostitute?"

Jacob Returns to Bethel

35 Then God said to Jacob, "Go up to Bethel and settle there, and build an altar there to God, who appeared to you when you were fleeing from your brother Esau."

[2]So Jacob said to his household and to all who were with him, "Get rid of the foreign gods you have with you, and purify yourselves and change your clothes. [3]Then come, let us go up to Bethel, where I will build an altar to God, who answered me in the day of my distress and who has been with me wherever I have gone." [4]So they gave Jacob all the foreign gods they had and the rings in their ears, and Jacob buried them under the oak at Shechem. [5]Then they set out, and the terror of God fell upon the towns all around them so that no one pursued them.

[6]Jacob and all the people with him came to Luz (that is, Bethel) in the land of Canaan. [7]There he built an altar, and he called the place El Bethel,[d] because it was there that God revealed himself to him when he was fleeing from his brother.

[8]Now Deborah, Rebekah's nurse, died and was buried under the oak below Bethel. So it was named Allon Bacuth.[e]

[9]After Jacob returned from Paddan Aram,[f] God appeared to him again and blessed him. [10]God said to him, "Your name is Jacob,[g] but you will no longer be

---

[a]10 Or *move about freely*; also in verse 21
[b]17 Hebrew *daughter*   [c]27 Or *because*   [d]7 *El Bethel* means *God of Bethel.*   [e]8 *Allon Bacuth* means *oak of weeping.*   [f]9 That is, Northwest Mesopotamia; also in verse 26   [g]10 *Jacob* means *he grasps the heel* (figuratively, *he deceives*).

called Jacob; your name will be Israel.*a*" So he named him Israel.

[11]And God said to him, "I am God Almighty*b*; be fruitful and increase in number. A nation and a community of nations will come from you, and kings will come from your body. [12]The land I gave to Abraham and Isaac I also give to you, and I will give this land to your descendants after you." [13]Then God went up from him at the place where he had talked with him.

[14]Jacob set up a stone pillar at the place where God had talked with him, and he poured out a drink offering on it; he also poured oil on it. [15]Jacob called the place where God had talked with him Bethel.*c*

The Deaths of Rachel and Isaac

[16]Then they moved on from Bethel. While they were still some distance from Ephrath, Rachel began to give birth and had great difficulty. [17]And as she was having great difficulty in childbirth, the midwife said to her, "Don't be afraid, for you have another son." [18]As she breathed her last—for she was dying—she named her son Ben-Oni.*d* But his father named him Benjamin.*e*

[19]So Rachel died and was buried on the way to Ephrath (that is, Bethlehem). [20]Over her tomb Jacob set up a pillar, and to this day that pillar marks Rachel's tomb.

[21]Israel moved on again and pitched his tent beyond Migdal Eder. [22]While Israel was living in that region, Reuben went in and slept with his father's concubine Bilhah, and Israel heard of it.

Jacob had twelve sons:

[23]The sons of Leah:
> Reuben the firstborn of Jacob,
> Simeon, Levi, Judah, Issachar and
> Zebulun.

[24]The sons of Rachel:
> Joseph and Benjamin.

[25]The sons of Rachel's maidservant Bilhah:
> Dan and Naphtali.

[26]The sons of Leah's maidservant Zilpah:
> Gad and Asher.

These were the sons of Jacob, who were born to him in Paddan Aram.

[27]Jacob came home to his father Isaac in Mamre, near Kiriath Arba (that is, Hebron), where Abraham and Isaac had stayed. [28]Isaac lived a hundred and eighty years. [29]Then he breathed his last and died and was gathered to his people, old and full of years. And his sons Esau and Jacob buried him.

Esau's Descendants

36 This is the account of Esau (that is, Edom).

[2]Esau took his wives from the women of Canaan: Adah daughter of Elon the Hittite, and Oholibamah daughter of Anah and granddaughter of Zibeon the Hivite— [3]also Basemath daughter of Ishmael and sister of Nebaioth.

[4]Adah bore Eliphaz to Esau, Basemath bore Reuel, [5]and Oholibamah bore Jeush, Jalam and Korah. These were the sons of Esau, who were born to him in Canaan.

[6]Esau took his wives and sons and daughters and all the members of his household, as well as his livestock and all his other animals and all the goods he had acquired in Canaan, and moved to a land some distance from his brother Jacob. [7]Their possessions were too great for them to remain together; the land where they were staying could not support them both because of their livestock. [8]So Esau (that is, Edom) settled in the hill country of Seir.

[9]This is the account of Esau the father of the Edomites in the hill country of Seir.

[10]These are the names of Esau's sons:
> Eliphaz, the son of Esau's wife
> Adah, and Reuel, the son of Esau's
> wife Basemath.

[11]The sons of Eliphaz:
> Teman, Omar, Zepho, Gatam and
> Kenaz.

[12]Esau's son Eliphaz also had a concubine named Timna, who bore him Amalek. These were grandsons of Esau's wife Adah.

[13]The sons of Reuel:
> Nahath, Zerah, Shammah and
> Mizzah. These were grandsons of
> Esau's wife Basemath.

[14]The sons of Esau's wife Oholibamah daughter of Anah and granddaughter of Zibeon, whom she bore to Esau:
> Jeush, Jalam and Korah.

---

a10 Israel means *he struggles with God.*
b11 Hebrew *El-Shaddai*   *c15 Bethel* means *house of God.*   *d18 Ben-Oni* means *son of my trouble.*
e18 Benjamin means *son of my right hand.*

¹⁵These were the chiefs among Esau's descendants:

The sons of Eliphaz the firstborn of Esau:
Chiefs Teman, Omar, Zepho, Kenaz, ¹⁶Korah,ᵃ Gatam and Amalek. These were the chiefs descended from Eliphaz in Edom; they were grandsons of Adah.
¹⁷The sons of Esau's son Reuel:
Chiefs Nahath, Zerah, Shammah and Mizzah. These were the chiefs descended from Reuel in Edom; they were grandsons of Esau's wife Basemath.
¹⁸The sons of Esau's wife Oholibamah:
Chiefs Jeush, Jalam and Korah. These were the chiefs descended from Esau's wife Oholibamah daughter of Anah.
¹⁹These were the sons of Esau (that is, Edom), and these were their chiefs.

²⁰These were the sons of Seir the Horite, who were living in the region:
Lotan, Shobal, Zibeon, Anah, ²¹Dishon, Ezer and Dishan. These sons of Seir in Edom were Horite chiefs.
²²The sons of Lotan:
Hori and Homam.ᵇ Timna was Lotan's sister.
²³The sons of Shobal:
Alvan, Manahath, Ebal, Shepho and Onam.
²⁴The sons of Zibeon:
Aiah and Anah. This is the Anah who discovered the hot springsᶜ in the desert while he was grazing the donkeys of his father Zibeon.
²⁵The children of Anah:
Dishon and Oholibamah daughter of Anah.
²⁶The sons of Dishonᵈ:
Hemdan, Eshban, Ithran and Keran.
²⁷The sons of Ezer:
Bilhan, Zaavan and Akan.
²⁸The sons of Dishan:
Uz and Aran.
²⁹These were the Horite chiefs:
Lotan, Shobal, Zibeon, Anah, ³⁰Dishon, Ezer and Dishan. These were the Horite chiefs, according to their divisions, in the land of Seir.

The Rulers of Edom

³¹These were the kings who reigned in Edom before any Israelite king reignedᵉ:
³²Bela son of Beor became king of Edom. His city was named Dinhabah.
³³When Bela died, Jobab son of Zerah from Bozrah succeeded him as king.
³⁴When Jobab died, Husham from the land of the Temanites succeeded him as king.
³⁵When Husham died, Hadad son of Bedad, who defeated Midian in the country of Moab, succeeded him as king. His city was named Avith.
³⁶When Hadad died, Samlah from Masrekah succeeded him as king.
³⁷When Samlah died, Shaul from Rehoboth on the riverᶠ succeeded him as king.
³⁸When Shaul died, Baal-Hanan son of Acbor succeeded him as king.
³⁹When Baal-Hanan son of Acbor died, Hadadᵍ succeeded him as king. His city was named Pau, and his wife's name was Mehetabel daughter of Matred, the daughter of Me-Zahab.

⁴⁰These were the chiefs descended from Esau, by name, according to their clans and regions:
Timna, Alvah, Jetheth, ⁴¹Oholibamah, Elah, Pinon, ⁴²Kenaz, Teman, Mibzar, ⁴³Magdiel and Iram. These were the chiefs of Edom, according to their settlements in the land they occupied.

This was Esau the father of the Edomites.

Joseph's Dreams

37 Jacob lived in the land where his father had stayed, the land of Canaan.

²This is the account of Jacob.

Joseph, a young man of seventeen, was tending the flocks with his brothers, the sons of Bilhah and the sons of Zilpah, his father's wives, and he brought their father a bad report about them.
³Now Israel loved Joseph more than any of his other sons, because he had been

---

ᵃ16 Masoretic Text; Samaritan Pentateuch (see also Gen. 36:11 and 1 Chron. 1:36) does not have *Korah.*   ᵇ22 Hebrew *Hemam,* a variant of *Homam* (see 1 Chron. 1:39)   ᶜ24 Vulgate; Syriac *discovered water;* the meaning of the Hebrew for this word is uncertain.   ᵈ26 Hebrew *Dishan,* a variant of *Dishon*   ᵉ31 Or *before an Israelite king reigned over them*   ᶠ37 Possibly the Euphrates   ᵍ39 Many manuscripts of the Masoretic Text, Samaritan Pentateuch and Syriac (see also 1 Chron. 1:50); most manuscripts of the Masoretic Text *Hadar*

Separate and Equal

Key Verse: *"[Joseph's] brothers were jealous of him, but his father kept the matter in mind."* Genesis 37:11

Text: Genesis 37:1–11 *(Dad or child reads the text.)*

DAD READS: What's your favorite soft drink? Your favorite sports team? Toothpaste? Pizza topping? Nearly everyone has a favorite everything. In fact, we are so consistent with some of our favorite things that they are held in computers and automatically assigned to us. My travel agent, for example, never asks me if I want a window seat or one on the aisle. My computer record tells him which one is my favorite. Favorite things are good in most areas of life. Having favorite children, however, isn't one of them.

Child reads: Children are like snowflakes; no two are alike. In fact, parents with more than one child sometimes can't believe that these children could have possibly come from the same dad and mom!

DAD READS: It's only natural to feel a tug of greater affection toward certain members of our family—natural, but *wrong*. Today's verses remind us of what can happen when a dad favors one of his children over the rest. It's a recipe for absolute disaster. Because of what Jacob did in showing special affection for Joseph, he set this boy up to be hated by the rest of the family.

Child reads: One message that fills the pages of our Bible: God's love and grace come in equal and full measure to everyone. No matter what his children do, he gives each one of us every bit of love he has.

DAD READS: The parable Jesus told of the landowner (Matthew 20) helps us to understand this truth. The man hired some workers at 6 o'clock in the morning, promising them a certain wage for twelve hours of work. Then, because there was more to be done than these men could do, the landowner hired more helpers at 9 o'clock; more at noon; more at 3 o'clock; and, finally, a few at 5 o'clock, only one hour before the end of the day. When closing time came, the landowner paid everyone the same amount he had promised to the folks who had been working all day. They were understandably upset, forgetting that the only thing that should have mattered was the landowner's promise to them, not what the others were paid. Jesus drove the point home: God's grace is available to each of us. It's also full and equal, regardless of what we deserve, based on our performance that day.

Child reads: On the days when I am really feeling good because I have been a model kid, it's easy for me to feel like I'm better than the others in my family. On other days when I know that I have not been good, I am thankful for God's grace because I really deserve much less.

DAD READS: Once again, our heavenly Father gives us a perfect example to follow. Let's thank him for this:

Our Father in heaven, thank you for your grace. Thank you for loving all of us all the time. Thank you for not having favorites in your family. Please help us to learn to love each other this way in our family. In Jesus' name, Amen.

For your next devotional reading, go to page 53.

born to him in his old age; and he made a richly ornamented*a* robe for him. **4**When his brothers saw that their father loved him more than any of them, they hated him and could not speak a kind word to him.

5Joseph had a dream, and when he told it to his brothers, they hated him all the more. **6**He said to them, "Listen to this dream I had: **7**We were binding sheaves of grain out in the field when suddenly my sheaf rose and stood upright, while your sheaves gathered around mine and bowed down to it."

8His brothers said to him, "Do you intend to reign over us? Will you actually rule us?" And they hated him all the more because of his dream and what he had said.

9Then he had another dream, and he told it to his brothers. "Listen," he said, "I had another dream, and this time the sun and moon and eleven stars were bowing down to me."

10When he told his father as well as his brothers, his father rebuked him and said, "What is this dream you had? Will your mother and I and your brothers actually come and bow down to the ground before you?" **11**His brothers were jealous of him, but his father kept the matter in mind.

Joseph Sold by His Brothers

12Now his brothers had gone to graze their father's flocks near Shechem, **13**and Israel said to Joseph, "As you know, your brothers are grazing the flocks near Shechem. Come, I am going to send you to them."

"Very well," he replied.

14So he said to him, "Go and see if all is well with your brothers and with the

a3 The meaning of the Hebrew for *richly ornamented* is uncertain; also in verses 23 and 32.

My Son, the Miniature Me
Jacob, the Biased Father

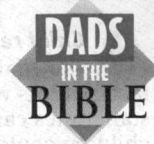

"When his brothers saw that their father loved [Joseph] more than any of them, they hated him and could not speak a kind word to him" (37:4).

Text: Genesis 37

As a father, you know that treating your children equally can be a major challenge. In his later years, Jacob gave us a strong reminder of what happens when a dad doesn't deal evenly with his family.

Joseph, Jacob's eleventh son, must have made his aged father very proud. He worked hard in the fields and brought Jacob the inside scoop on the rest of his family. Jacob allowed young Joseph to become his personal confidant and openly rewarded him for the special place he had found in his old father's heart.

Joseph's brothers reacted predictably. Their father's foolish indiscretion practically forced them to hate their little brother.

Treating your children with an equal amount of love, attention and discipline will foster the best possible relationship they could ever have with each other. Affectionately singling one of your children out—perhaps the one who, by some quirk of genetic fate, will become the scholar or the athlete you never were—will sentence your children to rivalry and bitterness.

Please do not miss the lesson to be learned by Jacob's gross error, and don't think for a moment that you and your family are exempt from this situation. Pour equal amounts of father-love onto your children. Find places where each one can excel. Celebrate their differences and their unique accomplishments, even if doing so seems foreign to you.

Each of your children must experience the full measure of their father's love. If they don't, they'll find a way to get your attention in other ways . . . such as selling "dad's favorite" off to total strangers. I'm sure this is not the kind of family Jacob had hoped for. Please do everything in your power to make sure this doesn't happen to yours.

For a complete listing of Dads in the Bible, turn to page 1434.

flocks, and bring word back to me." Then he sent him off from the Valley of Hebron.

When Joseph arrived at Shechem, ¹⁵a man found him wandering around in the fields and asked him, "What are you looking for?"

¹⁶He replied, "I'm looking for my brothers. Can you tell me where they are grazing their flocks?"

¹⁷"They have moved on from here," the man answered. "I heard them say, 'Let's go to Dothan.' "

So Joseph went after his brothers and found them near Dothan. ¹⁸But they saw him in the distance, and before he reached them, they plotted to kill him.

¹⁹"Here comes that dreamer!" they said to each other. ²⁰"Come now, let's kill him and throw him into one of these cisterns and say that a ferocious animal devoured him. Then we'll see what comes of his dreams."

²¹When Reuben heard this, he tried to rescue him from their hands. "Let's not take his life," he said. ²²"Don't shed any blood. Throw him into this cistern here in the desert, but don't lay a hand on him." Reuben said this to rescue him from them and take him back to his father.

²³So when Joseph came to his brothers, they stripped him of his robe—the richly ornamented robe he was wearing— ²⁴and they took him and threw him into the cistern. Now the cistern was empty; there was no water in it.

²⁵As they sat down to eat their meal, they looked up and saw a caravan of Ishmaelites coming from Gilead. Their camels were loaded with spices, balm and myrrh, and they were on their way to take them down to Egypt.

²⁶Judah said to his brothers, "What will we gain if we kill our brother and cover up his blood? ²⁷Come, let's sell him to the Ishmaelites and not lay our hands on him; after all, he is our brother, our own flesh and blood." His brothers agreed.

²⁸So when the Midianite merchants came by, his brothers pulled Joseph up out of the cistern and sold him for twenty shekels*a* of silver to the Ishmaelites, who took him to Egypt.

²⁹When Reuben returned to the cistern and saw that Joseph was not there, he tore his clothes. ³⁰He went back to his brothers and said, "The boy isn't there! Where can I turn now?"

³¹Then they got Joseph's robe, slaughtered a goat and dipped the robe in the blood. ³²They took the ornamented robe

back to their father and said, "We found this. Examine it to see whether it is your son's robe."

³³He recognized it and said, "It is my son's robe! Some ferocious animal has devoured him. Joseph has surely been torn to pieces."

³⁴Then Jacob tore his clothes, put on sackcloth and mourned for his son many days. ³⁵All his sons and daughters came to comfort him, but he refused to be comforted. "No," he said, "in mourning will I go down to the grave*b* to my son." So his father wept for him.

³⁶Meanwhile, the Midianites*c* sold Joseph in Egypt to Potiphar, one of Pharaoh's officials, the captain of the guard.

Judah and Tamar

38 At that time, Judah left his brothers and went down to stay with a man of Adullam named Hirah. ²There Judah met the daughter of a Canaanite man named Shua. He married her and lay with her; ³she became pregnant and gave birth to a son, who was named Er. ⁴She conceived again and gave birth to a son and named him Onan. ⁵She gave birth to still another son and named him Shelah. It was at Kezib that she gave birth to him.

⁶Judah got a wife for Er, his firstborn, and her name was Tamar. ⁷But Er, Judah's firstborn, was wicked in the LORD's sight; so the LORD put him to death.

⁸Then Judah said to Onan, "Lie with your brother's wife and fulfill your duty to her as a brother-in-law to produce offspring for your brother." ⁹But Onan knew that the offspring would not be his; so whenever he lay with his brother's wife, he spilled his semen on the ground to keep from producing offspring for his brother. ¹⁰What he did was wicked in the LORD's sight; so he put him to death also.

¹¹Judah then said to his daughter-in-law Tamar, "Live as a widow in your father's house until my son Shelah grows up." For he thought, "He may die too, just like his brothers." So Tamar went to live in her father's house.

¹²After a long time Judah's wife, the daughter of Shua, died. When Judah had recovered from his grief, he went up to Timnah, to the men who were shearing

---

a28 That is, about 8 ounces (about 0.2 kilogram)
b35 Hebrew *Sheol*   *c36* Samaritan Pentateuch, Septuagint, Vulgate and Syriac (see also verse 28); Masoretic Text *Medanites*

his sheep, and his friend Hirah the Adullamite went with him.

[13]When Tamar was told, "Your father-in-law is on his way to Timnah to shear his sheep," [14]she took off her widow's clothes, covered herself with a veil to disguise herself, and then sat down at the entrance to Enaim, which is on the road to Timnah. For she saw that, though Shelah had now grown up, she had not been given to him as his wife.

[15]When Judah saw her, he thought she was a prostitute, for she had covered her face. [16]Not realizing that she was his daughter-in-law, he went over to her by the roadside and said, "Come now, let me sleep with you."

"And what will you give me to sleep with you?" she asked.

[17]"I'll send you a young goat from my flock," he said.

"Will you give me something as a pledge until you send it?" she asked.

[18]He said, "What pledge should I give you?"

"Your seal and its cord, and the staff in your hand," she answered. So he gave them to her and slept with her, and she became pregnant by him. [19]After she left, she took off her veil and put on her widow's clothes again.

[20]Meanwhile Judah sent the young goat by his friend the Adullamite in order to get his pledge back from the woman, but he did not find her. [21]He asked the men who lived there, "Where is the shrine prostitute who was beside the road at Enaim?"

"There hasn't been any shrine prostitute here," they said.

[22]So he went back to Judah and said, "I didn't find her. Besides, the men who lived there said, 'There hasn't been any shrine prostitute here.'"

[23]Then Judah said, "Let her keep what she has, or we will become a laughingstock. After all, I did send her this young goat, but you didn't find her."

[24]About three months later Judah was told, "Your daughter-in-law Tamar is guilty of prostitution, and as a result she is now pregnant."

Judah said, "Bring her out and have her burned to death!"

[25]As she was being brought out, she sent a message to her father-in-law. "I am pregnant by the man who owns these," she said. And she added, "See if you recognize whose seal and cord and staff these are."

[26]Judah recognized them and said, "She is more righteous than I, since I wouldn't give her to my son Shelah." And he did not sleep with her again.

[27]When the time came for her to give birth, there were twin boys in her womb. [28]As she was giving birth, one of them put out his hand; so the midwife took a scarlet thread and tied it on his wrist and said, "This one came out first." [29]But when he drew back his hand, his brother came out, and she said, "So this is how you have broken out!" And he was named Perez.[a] [30]Then his brother, who had the scarlet thread on his wrist, came out and he was given the name Zerah.[b]

Joseph and Potiphar's Wife

39 Now Joseph had been taken down to Egypt. Potiphar, an Egyptian who was one of Pharaoh's officials, the captain of the guard, bought him from the Ishmaelites who had taken him there.

[2]The LORD was with Joseph and he prospered, and he lived in the house of his Egyptian master. [3]When his master saw that the LORD was with him and that the LORD gave him success in everything he did, [4]Joseph found favor in his eyes and became his attendant. Potiphar put him in charge of his household, and he entrusted to his care everything he owned. [5]From the time he put him in charge of his household and of all that he owned, the LORD blessed the household of the Egyptian because of Joseph. The blessing of the LORD was on everything Potiphar had, both in the house and in the field. [6]So he left in Joseph's care everything he had; with Joseph in charge, he did not concern himself with anything except the food he ate.

Now Joseph was well-built and handsome, [7]and after a while his master's wife took notice of Joseph and said, "Come to bed with me!"

[8]But he refused. "With me in charge," he told her, "my master does not concern himself with anything in the house; everything he owns he has entrusted to my care. [9]No one is greater in this house than I am. My master has withheld nothing from me except you, because you are his wife. How then could I do such a wicked thing and sin against God?" [10]And though she spoke to Joseph day after day, he

[a]29 Perez means breaking out.   [b]30 Zerah can mean scarlet or brightness.

Tell Bobbie "Hello" for Me

The seat belt light went off, and the flight attendant gave her predictable announcement about our being "free to move about the cabin." It was only then that I noticed the attractive woman sitting in the seat next to me.

She looked to be about my age. Her tailored navy suit and crisply starched blouse spoke of her success in business. I turned and said "hello." She looked up from the book she was reading and smiled, returning my greeting.

Over the next hour we talked. She was single—a stockbroker who lived in Northern Virginia. She worked for a large firm across the Potomac in the shadow of the Capitol Building. She was headed home after several days of meetings in Chicago. I asked her where she had grown up. She told me of her parents and siblings. I was curious about her education and her work. She was willing to talk about her schooling, her career, and even her fears and dreams. Our talk was effortless, moving seamlessly from laughter to expressions of deep feelings, then back to laughter again.

Ten minutes into the conversation, I felt my pulse slowly begin to quicken. This was more than simply an information-gathering experience. I felt myself, mysteriously but unmistakably, being attracted to my airplane companion. Her beauty was matched by her tenderness and willingness to disclose some of her deepest feelings. In spite of the fact that I considered myself to be a happily married man, I was taken by this intelligent and extremely articulate woman.

And I knew, presumptuous though it may sound, that she was feeling the same. Her willingness to talk openly about her failures and aspirations were a clue. Her occasional touches sealed it.

Until the captain informed us that we were "beginning our descent into the Washington area" we only talked about her. In fact, she had just suggested that since my hotel was close to the airport and her car was in long-term parking, she'd be happy to give me a ride.

DAILY INSIGHT

MONDAY

Passage:
Genesis 39:1–12

Verse:
Genesis 39:12

For a few minutes we sat in silence. I'm not sure what she was thinking, but I know that my mind was in a swirl. Then turning to me, she asked, "Tell me about you, Robert."

My mind raced through the options. I was alone in a city where anonymity is a sacrament. Like Joseph in Egypt, I was a grown man with the freedom to make any choice I wanted to make. I would probably never be found out. At the same time, eight hundred miles behind me was a family who loved me. I glanced at my watch. It was bedtime. I could envision Bobbie tenderly tucking our two little girls in with a prayer, a kiss, and an "I love you." I could see her crawling into our bed, exhausted from a busy day. I knew she was thinking about me.

"I'm in the publishing business," I finally said. "It's a wonderful career, and I love what I'm doing." I paused for just a moment. "And I have a precious wife named Bobbie and two young daughters who really love their Daddy." I reached into my briefcase and pulled out my day planner. Opening to the last few pages, I showed my traveling companion pictures of Bobbie and the girls.

Until the plane's wheels screeched our welcome to National Airport, I talked about my home—how I had met Bobbie, how much we loved each other, and what I enjoyed doing with Missy and Julie. I talked nonstop. My friend was genuinely interested in every detail.

As we stood to leave the plane, I thanked her for her offer to take me to my hotel. I told her that I would be happy to take the shuttle. She understood. "Thanks for telling me about your life," she said as I pulled my case from the overhead compartment. "I wish more men loved their families like you do." Then, as an afterthought, she added, "Tell Bobbie 'hello' for me."

"Thank you, Father in heaven," I remember praying that night as I slipped into bed. "Thank you for a family who loves me so much that they gave their lives to save mine tonight."

For your next devotional reading, go to page 56.

refused to go to bed with her or even be with her.

[11]One day he went into the house to attend to his duties, and none of the household servants was inside. [12]She caught him by his cloak and said, "Come to bed with me!" But he left his cloak in her hand and ran out of the house.

[13]When she saw that he had left his cloak in her hand and had run out of the house, [14]she called her household servants. "Look," she said to them, "this Hebrew has been brought to us to make sport of us! He came in here to sleep with me, but I screamed. [15]When he heard me scream for help, he left his cloak beside me and ran out of the house."

[16]She kept his cloak beside her until his master came home. [17]Then she told him this story: "That Hebrew slave you brought us came to me to make sport of me. [18]But as soon as I screamed for help, he left his cloak beside me and ran out of the house."

[19]When his master heard the story his wife told him, saying, "This is how your slave treated me," he burned with anger. [20]Joseph's master took him and put him in prison, the place where the king's prisoners were confined.

But while Joseph was there in the prison, [21]the LORD was with him; he showed him kindness and granted him favor in the eyes of the prison warden. [22]So the warden put Joseph in charge of all those held in the prison, and he was made responsible for all that was done there. [23]The warden paid no attention to anything under Joseph's care, because the LORD was with Joseph and gave him success in whatever he did.

The Cupbearer and the Baker

40 Some time later, the cupbearer and the baker of the king of Egypt offended their master, the king of Egypt. [2]Pharaoh was angry with his two officials, the chief cupbearer and the chief baker, [3]and put them in custody in the house of the captain of the guard, in the same prison where Joseph was confined. [4]The captain of the guard assigned them to Joseph, and he attended them.

After they had been in custody for some time, [5]each of the two men—the cupbearer and the baker of the king of Egypt, who were being held in prison—had a dream the same night, and each dream had a meaning of its own.

[6]When Joseph came to them the next morning, he saw that they were dejected. [7]So he asked Pharaoh's officials who were in custody with him in his master's house, "Why are your faces so sad today?"

[8]"We both had dreams," they answered, "but there is no one to interpret them."

Then Joseph said to them, "Do not interpretations belong to God? Tell me your dreams."

[9]So the chief cupbearer told Joseph his dream. He said to him, "In my dream I saw a vine in front of me, [10]and on the vine were three branches. As soon as it budded, it blossomed, and its clusters ripened into grapes. [11]Pharaoh's cup was in my hand, and I took the grapes, squeezed them into Pharaoh's cup and put the cup in his hand."

[12]"This is what it means," Joseph said to him. "The three branches are three days. [13]Within three days Pharaoh will lift up your head and restore you to your position, and you will put Pharaoh's cup in his hand, just as you used to do when you were his cupbearer. [14]But when all goes well with you, remember me and show me kindness; mention me to Pharaoh and get me out of this prison. [15]For I was forcibly carried off from the land of the Hebrews, and even here I have done nothing to deserve being put in a dungeon."

[16]When the chief baker saw that Joseph had given a favorable interpretation, he said to Joseph, "I too had a dream: On my head were three baskets of bread.[a] [17]In the top basket were all kinds of baked goods for Pharaoh, but the birds were eating them out of the basket on my head."

[18]"This is what it means," Joseph said. "The three baskets are three days. [19]Within three days Pharaoh will lift off your head and hang you on a tree.[b] And the birds will eat away your flesh."

[20]Now the third day was Pharaoh's birthday, and he gave a feast for all his officials. He lifted up the heads of the chief cupbearer and the chief baker in the presence of his officials: [21]He restored the chief cupbearer to his position, so that he once again put the cup into Pharaoh's hand, [22]but he hanged[c] the chief baker, just as Joseph had said to them in his interpretation.

[23]The chief cupbearer, however, did not remember Joseph; he forgot him.

---

[a]16 Or *three wicker baskets*   [b]19 Or *and impale you on a pole*   [c]22,13 Or *impaled*

Pharaoh's Dreams

41 When two full years had passed, Pharaoh had a dream: He was standing by the Nile, ²when out of the river there came up seven cows, sleek and fat, and they grazed among the reeds. ³After them, seven other cows, ugly and gaunt, came up out of the Nile and stood beside those on the riverbank. ⁴And the cows that were ugly and gaunt ate up the seven sleek, fat cows. Then Pharaoh woke up.

⁵He fell asleep again and had a second dream: Seven heads of grain, healthy and good, were growing on a single stalk. ⁶After them, seven other heads of grain sprouted—thin and scorched by the east wind. ⁷The thin heads of grain swallowed up the seven healthy, full heads. Then Pharaoh woke up; it had been a dream.

⁸In the morning his mind was troubled, so he sent for all the magicians and wise men of Egypt. Pharaoh told them his dreams, but no one could interpret them for him.

⁹Then the chief cupbearer said to Pharaoh, "Today I am reminded of my shortcomings. ¹⁰Pharaoh was once angry with his servants, and he imprisoned me and the chief baker in the house of the captain of the guard. ¹¹Each of us had a dream the same night, and each dream had a meaning of its own. ¹²Now a young Hebrew was there with us, a servant of the captain of the guard. We told him our dreams, and he interpreted them for us, giving each man the interpretation of his dream. ¹³And things turned out exactly as he interpreted them to us: I was restored to my position, and the other man was hanged.ᶜ"

¹⁴So Pharaoh sent for Joseph, and he was quickly brought from the dungeon. When he had shaved and changed his clothes, he came before Pharaoh.

¹⁵Pharaoh said to Joseph, "I had a dream, and no one can interpret it. But I have heard it said of you that when you hear a dream you can interpret it."

¹⁶"I cannot do it," Joseph replied to Pharaoh, "but God will give Pharaoh the answer he desires."

¹⁷Then Pharaoh said to Joseph, "In my dream I was standing on the bank of the Nile, ¹⁸when out of the river there came up seven cows, fat and sleek, and they grazed among the reeds. ¹⁹After them, seven other cows came up—scrawny and very ugly and lean. I had never seen such ugly cows in all the land of Egypt. ²⁰The lean, ugly cows ate up the seven fat cows that came up first. ²¹But even after they ate them, no one could tell that they had done so; they looked just as ugly as before. Then I woke up.

²²"In my dreams I also saw seven heads of grain, full and good, growing on a single stalk. ²³After them, seven other heads sprouted—withered and thin and scorched by the east wind. ²⁴The thin heads of grain swallowed up the seven good heads. I told this to the magicians, but none could explain it to me."

²⁵Then Joseph said to Pharaoh, "The dreams of Pharaoh are one and the same. God has revealed to Pharaoh what he is about to do. ²⁶The seven good cows are seven years, and the seven good heads of grain are seven years; it is one and the same dream. ²⁷The seven lean, ugly cows that came up afterward are seven years, and so are the seven worthless heads of grain scorched by the east wind: They are seven years of famine.

²⁸"It is just as I said to Pharaoh: God has shown Pharaoh what he is about to do. ²⁹Seven years of great abundance are coming throughout the land of Egypt, ³⁰but seven years of famine will follow them. Then all the abundance in Egypt will be forgotten, and the famine will ravage the land. ³¹The abundance in the land will not be remembered, because the famine that follows it will be so severe. ³²The reason the dream was given to Pharaoh in two forms is that the matter has been firmly decided by God, and God will do it soon.

³³"And now let Pharaoh look for a discerning and wise man and put him in charge of the land of Egypt. ³⁴Let Pharaoh appoint commissioners over the land to take a fifth of the harvest of Egypt during the seven years of abundance. ³⁵They should collect all the food of these good years that are coming and store up the grain under the authority of Pharaoh, to be kept in the cities for food. ³⁶This food should be held in reserve for the country, to be used during the seven years of famine that will come upon Egypt, so that the country may not be ruined by the famine."

³⁷The plan seemed good to Pharaoh and to all his officials. ³⁸So Pharaoh asked them, "Can we find anyone like this man, one in whom is the spirit of Godᵃ?"

³⁹Then Pharaoh said to Joseph, "Since

ᵃ38 Or of the gods

God has made all this known to you, there is no one so discerning and wise as you. [40]You shall be in charge of my palace, and all my people are to submit to your orders. Only with respect to the throne will I be greater than you."

Joseph in Charge of Egypt

[41]So Pharaoh said to Joseph, "I hereby put you in charge of the whole land of Egypt." [42]Then Pharaoh took his signet ring from his finger and put it on Joseph's finger. He dressed him in robes of fine linen and put a gold chain around his neck. [43]He had him ride in a chariot as his second-in-command,[a] and men shouted before him, "Make way[b]!" Thus he put him in charge of the whole land of Egypt.

[44]Then Pharaoh said to Joseph, "I am Pharaoh, but without your word no one will lift hand or foot in all Egypt." [45]Phar-

aoh gave Joseph the name Zaphenath-Paneah and gave him Asenath daughter of Potiphera, priest of On,[c] to be his wife. And Joseph went throughout the land of Egypt. [46]Joseph was thirty years old when he entered the service of Pharaoh king of Egypt. And Joseph went out from Pharaoh's presence and traveled throughout Egypt. [47]During the seven years of abundance the land produced plentifully. [48]Joseph collected all the food produced in those seven years of abundance in Egypt and stored it in the cities. In each city he put the food grown in the fields surrounding it. [49]Joseph stored up huge quantities of grain, like the sand of the sea; it was so much that he stopped keeping records because it was beyond measure.

[a]43 Or *in the chariot of his second-in-command*; or *in his second chariot*   [b]43 Or *Bow down*   [c]45 That is, Heliopolis; also in verse 50

Sandwiches, Rocket Ships, and Money in the Bank

DAILY INSIGHT

Early every morning, in kitchens around the world, people prepare and pack lunches for themselves. This job isn't all that easy to do; for most of us, the smell of peanut butter, bologna, or pickles at 6:30 a.m. is pretty disgusting. Even the *thought* of such food that early in the morning can give you a queasy feeling. But if you want lunch, you're going to have to prepare for it before you're hungry.

When NASA prepares to launch a rocket to meet up with Mars or Saturn, the engineers don't aim their space crafts at the planet. They aim them where the celestial body will be by the time their module gets there. It's the same as a quarterback throwing a pass to the spot where his receiver will be by the time the ball arrives.

In business, and in life, this type of behavior is called *strategic planning*—doing something before you need to so that when the need actually arises, you'll be ready. This takes discipline. It's thankless and hard work.

The leadership story of Joseph in Egypt is an incredible one. His rise from prison to

TUESDAY

Passage:
Genesis 41:33–41, 53–57

Verse:
Genesis 41:41

power is one of the greatest accounts of strategic planning in history. Joseph was disciplined enough to save resources during prosperous times so his nation would have "money in the bank" for the famine. Can you imagine the people who must have tried to talk Joseph out of his strategy during those first seven years of prosperity? "Come on, Joseph, let's eat all the good stuff *now*. What are we waiting for?"

The task of being a good father is this: Do things for your children now that are not based on where your children are, but on where they're going to be. Make investments of discipline, tenderness, and instruction, not because your children will applaud your efforts today (you may hear cries of, "C'mon Dad, chill out"), but because in the future, they're going to need to cash in on the investment you've made today.

By the way, if this sounds like a lot of thankless work, remember Joseph's word to the Pharaoh who asked him for his advice: "I cannot do it ... but God will" (41:16).

For your next devotional reading, go to page 60.

⁵⁰Before the years of famine came, two sons were born to Joseph by Asenath daughter of Potiphera, priest of On. ⁵¹Joseph named his firstborn Manasseh*ᵃ* and said, "It is because God has made me forget all my trouble and all my father's household." ⁵²The second son he named Ephraim*ᵇ* and said, "It is because God has made me fruitful in the land of my suffering."

⁵³The seven years of abundance in Egypt came to an end, ⁵⁴and the seven years of famine began, just as Joseph had said. There was famine in all the other lands, but in the whole land of Egypt there was food. ⁵⁵When all Egypt began to feel the famine, the people cried to Pharaoh for food. Then Pharaoh told all the Egyptians, "Go to Joseph and do what he tells you."

⁵⁶When the famine had spread over the whole country, Joseph opened the storehouses and sold grain to the Egyptians, for the famine was severe throughout Egypt. ⁵⁷And all the countries came to Egypt to buy grain from Joseph, because the famine was severe in all the world.

Joseph's Brothers Go to Egypt

42 When Jacob learned that there was grain in Egypt, he said to his sons, "Why do you just keep looking at each other?" ²He continued, "I have heard that there is grain in Egypt. Go down there and buy some for us, so that we may live and not die."

³Then ten of Joseph's brothers went down to buy grain from Egypt. ⁴But Jacob did not send Benjamin, Joseph's brother, with the others, because he was afraid that harm might come to him. ⁵So Israel's sons were among those who went to buy grain, for the famine was in the land of Canaan also.

⁶Now Joseph was the governor of the land, the one who sold grain to all its people. So when Joseph's brothers arrived, they bowed down to him with their faces to the ground. ⁷As soon as Joseph saw his brothers, he recognized them, but he pretended to be a stranger and spoke harshly to them. "Where do you come from?" he asked.

"From the land of Canaan," they replied, "to buy food."

⁸Although Joseph recognized his brothers, they did not recognize him. ⁹Then he remembered his dreams about them and said to them, "You are spies! You have come to see where our land is unprotected."

¹⁰"No, my lord," they answered. "Your servants have come to buy food. ¹¹We are all the sons of one man. Your servants are honest men, not spies."

¹²"No!" he said to them. "You have come to see where our land is unprotected."

¹³But they replied, "Your servants were twelve brothers, the sons of one man, who lives in the land of Canaan. The youngest is now with our father, and one is no more."

¹⁴Joseph said to them, "It is just as I told you: You are spies! ¹⁵And this is how you will be tested: As surely as Pharaoh lives, you will not leave this place unless your youngest brother comes here. ¹⁶Send one of your number to get your brother; the rest of you will be kept in prison, so that your words may be tested to see if you are telling the truth. If you are not, then as surely as Pharaoh lives, you are spies!" ¹⁷And he put them all in custody for three days.

¹⁸On the third day, Joseph said to them, "Do this and you will live, for I fear God: ¹⁹If you are honest men, let one of your brothers stay here in prison, while the rest of you go and take grain back for your starving households. ²⁰But you must bring your youngest brother to me, so that your words may be verified and that you may not die." This they proceeded to do.

²¹They said to one another, "Surely we are being punished because of our brother. We saw how distressed he was when he pleaded with us for his life, but we would not listen; that's why this distress has come upon us."

²²Reuben replied, "Didn't I tell you not to sin against the boy? But you wouldn't listen! Now we must give an accounting for his blood." ²³They did not realize that Joseph could understand them, since he was using an interpreter.

²⁴He turned away from them and began to weep, but then turned back and spoke to them again. He had Simeon taken from them and bound before their eyes.

²⁵Joseph gave orders to fill their bags with grain, to put each man's silver back in his sack, and to give them provisions for their journey. After this was done for

ᵃ51 Manasseh sounds like and may be derived from the Hebrew for *forget*.   *ᵇ52 Ephraim* sounds like the Hebrew for *twice fruitful*.

them, ²⁶they loaded their grain on their donkeys and left.

²⁷At the place where they stopped for the night one of them opened his sack to get feed for his donkey, and he saw his silver in the mouth of his sack. ²⁸"My silver has been returned," he said to his brothers. "Here it is in my sack."

Their hearts sank and they turned to each other trembling and said, "What is this that God has done to us?"

²⁹When they came to their father Jacob in the land of Canaan, they told him all that had happened to them. They said, ³⁰"The man who is lord over the land spoke harshly to us and treated us as though we were spying on the land. ³¹But we said to him, 'We are honest men; we are not spies. ³²We were twelve brothers, sons of one father. One is no more, and the youngest is now with our father in Canaan.'

³³"Then the man who is lord over the land said to us, 'This is how I will know whether you are honest men: Leave one of your brothers here with me, and take food for your starving households and go. ³⁴But bring your youngest brother to me so I will know that you are not spies but honest men. Then I will give your brother back to you, and you can trade^a in the land.' "

³⁵As they were emptying their sacks, there in each man's sack was his pouch of silver! When they and their father saw the money pouches, they were frightened. ³⁶Their father Jacob said to them, "You have deprived me of my children. Joseph is no more and Simeon is no more, and now you want to take Benjamin. Everything is against me!"

³⁷Then Reuben said to his father, "You may put both of my sons to death if I do not bring him back to you. Entrust him to my care, and I will bring him back."

³⁸But Jacob said, "My son will not go down there with you; his brother is dead and he is the only one left. If harm comes to him on the journey you are taking, you will bring my gray head down to the grave^b in sorrow."

The Second Journey to Egypt

43 Now the famine was still severe in the land. ²So when they had eaten all the grain they had brought from Egypt, their father said to them, "Go back and buy us a little more food." ³But Judah said to him, "The man

warned us solemnly, 'You will not see my face again unless your brother is with you.' ⁴If you will send our brother along with us, we will go down and buy food for you. ⁵But if you will not send him, we will not go down, because the man said to us, 'You will not see my face again unless your brother is with you.' "

⁶Israel asked, "Why did you bring this trouble on me by telling the man you had another brother?"

⁷They replied, "The man questioned us closely about ourselves and our family. 'Is your father still living?' he asked us. 'Do you have another brother?' We simply answered his questions. How were we to know he would say, 'Bring your brother down here'?"

⁸Then Judah said to Israel his father, "Send the boy along with me and we will go at once, so that we and you and our children may live and not die. ⁹I myself will guarantee his safety; you can hold me personally responsible for him. If I do not bring him back to you and set him here before you, I will bear the blame before you all my life. ¹⁰As it is, if we had not delayed, we could have gone and returned twice."

¹¹Then their father Israel said to them, "If it must be, then do this: Put some of the best products of the land in your bags and take them down to the man as a gift— a little balm and a little honey, some spices and myrrh, some pistachio nuts and almonds. ¹²Take double the amount of silver with you, for you must return the silver that was put back into the mouths of your sacks. Perhaps it was a mistake. ¹³Take your brother also and go back to the man at once. ¹⁴And may God Almighty^c grant you mercy before the man so that he will let your other brother and Benjamin come back with you. As for me, if I am bereaved, I am bereaved."

¹⁵So the men took the gifts and double the amount of silver, and Benjamin also. They hurried down to Egypt and presented themselves to Joseph. ¹⁶When Joseph saw Benjamin with them, he said to the steward of his house, "Take these men to my house, slaughter an animal and prepare dinner; they are to eat with me at noon."

¹⁷The man did as Joseph told him and took the men to Joseph's house. ¹⁸Now the men were frightened when they were tak-

^a34 Or *move about freely*   ^b38 Hebrew *Sheol*
^c14 Hebrew *El-Shaddai*

en to his house. They thought, "We were brought here because of the silver that was put back into our sacks the first time. He wants to attack us and overpower us and seize us as slaves and take our donkeys."

¹⁹So they went up to Joseph's steward and spoke to him at the entrance to the house. ²⁰"Please, sir," they said, "we came down here the first time to buy food. ²¹But at the place where we stopped for the night we opened our sacks and each of us found his silver—the exact weight—in the mouth of his sack. So we have brought it back with us. ²²We have also brought additional silver with us to buy food. We don't know who put our silver in our sacks."

²³"It's all right," he said. "Don't be afraid. Your God, the God of your father, has given you treasure in your sacks; I received your silver." Then he brought Simeon out to them.

²⁴The steward took the men into Joseph's house, gave them water to wash their feet and provided fodder for their donkeys. ²⁵They prepared their gifts for Joseph's arrival at noon, because they had heard that they were to eat there.

²⁶When Joseph came home, they presented to him the gifts they had brought into the house, and they bowed down before him to the ground. ²⁷He asked them how they were, and then he said, "How is your aged father you told me about? Is he still living?"

²⁸They replied, "Your servant our father is still alive and well." And they bowed low to pay him honor.

²⁹As he looked about and saw his brother Benjamin, his own mother's son, he asked, "Is this your youngest brother, the one you told me about?" And he said, "God be gracious to you, my son."

³⁰Deeply moved at the sight of his brother, Joseph hurried out and looked for a place to weep. He went into his private room and wept there.

³¹After he had washed his face, he came out and, controlling himself, said, "Serve the food."

³²They served him by himself, the brothers by themselves, and the Egyptians who ate with him by themselves, because Egyptians could not eat with Hebrews, for that is detestable to Egyptians. ³³The men had been seated before him in the order of their ages, from the firstborn to the youngest; and they looked at each other in astonishment. ³⁴When portions were served to them from Joseph's table, Benjamin's portion was five times as much as anyone else's. So they feasted and drank freely with him.

A Silver Cup in a Sack

44 Now Joseph gave these instructions to the steward of his house: "Fill the men's sacks with as much food as they can carry, and put each man's silver in the mouth of his sack. ²Then put my cup, the silver one, in the mouth of the youngest one's sack, along with the silver for his grain." And he did as Joseph said.

³As morning dawned, the men were sent on their way with their donkeys. ⁴They had not gone far from the city when Joseph said to his steward, "Go after those men at once, and when you catch up with them, say to them, 'Why have you repaid good with evil? ⁵Isn't this the cup my master drinks from and also uses for divination? This is a wicked thing you have done.' "

⁶When he caught up with them, he repeated these words to them. ⁷But they said to him, "Why does my lord say such things? Far be it from your servants to do anything like that! ⁸We even brought back to you from the land of Canaan the silver we found inside the mouths of our sacks. So why would we steal silver or gold from your master's house? ⁹If any of your servants is found to have it, he will die; and the rest of us will become my lord's slaves."

¹⁰"Very well, then," he said, "let it be as you say. Whoever is found to have it will become my slave; the rest of you will be free from blame."

¹¹Each of them quickly lowered his sack to the ground and opened it. ¹²Then the steward proceeded to search, beginning with the oldest and ending with the youngest. And the cup was found in Benjamin's sack. ¹³At this, they tore their clothes. Then they all loaded their donkeys and returned to the city.

¹⁴Joseph was still in the house when Judah and his brothers came in, and they threw themselves to the ground before him. ¹⁵Joseph said to them, "What is this you have done? Don't you know that a man like me can find things out by divination?"

¹⁶"What can we say to my lord?" Judah replied. "What can we say? How can we prove our innocence? God has uncovered your servants' guilt. We are now my lord's

slaves—we ourselves and the one who was found to have the cup."

[17]But Joseph said, "Far be it from me to do such a thing! Only the man who was found to have the cup will become my slave. The rest of you, go back to your father in peace."

[18]Then Judah went up to him and said: "Please, my lord, let your servant speak a word to my lord. Do not be angry with your servant, though you are equal to Pharaoh himself. [19]My lord asked his servants, 'Do you have a father or a brother?' [20]And we answered, 'We have an aged father, and there is a young son born to him in his old age. His brother is dead, and he is the only one of his mother's sons left, and his father loves him.'

[21]"Then you said to your servants, 'Bring him down to me so I can see him for myself.' [22]And we said to my lord, 'The boy cannot leave his father; if he leaves

It's Always Something

The wedding guests were in place. The grandparents were properly seated in the second row. The mother of the bride had just been escorted to the first row, across the aisle from the groom's mother and dad. The air was filled with the kind of indescribable excitement that only a wedding could bring.

This was especially true for me, since I was the dad at the back of the church with our Missy on my arm. She had waited a lifetime for this very moment.

The pastor and our future son-in-law were preparing to enter the church from one of the sanctuary's front doors on the organist's cue. They checked to be sure that everything was in place. It was, including the wireless microphone clipped to the minister's robe. Unfortunately, the minister didn't know that the mike was on!

"Well, Jon," Reverend DeVries joked to the anxious groom, "You can still back out." Of course, neither man had any idea that this very private conversation was being broadcast to almost six hundred people. The congregation held its collective breath.

"No way," was all Jon said.

An audible snicker passed over the seated guests like a wave. My wife sighed in relief. The color returned to the faces of Jon's parents.

Has this ever happened to you? You have done everything in your power to do the right thing. No stone is left unturned. In your opinion, the plan is as perfect as a plan could be. Nothing could have de-

DAILY INSIGHT

WEDNESDAY

Passage:
Genesis 44:1–16

Verse:
Genesis 44:16

scribed our daughter's wedding better than this. But in spite of all of this detailed planning, the technician in the sound booth turned the microphone on too early. It could have been an embarrassing disaster.

That's what happened to the men in this story. Joseph's brothers had followed his instructions to perfection. They had done everything exactly as they were told. But Joseph's servant had slipped a silver chalice into Benjamin's sack of grain, and now these men were being accused of stealing. They knew they were innocent, but they returned to Egypt and threw themselves at Joseph's feet, begging for his mercy.

Isn't it interesting that, even though they were not guilty of this particular charge, they knew they still needed forgiveness? Because of other things they had done—selling their brother like a used car, for one thing—they still needed Joseph's mercy.

Well, our merciful heavenly Father has a little message for us. Regardless of how well you and I have planned this day, something will probably go wrong. One of those little unexpected things will pop up, and we'll be faced with a little—or perhaps a substantial—detour. Count on it. And the lesson to be learned is the one these men learned that day: Perfection is unachievable. God's mercy is always necessary for our inescapable sinfulness ... impeccable plans and all.

For your next devotional reading, go to page 62.

him, his father will die.' [23]But you told your servants, 'Unless your youngest brother comes down with you, you will not see my face again.' [24]When we went back to your servant my father, we told him what my lord had said.

[25]"Then our father said, 'Go back and buy a little more food.' [26]But we said, 'We cannot go down. Only if our youngest brother is with us will we go. We cannot see the man's face unless our youngest brother is with us.'

[27]"Your servant my father said to us, 'You know that my wife bore me two sons. [28]One of them went away from me, and I said, "He has surely been torn to pieces." And I have not seen him since. [29]If you take this one from me too and harm comes to him, you will bring my gray head down to the grave[a] in misery.'

[30]"So now, if the boy is not with us when I go back to your servant my father and if my father, whose life is closely bound up with the boy's life, [31]sees that the boy isn't there, he will die. Your servants will bring the gray head of our father down to the grave in sorrow. [32]Your servant guaranteed the boy's safety to my father. I said, 'If I do not bring him back to you, I will bear the blame before you, my father, all my life!'

[33]"Now then, please let your servant remain here as my lord's slave in place of the boy, and let the boy return with his brothers. [34]How can I go back to my father if the boy is not with me? No! Do not let me see the misery that would come upon my father."

Joseph Makes Himself Known

45 Then Joseph could no longer control himself before all his attendants, and he cried out, "Have everyone leave my presence!" So there was no one with Joseph when he made himself known to his brothers. [2]And he wept so loudly that the Egyptians heard him, and Pharaoh's household heard about it.

[3]Joseph said to his brothers, "I am Joseph! Is my father still living?" But his brothers were not able to answer him, because they were terrified at his presence.

[4]Then Joseph said to his brothers, "Come close to me." When they had done so, he said, "I am your brother Joseph, the one you sold into Egypt! [5]And now, do not be distressed and do not be angry with yourselves for selling me here, because it was to save lives that God sent me ahead

of you. [6]For two years now there has been famine in the land, and for the next five years there will not be plowing and reaping. [7]But God sent me ahead of you to preserve for you a remnant on earth and to save your lives by a great deliverance.[b]

[8]"So then, it was not you who sent me here, but God. He made me father to Pharaoh, lord of his entire household and ruler of all Egypt. [9]Now hurry back to my father and say to him, 'This is what your son Joseph says: God has made me lord of all Egypt. Come down to me; don't delay. [10]You shall live in the region of Goshen and be near me—you, your children and grandchildren, your flocks and herds, and all you have. [11]I will provide for you there, because five years of famine are still to come. Otherwise you and your household and all who belong to you will become destitute.'

[12]"You can see for yourselves, and so can my brother Benjamin, that it is really I who am speaking to you. [13]Tell my father about all the honor accorded me in Egypt and about everything you have seen. And bring my father down here quickly."

[14]Then he threw his arms around his brother Benjamin and wept, and Benjamin embraced him, weeping. [15]And he kissed all his brothers and wept over them. Afterward his brothers talked with him.

[16]When the news reached Pharaoh's palace that Joseph's brothers had come, Pharaoh and all his officials were pleased. [17]Pharaoh said to Joseph, "Tell your brothers, 'Do this: Load your animals and return to the land of Canaan, [18]and bring your father and your families back to me. I will give you the best of the land of Egypt and you can enjoy the fat of the land.'

[19]"You are also directed to tell them, 'Do this: Take some carts from Egypt for your children and your wives, and get your father and come. [20]Never mind about your belongings, because the best of all Egypt will be yours.' "

[21]So the sons of Israel did this. Joseph gave them carts, as Pharaoh had commanded, and he also gave them provisions for their journey. [22]To each of them he gave new clothing, but to Benjamin he gave three hundred shekels[c] of silver and five sets of clothes. [23]And this is what he sent to his father: ten donkeys loaded

a29 Hebrew *Sheol*; also in verse 31   b7 Or *save you as a great band of survivors*   c22 That is, about 7 1/2 pounds (about 3.5 kilograms)

with the best things of Egypt, and ten female donkeys loaded with grain and bread and other provisions for his journey. ²⁴Then he sent his brothers away, and as they were leaving he said to them, "Don't quarrel on the way!"

²⁵So they went up out of Egypt and came to their father Jacob in the land of Canaan. ²⁶They told him, "Joseph is still alive! In fact, he is ruler of all Egypt." Jacob was stunned; he did not believe them. ²⁷But when they told him everything Joseph had said to them, and when he saw the carts Joseph had sent to carry him back, the spirit of their father Jacob revived. ²⁸And Israel said, "I'm convinced!

My son Joseph is still alive. I will go and see him before I die."

Jacob Goes to Egypt

46 So Israel set out with all that was his, and when he reached Beersheba, he offered sacrifices to the God of his father Isaac.

²And God spoke to Israel in a vision at night and said, "Jacob! Jacob!"

"Here I am," he replied.

³"I am God, the God of your father," he said. "Do not be afraid to go down to Egypt, for I will make you into a great nation there. ⁴I will go down to Egypt with

A Relationship Fixer-Upper

The word "restoration" is one of my favorites. I love the idea of taking something old and broken and making it like new.

One of the clerks at the Home Depot where I do most of my shopping owns a '56 Ford pickup. When I see it in the employee's parking area, I can't help but stare. It's one of the most beautifully restored vehicles I've ever seen, complete with its mid-fifties turquoise finish. Even though it's a truck, my suspicion is that the owner would rather die than to put anything in the bed that might scratch it.

The passage today talks about a different kind of restoration—a relationship fixer-upper. What Joseph's brothers had done to him was horrible. Their hostility toward Joseph as a teenager had led them to sell him. They had actually wanted to kill him, but changed their minds when the opportunity to exchange him for cash presented itself!

Joseph, however, wasn't entirely without blame. He had earned this relationship with his brothers by being an arrogant, spoiled brat and by shamelessly strutting his stuff in their faces.

This passage takes us to a scene almost thirty years later. All of these men have faced untold hardships. Things haven't turned out according to plan for any of

DAILY INSIGHT

THURSDAY

Passage:
Genesis 45:1–15

Verse:
Genesis 45:15

them. Maturity has taken root. And now Joseph stands in front of his brothers like my Home Depot friend must have stood in front of his rusted, old pickup muttering to himself, "This one could use some serious restoration."

Can you picture these grown men, embracing each other? Today's verse (45:15) tells us that they wept openly, probably with regret for the years that had passed without making things right, but filled with sheer delight over the sparkling new finish on their friendship.

My favorite part of this story is what they did after their broken relationship had been restored: *they talked.* There was so much ground to cover, so much to say. They couldn't wait to get reacquainted. Conversation after restoration is sheer delight.

Which of your relationships needs to be restored? Which one is covered with the rust of silence and bitterness? Picture what it might be like to confess your wrongdoing, forgive them for their part, then sit down over coffee in luxurious conversation.

Wouldn't it be great if people would gaze at this healing, like I do when I see that turquoise pickup? "What a tremendous restoration," they'd say.

For your next devotional reading, go to page 68.

Conversation: Just Keep Talking

"[Joseph] kissed all his brothers and wept over them.
Afterward his brothers talked with him."
Genesis 45:15

The most precious connection between human beings is the bridge of conversation. This is especially true between you and your children.

If you have small children, communication can be difficult. After all, you live in a world that's foreign to your son or daughter. You've got pressure at work and are struggling to make ends meet. She's got a dolly who scraped her knee. He's got a truck that lost a wheel. So you'll have to find some things to discuss and places to discuss them.

No problem. A good friend taught me a fathering lesson very early. "On the weekends, never go anywhere alone," he told me. This simple advice had wonderful consequences. I took his advice, and when I ran errands on the weekends, I almost always took one or both of my kids along.

And as we would drive along, I'd ask them questions. "Look over there in that field. Have you ever seen so many cows? I wonder how many there are?" They'd look and start counting. Or we'd play games. "Between here and the store," I'd say, "let's count how many trucks we pass." Or I'd try and make them imagine, "If you were an animal in the zoo, what animal would you like to be?" Early in our lives together, we built conversation bridges, a connection of words that inextricably bound us together.

In describing good conversation, Dr. James Dobson uses the helpful illustration of playing catch with a tennis ball. When you want to speak to your son, you throw him a question. When he answers, he's throwing a response back. Once you've caught the response, you toss him another question. This is a good model to use as you teach your child how to carry on a conversation. Use role play and practice regularly. Teach your child to listen so he or she can ask a question that follows what you've just said.

Or try this strategy. Little children are famous for indecipherable drawings. When you see one, don't cut off conversation with a quick, "That's nice, sweetie," or "What is it?" Rather, draw out a conversation by saying, "Tell me about your picture, Jennifer." Jennifer will describe what she sees—which, of course, is all that matters. As she talks, listen carefully so you can say, "That's so interesting that you colored that pony orange. Can you tell me why you chose that color?"

Hear that tennis ball bouncing back and forth? Your child is learning to speak, to accurately express her thoughts. And you're learning to listen so you can catch a glimpse of who this little person really is. When Jennifer comes home from high school after a verbal bout with one of her classmates, sixteen-year-old Jennifer will never talk to you about it unless, when she was small and the stakes were not quite as high, you taught her how.

Finally, make mealtime a priority. When I was a kid, holidays were filled with great dinner-table conversation. In looking back on those great feasts, I recall that my mother always did her best to add onto our primary dining room table. "Since we're a family," she'd say, "we're going to all eat together at the big table. No 'kids table' in the other room."

She was right. As children, my three brothers, two sisters, and I learned the importance of conversation. We learned that the dinner table wasn't a conveyor belt covered with food. We were taught that sitting down to a meal was an important time of conversation and listening.

Teach your kids to talk to you. Open conversation will be the lifeline that will keep your kids from emotionally hiding from you and your wife. It will allow you to learn who your children really are and will give you a vehicle to tell them about yourself. Teaching your children the art of conversation will introduce them to a world of other adults who will honor them because of their ability to talk and listen.

you, and I will surely bring you back again. And Joseph's own hand will close your eyes."

[5]Then Jacob left Beersheba, and Israel's sons took their father Jacob and their children and their wives in the carts that Pharaoh had sent to transport him. [6]They also took with them their livestock and the possessions they had acquired in Canaan, and Jacob and all his offspring went to Egypt. [7]He took with him to Egypt his sons and grandsons and his daughters and granddaughters—all his offspring.

[8]These are the names of the sons of Israel (Jacob and his descendants) who went to Egypt:

Reuben the firstborn of Jacob.
[9] The sons of Reuben:
   Hanoch, Pallu, Hezron and Carmi.
[10] The sons of Simeon:
   Jemuel, Jamin, Ohad, Jakin, Zohar and Shaul the son of a Canaanite woman.
[11] The sons of Levi:
   Gershon, Kohath and Merari.
[12] The sons of Judah:
   Er, Onan, Shelah, Perez and Zerah (but Er and Onan had died in the land of Canaan).
   The sons of Perez:
   Hezron and Hamul.
[13] The sons of Issachar:
   Tola, Puah,[a] Jashub[b] and Shimron.
[14] The sons of Zebulun:
   Sered, Elon and Jahleel.
[15]These were the sons Leah bore to Jacob in Paddan Aram,[c] besides his daughter Dinah. These sons and daughters of his were thirty-three in all.

[16] The sons of Gad:
   Zephon,[d] Haggi, Shuni, Ezbon, Eri, Arodi and Areli.
[17] The sons of Asher:
   Imnah, Ishvah, Ishvi and Beriah.
   Their sister was Serah.
   The sons of Beriah:
   Heber and Malkiel.
[18]These were the children born to Jacob by Zilpah, whom Laban had given to his daughter Leah—sixteen in all.

[19]The sons of Jacob's wife Rachel:
   Joseph and Benjamin. [20]In Egypt, Manasseh and Ephraim were born to Joseph by Asenath daughter of Potiphera, priest of On.[e]
[21]The sons of Benjamin:
   Bela, Beker, Ashbel, Gera, Naaman, Ehi, Rosh, Muppim, Huppim and Ard.
[22]These were the sons of Rachel who were born to Jacob—fourteen in all.

[23]The son of Dan:
   Hushim.
[24]The sons of Naphtali:
   Jahziel, Guni, Jezer and Shillem.
[25]These were the sons born to Jacob by Bilhah, whom Laban had given to his daughter Rachel—seven in all.

[26]All those who went to Egypt with Jacob—those who were his direct descendants, not counting his sons' wives—numbered sixty-six persons. [27]With the two sons[f] who had been born to Joseph in Egypt, the members of Jacob's family, which went to Egypt, were seventy[g] in all.

[28]Now Jacob sent Judah ahead of him to Joseph to get directions to Goshen. When they arrived in the region of Goshen, [29]Joseph had his chariot made ready and went to Goshen to meet his father Israel. As soon as Joseph appeared before him, he threw his arms around his father[h] and wept for a long time.

[30]Israel said to Joseph, "Now I am ready to die, since I have seen for myself that you are still alive."

[31]Then Joseph said to his brothers and to his father's household, "I will go up and speak to Pharaoh and will say to him, 'My brothers and my father's household, who were living in the land of Canaan, have come to me. [32]The men are shepherds; they tend livestock, and they have brought along their flocks and herds and everything they own.' [33]When Pharaoh calls you in and asks, 'What is your occupation?' [34]you should answer, 'Your servants have tended livestock from our boyhood on, just as our fathers did.' Then you will be allowed to settle in the region of Goshen, for all shepherds are detestable to the Egyptians."

47 Joseph went and told Pharaoh, "My father and brothers, with their flocks and herds and everything they own, have

---

[a]13 Samaritan Pentateuch and Syriac (see also 1 Chron. 7:1); Masoretic Text *Puvah*
[b]13 Samaritan Pentateuch and some Septuagint manuscripts (see also Num. 26:24 and 1 Chron. 7:1); Masoretic Text *Iob*   [c]15 That is, Northwest Mesopotamia   [d]16 Samaritan Pentateuch and Septuagint (see also Num. 26:15); Masoretic Text *Ziphion*   [e]20 That is, Heliopolis   [f]27 Hebrew; Septuagint *the nine children*   [g]27 Hebrew (see also Exodus 1:5 and footnote); Septuagint (see also Acts 7:14) *seventy-five*   [h]29 Hebrew *around him*

come from the land of Canaan and are now in Goshen." [2]He chose five of his brothers and presented them before Pharaoh.

[3]Pharaoh asked the brothers, "What is your occupation?"

"Your servants are shepherds," they replied to Pharaoh, "just as our fathers were." [4]They also said to him, "We have come to live here awhile, because the famine is severe in Canaan and your servants' flocks have no pasture. So now, please let your servants settle in Goshen."

[5]Pharaoh said to Joseph, "Your father and your brothers have come to you, [6]and the land of Egypt is before you; settle your father and your brothers in the best part of the land. Let them live in Goshen. And if you know of any among them with special ability, put them in charge of my own livestock."

[7]Then Joseph brought his father Jacob in and presented him before Pharaoh. After Jacob blessed[a] Pharaoh, [8]Pharaoh asked him, "How old are you?"

[9]And Jacob said to Pharaoh, "The years of my pilgrimage are a hundred and thirty. My years have been few and difficult, and they do not equal the years of the pilgrimage of my fathers." [10]Then Jacob blessed[b] Pharaoh and went out from his presence.

[11]So Joseph settled his father and his brothers in Egypt and gave them property in the best part of the land, the district of Rameses, as Pharaoh directed. [12]Joseph also provided his father and his brothers and all his father's household with food, according to the number of their children.

Joseph and the Famine

[13]There was no food, however, in the whole region because the famine was severe; both Egypt and Canaan wasted away because of the famine. [14]Joseph collected all the money that was to be found in Egypt and Canaan in payment for the grain they were buying, and he brought it to Pharaoh's palace. [15]When the money of the people of Egypt and Canaan was gone, all Egypt came to Joseph and said, "Give us food. Why should we die before your eyes? Our money is used up."

[16]"Then bring your livestock," said Joseph. "I will sell you food in exchange for your livestock, since your money is gone." [17]So they brought their livestock to Joseph, and he gave them food in exchange for their horses, their sheep and goats, their cattle and donkeys. And he brought them through that year with food in exchange for all their livestock.

[18]When that year was over, they came to him the following year and said, "We cannot hide from our lord the fact that since our money is gone and our livestock belongs to you, there is nothing left for our lord except our bodies and our land. [19]Why should we perish before your eyes—we and our land as well? Buy us and our land in exchange for food, and we with our land will be in bondage to Pharaoh. Give us seed so that we may live and not die, and that the land may not become desolate."

[20]So Joseph bought all the land in Egypt for Pharaoh. The Egyptians, one and all, sold their fields, because the famine was too severe for them. The land became Pharaoh's, [21]and Joseph reduced the people to servitude,[c] from one end of Egypt to the other. [22]However, he did not buy the land of the priests, because they received a regular allotment from Pharaoh and had food enough from the allotment Pharaoh gave them. That is why they did not sell their land.

[23]Joseph said to the people, "Now that I have bought you and your land today for Pharaoh, here is seed for you so you can plant the ground. [24]But when the crop comes in, give a fifth of it to Pharaoh. The other four-fifths you may keep as seed for the fields and as food for yourselves and your households and your children."

[25]"You have saved our lives," they said. "May we find favor in the eyes of our lord; we will be in bondage to Pharaoh."

[26]So Joseph established it as a law concerning land in Egypt—still in force today—that a fifth of the produce belongs to Pharaoh. It was only the land of the priests that did not become Pharaoh's.

[27]Now the Israelites settled in Egypt in the region of Goshen. They acquired property there and were fruitful and increased greatly in number.

[28]Jacob lived in Egypt seventeen years, and the years of his life were a hundred and forty-seven. [29]When the time drew near for Israel to die, he called for his son Joseph and said to him, "If I have found favor in your eyes, put your hand under my thigh and promise that you will show

---

[a]7 Or greeted   [b]10 Or said farewell to
[c]21 Samaritan Pentateuch and Septuagint (see also Vulgate); Masoretic Text and he moved the people into the cities

me kindness and faithfulness. Do not bury me in Egypt, [30]but when I rest with my fathers, carry me out of Egypt and bury me where they are buried."

"I will do as you say," he said.

[31]"Swear to me," he said. Then Joseph swore to him, and Israel worshiped as he leaned on the top of his staff.[a]

Manasseh and Ephraim

48 Some time later Joseph was told, "Your father is ill." So he took his two sons Manasseh and Ephraim along with him. [2]When Jacob was told, "Your son Joseph has come to you," Israel rallied his strength and sat up on the bed.

[3]Jacob said to Joseph, "God Almighty[b] appeared to me at Luz in the land of Canaan, and there he blessed me [4]and said to me, 'I am going to make you fruitful and will increase your numbers. I will make you a community of peoples, and I will give this land as an everlasting possession to your descendants after you.'

[5]"Now then, your two sons born to you in Egypt before I came to you here will be reckoned as mine; Ephraim and Manasseh will be mine, just as Reuben and Simeon are mine. [6]Any children born to you after them will be yours; in the territory they inherit they will be reckoned under the names of their brothers. [7]As I was returning from Paddan,[c] to my sorrow Rachel died in the land of Canaan while we were still on the way, a little distance from Ephrath. So I buried her there beside the road to Ephrath" (that is, Bethlehem).

[8]When Israel saw the sons of Joseph, he asked, "Who are these?"

[9]"They are the sons God has given me here," Joseph said to his father.

Then Israel said, "Bring them to me so I may bless them."

[10]Now Israel's eyes were failing because of old age, and he could hardly see. So Joseph brought his sons close to him, and his father kissed them and embraced them.

[11]Israel said to Joseph, "I never expected to see your face again, and now God has allowed me to see your children too."

[12]Then Joseph removed them from Israel's knees and bowed down with his face to the ground. [13]And Joseph took both of them, Ephraim on his right toward Israel's left hand and Manasseh on his left toward Israel's right hand, and brought them close to him. [14]But Israel reached

out his right hand and put it on Ephraim's head, though he was the younger, and crossing his arms, he put his left hand on Manasseh's head, even though Manasseh was the firstborn.

[15]Then he blessed Joseph and said,

"May the God before whom my fathers
   Abraham and Isaac walked,
the God who has been my shepherd
   all my life to this day,
[16]the Angel who has delivered me from
      all harm
   —may he bless these boys.
May they be called by my name
   and the names of my fathers
      Abraham and Isaac,
and may they increase greatly
   upon the earth."

[17]When Joseph saw his father placing his right hand on Ephraim's head he was displeased; so he took hold of his father's hand to move it from Ephraim's head to Manasseh's head. [18]Joseph said to him, "No, my father, this one is the firstborn; put your right hand on his head."

[19]But his father refused and said, "I know, my son, I know. He too will become a people, and he too will become great. Nevertheless, his younger brother will be greater than he, and his descendants will become a group of nations." [20]He blessed them that day and said,

"In your[d] name will Israel pronounce
      this blessing:
   'May God make you like Ephraim
      and Manasseh.' "

So he put Ephraim ahead of Manasseh.

[21]Then Israel said to Joseph, "I am about to die, but God will be with you[e] and take you[e] back to the land of your[e] fathers. [22]And to you, as one who is over your brothers, I give the ridge of land[f] I took from the Amorites with my sword and my bow."

Jacob Blesses His Sons

49 Then Jacob called for his sons and said: "Gather around so I can tell you what will happen to you in days to come.

[2]"Assemble and listen, sons of Jacob;
   listen to your father Israel.

---

[a]31 Or *Israel bowed down at the head of his bed*
[b]3 Hebrew *El-Shaddai*   [c]7 That is, Northwest Mesopotamia   [d]20 The Hebrew is singular.
[e]21 The Hebrew is plural.   [f]22 Or *And to you I give one portion more than to your brothers—the portion*

³"Reuben, you are my firstborn,
  my might, the first sign of my
    strength,
  excelling in honor, excelling in
    power.
⁴Turbulent as the waters, you will no
    longer excel,
  for you went up onto your father's
    bed,
  onto my couch and defiled it.

⁵"Simeon and Levi are brothers—
  their swords*a* are weapons of
    violence.
⁶Let me not enter their council,
  let me not join their assembly,
for they have killed men in their anger
  and hamstrung oxen as they pleased.
⁷Cursed be their anger, so fierce,
  and their fury, so cruel!
I will scatter them in Jacob
  and disperse them in Israel.

⁸"Judah,*b* your brothers will praise you;
  your hand will be on the neck of your
    enemies;
  your father's sons will bow down to
    you.
⁹You are a lion's cub, O Judah;
  you return from the prey, my son.
Like a lion he crouches and lies down,
  like a lioness—who dares to rouse
    him?
¹⁰The scepter will not depart from Judah,
  nor the ruler's staff from between his
    feet,
until he comes to whom it belongs*c*
  and the obedience of the nations is
    his.
¹¹He will tether his donkey to a vine,
  his colt to the choicest branch;
he will wash his garments in wine,
  his robes in the blood of grapes.
¹²His eyes will be darker than wine,
  his teeth whiter than milk.*d*

¹³"Zebulun will live by the seashore
  and become a haven for ships;
  his border will extend toward Sidon.

¹⁴"Issachar is a rawboned*e* donkey
  lying down between two saddlebags.*f*
¹⁵When he sees how good is his resting
    place
  and how pleasant is his land,
he will bend his shoulder to the burden
  and submit to forced labor.

¹⁶"Dan*g* will provide justice for his people
  as one of the tribes of Israel.
¹⁷Dan will be a serpent by the roadside,
  a viper along the path,

that bites the horse's heels
  so that its rider tumbles backward.

¹⁸"I look for your deliverance, O LORD.

¹⁹"Gad*h* will be attacked by a band of
    raiders,
  but he will attack them at their heels.

²⁰"Asher's food will be rich;
  he will provide delicacies fit for a
    king.

²¹"Naphtali is a doe set free
  that bears beautiful fawns.*i*

²²"Joseph is a fruitful vine,
  a fruitful vine near a spring,
  whose branches climb over a wall.*j*
²³With bitterness archers attacked him;
  they shot at him with hostility.
²⁴But his bow remained steady,
  his strong arms stayed*k* limber,
because of the hand of the Mighty One
    of Jacob,
  because of the Shepherd, the Rock of
    Israel,
²⁵because of your father's God, who
    helps you,
  because of the Almighty,*l* who
    blesses you
with blessings of the heavens above,
  blessings of the deep that lies below,
  blessings of the breast and womb.
²⁶Your father's blessings are greater
  than the blessings of the ancient
    mountains,
  than*m* the bounty of the age-old hills.
Let all these rest on the head of Joseph,
  on the brow of the prince among*n*
    his brothers.

²⁷"Benjamin is a ravenous wolf;
  in the morning he devours the prey,
  in the evening he divides the
    plunder."

²⁸All these are the twelve tribes of Israel,
and this is what their father said to them
when he blessed them, giving each the
blessing appropriate to him.

---

a5 The meaning of the Hebrew for this word is
uncertain.   *b8 Judah* sounds like and may be
derived from the Hebrew for *praise*.   *c10* Or *until
Shiloh comes*; or *until he comes to whom tribute
belongs*   *d12* Or *will be dull from wine, / his teeth
white from milk*   *e14* Or *strong*   *f14* Or *campfires*
g16 Dan here means *he provides justice*.   *h19 Gad*
can mean *attack* and *band of raiders*.   *i21* Or *free; /
he utters beautiful words*   *j22* Or *Joseph is a wild
colt, / a wild colt near a spring, / a wild donkey on a
terraced hill*   *k23,24* Or *archers will attack . . . will
shoot . . . will remain . . . will stay*   *l25* Hebrew
Shaddai   *m26* Or *of my progenitors, / as great as*
n26 Or *the one separated from*

The Death of Jacob

²⁹Then he gave them these instructions: "I am about to be gathered to my people. Bury me with my fathers in the cave in the field of Ephron the Hittite, ³⁰the cave in the field of Machpelah, near Mamre in Canaan, which Abraham bought as a burial place from Ephron the Hittite, along with the field. ³¹There Abraham and his wife Sarah were buried, there Isaac and his wife Rebekah were buried, and there I buried Leah. ³²The field and the cave in it were bought from the Hittites.ᵃ"

³³When Jacob had finished giving instructions to his sons, he drew his feet up into the bed, breathed his last and was gathered to his people.

50 Joseph threw himself upon his father and wept over him and kissed him. ²Then Joseph directed the physicians in his service to embalm his father Israel. So the physicians embalmed him, ³taking a full forty days, for that was the time required for embalming. And the Egyptians mourned for him seventy days.

⁴When the days of mourning had passed, Joseph said to Pharaoh's court, "If I have found favor in your eyes, speak to Pharaoh for me. Tell him, ⁵'My father made me swear an oath and said, "I am about to die; bury me in the tomb I dug for myself in the land of Canaan." Now let me go up and bury my father; then I will return.' "

⁶Pharaoh said, "Go up and bury your father, as he made you swear to do."

⁷So Joseph went up to bury his father. All Pharaoh's officials accompanied him—the dignitaries of his court and all the dignitaries of Egypt— ⁸besides all the members

ᵃ2 Or *the sons of Heth*

Go Climb a Tower

DAILY INSIGHT

If you were to drive past the football practice field just behind our local high school, you would see a wooden tower standing probably eighteen to twenty feet in the air. There's certainly nothing fancy about this structure. It actually looks like it may have been built by the boys in wood shop.

My guess is that very few people who drive down Murray Lane ever see this tower, and even if they do, I doubt if they have any idea what it's for.

But you know, don't you? It's for the coaches during practice. Climbing up to the raised platform gives them a different look at various plays and strategies. It gives them perspective—something that can be a lot more difficult standing at ground level.

The next time you see a tower next to a practice field, see Joseph standing there. Perhaps God's greatest gift to this man whose story ends today was the ability to get up off the field of daily activities and disappointments and see things from a different viewpoint.

Many of us, faced with the failures and

FRIDAY

Passage:
Genesis 50:15–21

Verse:
Genesis 50:20

seemingly insurmountable challenges Joseph faced—despised by his brothers, sold like a dog, thrown into prison on a bum rap, working a nation out of bankruptcy—would have quit. But God helped Joseph to "look down" on these events and realize that, in God's sovereign mercy, each had happened for his own good and for the survival of his family. "You intended to harm me, but God intended it for good." Now there's a panoramic look.

What has happened to you and your family that makes you wonder if God knows what he's doing? How have these events affected you? Are they keeping you awake at night? Does anyone know? Are you on the field, squashed by a three-hundred-and-fifty-pound sophomore linebacker and trying to figure out what's going on, or are you in the tower of God's perspective?

Ask him to lift you up. He's the very same God who lifted Joseph, and he'll do it for you.

For your next devotional reading, go to page 72.

of Joseph's household and his brothers and those belonging to his father's household. Only their children and their flocks and herds were left in Goshen. ⁹Chariots and horsemen[a] also went up with him. It was a very large company.

¹⁰When they reached the threshing floor of Atad, near the Jordan, they lamented loudly and bitterly; and there Joseph observed a seven-day period of mourning for his father. ¹¹When the Canaanites who lived there saw the mourning at the threshing floor of Atad, they said, "The Egyptians are holding a solemn ceremony of mourning." That is why that place near the Jordan is called Abel Mizraim.[b]

¹²So Jacob's sons did as he had commanded them: ¹³They carried him to the land of Canaan and buried him in the cave in the field of Machpelah, near Mamre, which Abraham had bought as a burial place from Ephron the Hittite, along with the field. ¹⁴After burying his father, Joseph returned to Egypt, together with his brothers and all the others who had gone with him to bury his father.

Joseph Reassures His Brothers

¹⁵When Joseph's brothers saw that their father was dead, they said, "What if Joseph holds a grudge against us and pays us back for all the wrongs we did to him?" ¹⁶So they sent word to Joseph, saying, "Your father left these instructions before he died: ¹⁷'This is what you are to say to Joseph: I ask you to forgive your brothers the sins and the wrongs they committed in treating you so badly.' Now please forgive the sins of the servants of the God of your father." When their message came to him, Joseph wept.

¹⁸His brothers then came and threw themselves down before him. "We are your slaves," they said.

¹⁹But Joseph said to them, "Don't be afraid. Am I in the place of God? ²⁰You intended to harm me, but God intended it for good to accomplish what is now being done, the saving of many lives. ²¹So then, don't be afraid. I will provide for you and your children." And he reassured them and spoke kindly to them.

The Death of Joseph

²²Joseph stayed in Egypt, along with all his father's family. He lived a hundred and ten years ²³and saw the third generation of Ephraim's children. Also the children of Makir son of Manasseh were placed at birth on Joseph's knees.[c]

²⁴Then Joseph said to his brothers, "I am about to die. But God will surely come to your aid and take you up out of this land to the land he promised on oath to Abraham, Isaac and Jacob." ²⁵And Joseph made the sons of Israel swear an oath and said, "God will surely come to your aid, and then you must carry my bones up from this place."

²⁶So Joseph died at the age of a hundred and ten. And after they embalmed him, he was placed in a coffin in Egypt.

[a]9 Or *charioteers*   [b]11 *Abel Mizraim* means *mourning of the Egyptians.*   [c]23 That is, were counted as his

Moses tried to convince Pharaoh to release the millions of Israelites being held captive in his country. But Pharaoh was no fool. Why would he knowingly give up the cheap labor these slaves provided for his booming economy? So Pharaoh refused. Unfortunately for the Egyptians, letting the Israelites go wasn't just Moses' idea. It was also God's idea.

The book of Exodus is about discovering what it means to hear and to obey your heavenly Father. Listening to God may have something to do with moving in faith out of familiar surroundings and into strange new territory, as it did with Moses and his people; or it may mean being faithful right where you are. In either case, the stories in Exodus ought to make one lesson clear to dads everywhere: When it comes time to make a decision, a man can either obey God or plan on paying a handsome penalty.

Exodus

The Israelites Oppressed

1 These are the names of the sons of Israel who went to Egypt with Jacob, each with his family: ²Reuben, Simeon, Levi and Judah; ³Issachar, Zebulun and Benjamin; ⁴Dan and Naphtali; Gad and Asher. ⁵The descendants of Jacob numbered seventy[a] in all; Joseph was already in Egypt.

⁶Now Joseph and all his brothers and all that generation died, ⁷but the Israelites were fruitful and multiplied greatly and became exceedingly numerous, so that the land was filled with them.

⁸Then a new king, who did not know about Joseph, came to power in Egypt. ⁹"Look," he said to his people, "the Israelites have become much too numerous for us. ¹⁰Come, we must deal shrewdly with them or they will become even more numerous and, if war breaks out, will join our enemies, fight against us and leave the country."

¹¹So they put slave masters over them to oppress them with forced labor, and they built Pithom and Rameses as store cities for Pharaoh. ¹²But the more they were oppressed, the more they multiplied and spread; so the Egyptians came to dread the Israelites ¹³and worked them ruthlessly. ¹⁴They made their lives bitter with hard labor in brick and mortar and with all kinds of work in the fields; in all their hard labor the Egyptians used them ruthlessly.

¹⁵The king of Egypt said to the Hebrew midwives, whose names were Shiphrah and Puah, ¹⁶"When you help the Hebrew

a5 Masoretic Text (see also Gen. 46:27); Dead Sea Scrolls and Septuagint (see also Acts 7:14 and note at Gen. 46:27) *seventy-five*

women in childbirth and observe them on the delivery stool, if it is a boy, kill him; but if it is a girl, let her live." ¹⁷The midwives, however, feared God and did not do what the king of Egypt had told them to do; they let the boys live. ¹⁸Then the king of Egypt summoned the midwives and asked them, "Why have you done this? Why have you let the boys live?"

¹⁹The midwives answered Pharaoh, "Hebrew women are not like Egyptian women; they are vigorous and give birth before the midwives arrive."

²⁰So God was kind to the midwives and the people increased and became even more numerous. ²¹And because the midwives feared God, he gave them families of their own.

²²Then Pharaoh gave this order to all his people: "Every boy that is born*a* you must throw into the Nile, but let every girl live."

The Birth of Moses

2 Now a man of the house of Levi married a Levite woman, ²and she became pregnant and gave birth to a son. When she saw that he was a fine child, she hid him for three months. ³But when she could hide him no longer, she got a papyrus basket for him and coated it with tar and pitch. Then she placed the child in it and put it among the reeds along the bank of the Nile. ⁴His sister stood at a distance to see what would happen to him.

⁵Then Pharaoh's daughter went down to the Nile to bathe, and her attendants were walking along the river bank. She saw the basket among the reeds and sent her slave girl to get it. ⁶She opened it and saw the baby. He was crying, and she felt sorry for him. "This is one of the Hebrew babies," she said.

⁷Then his sister asked Pharaoh's daughter, "Shall I go and get one of the Hebrew women to nurse the baby for you?"

⁸"Yes, go," she answered. And the girl went and got the baby's mother. ⁹Pharaoh's daughter said to her, "Take this baby and nurse him for me, and I will pay you." So the woman took the baby and nursed him. ¹⁰When the child grew older, she took him to Pharaoh's daughter and he became her son. She named him Moses,*b* saying, "I drew him out of the water."

Moses Flees to Midian

¹¹One day, after Moses had grown up, he went out to where his own people were and watched them at their hard labor. He saw an Egyptian beating a Hebrew, one of his own people. ¹²Glancing this way and that and seeing no one, he killed the Egyptian and hid him in the sand. ¹³The next day he went out and saw two Hebrews fighting. He asked the one in the wrong, "Why are you hitting your fellow Hebrew?"

¹⁴The man said, "Who made you ruler and judge over us? Are you thinking of killing me as you killed the Egyptian?" Then Moses was afraid and thought, "What I did must have become known."

¹⁵When Pharaoh heard of this, he tried to kill Moses, but Moses fled from Pharaoh and went to live in Midian, where he sat down by a well. ¹⁶Now a priest of Midian had seven daughters, and they came to draw water and fill the troughs to water their father's flock. ¹⁷Some shepherds came along and drove them away, but Moses got up and came to their rescue and watered their flock.

¹⁸When the girls returned to Reuel their father, he asked them, "Why have you returned so early today?"

¹⁹They answered, "An Egyptian rescued us from the shepherds. He even drew water for us and watered the flock."

²⁰"And where is he?" he asked his daughters. "Why did you leave him? Invite him to have something to eat."

²¹Moses agreed to stay with the man, who gave his daughter Zipporah to Moses in marriage. ²²Zipporah gave birth to a son, and Moses named him Gershom,*c* saying, "I have become an alien in a foreign land."

²³During that long period, the king of Egypt died. The Israelites groaned in their slavery and cried out, and their cry for help because of their slavery went up to God. ²⁴God heard their groaning and he remembered his covenant with Abraham, with Isaac and with Jacob. ²⁵So God looked on the Israelites and was concerned about them.

Moses and the Burning Bush

3 Now Moses was tending the flock of Jethro his father-in-law, the priest of Midian, and he led the flock to the far side of the desert and came to Horeb, the mountain of God. ²There the angel of the

---

*a*22 Masoretic Text; Samaritan Pentateuch, Septuagint and Targums *born to the Hebrews*
*b*10 *Moses* sounds like the Hebrew for *draw out.*
*c*22 *Gershom* sounds like the Hebrew for *an alien there.*

Key Verse: *"But when she could hide him no longer, she got a papyrus basket for him and coated it with tar and pitch. Then she placed the child in it and put it among the reeds along the bank of the Nile."* Exodus 2:3

Text: Exodus 2:1–10 *(Dad or child reads the text.)*

QUIET
TIMES
WITH Dad

DAD READS: When a person owns things, he does his best to protect them by putting them in safe places. He keeps his money in a bank, his car in a garage, and his valuable papers in a safety deposit box. But a dad doesn't own his family. The Bible tells a dad to be a faithful caretaker, but his family belongs to God.

Child reads: The story we just read today is about a mother who loves her baby boy very much. In fact, she loves him so much that she's willing to let him go, trusting him into God's care. It's hard to imagine how hard it must have been for baby Moses' family to lay him in that basket, all alone on a busy river.

DAD READS: From the day you were born, I have had two very important jobs. My first job was to love you. This is a wonderful thing, and I do love you very much. The second job is a difficult one—it's the task of letting you go.

Child reads: When I was a little baby, my parents were with me all day. They knew exactly where I was and what I was doing. The older I became, the more time I spent away from home, either at school or with friends. My job is to be good, even when my dad isn't around. This gives him the confidence to know that letting me go is the right thing to do.

DAD READS: I want you to know that I love you and I trust you. And, like Moses' mother did, I will also trust God to protect and care for you— even when you're floating down a busy river far from home. Let me pray this prayer with you:

Dear Father in heaven, thank you for _____. Thank you that you have given me such love for him/her. Please help me to be like Moses' mother. Help me to trust in your care for _____, even when I cannot see where he/she is or what he/she is doing. Please continue to protect him/her and to give him/her wisdom to make choices that are pleasing to you. In Jesus' name, Amen.

For your next devotional reading, go to page 73.

LORD appeared to him in flames of fire from within a bush. Moses saw that though the bush was on fire it did not burn up. ³So Moses thought, "I will go over and see this strange sight—why the bush does not burn up."

⁴When the LORD saw that he had gone over to look, God called to him from within the bush, "Moses! Moses!"

And Moses said, "Here I am."

⁵"Do not come any closer," God said. "Take off your sandals, for the place where you are standing is holy ground." ⁶Then he said, "I am the God of your father, the God of Abraham, the God of Isaac and the God of Jacob." At this, Moses hid his face, because he was afraid to look at God.

⁷The LORD said, "I have indeed seen the misery of my people in Egypt. I have heard them crying out because of their slave drivers, and I am concerned about their suffering. ⁸So I have come down to rescue them from the hand of the Egyptians and to bring them up out of that land into a good and spacious land, a land flowing with milk and honey—the home of the Canaanites, Hittites, Amorites, Perizzites, Hivites and Jebusites. ⁹And now the cry of the Israelites has reached me, and I have seen the way the Egyptians are oppressing them. ¹⁰So now, go. I am sending you to Pharaoh to bring my people Israelites out of Egypt."

¹¹But Moses said to God, "Who am I,

The Bush is Still Burning

DAILY INSIGHT

MONDAY

Passage:
Exodus 3:1–10

Verse:
Exodus 3:5

Take a moment and think of the answer to this question: Who, in your opinion, is the most important person alive today? A brilliant thinker? A sports hero? A great military leader? An entrepreneurial billionaire?

Now imagine that you're sitting in your favorite restaurant with your wife. She leans forward and whispers, "The most important person in the world is sitting right over there."

Can you feel the excitement? Your heart would beat a little faster. Your confidence would rise just knowing that such a person had chosen your local hangout to eat a meal. Even if you never actually saw this person or heard the sound of his or her voice, your dining experience would be different simply because you were in his or her presence.

No matter whom you chose to be your "most important person in the world," that person cannot come close to comparing to the God of the universe. The One who, with the sound of his voice, created the heavens and the earth. The One who is never in the dark—never shocked or surprised. The One whose mercy and grace forgives our willful transgression.

Moses was having one of those at-the-office-minding-his-own-business days. He was innocently taking care of his father-in-law's sheep when he saw a bit of scrub brush burst into flames. As he approached, he saw that even though the bush was on fire, *it wasn't being burned.* If Moses thought this was amazing, he couldn't have possibly predicted what would happen next.

God spoke to Moses.

Take a moment and let that one sink in. God's voice was audibly heard. Can you imagine how Moses must have felt? Like you would have felt at your local restaurant ... soaked in pure adrenaline. The text (3:6) tells us that Moses was so overwhelmed that he covered his face. It's amazing that his heart didn't beat right out of his chest!

Now, here's the most incredible truth of this story. You and I are literally in God's presence right now. The most important Being who has ever lived is in this room. He is listening and watching. He knows our words, our thoughts, our actions, even our intentions. And his Word promises us that he loves us. Can you believe it?

Today, let the glow of the torching tumbleweed overwhelm you. Let it light your path. Let it purify your mind. Let it warm your chilly heart. Hey, the bush is still burning.

For your next devotional reading, go to page 75.

that I should go to Pharaoh and bring the Israelites out of Egypt?"

¹²And God said, "I will be with you. And this will be the sign to you that it is I who have sent you: When you have brought the people out of Egypt, you*ᵃ* will worship God on this mountain."

¹³Moses said to God, "Suppose I go to the Israelites and say to them, 'The God of your fathers has sent me to you,' and they ask me, 'What is his name?' Then what shall I tell them?"

¹⁴God said to Moses, "I AM WHO I AM.*ᵇ* This is what you are to say to the Israelites: 'I AM has sent me to you.' "

¹⁵God also said to Moses, "Say to the Israelites, 'The LORD,*ᶜ* the God of your fathers—the God of Abraham, the God of Isaac and the God of Jacob—has sent me to you.' This is my name forever, the name by which I am to be remembered from generation to generation.

¹⁶"Go, assemble the elders of Israel and say to them, 'The LORD, the God of your fathers—the God of Abraham, Isaac and Jacob—appeared to me and said: I have watched over you and have seen what has been done to you in Egypt. ¹⁷And I have promised to bring you up out of your misery in Egypt into the land of the Canaanites, Hittites, Amorites, Perizzites, Hivites and Jebusites—a land flowing with milk and honey.'

¹⁸"The elders of Israel will listen to you. Then you and the elders are to go to the king of Egypt and say to him, 'The LORD, the God of the Hebrews, has met with us. Let us take a three-day journey into the desert to offer sacrifices to the LORD our God.' ¹⁹But I know that the king of Egypt will not let you go unless a mighty hand compels him. ²⁰So I will stretch out my hand and strike the Egyptians with all the wonders that I will perform among them. After that, he will let you go.

²¹"And I will make the Egyptians favorably disposed toward this people, so that when you leave you will not go empty-handed. ²²Every woman is to ask her neighbor and any woman living in her house for articles of silver and gold and for clothing, which you will put on your sons and daughters. And so you will plunder the Egyptians."

Signs for Moses

4 Moses answered, "What if they do not believe me or listen to me and say, 'The LORD did not appear to you'?"

²Then the LORD said to him, "What is that in your hand?"

"A staff," he replied.

³The LORD said, "Throw it on the ground."

Moses threw it on the ground and it became a snake, and he ran from it. ⁴Then the LORD said to him, "Reach out your hand and take it by the tail." So Moses reached out and took hold of the snake and it turned back into a staff in his hand. ⁵"This," said the LORD, "is so that they may believe that the LORD, the God of their fathers—the God of Abraham, the God of Isaac and the God of Jacob—has appeared to you."

⁶Then the LORD said, "Put your hand inside your cloak." So Moses put his hand into his cloak, and when he took it out, it was leprous,*ᵈ* like snow.

⁷"Now put it back into your cloak," he said. So Moses put his hand back into his cloak, and when he took it out, it was restored, like the rest of his flesh.

⁸Then the LORD said, "If they do not believe you or pay attention to the first miraculous sign, they may believe the second. ⁹But if they do not believe these two signs or listen to you, take some water from the Nile and pour it on the dry ground. The water you take from the river will become blood on the ground."

¹⁰Moses said to the LORD, "O Lord, I have never been eloquent, neither in the past nor since you have spoken to your servant. I am slow of speech and tongue."

¹¹The LORD said to him, "Who gave man his mouth? Who makes him deaf or mute? Who gives him sight or makes him blind? Is it not I, the LORD? ¹²Now go; I will help you speak and will teach you what to say."

¹³But Moses said, "O Lord, please send someone else to do it."

¹⁴Then the LORD's anger burned against Moses and he said, "What about your brother, Aaron the Levite? I know he can speak well. He is already on his way to meet you, and his heart will be glad when he sees you. ¹⁵You shall speak to him and put words in his mouth; I will help both of you speak and will teach you what to do. ¹⁶He will speak to the people for you, and it will be as if he were your mouth and as if you were God to him. ¹⁷But take this staff

---

ᵃ12 The Hebrew is plural.   *ᵇ14* Or *I WILL BE WHAT I WILL BE*   *ᶜ15* The Hebrew for LORD sounds like and may be derived from the Hebrew for *I AM* in verse 14.   *ᵈ6* The Hebrew word was used for various diseases affecting the skin—not necessarily leprosy.

in your hand so you can perform miraculous signs with it."

Moses Returns to Egypt

18Then Moses went back to Jethro his father-in-law and said to him, "Let me go back to my own people in Egypt to see if any of them are still alive."

Jethro said, "Go, and I wish you well."

19Now the LORD had said to Moses in Midian, "Go back to Egypt, for all the men who wanted to kill you are dead." **20**So Moses took his wife and sons, put them on a donkey and started back to Egypt. And he took the staff of God in his hand.

21The LORD said to Moses, "When you return to Egypt, see that you perform before Pharaoh all the wonders I have given

you the power to do. But I will harden his heart so that he will not let the people go. **22**Then say to Pharaoh, 'This is what the LORD says: Israel is my firstborn son, **23**and I told you, "Let my son go, so he may worship me." But you refused to let him go; so I will kill your firstborn son.' "

24At a lodging place on the way, the LORD met ⌊Moses⌋*ᵃ* and was about to kill him. **25**But Zipporah took a flint knife, cut off her son's foreskin and touched ⌊Moses'⌋ feet with it.*ᵇ* "Surely you are a bridegroom of blood to me," she said. **26**So the LORD let him alone. (At that time she said "bridegroom of blood," referring to circumcision.)

ᵃ24 Or ⌊Moses' son⌋; Hebrew *him*   *ᵇ25* Or *and drew near* ⌊Moses'⌋ *feet*

Who Made Your Mouth?

I took my first crack at public speaking at age seven. It was the Christmas dinner party for my dad's business. One of the more creative—or sadistic—executives in the company decided that it would be a good idea to have a family talent show as the after-dinner program. This was the same ladder-climbing, brown-nosing executive who always tousled my hair and called me "the president's young man."

Somehow, my parents convinced me that my dramatic soliloquy of the words to "O, Little Town of Bethlehem," would be a show-stopper. And because parents are never wrong (!), I naively agreed to perform.

Like it was last month, I remember what it felt like to walk out on the stage, gaze around the room filled mostly with total strangers, and begin to speak: "O, little ... town of ... uh (swallow) ... Bethlehem, how still ... er ... uh (gasp) ... we see thee ... lie."

I could hardly breathe. My head was spinning out of control. Then dizziness was replaced by nausea. I remember wondering, *Will I ever get through this?* Amazingly, I lived to tell the story.

DAILY INSIGHT

TUESDAY

Passage:
Exodus 4:1–12

Verse:
Exodus 4:11

In the once-in-a-lifetime conversation with God we mentioned yesterday, Moses was told to give a speech—one that was much more difficult than reciting the lyrics to a familiar Christmas carol at a dinner party. God told Moses to stand in front of the powerful Pharaoh—the ruler of the greatest nation on earth—and *order* him to release the Israelites from captivity.

Who can blame Moses for arguing with God? Who wouldn't find himself spitless in the face of such an unbelievable assignment? After several minutes of dialogue, God delivered the clincher: "Hey Moses, who made your mouth?" (4:11).

The argument came to a screeching halt.

This just might be a day for such a dramatic reminder. No matter how tough the assignment—speaking, writing, thinking, creating—there isn't anything that God cannot accomplish through your mouth, your hands, your intellect, or your mind. After all, he made them. And he can make them work.

Take this truth with you today.

For your next devotional reading, go to page 82.

²⁷The LORD said to Aaron, "Go into the desert to meet Moses." So he met Moses at the mountain of God and kissed him. ²⁸Then Moses told Aaron everything the LORD had sent him to say, and also about all the miraculous signs he had commanded him to perform.

²⁹Moses and Aaron brought together all the elders of the Israelites, ³⁰and Aaron told them everything the LORD had said to Moses. He also performed the signs before the people, ³¹and they believed. And when they heard that the LORD was concerned about them and had seen their misery, they bowed down and worshiped.

Bricks Without Straw

5 Afterward Moses and Aaron went to Pharaoh and said, "This is what the LORD, the God of Israel, says: 'Let my people go, so that they may hold a festival to me in the desert.' "

²Pharaoh said, "Who is the LORD, that I should obey him and let Israel go? I do not know the LORD and I will not let Israel go." ³Then they said, "The God of the Hebrews has met with us. Now let us take a three-day journey into the desert to offer sacrifices to the LORD our God, or he may strike us with plagues or with the sword."

⁴But the king of Egypt said, "Moses and Aaron, why are you taking the people away from their labor? Get back to your work!" ⁵Then Pharaoh said, "Look, the people of the land are now numerous, and you are stopping them from working."

⁶That same day Pharaoh gave this order to the slave drivers and foremen in charge of the people: ⁷"You are no longer to supply the people with straw for making bricks; let them go and gather their own straw. ⁸But require them to make the same number of bricks as before; don't reduce the quota. They are lazy; that is why they are crying out, 'Let us go and sacrifice to our God.' ⁹Make the work harder for the men so that they keep working and pay no attention to lies."

¹⁰Then the slave drivers and the foremen went out and said to the people, "This is what Pharaoh says: 'I will not give you any more straw. ¹¹Go and get your own straw wherever you can find it, but your work will not be reduced at all.' " ¹²So the people scattered all over Egypt to gather stubble to use for straw. ¹³The slave drivers kept pressing them, saying, "Complete the work required of you for each

day, just as when you had straw." ¹⁴The Israelite foremen appointed by Pharaoh's slave drivers were beaten and were asked, "Why didn't you meet your quota of bricks yesterday or today, as before?"

¹⁵Then the Israelite foremen went and appealed to Pharaoh: "Why have you treated your servants this way? ¹⁶Your servants are given no straw, yet we are told, 'Make bricks!' Your servants are being beaten, but the fault is with your own people."

¹⁷Pharaoh said, "Lazy, that's what you are—lazy! That is why you keep saying, 'Let us go and sacrifice to the LORD.' ¹⁸Now get to work. You will not be given any straw, yet you must produce your full quota of bricks."

¹⁹The Israelite foremen realized they were in trouble when they were told, "You are not to reduce the number of bricks required of you for each day." ²⁰When they left Pharaoh, they found Moses and Aaron waiting to meet them, ²¹and they said, "May the LORD look upon you and judge you! You have made us a stench to Pharaoh and his officials and have put a sword in their hand to kill us."

God Promises Deliverance

²²Moses returned to the LORD and said, "O Lord, why have you brought trouble upon this people? Is this why you sent me? ²³Ever since I went to Pharaoh to speak in your name, he has brought trouble upon this people, and you have not rescued your people at all."

6 Then the LORD said to Moses, "Now you will see what I will do to Pharaoh: Because of my mighty hand he will let them go; because of my mighty hand he will drive them out of his country."

²God also said to Moses, "I am the LORD. ³I appeared to Abraham, to Isaac and to Jacob as God Almighty,ᵃ but by my name the LORDᵇ I did not make myself known to them.ᶜ ⁴I also established my covenant with them to give them the land of Canaan, where they lived as aliens. ⁵Moreover, I have heard the groaning of the Israelites, whom the Egyptians are enslaving, and I have remembered my covenant. ⁶"Therefore, say to the Israelites: 'I am the LORD, and I will bring you out from under the yoke of the Egyptians. I will free you from being slaves to them, and I will

---

ᵃ3 Hebrew *El-Shaddai* ᵇ3 See note at Exodus 3:15.
ᶜ3 Or *Almighty, and by my name the* LORD *did I not let myself be known to them?*

redeem you with an outstretched arm and with mighty acts of judgment. [7]I will take you as my own people, and I will be your God. Then you will know that I am the LORD your God, who brought you out from under the yoke of the Egyptians. [8]And I will bring you to the land I swore with uplifted hand to give to Abraham, to Isaac and to Jacob. I will give it to you as a possession. I am the LORD.' "

[9]Moses reported this to the Israelites, but they did not listen to him because of their discouragement and cruel bondage. [10]Then the LORD said to Moses, [11]"Go, tell Pharaoh king of Egypt to let the Israelites go out of his country."

[12]But Moses said to the LORD, "If the Israelites will not listen to me, why would Pharaoh listen to me, since I speak with faltering lips[a]?"

Family Record of Moses and Aaron

[13]Now the LORD spoke to Moses and Aaron about the Israelites and Pharaoh king of Egypt, and he commanded them to bring the Israelites out of Egypt.

[14]These were the heads of their families[b]:

The sons of Reuben the firstborn son of Israel were Hanoch and Pallu, Hezron and Carmi. These were the clans of Reuben.

[15]The sons of Simeon were Jemuel, Jamin, Ohad, Jakin, Zohar and Shaul the son of a Canaanite woman. These were the clans of Simeon.

[16]These were the names of the sons of Levi according to their records: Gershon, Kohath and Merari. Levi lived 137 years.

[17]The sons of Gershon, by clans, were Libni and Shimei.

[18]The sons of Kohath were Amram, Izhar, Hebron and Uzziel. Kohath lived 133 years.

[19]The sons of Merari were Mahli and Mushi.

These were the clans of Levi according to their records.

[20]Amram married his father's sister Jochebed, who bore him Aaron and Moses. Amram lived 137 years.

[21]The sons of Izhar were Korah, Nepheg and Zicri.

[22]The sons of Uzziel were Mishael, Elzaphan and Sithri.

[23]Aaron married Elisheba, daughter of Amminadab and sister of Nah-

shon, and she bore him Nadab and Abihu, Eleazar and Ithamar.

[24]The sons of Korah were Assir, Elkanah and Abiasaph. These were the Korahite clans.

[25]Eleazar son of Aaron married one of the daughters of Putiel, and she bore him Phinehas.

These were the heads of the Levite families, clan by clan.

[26]It was this same Aaron and Moses to whom the LORD said, "Bring the Israelites out of Egypt by their divisions." [27]They were the ones who spoke to Pharaoh king of Egypt about bringing the Israelites out of Egypt. It was the same Moses and Aaron.

Aaron to Speak for Moses

[28]Now when the LORD spoke to Moses in Egypt, [29]he said to him, "I am the LORD. Tell Pharaoh king of Egypt everything I tell you."

[30]But Moses said to the LORD, "Since I speak with faltering lips, why would Pharaoh listen to me?"

7 Then the LORD said to Moses, "See, I have made you like God to Pharaoh, and your brother Aaron will be your prophet. [2]You are to say everything I command you, and your brother Aaron is to tell Pharaoh to let the Israelites go out of his country. [3]But I will harden Pharaoh's heart, and though I multiply my miraculous signs and wonders in Egypt, [4]he will not listen to you. Then I will lay my hand on Egypt and with mighty acts of judgment I will bring out my divisions, my people the Israelites. [5]And the Egyptians will know that I am the LORD when I stretch out my hand against Egypt and bring the Israelites out of it."

[6]Moses and Aaron did just as the LORD commanded them. [7]Moses was eighty years old and Aaron eighty-three when they spoke to Pharaoh.

Aaron's Staff Becomes a Snake

[8]The LORD said to Moses and Aaron, [9]"When Pharaoh says to you, 'Perform a miracle,' then say to Aaron, 'Take your staff and throw it down before Pharaoh,' and it will become a snake."

[10]So Moses and Aaron went to Pharaoh

---

[a]12 Hebrew *I am uncircumcised of lips*; also in verse 30   [b]14 The Hebrew for *families* here and in verse 25 refers to units larger than clans.

and did just as the LORD commanded. Aaron threw his staff down in front of Pharaoh and his officials, and it became a snake. ¹¹Pharaoh then summoned wise men and sorcerers, and the Egyptian magicians also did the same things by their secret arts: ¹²Each one threw down his staff and it became a snake. But Aaron's staff swallowed up their staffs. ¹³Yet Pharaoh's heart became hard and he would not listen to them, just as the LORD had said.

The Plague of Blood

¹⁴Then the LORD said to Moses, "Pharaoh's heart is unyielding; he refuses to let the people go. ¹⁵Go to Pharaoh in the morning as he goes out to the water. Wait on the bank of the Nile to meet him, and take in your hand the staff that was changed into a snake. ¹⁶Then say to him, 'The LORD, the God of the Hebrews, has sent me to say to you: Let my people go, so that they may worship me in the desert. But until now you have not listened. ¹⁷This is what the LORD says: By this you will know that I am the LORD: With the staff that is in my hand I will strike the water of the Nile, and it will be changed into blood. ¹⁸The fish in the Nile will die, and the river will stink; the Egyptians will not be able to drink its water.' "

¹⁹The LORD said to Moses, "Tell Aaron, 'Take your staff and stretch out your hand over the waters of Egypt—over the streams and canals, over the ponds and all the reservoirs'—and they will turn to blood. Blood will be everywhere in Egypt, even in the wooden buckets and stone jars."

²⁰Moses and Aaron did just as the LORD had commanded. He raised his staff in the presence of Pharaoh and his officials and struck the water of the Nile, and all the water was changed into blood. ²¹The fish in the Nile died, and the river smelled so bad that the Egyptians could not drink its water. Blood was everywhere in Egypt.

²²But the Egyptian magicians did the same things by their secret arts, and Pharaoh's heart became hard; he would not listen to Moses and Aaron, just as the LORD had said. ²³Instead, he turned and went into his palace, and did not take even this to heart. ²⁴And all the Egyptians dug along the Nile to get drinking water, because they could not drink the water of the river.

The Plague of Frogs

²⁵Seven days passed after the LORD struck the Nile. **8** ¹Then the LORD said to Moses, "Go to Pharaoh and say to him, 'This is what the LORD says: Let my people go, so that they may worship me. ²If you refuse to let them go, I will plague your whole country with frogs. ³The Nile will teem with frogs. They will come up into your palace and your bedroom and onto your bed, into the houses of your officials and on your people, and into your ovens and kneading troughs. ⁴The frogs will go up on you and your people and all your officials.' "

⁵Then the LORD said to Moses, "Tell Aaron, 'Stretch out your hand with your staff over the streams and canals and ponds, and make frogs come up on the land of Egypt.' "

⁶So Aaron stretched out his hand over the waters of Egypt, and the frogs came up and covered the land. ⁷But the magicians did the same things by their secret arts; they also made frogs come up on the land of Egypt.

⁸Pharaoh summoned Moses and Aaron and said, "Pray to the LORD to take the frogs away from me and my people, and I will let your people go to offer sacrifices to the LORD."

⁹Moses said to Pharaoh, "I leave to you the honor of setting the time for me to pray for you and your officials and your people that you and your houses may be rid of the frogs, except for those that remain in the Nile."

¹⁰"Tomorrow," Pharaoh said.

Moses replied, "It will be as you say, so that you may know there is no one like the LORD our God. ¹¹The frogs will leave you and your houses, your officials and your people; they will remain only in the Nile."

¹²After Moses and Aaron left Pharaoh, Moses cried out to the LORD about the frogs he had brought on Pharaoh. ¹³And the LORD did what Moses asked. The frogs died in the houses, in the courtyards and in the fields. ¹⁴They were piled into heaps, and the land reeked of them. ¹⁵But when Pharaoh saw that there was relief, he hardened his heart and would not listen to Moses and Aaron, just as the LORD had said.

The Plague of Gnats

¹⁶Then the LORD said to Moses, "Tell Aaron, 'Stretch out your staff and strike

the dust of the ground,' and throughout the land of Egypt the dust will become gnats." ¹⁷They did this, and when Aaron stretched out his hand with the staff and struck the dust of the ground, gnats came upon men and animals. All the dust throughout the land of Egypt became gnats. ¹⁸But when the magicians tried to produce gnats by their secret arts, they could not. And the gnats were on men and animals.

¹⁹The magicians said to Pharaoh, "This is the finger of God." But Pharaoh's heart was hard and he would not listen, just as the LORD had said.

The Plague of Flies

²⁰Then the LORD said to Moses, "Get up early in the morning and confront Pharaoh as he goes to the water and say to him, 'This is what the LORD says: Let my people go, so that they may worship me. ²¹If you do not let my people go, I will send swarms of flies on you and your officials, on your people and into your houses. The houses of the Egyptians will be full of flies, and even the ground where they are.

²²" 'But on that day I will deal differently with the land of Goshen, where my people live; no swarms of flies will be there, so that you will know that I, the LORD, am in this land. ²³I will make a distinction[a] between my people and your people. This miraculous sign will occur tomorrow.' "

²⁴And the LORD did this. Dense swarms of flies poured into Pharaoh's palace and into the houses of his officials, and throughout Egypt the land was ruined by the flies.

²⁵Then Pharaoh summoned Moses and Aaron and said, "Go, sacrifice to your God here in the land."

²⁶But Moses said, "That would not be right. The sacrifices we offer the LORD our God would be detestable to the Egyptians. And if we offer sacrifices that are detestable in their eyes, will they not stone us? ²⁷We must take a three-day journey into the desert to offer sacrifices to the LORD our God, as he commands us."

²⁸Pharaoh said, "I will let you go to offer sacrifices to the LORD your God in the desert, but you must not go very far. Now pray for me."

²⁹Moses answered, "As soon as I leave you, I will pray to the LORD, and tomorrow the flies will leave Pharaoh and his officials and his people. Only be sure that Pharaoh does not act deceitfully again by not letting the people go to offer sacrifices to the LORD."

³⁰Then Moses left Pharaoh and prayed to the LORD, ³¹and the LORD did what Moses asked: The flies left Pharaoh and his officials and his people; not a fly remained. ³²But this time also Pharaoh hardened his heart and would not let the people go.

The Plague on Livestock

9 Then the LORD said to Moses, "Go to Pharaoh and say to him, 'This is what the LORD, the God of the Hebrews, says: "Let my people go, so that they may worship me." ²If you refuse to let them go and continue to hold them back, ³the hand of the LORD will bring a terrible plague on your livestock in the field—on your horses and donkeys and camels and on your cattle and sheep and goats. ⁴But the LORD will make a distinction between the livestock of Israel and that of Egypt, so that no animal belonging to the Israelites will die.' "

⁵The LORD set a time and said, "Tomorrow the LORD will do this in the land." ⁶And the next day the LORD did it: All the livestock of the Egyptians died, but not one animal belonging to the Israelites died. ⁷Pharaoh sent men to investigate and found that not even one of the animals of the Israelites had died. Yet his heart was unyielding and he would not let the people go.

The Plague of Boils

⁸Then the LORD said to Moses and Aaron, "Take handfuls of soot from a furnace and have Moses toss it into the air in the presence of Pharaoh. ⁹It will become fine dust over the whole land of Egypt, and festering boils will break out on men and animals throughout the land."

¹⁰So they took soot from a furnace and stood before Pharaoh. Moses tossed it into the air, and festering boils broke out on men and animals. ¹¹The magicians could not stand before Moses because of the boils that were on them and on all the Egyptians. ¹²But the LORD hardened Pharaoh's heart and he would not listen to Moses and Aaron, just as the LORD had said to Moses.

---

[a]23 Septuagint and Vulgate; Hebrew *will put a deliverance*

The Plague of Hail

[13]Then the LORD said to Moses, "Get up early in the morning, confront Pharaoh and say to him, 'This is what the LORD, the God of the Hebrews, says: Let my people go, so that they may worship me, [14]or this time I will send the full force of my plagues against you and against your officials and your people, so you may know that there is no one like me in all the earth. [15]For by now I could have stretched out my hand and struck you and your people with a plague that would have wiped you off the earth. [16]But I have raised you up[a] for this very purpose, that I might show you my power and that my name might be proclaimed in all the earth. [17]You still set yourself against my people and will not let them go. [18]Therefore, at this time tomorrow I will send the worst hailstorm that has ever fallen on Egypt, from the day it was founded till now. [19]Give an order now to bring your livestock and everything you have in the field to a place of shelter, because the hail will fall on every man and animal that has not been brought in and is still out in the field, and they will die.' "

[20]Those officials of Pharaoh who feared the word of the LORD hurried to bring their slaves and their livestock inside. [21]But those who ignored the word of the LORD left their slaves and livestock in the field.

[22]Then the LORD said to Moses, "Stretch out your hand toward the sky so that hail will fall all over Egypt—on men and animals and on everything growing in the fields of Egypt." [23]When Moses stretched out his staff toward the sky, the LORD sent thunder and hail, and lightning flashed down to the ground. So the LORD rained hail on the land of Egypt; [24]hail fell and lightning flashed back and forth. It was the worst storm in all the land of Egypt since it had become a nation. [25]Throughout Egypt hail struck everything in the fields—both men and animals; it beat down everything growing in the fields and stripped every tree. [26]The only place it did not hail was the land of Goshen, where the Israelites were.

[27]Then Pharaoh summoned Moses and Aaron. "This time I have sinned," he said to them. "The LORD is in the right, and I and my people are in the wrong. [28]Pray to the LORD, for we have had enough thunder and hail. I will let you go; you don't have to stay any longer."

[29]Moses replied, "When I have gone out of the city, I will spread out my hands in prayer to the LORD. The thunder will stop and there will be no more hail, so you may know that the earth is the LORD's. [30]But I know that you and your officials still do not fear the LORD God."

[31](The flax and barley were destroyed, since the barley had headed and the flax was in bloom. [32]The wheat and spelt, however, were not destroyed, because they ripen later.)

[33]Then Moses left Pharaoh and went out of the city. He spread out his hands toward the LORD; the thunder and hail stopped, and the rain no longer poured down on the land. [34]When Pharaoh saw that the rain and hail and thunder had stopped, he sinned again: He and his officials hardened their hearts. [35]So Pharaoh's heart was hard and he would not let the Israelites go, just as the LORD had said through Moses.

The Plague of Locusts

10 Then the LORD said to Moses, "Go to Pharaoh, for I have hardened his heart and the hearts of his officials so that I may perform these miraculous signs of mine among them [2]that you may tell your children and grandchildren how I dealt harshly with the Egyptians and how I performed my signs among them, and that you may know that I am the LORD."

[3]So Moses and Aaron went to Pharaoh and said to him, "This is what the LORD, the God of the Hebrews, says: 'How long will you refuse to humble yourself before me? Let my people go, so that they may worship me. [4]If you refuse to let them go, I will bring locusts into your country tomorrow. [5]They will cover the face of the ground so that it cannot be seen. They will devour what little you have left after the hail, including every tree that is growing in your fields. [6]They will fill your houses and those of all your officials and all the Egyptians—something neither your fathers nor your forefathers have ever seen from the day they settled in this land till now.' " Then Moses turned and left Pharaoh.

[7]Pharaoh's officials said to him, "How long will this man be a snare to us? Let the people go, so that they may worship the LORD their God. Do you not yet realize that Egypt is ruined?"

[a]16 Or *have spared you*

[8]Then Moses and Aaron were brought back to Pharaoh. "Go, worship the LORD your God," he said. "But just who will be going?"

[9]Moses answered, "We will go with our young and old, with our sons and daughters, and with our flocks and herds, because we are to celebrate a festival to the LORD."

[10]Pharaoh said, "The LORD be with you—if I let you go, along with your women and children! Clearly you are bent on evil.[a] [11]No! Have only the men go; and worship the LORD, since that's what you have been asking for." Then Moses and Aaron were driven out of Pharaoh's presence.

[12]And the LORD said to Moses, "Stretch out your hand over Egypt so that locusts will swarm over the land and devour everything growing in the fields, everything left by the hail."

[13]So Moses stretched out his staff over Egypt, and the LORD made an east wind blow across the land all that day and all that night. By morning the wind had brought the locusts; [14]they invaded all Egypt and settled down in every area of the country in great numbers. Never before had there been such a plague of locusts, nor will there ever be again. [15]They covered all the ground until it was black. They devoured all that was left after the hail—everything growing in the fields and the fruit on the trees. Nothing green remained on tree or plant in all the land of Egypt.

[16]Pharaoh quickly summoned Moses and Aaron and said, "I have sinned against the LORD your God and against you. [17]Now forgive my sin once more and pray to the LORD your God to take this deadly plague away from me."

[18]Moses then left Pharaoh and prayed to the LORD. [19]And the LORD changed the wind to a very strong west wind, which caught up the locusts and carried them into the Red Sea.[b] Not a locust was left anywhere in Egypt. [20]But the LORD hardened Pharaoh's heart, and he would not let the Israelites go.

The Plague of Darkness

[21]Then the LORD said to Moses, "Stretch out your hand toward the sky so that darkness will spread over Egypt—darkness that can be felt." [22]So Moses stretched out his hand toward the sky, and total dark-

[a]10 Or *Be careful, trouble is in store for you!*
[b]19 Hebrew *Yam Suph*; that is, Sea of Reeds

HEY DAD

If God hardened Pharaoh's heart, why did God punish him for not letting the Israelites go?

Text: Exodus 10:27

Why did God harden Pharaoh's heart against the last few plagues, then punish him for not letting the Israelites go? Wasn't he stripping Pharaoh of his free will? At first, it would seem so. But think about this situation a bit further.

Let's say you kidnapped a rich man's young son. The rich man pled with you to return his child, but you refused. Then the rich man caught you off guard, put a gun to your head, and told you to return the child. Terrified, you quickly released his son. Now, did you return the son of your own free will? Hardly.

But let's say that for some reason, you weren't scared of the gun at all. Yet you realized, by this man's drastic measure, that you were wrong—or at least that he had the upper hand. So, unafraid, you would tell the child to get his things and go with his father. At that point, you would be *choosing* to do the right thing.

Do you see the point? There's no way of knowing exactly why God did what he did with Pharaoh. But one possibility is that God hardened Pharaoh's heart because he wanted Pharaoh to acknowledge God's power with his *mind*, not simply out of terror. God didn't want a knee-jerk reaction from the arrogant ruler. He wanted the glory that he deserved. And glory, he got.

QUESTIONS KIDS ASK

For a complete listing of Questions Kids Ask, turn to page 1435.

ness covered all Egypt for three days. [23]No one could see anyone else or leave his place for three days. Yet all the Israelites had light in the places where they lived.

[24]Then Pharaoh summoned Moses and said, "Go, worship the LORD. Even your women and children may go with you; only leave your flocks and herds behind."

[25]But Moses said, "You must allow us to have sacrifices and burnt offerings to present to the LORD our God. [26]Our livestock too must go with us; not a hoof is to be left behind. We have to use some of them in worshiping the LORD our God, and until we get there we will not know what we are to use to worship the LORD."

[27]But the LORD hardened Pharaoh's heart, and he was not willing to let them go. [28]Pharaoh said to Moses, "Get out of my sight! Make sure you do not appear before me again! The day you see my face you will die."

[29]"Just as you say," Moses replied, "I will never appear before you again."

The Plague on the Firstborn

11 Now the LORD had said to Moses, "I will bring one more plague on Pharaoh and on Egypt. After that, he will let you go from here, and when he does, he will drive you out completely. [2]Tell the

---

A Little Light Goes a Long Way

DAILY INSIGHT

WEDNESDAY

Passage:
Exodus 10:21–29

Verse:
Exodus 10:23

It's the middle of the night and you're wakened by a tiny beeping sound. You glance at your night stand clock, but you see nothing. You've heard thunderstorms rumble through during the past several hours, and even though you're pretty groggy, you conclude that the electricity is out.

As you lie there, listening to that little electronic sound, you wrack your brain for what it might be. Glancing over at your slumbering wife, you wish for the gift of sound sleep she was given at birth. You get up to investigate.

Beginning your journey through your dark house, you don't recall ever being surrounded by such blackness. Here you are, in the familiarity of your own home, inching forward and groping for doorways and furniture. (An infrared video tape of this mid-night walk would make for great comedy … later on.)

As the beeping sound gets louder, your heart is filled with a mix of fear and dread. *What could that be?* Soon you discover that the sound is coming from a smoke alarm, which is telling you that the power is out and the battery is low. *I'd better get that changed in the morning,* you think to yourself. You snap off the cover and disconnect the battery, thankful that the other alarms in the house are in good working order.

Turning around, you shuffle and grope your way back to bed.

Because of the Pharaoh's stubbornness, God visited his nation with ten terrible plagues, the ninth of which was darkness. For three full days, people shuffled and groped around Egypt, trying to survive this awful night.

What a graphic picture this is of what it would be like to live without God. In fact, it *is* a picture of the world in which we live … lost men and women, fearfully groping their way through life, hoping to touch safety while avoiding open stairwells.

Perhaps the most amazing part of this story is that God's people—those families that honored him—had light in their homes (10:23b). If there were ever a powerful reminder of what your home must be in the middle of a dark world, it's this one: Make your home a place where light shines. Invite lost people to visit. Show them the joy of living free from fear. Open your doors and windows and let the light chase the darkness from your neighborhood.

And take this light with you today. It doesn't take very much of it to change everything.

For your next devotional reading, go to page 86.

people that men and women alike are to ask their neighbors for articles of silver and gold." ³(The LORD made the Egyptians favorably disposed toward the people, and Moses himself was highly regarded in Egypt by Pharaoh's officials and by the people.)

⁴So Moses said, "This is what the LORD says: 'About midnight I will go throughout Egypt. ⁵Every firstborn son in Egypt will die, from the firstborn son of Pharaoh, who sits on the throne, to the firstborn son of the slave girl, who is at her hand mill, and all the firstborn of the cattle as well. ⁶There will be loud wailing throughout Egypt—worse than there has ever been or ever will be again. ⁷But among the Israelites not a dog will bark at any man or animal.' Then you will know that the LORD makes a distinction between Egypt and

Israel. ⁸All these officials of yours will come to me, bowing down before me and saying, 'Go, you and all the people who follow you!' After that I will leave." Then Moses, hot with anger, left Pharaoh.

⁹The LORD had said to Moses, "Pharaoh will refuse to listen to you—so that my wonders may be multiplied in Egypt." ¹⁰Moses and Aaron performed all these wonders before Pharaoh, but the LORD hardened Pharaoh's heart, and he would not let the Israelites go out of his country.

The Passover

12 The LORD said to Moses and Aaron in Egypt, ²"This month is to be for you the first month, the first month of your year. ³Tell the whole community of Israel that on the tenth day of this month each

Dig Your Heels in and Die
Pharaoh, the Stubborn Father

DADS
IN THE
BIBLE

"Pharaoh and all his officials and all the Egyptians got up during the night, and there was loud wailing in Egypt, for there was not a house without someone dead" (12:30).

Text: Exodus 11:1–10, 12:29–30

Go with me to the most beautiful structure on the face of the earth—the opulently decorated palace in Egypt, home of the most powerful man in the known world. Tonight this king, this father who has everything, this Pharaoh of Egypt, is in a living hell.

The Hebrews had held residence in Egypt for centuries. They lived for a time as the Pharaoh's guests, but as years had passed and power had traded hands, their position in Egypt had changed dramatically. Now the Hebrews lived as slaves, a cheap labor source for the Pharaoh's many building projects.

Moses, a man who had been raised up in the same household as the current Pharaoh, had repeatedly demanded that his stepbrother release these slaves. Not wanting to irreparably damage his administration's fiscal prowess, Pharaoh said "No" to Moses time and time again, despite the obvious power of Moses' God—the God of the plagues.

What this headstrong man never counted on was the price he was about to pay for his obstinacy. He never thought that the decisions he made "at the office" would take such a deadly toll on his family.

The lessons to be learned by this stiff-necked father are lessons of priorities, civility, perspective on life, and love for family over personal gain. What he was unwilling to give cost him something he thought he would never lose.

The opening picture of this lavish palace is gut-wrenching and pitiful. Standing on the precious marble floor, under a canopy of shining frescos and flashing gold, stands a dad with his dead son draped across his arms.

Was it worth the price you paid to hold out for your business, Pharaoh? Are you glad you made these decisions at the peril of your family? Do you wish you had listened to your heart?

Now, what are you going to do, Dad?

For a complete listing of Dads in the Bible, turn to page 1434.

man is to take a lamb*a* for his family, one for each household. **⁴**If any household is too small for a whole lamb, they must share one with their nearest neighbor, having taken into account the number of people there are. You are to determine the amount of lamb needed in accordance with what each person will eat. **⁵**The animals you choose must be year-old males without defect, and you may take them from the sheep or the goats. **⁶**Take care of them until the fourteenth day of the month, when all the people of the community of Israel must slaughter them at twilight. **⁷**Then they are to take some of the blood and put it on the sides and tops of the doorframes of the houses where they eat the lambs. **⁸**That same night they are to eat the meat roasted over the fire, along with bitter herbs, and bread made without yeast. **⁹**Do not eat the meat raw or cooked in water, but roast it over the fire—head, legs and inner parts. **¹⁰**Do not leave any of it till morning; if some is left till morning, you must burn it. **¹¹**This is how you are to eat it: with your cloak tucked into your belt, your sandals on your feet and your staff in your hand. Eat it in haste; it is the LORD's Passover.

¹²"On that same night I will pass through Egypt and strike down every firstborn—both men and animals—and I will bring judgment on all the gods of Egypt. I am the LORD. **¹³**The blood will be a sign for you on the houses where you are; and when I see the blood, I will pass over you. No destructive plague will touch you when I strike Egypt.

¹⁴"This is a day you are to commemorate; for the generations to come you shall celebrate it as a festival to the LORD—a lasting ordinance. **¹⁵**For seven days you are to eat bread made without yeast. On the first day remove the yeast from your houses, for whoever eats anything with yeast in it from the first day through the seventh must be cut off from Israel. **¹⁶**On the first day hold a sacred assembly, and another one on the seventh day. Do no work at all on these days, except to prepare food for everyone to eat—that is all you may do.

¹⁷"Celebrate the Feast of Unleavened Bread, because it was on this very day that I brought your divisions out of Egypt. Celebrate this day as a lasting ordinance for the generations to come. **¹⁸**In the first month you are to eat bread made without yeast, from the evening of the fourteenth day until the evening of the twenty-first

day. **¹⁹**For seven days no yeast is to be found in your houses. And whoever eats anything with yeast in it must be cut off from the community of Israel, whether he is an alien or native-born. **²⁰**Eat nothing made with yeast. Wherever you live, you must eat unleavened bread."

²¹Then Moses summoned all the elders of Israel and said to them, "Go at once and select the animals for your families and slaughter the Passover lamb. **²²**Take a bunch of hyssop, dip it into the blood in the basin and put some of the blood on the top and on both sides of the doorframe. Not one of you shall go out the door of his house until morning. **²³**When the LORD goes through the land to strike down the Egyptians, he will see the blood on the top and sides of the doorframe and will pass over that doorway, and he will not permit the destroyer to enter your houses and strike you down.

²⁴"Obey these instructions as a lasting ordinance for you and your descendants. **²⁵**When you enter the land that the LORD will give you as he promised, observe this ceremony. **²⁶**And when your children ask you, 'What does this ceremony mean to you?' **²⁷**then tell them, 'It is the Passover sacrifice to the LORD, who passed over the houses of the Israelites in Egypt and spared our homes when he struck down the Egyptians.' " Then the people bowed down and worshiped. **²⁸**The Israelites did just what the LORD commanded Moses and Aaron.

²⁹At midnight the LORD struck down all the firstborn in Egypt, from the firstborn of Pharaoh, who sat on the throne, to the firstborn of the prisoner, who was in the dungeon, and the firstborn of all the livestock as well. **³⁰**Pharaoh and all his officials and all the Egyptians got up during the night, and there was loud wailing in Egypt, for there was not a house without someone dead.

The Exodus

³¹During the night Pharaoh summoned Moses and Aaron and said, "Up! Leave my people, you and the Israelites! Go, worship the LORD as you have requested. **³²**Take your flocks and herds, as you have said, and go. And also bless me."

³³The Egyptians urged the people to hurry and leave the country. "For otherwise," they said, "we will all die!" **³⁴**So the

---

a3 The Hebrew word can mean lamb or kid; also in verse 4.

people took their dough before the yeast was added, and carried it on their shoulders in kneading troughs wrapped in clothing. ³⁵The Israelites did as Moses instructed and asked the Egyptians for articles of silver and gold and for clothing. ³⁶The LORD had made the Egyptians favorably disposed toward the people, and they gave them what they asked for; so they plundered the Egyptians.

³⁷The Israelites journeyed from Rameses to Succoth. There were about six hundred thousand men on foot, besides women and children. ³⁸Many other people went up with them, as well as large droves of livestock, both flocks and herds. ³⁹With the dough they had brought from Egypt, they baked cakes of unleavened bread. The dough was without yeast because they had been driven out of Egypt and did not have time to prepare food for themselves.

⁴⁰Now the length of time the Israelite people lived in Egypt*a* was 430 years. ⁴¹At the end of the 430 years, to the very day, all the LORD's divisions left Egypt. ⁴²Because the LORD kept vigil that night to bring them out of Egypt, on this night all the Israelites are to keep vigil to honor the LORD for the generations to come.

Passover Restrictions

⁴³The LORD said to Moses and Aaron, "These are the regulations for the Passover:

"No foreigner is to eat of it. ⁴⁴Any slave you have bought may eat of it after you have circumcised him, ⁴⁵but a temporary resident and a hired worker may not eat of it.

⁴⁶"It must be eaten inside one house; take none of the meat outside the house. Do not break any of the bones. ⁴⁷The whole community of Israel must celebrate it.

⁴⁸"An alien living among you who wants to celebrate the LORD's Passover must have all the males in his household circumcised; then he may take part like one born in the land. No uncircumcised male may eat of it. ⁴⁹The same law applies to the native-born and to the alien living among you."

⁵⁰All the Israelites did just what the LORD had commanded Moses and Aaron. ⁵¹And on that very day the LORD brought the Israelites out of Egypt by their divisions.

Consecration of the Firstborn

13 The LORD said to Moses, ²"Consecrate to me every firstborn male. The first offspring of every womb among the Israelites belongs to me, whether man or animal."

³Then Moses said to the people, "Commemorate this day, the day you came out of Egypt, out of the land of slavery, because the LORD brought you out of it with a mighty hand. Eat nothing containing yeast. ⁴Today, in the month of Abib, you are leaving. ⁵When the LORD brings you into the land of the Canaanites, Hittites, Amorites, Hivites and Jebusites—the land he swore to your forefathers to give you, a land flowing with milk and honey—you are to observe this ceremony in this month: ⁶For seven days eat bread made without yeast and on the seventh day hold a festival to the LORD. ⁷Eat unleavened bread during those seven days; nothing with yeast in it is to be seen among you, nor shall any yeast be seen anywhere within your borders. ⁸On that day tell your son, 'I do this because of what the LORD did for me when I came out of Egypt.' ⁹This observance will be for you like a sign on your hand and a reminder on your forehead that the law of the LORD is to be on your lips. For the LORD brought you out of Egypt with his mighty hand. ¹⁰You must keep this ordinance at the appointed time year after year.

¹¹"After the LORD brings you into the land of the Canaanites and gives it to you, as he promised on oath to you and your forefathers, ¹²you are to give over to the LORD the first offspring of every womb. All the firstborn males of your livestock belong to the LORD. ¹³Redeem with a lamb every firstborn donkey, but if you do not redeem it, break its neck. Redeem every firstborn among your sons.

¹⁴"In days to come, when your son asks you, 'What does this mean?' say to him, 'With a mighty hand the LORD brought us out of Egypt, out of the land of slavery. ¹⁵When Pharaoh stubbornly refused to let us go, the LORD killed every firstborn in Egypt, both man and animal. This is why I sacrifice to the LORD the first male offspring of every womb and redeem each of my firstborn sons.' ¹⁶And it will be like a sign on your hand and a symbol on your forehead that the LORD brought us out of Egypt with his mighty hand."

a40 Masoretic Text; Samaritan Pentateuch and Septuagint *Egypt and Canaan*

Crossing the Sea

17When Pharaoh let the people go, God did not lead them on the road through the Philistine country, though that was shorter. For God said, "If they face war, they might change their minds and return to Egypt." **18**So God led the people around by the desert road toward the Red Sea.*ᵃ* The Israelites went up out of Egypt armed for battle.

19Moses took the bones of Joseph with him because Joseph had made the sons of Israel swear an oath. He had said, "God will surely come to your aid, and then you must carry my bones up with you from this place."*ᵇ*

20After leaving Succoth they camped at Etham on the edge of the desert. **21**By day the LORD went ahead of them in a pillar of cloud to guide them on their way and by night in a pillar of fire to give them light, so that they could travel by day or night. **22**Neither the pillar of cloud by day nor the pillar of fire by night left its place in front of the people.

14 Then the LORD said to Moses, **2**"Tell the Israelites to turn back and encamp near Pi Hahiroth, between Migdol and the sea. They are to encamp by the sea, directly opposite Baal Zephon. **3**Pharaoh will think, 'The Israelites are wandering around the land in confusion,

ᵃ18 Hebrew Yam Suph; that is, Sea of Reeds
ᵇ19 See Gen. 50:25.

Reverend Dad

When I was in grade school, Memorial Day was my favorite holiday. Incredible though this may sound, I even preferred it to Christmas and Thanksgiving. I grew up in a large family where Christmas presents were quite practical—gloves, usually—rather than fun, and where Thanksgiving meant that my job was to drag every chair in the county into the dining room.

I *wish* I could report that Memorial Day was so special to me because it reminded me of those who had given their lives so I could live in the luxury of freedom. I *wish* I could say that it reminded me of the courage of great men and women who stood firmly to their convictions, no matter what the cost.

Actually, Memorial Day was my favorite because I played in the marching band, and school was almost over for the whole summer.

Now that I'm older, I still have a deep love for the day our nation sets aside to remember the faithfulness of courageous and fallen soldiers. But now it's for different reasons. It's a humbling thing to realize that people—total strangers—spilled their blood for me.

God's people had a similar event in their tradition. God's promises had been so visible to the Jews that, every year, they set

DAILY INSIGHT

THURSDAY

Passage:
Exodus 13:1–10

Verses:
Exodus 13:8–9

a week aside to remember and be grateful. Even today, Passover is a time when the children of Israel recall his goodness. And today's reading announces God's Passover requirement to fathers, "Tell your son, 'I do this because of what the LORD did for me' " (13:8).

Jewish tradition has a very, very important lesson to teach dads. Please don't miss this. *You are the priest in your home.* Tell your children about God's faithfulness in your life. Demonstrate what his love looks like when it's lived out in a person's life. Introduce your loved ones to God's amazing grace. Bring your family to their own personal experience of saving faith.

Yes, most of us have the privilege of being members of a church fellowship. Weekly, we are ministered to by men and women, called of God to teach and challenge us. But, these professionals have not taken us off the hook. Their job is not to assume this special role in our homes. This one is ours.

We have no choice but to live our lives as an example. We must teach our children God's ways, remind them of his faithfulness, and show them his grace.

For your next devotional reading, go to page 87.

hemmed in by the desert.' ⁴And I will harden Pharaoh's heart, and he will pursue them. But I will gain glory for myself through Pharaoh and all his army, and the Egyptians will know that I am the LORD." So the Israelites did this.

⁵When the king of Egypt was told that the people had fled, Pharaoh and his officials changed their minds about them and said, "What have we done? We have let the Israelites go and have lost their services!" ⁶So he had his chariot made ready and took his army with him. ⁷He took six hundred of the best chariots, along with all the other chariots of Egypt, with officers over all of them. ⁸The LORD hardened the heart of Pharaoh king of Egypt, so that he pursued the Israelites, who were marching out boldly. ⁹The Egyptians—all Pharaoh's horses and chariots, horsemen*a* and troops—pursued the Israelites and overtook them as they camped by the sea near Pi Hahiroth, opposite Baal Zephon.

¹⁰As Pharaoh approached, the Israelites looked up, and there were the Egyptians, marching after them. They were terrified and cried out to the LORD. ¹¹They said to Moses, "Was it because there were no graves in Egypt that you brought us to the desert to die? What have you done to us by

*a*9 Or *charioteers*; also in verses 17, 18, 23, 26 and 28

Are We There Yet?

DAILY INSIGHT

FRIDAY

Passage:
Exodus 14:10–18

Verse:
Exodus 14:13

Being a good dad is a very tough job. Given a choice, every dad would prefer being liked by his family to not being liked. "Dad, you're the greatest," feels a lot better than, "C'mon Dad, you can do better than this."

Unfortunately, there are many times in the lives of families when the dad would come in dead last on his kids' "Dad of the Year" nominee list. Leadership can be like that. If being applauded by the family for every single activity was the goal, then there would never be a "Please sit up straight at the table," "You will not speak to your little brother like that," or "Yes, we *are* going to church. Church is something we do as a family." Chaos would replace order, and in the long run, Dad would be charged with abandoning his post.

So either way, we're going to get it. We'll either be unpopular because we've been tough or guilty of not doing our jobs. As I said, being a dad is not easy.

Poor Moses knew something about this. He had just been personally responsible for the release of over two million Jews from captivity, no small job. But now these people—his family—were being squeezed between the Red Sea and the entire Egyptian army. And they were very upset at Moses. "How could you have done this to us?" and "This is all your fault," they moaned.

And don't you know that Moses was frustrated and angry at his family. "After all I've done for you, and all you do is *complain*?" Sound familiar?

Today's verse (14:13) is a keeper. In fact, it might be worth jotting this one down and putting it on the mirror where you shave. Moses stands in front of his people and he gives them a little talk: Don't be afraid, hold steady, and watch God do his thing.

Moses' confident response begs a question, doesn't it? Given what looked like the ultimate rock-and-a-hard-place, how could he possibly have been so sure? The answer lies in the chapters leading up to this amazing story. Moses had kept in close contact with the Lord. Moses' assurance didn't come from having read the latest in motivational literature. It came from God himself.

This might be a best-dad-in-the-world day at your house. Your children may kneel at their beds tonight and thank God for giving them such a spectacular father. Or maybe not. The secret to your success as a dad doesn't depend on how pleased your children are with your decisions. The key is in who is calling the shots for you.

For your next devotional reading, go to page 90.

bringing us out of Egypt? [12]Didn't we say to you in Egypt, 'Leave us alone; let us serve the Egyptians'? It would have been better for us to serve the Egyptians than to die in the desert!"

[13]Moses answered the people, "Do not be afraid. Stand firm and you will see the deliverance the LORD will bring you today. The Egyptians you see today you will never see again. [14]The LORD will fight for you; you need only to be still."

[15]Then the LORD said to Moses, "Why are you crying out to me? Tell the Israelites to move on. [16]Raise your staff and stretch out your hand over the sea to divide the water so that the Israelites can go through the sea on dry ground. [17]I will harden the hearts of the Egyptians so that they will go in after them. And I will gain glory through Pharaoh and all his army, through his chariots and his horsemen. [18]The Egyptians will know that I am the LORD when I gain glory through Pharaoh, his chariots and his horsemen."

[19]Then the angel of God, who had been traveling in front of Israel's army, withdrew and went behind them. The pillar of cloud also moved from in front and stood behind them, [20]coming between the armies of Egypt and Israel. Throughout the night the cloud brought darkness to the one side and light to the other side; so neither went near the other all night long.

[21]Then Moses stretched out his hand over the sea, and all that night the LORD drove the sea back with a strong east wind and turned it into dry land. The waters were divided, [22]and the Israelites went through the sea on dry ground, with a wall of water on their right and on their left.

[23]The Egyptians pursued them, and all Pharaoh's horses and chariots and horsemen followed them into the sea. [24]During the last watch of the night the LORD looked down from the pillar of fire and cloud at the Egyptian army and threw it into confusion. [25]He made the wheels of their chariots come off[a] so that they had difficulty driving. And the Egyptians said, "Let's get away from the Israelites! The LORD is fighting for them against Egypt."

[26]Then the LORD said to Moses, "Stretch out your hand over the sea so that the waters may flow back over the Egyptians and their chariots and horsemen." [27]Moses stretched out his hand over the sea, and at daybreak the sea went back to its place. The Egyptians were fleeing toward[b] it, and the LORD swept them into the sea. [28]The water flowed back and covered the chari-

ots and horsemen—the entire army of Pharaoh that had followed the Israelites into the sea. Not one of them survived.

[29]But the Israelites went through the sea on dry ground, with a wall of water on their right and on their left. [30]That day the LORD saved Israel from the hands of the Egyptians, and Israel saw the Egyptians lying dead on the shore. [31]And when the Israelites saw the great power the LORD displayed against the Egyptians, the people feared the LORD and put their trust in him and in Moses his servant.

The Song of Moses and Miriam

15 Then Moses and the Israelites sang this song to the LORD:

"I will sing to the LORD,
    for he is highly exalted.
The horse and its rider
    he has hurled into the sea.
[2]The LORD is my strength and my song;
    he has become my salvation.
He is my God, and I will praise him,
    my father's God, and I will exalt him.
[3]The LORD is a warrior;
    the LORD is his name.
[4]Pharaoh's chariots and his army
    he has hurled into the sea.
The best of Pharaoh's officers
    are drowned in the Red Sea.[c]
[5]The deep waters have covered them;
    they sank to the depths like a stone.

[6]"Your right hand, O LORD,
    was majestic in power.
Your right hand, O LORD,
    shattered the enemy.
[7]In the greatness of your majesty
    you threw down those who opposed you.
You unleashed your burning anger;
    it consumed them like stubble.
[8]By the blast of your nostrils
    the waters piled up.
The surging waters stood firm like a wall;
    the deep waters congealed in the heart of the sea.

[9]"The enemy boasted,
    'I will pursue, I will overtake them.
I will divide the spoils;
    I will gorge myself on them.
I will draw my sword

---

[a]25 Or *He jammed the wheels of their chariots* (see Samaritan Pentateuch, Septuagint and Syriac) [b]27 Or *from*   [c]4 Hebrew *Yam Suph*; that is, Sea of Reeds; also in verse 22

and my hand will destroy them.'
[10] But you blew with your breath,
    and the sea covered them.
They sank like lead
    in the mighty waters.

[11] "Who among the gods is like you,
    O Lord?
Who is like you—
    majestic in holiness,
    awesome in glory,
    working wonders?
[12] You stretched out your right hand
    and the earth swallowed them.

[13] "In your unfailing love you will lead
    the people you have redeemed.
In your strength you will guide them
    to your holy dwelling.
[14] The nations will hear and tremble;
    anguish will grip the people of
      Philistia.
[15] The chiefs of Edom will be terrified,
    the leaders of Moab will be seized
      with trembling,
the people[a] of Canaan will melt away;
[16]   terror and dread will fall upon
      them.
By the power of your arm
    they will be as still as a stone—
until your people pass by, O Lord,
    until the people you bought[b] pass by.
[17] You will bring them in and plant them
    on the mountain of your
      inheritance—
the place, O Lord, you made for your
      dwelling,
    the sanctuary, O Lord, your hands
      established.
[18] The Lord will reign
    for ever and ever."

[19] When Pharaoh's horses, chariots and horsemen[c] went into the sea, the Lord brought the waters of the sea back over them, but the Israelites walked through the sea on dry ground. [20] Then Miriam the prophetess, Aaron's sister, took a tambourine in her hand, and all the women followed her, with tambourines and dancing. [21] Miriam sang to them:

"Sing to the Lord,
    for he is highly exalted.
The horse and its rider
    he has hurled into the sea."

The Waters of Marah and Elim

[22] Then Moses led Israel from the Red Sea and they went into the Desert of Shur. For three days they traveled in the desert without finding water. [23] When they came to Marah, they could not drink its water because it was bitter. (That is why the place is called Marah.[d]) [24] So the people grumbled against Moses, saying, "What are we to drink?"

[25] Then Moses cried out to the Lord, and the Lord showed him a piece of wood. He threw it into the water, and the water became sweet.

There the Lord made a decree and a law for them, and there he tested them. [26] He said, "If you listen carefully to the voice of the Lord your God and do what is right in his eyes, if you pay attention to his commands and keep all his decrees, I will not bring on you any of the diseases I brought on the Egyptians, for I am the Lord, who heals you."

[27] Then they came to Elim, where there were twelve springs and seventy palm trees, and they camped there near the water.

Manna and Quail

16 The whole Israelite community set out from Elim and came to the Desert of Sin, which is between Elim and Sinai, on the fifteenth day of the second month after they had come out of Egypt. [2] In the desert the whole community grumbled against Moses and Aaron. [3] The Israelites said to them, "If only we had died by the Lord's hand in Egypt! There we sat around pots of meat and ate all the food we wanted, but you have brought us out into this desert to starve this entire assembly to death."

[4] Then the Lord said to Moses, "I will rain down bread from heaven for you. The people are to go out each day and gather enough for that day. In this way I will test them and see whether they will follow my instructions. [5] On the sixth day they are to prepare what they bring in, and that is to be twice as much as they gather on the other days."

[6] So Moses and Aaron said to all the Israelites, "In the evening you will know that it was the Lord who brought you out of Egypt, [7] and in the morning you will see the glory of the Lord, because he has heard your grumbling against him. Who are we, that you should grumble against us?" [8] Moses also said, "You will know that it was the Lord when he gives you meat to

---

[a]15 Or *rulers*   [b]16 Or *created*   [c]19 Or *charioteers*
[d]23 *Marah* means *bitter*.

What's for Dinner?

Key Verse: *Moses said to them, "It is the bread the LORD has given you to eat. This is what the LORD has commanded: 'Each one is to gather as much as he needs.'"* Exodus 16:15b–16a

Text: Exodus 16:4–16 *(Dad or child reads the text.)*

QUIET
TIMES
WITH Dad

DAD READS: Sometimes, during the winter, people turn on the television and hear the news that a big storm is coming. Soon the roads may be closed and people will probably be stuck in their homes. Because of this threatening weather report, people jump in their cars and drive to their local grocery stores. They fill their carts with more milk and bread than they'll ever need—unless the storm lasts for two months or unless they plan to feed their whole neighborhood! Because these people have taken more than their "share," others who get to the grocery store later may find the shelves empty.

Child reads: Families are about sharing. The story we read today is about a great big family who has been told not to take more than its share of food. If some do, two bad things will happen: the extra food they take will get rotten, and some of the rest of the family may not get enough to eat.

DAD READS: Sharing is a lot of hard work. It's easier for all of us in our family to just grab whatever we want, letting the rest of the family take care of themselves. But when we do this, two bad things will happen: the things we take, because we're greedy, will not make us happy—they'll spoil; and others in our family might have to go without. This is not the way to have a happy family.

Child reads: Sharing is also a lot of fun. It makes me feel good when I know that I have been kind to others and not taken more than my share. I don't want the things I take to spoil, and I don't want anyone to be hungry because I have been selfish and greedy.

DAD READS: I want you to know that I don't want to be selfish either. I want to be a loving and a generous dad. I never want to take more than my share so that everyone has plenty.

Child reads: This is the kind of family we want. Let's pray that God will help us to have generous and giving hearts. Let me pray this prayer with you:

Dear Father in heaven, thank you for the fun of sharing. Forgive us for taking more than our share—with our families and with our friends. Thank you for providing good things for us to enjoy. Please always help us to remember that all of these things are gifts from you. Thank you for being such a generous heavenly Father. In Jesus' name, Amen.

For your next devotional reading, go to page 92.

eat in the evening and all the bread you want in the morning, because he has heard your grumbling against him. Who are we? You are not grumbling against us, but against the LORD."

⁹Then Moses told Aaron, "Say to the entire Israelite community, 'Come before the LORD, for he has heard your grumbling.' "

¹⁰While Aaron was speaking to the whole Israelite community, they looked toward the desert, and there was the glory of the LORD appearing in the cloud.

¹¹The LORD said to Moses, ¹²"I have heard the grumbling of the Israelites. Tell them, 'At twilight you will eat meat, and in the morning you will be filled with bread. Then you will know that I am the LORD your God.' "

¹³That evening quail came and covered the camp, and in the morning there was a layer of dew around the camp. ¹⁴When the dew was gone, thin flakes like frost on the ground appeared on the desert floor. ¹⁵When the Israelites saw it, they said to each other, "What is it?" For they did not know what it was.

Moses said to them, "It is the bread the LORD has given you to eat. ¹⁶This is what the LORD has commanded: 'Each one is to gather as much as he needs. Take an omer*a* for each person you have in your tent.' "

¹⁷The Israelites did as they were told; some gathered much, some little. ¹⁸And when they measured it by the omer, he who gathered much did not have too much, and he who gathered little did not have too little. Each one gathered as much as he needed.

¹⁹Then Moses said to them, "No one is to keep any of it until morning."

²⁰However, some of them paid no attention to Moses; they kept part of it until morning, but it was full of maggots and began to smell. So Moses was angry with them.

²¹Each morning everyone gathered as much as he needed, and when the sun grew hot, it melted away. ²²On the sixth day, they gathered twice as much—two omers*b* for each person—and the leaders of the community came and reported this to Moses. ²³He said to them, "This is what the LORD commanded: 'Tomorrow is to be a day of rest, a holy Sabbath to the LORD. So bake what you want to bake and boil what you want to boil. Save whatever is left and keep it until morning.' "

²⁴So they saved it until morning, as Moses commanded, and it did not stink or get maggots in it. ²⁵"Eat it today," Moses said, "because today is a Sabbath to the LORD. You will not find any of it on the ground today. ²⁶Six days you are to gather it, but on the seventh day, the Sabbath, there will not be any."

²⁷Nevertheless, some of the people went out on the seventh day to gather it, but they found none. ²⁸Then the LORD said to Moses, "How long will you*c* refuse to keep my commands and my instructions? ²⁹Bear in mind that the LORD has given you the Sabbath; that is why on the sixth day he gives you bread for two days. Everyone is to stay where he is on the seventh day; no one is to go out." ³⁰So the people rested on the seventh day.

³¹The people of Israel called the bread manna.*d* It was white like coriander seed and tasted like wafers made with honey. ³²Moses said, "This is what the LORD has commanded: 'Take an omer of manna and keep it for the generations to come, so they can see the bread I gave you to eat in the desert when I brought you out of Egypt.' "

³³So Moses said to Aaron, "Take a jar and put an omer of manna in it. Then place it before the LORD to be kept for the generations to come."

³⁴As the LORD commanded Moses, Aaron put the manna in front of the Testimony, that it might be kept. ³⁵The Israelites ate manna forty years, until they came to a land that was settled; they ate manna until they reached the border of Canaan.

³⁶(An omer is one tenth of an ephah.)

Water From the Rock

17 The whole Israelite community set out from the Desert of Sin, traveling from place to place as the LORD commanded. They camped at Rephidim, but there was no water for the people to drink. ²So they quarreled with Moses and said, "Give us water to drink."

Moses replied, "Why do you quarrel with me? Why do you put the LORD to the test?"

³But the people were thirsty for water there, and they grumbled against Moses. They said, "Why did you bring us up out of Egypt to make us and our children and livestock die of thirst?"

---

a16 That is, probably about 2 quarts (about 2 liters); also in verses 18, 32, 33 and 36   *b22* That is, probably about 4 quarts (about 4.5 liters)   *c28* The Hebrew is plural.   *d31 Manna* means *What is it?* (see verse 15).

⁴Then Moses cried out to the LORD, "What am I to do with these people? They are almost ready to stone me."

⁵The LORD answered Moses, "Walk on ahead of the people. Take with you some of the elders of Israel and take in your hand the staff with which you struck the Nile, and go. ⁶I will stand there before you by the rock at Horeb. Strike the rock, and water will come out of it for the people to drink." So Moses did this in the sight of the elders of Israel. ⁷And he called the place Massah^a and Meribah^b because the Israelites quarreled and because they tested the LORD saying, "Is the LORD among us or not?"

The Amalekites Defeated

⁸The Amalekites came and attacked the Israelites at Rephidim. ⁹Moses said to Joshua, "Choose some of our men and go out to fight the Amalekites. Tomorrow I will stand on top of the hill with the staff of God in my hands."

¹⁰So Joshua fought the Amalekites as Moses had ordered, and Moses, Aaron and Hur went to the top of the hill. ¹¹As long as Moses held up his hands, the Israelites were winning, but whenever he lowered his hands, the Amalekites were winning. ¹²When Moses' hands grew tired, they took a stone and put it under him and he sat on it. Aaron and Hur held his hands up—one on one side, one on the other—so that his hands remained steady till sunset. ¹³So Joshua overcame the Amalekite army with the sword.

¹⁴Then the LORD said to Moses, "Write this on a scroll as something to be remembered and make sure that Joshua hears it, because I will completely blot

^a7 Massah means testing.   ^b7 Meribah means quarreling.

No Lone Rangers here

DAILY INSIGHT

"With a cloud of dust and a hearty, 'Hi-Yo, Silver!'"

This is the way one of my favorite black and white television programs began. The Lone Ranger, starring Clayton Moore, was about a good guy who dressed in white but wore a black mask. A real metaphor mix, if you know what I mean. However, this wasn't even the starkest paradox in the program. The Lone Ranger never went anywhere alone; he always took his faithful companion, Tonto, along. He was not, in fact, a *lone* ranger! How disillusioning this must be for all those dropouts who refer to themselves as "Lone Rangers!"

God never intended for you and me to do our jobs as dads all by ourselves. Believe it or not, he has surrounded us with faithful sidekicks and partners. Certainly, our wives help us to be better fathers. Youth ministers, extended family, neighbors … many of these people are only a phone call away from helping with the daunting task of effective fathering.

The Israelites were in a battle with the

MONDAY

Passage:
Exodus 17:8–16

Verse:
Exodus 17:12

Amalekites, and they needed an ally. It was one of those fights that could have gone either way. As the field commander, Moses discovered that when he held his hands high, his army prevailed. But when his arms grew tired and fell to his side, his army lost ground. So, Moses' two lieutenants, Aaron and Hur, stood next to him and held his hands high for him. As a result, the Israelites prevailed.

Isn't this a spectacular picture? The man charged with being the leader—the father—of his people gives his family a victory by asking his friends to help. There's no indication that this was hard for Moses to do. We don't know if he had to swallow his pride and admit that his arms were tired, too heavy to hold up by himself. All we know is that he got the help he needed and saved his family.

You are not the Lone Ranger. You cannot do your job as a dad all alone. You aren't even supposed to try. Just remember that even the Lone Ranger wasn't a lone ranger.

For your next devotional reading, go to page 98.

out the memory of Amalek from under heaven."

¹⁵Moses built an altar and called it The LORD is my Banner. ¹⁶He said, "For hands were lifted up to the throne of the LORD. The*ª* LORD will be at war against the Amalekites from generation to generation."

Jethro Visits Moses

18 Now Jethro, the priest of Midian and father-in-law of Moses, heard of everything God had done for Moses and for his people Israel, and how the LORD had brought Israel out of Egypt.

²After Moses had sent away his wife Zipporah, his father-in-law Jethro received her ³and her two sons. One son was named Gershom,*ᵇ* for Moses said, "I have become an alien in a foreign land"; ⁴and the other was named Eliezer,*ᶜ* for he said, "My father's God was my helper; he saved me from the sword of Pharaoh."

⁵Jethro, Moses' father-in-law, together with Moses' sons and wife, came to him in the desert, where he was camped near the mountain of God. ⁶Jethro had sent word to him, "I, your father-in-law Jethro, am coming to you with your wife and her two sons."

⁷So Moses went out to meet his father-in-law and bowed down and kissed him. They greeted each other and then went into the tent. ⁸Moses told his father-in-law about everything the LORD had done to Pharaoh and the Egyptians for Israel's sake and about all the hardships they had met along the way and how the LORD had saved them.

⁹Jethro was delighted to hear about all the good things the LORD had done for Israel in rescuing them from the hand of the Egyptians. ¹⁰He said, "Praise be to the LORD, who rescued you from the hand of the Egyptians and of Pharaoh, and who rescued the people from the hand of the Egyptians. ¹¹Now I know that the LORD is greater than all other gods, for he did this to those who had treated Israel arrogantly." ¹²Then Jethro, Moses' father-in-law, brought a burnt offering and other sacrifices to God, and Aaron came with all the elders of Israel to eat bread with Moses' father-in-law in the presence of God.

¹³The next day Moses took his seat to serve as judge for the people, and they stood around him from morning till evening. ¹⁴When his father-in-law saw all that Moses was doing for the people, he said, "What is this you are doing for the people? Why do you alone sit as judge, while all these people stand around you from morning till evening?"

¹⁵Moses answered him, "Because the people come to me to seek God's will. ¹⁶Whenever they have a dispute, it is brought to me, and I decide between the parties and inform them of God's decrees and laws."

¹⁷Moses' father-in-law replied, "What you are doing is not good. ¹⁸You and these people who come to you will only wear yourselves out. The work is too heavy for you; you cannot handle it alone. ¹⁹Listen now to me and I will give you some advice, and may God be with you. You must be the people's representative before God and bring their disputes to him. ²⁰Teach them the decrees and laws, and show them the way to live and the duties they are to perform. ²¹But select capable men from all the people—men who fear God, trustworthy men who hate dishonest gain—and appoint them as officials over thousands, hundreds, fifties and tens. ²²Have them serve as judges for the people at all times, but have them bring every difficult case to you; the simple cases they can decide themselves. That will make your load lighter, because they will share it with you. ²³If you do this and God so commands, you will be able to stand the strain, and all these people will go home satisfied."

²⁴Moses listened to his father-in-law and did everything he said. ²⁵He chose capable men from all Israel and made them leaders of the people, officials over thousands, hundreds, fifties and tens. ²⁶They served as judges for the people at all times. The difficult cases they brought to Moses, but the simple ones they decided themselves.

²⁷Then Moses sent his father-in-law on his way, and Jethro returned to his own country.

At Mount Sinai

19 In the third month after the Israelites left Egypt—on the very day—they came to the Desert of Sinai. ²After they set out from Rephidim, they entered the Desert of Sinai, and Israel camped there in the desert in front of the mountain. ³Then Moses went up to God, and the

---

ª16 Or *"Because a hand was against the throne of the LORD, the   ᵇ3 Gershom* sounds like the Hebrew for *an alien there.   ᶜ4 Eliezer* means *my God is helper.*

LORD called to him from the mountain and said, "This is what you are to say to the house of Jacob and what you are to tell the people of Israel: **4**'You yourselves have seen what I did to Egypt, and how I carried you on eagles' wings and brought you to myself. **5**Now if you obey me fully and keep my covenant, then out of all nations you will be my treasured possession. Although the whole earth is mine, **6**you*a* will be for me a kingdom of priests and a holy nation.' These are the words you are to speak to the Israelites."

7So Moses went back and summoned the elders of the people and set before them all the words the LORD had commanded him to speak. **8**The people all responded together, "We will do everything the LORD has said." So Moses brought their answer back to the LORD.

9The LORD said to Moses, "I am going to come to you in a dense cloud, so that the people will hear me speaking with you and will always put their trust in you." Then Moses told the LORD what the people had said.

10And the LORD said to Moses, "Go to the people and consecrate them today and tomorrow. Have them wash their clothes **11**and be ready by the third day, because on that day the LORD will come down on Mount Sinai in the sight of all the people. **12**Put limits for the people around the mountain and tell them, 'Be careful that you do not go up the mountain or touch the foot of it. Whoever touches the mountain shall surely be put to death. **13**He shall surely be stoned or shot with arrows; not a hand is to be laid on him. Whether man or animal, he shall not be permitted to live.' Only when the ram's horn sounds a long blast may they go up to the mountain."

14After Moses had gone down the mountain to the people, he consecrated them, and they washed their clothes. **15**Then he said to the people, "Prepare yourselves for the third day. Abstain from sexual relations."

16On the morning of the third day there was thunder and lightning, with a thick cloud over the mountain, and a very loud trumpet blast. Everyone in the camp trembled. **17**Then Moses led the people out of the camp to meet with God, and they stood at the foot of the mountain. **18**Mount Sinai was covered with smoke, because the LORD descended on it in fire. The smoke billowed up from it like smoke from a furnace, the whole mountain*b*

trembled violently, **19**and the sound of the trumpet grew louder and louder. Then Moses spoke and the voice of God answered him.*c*

20The LORD descended to the top of Mount Sinai and called Moses to the top of the mountain. So Moses went up **21**and the LORD said to him, "Go down and warn the people so they do not force their way through to see the LORD and many of them perish. **22**Even the priests, who approach the LORD, must consecrate themselves, or the LORD will break out against them."

23Moses said to the LORD, "The people cannot come up Mount Sinai, because you yourself warned us, 'Put limits around the mountain and set it apart as holy.' "

24The LORD replied, "Go down and bring Aaron up with you. But the priests and the people must not force their way through to come up to the LORD, or he will break out against them."

25So Moses went down to the people and told them.

The Ten Commandments

20 And God spoke all these words:

2 "I am the LORD your God, who brought you out of Egypt, out of the land of slavery.

3 "You shall have no other gods before*d* me.

4 "You shall not make for yourself an idol in the form of anything in heaven above or on the earth beneath or in the waters below. **5**You shall not bow down to them or worship them; for I, the LORD your God, am a jealous God, punishing the children for the sin of the fathers to the third and fourth generation of those who hate me, **6**but showing love to a thousand generations of those who love me and keep my commandments.

7 "You shall not misuse the name of the LORD your God, for the LORD will not hold anyone guiltless who misuses his name.

---

a5,6 Or possession, for the whole earth is mine.
6You   b18 Most Hebrew manuscripts; a few Hebrew manuscripts and Septuagint all the people   c19 Or and God answered him with thunder   d3 Or besides

[8] "Remember the Sabbath day by keeping it holy. [9] Six days you shall labor and do all your work, [10] but the seventh day is a Sabbath to the LORD your God. On it you shall not do any work, neither you, nor your son or daughter, nor your manservant or maidservant, nor your animals, nor the alien within your gates. [11] For in six days the LORD made the heavens and the earth, the sea, and all that is in them, but he rested on the seventh day. Therefore the LORD blessed the Sabbath day and made it holy.

[12] "Honor your father and your mother, so that you may live long in the land the LORD your God is giving you.

[13] "You shall not murder.

[14] "You shall not commit adultery.

[15] "You shall not steal.

[16] "You shall not give false testimony against your neighbor.

[17] "You shall not covet your neighbor's house. You shall not covet your neighbor's wife, or his manservant or maidservant, his ox or donkey, or anything that belongs to your neighbor."

[18] When the people saw the thunder and lightning and heard the trumpet and saw the mountain in smoke, they trembled with fear. They stayed at a distance [19] and said to Moses, "Speak to us yourself and we will listen. But do not have God speak to us or we will die."

[20] Moses said to the people, "Do not be afraid. God has come to test you, so that the fear of God will be with you to keep you from sinning."

[21] The people remained at a distance, while Moses approached the thick darkness where God was.

Idols and Altars

[22] Then the LORD said to Moses, "Tell the Israelites this: 'You have seen for yourselves that I have spoken to you from heaven: [23] Do not make any gods to be alongside me; do not make for yourselves gods of silver or gods of gold.

[24] " 'Make an altar of earth for me and sacrifice on it your burnt offerings and fellowship offerings,[a] your sheep and goats and your cattle. Wherever I cause my name to be honored, I will come to you and bless you. [25] If you make an altar of stones for me, do not build it with dressed stones, for you will defile it if you use a tool on it. [26] And do not go up to my altar on steps, lest your nakedness be exposed on it.'

21 "These are the laws you are to set before them:

Hebrew Servants

[2] "If you buy a Hebrew servant, he is to serve you for six years. But in the seventh

---

[a]24 Traditionally *peace offerings*

HEY DAD

What does it mean to "misuse" God's name?

Text: Exodus 20:7

How can we misuse God's name? Some people actually use his name as a curse word. This shows blatant disrespect for God. We can also misuse the Lord's name by making flippant promises in his name.

To give you an idea of how sacred God's name is, we can look at the Jewish festival of *Yom Kippur*, or the Day of Atonement. On this day each year, the high priest went before the Lord to offer sacrifices on behalf of all the people. It was only during this annual ceremony and in this atmosphere of awe and respect that the name of the LORD, YHWH, would be spoken out loud. At the end of each confession of sin, the priest would say the name of the LORD. At no other time during the year was this hallowed name ever spoken.

The point for us today is that the name of the Lord is sacred and awesome. We must treat it with the utmost respect.

QUESTIONS KIDS ASK

For a complete listing of Questions Kids Ask, turn to page 1435.

year, he shall go free, without paying anything. ³If he comes alone, he is to go free alone; but if he has a wife when he comes, she is to go with him. ⁴If his master gives him a wife and she bears him sons or daughters, the woman and her children shall belong to her master, and only the man shall go free.

⁵"But if the servant declares, 'I love my master and my wife and children and do not want to go free,' ⁶then his master must take him before the judges.ᵃ He shall take him to the door or the doorpost and pierce his ear with an awl. Then he will be his servant for life.

⁷"If a man sells his daughter as a servant, she is not to go free as menservants do. ⁸If she does not please the master who has selected her for himself,ᵇ he must let her be redeemed. He has no right to sell her to foreigners, because he has broken faith with her. ⁹If he selects her for his son, he must grant her the rights of a daughter. ¹⁰If he marries another woman, he must not deprive the first one of her food, clothing and marital rights. ¹¹If he does not provide her with these three things, she is to go free, without any payment of money.

Personal Injuries

¹²"Anyone who strikes a man and kills him shall surely be put to death. ¹³However, if he does not do it intentionally, but God lets it happen, he is to flee to a place I will designate. ¹⁴But if a man schemes and kills another man deliberately, take him away from my altar and put him to death.

¹⁵"Anyone who attacksᶜ his father or his mother must be put to death.

¹⁶"Anyone who kidnaps another and either sells him or still has him when he is caught must be put to death.

¹⁷"Anyone who curses his father or mother must be put to death.

¹⁸"If men quarrel and one hits the other with a stone or with his fistᵈ and he does not die but is confined to bed, ¹⁹the one who struck the blow will not be held responsible if the other gets up and walks around outside with his staff; however, he must pay the injured man for the loss of his time and see that he is completely healed.

²⁰"If a man beats his male or female slave with a rod and the slave dies as a direct result, he must be punished, ²¹but he is not to be punished if the slave gets up after a day or two, since the slave is his property.

²²"If men who are fighting hit a pregnant woman and she gives birth prematurelyᵉ but there is no serious injury, the offender must be fined whatever the woman's husband demands and the court allows. ²³But if there is serious injury, you are to take life for life, ²⁴eye for eye, tooth for tooth, hand for hand, foot for foot, ²⁵burn for burn, wound for wound, bruise for bruise.

²⁶"If a man hits a manservant or maidservant in the eye and destroys it, he must let the servant go free to compensate for the eye. ²⁷And if he knocks out the tooth of a manservant or maidservant, he must let the servant go free to compensate for the tooth.

²⁸"If a bull gores a man or a woman to death, the bull must be stoned to death, and its meat must not be eaten. But the owner of the bull will not be held responsible. ²⁹If, however, the bull has had the habit of goring and the owner has been warned but has not kept it penned up and it kills a man or woman, the bull must be stoned and the owner also must be put to death. ³⁰However, if payment is demanded of him, he may redeem his life by paying whatever is demanded. ³¹This law also applies if the bull gores a son or daughter. ³²If the bull gores a male or female slave, the owner must pay thirty shekelsᶠ of silver to the master of the slave, and the bull must be stoned.

³³"If a man uncovers a pit or digs one and fails to cover it and an ox or a donkey falls into it, ³⁴the owner of the pit must pay for the loss; he must pay its owner, and the dead animal will be his.

³⁵"If a man's bull injures the bull of another and it dies, they are to sell the live one and divide both the money and the dead animal equally. ³⁶However, if it was known that the bull had the habit of goring, yet the owner did not keep it penned up, the owner must pay, animal for animal, and the dead animal will be his.

Protection of Property

22 "If a man steals an ox or a sheep and slaughters it or sells it, he must pay back five head of cattle for the ox and four sheep for the sheep.

²"If a thief is caught breaking in and is struck so that he dies, the defender is not guilty of bloodshed; ³but if it happensᵍ after sunrise, he is guilty of bloodshed.

ᵃ6 Or *before God*   ᵇ8 Or *master so that he does not choose her*   ᶜ15 Or *kills*   ᵈ18 Or *with a tool*   ᵉ22 Or *she has a miscarriage*   ᶠ32 That is, about 12 ounces (about 0.3 kilogram)   ᵍ3 Or *if he strikes him*

"A thief must certainly make restitution, but if he has nothing, he must be sold to pay for his theft.

4 "If the stolen animal is found alive in his possession—whether ox or donkey or sheep—he must pay back double.

5 "If a man grazes his livestock in a field or vineyard and lets them stray and they graze in another man's field, he must make restitution from the best of his own field or vineyard.

6 "If a fire breaks out and spreads into thornbushes so that it burns shocks of grain or standing grain or the whole field, the one who started the fire must make restitution.

7 "If a man gives his neighbor silver or goods for safekeeping and they are stolen from the neighbor's house, the thief, if he is caught, must pay back double. **8** But if the thief is not found, the owner of the house must appear before the judges*a* to determine whether he has laid his hands on the other man's property. **9** In all cases of illegal possession of an ox, a donkey, a sheep, a garment, or any other lost property about which somebody says, 'This is mine,' both parties are to bring their cases before the judges. The one whom the judges declare*b* guilty must pay back double to his neighbor.

10 "If a man gives a donkey, an ox, a sheep or any other animal to his neighbor for safekeeping and it dies or is injured or is taken away while no one is looking, **11** the issue between them will be settled by the taking of an oath before the LORD that the neighbor did not lay hands on the other person's property. The owner is to accept this, and no restitution is required. **12** But if the animal was stolen from the neighbor, he must make restitution to the owner. **13** If it was torn to pieces by a wild animal, he shall bring in the remains as evidence and he will not be required to pay for the torn animal.

14 "If a man borrows an animal from his neighbor and it is injured or dies while the owner is not present, he must make restitution. **15** But if the owner is with the animal, the borrower will not have to pay. If the animal was hired, the money paid for the hire covers the loss.

Social Responsibility

16 "If a man seduces a virgin who is not pledged to be married and sleeps with her, he must pay the bride-price, and she shall be his wife. **17** If her father absolutely refuses to give her to him, he must still pay the bride-price for virgins.

18 "Do not allow a sorceress to live.

19 "Anyone who has sexual relations with an animal must be put to death.

20 "Whoever sacrifices to any god other than the LORD must be destroyed.*c*

21 "Do not mistreat an alien or oppress him, for you were aliens in Egypt.

22 "Do not take advantage of a widow or an orphan. **23** If you do and they cry out to me, I will certainly hear their cry. **24** My anger will be aroused, and I will kill you with the sword; your wives will become widows and your children fatherless.

25 "If you lend money to one of my people among you who is needy, do not be like a moneylender; charge him no interest.*d* **26** If you take your neighbor's cloak as a pledge, return it to him by sunset, **27** because his cloak is the only covering he has for his body. What else will he sleep in? When he cries out to me, I will hear, for I am compassionate.

28 "Do not blaspheme God*e* or curse the ruler of your people.

29 "Do not hold back offerings from your granaries or your vats.*f*

"You must give me the firstborn of your sons. **30** Do the same with your cattle and your sheep. Let them stay with their mothers for seven days, but give them to me on the eighth day.

31 "You are to be my holy people. So do not eat the meat of an animal torn by wild beasts; throw it to the dogs.

Laws of Justice and Mercy

23 "Do not spread false reports. Do not help a wicked man by being a malicious witness.

2 "Do not follow the crowd in doing wrong. When you give testimony in a lawsuit, do not pervert justice by siding with the crowd, **3** and do not show favoritism to a poor man in his lawsuit.

4 "If you come across your enemy's ox or donkey wandering off, be sure to take it back to him. **5** If you see the donkey of someone who hates you fallen down under its load, do not leave it there; be sure you help him with it.

6 "Do not deny justice to your poor

---

*a*8 Or *before God*; also in verse 9   *b*9 Or *whom God declares*   *c*20 The Hebrew term refers to the irrevocable giving over of things or persons to the LORD, often by totally destroying them.   *d*25 Or *excessive interest*   *e*28 Or *Do not revile the judges*   *f*29 The meaning of the Hebrew for this phrase is uncertain.

people in their lawsuits. ⁷Have nothing to do with a false charge and do not put an innocent or honest person to death, for I will not acquit the guilty.

⁸"Do not accept a bribe, for a bribe blinds those who see and twists the words of the righteous.

⁹"Do not oppress an alien; you yourselves know how it feels to be aliens, because you were aliens in Egypt.

Sabbath Laws

¹⁰"For six years you are to sow your fields and harvest the crops, ¹¹but during the seventh year let the land lie unplowed and unused. Then the poor among your people may get food from it, and the wild animals may eat what they leave. Do the same with your vineyard and your olive grove.

¹²"Six days do your work, but on the seventh day do not work, so that your ox and your donkey may rest and the slave born in your household, and the alien as well, may be refreshed.

¹³"Be careful to do everything I have said to you. Do not invoke the names of other gods; do not let them be heard on your lips.

The Three Annual Festivals

¹⁴"Three times a year you are to celebrate a festival to me.

Just Say "No"

DAILY INSIGHT

TUESDAY

Passage:
Exodus 23:1–9

Verse:
Exodus 23:2a

Not a single one of us would have been so stupid by ourselves. But there's just something about a bunch of young men getting fired up together.

When I was in college, I had the fun of finding a group of wonderful guys to be my friends. We lived in the same wing of the dormitory for several years, we played every intramural sport together, and we even had a name: The Association. Most everyone on our small campus knew who we were. We were—and, in many cases, still are—truly good friends.

Every once in a while— usually during an unusually stressful time, like final exam week—we'd find ourselves in someone's room, joking around with each other and, essentially, just blowing off a little of that if-we-fail-we're-going-to-Vietnam steam.

Someone would suggest that we go out for pizza, and like the lemmings traipsing to the sea, we'd go. Or someone would suggest that we get out a deck of cards and play hearts, which we would do ... for several, precious hours. Occasionally an idea would come up that was not quite as benign as pizza or cards. And, often, we'd all pile into our cars and go do whatever it was ... not illegal things, mind you, just stupid stuff.

If you have been reading the past several chapters in Exodus, you know about this list of pretty tough rules for the Israelites to follow. I'm sure listening to this list was as stressful to these people as getting ready for finals was for us. As we're getting down toward the end of the list of laws, we bump into something pretty simple—and powerful. Something that sounds like it could have been written for my college experience: *Do not follow the crowd in doing wrong* (23:2a).

As young men, we all faced this temptation. As adults, the pull toward doing wrong because our entire culture seems to be doing it—shaving the truth just a bit, saying regretful things, the temptation toward moral failure—is still pretty overwhelming. And of course, our children face this terrible temptation, as well.

So what's the Bible's persuasive advice for this dilemma? It's a simple, "don't." No explanation necessary. Just "don't." The writer of these words knew what we know. Following a crowd to do wrong things is stupid. So, don't do it. Set an example for your family and stand for what you know is right. Encourage your kids to do the same. You'll both be so happy you did.

For your next devotional reading, go to page 108.

¹⁵"Celebrate the Feast of Unleavened Bread; for seven days eat bread made without yeast, as I commanded you. Do this at the appointed time in the month of Abib, for in that month you came out of Egypt.

"No one is to appear before me empty-handed.

¹⁶"Celebrate the Feast of Harvest with the firstfruits of the crops you sow in your field.

"Celebrate the Feast of Ingathering at the end of the year, when you gather in your crops from the field.

¹⁷"Three times a year all the men are to appear before the Sovereign LORD.

¹⁸"Do not offer the blood of a sacrifice to me along with anything containing yeast.

"The fat of my festival offerings must not be kept until morning.

¹⁹"Bring the best of the firstfruits of your soil to the house of the LORD your God.

"Do not cook a young goat in its mother's milk.

God's Angel to Prepare the Way

²⁰"See, I am sending an angel ahead of you to guard you along the way and to bring you to the place I have prepared. ²¹Pay attention to him and listen to what he says. Do not rebel against him; he will not forgive your rebellion, since my Name is in him. ²²If you listen carefully to what he says and do all that I say, I will be an enemy to your enemies and will oppose those who oppose you. ²³My angel will go ahead of you and bring you into the land of the Amorites, Hittites, Perizzites, Canaanites, Hivites and Jebusites, and I will wipe them out. ²⁴Do not bow down before their gods or worship them or follow their practices. You must demolish them and break their sacred stones to pieces. ²⁵Worship the LORD your God, and his blessing will be on your food and water. I will take away sickness from among you, ²⁶and none will miscarry or be barren in your land. I will give you a full life span.

²⁷"I will send my terror ahead of you and throw into confusion every nation you encounter. I will make all your enemies turn their backs and run. ²⁸I will send the hornet ahead of you to drive the Hivites, Canaanites and Hittites out of your way. ²⁹But I will not drive them out in a single year, because the land would become desolate and the wild animals too numerous for you. ³⁰Little by little I will drive them out before you, until you have increased enough to take possession of the land.

³¹"I will establish your borders from the Red Sea*a* to the Sea of the Philistines,*b* and from the desert to the River.*c* I will hand over to you the people who live in the land and you will drive them out before you. ³²Do not make a covenant with them or with their gods. ³³Do not let them live in your land, or they will cause you to sin against me, because the worship of their gods will certainly be a snare to you."

The Covenant Confirmed

24 Then he said to Moses, "Come up to the LORD, you and Aaron, Nadab and Abihu, and seventy of the elders of Israel. You are to worship at a distance, ²but Moses alone is to approach the LORD; the others must not come near. And the people may not come up with him."

³When Moses went and told the people all the LORD's words and laws, they responded with one voice, "Everything the LORD has said we will do." ⁴Moses then wrote down everything the LORD had said.

He got up early the next morning and built an altar at the foot of the mountain and set up twelve stone pillars representing the twelve tribes of Israel. ⁵Then he sent young Israelite men, and they offered burnt offerings and sacrificed young bulls as fellowship offerings*d* to the LORD. ⁶Moses took half of the blood and put it in bowls, and the other half he sprinkled on the altar. ⁷Then he took the Book of the Covenant and read it to the people. They responded, "We will do everything the LORD has said; we will obey."

⁸Moses then took the blood, sprinkled it on the people and said, "This is the blood of the covenant that the LORD has made with you in accordance with all these words."

⁹Moses and Aaron, Nadab and Abihu, and the seventy elders of Israel went up ¹⁰and saw the God of Israel. Under his feet was something like a pavement made of sapphire,*e* clear as the sky itself. ¹¹But God did not raise his hand against these leaders of the Israelites; they saw God, and they ate and drank.

¹²The LORD said to Moses, "Come up to

---

a31 Hebrew *Yam Suph*; that is, Sea of Reeds
b31 That is, the Mediterranean   *c31* That is, the Euphrates   *d5* Traditionally *peace offerings*
e10 Or *lapis lazuli*

me on the mountain and stay here, and I will give you the tablets of stone, with the law and commands I have written for their instruction."

¹³Then Moses set out with Joshua his aide, and Moses went up on the mountain of God. ¹⁴He said to the elders, "Wait here for us until we come back to you. Aaron and Hur are with you, and anyone involved in a dispute can go to them."

¹⁵When Moses went up on the mountain, the cloud covered it, ¹⁶and the glory of the LORD settled on Mount Sinai. For six days the cloud covered the mountain, and on the seventh day the LORD called to Moses from within the cloud. ¹⁷To the Israelites the glory of the LORD looked like a consuming fire on top of the mountain. ¹⁸Then Moses entered the cloud as he went on up the mountain. And he stayed on the mountain forty days and forty nights.

Offerings for the Tabernacle

25 The LORD said to Moses, ²"Tell the Israelites to bring me an offering. You are to receive the offering for me from each man whose heart prompts him to give. ³These are the offerings you are to receive from them: gold, silver and bronze; ⁴blue, purple and scarlet yarn and fine linen; goat hair; ⁵ram skins dyed red and hides of sea cows*a*; acacia wood; ⁶olive oil for the light; spices for the anointing oil and for the fragrant incense; ⁷and onyx stones and other gems to be mounted on the ephod and breastpiece.

⁸"Then have them make a sanctuary for me, and I will dwell among them. ⁹Make this tabernacle and all its furnishings exactly like the pattern I will show you.

The Ark

¹⁰"Have them make a chest of acacia wood—two and a half cubits long, a cubit and a half wide, and a cubit and a half high.*b* ¹¹Overlay it with pure gold, both inside and out, and make a gold molding around it. ¹²Cast four gold rings for it and fasten them to its four feet, with two rings on one side and two rings on the other. ¹³Then make poles of acacia wood and overlay them with gold. ¹⁴Insert the poles into the rings on the sides of the chest to

a5 That is, dugongs   *b10* That is, about 3 3/4 feet (about 1.1 meters) long and 2 1/4 feet (about 0.7 meter) wide and high

HEY DAD

How did we get the Bible if it was written so long ago?

QUESTIONS KIDS ASK

Text: Exodus 24:3–4

These verses talk about Moses writing down God's words; chances are good that he used either parchment or papyrus. The Bible has existed for thousands of years—long before anyone invented paper. "The earliest books of the Bible were written on flat tablets of clay or on dried, scraped animal skins (called parchment) or perhaps on papyrus, made of the grass-like papyrus plant" (Van der Maas, 235).

For many years, priests and teachers copied the sacred words of the Scripture by hand, so there were very few copies of the Bible. Thousands of years later Johann Gutenberg invented the printing press in 1450 AD. This invention made the Bible accessible and affordable to many more people.

But another problem still existed: Most people couldn't read the Bible in the languages in which it was written (Hebrew, Aramaic, and Greek). So God used translators to put his message into languages people could understand.

God wants us to know him so much that he worked through history so that we could read his words to us in our own language today. Isn't that wonderful?

Van der Maas, E. (1994). Adventure Bible Handbook. *Grand Rapids, Michigan: Zondervan Publishing House.*

For a complete listing of Questions Kids Ask, turn to page 1435.

carry it. ¹⁵The poles are to remain in the rings of this ark; they are not to be removed. ¹⁶Then put in the ark the Testimony, which I will give you.

¹⁷"Make an atonement cover[a] of pure gold—two and a half cubits long and a cubit and a half wide.[b] ¹⁸And make two cherubim out of hammered gold at the ends of the cover. ¹⁹Make one cherub on one end and the second cherub on the other; make the cherubim of one piece with the cover, at the two ends. ²⁰The cherubim are to have their wings spread upward, overshadowing the cover with them. The cherubim are to face each other, looking toward the cover. ²¹Place the cover on top of the ark and put in the ark the Testimony, which I will give you. ²²There, above the cover between the two cherubim that are over the ark of the Testimony, I will meet with you and give you all my commands for the Israelites.

The Table

²³"Make a table of acacia wood—two cubits long, a cubit wide and a cubit and a half high.[c] ²⁴Overlay it with pure gold and make a gold molding around it. ²⁵Also make around it a rim a handbreadth[d] wide and put a gold molding on the rim. ²⁶Make four gold rings for the table and fasten them to the four corners, where the four legs are. ²⁷The rings are to be close to the rim to hold the poles used in carrying the table. ²⁸Make the poles of acacia wood, overlay them with gold and carry the table with them. ²⁹And make its plates and dishes of pure gold, as well as its pitchers and bowls for the pouring out of offerings. ³⁰Put the bread of the Presence on this table to be before me at all times.

The Lampstand

³¹"Make a lampstand of pure gold and hammer it out, base and shaft; its flower-like cups, buds and blossoms shall be of one piece with it. ³²Six branches are to extend from the sides of the lampstand—three on one side and three on the other. ³³Three cups shaped like almond flowers with buds and blossoms are to be on one branch, three on the next branch, and the same for all six branches extending from the lampstand. ³⁴And on the lampstand there are to be four cups shaped like almond flowers with buds and blossoms. ³⁵One bud shall be under the first pair of branches extending from the lampstand, a second bud under the second pair, and

a third bud under the third pair—six branches in all. ³⁶The buds and branches shall all be of one piece with the lampstand, hammered out of pure gold.

³⁷"Then make its seven lamps and set them up on it so that they light the space in front of it. ³⁸Its wick trimmers and trays are to be of pure gold. ³⁹A talent[e] of pure gold is to be used for the lampstand and all these accessories. ⁴⁰See that you make them according to the pattern shown you on the mountain.

The Tabernacle

26 "Make the tabernacle with ten curtains of finely twisted linen and blue, purple and scarlet yarn, with cherubim worked into them by a skilled craftsman. ²All the curtains are to be the same size—twenty-eight cubits long and four cubits wide.[f] ³Join five of the curtains together, and do the same with the other five. ⁴Make loops of blue material along the edge of the end curtain in one set, and do the same with the end curtain in the other set. ⁵Make fifty loops on one curtain and fifty loops on the end curtain of the other set, with the loops opposite each other. ⁶Then make fifty gold clasps and use them to fasten the curtains together so that the tabernacle is a unit.

⁷"Make curtains of goat hair for the tent over the tabernacle—eleven altogether. ⁸All eleven curtains are to be the same size—thirty cubits long and four cubits wide.[g] ⁹Join five of the curtains together into one set and the other six into another set. Fold the sixth curtain double at the front of the tent. ¹⁰Make fifty loops along the edge of the end curtain in one set and also along the edge of the end curtain in the other set. ¹¹Then make fifty bronze clasps and put them in the loops to fasten the tent together as a unit. ¹²As for the additional length of the tent curtains, the half curtain that is left over is to hang down at the rear of the tabernacle. ¹³The tent curtains will be a cubit[h] longer on

---

[a]17 Traditionally *a mercy seat* [b]17 That is, about 3 3/4 feet (about 1.1 meters) long and 2 1/4 feet (about 0.7 meter) wide [c]23 That is, about 3 feet (about 0.9 meter) long and 1 1/2 feet (about 0.5 meter) wide and 2 1/4 feet (about 0.7 meter) high [d]25 That is, about 3 inches (about 8 centimeters) [e]39 That is, about 75 pounds (about 34 kilograms) [f]2 That is, about 42 feet (about 12.5 meters) long and 6 feet (about 1.8 meters) wide [g]8 That is, about 45 feet (about 13.5 meters) long and 6 feet (about 1.8 meters) wide [h]13 That is, about 1 1/2 feet (about 0.5 meter)

both sides; what is left will hang over the sides of the tabernacle so as to cover it. [14]Make for the tent a covering of ram skins dyed red, and over that a covering of hides of sea cows.[a]

[15]"Make upright frames of acacia wood for the tabernacle. [16]Each frame is to be ten cubits long and a cubit and a half wide,[b] [17]with two projections set parallel to each other. Make all the frames of the tabernacle in this way. [18]Make twenty frames for the south side of the tabernacle [19]and make forty silver bases to go under them—two bases for each frame, one under each projection. [20]For the other side, the north side of the tabernacle, make twenty frames [21]and forty silver bases—two under each frame. [22]Make six frames for the far end, that is, the west end of the tabernacle, [23]and make two frames for the corners at the far end. [24]At these two corners they must be double from the bottom all the way to the top, and fitted into a single ring; both shall be like that. [25]So there will be eight frames and sixteen silver bases—two under each frame.

[26]"Also make crossbars of acacia wood: five for the frames on one side of the tabernacle, [27]five for those on the other side, and five for the frames on the west, at the far end of the tabernacle. [28]The center crossbar is to extend from end to end at the middle of the frames. [29]Overlay the frames with gold and make gold rings to hold the crossbars. Also overlay the crossbars with gold.

[30]"Set up the tabernacle according to the plan shown you on the mountain.

[31]"Make a curtain of blue, purple and scarlet yarn and finely twisted linen, with cherubim worked into it by a skilled craftsman. [32]Hang it with gold hooks on four posts of acacia wood overlaid with gold and standing on four silver bases. [33]Hang the curtain from the clasps and place the ark of the Testimony behind the curtain. The curtain will separate the Holy Place from the Most Holy Place. [34]Put the atonement cover on the ark of the Testimony in the Most Holy Place. [35]Place the table outside the curtain on the north side of the tabernacle and put the lampstand opposite it on the south side.

[36]"For the entrance to the tent make a curtain of blue, purple and scarlet yarn and finely twisted linen—the work of an embroiderer. [37]Make gold hooks for this curtain and five posts of acacia wood overlaid with gold. And cast five bronze bases for them.

The Altar of Burnt Offering

27 "Build an altar of acacia wood, three cubits[c] high; it is to be square, five cubits long and five cubits wide.[d] [2]Make a horn at each of the four corners, so that the horns and the altar are of one piece, and overlay the altar with bronze. [3]Make all its utensils of bronze—its pots to remove the ashes, and its shovels, sprinkling bowls, meat forks and firepans. [4]Make a grating for it, a bronze network, and make a bronze ring at each of the four corners of the network. [5]Put it under the ledge of the altar so that it is halfway up the altar. [6]Make poles of acacia wood for the altar and overlay them with bronze. [7]The poles are to be inserted into the rings so they will be on two sides of the altar when it is carried. [8]Make the altar hollow, out of boards. It is to be made just as you were shown on the mountain.

The Courtyard

[9]"Make a courtyard for the tabernacle. The south side shall be a hundred cubits[e] long and is to have curtains of finely twisted linen, [10]with twenty posts and twenty bronze bases and with silver hooks and bands on the posts. [11]The north side shall also be a hundred cubits long and is to have curtains, with twenty posts and twenty bronze bases and with silver hooks and bands on the posts.

[12]"The west end of the courtyard shall be fifty cubits[f] wide and have curtains, with ten posts and ten bases. [13]On the east end, toward the sunrise, the courtyard shall also be fifty cubits wide. [14]Curtains fifteen cubits[g] long are to be on one side of the entrance, with three posts and three bases, [15]and curtains fifteen cubits long are to be on the other side, with three posts and three bases.

[16]"For the entrance to the courtyard, provide a curtain twenty cubits[h] long, of blue, purple and scarlet yarn and finely twisted linen—the work of an embroiderer—with four posts and four bases. [17]All the posts around the courtyard are to

---

[a]14 That is, dugongs   [b]16 That is, about 15 feet (about 4.5 meters) long and 2 1/4 feet (about 0.7 meter) wide   [c]1 That is, about 4 1/2 feet (about 1.3 meters)   [d]1 That is, about 7 1/2 feet (about 2.3 meters) long and wide   [e]9 That is, about 150 feet (about 46 meters); also in verse 11   [f]12 That is, about 75 feet (about 23 meters); also in verse 13   [g]14 That is, about 22 1/2 feet (about 6.9 meters); also in verse 15   [h]16 That is, about 30 feet (about 9 meters)

have silver bands and hooks, and bronze bases. [18]The courtyard shall be a hundred cubits long and fifty cubits wide,[a] with curtains of finely twisted linen five cubits[b] high, and with bronze bases. [19]All the other articles used in the service of the tabernacle, whatever their function, including all the tent pegs for it and those for the courtyard, are to be of bronze.

Oil for the Lampstand

[20]"Command the Israelites to bring you clear oil of pressed olives for the light so that the lamps may be kept burning. [21]In the Tent of Meeting, outside the curtain that is in front of the Testimony, Aaron and his sons are to keep the lamps burning before the LORD from evening till morning. This is to be a lasting ordinance among the Israelites for the generations to come.

The Priestly Garments

28 "Have Aaron your brother brought to you from among the Israelites, along with his sons Nadab and Abihu, Eleazar and Ithamar, so they may serve me as priests. [2]Make sacred garments for your brother Aaron, to give him dignity and honor. [3]Tell all the skilled men to whom I have given wisdom in such matters that they are to make garments for Aaron, for his consecration, so he may serve me as priest. [4]These are the garments they are to make: a breastpiece, an ephod, a robe, a woven tunic, a turban and a sash. They are to make these sacred garments for your brother Aaron and his sons, so they may serve me as priests. [5]Have them use gold, and blue, purple and scarlet yarn, and fine linen.

The Ephod

[6]"Make the ephod of gold, and of blue, purple and scarlet yarn, and of finely twisted linen—the work of a skilled craftsman. [7]It is to have two shoulder pieces attached to two of its corners, so it can be fastened. [8]Its skillfully woven waistband is to be like it—of one piece with the ephod and made with gold, and with blue, purple and scarlet yarn, and with finely twisted linen.

[9]"Take two onyx stones and engrave on them the names of the sons of Israel [10]in the order of their birth—six names on one stone and the remaining six on the other. [11]Engrave the names of the sons of Israel

on the two stones the way a gem cutter engraves a seal. Then mount the stones in gold filigree settings [12]and fasten them on the shoulder pieces of the ephod as memorial stones for the sons of Israel. Aaron is to bear the names on his shoulders as a memorial before the LORD. [13]Make gold filigree settings [14]and two braided chains of pure gold, like a rope, and attach the chains to the settings.

The Breastpiece

[15]"Fashion a breastpiece for making decisions—the work of a skilled craftsman. Make it like the ephod: of gold, and of blue, purple and scarlet yarn, and of finely twisted linen. [16]It is to be square—a span[c] long and a span wide—and folded double. [17]Then mount four rows of precious stones on it. In the first row there shall be a ruby, a topaz and a beryl; [18]in the second row a turquoise, a sapphire[d] and an emerald; [19]in the third row a jacinth, an agate and an amethyst; [20]in the fourth row a chrysolite, an onyx and a jasper.[e] Mount them in gold filigree settings. [21]There are to be twelve stones, one for each of the names of the sons of Israel, each engraved like a seal with the name of one of the twelve tribes.

[22]"For the breastpiece make braided chains of pure gold, like a rope. [23]Make two gold rings for it and fasten them to two corners of the breastpiece. [24]Fasten the two gold chains to the rings at the corners of the breastpiece, [25]and the other ends of the chains to the two settings, attaching them to the shoulder pieces of the ephod at the front. [26]Make two gold rings and attach them to the other two corners of the breastpiece on the inside edge next to the ephod. [27]Make two more gold rings and attach them to the bottom of the shoulder pieces on the front of the ephod, close to the seam just above the waistband of the ephod. [28]The rings of the breastpiece are to be tied to the rings of the ephod with blue cord, connecting it to the waistband, so that the breastpiece will not swing out from the ephod.

[29]"Whenever Aaron enters the Holy Place, he will bear the names of the sons of Israel over his heart on the breastpiece

of decision as a continuing memorial before the LORD. [30]Also put the Urim and the Thummim in the breastpiece, so they may be over Aaron's heart whenever he enters the presence of the LORD. Thus Aaron will always bear the means of making decisions for the Israelites over his heart before the LORD.

Other Priestly Garments

[31]"Make the robe of the ephod entirely of blue cloth, [32]with an opening for the head in its center. There shall be a woven edge like a collar[a] around this opening, so that it will not tear. [33]Make pomegranates of blue, purple and scarlet yarn around the hem of the robe, with gold bells between them. [34]The gold bells and the pomegranates are to alternate around the hem of the robe. [35]Aaron must wear it when he ministers. The sound of the bells will be heard when he enters the Holy Place before the LORD and when he comes out, so that he will not die.

[36]"Make a plate of pure gold and engrave on it as on a seal: HOLY TO THE LORD. [37]Fasten a blue cord to it to attach it to the turban; it is to be on the front of the turban. [38]It will be on Aaron's forehead, and he will bear the guilt involved in the sacred gifts the Israelites consecrate, whatever their gifts may be. It will be on Aaron's forehead continually so that they will be acceptable to the LORD.

[39]"Weave the tunic of fine linen and make the turban of fine linen. The sash is to be the work of an embroiderer. [40]Make tunics, sashes and headbands for Aaron's sons, to give them dignity and honor. [41]After you put these clothes on your brother Aaron and his sons, anoint and ordain them. Consecrate them so they may serve me as priests.

[42]"Make linen undergarments as a covering for the body, reaching from the waist to the thigh. [43]Aaron and his sons must wear them whenever they enter the Tent of Meeting or approach the altar to minister in the Holy Place, so that they will not incur guilt and die.

"This is to be a lasting ordinance for Aaron and his descendants.

Consecration of the Priests

29 "This is what you are to do to consecrate them, so they may serve me as priests: Take a young bull and two rams without defect. [2]And from fine wheat flour, without yeast, make bread, and cakes mixed with oil, and wafers spread with oil. [3]Put them in a basket and present them in it—along with the bull and the two rams. [4]Then bring Aaron and his sons to the entrance to the Tent of Meeting and wash them with water. [5]Take the garments and dress Aaron with the tunic, the robe of the ephod, the ephod itself and the breastpiece. Fasten the ephod on him by its skillfully woven waistband. [6]Put the turban on his head and attach the sacred diadem to the turban. [7]Take the anointing oil and anoint him by pouring it on his head. [8]Bring his sons and dress them in tunics [9]and put headbands on them. Then tie sashes on Aaron and his sons.[b] The priesthood is theirs by a lasting ordinance. In this way you shall ordain Aaron and his sons.

[10]"Bring the bull to the front of the Tent of Meeting, and Aaron and his sons shall lay their hands on its head. [11]Slaughter it in the LORD's presence at the entrance to the Tent of Meeting. [12]Take some of the bull's blood and put it on the horns of the altar with your finger, and pour out the rest of it at the base of the altar. [13]Then take all the fat around the inner parts, the covering of the liver, and both kidneys with the fat on them, and burn them on the altar. [14]But burn the bull's flesh and its hide and its offal outside the camp. It is a sin offering.

[15]"Take one of the rams, and Aaron and his sons shall lay their hands on its head. [16]Slaughter it and take the blood and sprinkle it against the altar on all sides. [17]Cut the ram into pieces and wash the inner parts and the legs, putting them with the head and the other pieces. [18]Then burn the entire ram on the altar. It is a burnt offering to the LORD, a pleasing aroma, an offering made to the LORD by fire.

[19]"Take the other ram, and Aaron and his sons shall lay their hands on its head. [20]Slaughter it, take some of its blood and put it on the lobes of the right ears of Aaron and his sons, on the thumbs of their right hands, and on the big toes of their right feet. Then sprinkle blood against the altar on all sides. [21]And take some of the blood on the altar and some of the anointing oil and sprinkle it on Aaron and his garments and on his sons and their garments. Then he and his sons and their garments will be consecrated.

---

[a]32 The meaning of the Hebrew for this word is uncertain.   [b]9 Hebrew; Septuagint *on them*

²²"Take from this ram the fat, the fat tail, the fat around the inner parts, the covering of the liver, both kidneys with the fat on them, and the right thigh. (This is the ram for the ordination.) ²³From the basket of bread made without yeast, which is before the LORD, take a loaf, and a cake made with oil, and a wafer. ²⁴Put all these in the hands of Aaron and his sons and wave them before the LORD as a wave offering. ²⁵Then take them from their hands and burn them on the altar along with the burnt offering for a pleasing aroma to the LORD, an offering made to the LORD by fire. ²⁶After you take the breast of the ram for Aaron's ordination, wave it before the LORD as a wave offering, and it will be your share.

²⁷"Consecrate those parts of the ordination ram that belong to Aaron and his sons: the breast that was waved and the thigh that was presented. ²⁸This is always to be the regular share from the Israelites for Aaron and his sons. It is the contribution the Israelites are to make to the LORD from their fellowship offerings.ᵃ

²⁹"Aaron's sacred garments will belong to his descendants so that they can be anointed and ordained in them. ³⁰The son who succeeds him as priest and comes to the Tent of Meeting to minister in the Holy Place is to wear them seven days.

³¹"Take the ram for the ordination and cook the meat in a sacred place. ³²At the entrance to the Tent of Meeting, Aaron and his sons are to eat the meat of the ram and the bread that is in the basket. ³³They are to eat these offerings by which atonement was made for their ordination and consecration. But no one else may eat them, because they are sacred. ³⁴And if any of the meat of the ordination ram or any bread is left over till morning, burn it up. It must not be eaten, because it is sacred.

³⁵"Do for Aaron and his sons everything I have commanded you, taking seven days to ordain them. ³⁶Sacrifice a bull each day as a sin offering to make atonement. Purify the altar by making atonement for it, and anoint it to consecrate it. ³⁷For seven days make atonement for the altar and consecrate it. Then the altar will be most holy, and whatever touches it will be holy.

³⁸"This is what you are to offer on the altar regularly each day: two lambs a year old. ³⁹Offer one in the morning and the other at twilight. ⁴⁰With the first lamb offer a tenth of an ephahᵇ of fine flour mixed with a quarter of a hinᶜ of oil from pressed olives, and a quarter of a hin of wine as a drink offering. ⁴¹Sacrifice the other lamb at twilight with the same grain offering and its drink offering as in the morning—a pleasing aroma, an offering made to the LORD by fire.

⁴²"For the generations to come this burnt offering is to be made regularly at the entrance to the Tent of Meeting before the LORD. There I will meet you and speak to you; ⁴³there also I will meet with the Israelites, and the place will be consecrated by my glory.

⁴⁴"So I will consecrate the Tent of Meeting and the altar and will consecrate Aaron and his sons to serve me as priests. ⁴⁵Then I will dwell among the Israelites and be their God. ⁴⁶They will know that I am the LORD their God, who brought them out of Egypt so that I might dwell among them. I am the LORD their God.

The Altar of Incense

30 "Make an altar of acacia wood for burning incense. ²It is to be square, a cubit long and a cubit wide, and two cubits highᵈ—its horns of one piece with it. ³Overlay the top and all the sides and the horns with pure gold, and make a gold molding around it. ⁴Make two gold rings for the altar below the molding—two on opposite sides—to hold the poles used to carry it. ⁵Make the poles of acacia wood and overlay them with gold. ⁶Put the altar in front of the curtain that is before the ark of the Testimony—before the atonement cover that is over the Testimony—where I will meet with you.

⁷"Aaron must burn fragrant incense on the altar every morning when he tends the lamps. ⁸He must burn incense again when he lights the lamps at twilight so incense will burn regularly before the LORD for the generations to come. ⁹Do not offer on this altar any other incense or any burnt offering or grain offering, and do not pour a drink offering on it. ¹⁰Once a year Aaron shall make atonement on its horns. This annual atonement must be made with the blood of the atoning sin offering for the generations to come. It is most holy to the LORD."

ᵃ28 Traditionally *peace offerings*   ᵇ40 That is, probably about 2 quarts (about 2 liters)   ᶜ40 That is, probably about 1 quart (about 1 liter)   ᵈ2 That is, about 1 1/2 feet (about 0.5 meter) long and wide and about 3 feet (about 0.9 meter) high

Atonement Money

¹¹Then the LORD said to Moses, ¹²"When you take a census of the Israelites to count them, each one must pay the LORD a ransom for his life at the time he is counted. Then no plague will come on them when you number them. ¹³Each one who crosses over to those already counted is to give a half shekel,ᵃ according to the sanctuary shekel, which weighs twenty gerahs. This half shekel is an offering to the LORD. ¹⁴All who cross over, those twenty years old or more, are to give an offering to the LORD. ¹⁵The rich are not to give more than a half shekel and the poor are not to give less when you make the offering to the LORD to atone for your lives. ¹⁶Receive the atonement money from the Israelites and use it for the service of the Tent of Meeting. It will be a memorial for the Israelites before the LORD, making atonement for your lives."

Basin for Washing

¹⁷Then the LORD said to Moses, ¹⁸"Make a bronze basin, with its bronze stand, for washing. Place it between the Tent of Meeting and the altar, and put water in it. ¹⁹Aaron and his sons are to wash their hands and feet with water from it. ²⁰Whenever they enter the Tent of Meeting, they shall wash with water so that they will not die. Also, when they approach the altar to minister by presenting an offering made to the LORD by fire, ²¹they shall wash their hands and feet so that they will not die. This is to be a lasting ordinance for Aaron and his descendants for the generations to come."

Anointing Oil

²²Then the LORD said to Moses, ²³"Take the following fine spices: 500 shekelsᵇ of liquid myrrh, half as much (that is, 250 shekels) of fragrant cinnamon, 250 shekels of fragrant cane, ²⁴500 shekels of cassia—all according to the sanctuary shekel—and a hinᶜ of olive oil. ²⁵Make these into a sacred anointing oil, a fragrant blend, the work of a perfumer. It will be the sacred anointing oil. ²⁶Then use it to anoint the Tent of Meeting, the ark of the Testimony, ²⁷the table and all its articles, the lampstand and its accessories, the altar of incense, ²⁸the altar of burnt offering and all its utensils, and the basin with its stand. ²⁹You shall consecrate

them so they will be most holy, and whatever touches them will be holy.

³⁰"Anoint Aaron and his sons and consecrate them so they may serve me as priests. ³¹Say to the Israelites, 'This is to be my sacred anointing oil for the generations to come. ³²Do not pour it on men's bodies and do not make any oil with the same formula. It is sacred, and you are to consider it sacred. ³³Whoever makes perfume like it and whoever puts it on anyone other than a priest must be cut off from his people.'"

Incense

³⁴Then the LORD said to Moses, "Take fragrant spices—gum resin, onycha and galbanum—and pure frankincense, all in equal amounts, ³⁵and make a fragrant blend of incense, the work of a perfumer. It is to be salted and pure and sacred. ³⁶Grind some of it to powder and place it in front of the Testimony in the Tent of Meeting, where I will meet with you. It shall be most holy to you. ³⁷Do not make any incense with this formula for yourselves; consider it holy to the LORD. ³⁸Whoever makes any like it to enjoy its fragrance must be cut off from his people."

Bezalel and Oholiab

31 Then the LORD said to Moses, ²"See, I have chosen Bezalel son of Uri, the son of Hur, of the tribe of Judah, ³and I have filled him with the Spirit of God, with skill, ability and knowledge in all kinds of crafts— ⁴to make artistic designs for work in gold, silver and bronze, ⁵to cut and set stones, to work in wood, and to engage in all kinds of craftsmanship. ⁶Moreover, I have appointed Oholiab son of Ahisamach, of the tribe of Dan, to help him. Also I have given skill to all the craftsmen to make everything I have commanded you: ⁷the Tent of Meeting, the ark of the Testimony with the atonement cover on it, and all the other furnishings of the tent— ⁸the table and its articles, the pure gold lampstand and all its accessories, the altar of incense, ⁹the altar of burnt offering and all its utensils, the basin with its stand— ¹⁰and also the woven garments, both the sacred garments for Aaron the priest and the gar-

ᵃ13 That is, about 1/5 ounce (about 6 grams); also in verse 15   ᵇ23 That is, about 12 1/2 pounds (about 6 kilograms)   ᶜ24 That is, probably about 4 quarts (about 4 liters)

ments for his sons when they serve as priests, **11**and the anointing oil and fragrant incense for the Holy Place. They are to make them just as I commanded you."

The Sabbath

12Then the LORD said to Moses, **13**"Say to the Israelites, 'You must observe my Sabbaths. This will be a sign between me and you for the generations to come, so you may know that I am the LORD, who makes you holy.*a*

14" 'Observe the Sabbath, because it is holy to you. Anyone who desecrates it must be put to death; whoever does any work on that day must be cut off from his people. **15**For six days, work is to be done, but the seventh day is a Sabbath of rest, holy to the LORD. Whoever does any work on the Sabbath day must be put to death. **16**The Israelites are to observe the Sabbath, celebrating it for the generations to come as a lasting covenant. **17**It will be a sign between me and the Israelites forever, for in six days the LORD made the heavens and the earth, and on the seventh day he abstained from work and rested.' "

18When the LORD finished speaking to Moses on Mount Sinai, he gave him the two tablets of the Testimony, the tablets of stone inscribed by the finger of God.

The Golden Calf

32 When the people saw that Moses was so long in coming down from the mountain, they gathered around Aaron and said, "Come, make us gods*b* who will go before us. As for this fellow Moses who brought us up out of Egypt, we don't know what has happened to him."

2Aaron answered them, "Take off the gold earrings that your wives, your sons and your daughters are wearing, and bring them to me." **3**So all the people took off their earrings and brought them to Aaron. **4**He took what they handed him and made it into an idol cast in the shape of a calf, fashioning it with a tool. Then they said, "These are your gods,*c* O Israel, who brought you up out of Egypt."

5When Aaron saw this, he built an altar in front of the calf and announced, "Tomorrow there will be a festival to the LORD." **6**So the next day the people rose early and sacrificed burnt offerings and presented fellowship offerings.*d* Afterward they sat down to eat and drink and got up to indulge in revelry.

7Then the LORD said to Moses, "Go down, because your people, whom you brought up out of Egypt, have become corrupt. **8**They have been quick to turn away from what I commanded them and have made themselves an idol cast in the shape of a calf. They have bowed down to it and sacrificed to it and have said, 'These are your gods, O Israel, who brought you up out of Egypt.'

9"I have seen these people," the LORD said to Moses, "and they are a stiff-necked people. **10**Now leave me alone so that my anger may burn against them and that I may destroy them. Then I will make you into a great nation."

11But Moses sought the favor of the LORD his God. "O LORD," he said, "why should your anger burn against your people, whom you brought out of Egypt with great power and a mighty hand? **12**Why should the Egyptians say, 'It was with evil intent that he brought them out, to kill them in the mountains and to wipe them off the face of the earth'? Turn from your fierce anger; relent and do not bring disaster on your people. **13**Remember your servants Abraham, Isaac and Israel, to whom you swore by your own self: 'I will make your descendants as numerous as the stars in the sky and I will give your descendants all this land I promised them, and it will be their inheritance forever.' " **14**Then the LORD relented and did not bring on his people the disaster he had threatened.

15Moses turned and went down the mountain with the two tablets of the Testimony in his hands. They were inscribed on both sides, front and back. **16**The tablets were the work of God; the writing was the writing of God, engraved on the tablets.

17When Joshua heard the noise of the people shouting, he said to Moses, "There is the sound of war in the camp."

18Moses replied:

"It is not the sound of victory,
    it is not the sound of defeat;
    it is the sound of singing that I hear."

19When Moses approached the camp and saw the calf and the dancing, his anger burned and he threw the tablets out of his hands, breaking them to pieces at the

---

a13 Or *who sanctifies you;* or *who sets you apart as holy*   *b1* Or *a god;* also in verses 23 and 31   *c4* Or *This is your god;* also in verse 8   *d6* Traditionally *peace offerings*

foot of the mountain. ²⁰And he took the calf they had made and burned it in the fire; then he ground it to powder, scattered it on the water and made the Israelites drink it.

²¹He said to Aaron, "What did these people do to you, that you led them into such great sin?"

²²"Do not be angry, my lord," Aaron answered. "You know how prone these people are to evil. ²³They said to me, 'Make us gods who will go before us. As for this fellow Moses who brought us up out of Egypt, we don't know what has happened to him.' ²⁴So I told them, 'Whoever has any gold jewelry, take it off.' Then they gave me the gold, and I threw it into the fire, and out came this calf!"

²⁵Moses saw that the people were running wild and that Aaron had let them get out of control and so become a laughingstock to their enemies. ²⁶So he stood at the entrance to the camp and said, "Whoever is for the LORD, come to me." And all the Levites rallied to him.

²⁷Then he said to them, "This is what the LORD, the God of Israel, says: 'Each man strap a sword to his side. Go back and forth through the camp from one end to the other, each killing his brother and friend and neighbor.' " ²⁸The Levites did as Moses commanded, and that day about three thousand of the people died. ²⁹Then Moses said, "You have been set apart to the LORD today, for you were against your own sons and brothers, and he has blessed you this day."

³⁰The next day Moses said to the people, "You have committed a great sin. But now I will go up to the LORD; perhaps I can make atonement for your sin."

³¹So Moses went back to the LORD and said, "Oh, what a great sin these people have committed! They have made themselves gods of gold. ³²But now, please forgive their sin—but if not, then blot me out of the book you have written."

³³The LORD replied to Moses, "Whoever has sinned against me I will blot out of my book. ³⁴Now go, lead the people to the

Don't Make Me Laugh

DAILY
INSIGHT

WEDNESDAY

Passage:
Exodus 32:19–25

Verse:
Exodus 32:25

Turn on the television any night of the week, and you'll find a comedy that has something to do with a family. Many of the folks who write these programs have researched what would make the viewing audience laugh. Through focus groups and pilot shows, they have carefully studied what to do on the screen that will make us smile.

One of the reoccurring themes in these programs is the clumsy, indecisive and very confused dad. He may be quite successful in business, but get him home and his IQ drops to room temperature. The moment he sets his briefcase or lunch bucket down, this poor guy is overwhelmed by his demanding wife and unmanageable, loudmouthed children. Sometimes we sit and laugh at this foolish man in spite of ourselves.

Israel's enemies were also laughing. And like our laughter at bumbling dads on TV, their entertainment was the result of Aaron's atrocious leadership of God's fami-

ly. Moses was on a business trip to visit with God and he had left Aaron in charge.

And with Moses the lawmaker gone, the Israelites saw an opportunity for some good, old-fashioned complaining. "Give us handmade gods," they whined. "We're tired of worshiping a God we can't see."

So Aaron gave into the pressure and let them build an idol—a make-believe god. The out-of-control Israelite family became comic relief for everyone (32:25). "How funny it is," these other nations must have said, "to see a family where the children make the rules."

Your neighbors have enough on television to keep them in stitches. So at your house, you be the dad. In spite of the temptation to let your family's complaining and whining win out over your solid leadership, don't let your home make your neighbors laugh.

For your next devotional reading, go to page 111.

place I spoke of, and my angel will go before you. However, when the time comes for me to punish, I will punish them for their sin."

³⁵And the LORD struck the people with a plague because of what they did with the calf Aaron had made.

33 Then the LORD said to Moses, "Leave this place, you and the people you brought up out of Egypt, and go up to the land I promised on oath to Abraham, Isaac and Jacob, saying, 'I will give it to your descendants.' ²I will send an angel before you and drive out the Canaanites, Amorites, Hittites, Perizzites, Hivites and Jebusites. ³Go up to the land flowing with milk and honey. But I will not go with you, because you are a stiff-necked people and I might destroy you on the way."

⁴When the people heard these distressing words, they began to mourn and no one put on any ornaments. ⁵For the LORD had said to Moses, "Tell the Israelites, 'You are a stiff-necked people. If I were to go with you even for a moment, I might destroy you. Now take off your ornaments and I will decide what to do with you.' " ⁶So the Israelites stripped off their ornaments at Mount Horeb.

The Tent of Meeting

⁷Now Moses used to take a tent and pitch it outside the camp some distance away, calling it the "tent of meeting." Anyone inquiring of the LORD would go to the tent of meeting outside the camp. ⁸And whenever Moses went out to the tent, all the people rose and stood at the entrances to their tents, watching Moses until he entered the tent. ⁹As Moses went into the tent, the pillar of cloud would come down and stay at the entrance, while the LORD spoke with Moses. ¹⁰Whenever the people saw the pillar of cloud standing at the entrance to the tent, they all stood and worshiped, each at the entrance to his tent. ¹¹The LORD would speak to Moses face to face, as a man speaks with his friend. Then Moses would return to the camp, but his young aide Joshua son of Nun did not leave the tent.

Moses and the Glory of the LORD

¹²Moses said to the LORD, "You have been telling me, 'Lead these people,' but you have not let me know whom you will send with me. You have said, 'I know you by name and you have found favor with me.' ¹³If you are pleased with me, teach me your ways so I may know you and continue to find favor with you. Remember that this nation is your people."

¹⁴The LORD replied, "My Presence will go with you, and I will give you rest."

¹⁵Then Moses said to him, "If your Presence does not go with us, do not send us up from here. ¹⁶How will anyone know that you are pleased with me and with your people unless you go with us? What else will distinguish me and your people from all the other people on the face of the earth?"

¹⁷And the LORD said to Moses, "I will do the very thing you have asked, because I am pleased with you and I know you by name."

¹⁸Then Moses said, "Now show me your glory."

¹⁹And the LORD said, "I will cause all my goodness to pass in front of you, and I will proclaim my name, the LORD, in your presence. I will have mercy on whom I will have mercy, and I will have compassion on whom I will have compassion. ²⁰But," he said, "you cannot see my face, for no one may see me and live."

²¹Then the LORD said, "There is a place near me where you may stand on a rock. ²²When my glory passes by, I will put you in a cleft in the rock and cover you with my hand until I have passed by. ²³Then I will remove my hand and you will see my back; but my face must not be seen."

The New Stone Tablets

34 The LORD said to Moses, "Chisel out two stone tablets like the first ones, and I will write on them the words that were on the first tablets, which you broke. ²Be ready in the morning, and then come up on Mount Sinai. Present yourself to me there on top of the mountain. ³No one is to come with you or be seen anywhere on the mountain; not even the flocks and herds may graze in front of the mountain."

⁴So Moses chiseled out two stone tablets like the first ones and went up Mount Sinai early in the morning, as the LORD had commanded him; and he carried the two stone tablets in his hands. ⁵Then the LORD came down in the cloud and stood there with him and proclaimed his name, the LORD. ⁶And he passed in front of Moses, proclaiming, "The LORD, the LORD, the compassionate and gracious God, slow to anger, abounding in love and faithfulness, ⁷maintaining love to thousands, and

forgiving wickedness, rebellion and sin. Yet he does not leave the guilty unpunished; he punishes the children and their children for the sin of the fathers to the third and fourth generation."

8Moses bowed to the ground at once and worshiped. **9**"O Lord, if I have found favor in your eyes," he said, "then let the Lord go with us. Although this is a stiff-necked people, forgive our wickedness and our sin, and take us as your inheritance."

10Then the LORD said: "I am making a covenant with you. Before all your people I will do wonders never before done in any nation in all the world. The people you live among will see how awesome is the work that I, the LORD, will do for you. **11**Obey what I command you today. I will drive out before you the Amorites, Canaanites, Hittites, Perizzites, Hivites and Jebusites. **12**Be careful not to make a treaty with those who live in the land where you are going, or they will be a snare among you. **13**Break down their altars, smash their sacred stones and cut down their Asherah poles.*a* **14**Do not worship any other god, for the LORD, whose name is Jealous, is a jealous God.

15"Be careful not to make a treaty with those who live in the land; for when they prostitute themselves to their gods and sacrifice to them, they will invite you and you will eat their sacrifices. **16**And when you choose some of their daughters as wives for your sons and those daughters prostitute themselves to their gods, they will lead your sons to do the same.

17"Do not make cast idols.

18"Celebrate the Feast of Unleavened Bread. For seven days eat bread made without yeast, as I commanded you. Do this at the appointed time in the month of Abib, for in that month you came out of Egypt.

19"The first offspring of every womb belongs to me, including all the firstborn males of your livestock, whether from herd or flock. **20**Redeem the firstborn donkey with a lamb, but if you do not redeem it, break its neck. Redeem all your firstborn sons.

"No one is to appear before me empty-handed.

21"Six days you shall labor, but on the seventh day you shall rest; even during the plowing season and harvest you must rest.

22"Celebrate the Feast of Weeks with the firstfruits of the wheat harvest, and the

Feast of Ingathering at the turn of the year.*b* **23**Three times a year all your men are to appear before the Sovereign LORD, the God of Israel. **24**I will drive out nations before you and enlarge your territory, and no one will covet your land when you go up three times each year to appear before the LORD your God.

25"Do not offer the blood of a sacrifice to me along with anything containing yeast, and do not let any of the sacrifice from the Passover Feast remain until morning.

26"Bring the best of the firstfruits of your soil to the house of the LORD your God.

"Do not cook a young goat in its mother's milk."

27Then the LORD said to Moses, "Write down these words, for in accordance with these words I have made a covenant with you and with Israel." **28**Moses was there with the LORD forty days and forty nights without eating bread or drinking water. And he wrote on the tablets the words of the covenant—the Ten Commandments.

The Radiant Face of Moses

29When Moses came down from Mount Sinai with the two tablets of the Testimony in his hands, he was not aware that his face was radiant because he had spoken with the LORD. **30**When Aaron and all the Israelites saw Moses, his face was radiant, and they were afraid to come near him. **31**But Moses called to them; so Aaron and all the leaders of the community came back to him, and he spoke to them. **32**Afterward all the Israelites came near him, and he gave them all the commands the LORD had given him on Mount Sinai.

33When Moses finished speaking to them, he put a veil over his face. **34**But whenever he entered the LORD's presence to speak with him, he removed the veil until he came out. And when he came out and told the Israelites what he had been commanded, **35**they saw that his face was radiant. Then Moses would put the veil back over his face until he went in to speak with the LORD.

Sabbath Regulations

35 Moses assembled the whole Israelite community and said to them, "These are the things the LORD has commanded

---

*a13 That is, symbols of the goddess Asherah
*b22 That is, in the fall

you to do: ²For six days, work is to be done, but the seventh day shall be your holy day, a Sabbath of rest to the LORD. Whoever does any work on it must be put to death. ³Do not light a fire in any of your dwellings on the Sabbath day."

Materials for the Tabernacle

⁴Moses said to the whole Israelite community, "This is what the LORD has commanded: ⁵From what you have, take an offering for the LORD. Everyone who is willing is to bring to the LORD an offering

of gold, silver and bronze; ⁶blue, purple and scarlet yarn and fine linen; goat hair; ⁷ram skins dyed red and hides of sea cows ᵃ; acacia wood; ⁸olive oil for the light; spices for the anointing oil and for the fragrant incense; ⁹and onyx stones and other gems to be mounted on the ephod and breastpiece.

¹⁰"All who are skilled among you are to come and make everything the LORD has commanded: ¹¹the tabernacle with its

ᵃ7 That is, dugongs; also in verse 23

It's in Giving that We Receive

DAILY INSIGHT

THURSDAY

Passage:
Exodus 35:4–21

Verses:
Exodus 35:4–5

My mother told me that our local newspaper was looking for "paper boys." And she was pretty sure that there was an opening to deliver newspapers in our own neighborhood. I was only in the third grade, but entrepreneurial blood was already coursing through my veins, so I pedaled my bicycle downtown to apply for the job.

A few days later the phone call came, and I had my first job. The following Monday, after school, I rode to the newspaper office, picked up my allotment of papers, and rode back home. After rolling the newspapers and slipping a rubber band around each one, I lifted the canvas bag over my shoulder and was off to make my one-and-a-half cents per paper. This story, along with the one about trudging to school in three feet of snow with my feet bound in rags, is part of our family's folklore. Just ask our long-suffering daughters.

Anyway, for the first time in my life, I knew what it was to have "my own money." I felt independent and free. If I wanted to, I could stop at Frederick's Drug Store and buy a Dr. Pepper and bubble gum—without asking my parents' permission. I had *earned* this money, and it was mine to spend.

The problem was that once I had spent my money at Frederick's, it was gone. And what I had spent my money on was also soon gone. So in order to be able to splurge at the drug store again, I had to fill my canvas bag with more copies of The Daily

Journal and pedal from house to house again. I remember, even at this very early age, feeling the dread.

Forty years later, I was sitting in the sanctuary of a small, rural church planted in the fertile hills of Lancaster County, Pennsylvania. My family and I were there for my maternal grandfather's funeral service. One of his sons, my uncle Eber, was reading something my grandfather had written. "I leave to my family something more valuable than money. I leave them something they will not need to divide. I leave my family my love for them and my faith in Jesus Christ, something each one can enjoy in full." My eyes welled up with tears as I remembered this wise, faithful and generous man.

Today's text invites "everyone who is willing" to bring a portion of what they earn to the Lord as an offering. Why? Because the money we give away is the money that brings us the most happiness. There's no dread in this expenditure. And because giving reminds us that life's most precious possessions are not those things we can see, but the intangibles of love and family and faith.

Fill your bank account with "funds" that don't disappear once they're spent. Fill it with the stuff that will multiply when it's divided.

For your next devotional reading, go to page 122.

tent and its covering, clasps, frames, crossbars, posts and bases; [12]the ark with its poles and the atonement cover and the curtain that shields it; [13]the table with its poles and all its articles and the bread of the Presence; [14]the lampstand that is for light with its accessories, lamps and oil for the light; [15]the altar of incense with its poles, the anointing oil and the fragrant incense; the curtain for the doorway at the entrance to the tabernacle; [16]the altar of burnt offering with its bronze grating, its poles and all its utensils; the bronze basin with its stand; [17]the curtains of the courtyard with its posts and bases, and the curtain for the entrance to the courtyard; [18]the tent pegs for the tabernacle and for the courtyard, and their ropes; [19]the woven garments worn for ministering in the sanctuary—both the sacred garments for Aaron the priest and the garments for his sons when they serve as priests."

[20]Then the whole Israelite community withdrew from Moses' presence, [21]and everyone who was willing and whose heart moved him came and brought an offering to the LORD for the work on the Tent of Meeting, for all its service, and for the sacred garments. [22]All who were willing, men and women alike, came and brought gold jewelry of all kinds: brooches, earrings, rings and ornaments. They all presented their gold as a wave offering to the LORD. [23]Everyone who had blue, purple or scarlet yarn or fine linen, or goat hair, ram skins dyed red or hides of sea cows brought them. [24]Those presenting an offering of silver or bronze brought it as an offering to the LORD, and everyone who had acacia wood for any part of the work brought it. [25]Every skilled woman spun with her hands and brought what she had spun—blue, purple or scarlet yarn or fine linen. [26]And all the women who were willing and had the skill spun the goat hair. [27]The leaders brought onyx stones and other gems to be mounted on the ephod and breastpiece. [28]They also brought spices and olive oil for the light and for the anointing oil and for the fragrant incense. [29]All the Israelite men and women who were willing brought to the LORD freewill offerings for all the work the LORD through Moses had commanded them to do.

Bezalel and Oholiab

[30]Then Moses said to the Israelites, "See, the LORD has chosen Bezalel son of Uri, the son of Hur, of the tribe of Judah, [31]and he has filled him with the Spirit of God, with skill, ability and knowledge in all kinds of crafts— [32]to make artistic designs for work in gold, silver and bronze, [33]to cut and set stones, to work in wood and to engage in all kinds of artistic craftsmanship. [34]And he has given both him and Oholiab son of Ahisamach, of the tribe of Dan, the ability to teach others. [35]He has filled them with skill to do all kinds of work as craftsmen, designers, embroiderers in blue, purple and scarlet yarn and fine linen, and weavers—all of them master craftsmen and designers.

36 [1]So Bezalel, Oholiab and every skilled person to whom the LORD has given skill and ability to know how to carry out all the work of constructing the sanctuary are to do the work just as the LORD has commanded."

[2]Then Moses summoned Bezalel and Oholiab and every skilled person to whom the LORD had given ability and who was willing to come and do the work. [3]They received from Moses all the offerings the Israelites had brought to carry out the work of constructing the sanctuary. And the people continued to bring freewill offerings morning after morning. [4]So all the skilled craftsmen who were doing all the work on the sanctuary left their work [5]and said to Moses, "The people are bringing more than enough for doing the work the LORD commanded to be done." [6]Then Moses gave an order and they sent this word throughout the camp: "No man or woman is to make anything else as an offering for the sanctuary." And so the people were restrained from bringing more, [7]because what they already had was more than enough to do all the work.

The Tabernacle

[8]All the skilled men among the workmen made the tabernacle with ten curtains of finely twisted linen and blue, purple and scarlet yarn, with cherubim worked into them by a skilled craftsman. [9]All the curtains were the same size—twenty-eight cubits long and four cubits wide.[a] [10]They joined five of the curtains together and did the same with the other five. [11]Then they made loops of blue material along the edge of the end curtain in one set, and the same was done with the

---

[a]9 That is, about 42 feet (about 12.5 meters) long and 6 feet (about 1.8 meters) wide

end curtain in the other set. [12]They also made fifty loops on one curtain and fifty loops on the end curtain of the other set, with the loops opposite each other. [13]Then they made fifty gold clasps and used them to fasten the two sets of curtains together so that the tabernacle was a unit.

[14]They made curtains of goat hair for the tent over the tabernacle—eleven altogether. [15]All eleven curtains were the same size—thirty cubits long and four cubits wide.[a] [16]They joined five of the curtains into one set and the other six into another set. [17]Then they made fifty loops along the edge of the end curtain in one set and also along the edge of the end curtain in the other set. [18]They made fifty bronze clasps to fasten the tent together as a unit. [19]Then they made for the tent a covering of ram skins dyed red, and over that a covering of hides of sea cows.[b]

[20]They made upright frames of acacia wood for the tabernacle. [21]Each frame was ten cubits long and a cubit and a half wide,[c] [22]with two projections set parallel to each other. They made all the frames of the tabernacle in this way. [23]They made twenty frames for the south side of the tabernacle [24]and made forty silver bases to go under them—two bases for each frame, one under each projection. [25]For the other side, the north side of the tabernacle, they made twenty frames [26]and forty silver bases—two under each frame. [27]They made six frames for the far end, that is, the west end of the tabernacle, [28]and two frames were made for the corners of the tabernacle at the far end. [29]At these two corners the frames were double from the bottom all the way to the top and fitted into a single ring; both were made alike. [30]So there were eight frames and sixteen silver bases—two under each frame.

[31]They also made crossbars of acacia wood: five for the frames on one side of the tabernacle, [32]five for those on the other side, and five for the frames on the west, at the far end of the tabernacle. [33]They made the center crossbar so that it extended from end to end at the middle of the frames. [34]They overlaid the frames with gold and made gold rings to hold the crossbars. They also overlaid the crossbars with gold.

[35]They made the curtain of blue, purple and scarlet yarn and finely twisted linen, with cherubim worked into it by a skilled craftsman. [36]They made four posts of acacia wood for it and overlaid them with gold. They made gold hooks for them and cast their four silver bases. [37]For the entrance to the tent they made a curtain of blue, purple and scarlet yarn and finely twisted linen—the work of an embroiderer; [38]and they made five posts with hooks for them. They overlaid the tops of the posts and their bands with gold and made their five bases of bronze.

The Ark

37 Bezalel made the ark of acacia wood—two and a half cubits long, a cubit and a half wide, and a cubit and a half high.[d] [2]He overlaid it with pure gold, both inside and out, and made a gold molding around it. [3]He cast four gold rings for it and fastened them to its four feet, with two rings on one side and two rings on the other. [4]Then he made poles of acacia wood and overlaid them with gold. [5]And he inserted the poles into the rings on the sides of the ark to carry it.

[6]He made the atonement cover of pure gold—two and a half cubits long and a cubit and a half wide.[e] [7]Then he made two cherubim out of hammered gold at the ends of the cover. [8]He made one cherub on one end and the second cherub on the other; at the two ends he made them of one piece with the cover. [9]The cherubim had their wings spread upward, overshadowing the cover with them. The cherubim faced each other, looking toward the cover.

The Table

[10]They[f] made the table of acacia wood—two cubits long, a cubit wide, and a cubit and a half high.[g] [11]Then they overlaid it with pure gold and made a gold molding around it. [12]They also made around it a rim a handbreadth[h] wide and put a gold molding on the rim. [13]They cast four gold rings for the table and fastened them to the four corners, where the four legs were. [14]The rings were put close to the rim to hold the poles used in carrying the

---

[a]15 That is, about 45 feet (about 13.5 meters) long and 6 feet (about 1.8 meters) wide   [b]19 That is, dugongs   [c]21 That is, about 15 feet (about 4.5 meters) long and 2 1/4 feet (about 0.7 meter) wide   [d]1 That is, about 3 3/4 feet (about 1.1 meters) long and 2 1/4 feet (about 0.7 meter) wide and high   [e]6 That is, about 3 3/4 feet (about 1.1 meters) long and 2 1/4 feet (about 0.7 meter) wide   [f]10 Or He; also in verses 11-29   [g]10 That is, about 3 feet (about 0.9 meter) long, 1 1/2 feet (about 0.5 meter) wide, and 2 1/4 feet (about 0.7 meter) high   [h]12 That is, about 3 inches (about 8 centimeters)

table. ¹⁵The poles for carrying the table were made of acacia wood and were overlaid with gold. ¹⁶And they made from pure gold the articles for the table—its plates and dishes and bowls and its pitchers for the pouring out of drink offerings.

The Lampstand

¹⁷They made the lampstand of pure gold and hammered it out, base and shaft; its flowerlike cups, buds and blossoms were of one piece with it. ¹⁸Six branches extended from the sides of the lampstand—three on one side and three on the other. ¹⁹Three cups shaped like almond flowers with buds and blossoms were on one branch, three on the next branch and the same for all six branches extending from the lampstand. ²⁰And on the lampstand were four cups shaped like almond flowers with buds and blossoms. ²¹One bud was under the first pair of branches extending from the lampstand, a second bud under the second pair, and a third bud under the third pair—six branches in all. ²²The buds and the branches were all of one piece with the lampstand, hammered out of pure gold.

²³They made its seven lamps, as well as its wick trimmers and trays, of pure gold. ²⁴They made the lampstand and all its accessories from one talent[a] of pure gold.

The Altar of Incense

²⁵They made the altar of incense out of acacia wood. It was square, a cubit long and a cubit wide, and two cubits high[b]— its horns of one piece with it. ²⁶They overlaid the top and all the sides and the horns with pure gold, and made a gold molding around it. ²⁷They made two gold rings below the molding—two on opposite sides—to hold the poles used to carry it. ²⁸They made the poles of acacia wood and overlaid them with gold.

²⁹They also made the sacred anointing oil and the pure, fragrant incense—the work of a perfumer.

The Altar of Burnt Offering

38 They[c] built the altar of burnt offering of acacia wood, three cubits[d] high; it was square, five cubits long and five cubits wide.[e] ²They made a horn at each of the four corners, so that the horns and the altar were of one piece, and they overlaid the altar with bronze. ³They made all its utensils of bronze—its pots, shovels, sprinkling bowls, meat forks and firepans. ⁴They made a grating for the altar, a bronze network, to be under its ledge, halfway up the altar. ⁵They cast bronze rings to hold the poles for the four corners of the bronze grating. ⁶They made the poles of acacia wood and overlaid them with bronze. ⁷They inserted the poles into the rings so they would be on the sides of the altar for carrying it. They made it hollow, out of boards.

Basin for Washing

⁸They made the bronze basin and its bronze stand from the mirrors of the women who served at the entrance to the Tent of Meeting.

The Courtyard

⁹Next they made the courtyard. The south side was a hundred cubits[f] long and had curtains of finely twisted linen, ¹⁰with twenty posts and twenty bronze bases, and with silver hooks and bands on the posts. ¹¹The north side was also a hundred cubits long and had twenty posts and twenty bronze bases, with silver hooks and bands on the posts.

¹²The west end was fifty cubits[g] wide and had curtains, with ten posts and ten bases, with silver hooks and bands on the posts. ¹³The east end, toward the sunrise, was also fifty cubits wide. ¹⁴Curtains fifteen cubits[h] long were on one side of the entrance, with three posts and three bases, ¹⁵and curtains fifteen cubits long were on the other side of the entrance to the courtyard, with three posts and three bases. ¹⁶All the curtains around the courtyard were of finely twisted linen. ¹⁷The bases for the posts were bronze. The hooks and bands on the posts were silver, and their tops were overlaid with silver; so all the posts of the courtyard had silver bands.

¹⁸The curtain for the entrance to the courtyard was of blue, purple and scarlet yarn and finely twisted linen—the work of an embroiderer. It was twenty cubits[i] long

---

[a]24 That is, about 75 pounds (about 34 kilograms)   [b]25 That is, about 1 1/2 feet (about 0.5 meter) long and wide, and about 3 feet (about 0.9 meter) high   [c]1 Or He; also in verses 2-9   [d]1 That is, about 4 1/2 feet (about 1.3 meters)   [e]1 That is, about 7 1/2 feet (about 2.3 meters) long and wide   [f]9 That is, about 150 feet (about 46 meters)   [g]12 That is, about 75 feet (about 23 meters)   [h]14 That is, about 22 1/2 feet (about 6.9 meters)   [i]18 That is, about 30 feet (about 9 meters)

and, like the curtains of the courtyard, five cubits[a] high, [19]with four posts and four bronze bases. Their hooks and bands were silver, and their tops were overlaid with silver. [20]All the tent pegs of the tabernacle and of the surrounding courtyard were bronze.

The Materials Used

[21]These are the amounts of the materials used for the tabernacle, the tabernacle of the Testimony, which were recorded at Moses' command by the Levites under the direction of Ithamar son of Aaron, the priest. [22](Bezalel son of Uri, the son of Hur, of the tribe of Judah, made everything the LORD commanded Moses; [23]with him was Oholiab son of Ahisamach, of the tribe of Dan—a craftsman and designer, and an embroiderer in blue, purple and scarlet yarn and fine linen.) [24]The total amount of the gold from the wave offering used for all the work on the sanctuary was 29 talents and 730 shekels,[b] according to the sanctuary shekel. [25]The silver obtained from those of the community who were counted in the census was 100 talents and 1,775 shekels,[c] according to the sanctuary shekel— [26]one beka per person, that is, half a shekel,[d] according to the sanctuary shekel, from everyone who had crossed over to those counted, twenty years old or more, a total of 603,550 men. [27]The 100 talents[e] of silver were used to cast the bases for the sanctuary and for the curtain—100 bases from the 100 talents, one talent for each base. [28]They used the 1,775 shekels[f] to make the hooks for the posts, to overlay the tops of the posts, and to make their bands. [29]The bronze from the wave offering was 70 talents and 2,400 shekels.[g] [30]They used it to make the bases for the entrance to the Tent of Meeting, the bronze altar with its bronze grating and all its utensils, [31]the bases for the surrounding courtyard and those for its entrance and all the tent pegs for the tabernacle and those for the surrounding courtyard.

The Priestly Garments

39 From the blue, purple and scarlet yarn they made woven garments for ministering in the sanctuary. They also made sacred garments for Aaron, as the LORD commanded Moses.

The Ephod

[2]They[h] made the ephod of gold, and of blue, purple and scarlet yarn, and of finely twisted linen. [3]They hammered out thin sheets of gold and cut strands to be worked into the blue, purple and scarlet yarn and fine linen—the work of a skilled craftsman. [4]They made shoulder pieces for the ephod, which were attached to two of its corners, so it could be fastened. [5]Its skillfully woven waistband was like it—of one piece with the ephod and made with gold, and with blue, purple and scarlet yarn, and with finely twisted linen, as the LORD commanded Moses.

[6]They mounted the onyx stones in gold filigree settings and engraved them like a seal with the names of the sons of Israel. [7]Then they fastened them on the shoulder pieces of the ephod as memorial stones for the sons of Israel, as the LORD commanded Moses.

The Breastpiece

[8]They fashioned the breastpiece—the work of a skilled craftsman. They made it like the ephod: of gold, and of blue, purple and scarlet yarn, and of finely twisted linen. [9]It was square—a span[i] long and a span wide—and folded double. [10]Then they mounted four rows of precious stones on it. In the first row there was a ruby, a topaz and a beryl; [11]in the second row a turquoise, a sapphire[j] and an emerald; [12]in the third row a jacinth, an agate and an amethyst; [13]in the fourth row a chrysolite, an onyx and a jasper.[k] They were mounted in gold filigree settings. [14]There were twelve stones, one for each of the names of the sons of Israel, each engraved like a seal with the name of one of the twelve tribes.

[15]For the breastpiece they made braided chains of pure gold, like a rope. [16]They made two gold filigree settings and two gold rings, and fastened the rings to two of the corners of the breastpiece. [17]They

[a]18 That is, about 7 1/2 feet (about 2.3 meters)
[b]24 The weight of the gold was a little over one ton (about 1 metric ton).   [c]25 The weight of the silver was a little over 3 3/4 tons (about 3.4 metric tons).
[d]26 That is, about 1/5 ounce (about 5.5 grams)
[e]27 That is, about 3 3/4 tons (about 3.4 metric tons)   [f]28 That is, about 45 pounds (about 20 kilograms)   [g]29 The weight of the bronze was about 2 1/2 tons (about 2.4 metric tons).   [h]2 Or He; also in verses 7, 8 and 22   [i]9 That is, about 9 inches (about 22 centimeters)   [j]11 Or lapis lazuli   [k]13 The precise identification of some of these precious stones is uncertain.

fastened the two gold chains to the rings at the corners of the breastpiece, ¹⁸and the other ends of the chains to the two settings, attaching them to the shoulder pieces of the ephod at the front. ¹⁹They made two gold rings and attached them to the other two corners of the breastpiece on the inside edge next to the ephod. ²⁰Then they made two more gold rings and attached them to the bottom of the shoulder pieces on the front of the ephod, close to the seam just above the waistband of the ephod. ²¹They tied the rings of the breastpiece to the rings of the ephod with blue cord, connecting it to the waistband so that the breastpiece would not swing out from the ephod—as the LORD commanded Moses.

Other Priestly Garments

²²They made the robe of the ephod entirely of blue cloth—the work of a weaver— ²³with an opening in the center of the robe like the opening of a collar,ᵃ and a band around this opening, so that it would not tear. ²⁴They made pomegranates of blue, purple and scarlet yarn and finely twisted linen around the hem of the robe. ²⁵And they made bells of pure gold and attached them around the hem between the pomegranates. ²⁶The bells and pomegranates alternated around the hem of the robe to be worn for ministering, as the LORD commanded Moses.

²⁷For Aaron and his sons, they made tunics of fine linen—the work of a weaver— ²⁸and the turban of fine linen, the linen headbands and the undergarments of finely twisted linen. ²⁹The sash was of finely twisted linen and blue, purple and scarlet yarn—the work of an embroiderer—as the LORD commanded Moses.

³⁰They made the plate, the sacred diadem, out of pure gold and engraved on it, like an inscription on a seal: HOLY TO THE LORD. ³¹Then they fastened a blue cord to it to attach it to the turban, as the LORD commanded Moses.

Moses Inspects the Tabernacle

³²So all the work on the tabernacle, the Tent of Meeting, was completed. The Israelites did everything just as the LORD commanded Moses. ³³Then they brought the tabernacle to Moses: the tent and all its furnishings, its clasps, frames, crossbars, posts and bases; ³⁴the covering of ram skins dyed red, the covering of hides of sea cowsᵇ and the shielding curtain;

³⁵the ark of the Testimony with its poles and the atonement cover; ³⁶the table with all its articles and the bread of the Presence; ³⁷the pure gold lampstand with its row of lamps and all its accessories, and the oil for the light; ³⁸the gold altar, the anointing oil, the fragrant incense, and the curtain for the entrance to the tent; ³⁹the bronze altar with its bronze grating, its poles and all its utensils; the basin with its stand; ⁴⁰the curtains of the courtyard with its posts and bases, and the curtain for the entrance to the courtyard; the ropes and tent pegs for the courtyard; all the furnishings for the tabernacle, the Tent of Meeting; ⁴¹and the woven garments worn for ministering in the sanctuary, both the sacred garments for Aaron the priest and the garments for his sons when serving as priests.

⁴²The Israelites had done all the work just as the LORD had commanded Moses. ⁴³Moses inspected the work and saw that they had done it just as the LORD had commanded. So Moses blessed them.

Setting Up the Tabernacle

40 Then the LORD said to Moses: ²"Set up the tabernacle, the Tent of Meeting, on the first day of the first month. ³Place the ark of the Testimony in it and shield the ark with the curtain. ⁴Bring in the table and set out what belongs on it. Then bring in the lampstand and set up its lamps. ⁵Place the gold altar of incense in front of the ark of the Testimony and put the curtain at the entrance to the tabernacle.

⁶"Place the altar of burnt offering in front of the entrance to the tabernacle, the Tent of Meeting; ⁷place the basin between the Tent of Meeting and the altar and put water in it. ⁸Set up the courtyard around it and put the curtain at the entrance to the courtyard.

⁹"Take the anointing oil and anoint the tabernacle and everything in it; consecrate it and all its furnishings, and it will be holy. ¹⁰Then anoint the altar of burnt offering and all its utensils; consecrate the altar, and it will be most holy. ¹¹Anoint the basin and its stand and consecrate them.

¹²"Bring Aaron and his sons to the entrance to the Tent of Meeting and wash them with water. ¹³Then dress Aaron in

---

ᵃ23 The meaning of the Hebrew for this word is uncertain.   ᵇ34 That is, dugongs

the sacred garments, anoint him and consecrate him so he may serve me as priest. ¹⁴Bring his sons and dress them in tunics. ¹⁵Anoint them just as you anointed their father, so they may serve me as priests. Their anointing will be to a priesthood that will continue for all generations to come." ¹⁶Moses did everything just as the LORD commanded him.

¹⁷So the tabernacle was set up on the first day of the first month in the second year. ¹⁸When Moses set up the tabernacle, he put the bases in place, erected the frames, inserted the crossbars and set up the posts. ¹⁹Then he spread the tent over the tabernacle and put the covering over the tent, as the LORD commanded him.

²⁰He took the Testimony and placed it in the ark, attached the poles to the ark and put the atonement cover over it. ²¹Then he brought the ark into the tabernacle and hung the shielding curtain and shielded the ark of the Testimony, as the LORD commanded him.

²²Moses placed the table in the Tent of Meeting on the north side of the tabernacle outside the curtain ²³and set out the bread on it before the LORD, as the LORD commanded him.

²⁴He placed the lampstand in the Tent of Meeting opposite the table on the south side of the tabernacle ²⁵and set up the lamps before the LORD, as the LORD commanded him.

²⁶Moses placed the gold altar in the Tent of Meeting in front of the curtain ²⁷and burned fragrant incense on it, as the LORD commanded him. ²⁸Then he put up the curtain at the entrance to the tabernacle.

²⁹He set the altar of burnt offering near the entrance to the tabernacle, the Tent of Meeting, and offered on it burnt offerings and grain offerings, as the LORD commanded him.

³⁰He placed the basin between the Tent of Meeting and the altar and put water in it for washing, ³¹and Moses and Aaron and his sons used it to wash their hands and feet. ³²They washed whenever they entered the Tent of Meeting or approached the altar, as the LORD commanded Moses.

³³Then Moses set up the courtyard around the tabernacle and altar and put up the curtain at the entrance to the courtyard. And so Moses finished the work.

The Glory of the LORD

³⁴Then the cloud covered the Tent of Meeting, and the glory of the LORD filled the tabernacle. ³⁵Moses could not enter the Tent of Meeting because the cloud had settled upon it, and the glory of the LORD filled the tabernacle.

³⁶In all the travels of the Israelites, whenever the cloud lifted from above the tabernacle, they would set out; ³⁷but if the cloud did not lift, they did not set out—until the day it lifted. ³⁸So the cloud of the LORD was over the tabernacle by day, and fire was in the cloud by night, in the sight of all the house of Israel during all their travels.

We don't know very much about how the Israelites worshiped God during their captivity in Egypt, but it's safe to say that after living in a foreign land for generations, they had probably slipped into some bad spiritual habits. The book of Leviticus describes how God, through Moses, got these people back on track in their relationship with him. And, although some of the particulars listed here may seem strange, the message of this book ought to be clear. God takes our relationship with him very seriously. He's not pleased when we saunter through church every couple of weeks and casually tip our hats to him. He's the Sovereign Lord of the universe, and he deserves our disciplined worship.

Moving out of Egypt was no excuse for the Israelites to get sloppy with their spiritual discipline. For the Israelites, there was no postponement of regular religious rituals. There are no excuses for us either.

Leviticus

The Burnt Offering

1 The LORD called to Moses and spoke to him from the Tent of Meeting. He said, ²"Speak to the Israelites and say to them: 'When any of you brings an offering to the LORD, bring as your offering an animal from either the herd or the flock.

³" 'If the offering is a burnt offering from the herd, he is to offer a male without defect. He must present it at the entrance to the Tent of Meeting so that it*a* will be acceptable to the LORD. ⁴He is to lay his hand on the head of the burnt offering, and it will be accepted on his behalf to make atonement for him. ⁵He is to slaughter the young bull before the LORD, and then Aaron's sons the priests shall bring the blood and sprinkle it against the altar on all sides at the entrance to the

Tent of Meeting. ⁶He is to skin the burnt offering and cut it into pieces. ⁷The sons of Aaron the priest are to put fire on the altar and arrange wood on the fire. ⁸Then Aaron's sons the priests shall arrange the pieces, including the head and the fat, on the burning wood that is on the altar. ⁹He is to wash the inner parts and the legs with water, and the priest is to burn all of it on the altar. It is a burnt offering, an offering made by fire, an aroma pleasing to the LORD.

¹⁰" 'If the offering is a burnt offering from the flock, from either the sheep or the goats, he is to offer a male without defect. ¹¹He is to slaughter it at the north side of the altar before the LORD, and Aaron's sons the priests shall sprinkle its

a3 Or he

blood against the altar on all sides. ¹²He is to cut it into pieces, and the priest shall arrange them, including the head and the fat, on the burning wood that is on the altar. ¹³He is to wash the inner parts and the legs with water, and the priest is to bring all of it and burn it on the altar. It is a burnt offering, an offering made by fire, an aroma pleasing to the LORD.

¹⁴" 'If the offering to the LORD is a burnt offering of birds, he is to offer a dove or a young pigeon. ¹⁵The priest shall bring it to the altar, wring off the head and burn it on the altar; its blood shall be drained out on the side of the altar. ¹⁶He is to remove the crop with its contents*a* and throw it to the east side of the altar, where the ashes are. ¹⁷He shall tear it open by the wings, not severing it completely, and then the priest shall burn it on the wood that is on the fire on the altar. It is a burnt offering, an offering made by fire, an aroma pleasing to the LORD.

The Grain Offering

2 " 'When someone brings a grain offering to the LORD, his offering is to be of fine flour. He is to pour oil on it, put incense on it ²and take it to Aaron's sons the priests. The priest shall take a handful of the fine flour and oil, together with all the incense, and burn this as a memorial portion on the altar, an offering made by fire, an aroma pleasing to the LORD. ³The rest of the grain offering belongs to Aaron and his sons; it is a most holy part of the offerings made to the LORD by fire.

⁴" 'If you bring a grain offering baked in an oven, it is to consist of fine flour: cakes made without yeast and mixed with oil, or*b* wafers made without yeast and spread with oil. ⁵If your grain offering is prepared on a griddle, it is to be made of fine flour mixed with oil, and without yeast. ⁶Crumble it and pour oil on it; it is a grain offering. ⁷If your grain offering is cooked in a pan, it is to be made of fine flour and oil. ⁸Bring the grain offering made of these things to the LORD; present it to the priest, who shall take it to the altar. ⁹He shall take out the memorial portion from the grain offering and burn it on the altar as an offering made by fire, an aroma pleasing to the LORD. ¹⁰The rest of the grain offering belongs to Aaron and his sons; it is a most holy part of the offerings made to the LORD by fire.

¹¹" 'Every grain offering you bring to the LORD must be made without yeast, for you are not to burn any yeast or honey in an offering made to the LORD by fire. ¹²You may bring them to the LORD as an offering of the firstfruits, but they are not to be offered on the altar as a pleasing aroma. ¹³Season all your grain offerings with salt. Do not leave the salt of the covenant of your God out of your grain offerings; add salt to all your offerings.

¹⁴" 'If you bring a grain offering of firstfruits to the LORD, offer crushed heads of new grain roasted in the fire. ¹⁵Put oil and incense on it; it is a grain offering. ¹⁶The priest shall burn the memorial portion of the crushed grain and the oil, together with all the incense, as an offering made to the LORD by fire.

The Fellowship Offering

3 " 'If someone's offering is a fellowship offering,*c* and he offers an animal from the herd, whether male or female, he is to present before the LORD an animal without defect. ²He is to lay his hand on the head of his offering and slaughter it at the entrance to the Tent of Meeting. Then Aaron's sons the priests shall sprinkle the blood against the altar on all sides. ³From the fellowship offering he is to bring a sacrifice made to the LORD by fire: all the fat that covers the inner parts or is connected to them, ⁴both kidneys with the fat on them near the loins, and the covering of the liver, which he will remove with the kidneys. ⁵Then Aaron's sons are to burn it on the altar on top of the burnt offering that is on the burning wood, as an offering made by fire, an aroma pleasing to the LORD.

⁶" 'If he offers an animal from the flock as a fellowship offering to the LORD, he is to offer a male or female without defect. ⁷If he offers a lamb, he is to present it before the LORD. ⁸He is to lay his hand on the head of his offering and slaughter it in front of the Tent of Meeting. Then Aaron's sons shall sprinkle its blood against the altar on all sides. ⁹From the fellowship offering he is to bring a sacrifice made to the LORD by fire: its fat, the entire fat tail cut off close to the backbone, all the fat that covers the inner parts or is connected to them, ¹⁰both kidneys with the fat on them near the loins, and the covering of the liver, which he will remove with the

---

a16 Or *crop and the feathers*; the meaning of the Hebrew for this word is uncertain.   *b4* Or *and*   *c1* Traditionally *peace offering*; also in verses 3, 6 and 9

kidneys. [11]The priest shall burn them on the altar as food, an offering made to the LORD by fire.

[12]" 'If his offering is a goat, he is to present it before the LORD. [13]He is to lay his hand on its head and slaughter it in front of the Tent of Meeting. Then Aaron's sons shall sprinkle its blood against the altar on all sides. [14]From what he offers he is to make this offering to the LORD by fire: all the fat that covers the inner parts or is connected to them, [15]both kidneys with the fat on them near the loins, and the covering of the liver, which he will remove with the kidneys. [16]The priest shall burn them on the altar as food, an offering made by fire, a pleasing aroma. All the fat is the LORD's.

[17]" 'This is a lasting ordinance for the generations to come, wherever you live: You must not eat any fat or any blood.' "

The Sin Offering

4 The LORD said to Moses, [2]"Say to the Israelites: 'When anyone sins unintentionally and does what is forbidden in any of the LORD's commands—

[3]" 'If the anointed priest sins, bringing guilt on the people, he must bring to the LORD a young bull without defect as a sin offering for the sin he has committed. [4]He is to present the bull at the entrance to the Tent of Meeting before the LORD. He is to lay his hand on its head and slaughter it before the LORD. [5]Then the anointed priest shall take some of the bull's blood and carry it into the Tent of Meeting. [6]He is to dip his finger into the blood and sprinkle some of it seven times before the LORD, in front of the curtain of the sanctuary. [7]The priest shall then put some of the blood on the horns of the altar of fragrant incense that is before the LORD in the Tent of Meeting. The rest of the bull's blood he shall pour out at the base of the altar of burnt offering at the entrance to the Tent of Meeting. [8]He shall remove all the fat from the bull of the sin offering—the fat that covers the inner parts or is connected to them, [9]both kidneys with the fat on them near the loins, and the covering of the liver, which he will remove with the kidneys— [10]just as the fat is removed from the ox[a] sacrificed as a fellowship offering.[b] Then the priest shall burn them on the altar of burnt offering. [11]But the hide of the bull and all its flesh, as well as the head and legs, the inner parts and offal— [12]that is, all the rest of the bull—he must take outside the camp to a place ceremonially clean, where the ashes are thrown, and burn it in a wood fire on the ash heap.

[13]" 'If the whole Israelite community sins unintentionally and does what is forbidden in any of the LORD's commands, even though the community is unaware of the matter, they are guilty. [14]When they become aware of the sin they committed, the assembly must bring a young bull as a sin offering and present it before the Tent of Meeting. [15]The elders of the community are to lay their hands on the bull's head before the LORD, and the bull shall be slaughtered before the LORD. [16]Then the anointed priest is to take some of the bull's blood into the Tent of Meeting. [17]He shall dip his finger into the blood and sprinkle it before the LORD seven times in front of the curtain. [18]He is to put some of the blood on the horns of the altar that is before the LORD in the Tent of Meeting. The rest of the blood he shall pour out at the base of the altar of burnt offering at the entrance to the Tent of Meeting. [19]He shall remove all the fat from it and burn it on the altar, [20]and do with this bull just as he did with the bull for the sin offering. In this way the priest will make atonement for them, and they will be forgiven. [21]Then he shall take the bull outside the camp and burn it as he burned the first bull. This is the sin offering for the community.

[22]" 'When a leader sins unintentionally and does what is forbidden in any of the commands of the LORD his God, he is guilty. [23]When he is made aware of the sin he committed, he must bring as his offering a male goat without defect. [24]He is to lay his hand on the goat's head and slaughter it at the place where the burnt offering is slaughtered before the LORD. It is a sin offering. [25]Then the priest shall take some of the blood of the sin offering with his finger and put it on the horns of the altar of burnt offering and pour out the rest of the blood at the base of the altar. [26]He shall burn all the fat on the altar as he burned the fat of the fellowship offering. In this way the priest will make atonement for the man's sin, and he will be forgiven.

[27]" 'If a member of the community sins unintentionally and does what is forbid-

---

[a]10 The Hebrew word can include both male and female.   [b]10 Traditionally *peace offering*; also in verses 26, 31 and 35

den in any of the LORD's commands, he is guilty. ²⁸When he is made aware of the sin he committed, he must bring as his offering for the sin he committed a female goat without defect. ²⁹He is to lay his hand on the head of the sin offering and slaughter it at the place of the burnt offering. ³⁰Then the priest is to take some of the blood with his finger and put it on the horns of the altar of burnt offering and pour out the rest of the blood at the base of the altar. ³¹He shall remove all the fat, just as the fat is removed from the fellowship offering, and the priest shall burn it on the altar as an aroma pleasing to the LORD. In this way the priest will make atonement for him, and he will be forgiven.

³²" 'If he brings a lamb as his sin offering, he is to bring a female without defect. ³³He is to lay his hand on its head and slaughter it for a sin offering at the place where the burnt offering is slaughtered. ³⁴Then the priest shall take some of the blood of the sin offering with his finger and put it on the horns of the altar of burnt offering and pour out the rest of the blood at the base of the altar. ³⁵He shall remove all the fat, just as the fat is removed from the lamb of the fellowship offering, and the priest shall burn it on the altar on top of the offerings made to the LORD by fire. In this way the priest will make atonement for him for the sin he has committed, and he will be forgiven.

5 " 'If a person sins because he does not speak up when he hears a public charge to testify regarding something he has seen or learned about, he will be held responsible.

²" 'Or if a person touches anything ceremonially unclean—whether the carcasses of unclean wild animals or of unclean livestock or of unclean creatures that move along the ground—even though he is unaware of it, he has become unclean and is guilty.

³" 'Or if he touches human uncleanness—anything that would make him unclean—even though he is unaware of it, when he learns of it he will be guilty.

⁴" 'Or if a person thoughtlessly takes an oath to do anything, whether good or evil—in any matter one might carelessly swear about—even though he is unaware of it, in any case when he learns of it he will be guilty.

⁵" 'When anyone is guilty in any of these ways, he must confess in what way he has sinned ⁶and, as a penalty for the sin he has committed, he must bring to the LORD a female lamb or goat from the flock as a sin offering; and the priest shall make atonement for him for his sin.

⁷" 'If he cannot afford a lamb, he is to bring two doves or two young pigeons to the LORD as a penalty for his sin—one for a sin offering and the other for a burnt offering. ⁸He is to bring them to the priest, who shall first offer the one for the sin offering. He is to wring its head from its neck, not severing it completely, ⁹and is to sprinkle some of the blood of the sin offering against the side of the altar; the rest of the blood must be drained out at the base of the altar. It is a sin offering. ¹⁰The priest shall then offer the other as a burnt offering in the prescribed way and make atonement for him for the sin he has committed, and he will be forgiven.

¹¹" 'If, however, he cannot afford two doves or two young pigeons, he is to bring as an offering for his sin a tenth of an ephah*ᵃ* of fine flour for a sin offering. He must not put oil or incense on it, because it is a sin offering. ¹²He is to bring it to the priest, who shall take a handful of it as a memorial portion and burn it on the altar on top of the offerings made to the LORD by fire. It is a sin offering. ¹³In this way the priest will make atonement for him for any of these sins he has committed, and he will be forgiven. The rest of the offering will belong to the priest, as in the case of the grain offering.' "

The Guilt Offering

¹⁴The LORD said to Moses: ¹⁵"When a person commits a violation and sins unintentionally in regard to any of the LORD's holy things, he is to bring to the LORD as a penalty a ram from the flock, one without defect and of the proper value in silver, according to the sanctuary shekel.*ᵇ* It is a guilt offering. ¹⁶He must make restitution for what he has failed to do in regard to the holy things, add a fifth of the value to that and give it all to the priest, who will make atonement for him with the ram as a guilt offering, and he will be forgiven.

¹⁷"If a person sins and does what is forbidden in any of the LORD's commands, even though he does not know it, he is guilty and will be held responsible. ¹⁸He is to bring to the priest as a guilt offering a

ᵃ11 That is, probably about 2 quarts (about 2 liters)
ᵇ15 That is, about 2/5 ounce (about 11.5 grams)

ram from the flock, one without defect and of the proper value. In this way the priest will make atonement for him for the wrong he has committed unintentionally, and he will be forgiven. ¹⁹It is a guilt offering; he has been guilty of*ᵃ* wrongdoing against the LORD."

6 The LORD said to Moses: ²"If anyone sins and is unfaithful to the LORD by deceiving his neighbor about something entrusted to him or left in his care or stolen, or if he cheats him, ³or if he finds lost property and lies about it, or if he swears falsely, or if he commits any such sin that people may do— ⁴when he thus sins and becomes guilty, he must return what he has stolen or taken by extortion, or what was entrusted to him, or the lost property he found, ⁵or whatever it was he swore falsely about. He must make restitution in full, add a fifth of the value to it and give it all to the owner on the day he presents his guilt offering. ⁶And as a penalty he must bring to the priest, that is, to the LORD, his guilt offering, a ram from the flock, one without defect and of the proper value. ⁷In this way the priest will make atonement for him before the LORD, and he will be forgiven for any of these things he did that made him guilty."

ᵃ19 Or has made full expiation for his

Nice Pipes

You and I are copper pipes in the crawl space of life.

In the fall of 1997, our younger daughter bought her first house. It was a little two-bedroom, one-bath beauty about fifteen minutes from our home. The first time I walked through this solid structure, built in the early 50's, I told Julie that I'd be happy to help her remodel the bathroom. She could live at our house until the work was completed. I didn't need to ask twice.

I can only imagine what the neighbors must have thought when, on her first day of possession, they saw Julie, my nephew Erik and me walking into the house with crowbars and a sledgehammer. Over the next two months, Julie and I spent every spare moment at the house.

Because we had decided to move the toilet from one corner of the bathroom to the other and exchange the cast iron tub for a full-sized shower, I had a lot of plumbing work to do. I spent many hours on my knees in the crawl space under the house, cutting, fitting, and melting solder to secure new copper water-supply pipes. "Left is hot, right is cold," I whispered to myself a few hundred times.

Have you ever thought about how you and I are like those copper pipes? You

FRIDAY
Passage:
Leviticus 6:1–7
Verse:
Leviticus 6:7

haven't? Okay then, see if this makes sense to you.

A pipe's only responsibility is to take what it is given—hot or cold water—and faithfully pass it safely through to its destination. Of course, there is a lot to be said about enhancing what it's been given—as in the parable of the talents in the Gospels—and we'll talk about that later. But, for now, let's focus on this idea: Everything we "own" has been given to us—our talents, abilities, and possessions. Our job is to faithfully take these things and bring them as gifts to our heavenly Father who knows exactly what to do with them.

Today's text, and the chapters that surround it, make this truth very clear. At a very early age, Jewish children must have learned the way to the temple because they and their parents were constantly commanded to bring things to the Lord. Day after day, experience upon experience, he blesses the gifts, and he forgives the transgressions.

Take a wire brush to the clogs. Patch the dripping seams. Bring what you have been given to your Father without any impediments. He knows what to do with all of them.

For your next devotional reading, go to page 128.

The Burnt Offering

8The LORD said to Moses: **9**"Give Aaron and his sons this command: 'These are the regulations for the burnt offering: The burnt offering is to remain on the altar hearth throughout the night, till morning, and the fire must be kept burning on the altar. **10**The priest shall then put on his linen clothes, with linen undergarments next to his body, and shall remove the ashes of the burnt offering that the fire has consumed on the altar and place them beside the altar. **11**Then he is to take off these clothes and put on others, and carry the ashes outside the camp to a place that is ceremonially clean. **12**The fire on the altar must be kept burning; it must not go out. Every morning the priest is to add firewood and arrange the burnt offering on the fire and burn the fat of the fellowship offerings[a] on it. **13**The fire must be kept burning on the altar continuously; it must not go out.

The Grain Offering

14" 'These are the regulations for the grain offering: Aaron's sons are to bring it before the LORD, in front of the altar. **15**The priest is to take a handful of fine flour and oil, together with all the incense on the grain offering, and burn the memorial portion on the altar as an aroma pleasing to the LORD. **16**Aaron and his sons shall eat the rest of it, but it is to be eaten without yeast in a holy place; they are to eat it in the courtyard of the Tent of Meeting. **17**It must not be baked with yeast; I have given it as their share of the offerings made to me by fire. Like the sin offering and the guilt offering, it is most holy. **18**Any male descendant of Aaron may eat it. It is his regular share of the offerings made to the LORD by fire for the generations to come. Whatever touches them will become holy.[b] ' "

19The LORD also said to Moses, **20**"This is the offering Aaron and his sons are to bring to the LORD on the day he[c] is anointed: a tenth of an ephah[d] of fine flour as a regular grain offering, half of it in the morning and half in the evening. **21**Prepare it with oil on a griddle; bring it well-mixed and present the grain offering broken[e] in pieces as an aroma pleasing to the LORD. **22**The son who is to succeed him as anointed priest shall prepare it. It is the LORD's regular share and is to be burned

a12 Traditionally *peace offerings* *b18* Or *Whoever touches them must be holy*; similarly in verse 27 *c20* Or *each* *d20* That is, probably about 2 quarts (about 2 liters) *e21* The meaning of the Hebrew for this word is uncertain.

HEY DAD
Does the Bible say we have to change our underwear?

Text: Leviticus 6:10–11

There's not a rule in the Bible that says we have to change our underwear (though "honor your father and your mother" [Exodus 20:12] pretty much covers it). But, believe it or not, God actually required the priests to change their underwear at certain times.

This rule required a priest to put on clean linen clothes and undergarments every time he removed the ashes of the burnt offering from the altar. After the priest removed the ashes, he had to change his clothes again to take the ashes outside the camp. The priest made this burnt offering every morning and every evening, so God must really be concerned about clean underwear, right? Actually, the reason he made priests change their clothes went much deeper than that.

Linen was a very special fabric; garments made from linen were more expensive than regular clothes. When the priest put on linen garments and undergarments to remove the ashes, he was showing reverence to God. His fine clothes showed that he was giving his best to please God. He had to change his clothes before leaving the tabernacle because these special linen garments were considered pure and holy. If he wore them outside the tabernacle, the clothes would then be considered "unclean."

So listen to your father and mother. God cares about clean underwear, too!

For a complete listing of Questions Kids Ask, turn to page 1435.

completely. **23**Every grain offering of a priest shall be burned completely; it must not be eaten."

The Sin Offering

24The LORD said to Moses, **25**"Say to Aaron and his sons: 'These are the regulations for the sin offering: The sin offering is to be slaughtered before the LORD in the place the burnt offering is slaughtered; it is most holy. **26**The priest who offers it shall eat it; it is to be eaten in a holy place, in the courtyard of the Tent of Meeting. **27**Whatever touches any of the flesh will become holy, and if any of the blood is spattered on a garment, you must wash it in a holy place. **28**The clay pot the meat is cooked in must be broken; but if it is cooked in a bronze pot, the pot is to be scoured and rinsed with water. **29**Any male in a priest's family may eat it; it is most holy. **30**But any sin offering whose blood is brought into the Tent of Meeting to make atonement in the Holy Place must not be eaten; it must be burned.

The Guilt Offering

7 " 'These are the regulations for the guilt offering, which is most holy: **2**The guilt offering is to be slaughtered in the place where the burnt offering is slaughtered, and its blood is to be sprinkled against the altar on all sides. **3**All its fat shall be offered: the fat tail and the fat that covers the inner parts, **4**both kidneys with the fat on them near the loins, and the covering of the liver, which is to be removed with the kidneys. **5**The priest shall burn them on the altar as an offering made to the LORD by fire. It is a guilt offering. **6**Any male in a priest's family may eat it, but it must be eaten in a holy place; it is most holy.

7" 'The same law applies to both the sin offering and the guilt offering: They belong to the priest who makes atonement with them. **8**The priest who offers a burnt offering for anyone may keep its hide for himself. **9**Every grain offering baked in an oven or cooked in a pan or on a griddle belongs to the priest who offers it, **10**and every grain offering, whether mixed with oil or dry, belongs equally to all the sons of Aaron.

The Fellowship Offering

11" 'These are the regulations for the fellowship offering[a] a person may present to the LORD:

12" 'If he offers it as an expression of thankfulness, then along with this thank offering he is to offer cakes of bread made without yeast and mixed with oil, wafers made without yeast and spread with oil, and cakes of fine flour well-kneaded and mixed with oil. **13**Along with his fellowship offering of thanksgiving he is to present an offering with cakes of bread made with yeast. **14**He is to bring one of each kind as an offering, a contribution to the LORD; it belongs to the priest who sprinkles the blood of the fellowship offerings. **15**The meat of his fellowship offering of thanksgiving must be eaten on the day it is offered; he must leave none of it till morning.

16" 'If, however, his offering is the result of a vow or is a freewill offering, the sacrifice shall be eaten on the day he offers it, but anything left over may be eaten on the next day. **17**Any meat of the sacrifice left over till the third day must be burned up. **18**If any meat of the fellowship offering is eaten on the third day, it will not be accepted. It will not be credited to the one who offered it, for it is impure; the person who eats any of it will be held responsible.

19" 'Meat that touches anything ceremonially unclean must not be eaten; it must be burned up. As for other meat, anyone ceremonially clean may eat it. **20**But if anyone who is unclean eats any meat of the fellowship offering belonging to the LORD, that person must be cut off from his people. **21**If anyone touches something unclean—whether human uncleanness or an unclean animal or any unclean, detestable thing—and then eats any of the meat of the fellowship offering belonging to the LORD, that person must be cut off from his people.' "

Eating Fat and Blood Forbidden

22The LORD said to Moses, **23**"Say to the Israelites: 'Do not eat any of the fat of cattle, sheep or goats. **24**The fat of an animal found dead or torn by wild animals may be used for any other purpose, but you must not eat it. **25**Anyone who eats the fat of an animal from which an offering by fire may be[b] made to the LORD must be cut off from his people. **26**And wherever you live, you must not eat the blood of any bird or animal. **27**If anyone eats blood, that person must be cut off from his people.' "

---

a11 Traditionally *peace offering;* also in verses 13-37   *b25* Or *fire is*

The Priests' Share

²⁸The LORD said to Moses, ²⁹"Say to the Israelites: 'Anyone who brings a fellowship offering to the LORD is to bring part of it as his sacrifice to the LORD. ³⁰With his own hands he is to bring the offering made to the LORD by fire; he is to bring the fat, together with the breast, and wave the breast before the LORD as a wave offering. ³¹The priest shall burn the fat on the altar, but the breast belongs to Aaron and his sons. ³²You are to give the right thigh of your fellowship offerings to the priest as a contribution. ³³The son of Aaron who offers the blood and the fat of the fellowship offering shall have the right thigh as his share. ³⁴From the fellowship offerings of the Israelites, I have taken the breast that is waved and the thigh that is presented and have given them to Aaron the priest and his sons as their regular share from the Israelites.' "

³⁵This is the portion of the offerings made to the LORD by fire that were allotted to Aaron and his sons on the day they were presented to serve the LORD as priests. ³⁶On the day they were anointed, the LORD commanded that the Israelites give this to them as their regular share for the generations to come.

³⁷These, then, are the regulations for the burnt offering, the grain offering, the sin offering, the guilt offering, the ordination offering and the fellowship offering, ³⁸which the LORD gave Moses on Mount Sinai on the day he commanded the Israelites to bring their offerings to the LORD, in the Desert of Sinai.

The Ordination of Aaron and His Sons

8 The LORD said to Moses, ²"Bring Aaron and his sons, their garments, the anointing oil, the bull for the sin offering, the two rams and the basket containing bread made without yeast, ³and gather the entire assembly at the entrance to the Tent of Meeting." ⁴Moses did as the LORD commanded him, and the assembly gathered at the entrance to the Tent of Meeting.

⁵Moses said to the assembly, "This is what the LORD has commanded to be done." ⁶Then Moses brought Aaron and his sons forward and washed them with water. ⁷He put the tunic on Aaron, tied the sash around him, clothed him with the robe and put the ephod on him. He also tied the ephod to him by its skillfully woven waistband; so it was fastened on him. ⁸He placed the breastpiece on him and put the Urim and Thummim in the breastpiece. ⁹Then he placed the turban on Aaron's head and set the gold plate, the sacred diadem, on the front of it, as the LORD commanded Moses.

¹⁰Then Moses took the anointing oil and anointed the tabernacle and everything in it, and so consecrated them. ¹¹He sprinkled some of the oil on the altar seven times, anointing the altar and all its utensils and the basin with its stand, to consecrate them. ¹²He poured some of the anointing oil on Aaron's head and anointed him to consecrate him. ¹³Then he brought Aaron's sons forward, put tunics on them, tied sashes around them and put headbands on them, as the LORD commanded Moses.

¹⁴He then presented the bull for the sin offering, and Aaron and his sons laid their hands on its head. ¹⁵Moses slaughtered the bull and took some of the blood, and with his finger he put it on all the horns of the altar to purify the altar. He poured out the rest of the blood at the base of the altar. So he consecrated it to make atonement for it. ¹⁶Moses also took all the fat around the inner parts, the covering of the liver, and both kidneys and their fat, and burned it on the altar. ¹⁷But the bull with its hide and its flesh and its offal he burned up outside the camp, as the LORD commanded Moses.

¹⁸He then presented the ram for the burnt offering, and Aaron and his sons laid their hands on its head. ¹⁹Then Moses slaughtered the ram and sprinkled the blood against the altar on all sides. ²⁰He cut the ram into pieces and burned the head, the pieces and the fat. ²¹He washed the inner parts and the legs with water and burned the whole ram on the altar as a burnt offering, a pleasing aroma, an offering made to the LORD by fire, as the LORD commanded Moses.

²²He then presented the other ram, the ram for the ordination, and Aaron and his sons laid their hands on its head. ²³Moses slaughtered the ram and took some of its blood and put it on the lobe of Aaron's right ear, on the thumb of his right hand and on the big toe of his right foot. ²⁴Moses also brought Aaron's sons forward and put some of the blood on the lobes of their right ears, on the thumbs of their right hands and on the big toes of their right feet. Then he sprinkled blood against the altar on all sides. ²⁵He took the fat, the fat

tail, all the fat around the inner parts, the covering of the liver, both kidneys and their fat and the right thigh. **26**Then from the basket of bread made without yeast, which was before the LORD, he took a cake of bread, and one made with oil, and a wafer; he put these on the fat portions and on the right thigh. **27**He put all these in the hands of Aaron and his sons and waved them before the LORD as a wave offering. **28**Then Moses took them from their hands and burned them on the altar on top of the burnt offering as an ordination offering, a pleasing aroma, an offering made to the LORD by fire. **29**He also took the breast—Moses' share of the ordination ram—and waved it before the LORD as a wave offering, as the LORD commanded Moses.

30Then Moses took some of the anointing oil and some of the blood from the altar and sprinkled them on Aaron and his garments and on his sons and their garments. So he consecrated Aaron and his garments and his sons and their garments. **31**Moses then said to Aaron and his sons, "Cook the meat at the entrance to the Tent of Meeting and eat it there with the bread from the basket of ordination offerings, as I commanded, saying,*a* 'Aaron and his sons are to eat it.' **32**Then burn

up the rest of the meat and the bread. **33**Do not leave the entrance to the Tent of Meeting for seven days, until the days of your ordination are completed, for your ordination will last seven days. **34**What has been done today was commanded by the LORD to make atonement for you. **35**You must stay at the entrance to the Tent of Meeting day and night for seven days and do what the LORD requires, so you will not die; for that is what I have been commanded." **36**So Aaron and his sons did everything the LORD commanded through Moses.

The Priests Begin Their Ministry

9 On the eighth day Moses summoned Aaron and his sons and the elders of Israel. **2**He said to Aaron, "Take a bull calf for your sin offering and a ram for your burnt offering, both without defect, and present them before the LORD. **3**Then say to the Israelites: 'Take a male goat for a sin offering, a calf and a lamb—both a year old and without defect—for a burnt offering, **4**and an ox*b* and a ram for a fellowship offering*c* to sacrifice before the LORD, to-

a31 Or I was commanded: *b4 The Hebrew word can include both male and female; also in verses 18 and 19.*   *c4 Traditionally peace offering; also in verses 18 and 22*

Do we still have to obey the rules of the Old Testament?

Text: Leviticus 9:7

When Jesus came, many of the rules in the Old Testament became unnecessary. For instance, people did not need to offer animals as sacrifices anymore because Jesus became the ultimate sacrifice when he died on the cross. Dietary rules and circumcision were also declared non-essential to the Christian faith (Acts 15:5–21).

But Jesus did not make the Old Testament outdated and obsolete. He came, not to do away with the law, but to fulfill it! He showed us the actual intent of the law. In many ways, Jesus' teaching requires *more* of us than the Old Testament laws because he wasn't just concerned with our actions; he was also concerned with our hearts. For example, the Old Testament said, "eye for eye, tooth for tooth" in reference to punishment for evil (Deuteronomy 19:21), but Jesus teaches us to love our enemies and to pray for those who persecute us (Matthew 5:44).

God gave the Old Testament rules to his people for many good reasons. He wanted them to demonstrate to others in the world that they were different, set apart for God's service. These rules for worship and hygiene fit the bill at the time. Now that Jesus has come, many of those rules are obsolete. But he still calls us to live lives that demonstrate that we are his people—set apart to do God's work in the world.

For a complete listing of Questions Kids Ask, turn to page 1435.

gether with a grain offering mixed with oil. For today the LORD will appear to you.' "

⁵They took the things Moses commanded to the front of the Tent of Meeting, and the entire assembly came near and stood before the LORD. ⁶Then Moses said, "This is what the LORD has commanded you to do, so that the glory of the LORD may appear to you."

⁷Moses said to Aaron, "Come to the altar and sacrifice your sin offering and your burnt offering and make atonement for yourself and the people; sacrifice the offering that is for the people and make atonement for them, as the LORD has commanded."

⁸So Aaron came to the altar and slaughtered the calf as a sin offering for himself. ⁹His sons brought the blood to him, and he dipped his finger into the blood and put it on the horns of the altar; the rest of the blood he poured out at the base of the altar. ¹⁰On the altar he burned the fat, the kidneys and the covering of the liver from the sin offering, as the LORD commanded Moses; ¹¹the flesh and the hide he burned up outside the camp.

¹²Then he slaughtered the burnt offering. His sons handed him the blood, and he sprinkled it against the altar on all sides. ¹³They handed him the burnt offering piece by piece, including the head, and he burned them on the altar. ¹⁴He washed the inner parts and the legs and burned them on top of the burnt offering on the altar.

¹⁵Aaron then brought the offering that was for the people. He took the goat for the people's sin offering and slaughtered it and offered it for a sin offering as he did with the first one. ¹⁶He brought the burnt offering and offered it in the prescribed way. ¹⁷He also brought the grain offering, took a handful of it and burned it on the altar in addition to the morning's burnt offering.

¹⁸He slaughtered the ox and the ram as the fellowship offering for the people. His sons handed him the blood, and he sprinkled it against the altar on all sides. ¹⁹But the fat portions of the ox and the ram—the fat tail, the layer of fat, the kidneys and the covering of the liver— ²⁰these they laid on the breasts, and then Aaron burned the fat on the altar. ²¹Aaron waved the breasts and the right thigh before the LORD as a wave offering, as Moses commanded.

²²Then Aaron lifted his hands toward the people and blessed them. And having sacrificed the sin offering, the burnt offering and the fellowship offering, he stepped down.

²³Moses and Aaron then went into the Tent of Meeting. When they came out, they blessed the people; and the glory of the LORD appeared to all the people. ²⁴Fire came out from the presence of the LORD and consumed the burnt offering and the fat portions on the altar. And when all the people saw it, they shouted for joy and fell facedown.

The Death of Nadab and Abihu

10 Aaron's sons Nadab and Abihu took their censers, put fire in them and added incense; and they offered unauthorized fire before the LORD, contrary to his command. ²So fire came out from the presence of the LORD and consumed them, and they died before the LORD. ³Moses then said to Aaron, "This is what the LORD spoke of when he said:

" 'Among those who approach me
    I will show myself holy;
in the sight of all the people
    I will be honored.' "

Aaron remained silent.

⁴Moses summoned Mishael and Elzaphan, sons of Aaron's uncle Uzziel, and said to them, "Come here; carry your cousins outside the camp, away from the front of the sanctuary." ⁵So they came and carried them, still in their tunics, outside the camp, as Moses ordered.

⁶Then Moses said to Aaron and his sons Eleazar and Ithamar, "Do not let your hair become unkempt,ᵃ and do not tear your clothes, or you will die and the LORD will be angry with the whole community. But your relatives, all the house of Israel, may mourn for those the LORD has destroyed by fire. ⁷Do not leave the entrance to the Tent of Meeting or you will die, because the LORD's anointing oil is on you." So they did as Moses said.

⁸Then the LORD said to Aaron, ⁹"You and your sons are not to drink wine or other fermented drink whenever you go into the Tent of Meeting, or you will die. This is a lasting ordinance for the generations to come. ¹⁰You must distinguish between the holy and the common, between the unclean and the clean, ¹¹and you must teach the Israelites all the decrees the LORD has given them through Moses."

ᵃ6 Or *Do not uncover your heads*

An Important Meeting

Key Verse: *"Moses then said to Aaron, 'This is what the LORD spoke of when he said: "Among those who approach me I will show myself holy; in the sight of all the people I will be honored." '"* Leviticus 10:3

Text: Leviticus 10:1–3 *(Dad or child reads the text.)*

QUIET TIMES WITH Dad

DAD READS: If you could spend this afternoon with anyone in the whole world, who would it be? I'm talking about someone you have never actually met but someone whom you really like and respect.

Child reads: That would be great. I can't imagine how much fun it would be to tell my friends all about it.

DAD READS: Let's say that you are going to meet with this person at exactly 1:00 p.m. at the airport. They are flying into our town just to see you. Can you imagine how excited you would feel, standing in the airport, waiting for him or her to step off the plane?

Child reads: My heart would be beating so fast, just knowing that this person and I were actually going to spend the afternoon together! I would be on my best behavior, that's for sure.

DAD READS: The short story we read today is one of those difficult but very important Bible stories. It's about Aaron's two sons who were going to spend some time with God, but they didn't use their best manners. They forgot that they were going to be with the One who created the universe. And when they realized that they weren't ready to be with him, they actually dropped dead. Can you imagine such a thing?

Child reads: It would be like, when I met this important person, I said something rude like,

"You don't look as good as I thought you would, and by the way you're late. Don't you know how important I am? I don't like to wait for anyone." If I would say something so foolish to this person and then realize who I was talking to, I would almost feel bad enough to die!

DAD READS: The lesson from this story is a very important one. When we come into God's presence, like when we pray, we cannot forget that he is even more important than the most important person in the world. And we don't even have to wait until 1:00 p.m. this afternoon to talk to him. Isn't that wonderful?

Child reads: Yes it is. I want to always remember who God is when I speak to him. Let me pray this prayer with you:

Our Father in heaven, thank you for being such an awesome God. Please forgive my dad and me for the times when we forget who you are when we talk to you. We know that you're the most important person who ever was. And we also want to remember that you love us as a Father. We love you and we thank you for who you are. In Jesus' name, Amen.

For your next devotional reading, go to page 143.

¹²Moses said to Aaron and his remaining sons, Eleazar and Ithamar, "Take the grain offering left over from the offerings made to the LORD by fire and eat it prepared without yeast beside the altar, for it is most holy. ¹³Eat it in a holy place, because it is your share and your sons' share of the offerings made to the LORD by fire; for so I have been commanded. ¹⁴But you and your sons and your daughters may eat the breast that was waved and the thigh that was presented. Eat them in a ceremonially clean place; they have been given to you and your children as your share of the Israelites' fellowship offerings.[a] ¹⁵The thigh that was presented and the breast that was waved must be brought with the fat portions of the offerings made by fire, to be waved before the LORD as a wave offering. This will be the regular share for you and your children, as the LORD has commanded."

¹⁶When Moses inquired about the goat of the sin offering and found that it had been burned up, he was angry with Eleazar and Ithamar, Aaron's remaining sons, and asked, ¹⁷"Why didn't you eat the sin offering in the sanctuary area? It is most holy; it was given to you to take away the guilt of the community by making atonement for them before the LORD. ¹⁸Since its blood was not taken into the Holy Place, you should have eaten the goat in the sanctuary area, as I commanded."

¹⁹Aaron replied to Moses, "Today they sacrificed their sin offering and their burnt offering before the LORD, but such things as this have happened to me. Would the LORD have been pleased if I had eaten the sin offering today?" ²⁰When Moses heard this, he was satisfied.

a14 Traditionally *peace offerings*

Your Children Belong to God
Aaron, the Second-string Father

DADS
IN THE
BIBLE

"Moses then said to Aaron, 'This is what the LORD spoke of when he said: "Among those who approach me I will show myself holy; in the sight of all the people I will be honored." ' Aaron remained silent" (10:3).

Text: Leviticus 10

Who is your children's most important father? Now there's an odd question. Seriously, your children actually have two fathers: you and God. Are both of these fathers important? Yes. Do both of these fathers love their children? Yes. Should children obey one father over the other?

Now wait a minute. The answers to the first two questions were easy, but what's the answer to the third question? Whom should your children obey—the dad they *can* see or their Father in heaven whom they *can't* see? Aaron's two sons provide us with the answer to this third question.

Nadab and Abihu were career ministers—priests to the Jews. One day these two men did the unthinkable: they "offered unauthorized fire before the LORD." The exact nature of their violation remains unclear, but we do know that they were working "contrary to [God's] command." As professionals, they took the law into their own hands and dared God to call them on it.

Imagine Aaron's reaction as he saw fire pouring out over his sons, consuming them instantaneously. Except for the death of a spouse, there is no grief to compare with the death of a child—much less *two* children in the same incident. Aaron was reminded on that treacherous day that his sons were first accountable to God, then to him as their father.

Because of their blatant disobedience, God told Aaron that he could not mourn. Instead, he told Aaron to consecrate himself and to "teach the Israelites all the decrees" of the Lord (v. 11). "Fathers," Aaron may have said as he took up his charge, "you are only caretakers. Your children are not yours first. They belong to God. Teach your children well, and be sure they are listening to *God's* voice and living in obedience to him."

For a complete listing of Dads in the Bible, turn to page 1434.

Clean and Unclean Food

11 The LORD said to Moses and Aaron, ²"Say to the Israelites: 'Of all the animals that live on land, these are the ones you may eat: ³You may eat any animal that has a split hoof completely divided and that chews the cud.

⁴" 'There are some that only chew the cud or only have a split hoof, but you must not eat them. The camel, though it chews the cud, does not have a split hoof; it is ceremonially unclean for you. ⁵The coney,ᵃ though it chews the cud, does not have a split hoof; it is unclean for you. ⁶The rabbit, though it chews the cud, does not have a split hoof; it is unclean for you. ⁷And the pig, though it has a split hoof completely divided, does not chew the cud; it is unclean for you. ⁸You must not eat their meat or touch their carcasses; they are unclean for you.

⁹" 'Of all the creatures living in the water of the seas and the streams, you may eat any that have fins and scales. ¹⁰But all creatures in the seas or streams that do not have fins and scales—whether among all the swarming things or among all the other living creatures in the water—you are to detest. ¹¹And since you are to detest them, you must not eat their meat and you must detest their carcasses. ¹²Anything living in the water that does not have fins and scales is to be detestable to you.

¹³" 'These are the birds you are to detest and not eat because they are detestable: the eagle, the vulture, the black vulture, ¹⁴the red kite, any kind of black kite, ¹⁵any kind of raven, ¹⁶the horned owl, the screech owl, the gull, any kind of hawk, ¹⁷the little owl, the cormorant, the great owl, ¹⁸the white owl, the desert owl, the osprey, ¹⁹the stork, any kind of heron, the hoopoe and the bat.ᵇ

²⁰" 'All flying insects that walk on all fours are to be detestable to you. ²¹There are, however, some winged creatures that walk on all fours that you may eat: those that have jointed legs for hopping on the ground. ²²Of these you may eat any kind of locust, katydid, cricket or grasshopper. ²³But all other winged creatures that have four legs you are to detest.

²⁴" 'You will make yourselves unclean by these; whoever touches their carcasses will be unclean till evening. ²⁵Whoever picks up one of their carcasses must wash his clothes, and he will be unclean till evening.

²⁶" 'Every animal that has a split hoof not completely divided or that does not chew the cud is unclean for you; whoever touches the carcass of, any of them will be unclean. ²⁷Of all the animals that walk on all fours, those that walk on their paws are unclean for you; whoever touches their carcasses will be unclean till evening. ²⁸Anyone who picks up their carcasses must wash his clothes, and he will be unclean till evening. They are unclean for you.

²⁹" 'Of the animals that move about on the ground, these are unclean for you: the weasel, the rat, any kind of great lizard, ³⁰the gecko, the monitor lizard, the wall lizard, the skink and the chameleon. ³¹Of all those that move along the ground, these are unclean for you. Whoever touches them when they are dead will be unclean till evening. ³²When one of them dies and falls on something, that article, whatever its use, will be unclean, whether it is made of wood, cloth, hide or sackcloth. Put it in water; it will be unclean till evening, and then it will be clean. ³³If one of them falls into a clay pot, everything in it will be unclean, and you must break the pot. ³⁴Any food that could be eaten but has water on it from such a pot is unclean, and any liquid that could be drunk from it is unclean. ³⁵Anything that one of their carcasses falls on becomes unclean; an oven or cooking pot must be broken up. They are unclean, and you are to regard them as unclean. ³⁶A spring, however, or a cistern for collecting water remains clean, but anyone who touches one of these carcasses is unclean. ³⁷If a carcass falls on any seeds that are to be planted, they remain clean. ³⁸But if water has been put on the seed and a carcass falls on it, it is unclean for you.

³⁹" 'If an animal that you are allowed to eat dies, anyone who touches the carcass will be unclean till evening. ⁴⁰Anyone who eats some of the carcass must wash his clothes, and he will be unclean till evening. Anyone who picks up the carcass must wash his clothes, and he will be unclean till evening.

⁴¹" 'Every creature that moves about on the ground is detestable; it is not to be eaten. ⁴²You are not to eat any creature that moves about on the ground, whether it moves on its belly or walks on all fours

---

ᵃ5 That is, the hyrax or rock badger   ᵇ19 The precise identification of some of the birds, insects and animals in this chapter is uncertain.

or on many feet; it is detestable. **43**Do not defile yourselves by any of these creatures. Do not make yourselves unclean by means of them or be made unclean by them. **44**I am the LORD your God; consecrate yourselves and be holy, because I am holy. Do not make yourselves unclean by any creature that moves about on the ground. **45**I am the LORD who brought you up out of Egypt to be your God; therefore be holy, because I am holy.

46" 'These are the regulations concerning animals, birds, every living thing that moves in the water and every creature that moves about on the ground. **47**You must distinguish between the unclean and the clean, between living creatures that may be eaten and those that may not be eaten.' "

Purification After Childbirth

12 The LORD said to Moses, **2**"Say to the Israelites: 'A woman who becomes pregnant and gives birth to a son will be ceremonially unclean for seven days, just as she is unclean during her monthly period. **3**On the eighth day the boy is to be circumcised. **4**Then the woman must wait thirty-three days to be purified from her bleeding. She must not touch anything sacred or go to the sanctuary until the days of her purification are over. **5**If she gives birth to a daughter, for two weeks the woman will be unclean, as during her period. Then she must wait sixty-six days to be purified from her bleeding.

6" 'When the days of her purification for a son or daughter are over, she is to bring to the priest at the entrance to the Tent of Meeting a year-old lamb for a burnt offering and a young pigeon or a dove for a sin offering. **7**He shall offer them before the LORD to make atonement for her, and then she will be ceremonially clean from her flow of blood.

" 'These are the regulations for the woman who gives birth to a boy or a girl. **8**If she cannot afford a lamb, she is to bring two doves or two young pigeons, one for a burnt offering and the other for a sin offering. In this way the priest will make atonement for her, and she will be clean.' "

Regulations About Infectious Skin Diseases

13 The LORD said to Moses and Aaron, **2**"When anyone has a swelling or a rash or a bright spot on his skin that may become an infectious skin disease,*a* he

must be brought to Aaron the priest or to one of his sons*b* who is a priest. **3**The priest is to examine the sore on his skin, and if the hair in the sore has turned white and the sore appears to be more than skin deep,*c* it is an infectious skin disease. When the priest examines him, he shall pronounce him ceremonially unclean. **4**If the spot on his skin is white but does not appear to be more than skin deep and the hair in it has not turned white, the priest is to put the infected person in isolation for seven days. **5**On the seventh day the priest is to examine him, and if he sees that the sore is unchanged and has not spread in the skin, he is to keep him in isolation another seven days. **6**On the seventh day the priest is to examine him again, and if the sore has faded and has not spread in the skin, the priest shall pronounce him clean; it is only a rash. The man must wash his clothes, and he will be clean. **7**But if the rash does spread in his skin after he has shown himself to the priest to be pronounced clean, he must appear before the priest again. **8**The priest is to examine him, and if the rash has spread in the skin, he shall pronounce him unclean; it is an infectious disease.

9"When anyone has an infectious skin disease, he must be brought to the priest. **10**The priest is to examine him, and if there is a white swelling in the skin that has turned the hair white and if there is raw flesh in the swelling, **11**it is a chronic skin disease and the priest shall pronounce him unclean. He is not to put him in isolation, because he is already unclean.

12"If the disease breaks out all over his skin and, so far as the priest can see, it covers all the skin of the infected person from head to foot, **13**the priest is to examine him, and if the disease has covered his whole body, he shall pronounce that person clean. Since it has all turned white, he is clean. **14**But whenever raw flesh appears on him, he will be unclean. **15**When the priest sees the raw flesh, he shall pronounce him unclean. The raw flesh is unclean; he has an infectious disease. **16**Should the raw flesh change and turn white, he must go to the priest. **17**The priest is to examine him, and if the sores have turned white, the priest shall pronounce

*a*2 Traditionally *leprosy*; the Hebrew word was used for various diseases affecting the skin—not necessarily leprosy; also elsewhere in this chapter. *b*2 Or *descendants* *c*3 Or *be lower than the rest of the skin*; also elsewhere in this chapter the infected person clean; then he will be clean.

¹⁸"When someone has a boil on his skin and it heals, ¹⁹and in the place where the boil was, a white swelling or reddish-white spot appears, he must present himself to the priest. ²⁰The priest is to examine it, and if it appears to be more than skin deep and the hair in it has turned white, the priest shall pronounce him unclean. It is an infectious skin disease that has broken out where the boil was. ²¹But if, when the priest examines it, there is no white hair in it and it is not more than skin deep and has faded, then the priest is to put him in isolation for seven days. ²²If it is spreading in the skin, the priest shall pronounce him unclean; it is infectious. ²³But if the spot is unchanged and has not spread, it is only a scar from the boil, and the priest shall pronounce him clean.

²⁴"When someone has a burn on his skin and a reddish-white or white spot appears in the raw flesh of the burn, ²⁵the priest is to examine the spot, and if the hair in it has turned white, and it appears to be more than skin deep, it is an infectious disease that has broken out in the burn. The priest shall pronounce him unclean; it is an infectious skin disease. ²⁶But if the priest examines it and there is no white hair in the spot and if it is not more than skin deep and has faded, then the priest is to put him in isolation for seven days. ²⁷On the seventh day the priest is to examine him, and if it is spreading in the skin, the priest shall pronounce him unclean; it is an infectious skin disease. ²⁸If, however, the spot is unchanged and has not spread in the skin but has faded, it is a swelling from the burn, and the priest shall pronounce him clean; it is only a scar from the burn.

²⁹"If a man or woman has a sore on the head or on the chin, ³⁰the priest is to examine the sore, and if it appears to be more than skin deep and the hair in it is yellow and thin, the priest shall pronounce that person unclean; it is an itch, an infectious disease of the head or chin. ³¹But if, when the priest examines this kind of sore, it does not seem to be more than skin deep and there is no black hair in it, then the priest is to put the infected person in isolation for seven days. ³²On the seventh day the priest is to examine the sore, and if the itch has not spread and there is no yellow hair in it and it does not appear to be more than skin deep, ³³he

must be shaved except for the diseased area, and the priest is to keep him in isolation another seven days. ³⁴On the seventh day the priest is to examine the itch, and if it has not spread in the skin and appears to be no more than skin deep, the priest shall pronounce him clean. He must wash his clothes, and he will be clean. ³⁵But if the itch does spread in the skin after he is pronounced clean, ³⁶the priest is to examine him, and if the itch has spread in the skin, the priest does not need to look for yellow hair; the person is unclean. ³⁷If, however, in his judgment it is unchanged and black hair has grown in it, the itch is healed. He is clean, and the priest shall pronounce him clean.

³⁸"When a man or woman has white spots on the skin, ³⁹the priest is to examine them, and if the spots are dull white, it is a harmless rash that has broken out on the skin; that person is clean.

⁴⁰"When a man has lost his hair and is bald, he is clean. ⁴¹If he has lost his hair from the front of his scalp and has a bald forehead, he is clean. ⁴²But if he has a reddish-white sore on his bald head or forehead, it is an infectious disease breaking out on his head or forehead. ⁴³The priest is to examine him, and if the swollen sore on his head or forehead is reddish-white like an infectious skin disease, ⁴⁴the man is diseased and is unclean. The priest shall pronounce him unclean because of the sore on his head.

⁴⁵"The person with such an infectious disease must wear torn clothes, let his hair be unkempt,ᵃ cover the lower part of his face and cry out, 'Unclean! Unclean!' ⁴⁶As long as he has the infection he remains unclean. He must live alone; he must live outside the camp.

Regulations About Mildew

⁴⁷"If any clothing is contaminated with mildew—any woolen or linen clothing, ⁴⁸any woven or knitted material of linen or wool, any leather or anything made of leather— ⁴⁹and if the contamination in the clothing, or leather, or woven or knitted material, or any leather article, is greenish or reddish, it is a spreading mildew and must be shown to the priest. ⁵⁰The priest is to examine the mildew and isolate the affected article for seven days. ⁵¹On the seventh day he is to examine it, and if the mildew has spread in the cloth-

ᵃ45 Or *clothes, uncover his head*

ing, or the woven or knitted material, or the leather, whatever its use, it is a destructive mildew; the article is unclean. ⁵²He must burn up the clothing, or the woven or knitted material of wool or linen, or any leather article that has the contamination in it, because the mildew is destructive; the article must be burned up.

⁵³"But if, when the priest examines it, the mildew has not spread in the clothing, or the woven or knitted material, or the leather article, ⁵⁴he shall order that the contaminated article be washed. Then he is to isolate it for another seven days. ⁵⁵After the affected article has been washed, the priest is to examine it, and if the mildew has not changed its appearance, even though it has not spread, it is unclean. Burn it with fire, whether the mildew has affected one side or the other. ⁵⁶If, when the priest examines it, the mildew has faded after the article has been washed, he is to tear the contaminated part out of the clothing, or the leather, or the woven or knitted material. ⁵⁷But if it reappears in the clothing, or in the woven or knitted material, or in the leather article, it is spreading, and whatever has the mildew must be burned with fire. ⁵⁸The clothing, or the woven or knitted material, or any leather article that has been washed and is rid of the mildew, must be washed again, and it will be clean."

⁵⁹These are the regulations concerning contamination by mildew in woolen or linen clothing, woven or knitted material, or any leather article, for pronouncing them clean or unclean.

Cleansing From Infectious Skin Diseases

14 The LORD said to Moses, ²"These are the regulations for the diseased person at the time of his ceremonial cleansing, when he is brought to the priest: ³The priest is to go outside the camp and examine him. If the person has been healed of his infectious skin disease,ᵃ ⁴the priest shall order that two live clean birds and some cedar wood, scarlet yarn and hyssop be brought for the one to be cleansed. ⁵Then the priest shall order that one of the birds be killed over fresh water in a clay pot. ⁶He is then to take the live bird and dip it, together with the cedar wood, the scarlet yarn and the hyssop, into the blood of the bird that was killed over the fresh water. ⁷Seven times he shall sprinkle the one to be cleansed of the in-

fectious disease and pronounce him clean. Then he is to release the live bird in the open fields.

⁸"The person to be cleansed must wash his clothes, shave off all his hair and bathe with water; then he will be ceremonially clean. After this he may come into the camp, but he must stay outside his tent for seven days. ⁹On the seventh day he must shave off all his hair; he must shave his head, his beard, his eyebrows and the rest of his hair. He must wash his clothes and bathe himself with water, and he will be clean.

¹⁰"On the eighth day he must bring two male lambs and one ewe lamb a year old, each without defect, along with three-tenths of an ephahᵇ of fine flour mixed with oil for a grain offering, and one logᶜ of oil. ¹¹The priest who pronounces him clean shall present both the one to be cleansed and his offerings before the LORD at the entrance to the Tent of Meeting.

¹²"Then the priest is to take one of the male lambs and offer it as a guilt offering, along with the log of oil; he shall wave them before the LORD as a wave offering. ¹³He is to slaughter the lamb in the holy place where the sin offering and the burnt offering are slaughtered. Like the sin offering, the guilt offering belongs to the priest; it is most holy. ¹⁴The priest is to take some of the blood of the guilt offering and put it on the lobe of the right ear of the one to be cleansed, on the thumb of his right hand and on the big toe of his right foot. ¹⁵The priest shall then take some of the log of oil, pour it in the palm of his own left hand, ¹⁶dip his right forefinger into the oil in his palm, and with his finger sprinkle some of it before the LORD seven times. ¹⁷The priest is to put some of the oil remaining in his palm on the lobe of the right ear of the one to be cleansed, on the thumb of his right hand and on the big toe of his right foot, on top of the blood of the guilt offering. ¹⁸The rest of the oil in his palm the priest shall put on the head of the one to be cleansed and make atonement for him before the LORD.

¹⁹"Then the priest is to sacrifice the sin offering and make atonement for the one to be cleansed from his uncleanness.

ᵃ3 Traditionally *leprosy*; the Hebrew word was used for various diseases affecting the skin—not necessarily leprosy; also elsewhere in this chapter. ᵇ10 That is, probably about 6 quarts (about 6.5 liters) ᶜ10 That is, probably about 2/3 pint (about 0.3 liter); also in verses 12, 15, 21 and 24

After that, the priest shall slaughter the burnt offering **20**and offer it on the altar, together with the grain offering, and make atonement for him, and he will be clean.

21"If, however, he is poor and cannot afford these, he must take one male lamb as a guilt offering to be waved to make atonement for him, together with a tenth of an ephah*a* of fine flour mixed with oil for a grain offering, a log of oil, **22**and two doves or two young pigeons, which he can afford, one for a sin offering and the other for a burnt offering.

23"On the eighth day he must bring them for his cleansing to the priest at the entrance to the Tent of Meeting, before the LORD. **24**The priest is to take the lamb for the guilt offering, together with the log of oil, and wave them before the LORD as a wave offering. **25**He shall slaughter the lamb for the guilt offering and take some of its blood and put it on the lobe of the right ear of the one to be cleansed, on the thumb of his right hand and on the big toe of his right foot. **26**The priest is to pour some of the oil into the palm of his own left hand, **27**and with his right forefinger sprinkle some of the oil from his palm seven times before the LORD. **28**Some of the oil in his palm he is to put on the same places he put the blood of the guilt offering—on the lobe of the right ear of the one to be cleansed, on the thumb of his right hand and on the big toe of his right foot. **29**The rest of the oil in his palm the priest shall put on the head of the one to be cleansed, to make atonement for him before the LORD. **30**Then he shall sacrifice the doves or the young pigeons, which the person can afford, **31**one*b* as a sin offering and the other as a burnt offering, together with the grain offering. In this way the priest will make atonement before the LORD on behalf of the one to be cleansed."

32These are the regulations for anyone who has an infectious skin disease and who cannot afford the regular offerings for his cleansing.

Cleansing From Mildew

33The LORD said to Moses and Aaron, **34**"When you enter the land of Canaan, which I am giving you as your possession, and I put a spreading mildew in a house in that land, **35**the owner of the house must go and tell the priest, 'I have seen something that looks like mildew in my house.' **36**The priest is to order the house

to be emptied before he goes in to examine the mildew, so that nothing in the house will be pronounced unclean. After this the priest is to go in and inspect the house. **37**He is to examine the mildew on the walls, and if it has greenish or reddish depressions that appear to be deeper than the surface of the wall, **38**the priest shall go out the doorway of the house and close it up for seven days. **39**On the seventh day the priest shall return to inspect the house. If the mildew has spread on the walls, **40**he is to order that the contaminated stones be torn out and thrown into an unclean place outside the town. **41**He must have all the inside walls of the house scraped and the material that is scraped off dumped into an unclean place outside the town. **42**Then they are to take other stones to replace these and take new clay and plaster the house.

43"If the mildew reappears in the house after the stones have been torn out and the house scraped and plastered, **44**the priest is to go and examine it and, if the mildew has spread in the house, it is a destructive mildew; the house is unclean. **45**It must be torn down—its stones, timbers and all the plaster—and taken out of the town to an unclean place.

46"Anyone who goes into the house while it is closed up will be unclean till evening. **47**Anyone who sleeps or eats in the house must wash his clothes.

48"But if the priest comes to examine it and the mildew has not spread after the house has been plastered, he shall pronounce the house clean, because the mildew is gone. **49**To purify the house he is to take two birds and some cedar wood, scarlet yarn and hyssop. **50**He shall kill one of the birds over fresh water in a clay pot. **51**Then he is to take the cedar wood, the hyssop, the scarlet yarn and the live bird, dip them into the blood of the dead bird and the fresh water, and sprinkle the house seven times. **52**He shall purify the house with the bird's blood, the fresh water, the live bird, the cedar wood, the hyssop and the scarlet yarn. **53**Then he is to release the live bird in the open fields outside the town. In this way he will make atonement for the house, and it will be clean."

54These are the regulations for any infectious skin disease, for an itch, **55**for mil-

a21 That is, probably about 2 quarts (about 2 liters) b31 Septuagint and Syriac; Hebrew 31such as the person can afford, one

dew in clothing or in a house, **56**and for a swelling, a rash or a bright spot, **57**to determine when something is clean or unclean.

These are the regulations for infectious skin diseases and mildew.

Discharges Causing Uncleanness

15 The LORD said to Moses and Aaron, **2**"Speak to the Israelites and say to them: 'When any man has a bodily discharge, the discharge is unclean. **3**Whether it continues flowing from his body or is blocked, it will make him unclean. This is how his discharge will bring about uncleanness:

4" 'Any bed the man with a discharge lies on will be unclean, and anything he sits on will be unclean. **5**Anyone who touches his bed must wash his clothes and bathe with water, and he will be unclean till evening. **6**Whoever sits on anything that the man with a discharge sat on must wash his clothes and bathe with water, and he will be unclean till evening.

7" 'Whoever touches the man who has a discharge must wash his clothes and bathe with water, and he will be unclean till evening.

8" 'If the man with the discharge spits on someone who is clean, that person must wash his clothes and bathe with water, and he will be unclean till evening.

9" 'Everything the man sits on when riding will be unclean, **10**and whoever touches any of the things that were under him will be unclean till evening; whoever picks up those things must wash his clothes and bathe with water, and he will be unclean till evening.

11" 'Anyone the man with a discharge touches without rinsing his hands with water must wash his clothes and bathe with water, and he will be unclean till evening.

12" 'A clay pot that the man touches must be broken, and any wooden article is to be rinsed with water.

13" 'When a man is cleansed from his discharge, he is to count off seven days for his ceremonial cleansing; he must wash his clothes and bathe himself with fresh water, and he will be clean. **14**On the eighth day he must take two doves or two young pigeons and come before the LORD to the entrance to the Tent of Meeting and give them to the priest. **15**The priest is to sacrifice them, the one for a sin offering and the other for a burnt offering. In this

way he will make atonement before the LORD for the man because of his discharge.

16" 'When a man has an emission of semen, he must bathe his whole body with water, and he will be unclean till evening. **17**Any clothing or leather that has semen on it must be washed with water, and it will be unclean till evening. **18**When a man lies with a woman and there is an emission of semen, both must bathe with water, and they will be unclean till evening.

19" 'When a woman has her regular flow of blood, the impurity of her monthly period will last seven days, and anyone who touches her will be unclean till evening.

20" 'Anything she lies on during her period will be unclean, and anything she sits on will be unclean. **21**Whoever touches her bed must wash his clothes and bathe with water, and he will be unclean till evening. **22**Whoever touches anything she sits on must wash his clothes and bathe with water, and he will be unclean till evening. **23**Whether it is the bed or anything she was sitting on, when anyone touches it, he will be unclean till evening.

24" 'If a man lies with her and her monthly flow touches him, he will be unclean for seven days; any bed he lies on will be unclean.

25" 'When a woman has a discharge of blood for many days at a time other than her monthly period or has a discharge that continues beyond her period, she will be unclean as long as she has the discharge, just as in the days of her period. **26**Any bed she lies on while her discharge continues will be unclean, as is her bed during her monthly period, and anything she sits on will be unclean, as during her period. **27**Whoever touches them will be unclean; he must wash his clothes and bathe with water, and he will be unclean till evening.

28" 'When she is cleansed from her discharge, she must count off seven days, and after that she will be ceremonially clean. **29**On the eighth day she must take two doves or two young pigeons and bring them to the priest at the entrance to the Tent of Meeting. **30**The priest is to sacrifice one for a sin offering and the other for a burnt offering. In this way he will make atonement for her before the LORD for the uncleanness of her discharge.

31" 'You must keep the Israelites separate from things that make them unclean, so they will not die in their uncleanness for defiling my dwelling place,[a] which is among them.' "

³²These are the regulations for a man with a discharge, for anyone made unclean by an emission of semen, ³³for a woman in her monthly period, for a man or a woman with a discharge, and for a man who lies with a woman who is ceremonially unclean.

The Day of Atonement

16 The LORD spoke to Moses after the death of the two sons of Aaron who died when they approached the LORD. ²The LORD said to Moses: "Tell your brother Aaron not to come whenever he chooses into the Most Holy Place behind the curtain in front of the atonement cover on the ark, or else he will die, because I appear in the cloud over the atonement cover.

³"This is how Aaron is to enter the sanctuary area: with a young bull for a sin offering and a ram for a burnt offering. ⁴He is to put on the sacred linen tunic, with linen undergarments next to his body; he is to tie the linen sash around him and put on the linen turban. These are sacred garments; so he must bathe himself with water before he puts them on. ⁵From the Israelite community he is to take two male goats for a sin offering and a ram for a burnt offering.

⁶"Aaron is to offer the bull for his own sin offering to make atonement for himself and his household. ⁷Then he is to take the two goats and present them before the LORD at the entrance to the Tent of Meeting. ⁸He is to cast lots for the two goats—one lot for the LORD and the other for the scapegoat.[b] ⁹Aaron shall bring the goat whose lot falls to the LORD and sacrifice it for a sin offering. ¹⁰But the goat chosen by lot as the scapegoat shall be presented alive before the LORD to be used for making atonement by sending it into the desert as a scapegoat.

¹¹"Aaron shall bring the bull for his own sin offering to make atonement for himself and his household, and he is to slaughter the bull for his own sin offering. ¹²He is to take a censer full of burning coals from the altar before the LORD and two handfuls of finely ground fragrant incense and take them behind the curtain. ¹³He is to put the incense on the fire before the LORD, and the smoke of the incense will conceal the atonement cover above the Testimony, so that he will not

die. ¹⁴He is to take some of the bull's blood and with his finger sprinkle it on the front of the atonement cover; then he shall sprinkle some of it with his finger seven times before the atonement cover.

¹⁵"He shall then slaughter the goat for the sin offering for the people and take its blood behind the curtain and do with it as he did with the bull's blood: He shall sprinkle it on the atonement cover and in front of it. ¹⁶In this way he will make atonement for the Most Holy Place because of the uncleanness and rebellion of the Israelites, whatever their sins have been. He is to do the same for the Tent of Meeting, which is among them in the midst of their uncleanness. ¹⁷No one is to be in the Tent of Meeting from the time Aaron goes in to make atonement in the Most Holy Place until he comes out, having made atonement for himself, his household and the whole community of Israel.

¹⁸"Then he shall come out to the altar that is before the LORD and make atonement for it. He shall take some of the bull's blood and some of the goat's blood and put it on all the horns of the altar. ¹⁹He shall sprinkle some of the blood on it with his finger seven times to cleanse it and to consecrate it from the uncleanness of the Israelites.

²⁰"When Aaron has finished making atonement for the Most Holy Place, the Tent of Meeting and the altar, he shall bring forward the live goat. ²¹He is to lay both hands on the head of the live goat and confess over it all the wickedness and rebellion of the Israelites—all their sins—and put them on the goat's head. He shall send the goat away into the desert in the care of a man appointed for the task. ²²The goat will carry on itself all their sins to a solitary place; and the man shall release it in the desert.

²³"Then Aaron is to go into the Tent of Meeting and take off the linen garments he put on before he entered the Most Holy Place, and he is to leave them there. ²⁴He shall bathe himself with water in a holy place and put on his regular garments. Then he shall come out and sacrifice the burnt offering for himself and the burnt offering for the people, to make atonement for himself and for the people. ²⁵He shall also burn the fat of the sin offering on the altar.

ᵃ31 Or *my tabernacle*   ᵇ8 That is, the goat of removal; Hebrew *azazel*; also in verses 10 and 26

²⁶"The man who releases the goat as a scapegoat must wash his clothes and bathe himself with water; afterward he may come into the camp. ²⁷The bull and the goat for the sin offerings, whose blood was brought into the Most Holy Place to make atonement, must be taken outside the camp; their hides, flesh and offal are to be burned up. ²⁸The man who burns them must wash his clothes and bathe himself with water; afterward he may come into the camp.

²⁹"This is to be a lasting ordinance for you: On the tenth day of the seventh month you must deny yourselves[a] and not do any work—whether native-born or an alien living among you— ³⁰because on this day atonement will be made for you, to cleanse you. Then, before the LORD, you will be clean from all your sins. ³¹It is a sabbath of rest, and you must deny yourselves; it is a lasting ordinance. ³²The priest who is anointed and ordained to succeed his father as high priest is to make atonement. He is to put on the sacred linen garments ³³and make atonement for the Most Holy Place, for the Tent of Meeting and the altar, and for the priests and all the people of the community.

³⁴"This is to be a lasting ordinance for you: Atonement is to be made once a year for all the sins of the Israelites."

And it was done, as the LORD commanded Moses.

Eating Blood Forbidden

17 The LORD said to Moses, ²"Speak to Aaron and his sons and to all the Israelites and say to them: 'This is what the LORD has commanded: ³Any Israelite who sacrifices an ox,[b] a lamb or a goat in the camp or outside of it ⁴instead of bringing it to the entrance to the Tent of Meeting to present it as an offering to the LORD in front of the tabernacle of the LORD—that man shall be considered guilty of bloodshed; he has shed blood and must be cut off from his people. ⁵This is so the Israelites will bring to the LORD the sacrifices they are now making in the open fields. They must bring them to the priest, that is, to the LORD, at the entrance to the Tent of Meeting and sacrifice them as fellowship offerings.[c] ⁶The priest is to sprinkle the blood against the altar of the LORD at the entrance to the Tent of Meeting and burn the fat as an aroma pleasing to the LORD. ⁷They must no longer offer any of their sacrifices to the goat idols[d] to whom they prostitute themselves. This is to be a lasting ordinance for them and for the generations to come.'

⁸"Say to them: 'Any Israelite or any alien living among them who offers a burnt offering or sacrifice ⁹and does not bring it to the entrance to the Tent of Meeting to sacrifice it to the LORD—that man must be cut off from his people.

¹⁰"'Any Israelite or any alien living among them who eats any blood—I will set my face against that person who eats blood and will cut him off from his people. ¹¹For the life of a creature is in the blood, and I have given it to you to make atonement for yourselves on the altar; it is the blood that makes atonement for one's life. ¹²Therefore I say to the Israelites, "None of you may eat blood, nor may an alien living among you eat blood."

¹³"'Any Israelite or any alien living among you who hunts any animal or bird that may be eaten must drain out the blood and cover it with earth, ¹⁴because the life of every creature is its blood. That is why I have said to the Israelites, "You must not eat the blood of any creature, because the life of every creature is its blood; anyone who eats it must be cut off."

¹⁵"'Anyone, whether native-born or alien, who eats anything found dead or torn by wild animals must wash his clothes and bathe with water, and he will be ceremonially unclean till evening; then he will be clean. ¹⁶But if he does not wash his clothes and bathe himself, he will be held responsible.' "

Unlawful Sexual Relations

18 The LORD said to Moses, ²"Speak to the Israelites and say to them: 'I am the LORD your God. ³You must not do as they do in Egypt, where you used to live, and you must not do as they do in the land of Canaan, where I am bringing you. Do not follow their practices. ⁴You must obey my laws and be careful to follow my decrees. I am the LORD your God. ⁵Keep my decrees and laws, for the man who obeys them will live by them. I am the LORD.

⁶"'No one is to approach any close relative to have sexual relations. I am the LORD.

---

[a]29 Or *must fast*; also in verse 31   [b]3 The Hebrew word can include both male and female.
[c]5 Traditionally *peace offerings*   [d]7 Or *demons*

⁷" 'Do not dishonor your father by having sexual relations with your mother. She is your mother; do not have relations with her.

⁸" 'Do not have sexual relations with your father's wife; that would dishonor your father.

⁹" 'Do not have sexual relations with your sister, either your father's daughter or your mother's daughter, whether she was born in the same home or elsewhere.

¹⁰" 'Do not have sexual relations with your son's daughter or your daughter's daughter; that would dishonor you.

¹¹" 'Do not have sexual relations with the daughter of your father's wife, born to your father; she is your sister.

¹²" 'Do not have sexual relations with your father's sister; she is your father's close relative.

¹³" 'Do not have sexual relations with your mother's sister, because she is your mother's close relative.

¹⁴" 'Do not dishonor your father's brother by approaching his wife to have sexual relations; she is your aunt.

¹⁵" 'Do not have sexual relations with your daughter-in-law. She is your son's wife; do not have relations with her.

¹⁶" 'Do not have sexual relations with your brother's wife; that would dishonor your brother.

¹⁷" 'Do not have sexual relations with both a woman and her daughter. Do not have sexual relations with either her son's daughter or her daughter's daughter; they are her close relatives. That is wickedness.

¹⁸" 'Do not take your wife's sister as a rival wife and have sexual relations with her while your wife is living.

¹⁹" 'Do not approach a woman to have sexual relations during the uncleanness of her monthly period.

²⁰" 'Do not have sexual relations with your neighbor's wife and defile yourself with her.

²¹" 'Do not give any of your children to be sacrificed[a] to Molech, for you must not profane the name of your God. I am the LORD.

²²" 'Do not lie with a man as one lies with a woman; that is detestable.

²³" 'Do not have sexual relations with an animal and defile yourself with it. A woman must not present herself to an animal to have sexual relations with it; that is a perversion.

²⁴" 'Do not defile yourselves in any of these ways, because this is how the nations that I am going to drive out before you became defiled. ²⁵Even the land was defiled; so I punished it for its sin, and the land vomited out its inhabitants. ²⁶But you must keep my decrees and my laws. The native-born and the aliens living among you must not do any of these detestable things, ²⁷for all these things were done by the people who lived in the land before you, and the land became defiled. ²⁸And if you defile the land, it will vomit you out as it vomited out the nations that were before you.

²⁹" 'Everyone who does any of these detestable things—such persons must be cut off from their people. ³⁰Keep my requirements and do not follow any of the detestable customs that were practiced before you came and do not defile yourselves with them. I am the LORD your God.' "

Various Laws

19 The LORD said to Moses, ²"Speak to the entire assembly of Israel and say to them: 'Be holy because I, the LORD your God, am holy.

³" 'Each of you must respect his mother and father, and you must observe my Sabbaths. I am the LORD your God.

⁴" 'Do not turn to idols or make gods of cast metal for yourselves. I am the LORD your God.

⁵" 'When you sacrifice a fellowship offering[b] to the LORD, sacrifice it in such a way that it will be accepted on your behalf. ⁶It shall be eaten on the day you sacrifice it or on the next day; anything left over until the third day must be burned up. ⁷If any of it is eaten on the third day, it is impure and will not be accepted. ⁸Whoever eats it will be held responsible because he has desecrated what is holy to the LORD; that person must be cut off from his people.

⁹" 'When you reap the harvest of your land, do not reap to the very edges of your field or gather the gleanings of your harvest. ¹⁰Do not go over your vineyard a second time or pick up the grapes that have fallen. Leave them for the poor and the alien. I am the LORD your God.

¹¹" 'Do not steal.

" 'Do not lie.

" 'Do not deceive one another.

¹²" 'Do not swear falsely by my name and so profane the name of your God. I am the LORD.

---

[a]21 Or *to be passed through the fire*
[b]5 Traditionally *peace offering*

¹³" 'Do not defraud your neighbor or rob him.

" 'Do not hold back the wages of a hired man overnight.

¹⁴" 'Do not curse the deaf or put a stumbling block in front of the blind, but fear your God. I am the LORD.

¹⁵" 'Do not pervert justice; do not show partiality to the poor or favoritism to the great, but judge your neighbor fairly.

¹⁶" 'Do not go about spreading slander among your people.

" 'Do not do anything that endangers your neighbor's life. I am the LORD.

¹⁷" 'Do not hate your brother in your heart. Rebuke your neighbor frankly so you will not share in his guilt.

¹⁸" 'Do not seek revenge or bear a grudge against one of your people, but love your neighbor as yourself. I am the LORD.

¹⁹" 'Keep my decrees.

" 'Do not mate different kinds of animals.

" 'Do not plant your field with two kinds of seed.

" 'Do not wear clothing woven of two kinds of material.

²⁰" 'If a man sleeps with a woman who is a slave girl promised to another man but who has not been ransomed or given her freedom, there must be due punishment. Yet they are not to be put to death, because she had not been freed. ²¹The man, however, must bring a ram to the entrance to the Tent of Meeting for a guilt offering to the LORD. ²²With the ram of the guilt offering the priest is to make atonement for him before the LORD for the sin he has committed, and his sin will be forgiven.

²³" 'When you enter the land and plant any kind of fruit tree, regard its fruit as forbidden.ᵃ For three years you are to consider it forbiddenᵃ; it must not be eaten. ²⁴In the fourth year all its fruit will be holy, an offering of praise to the LORD. ²⁵But in the fifth year you may eat its fruit. In this way your harvest will be increased. I am the LORD your God.

²⁶" 'Do not eat any meat with the blood still in it.

" 'Do not practice divination or sorcery.

²⁷" 'Do not cut the hair at the sides of your head or clip off the edges of your beard.

²⁸" 'Do not cut your bodies for the dead or put tattoo marks on yourselves. I am the LORD.

²⁹" 'Do not degrade your daughter by making her a prostitute, or the land will turn to prostitution and be filled with wickedness.

³⁰" 'Observe my Sabbaths and have reverence for my sanctuary. I am the LORD.

³¹" 'Do not turn to mediums or seek out spiritists, for you will be defiled by them. I am the LORD your God.

³²" 'Rise in the presence of the aged, show respect for the elderly and revere your God. I am the LORD.

³³" 'When an alien lives with you in your land, do not mistreat him. ³⁴The alien living with you must be treated as one of your native-born. Love him as yourself, for you were aliens in Egypt. I am the LORD your God.

³⁵" 'Do not use dishonest standards when measuring length, weight or quantity. ³⁶Use honest scales and honest weights, an honest ephahᵇ and an honest hin.ᶜ I am the LORD your God, who brought you out of Egypt.

³⁷" 'Keep all my decrees and all my laws and follow them. I am the LORD.' "

Punishments for Sin

20 The LORD said to Moses, ²"Say to the Israelites: 'Any Israelite or any alien living in Israel who givesᵈ any of his children to Molech must be put to death. The people of the community are to stone him. ³I will set my face against that man and I will cut him off from his people; for by giving his children to Molech, he has defiled my sanctuary and profaned my holy name. ⁴If the people of the community close their eyes when that man gives one of his children to Molech and they fail to put him to death, ⁵I will set my face against that man and his family and will cut off from their people both him and all who follow him in prostituting themselves to Molech.

⁶" 'I will set my face against the person who turns to mediums and spiritists to prostitute himself by following them, and I will cut him off from his people.

⁷" 'Consecrate yourselves and be holy, because I am the LORD your God. ⁸Keep my decrees and follow them. I am the LORD, who makes you holy.ᵉ

⁹" 'If anyone curses his father or mother, he must be put to death. He has cursed his father or his mother, and his blood will be on his own head.

ᵃ23 Hebrew *uncircumcised*   ᵇ36 An ephah was a dry measure.   ᶜ36 A hin was a liquid measure.
ᵈ2 Or *sacrifices*; also in verses 3 and 4   ᵉ8 Or *who sanctifies you*; or *who sets you apart as holy*

¹⁰" 'If a man commits adultery with another man's wife—with the wife of his neighbor—both the adulterer and the adulteress must be put to death.

¹¹" 'If a man sleeps with his father's wife, he has dishonored his father. Both the man and the woman must be put to death; their blood will be on their own heads.

¹²" 'If a man sleeps with his daughter-in-law, both of them must be put to death. What they have done is a perversion; their blood will be on their own heads.

¹³" 'If a man lies with a man as one lies with a woman, both of them have done what is detestable. They must be put to death; their blood will be on their own heads.

¹⁴" 'If a man marries both a woman and her mother, it is wicked. Both he and they must be burned in the fire, so that no wickedness will be among you.

¹⁵" 'If a man has sexual relations with an animal, he must be put to death, and you must kill the animal.

¹⁶" 'If a woman approaches an animal to have sexual relations with it, kill both the woman and the animal. They must be put to death; their blood will be on their own heads.

¹⁷" 'If a man marries his sister, the daughter of either his father or his mother, and they have sexual relations, it is a disgrace. They must be cut off before the eyes of their people. He has dishonored his sister and will be held responsible.

¹⁸" 'If a man lies with a woman during her monthly period and has sexual relations with her, he has exposed the source of her flow, and she has also uncovered it. Both of them must be cut off from their people.

¹⁹" 'Do not have sexual relations with the sister of either your mother or your father, for that would dishonor a close relative; both of you would be held responsible.

²⁰" 'If a man sleeps with his aunt, he has dishonored his uncle. They will be held responsible; they will die childless.

²¹" 'If a man marries his brother's wife, it is an act of impurity; he has dishonored his brother. They will be childless.

²²" 'Keep all my decrees and laws and follow them, so that the land where I am bringing you to live may not vomit you out. ²³You must not live according to the customs of the nations I am going to drive out before you. Because they did all these things, I abhorred them. ²⁴But I said to

you, "You will possess their land; I will give it to you as an inheritance, a land flowing with milk and honey." I am the LORD your God, who has set you apart from the nations.

²⁵" 'You must therefore make a distinction between clean and unclean animals and between unclean and clean birds. Do not defile yourselves by any animal or bird or anything that moves along the ground—those which I have set apart as unclean for you. ²⁶You are to be holy to me^a because I, the LORD, am holy, and I have set you apart from the nations to be my own.

²⁷" 'A man or woman who is a medium or spiritist among you must be put to death. You are to stone them; their blood will be on their own heads.' "

Rules for Priests

21 The LORD said to Moses, "Speak to the priests, the sons of Aaron, and say to them: 'A priest must not make himself ceremonially unclean for any of his people who die, ²except for a close relative, such as his mother or father, his son or daughter, his brother, ³or an unmarried sister who is dependent on him since she has no husband—for her he may make himself unclean. ⁴He must not make himself unclean for people related to him by marriage,^b and so defile himself.

⁵" 'Priests must not shave their heads or shave off the edges of their beards or cut their bodies. ⁶They must be holy to their God and must not profane the name of their God. Because they present the offerings made to the LORD by fire, the food of their God, they are to be holy.

⁷" 'They must not marry women defiled by prostitution or divorced from their husbands, because priests are holy to their God. ⁸Regard them as holy, because they offer up the food of your God. Consider them holy, because I the LORD am holy—I who make you holy.^c

⁹" 'If a priest's daughter defiles herself by becoming a prostitute, she disgraces her father; she must be burned in the fire.

¹⁰" 'The high priest, the one among his brothers who has had the anointing oil poured on his head and who has been ordained to wear the priestly garments, must not let his hair become unkempt^d or tear his clothes. ¹¹He must not enter a

---

^a26 Or *be my holy ones*   ^b4 Or *unclean as a leader among his people*   ^c8 Or *who sanctify you*; or *who set you apart as holy*   ^d10 Or *not uncover his head*

place where there is a dead body. He must not make himself unclean, even for his father or mother, ¹²nor leave the sanctuary of his God or desecrate it, because he has been dedicated by the anointing oil of his God. I am the LORD.

¹³" 'The woman he marries must be a virgin. ¹⁴He must not marry a widow, a divorced woman, or a woman defiled by prostitution, but only a virgin from his own people, ¹⁵so he will not defile his offspring among his people. I am the LORD, who makes him holy.ᵃ' "

¹⁶The LORD said to Moses, ¹⁷"Say to Aaron: 'For the generations to come none of your descendants who has a defect may come near to offer the food of his God. ¹⁸No man who has any defect may come near: no man who is blind or lame, disfigured or deformed; ¹⁹no man with a crippled foot or hand, ²⁰or who is hunchbacked or dwarfed, or who has any eye defect, or who has festering or running sores or damaged testicles. ²¹No descendant of Aaron the priest who has any defect is to come near to present the offerings made to the LORD by fire. He has a defect; he must not come near to offer the food of his God. ²²He may eat the most holy food of his God, as well as the holy food; ²³yet because of his defect, he must not go near the curtain or approach the altar, and so desecrate my sanctuary. I am the LORD, who makes them holy.ᵇ' "

²⁴So Moses told this to Aaron and his sons and to all the Israelites.

22 The LORD said to Moses, ²"Tell Aaron and his sons to treat with respect the sacred offerings the Israelites consecrate to me, so they will not profane my holy name. I am the LORD.

³"Say to them: 'For the generations to come, if any of your descendants is ceremonially unclean and yet comes near the sacred offerings that the Israelites consecrate to the LORD, that person must be cut off from my presence. I am the LORD.

⁴" 'If a descendant of Aaron has an infectious skin diseaseᶜ or a bodily discharge, he may not eat the sacred offerings until he is cleansed. He will also be unclean if he touches something defiled by a corpse or by anyone who has an emission of semen, ⁵or if he touches any crawling thing that makes him unclean, or any person who makes him unclean, whatever the uncleanness may be. ⁶The one who touches any such thing will be unclean till evening. He must not eat any

of the sacred offerings unless he has bathed himself with water. ⁷When the sun goes down, he will be clean, and after that he may eat the sacred offerings, for they are his food. ⁸He must not eat anything found dead or torn by wild animals, and so become unclean through it. I am the LORD.

⁹" 'The priests are to keep my requirements so that they do not become guilty and die for treating them with contempt. I am the LORD, who makes them holy.ᵈ

¹⁰" 'No one outside a priest's family may eat the sacred offering, nor may the guest of a priest or his hired worker eat it. ¹¹But if a priest buys a slave with money, or if a slave is born in his household, that slave may eat his food. ¹²If a priest's daughter marries anyone other than a priest, she may not eat any of the sacred contributions. ¹³But if a priest's daughter becomes a widow or is divorced, yet has no children, and she returns to live in her father's house as in her youth, she may eat of her father's food. No unauthorized person, however, may eat any of it.

¹⁴" 'If anyone eats a sacred offering by mistake, he must make restitution to the priest for the offering and add a fifth of the value to it. ¹⁵The priests must not desecrate the sacred offerings the Israelites present to the LORD ¹⁶by allowing them to eat the sacred offerings and so bring upon them guilt requiring payment. I am the LORD, who makes them holy.' "

Unacceptable Sacrifices

¹⁷The LORD said to Moses, ¹⁸"Speak to Aaron and his sons and to all the Israelites and say to them: 'If any of you—either an Israelite or an alien living in Israel—presents a gift for a burnt offering to the LORD, either to fulfill a vow or as a freewill offering, ¹⁹you must present a male without defect from the cattle, sheep or goats in order that it may be accepted on your behalf. ²⁰Do not bring anything with a defect, because it will not be accepted on your behalf. ²¹When anyone brings from the herd or flock a fellowship offeringᵉ to the LORD to fulfill a special vow or as a freewill offering, it must be without defect

---

ᵃ15 Or *who sanctifies him*; or *who sets him apart as holy*   ᵇ23 Or *who sanctifies them*; or *who sets them apart as holy*   ᶜ4 Traditionally *leprosy*; the Hebrew word was used for various diseases affecting the skin—not necessarily leprosy.   ᵈ9 Or *who sanctifies them*; or *who sets them apart as holy*; also in verse 16   ᵉ21 Traditionally *peace offering*

or blemish to be acceptable. ²²Do not offer to the LORD the blind, the injured or the maimed, or anything with warts or festering or running sores. Do not place any of these on the altar as an offering made to the LORD by fire. ²³You may, however, present as a freewill offering an ox*a* or a sheep that is deformed or stunted, but it will not be accepted in fulfillment of a vow. ²⁴You must not offer to the LORD an animal whose testicles are bruised, crushed, torn or cut. You must not do this in your own land, ²⁵and you must not accept such animals from the hand of a foreigner and offer them as the food of your God. They will not be accepted on your behalf, because they are deformed and have defects.' "

²⁶The LORD said to Moses, ²⁷"When a calf, a lamb or a goat is born, it is to remain with its mother for seven days. From the eighth day on, it will be acceptable as an offering made to the LORD by fire. ²⁸Do not slaughter a cow or a sheep and its young on the same day.

²⁹"When you sacrifice a thank offering to the LORD, sacrifice it in such a way that it will be accepted on your behalf. ³⁰It must be eaten that same day; leave none of it till morning. I am the LORD.

³¹"Keep my commands and follow them. I am the LORD. ³²Do not profane my holy name. I must be acknowledged as holy by the Israelites. I am the LORD, who makes*b* you holy*c* ³³and who brought you out of Egypt to be your God. I am the LORD."

23 The LORD said to Moses, ²"Speak to the Israelites and say to them: 'These are my appointed feasts, the appointed feasts of the LORD, which you are to proclaim as sacred assemblies.

The Sabbath

³" 'There are six days when you may work, but the seventh day is a Sabbath of rest, a day of sacred assembly. You are not to do any work; wherever you live, it is a Sabbath to the LORD.

The Passover and Unleavened Bread

⁴" 'These are the LORD's appointed feasts, the sacred assemblies you are to proclaim at their appointed times: ⁵The LORD's Passover begins at twilight on the fourteenth day of the first month. ⁶On the fifteenth day of that month the LORD's Feast of Unleavened Bread begins; for

seven days you must eat bread made without yeast. ⁷On the first day hold a sacred assembly and do no regular work. ⁸For seven days present an offering made to the LORD by fire. And on the seventh day hold a sacred assembly and do no regular work.' "

Firstfruits

⁹The LORD said to Moses, ¹⁰"Speak to the Israelites and say to them: 'When you enter the land I am going to give you and you reap its harvest, bring to the priest a sheaf of the first grain you harvest. ¹¹He is to wave the sheaf before the LORD so it will be accepted on your behalf; the priest is to wave it on the day after the Sabbath. ¹²On the day you wave the sheaf, you must sacrifice as a burnt offering to the LORD a lamb a year old without defect, ¹³together with its grain offering of two-tenths of an ephah*d* of fine flour mixed with oil—an offering made to the LORD by fire, a pleasing aroma—and its drink offering of a quarter of a hin*e* of wine. ¹⁴You must not eat any bread, or roasted or new grain, until the very day you bring this offering to your God. This is to be a lasting ordinance for the generations to come, wherever you live.

Feast of Weeks

¹⁵" 'From the day after the Sabbath, the day you brought the sheaf of the wave offering, count off seven full weeks. ¹⁶Count off fifty days up to the day after the seventh Sabbath, and then present an offering of new grain to the LORD. ¹⁷From wherever you live, bring two loaves made of two-tenths of an ephah of fine flour, baked with yeast, as a wave offering of firstfruits to the LORD. ¹⁸Present with this bread seven male lambs, each a year old and without defect, one young bull and two rams. They will be a burnt offering to the LORD, together with their grain offerings and drink offerings—an offering made by fire, an aroma pleasing to the LORD. ¹⁹Then sacrifice one male goat for a sin offering and two lambs, each a year old, for a fellowship offering.*f* ²⁰The priest is to wave the two lambs before the LORD as a wave offering, together with the

---

*a*23 The Hebrew word can include both male and female.   *b*32 Or *made*   *c*32 Or *who sanctifies you*; or *who sets you apart as holy*   *d*13 That is, probably about 4 quarts (about 4.5 liters); also in verse 17   *e*13 That is, probably about 1 quart (about 1 liter)   *f*19 Traditionally *peace offering*

bread of the firstfruits. They are a sacred offering to the LORD for the priest. ²¹On that same day you are to proclaim a sacred assembly and do no regular work. This is to be a lasting ordinance for the generations to come, wherever you live.

²² " 'When you reap the harvest of your land, do not reap to the very edges of your field or gather the gleanings of your harvest. Leave them for the poor and the alien. I am the LORD your God.' "

Feast of Trumpets

²³The LORD said to Moses, ²⁴"Say to the Israelites: 'On the first day of the seventh month you are to have a day of rest, a sacred assembly commemorated with trumpet blasts. ²⁵Do no regular work, but present an offering made to the LORD by fire.' "

Day of Atonement

²⁶The LORD said to Moses, ²⁷"The tenth day of this seventh month is the Day of Atonement. Hold a sacred assembly and deny yourselves,ᵃ and present an offering made to the LORD by fire. ²⁸Do no work on that day, because it is the Day of Atonement, when atonement is made for you before the LORD your God. ²⁹Anyone who does not deny himself on that day must be cut off from his people. ³⁰I will destroy from among his people anyone who does any work on that day. ³¹You shall do no work at all. This is to be a lasting ordinance for the generations to come, wherever you live. ³²It is a sabbath of rest for you, and you must deny yourselves. From the evening of the ninth day of the month

ᵃ27 Or and fast; also in verses 29 and 32

Paper Clips and Other Sacrifices

DAILY INSIGHT

MONDAY

Passage:
Leviticus 23:9–14

Verses:
Leviticus 23:9–10

During the years when I worked in large corporations, I learned some important things about how people mistreated the company's assets. Actually, I'm not talking about people who had direct access to the corporations' balance sheet. I'm not even talking about folks who had anything to do with finance at all.

The problem was paper clips. I'm serious. People threw paper clips away. They'd finish reading a document that had several pages clipped together. Then they'd throw the whole thing away, clip and all.

My boss, who was a stickler for details, and I had a talk about paper clips. We decided that folks who didn't feel that it was their job to take a moment and slip off the clip, probably wouldn't take care of more significant assets if they had access to them.

Now, I know that an overspent paper clip budget has rarely been the reason for a corporation's financial demise. In fact, I can't even imagine that tossed paper clips have even shown up on any office manager's financials at all. The point, however, is this: Paper clips are symbols. When employees throw them away, they're "telling" their employer that it's not their job to look out for paper clips. They have other, more important things to do than to look out for something that's of no concern to them.

Today's text makes a powerful statement about taking care of more than just our own things. In fact, it helps us to see that we have a tremendous responsibility to take ownership of the things that surround us. The Bible calls this "stewardship," and it's one of the most often repeated charges to God's people.

When the people were commanded to bring a portion of their harvest to the priest, this was intended to be a symbol to them that everything they enjoyed was to be treated with special attention. They were not owners, only caretakers.

This truth also applies to you and me today. Everything—our careers, our possessions, our families—belongs to the Lord. He has only put these things under our temporary watch. And he wants us to be good caretakers.

For your next devotional reading, go to page 145.

until the following evening you are to observe your sabbath."

Feast of Tabernacles

[33]The LORD said to Moses, [34]"Say to the Israelites: 'On the fifteenth day of the seventh month the LORD's Feast of Tabernacles begins, and it lasts for seven days. [35]The first day is a sacred assembly; do no regular work. [36]For seven days present offerings made to the LORD by fire, and on the eighth day hold a sacred assembly and present an offering made to the LORD by fire. It is the closing assembly; do no regular work.

[37](" 'These are the LORD's appointed feasts, which you are to proclaim as sacred assemblies for bringing offerings made to the LORD by fire—the burnt offerings and grain offerings, sacrifices and drink offerings required for each day. [38]These offerings are in addition to those for the LORD's Sabbaths and[a] in addition to your gifts and whatever you have vowed and all the freewill offerings you give to the LORD.)

[39]" 'So beginning with the fifteenth day of the seventh month, after you have gathered the crops of the land, celebrate the festival to the LORD for seven days; the first day is a day of rest, and the eighth day also is a day of rest. [40]On the first day you are to take choice fruit from the trees, and palm fronds, leafy branches and poplars, and rejoice before the LORD your God for seven days. [41]Celebrate this as a festival to the LORD for seven days each year. This is to be a lasting ordinance for the generations to come; celebrate it in the seventh month. [42]Live in booths for seven days: All native-born Israelites are to live in booths [43]so your descendants will know that I had the Israelites live in booths when I brought them out of Egypt. I am the LORD your God.' "

[44]So Moses announced to the Israelites the appointed feasts of the LORD.

Oil and Bread Set Before the LORD

24 The LORD said to Moses, [2]"Command the Israelites to bring you clear oil of pressed olives for the light so that the lamps may be kept burning continually. [3]Outside the curtain of the Testimony in the Tent of Meeting, Aaron is to tend the lamps before the LORD from evening till morning, continually. This is to be a lasting ordinance for the generations to come. [4]The lamps on the pure gold lamp-

stand before the LORD must be tended continually.

[5]"Take fine flour and bake twelve loaves of bread, using two-tenths of an ephah[b] for each loaf. [6]Set them in two rows, six in each row, on the table of pure gold before the LORD. [7]Along each row put some pure incense as a memorial portion to represent the bread and to be an offering made to the LORD by fire. [8]This bread is to be set out before the LORD regularly, Sabbath after Sabbath, on behalf of the Israelites, as a lasting covenant. [9]It belongs to Aaron and his sons, who are to eat it in a holy place, because it is a most holy part of their regular share of the offerings made to the LORD by fire."

A Blasphemer Stoned

[10]Now the son of an Israelite mother and an Egyptian father went out among the Israelites, and a fight broke out in the camp between him and an Israelite. [11]The son of the Israelite woman blasphemed the Name with a curse; so they brought him to Moses. (His mother's name was Shelomith, the daughter of Dibri the Danite.) [12]They put him in custody until the will of the LORD should be made clear to them.

[13]Then the LORD said to Moses: [14]"Take the blasphemer outside the camp. All those who heard him are to lay their hands on his head, and the entire assembly is to stone him. [15]Say to the Israelites: 'If anyone curses his God, he will be held responsible; [16]anyone who blasphemes the name of the LORD must be put to death. The entire assembly must stone him. Whether an alien or native-born, when he blasphemes the Name, he must be put to death.

[17]" 'If anyone takes the life of a human being, he must be put to death. [18]Anyone who takes the life of someone's animal must make restitution—life for life. [19]If anyone injures his neighbor, whatever he has done must be done to him: [20]fracture for fracture, eye for eye, tooth for tooth. As he has injured the other, so is he to be injured. [21]Whoever kills an animal must make restitution, but whoever kills a man must be put to death. [22]You are to have the same law for the alien and the native-born. I am the LORD your God.' "

[23]Then Moses spoke to the Israelites,

---

[a]38 Or *These feasts are in addition to the LORD's Sabbaths, and these offerings are* [b]5 That is, probably about 4 quarts (about 4.5 liters)

and they took the blasphemer outside the camp and stoned him. The Israelites did as the LORD commanded Moses.

The Sabbath Year

25 The LORD said to Moses on Mount Sinai, [2]"Speak to the Israelites and say to them: 'When you enter the land I am going to give you, the land itself must observe a sabbath to the LORD. [3]For six years sow your fields, and for six years prune your vineyards and gather their crops. [4]But in the seventh year the land is to have a sabbath of rest, a sabbath to the LORD. Do not sow your fields or prune your vine-

yards. [5]Do not reap what grows of itself or harvest the grapes of your untended vines. The land is to have a year of rest. [6]Whatever the land yields during the sabbath year will be food for you—for yourself, your manservant and maidservant, and the hired worker and temporary resident who live among you, [7]as well as for your livestock and the wild animals in your land. Whatever the land produces may be eaten.

The Year of Jubilee

[8]" 'Count off seven sabbaths of years— seven times seven years—so that the

Be Fairly Tough

One of the necessary responsibilities of being a dad is disciplining your children. And one of the most important things to remember about issuing discipline is that the punishment must be fair. Make sure the penalty fits the infraction.

I was eleven and my brother, Ken, was thirteen. We had to run an errand for my mother and were about to ride into town on our bikes when we decided to ask if we could take our twin brother and sister along. Debbie and Dan were only three, and we loved to carry them on our bicycles. We asked my mother if we could take the twins along with us. She said "no." We begged. She said "no," again. We begged some more, and she reluctantly gave in.

Before we got to downtown Wheaton, Debbie's foot got caught in Ken's front wheel spokes. Dan and I were scooting along when it dawned on me that Ken wasn't close by. I stopped, turned around, and saw Ken bending over Debbie, who was lying on the street along with the bicycle. I panicked, realizing that we had coerced my mother into letting us bring the kids along. Punishment was absolutely inevitable.

A kind motorist saw what had happened and offered to drive Debbie to Dr. Wynegarden's office. She had no broken bones, but her treatment and medication

DAILY INSIGHT

TUESDAY
Passage:
Leviticus 24:17–22
Verses:
Leviticus 24:19–21

cost nineteen dollars. Our punishment was to pay the doctor's bill with our own money. As a result, Ken and I started a car wash business—one dollar for a regular car, twenty-five cents extra for white walls.

I suppose our mother could have spanked us, grounded us or taken away some privileges. But reflecting on what she did, the punishment seems to me a perfect match to the offense. As Ken and I worked on these cars, inching toward our nineteen dollar goal, we talked about how foolish we had been to push our mother, how fortunate we were that Debbie's injury wasn't more severe, and how careful we would be in the future.

Today's text sends a very simple message: Be sure punishment is fair. Make certain that it matches the crime. If it does, it will be memorable. Don't be guilty of overreacting to your children's offense because it has embarrassed you or made you angry. Take a moment and be certain that what you do creates a memory for your child that fixes the problem. If they remember their dad having a fit, they'll probably forget what they did to set you off.

Being a good dad requires that you be a sound disciplinarian. Just be sure that you're doing it right.

For your next devotional reading, go to page 153.

seven sabbaths of years amount to a period of forty-nine years. ⁹Then have the trumpet sounded everywhere on the tenth day of the seventh month; on the Day of Atonement sound the trumpet throughout your land. ¹⁰Consecrate the fiftieth year and proclaim liberty throughout the land to all its inhabitants. It shall be a jubilee for you; each one of you is to return to his family property and each to his own clan. ¹¹The fiftieth year shall be a jubilee for you; do not sow and do not reap what grows of itself or harvest the untended vines. ¹²For it is a jubilee and is to be holy for you; eat only what is taken directly from the fields.

¹³ 'In this Year of Jubilee everyone is to return to his own property.

¹⁴" 'If you sell land to one of your countrymen or buy any from him, do not take advantage of each other. ¹⁵You are to buy from your countryman on the basis of the number of years since the Jubilee. And he is to sell to you on the basis of the number of years left for harvesting crops. ¹⁶When the years are many, you are to increase the price, and when the years are few, you are to decrease the price, because what he is really selling you is the number of crops. ¹⁷Do not take advantage of each other, but fear your God. I am the LORD your God.

¹⁸" 'Follow my decrees and be careful to obey my laws, and you will live safely in the land. ¹⁹Then the land will yield its fruit, and you will eat your fill and live there in safety. ²⁰You may ask, "What will we eat in the seventh year if we do not plant or harvest our crops?" ²¹I will send you such a blessing in the sixth year that the land will yield enough for three years. ²²While you plant during the eighth year, you will eat from the old crop and will continue to eat from it until the harvest of the ninth year comes in.

²³" 'The land must not be sold permanently, because the land is mine and you are but aliens and my tenants. ²⁴Throughout the country that you hold as a possession, you must provide for the redemption of the land.

²⁵" 'If one of your countrymen becomes poor and sells some of his property, his nearest relative is to come and redeem what his countryman has sold. ²⁶If, however, a man has no one to redeem it for him but he himself prospers and acquires sufficient means to redeem it, ²⁷he is to determine the value for the years since he sold it and refund the balance to the man

to whom he sold it; he can then go back to his own property. ²⁸But if he does not acquire the means to repay him, what he sold will remain in the possession of the buyer until the Year of Jubilee. It will be returned in the Jubilee, and he can then go back to his property.

²⁹" 'If a man sells a house in a walled city, he retains the right of redemption a full year after its sale. During that time he may redeem it. ³⁰If it is not redeemed before a full year has passed, the house in the walled city shall belong permanently to the buyer and his descendants. It is not to be returned in the Jubilee. ³¹But houses in villages without walls around them are to be considered as open country. They can be redeemed, and they are to be returned in the Jubilee.

³²" 'The Levites always have the right to redeem their houses in the Levitical towns, which they possess. ³³So the property of the Levites is redeemable—that is, a house sold in any town they hold—and is to be returned in the Jubilee, because the houses in the towns of the Levites are their property among the Israelites. ³⁴But the pastureland belonging to their towns must not be sold; it is their permanent possession.

³⁵" 'If one of your countrymen becomes poor and is unable to support himself among you, help him as you would an alien or a temporary resident, so he can continue to live among you. ³⁶Do not take interest of any kind*a* from him, but fear your God, so that your countryman may continue to live among you. ³⁷You must not lend him money at interest or sell him food at a profit. ³⁸I am the LORD your God, who brought you out of Egypt to give you the land of Canaan and to be your God.

³⁹" 'If one of your countrymen becomes poor among you and sells himself to you, do not make him work as a slave. ⁴⁰He is to be treated as a hired worker or a temporary resident among you; he is to work for you until the Year of Jubilee. ⁴¹Then he and his children are to be released, and he will go back to his own clan and to the property of his forefathers. ⁴²Because the Israelites are my servants, whom I brought out of Egypt, they must not be sold as slaves. ⁴³Do not rule over them ruthlessly, but fear your God.

⁴⁴" 'Your male and female slaves are to come from the nations around you; from

a36 Or take excessive interest; *similarly in verse 37*

them you may buy slaves. ⁴⁵You may also buy some of the temporary residents living among you and members of their clans born in your country, and they will become your property. ⁴⁶You can will them to your children as inherited property and can make them slaves for life, but you must not rule over your fellow Israelites ruthlessly.

⁴⁷" 'If an alien or a temporary resident among you becomes rich and one of your countrymen becomes poor and sells himself to the alien living among you or to a member of the alien's clan, ⁴⁸he retains the right of redemption after he has sold himself. One of his relatives may redeem him: ⁴⁹An uncle or a cousin or any blood relative in his clan may redeem him. Or if he prospers, he may redeem himself. ⁵⁰He and his buyer are to count the time from the year he sold himself up to the Year of Jubilee. The price for his release is to be based on the rate paid to a hired man for that number of years. ⁵¹If many years remain, he must pay for his redemption a larger share of the price paid for him. ⁵²If only a few years remain until the Year of Jubilee, he is to compute that and pay for his redemption accordingly. ⁵³He is to be treated as a man hired from year to year; you must see to it that his owner does not rule over him ruthlessly.

⁵⁴" 'Even if he is not redeemed in any of these ways, he and his children are to be released in the Year of Jubilee, ⁵⁵for the Israelites belong to me as servants. They are my servants, whom I brought out of Egypt. I am the LORD your God.

Reward for Obedience

26 " 'Do not make idols or set up an image or a sacred stone for yourselves, and do not place a carved stone in your land to bow down before it. I am the LORD your God.

²" 'Observe my Sabbaths and have reverence for my sanctuary. I am the LORD.

³" 'If you follow my decrees and are careful to obey my commands, ⁴I will send you rain in its season, and the ground will yield its crops and the trees of the field their fruit. ⁵Your threshing will continue until grape harvest and the grape harvest will continue until planting, and you will eat all the food you want and live in safety in your land.

⁶" 'I will grant peace in the land, and you will lie down and no one will make you afraid. I will remove savage beasts from the land, and the sword will not pass through your country. ⁷You will pursue your enemies, and they will fall by the sword before you. ⁸Five of you will chase a hundred, and a hundred of you will chase ten thousand, and your enemies will fall by the sword before you.

⁹" 'I will look on you with favor and make you fruitful and increase your numbers, and I will keep my covenant with you. ¹⁰You will still be eating last year's harvest when you will have to move it out to make room for the new. ¹¹I will put my dwelling place*a* among you, and I will not abhor you. ¹²I will walk among you and be

a11 Or *my tabernacle*

HEY DAD
Does God want me to be afraid of him?

Text: Leviticus 25:36

God doesn't want us to be afraid of him like we'd be afraid of something mean or evil. But he does want us to fear him—kind of like we fear police officers.

What does that mean? Well, police officers are good people. They protect us from those who might want to hurt us or steal from us. They're able to protect us because they have the authority to punish people who break the law. Because we "fear" the authority of a police officer and don't want him or her to punish us, we don't break the law.

To "fear" God means to be in awe of him, to recognize his authority and to respect and honor him. But he doesn't want us to run from him. He loves us dearly. A philosopher once said wisely, "He who truly fears a thing runs from it, but he who truly fears God, flees unto him." Isn't this wonderful?

For a complete listing of Dads in the Bible, turn to page 1434.

your God, and you will be my people. [13]I am the LORD your God, who brought you out of Egypt so that you would no longer be slaves to the Egyptians; I broke the bars of your yoke and enabled you to walk with heads held high.

Punishment for Disobedience

[14]" 'But if you will not listen to me and carry out all these commands, [15]and if you reject my decrees and abhor my laws and fail to carry out all my commands and so violate my covenant, [16]then I will do this to you: I will bring upon you sudden terror, wasting diseases and fever that will destroy your sight and drain away your life. You will plant seed in vain, because your enemies will eat it. [17]I will set my face against you so that you will be defeated by your enemies; those who hate you will rule over you, and you will flee even when no one is pursuing you.

[18]" 'If after all this you will not listen to me, I will punish you for your sins seven times over. [19]I will break down your stubborn pride and make the sky above you like iron and the ground beneath you like bronze. [20]Your strength will be spent in vain, because your soil will not yield its crops, nor will the trees of the land yield their fruit.

[21]" 'If you remain hostile toward me and refuse to listen to me, I will multiply your afflictions seven times over, as your sins deserve. [22]I will send wild animals against you, and they will rob you of your children, destroy your cattle and make you so few in number that your roads will be deserted.

[23]" 'If in spite of these things you do not accept my correction but continue to be hostile toward me, [24]I myself will be hostile toward you and will afflict you for your sins seven times over. [25]And I will bring the sword upon you to avenge the breaking of the covenant. When you withdraw into your cities, I will send a plague among you, and you will be given into enemy hands. [26]When I cut off your supply of bread, ten women will be able to bake your bread in one oven, and they will dole out the bread by weight. You will eat, but you will not be satisfied.

[27]" 'If in spite of this you still do not listen to me but continue to be hostile toward me, [28]then in my anger I will be hostile toward you, and I myself will punish you for your sins seven times over. [29]You will eat the flesh of your sons and the flesh of your daughters. [30]I will destroy your high places, cut down your incense altars and pile your dead bodies on the lifeless forms of your idols, and I will abhor you. [31]I will turn your cities into ruins and lay waste your sanctuaries, and I will take no delight in the pleasing aroma of your offerings. [32]I will lay waste the land, so that your enemies who live there will be appalled. [33]I will scatter you among the nations and will draw out my sword and pursue you. Your land will be laid waste, and your cities will lie in ruins. [34]Then the land will enjoy its sabbath years all the time that it lies desolate and you are in the country of your enemies; then the land will rest and enjoy its sabbaths. [35]All the time that it lies desolate, the land will have the rest it did not have during the sabbaths you lived in it.

[36]" 'As for those of you who are left, I will make their hearts so fearful in the lands of their enemies that the sound of a wind-blown leaf will put them to flight. They will run as though fleeing from the sword, and they will fall, even though no one is pursuing them. [37]They will stumble over one another as though fleeing from the sword, even though no one is pursuing them. So you will not be able to stand before your enemies. [38]You will perish among the nations; the land of your enemies will devour you. [39]Those of you who are left will waste away in the lands of their enemies because of their sins; also because of their fathers' sins they will waste away.

[40]" 'But if they will confess their sins and the sins of their fathers—their treachery against me and their hostility toward me, [41]which made me hostile toward them so that I sent them into the land of their enemies—then when their uncircumcised hearts are humbled and they pay for their sin, [42]I will remember my covenant with Jacob and my covenant with Isaac and my covenant with Abraham, and I will remember the land. [43]For the land will be deserted by them and will enjoy its sabbaths while it lies desolate without them. They will pay for their sins because they rejected my laws and abhorred my decrees. [44]Yet in spite of this, when they are in the land of their enemies, I will not reject them or abhor them so as to destroy them completely, breaking my covenant with them. I am the LORD their God. [45]But for their sake I will remember the covenant with their ancestors whom I brought out of Egypt in

the sight of the nations to be their God. I am the LORD.' "

46These are the decrees, the laws and the regulations that the LORD established on Mount Sinai between himself and the Israelites through Moses.

Redeeming What Is the LORD's

27 The LORD said to Moses, **2**"Speak to the Israelites and say to them: 'If anyone makes a special vow to dedicate persons to the LORD by giving equivalent values, **3**set the value of a male between the ages of twenty and sixty at fifty shekels*a* of silver, according to the sanctuary shekel*b*; **4**and if it is a female, set her value at thirty shekels.*c* **5**If it is a person between the ages of five and twenty, set the value of a male at twenty shekels*d* and of a female at ten shekels.*e* **6**If it is a person between one month and five years, set the value of a male at five shekels*f* of silver and that of a female at three shekels*g* of silver. **7**If it is a person sixty years old or more, set the value of a male at fifteen shekels*h* and of a female at ten shekels. **8**If anyone making the vow is too poor to pay the specified amount, he is to present the person to the priest, who will set the value for him according to what the man making the vow can afford.

9" 'If what he vowed is an animal that is acceptable as an offering to the LORD, such an animal given to the LORD becomes holy. **10**He must not exchange it or substitute a good one for a bad one, or a bad one for a good one; if he should substitute one animal for another, both it and the substitute become holy. **11**If what he vowed is a ceremonially unclean animal—one that is not acceptable as an offering to the LORD—the animal must be presented to the priest, **12**who will judge its quality as good or bad. Whatever value the priest then sets, that is what it will be. **13**If the owner wishes to redeem the animal, he must add a fifth to its value.

14" 'If a man dedicates his house as something holy to the LORD, the priest will judge its quality as good or bad. Whatever value the priest then sets, so it will remain. **15**If the man who dedicates his house redeems it, he must add a fifth to its value, and the house will again become his.

16" 'If a man dedicates to the LORD part of his family land, its value is to be set according to the amount of seed required for it—fifty shekels of silver to a homer*i* of

barley seed. **17**If he dedicates his field during the Year of Jubilee, the value that has been set remains. **18**But if he dedicates his field after the Jubilee, the priest will determine the value according to the number of years that remain until the next Year of Jubilee, and its set value will be reduced. **19**If the man who dedicates the field wishes to redeem it, he must add a fifth to its value, and the field will again become his. **20**If, however, he does not redeem the field, or if he has sold it to someone else, it can never be redeemed. **21**When the field is released in the Jubilee, it will become holy, like a field devoted to the LORD; it will become the property of the priests.*j*

22" 'If a man dedicates to the LORD a field he has bought, which is not part of his family land, **23**the priest will determine its value up to the Year of Jubilee, and the man must pay its value on that day as something holy to the LORD. **24**In the Year of Jubilee the field will revert to the person from whom he bought it, the one whose land it was. **25**Every value is to be set according to the sanctuary shekel, twenty gerahs to the shekel.

26" 'No one, however, may dedicate the firstborn of an animal, since the firstborn already belongs to the LORD; whether an ox*k* or a sheep, it is the LORD's. **27**If it is one of the unclean animals, he may buy it back at its set value, adding a fifth of the value to it. If he does not redeem it, it is to be sold at its set value.

28" 'But nothing that a man owns and devotes*l* to the LORD—whether man or animal or family land—may be sold or redeemed; everything so devoted is most holy to the LORD.

29" 'No person devoted to destruction*m* may be ransomed; he must be put to death.

30" 'A tithe of everything from the land,

a3 That is, about 1 1/4 pounds (about 0.6 kilogram); also in verse 16   *b3* That is, about 2/5 ounce (about 11.5 grams); also in verse 25   *c4* That is, about 12 ounces (about 0.3 kilogram)   *d5* That is, about 8 ounces (about 0.2 kilogram)   *e5* That is, about 4 ounces (about 110 grams); also in verse 7   *f6* That is, about 2 ounces (about 55 grams)   *g6* That is, about 1 1/4 ounces (about 35 grams)   *h7* That is, about 6 ounces (about 170 grams)   *i16* That is, probably about 6 bushels (about 220 liters)   *j21* Or *priest*   *k26* The Hebrew word can include both male and female.   *l28* The Hebrew term refers to the irrevocable giving over of things or persons to the LORD.   *m29* The Hebrew term refers to the irrevocable giving over of things or persons to the LORD, often by totally destroying them.

whether grain from the soil or fruit from the trees, belongs to the LORD; it is holy to the LORD. ³¹If a man redeems any of his tithe, he must add a fifth of the value to it. ³²The entire tithe of the herd and flock— every tenth animal that passes under the shepherd's rod—will be holy to the LORD. ³³He must not pick out the good from the bad or make any substitution. If he does make a substitution, both the animal and its substitute become holy and cannot be redeemed.' "

³⁴These are the commands the LORD gave Moses on Mount Sinai for the Israelites.

"Follow the Leader" may be the name of a child's game, but for the Israelites, it was serious business. These people—a couple million of them—were stuck between captivity in Egypt and a new life in the promised land. For forty years they lived from day to day, not knowing where they were going. They felt lost, they acted lost, they grumbled and complained like they were lost . . . but they *weren't* lost.

God knew exactly where the Israelites were. He knew why they were there, how long they were going to be there, and where they were going. God even provided a huge cloud to follow during the day and a fireball to follow for late-night trips.

Following God every day in spite of feeling completely lost is the story of the book of Numbers. It was also what Jesus, God's precious Son, told his disciples—and us as well— to do. "Follow me," Jesus said. And since the typical dad would rather not take time to stop and ask for directions anyway, this is good news.

Numbers

The Census

1 The LORD spoke to Moses in the Tent of Meeting in the Desert of Sinai on the first day of the second month of the second year after the Israelites came out of Egypt. He said: [2]"Take a census of the whole Israelite community by their clans and families, listing every man by name, one by one. [3]You and Aaron are to number by their divisions all the men in Israel twenty years old or more who are able to serve in the army. [4]One man from each tribe, each the head of his family, is to help you. [5]These are the names of the men who are to assist you:

from Reuben, Elizur son of Shedeur;
[6] from Simeon, Shelumiel son of Zuri-shaddai;

[7] from Judah, Nahshon son of Ammin-adab;
[8] from Issachar, Nethanel son of Zuar;
[9] from Zebulun, Eliab son of Helon;
[10]from the sons of Joseph:
 from Ephraim, Elishama son of Ammihud;
 from Manasseh, Gamaliel son of Pedahzur;
[11]from Benjamin, Abidan son of Gide-oni;
[12]from Dan, Ahiezer son of Ammishad-dai;
[13]from Asher, Pagiel son of Ocran;
[14]from Gad, Eliasaph son of Deuel;
[15]from Naphtali, Ahira son of Enan."

[16]These were the men appointed from the community, the leaders of their

ancestral tribes. They were the heads of the clans of Israel.

¹⁷Moses and Aaron took these men whose names had been given, ¹⁸and they called the whole community together on the first day of the second month. The people indicated their ancestry by their clans and families, and the men twenty years old or more were listed by name, one by one, ¹⁹as the LORD commanded Moses. And so he counted them in the Desert of Sinai:

²⁰From the descendants of Reuben the firstborn son of Israel:
All the men twenty years old or more who were able to serve in the army were listed by name, one by one, according to the records of their clans and families. ²¹The number from the tribe of Reuben was 46,500.

²²From the descendants of Simeon:
All the men twenty years old or more who were able to serve in the army were counted and listed by name, one by one, according to the records of their clans and families. ²³The number from the tribe of Simeon was 59,300.

²⁴From the descendants of Gad:
All the men twenty years old or more who were able to serve in the army were listed by name, according to the records of their clans and families. ²⁵The number from the tribe of Gad was 45,650.

²⁶From the descendants of Judah:
All the men twenty years old or more who were able to serve in the army were listed by name, according to the records of their clans and families. ²⁷The number from the tribe of Judah was 74,600.

²⁸From the descendants of Issachar:
All the men twenty years old or more who were able to serve in the army were listed by name, according to the records of their clans and families. ²⁹The number from the tribe of Issachar was 54,400.

³⁰From the descendants of Zebulun:
All the men twenty years old or more who were able to serve in the army were listed by name, according to the records of their clans and families. ³¹The number from the tribe of Zebulun was 57,400.

³²From the sons of Joseph:
From the descendants of Ephraim:
All the men twenty years old or more who were able to serve in the army were listed by name, according to the records of their clans and families. ³³The number from the tribe of Ephraim was 40,500.

³⁴From the descendants of Manasseh:
All the men twenty years old or more who were able to serve in the army were listed by name, according to the records of their clans and families. ³⁵The number from the tribe of Manasseh was 32,200.

³⁶From the descendants of Benjamin:
All the men twenty years old or more who were able to serve in the army were listed by name, according to the records of their clans and families. ³⁷The number from the tribe of Benjamin was 35,400.

³⁸From the descendants of Dan:
All the men twenty years old or more who were able to serve in the army were listed by name, according to the records of their clans and families. ³⁹The number from the tribe of Dan was 62,700.

⁴⁰From the descendants of Asher:
All the men twenty years old or more who were able to serve in the army were listed by name, according to the records of their clans and families. ⁴¹The number from the tribe of Asher was 41,500.

⁴²From the descendants of Naphtali:
All the men twenty years old or more who were able to serve in the army were listed by name, according to the records of their clans and families. ⁴³The number from the tribe of Naphtali was 53,400.

⁴⁴These were the men counted by Moses and Aaron and the twelve leaders of Israel, each one representing his family. ⁴⁵All the Israelites twenty years old or more who were able to serve in Israel's army were counted according to their families. ⁴⁶The total number was 603,550.

⁴⁷The families of the tribe of Levi, however, were not counted along with the others. ⁴⁸The LORD had said to Moses: ⁴⁹"You must not count the tribe of Levi or include them in the census of the other Israelites. ⁵⁰Instead, appoint the Levites

to be in charge of the tabernacle of the Testimony—over all its furnishings and everything belonging to it. They are to carry the tabernacle and all its furnishings; they are to take care of it and encamp around it. ⁵¹Whenever the tabernacle is to move, the Levites are to take it down, and whenever the tabernacle is to be set up, the Levites shall do it. Anyone else who goes near it shall be put to death. ⁵²The Israelites are to set up their tents by divisions, each man in his own camp under his own standard. ⁵³The Levites, however, are to set up their tents around the tabernacle of the Testimony so that wrath will not fall on the Israelite community. The Levites are to be responsible for the care of the tabernacle of the Testimony."

⁵⁴The Israelites did all this just as the LORD commanded Moses.

The Arrangement of the Tribal Camps

2 The LORD said to Moses and Aaron: ²"The Israelites are to camp around the Tent of Meeting some distance from it, each man under his standard with the banners of his family."

³On the east, toward the sunrise, the divisions of the camp of Judah are to encamp under their standard. The leader of the people of Judah is Nahshon son of Amminadab. ⁴His division numbers 74,600.

⁵The tribe of Issachar will camp next to them. The leader of the people of Issachar is Nethanel son of Zuar. ⁶His division numbers 54,400.

⁷The tribe of Zebulun will be next. The leader of the people of Zebulun is Eliab son of Helon. ⁸His division numbers 57,400.

A High Calling

DAILY INSIGHT

When was the last time you curled up on your favorite easy chair with a good ... *telephone directory*? Today's reading appears to be about as stemwinding an experience.

It's the census ... the actual counting of the children of Israel. God had asked Moses to select one person from each tribe to help him do the tallying, which he did. But at the end of the first chapter (1:49) the Lord asked Moses not to count Levi's family. He told Moses that this family had been set apart for a sacred responsibility. The Levites were to take care of the tabernacle—the Israelites' house of worship. And they were to conduct the official ceremonies that corporately brought the people into the presence of the Almighty. So they were not even to be counted—they were *that* extraordinary.

Although, in your home, you are to be the priest—just like in Jewish homes around the world—there is something very special about the professional in ministry. This is a person who has been uniquely called of God to take care of the local church, to provide leadership for corporate

WEDNESDAY

Passage:
Numbers 1:44–54

Verses:
Numbers 1:47–50

worship, and to set an example of godly living. This is a very challenging and, at times, troublesome occupation.

Unfortunately, because your children have access to television programming, they're going to see some pretty unusual characters who may give them the wrong impression of what this ministry calling looks like. Fortunately your community has wonderful examples of what ministry should definitely look like ... men and women who faithfully tend to the needs of families like yours.

Most of what your children learn will be *caught*, not *taught*. Because this is true, let them catch your love for your church, your support of your ministry team, and your giving. Let your children overhear you expressing appreciation for the positive impact your church has in your life.

As church members, we are blessed with people who are called of God to vocational ministry. These are our shepherds. Involve your family in faithfully praying for your pastoral staff and supporting your church.

For your next devotional reading, go to page 163.

⁹All the men assigned to the camp of Judah, according to their divisions, number 186,400. They will set out first.

¹⁰On the south will be the divisions of the camp of Reuben under their standard. The leader of the people of Reuben is Elizur son of Shedeur. ¹¹His division numbers 46,500.
¹²The tribe of Simeon will camp next to them. The leader of the people of Simeon is Shelumiel son of Zurishaddai. ¹³His division numbers 59,300.
¹⁴The tribe of Gad will be next. The leader of the people of Gad is Eliasaph son of Deuel.ᵃ ¹⁵His division numbers 45,650.
¹⁶All the men assigned to the camp of Reuben, according to their divisions, number 151,450. They will set out second.

¹⁷Then the Tent of Meeting and the camp of the Levites will set out in the middle of the camps. They will set out in the same order as they encamp, each in his own place under his standard.

¹⁸On the west will be the divisions of the camp of Ephraim under their standard. The leader of the people of Ephraim is Elishama son of Ammihud. ¹⁹His division numbers 40,500.
²⁰The tribe of Manasseh will be next to them. The leader of the people of Manasseh is Gamaliel son of Pedahzur. ²¹His division numbers 32,200.
²²The tribe of Benjamin will be next. The leader of the people of Benjamin is Abidan son of Gideoni. ²³His division numbers 35,400.
²⁴All the men assigned to the camp of Ephraim, according to their divisions, number 108,100. They will set out third.

²⁵On the north will be the divisions of the camp of Dan, under their standard. The leader of the people of Dan is Ahiezer son of Ammishaddai. ²⁶His division numbers 62,700.
²⁷The tribe of Asher will camp next to them. The leader of the people of Asher is Pagiel son of Ocran. ²⁸His division numbers 41,500.
²⁹The tribe of Naphtali will be next. The leader of the people of Naphtali is Ahira son of Enan. ³⁰His division numbers 53,400.

³¹All the men assigned to the camp of Dan number 157,600. They will set out last, under their standards.

³²These are the Israelites, counted according to their families. All those in the camps, by their divisions, number 603,550. ³³The Levites, however, were not counted along with the other Israelites, as the LORD commanded Moses.

³⁴So the Israelites did everything the LORD commanded Moses; that is the way they encamped under their standards, and that is the way they set out, each with his clan and family.

The Levites

3 This is the account of the family of Aaron and Moses at the time the LORD talked with Moses on Mount Sinai.
²The names of the sons of Aaron were Nadab the firstborn and Abihu, Eleazar and Ithamar. ³Those were the names of Aaron's sons, the anointed priests, who were ordained to serve as priests. ⁴Nadab and Abihu, however, fell dead before the LORD when they made an offering with unauthorized fire before him in the Desert of Sinai. They had no sons; so only Eleazar and Ithamar served as priests during the lifetime of their father Aaron.

⁵The LORD said to Moses, ⁶"Bring the tribe of Levi and present them to Aaron the priest to assist him. ⁷They are to perform duties for him and for the whole community at the Tent of Meeting by doing the work of the tabernacle. ⁸They are to take care of all the furnishings of the Tent of Meeting, fulfilling the obligations of the Israelites by doing the work of the tabernacle. ⁹Give the Levites to Aaron and his sons; they are the Israelites who are to be given wholly to him.ᵇ ¹⁰Appoint Aaron and his sons to serve as priests; anyone else who approaches the sanctuary must be put to death."
¹¹The LORD also said to Moses, ¹²"I have taken the Levites from among the Israelites in place of the first male offspring of every Israelite woman. The Levites are mine, ¹³for all the firstborn are mine. When I struck

ᵃ14 Many manuscripts of the Masoretic Text, Samaritan Pentateuch and Vulgate (see also Num. 1:14); most manuscripts of the Masoretic Text *Reuel* ᵇ9 Most manuscripts of the Masoretic Text; some manuscripts of the Masoretic Text, Samaritan Pentateuch and Septuagint (see also Num. 8:16) *to me* down all the firstborn in Egypt, I set apart for myself every firstborn in Israel, whether man or animal. They are to be mine. I am the LORD."

¹⁴The LORD said to Moses in the Desert of Sinai, ¹⁵"Count the Levites by their families and clans. Count every male a month old or more." ¹⁶So Moses counted them, as he was commanded by the word of the LORD.

¹⁷These were the names of the sons of Levi:
Gershon, Kohath and Merari.
¹⁸These were the names of the Gershonite clans:
Libni and Shimei.
¹⁹The Kohathite clans:
Amram, Izhar, Hebron and Uzziel.
²⁰The Merarite clans:
Mahli and Mushi.
These were the Levite clans, according to their families.

²¹To Gershon belonged the clans of the Libnites and Shimeites; these were the Gershonite clans. ²²The number of all the males a month old or more who were counted was 7,500. ²³The Gershonite clans were to camp on the west, behind the tabernacle. ²⁴The leader of the families of the Gershonites was Eliasaph son of Lael. ²⁵At the Tent of Meeting the Gershonites were responsible for the care of the tabernacle and tent, its coverings, the curtain at the entrance to the Tent of Meeting, ²⁶the curtains of the courtyard, the curtain at the entrance to the courtyard surrounding the tabernacle and altar, and the ropes—and everything related to their use.

²⁷To Kohath belonged the clans of the Amramites, Izharites, Hebronites and Uzzielites; these were the Kohathite clans. ²⁸The number of all the males a month old or more was 8,600.ᵃ The Kohathites were responsible for the care of the sanctuary. ²⁹The Kohathite clans were to camp on the south side of the tabernacle. ³⁰The leader of the families of the Kohathite clans was Elizaphan son of Uzziel. ³¹They were responsible for the care of the ark, the table, the lampstand, the altars, the articles of the sanctuary used in ministering, the curtain, and everything related to their use. ³²The chief leader of the Levites was Eleazar son of Aaron, the priest. He was appointed over those who were responsible for the care of the sanctuary.

³³To Merari belonged the clans of the Mahlites and the Mushites; these were the Merarite clans. ³⁴The number of all the males a month old or more who were counted was 6,200. ³⁵The leader of the families of the Merarite clans was Zuriel son of Abihail; they were to camp on the north side of the tabernacle. ³⁶The Merarites were appointed to take care of the frames of the tabernacle, its crossbars, posts, bases, all its equipment, and everything related to their use, ³⁷as well as the posts of the surrounding courtyard with their bases, tent pegs and ropes.

³⁸Moses and Aaron and his sons were to camp to the east of the tabernacle, toward the sunrise, in front of the Tent of Meeting. They were responsible for the care of the sanctuary on behalf of the Israelites. Anyone else who approached the sanctuary was to be put to death.

³⁹The total number of Levites counted at the LORD's command by Moses and Aaron according to their clans, including every male a month old or more, was 22,000.

⁴⁰The LORD said to Moses, "Count all the firstborn Israelite males who are a month old or more and make a list of their names. ⁴¹Take the Levites for me in place of all the firstborn of the Israelites, and the livestock of the Levites in place of all the firstborn of the livestock of the Israelites. I am the LORD."

⁴²So Moses counted all the firstborn of the Israelites, as the LORD commanded him. ⁴³The total number of firstborn males a month old or more, listed by name, was 22,273.

⁴⁴The LORD also said to Moses, ⁴⁵"Take the Levites in place of all the firstborn of Israel, and the livestock of the Levites in place of their livestock. The Levites are to be mine. I am the LORD. ⁴⁶To redeem the 273 firstborn Israelites who exceed the number of the Levites, ⁴⁷collect five shekelsᵇ for each one, according to the sanctuary shekel, which weighs twenty gerahs. ⁴⁸Give the money for the redemption of the additional Israelites to Aaron and his sons."

⁴⁹So Moses collected the redemption money from those who exceeded the number redeemed by the Levites. ⁵⁰From

ᵃ28 Hebrew; some Septuagint manuscripts 8,300
ᵇ47 That is, about 2 ounces (about 55 grams)

the firstborn of the Israelites he collected silver weighing 1,365 shekels,[a] according to the sanctuary shekel. [51]Moses gave the redemption money to Aaron and his sons, as he was commanded by the word of the LORD.

The Kohathites

4 The LORD said to Moses and Aaron: [2]"Take a census of the Kohathite branch of the Levites by their clans and families. [3]Count all the men from thirty to fifty years of age who come to serve in the work in the Tent of Meeting.

[4]"This is the work of the Kohathites in the Tent of Meeting: the care of the most holy things. [5]When the camp is to move, Aaron and his sons are to go in and take down the shielding curtain and cover the ark of the Testimony with it. [6]Then they are to cover this with hides of sea cows,[b] spread a cloth of solid blue over that and put the poles in place.

[7]"Over the table of the Presence they are to spread a blue cloth and put on it the plates, dishes and bowls, and the jars for drink offerings; the bread that is continually there is to remain on it. [8]Over these they are to spread a scarlet cloth, cover that with hides of sea cows and put its poles in place.

[9]"They are to take a blue cloth and cover the lampstand that is for light, together with its lamps, its wick trimmers and trays, and all its jars for the oil used to supply it. [10]Then they are to wrap it and all its accessories in a covering of hides of sea cows and put it on a carrying frame.

[11]"Over the gold altar they are to spread a blue cloth and cover that with hides of sea cows and put its poles in place. [12]"They are to take all the articles used for ministering in the sanctuary, wrap them in a blue cloth, cover that with hides of sea cows and put them on a carrying frame.

[13]"They are to remove the ashes from the bronze altar and spread a purple cloth over it. [14]Then they are to place on it all the utensils used for ministering at the altar, including the firepans, meat forks, shovels and sprinkling bowls. Over it they are to spread a covering of hides of sea cows and put its poles in place.

[15]"After Aaron and his sons have finished covering the holy furnishings and all the holy articles, and when the camp is ready to move, the Kohathites are to come to do the carrying. But they must not

touch the holy things or they will die. The Kohathites are to carry those things that are in the Tent of Meeting.

[16]"Eleazar son of Aaron, the priest, is to have charge of the oil for the light, the fragrant incense, the regular grain offering and the anointing oil. He is to be in charge of the entire tabernacle and everything in it, including its holy furnishings and articles."

[17]The LORD said to Moses and Aaron, [18]"See that the Kohathite tribal clans are not cut off from the Levites. [19]So that they may live and not die when they come near the most holy things, do this for them: Aaron and his sons are to go into the sanctuary and assign to each man his work and what he is to carry. [20]But the Kohathites must not go in to look at the holy things, even for a moment, or they will die."

The Gershonites

[21]The LORD said to Moses, [22]"Take a census also of the Gershonites by their families and clans. [23]Count all the men from thirty to fifty years of age who come to serve in the work at the Tent of Meeting.

[24]"This is the service of the Gershonite clans as they work and carry burdens: [25]They are to carry the curtains of the tabernacle, the Tent of Meeting, its covering and the outer covering of hides of sea cows, the curtains for the entrance to the Tent of Meeting, [26]the curtains of the courtyard surrounding the tabernacle and altar, the curtain for the entrance, the ropes and all the equipment used in its service. The Gershonites are to do all that needs to be done with these things. [27]All their service, whether carrying or doing other work, is to be done under the direction of Aaron and his sons. You shall assign to them as their responsibility all they are to carry. [28]This is the service of the Gershonite clans at the Tent of Meeting. Their duties are to be under the direction of Ithamar son of Aaron, the priest.

The Merarites

[29]"Count the Merarites by their clans and families. [30]Count all the men from thirty to fifty years of age who come to serve in the work at the Tent of Meeting. [31]This is their duty as they perform service

a50 That is, about 35 pounds (about 15.5 kilograms)
b6 That is, dugongs; also in verses 8, 10, 11, 12, 14 and 25

at the Tent of Meeting: to carry the frames of the tabernacle, its crossbars, posts and bases, ³²as well as the posts of the surrounding courtyard with their bases, tent pegs, ropes, all their equipment and everything related to their use. Assign to each man the specific things he is to carry. ³³This is the service of the Merarite clans as they work at the Tent of Meeting under the direction of Ithamar son of Aaron, the priest."

The Numbering of the Levite Clans

³⁴Moses, Aaron and the leaders of the community counted the Kohathites by their clans and families. ³⁵All the men from thirty to fifty years of age who came to serve in the work in the Tent of Meeting, ³⁶counted by clans, were 2,750. ³⁷This was the total of all those in the Kohathite clans who served in the Tent of Meeting. Moses and Aaron counted them according to the LORD's command through Moses.

³⁸The Gershonites were counted by their clans and families. ³⁹All the men from thirty to fifty years of age who came to serve in the work at the Tent of Meeting, ⁴⁰counted by their clans and families, were 2,630. ⁴¹This was the total of those in the Gershonite clans who served at the Tent of Meeting. Moses and Aaron counted them according to the LORD's command.

⁴²The Merarites were counted by their clans and families. ⁴³All the men from thirty to fifty years of age who came to serve in the work at the Tent of Meeting, ⁴⁴counted by their clans, were 3,200. ⁴⁵This was the total of those in the Merarite clans. Moses and Aaron counted them according to the LORD's command through Moses.

⁴⁶So Moses, Aaron and the leaders of Israel counted all the Levites by their clans and families. ⁴⁷All the men from thirty to fifty years of age who came to do the work of serving and carrying the Tent of Meeting ⁴⁸numbered 8,580. ⁴⁹At the LORD's command through Moses, each was assigned his work and told what to carry.

Thus they were counted, as the LORD commanded Moses.

The Purity of the Camp

5 The LORD said to Moses, ²"Command the Israelites to send away from the camp anyone who has an infectious skin disease[a] or a discharge of any kind, or who

is ceremonially unclean because of a dead body. ³Send away male and female alike; send them outside the camp so they will not defile their camp, where I dwell among them." ⁴The Israelites did this; they sent them outside the camp. They did just as the LORD had instructed Moses.

Restitution for Wrongs

⁵The LORD said to Moses, ⁶"Say to the Israelites: 'When a man or woman wrongs another in any way[b] and so is unfaithful to the LORD, that person is guilty ⁷and must confess the sin he has committed. He must make full restitution for his wrong, add one fifth to it and give it all to the person he has wronged. ⁸But if that person has no close relative to whom restitution can be made for the wrong, the restitution belongs to the LORD and must be given to the priest, along with the ram with which atonement is made for him. ⁹All the sacred contributions the Israelites bring to a priest will belong to him. ¹⁰Each man's sacred gifts are his own, but what he gives to the priest will belong to the priest.' "

The Test for an Unfaithful Wife

¹¹Then the LORD said to Moses, ¹²"Speak to the Israelites and say to them: 'If a man's wife goes astray and is unfaithful to him ¹³by sleeping with another man, and this is hidden from her husband and her impurity is undetected (since there is no witness against her and she has not been caught in the act), ¹⁴and if feelings of jealousy come over her husband and he suspects his wife and she is impure—or if he is jealous and suspects her even though she is not impure— ¹⁵then he is to take his wife to the priest. He must also take an offering of a tenth of an ephah[c] of barley flour on her behalf. He must not pour oil on it or put incense on it, because it is a grain offering for jealousy, a reminder offering to draw attention to guilt.

¹⁶" 'The priest shall bring her and have her stand before the LORD. ¹⁷Then he shall take some holy water in a clay jar and put some dust from the tabernacle floor into the water. ¹⁸After the priest has had the woman stand before the LORD, he shall loosen her hair and place in her hands the

---

a2 Traditionally leprosy; *the Hebrew word was used for various diseases affecting the skin—not necessarily leprosy.* *b6 Or* woman commits any wrong common to mankind *c15 That is, probably about 2 quarts (about 2 liters)*

reminder offering, the grain offering for jealousy, while he himself holds the bitter water that brings a curse. ¹⁹Then the priest shall put the woman under oath and say to her, "If no other man has slept with you and you have not gone astray and become impure while married to your husband, may this bitter water that brings a curse not harm you. ²⁰But if you have gone astray while married to your husband and you have defiled yourself by sleeping with a man other than your husband"— ²¹here the priest is to put the woman under this curse of the oath— "may the LORD cause your people to curse and denounce you when he causes your thigh to waste away and your abdomen to swell.ᵃ ²²May this water that brings a curse enter your body so that your abdomen swells and your thigh wastes away.ᵇ"

" 'Then the woman is to say, "Amen. So be it."

²³" 'The priest is to write these curses on a scroll and then wash them off into the bitter water. ²⁴He shall have the woman drink the bitter water that brings a curse, and this water will enter her and cause bitter suffering. ²⁵The priest is to take from her hands the grain offering for jealousy, wave it before the LORD and bring it to the altar. ²⁶The priest is then to take a handful of the grain offering as a memorial offering and burn it on the altar; after that, he is to have the woman drink the water. ²⁷If she has defiled herself and been unfaithful to her husband, then when she is made to drink the water that brings a curse, it will go into her and cause bitter suffering; her abdomen will swell and her thigh waste away,ᶜ and she will become accursed among her people. ²⁸If, however, the woman has not defiled herself and is free from impurity, she will be cleared of guilt and will be able to have children.

²⁹" 'This, then, is the law of jealousy when a woman goes astray and defiles herself while married to her husband, ³⁰or when feelings of jealousy come over a man because he suspects his wife. The priest is to have her stand before the LORD and is to apply this entire law to her. ³¹The husband will be innocent of any wrongdoing, but the woman will bear the consequences of her sin.' "

The Nazirite

6 The LORD said to Moses, ²"Speak to the Israelites and say to them: 'If a man or woman wants to make a special vow, a vow of separation to the LORD as a Nazirite, ³he must abstain from wine and other fermented drink and must not drink vinegar made from wine or from other fermented drink. He must not drink grape juice or eat grapes or raisins. ⁴As long as he is a Nazirite, he must not eat anything that comes from the grapevine, not even the seeds or skins.

⁵" 'During the entire period of his vow of separation no razor may be used on his head. He must be holy until the period of his separation to the LORD is over; he must let the hair of his head grow long. ⁶Throughout the period of his separation to the LORD he must not go near a dead body. ⁷Even if his own father or mother or brother or sister dies, he must not make himself ceremonially unclean on account of them, because the symbol of his separation to God is on his head. ⁸Throughout the period of his separation he is consecrated to the LORD.

⁹" 'If someone dies suddenly in his presence, thus defiling the hair he has dedicated, he must shave his head on the day of his cleansing—the seventh day. ¹⁰Then on the eighth day he must bring two doves or two young pigeons to the priest at the entrance to the Tent of Meeting. ¹¹The priest is to offer one as a sin offering and the other as a burnt offering to make atonement for him because he sinned by being in the presence of the dead body. That same day he is to consecrate his head. ¹²He must dedicate himself to the LORD for the period of his separation and must bring a year-old male lamb as a guilt offering. The previous days do not count, because he became defiled during his separation.

¹³" 'Now this is the law for the Nazirite when the period of his separation is over. He is to be brought to the entrance to the Tent of Meeting. ¹⁴There he is to present his offerings to the LORD: a year-old male lamb without defect for a burnt offering, a year-old ewe lamb without defect for a sin offering, a ram without defect for a fellowship offering,ᵈ ¹⁵together with their grain offerings and drink offerings, and a basket of bread made without yeast—cakes made of fine flour mixed with oil, and wafers spread with oil.

ᵃ21 Or *causes you to have a miscarrying womb and barrenness* ᵇ22 Or *body and cause you to be barren and have a miscarrying womb* ᶜ27 Or *suffering; she will have barrenness and a miscarrying womb* ᵈ14 Traditionally *peace offering*; also in verses 17 and 18

[16] " 'The priest is to present them before the LORD and make the sin offering and the burnt offering. [17]He is to present the basket of unleavened bread and is to sacrifice the ram as a fellowship offering to the LORD, together with its grain offering and drink offering.

[18] " 'Then at the entrance to the Tent of Meeting, the Nazirite must shave off the hair that he dedicated. He is to take the hair and put it in the fire that is under the sacrifice of the fellowship offering.

[19] " 'After the Nazirite has shaved off the hair of his dedication, the priest is to place in his hands a boiled shoulder of the ram, and a cake and a wafer from the basket, both made without yeast. [20]The priest shall then wave them before the LORD as a wave offering; they are holy and belong to the priest, together with the breast that was waved and the thigh that was presented. After that, the Nazirite may drink wine.

[21] " 'This is the law of the Nazirite who vows his offering to the LORD in accordance with his separation, in addition to whatever else he can afford. He must fulfill the vow he has made, according to the law of the Nazirite.' "

The Priestly Blessing

[22]The LORD said to Moses, [23]"Tell Aaron and his sons, 'This is how you are to bless the Israelites. Say to them:

[24] " ' "The LORD bless you
　　and keep you;
[25] the LORD make his face shine upon you
　　and be gracious to you;
[26] the LORD turn his face toward you
　　and give you peace." '

[27]"So they will put my name on the Israelites, and I will bless them."

Offerings at the Dedication of the Tabernacle

7 When Moses finished setting up the tabernacle, he anointed it and consecrated it and all its furnishings. He also anointed and consecrated the altar and all its utensils. [2]Then the leaders of Israel, the heads of families who were the tribal leaders in charge of those who were counted, made offerings. [3]They brought as their gifts before the LORD six covered carts and twelve oxen—an ox from each leader and a cart from every two. These they presented before the tabernacle.

[4]The LORD said to Moses, [5]"Accept these from them, that they may be used in the work at the Tent of Meeting. Give them to the Levites as each man's work requires."

[6]So Moses took the carts and oxen and gave them to the Levites. [7]He gave two carts and four oxen to the Gershonites, as their work required, [8]and he gave four carts and eight oxen to the Merarites, as their work required. They were all under the direction of Ithamar son of Aaron, the priest. [9]But Moses did not give any to the Kohathites, because they were to carry on their shoulders the holy things, for which they were responsible.

[10]When the altar was anointed, the leaders brought their offerings for its dedication and presented them before the altar. [11]For the LORD had said to Moses, "Each day one leader is to bring his offering for the dedication of the altar."

[12]The one who brought his offering on the first day was Nahshon son of Amminadab of the tribe of Judah.

[13]His offering was one silver plate weighing a hundred and thirty shekels,[a] and one silver sprinkling bowl weighing seventy shekels,[b] both according to the sanctuary shekel, each filled with fine flour mixed with oil as a grain offering; [14]one gold dish weighing ten shekels,[c] filled with incense; [15]one young bull, one ram and one male lamb a year old, for a burnt offering; [16]one male goat for a sin offering; [17]and two oxen, five rams, five male goats and five male lambs a year old, to be sacrificed as a fellowship offering.[d] This was the offering of Nahshon son of Amminadab.

[18]On the second day Nethanel son of Zuar, the leader of Issachar, brought his offering.

[19]The offering he brought was one silver plate weighing a hundred and thirty shekels, and one silver sprinkling bowl weighing seventy shekels, both according to the sanctuary shekel, each filled with fine flour mixed with oil as a grain offering; [20]one gold dish weighing ten shekels, filled with incense; [21]one young bull, one ram and one male lamb a year

---

[a]13 That is, about 3 1/4 pounds (about 1.5 kilograms); also elsewhere in this chapter [b]13 That is, about 1 3/4 pounds (about 0.8 kilogram); also elsewhere in this chapter   [c]14 That is, about 4 ounces (about 110 grams); also elsewhere in this chapter   [d]17 Traditionally *peace offering*; also elsewhere in this chapter

old, for a burnt offering; ²²one male goat for a sin offering; ²³and two oxen, five rams, five male goats and five male lambs a year old, to be sacrificed as a fellowship offering. This was the offering of Nethanel son of Zuar.

²⁴On the third day, Eliab son of Helon, the leader of the people of Zebulun, brought his offering.
  ²⁵His offering was one silver plate weighing a hundred and thirty shekels, and one silver sprinkling bowl weighing seventy shekels, both according to the sanctuary shekel, each filled with fine flour mixed with oil as a grain offering; ²⁶one gold dish weighing ten shekels, filled with incense; ²⁷one young bull, one ram and one male lamb a year old, for a burnt offering; ²⁸one male goat for a sin offering; ²⁹and two oxen, five rams, five male goats and five male lambs a year old, to be sacrificed as a fellowship offering. This was the offering of Eliab son of Helon.

³⁰On the fourth day Elizur son of Shedeur, the leader of the people of Reuben, brought his offering.
  ³¹His offering was one silver plate weighing a hundred and thirty shekels, and one silver sprinkling bowl weighing seventy shekels, both according to the sanctuary shekel, each filled with fine flour mixed with oil as a grain offering; ³²one gold dish weighing ten shekels, filled with incense; ³³one young bull, one ram and one male lamb a year old, for a burnt offering; ³⁴one male goat for a sin offering; ³⁵and two oxen, five rams, five male goats and five male lambs a year old, to be sacrificed as a fellowship offering. This was the offering of Elizur son of Shedeur.

³⁶On the fifth day Shelumiel son of Zurishaddai, the leader of the people of Simeon, brought his offering.
  ³⁷His offering was one silver plate weighing a hundred and thirty shekels, and one silver sprinkling bowl weighing seventy shekels, both according to the sanctuary shekel, each filled with fine flour mixed with oil as a grain offering; ³⁸one gold dish weighing ten shekels, filled with incense; ³⁹one young bull, one ram and one male lamb a year old, for a burnt

offering; ⁴⁰one male goat for a sin offering; ⁴¹and two oxen, five rams, five male goats and five male lambs a year old, to be sacrificed as a fellowship offering. This was the offering of Shelumiel son of Zurishaddai.

⁴²On the sixth day Eliasaph son of Deuel, the leader of the people of Gad, brought his offering.
  ⁴³His offering was one silver plate weighing a hundred and thirty shekels, and one silver sprinkling bowl weighing seventy shekels, both according to the sanctuary shekel, each filled with fine flour mixed with oil as a grain offering; ⁴⁴one gold dish weighing ten shekels, filled with incense; ⁴⁵one young bull, one ram and one male lamb a year old, for a burnt offering; ⁴⁶one male goat for a sin offering; ⁴⁷and two oxen, five rams, five male goats and five male lambs a year old, to be sacrificed as a fellowship offering. This was the offering of Eliasaph son of Deuel.

⁴⁸On the seventh day Elishama son of Ammihud, the leader of the people of Ephraim, brought his offering.
  ⁴⁹His offering was one silver plate weighing a hundred and thirty shekels, and one silver sprinkling bowl weighing seventy shekels, both according to the sanctuary shekel, each filled with fine flour mixed with oil as a grain offering; ⁵⁰one gold dish weighing ten shekels, filled with incense; ⁵¹one young bull, one ram and one male lamb a year old, for a burnt offering; ⁵²one male goat for a sin offering; ⁵³and two oxen, five rams, five male goats and five male lambs a year old, to be sacrificed as a fellowship offering. This was the offering of Elishama son of Ammihud.

⁵⁴On the eighth day Gamaliel son of Pedahzur, the leader of the people of Manasseh, brought his offering.
  ⁵⁵His offering was one silver plate weighing a hundred and thirty shekels, and one silver sprinkling bowl weighing seventy shekels, both according to the sanctuary shekel, each filled with fine flour mixed with oil as a grain offering; ⁵⁶one gold dish weighing ten shekels, filled with incense; ⁵⁷one young bull, one ram and one male lamb a year old, for a burnt offering; ⁵⁸one male goat for a sin of-

fering; [59]and two oxen, five rams, five male goats and five male lambs a year old, to be sacrificed as a fellowship offering. This was the offering of Gamaliel son of Pedahzur.

[60]On the ninth day Abidan son of Gideoni, the leader of the people of Benjamin, brought his offering.

[61]His offering was one silver plate weighing a hundred and thirty shekels, and one silver sprinkling bowl weighing seventy shekels, both according to the sanctuary shekel, each filled with fine flour mixed with oil as a grain offering; [62]one gold dish weighing ten shekels, filled with incense; [63]one young bull, one ram and one male lamb a year old, for a burnt offering; [64]one male goat for a sin offering; [65]and two oxen, five rams, five male goats and five male lambs a year old, to be sacrificed as a fellowship offering. This was the offering of Abidan son of Gideoni.

[66]On the tenth day Ahiezer son of Ammishaddai, the leader of the people of Dan, brought his offering.

[67]His offering was one silver plate weighing a hundred and thirty shekels, and one silver sprinkling bowl weighing seventy shekels, both according to the sanctuary shekel, each filled with fine flour mixed with oil as a grain offering; [68]one gold dish weighing ten shekels, filled with incense; [69]one young bull, one ram and one male lamb a year old, for a burnt offering; [70]one male goat for a sin offering; [71]and two oxen, five rams, five male goats and five male lambs a year old, to be sacrificed as a fellowship offering. This was the offering of Ahiezer son of Ammishaddai.

[72]On the eleventh day Pagiel son of Ocran, the leader of the people of Asher, brought his offering.

[73]His offering was one silver plate weighing a hundred and thirty shekels, and one silver sprinkling bowl weighing seventy shekels, both according to the sanctuary shekel, each filled with fine flour mixed with oil as a grain offering; [74]one gold dish weighing ten shekels, filled with incense; [75]one young bull, one ram and one male lamb a year old, for a burnt offering; [76]one male goat for a sin offering; [77]and two oxen, five rams, five male goats and five male lambs a year old, to be sacrificed as a fellowship offering. This was the offering of Pagiel son of Ocran.

[78]On the twelfth day Ahira son of Enan, the leader of the people of Naphtali, brought his offering.

[79]His offering was one silver plate weighing a hundred and thirty shekels, and one silver sprinkling bowl weighing seventy shekels, both according to the sanctuary shekel, each filled with fine flour mixed with oil as a grain offering; [80]one gold dish weighing ten shekels, filled with incense; [81]one young bull, one ram and one male lamb a year old, for a burnt offering; [82]one male goat for a sin offering; [83]and two oxen, five rams, five male goats and five male lambs a year old, to be sacrificed as a fellowship offering. This was the offering of Ahira son of Enan.

[84]These were the offerings of the Israelite leaders for the dedication of the altar when it was anointed: twelve silver plates, twelve silver sprinkling bowls and twelve gold dishes. [85]Each silver plate weighed a hundred and thirty shekels, and each sprinkling bowl seventy shekels. Altogether, the silver dishes weighed two thousand four hundred shekels,[a] according to the sanctuary shekel. [86]The twelve gold dishes filled with incense weighed ten shekels each, according to the sanctuary shekel. Altogether, the gold dishes weighed a hundred and twenty shekels.[b] [87]The total number of animals for the burnt offering came to twelve young bulls, twelve rams and twelve male lambs a year old, together with their grain offering. Twelve male goats were used for the sin offering. [88]The total number of animals for the sacrifice of the fellowship offering came to twenty-four oxen, sixty rams, sixty male goats and sixty male lambs a year old. These were the offerings for the dedication of the altar after it was anointed.

[89]When Moses entered the Tent of Meeting to speak with the LORD, he heard the voice speaking to him from between the two cherubim above the atonement cover on the ark of the Testimony. And he spoke with him.

---

[a]85 That is, about 60 pounds (about 28 kilograms)
[b]86 That is, about 3 pounds (about 1.4 kilograms)

Setting Up the Lamps

8 The LORD said to Moses, [2]"Speak to Aaron and say to him, 'When you set up the seven lamps, they are to light the area in front of the lampstand.' "

[3]Aaron did so; he set up the lamps so that they faced forward on the lampstand, just as the LORD commanded Moses. [4]This is how the lampstand was made: It was made of hammered gold—from its base to its blossoms. The lampstand was made exactly like the pattern the LORD had shown Moses.

The Setting Apart of the Levites

[5]The LORD said to Moses: [6]"Take the Levites from among the other Israelites and make them ceremonially clean. [7]To purify them, do this: Sprinkle the water of cleansing on them; then have them shave their whole bodies and wash their clothes, and so purify themselves. [8]Have them take a young bull with its grain offering of fine flour mixed with oil; then you are to take a second young bull for a sin offering. [9]Bring the Levites to the front of the Tent of Meeting and assemble the whole Israelite community. [10]You are to bring the Levites before the LORD, and the Israelites are to lay their hands on them. [11]Aaron is to present the Levites before the LORD as a wave offering from the Israelites, so that they may be ready to do the work of the LORD.

[12]"After the Levites lay their hands on the heads of the bulls, use the one for a sin offering to the LORD and the other for a burnt offering, to make atonement for the Levites. [13]Have the Levites stand in front of Aaron and his sons and then present them as a wave offering to the LORD. [14]In this way you are to set the Levites apart from the other Israelites, and the Levites will be mine.

[15]"After you have purified the Levites and presented them as a wave offering, they are to come to do their work at the Tent of Meeting. [16]They are the Israelites who are to be given wholly to me. I have taken them as my own in place of the firstborn, the first male offspring from every Israelite woman. [17]Every firstborn male in Israel, whether man or animal, is mine. When I struck down all the firstborn in Egypt, I set them apart for myself. [18]And I have taken the Levites in place of all the firstborn sons in Israel. [19]Of all the Israelites, I have given the Levites as gifts to Aaron and his sons to do the work at the Tent of Meeting on behalf of the Israelites and to make atonement for them so that no plague will strike the Israelites when they go near the sanctuary."

[20]Moses, Aaron and the whole Israelite community did with the Levites just as the LORD commanded Moses. [21]The Levites purified themselves and washed their clothes. Then Aaron presented them as a wave offering before the LORD and made atonement for them to purify them. [22]After that, the Levites came to do their work at the Tent of Meeting under the supervision of Aaron and his sons. They did with the Levites just as the LORD commanded Moses.

[23]The LORD said to Moses, [24]"This applies to the Levites: Men twenty-five years old or more shall come to take part in the work at the Tent of Meeting, [25]but at the age of fifty, they must retire from their regular service and work no longer. [26]They may assist their brothers in performing their duties at the Tent of Meeting, but they themselves must not do the work. This, then, is how you are to assign the responsibilities of the Levites."

The Passover

9 The LORD spoke to Moses in the Desert of Sinai in the first month of the second year after they came out of Egypt. He said, [2]"Have the Israelites celebrate the Passover at the appointed time. [3]Celebrate it at the appointed time, at twilight on the fourteenth day of this month, in accordance with all its rules and regulations."

[4]So Moses told the Israelites to celebrate the Passover, [5]and they did so in the Desert of Sinai at twilight on the fourteenth day of the first month. The Israelites did everything just as the LORD commanded Moses.

[6]But some of them could not celebrate the Passover on that day because they were ceremonially unclean on account of a dead body. So they came to Moses and Aaron that same day [7]and said to Moses, "We have become unclean because of a dead body, but why should we be kept from presenting the LORD's offering with the other Israelites at the appointed time?"

[8]Moses answered them, "Wait until I find out what the LORD commands concerning you."

[9]Then the LORD said to Moses, [10]"Tell

the Israelites: 'When any of you or your descendants are unclean because of a dead body or are away on a journey, they may still celebrate the LORD's Passover. ¹¹They are to celebrate it on the fourteenth day of the second month at twilight. They are to eat the lamb, together with unleavened bread and bitter herbs. ¹²They must not leave any of it till morning or break any of its bones. When they celebrate the Passover, they must follow all the regulations. ¹³But if a man who is ceremonially clean and not on a journey fails to celebrate the Passover, that person must be cut off from his people because he did not present the LORD's offering at the appointed time. That man will bear the consequences of his sin.

¹⁴" 'An alien living among you who wants to celebrate the LORD's Passover must do so in accordance with its rules and regulations. You must have the same regulations for the alien and the native-born.' "

The Cloud Above the Tabernacle

¹⁵On the day the tabernacle, the Tent of the Testimony, was set up, the cloud covered it. From evening till morning the

Follow Him

DAILY INSIGHT

THURSDAY

Passage:
Numbers 9:9–23

Verse:
Numbers 9:23

What is it about men and directions? I know that this isn't universally true, but most men do not like to stop and ask for directions, even when they're hopelessly lost. And this isn't only true of hard-driving—no pun intended—"Type A" personality men. I know a true gentleman, a soft-spoken man, who has had a pleading wife and a back seat full of sobbing children, begging him to stop and ask. And he didn't stop.

This has been a problem with men for centuries. Perhaps the gene connected to this trait came to some of us from the early explorers. These men were knighted by some queen who, standing in her bedroom slippers, sent them out toward the horizon to find new lands. Even Christopher Columbus thought he was in the West Indies, but because he didn't stop and ask a flounder in the mid-Atlantic, he wound up a couple of miles north of Dover, Delaware. Thank goodness he didn't ask. America still may be undiscovered.

Now, I want you to imagine this. For forty years, the Israelites lived out of suitcases. They had no itinerary. No idea where they were going next. Except for a large cloud cluster that hung over the tabernacle during the day that turned to fire at night, they were completely lost.

Can you imagine how this must have felt for these people? They had no idea where they were going. Sometimes the cloud/fire would hang over the tabernacle for a year, and sometimes it would only stop for a day or two. The men in this huge Jewish family discovered what millions of wives would discover in the centuries to follow … what it was like to ride along without the driver asking for directions. God didn't seem to have a plan. "I'm tired of wandering around here," the people must have said to each other. "Why doesn't God make up his mind?"

There is a principle here that cannot be missed. Please listen carefully. A thousand years later, God's Son would look into the faces of ordinary men and say, "Follow me." And the Scripture tells us that they did exactly that. They left their businesses and their familiar, safe surroundings and followed him. They had no idea where he was going, they simply did what he asked them to do.

Do you know where God is taking you? You don't? Has he revealed his exact plan for you and your family? He hasn't? And will there probably be a few surprises around the corner that will cause you to wonder where he's going? Yes, probably.

But this is exactly the point. God knows. He's not lost. Trust him.

For your next devotional reading, go to page 168.

cloud above the tabernacle looked like fire. [16]That is how it continued to be; the cloud covered it, and at night it looked like fire. [17]Whenever the cloud lifted from above the Tent, the Israelites set out; wherever the cloud settled, the Israelites encamped. [18]At the LORD's command the Israelites set out, and at his command they encamped. As long as the cloud stayed over the tabernacle, they remained in camp. [19]When the cloud remained over the tabernacle a long time, the Israelites obeyed the LORD's order and did not set out. [20]Sometimes the cloud was over the tabernacle only a few days; at the LORD's command they would encamp, and then at his command they would set out. [21]Sometimes the cloud stayed only from evening till morning, and when it lifted in the morning, they set out. Whether by day or by night, whenever the cloud lifted, they set out. [22]Whether the cloud stayed over the tabernacle for two days or a month or a year, the Israelites would remain in camp and not set out; but when it lifted, they would set out. [23]At the LORD's command they encamped, and at the LORD's command they set out. They obeyed the LORD's order, in accordance with his command through Moses.

The Silver Trumpets

10 The LORD said to Moses: [2]"Make two trumpets of hammered silver, and use them for calling the community together and for having the camps set out. [3]When both are sounded, the whole community is to assemble before you at the entrance to the Tent of Meeting. [4]If only one is sounded, the leaders—the heads of the clans of Israel—are to assemble before you. [5]When a trumpet blast is sounded, the tribes camping on the east are to set out. [6]At the sounding of a second blast, the camps on the south are to set out. The blast will be the signal for setting out. [7]To gather the assembly, blow the trumpets, but not with the same signal.

[8]"The sons of Aaron, the priests, are to blow the trumpets. This is to be a lasting ordinance for you and the generations to come. [9]When you go into battle in your own land against an enemy who is oppressing you, sound a blast on the trumpets. Then you will be remembered by the LORD your God and rescued from your enemies. [10]Also at your times of rejoicing— your appointed feasts and New Moon festivals—you are to sound the trumpets

over your burnt offerings and fellowship offerings,[a] and they will be a memorial for you before your God. I am the LORD your God."

The Israelites Leave Sinai

[11]On the twentieth day of the second month of the second year, the cloud lifted from above the tabernacle of the Testimony. [12]Then the Israelites set out from the Desert of Sinai and traveled from place to place until the cloud came to rest in the Desert of Paran. [13]They set out, this first time, at the LORD's command through Moses.

[14]The divisions of the camp of Judah went first, under their standard. Nahshon son of Amminadab was in command. [15]Nethanel son of Zuar was over the division of the tribe of Issachar, [16]and Eliab son of Helon was over the division of the tribe of Zebulun. [17]Then the tabernacle was taken down, and the Gershonites and Merarites, who carried it, set out.

[18]The divisions of the camp of Reuben went next, under their standard. Elizur son of Shedeur was in command. [19]Shelumiel son of Zurishaddai was over the division of the tribe of Simeon, [20]and Eliasaph son of Deuel was over the division of the tribe of Gad. [21]Then the Kohathites set out, carrying the holy things. The tabernacle was to be set up before they arrived. [22]The divisions of the camp of Ephraim went next, under their standard. Elishama son of Ammihud was in command. [23]Gamaliel son of Pedahzur was over the division of the tribe of Manasseh, [24]and Abidan son of Gideoni was over the division of the tribe of Benjamin.

[25]Finally, as the rear guard for all the units, the divisions of the camp of Dan set out, under their standard. Ahiezer son of Ammishaddai was in command. [26]Pagiel son of Ocran was over the division of the tribe of Asher, [27]and Ahira son of Enan was over the division of the tribe of Naphtali. [28]This was the order of march for the Israelite divisions as they set out.

[29]Now Moses said to Hobab son of Reuel the Midianite, Moses' father-in-law, "We are setting out for the place about which the LORD said, 'I will give it to you.' Come with us and we will treat you well, for the LORD has promised good things to Israel."

[30]He answered, "No, I will not go; I am

[a]10 Traditionally *peace offerings*

going back to my own land and my own people."

³¹But Moses said, "Please do not leave us. You know where we should camp in the desert, and you can be our eyes. ³²If you come with us, we will share with you whatever good things the LORD gives us."

³³So they set out from the mountain of the LORD and traveled for three days. The ark of the covenant of the LORD went before them during those three days to find them a place to rest. ³⁴The cloud of the LORD was over them by day when they set out from the camp.

³⁵Whenever the ark set out, Moses said,

"Rise up, O LORD!
    May your enemies be scattered;
    may your foes flee before you."

³⁶Whenever it came to rest, he said,

"Return, O LORD,
    to the countless thousands of Israel."

Fire From the LORD

11 Now the people complained about their hardships in the hearing of the LORD, and when he heard them his anger was aroused. Then fire from the LORD burned among them and consumed some of the outskirts of the camp. ²When the people cried out to Moses, he prayed to the LORD and the fire died down. ³So that place was called Taberah,ᵃ because fire from the LORD had burned among them.

Quail From the LORD

⁴The rabble with them began to crave other food, and again the Israelites started wailing and said, "If only we had meat to eat! ⁵We remember the fish we ate in Egypt at no cost—also the cucumbers, melons, leeks, onions and garlic. ⁶But now we have lost our appetite; we never see anything but this manna!"

⁷The manna was like coriander seed and looked like resin. ⁸The people went around gathering it, and then ground it in a handmill or crushed it in a mortar. They cooked it in a pot or made it into cakes. And it tasted like something made with olive oil. ⁹When the dew settled on the camp at night, the manna also came down.

¹⁰Moses heard the people of every family wailing, each at the entrance to his tent. The LORD became exceedingly angry, and Moses was troubled. ¹¹He asked the LORD, "Why have you brought this trouble on your servant? What have I done to displease you that you put the burden of all these people on me? ¹²Did I conceive all these people? Did I give them birth? Why do you tell me to carry them in my arms, as a nurse carries an infant, to the land you promised on oath to their forefathers? ¹³Where can I get meat for all these people? They keep wailing to me, 'Give us meat to eat!' ¹⁴I cannot carry all these people by myself; the burden is too heavy for me. ¹⁵If this is how you are going to treat me, put me to death right now—if I have found favor in your eyes—and do not let me face my own ruin."

¹⁶The LORD said to Moses: "Bring me seventy of Israel's elders who are known to you as leaders and officials among the people. Have them come to the Tent of Meeting, that they may stand there with you. ¹⁷I will come down and speak with you there, and I will take of the Spirit that is on you and put the Spirit on them. They will help you carry the burden of the people so that you will not have to carry it alone.

¹⁸"Tell the people: 'Consecrate yourselves in preparation for tomorrow, when you will eat meat. The LORD heard you when you wailed, "If only we had meat to eat! We were better off in Egypt!" Now the LORD will give you meat, and you will eat it. ¹⁹You will not eat it for just one day, or two days, or five, ten or twenty days, ²⁰but for a whole month—until it comes out of your nostrils and you loathe it—because you have rejected the LORD, who is among you, and have wailed before him, saying, "Why did we ever leave Egypt?" ' "

²¹But Moses said, "Here I am among six hundred thousand men on foot, and you say, 'I will give them meat to eat for a whole month!' ²²Would they have enough if flocks and herds were slaughtered for them? Would they have enough if all the fish in the sea were caught for them?"

²³The LORD answered Moses, "Is the LORD's arm too short? You will now see whether or not what I say will come true for you."

²⁴So Moses went out and told the people what the LORD had said. He brought together seventy of their elders and had them stand around the Tent. ²⁵Then the LORD came down in the cloud and spoke with him, and he took of the Spirit that was on him and put the Spirit on the

---

ᵃ3 *Taberah* means *burning.*

seventy elders. When the Spirit rested on them, they prophesied, but they did not do so again.[a]

[26]However, two men, whose names were Eldad and Medad, had remained in the camp. They were listed among the elders, but did not go out to the Tent. Yet the Spirit also rested on them, and they prophesied in the camp. [27]A young man ran and told Moses, "Eldad and Medad are prophesying in the camp."

[28]Joshua son of Nun, who had been Moses' aide since youth, spoke up and said, "Moses, my lord, stop them!"

[29]But Moses replied, "Are you jealous for my sake? I wish that all the LORD's people were prophets and that the LORD would put his Spirit on them!" [30]Then Moses and the elders of Israel returned to the camp.

[31]Now a wind went out from the LORD and drove quail in from the sea. It brought them[b] down all around the camp to about three feet[c] above the ground, as far as a day's walk in any direction. [32]All that day and night and all the next day the people went out and gathered quail. No one gathered less than ten homers.[d] Then they spread them out all around the camp. [33]But while the meat was still between their teeth and before it could be consumed, the anger of the LORD burned against the people, and he struck them with a severe plague. [34]Therefore the place was named Kibroth Hattaavah,[e] because there they buried the people who had craved other food.

[35]From Kibroth Hattaavah the people traveled to Hazeroth and stayed there.

Miriam and Aaron Oppose Moses

12 Miriam and Aaron began to talk against Moses because of his Cushite wife, for he had married a Cushite. [2]"Has the LORD spoken only through Moses?" they asked. "Hasn't he also spoken through us?" And the LORD heard this.

[3](Now Moses was a very humble man, more humble than anyone else on the face of the earth.)

[4]At once the LORD said to Moses, Aaron and Miriam, "Come out to the Tent of Meeting, all three of you." So the three of them came out. [5]Then the LORD came down in a pillar of cloud; he stood at the entrance to the Tent and summoned Aaron and Miriam. When both of them stepped forward, [6]he said, "Listen to my words:

"When a prophet of the LORD is among you,
    I reveal myself to him in visions,
    I speak to him in dreams.
[7]But this is not true of my servant Moses;
    he is faithful in all my house.
[8]With him I speak face to face,
    clearly and not in riddles;
    he sees the form of the LORD.
Why then were you not afraid
    to speak against my servant Moses?"

[9]The anger of the LORD burned against them, and he left them.

[10]When the cloud lifted from above the Tent, there stood Miriam—leprous,[f] like snow. Aaron turned toward her and saw that she had leprosy; [11]and he said to Moses, "Please, my lord, do not hold against us the sin we have so foolishly committed. [12]Do not let her be like a stillborn infant coming from its mother's womb with its flesh half eaten away."

[13]So Moses cried out to the LORD, "O God, please heal her!"

[14]The LORD replied to Moses, "If her father had spit in her face, would she not have been in disgrace for seven days? Confine her outside the camp for seven days; after that she can be brought back." [15]So Miriam was confined outside the camp for seven days, and the people did not move on till she was brought back.

[16]After that, the people left Hazeroth and encamped in the Desert of Paran.

Exploring Canaan

13 The LORD said to Moses, [2]"Send some men to explore the land of Canaan, which I am giving to the Israelites. From each ancestral tribe send one of its leaders."

[3]So at the LORD's command Moses sent them out from the Desert of Paran. All of them were leaders of the Israelites. [4]These are their names:

from the tribe of Reuben, Shammua son of Zaccur;
[5]from the tribe of Simeon, Shaphat son of Hori;

---

[a]25 Or *prophesied and continued to do so*   [b]31 Or *They flew*   [c]31 Hebrew *two cubits* (about 1 meter)   [d]32 That is, probably about 60 bushels (about 2.2 kiloliters)   [e]34 *Kibroth Hattaavah* means *graves of craving.*   [f]10 The Hebrew word was used for various diseases affecting the skin—not necessarily leprosy.

⁶from the tribe of Judah, Caleb son of Jephunneh;
⁷from the tribe of Issachar, Igal son of Joseph;
⁸from the tribe of Ephraim, Hoshea son of Nun;
⁹from the tribe of Benjamin, Palti son of Raphu;
¹⁰from the tribe of Zebulun, Gaddiel son of Sodi;
¹¹from the tribe of Manasseh (a tribe of Joseph), Gaddi son of Susi;
¹²from the tribe of Dan, Ammiel son of Gemalli;
¹³from the tribe of Asher, Sethur son of Michael;
¹⁴from the tribe of Naphtali, Nahbi son of Vophsi;
¹⁵from the tribe of Gad, Geuel son of Maki.

¹⁶These are the names of the men Moses sent to explore the land. (Moses gave Hoshea son of Nun the name Joshua.)

¹⁷When Moses sent them to explore Canaan, he said, "Go up through the Negev and on into the hill country. ¹⁸See what the land is like and whether the people who live there are strong or weak, few or many. ¹⁹What kind of land do they live in? Is it good or bad? What kind of towns do they live in? Are they unwalled or fortified? ²⁰How is the soil? Is it fertile or poor? Are there trees on it or not? Do your best to bring back some of the fruit of the land." (It was the season for the first ripe grapes.)

²¹So they went up and explored the land from the Desert of Zin as far as Rehob, toward Lebo*a* Hamath. ²²They went up through the Negev and came to Hebron, where Ahiman, Sheshai and Talmai, the descendants of Anak, lived. (Hebron had been built seven years before Zoan in Egypt.) ²³When they reached the Valley of Eshcol,*b* they cut off a branch bearing a single cluster of grapes. Two of them carried it on a pole between them, along with some pomegranates and figs. ²⁴That place was called the Valley of Eshcol because of the cluster of grapes the Israelites cut off there. ²⁵At the end of forty days they returned from exploring the land.

Report on the Exploration

²⁶They came back to Moses and Aaron and the whole Israelite community at Kadesh in the Desert of Paran. There they reported to them and to the whole assembly and showed them the fruit of the land.

²⁷They gave Moses this account: "We went into the land to which you sent us, and it does flow with milk and honey! Here is its fruit. ²⁸But the people who live there are powerful, and the cities are fortified and very large. We even saw descendants of Anak there. ²⁹The Amalekites live in the Negev; the Hittites, Jebusites and Amorites live in the hill country; and the Canaanites live near the sea and along the Jordan."

³⁰Then Caleb silenced the people before Moses and said, "We should go up and take possession of the land, for we can certainly do it."

³¹But the men who had gone up with him said, "We can't attack those people; they are stronger than we are." ³²And they spread among the Israelites a bad report about the land they had explored. They said, "The land we explored devours those living in it. All the people we saw there are of great size. ³³We saw the Nephilim there (the descendants of Anak come from the Nephilim). We seemed like grasshoppers in our own eyes, and we looked the same to them."

The People Rebel

14 That night all the people of the community raised their voices and wept aloud. ²All the Israelites grumbled against Moses and Aaron, and the whole assembly said to them, "If only we had died in Egypt! Or in this desert! ³Why is the LORD bringing us to this land only to let us fall by the sword? Our wives and children will be taken as plunder. Wouldn't it be better for us to go back to Egypt?" ⁴And they said to each other, "We should choose a leader and go back to Egypt."

⁵Then Moses and Aaron fell facedown in front of the whole Israelite assembly gathered there. ⁶Joshua son of Nun and Caleb son of Jephunneh, who were among those who had explored the land, tore their clothes ⁷and said to the entire Israelite assembly, "The land we passed through and explored is exceedingly good. ⁸If the LORD is pleased with us, he will lead us into that land, a land flowing with milk and honey, and will give it to us. ⁹Only do not rebel against the LORD. And do not be afraid of the people of the land, because we will swallow them up. Their protection is gone, but the LORD is with us. Do not be afraid of them."

a21 Or toward the entrance to   b23 Eshcol means cluster; also in verse 24.

[10]But the whole assembly talked about stoning them. Then the glory of the LORD appeared at the Tent of Meeting to all the Israelites. [11]The LORD said to Moses, "How long will these people treat me with contempt? How long will they refuse to believe in me, in spite of all the miraculous signs I have performed among them? [12]I will strike them down with a plague and destroy them, but I will make you into a nation greater and stronger than they."

[13]Moses said to the LORD, "Then the Egyptians will hear about it! By your power you brought these people up from among them. [14]And they will tell the inhabitants of this land about it. They have already heard that you, O LORD, are with these people and that you, O LORD, have been seen face to face, that your cloud stays over them, and that you go before them in a pillar of cloud by day and a pillar of fire by night. [15]If you put these people to death all at one time, the nations who have heard this report about you will say, [16]'The LORD was not able to bring these people into the land he promised them on oath; so he slaughtered them in the desert.'

[17]"Now may the Lord's strength be displayed, just as you have declared: [18]'The LORD is slow to anger, abounding in love and forgiving sin and rebellion. Yet he does not leave the guilty unpunished; he punishes the children for the sin of the fathers to the third and fourth generation.' [19]In accordance with your great love, forgive the sin of these people, just as you have pardoned them from the time they left Egypt until now."

[20]The LORD replied, "I have forgiven them, as you asked. [21]Nevertheless, as surely as I live and as surely as the glory of the LORD fills the whole earth, [22]not one of the men who saw my glory and the miraculous signs I performed in Egypt and in the desert but who disobeyed me and tested me ten times— [23]not one of them will ever see the land I promised on oath to their forefathers. No one who has treated me with contempt will ever see it. [24]But because my servant Caleb has a different spirit and follows me wholeheart-

Take It. It's Yours.

DAILY INSIGHT

FRIDAY

Passage:
Numbers 14:1–9

Verse:
Numbers 14:8

Do you let your kids hang around the Christmas tree, scoping out the presents? Whether or not you allow this in your home, the undeniable truth is that all children want to know what's under there with their name on it.

You can see them, circling the brightly wrapped packages like hungry cats stealthily stalking unsuspecting mice.

Moses called together twelve men. He told them to sneak into the promised land, shake it a few times, and come back with a report of what they thought was inside. The men came back with good news and bad news. "It's an incredible place all right," they told the people, "but it couldn't be for us."

"Good gift," they might as well have been saying, "but the wrong name is on the tag."

I have a question: Does this story say something important about Canaan or the men who visited it? Can you see it? These poor men saw God's spectacular provision and said to themselves, "This place is too incredible for us. We don't deserve a homeland so fine—not to mention that it already has some giants' name on it!"

But two courageous men stepped forward (14:6–8). Daring to challenge the bad report from the cowards, Joshua and Caleb announced to the people, "[The LORD] will lead us into that land ... do not rebel ... do not be afraid."

God's promises are sure. Even though we may look at his good gifts and find it hard to believe that God could provide something so fine for someone so undeserving, they are truly ours anyway. His gifts are ours because *he said* they are. Celebrate his goodness today.

For your next devotional reading, go to page 178.

edly, I will bring him into the land he went to, and his descendants will inherit it. ²⁵Since the Amalekites and Canaanites are living in the valleys, turn back tomorrow and set out toward the desert along the route to the Red Sea.ᵃ"

²⁶The LORD said to Moses and Aaron: ²⁷"How long will this wicked community grumble against me? I have heard the complaints of these grumbling Israelites. ²⁸So tell them, 'As surely as I live, declares the LORD, I will do to you the very things I heard you say: ²⁹In this desert your bodies will fall—every one of you twenty years old or more who was counted in the census and who has grumbled against me. ³⁰Not one of you will enter the land I swore with uplifted hand to make your home, except Caleb son of Jephunneh and Joshua son of Nun. ³¹As for your children that you said would be taken as plunder, I will bring them in to enjoy the land you have rejected. ³²But you—your bodies will fall in this desert. ³³Your children will be shepherds here for forty years, suffering for your unfaithfulness, until the last of your bodies lies in the desert. ³⁴For forty years—one year for each of the forty days you explored the land—you will suffer for your sins and know what it is like to have me against you.' ³⁵I, the LORD, have spoken, and I will surely do these things to this whole wicked community, which has banded together against me. They will meet their end in this desert; here they will die."

³⁶So the men Moses had sent to explore the land, who returned and made the whole community grumble against him by spreading a bad report about it—³⁷these men responsible for spreading the bad report about the land were struck down and died of a plague before the LORD. ³⁸Of the men who went to explore the land, only Joshua son of Nun and Caleb son of Jephunneh survived.

³⁹When Moses reported this to all the Israelites, they mourned bitterly. ⁴⁰Early the next morning they went up toward the high hill country. "We have sinned," they said. "We will go up to the place the LORD promised."

⁴¹But Moses said, "Why are you disobeying the LORD's command? This will not succeed! ⁴²Do not go up, because the LORD is not with you. You will be defeated by your enemies, ⁴³for the Amalekites and Canaanites will face you there. Because you have turned away from the LORD, he

will not be with you and you will fall by the sword."

⁴⁴Nevertheless, in their presumption they went up toward the high hill country, though neither Moses nor the ark of the LORD's covenant moved from the camp. ⁴⁵Then the Amalekites and Canaanites who lived in that hill country came down and attacked them and beat them down all the way to Hormah.

Supplementary Offerings

15 The LORD said to Moses, ²"Speak to the Israelites and say to them: 'After you enter the land I am giving you as a home ³and you present to the LORD offerings made by fire, from the herd or the flock, as an aroma pleasing to the LORD—whether burnt offerings or sacrifices, for special vows or freewill offerings or festival offerings— ⁴then the one who brings his offering shall present to the LORD a grain offering of a tenth of an ephahᵇ of fine flour mixed with a quarter of a hinᶜ of oil. ⁵With each lamb for the burnt offering or the sacrifice, prepare a quarter of a hin of wine as a drink offering.

⁶" 'With a ram prepare a grain offering of two-tenths of an ephahᵈ of fine flour mixed with a third of a hinᵉ of oil, ⁷and a third of a hin of wine as a drink offering. Offer it as an aroma pleasing to the LORD.

⁸" 'When you prepare a young bull as a burnt offering or sacrifice, for a special vow or a fellowship offeringᶠ to the LORD, ⁹bring with the bull a grain offering of three-tenths of an ephahᵍ of fine flour mixed with half a hinʰ of oil. ¹⁰Also bring half a hin of wine as a drink offering. It will be an offering made by fire, an aroma pleasing to the LORD. ¹¹Each bull or ram, each lamb or young goat, is to be prepared in this manner. ¹²Do this for each one, for as many as you prepare.

¹³" 'Everyone who is native-born must do these things in this way when he brings an offering made by fire as an aroma pleasing to the LORD. ¹⁴For the generations to come, whenever an alien or anyone else living among you presents

---

ᵃ25 Hebrew *Yam Suph*; that is, Sea of Reeds
ᵇ4 That is, probably about 2 quarts (about 2 liters)
ᶜ4 That is, probably about 1 quart (about 1 liter); also in verse 5   ᵈ6 That is, probably about 4 quarts (about 4.5 liters)   ᵉ6 That is, probably about 1 1/4 quarts (about 1.2 liters); also in verse 7
ᶠ8 Traditionally *peace offering*   ᵍ9 That is, probably about 6 quarts (about 6.5 liters)   ʰ9 That is, probably about 2 quarts (about 2 liters); also in verse 10

an offering made by fire as an aroma pleasing to the LORD, he must do exactly as you do. [15]The community is to have the same rules for you and for the alien living among you; this is a lasting ordinance for the generations to come. You and the alien shall be the same before the LORD: [16]The same laws and regulations will apply both to you and to the alien living among you.' "

[17]The LORD said to Moses, [18]"Speak to the Israelites and say to them: 'When you enter the land to which I am taking you [19]and you eat the food of the land, present a portion as an offering to the LORD. [20]Present a cake from the first of your ground meal and present it as an offering from the threshing floor. [21]Throughout the generations to come you are to give this offering to the LORD from the first of your ground meal.

Offerings for Unintentional Sins

[22]" 'Now if you unintentionally fail to keep any of these commands the LORD gave Moses— [23]any of the LORD's commands to you through him, from the day the LORD gave them and continuing through the generations to come— [24]and if this is done unintentionally without the community being aware of it, then the whole community is to offer a young bull for a burnt offering as an aroma pleasing to the LORD, along with its prescribed grain offering and drink offering, and a male goat for a sin offering. [25]The priest is to make atonement for the whole Israelite community, and they will be forgiven, for it was not intentional and they have brought to the LORD for their wrong an offering made by fire and a sin offering. [26]The whole Israelite community and the aliens living among them will be forgiven, because all the people were involved in the unintentional wrong.

[27]" 'But if just one person sins unintentionally, he must bring a year-old female goat for a sin offering. [28]The priest is to make atonement before the LORD for the one who erred by sinning unintentionally, and when atonement has been made for him, he will be forgiven. [29]One and the same law applies to everyone who sins unintentionally, whether he is a native-born Israelite or an alien.

[30]" 'But anyone who sins defiantly, whether native-born or alien, blasphemes the LORD, and that person must be cut off from his people. [31]Because he

has despised the LORD's word and broken his commands, that person must surely be cut off; his guilt remains on him.' "

The Sabbath-Breaker Put to Death

[32]While the Israelites were in the desert, a man was found gathering wood on the Sabbath day. [33]Those who found him gathering wood brought him to Moses and Aaron and the whole assembly, [34]and they kept him in custody, because it was not clear what should be done to him. [35]Then the LORD said to Moses, "The man must die. The whole assembly must stone him outside the camp." [36]So the assembly took him outside the camp and stoned him to death, as the LORD commanded Moses.

Tassels on Garments

[37]The LORD said to Moses, [38]"Speak to the Israelites and say to them: 'Throughout the generations to come you are to make tassels on the corners of your garments, with a blue cord on each tassel. [39]You will have these tassels to look at and so you will remember all the commands of the LORD, that you may obey them and not prostitute yourselves by going after the lusts of your own hearts and eyes. [40]Then you will remember to obey all my commands and will be consecrated to your God. [41]I am the LORD your God, who brought you out of Egypt to be your God. I am the LORD your God.' "

Korah, Dathan and Abiram

16 Korah son of Izhar, the son of Kohath, the son of Levi, and certain Reubenites—Dathan and Abiram, sons of Eliab, and On son of Peleth—became insolent[a] [2]and rose up against Moses. With them were 250 Israelite men, well-known community leaders who had been appointed members of the council. [3]They came as a group to oppose Moses and Aaron and said to them, "You have gone too far! The whole community is holy, every one of them, and the LORD is with them. Why then do you set yourselves above the LORD's assembly?"

[4]When Moses heard this, he fell facedown. [5]Then he said to Korah and all his followers: "In the morning the LORD will show who belongs to him and who is holy, and he will have that person come near

---

[a]1 Or Peleth—took men

him. The man he chooses he will cause to come near him. ⁶You, Korah, and all your followers are to do this: Take censers ⁷and tomorrow put fire and incense in them before the LORD. The man the LORD chooses will be the one who is holy. You Levites have gone too far!"

⁸Moses also said to Korah, "Now listen, you Levites! ⁹Isn't it enough for you that the God of Israel has separated you from the rest of the Israelite community and brought you near himself to do the work at the LORD's tabernacle and to stand before the community and minister to them? ¹⁰He has brought you and all your fellow Levites near himself, but now you are trying to get the priesthood too. ¹¹It is against the LORD that you and all your followers have banded together. Who is Aaron that you should grumble against him?"

¹²Then Moses summoned Dathan and Abiram, the sons of Eliab. But they said, "We will not come! ¹³Isn't it enough that you have brought us up out of a land flowing with milk and honey to kill us in the desert? And now you also want to lord it over us? ¹⁴Moreover, you haven't brought us into a land flowing with milk and honey or given us an inheritance of fields and vineyards. Will you gouge out the eyes of*a* these men? No, we will not come!"

¹⁵Then Moses became very angry and said to the LORD, "Do not accept their offering. I have not taken so much as a donkey from them, nor have I wronged any of them."

¹⁶Moses said to Korah, "You and all your followers are to appear before the LORD tomorrow—you and they and Aaron. ¹⁷Each man is to take his censer and put incense in it—250 censers in all—and present it before the LORD. You and Aaron are to present your censers also." ¹⁸So each man took his censer, put fire and incense in it, and stood with Moses and Aaron at the entrance to the Tent of Meeting. ¹⁹When Korah had gathered all his followers in opposition to them at the entrance to the Tent of Meeting, the glory of the LORD appeared to the entire assembly. ²⁰The LORD said to Moses and Aaron, ²¹"Separate yourselves from this assembly so I can put an end to them at once."

²²But Moses and Aaron fell facedown and cried out, "O God, God of the spirits of all mankind, will you be angry with the entire assembly when only one man sins?"

²³Then the LORD said to Moses, ²⁴"Say to the assembly, 'Move away from the tents of Korah, Dathan and Abiram.' "

²⁵Moses got up and went to Dathan and Abiram, and the elders of Israel followed him. ²⁶He warned the assembly, "Move back from the tents of these wicked men! Do not touch anything belonging to them, or you will be swept away because of all their sins." ²⁷So they moved away from the tents of Korah, Dathan and Abiram. Dathan and Abiram had come out and were standing with their wives, children and little ones at the entrances to their tents.

²⁸Then Moses said, "This is how you will know that the LORD has sent me to do all these things and that it was not my idea: ²⁹If these men die a natural death and experience only what usually happens to men, then the LORD has not sent me. ³⁰But if the LORD brings about something totally new, and the earth opens its mouth and swallows them, with everything that belongs to them, and they go down alive into the grave,*b* then you will know that these men have treated the LORD with contempt."

³¹As soon as he finished saying all this, the ground under them split apart ³²and the earth opened its mouth and swallowed them, with their households and all Korah's men and all their possessions. ³³They went down alive into the grave, with everything they owned; the earth closed over them, and they perished and were gone from the community. ³⁴At their cries, all the Israelites around them fled, shouting, "The earth is going to swallow us too!"

³⁵And fire came out from the LORD and consumed the 250 men who were offering the incense.

³⁶The LORD said to Moses, ³⁷"Tell Eleazar son of Aaron, the priest, to take the censers out of the smoldering remains and scatter the coals some distance away, for the censers are holy— ³⁸the censers of the men who sinned at the cost of their lives. Hammer the censers into sheets to overlay the altar, for they were presented before the LORD and have become holy. Let them be a sign to the Israelites."

³⁹So Eleazar the priest collected the bronze censers brought by those who had been burned up, and he had them hammered out to overlay the altar, ⁴⁰as the LORD directed him through Moses. This

a14 Or *you make slaves of*; or *you deceive*
b30 Hebrew *Sheol*; also in verse 33

was to remind the Israelites that no one except a descendant of Aaron should come to burn incense before the LORD, or he would become like Korah and his followers.

⁴¹The next day the whole Israelite community grumbled against Moses and Aaron. "You have killed the LORD's people," they said.

⁴²But when the assembly gathered in opposition to Moses and Aaron and turned toward the Tent of Meeting, suddenly the cloud covered it and the glory of the LORD appeared. ⁴³Then Moses and Aaron went to the front of the Tent of Meeting, ⁴⁴and the LORD said to Moses, ⁴⁵"Get away from this assembly so I can put an end to them at once." And they fell facedown.

⁴⁶Then Moses said to Aaron, "Take your censer and put incense in it, along with fire from the altar, and hurry to the assembly to make atonement for them. Wrath has come out from the LORD; the plague has started." ⁴⁷So Aaron did as Moses said, and ran into the midst of the assembly. The plague had already started among the people, but Aaron offered the incense and made atonement for them. ⁴⁸He stood between the living and the dead, and the plague stopped. ⁴⁹But 14,700 people died from the plague, in addition to those who had died because of Korah. ⁵⁰Then Aaron returned to Moses at the entrance to the Tent of Meeting, for the plague had stopped.

The Budding of Aaron's Staff

17 The LORD said to Moses, ²"Speak to the Israelites and get twelve staffs from them, one from the leader of each of their ancestral tribes. Write the name of each man on his staff. ³On the staff of Levi write Aaron's name, for there must be one staff for the head of each ancestral tribe. ⁴Place them in the Tent of Meeting in front of the Testimony, where I meet with you. ⁵The staff belonging to the man I choose will sprout, and I will rid myself of this constant grumbling against you by the Israelites."

⁶So Moses spoke to the Israelites, and their leaders gave him twelve staffs, one for the leader of each of their ancestral tribes, and Aaron's staff was among them. ⁷Moses placed the staffs before the LORD in the Tent of the Testimony.

⁸The next day Moses entered the Tent of the Testimony and saw that Aaron's staff, which represented the house of Levi, had not only sprouted but had budded, blossomed and produced almonds. ⁹Then Moses brought out all the staffs from the LORD's presence to all the Israelites. They looked at them, and each man took his own staff.

¹⁰The LORD said to Moses, "Put back Aaron's staff in front of the Testimony, to be kept as a sign to the rebellious. This will put an end to their grumbling against me, so that they will not die." ¹¹Moses did just as the LORD commanded him.

¹²The Israelites said to Moses, "We will die! We are lost, we are all lost! ¹³Anyone who even comes near the tabernacle of the LORD will die. Are we all going to die?"

Duties of Priests and Levites

18 The LORD said to Aaron, "You, your sons and your father's family are to bear the responsibility for offenses against the sanctuary, and you and your sons alone are to bear the responsibility for offenses against the priesthood. ²Bring your fellow Levites from your ancestral tribe to join you and assist you when you and your sons minister before the Tent of the Testimony. ³They are to be responsible to you and are to perform all the duties of the Tent, but they must not go near the furnishings of the sanctuary or the altar, or both they and you will die. ⁴They are to join you and be responsible for the care of the Tent of Meeting—all the work at the Tent—and no one else may come near where you are.

⁵"You are to be responsible for the care of the sanctuary and the altar, so that wrath will not fall on the Israelites again. ⁶I myself have selected your fellow Levites from among the Israelites as a gift to you, dedicated to the LORD to do the work at the Tent of Meeting. ⁷But only you and your sons may serve as priests in connection with everything at the altar and inside the curtain. I am giving you the service of the priesthood as a gift. Anyone else who comes near the sanctuary must be put to death."

Offerings for Priests and Levites

⁸Then the LORD said to Aaron, "I myself have put you in charge of the offerings presented to me; all the holy offerings the Israelites give me I give to you and your sons as your portion and regular share. ⁹You are to have the part of the most holy offerings that is kept from the fire. From

all the gifts they bring me as most holy offerings, whether grain or sin or guilt offerings, that part belongs to you and your sons. ¹⁰Eat it as something most holy; every male shall eat it. You must regard it as holy.

¹¹"This also is yours: whatever is set aside from the gifts of all the wave offerings of the Israelites. I give this to you and your sons and daughters as your regular share. Everyone in your household who is ceremonially clean may eat it.

¹²"I give you all the finest olive oil and all the finest new wine and grain they give the LORD as the firstfruits of their harvest. ¹³All the land's firstfruits that they bring to the LORD will be yours. Everyone in your household who is ceremonially clean may eat it.

¹⁴"Everything in Israel that is devoted*a* to the LORD is yours. ¹⁵The first offspring of every womb, both man and animal, that is offered to the LORD is yours. But you must redeem every firstborn son and every firstborn male of unclean animals. ¹⁶When they are a month old, you must redeem them at the redemption price set at five shekels*b* of silver, according to the sanctuary shekel, which weighs twenty gerahs.

¹⁷"But you must not redeem the firstborn of an ox, a sheep or a goat; they are holy. Sprinkle their blood on the altar and burn their fat as an offering made by fire, an aroma pleasing to the LORD. ¹⁸Their meat is to be yours, just as the breast of the wave offering and the right thigh are yours. ¹⁹Whatever is set aside from the holy offerings the Israelites present to the LORD I give to you and your sons and daughters as your regular share. It is an everlasting covenant of salt before the LORD for both you and your offspring."

²⁰The LORD said to Aaron, "You will have no inheritance in their land, nor will you have any share among them; I am your share and your inheritance among the Israelites.

²¹"I give to the Levites all the tithes in Israel as their inheritance in return for the work they do while serving at the Tent of Meeting. ²²From now on the Israelites must not go near the Tent of Meeting, or they will bear the consequences of their sin and will die. ²³It is the Levites who are to do the work at the Tent of Meeting and bear the responsibility for offenses against it. This is a lasting ordinance for the generations to come. They will receive no inheritance among the Israelites. ²⁴Instead, I give to the Levites as their inheritance the tithes that the Israelites present as an offering to the LORD. That is why I said concerning them: 'They will have no inheritance among the Israelites.'"

²⁵The LORD said to Moses, ²⁶"Speak to the Levites and say to them: 'When you receive from the Israelites the tithe I give you as your inheritance, you must present a tenth of that tithe as the LORD's offering. ²⁷Your offering will be reckoned to you as grain from the threshing floor or juice from the winepress. ²⁸In this way you also will present an offering to the LORD from all the tithes you receive from the Israelites. From these tithes you must give the LORD's portion to Aaron the priest. ²⁹You must present as the LORD's portion the best and holiest part of everything given to you.'

³⁰"Say to the Levites: 'When you present the best part, it will be reckoned to you as the product of the threshing floor or the winepress. ³¹You and your households may eat the rest of it anywhere, for it is your wages for your work at the Tent of Meeting. ³²By presenting the best part of it you will not be guilty in this matter; then you will not defile the holy offerings of the Israelites, and you will not die.'"

The Water of Cleansing

19 The LORD said to Moses and Aaron: ²"This is a requirement of the law that the LORD has commanded: Tell the Israelites to bring you a red heifer without defect or blemish and that has never been under a yoke. ³Give it to Eleazar the priest; it is to be taken outside the camp and slaughtered in his presence. ⁴Then Eleazar the priest is to take some of its blood on his finger and sprinkle it seven times toward the front of the Tent of Meeting. ⁵While he watches, the heifer is to be burned—its hide, flesh, blood and offal. ⁶The priest is to take some cedar wood, hyssop and scarlet wool and throw them onto the burning heifer. ⁷After that, the priest must wash his clothes and bathe himself with water. He may then come into the camp, but he will be ceremonially unclean till evening. ⁸The man who burns it must also wash his clothes and bathe with water, and he too will be unclean till evening.

⁹"A man who is clean shall gather up the

---

a14 The Hebrew term refers to the irrevocable giving over of things or persons to the LORD.
b16 That is, about 2 ounces (about 55 grams)

ashes of the heifer and put them in a ceremonially clean place outside the camp. They shall be kept by the Israelite community for use in the water of cleansing; it is for purification from sin. [10]The man who gathers up the ashes of the heifer must also wash his clothes, and he too will be unclean till evening. This will be a lasting ordinance both for the Israelites and for the aliens living among them.

[11]"Whoever touches the dead body of anyone will be unclean for seven days. [12]He must purify himself with the water on the third day and on the seventh day; then he will be clean. But if he does not purify himself on the third and seventh days, he will not be clean. [13]Whoever touches the dead body of anyone and fails to purify himself defiles the LORD's tabernacle. That person must be cut off from Israel. Because the water of cleansing has not been sprinkled on him, he is unclean; his uncleanness remains on him.

[14]"This is the law that applies when a person dies in a tent: Anyone who enters the tent and anyone who is in it will be unclean for seven days, [15]and every open container without a lid fastened on it will be unclean.

[16]"Anyone out in the open who touches someone who has been killed or someone who has died a natural death, or anyone who touches a human bone or a grave, will be unclean for seven days.

[17]"For the unclean person, put some ashes from the burned purification offering into a jar and pour fresh water over them. [18]Then a man who is ceremonially clean is to take some hyssop, dip it in the water and sprinkle the tent and all the furnishings and the people who were there. He must also sprinkle anyone who has touched a human bone or a grave or someone who has been killed or someone who has died a natural death. [19]The man who is clean is to sprinkle the unclean person on the third and seventh days, and on the seventh day he is to purify him. The person being cleansed must wash his clothes and bathe with water, and that evening he will be clean. [20]But if a person who is unclean does not purify himself, he must be cut off from the community, because he has defiled the sanctuary of the LORD. The water of cleansing has not been sprinkled on him, and he is unclean. [21]This is a lasting ordinance for them.

"The man who sprinkles the water of cleansing must also wash his clothes, and anyone who touches the water of cleansing will be unclean till evening. [22]Anything that an unclean person touches becomes unclean, and anyone who touches it becomes unclean till evening."

Who invented baptism?

Text: Numbers 19:18–19

John the Baptist is well known and even named for the ceremonial immersions he performed. But John was not the first to practice this idea of symbolic cleansing. God had imprinted baptism on the hearts of the Israelites long before Christ came to cleanse humankind from sin. "Washings of purification were extensively practiced in Judaism for a variety of reasons" (Ward, 200). By tradition, all devout Jews washed their hands thoroughly before praying or eating. *Mikvehs,* or ritual baths, were also common.

There was, however, a significant difference between John's baptisms and the cleansing rituals Israelites had practiced. "For John, this baptism was not one washing in a series of ongoing purifications, but a unique seal that marked those who repented as belonging to the renewed people of God, prepared for God's intervention in the world" (Ward, 200).

With Christ's arrival, the cleansings that had for years been Jewish rituals now reached a new level of meaning—one we still honor today.

Ward, K. (Ed.). (1987). Jesus and His Times. Pleasantville, New York: The Reader's Digest Association.

For a complete listing of Questions Kids Ask, turn to page 1435.

Water From the Rock

20 In the first month the whole Israelite community arrived at the Desert of Zin, and they stayed at Kadesh. There Miriam died and was buried.

²Now there was no water for the community, and the people gathered in opposition to Moses and Aaron. ³They quarreled with Moses and said, "If only we had died when our brothers fell dead before the LORD! ⁴Why did you bring the LORD's community into this desert, that we and our livestock should die here? ⁵Why did you bring us up out of Egypt to this terrible place? It has no grain or figs, grapevines or pomegranates. And there is no water to drink!"

⁶Moses and Aaron went from the assembly to the entrance to the Tent of Meeting and fell facedown, and the glory of the LORD appeared to them. ⁷The LORD said to Moses, ⁸"Take the staff, and you and your brother Aaron gather the assembly together. Speak to that rock before their eyes and it will pour out its water. You will bring water out of the rock for the community so they and their livestock can drink."

⁹So Moses took the staff from the LORD's presence, just as he commanded him. ¹⁰He and Aaron gathered the assembly together in front of the rock and Moses said to them, "Listen, you rebels, must we bring you water out of this rock?" ¹¹Then Moses raised his arm and struck the rock twice with his staff. Water gushed out, and the community and their livestock drank.

¹²But the LORD said to Moses and Aaron, "Because you did not trust in me enough to honor me as holy in the sight of the Israelites, you will not bring this community into the land I give them."

¹³These were the waters of Meribah,ᵃ where the Israelites quarreled with the LORD and where he showed himself holy among them.

Edom Denies Israel Passage

¹⁴Moses sent messengers from Kadesh to the king of Edom, saying:

"This is what your brother Israel says: You know about all the hardships that have come upon us. ¹⁵Our forefathers went down into Egypt, and we lived there many years. The Egyptians mistreated us and our fathers, ¹⁶but when we cried out to the LORD, he heard our cry and sent an angel and brought us out of Egypt.

"Now we are here at Kadesh, a town on the edge of your territory. ¹⁷Please let us pass through your country. We will not go through any field or vineyard, or drink water from

ᵃ13 *Meribah* means *quarreling.*

HEY DAD

Why was God so harsh with Moses when Moses struck the rock?

Text: Numbers 20:10–12

Although God is sovereign and is entitled to do whatever he wants, whenever he wants, the punishment certainly doesn't seem to match the crime in this case.

Moses had been God's obedient servant while the Israelites complained, rebelled and grew angry with God. Yet God told Moses he would never enter the promised land for what appears to be one angry outburst. So, the prophet struck the rock instead of speaking to it. Is that really so bad?

From God's response, we can see that what Moses did *was* that bad. But maybe there's more to Moses' action than simply striking the rock. Some scholars suggest that his sin went much deeper than that. Notice the prophet's words in verse 10, "Listen, you rebels, must we bring you water out of this rock?" These scholars say that when Moses used the word "we," he was referring to himself and Aaron, not to God. If this is the case, Moses was taking the credit for God's miracle.

Whatever the case, God was angry with Moses because his actions shamed God in front of the people. God said to Moses, "You did not trust in me enough to honor me as holy in the sight of the Israelites." In light of that reasoning, God was actually very merciful with Moses.

For a complete listing of Questions Kids Ask, turn to page 1435.

any well. We will travel along the king's highway and not turn to the right or to the left until we have passed through your territory."

[18]But Edom answered:

"You may not pass through here; if you try, we will march out and attack you with the sword."

[19]The Israelites replied:

"We will go along the main road, and if we or our livestock drink any of your water, we will pay for it. We only want to pass through on foot—nothing else."

[20]Again they answered:

"You may not pass through."

Then Edom came out against them with a large and powerful army. [21]Since Edom refused to let them go through their territory, Israel turned away from them.

The Death of Aaron

[22]The whole Israelite community set out from Kadesh and came to Mount Hor. [23]At Mount Hor, near the border of Edom, the LORD said to Moses and Aaron, [24]"Aaron will be gathered to his people. He will not enter the land I give the Israelites, because both of you rebelled against my command at the waters of Meribah. [25]Get Aaron and his son Eleazar and take them up Mount Hor. [26]Remove Aaron's garments and put them on his son Eleazar, for Aaron will be gathered to his people; he will die there."

[27]Moses did as the LORD commanded: They went up Mount Hor in the sight of the whole community. [28]Moses removed Aaron's garments and put them on his son Eleazar. And Aaron died there on top of the mountain. Then Moses and Eleazar came down from the mountain, [29]and when the whole community learned that Aaron had died, the entire house of Israel mourned for him thirty days.

Arad Destroyed

21 When the Canaanite king of Arad, who lived in the Negev, heard that Israel was coming along the road to Atharim, he attacked the Israelites and captured some of them. [2]Then Israel made this vow to the LORD: "If you will deliver these people into our hands, we will totally destroy[a] their cities." [3]The LORD lis-

tened to Israel's plea and gave the Canaanites over to them. They completely destroyed them and their towns; so the place was named Hormah.[b]

The Bronze Snake

[4]They traveled from Mount Hor along the route to the Red Sea,[c] to go around Edom. But the people grew impatient on the way; [5]they spoke against God and against Moses, and said, "Why have you brought us up out of Egypt to die in the desert? There is no bread! There is no water! And we detest this miserable food!"

[6]Then the LORD sent venomous snakes among them; they bit the people and many Israelites died. [7]The people came to Moses and said, "We sinned when we spoke against the LORD and against you. Pray that the LORD will take the snakes away from us." So Moses prayed for the people.

[8]The LORD said to Moses, "Make a snake and put it up on a pole; anyone who is bitten can look at it and live." [9]So Moses made a bronze snake and put it up on a pole. Then when anyone was bitten by a snake and looked at the bronze snake, he lived.

The Journey to Moab

[10]The Israelites moved on and camped at Oboth. [11]Then they set out from Oboth and camped in Iye Abarim, in the desert that faces Moab toward the sunrise. [12]From there they moved on and camped in the Zered Valley. [13]They set out from there and camped alongside the Arnon, which is in the desert extending into Amorite territory. The Arnon is the border of Moab, between Moab and the Amorites. [14]That is why the Book of the Wars of the LORD says:

" . . . Waheb in Suphah[d] and the ravines,
   the Arnon [15]and[e] the slopes of the
      ravines
that lead to the site of Ar
   and lie along the border of Moab."

[16]From there they continued on to Beer, the well where the LORD said to Moses,

---

[a]2 The Hebrew term refers to the irrevocable giving over of things or persons to the LORD, often by totally destroying them; also in verse 3.
[b]3 Hormah means *destruction*.   [c]4 Hebrew *Yam Suph*; that is, Sea of Reeds   [d]14 The meaning of the Hebrew for this phrase is uncertain.   [e]14,15 Or *"I have been given from Suphah and the ravines / of the Arnon* [15]*to*

"Gather the people together and I will give them water."

[17] Then Israel sang this song:

"Spring up, O well!
    Sing about it,
[18] about the well that the princes dug,
    that the nobles of the people sank—
    the nobles with scepters and staffs."

Then they went from the desert to Mattanah, [19] from Mattanah to Nahaliel, from Nahaliel to Bamoth, [20] and from Bamoth to the valley in Moab where the top of Pisgah overlooks the wasteland.

Defeat of Sihon and Og

[21] Israel sent messengers to say to Sihon king of the Amorites:

[22] "Let us pass through your country. We will not turn aside into any field or vineyard, or drink water from any well. We will travel along the king's highway until we have passed through your territory."

[23] But Sihon would not let Israel pass through his territory. He mustered his entire army and marched out into the desert against Israel. When he reached Jahaz, he fought with Israel. [24] Israel, however, put him to the sword and took over his land from the Arnon to the Jabbok, but only as far as the Ammonites, because their border was fortified. [25] Israel captured all the cities of the Amorites and occupied them, including Heshbon and all its surrounding settlements. [26] Heshbon was the city of Sihon king of the Amorites, who had fought against the former king of Moab and had taken from him all his land as far as the Arnon.

[27] That is why the poets say:

"Come to Heshbon and let it be rebuilt;
    let Sihon's city be restored.

[28] "Fire went out from Heshbon,
    a blaze from the city of Sihon.
It consumed Ar of Moab,
    the citizens of Arnon's heights.
[29] Woe to you, O Moab!
    You are destroyed, O people of
        Chemosh!
He has given up his sons as fugitives
    and his daughters as captives
    to Sihon king of the Amorites.

[30] "But we have overthrown them;
    Heshbon is destroyed all the way to
        Dibon.

We have demolished them as far as
        Nophah,
    which extends to Medeba."

[31] So Israel settled in the land of the Amorites.

[32] After Moses had sent spies to Jazer, the Israelites captured its surrounding settlements and drove out the Amorites who were there. [33] Then they turned and went up along the road toward Bashan, and Og king of Bashan and his whole army marched out to meet them in battle at Edrei.

[34] The LORD said to Moses, "Do not be afraid of him, for I have handed him over to you, with his whole army and his land. Do to him what you did to Sihon king of the Amorites, who reigned in Heshbon."

[35] So they struck him down, together with his sons and his whole army, leaving them no survivors. And they took possession of his land.

Balak Summons Balaam

22 Then the Israelites traveled to the plains of Moab and camped along the Jordan across from Jericho.[a]

[2] Now Balak son of Zippor saw all that Israel had done to the Amorites, [3] and Moab was terrified because there were so many people. Indeed, Moab was filled with dread because of the Israelites.

[4] The Moabites said to the elders of Midian, "This horde is going to lick up everything around us, as an ox licks up the grass of the field."

So Balak son of Zippor, who was king of Moab at that time, [5] sent messengers to summon Balaam son of Beor, who was at Pethor, near the River,[b] in his native land. Balak said:

"A people has come out of Egypt; they cover the face of the land and have settled next to me. [6] Now come and put a curse on these people, because they are too powerful for me. Perhaps then I will be able to defeat them and drive them out of the country. For I know that those you bless are blessed, and those you curse are cursed."

[7] The elders of Moab and Midian left, taking with them the fee for divination.

---

[a]1 Hebrew *Jordan of Jericho*; possibly an ancient name for the Jordan River   [b]5 That is, the Euphrates

What Does God's Voice Sound like?

Key Verse: *"Then the LORD opened Balaam's eyes, and he saw the angel of the LORD standing in the road with his sword drawn. So he bowed low and fell facedown."* Numbers 22:31

Text: Numbers 22:21–31 *(Dad or child reads the text.)*

QUIET **TIMES** WITH Dad

DAD READS: Do you know what my voice sounds like? What a silly question. Of course you do. When we're in a crowd and I call your name, you recognize my voice because you have heard it many times.

Child reads: Yes, I know what your voice sounds like. It's very familiar to me. But what does God's voice sound like?

DAD READS: Today's verses tell an unbelievable story about how God speaks and what his voice sounds like. It's the story of Balaam, a man who tried to disobey God. Even though God gave him permission to take a trip on his donkey, God knew that he was going to do the wrong thing. So he sent an angel to stop the man, and the angel appeared in front of Balaam's donkey. Balaam tried to get the donkey to move, but the donkey would not budge. That made Balaam very angry. So Balaam took a stick and beat the donkey, but the donkey still refused to budge.

Child reads: Then God did a very funny thing. He made the donkey talk to Balaam. Can you imagine how surprised Balaam must have been when God talked to him through his animal?

DAD READS: This Bible story tells us something very important about God and his voice. It tells us that when God wants to speak to us, he will use whatever "voice" he chooses—a voice that will get our attention. Sometimes God speaks through the Bible. Sometimes he speaks through our minister at church. Sometimes

he speaks through our family or our friends. Sometimes he speaks to us through things that happen to us. But we must always remember that when God wants to speak to us, he *will* speak to us. If we aren't listening at first, he will not give up until we hear his voice.

Child reads: I want to hear God's voice, and I want to obey it. I don't want to be stubborn, like Balaam. I want God to know that I will do my best to be listening when he speaks to me.

DAD READS: I also want to hear God's voice. I don't want to ever be so busy that I miss it the first time he speaks. Let me pray this prayer with you:

Our Father in heaven, thank you for speaking to us. Thank you for not giving up on us when we act like we're not listening. Please give us ears to hear your voice. Then please help us to obey. We love you and we thank you for your persistent love. In Jesus' name, Amen.

For your next devotional reading, go to page 188.

When they came to Balaam, they told him what Balak had said.

[8]"Spend the night here," Balaam said to them, "and I will bring you back the answer the LORD gives me." So the Moabite princes stayed with him.

[9]God came to Balaam and asked. "Who are these men with you?"

[10]Balaam said to God, "Balak son of Zippor, king of Moab, sent me this message: [11]'A people that has come out of Egypt covers the face of the land. Now come and put a curse on them for me. Perhaps then I will be able to fight them and drive them away.' "

[12]But God said to Balaam, "Do not go with them. You must not put a curse on those people, because they are blessed."

[13]The next morning Balaam got up and said to Balak's princes, "Go back to your own country, for the LORD has refused to let me go with you."

[14]So the Moabite princes returned to Balak and said, "Balaam refused to come with us."

[15]Then Balak sent other princes, more numerous and more distinguished than the first. [16]They came to Balaam and said:

"This is what Balak son of Zippor says: Do not let anything keep you from coming to me, [17]because I will reward you handsomely and do whatever you say. Come and put a curse on these people for me."

[18]But Balaam answered them, "Even if Balak gave me his palace filled with silver and gold, I could not do anything great or small to go beyond the command of the LORD my God. [19]Now stay here tonight as the others did, and I will find out what else the LORD will tell me."

[20]That night God came to Balaam and said, "Since these men have come to summon you, go with them, but do only what I tell you."

Balaam's Donkey

[21]Balaam got up in the morning, saddled his donkey and went with the princes of Moab. [22]But God was very angry when he went, and the angel of the LORD stood in the road to oppose him. Balaam was riding on his donkey, and his two servants were with him. [23]When the donkey saw the angel of the LORD standing in the road with a drawn sword in his hand, she turned off the road into a field. Balaam beat her to get her back on the road.

[24]Then the angel of the LORD stood in a narrow path between two vineyards, with walls on both sides. [25]When the donkey saw the angel of the LORD, she pressed close to the wall, crushing Balaam's foot against it. So he beat her again.

[26]Then the angel of the LORD moved on ahead and stood in a narrow place where there was no room to turn, either to the right or to the left. [27]When the donkey saw the angel of the LORD, she lay down under Balaam, and he was angry and beat her with his staff. [28]Then the LORD opened the donkey's mouth, and she said to Balaam, "What have I done to you to make you beat me these three times?"

[29]Balaam answered the donkey, "You have made a fool of me! If I had a sword in my hand, I would kill you right now."

[30]The donkey said to Balaam, "Am I not your own donkey, which you have always ridden, to this day? Have I been in the habit of doing this to you?"

"No," he said.

[31]Then the LORD opened Balaam's eyes, and he saw the angel of the LORD standing in the road with his sword drawn. So he bowed low and fell facedown.

[32]The angel of the LORD asked him, "Why have you beaten your donkey these three times? I have come here to oppose you because your path is a reckless one before me.[a] [33]The donkey saw me and turned away from me these three times. If she had not turned away, I would certainly have killed you by now, but I would have spared her."

[34]Balaam said to the angel of the LORD, "I have sinned. I did not realize you were standing in the road to oppose me. Now if you are displeased, I will go back."

[35]The angel of the LORD said to Balaam, "Go with the men, but speak only what I tell you." So Balaam went with the princes of Balak.

[36]When Balak heard that Balaam was coming, he went out to meet him at the Moabite town on the Arnon border, at the edge of his territory. [37]Balak said to Balaam, "Did I not send you an urgent summons? Why didn't you come to me? Am I really not able to reward you?"

[38]"Well, I have come to you now," Balaam replied. "But can I say just anything? I must speak only what God puts in my mouth."

[39]Then Balaam went with Balak to

---

[a]32 The meaning of the Hebrew for this clause is uncertain.

Kiriath Huzoth. **⁴⁰**Balak sacrificed cattle and sheep, and gave some to Balaam and the princes who were with him. **⁴¹**The next morning Balak took Balaam up to Bamoth Baal, and from there he saw part of the people.

Balaam's First Oracle

23 Balaam said, "Build me seven altars here, and prepare seven bulls and seven rams for me." **²**Balak did as Balaam said, and the two of them offered a bull and a ram on each altar.

³Then Balaam said to Balak, "Stay here beside your offering while I go aside. Perhaps the LORD will come to meet with me. Whatever he reveals to me I will tell you." Then he went off to a barren height.

⁴God met with him, and Balaam said, "I have prepared seven altars, and on each altar I have offered a bull and a ram."

⁵The LORD put a message in Balaam's mouth and said, "Go back to Balak and give him this message."

⁶So he went back to him and found him standing beside his offering, with all the princes of Moab. **⁷**Then Balaam uttered his oracle:

"Balak brought me from Aram,
  the king of Moab from the eastern
    mountains.
'Come,' he said, 'curse Jacob for me;
  come, denounce Israel.'
⁸How can I curse
  those whom God has not cursed?
 How can I denounce
  those whom the LORD has not
    denounced?
⁹From the rocky peaks I see them,
  from the heights I view them.
 I see a people who live apart
  and do not consider themselves one
    of the nations.
¹⁰Who can count the dust of Jacob
  or number the fourth part of Israel?
 Let me die the death of the righteous,
  and may my end be like theirs!"

¹¹Balak said to Balaam, "What have you done to me? I brought you to curse my enemies, but you have done nothing but bless them!"

¹²He answered, "Must I not speak what the LORD puts in my mouth?"

Balaam's Second Oracle

¹³Then Balak said to him, "Come with me to another place where you can see them; you will see only a part but not all of them. And from there, curse them for me." **¹⁴**So he took him to the field of Zophim on the top of Pisgah, and there he built seven altars and offered a bull and a ram on each altar.

¹⁵Balaam said to Balak, "Stay here beside your offering while I meet with him over there."

¹⁶The LORD met with Balaam and put a message in his mouth and said, "Go back to Balak and give him this message."

¹⁷So he went to him and found him standing beside his offering, with the princes of Moab. Balak asked him, "What did the LORD say?"

¹⁸Then he uttered his oracle:

"Arise, Balak, and listen;
  hear me, son of Zippor.
¹⁹God is not a man, that he should lie,
  nor a son of man, that he should
    change his mind.
 Does he speak and then not act?
 Does he promise and not fulfill?
²⁰I have received a command to bless;
  he has blessed, and I cannot
    change it.
²¹"No misfortune is seen in Jacob,
  no misery observed in Israel.[a]
 The LORD their God is with them;
  the shout of the King is among them.
²²God brought them out of Egypt;
  they have the strength of a wild ox.
²³There is no sorcery against Jacob,
  no divination against Israel.
 It will now be said of Jacob
  and of Israel, 'See what God has
    done!'
²⁴The people rise like a lioness;
  they rouse themselves like a lion
 that does not rest till he devours his
    prey
  and drinks the blood of his victims."

²⁵Then Balak said to Balaam, "Neither curse them at all nor bless them at all!"

²⁶Balaam answered, "Did I not tell you I must do whatever the LORD says?"

Balaam's Third Oracle

²⁷Then Balak said to Balaam, "Come, let me take you to another place. Perhaps it will please God to let you curse them for me from there." **²⁸**And Balak took Balaam to the top of Peor, overlooking the wasteland.

²⁹Balaam said, "Build me seven altars

---

[a]21 Or *He has not looked on Jacob's offenses / or on the wrongs found in Israel.*

here, and prepare seven bulls and seven rams for me." ³⁰Balak did as Balaam had said, and offered a bull and a ram on each altar.

24 Now when Balaam saw that it pleased the LORD to bless Israel, he did not resort to sorcery as at other times, but turned his face toward the desert. ²When Balaam looked out and saw Israel encamped tribe by tribe, the Spirit of God came upon him ³and he uttered his oracle:

"The oracle of Balaam son of Beor,
　the oracle of one whose eye sees
　　clearly,
⁴ the oracle of one who hears the words
　　of God,
　who sees a vision from the Almighty,^a
　who falls prostrate, and whose eyes
　　are opened:

⁵ "How beautiful are your tents, O Jacob,
　your dwelling places, O Israel!

⁶ "Like valleys they spread out,
　like gardens beside a river,
like aloes planted by the LORD,
　like cedars beside the waters.
⁷ Water will flow from their buckets;
　their seed will have abundant water.

"Their king will be greater than Agag;
　their kingdom will be exalted.

⁸ "God brought them out of Egypt;
　they have the strength of a wild ox.
They devour hostile nations
　and break their bones in pieces;
　with their arrows they pierce them.
⁹ Like a lion they crouch and lie down,
　like a lioness—who dares to rouse
　　them?

"May those who bless you be blessed
　and those who curse you be cursed!"

¹⁰Then Balak's anger burned against Balaam. He struck his hands together and said to him, "I summoned you to curse my enemies, but you have blessed them these three times. ¹¹Now leave at once and go home! I said I would reward you handsomely, but the LORD has kept you from being rewarded."

¹²Balaam answered Balak, "Did I not tell the messengers you sent me, ¹³'Even if Balak gave me his palace filled with silver and gold, I could not do anything of my own accord, good or bad, to go beyond the command of the LORD—and I must say only what the LORD says'? ¹⁴Now I am going back to my people, but come, let me warn you of what this people will do to your people in days to come."

Balaam's Fourth Oracle

¹⁵Then he uttered his oracle:

"The oracle of Balaam son of Beor,
　the oracle of one whose eye sees
　　clearly,
¹⁶ the oracle of one who hears the words
　　of God,
　who has knowledge from the Most
　　High,
　who sees a vision from the Almighty,
　who falls prostrate, and whose eyes
　　are opened:
¹⁷ "I see him, but not now;
　I behold him, but not near.
A star will come out of Jacob;
　a scepter will rise out of Israel.
He will crush the foreheads of Moab,
　the skulls^b of^c all the sons of Sheth.^d
¹⁸ Edom will be conquered;
　Seir, his enemy, will be conquered,
　but Israel will grow strong.
¹⁹ A ruler will come out of Jacob
　and destroy the survivors of the
　　city."

Balaam's Final Oracles

²⁰Then Balaam saw Amalek and uttered his oracle:

"Amalek was first among the nations,
　but he will come to ruin at last."

²¹Then he saw the Kenites and uttered his oracle:

"Your dwelling place is secure,
　your nest is set in a rock;
²² yet you Kenites will be destroyed
　when Asshur takes you captive."

²³Then he uttered his oracle:

"Ah, who can live when God does this?^e
²⁴　Ships will come from the shores of
　　Kittim;
　they will subdue Asshur and Eber,
　but they too will come to ruin."

²⁵Then Balaam got up and returned home and Balak went his own way.

---

^a4 Hebrew *Shaddai*; also in verse 16
^b17 Samaritan Pentateuch (see also Jer. 48:45); the meaning of the word in the Masoretic Text is uncertain.　^c17 Or possibly *Moab, / batter*　^d17 Or *all the noisy boasters*　^e23 Masoretic Text; with a different word division of the Hebrew *A people will gather from the north.*

Moab Seduces Israel

25 While Israel was staying in Shittim, the men began to indulge in sexual immorality with Moabite women, **²**who invited them to the sacrifices to their gods. The people ate and bowed down before these gods. **³**So Israel joined in worshiping the Baal of Peor. And the LORD's anger burned against them.

⁴The LORD said to Moses, "Take all the leaders of these people, kill them and expose them in broad daylight before the LORD, so that the LORD's fierce anger may turn away from Israel."

⁵So Moses said to Israel's judges, "Each of you must put to death those of your men who have joined in worshiping the Baal of Peor."

⁶Then an Israelite man brought to his family a Midianite woman right before the eyes of Moses and the whole assembly of Israel while they were weeping at the entrance to the Tent of Meeting. **⁷**When Phinehas son of Eleazar, the son of Aaron, the priest, saw this, he left the assembly, took a spear in his hand **⁸**and followed the Israelite into the tent. He drove the spear through both of them—through the Israelite and into the woman's body. Then the plague against the Israelites was stopped; **⁹**but those who died in the plague numbered 24,000.

¹⁰The LORD said to Moses, **¹¹**"Phinehas son of Eleazar, the son of Aaron, the priest, has turned my anger away from the Israelites; for he was as zealous as I am for my honor among them, so that in my zeal I did not put an end to them. **¹²**Therefore tell him I am making my covenant of peace with him. **¹³**He and his descendants will have a covenant of a lasting priesthood, because he was zealous for the honor of his God and made atonement for the Israelites."

¹⁴The name of the Israelite who was killed with the Midianite woman was Zimri son of Salu, the leader of a Simeonite family. **¹⁵**And the name of the Midianite woman who was put to death was Cozbi daughter of Zur, a tribal chief of a Midianite family.

¹⁶The LORD said to Moses, **¹⁷**"Treat the Midianites as enemies and kill them, **¹⁸**because they treated you as enemies when they deceived you in the affair of Peor and their sister Cozbi, the daughter of a Midianite leader, the woman who was killed when the plague came as a result of Peor."

The Second Census

26 After the plague the LORD said to Moses and Eleazar son of Aaron, the priest, **²**"Take a census of the whole Israel-

HEY DAD
What's an "idol"?

Text: Numbers 25:3–5

An idol is something that a person worships instead of God. In the Old Testament, people actually made idols in the shape of statues and prayed to them as if they were gods. (In some places, people still do this today.)

God gets very angry when people worship idols. Can you imagine how you would feel if you did something wonderful for a friend and that friend ignored you, went up to a stuffed animal and started thanking the stuffed animal? How absurd!

The book of Numbers tells us about a time when the Israelites began to worship an idol called Baal. Enraged, God ordered Moses to have all of the men who worshiped Baal killed and exposed "in broad daylight before the LORD" (v. 4). Remember, this idol wasn't alive; it couldn't answer prayers; it was just a man-made statue. God was insulted when his people, who had seen his great might, chose to pray to a statue instead of to him. How foolish they were!

We might not be able to imagine praying to a statue, but an idol can be anything that we put ahead of God—money, other people, or our own desires. If we put anything other than God in first place, we'll be as foolish as those people who worshiped Baal—and that's foolish!

QUESTIONS KIDS ASK

For a complete listing of Questions Kids Ask, turn to page 1435.

ite community by families—all those twenty years old or more who are able to serve in the army of Israel." ³So on the plains of Moab by the Jordan across from Jericho,ᵃ Moses and Eleazar the priest spoke with them and said, ⁴"Take a census of the men twenty years old or more, as the LORD commanded Moses."

These were the Israelites who came out of Egypt:

⁵The descendants of Reuben, the first-born son of Israel, were:
through Hanoch, the Hanochite clan;
through Pallu, the Palluite clan;
⁶ through Hezron, the Hezronite clan;
through Carmi, the Carmite clan.
⁷These were the clans of Reuben; those numbered were 43,730.

⁸The son of Pallu was Eliab, ⁹and the sons of Eliab were Nemuel, Dathan and Abiram. The same Dathan and Abiram were the community officials who rebelled against Moses and Aaron and were among Korah's followers when they rebelled against the LORD. ¹⁰The earth opened its mouth and swallowed them along with Korah, whose followers died when the fire devoured the 250 men. And they served as a warning sign. ¹¹The line of Korah, however, did not die out.

¹²The descendants of Simeon by their clans were:
through Nemuel, the Nemuelite clan;
through Jamin, the Jaminite clan;
through Jakin, the Jakinite clan;
¹³ through Zerah, the Zerahite clan;
through Shaul, the Shaulite clan.
¹⁴These were the clans of Simeon; there were 22,200 men.

¹⁵The descendants of Gad by their clans were:
through Zephon, the Zephonite clan;
through Haggi, the Haggite clan;
through Shuni, the Shunite clan;
¹⁶ through Ozni, the Oznite clan;
through Eri, the Erite clan;
¹⁷ through Arodi,ᵇ the Arodite clan;
through Areli, the Arelite clan.
¹⁸These were the clans of Gad; those numbered were 40,500.

¹⁹Er and Onan were sons of Judah, but they died in Canaan.
²⁰The descendants of Judah by their clans were:
through Shelah, the Shelanite clan;
through Perez, the Perezite clan;

through Zerah, the Zerahite clan.
²¹The descendants of Perez were:
through Hezron, the Hezronite clan;
through Hamul, the Hamulite clan.
²²These were the clans of Judah; those numbered were 76,500.

²³The descendants of Issachar by their clans were:
through Tola, the Tolaite clan;
through Puah, the Puiteᶜ clan;
²⁴ through Jashub, the Jashubite clan;
through Shimron, the Shimronite clan.
²⁵These were the clans of Issachar; those numbered were 64,300.

²⁶The descendants of Zebulun by their clans were:
through Sered, the Seredite clan;
through Elon, the Elonite clan;
through Jahleel, the Jahleelite clan.
²⁷These were the clans of Zebulun; those numbered were 60,500.

²⁸The descendants of Joseph by their clans through Manasseh and Ephraim were:

²⁹The descendants of Manasseh:
through Makir, the Makirite clan (Makir was the father of Gilead);
through Gilead, the Gileadite clan.
³⁰These were the descendants of Gilead:
through Iezer, the Iezerite clan;
through Helek, the Helekite clan;
³¹ through Asriel, the Asrielite clan;
through Shechem, the Shechemite clan;
³² through Shemida, the Shemidaite clan;
through Hepher, the Hepherite clan.
³³(Zelophehad son of Hepher had no sons; he had only daughters, whose names were Mahlah, Noah, Hoglah, Milcah and Tirzah.)
³⁴These were the clans of Manasseh; those numbered were 52,700.

³⁵These were the descendants of Ephraim by their clans:

ᵃ3 Hebrew *Jordan of Jericho*; possibly an ancient name for the Jordan River; also in verse 63   ᵇ17 Samaritan Pentateuch and Syriac (see also Gen. 46:16); Masoretic Text *Arod*   ᶜ23 Samaritan Pentateuch, Septuagint, Vulgate and Syriac (see also 1 Chron. 7:1); Masoretic Text *through Puvah, the Punite*

through Shuthelah, the Shuthelahite
clan;
through Beker, the Bekerite clan;
through Tahan, the Tahanite clan.
³⁶These were the descendants of Shuthelah:
through Eran, the Eranite clan.
³⁷These were the clans of Ephraim; those
numbered were 32,500.

These were the descendants of Joseph by
their clans.

³⁸The descendants of Benjamin by their
clans were:
through Bela, the Belaite clan;
through Ashbel, the Ashbelite clan;
through Ahiram, the Ahiramite clan;
³⁹through Shupham,ᵃ the Shuphamite
clan;
through Hupham, the Huphamite
clan.
⁴⁰The descendants of Bela through Ard
and Naaman were:
through Ard,ᵇ the Ardite clan;
through Naaman, the Naamite
clan.
⁴¹These were the clans of Benjamin; those
numbered were 45,600.

⁴²These were the descendants of Dan by
their clans:
through Shuham, the Shuhamite clan.
These were the clans of Dan: ⁴³All of them
were Shuhamite clans; and those numbered were 64,400.

⁴⁴The descendants of Asher by their clans
were:
through Imnah, the Imnite clan;
through Ishvi, the Ishvite clan;
through Beriah, the Beriite clan;
⁴⁵and through the descendants of Beriah:
through Heber, the Heberite clan;
through Malkiel, the Malkielite
clan.
⁴⁶(Asher had a daughter named Serah.)
⁴⁷These were the clans of Asher; those
numbered were 53,400.

⁴⁸The descendants of Naphtali by their
clans were:
through Jahzeel, the Jahzeelite clan;
through Guni, the Gunite clan;
⁴⁹through Jezer, the Jezerite clan;
through Shillem, the Shillemite clan.
⁵⁰These were the clans of Naphtali; those
numbered were 45,400.

⁵¹The total number of the men of Israel
was 601,730.

⁵²The LORD said to Moses, ⁵³"The land is
to be allotted to them as an inheritance
based on the number of names. ⁵⁴To a
larger group give a larger inheritance, and
to a smaller group a smaller one; each is
to receive its inheritance according to the
number of those listed. ⁵⁵Be sure that the
land is distributed by lot. What each
group inherits will be according to the
names for its ancestral tribe. ⁵⁶Each inheritance is to be distributed by lot among
the larger and smaller groups."

⁵⁷These were the Levites who were
counted by their clans:
through Gershon, the Gershonite
clan;
through Kohath, the Kohathite clan;
through Merari, the Merarite clan.
⁵⁸These also were Levite clans:
the Libnite clan,
the Hebronite clan,
the Mahlite clan,
the Mushite clan,
the Korahite clan.
(Kohath was the forefather of Amram; ⁵⁹the name of Amram's wife was
Jochebed, a descendant of Levi, who
was born to the Levitesᶜ in Egypt. To
Amram she bore Aaron, Moses and
their sister Miriam. ⁶⁰Aaron was the
father of Nadab and Abihu, Eleazar
and Ithamar. ⁶¹But Nadab and Abihu
died when they made an offering before the LORD with unauthorized
fire.)

⁶²All the male Levites a month old or more
numbered 23,000. They were not counted
along with the other Israelites because
they received no inheritance among
them.

⁶³These are the ones counted by Moses
and Eleazar the priest when they counted
the Israelites on the plains of Moab by the
Jordan across from Jericho. ⁶⁴Not one of
them was among those counted by Moses
and Aaron the priest when they counted
the Israelites in the Desert of Sinai. ⁶⁵For
the LORD had told those Israelites they
would surely die in the desert, and not
one of them was left except Caleb son of
Jephunneh and Joshua son of Nun.

ᵃ39 A few manuscripts of the Masoretic Text,
Samaritan Pentateuch, Vulgate and Syriac (see also
Septuagint); most manuscripts of the Masoretic
Text *Shephupham*   ᵇ40 Samaritan Pentateuch and
Vulgate (see also Septuagint); Masoretic Text does
not have *through Ard*.   ᶜ59 Or *Jochebed, a
daughter of Levi, who was born to Levi*

Zelophehad's Daughters

27 The daughters of Zelophehad son of Hepher, the son of Gilead, the son of Makir, the son of Manasseh, belonged to the clans of Manasseh son of Joseph. The names of the daughters were Mahlah, Noah, Hoglah, Milcah and Tirzah. They approached ²the entrance to the Tent of Meeting and stood before Moses, Eleazar the priest, the leaders and the whole assembly, and said, ³"Our father died in the desert. He was not among Korah's followers, who banded together against the LORD, but he died for his own sin and left no sons. ⁴Why should our father's name disappear from his clan because he had no son? Give us property among our father's relatives."

⁵So Moses brought their case before the LORD ⁶and the LORD said to him, ⁷"What Zelophehad's daughters are saying is right. You must certainly give them property as an inheritance among their father's relatives and turn their father's inheritance over to them.

⁸"Say to the Israelites, 'If a man dies and leaves no son, turn his inheritance over to his daughter. ⁹If he has no daughter, give his inheritance to his brothers. ¹⁰If he has no brothers, give his inheritance to his father's brothers. ¹¹If his father had no brothers, give his inheritance to the nearest relative in his clan, that he may possess it. This is to be a legal requirement for the Israelites, as the LORD commanded Moses.'"

Joshua to Succeed Moses

¹²Then the LORD said to Moses, "Go up this mountain in the Abarim range and see the land I have given the Israelites. ¹³After you have seen it, you too will be gathered to your people, as your brother Aaron was, ¹⁴for when the community rebelled at the waters in the Desert of Zin, both of you disobeyed my command to honor me as holy before their eyes." (These were the waters of Meribah Kadesh, in the Desert of Zin.)

¹⁵Moses said to the LORD, ¹⁶"May the LORD, the God of the spirits of all mankind, appoint a man over this community ¹⁷to go out and come in before them, one who will lead them out and bring them in, so the LORD's people will not be like sheep without a shepherd."

¹⁸So the LORD said to Moses, "Take Joshua son of Nun, a man in whom is the spirit,ᵃ and lay your hand on him. ¹⁹Have him stand before Eleazar the priest and the entire assembly and commission him in their presence. ²⁰Give him some of your authority so the whole Israelite community will obey him. ²¹He is to stand before Eleazar the priest, who will obtain decisions for him by inquiring of the Urim before the LORD. At his command he and the entire community of the Israelites will go out, and at his command they will come in."

²²Moses did as the LORD commanded him. He took Joshua and had him stand before Eleazar the priest and the whole assembly. ²³Then he laid his hands on him and commissioned him, as the LORD instructed through Moses.

Daily Offerings

28 The LORD said to Moses, ²"Give this command to the Israelites and say to them: 'See that you present to me at the appointed time the food for my offerings made by fire, as an aroma pleasing to me.' ³Say to them: 'This is the offering made by fire that you are to present to the LORD: two lambs a year old without defect, as a regular burnt offering each day. ⁴Prepare one lamb in the morning and the other at twilight, ⁵together with a grain offering of a tenth of an ephahᵇ of fine flour mixed with a quarter of a hinᶜ of oil from pressed olives. ⁶This is the regular burnt offering instituted at Mount Sinai as a pleasing aroma, an offering made to the LORD by fire. ⁷The accompanying drink offering is to be a quarter of a hin of fermented drink with each lamb. Pour out the drink offering to the LORD at the sanctuary. ⁸Prepare the second lamb at twilight, along with the same kind of grain offering and drink offering that you prepare in the morning. This is an offering made by fire, an aroma pleasing to the LORD.

Sabbath Offerings

⁹"'On the Sabbath day, make an offering of two lambs a year old without defect, together with its drink offering and a grain offering of two-tenths of an ephahᵈ of fine flour mixed with oil. ¹⁰This is the

ᵃ18 Or Spirit   ᵇ5 That is, probably about 2 quarts (about 2 liters); also in verses 13, 21 and 29
ᶜ5 That is, probably about 1 quart (about 1 liter); also in verses 7 and 14   ᵈ9 That is, probably about 4 quarts (about 4.5 liters); also in verses 12, 20 and 28

burnt offering for every Sabbath, in addition to the regular burnt offering and its drink offering.

Monthly Offerings

11" 'On the first of every month, present to the LORD a burnt offering of two young bulls, one ram and seven male lambs a year old, all without defect. **12**With each bull there is to be a grain offering of three-tenths of an ephah[a] of fine flour mixed with oil; with the ram, a grain offering of two-tenths of an ephah of fine flour mixed with oil; **13**and with each lamb, a grain offering of a tenth of an ephah of fine flour mixed with oil. This is for a burnt offering, a pleasing aroma, an offering made to the LORD by fire. **14**With each bull there is to be a drink offering of half a hin[b] of wine; with the ram, a third of a hin[c]; and with each lamb, a quarter of a hin. This is the monthly burnt offering to be made at each new moon during the year. **15**Besides the regular burnt offering with its drink offering, one male goat is to be presented to the LORD as a sin offering.

The Passover

16" 'On the fourteenth day of the first month the LORD's Passover is to be held. **17**On the fifteenth day of this month there is to be a festival; for seven days eat bread made without yeast. **18**On the first day hold a sacred assembly and do no regular work. **19**Present to the LORD an offering made by fire, a burnt offering of two young bulls, one ram and seven male lambs a year old, all without defect. **20**With each bull prepare a grain offering of three-tenths of an ephah of fine flour mixed with oil; with the ram, two-tenths; **21**and with each of the seven lambs, one-tenth. **22**Include one male goat as a sin offering to make atonement for you. **23**Prepare these in addition to the regular morning burnt offering. **24**In this way prepare the food for the offering made by fire every day for seven days as an aroma pleasing to the LORD; it is to be prepared in addition to the regular burnt offering and its drink offering. **25**On the seventh day hold a sacred assembly and do no regular work.

Feast of Weeks

26" 'On the day of firstfruits, when you present to the LORD an offering of new grain during the Feast of Weeks, hold a sacred assembly and do no regular work. **27**Present a burnt offering of two young bulls, one ram and seven male lambs a year old as an aroma pleasing to the LORD. **28**With each bull there is to be a grain offering of three-tenths of an ephah of fine flour mixed with oil; with the ram, two-tenths; **29**and with each of the seven lambs, one-tenth. **30**Include one male goat to make atonement for you. **31**Prepare these together with their drink offerings, in addition to the regular burnt offering and its grain offering. Be sure the animals are without defect.

Feast of Trumpets

29 " 'On the first day of the seventh month hold a sacred assembly and do no regular work. It is a day for you to sound the trumpets. **2**As an aroma pleasing to the LORD, prepare a burnt offering of one young bull, one ram and seven male lambs a year old, all without defect. **3**With the bull prepare a grain offering of three-tenths of an ephah[d] of fine flour mixed with oil; with the ram, two-tenths[e]; **4**and with each of the seven lambs, one-tenth.[f] **5**Include one male goat as a sin offering to make atonement for you. **6**These are in addition to the monthly and daily burnt offerings with their grain offerings and drink offerings as specified. They are offerings made to the LORD by fire—a pleasing aroma.

Day of Atonement

7" 'On the tenth day of this seventh month hold a sacred assembly. You must deny yourselves[g] and do no work. **8**Present as an aroma pleasing to the LORD a burnt offering of one young bull, one ram and seven male lambs a year old, all without defect. **9**With the bull prepare a grain offering of three-tenths of an ephah of fine flour mixed with oil; with the ram, two-tenths; **10**and with each of the seven lambs, one-tenth. **11**Include one male goat as a sin offering, in addition to the sin offering for atonement and the regular

---

*a*12 That is, probably about 6 quarts (about 6.5 liters); also in verses 20 and 28   *b*14 That is, probably about 2 quarts (about 2 liters)   *c*14 That is, probably about 1 1/4 quarts (about 1.2 liters)   *d*3 That is, probably about 6 quarts (about 6.5 liters); also in verses 9 and 14   *e*3 That is, probably about 4 quarts (about 4.5 liters); also in verses 9 and 14   *f*4 That is, probably about 2 quarts (about 2 liters); also in verses 10 and 15   *g*7 Or *must fast*

burnt offering with its grain offering, and their drink offerings.

Feast of Tabernacles

¹²" 'On the fifteenth day of the seventh month, hold a sacred assembly and do no regular work. Celebrate a festival to the LORD for seven days. ¹³Present an offering made by fire as an aroma pleasing to the LORD, a burnt offering of thirteen young bulls, two rams and fourteen male lambs a year old, all without defect. ¹⁴With each of the thirteen bulls prepare a grain offering of three-tenths of an ephah of fine flour mixed with oil; with each of the two rams, two-tenths; ¹⁵and with each of the fourteen lambs, one-tenth. ¹⁶Include one male goat as a sin offering, in addition to the regular burnt offering with its grain offering and drink offering.

¹⁷" 'On the second day prepare twelve young bulls, two rams and fourteen male lambs a year old, all without defect. ¹⁸With the bulls, rams and lambs, prepare their grain offerings and drink offerings according to the number specified. ¹⁹Include one male goat as a sin offering, in addition to the regular burnt offering with its grain offering, and their drink offerings.

²⁰" 'On the third day prepare eleven bulls, two rams and fourteen male lambs a year old, all without defect. ²¹With the bulls, rams and lambs, prepare their grain offerings and drink offerings according to the number specified. ²²Include one male goat as a sin offering, in addition to the regular burnt offering with its grain offering and drink offering.

²³" 'On the fourth day prepare ten bulls, two rams and fourteen male lambs a year old, all without defect. ²⁴With the bulls, rams and lambs, prepare their grain offerings and drink offerings according to the number specified. ²⁵Include one male goat as a sin offering, in addition to the regular burnt offering with its grain offering and drink offering.

²⁶" 'On the fifth day prepare nine bulls, two rams and fourteen male lambs a year old, all without defect. ²⁷With the bulls, rams and lambs, prepare their grain offerings and drink offerings according to the number specified. ²⁸Include one male goat as a sin offering, in addition to the regular burnt offering with its grain offering and drink offering.

²⁹" 'On the sixth day prepare eight bulls, two rams and fourteen male lambs a year

old, all without defect. ³⁰With the bulls, rams and lambs, prepare their grain offerings and drink offerings according to the number specified. ³¹Include one male goat as a sin offering, in addition to the regular burnt offering with its grain offering and drink offering.

³²" 'On the seventh day prepare seven bulls, two rams and fourteen male lambs a year old, all without defect. ³³With the bulls, rams and lambs, prepare their grain offerings and drink offerings according to the number specified. ³⁴Include one male goat as a sin offering, in addition to the regular burnt offering with its grain offering and drink offering.

³⁵" 'On the eighth day hold an assembly and do no regular work. ³⁶Present an offering made by fire as an aroma pleasing to the LORD, a burnt offering of one bull, one ram and seven male lambs a year old, all without defect. ³⁷With the bull, the ram and the lambs, prepare their grain offerings and drink offerings according to the number specified. ³⁸Include one male goat as a sin offering, in addition to the regular burnt offering with its grain offering and drink offering.

³⁹" 'In addition to what you vow and your freewill offerings, prepare these for the LORD at your appointed feasts: your burnt offerings, grain offerings, drink offerings and fellowship offerings.ᵃ' "

⁴⁰Moses told the Israelites all that the LORD commanded him.

Vows

30 Moses said to the heads of the tribes of Israel: "This is what the LORD commands: ²When a man makes a vow to the LORD or takes an oath to obligate himself by a pledge, he must not break his word but must do everything he said.

³"When a young woman still living in her father's house makes a vow to the LORD or obligates herself by a pledge ⁴and her father hears about her vow or pledge but says nothing to her, then all her vows and every pledge by which she obligated herself will stand. ⁵But if her father forbids her when he hears about it, none of her vows or the pledges by which she obligated herself will stand; the LORD will release her because her father has forbidden her.

⁶"If she marries after she makes a vow or after her lips utter a rash promise by

ᵃ39 Traditionally *peace offerings*

which she obligates herself ⁷and her husband hears about it but says nothing to her, then her vows or the pledges by which she obligated herself will stand. ⁸But if her husband forbids her when he hears about it, he nullifies the vow that obligates her or the rash promise by which she obligates herself, and the LORD will release her.

⁹"Any vow or obligation taken by a widow or divorced woman will be binding on her.

¹⁰"If a woman living with her husband makes a vow or obligates herself by a pledge under oath ¹¹and her husband hears about it but says nothing to her and does not forbid her, then all her vows or the pledges by which she obligated herself will stand. ¹²But if her husband nullifies them when he hears about them, then none of the vows or pledges that came from her lips will stand. Her husband has nullified them, and the LORD will release her. ¹³Her husband may confirm or nullify any vow she makes or any sworn pledge to deny herself. ¹⁴But if her husband says nothing to her about it from day to day, then he confirms all her vows or the pledges binding on her. He confirms them by saying nothing to her when he

Words that Live Together

DAILY INSIGHT

MONDAY

Passage:
Numbers 30:3–8

Verse:
Numbers 30:2

It had been a very long time since I had bought a new car. Given all the obligations of the past several years—college tuition, to name a monster—I had opted to drive my car a lot longer than I really wanted to.

But now my wife and I saw our way clear to trade up for a new car. We set the appointment with the salesman for mid-afternoon. All morning, even though I had some important meetings to attend, I could hardly concentrate—you know the feeling.

The salesman seemed competent. I narrowed my options from a parking lot full of cars, and we had a deal. Almost. You see, there were a few additional things I wanted, including the upgraded radio, the traction package … Oh, and a little better price.

The salesman made a few notes on his sales sheet and then gave me the inevitable, "I'll have to check with the sales manager."

"I knew it," I muttered when the salesman was out of sight. "Why do these guys always do this? I wasn't asking for that much. Why don't they make these decisions on their own?"

The text today is a very interesting one. In the culture of the day, a husband or a dad actually had the power to reverse a vow his wife or his daughter had made if he didn't agree with what she had promised.

Setting aside, for a moment, how different this culture was from our own, there is an interesting principle at work here—an idea that carries a critical message for dads. In a family, no one person lives in isolation. Our bodies not only inhabit the same dwelling, our words also live together! Your promises affect your loved ones. And every promise your family makes has an impact on you.

Just like the car salesman's agreement has an effect on the dealership's profits, the things we commit to in a family have an impact on our family's "bottom line."

You may be about to make a very important decision. Technically, you have the authority as a dad to do what you think is right, then report what you've done to your wife and family. But, remembering that one person's commitments affect the whole family, take your decision to your family before you sign anything. Ask them for their help. Listen carefully to their input.

Someday your children will make life-altering decisions—college, vocation, or marriage partner. They'll remember that you came to them with your big decisions, so it will only be natural for them to come to you with theirs.

For your next devotional reading, go to page 200.

hears about them. ¹⁵If, however, he nullifies them some time after he hears about them, then he is responsible for her guilt."

¹⁶These are the regulations the LORD gave Moses concerning relationships between a man and his wife, and between a father and his young daughter still living in his house.

Vengeance on the Midianites

31 The LORD said to Moses, ²"Take vengeance on the Midianites for the Israelites. After that, you will be gathered to your people."

³So Moses said to the people, "Arm some of your men to go to war against the Midianites and to carry out the LORD's vengeance on them. ⁴Send into battle a thousand men from each of the tribes of Israel." ⁵So twelve thousand men armed for battle, a thousand from each tribe, were supplied from the clans of Israel. ⁶Moses sent them into battle, a thousand from each tribe, along with Phinehas son of Eleazar, the priest, who took with him articles from the sanctuary and the trumpets for signaling.

⁷They fought against Midian, as the LORD commanded Moses, and killed every man. ⁸Among their victims were Evi, Rekem, Zur, Hur and Reba—the five kings of Midian. They also killed Balaam son of Beor with the sword. ⁹The Israelites captured the Midianite women and children and took all the Midianite herds, flocks and goods as plunder. ¹⁰They burned all the towns where the Midianites had settled, as well as all their camps. ¹¹They took all the plunder and spoils, including the people and animals, ¹²and brought the captives, spoils and plunder to Moses and Eleazar the priest and the Israelite assembly at their camp on the plains of Moab, by the Jordan across from Jericho.ᵃ

¹³Moses, Eleazar the priest and all the leaders of the community went to meet them outside the camp. ¹⁴Moses was angry with the officers of the army—the commanders of thousands and commanders of hundreds—who returned from the battle.

¹⁵"Have you allowed all the women to live?" he asked them. ¹⁶"They were the ones who followed Balaam's advice and were the means of turning the Israelites away from the LORD in what happened at Peor, so that a plague struck the LORD's people. ¹⁷Now kill all the boys. And kill every woman who has slept with a man, ¹⁸but save for yourselves every girl who has never slept with a man.

¹⁹"All of you who have killed anyone or touched anyone who was killed must stay outside the camp seven days. On the third and seventh days you must purify yourselves and your captives. ²⁰Purify every garment as well as everything made of leather, goat hair or wood."

²¹Then Eleazar the priest said to the soldiers who had gone into battle, "This is the requirement of the law that the LORD gave Moses: ²²Gold, silver, bronze, iron, tin, lead ²³and anything else that can withstand fire must be put through the fire, and then it will be clean. But it must also be purified with the water of cleansing. And whatever cannot withstand fire must be put through that water. ²⁴On the seventh day wash your clothes and you will be clean. Then you may come into the camp."

Dividing the Spoils

²⁵The LORD said to Moses, ²⁶"You and Eleazar the priest and the family heads of the community are to count all the people and animals that were captured. ²⁷Divide the spoils between the soldiers who took part in the battle and the rest of the community. ²⁸From the soldiers who fought in the battle, set apart as tribute for the LORD one out of every five hundred, whether persons, cattle, donkeys, sheep or goats. ²⁹Take this tribute from their half share and give it to Eleazar the priest as the LORD's part. ³⁰From the Israelites' half, select one out of every fifty, whether persons, cattle, donkeys, sheep, goats or other animals. Give them to the Levites, who are responsible for the care of the LORD's tabernacle." ³¹So Moses and Eleazar the priest did as the LORD commanded Moses.

³²The plunder remaining from the spoils that the soldiers took was 675,000 sheep, ³³72,000 cattle, ³⁴61,000 donkeys ³⁵and 32,000 women who had never slept with a man.

³⁶The half share of those who fought in the battle was:

337,500 sheep, ³⁷of which the tribute for the LORD was 675;
³⁸36,000 cattle, of which the tribute for the LORD was 72;

ᵃ12 Hebrew *Jordan of Jericho*; possibly an ancient name for the Jordan River

²¹They left Libnah and camped at Rissah. ²²They left Rissah and camped at Kehelathah. ²³They left Kehelathah and camped at Mount Shepher. ²⁴They left Mount Shepher and camped at Haradah. ²⁵They left Haradah and camped at Makheloth. ²⁶They left Makheloth and camped at Tahath. ²⁷They left Tahath and camped at Terah. ²⁸They left Terah and camped at Mithcah. ²⁹They left Mithcah and camped at Hashmonah. ³⁰They left Hashmonah and camped at Moseroth. ³¹They left Moseroth and camped at Bene Jaakan. ³²They left Bene Jaakan and camped at Hor Haggidgad. ³³They left Hor Haggidgad and camped at Jotbathah. ³⁴They left Jotbathah and camped at Abronah. ³⁵They left Abronah and camped at Ezion Geber. ³⁶They left Ezion Geber and camped at Kadesh, in the Desert of Zin.

³⁷They left Kadesh and camped at Mount Hor, on the border of Edom. ³⁸At the LORD's command Aaron the priest went up Mount Hor, where he died on the first day of the fifth month of the fortieth year after the Israelites came out of Egypt. ³⁹Aaron was a hundred and twenty-three years old when he died on Mount Hor. ⁴⁰The Canaanite king of Arad, who lived in the Negev of Canaan, heard that the Israelites were coming.

⁴¹They left Mount Hor and camped at Zalmonah. ⁴²They left Zalmonah and camped at Punon. ⁴³They left Punon and camped at Oboth. ⁴⁴They left Oboth and camped at Iye Abarim, on the border of Moab. ⁴⁵They left Iyim[a] and camped at Dibon Gad. ⁴⁶They left Dibon Gad and camped at Almon Diblathaim. ⁴⁷They left Almon Diblathaim and camped in the mountains of Abarim, near Nebo.

⁴⁸They left the mountains of Abarim and camped on the plains of Moab by the Jordan across from Jericho.[b] ⁴⁹There on the plains of Moab they camped along the Jordan from Beth Jeshimoth to Abel Shittim.

⁵⁰On the plains of Moab by the Jordan across from Jericho the LORD said to Moses, ⁵¹"Speak to the Israelites and say to them: 'When you cross the Jordan into Canaan, ⁵²drive out all the inhabitants of the land before you. Destroy all their carved images and their cast idols, and demolish all their high places. ⁵³Take possession of the land and settle in it, for I have given you the land to possess. ⁵⁴Distribute the land by lot, according to your clans. To a larger group give a larger inheritance, and to a smaller group a smaller one. Whatever falls to them by lot will be theirs. Distribute it according to your ancestral tribes.

⁵⁵"'But if you do not drive out the inhabitants of the land, those you allow to remain will become barbs in your eyes and thorns in your sides. They will give you trouble in the land where you will live. ⁵⁶And then I will do to you what I plan to do to them.'"

Boundaries of Canaan

34 The LORD said to Moses, ²"Command the Israelites and say to them: 'When you enter Canaan, the land that will be allotted to you as an inheritance will have these boundaries:

³"'Your southern side will include some of the Desert of Zin along the border of Edom. On the east, your southern boundary will start from the end of the Salt Sea,[c] ⁴cross south of Scorpion[d] Pass, continue on to Zin and go south of Kadesh Barnea. Then it will go to Hazar Addar and over to Azmon, ⁵where it will turn, join the Wadi of Egypt and end at the Sea.[e]

⁶"'Your western boundary will be the coast of the Great Sea. This will be your boundary on the west.

⁷"'For your northern boundary, run a line from the Great Sea to Mount Hor ⁸and from Mount Hor to Lebo[f] Hamath.

---

[a]45 That is, Iye Abarim   [b]48 Hebrew *Jordan of Jericho;* possibly an ancient name for the Jordan River; also in verse 50   [c]3 That is, the Dead Sea; also in verse 12   [d]4 Hebrew *Akrabbim*   [e]5 That is, the Mediterranean; also in verses 6 and 7   [f]8 Or *to the entrance to*

Then the boundary will go to Zedad, [9]continue to Ziphron and end at Hazar Enan. This will be your boundary on the north.

[10]" 'For your eastern boundary, run a line from Hazar Enan to Shepham. [11]The boundary will go down from Shepham to Riblah on the east side of Ain and continue along the slopes east of the Sea of Kinnereth.[a] [12]Then the boundary will go down along the Jordan and end at the Salt Sea.

" 'This will be your land, with its boundaries on every side.' "

[13]Moses commanded the Israelites: "Assign this land by lot as an inheritance. The LORD has ordered that it be given to the nine and a half tribes, [14]because the families of the tribe of Reuben, the tribe of Gad and the half-tribe of Manasseh have received their inheritance. [15]These two and a half tribes have received their inheritance on the east side of the Jordan of Jericho,[b] toward the sunrise."

[16]The LORD said to Moses, [17]"These are the names of the men who are to assign the land for you as an inheritance: Eleazar the priest and Joshua son of Nun. [18]And appoint one leader from each tribe to help assign the land. [19]These are their names:

Caleb son of Jephunneh,
    from the tribe of Judah;
[20]Shemuel son of Ammihud,
    from the tribe of Simeon;
[21]Elidad son of Kislon,
    from the tribe of Benjamin;
[22]Bukki son of Jogli,
    the leader from the tribe of Dan;
[23]Hanniel son of Ephod,
    the leader from the tribe of Manasseh son of Joseph;
[24]Kemuel son of Shiphtan,
    the leader from the tribe of Ephraim son of Joseph;
[25]Elizaphan son of Parnach,
    the leader from the tribe of Zebulun;
[26]Paltiel son of Azzan,
    the leader from the tribe of Issachar;
[27]Ahihud son of Shelomi,
    the leader from the tribe of Asher;
[28]Pedahel son of Ammihud,
    the leader from the tribe of Naphtali."

[29]These are the men the LORD commanded to assign the inheritance to the Israelites in the land of Canaan.

Towns for the Levites

35 On the plains of Moab by the Jordan across from Jericho,[c] the LORD said to Moses, [2]"Command the Israelites to give the Levites towns to live in from the inheritance the Israelites will possess. And give them pasturelands around the towns. [3]Then they will have towns to live in and pasturelands for their cattle, flocks and all their other livestock.

[4]"The pasturelands around the towns that you give the Levites will extend out fifteen hundred feet[d] from the town wall. [5]Outside the town, measure three thousand feet[e] on the east side, three thousand on the south side, three thousand on the west and three thousand on the north, with the town in the center. They will have this area as pastureland for the towns.

Cities of Refuge

[6]"Six of the towns you give the Levites will be cities of refuge, to which a person who has killed someone may flee. In addition, give them forty-two other towns. [7]In all you must give the Levites forty-eight towns, together with their pasturelands. [8]The towns you give the Levites from the land the Israelites possess are to be given in proportion to the inheritance of each tribe: Take many towns from a tribe that has many, but few from one that has few."

[9]Then the LORD said to Moses: [10]"Speak to the Israelites and say to them: 'When you cross the Jordan into Canaan, [11]select some towns to be your cities of refuge, to which a person who has killed someone accidentally may flee. [12]They will be places of refuge from the avenger, so that a person accused of murder may not die before he stands trial before the assembly. [13]These six towns you give will be your cities of refuge. [14]Give three on this side of the Jordan and three in Canaan as cities of refuge. [15]These six towns will be a place of refuge for Israelites, aliens and any other people living among them, so that anyone who has killed another accidentally can flee there.

[16]" 'If a man strikes someone with an iron object so that he dies, he is a murderer; the murderer shall be put to death.

[a]11 That is, Galilee   [b]15 Jordan of Jericho was possibly an ancient name for the Jordan River.   [c]1 Hebrew Jordan of Jericho; possibly an ancient name for the Jordan River   [d]4 Hebrew a thousand cubits (about 450 meters)   [e]5 Hebrew two thousand cubits (about 900 meters)

[17] Or if anyone has a stone in his hand that could kill, and he strikes someone so that he dies, he is a murderer; the murderer shall be put to death. [18] Or if anyone has a wooden object in his hand that could kill, and he hits someone so that he dies, he is a murderer; the murderer shall be put to death. [19] The avenger of blood shall put the murderer to death; when he meets him, he shall put him to death. [20] If anyone with malice aforethought shoves another or throws something at him intentionally so that he dies [21] or if in hostility he hits him with his fist so that he dies, that person shall be put to death; he is a murderer. The avenger of blood shall put the murderer to death when he meets him.

[22] "'But if without hostility someone suddenly shoves another or throws something at him unintentionally [23] or, without seeing him, drops a stone on him that could kill him, and he dies, then since he was not his enemy and he did not intend to harm him, [24] the assembly must judge between him and the avenger of blood according to these regulations. [25] The assembly must protect the one accused of murder from the avenger of blood and send him back to the city of refuge to which he fled. He must stay there until the death of the high priest, who was anointed with the holy oil.

[26] "'But if the accused ever goes outside the limits of the city of refuge to which he has fled [27] and the avenger of blood finds him outside the city, the avenger of blood may kill the accused without being guilty of murder. [28] The accused must stay in his city of refuge until the death of the high priest; only after the death of the high priest may he return to his own property.

[29] "'These are to be legal requirements for you throughout the generations to come, wherever you live.

[30] "'Anyone who kills a person is to be put to death as a murderer only on the testimony of witnesses. But no one is to be put to death on the testimony of only one witness.

[31] "'Do not accept a ransom for the life of a murderer, who deserves to die. He must surely be put to death.

[32] "'Do not accept a ransom for anyone who has fled to a city of refuge and so allow him to go back and live on his own land before the death of the high priest.

[33] "'Do not pollute the land where you are. Bloodshed pollutes the land, and atonement cannot be made for the land on which blood has been shed, except by the blood of the one who shed it. [34] Do not defile the land where you live and where I dwell, for I, the LORD, dwell among the Israelites.' "

Inheritance of Zelophehad's Daughters

36 The family heads of the clan of Gilead son of Makir, the son of Manasseh, who were from the clans of the descendants of Joseph, came and spoke before Moses and the leaders, the heads of the Israelite families. [2] They said, "When the LORD commanded my lord to give the land as an inheritance to the Israelites by lot, he ordered you to give the inheritance of our brother Zelophehad to his daughters. [3] Now suppose they marry men from other Israelite tribes; then their inheritance will be taken from our ancestral inheritance and added to that of the tribe they marry into. And so part of the inheritance allotted to us will be taken away. [4] When the Year of Jubilee for the Israelites comes, their inheritance will be added to that of the tribe into which they marry, and their property will be taken from the tribal inheritance of our forefathers."

[5] Then at the LORD's command Moses gave this order to the Israelites: "What the tribe of the descendants of Joseph is saying is right. [6] This is what the LORD commands for Zelophehad's daughters: They may marry anyone they please as long as they marry within the tribal clan of their father. [7] No inheritance in Israel is to pass from tribe to tribe, for every Israelite shall keep the tribal land inherited from his forefathers. [8] Every daughter who inherits land in any Israelite tribe must marry someone in her father's tribal clan, so that every Israelite will possess the inheritance of his fathers. [9] No inheritance may pass from tribe to tribe, for each Israelite tribe is to keep the land it inherits."

[10] So Zelophehad's daughters did as the LORD commanded Moses. [11] Zelophehad's daughters—Mahlah, Tirzah, Hoglah, Milcah and Noah—married their cousins on their father's side. [12] They married within the clans of the descendants of Manasseh son of Joseph, and their inheritance remained in their father's clan and tribe.

[13] These are the commands and regulations the LORD gave through Moses to the Israelites on the plains of Moab by the Jordan across from Jericho.[a]

---

[a] 13 Hebrew *Jordan of Jericho*; possibly an ancient name for the Jordan River

Life would be so much easier without rules. We could drive as fast as we wanted, we could eat chocolate candy for breakfast every day, we could be as promiscuous as we felt, and we could tell our families that they could do whatever they wanted because that's what we were going to do.

Of course, this doesn't sound like a good time at all, does it? Societies and families need rules to survive. Without them, chaos and unhappiness takes over. The book of Deuteronomy was intended to be a guidebook for God's family, the Israelites. Sure, sometimes it may read like the tax code from the Internal Revenue Service, but every word is there for a good reason. Families who live together—like the Israelites' and like yours—need rules. They may squirm a little; you may not be applauded every time you enforce them, but guidelines make your family feel happy and safe. Just ask a couple million people who wandered around in the desert for forty years.

Deuteronomy

The Command to Leave Horeb

1 These are the words Moses spoke to all Israel in the desert east of the Jordan— that is, in the Arabah—opposite Suph, between Paran and Tophel, Laban, Hazeroth and Dizahab. ²(It takes eleven days to go from Horeb to Kadesh Barnea by the Mount Seir road.)

³In the fortieth year, on the first day of the eleventh month, Moses proclaimed to the Israelites all that the LORD had commanded him concerning them. ⁴This was after he had defeated Sihon king of the Amorites, who reigned in Heshbon, and at Edrei had defeated Og king of Bashan, who reigned in Ashtaroth.

⁵East of the Jordan in the territory of Moab, Moses began to expound this law, saying:

⁶The LORD our God said to us at Horeb, "You have stayed long enough at this mountain. ⁷Break camp and advance into the hill country of the Amorites; go to all the neighboring peoples in the Arabah, in the mountains, in the western foothills, in the Negev and along the coast, to the land of the Canaanites and to Lebanon, as far as the great river, the Euphrates. ⁸See, I have given you this land. Go in and take possession of the land that the LORD swore he would give to your fathers—to Abraham, Isaac and Jacob—and to their descendants after them."

The Appointment of Leaders

⁹At that time I said to you, "You are too heavy a burden for me to carry alone. ¹⁰The LORD your God has increased your

numbers so that today you are as many as the stars in the sky. [11]May the LORD, the God of your fathers, increase you a thousand times and bless you as he has promised! [12]But how can I bear your problems and your burdens and your disputes all by myself? [13]Choose some wise, understanding and respected men from each of your tribes, and I will set them over you."

[14]You answered me, "What you propose to do is good."

[15]So I took the leading men of your tribes, wise and respected men, and appointed them to have authority over you—as commanders of thousands, of hundreds, of fifties and of tens and as tribal officials. [16]And I charged your judges at that time: Hear the disputes between your brothers and judge fairly, whether the case is between brother Israelites or between one of them and an alien. [17]Do not show partiality in judging; hear both small and great alike. Do not be afraid of any man, for judgment belongs to God. Bring me any case too hard for you, and I will hear it. [18]And at that time I told you everything you were to do.

Spies Sent Out

[19]Then, as the LORD our God commanded us, we set out from Horeb and went toward the hill country of the Amorites through all that vast and dreadful desert that you have seen, and so we reached Kadesh Barnea. [20]Then I said to you, "You have reached the hill country of the Amorites, which the LORD our God is giving us. [21]See, the LORD your God has given you the land. Go up and take possession of it as the LORD, the God of your fathers, told you. Do not be afraid; do not be discouraged."

[22]Then all of you came to me and said, "Let us send men ahead to spy out the land for us and bring back a report about the route we are to take and the towns we will come to."

[23]The idea seemed good to me; so I selected twelve of you, one man from each tribe. [24]They left and went up into the hill country, and came to the Valley of Eshcol and explored it. [25]Taking with them some of the fruit of the land, they brought it down to us and reported, "It is a good land that the LORD our God is giving us."

Rebellion Against the LORD

[26]But you were unwilling to go up; you rebelled against the command of the LORD your God. [27]You grumbled in your tents and said, "The LORD hates us; so he brought us out of Egypt to deliver us into the hands of the Amorites to destroy us. [28]Where can we go? Our brothers have made us lose heart. They say, 'The people are stronger and taller than we are; the cities are large, with walls up to the sky. We even saw the Anakites there.' "

[29]Then I said to you, "Do not be terrified; do not be afraid of them. [30]The LORD your God, who is going before you, will fight for you, as he did for you in Egypt, before your very eyes, [31]and in the desert. There you saw how the LORD your God carried you, as a father carries his son, all the way you went until you reached this place."

[32]In spite of this, you did not trust in the LORD your God, [33]who went ahead of you on your journey, in fire by night and in a cloud by day, to search out places for you to camp and to show you the way you should go.

[34]When the LORD heard what you said, he was angry and solemnly swore: [35]"Not a man of this evil generation shall see the good land I swore to give your forefathers, [36]except Caleb son of Jephunneh. He will see it, and I will give him and his descendants the land he set his feet on, because he followed the LORD wholeheartedly."

[37]Because of you the LORD became angry with me also and said, "You shall not enter it, either. [38]But your assistant, Joshua son of Nun, will enter it. Encourage him, because he will lead Israel to inherit it. [39]And the little ones that you said would be taken captive, your children who do not yet know good from bad—they will enter the land. I will give it to them and they will take possession of it. [40]But as for you, turn around and set out toward the desert along the route to the Red Sea.[a]"

[41]Then you replied, "We have sinned against the LORD. We will go up and fight, as the LORD our God commanded us." So every one of you put on his weapons, thinking it easy to go up into the hill country.

[42]But the LORD said to me, "Tell them, 'Do not go up and fight, because I will not be with you. You will be defeated by your enemies.' "

[43]So I told you, but you would not listen. You rebelled against the LORD's command and in your arrogance you

---

[a]40 Hebrew *Yam Suph*; that is, Sea of Reeds

marched up into the hill country. ⁴⁴The Amorites who lived in those hills came out against you; they chased you like a swarm of bees and beat you down from Seir all the way to Hormah. ⁴⁵You came back and wept before the LORD, but he paid no attention to your weeping and turned a deaf ear to you. ⁴⁶And so you stayed in Kadesh many days—all the time you spent there.

Wanderings in the Desert

2 Then we turned back and set out toward the desert along the route to the Red Sea,ᵃ as the LORD had directed me. For a long time we made our way around the hill country of Seir.

²Then the LORD said to me, ³"You have made your way around this hill country long enough; now turn north. ⁴Give the people these orders: 'You are about to pass through the territory of your brothers the descendants of Esau, who live in Seir. They will be afraid of you, but be very careful. ⁵Do not provoke them to war, for I will not give you any of their land, not even enough to put your foot on. I have given Esau the hill country of Seir as his own. ⁶You are to pay them in silver for the food you eat and the water you drink.' "

⁷The LORD your God has blessed you in all the work of your hands. He has watched over your journey through this vast desert. These forty years the LORD your God has been with you, and you have not lacked anything.

⁸So we went on past our brothers the descendants of Esau, who live in Seir. We turned from the Arabah road, which comes up from Elath and Ezion Geber, and traveled along the desert road of Moab.

⁹Then the LORD said to me, "Do not harass the Moabites or provoke them to war, for I will not give you any part of their land. I have given Ar to the descendants of Lot as a possession."

¹⁰(The Emites used to live there—a people strong and numerous, and as tall as the Anakites. ¹¹Like the Anakites, they too were considered Rephaites, but the Moabites called them Emites. ¹²Horites used to live in Seir, but the descendants of Esau drove them out. They destroyed the Horites from before them and settled in their place, just as Israel did in the land the LORD gave them as their possession.)

¹³And the LORD said, "Now get up and cross the Zered Valley." So we crossed the valley.

¹⁴Thirty-eight years passed from the time we left Kadesh Barnea until we crossed the Zered Valley. By then, that entire generation of fighting men had perished from the camp, as the LORD had sworn to them. ¹⁵The LORD's hand was against them until he had completely eliminated them from the camp.

¹⁶Now when the last of these fighting men among the people had died, ¹⁷the LORD said to me, ¹⁸"Today you are to pass by the region of Moab at Ar. ¹⁹When you come to the Ammonites, do not harass them or provoke them to war, for I will not give you possession of any land belonging to the Ammonites. I have given it as a possession to the descendants of Lot."

²⁰(That too was considered a land of the Rephaites, who used to live there; but the Ammonites called them Zamzummites. ²¹They were a people strong and numerous, and as tall as the Anakites. The LORD destroyed them from before the Ammonites, who drove them out and settled in their place. ²²The LORD had done the same for the descendants of Esau, who lived in Seir, when he destroyed the Horites from before them. They drove them out and have lived in their place to this day. ²³And as for the Avvites who lived in villages as far as Gaza, the Caphtorites coming out from Caphtorᵇ destroyed them and settled in their place.)

Defeat of Sihon King of Heshbon

²⁴"Set out now and cross the Arnon Gorge. See, I have given into your hand Sihon the Amorite, king of Heshbon, and his country. Begin to take possession of it and engage him in battle. ²⁵This very day I will begin to put the terror and fear of you on all the nations under heaven. They will hear reports of you and will tremble and be in anguish because of you."

²⁶From the desert of Kedemoth I sent messengers to Sihon king of Heshbon offering peace and saying, ²⁷"Let us pass through your country. We will stay on the main road; we will not turn aside to the right or to the left. ²⁸Sell us food to eat and water to drink for their price in silver. Only let us pass through on foot— ²⁹as the descendants of Esau, who live in Seir, and the Moabites, who live in Ar, did for us—

ᵃ1 Hebrew *Yam Suph*; that is, Sea of Reeds
ᵇ23 That is, Crete

until we cross the Jordan into the land the LORD our God is giving us." [30]But Sihon king of Heshbon refused to let us pass through. For the LORD your God had made his spirit stubborn and his heart obstinate in order to give him into your hands, as he has now done.

[31]The LORD said to me, "See, I have begun to deliver Sihon and his country over to you. Now begin to conquer and possess his land."

[32]When Sihon and all his army came out to meet us in battle at Jahaz, [33]the LORD our God delivered him over to us and we struck him down, together with his sons and his whole army. [34]At that time we took all his towns and completely destroyed[a] them—men, women and children. We left no survivors. [35]But the livestock and the plunder from the towns we had captured we carried off for ourselves. [36]From Aroer on the rim of the Arnon Gorge, and from the town in the gorge, even as far as Gilead, not one town was too strong for us. The LORD our God gave us all of them. [37]But in accordance with the command of the LORD our God, you did not encroach on any of the land of the Ammonites, neither the land along the course of the Jabbok nor that around the towns in the hills.

Defeat of Og King of Bashan

3 Next we turned and went up along the road toward Bashan, and Og king of Bashan with his whole army marched out to meet us in battle at Edrei. [2]The LORD said to me, "Do not be afraid of him, for I have handed him over to you with his whole army and his land. Do to him what you did to Sihon king of the Amorites, who reigned in Heshbon."

[3]So the LORD our God also gave into our hands Og king of Bashan and all his army. We struck them down, leaving no survivors. [4]At that time we took all his cities. There was not one of the sixty cities that we did not take from them—the whole region of Argob, Og's kingdom in Bashan. [5]All these cities were fortified with high walls and with gates and bars, and there were also a great many unwalled villages. [6]We completely destroyed[a] them, as we had done with Sihon king of Heshbon, destroying[a] every city—men, women and children. [7]But all the livestock and the plunder from their cities we carried off for ourselves.

[8]So at that time we took from these two kings of the Amorites the territory east of the Jordan, from the Arnon Gorge as far as Mount Hermon. [9](Hermon is called Sirion by the Sidonians; the Amorites call it Senir.) [10]We took all the towns on the plateau, and all Gilead, and all Bashan as far as Salecah and Edrei, towns of Og's kingdom in Bashan. [11](Only Og king of Bashan was left of the remnant of the Rephaites. His bed[b] was made of iron and was more than thirteen feet long and six feet wide.[c] It is still in Rabbah of the Ammonites.)

Division of the Land

[12]Of the land that we took over at that time, I gave the Reubenites and the Gadites the territory north of Aroer by the Arnon Gorge, including half the hill country of Gilead, together with its towns. [13]The rest of Gilead and also all of Bashan, the kingdom of Og, I gave to the half tribe of Manasseh. (The whole region of Argob in Bashan used to be known as a land of the Rephaites. [14]Jair, a descendant of Manasseh, took the whole region of Argob as far as the border of the Geshurites and the Maacathites; it was named after him, so that to this day Bashan is called Havvoth Jair.[d]) [15]And I gave Gilead to Makir. [16]But to the Reubenites and the Gadites I gave the territory extending from Gilead down to the Arnon Gorge (the middle of the gorge being the border) and out to the Jabbok River, which is the border of the Ammonites. [17]Its western border was the Jordan in the Arabah, from Kinnereth to the Sea of the Arabah (the Salt Sea[e]), below the slopes of Pisgah.

[18]I commanded you at that time: "The LORD your God has given you this land to take possession of it. But all your able-bodied men, armed for battle, must cross over ahead of your brother Israelites. [19]However, your wives, your children and your livestock (I know you have much livestock) may stay in the towns I have given you, [20]until the LORD gives rest to your brothers as he has to you, and they too have taken over the land that the LORD your God is giving them, across the Jordan. After that, each of you may go back to the possession I have given you."

---

[a]34,6 The Hebrew term refers to the irrevocable giving over of things or persons to the LORD, often by totally destroying them.   [b]11 Or *sarcophagus*   [c]11 Hebrew *nine cubits long and four cubits wide* (about 4 meters long and 1.8 meters wide)   [d]14 Or *called the settlements of Jair*   [e]17 That is, the Dead Sea

Moses Forbidden to Cross the Jordan

²¹At that time I commanded Joshua: "You have seen with your own eyes all that the LORD your God has done to these two kings. The LORD will do the same to all the kingdoms over there where you are going. ²²Do not be afraid of them; the LORD your God himself will fight for you."

²³At that time I pleaded with the LORD: ²⁴"O Sovereign LORD, you have begun to show to your servant your greatness and your strong hand. For what god is there in heaven or on earth who can do the deeds and mighty works you do? ²⁵Let me go over and see the good land beyond the Jordan—that fine hill country and Lebanon."

²⁶But because of you the LORD was angry with me and would not listen to me. "That is enough," the LORD said. "Do not speak to me anymore about this matter. ²⁷Go up to the top of Pisgah and look west and north and south and east. Look at the land with your own eyes, since you are not going to cross this Jordan. ²⁸But commission Joshua, and encourage and strengthen him, for he will lead this people across and will cause them to inherit the land that you will see." ²⁹So we stayed in the valley near Beth Peor.

Obedience Commanded

4 Hear now, O Israel, the decrees and laws I am about to teach you. Follow them so that you may live and may go in and take possession of the land that the LORD, the God of your fathers, is giving you. ²Do not add to what I command you and do not subtract from it, but keep the commands of the LORD your God that I give you.

³You saw with your own eyes what the LORD did at Baal Peor. The LORD your God destroyed from among you everyone who followed the Baal of Peor, ⁴but all of you who held fast to the LORD your God are still alive today.

⁵See, I have taught you decrees and laws as the LORD my God commanded me, so that you may follow them in the land you are entering to take possession of it. ⁶Observe them carefully, for this will show your wisdom and understanding to the nations, who will hear about all these decrees and say, "Surely this great nation is a wise and understanding people." ⁷What other nation is so great as to have their gods near them the way the LORD

our God is near us whenever we pray to him? ⁸And what other nation is so great as to have such righteous decrees and laws as this body of laws I am setting before you today?

⁹Only be careful, and watch yourselves closely so that you do not forget the things your eyes have seen or let them slip from your heart as long as you live. Teach them to your children and to their children after them. ¹⁰Remember the day you stood before the LORD your God at Horeb, when he said to me, "Assemble the people before me to hear my words so that they may learn to revere me as long as they live in the land and may teach them to their children." ¹¹You came near and stood at the foot of the mountain while it blazed with fire to the very heavens, with black clouds and deep darkness. ¹²Then the LORD spoke to you out of the fire. You heard the sound of words but saw no form; there was only a voice. ¹³He declared to you his covenant, the Ten Commandments, which he commanded you to follow and then wrote them on two stone tablets. ¹⁴And the LORD directed me at that time to teach you the decrees and laws you are to follow in the land that you are crossing the Jordan to possess.

Idolatry Forbidden

¹⁵You saw no form of any kind the day the LORD spoke to you at Horeb out of the fire. Therefore watch yourselves very carefully, ¹⁶so that you do not become corrupt and make for yourselves an idol, an image of any shape, whether formed like a man or a woman, ¹⁷or like any animal on earth or any bird that flies in the air, ¹⁸or like any creature that moves along the ground or any fish in the waters below. ¹⁹And when you look up to the sky and see the sun, the moon and the stars—all the heavenly array—do not be enticed into bowing down to them and worshiping things the LORD your God has apportioned to all the nations under heaven. ²⁰But as for you, the LORD took you and brought you out of the iron-smelting furnace, out of Egypt, to be the people of his inheritance, as you now are.

²¹The LORD was angry with me because of you, and he solemnly swore that I would not cross the Jordan and enter the good land the LORD your God is giving you as your inheritance. ²²I will die in this land; I will not cross the Jordan; but you are about to cross over and take possession of

that good land. ²³Be careful not to forget the covenant of the LORD your God that he made with you; do not make for yourselves an idol in the form of anything the LORD your God has forbidden. ²⁴For the LORD your God is a consuming fire, a jealous God.

²⁵After you have had children and grandchildren and have lived in the land a long time—if you then become corrupt and make any kind of idol, doing evil in the eyes of the LORD your God and provoking him to anger, ²⁶I call heaven and earth as witnesses against you this day that you will quickly perish from the land that you are crossing the Jordan to pos-

sess. You will not live there long but will certainly be destroyed. ²⁷The LORD will scatter you among the peoples, and only a few of you will survive among the nations to which the LORD will drive you. ²⁸There you will worship man-made gods of wood and stone, which cannot see or hear or eat or smell. ²⁹But if from there you seek the LORD your God, you will find him if you look for him with all your heart and with all your soul. ³⁰When you are in distress and all these things have happened to you, then in later days you will return to the LORD your God and obey him. ³¹For the LORD your God is a merciful God; he will not abandon or destroy you or forget

Listen Up, Boys

DAILY INSIGHT

Did you ever go to summer camp as a kid? And if you did, do you remember the first night when the camp director—I think those guys slept and showered with whistles around their necks and clipboards under their arms—stood up and announced the camp rules? On and on he would drone about not swimming alone, no leaving the camp grounds without permission, mess hall "etiquette"—something about how to scrape excess food off plates into coffee cans, and the most important rule ... no boys in the girls' cabins. And it seemed like all the rules were for the boys and not for the girls. Remember?

The last thing the director said really sounded crazy. "If you follow these rules, you will have a great time here at camp."

By the time the director was finished, you sat there thinking, *Hey, this doesn't sound like a whole lot of fun. They've got way too many rules at this camp. Is this prison or summer camp? What could he possibly mean about having a "good time by following the rules"?*

Now, try to remember how you felt about the camp the day you were leaving. You were saying good-bye to guys you had met. You were telling each other that this was the best week of your life. You were remembering the great times you'd had

TUESDAY

Passage:
Deuteronomy 4:25–31

Verse:
Deuteronomy 4:29

together. You were promising to write letters to each other ... Oh, *sure* you would!

You had completely forgotten how you felt after the camp director laid down the law on opening night. Only a few guys had actually disobeyed, and sure enough, they experienced the pleasure of having their parents drive up to take them home. Following rules, you concluded, *does* make for good experiences. What a great lesson to learn as a youngster.

The Israelites were about to cross the Jordan River and enter the promised land. Before they did, Moses put on his whistle and tucked his clipboard under his arm for a little speech. He warned them of what would happen to them if they disobeyed God's laws—much worse than being sent home from camp. And then he gave them an incredible promise: "If, in your new home, you truly decide to seek God, you'll find him" (4:29).

Can there be a higher goal for our homes? Can there be a greater reward for doing what's right and following God's rules? I don't think so. Don't let the rules bog you down. The rewards of obeying them—living in a home where God lives—are well worth it.

For your next devotional reading, go to page 203.

the covenant with your forefathers, which he confirmed to them by oath.

The Lord Is God

[32]Ask now about the former days, long before your time, from the day God created man on the earth; ask from one end of the heavens to the other. Has anything so great as this ever happened, or has anything like it ever been heard of ? [33]Has any other people heard the voice of God[a] speaking out of fire, as you have, and lived? [34]Has any god ever tried to take for himself one nation out of another nation, by testings, by miraculous signs and wonders, by war, by a mighty hand and an outstretched arm, or by great and awesome deeds, like all the things the Lord your God did for you in Egypt before your very eyes?

[35]You were shown these things so that you might know that the Lord is God; besides him there is no other. [36]From heaven he made you hear his voice to discipline you. On earth he showed you his great fire, and you heard his words from out of the fire. [37]Because he loved your forefathers and chose their descendants after them, he brought you out of Egypt by his Presence and his great strength, [38]to drive out before you nations greater and stronger than you and to bring you into their land to give it to you for your inheritance, as it is today.

[39]Acknowledge and take to heart this day that the Lord is God in heaven above and on the earth below. There is no other. [40]Keep his decrees and commands, which I am giving you today, so that it may go well with you and your children after you and that you may live long in the land the Lord your God gives you for all time.

Cities of Refuge

[41]Then Moses set aside three cities east of the Jordan, [42]to which anyone who had killed a person could flee if he had unintentionally killed his neighbor without malice aforethought. He could flee into one of these cities and save his life. [43]The cities were these: Bezer in the desert plateau, for the Reubenites; Ramoth in Gilead, for the Gadites; and Golan in Bashan, for the Manassites.

Introduction to the Law

[44]This is the law Moses set before the Israelites. [45]These are the stipulations, decrees and laws Moses gave them when they came out of Egypt [46]and were in the valley near Beth Peor east of the Jordan, in the land of Sihon king of the Amorites, who reigned in Heshbon and was defeated by Moses and the Israelites as they came out of Egypt. [47]They took possession of his land and the land of Og king of Bashan, the two Amorite kings east of the Jordan. [48]This land extended from Aroer on the rim of the Arnon Gorge to Mount Siyon[b] (that is, Hermon), [49]and included all the Arabah east of the Jordan, as far as the Sea of the Arabah,[c] below the slopes of Pisgah.

The Ten Commandments

5 Moses summoned all Israel and said: Hear, O Israel, the decrees and laws I declare in your hearing today. Learn them and be sure to follow them. [2]The Lord our God made a covenant with us at Horeb. [3]It was not with our fathers that the Lord made this covenant, but with us, with all of us who are alive here today. [4]The Lord spoke to you face to face out of the fire on the mountain. [5](At that time I stood between the Lord and you to declare to you the word of the Lord, because you were afraid of the fire and did not go up the mountain.) And he said:

[6]"I am the Lord your God, who brought you out of Egypt, out of the land of slavery.

[7]"You shall have no other gods before[d] me.

[8]"You shall not make for yourself an idol in the form of anything in heaven above or on the earth beneath or in the waters below. [9]You shall not bow down to them or worship them; for I, the Lord your God, am a jealous God, punishing the children for the sin of the fathers to the third and fourth generation of those who hate me, [10]but showing love to a thousand generations of those who love me and keep my commandments.

[11]"You shall not misuse the name of the Lord your God, for the Lord will not hold anyone guiltless who misuses his name.

[a]33 Or of a god   [b]48 Hebrew; Syriac (see also Deut. 3:9) Sirion   [c]49 That is, the Dead Sea   [d]7 Or besides

¹² "Observe the Sabbath day by keeping it holy, as the LORD your God has commanded you. ¹³Six days you shall labor and do all your work, ¹⁴but the seventh day is a Sabbath to the LORD your God. On it you shall not do any work, neither you, nor your son or daughter, nor your manservant or maidservant, nor your ox, your donkey or any of your animals, nor the alien within your gates, so that your manservant and maidservant may rest, as you do. ¹⁵Remember that you were slaves in Egypt and that the LORD your God brought you out of there with a mighty hand and an outstretched arm. Therefore the LORD your God has commanded you to observe the Sabbath day.

¹⁶ "Honor your father and your mother, as the LORD your God has commanded you, so that you may live long and that it may go well with you in the land the LORD your God is giving you.

¹⁷ "You shall not murder.

¹⁸ "You shall not commit adultery.

¹⁹ "You shall not steal.

²⁰ "You shall not give false testimony against your neighbor.

²¹ "You shall not covet your neighbor's wife. You shall not set your desire on your neighbor's house or land, his manservant or maidservant, his ox or donkey, or anything that belongs to your neighbor."

²²These are the commandments the LORD proclaimed in a loud voice to your whole assembly there on the mountain from out of the fire, the cloud and the deep darkness; and he added nothing more. Then he wrote them on two stone tablets and gave them to me. ²³When you heard the voice out of the darkness, while the mountain was ablaze with fire, all the leading men of your tribes and your elders came to me. ²⁴And you said, "The LORD our God has shown us his glory and his majesty, and we have heard his voice from the fire. Today we have seen that a man can live even if God speaks with him. ²⁵But now, why should we die? This great fire will consume us, and we will die if we hear the voice of the LORD our God any longer. ²⁶For what mortal man has ever heard the voice of the living God speaking out of fire, as we have, and survived? ²⁷Go near and listen to all

HEY DAD

Why is it okay for God to be jealous?

Text: Deuteronomy 5:8–10

The Bible leaves no room for doubt: God is a jealous God. He makes it clear that all glory should go to him, not to any lifeless idol. Nor does he want men to steal the glory that is due him: Time after time we see kings in the Old Testament become proud of their success only to lose the crown. God wants the credit. This is non-negotiable.

But why is it okay for God to be self-centered and jealous when self-centeredness is a sin for people? Theologian R.C. Sproul gives a simple and insightful explanation. He reminds us that as God's creation we are to be God-centered, not self-centered. We are imperfect, sinful and deeply flawed. But God is holy. He is perfect. He is completely good, and therefore we are to focus on him.

However, when God is self-centered, he is also God-centered. For him to focus on anything other than himself would actually be a fault (Sproul, 22). Though it may seem to be an imperfection, God's self-centeredness, his jealousy, is actually one more reason why he's worthy of our worship.

Sproul, R.C. (1996). The Invisible Hand: Do All Things Really Work for Good? *Dallas, Texas: Word Publishing.*

For a complete listing of Questions Kids Ask, turn to page 1435.

that the LORD our God says. Then tell us whatever the LORD our God tells you. We will listen and obey."

²⁸The LORD heard you when you spoke to me and the LORD said to me, "I have heard what this people said to you. Everything they said was good. ²⁹Oh, that their hearts would be inclined to fear me and keep all my commands always, so that it might go well with them and their children forever!

³⁰"Go, tell them to return to their tents. ³¹But you stay here with me so that I may give you all the commands, decrees and laws you are to teach them to follow in the land I am giving them to possess."

³²So be careful to do what the LORD your God has commanded you; do not turn aside to the right or to the left. ³³Walk in all the way that the LORD your God has commanded you, so that you may live and prosper and prolong your days in the land that you will possess.

Love the LORD Your God

6 These are the commands, decrees and laws the LORD your God directed me to teach you to observe in the land that you are crossing the Jordan to possess, ²so that you, your children and their children after them may fear the LORD your God as long as you live by keeping all his decrees and commands that I give you, and so that you may enjoy long life. ³Hear, O Israel, and be careful to obey so that it may go well with you and that you may increase greatly in a land flowing with milk and honey, just as the LORD, the God of your fathers, promised you.

First Things First

DAILY INSIGHT

WEDNESDAY

Passage:
Deuteronomy 5:6–29

Verse:
Deuteronomy 5:29

My first job out of college was in youth ministry. I hadn't begun with this in mind; during my first several undergraduate years, I thought I was getting ready for something related to medicine. But my heart was drawn to youth ministry, so for almost eight years, youth ministry is what I did.

During the process of training for this specialized ministry, I remember a particular class taught by a very successful and well-known youth-ministry veteran. I remember looking forward to this class and the chance to write down all the techniques this man was going to give our group … clues on how to run an effective youth program.

When the man stood to speak, he made a few opening remarks I'll never forget. He told us that successful youth ministry was not, primarily, about learning methodology. There were many frustrated and unsuccessful youth ministers around the country who were veritable textbooks on meeting planning, special event coordination, and even Bible knowledge. "The thing that will decide your success as a youth minister," this wise teacher finally said, "is whether or not your really love teenagers."

I remember being stunned by this simple and profound statement. But in the years that followed, I clearly learned its truth.

Today's text includes The Ten Commandments. Moses brought this famous list of do's and don'ts down from the mountain, chiseled in stone. And these commandments are as relevant and important to obey right now as they were centuries ago.

But tucked into this chapter is a very important truth (5:29). Moses told the people that the Lord first wanted their hearts to be drawn to him. First he wanted their love, then their respect (fear), and *then* their obedience.

Living for God is not, primarily, about technique. It's not about collecting gold stars for good behavior. Living for God is about loving him, respecting his ways, and wanting to obey him. The best news is that once these things are in place, the part about obeying the commandments actually comes much more easily than you'd think.

For your next devotional reading, go to page 204.

⁴Hear, O Israel: The Lᴏʀᴅ our God, the Lᴏʀᴅ is one.ᵃ ⁵Love the Lᴏʀᴅ your God with all your heart and with all your soul and with all your strength. ⁶These commandments that I give you today are to be upon your hearts. ⁷Impress them on your children. Talk about them when you sit at home and when you walk along the road, when you lie down and when you get up. ⁸Tie them as symbols on your hands and bind them on your foreheads. ⁹Write them on the doorframes of your houses and on your gates.

¹⁰When the Lᴏʀᴅ your God brings you into the land he swore to your fathers, to Abraham, Isaac and Jacob, to give you—a land with large, flourishing cities you did not build, ¹¹houses filled with all kinds of good things you did not provide, wells you did not dig, and vineyards and olive groves you did not plant—then when you eat and are satisfied, ¹²be careful that you do not forget the Lᴏʀᴅ, who brought you out of Egypt, out of the land of slavery.

¹³Fear the Lᴏʀᴅ your God, serve him only and take your oaths in his name. ¹⁴Do not follow other gods, the gods of the peoples around you; ¹⁵for the Lᴏʀᴅ your God, who is among you, is a jealous God and his anger will burn against you, and he will destroy you from the face of the land. ¹⁶Do not test the Lᴏʀᴅ your God as you did at Massah. ¹⁷Be sure to keep the commands of the Lᴏʀᴅ your God and the stipulations and decrees he has given you. ¹⁸Do what is right and good in the Lᴏʀᴅ's sight, so that it may go well with you and you may go in and take over the good land that the Lᴏʀᴅ promised on oath to your forefathers, ¹⁹thrusting out all your enemies before you, as the Lᴏʀᴅ said.

²⁰In the future, when your son asks you, "What is the meaning of the stipulations,

ᵃ4 Or The Lᴏʀᴅ our God is one Lᴏʀᴅ; or The Lᴏʀᴅ is our God, the Lᴏʀᴅ is one; or The Lᴏʀᴅ is our God, the Lᴏʀᴅ alone

Include God in Everything

DAILY INSIGHT

THURSDAY

Passage:
Deuteronomy 6:4–13

Verses:
Deuteronomy 6:7–9

"Look at that beautiful tree over there. Can you believe how colorful the leaves are this time of year? Isn't God incredible to create such a thing?"

One of the things I resolved to do when our daughters were little girls was to take them along with me on weekend errands. Going to the hardware store with them on a Saturday morning was a huge bonding opportunity. I would (encourage them to) turn off the TV cartoons, help them with their blue jeans and sweaters, and put them in the car with me.

Driving to the store gave us a special opportunity to talk. I would ask them about their week at school. I'd tell them about my work week. We'd count trucks or look for horses on the hillsides. Then sometimes I'd say something about God … nothing heavy or doctrinally deep, just something about how wonderful he is. The girls would acknowledge that what I had said was true, then we'd go on with the conversation. No reference was made to our minister's particularly insightful sermon the previous week.

The simple comment about God was enough.

After delivering the Ten Commandments and encouraging the people to love God, Moses told parents to talk about God at home. He told them to begin each day celebrating God's goodness, whether at home or elsewhere. He seemed to be telling the Israelites, "Include God in everything. Don't do anything or go anywhere without him."

Make your faith—and the demonstration of it—as normal as going to work, as common as picking up a few groceries on your way home, and as natural as commenting on the score of last week's ball game.

The secret of living the Christian life is loving God, obeying his commandments, and weaving him into the fabric of your family's life. Talk about God today just as you would talk about your career, your friends or your family. He wants to be included in everything.

For your next devotional reading, go to page 206.

decrees and laws the LORD our God has commanded you?" ²¹tell him: "We were slaves of Pharaoh in Egypt, but the LORD brought us out of Egypt with a mighty hand. ²²Before our eyes the LORD sent miraculous signs and wonders—great and terrible—upon Egypt and Pharaoh and his whole household. ²³But he brought us out from there to bring us in and give us the land that he promised on oath to our forefathers. ²⁴The LORD commanded us to obey all these decrees and to fear the LORD our God, so that we might always prosper and be kept alive, as is the case today. ²⁵And if we are careful to obey all this law before the LORD our God, as he has commanded us, that will be our righteousness."

Driving Out the Nations

7 When the LORD your God brings you into the land you are entering to possess and drives out before you many nations—the Hittites, Girgashites, Amorites, Canaanites, Perizzites, Hivites and Jebusites, seven nations larger and stronger than you— ²and when the LORD your God has delivered them over to you and you have defeated them, then you must destroy them totally.[a] Make no treaty with them, and show them no mercy. ³Do not intermarry with them. Do not give your daughters to their sons or take their daughters for your sons, ⁴for they will turn your sons away from following me to serve other gods, and the LORD's anger will burn against you and will quickly destroy you. ⁵This is what you are to do to them: Break down their altars, smash their sacred stones, cut down their Asherah poles[b] and burn their idols in the fire. ⁶For you are a people holy to the LORD your God. The LORD your God has chosen you out of all the peoples on the face of the earth to be his people, his treasured possession.

⁷The LORD did not set his affection on you and choose you because you were more numerous than other peoples, for you were the fewest of all peoples. ⁸But it was because the LORD loved you and kept the oath he swore to your forefathers that he brought you out with a mighty hand and redeemed you from the land of slavery, from the power of Pharaoh king of Egypt. ⁹Know therefore that the LORD your God is God; he is the faithful God, keeping his covenant of love to a thousand generations of those who love him and keep his commands. ¹⁰But

those who hate him he will repay to
  their face by destruction;
he will not be slow to repay to their
  face those who hate him.

¹¹Therefore, take care to follow the commands, decrees and laws I give you today.

¹²If you pay attention to these laws and are careful to follow them, then the LORD your God will keep his covenant of love with you, as he swore to your forefathers. ¹³He will love you and bless you and increase your numbers. He will bless the fruit of your womb, the crops of your land—your grain, new wine and oil—the calves of your herds and the lambs of your flocks in the land that he swore to your forefathers to give you. ¹⁴You will be blessed more than any other people; none of your men or women will be childless, nor any of your livestock without young. ¹⁵The LORD will keep you free from every disease. He will not inflict on you the horrible diseases you knew in Egypt, but he will inflict them on all who hate you. ¹⁶You must destroy all the peoples the LORD your God gives over to you. Do not look on them with pity and do not serve their gods, for that will be a snare to you.

¹⁷You may say to yourselves, "These nations are stronger than we are. How can we drive them out?" ¹⁸But do not be afraid of them; remember well what the LORD your God did to Pharaoh and to all Egypt. ¹⁹You saw with your own eyes the great trials, the miraculous signs and wonders, the mighty hand and outstretched arm, with which the LORD your God brought you out. The LORD your God will do the same to all the peoples you now fear. ²⁰Moreover, the LORD your God will send the hornet among them until even the survivors who hide from you have perished. ²¹Do not be terrified by them, for the LORD your God, who is among you, is a great and awesome God. ²²The LORD your God will drive out those nations before you, little by little. You will not be allowed to eliminate them all at once, or the wild animals will multiply around you. ²³But the LORD your God will deliver them over to you, throwing them into great confusion until they are destroyed. ²⁴He will give their kings into your hand, and you will wipe out their names from under

---

[a]2 The Hebrew term refers to the irrevocable giving over of things or persons to the LORD, often by totally destroying them; also in verse 26.   [b]5 That is, symbols of the goddess Asherah; here and elsewhere in Deuteronomy

heaven. No one will be able to stand up against you; you will destroy them. **25**The images of their gods you are to burn in the fire. Do not covet the silver and gold on them, and do not take it for yourselves, or you will be ensnared by it, for it is detestable to the LORD your God. **26**Do not bring a detestable thing into your house or you, like it, will be set apart for destruction. Utterly abhor and detest it, for it is set apart for destruction.

Do Not Forget the LORD

8 Be careful to follow every command I am giving you today, so that you may live and increase and may enter and possess the land that the LORD promised on oath to your forefathers. **2**Remember how the LORD your God led you all the way in the desert these forty years, to humble you and to test you in order to know what was in your heart, whether or not you would keep his commands. **3**He humbled you, causing you to hunger and then feeding you with manna, which neither you nor your fathers had known, to teach you that man does not live on bread alone but on every word that comes from the mouth of the LORD. **4**Your clothes did not wear out and your feet did not swell during these forty years. **5**Know then in your heart that as a man disciplines his son, so the LORD your God disciplines you.

Give Me Patience ... Right Now

DAILY INSIGHT

FRIDAY
Passage:
Deuteronomy 8:1–9
Verse:
Deuteronomy 8:5

On a scale of one to ten, how would you rate your ability to be patient?

Being born north of the Mason-Dixon line made me a Yankee by birth. Growing up in Chicago indelibly marked me as a northerner . . . a mid-westerner, through and through. But in 1979 we moved south to Texas. Then in 1984, we moved to Tennessee. Frankly, we've grown accustomed to the South.

One of the things we've discovered while living here are the two-lane roads that wind through southern counties everywhere. These roads were trails, built by early settlers and used as party games like "Twister" and "Charades." Guests would be dispatched to a certain destination, being given an allotted time to return to the party. All the small, roadside graveyards ought to give you a clue as to what happened to some of these guests. You've never been lost like you'll get lost on these narrow roads.

At any rate, one of the features of these roads is the double yellow lines that grace every one. This means that if you're in a hurry, you'd better hope you don't get behind someone who doesn't really care about your hasty trip.

I have literally spent miles traveling closer to the car in front of me than his

"Don't Worry, Be Happy" bumper sticker. This has been a great conversation starter between my wife and me many times.

I score a two or three on the above patience quiz. How about you?

If you haven't already, read Deuteronomy 8—the whole chapter. Please take special note of today's key verse (8:5). Here Moses told the people that all they'd been through, including forty years of waiting in the desert, was exactly the discipline their heavenly Father knew they needed.

The lesson of this exhortation? Follow him. Do not be anxious. Be patient. If you try to pass him on a double-yellow line, you will be destroyed.

As whimsical as it might be to think about my impatient desperation on these little roads around my home, there's nothing more sobering than this truth: Follow your heavenly Father. He may be moving as fast as you can handle, or he may be crawling at a snail's pace. In either case, he knows exactly what he's doing.

Once you've learned this kind of discipline and patience, then teach your children. Chances are, they're right on your bumper waiting for your next move.

For your next devotional reading, go to page 209.

⁶Observe the commands of the LORD your God, walking in his ways and revering him. ⁷For the LORD your God is bringing you into a good land—a land with streams and pools of water, with springs flowing in the valleys and hills; ⁸a land with wheat and barley, vines and fig trees, pomegranates, olive oil and honey; ⁹a land where bread will not be scarce and you will lack nothing; a land where the rocks are iron and you can dig copper out of the hills.

¹⁰When you have eaten and are satisfied, praise the LORD your God for the good land he has given you. ¹¹Be careful that you do not forget the LORD your God, failing to observe his commands, his laws and his decrees that I am giving you this day. ¹²Otherwise, when you eat and are satisfied, when you build fine houses and settle down, ¹³and when your herds and flocks grow large and your silver and gold increase and all you have is multiplied, ¹⁴then your heart will become proud and you will forget the LORD your God, who brought you out of Egypt, out of the land of slavery. ¹⁵He led you through the vast and dreadful desert, that thirsty and waterless land, with its venomous snakes and scorpions. He brought you water out of hard rock. ¹⁶He gave you manna to eat in the desert, something your fathers had never known, to humble and to test you so that in the end it might go well with you. ¹⁷You may say to yourself, "My power and the strength of my hands have produced this wealth for me." ¹⁸But remember the LORD your God, for it is he who gives you the ability to produce wealth, and so confirms his covenant, which he swore to your forefathers, as it is today.

¹⁹If you ever forget the LORD your God and follow other gods and worship and bow down to them, I testify against you today that you will surely be destroyed. ²⁰Like the nations the LORD destroyed before you, so you will be destroyed for not obeying the LORD your God.

Not Because of Israel's Righteousness

9 Hear, O Israel. You are now about to cross the Jordan to go in and dispossess nations greater and stronger than you, with large cities that have walls up to the sky. ²The people are strong and tall—Anakites! You know about them and have heard it said: "Who can stand up against the Anakites?" ³But be assured today that the LORD your God is the one who goes across ahead of you like a devouring fire. He will destroy them; he will subdue them before you. And you will drive them out and annihilate them quickly, as the LORD has promised you.

⁴After the LORD your God has driven them out before you, do not say to yourself, "The LORD has brought me here to take possession of this land because of my righteousness." No, it is on account of the wickedness of these nations that the LORD is going to drive them out before you. ⁵It is not because of your righteousness or your integrity that you are going in to take possession of their land; but on account of the wickedness of these nations, the LORD your God will drive them out before you, to accomplish what he swore to your fathers, to Abraham, Isaac and Jacob. ⁶Understand, then, that it is not because of your righteousness that the LORD your God is giving you this good land to possess, for you are a stiff-necked people.

The Golden Calf

⁷Remember this and never forget how you provoked the LORD your God to anger in the desert. From the day you left Egypt until you arrived here, you have been rebellious against the LORD. ⁸At Horeb you aroused the LORD's wrath so that he was angry enough to destroy you. ⁹When I went up on the mountain to receive the tablets of stone, the tablets of the covenant that the LORD had made with you, I stayed on the mountain forty days and forty nights; I ate no bread and drank no water. ¹⁰The LORD gave me two stone tablets inscribed by the finger of God. On them were all the commandments the LORD proclaimed to you on the mountain out of the fire, on the day of the assembly.

¹¹At the end of the forty days and forty nights, the LORD gave me the two stone tablets, the tablets of the covenant. ¹²Then the LORD told me, "Go down from here at once, because your people whom you brought out of Egypt have become corrupt. They have turned away quickly from what I commanded them and have made a cast idol for themselves."

¹³And the LORD said to me, "I have seen this people, and they are a stiff-necked people indeed! ¹⁴Let me alone, so that I may destroy them and blot out their name from under heaven. And I will make you into a nation stronger and more numerous than they."

¹⁵So I turned and went down from the mountain while it was ablaze with fire. And the two tablets of the covenant were in my hands.ᵃ ¹⁶When I looked, I saw that you had sinned against the LORD your God; you had made for yourselves an idol cast in the shape of a calf. You had turned aside quickly from the way that the LORD had commanded you. ¹⁷So I took the two tablets and threw them out of my hands, breaking them to pieces before your eyes.

¹⁸Then once again I fell prostrate before the LORD for forty days and forty nights; I ate no bread and drank no water, because of all the sin you had committed, doing what was evil in the LORD's sight and so provoking him to anger. ¹⁹I feared the anger and wrath of the LORD, for he was angry enough with you to destroy you. But again the LORD listened to me. ²⁰And the LORD was angry enough with Aaron to destroy him, but at that time I prayed for Aaron too. ²¹Also I took that sinful thing of yours, the calf you had made, and burned it in the fire. Then I crushed it and ground it to powder as fine as dust and threw the dust into a stream that flowed down the mountain.

²²You also made the LORD angry at Taberah, at Massah and at Kibroth Hattaavah. ²³And when the LORD sent you out from Kadesh Barnea, he said, "Go up and take possession of the land I have given you." But you rebelled against the command of the LORD your God. You did not trust him or obey him. ²⁴You have been rebellious against the LORD ever since I have known you.

²⁵I lay prostrate before the LORD those forty days and forty nights because the LORD had said he would destroy you. ²⁶I prayed to the LORD and said, "O Sovereign LORD, do not destroy your people, your own inheritance that you redeemed by your great power and brought out of Egypt with a mighty hand. ²⁷Remember your servants Abraham, Isaac and Jacob. Overlook the stubbornness of this people, their wickedness and their sin. ²⁸Otherwise, the country from which you brought us will say, 'Because the LORD was not able to take them into the land he had promised them, and because he hated them, he brought them out to put them to death in the desert.' ²⁹But they are your people, your inheritance that you brought out by your great power and your outstretched arm."

Tablets Like the First Ones

10 At that time the LORD said to me, "Chisel out two stone tablets like the first ones and come up to me on the mountain. Also make a wooden chest.ᵇ ²I will write on the tablets the words that were on the first tablets, which you broke. Then you are to put them in the chest."

³So I made the ark out of acacia wood and chiseled out two stone tablets like the first ones, and I went up on the mountain with the two tablets in my hands. ⁴The LORD wrote on these tablets what he had written before, the Ten Commandments he had proclaimed to you on the mountain, out of the fire, on the day of the assembly. And the LORD gave them to me. ⁵Then I came back down the mountain and put the tablets in the ark I had made, as the LORD commanded me, and they are there now.

⁶(The Israelites traveled from the wells of the Jaakanites to Moserah. There Aaron died and was buried, and Eleazar his son succeeded him as priest. ⁷From there they traveled to Gudgodah and on to Jotbathah, a land with streams of water. ⁸At that time the LORD set apart the tribe of Levi to carry the ark of the covenant of the LORD, to stand before the LORD to minister and to pronounce blessings in his name, as they still do today. ⁹That is why the Levites have no share or inheritance among their brothers; the LORD is their inheritance, as the LORD your God told them.)

¹⁰Now I had stayed on the mountain forty days and nights, as I did the first time, and the LORD listened to me at this time also. It was not his will to destroy you. ¹¹"Go," the LORD said to me, "and lead the people on their way, so that they may enter and possess the land that I swore to their fathers to give them."

Fear the LORD

¹²And now, O Israel, what does the LORD your God ask of you but to fear the LORD your God, to walk in all his ways, to love him, to serve the LORD your God with all your heart and with all your soul, ¹³and to observe the LORD's commands and decrees that I am giving you today for your own good?

¹⁴To the LORD your God belong the heavens, even the highest heavens, the earth and everything in it. ¹⁵Yet the LORD

ᵃ15 Or And I had the two tablets of the covenant with me, one in each hand   ᵇ1 That is, an ark

Rules that Help Us to Enjoy Life

Key Verse: *"Observe the LORD's commands and decrees that I am giving you today [they are] for your own good."* Deuteronomy 10:13

Text: Deuteronomy 10:12–14 *(Dad or child reads the text.)*

QUIET TIMES WITH Dad

DAD READS: What if we lived in a place where there were no rules—a place where everyone did exactly what they felt like doing and no one ever tried to stop them? If I felt like driving one hundred miles an hour on our street, I could do it. If I didn't want to go to work, no one would make me. If I wanted to go to a sporting goods store and take a new set of golf clubs without paying for them, no one would try to stop me.

Child reads: If we lived in such a place, no one could make me go to school if I didn't want to. And if I didn't like someone, I could just hit him or her and no one would punish me for it. If I wanted to eat only candy, ice cream, and cake, my mother wouldn't try to get me to eat anything else. I wouldn't even have to brush my teeth if I didn't want to.

DAD READS: Sometimes it seems like there are too many rules to follow. Sometimes living in a place like we've just been talking about sounds pretty good. But we both know that if we really lived in a place like this, life would be hard. Everyone else would have the same freedom, and could take from us whatever they wanted. Everything would be upside down. And it really wouldn't be very much fun.

Child reads: The Bible gives us many rules to follow, like the Ten Commandments. And even though it seems like there are lots and lots of rules, today's verse says something very important. It says that these rules are for our own good.

DAD READS: That's right. Rules are like riverbanks. They keep the water flowing in the right direction. Without sides, a river becomes a smelly swamp. Without rules, life falls apart. It becomes miserable and confusing. That's why, even in our family, there are certain rules. Following these rules actually helps us to enjoy our life together. The rules are not meant to take away our fun; instead, they make fun possible.

Child reads: Even though I don't usually think about it like this, I *am* thankful that we have rules. I'm glad that you don't let us do whatever we want. And I'm glad for you that your life has rules, too.

DAD READS: We both must remember that because God made us and knows everything about us, the Bible's commandments are actually rules to make our lives better, not worse. I'm glad that God has given our lives riverbanks so they can flow in the right direction and be productive. Let me take a moment to thank him for this:

Our Father in heaven, thank you for rules. Thank you that you have not given us laws and commandments to make our lives miserable, but to give our lives greater joy. Please help us to remember this and please help us to be more and more obedient every day. In Jesus' name, Amen.

For your next devotional reading, go to page 217.

set his affection on your forefathers and loved them, and he chose you, their descendants, above all the nations, as it is today. [16]Circumcise your hearts, therefore, and do not be stiff-necked any longer. [17]For the LORD your God is God of gods and Lord of lords, the great God, mighty and awesome, who shows no partiality and accepts no bribes. [18]He defends the cause of the fatherless and the widow, and loves the alien, giving him food and clothing. [19]And you are to love those who are aliens, for you yourselves were aliens in Egypt. [20]Fear the LORD your God and serve him. Hold fast to him and take your oaths in his name. [21]He is your praise; he is your God, who performed for you those great and awesome wonders you saw with your own eyes. [22]Your forefathers who went down into Egypt were seventy in all, and now the LORD your God has made you as numerous as the stars in the sky.

Love and Obey the LORD

11 Love the LORD your God and keep his requirements, his decrees, his laws and his commands always. [2]Remember today that your children were not the ones who saw and experienced the discipline of the LORD your God: his majesty, his mighty hand, his outstretched arm; [3]the signs he performed and the things he did in the heart of Egypt, both to Pharaoh king of Egypt and to his whole country; [4]what he did to the Egyptian army, to its horses and chariots, how he overwhelmed them with the waters of the Red Sea[a] as they were pursuing you, and how the LORD brought lasting ruin on them. [5]It was not your children who saw what he did for you in the desert until you arrived at this place, [6]and what he did to Dathan and Abiram, sons of Eliab the Reubenite, when the earth opened its mouth right in the middle of all Israel and swallowed them up with their households, their tents and every living thing that belonged to them. [7]But it was your own eyes that saw all these great things the LORD has done.

[8]Observe therefore all the commands I am giving you today, so that you may have the strength to go in and take over the land that you are crossing the Jordan to possess, [9]and so that you may live long in the land that the LORD swore to your forefathers to give to them and their descendants, a land flowing with milk and honey. [10]The land you are entering to take over is not like the land of Egypt, from which you have come, where you planted your seed and irrigated it by foot as in a vegetable garden. [11]But the land you are crossing the Jordan to take possession of is a land of mountains and valleys that drinks rain from heaven. [12]It is a land the LORD your God cares for; the eyes of the LORD your God are continually on it from the beginning of the year to its end.

[13]So if you faithfully obey the commands I am giving you today—to love the LORD your God and to serve him with all your heart and with all your soul— [14]then I will send rain on your land in its season, both autumn and spring rains, so that you may gather in your grain, new wine and oil. [15]I will provide grass in the fields for your cattle, and you will eat and be satisfied.

[16]Be careful, or you will be enticed to turn away and worship other gods and bow down to them. [17]Then the LORD's anger will burn against you, and he will shut the heavens so that it will not rain and the ground will yield no produce, and you will soon perish from the good land the LORD is giving you. [18]Fix these words of mine in your hearts and minds; tie them as symbols on your hands and bind them on your foreheads. [19]Teach them to your children, talking about them when you sit at home and when you walk along the road, when you lie down and when you get up. [20]Write them on the doorframes of your houses and on your gates, [21]so that your days and the days of your children may be many in the land that the LORD swore to give your forefathers, as many as the days that the heavens are above the earth.

[22]If you carefully observe all these commands I am giving you to follow—to love the LORD your God, to walk in all his ways and to hold fast to him— [23]then the LORD will drive out all these nations before you, and you will dispossess nations larger and stronger than you. [24]Every place where you set your foot will be yours: Your territory will extend from the desert to Lebanon, and from the Euphrates River to the western sea.[b] [25]No man will be able to stand against you. The LORD your God, as he promised you, will put the terror and fear of you on the whole land, wherever you go.

[26]See, I am setting before you today a blessing and a curse— [27]the blessing if

---

[a]4 Hebrew Yam Suph; that is, Sea of Reeds
[b]24 That is, the Mediterranean

you obey the commands of the LORD your God that I am giving you today; ²⁸the curse if you disobey the commands of the LORD your God and turn from the way that I command you today by following other gods, which you have not known. ²⁹When the LORD your God has brought you into the land you are entering to possess, you are to proclaim on Mount Gerizim the blessings, and on Mount Ebal the curses. ³⁰As you know, these mountains are across the Jordan, west of the road,ᵃ toward the setting sun, near the great trees of Moreh, in the territory of those Canaanites living in the Arabah in the vicinity of Gilgal. ³¹You are about to cross the Jordan to enter and take possession of the land the LORD your God is giving you. When you have taken it over and are living there, ³²be sure that you obey all the decrees and laws I am setting before you today.

The One Place of Worship

12 These are the decrees and laws you must be careful to follow in the land that the LORD, the God of your fathers, has given you to possess—as long as you live in the land. ²Destroy completely all the places on the high mountains and on the hills and under every spreading tree where the nations you are dispossessing worship their gods. ³Break down their altars, smash their sacred stones and burn their Asherah poles in the fire; cut down the idols of their gods and wipe out their names from those places.

⁴You must not worship the LORD your God in their way. ⁵But you are to seek the place the LORD your God will choose from among all your tribes to put his Name there for his dwelling. To that place you must go; ⁶there bring your burnt offerings and sacrifices, your tithes and special gifts, what you have vowed to give and your freewill offerings, and the firstborn of your herds and flocks. ⁷There, in the presence of the LORD your God, you and your families shall eat and shall rejoice in everything you have put your hand to, because the LORD your God has blessed you.

⁸You are not to do as we do here today, everyone as he sees fit, ⁹since you have not yet reached the resting place and the inheritance the LORD your God is giving you. ¹⁰But you will cross the Jordan and settle in the land the LORD your God is giving you as an inheritance, and he will give you rest from all your enemies around

you so that you will live in safety. ¹¹Then to the place the LORD your God will choose as a dwelling for his Name—there you are to bring everything I command you: your burnt offerings and sacrifices, your tithes and special gifts, and all the choice possessions you have vowed to the LORD. ¹²And there rejoice before the LORD your God, you, your sons and daughters, your menservants and maidservants, and the Levites from your towns, who have no allotment or inheritance of their own. ¹³Be careful not to sacrifice your burnt offerings anywhere you please. ¹⁴Offer them only at the place the LORD will choose in one of your tribes, and there observe everything I command you.

¹⁵Nevertheless, you may slaughter your animals in any of your towns and eat as much of the meat as you want, as if it were gazelle or deer, according to the blessing the LORD your God gives you. Both the ceremonially unclean and the clean may eat it. ¹⁶But you must not eat the blood; pour it out on the ground like water. ¹⁷You must not eat in your own towns the tithe of your grain and new wine and oil, or the firstborn of your herds and flocks, or whatever you have vowed to give, or your freewill offerings or special gifts. ¹⁸Instead, you are to eat them in the presence of the LORD your God at the place the LORD your God will choose—you, your sons and daughters, your menservants and maidservants, and the Levites from your towns—and you are to rejoice before the LORD your God in everything you put your hand to. ¹⁹Be careful not to neglect the Levites as long as you live in your land.

²⁰When the LORD your God has enlarged your territory as he promised you, and you crave meat and say, "I would like some meat," then you may eat as much of it as you want. ²¹If the place where the LORD your God chooses to put his Name is too far away from you, you may slaughter animals from the herds and flocks the LORD has given you, as I have commanded you, and in your own towns you may eat as much of them as you want. ²²Eat them as you would gazelle or deer. Both the ceremonially unclean and the clean may eat. ²³But be sure you do not eat the blood, because the blood is the life, and you must not eat the life with the meat. ²⁴You must not eat the blood; pour it out on the ground like water. ²⁵Do not

ᵃ30 Or *Jordan, westward*

eat it, so that it may go well with you and your children after you, because you will be doing what is right in the eyes of the LORD.

²⁶But take your consecrated things and whatever you have vowed to give, and go to the place the LORD will choose. ²⁷Present your burnt offerings on the altar of the LORD your God, both the meat and the blood. The blood of your sacrifices must be poured beside the altar of the LORD your God, but you may eat the meat. ²⁸Be careful to obey all these regulations I am giving you, so that it may always go well with you and your children after you, because you will be doing what is good and right in the eyes of the LORD your God.

²⁹The LORD your God will cut off before you the nations you are about to invade and dispossess. But when you have driven them out and settled in their land, ³⁰and after they have been destroyed before you, be careful not to be ensnared by inquiring about their gods, saying, "How do these nations serve their gods? We will do the same." ³¹You must not worship the LORD your God in their way, because in worshiping their gods, they do all kinds of detestable things the LORD hates. They even burn their sons and daughters in the fire as sacrifices to their gods.

³²See that you do all I command you; do not add to it or take away from it.

Worshiping Other Gods

13 If a prophet, or one who foretells by dreams, appears among you and announces to you a miraculous sign or wonder, ²and if the sign or wonder of which he has spoken takes place, and he says, "Let us follow other gods" (gods you have not known) "and let us worship them," ³you must not listen to the words of that prophet or dreamer. The LORD your God is testing you to find out whether you love him with all your heart and with all your soul. ⁴It is the LORD your God you must follow, and him you must revere. Keep his commands and obey him; serve him and hold fast to him. ⁵That prophet or dreamer must be put to death, because he preached rebellion against the LORD your God, who brought you out of Egypt and redeemed you from the land of slavery; he has tried to turn you from the way the LORD your God commanded you to follow. You must purge the evil from among you.

⁶If your very own brother, or your son or daughter, or the wife you love, or your closest friend secretly entices you, saying, "Let us go and worship other gods" (gods that neither you nor your fathers have known, ⁷gods of the peoples around you, whether near or far, from one end of the land to the other), ⁸do not yield to him or listen to him. Show him no pity. Do not spare him or shield him. ⁹You must certainly put him to death. Your hand must be the first in putting him to death, and then the hands of all the people. ¹⁰Stone him to death, because he tried to turn you away from the LORD your God, who brought you out of Egypt, out of the land of slavery. ¹¹Then all Israel will hear and be afraid, and no one among you will do such an evil thing again.

¹²If you hear it said about one of the towns the LORD your God is giving you to live in ¹³that wicked men have arisen among you and have led the people of their town astray, saying, "Let us go and worship other gods" (gods you have not known), ¹⁴then you must inquire, probe and investigate it thoroughly. And if it is true and it has been proved that this detestable thing has been done among you, ¹⁵you must certainly put to the sword all who live in that town. Destroy it completely,ᵃ both its people and its livestock. ¹⁶Gather all the plunder of the town into the middle of the public square and completely burn the town and all its plunder as a whole burnt offering to the LORD your God. It is to remain a ruin forever, never to be rebuilt. ¹⁷None of those condemned thingsᵃ shall be found in your hands, so that the LORD will turn from his fierce anger; he will show you mercy, have compassion on you, and increase your numbers, as he promised on oath to your forefathers, ¹⁸because you obey the LORD your God, keeping all his commands that I am giving you today and doing what is right in his eyes.

Clean and Unclean Food

14 You are the children of the LORD your God. Do not cut yourselves or shave the front of your heads for the dead, ²for you are a people holy to the LORD your God. Out of all the peoples on the face of the earth, the LORD has chosen you to be his treasured possession.

³Do not eat any detestable thing.

ᵃ15,17 The Hebrew term refers to the irrevocable giving over of things or persons to the LORD, often by totally destroying them.

⁴These are the animals you may eat: the ox, the sheep, the goat, ⁵the deer, the gazelle, the roe deer, the wild goat, the ibex, the antelope and the mountain sheep.ᵃ ⁶You may eat any animal that has a split hoof divided in two and that chews the cud. ⁷However, of those that chew the cud or that have a split hoof completely divided you may not eat the camel, the rabbit or the coney.ᵇ Although they chew the cud, they do not have a split hoof; they are ceremonially unclean for you. ⁸The pig is also unclean; although it has a split hoof, it does not chew the cud. You are not to eat their meat or touch their carcasses.

⁹Of all the creatures living in the water, you may eat any that has fins and scales. ¹⁰But anything that does not have fins and scales you may not eat; for you it is unclean.

¹¹You may eat any clean bird. ¹²But these you may not eat: the eagle, the vulture, the black vulture, ¹³the red kite, the black kite, any kind of falcon, ¹⁴any kind of raven, ¹⁵the horned owl, the screech owl, the gull, any kind of hawk, ¹⁶the little owl, the great owl, the white owl, ¹⁷the desert owl, the osprey, the cormorant, ¹⁸the stork, any kind of heron, the hoopoe and the bat.

¹⁹All flying insects that swarm are unclean to you; do not eat them. ²⁰But any winged creature that is clean you may eat.

²¹Do not eat anything you find already dead. You may give it to an alien living in any of your towns, and he may eat it, or you may sell it to a foreigner. But you are a people holy to the LORD your God.

Do not cook a young goat in its mother's milk.

Tithes

²²Be sure to set aside a tenth of all that your fields produce each year. ²³Eat the tithe of your grain, new wine and oil, and the firstborn of your herds and flocks in the presence of the LORD your God at the place he will choose as a dwelling for his Name, so that you may learn to revere the LORD your God always. ²⁴But if that place is too distant and you have been blessed by the LORD your God and cannot carry your tithe (because the place where the LORD will choose to put his Name is so far away), ²⁵then exchange your tithe for silver, and take the silver with you and go to the place the LORD your God will choose. ²⁶Use the silver to buy whatever you like: cattle, sheep, wine or other fermented

drink, or anything you wish. Then you and your household shall eat there in the presence of the LORD your God and rejoice. ²⁷And do not neglect the Levites living in your towns, for they have no allotment or inheritance of their own.

²⁸At the end of every three years, bring all the tithes of that year's produce and store it in your towns, ²⁹so that the Levites (who have no allotment or inheritance of their own) and the aliens, the fatherless and the widows who live in your towns may come and eat and be satisfied, and so that the LORD your God may bless you in all the work of your hands.

The Year for Canceling Debts

15 At the end of every seven years you must cancel debts. ²This is how it is to be done: Every creditor shall cancel the loan he has made to his fellow Israelite. He shall not require payment from his fellow Israelite or brother, because the LORD's time for canceling debts has been proclaimed. ³You may require payment from a foreigner, but you must cancel any debt your brother owes you. ⁴However, there should be no poor among you, for in the land the LORD your God is giving you to possess as your inheritance, he will richly bless you, ⁵if only you fully obey the LORD your God and are careful to follow all these commands I am giving you today. ⁶For the LORD your God will bless you as he has promised, and you will lend to many nations but will borrow from none. You will rule over many nations but none will rule over you.

⁷If there is a poor man among your brothers in any of the towns of the land that the LORD your God is giving you, do not be hardhearted or tightfisted toward your poor brother. ⁸Rather be openhanded and freely lend him whatever he needs. ⁹Be careful not to harbor this wicked thought: "The seventh year, the year for canceling debts, is near," so that you do not show ill will toward your needy brother and give him nothing. He may then appeal to the LORD against you, and you will be found guilty of sin. ¹⁰Give generously to him and do so without a grudging heart; then because of this the LORD your God will bless you in all your work and in everything you put your hand to. ¹¹There will always be poor people in the

---

ᵃ5 The precise identification of some of the birds and animals in this chapter is uncertain.   ᵇ7 That is, the hyrax or rock badger

land. Therefore I command you to be openhanded toward your brothers and toward the poor and needy in your land.

Freeing Servants

[12]If a fellow Hebrew, a man or a woman, sells himself to you and serves you six years, in the seventh year you must let him go free. [13]And when you release him, do not send him away empty-handed. [14]Supply him liberally from your flock, your threshing floor and your winepress. Give to him as the LORD your God has blessed you. [15]Remember that you were slaves in Egypt and the LORD your God redeemed you. That is why I give you this command today.

[16]But if your servant says to you, "I do not want to leave you," because he loves you and your family and is well off with you, [17]then take an awl and push it through his ear lobe into the door, and he will become your servant for life. Do the same for your maidservant.

[18]Do not consider it a hardship to set your servant free, because his service to you these six years has been worth twice as much as that of a hired hand. And the LORD your God will bless you in everything you do.

The Firstborn Animals

[19]Set apart for the LORD your God every firstborn male of your herds and flocks. Do not put the firstborn of your oxen to work, and do not shear the firstborn of your sheep. [20]Each year you and your family are to eat them in the presence of the LORD your God at the place he will choose. [21]If an animal has a defect, is lame or blind, or has any serious flaw, you must not sacrifice it to the LORD your God. [22]You are to eat it in your own towns. Both the ceremonially unclean and the clean may eat it, as if it were gazelle or deer. [23]But you must not eat the blood; pour it out on the ground like water.

Passover

16 Observe the month of Abib and celebrate the Passover of the LORD your God, because in the month of Abib he brought you out of Egypt by night. [2]Sacrifice as the Passover to the LORD your God an animal from your flock or herd at the place the LORD will choose as a dwelling for his Name. [3]Do not eat it with bread made with yeast, but for seven days eat

unleavened bread, the bread of affliction, because you left Egypt in haste—so that all the days of your life you may remember the time of your departure from Egypt. [4]Let no yeast be found in your possession in all your land for seven days. Do not let any of the meat you sacrifice on the evening of the first day remain until morning.

[5]You must not sacrifice the Passover in any town the LORD your God gives you [6]except in the place he will choose as a dwelling for his Name. There you must sacrifice the Passover in the evening, when the sun goes down, on the anniversary[a] of your departure from Egypt. [7]Roast it and eat it at the place the LORD your God will choose. Then in the morning return to your tents. [8]For six days eat unleavened bread and on the seventh day hold an assembly to the LORD your God and do no work.

Feast of Weeks

[9]Count off seven weeks from the time you begin to put the sickle to the standing grain. [10]Then celebrate the Feast of Weeks to the LORD your God by giving a freewill offering in proportion to the blessings the LORD your God has given you. [11]And rejoice before the LORD your God at the place he will choose as a dwelling for his Name—you, your sons and daughters, your menservants and maidservants, the Levites in your towns, and the aliens, the fatherless and the widows living among you. [12]Remember that you were slaves in Egypt, and follow carefully these decrees.

Feast of Tabernacles

[13]Celebrate the Feast of Tabernacles for seven days after you have gathered the produce of your threshing floor and your winepress. [14]Be joyful at your Feast—you, your sons and daughters, your menservants and maidservants, and the Levites, the aliens, the fatherless and the widows who live in your towns. [15]For seven days celebrate the Feast to the LORD your God at the place the LORD will choose. For the LORD your God will bless you in all your harvest and in all the work of your hands, and your joy will be complete. [16]Three times a year all your men must appear before the LORD your God at the place he will choose: at the Feast of Unleavened Bread, the Feast of Weeks and

a6 Or down, at the time of day

the Feast of Tabernacles. No man should appear before the LORD empty-handed: [17]Each of you must bring a gift in proportion to the way the LORD your God has blessed you.

Judges

[18]Appoint judges and officials for each of your tribes in every town the LORD your God is giving you, and they shall judge the people fairly. [19]Do not pervert justice or show partiality. Do not accept a bribe, for a bribe blinds the eyes of the wise and twists the words of the righteous. [20]Follow justice and justice alone, so that you may live and possess the land the LORD your God is giving you.

Worshiping Other Gods

[21]Do not set up any wooden Asherah pole[a] beside the altar you build to the LORD your God, [22]and do not erect a sacred stone, for these the LORD your God hates.

17 Do not sacrifice to the LORD your God an ox or a sheep that has any defect or flaw in it, for that would be detestable to him.

[2]If a man or woman living among you in one of the towns the LORD gives you is found doing evil in the eyes of the LORD your God in violation of his covenant, [3]and contrary to my command has worshiped other gods, bowing down to them or to the sun or the moon or the stars of the sky, [4]and this has been brought to your attention, then you must investigate it thoroughly. If it is true and it has been proved that this detestable thing has been done in Israel, [5]take the man or woman who has done this evil deed to your city gate and stone that person to death. [6]On the testimony of two or three witnesses a man shall be put to death, but no one shall be put to death on the testimony of only one witness. [7]The hands of the witnesses must be the first in putting him to death, and then the hands of all the people. You must purge the evil from among you.

Law Courts

[8]If cases come before your courts that are too difficult for you to judge—whether bloodshed, lawsuits or assaults—take them to the place the LORD your God will choose. [9]Go to the priests, who are Levites, and to the judge who is in office at that time. Inquire of them and they will give you the verdict. [10]You must act according to the decisions they give you at the place the LORD will choose. Be careful to do everything they direct you to do. [11]Act according to the law they teach you and the decisions they give you. Do not turn aside from what they tell you, to the right or to the left. [12]The man who shows contempt for the judge or for the priest who stands ministering there to the LORD your God must be put to death. You must purge the evil from Israel. [13]All the people will hear and be afraid, and will not be contemptuous again.

The King

[14]When you enter the land the LORD your God is giving you and have taken possession of it and settled in it, and you say, "Let us set a king over us like all the nations around us," [15]be sure to appoint over you the king the LORD your God chooses. He must be from among your own brothers. Do not place a foreigner over you, one who is not a brother Israelite. [16]The king, moreover, must not acquire great numbers of horses for himself or make the people return to Egypt to get more of them, for the LORD has told you, "You are not to go back that way again." [17]He must not take many wives, or his heart will be led astray. He must not accumulate large amounts of silver and gold.

[18]When he takes the throne of his kingdom, he is to write for himself on a scroll a copy of this law, taken from that of the priests, who are Levites. [19]It is to be with him, and he is to read it all the days of his life so that he may learn to revere the LORD his God and follow carefully all the words of this law and these decrees [20]and not consider himself better than his brothers and turn from the law to the right or to the left. Then he and his descendants will reign a long time over his kingdom in Israel.

Offerings for Priests and Levites

18 The priests, who are Levites—indeed the whole tribe of Levi—are to have no allotment or inheritance with Israel. They shall live on the offerings made to the LORD by fire, for that is their inheritance. [2]They shall have no inheritance among their brothers; the LORD is their inheritance, as he promised them.

[a]21 Or *Do not plant any tree dedicated to Asherah*

³This is the share due the priests from the people who sacrifice a bull or a sheep: the shoulder, the jowls and the inner parts. ⁴You are to give them the firstfruits of your grain, new wine and oil, and the first wool from the shearing of your sheep, ⁵for the LORD your God has chosen them and their descendants out of all your tribes to stand and minister in the LORD's name always.

⁶If a Levite moves from one of your towns anywhere in Israel where he is living, and comes in all earnestness to the place the LORD will choose, ⁷he may minister in the name of the LORD his God like all his fellow Levites who serve there in the presence of the LORD. ⁸He is to share equally in their benefits, even though he has received money from the sale of family possessions.

Detestable Practices

⁹When you enter the land the LORD your God is giving you, do not learn to imitate the detestable ways of the nations there. ¹⁰Let no one be found among you who sacrifices his son or daughter inᵃ the fire, who practices divination or sorcery, interprets omens, engages in witchcraft, ¹¹or casts spells, or who is a medium or spiritist or who consults the dead. ¹²Anyone who does these things is detestable to the LORD, and because of these detestable practices the LORD your God will drive out those nations before you. ¹³You must be blameless before the LORD your God.

The Prophet

¹⁴The nations you will dispossess listen to those who practice sorcery or divination. But as for you, the LORD your God has not permitted you to do so. ¹⁵The LORD your God will raise up for you a prophet like me from among your own brothers. You must listen to him. ¹⁶For this is what you asked of the LORD your God at Horeb on the day of the assembly when you said, "Let us not hear the voice of the LORD our God nor see this great fire anymore, or we will die."

¹⁷The LORD said to me: "What they say is good. ¹⁸I will raise up for them a prophet like you from among their brothers; I will put my words in his mouth, and he will tell them everything I command him. ¹⁹If anyone does not listen to my words that the prophet speaks in my name, I myself will call him to account. ²⁰But a prophet who presumes to speak in my name anything I have not commanded him to say, or a prophet who speaks in the name of other gods, must be put to death."

²¹You may say to yourselves, "How can we know when a message has not been spoken by the LORD?" ²²If what a prophet proclaims in the name of the LORD does not take place or come true, that is a message the LORD has not spoken. That prophet has spoken presumptuously. Do not be afraid of him.

Cities of Refuge

19 When the LORD your God has destroyed the nations whose land he is giving you, and when you have driven them out and settled in their towns and houses, ²then set aside for yourselves three cities centrally located in the land the LORD your God is giving you to possess. ³Build roads to them and divide into three parts the land the LORD your God is giving you as an inheritance, so that anyone who kills a man may flee there.

⁴This is the rule concerning the man who kills another and flees there to save his life—one who kills his neighbor unintentionally, without malice aforethought. ⁵For instance, a man may go into the forest with his neighbor to cut wood, and as he swings his ax to fell a tree, the head may fly off and hit his neighbor and kill him. That man may flee to one of these cities and save his life. ⁶Otherwise, the avenger of blood might pursue him in a rage, overtake him if the distance is too great, and kill him even though he is not deserving of death, since he did it to his neighbor without malice aforethought. ⁷This is why I command you to set aside for yourselves three cities.

⁸If the LORD your God enlarges your territory, as he promised on oath to your forefathers, and gives you the whole land he promised them, ⁹because you carefully follow all these laws I command you today—to love the LORD your God and to walk always in his ways—then you are to set aside three more cities. ¹⁰Do this so that innocent blood will not be shed in your land, which the LORD your God is giving you as your inheritance, and so that you will not be guilty of bloodshed.

¹¹But if a man hates his neighbor and lies in wait for him, assaults and kills him,

ᵃ10 Or *who makes his son or daughter pass through*

and then flees to one of these cities, ¹²the elders of his town shall send for him, bring him back from the city, and hand him over to the avenger of blood to die. ¹³Show him no pity. You must purge from Israel the guilt of shedding innocent blood, so that it may go well with you.

¹⁴Do not move your neighbor's boundary stone set up by your predecessors in the inheritance you receive in the land the LORD your God is giving you to possess.

Witnesses

¹⁵One witness is not enough to convict a man accused of any crime or offense he may have committed. A matter must be established by the testimony of two or three witnesses.

¹⁶If a malicious witness takes the stand to accuse a man of a crime, ¹⁷the two men involved in the dispute must stand in the presence of the LORD before the priests and the judges who are in office at the time. ¹⁸The judges must make a thorough investigation, and if the witness proves to be a liar, giving false testimony against his brother, ¹⁹then do to him as he intended to do to his brother. You must purge the evil from among you. ²⁰The rest of the people will hear of this and be afraid, and never again will such an evil thing be done among you. ²¹Show no pity: life for life, eye for eye, tooth for tooth, hand for hand, foot for foot.

Going to War

20 When you go to war against your enemies and see horses and chariots and an army greater than yours, do not be afraid of them, because the LORD your God, who brought you up out of Egypt, will be with you. ²When you are about to

Safe at Home

You don't have to be a big baseball fan to envision a base runner waiting for the pitcher to deliver. He bobs and dances just a few feet from the safety of the first-base bag, hoping to get a head start toward second base, but also hoping to avoid being thrown out by a pitcher with a good pick-off move.

We tend to be like that base runner, spending most of our time away from safe zones. We're usually a few feet from the bag, trying to move ahead and yet desperately hoping to avoid getting caught off base. The external pressure and internal tension of living in this place can be exhausting.

Today's interesting text is about Biblical places that were like the safety of standing on the first-base bag. These places were often referred to as "the cities of refuge." God asked Moses to establish these cities as "safe places" for people who were wrongly accused of murder, but who were, nonetheless, under the threat of danger by their accusers. Now, don't get the wrong idea about these places of refuge. If you read ahead (19:11–13) you'll see that these

MONDAY

Passage:
Deuteronomy 19:1–10

Verse:
Deuteronomy 19:10

cities weren't intended to shelter real criminals. The law applied here just like everywhere else.

Imagine such a place where the truth about you was all that mattered; a place where no one pretended and no one jumped to premature and inaccurate conclusions. This would be a place where you could be who you really are without the pressure to be someone else. It would be a place where you were loved and appreciated, not because of your activity or your capability, but simply because you were you.

If there were ever an apt description of what your home ought to feel like to each member of your family, it's this one. Your home ought to be a place of refuge, a tender place of welcome and safety. Make it a dwelling where there is no need for pretense and no reward for performance; where the inhabitants are nurtured without suffocation, disciplined without disrespect, and loved without limits.

Cities of refuge ... what a great idea. Build your home like this.

For your next devotional reading, go to page 219.

go into battle, the priest shall come forward and address the army. ³He shall say: "Hear, O Israel, today you are going into battle against your enemies. Do not be fainthearted or afraid; do not be terrified or give way to panic before them. ⁴For the LORD your God is the one who goes with you to fight for you against your enemies to give you victory."

⁵The officers shall say to the army: "Has anyone built a new house and not dedicated it? Let him go home, or he may die in battle and someone else may dedicate it. ⁶Has anyone planted a vineyard and not begun to enjoy it? Let him go home, or he may die in battle and someone else enjoy it. ⁷Has anyone become pledged to a woman and not married her? Let him go home, or he may die in battle and someone else marry her." ⁸Then the officers shall add, "Is any man afraid or fainthearted? Let him go home so that his brothers will not become disheartened too." ⁹When the officers have finished speaking to the army, they shall appoint commanders over it.

¹⁰When you march up to attack a city, make its people an offer of peace. ¹¹If they accept and open their gates, all the people in it shall be subject to forced labor and shall work for you. ¹²If they refuse to make peace and they engage you in battle, lay siege to that city. ¹³When the LORD your God delivers it into your hand, put to the sword all the men in it. ¹⁴As for the women, the children, the livestock and everything else in the city, you may take these as plunder for yourselves. And you may use the plunder the LORD your God gives you from your enemies. ¹⁵This is how you are to treat all the cities that are at a distance from you and do not belong to the nations nearby.

¹⁶However, in the cities of the nations the LORD your God is giving you as an inheritance, do not leave alive anything that breathes. ¹⁷Completely destroy[a] them—the Hittites, Amorites, Canaanites, Perizzites, Hivites and Jebusites—as the LORD your God has commanded you. ¹⁸Otherwise, they will teach you to follow all the detestable things they do in worshiping their gods, and you will sin against the LORD your God.

¹⁹When you lay siege to a city for a long time, fighting against it to capture it, do not destroy its trees by putting an ax to them, because you can eat their fruit. Do not cut them down. Are the trees of the field people, that you should besiege

them?[b] ²⁰However, you may cut down trees that you know are not fruit trees and use them to build siege works until the city at war with you falls.

Atonement for an Unsolved Murder

21 If a man is found slain, lying in a field in the land the LORD your God is giving you to possess, and it is not known who killed him, ²your elders and judges shall go out and measure the distance from the body to the neighboring towns. ³Then the elders of the town nearest the body shall take a heifer that has never been worked and has never worn a yoke ⁴and lead her down to a valley that has not been plowed or planted and where there is a flowing stream. There in the valley they are to break the heifer's neck. ⁵The priests, the sons of Levi, shall step forward, for the LORD your God has chosen them to minister and to pronounce blessings in the name of the LORD and to decide all cases of dispute and assault. ⁶Then all the elders of the town nearest the body shall wash their hands over the heifer whose neck was broken in the valley, ⁷and they shall declare: "Our hands did not shed this blood, nor did our eyes see it done. ⁸Accept this atonement for your people Israel, whom you have redeemed, O LORD, and do not hold your people guilty of the blood of an innocent man." And the bloodshed will be atoned for. ⁹So you will purge from yourselves the guilt of shedding innocent blood, since you have done what is right in the eyes of the LORD.

Marrying a Captive Woman

¹⁰When you go to war against your enemies and the LORD your God delivers them into your hands and you take captives, ¹¹if you notice among the captives a beautiful woman and are attracted to her, you may take her as your wife. ¹²Bring her into your home and have her shave her head, trim her nails ¹³and put aside the clothes she was wearing when captured. After she has lived in your house and mourned her father and mother for a full month, then you may go to her and be her husband and she shall be your wife. ¹⁴If

---

[a]17 The Hebrew term refers to the irrevocable giving over of things or persons to the LORD, often by totally destroying them.   [b]19 Or *down to use in the siege, for the fruit trees are for the benefit of man.*

you are not pleased with her, let her go wherever she wishes. You must not sell her or treat her as a slave, since you have dishonored her.

The Right of the Firstborn

¹⁵If a man has two wives, and he loves one but not the other, and both bear him sons but the firstborn is the son of the wife he does not love, ¹⁶when he wills his property to his sons, he must not give the rights of the firstborn to the son of the wife he loves in preference to his actual firstborn, the son of the wife he does not love. ¹⁷He must acknowledge the son of his unloved wife as the firstborn by giving him a double share of all he has. That son is the first sign of his father's strength. The right of the firstborn belongs to him.

A Rebellious Son

¹⁸If a man has a stubborn and rebellious son who does not obey his father and mother and will not listen to them when they discipline him, ¹⁹his father and mother shall take hold of him and bring him to the elders at the gate of his town. ²⁰They shall say to the elders, "This son of ours is stubborn and rebellious. He will not obey us. He is a profligate and a drunkard." ²¹Then all the men of his town shall stone him to death. You must purge

Tender and Very Tough

DAILY INSIGHT

TUESDAY

Passage:
Deuteronomy 21:18–21

Verse:
Deuteronomy 21:20

In 1954, William Golding wrote a book that most of us had to read in high school. *The Lord of the Flies* was the story of seven boys who, due to a sequence of unforeseen circumstances, were given free reign on a small island. It was interesting to watch what the strong boys—like Ralph—did to the weak ones—like Piggy. What the thinkers—like Simon—did with the bullies—like Roger. Ultimately, the experiment became a disaster.

I have a few friends who, soon after they were married, made a conscious decision not to have children. The reason for this dramatic decision was common among these folks: *They had met a few kids!* I'm not kidding. These couples had visited the homes of friends who had small children. They saw what it looked like when parents let their little ones run the house and, like the boys in Golding's classic, it was a disaster. These children were disobedient and loud-mouthed. And their parents refused to take decisive action to stop them.

Today's verses are incredibly sobering, aren't they? In fact, some people would just as soon strike them from the Bible. How could the Scripture promote such a severe penalty for naughty children? In the New Testament, Jesus gives us a clue. He tells the people that if their eye causes them to sin, they should gouge it out. If their hand leads them to wrongdoing, they should cut it off. Then he gives a pointed explanation: "It is better for you to lose one part of your body than for your whole body to go into hell" (Matthew 5:30).

Here's the message: As ridiculous as it sounds to somehow eliminate one of your children because of his or her rebellion, it's even more preposterous to ignore a child whose behavior is tearing your family apart.

And here's the application: If you have a child whose activity is ruining your family, deal with it. Treat it as if this child had a terminal illness. Better yet, act as though this child is at the wheel of the family van—with everyone aboard—recklessly headed toward a precipice. It will not fix itself or go away. You're in charge here … take charge.

Sometimes love is tender and warm. Sometimes it's soothing and encouraging. And sometimes love is tough. Sometimes our love for each member of our family—and for our family as a whole—forces us into decisive action. And sometimes this action causes pain.

A godly father is tender. And a godly father is this kind of tough. Such action is for everyone's good.

For your next devotional reading, go to page 227.

the evil from among you. All Israel will hear of it and be afraid.

Various Laws

²²If a man guilty of a capital offense is put to death and his body is hung on a tree, ²³you must not leave his body on the tree overnight. Be sure to bury him that same day, because anyone who is hung on a tree is under God's curse. You must not desecrate the land the LORD your God is giving you as an inheritance.

22 If you see your brother's ox or sheep straying, do not ignore it but be sure to take it back to him. ²If the brother does not live near you or if you do not know who he is, take it home with you and keep it until he comes looking for it. Then give it back to him. ³Do the same if you find your brother's donkey or his cloak or anything he loses. Do not ignore it.

⁴If you see your brother's donkey or his ox fallen on the road, do not ignore it. Help him get it to its feet.

⁵A woman must not wear men's clothing, nor a man wear women's clothing, for the LORD your God detests anyone who does this.

⁶If you come across a bird's nest beside the road, either in a tree or on the ground, and the mother is sitting on the young or on the eggs, do not take the mother with the young. ⁷You may take the young, but be sure to let the mother go, so that it may go well with you and you may have a long life.

⁸When you build a new house, make a parapet around your roof so that you may not bring the guilt of bloodshed on your house if someone falls from the roof.

⁹Do not plant two kinds of seed in your vineyard; if you do, not only the crops you plant but also the fruit of the vineyard will be defiled.ᵃ

¹⁰Do not plow with an ox and a donkey yoked together.

¹¹Do not wear clothes of wool and linen woven together.

¹²Make tassels on the four corners of the cloak you wear.

Marriage Violations

¹³If a man takes a wife and, after lying with her, dislikes her ¹⁴and slanders her and gives her a bad name, saying, "I married this woman, but when I approached her, I did not find proof of her virginity," ¹⁵then the girl's father and mother shall bring proof that she was a virgin to the town elders at the gate. ¹⁶The girl's father will say to the elders, "I gave my daughter in marriage to this man, but he dislikes her. ¹⁷Now he has slandered her and said, 'I did not find your daughter to be a virgin.' But here is the proof of my daughter's virginity." Then her parents shall display the cloth before the elders of the town, ¹⁸and the elders shall take the man and punish him. ¹⁹They shall fine him a hundred shekels of silverᵇ and give them to the girl's father, because this man has given an Israelite virgin a bad name. She shall continue to be his wife; he must not divorce her as long as he lives.

²⁰If, however, the charge is true and no proof of the girl's virginity can be found, ²¹she shall be brought to the door of her father's house and there the men of her town shall stone her to death. She has done a disgraceful thing in Israel by being promiscuous while still in her father's house. You must purge the evil from among you.

²²If a man is found sleeping with another man's wife, both the man who slept with her and the woman must die. You must purge the evil from Israel.

²³If a man happens to meet in a town a virgin pledged to be married and he sleeps with her, ²⁴you shall take both of them to the gate of that town and stone them to death—the girl because she was in a town and did not scream for help, and the man because he violated another man's wife. You must purge the evil from among you.

²⁵But if out in the country a man happens to meet a girl pledged to be married and rapes her, only the man who has done this shall die. ²⁶Do nothing to the girl; she has committed no sin deserving death. This case is like that of someone who attacks and murders his neighbor, ²⁷for the man found the girl out in the country, and though the betrothed girl screamed, there was no one to rescue her.

²⁸If a man happens to meet a virgin who is not pledged to be married and rapes her and they are discovered, ²⁹he shall pay the girl's father fifty shekels of silver.ᶜ He must marry the girl, for he has violated her. He can never divorce her as long as he lives.

³⁰A man is not to marry his father's wife; he must not dishonor his father's bed.

ᵃ9 Or *be forfeited to the sanctuary*   ᵇ19 That is, about 2 1/2 pounds (about 1 kilogram)   ᶜ29 That is, about 1 1/4 pounds (about 0.6 kilogram)

Exclusion From the Assembly

23 No one who has been emasculated by crushing or cutting may enter the assembly of the LORD.

²No one born of a forbidden marriage*a* nor any of his descendants may enter the assembly of the LORD, even down to the tenth generation.

³No Ammonite or Moabite or any of his descendants may enter the assembly of the LORD, even down to the tenth generation. ⁴For they did not come to meet you with bread and water on your way when you came out of Egypt, and they hired Balaam son of Beor from Pethor in Aram Naharaim*b* to pronounce a curse on you. ⁵However, the LORD your God would not listen to Balaam but turned the curse into a blessing for you, because the LORD your God loves you. ⁶Do not seek a treaty of friendship with them as long as you live.

⁷Do not abhor an Edomite, for he is your brother. Do not abhor an Egyptian, because you lived as an alien in his country. ⁸The third generation of children born to them may enter the assembly of the LORD.

Uncleanness in the Camp

⁹When you are encamped against your enemies, keep away from everything impure. ¹⁰If one of your men is unclean because of a nocturnal emission, he is to go outside the camp and stay there. ¹¹But as evening approaches he is to wash himself, and at sunset he may return to the camp.

¹²Designate a place outside the camp where you can go to relieve yourself. ¹³As part of your equipment have something to dig with, and when you relieve yourself, dig a hole and cover up your excrement. ¹⁴For the LORD your God moves about in your camp to protect you and to deliver your enemies to you. Your camp must be holy, so that he will not see among you anything indecent and turn away from you.

Miscellaneous Laws

¹⁵If a slave has taken refuge with you, do not hand him over to his master. ¹⁶Let him live among you wherever he likes and in whatever town he chooses. Do not oppress him.

¹⁷No Israelite man or woman is to become a shrine prostitute. ¹⁸You must not bring the earnings of a female prostitute or of a male prostitute*c* into the house of the LORD your God to pay any vow, because the LORD your God detests them both.

¹⁹Do not charge your brother interest, whether on money or food or anything else that may earn interest. ²⁰You may charge a foreigner interest, but not a brother Israelite, so that the LORD your God may bless you in everything you put your hand to in the land you are entering to possess.

²¹If you make a vow to the LORD your God, do not be slow to pay it, for the LORD your God will certainly demand it of you and you will be guilty of sin. ²²But if you refrain from making a vow, you will not be guilty. ²³Whatever your lips utter you must be sure to do, because you made your vow freely to the LORD your God with your own mouth.

²⁴If you enter your neighbor's vineyard, you may eat all the grapes you want, but do not put any in your basket. ²⁵If you enter your neighbor's grainfield, you may pick kernels with your hands, but you must not put a sickle to his standing grain.

24 If a man marries a woman who becomes displeasing to him because he finds something indecent about her, and he writes her a certificate of divorce, gives it to her and sends her from his house, ²and if after she leaves his house she becomes the wife of another man, ³and her second husband dislikes her and writes her a certificate of divorce, gives it to her and sends her from his house, or if he dies, ⁴then her first husband, who divorced her, is not allowed to marry her again after she has been defiled. That would be detestable in the eyes of the LORD. Do not bring sin upon the land the LORD your God is giving you as an inheritance.

⁵If a man has recently married, he must not be sent to war or have any other duty laid on him. For one year he is to be free to stay at home and bring happiness to the wife he has married.

⁶Do not take a pair of millstones—not even the upper one—as security for a debt, because that would be taking a man's livelihood as security.

⁷If a man is caught kidnapping one of his brother Israelites and treats him as a slave or sells him, the kidnapper must die. You must purge the evil from among you.

a2 Or *one of illegitimate birth*   *b4* That is, Northwest Mesopotamia   *c18* Hebrew *of a dog*

[8]In cases of leprous[a] diseases be very careful to do exactly as the priests, who are Levites, instruct you. You must follow carefully what I have commanded them. [9]Remember what the LORD your God did to Miriam along the way after you came out of Egypt.

[10]When you make a loan of any kind to your neighbor, do not go into his house to get what he is offering as a pledge. [11]Stay outside and let the man to whom you are making the loan bring the pledge out to you. [12]If the man is poor, do not go to sleep with his pledge in your possession. [13]Return his cloak to him by sunset so that he may sleep in it. Then he will thank you, and it will be regarded as a righteous act in the sight of the LORD your God.

[14]Do not take advantage of a hired man who is poor and needy, whether he is a brother Israelite or an alien living in one of your towns. [15]Pay him his wages each day before sunset, because he is poor and is counting on it. Otherwise he may cry to the LORD against you, and you will be guilty of sin.

[16]Fathers shall not be put to death for their children, nor children put to death for their fathers; each is to die for his own sin.

[17]Do not deprive the alien or the fatherless of justice, or take the cloak of the widow as a pledge. [18]Remember that you were slaves in Egypt and the LORD your God redeemed you from there. That is why I command you to do this.

[19]When you are harvesting in your field and you overlook a sheaf, do not go back to get it. Leave it for the alien, the fatherless and the widow, so that the LORD your God may bless you in all the work of your hands. [20]When you beat the olives from your trees, do not go over the branches a second time. Leave what remains for the alien, the fatherless and the widow. [21]When you harvest the grapes in your vineyard, do not go over the vines again. Leave what remains for the alien, the fatherless and the widow. [22]Remember that you were slaves in Egypt. That is why I command you to do this.

25 When men have a dispute, they are to take it to court and the judges will decide the case, acquitting the innocent and condemning the guilty. [2]If the guilty man deserves to be beaten, the judge shall make him lie down and have him flogged in his presence with the number of lashes his crime deserves, [3]but he must not give him more than forty lashes. If he is flogged more than that, your brother will be degraded in your eyes.

[4]Do not muzzle an ox while it is treading out the grain.

[5]If brothers are living together and one of them dies without a son, his widow must not marry outside the family. Her husband's brother shall take her and marry her and fulfill the duty of a brother-in-law to her. [6]The first son she bears shall carry on the name of the dead brother so that his name will not be blotted out from Israel.

[7]However, if a man does not want to marry his brother's wife, she shall go to the elders at the town gate and say, "My husband's brother refuses to carry on his brother's name in Israel. He will not fulfill the duty of a brother-in-law to me." [8]Then the elders of his town shall summon him and talk to him. If he persists in saying, "I do not want to marry her," [9]his brother's widow shall go up to him in the presence of the elders, take off one of his sandals, spit in his face and say, "This is what is done to the man who will not build up his brother's family line." [10]That man's line shall be known in Israel as The Family of the Unsandaled.

[11]If two men are fighting and the wife of one of them comes to rescue her husband from his assailant, and she reaches out and seizes him by his private parts, [12]you shall cut off her hand. Show her no pity.

[13]Do not have two differing weights in your bag—one heavy, one light. [14]Do not have two differing measures in your house—one large, one small. [15]You must have accurate and honest weights and measures, so that you may live long in the land the LORD your God is giving you. [16]For the LORD your God detests anyone who does these things, anyone who deals dishonestly.

[17]Remember what the Amalekites did to you along the way when you came out of Egypt. [18]When you were weary and worn out, they met you on your journey and cut off all who were lagging behind; they had no fear of God. [19]When the LORD your God gives you rest from all the enemies around you in the land he is giving you to possess as an inheritance, you shall blot out the memory of Amalek from under heaven. Do not forget!

Firstfruits and Tithes

26 When you have entered the land the LORD your God is giving you as an in-

---

[a]8 The Hebrew word was used for various diseases affecting the skin—not necessarily leprosy.

heritance and have taken possession of it and settled in it, ²take some of the first-fruits of all that you produce from the soil of the land the LORD your God is giving you and put them in a basket. Then go to the place the LORD your God will choose as a dwelling for his Name ³and say to the priest in office at the time, "I declare today to the LORD your God that I have come to the land the LORD swore to our forefathers to give us." ⁴The priest shall take the basket from your hands and set it down in front of the altar of the LORD your God. ⁵Then you shall declare before the LORD your God: "My father was a wandering Aramean, and he went down into Egypt with a few people and lived there and became a great nation, powerful and numerous. ⁶But the Egyptians mistreated us and made us suffer, putting us to hard labor. ⁷Then we cried out to the LORD, the God of our fathers, and the LORD heard our voice and saw our misery, toil and oppression. ⁸So the LORD brought us out of Egypt with a mighty hand and an outstretched arm, with great terror and with miraculous signs and wonders. ⁹He brought us to this place and gave us this land, a land flowing with milk and honey; ¹⁰and now I bring the firstfruits of the soil that you, O LORD, have given me." Place the basket before the LORD your God and bow down before him. ¹¹And you and the Levites and the aliens among you shall rejoice in all the good things the LORD your God has given to you and your household.

¹²When you have finished setting aside a tenth of all your produce in the third year, the year of the tithe, you shall give it to the Levite, the alien, the fatherless and the widow, so that they may eat in your towns and be satisfied. ¹³Then say to the LORD your God: "I have removed from my house the sacred portion and have given it to the Levite, the alien, the fatherless and the widow, according to all you commanded. I have not turned aside from your commands nor have I forgotten any of them. ¹⁴I have not eaten any of the sacred portion while I was in mourning, nor have I removed any of it while I was unclean, nor have I offered any of it to the dead. I have obeyed the LORD my God; I have done everything you commanded me. ¹⁵Look down from heaven, your holy dwelling place, and bless your people Israel and the land you have given us as you promised on oath to our forefathers, a land flowing with milk and honey."

Follow the LORD's Commands

¹⁶The LORD your God commands you this day to follow these decrees and laws; carefully observe them with all your heart and with all your soul. ¹⁷You have declared this day that the LORD is your God and that you will walk in his ways, that you will keep his decrees, commands and laws, and that you will obey him. ¹⁸And the LORD has declared this day that you are his people, his treasured possession as he promised, and that you are to keep all his commands. ¹⁹He has declared that he will set you in praise, fame and honor high above all the nations he has made and that you will be a people holy to the LORD your God, as he promised.

The Altar on Mount Ebal

27 Moses and the elders of Israel commanded the people: "Keep all these commands that I give you today. ²When you have crossed the Jordan into the land the LORD your God is giving you, set up some large stones and coat them with plaster. ³Write on them all the words of this law when you have crossed over to enter the land the LORD your God is giving you, a land flowing with milk and honey, just as the LORD, the God of your fathers, promised you. ⁴And when you have crossed the Jordan, set up these stones on Mount Ebal, as I command you today, and coat them with plaster. ⁵Build there an altar to the LORD your God, an altar of stones. Do not use any iron tool upon them. ⁶Build the altar of the LORD your God with fieldstones and offer burnt offerings on it to the LORD your God. ⁷Sacrifice fellowship offerings*ᵃ* there, eating them and rejoicing in the presence of the LORD your God. ⁸And you shall write very clearly all the words of this law on these stones you have set up."

Curses From Mount Ebal

⁹Then Moses and the priests, who are Levites, said to all Israel, "Be silent, O Israel, and listen! You have now become the people of the LORD your God. ¹⁰Obey the LORD your God and follow his commands and decrees that I give you today."

¹¹On the same day Moses commanded the people:

¹²When you have crossed the Jordan,

ᵃ7 Traditionally *peace offerings*

these tribes shall stand on Mount Gerizim to bless the people: Simeon, Levi, Judah, Issachar, Joseph and Benjamin. [13]And these tribes shall stand on Mount Ebal to pronounce curses: Reuben, Gad, Asher, Zebulun, Dan and Naphtali.

[14]The Levites shall recite to all the people of Israel in a loud voice:

[15]"Cursed is the man who carves an image or casts an idol—a thing detestable to the LORD, the work of the craftsman's hands—and sets it up in secret."

Then all the people shall say, "Amen!"

[16]"Cursed is the man who dishonors his father or his mother."

Then all the people shall say, "Amen!"

[17]"Cursed is the man who moves his neighbor's boundary stone."

Then all the people shall say, "Amen!"

[18]"Cursed is the man who leads the blind astray on the road."

Then all the people shall say, "Amen!"

[19]"Cursed is the man who withholds justice from the alien, the fatherless or the widow."

Then all the people shall say, "Amen!"

[20]"Cursed is the man who sleeps with his father's wife, for he dishonors his father's bed."

Then all the people shall say, "Amen!"

[21]"Cursed is the man who has sexual relations with any animal."

Then all the people shall say, "Amen!"

[22]"Cursed is the man who sleeps with his sister, the daughter of his father or the daughter of his mother."

Then all the people shall say, "Amen!"

[23]"Cursed is the man who sleeps with his mother-in-law."

Then all the people shall say, "Amen!"

[24]"Cursed is the man who kills his neighbor secretly."

Then all the people shall say, "Amen!"

[25]"Cursed is the man who accepts a bribe to kill an innocent person."

Then all the people shall say, "Amen!"

[26]"Cursed is the man who does not uphold the words of this law by carrying them out."

Then all the people shall say, "Amen!"

Blessings for Obedience

28 If you fully obey the LORD your God and carefully follow all his commands I give you today, the LORD your God will set you high above all the nations on earth. [2]All these blessings will come upon you and accompany you if you obey the LORD your God:

[3]You will be blessed in the city and blessed in the country.

[4]The fruit of your womb will be blessed, and the crops of your land and the young of your livestock—the calves of your herds and the lambs of your flocks.

[5]Your basket and your kneading trough will be blessed.

[6]You will be blessed when you come in and blessed when you go out.

[7]The LORD will grant that the enemies who rise up against you will be defeated before you. They will come at you from one direction but flee from you in seven.

[8]The LORD will send a blessing on your barns and on everything you put your hand to. The LORD your God will bless you in the land he is giving you.

[9]The LORD will establish you as his holy people, as he promised you on oath, if you keep the commands of the LORD your God and walk in his ways. [10]Then all the peoples on earth will see that you are called by the name of the LORD, and they will fear you. [11]The LORD will grant you abundant prosperity—in the fruit of your womb, the young of your livestock and the crops of your ground—in the land he swore to your forefathers to give you.

[12]The LORD will open the heavens, the storehouse of his bounty, to send rain on your land in season and to bless all the work of your hands. You will lend to many nations but will borrow from none. [13]The LORD will make you the head, not the tail. If you pay attention to the commands of the LORD your God that I give you this day and carefully follow them, you will always be at the top, never at the bottom. [14]Do not turn aside from any of the commands I give you today, to the right or to the left, following other gods and serving them.

Curses for Disobedience

15However, if you do not obey the LORD your God and do not carefully follow all his commands and decrees I am giving you today, all these curses will come upon you and overtake you:

16You will be cursed in the city and cursed in the country.

17Your basket and your kneading trough will be cursed.

18The fruit of your womb will be cursed, and the crops of your land, and the calves of your herds and the lambs of your flocks.

19You will be cursed when you come in and cursed when you go out.

20The LORD will send on you curses, confusion and rebuke in everything you put your hand to, until you are destroyed and come to sudden ruin because of the evil you have done in forsaking him.*a* **21**The LORD will plague you with diseases until he has destroyed you from the land you are entering to possess. **22**The LORD will strike you with wasting disease, with fever and inflammation, with scorching heat and drought, with blight and mildew, which will plague you until you perish. **23**The sky over your head will be bronze, the ground beneath you iron. **24**The LORD will turn the rain of your country into dust and powder; it will come down from the skies until you are destroyed.

25The LORD will cause you to be defeated before your enemies. You will come at them from one direction but flee from them in seven, and you will become a thing of horror to all the kingdoms on earth. **26**Your carcasses will be food for all the birds of the air and the beasts of the earth, and there will be no one to frighten them away. **27**The LORD will afflict you with the boils of Egypt and with tumors, festering sores and the itch, from which you cannot be cured. **28**The LORD will afflict you with madness, blindness and confusion of mind. **29**At midday you will grope about like a blind man in the dark. You will be unsuccessful in everything you do; day after day you will be oppressed and robbed, with no one to rescue you.

30You will be pledged to be married to a woman, but another will take her and ravish her. You will build a house, but you will not live in it. You will plant a vineyard, but you will not even begin to enjoy its fruit. **31**Your ox will be slaughtered before your eyes, but you will eat none of it. Your donkey will be forcibly taken from you and will not be returned. Your sheep will be given to your enemies, and no one will rescue them. **32**Your sons and daughters will be given to another nation, and you will wear out your eyes watching for them day after day, powerless to lift a hand. **33**A people that you do not know will eat what your land and labor produce, and you will have nothing but cruel oppression all your days. **34**The sights you see will drive you mad. **35**The LORD will afflict your knees and legs with painful boils that cannot be cured, spreading from the soles of your feet to the top of your head.

36The LORD will drive you and the king you set over you to a nation unknown to you or your fathers. There you will worship other gods, gods of wood and stone. **37**You will become a thing of horror and an object of scorn and ridicule to all the nations where the LORD will drive you.

38You will sow much seed in the field but you will harvest little, because locusts will devour it. **39**You will plant vineyards and cultivate them but you will not drink the wine or gather the grapes, because worms will eat them. **40**You will have olive trees throughout your country but you will not use the oil, because the olives will drop off. **41**You will have sons and daughters but you will not keep them, because they will go into captivity. **42**Swarms of locusts will take over all your trees and the crops of your land.

43The alien who lives among you will rise above you higher and higher, but you will sink lower and lower. **44**He will lend to you, but you will not lend to him. He will be the head, but you will be the tail.

45All these curses will come upon you. They will pursue you and overtake you until you are destroyed, because you did not obey the LORD your God and observe the commands and decrees he gave you. **46**They will be a sign and a wonder to you and your descendants forever. **47**Because you did not serve the LORD your God joyfully and gladly in the time of prosperity, **48**therefore in hunger and thirst, in nakedness and dire poverty, you will serve the enemies the LORD sends against you. He will put an iron yoke on your neck until he has destroyed you.

49The LORD will bring a nation against you from far away, from the ends of the earth, like an eagle swooping down, a

a20 Hebrew me

nation whose language you will not understand, [50]a fierce-looking nation without respect for the old or pity for the young. [51]They will devour the young of your livestock and the crops of your land until you are destroyed. They will leave you no grain, new wine or oil, nor any calves of your herds or lambs of your flocks until you are ruined. [52]They will lay siege to all the cities throughout your land until the high fortified walls in which you trust fall down. They will besiege all the cities throughout the land the LORD your God is giving you.

[53]Because of the suffering that your enemy will inflict on you during the siege, you will eat the fruit of the womb, the flesh of the sons and daughters the LORD your God has given you. [54]Even the most gentle and sensitive man among you will have no compassion on his own brother or the wife he loves or his surviving children, [55]and he will not give to one of them any of the flesh of his children that he is eating. It will be all he has left because of the suffering your enemy will inflict on you during the siege of all your cities. [56]The most gentle and sensitive woman among you—so sensitive and gentle that she would not venture to touch the ground with the sole of her foot—will begrudge the husband she loves and her own son or daughter [57]the afterbirth from her womb and the children she bears. For she intends to eat them secretly during the siege and in the distress that your enemy will inflict on you in your cities.

[58]If you do not carefully follow all the words of this law, which are written in this book, and do not revere this glorious and awesome name—the LORD your God— [59]the LORD will send fearful plagues on you and your descendants, harsh and prolonged disasters, and severe and lingering illnesses. [60]He will bring upon you all the diseases of Egypt that you dreaded, and they will cling to you. [61]The LORD will also bring on you every kind of sickness and disaster not recorded in this Book of the Law, until you are destroyed. [62]You who were as numerous as the stars in the sky will be left but few in number, because you did not obey the LORD your God. [63]Just as it pleased the LORD to make you prosper and increase in number, so it will please him to ruin and destroy you. You will be uprooted from the land you are entering to possess.

[64]Then the LORD will scatter you among all nations, from one end of the earth to the other. There you will worship other gods—gods of wood and stone, which neither you nor your fathers have known. [65]Among those nations you will find no repose, no resting place for the sole of your foot. There the LORD will give you an anxious mind, eyes weary with longing, and a despairing heart. [66]You will live in constant suspense, filled with dread both night and day, never sure of your life. [67]In the morning you will say, "If only it were evening!" and in the evening, "If only it were morning!"—because of the terror that will fill your hearts and the sights that your eyes will see. [68]The LORD will send you back in ships to Egypt on a journey I said you should never make again. There you will offer yourselves for sale to your enemies as male and female slaves, but no one will buy you.

Renewal of the Covenant

29 These are the terms of the covenant the LORD commanded Moses to make with the Israelites in Moab, in addition to the covenant he had made with them at Horeb.

[2]Moses summoned all the Israelites and said to them:

Your eyes have seen all that the LORD did in Egypt to Pharaoh, to all his officials and to all his land. [3]With your own eyes you saw those great trials, those miraculous signs and great wonders. [4]But to this day the LORD has not given you a mind that understands or eyes that see or ears that hear. [5]During the forty years that I led you through the desert, your clothes did not wear out, nor did the sandals on your feet. [6]You ate no bread and drank no wine or other fermented drink. I did this so that you might know that I am the LORD your God.

[7]When you reached this place, Sihon king of Heshbon and Og king of Bashan came out to fight against us, but we defeated them. [8]We took their land and gave it as an inheritance to the Reubenites, the Gadites and the half-tribe of Manasseh.

[9]Carefully follow the terms of this covenant, so that you may prosper in everything you do. [10]All of you are standing today in the presence of the LORD your God—your leaders and chief men, your elders and officials, and all the other men of Israel, [11]together with your children and your wives, and the aliens living in your camps who chop your wood and carry your water. [12]You are standing here

in order to enter into a covenant with the LORD your God, a covenant the LORD is making with you this day and sealing with an oath, **13**to confirm you this day as his people, that he may be your God as he promised you and as he swore to your fathers, Abraham, Isaac and Jacob. **14**I am making this covenant, with its oath, not only with you **15**who are standing here with us today in the presence of the LORD our God but also with those who are not here today.

16You yourselves know how we lived in Egypt and how we passed through the countries on the way here. **17**You saw among them their detestable images and idols of wood and stone, of silver and gold. **18**Make sure there is no man or woman, clan or tribe among you today whose heart turns away from the LORD our God to go and worship the gods of those nations; make sure there is no root among you that produces such bitter poison.

19When such a person hears the words of this oath, he invokes a blessing on himself and therefore thinks, "I will be safe, even though I persist in going my own way." This will bring disaster on the watered land as well as the dry.*a* **20**The LORD will never be willing to forgive him; his wrath and zeal will burn against that man. All the curses written in this book will fall upon him, and the LORD will blot out his name from under heaven. **21**The LORD will single him out from all the tribes of Israel for disaster, according to all the curses of the covenant written in this Book of the Law.

22Your children who follow you in later generations and foreigners who come from distant lands will see the calamities that have fallen on the land and the diseases with which the LORD has afflicted it. **23**The whole land will be a burning waste of salt and sulfur—nothing planted,

a19 Or way, in order to add drunkenness to thirst."

Your Family's Highlight Video

DAILY INSIGHT

Your house is on fire. All the members of your family, including the pets, are safely out, and the fire chief tells you that you can make one last trip into the house before it's too late. What would you retrieve?

Many of us would grab the photo albums. Nearly everything else can be replaced, but if the family pictures are destroyed, there's no bringing them back. They're absolutely irreplaceable.

A few months before our daughter's wedding, I decided to put together a walk-down-memory-lane slide show. So for several hours, I paged through our old photos. Magically, twenty-five years were compressed into what seemed like no time at all. I saw special birthday celebrations, memorable vacations, leg casts from various accidents or surgeries, and building projects. For several weeks following my pictorial review, I played the role of our family's historian. Because I had taken time to review the past, I was a veritable walking family highlight video.

WEDNESDAY
Passage:
Deuteronomy 29:22–29
Verse:
Deuteronomy 29:29

This passage makes me think that Moses had spent some time thumbing through the Israelites' photo albums. And because he had this unique historical overview in mind, he delivered some stout warnings about the future. It was as though he was saying, "I know how God punishes for sin ... I've seen him do it in the past. If we don't obey him tomorrow, we'll suffer as we did yesterday."

Then he adds an interesting footnote (29:29). He reminds the people that God is still God. Many of the "why" and "how" questions will never be answered. But, he tells them, the things that we do know, the experiences we have had, belong to us. We must learn from them. We must follow them.

If we as dads remember the past, there are plenty of lessons hidden there. Then we must show these truths to our children.

For your next devotional reading, go to page 228.

nothing sprouting, no vegetation growing on it. It will be like the destruction of Sodom and Gomorrah, Admah and Zeboiim, which the LORD overthrew in fierce anger. **24**All the nations will ask: "Why has the LORD done this to this land? Why this fierce, burning anger?"

25And the answer will be: "It is because this people abandoned the covenant of the LORD, the God of their fathers, the covenant he made with them when he brought them out of Egypt. **26**They went off and worshiped other gods and bowed down to them, gods they did not know, gods he had not given them. **27**Therefore the LORD's anger burned against this land, so that he brought on it all the curses written in this book. **28**In furious anger and in great wrath the LORD uprooted them from their land and thrust them into another land, as it is now."

29The secret things belong to the LORD our God, but the things revealed belong to us and to our children forever, that we may follow all the words of this law.

Prosperity After Turning to the LORD

30 When all these blessings and curses I have set before you come upon you and you take them to heart wherever the LORD your God disperses you among the nations, **2**and when you and your children return to the LORD your God and obey him with all your heart and with all your soul according to everything I command you today, **3**then the LORD your God will restore your fortunes[a] and have compassion on you and gather you again from all the nations where he scattered you. **4**Even

a 3 Or will bring you back from captivity

Truth You Can Count on

Let's take a little journey back to geometry class. We're going to discuss postulates. Remember them? You start with a common belief, add a truth, and come to a conclusion that is the natural result of mixing these two elements.

For example, let's start with a triangle. You might remember that the angles of a triangle always add up to one hundred and eighty degrees. So here we go with a postulate: we have a triangle and one of the angles is ninety degrees. If the second angle is forty-five degrees, then the last angle is also forty-five degrees. Since the first two things are true, then the third thing must also be true.

Now let's try a family postulate. If I am married and if my wife gives birth to a baby, then I am a father. If I make a rule and my son or daughter disobeys me, then I have some disciplining work to do. Since the first part of each statement is true, and since the second part of each statement is also true, then the combination of the first and second parts make each conclusion true for sure. See how these work?

In today's reading we have an amazing

DAILY INSIGHT

THURSDAY

Passage:
Deuteronomy 30:1–11

Verse:
Deuteronomy 30:11

postulate. It starts with verse one and ends with verse three. Moses presented this amazing postulate to the Israelites in terms they could clearly understand: Since God can be taken at his word, if he finds you obedient to his law, then he will "restore your fortunes ... have compassion on you ... and gather you again from all the nations."

Over the next few verses, you'll see that there's an unequivocal promise of prosperity. While theologians will arm-wrestle over the kind of "prosperity" God is referring to here, it's indisputable that he does promise the kind of success that is consistent within his economy—where a private jet can be purchased with a single paycheck, a foreign import can be bought with lunch money, and a happy family is a priceless treasure.

And don't you just love today's verse (30:11)? Read that verse again. All of this is not too difficult. It's not unreachable. It's something we can believe because we know it's true. Take that with you today.

For your next devotional reading, go to page 234.

if you have been banished to the most distant land under the heavens, from there the LORD your God will gather you and bring you back. [5]He will bring you to the land that belonged to your fathers, and you will take possession of it. He will make you more prosperous and numerous than your fathers. [6]The LORD your God will circumcise your hearts and the hearts of your descendants, so that you may love him with all your heart and with all your soul, and live. [7]The LORD your God will put all these curses on your enemies who hate and persecute you. [8]You will again obey the LORD and follow all his commands I am giving you today. [9]Then the LORD your God will make you most prosperous in all the work of your hands and in the fruit of your womb, the young of your livestock and the crops of your land. The LORD will again delight in you and make you prosperous, just as he delighted in your fathers, [10]if you obey the LORD your God and keep his commands and decrees that are written in this Book of the Law and turn to the LORD your God with all your heart and with all your soul.

The Offer of Life or Death

[11]Now what I am commanding you today is not too difficult for you or beyond your reach. [12]It is not up in heaven, so that you have to ask, "Who will ascend into heaven to get it and proclaim it to us so we may obey it?" [13]Nor is it beyond the sea, so that you have to ask, "Who will cross the sea to get it and proclaim it to us so we may obey it?" [14]No, the word is very near you; it is in your mouth and in your heart so you may obey it.

[15]See, I set before you today life and prosperity, death and destruction. [16]For I command you today to love the LORD your God, to walk in his ways, and to keep his commands, decrees and laws; then you will live and increase, and the LORD your God will bless you in the land you are entering to possess.

[17]But if your heart turns away and you are not obedient, and if you are drawn away to bow down to other gods and worship them, [18]I declare to you this day that you will certainly be destroyed. You will not live long in the land you are crossing the Jordan to enter and possess.

[19]This day I call heaven and earth as witnesses against you that I have set before you life and death, blessings and curses. Now choose life, so that you and

your children may live [20]and that you may love the LORD your God, listen to his voice, and hold fast to him. For the LORD is your life, and he will give you many years in the land he swore to give to your fathers, Abraham, Isaac and Jacob.

Joshua to Succeed Moses

31 Then Moses went out and spoke these words to all Israel: [2]"I am now a hundred and twenty years old and I am no longer able to lead you. The LORD has said to me, 'You shall not cross the Jordan.' [3]The LORD your God himself will cross over ahead of you. He will destroy these nations before you, and you will take possession of their land. Joshua also will cross over ahead of you, as the LORD said. [4]And the LORD will do to them what he did to Sihon and Og, the kings of the Amorites, whom he destroyed along with their land. [5]The LORD will deliver them to you, and you must do to them all that I have commanded you. [6]Be strong and courageous. Do not be afraid or terrified because of them, for the LORD your God goes with you; he will never leave you nor forsake you."

[7]Then Moses summoned Joshua and said to him in the presence of all Israel, "Be strong and courageous, for you must go with this people into the land that the LORD swore to their forefathers to give them, and you must divide it among them as their inheritance. [8]The LORD himself goes before you and will be with you; he will never leave you nor forsake you. Do not be afraid; do not be discouraged."

The Reading of the Law

[9]So Moses wrote down this law and gave it to the priests, the sons of Levi, who carried the ark of the covenant of the LORD, and to all the elders of Israel. [10]Then Moses commanded them: "At the end of every seven years, in the year for canceling debts, during the Feast of Tabernacles, [11]when all Israel comes to appear before the LORD your God at the place he will choose, you shall read this law before them in their hearing. [12]Assemble the people—men, women and children, and the aliens living in your towns—so they can listen and learn to fear the LORD your God and follow carefully all the words of this law. [13]Their children, who do not know this law, must hear it and learn to fear the LORD your God as long as you live in the land you are crossing the Jordan to possess."

Israel's Rebellion Predicted

14The LORD said to Moses, "Now the day of your death is near. Call Joshua and present yourselves at the Tent of Meeting, where I will commission him." So Moses and Joshua came and presented themselves at the Tent of Meeting.

15Then the LORD appeared at the Tent in a pillar of cloud, and the cloud stood over the entrance to the Tent. **16**And the LORD said to Moses: "You are going to rest with your fathers, and these people will soon prostitute themselves to the foreign gods of the land they are entering. They will forsake me and break the covenant I made with them. **17**On that day I will become angry with them and forsake them; I will hide my face from them, and they will be destroyed. Many disasters and difficulties will come upon them, and on that day they will ask, 'Have not these disasters come upon us because our God is not with us?' **18**And I will certainly hide my face on that day because of all their wickedness in turning to other gods.

19"Now write down for yourselves this song and teach it to the Israelites and have them sing it, so that it may be a witness for me against them. **20**When I have brought them into the land flowing with milk and honey, the land I promised on oath to their forefathers, and when they eat their fill and thrive, they will turn to other gods and worship them, rejecting me and breaking my covenant. **21**And when many disasters and difficulties come upon them, this song will testify against them, because it will not be forgotten by their descendants. I know what they are disposed to do, even before I bring them into the land I promised them on oath." **22**So Moses wrote down this song that day and taught it to the Israelites.

23The LORD gave this command to Joshua son of Nun: "Be strong and courageous, for you will bring the Israelites into the land I promised them on oath, and I myself will be with you."

24After Moses finished writing in a book the words of this law from beginning to end, **25**he gave this command to the Levites who carried the ark of the covenant of the LORD: **26**"Take this Book of the Law and place it beside the ark of the covenant of the LORD your God. There it will remain as a witness against you. **27**For I know how rebellious and stiff-necked you are. If you have been rebellious against the LORD while I am still alive and with you, how

much more will you rebel after I die! **28**Assemble before me all the elders of your tribes and all your officials, so that I can speak these words in their hearing and call heaven and earth to testify against them. **29**For I know that after my death you are sure to become utterly corrupt and to turn from the way I have commanded you. In days to come, disaster will fall upon you because you will do evil in the sight of the LORD and provoke him to anger by what your hands have made."

The Song of Moses

30And Moses recited the words of this song from beginning to end in the hearing of the whole assembly of Israel:

32 Listen, O heavens, and I will speak;
　　hear, O earth, the words of my
　　　mouth.
2 Let my teaching fall like rain
　　and my words descend like dew,
　like showers on new grass,
　　like abundant rain on tender plants.

3 I will proclaim the name of the LORD.
　　Oh, praise the greatness of our God!
4 He is the Rock, his works are perfect,
　　and all his ways are just.
A faithful God who does no wrong,
　　upright and just is he.

5 They have acted corruptly toward him;
　　to their shame they are no longer his
　　　children,
　but a warped and crooked
　　　generation.*a*
6 Is this the way you repay the LORD,
　　O foolish and unwise people?
Is he not your Father, your Creator,*b*
　　who made you and formed you?

7 Remember the days of old;
　　consider the generations long past.
Ask your father and he will tell you,
　　your elders, and they will explain to
　　　you.
8 When the Most High gave the nations
　　their inheritance,
　when he divided all mankind,
　he set up boundaries for the peoples
　　according to the number of the sons
　　　of Israel.*c*
9 For the LORD's portion is his people,
　　Jacob his allotted inheritance.

---

*a*5 Or *Corrupt are they and not his children, / a generation warped and twisted to their shame*
*b*6 Or *Father, who bought you*   *c*8 Masoretic Text; Dead Sea Scrolls (see also Septuagint) *sons of God*

¹⁰In a desert land he found him,
  in a barren and howling waste.
He shielded him and cared for him;
  he guarded him as the apple of his
  eye,
¹¹like an eagle that stirs up its nest
  and hovers over its young,
that spreads its wings to catch them
  and carries them on its pinions.
¹²The LORD alone led him;
  no foreign god was with him.

¹³He made him ride on the heights of the
  land
  and fed him with the fruit of the
  fields.
He nourished him with honey from the
  rock,
  and with oil from the flinty crag,
¹⁴with curds and milk from herd and flock
  and with fattened lambs and goats,
with choice rams of Bashan
  and the finest kernels of wheat.
You drank the foaming blood of the
  grape.

¹⁵Jeshurun[a] grew fat and kicked;
  filled with food, he became heavy
  and sleek.
He abandoned the God who made him
  and rejected the Rock his Savior.
¹⁶They made him jealous with their
  foreign gods
  and angered him with their
  detestable idols.
¹⁷They sacrificed to demons, which are
  not God—
  gods they had not known,
  gods that recently appeared,
  gods your fathers did not fear.
¹⁸You deserted the Rock, who fathered
  you;
  you forgot the God who gave you
  birth.

¹⁹The LORD saw this and rejected them
  because he was angered by his sons
  and daughters.
²⁰"I will hide my face from them," he
  said,
  "and see what their end will be;
for they are a perverse generation,
  children who are unfaithful.
²¹They made me jealous by what is no
  god
  and angered me with their worthless
  idols.
I will make them envious by those who
  are not a people;
  I will make them angry by a nation
  that has no understanding.

²²For a fire has been kindled by my
  wrath,
  one that burns to the realm of death[b]
  below.
It will devour the earth and its
  harvests
  and set afire the foundations of the
  mountains.

²³"I will heap calamities upon them
  and spend my arrows against them.
²⁴I will send wasting famine against
  them,
  consuming pestilence and deadly
  plague;
I will send against them the fangs of
  wild beasts,
  the venom of vipers that glide in the
  dust.
²⁵In the street the sword will make them
  childless;
  in their homes terror will reign.
Young men and young women will
  perish,
  infants and gray-haired men.
²⁶I said I would scatter them
  and blot out their memory from
  mankind,
²⁷but I dreaded the taunt of the enemy,
  lest the adversary misunderstand
and say, 'Our hand has triumphed;
  the LORD has not done all this.' "

²⁸They are a nation without sense,
  there is no discernment in them.
²⁹If only they were wise and would
  understand this
  and discern what their end will be!
³⁰How could one man chase a thousand,
  or two put ten thousand to flight,
unless their Rock had sold them,
  unless the LORD had given them up?
³¹For their rock is not like our Rock,
  as even our enemies concede.
³²Their vine comes from the vine of
  Sodom
  and from the fields of Gomorrah.
Their grapes are filled with poison,
  and their clusters with bitterness.
³³Their wine is the venom of serpents,
  the deadly poison of cobras.

³⁴"Have I not kept this in reserve
  and sealed it in my vaults?
³⁵It is mine to avenge; I will repay.
  In due time their foot will slip;
  their day of disaster is near
  and their doom rushes upon them."

---

a15 *Jeshurun* means *the upright one,* that is, Israel.
b22 Hebrew *to Sheol*

³⁶ The LORD will judge his people
   and have compassion on his
      servants
 when he sees their strength is gone
   and no one is left, slave or free.
³⁷ He will say: "Now where are their gods,
      the rock they took refuge in,
³⁸ the gods who ate the fat of their
      sacrifices
   and drank the wine of their drink
      offerings?
 Let them rise up to help you!
 Let them give you shelter!

³⁹ "See now that I myself am He!
   There is no god besides me.
 I put to death and I bring to life,
 I have wounded and I will heal,
   and no one can deliver out of my
      hand.
⁴⁰ I lift my hand to heaven and declare:
   As surely as I live forever,
⁴¹ when I sharpen my flashing sword
   and my hand grasps it in judgment,
 I will take vengeance on my adversaries
   and repay those who hate me.
⁴² I will make my arrows drunk with
      blood,
   while my sword devours flesh:
 the blood of the slain and the captives,
   the heads of the enemy leaders."

⁴³ Rejoice, O nations, with his people,ᵃ·ᵇ
   for he will avenge the blood of his
      servants;
 he will take vengeance on his enemies
   and make atonement for his land
      and people.

⁴⁴ Moses came with Joshuaᶜ son of Nun
and spoke all the words of this song in the
hearing of the people. ⁴⁵ When Moses finished reciting all these words to all Israel,
⁴⁶ he said to them, "Take to heart all the
words I have solemnly declared to you
this day, so that you may command your
children to obey carefully all the words of
this law. ⁴⁷ They are not just idle words for
you—they are your life. By them you will
live long in the land you are crossing the
Jordan to possess."

Moses to Die on Mount Nebo

⁴⁸ On that same day the LORD told Moses, ⁴⁹ "Go up into the Abarim Range to
Mount Nebo in Moab, across from Jericho, and view Canaan, the land I am
giving the Israelites as their own possession. ⁵⁰ There on the mountain that you
have climbed you will die and be gathered
to your people, just as your brother Aaron

died on Mount Hor and was gathered to
his people. ⁵¹ This is because both of you
broke faith with me in the presence of the
Israelites at the waters of Meribah Kadesh
in the Desert of Zin and because you did
not uphold my holiness among the Israelites. ⁵² Therefore, you will see the land only
from a distance; you will not enter the
land I am giving to the people of Israel."

Moses Blesses the Tribes

33 This is the blessing that Moses the
man of God pronounced on the Israelites before his death. ²He said:

 "The LORD came from Sinai
   and dawned over them from Seir;
   he shone forth from Mount Paran.
 He came withᵈ myriads of holy ones
   from the south, from his mountain
      slopes.ᵉ
³ Surely it is you who love the people;
   all the holy ones are in your hand.
 At your feet they all bow down,
   and from you receive instruction,
⁴ the law that Moses gave us,
   the possession of the assembly of
      Jacob.
⁵ He was king over Jeshurunᶠ
   when the leaders of the people
      assembled,
   along with the tribes of Israel.

⁶ "Let Reuben live and not die,
   norᵍ his men be few."

⁷ And this he said about Judah:

 "Hear, O LORD, the cry of Judah;
   bring him to his people.
 With his own hands he defends his
      cause.
 Oh, be his help against his foes!"

⁸ About Levi he said:

 "Your Thummim and Urim belong
   to the man you favored.
 You tested him at Massah;
   you contended with him at the
      waters of Meribah.
⁹ He said of his father and mother,
   'I have no regard for them.'
 He did not recognize his brothers
   or acknowledge his own children,

ᵃ43 Or *Make his people rejoice, O nations*
ᵇ43 Masoretic Text; Dead Sea Scrolls (see also
Septuagint) *people, / and let all the angels worship
him /*   ᶜ44 Hebrew *Hoshea,* a variant of *Joshua*
ᵈ2 Or *from*   ᵉ2 The meaning of the Hebrew for this
phrase is uncertain.   ᶠ5 *Jeshurun* means *the
upright one,* that is, Israel; also in verse 26.
ᵍ6 Or *but let*

but he watched over your word
and guarded your covenant.
[10] He teaches your precepts to Jacob
and your law to Israel.
He offers incense before you
and whole burnt offerings on your
altar.
[11] Bless all his skills, O LORD,
and be pleased with the work of his
hands.
Smite the loins of those who rise up
against him;
strike his foes till they rise no more."

[12] About Benjamin he said:

"Let the beloved of the LORD rest secure
in him,
for he shields him all day long,
and the one the LORD loves rests
between his shoulders."

[13] About Joseph he said:

"May the LORD bless his land
with the precious dew from heaven
above
and with the deep waters that lie
below;
[14] with the best the sun brings forth
and the finest the moon can yield;
[15] with the choicest gifts of the ancient
mountains
and the fruitfulness of the
everlasting hills;
[16] with the best gifts of the earth and its
fullness
and the favor of him who dwelt in
the burning bush.
Let all these rest on the head of Joseph,

on the brow of the prince among[a] his
brothers.
[17] In majesty he is like a firstborn bull;
his horns are the horns of a wild ox.
With them he will gore the nations,
even those at the ends of the earth.
Such are the ten thousands of Ephraim;
such are the thousands of
Manasseh."

[18] About Zebulun he said:

"Rejoice, Zebulun, in your going out,
and you, Issachar, in your tents.
[19] They will summon peoples to the
mountain
and there offer sacrifices of
righteousness;
they will feast on the abundance of the
seas,
on the treasures hidden in the sand."

[20] About Gad he said:

"Blessed is he who enlarges Gad's
domain!
Gad lives there like a lion,
tearing at arm or head.
[21] He chose the best land for himself;
the leader's portion was kept for him.
When the heads of the people
assembled,
he carried out the LORD's righteous
will,
and his judgments concerning
Israel."

[22] About Dan he said:

[a]16 Or of the one separated from

HEY DAD
How big is God?

Text: Deuteronomy 33:26, 27a

We cannot even begin to imagine how big God is, but the Bible gives us some
clues that may help us start thinking in the right direction. It says that God "rides
on the heavens" to help us, and he "[rides] on the clouds in his majesty." God is so
big he can ride on the heavens like we might ride on a pony or a bicycle.

When we think of how vast the universe is, we begin to get a picture of how big
God is. The earth, as enormous as it is compared to one person, is one of nine
planets in our solar system. Our solar system makes up a tiny part of our galaxy,
the Milky Way. And our galaxy is only one of billions of heavenly galaxies. Think about this
again: God can ride on the heavens! That's big.

God is big enough to be everywhere in the universe. But, amazingly, God is still concerned
about the events of our daily lives. Isn't that wonderful?

For a complete listing of Questions Kids Ask, turn to page 1435.

QUESTIONS KIDS ASK

"Dan is a lion's cub,
    springing out of Bashan."

²³About Naphtali he said:

"Naphtali is abounding with the favor
        of the LORD
    and is full of his blessing;
    he will inherit southward to the
        lake."

²⁴About Asher he said:

"Most blessed of sons is Asher;
    let him be favored by his brothers,
    and let him bathe his feet in oil.
²⁵ The bolts of your gates will be iron and
        bronze,
    and your strength will equal your
        days.

²⁶ "There is no one like the God of
        Jeshurun,
    who rides on the heavens to help you
    and on the clouds in his majesty.
²⁷ The eternal God is your refuge,
    and underneath are the everlasting
        arms.
    He will drive out your enemy before
        you,
    saying, 'Destroy him!'
²⁸ So Israel will live in safety alone;
    Jacob's spring is secure
in a land of grain and new wine,
    where the heavens drop dew.
²⁹ Blessed are you, O Israel!
    Who is like you,
    a people saved by the LORD?
He is your shield and helper

Rest in Peace

DAILY INSIGHT

FRIDAY

Passage:
Deuteronomy 34:1–12

Verse:
Deuteronomy 34:12

Can we talk? Are we alone? Good, because there's something I need to say to you and it would be better if there were no distractions.

You and I are going to die. Take just a moment and let this sink in. Someday our eyes will close, we will draw our last breaths of air, and our hearts will strike their last beats. Our lives will be over.

A day later, our loved ones will sit down with a minister to discuss our funeral service. They'll decide which hymns should be sung and who will deliver the eulogy. Prior to this service, there will be a time of visitation when people will file past our caskets. They'll stop and gaze at our bodies. Some will shed tears. The brave ones will touch our cold hands.

Regardless of how old we are today and how healthy and strong we might be feeling at this moment, this is going to happen to you and me.

Death happened to Moses. Today's verses tell us about it. And we read some pretty remarkable things that were said about this man when he died. "No prophet has risen in Israel like Moses, whom the LORD knew face to face" (v. 10). "No one has ever shown the mighty power or performed the awesome deeds that Moses did" (v. 12).

We also read some sobering messages about Moses' death. In spite of his tireless leadership—from the brave days back in Egypt to standing on the cusp of Canaan—Moses was not allowed to actually set foot in the promised land. Because of his public display of disobedience to God (Numbers 20:1–12), God only allowed Moses to see the land from a distance.

It's pretty amazing, isn't it? A man's entire life compressed into just a few words. It hardly seems fair, but that's just the way it is.

So, back to our funerals. What will people say about us? What are we going to do today that will be completely forgotten when we're gone, and what will be remembered? What trivial things should we overlook today and to what should we pay special attention?

Live today with a new perspective. Fill your heart with thanksgiving to God for his goodness. Take an extra moment to tell your family how much you love them. Remind the people you work with how grateful you are for their hard work. If you live for many more years, these things will still make for a special day. But, just in case you don't have a tomorrow, imagine how grateful these people will be.

For your next devotional reading, go to page 237.

and your glorious sword.
Your enemies will cower before you,
    and you will trample down their high
        places.*"

The Death of Moses

34 Then Moses climbed Mount Nebo
    from the plains of Moab to the top of
Pisgah, across from Jerichc. There the
LORD showed him the whole land—from
Gilead to Dan, **2**all of Naphtali, the territory of Ephraim and Manasseh, all the
land of Judah as far as the western sea,*
3the Negev and the whole region from the
Valley of Jericho, the City of Palms, as far
as Zoar. **4**Then the LORD said to him, "This
is the land I promised on oath to Abraham, Isaac and Jacob when I said, 'I will
give it to your descendants.' I have let you
see it with your eyes, but you will not
cross over into it."

5And Moses the servant of the LORD
died there in Moab, as the LORD had said.
6He buried him* in Moab, in the valley opposite Beth Peor, but to this day no one
knows where his grave is. **7**Moses was a
hundred and twenty years old when he
died, yet his eyes were not weak nor his
strength gone. **8**The Israelites grieved for
Moses in the plains of Moab thirty days,
until the time of weeping and mourning
was over.

9Now Joshua son of Nun was filled with
the spirit* of wisdom because Moses had
laid his hands on him. So the Israelites listened to him and did what the LORD had
commanded Moses.

10Since then, no prophet has risen in Israel like Moses, whom the LORD knew face
to face, **11**who did all those miraculous
signs and wonders the LORD sent him to
do in Egypt—to Pharaoh and to all his officials and to his whole land. **12**For no one
has ever shown the mighty power or performed the awesome deeds that Moses
did in the sight of all Israel.

---

*a*29 Or *will tread upon their bodies*   *b*2 That is, the
Mediterranean   *c*6 Or *He was buried*   *d*9 Or *Spirit*

There may be no more thrilling words for a father to hear than, "Daddy's home!" Whether it's been a full day away at work or a week-long business trip, there really is no place like home. Having been away from home for a few hundred years, the Israelites had been on a fairly significant journey! But now they were back in Canaan, the land of their forefathers, the land in which God had promised them they would resettle.

Can you imagine the celebration when Joshua stood in front of the Israelites and shouted, "Welcome home!" These people, who had for generations only heard about this wonderful place, were now going to be able to settle down. They would have their own land, their own possessions, a place that they and their families could "home." Can you imagine the joy? The book of Joshua contains the celebration of this precious place—a place of protection and security for the children of Israel … and for your children.

Joshua

The LORD Commands Joshua

1 After the death of Moses the servant of the LORD, the LORD said to Joshua son of Nun, Moses' aide: ²"Moses my servant is dead. Now then, you and all these people, get ready to cross the Jordan River into the land I am about to give to them—to the Israelites. ³I will give you every place where you set your foot, as I promised Moses. ⁴Your territory will extend from the desert to Lebanon, and from the great river, the Euphrates—all the Hittite country—to the Great Sea*a* on the west. ⁵No one will be able to stand up against you all the days of your life. As I was with Moses, so I will be with you; I will never leave you nor forsake you.

⁶"Be strong and courageous, because you will lead these people to inherit the land I swore to their forefathers to give them. ⁷Be strong and very courageous. Be careful to obey all the law my servant Moses gave you; do not turn from it to the right or to the left, that you may be successful wherever you go. ⁸Do not let this Book of the Law depart from your mouth; meditate on it day and night, so that you may be careful to do everything written in it. Then you will be prosperous and successful. ⁹Have I not commanded you? Be strong and courageous. Do not be terrified; do not be discouraged, for the LORD your God will be with you wherever you go."

¹⁰So Joshua ordered the officers of the people: ¹¹"Go through the camp and tell the people, 'Get your supplies ready.

a4 That is, the Mediterranean

Passing Our Faith Along

Key Verse: *"Do not let this Book of the Law depart from your mouth; meditate on it day and night."* Joshua 1:8

Text: Joshua 1:1–9 *(Dad or child reads the text.)*

QUIET TIMES with Dad

DAD READS: Relay races are fun to watch. In normal running events, all that matters is how fast a person can run. But in a relay race, the fastest runners may lose the race if they make a mistake handing the baton from one person to the next.

Child reads: When athletes who are going to run a relay race practice, they need to make sure they have worked on passing the baton. Even if they're ready to run, they could lose the race because they have not practiced giving the baton to the next runner.

DAD READS: Sometimes life is like a relay race. When I ask you to take over a chore for me, such as feeding the dog every day, I am "handing you the baton" and trusting that you'll do a good job. A man who retires from his business and leaves it to his son or daughter is, in a way, passing the baton to his child. And when a person dies, he or she passes the baton to family members.

Child reads: When Moses died, he passed his baton to a man named Joshua. Joshua was a great leader, just like Moses. He loved God and wanted the people to love God, too. And since Moses was gone, he was the new leader of God's people. Now the baton was his to carry.

DAD READS: In Joshua's first speech to the Israelites, he told them something very important. He reminded them that knowing and obeying God's law was the most important thing they could do. What a wise thing this was to say!

Child reads: I know how important the Bible is to you and me. I know that what we're doing right now is just like putting money in our spiritual banks . . . it helps us to be ready for the times when we need God's help and wisdom.

DAD READS: You're right. I don't want to wait to begin passing this wonderful baton to you. I'm so glad that we are spending time together in God's Word right now. It's kind of like carrying the baton together for a while. I like that idea.

Child reads: Me, too. I know that I can learn a lot of good things from my dad. Thank you for starting to pass your baton to me now. Let me pray this prayer with you:

Our Father in heaven, thank you for my dad. And thank you for helping him to start passing his spiritual baton to me now. Please help us both to learn more about you in the Bible. Thank you for all the promises you have for us in your Word. Give us the strength to be obedient. In Jesus' name, Amen.

For your next devotional reading, go to page 240.

Three days from now you will cross the Jordan here to go in and take possession of the land the LORD your God is giving you for your own.' "

¹²But to the Reubenites, the Gadites and the half-tribe of Manasseh, Joshua said, ¹³"Remember the command that Moses the servant of the LORD gave you: 'The LORD your God is giving you rest and has granted you this land.' ¹⁴Your wives, your children and your livestock may stay in the land that Moses gave you east of the Jordan, but all your fighting men, fully armed, must cross over ahead of your brothers. You are to help your brothers ¹⁵until the LORD gives them rest, as he has done for you, and until they too have taken possession of the land that the LORD your God is giving them. After that, you may go back and occupy your own land, which Moses the servant of the LORD gave you east of the Jordan toward the sunrise."

¹⁶Then they answered Joshua, "Whatever you have commanded us we will do, and wherever you send us we will go. ¹⁷Just as we fully obeyed Moses, so we will obey you. Only may the LORD your God be with you as he was with Moses. ¹⁸Whoever rebels against your word and does not obey your words, whatever you may com-

mand them, will be put to death. Only be strong and courageous!"

Rahab and the Spies

2 Then Joshua son of Nun secretly sent two spies from Shittim. "Go, look over the land," he said, "especially Jericho." So they went and entered the house of a prostitute*a* named Rahab and stayed there.

²The king of Jericho was told, "Look! Some of the Israelites have come here tonight to spy out the land." ³So the king of Jericho sent this message to Rahab: "Bring out the men who came to you and entered your house, because they have come to spy out the whole land."

⁴But the woman had taken the two men and hidden them. She said, "Yes, the men came to me, but I did not know where they had come from. ⁵At dusk, when it was time to close the city gate, the men left. I don't know which way they went. Go after them quickly. You may catch up with them." ⁶(But she had taken them up to the roof and hidden them under the stalks of flax she had laid out on the roof.) ⁷So the men set out in pursuit of the spies on the

---

a1 Or possibly *an innkeeper*

HEY DAD

Why do we have to follow so many rules?

Text: Joshua 1:7–9

The Israelites sometimes wondered why they had to follow God's rules. But the book of Joshua makes it clear: God gave them rules to follow "that you may be successful wherever you go" (v. 7).

To a child, some rules may seem pointless. Why chew with your mouth closed? Why say "Yes, Sir" or "No, Ma'am"? But good manners prove useful later in life. Even in Moses' day, parents had rules like these. Egyptian fathers taught their sons "wisdom texts." For example, "If you dine with a great man, 'take what he may give, when it is set before thy nose ... speak only when he addresses thee. Laugh after he laughs, and it will be very pleasing to his heart' " (Wilson, 112).

God also gave his people in the Bible rules to protect them—for example, God commanded them not to eat unclean food. He didn't want his children to get sick. For the same reason, parents still make children wash their hands before eating.

Rules govern our society, and learning to follow the rules as a child makes it much easier to be successful as an adult. For thousands of years, parents have understood this. In the same way, God understands that we must learn to follow his rules. And so he gives us lots of behavioral guidelines for a reason: "that [we] may be successful wherever [we] go."

Wilson, John A. (1967). "The World of Moses" in Everyday Life in Bible Times, ed. M. Severy. Washington, D.C.: National Geographic Society.

For a complete listing of Questions Kids Ask, turn to page 1435.

road that leads to the fords of the Jordan, and as soon as the pursuers had gone out, the gate was shut.

⁸Before the spies lay down for the night, she went up on the roof ⁹and said to them, "I know that the LORD has given this land to you and that a great fear of you has fallen on us, so that all who live in this country are melting in fear because of you. ¹⁰We have heard how the LORD dried up the water of the Red Sea*ᵉ* for you when you came out of Egypt, and what you did to Sihon and Og, the two kings of the Amorites east of the Jordan, whom you completely destroyed.*ᵇ* ¹¹When we heard of it, our hearts melted and everyone's courage failed because of you, for the LORD your God is God in heaven above and on the earth below. ¹²Now then, please swear to me by the LORD that you will show kindness to my family, because I have shown kindness to you. Give me a sure sign ¹³that you will spare the lives of my father and mother, my brothers and sisters, and all who belong to them, and that you will save us from death."

¹⁴"Our lives for your lives!" the men assured her. "If you don't tell what we are doing, we will treat you kindly and faithfully when the LORD gives us the land."

¹⁵So she let them down by a rope through the window, for the house she lived in was part of the city wall. ¹⁶Now she had said to them, "Go to the hills so the pursuers will not find you. Hide yourselves there three days until they return and then go on your way."

¹⁷The men said to her, "This oath you made us swear will not be binding on us ¹⁸unless, when we enter the land, you have tied this scarlet cord in the window through which you let us down, and unless you have brought your father and mother, your brothers and all your family into your house. ¹⁹If anyone goes outside your house into the street, his blood will be on his own head; we will not be responsible. As for anyone who is in the house with you, his blood will be on our head if a hand is laid on him. ²⁰But if you tell what we are doing, we will be released from the oath you made us swear."

²¹"Agreed," she replied. "Let it be as you say." So she sent them away and they departed. And she tied the scarlet cord in the window.

²²When they left, they went into the hills and stayed there three days, until the pursuers had searched all along the road and returned without finding them.

²³Then the two men started back. They went down out of the hills, forded the river and came to Joshua son of Nun and told him everything that had happened to them. ²⁴They said to Joshua, "The LORD has surely given the whole land into our hands; all the people are melting in fear because of us."

Crossing the Jordan

3 Early in the morning Joshua and all the Israelites set out from Shittim and went to the Jordan, where they camped before crossing over. ²After three days the officers went throughout the camp, ³giving orders to the people: "When you see the ark of the covenant of the LORD your God, and the priests, who are Levites, carrying it, you are to move out from your positions and follow it. ⁴Then you will know which way to go, since you have never been this way before. But keep a distance of about a thousand yards*ᶜ* between you and the ark; do not go near it."

⁵Joshua told the people, "Consecrate yourselves, for tomorrow the LORD will do amazing things among you."

⁶Joshua said to the priests, "Take up the ark of the covenant and pass on ahead of the people." So they took it up and went ahead of them.

⁷And the LORD said to Joshua, "Today I will begin to exalt you in the eyes of all Israel, so they may know that I am with you as I was with Moses. ⁸Tell the priests who carry the ark of the covenant: 'When you reach the edge of the Jordan's waters, go and stand in the river.' "

⁹Joshua said to the Israelites, "Come here and listen to the words of the LORD your God. ¹⁰This is how you will know that the living God is among you and that he will certainly drive out before you the Canaanites, Hittites, Hivites, Perizzites, Girgashites, Amorites and Jebusites. ¹¹See, the ark of the covenant of the Lord of all the earth will go into the Jordan ahead of you. ¹²Now then, choose twelve men from the tribes of Israel, one from each tribe. ¹³And as soon as the priests who carry the ark of the LORD—the Lord of all the earth—set foot in the Jordan, its waters flowing downstream will be cut off and stand up in a heap."

ᵃ10 Hebrew *Yam Suph*; that is, Sea of Reeds
ᵇ10 The Hebrew term refers to the irrevocable giving over of things or persons to the LORD, often by totally destroying them.   *ᶜ4* Hebrew *about two thousand cubits* (about 900 meters)

¹⁴So when the people broke camp to cross the Jordan, the priests carrying the ark of the covenant went ahead of them. ¹⁵Now the Jordan is at flood stage all during harvest. Yet as soon as the priests who carried the ark reached the Jordan and their feet touched the water's edge, ¹⁶the water from upstream stopped flowing. It piled up in a heap a great distance away, at a town called Adam in the vicinity of Zarethan, while the water flowing down to the Sea of the Arabah (the Salt Sea*)

was completely cut off. So the people crossed over opposite Jericho. ¹⁷The priests who carried the ark of the covenant of the LORD stood firm on dry ground in the middle of the Jordan, while all Israel passed by until the whole nation had completed the crossing on dry ground.

4 When the whole nation had finished crossing the Jordan, the LORD said to

*16 That is, the Dead Sea

Your Own Personal Skyscraper

DAILY INSIGHT

The next time you drive into a major city, take a look at the skyline. Many cities of the world are recognizable by one-of-a-kind structures that are easily visible from a great distance. The twin towers of the World Trade Center tell you that you're near New York City. The skyscraper that comes to a point could only mean you're in San Francisco looking at the TransAmerica Building. Around the world, great structures like the Eiffel Tower and Big Ben let you know that you're in Paris or London.

You may have never thought of it this way, but every one of these buildings is a concrete, brick, marble, steel and glass memorial to someone. If it weren't for a single visionary who spearheaded the creation of these free-standing monsters, they simply wouldn't exist. Another way of saying this is that every single skyscraper in the world could be wearing someone's name … actually, some of them already do! Each structure reminds passers-by of someone.

Now let's take a drive down your street and survey the "skyline." Of course, your house isn't visible from a great distance, but it *does* have someone's name on it. Your home represents something or someone to every person who drives past. Here's the question for the day: "Who does your house remind people of?"

The only thing standing between the Israelites and their home was the Jordan River. So, just as he had done when they

MONDAY

Passage:
Joshua 3:14–4:7

Verse:
Joshua 4:7b

were faced with the daunting Red Sea, God drew back the water like a curtain and the people walked across on a dry riverbed.

To mark the significance of this amazing miracle, Joshua instructed the tribes to build a monument out of twelve stones from the riverbed. From that day forward, anyone who saw these rocks thought about God. For centuries, dads could bring their children to this site. "Before you were born," they might say, "God opened the way so that our people could walk across the river on dry land. And he gave us our beautiful homeland. And do you know what else?" Children would wait for the inevitable answer, "God also loves us."

Can't you see these dads, hand-in-hand with their sons and daughters, standing there in front of the stones recalling God's goodness?

When your neighbors take their children for a walk and stand in front of your house, what do they say? Who does your place remind them of? Does your home speak to them of your attempts to make a name for yourself, or does it represent a place of welcome and kindness? Does it remind them of the God you love and serve, or is it only a house with your family name on the mailbox?

Put God's name on your house. Let it remind your neighbors of his love and goodness. Impress them with the One who is in the process of building you.

For your next devotional reading, go to page 255.

Joshua, ²"Choose twelve men from among the people, one from each tribe, ³and tell them to take up twelve stones from the middle of the Jordan from right where the priests stood and to carry them over with you and put them down at the place where you stay tonight."

⁴So Joshua called together the twelve men he had appointed from the Israelites, one from each tribe, ⁵and said to them, "Go over before the ark of the LORD your God into the middle of the Jordan. Each of you is to take up a stone on his shoulder, according to the number of the tribes of the Israelites, ⁶to serve as a sign among you. In the future, when your children ask you, 'What do these stones mean?' ⁷tell them that the flow of the Jordan was cut off before the ark of the covenant of the LORD. When it crossed the Jordan, the waters of the Jordan were cut off. These stones are to be a memorial to the people of Israel forever."

⁸So the Israelites did as Joshua commanded them. They took twelve stones from the middle of the Jordan, according to the number of the tribes of the Israelites, as the LORD had told Joshua; and they carried them over with them to their camp, where they put them down. ⁹Joshua set up the twelve stones that had been[a] in the middle of the Jordan at the spot where the priests who carried the ark of the covenant had stood. And they are there to this day.

¹⁰Now the priests who carried the ark remained standing in the middle of the Jordan until everything the LORD had commanded Joshua was done by the people, just as Moses had directed Joshua. The people hurried over, ¹¹and as soon as all of them had crossed, the ark of the LORD and the priests came to the other side while the people watched. ¹²The men of Reuben, Gad and the half-tribe of Manasseh crossed over, armed, in front of the Israelites, as Moses had directed them. ¹³About forty thousand armed for battle crossed over before the LORD to the plains of Jericho for war.

¹⁴That day the LORD exalted Joshua in the sight of all Israel; and they revered him all the days of his life, just as they had revered Moses.

¹⁵Then the LORD said to Joshua, ¹⁶"Command the priests carrying the ark of the Testimony to come up out of the Jordan."

¹⁷So Joshua commanded the priests, "Come up out of the Jordan."

¹⁸And the priests came up out of the river carrying the ark of the covenant of the LORD. No sooner had they set their feet on the dry ground than the waters of the Jordan returned to their place and ran at flood stage as before.

¹⁹On the tenth day of the first month the people went up from the Jordan and camped at Gilgal on the eastern border of Jericho. ²⁰And Joshua set up at Gilgal the twelve stones they had taken out of the Jordan. ²¹He said to the Israelites, "In the future when your descendants ask their fathers, 'What do these stones mean?' ²²tell them, 'Israel crossed the Jordan on dry ground.' ²³For the LORD your God dried up the Jordan before you until you had crossed over. The LORD your God did to the Jordan just what he had done to the Red Sea[b] when he dried it up before us until we had crossed over. ²⁴He did this so that all the peoples of the earth might know that the hand of the LORD is powerful and so that you might always fear the LORD your God."

Circumcision at Gilgal

5 Now when all the Amorite kings west of the Jordan and all the Canaanite kings along the coast heard how the LORD had dried up the Jordan before the Israelites until we had crossed over, their hearts melted and they no longer had the courage to face the Israelites.

²At that time the LORD said to Joshua, "Make flint knives and circumcise the Israelites again." ³So Joshua made flint knives and circumcised the Israelites at Gibeath Haaraloth.[c]

⁴Now this is why he did so: All those who came out of Egypt—all the men of military age—died in the desert on the way after leaving Egypt. ⁵All the people that came out had been circumcised, but all the people born in the desert during the journey from Egypt had not. ⁶The Israelites had moved about in the desert forty years until all the men who were of military age when they left Egypt had died, since they had not obeyed the LORD. For the LORD had sworn to them that they would not see the land that he had solemnly promised their fathers to give us, a land flowing with milk and honey. ⁷So he raised up their sons in their place, and these were the ones Joshua circumcised.

[a]9 Or *Joshua also set up twelve stones*
[b]23 Hebrew *Yam Suph*; that is, Sea of Reeds
[c]3 *Gibeath Haaraloth* means *hill of foreskins.*

They were still uncircumcised because they had not been circumcised on the way. **8**And after the whole nation had been circumcised, they remained where they were in camp until they were healed. **9**Then the LORD said to Joshua, "Today I have rolled away the reproach of Egypt from you." So the place has been called Gilgal*a* to this day.

10On the evening of the fourteenth day of the month, while camped at Gilgal on the plains of Jericho, the Israelites celebrated the Passover. **11**The day after the Passover, that very day, they ate some of the produce of the land: unleavened bread and roasted grain. **12**The manna stopped the day after*b* they ate this food from the land; there was no longer any manna for the Israelites, but that year they ate of the produce of Canaan.

The Fall of Jericho

13Now when Joshua was near Jericho, he looked up and saw a man standing in front of him with a drawn sword in his hand. Joshua went up to him and asked, "Are you for us or for our enemies?"

14"Neither," he replied, "but as commander of the army of the LORD I have now come." Then Joshua fell facedown to the ground in reverence, and asked him, "What message does my Lord*c* have for his servant?"

15The commander of the LORD's army replied, "Take off your sandals, for the place where you are standing is holy." And Joshua did so.

6 Now Jericho was tightly shut up because of the Israelites. No one went out and no one came in.

2Then the LORD said to Joshua, "See, I have delivered Jericho into your hands, along with its king and its fighting men. **3**March around the city once with all the armed men. Do this for six days. **4**Have seven priests carry trumpets of rams' horns in front of the ark. On the seventh day, march around the city seven times, with the priests blowing the trumpets. **5**When you hear them sound a long blast on the trumpets, have all the people give a loud shout; then the wall of the city will collapse and the people will go up, every man straight in."

6So Joshua son of Nun called the priests and said to them, "Take up the ark of the covenant of the LORD and have seven priests carry trumpets in front of it." **7**And he ordered the people, "Advance! March

around the city, with the armed guard going ahead of the ark of the LORD."

8When Joshua had spoken to the people, the seven priests carrying the seven trumpets before the LORD went forward, blowing their trumpets, and the ark of the LORD's covenant followed them. **9**The armed guard marched ahead of the priests who blew the trumpets, and the rear guard followed the ark. All this time the trumpets were sounding. **10**But Joshua had commanded the people, "Do not give a war cry, do not raise your voices, do not say a word until the day I tell you to shout. Then shout!" **11**So he had the ark of the LORD carried around the city, circling it once. Then the people returned to camp and spent the night there.

12Joshua got up early the next morning and the priests took up the ark of the LORD. **13**The seven priests carrying the seven trumpets went forward, marching before the ark of the LORD and blowing the trumpets. The armed men went ahead of them and the rear guard followed the ark of the LORD, while the trumpets kept sounding. **14**So on the second day they marched around the city once and returned to the camp. They did this for six days.

15On the seventh day, they got up at daybreak and marched around the city seven times in the same manner, except that on that day they circled the city seven times. **16**The seventh time around, when the priests sounded the trumpet blast, Joshua commanded the people, "Shout! For the LORD has given you the city! **17**The city and all that is in it are to be devoted*d* to the LORD. Only Rahab the prostitute*e* and all who are with her in her house shall be spared, because she hid the spies we sent. **18**But keep away from the devoted things, so that you will not bring about your own destruction by taking any of them. Otherwise you will make the camp of Israel liable to destruction and bring trouble on it. **19**All the silver and gold and the articles of bronze and iron are sacred to the LORD and must go into his treasury."

20When the trumpets sounded, the people shouted, and at the sound of the trumpet, when the people gave a loud

a9 Gilgal sounds like the Hebrew for *roll.* *b12* Or *the day* *c14* Or *lord* *d17* The Hebrew term refers to the irrevocable giving over of things or persons to the LORD, often by totally destroying them; also in verses 18 and 21. *e17* Or possibly *innkeeper*; also in verses 22 and 25

shout, the wall collapsed; so every man charged straight in, and they took the city. [21]They devoted the city to the LORD and destroyed with the sword every living thing in it—men and women, young and old, cattle, sheep and donkeys.

[22]Joshua said to the two men who had spied out the land, "Go into the prostitute's house and bring her out and all who belong to her, in accordance with your oath to her." [23]So the young men who had done the spying went in and brought out Rahab, her father and mother and brothers and all who belonged to her. They brought out her entire family and put them in a place outside the camp of Israel.

[24]Then they burned the whole city and everything in it, but they put the silver and gold and the articles of bronze and iron into the treasury of the LORD's house. [25]But Joshua spared Rahab the prostitute, with her family and all who belonged to her, because she hid the men Joshua had sent as spies to Jericho—and she lives among the Israelites to this day.

[26]At that time Joshua pronounced this solemn oath: "Cursed before the LORD is the man who undertakes to rebuild this city, Jericho:

"At the cost of his firstborn son
  will he lay its foundations;
at the cost of his youngest
  will he set up its gates."

[27]So the LORD was with Joshua, and his fame spread throughout the land.

Achan's Sin

7 But the Israelites acted unfaithfully in regard to the devoted things[a]; Achan son of Carmi, the son of Zimri,[b] the son of Zerah, of the tribe of Judah, took some of them. So the LORD's anger burned against Israel.

[2]Now Joshua sent men from Jericho to Ai, which is near Beth Aven to the east of Bethel, and told them, "Go up and spy out the region." So the men went up and spied out Ai.

[3]When they returned to Joshua, they said, "Not all the people will have to go up against Ai. Send two or three thousand men to take it and do not weary all the people, for only a few men are there." [4]So about three thousand men went up; but they were routed by the men of Ai, [5]who killed about thirty-six of them. They chased the Israelites from the city gate as

far as the stone quarries[c] and struck them down on the slopes. At this the hearts of the people melted and became like water.

[6]Then Joshua tore his clothes and fell facedown to the ground before the ark of the LORD, remaining there till evening. The elders of Israel did the same, and sprinkled dust on their heads. [7]And Joshua said, "Ah, Sovereign LORD, why did you ever bring this people across the Jordan to deliver us into the hands of the Amorites to destroy us? If only we had been content to stay on the other side of the Jordan! [8]O Lord, what can I say, now that Israel has been routed by its enemies? [9]The Canaanites and the other people of the country will hear about this and they will surround us and wipe out our name from the earth. What then will you do for your own great name?"

[10]The LORD said to Joshua, "Stand up! What are you doing down on your face? [11]Israel has sinned; they have violated my covenant, which I commanded them to keep. They have taken some of the devoted things; they have stolen, they have lied, they have put them with their own possessions. [12]That is why the Israelites cannot stand against their enemies; they turn their backs and run because they have been made liable to destruction. I will not be with you anymore unless you destroy whatever among you is devoted to destruction.

[13]"Go, consecrate the people. Tell them, 'Consecrate yourselves in preparation for tomorrow; for this is what the LORD, the God of Israel, says: That which is devoted is among you, O Israel. You cannot stand against your enemies until you remove it.

[14]" 'In the morning, present yourselves tribe by tribe. The tribe that the LORD takes shall come forward clan by clan; the clan that the LORD takes shall come forward family by family; and the family that the LORD takes shall come forward man by man. [15]He who is caught with the devoted things shall be destroyed by fire, along with all that belongs to him. He has violated the covenant of the LORD and has done a disgraceful thing in Israel!' "

[16]Early the next morning Joshua had Israel come forward by tribes, and Judah

---

[a]1 The Hebrew term refers to the irrevocable giving over of things or persons to the LORD, often by totally destroying them; also in verses 11, 12, 13 and 15.   [b]1 See Septuagint and 1 Chron. 2:6; Hebrew *Zabdi*; also in verses 17 and 18.   [c]5 Or *as far as Shebarim*

was taken. ¹⁷The clans of Judah came forward, and he took the Zerahites. He had the clan of the Zerahites come forward by families, and Zimri was taken. ¹⁸Joshua had his family come forward man by man, and Achan son of Carmi, the son of Zimri, the son of Zerah, of the tribe of Judah, was taken.

¹⁹Then Joshua said to Achan, "My son, give glory to the LORD,ᵃ the God of Israel, and give him the praise.ᵇ Tell me what you have done; do not hide it from me."

²⁰Achan replied, "It is true! I have sinned against the LORD, the God of Israel. This is what I have done: ²¹When I saw in the plunder a beautiful robe from Babylonia,ᶜ two hundred shekelsᵈ of silver and a wedge of gold weighing fifty shekels,ᵉ I coveted them and took them. They

are hidden in the ground inside my tent, with the silver underneath."

²²So Joshua sent messengers, and they ran to the tent, and there it was, hidden in his tent, with the silver underneath. ²³They took the things from the tent, brought them to Joshua and all the Israelites and spread them out before the LORD.

²⁴Then Joshua, together with all Israel, took Achan son of Zerah, the silver, the robe, the gold wedge, his sons and daughters, his cattle, donkeys and sheep, his tent and all that he had, to the Valley of Achor. ²⁵Joshua said, "Why have you

ᵃ19 A solemn charge to tell the truth   ᵇ19 Or *and confess to him*   ᶜ21 Hebrew *Shinar*   ᵈ21 That is, about 5 pounds (about 2.3 kilograms)   ᵉ21 That is, about 1 1/4 pounds (about 0.6 kilogram)

There's No Such Thing as a Secret Sin
Achan, the Disobedient Father

"Achan replied, 'It is true! I have sinned against the LORD, the God of Israel. This is what I have done . . .'" (7:20).

Text: Joshua 7

Achan had participated in one of the more famous victories in the Bible—God's defeat of the fortified city of Jericho. Because this had been such a dramatic display of divine intervention, God told Joshua that the people were not to take any plunder for themselves. The silver, gold and anything else of value was God's and was to be taken to the temple. But Achan couldn't resist, and he hid some of the glittering contraband under his tent.

Achan should have known that no hiding place is secret enough to escape God's vision. After Joshua's quick and intensive investigation, Achan found himself standing accused in the presence of this great leader. Not only was Achan guilty of disobeying God's commands, but his disobedience had also caused the deaths of thirty-six fighting men. His pathetic and public admission of guilt (vv. 20–21) has served as a prototype for thousands throughout the centuries who have been caught in similar treachery.

So Joshua took "Achan . . . the silver, the robe, the gold wedge, his sons and daughters, his cattle, donkeys and sheep, his tent and all that he had, to the Valley of Achor." In front of all the people, Achan and his entire family were killed; his precious possessions were burned, and he himself was buried under a mountain of rocks.

The lesson here is brutally clear. Any dad who doesn't think that his own sin will make an indelible mark on his whole family needs to read Achan's story. God sees everything we do, every sin that we commit in "secret." Sometimes God's judgment rains down on us and on our families like an avalanche, shattering us and them in the process. At other times, sin festers like an infection that destroys from the inside out.

But through the power of God's Spirit, we can spare our families and ourselves from this kind of destruction. Notice that Achan was the only one who disobeyed God's command among the thousands of Israelites who witnessed Jericho's defeat. By confessing our sins (1 John 1:9) and relying on God's strength instead of our own, we can honor God and live worthy of our calling as fathers and as Christians.

Be obedient and faithful. A whole generation's very life depends on it.

For a complete listing of Dads in the Bible, turn to page 1434.

brought this trouble on us? The LORD will bring trouble on you today."

Then all Israel stoned him, and after they had stoned the rest, they burned them. **26**Over Achan they heaped up a large pile of rocks, which remains to this day. Then the LORD turned from his fierce anger. Therefore that place has been called the Valley of Achor*a* ever since.

Ai Destroyed

8 Then the LORD said to Joshua, "Do not be afraid; do not be discouraged. Take the whole army with you, and go up and attack Ai. For I have delivered into your hands the king of Ai, his people, his city and his land. **2**You shall do to Ai and its king as you did to Jericho and its king, except that you may carry off their plunder and livestock for yourselves. Set an ambush behind the city."

3So Joshua and the whole army moved out to attack Ai. He chose thirty thousand of his best fighting men and sent them out at night **4**with these orders: "Listen carefully. You are to set an ambush behind the city. Don't go very far from it. All of you be on the alert. **5**I and all those with me will advance on the city, and when the men come out against us, as they did before, we will flee from them. **6**They will pursue us until we have lured them away from the city, for they will say, 'They are running away from us as they did before.' So when we flee from them, **7**you are to rise up from ambush and take the city. The LORD your God will give it into your hand. **8**When you have taken the city, set it on fire. Do what the LORD has commanded. See to it; you have my orders."

9Then Joshua sent them off, and they went to the place of ambush and lay in wait between Bethel and Ai, to the west of Ai—but Joshua spent that night with the people.

10Early the next morning Joshua mustered his men, and he and the leaders of Israel marched before them to Ai. **11**The entire force that was with him marched up and approached the city and arrived in front of it. They set up camp north of Ai, with the valley between them and the city. **12**Joshua had taken about five thousand men and set them in ambush between Bethel and Ai, to the west of the city. **13**They had the soldiers take up their positions—all those in the camp to the north of the city and the ambush to the west of it. That night Joshua went into the valley.

14When the king of Ai saw this, he and all the men of the city hurried out early in the morning to meet Israel in battle at a certain place overlooking the Arabah. But he did not know that an ambush had been set against him behind the city. **15**Joshua and all Israel let themselves be driven back before them, and they fled toward the desert. **16**All the men of Ai were called to pursue them, and they pursued Joshua and were lured away from the city. **17**Not a man remained in Ai or Bethel who did not go after Israel. They left the city open and went in pursuit of Israel.

18Then the LORD said to Joshua, "Hold out toward Ai the javelin that is in your hand, for into your hand I will deliver the city." So Joshua held out his javelin toward Ai. **19**As soon as he did this, the men in the ambush rose quickly from their position and rushed forward. They entered the city and captured it and quickly set it on fire.

20The men of Ai looked back and saw the smoke of the city rising against the sky, but they had no chance to escape in any direction, for the Israelites who had been fleeing toward the desert had turned back against their pursuers. **21**For when Joshua and all Israel saw that the ambush had taken the city and that smoke was going up from the city, they turned around and attacked the men of Ai. **22**The men of the ambush also came out of the city against them, so that they were caught in the middle, with Israelites on both sides. Israel cut them down, leaving them neither survivors nor fugitives. **23**But they took the king of Ai alive and brought him to Joshua.

24When Israel had finished killing all the men of Ai in the fields and in the desert where they had chased them, and when every one of them had been put to the sword, all the Israelites returned to Ai and killed those who were in it. **25**Twelve thousand men and women fell that day— all the people of Ai. **26**For Joshua did not draw back the hand that held out his javelin until he had destroyed*b* all who lived in Ai. **27**But Israel did carry off for themselves the livestock and plunder of this city, as the LORD had instructed Joshua.

28So Joshua burned Ai and made it a permanent heap of ruins, a desolate place to this day. **29**He hung the king of Ai on a

---

a26 Achor means *trouble.* *b26* The Hebrew term refers to the irrevocable giving over of things or persons to the LORD, often by totally destroying them.

tree and left him there until evening. At sunset, Joshua ordered them to take his body from the tree and throw it down at the entrance of the city gate. And they raised a large pile of rocks over it, which remains to this day.

The Covenant Renewed at Mount Ebal

30Then Joshua built on Mount Ebal an altar to the LORD, the God of Israel, **31**as Moses the servant of the LORD had commanded the Israelites. He built it according to what is written in the Book of the Law of Moses—an altar of uncut stones, on which no iron tool had been used. On it they offered to the LORD burnt offerings and sacrificed fellowship offerings.*a* **32**There, in the presence of the Israelites, Joshua copied on stones the law of Moses, which he had written. **33**All Israel, aliens and citizens alike, with their elders, officials and judges, were standing on both sides of the ark of the covenant of the LORD, facing those who carried it— the priests, who were Levites. Half of the people stood in front of Mount Gerizim and half of them in front of Mount Ebal, as Moses the servant of the LORD had formerly commanded when he gave instructions to bless the people of Israel.

34Afterward, Joshua read all the words of the law—the blessings and the curses— just as it is written in the Book of the Law. **35**There was not a word of all that Moses had commanded that Joshua did not read to the whole assembly of Israel, including the women and children, and the aliens who lived among them.

The Gibeonite Deception

9 Now when all the kings west of the Jordan heard about these things—those in the hill country, in the western foothills, and along the entire coast of the Great Sea*b* as far as Lebanon (the kings of the Hittites, Amorites, Canaanites, Perizzites, Hivites and Jebusites)— **2**they came together to make war against Joshua and Israel.

3However, when the people of Gibeon heard what Joshua had done to Jericho and Ai, **4**they resorted to a ruse: They went as a delegation whose donkeys were loaded*c* with worn-out sacks and old wineskins, cracked and mended. **5**The men put worn and patched sandals on their feet and wore old clothes. All the bread of their food supply was dry and moldy. **6**Then they went to Joshua in the camp at Gilgal and said to him and the men of Israel, "We have come from a distant country; make a treaty with us."

7The men of Israel said to the Hivites, "But perhaps you live near us. How then can we make a treaty with you?"

8"We are your servants," they said to Joshua.

But Joshua asked, "Who are you and where do you come from?"

9They answered: "Your servants have come from a very distant country because of the fame of the LORD your God. For we have heard reports of him: all that he did in Egypt, **10**and all that he did to the two kings of the Amorites east of the Jordan— Sihon king of Heshbon, and Og king of Bashan, who reigned in Ashtaroth. **11**And our elders and all those living in our country said to us, 'Take provisions for your journey; go and meet them and say to them, "We are your servants; make a treaty with us." ' **12**This bread of ours was warm when we packed it at home on the day we left to come to you. But now see how dry and moldy it is. **13**And these wineskins that we filled were new, but see how cracked they are. And our clothes and sandals are worn out by the very long journey."

14The men of Israel sampled their provisions but did not inquire of the LORD. **15**Then Joshua made a treaty of peace with them to let them live, and the leaders of the assembly ratified it by oath.

16Three days after they made the treaty with the Gibeonites, the Israelites heard that they were neighbors, living near them. **17**So the Israelites set out and on the third day came to their cities: Gibeon, Kephirah, Beeroth and Kiriath Jearim. **18**But the Israelites did not attack them, because the leaders of the assembly had sworn an oath to them by the LORD, the God of Israel.

The whole assembly grumbled against the leaders, **19**but all the leaders answered, "We have given them our oath by the LORD, the God of Israel, and we cannot touch them now. **20**This is what we will do to them: We will let them live, so that wrath will not fall on us for breaking the oath we swore to them." **21**They continued, "Let them live, but let them be woodcutters and water carriers for the entire

a31 Traditionally *peace offerings*   *b1* That is, the Mediterranean   *c4* Most Hebrew manuscripts; some Hebrew manuscripts, Vulgate and Syriac (see also Septuagint) *They prepared provisions and loaded their donkeys*

community." So the leaders' promise to them was kept.

²²Then Joshua summoned the Gibeonites and said, "Why did you deceive us by saying, 'We live a long way from you,' while actually you live near us? ²³You are now under a curse: You will never cease to serve as woodcutters and water carriers for the house of my God."

²⁴They answered Joshua, "Your servants were clearly told how the LORD your God had commanded his servant Moses to give you the whole land and to wipe out all its inhabitants from before you. So we feared for our lives because of you, and that is why we did this. ²⁵We are now in your hands. Do to us whatever seems good and right to you."

²⁶So Joshua saved them from the Israelites, and they did not kill them. ²⁷That day he made the Gibeonites woodcutters and water carriers for the community and for the altar of the LORD at the place the LORD would choose. And that is what they are to this day.

The Sun Stands Still

10 Now Adoni-Zedek king of Jerusalem heard that Joshua had taken Ai and totally destroyed[a] it, doing to Ai and its king as he had done to Jericho and its king, and that the people of Gibeon had made a treaty of peace with Israel and were living near them. ²He and his people were very much alarmed at this, because Gibeon was an important city, like one of the royal cities; it was larger than Ai, and all its men were good fighters. ³So Adoni-Zedek king of Jerusalem appealed to Hoham king of Hebron, Piram king of Jarmuth, Japhia king of Lachish and Debir king of Eglon. ⁴"Come up and help me attack Gibeon," he said, "because it has made peace with Joshua and the Israelites."

⁵Then the five kings of the Amorites—the kings of Jerusalem, Hebron, Jarmuth, Lachish and Eglon—joined forces. They moved up with all their troops and took up positions against Gibeon and attacked it.

⁶The Gibeonites then sent word to Joshua in the camp at Gilgal: "Do not abandon your servants. Come up to us quickly and save us! Help us, because all the Amorite kings from the hill country have joined forces against us."

⁷So Joshua marched up from Gilgal with his entire army, including all the best

fighting men. ⁸The LORD said to Joshua, "Do not be afraid of them; I have given them into your hand. Not one of them will be able to withstand you."

⁹After an all-night march from Gilgal, Joshua took them by surprise. ¹⁰The LORD threw them into confusion before Israel, who defeated them in a great victory at Gibeon. Israel pursued them along the road going up to Beth Horon and cut them down all the way to Azekah and Makkedah. ¹¹As they fled before Israel on the road down from Beth Horon to Azekah, the LORD hurled large hailstones down on them from the sky, and more of them died from the hailstones than were killed by the swords of the Israelites.

¹²On the day the LORD gave the Amorites over to Israel, Joshua said to the LORD in the presence of Israel:

"O sun, stand still over Gibeon,
    O moon, over the Valley of Aijalon."
¹³So the sun stood still,
    and the moon stopped,
    till the nation avenged itself on[b] its
        enemies,

as it is written in the Book of Jashar.

The sun stopped in the middle of the sky and delayed going down about a full day. ¹⁴There has never been a day like it before or since, a day when the LORD listened to a man. Surely the LORD was fighting for Israel!

¹⁵Then Joshua returned with all Israel to the camp at Gilgal.

Five Amorite Kings Killed

¹⁶Now the five kings had fled and hidden in the cave at Makkedah. ¹⁷When Joshua was told that the five kings had been found hiding in the cave at Makkedah, ¹⁸he said, "Roll large rocks up to the mouth of the cave, and post some men there to guard it. ¹⁹But don't stop! Pursue your enemies, attack them from the rear and don't let them reach their cities, for the LORD your God has given them into your hand."

²⁰So Joshua and the Israelites destroyed them completely—almost to a man—but the few who were left reached their fortified cities. ²¹The whole army then returned safely to Joshua in the camp at

---

[a]1 The Hebrew term refers to the irrevocable giving over of things or persons to the LORD, often by totally destroying them; also in verses 28, 35, 37, 39 and 40.   [b]13 Or *nation triumphed over*

Makkedah, and no one uttered a word against the Israelites.

²²Joshua said, "Open the mouth of the cave and bring those five kings out to me." ²³So they brought the five kings out of the cave—the kings of Jerusalem, Hebron, Jarmuth, Lachish and Eglon. ²⁴When they had brought these kings to Joshua, he summoned all the men of Israel and said to the army commanders who had come with him, "Come here and put your feet on the necks of these kings." So they came forward and placed their feet on their necks.

²⁵Joshua said to them, "Do not be afraid; do not be discouraged. Be strong and courageous. This is what the LORD will do to all the enemies you are going to fight." ²⁶Then Joshua struck and killed the kings and hung them on five trees, and they were left hanging on the trees until evening.

²⁷At sunset Joshua gave the order and they took them down from the trees and threw them into the cave where they had been hiding. At the mouth of the cave they placed large rocks, which are there to this day.

²⁸That day Joshua took Makkedah. He put the city and its king to the sword and totally destroyed everyone in it. He left no survivors. And he did to the king of Makkedah as he had done to the king of Jericho.

Southern Cities Conquered

²⁹Then Joshua and all Israel with him moved on from Makkedah to Libnah and attacked it. ³⁰The LORD also gave that city and its king into Israel's hand. The city and everyone in it Joshua put to the sword. He left no survivors there. And he did to its king as he had done to the king of Jericho.

³¹Then Joshua and all Israel with him moved on from Libnah to Lachish; he took up positions against it and attacked it. ³²The LORD handed Lachish over to Israel, and Joshua took it on the second day. The city and everyone in it he put to the sword, just as he had done to Libnah. ³³Meanwhile, Horam king of Gezer had come up to help Lachish, but Joshua defeated him and his army—until no survivors were left.

³⁴Then Joshua and all Israel with him moved on from Lachish to Eglon; they took up positions against it and attacked it. ³⁵They captured it that same day and put it to the sword and totally destroyed everyone in it, just as they had done to Lachish.

³⁶Then Joshua and all Israel with him went up from Eglon to Hebron and attacked it. ³⁷They took the city and put it to the sword, together with its king, its villages and everyone in it. They left no survivors. Just as at Eglon, they totally destroyed it and everyone in it.

³⁸Then Joshua and all Israel with him turned around and attacked Debir. ³⁹They took the city, its king and its villages, and put them to the sword. Everyone in it they totally destroyed. They left no survivors. They did to Debir and its king as they had done to Libnah and its king and to Hebron.

⁴⁰So Joshua subdued the whole region, including the hill country, the Negev, the western foothills and the mountain slopes, together with all their kings. He left no survivors. He totally destroyed all who breathed, just as the LORD, the God of Israel, had commanded. ⁴¹Joshua subdued them from Kadesh Barnea to Gaza and from the whole region of Goshen to Gibeon. ⁴²All these kings and their lands Joshua conquered in one campaign, because the LORD, the God of Israel, fought for Israel.

⁴³Then Joshua returned with all Israel to the camp at Gilgal.

Northern Kings Defeated

11 When Jabin king of Hazor heard of this, he sent word to Jobab king of Madon, to the kings of Shimron and Acshaph, ²and to the northern kings who were in the mountains, in the Arabah south of Kinnereth, in the western foothills and in Naphoth Dor*a* on the west; ³to the Canaanites in the east and west; to the Amorites, Hittites, Perizzites and Jebusites in the hill country; and to the Hivites below Hermon in the region of Mizpah. ⁴They came out with all their troops and a large number of horses and chariots—a huge army, as numerous as the sand on the seashore. ⁵All these kings joined forces and made camp together at the Waters of Merom, to fight against Israel.

⁶The LORD said to Joshua, "Do not be afraid of them, because by this time tomorrow I will hand all of them over to Israel, slain. You are to hamstring their horses and burn their chariots."

⁷So Joshua and his whole army came

a2 Or in the heights of Dor

against them suddenly at the Waters of Merom and attacked them, [8]and the LORD gave them into the hand of Israel. They defeated them and pursued them all the way to Greater Sidon, to Misrephoth Maim, and to the Valley of Mizpah on the east, until no survivors were left. [9]Joshua did to them as the LORD had directed: He hamstrung their horses and burned their chariots.

[10]At that time Joshua turned back and captured Hazor and put its king to the sword. (Hazor had been the head of all these kingdoms.) [11]Everyone in it they put to the sword. They totally destroyed[a] them, not sparing anything that breathed, and he burned up Hazor itself.

[12]Joshua took all these royal cities and their kings and put them to the sword. He totally destroyed them, as Moses the servant of the LORD had commanded. [13]Yet Israel did not burn any of the cities built on their mounds—except Hazor, which Joshua burned. [14]The Israelites carried off for themselves all the plunder and livestock of these cities, but all the people they put to the sword until they completely destroyed them, not sparing anyone that breathed. [15]As the LORD commanded his servant Moses, so Moses commanded Joshua, and Joshua did it; he left nothing undone of all that the LORD commanded Moses.

[16]So Joshua took this entire land: the hill country, all the Negev, the whole region of Goshen, the western foothills, the Arabah and the mountains of Israel with their foothills, [17]from Mount Halak, which rises toward Seir, to Baal Gad in the Valley of Lebanon below Mount Hermon. He captured all their kings and struck them down, putting them to death. [18]Joshua waged war against all these kings for a long time. [19]Except for the Hivites living in Gibeon, not one city made a treaty of peace with the Israelites, who took them all in battle. [20]For it was the LORD himself who hardened their hearts to wage war against Israel, so that he might destroy them totally, exterminating them without mercy, as the LORD had commanded Moses.

[21]At that time Joshua went and destroyed the Anakites from the hill country: from Hebron, Debir and Anab, from all the hill country of Judah, and from all the hill country of Israel. Joshua totally destroyed them and their towns. [22]No Anakites were left in Israelite territory; only in Gaza, Gath and Ashdod did any survive. [23]So Joshua took the entire land, just as the LORD had directed Moses, and he gave it as an inheritance to Israel according to their tribal divisions.

Then the land had rest from war.

List of Defeated Kings

12 These are the kings of the land whom the Israelites had defeated and whose territory they took over east of the Jordan, from the Arnon Gorge to Mount Hermon, including all the eastern side of the Arabah:

[2]Sihon king of the Amorites,
who reigned in Heshbon. He ruled from Aroer on the rim of the Arnon Gorge—from the middle of the gorge—to the Jabbok River, which is the border of the Ammonites. This included half of Gilead. [3]He also ruled over the eastern Arabah from the Sea of Kinnereth[b] to the Sea of the Arabah (the Salt Sea[c]), to Beth Jeshimoth, and then southward below the slopes of Pisgah.

[4]And the territory of Og king of Bashan, one of the last of the Rephaites, who reigned in Ashtaroth and Edrei. [5]He ruled over Mount Hermon, Salecah, all of Bashan to the border of the people of Geshur and Maacah, and half of Gilead to the border of Sihon king of Heshbon.

[6]Moses, the servant of the LORD, and the Israelites conquered them. And Moses the servant of the LORD gave their land to the Reubenites, the Gadites and the half-tribe of Manasseh to be their possession.

[7]These are the kings of the land that Joshua and the Israelites conquered on the west side of the Jordan, from Baal Gad in the Valley of Lebanon to Mount Halak, which rises toward Seir (their lands Joshua gave as an inheritance to the tribes of Israel according to their tribal divisions— [8]the hill country, the western foothills, the Arabah, the mountain slopes, the desert and the Negev—the lands of the Hittites, Amorites, Canaanites, Perizzites, Hivites and Jebusites):

[9]the king of Jericho   one
the king of Ai (near Bethel)   one

---

[a]11 The Hebrew term refers to the irrevocable giving over of things or persons to the LORD, often by totally destroying them; also in verses 12, 20 and 21.   [b]3 That is, Galilee   [c]3 That is, the Dead Sea

¹⁰the king of Jerusalem   one
    the king of Hebron   one
¹¹the king of Jarmuth   one
    the king of Lachish   one
¹²the king of Eglon   one
    the king of Gezer   one
¹³the king of Debir   one
    the king of Geder   one
¹⁴the king of Hormah   one
    the king of Arad   one
¹⁵the king of Libnah   one
    the king of Adullam   one
¹⁶the king of Makkedah   one
    the king of Bethel   one
¹⁷the king of Tappuah   one
    the king of Hepher   one
¹⁸the king of Aphek   one
    the king of Lasharon   one
¹⁹the king of Madon   one
    the king of Hazor   one
²⁰the king of Shimron Meron   one
    the king of Acshaph   one
²¹the king of Taanach   one
    the king of Megiddo   one
²²the king of Kedesh   one
    the king of Jokneam in Carmel   one
²³the king of Dor
    (in Naphoth Dor^a)   one
    the king of Goyim in Gilgal   one
²⁴the king of Tirzah   one
thirty-one kings in all.

Land Still to Be Taken

13 When Joshua was old and well advanced in years, the LORD said to him, "You are very old, and there are still very large areas of land to be taken over.

²"This is the land that remains: all the regions of the Philistines and Geshurites: ³from the Shihor River on the east of Egypt to the territory of Ekron on the north, all of it counted as Canaanite (the territory of the five Philistine rulers in Gaza, Ashdod, Ashkelon, Gath and Ekron—that of the Avvites); ⁴from the south, all the land of the Canaanites, from Arah of the Sidonians as far as Aphek, the region of the Amorites, ⁵the area of the Gebalites^b; and all Lebanon to the east, from Baal Gad below Mount Hermon to Lebo^c Hamath.

⁶"As for all the inhabitants of the mountain regions from Lebanon to Misrephoth Maim, that is, all the Sidonians, I myself will drive them out before the Israelites. Be sure to allocate this land to Israel for an inheritance, as I have instructed you,

⁷and divide it as an inheritance among the nine tribes and half of the tribe of Manasseh."

Division of the Land East of the Jordan

⁸The other half of Manasseh,^d the Reubenites and the Gadites had received the inheritance that Moses had given them east of the Jordan, as he, the servant of the LORD, had assigned it to them.

⁹It extended from Aroer on the rim of the Arnon Gorge, and from the town in the middle of the gorge, and included the whole plateau of Medeba as far as Dibon, ¹⁰and all the towns of Sihon king of the Amorites, who ruled in Heshbon, out to the border of the Ammonites. ¹¹It also included Gilead, the territory of the people of Geshur and Maacah, all of Mount Hermon and all Bashan as far as Salecah— ¹²that is, the whole kingdom of Og in Bashan, who had reigned in Ashtaroth and Edrei and had survived as one of the last of the Rephaites. Moses had defeated them and taken over their land. ¹³But the Israelites did not drive out the people of Geshur and Maacah, so they continue to live among the Israelites to this day.

¹⁴But to the tribe of Levi he gave no inheritance, since the offerings made by fire to the LORD, the God of Israel, are their inheritance, as he promised them.

¹⁵This is what Moses had given to the tribe of Reuben, clan by clan:

¹⁶The territory from Aroer on the rim of the Arnon Gorge, and from the town in the middle of the gorge, and the whole plateau past Medeba ¹⁷to Heshbon and all its towns on the plateau, including Dibon, Bamoth Baal, Beth Baal Meon, ¹⁸Jahaz, Kedemoth, Mephaath, ¹⁹Kiriathaim, Sibmah, Zereth Shahar on the hill in the valley, ²⁰Beth Peor, the slopes of Pisgah, and Beth Jeshimoth ²¹—all the towns on the plateau and the entire realm of Sihon king of the Amorites, who ruled at Heshbon. Moses had defeated him and the Midianite chiefs, Evi, Rekem, Zur, Hur and Reba—princes allied with Sihon—who lived in that

---

^a23 Or *in the heights of Dor* ^b5 That is, the area of Byblos ^c5 Or *to the entrance to* ^d8 Hebrew *With it* (that is, with the other half of Manasseh)

country. ²²In addition to those slain in battle, the Israelites had put to the sword Balaam son of Beor, who practiced divination. ²³The boundary of the Reubenites was the bank of the Jordan. These towns and their villages were the inheritance of the Reubenites, clan by clan.

²⁴This is what Moses had given to the tribe of Gad, clan by clan:

²⁵The territory of Jazer, all the towns of Gilead and half the Ammonite country as far as Aroer, near Rabbah; ²⁶and from Heshbon to Ramath Mizpah and Betonim, and from Mahanaim to the territory of Debir; ²⁷and in the valley, Beth Haram, Beth Nimrah, Succoth and Zaphon with the rest of the realm of Sihon king of Heshbon (the east side of the Jordan, the territory up to the end of the Sea of Kinnereth*ª*). ²⁸These towns and their villages were the inheritance of the Gadites, clan by clan.

²⁹This is what Moses had given to the half-tribe of Manasseh, that is, to half the family of the descendants of Manasseh, clan by clan:

³⁰The territory extending from Mahanaim and including all of Bashan, the entire realm of Og king of Bashan—all the settlements of Jair in Bashan, sixty towns, ³¹half of Gilead, and Ashtaroth and Edrei (the royal cities of Og in Bashan). This was for the descendants of Makir son of Manasseh—for half of the sons of Makir, clan by clan.

³²This is the inheritance Moses had given when he was in the plains of Moab across the Jordan east of Jericho. ³³But to the tribe of Levi, Moses had given no inheritance; the LORD, the God of Israel, is their inheritance, as he promised them.

Division of the Land West of the Jordan

14 Now these are the areas the Israelites received as an inheritance in the land of Canaan, which Eleazar the priest, Joshua son of Nun and the heads of the tribal clans of Israel allotted to them. ²Their inheritances were assigned by lot to the nine-and-a-half tribes, as the LORD had commanded through Moses. ³Moses had granted the two-and-a-half tribes their inheritance east of the Jordan but had not granted the Levites an inheritance among

the rest, ⁴for the sons of Joseph had become two tribes—Manasseh and Ephraim. The Levites received no share of the land but only towns to live in, with pasturelands for their flocks and herds. ⁵So the Israelites divided the land, just as the LORD had commanded Moses.

Hebron Given to Caleb

⁶Now the men of Judah approached Joshua at Gilgal, and Caleb son of Jephunneh the Kenizzite said to him, "You know what the LORD said to Moses the man of God at Kadesh Barnea about you and me. ⁷I was forty years old when Moses the servant of the LORD sent me from Kadesh Barnea to explore the land. And I brought him back a report according to my convictions, ⁸but my brothers who went up with me made the hearts of the people melt with fear. I, however, followed the LORD my God wholeheartedly. ⁹So on that day Moses swore to me, 'The land on which your feet have walked will be your inheritance and that of your children forever, because you have followed the LORD my God wholeheartedly.'*ᵇ*

¹⁰"Now then, just as the LORD promised, he has kept me alive for forty-five years since the time he said this to Moses, while Israel moved about in the desert. So here I am today, eighty-five years old! ¹¹I am still as strong today as the day Moses sent me out; I'm just as vigorous to go out to battle now as I was then. ¹²Now give me this hill country that the LORD promised me that day. You yourself heard then that the Anakites were there and their cities were large and fortified, but, the LORD helping me, I will drive them out just as he said."

¹³Then Joshua blessed Caleb son of Jephunneh and gave him Hebron as his inheritance. ¹⁴So Hebron has belonged to Caleb son of Jephunneh the Kenizzite ever since, because he followed the LORD, the God of Israel, wholeheartedly. ¹⁵(Hebron used to be called Kiriath Arba after Arba, who was the greatest man among the Anakites.)

Then the land had rest from war.

Allotment for Judah

15 The allotment for the tribe of Judah, clan by clan, extended down to the territory of Edom, to the Desert of Zin in the extreme south.

²Their southern boundary started

ª27 That is, Galilee   ᵇ9 Deut. 1:36

from the bay at the southern end of the Salt Sea,[a] [3]crossed south of Scorpion[b] Pass, continued on to Zin and went over to the south of Kadesh Barnea. Then it ran past Hezron up to Addar and curved around to Karka. [4]It then passed along to Azmon and joined the Wadi of Egypt, ending at the sea. This is their[c] southern boundary.

[5]The eastern boundary is the Salt Sea as far as the mouth of the Jordan.

The northern boundary started from the bay of the sea at the mouth of the Jordan, [6]went up to Beth Hoglah and continued north of Beth Arabah to the Stone of Bohan son of Reuben. [7]The boundary then went up to Debir from the Valley of Achor and turned north to Gilgal, which faces the Pass of Adummim south of the gorge. It continued along to the waters of En Shemesh and came out at En Rogel. [8]Then it ran up the Valley of Ben Hinnom along the southern slope of the Jebusite city (that is, Jerusalem). From there it climbed to the top of the hill west of the Hinnom Valley at the northern end of the Valley of Rephaim. [9]From the hilltop the boundary headed toward the spring of the waters of Nephtoah, came out at the towns of Mount Ephron and went down toward Baalah (that is, Kiriath Jearim). [10]Then it curved westward from Baalah to Mount Seir, ran along the northern slope of Mount Jearim (that is, Kesalon), continued down to Beth Shemesh and crossed to Timnah. [11]It went to the northern slope of Ekron, turned toward Shikkeron, passed along to Mount Baalah and reached Jabneel. The boundary ended at the sea.

[12]The western boundary is the coastline of the Great Sea.[d]

These are the boundaries around the people of Judah by their clans.

[13]In accordance with the LORD's command to him, Joshua gave to Caleb son of Jephunneh a portion in Judah—Kiriath Arba, that is, Hebron. (Arba was the forefather of Anak.) [14]From Hebron Caleb drove out the three Anakites—Sheshai, Ahiman and Talmai—descendants of Anak. [15]From there he marched against the people living in Debir (formerly called Kiriath Sepher). [16]And Caleb said, "I will give my daughter Acsah in marriage to the

man who attacks and captures Kiriath Sepher." [17]Othniel son of Kenaz, Caleb's brother, took it; so Caleb gave his daughter Acsah to him in marriage. [18]One day when she came to Othniel, she urged him[e] to ask her father for a field. When she got off her donkey, Caleb asked her, "What can I do for you?"

[19]She replied, "Do me a special favor. Since you have given me land in the Negev, give me also springs of water." So Caleb gave her the upper and lower springs.

[20]This is the inheritance of the tribe of Judah, clan by clan:

[21]The southernmost towns of the tribe of Judah in the Negev toward the boundary of Edom were:

Kabzeel, Eder, Jagur, [22]Kinah, Dimonah, Adadah, [23]Kedesh, Hazor, Ithnan, [24]Ziph, Telem, Bealoth, [25]Hazor Hadattah, Kerioth Hezron (that is, Hazor), [26]Amam, Shema, Moladah, [27]Hazar Gaddah, Heshmon, Beth Pelet, [28]Hazar Shual, Beersheba, Biziothiah, [29]Baalah, Iim, Ezem, [30]Eltolad, Kesil, Hormah, [31]Ziklag, Madmannah, Sansannah, [32]Lebaoth, Shilhim, Ain and Rimmon—a total of twenty-nine towns and their villages.

[33]In the western foothills:

Eshtaol, Zorah, Ashnah, [34]Zanoah, En Gannim, Tappuah, Enam, [35]Jarmuth, Adullam, Socoh, Azekah, [36]Shaaraim, Adithaim and Gederah (or Gederothaim)[f]—fourteen towns and their villages.

[37]Zenan, Hadashah, Migdal Gad, [38]Dilean, Mizpah, Joktheel, [39]Lachish, Bozkath, Eglon, [40]Cabbon, Lahmas, Kitlish, [41]Gederoth, Beth Dagon, Naamah and Makkedah—sixteen towns and their villages.

[42]Libnah, Ether, Ashan, [43]Iphtah, Ashnah, Nezib, [44]Keilah, Aczib and Mareshah—nine towns and their villages.

[45]Ekron, with its surrounding settlements and villages; [46]west of Ekron, all that were in the vicinity of Ashdod, together with their villages; [47]Ashdod, its surrounding settle-

---

[a]2 That is, the Dead Sea; also in verse 5   [b]3 Hebrew *Akrabbim*   [c]4 Hebrew *your*   [d]12 That is, the Mediterranean; also in verse 47   [e]18 Hebrew and some Septuagint manuscripts; other Septuagint manuscripts (see also note at Judges 1:14) *Othniel, he urged her*   [f]36 Or *Gederah and Gederothaim*

ments and villages; and Gaza, its settlements and villages, as far as the Wadi of Egypt and the coastline of the Great Sea.

⁴⁸In the hill country:

Shamir, Jattir, Socoh, ⁴⁹Dannah, Kiriath Sannah (that is, Debir), ⁵⁰Anab, Eshtemoh, Anim, ⁵¹Goshen, Holon and Giloh—eleven towns and their villages.

⁵²Arab, Dumah, Eshan, ⁵³Janim, Beth Tappuah, Aphekah, ⁵⁴Humtah, Kiriath Arba (that is, Hebron) and Zior—nine towns and their villages.

⁵⁵Maon, Carmel, Ziph, Juttah, ⁵⁶Jezreel, Jokdeam, Zanoah, ⁵⁷Kain, Gibeah and Timnah—ten towns and their villages.

⁵⁸Halhul, Beth Zur, Gedor, ⁵⁹Maarath, Beth Anoth and Eltekon—six towns and their villages.

⁶⁰Kiriath Baal (that is, Kiriath Jearim) and Rabbah—two towns and their villages.

⁶¹In the desert:

Beth Arabah, Middin, Secacah, ⁶²Nibshan, the City of Salt and En Gedi—six towns and their villages.

⁶³Judah could not dislodge the Jebusites, who were living in Jerusalem; to this day the Jebusites live there with the people of Judah.

Allotment for Ephraim and Manasseh

16 The allotment for Joseph began at the Jordan of Jericho,ᵃ east of the waters of Jericho, and went up from there through the desert into the hill country of Bethel. ²It went on from Bethel (that is, Luz),ᵇ crossed over to the territory of the Arkites in Ataroth, ³descended westward to the territory of the Japhletites as far as the region of Lower Beth Horon and on to Gezer, ending at the sea.

⁴So Manasseh and Ephraim, the descendants of Joseph, received their inheritance.

⁵This was the territory of Ephraim, clan by clan:

The boundary of their inheritance went from Ataroth Addar in the east to Upper Beth Horon ⁶and continued to the sea. From Micmethath on the north it curved eastward to Taanath Shiloh, passing by it to Janoah on the east. ⁷Then it went down from Janoah to Ataroth and Naarah, touched

Jericho and came out at the Jordan. ⁸From Tappuah the border went west to the Kanah Ravine and ended at the sea. This was the inheritance of the tribe of the Ephraimites, clan by clan. ⁹It also included all the towns and their villages that were set aside for the Ephraimites within the inheritance of the Manassites.

¹⁰They did not dislodge the Canaanites living in Gezer; to this day the Canaanites live among the people of Ephraim but are required to do forced labor.

17 This was the allotment for the tribe of Manasseh as Joseph's firstborn, that is, for Makir, Manasseh's firstborn. Makir was the ancestor of the Gileadites, who had received Gilead and Bashan because the Makirites were great soldiers. ²So this allotment was for the rest of the people of Manasseh—the clans of Abiezer, Helek, Asriel, Shechem, Hepher and Shemida. These are the other male descendants of Manasseh son of Joseph by their clans.

³Now Zelophehad son of Hepher, the son of Gilead, the son of Makir, the son of Manasseh, had no sons but only daughters, whose names were Mahlah, Noah, Hoglah, Milcah and Tirzah. ⁴They went to Eleazar the priest, Joshua son of Nun, and the leaders and said, "The LORD commanded Moses to give us an inheritance among our brothers." So Joshua gave them an inheritance along with the brothers of their father, according to the LORD's command. ⁵Manasseh's share consisted of ten tracts of land besides Gilead and Bashan east of the Jordan, ⁶because the daughters of the tribe of Manasseh received an inheritance among the sons. The land of Gilead belonged to the rest of the descendants of Manasseh.

⁷The territory of Manasseh extended from Asher to Micmethath east of Shechem. The boundary ran southward from there to include the people living at En Tappuah. ⁸Manasseh had the land of Tappuah, but Tappuah itself, on the boundary of Manasseh, belonged to the Ephraimites.) ⁹Then the boundary continued south to the Kanah Ravine. There were towns belonging to Ephraim lying among the towns of Manasseh, but the boundary of Manasseh was the northern side of the ravine and

ended at the sea. **10**On the south the land belonged to Ephraim, on the north to Manasseh. The territory of Manasseh reached the sea and bordered Asher on the north and Issachar on the east.

11Within Issachar and Asher, Manasseh also had Beth Shan, Ibleam and the people of Dor, Endor, Taanach and Megiddo, together with their surrounding settlements (the third in the list is Naphoth*a*).

12Yet the Manassites were not able to occupy these towns, for the Canaanites were determined to live in that region. **13**However, when the Israelites grew stronger, they subjected the Canaanites to forced labor but did not drive them out completely.

14The people of Joseph said to Joshua, "Why have you given us only one allotment and one portion for an inheritance? We are a numerous people and the LORD has blessed us abundantly."

15"If you are so numerous," Joshua answered, "and if the hill country of Ephraim is too small for you, go up into the forest and clear land for yourselves there in the land of the Perizzites and Rephaites."

16The people of Joseph replied, "The hill country is not enough for us, and all the Canaanites who live in the plain have iron chariots, both those in Beth Shan and its settlements and those in the Valley of Jezreel."

17But Joshua said to the house of Joseph—to Ephraim and Manasseh—"You are numerous and very powerful. You will have not only one allotment **18**but the forested hill country as well. Clear it, and its farthest limits will be yours; though the Canaanites have iron chariots and though they are strong, you can drive them out."

Division of the Rest of the Land

18 The whole assembly of the Israelites gathered at Shiloh and set up the Tent of Meeting there. The country was brought under their control, **2**but there were still seven Israelite tribes who had not yet received their inheritance.

3So Joshua said to the Israelites: "How long will you wait before you begin to take possession of the land that the LORD, the God of your fathers, has given you? **4**Appoint three men from each tribe. I will send them out to make a survey of the land and to write a description of it, according to the inheritance of each. Then

they will return to me. **5**You are to divide the land into seven parts. Judah is to remain in its territory on the south and the house of Joseph in its territory on the north. **6**After you have written descriptions of the seven parts of the land, bring them here to me and I will cast lots for you in the presence of the LORD our God. **7**The Levites, however, do not get a portion among you, because the priestly service of the LORD is their inheritance. And Gad, Reuben and the half-tribe of Manasseh have already received their inheritance on the east side of the Jordan. Moses the servant of the LORD gave it to them."

8As the men started on their way to map out the land, Joshua instructed them, "Go and make a survey of the land and write a description of it. Then return to me, and I will cast lots for you here at Shiloh in the presence of the LORD." **9**So the men left and went through the land. They wrote its description on a scroll, town by town, in seven parts, and returned to Joshua in the camp at Shiloh. **10**Joshua then cast lots for them in Shiloh in the presence of the LORD, and there he distributed the land to the Israelites according to their tribal divisions.

Allotment for Benjamin

11The lot came up for the tribe of Benjamin, clan by clan. Their allotted territory lay between the tribes of Judah and Joseph:

12On the north side their boundary began at the Jordan, passed the northern slope of Jericho and headed west into the hill country, coming out at the desert of Beth Aven. **13**From there it crossed to the south slope of Luz (that is, Bethel) and went down to Ataroth Addar on the hill south of Lower Beth Horon.

14From the hill facing Beth Horon on the south the boundary turned south along the western side and came out at Kiriath Baal (that is, Kiriath Jearim), a town of the people of Judah. This was the western side.

15The southern side began at the outskirts of Kiriath Jearim on the west, and the boundary came out at the spring of the waters of Nephtoah. **16**The boundary went down to the foot of the hill facing the Valley of Ben Hinnom, north of the Valley of Reph-

a11 That is, Naphoth Dor

aim. It continued down the Hinnom Valley along the southern slope of the Jebusite city and so to En Rogel. [17]It then curved north, went to En Shemesh, continued to Geliloth, which faces the Pass of Adummim, and ran down to the Stone of Bohan son of Reuben. [18]It continued to the northern slope of Beth Arabah[a] and on down into the Arabah. [19]It then went to the northern slope of Beth Hoglah and came out at the northern bay of the Salt Sea,[b] at the mouth of the Jordan in the south. This was the southern boundary.

[20]The Jordan formed the boundary on the eastern side.

These were the boundaries that marked out the inheritance of the clans of Benjamin on all sides.

[21]The tribe of Benjamin, clan by clan, had the following cities:

Jericho, Beth Hoglah, Emek Keziz, [22]Beth Arabah, Zemaraim, Bethel, [23]Avvim, Parah, Ophrah, [24]Kephar Ammoni, Ophni and Geba—twelve towns and their villages.

[a]18 Septuagint; Hebrew *slope facing the Arabah*
[b]19 That is, the Dead Sea

A Special Place for Everyone

DAILY INSIGHT

TUESDAY

Passage:
Joshua 18:1–7

Verse:
Joshua 18:4

When you stop and think about it, our children have no business referring to the place where they sleep and keep their stuff as "my room." In fact, as parents, we're at fault because from the time we first carry them home from the hospital we call the nursery "the baby's room."

Come on, let's get serious. How much of a contribution have these children made to the mortgage? And what are your expectations for their help with the utilities over the next few years? In fact, we call their space by their name even before they can pick up their own socks and toys—if they ever do! Does this make any sense and is this right?

Yes, and absolutely yes.

Just as parents assign bedrooms to their children, Joshua had the job of assigning land to the Israelite families. Like our forefathers who set the boundaries between states, counties and cities, he drew lines in the land and told them, "This land belongs to you. You are a part of the whole nation, but you still own something that's truly yours."

This is a story about acres of land, and about square feet in your home. Like these Israelite families, our children deserve their own territory. But the story is also about the emotional ownership of private space. This is a critical thing for us to understand.

As a parent in your house, you technically have the right to go anywhere you want. After all, you and your wife own the place. But you *don't* go anywhere you want. You knock on a closed door. You ask your child's permission to enter. And you only come in when that permission is freely granted. You honor this sacred boundary.

In the same way, as the dad, you might have the right to push your way into your son or daughter's life, but you don't do that. You tenderly honor your children's right to privacy—to only allow you into the areas of their lives that they have invited you to freely enter. Your love for them earns you entrance.

However, if you try to force your way in, you will pay a dear price.

I love the picture of Joshua, standing at a map of Canaan, awarding land to his family—honoring them by declaring it "their own land," in spite of the fact that they didn't actually pay anything for it. I also love the picture of you and me giving our children their own safe place in our home—a physical and emotional territory with their name on it.

As the father of your household, don't act like a landlord. Rather, earn the love and respect of your family by respecting and loving each one individually.

For your next devotional reading, go to page 262.

[25]Gibeon, Ramah, Beeroth, [26]Mizpah, Kephirah, Mozah, [27]Rekem, Irpeel, Taralah, [28]Zelah, Haeleph, the Jebusite city (that is, Jerusalem), Gibeah and Kiriath—fourteen towns and their villages.

This was the inheritance of Benjamin for its clans.

Allotment for Simeon

19 The second lot came out for the tribe of Simeon, clan by clan. Their inheritance lay within the territory of Judah. [2]It included:

Beersheba (or Sheba),[a] Moladah, [3]Hazar Shual, Balah, Ezem, [4]Eltolad, Bethul, Hormah, [5]Ziklag, Beth Marcaboth, Hazar Susah, [6]Beth Lebaoth and Sharuhen—thirteen towns and their villages;

[7]Ain, Rimmon, Ether and Ashan—four towns and their villages— [8]and all the villages around these towns as far as Baalath Beer (Ramah in the Negev).

This was the inheritance of the tribe of the Simeonites, clan by clan. [9]The inheritance of the Simeonites was taken from the share of Judah, because Judah's portion was more than they needed. So the Simeonites received their inheritance within the territory of Judah.

Allotment for Zebulun

[10]The third lot came up for Zebulun, clan by clan:

The boundary of their inheritance went as far as Sarid. [11]Going west it ran to Maralah, touched Dabbesheth, and extended to the ravine near Jokneam. [12]It turned east from Sarid toward the sunrise to the territory of Kisloth Tabor and went on to Daberath and up to Japhia. [13]Then it continued eastward to Gath Hepher and Eth Kazin; it came out at Rimmon and turned toward Neah. [14]There the boundary went around on the north to Hannathon and ended at the Valley of Iphtah El. [15]Included were Kattath, Nahalal, Shimron, Idalah and Bethlehem. There were twelve towns and their villages.

[16]These towns and their villages were the inheritance of Zebulun, clan by clan.

Allotment for Issachar

[17]The fourth lot came out for Issachar, clan by clan. [18]Their territory included:

Jezreel, Kesulloth, Shunem,

[a]2 Or *Beersheba, Sheba*; 1 Chron. 4:28 does not have *Sheba*.

HEY DAD

Why is the Dead Sea dead?

Text: Joshua 18:19

The Dead Sea is called "dead" for several reasons. First, this sea is actually a dead end. Several rivers flow into it, but with no exits, the water stays put. Under the hot sun, the water evaporates, leaving behind salt and minerals. The remaining seawater is made up of more than twenty-five percent salt and minerals (as compared to the six percent mineral content of typical ocean water). The high salt content in the Dead Sea makes it impossible for most marine life to survive there. So this dead end is, quite literally, dead.

The Dead Sea, also known as the Salt Sea in the Bible, marks the lowest point on earth. The water level begins an incredible 1,300 feet below sea level. Many scholars believe that the destroyed cities of Sodom and Gomorrah lie beneath the southern tip of the sea (Lockyer, 288). So these briny waters may actually conceal the graves of ancient people who learned too late not to provoke God's wrath.

Rich with history and full of archeological promise, the aptly named Dead Sea remains one of the earth's great mysteries.

Lockyer, H. (Ed.). (1986). *Nelson's Illustrated Bible Dictionary*. *Nashville: Thomas Nelson Publishers*.

For a complete listing of Questions Kids Ask, turn to page 1435.

[19]Hapharaim, Shion, Anaharath, [20]Rabbith, Kishion, Ebez, [21]Remeth, En Gannim, En Haddah and Beth Pazzez. [22]The boundary touched Tabor, Shahazumah and Beth Shemesh, and ended at the Jordan. There were sixteen towns and their villages. [23]These towns and their villages were the inheritance of the tribe of Issachar, clan by clan.

Allotment for Asher

[24]The fifth lot came out for the tribe of Asher, clan by clan. [25]Their territory included:

Helkath, Hali, Beten, Acshaph, [26]Allammelech, Amad and Mishal. On the west the boundary touched Carmel and Shihor Libnath. [27]It then turned east toward Beth Dagon, touched Zebulun and the Valley of Iphtah El, and went north to Beth Emek and Neiel, passing Cabul on the left. [28]It went to Abdon,[a] Rehob, Hammon and Kanah, as far as Greater Sidon. [29]The boundary then turned back toward Ramah and went to the fortified city of Tyre, turned toward Hosah and came out at the sea in the region of Aczib, [30]Ummah, Aphek and Rehob. There were twenty-two towns and their villages.
[31]These towns and their villages were the inheritance of the tribe of Asher, clan by clan.

Allotment for Naphtali

[32]The sixth lot came out for Naphtali, clan by clan:

[33]Their boundary went from Heleph and the large tree in Zaanannim, passing Adami Nekeb and Jabneel to Lakkum and ending at the Jordan. [34]The boundary ran west through Aznoth Tabor and came out at Hukkok. It touched Zebulun on the south, Asher on the west and the Jordan[b] on the east. [35]The fortified cities were Ziddim, Zer, Hammath, Rakkath, Kinnereth, [36]Adamah, Ramah, Hazor, [37]Kedesh, Edrei, En Hazor, [38]Iron, Migdal El, Horem, Beth Anath and Beth Shemesh. There were nineteen towns and their villages.
[39]These towns and their villages were the inheritance of the tribe of Naphtali, clan by clan.

Allotment for Dan

[40]The seventh lot came out for the tribe of Dan, clan by clan. [41]The territory of their inheritance included:

Zorah, Eshtaol, Ir Shemesh, [42]Shaalabbin, Aijalon, Ithlah, [43]Elon, Timnah, Ekron, [44]Eltekeh, Gibbethon, Baalath, [45]Jehud, Bene Berak, Gath Rimmon, [46]Me Jarkon and Rakkon, with the area facing Joppa.
[47](But the Danites had difficulty taking possession of their territory, so they went up and attacked Leshem, took it, put it to the sword and occupied it. They settled in Leshem and named it Dan after their forefather.)
[48]These towns and their villages were the inheritance of the tribe of Dan, clan by clan.

Allotment for Joshua

[49]When they had finished dividing the land into its allotted portions, the Israelites gave Joshua son of Nun an inheritance among them, [50]as the LORD had commanded. They gave him the town he asked for—Timnath Serah[c] in the hill country of Ephraim. And he built up the town and settled there.
[51]These are the territories that Eleazar the priest, Joshua son of Nun and the heads of the tribal clans of Israel assigned by lot at Shiloh in the presence of the LORD at the entrance to the Tent of Meeting. And so they finished dividing the land.

Cities of Refuge

20 Then the LORD said to Joshua: [2]"Tell the Israelites to designate the cities of refuge, as I instructed you through Moses, [3]so that anyone who kills a person accidentally and unintentionally may flee there and find protection from the avenger of blood.
[4]"When he flees to one of these cities, he is to stand in the entrance of the city gate and state his case before the elders of that city. Then they are to admit him into their city and give him a place to live with them. [5]If the avenger of blood pursues him, they must not surrender the one accused, because he killed his neighbor

---

[a]28 Some Hebrew manuscripts (see also Joshua 21:30); most Hebrew manuscripts Ebron
[b]34 Septuagint; Hebrew west, and Judah, the Jordan,   [c]50 Also known as Timnath Heres (see Judges 2:9)

unintentionally and without malice aforethought. **6**He is to stay in that city until he has stood trial before the assembly and until the death of the high priest who is serving at that time. Then he may go back to his own home in the town from which he fled."

7So they set apart Kedesh in Galilee in the hill country of Naphtali, Shechem in the hill country of Ephraim, and Kiriath Arba (that is, Hebron) in the hill country of Judah. **8**On the east side of the Jordan of Jericho*a* they designated Bezer in the desert on the plateau in the tribe of Reuben, Ramoth in Gilead in the tribe of Gad, and Golan in Bashan in the tribe of Manasseh. **9**Any of the Israelites or any alien living among them who killed someone accidentally could flee to these designated cities and not be killed by the avenger of blood prior to standing trial before the assembly.

Towns for the Levites

21 Now the family heads of the Levites approached Eleazar the priest, Joshua son of Nun, and the heads of the other tribal families of Israel **2**at Shiloh in Canaan and said to them, "The LORD commanded through Moses that you give us towns to live in, with pasturelands for our livestock." **3**So, as the LORD had commanded, the Israelites gave the Levites the following towns and pasturelands out of their own inheritance:

4The first lot came out for the Kohathites, clan by clan. The Levites who were descendants of Aaron the priest were allotted thirteen towns from the tribes of Judah, Simeon and Benjamin. **5**The rest of Kohath's descendants were allotted ten towns from the clans of the tribes of Ephraim, Dan and half of Manasseh.

6The descendants of Gershon were allotted thirteen towns from the clans of the tribes of Issachar, Asher, Naphtali and the half-tribe of Manasseh in Bashan.

7The descendants of Merari, clan by clan, received twelve towns from the tribes of Reuben, Gad and Zebulun.

8So the Israelites allotted to the Levites these towns and their pasturelands, as the LORD had commanded through Moses.

9From the tribes of Judah and Simeon they allotted the following towns by name **10**(these towns were assigned to the descendants of Aaron who were from the Kohathite clans of the Levites, because the first lot fell to them):

11They gave them Kiriath Arba (that is, Hebron), with its surrounding pastureland, in the hill country of Judah. (Arba was the forefather of Anak.) **12**But the fields and villages around the city they had given to Caleb son of Jephunneh as his possession.

13So to the descendants of Aaron the priest they gave Hebron (a city of refuge for one accused of murder), Libnah, **14**Jattir, Eshtemoa, **15**Holon, Debir, **16**Ain, Juttah and Beth Shemesh, together with their pasturelands—nine towns from these two tribes. **17**And from the tribe of Benjamin they gave them Gibeon, Geba, **18**Anathoth and Almon, together with their pasturelands—four towns. **19**All the towns for the priests, the descendants of Aaron, were thirteen, together with their pasturelands.

20The rest of the Kohathite clans of the Levites were allotted towns from the tribe of Ephraim:

21In the hill country of Ephraim they were given Shechem (a city of refuge for one accused of murder) and Gezer, **22**Kibzaim and Beth Horon, together with their pasturelands—four towns.

23Also from the tribe of Dan they received Eltekeh, Gibbethon, **24**Aijalon and Gath Rimmon, together with their pasturelands—four towns.

25From half the tribe of Manasseh they received Taanach and Gath Rimmon, together with their pasturelands—two towns. **26**All these ten towns and their pasturelands were given to the rest of the Kohathite clans.

27The Levite clans of the Gershonites were given:
from the half-tribe of Manasseh,
Golan in Bashan (a city of refuge for one accused of murder) and Be Eshtarah, together with their pasturelands—two towns;
28from the tribe of Issachar,
Kishion, Daberath, **29**Jarmuth and En Gannim, together with their pasturelands—four towns;
30from the tribe of Asher,
Mishal, Abdon, **31**Helkath and Rehob,

a8 Jordan of Jericho was possibly an ancient name for the Jordan River.

together with their pasturelands—four towns;

³²from the tribe of Naphtali,
Kedesh in Galilee (a city of refuge for one accused of murder), Hammoth Dor and Kartan, together with their pasturelands—three towns.

³³All the towns of the Gershonite clans were thirteen, together with their pasturelands.

³⁴The Merarite clans (the rest of the Levites) were given:
from the tribe of Zebulun,
Jokneam, Kartah, ³⁵Dimnah and Nahalal, together with their pasturelands—four towns;
³⁶from the tribe of Reuben,
Bezer, Jahaz, ³⁷Kedemoth and Mephaath, together with their pasturelands—four towns;
³⁸from the tribe of Gad,
Ramoth in Gilead (a city of refuge for one accused of murder), Mahanaim, ³⁹Heshbon and Jazer, together with their pasturelands—four towns in all.

⁴⁰All the towns allotted to the Merarite clans, who were the rest of the Levites, were twelve.

⁴¹The towns of the Levites in the territory held by the Israelites were forty-eight in all, together with their pasturelands. ⁴²Each of these towns had pasturelands surrounding it; this was true for all these towns.

⁴³So the LORD gave Israel all the land he had sworn to give their forefathers, and they took possession of it and settled there. ⁴⁴The LORD gave them rest on every side, just as he had sworn to their forefathers. Not one of their enemies withstood them; the LORD handed all their enemies over to them. ⁴⁵Not one of all the LORD's good promises to the house of Israel failed; every one was fulfilled.

Eastern Tribes Return Home

22 Then Joshua summoned the Reubenites, the Gadites and the half-tribe of Manasseh ²and said to them, "You have done all that Moses the servant of the LORD commanded, and you have obeyed me in everything I commanded. ³For a long time now—to this very day—you have not deserted your brothers but have carried out the mission the LORD your God gave you. ⁴Now that the LORD your God has given your brothers rest as he promised, return to your homes in the land that Moses the servant of the LORD gave you on the other side of the Jordan. ⁵But be very careful to keep the commandment and the law that Moses servant of the LORD gave you: to love the LORD your God, to walk in all his ways, to obey his commands, to hold fast to him and to serve him with all your heart and all your soul."

⁶Then Joshua blessed them and sent them away, and they went to their homes. ⁷(To the half-tribe of Manasseh Moses had given land in Bashan, and to the other half of the tribe Joshua gave land on the west side of the Jordan with their brothers.) When Joshua sent them home, he blessed them, ⁸saying, "Return to your homes with your great wealth—with large herds of livestock, with silver, gold, bronze and iron, and a great quantity of clothing—and divide with your brothers the plunder from your enemies."

⁹So the Reubenites, the Gadites and the half-tribe of Manasseh left the Israelites at Shiloh in Canaan to return to Gilead, their own land, which they had acquired in accordance with the command of the LORD through Moses.

¹⁰When they came to Geliloth near the Jordan in the land of Canaan, the Reubenites, the Gadites and the half-tribe of Manasseh built an imposing altar there by the Jordan. ¹¹And when the Israelites heard that they had built the altar on the border of Canaan at Geliloth near the Jordan on the Israelite side, ¹²the whole assembly of Israel gathered at Shiloh to go to war against them.

¹³So the Israelites sent Phinehas son of Eleazar, the priest, to the land of Gilead—to Reuben, Gad and the half-tribe of Manasseh. ¹⁴With him they sent ten of the chief men, one for each of the tribes of Israel, each the head of a family division among the Israelite clans.

¹⁵When they went to Gilead—to Reuben, Gad and the half-tribe of Manasseh—they said to them: ¹⁶"The whole assembly of the LORD says: 'How could you break faith with the God of Israel like this? How could you turn away from the LORD and build yourselves an altar in rebellion against him now? ¹⁷Was not the sin of Peor enough for us? Up to this very day we have not cleansed ourselves from that sin, even though a plague fell on the community of the LORD! ¹⁸And are you now turning away from the LORD?

" 'If you rebel against the LORD today, tomorrow he will be angry with the whole community of Israel. ¹⁹If the land you possess is defiled, come over to the LORD's land, where the LORD's tabernacle stands, and share the land with us. But do not rebel against the LORD or against us by building an altar for yourselves, other than the altar of the LORD our God. ²⁰When Achan son of Zerah acted unfaithfully regarding the devoted things,ᵃ did not wrath come upon the whole community of Israel? He was not the only one who died for his sin.' "

²¹Then Reuben, Gad and the half-tribe of Manasseh replied to the heads of the clans of Israel: ²²"The Mighty One, God, the LORD! The Mighty One, God, the LORD! He knows! And let Israel know! If this has been in rebellion or disobedience to the LORD, do not spare us this day. ²³If we have built our own altar to turn away from the LORD and to offer burnt offerings and grain offerings, or to sacrifice fellowship offeringsᵇ on it, may the LORD himself call us to account.

²⁴"No! We did it for fear that some day your descendants might say to ours, 'What do you have to do with the LORD, the God of Israel? ²⁵The LORD has made the Jordan a boundary between us and you—you Reubenites and Gadites! You have no share in the LORD.' So your descendants might cause ours to stop fearing the LORD.

²⁶"That is why we said, 'Let us get ready and build an altar—but not for burnt offerings or sacrifices.' ²⁷On the contrary, it is to be a witness between us and you and the generations that follow, that we will worship the LORD at his sanctuary with our burnt offerings, sacrifices and fellowship offerings. Then in the future your descendants will not be able to say to ours, 'You have no share in the LORD.'

²⁸"And we said, 'If they ever say this to us, or to our descendants, we will answer: Look at the replica of the LORD's altar, which our fathers built, not for burnt offerings and sacrifices, but as a witness between us and you.'

²⁹"Far be it from us to rebel against the LORD and turn away from him today by building an altar for burnt offerings, grain offerings and sacrifices, other than the altar of the LORD our God that stands before his tabernacle."

³⁰When Phinehas the priest and the leaders of the community—the heads of the clans of the Israelites—heard what Reuben, Gad and Manasseh had to say, they were pleased. ³¹And Phinehas son of Eleazar, the priest, said to Reuben, Gad and Manasseh, "Today we know that the LORD is with us, because you have not acted unfaithfully toward the LORD in this matter. Now you have rescued the Israelites from the LORD's hand."

³²Then Phinehas son of Eleazar, the priest, and the leaders returned to Canaan from their meeting with the Reubenites and Gadites in Gilead and reported to the Israelites. ³³They were glad to hear the report and praised God. And they talked no more about going to war against them to devastate the country where the Reubenites and the Gadites lived.

³⁴And the Reubenites and the Gadites gave the altar this name: A Witness Between Us that the LORD is God.

Joshua's Farewell to the Leaders

23 After a long time had passed and the LORD had given Israel rest from all their enemies around them, Joshua, by then old and well advanced in years, ²summoned all Israel—their elders, leaders, judges and officials—and said to them: "I am old and well advanced in years. ³You yourselves have seen everything the LORD your God has done to all these nations for your sake; it was the LORD your God who fought for you. ⁴Remember how I have allotted as an inheritance for your tribes all the land of the nations that remain—the nations I conquered—between the Jordan and the Great Seaᶜ in the west. ⁵The LORD your God himself will drive them out of your way. He will push them out before you, and you will take possession of their land, as the LORD your God promised you.

⁶"Be very strong; be careful to obey all that is written in the Book of the Law of Moses, without turning aside to the right or to the left. ⁷Do not associate with these nations that remain among you; do not invoke the names of their gods or swear by them. You must not serve them or bow down to them. ⁸But you are to hold fast to the LORD your God, as you have until now.

⁹"The LORD has driven out before you great and powerful nations; to this day no one has been able to withstand you. ¹⁰One of you routs a thousand, because the

ᵃ20 The Hebrew term refers to the irrevocable giving over of things or persons to the LORD, often by totally destroying them.   ᵇ23 Traditionally peace offerings; also in verse 27   ᶜ4 That is, the Mediterranean

LORD your God fights for you, just as he promised. ¹¹So be very careful to love the LORD your God.

¹²"But if you turn away and ally yourselves with the survivors of these nations that remain among you and if you intermarry with them and associate with them, ¹³then you may be sure that the LORD your God will no longer drive out these nations before you. Instead, they will become snares and traps for you, whips on your backs and thorns in your eyes, until you perish from this good land, which the LORD your God has given you.

¹⁴"Now I am about to go the way of all the earth. You know with all your heart and soul that not one of all the good promises the LORD your God gave you has failed. Every promise has been fulfilled; not one has failed. ¹⁵But just as every good promise of the LORD your God has come true, so the LORD will bring on you all the evil he has threatened, until he has destroyed you from this good land he has given you. ¹⁶If you violate the covenant of the LORD your God, which he commanded you, and go and serve other gods and bow down to them, the LORD's anger will burn against you, and you will quickly perish from the good land he has given you."

The Covenant Renewed at Shechem

24 Then Joshua assembled all the tribes of Israel at Shechem. He summoned the elders, leaders, judges and officials of Israel, and they presented themselves before God.

²Joshua said to all the people, "This is what the LORD, the God of Israel, says: 'Long ago your forefathers, including Terah the father of Abraham and Nahor, lived beyond the River[a] and worshiped other gods. ³But I took your father Abraham from the land beyond the River and led him throughout Canaan and gave him many descendants. I gave him Isaac, ⁴and to Isaac I gave Jacob and Esau. I assigned the hill country of Seir to Esau, but Jacob and his sons went down to Egypt.

⁵" 'Then I sent Moses and Aaron, and I afflicted the Egyptians by what I did there, and I brought you out. ⁶When I brought your fathers out of Egypt, you came to the sea, and the Egyptians pursued them with chariots and horsemen[b] as far as the Red Sea.[c] ⁷But they cried to the LORD for help, and he put darkness between you and the Egyptians; he brought the sea over them

and covered them. You saw with your own eyes what I did to the Egyptians. Then you lived in the desert for a long time.

⁸" 'I brought you to the land of the Amorites who lived east of the Jordan. They fought against you, but I gave them into your hands. I destroyed them from before you, and you took possession of their land. ⁹When Balak son of Zippor, the king of Moab, prepared to fight against Israel, he sent for Balaam son of Beor to put a curse on you. ¹⁰But I would not listen to Balaam, so he blessed you again and again, and I delivered you out of his hand.

¹¹" 'Then you crossed the Jordan and came to Jericho. The citizens of Jericho fought against you, as did also the Amorites, Perizzites, Canaanites, Hittites, Girgashites, Hivites and Jebusites, but I gave them into your hands. ¹²I sent the hornet ahead of you, which drove them out before you—also the two Amorite kings. You did not do it with your own sword and bow. ¹³So I gave you a land on which you did not toil and cities you did not build; and you live in them and eat from vineyards and olive groves that you did not plant.'

¹⁴"Now fear the LORD and serve him with all faithfulness. Throw away the gods your forefathers worshiped beyond the River and in Egypt, and serve the LORD. ¹⁵But if serving the LORD seems undesirable to you, then choose for yourselves this day whom you will serve, whether the gods your forefathers served beyond the River, or the gods of the Amorites, in whose land you are living. But as for me and my household, we will serve the LORD."

¹⁶Then the people answered, "Far be it from us to forsake the LORD to serve other gods! ¹⁷It was the LORD our God himself who brought us and our fathers up out of Egypt, from that land of slavery, and performed those great signs before our eyes. He protected us on our entire journey and among all the nations through which we traveled. ¹⁸And the LORD drove out before us all the nations, including the Amorites, who lived in the land. We too will serve the LORD, because he is our God."

¹⁹Joshua said to the people, "You are not able to serve the LORD. He is a holy God; he is a jealous God. He will not forgive your rebellion and your sins. ²⁰If you

---

a2 That is, the Euphrates; also in verses 3, 14 and 15   *b6* Or *charioteers*   *c6* Hebrew *Yam Suph*; that is, Sea of Reeds

forsake the LORD and serve foreign gods, he will turn and bring disaster on you and make an end of you, after he has been good to you."

²¹But the people said to Joshua, "No! We will serve the LORD."

²²Then Joshua said, "You are witnesses against yourselves that you have chosen to serve the LORD."

"Yes, we are witnesses," they replied.

²³"Now then," said Joshua, "throw away the foreign gods that are among you and yield your hearts to the LORD, the God of Israel."

²⁴And the people said to Joshua, "We will serve the LORD our God and obey him."

²⁵On that day Joshua made a covenant for the people, and there at Shechem he drew up for them decrees and laws. ²⁶And Joshua recorded these things in the Book of the Law of God. Then he took a large stone and set it up there under the oak near the holy place of the LORD.

²⁷"See!" he said to all the people. "This stone will be a witness against us. It has heard all the words the LORD has said to us. It will be a witness against you if you are untrue to your God."

Buried in the Promised Land

²⁸Then Joshua sent the people away, each to his own inheritance.

²⁹After these things, Joshua son of Nun, the servant of the LORD, died at the age of a hundred and ten. ³⁰And they buried him in the land of his inheritance, at Timnath Serah[a] in the hill country of Ephraim, north of Mount Gaash.

³¹Israel served the LORD throughout the lifetime of Joshua and of the elders who outlived him and who had experienced everything the LORD had done for Israel.

³²And Joseph's bones, which the Israelites had brought up from Egypt, were buried at Shechem in the tract of land that Jacob bought for a hundred pieces of

[a]30 Also known as *Timnath Heres* (see Judges 2:9)

Have It Your Way

DAILY INSIGHT

Most every business has its own slogan. From small, family-owned restaurants: "The best chili in this here county," to major airlines: "Something special in the air," companies like to summarize who they are in just a few memorable words.

Actually, the companies who create them can *own* these slogans. When you see the tiny letters "SM" next to one of these, it means that no one else can use it. Even though "You deserve a break today" would fit nicely on your restaurant's sign, you can't use it. And even though "Quality is job #1" would be a great slogan for General Motors to use, Ford already has their "SM" on it.

Almost three thousand years ago, it dawned on Joshua that he needed a few words to set his family apart. "What could I say," he must have thought, "to distinguish our family from other families? And what words would remind our own clan of who

WEDNESDAY

Passage:
Joshua 24:14–18

Verse:
Joshua 24:15b

they are?" So Joshua came up with history's first family slogan: "As for me and my house, we will serve the LORD."

Even if he had hired a New York advertising agency, I doubt if they could have come up with a better one. Don't you agree?

Now here's a great piece of news. If you'll look closely at this verse (24:15b) in your Bible, you'll not see the "SM" anywhere. Under consultation with his lawyer, I'm sure, Joshua decided not to copyright his family's slogan. He decided to leave it in the public domain so that you and I could use it for our own homes if we wanted to.

Your family needs a slogan … a phrase that sets it apart from other families. Go ahead and write one for your clan. If you have a hard time with this, don't worry. It's okay with Joshua if you use the one he came up with. It's free and it's yours.

For your next devotional reading, go to page 268.
For your next devotional reading, go to page 268.

silver*a* from the sons of Hamor, the father of Shechem. This became the inheritance of Joseph's descendants.

³³And Eleazar son of Aaron died and was buried at Gibeah, which had been al-

lotted to his son Phinehas in the hill country of Ephraim.

a32 Hebrew *hundred kesitahs*; a kesitah was a unit of money of unknown weight and value.

When children challenge their dads to a game of "who's the boss around here," they should lose . . . every time. Your authority in your home is something God established a long time ago with his own children. When they obeyed, they were rewarded. When they disobeyed, they were punished. The book of Judges clearly establishes this model as God deals swiftly and fairly with the Israelites. However, what you'll notice as you read this book is that God usually chose to issue his authority by way of his appointed associates: his judges. When Deborah, Gideon, Jephthah or Samson spoke, they spoke on behalf of their heavenly Father—and with his complete sanction.

What a privilege it must have been for these people to be God's representatives! Actually, this is exactly like the privilege of being a dad, God's ambassador to *your* family.

Judges

Israel Fights the Remaining Canaanites

1 After the death of Joshua, the Israelites asked the LORD, "Who will be the first to go up and fight for us against the Canaanites?"

²The LORD answered, "Judah is to go; I have given the land into their hands."

³Then the men of Judah said to the Simeonites their brothers, "Come up with us into the territory allotted to us, to fight against the Canaanites. We in turn will go with you into yours." So the Simeonites went with them.

⁴When Judah attacked, the LORD gave the Canaanites and Perizzites into their hands and they struck down ten thousand men at Bezek. ⁵It was there that they found Adoni-Bezek and fought against him, putting to rout the Canaanites and Perizzites. ⁶Adoni-Bezek fled, but they chased him and caught him, and cut off his thumbs and big toes.

⁷Then Adoni-Bezek said, "Seventy kings with their thumbs and big toes cut off have picked up scraps under my table. Now God has paid me back for what I did to them." They brought him to Jerusalem, and he died there.

⁸The men of Judah attacked Jerusalem also and took it. They put the city to the sword and set it on fire.

⁹After that, the men of Judah went down to fight against the Canaanites living in the hill country, the Negev and the western foothills. ¹⁰They advanced against the Canaanites living in Hebron (formerly called Kiriath Arba) and defeated Sheshai, Ahiman and Talmai.

¹¹From there they advanced against the people living in Debir (formerly called Kiriath Sepher). ¹²And Caleb said, "I will

give my daughter Acsah in marriage to the man who attacks and captures Kiriath Sepher." **¹³**Othniel son of Kenaz, Caleb's younger brother, took it; so Caleb gave his daughter Acsah to him in marriage.

¹⁴One day when she came to Othniel, she urged him*ᵃ* to ask her father for a field. When she got off her donkey, Caleb asked her, "What can I do for you?"

¹⁵She replied, "Do me a special favor. Since you have given me land in the Negev, give me also springs of water." Then Caleb gave her the upper and lower springs.

¹⁶The descendants of Moses' father-in-law, the Kenite, went up from the City of Palms*ᵇ* with the men of Judah to live among the people of the Desert of Judah in the Negev near Arad.

¹⁷Then the men of Judah went with the Simeonites their brothers and attacked the Canaanites living in Zephath, and they totally destroyed*ᶜ* the city. Therefore it was called Hormah.*ᵈ* **¹⁸**The men of Judah also took*ᵉ* Gaza, Ashkelon and Ekron—each city with its territory.

¹⁹The LORD was with the men of Judah. They took possession of the hill country, but they were unable to drive the people from the plains, because they had iron chariots. **²⁰**As Moses had promised, Hebron was given to Caleb, who drove from it the three sons of Anak. **²¹**The Benjamites, however, failed to dislodge the Jebusites, who were living in Jerusalem; to this day the Jebusites live there with the Benjamites.

²²Now the house of Joseph attacked Bethel, and the LORD was with them. **²³**When they sent men to spy out Bethel (formerly called Luz), **²⁴**the spies saw a man coming out of the city and they said to him, "Show us how to get into the city and we will see that you are treated well." **²⁵**So he showed them, and they put the city to the sword but spared the man and his whole family. **²⁶**He then went to the land of the Hittites, where he built a city and called it Luz, which is its name to this day.

²⁷But Manasseh did not drive out the people of Beth Shan or Taanach or Dor or Ibleam or Megiddo and their surrounding settlements, for the Canaanites were determined to live in that land. **²⁸**When Israel became strong, they pressed the Canaanites into forced labor but never drove them out completely. **²⁹**Nor did Ephraim drive out the Canaanites living in Gezer, but the Canaanites continued to live there among them. **³⁰**Neither did Zebulun drive out the Canaanites living in Kitron or Nahalol, who remained among them; but they did subject them to forced labor. **³¹**Nor did Asher drive out those living in Acco or Sidon or Ahlab or Aczib or Helbah or Aphek or Rehob, **³²**and because of this the people of Asher lived among the Canaanite inhabitants of the land. **³³**Neither did Naphtali drive out those living in Beth Shemesh or Beth Anath; but the Naphtalites too lived among the Canaanite inhabitants of the land, and those living in Beth Shemesh and Beth Anath became forced laborers for them. **³⁴**The Amorites confined the Danites to the hill country, not allowing them to come down into the plain. **³⁵**And the Amorites were determined also to hold out in Mount Heres, Aijalon and Shaalbim, but when the power of the house of Joseph increased, they too were pressed into forced labor. **³⁶**The boundary of the Amorites was from Scorpion*ᶠ* Pass to Sela and beyond.

The Angel of the LORD at Bokim

2 The angel of the LORD went up from Gilgal to Bokim and said, "I brought you up out of Egypt and led you into the land that I swore to give to your forefathers. I said, 'I will never break my covenant with you, **²**and you shall not make a covenant with the people of this land, but you shall break down their altars.' Yet you have disobeyed me. Why have you done this? **³**Now therefore I tell you that I will not drive them out before you; they will be thorns in your sides and their gods will be a snare to you."

⁴When the angel of the LORD had spoken these things to all the Israelites, the people wept aloud, **⁵**and they called that place Bokim.*ᵍ* There they offered sacrifices to the LORD.

Disobedience and Defeat

⁶After Joshua had dismissed the Israelites, they went to take possession of the land, each to his own inheritance. **⁷**The people served the LORD throughout the lifetime of Joshua and of the elders who outlived him and who had seen all

---

ᵃ14 Hebrew; Septuagint and Vulgate *Othniel, he urged her*   *ᵇ16* That is, Jericho   *ᶜ17* The Hebrew term refers to the irrevocable giving over of things or persons to the LORD, often by totally destroying them.   *ᵈ17 Hormah* means *destruction.*
ᵉ18 Hebrew; Septuagint *Judah did not take*
ᶠ36 Hebrew *Akrabbim*   *ᵍ5 Bokim* means *weepers.*

the great things the LORD had done for Israel.

[8]Joshua son of Nun, the servant of the LORD, died at the age of a hundred and ten. [9]And they buried him in the land of his inheritance, at Timnath Heres[a] in the hill country of Ephraim, north of Mount Gaash.

[10]After that whole generation had been gathered to their fathers, another generation grew up, who knew neither the LORD nor what he had done for Israel. [11]Then the Israelites did evil in the eyes of the LORD and served the Baals. [12]They forsook the LORD, the God of their fathers, who had brought them out of Egypt. They followed and worshiped various gods of the peoples around them. They provoked the LORD to anger [13]because they forsook him and served Baal and the Ashtoreths. [14]In his anger against Israel the LORD handed them over to raiders who plundered them. He sold them to their enemies all around, whom they were no longer able to resist. [15]Whenever Israel went out to fight, the hand of the LORD was against them to defeat them, just as he had sworn to them. They were in great distress.

[16]Then the LORD raised up judges,[b] who saved them out of the hands of these raiders. [17]Yet they would not listen to their judges but prostituted themselves to other gods and worshiped them. Unlike their fathers, they quickly turned from the way in which their fathers had walked, the way of obedience to the LORD's commands. [18]Whenever the LORD raised up a judge for them, he was with the judge and saved them out of the hands of their enemies as long as the judge lived; for the LORD had compassion on them as they groaned under those who oppressed and afflicted them. [19]But when the judge died, the people returned to ways even more corrupt than those of their fathers, following other gods and serving and worshiping them. They refused to give up their evil practices and stubborn ways.

[20]Therefore the LORD was very angry with Israel and said, "Because this nation has violated the covenant that I laid down for their forefathers and has not listened to me, [21]I will no longer drive out before them any of the nations Joshua left when he died. [22]I will use them to test Israel and see whether they will keep the way of the LORD and walk in it as their forefathers did." [23]The LORD had allowed those nations to remain; he did not drive them out

at once by giving them into the hands of Joshua.

3 These are the nations the LORD left to test all those Israelites who had not experienced any of the wars in Canaan [2](he did this only to teach warfare to the descendants of the Israelites who had not had previous battle experience): [3]the five rulers of the Philistines, all the Canaanites, the Sidonians, and the Hivites living in the Lebanon mountains from Mount Baal Hermon to Lebo[c] Hamath. [4]They were left to test the Israelites to see whether they would obey the LORD's commands, which he had given their forefathers through Moses.

[5]The Israelites lived among the Canaanites, Hittites, Amorites, Perizzites, Hivites and Jebusites. [6]They took their daughters in marriage and gave their own daughters to their sons, and served their gods.

Othniel

[7]The Israelites did evil in the eyes of the LORD; they forgot the LORD their God and served the Baals and the Asherahs. [8]The anger of the LORD burned against Israel so that he sold them into the hands of Cushan-Rishathaim king of Aram Naharaim,[d] to whom the Israelites were subject for eight years. [9]But when they cried out to the LORD, he raised up for them a deliverer, Othniel son of Kenaz, Caleb's younger brother, who saved them. [10]The Spirit of the LORD came upon him, so that he became Israel's judge[e] and went to war. The LORD gave Cushan-Rishathaim king of Aram into the hands of Othniel, who overpowered him. [11]So the land had peace for forty years, until Othniel son of Kenaz died.

Ehud

[12]Once again the Israelites did evil in the eyes of the LORD, and because they did this evil the LORD gave Eglon king of Moab power over Israel. [13]Getting the Ammonites and Amalekites to join him, Eglon came and attacked Israel, and they took possession of the City of Palms.[f] [14]The Israelites were subject to Eglon king of Moab for eighteen years.

[15]Again the Israelites cried out to the

---

[a]9 Also known as Timnath Serah (see Joshua 19:50 and 24:30)   [b]16 Or leaders; similarly in verses 17-19   [c]3 Or to the entrance to   [d]8 That is, Northwest Mesopotamia   [e]10 Or leader   [f]13 That is, Jericho

LORD, and he gave them a deliverer— Ehud, a left-handed man, the son of Gera the Benjamite. The Israelites sent him with tribute to Eglon king of Moab. ¹⁶Now Ehud had made a double-edged sword about a foot and a half*a* long, which he strapped to his right thigh under his clothing. ¹⁷He presented the tribute to Eglon king of Moab, who was a very fat man. ¹⁸After Ehud had presented the tribute, he sent on their way the men who had carried it. ¹⁹At the idols*b* near Gilgal he himself turned back and said, "I have a secret message for you, O king."

The king said, "Quiet!" And all his attendants left him.

²⁰Ehud then approached him while he was sitting alone in the upper room of his summer palace*c* and said, "I have a message from God for you." As the king rose from his seat, ²¹Ehud reached with his left hand, drew the sword from his right thigh and plunged it into the king's belly. ²²Even the handle sank in after the blade, which came out his back. Ehud did not pull the sword out, and the fat closed in over it. ²³Then Ehud went out to the porch*d*; he shut the doors of the upper room behind him and locked them.

²⁴After he had gone, the servants came and found the doors of the upper room locked. They said, "He must be relieving himself in the inner room of the house." ²⁵They waited to the point of embarrassment, but when he did not open the doors of the room, they took a key and unlocked them. There they saw their lord fallen to the floor, dead.

²⁶While they waited, Ehud got away. He passed by the idols and escaped to Seirah. ²⁷When he arrived there, he blew a trumpet in the hill country of Ephraim, and the Israelites went down with him from the hills, with him leading them.

²⁸"Follow me," he ordered, "for the LORD has given Moab, your enemy, into your hands." So they followed him down and, taking possession of the fords of the Jordan that led to Moab, they allowed no one to cross over. ²⁹At that time they struck down about ten thousand Moabites, all vigorous and strong; not a man escaped. ³⁰That day Moab was made subject to Israel, and the land had peace for eighty years.

Shamgar

³¹After Ehud came Shamgar son of Anath, who struck down six hundred Philistines with an oxgoad. He too saved Israel.

Deborah

4 After Ehud died, the Israelites once again did evil in the eyes of the LORD. ²So the LORD sold them into the hands of Jabin, a king of Canaan, who reigned in Hazor. The commander of his army was Sisera, who lived in Harosheth Haggoyim. ³Because he had nine hundred iron chariots and had cruelly oppressed the Israelites for twenty years, they cried to the LORD for help.

⁴Deborah, a prophetess, the wife of Lappidoth, was leading*e* Israel at that time. ⁵She held court under the Palm of Deborah between Ramah and Bethel in the hill country of Ephraim, and the Israelites came to her to have their disputes decided. ⁶She sent for Barak son of Abinoam from Kedesh in Naphtali and said to him, "The LORD, the God of Israel, commands you: 'Go, take with you ten thousand men of Naphtali and Zebulun and lead the way to Mount Tabor. ⁷I will lure Sisera, the commander of Jabin's army, with his chariots and his troops to the Kishon River and give him into your hands.' "

⁸Barak said to her, "If you go with me, I will go; but if you don't go with me, I won't go."

⁹"Very well," Deborah said, "I will go with you. But because of the way you are going about this,*f* the honor will not be yours, for the LORD will hand Sisera over to a woman." So Deborah went with Barak to Kedesh, ¹⁰where he summoned Zebulun and Naphtali. Ten thousand men followed him, and Deborah also went with him.

¹¹Now Heber the Kenite had left the other Kenites, the descendants of Hobab, Moses' brother-in-law,*g* and pitched his tent by the great tree in Zaanannim near Kedesh.

¹²When they told Sisera that Barak son of Abinoam had gone up to Mount Tabor, ¹³Sisera gathered together his nine hundred iron chariots and all the men with him, from Harosheth Haggoyim to the Kishon River.

---

*a*16 Hebrew *a cubit* (about 0.5 meter)   *b*19 Or *the stone quarries*; also in verse 26   *c*20 The meaning of the Hebrew for this phrase is uncertain.   *d*23 The meaning of the Hebrew for this word is uncertain.   *e*4 Traditionally *judging*   *f*9 Or *But on the expedition you are undertaking*   *g*11 Or *father-in-law*

¹⁴Then Deborah said to Barak, "Go! This is the day the LORD has given Sisera into your hands. Has not the LORD gone ahead of you?" So Barak went down Mount Tabor, followed by ten thousand men. ¹⁵At Barak's advance, the LORD routed Sisera and all his chariots and army by the sword, and Sisera abandoned his chariot and fled on foot. ¹⁶But Barak pursued the chariots and army as far as Harosheth Haggoyim. All the troops of Sisera fell by the sword; not a man was left.

¹⁷Sisera, however, fled on foot to the tent of Jael, the wife of Heber the Kenite, because there were friendly relations between Jabin king of Hazor and the clan of Heber the Kenite.

¹⁸Jael went out to meet Sisera and said to him, "Come, my lord, come right in. Don't be afraid." So he entered her tent, and she put a covering over him.

¹⁹"I'm thirsty," he said. "Please give me some water." She opened a skin of milk, gave him a drink, and covered him up.

²⁰"Stand in the doorway of the tent," he told her. "If someone comes by and asks you, 'Is anyone here?' say 'No.'"

²¹But Jael, Heber's wife, picked up a tent peg and a hammer and went quietly to him while he lay fast asleep, exhausted. She drove the peg through his temple into the ground, and he died.

²²Barak came by in pursuit of Sisera, and Jael went out to meet him. "Come," she said, "I will show you the man you're looking for." So he went in with her, and there lay Sisera with the tent peg through his temple—dead.

²³On that day God subdued Jabin, the Canaanite king, before the Israelites. ²⁴And the hand of the Israelites grew stronger and stronger against Jabin, the Canaanite king, until they destroyed him.

The Song of Deborah

5 On that day Deborah and Barak son of Abinoam sang this song:

² "When the princes in Israel take the lead,
   when the people willingly offer themselves—
   praise the LORD!

Hey, Honey, What Do You Think?

Sometimes the best man for the job is … *a woman*!

This may or may not be a hard thing for you to hear, but the best advice you'll ever get on being a good dad may come from someone who will never be a father; someone who will never hear anyone call her "Daddy." It's your wife.

How is this possible?

Let's start with a question. How did you learn how to be a dad? Well, for the most part you learned by watching dads—especially your own—do their fathering thing. There were things you saw your dad do that you have tried to repeat. And there are probably things you observed in your dad that you are trying to avoid. In either case, you learned by watching a dad in action.

Your wife also had a dad. She also observed the things he did well … and not so well. And your wife actually has a better memory than you. Even though there are

DAILY INSIGHT

THURSDAY

Passage:
Judges 4:4–10

Verse:
Judges 4:7

plenty of studies that confirm this, you already know it, because she probably doesn't need a shopping list as badly as you do!

In today's text, Barak learned a valuable lesson. He should have listened to Deborah. God had chosen her to do some pretty incredible things in his name, and she knew what she was talking about. But Barak did not handle himself properly in the face of her counsel and lost the respect of the people. Eventually, he had to do the dangerous work of fighting the battle without getting any credit for the victory.

Silly Barak. Next time he'll know.

God has given women special insight, discernment, and wisdom. Consulting your wife on fatherly matters just might be the smartest thing you do as a dad.

For your next devotional reading, go to page 272.

³"Hear this, you kings! Listen, you
    rulers!
  I will sing to*a* the LORD, I will sing;
  I will make music to*b* the LORD, the
    God of Israel.

⁴"O LORD, when you went out from Seir,
  when you marched from the land of
    Edom,
the earth shook, the heavens poured,
  the clouds poured down water.
⁵The mountains quaked before the
    LORD, the One of Sinai,
  before the LORD, the God of Israel.

⁶"In the days of Shamgar son of Anath,
  in the days of Jael, the roads were
    abandoned;
  travelers took to winding paths.
⁷Village life*c* in Israel ceased,
  ceased until I,*d* Deborah, arose,
  arose a mother in Israel.
⁸When they chose new gods,
  war came to the city gates,
and not a shield or spear was seen
  among forty thousand in Israel.
⁹My heart is with Israel's princes,
  with the willing volunteers among
    the people.
  Praise the LORD!

¹⁰"You who ride on white donkeys,
  sitting on your saddle blankets,
  and you who walk along the road,
consider ¹¹the voice of the singers*e* at
  the watering places.
  They recite the righteous acts of the
    LORD,
  the righteous acts of his warriors*f* in
    Israel.

  "Then the people of the LORD
  went down to the city gates.
¹²'Wake up, wake up, Deborah!
  Wake up, wake up, break out in song!
Arise, O Barak!
  Take captive your captives, O son of
    Abinoam.'

¹³"Then the men who were left
  came down to the nobles;
the people of the LORD
  came to me with the mighty.
¹⁴Some came from Ephraim, whose roots
  were in Amalek;
  Benjamin was with the people who
    followed you.
From Makir captains came down,
  from Zebulun those who bear a
    commander's staff.
¹⁵The princes of Issachar were with
  Deborah;

yes, Issachar was with Barak,
  rushing after him into the valley.
In the districts of Reuben
  there was much searching of heart.
¹⁶Why did you stay among the
    campfires*g*
  to hear the whistling for the flocks?
In the districts of Reuben
  there was much searching of heart.
¹⁷Gilead stayed beyond the Jordan.
  And Dan, why did he linger by the
    ships?
Asher remained on the coast
  and stayed in his coves.
¹⁸The people of Zebulun risked their very
    lives;
  so did Naphtali on the heights of the
    field.

¹⁹"Kings came, they fought;
  the kings of Canaan fought
at Taanach by the waters of Megiddo,
  but they carried off no silver, no
    plunder.
²⁰From the heavens the stars fought,
  from their courses they fought
    against Sisera.
²¹The river Kishon swept them away,
  the age-old river, the river Kishon.
  March on, my soul; be strong!
²²Then thundered the horses' hoofs—
  galloping, galloping go his mighty
    steeds.
²³'Curse Meroz,' said the angel of the
    LORD.
  'Curse its people bitterly,
because they did not come to help the
    LORD,
  to help the LORD against the mighty.'

²⁴"Most blessed of women be Jael,
  the wife of Heber the Kenite,
  most blessed of tent-dwelling
    women.
²⁵He asked for water, and she gave him
    milk;
  in a bowl fit for nobles she brought
    him curdled milk.
²⁶Her hand reached for the tent peg,
  her right hand for the workman's
    hammer.
  She struck Sisera, she crushed his head,
  she shattered and pierced his
    temple.
²⁷At her feet he sank,
  he fell; there he lay.

---

*a*3 Or *of*   *b*3 Or *I with song I will praise*   *c*7 Or
Warriors   *d*7 Or *you*   *e*11 Or *archers*; the meaning
of the Hebrew for this word is uncertain.
*f*11 Or *villagers*   *g*16 Or *saddlebags*

At her feet he sank, he fell;
  where he sank, there he fell—dead.

28 "Through the window peered Sisera's
  mother;
  behind the lattice she cried out,
'Why is his chariot so long in coming?
  Why is the clatter of his chariots
  delayed?'
29 The wisest of her ladies answer her;
  indeed, she keeps saying to herself,
30 'Are they not finding and dividing the
  spoils:
a girl or two for each man,
  colorful garments as plunder for
  Sisera,
  colorful garments embroidered,
  highly embroidered garments for my
  neck—
all this as plunder?'

31 "So may all your enemies perish,
  O LORD!
But may they who love you be like
  the sun
  when it rises in its strength."

Then the land had peace forty years.

Gideon

6 Again the Israelites did evil in the eyes
of the LORD, and for seven years he
gave them into the hands of the Midianites. ²Because the power of Midian was so
oppressive, the Israelites prepared shelters for themselves in mountain clefts,
caves and strongholds. ³Whenever the
Israelites planted their crops, the Midianites, Amalekites and other eastern
peoples invaded the country. ⁴They
camped on the land and ruined the crops
all the way to Gaza and did not spare a
living thing for Israel, neither sheep nor
cattle nor donkeys. ⁵They came up with
their livestock and their tents like swarms
of locusts. It was impossible to count the
men and their camels; they invaded the
land to ravage it. ⁶Midian so impover-
ished the Israelites that they cried out to
the LORD for help.

⁷When the Israelites cried to the LORD
because of Midian, ⁸he sent them a
prophet, who said, "This is what the LORD,
the God of Israel, says: I brought you up
out of Egypt, out of the land of slavery. ⁹I
snatched you from the power of Egypt
and from the hand of all your oppressors.
I drove them from before you and gave
you their land. ¹⁰I said to you, 'I am the
LORD your God; do not worship the gods

of the Amorites, in whose land you live.'
But you have not listened to me."

¹¹The angel of the LORD came and sat
down under the oak in Ophrah that belonged to Joash the Abiezrite, where his
son Gideon was threshing wheat in a
winepress to keep it from the Midianites.
¹²When the angel of the LORD appeared to
Gideon, he said, "The LORD is with you,
mighty warrior."

¹³"But sir," Gideon replied, "if the LORD
is with us, why has all this happened to
us? Where are all his wonders that our fathers told us about when they said, 'Did
not the LORD bring us up out of Egypt?'
But now the LORD has abandoned us and
put us into the hand of Midian."

¹⁴The LORD turned to him and said, "Go
in the strength you have and save Israel
out of Midian's hand. Am I not sending
you?"

¹⁵"But Lord,ᵃ" Gideon asked, "how can I
save Israel? My clan is the weakest in Manasseh, and I am the least in my family."

¹⁶The LORD answered, "I will be with
you, and you will strike down all the Midianites together."

¹⁷Gideon replied, "If now I have found
favor in your eyes, give me a sign that it is
really you talking to me. ¹⁸Please do not go
away until I come back and bring my offering and set it before you."

And the LORD said, "I will wait until you
return."

¹⁹Gideon went in, prepared a young
goat, and from an ephahᵇ of flour he made
bread without yeast. Putting the meat in a
basket and its broth in a pot, he brought
them out and offered them to him under
the oak.

²⁰The angel of God said to him, "Take
the meat and the unleavened bread, place
them on this rock, and pour out the
broth." And Gideon did so. ²¹With the tip
of the staff that was in his hand, the angel
of the LORD touched the meat and the unleavened bread. Fire flared from the rock,
consuming the meat and the bread. And
the angel of the LORD disappeared.
²²When Gideon realized that it was the
angel of the LORD, he exclaimed, "Ah, Sovereign LORD! I have seen the angel of the
LORD face to face!"

²³But the LORD said to him, "Peace! Do
not be afraid. You are not going to die."

²⁴So Gideon built an altar to the LORD
there and called it The LORD is Peace. To

ᵃ15 Or sir   ᵇ19 That is, probably about 3/5 bushel
(about 22 liters)

this day it stands in Ophrah of the Abiezrites. ²⁵That same night the LORD said to him, "Take the second bull from your father's herd, the one seven years old.ᵃ Tear down your father's altar to Baal and cut down the Asherah poleᵇ beside it. ²⁶Then build a proper kind ofᶜ altar to the LORD your God on the top of this height. Using the wood of the Asherah pole that you cut down, offer the secondᵈ bull as a burnt offering."

²⁷So Gideon took ten of his servants and did as the LORD told him. But because he was afraid of his family and the men of the town, he did it at night rather than in the daytime.

²⁸In the morning when the men of the town got up, there was Baal's altar, demolished, with the Asherah pole beside it cut down and the second bull sacrificed on the newly built altar!

²⁹They asked each other, "Who did this?"

When they carefully investigated, they were told, "Gideon son of Joash did it."

³⁰The men of the town demanded of Joash, "Bring out your son. He must die, because he has broken down Baal's altar and cut down the Asherah pole beside it."

³¹But Joash replied to the hostile crowd around him, "Are you going to plead Baal's cause? Are you trying to save him? Whoever fights for him shall be put to death by morning! If Baal really is a god, he can defend himself when someone breaks down his altar." ³²So that day they called Gideon "Jerub-Baal,ᵉ" saying, "Let Baal contend with him," because he broke down Baal's altar.

³³Now all the Midianites, Amalekites and other eastern peoples joined forces and crossed over the Jordan and camped in the Valley of Jezreel. ³⁴Then the Spirit of the LORD came upon Gideon, and he blew a trumpet, summoning the Abiezrites to follow him. ³⁵He sent messengers throughout Manasseh, calling them to arms, and also into Asher, Zebulun and Naphtali, so that they too went up to meet them.

³⁶Gideon said to God, "If you will save Israel by my hand as you have promised— ³⁷look, I will place a wool fleece on the threshing floor. If there is dew only on the fleece and all the ground is dry, then I will know that you will save Israel by my hand, as you said." ³⁸And that is what happened. Gideon rose early the next day; he squeezed the fleece and wrung out the dew—a bowlful of water.

³⁹Then Gideon said to God, "Do not be angry with me. Let me make just one more request. Allow me one more test with the fleece. This time make the fleece dry and the ground covered with dew." ⁴⁰That night God did so. Only the fleece was dry; all the ground was covered with dew.

Gideon Defeats the Midianites

7 Early in the morning, Jerub-Baal (that is, Gideon) and all his men camped at the spring of Harod. The camp of Midian was north of them in the valley near the hill of Moreh. ²The LORD said to Gideon, "You have too many men for me to deliver Midian into their hands. In order that Israel may not boast against me that her own strength has saved her, ³announce now to the people, 'Anyone who trembles with fear may turn back and leave Mount Gilead.' " So twenty-two thousand men left, while ten thousand remained.

⁴But the LORD said to Gideon, "There are still too many men. Take them down to the water, and I will sift them for you there. If I say, 'This one shall go with you,' he shall go; but if I say, 'This one shall not go with you,' he shall not go."

⁵So Gideon took the men down to the water. There the LORD told him, "Separate those who lap the water with their tongues like a dog from those who kneel down to drink." ⁶Three hundred men lapped with their hands to their mouths. All the rest got down on their knees to drink.

⁷The LORD said to Gideon, "With the three hundred men that lapped I will save you and give the Midianites into your hands. Let all the other men go, each to his own place." ⁸So Gideon sent the rest of the Israelites to their tents but kept the three hundred, who took over the provisions and trumpets of the others.

Now the camp of Midian lay below him in the valley. ⁹During that night the LORD said to Gideon, "Get up, go down against the camp, because I am going to give it into your hands. ¹⁰If you are afraid to attack, go down to the camp with your servant Purah ¹¹and listen to what they are saying. Afterward, you will be encouraged

---

ᵃ25 Or *Take a full-grown, mature bull from your father's herd*   ᵇ25 That is, a symbol of the goddess Asherah; here and elsewhere in Judges   ᶜ26 Or *build with layers of stone an*   ᵈ26 Or *full-grown*; also in verse 28   ᵉ32 *Jerub-Baal* means *let Baal contend.*

to attack the camp." So he and Purah his servant went down to the outposts of the camp. ¹²The Midianites, the Amalekites and all the other eastern peoples had settled in the valley, thick as locusts. Their camels could no more be counted than the sand on the seashore. ¹³Gideon arrived just as a man was telling a friend his dream. "I had a dream," he was saying. "A round loaf of barley bread came tumbling into the Midianite camp. It struck the tent with such force that the tent overturned and collapsed."

¹⁴His friend responded, "This can be nothing other than the sword of Gideon son of Joash, the Israelite. God has given the Midianites and the whole camp into his hands."

¹⁵When Gideon heard the dream and its interpretation, he worshiped God. He returned to the camp of Israel and called out, "Get up! The LORD has given the Midianite camp into your hands." ¹⁶Dividing the three hundred men into three companies, he placed trumpets and empty jars in the hands of all of them, with torches inside.

Against All Odds

DAILY INSIGHT

FRIDAY

Passage:
Judges 7:1–8,19–21

Verse:
Judges 7:21

Don't you love cheering for the underdog? In pro basketball, we're pulling for the five-foot three-inch Muggsy Bouges as he brilliantly negotiates his way in a land of giants. In golf, it's Tiger Woods, the 21-year-old rookie, at the 1997 Masters. In hockey, it's the American boys against the Soviets in the 1980 Olympic Games. In baseball, it's the 1969 Mets or the 1988 Dodgers. We love to watch these courageous athletes in the face of what shouldn't be, doing the impossible and winning!

The story today is one of the most incredible, against-all-odds stories in history. Gideon has a battle scheduled against the formidable Midianites. They're the New York Yankees of the sixties; the Miami Dolphins of the seventies; the Chicago Bulls of the nineties. They're tough, they're big, and they're very good … not to mention that there are *three times as many of them* as there are in Gideon's army!

Then God has a little chat with Gideon (vv. 2–8). "This is *my* battle," God tells a trembling Gideon, "And I want everyone to know it for sure." He instructs Gideon to slash his roster to a bare-bones count of three hundred brave soldiers.

If they were underdogs against one hundred thousand Midianite troops at the beginning of this story, imagine what they are now! Nonetheless, because Gideon's men obey God and "hold their positions" (v. 21), the Scripture tells us that all the

Midianites run. To make it really incredible, they *cry* as they run. Can you hear this? One hundred thousand grown men running and crying like kids fleeing from a sandbox bully. Unbelievable.

The story of Gideon is another spectacular Biblical account. But here's the message for you and me: *We're underdogs in a huge way.* Picture for a moment all the people in your world who think you're wasting your time right now, reading God's Word, listening to his voice, then committing yourself to obedient living. "It's understandable," they might say, "to attend church (when you have the time), but to take God seriously? To deeply desire to trust him and live for him and lead your family in his ways? What are you, some kind of religious fanatic?"

But you quietly take refuge in the God of the Bible. This is the One who faithfully led Gideon to victory against the Midianites. The One who promises courage for today and hope for tomorrow. The One who gives wisdom in the face of every challenge a man faces—at work, at home, in his own heart. And you feel a new sense of expectation … against the odds.

Just like Gideon, even though you're an underdog, you have the assurance of God's presence. With this confidence, you can go for it. I can't wait to see the highlight films. This is going to be good.

For your next devotional reading, go to page 282.

¹⁷"Watch me," he told them. "Follow my lead. When I get to the edge of the camp, do exactly as I do. ¹⁸When I and all who are with me blow our trumpets, then from all around the camp blow yours and shout, 'For the LORD and for Gideon.' "

¹⁹Gideon and the hundred men with him reached the edge of the camp at the beginning of the middle watch, just after they had changed the guard. They blew their trumpets and broke the jars that were in their hands. ²⁰The three companies blew the trumpets and smashed the jars. Grasping the torches in their left hands and holding in their right hands the trumpets they were to blow, they shouted, "A sword for the LORD and for Gideon!" ²¹While each man held his position around the camp, all the Midianites ran, crying out as they fled.

²²When the three hundred trumpets sounded, the LORD caused the men throughout the camp to turn on each other with their swords. The army fled to Beth Shittah toward Zererah as far as the border of Abel Meholah near Tabbath. ²³Israelites from Naphtali, Asher and all Manasseh were called out, and they pursued the Midianites. ²⁴Gideon sent messengers throughout the hill country of Ephraim, saying, "Come down against the Midianites and seize the waters of the Jordan ahead of them as far as Beth Barah."

So all the men of Ephraim were called out and they took the waters of the Jordan as far as Beth Barah. ²⁵They also captured two of the Midianite leaders, Oreb and Zeeb. They killed Oreb at the rock of Oreb, and Zeeb at the winepress of Zeeb. They pursued the Midianites and brought the heads of Oreb and Zeeb to Gideon, who was by the Jordan.

Zebah and Zalmunna

8 Now the Ephraimites asked Gideon, "Why have you treated us like this? Why didn't you call us when you went to fight Midian?" And they criticized him sharply.

²But he answered them, "What have I accomplished compared to you? Aren't the gleanings of Ephraim's grapes better than the full grape harvest of Abiezer? ³God gave Oreb and Zeeb, the Midianite leaders, into your hands. What was I able to do compared to you?" At this, their resentment against him subsided.

⁴Gideon and his three hundred men, exhausted yet keeping up the pursuit,

came to the Jordan and crossed it. ⁵He said to the men of Succoth, "Give my troops some bread; they are worn out, and I am still pursuing Zebah and Zalmunna, the kings of Midian."

⁶But the officials of Succoth said, "Do you already have the hands of Zebah and Zalmunna in your possession? Why should we give bread to your troops?"

⁷Then Gideon replied, "Just for that, when the LORD has given Zebah and Zalmunna into my hand, I will tear your flesh with desert thorns and briers."

⁸From there he went up to Peniel[a] and made the same request of them, but they answered as the men of Succoth had. ⁹So he said to the men of Peniel, "When I return in triumph, I will tear down this tower."

¹⁰Now Zebah and Zalmunna were in Karkor with a force of about fifteen thousand men, all that were left of the armies of the eastern peoples; a hundred and twenty thousand swordsmen had fallen. ¹¹Gideon went up by the route of the nomads east of Nobah and Jogbehah and fell upon the unsuspecting army. ¹²Zebah and Zalmunna, the two kings of Midian, fled, but he pursued them and captured them, routing their entire army.

¹³Gideon son of Joash then returned from the battle by the Pass of Heres. ¹⁴He caught a young man of Succoth and questioned him, and the young man wrote down for him the names of the seventy-seven officials of Succoth, the elders of the town. ¹⁵Then Gideon came and said to the men of Succoth, "Here are Zebah and Zalmunna, about whom you taunted me by saying, 'Do you already have the hands of Zebah and Zalmunna in your possession? Why should we give bread to your exhausted men?' " ¹⁶He took the elders of the town and taught the men of Succoth a lesson by punishing them with desert thorns and briers. ¹⁷He also pulled down the tower of Peniel and killed the men of the town.

¹⁸Then he asked Zebah and Zalmunna, "What kind of men did you kill at Tabor?"

"Men like you," they answered, "each one with the bearing of a prince."

¹⁹Gideon replied, "Those were my brothers, the sons of my own mother. As surely as the LORD lives, if you had spared their lives, I would not kill you." ²⁰Turning to Jether, his oldest son, he said, "Kill

a8 Hebrew Penuel, a variant of Peniel: also in verses 9 and 17 them!" But Jether did not draw his sword, because he was only a boy and was afraid.

²¹Zebah and Zalmunna said, "Come, do it yourself. 'As is the man, so is his strength.'" So Gideon stepped forward and killed them, and took the ornaments off their camels' necks.

Gideon's Ephod

²²The Israelites said to Gideon, "Rule over us—you, your son and your grandson—because you have saved us out of the hand of Midian."

²³But Gideon told them, "I will not rule over you, nor will my son rule over you. The LORD will rule over you." ²⁴And he said, "I do have one request, that each of you give me an earring from your share of the plunder." (It was the custom of the Ishmaelites to wear gold earrings.)

²⁵They answered, "We'll be glad to give them." So they spread out a garment, and each man threw a ring from his plunder onto it. ²⁶The weight of the gold rings he asked for came to seventeen hundred shekels,ᵃ not counting the ornaments, the pendants and the purple garments worn by the kings of Midian or the chains that were on their camels' necks. ²⁷Gideon made the gold into an ephod, which he placed in Ophrah, his town. All Israel prostituted themselves by worshiping it there, and it became a snare to Gideon and his family.

Gideon's Death

²⁸Thus Midian was subdued before the Israelites and did not raise its head again. During Gideon's lifetime, the land enjoyed peace forty years.

²⁹Jerub-Baal son of Joash went back home to live. ³⁰He had seventy sons of his own, for he had many wives. ³¹His concubine, who lived in Shechem, also bore him a son, whom he named Abimelech. ³²Gideon son of Joash died at a good old age and was buried in the tomb of his father Joash in Ophrah of the Abiezrites.

³³No sooner had Gideon died than the Israelites again prostituted themselves to the Baals. They set up Baal-Berith as their god and ³⁴did not remember the LORD their God, who had rescued them from the hands of all their enemies on every side. ³⁵They also failed to show kindness to the family of Jerub-Baal (that is, Gideon) for all the good things he had done for them.

Abimelech

9 Abimelech son of Jerub-Baal went to his mother's brothers in Shechem and said to them and to all his mother's clan, ²"Ask all the citizens of Shechem, 'Which is better for you: to have all seventy of Jerub-Baal's sons rule over you, or just one man?' Remember, I am your flesh and blood."

³When the brothers repeated all this to the citizens of Shechem, they were inclined to follow Abimelech, for they said, "He is our brother." ⁴They gave him seventy shekelsᵇ of silver from the temple of Baal-Berith, and Abimelech used it to hire reckless adventurers, who became his followers. ⁵He went to his father's home in Ophrah and on one stone murdered his seventy brothers, the sons of Jerub-Baal. But Jotham, the youngest son of Jerub-Baal, escaped by hiding. ⁶Then all the citizens of Shechem and Beth Millo gathered beside the great tree at the pillar in Shechem to crown Abimelech king.

⁷When Jotham was told about this, he climbed up on the top of Mount Gerizim and shouted to them, "Listen to me, citizens of Shechem, so that God may listen to you. ⁸One day the trees went out to anoint a king for themselves. They said to the olive tree, 'Be our king.'

⁹"But the olive tree answered, 'Should I give up my oil, by which both gods and men are honored, to hold sway over the trees?'

¹⁰"Next, the trees said to the fig tree, 'Come and be our king.'

¹¹"But the fig tree replied, 'Should I give up my fruit, so good and sweet, to hold sway over the trees?'

¹²"Then the trees said to the vine, 'Come and be our king.'

¹³"But the vine answered, 'Should I give up my wine, which cheers both gods and men, to hold sway over the trees?'

¹⁴"Finally all the trees said to the thornbush, 'Come and be our king.'

¹⁵"The thornbush said to the trees, 'If you really want to anoint me king over you, come and take refuge in my shade; but if not, then let fire come out of the thornbush and consume the cedars of Lebanon!'

¹⁶"Now if you have acted honorably and in good faith when you made Abimelech

---

ᵃ26 That is, about 43 pounds (about 19.5 kilograms)   ᵇ4 That is, about 1 3/4 pounds (about 0.8 kilogram) king, and if you have been fair to Jerub-Baal and his family, and if you have treated him as he deserves— [17]and to think that my father fought for you, risked his life to rescue you from the hand of Midian [18](but today you have revolted against my father's family, murdered his seventy sons on a single stone, and made Abimelech, the son of his slave girl, king over the citizens of Shechem because he is your brother)— [19]if then you have acted honorably and in good faith toward Jerub-Baal and his family today, may Abimelech be your joy, and may you be his, too! [20]But if you have not, let fire come out from Abimelech and consume you, citizens of Shechem and Beth Millo, and let fire come out from you, citizens of Shechem and Beth Millo, and consume Abimelech!"

[21]Then Jotham fled, escaping to Beer, and he lived there because he was afraid of his brother Abimelech.

[22]After Abimelech had governed Israel three years, [23]God sent an evil spirit between Abimelech and the citizens of Shechem, who acted treacherously against Abimelech. [24]God did this in order that the crime against Jerub-Baal's seventy sons, the shedding of their blood, might be avenged on their brother Abimelech and on the citizens of Shechem, who had helped him murder his brothers. [25]In opposition to him these citizens of Shechem set men on the hilltops to ambush and rob everyone who passed by, and this was reported to Abimelech.

[26]Now Gaal son of Ebed moved with his brothers into Shechem, and its citizens put their confidence in him. [27]After they had gone out into the fields and gathered the grapes and trodden them, they held a festival in the temple of their god. While they were eating and drinking, they cursed Abimelech. [28]Then Gaal son of Ebed said, "Who is Abimelech, and who is Shechem, that we should be subject to him? Isn't he Jerub-Baal's son, and isn't Zebul his deputy? Serve the men of Hamor, Shechem's father! Why should we serve Abimelech? [29]If only this people were under my command! Then I would get rid of him. I would say to Abimelech, 'Call out your whole army!' "[a]

[30]When Zebul the governor of the city heard what Gaal son of Ebed said, he was very angry. [31]Under cover he sent messengers to Abimelech, saying, "Gaal son of Ebed and his brothers have come to Shechem and are stirring up the city against you. [32]Now then, during the night you and your men should come and lie in wait in the fields. [33]In the morning at sunrise, advance against the city. When Gaal and his men come out against you, do whatever your hand finds to do."

[34]So Abimelech and all his troops set out by night and took up concealed positions near Shechem in four companies. [35]Now Gaal son of Ebed had gone out and was standing at the entrance to the city gate just as Abimelech and his soldiers came out from their hiding place.

[36]When Gaal saw them, he said to Zebul, "Look, people are coming down from the tops of the mountains!"

Zebul replied, "You mistake the shadows of the mountains for men."

[37]But Gaal spoke up again: "Look, people are coming down from the center of the land, and a company is coming from the direction of the soothsayers' tree."

[38]Then Zebul said to him, "Where is your big talk now, you who said, 'Who is Abimelech that we should be subject to him?' Aren't these the men you ridiculed? Go out and fight them!"

[39]So Gaal led out[b] the citizens of Shechem and fought Abimelech. [40]Abimelech chased him, and many fell wounded in the flight—all the way to the entrance to the gate. [41]Abimelech stayed in Arumah, and Zebul drove Gaal and his brothers out of Shechem.

[42]The next day the people of Shechem went out to the fields, and this was reported to Abimelech. [43]So he took his men, divided them into three companies and set an ambush in the fields. When he saw the people coming out of the city, he rose to attack them. [44]Abimelech and the companies with him rushed forward to a position at the entrance to the city gate. Then two companies rushed upon those in the fields and struck them down. [45]All that day Abimelech pressed his attack against the city until he had captured it and killed its people. Then he destroyed the city and scattered salt over it.

[46]On hearing this, the citizens in the tower of Shechem went into the stronghold of the temple of El-Berith. [47]When Abimelech heard that they had assembled there, [48]he and all his men went up Mount Zalmon. He took an ax and cut off some

---

[a]29 Septuagint; Hebrew *him." Then he said to Abimelech, "Call out your whole army!"*   [b]39 Or *Gaal went out in the sight of*

branches, which he lifted to his shoulders. He ordered the men with him, "Quick! Do what you have seen me do!" [49]So all the men cut branches and followed Abimelech. They piled them against the stronghold and set it on fire over the people inside. So all the people in the tower of Shechem, about a thousand men and women, also died.

[50]Next Abimelech went to Thebez and besieged it and captured it. [51]Inside the city, however, was a strong tower, to which all the men and women—all the people of the city—fled. They locked themselves in and climbed up on the tower roof. [52]Abimelech went to the tower and stormed it. But as he approached the entrance to the tower to set it on fire, [53]a woman dropped an upper millstone on his head and cracked his skull.

[54]Hurriedly he called to his armor-bearer, "Draw your sword and kill me, so that they can't say, 'A woman killed him.' " So his servant ran him through, and he died. [55]When the Israelites saw that Abimelech was dead, they went home.

[56]Thus God repaid the wickedness that Abimelech had done to his father by murdering his seventy brothers. [57]God also made the men of Shechem pay for all their wickedness. The curse of Jotham son of Jerub-Baal came on them.

Tola

10 After the time of Abimelech a man of Issachar, Tola son of Puah, the son of Dodo, rose to save Israel. He lived in Shamir, in the hill country of Ephraim. [2]He led[a] Israel twenty-three years; then he died, and was buried in Shamir.

Jair

[3]He was followed by Jair of Gilead, who led Israel twenty-two years. [4]He had had thirty sons, who rode thirty donkeys. They controlled thirty towns in Gilead, which to this day are called Havvoth Jair.[b] [5]When Jair died, he was buried in Kamon.

Jephthah

[6]Again the Israelites did evil in the eyes of the LORD. They served the Baals and the Ashtoreths, and the gods of Aram, the gods of Sidon, the gods of Moab, the gods of the Ammonites and the gods of the Philistines. And because the Israelites forsook the LORD and no longer served him, [7]he became angry with them. He sold

them into the hands of the Philistines and the Ammonites, [8]who that year shattered and crushed them. For eighteen years they oppressed all the Israelites on the east side of the Jordan in Gilead, the land of the Amorites. [9]The Ammonites also crossed the Jordan to fight against Judah, Benjamin and the house of Ephraim; and Israel was in great distress. [10]Then the Israelites cried out to the LORD, "We have sinned against you, forsaking our God and serving the Baals."

[11]The LORD replied, "When the Egyptians, the Amorites, the Ammonites, the Philistines, [12]the Sidonians, the Amalekites and the Maonites[c] oppressed you and you cried to me for help, did I not save you from their hands? [13]But you have forsaken me and served other gods, so I will no longer save you. [14]Go and cry out to the gods you have chosen. Let them save you when you are in trouble!"

[15]But the Israelites said to the LORD, "We have sinned. Do with us whatever you think best, but please rescue us now." [16]Then they got rid of the foreign gods among them and served the LORD. And he could bear Israel's misery no longer.

[17]When the Ammonites were called to arms and camped in Gilead, the Israelites assembled and camped at Mizpah. [18]The leaders of the people of Gilead said to each other, "Whoever will launch the attack against the Ammonites will be the head of all those living in Gilead."

11 Jephthah the Gileadite was a mighty warrior. His father was Gilead; his mother was a prostitute. [2]Gilead's wife also bore him sons, and when they were grown up, they drove Jephthah away. "You are not going to get any inheritance in our family," they said, "because you are the son of another woman." [3]So Jephthah fled from his brothers and settled in the land of Tob, where a group of adventurers gathered around him and followed him.

[4]Some time later, when the Ammonites made war on Israel, [5]the elders of Gilead went to get Jephthah from the land of Tob. [6]"Come," they said, "be our commander, so we can fight the Ammonites."

[7]Jephthah said to them, "Didn't you hate me and drive me from my father's house? Why do you come to me now, when you're in trouble?"

[8]The elders of Gilead said to him, "Nev-

a2 Traditionally judged; also in verse 3   b4 Or called the settlements of Jair c12 Hebrew; some Septuagint manuscripts Midianites ertheless, we are turning to you now; come with us to fight the Ammonites, and you will be our head over all who live in Gilead."

⁹Jephthah answered, "Suppose you take me back to fight the Ammonites and the LORD gives them to me—will I really be your head?"

¹⁰The elders of Gilead replied, "The LORD is our witness; we will certainly do as you say." ¹¹So Jephthah went with the elders of Gilead, and the people made him head and commander over them. And he repeated all his words before the LORD in Mizpah.

¹²Then Jephthah sent messengers to the Ammonite king with the question: "What do you have against us that you have attacked our country?"

¹³The king of the Ammonites answered Jephthah's messengers, "When Israel came up out of Egypt, they took away my land from the Arnon to the Jabbok, all the way to the Jordan. Now give it back peaceably."

¹⁴Jephthah sent back messengers to the Ammonite king, ¹⁵saying:

"This is what Jephthah says: Israel did not take the land of Moab or the land of the Ammonites. ¹⁶But when they came up out of Egypt, Israel went through the desert to the Red Sea[a] and on to Kadesh. ¹⁷Then Israel sent messengers to the king of Edom, saying, 'Give us permission to go through your country,' but the king of Edom would not listen. They sent also to the king of Moab, and he refused. So Israel stayed at Kadesh.

¹⁸"Next they traveled through the desert, skirted the lands of Edom and Moab, passed along the eastern side of the country of Moab, and camped on the other side of the Arnon. They did not enter the territory of Moab, for the Arnon was its border.

¹⁹"Then Israel sent messengers to Sihon king of the Amorites, who ruled in Heshbon, and said to him, 'Let us pass through your country to our own place.' ²⁰Sihon, however, did not trust Israel[b] to pass through his territory. He mustered all his men and encamped at Jahaz and fought with Israel.

²¹"Then the LORD, the God of Israel, gave Sihon and all his men into Israel's hands, and they defeated them. Israel took over all the land of the Amorites who lived in that country, ²²capturing all of it from the Arnon to the Jabbok and from the desert to the Jordan.

²³"Now since the LORD, the God of Israel, has driven the Amorites out before his people Israel, what right have you to take it over? ²⁴Will you not take what your god Chemosh gives you? Likewise, whatever the LORD our God has given us, we will possess. ²⁵Are you better than Balak son of Zippor, king of Moab? Did he ever quarrel with Israel or fight with them? ²⁶For three hundred years Israel occupied Heshbon, Aroer, the surrounding settlements and all the towns along the Arnon. Why didn't you retake them during that time? ²⁷I have not wronged you, but you are doing me wrong by waging war against me. Let the LORD, the Judge,[c] decide the dispute this day between the Israelites and the Ammonites."

²⁸The king of Ammon, however, paid no attention to the message Jephthah sent him.

²⁹Then the Spirit of the LORD came upon Jephthah. He crossed Gilead and Manasseh, passed through Mizpah of Gilead, and from there he advanced against the Ammonites. ³⁰And Jephthah made a vow to the LORD: "If you give the Ammonites into my hands, ³¹whatever comes out of the door of my house to meet me when I return in triumph from the Ammonites will be the LORD's, and I will sacrifice it as a burnt offering."

³²Then Jephthah went over to fight the Ammonites, and the LORD gave them into his hands. ³³He devastated twenty towns from Aroer to the vicinity of Minnith, as far as Abel Keramim. Thus Israel subdued Ammon.

³⁴When Jephthah returned to his home in Mizpah, who should come out to meet him but his daughter, dancing to the sound of tambourines! She was an only child. Except for her he had neither son nor daughter. ³⁵When he saw her, he tore his clothes and cried, "Oh! My daughter! You have made me miserable and wretched, because I have made a vow to the LORD that I cannot break."

³⁶"My father," she replied, "you have given your word to the LORD. Do to me

---

a16 Hebrew *Yam Suph*; that is, Sea of Reeds   *b20* Or *however, would not make an agreement for Israel*   *c27* Or *Ruler* just as you promised, now that the LORD has avenged you of your enemies, the Ammonites. **37**But grant me this one request," she said. "Give me two months to roam the hills and weep with my friends, because I will never marry."

38"You may go," he said. And he let her go for two months. She and the girls went into the hills and wept because she would never marry. **39**After the two months, she returned to her father and he did to her as he had vowed. And she was a virgin.

From this comes the Israelite custom **40**that each year the young women of Israel go out for four days to commemorate the daughter of Jephthah the Gileadite.

Jephthah and Ephraim

12 The men of Ephraim called out their forces, crossed over to Zaphon and said to Jephthah, "Why did you go to fight the Ammonites without calling us to go with you? We're going to burn down your house over your head."

2Jephthah answered, "I and my people were engaged in a great struggle with the Ammonites, and although I called, you didn't save me out of their hands. **3**When I saw that you wouldn't help, I took my life in my hands and crossed over to fight the Ammonites, and the LORD gave me the victory over them. Now why have you come up today to fight me?"

4Jephthah then called together the men of Gilead and fought against Ephraim. The Gileadites struck them down because the Ephraimites had said, "You Gileadites are renegades from Ephraim and Manasseh." **5**The Gileadites captured the fords of the Jordan leading to Ephraim, and whenever a survivor of Ephraim said, "Let me cross over," the men of Gilead asked him, "Are you an Ephraimite?" If he replied, "No," **6**they said, "All right, say 'Shibboleth.'" If he said, "Sibboleth," because he could not pronounce the word correctly, they seized him and killed him at the fords of the Jordan. Forty-two thousand Ephraimites were killed at that time.

7Jephthah led*a* Israel six years. Then Jephthah the Gileadite died, and was buried in a town in Gilead.

Ibzan, Elon and Abdon

8After him, Ibzan of Bethlehem led Israel. **9**He had thirty sons and thirty daughters. He gave his daughters away in marriage to those outside his clan, and for his sons he brought in thirty young women as wives from outside his clan. Ibzan led Israel seven years. **10**Then Ibzan died, and was buried in Bethlehem.

11After him, Elon the Zebulunite led Israel ten years. **12**Then Elon died, and was buried in Aijalon in the land of Zebulun.

13After him, Abdon son of Hillel, from Pirathon, led Israel. **14**He had forty sons and thirty grandsons, who rode on seventy donkeys. He led Israel eight years. **15**Then Abdon son of Hillel died, and was buried at Pirathon in Ephraim, in the hill country of the Amalekites.

The Birth of Samson

13 Again the Israelites did evil in the eyes of the LORD, so the LORD delivered them into the hands of the Philistines for forty years.

2A certain man of Zorah, named Manoah, from the clan of the Danites, had a wife who was sterile and remained childless. **3**The angel of the LORD appeared to her and said, "You are sterile and childless, but you are going to conceive and have a son. **4**Now see to it that you drink no wine or other fermented drink and that you do not eat anything unclean, **5**because you will conceive and give birth to a son. No razor may be used on his head, because the boy is to be a Nazirite, set apart to God from birth, and he will begin the deliverance of Israel from the hands of the Philistines."

6Then the woman went to her husband and told him, "A man of God came to me. He looked like an angel of God, very awesome. I didn't ask him where he came from, and he didn't tell me his name. **7**But he said to me, 'You will conceive and give birth to a son. Now then, drink no wine or other fermented drink and do not eat anything unclean, because the boy will be a Nazirite of God from birth until the day of his death.'"

8Then Manoah prayed to the LORD: "O Lord, I beg you, let the man of God you sent to us come again to teach us how to bring up the boy who is to be born."

9God heard Manoah, and the angel of God came again to the woman while she was out in the field; but her husband Manoah was not with her. **10**The woman hurried to tell her husband, "He's here! The man who appeared to me the other day!"

11Manoah got up and followed his wife.

---

a7 Traditionally judged; also in verses 8-14

When he came to the man, he said, "Are you the one who talked to my wife?"

"I am," he said.

[12]So Manoah asked him, "When your words are fulfilled, what is to be the rule for the boy's life and work?"

[13]The angel of the LORD answered, "Your wife must do all that I have told her. [14]She must not eat anything that comes from the grapevine, nor drink any wine or other fermented drink nor eat anything unclean. She must do everything I have commanded her."

[15]Manoah said to the angel of the LORD, "We would like you to stay until we prepare a young goat for you."

[16]The angel of the LORD replied, "Even though you detain me, I will not eat any of your food. But if you prepare a burnt offering, offer it to the LORD." (Manoah did not realize that it was the angel of the LORD.)

[17]Then Manoah inquired of the angel of the LORD, "What is your name, so that we may honor you when your word comes true?"

[18]He replied, "Why do you ask my name? It is beyond understanding.[a]" [19]Then Manoah took a young goat, together with the grain offering, and sacrificed it on a rock to the LORD. And the LORD did an amazing thing while Manoah and his wife watched: [20]As the flame blazed up from the altar toward heaven, the angel of the LORD ascended in the flame. Seeing this, Manoah and his wife fell with their faces to the ground. [21]When the angel of the LORD did not show himself again to Manoah and his wife, Manoah realized that it was the angel of the LORD.

[22]"We are doomed to die!" he said to his wife. "We have seen God!"

[23]But his wife answered, "If the LORD had meant to kill us, he would not have accepted a burnt offering and grain offering from our hands, nor shown us all these things or now told us this."

[24]The woman gave birth to a boy and named him Samson. He grew and the LORD blessed him, [25]and the Spirit of the LORD began to stir him while he was in Mahaneh Dan, between Zorah and Eshtaol.

Samson's Marriage

14 Samson went down to Timnah and saw there a young Philistine woman. [2]When he returned, he said to his father and mother, "I have seen a Philistine woman in Timnah; now get her for me as my wife."

[3]His father and mother replied, "Isn't there an acceptable woman among your relatives or among all our people? Must you go to the uncircumcised Philistines to get a wife?"

But Samson said to his father, "Get her for me. She's the right one for me." [4](His parents did not know that this was from the LORD, who was seeking an occasion to confront the Philistines; for at that time they were ruling over Israel.) [5]Samson went down to Timnah together with his father and mother. As they approached the vineyards of Timnah, suddenly a young lion came roaring toward him. [6]The Spirit of the LORD came upon him in power so that he tore the lion apart with his bare hands as he might have torn a young goat. But he told neither his father nor his mother what he had done. [7]Then he went down and talked with the woman, and he liked her.

[8]Some time later, when he went back to marry her, he turned aside to look at the lion's carcass. In it was a swarm of bees and some honey, [9]which he scooped out with his hands and ate as he went along. When he rejoined his parents, he gave them some, and they too ate it. But he did not tell them that he had taken the honey from the lion's carcass.

[10]Now his father went down to see the woman. And Samson made a feast there, as was customary for bridegrooms. [11]When he appeared, he was given thirty companions.

[12]"Let me tell you a riddle," Samson said to them. "If you can give me the answer within the seven days of the feast, I will give you thirty linen garments and thirty sets of clothes. [13]If you can't tell me the answer, you must give me thirty linen garments and thirty sets of clothes."

"Tell us your riddle," they said. "Let's hear it."

[14]He replied,

"Out of the eater, something to eat;
  out of the strong, something sweet."

For three days they could not give the answer.

[15]On the fourth[b] day, they said to Samson's wife, "Coax your husband into explaining the riddle for us, or we will

[a]18 Or *is wonderful*   [b]15 Some Septuagint manuscripts and Syriac; Hebrew *seventh*

burn you and your father's household to death. Did you invite us here to rob us?"

[16]Then Samson's wife threw herself on him, sobbing, "You hate me! You don't really love me. You've given my people a riddle, but you haven't told me the answer."

"I haven't even explained it to my father or mother," he replied, "so why should I explain it to you?" [17]She cried the whole seven days of the feast. So on the seventh day he finally told her, because she continued to press him. She in turn explained the riddle to her people.

[18]Before sunset on the seventh day the men of the town said to him,

"What is sweeter than honey?
    What is stronger than a lion?"

Samson said to them,

"If you had not plowed with my heifer,
    you would not have solved my
        riddle."

[19]Then the Spirit of the LORD came upon him in power. He went down to Ashkelon, struck down thirty of their men, stripped them of their belongings and gave their clothes to those who had explained the riddle. Burning with anger, he went up to his father's house. [20]And Samson's wife was given to the friend who had attended him at his wedding.

Samson's Vengeance on the Philistines

15 Later on, at the time of wheat harvest, Samson took a young goat and went to visit his wife. He said, "I'm going to my wife's room." But her father would not let him go in.

[2]"I was so sure you thoroughly hated her," he said, "that I gave her to your friend. Isn't her younger sister more attractive? Take her instead."

[3]Samson said to them, "This time I have a right to get even with the Philistines; I will really harm them." [4]So he went out and caught three hundred foxes and tied them tail to tail in pairs. He then fastened a torch to every pair of tails, [5]lit the torches and let the foxes loose in the standing grain of the Philistines. He burned up the shocks and standing grain, together with the vineyards and olive groves.

[6]When the Philistines asked, "Who did this?" they were told, "Samson, the Timnite's son-in-law, because his wife was given to his friend."

So the Philistines went up and burned her and her father to death. [7]Samson said to them, "Since you've acted like this, I won't stop until I get my revenge on you." [8]He attacked them viciously and slaughtered many of them. Then he went down and stayed in a cave in the rock of Etam.

[9]The Philistines went up and camped in Judah, spreading out near Lehi. [10]The men of Judah asked, "Why have you come to fight us?"

"We have come to take Samson prisoner," they answered, "to do to him as he did to us."

[11]Then three thousand men from Judah went down to the cave in the rock of Etam and said to Samson, "Don't you realize that the Philistines are rulers over us? What have you done to us?"

He answered, "I merely did to them what they did to me."

[12]They said to him, "We've come to tie you up and hand you over to the Philistines."

Samson said, "Swear to me that you won't kill me yourselves."

[13]"Agreed," they answered. "We will only tie you up and hand you over to them. We will not kill you." So they bound him with two new ropes and led him up from the rock. [14]As he approached Lehi, the Philistines came toward him shouting. The Spirit of the LORD came upon him in power. The ropes on his arms became like charred flax, and the bindings dropped from his hands. [15]Finding a fresh jawbone of a donkey, he grabbed it and struck down a thousand men.

[16]Then Samson said,

"With a donkey's jawbone
    I have made donkeys of them.[a]
With a donkey's jawbone
    I have killed a thousand men."

[17]When he finished speaking, he threw away the jawbone; and the place was called Ramath Lehi.[b]

[18]Because he was very thirsty, he cried out to the LORD, "You have given your servant this great victory. Must I now die of thirst and fall into the hands of the uncircumcised?" [19]Then God opened up the hollow place in Lehi, and water came out of it. When Samson drank, his strength returned and he revived. So the spring was called En Hakkore,[c] and it is still there in Lehi.

---

[a]16 Or *made a heap or two*; the Hebrew for *donkey* sounds like the Hebrew for *heap*.   [b]17 *Ramath Lehi* means *jawbone hill*.   [c]19 *En Hakkore* means *caller's spring*.

[20]Samson led[a] Israel for twenty years in the days of the Philistines.

Samson and Delilah

16 One day Samson went to Gaza, where he saw a prostitute. He went in to spend the night with her. [2]The people of Gaza were told, "Samson is here!" So they surrounded the place and lay in wait for him all night at the city gate. They made no move during the night, saying, "At dawn we'll kill him."

[3]But Samson lay there only until the middle of the night. Then he got up and took hold of the doors of the city gate, together with the two posts, and tore them loose, bar and all. He lifted them to his shoulders and carried them to the top of the hill that faces Hebron.

[4]Some time later, he fell in love with a woman in the Valley of Sorek whose name was Delilah. [5]The rulers of the Philistines went to her and said, "See if you can lure him into showing you the secret of his great strength and how we can overpower him so we may tie him up and subdue him. Each one of us will give you eleven hundred shekels[b] of silver."

[6]So Delilah said to Samson, "Tell me the secret of your great strength and how you can be tied up and subdued."

[7]Samson answered her, "If anyone ties me with seven fresh thongs[c] that have not been dried, I'll become as weak as any other man."

[8]Then the rulers of the Philistines brought her seven fresh thongs that had not been dried, and she tied him with them. [9]With men hidden in the room, she called to him, "Samson, the Philistines are upon you!" But he snapped the thongs as easily as a piece of string snaps when it comes close to a flame. So the secret of his strength was not discovered.

[10]Then Delilah said to Samson, "You have made a fool of me; you lied to me. Come now, tell me how you can be tied."

[11]He said, "If anyone ties me securely with new ropes that have never been used, I'll become as weak as any other man."

[12]So Delilah took new ropes and tied him with them. Then, with men hidden in the room, she called to him, "Samson, the Philistines are upon you!" But he snapped the ropes off his arms as if they were threads.

[13]Delilah then said to Samson, "Until now, you have been making a fool of me and lying to me. Tell me how you can be tied."

[a]20 Traditionally *judged*   [b]5 That is, about 28 pounds (about 13 kilograms)   [c]7 Or *bowstrings*; also in verses 8 and 9

HEY DAD
Why was Samson's hair so strong?

Text: Judges 16:13–14

Samson's strength wasn't literally in his hair! But before Samson was born, God told his parents that Samson was to be a Nazirite, a special servant of God. Nazirites were set apart from others by their appearance and behavior. For example, Nazirites weren't allowed to drink wine or anything fermented, and they weren't allowed to cut their hair—or, if they were men, trim their beards (women could be Nazirites, too).

A Nazirite wasn't a hermit, a priest, or part of a certain tribe. He or she was simply a person who made a voluntary vow to dedicate his or her life to God and be set apart from the world. Samson was one of only two people in the Bible whose parents made this vow for him. (The other person was Samuel.)

So while Samson's hair didn't actually give rise to his strength, his long hair was the outward evidence of his commitment to and special bond with God. Samson's strength came from God, and he would continue to possess it only as long as he remained a Nazirite. When Delilah cut his hair, that bond was broken, and Samson became an ordinary man. God's strength and Spirit left him for a time. (But see vv. 28–30 for the dramatic ending of this story!)

For a complete listing of Questions Kids Ask, turn to page 1435.

Samson's Expensive Haircut

Key Verse: *"Having put him to sleep on her lap, she called a man to shave off the seven braids of his hair, and so began to subdue him. And his strength left him."* Judges 16:19

Text: Judges 16:4–20 *(Dad or child reads the text.)*

QUIET TIMES WITH Dad

DAD READS: When I was your age, sometimes my friends would invite me to do things I knew my parents wouldn't approve of. I remember feeling a lot of pressure because I wanted my friends to like me, but I also wanted to obey my dad and mother. Even as an adult, I am tempted to do things that disappoint my heavenly Father.

Child reads: I know what you're talking about. I know what this pressure feels like. Sometimes my friends want me to join in when they do things that I know would make you unhappy.

DAD READS: Today's verses tell the story about a man whom God had specially appointed to be a leader of the Israelites. Samson was a judge over Israel, one of the few whom God had asked to help his people to be obedient to his voice. During his life, Samson made some very bad decisions. One of them was loving a woman named Delilah who didn't really love Samson. She also didn't believe in God.

Child reads: Delilah acted like she was Samson's friend, but she really wanted to hurt him. She wanted to find the secret to his strength so she could tell Israel's enemies. Samson thought she was playing a game, but she was very serious. Because of what Samson let Delilah do, he lost all of his power.

DAD READS: This is such a sad story. It tells us that even people who are leaders can do foolish things. And because lots of people listen to them, many people are hurt by their disobedience to God. If you and I could have talked to Samson before he made his mistake, we would have told him to be very careful when he chose his friends, especially his wife.

Child reads: And we would have told him not to let Delilah talk him into telling her the secret about his hair, no matter how much she begged. Choosing good friends and not letting people talk us into things that are wrong are two lessons you and I can learn from Samson.

DAD READS: You're right. Let's tell God that we want his strength to help us make good decisions. Let me pray this prayer with you:

Our Father in heaven, thank you for reminding us today of what can happen when we listen to others and not to you. Forgive us for the times when we give in to those who want us to do things that disappoint you. Thank you for loving us and for promising to help us, even in difficult situations. In Jesus' name, *Amen.*

For your next devotional reading, go to page 290.

He replied, "If you weave the seven braids of my head into the fabric on the loom, and tighten it with the pin, I'll become as weak as any other man." So while he was sleeping, Delilah took the seven braids of his head, wove them into the fabric [14]and[a] tightened it with the pin.

Again she called to him, "Samson, the Philistines are upon you!" He awoke from his sleep and pulled up the pin and the loom, with the fabric.

[15]Then she said to him, "How can you say, 'I love you,' when you won't confide in me? This is the third time you have made a fool of me and haven't told me the secret of your great strength." [16]With such nagging she prodded him day after day until he was tired to death.

[17]So he told her everything. "No razor has ever been used on my head," he said, "because I have been a Nazirite set apart to God since birth. If my head were shaved, my strength would leave me, and I would become as weak as any other man."

[18]When Delilah saw that he had told her everything, she sent word to the rulers of the Philistines, "Come back once more; he has told me everything." So the rulers of the Philistines returned with the silver in their hands. [19]Having put him to sleep on her lap, she called a man to shave off the seven braids of his hair, and so began to subdue him.[b] And his strength left him.

[20]Then she called, "Samson, the Philistines are upon you!"

He awoke from his sleep and thought, "I'll go out as before and shake myself free." But he did not know that the LORD had left him.

[21]Then the Philistines seized him, gouged out his eyes and took him down to Gaza. Binding him with bronze shackles, they set him to grinding in the prison. [22]But the hair on his head began to grow again after it had been shaved.

The Death of Samson

[23]Now the rulers of the Philistines assembled to offer a great sacrifice to Dagon their god and to celebrate, saying, "Our god has delivered Samson, our enemy, into our hands."

[24]When the people saw him, they praised their god, saying,

"Our god has delivered our enemy
    into our hands,
the one who laid waste our land
    and multiplied our slain."

[25]While they were in high spirits, they shouted, "Bring out Samson to entertain us." So they called Samson out of the prison, and he performed for them.

When they stood him among the pillars, [26]Samson said to the servant who held his hand, "Put me where I can feel the pillars that support the temple, so that I may lean against them." [27]Now the temple was crowded with men and women; all the rulers of the Philistines were there, and on the roof were about three thousand men and women watching Samson perform. [28]Then Samson prayed to the LORD, "O Sovereign LORD, remember me. O God, please strengthen me just once more, and let me with one blow get revenge on the Philistines for my two eyes." [29]Then Samson reached toward the two central pillars on which the temple stood. Bracing himself against them, his right hand on the one and his left hand on the other, [30]Samson said, "Let me die with the Philistines!" Then he pushed with all his might, and down came the temple on the rulers and all the people in it. Thus he killed many more when he died than while he lived.

[31]Then his brothers and his father's whole family went down to get him. They brought him back and buried him between Zorah and Eshtaol in the tomb of Manoah his father. He had led[c] Israel twenty years.

Micah's Idols

17 Now a man named Micah from the hill country of Ephraim [2]said to his mother, "The eleven hundred shekels[d] of silver that were taken from you and about which I heard you utter a curse—I have that silver with me; I took it."

Then his mother said, "The LORD bless you, my son!"

[3]When he returned the eleven hundred shekels of silver to his mother, she said, "I solemnly consecrate my silver to the LORD for my son to make a carved image and a cast idol. I will give it back to you."

[4]So he returned the silver to his mother, and she took two hundred shekels[e] of silver and gave them to a silversmith, who

---

[a]13,14 Some Septuagint manuscripts; Hebrew ". I can if you weave the seven braids of my head into the fabric on the loom." [14]So she   [b]19 Hebrew; some Septuagint manuscripts and he began to weaken   [c]31 Traditionally judged   [d]2 That is, about 28 pounds (about 13 kilograms)   [e]4 That is, about 5 pounds (about 2.3 kilograms)

made them into the image and the idol. And they were put in Micah's house.

⁵Now this man Micah had a shrine, and he made an ephod and some idols and installed one of his sons as his priest. ⁶In those days Israel had no king; everyone did as he saw fit.

⁷A young Levite from Bethlehem in Judah, who had been living within the clan of Judah, ⁸left that town in search of some other place to stay. On his way*ᵃ* he came to Micah's house in the hill country of Ephraim.

⁹Micah asked him, "Where are you from?"

"I'm a Levite from Bethlehem in Judah," he said, "and I'm looking for a place to stay."

¹⁰Then Micah said to him, "Live with me and be my father and priest, and I'll give you ten shekels*ᵇ* of silver a year, your clothes and your food." ¹¹So the Levite agreed to live with him, and the young man was to him like one of his sons. ¹²Then Micah installed the Levite, and the young man became his priest and lived in his house. ¹³And Micah said, "Now I know that the LORD will be good to me, since this Levite has become my priest."

Danites Settle in Laish

18 In those days Israel had no king. And in those days the tribe of the Danites was seeking a place of their own where they might settle, because they had not yet come into an inheritance among the tribes of Israel. ²So the Danites sent five warriors from Zorah and Eshtaol to spy out the land and explore it. These men represented all their clans. They told them, "Go, explore the land."

The men entered the hill country of Ephraim and came to the house of Micah, where they spent the night. ³When they were near Micah's house, they recognized the voice of the young Levite; so they turned in there and asked him, "Who brought you here? What are you doing in this place? Why are you here?"

⁴He told them what Micah had done for him, and said, "He has hired me and I am his priest."

⁵Then they said to him, "Please inquire of God to learn whether our journey will be successful."

⁶The priest answered them, "Go in peace. Your journey has the LORD's approval."

⁷So the five men left and came to Laish, where they saw that the people were living in safety, like the Sidonians, unsuspecting and secure. And since their land lacked nothing, they were prosperous.*ᶜ* Also, they lived a long way from the Sidonians and had no relationship with anyone else.*ᵈ*

⁸When they returned to Zorah and Eshtaol, their brothers asked them, "How did you find things?"

⁹They answered, "Come on, let's attack them! We have seen that the land is very good. Aren't you going to do something? Don't hesitate to go there and take it over. ¹⁰When you get there, you will find an unsuspecting people and a spacious land that God has put into your hands, a land that lacks nothing whatever."

¹¹Then six hundred men from the clan of the Danites, armed for battle, set out from Zorah and Eshtaol. ¹²On their way they set up camp near Kiriath Jearim in Judah. This is why the place west of Kiriath Jearim is called Mahaneh Dan*ᵉ* to this day. ¹³From there they went on to the hill country of Ephraim and came to Micah's house.

¹⁴Then the five men who had spied out the land of Laish said to their brothers, "Do you know that one of these houses has an ephod, other household gods, a carved image and a cast idol? Now you know what to do." ¹⁵So they turned in there and went to the house of the young Levite at Micah's place and greeted him. ¹⁶The six hundred Danites, armed for battle, stood at the entrance to the gate. ¹⁷The five men who had spied out the land went inside and took the carved image, the ephod, the other household gods and the cast idol while the priest and the six hundred armed men stood at the entrance to the gate.

¹⁸When these men went into Micah's house and took the carved image, the ephod, the other household gods and the cast idol, the priest said to them, "What are you doing?"

¹⁹They answered him, "Be quiet! Don't say a word. Come with us, and be our father and priest. Isn't it better that you serve a tribe and clan in Israel as priest rather than just one man's household?" ²⁰Then the priest was glad. He took the

---

ᵃ8 Or *To carry on his profession*   *ᵇ10* That is, about 4 ounces (about 110 grams)   *ᶜ7* The meaning of the Hebrew for this clause is uncertain.   *ᵈ7* Hebrew; some Septuagint manuscripts *with the Arameans*   *ᵉ12* Mahaneh Dan means *Dan's camp.*

ephod, the other household gods and the carved image and went along with the people. ²¹Putting their little children, their livestock and their possessions in front of them, they turned away and left.

²²When they had gone some distance from Micah's house, the men who lived near Micah were called together and overtook the Danites. ²³As they shouted after them, the Danites turned and said to Micah, "What's the matter with you that you called out your men to fight?"

²⁴He replied, "You took the gods I made, and my priest, and went away. What else do I have? How can you ask, 'What's the matter with you?' "

²⁵The Danites answered, "Don't argue with us, or some hot-tempered men will attack you, and you and your family will lose your lives." ²⁶So the Danites went their way, and Micah, seeing that they were too strong for him, turned around and went back home.

²⁷Then they took what Micah had made, and his priest, and went on to Laish, against a peaceful and unsuspecting people. They attacked them with the sword and burned down their city. ²⁸There was no one to rescue them because they lived a long way from Sidon and had no relationship with anyone else. The city was in a valley near Beth Rehob.

The Danites rebuilt the city and settled there. ²⁹They named it Dan after their forefather Dan, who was born to Israel—though the city used to be called Laish. ³⁰There the Danites set up for themselves the idols, and Jonathan son of Gershom, the son of Moses,ᵃ and his sons were priests for the tribe of Dan until the time of the captivity of the land. ³¹They continued to use the idols Micah had made, all the time the house of God was in Shiloh.

A Levite and His Concubine

19 In those days Israel had no king. Now a Levite who lived in a remote area in the hill country of Ephraim took a concubine from Bethlehem in Judah. ²But she was unfaithful to him. She left him and went back to her father's house in Bethlehem, Judah. After she had been there four months, ³her husband went to her to persuade her to return. He had with him his servant and two donkeys. She took him into her father's house, and when her father saw him, he gladly welcomed him. ⁴His father-in-law, the girl's father, prevailed upon him to stay; so he remained

with him three days, eating and drinking, and sleeping there.

⁵On the fourth day they got up early and he prepared to leave, but the girl's father said to his son-in-law, "Refresh yourself with something to eat; then you can go." ⁶So the two of them sat down to eat and drink together. Afterward the girl's father said, "Please stay tonight and enjoy yourself." ⁷And when the man got up to go, his father-in-law persuaded him, so he stayed there that night. ⁸On the morning of the fifth day, when he rose to go, the girl's father said, "Refresh yourself. Wait till afternoon!" So the two of them ate together.

⁹Then when the man, with his concubine and his servant, got up to leave, his father-in-law, the girl's father, said, "Now look, it's almost evening. Spend the night here; the day is nearly over. Stay and enjoy yourself. Early tomorrow morning you can get up and be on your way home." ¹⁰But, unwilling to stay another night, the man left and went toward Jebus (that is, Jerusalem), with his two saddled donkeys and his concubine.

¹¹When they were near Jebus and the day was almost gone, the servant said to his master, "Come, let's stop at this city of the Jebusites and spend the night."

¹²His master replied, "No. We won't go into an alien city, whose people are not Israelites. We will go on to Gibeah." ¹³He added, "Come, let's try to reach Gibeah or Ramah and spend the night in one of those places." ¹⁴So they went on, and the sun set as they neared Gibeah in Benjamin. ¹⁵There they stopped to spend the night. They went and sat in the city square, but no one took them into his home for the night.

¹⁶That evening an old man from the hill country of Ephraim, who was living in Gibeah (the men of the place were Benjamites), came in from his work in the fields. ¹⁷When he looked and saw the traveler in the city square, the old man asked, "Where are you going? Where did you come from?"

¹⁸He answered, "We are on our way from Bethlehem in Judah to a remote area in the hill country of Ephraim where I live. I have been to Bethlehem in Judah and now I am going to the house of the LORD. No one has taken me into his house. ¹⁹We

---

ᵃ30 An ancient Hebrew scribal tradition, some Septuagint manuscripts and Vulgate; Masoretic Text *Manasseh*

have both straw and fodder for our donkeys and bread and wine for ourselves your servants—me, your maidservant, and the young man with us. We don't need anything."

[20]"You are welcome at my house," the old man said. "Let me supply whatever you need. Only don't spend the night in the square." [21]So he took him into his house and fed his donkeys. After they had washed their feet, they had something to eat and drink.

[22]While they were enjoying themselves, some of the wicked men of the city surrounded the house. Pounding on the door, they shouted to the old man who owned the house, "Bring out the man who came to your house so we can have sex with him."

[23]The owner of the house went outside and said to them, "No, my friends, don't be so vile. Since this man is my guest, don't do this disgraceful thing. [24]Look, here is my virgin daughter, and his concubine. I will bring them out to you now, and you can use them and do to them whatever you wish. But to this man, don't do such a disgraceful thing."

[25]But the men would not listen to him. So the man took his concubine and sent her outside to them, and they raped her and abused her throughout the night, and at dawn they let her go. [26]At daybreak the woman went back to the house where her master was staying, fell down at the door and lay there until daylight.

[27]When her master got up in the morning and opened the door of the house and stepped out to continue on his way, there lay his concubine, fallen in the doorway of the house, with her hands on the threshold. [28]He said to her, "Get up; let's go." But there was no answer. Then the man put her on his donkey and set out for home.

[29]When he reached home, he took a knife and cut up his concubine, limb by limb, into twelve parts and sent them into all the areas of Israel. [30]Everyone who saw it said, "Such a thing has never been seen or done, not since the day the Israelites came up out of Egypt. Think about it! Consider it! Tell us what to do!"

Israelites Fight the Benjamites

20 Then all the Israelites from Dan to Beersheba and from the land of Gilead came out as one man and assembled before the LORD in Mizpah. [2]The leaders of all the people of the tribes of Israel took their places in the assembly of the people of God, four hundred thousand soldiers armed with swords. [3](The Benjamites heard that the Israelites had gone up to Mizpah.) Then the Israelites said, "Tell us how this awful thing happened."

[4]So the Levite, the husband of the murdered woman, said, "I and my concubine came to Gibeah in Benjamin to spend the night. [5]During the night the men of Gibeah came after me and surrounded the house, intending to kill me. They raped my concubine, and she died. [6]I took my concubine, cut her into pieces and sent one piece to each region of Israel's inheritance, because they committed this lewd and disgraceful act in Israel. [7]Now, all you Israelites, speak up and give your verdict."

[8]All the people rose as one man, saying, "None of us will go home. No, not one of us will return to his house. [9]But now this is what we'll do to Gibeah: We'll go up against it as the lot directs. [10]We'll take ten men out of every hundred from all the tribes of Israel, and a hundred from a thousand, and a thousand from ten thousand, to get provisions for the army. Then, when the army arrives at Gibeah[a] in Benjamin, it can give them what they deserve for all this vileness done in Israel." [11]So all the men of Israel got together and united as one man against the city.

[12]The tribes of Israel sent men throughout the tribe of Benjamin, saying, "What about this awful crime that was committed among you? [13]Now surrender those wicked men of Gibeah so that we may put them to death and purge the evil from Israel."

But the Benjamites would not listen to their fellow Israelites. [14]From their towns they came together at Gibeah to fight against the Israelites. [15]At once the Benjamites mobilized twenty-six thousand swordsmen from their towns, in addition to seven hundred chosen men from those living in Gibeah. [16]Among all these soldiers there were seven hundred chosen men who were left-handed, each of whom could sling a stone at a hair and not miss.

[17]Israel, apart from Benjamin, mustered four hundred thousand swordsmen, all of them fighting men.

[18]The Israelites went up to Bethel[b] and

---

[a]10 One Hebrew manuscript; most Hebrew manuscripts *Geba*, a variant of *Gibeah*   [b]18 Or *to the house of God*; also in verse 26

inquired of God. They said, "Who of us shall go first to fight against the Benjamites?"

The LORD replied, "Judah shall go first."

¹⁹The next morning the Israelites got up and pitched camp near Gibeah. ²⁰The men of Israel went out to fight the Benjamites and took up battle positions against them at Gibeah. ²¹The Benjamites came out of Gibeah and cut down twenty-two thousand Israelites on the battlefield that day. ²²But the men of Israel encouraged one another and again took up their positions where they had stationed themselves the first day. ²³The Israelites went up and wept before the LORD until evening, and they inquired of the LORD. They said, "Shall we go up again to battle against the Benjamites, our brothers?"

The LORD answered, "Go up against them."

²⁴Then the Israelites drew near to Benjamin the second day. ²⁵This time, when the Benjamites came out from Gibeah to oppose them, they cut down another eighteen thousand Israelites, all of them armed with swords.

²⁶Then the Israelites, all the people, went up to Bethel, and there they sat weeping before the LORD. They fasted that day until evening and presented burnt offerings and fellowship offeringsᵃ to the LORD. ²⁷And the Israelites inquired of the LORD. (In those days the ark of the covenant of God was there, ²⁸with Phinehas son of Eleazar, the son of Aaron, ministering before it.) They asked, "Shall we go up again to battle with Benjamin our brother, or not?"

The LORD responded, "Go, for tomorrow I will give them into your hands."

²⁹Then Israel set an ambush around Gibeah. ³⁰They went up against the Benjamites on the third day and took up positions against Gibeah as they had done before. ³¹The Benjamites came out to meet them and were drawn away from the city. They began to inflict casualties on the Israelites as before, so that about thirty men fell in the open field and on the roads—the one leading to Bethel and the other to Gibeah.

³²While the Benjamites were saying, "We are defeating them as before," the Israelites were saying, "Let's retreat and draw them away from the city to the roads."

³³All the men of Israel moved from their places and took up positions at Baal Tamar, and the Israelite ambush charged out of its place on the westᵇ of Gibeah.ᶜ ³⁴Then ten thousand of Israel's finest men made a frontal attack on Gibeah. The fighting was so heavy that the Benjamites did not realize how near disaster was. ³⁵The LORD defeated Benjamin before Israel, and on that day the Israelites struck down 25,100 Benjamites, all armed with swords. ³⁶Then the Benjamites saw that they were beaten.

Now the men of Israel had given way before Benjamin, because they relied on the ambush they had set near Gibeah. ³⁷The men who had been in ambush made a sudden dash into Gibeah, spread out and put the whole city to the sword. ³⁸The men of Israel had arranged with the ambush that they should send up a great cloud of smoke from the city, ³⁹and then the men of Israel would turn in the battle.

The Benjamites had begun to inflict casualties on the men of Israel (about thirty), and they said, "We are defeating them as in the first battle." ⁴⁰But when the column of smoke began to rise from the city, the Benjamites turned and saw the smoke of the whole city going up into the sky. ⁴¹Then the men of Israel turned on them, and the men of Benjamin were terrified, because they realized that disaster had come upon them. ⁴²So they fled before the Israelites in the direction of the desert, but they could not escape the battle. And the men of Israel who came out of the towns cut them down there. ⁴³They surrounded the Benjamites, chased them and easilyᵈ overran them in the vicinity of Gibeah on the east. ⁴⁴Eighteen thousand Benjamites fell, all of them valiant fighters. ⁴⁵As they turned and fled toward the desert to the rock of Rimmon, the Israelites cut down five thousand men along the roads. They kept pressing after the Benjamites as far as Gidom and struck down two thousand more.

⁴⁶On that day twenty-five thousand Benjamite swordsmen fell, all of them valiant fighters. ⁴⁷But six hundred men turned and fled into the desert to the rock of Rimmon, where they stayed four months. ⁴⁸The men of Israel went back to Benjamin and put all the towns to the sword, including the animals and everything else they found. All the towns they came across they set on fire.

ᵃ26 Traditionally *peace offerings*   ᵇ33 Some Septuagint manuscripts and Vulgate; the meaning of the Hebrew for this word is uncertain.
ᶜ33 Hebrew *Geba*, a variant of *Gibeah*   ᵈ43 The meaning of the Hebrew for this word is uncertain.

Wives for the Benjamites

21 The men of Israel had taken an oath at Mizpah: "Not one of us will give his daughter in marriage to a Benjamite."

2The people went to Bethel,*a* where they sat before God until evening, raising their voices and weeping bitterly. **3**"O LORD, the God of Israel," they cried, "why has this happened to Israel? Why should one tribe be missing from Israel today?"

4Early the next day the people built an altar and presented burnt offerings and fellowship offerings.*b*

5Then the Israelites asked, "Who from all the tribes of Israel has failed to assemble before the LORD?" For they had taken a solemn oath that anyone who failed to assemble before the LORD at Mizpah should certainly be put to death.

6Now the Israelites grieved for their brothers, the Benjamites. "Today one tribe is cut off from Israel," they said. **7**"How can we provide wives for those who are left, since we have taken an oath by the LORD not to give them any of our daughters in marriage?" **8**Then they asked, "Which one of the tribes of Israel failed to assemble before the LORD at Mizpah?" They discovered that no one from Jabesh Gilead had come to the camp for the assembly. **9**For when they counted the people, they found that none of the people of Jabesh Gilead were there.

10So the assembly sent twelve thousand fighting men with instructions to go to Jabesh Gilead and put to the sword those living there, including the women and children. **11**"This is what you are to do," they said. "Kill every male and every woman who is not a virgin." **12**They found among the people living in Jabesh Gilead four hundred young women who had never slept with a man, and they took them to the camp at Shiloh in Canaan.

13Then the whole assembly sent an offer of peace to the Benjamites at the rock

of Rimmon. **14**So the Benjamites returned at that time and were given the women of Jabesh Gilead who had been spared. But there were not enough for all of them.

15The people grieved for Benjamin, because the LORD had made a gap in the tribes of Israel. **16**And the elders of the assembly said, "With the women of Benjamin destroyed, how shall we provide wives for the men who are left? **17**The Benjamite survivors must have heirs," they said, "so that a tribe of Israel will not be wiped out. **18**We can't give them our daughters as wives, since we Israelites have taken this oath: 'Cursed be anyone who gives a wife to a Benjamite.' **19**But look, there is the annual festival of the LORD in Shiloh, to the north of Bethel, and east of the road that goes from Bethel to Shechem, and to the south of Lebonah."

20So they instructed the Benjamites, saying, "Go and hide in the vineyards **21**and watch. When the girls of Shiloh come out to join in the dancing, then rush from the vineyards and each of you seize a wife from the girls of Shiloh and go to the land of Benjamin. **22**When their fathers or brothers complain to us, we will say to them, 'Do us a kindness by helping them, because we did not get wives for them during the war, and you are innocent, since you did not give your daughters to them.' "

23So that is what the Benjamites did. While the girls were dancing, each man caught one and carried her off to be his wife. Then they returned to their inheritance and rebuilt the towns and settled in them.

24At that time the Israelites left that place and went home to their tribes and clans, each to his own inheritance.

25In those days Israel had no king; everyone did as he saw fit.

*a*2 Or *to the house of God*   *b*4 Traditionally *peace offerings*

Family relationships can be a real challenge. Yours is no exception. Not only are there daily hazards of living in a confined space with people who are very, very different from each other, but there are also the challenges of coping with extended family—your parents and siblings and their families, and your wife's parents and siblings and their families. Then, as time goes by, each of your children will grow up, marry some lucky person, and suddenly, *you* will become an in-law!

It's no small challenge to keep all of these connections intact. Happily, tucked away in the book of Ruth is the tender account of a family who successfully negotiated the potentially treacherous waters of living in an extended family. Even though keeping every family relationship strong is a tall order, it *can* be done. This book gives us some important evidence.

Ruth

Naomi and Ruth

In the days when the judges ruled,[a] there was a famine in the land, and a man from Bethlehem in Judah, together with his wife and two sons, went to live for a while in the country of Moab. [2]The man's name was Elimelech, his wife's name Naomi, and the names of his two sons were Mahlon and Kilion. They were Ephrathites from Bethlehem, Judah. And they went to Moab and lived there.

[3]Now Elimelech, Naomi's husband, died, and she was left with her two sons. [4]They married Moabite women, one named Orpah and the other Ruth. After they had lived there about ten years, [5]both Mahlon and Kilion also died, and Naomi was left without her two sons and her husband.

[6]When she heard in Moab that the LORD had come to the aid of his people by

providing food for them, Naomi and her daughters-in-law prepared to return home from there. [7]With her two daughters-in-law she left the place where she had been living and set out on the road that would take them back to the land of Judah.

[8]Then Naomi said to her two daughters-in-law, "Go back, each of you, to your mother's home. May the LORD show kindness to you, as you have shown to your dead and to me. [9]May the LORD grant that each of you will find rest in the home of another husband."

Then she kissed them and they wept aloud [10]and said to her, "We will go back with you to your people."

[11]But Naomi said, "Return home, my daughters. Why would you come with me? Am I going to have any more sons, who could become your husbands? [12]Return

[a]1 Traditionally *judged*

home, my daughters; I am too old to have another husband. Even if I thought there was still hope for me—even if I had a husband tonight and then gave birth to sons— ¹³would you wait until they grew up? Would you remain unmarried for them? No, my daughters. It is more bitter for me than for you, because the LORD's hand has gone out against me!"

¹⁴At this they wept again. Then Orpah kissed her mother-in-law good-by, but Ruth clung to her.

¹⁵"Look," said Naomi, "your sister-in-law is going back to her people and her gods. Go back with her."

¹⁶But Ruth replied, "Don't urge me to leave you or to turn back from you. Where you go I will go, and where you stay I will stay. Your people will be my people and your God my God. ¹⁷Where you die I will die, and there I will be buried. May the LORD deal with me, be it ever so severely, if anything but death separates you and me." ¹⁸When Naomi realized that Ruth

No Trouble with the In-laws

DAILY INSIGHT

MONDAY

Passage:
Ruth 1:1–18

Verse:
Ruth 1:16

Strange and strained relationships with in-laws are, of course, the subject of many jokes. In fact, it's hard to say the words, "mother-in-law" without it sounding cynical. But when you got married, were you ready for the in-laws?

When we got married, Bobbie and I decided to live in the Chicago area. This meant that we would live within easy driving distance of my parents. I was pleased when I saw the relationship between my wife and my parents growing stronger. I soon realized that the best insurance policy for a good relationship between in-laws is a good relationship between parents and their married children. If I had any hope that Bobbie would form a special bond with my own dad and mother, I had to be sure my own relationship with them was intact.

Naomi's sons must have known this as well, because the relationship between Ruth and Naomi is one of the most tender and beautiful in all of Scripture. And, even though Naomi convinced Orpah to return home, she initially chose to stay with her mother-in-law as well. Take a moment to read Ruth's plea to Naomi (vv. 16–17). It's such a tender speech that it's often used in wedding ceremonies to affirm a bride and groom's commitment to each other.

Someday your children will get married. Promising to love and cherish someone else, they'll actually leave your house and move in with their new spouse. Then you'll face the challenge of building a relationship with a brand new member of your family—an in-law.

Many family relationships, once children get married, escalate into a battle. Fiercely loyal to their own spouses, grown children sometimes begin to build walls between themselves and their parents. Act to prevent this from happening at all costs. After a lifetime of loving your precious children, you don't want to feel as if they've been ripped from your heart.

How do you do this? By following Naomi's example and loving your children with an open hand. Given the loss of her own husband and the death of her sons, she might have tried to coerce these women into staying with her. "Who's going to take care of me?" she could have whined. Instead, she encouraged them to leave, to return to their own families. This, of course, drew them to her all the more.

The choice your children make for their spouses is a colossal one. And the importance of your relationship to these new family members is no less immense. How can you get ready for this? Continue tenderly loving your children while you have them; then, as they grow older, open your hand so that their reciprocal love is invited, not forced.

Today, pray that God will bless and protect your children's spouses, wherever they are. Pray also that God will prepare you for a wonderful relationship with them.

For your next devotional reading, go to page 295.

was determined to go with her, she stopped urging her.

¹⁹So the two women went on until they came to Bethlehem. When they arrived in Bethlehem, the whole town was stirred because of them, and the women exclaimed, "Can this be Naomi?"

²⁰"Don't call me Naomi,^{*a*}" she told them. "Call me Mara,^{*b*} because the Almighty^{*c*} has made my life very bitter. ²¹I went away full, but the LORD has brought me back empty. Why call me Naomi? The LORD has afflicted^{*d*} me; the Almighty has brought misfortune upon me."

²²So Naomi returned from Moab accompanied by Ruth the Moabitess, her daughter-in-law, arriving in Bethlehem as the barley harvest was beginning.

Ruth Meets Boaz

2 Now Naomi had a relative on her husband's side, from the clan of Elimelech, a man of standing, whose name was Boaz.

²And Ruth the Moabitess said to Naomi, "Let me go to the fields and pick up the leftover grain behind anyone in whose eyes I find favor."

Naomi said to her, "Go ahead, my daughter." ³So she went out and began to glean in the fields behind the harvesters. As it turned out, she found herself working in a field belonging to Boaz, who was from the clan of Elimelech.

⁴Just then Boaz arrived from Bethlehem and greeted the harvesters, "The LORD be with you!"

"The LORD bless you!" they called back.

⁵Boaz asked the foreman of his harvesters, "Whose young woman is that?"

⁶The foreman replied, "She is the Moabitess who came back from Moab with Naomi. ⁷She said, 'Please let me glean and gather among the sheaves behind the harvesters.' She went into the field and has worked steadily from morning till now, except for a short rest in the shelter."

⁸So Boaz said to Ruth, "My daughter, listen to me. Don't go and glean in another field and don't go away from here. Stay here with my servant girls. ⁹Watch the field where the men are harvesting, and follow along after the girls. I have told the men not to touch you. And whenever you are thirsty, go and get a drink from the water jars the men have filled."

¹⁰At this, she bowed down with her face to the ground. She exclaimed, "Why have

I found such favor in your eyes that you notice me—a foreigner?"

¹¹Boaz replied, "I've been told all about what you have done for your mother-in-law since the death of your husband—how you left your father and mother and your homeland and came to live with a people you did not know before. ¹²May the LORD repay you for what you have done. May you be richly rewarded by the LORD, the God of Israel, under whose wings you have come to take refuge."

¹³"May I continue to find favor in your eyes, my lord," she said. "You have given me comfort and have spoken kindly to your servant—though I do not have the standing of one of your servant girls."

¹⁴At mealtime Boaz said to her, "Come over here. Have some bread and dip it in the wine vinegar."

When she sat down with the harvesters, he offered her some roasted grain. She ate all she wanted and had some left over. ¹⁵As she got up to glean, Boaz gave orders to his men, "Even if she gathers among the sheaves, don't embarrass her. ¹⁶Rather, pull out some stalks for her from the bundles and leave them for her to pick up, and don't rebuke her."

¹⁷So Ruth gleaned in the field until evening. Then she threshed the barley she had gathered, and it amounted to about an ephah.^{*e*} ¹⁸She carried it back to town, and her mother-in-law saw how much she had gathered. Ruth also brought out and gave her what she had left over after she had eaten enough.

¹⁹Her mother-in-law asked her, "Where did you glean today? Where did you work? Blessed be the man who took notice of you!"

Then Ruth told her mother-in-law about the one at whose place she had been working. "The name of the man I worked with today is Boaz," she said.

²⁰"The LORD bless him!" Naomi said to her daughter-in-law. "He has not stopped showing his kindness to the living and the dead." She added, "That man is our close relative; he is one of our kinsman-redeemers."

²¹Then Ruth the Moabitess said, "He even said to me, 'Stay with my workers until they finish harvesting all my grain.' "

²²Naomi said to Ruth her daughter-in-law, "It will be good for you, my daughter,

---

^{*a*}20 *Naomi* means *pleasant*; also in verse 21.
^{*b*}20 *Mara* means *bitter.*   ^{*c*}20 Hebrew *Shaddai*; also in verse 21   ^{*d*}21 Or *has testified against*   ^{*e*}17 That is, probably about 3/5 bushel (about 22 liters)

to go with his girls, because in someone else's field you might be harmed."

²³So Ruth stayed close to the servant girls of Boaz to glean until the barley and wheat harvests were finished. And she lived with her mother-in-law.

Ruth and Boaz at the Threshing Floor

3 One day Naomi her mother-in-law said to her, "My daughter, should I not try to find a home*a* for you, where you will be well provided for? ²Is not Boaz, with whose servant girls you have been, a kinsman of ours? Tonight he will be winnowing barley on the threshing floor. ³Wash and perfume yourself, and put on your best clothes. Then go down to the threshing floor, but don't let him know you are there until he has finished eating and drinking. ⁴When he lies down, note the place where he is lying. Then go and uncover his feet and lie down. He will tell you what to do."

⁵"I will do whatever you say," Ruth answered. ⁶So she went down to the threshing floor and did everything her mother-in-law told her to do.

⁷When Boaz had finished eating and drinking and was in good spirits, he went over to lie down at the far end of the grain pile. Ruth approached quietly, uncovered his feet and lay down. ⁸In the middle of the night something startled the man, and he turned and discovered a woman lying at his feet.

⁹"Who are you?" he asked.

"I am your servant Ruth," she said. "Spread the corner of your garment over me, since you are a kinsman-redeemer."

¹⁰"The LORD bless you, my daughter," he replied. "This kindness is greater than that which you showed earlier: You have not run after the younger men, whether rich or poor. ¹¹And now, my daughter, don't be afraid. I will do for you all you ask. All my fellow townsmen know that you are a woman of noble character. ¹²Although it is true that I am near of kin, there is a kinsman-redeemer nearer than I. ¹³Stay here for the night, and in the morning if he wants to redeem, good; let him redeem. But if he is not willing, as surely as the LORD lives I will do it. Lie here until morning."

¹⁴So she lay at his feet until morning, but got up before anyone could be recognized; and he said, "Don't let it be known that a woman came to the threshing floor."

¹⁵He also said, "Bring me the shawl you are wearing and hold it out." When she did so, he poured into it six measures of

a1 Hebrew *find rest* (see Ruth 1:9)

HEY DAD

In the Old Testament, could people who weren't Israelites worship God?

Text: Ruth 4:13–17

Yes! God has always welcomed the praise of all people, but in the Old Testament, Israel was the only nation who followed and worshiped the true God. God hadn't revealed himself to everyone yet, but when members of another nation truly wanted to worship God, he gladly received them.

Ruth, for example, was from Moab. She came from a nation that worshiped idols, but she married an Israelite. When her husband died, Ruth returned with her mother-in-law to Israel and vowed that she would regard the Israelites as her own people and would faithfully serve their God. She kept her vow and proved to be a loyal and noble woman.

How did God feel about this? Well, he not only allowed Ruth to worship him and become one of his people, he chose her to be an ancestor of King David, and eventually of Jesus himself.

When God chose Ruth for this incredible honor, he showed us that, even in the Old Testament, his love was for all people. How interesting it is that Christ, the one who would bring the message of grace to all nations, had a non-Jewish woman in his family tree. Was this a coincidence? Not likely.

For a complete listing of Questions Kids Ask, turn to page 1435.

barley and put it on her. Then he[a] went back to town.

[16]When Ruth came to her mother-in-law, Naomi asked, "How did it go, my daughter?"

Then she told her everything Boaz had done for her [17]and added, "He gave me these six measures of barley, saying, 'Don't go back to your mother-in-law empty-handed.' "

[18]Then Naomi said, "Wait, my daughter, until you find out what happens. For the man will not rest until the matter is settled today."

Boaz Marries Ruth

4 Meanwhile Boaz went up to the town gate and sat there. When the kinsman-redeemer he had mentioned came along, Boaz said, "Come over here, my friend, and sit down." So he went over and sat down.

[2]Boaz took ten of the elders of the town and said, "Sit here," and they did so. [3]Then he said to the kinsman-redeemer, "Naomi, who has come back from Moab, is selling the piece of land that belonged to our brother Elimelech. [4]I thought I should bring the matter to your attention and suggest that you buy it in the presence of these seated here and in the presence of the elders of my people. If you will redeem it, do so. But if you[b] will not, tell me, so I will know. For no one has the right to do it except you, and I am next in line."

"I will redeem it," he said.

[5]Then Boaz said, "On the day you buy the land from Naomi and from Ruth the Moabitess, you acquire[c] the dead man's widow, in order to maintain the name of the dead with his property."

[6]At this, the kinsman-redeemer said, "Then I cannot redeem it because I might endanger my own estate. You redeem it yourself. I cannot do it."

[7](Now in earlier times in Israel, for the redemption and transfer of property to become final, one party took off his sandal and gave it to the other. This was the method of legalizing transactions in Israel.)

[8]So the kinsman-redeemer said to Boaz, "Buy it yourself." And he removed his sandal.

[9]Then Boaz announced to the elders and all the people, "Today you are witnesses that I have bought from Naomi all the property of Elimelech, Kilion and Mahlon. [10]I have also acquired Ruth the Moabitess, Mahlon's widow, as my wife, in order to maintain the name of the dead with his property, so that his name will not disappear from among his family or from the town records. Today you are witnesses!"

[11]Then the elders and all those at the gate said, "We are witnesses. May the LORD make the woman who is coming into your home like Rachel and Leah, who together built up the house of Israel. May you have standing in Ephrathah and be famous in Bethlehem. [12]Through the offspring the LORD gives you by this young woman, may your family be like that of Perez, whom Tamar bore to Judah."

The Genealogy of David

[13]So Boaz took Ruth and she became his wife. Then he went to her, and the LORD enabled her to conceive, and she gave birth to a son. [14]The women said to Naomi: "Praise be to the LORD, who this day has not left you without a kinsman-redeemer. May he become famous throughout Israel! [15]He will renew your life and sustain you in your old age. For your daughter-in-law, who loves you and who is better to you than seven sons, has given him birth."

[16]Then Naomi took the child, laid him in her lap and cared for him. [17]The women living there said, "Naomi has a son." And they named him Obed. He was the father of Jesse, the father of David.

[18]This, then, is the family line of Perez:

Perez was the father of Hezron,
[19] Hezron the father of Ram,
  Ram the father of Amminadab,
[20] Amminadab the father of Nahshon,
  Nahshon the father of Salmon,[d]
[21] Salmon the father of Boaz,
  Boaz the father of Obed,
[22] Obed the father of Jesse,
  and Jesse the father of David.

[a]15 Most Hebrew manuscripts; many Hebrew manuscripts, Vulgate and Syriac she   [b]4 Many Hebrew manuscripts, Septuagint, Vulgate and Syriac; most Hebrew manuscripts he   [c]5 Hebrew; Vulgate and Syriac Naomi, you acquire Ruth the Moabitess,   [d]20 A few Hebrew manuscripts, some Septuagint manuscripts and Vulgate (see also verse 21 and Septuagint of 1 Chron. 2:11); most Hebrew manuscripts Salma

Children change their parents' lives. Have you noticed this? Have you experienced this, too? Of course you have.

Once you bring that little bundle home from the hospital, nothing is ever the same. This little, unique, precious human being is a blessing from God; there's no doubting that. But even if you're the perfect dad, this child is a free agent . . . an individual with a will of his own. As he grows up, he will listen to your advice, watch your example of character and consistency, and then make up his own mind about his friends, his habits, his vocation, and his own spouse and family.

The book of 1 Samuel tells us of the blessing and the challenge of children. This book is also a reminder that the one sure thing we can always do for our kids—the one thing that will ensure their protection and their constant guidance—is to pray for them. Now *there's* something every dad can do.

1 Samuel

The Birth of Samuel

1 There was a certain man from Ramathaim, a Zuphite*a* from the hill country of Ephraim, whose name was Elkanah son of Jeroham, the son of Elihu, the son of Tohu, the son of Zuph, an Ephraimite. ²He had two wives; one was called Hannah and the other Peninnah. Peninnah had children, but Hannah had none.

³Year after year this man went up from his town to worship and sacrifice to the LORD Almighty at Shiloh, where Hophni and Phinehas, the two sons of Eli, were priests of the LORD. ⁴Whenever the day came for Elkanah to sacrifice, he would give portions of the meat to his wife Peninnah and to all her sons and daughters. ⁵But to Hannah he gave a double portion because he loved her, and the LORD had closed her womb. ⁶And because the LORD had closed her womb, her rival kept provoking her in order to irritate her. ⁷This went on year after year. Whenever Hannah went up to the house of the LORD, her rival provoked her till she wept and would not eat. ⁸Elkanah her husband would say to her, "Hannah, why are you weeping? Why don't you eat? Why are you downhearted? Don't I mean more to you than ten sons?"

⁹Once when they had finished eating and drinking in Shiloh, Hannah stood up. Now Eli the priest was sitting on a chair by the doorpost of the LORD's temple.*b* ¹⁰In bitterness of soul Hannah wept much and

a1 Or from Ramathaim Zuphim *b9 That is, tabernacle*

prayed to the LORD. ¹¹And she made a vow, saying, "O LORD Almighty, if you will only look upon your servant's misery and remember me, and not forget your servant but give her a son, then I will give him to the LORD for all the days of his life, and no razor will ever be used on his head."

¹²As she kept on praying to the LORD, Eli observed her mouth. ¹³Hannah was praying in her heart, and her lips were moving but her voice was not heard. Eli thought she was drunk ¹⁴and said to her, "How long will you keep on getting drunk? Get rid of your wine."

¹⁵"Not so, my lord," Hannah replied, "I am a woman who is deeply troubled. I have not been drinking wine or beer; I was pouring out my soul to the LORD. ¹⁶Do not take your servant for a wicked woman; I have been praying here out of my great anguish and grief."

¹⁷Eli answered, "Go in peace, and may the God of Israel grant you what you have asked of him."

¹⁸She said, "May your servant find favor in your eyes." Then she went her way and ate something, and her face was no longer downcast.

¹⁹Early the next morning they arose and worshiped before the LORD and then went back to their home at Ramah. Elkanah lay with Hannah his wife, and the LORD remembered her. ²⁰So in the course of time Hannah conceived and gave birth to a son. She named him Samuel,ᵃ saying, "Because I asked the LORD for him."

ᵃ20 Samuel sounds like the Hebrew for heard of God.

The Blessing of Children

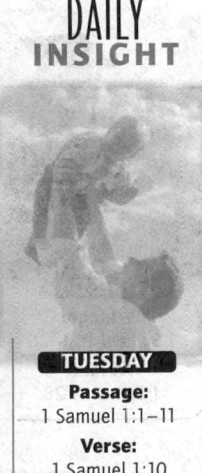

DAILY INSIGHT

TUESDAY

Passage:
1 Samuel 1:1–11

Verse:
1 Samuel 1:10

Even though I like saving money by flying one of the low-cost air carriers, I truly prefer having a boarding pass that tells me which seat is going to be mine for a flight. As you may know, one of the "features" of the low-cost airlines is the cattle-like crowding onto the plane to find a desirable seat.

Over the years that I've flown on these open-seating airplanes, I've discovered something interesting having to do with children. When someone boards the plane with a small kid or two in hand, I've watched the already seated passengers as the family slowly progresses down the aisle. One can almost hear these people, faced with the specter of flying next to a little person, silently pleading with the parents not to select their row. As the parents and children pass by, there's an audible sigh from these adults.

Kids are a bunch of trouble. Have you noticed this? They're usually demanding, noisy, and messy. Basically, they disrupt our serene, adult lives. To some, they're a contemptuous intrusion. And we get no help from a culture that, at times, seems quite preoccupied with not having them.

But amazingly, once we have children of our own, we discover how truly precious they are. We would, in fact, give our lives for them. We literally can't imagine life without them.

Hannah had no children and she desperately wanted a son. Her husband, Elkanah, not fully understanding why kids were so important, tried to encourage Hannah by asking her if he wasn't more valuable to her than ten sons (1:8). Hannah answered him with merciless silence. Sorry Elkanah, nice try.

The message that children are a blessing from God fills the pages of your Bible. Having them is God's way of reminding you of his presence and faithfulness. In a word, you are blessed. Your child is proof of this fact.

Today we need to celebrate God's goodness by thanking him for this visible blessing. And we must also seek his forgiveness for the times when we have found ourselves complaining about the demands, the noise and the mess. We both know how much our children mean to us.

"Thank you, heavenly Father, for this blessing."

For your next devotional reading, go to page 296.

Hannah Dedicates Samuel

²¹When the man Elkanah went up with all his family to offer the annual sacrifice to the LORD and to fulfill his vow, ²²Hannah did not go. She said to her husband, "After the boy is weaned, I will take him and present him before the LORD, and he will live there always."

²³"Do what seems best to you," Elkanah her husband told her. "Stay here until you have weaned him; only may the LORD make good his*ª* word." So the woman stayed at home and nursed her son until she had weaned him.

²⁴After he was weaned, she took the boy with her, young as he was, along with a three-year-old bull,*ᵇ* an ephah*ᶜ* of flour and a skin of wine, and brought him to the house of the LORD at Shiloh. ²⁵When they had slaughtered the bull, they brought the boy to Eli, ²⁶and she said to him, "As surely as you live, my lord, I am the woman who stood here beside you praying to the LORD. ²⁷I prayed for this child, and the LORD has granted me what I asked of him. ²⁸So now I give him to the LORD. For his whole life he will be given over to the LORD." And he worshiped the LORD there.

ª23 Masoretic Text; Dead Sea Scrolls, Septuagint and Syriac *your*   *ᵇ24* Dead Sea Scrolls, Septuagint and Syriac; Masoretic Text *with three bulls*   *ᶜ24* That is, probably about 3/5 bushel (about 22 liters)

Green Stamps and Your Kids

DAILY INSIGHT

WEDNESDAY

Passage:
1 Samuel 1:21–28

Verse:
1 Samuel 1:28

Trading stamps used to be a big deal. I can remember going to the grocery store with my mother and seeing the cashier give her S&H Green Stamps in proportion to the amount she had spent on her order. I can also remember my mother asking me to paste these stamps into a book. But collecting the stamps and putting them in the book didn't mean anything until they were taken to a "redemption center" and exchanged for valuable merchandise.

For centuries, Christian parents have brought their children to their churches for a special ceremony, just like my mother took those Green Stamp books to a place that knew what to do with them.

Some churches call it "baby dedication." Some call it "christening" or "infant baptism," but it's essentially the same thing: the parents are there to publicly acknowledge that this little person is a blessing ... a gift on loan from God. And they are promising to bring him or her up in the faith. This takes place in front of people they know who love them enough to remind them of this promise—family and friends who would, at some later time, dare to challenge their activity when it seems to be drifting from this visible pledge.

"Excuse me, but I couldn't help but overhear what you just said to your child," they might courageously say. "I happened to be at the church when you promised God and your friends that you'd be a living example of what it means to be a godly person. Perhaps you ought to take a minute and ask your child's forgiveness ... and please do it right away."

Hannah brought Samuel to the temple as a small child. We're not sure if Elkanah was also there with her, but if he was, he was part of this blessing. In any case, Hannah's promise (1:28) to "give him to the LORD" is a tremendous model for us and our children. In fact, even the priest who performed the ceremony took note, promising to do his part in raising young Samuel to become a man of God.

When you bring your child to the front of your church and, together with your wife, present him or her to the Lord, you are promising to be a godly example for this child. You are asking your minister and your friends to do the same. And you are putting the world on notice: "I'm going to be a Christian father; I need some help from you, and I expect us to hold each other accountable on this one."

Bring your child to the redemption center. What a great idea.

For your next devotional reading, go to page 303.

Hannah's Prayer

2 Then Hannah prayed and said:

"My heart rejoices in the LORD;
   in the LORD my horn*a* is lifted high.
My mouth boasts over my enemies,
   for I delight in your deliverance.

2 "There is no one holy*b* like the LORD;
   there is no one besides you;
   there is no Rock like our God.

3 "Do not keep talking so proudly
   or let your mouth speak such
      arrogance,
for the LORD is a God who knows,
   and by him deeds are weighed.

4 "The bows of the warriors are broken,
   but those who stumbled are armed
      with strength.
5 Those who were full hire themselves
      out for food,
   but those who were hungry hunger
      no more.
She who was barren has borne seven
      children,
   but she who has had many sons
      pines away.

6 "The LORD brings death and makes
      alive;
   he brings down to the grave*c* and
      raises up.
7 The LORD sends poverty and wealth;
   he humbles and he exalts.
8 He raises the poor from the dust
   and lifts the needy from the ash heap;
he seats them with princes
   and has them inherit a throne of
      honor.

"For the foundations of the earth are
      the LORD's;
   upon them he has set the world.
9 He will guard the feet of his saints,
   but the wicked will be silenced in
      darkness.

"It is not by strength that one prevails;
10   those who oppose the LORD will be
      shattered.
He will thunder against them from
      heaven;
   the LORD will judge the ends of the
      earth.

"He will give strength to his king
   and exalt the horn of his anointed."

11 Then Elkanah went home to Ramah,
but the boy ministered before the LORD
under Eli the priest.

Eli's Wicked Sons

12 Eli's sons were wicked men; they had
no regard for the LORD. **13** Now it was the
practice of the priests with the people that
whenever anyone offered a sacrifice and
while the meat was being boiled, the servant of the priest would come with a
three-pronged fork in his hand. **14** He
would plunge it into the pan or kettle or
caldron or pot, and the priest would take
for himself whatever the fork brought up.
This is how they treated all the Israelites
who came to Shiloh. **15** But even before the
fat was burned, the servant of the priest
would come and say to the man who was
sacrificing, "Give the priest some meat to
roast; he won't accept boiled meat from
you, but only raw."

16 If the man said to him, "Let the fat be
burned up first, and then take whatever
you want," the servant would then answer, "No, hand it over now; if you don't,
I'll take it by force."

17 This sin of the young men was very
great in the LORD's sight, for they*d* were
treating the LORD's offering with contempt.

18 But Samuel was ministering before
the LORD—a boy wearing a linen ephod.
19 Each year his mother made him a little
robe and took it to him when she went up
with her husband to offer the annual sacrifice. **20** Eli would bless Elkanah and his
wife, saying, "May the LORD give you children by this woman to take the place of
the one she prayed for and gave to the
LORD." Then they would go home. **21** And
the LORD was gracious to Hannah; she
conceived and gave birth to three sons
and two daughters. Meanwhile, the boy
Samuel grew up in the presence of the
LORD.

22 Now Eli, who was very old, heard
about everything his sons were doing to
all Israel and how they slept with the
women who served at the entrance to the
Tent of Meeting. **23** So he said to them,
"Why do you do such things? I hear from
all the people about these wicked deeds of
yours. **24** No, my sons; it is not a good report
that I hear spreading among the LORD's
people. **25** If a man sins against another
man, God*e* may mediate for him; but if a
man sins against the LORD, who will intercede for him?" His sons, however, did not
listen to their father's rebuke, for it was
the LORD's will to put them to death.

---

a1 Horn here symbolizes strength; also in verse 10.
b2 Or *no Holy One*   *c6* Hebrew *Sheol*   *d17* Or *men*
e25 Or *the judges*

26And the boy Samuel continued to grow in stature and in favor with the LORD and with men.

Prophecy Against the House of Eli

27Now a man of God came to Eli and said to him, "This is what the LORD says: 'Did I not clearly reveal myself to your father's house when they were in Egypt under Pharaoh? **28**I chose your father out of all the tribes of Israel to be my priest, to go up to my altar, to burn incense, and to wear an ephod in my presence. I also gave your father's house all the offerings made with fire by the Israelites. **29**Why do you*a* scorn my sacrifice and offering that I prescribed for my dwelling? Why do you honor your sons more than me by fattening yourselves on the choice parts of every offering made by my people Israel?' **30**"Therefore the LORD, the God of Israel, declares: 'I promised that your house

and your father's house would minister before me forever.' But now the LORD declares: 'Far be it from me! Those who honor me I will honor, but those who despise me will be disdained. **31**The time is coming when I will cut short your strength and the strength of your father's house, so that there will not be an old man in your family line **32**and you will see distress in my dwelling. Although good will be done to Israel, in your family line there will never be an old man. **33**Every one of you that I do not cut off from my altar will be spared only to blind your eyes with tears and to grieve your heart, and all your descendants will die in the prime of life.

34" 'And what happens to your two sons, Hophni and Phinehas, will be a sign to you—they will both die on the same day. **35**I will raise up for myself a faithful priest,

a29 The Hebrew is plural.

Those Preacher's Kids
Eli, the Passive Father

"This sin of the young men was very great in the LORD's sight, for they were treating the LORD's offering with contempt" (2:17).

Text: 1 Samuel 2:12–26

Everybody knew Eli's sons. After all, they were the children of one of the most prominent men in Israel. But these sons were more *in*famous than they were famous. Their bad reputation had literally spread throughout Israel.

Having graduated far beyond running around the temple and making a general nuisance of themselves, these incorrigibles dared to tamper with the sacred rites and rituals that directed Israel's worship. What's worse, they seduced the women who served as ushers for those who had come to the temple. To put it bluntly, these young men were a disgrace to Eli.

Inevitably—because fathers eventually do find out what's going on—the aging Eli called his sons together. "Why do you do such things?" the priest complained. "I hear from all the people about these wicked deeds of yours . . . it is not a good report." But Eli's sons were unfazed by their father's benign admonition. They had probably heard this same speech many times before.

When his children were growing up, Eli was probably a very busy man—just ask any clergyman who heads up a large congregation. The demands of the ministry are relentless. Calling parishioners to personal account can be completely exhausting. Unfortunately for Eli's sons, their dad had evidently used up his wisdom and good judgment at the office. When he got home, he had none left for his most important charge . . . his own family.

The story of Eli's failure as a father is a bitter reminder that a man's most important task is the consistent, thankless and at times painful regulation of his own household. Eli's error cost his boys their lives. No occupation, not even the priesthood, could ever be worth such a price.

For a complete listing of Dads in the Bible, turn to page 1434.

who will do according to what is in my heart and mind. I will firmly establish his house, and he will minister before my anointed one always. **36**Then everyone left in your family line will come and bow down before him for a piece of silver and a crust of bread and plead, "Appoint me to some priestly office so I can have food to eat." ' "

The LORD Calls Samuel

3 The boy Samuel ministered before the LORD under Eli. In those days the word of the LORD was rare; there were not many visions.

2One night Eli, whose eyes were becoming so weak that he could barely see, was lying down in his usual place. **3**The lamp of God had not yet gone out, and Samuel was lying down in the temple[a] of the LORD, where the ark of God was. **4**Then the LORD called Samuel.

Samuel answered, "Here I am." **5**And he ran to Eli and said, "Here I am; you called me."

But Eli said, "I did not call; go back and lie down." So he went and lay down.

6Again the LORD called, "Samuel!" And Samuel got up and went to Eli and said, "Here I am; you called me."

"My son," Eli said, "I did not call; go back and lie down."

7Now Samuel did not yet know the LORD: The word of the LORD had not yet been revealed to him.

8The LORD called Samuel a third time, and Samuel got up and went to Eli and said, "Here I am; you called me."

Then Eli realized that the LORD was calling the boy. **9**So Eli told Samuel, "Go and lie down, and if he calls you, say, 'Speak, LORD, for your servant is listening.' " So Samuel went and lay down in his place.

10The LORD came and stood there, calling as at the other times, "Samuel! Samuel!"

Then Samuel said, "Speak, for your servant is listening."

11And the LORD said to Samuel: "See, I am about to do something in Israel that will make the ears of everyone who hears of it tingle. **12**At that time I will carry out against Eli everything I spoke against his family—from beginning to end. **13**For I told him that I would judge his family forever because of the sin he knew about; his sons made themselves contemptible,[b] and he failed to restrain them. **14**There-

fore, I swore to the house of Eli, 'The guilt of Eli's house will never be atoned for by sacrifice or offering.' "

15Samuel lay down until morning and then opened the doors of the house of the LORD. He was afraid to tell Eli the vision, **16**but Eli called him and said, "Samuel, my son."

Samuel answered, "Here I am."

17"What was it he said to you?" Eli asked. "Do not hide it from me. May God deal with you, be it ever so severely, if you hide from me anything he told you." **18**So Samuel told him everything, hiding nothing from him. Then Eli said, "He is the LORD; let him do what is good in his eyes."

19The LORD was with Samuel as he grew up, and he let none of his words fall to the ground. **20**And all Israel from Dan to Beersheba recognized that Samuel was attested as a prophet of the LORD. **21**The LORD continued to appear at Shiloh, and there he revealed himself to Samuel through his word.

4 And Samuel's word came to all Israel.

The Philistines Capture the Ark

Now the Israelites went out to fight against the Philistines. The Israelites camped at Ebenezer, and the Philistines at Aphek. **2**The Philistines deployed their forces to meet Israel, and as the battle spread, Israel was defeated by the Philistines, who killed about four thousand of them on the battlefield. **3**When the soldiers returned to camp, the elders of Israel asked, "Why did the LORD bring defeat upon us today before the Philistines? Let us bring the ark of the LORD's covenant from Shiloh, so that it[c] may go with us and save us from the hand of our enemies."

4So the people sent men to Shiloh, and they brought back the ark of the covenant of the LORD Almighty, who is enthroned between the cherubim. And Eli's two sons, Hophni and Phinehas, were there with the ark of the covenant of God.

5When the ark of the LORD's covenant came into the camp, all Israel raised such a great shout that the ground shook. **6**Hearing the uproar, the Philistines asked, "What's all this shouting in the Hebrew camp?"

When they learned that the ark of the

---

a3 That is, tabernacle   *b13* Masoretic Text; an ancient Hebrew scribal tradition and Septuagint *sons blasphemed God*   *c3* Or *he*

LORD had come into the camp, [7]the Philistines were afraid. "A god has come into the camp," they said. "We're in trouble! Nothing like this has happened before. [8]Woe to us! Who will deliver us from the hand of these mighty gods? They are the gods who struck the Egyptians with all kinds of plagues in the desert. [9]Be strong, Philistines! Be men, or you will be subject to the Hebrews, as they have been to you. Be men, and fight!"

[10]So the Philistines fought, and the Israelites were defeated and every man fled to his tent. The slaughter was very great; Israel lost thirty thousand foot soldiers. [11]The ark of God was captured, and Eli's two sons, Hophni and Phinehas, died.

Death of Eli

[12]That same day a Benjamite ran from the battle line and went to Shiloh, his clothes torn and dust on his head. [13]When he arrived, there was Eli sitting on his chair by the side of the road, watching, because his heart feared for the ark of God. When the man entered the town and told what had happened, the whole town sent up a cry.

[14]Eli heard the outcry and asked, "What is the meaning of this uproar?"

The man hurried over to Eli, [15]who was ninety-eight years old and whose eyes were set so that he could not see. [16]He told Eli, "I have just come from the battle line; I fled from it this very day."

Eli asked, "What happened, my son?"

[17]The man who brought the news replied, "Israel fled before the Philistines, and the army has suffered heavy losses. Also your two sons, Hophni and Phinehas, are dead, and the ark of God has been captured."

[18]When he mentioned the ark of God, Eli fell backward off his chair by the side of the gate. His neck was broken and he died, for he was an old man and heavy. He had led[a] Israel forty years.

[19]His daughter-in-law, the wife of Phinehas, was pregnant and near the time of delivery. When she heard the news that the ark of God had been captured and that her father-in-law and her husband were dead, she went into labor and gave birth, but was overcome by her labor pains. [20]As she was dying, the women attending her said, "Don't despair; you have given birth to a son." But she did not respond or pay any attention.

[21]She named the boy Ichabod,[b] saying,

"The glory has departed from Israel"— because of the capture of the ark of God and the deaths of her father-in-law and her husband. [22]She said, "The glory has departed from Israel, for the ark of God has been captured."

The Ark in Ashdod and Ekron

5 After the Philistines had captured the ark of God, they took it from Ebenezer to Ashdod. [2]Then they carried the ark into Dagon's temple and set it beside Dagon. [3]When the people of Ashdod rose early the next day, there was Dagon, fallen on his face on the ground before the ark of the LORD! They took Dagon and put him back in his place. [4]But the following morning when they rose, there was Dagon, fallen on his face on the ground before the ark of the LORD! His head and hands had been broken off and were lying on the threshold; only his body remained. [5]That is why to this day neither the priests of Dagon nor any others who enter Dagon's temple at Ashdod step on the threshold.

[6]The LORD's hand was heavy upon the people of Ashdod and its vicinity; he brought devastation upon them and afflicted them with tumors.[c] [7]When the men of Ashdod saw what was happening, they said, "The ark of the god of Israel must not stay here with us, because his hand is heavy upon us and upon Dagon our god." [8]So they called together all the rulers of the Philistines and asked them, "What shall we do with the ark of the god of Israel?"

They answered, "Have the ark of the god of Israel moved to Gath." So they moved the ark of the God of Israel.

[9]But after they had moved it, the LORD's hand was against that city, throwing it into a great panic. He afflicted the people of the city, both young and old, with an outbreak of tumors.[d] [10]So they sent the ark of God to Ekron.

As the ark of God was entering Ekron, the people of Ekron cried out, "They have brought the ark of the god of Israel around to us to kill us and our people." [11]So they called together all the rulers of the Philistines and said, "Send the ark of the god of Israel away; let it go back to its own place,

---

[a]18 Traditionally judged   [b]21 Ichabod means no glory.   [c]6 Hebrew; Septuagint and Vulgate tumors. And rats appeared in their land, and death and destruction were throughout the city   [d]9 Or with tumors in the groin (see Septuagint)

or it[a] will kill us and our people." For death had filled the city with panic; God's hand was very heavy upon it. [12]Those who did not die were afflicted with tumors, and the outcry of the city went up to heaven.

The Ark Returned to Israel

6 When the ark of the LORD had been in Philistine territory seven months, [2]the Philistines called for the priests and the diviners and said, "What shall we do with the ark of the LORD? Tell us how we should send it back to its place."

[3]They answered, "If you return the ark of the god of Israel, do not send it away empty, but by all means send a guilt offering to him. Then you will be healed, and you will know why his hand has not been lifted from you."

[4]The Philistines asked, "What guilt offering should we send to him?"

They replied, "Five gold tumors and five gold rats, according to the number of the Philistine rulers, because the same plague has struck both you and your rulers. [5]Make models of the tumors and of the rats that are destroying the country, and pay honor to Israel's god. Perhaps he will lift his hand from you and your gods and your land. [6]Why do you harden your hearts as the Egyptians and Pharaoh did? When he[b] treated them harshly, did they not send the Israelites out so they could go on their way?

[7]"Now then, get a new cart ready, with two cows that have calved and have never been yoked. Hitch the cows to the cart, but take their calves away and pen them up. [8]Take the ark of the LORD and put it on the cart, and in a chest beside it put the gold objects you are sending back to him as a guilt offering. Send it on its way, [9]but keep watching it. If it goes up to its own territory, toward Beth Shemesh, then the LORD has brought this great disaster on us. But if it does not, then we will know that it was not his hand that struck us and that it happened to us by chance."

[10]So they did this. They took two such cows and hitched them to the cart and penned up their calves. [11]They placed the ark of the LORD on the cart and along with it the chest containing the gold rats and the models of the tumors. [12]Then the cows went straight up toward Beth Shemesh, keeping on the road and lowing all the way; they did not turn to the right or to the left. The rulers of the Philistines followed them as far as the border of Beth Shemesh.

[13]Now the people of Beth Shemesh were harvesting their wheat in the valley, and when they looked up and saw the ark, they rejoiced at the sight. [14]The cart came to the field of Joshua of Beth Shemesh, and there it stopped beside a large rock. The people chopped up the wood of the cart and sacrificed the cows as a burnt offering to the LORD. [15]The Levites took down the ark of the LORD, together with the chest containing the gold objects, and placed them on the large rock. On that day the people of Beth Shemesh offered burnt offerings and made sacrifices to the LORD. [16]The five rulers of the Philistines saw all this and then returned that same day to Ekron.

[17]These are the gold tumors the Philistines sent as a guilt offering to the LORD—one each for Ashdod, Gaza, Ashkelon, Gath and Ekron. [18]And the number of the gold rats was according to the number of Philistine towns belonging to the five rulers—the fortified towns with their country villages. The large rock, on which[c] they set the ark of the LORD, is a witness to this day in the field of Joshua of Beth Shemesh.

[19]But God struck down some of the men of Beth Shemesh, putting seventy[d] of them to death because they had looked into the ark of the LORD. The people mourned because of the heavy blow the LORD had dealt them, [20]and the men of Beth Shemesh asked, "Who can stand in the presence of the LORD, this holy God? To whom will the ark go up from here?"

[21]Then they sent messengers to the people of Kiriath Jearim, saying, "The Philistines have returned the ark of the LORD. Come down and take it up to your place." **7** [1]So the men of Kiriath Jearim came and took up the ark of the LORD. They took it to Abinadab's house on the hill and consecrated Eleazar his son to guard the ark of the LORD.

Samuel Subdues the Philistines at Mizpah

[2]It was a long time, twenty years in all, that the ark remained at Kiriath Jearim, and all the people of Israel mourned and sought after the LORD. [3]And Samuel said

---

[a]11 Or he [b]6 That is, God [c]18 A few Hebrew manuscripts (see also Septuagint); most Hebrew manuscripts *villages as far as Greater Abel, where* [d]19 A few Hebrew manuscripts; most Hebrew manuscripts and Septuagint *50,070*

to the whole house of Israel, "If you are returning to the LORD with all your hearts, then rid yourselves of the foreign gods and the Ashtoreths and commit yourselves to the LORD and serve him only, and he will deliver you out of the hand of the Philistines." [4]So the Israelites put away their Baals and Ashtoreths, and served the LORD only.

[5]Then Samuel said, "Assemble all Israel at Mizpah and I will intercede with the LORD for you." [6]When they had assembled at Mizpah, they drew water and poured it out before the LORD. On that day they fasted and there they confessed, "We have sinned against the LORD." And Samuel was leader[a] of Israel at Mizpah.

[7]When the Philistines heard that Israel had assembled at Mizpah, the rulers of the Philistines came up to attack them. And when the Israelites heard of it, they were afraid because of the Philistines. [8]They said to Samuel, "Do not stop crying out to the LORD our God for us, that he may rescue us from the hand of the Philistines." [9]Then Samuel took a suckling lamb and offered it up as a whole burnt offering to the LORD. He cried out to the LORD on Israel's behalf, and the LORD answered him.

[10]While Samuel was sacrificing the burnt offering, the Philistines drew near to engage Israel in battle. But that day the LORD thundered with loud thunder against the Philistines and threw them into such a panic that they were routed before the Israelites. [11]The men of Israel rushed out of Mizpah and pursued the Philistines, slaughtering them along the way to a point below Beth Car.

[12]Then Samuel took a stone and set it up between Mizpah and Shen. He named it Ebenezer,[b] saying, "Thus far has the LORD helped us." [13]So the Philistines were subdued and did not invade Israelite territory again.

Throughout Samuel's lifetime, the hand of the LORD was against the Philistines. [14]The towns from Ekron to Gath that the Philistines had captured from Israel were restored to her, and Israel delivered the neighboring territory from the power of the Philistines. And there was peace between Israel and the Amorites.

[15]Samuel continued as judge over Israel all the days of his life. [16]From year to year he went on a circuit from Bethel to Gilgal to Mizpah, judging Israel in all those places. [17]But he always went back to Ra-

mah, where his home was, and there he also judged Israel. And he built an altar there to the LORD.

Israel Asks for a King

8 When Samuel grew old, he appointed his sons as judges for Israel. [2]The name of his firstborn was Joel and the name of his second was Abijah, and they served at Beersheba. [3]But his sons did not walk in his ways. They turned aside after dishonest gain and accepted bribes and perverted justice.

[4]So all the elders of Israel gathered together and came to Samuel at Ramah. [5]They said to him, "You are old, and your sons do not walk in your ways; now appoint a king to lead[c] us, such as all the other nations have."

[6]But when they said, "Give us a king to lead us," this displeased Samuel; so he prayed to the LORD. [7]And the LORD told him: "Listen to all that the people are saying to you; it is not you they have rejected, but they have rejected me as their king. [8]As they have done from the day I brought them up out of Egypt until this day, forsaking me and serving other gods, so they are doing to you. [9]Now listen to them; but warn them solemnly and let them know what the king who will reign over them will do."

[10]Samuel told all the words of the LORD to the people who were asking him for a king. [11]He said, "This is what the king who will reign over you will do: He will take your sons and make them serve with his chariots and horses, and they will run in front of his chariots. [12]Some he will assign to be commanders of thousands and commanders of fifties, and others to plow his ground and reap his harvest, and still others to make weapons of war and equipment for his chariots. [13]He will take your daughters to be perfumers and cooks and bakers. [14]He will take the best of your fields and vineyards and olive groves and give them to his attendants. [15]He will take a tenth of your grain and of your vintage and give it to his officials and attendants. [16]Your menservants and maidservants and the best of your cattle[d] and donkeys he will take for his own use. [17]He will take a tenth of your flocks, and you yourselves will become his slaves.

---

[a]6 Traditionally *judge*   [b]12 Ebenezer means *stone of help.*   [c]5 Traditionally *judge*; also in verses 6 and 20   [d]16 Septuagint; Hebrew *young men*

¹⁸When that day comes, you will cry out for relief from the king you have chosen, and the LORD will not answer you in that day."

¹⁹But the people refused to listen to Samuel. "No!" they said. "We want a king over us. ²⁰Then we will be like all the other nations, with a king to lead us and to go out before us and fight our battles."

²¹When Samuel heard all that the people said, he repeated it before the LORD.

²²The LORD answered, "Listen to them and give them a king."

Then Samuel said to the men of Israel, "Everyone go back to his town."

Samuel Anoints Saul

9 There was a Benjamite, a man of standing, whose name was Kish son of Abiel, the son of Zeror, the son of Becorath, the son of Aphiah of Benjamin.

Balloons—the Soaring and the Popping Kind

"Gentlemen, start your engines!" If you've ever been to Indianapolis Motor Speedway on Memorial Day, you can probably still feel the rush of the moment when the announcer says these words to forty-four anxious drivers. At that moment, thousands of helium-filled balloons are released.

At first the balloons seem to hang together on their journey skyward. But soon the breeze and the varying amounts of helium in each balloon separate them—just a little at first. Eventually these balloons drift apart.

Most of these brightly colored delights soar higher and higher. A few, however, have difficulty flying. Instead of sailing upward, they may hover near the treetops. Some will even brush along high-tension electrical wires, exploding with a pathetic pop.

Isn't it interesting that these balloons from the same group, filled with the same kind of helium, and released at the same moment, could have such diverse results?

Children can be like these balloons. Regardless of a dad's best efforts, some are the hovering kind rather than the soaring kind. This can be an incredible frustration, especially for parents with more than one child who have experienced very different results in each one—the same parents, basically the same external influences but greatly diverse outcomes.

We don't know what kind of dad Samuel was. We do know that he grew up in the temple and was exposed to Eli's rebellious

DAILY INSIGHT

THURSDAY

Passage:
1 Samuel 8:1–3

Verse:
1 Samuel 8:3

sons. We can assume that he observed Eli's fathering techniques and tried to learn from his elder's mistakes. But still Samuel's two sons, Joel and Abijah, "did not walk in his ways." Can you imagine how embarrassed Samuel must have been?

The critical message in these verses today is that every child is a free agent. Please pay special attention to this; it may be an encouragement to you or another dad you know. As the dad, you pour everything you can into your children. You make mistakes, and you also do some things correctly. But, like those balloons on race day, you eventually turn your children loose. Some soar skyward, making their parents proud. Others struggle near the treetops and power lines. The popping sounds spell the deepest levels of grief their parents could ever know.

Parenting is a stewardship. We care for our children, but we do not own them. We cannot control their minds or their hearts. We teach them, discipline them and love them, and then we turn them loose. If you or one of your friends is drowning in guilt and pain over a child's rebellion, this message is for you and them.

Someday you will completely release your children. What they do with their lives will be completely up to them. All you will be able to do is pray ... which, according to God's promises for you, will be enough.

For your next devotional reading, go to page 308.

[2]He had a son named Saul, an impressive young man without equal among the Israelites—a head taller than any of the others.

[3]Now the donkeys belonging to Saul's father Kish were lost, and Kish said to his son Saul, "Take one of the servants with you and go and look for the donkeys." [4]So he passed through the hill country of Ephraim and through the area around Shalisha, but they did not find them. They went on into the district of Shaalim, but the donkeys were not there. Then he passed through the territory of Benjamin, but they did not find them.

[5]When they reached the district of Zuph, Saul said to the servant who was with him, "Come, let's go back, or my father will stop thinking about the donkeys and start worrying about us."

[6]But the servant replied, "Look, in this town there is a man of God; he is highly respected, and everything he says comes true. Let's go there now. Perhaps he will tell us what way to take."

[7]Saul said to his servant, "If we go, what can we give the man? The food in our sacks is gone. We have no gift to take to the man of God. What do we have?"

[8]The servant answered him again. "Look," he said, "I have a quarter of a shekel[a] of silver. I will give it to the man of God so that he will tell us what way to take." [9](Formerly in Israel, if a man went to inquire of God, he would say, "Come, let us go to the seer," because the prophet of today used to be called a seer.)

[10]"Good," Saul said to his servant. "Come, let's go." So they set out for the town where the man of God was.

[11]As they were going up the hill to the town, they met some girls coming out to draw water, and they asked them, "Is the seer here?"

[12]"He is," they answered. "He's ahead of you. Hurry now; he has just come to our town today, for the people have a sacrifice at the high place. [13]As soon as you enter the town, you will find him before he goes up to the high place to eat. The people will not begin eating until he comes, because he must bless the sacrifice; afterward, those who are invited will eat. Go up now; you should find him about this time."

[14]They went up to the town, and as they were entering it, there was Samuel, coming toward them on his way up to the high place.

[15]Now the day before Saul came, the LORD had revealed this to Samuel: [16]"About this time tomorrow I will send you a man from the land of Benjamin. Anoint him leader over my people Israel; he will deliver my people from the hand of the Philistines. I have looked upon my people, for their cry has reached me."

[17]When Samuel caught sight of Saul, the LORD said to him, "This is the man I spoke to you about; he will govern my people."

[18]Saul approached Samuel in the gateway and asked, "Would you please tell me where the seer's house is?"

[19]"I am the seer," Samuel replied. "Go up ahead of me to the high place, for today you are to eat with me, and in the morning I will let you go and will tell you all that is in your heart. [20]As for the donkeys you lost three days ago, do not worry about them; they have been found. And to whom is all the desire of Israel turned, if not to you and all your father's family?"

[21]Saul answered, "But am I not a Benjamite, from the smallest tribe of Israel, and is not my clan the least of all the clans of the tribe of Benjamin? Why do you say such a thing to me?"

[22]Then Samuel brought Saul and his servant into the hall and seated them at the head of those who were invited—about thirty in number. [23]Samuel said to the cook, "Bring the piece of meat I gave you, the one I told you to lay aside."

[24]So the cook took up the leg with what was on it and set it in front of Saul. Samuel said, "Here is what has been kept for you. Eat, because it was set aside for you for this occasion, from the time I said, 'I have invited guests.'" And Saul dined with Samuel that day.

[25]After they came down from the high place to the town, Samuel talked with Saul on the roof of his house. [26]They rose about daybreak and Samuel called to Saul on the roof, "Get ready, and I will send you on your way." When Saul got ready, he and Samuel went outside together. [27]As they were going down to the edge of the town, Samuel said to Saul, "Tell the servant to go on ahead of us"—and the servant did so—"but you stay here awhile, so that I may give you a message from God."

10 Then Samuel took a flask of oil and poured it on Saul's head and kissed him, saying, "Has not the LORD anointed

---

[a]8 That is, about 1/10 ounce (about 3 grams)

you leader over his inheritance?ᵃ ²When you leave me today, you will meet two men near Rachel's tomb, at Zelzah on the border of Benjamin. They will say to you, 'The donkeys you set out to look for have been found. And now your father has stopped thinking about them and is worried about you. He is asking, "What shall I do about my son?" '

³"Then you will go on from there until you reach the great tree of Tabor. Three men going up to God at Bethel will meet you there. One will be carrying three young goats, another three loaves of bread, and another a skin of wine. ⁴They will greet you and offer you two loaves of bread, which you will accept from them.

⁵"After that you will go to Gibeah of God, where there is a Philistine outpost. As you approach the town, you will meet a procession of prophets coming down from the high place with lyres, tambourines, flutes and harps being played before them, and they will be prophesying. ⁶The Spirit of the LORD will come upon you in power, and you will prophesy with them; and you will be changed into a different person. ⁷Once these signs are fulfilled, do whatever your hand finds to do, for God is with you.

⁸"Go down ahead of me to Gilgal. I will surely come down to you to sacrifice burnt offerings and fellowship offerings,ᵇ but you must wait seven days until I come to you and tell you what you are to do."

Saul Made King

⁹As Saul turned to leave Samuel, God changed Saul's heart, and all these signs were fulfilled that day. ¹⁰When they arrived at Gibeah, a procession of prophets met him; the Spirit of God came upon him in power, and he joined in their prophesying. ¹¹When all those who had formerly known him saw him prophesying with the prophets, they asked each other, "What is this that has happened to the son of Kish? Is Saul also among the prophets?"

¹²A man who lived there answered, "And who is their father?" So it became a saying: "Is Saul also among the prophets?" ¹³After Saul stopped prophesying, he went to the high place.

¹⁴Now Saul's uncle asked him and his servant, "Where have you been?"

"Looking for the donkeys," he said. "But when we saw they were not to be found, we went to Samuel."

¹⁵Saul's uncle said, "Tell me what Samuel said to you."

¹⁶Saul replied, "He assured us that the donkeys had been found." But he did not tell his uncle what Samuel had said about the kingship.

¹⁷Samuel summoned the people of Israel to the LORD at Mizpah ¹⁸and said to them, "This is what the LORD, the God of Israel, says: 'I brought Israel up out of Egypt, and I delivered you from the power of Egypt and all the kingdoms that oppressed you.' ¹⁹But you have now rejected your God, who saves you out of all your calamities and distresses. And you have said, 'No, set a king over us.' So now present yourselves before the LORD by your tribes and clans."

²⁰When Samuel brought all the tribes of Israel near, the tribe of Benjamin was chosen. ²¹Then he brought forward the tribe of Benjamin, clan by clan, and Matri's clan was chosen. Finally Saul son of Kish was chosen. But when they looked for him, he was not to be found. ²²So they inquired further of the LORD, "Has the man come here yet?"

And the LORD said, "Yes, he has hidden himself among the baggage."

²³They ran and brought him out, and as he stood among the people he was a head taller than any of the others. ²⁴Samuel said to all the people, "Do you see the man the LORD has chosen? There is no one like him among all the people."

Then the people shouted, "Long live the king!"

²⁵Samuel explained to the people the regulations of the kingship. He wrote them down on a scroll and deposited it before the LORD. Then Samuel dismissed the people, each to his own home. ²⁶Saul also went to his home in Gibeah, accompanied by valiant men whose hearts God had touched. ²⁷But some troublemakers said, "How can this fellow save us?" They despised him and brought him no gifts. But Saul kept silent.

Saul Rescues the City of Jabesh

11 Nahash the Ammonite went up and besieged Jabesh Gilead. And all the men of Jabesh said to him, "Make a treaty with us, and we will be subject to you."

ᵃ1 Hebrew; Septuagint and Vulgate *over his people Israel? You will reign over the LORD's people and save them from the power of their enemies round about. And this will be a sign to you that the LORD has anointed you leader over his inheritance:* ᵇ8 Traditionally *peace offerings*

²But Nahash the Ammonite replied, "I will make a treaty with you only on the condition that I gouge out the right eye of every one of you and so bring disgrace on all Israel."

³The elders of Jabesh said to him, "Give us seven days so we can send messengers throughout Israel; if no one comes to rescue us, we will surrender to you."

⁴When the messengers came to Gibeah of Saul and reported these terms to the people, they all wept aloud. ⁵Just then Saul was returning from the fields, behind his oxen, and he asked, "What is wrong with the people? Why are they weeping?" Then they repeated to him what the men of Jabesh had said.

⁶When Saul heard their words, the Spirit of God came upon him in power, and he burned with anger. ⁷He took a pair of oxen, cut them into pieces, and sent the pieces by messengers throughout Israel, proclaiming, "This is what will be done to the oxen of anyone who does not follow Saul and Samuel." Then the terror of the LORD fell on the people, and they turned out as one man. ⁸When Saul mustered them at Bezek, the men of Israel numbered three hundred thousand and the men of Judah thirty thousand.

⁹They told the messengers who had come, "Say to the men of Jabesh Gilead, 'By the time the sun is hot tomorrow, you will be delivered.' " When the messengers went and reported this to the men of Jabesh, they were elated. ¹⁰They said to the Ammonites, "Tomorrow we will surrender to you, and you can do to us whatever seems good to you."

¹¹The next day Saul separated his men into three divisions; during the last watch of the night they broke into the camp of the Ammonites and slaughtered them until the heat of the day. Those who survived were scattered, so that no two of them were left together.

Saul Confirmed as King

¹²The people then said to Samuel, "Who was it that asked, 'Shall Saul reign over us?' Bring these men to us and we will put them to death."

¹³But Saul said, "No one shall be put to death today, for this day the LORD has rescued Israel."

¹⁴Then Samuel said to the people, "Come, let us go to Gilgal and there reaffirm the kingship." ¹⁵So all the people went to Gilgal and confirmed Saul as king

in the presence of the LORD. There they sacrificed fellowship offerings[a] before the LORD, and Saul and all the Israelites held a great celebration.

Samuel's Farewell Speech

12 Samuel said to all Israel, "I have listened to everything you said to me and have set a king over you. ²Now you have a king as your leader. As for me, I am old and gray, and my sons are here with you. I have been your leader from my youth until this day. ³Here I stand. Testify against me in the presence of the LORD and his anointed. Whose ox have I taken? Whose donkey have I taken? Whom have I cheated? Whom have I oppressed? From whose hand have I accepted a bribe to make me shut my eyes? If I have done any of these, I will make it right."

⁴"You have not cheated or oppressed us," they replied. "You have not taken anything from anyone's hand."

⁵Samuel said to them, "The LORD is witness against you, and also his anointed is witness this day, that you have not found anything in my hand."

"He is witness," they said.

⁶Then Samuel said to the people, "It is the LORD who appointed Moses and Aaron and brought your forefathers up out of Egypt. ⁷Now then, stand here, because I am going to confront you with evidence before the LORD as to all the righteous acts performed by the LORD for you and your fathers.

⁸"After Jacob entered Egypt, they cried to the LORD for help, and the LORD sent Moses and Aaron, who brought your forefathers out of Egypt and settled them in this place.

⁹"But they forgot the LORD their God; so he sold them into the hand of Sisera, the commander of the army of Hazor, and into the hands of the Philistines and the king of Moab, who fought against them. ¹⁰They cried out to the LORD and said, 'We have sinned; we have forsaken the LORD and served the Baals and the Ashtoreths. But now deliver us from the hands of our enemies, and we will serve you.' ¹¹Then the LORD sent Jerub-Baal,[b] Barak,[c] Jephthah and Samuel,[d] and he delivered you from the hands of your enemies on every side, so that you lived securely.

---

*a*15 Traditionally *peace offerings*   *b*11 Also called *Gideon*   *c*11 Some Septuagint manuscripts and Syriac; Hebrew *Bedan*   *d*11 Hebrew; some Septuagint manuscripts and Syriac *Samson*

¹²"But when you saw that Nahash king of the Ammonites was moving against you, you said to me, 'No, we want a king to rule over us'—even though the LORD your God was your king. ¹³Now here is the king you have chosen, the one you asked for; see, the LORD has set a king over you. ¹⁴If you fear the LORD and serve and obey him and do not rebel against his commands, and if both you and the king who reigns over you follow the LORD your God—good! ¹⁵But if you do not obey the LORD, and if you rebel against his commands, his hand will be against you, as it was against your fathers.

¹⁶"Now then, stand still and see this great thing the LORD is about to do before your eyes! ¹⁷Is it not wheat harvest now? I will call upon the LORD to send thunder and rain. And you will realize what an evil thing you did in the eyes of the LORD when you asked for a king."

¹⁸Then Samuel called upon the LORD, and that same day the LORD sent thunder and rain. So all the people stood in awe of the LORD and of Samuel.

¹⁹The people all said to Samuel, "Pray to the LORD your God for your servants so that we will not die, for we have added to all our other sins the evil of asking for a king."

²⁰"Do not be afraid," Samuel replied. "You have done all this evil; yet do not turn away from the LORD, but serve the LORD with all your heart. ²¹Do not turn away after useless idols. They can do you no good, nor can they rescue you, because they are useless. ²²For the sake of his great name the LORD will not reject his people, because the LORD was pleased to make you his own. ²³As for me, far be it from me that I should sin against the LORD by failing to pray for you. And I will teach you the way that is good and right. ²⁴But be sure to fear the LORD and serve him faithfully with all your heart; consider what great things he has done for you. ²⁵Yet if you persist in doing evil, both you and your king will be swept away."

Samuel Rebukes Saul

13 Saul was ˎthirty,ᵃ years old when he became king, and he reigned over Israel ˎfortyˍᵇ two years.

²Saulᶜ chose three thousand men from Israel; two thousand were with him at Micmash and in the hill country of Bethel, and a thousand were with Jonathan at Gibeah in Benjamin. The rest of the men he sent back to their homes.

³Jonathan attacked the Philistine outpost at Geba, and the Philistines heard about it. Then Saul had the trumpet blown throughout the land and said, "Let the Hebrews hear!" ⁴So all Israel heard the news: "Saul has attacked the Philistine outpost, and now Israel has become a stench to the Philistines." And the people were summoned to join Saul at Gilgal.

⁵The Philistines assembled to fight Israel, with three thousandᵈ chariots, six thousand charioteers, and soldiers as numerous as the sand on the seashore. They went up and camped at Micmash, east of Beth Aven. ⁶When the men of Israel saw that their situation was critical and that their army was hard pressed, they hid in caves and thickets, among the rocks, and in pits and cisterns. ⁷Some Hebrews even crossed the Jordan to the land of Gad and Gilead.

Saul remained at Gilgal, and all the troops with him were quaking with fear. ⁸He waited seven days, the time set by Samuel; but Samuel did not come to Gilgal, and Saul's men began to scatter. ⁹So he said, "Bring me the burnt offering and the fellowship offerings.ᵉ" And Saul offered up the burnt offering. ¹⁰Just as he finished making the offering, Samuel arrived, and Saul went out to greet him.

¹¹"What have you done?" asked Samuel.

Saul replied, "When I saw that the men were scattering, and that you did not come at the set time, and that the Philistines were assembling at Micmash, ¹²I thought, 'Now the Philistines will come down against me at Gilgal, and I have not sought the LORD's favor.' So I felt compelled to offer the burnt offering."

¹³"You acted foolishly," Samuel said. "You have not kept the command the LORD your God gave you; if you had, he would have established your kingdom over Israel for all time. ¹⁴But now your kingdom will not endure; the LORD has sought out a man after his own heart and appointed him leader of his people, because you have not kept the LORD's command."

ᵃ1 A few late manuscripts of the Septuagint; Hebrew does not have *thirty*.   ᵇ1 See the round number in Acts 13:21; Hebrew does not have *forty-*.   ᶜ1,2 Or *and when he had reigned over Israel two years,* ²*he*   ᵈ5 Some Septuagint manuscripts and Syriac; Hebrew *thirty thousand*   ᵉ9 Traditionally *peace offerings*

¹⁵Then Samuel left Gilgal*ᵃ* and went up to Gibeah in Benjamin, and Saul counted the men who were with him. They numbered about six hundred.

Israel Without Weapons

¹⁶Saul and his son Jonathan and the men with them were staying in Gibeah*ᵇ* in Benjamin, while the Philistines camped at Micmash. ¹⁷Raiding parties went out from the Philistine camp in three detachments. One turned toward Ophrah in the

vicinity of Shual, ¹⁸another toward Beth Horon, and the third toward the borderland overlooking the Valley of Zeboim facing the desert.

¹⁹Not a blacksmith could be found in the whole land of Israel, because the Philistines had said, "Otherwise the Hebrews

ᵃ15 Hebrew; Septuagint Gilgal and went his way; the rest of the people went after Saul to meet the army, and they went out of Gilgal   ᵇ16 Two Hebrew manuscripts; most Hebrew manuscripts Geba, a variant of Gibeah

A Not-So-Happy Meal

DAILY INSIGHT

FRIDAY

Passage:
1 Samuel 13:1–15

Verses:
1 Samuel 13:13–14

My associate and I had spent most of the day in the air or in airport terminals waiting for flights. I don't quite know why this is true, but days like this make me very tired. Interestingly enough, they also make me very hungry. Perhaps it's because there are so many food vendors at airports and such little food on airplanes!

In any case, finally—and happily—we arrived at our destination. A colleague met us at the airport and whisked us off to dinner. *Oh, boy,* I thought, *I'm starved.*

In a few minutes, our car pulled into … *Hey, what's going on here … this looks like … those are golden arches!* Sure enough, kind of as a joke, our host had decided to take us to the local McDonald's for appetizers. Our host ordered a Happy Meal for each of us, and we sat down to enjoy a baby cheeseburger, a few fries, a miniature drink, and, of course, a little toy. Just as soon as we had finished, we loaded back in the car and were driven to the "real" restaurant for a wonderful meal.

Unfortunately, for me, I had left my voracious appetite and longing for a great dinner back in fast-food land. I remember thinking to myself when our waitress brought my spectacularly presented, grilled swordfish, *I wish I had waited for this.*

King Saul was very anxious. He and his troops were up to their shoulders in a battle at Gilgal. Saul knew it was time to stop and worship the God who had prom-

ised to bring him through the conflict. Samuel had promised to come and perform the service, and Saul knew the law—only God's anointed prophet had the right to do the sacrifice. *But where was Samuel?* He was late, and Saul had had enough. He ordered the elements delivered to him and performed the service himself. Just as he finished, Samuel showed up.

"What have you done, Saul?" Samuel asked. "How foolish could you be?" At that moment, Saul must have been filled with tremendous regret. *I wish I had waited,* he must have whispered to himself.

In reading this story, it's easy for you and me to understand both sides. True, Saul should not have jumped the gun, but he had a battle to fight and waiting was the *last* thing he wanted to do. Still, Saul traded God's best to suit his own needs. This action cost Saul God's blessing … and eventually his position as king.

Sometimes God calls us to action. But sometimes he asks us to wait. "If you move now," God seems to be saying, "You'll be denying yourself the luxury of experiencing my best."

Waiting is tough. But satisfying yourself with a kiddie meal and missing out on savory grilled swordfish is worse. Learn from Saul. Experiencing God's finest is always worth the wait.

For your next devotional reading, go to page 310.

will make swords or spears!" [20]So all Israel went down to the Philistines to have their plowshares, mattocks, axes and sickles[a] sharpened. [21]The price was two thirds of a shekel[b] for sharpening plowshares and mattocks, and a third of a shekel[c] for sharpening forks and axes and for re-pointing goads.

[22]So on the day of the battle not a soldier with Saul and Jonathan had a sword or spear in his hand; only Saul and his son Jonathan had them.

Jonathan Attacks the Philistines

[23]Now a detachment of Philistines had gone out to the pass at Micmash. **14** [1]One day Jonathan son of Saul said to the young man bearing his armor, "Come, let's go over to the Philistine outpost on the other side." But he did not tell his father.

[2]Saul was staying on the outskirts of Gibeah under a pomegranate tree in Migron. With him were about six hundred men, [3]among whom was Ahijah, who was wearing an ephod. He was a son of Ichabod's brother Ahitub son of Phinehas, the son of Eli, the LORD's priest in Shiloh. No one was aware that Jonathan had left.

[4]On each side of the pass that Jonathan intended to cross to reach the Philistine outpost was a cliff; one was called Bozez, and the other Seneh. [5]One cliff stood to the north toward Micmash, the other to the south toward Geba.

[6]Jonathan said to his young armor-bearer, "Come, let's go over to the outpost of those uncircumcised fellows. Perhaps the LORD will act in our behalf. Nothing can hinder the LORD from saving, whether by many or by few."

[7]"Do all that you have in mind," his armor-bearer said. "Go ahead; I am with you heart and soul."

[8]Jonathan said, "Come, then; we will cross over toward the men and let them see us. [9]If they say to us, 'Wait there until we come to you,' we will stay where we are and not go up to them. [10]But if they say, 'Come up to us,' we will climb up, because that will be our sign that the LORD has given them into our hands."

[11]So both of them showed themselves to the Philistine outpost. "Look!" said the Philistines. "The Hebrews are crawling out of the holes they were hiding in." [12]The men of the outpost shouted to Jonathan and his armor-bearer, "Come up to us and we'll teach you a lesson."

So Jonathan said to his armor-bearer, "Climb up after me; the LORD has given them into the hand of Israel."

[13]Jonathan climbed up, using his hands and feet, with his armor-bearer right behind him. The Philistines fell before Jonathan, and his armor-bearer followed and killed behind him. [14]In that first attack Jonathan and his armor-bearer killed some twenty men in an area of about half an acre.[d]

Israel Routs the Philistines

[15]Then panic struck the whole army—those in the camp and field, and those in the outposts and raiding parties—and the ground shook. It was a panic sent by God.[e]

[16]Saul's lookouts at Gibeah in Benjamin saw the army melting away in all directions. [17]Then Saul said to the men who were with him, "Muster the forces and see who has left us." When they did, it was Jonathan and his armor-bearer who were not there.

[18]Saul said to Ahijah, "Bring the ark of God." (At that time it was with the Israelites.)[f] [19]While Saul was talking to the priest, the tumult in the Philistine camp increased more and more. So Saul said to the priest, "Withdraw your hand."

[20]Then Saul and all his men assembled and went to the battle. They found the Philistines in total confusion, striking each other with their swords. [21]Those Hebrews who had previously been with the Philistines and had gone up with them to their camp went over to the Israelites who were with Saul and Jonathan. [22]When all the Israelites who had hidden in the hill country of Ephraim heard that the Philistines were on the run, they joined the battle in hot pursuit. [23]So the LORD rescued Israel that day, and the battle moved on beyond Beth Aven.

Jonathan Eats Honey

[24]Now the men of Israel were in distress that day, because Saul had bound the people under an oath, saying, "Cursed be any man who eats food before evening comes, before I have avenged myself on

[a]20 Septuagint; Hebrew *plowshares*   [b]21 Hebrew *pim*; that is, about 1/4 ounce (about 8 grams)   [c]21 That is, about 1/8 ounce (about 4 grams)   [d]14 Hebrew *half a yoke*; a "yoke" was the land plowed by a yoke of oxen in one day.   [e]15 Or *a terrible panic*   [f]18 Hebrew; Septuagint *"Bring the ephod." (At that time he wore the ephod before the Israelites.)*

Plenty of Speed Limit Signs

Key Verse: *"But Jonathan had not heard that his father had bound the people with the oath, so he reached out the end of the staff that was in his hand and dipped it into the honeycomb."* 1 Samuel 14:27

Text: 1 Samuel 14:24–28 *(Dad or child reads the text.)*

QUIET
TIMES
WITH Dad

DAD READS: One of the most difficult things for me to do when I'm driving is to obey the speed limit. Sometimes I go too fast because I'm in a hurry, and sometimes I go too fast because I don't remember what the limit is. That's why, when we drive through our town, the speed limit signs are placed every few hundred yards, just to be sure that everyone knows how fast they can go.

Child reads: The police in our town don't want anyone to be able to say, "I didn't know what the speed limit was." Maybe that's why they put up all those signs.

DAD READS: I'm sure you're right. If we're expected to obey the law, it's only fair that we know what the laws are. Today's story is about a father and a son. Saul, the father, made a rule that no one was to eat until the end of the day. But Jonathan, his son, didn't hear him make the rule. So when Jonathan saw something good to eat, he helped himself.

Child reads: I know that it's important for me to be obedient. Sometimes it's hard for me to always do what you want me to do, but I know that I should. Jonathan disobeyed his dad, but he was really innocent, because Saul had not told him the rules. If a dad doesn't make sure his child knows the rules, how can he expect him to obey them?

DAD READS: You're right. It's only fair that dads—and moms, too—tell their children what they want them to do.

And it's not fair if they just expect their kids to obey if the rules aren't clear. I always want to be fair with you. I know how unhappy I would feel if I got a ticket for speeding because the policeman had not put up a sign. I never want you to be punished because I failed to talk to you about the rules.

Child reads: Thank you for telling me this. Thank you for wanting to be fair. I'm glad that the Bible makes sure that we always understand what God wants us to do. His laws are clear. I'm glad that you read God's Word so that you understand what God expects of you. I'm glad that, as my dad, you can help me to learn God's ways, too.

DAD READS: I need to always remember how important it is to be obedient to God before I can ask my children to be obedient to me. Let me pray this prayer with you:

Our Father in heaven, thank you for making your laws so clear to me. Forgive me when I disobey. Help me to always take time to tell my children what I want before expecting them to obey. And help me to be more forgiving. Thank you for giving all of us hearts to love and honor each other. In Jesus' name, Amen.

For your next devotional reading, go to page 314.

my enemies!" So none of the troops tasted food.

[25]The entire army[a] entered the woods, and there was honey on the ground. [26]When they went into the woods, they saw the honey oozing out, yet no one put his hand to his mouth, because they feared the oath. [27]But Jonathan had not heard that his father had bound the people with the oath, so he reached out the end of the staff that was in his hand and dipped it into the honeycomb. He raised his hand to his mouth, and his eyes brightened.[b] [28]Then one of the soldiers told him, "Your father bound the army under a strict oath, saying, 'Cursed be any man who eats food today!' That is why the men are faint."

[29]Jonathan said, "My father has made trouble for the country. See how my eyes brightened[c] when I tasted a little of this honey. [30]How much better it would have been if the men had eaten today some of the plunder they took from their enemies. Would not the slaughter of the Philistines have been even greater?"

[31]That day, after the Israelites had struck down the Philistines from Micmash to Aijalon, they were exhausted. [32]They pounced on the plunder and, taking sheep, cattle and calves, they butchered them on the ground and ate them, together with the blood. [33]Then someone said to Saul, "Look, the men are sinning against the LORD by eating meat that has blood in it."

"You have broken faith," he said. "Roll a large stone over here at once." [34]Then he said, "Go out among the men and tell them, 'Each of you bring me your cattle and sheep, and slaughter them here and eat them. Do not sin against the LORD by eating meat with blood still in it.' "

So everyone brought his ox that night and slaughtered it there. [35]Then Saul built an altar to the LORD; it was the first time he had done this.

[36]Saul said, "Let us go down after the Philistines by night and plunder them till dawn, and let us not leave one of them alive."

"Do whatever seems best to you," they replied.

But the priest said, "Let us inquire of God here."

[37]So Saul asked God, "Shall I go down after the Philistines? Will you give them into Israel's hand?" But God did not answer him that day.

[38]Saul therefore said, "Come here, all you who are leaders of the army, and let us find out what sin has been committed today. [39]As surely as the LORD who rescues Israel lives, even if it lies with my son Jonathan, he must die." But not one of the men said a word.

[40]Saul then said to all the Israelites, "You stand over there; I and Jonathan my son will stand over here."

"Do what seems best to you," the men replied.

[41]Then Saul prayed to the LORD, the God of Israel, "Give me the right answer."[d] And Jonathan and Saul were taken by lot, and the men were cleared. [42]Saul said, "Cast the lot between me and Jonathan my son." And Jonathan was taken.

[43]Then Saul said to Jonathan, "Tell me what you have done."

So Jonathan told him, "I merely tasted a little honey with the end of my staff. And now must I die?"

[44]Saul said, "May God deal with me, be it ever so severely, if you do not die, Jonathan."

[45]But the men said to Saul, "Should Jonathan die—he who has brought about this great deliverance in Israel? Never! As surely as the LORD lives, not a hair of his head will fall to the ground, for he did this today with God's help." So the men rescued Jonathan, and he was not put to death.

[46]Then Saul stopped pursuing the Philistines, and they withdrew to their own land.

[47]After Saul had assumed rule over Israel, he fought against their enemies on every side: Moab, the Ammonites, Edom, the kings[e] of Zobah, and the Philistines. Wherever he turned, he inflicted punishment on them.[f] [48]He fought valiantly and defeated the Amalekites, delivering Israel from the hands of those who had plundered them.

Saul's Family

[49]Saul's sons were Jonathan, Ishvi and Malki-Shua. The name of his older daughter was Merab, and that of the younger was Michal. [50]His wife's name was Ahinoam daughter of Ahimaaz. The name of the

---

a25 Or *Now all the people of the land*   *b27* Or *his strength was renewed*   *c29* Or *my strength was renewed*   *d41* Hebrew; Septuagint *"Why have you not answered your servant today? If the fault is in me or my son Jonathan, respond with Urim, but if the men of Israel are at fault, respond with Thummim."*   *e47* Masoretic Text; Dead Sea Scrolls and Septuagint *king*   *f47* Hebrew; Septuagint *he was victorious*

commander of Saul's army was Abner son of Ner, and Ner was Saul's uncle. [51]Saul's father Kish and Abner's father Ner were sons of Abiel.

[52]All the days of Saul there was bitter war with the Philistines, and whenever Saul saw a mighty or brave man, he took him into his service.

The Lord Rejects Saul as King

15 Samuel said to Saul, "I am the one the Lord sent to anoint you king over his people Israel; so listen now to the message from the Lord. [2]This is what the Lord Almighty says: 'I will punish the Amalekites for what they did to Israel when they waylaid them as they came up from Egypt. [3]Now go, attack the Amalekites and totally destroy[a] everything that belongs to them. Do not spare them; put to death men and women, children and infants, cattle and sheep, camels and donkeys.' "

[4]So Saul summoned the men and mustered them at Telaim—two hundred thousand foot soldiers and ten thousand men from Judah. [5]Saul went to the city of Amalek and set an ambush in the ravine. [6]Then he said to the Kenites, "Go away, leave the Amalekites so that I do not destroy you along with them; for you showed kindness to all the Israelites when they came up out of Egypt." So the Kenites moved away from the Amalekites.

[7]Then Saul attacked the Amalekites all the way from Havilah to Shur, to the east of Egypt. [8]He took Agag king of the Amalekites alive, and all his people he totally destroyed with the sword. [9]But Saul and the army spared Agag and the best of the sheep and cattle, the fat calves[b] and lambs—everything that was good. These they were unwilling to destroy completely, but everything that was despised and weak they totally destroyed.

[10]Then the word of the Lord came to Samuel: [11]"I am grieved that I have made Saul king, because he has turned away from me and has not carried out my instructions." Samuel was troubled, and he cried out to the Lord all that night.

[12]Early in the morning Samuel got up and went to meet Saul, but he was told, "Saul has gone to Carmel. There he has set up a monument in his own honor and has turned and gone on down to Gilgal."

[13]When Samuel reached him, Saul said, "The Lord bless you! I have carried out the Lord's instructions."

[14]But Samuel said, "What then is this bleating of sheep in my ears? What is this lowing of cattle that I hear?"

[15]Saul answered, "The soldiers brought them from the Amalekites; they spared the best of the sheep and cattle to sacrifice to the Lord your God, but we totally destroyed the rest."

[16]"Stop!" Samuel said to Saul. "Let me tell you what the Lord said to me last night."

"Tell me," Saul replied.

[17]Samuel said, "Although you were once small in your own eyes, did you not become the head of the tribes of Israel? The Lord anointed you king over Israel. [18]And he sent you on a mission, saying, 'Go and completely destroy those wicked people, the Amalekites; make war on them until you have wiped them out.' [19]Why did you not obey the Lord? Why did you pounce on the plunder and do evil in the eyes of the Lord?"

[20]"But I did obey the Lord," Saul said. "I went on the mission the Lord assigned me. I completely destroyed the Amalekites and brought back Agag their king. [21]The soldiers took sheep and cattle from the plunder, the best of what was devoted to God, in order to sacrifice them to the Lord your God at Gilgal."

[22]But Samuel replied:

"Does the Lord delight in burnt
    offerings and sacrifices
    as much as in obeying the voice of
      the Lord?
To obey is better than sacrifice,
    and to heed is better than the fat of
      rams.
[23]For rebellion is like the sin of divination,
    and arrogance like the evil of
      idolatry.
Because you have rejected the word of
      the Lord,
    he has rejected you as king."

[24]Then Saul said to Samuel, "I have sinned. I violated the Lord's command and your instructions. I was afraid of the people and so I gave in to them. [25]Now I beg you, forgive my sin and come back with me, so that I may worship the Lord."

[26]But Samuel said to him, "I will not go back with you. You have rejected the word of the Lord, and the Lord has rejected you as king over Israel!"

---

[a]3 The Hebrew term refers to the irrevocable giving over of things or persons to the Lord, often by totally destroying them; also in verses 8, 9, 15, 18, 20 and 21.   [b]9 Or *the grown bulls*; the meaning of the Hebrew for this phrase is uncertain.

²⁷As Samuel turned to leave, Saul caught hold of the hem of his robe, and it tore. ²⁸Samuel said to him, "The LORD has torn the kingdom of Israel from you today and has given it to one of your neighbors—to one better than you. ²⁹He who is the Glory of Israel does not lie or change his mind; for he is not a man, that he should change his mind."

³⁰Saul replied, "I have sinned. But please honor me before the elders of my people and before Israel; come back with me, so that I may worship the LORD your God." ³¹So Samuel went back with Saul, and Saul worshiped the LORD.

³²Then Samuel said, "Bring me Agag king of the Amalekites."

Agag came to him confidently,ᵃ thinking, "Surely the bitterness of death is past."

³³But Samuel said,

"As your sword has made women
            childless,
    so will your mother be childless
            among women."

And Samuel put Agag to death before the LORD at Gilgal.

³⁴Then Samuel left for Ramah, but Saul went up to his home in Gibeah of Saul. ³⁵Until the day Samuel died, he did not go to see Saul again, though Samuel mourned for him. And the LORD was grieved that he had made Saul king over Israel.

Samuel Anoints David

16 The LORD said to Samuel, "How long will you mourn for Saul, since I have rejected him as king over Israel? Fill your horn with oil and be on your way; I am sending you to Jesse of Bethlehem. I have chosen one of his sons to be king."

²But Samuel said, "How can I go? Saul will hear about it and kill me."

The LORD said, "Take a heifer with you and say, 'I have come to sacrifice to the LORD.' ³Invite Jesse to the sacrifice, and I will show you what to do. You are to anoint for me the one I indicate."

⁴Samuel did what the LORD said. When he arrived at Bethlehem, the elders of the town trembled when they met him. They asked, "Do you come in peace?"

⁵Samuel replied, "Yes, in peace; I have come to sacrifice to the LORD. Consecrate yourselves and come to the sacrifice with me." Then he consecrated Jesse and his sons and invited them to the sacrifice.

⁶When they arrived, Samuel saw Eliab and thought, "Surely the LORD's anointed stands here before the LORD."

⁷But the LORD said to Samuel, "Do not consider his appearance or his height, for I have rejected him. The LORD does not look at the things man looks at. Man looks at the outward appearance, but the LORD looks at the heart."

⁸Then Jesse called Abinadab and had him pass in front of Samuel. But Samuel said, "The LORD has not chosen this one either." ⁹Jesse then had Shammah pass by, but Samuel said, "Nor has the LORD chosen this one." ¹⁰Jesse had seven of his sons pass before Samuel, but Samuel said to him, "The LORD has not chosen these." ¹¹So he asked Jesse, "Are these all the sons you have?"

"There is still the youngest," Jesse answered, "but he is tending the sheep."

Samuel said, "Send for him; we will not sit downᵇ until he arrives."

¹²So he sent and had him brought in. He was ruddy, with a fine appearance and handsome features.

Then the LORD said, "Rise and anoint him; he is the one."

¹³So Samuel took the horn of oil and anointed him in the presence of his brothers, and from that day on the Spirit of the LORD came upon David in power. Samuel then went to Ramah.

David in Saul's Service

¹⁴Now the Spirit of the LORD had departed from Saul, and an evilᶜ spirit from the LORD tormented him.

¹⁵Saul's attendants said to him, "See, an evil spirit from God is tormenting you. ¹⁶Let our lord command his servants here to search for someone who can play the harp. He will play when the evil spirit from God comes upon you, and you will feel better."

¹⁷So Saul said to his attendants, "Find someone who plays well and bring him to me."

¹⁸One of the servants answered, "I have seen a son of Jesse of Bethlehem who knows how to play the harp. He is a brave man and a warrior. He speaks well and is a fine-looking man. And the LORD is with him."

¹⁹Then Saul sent messengers to Jesse and said, "Send me your son David, who

---

ᵃ32 Or him trembling, yet   ᵇ11 Some Septuagint manuscripts; Hebrew not gather around   ᶜ14 Or injurious; also in verses 15, 16 and 23 is with the sheep." **20**So Jesse took a donkey loaded with bread, a skin of wine and a young goat and sent them with his son David to Saul.

21David came to Saul and entered his service. Saul liked him very much, and David became one of his armor-bearers. **22**Then Saul sent word to Jesse, saying, "Allow David to remain in my service, for I am pleased with him."

23Whenever the spirit from God came upon Saul, David would take his harp and play. Then relief would come to Saul; he would feel better, and the evil spirit would leave him.

David and Goliath

17 Now the Philistines gathered their forces for war and assembled at Socoh in Judah. They pitched camp at Ephes Dammim, between Socoh and Azekah. **2**Saul and the Israelites assembled and camped in the Valley of Elah and drew up their battle line to meet the Philistines. **3**The Philistines occupied one hill and the Israelites another, with the valley between them.

4A champion named Goliath, who was from Gath, came out of the Philistine camp. He was over nine feet[a] tall. **5**He had a bronze helmet on his head and wore a coat of scale armor of bronze weighing five thousand shekels[b]; **6**on his legs he wore bronze greaves, and a bronze javelin was slung on his back. **7**His spear shaft

[a]4 Hebrew *was six cubits and a span* (about 3 meters)   [b]5 That is, about 125 pounds (about 57 kilograms)

A Beautiful Heart

DAILY INSIGHT

MONDAY

Passage:
1 Samuel 16:1–7

Verse:
1 Samuel 16:7

Beautiful people are everywhere. Newsstand magazine covers are a veritable banquet of this month's most attractive faces. But who are these people, and why are they so beautiful? Is it because they have straight teeth and flawless complexions? Are they so attractive because of their prowess on the silver screen or the athletic field? Or is it their power and wealth that make them so handsome?

Whatever the reason, it's safe to say that our culture is completely infatuated with such people. And it's also safe to say that it's impossible for you and me not to be impressed by their seeming flawlessness.

The Israelites were also impressed by a beautiful person. The Scripture tells us that Saul was tall and handsome and that he stood out in a crowd. People noticed Saul. In our day, he would've been a sure candidate for People Magazine's "Fifty Most Beautiful People in the World" issue. But God was not happy with Saul. In fact, our text today tells us that God had rejected him as king over Israel (16:1). Saul's impressive exterior did not dazzle the Creator of the universe, because the king's constitution had become completely corrupt.

So God asked Samuel to go find another king. This time, however, the Lord told Samuel to look on the *inside*, at the character of the man, and not at how photogenic he might be on the cover of the inauguration program.

Think for a second about how much effort you and I exert on our outsides. Shaving, grooming, deodorizing and dressing takes time. We also try to eat right and exercise so we look acceptable in spite of our age. But to God, we're completely transparent. When he looks at us, he is able to look through all the externals, directly into who we are—our thoughts, our motives, our desires ... our hearts.

The message today is certainly not meant to say we should ignore our bodies. They are, after all, the temples where God's Spirit lives. However, the challenge is to spend at least as much time working on who we *are* as we do working on what we look like.

Taking time each day to read God's Word and listen to his voice is certainly a great start toward becoming a beautiful person on the inside. Congratulations, you're right on track.

For your next devotional reading, go to page 323.

was like a weaver's rod, and its iron point weighed six hundred shekels.[a] His shield bearer went ahead of him.

[8]Goliath stood and shouted to the ranks of Israel, "Why do you come out and line up for battle? Am I not a Philistine, and are you not the servants of Saul? Choose a man and have him come down to me. [9]If he is able to fight and kill me, we will become your subjects; but if I overcome him and kill him, you will become our subjects and serve us." [10]Then the Philistine said, "This day I defy the ranks of Israel! Give me a man and let us fight each other." [11]On hearing the Philistine's words, Saul and all the Israelites were dismayed and terrified.

[12]Now David was the son of an Ephrathite named Jesse, who was from Bethlehem in Judah. Jesse had eight sons, and in Saul's time he was old and well advanced in years. [13]Jesse's three oldest sons had followed Saul to the war: The firstborn was Eliab; the second, Abinadab; and the third, Shammah. [14]David was the youngest. The three oldest followed Saul, [15]but David went back and forth from Saul to tend his father's sheep at Bethlehem.

[16]For forty days the Philistine came forward every morning and evening and took his stand.

[17]Now Jesse said to his son David, "Take this ephah[b] of roasted grain and these ten loaves of bread for your brothers and hurry to their camp. [18]Take along these ten cheeses to the commander of their unit.[c] See how your brothers are and bring back some assurance[d] from them. [19]They are with Saul and all the men of Israel in the Valley of Elah, fighting against the Philistines."

[20]Early in the morning David left the flock with a shepherd, loaded up and set out, as Jesse had directed. He reached the camp as the army was going out to its battle positions, shouting the war cry. [21]Israel and the Philistines were drawing up their lines facing each other. [22]David left his things with the keeper of supplies, ran to the battle lines and greeted his brothers. [23]As he was talking with them, Goliath, the Philistine champion from Gath, stepped out from his lines and shouted his usual defiance, and David heard it. [24]When the Israelites saw the man, they all ran from him in great fear.

[25]Now the Israelites had been saying, "Do you see how this man keeps coming out? He comes out to defy Israel. The king will give great wealth to the man who kills him. He will also give him his daughter in marriage and will exempt his father's family from taxes in Israel."

[26]David asked the men standing near him, "What will be done for the man who kills this Philistine and removes this disgrace from Israel? Who is this uncircumcised Philistine that he should defy the armies of the living God?"

[27]They repeated to him what they had been saying and told him, "This is what will be done for the man who kills him."

[28]When Eliab, David's oldest brother, heard him speaking with the men, he burned with anger at him and asked, "Why have you come down here? And with whom did you leave those few sheep in the desert? I know how conceited you are and how wicked your heart is; you came down only to watch the battle."

[29]"Now what have I done?" said David. "Can't I even speak?" [30]He then turned away to someone else and brought up the same matter, and the men answered him as before. [31]What David said was overheard and reported to Saul, and Saul sent for him.

[32]David said to Saul, "Let no one lose heart on account of this Philistine; your servant will go and fight him."

[33]Saul replied, "You are not able to go out against this Philistine and fight him; you are only a boy, and he has been a fighting man from his youth."

[34]But David said to Saul, "Your servant has been keeping his father's sheep. When a lion or a bear came and carried off a sheep from the flock, [35]I went after it, struck it and rescued the sheep from its mouth. When it turned on me, I seized it by its hair, struck it and killed it. [36]Your servant has killed both the lion and the bear; this uncircumcised Philistine will be like one of them, because he has defied the armies of the living God. [37]The LORD who delivered me from the paw of the lion and the paw of the bear will deliver me from the hand of this Philistine."

Saul said to David, "Go, and the LORD be with you."

[38]Then Saul dressed David in his own tunic. He put a coat of armor on him and a bronze helmet on his head. [39]David fastened on his sword over the tunic and tried walking around, because he was not used to them.

[a]7 That is, about 15 pounds (about 7 kilograms)   [b]17 That is, probably about 3/5 bushel (about 22 liters)   [c]18 Hebrew *thousand*   [d]18 Or *some token*; or *some pledge of spoils*

"I cannot go in these," he said to Saul, "because I am not used to them." So he took them off. [40]Then he took his staff in his hand, chose five smooth stones from the stream, put them in the pouch of his shepherd's bag and, with his sling in his hand, approached the Philistine.

[41]Meanwhile, the Philistine, with his shield bearer in front of him, kept coming closer to David. [42]He looked David over and saw that he was only a boy, ruddy and handsome, and he despised him. [43]He said to David, "Am I a dog, that you come at me with sticks?" And the Philistine cursed David by his gods. [44]"Come here," he said, "and I'll give your flesh to the birds of the air and the beasts of the field!"

[45]David said to the Philistine, "You come against me with sword and spear and javelin, but I come against you in the name of the LORD Almighty, the God of the armies of Israel, whom you have defied. [46]This day the LORD will hand you over to me, and I'll strike you down and cut off your head. Today I will give the carcasses of the Philistine army to the birds of the air and the beasts of the earth, and the whole world will know that there is a God in Israel. [47]All those gathered here will know that it is not by sword or spear that the LORD saves; for the battle is the LORD's, and he will give all of you into our hands."

[48]As the Philistine moved closer to attack him, David ran quickly toward the battle line to meet him. [49]Reaching into his bag and taking out a stone, he slung it and struck the Philistine on the forehead. The stone sank into his forehead, and he fell facedown on the ground.

[50]So David triumphed over the Philistine with a sling and a stone; without a sword in his hand he struck down the Philistine and killed him.

[51]David ran and stood over him. He took hold of the Philistine's sword and drew it from the scabbard. After he killed him, he cut off his head with the sword.

When the Philistines saw that their hero was dead, they turned and ran. [52]Then the men of Israel and Judah surged forward with a shout and pursued the Philistines to the entrance of Gath[a] and to the gates of Ekron. Their dead were strewn along the Shaaraim road to Gath and Ekron. [53]When the Israelites returned from chasing the Philistines, they plundered their camp. [54]David took the Philistine's head and brought it to Jerusalem, and he put the Philistine's weapons in his own tent.

[55]As Saul watched David going out to meet the Philistine, he said to Abner, commander of the army, "Abner, whose son is that young man?"

Abner replied, "As surely as you live, O king, I don't know."

[56]The king said, "Find out whose son this young man is."

[57]As soon as David returned from killing the Philistine, Abner took him and brought him before Saul, with David still holding the Philistine's head.

[58]"Whose son are you, young man?" Saul asked him.

David said, "I am the son of your servant Jesse of Bethlehem."

Saul's Jealousy of David

18 After David had finished talking with Saul, Jonathan became one in spirit with David, and he loved him as himself. [2]From that day Saul kept David with him and did not let him return to his father's house. [3]And Jonathan made a covenant with David because he loved him as himself. [4]Jonathan took off the robe he was wearing and gave it to David, along with his tunic, and even his sword, his bow and his belt.

[5]Whatever Saul sent him to do, David did it so successfully[b] that Saul gave him a high rank in the army. This pleased all the people, and Saul's officers as well.

[6]When the men were returning home after David had killed the Philistine, the women came out from all the towns of Israel to meet King Saul with singing and dancing, with joyful songs and with tambourines and lutes. [7]As they danced, they sang:

"Saul has slain his thousands,
    and David his tens of thousands."

[8]Saul was very angry; this refrain galled him. "They have credited David with tens of thousands," he thought, "but me with only thousands. What more can he get but the kingdom?" [9]And from that time on Saul kept a jealous eye on David.

[10]The next day an evil[c] spirit from God came forcefully upon Saul. He was prophesying in his house, while David was playing the harp, as he usually did. Saul had a spear in his hand [11]and he hurled it, saying to himself, "I'll pin David to the wall." But David eluded him twice.

---

[a]52 Some Septuagint manuscripts; Hebrew *a valley*
[b]5 Or *wisely*   [c]10 Or *injurious*

¹²Saul was afraid of David, because the LORD was with David but had left Saul. ¹³So he sent David away from him and gave him command over a thousand men, and David led the troops in their campaigns. ¹⁴In everything he did he had great success,ᵃ because the LORD was with him. ¹⁵When Saul saw how successfulᵇ he was, he was afraid of him. ¹⁶But all Israel and Judah loved David, because he led them in their campaigns.

¹⁷Saul said to David, "Here is my older daughter Merab. I will give her to you in marriage; only serve me bravely and fight the battles of the LORD." For Saul said to himself, "I will not raise a hand against him. Let the Philistines do that!"

¹⁸But David said to Saul, "Who am I, and what is my family or my father's clan in Israel, that I should become the king's son-in-law?" ¹⁹Soᶜ when the time came for Merab, Saul's daughter, to be given to David, she was given in marriage to Adriel of Meholah.

²⁰Now Saul's daughter Michal was in love with David, and when they told Saul about it, he was pleased. ²¹"I will give her to him," he thought, "so that she may be a snare to him and so that the hand of the Philistines may be against him." So Saul said to David, "Now you have a second opportunity to become my son-in-law."

²²Then Saul ordered his attendants: "Speak to David privately and say, 'Look, the king is pleased with you, and his attendants all like you; now become his son-in-law.'"

²³They repeated these words to David. But David said, "Do you think it is a small matter to become the king's son-in-law? I'm only a poor man and little known." ²⁴When Saul's servants told him what David had said, ²⁵Saul replied, "Say to David, 'The king wants no other price for the bride than a hundred Philistine foreskins, to take revenge on his enemies.'" Saul's plan was to have David fall by the hands of the Philistines.

²⁶When the attendants told David these things, he was pleased to become the king's son-in-law. So before the allotted time elapsed, ²⁷David and his men went out and killed two hundred Philistines. He brought their foreskins and presented the full number to the king so that he might become the king's son-in-law. Then Saul gave him his daughter Michal in marriage.

²⁸When Saul realized that the LORD was with David and that his daughter Michal loved David, ²⁹Saul became still more afraid of him, and he remained his enemy the rest of his days.

³⁰The Philistine commanders continued to go out to battle, and as often as they did, David met with more successᵈ than the rest of Saul's officers, and his name became well known.

Saul Tries to Kill David

19 Saul told his son Jonathan and all the attendants to kill David. But Jonathan was very fond of David ²and warned him, "My father Saul is looking for a chance to kill you. Be on your guard tomorrow morning; go into hiding and stay there. ³I will go out and stand with my father in the field where you are. I'll speak to him about you and will tell you what I find out."

⁴Jonathan spoke well of David to Saul his father and said to him, "Let not the king do wrong to his servant David; he has not wronged you, and what he has done has benefited you greatly. ⁵He took his life in his hands when he killed the Philistine. The LORD won a great victory for all Israel, and you saw it and were glad. Why then would you do wrong to an innocent man like David by killing him for no reason?"

⁶Saul listened to Jonathan and took this oath: "As surely as the LORD lives, David will not be put to death."

⁷So Jonathan called David and told him the whole conversation. He brought him to Saul, and David was with Saul as before.

⁸Once more war broke out, and David went out and fought the Philistines. He struck them with such force that they fled before him.

⁹But an evilᵉ spirit from the LORD came upon Saul as he was sitting in his house with his spear in his hand. While David was playing the harp, ¹⁰Saul tried to pin him to the wall with his spear, but David eluded him as Saul drove the spear into the wall. That night David made good his escape.

¹¹Saul sent men to David's house to watch it and to kill him in the morning. But Michal, David's wife, warned him, "If you don't run for your life tonight, tomorrow you'll be killed." ¹²So Michal let David down through a window, and he fled and escaped. ¹³Then Michal took an idolᶠ and

---

ᵃ14 Or he was very wise   ᵇ15 Or wise   ᶜ19 Or However,   ᵈ30 Or David acted more wisely   ᵉ9 Or injurious   ᶠ13 Hebrew teraphim; also in verse 16

laid it on the bed, covering it with a garment and putting some goats' hair at the head.

¹⁴When Saul sent the men to capture David, Michal said, "He is ill."

¹⁵Then Saul sent the men back to see David and told them, "Bring him up to me in his bed so that I may kill him." ¹⁶But when the men entered, there was the idol in the bed, and at the head was some goats' hair.

¹⁷Saul said to Michal, "Why did you deceive me like this and send my enemy away so that he escaped?"

Michal told him, "He said to me, 'Let me get away. Why should I kill you?' "

¹⁸When David had fled and made his escape, he went to Samuel at Ramah and told him all that Saul had done to him. Then he and Samuel went to Naioth and stayed there. ¹⁹Word came to Saul: "David is in Naioth at Ramah"; ²⁰so he sent men to capture him. But when they saw a group of prophets prophesying, with Samuel standing there as their leader, the Spirit of God came upon Saul's men and they also prophesied. ²¹Saul was told about it, and he sent more men, and they prophesied too. Saul sent men a third time, and they also prophesied. ²²Finally, he himself left for Ramah and went to the great cistern at Secu. And he asked, "Where are Samuel and David?"

"Over in Naioth at Ramah," they said.

²³So Saul went to Naioth at Ramah. But the Spirit of God came even upon him, and he walked along prophesying until he came to Naioth. ²⁴He stripped off his robes and also prophesied in Samuel's presence. He lay that way all that day and night. This is why people say, "Is Saul also among the prophets?"

David and Jonathan

20 Then David fled from Naioth at Ramah and went to Jonathan and asked, "What have I done? What is my crime? How have I wronged your father, that he is trying to take my life?"

²"Never!" Jonathan replied. "You are not going to die! Look, my father doesn't do anything, great or small, without confiding in me. Why would he hide this from me? It's not so!"

³But David took an oath and said, "Your father knows very well that I have found favor in your eyes, and he has said to himself, 'Jonathan must not know this or he will be grieved.' Yet as surely as the LORD

lives and as you live, there is only a step between me and death."

⁴Jonathan said to David, "Whatever you want me to do, I'll do for you."

⁵So David said, "Look, tomorrow is the New Moon festival, and I am supposed to dine with the king; but let me go and hide in the field until the evening of the day after tomorrow. ⁶If your father misses me at all, tell him, 'David earnestly asked my permission to hurry to Bethlehem, his hometown, because an annual sacrifice is being made there for his whole clan.' ⁷If he says, 'Very well,' then your servant is safe. But if he loses his temper, you can be sure that he is determined to harm me. ⁸As for you, show kindness to your servant, for you have brought him into a covenant with you before the LORD. If I am guilty, then kill me yourself! Why hand me over to your father?"

⁹"Never!" Jonathan said. "If I had the least inkling that my father was determined to harm you, wouldn't I tell you?"

¹⁰David asked, "Who will tell me if your father answers you harshly?"

¹¹"Come," Jonathan said, "let's go out into the field." So they went there together.

¹²Then Jonathan said to David: "By the LORD, the God of Israel, I will surely sound out my father by this time the day after tomorrow! If he is favorably disposed toward you, will I not send you word and let you know? ¹³But if my father is inclined to harm you, may the LORD deal with me, be it ever so severely, if I do not let you know and send you away safely. May the LORD be with you as he has been with my father. ¹⁴But show me unfailing kindness like that of the LORD as long as I live, so that I may not be killed, ¹⁵and do not ever cut off your kindness from my family—not even when the LORD has cut off every one of David's enemies from the face of the earth."

¹⁶So Jonathan made a covenant with the house of David, saying, "May the LORD call David's enemies to account." ¹⁷And Jonathan had David reaffirm his oath out of love for him, because he loved him as he loved himself.

¹⁸Then Jonathan said to David: "Tomorrow is the New Moon festival. You will be missed, because your seat will be empty. ¹⁹The day after tomorrow, toward evening, go to the place where you hid when this trouble began, and wait by the stone Ezel. ²⁰I will shoot three arrows to the side of it, as though I were shooting at a target.

²¹Then I will send a boy and say, 'Go, find the arrows.' If I say to him, 'Look, the arrows are on this side of you; bring them here,' then come, because, as surely as the LORD lives, you are safe; there is no danger. ²²But if I say to the boy, 'Look, the arrows are beyond you,' then you must go, because the LORD has sent you away. ²³And about the matter you and I discussed—remember, the LORD is witness between you and me forever."

²⁴So David hid in the field, and when the New Moon festival came, the king sat down to eat. ²⁵He sat in his customary place by the wall, opposite Jonathan,ᵃ and Abner sat next to Saul, but David's place was empty. ²⁶Saul said nothing that day, for he thought, "Something must have happened to David to make him ceremonially unclean—surely he is unclean." ²⁷But the next day, the second day of the month, David's place was empty again. Then Saul said to his son Jonathan, "Why hasn't the son of Jesse come to the meal, either yesterday or today?"

²⁸Jonathan answered, "David earnestly asked me for permission to go to Bethlehem. ²⁹He said, 'Let me go, because our family is observing a sacrifice in the town and my brother has ordered me to be there. If I have found favor in your eyes, let me get away to see my brothers.' That is why he has not come to the king's table."

³⁰Saul's anger flared up at Jonathan and he said to him, "You son of a perverse and rebellious woman! Don't I know that you have sided with the son of Jesse to your own shame and to the shame of the mother who bore you? ³¹As long as the son of Jesse lives on this earth, neither you nor your kingdom will be established. Now send and bring him to me, for he must die!"

³²"Why should he be put to death? What has he done?" Jonathan asked his father. ³³But Saul hurled his spear at him to kill him. Then Jonathan knew that his father intended to kill David.

³⁴Jonathan got up from the table in fierce anger; on that second day of the month he did not eat, because he was grieved at his father's shameful treatment of David.

³⁵In the morning Jonathan went out to the field for his meeting with David. He had a small boy with him, ³⁶and he said to the boy, "Run and find the arrows I shoot." As the boy ran, he shot an arrow beyond him. ³⁷When the boy came to the place where Jonathan's arrow had fallen, Jonathan called out after him, "Isn't the arrow beyond you?" ³⁸Then he shouted, "Hurry! Go quickly! Don't stop!" The boy picked up the arrow and returned to his master. ³⁹(The boy knew nothing of all this; only Jonathan and David knew.) ⁴⁰Then Jonathan gave his weapons to the boy and said, "Go, carry them back to town."

⁴¹After the boy had gone, David got up from the south side ₍of the stone₎ and bowed down before Jonathan three times, with his face to the ground. Then they kissed each other and wept together—but David wept the most.

⁴²Jonathan said to David, "Go in peace, for we have sworn friendship with each other in the name of the LORD, saying, 'The LORD is witness between you and me, and between your descendants and my descendants forever.' " Then David left, and Jonathan went back to the town.

David at Nob

21 David went to Nob, to Ahimelech the priest. Ahimelech trembled when he met him, and asked, "Why are you alone? Why is no one with you?"

²David answered Ahimelech the priest, "The king charged me with a certain matter and said to me, 'No one is to know anything about your mission and your instructions.' As for my men, I have told them to meet me at a certain place. ³Now then, what do you have on hand? Give me five loaves of bread, or whatever you can find."

⁴But the priest answered David, "I don't have any ordinary bread on hand; however, there is some consecrated bread here—provided the men have kept themselves from women."

⁵David replied, "Indeed women have been kept from us, as usual wheneverᵇ I set out. The men's thingsᶜ are holy even on missions that are not holy. How much more so today!" ⁶So the priest gave him the consecrated bread, since there was no bread there except the bread of the Presence that had been removed from before the LORD and replaced by hot bread on the day it was taken away.

⁷Now one of Saul's servants was there that day, detained before the LORD; he was Doeg the Edomite, Saul's head shepherd.

⁸David asked Ahimelech, "Don't you

ᵃ25 Septuagint; Hebrew wall. Jonathan arose
ᵇ5 Or from us in the past few days since
ᶜ5 Or bodies

have a spear or a sword here? I haven't brought my sword or any other weapon, because the king's business was urgent." [9]The priest replied, "The sword of Goliath the Philistine, whom you killed in the Valley of Elah, is here; it is wrapped in a cloth behind the ephod. If you want it, take it; there is no sword here but that one."

David said, "There is none like it; give it to me."

David at Gath

[10]That day David fled from Saul and went to Achish king of Gath. [11]But the servants of Achish said to him, "Isn't this David, the king of the land? Isn't he the one they sing about in their dances:

" 'Saul has slain his thousands,
    and David his tens of thousands'?"

[12]David took these words to heart and was very much afraid of Achish king of Gath. [13]So he pretended to be insane in their presence; and while he was in their hands he acted like a madman, making marks on the doors of the gate and letting saliva run down his beard.

[14]Achish said to his servants, "Look at the man! He is insane! Why bring him to me? [15]Am I so short of madmen that you have to bring this fellow here to carry on like this in front of me? Must this man come into my house?"

David at Adullam and Mizpah

22 David left Gath and escaped to the cave of Adullam. When his brothers and his father's household heard about it, they went down to him there. [2]All those who were in distress or in debt or discontented gathered around him, and he became their leader. About four hundred men were with him.

[3]From there David went to Mizpah in Moab and said to the king of Moab, "Would you let my father and mother come and stay with you until I learn what God will do for me?" [4]So he left them with the king of Moab, and they stayed with him as long as David was in the stronghold.

[5]But the prophet Gad said to David, "Do not stay in the stronghold. Go into the land of Judah." So David left and went to the forest of Hereth.

Saul Kills the Priests of Nob

[6]Now Saul heard that David and his men had been discovered. And Saul, spear in hand, was seated under the tamarisk tree on the hill at Gibeah, with all his officials standing around him. [7]Saul said to them, "Listen, men of Benjamin! Will the son of Jesse give all of you fields and vineyards? Will he make all of you commanders of thousands and commanders of hundreds? [8]Is that why you have all conspired against me? No one tells me when my son makes a covenant with the son of Jesse. None of you is concerned about me or tells me that my son has incited my servant to lie in wait for me, as he does today."

[9]But Doeg the Edomite, who was standing with Saul's officials, said, "I saw the son of Jesse come to Ahimelech son of Ahitub at Nob. [10]Ahimelech inquired of the LORD for him; he also gave him provisions and the sword of Goliath the Philistine."

[11]Then the king sent for the priest Ahimelech son of Ahitub and his father's whole family, who were the priests at Nob, and they all came to the king. [12]Saul said, "Listen now, son of Ahitub."

"Yes, my lord," he answered.

[13]Saul said to him, "Why have you conspired against me, you and the son of Jesse, giving him bread and a sword and inquiring of God for him, so that he has rebelled against me and lies in wait for me, as he does today?"

[14]Ahimelech answered the king, "Who of all your servants is as loyal as David, the king's son-in-law, captain of your bodyguard and highly respected in your household? [15]Was that day the first time I inquired of God for him? Of course not! Let not the king accuse your servant or any of his father's family, for your servant knows nothing at all about this whole affair."

[16]But the king said, "You will surely die, Ahimelech, you and your father's whole family."

[17]Then the king ordered the guards at his side: "Turn and kill the priests of the LORD, because they too have sided with David. They knew he was fleeing, yet they did not tell me."

But the king's officials were not willing to raise a hand to strike the priests of the LORD.

[18]The king then ordered Doeg, "You turn and strike down the priests." So Doeg the Edomite turned and struck them down. That day he killed eighty-five men who wore the linen ephod. [19]He also put to the sword Nob, the town of the priests,

with its men and women, its children and infants, and its cattle, donkeys and sheep. ²⁰But Abiathar, a son of Ahimelech son of Ahitub, escaped and fled to join David. ²¹He told David that Saul had killed the priests of the LORD. ²²Then David said to Abiathar: "That day, when Doeg the Edomite was there, I knew he would be sure to tell Saul. I am responsible for the death of your father's whole family. ²³Stay with me; don't be afraid; the man who is seeking your life is seeking mine also. You will be safe with me."

David Saves Keilah

23 When David was told, "Look, the Philistines are fighting against Keilah and are looting the threshing floors," ²he inquired of the LORD, saying, "Shall I go and attack these Philistines?"

The LORD answered him, "Go, attack the Philistines and save Keilah."

³But David's men said to him, "Here in Judah we are afraid. How much more, then, if we go to Keilah against the Philistine forces!"

⁴Once again David inquired of the LORD, and the LORD answered him, "Go down to Keilah, for I am going to give the Philistines into your hand." ⁵So David and his men went to Keilah, fought the Philistines and carried off their livestock. He inflicted heavy losses on the Philistines and saved the people of Keilah. ⁶(Now Abiathar son of Ahimelech had brought the ephod down with him when he fled to David at Keilah.)

Saul Pursues David

⁷Saul was told that David had gone to Keilah, and he said, "God has handed him over to me, for David has imprisoned himself by entering a town with gates and bars." ⁸And Saul called up all his forces for battle, to go down to Keilah to besiege David and his men.

⁹When David learned that Saul was plotting against him, he said to Abiathar the priest, "Bring the ephod." ¹⁰David said, "O LORD, God of Israel, your servant has heard definitely that Saul plans to come to Keilah and destroy the town on account of me. ¹¹Will the citizens of Keilah surrender me to him? Will Saul come down, as your servant has heard? O LORD, God of Israel, tell your servant."

And the LORD said, "He will."

¹²Again David asked, "Will the citizens of Keilah surrender me and my men to Saul?"

And the LORD said, "They will."

¹³So David and his men, about six hundred in number, left Keilah and kept moving from place to place. When Saul was told that David had escaped from Keilah, he did not go there.

¹⁴David stayed in the desert strongholds and in the hills of the Desert of Ziph. Day after day Saul searched for him, but God did not give David into his hands. ¹⁵While David was at Horesh in the Desert of Ziph, he learned that Saul had come out to take his life. ¹⁶And Saul's son Jonathan went to David at Horesh and helped him find strength in God. ¹⁷"Don't be afraid," he said. "My father Saul will not lay a hand on you. You will be king over Israel, and I will be second to you. Even my father Saul knows this." ¹⁸The two of them made a covenant before the LORD. Then Jonathan went home, but David remained at Horesh.

¹⁹The Ziphites went up to Saul at Gibeah and said, "Is not David hiding among us in the strongholds at Horesh, on the hill of Hakilah, south of Jeshimon? ²⁰Now, O king, come down whenever it pleases you to do so, and we will be responsible for handing him over to the king."

²¹Saul replied, "The LORD bless you for your concern for me. ²²Go and make further preparation. Find out where David usually goes and who has seen him there. They tell me he is very crafty. ²³Find out about all the hiding places he uses and come back to me with definite information.^a Then I will go with you; if he is in the area, I will track him down among all the clans of Judah."

²⁴So they set out and went to Ziph ahead of Saul. Now David and his men were in the Desert of Maon, in the Arabah south of Jeshimon. ²⁵Saul and his men began the search, and when David was told about it, he went down to the rock and stayed in the Desert of Maon. When Saul heard this, he went into the Desert of Maon in pursuit of David.

²⁶Saul was going along one side of the mountain, and David and his men were on the other side, hurrying to get away from Saul. As Saul and his forces were closing in on David and his men to capture them, ²⁷a messenger came to Saul, saying, "Come quickly! The Philistines are raiding the land." ²⁸Then Saul broke off

^a23 Or *me at Nacon*

his pursuit of David and went to meet the Philistines. That is why they call this place Sela Hammahlekoth.*ᵃ ²⁹And David went up from there and lived in the strongholds of En Gedi.

David Spares Saul's Life

24 After Saul returned from pursuing the Philistines, he was told, "David is in the Desert of En Gedi." ²So Saul took three thousand chosen men from all Israel and set out to look for David and his men near the Crags of the Wild Goats.

³He came to the sheep pens along the way; a cave was there, and Saul went in to relieve himself. David and his men were far back in the cave. ⁴The men said, "This is the day the LORD spoke of when he said*ᵇ to you, 'I will give your enemy into your hands for you to deal with as you wish.' " Then David crept up unnoticed and cut off a corner of Saul's robe.

⁵Afterward, David was conscience-stricken for having cut off a corner of his robe. ⁶He said to his men, "The LORD forbid that I should do such a thing to my master, the LORD's anointed, or lift my hand against him; for he is the anointed of the LORD." ⁷With these words David rebuked his men and did not allow them to attack Saul. And Saul left the cave and went his way.

⁸Then David went out of the cave and called out to Saul, "My lord the king!" When Saul looked behind him, David bowed down and prostrated himself with his face to the ground. ⁹He said to Saul, "Why do you listen when men say, 'David is bent on harming you'? ¹⁰This day you have seen with your own eyes how the LORD delivered you into my hands in the cave. Some urged me to kill you, but I spared you; I said, 'I will not lift my hand against my master, because he is the LORD's anointed.' ¹¹See, my father, look at this piece of your robe in my hand! I cut off the corner of your robe but did not kill you. Now understand and recognize that I am not guilty of wrongdoing or rebellion. I have not wronged you, but you are hunting me down to take my life. ¹²May the LORD judge between you and me. And may the LORD avenge the wrongs you have done to me, but my hand will not touch you. ¹³As the old saying goes, 'From evildoers come evil deeds,' so my hand will not touch you.

¹⁴"Against whom has the king of Israel come out? Whom are you pursuing? A dead dog? A flea? ¹⁵May the LORD be our judge and decide between us. May he consider my cause and uphold it; may he vindicate me by delivering me from your hand."

¹⁶When David finished saying this, Saul asked, "Is that your voice, David my son?" And he wept aloud. ¹⁷"You are more righteous than I," he said. "You have treated me well, but I have treated you badly. ¹⁸You have just now told me of the good you did to me; the LORD delivered me into your hands, but you did not kill me. ¹⁹When a man finds his enemy, does he let him get away unharmed? May the LORD reward you well for the way you treated me today. ²⁰I know that you will surely be king and that the kingdom of Israel will be established in your hands. ²¹Now swear to me by the LORD that you will not cut off my descendants or wipe out my name from my father's family."

²²So David gave his oath to Saul. Then Saul returned home, but David and his men went up to the stronghold.

David, Nabal and Abigail

25 Now Samuel died, and all Israel assembled and mourned for him; and they buried him at his home in Ramah.

Then David moved down into the Desert of Maon.*ᶜ ²A certain man in Maon, who had property there at Carmel, was very wealthy. He had a thousand goats and three thousand sheep, which he was shearing in Carmel. ³His name was Nabal and his wife's name was Abigail. She was an intelligent and beautiful woman, but her husband, a Calebite, was surly and mean in his dealings.

⁴While David was in the desert, he heard that Nabal was shearing sheep. ⁵So he sent ten young men and said to them, "Go up to Nabal at Carmel and greet him in my name. ⁶Say to him: 'Long life to you! Good health to you and your household! And good health to all that is yours!

⁷"'Now I hear that it is sheep-shearing time. When your shepherds were with us, we did not mistreat them, and the whole time they were at Carmel nothing of theirs was missing. ⁸Ask your own servants and they will tell you. Therefore be favorable toward my young men, since we come at a festive time. Please give your servants and

---

ᵃ28 Sela Hammahlekoth means *rock of parting.*
ᵇ4 Or *"Today the LORD is saying*   *ᶜ1* Some Septuagint manuscripts; Hebrew *Paran*

your son David whatever you can find for them.'"

⁹When David's men arrived, they gave Nabal this message in David's name. Then they waited.

¹⁰Nabal answered David's servants, "Who is this David? Who is this son of Jesse? Many servants are breaking away from their masters these days. ¹¹Why should I take my bread and water, and the meat I have slaughtered for my shearers, and give it to men coming from who knows where?"

¹²David's men turned around and went back. When they arrived, they reported every word. ¹³David said to his men, "Put on your swords!" So they put on their swords, and David put on his. About four hundred men went up with David, while two hundred stayed with the supplies.

Surly to Bed, Surly to Rise

DAILY INSIGHT

TUESDAY

Passage:
1 Samuel 25

Verses:
1 Samuel 25:2–3

Working with William was no picnic. Although I didn't answer directly to him, he held such a position of power and influence in the company that his abrupt and unfriendly style had an effect on everyone who worked there. People feared William.

I had never known anyone quite like him. To be sure, at times my colleagues went through phases of unusual pressure and responded by being a little cantankerous. I guess I've been guilty of the same. But for William, being surly was terminal.

As a fairly young—and pretty naïve—man when I joined the company, and being drawn to unusual challenges, I figured I could change William. Silly boy. Okay, I'll admit that there were moments when I saw the softer side of the man, even once receiving a memorandum from him that was actually quite kind. But when I thanked him for the memo, William shrugged and brusquely slithered back to his cell.

Today's passage describes a character that makes William look like Prince Charming. Nabal was, to be blunt, an absolute idiot. And amazingly, he was married to an angel. David's men called on the wealthy and irritable landowner to request a small contribution in return for protecting his flocks and his profits. Being his usual delightful self, Nabal ordered David's men off his land.

Enter Abigail, Nabal's wife. When she heard what had happened, she immediately realized the danger their family was facing. David wouldn't take this insult, and she knew it. So in order to protect her merciless husband, she prepared a huge peace offering (25:18) to present to David, hoping to assuage his fury.

Seeing Abigail's gifts and hearing her plea for mercy, David pardoned her and her undeserving husband. The next morning, when Abigail told the ungrateful Nabal—hung over from a raucous party the night before—what she had done on his behalf, he dropped dead. Sleep well, old man.

Do you know someone like Nabal? Do you work with someone like Nabal? Are you related to someone like Nabal? Today's story gives you some great advice. First, you will probably not change your Nabal. Whatever has caused him to be like this, your chances of fixing him are slim to none. You are not responsible for his behavior. You are, however, responsible for *yours*.

Although some may charge Abigail with enabling Nabal to be such a fool, I admire her attitude. I like what she did. Abigail decided that, no matter how much Nabal was going to be Nabal, she was not going to let *him* change *her*. She was going to enjoy life as a loving, caring and generous person. Imagine the daily challenge she faced with no encouragement from her husband.

But God rewarded her by taking the old buzzard out. In fact, her faithfulness and determination got her a throne right next to the king. Don't you just love this story?

For your next devotional reading, go to page 337.

¹⁴One of the servants told Nabal's wife Abigail: "David sent messengers from the desert to give our master his greetings, but he hurled insults at them. ¹⁵Yet these men were very good to us. They did not mistreat us, and the whole time we were out in the fields near them nothing was missing. ¹⁶Night and day they were a wall around us all the time we were herding our sheep near them. ¹⁷Now think it over and see what you can do, because disaster is hanging over our master and his whole household. He is such a wicked man that no one can talk to him."

¹⁸Abigail lost no time. She took two hundred loaves of bread, two skins of wine, five dressed sheep, five seahs*a* of roasted grain, a hundred cakes of raisins and two hundred cakes of pressed figs, and loaded them on donkeys. ¹⁹Then she told her servants, "Go on ahead; I'll follow you." But she did not tell her husband Nabal.

²⁰As she came riding her donkey into a mountain ravine, there were David and his men descending toward her, and she met them. ²¹David had just said, "It's been useless—all my watching over this fellow's property in the desert so that nothing of his was missing. He has paid me back evil for good. ²²May God deal with David,*b* be it ever so severely, if by morning I leave alive one male of all who belong to him!"

²³When Abigail saw David, she quickly got off her donkey and bowed down before David with her face to the ground. ²⁴She fell at his feet and said: "My lord, let the blame be on me alone. Please let your servant speak to you; hear what your servant has to say. ²⁵May my lord pay no attention to that wicked man Nabal. He is just like his name—his name is Fool, and folly goes with him. But as for me, your servant, I did not see the men my master sent.

²⁶"Now since the LORD has kept you, my master, from bloodshed and from avenging yourself with your own hands, as surely as the LORD lives and as you live, may your enemies and all who intend to harm my master be like Nabal. ²⁷And let this gift, which your servant has brought to my master, be given to the men who follow you. ²⁸Please forgive your servant's offense, for the LORD will certainly make a lasting dynasty for my master, because he fights the LORD's battles. Let no wrongdoing be found in you as long as you live. ²⁹Even though someone is pursuing you

to take your life, the life of my master will be bound securely in the bundle of the living by the LORD your God. But the lives of your enemies he will hurl away as from the pocket of a sling. ³⁰When the LORD has done for my master every good thing he promised concerning him and has appointed him leader over Israel, ³¹my master will not have on his conscience the staggering burden of needless bloodshed or of having avenged himself. And when the LORD has brought my master success, remember your servant."

³²David said to Abigail, "Praise be to the LORD, the God of Israel, who has sent you today to meet me. ³³May you be blessed for your good judgment and for keeping me from bloodshed this day and from avenging myself with my own hands. ³⁴Otherwise, as surely as the LORD, the God of Israel, lives, who has kept me from harming you, if you had not come quickly to meet me, not one male belonging to Nabal would have been left alive by daybreak."

³⁵Then David accepted from her hand what she had brought him and said, "Go home in peace. I have heard your words and granted your request."

³⁶When Abigail went to Nabal, he was in the house holding a banquet like that of a king. He was in high spirits and very drunk. So she told him nothing until daybreak. ³⁷Then in the morning, when Nabal was sober, his wife told him all these things, and his heart failed him and he became like a stone. ³⁸About ten days later, the LORD struck Nabal and he died.

³⁹When David heard that Nabal was dead, he said, "Praise be to the LORD, who has upheld my cause against Nabal for treating me with contempt. He has kept his servant from doing wrong and has brought Nabal's wrongdoing down on his own head."

Then David sent word to Abigail, asking her to become his wife. ⁴⁰His servants went to Carmel and said to Abigail, "David has sent us to you to take you to become his wife."

⁴¹She bowed down with her face to the ground and said, "Here is your maidservant, ready to serve you and wash the feet of my master's servants." ⁴²Abigail quickly got on a donkey and, attended by her five maids, went with David's messengers and

---

a18 That is, probably about a bushel (about 37 liters)   *b22* Some Septuagint manuscripts; Hebrew *with David's enemies*

became his wife. ⁴³David had also married Ahinoam of Jezreel, and they both were his wives. ⁴⁴But Saul had given his daughter Michal, David's wife, to Paltiel*ᵃ* son of Laish, who was from Gallim.

David Again Spares Saul's Life

26 The Ziphites went to Saul at Gibeah and said, "Is not David hiding on the hill of Hakilah, which faces Jeshimon?" ²So Saul went down to the Desert of Ziph, with his three thousand chosen men of Israel, to search there for David. ³Saul made his camp beside the road on the hill of Hakilah facing Jeshimon, but David stayed in the desert. When he saw that Saul had followed him there, ⁴he sent out scouts and learned that Saul had definitely arrived.*ᵇ*

⁵Then David set out and went to the place where Saul had camped. He saw where Saul and Abner son of Ner, the commander of the army, had lain down. Saul was lying inside the camp, with the army encamped around him.

⁶David then asked Ahimelech the Hittite and Abishai son of Zeruiah, Joab's brother, "Who will go down into the camp with me to Saul?"

"I'll go with you," said Abishai.

⁷So David and Abishai went to the army by night, and there was Saul, lying asleep inside the camp with his spear stuck in the ground near his head. Abner and the soldiers were lying around him.

⁸Abishai said to David, "Today God has delivered your enemy into your hands. Now let me pin him to the ground with one thrust of my spear; I won't strike him twice."

⁹But David said to Abishai, "Don't destroy him! Who can lay a hand on the LORD's anointed and be guiltless? ¹⁰As surely as the LORD lives," he said, "the LORD himself will strike him; either his time will come and he will die, or he will go into battle and perish. ¹¹But the LORD forbid that I should lay a hand on the LORD's anointed. Now get the spear and water jug that are near his head, and let's go."

¹²So David took the spear and water jug near Saul's head, and they left. No one saw or knew about it, nor did anyone wake up. They were all sleeping, because the LORD had put them into a deep sleep.

¹³Then David crossed over to the other side and stood on top of the hill some distance away; there was a wide space between them. ¹⁴He called out to the army and to Abner son of Ner, "Aren't you going to answer me, Abner?"

Abner replied, "Who are you who calls to the king?"

¹⁵David said, "You're a man, aren't you? And who is like you in Israel? Why didn't you guard your lord the king? Someone came to destroy your lord the king. ¹⁶What you have done is not good. As surely as the LORD lives, you and your men deserve to die, because you did not guard your master, the LORD's anointed. Look around you. Where are the king's spear and water jug that were near his head?"

¹⁷Saul recognized David's voice and said, "Is that your voice, David my son?"

David replied, "Yes it is, my lord the king." ¹⁸And he added, "Why is my lord pursuing his servant? What have I done, and what wrong am I guilty of? ¹⁹Now let my lord the king listen to his servant's words. If the LORD has incited you against me, then may he accept an offering. If, however, men have done it, may they be cursed before the LORD! They have now driven me from my share in the LORD's inheritance and have said, 'Go, serve other gods.' ²⁰Now do not let my blood fall to the ground far from the presence of the LORD. The king of Israel has come out to look for a flea—as one hunts a partridge in the mountains."

²¹Then Saul said, "I have sinned. Come back, David my son. Because you considered my life precious today, I will not try to harm you again. Surely I have acted like a fool and have erred greatly."

²²"Here is the king's spear," David answered. "Let one of your young men come over and get it. ²³The LORD rewards every man for his righteousness and faithfulness. The LORD delivered you into my hands today, but I would not lay a hand on the LORD's anointed. ²⁴As surely as I valued your life today, so may the LORD value my life and deliver me from all trouble."

²⁵Then Saul said to David, "May you be blessed, my son David; you will do great things and surely triumph."

So David went on his way, and Saul returned home.

David Among the Philistines

27 But David thought to himself, "One of these days I will be destroyed by the

---

*ᵃ*44 Hebrew *Palti*, a variant of *Paltiel*   *ᵇ*4 Or *had come to Nacon* hand of Saul. The best thing I can do is to escape to the land of the Philistines. Then Saul will give up searching for me anywhere in Israel, and I will slip out of his hand."

²So David and the six hundred men with him left and went over to Achish son of Maoch king of Gath. ³David and his men settled in Gath with Achish. Each man had his family with him, and David had his two wives: Ahinoam of Jezreel and Abigail of Carmel, the widow of Nabal. ⁴When Saul was told that David had fled to Gath, he no longer searched for him.

⁵Then David said to Achish, "If I have found favor in your eyes, let a place be assigned to me in one of the country towns, that I may live there. Why should your servant live in the royal city with you?"

⁶So on that day Achish gave him Ziklag, and it has belonged to the kings of Judah ever since. ⁷David lived in Philistine territory a year and four months.

⁸Now David and his men went up and raided the Geshurites, the Girzites and the Amalekites. (From ancient times these peoples had lived in the land extending to Shur and Egypt.) ⁹Whenever David attacked an area, he did not leave a man or woman alive, but took sheep and cattle, donkeys and camels, and clothes. Then he returned to Achish.

¹⁰When Achish asked, "Where did you go raiding today?" David would say, "Against the Negev of Judah" or "Against the Negev of Jerahmeel" or "Against the Negev of the Kenites." ¹¹He did not leave a man or woman alive to be brought to Gath, for he thought, "They might inform on us and say, 'This is what David did.' " And such was his practice as long as he lived in Philistine territory. ¹²Achish trusted David and said to himself, "He has become so odious to his people, the Israelites, that he will be my servant forever."

Saul and the Witch of Endor

28 In those days the Philistines gathered their forces to fight against Israel. Achish said to David, "You must understand that you and your men will accompany me in the army."

²David said, "Then you will see for yourself what your servant can do."

Achish replied, "Very well, I will make you my bodyguard for life."

³Now Samuel was dead, and all Israel had mourned for him and buried him in his own town of Ramah. Saul had expelled

HEY DAD
Are witches real?

Text: 1 Samuel 28:1-24

QUESTIONS KIDS ASK

While we might like to tell our children witches really don't exist, the Bible says King Saul once visited a witch. Saul was afraid of the Philistines, and the Lord wouldn't answer him about the outcome of the battle he was fighting. So he dressed in such a way that no one would recognize him and went to visit a woman called the witch of Endor.

Once there, Saul asked the witch to contact the spirit of the prophet Samuel. Saul thought that Samuel might tell him the things that God had not revealed. But when Samuel's spirit returned he scolded Saul, saying that if the Lord wouldn't answer him, there was no need to call the Lord's prophet.

Pretty scary stuff, right? Here's a disguised king visiting a witch in the middle of the night and a dead prophet coming back to foretell the king's doom. Not exactly recommended bedtime reading.

But the point of this encounter isn't scary at all. God is in control. God allowed the witch of Endor to call Samuel's spirit back from the dead. What did Saul gain from the experience? The knowledge that he had again broken God's law, and a message that God was going to give him over to the Philistines.

So, whether you're consoling a frightened little one or fascinating a curious older child, remind them that, witches or no witches, God is in control.

Maybe this story isn't so scary after all.

For a complete listing of Questions Kids Ask, turn to page 1435.

the mediums and spiritists from the land.

⁴The Philistines assembled and came and set up camp at Shunem, while Saul gathered all the Israelites and set up camp at Gilboa. ⁵When Saul saw the Philistine army, he was afraid; terror filled his heart. ⁶He inquired of the LORD, but the LORD did not answer him by dreams or Urim or prophets. ⁷Saul then said to his attendants, "Find me a woman who is a medium, so I may go and inquire of her."

"There is one in Endor," they said.

⁸So Saul disguised himself, putting on other clothes, and at night he and two men went to the woman. "Consult a spirit for me," he said, "and bring up for me the one I name."

⁹But the woman said to him, "Surely you know what Saul has done. He has cut off the mediums and spiritists from the land. Why have you set a trap for my life to bring about my death?"

¹⁰Saul swore to her by the LORD, "As surely as the LORD lives, you will not be punished for this."

¹¹Then the woman asked, "Whom shall I bring up for you?"

"Bring up Samuel," he said.

¹²When the woman saw Samuel, she cried out at the top of her voice and said to Saul, "Why have you deceived me? You are Saul!"

¹³The king said to her, "Don't be afraid. What do you see?"

The woman said, "I see a spirit*ᵃ* coming up out of the ground."

¹⁴"What does he look like?" he asked.

"An old man wearing a robe is coming up," she said.

Then Saul knew it was Samuel, and he bowed down and prostrated himself with his face to the ground.

¹⁵Samuel said to Saul, "Why have you disturbed me by bringing me up?"

"I am in great distress," Saul said. "The Philistines are fighting against me, and God has turned away from me. He no longer answers me, either by prophets or by dreams. So I have called on you to tell me what to do."

¹⁶Samuel said, "Why do you consult me, now that the LORD has turned away from you and become your enemy? ¹⁷The LORD has done what he predicted through me. The LORD has torn the kingdom out of your hands and given it to one of your neighbors—to David. ¹⁸Because you did not obey the LORD or carry out his fierce wrath against the Amalekites, the LORD

has done this to you today. ¹⁹The LORD will hand over both Israel and you to the Philistines, and tomorrow you and your sons will be with me. The LORD will also hand over the army of Israel to the Philistines."

²⁰Immediately Saul fell full length on the ground, filled with fear because of Samuel's words. His strength was gone, for he had eaten nothing all that day and night.

²¹When the woman came to Saul and saw that he was greatly shaken, she said, "Look, your maidservant has obeyed you. I took my life in my hands and did what you told me to do. ²²Now please listen to your servant and let me give you some food so you may eat and have the strength to go on your way."

²³He refused and said, "I will not eat."

But his men joined the woman in urging him, and he listened to them. He got up from the ground and sat on the couch.

²⁴The woman had a fattened calf at the house, which she butchered at once. She took some flour, kneaded it and baked bread without yeast. ²⁵Then she set it before Saul and his men, and they ate. That same night they got up and left.

Achish Sends David Back to Ziklag

29 The Philistines gathered all their forces at Aphek, and Israel camped by the spring in Jezreel. ²As the Philistine rulers marched with their units of hundreds and thousands, David and his men were marching at the rear with Achish. ³The commanders of the Philistines asked, "What about these Hebrews?"

Achish replied, "Is this not David, who was an officer of Saul king of Israel? He has already been with me for over a year, and from the day he left Saul until now, I have found no fault in him."

⁴But the Philistine commanders were angry with him and said, "Send the man back, that he may return to the place you assigned him. He must not go with us into battle, or he will turn against us during the fighting. How better could he regain his master's favor than by taking the heads of our own men? ⁵Isn't this the David they sang about in their dances:

" 'Saul has slain his thousands,
    and David his tens of thousands'?"

⁶So Achish called David and said to him, "As surely as the LORD lives, you have been reliable, and I would be pleased to

ᵃ13 Or *see spirits*; or *see gods*

have you serve with me in the army. From the day you came to me until now, I have found no fault in you, but the rulers don't approve of you. ⁷Turn back and go in peace; do nothing to displease the Philistine rulers."

⁸"But what have I done?" asked David. "What have you found against your servant from the day I came to you until now? Why can't I go and fight against the enemies of my lord the king?"

⁹Achish answered, "I know that you have been as pleasing in my eyes as an angel of God; nevertheless, the Philistine commanders have said, 'He must not go up with us into battle.' ¹⁰Now get up early, along with your master's servants who have come with you, and leave in the morning as soon as it is light."

¹¹So David and his men got up early in the morning to go back to the land of the Philistines, and the Philistines went up to Jezreel.

David Destroys the Amalekites

30 David and his men reached Ziklag on the third day. Now the Amalekites had raided the Negev and Ziklag. They had attacked Ziklag and burned it, ²and had taken captive the women and all who were in it, both young and old. They killed none of them, but carried them off as they went on their way.

³When David and his men came to Ziklag, they found it destroyed by fire and their wives and sons and daughters taken captive. ⁴So David and his men wept aloud until they had no strength left to weep. ⁵David's two wives had been captured—Ahinoam of Jezreel and Abigail, the widow of Nabal of Carmel. ⁶David was greatly distressed because the men were talking of stoning him; each one was bitter in spirit because of his sons and daughters. But David found strength in the LORD his God.

⁷Then David said to Abiathar the priest, the son of Ahimelech, "Bring me the ephod." Abiathar brought it to him, ⁸and David inquired of the LORD, "Shall I pursue this raiding party? Will I overtake them?"

"Pursue them," he answered. "You will certainly overtake them and succeed in the rescue."

⁹David and the six hundred men with him came to the Besor Ravine, where some stayed behind, ¹⁰for two hundred men were too exhausted to cross the ra-

vine. But David and four hundred men continued the pursuit.

¹¹They found an Egyptian in a field and brought him to David. They gave him water to drink and food to eat— ¹²part of a cake of pressed figs and two cakes of raisins. He ate and was revived, for he had not eaten any food or drunk any water for three days and three nights.

¹³David asked him, "To whom do you belong, and where do you come from?"

He said, "I am an Egyptian, the slave of an Amalekite. My master abandoned me when I became ill three days ago. ¹⁴We raided the Negev of the Kerethites and the territory belonging to Judah and the Negev of Caleb. And we burned Ziklag."

¹⁵David asked him, "Can you lead me down to this raiding party?"

He answered, "Swear to me before God that you will not kill me or hand me over to my master, and I will take you down to them."

¹⁶He led David down, and there they were, scattered over the countryside, eating, drinking and reveling because of the great amount of plunder they had taken from the land of the Philistines and from Judah. ¹⁷David fought them from dusk until the evening of the next day, and none of them got away, except four hundred young men who rode off on camels and fled. ¹⁸David recovered everything the Amalekites had taken, including his two wives. ¹⁹Nothing was missing: young or old, boy or girl, plunder or anything else they had taken. David brought everything back. ²⁰He took all the flocks and herds, and his men drove them ahead of the other livestock, saying, "This is David's plunder."

²¹Then David came to the two hundred men who had been too exhausted to follow him and who were left behind at the Besor Ravine. They came out to meet David and the people with him. As David and his men approached, he greeted them. ²²But all the evil men and troublemakers among David's followers said, "Because they did not go out with us, we will not share with them the plunder we recovered. However, each man may take his wife and children and go."

²³David replied, "No, my brothers, you must not do that with what the LORD has given us. He has protected us and handed over to us the forces that came against us. ²⁴Who will listen to what you say? The share of the man who stayed with the supplies is to be the same as that of him

who went down to the battle. All will share alike." ²⁵David made this a statute and ordinance for Israel from that day to this.

²⁶When David arrived in Ziklag, he sent some of the plunder to the elders of Judah, who were his friends, saying, "Here is a present for you from the plunder of the LORD's enemies."

²⁷He sent it to those who were in Bethel, Ramoth Negev and Jattir; ²⁸to those in Aroer, Siphmoth, Eshtemoa ²⁹and Racal; to those in the towns of the Jerahmeelites and the Kenites; ³⁰to those in Hormah, Bor Ashan, Athach ³¹and Hebron; and to those in all the other places where David and his men had roamed.

Saul Takes His Life

31 Now the Philistines fought against Israel; the Israelites fled before them, and many fell slain on Mount Gilboa. ²The Philistines pressed hard after Saul and his sons, and they killed his sons Jonathan, Abinadab and Malki-Shua. ³The fighting grew fierce around Saul, and when the archers overtook him, they wounded him critically.

⁴Saul said to his armor-bearer, "Draw your sword and run me through, or these uncircumcised fellows will come and run me through and abuse me."

But his armor-bearer was terrified and would not do it; so Saul took his own sword and fell on it. ⁵When the armor-bearer saw that Saul was dead, he too fell on his sword and died with him. ⁶So Saul and his three sons and his armor-bearer and all his men died together that same day.

⁷When the Israelites along the valley and those across the Jordan saw that the Israelite army had fled and that Saul and his sons had died, they abandoned their towns and fled. And the Philistines came and occupied them.

⁸The next day, when the Philistines came to strip the dead, they found Saul and his three sons fallen on Mount Gilboa. ⁹They cut off his head and stripped off his armor, and they sent messengers throughout the land of the Philistines to proclaim the news in the temple of their idols and among their people. ¹⁰They put his armor in the temple of the Ashtoreths and fastened his body to the wall of Beth Shan.

¹¹When the people of Jabesh Gilead heard of what the Philistines had done to Saul, ¹²all their valiant men journeyed through the night to Beth Shan. They took down the bodies of Saul and his sons from the wall of Beth Shan and went to Jabesh, where they burned them. ¹³Then they took their bones and buried them under a tamarisk tree at Jabesh, and they fasted seven days.

There may be no one in the Bible we know more about than David, with the possible exception of Jesus, God's Son. Second Samuel tells us about David in great detail. We learn of his dreams, his physical strength, his leadership skills, his moral failings, his troubled family, and the depth of his character. It's all here … certainly much more information than you and I would prefer to have in print about ourselves. But, as you read the story of this man-king, father, and sinner, you'll discover the secrets to his success: his ability to confess his own sinfulness and his desire to know God.

There are many things we can learn from David, as well as many things we can avoid because of the consequences he was forced to deal with. And they are lessons worth learning. After all, wouldn't you be pleased to share David's epitaph: "A man after [God's] own heart" (1 Samuel 13:14; Acts 13:22)?

2 Samuel

David Hears of Saul's Death

1 After the death of Saul, David returned from defeating the Amalekites and stayed in Ziklag two days. ²On the third day a man arrived from Saul's camp, with his clothes torn and with dust on his head. When he came to David, he fell to the ground to pay him honor.

³"Where have you come from?" David asked him.

He answered, "I have escaped from the Israelite camp."

⁴"What happened?" David asked. "Tell me."

He said, "The men fled from the battle. Many of them fell and died. And Saul and his son Jonathan are dead."

⁵Then David said to the young man who brought him the report, "How do you know that Saul and his son Jonathan are dead?"

⁶"I happened to be on Mount Gilboa," the young man said, "and there was Saul, leaning on his spear, with the chariots and riders almost upon him. ⁷When he turned around and saw me, he called out to me, and I said, 'What can I do?'

⁸"He asked me, 'Who are you?'

" 'An Amalekite,' I answered.

⁹"Then he said to me, 'Stand over me and kill me! I am in the throes of death, but I'm still alive.'

¹⁰"So I stood over him and killed him, because I knew that after he had fallen he could not survive. And I took the crown that was on his head and the band on his arm and have brought them here to my lord."

¹¹Then David and all the men with him took hold of their clothes and tore them. ¹²They mourned and wept and fasted till evening for Saul and his son Jonathan, and for the army of the LORD and the

house of Israel, because they had fallen by the sword. ¹³David said to the young man who brought him the report "Where are you from?"

"I am the son of an alien, an Amalekite," he answered.

¹⁴David asked him, "Why were you not afraid to lift your hand to destroy the LORD's anointed?"

¹⁵Then David called one of his men and said, "Go, strike him down!" So he struck him down, and he died. ¹⁶For David had said to him, "Your blood be on your own head. Your own mouth testified against you when you said, 'I killed the LORD's anointed.' "

David's Lament for Saul and Jonathan

¹⁷David took up this lament concerning Saul and his son Jonathan, ¹⁸and ordered that the men of Judah be taught this lament of the bow (it is written in the Book of Jashar):

¹⁹ "Your glory, O Israel, lies slain on your heights.
    How the mighty have fallen!

²⁰ "Tell it not in Gath,
    proclaim it not in the streets of Ashkelon,
    lest the daughters of the Philistines be glad,
    lest the daughters of the uncircumcised rejoice.

²¹ "O mountains of Gilboa,
    may you have neither dew nor rain,
    nor fields that yield offerings of grain.
For there the shield of the mighty was defiled,
    the shield of Saul—no longer rubbed with oil.
²² From the blood of the slain,
    from the flesh of the mighty,
the bow of Jonathan did not turn back,
    the sword of Saul did not return unsatisfied.

²³ "Saul and Jonathan—
    in life they were loved and gracious,
    and in death they were not parted.
They were swifter than eagles,
    they were stronger than lions.

²⁴ "O daughters of Israel,
    weep for Saul,
who clothed you in scarlet and finery,
    who adorned your garments with ornaments of gold.

²⁵ "How the mighty have fallen in battle!
    Jonathan lies slain on your heights.
²⁶ I grieve for you, Jonathan my brother;
    you were very dear to me.
Your love for me was wonderful,
    more wonderful than that of women.

²⁷ "How the mighty have fallen!
    The weapons of war have perished!"

David Anointed King Over Judah

In the course of time, David inquired of the LORD. "Shall I go up to one of the towns of Judah?" he asked.

The LORD said, "Go up."

David asked, "Where shall I go?"

"To Hebron," the LORD answered.

²So David went up there with his two wives, Ahinoam of Jezreel and Abigail, the widow of Nabal of Carmel. ³David also took the men who were with him, each with his family, and they settled in Hebron and its towns. ⁴Then the men of Judah came to Hebron and there they anointed David king over the house of Judah.

When David was told that it was the men of Jabesh Gilead who had buried Saul, ⁵he sent messengers to the men of Jabesh Gilead to say to them, "The LORD bless you for showing this kindness to Saul your master by burying him. ⁶May the LORD now show you kindness and faithfulness, and I too will show you the same favor because you have done this. ⁷Now then, be strong and brave, for Saul your master is dead, and the house of Judah has anointed me king over them."

War Between the Houses of David and Saul

⁸Meanwhile, Abner son of Ner, the commander of Saul's army, had taken Ish-Bosheth son of Saul and brought him over to Mahanaim. ⁹He made him king over Gilead, Ashuri[a] and Jezreel, and also over Ephraim, Benjamin and all Israel.

¹⁰Ish-Bosheth son of Saul was forty years old when he became king over Israel, and he reigned two years. The house of Judah, however, followed David. ¹¹The length of time David was king in Hebron over the house of Judah was seven years and six months.

¹²Abner son of Ner, together with the men of Ish-Bosheth son of Saul, left Mahanaim and went to Gibeon. ¹³Joab son of Zeruiah and David's men went out and

a9 Or Asher

met them at the pool of Gibeon. One group sat down on one side of the pool and one group on the other side. ¹⁴Then Abner said to Joab, "Let's have some of the young men get up and fight hand to hand in front of us."

"All right, let them do it," Joab said.

¹⁵So they stood up and were counted off—twelve men for Benjamin and Ish-Bosheth son of Saul, and twelve for David. ¹⁶Then each man grabbed his opponent by the head and thrust his dagger into his opponent's side, and they fell down together. So that place in Gibeon was called Helkath Hazzurim.ᵃ

¹⁷The battle that day was very fierce, and Abner and the men of Israel were defeated by David's men.

¹⁸The three sons of Zeruiah were there: Joab, Abishai and Asahel. Now Asahel was as fleet-footed as a wild gazelle. ¹⁹He chased Abner, turning neither to the right nor to the left as he pursued him. ²⁰Abner looked behind him and asked, "Is that you, Asahel?"

"It is," he answered.

²¹Then Abner said to him, "Turn aside to the right or to the left; take on one of the young men and strip him of his weapons." But Asahel would not stop chasing him.

²²Again Abner warned Asahel, "Stop chasing me! Why should I strike you down? How could I look your brother Joab in the face?"

²³But Asahel refused to give up the pursuit; so Abner thrust the butt of his spear into Asahel's stomach, and the spear came out through his back. He fell there and died on the spot. And every man stopped when he came to the place where Asahel had fallen and died.

²⁴But Joab and Abishai pursued Abner, and as the sun was setting, they came to the hill of Ammah, near Giah on the way to the wasteland of Gibeon. ²⁵Then the men of Benjamin rallied behind Abner. They formed themselves into a group and took their stand on top of a hill.

²⁶Abner called out to Joab, "Must the sword devour forever? Don't you realize that this will end in bitterness? How long before you order your men to stop pursuing their brothers?"

²⁷Joab answered, "As surely as God lives, if you had not spoken, the men would have continued the pursuit of their brothers until morning.ᵇ"

²⁸So Joab blew the trumpet, and all the men came to a halt; they no longer

pursued Israel, nor did they fight anymore.

²⁹All that night Abner and his men marched through the Arabah. They crossed the Jordan, continued through the whole Bithronᶜ and came to Mahanaim.

³⁰Then Joab returned from pursuing Abner and assembled all his men. Besides Asahel, nineteen of David's men were found missing. ³¹But David's men had killed three hundred and sixty Benjamites who were with Abner. ³²They took Asahel and buried him in his father's tomb at Bethlehem. Then Joab and his men marched all night and arrived at Hebron by daybreak.

3 The war between the house of Saul and the house of David lasted a long time. David grew stronger and stronger, while the house of Saul grew weaker and weaker.

²Sons were born to David in Hebron:

His firstborn was Amnon the son of Ahinoam of Jezreel;
³his second, Kileab the son of Abigail the widow of Nabal of Carmel;
the third, Absalom the son of Maacah daughter of Talmai king of Geshur;
⁴the fourth, Adonijah the son of Haggith;
the fifth, Shephatiah the son of Abital;
⁵and the sixth, Ithream the son of David's wife Eglah.
These were born to David in Hebron.

Abner Goes Over to David

⁶During the war between the house of Saul and the house of David, Abner had been strengthening his own position in the house of Saul. ⁷Now Saul had had a concubine named Rizpah daughter of Aiah. And Ish-Bosheth said to Abner, "Why did you sleep with my father's concubine?"

⁸Abner was very angry because of what Ish-Bosheth said and he answered, "Am I a dog's head—on Judah's side? This very day I am loyal to the house of your father

ᵃ16 *Helkath Hazzurim* means *field of daggers* or *field of hostilities.*   ᵇ27 Or *spoken this morning, the men would not have taken up the pursuit of their brothers*; or *spoken, the men would have given up the pursuit of their brothers by morning*   ᶜ29 Or *morning*; or *ravine*; the meaning of the Hebrew for this word is uncertain.

Saul and to his family and friends. I haven't handed you over to David. Yet now you accuse me of an offense involving this woman! [9]May God deal with Abner, be it ever so severely, if I do not do for David what the LORD promised him on oath [10]and transfer the kingdom from the house of Saul and establish David's throne over Israel and Judah from Dan to Beersheba." [11]Ish-Bosheth did not dare to say another word to Abner, because he was afraid of him.

[12]Then Abner sent messengers on his behalf to say to David, "Whose land is it? Make an agreement with me, and I will help you bring all Israel over to you."

[13]"Good," said David. "I will make an agreement with you. But I demand one thing of you: Do not come into my presence unless you bring Michal daughter of Saul when you come to see me." [14]Then David sent messengers to Ish-Bosheth son of Saul, demanding, "Give me my wife Michal, whom I betrothed to myself for the price of a hundred Philistine foreskins."

[15]So Ish-Bosheth gave orders and had her taken away from her husband Paltiel son of Laish. [16]Her husband, however, went with her, weeping behind her all the way to Bahurim. Then Abner said to him, "Go back home!" So he went back.

[17]Abner conferred with the elders of Israel and said, "For some time you have wanted to make David your king. [18]Now do it! For the LORD promised David, 'By my servant David I will rescue my people Israel from the hand of the Philistines and from the hand of all their enemies.'"

[19]Abner also spoke to the Benjamites in person. Then he went to Hebron to tell David everything that Israel and the whole house of Benjamin wanted to do. [20]When Abner, who had twenty men with him, came to David at Hebron, David prepared a feast for him and his men. [21]Then Abner said to David, "Let me go at once and assemble all Israel for my lord the king, so that they may make a compact with you, and that you may rule over all that your heart desires." So David sent Abner away, and he went in peace.

Joab Murders Abner

[22]Just then David's men and Joab returned from a raid and brought with them a great deal of plunder. But Abner was no longer with David in Hebron, because David had sent him away, and he had gone in peace. [23]When Joab and all the soldiers with him arrived, he was told that Abner son of Ner had come to the king and that the king had sent him away and that he had gone in peace.

[24]So Joab went to the king and said, "What have you done? Look, Abner came to you. Why did you let him go? Now he is gone! [25]You know Abner son of Ner; he came to deceive you and observe your movements and find out everything you are doing."

[26]Joab then left David and sent messengers after Abner, and they brought him back from the well of Sirah. But David did not know it. [27]Now when Abner returned to Hebron, Joab took him aside into the gateway, as though to speak with him privately. And there, to avenge the blood of his brother Asahel, Joab stabbed him in the stomach, and he died.

[28]Later, when David heard about this, he said, "I and my kingdom are forever innocent before the LORD concerning the blood of Abner son of Ner. [29]May his blood fall upon the head of Joab and upon all his father's house! May Joab's house never be without someone who has a running sore or leprosy[a] or who leans on a crutch or who falls by the sword or who lacks food."

[30](Joab and his brother Abishai murdered Abner because he had killed their brother Asahel in the battle at Gibeon.)

[31]Then David said to Joab and all the people with him, "Tear your clothes and put on sackcloth and walk in mourning in front of Abner." King David himself walked behind the bier. [32]They buried Abner in Hebron, and the king wept aloud at Abner's tomb. All the people wept also.

[33]The king sang this lament for Abner:

"Should Abner have died as the lawless die?
[34]   Your hands were not bound,
        your feet were not fettered.
You fell as one falls before wicked men."

And all the people wept over him again. [35]Then they all came and urged David to eat something while it was still day; but David took an oath, saying, "May God deal with me, be it ever so severely, if I taste bread or anything else before the sun sets!"

[36]All the people took note and were

---

[a]29 The Hebrew word was used for various diseases affecting the skin—not necessarily leprosy.

pleased; indeed, everything the king did pleased them. [37]So on that day all the people and all Israel knew that the king had no part in the murder of Abner son of Ner.

[38]Then the king said to his men, "Do you not realize that a prince and a great man has fallen in Israel this day? [39]And today, though I am the anointed king, I am weak, and these sons of Zeruiah are too strong for me. May the LORD repay the evildoer according to his evil deeds!"

Ish-Bosheth Murdered

4 When Ish-Bosheth son of Saul heard that Abner had died in Hebron, he lost courage, and all Israel became alarmed. [2]Now Saul's son had two men who were leaders of raiding bands. One was named Baanah and the other Recab; they were sons of Rimmon the Beerothite from the tribe of Benjamin—Beeroth is considered part of Benjamin, [3]because the people of Beeroth fled to Gittaim and have lived there as aliens to this day.

[4](Jonathan son of Saul had a son who was lame in both feet. He was five years old when the news about Saul and Jonathan came from Jezreel. His nurse picked him up and fled, but as she hurried to leave, he fell and became crippled. His name was Mephibosheth.)

[5]Now Recab and Baanah, the sons of Rimmon the Beerothite, set out for the house of Ish-Bosheth, and they arrived there in the heat of the day while he was taking his noonday rest. [6]They went into the inner part of the house as if to get some wheat, and they stabbed him in the stomach. Then Recab and his brother Baanah slipped away.

[7]They had gone into the house while he was lying on the bed in his bedroom. After they stabbed and killed him, they cut off his head. Taking it with them, they traveled all night by way of the Arabah. [8]They brought the head of Ish-Bosheth to David at Hebron and said to the king, "Here is the head of Ish-Bosheth son of Saul, your enemy, who tried to take your life. This day the LORD has avenged my lord the king against Saul and his offspring."

[9]David answered Recab and his brother Baanah, the sons of Rimmon the Beerothite, "As surely as the LORD lives, who has delivered me out of all trouble, [10]when a man told me, 'Saul is dead,' and thought he was bringing good news, I seized him and put him to death in Ziklag. That was

the reward I gave him for his news! [11]How much more—when wicked men have killed an innocent man in his own house and on his own bed—should I not now demand his blood from your hand and rid the earth of you!"

[12]So David gave an order to his men, and they killed them. They cut off their hands and feet and hung the bodies by the pool in Hebron. But they took the head of Ish-Bosheth and buried it in Abner's tomb at Hebron.

David Becomes King Over Israel

5 All the tribes of Israel came to David at Hebron and said, "We are your own flesh and blood. [2]In the past, while Saul was king over us, you were the one who led Israel on their military campaigns. And the LORD said to you, 'You will shepherd my people Israel, and you will become their ruler.' "

[3]When all the elders of Israel had come to King David at Hebron, the king made a compact with them at Hebron before the LORD, and they anointed David king over Israel.

[4]David was thirty years old when he became king, and he reigned forty years. [5]In Hebron he reigned over Judah seven years and six months, and in Jerusalem he reigned over all Israel and Judah thirty-three years.

David Conquers Jerusalem

[6]The king and his men marched to Jerusalem to attack the Jebusites, who lived there. The Jebusites said to David, "You will not get in here; even the blind and the lame can ward you off." They thought, "David cannot get in here." [7]Nevertheless, David captured the fortress of Zion, the City of David.

[8]On that day, David said, "Anyone who conquers the Jebusites will have to use the water shaft[a] to reach those 'lame and blind' who are David's enemies.[b]" That is why they say, "The 'blind and lame' will not enter the palace."

[9]David then took up residence in the fortress and called it the City of David. He built up the area around it, from the supporting terraces[c] inward. [10]And he became more and more powerful, because the LORD God Almighty was with him.

[11]Now Hiram king of Tyre sent messen-

---

[a]8 Or use scaling hooks   [b]8 Or are hated by David
[c]9 Or the Millo

gers to David, along with cedar logs and carpenters and stonemasons, and they built a palace for David. ¹²And David knew that the LORD had established him as king over Israel and had exalted his kingdom for the sake of his people Israel.

¹³After he left Hebron, David took more concubines and wives in Jerusalem, and more sons and daughters were born to him. ¹⁴These are the names of the children born to him there: Shammua, Shobab, Nathan, Solomon, ¹⁵Ibhar, Elishua, Nepheg, Japhia, ¹⁶Elishama, Eliada and Eliphelet.

David Defeats the Philistines

¹⁷When the Philistines heard that David had been anointed king over Israel, they went up in full force to search for him, but David heard about it and went down to the stronghold. ¹⁸Now the Philistines had come and spread out in the Valley of Rephaim; ¹⁹so David inquired of the LORD, "Shall I go and attack the Philistines? Will you hand them over to me?"

The LORD answered him, "Go, for I will surely hand the Philistines over to you."

²⁰So David went to Baal Perazim, and there he defeated them. He said, "As waters break out, the LORD has broken out against my enemies before me." So that place was called Baal Perazim.ᵃ ²¹The Philistines abandoned their idols there, and David and his men carried them off.

²²Once more the Philistines came up and spread out in the Valley of Rephaim; ²³so David inquired of the LORD, and he answered, "Do not go straight up, but circle around behind them and attack them in front of the balsam trees. ²⁴As soon as you hear the sound of marching in the tops of the balsam trees, move quickly, because that will mean the LORD has gone out in front of you to strike the Philistine army." ²⁵So David did as the LORD commanded him, and he struck down the Philistines all the way from Gibeonᵇ to Gezer.

The Ark Brought to Jerusalem

6 David again brought together out of Israel chosen men, thirty thousand in all. ²He and all his men set out from Baalah of Judahᶜ to bring up from there the ark of God, which is called by the Name,ᵈ the name of the LORD Almighty, who is enthroned between the cherubim that are on the ark. ³They set the ark of God on a

new cart and brought it from the house of Abinadab, which was on the hill. Uzzah and Ahio, sons of Abinadab, were guiding the new cart ⁴with the ark of God on it,ᵉ and Ahio was walking in front of it. ⁵David and the whole house of Israel were celebrating with all their might before the LORD, with songsᶠ and with harps, lyres, tambourines, sistrums and cymbals.

⁶When they came to the threshing floor of Nacon, Uzzah reached out and took hold of the ark of God, because the oxen stumbled. ⁷The LORD's anger burned against Uzzah because of his irreverent act; therefore God struck him down and he died there beside the ark of God.

⁸Then David was angry because the LORD's wrath had broken out against Uzzah, and to this day that place is called Perez Uzzah.ᵍ

⁹David was afraid of the LORD that day and said, "How can the ark of the LORD ever come to me?" ¹⁰He was not willing to take the ark of the LORD to be with him in the City of David. Instead, he took it aside to the house of Obed-Edom the Gittite. ¹¹The ark of the LORD remained in the house of Obed-Edom the Gittite for three months, and the LORD blessed him and his entire household.

¹²Now King David was told, "The LORD has blessed the household of Obed-Edom and everything he has, because of the ark of God." So David went down and brought up the ark of God from the house of Obed-Edom to the City of David with rejoicing. ¹³When those who were carrying the ark of the LORD had taken six steps, he sacrificed a bull and a fattened calf. ¹⁴David, wearing a linen ephod, danced before the LORD with all his might, ¹⁵while he and the entire house of Israel brought up the ark of the LORD with shouts and the sound of trumpets.

¹⁶As the ark of the LORD was entering the City of David, Michal daughter of Saul watched from a window. And when she saw King David leaping and dancing

ᵃ20 Baal Perazim means the lord who breaks out. ᵇ25 Septuagint (see also 1 Chron. 14:16); Hebrew Geba ᶜ2 That is, Kiriath Jearim; Hebrew Baale Judah, a variant of Baalah of Judah ᵈ2 Hebrew; Septuagint and Vulgate do not have the Name. ᵉ3,4 Dead Sea Scrolls and some Septuagint manuscripts; Masoretic Text cart ⁴and they brought it with the ark of God from the house of Abinadab, which was on the hill ᶠ5 See Dead Sea Scrolls, Septuagint and 1 Chronicles 13:8; Masoretic Text celebrating before the LORD with all kinds of instruments made of pine. ᵍ8 Perez Uzzah means outbreak against Uzzah.

before the LORD, she despised him in her heart.

[17]They brought the ark of the LORD and set it in its place inside the tent that David had pitched for it, and David sacrificed burnt offerings and fellowship offerings[a] before the LORD. [18]After he had finished sacrificing the burnt offerings and fellowship offerings, he blessed the people in the name of the LORD Almighty. [19]Then he gave a loaf of bread, a cake of dates and a cake of raisins to each person in the whole crowd of Israelites, both men and women. And all the people went to their homes.

[20]When David returned home to bless his household, Michal daughter of Saul came out to meet him and said, "How the king of Israel has distinguished himself today, disrobing in the sight of the slave girls of his servants as any vulgar fellow would!"

[21]David said to Michal, "It was before the LORD, who chose me rather than your father or anyone from his house when he appointed me ruler over the LORD's people Israel—I will celebrate before the LORD. [22]I will become even more undignified than this, and I will be humiliated in my own eyes. But by these slave girls you spoke of, I will be held in honor."

[23]And Michal daughter of Saul had no children to the day of her death.

God's Promise to David

7 After the king was settled in his palace and the LORD had given him rest from all his enemies around him, [2]he said to Nathan the prophet, "Here I am, living in a palace of cedar, while the ark of God remains in a tent."

[3]Nathan replied to the king, "Whatever you have in mind, go ahead and do it, for the LORD is with you."

[4]That night the word of the LORD came to Nathan, saying:

[a]17 Traditionally *peace offerings*; also in verse 18

"That's My Kid Out There"
God, the Long-suffering Father

"The LORD declares to you that the LORD himself will establish a house for you . . . I will raise up your offspring to succeed you" (7:11–12).

Text: 2 Samuel 7

Every Saturday morning, all over the country, you'll find dads standing along the sidelines of soccer fields, baseball diamonds, hockey rinks, and tennis and basketball courts. Why are these dads doing this, especially in light of all the other things they could be doing with their precious weekends? The answer should be obvious: These patient fathers have a child on the field, on the ice, or on the court. "That's my kid out there," a typical dad will boast. "I'm not going anywhere until the game is over."

The Bible calls this "long-suffering." The word refers to a patient father, waiting tirelessly for his child to learn the lessons that life has to offer: the benefits of teamwork, rewards for fair play, consequences for disregarding the rules. But rather than going home to watch seasoned professionals play the same sports on television, he stands faithfully by, cheering for his own children.

What we have here is a perfect metaphor for our heavenly Father. God sent a message to David by way of Nathan, a promise that God himself would establish and bless David's family. Our heavenly father was willing to stand by David. He was willing to give him a son to succeed him. He was willing to love and discipline both David and his son. He does much the same thing for you and me.

Could God go elsewhere to see a better performance than the one his children are giving him? Yes. But would he rather watch his angels scrimmage or observe the heavenly hosts flawlessly control a soccer ball? No, actually, he wouldn't. Our God cheers for his children. He stands by while we struggle and complain. He celebrates each victory with us. And his long-suffering is sure.

For a complete listing of Dads in the Bible, turn to page 1434.

⁵"Go and tell my servant David, 'This is what the LORD says: Are you the one to build me a house to dwell in? ⁶I have not dwelt in a house from the day I brought the Israelites up out of Egypt to this day. I have been moving from place to place with a tent as my dwelling. ⁷Wherever I have moved with all the Israelites, did I ever say to any of their rulers whom I commanded to shepherd my people Israel, "Why have you not built me a house of cedar?"'

⁸"Now then, tell my servant David, 'This is what the LORD Almighty says: I took you from the pasture and from following the flock to be ruler over my people Israel. ⁹I have been with you wherever you have gone, and I have cut off all your enemies from before you. Now I will make your name great, like the names of the greatest men of the earth. ¹⁰And I will provide a place for my people Israel and will plant them so that they can have a home of their own and no longer be disturbed. Wicked people will not oppress them anymore, as they did at the beginning ¹¹and have done ever since the time I appointed leaders*a* over my people Israel. I will also give you rest from all your enemies.

"'The LORD declares to you that the LORD himself will establish a house for you: ¹²When your days are

---

a11 Traditionally *judges*

The Impossible Dream

DAILY INSIGHT

WEDNESDAY

Passage:
2 Samuel 7:5–29

Verses:
2 Samuel 7:27–29

Behind my parents' house, my dad had built a swing set. It was the deluxe model with three swings and a "sky glider." An incredibly frugal man, my dad must have been overwhelmingly inspired to invest in the above-average edition. In any case, on warm summer nights, sometimes I would slip out of the house and sit on one of the swings. A fairly quiet boy, I rarely disclosed this kind of stuff to anyone, but all alone under a crystal night sky, I'd rock back and forth on the chain-suspended wooden swing and dream about the future.

For so many years, girls were other-worldly to me. Sure, I had an older sister and a younger sister and got along great with both of them. But they were my *sisters*. They weren't really "girls"—not like the mysterious and seemingly unapproachable girls at school. Sitting on the old swing set, I wondered if there was a girl out there for me. I thought about what it would be like to live with, sleep with and have babies with this girl. Such thoughts actually made a boy's heartbeat audible to an ordinarily inanimate swing set on a summer night.

A family of my very own? I could hardly allow myself to dream such a dream. Did this ever happen to you?

But here we are, you and I, decades later. And, as incredible as our dreams seemed at the time, they have literally come true. You and I *do* have families of our very own. Can you believe it?

The prophet Nathan had a message from God for David. "The LORD declares to you that the LORD himself will establish a house for you" (7:11b). It was as though God was saying to David, "I'm going to find a gift for the 'king who has everything.' It will become your most precious possession." Completely overwhelmed by God's covenant, David made a promise of his own. "I will build a house for you" (7:27).

This very moment could be one of the most important you have ever known as a dad. Please focus on the following words as though your life depended on them.

Your family is one of God's most spectacular gifts to you. Before the foundation of time, he chose you to be a dad. Not every man gets this privilege, but you do. You have a family of your very own … the fulfillment of a dream you barely had the courage to dream.

Now, build your house for God.

For your next devotional reading, go to page 341.

over and you rest with your fathers, I will raise up your offspring to succeed you, who will come from your own body, and I will establish his kingdom. [13]He is the one who will build a house for my Name, and I will establish the throne of his kingdom forever. [14]I will be his father, and he will be my son. When he does wrong, I will punish him with the rod of men, with floggings inflicted by men. [15]But my love will never be taken away from him, as I took it away from Saul, whom I removed from before you. [16]Your house and your kingdom will endure forever before me[a]; your throne will be established forever.' "

[17]Nathan reported to David all the words of this entire revelation.

David's Prayer

[18]Then King David went in and sat before the LORD, and he said:

"Who am I, O Sovereign LORD, and what is my family, that you have brought me this far? [19]And as if this were not enough in your sight, O Sovereign LORD, you have also spoken about the future of the house of your servant. Is this your usual way of dealing with man, O Sovereign LORD?

[20]"What more can David say to you? For you know your servant, O Sovereign LORD. [21]For the sake of your word and according to your will, you have done this great thing and made it known to your servant.

[22]"How great you are, O Sovereign LORD! There is no one like you, and there is no God but you, as we have heard with our own ears. [23]And who is like your people Israel—the one nation on earth that God went out to redeem as a people for himself, and to make a name for himself, and to perform great and awesome wonders by driving out nations and their gods from before your people, whom you redeemed from Egypt?[b] [24]You have established your people Israel as your very own forever, and you, O LORD, have become their God.

[25]"And now, LORD God, keep forever the promise you have made concerning your servant and his house. Do as you promised, [26]so that your name will be great forever. Then

men will say, 'The LORD Almighty is God over Israel!' And the house of your servant David will be established before you.

[27]"O LORD Almighty, God of Israel, you have revealed this to your servant, saying, 'I will build a house for you.' So your servant has found courage to offer you this prayer. [28]O Sovereign LORD, you are God! Your words are trustworthy, and you have promised these good things to your servant. [29]Now be pleased to bless the house of your servant, that it may continue forever in your sight; for you, O Sovereign LORD, have spoken, and with your blessing the house of your servant will be blessed forever."

David's Victories

8 In the course of time, David defeated the Philistines and subdued them, and he took Metheg Ammah from the control of the Philistines.

[2]David also defeated the Moabites. He made them lie down on the ground and measured them off with a length of cord. Every two lengths of them were put to death, and the third length was allowed to live. So the Moabites became subject to David and brought tribute.

[3]Moreover, David fought Hadadezer son of Rehob, king of Zobah, when he went to restore his control along the Euphrates River. [4]David captured a thousand of his chariots, seven thousand charioteers[c] and twenty thousand foot soldiers. He hamstrung all but a hundred of the chariot horses.

[5]When the Arameans of Damascus came to help Hadadezer king of Zobah, David struck down twenty-two thousand of them. [6]He put garrisons in the Aramean kingdom of Damascus, and the Arameans became subject to him and brought tribute. The LORD gave David victory wherever he went.

[7]David took the gold shields that belonged to the officers of Hadadezer and brought them to Jerusalem. [8]From Tebah[d]

---

[a]16 Some Hebrew manuscripts and Septuagint; most Hebrew manuscripts *you*   [b]23 See Septuagint and 1 Chron. 17:21; Hebrew *wonders for your land and before your people, whom you redeemed from Egypt, from the nations and their gods.*   [c]4 Septuagint (see also Dead Sea Scrolls and 1 Chron. 18:4); Masoretic Text *captured seventeen hundred of his charioteers*   [d]8 See some Septuagint manuscripts (see also 1 Chron. 18:8); Hebrew *Betah.*

and Berothai, towns that belonged to Hadadezer, King David took a great quantity of bronze.

⁹When Tou[a] king of Hamath heard that David had defeated the entire army of Hadadezer, ¹⁰he sent his son Joram[b] to King David to greet him and congratulate him on his victory in battle over Hadadezer, who had been at war with Tou. Joram brought with him articles of silver and gold and bronze.

¹¹King David dedicated these articles to the LORD, as he had done with the silver and gold from all the nations he had subdued: ¹²Edom[c] and Moab, the Ammonites and the Philistines, and Amalek. He also dedicated the plunder taken from Hadadezer son of Rehob, king of Zobah.

¹³And David became famous after he returned from striking down eighteen thousand Edomites[d] in the Valley of Salt.

¹⁴He put garrisons throughout Edom, and all the Edomites became subject to David. The LORD gave David victory wherever he went.

David's Officials

¹⁵David reigned over all Israel, doing what was just and right for all his people. ¹⁶Joab son of Zeruiah was over the army; Jehoshaphat son of Ahilud was recorder; ¹⁷Zadok son of Ahitub and Ahimelech son of Abiathar were priests; Seraiah was secretary; ¹⁸Benaiah son of Jehoiada was over the Kerethites and Pelethites; and David's sons were royal advisers.[e]

David and Mephibosheth

9 David asked, "Is there anyone still left of the house of Saul to whom I can show kindness for Jonathan's sake?"

²Now there was a servant of Saul's household named Ziba. They called him to appear before David, and the king said to him, "Are you Ziba?"

"Your servant," he replied.

³The king asked, "Is there no one still left of the house of Saul to whom I can show God's kindness?"

Ziba answered the king, "There is still a son of Jonathan; he is crippled in both feet."

⁴"Where is he?" the king asked.

Ziba answered, "He is at the house of Makir son of Ammiel in Lo Debar."

⁵So King David had him brought from Lo Debar, from the house of Makir son of Ammiel.

⁶When Mephibosheth son of Jonathan,

the son of Saul, came to David, he bowed down to pay him honor.

David said, "Mephibosheth!"

"Your servant," he replied.

⁷"Don't be afraid," David said to him, "for I will surely show you kindness for the sake of your father Jonathan. I will restore to you all the land that belonged to your grandfather Saul, and you will always eat at my table."

⁸Mephibosheth bowed down and said, "What is your servant, that you should notice a dead dog like me?"

⁹Then the king summoned Ziba, Saul's servant, and said to him, "I have given your master's grandson everything that belonged to Saul and his family. ¹⁰You and your sons and your servants are to farm the land for him and bring in the crops, so that your master's grandson may be provided for. And Mephibosheth, grandson of your master, will always eat at my table." (Now Ziba had fifteen sons and twenty servants.)

¹¹Then Ziba said to the king, "Your servant will do whatever my lord the king commands his servant to do." So Mephibosheth ate at David's[f] table like one of the king's sons.

¹²Mephibosheth had a young son named Mica, and all the members of Ziba's household were servants of Mephibosheth. ¹³And Mephibosheth lived in Jerusalem, because he always ate at the king's table, and he was crippled in both feet.

David Defeats the Ammonites

10 In the course of time, the king of the Ammonites died, and his son Hanun succeeded him as king. ²David thought, "I will show kindness to Hanun son of Nahash, just as his father showed kindness to me." So David sent a delegation to express his sympathy to Hanun concerning his father.

When David's men came to the land of the Ammonites, ³the Ammonite nobles said to Hanun their lord, "Do you think David is honoring your father by sending men to you to express sympathy? Hasn't David sent them to you to explore the

---

[a]9 Hebrew *Toi*, a variant of *Tou*; also in verse 10   [b]10 A variant of *Hadoram*   [c]12 Some Hebrew manuscripts, Septuagint and Syriac (see also 1 Chron. 18:11); most Hebrew manuscripts *Aram*   [d]13 A few Hebrew manuscripts, Septuagint and Syriac (see also 1 Chron. 18:12); most Hebrew manuscripts *Aram* (that is, Arameans)   [e]18 Or *were priests*   [f]11 Septuagint; Hebrew *my*

city and spy it out and overthrow it?" ⁴So Hanun seized David's men, shaved off half of each man's beard, cut off their garments in the middle at the buttocks, and sent them away.

⁵When David was told about this, he sent messengers to meet the men, for they were greatly humiliated. The king said, "Stay at Jericho till your beards have grown, and then come back."

⁶When the Ammonites realized that they had become a stench in David's nostrils, they hired twenty thousand Aramean foot soldiers from Beth Rehob and Zobah, as well as the king of Maacah with a thousand men, and also twelve thousand men from Tob.

⁷On hearing this, David sent Joab out with the entire army of fighting men. ⁸The Ammonites came out and drew up in battle formation at the entrance to their city gate, while the Arameans of Zobah and Rehob and the men of Tob and Maacah were by themselves in the open country.

⁹Joab saw that there were battle lines in front of him and behind him; so he selected some of the best troops in Israel and deployed them against the Arameans. ¹⁰He put the rest of the men under the command of Abishai his brother and deployed them against the Ammonites. ¹¹Joab said, "If the Arameans are too strong for me, then you are to come to my rescue; but if the Ammonites are too strong for you, then I will come to rescue you. ¹²Be strong and let us fight bravely for our people and the cities of our God. The LORD will do what is good in his sight."

¹³Then Joab and the troops with him advanced to fight the Arameans, and they fled before him. ¹⁴When the Ammonites saw that the Arameans were fleeing, they fled before Abishai and went inside the city. So Joab returned from fighting the Ammonites and came to Jerusalem.

¹⁵After the Arameans saw that they had been routed by Israel, they regrouped. ¹⁶Hadadezer had Arameans brought from beyond the River*a*; they went to Helam, with Shobach the commander of Hadadezer's army leading them.

¹⁷When David was told of this, he gathered all Israel, crossed the Jordan and went to Helam. The Arameans formed their battle lines to meet David and fought against him. ¹⁸But they fled before Israel, and David killed seven hundred of their charioteers and forty thousand of their foot soldiers.*b* He also struck down

Shobach the commander of their army, and he died there. ¹⁹When all the kings who were vassals of Hadadezer saw that they had been defeated by Israel, they made peace with the Israelites and became subject to them.

So the Arameans were afraid to help the Ammonites anymore.

David and Bathsheba

11 In the spring, at the time when kings go off to war, David sent Joab out with the king's men and the whole Israelite army. They destroyed the Ammonites and besieged Rabbah. But David remained in Jerusalem.

²One evening David got up from his bed and walked around on the roof of the palace. From the roof he saw a woman bathing. The woman was very beautiful, ³and David sent someone to find out about her. The man said, "Isn't this Bathsheba, the daughter of Eliam and the wife of Uriah the Hittite?" ⁴Then David sent messengers to get her. She came to him, and he slept with her. (She had purified herself from her uncleanness.) Then*c* she went back home. ⁵The woman conceived and sent word to David, saying, "I am pregnant."

⁶So David sent this word to Joab: "Send me Uriah the Hittite." And Joab sent him to David. ⁷When Uriah came to him, David asked him how Joab was, how the soldiers were and how the war was going. ⁸Then David said to Uriah, "Go down to your house and wash your feet." So Uriah left the palace, and a gift from the king was sent after him. ⁹But Uriah slept at the entrance to the palace with all his master's servants and did not go down to his house.

¹⁰When David was told, "Uriah did not go home," he asked him, "Haven't you just come from a distance? Why didn't you go home?"

¹¹Uriah said to David, "The ark and Israel and Judah are staying in tents, and my master Joab and my lord's men are camped in the open fields. How could I go to my house to eat and drink and lie with my wife? As surely as you live, I will not do such a thing!"

¹²Then David said to him, "Stay here one more day, and tomorrow I will send

a16 That is, the Euphrates   b18 Some Septuagint manuscripts (see also 1 Chron. 19:18); Hebrew horsemen   c4 Or with her. When she purified herself from her uncleanness,

you back." So Uriah remained in Jerusalem that day and the next. [13]At David's invitation, he ate and drank with him, and David made him drunk. But in the evening Uriah went out to sleep on his mat among his master's servants; he did not go home.

[14]In the morning David wrote a letter to Joab and sent it with Uriah. [15]In it he wrote, "Put Uriah in the front line where the fighting is fiercest. Then withdraw from him so he will be struck down and die."

[16]So while Joab had the city under siege, he put Uriah at a place where he knew the strongest defenders were. [17]When the men of the city came out and fought against Joab, some of the men in David's army fell; moreover, Uriah the Hittite died.

[18]Joab sent David a full account of the battle. [19]He instructed the messenger:

Great Game, Dad

DAILY INSIGHT

THURSDAY

Passage:
2 Samuel 11:1–17

Verses:
2 Samuel 11:2–4

When our daughters were quite young, one of the things we tried to do during mealtime was to have fun together—in addition, of course, to eating our food in a basically well-mannered way. Thanks to a very creative wife, we had already learned to play the "what-was-our-happiest-thing-today" and "what-was-our-saddest-thing-today" games. Dinner had become a great time of learning about each other and, as I said, fun.

One evening I had an idea. "Let's play the 'no' game." My family looked at me as though I had just suggested that we follow a house painter around to watch his paint dry. "I'm serious," I said, trying to get more than blank stares. "It'll be fun."

I explained. "Between now and tomorrow night, let's all say 'no' to something. It doesn't have to be something bad, only something we'd *like* to do but something we decide *not* to do. Let's just see if we can say 'no.'"

The next evening we gave our reports. I had said "no" to dessert at a luncheon meeting. Missy had said "no" to talking too long on the phone. Julie had said "no" to an extra thirty minutes of television. Following each report, the rest of the family celebrated. My game was a hit. Why? Because we had discovered that a great deal of joy comes with knowing one has the power to voluntarily govern oneself, to say "no" when one could say "yes."

The story of David and Bathsheba is one of the most famous in all of the Bible.

Because of its lurid script, Hollywood has done more than its share of reenactments. And for centuries, preachers have capitalized on its powerful message of the wages of impurity. But, at least for me, the most important message in this story is David's pathetic inability to say "no."

Kings have spectacular privileges, and David was no exception. Most of them live with very few unfulfilled physical needs. They have the luxury of saying "yes" to everything. For David, this particular day included: "I think I'll take a vacation from battle." "I feel like going for a little walk." "I believe I'll have that woman over there." No one said "no," including the king himself.

But losing the ability to say "no" means losing everything. In doing so, we become whimpering and pitiful victims. The strength—and pleasure—of living a disciplined life atrophies into uselessness.

As men, you and I are faced with myriad opportunities and temptations—inconsequential ones and life-changing ones. When those chances begin to take charge because we have lost the will to turn away, everything in our world crumbles.

Even if your family never plays the " 'no' game," try a few rounds on your own. Experience the sheer pleasure of knowing you actually have the strength to make yourself do the right thing. Especially when "no one" is watching.

For your next devotional reading, go to page 351.

"When you have finished giving the king this account of the battle, [20]the king's anger may flare up, and he may ask you, 'Why did you get so close to the city to fight? Didn't you know they would shoot arrows from the wall? [21]Who killed Abimelech son of Jerub-Besheth[a]? Didn't a woman throw an upper millstone on him from the wall, so that he died in Thebez? Why did you get so close to the wall?' If he asks you this, then say to him, 'Also, your servant Uriah the Hittite is dead.' "

[22]The messenger set out, and when he arrived he told David everything Joab had sent him to say. [23]The messenger said to David, "The men overpowered us and came out against us in the open, but we drove them back to the entrance to the city gate. [24]Then the archers shot arrows at your servants from the wall, and some of the king's men died. Moreover, your servant Uriah the Hittite is dead."

[25]David told the messenger, "Say this to Joab: 'Don't let this upset you; the sword devours one as well as another. Press the attack against the city and destroy it.' Say this to encourage Joab."

[26]When Uriah's wife heard that her husband was dead, she mourned for him. [27]After the time of mourning was over, David had her brought to his house, and she became his wife and bore him a son. But the thing David had done displeased the LORD.

Nathan Rebukes David

12 The LORD sent Nathan to David. When he came to him, he said, "There were two men in a certain town, one rich and the other poor. [2]The rich man had a very large number of sheep and cattle, [3]but the

[a]21 Also known as *Jerub-Baal* (that is, Gideon)

The Little Boy Without a Name
David, the Adulterous Father

DADS
IN THE
BIBLE

"Nathan said to David, 'You are the man! . . . This is what the LORD says: "Out of your own household I am going to bring calamity upon you" ' " (12:7, 11).

Text: 2 Samuel 11, 12

David's kingdom was renowned. His military prowess was unmistakable. He was certainly the most powerful man he knew. David was even the master of his schedule. It was spring, "when kings go off to war," but David sent Joab in his place (11:1).

With a little extra time on his hands, David saw something he didn't think he would ever see: something that he wanted that he couldn't have . . . a beautiful woman . . . someone else's wife. Burning with desire, "David sent messengers to get her" (11:4). The result of David's adultery was the murder of Bathsheba's husband, the conception of a little boy, and the horror of God's judgment.

Don't you wonder if, between the time he sent for Bathsheba and the time he slept with her, the potential cost of his own foolishness ever crossed David's mind? Didn't his heart burn with the certain consequences of crossing this line?

We don't know the answers to these questions, but we do know that David paid a horrible price for his sin. Not only did Nathan the prophet level the king's soul with the treachery of his flagrant disobedience, but God also took David's son . . . the little boy without a name.

If David had known what was going to happen as a direct result of his actions, he wouldn't have gone through with them. And if David could consult with every man who is choosing the same path he did, he would plead with him to stop. "Don't go through with this," he would beg. "One day I buried a little boy without a name. This child paid the price for my sin. I wish I had died instead."

Adultery brings with it a guarantee of pain. If you're fortunate, it will only be your own. Chances are, however, it will bring searing pain to your family, too. What could ever be worth this?

For a complete listing of Dads in the Bible, turn to page 1434.

poor man had nothing except one little ewe lamb he had bought. He raised it, and it grew up with him and his children. It shared his food, drank from his cup and even slept in his arms. It was like a daughter to him.

⁴"Now a traveler came to the rich man, but the rich man refrained from taking one of his own sheep or cattle to prepare a meal for the traveler who had come to him. Instead, he took the ewe lamb that belonged to the poor man and prepared it for the one who had come to him."

⁵David burned with anger against the man and said to Nathan, "As surely as the LORD lives, the man who did this deserves to die! ⁶He must pay for that lamb four times over, because he did such a thing and had no pity."

⁷Then Nathan said to David, "You are the man! This is what the LORD, the God of Israel, says: 'I anointed you king over Israel, and I delivered you from the hand of Saul. ⁸I gave your master's house to you, and your master's wives into your arms. I gave you the house of Israel and Judah. And if all this had been too little, I would have given you even more. ⁹Why did you despise the word of the LORD by doing what is evil in his eyes? You struck down Uriah the Hittite with the sword and took his wife to be your own. You killed him with the sword of the Ammonites. ¹⁰Now, therefore, the sword will never depart from your house, because you despised me and took the wife of Uriah the Hittite to be your own.'

¹¹"This is what the LORD says: 'Out of your own household I am going to bring calamity upon you. Before your very eyes I will take your wives and give them to one who is close to you, and he will lie with your wives in broad daylight. ¹²You did it in secret, but I will do this thing in broad daylight before all Israel.' "

¹³Then David said to Nathan, "I have sinned against the LORD."

Nathan replied, "The LORD has taken away your sin. You are not going to die. ¹⁴But because by doing this you have made the enemies of the LORD show utter contempt,ᵃ the son born to you will die."

¹⁵After Nathan had gone home, the LORD struck the child that Uriah's wife had borne to David, and he became ill. ¹⁶David pleaded with God for the child. He fasted and went into his house and spent the nights lying on the ground. ¹⁷The elders of his household stood

ᵃ14 Masoretic Text; an ancient Hebrew scribal tradition *this you have shown utter contempt for the LORD*

HEY DAD

If I'm forgiven, why am I still grounded?

QUESTIONS Kids

ASK

Text: 2 Samuel 12:13-23

The principle of sowing and reaping is a lesson we all sometimes forget. It's tempting to believe and hope that if God forgives us, he will also removes the consequences of our sinful actions. David learned that this wasn't always the case. God forgave David, but he still took the life of his baby boy.

Let's say a man was involved in a car accident that clearly wasn't his fault. The driver who smashed into him probably apologized more than once while waiting for the police to arrive. And the man was quick to forgive the offender. "That's okay. These things happen," he may have heard himself saying.

But would he have said, "And hey, don't worry about that repair bill. I've got some extra money stored away, and I don't mind paying for it myself"? Probably not.

Sometimes God chooses to pick up our "repair bill;" sometimes he doesn't. He's faithful to forgive us, but our actions have consequences. Period.

So if your daughter pouts when she learns she's still going to have to apologize to her mother, or if your son balks at the fact that he's going to have to pay for that broken window, stand firm. Remind him or her that you're simply following the example of the perfect Father. "Yes, I love you. Yes, you're forgiven. Now, roll up your sleeves. You've got work to do."

For a complete listing of Questions Kids Ask, turn to page 1435.

beside him to get him up from the ground, but he refused, and he would not eat any food with them.

[18]On the seventh day the child died. David's servants were afraid to tell him that the child was dead, for they thought, "While the child was still living, we spoke to David but he would not listen to us. How can we tell him the child is dead? He may do something desperate."

[19]David noticed that his servants were whispering among themselves and he realized the child was dead. "Is the child dead?" he asked.

"Yes," they replied, "he is dead."

[20]Then David got up from the ground. After he had washed, put on lotions and changed his clothes, he went into the house of the LORD and worshiped. Then he went to his own house, and at his request they served him food, and he ate.

[21]His servants asked him, "Why are you acting this way? While the child was alive, you fasted and wept, but now that the child is dead, you get up and eat!"

[22]He answered, "While the child was still alive, I fasted and wept. I thought, 'Who knows? The LORD may be gracious to me and let the child live.' [23]But now that he is dead, why should I fast? Can I bring him back again? I will go to him, but he will not return to me."

[24]Then David comforted his wife Bathsheba, and he went to her and lay with her. She gave birth to a son, and they named him Solomon. The LORD loved him; [25]and because the LORD loved him, he sent word through Nathan the prophet to name him Jedidiah.[a]

[26]Meanwhile Joab fought against Rabbah of the Ammonites and captured the royal citadel. [27]Joab then sent messengers to David, saying, "I have fought against Rabbah and taken its water supply. [28]Now muster the rest of the troops and besiege the city and capture it. Otherwise I will take the city, and it will be named after me."

[29]So David mustered the entire army and went to Rabbah, and attacked and captured it. [30]He took the crown from the head of their king[b]—its weight was a talent[c] of gold, and it was set with precious stones—and it was placed on David's head. He took a great quantity of plunder from the city [31]and brought out the people who were there, consigning them to labor with saws and with iron picks and axes, and he made them work at brickmaking.[d] He did this to all the Am-

monite towns. Then David and his entire army returned to Jerusalem.

Amnon and Tamar

13 In the course of time, Amnon son of David fell in love with Tamar, the beautiful sister of Absalom son of David. [2]Amnon became frustrated to the point of illness on account of his sister Tamar, for she was a virgin, and it seemed impossible for him to do anything to her.

[3]Now Amnon had a friend named Jonadab son of Shimeah, David's brother. Jonadab was a very shrewd man. [4]He asked Amnon, "Why do you, the king's son, look so haggard morning after morning? Won't you tell me?"

Amnon said to him, "I'm in love with Tamar, my brother Absalom's sister."

[5]"Go to bed and pretend to be ill," Jonadab said. "When your father comes to see you, say to him, 'I would like my sister Tamar to come and give me something to eat. Let her prepare the food in my sight so I may watch her and then eat it from her hand.' "

[6]So Amnon lay down and pretended to be ill. When the king came to see him, Amnon said to him, "I would like my sister Tamar to come and make some special bread in my sight, so I may eat from her hand."

[7]David sent word to Tamar at the palace: "Go to the house of your brother Amnon and prepare some food for him." [8]So Tamar went to the house of her brother Amnon, who was lying down. She took some dough, kneaded it, made the bread in his sight and baked it. [9]Then she took the pan and served him the bread, but he refused to eat.

"Send everyone out of here," Amnon said. So everyone left him. [10]Then Amnon said to Tamar, "Bring the food here into my bedroom so I may eat from your hand." And Tamar took the bread she had prepared and brought it to her brother Amnon in his bedroom. [11]But when she took it to him to eat, he grabbed her and said, "Come to bed with me, my sister."

[12]"Don't, my brother!" she said to him. "Don't force me. Such a thing should not be done in Israel! Don't do this wicked thing. [13]What about me? Where could I get rid of my disgrace? And what about you?

---

[a]25 Jedidiah means loved by the LORD.   [b]30 Or of Milcom (that is, Molech)   [c]30 That is, about 75 pounds (about 34 kilograms)   [d]31 The meaning of the Hebrew for this clause is uncertain.

You would be like one of the wicked fools in Israel. Please speak to the king; he will not keep me from being married to you." [14]But he refused to listen to her, and since he was stronger than she, he raped her.

[15]Then Amnon hated her with intense hatred. In fact, he hated her more than he had loved her. Amnon said to her, "Get up and get out!"

[16]"No!" she said to him. "Sending me away would be a greater wrong than what you have already done to me."

But he refused to listen to her. [17]He called his personal servant and said, "Get this woman out of here and bolt the door after her." [18]So his servant put her out and bolted the door after her. She was wearing a richly ornamented[a] robe, for this was the kind of garment the virgin daughters of the king wore. [19]Tamar put ashes on her head and tore the ornamented[b] robe she was wearing. She put her hand on her head and went away, weeping aloud as she went.

[20]Her brother Absalom said to her, "Has that Amnon, your brother, been with you? Be quiet now, my sister; he is your brother. Don't take this thing to heart." And Tamar lived in her brother Absalom's house, a desolate woman.

[21]When King David heard all this, he was furious. [22]Absalom never said a word to Amnon, either good or bad; he hated Amnon because he had disgraced his sister Tamar.

Absalom Kills Amnon

[23]Two years later, when Absalom's sheepshearers were at Baal Hazor near the border of Ephraim, he invited all the king's sons to come there. [24]Absalom went to the king and said, "Your servant has had shearers come. Will the king and his officials please join me?"

[25]"No, my son," the king replied. "All of us should not go; we would only be a

---

[a]18 The meaning of the Hebrew for this phrase is uncertain.   [b]19 The meaning of the Hebrew for this word is uncertain.

Life Without Consequences
David, the Neglectful Father

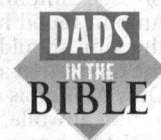
DADS
IN THE
BIBLE

"A messenger came and told David, 'The hearts of the men of Israel are with Absalom.' Then David said . . . 'Come! We must flee, or none of us will escape from Absalom' " (15:13–14).

Text: 2 Samuel 13, 19

In many ways, Absalom was as gifted as his father, King David. He was a great strategist, a natural-born leader, and he had a wonderful way with the people. But Absalom was leading a rebellion against his father, and David was unwilling to confront his boy. This unwillingness perilously divided the kingdom. Many followed Absalom; others remained loyal to David.

David was vulnerable because of his own sin. His poor example of self-discipline kept him from being the father his son, Absalom, desperately needed. He was afraid to challenge his son, and as a result, he lost him forever.

Confronting children with their failures is one of the most difficult aspects of being a father. "Who do you think you are?" they may snap back at their dads. "You're not so perfect yourself." Of course, they would be right. However, God has given a dad the privilege and the responsibility of being a leader, of lovingly but directly dealing with his children's rebellion. They do this, not because they are perfect, but because it is their responsibility—their calling—as fathers. Dads who neglect this responsibility invite the division of their relatives and friends.

What happened to Absalom could have been averted if David had not neglected his duty. David's mournful cry (18:33) reflects the agonizing pain this situation brought with it. Put yourself, for a moment, in David's place. What can you do today to ensure that you and your children will never face the same situation?

For a complete listing of Dads in the Bible, turn to page 1434.

burden to you." Although Absalom urged him, he still refused to go, but gave him his blessing.

26Then Absalom said, "If not, please let my brother Amnon come with us."

The king asked him, "Why should he go with you?" **27**But Absalom urged him, so he sent with him Amnon and the rest of the king's sons.

28Absalom ordered his men, "Listen! When Amnon is in high spirits from drinking wine and I say to you, 'Strike Amnon down,' then kill him. Don't be afraid. Have not I given you this order? Be strong and brave." **29**So Absalom's men did to Amnon what Absalom had ordered. Then all the king's sons got up, mounted their mules and fled.

30While they were on their way, the report came to David: "Absalom has struck down all the king's sons; not one of them is left." **31**The king stood up, tore his clothes and lay down on the ground; and all his servants stood by with their clothes torn.

32But Jonadab son of Shimeah, David's brother, said, "My lord should not think that they killed all the princes; only Amnon is dead. This has been Absalom's expressed intention ever since the day Amnon raped his sister Tamar. **33**My lord the king should not be concerned about the report that all the king's sons are dead. Only Amnon is dead."

34Meanwhile, Absalom had fled.

Now the man standing watch looked up and saw many people on the road west of him, coming down the side of the hill. The watchman went and told the king, "I see men in the direction of Horonaim, on the side of the hill."[a]

35Jonadab said to the king, "See, the king's sons are here; it has happened just as your servant said."

36As he finished speaking, the king's sons came in, wailing loudly. The king, too, and all his servants wept very bitterly.

37Absalom fled and went to Talmai son of Ammihud, the king of Geshur. But King David mourned for his son every day.

38After Absalom fled and went to Geshur, he stayed there three years. **39**And the spirit of the king[b] longed to go to Absalom, for he was consoled concerning Amnon's death.

Absalom Returns to Jerusalem

14 Joab son of Zeruiah knew that the king's heart longed for Absalom. **2**So Joab sent someone to Tekoa and had a wise woman brought from there. He said to her, "Pretend you are in mourning. Dress in mourning clothes, and don't use any cosmetic lotions. Act like a woman who has spent many days grieving for the dead. **3**Then go to the king and speak these words to him." And Joab put the words in her mouth.

4When the woman from Tekoa went[c] to the king, she fell with her face to the ground to pay him honor, and she said, "Help me, O king!"

5The king asked her, "What is troubling you?"

She said, "I am indeed a widow; my husband is dead. **6**I your servant had two sons. They got into a fight with each other in the field, and no one was there to separate them. One struck the other and killed him. **7**Now the whole clan has risen up against your servant; they say, 'Hand over the one who struck his brother down, so that we may put him to death for the life of his brother whom he killed; then we will get rid of the heir as well.' They would put out the only burning coal I have left, leaving my husband neither name nor descendant on the face of the earth."

8The king said to the woman, "Go home, and I will issue an order in your behalf."

9But the woman from Tekoa said to him, "My lord the king, let the blame rest on me and on my father's family, and let the king and his throne be without guilt."

10The king replied, "If anyone says anything to you, bring him to me, and he will not bother you again."

11She said, "Then let the king invoke the LORD his God to prevent the avenger of blood from adding to the destruction, so that my son will not be destroyed."

"As surely as the LORD lives," he said, "not one hair of your son's head will fall to the ground."

12Then the woman said, "Let your servant speak a word to my lord the king."

"Speak," he replied.

13The woman said, "Why then have you devised a thing like this against the people of God? When the king says this, does he not convict himself, for the king has not brought back his banished son?

---

a34 Septuagint; Hebrew does not have this sentence.   *b39* Dead Sea Scrolls and some Septuagint manuscripts; Masoretic Text *But the spirit of David the king*   *c4* Many Hebrew manuscripts, Septuagint, Vulgate and Syriac; most Hebrew manuscripts *spoke*

¹⁴Like water spilled on the ground, which cannot be recovered, so we must die. But God does not take away life; instead, he devises ways so that a banished person may not remain estranged from him.

¹⁵"And now I have come to say this to my lord the king because the people have made me afraid. Your servant thought, 'I will speak to the king; perhaps he will do what his servant asks. ¹⁶Perhaps the king will agree to deliver his servant from the hand of the man who is trying to cut off both me and my son from the inheritance God gave us.'

¹⁷"And now your servant says, 'May the word of my lord the king bring me rest, for my lord the king is like an angel of God in discerning good and evil. May the LORD your God be with you.'"

¹⁸Then the king said to the woman, "Do not keep from me the answer to what I am going to ask you."

"Let my lord the king speak," the woman said.

¹⁹The king asked, "Isn't the hand of Joab with you in all this?"

The woman answered, "As surely as you live, my lord the king, no one can turn to the right or to the left from anything my lord the king says. Yes, it was your servant Joab who instructed me to do this and who put all these words into the mouth of your servant. ²⁰Your servant Joab did this to change the present situation. My lord has wisdom like that of an angel of God—he knows everything that happens in the land."

²¹The king said to Joab, "Very well, I will do it. Go, bring back the young man Absalom."

²²Joab fell with his face to the ground to pay him honor, and he blessed the king. Joab said, "Today your servant knows that he has found favor in your eyes, my lord the king, because the king has granted his servant's request."

²³Then Joab went to Geshur and brought Absalom back to Jerusalem. ²⁴But the king said, "He must go to his own house; he must not see my face." So Absalom went to his own house and did not see the face of the king.

²⁵In all Israel there was not a man so highly praised for his handsome appearance as Absalom. From the top of his head to the sole of his foot there was no blemish in him. ²⁶Whenever he cut the hair of his head—he used to cut his hair from time to time when it became too heavy for him—he would weigh it, and its weight was two hundred shekels[a] by the royal standard.

²⁷Three sons and a daughter were born to Absalom. The daughter's name was Tamar, and she became a beautiful woman.

²⁸Absalom lived two years in Jerusalem without seeing the king's face. ²⁹Then Absalom sent for Joab in order to send him to the king, but Joab refused to come to him. So he sent a second time, but he refused to come. ³⁰Then he said to his servants, "Look, Joab's field is next to mine, and he has barley there. Go and set it on fire." So Absalom's servants set the field on fire.

³¹Then Joab did go to Absalom's house and he said to him, "Why have your servants set my field on fire?"

³²Absalom said to Joab, "Look, I sent word to you and said, 'Come here so I can send you to the king to ask, "Why have I come from Geshur? It would be better for me if I were still there!"' Now then, I want to see the king's face, and if I am guilty of anything, let him put me to death."

³³So Joab went to the king and told him this. Then the king summoned Absalom, and he came in and bowed down with his face to the ground before the king. And the king kissed Absalom.

Absalom's Conspiracy

15 In the course of time, Absalom provided himself with a chariot and horses and with fifty men to run ahead of him. ²He would get up early and stand by the side of the road leading to the city gate. Whenever anyone came with a complaint to be placed before the king for a decision, Absalom would call out to him, "What town are you from?" He would answer, "Your servant is from one of the tribes of Israel." ³Then Absalom would say to him, "Look, your claims are valid and proper, but there is no representative of the king to hear you." ⁴And Absalom would add, "If only I were appointed judge in the land! Then everyone who has a complaint or case could come to me and I would see that he gets justice."

⁵Also, whenever anyone approached him to bow down before him, Absalom would reach out his hand, take hold of him and kiss him. ⁶Absalom behaved in this way toward all the Israelites who came to the king asking for justice, and so he stole the hearts of the men of Israel.

ᵃ26 That is, about 5 pounds (about 2.3 kilograms)

[7]At the end of four[a] years, Absalom said to the king, "Let me go to Hebron and fulfill a vow I made to the LORD. [8]While your servant was living at Geshur in Aram, I made this vow: 'If the LORD takes me back to Jerusalem, I will worship the LORD in Hebron.[b]' "

[9]The king said to him, "Go in peace." So he went to Hebron.

[10]Then Absalom sent secret messengers throughout the tribes of Israel to say, "As soon as you hear the sound of the trumpets, then say, 'Absalom is king in Hebron.' " [11]Two hundred men from Jerusalem had accompanied Absalom. They had been invited as guests and went quite innocently, knowing nothing about the matter. [12]While Absalom was offering sacrifices, he also sent for Ahithophel the Gilonite, David's counselor, to come from Giloh, his hometown. And so the conspiracy gained strength, and Absalom's following kept on increasing.

David Flees

[13]A messenger came and told David, "The hearts of the men of Israel are with Absalom."

[14]Then David said to all his officials who were with him in Jerusalem, "Come! We must flee, or none of us will escape from Absalom. We must leave immediately, or he will move quickly to overtake us and bring ruin upon us and put the city to the sword."

[15]The king's officials answered him, "Your servants are ready to do whatever our lord the king chooses."

[16]The king set out, with his entire household following him; but he left ten concubines to take care of the palace. [17]So the king set out, with all the people following him, and they halted at a place some distance away. [18]All his men marched past him, along with all the Kerethites and Pelethites; and all the six hundred Gittites who had accompanied him from Gath marched before the king.

[19]The king said to Ittai the Gittite, "Why should you come along with us? Go back and stay with King Absalom. You are a foreigner, an exile from your homeland. [20]You came only yesterday. And today shall I make you wander about with us, when I do not know where I am going? Go back, and take your countrymen. May kindness and faithfulness be with you."

[21]But Ittai replied to the king, "As surely as the LORD lives, and as my lord the king

lives, wherever my lord the king may be, whether it means life or death, there will your servant be."

[22]David said to Ittai, "Go ahead, march on." So Ittai the Gittite marched on with all his men and the families that were with him.

[23]The whole countryside wept aloud as all the people passed by. The king also crossed the Kidron Valley, and all the people moved on toward the desert.

[24]Zadok was there, too, and all the Levites who were with him were carrying the ark of the covenant of God. They set down the ark of God, and Abiathar offered sacrifices[c] until all the people had finished leaving the city.

[25]Then the king said to Zadok, "Take the ark of God back into the city. If I find favor in the LORD's eyes, he will bring me back and let me see it and his dwelling place again. [26]But if he says, 'I am not pleased with you,' then I am ready; let him do to me whatever seems good to him."

[27]The king also said to Zadok the priest, "Aren't you a seer? Go back to the city in peace, with your son Ahimaaz and Jonathan son of Abiathar. You and Abiathar take your two sons with you. [28]I will wait at the fords in the desert until word comes from you to inform me." [29]So Zadok and Abiathar took the ark of God back to Jerusalem and stayed there.

[30]But David continued up the Mount of Olives, weeping as he went; his head was covered and he was barefoot. All the people with him covered their heads too and were weeping as they went up. [31]Now David had been told, "Ahithophel is among the conspirators with Absalom." So David prayed, "O LORD, turn Ahithophel's counsel into foolishness."

[32]When David arrived at the summit, where people used to worship God, Hushai the Arkite was there to meet him, his robe torn and dust on his head. [33]David said to him, "If you go with me, you will be a burden to me. [34]But if you return to the city and say to Absalom, 'I will be your servant, O king; I was your father's servant in the past, but now I will be your servant,' then you can help me by frustrating Ahithophel's advice. [35]Won't the priests Zadok and Abiathar be there with you? Tell them anything you hear in the king's

---

[a]7 Some Septuagint manuscripts, Syriac and Josephus; Hebrew *forty*   [b]8 Some Septuagint manuscripts; Hebrew does not have *in Hebron.*   [c]24 Or *Abiathar went up*

palace. ³⁶Their two sons, Ahimaaz son of Zadok and Jonathan son of Abiathar, are there with them. Send them to me with anything you hear."

³⁷So David's friend Hushai arrived at Jerusalem as Absalom was entering the city.

David and Ziba

16 When David had gone a short distance beyond the summit, there was Ziba, the steward of Mephibosheth, waiting to meet him. He had a string of donkeys saddled and loaded with two hundred loaves of bread, a hundred cakes of raisins, a hundred cakes of figs and a skin of wine.

²The king asked Ziba, "Why have you brought these?"

Ziba answered, "The donkeys are for the king's household to ride on, the bread and fruit are for the men to eat, and the wine is to refresh those who become exhausted in the desert."

³The king then asked, "Where is your master's grandson?"

Ziba said to him, "He is staying in Jerusalem, because he thinks, 'Today the house of Israel will give me back my grandfather's kingdom.' "

⁴Then the king said to Ziba, "All that belonged to Mephibosheth is now yours."

"I humbly bow," Ziba said. "May I find favor in your eyes, my lord the king."

Shimei Curses David

⁵As King David approached Bahurim, a man from the same clan as Saul's family came out from there. His name was Shimei son of Gera, and he cursed as he came out. ⁶He pelted David and all the king's officials with stones, though all the troops and the special guard were on David's right and left. ⁷As he cursed, Shimei said, "Get out, get out, you man of blood, you scoundrel! ⁸The LORD has repaid you for all the blood you shed in the household of Saul, in whose place you have reigned. The LORD has handed the kingdom over to your son Absalom. You have come to ruin because you are a man of blood!"

⁹Then Abishai son of Zeruiah said to the king, "Why should this dead dog curse my lord the king? Let me go over and cut off his head."

¹⁰But the king said, "What do you and I have in common, you sons of Zeruiah? If he is cursing because the LORD said to

him, 'Curse David,' who can ask, 'Why do you do this?' "

¹¹David then said to Abishai and all his officials, "My son, who is of my own flesh, is trying to take my life. How much more, then, this Benjamite! Leave him alone; let him curse, for the LORD has told him to. ¹²It may be that the LORD will see my distress and repay me with good for the cursing I am receiving today."

¹³So David and his men continued along the road while Shimei was going along the hillside opposite him, cursing as he went and throwing stones at him and showering him with dirt. ¹⁴The king and all the people with him arrived at their destination exhausted. And there he refreshed himself.

The Advice of Hushai and Ahithophel

¹⁵Meanwhile, Absalom and all the men of Israel came to Jerusalem, and Ahithophel was with him. ¹⁶Then Hushai the Arkite, David's friend, went to Absalom and said to him, "Long live the king! Long live the king!"

¹⁷Absalom asked Hushai, "Is this the love you show your friend? Why didn't you go with your friend?"

¹⁸Hushai said to Absalom, "No, the one chosen by the LORD, by these people, and by all the men of Israel—his I will be, and I will remain with him. ¹⁹Furthermore, whom should I serve? Should I not serve the son? Just as I served your father, so I will serve you."

²⁰Absalom said to Ahithophel, "Give us your advice. What should we do?"

²¹Ahithophel answered, "Lie with your father's concubines whom he left to take care of the palace. Then all Israel will hear that you have made yourself a stench in your father's nostrils, and the hands of everyone with you will be strengthened." ²²So they pitched a tent for Absalom on the roof, and he lay with his father's concubines in the sight of all Israel.

²³Now in those days the advice Ahithophel gave was like that of one who inquires of God. That was how both David and Absalom regarded all of Ahithophel's advice.

17 Ahithophel said to Absalom, "I would*ᵃ* choose twelve thousand men and set out tonight in pursuit of David. ²I would*ᵇ* attack him while he is weary and weak. I would*ᵇ* strike him with terror, and then all the people with him will flee. I would*ᵇ*

ᵃ1 Or *Let me*   *ᵇ2* Or *will*

strike down only the king ³and bring all the people back to you. The death of the man you seek will mean the return of all; all the people will be unharmed." ⁴This plan seemed good to Absalom and to all the elders of Israel.

⁵But Absalom said, "Summon also Hushai the Arkite, so we can hear what he has to say." ⁶When Hushai came to him, Absalom said, "Ahithophel has given this advice. Should we do what he says? If not, give us your opinion."

⁷Hushai replied to Absalom, "The advice Ahithophel has given is not good this time. ⁸You know your father and his men; they are fighters, and as fierce as a wild bear robbed of her cubs. Besides, your father is an experienced fighter; he will not spend the night with the troops. ⁹Even now, he is hidden in a cave or some other place. If he should attack your troops first,ᵃ whoever hears about it will say, 'There has been a slaughter among the troops who follow Absalom.' ¹⁰Then even the bravest soldier, whose heart is like the heart of a lion, will melt with fear, for all Israel knows that your father is a fighter and that those with him are brave.

¹¹"So I advise you: Let all Israel, from Dan to Beersheba—as numerous as the sand on the seashore—be gathered to you, with you yourself leading them into battle. ¹²Then we will attack him wherever he may be found, and we will fall on him as dew settles on the ground. Neither he nor any of his men will be left alive. ¹³If he withdraws into a city, then all Israel will bring ropes to that city, and we will drag it down to the valley until not even a piece of it can be found."

¹⁴Absalom and all the men of Israel said, "The advice of Hushai the Arkite is better than that of Ahithophel." For the LORD had determined to frustrate the good advice of Ahithophel in order to bring disaster on Absalom.

¹⁵Hushai told Zadok and Abiathar, the priests, "Ahithophel has advised Absalom and the elders of Israel to do such and such, but I have advised them to do so and so. ¹⁶Now send a message immediately and tell David, 'Do not spend the night at the fords in the desert; cross over without fail, or the king and all the people with him will be swallowed up.' "

¹⁷Jonathan and Ahimaaz were staying at En Rogel. A servant girl was to go and inform them, and they were to go and tell King David, for they could not risk being seen entering the city. ¹⁸But a young man saw them and told Absalom. So the two of them left quickly and went to the house of a man in Bahurim. He had a well in his courtyard, and they climbed down into it. ¹⁹His wife took a covering and spread it out over the opening of the well and scattered grain over it. No one knew anything about it.

²⁰When Absalom's men came to the woman at the house, they asked, "Where are Ahimaaz and Jonathan?"

The woman answered them, "They crossed over the brook."ᵇ The men searched but found no one, so they returned to Jerusalem. ²¹After the men had gone, the two climbed out of the well and went to inform King David. They said to him, "Set out and cross the river at once; Ahithophel has advised such and such against you." ²²So David and all the people with him set out and crossed the Jordan. By daybreak, no one was left who had not crossed the Jordan.

²³When Ahithophel saw that his advice had not been followed, he saddled his donkey and set out for his house in his hometown. He put his house in order and then hanged himself. So he died and was buried in his father's tomb.

²⁴David went to Mahanaim, and Absalom crossed the Jordan with all the men of Israel. ²⁵Absalom had appointed Amasa over the army in place of Joab. Amasa was the son of a man named Jether,ᶜ an Israeliteᵈ who had married Abigail,ᵉ the daughter of Nahash and sister of Zeruiah the mother of Joab. ²⁶The Israelites and Absalom camped in the land of Gilead.

²⁷When David came to Mahanaim, Shobi son of Nahash from Rabbah of the Ammonites, and Makir son of Ammiel from Lo Debar, and Barzillai the Gileadite from Rogelim ²⁸brought bedding and bowls and articles of pottery. They also brought wheat and barley, flour and roasted grain, beans and lentils,ᶠ ²⁹honey and curds, sheep, and cheese from cows' milk for David and his people to eat. For they said, "The people have become hungry and tired and thirsty in the desert."

ᵃ9 Or *When some of the men fall at the first attack*
ᵇ20 Or *"They passed by the sheep pen toward the water."*   ᶜ25 Hebrew *Ithra,* a variant of *Jether*
ᵈ25 Hebrew and some Septuagint manuscripts; other Septuagint manuscripts (see also 1 Chron. 2:17) *Ishmaelite* or *Jezreelite*   ᵉ25 Hebrew *Abigal,* a variant of *Abigail*   ᶠ28 Most Septuagint manuscripts and Syriac; Hebrew *lentils, and roasted grain*

Absalom's Death

18 David mustered the men who were with him and appointed over them commanders of thousands and commanders of hundreds. ²David sent the troops out—a third under the command of Joab, a third under Joab's brother Abishai son of Zeruiah, and a third under Ittai the Gittite. The king told the troops, "I myself will surely march out with you."

³But the men said, "You must not go out; if we are forced to flee, they won't care about us. Even if half of us die, they won't

Love for a Lifetime

DAILY INSIGHT

FRIDAY
Passage:
2 Samuel 18:1–17, 25–33
Verse:
2 Samuel 18:5

Since my wife and I had no sons, and since our daughters opted for cheerleading and not for little league baseball or soccer, I never had the experience of standing behind the backstop or along the side lines while my child played on the field. However, having had the fun of watching my nephews play, I have seen many "out-of-bounds" dads. And what an interesting group they are.

Even though they express themselves differently, every single dad, if he could, would say to the coach, "Please take special care of my child. Give him more playing time than the rest of the children, and don't scold him when a ground ball scoots through his legs." Of course, most dads wouldn't stoop to begging like this, but it's what they really want. "After all," they'd say, "that's *my kid* out there." And I don't blame them.

Nor do I blame David for asking his senior commanding officers, headed toward a major battle, "Be gentle with the young man Absalom for my sake."

The fact is that Absalom didn't deserve special attention. He was literally in the process of leading an insurrection against his father, and he had apparently been successful in collecting some loyal troops. Unfortunately, his troops didn't save him from Joab, one of David's commanders. Finding the king's son caught in a tree by his long, thick hair, Joab plunged three javelins into Absalom's heart. So much for King David's heartfelt request.

When word came back to David that his son was dead, the king's heart was broken. "If only I had died instead of you," he sobbed.

Nothing is revealed in these verses about how much David knew of Absalom's plot. We can only surmise that he must have known something. After all, as with any good CEO, "nothing was hidden from the king."

So why did David weep? Why didn't he celebrate the demise of a traitor? The last four words of this chapter tell us everything … this dead man was David's beloved son.

The moment your child is conceived, you fall in love with this unknown person in your wife's womb. When he draws his first breath, the object of your affection is given a name, and you become "Dad." For the rest of your life you cheer for your child. Whether he's just holding his head up, rolling over on his own, eating solid food, standing, walking, making the pee wee soccer team … or shaking his fist in your face in open rebellion, he's yours and you love him.

You argue with him, you punish him, he breaks your heart, but you never stop loving him. He may even try to get you to stop loving him—and, for a time, he may be somewhat successful. But your heart will come back to loving him, nonetheless.

God has placed in our hearts a love for our children that cannot be broken. A love that is sustained through dropped fly balls and foolish, life-altering choices. A love that God himself has faithfully demonstrated to us, his rebellious and undeserving children.

Remove the conditions on your love. If you find this an unusually tough assignment, trust God with it. He's been there before—with you and with me.

For your next devotional reading, go to page 364.

care; but you are worth ten thousand of us.[a] It would be better now for you to give us support from the city."

[4]The king answered, "I will do whatever seems best to you."

So the king stood beside the gate while all the men marched out in units of hundreds and of thousands. [5]The king commanded Joab, Abishai and Ittai, "Be gentle with the young man Absalom for my sake." And all the troops heard the king giving orders concerning Absalom to each of the commanders.

[6]The army marched into the field to fight Israel, and the battle took place in the forest of Ephraim. [7]There the army of Israel was defeated by David's men, and the casualties that day were great—twenty thousand men. [8]The battle spread out over the whole countryside, and the forest claimed more lives that day than the sword.

[9]Now Absalom happened to meet David's men. He was riding his mule, and as the mule went under the thick branches of a large oak, Absalom's head got caught in the tree. He was left hanging in midair, while the mule he was riding kept on going.

[10]When one of the men saw this, he told Joab, "I just saw Absalom hanging in an oak tree."

[11]Joab said to the man who had told him this, "What! You saw him? Why didn't you strike him to the ground right there? Then I would have had to give you ten shekels[b] of silver and a warrior's belt."

[12]But the man replied, "Even if a thousand shekels[c] were weighed out into my hands, I would not lift my hand against the king's son. In our hearing the king commanded you and Abishai and Ittai, 'Protect the young man Absalom for my sake.[d]' [13]And if I had put my life in jeopardy[e]—and nothing is hidden from the king—you would have kept your distance from me."

[14]Joab said, "I'm not going to wait like this for you." So he took three javelins in his hand and plunged them into Absalom's heart while Absalom was still alive in the oak tree. [15]And ten of Joab's armor-bearers surrounded Absalom, struck him and killed him.

[16]Then Joab sounded the trumpet, and the troops stopped pursuing Israel, for Joab halted them. [17]They took Absalom, threw him into a big pit in the forest and piled up a large heap of rocks over him. Meanwhile, all the Israelites fled to their homes.

[18]During his lifetime Absalom had taken a pillar and erected it in the King's Valley as a monument to himself, for he thought, "I have no son to carry on the memory of my name." He named the pillar after himself, and it is called Absalom's Monument to this day.

David Mourns

[19]Now Ahimaaz son of Zadok said, "Let me run and take the news to the king that the Lord has delivered him from the hand of his enemies."

[20]"You are not the one to take the news today," Joab told him. "You may take the news another time, but you must not do so today, because the king's son is dead."

[21]Then Joab said to a Cushite, "Go, tell the king what you have seen." The Cushite bowed down before Joab and ran off.

[22]Ahimaaz son of Zadok again said to Joab, "Come what may, please let me run behind the Cushite."

But Joab replied, "My son, why do you want to go? You don't have any news that will bring you a reward."

[23]He said, "Come what may, I want to run."

So Joab said, "Run!" Then Ahimaaz ran by way of the plain[f] and outran the Cushite.

[24]While David was sitting between the inner and outer gates, the watchman went up to the roof of the gateway by the wall. As he looked out, he saw a man running alone. [25]The watchman called out to the king and reported it.

The king said, "If he is alone, he must have good news." And the man came closer and closer.

[26]Then the watchman saw another man running, and he called down to the gatekeeper, "Look, another man running alone!"

The king said, "He must be bringing good news, too."

[27]The watchman said, "It seems to me that the first one runs like Ahimaaz son of Zadok."

---

[a]3 Two Hebrew manuscripts, some Septuagint manuscripts and Vulgate; most Hebrew manuscripts care; for now there are ten thousand like us   [b]11 That is, about 4 ounces (about 115 grams)   [c]12 That is, about 25 pounds (about 11 kilograms)   [d]12 A few Hebrew manuscripts, Septuagint, Vulgate and Syriac; most Hebrew manuscripts may be translated Absalom, whoever you may be.   [e]13 Or Otherwise, if I had acted treacherously toward him   [f]23 That is, the plain of the Jordan

"He's a good man," the king said. "He comes with good news."

²⁸Then Ahimaaz called out to the king, "All is well!" He bowed down before the king with his face to the ground and said, "Praise be to the LORD your God! He has delivered up the men who lifted their hands against my lord the king."

²⁹The king asked, "Is the young man Absalom safe?"

Ahimaaz answered, "I saw great confusion just as Joab was about to send the king's servant and me, your servant, but I don't know what it was."

³⁰The king said, "Stand aside and wait here." So he stepped aside and stood there.

³¹Then the Cushite arrived and said, "My lord the king, hear the good news! The LORD has delivered you today from all who rose up against you."

³²The king asked the Cushite, "Is the young man Absalom safe?"

The Cushite replied, "May the enemies of my lord the king and all who rise up to harm you be like that young man."

³³The king was shaken. He went up to the room over the gateway and wept. As he went, he said: "O my son Absalom! My son, my son Absalom! If only I had died instead of you—O Absalom, my son, my son!"

19 Joab was told, "The king is weeping and mourning for Absalom." ²And for the whole army the victory that day was turned into mourning, because on that day the troops heard it said, "The king is grieving for his son." ³The men stole into the city that day as men steal in who are ashamed when they flee from battle. ⁴The king covered his face and cried aloud, "O my son Absalom! O Absalom, my son, my son!"

⁵Then Joab went into the house to the king and said, "Today you have humiliated all your men, who have just saved your life and the lives of your sons and daughters and the lives of your wives and concubines. ⁶You love those who hate you and hate those who love you. You have made it clear today that the commanders and their men mean nothing to you. I see that you would be pleased if Absalom were alive today and all of us were dead. ⁷Now go out and encourage your men. I swear by the LORD that if you don't go out, not a man will be left with you by nightfall. This will be worse for you than all the calamities that have come upon you from your youth till now."

⁸So the king got up and took his seat in the gateway. When the men were told, "The king is sitting in the gateway," they all came before him.

David Returns to Jerusalem

Meanwhile, the Israelites had fled to their homes. ⁹Throughout the tribes of Israel, the people were all arguing with each other, saying, "The king delivered us from the hand of our enemies; he is the one who rescued us from the hand of the Philistines. But now he has fled the country because of Absalom; ¹⁰and Absalom, whom we anointed to rule over us, has died in battle. So why do you say nothing about bringing the king back?"

¹¹King David sent this message to Zadok and Abiathar, the priests: "Ask the elders of Judah, 'Why should you be the last to bring the king back to his palace, since what is being said throughout Israel has reached the king at his quarters? ¹²You are my brothers, my own flesh and blood. So why should you be the last to bring back the king?' ¹³And say to Amasa, 'Are you not my own flesh and blood? May God deal with me, be it ever so severely, if from now on you are not the commander of my army in place of Joab.' "

¹⁴He won over the hearts of all the men of Judah as though they were one man. They sent word to the king, "Return, you and all your men." ¹⁵Then the king returned and went as far as the Jordan.

Now the men of Judah had come to Gilgal to go out and meet the king and bring him across the Jordan. ¹⁶Shimei son of Gera, the Benjamite from Bahurim, hurried down with the men of Judah to meet King David. ¹⁷With him were a thousand Benjamites, along with Ziba, the steward of Saul's household, and his fifteen sons and twenty servants. They rushed to the Jordan, where the king was. ¹⁸They crossed at the ford to take the king's household over and to do whatever he wished.

When Shimei son of Gera crossed the Jordan, he fell prostrate before the king ¹⁹and said to him, "May my lord not hold me guilty. Do not remember how your servant did wrong on the day my lord the king left Jerusalem. May the king put it out of his mind. ²⁰For I your servant know that I have sinned, but today I have come here as the first of the whole house of Joseph to come down and meet my lord the king."

²¹Then Abishai son of Zeruiah said, "Shouldn't Shimei be put to death for this? He cursed the LORD's anointed."

²²David replied, "What do you and I have in common, you sons of Zeruiah? This day you have become my adversaries! Should anyone be put to death in Israel today? Do I not know that today I am king over Israel?" ²³So the king said to Shimei, "You shall not die." And the king promised him on oath.

²⁴Mephibosheth, Saul's grandson, also went down to meet the king. He had not taken care of his feet or trimmed his mustache or washed his clothes from the day the king left until the day he returned safely. ²⁵When he came from Jerusalem to meet the king, the king asked him, "Why didn't you go with me, Mephibosheth?"

²⁶He said, "My lord the king, since I your servant am lame, I said, 'I will have my donkey saddled and will ride on it, so I can go with the king.' But Ziba my servant betrayed me. ²⁷And he has slandered your servant to my lord the king. My lord the king is like an angel of God; so do whatever pleases you. ²⁸All my grandfather's descendants deserved nothing but death from my lord the king, but you gave your servant a place among those who eat at your table. So what right do I have to make any more appeals to the king?"

²⁹The king said to him, "Why say more? I order you and Ziba to divide the fields."

³⁰Mephibosheth said to the king, "Let him take everything, now that my lord the king has arrived home safely."

³¹Barzillai the Gileadite also came down from Rogelim to cross the Jordan with the king and to send him on his way from there. ³²Now Barzillai was a very old man, eighty years of age. He had provided for the king during his stay in Mahanaim, for he was a very wealthy man. ³³The king said to Barzillai, "Cross over with me and stay with me in Jerusalem, and I will provide for you."

³⁴But Barzillai answered the king, "How many more years will I live, that I should go up to Jerusalem with the king? ³⁵I am now eighty years old. Can I tell the difference between what is good and what is not? Can your servant taste what he eats and drinks? Can I still hear the voices of men and women singers? Why should your servant be an added burden to my lord the king? ³⁶Your servant will cross over the Jordan with the king for a short distance, but why should the king reward me in this way? ³⁷Let your servant return,

that I may die in my own town near the tomb of my father and mother. But here is your servant Kimham. Let him cross over with my lord the king. Do for him whatever pleases you."

³⁸The king said, "Kimham shall cross over with me, and I will do for him whatever pleases you. And anything you desire from me I will do for you."

³⁹So all the people crossed the Jordan, and then the king crossed over. The king kissed Barzillai and gave him his blessing, and Barzillai returned to his home.

⁴⁰When the king crossed over to Gilgal, Kimham crossed with him. All the troops of Judah and half the troops of Israel had taken the king over.

⁴¹Soon all the men of Israel were coming to the king and saying to him, "Why did our brothers, the men of Judah, steal the king away and bring him and his household across the Jordan, together with all his men?"

⁴²All the men of Judah answered the men of Israel, "We did this because the king is closely related to us. Why are you angry about it? Have we eaten any of the king's provisions? Have we taken anything for ourselves?"

⁴³Then the men of Israel answered the men of Judah, "We have ten shares in the king; and besides, we have a greater claim on David than you have. So why do you treat us with contempt? Were we not the first to speak of bringing back our king?"

But the men of Judah responded even more harshly than the men of Israel.

Sheba Rebels Against David

20 Now a troublemaker named Sheba son of Bicri, a Benjamite, happened to be there. He sounded the trumpet and shouted,

"We have no share in David,
    no part in Jesse's son!
Every man to his tent, O Israel!"

²So all the men of Israel deserted David to follow Sheba son of Bicri. But the men of Judah stayed by their king all the way from the Jordan to Jerusalem.

³When David returned to his palace in Jerusalem, he took the ten concubines he had left to take care of the palace and put them in a house under guard. He provided for them, but did not lie with them. They were kept in confinement till the day of their death, living as widows.

⁴Then the king said to Amasa, "Sum-

mon the men of Judah to come to me within three days, and be here yourself." **5**But when Amasa went to summon Judah, he took longer than the time the king had set for him.

6David said to Abishai, "Now Sheba son of Bicri will do us more harm than Absalom did. Take your master's men and pursue him, or he will find fortified cities and escape from us." **7**So Joab's men and the Kerethites and Pelethites and all the mighty warriors went out under the command of Abishai. They marched out from Jerusalem to pursue Sheba son of Bicri.

8While they were at the great rock in Gibeon, Amasa came to meet them. Joab was wearing his military tunic, and strapped over it at his waist was a belt with a dagger in its sheath. As he stepped forward, it dropped out of its sheath.

9Joab said to Amasa, "How are you, my brother?" Then Joab took Amasa by the beard with his right hand to kiss him. **10**Amasa was not on his guard against the dagger in Joab's hand, and Joab plunged it into his belly, and his intestines spilled out on the ground. Without being stabbed again, Amasa died. Then Joab and his brother Abishai pursued Sheba son of Bicri.

11One of Joab's men stood beside Amasa and said, "Whoever favors Joab, and whoever is for David, let him follow Joab!" **12**Amasa lay wallowing in his blood in the middle of the road, and the man saw that all the troops came to a halt there. When he realized that everyone who came up to Amasa stopped, he dragged him from the road into a field and threw a garment over him. **13**After Amasa had been removed from the road, all the men went on with Joab to pursue Sheba son of Bicri.

14Sheba passed through all the tribes of Israel to Abel Beth Maacah*a* and through the entire region of the Berites, who gathered together and followed him. **15**All the troops with Joab came and besieged Sheba in Abel Beth Maacah. They built a siege ramp up to the city, and it stood against the outer fortifications. While they were battering the wall to bring it down, **16**a wise woman called from the city, "Listen! Listen! Tell Joab to come here so I can speak to him." **17**He went toward her, and she asked, "Are you Joab?"

"I am," he answered.

She said, "Listen to what your servant has to say."

"I'm listening," he said.

18She continued, "Long ago they used to say, 'Get your answer at Abel,' and that settled it. **19**We are the peaceful and faithful in Israel. You are trying to destroy a city that is a mother in Israel. Why do you want to swallow up the LORD's inheritance?"

20"Far be it from me!" Joab replied, "Far be it from me to swallow up or destroy! **21**That is not the case. A man named Sheba son of Bicri, from the hill country of Ephraim, has lifted up his hand against the king, against David. Hand over this one man, and I'll withdraw from the city."

The woman said to Joab, "His head will be thrown to you from the wall."

22Then the woman went to all the people with her wise advice, and they cut off the head of Sheba son of Bicri and threw it to Joab. So he sounded the trumpet, and his men dispersed from the city, each returning to his home. And Joab went back to the king in Jerusalem.

23Joab was over Israel's entire army; Benaiah son of Jehoiada was over the Kerethites and Pelethites; **24**Adoniram*b* was in charge of forced labor; Jehoshaphat son of Ahilud was recorder; **25**Sheva was secretary; Zadok and Abiathar were priests; **26**and Ira the Jairite was David's priest.

The Gibeonites Avenged

21 During the reign of David, there was a famine for three successive years; so David sought the face of the LORD. The LORD said, "It is on account of Saul and his blood-stained house; it is because he put the Gibeonites to death."

2The king summoned the Gibeonites and spoke to them. (Now the Gibeonites were not a part of Israel but were survivors of the Amorites; the Israelites had sworn to spare them, but Saul in his zeal for Israel and Judah had tried to annihilate them.) **3**David asked the Gibeonites, "What shall I do for you? How shall I make amends so that you will bless the LORD's inheritance?"

4The Gibeonites answered him, "We have no right to demand silver or gold from Saul or his family, nor do we have the right to put anyone in Israel to death."

"What do you want me to do for you?" David asked.

5They answered the king, "As for the man who destroyed us and plotted against us so that we have been decimated and

---

*a*14 Or *Abel, even Beth Maacah*; also in verse 15
*b*24 Some Septuagint manuscripts (see also 1 Kings 4:6 and 5:14); Hebrew *Adoram*

have no place anywhere in Israel, ⁶let seven of his male descendants be given to us to be killed and exposed before the LORD at Gibeah of Saul—the LORD's chosen one."

So the king said, "I will give them to you."

⁷The king spared Mephibosheth son of Jonathan, the son of Saul, because of the oath before the LORD between David and Jonathan son of Saul. ⁸But the king took Armoni and Mephibosheth, the two sons of Aiah's daughter Rizpah, whom she had borne to Saul, together with the five sons of Saul's daughter Merab,ᵃ whom she had borne to Adriel son of Barzillai the Meholathite. ⁹He handed them over to the Gibeonites, who killed and exposed them on a hill before the LORD. All seven of them fell together; they were put to death during the first days of the harvest, just as the barley harvest was beginning.

¹⁰Rizpah daughter of Aiah took sackcloth and spread it out for herself on a rock. From the beginning of the harvest till the rain poured down from the heavens on the bodies, she did not let the birds of the air touch them by day or the wild animals by night. ¹¹When David was told what Aiah's daughter Rizpah, Saul's concubine, had done, ¹²he went and took the bones of Saul and his son Jonathan from the citizens of Jabesh Gilead. (They had taken them secretly from the public square at Beth Shan, where the Philistines had hung them after they struck Saul down on Gilboa.) ¹³David brought the bones of Saul and his son Jonathan from there, and the bones of those who had been killed and exposed were gathered up.

¹⁴They buried the bones of Saul and his son Jonathan in the tomb of Saul's father Kish, at Zela in Benjamin, and did everything the king commanded. After that, God answered prayer in behalf of the land.

Wars Against the Philistines

¹⁵Once again there was a battle between the Philistines and Israel. David went down with his men to fight against the Philistines, and he became exhausted. ¹⁶And Ishbi-Benob, one of the descendants of Rapha, whose bronze spearhead weighed three hundred shekelsᵇ and who was armed with a new sword, said he would kill David. ¹⁷But Abishai son of Zeruiah came to David's rescue; he struck the

Philistine down and killed him. Then David's men swore to him, saying, "Never again will you go out with us to battle, so that the lamp of Israel will not be extinguished."

¹⁸In the course of time, there was another battle with the Philistines, at Gob. At that time Sibbecai the Hushathite killed Saph, one of the descendants of Rapha. ¹⁹In another battle with the Philistines at Gob, Elhanan son of Jaare-Oregimᶜ the Bethlehemite killed Goliathᵈ the Gittite, who had a spear with a shaft like a weaver's rod.

²⁰In still another battle, which took place at Gath, there was a huge man with six fingers on each hand and six toes on each foot—twenty-four in all. He also was descended from Rapha. ²¹When he taunted Israel, Jonathan son of Shimeah, David's brother, killed him.

²²These four were descendants of Rapha in Gath, and they fell at the hands of David and his men.

David's Song of Praise

22 David sang to the LORD the words of this song when the LORD delivered him from the hand of all his enemies and from the hand of Saul. ²He said:

"The LORD is my rock, my fortress and
      my deliverer;
³   my God is my rock, in whom I take
      refuge,
    my shield and the hornᵉ of my
      salvation.
    He is my stronghold, my refuge and my
      savior—
    from violent men you save me.
⁴I call to the LORD, who is worthy of
      praise,
    and I am saved from my enemies.

⁵"The waves of death swirled about me;
    the torrents of destruction
      overwhelmed me.
⁶The cords of the graveᶠ coiled around
      me;
    the snares of death confronted me.
⁷In my distress I called to the LORD;
    I called out to my God.

ᵃ8 Two Hebrew manuscripts, some Septuagint manuscripts and Syriac (see also 1 Samuel 18:19); most Hebrew and Septuagint manuscripts *Michal*   ᵇ16 That is, about 7 1/2 pounds (about 3.5 kilograms)   ᶜ19 Or *son of Jair the weaver*   ᵈ19 Hebrew and Septuagint; 1 Chron. 20:5 *son of Jair killed Lahmi the brother of Goliath*   ᵉ3 Horn here symbolizes strength.   ᶠ6 Hebrew *Sheol*

From his temple he heard my voice;
  my cry came to his ears.

⁸ "The earth trembled and quaked,
    the foundations of the heavens*a*
      shook;
    they trembled because he was angry.
⁹ Smoke rose from his nostrils;
    consuming fire came from his
      mouth,
    burning coals blazed out of it.
¹⁰ He parted the heavens and came down;
    dark clouds were under his feet.
¹¹ He mounted the cherubim and flew;
    he soared*b* on the wings of the wind.
¹² He made darkness his canopy around
      him—
    the dark*c* rain clouds of the sky.
¹³ Out of the brightness of his presence
    bolts of lightning blazed forth.
¹⁴ The LORD thundered from heaven;
    the voice of the Most High
      resounded.
¹⁵ He shot arrows and scattered the
      enemies,
    bolts of lightning and routed them.
¹⁶ The valleys of the sea were exposed
    and the foundations of the earth laid
      bare
  at the rebuke of the LORD,
    at the blast of breath from his nostrils.

¹⁷ "He reached down from on high and
      took hold of me;
    he drew me out of deep waters.
¹⁸ He rescued me from my powerful
      enemy,
    from my foes, who were too strong
      for me.
¹⁹ They confronted me in the day of my
      disaster,
    but the LORD was my support.
²⁰ He brought me out into a spacious
      place;
    he rescued me because he delighted
      in me.

²¹ "The LORD has dealt with me according
      to my righteousness;
    according to the cleanness of my
      hands he has rewarded me.
²² For I have kept the ways of the LORD;
    I have not done evil by turning from
      my God.
²³ All his laws are before me;
    I have not turned away from his
      decrees.
²⁴ I have been blameless before him
    and have kept myself from sin.
²⁵ The LORD has rewarded me according
      to my righteousness,

according to my cleanness*d* in his
      sight.

²⁶ "To the faithful you show yourself
      faithful,
    to the blameless you show yourself
      blameless,
²⁷ to the pure you show yourself pure,
    but to the crooked you show yourself
      shrewd.
²⁸ You save the humble,
    but your eyes are on the haughty to
      bring them low.
²⁹ You are my lamp, O LORD;
    the LORD turns my darkness into
      light.
³⁰ With your help I can advance against a
      troop*e*;
    with my God I can scale a wall.

³¹ "As for God, his way is perfect;
    the word of the LORD is flawless.
  He is a shield
    for all who take refuge in him.
³² For who is God besides the LORD?
    And who is the Rock except our God?
³³ It is God who arms me with strength*f*
    and makes my way perfect.
³⁴ He makes my feet like the feet of a
      deer;
    he enables me to stand on the
      heights.
³⁵ He trains my hands for battle;
    my arms can bend a bow of bronze.
³⁶ You give me your shield of victory;
    you stoop down to make me great.
³⁷ You broaden the path beneath me,
    so that my ankles do not turn.

³⁸ "I pursued my enemies and crushed
      them;
    I did not turn back till they were
      destroyed.
³⁹ I crushed them completely, and they
      could not rise;
    they fell beneath my feet.
⁴⁰ You armed me with strength for battle;
    you made my adversaries bow at my
      feet.
⁴¹ You made my enemies turn their backs
      in flight,
    and I destroyed my foes.

---

a8 Hebrew; Vulgate and Syriac (see also Psalm 18:7)
mountains   *b11* Many Hebrew manuscripts (see
also Psalm 18:10); most Hebrew manuscripts
appeared   *c12* Septuagint and Vulgate (see also
Psalm 18:11); Hebrew *massed*   *d25* Hebrew;
Septuagint and Vulgate (see also Psalm 18:24) *to
the cleanness of my hands*   *e30* Or *can run through
a barricade*   *f33* Dead Sea Scrolls, some Septuagint
manuscripts, Vulgate and Syriac (see also Psalm
18:32); Masoretic Text *who is my strong refuge*

42They cried for help, but there was no
one to save them—
to the LORD, but he did not answer.
43I beat them as fine as the dust of the
earth;
I pounded and trampled them like
mud in the streets.

44"You have delivered me from the
attacks of my people;
you have preserved me as the head
of nations.
People I did not know are subject to me,
45   and foreigners come cringing to me;
as soon as they hear me, they obey
me.
46They all lose heart;
they come trembling[a] from their
strongholds.

47"The LORD lives! Praise be to my Rock!
Exalted be God, the Rock, my Savior!
48He is the God who avenges me,
who puts the nations under me,
49   who sets me free from my enemies.
You exalted me above my foes;
from violent men you rescued me.
50Therefore I will praise you, O LORD,
among the nations;
I will sing praises to your name.
51He gives his king great victories;
he shows unfailing kindness to his
anointed,
to David and his descendants
forever."

The Last Words of David

23 These are the last words of David:

"The oracle of David son of Jesse,
the oracle of the man exalted by the
Most High,
the man anointed by the God of Jacob,
Israel's singer of songs[b].

2"The Spirit of the LORD spoke through
me;
his word was on my tongue.
3The God of Israel spoke,
the Rock of Israel said to me:
'When one rules over men in
righteousness,
when he rules in the fear of God,
4he is like the light of morning at sunrise
on a cloudless morning,
like the brightness after rain
that brings the grass from the earth.'

5"Is not my house right with God?
Has he not made with me an
everlasting covenant,

arranged and secured in every part?
Will he not bring to fruition my
salvation
and grant me my every desire?
6But evil men are all to be cast aside like
thorns,
which are not gathered with the
hand.
7Whoever touches thorns
uses a tool of iron or the shaft of a
spear;
they are burned up where they lie."

David's Mighty Men

8These are the names of David's mighty
men:

Josheb-Basshebeth,[c] a Tahkemonite,[d]
was chief of the Three; he raised his spear
against eight hundred men, whom he
killed[e] in one encounter.

9Next to him was Eleazar son of Dodai
the Ahohite. As one of the three mighty
men, he was with David when they taunted the Philistines gathered at Pas
Dammim,[f] for battle. Then the men of Israel retreated, **10**but he stood his ground
and struck down the Philistines till his
hand grew tired and froze to the sword.
The LORD brought about a great victory
that day. The troops returned to Eleazar,
but only to strip the dead.

11Next to him was Shammah son of
Agee the Hararite. When the Philistines
banded together at a place where there
was a field full of lentils, Israel's troops
fled from them. **12**But Shammah took his
stand in the middle of the field. He defended it and struck the Philistines down,
and the LORD brought about a great victory.

13During harvest time, three of the thirty chief men came down to David at the
cave of Adullam, while a band of Philistines was encamped in the Valley of Rephaim. **14**At that time David was in the
stronghold, and the Philistine garrison
was at Bethlehem. **15**David longed for water and said, "Oh, that someone would get
me a drink of water from the well near the

---

[a]46 Some Septuagint manuscripts and Vulgate (see
also Psalm 18:45); Masoretic Text *they arm
themselves.*   [b]1 Or *Israel's beloved singer*
[c]8 Hebrew; some Septuagint manuscripts suggest
Ish-Bosheth, that is, *Esh-Baal* (see also 1 Chron.
11:11 *Jashobeam*).   [d]8 Probably a variant of
Hacmonite (see 1 Chron. 11:11)   [e]8 Some
Septuagint manuscripts (see also 1 Chron. 11:11);
Hebrew and other Septuagint manuscripts *Three; it
was Adino the Eznite who killed eight hundred men*
[f]9 See 1 Chron. 11:13; Hebrew *gathered there.*

gate of Bethlehem!" [16]So the three mighty men broke through the Philistine lines, drew water from the well near the gate of Bethlehem and carried it back to David. But he refused to drink it; instead, he poured it out before the LORD. [17]"Far be it from me, O LORD, to do this!" he said. "Is it not the blood of men who went at the risk of their lives?" And David would not drink it.

Such were the exploits of the three mighty men.

[18]Abishai the brother of Joab son of Zeruiah was chief of the Three.[a] He raised his spear against three hundred men, whom he killed, and so he became as famous as the Three. [19]Was he not held in greater honor than the Three? He became their commander, even though he was not included among them.

[20]Benaiah son of Jehoiada was a valiant fighter from Kabzeel, who performed great exploits. He struck down two of Moab's best men. He also went down into a pit on a snowy day and killed a lion. [21]And he struck down a huge Egyptian. Although the Egyptian had a spear in his hand, Benaiah went against him with a club. He snatched the spear from the Egyptian's hand and killed him with his own spear. [22]Such were the exploits of Benaiah son of Jehoiada; he too was as famous as the three mighty men. [23]He was held in greater honor than any of the Thirty, but he was not included among the Three. And David put him in charge of his bodyguard.

[24]Among the Thirty were:
Asahel the brother of Joab,
Elhanan son of Dodo from Bethlehem,
[25]Shammah the Harodite,
Elika the Harodite,
[26]Helez the Paltite,
Ira son of Ikkesh from Tekoa,
[27]Abiezer from Anathoth,
Mebunnai[b] the Hushathite,
[28]Zalmon the Ahohite,
Maharai the Netophathite,
[29]Heled[c] son of Baanah the Netophathite,
Ithai son of Ribai from Gibeah in Benjamin,
[30]Benaiah the Pirathonite,
Hiddai[d] from the ravines of Gaash,
[31]Abi-Albon the Arbathite,
Azmaveth the Barhumite,
[32]Eliahba the Shaalbonite,
the sons of Jashen,

Jonathan [33]son of[e] Shammah the Hararite,
Ahiam son of Sharar[f] the Hararite,
[34]Eliphelet son of Ahasbai the Maacathite,
Eliam son of Ahithophel the Gilonite,
[35]Hezro the Carmelite,
Paarai the Arbite,
[36]Igal son of Nathan from Zobah,
the son of Hagri,[g]
[37]Zelek the Ammonite,
Naharai the Beerothite, the armorbearer of Joab son of Zeruiah,
[38]Ira the Ithrite,
Gareb the Ithrite
[39]and Uriah the Hittite.
There were thirty-seven in all.

David Counts the Fighting Men

24 Again the anger of the LORD burned against Israel, and he incited David against them, saying, "Go and take a census of Israel and Judah."

[2]So the king said to Joab and the army commanders[h] with him, "Go throughout the tribes of Israel from Dan to Beersheba and enroll the fighting men, so that I may know how many there are."

[3]But Joab replied to the king, "May the LORD your God multiply the troops a hundred times over, and may the eyes of my lord the king see it. But why does my lord the king want to do such a thing?"

[4]The king's word, however, overruled Joab and the army commanders; so they left the presence of the king to enroll the fighting men of Israel.

[5]After crossing the Jordan, they camped near Aroer, south of the town in the gorge, and then went through Gad and on to Jazer. [6]They went to Gilead and the region of Tahtim Hodshi, and on to Dan Jaan and around toward Sidon. [7]Then they went toward the fortress of Tyre and all the towns of the Hivites and Canaanites. Finally,

---

[a]18 Most Hebrew manuscripts (see also 1 Chron. 11:20); two Hebrew manuscripts and Syriac *Thirty* [b]27 Hebrew; some Septuagint manuscripts (see also 1 Chron. 11:29) *Sibbecai* [c]29 Some Hebrew manuscripts and Vulgate (see also 1 Chron. 11:30); most Hebrew manuscripts *Heleb* [d]30 Hebrew; some Septuagint manuscripts (see also 1 Chron. 11:32) *Hurai* [e]33 Some Septuagint manuscripts (see also 1 Chron. 11:34); Hebrew does not have *son of.* [f]33 Hebrew; some Septuagint manuscripts (see also 1 Chron. 11:35) *Sacar* [g]36 Some Septuagint manuscripts (see also 1 Chron. 11:38); Hebrew *Haggadi* [h]2 Septuagint (see also verse 4 and 1 Chron. 21:2); Hebrew *Joab the army commander*

they went on to Beersheba in the Negev of Judah.

⁸After they had gone through the entire land, they came back to Jerusalem at the end of nine months and twenty days.

⁹Joab reported the number of the fighting men to the king: In Israel there were eight hundred thousand able-bodied men who could handle a sword, and in Judah five hundred thousand.

¹⁰David was conscience-stricken after he had counted the fighting men, and he said to the LORD, "I have sinned greatly in what I have done. Now, O LORD, I beg you, take away the guilt of your servant. I have done a very foolish thing."

¹¹Before David got up the next morning, the word of the LORD had come to Gad the prophet, David's seer: ¹²"Go and tell David, 'This is what the LORD says: I am giving you three options. Choose one of them for me to carry out against you.' "

¹³So Gad went to David and said to him, "Shall there come upon you three^a years of famine in your land? Or three months of fleeing from your enemies while they pursue you? Or three days of plague in your land? Now then, think it over and decide how I should answer the one who sent me."

¹⁴David said to Gad, "I am in deep distress. Let us fall into the hands of the LORD, for his mercy is great; but do not let me fall into the hands of men."

¹⁵So the LORD sent a plague on Israel from that morning until the end of the time designated, and seventy thousand of the people from Dan to Beersheba died. ¹⁶When the angel stretched out his hand to destroy Jerusalem, the LORD was grieved because of the calamity and said to the angel who was afflicting the people, "Enough! Withdraw your hand." The angel of the LORD was then at the threshing floor of Araunah the Jebusite.

¹⁷When David saw the angel who was striking down the people, he said to the LORD, "I am the one who has sinned and done wrong. These are but sheep. What have they done? Let your hand fall upon me and my family."

David Builds an Altar

¹⁸On that day Gad went to David and said to him, "Go up and build an altar to the LORD on the threshing floor of Araunah the Jebusite." ¹⁹So David went up, as the LORD had commanded through Gad. ²⁰When Araunah looked and saw the king and his men coming toward him, he went out and bowed down before the king with his face to the ground.

²¹Araunah said, "Why has my lord the king come to his servant?"

"To buy your threshing floor," David answered, "so I can build an altar to the LORD, that the plague on the people may be stopped."

²²Araunah said to David, "Let my lord the king take whatever pleases him and offer it up. Here are oxen for the burnt offering, and here are threshing sledges and ox yokes for the wood. ²³O king, Araunah gives all this to the king." Araunah also said to him, "May the LORD your God accept you."

²⁴But the king replied to Araunah, "No, I insist on paying you for it. I will not sacrifice to the LORD my God burnt offerings that cost me nothing."

So David bought the threshing floor and the oxen and paid fifty shekels^b of silver for them. ²⁵David built an altar to the LORD there and sacrificed burnt offerings and fellowship offerings.^c Then the LORD answered prayer in behalf of the land, and the plague on Israel was stopped.

---

^a13 Septuagint (see also 1 Chron. 21:12); Hebrew *seven* ^b24 That is, about 1 1/4 pounds (about 0.6 kilogram) ^c25 Traditionally *peace offerings*

For many people who enjoy watching track and field meets, there is no more exciting event than the relay race. Most track coaches will tell you that this race, a thrilling combination of individual and team competition, is often won or lost in the exchange area. An athlete can waste his entire running effort if he's careless about the way he hands the baton to the next runner.

Reading the book of 1 Kings is like watching a relay race. We see crisp exchanges (such as the one from David to Solomon) and a few pretty sloppy ones (such as the one from Solomon to his sons). This book is a powerful reminder to dads that life's race has two parts: first, how well you run it; and second, how well you pass the baton to your children. In order to win, you've got to be proficient in both of these skills. Read this book as a coach's manual for success in life's relay race.

1 Kings

Adonijah Sets Himself Up as King

1 When King David was old and well advanced in years, he could not keep warm even when they put covers over him. [2]So his servants said to him, "Let us look for a young virgin to attend the king and take care of him. She can lie beside him so that our lord the king may keep warm."

[3]Then they searched throughout Israel for a beautiful girl and found Abishag, a Shunammite, and brought her to the king. [4]The girl was very beautiful; she took care of the king and waited on him, but the king had no intimate relations with her.

[5]Now Adonijah, whose mother was Haggith, put himself forward and said, "I will be king." So he got chariots and horses[a] ready, with fifty men to run ahead

of him. [6](His father had never interfered with him by asking, "Why do you behave as you do?" He was also very handsome and was born next after Absalom.)

[7]Adonijah conferred with Joab son of Zeruiah and with Abiathar the priest, and they gave him their support. [8]But Zadok the priest, Benaiah son of Jehoiada, Nathan the prophet, Shimei and Rei[b] and David's special guard did not join Adonijah.

[9]Adonijah then sacrificed sheep, cattle and fattened calves at the Stone of Zoheleth near En Rogel. He invited all his brothers, the king's sons, and all the men of Judah who were royal officials, [10]but he did not invite Nathan the prophet or Benaiah or the special guard or his brother Solomon.

a5 Or charioteers   *b8 Or and his friends*

¹¹Then Nathan asked Bathsheba, Solomon's mother, "Have you not heard that Adonijah, the son of Haggith, has become king without our lord David's knowing it? ¹²Now then, let me advise you how you can save your own life and the life of your son Solomon. ¹³Go in to King David and say to him, 'My lord the king, did you not swear to me your servant: "Surely Solomon your son shall be king after me, and he will sit on my throne"? Why then has Adonijah become king?' ¹⁴While you are still there talking to the king, I will come in and confirm what you have said."

¹⁵So Bathsheba went to see the aged king in his room, where Abishag the Shunammite was attending him. ¹⁶Bathsheba bowed low and knelt before the king.

"What is it you want?" the king asked.

¹⁷She said to him, "My lord, you yourself swore to me your servant by the LORD your God: 'Solomon your son shall be king after me, and he will sit on my throne.' ¹⁸But now Adonijah has become king, and you, my lord the king, do not know about it. ¹⁹He has sacrificed great numbers of cattle, fattened calves, and sheep, and has invited all the king's sons, Abiathar the priest and Joab the commander of the army, but he has not invited Solomon your servant. ²⁰My lord the king, the eyes of all Israel are on you, to learn from you who will sit on the throne of my lord the king after him. ²¹Otherwise, as soon as my lord the king is laid to rest with his fathers, I and my son Solomon will be treated as criminals."

²²While she was still speaking with the king, Nathan the prophet arrived. ²³And they told the king, "Nathan the prophet is here." So he went before the king and bowed with his face to the ground.

²⁴Nathan said, "Have you, my lord the king, declared that Adonijah shall be king after you, and that he will sit on your throne? ²⁵Today he has gone down and sacrificed great numbers of cattle, fattened calves, and sheep. He has invited all the king's sons, the commanders of the army and Abiathar the priest. Right now they are eating and drinking with him and saying, 'Long live King Adonijah!' ²⁶But me your servant, and Zadok the priest, and Benaiah son of Jehoiada, and your servant Solomon he did not invite. ²⁷Is this something my lord the king has done without letting his servants know who should sit on the throne of my lord the king after him?"

David Makes Solomon King

²⁸Then King David said, "Call in Bathsheba." So she came into the king's presence and stood before him.

²⁹The king then took an oath: "As surely as the LORD lives, who has delivered me out of every trouble, ³⁰I will surely carry out today what I swore to you by the LORD, the God of Israel: Solomon your son shall be king after me, and he will sit on my throne in my place."

³¹Then Bathsheba bowed low with her face to the ground and, kneeling before the king, said, "May my lord King David live forever!"

³²King David said, "Call in Zadok the priest, Nathan the prophet and Benaiah son of Jehoiada." When they came before the king, ³³he said to them: "Take your lord's servants with you and set Solomon my son on my own mule and take him down to Gihon. ³⁴There have Zadok the priest and Nathan the prophet anoint him king over Israel. Blow the trumpet and shout, 'Long live King Solomon!' ³⁵Then you are to go up with him, and he is to come and sit on my throne and reign in my place. I have appointed him ruler over Israel and Judah."

³⁶Benaiah son of Jehoiada answered the king, "Amen! May the LORD, the God of my lord the king, so declare it. ³⁷As the LORD was with my lord the king, so may he be with Solomon to make his throne even greater than the throne of my lord King David!"

³⁸So Zadok the priest, Nathan the prophet, Benaiah son of Jehoiada, the Kerethites and the Pelethites went down and put Solomon on King David's mule and escorted him to Gihon. ³⁹Zadok the priest took the horn of oil from the sacred tent and anointed Solomon. Then they sounded the trumpet and all the people shouted, "Long live King Solomon!" ⁴⁰And all the people went up after him, playing flutes and rejoicing greatly, so that the ground shook with the sound.

⁴¹Adonijah and all the guests who were with him heard it as they were finishing their feast. On hearing the sound of the trumpet, Joab asked, "What's the meaning of all the noise in the city?"

⁴²Even as he was speaking, Jonathan son of Abiathar the priest arrived. Adonijah said, "Come in. A worthy man like you must be bringing good news."

⁴³"Not at all!" Jonathan answered. "Our lord King David has made Solomon king.

⁴⁴The king has sent with him Zadok the priest, Nathan the prophet, Benaiah son of Jehoiada, the Kerethites and the Pelethites, and they have put him on the king's mule, ⁴⁵and Zadok the priest and Nathan the prophet have anointed him king at Gihon. From there they have gone up cheering, and the city resounds with it. That's the noise you hear. ⁴⁶Moreover, Solomon has taken his seat on the royal throne. ⁴⁷Also, the royal officials have come to congratulate our lord King David, saying, 'May your God make Solomon's name more famous than yours and his throne greater than yours!' And the king bowed in worship on his bed ⁴⁸and said, 'Praise be to the LORD, the God of Israel, who has allowed my eyes to see a successor on my throne today.' "

⁴⁹At this, all Adonijah's guests rose in alarm and dispersed. ⁵⁰But Adonijah, in fear of Solomon, went and took hold of the horns of the altar. ⁵¹Then Solomon was told, "Adonijah is afraid of King Solomon and is clinging to the horns of the altar. He says, 'Let King Solomon swear to me today that he will not put his servant to death with the sword.' "

⁵²Solomon replied, "If he shows himself to be a worthy man, not a hair of his head will fall to the ground; but if evil is found in him, he will die." ⁵³Then King Solomon sent men, and they brought him down from the altar. And Adonijah came and bowed down to King Solomon, and Solomon said, "Go to your home."

David's Charge to Solomon

2 When the time drew near for David to die, he gave a charge to Solomon his son.

²"I am about to go the way of all the earth," he said. "So be strong, show yourself a man, ³and observe what the LORD your God requires: Walk in his ways, and keep his decrees and commands, his laws and requirements, as written in the Law of Moses, so that you may prosper in all you do and wherever you go, ⁴and that the LORD may keep his promise to me: 'If your descendants watch how they live, and if they walk faithfully before me with all their heart and soul, you will never fail to have a man on the throne of Israel.'

⁵"Now you yourself know what Joab son of Zeruiah did to me—what he did to the two commanders of Israel's armies, Abner son of Ner and Amasa son of Jether. He killed them, shedding their blood in peacetime as if in battle, and with that blood stained the belt around his waist and the sandals on his feet. ⁶Deal with him according to your wisdom, but do not let his gray head go down to the grave*a* in peace.

⁷"But show kindness to the sons of Barzillai of Gilead and let them be among those who eat at your table. They stood by me when I fled from your brother Absalom.

⁸"And remember, you have with you Shimei son of Gera, the Benjamite from Bahurim, who called down bitter curses on me the day I went to Mahanaim. When he came down to meet me at the Jordan, I swore to him by the LORD: 'I will not put you to death by the sword.' ⁹But now, do not consider him innocent. You are a man of wisdom; you will know what to do to him. Bring his gray head down to the grave in blood."

¹⁰Then David rested with his fathers and was buried in the City of David. ¹¹He had reigned forty years over Israel—seven years in Hebron and thirty-three in Jerusalem. ¹²So Solomon sat on the throne of his father David, and his rule was firmly established.

Solomon's Throne Established

¹³Now Adonijah, the son of Haggith, went to Bathsheba, Solomon's mother. Bathsheba asked him, "Do you come peacefully?"

He answered, "Yes, peacefully." ¹⁴Then he added, "I have something to say to you."

"You may say it," she replied.

¹⁵"As you know," he said, "the kingdom was mine. All Israel looked to me as their king. But things changed, and the kingdom has gone to my brother; for it has come to him from the LORD. ¹⁶Now I have one request to make of you. Do not refuse me."

"You may make it," she said.

¹⁷So he continued, "Please ask King Solomon—he will not refuse you—to give me Abishag the Shunammite as my wife."

¹⁸"Very well," Bathsheba replied, "I will speak to the king for you."

¹⁹When Bathsheba went to King Solomon to speak to him for Adonijah, the king stood up to meet her, bowed down to her and sat down on his throne. He had a throne brought for the king's mother, and she sat down at his right hand.

---

a6 Hebrew *Sheol*; also in verse 9

Key Verse: *"Observe what the LORD your God requires: Walk in his ways, and keep his decrees and commands, his laws and requirements . . . . so that you may prosper in all you do and wherever you go."* 1 Kings 2:3

Text: 1 Kings 2:1–4 *(Dad or child reads the text.)*

QUIET
TIMES
WITH **Dad**

DAD READS: Have you ever seen a television show or a movie that shows a person who is about to die? His friends are gathered around him, and he's telling them some pretty important things.

Child reads: The words a dying person speaks will be remembered by those people standing there for the rest of their lives. These may be the most important things they have ever heard this person say.

DAD READS: King David was about to take his last breath. And Solomon was standing right there next to his dad. I'm sure that Solomon was very sad. He and his dad loved each other very much, and now they had to say good-bye. But before they did, David had a few things he wanted his son to remember. These are the words we read today . . . "My son, please follow God, please obey his laws, and then you will be successful."

Child reads: Just as David helped Solomon, I know that, for the rest of your life, you want to help me do these things. I know that you want me to follow God, to obey his laws, and to be successful, too.

DAD READS: Yes, I do—more than anything in the world. And I know that by doing these things myself, I am giving you something to follow—an

example on which to pattern your life. There is nothing more important that I can do with the rest of my life.

Child reads: I may be the luckiest kid alive to have a dad who wants to be a godly man. Thank you for giving me something to shoot for. I want to be a godly person, too. Let me pray this prayer with you:

Our Father in heaven, thank you for giving my dad and me time together. Thank you that, even though the words we have said to each other today are not his last words, they are still very, very important. Please help my dad and me to follow you and obey you. And thank you for giving us the kind of success that makes you happy. We love you. In Jesus' name, Amen.

For your next devotional reading, go to page 367.

²⁰"I have one small request to make of you," she said. "Do not refuse me."

The king replied, "Make it, my mother; I will not refuse you."

²¹So she said, "Let Abishag the Shunammite be given in marriage to your brother Adonijah."

²²King Solomon answered his mother, "Why do you request Abishag the Shunammite for Adonijah? You might as well request the kingdom for him—after all, he is my older brother—yes, for him and for Abiathar the priest and Joab son of Zeruiah!"

²³Then King Solomon swore by the LORD: "May God deal with me, be it ever so severely, if Adonijah does not pay with his life for this request! ²⁴And now, as surely as the LORD lives—he who has established me securely on the throne of my father David and has founded a dynasty for me as he promised—Adonijah shall be put to death today!" ²⁵So King Solomon gave orders to Benaiah son of Jehoiada, and he struck down Adonijah and he died.

²⁶To Abiathar the priest the king said, "Go back to your fields in Anathoth. You deserve to die, but I will not put you to death now, because you carried the ark of the Sovereign LORD before my father David and shared all my father's hardships." ²⁷So Solomon removed Abiathar from the priesthood of the LORD, fulfilling the word the LORD had spoken at Shiloh about the house of Eli.

²⁸When the news reached Joab, who had conspired with Adonijah though not with Absalom, he fled to the tent of the LORD and took hold of the horns of the altar. ²⁹King Solomon was told that Joab had fled to the tent of the LORD and was beside the altar. Then Solomon ordered Benaiah son of Jehoiada, "Go, strike him down!"

³⁰So Benaiah entered the tent of the LORD and said to Joab, "The king says, 'Come out!'"

But he answered, "No, I will die here."

Benaiah reported to the king, "This is how Joab answered me."

³¹Then the king commanded Benaiah, "Do as he says. Strike him down and bury him, and so clear me and my father's house of the guilt of the innocent blood that Joab shed. ³²The LORD will repay him for the blood he shed, because without the knowledge of my father David he attacked two men and killed them with the sword. Both of them—Abner son of Ner, commander of Israel's army, and Amasa son of Jether, commander of Judah's army—were better men and more upright than he. ³³May the guilt of their blood rest on the head of Joab and his descendants forever. But on David and his descendants, his house and his throne, may there be the LORD's peace forever."

³⁴So Benaiah son of Jehoiada went up and struck down Joab and killed him, and he was buried on his own land*ᵃ* in the desert. ³⁵The king put Benaiah son of Jehoiada over the army in Joab's position and replaced Abiathar with Zadok the priest.

³⁶Then the king sent for Shimei and said to him, "Build yourself a house in Jerusalem and live there, but do not go anywhere else. ³⁷The day you leave and cross the Kidron Valley, you can be sure you will die; your blood will be on your own head."

³⁸Shimei answered the king, "What you say is good. Your servant will do as my lord the king has said." And Shimei stayed in Jerusalem for a long time.

³⁹But three years later, two of Shimei's slaves ran off to Achish son of Maacah, king of Gath, and Shimei was told, "Your slaves are in Gath." ⁴⁰At this, he saddled his donkey and went to Achish at Gath in search of his slaves. So Shimei went away and brought the slaves back from Gath.

⁴¹When Solomon was told that Shimei had gone from Jerusalem to Gath and had returned, ⁴²the king summoned Shimei and said to him, "Did I not make you swear by the LORD and warn you, 'On the day you leave to go anywhere else, you can be sure you will die'? At that time you said to me, 'What you say is good. I will obey.' ⁴³Why then did you not keep your oath to the LORD and obey the command I gave you?"

⁴⁴The king also said to Shimei, "You know in your heart all the wrong you did to my father David. Now the LORD will repay you for your wrongdoing. ⁴⁵But King Solomon will be blessed, and David's throne will remain secure before the LORD forever."

⁴⁶Then the king gave the order to Benaiah son of Jehoiada, and he went out and struck Shimei down and killed him.

The kingdom was now firmly established in Solomon's hands.

ᵃ34 Or buried in his tomb

Solomon Asks for Wisdom

3 Solomon made an alliance with Pharaoh king of Egypt and married his daughter. He brought her to the City of David until he finished building his palace and the temple of the LORD, and the wall around Jerusalem. ²The people, however, were still sacrificing at the high places, because a temple had not yet been built for the Name of the LORD. ³Solomon showed his love for the LORD by walking according to the statutes of his father David, except that he offered sacrifices and burned incense on the high places.

⁴The king went to Gibeon to offer sacrifices, for that was the most important high place, and Solomon offered a thousand burnt offerings on that altar. ⁵At Gibeon the LORD appeared to Solomon during the night in a dream, and God said, "Ask for whatever you want me to give you."

⁶Solomon answered, "You have shown great kindness to your servant, my father David, because he was faithful to you and righteous and upright in heart. You have continued this great kindness to him and have given him a son to sit on his throne this very day.

⁷"Now, O LORD my God, you have made your servant king in place of my father David. But I am only a little child and do not know how to carry out my duties. ⁸Your servant is here among the people you have chosen, a great people, too numerous to count or number. ⁹So give your servant a discerning heart to govern your people and to distinguish between right and wrong. For who is able to govern this great people of yours?"

¹⁰The Lord was pleased that Solomon had asked for this. ¹¹So God said to him, "Since you have asked for this and not for long life or wealth for yourself, nor have asked for the death of your enemies but for discernment in administering justice, ¹²I will do what you have asked. I will give you a wise and discerning heart, so that there will never have been anyone like you, nor will there ever be. ¹³Moreover, I will give you what you have not asked for—both riches and honor—so that in your lifetime you will have no equal among kings. ¹⁴And if you walk in my ways and obey my statutes and commands as David your father did, I will give you a long life." ¹⁵Then Solomon awoke—and he realized it had been a dream.

He returned to Jerusalem, stood before the ark of the Lord's covenant and sacrificed burnt offerings and fellowship offerings.ᵃ Then he gave a feast for all his court.

ᵃ15 Traditionally *peace offerings*

HEY DAD

Is it wrong to be rich?

Text: 1 Kings 3:5-13

Wealth is a neutral thing. Having it doesn't make us any more righteous or any more sinful than we already are. But the Bible warns people who are rich not to put their hope in their wealth. Rather, people are to hope in God "who richly provides us with everything for our enjoyment" (1 Timothy 6:17).

In his first letter to Timothy, Paul is very careful to point out that our priorities count. If our priority is pleasing God and being thankful for what we already have, we're in great shape. Think about King Solomon. God gave him a blank check and told him to write in any amount. God's bank was willing to cover anything the king might want: a huge palace, lots of power, his own kingdom, world fame, or more gold and riches than he could ever spend. But Solomon didn't ask for money, prestige or power. Instead, he asked for wisdom and understanding so he could be a just ruler. This request delighted God, so God gave him wisdom plus riches, power and fame. Solomon's heart was right where God wanted it—on a search for godliness and contentment.

Rich and poor alike can be wealthy by God's standard. Following God and being satisfied in that journey are the keys.

For a complete listing of Questions Kids Ask, turn to page 1435.

QUESTIONS KIDS ASK

A Wise Ruling

16Now two prostitutes came to the king and stood before him. **17**One of them said, "My lord, this woman and I live in the same house. I had a baby while she was there with me. **18**The third day after my child was born, this woman also had a baby. We were alone; there was no one in the house but the two of us.

19"During the night this woman's son died because she lay on him. **20**So she got up in the middle of the night and took my son from my side while I your servant was asleep. She put him by her breast and put her dead son by my breast. **21**The next morning, I got up to nurse my son—and he was dead! But when I looked at him closely in the morning light, I saw that it wasn't the son I had borne."

22The other woman said, "No! The living one is my son; the dead one is yours."

But the first one insisted, "No! The dead one is yours; the living one is mine." And so they argued before the king.

23The king said, "This one says, 'My son is alive and your son is dead,' while that one says, 'No! Your son is dead and mine is alive.' "

24Then the king said, "Bring me a sword." So they brought a sword for the king. **25**He then gave an order: "Cut the living child in two and give half to one and half to the other."

26The woman whose son was alive was filled with compassion for her son and

The Family Referee

DAILY INSIGHT

MONDAY

Passage:
1 Kings 3:16–28

Verse:
1 Kings 3:28

Here are a few delightful, and perhaps familiar, statements with which to start your day:

- "No running through the dining room!"
- "My brother bit me!"
- "*Please* don't put peas in your nose."
- "Stephanie is sitting on *my* side."
- "But, *Daaaaaaaaad*!"

I don't think it was ever in our official fathering job description, but "family referee" is a role we're often called upon to perform. Our wives often get this call, too—and it's not a lot of fun.

Being a good referee can be a real challenge because, most of the time, we weren't there to see what happened. We have no video replay. We don't know who hit whom first. We don't know what may have provoked the conflict. We don't know who, if anyone, should be punished. So what's a dad to do?

Solomon was facing a tough situation. Yes, a situation even more difficult than dealing with a little boy who has just bitten his sister. Two women stood before him, both claiming to be the mother of the same child.

Like a skilled tennis player, Solomon smashed a cross-court winner. He answered the question, "Whose baby is this?" with the question, "Who loves this baby more?"

With his question, he got the answer he was looking for. The baby's real mother pled for its life.

Since we either have or will be called upon to be our families' referee, this story provides some great help. Wise Solomon gives us a clinic. *Settle as many disputes as you can without making the call yourself.* Listen carefully to the grievances. Make sure that you understand exactly what happened. Then ask some pointed questions. In fact, one of my favorites is, "Okay, if *you* were the dad, what would you do?"

"Cut my sister in two with your sword," would not be an acceptable answer, by the way.

One more thing. Nothing in this story indicates that Solomon was upset at all. In fact, can't you picture him shocking these two women with his aloof attitude? "Bring me my sword," Solomon said to his servant, probably in the same tone of voice as he would have asked for a refill of his coffee. The message here is pretty clear and simple: Stay cool. Be in control.

Be a good referee, one that keeps the game from getting out of control. You can do it. Actually, you look terrific in black and white stripes.

For your next devotional reading, go to page 380.

said to the king, "Please, my lord, give her the living baby! Don't kill him!"

But the other said, "Neither I nor you shall have him. Cut him in two!"

[27] Then the king gave his ruling: "Give the living baby to the first woman. Do not kill him; she is his mother."

[28] When all Israel heard the verdict the king had given, they held the king in awe, because they saw that he had wisdom from God to administer justice.

Solomon's Officials and Governors

4 So King Solomon ruled over all Israel. [2] And these were his chief officials:

Azariah son of Zadok—the priest;
[3] Elihoreph and Ahijah, sons of Shisha—secretaries;
Jehoshaphat son of Ahilud—recorder;
[4] Benaiah son of Jehoiada—commander in chief;
Zadok and Abiathar—priests;
[5] Azariah son of Nathan—in charge of the district officers;
Zabud son of Nathan—a priest and personal adviser to the king;
[6] Ahishar—in charge of the palace;
Adoniram son of Abda—in charge of forced labor.

[7] Solomon also had twelve district governors over all Israel, who supplied provisions for the king and the royal household. Each one had to provide supplies for one month in the year. [8] These are their names:

Ben-Hur—in the hill country of Ephraim;
[9] Ben-Deker—in Makaz, Shaalbim, Beth Shemesh and Elon Bethhanan;
[10] Ben-Hesed—in Arubboth (Socoh and all the land of Hepher were his);
[11] Ben-Abinadab—in Naphoth Dor[a] (he was married to Taphath daughter of Solomon);
[12] Baana son of Ahilud—in Taanach and Megiddo, and in all of Beth Shan next to Zarethan below Jezreel, from Beth Shan to Abel Meholah across to Jokmeam;
[13] Ben-Geber—in Ramoth Gilead (the settlements of Jair son of Manasseh in Gilead were his, as well as the district of Argob in Bashan and its sixty large walled cities with bronze gate bars);
[14] Ahinadab son of Iddo—in Mahanaim;
[15] Ahimaaz—in Naphtali (he had married Basemath daughter of Solomon);
[16] Baana son of Hushai—in Asher and in Aloth;
[17] Jehoshaphat son of Paruah—in Issachar;
[18] Shimei son of Ela—in Benjamin;
[19] Geber son of Uri—in Gilead (the country of Sihon king of the Amorites and the country of Og king of Bashan). He was the only governor over the district.

Solomon's Daily Provisions

[20] The people of Judah and Israel were as numerous as the sand on the seashore; they ate, they drank and they were happy. [21] And Solomon ruled over all the kingdoms from the River[b] to the land of the Philistines, as far as the border of Egypt. These countries brought tribute and were Solomon's subjects all his life.

[22] Solomon's daily provisions were thirty cors[c] of fine flour and sixty cors[d] of meal, [23] ten head of stall-fed cattle, twenty of pasture-fed cattle and a hundred sheep and goats, as well as deer, gazelles, roebucks and choice fowl. [24] For he ruled over all the kingdoms west of the River, from Tiphsah to Gaza, and had peace on all sides. [25] During Solomon's lifetime Judah and Israel, from Dan to Beersheba, lived in safety, each man under his own vine and fig tree.

[26] Solomon had four[e] thousand stalls for chariot horses, and twelve thousand horses.[f]

[27] The district officers, each in his month, supplied provisions for King Solomon and all who came to the king's table. They saw to it that nothing was lacking. [28] They also brought to the proper place their quotas of barley and straw for the chariot horses and the other horses.

Solomon's Wisdom

[29] God gave Solomon wisdom and very great insight, and a breadth of understanding as measureless as the sand on

[a]11 Or in the heights of Dor   [b]21 That is, the Euphrates; also in verse 24   [c]22 That is, probably about 185 bushels (about 6.6 kiloliters)   [d]22 That is, probably about 375 bushels (about 13.2 kiloliters)   [e]26 Some Septuagint manuscripts (see also 2 Chron. 9:25); Hebrew forty   [f]26 Or charioteers

the seashore. **30**Solomon's wisdom was greater than the wisdom of all the men of the East, and greater than all the wisdom of Egypt. **31**He was wiser than any other man, including Ethan the Ezrahite—wiser than Heman, Calcol and Darda, the sons of Mahol. And his fame spread to all the surrounding nations. **32**He spoke three thousand proverbs and his songs numbered a thousand and five. **33**He described plant life, from the cedar of Lebanon to the hyssop that grows out of walls. He also taught about animals and birds, reptiles and fish. **34**Men of all nations came to listen to Solomon's wisdom, sent by all the kings of the world, who had heard of his wisdom.

Preparations for Building the Temple

5 When Hiram king of Tyre heard that Solomon had been anointed king to succeed his father David, he sent his envoys to Solomon, because he had always been on friendly terms with David. **2**Solomon sent back this message to Hiram:

3"You know that because of the wars waged against my father David from all sides, he could not build a temple for the Name of the LORD his God until the LORD put his enemies under his feet. **4**But now the LORD my God has given me rest on every side, and there is no adversary or disaster. **5**I intend, therefore, to build a temple for the Name of the LORD my God, as the LORD told my father David, when he said, 'Your son whom I will put on the throne in your place will build the temple for my Name.'

6"So give orders that cedars of Lebanon be cut for me. My men will work with yours, and I will pay you for your men whatever wages you set. You know that we have no one so skilled in felling timber as the Sidonians."

7When Hiram heard Solomon's message, he was greatly pleased and said, "Praise be to the LORD today, for he has given David a wise son to rule over this great nation."

8So Hiram sent word to Solomon:

"I have received the message you sent me and will do all you want in providing the cedar and pine logs. **9**My men will haul them down from Lebanon to the sea, and I will float them in rafts by sea to the place you specify. There I will separate them and you can take them away. And you are to grant my wish by providing food for my royal household."

10In this way Hiram kept Solomon supplied with all the cedar and pine logs he wanted, **11**and Solomon gave Hiram twenty thousand cors*a* of wheat as food for his household, in addition to twenty thousand baths*b,c* of pressed olive oil. Solomon continued to do this for Hiram year after year. **12**The LORD gave Solomon wisdom, just as he had promised him. There were peaceful relations between Hiram and Solomon, and the two of them made a treaty.

13King Solomon conscripted laborers from all Israel—thirty thousand men. **14**He sent them off to Lebanon in shifts of ten thousand a month, so that they spent one month in Lebanon and two months at home. Adoniram was in charge of the forced labor. **15**Solomon had seventy thousand carriers and eighty thousand stonecutters in the hills, **16**as well as thirty-three hundred*d* foremen who supervised the project and directed the workmen. **17**At the king's command they removed from the quarry large blocks of quality stone to provide a foundation of dressed stone for the temple. **18**The craftsmen of Solomon and Hiram and the men of Gebal*e* cut and prepared the timber and stone for the building of the temple.

Solomon Builds the Temple

6 In the four hundred and eightieth*f* year after the Israelites had come out of Egypt, in the fourth year of Solomon's reign over Israel, in the month of Ziv, the second month, he began to build the temple of the LORD.

2The temple that King Solomon built for the LORD was sixty cubits long, twenty wide and thirty high.*g* **3**The portico at the front of the main hall of the temple extended the width of the temple, that is twenty cubits,*h* and projected ten cubits*i*

---

a11 That is, probably about 125,000 bushels (about 4,400 kiloliters)   *b11* Septuagint (see also 2 Chron. 2:10); Hebrew *twenty cors*   *c11* That is, about 115,000 gallons (about 440 kiloliters)   *d16* Hebrew; some Septuagint manuscripts (see also 2 Chron. 2:2, 18) *thirty-six hundred*   *e18* That is, Byblos   *f1* Hebrew; Septuagint *four hundred and fortieth*   *g2* That is, about 90 feet (about 27 meters) long and 30 feet (about 9 meters) wide and 45 feet (about 13.5 meters) high   *h3* That is, about 30 feet (about 9 meters)   *i3* That is, about 15 feet (about 4.5 meters)

from the front of the temple. ⁴He made narrow clerestory windows in the temple. ⁵Against the walls of the main hall and inner sanctuary he built a structure around the building, in which there were side rooms. ⁶The lowest floor was five cubits*a* wide, the middle floor six cubits*b* and the third floor seven.*c* He made offset ledges around the outside of the temple so that nothing would be inserted into the temple walls.

⁷In building the temple, only blocks dressed at the quarry were used, and no hammer, chisel or any other iron tool was heard at the temple site while it was being built.

⁸The entrance to the lowest*d* floor was on the south side of the temple; a stairway led up to the middle level and from there to the third. ⁹So he built the temple and completed it, roofing it with beams and cedar planks. ¹⁰And he built the side rooms all along the temple. The height of each was five cubits, and they were attached to the temple by beams of cedar.

¹¹The word of the Lord came to Solomon: ¹²"As for this temple you are building, if you follow my decrees, carry out my regulations and keep all my commands and obey them, I will fulfill through you the promise I gave to David your father. ¹³And I will live among the Israelites and will not abandon my people Israel."

¹⁴So Solomon built the temple and completed it. ¹⁵He lined its interior walls with cedar boards, paneling them from the floor of the temple to the ceiling, and covered the floor of the temple with planks of pine. ¹⁶He partitioned off twenty cubits*e* at the rear of the temple with cedar boards from floor to ceiling to form within the temple an inner sanctuary, the Most Holy Place. ¹⁷The main hall in front of this room was forty cubits*f* long. ¹⁸The inside of the temple was cedar, carved with gourds and open flowers. Everything was cedar; no stone was to be seen.

¹⁹He prepared the inner sanctuary within the temple to set the ark of the covenant of the Lord there. ²⁰The inner sanctuary was twenty cubits long, twenty wide and twenty high.*g* He overlaid the inside with pure gold, and he also overlaid the altar of cedar. ²¹Solomon covered the inside of the temple with pure gold, and he extended gold chains across the front of the inner sanctuary, which was overlaid with gold. ²²So he overlaid the whole interior with gold. He also overlaid with gold the altar that belonged to the inner sanctuary.

²³In the inner sanctuary he made a pair of cherubim of olive wood, each ten cubits*h* high. ²⁴One wing of the first cherub was five cubits long, and the other wing five cubits—ten cubits from wing tip to wing tip. ²⁵The second cherub also measured ten cubits, for the two cherubim were identical in size and shape. ²⁶The height of each cherub was ten cubits. ²⁷He placed the cherubim inside the innermost room of the temple, with their wings spread out. The wing of one cherub touched one wall, while the wing of the other touched the other wall, and their wings touched each other in the middle of the room. ²⁸He overlaid the cherubim with gold.

²⁹On the walls all around the temple, in both the inner and outer rooms, he carved cherubim, palm trees and open flowers. ³⁰He also covered the floors of both the inner and outer rooms of the temple with gold.

³¹For the entrance of the inner sanctuary he made doors of olive wood with five-sided jambs. ³²And on the two olive wood doors he carved cherubim, palm trees and open flowers, and overlaid the cherubim and palm trees with beaten gold. ³³In the same way he made four-sided jambs of olive wood for the entrance to the main hall. ³⁴He also made two pine doors, each having two leaves that turned in sockets. ³⁵He carved cherubim, palm trees and open flowers on them and overlaid them with gold hammered evenly over the carvings.

³⁶And he built the inner courtyard of three courses of dressed stone and one course of trimmed cedar beams.

³⁷The foundation of the temple of the Lord was laid in the fourth year, in the month of Ziv. ³⁸In the eleventh year in the month of Bul, the eighth month, the temple was finished in all its details according to its specifications. He had spent seven years building it.

Solomon Builds His Palace

7 It took Solomon thirteen years, however, to complete the construction of

---

a6 That is, about 7 1/2 feet (about 2.3 meters); also in verses 10 and 24   *b6* That is, about 9 feet (about 2.7 meters)   *c6* That is, about 10 1/2 feet (about 3.1 meters)   *d8* Septuagint; Hebrew *middle*   *e16* That is, about 30 feet (about 9 meters)   *f17* That is, about 60 feet (about 18 meters)   *g20* That is, about 30 feet (about 9 meters) long, wide and high   *h23* That is, about 15 feet (about 4.5 meters)

his palace. [2]He built the Palace of the Forest of Lebanon a hundred cubits long, fifty wide and thirty high,[a] with four rows of cedar columns supporting trimmed cedar beams. [3]It was roofed with cedar above the beams that rested on the columns—forty-five beams, fifteen to a row. [4]Its windows were placed high in sets of three, facing each other. [5]All the doorways had rectangular frames; they were in the front part in sets of three, facing each other.[b]

[6]He made a colonnade fifty cubits long and thirty wide.[c] In front of it was a portico, and in front of that were pillars and an overhanging roof.

[7]He built the throne hall, the Hall of Justice, where he was to judge, and he covered it with cedar from floor to ceiling.[d] [8]And the palace in which he was to live, set farther back, was similar in design. Solomon also made a palace like this hall for Pharaoh's daughter, whom he had married.

[9]All these structures, from the outside to the great courtyard and from foundation to eaves, were made of blocks of high-grade stone cut to size and trimmed with a saw on their inner and outer faces. [10]The foundations were laid with large stones of good quality, some measuring ten cubits[e] and some eight.[f] [11]Above were high-grade stones, cut to size, and cedar beams. [12]The great courtyard was surrounded by a wall of three courses of dressed stone and one course of trimmed cedar beams, as was the inner courtyard of the temple of the LORD with its portico.

The Temple's Furnishings

[13]King Solomon sent to Tyre and brought Huram,[g] [14]whose mother was a widow from the tribe of Naphtali and whose father was a man of Tyre and a craftsman in bronze. Huram was highly skilled and experienced in all kinds of bronze work. He came to King Solomon and did all the work assigned to him.

[15]He cast two bronze pillars, each eighteen cubits high and twelve cubits around,[h] by line. [16]He also made two capitals of cast bronze to set on the tops of the pillars; each capital was five cubits[i] high. [17]A network of interwoven chains festooned the capitals on top of the pillars, seven for each capital. [18]He made pomegranates in two rows[j] encircling each network to decorate the capitals on top of the pillars.[k] He did the same for each capital.

[19]The capitals on top of the pillars in the portico were in the shape of lilies, four cubits[l] high. [20]On the capitals of both pillars, above the bowl-shaped part next to the network, were the two hundred pomegranates in rows all around. [21]He erected the pillars at the portico of the temple. The pillar to the south he named Jakin[m] and the one to the north Boaz.[n] [22]The capitals on top were in the shape of lilies. And so the work on the pillars was completed.

[23]He made the Sea of cast metal, circular in shape, measuring ten cubits[o] from rim to rim and five cubits high. It took a line of thirty cubits[p] to measure around it. [24]Below the rim, gourds encircled it—ten to a cubit. The gourds were cast in two rows in one piece with the Sea.

[25]The Sea stood on twelve bulls, three facing north, three facing west, three facing south and three facing east. The Sea rested on top of them, and their hindquarters were toward the center. [26]It was a handbreadth[q] in thickness, and its rim was like the rim of a cup, like a lily blossom. It held two thousand baths.[r]

[27]He also made ten movable stands of bronze; each was four cubits long, four wide and three high.[s] [28]This is how the stands were made: They had side panels attached to uprights. [29]On the panels between the uprights were lions, bulls and cherubim—and on the uprights as well. Above and below the lions and bulls were wreaths of hammered work. [30]Each stand

[a]2 That is, about 150 feet (about 46 meters) long, 75 feet (about 23 meters) wide and 45 feet (about 13.5 meters) high [b]5 The meaning of the Hebrew for this verse is uncertain. [c]6 That is, about 75 feet (about 23 meters) long and 45 feet (about 13.5 meters) wide [d]7 Vulgate and Syriac; Hebrew floor [e]10 That is, about 15 feet (about 4.5 meters) [f]10 That is, about 12 feet (about 3.6 meters) [g]13 Hebrew Hiram, a variant of Huram; also in verses 40 and 45 [h]15 That is, about 27 feet (about 8.1 meters) high and 18 feet (about 5.4 meters) around [i]16 That is, about 7 1/2 feet (about 2.3 meters); also in verse 23 [j]18 Two Hebrew manuscripts and Septuagint; most Hebrew manuscripts made the pillars, and there were two rows [k]18 Many Hebrew manuscripts and Syriac; most Hebrew manuscripts pomegranates [l]19 That is, about 6 feet (about 1.8 meters); also in verse 38 [m]21 Jakin probably means he establishes. [n]21 Boaz probably means in him is strength. [o]23 That is, about 15 feet (about 4.5 meters) [p]23 That is, about 45 feet (about 13.5 meters) [q]26 That is, about 3 inches (about 8 centimeters) [r]26 That is, probably about 11,500 gallons (about 44 kiloliters); the Septuagint does not have this sentence. [s]27 That is, about 6 feet (about 1.8 meters) long and wide and about 4 1/2 feet (about 1.3 meters) high

had four bronze wheels with bronze axles, and each had a basin resting on four supports, cast with wreaths on each side. ³¹On the inside of the stand there was an opening that had a circular frame one cubit*a* deep. This opening was round, and with its basework it measured a cubit and a half.*b* Around its opening there was engraving. The panels of the stands were square, not round. ³²The four wheels were under the panels, and the axles of the wheels were attached to the stand. The diameter of each wheel was a cubit and a half. ³³The wheels were made like chariot wheels; the axles, rims, spokes and hubs were all of cast metal.

³⁴Each stand had four handles, one on each corner, projecting from the stand. ³⁵At the top of the stand there was a circular band half a cubit*c* deep. The supports and panels were attached to the top of the stand. ³⁶He engraved cherubim, lions and palm trees on the surfaces of the supports and on the panels, in every available space, with wreaths all around. ³⁷This is the way he made the ten stands. They were all cast in the same molds and were identical in size and shape.

³⁸He then made ten bronze basins, each holding forty baths*d* and measuring four cubits across, one basin to go on each of the ten stands. ³⁹He placed five of the stands on the south side of the temple and five on the north. He placed the Sea on the south side, at the southeast corner of the temple. ⁴⁰He also made the basins and shovels and sprinkling bowls.

So Huram finished all the work he had undertaken for King Solomon in the temple of the LORD:

⁴¹the two pillars;
the two bowl-shaped capitals on top of the pillars;
the two sets of network decorating the two bowl-shaped capitals on top of the pillars;
⁴²the four hundred pomegranates for the two sets of network (two rows of pomegranates for each network, decorating the bowl-shaped capitals on top of the pillars);
⁴³the ten stands with their ten basins;
⁴⁴the Sea and the twelve bulls under it;
⁴⁵the pots, shovels and sprinkling bowls.

All these objects that Huram made for King Solomon for the temple of the LORD were of burnished bronze. ⁴⁶The king had them cast in clay molds in the plain of the

Jordan between Succoth and Zarethan. ⁴⁷Solomon left all these things unweighed, because there were so many; the weight of the bronze was not determined.

⁴⁸Solomon also made all the furnishings that were in the LORD's temple:

the golden altar;
the golden table on which was the bread of the Presence;
⁴⁹the lampstands of pure gold (five on the right and five on the left, in front of the inner sanctuary);
the gold floral work and lamps and tongs;
⁵⁰the pure gold basins, wick trimmers, sprinkling bowls, dishes and censers;
and the gold sockets for the doors of the innermost room, the Most Holy Place, and also for the doors of the main hall of the temple.

⁵¹When all the work King Solomon had done for the temple of the LORD was finished, he brought in the things his father David had dedicated—the silver and gold and the furnishings—and he placed them in the treasuries of the LORD's temple.

The Ark Brought to the Temple

8 Then King Solomon summoned into his presence at Jerusalem the elders of Israel, all the heads of the tribes and the chiefs of the Israelite families, to bring up the ark of the LORD's covenant from Zion, the City of David. ²All the men of Israel came together to King Solomon at the time of the festival in the month of Ethanim, the seventh month.

³When all the elders of Israel had arrived, the priests took up the ark, ⁴and they brought up the ark of the LORD and the Tent of Meeting and all the sacred furnishings in it. The priests and Levites carried them up, ⁵and King Solomon and the entire assembly of Israel that had gathered about him were before the ark, sacrificing so many sheep and cattle that they could not be recorded or counted.

⁶The priests then brought the ark of the LORD's covenant to its place in the inner sanctuary of the temple, the Most Holy Place, and put it beneath the wings of the cherubim. ⁷The cherubim spread their

---

a31 That is, about 1 1/2 feet (about 0.5 meter)
b31 That is, about 2 1/4 feet (about 0.7 meter); also in verse 32   *c35* That is, about 3/4 foot (about 0.2 meter)   *d38* That is, about 230 gallons (about 880 liters)

wings over the place of the ark and over-shadowed the ark and its carrying poles. [8]These poles were so long that their ends could be seen from the Holy Place in front of the inner sanctuary, but not from outside the Holy Place; and they are still there today. [9]There was nothing in the ark except the two stone tablets that Moses had placed in it at Horeb, where the LORD made a covenant with the Israelites after they came out of Egypt.

[10]When the priests withdrew from the Holy Place, the cloud filled the temple of the LORD. [11]And the priests could not perform their service because of the cloud, for the glory of the LORD filled his temple.

[12]Then Solomon said, "The LORD has said that he would dwell in a dark cloud; [13]I have indeed built a magnificent temple for you, a place for you to dwell forever."

[14]While the whole assembly of Israel was standing there, the king turned around and blessed them. [15]Then he said:

"Praise be to the LORD, the God of Israel, who with his own hand has fulfilled what he promised with his own mouth to my father David. For he said, [16]'Since the day I brought my people Israel out of Egypt, I have not chosen a city in any tribe of Israel to have a temple built for my Name to be there, but I have chosen David to rule my people Israel.'

[17]"My father David had it in his heart to build a temple for the Name of the LORD, the God of Israel. [18]But the LORD said to my father David, 'Because it was in your heart to build a temple for my Name, you did well to have this in your heart. [19]Nevertheless, you are not the one to build the temple, but your son, who is your own flesh and blood—he is the one who will build the temple for my Name.'

[20]"The LORD has kept the promise he made: I have succeeded David my father and now I sit on the throne of Israel, just as the LORD promised, and I have built the temple for the Name of the LORD, the God of Israel. [21]I have provided a place there for the ark, in which is the covenant of the LORD that he made with our fathers when he brought them out of Egypt."

Solomon's Prayer of Dedication

[22]Then Solomon stood before the altar of the LORD in front of the whole assembly of Israel, spread out his hands toward heaven [23]and said:

"O LORD, God of Israel, there is no God like you in heaven above or on earth below—you who keep your covenant of love with your servants who continue wholeheartedly in your way. [24]You have kept your promise to your servant David my father; with your mouth you have promised and with your hand you have fulfilled it—as it is today.

[25]"Now LORD, God of Israel, keep for your servant David my father the promises you made to him when you said, 'You shall never fail to have a man to sit before me on the throne of Israel, if only your sons are careful in all they do to walk before me as you have done.' [26]And now, O God of Israel, let your word that you promised your servant David my father come true.

[27]"But will God really dwell on earth? The heavens, even the highest heaven, cannot contain you. How much less this temple I have built! [28]Yet give attention to your servant's prayer and his plea for mercy, O LORD my God. Hear the cry and the prayer that your servant is praying in your presence this day. [29]May your eyes be open toward this temple night and day, this place of which you said, 'My Name shall be there,' so that you will hear the prayer your servant prays toward this place. [30]Hear the supplication of your servant and of your people Israel when they pray toward this place. Hear from heaven, your dwelling place, and when you hear, forgive.

[31]"When a man wrongs his neighbor and is required to take an oath and he comes and swears the oath before your altar in this temple, [32]then hear from heaven and act. Judge between your servants, condemning the guilty and bringing down on his own head what he has done. Declare the innocent not guilty, and so establish his innocence.

[33]"When your people Israel have been defeated by an enemy because they have sinned against you, and when they turn back to you and confess your name, praying and making supplication to you in this temple,

34then hear from heaven and forgive the sin of your people Israel and bring them back to the land you gave to their fathers.

35"When the heavens are shut up and there is no rain because your people have sinned against you, and when they pray toward this place and confess your name and turn from their sin because you have afflicted them, **36**then hear from heaven and forgive the sin of your servants, your people Israel. Teach them the right way to live, and send rain on the land you gave your people for an inheritance.

37"When famine or plague comes to the land, or blight or mildew, locusts or grasshoppers, or when an enemy besieges them in any of their cities, whatever disaster or disease may come, **38**and when a prayer or plea is made by any of your people Israel—each one aware of the afflictions of his own heart, and spreading out his hands toward this temple— **39**then hear from heaven, your dwelling place. Forgive and act; deal with each man according to all he does, since you know his heart (for you alone know the hearts of all men), **40**so that they will fear you all the time they live in the land you gave our fathers.

41"As for the foreigner who does not belong to your people Israel but has come from a distant land because of your name— **42**for men will hear of your great name and your mighty hand and your outstretched arm—when he comes and prays toward this temple, **43**then hear from heaven, your dwelling place, and do whatever the foreigner asks of you, so that all the peoples of the earth may know your name and fear you, as do your own people Israel, and may know that this house I have built bears your Name.

44"When your people go to war against their enemies, wherever you send them, and when they pray to the LORD toward the city you have chosen and the temple I have built for your Name, **45**then hear from heaven their prayer and their plea, and uphold their cause.

46"When they sin against you—for there is no one who does not sin— and you become angry with them

and give them over to the enemy, who takes them captive to his own land, far away or near; **47**and if they have a change of heart in the land where they are held captive, and repent and plead with you in the land of their conquerors and say, 'We have sinned, we have done wrong, we have acted wickedly'; **48**and if they turn back to you with all their heart and soul in the land of their enemies who took them captive, and pray to you toward the land you gave their fathers, toward the city you have chosen and the temple I have built for your Name; **49**then from heaven, your dwelling place, hear their prayer and their plea, and uphold their cause. **50**And forgive your people, who have sinned against you; forgive all the offenses they have committed against you, and cause their conquerors to show them mercy; **51**for they are your people and your inheritance, whom you brought out of Egypt, out of that iron-smelting furnace.

52"May your eyes be open to your servant's plea and to the plea of your people Israel, and may you listen to them whenever they cry out to you. **53**For you singled them out from all the nations of the world to be your own inheritance, just as you declared through your servant Moses when you, O Sovereign LORD, brought our fathers out of Egypt."

54When Solomon had finished all these prayers and supplications to the LORD, he rose from before the altar of the LORD, where he had been kneeling with his hands spread out toward heaven. **55**He stood and blessed the whole assembly of Israel in a loud voice, saying:

56"Praise be to the LORD, who has given rest to his people Israel just as he promised. Not one word has failed of all the good promises he gave through his servant Moses. **57**May the LORD our God be with us as he was with our fathers; may he never leave us nor forsake us. **58**May he turn our hearts to him, to walk in all his ways and to keep the commands, decrees and regulations he gave our fathers. **59**And may these words of mine, which I have prayed before the LORD, be near to the LORD our God day and night, that he may uphold the cause of his servant and the cause of his people Israel according to each day's need, **⁶⁰**so that all the peoples of the earth may know that the LORD is God and that there is no other. **⁶¹**But your hearts must be fully committed to the LORD our God, to live by his decrees and obey his commands, as at this time."

The Dedication of the Temple

⁶²Then the king and all Israel with him offered sacrifices before the LORD. **⁶³**Solomon offered a sacrifice of fellowship offerings*ᵃ* to the LORD: twenty-two thousand cattle and a hundred and twenty thousand sheep and goats. So the king and all the Israelites dedicated the temple of the LORD.

⁶⁴On that same day the king consecrated the middle part of the courtyard in front of the temple of the LORD, and there he offered burnt offerings, grain offerings and the fat of the fellowship offerings, because the bronze altar before the LORD was too small to hold the burnt offerings, the grain offerings and the fat of the fellowship offerings.

⁶⁵So Solomon observed the festival at that time, and all Israel with him—a vast assembly, people from Lebo*ᵇ* Hamath to the Wadi of Egypt. They celebrated it before the LORD our God for seven days and seven days more, fourteen days in all. **⁶⁶**On the following day he sent the people away. They blessed the king and then went home, joyful and glad in heart for all the good things the LORD had done for his servant David and his people Israel.

The LORD Appears to Solomon

9 When Solomon had finished building the temple of the LORD and the royal palace, and had achieved all he had desired to do, **²**the LORD appeared to him a second time, as he had appeared to him at Gibeon. **³**The LORD said to him:

"I have heard the prayer and plea you have made before me; I have consecrated this temple, which you have built, by putting my Name there forever. My eyes and my heart will always be there.

⁴"As for you, if you walk before me in integrity of heart and uprightness, as David your father did, and do all I command and observe my decrees and laws, **⁵**I will establish your royal

throne over Israel forever, as I promised David your father when I said, 'You shall never fail to have a man on the throne of Israel.'

⁶"But if you*ᶜ* or your sons turn away from me and do not observe the commands and decrees I have given you*ᶜ* and go off to serve other gods and worship them, **⁷**then I will cut off Israel from the land I have given them and will reject this temple I have consecrated for my Name. Israel will then become a byword and an object of ridicule among all peoples. **⁸**And though this temple is now imposing, all who pass by will be appalled and will scoff and say, 'Why has the LORD done such a thing to this land and to this temple?' **⁹**People will answer, 'Because they have forsaken the LORD their God, who brought their fathers out of Egypt, and have embraced other gods, worshiping and serving them—that is why the LORD brought all this disaster on them.' "

Solomon's Other Activities

¹⁰At the end of twenty years, during which Solomon built these two buildings—the temple of the LORD and the royal palace— **¹¹**King Solomon gave twenty towns in Galilee to Hiram king of Tyre, because Hiram had supplied him with all the cedar and pine and gold he wanted. **¹²**But when Hiram went from Tyre to see the towns that Solomon had given him, he was not pleased with them. **¹³**"What kind of towns are these you have given me, my brother?" he asked. And he called them the Land of Cabul,*ᵈ* a name they have to this day. **¹⁴**Now Hiram had sent to the king 120 talents*ᵉ* of gold.

¹⁵Here is the account of the forced labor King Solomon conscripted to build the LORD's temple, his own palace, the supporting terraces,*ᶠ* the wall of Jerusalem, and Hazor, Megiddo and Gezer. **¹⁶**(Pharaoh king of Egypt had attacked and captured Gezer. He had set it on fire. He killed its Canaanite inhabitants and then gave it as a wedding gift to his daughter, Solomon's wife. **¹⁷**And Solomon rebuilt

ᵃ63 Traditionally *peace offerings;* also in verse 64   *ᵇ65* Or *from the entrance to*   *ᶜ6* The Hebrew is plural.   *ᵈ13 Cabul* sounds like the Hebrew for *good-for-nothing.*   *ᵉ14* That is, about 4 1/2 tons (about 4 metric tons)   *ᶠ15* Or *the Millo;* also in verse 24

Gezer.) He built up Lower Beth Horon, [18]Baalath, and Tadmor[a] in the desert, within his land, [19]as well as all his store cities and the towns for his chariots and for his horses[b]—whatever he desired to build in Jerusalem, in Lebanon and throughout all the territory he ruled.

[20]All the people left from the Amorites, Hittites, Perizzites, Hivites and Jebusites (these peoples were not Israelites), [21]that is, their descendants remaining in the land, whom the Israelites could not exterminate[c]—these Solomon conscripted for his slave labor force, as it is to this day. [22]But Solomon did not make slaves of any of the Israelites; they were his fighting men, his government officials, his officers, his captains, and the commanders of his chariots and charioteers. [23]They were also the chief officials in charge of Solomon's projects—550 officials supervising the men who did the work.

[24]After Pharaoh's daughter had come up from the City of David to the palace Solomon had built for her, he constructed the supporting terraces.

[25]Three times a year Solomon sacrificed burnt offerings and fellowship offerings[d] on the altar he had built for the LORD, burning incense before the LORD along with them, and so fulfilled the temple obligations.

[26]King Solomon also built ships at Ezion Geber, which is near Elath in Edom, on the shore of the Red Sea.[e] [27]And Hiram sent his men—sailors who knew the sea—to serve in the fleet with Solomon's men. [28]They sailed to Ophir and brought back 420 talents[f] of gold, which they delivered to King Solomon.

The Queen of Sheba Visits Solomon

10 When the queen of Sheba heard about the fame of Solomon and his relation to the name of the LORD, she came to test him with hard questions. [2]Arriving at Jerusalem with a very great caravan—with camels carrying spices, large quantities of gold, and precious stones—she came to Solomon and talked with him about all that she had on her mind. [3]Solomon answered all her questions; nothing was too hard for the king to explain to her. [4]When the queen of Sheba saw all the wisdom of Solomon and the palace he had built, [5]the food on his table, the seating of his officials, the attending servants in their robes, his cupbearers, and the burnt offerings he made at[g] the temple of the LORD, she was overwhelmed.

[6]She said to the king, "The report I heard in my own country about your achievements and your wisdom is true. [7]But I did not believe these things until I came and saw with my own eyes. Indeed, not even half was told me; in wisdom and wealth you have far exceeded the report I heard. [8]How happy your men must be! How happy your officials, who continually stand before you and hear your wisdom! [9]Praise be to the LORD your God, who has delighted in you and placed you on the throne of Israel. Because of the LORD's eternal love for Israel, he has made you king, to maintain justice and righteousness."

[10]And she gave the king 120 talents[h] of gold, large quantities of spices, and precious stones. Never again were so many spices brought in as those the queen of Sheba gave to King Solomon.

[11](Hiram's ships brought gold from Ophir; and from there they brought great cargoes of almugwood[i] and precious stones. [12]The king used the almugwood to make supports for the temple of the LORD and for the royal palace, and to make harps and lyres for the musicians. So much almugwood has never been imported or seen since that day.)

[13]King Solomon gave the queen of Sheba all she desired and asked for, besides what he had given her out of his royal bounty. Then she left and returned with her retinue to her own country.

Solomon's Splendor

[14]The weight of the gold that Solomon received yearly was 666 talents,[j] [15]not including the revenues from merchants and traders and from all the Arabian kings and the governors of the land.

[16]King Solomon made two hundred large shields of hammered gold; six hundred bekas[k] of gold went into each shield. [17]He also made three hundred small

---

[a]18 The Hebrew may also be read *Tamar.*   [b]19 Or *charioteers*   [c]21 The Hebrew term refers to the irrevocable giving over of things or persons to the LORD, often by totally destroying them. [d]25 Traditionally *peace offerings*   [e]26 Hebrew *Yam Suph*; that is, Sea of Reeds   [f]28 That is, about 16 tons (about 14.5 metric tons)   [g]5 Or *the ascent by which he went up to*   [h]10 That is, about 4 1/2 tons (about 4 metric tons)   [i]11 Probably a variant of *algumwood*; also in verse 12   [j]14 That is, about 25 tons (about 23 metric tons)   [k]16 That is, about 7 1/2 pounds (about 3.5 kilograms)

shields of hammered gold, with three minas*a* of gold in each shield. The king put them in the Palace of the Forest of Lebanon.
18Then the king made a great throne inlaid with ivory and overlaid with fine gold. **19**The throne had six steps, and its back had a rounded top. On both sides of the seat were armrests, with a lion standing beside each of them. **20**Twelve lions stood on the six steps, one at either end of each step. Nothing like it had ever been made for any other kingdom. **21**All King Solomon's goblets were gold, and all the household articles in the Palace of the Forest of Lebanon were pure gold. Nothing was made of silver, because silver was considered of little value in Solomon's days. **22**The king had a fleet of trading ships*b* at sea along with the ships of Hiram. Once every three years it returned, carrying gold, silver and ivory, and apes and baboons.
23King Solomon was greater in riches and wisdom than all the other kings of the earth. **24**The whole world sought audience with Solomon to hear the wisdom God had put in his heart. **25**Year after year, everyone who came brought a gift—articles of silver and gold, robes, weapons and spices, and horses and mules.

26Solomon accumulated chariots and horses; he had fourteen hundred chariots and twelve thousand horses,*c* which he kept in the chariot cities and also with him in Jerusalem. **27**The king made silver as common in Jerusalem as stones, and cedar as plentiful as sycamore-fig trees in the foothills. **28**Solomon's horses were imported from Egypt*d* and from Kue*e*—the royal merchants purchased them from Kue. **29**They imported a chariot from Egypt for six hundred shekels*f* of silver, and a horse for a hundred and fifty.*g* They also exported them to all the kings of the Hittites and of the Arameans.

Solomon's Wives

11 King Solomon, however, loved many foreign women besides Pharaoh's daughter—Moabites, Ammonites, Edomites, Sidonians and Hittites. **2**They were from nations about which the LORD had told the Israelites, "You must not intermarry with them, because they will surely

a17 That is, about 3 3/4 pounds (about 1.7 kilograms)   *b22* Hebrew *of ships of Tarshish*   *c26* Or *charioteers*   *d28* Or possibly *Muzur*, a region in Cilicia; also in verse 29   *e28* Probably *Cilicia*   *f29* That is, about 15 pounds (about 7 kilograms)   *g29* That is, about 3 3/4 pounds (about 1.7 kilograms)

HEY DAD

Why could men in the Old Testament have more than one wife?

Text: 1 Kings 11:3-4

God did not originally plan for a man to have more than one wife. Genesis 2:24 says that "a man will leave his father and mother and be united to his *wife* [not wives], and they will become one flesh."

Rabbi Joseph Telushkin, author of *Jewish Literacy,* is an expert on the laws of the Old Testament. In fact, as a Rabbi, the Old Testament is the only part of Scripture he regards as valid. He says that the 10th century Jewish ban on polygamy was probably influenced "by the curious fact that although the Torah law permitted polygamy, Torah narrative opposed it. Virtually every polygamous relationship described in the Bible is miserably unhappy" (p. 178).

When Abraham took Hagar as a concubine, she and Sarah grew to hate each other. King David had many wives, and his family was filled with strife. And as for Solomon, the wisest man in history … multiple wives were his downfall. King Solomon had *hundreds* of wives and concubines. 1 Kings 11:3 says Solomon's wives led him astray, and because he chose their false gods over the true God, his kingdom was ripped away from him.

Now, what do you think God was trying to get across here? Legal or illegal, having more than one wife is simply not a good idea.

Telushkin, Joseph (1991). Jewish Literacy: The Most Important Things to Know about the Jewish Religion, Its People, and Its History. *New York, NY: William Morrow and Company, Inc.*

For a complete listing of Questions Kids Ask, turn to page 1435.

turn your hearts after their gods." Nevertheless, Solomon held fast to them in love. ³He had seven hundred wives of royal birth and three hundred concubines, and his wives led him astray. ⁴As Solomon grew old, his wives turned his heart after other gods, and his heart was not fully devoted to the LORD his God, as the heart of David his father had been. ⁵He followed Ashtoreth the goddess of the Sidonians, and Molech*ᵃ* the detestable god of the Ammonites. ⁶So Solomon did evil in the eyes of the LORD; he did not follow the LORD completely, as David his father had done.

⁷On a hill east of Jerusalem, Solomon built a high place for Chemosh the detestable god of Moab, and for Molech the detestable god of the Ammonites. ⁸He did the same for all his foreign wives, who burned incense and offered sacrifices to their gods.

⁹The LORD became angry with Solomon because his heart had turned away from the LORD, the God of Israel, who had ap-

peared to him twice. ¹⁰Although he had forbidden Solomon to follow other gods, Solomon did not keep the LORD's command. ¹¹So the LORD said to Solomon, "Since this is your attitude and you have not kept my covenant and my decrees, which I commanded you, I will most certainly tear the kingdom away from you and give it to one of your subordinates. ¹²Nevertheless, for the sake of David your father, I will not do it during your lifetime. I will tear it out of the hand of your son. ¹³Yet I will not tear the whole kingdom from him, but will give him one tribe for the sake of David my servant and for the sake of Jerusalem, which I have chosen."

Solomon's Adversaries

¹⁴Then the LORD raised up against Solomon an adversary, Hadad the Edomite, from the royal line of Edom. ¹⁵Earlier when David was fighting with Edom, Joab

---

ᵃ5 Hebrew Milcom; also in verse 33

An Extra Season of Protection
David, the Hedge-building Father

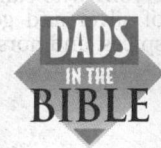
DADS
IN THE
BIBLE

"I will most certainly tear the kingdom away from you and give it to one of your subordinates. Nevertheless, for the sake of David your father, I will not do it during your lifetime" (11:11–12).

Text: 1 Kings 11

If you faithfully apply top-quality, weed-killing chemicals to your lawn, you'll enjoy the beauty of consistently dandelion-free turf around your home. Because a man in our neighborhood did this for many years, his lawn looked like a page out of a magazine.

When this neighbor moved, the new owner didn't seem to care about the weeds. During the first year that he lived there, I noticed only a few dandelions. But during the following seasons there was more yellow than green around his place. In fact, after a few years, we thought he may be growing dandelions commercially!

In a sense, the former owner of the house protected the lawn from weeds for the one who succeeded him. The new owner had a choice: Either keep up the regimen and enjoy the benefits, or stop it and allow the weeds to grow.

David was a bit like my old neighbor. His confession and godly obedience not only benefited him while he lived, it also became a "hedge of protection" for his son Solomon after his death.

As a dad, you have a responsibility to be God's man—at work, at home, and in the quietness of your own heart. This will bring tangible dividends to you during your lifetime. Your awareness of a life reconciled to God will be a great joy.

But this isn't the only benefit you will reap from living a godly life. By your godly example, you will be protecting your children as well—killing the weeds in their lawns, so to speak—long after you are gone. That ought to be enough to motivate you to walk the straight and narrow . . . just in case you needed some encouragement.

For a complete listing of Dads in the Bible, turn to page 1434.

the commander of the army, who had gone up to bury the dead, had struck down all the men in Edom. ¹⁶Joab and all the Israelites stayed there for six months, until they had destroyed all the men in Edom. ¹⁷But Hadad, still only a boy, fled to Egypt with some Edomite officials who had served his father. ¹⁸They set out from Midian and went to Paran. Then taking men from Paran with them, they went to Egypt, to Pharaoh king of Egypt, who gave Hadad a house and land and provided him with food.

¹⁹Pharaoh was so pleased with Hadad that he gave him a sister of his own wife, Queen Tahpenes, in marriage. ²⁰The sister of Tahpenes bore him a son named Genubath, whom Tahpenes brought up in the royal palace. There Genubath lived with Pharaoh's own children.

²¹While he was in Egypt, Hadad heard that David rested with his fathers and that Joab the commander of the army was also dead. Then Hadad said to Pharaoh, "Let me go, that I may return to my own country."

²²"What have you lacked here that you want to go back to your own country?" Pharaoh asked.

"Nothing," Hadad replied, "but do let me go!"

²³And God raised up against Solomon another adversary, Rezon son of Eliada, who had fled from his master, Hadadezer king of Zobah. ²⁴He gathered men around him and became the leader of a band of rebels when David destroyed the forces*ᵃ* of Zobah; the rebels went to Damascus, where they settled and took control. ²⁵Rezon was Israel's adversary as long as Solomon lived, adding to the trouble caused by Hadad. So Rezon ruled in Aram and was hostile toward Israel.

Jeroboam Rebels Against Solomon

²⁶Also, Jeroboam son of Nebat rebelled against the king. He was one of Solomon's officials, an Ephraimite from Zeredah, and his mother was a widow named Zeruah.

²⁷Here is the account of how he rebelled against the king: Solomon had built the supporting terraces*ᵇ* and had filled in the gap in the wall of the city of David his father. ²⁸Now Jeroboam was a man of standing, and when Solomon saw how well the young man did his work, he put him in charge of the whole labor force of the house of Joseph.

²⁹About that time Jeroboam was going out of Jerusalem, and Ahijah the prophet of Shiloh met him on the way, wearing a new cloak. The two of them were alone out in the country, ³⁰and Ahijah took hold of the new cloak he was wearing and tore it into twelve pieces. ³¹Then he said to Jeroboam, "Take ten pieces for yourself, for this is what the LORD, the God of Israel, says: 'See, I am going to tear the kingdom out of Solomon's hand and give you ten tribes. ³²But for the sake of my servant David and the city of Jerusalem, which I have chosen out of all the tribes of Israel, he will have one tribe. ³³I will do this because they have*ᶜ* forsaken me and worshiped Ashtoreth the goddess of the Sidonians, Chemosh the god of the Moabites, and Molech the god of the Ammonites, and have not walked in my ways, nor done what is right in my eyes, nor kept my statutes and laws as David, Solomon's father, did.

³⁴" 'But I will not take the whole kingdom out of Solomon's hand; I have made him ruler all the days of his life for the sake of David my servant, whom I chose and who observed my commands and statutes. ³⁵I will take the kingdom from his son's hands and give you ten tribes. ³⁶I will give one tribe to his son so that David my servant may always have a lamp before me in Jerusalem, the city where I chose to put my Name. ³⁷However, as for you, I will take you, and you will rule over all that your heart desires; you will be king over Israel. ³⁸If you do whatever I command you and walk in my ways and do what is right in my eyes by keeping my statutes and commands, as David my servant did, I will be with you. I will build you a dynasty as enduring as the one I built for David and will give Israel to you. ³⁹I will humble David's descendants because of this, but not forever.' "

⁴⁰Solomon tried to kill Jeroboam, but Jeroboam fled to Egypt, to Shishak the king, and stayed there until Solomon's death.

Solomon's Death

⁴¹As for the other events of Solomon's reign—all he did and the wisdom he displayed—are they not written in the book of the annals of Solomon? ⁴²Solomon reigned in Jerusalem over all Israel forty

---

ᵃ24 Hebrew *destroyed them*   *ᵇ27* Or *the Millo*
ᶜ33 Hebrew; Septuagint, Vulgate and Syriac *because he has*

years. ⁴³Then he rested with his fathers and was buried in the city of David his father. And Rehoboam his son succeeded him as king.

Israel Rebels Against Rehoboam

12 Rehoboam went to Shechem, for all the Israelites had gone there to make him king. ²When Jeroboam son of Nebat heard this (he was still in Egypt, where he had fled from King Solomon), he returned from*ᵃ* Egypt. ³So they sent for Jeroboam, and he and the whole assembly of Israel went to Rehoboam and said to him: ⁴"Your father put a heavy yoke on us, but now lighten the harsh labor and the heavy yoke he put on us, and we will serve you." ⁵Rehoboam answered, "Go away for three days and then come back to me." So the people went away.

⁶Then King Rehoboam consulted the

ᵃ2 Or he remained in

Headlines from Hell

Every morning, usually before dawn, our little dog, Bear, goes to the back door. She stands there for a moment, then she makes a little chirping sound. My wife calls it a "trill." Whatever it is, I know it's Bear's way of telling me that she needs to go on a field trip to the back yard.

I clip her leash on, open the garage door, and venture out into the darkness. While waiting for Bear to find the perfect blade of grass to water, I unroll the newspaper. The first thing I see is the headline: political news, sports results, crimes committed … whatever our local publisher decides should grab me first. The other day I got to thinking, *When I unroll this paper, what headline do I hate most to see?* Let me ask you the same question. Which headline do you dislike more than any other?

For me, the headline that hurts the most is an airline disaster. I'm gripped by pictures of small pieces of a once-airworthy ship that had been full of unsuspecting passengers. The tragedy always seems so needless.

The second worst headline for me is the news of another fallen leader—someone who had been respected by thousands, perhaps millions of people and who has, like a crippled airplane, needlessly fallen from grace. I always wonder how this really happened. I grieve for his horrified and embarrassed family. I speculate as to how this will affect others.

King Rehoboam, Solomon's son, had an

DAILY INSIGHT

TUESDAY
Passage:
1 Kings 12:1–15
Verse:
1 Kings 12:8

important decision to make. His first instinct was to consult his elders—veteran decision makers who knew the consequences of making both wise and foolish choices. Rehoboam got the counsel he was seeking, but he didn't like it. So he went to a bunch of his buddies—friends who had not only grown up with him, but who were also on his payroll.

They, too, gave Rehoboam advice. But this time it was just what the king wanted to hear. So, rejecting the wisdom of his elders, this foolish and indiscreet leader did what his *friends* told him to do.

To whom do you go for advice? Is there a person in your life who would dare to challenge your presuppositions and biases? Do you count on the counsel of someone who has the wisdom of advanced years and/or experience? Or do you only look for input that supports your own viewpoint?

Today's text ought to provide fair warning. One cool morning, the Israelites heard the following whispered headline: "Disgraced king flees town. Chief of staff murdered in cold blood."

I have a question: What person do you go to for answers to the tough questions? If someone's name doesn't immediately come to your mind, you may be in line for trouble. Find someone who loves you enough to tell you the truth. Please don't wait until you have a headline of your very own.

For your next devotional reading, go to page 386.

elders who had served his father Solomon during his lifetime. "How would you advise me to answer these people?" he asked.

[7]They replied, "If today you will be a servant to these people and serve them and give them a favorable answer, they will always be your servants."

[8]But Rehoboam rejected the advice the elders gave him and consulted the young men who had grown up with him and were serving him. [9]He asked them, "What is your advice? How should we answer these people who say to me, 'Lighten the yoke your father put on us'?"

[10]The young men who had grown up with him replied, "Tell these people who have said to you, 'Your father put a heavy yoke on us, but make our yoke lighter'— tell them, 'My little finger is thicker than my father's waist. [11]My father laid on you a heavy yoke; I will make it even heavier. My father scourged you with whips; I will scourge you with scorpions.' "

[12]Three days later Jeroboam and all the people returned to Rehoboam, as the king had said, "Come back to me in three days." [13]The king answered the people harshly. Rejecting the advice given him by the elders, [14]he followed the advice of the young men and said, "My father made your yoke heavy; I will make it even heavier. My father scourged you with whips; I will scourge you with scorpions." [15]So the king did not listen to the people, for this turn of events was from the LORD, to fulfill the word the LORD had spoken to Jeroboam son of Nebat through Ahijah the Shilonite.

[16]When all Israel saw that the king refused to listen to them, they answered the king:

"What share do we have in David,
    what part in Jesse's son?
To your tents, O Israel!
    Look after your own house,
        O David!"

So the Israelites went home. [17]But as for the Israelites who were living in the towns of Judah, Rehoboam still ruled over them.

[18]King Rehoboam sent out Adoniram,[a] who was in charge of forced labor, but all Israel stoned him to death. King Rehoboam, however, managed to get into his chariot and escape to Jerusalem. [19]So Israel has been in rebellion against the house of David to this day.

[20]When all the Israelites heard that Jeroboam had returned, they sent and called him to the assembly and made him king over all Israel. Only the tribe of Judah remained loyal to the house of David.

[21]When Rehoboam arrived in Jerusalem, he mustered the whole house of Judah and the tribe of Benjamin—a hundred and eighty thousand fighting men— to make war against the house of Israel and to regain the kingdom for Rehoboam son of Solomon.

[22]But this word of God came to Shemaiah the man of God: [23]"Say to Rehoboam son of Solomon king of Judah, to the whole house of Judah and Benjamin, and to the rest of the people, [24]'This is what the LORD says: Do not go up to fight against your brothers, the Israelites. Go home, every one of you, for this is my doing.' " So they obeyed the word of the LORD and went home again, as the LORD had ordered.

Golden Calves at Bethel and Dan

[25]Then Jeroboam fortified Shechem in the hill country of Ephraim and lived there. From there he went out and built up Peniel.[b]

[26]Jeroboam thought to himself, "The kingdom will now likely revert to the house of David. [27]If these people go up to offer sacrifices at the temple of the LORD in Jerusalem, they will again give their allegiance to their lord, Rehoboam king of Judah. They will kill me and return to King Rehoboam."

[28]After seeking advice, the king made two golden calves. He said to the people, "It is too much for you to go up to Jerusalem. Here are your gods, O Israel, who brought you up out of Egypt." [29]One he set up in Bethel, and the other in Dan. [30]And this thing became a sin; the people went even as far as Dan to worship the one there.

[31]Jeroboam built shrines on high places and appointed priests from all sorts of people, even though they were not Levites. [32]He instituted a festival on the fifteenth day of the eighth month, like the festival held in Judah, and offered sacrifices on the altar. This he did in Bethel, sacrificing to the calves he had made. And at Bethel he also installed priests at the high places he had made. [33]On the fifteenth day of the eighth month, a month of his own choosing, he offered sacrifices

---

[a]18 Some Septuagint manuscripts and Syriac (see also 1 Kings 4:6 and 5:14); Hebrew Adoram
[b]25 Hebrew Penuel, a variant of Peniel

on the altar he had built at Bethel. So he instituted the festival for the Israelites and went up to the altar to make offerings.

The Man of God From Judah

13 By the word of the LORD a man of God came from Judah to Bethel, as Jeroboam was standing by the altar to make an offering. ²He cried out against the altar by the word of the LORD: "O altar, altar! This is what the LORD says: 'A son named Josiah will be born to the house of David. On you he will sacrifice the priests of the high places who now make offerings here, and human bones will be burned on you.' " ³That same day the man of God gave a sign: "This is the sign the LORD has declared: The altar will be split apart and the ashes on it will be poured out."

⁴When King Jeroboam heard what the man of God cried out against the altar at Bethel, he stretched out his hand from the altar and said, "Seize him!" But the hand he stretched out toward the man shriveled up, so that he could not pull it back. ⁵Also, the altar was split apart and its ashes poured out according to the sign given by the man of God by the word of the LORD.

⁶Then the king said to the man of God, "Intercede with the LORD your God and pray for me that my hand may be restored." So the man of God interceded with the LORD, and the king's hand was restored and became as it was before. ⁷The king said to the man of God, "Come home with me and have something to eat, and I will give you a gift."

⁸But the man of God answered the king, "Even if you were to give me half your possessions, I would not go with you, nor would I eat bread or drink water here. ⁹For I was commanded by the word of the LORD: 'You must not eat bread or drink water or return by the way you came.' " ¹⁰So he took another road and did not return by the way he had come to Bethel.

¹¹Now there was a certain old prophet living in Bethel, whose sons came and told him all that the man of God had done there that day. They also told their father what he had said to the king. ¹²Their father asked them, "Which way did he go?" And his sons showed him which road the man of God from Judah had taken. ¹³So he said to his sons, "Saddle the donkey for me." And when they had saddled the donkey for him, he mounted it ¹⁴and rode after the man of God. He found him sitting under an oak tree and asked, "Are you the man of God who came from Judah?"

"I am," he replied.

¹⁵So the prophet said to him, "Come home with me and eat."

¹⁶The man of God said, "I cannot turn back and go with you, nor can I eat bread or drink water with you in this place. ¹⁷I have been told by the word of the LORD: 'You must not eat bread or drink water there or return by the way you came.' "

¹⁸The old prophet answered, "I too am a prophet, as you are. And an angel said to me by the word of the LORD: 'Bring him back with you to your house so that he may eat bread and drink water.' " (But he was lying to him.) ¹⁹So the man of God returned with him and ate and drank in his house.

²⁰While they were sitting at the table, the word of the LORD came to the old prophet who had brought him back. ²¹He cried out to the man of God who had come from Judah, "This is what the LORD says: 'You have defied the word of the LORD and have not kept the command the LORD your God gave you. ²²You came back and ate bread and drank water in the place where he told you not to eat or drink. Therefore your body will not be buried in the tomb of your fathers.' "

²³When the man of God had finished eating and drinking, the prophet who had brought him back saddled his donkey for him. ²⁴As he went on his way, a lion met him on the road and killed him, and his body was thrown down on the road, with both the donkey and the lion standing beside it. ²⁵Some people who passed by saw the body thrown down there, with the lion standing beside the body, and they went and reported it in the city where the old prophet lived.

²⁶When the prophet who had brought him back from his journey heard of it, he said, "It is the man of God who defied the word of the LORD. The LORD has given him over to the lion, which has mauled him and killed him, as the word of the LORD had warned him."

²⁷The prophet said to his sons, "Saddle the donkey for me," and they did so. ²⁸Then he went out and found the body thrown down on the road, with the donkey and the lion standing beside it. The lion had neither eaten the body nor mauled the donkey. ²⁹So the prophet picked up the body of the man of God, laid it on the donkey, and brought it back

to his own city to mourn for him and bury him. ³⁰Then he laid the body in his own tomb, and they mourned over him and said, "Oh, my brother!"

³¹After burying him, he said to his sons, "When I die, bury me in the grave where the man of God is buried; lay my bones beside his bones. ³²For the message he declared by the word of the LORD against the altar in Bethel and against all the shrines on the high places in the towns of Samaria will certainly come true."

³³Even after this, Jeroboam did not change his evil ways, but once more appointed priests for the high places from all sorts of people. Anyone who wanted to become a priest he consecrated for the high places. ³⁴This was the sin of the house of Jeroboam that led to its downfall and to its destruction from the face of the earth.

Ahijah's Prophecy Against Jeroboam

14 At that time Abijah son of Jeroboam became ill, ²and Jeroboam said to his wife, "Go, disguise yourself, so you won't be recognized as the wife of Jeroboam. Then go to Shiloh. Ahijah the prophet is there—the one who told me I would be king over this people. ³Take ten loaves of bread with you, some cakes and a jar of honey, and go to him. He will tell you what will happen to the boy." ⁴So Jeroboam's wife did what he said and went to Ahijah's house in Shiloh.

Now Ahijah could not see; his sight was gone because of his age. ⁵But the LORD had told Ahijah, "Jeroboam's wife is coming to ask you about her son, for he is ill, and you are to give her such and such an answer. When she arrives, she will pretend to be someone else."

⁶So when Ahijah heard the sound of her footsteps at the door, he said, "Come in, wife of Jeroboam. Why this pretense? I have been sent to you with bad news. ⁷Go, tell Jeroboam that this is what the LORD, the God of Israel, says: 'I raised you up from among the people and made you a leader over my people Israel. ⁸I tore the kingdom away from the house of David and gave it to you, but you have not been like my servant David, who kept my commands and followed me with all his heart, doing only what was right in my eyes. ⁹You have done more evil than all who lived before you. You have made for yourself other gods, idols made of metal; you have provoked me to anger and thrust me behind your back.

¹⁰" 'Because of this, I am going to bring disaster on the house of Jeroboam. I will cut off from Jeroboam every last male in Israel—slave or free. I will burn up the house of Jeroboam as one burns dung, until it is all gone. ¹¹Dogs will eat those belonging to Jeroboam who die in the city, and the birds of the air will feed on those who die in the country. The LORD has spoken!'

¹²"As for you, go back home. When you set foot in your city, the boy will die. ¹³All Israel will mourn for him and bury him. He is the only one belonging to Jeroboam who will be buried, because he is the only one in the house of Jeroboam in whom the LORD, the God of Israel, has found anything good.

¹⁴"The LORD will raise up for himself a king over Israel who will cut off the family of Jeroboam. This is the day! What? Yes, even now.ᵃ ¹⁵And the LORD will strike Israel, so that it will be like a reed swaying in the water. He will uproot Israel from this good land that he gave to their forefathers and scatter them beyond the River,ᵇ because they provoked the LORD to anger by making Asherah poles.ᶜ ¹⁶And he will give Israel up because of the sins Jeroboam has committed and has caused Israel to commit."

¹⁷Then Jeroboam's wife got up and left and went to Tirzah. As soon as she stepped over the threshold of the house, the boy died. ¹⁸They buried him, and all Israel mourned for him, as the LORD had said through his servant the prophet Ahijah.

¹⁹The other events of Jeroboam's reign, his wars and how he ruled, are written in the book of the annals of the kings of Israel. ²⁰He reigned for twenty-two years and then rested with his fathers. And Nadab his son succeeded him as king.

Rehoboam King of Judah

²¹Rehoboam son of Solomon was king in Judah. He was forty-one years old when he became king, and he reigned seventeen years in Jerusalem, the city the LORD had chosen out of all the tribes of Israel in which to put his Name. His mother's name was Naamah; she was an Ammonite. ²²Judah did evil in the eyes of the LORD.

ᵃ14 The meaning of the Hebrew for this sentence is uncertain.   ᵇ15 That is, the Euphrates   ᶜ15 That is, symbols of the goddess Asherah; here and elsewhere in 1 Kings

By the sins they committed they stirred up his jealous anger more than their fathers had done. [23]They also set up for themselves high places, sacred stones and Asherah poles on every high hill and under every spreading tree. [24]There were even male shrine prostitutes in the land; the people engaged in all the detestable practices of the nations the LORD had driven out before the Israelites.

[25]In the fifth year of King Rehoboam, Shishak king of Egypt attacked Jerusalem. [26]He carried off the treasures of the temple of the LORD and the treasures of the royal palace. He took everything, including all the gold shields Solomon had made. [27]So King Rehoboam made bronze shields to replace them and assigned these to the commanders of the guard on duty at the entrance to the royal palace. [28]Whenever the king went to the LORD's temple, the guards bore the shields, and afterward they returned them to the guardroom.

[29]As for the other events of Rehoboam's reign, and all he did, are they not written in the book of the annals of the kings of Judah? [30]There was continual warfare between Rehoboam and Jeroboam. [31]And Rehoboam rested with his fathers and was buried with them in the City of David. His mother's name was Naamah; she was an Ammonite. And Abijah[a] his son succeeded him as king.

Abijah King of Judah

15 In the eighteenth year of the reign of Jeroboam son of Nebat, Abijah[b] became king of Judah, [2]and he reigned in Jerusalem three years. His mother's name was Maacah daughter of Abishalom.[c]

[3]He committed all the sins his father had done before him; his heart was not fully devoted to the LORD his God, as the heart of David his forefather had been. [4]Nevertheless, for David's sake the LORD his God gave him a lamp in Jerusalem by raising up a son to succeed him and by making Jerusalem strong. [5]For David had done what was right in the eyes of the LORD and had not failed to keep any of the LORD's commands all the days of his life—except in the case of Uriah the Hittite.

[6]There was war between Rehoboam[d] and Jeroboam throughout ⌜Abijah's⌝ lifetime. [7]As for the other events of Abijah's reign, and all he did, are they not written in the book of the annals of the kings of Judah? There was war between Abijah and

Jeroboam. [8]And Abijah rested with his fathers and was buried in the City of David. And Asa his son succeeded him as king.

Asa King of Judah

[9]In the twentieth year of Jeroboam king of Israel, Asa became king of Judah, [10]and he reigned in Jerusalem forty-one years. His grandmother's name was Maacah daughter of Abishalom.

[11]Asa did what was right in the eyes of the LORD, as his father David had done. [12]He expelled the male shrine prostitutes from the land and got rid of all the idols his fathers had made. [13]He even deposed his grandmother Maacah from her position as queen mother, because she had made a repulsive Asherah pole. Asa cut the pole down and burned it in the Kidron Valley. [14]Although he did not remove the high places, Asa's heart was fully committed to the LORD all his life. [15]He brought into the temple of the LORD the silver and gold and the articles that he and his father had dedicated.

[16]There was war between Asa and Baasha king of Israel throughout their reigns. [17]Baasha king of Israel went up against Judah and fortified Ramah to prevent anyone from leaving or entering the territory of Asa king of Judah.

[18]Asa then took all the silver and gold that was left in the treasuries of the LORD's temple and of his own palace. He entrusted it to his officials and sent them to Ben-Hadad son of Tabrimmon, the son of Hezion, the king of Aram, who was ruling in Damascus. [19]"Let there be a treaty between me and you," he said, "as there was between my father and your father. See, I am sending you a gift of silver and gold. Now break your treaty with Baasha king of Israel so he will withdraw from me."

[20]Ben-Hadad agreed with King Asa and sent the commanders of his forces against the towns of Israel. He conquered Ijon, Dan, Abel Beth Maacah and all Kinnereth in addition to Naphtali. [21]When Baasha heard this, he stopped building Ramah and withdrew to Tirzah. [22]Then King Asa issued an order to all Judah—no one was exempt—and they carried away from Ra-

---

[a]31 Some Hebrew manuscripts and Septuagint (see also 2 Chron. 12:16); most Hebrew manuscripts *Abijam*   [b]1 Some Hebrew manuscripts and Septuagint (see also 2 Chron. 12:16); most Hebrew manuscripts *Abijam*; also in verses 7 and 8   [c]2 A variant of *Absalom*; also in verse 10   [d]6 Most Hebrew manuscripts; some Hebrew manuscripts and Syriac *Abijam* (that is, Abijah)

mah the stones and timber Baasha had been using there. With them King Asa built up Geba in Benjamin, and also Mizpah.

²³As for all the other events of Asa's reign, all his achievements, all he did and the cities he built, are they not written in the book of the annals of the kings of Judah? In his old age, however, his feet became diseased. ²⁴Then Asa rested with his fathers and was buried with them in the city of his father David. And Jehoshaphat his son succeeded him as king.

Nadab King of Israel

²⁵Nadab son of Jeroboam became king of Israel in the second year of Asa king of Judah, and he reigned over Israel two years. ²⁶He did evil in the eyes of the LORD, walking in the ways of his father and in his sin, which he had caused Israel to commit.

²⁷Baasha son of Ahijah of the house of Issachar plotted against him, and he struck him down at Gibbethon, a Philistine town, while Nadab and all Israel were besieging it. ²⁸Baasha killed Nadab in the third year of Asa king of Judah and succeeded him as king.

²⁹As soon as he began to reign, he killed Jeroboam's whole family. He did not leave Jeroboam anyone that breathed, but destroyed them all, according to the word of the LORD given through his servant Ahijah the Shilonite— ³⁰because of the sins Jeroboam had committed and had caused Israel to commit, and because he provoked the LORD, the God of Israel, to anger.

³¹As for the other events of Nadab's reign, and all he did, are they not written in the book of the annals of the kings of Israel? ³²There was war between Asa and Baasha king of Israel throughout their reigns.

Baasha King of Israel

³³In the third year of Asa king of Judah, Baasha son of Ahijah became king of all Israel in Tirzah, and he reigned twenty-four years. ³⁴He did evil in the eyes of the LORD, walking in the ways of Jeroboam and in his sin, which he had caused Israel to commit.

16 Then the word of the LORD came to Jehu son of Hanani against Baasha: ²"I lifted you up from the dust and made you leader of my people Israel, but you walked in the ways of Jeroboam and caused my people Israel to sin and to pro-

voke me to anger by their sins. ³So I am about to consume Baasha and his house, and I will make your house like that of Jeroboam son of Nebat. ⁴Dogs will eat those belonging to Baasha who die in the city, and the birds of the air will feed on those who die in the country."

⁵As for the other events of Baasha's reign, what he did and his achievements, are they not written in the book of the annals of the kings of Israel? ⁶Baasha rested with his fathers and was buried in Tirzah. And Elah his son succeeded him as king.

⁷Moreover, the word of the LORD came through the prophet Jehu son of Hanani to Baasha and his house, because of all the evil he had done in the eyes of the LORD, provoking him to anger by the things he did, and becoming like the house of Jeroboam—and also because he destroyed it.

Elah King of Israel

⁸In the twenty-sixth year of Asa king of Judah, Elah son of Baasha became king of Israel, and he reigned in Tirzah two years.

⁹Zimri, one of his officials, who had command of half his chariots, plotted against him. Elah was in Tirzah at the time, getting drunk in the home of Arza, the man in charge of the palace at Tirzah. ¹⁰Zimri came in, struck him down and killed him in the twenty-seventh year of Asa king of Judah. Then he succeeded him as king.

¹¹As soon as he began to reign and was seated on the throne, he killed off Baasha's whole family. He did not spare a single male, whether relative or friend. ¹²So Zimri destroyed the whole family of Baasha, in accordance with the word of the LORD spoken against Baasha through the prophet Jehu— ¹³because of all the sins Baasha and his son Elah had committed and had caused Israel to commit, so that they provoked the LORD, the God of Israel, to anger by their worthless idols. ¹⁴As for the other events of Elah's reign, and all he did, are they not written in the book of the annals of the kings of Israel?

Zimri King of Israel

¹⁵In the twenty-seventh year of Asa king of Judah, Zimri reigned in Tirzah seven days. The army was encamped near Gibbethon, a Philistine town. ¹⁶When the Israelites in the camp heard that Zimri had plotted against the king and murdered him, they proclaimed Omri, the

commander of the army, king over Israel that very day there in the camp. ¹⁷Then Omri and all the Israelites with him withdrew from Gibbethon and laid siege to Tirzah. ¹⁸When Zimri saw that the city was taken, he went into the citadel of the royal palace and set the palace on fire around him. So he died, ¹⁹because of the sins he had committed, doing evil in the eyes of the LORD and walking in the ways of Jeroboam and in the sin he had committed and had caused Israel to commit.

²⁰As for the other events of Zimri's reign, and the rebellion he carried out, are they not written in the book of the annals of the kings of Israel?

Beep, Beep

DAILY INSIGHT

WEDNESDAY

Passage:
1 Kings 16:1–20

Verses:
1 Kings 16:14–20

The drive from college to my folks' home in Chicago was exactly 212 miles. Depending on the time of day and, of course, the weather conditions, it usually took me four solid hours of driving. Late one spring afternoon, just before dusk, I was driving my 1962 Chevy Bel Aire north on state road 41, just south of West Lafayette, Indiana. All alone, I had the radio cranked up to windshield-cracking decibels. The Mammas and the Papas were belting out "Monday, Monday."

I can't tell you why I remember this incident so clearly, but I do. It happened just like this: The road was a double-yellow two lane highway, and there was very little traffic. The car in front of me was at least three-quarters of a mile away. Suddenly, out of the corner of my eye, no more than a hundred yards in front of me, I saw a little bird. It looked like one of those skinny road-runner-like birds, and it was crossing the road, lickety split.

The bird traversed the gravel shoulder, then scooted across my northbound lane without a problem. What he didn't see was a gigantic Kenworth eighteen-wheeler, bearing southward. The cab was massive—polished chrome exhaust pipes belching white smoke, wind spoilers, and running lights already illuminated.

Unfortunately for my little friend, the timing of his venture to the southbound lane coincided with the truck's journey to the same spot. Tragically, the exact center of the left front wheel met him mid-stride. Quite simply, the bird disappeared. In an instant he went from being a busy little creature to being a wet spot on highway 41, just south of West Lafayette. No feath-ers. No flopping around. Just gone.

Chapter sixteen of 1 Kings tells of five wicked men who ruled Israel. Except for Ahab, the last one in the chapter, these are names you've probably never heard before. In fact, today's verses tell us that there is so little worth remembering about these corrupt leaders that the Bible says almost nothing about them. What a sobering thought.

If you and I would have had the chance to interview these mighty kings during their reigns, I'll bet they'd have told us that they were pretty significant. "My administration is moving right along," each one might have told us … blind road runners, each one of them.

When these busy kings died, there were no feathers. No flopping around. Just a small wet spot in Hebrew history. What a shame.

You and I must achieve more than this. Our lives must count for something more than a smear in the history books of our family lineage. Our best efforts to live a life marked with integrity and mercy, hard work and tenderness, faithfulness and love will insure that our lives will be an encouragement to those who follow and remember … a model for our children and their children. God, through his Holy Spirit, promises to empower us to do just that if we ask for his help.

Run hard. Be good. Pray always. And whatever you do, please look both ways before crossing Highway 41 just south of West Lafayette.

For your next devotional reading, go to page 389.

Omri King of Israel

²¹Then the people of Israel were split into two factions; half supported Tibni son of Ginath for king, and the other half supported Omri. ²²But Omri's followers proved stronger than those of Tibni son of Ginath. So Tibni died and Omri became king.

²³In the thirty-first year of Asa king of Judah, Omri became king of Israel, and he reigned twelve years, six of them in Tirzah. ²⁴He bought the hill of Samaria from Shemer for two talents*a* of silver and built a city on the hill, calling it Samaria, after Shemer, the name of the former owner of the hill.

²⁵But Omri did evil in the eyes of the LORD and sinned more than all those before him. ²⁶He walked in all the ways of Jeroboam son of Nebat and in his sin, which he had caused Israel to commit, so that they provoked the LORD, the God of Israel, to anger by their worthless idols.

²⁷As for the other events of Omri's reign, what he did and the things he achieved, are they not written in the book of the annals of the kings of Israel? ²⁸Omri rested with his fathers and was buried in Samaria. And Ahab his son succeeded him as king.

Ahab Becomes King of Israel

²⁹In the thirty-eighth year of Asa king of Judah, Ahab son of Omri became king of Israel, and he reigned in Samaria over Israel twenty-two years. ³⁰Ahab son of Omri did more evil in the eyes of the LORD than any of those before him. ³¹He not only considered it trivial to commit the sins of Jeroboam son of Nebat, but he also married Jezebel daughter of Ethbaal king of the Sidonians, and began to serve Baal and worship him. ³²He set up an altar for Baal in the temple of Baal that he built in Samaria. ³³Ahab also made an Asherah pole and did more to provoke the LORD, the God of Israel, to anger than did all the kings of Israel before him.

³⁴In Ahab's time, Hiel of Bethel rebuilt Jericho. He laid its foundations at the cost of his firstborn son Abiram, and he set up its gates at the cost of his youngest son Segub, in accordance with the word of the LORD spoken by Joshua son of Nun.

Elijah Fed by Ravens

17 Now Elijah the Tishbite, from Tishbe*b* in Gilead, said to Ahab, "As the LORD, the God of Israel, lives, whom I serve, there will be neither dew nor rain in the next few years except at my word."

²Then the word of the LORD came to Elijah: ³"Leave here, turn eastward and hide in the Kerith Ravine, east of the Jordan. ⁴You will drink from the brook, and I have ordered the ravens to feed you there."

⁵So he did what the LORD had told him. He went to the Kerith Ravine, east of the Jordan, and stayed there. ⁶The ravens brought him bread and meat in the morning and bread and meat in the evening, and he drank from the brook.

The Widow at Zarephath

⁷Some time later the brook dried up because there had been no rain in the land. ⁸Then the word of the LORD came to him: ⁹"Go at once to Zarephath of Sidon and stay there. I have commanded a widow in that place to supply you with food." ¹⁰So he went to Zarephath. When he came to the town gate, a widow was there gathering sticks. He called to her and asked, "Would you bring me a little water in a jar so I may have a drink?" ¹¹As she was going to get it, he called, "And bring me, please, a piece of bread."

¹²"As surely as the LORD your God lives," she replied, "I don't have any bread—only a handful of flour in a jar and a little oil in a jug. I am gathering a few sticks to take home and make a meal for myself and my son, that we may eat it—and die."

¹³Elijah said to her, "Don't be afraid. Go home and do as you have said. But first make a small cake of bread for me from what you have and bring it to me, and then make something for yourself and your son. ¹⁴For this is what the LORD, the God of Israel, says: 'The jar of flour will not be used up and the jug of oil will not run dry until the day the LORD gives rain on the land.' "

¹⁵She went away and did as Elijah had told her. So there was food every day for Elijah and for the woman and her family. ¹⁶For the jar of flour was not used up and the jug of oil did not run dry, in keeping with the word of the LORD spoken by Elijah.

¹⁷Some time later the son of the woman who owned the house became ill. He grew worse and worse, and finally stopped breathing. ¹⁸She said to Elijah, "What do you have against me, man of God? Did

---

a24 That is, about 150 pounds (about 70 kilograms)
b1 Or *Tishbite, of the settlers*

you come to remind me of my sin and kill my son?"

¹⁹"Give me your son," Elijah replied. He took him from her arms, carried him to the upper room where he was staying, and laid him on his bed. ²⁰Then he cried out to the LORD, "O LORD my God, have you brought tragedy also upon this widow I am staying with, by causing her son to die?" ²¹Then he stretched himself out on the boy three times and cried to the LORD, "O LORD my God, let this boy's life return to him!"

²²The LORD heard Elijah's cry, and the boy's life returned to him, and he lived. ²³Elijah picked up the child and carried him down from the room into the house. He gave him to his mother and said, "Look, your son is alive!"

²⁴Then the woman said to Elijah, "Now I know that you are a man of God and that the word of the LORD from your mouth is the truth."

Elijah and Obadiah

18 After a long time, in the third year, the word of the LORD came to Elijah: "Go and present yourself to Ahab, and I will send rain on the land." ²So Elijah went to present himself to Ahab.

Now the famine was severe in Samaria, ³and Ahab had summoned Obadiah, who was in charge of his palace. (Obadiah was a devout believer in the LORD. ⁴While Jezebel was killing off the LORD's prophets, Obadiah had taken a hundred prophets and hidden them in two caves, fifty in each, and had supplied them with food and water.) ⁵Ahab had said to Obadiah, "Go through the land to all the springs and valleys. Maybe we can find some grass to keep the horses and mules alive so we will not have to kill any of our animals." ⁶So they divided the land they were to cover, Ahab going in one direction and Obadiah in another.

⁷As Obadiah was walking along, Elijah met him. Obadiah recognized him, bowed down to the ground, and said, "Is it really you, my lord Elijah?"

⁸"Yes," he replied. "Go tell your master, 'Elijah is here.' "

⁹"What have I done wrong," asked Obadiah, "that you are handing your servant over to Ahab to be put to death? ¹⁰As surely as the LORD your God lives, there is not a nation or kingdom where my master has not sent someone to look for you. And whenever a nation or kingdom claimed you were not there, he made them swear they could not find you. ¹¹But now you tell me to go to my master and say, 'Elijah is here.' ¹²I don't know where the Spirit of the LORD may carry you when I leave you. If I go and tell Ahab and he doesn't find you, he will kill me. Yet I your servant have worshiped the LORD since my youth. ¹³Haven't you heard, my lord, what I did while Jezebel was killing the prophets of the LORD? I hid a hundred of the LORD's prophets in two caves, fifty in each, and supplied them with food and water. ¹⁴And now you tell me to go to my master and say, 'Elijah is here.' He will kill me!"

¹⁵Elijah said, "As the LORD Almighty lives, whom I serve, I will surely present myself to Ahab today."

Elijah on Mount Carmel

¹⁶So Obadiah went to meet Ahab and told him, and Ahab went to meet Elijah. ¹⁷When he saw Elijah, he said to him, "Is that you, you troubler of Israel?"

¹⁸"I have not made trouble for Israel," Elijah replied. "But you and your father's family have. You have abandoned the LORD's commands and have followed the Baals. ¹⁹Now summon the people from all over Israel to meet me on Mount Carmel. And bring the four hundred and fifty prophets of Baal and the four hundred prophets of Asherah, who eat at Jezebel's table."

²⁰So Ahab sent word throughout all Israel and assembled the prophets on Mount Carmel. ²¹Elijah went before the people and said, "How long will you waver between two opinions? If the LORD is God, follow him; but if Baal is God, follow him."

But the people said nothing.

²²Then Elijah said to them, "I am the only one of the LORD's prophets left, but Baal has four hundred and fifty prophets. ²³Get two bulls for us. Let them choose one for themselves, and let them cut it into pieces and put it on the wood but not set fire to it. I will prepare the other bull and put it on the wood but not set fire to it. ²⁴Then you call on the name of your god, and I will call on the name of the LORD. The god who answers by fire—he is God."

Then all the people said, "What you say is good."

²⁵Elijah said to the prophets of Baal, "Choose one of the bulls and prepare it first, since there are so many of you. Call on the name of your god, but do not light

the fire." ²⁶So they took the bull given them and prepared it.

Then they called on the name of Baal from morning till noon. "O Baal, answer us!" they shouted. But there was no response; no one answered. And they danced around the altar they had made.

²⁷At noon Elijah began to taunt them. "Shout louder!" he said. "Surely he is a god! Perhaps he is deep in thought, or busy, or traveling. Maybe he is sleeping and must be awakened." ²⁸So they shout-

ed louder and slashed themselves with swords and spears, as was their custom, until their blood flowed. ²⁹Midday passed, and they continued their frantic prophesying until the time for the evening sacrifice. But there was no response, no one answered, no one paid attention.

³⁰Then Elijah said to all the people, "Come here to me." They came to him, and he repaired the altar of the LORD, which was in ruins. ³¹Elijah took twelve stones, one for each of the tribes descend-

Little Clouds Bring Great Rain

One of our friends spent several years teaching first grade. One evening over dinner, she told us the story of little Jason. This boy was an above-average student who got along with his classmates quite well and was kind and respectful to the teacher. Jason's problem was his hair. Although it certainly wasn't life-threatening, the lad's daily appearance became a real quandary to our friend.

"How could a bright youngster like Jason," she wondered, "look so absolutely awful?"

She waited for an opportunity to deal with the problem. And then it happened. On picture day, incredibly, Jason showed up for school impeccably coiffed. His teacher seized the moment like a kitten would a ball of yarn. "Jason, you look terrific," she told the surprised youngster. "You'd better strap on your running shoes, because every girl in our class will be chasing you today." Jason never again came to school with messy hair.

Who will ever be able to harness the power of an encouraging word?

The story preceding today's verses is a remarkable one. Elijah's courage and God's visible faithfulness are indelibly recorded here. But now it's time for rain. Imagine how thirsty everything must have been after *seven years* of drought! With a pat on the back, Elijah told King Ahab to hustle back to the palace; he'd heard "the sound of heavy rain." But as you read on, you realize there literally wasn't a cloud in the sky.

Elijah climbed to the top of Mount

DAILY INSIGHT

THURSDAY

Passage:
1 Kings 18:16–46

Verses:
1 Kings 18:41–46

Carmel to pray for rain. We see him with his face on the ground desperately pleading with God to answer his request. Periodically, he sent his servant to look into the western sky for rain clouds. Six times the servant came back to Elijah and told him there was nothing. Then on the seventh trip, the servant reported that there was "a cloud as small as a man's hand" rising from the sea. The average meteorologist wouldn't have paid attention, but this was all the encouragement Elijah needed. He hiked up his robe and ran "all the way to Jezreel."

Isn't this a great picture? ... the Creator of the universe sends a tiny cloud, followed by a torrential thunderstorm. And the believing man, making no attempt to dodge the raindrops splattering the dust or the puddles collecting on the roadway, dashes for town just ahead of the king.

One tiny cloud was all Elijah needed. Our teacher friend spoke one word of encouragement to Jason, and his behavior was completely transformed.

How about your children? Do they need such a word from their dad? And what about your wife? How long has it been since you spotted something special and told her how much you appreciated it?

Aren't you glad that God loves us enough to send little clouds to encourage us? Now, go and do likewise.

For your next devotional reading, go to page 398.

ed from Jacob, to whom the word of the LORD had come, saying, "Your name shall be Israel." ³²With the stones he built an altar in the name of the LORD, and he dug a trench around it large enough to hold two seahs*a* of seed. ³³He arranged the wood, cut the bull into pieces and laid it on the wood. Then he said to them, "Fill four large jars with water and pour it on the offering and on the wood."

³⁴"Do it again," he said, and they did it again.

"Do it a third time," he ordered, and they did it the third time. ³⁵The water ran down around the altar and even filled the trench.

³⁶At the time of sacrifice, the prophet Elijah stepped forward and prayed: "O LORD, God of Abraham, Isaac and Israel, let it be known today that you are God in Israel and that I am your servant and have done all these things at your command. ³⁷Answer me, O LORD, answer me, so these people will know that you, O LORD, are God, and that you are turning their hearts back again."

³⁸Then the fire of the LORD fell and burned up the sacrifice, the wood, the stones and the soil, and also licked up the water in the trench.

³⁹When all the people saw this, they fell prostrate and cried, "The LORD—he is God! The LORD—he is God!"

⁴⁰Then Elijah commanded them, "Seize the prophets of Baal. Don't let anyone get away!" They seized them, and Elijah had them brought down to the Kishon Valley and slaughtered there.

⁴¹And Elijah said to Ahab, "Go, eat and drink, for there is the sound of a heavy rain." ⁴²So Ahab went off to eat and drink, but Elijah climbed to the top of Carmel, bent down to the ground and put his face between his knees.

⁴³"Go and look toward the sea," he told his servant. And he went up and looked.

"There is nothing there," he said.

Seven times Elijah said, "Go back."

⁴⁴The seventh time the servant reported, "A cloud as small as a man's hand is rising from the sea."

So Elijah said, "Go and tell Ahab, 'Hitch up your chariot and go down before the rain stops you.' "

⁴⁵Meanwhile, the sky grew black with clouds, the wind rose, a heavy rain came on and Ahab rode off to Jezreel. ⁴⁶The power of the LORD came upon Elijah and, tucking his cloak into his belt, he ran ahead of Ahab all the way to Jezreel.

Elijah Flees to Horeb

19 Now Ahab told Jezebel everything Elijah had done and how he had killed all the prophets with the sword. ²So Jezebel sent a messenger to Elijah to say, "May the gods deal with me, be it ever so severely, if by this time tomorrow I do not make your life like that of one of them."

³Elijah was afraid*b* and ran for his life. When he came to Beersheba in Judah, he left his servant there, ⁴while he himself went a day's journey into the desert. He came to a broom tree, sat down under it and prayed that he might die. "I have had enough, LORD," he said. "Take my life; I am no better than my ancestors." ⁵Then he lay down under the tree and fell asleep.

All at once an angel touched him and said, "Get up and eat." ⁶He looked around, and there by his head was a cake of bread baked over hot coals, and a jar of water. He ate and drank and then lay down again.

⁷The angel of the LORD came back a second time and touched him and said, "Get up and eat, for the journey is too much for you." ⁸So he got up and ate and drank. Strengthened by that food, he traveled forty days and forty nights until he reached Horeb, the mountain of God. ⁹There he went into a cave and spent the night.

The LORD Appears to Elijah

And the word of the LORD came to him: "What are you doing here, Elijah?"

¹⁰He replied, "I have been very zealous for the LORD God Almighty. The Israelites have rejected your covenant, broken down your altars, and put your prophets to death with the sword. I am the only one left, and now they are trying to kill me too."

¹¹The LORD said, "Go out and stand on the mountain in the presence of the LORD, for the LORD is about to pass by."

Then a great and powerful wind tore the mountains apart and shattered the rocks before the LORD, but the LORD was not in the wind. After the wind there was an earthquake, but the LORD was not in the earthquake. ¹²After the earthquake came a fire, but the LORD was not in the fire. And after the fire came a gentle whisper. ¹³When Elijah heard it, he pulled his cloak over his face and went out and stood at the mouth of the cave.

a32 That is, probably about 13 quarts (about 15 liters)   *b3* Or *Elijah saw*

Then a voice said to him, "What are you doing here, Elijah?" ¹⁴He replied, "I have been very zealous for the LORD God Almighty. The Israelites have rejected your covenant, broken down your altars, and put your prophets to death with the sword. I am the only one left, and now they are trying to kill me too."

¹⁵The LORD said to him, "Go back the way you came, and go to the Desert of Damascus. When you get there, anoint Hazael king over Aram. ¹⁶Also, anoint Jehu son of Nimshi king over Israel, and anoint Elisha son of Shaphat from Abel Meholah to succeed you as prophet. ¹⁷Jehu will put to death any who escape the sword of Hazael, and Elisha will put to death any who escape the sword of Jehu. ¹⁸Yet I reserve seven thousand in Israel—all whose knees have not bowed down to Baal and all whose mouths have not kissed him."

The Call of Elisha

¹⁹So Elijah went from there and found Elisha son of Shaphat. He was plowing with twelve yoke of oxen, and he himself was driving the twelfth pair. Elijah went up to him and threw his cloak around him. ²⁰Elisha then left his oxen and ran after Elijah. "Let me kiss my father and mother good-by," he said, "and then I will come with you."

"Go back," Elijah replied. "What have I done to you?"

²¹So Elisha left him and went back. He took his yoke of oxen and slaughtered them. He burned the plowing equipment to cook the meat and gave it to the people, and they ate. Then he set out to follow Elijah and became his attendant.

Ben-Hadad Attacks Samaria

20 Now Ben-Hadad king of Aram mustered his entire army. Accompanied by thirty-two kings with their horses and chariots, he went up and besieged Samaria and attacked it. ²He sent messengers into the city to Ahab king of Israel, saying, "This is what Ben-Hadad says: ³'Your silver and gold are mine, and the best of your wives and children are mine.' "

⁴The king of Israel answered, "Just as you say, my lord the king. I and all I have are yours."

⁵The messengers came again and said, "This is what Ben-Hadad says: 'I sent to demand your silver and gold, your wives and your children. ⁶But about this time

tomorrow I am going to send my officials to search your palace and the houses of your officials. They will seize everything you value and carry it away.' "

⁷The king of Israel summoned all the elders of the land and said to them, "See how this man is looking for trouble! When he sent for my wives and my children, my silver and my gold, I did not refuse him."

⁸The elders and the people all answered, "Don't listen to him or agree to his demands."

⁹So he replied to Ben-Hadad's messengers, "Tell my lord the king, 'Your servant will do all you demanded the first time, but this demand I cannot meet.' " They left and took the answer back to Ben-Hadad.

¹⁰Then Ben-Hadad sent another message to Ahab: "May the gods deal with me, be it ever so severely, if enough dust remains in Samaria to give each of my men a handful."

¹¹The king of Israel answered, "Tell him: 'One who puts on his armor should not boast like one who takes it off.' "

¹²Ben-Hadad heard this message while he and the kings were drinking in their tents,^a and he ordered his men: "Prepare to attack." So they prepared to attack the city.

Ahab Defeats Ben-Hadad

¹³Meanwhile a prophet came to Ahab king of Israel and announced, "This is what the LORD says: 'Do you see this vast army? I will give it into your hand today, and then you will know that I am the LORD.' "

¹⁴"But who will do this?" asked Ahab.

The prophet replied, "This is what the LORD says: 'The young officers of the provincial commanders will do it.' "

"And who will start the battle?" he asked.

The prophet answered, "You will."

¹⁵So Ahab summoned the young officers of the provincial commanders, 232 men. Then he assembled the rest of the Israelites, 7,000 in all. ¹⁶They set out at noon while Ben-Hadad and the 32 kings allied with him were in their tents getting drunk. ¹⁷The young officers of the provincial commanders went out first.

Now Ben-Hadad had dispatched scouts, who reported, "Men are advancing from Samaria."

¹⁸He said, "If they have come out for

^a12 Or in Succoth; also in verse 16

peace, take them alive; if they have come out for war, take them alive.'"

¹⁹The young officers of the provincial commanders marched out of the city with the army behind them ²⁰and each one struck down his opponent. At that, the Arameans fled, with the Israelites in pursuit. But Ben-Hadad king of Aram escaped on horseback with some of his horsemen. ²¹The king of Israel advanced and overpowered the horses and chariots and inflicted heavy losses on the Arameans.

²²Afterward, the prophet came to the king of Israel and said, "Strengthen your position and see what must be done, because next spring the king of Aram will attack you again."

²³Meanwhile, the officials of the king of Aram advised him, "Their gods are gods of the hills. That is why they were too strong for us. But if we fight them on the plains, surely we will be stronger than they. ²⁴Do this: Remove all the kings from their commands and replace them with other officers. ²⁵You must also raise an army like the one you lost—horse for horse and chariot for chariot—so we can fight Israel on the plains. Then surely we will be stronger than they." He agreed with them and acted accordingly.

²⁶The next spring Ben-Hadad mustered the Arameans and went up to Aphek to fight against Israel. ²⁷When the Israelites were also mustered and given provisions, they marched out to meet them. The Israelites camped opposite them like two small flocks of goats, while the Arameans covered the countryside.

²⁸The man of God came up and told the king of Israel, "This is what the LORD says: 'Because the Arameans think the LORD is a god of the hills and not a god of the valleys, I will deliver this vast army into your hands, and you will know that I am the LORD.' "

²⁹For seven days they camped opposite each other, and on the seventh day the battle was joined. The Israelites inflicted a hundred thousand casualties on the Aramean foot soldiers in one day. ³⁰The rest of them escaped to the city of Aphek, where the wall collapsed on twenty-seven thousand of them. And Ben-Hadad fled to the city and hid in an inner room.

³¹His officials said to him, "Look, we have heard that the kings of the house of Israel are merciful. Let us go to the king of Israel with sackcloth around our waists and ropes around our heads. Perhaps he will spare your life."

³²Wearing sackcloth around their waists and ropes around their heads, they went to the king of Israel and said, "Your servant Ben-Hadad says: 'Please let me live.' "

The king answered, "Is he still alive? He is my brother."

³³The men took this as a good sign and were quick to pick up his word. "Yes, your brother Ben-Hadad!" they said.

"Go and get him," the king said. When Ben-Hadad came out, Ahab had him come up into his chariot.

³⁴"I will return the cities my father took from your father," Ben-Hadad offered. "You may set up your own market areas in Damascus, as my father did in Samaria."

⌐Ahab said,⌐ "On the basis of a treaty I will set you free." So he made a treaty with him, and let him go.

A Prophet Condemns Ahab

³⁵By the word of the LORD one of the sons of the prophets said to his companion, "Strike me with your weapon," but the man refused.

³⁶So the prophet said, "Because you have not obeyed the LORD, as soon as you leave me a lion will kill you." And after the man went away, a lion found him and killed him.

³⁷The prophet found another man and said, "Strike me, please." So the man struck him and wounded him. ³⁸Then the prophet went and stood by the road waiting for the king. He disguised himself with his headband down over his eyes. ³⁹As the king passed by, the prophet called out to him, "Your servant went into the thick of the battle, and someone came to me with a captive and said, 'Guard this man. If he is missing, it will be your life for his life, or you must pay a talent*ᵃ* of silver.' ⁴⁰While your servant was busy here and there, the man disappeared."

"That is your sentence," the king of Israel said. "You have pronounced it yourself."

⁴¹Then the prophet quickly removed the headband from his eyes, and the king of Israel recognized him as one of the prophets. ⁴²He said to the king, "This is what the LORD says: 'You have set free a man I had determined should die.'*ᵇ* Therefore it is your life for his life, your people

---

*ᵃ39 That is, about 75 pounds (about 34 kilograms)
*ᵇ42 The Hebrew term refers to the irrevocable giving over of things or persons to the LORD, often by totally destroying them.

for his people.' " ⁴³Sullen and angry, the king of Israel went to his palace in Samaria.

Naboth's Vineyard

21 Some time later there was an incident involving a vineyard belonging to Naboth the Jezreelite. The vineyard was in Jezreel, close to the palace of Ahab king of Samaria. ²Ahab said to Naboth, "Let me have your vineyard to use for a vegetable garden, since it is close to my palace. In exchange I will give you a better vineyard or, if you prefer, I will pay you whatever it is worth."

³But Naboth replied, "The LORD forbid that I should give you the inheritance of my fathers."

⁴So Ahab went home, sullen and angry because Naboth the Jezreelite had said, "I will not give you the inheritance of my fathers." He lay on his bed sulking and refused to eat.

⁵His wife Jezebel came in and asked him, "Why are you so sullen? Why won't you eat?"

⁶He answered her, "Because I said to Naboth the Jezreelite, 'Sell me your vineyard; or if you prefer, I will give you another vineyard in its place.' But he said, 'I will not give you my vineyard.' "

⁷Jezebel his wife said, "Is this how you act as king over Israel? Get up and eat! Cheer up. I'll get you the vineyard of Naboth the Jezreelite."

⁸So she wrote letters in Ahab's name, placed his seal on them, and sent them to the elders and nobles who lived in Naboth's city with him. ⁹In those letters she wrote:

"Proclaim a day of fasting and seat Naboth in a prominent place among the people. ¹⁰But seat two scoundrels opposite him and have them testify that he has cursed both God and the king. Then take him out and stone him to death."

¹¹So the elders and nobles who lived in Naboth's city did as Jezebel directed in the letters she had written to them. ¹²They proclaimed a fast and seated Naboth in a prominent place among the people. ¹³Then two scoundrels came and sat opposite him and brought charges against Naboth before the people, saying, "Naboth has cursed both God and the king." So they took him outside the city and stoned him to death. ¹⁴Then they sent word to Jezebel: "Naboth has been stoned and is dead."

¹⁵As soon as Jezebel heard that Naboth had been stoned to death, she said to Ahab, "Get up and take possession of the vineyard of Naboth the Jezreelite that he refused to sell you. He is no longer alive, but dead." ¹⁶When Ahab heard that Naboth was dead, he got up and went down to take possession of Naboth's vineyard.

¹⁷Then the word of the LORD came to Elijah the Tishbite: ¹⁸"Go down to meet Ahab king of Israel, who rules in Samaria. He is now in Naboth's vineyard, where he has gone to take possession of it. ¹⁹Say to him, 'This is what the LORD says: Have you not murdered a man and seized his property?' Then say to him, 'This is what the LORD says: In the place where dogs licked up Naboth's blood, dogs will lick up your blood—yes, yours!' "

²⁰Ahab said to Elijah, "So you have found me, my enemy!"

"I have found you," he answered, "because you have sold yourself to do evil in the eyes of the LORD. ²¹'I am going to bring disaster on you. I will consume your descendants and cut off from Ahab every last male in Israel—slave or free. ²²I will make your house like that of Jeroboam son of Nebat and that of Baasha son of Ahijah, because you have provoked me to anger and have caused Israel to sin.'

²³"And also concerning Jezebel the LORD says: 'Dogs will devour Jezebel by the wall ofᵃ Jezreel.'

²⁴"Dogs will eat those belonging to Ahab who die in the city, and the birds of the air will feed on those who die in the country."

²⁵(There was never a man like Ahab, who sold himself to do evil in the eyes of the LORD, urged on by Jezebel his wife. ²⁶He behaved in the vilest manner by going after idols, like the Amorites the LORD drove out before Israel.)

²⁷When Ahab heard these words, he tore his clothes, put on sackcloth and fasted. He lay in sackcloth and went around meekly.

²⁸Then the word of the LORD came to Elijah the Tishbite: ²⁹"Have you noticed how Ahab has humbled himself before me? Because he has humbled himself, I will not bring this disaster in his day, but I will bring it on his house in the days of his son."

ᵃ23 Most Hebrew manuscripts; a few Hebrew manuscripts, Vulgate and Syriac (see also 2 Kings 9:26) *the plot of ground at*

Micaiah Prophesies Against Ahab

22 For three years there was no war between Aram and Israel. ²But in the third year Jehoshaphat king of Judah went down to see the king of Israel. ³The king of Israel had said to his officials, "Don't you know that Ramoth Gilead belongs to us and yet we are doing nothing to retake it from the king of Aram?"

⁴So he asked Jehoshaphat, "Will you go with me to fight against Ramoth Gilead?"

Jehoshaphat replied to the king of Israel, "I am as you are, my people as your people, my horses as your horses." ⁵But Jehoshaphat also said to the king of Israel, "First seek the counsel of the LORD."

⁶So the king of Israel brought together the prophets—about four hundred men—and asked them, "Shall I go to war against Ramoth Gilead, or shall I refrain?"

"Go," they answered, "for the Lord will give it into the king's hand."

⁷But Jehoshaphat asked, "Is there not a prophet of the LORD here whom we can inquire of?"

⁸The king of Israel answered Jehoshaphat, "There is still one man through whom we can inquire of the LORD, but I hate him because he never prophesies anything good about me, but always bad. He is Micaiah son of Imlah."

"The king should not say that," Jehoshaphat replied.

⁹So the king of Israel called one of his officials and said, "Bring Micaiah son of Imlah at once."

¹⁰Dressed in their royal robes, the king of Israel and Jehoshaphat king of Judah were sitting on their thrones at the threshing floor by the entrance of the gate of Samaria, with all the prophets prophesying before them. ¹¹Now Zedekiah son of Kenaanah had made iron horns and he declared, "This is what the LORD says: 'With these you will gore the Arameans until they are destroyed.' "

¹²All the other prophets were prophesying the same thing. "Attack Ramoth Gilead and be victorious," they said, "for the LORD will give it into the king's hand."

¹³The messenger who had gone to summon Micaiah said to him, "Look, as one man the other prophets are predicting success for the king. Let your word agree with theirs, and speak favorably."

¹⁴But Micaiah said, "As surely as the LORD lives, I can tell him only what the LORD tells me."

¹⁵When he arrived, the king asked him,

"Micaiah, shall we go to war against Ramoth Gilead, or shall I refrain?"

"Attack and be victorious," he answered, "for the LORD will give it into the king's hand."

¹⁶The king said to him, "How many times must I make you swear to tell me nothing but the truth in the name of the LORD?"

¹⁷Then Micaiah answered, "I saw all Israel scattered on the hills like sheep without a shepherd, and the LORD said, 'These people have no master. Let each one go home in peace.' "

¹⁸The king of Israel said to Jehoshaphat, "Didn't I tell you that he never prophesies anything good about me, but only bad?"

¹⁹Micaiah continued, "Therefore hear the word of the LORD: I saw the LORD sitting on his throne with all the host of heaven standing around him on his right and on his left. ²⁰And the LORD said, 'Who will entice Ahab into attacking Ramoth Gilead and going to his death there?'

"One suggested this, and another that. ²¹Finally, a spirit came forward, stood before the LORD and said, 'I will entice him.'

²²" 'By what means?' the LORD asked.

" 'I will go out and be a lying spirit in the mouths of all his prophets,' he said.

" 'You will succeed in enticing him,' said the LORD. 'Go and do it.'

²³"So now the LORD has put a lying spirit in the mouths of all these prophets of yours. The LORD has decreed disaster for you."

²⁴Then Zedekiah son of Kenaanah went up and slapped Micaiah in the face. "Which way did the spirit from*a* the LORD go when he went from me to speak to you?" he asked.

²⁵Micaiah replied, "You will find out on the day you go to hide in an inner room."

²⁶The king of Israel then ordered, "Take Micaiah and send him back to Amon the ruler of the city and to Joash the king's son ²⁷and say, 'This is what the king says: Put this fellow in prison and give him nothing but bread and water until I return safely.' "

²⁸Micaiah declared, "If you ever return safely, the LORD has not spoken through me." Then he added, "Mark my words, all you people!"

Ahab Killed at Ramoth Gilead

²⁹So the king of Israel and Jehoshaphat king of Judah went up to Ramoth Gilead.

a24 Or Spirit of

30The king of Israel said to Jehoshaphat, "I will enter the battle in disguise, but you wear your royal robes." So the king of Israel disguised himself and went into battle.

31Now the king of Aram had ordered his thirty-two chariot commanders, "Do not fight with anyone, small or great, except the king of Israel." **32**When the chariot commanders saw Jehoshaphat, they thought, "Surely this is the king of Israel." So they turned to attack him, but when Jehoshaphat cried out, **33**the chariot commanders saw that he was not the king of Israel and stopped pursuing him.

34But someone drew his bow at random and hit the king of Israel between the sections of his armor. The king told his chariot driver, "Wheel around and get me out of the fighting. I've been wounded." **35**All day long the battle raged, and the king was propped up in his chariot facing the Arameans. The blood from his wound ran onto the floor of the chariot, and that evening he died. **36**As the sun was setting, a cry spread through the army: "Every man to his town; everyone to his land!"

37So the king died and was brought to Samaria, and they buried him there. **38**They washed the chariot at a pool in Samaria (where the prostitutes bathed),*a* and the dogs licked up his blood, as the word of the LORD had declared.

39As for the other events of Ahab's reign, including all he did, the palace he built and inlaid with ivory, and the cities he fortified, are they not written in the book of the annals of the kings of Israel? **40**Ahab rested with his fathers. And Ahaziah his son succeeded him as king.

Jehoshaphat King of Judah

41Jehoshaphat son of Asa became king of Judah in the fourth year of Ahab king of Israel. **42**Jehoshaphat was thirty-five years old when he became king, and he reigned

in Jerusalem twenty-five years. His mother's name was Azubah daughter of Shilhi. **43**In everything he walked in the ways of his father Asa and did not stray from them; he did what was right in the eyes of the LORD. The high places, however, were not removed, and the people continued to offer sacrifices and burn incense there. **44**Jehoshaphat was also at peace with the king of Israel.

45As for the other events of Jehoshaphat's reign, the things he achieved and his military exploits, are they not written in the book of the annals of the kings of Judah? **46**He rid the land of the rest of the male shrine prostitutes who remained there even after the reign of his father Asa. **47**There was then no king in Edom; a deputy ruled.

48Now Jehoshaphat built a fleet of trading ships*b* to go to Ophir for gold, but they never set sail—they were wrecked at Ezion Geber. **49**At that time Ahaziah son of Ahab said to Jehoshaphat, "Let my men sail with your men," but Jehoshaphat refused.

50Then Jehoshaphat rested with his fathers and was buried with them in the city of David his father. And Jehoram his son succeeded him.

Ahaziah King of Israel

51Ahaziah son of Ahab became king of Israel in Samaria in the seventeenth year of Jehoshaphat king of Judah, and he reigned over Israel two years. **52**He did evil in the eyes of the LORD, because he walked in the ways of his father and mother and in the ways of Jeroboam son of Nebat, who caused Israel to sin. **53**He served and worshiped Baal and provoked the LORD, the God of Israel, to anger, just as his father had done.

*a*38 Or *Samaria and cleaned the weapons*
*b*48 Hebrew *of ships of Tarshish*

If it wasn't so tragic, it could actually be comical. Almost every time a professional sports team achieves ultimate success—either in the Super Bowl, the NBA finals, the Stanley Cup finals, or the World Series—they soon find a way to dismantle what they've built, slowly but surely sliding to the basement of their division. Why don't these teams learn from the successes and mistakes of the past? Good question.

The book of 2 Kings continues the saga of men and nations, most of them disobedient to God's laws and unaffected by the inevitable repetition of the past. Because so many of these foolish people refused to learn from the errors of those who had gone before them, they found themselves living the same tragedy.

Your dad made mistakes. He probably did more than a few things right, as well. And he could have said the same about his dad. This is a book about learning from those mistakes or suffering the consequences of repeating them.

2 Kings

The Lord's Judgment on Ahaziah

1 After Ahab's death, Moab rebelled against Israel. ²Now Ahaziah had fallen through the lattice of his upper room in Samaria and injured himself. So he sent messengers, saying to them, "Go and consult Baal-Zebub, the god of Ekron, to see if I will recover from this injury."

³But the angel of the LORD said to Elijah the Tishbite, "Go up and meet the messengers of the king of Samaria and ask them, 'Is it because there is no God in Israel that you are going off to consult Baal-Zebub, the god of Ekron?' ⁴Therefore this is what the LORD says: 'You will not leave the bed you are lying on. You will certainly die!' " So Elijah went.

⁵When the messengers returned to the king, he asked them, "Why have you come back?"

⁶"A man came to meet us," they replied. "And he said to us, 'Go back to the king who sent you and tell him, "This is what the LORD says: Is it because there is no God in Israel that you are sending men to consult Baal-Zebub, the god of Ekron? Therefore you will not leave the bed you are lying on. You will certainly die!" ' "

⁷The king asked them, "What kind of man was it who came to meet you and told you this?"

⁸They replied, "He was a man with a garment of hair and with a leather belt around his waist."

The king said, "That was Elijah the Tishbite."

⁹Then he sent to Elijah a captain with

his company of fifty men. The captain went up to Elijah, who was sitting on the top of a hill, and said to him, "Man of God, the king says, 'Come down!' "

¹⁰Elijah answered the captain, "If I am a man of God, may fire come down from heaven and consume you and your fifty men!" Then fire fell from heaven and consumed the captain and his men.

¹¹At this the king sent to Elijah another captain with his fifty men. The captain said to him, "Man of God, this is what the king says, 'Come down at once!' "

¹²"If I am a man of God," Elijah replied, "may fire come down from heaven and consume you and your fifty men!" Then the fire of God fell from heaven and consumed him and his fifty men.

¹³So the king sent a third captain with his fifty men. This third captain went up and fell on his knees before Elijah. "Man of God," he begged, "please have respect for my life and the lives of these fifty men, your servants! ¹⁴See, fire has fallen from heaven and consumed the first two captains and all their men. But now have respect for my life!"

¹⁵The angel of the LORD said to Elijah, "Go down with him; do not be afraid of him." So Elijah got up and went down with him to the king.

¹⁶He told the king, "This is what the LORD says: Is it because there is no God in Israel for you to consult that you have sent messengers to consult Baal-Zebub, the god of Ekron? Because you have done this, you will never leave the bed you are lying on. You will certainly die!" ¹⁷So he died, according to the word of the LORD that Elijah had spoken.

Because Ahaziah had no son, Joram[a] succeeded him as king in the second year of Jehoram son of Jehoshaphat king of Judah. ¹⁸As for all the other events of Ahaziah's reign, and what he did, are they not written in the book of the annals of the kings of Israel?

Elijah Taken Up to Heaven

2 When the LORD was about to take Elijah up to heaven in a whirlwind, Elijah and Elisha were on their way from Gilgal. ²Elijah said to Elisha, "Stay here; the LORD has sent me to Bethel."

But Elisha said, "As surely as the LORD lives and as you live, I will not leave you." So they went down to Bethel.

³The company of the prophets at Bethel came out to Elisha and asked, "Do you know that the LORD is going to take your master from you today?"

"Yes, I know," Elisha replied, "but do not speak of it."

⁴Then Elijah said to him, "Stay here, Elisha; the LORD has sent me to Jericho."

And he replied, "As surely as the LORD lives and as you live, I will not leave you." So they went to Jericho.

⁵The company of the prophets at Jericho went up to Elisha and asked him, "Do you know that the LORD is going to take your master from you today?"

"Yes, I know," he replied, "but do not speak of it."

⁶Then Elijah said to him, "Stay here; the LORD has sent me to the Jordan."

And he replied, "As surely as the LORD lives and as you live, I will not leave you." So the two of them walked on.

⁷Fifty men of the company of the prophets went and stood at a distance, facing the place where Elijah and Elisha had stopped at the Jordan. ⁸Elijah took his cloak, rolled it up and struck the water with it. The water divided to the right and to the left, and the two of them crossed over on dry ground.

⁹When they had crossed, Elijah said to Elisha, "Tell me, what can I do for you before I am taken from you?"

"Let me inherit a double portion of your spirit," Elisha replied.

¹⁰"You have asked a difficult thing," Elijah said, "yet if you see me when I am taken from you, it will be yours—otherwise not."

¹¹As they were walking along and talking together, suddenly a chariot of fire and horses of fire appeared and separated the two of them, and Elijah went up to heaven in a whirlwind. ¹²Elisha saw this and cried out, "My father! My father! The chariots and horsemen of Israel!" And Elisha saw him no more. Then he took hold of his own clothes and tore them apart.

¹³He picked up the cloak that had fallen from Elijah and went back and stood on the bank of the Jordan. ¹⁴Then he took the cloak that had fallen from him and struck the water with it. "Where now is the LORD, the God of Elijah?" he asked. When he struck the water, it divided to the right and to the left, and he crossed over.

¹⁵The company of the prophets from Jericho, who were watching, said, "The

a17 Hebrew Jehoram, a variant of Joram

spirit of Elijah is resting on Elisha." And they went to meet him and bowed to the ground before him. [16]"Look," they said, "we your servants have fifty able men. Let them go and look for your master. Perhaps the Spirit of the LORD has picked him up and set him down on some mountain or in some valley."

"No," Elisha replied, "do not send them."

[17]But they persisted until he was too ashamed to refuse. So he said, "Send them." And they sent fifty men, who searched for three days but did not find him. [18]When they returned to Elisha, who was staying in Jericho, he said to them, "Didn't I tell you not to go?"

Healing of the Water

[19]The men of the city said to Elisha, "Look, our lord, this town is well situated, as you can see, but the water is bad and the land is unproductive."

[20]"Bring me a new bowl," he said, "and put salt in it." So they brought it to him.

[21]Then he went out to the spring and threw the salt into it, saying, "This is what the LORD says: 'I have healed this water. Never again will it cause death or make the land unproductive.' " [22]And the water has remained wholesome to this day, according to the word Elisha had spoken.

Hey, Brother

DAILY INSIGHT

My brother Ken and I are good friends. But when we were growing up, we were inseparable. In many ways, we were—and still are—as different as night and day, but as little children, we did everything together. For many years, our parents had a photograph hanging in their home that my dad took of Ken and me, sticking our heads out of a ship's porthole. Our arms were wrapped around each other's heads; the expressions on our faces clearly underscored the special friendship we enjoyed.

Once, when we were little boys, we found a dead bird. We gently placed the bird on a window sill, knelt down, and prayed for God to bring it to life. Actually, I don't recall being disappointed that the bird laid there motionless. Knowing Ken, he probably turned the disappointment into a lesson on God's sovereignty.

Elijah and Elisha had this same kind of friendship. I've often wondered if their relationship was founded because people called them by each other's names—like parents who give all their children names beginning with the same letter. Regardless of how it came to be, these men were great friends.

For a moment, let's remember what Elijah and Elisha did for a living. As

FRIDAY
Passage:
2 Kings 2:1–6

Verse:
2 Kings 2:6b

prophets, their jobs essentially consisted of two things: living lives worth examining and telling people of God's judgment and grace. In today's nomenclature, Elijah and Elisha were just like men who are brothers in Christ.

Do you have a Christian brother? Is there someone who, along with you, is committed to living a life of obedience to God's Word? Do you have a friend who readily and naturally reminds others of their need for God's grace? If you have such a soul-brother, then you know exactly why Elijah and Elisha were so close. You are also very fortunate.

Several days ago, when we learned of Rehoboam's lack of sound accountability, we were challenged to find a mentor—an elder in the faith—who was willing to give us good advice. The task today is to find a Christian brother ... someone who knows you and (still) loves you. A man who will refuse to leave your side, no matter what.

And once you've found such a friend, be sure each member of your family has an Elisha. Let your life be an example of how important, refreshing, and healthy a deep, Christian friendship can be.

For your next devotional reading, go to page 403.

Elisha Is Jeered

²³From there Elisha went up to Bethel. As he was walking along the road, some youths came out of the town and jeered at him. "Go on up, you baldhead!" they said. "Go on up, you baldhead!" ²⁴He turned around, looked at them and called down a curse on them in the name of the LORD. Then two bears came out of the woods and mauled forty-two of the youths. ²⁵And he went on to Mount Carmel and from there returned to Samaria.

Moab Revolts

3 Joram*a* son of Ahab became king of Israel in Samaria in the eighteenth year of Jehoshaphat king of Judah, and he reigned twelve years. ²He did evil in the eyes of the LORD, but not as his father and mother had done. He got rid of the sacred stone of Baal that his father had made. ³Nevertheless he clung to the sins of Jeroboam son of Nebat, which he had caused Israel to commit; he did not turn away from them.

⁴Now Mesha king of Moab raised sheep, and he had to supply the king of Israel with a hundred thousand lambs and with the wool of a hundred thousand rams. ⁵But after Ahab died, the king of Moab rebelled against the king of Israel. ⁶So at that time King Joram set out from Samaria and mobilized all Israel. ⁷He also sent this message to Jehoshaphat king of Judah: "The king of Moab has rebelled against

me. Will you go with me to fight against Moab?"

"I will go with you," he replied. "I am as you are, my people as your people, my horses as your horses."

⁸"By what route shall we attack?" he asked.

"Through the Desert of Edom," he answered.

⁹So the king of Israel set out with the king of Judah and the king of Edom. After a roundabout march of seven days, the army had no more water for themselves or for the animals with them.

¹⁰"What!" exclaimed the king of Israel. "Has the LORD called us three kings together only to hand us over to Moab?"

¹¹But Jehoshaphat asked, "Is there no prophet of the LORD here, that we may inquire of the LORD through him?"

An officer of the king of Israel answered, "Elisha son of Shaphat is here. He used to pour water on the hands of Elijah.*b*"

¹²Jehoshaphat said, "The word of the LORD is with him." So the king of Israel and Jehoshaphat and the king of Edom went down to him.

¹³Elisha said to the king of Israel, "What do we have to do with each other? Go to the prophets of your father and the prophets of your mother."

"No," the king of Israel answered,

a1 Hebrew *Jehoram,* a variant of *Joram*; also in verse 6   *b11* That is, he was Elijah's personal servant.

HEY DAD

Why did Elisha make bears attack those boys?

Text: 2 Kings 2:23-24

The boys' punishment in this narrative does seem a bit harsh. These young people were just making fun of Elisha's bald head. Kids will be kids, right? One wouldn't think a bear attack would be the fair punishment for that behavior.

But there's a deeper meaning involved in this jeering than meets the eye. Among a people who valued a full head of hair as a sign of vigor and strength, these young people were letting Elisha know that they thought he was weak and powerless. They were expressing their utter disdain for God's representative. That implication, besides the fact that Elisha may have felt threatened by the number of hostile individuals taunting him, prompted Elisha to call down this curse. The sight of the bears bounding out of the woods and mauling forty-two of these young men would not soon be forgotten by those who survived.

Elisha was one of God's right-hand men. And threatening and jeering one of God's right-hand men is never a smart move.

For a complete listing of Questions Kids Ask, turn to page 1435.

"because it was the LORD who called us three kings together to hand us over to Moab."

¹⁴Elisha said, "As surely as the LORD Almighty lives, whom I serve, if I did not have respect for the presence of Jehoshaphat king of Judah, I would not look at you or even notice you. ¹⁵But now bring me a harpist."

While the harpist was playing, the hand of the LORD came upon Elisha ¹⁶and he said, "This is what the LORD says: Make this valley full of ditches. ¹⁷For this is what the LORD says: You will see neither wind nor rain, yet this valley will be filled with water, and you, your cattle and your other animals will drink. ¹⁸This is an easy thing in the eyes of the LORD; he will also hand Moab over to you. ¹⁹You will overthrow every fortified city and every major town. You will cut down every good tree, stop up all the springs, and ruin every good field with stones."

²⁰The next morning, about the time for offering the sacrifice, there it was—water flowing from the direction of Edom! And the land was filled with water.

²¹Now all the Moabites had heard that the kings had come to fight against them; so every man, young and old, who could bear arms was called up and stationed on the border. ²²When they got up early in the morning, the sun was shining on the water. To the Moabites across the way, the water looked red—like blood. ²³"That's blood!" they said. "Those kings must have fought and slaughtered each other. Now to the plunder, Moab!"

²⁴But when the Moabites came to the camp of Israel, the Israelites rose up and fought them until they fled. And the Israelites invaded the land and slaughtered the Moabites. ²⁵They destroyed the towns, and each man threw a stone on every good field until it was covered. They stopped up all the springs and cut down every good tree. Only Kir Hareseth was left with its stones in place, but men armed with slings surrounded it and attacked it as well.

²⁶When the king of Moab saw that the battle had gone against him, he took with him seven hundred swordsmen to break through to the king of Edom, but they failed. ²⁷Then he took his firstborn son, who was to succeed him as king, and offered him as a sacrifice on the city wall. The fury against Israel was great; they withdrew and returned to their own land.

The Widow's Oil

4 The wife of a man from the company of the prophets cried out to Elisha, "Your servant my husband is dead, and you know that he revered the LORD. But now his creditor is coming to take my two boys as his slaves."

²Elisha replied to her, "How can I help you? Tell me, what do you have in your house?"

"Your servant has nothing there at all," she said, "except a little oil."

³Elisha said, "Go around and ask all your neighbors for empty jars. Don't ask for just a few. ⁴Then go inside and shut the door behind you and your sons. Pour oil into all the jars, and as each is filled, put it to one side."

⁵She left him and afterward shut the door behind her and her sons. They brought the jars to her and she kept pouring. ⁶When all the jars were full, she said to her son, "Bring me another one."

But he replied, "There is not a jar left." Then the oil stopped flowing.

⁷She went and told the man of God, and he said, "Go, sell the oil and pay your debts. You and your sons can live on what is left."

The Shunammite's Son Restored to Life

⁸One day Elisha went to Shunem. And a well-to-do woman was there, who urged him to stay for a meal. So whenever he came by, he stopped there to eat. ⁹She said to her husband, "I know that this man who often comes our way is a holy man of God. ¹⁰Let's make a small room on the roof and put in it a bed and a table, a chair and a lamp for him. Then he can stay there whenever he comes to us."

¹¹One day when Elisha came, he went up to his room and lay down there. ¹²He said to his servant Gehazi, "Call the Shunammite." So he called her, and she stood before him. ¹³Elisha said to him, "Tell her, 'You have gone to all this trouble for us. Now what can be done for you? Can we speak on your behalf to the king or the commander of the army?' "

She replied, "I have a home among my own people."

¹⁴"What can be done for her?" Elisha asked.

Gehazi said, "Well, she has no son and her husband is old."

¹⁵Then Elisha said, "Call her." So he called her, and she stood in the doorway.

¹⁶"About this time next year," Elisha said, "you will hold a son in your arms."

"No, my lord," she objected. "Don't mislead your servant, O man of God!"

¹⁷But the woman became pregnant, and the next year about that same time she gave birth to a son, just as Elisha had told her.

¹⁸The child grew, and one day he went out to his father, who was with the reapers. ¹⁹"My head! My head!" he said to his father.

His father told a servant, "Carry him to his mother." ²⁰After the servant had lifted him up and carried him to his mother, the boy sat on her lap until noon, and then he died. ²¹She went up and laid him on the bed of the man of God, then shut the door and went out.

²²She called her husband and said, "Please send me one of the servants and a donkey so I can go to the man of God quickly and return."

²³"Why go to him today?" he asked. "It's not the New Moon or the Sabbath."

"It's all right," she said.

²⁴She saddled the donkey and said to her servant, "Lead on; don't slow down for me unless I tell you." ²⁵So she set out and came to the man of God at Mount Carmel.

When he saw her in the distance, the man of God said to his servant Gehazi, "Look! There's the Shunammite! ²⁶Run to meet her and ask her, 'Are you all right? Is your husband all right? Is your child all right?' "

"Everything is all right," she said.

²⁷When she reached the man of God at the mountain, she took hold of his feet. Gehazi came over to push her away, but the man of God said, "Leave her alone! She is in bitter distress, but the LORD has hidden it from me and has not told me why."

²⁸"Did I ask you for a son, my lord?" she said. "Didn't I tell you, 'Don't raise my hopes'?"

²⁹Elisha said to Gehazi, "Tuck your cloak into your belt, take my staff in your hand and run. If you meet anyone, do not greet him, and if anyone greets you, do not answer. Lay my staff on the boy's face."

³⁰But the child's mother said, "As surely as the LORD lives and as you live, I will not leave you." So he got up and followed her.

³¹Gehazi went on ahead and laid the staff on the boy's face, but there was no sound or response. So Gehazi went back to meet Elisha and told him, "The boy has not awakened."

³²When Elisha reached the house, there was the boy lying dead on his couch. ³³He went in, shut the door on the two of them and prayed to the LORD. ³⁴Then he got on the bed and lay upon the boy, mouth to mouth, eyes to eyes, hands to hands. As he stretched himself out upon him, the boy's body grew warm. ³⁵Elisha turned away and walked back and forth in the room and then got on the bed and stretched out upon him once more. The boy sneezed seven times and opened his eyes.

³⁶Elisha summoned Gehazi and said, "Call the Shunammite." And he did. When she came, he said, "Take your son." ³⁷She came in, fell at his feet and bowed to the ground. Then she took her son and went out.

Death in the Pot

³⁸Elisha returned to Gilgal and there was a famine in that region. While the company of the prophets was meeting with him, he said to his servant, "Put on the large pot and cook some stew for these men."

³⁹One of them went out into the fields to gather herbs and found a wild vine. He gathered some of its gourds and filled the fold of his cloak. When he returned, he cut them up into the pot of stew, though no one knew what they were. ⁴⁰The stew was poured out for the men, but as they began to eat it, they cried out, "O man of God, there is death in the pot!" And they could not eat it.

⁴¹Elisha said, "Get some flour." He put it into the pot and said, "Serve it to the people to eat." And there was nothing harmful in the pot.

Feeding of a Hundred

⁴²A man came from Baal Shalishah, bringing the man of God twenty loaves of barley bread baked from the first ripe grain, along with some heads of new grain. "Give it to the people to eat," Elisha said.

⁴³"How can I set this before a hundred men?" his servant asked.

But Elisha answered, "Give it to the people to eat. For this is what the LORD says: 'They will eat and have some left over.' " ⁴⁴Then he set it before them, and they ate and had some left over, according to the word of the LORD.

Naaman Healed of Leprosy

5 Now Naaman was commander of the army of the king of Aram. He was a great man in the sight of his master and highly regarded, because through him the LORD had given victory to Aram. He was a valiant soldier, but he had leprosy.[a]

2 Now bands from Aram had gone out and had taken captive a young girl from Israel, and she served Naaman's wife. 3 She said to her mistress, "If only my master would see the prophet who is in Samaria! He would cure him of his leprosy."

4 Naaman went to his master and told him what the girl from Israel had said. 5 "By all means, go," the king of Aram replied. "I will send a letter to the king of Israel." So Naaman left, taking with him ten talents[b] of silver, six thousand shekels[c] of gold and ten sets of clothing. 6 The letter that he took to the king of Israel read: "With this letter I am sending my servant Naaman to you so that you may cure him of his leprosy."

7 As soon as the king of Israel read the letter, he tore his robes and said, "Am I God? Can I kill and bring back to life? Why does this fellow send someone to me to be cured of his leprosy? See how he is trying to pick a quarrel with me!"

8 When Elisha the man of God heard that the king of Israel had torn his robes, he sent him this message: "Why have you torn your robes? Have the man come to me and he will know that there is a prophet in Israel." 9 So Naaman went with his horses and chariots and stopped at the door of Elisha's house. 10 Elisha sent a messenger to say to him, "Go, wash yourself seven times in the Jordan, and your flesh will be restored and you will be cleansed."

11 But Naaman went away angry and said, "I thought that he would surely come out to me and stand and call on the name of the LORD his God, wave his hand over the spot and cure me of my leprosy. 12 Are not Abana and Pharpar, the rivers of Damascus, better than any of the waters of Israel? Couldn't I wash in them and be cleansed?" So he turned and went off in a rage.

13 Naaman's servants went to him and said, "My father, if the prophet had told you to do some great thing, would you

---

[a]1 The Hebrew word was used for various diseases affecting the skin—not necessarily leprosy; also in verses 3, 6, 7, 11 and 27.   [b]5 That is, about 750 pounds (about 340 kilograms)   [c]5 That is, about 150 pounds (about 70 kilograms)

HEY DAD

Was Jesus the only person who healed people in the Bible?

Text: 2 Kings 5

Long before Jesus' ministry on earth, God supernaturally healed people through his prophets and other individuals. In today's reading, God used Elisha to heal a man named Naaman from his leprosy (2 Kings 5:13-14). In Jewish and Roman circles, "godly and divinely inspired men were believed to have the power to perform miraculous cures" (Ward, 232). And Jews were particularly receptive to these types of miracles, because they believed such things would signal their nation's release from foreign rule.

Although Jesus wasn't the first to perform miracles or heal people, his acts of healing were unique in several ways. First, Jesus didn't use "magical formulas or obscure rituals as other healers reportedly did. Rather than recite prayers and openly ask for healing power, Jesus often stressed the faith of the afflicted or of those who brought them to him" (Ward, 232). Second, during the act of healing, he often forgave the sick person's sin. No one before him had ever done such a thing. Finally, Jesus gave his disciples, through the Holy Spirit, the power to do the same mighty things he had done, including the power to heal others.

Jesus wasn't the first or only person in the Bible who healed people. But he was the only God-man whose healing power came from within, whose healings cleansed people of their sin, and who had the authority to give others the same power!

Ward, K. (Ed.). (1987). Jesus and His Times. Pleasantville, New York: The Reader's Digest Association.

For a complete listing of Questions Kids Ask, turn to page 1435.

The Powerful Faith of a Young Girl

Key Verse: *"[The young girl] said to her mistress, 'If only my master would see the prophet who is in Samaria! He would cure him of his leprosy.'"* 2 Kings 5:3

Text: 2 Kings 5:1–10 *(Dad or child reads the text.)*

QUIET
TIMES
WITH Dad

DAD READS: Naaman was a great military leader. When Captain Naaman told the thousands of troops in his army to go to battle, they would go, just because he told them to. He was *that* powerful. But Naaman had a serious problem. He had leprosy, the most terrible disease that anyone during those days could have. People who had leprosy had to leave their families and move to places where only people with this disease lived.

Child reads: There was a young girl who worked at the home of Captain Naaman and his wife. We don't know her name, but she must have been a very special girl. She loved God, and she knew that God could heal Naaman of this terrible disease. So she told Naaman's wife that if Naaman would go to God's prophet, he would be healed of his leprosy.

DAD READS: Naaman went to his king and told him what the little girl had said. The king wrote a letter to the King of Israel, telling him to cure Naaman of his leprosy. The King of Israel was very upset when he read the letter. He was afraid that if Naaman did not get cured, just as the little girl said he would, then Naaman's army might attack Israel. When Elisha heard about this, he told the King of Israel to send Naaman to him. He knew God would heal this great man's leprosy.

Child reads: There are four very important things we can learn from four people in this story. First, Naaman was sick, and there was nothing he could do about it. Second, there was a young girl who loved God and was brave enough to tell the people about him. Third, there was the King of Israel who did not have enough faith to believe God could heal

Naaman. And fourth, there was the prophet Elisha who obeyed God and healed Naaman.

DAD READS: Our world is filled with people who are just like these four people. There are many who are lost because they don't know God. And just like Captain Naaman, there is nothing they can do about it. There are people like the King of Israel who know about God, but they are afraid to really believe in him. There are people like Elisha who have seen God heal and are ready to call on his power to do it again and again.

Child reads: And there are people like the young girl who knew that her God could heal this important and powerful man. I want to have faith like that. I want to be able to tell my friends that I love such a wonderful God that can heal awful things like leprosy. And that he loves us so much that he can forgive our sins.

DAD READS: I want to have faith like that, too. Let me pray this prayer with you:

Our Father in heaven, thank you that we can believe in your love and healing power. Please help us to have that kind of faith in you. Help us to always remember that you, in grace and mercy, forgive our sins, too. And help us to be excited about telling our friends about you, because we know how great you are. We love you. In Jesus' name, **Amen.**

For your next devotional reading, go to page 418.

not have done it? How much more, then, when he tells you, 'Wash and be cleansed'!" [14]So he went down and dipped himself in the Jordan seven times, as the man of God had told him, and his flesh was restored and became clean like that of a young boy.

[15]Then Naaman and all his attendants went back to the man of God. He stood before him and said, "Now I know that there is no God in all the world except in Israel. Please accept now a gift from your servant."

[16]The prophet answered, "As surely as the LORD lives, whom I serve, I will not accept a thing." And even though Naaman urged him, he refused.

[17]"If you will not," said Naaman, "please let me, your servant, be given as much earth as a pair of mules can carry, for your servant will never again make burnt offerings and sacrifices to any other god but the LORD. [18]But may the LORD forgive your servant for this one thing: When my master enters the temple of Rimmon to bow down and he is leaning on my arm and I bow there also—when I bow down in the temple of Rimmon, may the LORD forgive your servant for this."

[19]"Go in peace," Elisha said.

After Naaman had traveled some distance, [20]Gehazi, the servant of Elisha the man of God, said to himself, "My master was too easy on Naaman, this Aramean, by not accepting from him what he brought. As surely as the LORD lives, I will run after him and get something from him."

[21]So Gehazi hurried after Naaman. When Naaman saw him running toward him, he got down from the chariot to meet him. "Is everything all right?" he asked.

[22]"Everything is all right," Gehazi answered. "My master sent me to say, 'Two young men from the company of the prophets have just come to me from the hill country of Ephraim. Please give them a talent[a] of silver and two sets of clothing.' "

[23]"By all means, take two talents," said Naaman. He urged Gehazi to accept them, and then tied up the two talents of silver in two bags, with two sets of clothing. He gave them to two of his servants, and they carried them ahead of Gehazi. [24]When Gehazi came to the hill, he took the things from the servants and put them away in the house. He sent the men away and they left. [25]Then he went in and stood before his master Elisha.

"Where have you been, Gehazi?" Elisha asked.

"Your servant didn't go anywhere," Gehazi answered.

[26]But Elisha said to him, "Was not my spirit with you when the man got down from his chariot to meet you? Is this the time to take money, or to accept clothes, olive groves, vineyards, flocks, herds, or menservants and maidservants? [27]Naaman's leprosy will cling to you and to your descendants forever." Then Gehazi went from Elisha's presence and he was leprous, as white as snow.

An Axhead Floats

6 The company of the prophets said to Elisha, "Look, the place where we meet with you is too small for us. [2]Let us go to the Jordan, where each of us can get a pole; and let us build a place there for us to live."

And he said, "Go."

[3]Then one of them said, "Won't you please come with your servants?"

"I will," Elisha replied. [4]And he went with them.

They went to the Jordan and began to cut down trees. [5]As one of them was cutting down a tree, the iron axhead fell into the water. "Oh, my lord," he cried out, "it was borrowed!"

[6]The man of God asked, "Where did it fall?" When he showed him the place, Elisha cut a stick and threw it there, and made the iron float. [7]"Lift it out," he said. Then the man reached out his hand and took it.

Elisha Traps Blinded Arameans

[8]Now the king of Aram was at war with Israel. After conferring with his officers, he said, "I will set up my camp in such and such a place."

[9]The man of God sent word to the king of Israel: "Beware of passing that place, because the Arameans are going down there." [10]So the king of Israel checked on the place indicated by the man of God. Time and again Elisha warned the king, so that he was on his guard in such places.

[11]This enraged the king of Aram. He summoned his officers and demanded of them, "Will you not tell me which of us is on the side of the king of Israel?"

---

[a]22 That is, about 75 pounds (about 34 kilograms)

¹²"None of us, my lord the king," said one of his officers, "but Elisha, the prophet who is in Israel, tells the king of Israel the very words you speak in your bedroom."

¹³"Go, find out where he is," the king ordered, "so I can send men and capture him." The report came back: "He is in Dothan." ¹⁴Then he sent horses and chariots and a strong force there. They went by night and surrounded the city.

¹⁵When the servant of the man of God got up and went out early the next morning, an army with horses and chariots had surrounded the city. "Oh, my lord, what shall we do?" the servant asked.

¹⁶"Don't be afraid," the prophet answered. "Those who are with us are more than those who are with them."

¹⁷And Elisha prayed, "O LORD, open his eyes so he may see." Then the LORD opened the servant's eyes, and he looked and saw the hills full of horses and chariots of fire all around Elisha.

¹⁸As the enemy came down toward him, Elisha prayed to the LORD, "Strike these people with blindness." So he struck them with blindness, as Elisha had asked.

¹⁹Elisha told them, "This is not the road and this is not the city. Follow me, and I will lead you to the man you are looking for." And he led them to Samaria.

²⁰After they entered the city, Elisha said, "LORD, open the eyes of these men so they can see." Then the LORD opened their eyes and they looked, and there they were, inside Samaria.

²¹When the king of Israel saw them, he asked Elisha, "Shall I kill them, my father? Shall I kill them?"

²²"Do not kill them," he answered. "Would you kill men you have captured with your own sword or bow? Set food and water before them so that they may eat and drink and then go back to their master." ²³So he prepared a great feast for them, and after they had finished eating and drinking, he sent them away, and they returned to their master. So the bands from Aram stopped raiding Israel's territory.

Famine in Besieged Samaria

²⁴Some time later, Ben-Hadad king of Aram mobilized his entire army and marched up and laid siege to Samaria. ²⁵There was a great famine in the city; the siege lasted so long that a donkey's head sold for eighty shekels^a of silver, and a quarter of a cab^b of seed pods^c for five shekels.^d

²⁶As the king of Israel was passing by on the wall, a woman cried to him, "Help me, my lord the king!"

²⁷The king replied, "If the LORD does not help you, where can I get help for you? From the threshing floor? From the winepress?" ²⁸Then he asked her, "What's the matter?"

She answered, "This woman said to me, 'Give up your son so we may eat him today, and tomorrow we'll eat my son.' ²⁹So we cooked my son and ate him. The next day I said to her, 'Give up your son so we may eat him,' but she had hidden him."

³⁰When the king heard the woman's words, he tore his robes. As he went along the wall, the people looked, and there, underneath, he had sackcloth on his body. ³¹He said, "May God deal with me, be it ever so severely, if the head of Elisha son of Shaphat remains on his shoulders today!"

³²Now Elisha was sitting in his house, and the elders were sitting with him. The king sent a messenger ahead, but before he arrived, Elisha said to the elders, "Don't you see how this murderer is sending someone to cut off my head? Look, when the messenger comes, shut the door and hold it shut against him. Is not the sound of his master's footsteps behind him?" ³³While he was still talking to them, the messenger came down to him. And the king said, "This disaster is from the LORD. Why should I wait for the LORD any longer?"

7 Elisha said, "Hear the word of the LORD. This is what the LORD says: About this time tomorrow, a seah^e of flour will sell for a shekel^f and two seahs^g of barley for a shekel at the gate of Samaria."

²The officer on whose arm the king was leaning said to the man of God, "Look, even if the LORD should open the floodgates of the heavens, could this happen?"

"You will see it with your own eyes," answered Elisha, "but you will not eat any of it!"

^a25 That is, about 2 pounds (about 1 kilogram)
^b25 That is, probably about 1/2 pint (about 0.3 liter)   ^c25 Or of dove's dung   ^d25 That is, about 2 ounces (about 55 grams)   ^e1 That is, probably about 7 quarts (about 7.3 liters); also in verses 16 and 13   ^f1 That is, about 2/5 ounce (about 11 grams); also in verses 16 and 18   ^g1 That is, probably about 13 quarts (about 15 liters); also in verses 16 and 18

The Siege Lifted

[3]Now there were four men with leprosy[a] at the entrance of the city gate. They said to each other, "Why stay here until we die? [4]If we say, 'We'll go into the city'—the famine is there, and we will die. And if we stay here, we will die. So let's go over to the camp of the Arameans and surrender. If they spare us, we live; if they kill us, then we die."

[5]At dusk they got up and went to the camp of the Arameans. When they reached the edge of the camp, not a man was there, [6]for the Lord had caused the Arameans to hear the sound of chariots and horses and a great army, so that they said to one another, "Look, the king of Israel has hired the Hittite and Egyptian kings to attack us!" [7]So they got up and fled in the dusk and abandoned their tents and their horses and donkeys. They left the camp as it was and ran for their lives.

[8]The men who had leprosy reached the edge of the camp and entered one of the tents. They ate and drank, and carried away silver, gold and clothes, and went off and hid them. They returned and entered another tent and took some things from it and hid them also.

[9]Then they said to each other, "We're not doing right. This is a day of good news and we are keeping it to ourselves. If we wait until daylight, punishment will overtake us. Let's go at once and report this to the royal palace."

[10]So they went and called out to the city gatekeepers and told them, "We went into the Aramean camp and not a man was there—not a sound of anyone—only tethered horses and donkeys, and the tents left just as they were." [11]The gatekeepers shouted the news, and it was reported within the palace.

[12]The king got up in the night and said to his officers, "I will tell you what the Arameans have done to us. They know we are starving; so they have left the camp to hide in the countryside, thinking, 'They will surely come out, and then we will take them alive and get into the city.' "

[13]One of his officers answered, "Have some men take five of the horses that are left in the city. Their plight will be like that of all the Israelites left here—yes, they will only be like all these Israelites who are doomed. So let us send them to find out what happened."

[14]So they selected two chariots with their horses, and the king sent them after the Aramean army. He commanded the drivers, "Go and find out what has happened." [15]They followed them as far as the Jordan, and they found the whole road strewn with the clothing and equipment the Arameans had thrown away in their headlong flight. So the messengers returned and reported to the king. [16]Then the people went out and plundered the camp of the Arameans. So a seah of flour sold for a shekel, and two seahs of barley sold for a shekel, as the LORD had said.

[17]Now the king had put the officer on whose arm he leaned in charge of the gate, and the people trampled him in the gateway, and he died, just as the man of God had foretold when the king came down to his house. [18]It happened as the man of God had said to the king: "About this time tomorrow, a seah of flour will sell for a shekel and two seahs of barley for a shekel at the gate of Samaria."

[19]The officer had said to the man of God, "Look, even if the LORD should open the floodgates of the heavens, could this happen?" The man of God had replied, "You will see it with your own eyes, but you will not eat any of it!" [20]And that is exactly what happened to him, for the people trampled him in the gateway, and he died.

The Shunammite's Land Restored

8 Now Elisha had said to the woman whose son he had restored to life, "Go away with your family and stay for a while wherever you can, because the LORD has decreed a famine in the land that will last seven years." [2]The woman proceeded to do as the man of God said. She and her family went away and stayed in the land of the Philistines seven years.

[3]At the end of the seven years she came back from the land of the Philistines and went to the king to beg for her house and land. [4]The king was talking to Gehazi, the servant of the man of God, and had said, "Tell me about all the great things Elisha has done." [5]Just as Gehazi was telling the king how Elisha had restored the dead to life, the woman whose son Elisha had brought back to life came to beg the king for her house and land.

Gehazi said, "This is the woman, my lord the king, and this is her son whom

---

[a]3 The Hebrew word is used for various diseases affecting the skin—not necessarily leprosy; also in verse 8.

Elisha restored to life." [6]The king asked the woman about it, and she told him.

Then he assigned an official to her case and said to him, "Give back everything that belonged to her, including all the income from her land from the day she left the country until now."

Hazael Murders Ben-Hadad

[7]Elisha went to Damascus, and Ben-Hadad king of Aram was ill. When the king was told, "The man of God has come all the way up here," [8]he said to Hazael, "Take a gift with you and go to meet the man of God. Consult the LORD through him; ask him, 'Will I recover from this illness?' "

[9]Hazael went to meet Elisha, taking with him as a gift forty camel-loads of all the finest wares of Damascus. He went in and stood before him, and said, "Your son Ben-Hadad king of Aram has sent me to ask, 'Will I recover from this illness?' "

[10]Elisha answered, "Go and say to him, 'You will certainly recover'; but[a] the LORD has revealed to me that he will in fact die."

[11]He stared at him with a fixed gaze until Hazael felt ashamed. Then the man of God began to weep.

[12]"Why is my lord weeping?" asked Hazael.

"Because I know the harm you will do to the Israelites," he answered. "You will set fire to their fortified places, kill their young men with the sword, dash their little children to the ground, and rip open their pregnant women."

[13]Hazael said, "How could your servant, a mere dog, accomplish such a feat?"

"The LORD has shown me that you will become king of Aram," answered Elisha.

[14]Then Hazael left Elisha and returned to his master. When Ben-Hadad asked, "What did Elisha say to you?" Hazael replied, "He told me that you would certainly recover." [15]But the next day he took a thick cloth, soaked it in water and spread it over the king's face, so that he died. Then Hazael succeeded him as king.

Jehoram King of Judah

[16]In the fifth year of Joram son of Ahab king of Israel, when Jehoshaphat was king of Judah, Jehoram son of Jehoshaphat began his reign as king of Judah. [17]He was thirty-two years old when he became king, and he reigned in Jerusalem eight years. [18]He walked in the ways of the kings of Israel, as the house of Ahab had done, for he married a daughter of Ahab. He did

evil in the eyes of the LORD. [19]Nevertheless, for the sake of his servant David, the LORD was not willing to destroy Judah. He had promised to maintain a lamp for David and his descendants forever.

[20]In the time of Jehoram, Edom rebelled against Judah and set up its own king. [21]So Jehoram[b] went to Zair with all his chariots. The Edomites surrounded him and his chariot commanders, but he rose up and broke through by night; his army, however, fled back home. [22]To this day Edom has been in rebellion against Judah. Libnah revolted at the same time.

[23]As for the other events of Jehoram's reign, and all he did, are they not written in the book of the annals of the kings of Judah? [24]Jehoram rested with his fathers and was buried with them in the City of David. And Ahaziah his son succeeded him as king.

Ahaziah King of Judah

[25]In the twelfth year of Joram son of Ahab king of Israel, Ahaziah son of Jehoram king of Judah began to reign. [26]Ahaziah was twenty-two years old when he became king, and he reigned in Jerusalem one year. His mother's name was Athaliah, a granddaughter of Omri king of Israel. [27]He walked in the ways of the house of Ahab and did evil in the eyes of the LORD, as the house of Ahab had done, for he was related by marriage to Ahab's family.

[28]Ahaziah went with Joram son of Ahab to war against Hazael king of Aram at Ramoth Gilead. The Arameans wounded Joram; [29]so King Joram returned to Jezreel to recover from the wounds the Arameans had inflicted on him at Ramoth[c] in his battle with Hazael king of Aram.

Then Ahaziah son of Jehoram king of Judah went down to Jezreel to see Joram son of Ahab, because he had been wounded.

Jehu Anointed King of Israel

9 The prophet Elisha summoned a man from the company of the prophets and said to him, "Tuck your cloak into your belt, take this flask of oil with you and go to Ramoth Gilead. [2]When you get there, look for Jehu son of Jehoshaphat, the son

---

[a]10 The Hebrew may also be read *Go and say, 'You will certainly not recover,' for.*   [b]21 Hebrew *Joram*, a variant of *Jehoram*; also in verses 23 and 24
[c]29 Hebrew *Ramah*, a variant of *Ramoth*

of Nimshi. Go to him, get him away from his companions and take him into an inner room. ³Then take the flask and pour the oil on his head and declare, 'This is what the LORD says: I anoint you king over Israel.' Then open the door and run; don't delay!"

⁴So the young man, the prophet, went to Ramoth Gilead. ⁵When he arrived, he found the army officers sitting together. "I have a message for you, commander," he said.

"For which of us?" asked Jehu.

"For you, commander," he replied.

⁶Jehu got up and went into the house. Then the prophet poured the oil on Jehu's head and declared, "This is what the LORD, the God of Israel, says: 'I anoint you king over the LORD's people Israel. ⁷You are to destroy the house of Ahab your master, and I will avenge the blood of my servants the prophets and the blood of all the LORD's servants shed by Jezebel. ⁸The whole house of Ahab will perish. I will cut off from Ahab every last male in Israel—slave or free. ⁹I will make the house of Ahab like the house of Jeroboam son of Nebat and like the house of Baasha son of Ahijah. ¹⁰As for Jezebel, dogs will devour her on the plot of ground at Jezreel, and no one will bury her.' " Then he opened the door and ran.

¹¹When Jehu went out to his fellow officers, one of them asked him, "Is everything all right? Why did this madman come to you?"

"You know the man and the sort of things he says," Jehu replied.

¹²"That's not true!" they said. "Tell us."

Jehu said, "Here is what he told me: 'This is what the LORD says: I anoint you king over Israel.' "

¹³They hurried and took their cloaks and spread them under him on the bare steps. Then they blew the trumpet and shouted, "Jehu is king!"

Jehu Kills Joram and Ahaziah

¹⁴So Jehu son of Jehoshaphat, the son of Nimshi, conspired against Joram. (Now Joram and all Israel had been defending Ramoth Gilead against Hazael king of Aram, ¹⁵but King Joram*ᵃ* had returned to Jezreel to recover from the wounds the Arameans had inflicted on him in the battle with Hazael king of Aram.) Jehu said, "If this is the way you feel, don't let anyone slip out of the city to go and tell the news in Jezreel." ¹⁶Then he got into his chariot and rode to Jezreel, because Joram was resting there and Ahaziah king of Judah had gone down to see him.

¹⁷When the lookout standing on the tower in Jezreel saw Jehu's troops approaching, he called out, "I see some troops coming."

"Get a horseman," Joram ordered. "Send him to meet them and ask, 'Do you come in peace?' "

¹⁸The horseman rode off to meet Jehu and said, "This is what the king says: 'Do you come in peace?' "

"What do you have to do with peace?" Jehu replied. "Fall in behind me."

The lookout reported, "The messenger has reached them, but he isn't coming back."

¹⁹So the king sent out a second horseman. When he came to them he said, "This is what the king says: 'Do you come in peace?' "

Jehu replied, "What do you have to do with peace? Fall in behind me."

²⁰The lookout reported, "He has reached them, but he isn't coming back either. The driving is like that of Jehu son of Nimshi—he drives like a madman."

²¹"Hitch up my chariot," Joram ordered. And when it was hitched up, Joram king of Israel and Ahaziah king of Judah rode out, each in his own chariot, to meet Jehu. They met him at the plot of ground that had belonged to Naboth the Jezreelite. ²²When Joram saw Jehu he asked, "Have you come in peace, Jehu?"

"How can there be peace," Jehu replied, "as long as all the idolatry and witchcraft of your mother Jezebel abound?"

²³Joram turned about and fled, calling out to Ahaziah, "Treachery, Ahaziah!"

²⁴Then Jehu drew his bow and shot Joram between the shoulders. The arrow pierced his heart and he slumped down in his chariot. ²⁵Jehu said to Bidkar, his chariot officer, "Pick him up and throw him on the field that belonged to Naboth the Jezreelite. Remember how you and I were riding together in chariots behind Ahab his father when the LORD made this prophecy about him: ²⁶'Yesterday I saw the blood of Naboth and the blood of his sons, declares the LORD, and I will surely make you pay for it on this plot of ground, declares the LORD.'ᵇ Now then, pick him up and throw him on that plot, in accordance with the word of the LORD."

ᵃ15 Hebrew *Jehoram*, a variant of *Joram*; also in verses 17 and 21-24   ᵇ26 See 1 Kings 21:19.

²⁷When Ahaziah king of Judah saw what had happened, he fled up the road to Beth Haggan.ᵃ Jehu chased him, shouting, "Kill him too!" They wounded him in his chariot on the way up to Gur near Ibleam, but he escaped to Megiddo and died there. ²⁸His servants took him by chariot to Jerusalem and buried him with his fathers in his tomb in the City of David. ²⁹(In the eleventh year of Joram son of Ahab, Ahaziah had become king of Judah.)

Jezebel Killed

³⁰Then Jehu went to Jezreel. When Jezebel heard about it, she painted her eyes, arranged her hair and looked out of a window. ³¹As Jehu entered the gate, she asked, "Have you come in peace, Zimri, you murderer of your master?"ᵇ ³²He looked up at the window and called out, "Who is on my side? Who?" Two or three eunuchs looked down at him. ³³"Throw her down!" Jehu said. So they threw her down, and some of her blood spattered the wall and the horses as they trampled her underfoot.

³⁴Jehu went in and ate and drank. "Take care of that cursed woman," he said, "and bury her, for she was a king's daughter." ³⁵But when they went out to bury her, they found nothing except her skull, her feet and her hands. ³⁶They went back and told Jehu, who said, "This is the word of the LORD that he spoke through his servant Elijah the Tishbite: On the plot of ground at Jezreel dogs will devour Jezebel's flesh.ᶜ ³⁷Jezebel's body will be like refuse on the ground in the plot at Jezreel, so that no one will be able to say, 'This is Jezebel.' "

Ahab's Family Killed

10 Now there were in Samaria seventy sons of the house of Ahab. So Jehu wrote letters and sent them to Samaria: to the officials of Jezreel,ᵈ to the elders and to the guardians of Ahab's children. He said, ²"As soon as this letter reaches you, since your master's sons are with you and you have chariots and horses, a fortified city and weapons, ³choose the best and most worthy of your master's sons and set him on his father's throne. Then fight for your master's house."

⁴But they were terrified and said, "If two kings could not resist him, how can we?" ⁵So the palace administrator, the city governor, the elders and the guardians sent this message to Jehu: "We are your servants and we will do anything you say.

We will not appoint anyone as king; you do whatever you think best."

⁶Then Jehu wrote them a second letter, saying, "If you are on my side and will obey me, take the heads of your master's sons and come to me in Jezreel by this time tomorrow."

Now the royal princes, seventy of them, were with the leading men of the city, who were rearing them. ⁷When the letter arrived, these men took the princes and slaughtered all seventy of them. They put their heads in baskets and sent them to Jehu in Jezreel. ⁸When the messenger arrived, he told Jehu, "They have brought the heads of the princes."

Then Jehu ordered, "Put them in two piles at the entrance of the city gate until morning."

⁹The next morning Jehu went out. He stood before all the people and said, "You are innocent. It was I who conspired against my master and killed him, but who killed all these? ¹⁰Know then, that not a word the LORD has spoken against the house of Ahab will fail. The LORD has done what he promised through his servant Elijah." ¹¹So Jehu killed everyone in Jezreel who remained of the house of Ahab, as well as all his chief men, his close friends and his priests, leaving him no survivor.

¹²Jehu then set out and went toward Samaria. At Beth Eked of the Shepherds, ¹³he met some relatives of Ahaziah king of Judah and asked, "Who are you?"

They said, "We are relatives of Ahaziah, and we have come down to greet the families of the king and of the queen mother."

¹⁴"Take them alive!" he ordered. So they took them alive and slaughtered them by the well of Beth Eked—forty-two men. He left no survivor.

¹⁵After he left there, he came upon Jehonadab son of Recab, who was on his way to meet him. Jehu greeted him and said, "Are you in accord with me, as I am with you?"

"I am," Jehonadab answered.

"If so," said Jehu, "give me your hand." So he did, and Jehu helped him up into the chariot. ¹⁶Jehu said, "Come with me and see my zeal for the LORD." Then he had him ride along in his chariot.

¹⁷When Jehu came to Samaria, he killed all who were left there of Ahab's family; he

---

ᵃ27 Or *fled by way of the garden house*   ᵇ31 Or *"Did Zimri have peace, who murdered his master?"*   ᶜ36 See 1 Kings 21:23.   ᵈ1 Hebrew; some Septuagint manuscripts and Vulgate *of the city*

destroyed them, according to the word of the LORD spoken to Elijah.

Ministers of Baal Killed

¹⁸Then Jehu brought all the people together and said to them, "Ahab served Baal a little; Jehu will serve him much. ¹⁹Now summon all the prophets of Baal, all his ministers and all his priests. See that no one is missing, because I am going to hold a great sacrifice for Baal. Anyone who fails to come will no longer live." But Jehu was acting deceptively in order to destroy the ministers of Baal. ²⁰Jehu said, "Call an assembly in honor of Baal." So they proclaimed it. ²¹Then he sent word throughout Israel, and all the ministers of Baal came; not one stayed away. They crowded into the temple of Baal until it was full from one end to the other. ²²And Jehu said to the keeper of the wardrobe, "Bring robes for all the ministers of Baal." So he brought out robes for them.

²³Then Jehu and Jehonadab son of Recab went into the temple of Baal. Jehu said to the ministers of Baal, "Look around and see that no servants of the LORD are here with you—only ministers of Baal." ²⁴So they went in to make sacrifices and burnt offerings. Now Jehu had posted eighty men outside with this warning: "If one of you lets any of the men I am placing in your hands escape, it will be your life for his life."

²⁵As soon as Jehu had finished making the burnt offering, he ordered the guards and officers: "Go in and kill them; let no one escape." So they cut them down with the sword. The guards and officers threw the bodies out and then entered the inner shrine of the temple of Baal. ²⁶They brought the sacred stone out of the temple of Baal and burned it. ²⁷They demolished the sacred stone of Baal and tore down the temple of Baal, and people have used it for a latrine to this day.

²⁸So Jehu destroyed Baal worship in Israel. ²⁹However, he did not turn away from the sins of Jeroboam son of Nebat, which he had caused Israel to commit—the worship of the golden calves at Bethel and Dan.

³⁰The LORD said to Jehu, "Because you have done well in accomplishing what is right in my eyes and have done to the house of Ahab all I had in mind to do, your descendants will sit on the throne of Israel to the fourth generation." ³¹Yet Jehu

was not careful to keep the law of the LORD, the God of Israel, with all his heart. He did not turn away from the sins of Jeroboam, which he had caused Israel to commit.

³²In those days the LORD began to reduce the size of Israel. Hazael overpowered the Israelites throughout their territory ³³east of the Jordan in all the land of Gilead (the region of Gad, Reuben and Manasseh), from Aroer by the Arnon Gorge through Gilead to Bashan.

³⁴As for the other events of Jehu's reign, all he did, and all his achievements, are they not written in the book of the annals of the kings of Israel?

³⁵Jehu rested with his fathers and was buried in Samaria. And Jehoahaz his son succeeded him as king. ³⁶The time that Jehu reigned over Israel in Samaria was twenty-eight years.

Athaliah and Joash

11 When Athaliah the mother of Ahaziah saw that her son was dead, she proceeded to destroy the whole royal family. ²But Jehosheba, the daughter of King Jehoram[a] and sister of Ahaziah, took Joash son of Ahaziah and stole him away from among the royal princes, who were about to be murdered. She put him and his nurse in a bedroom to hide him from Athaliah; so he was not killed. ³He remained hidden with his nurse at the temple of the LORD for six years while Athaliah ruled the land.

⁴In the seventh year Jehoiada sent for the commanders of units of a hundred, the Carites and the guards and had them brought to him at the temple of the LORD. He made a covenant with them and put them under oath at the temple of the LORD. Then he showed them the king's son. ⁵He commanded them, saying, "This is what you are to do: You who are in the three companies that are going on duty on the Sabbath—a third of you guarding the royal palace, ⁶a third at the Sur Gate, and a third at the gate behind the guard, who take turns guarding the temple—⁷and you who are in the other two companies that normally go off Sabbath duty are all to guard the temple for the king. ⁸Station yourselves around the king, each man with his weapon in his hand. Anyone who approaches your ranks[b] must be put

---

[a]2 Hebrew *Joram*, a variant of *Jehoram*   [b]8 Or *approaches the precincts*

to death. Stay close to the king wherever he goes."

⁹The commanders of units of a hundred did just as Jehoiada the priest ordered. Each one took his men—those who were going on duty on the Sabbath and those who were going off duty—and came to Jehoiada the priest. ¹⁰Then he gave the commanders the spears and shields that had belonged to King David and that were in the temple of the LORD. ¹¹The guards, each with his weapon in his hand, stationed themselves around the king—near the altar and the temple, from the south side to the north side of the temple.

¹²Jehoiada brought out the king's son and put the crown on him; he presented him with a copy of the covenant and proclaimed him king. They anointed him, and the people clapped their hands and shouted, "Long live the king!"

¹³When Athaliah heard the noise made by the guards and the people, she went to the people at the temple of the LORD. ¹⁴She looked and there was the king, standing by the pillar, as the custom was. The officers and the trumpeters were beside the king, and all the people of the land were rejoicing and blowing trumpets. Then Athaliah tore her robes and called out, "Treason! Treason!"

¹⁵Jehoiada the priest ordered the commanders of units of a hundred, who were in charge of the troops: "Bring her out between the ranks*ᵃ* and put to the sword anyone who follows her." For the priest had said, "She must not be put to death in the temple of the LORD." ¹⁶So they seized her as she reached the place where the horses enter the palace grounds, and there she was put to death.

¹⁷Jehoiada then made a covenant between the LORD and the king and people that they would be the LORD's people. He also made a covenant between the king and the people. ¹⁸All the people of the land went to the temple of Baal and tore it down. They smashed the altars and idols to pieces and killed Mattan the priest of Baal in front of the altars.

Then Jehoiada the priest posted guards at the temple of the LORD. ¹⁹He took with him the commanders of hundreds, the Carites, the guards and all the people of the land, and together they brought the king down from the temple of the LORD and went into the palace, entering by way of the gate of the guards. The king then took his place on the royal throne, ²⁰and all the people of the land rejoiced. And the

city was quiet, because Athaliah had been slain with the sword at the palace. ²¹Joash*ᵇ* was seven years old when he began to reign.

Joash Repairs the Temple

12 In the seventh year of Jehu, Joash*ᶜ* became king, and he reigned in Jerusalem forty years. His mother's name was Zibiah; she was from Beersheba. ²Joash did what was right in the eyes of the LORD all the years Jehoiada the priest instructed him. ³The high places, however, were not removed; the people continued to offer sacrifices and burn incense there.

⁴Joash said to the priests, "Collect all the money that is brought as sacred offerings to the temple of the LORD—the money collected in the census, the money received from personal vows and the money brought voluntarily to the temple. ⁵Let every priest receive the money from one of the treasurers, and let it be used to repair whatever damage is found in the temple."

⁶But by the twenty-third year of King Joash the priests still had not repaired the temple. ⁷Therefore King Joash summoned Jehoiada the priest and the other priests and asked them, "Why aren't you repairing the damage done to the temple? Take no more money from your treasurers, but hand it over for repairing the temple." ⁸The priests agreed that they would not collect any more money from the people and that they would not repair the temple themselves.

⁹Jehoiada the priest took a chest and bored a hole in its lid. He placed it beside the altar, on the right side as one enters the temple of the LORD. The priests who guarded the entrance put into the chest all the money that was brought to the temple of the LORD. ¹⁰Whenever they saw that there was a large amount of money in the chest, the royal secretary and the high priest came, counted the money that had been brought into the temple of the LORD and put it into bags. ¹¹When the amount had been determined, they gave the money to the men appointed to supervise the work on the temple. With it they paid those who worked on the temple of the LORD—the carpenters and builders, ¹²the masons and stonecutters. They purchased timber and dressed stone for the repair of

---

ᵃ15 Or *out from the precincts*   *ᵇ21* Hebrew *Jehoash*, a variant of *Joash*   *ᶜ1* Hebrew *Jehoash*, a variant of *Joash*; also in verses 2, 4, 6, 7 and 18

the temple of the LORD, and met all the other expenses of restoring the temple.

[13]The money brought into the temple was not spent for making silver basins, wick trimmers, sprinkling bowls, trumpets or any other articles of gold or silver for the temple of the LORD; [14]it was paid to the workmen, who used it to repair the temple. [15]They did not require an accounting from those to whom they gave the money to pay the workers, because they acted with complete honesty. [16]The money from the guilt offerings and sin offerings was not brought into the temple of the LORD; it belonged to the priests.

[17]About this time Hazael king of Aram went up and attacked Gath and captured it. Then he turned to attack Jerusalem. [18]But Joash king of Judah took all the sacred objects dedicated by his fathers—Jehoshaphat, Jehoram and Ahaziah, the kings of Judah—and the gifts he himself had dedicated and all the gold found in the treasuries of the temple of the LORD and of the royal palace, and he sent them to Hazael king of Aram, who then withdrew from Jerusalem.

[19]As for the other events of the reign of Joash, and all he did, are they not written in the book of the annals of the kings of Judah? [20]His officials conspired against him and assassinated him at Beth Millo, on the road down to Silla. [21]The officials who murdered him were Jozabad son of Shimeath and Jehozabad son of Shomer. He died and was buried with his fathers in the City of David. And Amaziah his son succeeded him as king.

Jehoahaz King of Israel

13 In the twenty-third year of Joash son of Ahaziah king of Judah, Jehoahaz son of Jehu became king of Israel in Samaria, and he reigned seventeen years. [2]He did evil in the eyes of the LORD by following the sins of Jeroboam son of Nebat, which he had caused Israel to commit, and he did not turn away from them. [3]So the LORD's anger burned against Israel, and for a long time he kept them under the power of Hazael king of Aram and Ben-Hadad his son.

[4]Then Jehoahaz sought the LORD's favor, and the LORD listened to him, for he saw how severely the king of Aram was oppressing Israel. [5]The LORD provided a deliverer for Israel, and they escaped from the power of Aram. So the Israelites lived in their own homes as they had before.

[6]But they did not turn away from the sins of the house of Jeroboam, which he had caused Israel to commit; they continued in them. Also, the Asherah pole[a] remained standing in Samaria.

[7]Nothing had been left of the army of Jehoahaz except fifty horsemen, ten chariots and ten thousand foot soldiers, for the king of Aram had destroyed the rest and made them like the dust at threshing time.

[8]As for the other events of the reign of Jehoahaz, all he did and his achievements, are they not written in the book of the annals of the kings of Israel? [9]Jehoahaz rested with his fathers and was buried in Samaria. And Jehoash[b] his son succeeded him as king.

Jehoash King of Israel

[10]In the thirty-seventh year of Joash king of Judah, Jehoash son of Jehoahaz became king of Israel in Samaria, and he reigned sixteen years. [11]He did evil in the eyes of the LORD and did not turn away from any of the sins of Jeroboam son of Nebat, which he had caused Israel to commit; he continued in them.

[12]As for the other events of the reign of Jehoash, all he did and his achievements, including his war against Amaziah king of Judah, are they not written in the book of the annals of the kings of Israel? [13]Jehoash rested with his fathers, and Jeroboam succeeded him on the throne. Jehoash was buried in Samaria with the kings of Israel.

[14]Now Elisha was suffering from the illness from which he died. Jehoash king of Israel went down to see him and wept over him. "My father! My father!" he cried. "The chariots and horsemen of Israel!"

[15]Elisha said, "Get a bow and some arrows," and he did so. [16]"Take the bow in your hands," he said to the king of Israel. When he had taken it, Elisha put his hands on the king's hands.

[17]"Open the east window," he said, and he opened it. "Shoot!" Elisha said, and he shot. "The LORD's arrow of victory, the arrow of victory over Aram!" Elisha declared. "You will completely destroy the Arameans at Aphek."

[18]Then he said, "Take the arrows," and the king took them. Elisha told him,

a6 That is, a symbol of the goddess Asherah; here and elsewhere in 2 Kings   b9 Hebrew Joash, a variant of Jehoash; also in verses 12-14 and 25

"Strike the ground." He struck it three times and stopped. [19]The man of God was angry with him and said, "You should have struck the ground five or six times; then you would have defeated Aram and completely destroyed it. But now you will defeat it only three times."

[20]Elisha died and was buried.

Now Moabite raiders used to enter the country every spring. [21]Once while some Israelites were burying a man, suddenly they saw a band of raiders; so they threw the man's body into Elisha's tomb. When the body touched Elisha's bones, the man came to life and stood up on his feet.

[22]Hazael king of Aram oppressed Israel throughout the reign of Jehoahaz. [23]But the LORD was gracious to them and had compassion and showed concern for them because of his covenant with Abraham, Isaac and Jacob. To this day he has been unwilling to destroy them or banish them from his presence.

[24]Hazael king of Aram died, and Ben-Hadad his son succeeded him as king. [25]Then Jehoash son of Jehoahaz recaptured from Ben-Hadad son of Hazael the towns he had taken in battle from his father Jehoahaz. Three times Jehoash defeated him, and so he recovered the Israelite towns.

Amaziah King of Judah

14 In the second year of Jehoash[a] son of Jehoahaz king of Israel, Amaziah son of Joash king of Judah began to reign. [2]He was twenty-five years old when he became king, and he reigned in Jerusalem twenty-nine years. His mother's name was Jehoaddin; she was from Jerusalem. [3]He did what was right in the eyes of the LORD, but not as his father David had done. In everything he followed the example of his father Joash. [4]The high places, however, were not removed; the people continued to offer sacrifices and burn incense there.

[5]After the kingdom was firmly in his grasp, he executed the officials who had murdered his father the king. [6]Yet he did not put the sons of the assassins to death, in accordance with what is written in the Book of the Law of Moses where the LORD commanded: "Fathers shall not be put to death for their children, nor children put to death for their fathers; each is to die for his own sins."[b]

[7]He was the one who defeated ten thousand Edomites in the Valley of Salt and captured Sela in battle, calling it Joktheel, the name it has to this day.

[8]Then Amaziah sent messengers to Jehoash son of Jehoahaz, the son of Jehu, king of Israel, with the challenge: "Come, meet me face to face."

[9]But Jehoash king of Israel replied to Amaziah king of Judah: "A thistle in Lebanon sent a message to a cedar in Lebanon, 'Give your daughter to my son in marriage.' Then a wild beast in Lebanon came along and trampled the thistle underfoot. [10]You have indeed defeated Edom and now you are arrogant. Glory in your victory, but stay at home! Why ask for trouble and cause your own downfall and that of Judah also?"

[11]Amaziah, however, would not listen, so Jehoash king of Israel attacked. He and Amaziah king of Judah faced each other at Beth Shemesh in Judah. [12]Judah was routed by Israel, and every man fled to his home. [13]Jehoash king of Israel captured Amaziah king of Judah, the son of Joash, the son of Ahaziah, at Beth Shemesh. Then Jehoash went to Jerusalem and broke down the wall of Jerusalem from the Ephraim Gate to the Corner Gate—a section about six hundred feet long.[c] [14]He took all the gold and silver and all the articles found in the temple of the LORD and in the treasuries of the royal palace. He also took hostages and returned to Samaria.

[15]As for the other events of the reign of Jehoash, what he did and his achievements, including his war against Amaziah king of Judah, are they not written in the book of the annals of the kings of Israel? [16]Jehoash rested with his fathers and was buried in Samaria with the kings of Israel. And Jeroboam his son succeeded him as king.

[17]Amaziah son of Joash king of Judah lived for fifteen years after the death of Jehoash son of Jehoahaz king of Israel. [18]As for the other events of Amaziah's reign, are they not written in the book of the annals of the kings of Judah?

[19]They conspired against him in Jerusalem, and he fled to Lachish, but they sent men after him to Lachish and killed him there. [20]He was brought back by horse and was buried in Jerusalem with his fathers, in the City of David.

[21]Then all the people of Judah took

---

[a]1 Hebrew *Joash*, a variant of *Jehoash*; also in verses 13, 23 and 27   [b]6 Deut. 24:16   [c]13 Hebrew *four hundred cubits* (about 180 meters)

Azariah,*a* who was sixteen years old, and made him king in place of his father Amaziah. **22**He was the one who rebuilt Elath and restored it to Judah after Amaziah rested with his fathers.

Jeroboam II King of Israel

23In the fifteenth year of Amaziah son of Joash king of Judah, Jeroboam son of Jehoash king of Israel became king in Samaria, and he reigned forty-one years. **24**He did evil in the eyes of the LORD and did not turn away from any of the sins of Jeroboam son of Nebat, which he had caused Israel to commit. **25**He was the one who restored the boundaries of Israel from Lebo*b* Hamath to the Sea of the Arabah,*c* in accordance with the word of the LORD, the God of Israel, spoken through his servant Jonah son of Amittai, the prophet from Gath Hepher.

26The LORD had seen how bitterly everyone in Israel, whether slave or free, was suffering; there was no one to help them. **27**And since the LORD had not said he would blot out the name of Israel from under heaven, he saved them by the hand of Jeroboam son of Jehoash.

28As for the other events of Jeroboam's reign, all he did, and his military achievements, including how he recovered for Israel both Damascus and Hamath, which had belonged to Yaudi,*d* are they not written in the book of the annals of the kings of Israel? **29**Jeroboam rested with his fathers, the kings of Israel. And Zechariah his son succeeded him as king.

Azariah King of Judah

15 In the twenty-seventh year of Jeroboam king of Israel, Azariah son of Amaziah king of Judah began to reign. **2**He was sixteen years old when he became king, and he reigned in Jerusalem fifty-two years. His mother's name was Jecoliah; she was from Jerusalem. **3**He did what was right in the eyes of the LORD, just as his father Amaziah had done. **4**The high places, however, were not removed; the people continued to offer sacrifices and burn incense there.

5The LORD afflicted the king with leprosy*e* until the day he died, and he lived in a separate house.*f* Jotham the king's son had charge of the palace and governed the people of the land.

6As for the other events of Azariah's reign, and all he did, are they not written in the book of the annals of the kings of

Judah? **7**Azariah rested with his fathers and was buried near them in the City of David. And Jotham his son succeeded him as king.

Zechariah King of Israel

8In the thirty-eighth year of Azariah king of Judah, Zechariah son of Jeroboam became king of Israel in Samaria, and he reigned six months. **9**He did evil in the eyes of the LORD, as his fathers had done. He did not turn away from the sins of Jeroboam son of Nebat, which he had caused Israel to commit.

10Shallum son of Jabesh conspired against Zechariah. He attacked him in front of the people,*g* assassinated him and succeeded him as king. **11**The other events of Zechariah's reign are written in the book of the annals of the kings of Israel. **12**So the word of the LORD spoken to Jehu was fulfilled: "Your descendants will sit on the throne of Israel to the fourth generation."*h*

Shallum King of Israel

13Shallum son of Jabesh became king in the thirty-ninth year of Uzziah king of Judah, and he reigned in Samaria one month. **14**Then Menahem son of Gadi went from Tirzah up to Samaria. He attacked Shallum son of Jabesh in Samaria, assassinated him and succeeded him as king.

15The other events of Shallum's reign, and the conspiracy he led, are written in the book of the annals of the kings of Israel.

16At that time Menahem, starting out from Tirzah, attacked Tiphsah and everyone in the city and its vicinity, because they refused to open their gates. He sacked Tiphsah and ripped open all the pregnant women.

Menahem King of Israel

17In the thirty-ninth year of Azariah king of Judah, Menahem son of Gadi became king of Israel, and he reigned in Samaria ten years. **18**He did evil in the eyes of the LORD. During his entire reign he did

*a*21 Also called *Uzziah*   *b*25 Or *from the entrance to*   *c*25 That is, the Dead Sea   *d*28 Or *Judah*   *e*5 The Hebrew word was used for various diseases affecting the skin—not necessarily leprosy.   *f*5 Or *in a house where he was relieved of responsibility*   *g*10 Hebrew; some Septuagint manuscripts *in Ibleam*   *h*12 2 Kings 10:30

not turn away from the sins of Jeroboam son of Nebat, which he had caused Israel to commit.

¹⁹Then Pul[a] king of Assyria invaded the land, and Menahem gave him a thousand talents[b] of silver to gain his support and strengthen his own hold on the kingdom. ²⁰Menahem exacted this money from Israel. Every wealthy man had to contribute fifty shekels[c] of silver to be given to the king of Assyria. So the king of Assyria withdrew and stayed in the land no longer.

²¹As for the other events of Menahem's reign, and all he did, are they not written in the book of the annals of the kings of Israel? ²²Menahem rested with his fathers. And Pekahiah his son succeeded him as king.

Pekahiah King of Israel

²³In the fiftieth year of Azariah king of Judah, Pekahiah son of Menahem became king of Israel in Samaria, and he reigned two years. ²⁴Pekahiah did evil in the eyes of the LORD. He did not turn away from the sins of Jeroboam son of Nebat, which he had caused Israel to commit. ²⁵One of his chief officers, Pekah son of Remaliah, conspired against him. Taking fifty men of Gilead with him, he assassinated Pekahiah, along with Argob and Arieh, in the citadel of the royal palace at Samaria. So Pekah killed Pekahiah and succeeded him as king.

²⁶The other events of Pekahiah's reign, and all he did, are written in the book of the annals of the kings of Israel.

Pekah King of Israel

²⁷In the fifty-second year of Azariah king of Judah, Pekah son of Remaliah became king of Israel in Samaria, and he reigned twenty years. ²⁸He did evil in the eyes of the LORD. He did not turn away from the sins of Jeroboam son of Nebat, which he had caused Israel to commit.

²⁹In the time of Pekah king of Israel, Tiglath-Pileser king of Assyria came and took Ijon, Abel Beth Maacah, Janoah, Kedesh and Hazor. He took Gilead and Galilee, including all the land of Naphtali, and deported the people to Assyria. ³⁰Then Hoshea son of Elah conspired against Pekah son of Remaliah. He attacked and assassinated him, and then succeeded him as king in the twentieth year of Jotham son of Uzziah.

³¹As for the other events of Pekah's reign, and all he did, are they not written in the book of the annals of the kings of Israel?

Jotham King of Judah

³²In the second year of Pekah son of Remaliah king of Israel, Jotham son of Uzziah king of Judah began to reign. ³³He was twenty-five years old when he became king, and he reigned in Jerusalem sixteen years. His mother's name was Jerusha daughter of Zadok. ³⁴He did what was right in the eyes of the LORD, just as his father Uzziah had done. ³⁵The high places, however, were not removed; the people continued to offer sacrifices and burn incense there. Jotham rebuilt the Upper Gate of the temple of the LORD.

³⁶As for the other events of Jotham's reign, and what he did, are they not written in the book of the annals of the kings of Judah? ³⁷(In those days the LORD began to send Rezin king of Aram and Pekah son of Remaliah against Judah.) ³⁸Jotham rested with his fathers and was buried with them in the City of David, the city of his father. And Ahaz his son succeeded him as king.

Ahaz King of Judah

16 In the seventeenth year of Pekah son of Remaliah, Ahaz son of Jotham king of Judah began to reign. ²Ahaz was twenty years old when he became king, and he reigned in Jerusalem sixteen years. Unlike David his father, he did not do what was right in the eyes of the LORD his God. ³He walked in the ways of the kings of Israel and even sacrificed his son in[d] the fire, following the detestable ways of the nations the LORD had driven out before the Israelites. ⁴He offered sacrifices and burned incense at the high places, on the hilltops and under every spreading tree.

⁵Then Rezin king of Aram and Pekah son of Remaliah king of Israel marched up to fight against Jerusalem and besieged Ahaz, but they could not overpower him. ⁶At that time, Rezin king of Aram recovered Elath for Aram by driving out the men of Judah. Edomites then moved into Elath and have lived there to this day. ⁷Ahaz sent messengers to say to

a19 Also called *Tiglath-Pileser*   b19 That is, about 37 tons (about 34 metric tons)   c20 That is, about 1 1/4 pounds (about 0.6 kilogram)   d3 Or *even made his son pass through*

Tiglath-Pileser king of Assyria, "I am your servant and vassal. Come up and save me out of the hand of the king of Aram and of the king of Israel, who are attacking me." [8]And Ahaz took the silver and gold found in the temple of the LORD and in the treasuries of the royal palace and sent it as a gift to the king of Assyria. [9]The king of Assyria complied by attacking Damascus and capturing it. He deported its inhabitants to Kir and put Rezin to death.

[10]Then King Ahaz went to Damascus to meet Tiglath-Pileser king of Assyria. He saw an altar in Damascus and sent to Uriah the priest a sketch of the altar, with detailed plans for its construction. [11]So Uriah the priest built an altar in accordance with all the plans that King Ahaz had sent from Damascus and finished it before King Ahaz returned. [12]When the king came back from Damascus and saw the altar, he approached it and presented offerings[a] on it. [13]He offered up his burnt offering and grain offering, poured out his drink offering, and sprinkled the blood of his fellowship offerings[b] on the altar. [14]The bronze altar that stood before the LORD he brought from the front of the temple—from between the new altar and the temple of the LORD—and put it on the north side of the new altar.

[15]King Ahaz then gave these orders to Uriah the priest: "On the large new altar, offer the morning burnt offering and the evening grain offering, the king's burnt offering and his grain offering, and the burnt offering of all the people of the land, and their grain offering and their drink offering. Sprinkle on the altar all the blood of the burnt offerings and sacrifices. But I will use the bronze altar for seeking guidance." [16]And Uriah the priest did just as King Ahaz had ordered.

[17]King Ahaz took away the side panels and removed the basins from the movable stands. He removed the Sea from the bronze bulls that supported it and set it on a stone base. [18]He took away the Sabbath canopy[c] that had been built at the temple and removed the royal entryway outside the temple of the LORD, in deference to the king of Assyria.

[19]As for the other events of the reign of Ahaz, and what he did, are they not written in the book of the annals of the kings of Judah? [20]Ahaz rested with his fathers and was buried with them in the City of David. And Hezekiah his son succeeded him as king.

Hoshea Last King of Israel

17 In the twelfth year of Ahaz king of Judah, Hoshea son of Elah became king of Israel in Samaria, and he reigned nine years. [2]He did evil in the eyes of the LORD, but not like the kings of Israel who preceded him.

[3]Shalmaneser king of Assyria came up to attack Hoshea, who had been Shalmaneser's vassal and had paid him tribute. [4]But the king of Assyria discovered that Hoshea was a traitor, for he had sent envoys to So[d] king of Egypt, and he no longer paid tribute to the king of Assyria, as he had done year by year. Therefore Shalmaneser seized him and put him in prison. [5]The king of Assyria invaded the entire land, marched against Samaria and laid siege to it for three years. [6]In the ninth year of Hoshea, the king of Assyria captured Samaria and deported the Israelites to Assyria. He settled them in Halah, in Gozan on the Habor River and in the towns of the Medes.

Israel Exiled Because of Sin

[7]All this took place because the Israelites had sinned against the LORD their God, who had brought them up out of Egypt from under the power of Pharaoh king of Egypt. They worshiped other gods [8]and followed the practices of the nations the LORD had driven out before them, as well as the practices that the kings of Israel had introduced. [9]The Israelites secretly did things against the LORD their God that were not right. From watchtower to fortified city they built themselves high places in all their towns. [10]They set up sacred stones and Asherah poles on every high hill and under every spreading tree. [11]At every high place they burned incense, as the nations whom the LORD had driven out before them had done. They did wicked things that provoked the LORD to anger. [12]They worshiped idols, though the LORD had said, "You shall not do this."[e] [13]The LORD warned Israel and Judah through all his prophets and seers: "Turn from your evil ways. Observe my commands and decrees, in accordance with the entire Law that I commanded your fathers to obey and that I delivered to you through my servants the prophets."

---

[a]12 Or *and went up*   [b]13 Traditionally *peace offerings*   [c]18 Or *the dais of his throne* (see Septuagint)   [d]4 Or *to Sais, to the*; *So* is possibly an abbreviation for *Osorkon*.   [e]12 Exodus 20:4, 5

[14]But they would not listen and were as stiff-necked as their fathers, who did not trust in the LORD their God. [15]They rejected his decrees and the covenant he had made with their fathers and the warnings he had given them. They followed worthless idols and themselves became worthless. They imitated the nations around them although the LORD had ordered them, "Do not do as they do," and they did the things the LORD had forbidden them to do.

[16]They forsook all the commands of the LORD their God and made for themselves two idols cast in the shape of calves, and an Asherah pole. They bowed down to all the starry hosts, and they worshiped Baal. [17]They sacrificed their sons and daughters in[a] the fire. They practiced divination and sorcery and sold themselves to do evil in the eyes of the LORD, provoking him to anger.

[18]So the LORD was very angry with Israel and removed them from his presence. Only the tribe of Judah was left, [19]and even Judah did not keep the commands of the LORD their God. They followed the practices Israel had introduced. [20]Therefore the LORD rejected all the people of Israel; he afflicted them and gave them into the hands of plunderers, until he thrust them from his presence.

[21]When he tore Israel away from the house of David, they made Jeroboam son of Nebat their king. Jeroboam enticed Israel away from following the LORD and caused them to commit a great sin. [22]The Israelites persisted in all the sins of Jeroboam and did not turn away from them [23]until the LORD removed them from his presence, as he had warned through all his servants the prophets. So the people of Israel were taken from their homeland into exile in Assyria, and they are still there.

Samaria Resettled

[24]The king of Assyria brought people from Babylon, Cuthah, Avva, Hamath and Sepharvaim and settled them in the towns of Samaria to replace the Israelites. They took over Samaria and lived in its towns. [25]When they first lived there, they did not worship the LORD; so he sent lions among them and they killed some of the people. [26]It was reported to the king of Assyria: "The people you deported and resettled in the towns of Samaria do not know what the god of that country requires. He has sent lions among them, which are killing them off, because the people do not know what he requires."

[27]Then the king of Assyria gave this order: "Have one of the priests you took captive from Samaria go back to live there and teach the people what the god of the land requires." [28]So one of the priests who had been exiled from Samaria came to live in Bethel and taught them how to worship the LORD.

[29]Nevertheless, each national group made its own gods in the several towns where they settled, and set them up in the shrines the people of Samaria had made at the high places. [30]The men from Babylon made Succoth Benoth, the men from Cuthah made Nergal, and the men from Hamath made Ashima; [31]the Avvites made Nibhaz and Tartak, and the Sepharvites burned their children in the fire as sacrifices to Adrammelech and Anammelech, the gods of Sepharvaim. [32]They worshiped the LORD, but they also appointed all sorts of their own people to officiate for them as priests in the shrines at the high places. [33]They worshiped the LORD, but they also served their own gods in accordance with the customs of the nations from which they had been brought.

[34]To this day they persist in their former practices. They neither worship the LORD nor adhere to the decrees and ordinances, the laws and commands that the LORD gave the descendants of Jacob, whom he named Israel. [35]When the LORD made a covenant with the Israelites, he commanded them: "Do not worship any other gods or bow down to them, serve them or sacrifice to them. [36]But the LORD, who brought you up out of Egypt with mighty power and outstretched arm, is the one you must worship. To him you shall bow down and to him offer sacrifices. [37]You must always be careful to keep the decrees and ordinances, the laws and commands he wrote for you. Do not worship other gods. [38]Do not forget the covenant I have made with you, and do not worship other gods. [39]Rather, worship the LORD your God; it is he who will deliver you from the hand of all your enemies."

[40]They would not listen, however, but persisted in their former practices. [41]Even while these people were worshiping the LORD, they were serving their idols. To this day their children and grandchildren continue to do as their fathers did.

[a]17 Or *They made their sons and daughters pass through*

Hezekiah King of Judah

18 In the third year of Hoshea son of Elah king of Israel, Hezekiah son of Ahaz king of Judah began to reign. [2]He was twenty-five years old when he became king, and he reigned in Jerusalem twenty-nine years. His mother's name was Abijah[a] daughter of Zechariah. [3]He did what was right in the eyes of the LORD, just as his father David had done. [4]He removed the high places, smashed the sacred stones and cut down the Asherah poles. He broke into pieces the bronze snake Moses had made, for up to that time the Israelites had been burning incense to it. (It was called[b] Nehushtan.[c])

[5]Hezekiah trusted in the LORD, the God of Israel. There was no one like him among all the kings of Judah, either before him or after him. [6]He held fast to the LORD and did not cease to follow him; he kept the commands the LORD had given Moses. [7]And the LORD was with him; he was successful in whatever he undertook. He rebelled against the king of Assyria

---

[a]2 Hebrew *Abi*, a variant of *Abijah*   [b]4 Or *He called it*   [c]4 *Nehushtan* sounds like the Hebrew for *bronze* and *snake* and *unclean thing.*

That's My Boy

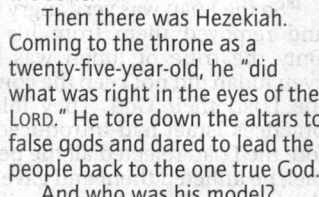

MONDAY

Passage:
2 Kings 18:1–8

Verse:
2 Kings 18:3

Some warm Saturday afternoon, take a drive up and down the residential streets of your town. Without a doubt, you'll see dads in their front yards playing pitch and catch or kicking a soccer ball back and forth to their children.

Usually, these faithful dads are just spending some good old "quality time" with their children. But sometimes the dads are motivated by something else. They want to teach their kids the fundamentals of a game. They want their kids to excel in this sport and someday make their dads proud. Who knows, they may even be thinking about a college scholarship!

There is absolutely nothing wrong with any of these motives. These kids are having fun with their dads, and that's good enough. And the lessons they learn—teamwork, unselfish play, rules of the game, the importance of physical fitness—can last a lifetime.

King David had high hopes for his offspring. As Israel's greatest earthly king, he worked hard to present an example that his children could imitate. And although he sometimes failed to please God, he always dealt with his failure in a God-honoring way. But after David left the throne of Israel, there were precious few good kings who followed. Many forgot their heritage and the lessons they should have learned from the past. Many completely forgot about God and his faithfulness to the Jews.

Then there was Hezekiah. Coming to the throne as a twenty-five-year-old, he "did what was right in the eyes of the LORD." He tore down the altars to false gods and dared to lead the people back to the one true God.

And who was his model? … his father David. Actually, David was not Hezekiah's father. He was, instead, his great grandfather times eight! But the text gives David credit for being the model whom Hezekiah followed. Imagine the implications of this. For ten generations, even though so many had ignored his example of godliness, people still remembered how David, the father, had faithfully taught and modeled to his son—and his son's sons—the "fundamentals" of the game of life.

Stop and think about it. The things that you are doing for your children through instruction and example will last for generations. The memory of your spiritual faithfulness and discipline will be like a snapshot of you playing ball with your child that will be pasted in mental scrapbooks for centuries to come.

As a young king, Hezekiah was blessed; he had David's example to follow. Give your children—and their children—the same blessing.

For your next devotional reading, go to page 424.

and did not serve him. [8]From watchtower to fortified city, he defeated the Philistines, as far as Gaza and its territory.

[9]In King Hezekiah's fourth year, which was the seventh year of Hoshea son of Elah king of Israel, Shalmaneser king of Assyria marched against Samaria and laid siege to it. [10]At the end of three years the Assyrians took it. So Samaria was captured in Hezekiah's sixth year, which was the ninth year of Hoshea king of Israel. [11]The king of Assyria deported Israel to Assyria and settled them in Halah, in Gozan on the Habor River and in towns of the Medes. [12]This happened because they had not obeyed the LORD their God, but had violated his covenant—all that Moses the servant of the LORD commanded. They neither listened to the commands nor carried them out.

[13]In the fourteenth year of King Hezekiah's reign, Sennacherib king of Assyria attacked all the fortified cities of Judah and captured them. [14]So Hezekiah king of Judah sent this message to the king of Assyria at Lachish: "I have done wrong. Withdraw from me, and I will pay whatever you demand of me." The king of Assyria exacted from Hezekiah king of Judah three hundred talents[a] of silver and thirty talents[b] of gold. [15]So Hezekiah gave him all the silver that was found in the temple of the LORD and in the treasuries of the royal palace.

[16]At this time Hezekiah king of Judah stripped off the gold with which he had covered the doors and doorposts of the temple of the LORD, and gave it to the king of Assyria.

Sennacherib Threatens Jerusalem

[17]The king of Assyria sent his supreme commander, his chief officer and his field commander with a large army, from Lachish to King Hezekiah at Jerusalem. They came up to Jerusalem and stopped at the aqueduct of the Upper Pool, on the road to the Washerman's Field. [18]They called for the king; and Eliakim son of Hilkiah the palace administrator, Shebna the secretary, and Joah son of Asaph the recorder went out to them.

[19]The field commander said to them, "Tell Hezekiah:

" 'This is what the great king, the king of Assyria, says: On what are you basing this confidence of yours? [20]You say you have strategy and military strength—but you speak only empty words. On whom are you depending, that you rebel against me? [21]Look now, you are depending on Egypt, that splintered reed of a staff, which pierces a man's hand and wounds him if he leans on it! Such is Pharaoh king of Egypt to all who depend on him. [22]And if you say to me, "We are depending on the LORD our God"—isn't he the one whose high places and altars Hezekiah removed, saying to Judah and Jerusalem, "You must worship before this altar in Jerusalem"?

[23]" 'Come now, make a bargain with my master, the king of Assyria: I will give you two thousand horses— if you can put riders on them! [24]How can you repulse one officer of the least of my master's officials, even though you are depending on Egypt for chariots and horsemen[c]? [25]Furthermore, have I come to attack and destroy this place without word from the LORD? The LORD himself told me to march against this country and destroy it.' "

[26]Then Eliakim son of Hilkiah, and Shebna and Joah said to the field commander, "Please speak to your servants in Aramaic, since we understand it. Don't speak to us in Hebrew in the hearing of the people on the wall."

[27]But the commander replied, "Was it only to your master and you that my master sent me to say these things, and not to the men sitting on the wall—who, like you, will have to eat their own filth and drink their own urine?"

[28]Then the commander stood and called out in Hebrew: "Hear the word of the great king, the king of Assyria! [29]This is what the king says: Do not let Hezekiah deceive you. He cannot deliver you from my hand. [30]Do not let Hezekiah persuade you to trust in the LORD when he says, 'The LORD will surely deliver us; this city will not be given into the hand of the king of Assyria.'

[31]"Do not listen to Hezekiah. This is what the king of Assyria says: Make peace with me and come out to me. Then every one of you will eat from his own vine and fig tree and drink water from his own cistern, [32]until I come and take you to a land like your own, a land of grain and new

[a]14 That is, about 11 tons (about 10 metric tons)
[b]14 That is, about 1 ton (about 1 metric ton)
[c]24 Or charioteers

wine, a land of bread and vineyards, a land of olive trees and honey. Choose life and not death!

"Do not listen to Hezekiah, for he is misleading you when he says, 'The LORD will deliver us.' ³³Has the god of any nation ever delivered his land from the hand of the king of Assyria? ³⁴Where are the gods of Hamath and Arpad? Where are the gods of Sepharvaim, Hena and Ivvah? Have they rescued Samaria from my hand? ³⁵Who of all the gods of these countries has been able to save his land from me? How then can the LORD deliver Jerusalem from my hand?"

³⁶But the people remained silent and said nothing in reply, because the king had commanded, "Do not answer him."

³⁷Then Eliakim son of Hilkiah the palace administrator, Shebna the secretary and Joah son of Asaph the recorder went to Hezekiah, with their clothes torn, and told him what the field commander had said.

Jerusalem's Deliverance Foretold

19 When King Hezekiah heard this, he tore his clothes and put on sackcloth and went into the temple of the LORD. ²He sent Eliakim the palace administrator, Shebna the secretary and the leading priests, all wearing sackcloth, to the prophet Isaiah son of Amoz. ³They told him, "This is what Hezekiah says: This day is a day of distress and rebuke and disgrace, as when children come to the point of birth and there is no strength to deliver them. ⁴It may be that the LORD your God will hear all the words of the field commander, whom his master, the king of Assyria, has sent to ridicule the living God, and that he will rebuke him for the words the LORD your God has heard. Therefore pray for the remnant that still survives."

⁵When King Hezekiah's officials came to Isaiah, ⁶Isaiah said to them, "Tell your master, 'This is what the LORD says: Do not be afraid of what you have heard—those words with which the underlings of the king of Assyria have blasphemed me. ⁷Listen! I am going to put such a spirit in him that when he hears a certain report, he will return to his own country, and there I will have him cut down with the sword.' "

⁸When the field commander heard that the king of Assyria had left Lachish, he withdrew and found the king fighting against Libnah.

⁹Now Sennacherib received a report that Tirhakah, the Cushite*ᵃ* king of Egypt, was marching out to fight against him. So he again sent messengers to Hezekiah with this word: ¹⁰"Say to Hezekiah king of Judah: Do not let the god you depend on deceive you when he says, 'Jerusalem will not be handed over to the king of Assyria.' ¹¹Surely you have heard what the kings of Assyria have done to all the countries, destroying them completely. And will you be delivered? ¹²Did the gods of the nations that were destroyed by my forefathers deliver them: the gods of Gozan, Haran, Rezeph and the people of Eden who were in Tel Assar? ¹³Where is the king of Hamath, the king of Arpad, the king of the city of Sepharvaim, or of Hena or Ivvah?"

Hezekiah's Prayer

¹⁴Hezekiah received the letter from the messengers and read it. Then he went up to the temple of the LORD and spread it out before the LORD. ¹⁵And Hezekiah prayed to the LORD: "O LORD, God of Israel, enthroned between the cherubim, you alone are God over all the kingdoms of the earth. You have made heaven and earth. ¹⁶Give ear, O LORD, and hear; open your eyes, O LORD, and see; listen to the words Sennacherib has sent to insult the living God.

¹⁷"It is true, O LORD, that the Assyrian kings have laid waste these nations and their lands. ¹⁸They have thrown their gods into the fire and destroyed them, for they were not gods but only wood and stone, fashioned by men's hands. ¹⁹Now, O LORD our God, deliver us from his hand, so that all kingdoms on earth may know that you alone, O LORD, are God."

Isaiah Prophesies Sennacherib's Fall

²⁰Then Isaiah son of Amoz sent a message to Hezekiah: "This is what the LORD, the God of Israel, says: I have heard your prayer concerning Sennacherib king of Assyria. ²¹This is the word that the LORD has spoken against him:

" 'The Virgin Daughter of Zion
    despises you and mocks you.
The Daughter of Jerusalem
    tosses her head as you flee.
²²Who is it you have insulted and
    blasphemed?

ᵃ9 That is, from the upper Nile region

Against whom have you raised your
voice
and lifted your eyes in pride?
Against the Holy One of Israel!
²³By your messengers
you have heaped insults on the Lord.
And you have said,
"With my many chariots
I have ascended the heights of the
mountains,
the utmost heights of Lebanon.
I have cut down its tallest cedars,
the choicest of its pines.
I have reached its remotest parts,
the finest of its forests.
²⁴I have dug wells in foreign lands
and drunk the water there.
With the soles of my feet
I have dried up all the streams of
Egypt."

²⁵" 'Have you not heard?
Long ago I ordained it.
In days of old I planned it;
now I have brought it to pass,
that you have turned fortified cities
into piles of stone.
²⁶Their people, drained of power,
are dismayed and put to shame.
They are like plants in the field,
like tender green shoots,
like grass sprouting on the roof,
scorched before it grows up.

²⁷" 'But I know where you stay
and when you come and go
and how you rage against me.
²⁸Because you rage against me
and your insolence has reached my
ears,
I will put my hook in your nose
and my bit in your mouth,
and I will make you return
by the way you came.'

²⁹"This will be the sign for you,
O Hezekiah:

"This year you will eat what grows by
itself,
and the second year what springs
from that.
But in the third year sow and reap,
plant vineyards and eat their fruit.
³⁰Once more a remnant of the house of
Judah
will take root below and bear fruit
above.
³¹For out of Jerusalem will come a
remnant,
and out of Mount Zion a band of
survivors.

The zeal of the LORD Almighty will accomplish this.

³²"Therefore this is what the LORD says
concerning the king of Assyria:

"He will not enter this city
or shoot an arrow here.
He will not come before it with shield
or build a siege ramp against it.
³³By the way that he came he will return;
he will not enter this city,
declares the LORD.
³⁴I will defend this city and save it,
for my sake and for the sake of David
my servant."

³⁵That night the angel of the LORD went
out and put to death a hundred and
eighty-five thousand men in the Assyrian
camp. When the people got up the next
morning—there were all the dead bodies!
³⁶So Sennacherib king of Assyria broke
camp and withdrew. He returned to Nineveh and stayed there.

³⁷One day while he was worshiping
in the temple of his god Nisroch, his
sons Adrammelech and Sharezer cut him
down with the sword, and they escaped to
the land of Ararat. And Esarhaddon his
son succeeded him as king.

Hezekiah's Illness

20 In those days Hezekiah became ill
and was at the point of death. The
prophet Isaiah son of Amoz went to him
and said, "This is what the LORD says: Put
your house in order, because you are going to die; you will not recover."

²Hezekiah turned his face to the wall
and prayed to the LORD, ³"Remember,
O LORD, how I have walked before you
faithfully and with wholehearted devotion and have done what is good in your
eyes." And Hezekiah wept bitterly.

⁴Before Isaiah had left the middle court,
the word of the LORD came to him: ⁵"Go
back and tell Hezekiah, the leader of my
people, 'This is what the LORD, the God of
your father David, says: I have heard your
prayer and seen your tears; I will heal you.
On the third day from now you will go up
to the temple of the LORD. ⁶I will add fifteen years to your life. And I will deliver
you and this city from the hand of the king
of Assyria. I will defend this city for my
sake and for the sake of my servant
David.' "

⁷Then Isaiah said, "Prepare a poultice of
figs." They did so and applied it to the
boil, and he recovered.

⁸Hezekiah had asked Isaiah, "What will be the sign that the LORD will heal me and that I will go up to the temple of the LORD on the third day from now?"

⁹Isaiah answered, "This is the LORD's sign to you that the LORD will do what he has promised: Shall the shadow go forward ten steps, or shall it go back ten steps?"

¹⁰"It is a simple matter for the shadow to go forward ten steps," said Hezekiah. "Rather, have it go back ten steps."

¹¹Then the prophet Isaiah called upon the LORD, and the LORD made the shadow go back the ten steps it had gone down on the stairway of Ahaz.

Envoys From Babylon

¹²At that time Merodach-Baladan son of Baladan king of Babylon sent Hezekiah letters and a gift, because he had heard of Hezekiah's illness. ¹³Hezekiah received the messengers and showed them all that was in his storehouses—the silver, the gold, the spices and the fine oil—his armory and everything found among his treasures. There was nothing in his palace or in all his kingdom that Hezekiah did not show them.

¹⁴Then Isaiah the prophet went to King Hezekiah and asked, "What did those men say, and where did they come from?"

"From a distant land," Hezekiah replied. "They came from Babylon."

¹⁵The prophet asked, "What did they see in your palace?"

"They saw everything in my palace," Hezekiah said. "There is nothing among my treasures that I did not show them."

¹⁶Then Isaiah said to Hezekiah, "Hear the word of the LORD: ¹⁷The time will surely come when everything in your palace, and all that your fathers have stored up until this day, will be carried off to Babylon. Nothing will be left, says the LORD. ¹⁸And some of your descendants, your own flesh and blood, that will be born to you, will be taken away, and they will become eunuchs in the palace of the king of Babylon."

¹⁹"The word of the LORD you have spoken is good," Hezekiah replied. For he thought, "Will there not be peace and security in my lifetime?"

²⁰As for the other events of Hezekiah's reign, all his achievements and how he made the pool and the tunnel by which he brought water into the city, are they not written in the book of the annals of the kings of Judah? ²¹Hezekiah rested with his fathers. And Manasseh his son succeeded him as king.

Manasseh King of Judah

21 Manasseh was twelve years old when he became king, and he reigned in Jerusalem fifty-five years. His mother's name was Hephzibah. ²He did evil in the eyes of the LORD, following the detestable practices of the nations the LORD had driven out before the Israelites. ³He rebuilt the high places his father Hezekiah had destroyed; he also erected altars to Baal and made an Asherah pole, as Ahab king of Israel had done. He bowed down to all the starry hosts and worshiped them. ⁴He built altars in the temple of the LORD, of which the LORD had said, "In Jerusalem I will put my Name." ⁵In both courts of the temple of the LORD, he built altars to all the starry hosts. ⁶He sacrificed his own son in*ᵃ* the fire, practiced sorcery and divination, and consulted mediums and spiritists. He did much evil in the eyes of the LORD, provoking him to anger.

⁷He took the carved Asherah pole he had made and put it in the temple, of which the LORD had said to David and to his son Solomon, "In this temple and in Jerusalem, which I have chosen out of all the tribes of Israel, I will put my Name forever. ⁸I will not again make the feet of the Israelites wander from the land I gave their forefathers, if only they will be careful to do everything I commanded them and will keep the whole Law that my servant Moses gave them." ⁹But the people did not listen. Manasseh led them astray, so that they did more evil than the nations the LORD had destroyed before the Israelites.

¹⁰The LORD said through his servants the prophets: ¹¹"Manasseh king of Judah has committed these detestable sins. He has done more evil than the Amorites who preceded him and has led Judah into sin with his idols. ¹²Therefore this is what the LORD, the God of Israel, says: I am going to bring such disaster on Jerusalem and Judah that the ears of everyone who hears of it will tingle. ¹³I will stretch out over Jerusalem the measuring line used against Samaria and the plumb line used against the house of Ahab. I will wipe out Jerusalem as one wipes a dish, wiping it and turning it upside down. ¹⁴I will forsake the remnant of my inheritance and

---

ᵃ6 Or He made his own son pass through

hand them over to their enemies. They will be looted and plundered by all their foes, [15]because they have done evil in my eyes and have provoked me to anger from the day their forefathers came out of Egypt until this day."

[16]Moreover, Manasseh also shed so much innocent blood that he filled Jerusalem from end to end—besides the sin that he had caused Judah to commit, so that they did evil in the eyes of the LORD.

[17]As for the other events of Manasseh's reign, and all he did, including the sin he committed, are they not written in the book of the annals of the kings of Judah? [18]Manasseh rested with his fathers and was buried in his palace garden, the garden of Uzza. And Amon his son succeeded him as king.

Amon King of Judah

[19]Amon was twenty-two years old when he became king, and he reigned in Jerusalem two years. His mother's name was Meshullemeth daughter of Haruz; she was from Jotbah. [20]He did evil in the eyes of the LORD, as his father Manasseh had done. [21]He walked in all the ways of his father; he worshiped the idols his father had worshiped, and bowed down to them. [22]He forsook the LORD, the God of his fathers, and did not walk in the way of the LORD.

[23]Amon's officials conspired against him and assassinated the king in his palace. [24]Then the people of the land killed all who had plotted against King Amon, and they made Josiah his son king in his place.

[25]As for the other events of Amon's reign, and what he did, are they not written in the book of the annals of the kings of Judah? [26]He was buried in his grave in the garden of Uzza. And Josiah his son succeeded him as king.

The Book of the Law Found

22 Josiah was eight years old when he became king, and he reigned in Jerusalem thirty-one years. His mother's name was Jedidah daughter of Adaiah; she was from Bozkath. [2]He did what was right in the eyes of the LORD and walked in all the ways of his father David, not turning aside to the right or to the left.

[3]In the eighteenth year of his reign, King Josiah sent the secretary, Shaphan son of Azaliah, the son of Meshullam, to the temple of the LORD. He said: [4]"Go up to Hilkiah the high priest and have him get ready the money that has been brought into the temple of the LORD, which the doorkeepers have collected from the people. [5]Have them entrust it to the men appointed to supervise the work on the temple. And have these men pay the workers who repair the temple of the LORD— [6]the carpenters, the builders and the masons. Also have them purchase timber and dressed stone to repair the temple. [7]But they need not account for the money entrusted to them, because they are acting faithfully."

[8]Hilkiah the high priest said to Shaphan the secretary, "I have found the Book of the Law in the temple of the LORD." He gave it to Shaphan, who read it. [9]Then Shaphan the secretary went to the king and reported to him: "Your officials have paid out the money that was in the temple of the LORD and have entrusted it to the workers and supervisors at the temple." [10]Then Shaphan the secretary informed the king, "Hilkiah the priest has given me a book." And Shaphan read from it in the presence of the king.

[11]When the king heard the words of the Book of the Law, he tore his robes. [12]He gave these orders to Hilkiah the priest, Ahikam son of Shaphan, Acbor son of Micaiah, Shaphan the secretary and Asaiah the king's attendant: [13]"Go and inquire of the LORD for me and for the people and for all Judah about what is written in this book that has been found. Great is the LORD's anger that burns against us because our fathers have not obeyed the words of this book; they have not acted in accordance with all that is written there concerning us."

[14]Hilkiah the priest, Ahikam, Acbor, Shaphan and Asaiah went to speak to the prophetess Huldah, who was the wife of Shallum son of Tikvah, the son of Harhas, keeper of the wardrobe. She lived in Jerusalem, in the Second District.

[15]She said to them, "This is what the LORD, the God of Israel, says: Tell the man who sent you to me, [16]'This is what the LORD says: I am going to bring disaster on this place and its people, according to everything written in the book the king of Judah has read. [17]Because they have forsaken me and burned incense to other gods and provoked me to anger by all the idols their hands have made,*a* my anger will burn against this place and will not be

---

a17 Or by everything they have done

quenched.' **18**Tell the king of Judah, who sent you to inquire of the LORD, 'This is what the LORD, the God of Israel, says concerning the words you heard: **19**Because your heart was responsive and you humbled yourself before the LORD when you heard what I have spoken against this place and its people, that they would become accursed and laid waste, and because you tore your robes and wept in my presence, I have heard you, declares the LORD. **20**Therefore I will gather you to your fathers, and you will be buried in peace. Your eyes will not see all the disaster I am going to bring on this place.' "

So they took her answer back to the king.

Josiah Renews the Covenant

23 Then the king called together all the elders of Judah and Jerusalem. **2**He went up to the temple of the LORD with the men of Judah, the people of Jerusalem, the priests and the prophets—all the people from the least to the greatest. He read in their hearing all the words of the Book of the Covenant, which had been found in the temple of the LORD. **3**The king stood by the pillar and renewed the covenant in the presence of the LORD—to follow the LORD and keep his commands, regulations and decrees with all his heart and all his soul, thus confirming the words of the covenant written in this

Could I Please Have a Receipt on That?

DAILY INSIGHT

TUESDAY

Passage:
2 Kings 22:3–7

Verse:
2 Kings 22:7

In the mid-seventies, I got my first job in sales. In addition to getting a good product to sell and a nice territory to sell it in, I received a travel expense budget. My boss explained the procedures for reporting money that I spent on the road. "Here's the form you fill out when you get back," he said, "and, by the way, the Internal Revenue Service does not require receipts for expenses less than twenty five dollars."

A few days later I was sitting on an airplane, headed for the west coast. I remember thinking, *Let's see. If I put a few less-than-twenty-dollar expenses in my reports for money I don't actually spend, this could really add up. After all, I'm working night and day for this company, and I'm not getting paid for all this extra time.*

Over the next few weeks, I discovered an interesting fact. And, although this dawned on me a long time ago, it's as fresh as if it had dashed across my mind last week. Here's the truth: You are who you are when no one's checking up on you.

King Josiah had given his secretary Shaphan an assignment. He had asked him to tell the high priest to take the donations the people had made at the temple and give them to the construction supervisors for parceling out to the workers. Then we

find an interesting post-script. Josiah tells Shaphan that the supervisors don't need to fill out expense reports. The king himself testifies that they are "acting faithfully."

I imagine the high priest said to these managers, "Spend the money carefully, but don't be concerned with keeping records. Our king trusts you, even when no one is checking up on you." Were these men tempted to slip a few shekels in their robes when they discovered that they weren't going to be audited? I doubt it. Rather, I imagine that these words motivated them to greater honesty. "Wow, the king trusts us with this money," they may have said to each other. "How could we do anything but be trustworthy?"

There are many different ways to motivate your children to be good when you're not around. You can read them a list of consequences they'll experience if they mess up. You can sit them down and interrogate them when they come home. Or you can tell them that you trust them to be honest, trustworthy, and faithful.

Which of these options do you suppose will get you the best results? Yeah, I do, too.

For your next devotional reading, go to page 441.

book. Then all the people pledged themselves to the covenant.

⁴The king ordered Hilkiah the high priest, the priests next in rank and the doorkeepers to remove from the temple of the LORD all the articles made for Baal and Asherah and all the starry hosts. He burned them outside Jerusalem in the fields of the Kidron Valley and took the ashes to Bethel. ⁵He did away with the pagan priests appointed by the kings of Judah to burn incense on the high places of the towns of Judah and on those around Jerusalem—those who burned incense to Baal, to the sun and moon, to the constellations and to all the starry hosts. ⁶He took the Asherah pole from the temple of the LORD to the Kidron Valley outside Jerusalem and burned it there. He ground it to powder and scattered the dust over the graves of the common people. ⁷He also tore down the quarters of the male shrine prostitutes, which were in the temple of the LORD and where women did weaving for Asherah.

⁸Josiah brought all the priests from the towns of Judah and desecrated the high places, from Geba to Beersheba, where the priests had burned incense. He broke down the shrines*a* at the gates—at the entrance to the Gate of Joshua, the city governor, which is on the left of the city gate. ⁹Although the priests of the high places did not serve at the altar of the LORD in Jerusalem, they ate unleavened bread with their fellow priests.

¹⁰He desecrated Topheth, which was in the Valley of Ben Hinnom, so no one could use it to sacrifice his son or daughter in*b* the fire to Molech. ¹¹He removed from the entrance to the temple of the LORD the horses that the kings of Judah had dedicated to the sun. They were in the court near the room of an official named Nathan-Melech. Josiah then burned the chariots dedicated to the sun.

¹²He pulled down the altars the kings of Judah had erected on the roof near the upper room of Ahaz, and the altars Manasseh had built in the two courts of the temple of the LORD. He removed them from there, smashed them to pieces and threw the rubble into the Kidron Valley. ¹³The king also desecrated the high places that were east of Jerusalem on the south of the Hill of Corruption—the ones Solomon king of Israel had built for Ashtoreth the vile goddess of the Sidonians, for Chemosh the vile god of Moab, and for Molech*c* the detestable god of the people

of Ammon. ¹⁴Josiah smashed the sacred stones and cut down the Asherah poles and covered the sites with human bones.

¹⁵Even the altar at Bethel, the high place made by Jeroboam son of Nebat, who had caused Israel to sin—even that altar and high place he demolished. He burned the high place and ground it to powder, and burned the Asherah pole also. ¹⁶Then Josiah looked around, and when he saw the tombs that were there on the hillside, he had the bones removed from them and burned on the altar to defile it, in accordance with the word of the LORD proclaimed by the man of God who foretold these things.

¹⁷The king asked, "What is that tombstone I see?"

The men of the city said, "It marks the tomb of the man of God who came from Judah and pronounced against the altar of Bethel the very things you have done to it."

¹⁸"Leave it alone," he said. "Don't let anyone disturb his bones." So they spared his bones and those of the prophet who had come from Samaria.

¹⁹Just as he had done at Bethel, Josiah removed and defiled all the shrines at the high places that the kings of Israel had built in the towns of Samaria that had provoked the LORD to anger. ²⁰Josiah slaughtered all the priests of those high places on the altars and burned human bones on them. Then he went back to Jerusalem.

²¹The king gave this order to all the people: "Celebrate the Passover to the LORD your God, as it is written in this Book of the Covenant." ²²Not since the days of the judges who led Israel, nor throughout the days of the kings of Israel and the kings of Judah, had any such Passover been observed. ²³But in the eighteenth year of King Josiah, this Passover was celebrated to the LORD in Jerusalem.

²⁴Furthermore, Josiah got rid of the mediums and spiritists, the household gods, the idols and all the other detestable things seen in Judah and Jerusalem. This he did to fulfill the requirements of the law written in the book that Hilkiah the priest had discovered in the temple of the LORD. ²⁵Neither before nor after Josiah was there a king like him who turned to the LORD as he did—with all his heart and with all his soul and with all his strength,

a8 Or high places   b10 Or to make his son or daughter pass through   c13 Hebrew Milcom

in accordance with all the Law of Moses.
²⁶Nevertheless, the LORD did not turn away from the heat of his fierce anger, which burned against Judah because of all that Manasseh had done to provoke him to anger. ²⁷So the LORD said, "I will remove Judah also from my presence as I removed Israel, and I will reject Jerusalem, the city I chose, and this temple, about which I said, 'There shall my Name be.'ᵃ"

²⁸As for the other events of Josiah's reign, and all he did, are they not written in the book of the annals of the kings of Judah?

²⁹While Josiah was king, Pharaoh Neco king of Egypt went up to the Euphrates River to help the king of Assyria. King Josiah marched out to meet him in battle, but Neco faced him and killed him at Megiddo. ³⁰Josiah's servants brought his body in a chariot from Megiddo to Jerusalem and buried him in his own tomb. And the people of the land took Jehoahaz son of Josiah and anointed him and made him king in place of his father.

Jehoahaz King of Judah

³¹Jehoahaz was twenty-three years old when he became king, and he reigned in Jerusalem three months. His mother's name was Hamutal daughter of Jeremiah; she was from Libnah. ³²He did evil in the eyes of the LORD, just as his fathers had done. ³³Pharaoh Neco put him in chains at Riblah in the land of Hamathᵇ so that he might not reign in Jerusalem, and he imposed on Judah a levy of a hundred talentsᶜ of silver and a talentᵈ of gold. ³⁴Pharaoh Neco made Eliakim son of Josiah king in place of his father Josiah and changed Eliakim's name to Jehoiakim. But he took Jehoahaz and carried him off to Egypt, and there he died. ³⁵Jehoiakim paid Pharaoh Neco the silver and gold he demanded. In order to do so, he taxed the land and exacted the silver and gold from the people of the land according to their assessments.

Jehoiakim King of Judah

³⁶Jehoiakim was twenty-five years old when he became king, and he reigned in Jerusalem eleven years. His mother's name was Zebidah daughter of Pedaiah; she was from Rumah. ³⁷And he did evil in the eyes of the LORD, just as his fathers had done.

24 During Jehoiakim's reign, Nebuchadnezzar king of Babylon invaded the land, and Jehoiakim became his vassal for three years. But then he changed his mind and rebelled against Nebuchadnezzar. ²The LORD sent Babylonian,ᵉ Aramean, Moabite and Ammonite raiders against him. He sent them to destroy Judah, in accordance with the word of the LORD proclaimed by his servants the prophets. ³Surely these things happened to Judah according to the LORD's command, in order to remove them from his presence because of the sins of Manasseh and all he had done, ⁴including the shedding of innocent blood. For he had filled Jerusalem with innocent blood, and the LORD was not willing to forgive.

⁵As for the other events of Jehoiakim's reign, and all he did, are they not written in the book of the annals of the kings of Judah? ⁶Jehoiakim rested with his fathers. And Jehoiachin his son succeeded him as king.

⁷The king of Egypt did not march out from his own country again, because the king of Babylon had taken all his territory, from the Wadi of Egypt to the Euphrates River.

Jehoiachin King of Judah

⁸Jehoiachin was eighteen years old when he became king, and he reigned in Jerusalem three months. His mother's name was Nehushta daughter of Elnathan; she was from Jerusalem. ⁹He did evil in the eyes of the LORD, just as his father had done.

¹⁰At that time the officers of Nebuchadnezzar king of Babylon advanced on Jerusalem and laid siege to it, ¹¹and Nebuchadnezzar himself came up to the city while his officers were besieging it. ¹²Jehoiachin king of Judah, his mother, his attendants, his nobles and his officials all surrendered to him.

In the eighth year of the reign of the king of Babylon, he took Jehoiachin prisoner. ¹³As the LORD had declared, Nebuchadnezzar removed all the treasures from the temple of the LORD and from the royal palace, and took away all the gold articles that Solomon king of Israel had made for the temple of the LORD. ¹⁴He car-

---

ᵃ27 1 Kings 8:29   ᵇ33 Hebrew; Septuagint (see also 2 Chron. 36:3) *Neco at Riblah in Hamath removed him*   ᶜ33 That is, about 3 3/4 tons (about 3.4 metric tons)   ᵈ33 That is, about 75 pounds (about 34 kilograms)   ᵉ2 Or *Chaldean*

ried into exile all Jerusalem: all the officers and fighting men, and all the craftsmen and artisans—a total of ten thousand. Only the poorest people of the land were left.

¹⁵Nebuchadnezzar took Jehoiachin captive to Babylon. He also took from Jerusalem to Babylon the king's mother, his wives, his officials and the leading men of the land. ¹⁶The king of Babylon also deported to Babylon the entire force of seven thousand fighting men, strong and fit for war, and a thousand craftsmen and artisans. ¹⁷He made Mattaniah, Jehoiachin's uncle, king in his place and changed his name to Zedekiah.

Zedekiah King of Judah

¹⁸Zedekiah was twenty-one years old when he became king, and he reigned in Jerusalem eleven years. His mother's name was Hamutal daughter of Jeremiah; she was from Libnah. ¹⁹He did evil in the eyes of the LORD, just as Jehoiakim had done. ²⁰It was because of the LORD's anger that all this happened to Jerusalem and Judah, and in the end he thrust them from his presence.

The Fall of Jerusalem

Now Zedekiah rebelled against the king of Babylon.

25 So in the ninth year of Zedekiah's reign, on the tenth day of the tenth month, Nebuchadnezzar king of Babylon marched against Jerusalem with his whole army. He encamped outside the city and built siege works all around it. ²The city was kept under siege until the eleventh year of King Zedekiah. ³By the ninth day of the ˻fourth˼ᵃ month the famine in the city had become so severe that there was no food for the people to eat. ⁴Then the city wall was broken through, and the whole army fled at night through the gate between the two walls near the king's garden, though the Babyloniansᵇ were surrounding the city. They fled toward the Arabah,ᶜ ⁵but the Babylonianᵈ army pursued the king and overtook him in the plains of Jericho. All his soldiers were separated from him and scattered, ⁶and he was captured. He was taken to the king of Babylon at Riblah, where sentence was pronounced on him. ⁷They killed the sons of Zedekiah before his eyes. Then they put out his eyes, bound him with bronze shackles and took him to Babylon.

⁸On the seventh day of the fifth month, in the nineteenth year of Nebuchadnezzar king of Babylon, Nebuzaradan commander of the imperial guard, an official of the king of Babylon, came to Jerusalem. ⁹He set fire to the temple of the LORD, the royal palace and all the houses of Jerusalem. Every important building he burned down. ¹⁰The whole Babylonian army, under the commander of the imperial guard, broke down the walls around Jerusalem. ¹¹Nebuzaradan the commander of the guard carried into exile the people who remained in the city, along with the rest of the populace and those who had gone over to the king of Babylon. ¹²But the commander left behind some of the poorest people of the land to work the vineyards and fields.

¹³The Babylonians broke up the bronze pillars, the movable stands and the bronze Sea that were at the temple of the LORD and they carried the bronze to Babylon. ¹⁴They also took away the pots, shovels, wick trimmers, dishes and all the bronze articles used in the temple service. ¹⁵The commander of the imperial guard took away the censers and sprinkling bowls—all that were made of pure gold or silver.

¹⁶The bronze from the two pillars, the Sea and the movable stands, which Solomon had made for the temple of the LORD, was more than could be weighed. ¹⁷Each pillar was twenty-seven feetᵉ high. The bronze capital on top of one pillar was four and a half feetᶠ high and was decorated with a network and pomegranates of bronze all around. The other pillar, with its network, was similar.

¹⁸The commander of the guard took as prisoners Seraiah the chief priest, Zephaniah the priest next in rank and the three doorkeepers. ¹⁹Of those still in the city, he took the officer in charge of the fighting men and five royal advisers. He also took the secretary who was chief officer in charge of conscripting the people of the land and sixty of his men who were found in the city. ²⁰Nebuzaradan the commander took them all and brought them to the king of Babylon at Riblah. ²¹There at Riblah, in the land of Hamath, the king had them executed.

So Judah went into captivity, away from her land.

ᵃ3 See Jer. 52:6.   ᵇ4 Or *Chaldeans*; also in verses 13, 25 and 26   ᶜ4 Or *the Jordan Valley*   ᵈ5 Or *Chaldean*; also in verses 10 and 24   ᵉ17 Hebrew *eighteen cubits* (about 8.1 meters)   ᶠ17 Hebrew *three cubits* (about 1.3 meters)

²²Nebuchadnezzar king of Babylon appointed Gedaliah son of Ahikam, the son of Shaphan, to be over the people he had left behind in Judah. ²³When all the army officers and their men heard that the king of Babylon had appointed Gedaliah as governor, they came to Gedaliah at Mizpah—Ishmael son of Nethaniah, Johanan son of Kareah, Seraiah son of Tanhumeth the Netophathite, Jaazaniah the son of the Maacathite, and their men. ²⁴Gedaliah took an oath to reassure them and their men. "Do not be afraid of the Babylonian officials," he said. "Settle down in the land and serve the king of Babylon, and it will go well with you."

²⁵In the seventh month, however, Ishmael son of Nethaniah, the son of Elishama, who was of royal blood, came with ten men and assassinated Gedaliah and also the men of Judah and the Babylonians who were with him at Mizpah.

²⁶At this, all the people from the least to the greatest, together with the army officers, fled to Egypt for fear of the Babylonians.

Jehoiachin Released

²⁷In the thirty-seventh year of the exile of Jehoiachin king of Judah, in the year Evil-Merodach[a] became king of Babylon, he released Jehoiachin from prison on the twenty-seventh day of the twelfth month. ²⁸He spoke kindly to him and gave him a seat of honor higher than those of the other kings who were with him in Babylon. ²⁹So Jehoiachin put aside his prison clothes and for the rest of his life ate regularly at the king's table. ³⁰Day by day the king gave Jehoiachin a regular allowance as long as he lived.

a27 Also called *Amel-Marduk*

> **"A** place for everything, and everything in its place."
> This is the credo of every compulsive perfectionist. Whether you
> identify yourself as one of these or not (the condition of your
> garage ought to give you a clue on this one), the book of
> 1 Chronicles introduces us to something for which the Israelites
> had longed for generations: a temple—a brick-and-mortar place
> for worship, a permanent dwelling for the Sovereign Lord. And
> even though God didn't hire David on as the general contractor
> for this great house of honor, the king was still overwhelmed by
> God's goodness in allowing his son Solomon to take up the task.
>
> Every dad has the privilege of building something special
> for God. It's not his local church building; it's his family. Each
> dad has the responsibility of building a home where people are
> treated with honor and love, a place where discipline is consis-
> tent and grace is abundant. What a privilege to build such a
> temple.

1 Chronicles

Historical Records From Adam to Abraham

To Noah's Sons

1 Adam, Seth, Enosh, ²Kenan, Mahalalel, Jared, ³Enoch, Methuselah, Lamech, Noah.

⁴The sons of Noah:*a*
Shem, Ham and Japheth.

The Japhethites

⁵The sons*b* of Japheth:
Gomer, Magog, Madai, Javan, Tubal, Meshech and Tiras.
⁶The sons of Gomer:
Ashkenaz, Riphath*c* and Togarmah.
⁷The sons of Javan:
Elishah, Tarshish, the Kittim and the Rodanim.

The Hamites

⁸The sons of Ham:
Cush, Mizraim,*d* Put and Canaan.
⁹The sons of Cush:
Seba, Havilah, Sabta, Raamah and Sabteca.
The sons of Raamah:
Sheba and Dedan.
¹⁰Cush was the father*e* of
Nimrod, who grew to be a mighty warrior on earth.

---

a4 Septuagint; Hebrew does not have *The sons of Noah:* *b5 Sons* may mean *descendants* or *successors* or *nations*; also in verses 6-10, 17 and 20. *c6* Many Hebrew manuscripts and Vulgate (see also Septuagint and Gen. 10:3); most Hebrew manuscripts *Diphath* *d8* That is, Egypt; also in verse 11 *e10 Father* may mean *ancestor* or *predecessor* or *founder*; also in verses 11, 13, 18 and 20.

11 Mizraim was the father of
the Ludites, Anamites, Lehabites,
Naphtuhites, **12** Pathrusites, Casluhites (from whom the Philistines
came) and Caphtorites.
13 Canaan was the father of
Sidon his firstborn,*a* and of the
Hittites, **14** Jebusites, Amorites, Girgashites, **15** Hivites, Arkites, Sinites,
16 Arvadites, Zemarites and Hamathites.

The Semites

17 The sons of Shem:
Elam, Asshur, Arphaxad, Lud and
Aram.
The sons of Aram*b*:
Uz, Hul, Gether and Meshech.
18 Arphaxad was the father of Shelah,
and Shelah the father of Eber.
19 Two sons were born to Eber:
One was named Peleg,*c* because in
his time the earth was divided; his
brother was named Joktan.
20 Joktan was the father of
Almodad, Sheleph, Hazarmaveth,
Jerah, **21** Hadoram, Uzal, Diklah,
22 Obal,*d* Abimael, Sheba, **23** Ophir,
Havilah and Jobab. All these were
sons of Joktan.

24 Shem, Arphaxad,*e* Shelah,
25 Eber, Peleg, Reu,
26 Serug, Nahor, Terah
27 and Abram (that is, Abraham).

The Family of Abraham

28 The sons of Abraham:
Isaac and Ishmael.

Descendants of Hagar

29 These were their descendants:
Nebaioth the firstborn of Ishmael,
Kedar, Adbeel, Mibsam, **30** Mishma,
Dumah, Massa, Hadad, Tema, **31** Je-
tur, Naphish and Kedemah. These
were the sons of Ishmael.

Descendants of Keturah

32 The sons born to Keturah, Abraham's
concubine:
Zimran, Jokshan, Medan, Midian,
Ishbak and Shuah.
The sons of Jokshan:
Sheba and Dedan.
33 The sons of Midian:
Ephah, Epher, Hanoch, Abida and
Eldaah.

All these were descendants of Keturah.

Descendants of Sarah

34 Abraham was the father of Isaac.
The sons of Isaac:
Esau and Israel.

Esau's Sons

35 The sons of Esau:
Eliphaz, Reuel, Jeush, Jalam and
Korah.
36 The sons of Eliphaz:
Teman, Omar, Zepho,*f* Gatam and
Kenaz;
by Timna: Amalek.*g*
37 The sons of Reuel:
Nahath, Zerah, Shammah and
Mizzah.

The People of Seir in Edom

38 The sons of Seir:
Lotan, Shobal, Zibeon, Anah, Di-
shon, Ezer and Dishan.
39 The sons of Lotan:
Hori and Homam. Timna was
Lotan's sister.
40 The sons of Shobal:
Alvan,*h* Manahath, Ebal, Shepho
and Onam.
The sons of Zibeon:
Aiah and Anah.
41 The son of Anah:
Dishon.
The sons of Dishon:
Hemdan,*i* Eshban, Ithran and
Keran.
42 The sons of Ezer:
Bilhan, Zaavan and Akan.*j*
The sons of Dishan*k*:
Uz and Aran.

---

*a*13 Or *of the Sidonians, the foremost*   *b*17 One
Hebrew manuscript and some Septuagint
manuscripts (see also Gen. 10:23); most Hebrew
manuscripts do not have this line.   *c*19 *Peleg*
means *division.*   *d*22 Some Hebrew manuscripts
and Syriac (see also Gen. 10:28); most Hebrew
manuscripts *Ebal*   *e*24 Hebrew; some Septuagint
manuscripts *Arphaxad, Cainan* (see also note at Gen.
11:10)   *f*36 Many Hebrew manuscripts, some
Septuagint manuscripts and Syriac (see also Gen.
36:11); most Hebrew manuscripts *Zephi*   *g*36 Some
Septuagint manuscripts (see also Gen. 36:12);
Hebrew *Gatam, Kenaz, Timna and Amalek*
*h*40 Many Hebrew manuscripts and some Septuagint
manuscripts (see also Gen. 36:23); most Hebrew
manuscripts *Alian*   *i*41 Many Hebrew manuscripts
and some Septuagint manuscripts (see also Gen.
36:26); most Hebrew manuscripts *Hamran*   *j*42 Many
Hebrew and Septuagint manuscripts (see also Gen.
36:27); most Hebrew manuscripts *Zaavan, Jaakan*
*k*42 Hebrew *Dishon,* a variant of *Dishan*

The Rulers of Edom

43These were the kings who reigned in Edom before any Israelite king reigned[a]:

Bela son of Beor, whose city was named Dinhabah.

44When Bela died, Jobab son of Zerah from Bozrah succeeded him as king.

45When Jobab died, Husham from the land of the Temanites succeeded him as king.

46When Husham died, Hadad son of Bedad, who defeated Midian in the country of Moab, succeeded him as king. His city was named Avith.

47When Hadad died, Samlah from Masrekah succeeded him as king.

48When Samlah died, Shaul from Rehoboth on the river[b] succeeded him as king.

49When Shaul died, Baal-Hanan son of Acbor succeeded him as king.

50When Baal-Hanan died, Hadad succeeded him as king. His city was named Pau,[c] and his wife's name was Mehetabel daughter of Matred, the daughter of Me-Zahab. **51**Hadad also died.

The chiefs of Edom were:

Timna, Alvah, Jetheth, **52**Oholibamah, Elah, Pinon, **53**Kenaz, Teman, Mibzar, **54**Magdiel and Iram. These were the chiefs of Edom.

Israel's Sons

2 These were the sons of Israel: Reuben, Simeon, Levi, Judah, Issachar, Zebulun, **2**Dan, Joseph, Benjamin, Naphtali, Gad and Asher.

Judah

To Hezron's Sons

3The sons of Judah:

Er, Onan and Shelah. These three were born to him by a Canaanite woman, the daughter of Shua. Er, Judah's firstborn, was wicked in the LORD's sight; so the LORD put him to death. **4**Tamar, Judah's daughter-in-law, bore him Perez and Zerah. Judah had five sons in all.

5The sons of Perez:

Hezron and Hamul.

6The sons of Zerah:

Zimri, Ethan, Heman, Calcol and Darda[d]—five in all.

7The son of Carmi:

Achar,[e] who brought trouble on Israel by violating the ban on taking devoted things.[f]

8The son of Ethan:

Azariah.

9The sons born to Hezron were:

Jerahmeel, Ram and Caleb.[g]

From Ram Son of Hezron

10Ram was the father of Amminadab, and Amminadab the father of Nahshon, the leader of the people of Judah. **11**Nahshon was the father of Salmon,[h] Salmon the father of Boaz, **12**Boaz the father of Obed and Obed the father of Jesse.

13Jesse was the father of Eliab his firstborn; the second son was Abinadab, the third Shimea, **14**the fourth Nethanel, the fifth Raddai, **15**the sixth Ozem and the seventh David. **16**Their sisters were Zeruiah and Abigail. Zeruiah's three sons were Abishai, Joab and Asahel. **17**Abigail was the mother of Amasa, whose father was Jether the Ishmaelite.

Caleb Son of Hezron

18Caleb son of Hezron had children by his wife Azubah (and by Jerioth). These were her sons: Jesher, Shobab and Ardon. **19**When Azubah died, Caleb married Ephrath, who bore him Hur. **20**Hur was the father of Uri, and Uri the father of Bezalel.

21Later, Hezron lay with the daughter of Makir the father of Gilead (he had married her when he was sixty years old), and she bore him Segub. **22**Segub was the father of

---

*a*43 Or *before an Israelite king reigned over them*   *b*48 Possibly the Euphrates   *c*50 Many Hebrew manuscripts, some Septuagint manuscripts, Vulgate and Syriac (see also Gen. 36:39); most Hebrew manuscripts *Pai*   *d*6 Many Hebrew manuscripts, some Septuagint manuscripts and Syriac (see also 1 Kings 4:31); most Hebrew manuscripts *Dara*   *e*7 *Achar* means *trouble; Achar* is called *Achan* in Joshua.   *f*7 The Hebrew term refers to the irrevocable giving over of things or persons to the LORD, often by totally destroying them.   *g*9 Hebrew *Kelubai,* a variant of *Caleb*   *h*11 Septuagint (see also Ruth 4:21); Hebrew *Salma*

Jair, who controlled twenty-three towns in Gilead. [23](But Geshur and Aram captured Havvoth Jair,[a] as well as Kenath with its surrounding settlements—sixty towns.) All these were descendants of Makir the father of Gilead.

[24]After Hezron died in Caleb Ephrathah, Abijah the wife of Hezron bore him Ashhur the father[b] of Tekoa.

Jerahmeel Son of Hezron

[25]The sons of Jerahmeel the firstborn of Hezron:
Ram his firstborn, Bunah, Oren, Ozem and[c] Ahijah. [26]Jerahmeel had another wife, whose name was Atarah; she was the mother of Onam.

[27]The sons of Ram the firstborn of Jerahmeel:
Maaz, Jamin and Eker.
[28]The sons of Onam:
Shammai and Jada.
The sons of Shammai:
Nadab and Abishur.
[29]Abishur's wife was named Abihail, who bore him Ahban and Molid.
[30]The sons of Nadab:
Seled and Appaim. Seled died without children.
[31]The son of Appaim:
Ishi, who was the father of Sheshan.
Sheshan was the father of Ahlai.
[32]The sons of Jada, Shammai's brother:
Jether and Jonathan. Jether died without children.
[33]The sons of Jonathan:
Peleth and Zaza.
These were the descendants of Jerahmeel.
[34]Sheshan had no sons—only daughters.
He had an Egyptian servant named Jarha. [35]Sheshan gave his daughter in marriage to his servant Jarha, and she bore him Attai.
[36]Attai was the father of Nathan,
Nathan the father of Zabad,
[37]Zabad the father of Ephlal,
Ephlal the father of Obed,
[38]Obed the father of Jehu,
Jehu the father of Azariah,
[39]Azariah the father of Helez,
Helez the father of Eleasah,
[40]Eleasah the father of Sismai,

Sismai the father of Shallum,
[41]Shallum the father of Jekamiah,
and Jekamiah the father of Elishama.

The Clans of Caleb

[42]The sons of Caleb the brother of Jerahmeel:
Mesha his firstborn, who was the father of Ziph, and his son Mareshah,[d] who was the father of Hebron.
[43]The sons of Hebron:
Korah, Tappuah, Rekem and Shema. [44]Shema was the father of Raham, and Raham the father of Jorkeam. Rekem was the father of Shammai. [45]The son of Shammai was Maon, and Maon was the father of Beth Zur.
[46]Caleb's concubine Ephah was the mother of Haran, Moza and Gazez. Haran was the father of Gazez.
[47]The sons of Jahdai:
Regem, Jotham, Geshan, Pelet, Ephah and Shaaph.
[48]Caleb's concubine Maacah was the mother of Sheber and Tirhanah. [49]She also gave birth to Shaaph the father of Madmannah and to Sheva the father of Macbenah and Gibea. Caleb's daughter was Acsah. [50]These were the descendants of Caleb.

The sons of Hur the firstborn of Ephrathah:
Shobal the father of Kiriath Jearim, [51]Salma the father of Bethlehem, and Hareph the father of Beth Gader.
[52]The descendants of Shobal the father of Kiriath Jearim were:
Haroeh, half the Manahathites, [53]and the clans of Kiriath Jearim: the Ithrites, Puthites, Shumathites and Mishraites. From these descended the Zorathites and Eshtaolites.
[54]The descendants of Salma:
Bethlehem, the Netophathites, Atroth Beth Joab, half the Manahathites, the Zorites, [55]and the clans of scribes[e] who lived at Jabez: the Ti-

---

[a]23 Or captured the settlements of Jair   [b]24 Father may mean civic leader or military leader; also in verses 42, 45, 49-52 and possibly elsewhere. [c]25 Or Oren and Ozem, by   [d]42 The meaning of the Hebrew for this phrase is uncertain.   [e]55 Or of the Sopherites

rathites, Shimeathites and Sucath-
ites. These are the Kenites who
came from Hammath, the father of
the house of Recab.[a]

The Sons of David

3 These were the sons of David born to
him in Hebron:
The firstborn was Amnon the son
of Ahinoam of Jezreel;
the second, Daniel the son of Abigail of Carmel;
²the third, Absalom the son of Maacah daughter of Talmai king of Geshur;
the fourth, Adonijah the son of
Haggith;
³the fifth, Shephatiah the son of
Abital;
and the sixth, Ithream, by his wife
Eglah.
⁴These six were born to David in
Hebron, where he reigned seven
years and six months.
David reigned in Jerusalem thirty-three
years, ⁵and these were the children born
to him there:
Shammua,[b] Shobab, Nathan and
Solomon. These four were by Bathsheba[c] daughter of Ammiel. ⁶There
were also Ibhar, Elishua,[d] Eliphelet, ⁷Nogah, Nepheg, Japhia,
⁸Elishama, Eliada and Eliphelet—
nine in all. ⁹All these were the sons
of David, besides his sons by his
concubines. And Tamar was their
sister.

The Kings of Judah

¹⁰Solomon's son was Rehoboam,
Abijah his son,
Asa his son,
Jehoshaphat his son,
¹¹Jehoram[e] his son,
Ahaziah his son,
Joash his son,
¹²Amaziah his son,
Azariah his son,
Jotham his son,
¹³Ahaz his son,
Hezekiah his son,
Manasseh his son,
¹⁴Amon his son,
Josiah his son.
¹⁵The sons of Josiah:
Johanan the firstborn,
Jehoiakim the second son,
Zedekiah the third,
Shallum the fourth.
¹⁶The successors of Jehoiakim:

Jehoiachin[f] his son,
and Zedekiah.

The Royal Line After the Exile

¹⁷The descendants of Jehoiachin the
captive:
Shealtiel his son, ¹⁸Malkiram, Pe-
daiah, Shenazzar, Jekamiah, Hosh-
ama and Nedabiah.
¹⁹The sons of Pedaiah:
Zerubbabel and Shimei.
The sons of Zerubbabel:
Meshullam and Hananiah.
Shelomith was their sister.
²⁰There were also five others:
Hashubah, Ohel, Berekiah, Hasa-
diah and Jushab-Hesed.
²¹The descendants of Hananiah:
Pelatiah and Jeshaiah, and the
sons of Rephaiah, of Arnan, of
Obadiah and of Shecaniah.
²²The descendants of Shecaniah:
Shemaiah and his sons:
Hattush, Igal, Bariah, Neariah and
Shaphat—six in all.
²³The sons of Neariah:
Elioenai, Hizkiah and Azrikam—
three in all.
²⁴The sons of Elioenai:
Hodaviah, Eliashib, Pelaiah, Akkub, Johanan, Delaiah and Ana-
ni—seven in all.

Other Clans of Judah

4 The descendants of Judah:
Perez, Hezron, Carmi, Hur and
Shobal.
²Reaiah son of Shobal was the father
of Jahath, and Jahath the father of
Ahumai and Lahad. These were
the clans of the Zorathites.
³These were the sons[g] of Etam:
Jezreel, Ishma and Idbash. Their
sister was named Hazzelelponi.
⁴Penuel was the father of Gedor,
and Ezer the father of Hushah.
These were the descendants of Hur,
the firstborn of Ephrathah and
father[h] of Bethlehem.

---

[a]55 Or *father of Beth Recab*   [b]5 Hebrew *Shimea*, a
variant of *Shammua*   [c]5 One Hebrew manuscript
and Vulgate (see also Septuagint and 2 Samuel
11:3); most Hebrew manuscripts *Bathshua*
[d]6 Two Hebrew manuscripts (see also 2 Samuel
5:15 and 1 Chron. 14:5); most Hebrew manuscripts
Elishama   [e]11 Hebrew *Joram*, a variant of *Jehoram*
[f]16 Hebrew *Jeconiah*, a variant of *Jehoiachin*; also
in verse 17   [g]3 Some Septuagint manuscripts (see
also Vulgate); Hebrew *father*   [h]4 *Father* may mean
civic leader or *military leader*; also in verses 12, 14,
17, 18 and possibly elsewhere.

⁵Ashhur the father of Tekoa had two wives, Helah and Naarah. ⁶Naarah bore him Ahuzzam, Hepher, Temeni and Haahashtari. These were the descendants of Naarah. ⁷The sons of Helah:

Zereth, Zohar, Ethnan, ⁸and Koz, who was the father of Anub and Hazzobebah and of the clans of Aharhel son of Harum.

⁹Jabez was more honorable than his brothers. His mother had named him Jabez,ᵃ saying, "I gave birth to him in pain." ¹⁰Jabez cried out to the God of Israel, "Oh, that you would bless me and enlarge my territory! Let your hand be with me, and keep me from harm so that I will be free from pain." And God granted his request.

¹¹Kelub, Shuhah's brother, was the father of Mehir, who was the father of Eshton. ¹²Eshton was the father of Beth Rapha, Paseah and Tehinnah the father of Ir Nahash.ᵇ These were the men of Recah.

¹³The sons of Kenaz:

Othniel and Seraiah.

The sons of Othniel:

Hathath and Meonothai.ᶜ ¹⁴Meonothai was the father of Ophrah.

Seraiah was the father of Joab,

the father of Ge Harashim.ᵈ It was called this because its people were craftsmen.

¹⁵The sons of Caleb son of Jephunneh:

Iru, Elah and Naam.

The son of Elah:

Kenaz.

¹⁶The sons of Jehallelel:

Ziph, Ziphah, Tiria and Asarel.

¹⁷The sons of Ezrah:

Jether, Mered, Epher and Jalon. One of Mered's wives gave birth to Miriam, Shammai and Ishbah the father of Eshtemoa. ¹⁸(His Judean wife gave birth to Jered the father of Gedor, Heber the father of Soco, and Jekuthiel the father of Zanoah.) These were the children of Pharaoh's daughter Bithiah, whom Mered had married.

¹⁹The sons of Hodiah's wife, the sister of Naham:

the father of Keilah the Garmite, and Eshtemoa the Maacathite.

²⁰The sons of Shimon:

Amnon, Rinnah, Ben-Hanan and Tilon.

The descendants of Ishi:

Zoheth and Ben-Zoheth.

²¹The sons of Shelah son of Judah:

Er the father of Lecah, Laadah the father of Mareshah and the clans of the linen workers at Beth Ashbea, ²²Jokim, the men of Cozeba, and Joash and Saraph, who ruled in Moab and Jashubi Lehem. (These records are from ancient times.) ²³They were the potters who lived at Netaim and Gederah; they stayed there and worked for the king.

Simeon

²⁴The descendants of Simeon:

Nemuel, Jamin, Jarib, Zerah and Shaul;

²⁵Shallum was Shaul's son, Mibsam his son and Mishma his son.

²⁶The descendants of Mishma:

Hammuel his son, Zaccur his son and Shimei his son.

²⁷Shimei had sixteen sons and six daughters, but his brothers did not have many children; so their entire clan did not become as numerous as the people of Judah. ²⁸They lived in Beersheba, Moladah, Hazar Shual, ²⁹Bilhah, Ezem, Tolad, ³⁰Bethuel, Hormah, Ziklag, ³¹Beth Marcaboth, Hazar Susim, Beth Biri and Shaaraim. These were their towns until the reign of David. ³²Their surrounding villages were Etam, Ain, Rimmon, Token and Ashan— five towns— ³³and all the villages around these towns as far as Baalath.ᵉ These were their settlements. And they kept a genealogical record.

³⁴Meshobab, Jamlech, Joshah son of Amaziah, ³⁵Joel, Jehu son of Joshibiah, the son of Seraiah, the son of Asiel, ³⁶also Elioenai, Jaakobah, Jeshohaiah, Asaiah, Adiel, Jesimiel, Benaiah, ³⁷and Ziza son of Shiphi, the son of Allon, the son of Jedaiah, the son of Shimri, the son of Shemaiah.

³⁸The men listed above by name were leaders of their clans. Their families increased greatly, ³⁹and they went to the outskirts of Gedor to the east of the valley in search of pasture for their flocks. ⁴⁰They found rich, good pasture, and the land

ᵃ9 *Jabez* sounds like the Hebrew for *pain*. ᵇ12 Or *of the city of Nahash* ᶜ13 Some Septuagint manuscripts and Vulgate; Hebrew does not have *and Meonothai*. ᵈ14 *Ge Harashim* means *valley of craftsmen*. ᵉ33 Some Septuagint manuscripts (see also Joshua 19:8); Hebrew *Baal*

was spacious, peaceful and quiet. Some Hamites had lived there formerly. **41**The men whose names were listed came in the days of Hezekiah king of Judah. They attacked the Hamites in their dwellings and also the Meunites who were there and completely destroyed[a] them, as is evident to this day. Then they settled in their place, because there was pasture for their flocks. **42**And five hundred of these Simeonites, led by Pelatiah, Neariah, Rephaiah and Uzziel, the sons of Ishi, invaded the hill country of Seir. **43**They killed the remaining Amalekites who had escaped, and they have lived there to this day.

Reuben

5 The sons of Reuben the firstborn of Israel (he was the firstborn, but when he defiled his father's marriage bed, his rights as firstborn were given to the sons of Joseph son of Israel; so he could not be listed in the genealogical record in accordance with his birthright, **2**and though Judah was the strongest of his brothers and a ruler came from him, the rights of the firstborn belonged to Joseph)— **3**the sons of Reuben the firstborn of Israel:

Hanoch, Pallu, Hezron and Carmi.
4The descendants of Joel:
Shemaiah his son, Gog his son, Shimei his son, **5**Micah his son, Reaiah his son, Baal his son, **6**and Beerah his son, whom Tiglath-Pileser[b] king of Assyria took into exile. Beerah was a leader of the Reubenites.
7Their relatives by clans, listed according to their genealogical records: Jeiel the chief, Zechariah, **8**and Bela son of Azaz, the son of Shema, the son of Joel. They settled in the area from Aroer to Nebo and Baal Meon. **9**To the east they occupied the land up to the edge of the desert that extends to the Euphrates River, because their livestock had increased in Gilead. **10**During Saul's reign they waged war against the Hagrites, who were defeated at their hands; they occupied the dwellings of the Hagrites throughout the entire region east of Gilead.

Gad

11The Gadites lived next to them in Bashan, as far as Salecah:

12Joel was the chief, Shapham the second, then Janai and Shaphat, in Bashan. **13**Their relatives, by families, were: Michael, Meshullam, Sheba, Jorai, Jacan, Zia and Eber—seven in all. **14**These were the sons of Abihail son of Huri, the son of Jaroah, the son of Gilead, the son of Michael, the son of Jeshishai, the son of Jahdo, the son of Buz. **15**Ahi son of Abdiel, the son of Guni, was head of their family.

16The Gadites lived in Gilead, in Bashan and its outlying villages, and on all the pasturelands of Sharon as far as they extended. **17**All these were entered in the genealogical records during the reigns of Jotham king of Judah and Jeroboam king of Israel.

18The Reubenites, the Gadites and the half-tribe of Manasseh had 44,760 men ready for military service—able-bodied men who could handle shield and sword, who could use a bow, and who were trained for battle. **19**They waged war against the Hagrites, Jetur, Naphish and Nodab. **20**They were helped in fighting them, and God handed the Hagrites and all their allies over to them, because they cried out to him during the battle. He answered their prayers, because they trusted in him. **21**They seized the livestock of the Hagrites—fifty thousand camels, two hundred fifty thousand sheep and two thousand donkeys. They also took one hundred thousand people captive, **22**and many others fell slain, because the battle was God's. And they occupied the land until the exile.

The Half-Tribe of Manasseh

23The people of the half-tribe of Manasseh were numerous; they settled in the land from Bashan to Baal Hermon, that is, to Senir (Mount Hermon). **24**These were the heads of their families: Epher, Ishi, Eliel, Azriel, Jeremiah, Hodaviah and Jahdiel. They were brave warriors, famous men, and heads of their families. **25**But they were unfaithful to the God of their fathers and prostituted themselves to the gods of the peoples of

---

[a]41 The Hebrew term refers to the irrevocable giving over of things or persons to the LORD, often by totally destroying them.   [b]6 Hebrew *Tilgath-Pilneser*, a variant of *Tiglath-Pileser*; also in verse 26

the land, whom God had destroyed before them. [26]So the God of Israel stirred up the spirit of Pul king of Assyria (that is, Tiglath-Pileser king of Assyria), who took the Reubenites, the Gadites and the half-tribe of Manasseh into exile. He took them to Halah, Habor, Hara and the river of Gozan, where they are to this day.

Levi

6 The sons of Levi:
Gershon, Kohath and Merari.
[2]The sons of Kohath:
Amram, Izhar, Hebron and Uzziel.
[3]The children of Amram:
Aaron, Moses and Miriam.
The sons of Aaron:
Nadab, Abihu, Eleazar and Ithamar.
[4]Eleazar was the father of Phinehas,
Phinehas the father of Abishua,
[5]Abishua the father of Bukki,
Bukki the father of Uzzi,
[6]Uzzi the father of Zerahiah,
Zerahiah the father of Meraioth,
[7]Meraioth the father of Amariah,
Amariah the father of Ahitub,
[8]Ahitub the father of Zadok,
Zadok the father of Ahimaaz,
[9]Ahimaaz the father of Azariah,
Azariah the father of Johanan,
[10]Johanan the father of Azariah (it was he who served as priest in the temple Solomon built in Jerusalem),
[11]Azariah the father of Amariah,
Amariah the father of Ahitub,
[12]Ahitub the father of Zadok,
Zadok the father of Shallum,
[13]Shallum the father of Hilkiah,
Hilkiah the father of Azariah,
[14]Azariah the father of Seraiah,
and Seraiah the father of Jehozadak.
[15]Jehozadak was deported when the LORD sent Judah and Jerusalem into exile by the hand of Nebuchadnezzar.

[16]The sons of Levi:
Gershon,[a] Kohath and Merari.
[17]These are the names of the sons of Gershon:
Libni and Shimei.
[18]The sons of Kohath:
Amram, Izhar, Hebron and Uzziel.
[19]The sons of Merari:
Mahli and Mushi.
These are the clans of the Levites

listed according to their fathers:
[20]Of Gershon:
Libni his son, Jehath his son,
Zimmah his son, [21]Joah his son,
Iddo his son, Zerah his son
and Jeatherai his son.
[22]The descendants of Kohath:
Amminadab his son, Korah his son,
Assir his son, [23]Elkanah his son,
Ebiasaph his son, Assir his son,
[24]Tahath his son, Uriel his son,
Uzziah his son and Shaul his son.
[25]The descendants of Elkanah:
Amasai, Ahimoth,
[26]Elkanah his son,[b] Zophai his son,
Nahath his son, [27]Eliab his son,
Jeroham his son, Elkanah his son
and Samuel his son.[c]
[28]The sons of Samuel:
Joel[d] the firstborn
and Abijah the second son.
[29]The descendants of Merari:
Mahli, Libni his son,
Shimei his son, Uzzah his son,
[30]Shimea his son, Haggiah his son
and Asaiah his son.

The Temple Musicians

[31]These are the men David put in charge of the music in the house of the LORD after the ark came to rest there. [32]They ministered with music before the tabernacle, the Tent of Meeting, until Solomon built the temple of the LORD in Jerusalem. They performed their duties according to the regulations laid down for them. [33]Here are the men who served, together with their sons:
From the Kohathites:
Heman, the musician,
the son of Joel, the son of Samuel,
[34]the son of Elkanah, the son of Jeroham,
the son of Eliel, the son of Toah,
[35]the son of Zuph, the son of Elkanah,
the son of Mahath, the son of Amasai,
[36]the son of Elkanah, the son of Joel,

---

[a]16 Hebrew *Gershom*, a variant of *Gershon*; also in verses 17, 20, 43, 62 and 71   [b]26 Some Hebrew manuscripts, Septuagint and Syriac; most Hebrew manuscripts *Ahimoth* [26]*and Elkanah. The sons of Elkanah:*   [c]27 Some Septuagint manuscripts (see also 1 Samuel 1:19,20 and 1 Chron. 6:33,34); Hebrew does not have *and Samuel his son.*
[d]28 Some Septuagint manuscripts and Syriac (see also 1 Samuel 8:2 and 1 Chron. 6:33); Hebrew does not have *Joel.*

the son of Azariah, the son of
Zephaniah,
[37] the son of Tahath, the son of Assir,
the son of Ebiasaph, the son of
Korah,
[38] the son of Izhar, the son of Kohath,
the son of Levi, the son of Israel;
[39] and Heman's associate Asaph, who
served at his right hand:
Asaph son of Berekiah, the son of
Shimea,
[40] the son of Michael, the son of
Baaseiah,[a]
the son of Malkijah, [41] the son of
Ethni,
the son of Zerah, the son of Adaiah,
[42] the son of Ethan, the son of
Zimmah,
the son of Shimei, [43] the son of
Jahath,
the son of Gershon, the son of
Levi;
[44] and from their associates, the Merarites, at his left hand:
Ethan son of Kishi, the son of Abdi,
the son of Malluch, [45] the son of
Hashabiah,
the son of Amaziah, the son of Hilkiah,
[46] the son of Amzi, the son of Bani,
the son of Shemer, [47] the son of
Mahli,
the son of Mushi, the son of Merari,
the son of Levi.

[48] Their fellow Levites were assigned to
all the other duties of the tabernacle, the
house of God. [49] But Aaron and his descendants were the ones who presented
offerings on the altar of burnt offering
and on the altar of incense in connection
with all that was done in the Most Holy
Place, making atonement for Israel, in accordance with all that Moses the servant
of God had commanded.

[50] These were the descendants of
Aaron:
Eleazar his son, Phinehas his son,
Abishua his son, [51] Bukki his son,
Uzzi his son, Zerahiah his son,
[52] Meraioth his son, Amariah his son,
Ahitub his son, [53] Zadok his son
and Ahimaaz his son.

[54] These were the locations of their
settlements allotted as their territory
(they were assigned to the descendants of
Aaron who were from the Kohathite clan,
because the first lot was for them):

[55] They were given Hebron in Judah
with its surrounding pasturelands.
[56] But the fields and villages around
the city were given to Caleb son of
Jephunneh.
[57] So the descendants of Aaron
were given Hebron (a city of refuge),
and Libnah,[b] Jattir, Eshtemoa, [58] Hi-
len, Debir, [59] Ashan, Juttah[c] and Beth
Shemesh, together with their pasturelands. [60] And from the tribe of
Benjamin they were given Gibeon,[d]
Geba, Alemeth and Anathoth, together with their pasturelands.
These towns, which were distributed among the Kohathite clans,
were thirteen in all.
[61] The rest of Kohath's descendants were
allotted ten towns from the clans of half
the tribe of Manasseh.
[62] The descendants of Gershon, clan by
clan, were allotted thirteen towns from
the tribes of Issachar, Asher and Naphtali,
and from the part of the tribe of Manasseh
that is in Bashan.
[63] The descendants of Merari, clan by
clan, were allotted twelve towns from the
tribes of Reuben, Gad and Zebulun.
[64] So the Israelites gave the Levites these
towns and their pasturelands. [65] From the
tribes of Judah, Simeon and Benjamin
they allotted the previously named towns.
[66] Some of the Kohathite clans were
given as their territory towns from the
tribe of Ephraim.
[67] In the hill country of Ephraim
they were given Shechem (a city of
refuge), and Gezer,[e] [68] Jokmeam, Beth
Horon, [69] Aijalon and Gath Rimmon,
together with their pasturelands.
[70] And from half the tribe of Manasseh the Israelites gave Aner and Bile-
am, together with their pasturelands,
to the rest of the Kohathite clans.

[71] The Gershonites received the following:
From the clan of the half-tribe of
Manasseh
they received Golan in Bashan and
also Ashtaroth, together with their
pasturelands;

---

[a]40 Most Hebrew manuscripts; some Hebrew
manuscripts, one Septuagint manuscript and
Syriac *Maaseiah*   [b]57 See Joshua 21:13; Hebrew
given the cities of refuge: Hebron, Libnah.
[c]59 Syriac (see also Septuagint and Joshua 21:16);
Hebrew does not have *Juttah.*   [d]60 See Joshua
21:17; Hebrew does not have *Gibeon.*   [e]67 See
Joshua 21:21; Hebrew *given the cities of refuge:
Shechem, Gezer.*

72 from the tribe of Issachar
they received Kedesh, Daberath,
73 Ramoth and Anem, together with
their pasturelands;
74 from the tribe of Asher
they received Mashal, Abdon,
75 Hukok and Rehob, together with
their pasturelands;
76 and from the tribe of Naphtali
they received Kedesh in Galilee,
Hammon and Kiriathaim, together with their pasturelands.

77 The Merarites (the rest of the Levites)
received the following:
From the tribe of Zebulun
they received Jokneam, Kartah,[a]
Rimmono and Tabor, together
with their pasturelands;
78 from the tribe of Reuben across the
Jordan east of Jericho
they received Bezer in the desert,
Jahzah, **79** Kedemoth and Mephaath, together with their pasturelands;
80 and from the tribe of Gad
they received Ramoth in Gilead,
Mahanaim, **81** Heshbon and Jazer,
together with their pasturelands.

Issachar

7 The sons of Issachar:
Tola, Puah, Jashub and Shimron—
four in all.
2 The sons of Tola:
Uzzi, Rephaiah, Jeriel, Jahmai, Ib-
sam and Samuel—heads of their
families. During the reign of David,
the descendants of Tola listed as
fighting men in their genealogy
numbered 22,600.
3 The son of Uzzi:
Izrahiah.
The sons of Izrahiah:
Michael, Obadiah, Joel and Isshiah. All five of them were chiefs.
4 According to their family genealogy, they had 36,000 men ready for
battle, for they had many wives
and children.
5 The relatives who were fighting men
belonging to all the clans of Issachar, as listed in their genealogy,
were 87,000 in all.

Benjamin

6 Three sons of Benjamin:
Bela, Beker and Jediael.

7 The sons of Bela:
Ezbon, Uzzi, Uzziel, Jerimoth and
Iri, heads of families—five in all.
Their genealogical record listed
22,034 fighting men.
8 The sons of Beker:
Zemirah, Joash, Eliezer, Elioenai,
Omri, Jeremoth, Abijah, Anathoth
and Alemeth. All these were the
sons of Beker. **9** Their genealogical
record listed the heads of families
and 20,200 fighting men.
10 The son of Jediael:
Bilhan.
The sons of Bilhan:
Jeush, Benjamin, Ehud, Kenaanah,
Zethan, Tarshish and Ahishahar.
11 All these sons of Jediael were
heads of families. There were
17,200 fighting men ready to go
out to war.
12 The Shuppites and Huppites were
the descendants of Ir, and the Hu-
shites the descendants of Aher.

Naphtali

13 The sons of Naphtali:
Jahziel, Guni, Jezer and Shillem[b]—
the descendants of Bilhah.

Manasseh

14 The descendants of Manasseh:
Asriel was his descendant through
his Aramean concubine. She gave
birth to Makir the father of Gilead.
15 Makir took a wife from among the
Huppites and Shuppites. His sister's
name was Maacah.
Another descendant was named
Zelophehad, who had only daughters.
16 Makir's wife Maacah gave birth
to a son and named him Peresh. His
brother was named Sheresh, and his
sons were Ulam and Rakem.
17 The son of Ulam:
Bedan.
These were the sons of Gilead son of
Makir, the son of Manasseh. **18** His
sister Hammoleketh gave birth to
Ishhod, Abiezer and Mahlah.
19 The sons of Shemida were:
Ahian, Shechem, Likhi and Aniam.

---

[a]77 See Septuagint and Joshua 21:34; Hebrew does
not have *Jokneam, Kartah.* [b]13 Some Hebrew and
Septuagint manuscripts (see also Gen. 46:24 and
Num. 26:49); most Hebrew manuscripts *Shallum*

Ephraim

²⁰ The descendants of Ephraim:
Shuthelah, Bered his son,
Tahath his son, Eleadah his son,
Tahath his son, ²¹ Zabad his son
and Shuthelah his son.
Ezer and Elead were killed by the
native-born men of Gath, when they
went down to seize their livestock.
²² Their father Ephraim mourned for
them many days, and his relatives
came to comfort him. ²³ Then he lay
with his wife again, and she became
pregnant and gave birth to a son. He
named him Beriah,ᵃ because there
had been misfortune in his family.
²⁴ His daughter was Sheerah, who
built Lower and Upper Beth Horon as
well as Uzzen Sheerah.

²⁵ Rephah was his son, Resheph his
son,ᵇ
Telah his son, Tahan his son,
²⁶ Ladan his son, Ammihud his son,
Elishama his son, ²⁷ Nun his son
and Joshua his son.

²⁸ Their lands and settlements included
Bethel and its surrounding villages, Naa-
ran to the east, Gezer and its villages to
the west, and Shechem and its villages all
the way to Ayyah and its villages. ²⁹ Along
the borders of Manasseh were Beth Shan,
Taanach, Megiddo and Dor, together with
their villages. The descendants of Joseph
son of Israel lived in these towns.

Asher

³⁰ The sons of Asher:
Imnah, Ishvah, Ishvi and Beriah.
Their sister was Serah.
³¹ The sons of Beriah:
Heber and Malkiel, who was the
father of Birzaith.
³² Heber was the father of Japhlet, Shomer and Hotham and of their sister
Shua.
³³ The sons of Japhlet:
Pasach, Bimhal and Ashvath.
These were Japhlet's sons.
³⁴ The sons of Shomer:
Ahi, Rohgah,ᶜ Hubbah and Aram.
³⁵ The sons of his brother Helem:
Zophah, Imna, Shelesh and Amal.
³⁶ The sons of Zophah:
Suah, Harnepher, Shual, Beri, Im-
rah, ³⁷ Bezer, Hod, Shamma, Shil-
shah, Ithranᵈ and Beera.
³⁸ The sons of Jether:
Jephunneh, Pispah and Ara.

³⁹ The sons of Ulla:
Arah, Hanniel and Rizia.

⁴⁰ All these were descendants of Asher—
heads of families, choice men, brave warriors and outstanding leaders. The
number of men ready for battle, as listed
in their genealogy, was 26,000.

The Genealogy of Saul the Benjamite

8 Benjamin was the father of Bela his
firstborn,
Ashbel the second son, Aharah the
third,
² Nohah the fourth and Rapha the
fifth.
³ The sons of Bela were:
Addar, Gera, Abihud,ᵉ ⁴ Abishua,
Naaman, Ahoah, ⁵ Gera, Shephu-
phan and Huram.
⁶ These were the descendants of Ehud,
who were heads of families of
those living in Geba and were deported to Manahath:
⁷ Naaman, Ahijah, and Gera, who
deported them and who was the
father of Uzza and Ahihud.
⁸ Sons were born to Shaharaim in
Moab after he had divorced his
wives Hushim and Baara. ⁹ By his
wife Hodesh he had Jobab, Zibia,
Mesha, Malcam, ¹⁰ Jeuz, Sakia and
Mirmah. These were his sons,
heads of families. ¹¹ By Hushim he
had Abitub and Elpaal.
¹² The sons of Elpaal:
Eber, Misham, Shemed (who built
Ono and Lod with its surrounding
villages), ¹³ and Beriah and Shema,
who were heads of families of
those living in Aijalon and who
drove out the inhabitants of Gath.
¹⁴ Ahio, Shashak, Jeremoth, ¹⁵ Zebadiah,
Arad, Eder, ¹⁶ Michael, Ishpah and
Joha were the sons of Beriah.
¹⁷ Zebadiah, Meshullam, Hizki, Heber,
¹⁸ Ishmerai, Izliah and Jobab were
the sons of Elpaal.
¹⁹ Jakim, Zicri, Zabdi, ²⁰ Elienai, Zillethai, Eliel, ²¹ Adaiah, Beraiah and
Shimrath were the sons of Shimei.
²² Ishpan, Eber, Eliel, ²³ Abdon, Zicri,
Hanan, ²⁴ Hananiah, Elam, Antho-
thijah, ²⁵ Iphdeiah and Penuel were
the sons of Shashak.

ᵃ23 *Beriah* sounds like the Hebrew for *misfortune.*
ᵇ25 Some Septuagint manuscripts; Hebrew does
not have *his son.*   ᶜ34 Or *of his brother Shomer:
Rohgah*   ᵈ37 Possibly a variant of *Jether*   ᵉ3 Or
Gera the father of Ehud

²⁶Shamsherai, Shehariah, Athaliah, ²⁷Jaareshiah, Elijah and Zicri were the sons of Jeroham.

²⁸All these were heads of families, chiefs as listed in their genealogy, and they lived in Jerusalem.

²⁹Jeiel*ᵃ* the father*ᵇ* of Gibeon lived in Gibeon.
His wife's name was Maacah, ³⁰and his firstborn son was Abdon, followed by Zur, Kish, Baal, Ner,*ᶜ* Nadab, ³¹Gedor, Ahio, Zeker ³²and Mikloth, who was the father of Shimeah. They too lived near their relatives in Jerusalem.

³³Ner was the father of Kish, Kish the father of Saul, and Saul the father of Jonathan, Malki-Shua, Abinadab and Esh-Baal.*ᵈ*

³⁴The son of Jonathan:
Merib-Baal,*ᵉ* who was the father of Micah.

³⁵The sons of Micah:
Pithon, Melech, Tarea and Ahaz.

³⁶Ahaz was the father of Jehoaddah, Jehoaddah was the father of Alemeth, Azmaveth and Zimri, and Zimri was the father of Moza. ³⁷Moza was the father of Binea; Raphah was his son, Eleasah his son and Azel his son.

³⁸Azel had six sons, and these were their names:
Azrikam, Bokeru, Ishmael, Sheariah, Obadiah and Hanan. All these were the sons of Azel.

³⁹The sons of his brother Eshek:
Ulam his firstborn, Jeush the second son and Eliphelet the third.
⁴⁰The sons of Ulam were brave warriors who could handle the bow. They had many sons and grandsons—150 in all.

All these were the descendants of Benjamin.

9 All Israel was listed in the genealogies recorded in the book of the kings of Israel.

The People in Jerusalem

The people of Judah were taken captive to Babylon because of their unfaithfulness. ²Now the first to resettle on their own property in their own towns were some Israelites, priests, Levites and temple servants.

³Those from Judah, from Benjamin, and from Ephraim and Manasseh who lived in Jerusalem were:

⁴Uthai son of Ammihud, the son of Omri, the son of Imri, the son of Bani, a descendant of Perez son of Judah.

⁵Of the Shilonites:
Asaiah the firstborn and his sons.

⁶Of the Zerahites:
Jeuel.
The people from Judah numbered 690.

⁷Of the Benjamites:
Sallu son of Meshullam, the son of Hodaviah, the son of Hassenuah;
⁸Ibneiah son of Jeroham; Elah son of Uzzi, the son of Micri; and Meshullam son of Shephatiah, the son of Reuel, the son of Ibnijah.
⁹The people from Benjamin, as listed in their genealogy, numbered 956. All these men were heads of their families.

¹⁰Of the priests:
Jedaiah; Jehoiarib; Jakin;
¹¹Azariah son of Hilkiah, the son of Meshullam, the son of Zadok, the son of Meraioth, the son of Ahitub, the official in charge of the house of God;
¹²Adaiah son of Jeroham, the son of Pashhur, the son of Malkijah; and Maasai son of Adiel, the son of Jahzerah, the son of Meshullam, the son of Meshillemith, the son of Immer.
¹³The priests, who were heads of families, numbered 1,760. They were able men, responsible for ministering in the house of God.

¹⁴Of the Levites:
Shemaiah son of Hasshub, the son of Azrikam, the son of Hashabiah, a Merarite; ¹⁵Bakbakkar, Heresh, Galal and Mattaniah son of Mica, the son of Zicri, the son of Asaph; ¹⁶Obadiah son of Shemaiah, the son of Galal, the son of Jeduthun; and Berekiah son of Asa, the son of Elkanah, who lived in the villages of the Netophathites.

¹⁷The gatekeepers:
Shallum, Akkub, Talmon, Ahiman

ᵃ29 Some Septuagint manuscripts (see also 1 Chron. 9:35); Hebrew does not have *Jeiel.* *ᵇ29 Father* may mean *civic leader* or *military leader.* *ᶜ30* Some Septuagint manuscripts (see also 1 Chron. 9:36); Hebrew does not have *Ner.* *ᵈ33* Also known as *Ish-Bosheth* *ᵉ34* Also known as *Mephibosheth*

and their brothers, Shallum their chief [18]being stationed at the King's Gate on the east, up to the present time. These were the gatekeepers belonging to the camp of the Levites. [19]Shallum son of Kore, the son of Ebiasaph, the son of Korah, and his fellow gatekeepers from his family (the Korahites) were responsible for guarding the thresholds of the Tent[a] just as their fathers had been responsible for guarding the entrance to the dwelling of the LORD. [20]In earlier times Phinehas son of Eleazar was in charge of the gatekeepers, and the LORD was with him. [21]Zechariah son of Meshelemiah was the gatekeeper at the entrance to the Tent of Meeting.

[22]Altogether, those chosen to be gatekeepers at the thresholds numbered 212. They were registered by genealogy in their villages. The gatekeepers had been assigned to their positions of trust by David and Samuel the seer. [23]They and their

a19 That is, the temple; also in verses 21 and 23

Double-Checking Dads

"At first I was insulted by what Randy did before going to bed every night," I heard my friend tell me, "but then it dawned on me that my husband was a door-checker."

Randy and Sandra had been married for only a few weeks. At the end of the day, just before retiring for the evening, Sandra would walk around their small, first-floor apartment, making sure all the doors and windows were locked. A few minutes later, while she was taking her makeup off and getting dressed for bed, Randy would make the rounds. He would go to each door and window, testing to be sure they were really locked.

This infuriated Sandra. *Who does he think he is?* she would fume. *Doesn't he think I know how to lock a door?* But like many newlyweds making the adjustment to married life, Sandra didn't say anything to Randy.

"Then one afternoon," Sandra told me, "almost a full year into our marriage, after Randy had called me from the bank where he worked, it hit me. Randy's job is to take care of people's money. They trust him because of the way he values their life savings. I was married to a professional door-checker … and, for the first time, I was thankful."

The Israelites were in trouble. Their enemies had surrounded them and were licking their chops over the possibility of capturing this fertile land and enslaving

DAILY INSIGHT

WEDNESDAY

Passage:
1 Chronicles 9:22–27

Verse:
1 Chronicles 9:27

these hard-working people. So two hundred and twelve men were charged with guarding the temple—the precious home of the God whom they loved. Day and night these sentinels stood guard, making sure that nothing happened to this sacred dwelling place. With the diligent protection of these gatekeepers, the Israelites slept peacefully.

You're way ahead of me, aren't you? Good.

One of the most important responsibilities you and I have as dads is to stand guard over our homes. We take very seriously the task of giving our families physical and emotional security.

This protection can take many forms. Of course, it includes our doing our best to guard our children's bodies—the right kind of safety seats in the car, instructions on hot stoves or how to deal with stray dogs. But our door-checking must also include standing guard over their emotions. As dads, our job is to provide a safe place for our children's inevitable broken hearts and shattered dreams.

Our children need to know that, even when they're sleeping, their dads are safeguarding them. We're doing our very best to insure their protection—outside and inside. Door-checking—it's one of the most important jobs we have to do.

For your next devotional reading, go to page 453.

descendants were in charge of guarding the gates of the house of the LORD—the house called the Tent. [24]The gatekeepers were on the four sides: east, west, north and south. [25]Their brothers in their villages had to come from time to time and share their duties for seven-day periods. [26]But the four principal gatekeepers, who were Levites, were entrusted with the responsibility for the rooms and treasuries in the house of God. [27]They would spend the night stationed around the house of God, because they had to guard it; and they had charge of the key for opening it each morning.

[28]Some of them were in charge of the articles used in the temple service; they counted them when they were brought in and when they were taken out. [29]Others were assigned to take care of the furnishings and all the other articles of the sanctuary, as well as the flour and wine, and the oil, incense and spices. [30]But some of the priests took care of mixing the spices. [31]A Levite named Mattithiah, the firstborn son of Shallum the Korahite, was entrusted with the responsibility for baking the offering bread. [32]Some of their Kohathite brothers were in charge of preparing for every Sabbath the bread set out on the table.

[33]Those who were musicians, heads of Levite families, stayed in the rooms of the temple and were exempt from other duties because they were responsible for the work day and night.

[34]All these were heads of Levite families, chiefs as listed in their genealogy, and they lived in Jerusalem.

The Genealogy of Saul

[35]Jeiel the father[a] of Gibeon lived in Gibeon.

His wife's name was Maacah, [36]and his firstborn son was Abdon, followed by Zur, Kish, Baal, Ner, Nadab, [37]Gedor, Ahio, Zechariah and Mikloth. [38]Mikloth was the father of Shimeam. They too lived near their relatives in Jerusalem.

[39]Ner was the father of Kish, Kish the father of Saul, and Saul the father of Jonathan, Malki-Shua, Abinadab and Esh-Baal.[b]

[40]The son of Jonathan:

Merib-Baal,[c] who was the father of Micah.

[41]The sons of Micah:

Pithon, Melech, Tahrea and Ahaz.[d]

[42]Ahaz was the father of Jadah, Jadah[e] was the father of Alemeth, Azmaveth and Zimri, and Zimri was the father of Moza. [43]Moza was the father of Binea; Rephaiah was his son, Eleasah his son and Azel his son.

[44]Azel had six sons, and these were their names:

Azrikam, Bokeru, Ishmael, Sheariah, Obadiah and Hanan. These were the sons of Azel.

Saul Takes His Life

10 Now the Philistines fought against Israel; the Israelites fled before them, and many fell slain on Mount Gilboa. [2]The Philistines pressed hard after Saul and his sons, and they killed his sons Jonathan, Abinadab and Malki-Shua. [3]The fighting grew fierce around Saul, and when the archers overtook him, they wounded him.

[4]Saul said to his armor-bearer, "Draw your sword and run me through, or these uncircumcised fellows will come and abuse me."

But his armor-bearer was terrified and would not do it; so Saul took his own sword and fell on it. [5]When the armor-bearer saw that Saul was dead, he too fell on his sword and died. [6]So Saul and his three sons died, and all his house died together.

[7]When all the Israelites in the valley saw that the army had fled and that Saul and his sons had died, they abandoned their towns and fled. And the Philistines came and occupied them.

[8]The next day, when the Philistines came to strip the dead, they found Saul and his sons fallen on Mount Gilboa. [9]They stripped him and took his head and his armor, and sent messengers throughout the land of the Philistines to proclaim the news among their idols and their people. [10]They put his armor in the temple of their gods and hung up his head in the temple of Dagon.

[11]When all the inhabitants of Jabesh Gilead heard of everything the Philistines had done to Saul, [12]all their valiant men

---

[a]35 *Father* may mean *civic leader* or *military leader.*
[b]39 Also known as *Ish-Bosheth*   [c]40 Also known as *Mephibosheth*   [d]41 Vulgate and Syriac (see also Septuagint and 1 Chron. 8:35); Hebrew does not have *and Ahaz.*   [e]42 Some Hebrew manuscripts and Septuagint (see also 1 Chron. 8:36); most Hebrew manuscripts *Jarah, Jarah*

went and took the bodies of Saul and his sons and brought them to Jabesh. Then they buried their bones under the great tree in Jabesh, and they fasted seven days. ¹³Saul died because he was unfaithful to the LORD; he did not keep the word of the LORD and even consulted a medium for guidance, ¹⁴and did not inquire of the LORD. So the LORD put him to death and turned the kingdom over to David son of Jesse.

David Becomes King Over Israel

11 All Israel came together to David at Hebron and said, "We are your own flesh and blood. ²In the past, even while Saul was king, you were the one who led Israel on their military campaigns. And the LORD your God said to you, 'You will shepherd my people Israel, and you will become their ruler.'"

³When all the elders of Israel had come to King David at Hebron, he made a compact with them at Hebron before the LORD, and they anointed David king over Israel, as the LORD had promised through Samuel.

David Conquers Jerusalem

⁴David and all the Israelites marched to Jerusalem (that is, Jebus). The Jebusites who lived there ⁵said to David, "You will not get in here." Nevertheless, David cap-tured the fortress of Zion, the City of David.

⁶David had said, "Whoever leads the attack on the Jebusites will become commander-in-chief." Joab son of Zeruiah went up first, and so he received the command.

⁷David then took up residence in the fortress, and so it was called the City of David. ⁸He built up the city around it, from the supporting terraces*a* to the surrounding wall, while Joab restored the rest of the city. ⁹And David became more and more powerful, because the LORD Almighty was with him.

David's Mighty Men

¹⁰These were the chiefs of David's mighty men—they, together with all Israel, gave his kingship strong support to extend it over the whole land, as the LORD had promised— ¹¹this is the list of David's mighty men:

Jashobeam,*b* a Hacmonite, was chief of the officers*c*; he raised his spear against three hundred men, whom he killed in one encounter.

¹²Next to him was Eleazar son of Dodai the Ahohite, one of the three mighty men. ¹³He was with David at Pas Dammim when the Philistines gathered there for

---

*a*8 Or *the Millo*   *b*11 Possibly a variant of *Jashob-Baal*   *c*11 Or *Thirty*; some Septuagint manuscripts *Three* (see also 2 Samuel 23:8)

HEY DAD

Who were the bravest people in the Bible?

Text: 1 Chronicles 11:10–21

The Bible is filled with stories of brave people, but there's one trio of men that we don't hear about very often. These three mighty men served under King David. These warriors were so valiant that the author of the first book of Chronicles includes their adventures in his records.

The Bible only names one of these men—Eleazar, son of Dodai. Instead of hailing each of them individually, the Scripture simply refers to them as "the Three." These soldiers were three of David's thirty chiefs, and they became famous for their bravery and for leading the Israelites to many victories over the Philistines.

You can read about their most famous exploit, however, in verses 15 through 19. Although it might seem odd that David would pour out the water that these men had worked so hard to obtain, the king was, in fact, acknowledging their bravery before God.

If you're looking for adventurous tales of fierce battles, valiant warriors and noble kings, you don't have to turn on after-school television or read the tales of Camelot. These and other great stories are in your Bible. Read them for yourself—you won't be disappointed.

QUESTIONS KIDS ASK

For a complete listing of Questions Kids Ask, turn to page 1435.

battle. At a place where there was a field full of barley, the troops fled from the Philistines. ¹⁴But they took their stand in the middle of the field. They defended it and struck the Philistines down, and the LORD brought about a great victory.

¹⁵Three of the thirty chiefs came down to David to the rock at the cave of Adullam, while a band of Philistines was encamped in the Valley of Rephaim. ¹⁶At that time David was in the stronghold, and the Philistine garrison was at Bethlehem. ¹⁷David longed for water and said, "Oh, that someone would get me a drink of water from the well near the gate of Bethlehem!" ¹⁸So the Three broke through the Philistine lines, drew water from the well near the gate of Bethlehem and carried it back to David. But he refused to drink it; instead, he poured it out before the LORD. ¹⁹"God forbid that I should do this!" he said. "Should I drink the blood of these men who went at the risk of their lives?" Because they risked their lives to bring it back, David would not drink it.

Such were the exploits of the three mighty men.

²⁰Abishai the brother of Joab was chief of the Three. He raised his spear against three hundred men, whom he killed, and so he became as famous as the Three. ²¹He was doubly honored above the Three and became their commander, even though he was not included among them.

²²Benaiah son of Jehoiada was a valiant fighter from Kabzeel, who performed great exploits. He struck down two of Moab's best men. He also went down into a pit on a snowy day and killed a lion. ²³And he struck down an Egyptian who was seven and a half feet*a* tall. Although the Egyptian had a spear like a weaver's rod in his hand, Benaiah went against him with a club. He snatched the spear from the Egyptian's hand and killed him with his own spear. ²⁴Such were the exploits of Benaiah son of Jehoiada; he too was as famous as the three mighty men. ²⁵He was held in greater honor than any of the Thirty, but he was not included among the Three. And David put him in charge of his bodyguard.

²⁶The mighty men were:
Asahel the brother of Joab,
Elhanan son of Dodo from Bethlehem,
²⁷Shammoth the Harorite,
Helez the Pelonite,
²⁸Ira son of Ikkesh from Tekoa,
Abiezer from Anathoth,
²⁹Sibbecai the Hushathite,
Ilai the Ahohite,
³⁰Maharai the Netophathite,
Heled son of Baanah the Netophathite,
³¹Ithai son of Ribai from Gibeah in Benjamin,
Benaiah the Pirathonite,
³²Hurai from the ravines of Gaash,
Abiel the Arbathite,
³³Azmaveth the Baharumite,
Eliahba the Shaalbonite,
³⁴the sons of Hashem the Gizonite,
Jonathan son of Shagee the Hararite,
³⁵Ahiam son of Sacar the Hararite,
Eliphal son of Ur,
³⁶Hepher the Mekerathite,
Ahijah the Pelonite,
³⁷Hezro the Carmelite,
Naarai son of Ezbai,
³⁸Joel the brother of Nathan,
Mibhar son of Hagri,
³⁹Zelek the Ammonite,
Naharai the Berothite, the armor-bearer of Joab son of Zeruiah,
⁴⁰Ira the Ithrite,
Gareb the Ithrite,
⁴¹Uriah the Hittite,
Zabad son of Ahlai,
⁴²Adina son of Shiza the Reubenite, who was chief of the Reubenites, and the thirty with him,
⁴³Hanan son of Maacah,
Joshaphat the Mithnite,
⁴⁴Uzzia the Ashterathite,
Shama and Jeiel the sons of Hotham the Aroerite,
⁴⁵Jediael son of Shimri,
his brother Joha the Tizite,
⁴⁶Eliel the Mahavite,
Jeribai and Joshaviah the sons of Elnaam,
Ithmah the Moabite,
⁴⁷Eliel, Obed and Jaasiel the Mezobaite.

Warriors Join David

12 These were the men who came to David at Ziklag, while he was banished from the presence of Saul son of Kish (they were among the warriors who helped him in battle; ²they were armed with bows and were able to shoot arrows or to sling stones right-handed or left-

*a23 Hebrew *five cubits* (about 2.3 meters)

handed; they were kinsmen of Saul from the tribe of Benjamin):

³Ahiezer their chief and Joash the sons of Shemaah the Gibeathite; Jeziel and Pelet the sons of Azmaveth; Beracah, Jehu the Anathothite, ⁴and Ishmaiah the Gibeonite, a mighty man among the Thirty, who was a leader of the Thirty; Jeremiah, Jahaziel, Johanan, Jozabad the Gederathite, ⁵Eluzai, Jerimoth, Bealiah, Shemariah and Shephatiah the Haruphite; ⁶Elkanah, Isshiah, Azarel, Joezer and Jashobeam the Korahites; ⁷and Joelah and Zebadiah the sons of Jeroham from Gedor.

⁸Some Gadites defected to David at his stronghold in the desert. They were brave warriors, ready for battle and able to handle the shield and spear. Their faces were the faces of lions, and they were as swift as gazelles in the mountains.

⁹Ezer was the chief,
  Obadiah the second in command,
    Eliab the third,
¹⁰Mishmannah the fourth, Jeremiah the fifth,
¹¹Attai the sixth, Eliel the seventh,
¹²Johanan the eighth, Elzabad the ninth,
¹³Jeremiah the tenth and Macbannai the eleventh.

¹⁴These Gadites were army commanders; the least was a match for a hundred, and the greatest for a thousand. ¹⁵It was they who crossed the Jordan in the first month when it was overflowing all its banks, and they put to flight everyone living in the valleys, to the east and to the west.

¹⁶Other Benjamites and some men from Judah also came to David in his stronghold. ¹⁷David went out to meet them and said to them, "If you have come to me in peace, to help me, I am ready to have you unite with me. But if you have come to betray me to my enemies when my hands are free from violence, may the God of our fathers see it and judge you."

¹⁸Then the Spirit came upon Amasai, chief of the Thirty, and he said:

"We are yours, O David!
  We are with you, O son of Jesse!
Success, success to you,
  and success to those who help you,
    for your God will help you."

So David received them and made them leaders of his raiding bands.

¹⁹Some of the men of Manasseh defected to David when he went with the Philistines to fight against Saul. (He and his men did not help the Philistines because, after consultation, their rulers sent him away. They said, "It will cost us our heads if he deserts to his master Saul.") ²⁰When David went to Ziklag, these were the men of Manasseh who defected to him: Adnah, Jozabad, Jediael, Michael, Jozabad, Elihu and Zillethai, leaders of units of a thousand in Manasseh. ²¹They helped David against raiding bands, for all of them were brave warriors, and they were commanders in his army. ²²Day after day men came to help David, until he had a great army, like the army of God.ᵃ

Others Join David at Hebron

²³These are the numbers of the men armed for battle who came to David at Hebron to turn Saul's kingdom over to him, as the LORD had said:
²⁴men of Judah, carrying shield and spear—6,800 armed for battle;
²⁵men of Simeon, warriors ready for battle—7,100;
²⁶men of Levi—4,600, ²⁷including Jehoiada, leader of the family of Aaron, with 3,700 men, ²⁸and Zadok, a brave young warrior, with 22 officers from his family;
²⁹men of Benjamin, Saul's kinsmen—3,000, most of whom had remained loyal to Saul's house until then;
³⁰men of Ephraim, brave warriors, famous in their own clans—20,800;
³¹men of half the tribe of Manasseh, designated by name to come and make David king—18,000;
³²men of Issachar, who understood the times and knew what Israel should do—200 chiefs, with all their relatives under their command;
³³men of Zebulun, experienced soldiers prepared for battle with every type of weapon, to help David with undivided loyalty—50,000;
³⁴men of Naphtali—1,000 officers, together with 37,000 men carrying shields and spears;
³⁵men of Dan, ready for battle—28,600;
³⁶men of Asher, experienced soldiers prepared for battle—40,000;
³⁷and from east of the Jordan, men of Reuben, Gad and the half-tribe of

ᵃ22 Or *a great and mighty army*

Manasseh, armed with every type of weapon—120,000.

[38]All these were fighting men who volunteered to serve in the ranks. They came to Hebron fully determined to make David king over all Israel. All the rest of the Israelites were also of one mind to make David king. [39]The men spent three days there with David, eating and drinking, for their families had supplied provisions for them. [40]Also, their neighbors from as far away as Issachar, Zebulun and Naphtali came bringing food on donkeys, camels, mules and oxen. There were plentiful supplies of flour, fig cakes, raisin cakes, wine, oil, cattle and sheep, for there was joy in Israel.

Bringing Back the Ark

13 David conferred with each of his officers, the commanders of thousands and commanders of hundreds. [2]He then said to the whole assembly of Israel, "If it seems good to you and if it is the will of the LORD our God, let us send word far and wide to the rest of our brothers throughout the territories of Israel, and also to the priests and Levites who are with them in their towns and pasturelands, to come and join us. [3]Let us bring the ark of our God back to us, for we did not inquire of[a] it[b] during the reign of Saul." [4]The whole assembly agreed to do this, because it seemed right to all the people.

[5]So David assembled all the Israelites, from the Shihor River in Egypt to Lebo[c] Hamath, to bring the ark of God from Kiriath Jearim. [6]David and all the Israelites with him went to Baalah of Judah (Kiriath Jearim) to bring up from there the ark of God the LORD, who is enthroned between the cherubim—the ark that is called by the Name.

[7]They moved the ark of God from Abinadab's house on a new cart, with Uzzah and Ahio guiding it. [8]David and all the Israelites were celebrating with all their might before God, with songs and with harps, lyres, tambourines, cymbals and trumpets.

[9]When they came to the threshing floor of Kidon, Uzzah reached out his hand to steady the ark, because the oxen stumbled. [10]The LORD's anger burned against Uzzah, and he struck him down because he had put his hand on the ark. So he died there before God.

[11]Then David was angry because the LORD's wrath had broken out against Uzzah, and to this day that place is called Perez Uzzah.[d]

[12]David was afraid of God that day and asked, "How can I ever bring the ark of God to me?" [13]He did not take the ark to be with him in the City of David. Instead, he took it aside to the house of Obed-Edom the Gittite. [14]The ark of God remained with the family of Obed-Edom in his house for three months, and the LORD blessed his household and everything he had.

David's House and Family

14 Now Hiram king of Tyre sent messengers to David, along with cedar logs, stonemasons and carpenters to build a palace for him. [2]And David knew that the LORD had established him as king over Israel and that his kingdom had been highly exalted for the sake of his people Israel.

[3]In Jerusalem David took more wives and became the father of more sons and daughters. [4]These are the names of the children born to him there: Shammua, Shobab, Nathan, Solomon, [5]Ibhar, Elishua, Elpelet, [6]Nogah, Nepheg, Japhia, [7]Elishama, Beeliada[e] and Eliphelet.

David Defeats the Philistines

[8]When the Philistines heard that David had been anointed king over all Israel, they went up in full force to search for him, but David heard about it and went out to meet them. [9]Now the Philistines had come and raided the Valley of Rephaim; [10]so David inquired of God: "Shall I go and attack the Philistines? Will you hand them over to me?"

The LORD answered him, "Go, I will hand them over to you."

[11]So David and his men went up to Baal Perazim, and there he defeated them. He said, "As waters break out, God has broken out against my enemies by my hand." So that place was called Baal Perazim.[f] [12]The Philistines had abandoned their gods there, and David gave orders to burn them in the fire.

[13]Once more the Philistines raided the valley; [14]so David inquired of God again, and God answered him, "Do not go straight up, but circle around them and

---

a3 Or we neglected   b3 Or him   c5 Or to the entrance to   d11 Perez Uzzah means outbreak against Uzzah.   e7 A variant of Eliada   f11 Baal Perazim means the lord who breaks out.

attack them in front of the balsam trees. [15]As soon as you hear the sound of marching in the tops of the balsam trees, move out to battle, because that will mean God has gone out in front of you to strike the Philistine army." [16]So David did as God commanded him, and they struck down the Philistine army, all the way from Gibeon to Gezer.

[17]So David's fame spread throughout every land, and the LORD made all the nations fear him.

The Ark Brought to Jerusalem

15 After David had constructed buildings for himself in the City of David, he prepared a place for the ark of God and pitched a tent for it. [2]Then David said, "No one but the Levites may carry the ark of God, because the LORD chose them to carry the ark of the LORD and to minister before him forever."

[3]David assembled all Israel in Jerusalem to bring up the ark of the LORD to the place he had prepared for it. [4]He called together the descendants of Aaron and the Levites:

[5]From the descendants of Kohath,
  Uriel the leader and 120 relatives;
[6]from the descendants of Merari,
  Asaiah the leader and 220 relatives;
[7]from the descendants of Gershon,[a]
  Joel the leader and 130 relatives;
[8]from the descendants of Elizaphan,
  Shemaiah the leader and 200 relatives;
[9]from the descendants of Hebron,
  Eliel the leader and 80 relatives;
[10]from the descendants of Uzziel,
  Amminadab the leader and 112 relatives.

[11]Then David summoned Zadok and Abiathar the priests, and Uriel, Asaiah, Joel, Shemaiah, Eliel and Amminadab the Levites. [12]He said to them, "You are the heads of the Levitical families; you and your fellow Levites are to consecrate yourselves and bring up the ark of the LORD, the God of Israel, to the place I have prepared for it. [13]It was because you, the Levites, did not bring it up the first time that the LORD our God broke out in anger against us. We did not inquire of him about how to do it in the prescribed way." [14]So the priests and Levites consecrated themselves in order to bring up the ark of the LORD, the God of Israel. [15]And the Levites carried the ark of God with the poles on their shoulders, as Moses had commanded in accordance with the word of the LORD.

[16]David told the leaders of the Levites to appoint their brothers as singers to sing joyful songs, accompanied by musical instruments: lyres, harps and cymbals.

[17]So the Levites appointed Heman son of Joel; from his brothers, Asaph son of Berekiah; and from their brothers the Merarites, Ethan son of Kushaiah; [18]and with them their brothers next in rank: Zechariah,[b] Jaaziel, Shemiramoth, Jehiel, Unni, Eliab, Benaiah, Maaseiah, Mattithiah, Eliphelehu, Mikneiah, Obed-Edom and Jeiel,[c] the gatekeepers.

[19]The musicians Heman, Asaph and Ethan were to sound the bronze cymbals; [20]Zechariah, Aziel, Shemiramoth, Jehiel, Unni, Eliab, Maaseiah and Benaiah were to play the lyres according to *alamoth*,[d] [21]and Mattithiah, Eliphelehu, Mikneiah, Obed-Edom, Jeiel and Azaziah were to play the harps, directing according to *sheminith*.[d] [22]Kenaniah the head Levite was in charge of the singing; that was his responsibility because he was skillful at it.

[23]Berekiah and Elkanah were to be doorkeepers for the ark. [24]Shebaniah, Joshaphat, Nethanel, Amasai, Zechariah, Benaiah and Eliezer the priests were to blow trumpets before the ark of God. Obed-Edom and Jehiah were also to be doorkeepers for the ark.

[25]So David and the elders of Israel and the commanders of units of a thousand went to bring up the ark of the covenant of the LORD from the house of Obed-Edom, with rejoicing. [26]Because God had helped the Levites who were carrying the ark of the covenant of the LORD, seven bulls and seven rams were sacrificed. [27]Now David was clothed in a robe of fine linen, as were all the Levites who were carrying the ark, and as were the singers, and Kenaniah, who was in charge of the singing of the choirs. David also wore a linen ephod. [28]So all Israel brought up the ark of the covenant of the LORD with shouts, with the sounding of rams' horns and trumpets, and of cymbals, and the playing of lyres and harps.

---

[a]7 Hebrew *Gershom,* a variant of *Gershon*
[b]18 Three Hebrew manuscripts and most Septuagint manuscripts (see also verse 20 and 1 Chron. 16:5); most Hebrew manuscripts *Zechariah son and* or *Zechariah, Ben and*
[c]18 Hebrew; Septuagint (see also verse 21) *Jeiel and Azaziah*   [d]20,21 Probably a musical term

²⁹As the ark of the covenant of the LORD was entering the City of David, Michal daughter of Saul watched from a window. And when she saw King David dancing and celebrating, she despised him in her heart.

16 They brought the ark of God and set it inside the tent that David had pitched for it, and they presented burnt offerings and fellowship offerings[a] before God. ²After David had finished sacrificing the burnt offerings and fellowship offerings, he blessed the people in the name of the LORD. ³Then he gave a loaf of bread, a cake of dates and a cake of raisins to each Israelite man and woman.

⁴He appointed some of the Levites to minister before the ark of the LORD, to make petition, to give thanks, and to praise the LORD, the God of Israel: ⁵Asaph was the chief, Zechariah second, then Jeiel, Shemiramoth, Jehiel, Mattithiah, Eliab, Benaiah, Obed-Edom and Jeiel. They were to play the lyres and harps, Asaph was to sound the cymbals, ⁶and Benaiah and Jahaziel the priests were to blow the trumpets regularly before the ark of the covenant of God.

David's Psalm of Thanks

⁷That day David first committed to Asaph and his associates this psalm of thanks to the LORD:

⁸Give thanks to the LORD, call on his name;
    make known among the nations
      what he has done.
⁹Sing to him, sing praise to him;
    tell of all his wonderful acts.
¹⁰Glory in his holy name;
    let the hearts of those who seek the
      LORD rejoice.
¹¹Look to the LORD and his strength;
    seek his face always.
¹²Remember the wonders he has done,
    his miracles, and the judgments he
      pronounced,
¹³O descendants of Israel his servant,
    O sons of Jacob, his chosen ones.
¹⁴He is the LORD our God;
    his judgments are in all the earth.
¹⁵He remembers[b] his covenant forever,
    the word he commanded, for a
      thousand generations,
¹⁶the covenant he made with Abraham,
    the oath he swore to Isaac.
¹⁷He confirmed it to Jacob as a decree,
    to Israel as an everlasting covenant:

¹⁸"To you I will give the land of Canaan
    as the portion you will inherit."
¹⁹When they were but few in number,
    few indeed, and strangers in it,
²⁰they[c] wandered from nation to nation,
    from one kingdom to another.
²¹He allowed no man to oppress them;
    for their sake he rebuked kings:
²²"Do not touch my anointed ones;
    do my prophets no harm."

²³Sing to the LORD, all the earth;
    proclaim his salvation day after day.
²⁴Declare his glory among the nations,
    his marvelous deeds among all
      peoples.
²⁵For great is the LORD and most worthy
      of praise;
    he is to be feared above all gods.
²⁶For all the gods of the nations are idols,
    but the LORD made the heavens.
²⁷Splendor and majesty are before him;
    strength and joy in his dwelling
      place.
²⁸Ascribe to the LORD, O families of
      nations,
    ascribe to the LORD glory and
      strength,
²⁹   ascribe to the LORD the glory due his
      name.
Bring an offering and come before him;
    worship the LORD in the splendor of
      his[d] holiness.
³⁰Tremble before him, all the earth!
    The world is firmly established; it
      cannot be moved.
³¹Let the heavens rejoice, let the earth be
      glad;
    let them say among the nations,
      "The LORD reigns!"
³²Let the sea resound, and all that is in it;
    let the fields be jubilant, and
      everything in them!
³³Then the trees of the forest will sing,
    they will sing for joy before the LORD,
    for he comes to judge the earth.

³⁴Give thanks to the LORD, for he is good;
    his love endures forever.
³⁵Cry out, "Save us, O God our Savior;
    gather us and deliver us from the
      nations,

---

a1 Traditionally *peace offerings*; also in verse 2
b15 Some Septuagint manuscripts (see also Psalm 105:8); Hebrew *Remember*   c18-20 One Hebrew manuscript, Septuagint and Vulgate (see also Psalm 105:12); most Hebrew manuscripts *inherit, /* ¹⁹*though you are but few in number, / few indeed, and strangers in it.* / ²⁰*They*   d29 Or *LORD with the splendor of*

that we may give thanks to your holy
name,
    that we may glory in your praise."
36 Praise be to the LORD, the God of Israel,
    from everlasting to everlasting.

Then all the people said "Amen" and
"Praise the LORD."

37 David left Asaph and his associates
before the ark of the covenant of the LORD
to minister there regularly, according to
each day's requirements. **38** He also left
Obed-Edom and his sixty-eight associates
to minister with them. Obed-Edom son of
Jeduthun, and also Hosah, were gatekeepers.

39 David left Zadok the priest and his fellow priests before the tabernacle of the
LORD at the high place in Gibeon **40** to
present burnt offerings to the LORD on the
altar of burnt offering regularly, morning
and evening, in accordance with everything written in the Law of the LORD,
which he had given Israel. **41** With them
were Heman and Jeduthun and the rest of
those chosen and designated by name to
give thanks to the LORD, "for his love endures forever." **42** Heman and Jeduthun
were responsible for the sounding of the
trumpets and cymbals and for the playing
of the other instruments for sacred song.
The sons of Jeduthun were stationed at
the gate.

43 Then all the people left, each for his
own home, and David returned home to
bless his family.

God's Promise to David

17 After David was settled in his palace,
he said to Nathan the prophet, "Here I
am, living in a palace of cedar, while the
ark of the covenant of the LORD is under a
tent."

2 Nathan replied to David, "Whatever
you have in mind, do it, for God is with
you."

3 That night the word of God came to
Nathan, saying:

4 "Go and tell my servant David,
'This is what the LORD says: You are
not the one to build me a house to
dwell in. **5** I have not dwelt in a house
from the day I brought Israel up out
of Egypt to this day. I have moved
from one tent site to another, from
one dwelling place to another.
6 Wherever I have moved with all the
Israelites, did I ever say to any of their
leaders*a* whom I commanded to
shepherd my people, "Why have you
not built me a house of cedar?" '
7 "Now then, tell my servant David,
'This is what the LORD Almighty says:

a6 Traditionally *judges*; also in verse 10

HEY DAD

Why was there so much fighting in the Old Testament?

Text: 1 Chronicles 16:18

The battles that the Old Testament records were caused by many of the same
reasons there's fighting in the Middle East today. The countries of Syria, Lebanon,
Jordan, Iraq, Kuwait, Saudi Arabia and Israel are located in the same area where
the Israelites and their enemies lived during Old Testament times. Just turn on the
nightly news and you'll find out about the endless conflict there.

    While this conflict exists for many reasons, at least one reason has remained
constant through the years. The people are fighting over the land. God picked the
very best part of the land and gave it to his chosen people. But the neighboring countries
wanted this land, too, because whoever controlled this strip of land would also control a
vital connection between Asia and Africa.

    God gave his children the best, and he protected them from upheaval and turmoil. All
other nations saw God's power in the way he protected and strengthened the Israelites. But
when the Israelites rebelled against him, God allowed the neighboring countries to capture
the land and, sometimes, the Israelites themselves.

    Let's take a lesson from the history of the Israelites. In all things—personal matters as
well as matters of state—it's best to be on the *Lord's* side.

For a complete listing of Questions Kids Ask, turn to page 1435.

QUESTIONS KIDS ASK

I took you from the pasture and from following the flock, to be ruler over my people Israel. [8]I have been with you wherever you have gone, and I have cut off all your enemies from before you. Now I will make your name like the names of the greatest men of the earth. [9]And I will provide a place for my people Israel and will plant them so that they can have a home of their own and no longer be disturbed. Wicked people will not oppress them anymore, as they did at the beginning [10]and have done ever since the time I appointed leaders over my people Israel. I will also subdue all your enemies.

" 'I declare to you that the LORD will build a house for you: [11]When your days are over and you go to be with your fathers, I will raise up your offspring to succeed you, one of your own sons, and I will establish his kingdom. [12]He is the one who will build a house for me, and I will establish his throne forever. [13]I will be his father, and he will be my son. I will never take my love away from him, as I took it away from your predecessor. [14]I will set him over my house and my kingdom forever; his throne will be established forever.' "

[15]Nathan reported to David all the words of this entire revelation.

David's Prayer

[16]Then King David went in and sat before the LORD, and he said:

"Who am I, O LORD God, and what is my family, that you have brought me this far? [17]And as if this were not enough in your sight, O God, you have spoken about the future of the house of your servant. You have looked on me as though I were the most exalted of men, O LORD God.

[18]"What more can David say to you for honoring your servant? For you know your servant, [19]O LORD. For the sake of your servant and according to your will, you have done this great thing and made known all these great promises.

[20]"There is no one like you, O LORD, and there is no God but you, as we have heard with our own ears. [21]And who is like your people Israel—

the one nation on earth whose God went out to redeem a people for himself, and to make a name for yourself, and to perform great and awesome wonders by driving out nations from before your people, whom you redeemed from Egypt? [22]You made your people Israel your very own forever, and you, O LORD, have become their God.

[23]"And now, LORD, let the promise you have made concerning your servant and his house be established forever. Do as you promised, [24]so that it will be established and that your name will be great forever. Then men will say, 'The LORD Almighty, the God over Israel, is Israel's God!' And the house of your servant David will be established before you.

[25]"You, my God, have revealed to your servant that you will build a house for him. So your servant has found courage to pray to you. [26]O LORD, you are God! You have promised these good things to your servant. [27]Now you have been pleased to bless the house of your servant, that it may continue forever in your sight; for you, O LORD, have blessed it, and it will be blessed forever."

David's Victories

18 In the course of time, David defeated the Philistines and subdued them, and he took Gath and its surrounding villages from the control of the Philistines.

[2]David also defeated the Moabites, and they became subject to him and brought tribute.

[3]Moreover, David fought Hadadezer king of Zobah, as far as Hamath, when he went to establish his control along the Euphrates River. [4]David captured a thousand of his chariots, seven thousand charioteers and twenty thousand foot soldiers. He hamstrung all but a hundred of the chariot horses.

[5]When the Arameans of Damascus came to help Hadadezer king of Zobah, David struck down twenty-two thousand of them. [6]He put garrisons in the Aramean kingdom of Damascus, and the Arameans became subject to him and brought tribute. The LORD gave David victory everywhere he went.

[7]David took the gold shields carried by the officers of Hadadezer and brought

them to Jerusalem. [8]From Tebah[a] and Cun, towns that belonged to Hadadezer, David took a great quantity of bronze, which Solomon used to make the bronze Sea, the pillars and various bronze articles.

[9]When Tou king of Hamath heard that David had defeated the entire army of Hadadezer king of Zobah, [10]he sent his son Hadoram to King David to greet him and congratulate him on his victory in battle over Hadadezer, who had been at war with Tou. Hadoram brought all kinds of articles of gold and silver and bronze.

[11]King David dedicated these articles to the LORD, as he had done with the silver and gold he had taken from all these nations: Edom and Moab, the Ammonites and the Philistines, and Amalek.

[12]Abishai son of Zeruiah struck down eighteen thousand Edomites in the Valley of Salt. [13]He put garrisons in Edom, and all the Edomites became subject to David. The LORD gave David victory everywhere he went.

David's Officials

[14]David reigned over all Israel, doing what was just and right for all his people. [15]Joab son of Zeruiah was over the army; Jehoshaphat son of Ahilud was recorder; [16]Zadok son of Ahitub and Ahimelech[b] son of Abiathar were priests; Shavsha was secretary; [17]Benaiah son of Jehoiada was over the Kerethites and Pelethites; and David's sons were chief officials at the king's side.

The Battle Against the Ammonites

19 In the course of time, Nahash king of the Ammonites died, and his son succeeded him as king. [2]David thought, "I will show kindness to Hanun son of Nahash, because his father showed kindness to me." So David sent a delegation to express his sympathy to Hanun concerning his father.

When David's men came to Hanun in the land of the Ammonites to express sympathy to him, [3]the Ammonite nobles said to Hanun, "Do you think David is honoring your father by sending men to you to express sympathy? Haven't his men come to you to explore and spy out the country and overthrow it?" [4]So Hanun seized David's men, shaved them, cut off their garments in the middle at the buttocks, and sent them away.

[5]When someone came and told David about the men, he sent messengers to meet them, for they were greatly humiliated. The king said, "Stay at Jericho till your beards have grown, and then come back."

[6]When the Ammonites realized that they had become a stench in David's nostrils, Hanun and the Ammonites sent a thousand talents[c] of silver to hire chariots and charioteers from Aram Naharaim,[d] Aram Maacah and Zobah. [7]They hired thirty-two thousand chariots and charioteers, as well as the king of Maacah with his troops, who came and camped near Medeba, while the Ammonites were mustered from their towns and moved out for battle.

[8]On hearing this, David sent Joab out with the entire army of fighting men. [9]The Ammonites came out and drew up in battle formation at the entrance to their city, while the kings who had come were by themselves in the open country.

[10]Joab saw that there were battle lines in front of him and behind him; so he selected some of the best troops in Israel and deployed them against the Arameans. [11]He put the rest of the men under the command of Abishai his brother, and they were deployed against the Ammonites. [12]Joab said, "If the Arameans are too strong for me, then you are to rescue me; but if the Ammonites are too strong for you, then I will rescue you. [13]Be strong and let us fight bravely for our people and the cities of our God. The LORD will do what is good in his sight."

[14]Then Joab and the troops with him advanced to fight the Arameans, and they fled before him. [15]When the Ammonites saw that the Arameans were fleeing, they too fled before his brother Abishai and went inside the city. So Joab went back to Jerusalem.

[16]After the Arameans saw that they had been routed by Israel, they sent messengers and had Arameans brought from beyond the River,[e] with Shophach the commander of Hadadezer's army leading them.

[17]When David was told of this, he gathered all Israel and crossed the Jordan; he advanced against them and formed his battle lines opposite them. David formed

[a]8 Hebrew *Tibhath*, a variant of *Tebah* [b]16 Some Hebrew manuscripts, Vulgate and Syriac (see also 2 Samuel 8:17); most Hebrew manuscripts *Abimelech* [c]6 That is, about 37 tons (about 34 metric tons) [d]6 That is, Northwest Mesopotamia [e]16 That is, the Euphrates

his lines to meet the Arameans in battle, and they fought against him. [18]But they fled before Israel, and David killed seven thousand of their charioteers and forty thousand of their foot soldiers. He also killed Shophach the commander of their army.

[19]When the vassals of Hadadezer saw that they had been defeated by Israel, they made peace with David and became subject to him.

So the Arameans were not willing to help the Ammonites anymore.

The Capture of Rabbah

20 In the spring, at the time when kings go off to war, Joab led out the armed forces. He laid waste the land of the Ammonites and went to Rabbah and besieged it, but David remained in Jerusalem. Joab attacked Rabbah and left it in ruins. [2]David took the crown from the head of their king[a]—its weight was found to be a talent[b] of gold, and it was set with precious stones—and it was placed on David's head. He took a great quantity of plunder from the city [3]and brought out the people who were there, consigning them to labor with saws and with iron picks and axes. David did this to all the Ammonite towns. Then David and his entire army returned to Jerusalem.

War With the Philistines

[4]In the course of time, war broke out with the Philistines, at Gezer. At that time Sibbecai the Hushathite killed Sippai, one of the descendants of the Rephaites, and the Philistines were subjugated.

[5]In another battle with the Philistines, Elhanan son of Jair killed Lahmi the brother of Goliath the Gittite, who had a spear with a shaft like a weaver's rod.

[6]In still another battle, which took place at Gath, there was a huge man with six fingers on each hand and six toes on each foot—twenty-four in all. He also was descended from Rapha. [7]When he taunted Israel, Jonathan son of Shimea, David's brother, killed him.

[8]These were descendants of Rapha in Gath, and they fell at the hands of David and his men.

David Numbers the Fighting Men

21 Satan rose up against Israel and incited David to take a census of Israel. [2]So David said to Joab and the command-

ers of the troops, "Go and count the Israelites from Beersheba to Dan. Then report back to me so that I may know how many there are."

[3]But Joab replied, "May the LORD multiply his troops a hundred times over. My lord the king, are they not all my lord's subjects? Why does my lord want to do this? Why should he bring guilt on Israel?"

[4]The king's word, however, overruled Joab; so Joab left and went throughout Israel and then came back to Jerusalem. [5]Joab reported the number of the fighting men to David: In all Israel there were one million one hundred thousand men who could handle a sword, including four hundred and seventy thousand in Judah.

[6]But Joab did not include Levi and Benjamin in the numbering, because the king's command was repulsive to him. [7]This command was also evil in the sight of God; so he punished Israel.

[8]Then David said to God, "I have sinned greatly by doing this. Now, I beg you, take away the guilt of your servant. I have done a very foolish thing."

[9]The LORD said to Gad, David's seer, [10]"Go and tell David, 'This is what the LORD says: I am giving you three options. Choose one of them for me to carry out against you.' "

[11]So Gad went to David and said to him, "This is what the LORD says: 'Take your choice: [12]three years of famine, three months of being swept away[c] before your enemies, with their swords overtaking you, or three days of the sword of the LORD—days of plague in the land, with the angel of the LORD ravaging every part of Israel.' Now then, decide how I should answer the one who sent me."

[13]David said to Gad, "I am in deep distress. Let me fall into the hands of the LORD, for his mercy is very great; but do not let me fall into the hands of men."

[14]So the LORD sent a plague on Israel, and seventy thousand men of Israel fell dead. [15]And God sent an angel to destroy Jerusalem. But as the angel was doing so, the LORD saw it and was grieved because of the calamity and said to the angel who was destroying the people, "Enough! Withdraw your hand." The angel of the LORD was then standing at the threshing floor of Araunah[d] the Jebusite.

a2 Or of Milcom, that is, Molech   b2 That is, about 75 pounds (about 34 kilograms)   c12 Hebrew; Septuagint and Vulgate (see also 2 Samuel 24:13) of fleeing   d15 Hebrew Ornan, a variant of Araunah; also in verses 18-28

¹⁶David looked up and saw the angel of the LORD standing between heaven and earth, with a drawn sword in his hand extended over Jerusalem. Then David and the elders, clothed in sackcloth, fell facedown.

¹⁷David said to God, "Was it not I who ordered the fighting men to be counted? I am the one who has sinned and done wrong. These are but sheep. What have they done? O LORD my God, let your hand fall upon me and my family,

but do not let this plague remain on your people."

¹⁸Then the angel of the LORD ordered Gad to tell David to go up and build an altar to the LORD on the threshing floor of Araunah the Jebusite. ¹⁹So David went up in obedience to the word that Gad had spoken in the name of the LORD.

²⁰While Araunah was threshing wheat, he turned and saw the angel; his four sons who were with him hid themselves. ²¹Then David approached, and when

Choosing Your Poison

DAILY INSIGHT

THURSDAY

Passage:
1 Chronicles 21:8–17

Verse:
1 Chronicles 21:16

"Wait until your father gets home," my mother would finally say after I would take her to the breaking point, "He'll deal with you."

Sam Wolgemuth wasn't a big man. I was only sixteen years old when I scooted past him in size. And even though he played baseball at the college level, my dad wasn't a particularly quick man. But my dad was strong. A spanking from my father was serious and memorable punishment. How well my brothers and I can remember how Dad, while gliding down the highway at seventy miles an hour, could find us in the back seat with his powerful hand. Unsuccessfully trying to escape by squeezing into the ash trays on the door handles, he would locate the soft flesh just under our thighs with a pinch that would throb for six to eight weeks.

Mother was always the disciplinarian of choice. We believed that we could finesse our way through her emotions, capturing a little mercy for our childhood transgressions. Now, I don't actually remember how old I was when it dawned on me that I was making a terrible choice. The physical pain of my dad's punishment was a walk in the park when compared to the emotional pain of knowing that I had disappointed my mother. Her downcast spirit and penetrating silence in response to my youthful deficiencies were torturous. Knowing I had hurt her made me long for the pain from my father's hand.

In today's passage, David was in line for

punishment, and he knew it. So God gave him a choice: three years of famine, three months of bludgeoning by his enemies, or three days of God's discipline. Believing that God would be merciful, David chose door number three.

Bad choice, David.

Even though God made David and his people pay a dear price, nothing was as awful as the moment when David saw God's fury in the form of a sword-carrying angel (21:16). When he realized that the gracious God of the universe was punishing his people, David fell on his face. In fact, David pled with the Lord to take him instead.

Our lives are filled with choices. From our choice of socks in the morning to decisions in lonely hotel rooms on the road, we're faced with options. Have you ever decided to do the wrong thing, determining that God's mercy would cover you? I have. This is a bad choice.

Does God forgive? Yes. Does his mercy endure forever? Of course it does. But is it ever worth it to choose to disappoint him? Never. The anguish of looking up and seeing his displeasure with my willful disobedience ought to have a profound and life-changing effect on what I do.

The message is pretty simple: It's far less painful for us to discipline ourselves than to count on God to do it for us. I'm quite sure that David would agree on this one.

For your next devotional reading, go to page 461.

Araunah looked and saw him, he left the threshing floor and bowed down before David with his face to the ground.

²²David said to him, "Let me have the site of your threshing floor so I can build an altar to the LORD, that the plague on the people may be stopped. Sell it to me at the full price."

²³Araunah said to David, "Take it! Let my lord the king do whatever pleases him. Look, I will give the oxen for the burnt offerings, the threshing sledges for the wood, and the wheat for the grain offering. I will give all this."

²⁴But King David replied to Araunah, "No, I insist on paying the full price. I will not take for the LORD what is yours, or sacrifice a burnt offering that costs me nothing."

²⁵So David paid Araunah six hundred shekels[a] of gold for the site. ²⁶David built an altar to the LORD there and sacrificed burnt offerings and fellowship offerings.[b] He called on the LORD, and the LORD answered him with fire from heaven on the altar of burnt offering.

²⁷Then the LORD spoke to the angel, and he put his sword back into its sheath. ²⁸At that time, when David saw that the LORD had answered him on the threshing floor of Araunah the Jebusite, he offered sacrifices there. ²⁹The tabernacle of the LORD, which Moses had made in the desert, and the altar of burnt offering were at that time on the high place at Gibeon. ³⁰But David could not go before it to inquire of God, because he was afraid of the sword of the angel of the LORD.

22 Then David said, "The house of the LORD God is to be here, and also the altar of burnt offering for Israel."

Preparations for the Temple

²So David gave orders to assemble the aliens living in Israel, and from among them he appointed stonecutters to prepare dressed stone for building the house of God. ³He provided a large amount of iron to make nails for the doors of the gateways and for the fittings, and more bronze than could be weighed. ⁴He also provided more cedar logs than could be counted, for the Sidonians and Tyrians had brought large numbers of them to David.

⁵David said, "My son Solomon is young and inexperienced, and the house to be built for the LORD should be of great magnificence and fame and splendor in the

sight of all the nations. Therefore I will make preparations for it." So David made extensive preparations before his death.

⁶Then he called for his son Solomon and charged him to build a house for the LORD, the God of Israel. ⁷David said to Solomon: "My son, I had it in my heart to build a house for the Name of the LORD my God. ⁸But this word of the LORD came to me: 'You have shed much blood and have fought many wars. You are not to build a house for my Name, because you have shed much blood on the earth in my sight. ⁹But you will have a son who will be a man of peace and rest, and I will give him rest from all his enemies on every side. His name will be Solomon,[c] and I will grant Israel peace and quiet during his reign. ¹⁰He is the one who will build a house for my Name. He will be my son, and I will be his father. And I will establish the throne of his kingdom over Israel forever.'

¹¹"Now, my son, the LORD be with you, and may you have success and build the house of the LORD your God, as he said you would. ¹²May the LORD give you discretion and understanding when he puts you in command over Israel, so that you may keep the law of the LORD your God. ¹³Then you will have success if you are careful to observe the decrees and laws that the LORD gave Moses for Israel. Be strong and courageous. Do not be afraid or discouraged.

¹⁴"I have taken great pains to provide for the temple of the LORD a hundred thousand talents[d] of gold, a million talents[e] of silver, quantities of bronze and iron too great to be weighed, and wood and stone. And you may add to them. ¹⁵You have many workmen: stonecutters, masons and carpenters, as well as men skilled in every kind of work ¹⁶in gold and silver, bronze and iron—craftsmen beyond number. Now begin the work, and the LORD be with you."

¹⁷Then David ordered all the leaders of Israel to help his son Solomon. ¹⁸He said to them, "Is not the LORD your God with you? And has he not granted you rest on every side? For he has handed the inhabitants of the land over to me, and the land is subject to the LORD and to his people.

---

[a]25 That is, about 15 pounds (about 7 kilograms)   [b]26 Traditionally *peace offerings*   [c]9 *Solomon* sounds like and may be derived from the Hebrew for *peace*.   [d]14 That is, about 3,750 tons (about 3,450 metric tons)   [e]14 That is, about 37,500 tons (about 34,500 metric tons)

[19]Now devote your heart and soul to seeking the LORD your God. Begin to build the sanctuary of the LORD God, so that you may bring the ark of the covenant of the LORD and the sacred articles belonging to God into the temple that will be built for the Name of the LORD."

The Levites

23 When David was old and full of years, he made his son Solomon king over Israel.

[2]He also gathered together all the leaders of Israel, as well as the priests and Levites. [3]The Levites thirty years old or more were counted, and the total number of men was thirty-eight thousand. [4]David said, "Of these, twenty-four thousand are to supervise the work of the temple of the LORD and six thousand are to be officials and judges. [5]Four thousand are to be gatekeepers and four thousand are to praise the LORD with the musical instruments I have provided for that purpose."

[6]David divided the Levites into groups corresponding to the sons of Levi: Gershon, Kohath and Merari.

Gershonites

[7]Belonging to the Gershonites:
Ladan and Shimei.
[8]The sons of Ladan:
Jehiel the first, Zetham and Joel—three in all.
[9]The sons of Shimei:
Shelomoth, Haziel and Haran—three in all.
These were the heads of the families of Ladan.
[10]And the sons of Shimei:
Jahath, Ziza,[a] Jeush and Beriah.
These were the sons of Shimei—four in all.
[11]Jahath was the first and Ziza the second, but Jeush and Beriah did not have many sons; so they were counted as one family with one assignment.

Kohathites

[12]The sons of Kohath:
Amram, Izhar, Hebron and Uzziel—four in all.
[13]The sons of Amram:
Aaron and Moses.
Aaron was set apart, he and his descendants forever, to consecrate the most holy things, to offer sacrifices before the LORD, to minister before him and to pronounce blessings in his name forever.
[14]The sons of Moses the man of God were counted as part of the tribe of Levi.
[15]The sons of Moses:
Gershom and Eliezer.
[16]The descendants of Gershom:
Shubael was the first.
[17]The descendants of Eliezer:
Rehabiah was the first.
Eliezer had no other sons, but the sons of Rehabiah were very numerous.
[18]The sons of Izhar:
Shelomith was the first.
[19]The sons of Hebron:
Jeriah the first, Amariah the second, Jahaziel the third and Jekameam the fourth.
[20]The sons of Uzziel:
Micah the first and Isshiah the second.

Merarites

[21]The sons of Merari:
Mahli and Mushi.
The sons of Mahli:
Eleazar and Kish.
[22]Eleazar died without having sons: he had only daughters. Their cousins, the sons of Kish, married them.
[23]The sons of Mushi:
Mahli, Eder and Jerimoth—three in all.

[24]These were the descendants of Levi by their families—the heads of families as they were registered under their names and counted individually, that is, the workers twenty years old or more who served in the temple of the LORD. [25]For David had said, "Since the LORD, the God of Israel, has granted rest to his people and has come to dwell in Jerusalem forever, [26]the Levites no longer need to carry the tabernacle or any of the articles used in its service." [27]According to the last instructions of David, the Levites were counted from those twenty years old or more.
[28]The duty of the Levites was to help Aaron's descendants in the service of the temple of the LORD: to be in charge of the

---

[a]10 One Hebrew manuscript, Septuagint and Vulgate (see also verse 11); most Hebrew manuscripts *Zina*

courtyards, the side rooms, the purification of all sacred things and the performance of other duties at the house of God. [29]They were in charge of the bread set out on the table, the flour for the grain offerings, the unleavened wafers, the baking and the mixing, and all measurements of quantity and size. [30]They were also to stand every morning to thank and praise the LORD. They were to do the same in the evening [31]and whenever burnt offerings were presented to the LORD on Sabbaths and at New Moon festivals and at appointed feasts. They were to serve before the LORD regularly in the proper number and in the way prescribed for them.

[32]And so the Levites carried out their responsibilities for the Tent of Meeting, for the Holy Place and, under their brothers the descendants of Aaron, for the service of the temple of the LORD.

The Divisions of Priests

24 These were the divisions of the sons of Aaron:

The sons of Aaron were Nadab, Abihu, Eleazar and Ithamar. [2]But Nadab and Abihu died before their father did, and they had no sons; so Eleazar and Ithamar served as the priests. [3]With the help of Zadok a descendant of Eleazar and Ahimelech a descendant of Ithamar, David separated them into divisions for their appointed order of ministering. [4]A larger number of leaders were found among Eleazar's descendants than among Ithamar's, and they were divided accordingly: sixteen heads of families from Eleazar's descendants and eight heads of families from Ithamar's descendants. [5]They divided them impartially by drawing lots, for there were officials of the sanctuary and officials of God among the descendants of both Eleazar and Ithamar.

[6]The scribe Shemaiah son of Nethanel, a Levite, recorded their names in the presence of the king and of the officials: Zadok the priest, Ahimelech son of Abiathar and the heads of families of the priests and of the Levites—one family being taken from Eleazar and then one from Ithamar.

[7]The first lot fell to Jehoiarib,
　　the second to Jedaiah,
[8]the third to Harim,
　　the fourth to Seorim,
[9]the fifth to Malkijah,
　　the sixth to Mijamin,
[10]the seventh to Hakkoz,
　　the eighth to Abijah,

[11]the ninth to Jeshua,
　　the tenth to Shecaniah,
[12]the eleventh to Eliashib,
　　the twelfth to Jakim,
[13]the thirteenth to Huppah,
　　the fourteenth to Jeshebeab,
[14]the fifteenth to Bilgah,
　　the sixteenth to Immer,
[15]the seventeenth to Hezir,
　　the eighteenth to Happizzez,
[16]the nineteenth to Pethahiah,
　　the twentieth to Jehezkel,
[17]the twenty-first to Jakin,
　　the twenty-second to Gamul,
[18]the twenty-third to Delaiah
　　and the twenty-fourth to Maaziah.

[19]This was their appointed order of ministering when they entered the temple of the LORD, according to the regulations prescribed for them by their forefather Aaron, as the LORD, the God of Israel, had commanded him.

The Rest of the Levites

[20]As for the rest of the descendants of Levi:

　　from the sons of Amram: Shubael;
　　　　from the sons of Shubael: Jehdeiah.
[21]As for Rehabiah, from his sons:
　　　　Isshiah was the first.
[22]From the Izharites: Shelomoth;
　　　　from the sons of Shelomoth: Jahath.
[23]The sons of Hebron: Jeriah the first,[a]
　　　　Amariah the second, Jahaziel the third and Jekameam the fourth.
[24]The son of Uzziel: Micah;
　　　　from the sons of Micah: Shamir.
[25]The brother of Micah: Isshiah;
　　　　from the sons of Isshiah: Zechariah.
[26]The sons of Merari: Mahli and Mushi.
　　　　The son of Jaaziah: Beno.
[27]The sons of Merari:
　　　　from Jaaziah: Beno, Shoham, Zaccur and Ibri.
[28]From Mahli: Eleazar, who had no sons.
[29]From Kish: the son of Kish:
　　　　Jerahmeel.
[30]And the sons of Mushi: Mahli, Eder and Jerimoth.

These were the Levites, according to their families. [31]They also cast lots, just as

---

[a]23 Two Hebrew manuscripts and some Septuagint manuscripts (see also 1 Chron. 23:19); most Hebrew manuscripts *The sons of Jeriah:*

their brothers the descendants of Aaron did, in the presence of King David and of Zadok, Ahimelech, and the heads of families of the priests and of the Levites. The families of the oldest brother were treated the same as those of the youngest.

The Singers

25 David, together with the commanders of the army, set apart some of the sons of Asaph, Heman and Jeduthun for the ministry of prophesying, accompanied by harps, lyres and cymbals. Here is the list of the men who performed this service:

²From the sons of Asaph:
Zaccur, Joseph, Nethaniah and Asarelah. The sons of Asaph were under the supervision of Asaph, who prophesied under the king's supervision.
³As for Jeduthun, from his sons:
Gedaliah, Zeri, Jeshaiah, Shimei,ᵃ Hashabiah and Mattithiah, six in all, under the supervision of their father Jeduthun, who prophesied, using the harp in thanking and praising the LORD.
⁴As for Heman, from his sons:
Bukkiah, Mattaniah, Uzziel, Shubael and Jerimoth; Hananiah, Hanani, Eliathah, Giddalti and Romamti-Ezer; Joshbekashah, Mallothi, Hothir and Mahazioth. ⁵All these were sons of Heman the king's seer. They were given him through the promises of God to exalt him.ᵇ God gave Heman fourteen sons and three daughters.

⁶All these men were under the supervision of their fathers for the music of the temple of the LORD, with cymbals, lyres and harps, for the ministry at the house of God. Asaph, Jeduthun and Heman were under the supervision of the king. ⁷Along with their relatives—all of them trained and skilled in music for the LORD—they numbered 288. ⁸Young and old alike, teacher as well as student, cast lots for their duties.

⁹The first lot, which was for Asaph, fell to Joseph,
his sons and relatives,ᶜ   12ᵈ
the second to Gedaliah,
he and his relatives and sons,   12
¹⁰the third to Zaccur,
his sons and relatives,   12
¹¹the fourth to Izri,ᵉ
his sons and relatives,   12

¹²the fifth to Nethaniah,
his sons and relatives,   12
¹³the sixth to Bukkiah,
his sons and relatives,   12
¹⁴the seventh to Jesarelah,ᶠ
his sons and relatives,   12
¹⁵the eighth to Jeshaiah,
his sons and relatives,   12
¹⁶the ninth to Mattaniah,
his sons and relatives,   12
¹⁷the tenth to Shimei,
his sons and relatives,   12
¹⁸the eleventh to Azarel,ᵍ
his sons and relatives,   12
¹⁹the twelfth to Hashabiah,
his sons and relatives,   12
²⁰the thirteenth to Shubael,
his sons and relatives,   12
²¹the fourteenth to Mattithiah,
his sons and relatives,   12
²²the fifteenth to Jerimoth,
his sons and relatives,   12
²³the sixteenth to Hananiah,
his sons and relatives,   12
²⁴the seventeenth to Joshbekashah,
his sons and relatives,   12
²⁵the eighteenth to Hanani,
his sons and relatives,   12
²⁶the nineteenth to Mallothi,
his sons and relatives,   12
²⁷the twentieth to Eliathah,
his sons and relatives,   12
²⁸the twenty-first to Hothir,
his sons and relatives,   12
²⁹the twenty-second to Giddalti,
his sons and relatives,   12
³⁰the twenty-third to Mahazioth,
his sons and relatives,   12
³¹the twenty-fourth to Romamti-Ezer,
his sons and relatives,   12

The Gatekeepers

26 The divisions of the gatekeepers:

From the Korahites: Meshelemiah son of Kore, one of the sons of Asaph.
²Meshelemiah had sons:

ᵃ3 One Hebrew manuscript and some Septuagint manuscripts (see also verse 17); most Hebrew manuscripts do not have *Shimei.* ᵇ5 Hebrew *exalt the horn* ᶜ9 See Septuagint; Hebrew does not have *his sons and relatives.* ᵈ9 See the total in verse 7; Hebrew does not have *twelve.* ᵉ11 A variant of *Zeri* ᶠ14 A variant of *Asarelah* ᵍ18 A variant of *Uzziel*

Zechariah the firstborn,
Jediael the second,
Zebadiah the third,
Jathniel the fourth,
[3] Elam the fifth,
Jehohanan the sixth
and Eliehoenai the seventh.
[4] Obed-Edom also had sons:
Shemaiah the firstborn,
Jehozabad the second,
Joah the third,
Sacar the fourth,
Nethanel the fifth,
[5] Ammiel the sixth,
Issachar the seventh
and Peullethai the eighth.
(For God had blessed Obed-Edom.)

[6] His son Shemaiah also had sons, who were leaders in their father's family because they were very capable men. [7] The sons of Shemaiah: Othni, Rephael, Obed and Elzabad; his relatives Elihu and Semakiah were also able men. [8] All these were descendants of Obed-Edom; they and their sons and their relatives were capable men with the strength to do the work—descendants of Obed-Edom, 62 in all.
[9] Meshelemiah had sons and relatives, who were able men—18 in all.

[10] Hosah the Merarite had sons: Shimri the first (although he was not the firstborn, his father had appointed him the first), [11] Hilkiah the second, Tabaliah the third and Zechariah the fourth. The sons and relatives of Hosah were 13 in all.

[12] These divisions of the gatekeepers, through their chief men, had duties for ministering in the temple of the LORD, just as their relatives had. [13] Lots were cast for each gate, according to their families, young and old alike.
[14] The lot for the East Gate fell to Shelemiah.[a] Then lots were cast for his son Zechariah, a wise counselor, and the lot for the North Gate fell to him. [15] The lot for the South Gate fell to Obed-Edom, and the lot for the storehouse fell to his sons. [16] The lots for the West Gate and the Shalleketh Gate on the upper road fell to Shuppim and Hosah.

Guard was alongside of guard: [17] There were six Levites a day on the east, four a day on the north, four a day on the south and two at a time at the storehouse. [18] As for the court to the west, there were four at the road and two at the court itself.

[19] These were the divisions of the gatekeepers who were descendants of Korah and Merari.

The Treasurers and Other Officials

[20] Their fellow Levites were[b] in charge of the treasuries of the house of God and the treasuries for the dedicated things. [21] The descendants of Ladan, who were Gershonites through Ladan and who were heads of families belonging to Ladan the Gershonite, were Jehieli, [22] the sons of Jehieli, Zetham and his brother Joel. They were in charge of the treasuries of the temple of the LORD.
[23] From the Amramites, the Izharites, the Hebronites and the Uzzielites:

[24] Shubael, a descendant of Gershom son of Moses, was the officer in charge of the treasuries. [25] His relatives through Eliezer: Rehabiah his son, Jeshaiah his son, Joram his son, Zicri his son and Shelomith his son. [26] Shelomith and his relatives were in charge of all the treasuries for the things dedicated by King David, by the heads of families who were the commanders of thousands and commanders of hundreds, and by the other army commanders. [27] Some of the plunder taken in battle they dedicated for the repair of the temple of the LORD. [28] And everything dedicated by Samuel the seer and by Saul son of Kish, Abner son of Ner and Joab son of Zeruiah, and all the other dedicated things were in the care of Shelomith and his relatives.
[29] From the Izharites: Kenaniah and his sons were assigned duties away from the temple, as officials and judges over Israel.
[30] From the Hebronites: Hashabiah and his relatives—seventeen hundred able men—were responsible in Israel west of the Jordan for all the work of the LORD and for the king's service. [31] As for the Hebronites, Jeriah was their chief according to the genealogical records of their families. In the fortieth year of David's reign a search was made in the records, and capable men among the Hebronites were found at Jazer in Gilead. [32] Jeriah had

---

[a]14 A variant of *Meshelemiah*   [b]20 Septuagint; Hebrew *As for the Levites, Ahijah was*

twenty-seven hundred relatives, who were able men and heads of families, and King David put them in charge of the Reubenites, the Gadites and the half-tribe of Manasseh for every matter pertaining to God and for the affairs of the king.

Army Divisions

27 This is the list of the Israelites—heads of families, commanders of thousands and commanders of hundreds, and their officers, who served the king in all that concerned the army divisions that were on duty month by month throughout the year. Each division consisted of 24,000 men.

²In charge of the first division, for the first month, was Jashobeam son of Zabdiel. There were 24,000 men in his division. ³He was a descendant of Perez and chief of all the army officers for the first month. ⁴In charge of the division for the second month was Dodai the Ahohite; Mikloth was the leader of his division. There were 24,000 men in his division. ⁵The third army commander, for the third month, was Benaiah son of Jehoiada the priest. He was chief and there were 24,000 men in his division. ⁶This was the Benaiah who was a mighty man among the Thirty and was over the Thirty. His son Ammizabad was in charge of his division. ⁷The fourth, for the fourth month, was Asahel the brother of Joab; his son Zebadiah was his successor. There were 24,000 men in his division. ⁸The fifth, for the fifth month, was the commander Shamhuth the Izrahite. There were 24,000 men in his division. ⁹The sixth, for the sixth month, was Ira the son of Ikkesh the Tekoite. There were 24,000 men in his division. ¹⁰The seventh, for the seventh month, was Helez the Pelonite, an Ephraimite. There were 24,000 men in his division. ¹¹The eighth, for the eighth month, was Sibbecai the Hushathite, a Zerahite. There were 24,000 men in his division. ¹²The ninth, for the ninth month, was Abiezer the Anathothite, a Benjamite. There were 24,000 men in his division. ¹³The tenth, for the tenth month, was Maharai the Netophathite, a Zerahite. There were 24,000 men in his division. ¹⁴The eleventh, for the eleventh month, was Benaiah the Pirathonite, an Ephraimite. There were 24,000 men in his division. ¹⁵The twelfth, for the twelfth month, was Heldai the Netophathite, from the family of Othniel. There were 24,000 men in his division.

Officers of the Tribes

¹⁶The officers over the tribes of Israel:

over the Reubenites: Eliezer son of Zicri;
over the Simeonites: Shephatiah son of Maacah;
¹⁷over Levi: Hashabiah son of Kemuel;
over Aaron: Zadok;
¹⁸over Judah: Elihu, a brother of David;
over Issachar: Omri son of Michael;
¹⁹over Zebulun: Ishmaiah son of Obadiah;
over Naphtali: Jerimoth son of Azriel;
²⁰over the Ephraimites: Hoshea son of Azaziah;
over half the tribe of Manasseh: Joel son of Pedaiah;
²¹over the half-tribe of Manasseh in Gilead: Iddo son of Zechariah;
over Benjamin: Jaasiel son of Abner;
²²over Dan: Azarel son of Jeroham.
These were the officers over the tribes of Israel.

²³David did not take the number of the men twenty years old or less, because the LORD had promised to make Israel as numerous as the stars in the sky. ²⁴Joab son of Zeruiah began to count the men but did not finish. Wrath came on Israel on account of this numbering, and the number was not entered in the book[a] of the annals of King David.

The King's Overseers

²⁵Azmaveth son of Adiel was in charge of the royal storehouses.
Jonathan son of Uzziah was in charge of the storehouses in the outlying districts, in the towns, the villages and the watchtowers.

[a]24 Septuagint; Hebrew number

²⁶Ezri son of Kelub was in charge of the field workers who farmed the land.

²⁷Shimei the Ramathite was in charge of the vineyards.

Zabdi the Shiphmite was in charge of the produce of the vineyards for the wine vats.

²⁸Baal-Hanan the Gederite was in charge of the olive and sycamore-fig trees in the western foothills.

Joash was in charge of the supplies of olive oil.

²⁹Shitrai the Sharonite was in charge of the herds grazing in Sharon.

Shaphat son of Adlai was in charge of the herds in the valleys.

³⁰Obil the Ishmaelite was in charge of the camels.

Jehdeiah the Meronothite was in charge of the donkeys.

³¹Jaziz the Hagrite was in charge of the flocks.

All these were the officials in charge of King David's property.

³²Jonathan, David's uncle, was a counselor, a man of insight and a scribe. Jehiel son of Hacmoni took care of the king's sons.

³³Ahithophel was the king's counselor. Hushai the Arkite was the king's friend.

³⁴Ahithophel was succeeded by Jehoiada son of Benaiah and by Abiathar.

Joab was the commander of the royal army.

David's Plans for the Temple

28 David summoned all the officials of Israel to assemble at Jerusalem: the officers over the tribes, the commanders of the divisions in the service of the king, the commanders of thousands and commanders of hundreds, and the officials in charge of all the property and livestock belonging to the king and his sons, together with the palace officials, the mighty men and all the brave warriors.

²King David rose to his feet and said: "Listen to me, my brothers and my people. I had it in my heart to build a house as a place of rest for the ark of the covenant of the LORD, for the footstool of our God, and I made plans to build it. ³But God said to me, 'You are not to build a house for my Name, because you are a warrior and have shed blood.'

⁴"Yet the LORD, the God of Israel, chose me from my whole family to be king over Israel forever. He chose Judah as leader, and from the house of Judah he chose my family, and from my father's sons he was pleased to make me king over all Israel. ⁵Of all my sons—and the LORD has given me many—he has chosen my son Solomon to sit on the throne of the kingdom of the LORD over Israel. ⁶He said to me: 'Solomon your son is the one who will build my house and my courts, for I have chosen him to be my son, and I will be his father. ⁷I will establish his kingdom forever if he is unswerving in carrying out my commands and laws, as is being done at this time.'

⁸"So now I charge you in the sight of all Israel and of the assembly of the LORD, and in the hearing of our God: Be careful to follow all the commands of the LORD your God, that you may possess this good land and pass it on as an inheritance to your descendants forever.

⁹"And you, my son Solomon, acknowledge the God of your father, and serve him with wholehearted devotion and with a willing mind, for the LORD searches every heart and understands every motive behind the thoughts. If you seek him, he will be found by you; but if you forsake him, he will reject you forever. ¹⁰Consider now, for the LORD has chosen you to build a temple as a sanctuary. Be strong and do the work."

¹¹Then David gave his son Solomon the plans for the portico of the temple, its buildings, its storerooms, its upper parts, its inner rooms and the place of atonement. ¹²He gave him the plans of all that the Spirit had put in his mind for the courts of the temple of the LORD and all the surrounding rooms, for the treasuries of the temple of God and for the treasuries for the dedicated things. ¹³He gave him instructions for the divisions of the priests and Levites, and for all the work of serving in the temple of the LORD, as well as for all the articles to be used in its service. ¹⁴He designated the weight of gold for all the gold articles to be used in various kinds of service, and the weight of silver for all the silver articles to be used in various kinds of service: ¹⁵the weight of gold for the gold lampstands and their lamps, with the weight for each lampstand and its lamps; and the weight of silver for each silver lampstand and its lamps, according to the use of each lampstand; ¹⁶the weight of gold for each table for consecrated bread; the weight of silver for the silver tables; ¹⁷the weight of pure gold for the forks, sprinkling bowls and pitchers; the weight of gold for each gold

dish; the weight of silver for each silver dish; ¹⁸and the weight of the refined gold for the altar of incense. He also gave him the plan for the chariot, that is, the cherubim of gold that spread their wings and shelter the ark of the covenant of the LORD.

¹⁹"All this," David said, "I have in writing from the hand of the LORD upon me, and he gave me understanding in all the details of the plan."

²⁰David also said to Solomon his son, "Be strong and courageous, and do the work. Do not be afraid or discouraged, for the LORD God, my God, is with you. He will not fail you or forsake you until all the work for the service of the temple of the LORD is finished. ²¹The divisions of the priests and Levites are ready for all the work on the temple of God, and every willing man skilled in any craft will help you in all the work. The officials and all the people will obey your every command."

Gifts for Building the Temple

29 Then King David said to the whole assembly: "My son Solomon, the one

A Monument with a Steeple

DAILY INSIGHT

FRIDAY

Passage:
1 Chronicles 28:1–10

Verse:
1 Chronicles 28:10

Visitors to Washington D.C. quickly find that the city features literally hundreds of memorials and monuments. The most familiar are the huge structures in memory of Washington, Lincoln, and Jefferson, and the smaller but incredibly emotional sites such as the black granite of the Vietnam Memorial. These are among the most visited and most photographed monuments in the world. But throughout the rest of the city, statues stand in every square, and countless plaques honor courageous and influential men and women. We see these places, and we are compelled to remember.

Believe it or not, your town also has many structures built for the purpose of helping us to remember. They come in a multiplicity of shapes and sizes. They are built with many different kinds of materials. Some are built on shoestring budgets, and some are built at a tremendous cost. They challenge us to remember God's tireless faithfulness and seamless grace.

These memorials are church buildings.

Perhaps you've never considered the idea that the churches that dot the landscape where you live are, in fact, memorials. Of course, the Bible makes it clear that "the church" is not a building, but an assembly of believers. But the buildings where these believers meet are powerful symbols for those who attend, as well as those who drive by. Each one could be called a brick and mortar monument to honor an almighty and sovereign God.

For decades, Israel's house of worship was portable. The collapsible tabernacle was made out of canvas and wood so it could be moved from place to place as the Israelites traveled in the wilderness. In this passage David announced to the people that his son, Solomon, was to build a temple—an ornate and permanent memorial to God's faithfulness. David was able to rise above his disappointment at not being chosen to build this structure himself (see 22:8–10), and he was grateful that God had chosen his son to do the work.

You have a church, a visible reminder of God's faithfulness to you and your family. Even though you may not be a professional in ministry, God has called you and your family to build this place up as a living memorial to him. He requires that you loyally worship here, that you participate in the life of your church with your time and treasure, and that you encourage those who are in leadership. Then, when it's time for you to move on, your children and grandchildren will pick up where you left off—committing themselves to worship, participation and encouragement.

The place where you go to visit with your Savior and his people is sacred. Don't forget it.

For your next devotional reading, go to page 465.

whom God has chosen, is young and inexperienced. The task is great, because this palatial structure is not for man but for the LORD God. ²With all my resources I have provided for the temple of my God— gold for the gold work, silver for the silver, bronze for the bronze, iron for the iron and wood for the wood, as well as onyx for the settings, turquoise,ᵃ stones of various colors, and all kinds of fine stone and marble—all of these in large quantities. ³Besides, in my devotion to the temple of my God I now give my personal treasures of gold and silver for the temple of my God, over and above everything I have provided for this holy temple: ⁴three thousand talentsᵇ of gold (gold of Ophir) and seven thousand talentsᶜ of refined silver, for the overlaying of the walls of the buildings, ⁵for the gold work and the silver work, and for all the work to be done by the craftsmen. Now, who is willing to consecrate himself today to the LORD?"

⁶Then the leaders of families, the officers of the tribes of Israel, the commanders of thousands and commanders of hundreds, and the officials in charge of the king's work gave willingly. ⁷They gave toward the work on the temple of God five thousand talentsᵈ and ten thousand daricsᵉ of gold, ten thousand talentsᶠ of silver, eighteen thousand talentsᵍ of bronze and a hundred thousand talentsʰ of iron. ⁸Any who had precious stones gave them to the treasury of the temple of the LORD in the custody of Jehiel the Gershonite. ⁹The people rejoiced at the willing response of their leaders, for they had given freely and wholeheartedly to the LORD. David the king also rejoiced greatly.

David's Prayer

¹⁰David praised the LORD in the presence of the whole assembly, saying,

"Praise be to you, O LORD,
    God of our father Israel,
    from everlasting to everlasting.
¹¹Yours, O LORD, is the greatness and the
        power
    and the glory and the majesty and
        the splendor,
    for everything in heaven and earth is
        yours.
Yours, O LORD, is the kingdom;
    you are exalted as head over all.
¹²Wealth and honor come from you;
    you are the ruler of all things.
In your hands are strength and power
    to exalt and give strength to all.

¹³Now, our God, we give you thanks,
    and praise your glorious name.

¹⁴"But who am I, and who are my people, that we should be able to give as generously as this? Everything comes from you, and we have given you only what comes from your hand. ¹⁵We are aliens and strangers in your sight, as were all our forefathers. Our days on earth are like a shadow, without hope. ¹⁶O LORD our God, as for all this abundance that we have provided for building you a temple for your Holy Name, it comes from your hand, and all of it belongs to you. ¹⁷I know, my God, that you test the heart and are pleased with integrity. All these things have I given willingly and with honest intent. And now I have seen with joy how willingly your people who are here have given to you. ¹⁸O LORD, God of our fathers Abraham, Isaac and Israel, keep this desire in the hearts of your people forever, and keep their hearts loyal to you. ¹⁹And give my son Solomon the wholehearted devotion to keep your commands, requirements and decrees and to do everything to build the palatial structure for which I have provided."

²⁰Then David said to the whole assembly, "Praise the LORD your God." So they all praised the LORD, the God of their fathers; they bowed low and fell prostrate before the LORD and the king.

Solomon Acknowledged as King

²¹The next day they made sacrifices to the LORD and presented burnt offerings to him: a thousand bulls, a thousand rams and a thousand male lambs, together with their drink offerings, and other sacrifices in abundance for all Israel. ²²They ate and drank with great joy in the presence of the LORD that day.

Then they acknowledged Solomon son of David as king a second time, anointing him before the LORD to be ruler and Zadok to be priest. ²³So Solomon sat on the throne of the LORD as king in place of his father David. He prospered and all Israel obeyed him. ²⁴All the officers and mighty

---

ᵃ2 The meaning of the Hebrew for this word is uncertain. ᵇ4 That is, about 110 tons (about 100 metric tons) ᶜ4 That is, about 260 tons (about 240 metric tons) ᵈ7 That is, about 190 tons (about 170 metric tons) ᵉ7 That is, about 185 pounds (about 84 kilograms) ᶠ7 That is, about 375 tons (about 345 metric tons) ᵍ7 That is, about 675 tons (about 610 metric tons) ʰ7 That is, about 3,750 tons (about 3,450 metric tons)

men, as well as all of King David's sons, pledged their submission to King Solomon.

²⁵The LORD highly exalted Solomon in the sight of all Israel and bestowed on him royal splendor such as no king over Israel ever had before.

The Death of David

²⁶David son of Jesse was king over all Israel. ²⁷He ruled over Israel forty years— seven in Hebron and thirty-three in Jerusalem. ²⁸He died at a good old age, having enjoyed long life, wealth and honor. His son Solomon succeeded him as king.

²⁹As for the events of King David's reign, from beginning to end, they are written in the records of Samuel the seer, the records of Nathan the prophet and the records of Gad the seer, ³⁰together with the details of his reign and power, and the circumstances that surrounded him and Israel and the kingdoms of all the other lands.

Life is full of "if's" and "then's." *If* you take this medicine, *then* your backache will subside. *If* you exercise three or four times a week, *then* your heart will stay strong. *If* you oil the mechanism on the swing set in your backyard every month for the rest of your life, *then* it won't rust and break, seriously injuring your children. *If* you invest conservatively, *then* you'll be less likely to lose everything overnight.

Second Chronicles offers one of the most important "if-then" promises ever made. The God of the universe expressed it to Solomon in the dead of night: "*If* my people, who are called by my name, will humble themselves and pray and seek my face and turn from their wicked ways, *then* will I hear from heaven and will forgive their sin and will heal their land" (7:14). This was true in the tenth century before Christ, and it's true for every tribe, every nation and every family today . . . even yours.

2 Chronicles

Solomon Asks for Wisdom

1 Solomon son of David established himself firmly over his kingdom, for the LORD his God was with him and made him exceedingly great.

²Then Solomon spoke to all Israel—to the commanders of thousands and commanders of hundreds, to the judges and to all the leaders in Israel, the heads of families— ³and Solomon and the whole assembly went to the high place at Gibeon, for God's Tent of Meeting was there, which Moses the LORD's servant had made in the desert. ⁴Now David had brought up the ark of God from Kiriath Jearim to the place he had prepared for it, because he had pitched a tent for it in Jerusalem. ⁵But the bronze altar that Bezalel son of Uri, the son of Hur, had made was in Gibeon in front of the tabernacle of the LORD; so Solomon and the assembly inquired of him there. ⁶Solomon went up to the bronze altar before the LORD in the Tent of Meeting and offered a thousand burnt offerings on it.

⁷That night God appeared to Solomon and said to him, "Ask for whatever you want me to give you."

⁸Solomon answered God, "You have shown great kindness to David my father and have made me king in his place. ⁹Now, LORD God, let your promise to my father David be confirmed, for you have made me king over a people who are as numerous as the dust of the earth. ¹⁰Give me wisdom and knowledge, that I may lead this people, for who is able to govern this great people of yours?"

The Gift We Really Want

Key Verse: *"Therefore wisdom and knowledge will be given [to] you."* 2 Chronicles 1:12

Text: 2 Chronicles 1:7–13 *(Dad or child reads the text.)*

QUIET TIMES WITH Dad

DAD READS: Let's say it's a week before your next birthday. I take you out to breakfast and tell you that because I love you very much, I'm going to do something special for this birthday. Then I say to you, "I want you to think of one thing that you want more than anything in the whole world. When you decide what that is, I'll give it to you. I promise."

Child reads: It would be pretty exciting to hear you make me that promise. I would probably spend a lot of time thinking and thinking about the one thing I wanted more than anything else.

DAD READS: In the verses we read today, Solomon was visited by a very special guest. It was nighttime and this visitor, his heavenly Father, promised to give him the one thing he really wanted. It wasn't Solomon's birthday, but it was still an exciting day. Solomon was the new king of Israel!

Child reads: Solomon must have thought about a lot of things he would really like to have—a beautiful palace to live in, a new chariot to drive, or lots of toys to play with on his days off.

DAD READS: You're right. I'm sure he thought of these things. But Solomon told God that what he really wanted was wisdom and knowledge. He wanted to be a good king and he knew that, without these two things, he would surely fail.

Child reads: What if it was a week before your birthday? And what if I came to you and told you that I would give you the one thing you wanted more than anything in the whole world? What would you ask for?

DAD READS: I'm sure I'd think about this for a long time, just like you would. I'd think about all kinds of things that I would like to have. But when it came time to decide, I would really want what Solomon wanted. I would want wisdom and knowledge to be the dad I know that God wants me to be.

Child reads: Even though it would be tempting for both of us to ask for houses, cars, or toys, I know that Solomon is a good example for us today. I know he made a good choice. Let me pray this prayer with you:

Our Father in heaven, thank you for Solomon. Thank you that he made such a good choice when you asked him what he really wanted. Please help my dad and me to always want your wisdom and knowledge more than anything else. Thank you for your promise that when we ask for these things, you will give them to us. In Jesus' name, Amen.

For your next devotional reading, go to page 471.

[11]God said to Solomon, "Since this is your heart's desire and you have not asked for wealth, riches or honor, nor for the death of your enemies, and since you have not asked for a long life but for wisdom and knowledge to govern my people over whom I have made you king, [12]therefore wisdom and knowledge will be given you. And I will also give you wealth, riches and honor, such as no king who was before you ever had and none after you will have."

[13]Then Solomon went to Jerusalem from the high place at Gibeon, from before the Tent of Meeting. And he reigned over Israel.

[14]Solomon accumulated chariots and horses; he had fourteen hundred chariots and twelve thousand horses,[a] which he kept in the chariot cities and also with him in Jerusalem. [15]The king made silver and gold as common in Jerusalem as stones, and cedar as plentiful as sycamore-fig trees in the foothills. [16]Solomon's horses were imported from Egypt[b] and from Kue[c]—the royal merchants purchased them from Kue. [17]They imported a chariot from Egypt for six hundred shekels[d] of silver, and a horse for a hundred and fifty.[e] They also exported them to all the kings of the Hittites and of the Arameans.

Preparations for Building the Temple

2 Solomon gave orders to build a temple for the Name of the LORD and a royal palace for himself. [2]He conscripted seventy thousand men as carriers and eighty thousand as stonecutters in the hills and thirty-six hundred as foremen over them. [3]Solomon sent this message to Hiram[f] king of Tyre:

"Send me cedar logs as you did for my father David when you sent him cedar to build a palace to live in. [4]Now I am about to build a temple for the Name of the LORD my God and to dedicate it to him for burning fragrant incense before him, for setting out the consecrated bread regularly, and for making burnt offerings every morning and evening and on Sabbaths and New Moons and at the appointed feasts of the LORD our God. This is a lasting ordinance for Israel.

[5]"The temple I am going to build will be great, because our God is greater than all other gods. [6]But who is able to build a temple for him, since the heavens, even the highest heavens, cannot contain him? Who then am I to build a temple for him, except as a place to burn sacrifices before him?

[7]"Send me, therefore, a man skilled to work in gold and silver, bronze and iron, and in purple, crimson and blue yarn, and experienced in the art of engraving, to work in Judah and Jerusalem with my skilled craftsmen, whom my father David provided.

[8]"Send me also cedar, pine and algum[g] logs from Lebanon, for I know that your men are skilled in cutting timber there. My men will work with yours [9]to provide me with plenty of lumber, because the temple I build must be large and magnificent. [10]I will give your servants, the woodsmen who cut the timber, twenty thousand cors[h] of ground wheat, twenty thousand cors of barley, twenty thousand baths[i] of wine and twenty thousand baths of olive oil."

[11]Hiram king of Tyre replied by letter to Solomon:

"Because the LORD loves his people, he has made you their king."

[12]And Hiram added:

"Praise be to the LORD, the God of Israel, who made heaven and earth! He has given King David a wise son, endowed with intelligence and discernment, who will build a temple for the LORD and a palace for himself.

[13]"I am sending you Huram-Abi, a man of great skill, [14]whose mother was from Dan and whose father was from Tyre. He is trained to work in gold and silver, bronze and iron, stone and wood, and with purple and blue and crimson yarn and fine linen. He is experienced in all kinds of engraving and can execute any design given to him. He will work with your craftsmen and with those of my lord, David your father.

---

[a]14 Or *charioteers*   [b]16 Or possibly *Muzur*, a region in Cilicia; also in verse 17   [c]16 Probably Cilicia   [d]17 That is, about 15 pounds (about 7 kilograms)   [e]17 That is, about 3 3/4 pounds (about 1.7 kilograms)   [f]3 Hebrew *Huram*, a variant of *Hiram*; also in verses 11 and 12   [g]8 Probably a variant of *almug*; possibly juniper   [h]10 That is, probably about 125,000 bushels (about 4,400 kiloliters)   [i]10 That is, probably about 115,000 gallons (about 440 kiloliters)

[15]"Now let my lord send his servants the wheat and barley and the olive oil and wine he promised, [16]and we will cut all the logs from Lebanon that you need and will float them in rafts by sea down to Joppa. You can then take them up to Jerusalem."

[17]Solomon took a census of all the aliens who were in Israel, after the census his father David had taken; and they were found to be 153,600. [18]He assigned 70,000 of them to be carriers and 80,000 to be stonecutters in the hills, with 3,600 foremen over them to keep the people working.

Solomon Builds the Temple

3 Then Solomon began to build the temple of the LORD in Jerusalem on Mount Moriah, where the LORD had appeared to his father David. It was on the threshing floor of Araunah[a] the Jebusite, the place provided by David. [2]He began building on the second day of the second month in the fourth year of his reign.

[3]The foundation Solomon laid for building the temple of God was sixty cubits long and twenty cubits wide[b] (using the cubit of the old standard). [4]The portico at the front of the temple was twenty cubits[c] long across the width of the building and twenty cubits[d] high.

He overlaid the inside with pure gold. [5]He paneled the main hall with pine and covered it with fine gold and decorated it with palm tree and chain designs. [6]He adorned the temple with precious stones. And the gold he used was gold of Parvaim. [7]He overlaid the ceiling beams, doorframes, walls and doors of the temple with gold, and he carved cherubim on the walls.

[8]He built the Most Holy Place, its length corresponding to the width of the temple—twenty cubits long and twenty cubits wide. He overlaid the inside with six hundred talents[e] of fine gold. [9]The gold nails weighed fifty shekels.[f] He also overlaid the upper parts with gold.

[10]In the Most Holy Place he made a pair of sculptured cherubim and overlaid them with gold. [11]The total wingspan of the cherubim was twenty cubits. One wing of the first cherub was five cubits[g] long and touched the temple wall, while its other wing, also five cubits long, touched the wing of the other cherub. [12]Similarly one wing of the second cherub was five cubits long and touched the

other temple wall, and its other wing, also five cubits long, touched the wing of the first cherub. [13]The wings of these cherubim extended twenty cubits. They stood on their feet, facing the main hall.[h]

[14]He made the curtain of blue, purple and crimson yarn and fine linen, with cherubim worked into it.

[15]In the front of the temple he made two pillars, which together were thirty-five cubits[i] long, each with a capital on top measuring five cubits. [16]He made interwoven chains[j] and put them on top of the pillars. He also made a hundred pomegranates and attached them to the chains. [17]He erected the pillars in the front of the temple, one to the south and one to the north. The one to the south he named Jakin[k] and the one to the north Boaz.[l]

The Temple's Furnishings

4 He made a bronze altar twenty cubits long, twenty cubits wide and ten cubits high.[m] [2]He made the Sea of cast metal, circular in shape, measuring ten cubits from rim to rim and five cubits[n] high. It took a line of thirty cubits[o] to measure around it. [3]Below the rim, figures of bulls encircled it—ten to a cubit.[p] The bulls were cast in two rows in one piece with the Sea.

[4]The Sea stood on twelve bulls, three facing north, three facing west, three facing south and three facing east. The Sea rested on top of them, and their hindquarters were toward the center. [5]It was a handbreadth[q] in thickness, and its rim was like the rim of a cup, like a lily blossom. It held three thousand baths.[r]

[a]1 Hebrew *Ornan*, a variant of *Araunah*   [b]3 That is, about 90 feet (about 27 meters) long and 30 feet (about 9 meters) wide   [c]4 That is, about 30 feet (about 9 meters); also in verses 8, 11 and 13   [d]4 Some Septuagint and Syriac manuscripts; Hebrew *and a hundred and twenty*   [e]8 That is, about 23 tons (about 21 metric tons)   [f]9 That is, about 1 1/4 pounds (about 0.6 kilogram)   [g]11 That is, about 7 1/2 feet (about 2.3 meters); also in verse 15   [h]13 Or *facing inward*   [i]15 That is, about 52 feet (about 16 meters)   [j]16 Or possibly *made chains in the inner sanctuary*; the meaning of the Hebrew for this phrase is uncertain.   [k]17 *Jakin* probably means *he establishes.*   [l]17 *Boaz* probably means *in him is strength.*   [m]1 That is, about 30 feet (about 9 meters) long and wide, and about 15 feet (about 4.5 meters) high   [n]2 That is, about 7 1/2 feet (about 2.3 meters)   [o]2 That is, about 45 feet (about 13.5 meters)   [p]3 That is, about 1 1/2 feet (about 0.5 meter)   [q]5 That is, about 3 inches (about 8 centimeters)   [r]5 That is, about 17,500 gallons (about 66 kiloliters)

⁶He then made ten basins for washing and placed five on the south side and five on the north. In them the things to be used for the burnt offerings were rinsed, but the Sea was to be used by the priests for washing.

⁷He made ten gold lampstands according to the specifications for them and placed them in the temple, five on the south side and five on the north.

⁸He made ten tables and placed them in the temple, five on the south side and five on the north. He also made a hundred gold sprinkling bowls.

⁹He made the courtyard of the priests, and the large court and the doors for the court, and overlaid the doors with bronze. ¹⁰He placed the Sea on the south side, at the southeast corner. ¹¹He also made the pots and shovels and sprinkling bowls.

So Huram finished the work he had undertaken for King Solomon in the temple of God:

¹²the two pillars;
  the two bowl-shaped capitals on top of the pillars;
  the two sets of network decorating the two bowl-shaped capitals on top of the pillars;
¹³the four hundred pomegranates for the two sets of network (two rows of pomegranates for each network, decorating the bowl-shaped capitals on top of the pillars);
¹⁴the stands with their basins;
¹⁵the Sea and the twelve bulls under it;
¹⁶the pots, shovels, meat forks and all related articles.

All the objects that Huram-Abi made for King Solomon for the temple of the LORD were of polished bronze. ¹⁷The king had them cast in clay molds in the plain of the Jordan between Succoth and Zarethan.ᵃ ¹⁸All these things that Solomon made amounted to so much that the weight of the bronze was not determined.

¹⁹Solomon also made all the furnishings that were in God's temple:

  the golden altar;
  the tables on which was the bread of the Presence;
²⁰the lampstands of pure gold with their lamps, to burn in front of the inner sanctuary as prescribed;
²¹the gold floral work and lamps and tongs (they were solid gold);
²²the pure gold wick trimmers, sprin-kling bowls, dishes and censers; and the gold doors of the temple: the inner doors to the Most Holy Place and the doors of the main hall.

5 When all the work Solomon had done for the temple of the LORD was finished, he brought in the things his father David had dedicated—the silver and gold and all the furnishings—and he placed them in the treasuries of God's temple.

The Ark Brought to the Temple

²Then Solomon summoned to Jerusalem the elders of Israel, all the heads of the tribes and the chiefs of the Israelite families, to bring up the ark of the LORD's covenant from Zion, the City of David. ³And all the men of Israel came together to the king at the time of the festival in the seventh month.

⁴When all the elders of Israel had arrived, the Levites took up the ark, ⁵and they brought up the ark and the Tent of Meeting and all the sacred furnishings in it. The priests, who were Levites, carried them up; ⁶and King Solomon and the entire assembly of Israel that had gathered about him were before the ark, sacrificing so many sheep and cattle that they could not be recorded or counted.

⁷The priests then brought the ark of the LORD's covenant to its place in the inner sanctuary of the temple, the Most Holy Place, and put it beneath the wings of the cherubim. ⁸The cherubim spread their wings over the place of the ark and covered the ark and its carrying poles. ⁹These poles were so long that their ends, extending from the ark, could be seen from in front of the inner sanctuary, but not from outside the Holy Place; and they are still there today. ¹⁰There was nothing in the ark except the two tablets that Moses had placed in it at Horeb, where the LORD made a covenant with the Israelites after they came out of Egypt.

¹¹The priests then withdrew from the Holy Place. All the priests who were there had consecrated themselves, regardless of their divisions. ¹²All the Levites who were musicians—Asaph, Heman, Jeduthun and their sons and relatives—stood on the east side of the altar, dressed in fine linen and playing cymbals, harps and lyres. They were accompanied by 120 priests sounding trumpets. ¹³The trum-

ᵃ17 Hebrew *Zeredatha*, a variant of *Zarethan*

peters and singers joined in unison, as with one voice, to give praise and thanks to the LORD. Accompanied by trumpets, cymbals and other instruments, they raised their voices in praise to the LORD and sang:

"He is good;
    his love endures forever."

Then the temple of the LORD was filled with a cloud, **14**and the priests could not perform their service because of the cloud, for the glory of the LORD filled the temple of God.

6 Then Solomon said, "The LORD has said that he would dwell in a dark cloud; **2**I have built a magnificent temple for you, a place for you to dwell forever."

3While the whole assembly of Israel was standing there, the king turned around and blessed them. **4**Then he said:

"Praise be to the LORD, the God of Israel, who with his hands has fulfilled what he promised with his mouth to my father David. For he said, **5**'Since the day I brought my people out of Egypt, I have not chosen a city in any tribe of Israel to have a temple built for my Name to be there, nor have I chosen anyone to be the leader over my people Israel. **6**But now I have chosen Jerusalem for my Name to be there, and I have chosen David to rule my people Israel.'

7"My father David had it in his heart to build a temple for the Name of the LORD, the God of Israel. **8**But the LORD said to my father David, 'Because it was in your heart to build a temple for my Name, you did well to have this in your heart. **9**Nevertheless, you are not the one to build the temple, but your son, who is your own flesh and blood—he is the one who will build the temple for my Name.'

10"The LORD has kept the promise he made. I have succeeded David my father and now I sit on the throne of Israel, just as the LORD promised, and I have built the temple for the Name of the LORD, the God of Israel. **11**There I have placed the ark, in which is the covenant of the LORD that he made with the people of Israel."

Solomon's Prayer of Dedication

12Then Solomon stood before the altar of the LORD in front of the whole assembly

of Israel and spread out his hands. **13**Now he had made a bronze platform, five cubits*a* long, five cubits wide and three cubits*b* high, and had placed it in the center of the outer court. He stood on the platform and then knelt down before the whole assembly of Israel and spread out his hands toward heaven. **14**He said:

"O LORD, God of Israel, there is no God like you in heaven or on earth— you who keep your covenant of love with your servants who continue wholeheartedly in your way. **15**You have kept your promise to your servant David my father; with your mouth you have promised and with your hand you have fulfilled it—as it is today.

16"Now LORD, God of Israel, keep for your servant David my father the promises you made to him when you said, 'You shall never fail to have a man to sit before me on the throne of Israel, if only your sons are careful in all they do to walk before me according to my law, as you have done.' **17**And now, O LORD, God of Israel, let your word that you promised your servant David come true.

18"But will God really dwell on earth with men? The heavens, even the highest heavens, cannot contain you. How much less this temple I have built! **19**Yet give attention to your servant's prayer and his plea for mercy, O LORD my God. Hear the cry and the prayer that your servant is praying in your presence. **20**May your eyes be open toward this temple day and night, this place of which you said you would put your Name there. May you hear the prayer your servant prays toward this place. **21**Hear the supplications of your servant and of your people Israel when they pray toward this place. Hear from heaven, your dwelling place; and when you hear, forgive.

22"When a man wrongs his neighbor and is required to take an oath and he comes and swears the oath before your altar in this temple, **23**then hear from heaven and act. Judge between your servants, repaying the guilty by bringing down on his own head what he has done.

a13 That is, about 7 1/2 feet (about 2.3 meters)
b13 That is, about 4 1/2 feet (about 1.3 meters)

Declare the innocent not guilty and so establish his innocence.

²⁴"When your people Israel have been defeated by an enemy because they have sinned against you and when they turn back and confess your name, praying and making supplication before you in this temple, ²⁵then hear from heaven and forgive the sin of your people Israel and bring them back to the land you gave to them and their fathers.

²⁶"When the heavens are shut up and there is no rain because your people have sinned against you, and when they pray toward this place and confess your name and turn from their sin because you have afflicted them, ²⁷then hear from heaven and forgive the sin of your servants, your people Israel. Teach them the right way to live, and send rain on the land you gave your people for an inheritance.

²⁸"When famine or plague comes to the land, or blight or mildew, locusts or grasshoppers, or when enemies besiege them in any of their cities, whatever disaster or disease may come, ²⁹and when a prayer or plea is made by any of your people Israel—each one aware of his afflictions and pains, and spreading out his hands toward this temple— ³⁰then hear from heaven, your dwelling place. Forgive, and deal with each man according to all he does, since you know his heart (for you alone know the hearts of men), ³¹so that they will fear you and walk in your ways all the time they live in the land you gave our fathers.

³²"As for the foreigner who does not belong to your people Israel but has come from a distant land because of your great name and your mighty hand and your outstretched arm—when he comes and prays toward this temple, ³³then hear from heaven, your dwelling place, and do whatever the foreigner asks of you, so that all the peoples of the earth may know your name and fear you, as do your own people Israel, and may know that this house I have built bears your Name.

³⁴"When your people go to war against their enemies, wherever you send them, and when they pray to you toward this city you have chosen and the temple I have built for your Name, ³⁵then hear from heaven their prayer and their plea, and uphold their cause.

³⁶"When they sin against you—for there is no one who does not sin—and you become angry with them and give them over to the enemy, who takes them captive to a land far away or near; ³⁷and if they have a change of heart in the land where they are held captive, and repent and plead with you in the land of their captivity and say, 'We have sinned, we have done wrong and acted wickedly'; ³⁸and if they turn back to you with all their heart and soul in the land of their captivity where they were taken, and pray toward the land you gave their fathers, toward the city you have chosen and toward the temple I have built for your Name; ³⁹then from heaven, your dwelling place, hear their prayer and their pleas, and uphold their cause. And forgive your people, who have sinned against you.

⁴⁰"Now, my God, may your eyes be open and your ears attentive to the prayers offered in this place.

⁴¹"Now arise, O LORD God, and come
    to your resting place,
  you and the ark of your might.
May your priests, O LORD God, be
    clothed with salvation,
  may your saints rejoice in your
    goodness.
⁴²O LORD God, do not reject your
    anointed one.
  Remember the great love
    promised to David your
    servant."

The Dedication of the Temple

7 When Solomon finished praying, fire came down from heaven and consumed the burnt offering and the sacrifices, and the glory of the LORD filled the temple. ²The priests could not enter the temple of the LORD because the glory of the LORD filled it. ³When all the Israelites saw the fire coming down and the glory of the LORD above the temple, they knelt on the pavement with their faces to the ground, and they worshiped and gave thanks to the LORD, saying,

"He is good;
  his love endures forever."

⁴Then the king and all the people offered sacrifices before the LORD. ⁵And King Solomon offered a sacrifice of twenty-two thousand head of cattle and a hundred and twenty thousand sheep and goats. So the king and all the people dedicated the temple of God. ⁶The priests took their positions, as did the Levites with the LORD's musical instruments, which King David had made for praising the LORD and which were used when he gave thanks, saying, "His love endures forever." Opposite the Levites, the priests blew their trumpets, and all the Israelites were standing.

⁷Solomon consecrated the middle part of the courtyard in front of the temple of the LORD, and there he offered burnt offerings and the fat of the fellowship offerings,ᵃ because the bronze altar he had made could not hold the burnt offerings, the grain offerings and the fat portions.

⁸So Solomon observed the festival at that time for seven days, and all Israel with him—a vast assembly, people from Leboᵇ Hamath to the Wadi of Egypt. ⁹On the eighth day they held an assembly, for they had celebrated the dedication of the altar for seven days and the festival for seven days more. ¹⁰On the twenty-third day of the seventh month he sent the people to their homes, joyful and glad in heart for the good things the LORD had done for David and Solomon and for his people Israel.

The LORD Appears to Solomon

¹¹When Solomon had finished the temple of the LORD and the royal palace, and had succeeded in carrying out all he had in mind to do in the temple of the LORD and in his own palace, ¹²the LORD appeared to him at night and said:

ᵃ7 Traditionally *peace offerings*   ᵇ8 Or *from the entrance to*

Are You for Real?

DAILY INSIGHT

How I love a good spy movie! And Hollywood does a great job of satisfying my taste for espionage. A common scene in these movies features a crafty spy stealing a military uniform. As the tempo of the music quickens, he or she slips unnoticed into a secret location and takes the chance to do his or her dastardly deeds. Within minutes, oil refineries or military installations light the sky as these dangerous frauds incinerate them.

This theme makes my heart pound. I have found myself wanting to call out loud in the theater, "Stop! He's not really who you think he is. He's not a soldier. He's an impostor. Run for your life!" Fortunately, I can wait until these movies are released on video, then shout to my heart's content in the privacy of our living room. My family graciously puts up with these outbursts … most of the time.

God spoke to King Solomon in the night and made an incredible promise. This covenant, however, had some serious

MONDAY

Passage:
2 Chronicles 7:11–22

Verse:
2 Chronicles 7:14

strings attached. God's nocturnal message to the monarch was clear. "*If* those who 'wear' my name will live humbly and obediently, *then* I will hear them, forgive them, and heal their land." God will not support those who claim to follow him but who work to sabotage his kingdom.

You and I are followers of the living God. In fact, we have chosen to take his name. We are Christians. We speak his name. We wear the uniform. In today's verses, God has spoken. Listen to him: *If* we refuse to be impostors, *if* we wear his name with integrity, *if* we walk humbly, and *if* we live obediently, *then* he will hear us and forgive us.

You and I have been drafted into God's army. We wear the uniform of the King of Kings. The battle for the minds of our children—and ours as well—is as hot as it has ever been. Be a real soldier. Deserve the outfit you wear. Be humble and obedient. Know God's presence and forgiveness. Then, watch him work miracles.

For your next devotional reading, go to page 476.

"I have heard your prayer and have chosen this place for myself as a temple for sacrifices.

[13]"When I shut up the heavens so that there is no rain, or command locusts to devour the land or send a plague among my people, [14]if my people, who are called by my name, will humble themselves and pray and seek my face and turn from their wicked ways, then will I hear from heaven and will forgive their sin and will heal their land. [15]Now my eyes will be open and my ears attentive to the prayers offered in this place. [16]I have chosen and consecrated this temple so that my Name may be there forever. My eyes and my heart will always be there.

[17]"As for you, if you walk before me as David your father did, and do all I command, and observe my decrees and laws, [18]I will establish your royal throne, as I covenanted with David your father when I said, 'You shall never fail to have a man to rule over Israel.'

[19]"But if you[a] turn away and forsake the decrees and commands I have given you[a] and go off to serve other gods and worship them, [20]then I will uproot Israel from my land, which I have given them, and will reject this temple I have consecrated for my Name. I will make it a byword and an object of ridicule among all peoples. [21]And though this temple is now so imposing, all who pass by will be appalled and say, 'Why has the LORD done such a thing to this land and to this temple?' [22]People will answer, 'Because they have forsaken the LORD, the God of their fathers, who brought them out of Egypt, and have embraced other gods, worshiping and serving them—that is why he brought all this disaster on them.' "

Solomon's Other Activities

8 At the end of twenty years, during which Solomon built the temple of the LORD and his own palace, [2]Solomon rebuilt the villages that Hiram[b] had given him, and settled Israelites in them. [3]Solomon then went to Hamath Zobah and captured it. [4]He also built up Tadmor in the desert and all the store cities he had built in Hamath. [5]He rebuilt Upper Beth Horon and Lower Beth Horon as fortified cities, with walls and with gates and bars, [6]as well as Baalath and all his store cities, and all the cities for his chariots and for his horses[c]—whatever he desired to build in Jerusalem, in Lebanon and throughout all the territory he ruled.

[7]All the people left from the Hittites, Amorites, Perizzites, Hivites and Jebusites (these peoples were not Israelites), [8]that is, their descendants remaining in the land, whom the Israelites had not destroyed—these Solomon conscripted for his slave labor force, as it is to this day. [9]But Solomon did not make slaves of the Israelites for his work; they were his fighting men, commanders of his captains, and commanders of his chariots and charioteers. [10]They were also King Solomon's chief officials—two hundred and fifty officials supervising the men.

[11]Solomon brought Pharaoh's daughter up from the City of David to the palace he had built for her, for he said, "My wife must not live in the palace of David king of Israel, because the places the ark of the LORD has entered are holy."

[12]On the altar of the LORD that he had built in front of the portico, Solomon sacrificed burnt offerings to the LORD, [13]according to the daily requirement for offerings commanded by Moses for Sabbaths, New Moons and the three annual feasts—the Feast of Unleavened Bread, the Feast of Weeks and the Feast of Tabernacles. [14]In keeping with the ordinance of his father David, he appointed the divisions of the priests for their duties, and the Levites to lead the praise and to assist the priests according to each day's requirement. He also appointed the gatekeepers by divisions for the various gates, because this was what David the man of God had ordered. [15]They did not deviate from the king's commands to the priests or to the Levites in any matter, including that of the treasuries. [16]All Solomon's work was carried out, from the day the foundation of the temple of the LORD was laid until its completion. So the temple of the LORD was finished.

[17]Then Solomon went to Ezion Geber and Elath on the coast of Edom. [18]And Hiram sent him ships commanded by his own officers, men who knew the sea. These, with Solomon's men, sailed to

---

[a]19 The Hebrew is plural.   [b]2 Hebrew *Huram*, a variant of *Hiram*; also in verse 18   [c]6 Or *charioteers*

Ophir and brought back four hundred and fifty talents[a] of gold, which they delivered to King Solomon.

The Queen of Sheba Visits Solomon

9 When the queen of Sheba heard of Solomon's fame, she came to Jerusalem to test him with hard questions. Arriving with a very great caravan—with camels carrying spices, large quantities of gold, and precious stones—she came to Solomon and talked with him about all she had on her mind. [2]Solomon answered all her questions; nothing was too hard for him to explain to her. [3]When the queen of Sheba saw the wisdom of Solomon, as well as the palace he had built, [4]the food on his table, the seating of his officials, the attending servants in their robes, the cupbearers in their robes and the burnt offerings he made at[b] the temple of the LORD, she was overwhelmed.

[5]She said to the king, "The report I heard in my own country about your achievements and your wisdom is true. [6]But I did not believe what they said until I came and saw with my own eyes. Indeed, not even half the greatness of your wisdom was told me; you have far exceeded the report I heard. [7]How happy your men must be! How happy your officials, who continually stand before you and hear your wisdom! [8]Praise be to the LORD your God, who has delighted in you and placed you on his throne as king to rule for the LORD your God. Because of the love of your God for Israel and his desire to uphold them forever, he has made you king over them, to maintain justice and righteousness."

[9]Then she gave the king 120 talents[c] of gold, large quantities of spices, and precious stones. There had never been such spices as those the queen of Sheba gave to King Solomon.

[10](The men of Hiram and the men of Solomon brought gold from Ophir; they also brought algumwood[d] and precious stones. [11]The king used the algumwood to make steps for the temple of the LORD and for the royal palace, and to make harps and lyres for the musicians. Nothing like them had ever been seen in Judah.)

[12]King Solomon gave the queen of Sheba all she desired and asked for; he gave her more than she had brought to him. Then she left and returned with her retinue to her own country.

Solomon's Splendor

[13]The weight of the gold that Solomon received yearly was 666 talents,[e] [14]not including the revenues brought in by merchants and traders. Also all the kings of Arabia and the governors of the land brought gold and silver to Solomon.

[15]King Solomon made two hundred large shields of hammered gold; six hundred bekas[f] of hammered gold went into each shield. [16]He also made three hundred small shields of hammered gold, with three hundred bekas[g] of gold in each shield. The king put them in the Palace of the Forest of Lebanon.

[17]Then the king made a great throne inlaid with ivory and overlaid with pure gold. [18]The throne had six steps, and a footstool of gold was attached to it. On both sides of the seat were armrests, with a lion standing beside each of them. [19]Twelve lions stood on the six steps, one at either end of each step. Nothing like it had ever been made for any other kingdom. [20]All King Solomon's goblets were gold, and all the household articles in the Palace of the Forest of Lebanon were pure gold. Nothing was made of silver, because silver was considered of little value in Solomon's day. [21]The king had a fleet of trading ships[h] manned by Hiram's[i] men. Once every three years it returned, carrying gold, silver and ivory, and apes and baboons.

[22]King Solomon was greater in riches and wisdom than all the other kings of the earth. [23]All the kings of the earth sought audience with Solomon to hear the wisdom God had put in his heart. [24]Year after year, everyone who came brought a gift—articles of silver and gold, and robes, weapons and spices, and horses and mules.

[25]Solomon had four thousand stalls for horses and chariots, and twelve thousand horses,[j] which he kept in the chariot cities and also with him in Jerusalem. [26]He ruled over all the kings from the River[k] to the land of the Philistines, as far as the border of Egypt. [27]The king made silver as

---

[a]18 That is, about 17 tons (about 16 metric tons)   [b]4 Or *the ascent by which he went up to*   [c]9 That is, about 4 1/2 tons (about 4 metric tons)   [d]10 Probably a variant of *almugwood*   [e]13 That is, about 25 tons (about 23 metric tons)   [f]15 That is, about 7 1/2 pounds (about 3.5 kilograms)   [g]16 That is, about 3 3/4 pounds (about 1.7 kilograms)   [h]21 Hebrew *of ships that could go to Tarshish*   [i]21 Hebrew *Huram*, a variant of *Hiram*   [j]25 Or *charioteers*   [k]26 That is, the Euphrates

common in Jerusalem as stones, and cedar as plentiful as sycamore-fig trees in the foothills. [28]Solomon's horses were imported from Egypt[a] and from all other countries.

Solomon's Death

[29]As for the other events of Solomon's reign, from beginning to end, are they not written in the records of Nathan the prophet, in the prophecy of Ahijah the Shilonite and in the visions of Iddo the seer concerning Jeroboam son of Nebat? [30]Solomon reigned in Jerusalem over all Israel forty years. [31]Then he rested with his fathers and was buried in the city of David his father. And Rehoboam his son succeeded him as king.

Israel Rebels Against Rehoboam

10 Rehoboam went to Shechem, for all the Israelites had gone there to make him king. [2]When Jeroboam son of Nebat heard this (he was in Egypt, where he had fled from King Solomon), he returned from Egypt. [3]So they sent for Jeroboam, and he and all Israel went to Rehoboam and said to him: [4]"Your father put a heavy yoke on us, but now lighten the harsh labor and the heavy yoke he put on us, and we will serve you."

[5]Rehoboam answered, "Come back to me in three days." So the people went away.

[6]Then King Rehoboam consulted the elders who had served his father Solomon during his lifetime. "How would you advise me to answer these people?" he asked.

[7]They replied, "If you will be kind to these people and please them and give them a favorable answer, they will always be your servants."

[8]But Rehoboam rejected the advice the elders gave him and consulted the young men who had grown up with him and were serving him. [9]He asked them, "What is your advice? How should we answer these people who say to me, 'Lighten the yoke your father put on us'?"

[10]The young men who had grown up with him replied, "Tell the people who have said to you, 'Your father put a heavy yoke on us, but make our yoke lighter'— tell them, 'My little finger is thicker than my father's waist. [11]My father laid on you a heavy yoke; I will make it even heavier. My father scourged you with whips; I will scourge you with scorpions.' "

[12]Three days later Jeroboam and all the people returned to Rehoboam, as the king had said, "Come back to me in three days." [13]The king answered them harshly. Rejecting the advice of the elders, [14]he followed the advice of the young men and said, "My father made your yoke heavy; I will make it even heavier. My father scourged you with whips; I will scourge you with scorpions." [15]So the king did not listen to the people, for this turn of events was from God, to fulfill the word the LORD had spoken to Jeroboam son of Nebat through Ahijah the Shilonite.

[16]When all Israel saw that the king refused to listen to them, they answered the king:

"What share do we have in David,
    what part in Jesse's son?
To your tents, O Israel!
    Look after your own house,
        O David!"

So all the Israelites went home. [17]But as for the Israelites who were living in the towns of Judah, Rehoboam still ruled over them.

[18]King Rehoboam sent out Adoniram,[b] who was in charge of forced labor, but the Israelites stoned him to death. King Rehoboam, however, managed to get into his chariot and escape to Jerusalem. [19]So Israel has been in rebellion against the house of David to this day.

11 When Rehoboam arrived in Jerusalem, he mustered the house of Judah and Benjamin—a hundred and eighty thousand fighting men—to make war against Israel and to regain the kingdom for Rehoboam.

[2]But this word of the LORD came to Shemaiah the man of God: [3]"Say to Rehoboam son of Solomon king of Judah and to all the Israelites in Judah and Benjamin, [4]'This is what the LORD says: Do not go up to fight against your brothers. Go home, every one of you, for this is my doing.' " So they obeyed the words of the LORD and turned back from marching against Jeroboam.

Rehoboam Fortifies Judah

[5]Rehoboam lived in Jerusalem and built up towns for defense in Judah: [6]Bethlehem, Etam, Tekoa, [7]Beth Zur, Soco, Adullam, [8]Gath, Mareshah, Ziph, [9]Adoraim, Lachish, Azekah, [10]Zorah, Aijalon and

---

[a]28 Or possibly *Muzur,* a region in Cilicia
[b]18 Hebrew *Hadoram,* a variant of *Adoniram*

Hebron. These were fortified cities in Judah and Benjamin. [11]He strengthened their defenses and put commanders in them, with supplies of food, olive oil and wine. [12]He put shields and spears in all the cities, and made them very strong. So Judah and Benjamin were his.

[13]The priests and Levites from all their districts throughout Israel sided with him. [14]The Levites even abandoned their pasturelands and property, and came to Judah and Jerusalem because Jeroboam and his sons had rejected them as priests of the LORD. [15]And he appointed his own priests for the high places and for the goat and calf idols he had made. [16]Those from every tribe of Israel who set their hearts on seeking the LORD, the God of Israel, followed the Levites to Jerusalem to offer sacrifices to the LORD, the God of their fathers. [17]They strengthened the kingdom of Judah and supported Rehoboam son of Solomon three years, walking in the ways of David and Solomon during this time.

Rehoboam's Family

[18]Rehoboam married Mahalath, who was the daughter of David's son Jerimoth and of Abihail, the daughter of Jesse's son Eliab. [19]She bore him sons: Jeush, Shemariah and Zaham. [20]Then he married Maacah daughter of Absalom, who bore him Abijah, Attai, Ziza and Shelomith. [21]Rehoboam loved Maacah daughter of Absalom more than any of his other wives and concubines. In all, he had eighteen wives and sixty concubines, twenty-eight sons and sixty daughters.

[22]Rehoboam appointed Abijah son of Maacah to be the chief prince among his brothers, in order to make him king. [23]He acted wisely, dispersing some of his sons throughout the districts of Judah and Benjamin, and to all the fortified cities. He gave them abundant provisions and took many wives for them.

Shishak Attacks Jerusalem

12 After Rehoboam's position as king was established and he had become strong, he and all Israel[a] with him abandoned the law of the LORD. [2]Because they had been unfaithful to the LORD, Shishak king of Egypt attacked Jerusalem in the fifth year of King Rehoboam. [3]With twelve hundred chariots and sixty thousand horsemen and the innumerable troops of Libyans, Sukkites and Cushites[b] that came

with him from Egypt, [4]he captured the fortified cities of Judah and came as far as Jerusalem.

[5]Then the prophet Shemaiah came to Rehoboam and to the leaders of Judah who had assembled in Jerusalem for fear of Shishak, and he said to them, "This is what the LORD says, 'You have abandoned me; therefore, I now abandon you to Shishak.' "

[6]The leaders of Israel and the king humbled themselves and said, "The LORD is just."

[7]When the LORD saw that they humbled themselves, this word of the LORD came to Shemaiah: "Since they have humbled themselves, I will not destroy them but will soon give them deliverance. My wrath will not be poured out on Jerusalem through Shishak. [8]They will, however, become subject to him, so that they may learn the difference between serving me and serving the kings of other lands."

[9]When Shishak king of Egypt attacked Jerusalem, he carried off the treasures of the temple of the LORD and the treasures of the royal palace. He took everything, including the gold shields Solomon had made. [10]So King Rehoboam made bronze shields to replace them and assigned these to the commanders of the guard on duty at the entrance to the royal palace. [11]Whenever the king went to the LORD's temple, the guards went with him, bearing the shields, and afterward they returned them to the guardroom. [12]Because Rehoboam humbled himself, the LORD's anger turned from him, and he was not totally destroyed. Indeed, there was some good in Judah.

[13]King Rehoboam established himself firmly in Jerusalem and continued as king. He was forty-one years old when he became king, and he reigned seventeen years in Jerusalem, the city the LORD had chosen out of all the tribes of Israel in which to put his Name. His mother's name was Naamah; she was an Ammonite. [14]He did evil because he had not set his heart on seeking the LORD.

[15]As for the events of Rehoboam's reign, from beginning to end, are they not written in the records of Shemaiah the prophet and of Iddo the seer that deal with genealogies? There was continual warfare between Rehoboam and Jeroboam. [16]Rehoboam rested with his fathers

---

[a]1 That is, Judah, as frequently in 2 Chronicles
[b]3 That is, people from the upper Nile region

and was buried in the City of David. And Abijah his son succeeded him as king.

Abijah King of Judah

13 In the eighteenth year of the reign of Jeroboam, Abijah became king of Judah, ²and he reigned in Jerusalem three years. His mother's name was Maacah,ᵃ a daughterᵇ of Uriel of Gibeah.

There was war between Abijah and Jeroboam. ³Abijah went into battle with a force of four hundred thousand able fighting men, and Jeroboam drew up a battle line against him with eight hundred thousand able troops.

⁴Abijah stood on Mount Zemaraim, in the hill country of Ephraim, and said, "Jeroboam and all Israel, listen to me! ⁵Don't you know that the LORD, the God of Israel, has given the kingship of Israel to David and his descendants forever by a

ᵃ2 Most Septuagint manuscripts and Syriac (see also 2 Chron. 11:20 and 1 Kings 15:2); Hebrew *Micaiah*   ᵇ2 Or *granddaughter*

Can Someone Give Me a Hand with This Thing?

DAILY INSIGHT

Stop for a moment and think of all the things that take two people to accomplish.

Several years ago I went to our local rental center—where I'm on a first-name basis with most of the clerks—and rented a de-thatcher for my lawn. After I had handed Mike the yellow copy of the invoice, he pulled out from the warehouse what looked like an oversized lawn mower. Once we had finished the paperwork, Mike pushed the machine to my waiting car. With him on one side and me on the other, we effortlessly lifted it into the trunk. Nothing to it.

When I got home, it dawned on me that I had a serious problem. There was no way I was ever going to get this thing out of my trunk without some help. But, being a guy and not wanting to admit my need for help, I checked to make sure my wife wasn't watching and tried to see if I could grip it in such a way that I could do it alone. No dice. It wasn't that the de-thatcher was so heavy, it was just that I couldn't get the proper grip to leverage it out of my car.

Fortunately, Vince and Adam, two teenagers who lived across the street, were home. Once I had enlisted their help, the machine was out of my trunk in a flash. Again, nothing to it … with the right kind of help.

King Solomon was dead. His son, Rehoboam, succeeded him to the throne of Israel. Solomon's other son, Jereboam,

TUESDAY

Passage:
2 Chronicles 12:1–8

Verse:
2 Chronicles 12:6

rebelled against his brother, pulling a portion of the nation with him. From that point until 1948, the single nation of Israel ceased to exist.

Imagine this tragedy. Two men—brothers who should have known better—take leave of their good senses and decide to go it alone. In fact, not only do they abandon each other, they desert the God of their fathers.

Something that could have been so successfully accomplished with the cooperation of two men falls apart, leaving the lives of millions of people in chaos for centuries. In fact, we read a perilously sobering judgment from God himself in this text. "You have abandoned me; therefore, I now abandon you" (12:5). It's as if God is saying to Rehoboam, "So you think you can lift this thing by yourself? Go ahead. Give it a shot." These are not words you and I should ever have to hear.

Solomon's two sons decided to go their own way. Instead of helping each other with the task of leading God's people, they let jealousy and pride cloud their minds. How foolish of them.

Don't abandon the companionship of a brother. And don't forget to secure your partnership with your heavenly Father every single day. Doing so only makes good sense because in this life, it doesn't pay to go it alone.

For your next devotional reading, go to page 488.

covenant of salt? [6]Yet Jeroboam son of Nebat, an official of Solomon son of David, rebelled against his master. [7]Some worthless scoundrels gathered around him and opposed Rehoboam son of Solomon when he was young and indecisive and not strong enough to resist them.

[8]"And now you plan to resist the kingdom of the LORD, which is in the hands of David's descendants. You are indeed a vast army and have with you the golden calves that Jeroboam made to be your gods. [9]But didn't you drive out the priests of the LORD, the sons of Aaron, and the Levites, and make priests of your own as the peoples of other lands do? Whoever comes to consecrate himself with a young bull and seven rams may become a priest of what are not gods.

[10]"As for us, the LORD is our God, and we have not forsaken him. The priests who serve the LORD are sons of Aaron, and the Levites assist them. [11]Every morning and evening they present burnt offerings and fragrant incense to the LORD. They set out the bread on the ceremonially clean table and light the lamps on the gold lampstand every evening. We are observing the requirements of the LORD our God. But you have forsaken him. [12]God is with us; he is our leader. His priests with their trumpets will sound the battle cry against you. Men of Israel, do not fight against the LORD, the God of your fathers, for you will not succeed."

[13]Now Jeroboam had sent troops around to the rear, so that while he was in front of Judah the ambush was behind them. [14]Judah turned and saw that they were being attacked at both front and rear. Then they cried out to the LORD. The priests blew their trumpets [15]and the men of Judah raised the battle cry. At the sound of their battle cry, God routed Jeroboam and all Israel before Abijah and Judah. [16]The Israelites fled before Judah, and God delivered them into their hands. [17]Abijah and his men inflicted heavy losses on them, so that there were five hundred thousand casualties among Israel's able men. [18]The men of Israel were subdued on that occasion, and the men of Judah were victorious because they relied on the LORD, the God of their fathers.

[19]Abijah pursued Jeroboam and took from him the towns of Bethel, Jeshanah and Ephron, with their surrounding villages. [20]Jeroboam did not regain power during the time of Abijah. And the LORD struck him down and he died.

[21]But Abijah grew in strength. He married fourteen wives and had twenty-two sons and sixteen daughters.

[22]The other events of Abijah's reign, what he did and what he said, are written in the annotations of the prophet Iddo.

14 And Abijah rested with his fathers and was buried in the City of David. Asa his son succeeded him as king, and in his days the country was at peace for ten years.

Asa King of Judah

[2]Asa did what was good and right in the eyes of the LORD his God. [3]He removed the foreign altars and the high places, smashed the sacred stones and cut down the Asherah poles.[a] [4]He commanded Judah to seek the LORD, the God of their fathers, and to obey his laws and commands. [5]He removed the high places and incense altars in every town in Judah, and the kingdom was at peace under him. [6]He built up the fortified cities of Judah, since the land was at peace. No one was at war with him during those years, for the LORD gave him rest.

[7]"Let us build up these towns," he said to Judah, "and put walls around them, with towers, gates and bars. The land is still ours, because we have sought the LORD our God; we sought him and he has given us rest on every side." So they built and prospered.

[8]Asa had an army of three hundred thousand men from Judah, equipped with large shields and with spears, and two hundred and eighty thousand from Benjamin, armed with small shields and with bows. All these were brave fighting men.

[9]Zerah the Cushite marched out against them with a vast army[b] and three hundred chariots, and came as far as Mareshah. [10]Asa went out to meet him, and they took up battle positions in the Valley of Zephathah near Mareshah.

[11]Then Asa called to the LORD his God and said, "LORD, there is no one like you to help the powerless against the mighty. Help us, O LORD our God, for we rely on you, and in your name we have come against this vast army. O LORD, you are our God; do not let man prevail against you."

---

[a]3 That is, symbols of the goddess Asherah; here and elsewhere in 2 Chronicles   [b]9 Hebrew *with an army of a thousand thousands* or *with an army of thousands upon thousands*

¹²The LORD struck down the Cushites before Asa and Judah. The Cushites fled, ¹³and Asa and his army pursued them as far as Gerar. Such a great number of Cushites fell that they could not recover; they were crushed before the LORD and his forces. The men of Judah carried off a large amount of plunder. ¹⁴They destroyed all the villages around Gerar, for the terror of the LORD had fallen upon them. They plundered all these villages, since there was much booty there. ¹⁵They also attacked the camps of the herdsmen and carried off droves of sheep and goats and camels. Then they returned to Jerusalem.

Asa's Reform

15 The Spirit of God came upon Azariah son of Oded. ²He went out to meet Asa and said to him, "Listen to me, Asa and all Judah and Benjamin. The LORD is with you when you are with him. If you seek him, he will be found by you, but if you forsake him, he will forsake you. ³For a long time Israel was without the true God, without a priest to teach and without the law. ⁴But in their distress they turned to the LORD, the God of Israel, and sought him, and he was found by them. ⁵In those days it was not safe to travel about, for all the inhabitants of the lands were in great turmoil. ⁶One nation was being crushed by another and one city by another, because God was troubling them with every kind of distress. ⁷But as for you, be strong and do not give up, for your work will be rewarded."

⁸When Asa heard these words and the prophecy of Azariah son of[a] Oded the prophet, he took courage. He removed the detestable idols from the whole land of Judah and Benjamin and from the towns he had captured in the hills of Ephraim. He repaired the altar of the LORD that was in front of the portico of the LORD's temple.

⁹Then he assembled all Judah and Benjamin and the people from Ephraim, Manasseh and Simeon who had settled among them, for large numbers had come over to him from Israel when they saw that the LORD his God was with him.

¹⁰They assembled at Jerusalem in the third month of the fifteenth year of Asa's reign. ¹¹At that time they sacrificed to the LORD seven hundred head of cattle and seven thousand sheep and goats from the plunder they had brought back. ¹²They

entered into a covenant to seek the LORD, the God of their fathers, with all their heart and soul. ¹³All who would not seek the LORD, the God of Israel, were to be put to death, whether small or great, man or woman. ¹⁴They took an oath to the LORD with loud acclamation, with shouting and with trumpets and horns. ¹⁵All Judah rejoiced about the oath because they had sworn it wholeheartedly. They sought God eagerly, and he was found by them. So the LORD gave them rest on every side.

¹⁶King Asa also deposed his grandmother Maacah from her position as queen mother, because she had made a repulsive Asherah pole. Asa cut the pole down, broke it up and burned it in the Kidron Valley. ¹⁷Although he did not remove the high places from Israel, Asa's heart was fully committed to the LORD all his life. ¹⁸He brought into the temple of God the silver and gold and the articles that he and his father had dedicated.

¹⁹There was no more war until the thirty-fifth year of Asa's reign.

Asa's Last Years

16 In the thirty-sixth year of Asa's reign Baasha king of Israel went up against Judah and fortified Ramah to prevent anyone from leaving or entering the territory of Asa king of Judah.

²Asa then took the silver and gold out of the treasuries of the LORD's temple and of his own palace and sent it to Ben-Hadad king of Aram, who was ruling in Damascus. ³"Let there be a treaty between me and you," he said, "as there was between my father and your father. See, I am sending you silver and gold. Now break your treaty with Baasha king of Israel so he will withdraw from me."

⁴Ben-Hadad agreed with King Asa and sent the commanders of his forces against the towns of Israel. They conquered Ijon, Dan, Abel Maim[b] and all the store cities of Naphtali. ⁵When Baasha heard this, he stopped building Ramah and abandoned his work. ⁶Then King Asa brought all the men of Judah, and they carried away from Ramah the stones and timber Baasha had been using. With them he built up Geba and Mizpah.

⁷At that time Hanani the seer came to Asa king of Judah and said to him: "Because you relied on the king of Aram and

a8 Vulgate and Syriac (see also Septuagint and verse 1); Hebrew does not have *Azariah son of*. b4 Also known as *Abel Beth Maacah*

not on the LORD your God, the army of the king of Aram has escaped from your hand. ⁸Were not the Cushites*a* and Libyans a mighty army with great numbers of chariots and horsemen*b*? Yet when you relied on the LORD, he delivered them into your hand. ⁹For the eyes of the LORD range throughout the earth to strengthen those whose hearts are fully committed to him. You have done a foolish thing, and from now on you will be at war."

¹⁰Asa was angry with the seer because of this; he was so enraged that he put him in prison. At the same time Asa brutally oppressed some of the people.

¹¹The events of Asa's reign, from beginning to end, are written in the book of the kings of Judah and Israel. ¹²In the thirty-ninth year of his reign Asa was afflicted with a disease in his feet. Though his disease was severe, even in his illness he did not seek help from the LORD, but only from the physicians. ¹³Then in the forty-first year of his reign Asa died and rested with his fathers. ¹⁴They buried him in the tomb that he had cut out for himself in the City of David. They laid him on a bier covered with spices and various blended perfumes, and they made a huge fire in his honor.

Jehoshaphat King of Judah

17 Jehoshaphat his son succeeded him as king and strengthened himself against Israel. ²He stationed troops in all the fortified cities of Judah and put garrisons in Judah and in the towns of Ephraim that his father Asa had captured.

³The LORD was with Jehoshaphat because in his early years he walked in the ways his father David had followed. He did not consult the Baals ⁴but sought the God of his father and followed his commands rather than the practices of Israel. ⁵The LORD established the kingdom under his control; and all Judah brought gifts to Jehoshaphat, so that he had great wealth and honor. ⁶His heart was devoted to the ways of the LORD; furthermore, he removed the high places and the Asherah poles from Judah.

⁷In the third year of his reign he sent his officials Ben-Hail, Obadiah, Zechariah, Nethanel and Micaiah to teach in the towns of Judah. ⁸With them were certain Levites—Shemaiah, Nethaniah, Zebadiah, Asahel, Shemiramoth, Jehonathan, Adonijah, Tobijah and Tob-Adonijah—and the priests Elishama and Jehoram.

⁹They taught throughout Judah, taking with them the Book of the Law of the LORD; they went around to all the towns of Judah and taught the people.

¹⁰The fear of the LORD fell on all the kingdoms of the lands surrounding Judah, so that they did not make war with Jehoshaphat. ¹¹Some Philistines brought Jehoshaphat gifts and silver as tribute, and the Arabs brought him flocks: seven thousand seven hundred rams and seven thousand seven hundred goats.

¹²Jehoshaphat became more and more powerful; he built forts and store cities in Judah ¹³and had large supplies in the towns of Judah. He also kept experienced fighting men in Jerusalem. ¹⁴Their enrollment by families was as follows:

From Judah, commanders of units of 1,000:
   Adnah the commander, with 300,000 fighting men;
¹⁵next, Jehohanan the commander, with 280,000;
¹⁶next, Amasiah son of Zicri, who volunteered himself for the service of the LORD, with 200,000.
¹⁷From Benjamin:
   Eliada, a valiant soldier, with 200,000 men armed with bows and shields;
¹⁸next, Jehozabad, with 180,000 men armed for battle.

¹⁹These were the men who served the king, besides those he stationed in the fortified cities throughout Judah.

Micaiah Prophesies Against Ahab

18 Now Jehoshaphat had great wealth and honor, and he allied himself with Ahab by marriage. ²Some years later he went down to visit Ahab in Samaria. Ahab slaughtered many sheep and cattle for him and the people with him and urged him to attack Ramoth Gilead. ³Ahab king of Israel asked Jehoshaphat king of Judah, "Will you go with me against Ramoth Gilead?"

Jehoshaphat replied, "I am as you are, and my people as your people; we will join you in the war." ⁴But Jehoshaphat also said to the king of Israel, "First seek the counsel of the LORD."

⁵So the king of Israel brought together the prophets—four hundred men—and

*a8 That is, people from the upper Nile region
b8 Or charioteers*

asked them, "Shall we go to war against Ramoth Gilead, or shall I refrain?"

"Go," they answered, "for God will give it into the king's hand."

⁶But Jehoshaphat asked, "Is there not a prophet of the LORD here whom we can inquire of?"

⁷The king of Israel answered Jehoshaphat, "There is still one man through whom we can inquire of the LORD, but I hate him because he never prophesies anything good about me, but always bad. He is Micaiah son of Imlah."

"The king should not say that," Jehoshaphat replied.

⁸So the king of Israel called one of his officials and said, "Bring Micaiah son of Imlah at once."

⁹Dressed in their royal robes, the king of Israel and Jehoshaphat king of Judah were sitting on their thrones at the threshing floor by the entrance to the gate of Samaria, with all the prophets prophesying before them. ¹⁰Now Zedekiah son of Kenaanah had made iron horns, and he declared, "This is what the LORD says: 'With these you will gore the Arameans until they are destroyed.' "

¹¹All the other prophets were prophesying the same thing. "Attack Ramoth Gilead and be victorious," they said, "for the LORD will give it into the king's hand."

¹²The messenger who had gone to summon Micaiah said to him, "Look, as one man the other prophets are predicting success for the king. Let your word agree with theirs, and speak favorably."

¹³But Micaiah said, "As surely as the LORD lives, I can tell him only what my God says."

¹⁴When he arrived, the king asked him, "Micaiah, shall we go to war against Ramoth Gilead, or shall I refrain?"

"Attack and be victorious," he answered, "for they will be given into your hand."

¹⁵The king said to him, "How many times must I make you swear to tell me nothing but the truth in the name of the LORD?"

¹⁶Then Micaiah answered, "I saw all Israel scattered on the hills like sheep without a shepherd, and the LORD said, 'These people have no master. Let each one go home in peace.' "

¹⁷The king of Israel said to Jehoshaphat, "Didn't I tell you that he never prophesies anything good about me, but only bad?"

¹⁸Micaiah continued, "Therefore hear the word of the LORD: I saw the LORD sitting on his throne with all the host of heaven standing on his right and on his left. ¹⁹And the LORD said, 'Who will entice Ahab king of Israel into attacking Ramoth Gilead and going to his death there?'

"One suggested this, and another that. ²⁰Finally, a spirit came forward, stood before the LORD and said, 'I will entice him.'

" 'By what means?' the LORD asked.

²¹" 'I will go and be a lying spirit in the mouths of all his prophets,' he said.

" 'You will succeed in enticing him,' said the LORD. 'Go and do it.'

²²"So now the LORD has put a lying spirit in the mouths of these prophets of yours. The LORD has decreed disaster for you."

²³Then Zedekiah son of Kenaanah went up and slapped Micaiah in the face. "Which way did the spirit from^a the LORD go when he went from me to speak to you?" he asked.

²⁴Micaiah replied, "You will find out on the day you go to hide in an inner room."

²⁵The king of Israel then ordered, "Take Micaiah and send him back to Amon the ruler of the city and to Joash the king's son, ²⁶and say, 'This is what the king says: Put this fellow in prison and give him nothing but bread and water until I return safely.' "

²⁷Micaiah declared, "If you ever return safely, the LORD has not spoken through me." Then he added, "Mark my words, all you people!"

Ahab Killed at Ramoth Gilead

²⁸So the king of Israel and Jehoshaphat king of Judah went up to Ramoth Gilead. ²⁹The king of Israel said to Jehoshaphat, "I will enter the battle in disguise, but you wear your royal robes." So the king of Israel disguised himself and went into battle.

³⁰Now the king of Aram had ordered his chariot commanders, "Do not fight with anyone, small or great, except the king of Israel." ³¹When the chariot commanders saw Jehoshaphat, they thought, "This is the king of Israel." So they turned to attack him, but Jehoshaphat cried out, and the LORD helped him. God drew them away from him, ³²for when the chariot commanders saw that he was not the king of Israel, they stopped pursuing him.

³³But someone drew his bow at random and hit the king of Israel between the sections of his armor. The king told the

^a23 Or *Spirit of*

chariot driver, "Wheel around and get me out of the fighting. I've been wounded." [34]All day long the battle raged, and the king of Israel propped himself up in his chariot facing the Arameans until evening. Then at sunset he died.

19 When Jehoshaphat king of Judah returned safely to his palace in Jerusalem, [2]Jehu the seer, the son of Hanani, went out to meet him and said to the king, "Should you help the wicked and love[a] those who hate the LORD? Because of this, the wrath of the LORD is upon you. [3]There is, however, some good in you, for you have rid the land of the Asherah poles and have set your heart on seeking God."

Jehoshaphat Appoints Judges

[4]Jehoshaphat lived in Jerusalem, and he went out again among the people from Beersheba to the hill country of Ephraim and turned them back to the LORD, the God of their fathers. [5]He appointed judges in the land, in each of the fortified cities of Judah. [6]He told them, "Consider carefully what you do, because you are not judging for man but for the LORD, who is with you whenever you give a verdict. [7]Now let the fear of the LORD be upon you. Judge carefully, for with the LORD our God there is no injustice or partiality or bribery."

[8]In Jerusalem also, Jehoshaphat appointed some of the Levites, priests and heads of Israelite families to administer the law of the LORD and to settle disputes. And they lived in Jerusalem. [9]He gave them these orders: "You must serve faithfully and wholeheartedly in the fear of the LORD. [10]In every case that comes before you from your fellow countrymen who live in the cities—whether bloodshed or other concerns of the law, commands, decrees or ordinances—you are to warn them not to sin against the LORD; otherwise his wrath will come on you and your brothers. Do this, and you will not sin. [11]"Amariah the chief priest will be over you in any matter concerning the LORD, and Zebadiah son of Ishmael, the leader of the tribe of Judah, will be over you in any matter concerning the king, and the Levites will serve as officials before you. Act with courage, and may the LORD be with those who do well."

Jehoshaphat Defeats Moab and Ammon

20 After this, the Moabites and Ammonites with some of the Meunites[b] came to make war on Jehoshaphat.

[2]Some men came and told Jehoshaphat, "A vast army is coming against you from Edom,[c] from the other side of the Sea.[d] It is already in Hazazon Tamar" (that is, En Gedi). [3]Alarmed, Jehoshaphat resolved to inquire of the LORD, and he proclaimed a fast for all Judah. [4]The people of Judah came together to seek help from the LORD; indeed, they came from every town in Judah to seek him.

[5]Then Jehoshaphat stood up in the assembly of Judah and Jerusalem at the temple of the LORD in the front of the new courtyard [6]and said:

"O LORD, God of our fathers, are you not the God who is in heaven? You rule over all the kingdoms of the nations. Power and might are in your hand, and no one can withstand you. [7]O our God, did you not drive out the inhabitants of this land before your people Israel and give it forever to the descendants of Abraham your friend? [8]They have lived in it and have built in it a sanctuary for your Name, saying, [9]'If calamity comes upon us, whether the sword of judgment, or plague or famine, we will stand in your presence before this temple that bears your Name and will cry out to you in our distress, and you will hear us and save us.'

[10]"But now here are men from Ammon, Moab and Mount Seir, whose territory you would not allow Israel to invade when they came from Egypt; so they turned away from them and did not destroy them. [11]See how they are repaying us by coming to drive us out of the possession you gave us as an inheritance. [12]O our God, will you not judge them? For we have no power to face this vast army that is attacking us. We do not know what to do, but our eyes are upon you."

[13]All the men of Judah, with their wives and children and little ones, stood there before the LORD.

[14]Then the Spirit of the LORD came upon Jahaziel son of Zechariah, the son of Benaiah, the son of Jeiel, the son of Mattaniah, a Levite and descendant of Asaph, as he stood in the assembly.

[a]2 Or *and make alliances with*   [b]1 Some Septuagint manuscripts; Hebrew *Ammonites*
[c]2 One Hebrew manuscript; most Hebrew manuscripts, Septuagint and Vulgate *Aram*
[d]2 That is, the Dead Sea

¹⁵He said: "Listen, King Jehoshaphat and all who live in Judah and Jerusalem! This is what the LORD says to you: 'Do not be afraid or discouraged because of this vast army. For the battle is not yours, but God's. ¹⁶Tomorrow march down against them. They will be climbing up by the Pass of Ziz, and you will find them at the end of the gorge in the Desert of Jeruel. ¹⁷You will not have to fight this battle. Take up your positions; stand firm and see the deliverance the LORD will give you, O Judah and Jerusalem. Do not be afraid; do not be discouraged. Go out to face them tomorrow, and the LORD will be with you.' "

¹⁸Jehoshaphat bowed with his face to the ground, and all the people of Judah and Jerusalem fell down in worship before the LORD. ¹⁹Then some Levites from the Kohathites and Korahites stood up and praised the LORD, the God of Israel, with very loud voice.

²⁰Early in the morning they left for the Desert of Tekoa. As they set out, Jehoshaphat stood and said, "Listen to me, Judah and people of Jerusalem! Have faith in the LORD your God and you will be upheld; have faith in his prophets and you will be successful." ²¹After consulting the people, Jehoshaphat appointed men to sing to the LORD and to praise him for the splendor of his*ᵃ* holiness as they went out at the head of the army, saying:

"Give thanks to the LORD,
    for his love endures forever."

²²As they began to sing and praise, the LORD set ambushes against the men of Ammon and Moab and Mount Seir who were invading Judah, and they were defeated. ²³The men of Ammon and Moab rose up against the men from Mount Seir to destroy and annihilate them. After they finished slaughtering the men from Seir, they helped to destroy one another.

²⁴When the men of Judah came to the place that overlooks the desert and looked toward the vast army, they saw only dead bodies lying on the ground; no one had escaped. ²⁵So Jehoshaphat and his men went to carry off their plunder, and they found among them a great amount of equipment and clothingᵇ and also articles of value—more than they could take away. There was so much plunder that it took three days to collect it. ²⁶On the fourth day they assembled in the Valley of Beracah, where they praised the LORD. This is why it is called the Valley of Beracahᶜ to this day.

²⁷Then, led by Jehoshaphat, all the men of Judah and Jerusalem returned joyfully to Jerusalem, for the LORD had given them cause to rejoice over their enemies. ²⁸They entered Jerusalem and went to the temple of the LORD with harps and lutes and trumpets.

²⁹The fear of God came upon all the kingdoms of the countries when they heard how the LORD had fought against the enemies of Israel. ³⁰And the kingdom of Jehoshaphat was at peace, for his God had given him rest on every side.

The End of Jehoshaphat's Reign

³¹So Jehoshaphat reigned over Judah. He was thirty-five years old when he became king of Judah, and he reigned in Jerusalem twenty-five years. His mother's name was Azubah daughter of Shilhi. ³²He walked in the ways of his father Asa and did not stray from them; he did what was right in the eyes of the LORD. ³³The high places, however, were not removed, and the people still had not set their hearts on the God of their fathers.

³⁴The other events of Jehoshaphat's reign, from beginning to end, are written in the annals of Jehu son of Hanani, which are recorded in the book of the kings of Israel.

³⁵Later, Jehoshaphat king of Judah made an alliance with Ahaziah king of Israel, who was guilty of wickedness. ³⁶He agreed with him to construct a fleet of trading ships.ᵈ After these were built at Ezion Geber, ³⁷Eliezer son of Dodavahu of Mareshah prophesied against Jehoshaphat, saying, "Because you have made an alliance with Ahaziah, the LORD will destroy what you have made." The ships were wrecked and were not able to set sail to trade.ᵉ

21 Then Jehoshaphat rested with his fathers and was buried with them in the City of David. And Jehoram his son succeeded him as king. ²Jehoram's brothers, the sons of Jehoshaphat, were Azariah, Jehiel, Zechariah, Azariahu, Michael and Shephatiah. All these were sons of Jehoshaphat king of Israel.ᶠ ³Their father had given them many gifts of silver and gold and articles of value, as well as fortified

---

ᵃ21 Or *him with the splendor of*   ᵇ25 Some Hebrew manuscripts and Vulgate; most Hebrew manuscripts *corpses*   ᶜ26 *Beracah* means *praise*.   ᵈ36 Hebrew *of ships that could go to Tarshish*   ᵉ37 Hebrew *sail for Tarshish*   ᶠ2 That is, Judah, as frequently in 2 Chronicles

cities in Judah, but he had given the kingdom to Jehoram because he was his firstborn son.

Jehoram King of Judah

⁴When Jehoram established himself firmly over his father's kingdom, he put all his brothers to the sword along with some of the princes of Israel. ⁵Jehoram was thirty-two years old when he became king, and he reigned in Jerusalem eight years. ⁶He walked in the ways of the kings of Israel, as the house of Ahab had done, for he married a daughter of Ahab. He did evil in the eyes of the LORD. ⁷Nevertheless, because of the covenant the LORD had made with David, the LORD was not willing to destroy the house of David. He had promised to maintain a lamp for him and his descendants forever.

⁸In the time of Jehoram, Edom rebelled against Judah and set up its own king. ⁹So Jehoram went there with his officers and all his chariots. The Edomites surrounded him and his chariot commanders, but he rose up and broke through by night. ¹⁰To this day Edom has been in rebellion against Judah.

Libnah revolted at the same time, because Jehoram had forsaken the LORD, the God of his fathers. ¹¹He had also built high places on the hills of Judah and had caused the people of Jerusalem to prostitute themselves and had led Judah astray. ¹²Jehoram received a letter from Elijah the prophet, which said:

"This is what the LORD, the God of your father David, says: 'You have not walked in the ways of your father Jehoshaphat or of Asa king of Judah. ¹³But you have walked in the ways of the kings of Israel, and you have led Judah and the people of Jerusalem to prostitute themselves, just as the house of Ahab did. You have also murdered your own brothers, members of your father's house, men who were better than you. ¹⁴So now the LORD is about to strike your people, your sons, your wives and everything that is yours, with a heavy blow. ¹⁵You yourself will be very ill with a lingering disease of the bowels, until the disease causes your bowels to come out.' "

¹⁶The LORD aroused against Jehoram the hostility of the Philistines and of the Arabs who lived near the Cushites. ¹⁷They attacked Judah, invaded it and carried off all the goods found in the king's palace, together with his sons and wives. Not a son was left to him except Ahaziah,ᵃ the youngest.

¹⁸After all this, the LORD afflicted Jehoram with an incurable disease of the bowels. ¹⁹In the course of time, at the end of the second year, his bowels came out because of the disease, and he died in great pain. His people made no fire in his honor, as they had for his fathers.

²⁰Jehoram was thirty-two years old when he became king, and he reigned in Jerusalem eight years. He passed away, to no one's regret, and was buried in the City of David, but not in the tombs of the kings.

Ahaziah King of Judah

22 The people of Jerusalem made Ahaziah, Jehoram's youngest son, king in his place, since the raiders, who came with the Arabs into the camp, had killed all the older sons. So Ahaziah son of Jehoram king of Judah began to reign.

²Ahaziah was twenty-twoᵇ years old when he became king, and he reigned in Jerusalem one year. His mother's name was Athaliah, a granddaughter of Omri.

³He too walked in the ways of the house of Ahab, for his mother encouraged him in doing wrong. ⁴He did evil in the eyes of the LORD, as the house of Ahab had done, for after his father's death they became his advisers, to his undoing. ⁵He also followed their counsel when he went with Joramᶜ son of Ahab king of Israel to war against Hazael king of Aram at Ramoth Gilead. The Arameans wounded Joram; ⁶so he returned to Jezreel to recover from the wounds they had inflicted on him at Ramothᵈ in his battle with Hazael king of Aram.

Then Ahaziahᵉ son of Jehoram king of Judah went down to Jezreel to see Joram son of Ahab because he had been wounded.

⁷Through Ahaziah's visit to Joram, God brought about Ahaziah's downfall. When Ahaziah arrived, he went out with Joram to meet Jehu son of Nimshi, whom the

ᵃ17 Hebrew *Jehoahaz*, a variant of *Ahaziah*
ᵇ2 Some Septuagint manuscripts and Syriac (see also 2 Kings 8:26); Hebrew *forty-two*   ᶜ5 Hebrew *Jehoram*, a variant of *Joram*; also in verses 6 and 7   ᵈ6 Hebrew *Ramah*, a variant of *Ramoth*   ᵉ6 Some Hebrew manuscripts, Septuagint, Vulgate and Syriac (see also 2 Kings 8:29); most Hebrew manuscripts *Azariah*

LORD had anointed to destroy the house of Ahab. [8]While Jehu was executing judgment on the house of Ahab, he found the princes of Judah and the sons of Ahaziah's relatives, who had been attending Ahaziah, and he killed them. [9]He then went in search of Ahaziah, and his men captured him while he was hiding in Samaria. He was brought to Jehu and put to death. They buried him, for they said, "He was a son of Jehoshaphat, who sought the LORD with all his heart." So there was no one in the house of Ahaziah powerful enough to retain the kingdom.

Athaliah and Joash

[10]When Athaliah the mother of Ahaziah saw that her son was dead, she proceeded to destroy the whole royal family of the house of Judah. [11]But Jehosheba,[a] the daughter of King Jehoram, took Joash son of Ahaziah and stole him away from among the royal princes who were about to be murdered and put him and his nurse in a bedroom. Because Jehosheba,[a] the daughter of King Jehoram and wife of the priest Jehoiada, was Ahaziah's sister, she hid the child from Athaliah so she could not kill him. [12]He remained hidden with them at the temple of God for six years while Athaliah ruled the land.

23 In the seventh year Jehoiada showed his strength. He made a covenant with the commanders of units of a hundred: Azariah son of Jeroham, Ishmael son of Jehohanan, Azariah son of Obed, Maaseiah son of Adaiah, and Elishaphat son of Zicri. [2]They went throughout Judah and gathered the Levites and the heads of Israelite families from all the towns. When they came to Jerusalem, [3]the whole assembly made a covenant with the king at the temple of God.

Jehoiada said to them, "The king's son shall reign, as the LORD promised concerning the descendants of David. [4]Now this is what you are to do: A third of you priests and Levites who are going on duty on the Sabbath are to keep watch at the doors, [5]a third of you at the royal palace and a third at the Foundation Gate, and all the other men are to be in the courtyards of the temple of the LORD. [6]No one is to enter the temple of the LORD except the priests and Levites on duty; they may enter because they are consecrated, but all the other men are to guard what the LORD has assigned to them.[b] [7]The Levites are to station themselves around the king, each

man with his weapons in his hand. Anyone who enters the temple must be put to death. Stay close to the king wherever he goes."

[8]The Levites and all the men of Judah did just as Jehoiada the priest ordered. Each one took his men—those who were going on duty on the Sabbath and those who were going off duty—for Jehoiada the priest had not released any of the divisions. [9]Then he gave the commanders of units of a hundred the spears and the large and small shields that had belonged to King David and that were in the temple of God. [10]He stationed all the men, each with his weapon in his hand, around the king—near the altar and the temple, from the south side to the north side of the temple.

[11]Jehoiada and his sons brought out the king's son and put the crown on him; they presented him with a copy of the covenant and proclaimed him king. They anointed him and shouted, "Long live the king!"

[12]When Athaliah heard the noise of the people running and cheering the king, she went to them at the temple of the LORD. [13]She looked, and there was the king, standing by his pillar at the entrance. The officers and the trumpeters were beside the king, and all the people of the land were rejoicing and blowing trumpets, and singers with musical instruments were leading the praises. Then Athaliah tore her robes and shouted, "Treason! Treason!"

[14]Jehoiada the priest sent out the commanders of units of a hundred, who were in charge of the troops, and said to them: "Bring her out between the ranks[c] and put to the sword anyone who follows her." For the priest had said, "Do not put her to death at the temple of the LORD." [15]So they seized her as she reached the entrance of the Horse Gate on the palace grounds, and there they put her to death.

[16]Jehoiada then made a covenant that he and the people and the king[d] would be the LORD's people. [17]All the people went to the temple of Baal and tore it down. They smashed the altars and idols and killed Mattan the priest of Baal in front of the altars.

[18]Then Jehoiada placed the oversight of

---

[a]11 Hebrew *Jehoshabeath*, a variant of *Jehosheba*
[b]6 Or *to observe the LORD's command, not to enter*
[c]14 Or *out from the precincts*   [d]16 Or *covenant between the LORD, and the people and the king that they* (see 2 Kings 11:17)

the temple of the LORD in the hands of the priests, who were Levites, to whom David had made assignments in the temple, to present the burnt offerings of the LORD as written in the Law of Moses, with rejoicing and singing, as David had ordered. ¹⁹He also stationed doorkeepers at the gates of the LORD's temple so that no one who was in any way unclean might enter.

²⁰He took with him the commanders of hundreds, the nobles, the rulers of the people and all the people of the land and brought the king down from the temple of the LORD. They went into the palace through the Upper Gate and seated the king on the royal throne, ²¹and all the people of the land rejoiced. And the city was quiet, because Athaliah had been slain with the sword.

Joash Repairs the Temple

24 Joash was seven years old when he became king, and he reigned in Jerusalem forty years. His mother's name was Zibiah; she was from Beersheba. ²Joash did what was right in the eyes of the LORD all the years of Jehoiada the priest. ³Jehoiada chose two wives for him, and he had sons and daughters.

⁴Some time later Joash decided to restore the temple of the LORD. ⁵He called together the priests and Levites and said to them, "Go to the towns of Judah and collect the money due annually from all Israel, to repair the temple of your God. Do it now." But the Levites did not act at once.

⁶Therefore the king summoned Jehoiada the chief priest and said to him, "Why haven't you required the Levites to bring in from Judah and Jerusalem the tax imposed by Moses the servant of the LORD and by the assembly of Israel for the Tent of the Testimony?"

⁷Now the sons of that wicked woman Athaliah had broken into the temple of God and had used even its sacred objects for the Baals.

⁸At the king's command, a chest was made and placed outside, at the gate of the temple of the LORD. ⁹A proclamation was then issued in Judah and Jerusalem that they should bring to the LORD the tax that Moses the servant of God had required of Israel in the desert. ¹⁰All the officials and all the people brought their contributions gladly, dropping them into the chest until it was full. ¹¹Whenever the chest was brought in by the Levites to the king's officials and they saw that there was a large amount of money, the royal secretary and the officer of the chief priest would come and empty the chest and carry it back to its place. They did this regularly and collected a great amount of money. ¹²The king and Jehoiada gave it to the men who carried out the work required for the temple of the LORD. They hired masons and carpenters to restore the LORD's temple, and also workers in iron and bronze to repair the temple.

¹³The men in charge of the work were diligent, and the repairs progressed under them. They rebuilt the temple of God according to its original design and reinforced it. ¹⁴When they had finished, they brought the rest of the money to the king and Jehoiada, and with it were made articles for the LORD's temple: articles for the service and for the burnt offerings, and also dishes and other objects of gold and silver. As long as Jehoiada lived, burnt offerings were presented continually in the temple of the LORD.

¹⁵Now Jehoiada was old and full of years, and he died at the age of a hundred and thirty. ¹⁶He was buried with the kings in the City of David, because of the good he had done in Israel for God and his temple.

The Wickedness of Joash

¹⁷After the death of Jehoiada, the officials of Judah came and paid homage to the king, and he listened to them. ¹⁸They abandoned the temple of the LORD, the God of their fathers, and worshiped Asherah poles and idols. Because of their guilt, God's anger came upon Judah and Jerusalem. ¹⁹Although the LORD sent prophets to the people to bring them back to him, and though they testified against them, they would not listen.

²⁰Then the Spirit of God came upon Zechariah son of Jehoiada the priest. He stood before the people and said, "This is what God says: 'Why do you disobey the LORD's commands? You will not prosper. Because you have forsaken the LORD, he has forsaken you.' "

²¹But they plotted against him, and by order of the king they stoned him to death in the courtyard of the LORD's temple. ²²King Joash did not remember the kindness Zechariah's father Jehoiada had shown him but killed his son, who said as he lay dying, "May the LORD see this and call you to account."

²³At the turn of the year,ᵃ the army of Aram marched against Joash; it invaded Judah and Jerusalem and killed all the leaders of the people. They sent all the plunder to their king in Damascus. ²⁴Although the Aramean army had come with only a few men, the LORD delivered into their hands a much larger army. Because Judah had forsaken the LORD, the God of their fathers, judgment was executed on Joash. ²⁵When the Arameans withdrew, they left Joash severely wounded. His officials conspired against him for murdering the son of Jehoiada the priest, and they killed him in his bed. So he died and was buried in the City of David, but not in the tombs of the kings.

²⁶Those who conspired against him were Zabad,ᵇ son of Shimeath an Ammonite woman, and Jehozabad, son of Shimrithᶜ a Moabite woman. ²⁷The account of his sons, the many prophecies about him, and the record of the restoration of the temple of God are written in the annotations on the book of the kings. And Amaziah his son succeeded him as king.

Amaziah King of Judah

25 Amaziah was twenty-five years old when he became king, and he reigned in Jerusalem twenty-nine years. His mother's name was Jehoaddinᵈ; she was from Jerusalem. ²He did what was right in the eyes of the LORD, but not wholeheartedly. ³After the kingdom was firmly in his control, he executed the officials who had murdered his father the king. ⁴Yet he did not put their sons to death, but acted in accordance with what is written in the Law, in the Book of Moses, where the LORD commanded: "Fathers shall not be put to death for their children, nor children put to death for their fathers; each is to die for his own sins."ᵉ

⁵Amaziah called the people of Judah together and assigned them according to their families to commanders of thousands and commanders of hundreds for all Judah and Benjamin. He then mustered those twenty years old or more and found that there were three hundred thousand men ready for military service, able to handle the spear and shield. ⁶He also hired a hundred thousand fighting men from Israel for a hundred talentsᶠ of silver.

⁷But a man of God came to him and said, "O king, these troops from Israel must not march with you, for the LORD is not with Israel—not with any of the people of Ephraim. ⁸Even if you go and fight courageously in battle, God will overthrow you before the enemy, for God has the power to help or to overthrow."

⁹Amaziah asked the man of God, "But what about the hundred talents I paid for these Israelite troops?"

The man of God replied, "The LORD can give you much more than that."

¹⁰So Amaziah dismissed the troops who had come to him from Ephraim and sent them home. They were furious with Judah and left for home in a great rage.

¹¹Amaziah then marshaled his strength and led his army to the Valley of Salt, where he killed ten thousand men of Seir. ¹²The army of Judah also captured ten thousand men alive, took them to the top of a cliff and threw them down so that all were dashed to pieces.

¹³Meanwhile the troops that Amaziah had sent back and had not allowed to take part in the war raided Judean towns from Samaria to Beth Horon. They killed three thousand people and carried off great quantities of plunder.

¹⁴When Amaziah returned from slaughtering the Edomites, he brought back the gods of the people of Seir. He set them up as his own gods, bowed down to them and burned sacrifices to them. ¹⁵The anger of the LORD burned against Amaziah, and he sent a prophet to him, who said, "Why do you consult this people's gods, which could not save their own people from your hand?"

¹⁶While he was still speaking, the king said to him, "Have we appointed you an adviser to the king? Stop! Why be struck down?"

So the prophet stopped but said, "I know that God has determined to destroy you, because you have done this and have not listened to my counsel."

¹⁷After Amaziah king of Judah consulted his advisers, he sent this challenge to Jehoashᵍ son of Jehoahaz, the son of Jehu, king of Israel: "Come, meet me face to face."

¹⁸But Jehoash king of Israel replied to Amaziah king of Judah: "A thistle in Lebanon sent a message to a cedar in Lebanon, 'Give your daughter to my son in mar-

---

ᵃ23 Probably in the spring   ᵇ26 A variant of Jozabad   ᶜ26 A variant of Shomer   ᵈ1 Hebrew Jehoaddan, a variant of Jehoaddin   ᵉ4 Deut. 24:16   ᶠ6 That is, about 3 3/4 tons (about 3.4 metric tons); also in verse 9   ᵍ17 Hebrew Joash, a variant of Jehoash; also in verses 18, 21, 23 and 25

riage.' Then a wild beast in Lebanon came along and trampled the thistle underfoot. ¹⁹You say to yourself that you have defeated Edom, and now you are arrogant and proud. But stay at home! Why ask for trouble and cause your own downfall and that of Judah also?"

²⁰Amaziah, however, would not listen, for God so worked that he might hand them over to Jehoash, because they sought the gods of Edom. ²¹So Jehoash king of Israel attacked. He and Amaziah king of Judah faced each other at Beth Shemesh in Judah. ²²Judah was routed by Israel, and every man fled to his home. ²³Jehoash king of Israel captured Amaziah king of Judah, the son of Joash, the son of Ahaziah,^a at Beth Shemesh. Then Jehoash brought him to Jerusalem and broke down the wall of Jerusalem from the Ephraim Gate to the Corner Gate—a section about six hundred feet^b long. ²⁴He took all the gold and silver and all the articles found in the temple of God that had been in the care of Obed-Edom, together with the palace treasures and the hostages, and returned to Samaria.

²⁵Amaziah son of Joash king of Judah lived for fifteen years after the death of Jehoash son of Jehoahaz king of Israel. ²⁶As for the other events of Amaziah's reign, from beginning to end, are they not written in the book of the kings of Judah and Israel? ²⁷From the time that Amaziah turned away from following the LORD, they conspired against him in Jerusalem and he fled to Lachish, but they sent men after him to Lachish and killed him there. ²⁸He was brought back by horse and was buried with his fathers in the City of Judah.

Uzziah King of Judah

26 Then all the people of Judah took Uzziah,^c who was sixteen years old, and made him king in place of his father Amaziah. ²He was the one who rebuilt Elath and restored it to Judah after Amaziah rested with his fathers.

³Uzziah was sixteen years old when he became king, and he reigned in Jerusalem fifty-two years. His mother's name was Jecoliah; she was from Jerusalem. ⁴He did what was right in the eyes of the LORD, just as his father Amaziah had done. ⁵He sought God during the days of Zechariah, who instructed him in the fear^d of God. As long as he sought the LORD, God gave him success.

⁶He went to war against the Philistines and broke down the walls of Gath, Jabneh and Ashdod. He then rebuilt towns near Ashdod and elsewhere among the Philistines. ⁷God helped him against the Philistines and against the Arabs who lived in Gur Baal and against the Meunites. ⁸The Ammonites brought tribute to Uzziah, and his fame spread as far as the border of Egypt, because he had become very powerful.

⁹Uzziah built towers in Jerusalem at the Corner Gate, at the Valley Gate and at the angle of the wall, and he fortified them. ¹⁰He also built towers in the desert and dug many cisterns, because he had much livestock in the foothills and in the plain. He had people working his fields and vineyards in the hills and in the fertile lands, for he loved the soil.

¹¹Uzziah had a well-trained army, ready to go out by divisions according to their numbers as mustered by Jeiel the secretary and Maaseiah the officer under the direction of Hananiah, one of the royal officials. ¹²The total number of family leaders over the fighting men was 2,600. ¹³Under their command was an army of 307,500 men trained for war, a powerful force to support the king against his enemies. ¹⁴Uzziah provided shields, spears, helmets, coats of armor, bows and slingstones for the entire army. ¹⁵In Jerusalem he made machines designed by skillful men for use on the towers and on the corner defenses to shoot arrows and hurl large stones. His fame spread far and wide, for he was greatly helped until he became powerful.

¹⁶But after Uzziah became powerful, his pride led to his downfall. He was unfaithful to the LORD his God, and entered the temple of the LORD to burn incense on the altar of incense. ¹⁷Azariah the priest with eighty other courageous priests of the LORD followed him in. ¹⁸They confronted him and said, "It is not right for you, Uzziah, to burn incense to the LORD. That is for the priests, the descendants of Aaron, who have been consecrated to burn incense. Leave the sanctuary, for you have been unfaithful; and you will not be honored by the LORD God."

¹⁹Uzziah, who had a censer in his hand ready to burn incense, became angry.

^a23 Hebrew *Jehoahaz,* a variant of *Ahaziah*
^b23 Hebrew *four hundred cubits* (about 180 meters)
^c1 Also called *Azariah*   ^d5 Many Hebrew manuscripts, Septuagint and Syriac; other Hebrew manuscripts *vision*

While he was raging at the priests in their presence before the incense altar in the LORD's temple, leprosy[a] broke out on his forehead. [20]When Azariah the chief priest and all the other priests looked at him, they saw that he had leprosy on his forehead, so they hurried him out. Indeed, he himself was eager to leave, because the LORD had afflicted him.

[21]King Uzziah had leprosy until the day he died. He lived in a separate house[b]—leprous, and excluded from the temple of the LORD. Jotham his son had charge of

[a]19 The Hebrew word was used for various diseases affecting the skin—not necessarily leprosy; also in verses 20, 21 and 23. [b]21 Or *in a house where he was relieved of responsibilities*

Don't Leave Home Without It

DAILY INSIGHT

A number of years ago, American Express ran an advertising campaign featuring Karl Malden, an actor who had made a name for himself portraying a hard-nosed detective on television. American Express wisely used this plain-clothed "lawman" to tell us that their traveler's checks were better than cash if you were out of town. After a dramatic recreation of a situation in which some hapless couple lost their money while on vacation, Malden stepped on camera and told us to use American Express traveler's checks because they could be "instantly" replaced if lost or stolen. Then he added those now-famous words, "Don't leave home without them."

In the fall of 1989, I was desperately trying to sell my business. Undercapitalization can be more powerful than strong, black coffee in robbing most entrepreneurs of a good night's sleep. I was such an entrepreneur. But I had a buyer—a local businessman who asked to see my numbers and who had arranged a special meeting with his top lieutenants to discuss the matter. On this particular morning, my business partner and I were invited to meet with this man and his advisers.

"This could be it," I said to my wife, Bobbie, over a bowl of granola and raisins. "I really think we have found someone to invest the cash we need." As she had so many times before, Bobbie carefully listened.

But as I was getting into my car for the twenty-minute trip to the meeting that day, Bobbie made a comment that penetrated my overly optimistic—and often naïve—

WEDNESDAY
Passage:
2 Chronicles 26:3–16
Verses:
2 Chronicles 26:6–8

demeanor. "Don't forget that this wealthy businessman is not your source," she warned. "If this deal doesn't have God's blessing, it'll be a waste of time."

I was stunned, even disappointed at her directness and her caution. However as I made my way through city traffic to the appointed meeting, I knew she was right. My wife had spoken with God's voice, and I knew it was a message for me.

Uzziah was only sixteen years old when he became king. At an age where other teenagers are out getting their driver's licenses, this young man took over the throne of Judah. In a very short time he set out, moving from one corner of his kingdom to another. Fortunately he took the God of his fathers with him. He didn't leave home without the Lord's protection.

Unfortunately, as was the case with so many of these kings, he forgot God (26:16) and bowed to the great god of presumption and self-sufficiency. Eventually, his "pride led to his downfall."

As a dad, you have the opportunity every day to leave home either with or without God's sovereign protection. Today might be one of those days. Ask God for wisdom. Seek his blessing. Take him with you. And if it feels like you're pushing for something out of fear, desperation, or just plain blind enthusiasm, slow down.

Remember what my wise wife said to me that cool spring morning. If this thing doesn't have God's blessing, it'll be a waste of your time.

For your next devotional reading, go to page 503.

the palace and governed the people of the land.

²²The other events of Uzziah's reign, from beginning to end, are recorded by the prophet Isaiah son of Amoz. ²³Uzziah rested with his fathers and was buried near them in a field for burial that belonged to the kings, for people said, "He had leprosy." And Jotham his son succeeded him as king.

Jotham King of Judah

27 Jotham was twenty-five years old when he became king, and he reigned in Jerusalem sixteen years. His mother's name was Jerusha daughter of Zadok. ²He did what was right in the eyes of the LORD, just as his father Uzziah had done, but unlike him he did not enter the temple of the LORD. The people, however, continued their corrupt practices. ³Jotham rebuilt the Upper Gate of the temple of the LORD and did extensive work on the wall at the hill of Ophel. ⁴He built towns in the Judean hills and forts and towers in the wooded areas.

⁵Jotham made war on the king of the Ammonites and conquered them. That year the Ammonites paid him a hundred talents*a* of silver, ten thousand cors*b* of wheat and ten thousand cors of barley. The Ammonites brought him the same amount also in the second and third years.

⁶Jotham grew powerful because he walked steadfastly before the LORD his God.

⁷The other events in Jotham's reign, including all his wars and the other things he did, are written in the book of the kings of Israel and Judah. ⁸He was twenty-five years old when he became king, and he reigned in Jerusalem sixteen years. ⁹Jotham rested with his fathers and was buried in the City of David. And Ahaz his son succeeded him as king.

Ahaz King of Judah

28 Ahaz was twenty years old when he became king, and he reigned in Jerusalem sixteen years. Unlike David his father, he did not do what was right in the eyes of the LORD. ²He walked in the ways of the kings of Israel and also made cast idols for worshiping the Baals. ³He burned sacrifices in the Valley of Ben Hinnom and sacrificed his sons in the fire, following the detestable ways of the nations the LORD had driven out before

the Israelites. ⁴He offered sacrifices and burned incense at the high places, on the hilltops and under every spreading tree.

⁵Therefore the LORD his God handed him over to the king of Aram. The Arameans defeated him and took many of his people as prisoners and brought them to Damascus.

He was also given into the hands of the king of Israel, who inflicted heavy casualties on him. ⁶In one day Pekah son of Remaliah killed a hundred and twenty thousand soldiers in Judah—because Judah had forsaken the LORD, the God of their fathers. ⁷Zicri, an Ephraimite warrior, killed Maaseiah the king's son, Azrikam the officer in charge of the palace, and Elkanah, second to the king. ⁸The Israelites took captive from their kinsmen two hundred thousand wives, sons and daughters. They also took a great deal of plunder, which they carried back to Samaria.

⁹But a prophet of the LORD named Oded was there, and he went out to meet the army when it returned to Samaria. He said to them, "Because the LORD, the God of your fathers, was angry with Judah, he gave them into your hand. But you have slaughtered them in a rage that reaches to heaven. ¹⁰And now you intend to make the men and women of Judah and Jerusalem your slaves. But aren't you also guilty of sins against the LORD your God? ¹¹Now listen to me! Send back your fellow countrymen you have taken as prisoners, for the LORD's fierce anger rests on you."

¹²Then some of the leaders in Ephraim—Azariah son of Jehohanan, Berekiah son of Meshillemoth, Jehizkiah son of Shallum, and Amasa son of Hadlai—confronted those who were arriving from the war. ¹³"You must not bring those prisoners here," they said, "or we will be guilty before the LORD. Do you intend to add to our sin and guilt? For our guilt is already great, and his fierce anger rests on Israel."

¹⁴So the soldiers gave up the prisoners and plunder in the presence of the officials and all the assembly. ¹⁵The men designated by name took the prisoners, and from the plunder they clothed all who were naked. They provided them with clothes and sandals, food and drink, and healing balm. All those who were weak they put on donkeys. So they took them

---

*a5 That is, about 3 3/4 tons (about 3.4 metric tons)
*b5 That is, probably about 62,000 bushels (about 2,200 kiloliters)

back to their fellow countrymen at Jericho, the City of Palms, and returned to Samaria.

[16]At that time King Ahaz sent to the king[a] of Assyria for help. [17]The Edomites had again come and attacked Judah and carried away prisoners, [18]while the Philistines had raided towns in the foothills and in the Negev of Judah. They captured and occupied Beth Shemesh, Aijalon and Gederoth, as well as Soco, Timnah and Gimzo, with their surrounding villages. [19]The LORD had humbled Judah because of Ahaz king of Israel,[b] for he had promoted wickedness in Judah and had been most unfaithful to the LORD. [20]Tiglath-Pileser[c] king of Assyria came to him, but he gave him trouble instead of help. [21]Ahaz took some of the things from the temple of the LORD and from the royal palace and from the princes and presented them to the king of Assyria, but that did not help him.

[22]In his time of trouble King Ahaz became even more unfaithful to the LORD. [23]He offered sacrifices to the gods of Damascus, who had defeated him; for he thought, "Since the gods of the kings of Aram have helped them, I will sacrifice to them so they will help me." But they were his downfall and the downfall of all Israel.

[24]Ahaz gathered together the furnishings from the temple of God and took them away.[d] He shut the doors of the LORD's temple and set up altars at every street corner in Jerusalem. [25]In every town in Judah he built high places to burn sacrifices to other gods and provoked the LORD, the God of his fathers, to anger.

[26]The other events of his reign and all his ways, from beginning to end, are written in the book of the kings of Judah and Israel. [27]Ahaz rested with his fathers and was buried in the city of Jerusalem, but he was not placed in the tombs of the kings of Israel. And Hezekiah his son succeeded him as king.

Hezekiah Purifies the Temple

29 Hezekiah was twenty-five years old when he became king, and he reigned in Jerusalem twenty-nine years. His mother's name was Abijah daughter of Zechariah. [2]He did what was right in the eyes of the LORD, just as his father David had done.

[3]In the first month of the first year of his reign, he opened the doors of the temple of the LORD and repaired them. [4]He

brought in the priests and the Levites, assembled them in the square on the east side [5]and said: "Listen to me, Levites! Consecrate yourselves now and consecrate the temple of the LORD, the God of your fathers. Remove all defilement from the sanctuary. [6]Our fathers were unfaithful; they did evil in the eyes of the LORD our God and forsook him. They turned their faces away from the LORD's dwelling place and turned their backs on him. [7]They also shut the doors of the portico and put out the lamps. They did not burn incense or present any burnt offerings at the sanctuary to the God of Israel. [8]Therefore, the anger of the LORD has fallen on Judah and Jerusalem; he has made them an object of dread and horror and scorn, as you can see with your own eyes. [9]This is why our fathers have fallen by the sword and why our sons and daughters and our wives are in captivity. [10]Now I intend to make a covenant with the LORD, the God of Israel, so that his fierce anger will turn away from us. [11]My sons, do not be negligent now, for the LORD has chosen you to stand before him and serve him, to minister before him and to burn incense."

[12]Then these Levites set to work:

    from the Kohathites,
        Mahath son of Amasai and Joel son
          of Azariah;
    from the Merarites,
        Kish son of Abdi and Azariah son
          of Jehallelel;
    from the Gershonites,
        Joah son of Zimmah and Eden son
          of Joah;
[13] from the descendants of Elizaphan,
        Shimri and Jeiel;
    from the descendants of Asaph,
        Zechariah and Mattaniah;
[14] from the descendants of Heman,
        Jehiel and Shimei;
    from the descendants of Jeduthun,
        Shemaiah and Uzziel.

[15]When they had assembled their brothers and consecrated themselves, they went in to purify the temple of the LORD, as the king had ordered, following the word of the LORD. [16]The priests went into the sanctuary of the LORD to purify it. They brought out to the courtyard of the LORD's temple everything unclean that

---

[a]16 One Hebrew manuscript, Septuagint and Vulgate (see also 2 Kings 16:7); most Hebrew manuscripts *kings*   [b]19 That is, Judah, as frequently in 2 Chronicles   [c]20 Hebrew *Tilgath-Pilneser*, a variant of *Tiglath-Pileser*   [d]24 Or *and cut them up*

they found in the temple of the LORD. The Levites took it and carried it out to the Kidron Valley. [17]They began the consecration on the first day of the first month, and by the eighth day of the month they reached the portico of the LORD. For eight more days they consecrated the temple of the LORD itself, finishing on the sixteenth day of the first month.

[18]Then they went in to King Hezekiah and reported: "We have purified the entire temple of the LORD, the altar of burnt offering with all its utensils, and the table for setting out the consecrated bread, with all its articles. [19]We have prepared and consecrated all the articles that King Ahaz removed in his unfaithfulness while he was king. They are now in front of the LORD's altar."

[20]Early the next morning King Hezekiah gathered the city officials together and went up to the temple of the LORD. [21]They brought seven bulls, seven rams, seven male lambs and seven male goats as a sin offering for the kingdom, for the sanctuary and for Judah. The king commanded the priests, the descendants of Aaron, to offer these on the altar of the LORD. [22]So they slaughtered the bulls, and the priests took the blood and sprinkled it on the altar; next they slaughtered the rams and sprinkled their blood on the altar; then they slaughtered the lambs and sprinkled their blood on the altar. [23]The goats for the sin offering were brought before the king and the assembly, and they laid their hands on them. [24]The priests then slaughtered the goats and presented their blood on the altar for a sin offering to atone for all Israel, because the king had ordered the burnt offering and the sin offering for all Israel.

[25]He stationed the Levites in the temple of the LORD with cymbals, harps and lyres in the way prescribed by David and Gad the king's seer and Nathan the prophet; this was commanded by the LORD through his prophets. [26]So the Levites stood ready with David's instruments, and the priests with their trumpets.

[27]Hezekiah gave the order to sacrifice the burnt offering on the altar. As the offering began, singing to the LORD began also, accompanied by trumpets and the instruments of David king of Israel. [28]The whole assembly bowed in worship, while the singers sang and the trumpeters played. All this continued until the sacrifice of the burnt offering was completed.

[29]When the offerings were finished, the king and everyone present with him knelt down and worshiped. [30]King Hezekiah and his officials ordered the Levites to praise the LORD with the words of David and of Asaph the seer. So they sang praises with gladness and bowed their heads and worshiped.

[31]Then Hezekiah said, "You have now dedicated yourselves to the LORD. Come and bring sacrifices and thank offerings to the temple of the LORD." So the assembly brought sacrifices and thank offerings, and all whose hearts were willing brought burnt offerings.

[32]The number of burnt offerings the assembly brought was seventy bulls, a hundred rams and two hundred male lambs—all of them for burnt offerings to the LORD. [33]The animals consecrated as sacrifices amounted to six hundred bulls and three thousand sheep and goats. [34]The priests, however, were too few to skin all the burnt offerings; so their kinsmen the Levites helped them until the task was finished and until other priests had been consecrated, for the Levites had been more conscientious in consecrating themselves than the priests had been. [35]There were burnt offerings in abundance, together with the fat of the fellowship offerings[a] and the drink offerings that accompanied the burnt offerings.

So the service of the temple of the LORD was reestablished. [36]Hezekiah and all the people rejoiced at what God had brought about for his people, because it was done so quickly.

Hezekiah Celebrates the Passover

30 Hezekiah sent word to all Israel and Judah and also wrote letters to Ephraim and Manasseh, inviting them to come to the temple of the LORD in Jerusalem and celebrate the Passover to the LORD, the God of Israel. [2]The king and his officials and the whole assembly in Jerusalem decided to celebrate the Passover in the second month. [3]They had not been able to celebrate it at the regular time because not enough priests had consecrated themselves and the people had not assembled in Jerusalem. [4]The plan seemed right both to the king and to the whole assembly. [5]They decided to send a proclamation throughout Israel, from Beersheba to Dan, calling the people to come to Jerusalem and celebrate the

[a]35 Traditionally *peace offerings*

Passover to the LORD, the God of Israel. It had not been celebrated in large numbers according to what was written. [6]At the king's command, couriers went throughout Israel and Judah with letters from the king and from his officials, which read:

"People of Israel, return to the LORD, the God of Abraham, Isaac and Israel, that he may return to you who are left, who have escaped from the hand of the kings of Assyria. [7]Do not be like your fathers and brothers, who were unfaithful to the LORD, the God of their fathers, so that he made them an object of horror, as you see. [8]Do not be stiff-necked, as your fathers were; submit to the LORD. Come to the sanctuary, which he has consecrated forever. Serve the LORD your God, so that his fierce anger will turn away from you. [9]If you return to the LORD, then your brothers and your children will be shown compassion by their captors and will come back to this land, for the LORD your God is gracious and compassionate. He will not turn his face from you if you return to him."

[10]The couriers went from town to town in Ephraim and Manasseh, as far as Zebulun, but the people scorned and ridiculed them. [11]Nevertheless, some men of Asher, Manasseh and Zebulun humbled themselves and went to Jerusalem. [12]Also in Judah the hand of God was on the people to give them unity of mind to carry out what the king and his officials had ordered, following the word of the LORD.

[13]A very large crowd of people assembled in Jerusalem to celebrate the Feast of Unleavened Bread in the second month. [14]They removed the altars in Jerusalem and cleared away the incense altars and threw them into the Kidron Valley.

[15]They slaughtered the Passover lamb on the fourteenth day of the second month. The priests and the Levites were ashamed and consecrated themselves and brought burnt offerings to the temple of the LORD. [16]Then they took up their regular positions as prescribed in the Law of Moses the man of God. The priests sprinkled the blood handed to them by the Levites. [17]Since many in the crowd had not consecrated themselves, the Levites had to kill the Passover lambs for all those who were not ceremonially clean and could not consecrate their lambs to the LORD. [18]Although most of the many people who came from Ephraim, Manasseh, Issachar and Zebulun had not purified themselves, yet they ate the Passover, contrary to what was written. But Hezekiah prayed for them, saying, "May the LORD, who is good, pardon everyone [19]who sets his heart on seeking God—the LORD, the God of his fathers—even if he is not clean according to the rules of the sanctuary." [20]And the LORD heard Hezekiah and healed the people.

[21]The Israelites who were present in Jerusalem celebrated the Feast of Unleavened Bread for seven days with great rejoicing, while the Levites and priests sang to the LORD every day, accompanied by the LORD's instruments of praise.[a] [22]Hezekiah spoke encouragingly to all the Levites, who showed good understanding of the service of the LORD. For the seven days they ate their assigned portion and offered fellowship offerings[b] and praised the LORD, the God of their fathers.

[23]The whole assembly then agreed to celebrate the festival seven more days; so for another seven days they celebrated joyfully. [24]Hezekiah king of Judah provided a thousand bulls and seven thousand sheep and goats for the assembly, and the officials provided them with a thousand bulls and ten thousand sheep and goats. A great number of priests consecrated themselves. [25]The entire assembly of Judah rejoiced, along with the priests and Levites and all who had assembled from Israel, including the aliens who had come from Israel and those who lived in Judah. [26]There was great joy in Jerusalem, for since the days of Solomon son of David king of Israel there had been nothing like this in Jerusalem. [27]The priests and the Levites stood to bless the people, and God heard them, for their prayer reached heaven, his holy dwelling place.

31 When all this had ended, the Israelites who were there went out to the towns of Judah, smashed the sacred stones and cut down the Asherah poles. They destroyed the high places and the altars throughout Judah and Benjamin and in Ephraim and Manasseh. After they had destroyed all of them, the Israelites returned to their own towns and to their own property.

[a]21 Or *priests praised the LORD every day with resounding instruments belonging to the LORD*
[b]22 Traditionally *peace offerings*

Contributions for Worship

2Hezekiah assigned the priests and Levites to divisions—each of them according to their duties as priests or Levites—to offer burnt offerings and fellowship offerings,[a] to minister, to give thanks and to sing praises at the gates of the LORD's dwelling. **3**The king contributed from his own possessions for the morning and evening burnt offerings and for the burnt offerings on the Sabbaths, New Moons and appointed feasts as written in the Law of the LORD. **4**He ordered the people living in Jerusalem to give the portion due the priests and Levites so they could devote themselves to the Law of the LORD. **5**As soon as the order went out, the Israelites generously gave the firstfruits of their grain, new wine, oil and honey and all that the fields produced. They brought a great amount, a tithe of everything. **6**The men of Israel and Judah who lived in the towns of Judah also brought a tithe of their herds and flocks and a tithe of the holy things dedicated to the LORD their God, and they piled them in heaps. **7**They began doing this in the third month and finished in the seventh month. **8**When Hezekiah and his officials came and saw the heaps, they praised the LORD and blessed his people Israel.

9Hezekiah asked the priests and Levites about the heaps; **10**and Azariah the chief priest, from the family of Zadok, answered, "Since the people began to bring their contributions to the temple of the LORD, we have had enough to eat and plenty to spare, because the LORD has blessed his people, and this great amount is left over."

11Hezekiah gave orders to prepare storerooms in the temple of the LORD, and this was done. **12**Then they faithfully brought in the contributions, tithes and dedicated gifts. Conaniah, a Levite, was in charge of these things, and his brother Shimei was next in rank. **13**Jehiel, Azaziah, Nahath, Asahel, Jerimoth, Jozabad, Eliel, Ismakiah, Mahath and Benaiah were supervisors under Conaniah and Shimei his brother, by appointment of King Hezekiah and Azariah the official in charge of the temple of God.

14Kore son of Imnah the Levite, keeper of the East Gate, was in charge of the freewill offerings given to God, distributing the contributions made to the LORD and also the consecrated gifts. **15**Eden, Miniamin, Jeshua, Shemaiah, Amariah and Shecaniah assisted him faithfully in the towns of the priests, distributing to their fellow priests according to their divisions, old and young alike.

16In addition, they distributed to the males three years old or more whose names were in the genealogical records—all who would enter the temple of the LORD to perform the daily duties of their various tasks, according to their responsibilities and their divisions. **17**And they distributed to the priests enrolled by their families in the genealogical records and likewise to the Levites twenty years old or more, according to their responsibilities and their divisions. **18**They included all the little ones, the wives, and the sons and daughters of the whole community listed in these genealogical records. For they were faithful in consecrating themselves.

19As for the priests, the descendants of Aaron, who lived on the farm lands around their towns or in any other towns, men were designated by name to distribute portions to every male among them and to all who were recorded in the genealogies of the Levites.

20This is what Hezekiah did throughout Judah, doing what was good and right and faithful before the LORD his God. **21**In everything that he undertook in the service of God's temple and in obedience to the law and the commands, he sought his God and worked wholeheartedly. And so he prospered.

Sennacherib Threatens Jerusalem

32 After all that Hezekiah had so faithfully done, Sennacherib king of Assyria came and invaded Judah. He laid siege to the fortified cities, thinking to conquer them for himself. **2**When Hezekiah saw that Sennacherib had come and that he intended to make war on Jerusalem, **3**he consulted with his officials and military staff about blocking off the water from the springs outside the city, and they helped him. **4**A large force of men assembled, and they blocked all the springs and the stream that flowed through the land. "Why should the kings[b] of Assyria come and find plenty of water?" they said. **5**Then he worked hard repairing all the broken sections of the wall and building towers on it. He built another wall outside that one and reinforced the supporting

<hr/>

[a]2 Traditionally *peace offerings*   [b]4 Hebrew; Septuagint and Syriac *king*

terraces[a] of the City of David. He also made large numbers of weapons and shields.

[6]He appointed military officers over the people and assembled them before him in the square at the city gate and encouraged them with these words: [7]"Be strong and courageous. Do not be afraid or discouraged because of the king of Assyria and the vast army with him, for there is a greater power with us than with him. [8]With him is only the arm of flesh, but with us is the LORD our God to help us and to fight our battles." And the people gained confidence from what Hezekiah the king of Judah said.

[9]Later, when Sennacherib king of Assyria and all his forces were laying siege to Lachish, he sent his officers to Jerusalem with this message for Hezekiah king of Judah and for all the people of Judah who were there:

[10]"This is what Sennacherib king of Assyria says: On what are you basing your confidence, that you remain in Jerusalem under siege? [11]When Hezekiah says, 'The LORD our God will save us from the hand of the king of Assyria,' he is misleading you, to let you die of hunger and thirst. [12]Did not Hezekiah himself remove this god's high places and altars, saying to Judah and Jerusalem, 'You must worship before one altar and burn sacrifices on it'?

[13]"Do you not know what I and my fathers have done to all the peoples of the other lands? Were the gods of those nations ever able to deliver their land from my hand? [14]Who of all the gods of these nations that my fathers destroyed has been able to save his people from me? How then can your god deliver you from my hand? [15]Now do not let Hezekiah deceive you and mislead you like this. Do not believe him, for no god of any nation or kingdom has been able to deliver his people from my hand or the hand of my fathers. How much less will your god deliver you from my hand!"

[16]Sennacherib's officers spoke further against the LORD God and against his servant Hezekiah. [17]The king also wrote letters insulting the LORD, the God of Israel, and saying this against him: "Just as the gods of the peoples of the other lands did not rescue their people from my hand, so the god of Hezekiah will not rescue his

people from my hand." [18]Then they called out in Hebrew to the people of Jerusalem who were on the wall, to terrify them and make them afraid in order to capture the city. [19]They spoke about the God of Jerusalem as they did about the gods of the other peoples of the world—the work of men's hands.

[20]King Hezekiah and the prophet Isaiah son of Amoz cried out in prayer to heaven about this. [21]And the LORD sent an angel, who annihilated all the fighting men and the leaders and officers in the camp of the Assyrian king. So he withdrew to his own land in disgrace. And when he went into the temple of his god, some of his sons cut him down with the sword.

[22]So the LORD saved Hezekiah and the people of Jerusalem from the hand of Sennacherib king of Assyria and from the hand of all others. He took care of them[b] on every side. [23]Many brought offerings to Jerusalem for the LORD and valuable gifts for Hezekiah king of Judah. From then on he was highly regarded by all the nations.

Hezekiah's Pride, Success and Death

[24]In those days Hezekiah became ill and was at the point of death. He prayed to the LORD, who answered him and gave him a miraculous sign. [25]But Hezekiah's heart was proud and he did not respond to the kindness shown him; therefore the LORD's wrath was on him and on Judah and Jerusalem. [26]Then Hezekiah repented of the pride of his heart, as did the people of Jerusalem; therefore the LORD's wrath did not come upon them during the days of Hezekiah.

[27]Hezekiah had very great riches and honor, and he made treasuries for his silver and gold and for his precious stones, spices, shields and all kinds of valuables. [28]He also made buildings to store the harvest of grain, new wine and oil; and he made stalls for various kinds of cattle, and pens for the flocks. [29]He built villages and acquired great numbers of flocks and herds, for God had given him very great riches.

[30]It was Hezekiah who blocked the upper outlet of the Gihon spring and channeled the water down to the west side of the City of David. He succeeded in everything he undertook. [31]But when envoys were sent by the rulers of Babylon to ask

[a]5 Or the Millo   [b]22 Hebrew; Septuagint and Vulgate He gave them rest

him about the miraculous sign that had occurred in the land, God left him to test him and to know everything that was in his heart.

³²The other events of Hezekiah's reign and his acts of devotion are written in the vision of the prophet Isaiah son of Amoz in the book of the kings of Judah and Israel. ³³Hezekiah rested with his fathers and was buried on the hill where the tombs of David's descendants are. All Judah and the people of Jerusalem honored him when he died. And Manasseh his son succeeded him as king.

Manasseh King of Judah

33 Manasseh was twelve years old when he became king, and he reigned in Jerusalem fifty-five years. ²He did evil in the eyes of the LORD, following the detestable practices of the nations the LORD had driven out before the Israelites. ³He rebuilt the high places his father Hezekiah had demolished; he also erected altars to the Baals and made Asherah poles. He bowed down to all the starry hosts and worshiped them. ⁴He built altars in the temple of the LORD, of which the LORD had said, "My Name will remain in Jerusalem forever." ⁵In both courts of the temple of the LORD, he built altars to all the starry hosts. ⁶He sacrificed his sons in*ᵃ* the fire in the Valley of Ben Hinnom, practiced sorcery, divination and witchcraft, and consulted mediums and spiritists. He did much evil in the eyes of the LORD, provoking him to anger.

⁷He took the carved image he had made and put it in God's temple, of which God had said to David and to his son Solomon, "In this temple and in Jerusalem, which I have chosen out of all the tribes of Israel, I will put my Name forever. ⁸I will not again make the feet of the Israelites leave the land I assigned to your forefathers, if only they will be careful to do everything I commanded them concerning all the laws, decrees and ordinances given through Moses." ⁹But Manasseh led Judah and the people of Jerusalem astray, so that they did more evil than the nations the LORD had destroyed before the Israelites.

¹⁰The LORD spoke to Manasseh and his people, but they paid no attention. ¹¹So the LORD brought against them the army commanders of the king of Assyria, who took Manasseh prisoner, put a hook in his nose, bound him with bronze shackles and took him to Babylon. ¹²In his distress

he sought the favor of the LORD his God and humbled himself greatly before the God of his fathers. ¹³And when he prayed to him, the LORD was moved by his entreaty and listened to his plea; so he brought him back to Jerusalem and to his kingdom. Then Manasseh knew that the LORD is God.

¹⁴Afterward he rebuilt the outer wall of the City of David, west of the Gihon spring in the valley, as far as the entrance of the Fish Gate and encircling the hill of Ophel; he also made it much higher. He stationed military commanders in all the fortified cities in Judah.

¹⁵He got rid of the foreign gods and removed the image from the temple of the LORD, as well as all the altars he had built on the temple hill and in Jerusalem; and he threw them out of the city. ¹⁶Then he restored the altar of the LORD and sacrificed fellowship offerings*ᵇ* and thank offerings on it, and told Judah to serve the LORD, the God of Israel. ¹⁷The people, however, continued to sacrifice at the high places, but only to the LORD their God.

¹⁸The other events of Manasseh's reign, including his prayer to his God and the words the seers spoke to him in the name of the LORD, the God of Israel, are written in the annals of the kings of Israel.*ᶜ* ¹⁹His prayer and how God was moved by his entreaty, as well as all his sins and unfaithfulness, and the sites where he built high places and set up Asherah poles and idols before he humbled himself—all are written in the records of the seers.*ᵈ* ²⁰Manasseh rested with his fathers and was buried in his palace. And Amon his son succeeded him as king.

Amon King of Judah

²¹Amon was twenty-two years old when he became king, and he reigned in Jerusalem two years. ²²He did evil in the eyes of the LORD, as his father Manasseh had done. Amon worshiped and offered sacrifices to all the idols Manasseh had made. ²³But unlike his father Manasseh, he did not humble himself before the LORD; Amon increased his guilt.

²⁴Amon's officials conspired against him and assassinated him in his palace.

ᵃ6 Or *He made his sons pass through*
ᵇ16 Traditionally *peace offerings*   *ᶜ18* That is, Judah, as frequently in 2 Chronicles   *ᵈ19* One Hebrew manuscript and Septuagint; most Hebrew manuscripts *of Hozai*

²⁵Then the people of the land killed all who had plotted against King Amon, and they made Josiah his son king in his place.

Josiah's Reforms

34 Josiah was eight years old when he became king, and he reigned in Jerusalem thirty-one years. ²He did what was right in the eyes of the LORD and walked in the ways of his father David, not turning aside to the right or to the left.

³In the eighth year of his reign, while he was still young, he began to seek the God of his father David. In his twelfth year he began to purge Judah and Jerusalem of high places, Asherah poles, carved idols and cast images. ⁴Under his direction the altars of the Baals were torn down; he cut to pieces the incense altars that were above them, and smashed the Asherah poles, the idols and the images. These he broke to pieces and scattered over the graves of those who had sacrificed to them. ⁵He burned the bones of the priests on their altars, and so he purged Judah and Jerusalem. ⁶In the towns of Manasseh, Ephraim and Simeon, as far as Naphtali, and in the ruins around them, ⁷he tore down the altars and the Asherah poles and crushed the idols to powder and cut to pieces all the incense altars throughout Israel. Then he went back to Jerusalem.

⁸In the eighteenth year of Josiah's reign, to purify the land and the temple, he sent Shaphan son of Azaliah and Maaseiah the ruler of the city, with Joah son of Joahaz, the recorder, to repair the temple of the LORD his God.

⁹They went to Hilkiah the high priest and gave him the money that had been brought into the temple of God, which the Levites who were the doorkeepers had collected from the people of Manasseh, Ephraim and the entire remnant of Israel and from all the people of Judah and Benjamin and the inhabitants of Jerusalem. ¹⁰Then they entrusted it to the men appointed to supervise the work on the LORD's temple. These men paid the workers who repaired and restored the temple. ¹¹They also gave money to the carpenters and builders to purchase dressed stone, and timber for joists and beams for the buildings that the kings of Judah had allowed to fall into ruin.

¹²The men did the work faithfully. Over them to direct them were Jahath and Obadiah, Levites descended from Merari, and Zechariah and Meshullam, descended from Kohath. The Levites—all who were skilled in playing musical instruments—¹³had charge of the laborers and supervised all the workers from job to job. Some of the Levites were secretaries, scribes and doorkeepers.

The Book of the Law Found

¹⁴While they were bringing out the money that had been taken into the temple of the LORD, Hilkiah the priest found the Book of the Law of the LORD that had been given through Moses. ¹⁵Hilkiah said to Shaphan the secretary, "I have found the Book of the Law in the temple of the LORD." He gave it to Shaphan.

¹⁶Then Shaphan took the book to the king and reported to him: "Your officials are doing everything that has been committed to them. ¹⁷They have paid out the money that was in the temple of the LORD and have entrusted it to the supervisors and workers." ¹⁸Then Shaphan the secretary informed the king, "Hilkiah the priest has given me a book." And Shaphan read from it in the presence of the king.

¹⁹When the king heard the words of the Law, he tore his robes. ²⁰He gave these orders to Hilkiah, Ahikam son of Shaphan, Abdon son of Micah,ᵃ Shaphan the secretary and Asaiah the king's attendant: ²¹"Go and inquire of the LORD for me and for the remnant in Israel and Judah about what is written in this book that has been found. Great is the LORD's anger that is poured out on us because our fathers have not kept the word of the LORD; they have not acted in accordance with all that is written in this book."

²²Hilkiah and those the king had sent with himᵇ went to speak to the prophetess Huldah, who was the wife of Shallum son of Tokhath,ᶜ the son of Hasrah,ᵈ keeper of the wardrobe. She lived in Jerusalem, in the Second District.

²³She said to them, "This is what the LORD, the God of Israel, says: Tell the man who sent you to me, ²⁴'This is what the LORD says: I am going to bring disaster on this place and its people—all the curses written in the book that has been read in the presence of the king of Judah. ²⁵Because they have forsaken me and burned

---

ᵃ20 Also called *Acbor son of Micaiah*   ᵇ22 One Hebrew manuscript, Vulgate and Syriac; most Hebrew manuscripts do not have *had sent with him.*   ᶜ22 Also called *Tikvah*   ᵈ22 Also called *Harhas*

incense to other gods and provoked me to anger by all that their hands have made,[a] my anger will be poured out on this place and will not be quenched.' ²⁶Tell the king of Judah, who sent you to inquire of the LORD, 'This is what the LORD, the God of Israel, says concerning the words you heard: ²⁷Because your heart was responsive and you humbled yourself before God when you heard what he spoke against this place and its people, and because you humbled yourself before me and tore your robes and wept in my presence, I have heard you, declares the LORD. ²⁸Now I will gather you to your fathers, and you will be buried in peace. Your eyes will not see all the disaster I am going to bring on this place and on those who live here.' "

So they took her answer back to the king.

²⁹Then the king called together all the elders of Judah and Jerusalem. ³⁰He went up to the temple of the LORD with the men of Judah, the people of Jerusalem, the priests and the Levites—all the people from the least to the greatest. He read in their hearing all the words of the Book of the Covenant, which had been found in the temple of the LORD. ³¹The king stood by his pillar and renewed the covenant in the presence of the LORD—to follow the LORD and keep his commands, regula-

tions and decrees with all his heart and all his soul, and to obey the words of the covenant written in this book.

³²Then he had everyone in Jerusalem and Benjamin pledge themselves to it; the people of Jerusalem did this in accordance with the covenant of God, the God of their fathers.

³³Josiah removed all the detestable idols from all the territory belonging to the Israelites, and he had all who were present in Israel serve the LORD their God. As long as he lived, they did not fail to follow the LORD, the God of their fathers.

Josiah Celebrates the Passover

35 Josiah celebrated the Passover to the LORD in Jerusalem, and the Passover lamb was slaughtered on the fourteenth day of the first month. ²He appointed the priests to their duties and encouraged them in the service of the LORD's temple. ³He said to the Levites, who instructed all Israel and who had been consecrated to the LORD: "Put the sacred ark in the temple that Solomon son of David king of Israel built. It is not to be carried about on your shoulders. Now serve the LORD your God and his people Israel. ⁴Prepare yourselves by families in your divisions, ac-

[a]25 Or *by everything they have done*

HEY DAD

Will God punish me when I sin—even if I don't know I'm sinning?

QUESTIONS KIDS ASK

Text: 2 Chronicles 34:14–33

God is a merciful God, and he sees when our hearts are right, even if we make a mistake. But if we sin because we haven't learned what God says in his Word, God will still hold us accountable.

As hard as it may be to believe, the Israelites at one time completely forgot about the Book of the Law God had given Moses. For all practical purposes, this book was lost. The Jews didn't teach their children the laws, and before long, the Israelites weren't following the rules at all! Yet, despite their ignorance, God was angry (v. 21). In God's eyes, broken rules are broken rules.

But when Josiah became king, he turned back to God. Soon after that, one of the priests found the Book of the Law that had been lost for so long (vv. 14–15). When King Josiah read the book, he wept because he knew his people had been sinning against God all the time that this book had been lost. After Josiah read from the Book of the Law (v. 30), he asked the people to "pledge themselves to it" (v. 32), and the people followed the Lord for as long as Josiah was king.

From this story we learn that God has mercy on us, but we'd better make sure we learn his rules, all the same. Only in obeying God's Word will we experience God's best for ourselves.

For a complete listing of Questions Kids Ask, turn to page 1435.

cording to the directions written by David king of Israel and by his son Solomon. 5"Stand in the holy place with a group of Levites for each subdivision of the families of your fellow countrymen, the lay people. 6Slaughter the Passover lambs, consecrate yourselves and prepare the lambs for your fellow countrymen, doing what the LORD commanded through Moses." 7Josiah provided for all the lay people who were there a total of thirty thousand sheep and goats for the Passover offerings, and also three thousand cattle—all from the king's own possessions.

8His officials also contributed voluntarily to the people and the priests and Levites. Hilkiah, Zechariah and Jehiel, the administrators of God's temple, gave the priests twenty-six hundred Passover offerings and three hundred cattle. 9Also Conaniah along with Shemaiah and Nethanel, his brothers, and Hashabiah, Jeiel and Jozabad, the leaders of the Levites, provided five thousand Passover offerings and five hundred head of cattle for the Levites.

10The service was arranged and the priests stood in their places with the Levites in their divisions as the king had ordered. 11The Passover lambs were slaughtered, and the priests sprinkled the blood handed to them, while the Levites skinned the animals. 12They set aside the burnt offerings to give them to the subdivisions of the families of the people to offer to the LORD, as is written in the Book of Moses. They did the same with the cattle. 13They roasted the Passover animals over the fire as prescribed, and boiled the holy offerings in pots, caldrons and pans and served them quickly to all the people. 14After this, they made preparations for themselves and for the priests, because the priests, the descendants of Aaron, were sacrificing the burnt offerings and the fat portions until nightfall. So the Levites made preparations for themselves and for the Aaronic priests.

15The musicians, the descendants of Asaph, were in the places prescribed by David, Asaph, Heman and Jeduthun the king's seer. The gatekeepers at each gate did not need to leave their posts, because their fellow Levites made the preparations for them.

16So at that time the entire service of the LORD was carried out for the celebration of the Passover and the offering of burnt offerings on the altar of the LORD, as King Josiah had ordered. 17The Israelites who were present celebrated the Passover at that time and observed the Feast of Unleavened Bread for seven days. 18The Passover had not been observed like this in Israel since the days of the prophet Samuel; and none of the kings of Israel had ever celebrated such a Passover as did Josiah, with the priests, the Levites and all Judah and Israel who were there with the people of Jerusalem. 19This Passover was celebrated in the eighteenth year of Josiah's reign.

The Death of Josiah

20After all this, when Josiah had set the temple in order, Neco king of Egypt went up to fight at Carchemish on the Euphrates, and Josiah marched out to meet him in battle. 21But Neco sent messengers to him, saying, "What quarrel is there between you and me, O king of Judah? It is not you I am attacking at this time, but the house with which I am at war. God has told me to hurry; so stop opposing God, who is with me, or he will destroy you."

22Josiah, however, would not turn away from him, but disguised himself to engage him in battle. He would not listen to what Neco had said at God's command but went to fight him on the plain of Megiddo.

23Archers shot King Josiah, and he told his officers, "Take me away; I am badly wounded." 24So they took him out of his chariot, put him in the other chariot he had and brought him to Jerusalem, where he died. He was buried in the tombs of his fathers, and all Judah and Jerusalem mourned for him.

25Jeremiah composed laments for Josiah, and to this day all the men and women singers commemorate Josiah in the laments. These became a tradition in Israel and are written in the Laments.

26The other events of Josiah's reign and his acts of devotion, according to what is written in the Law of the LORD— 27all the events, from beginning to end, are written in the book of the kings of Israel and **36** Judah. 1And the people of the land took Jehoahaz son of Josiah and made him king in Jerusalem in place of his father.

Jehoahaz King of Judah

2Jehoahaz[a] was twenty-three years old when he became king, and he reigned in

a2 Hebrew Joahaz, a variant of Jehoahaz; also in verse 4

Jerusalem three months. ³The king of Egypt dethroned him in Jerusalem and imposed on Judah a levy of a hundred talents*a* of silver and a talent*b* of gold. ⁴The king of Egypt made Eliakim, a brother of Jehoahaz, king over Judah and Jerusalem and changed Eliakim's name to Jehoiakim. But Neco took Eliakim's brother Jehoahaz and carried him off to Egypt.

Jehoiakim King of Judah

⁵Jehoiakim was twenty-five years old when he became king, and he reigned in Jerusalem eleven years. He did evil in the eyes of the LORD his God. ⁶Nebuchadnezzar king of Babylon attacked him and bound him with bronze shackles to take him to Babylon. ⁷Nebuchadnezzar also took to Babylon articles from the temple of the LORD and put them in his temple*c* there.

⁸The other events of Jehoiakim's reign, the detestable things he did and all that was found against him, are written in the book of the kings of Israel and Judah. And Jehoiachin his son succeeded him as king.

Jehoiachin King of Judah

⁹Jehoiachin was eighteen*d* years old when he became king, and he reigned in Jerusalem three months and ten days. He did evil in the eyes of the LORD. ¹⁰In the spring, King Nebuchadnezzar sent for him and brought him to Babylon, together with articles of value from the temple of the LORD, and he made Jehoiachin's uncle,*e* Zedekiah, king over Judah and Jerusalem.

Zedekiah King of Judah

¹¹Zedekiah was twenty-one years old when he became king, and he reigned in Jerusalem eleven years. ¹²He did evil in the eyes of the LORD his God and did not humble himself before Jeremiah the prophet, who spoke the word of the LORD. ¹³He also rebelled against King Nebuchadnezzar, who had made him take an oath in God's name. He became stiff-necked and hardened his heart and would not turn to the LORD, the God of Israel. ¹⁴Furthermore, all the leaders of the priests and the people became more and more unfaithful, following all the detestable practices of the nations and defiling

the temple of the LORD, which he had consecrated in Jerusalem.

The Fall of Jerusalem

¹⁵The LORD, the God of their fathers, sent word to them through his messengers again and again, because he had pity on his people and on his dwelling place. ¹⁶But they mocked God's messengers, despised his words and scoffed at his prophets until the wrath of the LORD was aroused against his people and there was no remedy. ¹⁷He brought up against them the king of the Babylonians,*f* who killed their young men with the sword in the sanctuary, and spared neither young man nor young woman, old man or aged. God handed all of them over to Nebuchadnezzar. ¹⁸He carried to Babylon all the articles from the temple of God, both large and small, and the treasures of the LORD's temple and the treasures of the king and his officials. ¹⁹They set fire to God's temple and broke down the wall of Jerusalem; they burned all the palaces and destroyed everything of value there.

²⁰He carried into exile to Babylon the remnant, who escaped from the sword, and they became servants to him and his sons until the kingdom of Persia came to power. ²¹The land enjoyed its sabbath rests; all the time of its desolation it rested, until the seventy years were completed in fulfillment of the word of the LORD spoken by Jeremiah.

²²In the first year of Cyrus king of Persia, in order to fulfill the word of the LORD spoken by Jeremiah, the LORD moved the heart of Cyrus king of Persia to make a proclamation throughout his realm and to put it in writing:

²³"This is what Cyrus king of Persia says:

" 'The LORD, the God of heaven, has given me all the kingdoms of the earth and he has appointed me to build a temple for him at Jerusalem in Judah. Anyone of his people among you—may the LORD his God be with him, and let him go up.' "

---

a3 That is, about 3 3/4 tons (about 3.4 metric tons)
b3 That is, about 75 pounds (about 34 kilograms)
c7 Or palace   d9 One Hebrew manuscript, some Septuagint manuscripts and Syriac (see also 2 Kings 24:8); most Hebrew manuscripts *eight*
e10 Hebrew *brother*, that is, relative (see 2 Kings 24:17)   *f17 Or Chaldeans*

The Gospel of Luke tells three familiar stories about a lost sheep, a lost coin, and a lost son ... three very precious things in the eyes of their owners. But in telling the story, Jesus let us in on this interesting truth: Wonderful things become even more special when one gets them back after they're lost.

This was true of the Jews' house of worship ... their priceless temple. After enduring generations of his people's disobedience, God had allowed them to be taken into captivity. Their beautiful temple had been looted and destroyed by hostile neighbors. Now, with the people freshly released from captivity in Babylon, Zerubbabel organized a massive rebuilding project. With every step toward reconstruction, the people rejoiced. What they thought they had lost was being reclaimed!

The book of Ezra is more than a story about the restoration of a building; it's also a powerful illustration of God's grace. Lost and broken things have something to hope for—forgiveness and restoration. This is good news for lost dads ... and lost kids, too.

Ezra

Cyrus Helps the Exiles to Return

1 In the first year of Cyrus king of Persia, in order to fulfill the word of the LORD spoken by Jeremiah, the LORD moved the heart of Cyrus king of Persia to make a proclamation throughout his realm and to put it in writing:

²"This is what Cyrus king of Persia says:

" 'The LORD, the God of heaven, has given me all the kingdoms of the earth and he has appointed me to build a temple for him at Jerusalem in Judah. ³Anyone of his people among you—may his God be with him, and let him go up to Jerusalem in Judah and build the temple of the LORD, the God of Israel, the God who is in Jerusalem. ⁴And the people of any place where survivors may now be living are to provide him with silver and gold, with goods and livestock, and with freewill offerings for the temple of God in Jerusalem.' "

⁵Then the family heads of Judah and Benjamin, and the priests and Levites—everyone whose heart God had moved—prepared to go up and build the house of the LORD in Jerusalem. ⁶All their neighbors assisted them with articles of silver and gold, with goods and livestock, and with valuable gifts, in addition to all the freewill offerings. ⁷Moreover, King Cyrus brought

out the articles belonging to the temple of the LORD, which Nebuchadnezzar had carried away from Jerusalem and had placed in the temple of his god.[a] [8]Cyrus king of Persia had them brought by Mithredath the treasurer, who counted them out to Sheshbazzar the prince of Judah.

[9]This was the inventory:

gold dishes	30
silver dishes	1,000
silver pans[b]	29
[10]gold bowls	30
matching silver bowls	410
other articles	1,000

[11]In all, there were 5,400 articles of gold and of silver. Sheshbazzar brought all these along when the exiles came up from Babylon to Jerusalem.

The List of the Exiles Who Returned

2 Now these are the people of the province who came up from the captivity of the exiles, whom Nebuchadnezzar king of Babylon had taken captive to Babylon (they returned to Jerusalem and Judah, each to his own town, [2]in company with Zerubbabel, Jeshua, Nehemiah, Seraiah, Reelaiah, Mordecai, Bilshan, Mispar, Bigvai, Rehum and Baanah):

The list of the men of the people of Israel:

[3]the descendants of Parosh	2,172
[4]of Shephatiah	372
[5]of Arah	775
[6]of Pahath-Moab (through the line of Jeshua and Joab)	2,812
[7]of Elam	1,254
[8]of Zattu	945
[9]of Zaccai	760
[10]of Bani	642
[11]of Bebai	623
[12]of Azgad	1,222
[13]of Adonikam	666
[14]of Bigvai	2,056
[15]of Adin	454
[16]of Ater (through Hezekiah)	98
[17]of Bezai	323
[18]of Jorah	112
[19]of Hashum	223
[20]of Gibbar	95
[21]the men of Bethlehem	123
[22]of Netophah	56
[23]of Anathoth	128
[24]of Azmaveth	42
[25]of Kiriath Jearim,[c] Kephirah and Beeroth	743
[26]of Ramah and Geba	621

[27]of Micmash	122
[28]of Bethel and Ai	223
[29]of Nebo	52
[30]of Magbish	156
[31]of the other Elam	1,254
[32]of Harim	320
[33]of Lod, Hadid and Ono	725
[34]of Jericho	345
[35]of Senaah	3,630

[36]The priests:

the descendants of Jedaiah (through the family of Jeshua)	973
[37]of Immer	1,052
[38]of Pashhur	1,247
[39]of Harim	1,017

[40]The Levites:

the descendants of Jeshua and Kadmiel (through the line of Hodaviah)	74

[41]The singers:

the descendants of Asaph	128

[42]The gatekeepers of the temple:

the descendants of Shallum, Ater, Talmon, Akkub, Hatita and Shobai	139

[43]The temple servants:

the descendants of
Ziha, Hasupha, Tabbaoth,
[44]Keros, Siaha, Padon,
[45]Lebanah, Hagabah, Akkub,
[46]Hagab, Shalmai, Hanan,
[47]Giddel, Gahar, Reaiah,
[48]Rezin, Nekoda, Gazzam,
[49]Uzza, Paseah, Besai,
[50]Asnah, Meunim, Nephussim,
[51]Bakbuk, Hakupha, Harhur,
[52]Bazluth, Mehida, Harsha,
[53]Barkos, Sisera, Temah,
[54]Neziah and Hatipha

[55]The descendants of the servants of Solomon:

the descendants of
Sotai, Hassophereth, Peruda,
[56]Jaala, Darkon, Giddel,
[57]Shephatiah, Hattil,
Pokereth-Hazzebaim and Ami

[58]The temple servants and the descendants of the servants of Solomon	392

---

[a]7 Or gods [b]9 The meaning of the Hebrew for this word is uncertain. [c]25 See Septuagint (see also Neh. 7:29); Hebrew Kiriath Arim.

[59]The following came up from the towns of Tel Melah, Tel Harsha, Kerub, Addon and Immer, but they could not show that their families were descended from Israel:

[60]The descendants of
Delaiah, Tobiah and Nekoda   652

[61]And from among the priests:

The descendants of
Hobaiah, Hakkoz and Barzillai (a man who had married a daughter of Barzillai the Gileadite and was called by that name).

[62]These searched for their family records, but they could not find them and so were excluded from the priesthood as unclean. [63]The governor ordered them not to eat any of the most sacred food until there was a priest ministering with the Urim and Thummim.

[64]The whole company numbered 42,360, [65]besides their 7,337 menservants and maidservants; and they also had 200 men and women singers. [66]They had 736 horses, 245 mules, [67]435 camels and 6,720 donkeys.

[68]When they arrived at the house of the LORD in Jerusalem, some of the heads of the families gave freewill offerings toward the rebuilding of the house of God on its site. [69]According to their ability they gave to the treasury for this work 61,000 drachmas[a] of gold, 5,000 minas[b] of silver and 100 priestly garments.

[70]The priests, the Levites, the singers, the gatekeepers and the temple servants settled in their own towns, along with some of the other people, and the rest of the Israelites settled in their towns.

Rebuilding the Altar

3 When the seventh month came and the Israelites had settled in their towns, the people assembled as one man in Jerusalem. [2]Then Jeshua son of Jozadak and his fellow priests and Zerubbabel son of Shealtiel and his associates began to build the altar of the God of Israel to sacrifice burnt offerings on it, in accordance with what is written in the Law of Moses the man of God. [3]Despite their fear of the peoples around them, they built the altar on its foundation and sacrificed burnt offerings on it to the LORD, both the morning and evening sacrifices. [4]Then in accordance

with what is written, they celebrated the Feast of Tabernacles with the required number of burnt offerings prescribed for each day. [5]After that, they presented the regular burnt offerings, the New Moon sacrifices and the sacrifices for all the appointed sacred feasts of the LORD, as well as those brought as freewill offerings to the LORD. [6]On the first day of the seventh month they began to offer burnt offerings to the LORD, though the foundation of the LORD's temple had not yet been laid.

Rebuilding the Temple

[7]Then they gave money to the masons and carpenters, and gave food and drink and oil to the people of Sidon and Tyre, so that they would bring cedar logs by sea from Lebanon to Joppa, as authorized by Cyrus king of Persia.

[8]In the second month of the second year after their arrival at the house of God in Jerusalem, Zerubbabel son of Shealtiel, Jeshua son of Jozadak and the rest of their brothers (the priests and the Levites and all who had returned from the captivity to Jerusalem) began the work, appointing Levites twenty years of age and older to supervise the building of the house of the LORD. [9]Jeshua and his sons and brothers and Kadmiel and his sons (descendants of Hodaviah[c]) and the sons of Henadad and their sons and brothers—all Levites—joined together in supervising those working on the house of God.

[10]When the builders laid the foundation of the temple of the LORD, the priests in their vestments and with trumpets, and the Levites (the sons of Asaph) with cymbals, took their places to praise the LORD, as prescribed by David king of Israel. [11]With praise and thanksgiving they sang to the LORD:

"He is good;
his love to Israel endures forever."

And all the people gave a great shout of praise to the LORD, because the foundation of the house of the LORD was laid. [12]But many of the older priests and Levites and family heads, who had seen the former temple, wept aloud when they saw the foundation of this temple being laid, while many others shouted for joy. [13]No one could distinguish the sound of the

---

[a]69 That is, about 1,100 pounds (about 500 kilograms)   [b]69 That is, about 3 tons (about 2.9 metric tons)   [c]9 Hebrew *Yehudah*, probably a variant of *Hodaviah*

shouts of joy from the sound of weeping, because the people made so much noise. And the sound was heard far away.

Opposition to the Rebuilding

4 When the enemies of Judah and Benjamin heard that the exiles were building a temple for the LORD, the God of Israel, ²they came to Zerubbabel and to the heads of the families and said, "Let us help you build because, like you, we seek your God and have been sacrificing to him since the time of Esarhaddon king of Assyria, who brought us here."

³But Zerubbabel, Jeshua and the rest of the heads of the families of Israel answered, "You have no part with us in building a temple to our God. We alone will build it for the LORD, the God of Israel, as King Cyrus, the king of Persia, commanded us."

⁴Then the peoples around them set out to discourage the people of Judah and

make them afraid to go on building.ᵃ ⁵They hired counselors to work against them and frustrate their plans during the entire reign of Cyrus king of Persia and down to the reign of Darius king of Persia.

Later Opposition Under Xerxes and Artaxerxes

⁶At the beginning of the reign of Xerxes,ᵇ they lodged an accusation against the people of Judah and Jerusalem.

⁷And in the days of Artaxerxes king of Persia, Bishlam, Mithredath, Tabeel and the rest of his associates wrote a letter to Artaxerxes. The letter was written in Aramaic script and in the Aramaic language.ᶜ,ᵈ

⁸Rehum the commanding officer and Shimshai the secretary wrote a letter

---

ᵃ4 Or *and troubled them as they built*   ᵇ6 Hebrew *Ahasuerus*, a variant of Xerxes' Persian name   ᶜ7 Or *written in Aramaic and translated*   ᵈ7 The text of Ezra 4:8—6:18 is in Aramaic.

Sticks and Stones

DAILY INSIGHT

When we were much younger, most of us heard the kids in the neighborhood chant, "Sticks and stones may break my bones, but words will never hurt me."

If you believe this, I've got some "prime" real estate in central Florida I'd like to talk to you about. It's nonsense. Why? Because words are powerful. And, at times, they can hurt deeply.

Our friend Zerubbabel and his crew were busily rebuilding the temple that once had been the center of Jewish life. Years of war had devastated this sacred place, and Zerubbabel was doing the right thing. Unfortunately, not everyone was enthusiastic about the work. Enemies of the Jews from neighboring countries tried to hurt Zerubbabel and his associates—not with fists or weapons, but with their words.

Oh yes, they took the job of discouraging the people seriously, and they did it well. They even sent in trained specialists ("counselors to work against them") to

THURSDAY

Passage:
Ezra 4:1–5

Verse:
Ezra 4:3

extract the enthusiasm and joy from these faithful people.

Did Zerubbabel understand the power of words? He sure did. He reminded the naysayers, "You have no part with us in building a temple to our God." And don't you suspect that he did this within earshot of his workers? He defended their cause and countered the cruel and discouraging words that might have weakened his people's hands.

You and I know about this. We've heard words that have frightened or weakened us. In turn, we also have the power of these "counselors"; our words can frighten our children and weaken the very ones we love.

But, thankfully, we also can choose to imitate Zerubbabel in speaking good words that will encourage our kids. We can literally reverse fearfulness and give our families strength—just with the things we say.

Choose your words carefully. They have unbelievable power.

For your next devotional reading, go to page 510.

against Jerusalem to Artaxerxes the king as follows:

[9]Rehum the commanding officer and Shimshai the secretary, together with the rest of their associates—the judges and officials over the men from Tripolis, Persia,[a] Erech and Babylon, the Elamites of Susa, [10]and the other people whom the great and honorable Ashurbanipal[b] deported and settled in the city of Samaria and elsewhere in Trans-Euphrates.

[11](This is a copy of the letter they sent him.)

To King Artaxerxes,

From your servants, the men of Trans-Euphrates:

[12]The king should know that the Jews who came up to us from you have gone to Jerusalem and are rebuilding that rebellious and wicked city. They are restoring the walls and repairing the foundations.
[13]Furthermore, the king should know that if this city is built and its walls are restored, no more taxes, tribute or duty will be paid, and the royal revenues will suffer. [14]Now since we are under obligation to the palace and it is not proper for us to see the king dishonored, we are sending this message to inform the king, [15]so that a search may be made in the archives of your predecessors. In these records you will find that this city is a rebellious city, troublesome to kings and provinces, a place of rebellion from ancient times. That is why this city was destroyed. [16]We inform the king that if this city is built and its walls are restored, you will be left with nothing in Trans-Euphrates.

[17]The king sent this reply:

To Rehum the commanding officer, Shimshai the secretary and the rest of their associates living in Samaria and elsewhere in Trans-Euphrates:

Greetings.

[18]The letter you sent us has been read and translated in my presence. [19]I issued an order and a search was made, and it was found that this city has a long history of revolt against kings and has been a place of rebellion and sedition. [20]Jerusalem has

had powerful kings ruling over the whole of Trans-Euphrates, and taxes, tribute and duty were paid to them. [21]Now issue an order to these men to stop work, so that this city will not be rebuilt until I so order. [22]Be careful not to neglect this matter. Why let this threat grow, to the detriment of the royal interests?

[23]As soon as the copy of the letter of King Artaxerxes was read to Rehum and Shimshai the secretary and their associates, they went immediately to the Jews in Jerusalem and compelled them by force to stop.

[24]Thus the work on the house of God in Jerusalem came to a standstill until the second year of the reign of Darius king of Persia.

Tattenai's Letter to Darius

5 Now Haggai the prophet and Zechariah the prophet, a descendant of Iddo, prophesied to the Jews in Judah and Jerusalem in the name of the God of Israel, who was over them. [2]Then Zerubbabel son of Shealtiel and Jeshua son of Jozadak set to work to rebuild the house of God in Jerusalem. And the prophets of God were with them, helping them.
[3]At that time Tattenai, governor of Trans-Euphrates, and Shethar-Bozenai and their associates went to them and asked, "Who authorized you to rebuild this temple and restore this structure?" [4]They also asked, "What are the names of the men constructing this building?"[c] [5]But the eye of their God was watching over the elders of the Jews, and they were not stopped until a report could go to Darius and his written reply be received.

[6]This is a copy of the letter that Tattenai, governor of Trans-Euphrates, and Shethar-Bozenai and their associates, the officials of Trans-Euphrates, sent to King Darius. [7]The report they sent him read as follows:

To King Darius:

Cordial greetings.

[8]The king should know that we went to the district of Judah, to the

---

[a]9 Or officials, magistrates and governors over the men from   [b]10 Aramaic Osnappar, a variant of Ashurbanipal   [c]4 See Septuagint; Aramaic [4]We told them the names of the men constructing this building.

temple of the great God. The people are building it with large stones and placing the timbers in the walls. The work is being carried on with diligence and is making rapid progress under their direction. **⁹**We questioned the elders and asked them, "Who authorized you to rebuild this temple and restore this structure?" **¹⁰**We also asked them their names, so that we could write down the names of their leaders for your information. **¹¹**This is the answer they gave us:

"We are the servants of the God of heaven and earth, and we are rebuilding the temple that was built many years ago, one that a great king of Israel built and finished. **¹²**But because our fathers angered the God of heaven, he handed them over to Nebuchadnezzar the Chaldean, king of Babylon, who destroyed this temple and deported the people to Babylon.

¹³"However, in the first year of Cyrus king of Babylon, King Cyrus issued a decree to rebuild this house of God. **¹⁴**He even removed from the temple*ᵃ* of Babylon the gold and silver articles of the house of God, which Nebuchadnezzar had taken from the temple in Jerusalem and brought to the temple*ᵃ* in Babylon.

"Then King Cyrus gave them to a man named Sheshbazzar, whom he had appointed governor, **¹⁵**and he told him, 'Take these articles and go and deposit them in the temple in Jerusalem. And rebuild the house of God on its site.' **¹⁶**So this Sheshbazzar came and laid the foundations of the house of God in Jerusalem. From that day to the present it has been under construction but is not yet finished."

¹⁷Now if it pleases the king, let a search be made in the royal archives of Babylon to see if King Cyrus did in fact issue a decree to rebuild this house of God in Jerusalem. Then let the king send us his decision in this matter.

The Decree of Darius

6 King Darius then issued an order, and they searched in the archives stored in the treasury at Babylon. **²**A scroll was found in the citadel of Ecbatana in the province of Media, and this was written on it:

Memorandum:

³In the first year of King Cyrus, the king issued a decree concerning the temple of God in Jerusalem:

Let the temple be rebuilt as a place to present sacrifices, and let its foundations be laid. It is to be ninety feet*ᵇ* high and ninety feet wide, **⁴**with three courses of large stones and one of timbers. The costs are to be paid by the royal treasury. **⁵**Also, the gold and silver articles of the house of God, which Nebuchadnezzar took from the temple in Jerusalem and brought to Babylon, are to be returned to their places in the temple in Jerusalem; they are to be deposited in the house of God.

⁶Now then, Tattenai, governor of Trans-Euphrates, and Shethar-Bozenai and you, their fellow officials of that province, stay away from there. **⁷**Do not interfere with the work on this temple of God. Let the governor of the Jews and the Jewish elders rebuild this house of God on its site.

⁸Moreover, I hereby decree what you are to do for these elders of the Jews in the construction of this house of God:

The expenses of these men are to be fully paid out of the royal treasury, from the revenues of Trans-Euphrates, so that the work will not stop. **⁹**Whatever is needed—young bulls, rams, male lambs for burnt offerings to the God of heaven, and wheat, salt, wine and oil, as requested by the priests in Jerusalem—must be given them daily without fail, **¹⁰**so that they may offer sacrifices pleasing to the God of heaven and pray for the well-being of the king and his sons.

¹¹Furthermore, I decree that if anyone changes this edict, a beam is to be pulled from his house and he is to be lifted up and impaled on it. And for this crime his house is to be made a pile of rubble. **¹²**May God, who has caused his Name to dwell there, overthrow any king or people who lifts a hand to change this decree or to destroy this temple in Jerusalem.

ᵃ14 Or palace   ᵇ3 Aramaic sixty cubits (about 27 meters)

I Darius have decreed it. Let it be carried out with diligence.

Completion and Dedication of the Temple

¹³Then, because of the decree King Darius had sent, Tattenai, governor of Trans-Euphrates, and Shethar-Bozenai and their associates carried it out with diligence. ¹⁴So the elders of the Jews continued to build and prosper under the preaching of Haggai the prophet and Zechariah, a descendant of Iddo. They finished building the temple according to the command of the God of Israel and the decrees of Cyrus, Darius and Artaxerxes, kings of Persia. ¹⁵The temple was completed on the third day of the month Adar, in the sixth year of the reign of King Darius.

¹⁶Then the people of Israel—the priests, the Levites and the rest of the exiles—celebrated the dedication of the house of God with joy. ¹⁷For the dedication of this house of God they offered a hundred bulls, two hundred rams, four hundred male lambs and, as a sin offering for all Israel, twelve male goats, one for each of the tribes of Israel. ¹⁸And they installed the priests in their divisions and the Levites in their groups for the service of God at Jerusalem, according to what is written in the Book of Moses.

The Passover

¹⁹On the fourteenth day of the first month, the exiles celebrated the Passover. ²⁰The priests and Levites had purified themselves and were all ceremonially clean. The Levites slaughtered the Passover lamb for all the exiles, for their brothers the priests and for themselves. ²¹So the Israelites who had returned from the exile ate it, together with all who had separated themselves from the unclean practices of their Gentile neighbors in order to seek the LORD, the God of Israel. ²²For seven days they celebrated with joy the Feast of Unleavened Bread, because the LORD had filled them with joy by changing the attitude of the king of Assyria, so that he assisted them in the work on the house of God, the God of Israel.

Ezra Comes to Jerusalem

7 After these things, during the reign of Artaxerxes king of Persia, Ezra son of Seraiah, the son of Azariah, the son of Hilkiah, ²the son of Shallum, the son of Za-

dok, the son of Ahitub, ³the son of Amariah, the son of Azariah, the son of Meraioth, ⁴the son of Zerahiah, the son of Uzzi, the son of Bukki, ⁵the son of Abishua, the son of Phinehas, the son of Eleazar, the son of Aaron the chief priest— ⁶this Ezra came up from Babylon. He was a teacher well versed in the Law of Moses, which the LORD, the God of Israel, had given. The king had granted him everything he asked, for the hand of the LORD his God was on him. ⁷Some of the Israelites, including priests, Levites, singers, gatekeepers and temple servants, also came up to Jerusalem in the seventh year of King Artaxerxes.

⁸Ezra arrived in Jerusalem in the fifth month of the seventh year of the king. ⁹He had begun his journey from Babylon on the first day of the first month, and he arrived in Jerusalem on the first day of the fifth month, for the gracious hand of his God was on him. ¹⁰For Ezra had devoted himself to the study and observance of the Law of the LORD, and to teaching its decrees and laws in Israel.

King Artaxerxes' Letter to Ezra

¹¹This is a copy of the letter King Artaxerxes had given to Ezra the priest and teacher, a man learned in matters concerning the commands and decrees of the LORD for Israel:

¹²ᵃArtaxerxes, king of kings,

To Ezra the priest, a teacher of the Law of the God of heaven:

Greetings.

¹³Now I decree that any of the Israelites in my kingdom, including priests and Levites, who wish to go to Jerusalem with you, may go. ¹⁴You are sent by the king and his seven advisers to inquire about Judah and Jerusalem with regard to the Law of your God, which is in your hand. ¹⁵Moreover, you are to take with you the silver and gold that the king and his advisers have freely given to the God of Israel, whose dwelling is in Jerusalem, ¹⁶together with all the silver and gold you may obtain from the province of Babylon, as well as the freewill offerings of the people and priests for the temple of their

ᵃ12 The text of Ezra 7:12-26 is in Aramaic.

God in Jerusalem. ¹⁷With this money be sure to buy bulls, rams and male lambs, together with their grain offerings and drink offerings, and sacrifice them on the altar of the temple of your God in Jerusalem.

¹⁸You and your brother Jews may then do whatever seems best with the rest of the silver and gold, in accordance with the will of your God. ¹⁹Deliver to the God of Jerusalem all the articles entrusted to you for worship in the temple of your God. ²⁰And anything else needed for the temple of your God that you may have occasion to supply, you may provide from the royal treasury.

²¹Now I, King Artaxerxes, order all the treasurers of Trans-Euphrates to provide with diligence whatever Ezra the priest, a teacher of the Law of the God of heaven, may ask of you— ²²up to a hundred talents*a* of silver, a hundred cors*b* of wheat, a hundred baths*c* of wine, a hundred baths*c* of olive oil, and salt without limit. ²³Whatever the God of heaven has prescribed, let it be done with diligence for the temple of the God of heaven. Why should there be wrath against the realm of the king and of his sons? ²⁴You are also to know that you have no authority to impose taxes, tribute or duty on any of the priests, Levites, singers, gatekeepers, temple servants or other workers at this house of God.

²⁵And you, Ezra, in accordance with the wisdom of your God, which you possess, appoint magistrates and judges to administer justice to all the people of Trans-Euphrates— all who know the laws of your God. And you are to teach any who do not know them. ²⁶Whoever does not obey the law of your God and the law of the king must surely be punished by death, banishment, confiscation of property, or imprisonment.

²⁷Praise be to the LORD, the God of our fathers, who has put it into the king's heart to bring honor to the house of the LORD in Jerusalem in this way ²⁸and who has extended his good favor to me before the king and his advisers and all the king's powerful officials. Because the hand of the LORD my God was on me, I took courage and gathered leading men from Israel to go up with me.

List of the Family Heads Returning With Ezra

8 These are the family heads and those registered with them who came up with me from Babylon during the reign of King Artaxerxes:

²of the descendants of Phinehas, Gershom;

of the descendants of Ithamar, Daniel;

of the descendants of David, Hattush ³of the descendants of Shecaniah;

of the descendants of Parosh, Zechariah, and with him were registered 150 men;

⁴of the descendants of Pahath-Moab, Eliehoenai son of Zerahiah, and with him 200 men;

⁵of the descendants of Zattu,*d* Shecaniah son of Jahaziel, and with him 300 men;

⁶of the descendants of Adin, Ebed son of Jonathan, and with him 50 men;

⁷of the descendants of Elam, Jeshaiah son of Athaliah, and with him 70 men;

⁸of the descendants of Shephatiah, Zebadiah son of Michael, and with him 80 men;

⁹of the descendants of Joab, Obadiah son of Jehiel, and with him 218 men;

¹⁰of the descendants of Bani,*e* Shelomith son of Josiphiah, and with him 160 men;

¹¹of the descendants of Bebai, Zechariah son of Bebai, and with him 28 men;

¹²of the descendants of Azgad, Johanan son of Hakkatan, and with him 110 men;

¹³of the descendants of Adonikam, the last ones, whose names were Eliphelet, Jeuel and Shemaiah, and with them 60 men;

¹⁴of the descendants of Bigvai, Uthai and Zaccur, and with them 70 men.

The Return to Jerusalem

¹⁵I assembled them at the canal that flows toward Ahava, and we camped there

a22 That is, about 3 3/4 tons (about 3.4 metric tons) *b22* That is, probably about 600 bushels (about 22 kiloliters) *c22* That is, probably about 600 gallons (about 2.2 kiloliters) *d5* Some Septuagint manuscripts (also 1 Esdras 8:32); Hebrew does not have *Zattu.* *e10* Some Septuagint manuscripts (also 1 Esdras 8:36); Hebrew does not have *Bani.*

three days. When I checked among the people and the priests, I found no Levites there. [16]So I summoned Eliezer, Ariel, Shemaiah, Elnathan, Jarib, Elnathan, Nathan, Zechariah and Meshullam, who were leaders, and Joiarib and Elnathan, who were men of learning, [17]and I sent them to Iddo, the leader in Casiphia. I told them what to say to Iddo and his kinsmen, the temple servants in Casiphia, so that they might bring attendants to us for the house of our God. [18]Because the gracious hand of our God was on us, they brought us Sherebiah, a capable man, from the descendants of Mahli son of Levi, the son of Israel, and Sherebiah's sons and brothers, 18 men; [19]and Hashabiah, together with Jeshaiah from the descendants of Merari, and his brothers and nephews, 20 men. [20]They also brought 220 of the temple servants—a body that David and the officials had established to assist the Levites. All were registered by name.

[21]There, by the Ahava Canal, I proclaimed a fast, so that we might humble ourselves before our God and ask him for a safe journey for us and our children, with all our possessions. [22]I was ashamed to ask the king for soldiers and horsemen to protect us from enemies on the road, because we had told the king, "The gracious hand of our God is on everyone who looks to him, but his great anger is against all who forsake him." [23]So we fasted and petitioned our God about this, and he answered our prayer.

[24]Then I set apart twelve of the leading priests, together with Sherebiah, Hashabiah and ten of their brothers, [25]and I weighed out to them the offering of silver and gold and the articles that the king, his advisers, his officials and all Israel present there had donated for the house of our God. [26]I weighed out to them 650 talents[a] of silver, silver articles weighing 100 talents,[b] 100 talents[b] of gold, [27]20 bowls of gold valued at 1,000 darics,[c] and two fine articles of polished bronze, as precious as gold.

[28]I said to them, "You as well as these articles are consecrated to the LORD. The silver and gold are a freewill offering to the LORD, the God of your fathers. [29]Guard them carefully until you weigh them out in the chambers of the house of the LORD in Jerusalem before the leading priests and the Levites and the family heads of Israel." [30]Then the priests and Levites received the silver and gold and sacred articles that had been weighed out to be taken to the house of our God in Jerusalem.

[31]On the twelfth day of the first month we set out from the Ahava Canal to go to Jerusalem. The hand of our God was on us, and he protected us from enemies and bandits along the way. [32]So we arrived in Jerusalem, where we rested three days.

[33]On the fourth day, in the house of our God, we weighed out the silver and gold and the sacred articles into the hands of Meremoth son of Uriah, the priest. Eleazar son of Phinehas was with him, and so were the Levites Jozabad son of Jeshua and Noadiah son of Binnui. [34]Everything was accounted for by number and weight, and the entire weight was recorded at that time.

[35]Then the exiles who had returned from captivity sacrificed burnt offerings to the God of Israel: twelve bulls for all Israel, ninety-six rams, seventy-seven male lambs and, as a sin offering, twelve male goats. All this was a burnt offering to the LORD. [36]They also delivered the king's orders to the royal satraps and to the governors of Trans-Euphrates, who then gave assistance to the people and to the house of God.

Ezra's Prayer About Intermarriage

9 After these things had been done, the leaders came to me and said, "The people of Israel, including the priests and the Levites, have not kept themselves separate from the neighboring peoples with their detestable practices, like those of the Canaanites, Hittites, Perizzites, Jebusites, Ammonites, Moabites, Egyptians and Amorites. [2]They have taken some of their daughters as wives for themselves and their sons, and have mingled the holy race with the peoples around them. And the leaders and officials have led the way in this unfaithfulness."

[3]When I heard this, I tore my tunic and cloak, pulled hair from my head and beard and sat down appalled. [4]Then everyone who trembled at the words of the God of Israel gathered around me because of this unfaithfulness of the exiles. And I sat there appalled until the evening sacrifice.

[5]Then, at the evening sacrifice, I rose

[a]26 That is, about 25 tons (about 22 metric tons)   [b]26 That is, about 3 3/4 tons (about 3.4 metric tons)   [c]27 That is, about 19 pounds (about 8.5 kilograms)

from my self-abasement, with my tunic and cloak torn, and fell on my knees with my hands spread out to the LORD my God ⁶and prayed:

⁷"O my God, I am too ashamed and disgraced to lift up my face to you, my God, because our sins are higher than our heads and our guilt has reached to the heavens. ⁷From the days of our forefathers until now, our guilt has been great. Because of our sins, we and our kings and our priests have been subjected to the sword and captivity, to pillage and humiliation at the hand of foreign kings, as it is today.

⁸"But now, for a brief moment, the LORD our God has been gracious in leaving us a remnant and giving us a firm place in his sanctuary, and so our God gives light to our eyes and a little relief in our bondage. ⁹Though we are slaves, our God has not deserted us in our bondage. He has shown us kindness in the sight of the kings of Persia: He has granted us new life to rebuild the house of our God and repair its ruins, and he has given us a wall of protection in Judah and Jerusalem.

¹⁰"But now, O our God, what can we say after this? For we have disregarded the commands ¹¹you gave through your servants the prophets when you said: 'The land you are entering to possess is a land polluted by the corruption of its peoples. By their detestable practices they have filled it with their impurity from one end to the other. ¹²Therefore, do not give your daughters in marriage to their sons or take their daughters for your sons. Do not seek a treaty of friendship with them at any time, that you may be strong and eat the good things of the land and leave it to your children as an everlasting inheritance.'

¹³"What has happened to us is a result of our evil deeds and our great guilt, and yet, our God, you have punished us less than our sins have deserved and have given us a remnant like this. ¹⁴Shall we again break your commands and intermarry with the peoples who commit such detestable practices? Would you not be angry enough with us to destroy us, leaving us no remnant or survivor?

¹⁵O LORD, God of Israel, you are righteous! We are left this day as a remnant. Here we are before you in our guilt, though because of it not one of us can stand in your presence."

The People's Confession of Sin

10 While Ezra was praying and confessing, weeping and throwing himself down before the house of God, a large crowd of Israelites—men, women and children—gathered around him. They too wept bitterly. ²Then Shecaniah son of Jehiel, one of the descendants of Elam, said to Ezra, "We have been unfaithful to our God by marrying foreign women from the peoples around us. But in spite of this, there is still hope for Israel. ³Now let us make a covenant before our God to send away all these women and their children, in accordance with the counsel of my lord and of those who fear the commands of our God. Let it be done according to the Law. ⁴Rise up; this matter is in your hands. We will support you, so take courage and do it."

⁵So Ezra rose up and put the leading priests and Levites and all Israel under oath to do what had been suggested. And they took the oath. ⁶Then Ezra withdrew from before the house of God and went to the room of Jehohanan son of Eliashib. While he was there, he ate no food and drank no water, because he continued to mourn over the unfaithfulness of the exiles.

⁷A proclamation was then issued throughout Judah and Jerusalem for all the exiles to assemble in Jerusalem. ⁸Anyone who failed to appear within three days would forfeit all his property, in accordance with the decision of the officials and elders, and would himself be expelled from the assembly of the exiles.

⁹Within the three days, all the men of Judah and Benjamin had gathered in Jerusalem. And on the twentieth day of the ninth month, all the people were sitting in the square before the house of God, greatly distressed by the occasion and because of the rain. ¹⁰Then Ezra the priest stood up and said to them, "You have been unfaithful; you have married foreign women, adding to Israel's guilt. ¹¹Now make confession to the LORD, the God of your fathers, and do his will. Separate yourselves from the peoples around you and from your foreign wives."

¹²The whole assembly responded with

a loud voice: "You are right! We must do as you say. ¹³But there are many people here and it is the rainy season; so we cannot stand outside. Besides, this matter cannot be taken care of in a day or two, because we have sinned greatly in this thing. ¹⁴Let our officials act for the whole assembly. Then let everyone in our towns who has married a foreign woman come at a set time, along with the elders and judges of each town, until the fierce anger of our God in this matter is turned away from us." ¹⁵Only Jonathan son of Asahel and Jahzeiah son of Tikvah, supported by Meshullam and Shabbethai the Levite, opposed this.

¹⁶So the exiles did as was proposed. Ezra the priest selected men who were family heads, one from each family division, and all of them designated by name.

Extra, Extra, Read all About It

DAILY INSIGHT

It can be a lot of fun to see your name in print … well, most of the time.

I was a senior at a Christian college. For the most part, the rules seemed fair, even to the most free-spirited among my friends. However, there was one rule that really ticked me off. A couple of times each semester, the college blocked students from leaving campus on weekends. The administration had good reasons for doing so—special scheduled meetings, activities and the like—but for we claustrophobics, our lovely school became a federal prison four times a year. On one of these weekends, right after my last class on Friday afternoon, I got in my 1962 Chevy Bel Aire and slipped through the gate.

A week later, one of the school's several newspapers picked up the story. Some clever investigative reporter—a sophomore, probably—wrote all about it. I still remember his exact words: "If Wolgemuth can leave campus, why can't we?"

I was furious. Actually, I was embarrassed, and being publicly humiliated really makes me mad. Nonetheless, I was guilty, and I had to face the college's discipline for my disobedience.

Ezra had a problem with his own rule-breaking people. During the time when the Jewish men were captives, they fell in love with non-Jewish women. God, through Moses, had commanded that they not marry outside of their faith. They knew the rules, and they knew they were breaking them—no innocence here.

This disobedience put Ezra on his face

FRIDAY

Passage:
Ezra 10:1–6

Verse:
Ezra 10:1

before the Lord. His open confession on behalf of his people became contagious, and many people joined him. In fact, they promised to do an incredibly painful thing … allow their wives and children to return to their own homeland. Imagine the trauma of having to say good-bye!

After prayer, Ezra ordered the scribes to make a list of those who had broken the law and printed it. The names of those who had sinned were right there in black and white. And not only was this list distributed among the people, it's right here in our Bibles thousands of years later. Pretty embarrassing stuff, wouldn't you say?

At the end of all time, God will open a book in which will be recorded everything you and I have done—the things everyone already knows about and those things that have survived in the corners of our private memories (see Rev. 20:12). There they will be in black and white. Pretty embarrassing stuff, wouldn't you say?

But there's good news about this printing. "If we confess our sins"—even the ones printed in this book—"[God] is faithful and just and will forgive us our sins and purify us from all unrighteousness" (1 John 1:9). Stamped across this particular printing of your name and mine will be these words: "Forgiven because of Jesus."

Take this. Confess it. Believe it. And don't worry about the school newspaper. You're in there all right, but it doesn't make any difference.

For your next devotional reading, go to page 516.

On the first day of the tenth month they sat down to investigate the cases, [17]and by the first day of the first month they finished dealing with all the men who had married foreign women.

Those Guilty of Intermarriage

[18]Among the descendants of the priests, the following had married foreign women:

From the descendants of Jeshua son of Jozadak, and his brothers: Maaseiah, Eliezer, Jarib and Gedaliah. [19](They all gave their hands in pledge to put away their wives, and for their guilt they each presented a ram from the flock as a guilt offering.)

[20]From the descendants of Immer:
Hanani and Zebadiah.

[21]From the descendants of Harim:
Maaseiah, Elijah, Shemaiah, Jehiel and Uzziah.

[22]From the descendants of Pashhur:
Elioenai, Maaseiah, Ishmael, Nethanel, Jozabad and Elasah.

[23]Among the Levites:

Jozabad, Shimei, Kelaiah (that is, Kelita), Pethahiah, Judah and Eliezer.

[24]From the singers:
Eliashib.
From the gatekeepers:
Shallum, Telem and Uri.

[25]And among the other Israelites:

From the descendants of Parosh:
Ramiah, Izziah, Malkijah, Mijamin, Eleazar, Malkijah and Benaiah.

[26]From the descendants of Elam:

Mattaniah, Zechariah, Jehiel, Abdi, Jeremoth and Elijah.

[27]From the descendants of Zattu:
Elioenai, Eliashib, Mattaniah, Jeremoth, Zabad and Aziza.

[28]From the descendants of Bebai:
Jehohanan, Hananiah, Zabbai and Athlai.

[29]From the descendants of Bani:
Meshullam, Malluch, Adaiah, Jashub, Sheal and Jeremoth.

[30]From the descendants of Pahath-Moab:
Adna, Kelal, Benaiah, Maaseiah, Mattaniah, Bezalel, Binnui and Manasseh.

[31]From the descendants of Harim:
Eliezer, Ishijah, Malkijah, Shemaiah, Shimeon, [32]Benjamin, Malluch and Shemariah.

[33]From the descendants of Hashum:
Mattenai, Mattattah, Zabad, Eliphelet, Jeremai, Manasseh and Shimei.

[34]From the descendants of Bani:
Maadai, Amram, Uel, [35]Benaiah, Bedeiah, Keluhi, [36]Vaniah, Meremoth, Eliashib, [37]Mattaniah, Mattenai and Jaasu.

[38]From the descendants of Binnui:[a]
Shimei, [39]Shelemiah, Nathan, Adaiah, [40]Macnadebai, Shashai, Sharai, [41]Azarel, Shelemiah, Shemariah, [42]Shallum, Amariah and Joseph.

[43]From the descendants of Nebo:
Jeiel, Mattithiah, Zabad, Zebina, Jaddai, Joel and Benaiah.

[44]All these had married foreign women, and some of them had children by these wives.[b]

[a]37,38 See Septuagint (also 1 Esdras 9:34); Hebrew *Jaasu* [38]*and Bani and Binnui,*   [b]44 Or *and they sent them away with their children*

YOU were an accomplice to a vicious lie when you were a kid. You defended yourself against other children with the chant, "Sticks and stones may break my bones, but words will never hurt me." But as you grew older, you learned that words have a powerful and sometimes devastating effect. Words can encourage, literally issuing strength to the hearer. Words can also discourage, rendering the recipient impotent.

Nehemiah's story is one of a courageous leader who risked a prestigious job to ask his superior, the King of Persia, to give him a leave of absence and allow him to organize the rebuilding of Jerusalem's walls. Given this permission, Nehemiah set out to accomplish this huge project. But right in the middle of the work, hecklers showed up. The people were discouraged, but Nehemiah spoke words of assurance that revived and empowered them.

Good words restore tired and frustrated people. This includes, of course, wives, children, family and friends.

Nehemiah

Nehemiah's Prayer

1 The words of Nehemiah son of Hacaliah:

In the month of Kislev in the twentieth year, while I was in the citadel of Susa, ²Hanani, one of my brothers, came from Judah with some other men, and I questioned them about the Jewish remnant that survived the exile, and also about Jerusalem.

³They said to me, "Those who survived the exile and are back in the province are in great trouble and disgrace. The wall of Jerusalem is broken down, and its gates have been burned with fire."

⁴When I heard these things, I sat down and wept. For some days I mourned and fasted and prayed before the God of heaven. ⁵Then I said:

"O LORD, God of heaven, the great and awesome God, who keeps his covenant of love with those who love him and obey his commands, ⁶let your ear be attentive and your eyes open to hear the prayer your servant is praying before you day and night for your servants, the people of Israel. I confess the sins we Israelites, including myself and my father's house, have committed against you. ⁷We have acted very wickedly toward you. We have not obeyed the commands, decrees and laws you gave your servant Moses.

⁸"Remember the instruction you

gave your servant Moses, saying, 'If you are unfaithful, I will scatter you among the nations, ⁹but if you return to me and obey my commands, then even if your exiled people are at the farthest horizon, I will gather them from there and bring them to the place I have chosen as a dwelling for my Name.'

¹⁰"They are your servants and your people, whom you redeemed by your great strength and your mighty hand. ¹¹O Lord, let your ear be attentive to the prayer of this your servant and to the prayer of your servants who delight in revering your name. Give your servant success today by granting him favor in the presence of this man."

I was cupbearer to the king.

Artaxerxes Sends Nehemiah to Jerusalem

2 In the month of Nisan in the twentieth year of King Artaxerxes, when wine was brought for him, I took the wine and gave it to the king. I had not been sad in his presence before; ²so the king asked me, "Why does your face look so sad when you are not ill? This can be nothing but sadness of heart."

I was very much afraid, ³but I said to the king, "May the king live forever! Why should my face not look sad when the city where my fathers are buried lies in ruins, and its gates have been destroyed by fire?"

⁴The king said to me, "What is it you want?"

Then I prayed to the God of heaven, ⁵and I answered the king, "If it pleases the king and if your servant has found favor in his sight, let him send me to the city in Judah where my fathers are buried so that I can rebuild it."

⁶Then the king, with the queen sitting beside him, asked me, "How long will your journey take, and when will you get back?" It pleased the king to send me; so I set a time.

⁷I also said to him, "If it pleases the king, may I have letters to the governors of Trans-Euphrates, so that they will provide me safe-conduct until I arrive in Judah? ⁸And may I have a letter to Asaph, keeper of the king's forest, so he will give me timber to make beams for the gates of the citadel by the temple and for the city wall and for the residence I will occupy?" And because the gracious hand of my God was upon me, the king granted my requests. ⁹So I went to the governors of Trans-Euphrates and gave them the king's letters. The king had also sent army officers and cavalry with me.

¹⁰When Sanballat the Horonite and Tobiah the Ammonite official heard about this, they were very much disturbed that someone had come to promote the welfare of the Israelites.

Nehemiah Inspects Jerusalem's Walls

¹¹I went to Jerusalem, and after staying there three days ¹²I set out during the night with a few men. I had not told anyone what my God had put in my heart to do for Jerusalem. There were no mounts with me except the one I was riding on.

¹³By night I went out through the Valley Gate toward the Jackalᵃ Well and the Dung Gate, examining the walls of Jerusalem, which had been broken down, and its gates, which had been destroyed by fire. ¹⁴Then I moved on toward the Fountain Gate and the King's Pool, but there was not enough room for my mount to get through; ¹⁵so I went up the valley by night, examining the wall. Finally, I turned back and reentered through the Valley Gate. ¹⁶The officials did not know where I had gone or what I was doing, because as yet I had said nothing to the Jews or the priests or nobles or officials or any others who would be doing the work. ¹⁷Then I said to them, "You see the trouble we are in: Jerusalem lies in ruins, and its gates have been burned with fire. Come, let us rebuild the wall of Jerusalem, and we will no longer be in disgrace." ¹⁸I also told them about the gracious hand of my God upon me and what the king had said to me.

They replied, "Let us start rebuilding." So they began this good work.

¹⁹But when Sanballat the Horonite, Tobiah the Ammonite official and Geshem the Arab heard about it, they mocked and ridiculed us. "What is this you are doing?" they asked. "Are you rebelling against the king?"

²⁰I answered them by saying, "The God of heaven will give us success. We his servants will start rebuilding, but as for you, you have no share in Jerusalem or any claim or historic right to it."

Builders of the Wall

3 Eliashib the high priest and his fellow priests went to work and rebuilt the

ᵃ13 Or Serpent or Fig

Sheep Gate. They dedicated it and set its doors in place, building as far as the Tower of the Hundred, which they dedicated, and as far as the Tower of Hananel. [2]The men of Jericho built the adjoining section, and Zaccur son of Imri built next to them.

[3]The Fish Gate was rebuilt by the sons of Hassenaah. They laid its beams and put its doors and bolts and bars in place. [4]Meremoth son of Uriah, the son of Hakkoz, repaired the next section. Next to him Meshullam son of Berekiah, the son of Meshezabel, made repairs, and next to him Zadok son of Baana also made repairs. [5]The next section was repaired by the men of Tekoa, but their nobles would not put their shoulders to the work under their supervisors.[a]

[6]The Jeshanah[b] Gate was repaired by Joiada son of Paseah and Meshullam son of Besodeiah. They laid its beams and put its doors and bolts and bars in place. [7]Next to them, repairs were made by men from Gibeon and Mizpah—Melatiah of Gibeon and Jadon of Meronoth—places under the authority of the governor of Trans-Euphrates. [8]Uzziel son of Harhaiah, one of the goldsmiths, repaired the next section; and Hananiah, one of the perfume-makers, made repairs next to that. They restored[c] Jerusalem as far as the Broad Wall. [9]Rephaiah son of Hur, ruler of a half-district of Jerusalem, repaired the next section. [10]Adjoining this, Jedaiah son of Harumaph made repairs opposite his house, and Hattush son of Hashabneiah made repairs next to him. [11]Malkijah son of Harim and Hasshub son of Pahath-Moab repaired another section and the Tower of the Ovens. [12]Shallum son of Hallohesh, ruler of a half-district of Jerusalem, repaired the next section with the help of his daughters.

[13]The Valley Gate was repaired by Hanun and the residents of Zanoah. They rebuilt it and put its doors and bolts and bars in place. They also repaired five hundred yards[d] of the wall as far as the Dung Gate.

[14]The Dung Gate was repaired by Malkijah son of Recab, ruler of the district of Beth Hakkerem. He rebuilt it and put its doors and bolts and bars in place.

[15]The Fountain Gate was repaired by Shallun son of Col-Hozeh, ruler of the district of Mizpah. He rebuilt it, roofing it over and putting its doors and bolts and bars in place. He also repaired the wall of the Pool of Siloam,[e] by the King's Garden, as far as the steps going down from the City of David. [16]Beyond him, Nehemiah son of Azbuk, ruler of a half-district of Beth Zur, made repairs up to a point opposite the tombs[f] of David, as far as the artificial pool and the House of the Heroes.

[17]Next to him, the repairs were made by the Levites under Rehum son of Bani. Beside him, Hashabiah, ruler of half the district of Keilah, carried out repairs for his district. [18]Next to him, the repairs were made by their countrymen under Binnui[g] son of Henadad, ruler of the other half-district of Keilah. [19]Next to him, Ezer son of Jeshua, ruler of Mizpah, repaired another section, from a point facing the ascent to the armory as far as the angle. [20]Next to him, Baruch son of Zabbai zealously repaired another section, from the angle to the entrance of the house of Eliashib the high priest. [21]Next to him, Meremoth son of Uriah, the son of Hakkoz, repaired another section, from the entrance of Eliashib's house to the end of it.

[22]The repairs next to him were made by the priests from the surrounding region. [23]Beyond them, Benjamin and Hasshub made repairs in front of their house; and next to them, Azariah son of Maaseiah, the son of Ananiah, made repairs beside his house. [24]Next to him, Binnui son of Henadad repaired another section, from Azariah's house to the angle and the corner, [25]and Palal son of Uzai worked opposite the angle and the tower projecting from the upper palace near the court of the guard. Next to him, Pedaiah son of Parosh [26]and the temple servants living on the hill of Ophel made repairs up to a point opposite the Water Gate toward the east and the projecting tower. [27]Next to them, the men of Tekoa repaired another section, from the great projecting tower to the wall of Ophel.

[28]Above the Horse Gate, the priests made repairs, each in front of his own house. [29]Next to them, Zadok son of Im-

[a]5 Or their Lord or the governor   [b]6 Or Old   [c]8 Or They left out part of   [d]13 Hebrew a thousand cubits (about 450 meters)   [e]15 Hebrew Shelah, a variant of Shiloah, that is, Siloam   [f]16 Hebrew; Septuagint, some Vulgate manuscripts and Syriac tomb   [g]18 Two Hebrew manuscripts and Syriac (see also Septuagint and verse 24); most Hebrew manuscripts Bavvai

mer made repairs opposite his house. Next to him, Shemaiah son of Shecaniah, the guard at the East Gate, made repairs. ³⁰Next to him, Hananiah son of Shelemiah, and Hanun, the sixth son of Zalaph, repaired another section. Next to them, Meshullam son of Berekiah made repairs opposite his living quarters. ³¹Next to him, Malkijah, one of the goldsmiths, made repairs as far as the house of the temple servants and the merchants, opposite the Inspection Gate, and as far as the room above the corner; ³²and between the room above the corner and the Sheep Gate the goldsmiths and merchants made repairs.

Opposition to the Rebuilding

4 When Sanballat heard that we were rebuilding the wall, he became angry and was greatly incensed. He ridiculed the Jews, ²and in the presence of his associates and the army of Samaria, he said, "What are those feeble Jews doing? Will they restore their wall? Will they offer sacrifices? Will they finish in a day? Can they bring the stones back to life from those heaps of rubble—burned as they are?"

³Tobiah the Ammonite, who was at his side, said, "What they are building—if even a fox climbed up on it, he would break down their wall of stones!"

⁴Hear us, O our God, for we are despised. Turn their insults back on their own heads. Give them over as plunder in a land of captivity. ⁵Do not cover up their guilt or blot out their sins from your sight, for they have thrown insults in the face of ᵃ the builders.

⁶So we rebuilt the wall till all of it reached half its height, for the people worked with all their heart.

⁷But when Sanballat, Tobiah, the Arabs, the Ammonites and the men of Ashdod heard that the repairs to Jerusalem's walls had gone ahead and that the gaps were being closed, they were very angry. ⁸They all plotted together to come and fight against Jerusalem and stir up trouble against it. ⁹But we prayed to our God and posted a guard day and night to meet this threat.

¹⁰Meanwhile, the people in Judah said, "The strength of the laborers is giving out, and there is so much rubble that we cannot rebuild the wall."

¹¹Also our enemies said, "Before they know it or see us, we will be right there among them and will kill them and put an end to the work."

¹²Then the Jews who lived near them came and told us ten times over, "Wherever you turn, they will attack us."

¹³Therefore I stationed some of the people behind the lowest points of the wall at the exposed places, posting them by families, with their swords, spears and bows. ¹⁴After I looked things over, I stood up and said to the nobles, the officials and the rest of the people, "Don't be afraid of them. Remember the Lord, who is great and awesome, and fight for your brothers, your sons and your daughters, your wives and your homes."

¹⁵When our enemies heard that we were aware of their plot and that God had frustrated it, we all returned to the wall, each to his own work.

¹⁶From that day on, half of my men did the work, while the other half were equipped with spears, shields, bows and armor. The officers posted themselves behind all the people of Judah ¹⁷who were building the wall. Those who carried materials did their work with one hand and held a weapon in the other, ¹⁸and each of the builders wore his sword at his side as he worked. But the man who sounded the trumpet stayed with me.

¹⁹Then I said to the nobles, the officials and the rest of the people, "The work is extensive and spread out, and we are widely separated from each other along the wall. ²⁰Wherever you hear the sound of the trumpet, join us there. Our God will fight for us!"

²¹So we continued the work with half the men holding spears, from the first light of dawn till the stars came out. ²²At that time I also said to the people, "Have every man and his helper stay inside Jerusalem at night, so they can serve us as guards by night and workmen by day." ²³Neither I nor my brothers nor my men nor the guards with me took off our clothes; each had his weapon, even when he went for water.ᵇ

Nehemiah Helps the Poor

5 Now the men and their wives raised a great outcry against their Jewish brothers. ²Some were saying, "We and our sons and daughters are numerous; in order for us to eat and stay alive, we must get grain."

ᵃ5 Or *have provoked you to anger before*   ᵇ23 The meaning of the Hebrew for this clause is uncertain.

Home on the Range

Key Verse: *"So we rebuilt the wall . . . for the people worked with all their heart."* Nehemiah 4:6

Text: Nehemiah 4:1–6 *(Dad or child reads the text.)*

QUIET
TIMES
WITH Dad

DAD READS: Remember the old song, "Home on the Range"? People have sung this song around campfires for many, many years. The first verse of the song includes this interesting little phrase: "Where seldom is heard a discouraging word and the skies are not cloudy all day." I want our home to be like that.

Child reads: Harmful words can take all the fun out of life. In fact, mean words can make people feel sick, just like they have the flu.

DAD READS: In the verses we read today, people were hard at work fixing a wall around the city of Jerusalem that had been broken down by years of war and neglect. Many of the stones were broken and charred. So a man named Nehemiah decided to gather some of his friends together and rebuild this wall.

Child reads: But there were other men who didn't want Nehemiah to fix the wall. They walked around while the people worked and they mocked them. They said nasty and unkind things, like "even [if] a fox climbed up on it, he would break down [your] wall of stones." If I was working on this wall, those words would make me feel bad.

DAD READS: Me too. Hard work is difficult enough without cruel words. This is why I want a "home on the range." I want to live in a home where the words we speak to each other are encouraging words, not discouraging words.

Child reads: I would love it if my family would always look for ways to build me up with the things they say. This would make living in our house even better than it already is!

DAD READS: Today I am going to make you a promise. I promise that I'll do my very best to speak more kind and uplifting words to you. Even though I know that I will need to correct you at times, I promise that I will also look for more chances to say things that encourage, not discourage, you.

Child reads: Thank you for saying this. I want to learn this lesson from you and try to say more kind things to my family, too. Let me pray this prayer with you:

Our Father in heaven, thank you for encouraging words. Thank you for this story about Nehemiah so we can remember how wonderful good words can be. Please help my dad to keep his promise and to speak more encouraging words to our family. And help me to learn this lesson from my dad. In Jesus' name, Amen.

For your next devotional reading, go to page 520.

³Others were saying, "We are mortgaging our fields, our vineyards and our homes to get grain during the famine."

⁴Still others were saying, "We have had to borrow money to pay the king's tax on our fields and vineyards. ⁵Although we are of the same flesh and blood as our countrymen and though our sons are as good as theirs, yet we have to subject our sons and daughters to slavery. Some of our daughters have already been enslaved, but we are powerless, because our fields and our vineyards belong to others."

⁶When I heard their outcry and these charges, I was very angry. ⁷I pondered them in my mind and then accused the nobles and officials. I told them, "You are exacting usury from your own countrymen!" So I called together a large meeting to deal with them ⁸and said: "As far as possible, we have bought back our Jewish brothers who were sold to the Gentiles. Now you are selling your brothers, only for them to be sold back to us!" They kept quiet, because they could find nothing to say.

⁹So I continued, "What you are doing is not right. Shouldn't you walk in the fear of our God to avoid the reproach of our Gentile enemies? ¹⁰I and my brothers and my men are also lending the people money and grain. But let the exacting of usury stop! ¹¹Give back to them immediately their fields, vineyards, olive groves and houses, and also the usury you are charging them—the hundredth part of the money, grain, new wine and oil."

¹²"We will give it back," they said. "And we will not demand anything more from them. We will do as you say."

Then I summoned the priests and made the nobles and officials take an oath to do what they had promised. ¹³I also shook out the folds of my robe and said, "In this way may God shake out of his house and possessions every man who does not keep this promise. So may such a man be shaken out and emptied!"

At this the whole assembly said, "Amen," and praised the LORD. And the people did as they had promised.

¹⁴Moreover, from the twentieth year of King Artaxerxes, when I was appointed to be their governor in the land of Judah, until his thirty-second year—twelve years—neither I nor my brothers ate the food allotted to the governor. ¹⁵But the earlier governors—those preceding me—placed a heavy burden on the people and took forty shekels[a] of silver from them in addition to food and wine. Their assistants also lorded it over the people. But out of reverence for God I did not act like that. ¹⁶Instead, I devoted myself to the work on this wall. All my men were assembled there for the work; we[b] did not acquire any land.

¹⁷Furthermore, a hundred and fifty Jews and officials ate at my table, as well as those who came to us from the surrounding nations. ¹⁸Each day one ox, six choice sheep and some poultry were prepared for me, and every ten days an abundant supply of wine of all kinds. In spite of all this, I never demanded the food allotted to the governor, because the demands were heavy on these people.

¹⁹Remember me with favor, O my God, for all I have done for these people.

Further Opposition to the Rebuilding

6 When word came to Sanballat, Tobiah, Geshem the Arab and the rest of our enemies that I had rebuilt the wall and not a gap was left in it—though up to that time I had not set the doors in the gates— ²Sanballat and Geshem sent me this message: "Come, let us meet together in one of the villages[c] on the plain of Ono."

But they were scheming to harm me; ³so I sent messengers to them with this reply: "I am carrying on a great project and cannot go down. Why should the work stop while I leave it and go down to you?" ⁴Four times they sent me the same message, and each time I gave them the same answer.

⁵Then, the fifth time, Sanballat sent his aide to me with the same message, and in his hand was an unsealed letter ⁶in which was written:

"It is reported among the nations—and Geshem[d] says it is true—that you and the Jews are plotting to revolt, and therefore you are building the wall. Moreover, according to these reports you are about to become their king ⁷and have even appointed prophets to make this proclamation about you in Jerusalem: 'There is a king in Judah!' Now this report will get back to the king; so come, let us confer together."

ᵃ15 That is, about 1 pound (about 0.5 kilogram) ᵇ16 Most Hebrew manuscripts; some Hebrew manuscripts, Septuagint, Vulgate and Syriac *I* ᶜ2 Or *in Kephirim*   ᵈ6 Hebrew *Gashmu*, a variant of *Geshem*

[8]I sent him this reply: "Nothing like what you are saying is happening; you are just making it up out of your head."

[9]They were all trying to frighten us, thinking, "Their hands will get too weak for the work, and it will not be completed."

But I prayed, "Now strengthen my hands."

[10]One day I went to the house of Shemaiah son of Delaiah, the son of Mehetabel, who was shut in at his home. He said, "Let us meet in the house of God, inside the temple, and let us close the temple doors, because men are coming to kill you—by night they are coming to kill you."

[11]But I said, "Should a man like me run away? Or should one like me go into the temple to save his life? I will not go!" [12]I realized that God had not sent him, but that he had prophesied against me because Tobiah and Sanballat had hired him. [13]He had been hired to intimidate me so that I would commit a sin by doing this, and then they would give me a bad name to discredit me.

[14]Remember Tobiah and Sanballat, O my God, because of what they have done; remember also the prophetess Noadiah and the rest of the prophets who have been trying to intimidate me.

The Completion of the Wall

[15]So the wall was completed on the twenty-fifth of Elul, in fifty-two days. [16]When all our enemies heard about this, all the surrounding nations were afraid and lost their self-confidence, because they realized that this work had been done with the help of our God.

[17]Also, in those days the nobles of Judah were sending many letters to Tobiah, and replies from Tobiah kept coming to them. [18]For many in Judah were under oath to him, since he was son-in-law to Shecaniah son of Arah, and his son Jehohanan had married the daughter of Meshullam son of Berekiah. [19]Moreover, they kept reporting to me his good deeds and then telling him what I said. And Tobiah sent letters to intimidate me.

7 After the wall had been rebuilt and I had set the doors in place, the gatekeepers and the singers and the Levites were appointed. [2]I put in charge of Jerusalem my brother Hanani, along with[a] Hananiah the commander of the citadel, because he was a man of integrity and feared God more than most men do. [3]I said to them, "The gates of Jerusalem are not to be opened until the sun is hot. While the gatekeepers are still on duty, have them shut the doors and bar them. Also appoint residents of Jerusalem as guards, some at their posts and some near their own houses."

The List of the Exiles Who Returned

[4]Now the city was large and spacious, but there were few people in it, and the houses had not yet been rebuilt. [5]So my God put it into my heart to assemble the nobles, the officials and the common people for registration by families. I found the genealogical record of those who had been the first to return. This is what I found written there:

[6]These are the people of the province who came up from the captivity of the exiles whom Nebuchadnezzar king of Babylon had taken captive (they returned to Jerusalem and Judah, each to his own town, [7]in company with Zerubbabel, Jeshua, Nehemiah, Azariah, Raamiah, Nahamani, Mordecai, Bilshan, Mispereth, Bigvai, Nehum and Baanah):

The list of the men of Israel:

[8]the descendants of Parosh	2,172
[9]of Shephatiah	372
[10]of Arah	652
[11]of Pahath-Moab (through the line of Jeshua and Joab)	2,818
[12]of Elam	1,254
[13]of Zattu	845
[14]of Zaccai	760
[15]of Binnui	648
[16]of Bebai	628
[17]of Azgad	2,322
[18]of Adonikam	667
[19]of Bigvai	2,067
[20]of Adin	655
[21]of Ater (through Hezekiah)	98
[22]of Hashum	328
[23]of Bezai	324
[24]of Hariph	112
[25]of Gibeon	95
[26]the men of Bethlehem and Netophah	188
[27]of Anathoth	128
[28]of Beth Azmaveth	42
[29]of Kiriath Jearim,	

a2 Or Hanani, that is,

Kephirah and Beeroth 743
³⁰ of Ramah and Geba 621
³¹ of Micmash 122
³² of Bethel and Ai 123
³³ of the other Nebo 52
³⁴ of the other Elam 1,254
³⁵ of Harim 320
³⁶ of Jericho 345
³⁷ of Lod, Hadid and Ono 721
³⁸ of Senaah 3,930

³⁹The priests:

the descendants of Jedaiah
(through the family of
Jeshua) 973
⁴⁰ of Immer 1,052
⁴¹ of Pashhur 1,247
⁴² of Harim 1,017

⁴³The Levites:

the descendants of Jeshua
(through Kadmiel through
the line of Hodaviah) 74

⁴⁴The singers:

the descendants of Asaph 148

⁴⁵The gatekeepers:

the descendants of
Shallum, Ater, Talmon,
Akkub, Hatita and Shobai 138

⁴⁶The temple servants:

the descendants of
Ziha, Hasupha, Tabbaoth,
⁴⁷ Keros, Sia, Padon,
⁴⁸ Lebana, Hagaba, Shalmai,
⁴⁹ Hanan, Giddel, Gahar,
⁵⁰ Reaiah, Rezin, Nekoda,
⁵¹ Gazzam, Uzza, Paseah,
⁵² Besai, Meunim, Nephussim,
⁵³ Bakbuk, Hakupha, Harhur,
⁵⁴ Bazluth, Mehida, Harsha,
⁵⁵ Barkos, Sisera, Temah,
⁵⁶ Neziah and Hatipha

⁵⁷The descendants of the servants of
Solomon:

the descendants of
Sotai, Sophereth, Perida,
⁵⁸ Jaala, Darkon, Giddel,
⁵⁹ Shephatiah, Hattil,
Pokereth-Hazzebaim and Amon

⁶⁰ The temple servants and the
descendants of the servants
of Solomon 392

⁶¹The following came up from the
towns of Tel Melah, Tel Harsha, Kerub, Addon and Immer, but they

could not show that their families
were descended from Israel:

⁶² the descendants of
Delaiah, Tobiah and Nekoda 642

⁶³And from among the priests:

the descendants of
Hobaiah, Hakkoz and Barzillai (a
man who had married a daughter
of Barzillai the Gileadite and was
called by that name).
⁶⁴These searched for their family
records, but they could not find them
and so were excluded from the
priesthood as unclean. ⁶⁵The governor, therefore, ordered them not to
eat any of the most sacred food until
there should be a priest ministering
with the Urim and Thummim.

⁶⁶The whole company numbered
42,360, ⁶⁷besides their 7,337 menservants and maidservants; and they
also had 245 men and women singers.
⁶⁸There were 736 horses, 245 mules,ᵃ
⁶⁹435 camels and 6,720 donkeys.

⁷⁰Some of the heads of the families
contributed to the work. The governor gave to the treasury 1,000
drachmasᵇ of gold, 50 bowls and 530
garments for priests. ⁷¹Some of the
heads of the families gave to the treasury for the work 20,000 drachmasᶜ
of gold and 2,200 minasᵈ of silver.
⁷²The total given by the rest of the
people was 20,000 drachmas of gold,
2,000 minasᵉ of silver and 67 garments for priests.
⁷³The priests, the Levites, the gatekeepers, the singers and the temple
servants, along with certain of the
people and the rest of the Israelites,
settled in their own towns.

Ezra Reads the Law

When the seventh month came and the
Israelites had settled in their towns,
8 ¹all the people assembled as one man
in the square before the Water Gate.
They told Ezra the scribe to bring out the
Book of the Law of Moses, which the LORD
had commanded for Israel.

ᵃ68 Some Hebrew manuscripts (see also Ezra 2:66);
most Hebrew manuscripts do not have this verse.
ᵇ70 That is, about 19 pounds (about 8.5 kilograms)
ᶜ71 That is, about 375 pounds (about 170
kilograms); also in verse 72   ᵈ71 That is, about
1 1/3 tons (about 1.2 metric tons)   ᵉ72 That is,
about 1 1/4 tons (about 1.1 metric tons)

²So on the first day of the seventh month Ezra the priest brought the Law before the assembly, which was made up of men and women and all who were able to understand. ³He read it aloud from daybreak till noon as he faced the square before the Water Gate in the presence of the men, women and others who could understand. And all the people listened attentively to the Book of the Law.

⁴Ezra the scribe stood on a high wooden platform built for the occasion. Beside him on his right stood Mattithiah, Shema, Anaiah, Uriah, Hilkiah and Maaseiah; and on his left were Pedaiah, Mishael, Malkijah, Hashum, Hashbaddanah, Zechariah and Meshullam.

⁵Ezra opened the book. All the people could see him because he was standing above them; and as he opened it, the people all stood up. ⁶Ezra praised the LORD, the great God; and all the people lifted their hands and responded, "Amen! Amen!" Then they bowed down and worshiped the LORD with their faces to the ground.

Homecoming

DAILY INSIGHT

Hitchhiking was something I would never do.

As a small boy, I can recall our family car speeding past men standing on the shoulder of the highway with their thumb in the air. I recall my parents making comments about the dangers of such a thing. So hitchhiking went on my "don't-do" list.

Six weeks into my freshman year in college, I took hitchhiking off the "don't-do" list. I felt like a nine-year-old at Boy Scout camp. I was so homesick for my dad and mother, it was as though my heart was in a vise. Of course, no one at school knew about this. It's not cool for a semi-grown, prideful young man to admit that he misses his parents and just wants to go home ... although many of my buddies were probably homesick, too.

So I made a sign that read, "College student to Chicago," put on a clean white shirt and tie, walked to Highway 22 right in front of our college, took a deep breath, and stuck out my thumb.

To say that the next several hours were interesting would be an understatement. But thankfully, there were no criminals and no perverts. Only good people who felt sorry for this woeful boy, longing for his home.

Dusk was settling on the old neighborhood when my last ride dropped me off just a block from our house. Duffel bag in hand, my pace was somewhere between a speed

MONDAY

Passage:
Nehemiah 8:1–12

Verse:
Nehemiah 8:10

walk and a dead run. I was almost home. Moments later I burst through the front door, wrapping my arms around my precious mother who had no idea that her son was coming home—much less *how* her son was getting home! Our tears said it all.

I will never forget the feeling of being home—the back yard where I had played touch football with Roger Morris, Larry Strandquist, and Bobby Shemanski; the picture window I had perforated with my BB gun; the kitchen where our family had been whole; the home-cooked meal on the table. My homesickness had been miraculously and instantaneously healed.

The Israelites were home, too. After years of exile and slavery, they were back, surrounded by friends and familiar places. And, of course, they were overcome with sheer delight.

Ezra stood up on a high platform in front of the happy throng, opened the book of the law, and began reading. When the people heard God's Word again—after years of being denied its public reading—they threw their hands up in celebration, then they fell to the ground in worship, then they wept like college boys, ecstatic to be home.

Every new day can be a homecoming. God invites you to leave your isolation and to bask in the delight of his presence. Wrap your tired arms around this invitation. Welcome home, lonely boy.

For your next devotional reading, go to page 531.

⁷The Levites—Jeshua, Bani, Sherebiah, Jamin, Akkub, Shabbethai, Hodiah, Maaseiah, Kelita, Azariah, Jozabad, Hanan and Pelaiah—instructed the people in the Law while the people were standing there. ⁸They read from the Book of the Law of God, making it clear*a* and giving the meaning so that the people could understand what was being read.

⁹Then Nehemiah the governor, Ezra the priest and scribe, and the Levites who were instructing the people said to them all, "This day is sacred to the LORD your God. Do not mourn or weep." For all the people had been weeping as they listened to the words of the Law.

¹⁰Nehemiah said, "Go and enjoy choice food and sweet drinks, and send some to those who have nothing prepared. This day is sacred to our Lord. Do not grieve, for the joy of the LORD is your strength."

¹¹The Levites calmed all the people, saying, "Be still, for this is a sacred day. Do not grieve."

¹²Then all the people went away to eat and drink, to send portions of food and to celebrate with great joy, because they now understood the words that had been made known to them.

¹³On the second day of the month, the heads of all the families, along with the priests and the Levites, gathered around Ezra the scribe to give attention to the words of the Law. ¹⁴They found written in the Law, which the LORD had commanded through Moses, that the Israelites were to live in booths during the feast of the seventh month ¹⁵and that they should proclaim this word and spread it throughout their towns and in Jerusalem: "Go out into the hill country and bring back branches from olive and wild olive trees, and from myrtles, palms and shade trees, to make booths"—as it is written.*b*

¹⁶So the people went out and brought back branches and built themselves booths on their own roofs, in their courtyards, in the courts of the house of God and in the square by the Water Gate and the one by the Gate of Ephraim. ¹⁷The whole company that had returned from exile built booths and lived in them. From the days of Joshua son of Nun until that day, the Israelites had not celebrated it like this. And their joy was very great.

¹⁸Day after day, from the first day to the last, Ezra read from the Book of the Law of God. They celebrated the feast for seven

a8 Or *God, translating it*   *b15* See Lev. 23:37-40.

HEY DAD

Why do we have to read the Old Testament? Isn't that outdated now?

Text: Nehemiah 8:14, 16–17

The Old Testament is absolutely *not* outdated! The Old Testament has something to say to all of us today; it helps us see how we fit into God's plan. God has been carrying out this master plan since he created Adam and Eve. And God wants us to remember what he's done in the past so we can see that he has big plans for the future.

The Israelites participated in an interesting ritual to remember God's faithfulness to them. They celebrated the Feast of Tabernacles in the seventh month of every year.

During this Feast, the Israelites remembered how God had been with their ancestors as they wandered for forty years in the desert. During this feast, the Israelites actually made "booths" out of palm and willow trees. They lived in these booths for seven days so they could remember how it felt for their ancestors to live in the desert with no permanent homes. This became a powerful reminder to the people of God's faithfulness, and ensured that their children would hear and remember the story as well.

When we read this and other Old Testament stories, we're just like those children. We discover that God has been faithful to his people for many, many centuries. What celebrations do you participate in to remember God's faithfulness to you?

For a complete listing of Questions Kids Ask, turn to page 1435.

QUESTIONS KIDS ASK

days, and on the eighth day, in accordance with the regulation, there was an assembly.

The Israelites Confess Their Sins

9 On the twenty-fourth day of the same month, the Israelites gathered together, fasting and wearing sackcloth and having dust on their heads. ²Those of Israelite descent had separated themselves from all foreigners. They stood in their places and confessed their sins and the wickedness of their fathers. ³They stood where they were and read from the Book of the Law of the LORD their God for a quarter of the day, and spent another quarter in confession and in worshiping the LORD their God. ⁴Standing on the stairs were the Levites—Jeshua, Bani, Kadmiel, Shebaniah, Bunni, Sherebiah, Bani and Kenani—who called with loud voices to the LORD their God. ⁵And the Levites—Jeshua, Kadmiel, Bani, Hashabneiah, Sherebiah, Hodiah, Shebaniah and Pethahiah—said: "Stand up and praise the LORD your God, who is from everlasting to everlasting.ᵃ"

"Blessed be your glorious name, and may it be exalted above all blessing and praise. ⁶You alone are the LORD. You made the heavens, even the highest heavens, and all their starry host, the earth and all that is on it, the seas and all that is in them. You give life to everything, and the multitudes of heaven worship you.

⁷"You are the LORD God, who chose Abram and brought him out of Ur of the Chaldeans and named him Abraham. ⁸You found his heart faithful to you, and you made a covenant with him to give to his descendants the land of the Canaanites, Hittites, Amorites, Perizzites, Jebusites and Girgashites. You have kept your promise because you are righteous.

⁹"You saw the suffering of our forefathers in Egypt; you heard their cry at the Red Sea.ᵇ ¹⁰You sent miraculous signs and wonders against Pharaoh, against all his officials and all the people of his land, for you knew how arrogantly the Egyptians treated them. You made a name for yourself, which remains to this day. ¹¹You divided the sea before them, so that they passed through it on dry ground, but you hurled their pursuers into the depths, like a stone into mighty waters. ¹²By day you led them with a pillar of cloud, and by night with a pillar of fire to give them light on the way they were to take.

¹³"You came down on Mount Sinai; you spoke to them from heaven. You gave them regulations and laws that are just and right, and decrees and commands that are good. ¹⁴You made known to them your holy Sabbath and gave them commands, decrees and laws through your servant Moses. ¹⁵In their hunger you gave them bread from heaven and in their thirst you brought them water from the rock; you told them to go in and take possession of the land you had sworn with uplifted hand to give them.

¹⁶"But they, our forefathers, became arrogant and stiff-necked, and did not obey your commands. ¹⁷They refused to listen and failed to remember the miracles you performed among them. They became stiff-necked and in their rebellion appointed a leader in order to return to their slavery. But you are a forgiving God, gracious and compassionate, slow to anger and abounding in love. Therefore you did not desert them, ¹⁸even when they cast for themselves an image of a calf and said, 'This is your god, who brought you up out of Egypt,' or when they committed awful blasphemies.

¹⁹"Because of your great compassion you did not abandon them in the desert. By day the pillar of cloud did not cease to guide them on their path, nor the pillar of fire by night to shine on the way they were to take. ²⁰You gave your good Spirit to instruct them. You did not withhold your manna from their mouths, and you gave them water for their thirst. ²¹For forty years you sustained them in the desert; they lacked nothing, their clothes did not wear out nor did their feet become swollen.

²²"You gave them kingdoms and nations, allotting to them even the remotest frontiers. They took over the country of Sihonᶜ king of Heshbon and the country of Og king of

---

ᵃ5 Or *God for ever and ever*   ᵇ9 Hebrew *Yam Suph*; that is, Sea of Reeds   ᶜ22 One Hebrew manuscript and Septuagint; most Hebrew manuscripts *Sihon, that is, the country of the*

Bashan. ²³You made their sons as numerous as the stars in the sky, and you brought them into the land that you told their fathers to enter and possess. ²⁴Their sons went in and took possession of the land. You subdued before them the Canaanites, who lived in the land; you handed the Canaanites over to them, along with their kings and the peoples of the land, to deal with them as they pleased. ²⁵They captured fortified cities and fertile land; they took possession of houses filled with all kinds of good things, wells already dug, vineyards, olive groves and fruit trees in abundance. They ate to the full and were well-nourished; they reveled in your great goodness.

²⁶"But they were disobedient and rebelled against you; they put your law behind their backs. They killed your prophets, who had admonished them in order to turn them back to you; they committed awful blasphemies. ²⁷So you handed them over to their enemies, who oppressed them. But when they were oppressed they cried out to you. From heaven you heard them, and in your great compassion you gave them deliverers, who rescued them from the hand of their enemies.

²⁸"But as soon as they were at rest, they again did what was evil in your sight. Then you abandoned them to the hand of their enemies so that they ruled over them. And when they cried out to you again, you heard from heaven, and in your compassion you delivered them time after time.

²⁹"You warned them to return to your law, but they became arrogant and disobeyed your commands. They sinned against your ordinances, by which a man will live if he obeys them. Stubbornly they turned their backs on you, became stiff-necked and refused to listen. ³⁰For many years you were patient with them. By your Spirit you admonished them through your prophets. Yet they paid no attention, so you handed them over to the neighboring peoples. ³¹But in your great mercy you did not put an end to them or abandon them, for you are a gracious and merciful God.

³²"Now therefore, O our God, the

great, mighty and awesome God, who keeps his covenant of love, do not let all this hardship seem trifling in your eyes—the hardship that has come upon us, upon our kings and leaders, upon our priests and prophets, upon our fathers and all your people, from the days of the kings of Assyria until today. ³³In all that has happened to us, you have been just; you have acted faithfully, while we did wrong. ³⁴Our kings, our leaders, our priests and our fathers did not follow your law; they did not pay attention to your commands or the warnings you gave them. ³⁵Even while they were in their kingdom, enjoying your great goodness to them in the spacious and fertile land you gave them, they did not serve you or turn from their evil ways.

³⁶"But see, we are slaves today, slaves in the land you gave our forefathers so they could eat its fruit and the other good things it produces. ³⁷Because of our sins, its abundant harvest goes to the kings you have placed over us. They rule over our bodies and our cattle as they please. We are in great distress.

The Agreement of the People

³⁸"In view of all this, we are making a binding agreement, putting it in writing, and our leaders, our Levites and our priests are affixing their seals to it."

10 Those who sealed it were:

Nehemiah the governor, the son of Hacaliah.

Zedekiah, ²Seraiah, Azariah, Jeremiah,
³Pashhur, Amariah, Malkijah,
⁴Hattush, Shebaniah, Malluch,
⁵Harim, Meremoth, Obadiah,
⁶Daniel, Ginnethon, Baruch,
⁷Meshullam, Abijah, Mijamin,
⁸Maaziah, Bilgai and Shemaiah.
These were the priests.

⁹The Levites:

Jeshua son of Azaniah, Binnui of the sons of Henadad, Kadmiel,
¹⁰and their associates: Shebaniah, Hodiah, Kelita, Pelaiah, Hanan,
¹¹Mica, Rehob, Hashabiah,
¹²Zaccur, Sherebiah, Shebaniah,
¹³Hodiah, Bani and Beninu.

[14]The leaders of the people:

> Parosh, Pahath-Moab, Elam, Zattu, Bani,
> [15]Bunni, Azgad, Bebai,
> [16]Adonijah, Bigvai, Adin,
> [17]Ater, Hezekiah, Azzur,
> [18]Hodiah, Hashum, Bezai,
> [19]Hariph, Anathoth, Nebai,
> [20]Magpiash, Meshullam, Hezir,
> [21]Meshezabel, Zadok, Jaddua,
> [22]Pelatiah, Hanan, Anaiah,
> [23]Hoshea, Hananiah, Hasshub,
> [24]Hallohesh, Pilha, Shobek,
> [25]Rehum, Hashabnah, Maaseiah,
> [26]Ahiah, Hanan, Anan,
> [27]Malluch, Harim and Baanah.

[28]"The rest of the people—priests, Levites, gatekeepers, singers, temple servants and all who separated themselves from the neighboring peoples for the sake of the Law of God, together with their wives and all their sons and daughters who are able to understand— [29]all these now join their brothers the nobles, and bind themselves with a curse and an oath to follow the Law of God given through Moses the servant of God and to obey carefully all the commands, regulations and decrees of the LORD our Lord.

[30]"We promise not to give our daughters in marriage to the peoples around us or take their daughters for our sons.

[31]"When the neighboring peoples bring merchandise or grain to sell on the Sabbath, we will not buy from them on the Sabbath or on any holy day. Every seventh year we will forgo working the land and will cancel all debts.

[32]"We assume the responsibility for carrying out the commands to give a third of a shekel[a] each year for the service of the house of our God: [33]for the bread set out on the table; for the regular grain offerings and burnt offerings; for the offerings on the Sabbaths, New Moon festivals and appointed feasts; for the holy offerings; for sin offerings to make atonement for Israel; and for all the duties of the house of our God.

[34]"We—the priests, the Levites and the people—have cast lots to determine when each of our families is to bring to the house of our God at set times each year a contribution of wood to burn on the altar of the LORD our God, as it is written in the Law.

[35]"We also assume responsibility for bringing to the house of the LORD each year the firstfruits of our crops and of every fruit tree.

[36]"As it is also written in the Law, we will bring the firstborn of our sons and of our cattle, of our herds and of our flocks to the house of our God, to the priests ministering there.

[37]"Moreover, we will bring to the storerooms of the house of our God, to the priests, the first of our ground meal, of our grain offerings, of the fruit of all our trees and of our new wine and oil. And we will bring a tithe of our crops to the Levites, for it is the Levites who collect the tithes in all the towns where we work. [38]A priest descended from Aaron is to accompany the Levites when they receive the tithes, and the Levites are to bring a tenth of the tithes up to the house of our God, to the storerooms of the treasury. [39]The people of Israel, including the Levites, are to bring their contributions of grain, new wine and oil to the storerooms where the articles for the sanctuary are kept and where the ministering priests, the gatekeepers and the singers stay.

"We will not neglect the house of our God."

The New Residents of Jerusalem

11 Now the leaders of the people settled in Jerusalem, and the rest of the people cast lots to bring one out of every ten to live in Jerusalem, the holy city, while the remaining nine were to stay in their own towns. [2]The people commended all the men who volunteered to live in Jerusalem.

[3]These are the provincial leaders who settled in Jerusalem (now some Israelites, priests, Levites, temple servants and descendants of Solomon's servants lived in the towns of Judah, each on his own property in the various towns, [4]while other people from both Judah and Benjamin lived in Jerusalem):

From the descendants of Judah:

Athaiah son of Uzziah, the son of Zechariah, the son of Amariah, the

---

[a]32 That is, about 1/8 ounce (about 4 grams)

son of Shephatiah, the son of Mahalalel, a descendant of Perez; [5]and Maaseiah son of Baruch, the son of Col-Hozeh, the son of Hazaiah, the son of Adaiah, the son of Joiarib, the son of Zechariah, a descendant of Shelah. [6]The descendants of Perez who lived in Jerusalem totaled 468 able men.

[7]From the descendants of Benjamin:

Sallu son of Meshullam, the son of Joed, the son of Pedaiah, the son of Kolaiah, the son of Maaseiah, the son of Ithiel, the son of Jeshaiah, [8]and his followers, Gabbai and Sallai—928 men. [9]Joel son of Zicri was their chief officer, and Judah son of Hassenuah was over the Second District of the city.

[10]From the priests:

Jedaiah; the son of Joiarib; Jakin; [11]Seraiah son of Hilkiah, the son of Meshullam, the son of Zadok, the son of Meraioth, the son of Ahitub, supervisor in the house of God, [12]and their associates, who carried on work for the temple—822 men; Adaiah son of Jeroham, the son of Pelaliah, the son of Amzi, the son of Zechariah, the son of Pashhur, the son of Malkijah, [13]and his associates, who were heads of families—242 men; Amashsai son of Azarel, the son of Ahzai, the son of Meshillemoth, the son of Immer, [14]and his[a] associates, who were able men—128. Their chief officer was Zabdiel son of Haggedolim.

[15]From the Levites:

Shemaiah son of Hasshub, the son of Azrikam, the son of Hashabiah, the son of Bunni; [16]Shabbethai and Jozabad, two of the heads of the Levites, who had charge of the outside work of the house of God; [17]Mattaniah son of Mica, the son of Zabdi, the son of Asaph, the director who led in thanksgiving and prayer; Bakbukiah, second among his associates; and Abda son of Shammua, the son of Galal, the son of Jeduthun. [18]The Levites in the holy city totaled 284.

[19]The gatekeepers:

Akkub, Talmon and their associates, who kept watch at the gates—172 men.

[20]The rest of the Israelites, with the priests and Levites, were in all the towns of Judah, each on his ancestral property. [21]The temple servants lived on the hill of Ophel, and Ziha and Gishpa were in charge of them.

[22]The chief officer of the Levites in Jerusalem was Uzzi son of Bani, the son of Hashabiah, the son of Mattaniah, the son of Mica. Uzzi was one of Asaph's descendants, who were the singers responsible for the service of the house of God. [23]The singers were under the king's orders, which regulated their daily activity. [24]Pethahiah son of Meshezabel, one of the descendants of Zerah son of Judah, was the king's agent in all affairs relating to the people.

[25]As for the villages with their fields, some of the people of Judah lived in Kiriath Arba and its surrounding settlements, in Dibon and its settlements, in Jekabzeel and its villages, [26]in Jeshua, in Moladah, in Beth Pelet, [27]in Hazar Shual, in Beersheba and its settlements, [28]in Ziklag, in Meconah and its settlements, [29]in En Rimmon, in Zorah, in Jarmuth, [30]Zanoah, Adullam and their villages, in Lachish and its fields, and in Azekah and its settlements. So they were living all the way from Beersheba to the Valley of Hinnom.

[31]The descendants of the Benjamites from Geba lived in Micmash, Aija, Bethel and its settlements, [32]in Anathoth, Nob and Ananiah, [33]in Hazor, Ramah and Gittaim, [34]in Hadid, Zeboim and Neballat, [35]in Lod and Ono, and in the Valley of the Craftsmen.

[36]Some of the divisions of the Levites of Judah settled in Benjamin.

Priests and Levites

12 These were the priests and Levites who returned with Zerubbabel son of Shealtiel and with Jeshua:

Seraiah, Jeremiah, Ezra,
[2] Amariah, Malluch, Hattush,
[3] Shecaniah, Rehum, Meremoth,
[4] Iddo, Ginnethon,[b] Abijah,
[5] Mijamin,[c] Moadiah, Bilgah,
[6] Shemaiah, Joiarib, Jedaiah,
[7] Sallu, Amok, Hilkiah and Jedaiah.

These were the leaders of the priests and their associates in the days of Jeshua.

[8]The Levites were Jeshua, Binnui,

---

[a]14 Most Septuagint manuscripts; Hebrew *their*
[b]4 Many Hebrew manuscripts and Vulgate (see also Neh. 12:16); most Hebrew manuscripts *Ginnethoi*
[c]5 A variant of *Miniamin*

Kadmiel, Sherebiah, Judah, and also Mattaniah, who, together with his associates, was in charge of the songs of thanksgiving. [9]Bakbukiah and Unni, their associates, stood opposite them in the services. [10]Jeshua was the father of Joiakim, Joiakim the father of Eliashib, Eliashib the father of Joiada, [11]Joiada the father of Jonathan, and Jonathan the father of Jaddua.

[12]In the days of Joiakim, these were the heads of the priestly families:

of Seraiah's family, Meraiah;
of Jeremiah's, Hananiah;
[13]of Ezra's, Meshullam;
of Amariah's, Jehohanan;
[14]of Malluch's, Jonathan;
of Shecaniah's,[a] Joseph;
[15]of Harim's, Adna;
of Meremoth's,[b] Helkai;
[16]of Iddo's, Zechariah;
of Ginnethon's, Meshullam;
[17]of Abijah's, Zicri;
of Miniamin's and of Moadiah's, Piltai;
[18]of Bilgah's, Shammua;
of Shemaiah's, Jehonathan;
[19]of Joiarib's, Mattenai;
of Jedaiah's, Uzzi;
[20]of Sallu's, Kallai;
of Amok's, Eber;
[21]of Hilkiah's, Hashabiah;
of Jedaiah's, Nethanel.

[22]The family heads of the Levites in the days of Eliashib, Joiada, Johanan and Jaddua, as well as those of the priests, were recorded in the reign of Darius the Persian. [23]The family heads among the descendants of Levi up to the time of Johanan son of Eliashib were recorded in the book of the annals. [24]And the leaders of the Levites were Hashabiah, Sherebiah, Jeshua son of Kadmiel, and their associates, who stood opposite them to give praise and thanksgiving, one section responding to the other, as prescribed by David the man of God.

[25]Mattaniah, Bakbukiah, Obadiah, Meshullam, Talmon and Akkub were gatekeepers who guarded the storerooms at the gates. [26]They served in the days of Joiakim son of Jeshua, the son of Jozadak, and in the days of Nehemiah the governor and of Ezra the priest and scribe.

Dedication of the Wall of Jerusalem

[27]At the dedication of the wall of Jerusalem, the Levites were sought out from where they lived and were brought to Jerusalem to celebrate joyfully the dedication with songs of thanksgiving and with the music of cymbals, harps and lyres. [28]The singers also were brought together from the region around Jerusalem—from the villages of the Netophathites, [29]from Beth Gilgal, and from the area of Geba and Azmaveth, for the singers had built villages for themselves around Jerusalem. [30]When the priests and Levites had purified themselves ceremonially, they purified the people, the gates and the wall.

[31]I had the leaders of Judah go up on top[c] of the wall. I also assigned two large choirs to give thanks. One was to proceed on top[d] of the wall to the right, toward the Dung Gate. [32]Hoshaiah and half the leaders of Judah followed them, [33]along with Azariah, Ezra, Meshullam, [34]Judah, Benjamin, Shemaiah, Jeremiah, [35]as well as some priests with trumpets, and also Zechariah son of Jonathan, the son of Shemaiah, the son of Mattaniah, the son of Micaiah, the son of Zaccur, the son of Asaph, [36]and his associates—Shemaiah, Azarel, Milalai, Gilalai, Maai, Nethanel, Judah and Hanani—with musical instruments prescribed by David the man of God. Ezra the scribe led the procession. [37]At the Fountain Gate they continued directly up the steps of the City of David on the ascent to the wall and passed above the house of David to the Water Gate on the east.

[38]The second choir proceeded in the opposite direction. I followed them on top[e] of the wall, together with half the people—past the Tower of the Ovens to the Broad Wall, [39]over the Gate of Ephraim, the Jeshanah[f] Gate, the Fish Gate, the Tower of Hananel and the Tower of the Hundred, as far as the Sheep Gate. At the Gate of the Guard they stopped.

[40]The two choirs that gave thanks then took their places in the house of God; so did I, together with half the officials, [41]as well as the priests—Eliakim, Maaseiah, Miniamin, Micaiah, Elioenai, Zechariah and Hananiah with their trumpets—[42]and also Maaseiah, Shemaiah, Eleazar, Uzzi, Jehohanan, Malkijah, Elam and Ezer. The choirs sang under the direction

of Jezrahiah. ⁴³And on that day they offered great sacrifices, rejoicing because God had given them great joy. The women and children also rejoiced. The sound of rejoicing in Jerusalem could be heard far away.

⁴⁴At that time men were appointed to be in charge of the storerooms for the contributions, firstfruits and tithes. From the fields around the towns they were to bring into the storerooms the portions required by the Law for the priests and the Levites, for Judah was pleased with the ministering priests and Levites. ⁴⁵They performed the service of their God and the service of purification, as did also the singers and gatekeepers, according to the commands of David and his son Solomon. ⁴⁶For long ago, in the days of David and Asaph, there had been directors for the singers and for the songs of praise and thanksgiving to God. ⁴⁷So in the days of Zerubbabel and of Nehemiah, all Israel contributed the daily portions for the singers and gatekeepers. They also set aside the portion for the other Levites, and the Levites set aside the portion for the descendants of Aaron.

Nehemiah's Final Reforms

13 On that day the Book of Moses was read aloud in the hearing of the people and there it was found written that no Ammonite or Moabite should ever be admitted into the assembly of God, ²because they had not met the Israelites with food and water but had hired Balaam to call a curse down on them. (Our God, however, turned the curse into a blessing.) ³When the people heard this law, they excluded from Israel all who were of foreign descent.

⁴Before this, Eliashib the priest had been put in charge of the storerooms of the house of our God. He was closely associated with Tobiah, ⁵and he had provided him with a large room formerly used to store the grain offerings and incense and temple articles, and also the tithes of grain, new wine and oil prescribed for the Levites, singers and gatekeepers, as well as the contributions for the priests.

⁶But while all this was going on, I was not in Jerusalem, for in the thirty-second year of Artaxerxes king of Babylon I had returned to the king. Some time later I asked his permission ⁷and came back to Jerusalem. Here I learned about the evil thing Eliashib had done in providing To-

biah a room in the courts of the house of God. ⁸I was greatly displeased and threw all Tobiah's household goods out of the room. ⁹I gave orders to purify the rooms, and then I put back into them the equipment of the house of God, with the grain offerings and the incense.

¹⁰I also learned that the portions assigned to the Levites had not been given to them, and that all the Levites and singers responsible for the service had gone back to their own fields. ¹¹So I rebuked the officials and asked them, "Why is the house of God neglected?" Then I called them together and stationed them at their posts.

¹²All Judah brought the tithes of grain, new wine and oil into the storerooms. ¹³I put Shelemiah the priest, Zadok the scribe, and a Levite named Pedaiah in charge of the storerooms and made Hanan son of Zaccur, the son of Mattaniah, their assistant, because these men were considered trustworthy. They were made responsible for distributing the supplies to their brothers.

¹⁴Remember me for this, O my God, and do not blot out what I have so faithfully done for the house of my God and its services.

¹⁵In those days I saw men in Judah treading winepresses on the Sabbath and bringing in grain and loading it on donkeys, together with wine, grapes, figs and all other kinds of loads. And they were bringing all this into Jerusalem on the Sabbath. Therefore I warned them against selling food on that day. ¹⁶Men from Tyre who lived in Jerusalem were bringing in fish and all kinds of merchandise and selling them in Jerusalem on the Sabbath to the people of Judah. ¹⁷I rebuked the nobles of Judah and said to them, "What is this wicked thing you are doing—desecrating the Sabbath day? ¹⁸Didn't your forefathers do the same things, so that our God brought all this calamity upon us and upon this city? Now you are stirring up more wrath against Israel by desecrating the Sabbath."

¹⁹When evening shadows fell on the gates of Jerusalem before the Sabbath, I ordered the doors to be shut and not opened until the Sabbath was over. I stationed some of my own men at the gates so that no load could be brought in on the Sabbath day. ²⁰Once or twice the merchants and sellers of all kinds of goods spent the night outside Jerusalem. ²¹But I

warned them and said, "Why do you spend the night by the wall? If you do this again, I will lay hands on you." From that time on they no longer came on the Sabbath. ²²Then I commanded the Levites to purify themselves and go and guard the gates in order to keep the Sabbath day holy.

Remember me for this also, O my God, and show mercy to me according to your great love.

²³Moreover, in those days I saw men of Judah who had married women from Ashdod, Ammon and Moab. ²⁴Half of their children spoke the language of Ashdod or the language of one of the other peoples, and did not know how to speak the language of Judah. ²⁵I rebuked them and called curses down on them. I beat some of the men and pulled out their hair. I made them take an oath in God's name and said: "You are not to give your daughters in marriage to their sons, nor are you to take their daughters in marriage for your sons or for yourselves. ²⁶Was it not

because of marriages like these that Solomon king of Israel sinned? Among the many nations there was no king like him. He was loved by his God, and God made him king over all Israel, but even he was led into sin by foreign women. ²⁷Must we hear now that you too are doing all this terrible wickedness and are being unfaithful to our God by marrying foreign women?"

²⁸One of the sons of Joiada son of Eliashib the high priest was son-in-law to Sanballat the Horonite. And I drove him away from me.

²⁹Remember them, O my God, because they defiled the priestly office and the covenant of the priesthood and of the Levites.

³⁰So I purified the priests and the Levites of everything foreign, and assigned them duties, each to his own task. ³¹I also made provision for contributions of wood at designated times, and for the firstfruits.

Remember me with favor, O my God.

God's provision sometimes shows up in unlikely forms. The Bible is full of accounts of God's faithfulness, his discipline, or his charity being delivered in unusual packages. From a godless Pharaoh, to Balaam's donkey, to a tiny baby lying in a feedbox, God's messages sometimes come in unexpected ways.

The story of Esther is this kind of surprise. Right in the middle of a heavily male-dominated culture, God provided his people with a redeemer in the form of a courageous Jewish woman—one whom he had miraculously made queen of a pagan empire. In this context, cultural historians might ask, "What in the world is going on here—the Sovereign God's redemption coming through a woman?" This book is a powerful reminder that whenever and however he chooses to do so, God will speak, and he will act. His message will be delivered exactly as he wants it to be delivered.

As a dad, remember Jesus' instruction that sometimes God's voice will even come to you through your children (Matthew 21:16). Listen closely to your family members; at various times and in surprising ways, they will become God's messengers to you.

Esther

Queen Vashti Deposed

1 This is what happened during the time of Xerxes,[a] the Xerxes who ruled over 127 provinces stretching from India to Cush[b]: ²At that time King Xerxes reigned from his royal throne in the citadel of Susa, ³and in the third year of his reign he gave a banquet for all his nobles and officials. The military leaders of Persia and Media, the princes, and the nobles of the provinces were present.

⁴For a full 180 days he displayed the vast wealth of his kingdom and the splendor and glory of his majesty. ⁵When these days were over, the king gave a banquet, lasting seven days, in the enclosed garden of the king's palace, for all the people from the least to the greatest, who were in the citadel of Susa. ⁶The garden had hangings of white and blue linen, fastened with cords of white linen and purple material

---

a1 Hebrew *Ahasuerus*, a variant of Xerxes' Persian name; here and throughout Esther   *b1* That is, the upper Nile region

to silver rings on marble pillars. There were couches of gold and silver on a mosaic pavement of porphyry, marble, mother-of-pearl and other costly stones. ⁷Wine was served in goblets of gold, each one different from the other, and the royal wine was abundant, in keeping with the king's liberality. ⁸By the king's command each guest was allowed to drink in his own way, for the king instructed all the wine stewards to serve each man what he wished.

⁹Queen Vashti also gave a banquet for the women in the royal palace of King Xerxes.

¹⁰On the seventh day, when King Xerxes was in high spirits from wine, he commanded the seven eunuchs who served him—Mehuman, Biztha, Harbona, Bigtha, Abagtha, Zethar and Carcas— ¹¹to bring before him Queen Vashti, wearing her royal crown, in order to display her beauty to the people and nobles, for she was lovely to look at. ¹²But when the attendants delivered the king's command, Queen Vashti refused to come. Then the king became furious and burned with anger.

¹³Since it was customary for the king to consult experts in matters of law and justice, he spoke with the wise men who understood the times ¹⁴and were closest to the king—Carshena, Shethar, Admatha, Tarshish, Meres, Marsena and Memucan, the seven nobles of Persia and Media who had special access to the king and were highest in the kingdom.

¹⁵"According to law, what must be done to Queen Vashti?" he asked. "She has not obeyed the command of King Xerxes that the eunuchs have taken to her."

¹⁶Then Memucan replied in the presence of the king and the nobles, "Queen Vashti has done wrong, not only against the king but also against all the nobles and the peoples of all the provinces of King Xerxes. ¹⁷For the queen's conduct will become known to all the women, and so they will despise their husbands and say, 'King Xerxes commanded Queen Vashti to be brought before him, but she would not come.' ¹⁸This very day the Persian and Median women of the nobility who have heard about the queen's conduct will respond to all the king's nobles in the same way. There will be no end of disrespect and discord.

¹⁹"Therefore, if it pleases the king, let him issue a royal decree and let it be written in the laws of Persia and Media, which

cannot be repealed, that Vashti is never again to enter the presence of King Xerxes. Also let the king give her royal position to someone else who is better than she. ²⁰Then when the king's edict is proclaimed throughout all his vast realm, all the women will respect their husbands, from the least to the greatest."

²¹The king and his nobles were pleased with this advice, so the king did as Memucan proposed. ²²He sent dispatches to all parts of the kingdom, to each province in its own script and to each people in its own language, proclaiming in each people's tongue that every man should be ruler over his own household.

Esther Made Queen

2 Later when the anger of King Xerxes had subsided, he remembered Vashti and what she had done and what he had decreed about her. ²Then the king's personal attendants proposed, "Let a search be made for beautiful young virgins for the king. ³Let the king appoint commissioners in every province of his realm to bring all these beautiful girls into the harem at the citadel of Susa. Let them be placed under the care of Hegai, the king's eunuch, who is in charge of the women; and let beauty treatments be given to them. ⁴Then let the girl who pleases the king be queen instead of Vashti." This advice appealed to the king, and he followed it.

⁵Now there was in the citadel of Susa a Jew of the tribe of Benjamin, named Mordecai son of Jair, the son of Shimei, the son of Kish, ⁶who had been carried into exile from Jerusalem by Nebuchadnezzar king of Babylon, among those taken captive with Jehoiachin*ᵃ* king of Judah. ⁷Mordecai had a cousin named Hadassah, whom he had brought up because she had neither father nor mother. This girl, who was also known as Esther, was lovely in form and features, and Mordecai had taken her as his own daughter when her father and mother died.

⁸When the king's order and edict had been proclaimed, many girls were brought to the citadel of Susa and put under the care of Hegai. Esther also was taken to the king's palace and entrusted to Hegai, who had charge of the harem. ⁹The girl pleased him and won his favor. Immediately he provided her with her beauty

---

ᵃ6 Hebrew Jeconiah, a variant of Jehoiachin

treatments and special food. He assigned to her seven maids selected from the king's palace and moved her and her maids into the best place in the harem.

[10] Esther had not revealed her nationality and family background, because Mordecai had forbidden her to do so. [11] Every day he walked back and forth near the courtyard of the harem to find out how Esther was and what was happening to her.

[12] Before a girl's turn came to go in to King Xerxes, she had to complete twelve months of beauty treatments prescribed for the women, six months with oil of myrrh and six with perfumes and cosmetics. [13] And this is how she would go to the king: Anything she wanted was given her to take with her from the harem to the king's palace. [14] In the evening she would go there and in the morning return to another part of the harem to the care of Shaashgaz, the king's eunuch who was in charge of the concubines. She would not return to the king unless he was pleased with her and summoned her by name.

Just a Little, Unfortunate Kid

DAILY INSIGHT

TUESDAY

Passage:
Esther 2:1–7

Verse:
Esther 2:7

A child huddled in a corner near the grade school's front door, trying to keep warm against the chilly morning air. On his way to the factory, as he had to do every morning, Michelle's daddy had dropped her off an hour before school started.

On this particular Texas morning, my wife, Bobbie, was taking her morning walk. Not on her regular route, this time her pre-dawn journey took her past Midway school. And as she paced by the front door, the shadowed little girl caught her eye. She stopped. "What are you doing here?" Bobbie asked.

Michelle shyly told her the story … single dad trying to make ends meet, early morning shift at the plant, and once again, waiting for the school doors to open.

A few minutes later, Bobbie walked through the front door of our home, Michelle in tow. For the next few years, our home became Michelle's "home." We partnered with her dad to give her a family she could come home to—a surrogate mother and dad to fill in the gaps. She also got two "sisters" as a bonus who loved her very much.

Esther was something like that young girl. Alone in the world, Esther had lost her parents. We don't know how they died, but we do know that, because of Mordecai's compassion, Esther was given a place to live—a home and a family.

This is an incredible story. A beautiful Jewish girl, Esther the orphan was eventually selected to be the wife of Xerxes, the powerful Persian king. And as part of his wonderful plan, God used Esther to bring mercy to the Jews.

How could Mordecai ever have known that this orphan girl would be queen? Of course, he couldn't have known. All he knew was that she needed a home, and he gladly provided it for her. Imagine how proud his other children must have been to have their adopted sister reign as the first lady of Babylon. And imagine how happy they were with their dad for having taken this little girl into their home.

Whom does your family need to adopt? What child's life could be transformed by your compassion? Is there an orphaned or unfortunate little one out there who could bring such happiness to your clan?

You're probably thinking, *I don't know any kids like this.* Well, with all due respect, it's because you're not looking. There are needy children everywhere. They're in your town, and they're around the world. There are dozens of organizations who will help you and your family find a Michelle of your own, either at home or abroad.

Do this for a youngster in need. Queen Esther had someone like you to thank for her life and her success. And do this for your family. They'll never be the same.

For your next devotional reading, go to page 534.

[15]When the turn came for Esther (the girl Mordecai had adopted, the daughter of his uncle Abihail) to go to the king, she asked for nothing other than what Hegai, the king's eunuch who was in charge of the harem, suggested. And Esther won the favor of everyone who saw her. [16]She was taken to King Xerxes in the royal residence in the tenth month, the month of Tebeth, in the seventh year of his reign.

[17]Now the king was attracted to Esther more than to any of the other women, and she won his favor and approval more than any of the other virgins. So he set a royal crown on her head and made her queen instead of Vashti. [18]And the king gave a great banquet, Esther's banquet, for all his nobles and officials. He proclaimed a holiday throughout the provinces and distributed gifts with royal liberality.

Mordecai Uncovers a Conspiracy

[19]When the virgins were assembled a second time, Mordecai was sitting at the king's gate. [20]But Esther had kept secret her family background and nationality just as Mordecai had told her to do, for she continued to follow Mordecai's instructions as she had done when he was bringing her up.

[21]During the time Mordecai was sitting at the king's gate, Bigthana[a] and Teresh, two of the king's officers who guarded the doorway, became angry and conspired to assassinate King Xerxes. [22]But Mordecai found out about the plot and told Queen Esther, who in turn reported it to the king, giving credit to Mordecai. [23]And when the report was investigated and found to be true, the two officials were hanged on a gallows.[b] All this was recorded in the book of the annals in the presence of the king.

Haman's Plot to Destroy the Jews

3 After these events, King Xerxes honored Haman son of Hammedatha, the Agagite, elevating him and giving him a seat of honor higher than that of all the other nobles. [2]All the royal officials at the king's gate knelt down and paid honor to Haman, for the king had commanded this

[a]21 Hebrew *Bigthan*, a variant of *Bigthana*
[b]23 Or *were hung* (or *impaled*) *on poles*; similarly elsewhere in Esther

Fathering Children God's Other Way
Mordecai, the Adoptive Father

"Mordecai had taken [Esther] as his own daughter when her father and mother died" (2:7).

Text: Esther 2

Some dads have the privilege of getting children in a way that departs from the "traditional" method: through the miracle of adoption. One dad told me that, when he sat his daughter down to tell her of the circumstances of her adoption, he said, "Some dads go to the hospital and God gives them a child. But you're special. God helped your mother and dad to *choose* you. We could have picked many, many other children, but we picked *you*."

Today's passage tells just such a story. When a beautiful little girl named Hadassah (Esther) had lost her mother and father, her older cousin, a man named Mordecai, took her in. Not only did he give her a home, he literally adopted her as his own.

This girl went on to become the queen of Persia, the most powerful nation on earth at the time. And because of Mordecai's love and compassion, this little-girl-turned-queen saved her people, the Jews, from destruction. How could he have ever known that his act of mercy, his adoption and loving care for Esther, would result in his own salvation from a treacherous plot? He couldn't have. But his example gave Esther the strength and courage to stand for what she knew was right when she most needed to.

Parents of adopted children will tell you that God gives them a special love for these little ones they have chosen. What an awesome picture this is of our Savior's love for us.

Thanks, Mordecai, for your obedience.

For a complete listing of Dads in the Bible, turn to page 1434.

concerning him. But Mordecai would not kneel down or pay him honor.

³Then the royal officials at the king's gate asked Mordecai, "Why do you disobey the king's command?" ⁴Day after day they spoke to him but he refused to comply. Therefore they told Haman about it to see whether Mordecai's behavior would be tolerated, for he had told them he was a Jew.

⁵When Haman saw that Mordecai would not kneel down or pay him honor, he was enraged. ⁶Yet having learned who Mordecai's people were, he scorned the idea of killing only Mordecai. Instead Haman looked for a way to destroy all Mordecai's people, the Jews, throughout the whole kingdom of Xerxes.

⁷In the twelfth year of King Xerxes, in the first month, the month of Nisan, they cast the *pur* (that is, the lot) in the presence of Haman to select a day and month. And the lot fell on*a* the twelfth month, the month of Adar.

⁸Then Haman said to King Xerxes, "There is a certain people dispersed and scattered among the peoples in all the provinces of your kingdom whose customs are different from those of all other people and who do not obey the king's laws; it is not in the king's best interest to tolerate them. ⁹If it pleases the king, let a decree be issued to destroy them, and I will put ten thousand talents*b* of silver into the royal treasury for the men who carry out this business."

¹⁰So the king took his signet ring from his finger and gave it to Haman son of Hammedatha, the Agagite, the enemy of the Jews. ¹¹"Keep the money," the king said to Haman, "and do with the people as you please."

¹²Then on the thirteenth day of the first month the royal secretaries were summoned. They wrote out in the script of each province and in the language of each people all Haman's orders to the king's satraps, the governors of the various provinces and the nobles of the various peoples. These were written in the name of King Xerxes himself and sealed with his own ring. ¹³Dispatches were sent by couriers to all the king's provinces with the order to destroy, kill and annihilate all the Jews—young and old, women and little children—on a single day, the thirteenth day of the twelfth month, the month of Adar, and to plunder their goods. ¹⁴A copy of the text of the edict was to be issued as law in every province and made known to the people of every nationality so they would be ready for that day.

a7 Septuagint; Hebrew does not have *And the lot fell on*.   *b9* That is, about 375 tons (about 345 metric tons)

HEY DAD

Why aren't we supposed to judge others?

Text: Esther 2:20

We're not supposed to judge others for one reason: God is God, and we're not. Consider the story of Esther. From all outward appearances, Esther could have been a traitor to the Jews. She married a Gentile king, she changed her name to "Esther" from her Jewish name "Hadassah," and she even hid her nationality from the king and his advisers.

Can't you just hear the whispers in the Israelite community? "That Hadassah sure has gotten a big head, hasn't she?" "Who does she think she *is* anyway? Is she too good for us now?" "She wins some beauty pageant, and now she's willingly submitting to that pagan king." "She hasn't even told him that she's a Jew! I would *never* do what she's doing!"

But Esther went on to become one of the greatest heroines in Jewish history. Through her bravery, her obedience to God, and her willingness to listen to Mordecai's wise counsel, Esther helped save her entire nation.

God knew Esther's heart, and he knows our hearts, too. Look at that statement again: *He knows our hearts, too.* Now *there's* a good reason to be quick to have mercy and to be slow to judge!

For a complete listing of Questions Kids Ask, turn to page 1435.

¹⁵Spurred on by the king's command, the couriers went out, and the edict was issued in the citadel of Susa. The king and Haman sat down to drink, but the city of Susa was bewildered.

Mordecai Persuades Esther to Help

4 When Mordecai learned of all that had been done, he tore his clothes, put on sackcloth and ashes, and went out into the city, wailing loudly and bitterly. ²But he went only as far as the king's gate, because no one clothed in sackcloth was allowed to enter it. ³In every province to which the edict and order of the king came, there was great mourning among the Jews, with fasting, weeping and wailing. Many lay in sackcloth and ashes.

⁴When Esther's maids and eunuchs came and told her about Mordecai, she was in great distress. She sent clothes for him to put on instead of his sackcloth, but he would not accept them. ⁵Then Esther summoned Hathach, one of the king's eunuchs assigned to attend her, and ordered him to find out what was troubling Mordecai and why.

⁶So Hathach went out to Mordecai in the open square of the city in front of the king's gate. ⁷Mordecai told him everything that had happened to him, including the exact amount of money Haman had promised to pay into the royal treasury for

Trumpets, Banjos, and Good Timing

DAILY INSIGHT

WEDNESDAY

Passage:
Esther 4:1–17

Verse:
Esther 4:14

As a teenager, I played a *man's* instrument, the trumpet, in the marching band. I sat in the third chair, next to Mary Kay Warren and Mary Lee Babb. They were both very good players and they were both girls. Oh, the things we learned as kids.

Throughout the fall, our band would practice for home football games. Arthur Sweet, the director, would first teach us the music, then he would show us, on the blackboard, what the various formations would be—a banjo for "Way Down upon the Swanee River," or the Empire State Building for the Broadway medley. Then we'd go to the football field and practice. Over and over we'd go through the steps, making sure our banjo really looked like a banjo and making sure we didn't knock each other down in the transition from our award-winning "block formation."

Precision and good timing were Mr. Sweet's plan, and so we practiced until we were ready. The problem for those of us in the band was that, standing on the field, we couldn't tell a banjo from a duck. So Mr. Sweet would stand on a high platform with a bullhorn, directing our every move. For him, close wasn't good enough. It had to be *perfect.*

Before the beginning of time, God knew that King Xerxes would be a volatile man.

God knew that, because his first wife would disobey him, he would throw her out of the palace. Years before this, God had put a beautiful little orphan girl in Mordecai's way, and he gave this young girl a home. Then God gave this same young woman, Esther, favor in Xerxes' eyes; she became queen of Persia. Each detail was part of God's wonderful plan.

God also knew that Xerxes would take the advice of his evil adviser, Haman, and order the destruction of every Jew. What if Esther hadn't been there? But she was. And what if Xerxes had not listened to her plea for mercy for her people? But he did. Precision and timing are God's great forte. Mr. Sweet wasn't the only one.

How often have you and I looked at our circumstances and wondered, *What is God up to*? Unfortunately, we're on the field, and we can't tell a banjo from a duck. But God sees the whole picture. With flawless perfection, his ways are unfolding one step at a time. So as mere mortals—third chair trumpet players at best—our great challenge is to trust him.

God's timing is perfect. No one knew this better than Queen Esther. Now, take this truth for yourself and trust him.

For your next devotional reading, go to page 540.

the destruction of the Jews. [8]He also gave him a copy of the text of the edict for their annihilation, which had been published in Susa, to show to Esther and explain it to her, and he told him to urge her to go into the king's presence to beg for mercy and plead with him for her people.

[9]Hathach went back and reported to Esther what Mordecai had said. [10]Then she instructed him to say to Mordecai, [11]"All the king's officials and the people of the royal provinces know that for any man or woman who approaches the king in the inner court without being summoned the king has but one law: that he be put to death. The only exception to this is for the king to extend the gold scepter to him and spare his life. But thirty days have passed since I was called to go to the king."

[12]When Esther's words were reported to Mordecai, [13]he sent back this answer: "Do not think that because you are in the king's house you alone of all the Jews will escape. [14]For if you remain silent at this time, relief and deliverance for the Jews will arise from another place, but you and your father's family will perish. And who knows but that you have come to royal position for such a time as this?"

[15]Then Esther sent this reply to Mordecai: [16]"Go, gather together all the Jews who are in Susa, and fast for me. Do not eat or drink for three days, night or day. I and my maids will fast as you do. When this is done, I will go to the king, even though it is against the law. And if I perish, I perish."

[17]So Mordecai went away and carried out all of Esther's instructions.

Esther's Request to the King

5 On the third day Esther put on her royal robes and stood in the inner court of the palace, in front of the king's hall. The king was sitting on his royal throne in the hall, facing the entrance. [2]When he saw Queen Esther standing in the court, he was pleased with her and held out to her the gold scepter that was in his hand. So Esther approached and touched the tip of the scepter.

[3]Then the king asked, "What is it, Queen Esther? What is your request? Even up to half the kingdom, it will be given you."

[4]"If it pleases the king," replied Esther, "let the king, together with Haman, come today to a banquet I have prepared for him."

[5]"Bring Haman at once," the king said, "so that we may do what Esther asks."

So the king and Haman went to the banquet Esther had prepared. [6]As they were drinking wine, the king again asked Esther, "Now what is your petition? It will be given you. And what is your request? Even up to half the kingdom, it will be granted."

[7]Esther replied, "My petition and my request is this: [8]If the king regards me with favor and if it pleases the king to grant my petition and fulfill my request, let the king and Haman come tomorrow to the banquet I will prepare for them. Then I will answer the king's question."

Haman's Rage Against Mordecai

[9]Haman went out that day happy and in high spirits. But when he saw Mordecai at the king's gate and observed that he neither rose nor showed fear in his presence, he was filled with rage against Mordecai. [10]Nevertheless, Haman restrained himself and went home.

Calling together his friends and Zeresh, his wife, [11]Haman boasted to them about his vast wealth, his many sons, and all the ways the king had honored him and how he had elevated him above the other nobles and officials. [12]"And that's not all," Haman added. "I'm the only person Queen Esther invited to accompany the king to the banquet she gave. And she has invited me along with the king tomorrow. [13]But all this gives me no satisfaction as long as I see that Jew Mordecai sitting at the king's gate."

[14]His wife Zeresh and all his friends said to him, "Have a gallows built, seventy-five feet[a] high, and ask the king in the morning to have Mordecai hanged on it. Then go with the king to the dinner and be happy." This suggestion delighted Haman, and he had the gallows built.

Mordecai Honored

6 That night the king could not sleep; so he ordered the book of the chronicles, the record of his reign, to be brought in and read to him. [2]It was found recorded there that Mordecai had exposed Bigthana and Teresh, two of the king's officers who guarded the doorway, who had conspired to assassinate King Xerxes.

[3]"What honor and recognition has Mordecai received for this?" the king asked.

[a]14 Hebrew *fifty cubits* (about 23 meters)

"Nothing has been done for him," his attendants answered.

[4]The king said, "Who is in the court?" Now Haman had just entered the outer court of the palace to speak to the king about hanging Mordecai on the gallows he had erected for him.

[5]His attendants answered, "Haman is standing in the court."

"Bring him in," the king ordered.

[6]When Haman entered, the king asked him, "What should be done for the man the king delights to honor?"

Now Haman thought to himself, "Who is there that the king would rather honor than me?" [7]So he answered the king, "For the man the king delights to honor, [8]have them bring a royal robe the king has worn and a horse the king has ridden, one with a royal crest placed on its head. [9]Then let the robe and horse be entrusted to one of the king's most noble princes. Let them robe the man the king delights to honor, and lead him on the horse through the city streets, proclaiming before him, 'This is what is done for the man the king delights to honor!' "

[10]"Go at once," the king commanded Haman. "Get the robe and the horse and do just as you have suggested for Mordecai the Jew, who sits at the king's gate. Do not neglect anything you have recommended."

[11]So Haman got the robe and the horse. He robed Mordecai, and led him on horseback through the city streets, proclaiming before him, "This is what is done for the man the king delights to honor!"

[12]Afterward Mordecai returned to the king's gate. But Haman rushed home, with his head covered in grief, [13]and told Zeresh his wife and all his friends everything that had happened to him.

His advisers and his wife Zeresh said to him, "Since Mordecai, before whom your downfall has started, is of Jewish origin, you cannot stand against him—you will surely come to ruin!" [14]While they were still talking with him, the king's eunuchs arrived and hurried Haman away to the banquet Esther had prepared.

Haman Hanged

7 So the king and Haman went to dine with Queen Esther, [2]and as they were drinking wine on that second day, the king again asked, "Queen Esther, what is your petition? It will be given you. What is

your request? Even up to half the kingdom, it will be granted."

[3]Then Queen Esther answered, "If I have found favor with you, O king, and if it pleases your majesty, grant me my life—this is my petition. And spare my people—this is my request. [4]For I and my people have been sold for destruction and slaughter and annihilation. If we had merely been sold as male and female slaves, I would have kept quiet, because no such distress would justify disturbing the king.[a]"

[5]King Xerxes asked Queen Esther, "Who is he? Where is the man who has dared to do such a thing?"

[6]Esther said, "The adversary and enemy is this vile Haman."

Then Haman was terrified before the king and queen. [7]The king got up in a rage, left his wine and went out into the palace garden. But Haman, realizing that the king had already decided his fate, stayed behind to beg Queen Esther for his life.

[8]Just as the king returned from the palace garden to the banquet hall, Haman was falling on the couch where Esther was reclining.

The king exclaimed, "Will he even molest the queen while she is with me in the house?"

As soon as the word left the king's mouth, they covered Haman's face. [9]Then Harbona, one of the eunuchs attending the king, said, "A gallows seventy-five feet[b] high stands by Haman's house. He had it made for Mordecai, who spoke up to help the king."

The king said, "Hang him on it!" [10]So they hanged Haman on the gallows he had prepared for Mordecai. Then the king's fury subsided.

The King's Edict in Behalf of the Jews

8 That same day King Xerxes gave Queen Esther the estate of Haman, the enemy of the Jews. And Mordecai came into the presence of the king, for Esther had told how he was related to her. [2]The king took off his signet ring, which he had reclaimed from Haman, and presented it to Mordecai. And Esther appointed him over Haman's estate.

[3]Esther again pleaded with the king, falling at his feet and weeping. She

a4 Or quiet, but the compensation our adversary offers cannot be compared with the loss the king would suffer *b9 Hebrew fifty cubits* (about 23 meters)

begged him to put an end to the evil plan of Haman the Agagite, which he had devised against the Jews. ⁴Then the king extended the gold scepter to Esther and she arose and stood before him.

⁵"If it pleases the king," she said, "and if he regards me with favor and thinks it the right thing to do, and if he is pleased with me, let an order be written overruling the dispatches that Haman son of Hammedatha, the Agagite, devised and wrote to destroy the Jews in all the king's provinces. ⁶For how can I bear to see disaster fall on my people? How can I bear to see the destruction of my family?"

⁷King Xerxes replied to Queen Esther and to Mordecai the Jew, "Because Haman attacked the Jews, I have given his estate to Esther, and they have hanged him on the gallows. ⁸Now write another decree in the king's name in behalf of the Jews as seems best to you, and seal it with the king's signet ring—for no document written in the king's name and sealed with his ring can be revoked."

⁹At once the royal secretaries were summoned—on the twenty-third day of the third month, the month of Sivan. They wrote out all Mordecai's orders to the Jews, and to the satraps, governors and nobles of the 127 provinces stretching from India to Cush.^a These orders were written in the script of each province and the language of each people and also to the Jews in their own script and language. ¹⁰Mordecai wrote in the name of King Xerxes, sealed the dispatches with the king's signet ring, and sent them by mounted couriers, who rode fast horses especially bred for the king.

¹¹The king's edict granted the Jews in every city the right to assemble and protect themselves; to destroy, kill and annihilate any armed force of any nationality or province that might attack them and their women and children; and to plunder the property of their enemies. ¹²The day appointed for the Jews to do this in all the provinces of King Xerxes was the thirteenth day of the twelfth month, the month of Adar. ¹³A copy of the text of the edict was to be issued as law in every province and made known to the people of every nationality so that the Jews would be ready on that day to avenge themselves on their enemies.

¹⁴The couriers, riding the royal horses, raced out, spurred on by the king's command. And the edict was also issued in the citadel of Susa.

¹⁵Mordecai left the king's presence wearing royal garments of blue and white, a large crown of gold and a purple robe of fine linen. And the city of Susa held a joyous celebration. ¹⁶For the Jews it was a time of happiness and joy, gladness and honor. ¹⁷In every province and in every city, wherever the edict of the king went, there was joy and gladness among the Jews, with feasting and celebrating. And many people of other nationalities became Jews because fear of the Jews had seized them.

Triumph of the Jews

9 On the thirteenth day of the twelfth month, the month of Adar, the edict commanded by the king was to be carried out. On this day the enemies of the Jews had hoped to overpower them, but now the tables were turned and the Jews got the upper hand over those who hated them. ²The Jews assembled in their cities in all the provinces of King Xerxes to attack those seeking their destruction. No one could stand against them, because the people of all the other nationalities were afraid of them. ³And all the nobles of the provinces, the satraps, the governors and the king's administrators helped the Jews, because fear of Mordecai had seized them. ⁴Mordecai was prominent in the palace; his reputation spread throughout the provinces, and he became more and more powerful.

⁵The Jews struck down all their enemies with the sword, killing and destroying them, and they did what they pleased to those who hated them. ⁶In the citadel of Susa, the Jews killed and destroyed five hundred men. ⁷They also killed Parshandatha, Dalphon, Aspatha, ⁸Poratha, Adalia, Aridatha, ⁹Parmashta, Arisai, Aridai and Vaizatha, ¹⁰the ten sons of Haman son of Hammedatha, the enemy of the Jews. But they did not lay their hands on the plunder.

¹¹The number of those slain in the citadel of Susa was reported to the king that same day. ¹²The king said to Queen Esther, "The Jews have killed and destroyed five hundred men and the ten sons of Haman in the citadel of Susa. What have they done in the rest of the king's provinces? Now what is your petition? It will be given you. What is your request? It will also be granted."

---

^a9 That is, the upper Nile region

¹³"If it pleases the king," Esther answered, "give the Jews in Susa permission to carry out this day's edict tomorrow also, and let Haman's ten sons be hanged on gallows."

¹⁴So the king commanded that this be done. An edict was issued in Susa, and they hanged the ten sons of Haman. ¹⁵The Jews in Susa came together on the fourteenth day of the month of Adar, and they put to death in Susa three hundred men, but they did not lay their hands on the plunder.

¹⁶Meanwhile, the remainder of the Jews who were in the king's provinces also assembled to protect themselves and get relief from their enemies. They killed seventy-five thousand of them but did not lay their hands on the plunder. ¹⁷This happened on the thirteenth day of the month of Adar, and on the fourteenth they rested and made it a day of feasting and joy.

Purim Celebrated

¹⁸The Jews in Susa, however, had assembled on the thirteenth and fourteenth, and then on the fifteenth they rested and made it a day of feasting and joy. ¹⁹That is why rural Jews—those living in villages—observe the fourteenth of the month of Adar as a day of joy and feasting, a day for giving presents to each other.

²⁰Mordecai recorded these events, and he sent letters to all the Jews throughout the provinces of King Xerxes, near and far, ²¹to have them celebrate annually the fourteenth and fifteenth days of the month of Adar ²²as the time when the Jews got relief from their enemies, and as the month when their sorrow was turned into joy and their mourning into a day of celebration. He wrote them to observe the days as days of feasting and joy and giving presents of food to one another and gifts to the poor.

²³So the Jews agreed to continue the celebration they had begun, doing what Mordecai had written to them. ²⁴For Haman son of Hammedatha, the Agagite, the enemy of all the Jews, had plotted against the Jews to destroy them and had cast the *pur* (that is, the lot) for their ruin and destruction. ²⁵But when the plot came to the king's attention,[a] he issued written orders that the evil scheme Haman had devised against the Jews should come back onto his own head, and that he and his sons should be hanged on the gallows. ²⁶(Therefore these days were called Purim, from the word *pur.*) Because of everything written in this letter and because of what they had seen and what had happened to them, ²⁷the Jews took it upon themselves to establish the custom that they and their descendants and all who join them should without fail observe these two days every year, in the way prescribed and at the time appointed. ²⁸These days should be remembered and observed in every generation by every family, and in every province and in every city. And these days of Purim should never cease to be celebrated by the Jews, nor should the memory of them die out among their descendants.

²⁹So Queen Esther, daughter of Abihail, along with Mordecai the Jew, wrote with full authority to confirm this second letter concerning Purim. ³⁰And Mordecai sent letters to all the Jews in the 127 provinces of the kingdom of Xerxes—words of goodwill and assurance— ³¹to establish these days of Purim at their designated times, as Mordecai the Jew and Queen Esther had decreed for them, and as they had established for themselves and their descendants in regard to their times of fasting and lamentation. ³²Esther's decree confirmed these regulations about Purim, and it was written down in the records.

The Greatness of Mordecai

10 King Xerxes imposed tribute throughout the empire, to its distant shores. ²And all his acts of power and might, together with a full account of the greatness of Mordecai to which the king had raised him, are they not written in the book of the annals of the kings of Media and Persia? ³Mordecai the Jew was second in rank to King Xerxes, preeminent among the Jews, and held in high esteem by his many fellow Jews, because he worked for the good of his people and spoke up for the welfare of all the Jews.

―――――――――

a25 Or *when Esther came before the king*

Job's story is one of the most famous in the Bible. Cynics have pointed to it to affirm their presuppositions about how unfair God is, in spite of an innocent man's obedience. Sometimes even the most faithful believers have scratched their heads in bewilderment. How could so many terrible things have happened to this nearly flawless man?

Like most Biblical accounts, the message here isn't so much about Job and his family; this story is about God. Perhaps the most important lesson to be learned from Job's life is this one: The sooner we deal with who God really is and who we are in contrast to him, the wiser and more satisfied we'll be. If we want to learn this early in life, then the remainder of our lives will be rewarded—we'll be prosperous in God's almighty economy. If we wait until we're old men to make this discovery, we'll literally waste decades of potential usefulness and peace.

Job

Prologue

1 In the land of Uz there lived a man whose name was Job. This man was blameless and upright; he feared God and shunned evil. ²He had seven sons and three daughters, ³and he owned seven thousand sheep, three thousand camels, five hundred yoke of oxen and five hundred donkeys, and had a large number of servants. He was the greatest man among all the people of the East.

⁴His sons used to take turns holding feasts in their homes, and they would invite their three sisters to eat and drink with them. ⁵When a period of feasting had run its course, Job would send and have them purified. Early in the morning he would sacrifice a burnt offering for each of them, thinking, "Perhaps my children have sinned and cursed God in their hearts." This was Job's regular custom.

Job's First Test

⁶One day the angels*ᵃ* came to present themselves before the LORD, and Satan*ᵇ* also came with them. ⁷The LORD said to Satan, "Where have you come from?"

Satan answered the LORD, "From roaming through the earth and going back and forth in it."

⁸Then the LORD said to Satan, "Have you considered my servant Job? There is no one on earth like him; he is blameless and upright, a man who fears God and shuns evil."

⁹"Does Job fear God for nothing?" Satan replied. ¹⁰"Have you not put a hedge around him and his household and everything he has? You have blessed the work of his hands, so that his flocks and herds are

ᵃ6 Hebrew the sons of God ᵇ6 Satan means accuser.

spread throughout the land. ¹¹But stretch out your hand and strike everything he has, and he will surely curse you to your face."

¹²The LORD said to Satan, "Very well, then, everything he has is in your hands, but on the man himself do not lay a finger."

Then Satan went out from the presence of the LORD.

¹³One day when Job's sons and daughters were feasting and drinking wine at the oldest brother's house, ¹⁴a messenger came to Job and said, "The oxen were plowing and the donkeys were grazing nearby, ¹⁵and the Sabeans attacked and carried them off. They put the servants to the sword, and I am the only one who has escaped to tell you!"

¹⁶While he was still speaking, another messenger came and said, "The fire of God fell from the sky and burned up the sheep and the servants, and I am the only one who has escaped to tell you!"

¹⁷While he was still speaking, another messenger came and said, "The Chaldeans formed three raiding parties and swept down on your camels and carried

They're Gifts. Every One of Them.

DAILY INSIGHT

THURSDAY

Passage:
Job 1:13–22

Verse:
Job 1:21

It's 5:45 A.M. Your alarm is set to go off in exactly fifteen minutes, but on this particular day, it doesn't matter. Why? Because today someone—apparently with an IQ similar to that of a carrot—rings your doorbell.

In an instant, it's as though the circus has come to your living room. The dog is in a frenzy, your wife has bolted for her robe, the baby is wailing, and your heart is fully aerobic. To say the least, you're furious. "Who, in the name of good sense, could this be?" you sneer.

The man at the door is dressed in a tidy navy suit and light brown trench coat. His precise, narrow face and pasty complexion make it immediately clear to you that he has spent no time in the National Hockey League. *A bill collector*, you think to yourself.

"Good morning," the man speaks in a quiet but confident voice. "I am truly sorry to have wakened you this early, but I have something to give you." With that, he hands you a crisp white envelope, turns on his polished heel and walks away. You stand there stunned for a moment, then tear open the envelope. Inside is a crisp one hundred dollar bill. There's nothing else inside … no note, no explanation … just the money.

The next morning, at exactly 5:45, the doorbell rings and every detail of yesterday's story is repeated. Despite your questions and an offer of coffee and a danish, the strange little man makes his deposit with a pleasant smile and abruptly walks away. Incredibly, this happens every morning, like clock work—one hundred dollars a day.

A few weeks into this experience you are fully awake by 5:45, knowing the gift is on its way. In a few months, you are fully expecting the money to come. In fact, you have bought a car and told your banker that you "earn" an extra three thousand dollars a month!

At the end of a year, without explanation, the strange little man stops coming to your house. Even though you neither knew him nor understood why the gifts were delivered, they both are gone. Despite your curiosity, you can't help but resent the fact that, every morning, this man fails to show up to give you "your" money.

Job lost everything … his oxen, his donkeys, his servants, his sheep, his camels, his family. But he realized that everything that he "owned" was a gift in the first place. And now they were gone. For Job, the early morning doorbell stopped ringing.

What did Job do? The only thing he could do: He mourned, he thanked God for giving all these incredible things to him for a while, and then Job got on with his life. What a story.

For your next devotional reading, go to page 543.

them off. They put the servants to the sword, and I am the only one who has escaped to tell you!"

[18]While he was still speaking, yet another messenger came and said, "Your sons and daughters were feasting and drinking wine at the oldest brother's house, [19]when suddenly a mighty wind swept in from the desert and struck the four corners of the house. It collapsed on them and they are dead, and I am the only one who has escaped to tell you!"

[20]At this, Job got up and tore his robe and shaved his head. Then he fell to the ground in worship [21]and said:

"Naked I came from my mother's womb,
    and naked I will depart.[a]
The LORD gave and the LORD has taken
        away;
    may the name of the LORD be
        praised."

[22]In all this, Job did not sin by charging God with wrongdoing.

Job's Second Test

2 On another day the angels[b] came to present themselves before the LORD, and Satan also came with them to present himself before him. [2]And the LORD said to Satan, "Where have you come from?"

Satan answered the LORD, "From roaming through the earth and going back and forth in it."

[3]Then the LORD said to Satan, "Have you considered my servant Job? There is no one on earth like him; he is blameless and upright, a man who fears God and shuns evil. And he still maintains his integrity, though you incited me against him to ruin him without any reason."

[4]"Skin for skin!" Satan replied. "A man will give all he has for his own life. [5]But stretch out your hand and strike his flesh and bones, and he will surely curse you to your face."

[6]The LORD said to Satan, "Very well, then, he is in your hands; but you must spare his life."

[7]So Satan went out from the presence of the LORD and afflicted Job with painful sores from the soles of his feet to the top of his head. [8]Then Job took a piece of broken pottery and scraped himself with it as he sat among the ashes.

[a]21 Or *will return there* [b]1 Hebrew *the sons of God*

HEY DAD

Why do good people suffer?

Text: Job 1:8–12

Job is the most famous example of a Biblical character who suffered. But why Job? Of all people, why did this blameless man (v. 1) suffer so much? The reason, though it may be hard to see, is simple: In allowing Job to suffer, God proved that Job's love for him was pure. Satan argued that Job only loved God because God blessed him so richly. So God allowed Satan to take almost everything Job had: his riches, his family, and his health. Yet Job proved faithful; he never cursed God or blamed him for what had happened (v. 22).

Several verses in the New Testament shed light on this perplexing question. Hebrews 12:10-11 tells us that sometimes God uses pain to discipline us and turn us away from doing wrong things. James 1:2-4 says that sometimes God uses pain to help us grow up. These trials test our faith and help us develop perseverance "that [we] may be mature and complete, not lacking anything." So, as strange as it may seem, many times we have to suffer before we can experience complete and full lives. Finally, the apostle Paul moves us beyond the question of why and gives us an example of trust in God through the pain and trials of life: "I have learned the secret of being content in any and every situation ... I can do everything through him who gives me strength" (Philippians 4:12, 13).

Still today we see many examples of "good" people who suffer. And although *God* knows what's in his people's hearts, these types of trials allow them to discover—and to demonstrate to those watching—that God is worthy of their love regardless of their outward circumstances.

QUESTIONS KIDS ASK

For a complete listing of Questions Kids Ask, turn to page 1435.

[9]His wife said to him, "Are you still holding on to your integrity? Curse God and die!"

[10]He replied, "You are talking like a foolish[a] woman. Shall we accept good from God, and not trouble?"

In all this, Job did not sin in what he said.

Job's Three Friends

[11]When Job's three friends, Eliphaz the Temanite, Bildad the Shuhite and Zophar the Naamathite, heard about all the troubles that had come upon him, they set out from their homes and met together by agreement to go and sympathize with him and comfort him. [12]When they saw him from a distance, they could hardly recognize him; they began to weep aloud, and they tore their robes and sprinkled dust on their heads. [13]Then they sat on the ground with him for seven days and seven nights. No one said a word to him, because they saw how great his suffering was.

Job Speaks

3 After this, Job opened his mouth and cursed the day of his birth. [2]He said:

[3]"May the day of my birth perish,
 and the night it was said, 'A boy is
  born!'
[4]That day—may it turn to darkness;
 may God above not care about it;
 may no light shine upon it.
[5]May darkness and deep shadow[b] claim
  it once more;
 may a cloud settle over it;
 may blackness overwhelm its light.
[6]That night—may thick darkness
  seize it;
 may it not be included among the
  days of the year
 nor be entered in any of the
  months.
[7]May that night be barren;
 may no shout of joy be heard in it.

[a]10 The Hebrew word rendered *foolish* denotes moral deficiency.   [b]5 Or *and the shadow of death*

Prayer: Good for You, Good for Them
Job, the Praying Father

"Early in the morning he would sacrifice a burnt offering for each of [his sons and daughters] . . . This was Job's regular custom" (1:5).

DADS
IN THE
BIBLE

Text: Job 1

During the Hebrew temple rituals, sometimes the priest faced the people to tell them the news God had for them. "Hear the word of the Lord," he would cry. At other times the priest turned his back on the people and faced the altar, the symbol for the presence of God Almighty. In this position, he might raise his hands and, like an attorney before a judge, plead his people's case.

The Bible tells us that Job did this same thing for his children.

Of course, you remember the rest of the story, how God spoke about Job to Satan, saying, "There is no one on earth like him; he is blameless and upright, a man who fears God and shuns evil" (1:8). Perhaps one of the things that so impressed God about this man was the way he faithfully prayed for his children.

How often do your children see you face the altar and plead their case? "Father in heaven, please protect Missy today in school. Guard her mind and her actions. Talk to her through her friends who love you, and keep her from those who would turn her away from your love."

As Missy hears her dad hold her up before the throne of God, the chills run down her spine. *My dad is praying for me.* These words will roll over and over again in her mind. Over the course of the years, these prayers could change her life.

Pray for your children. Lift them up before the Father and seek his protection and blessing on their lives. This will be a powerful thing—both for you and for them.

For a complete listing of Dads in the Bible, turn to page 1434.

⁸May those who curse days*ᵃ* curse that
day,
those who are ready to rouse
Leviathan.
⁹May its morning stars become dark;
may it wait for daylight in vain
and not see the first rays of dawn,
¹⁰for it did not shut the doors of the
womb on me
to hide trouble from my eyes.

¹¹"Why did I not perish at birth,
and die as I came from the womb?
¹²Why were there knees to receive me
and breasts that I might be nursed?
¹³For now I would be lying down in
peace;
I would be asleep and at rest
¹⁴with kings and counselors of the
earth,
who built for themselves places now
lying in ruins,
¹⁵with rulers who had gold,
who filled their houses with silver.
¹⁶Or why was I not hidden in the ground
like a stillborn child,
like an infant who never saw the
light of day?
¹⁷There the wicked cease from turmoil,
and there the weary are at rest.
¹⁸Captives also enjoy their ease;
they no longer hear the slave driver's
shout.
¹⁹The small and the great are there,
and the slave is freed from his master.

²⁰"Why is light given to those in misery,
and life to the bitter of soul,

ᵃ8 Or the sea

Articulate Silence

My precious friend, Kip Jordon, was dead. He was a man just a few years older than me, and his ailing liver had simply shut down. His family had rushed him to the hospital, but in only a few hours he was gone.

The next few days were filled with the hurried plans of shocked and disbelieving friends. "How could this be?" we said to each other. "How could this have happened? Not Kip. Not now."

Our family—and many other friends—made the arrangements to fly to Dallas for the funeral service. Although we didn't know what we'd say to these lifelong friends, we couldn't wait to see Kip's wife, Kathy, and their two sons, Kelly and Karl.

On Sunday afternoon we were reunited. And although there were so many things to be said, we actually said very little. We held each other. We wept openly. We stood silently by while other dear friends did the same. And then we came home.

Over the next several weeks, we talked to Kathy. She thanked us—and all the others—for taking time to come. She thanked us for our prayers and our consolation. But amazingly, very few words had ever been spoken that day in Dallas.

DAILY INSIGHT

FRIDAY
Passage:
Job 2:1–13
Verse:
Job 2:13

Job's friends heard what had happened to their comrade, so they paid him a visit. The text tells us that, for seven long days, these three men sat on the ground with Job and didn't speak a single word. Could these friends have said anything to Job? Did they have any "helpful" advice to share? Even though they didn't divulge any of this wisdom, did Job feel supported and comforted by these men? Was he grateful for their friendship and their articulate silence?

Yes, four times yes.

In many ways, knowing what to do with the pain of a friend is more difficult than knowing what to do with your own suffering. Sometimes verbal advice is in order. But sometimes, silent presence is the most appropriate action.

The next time one of your friends is in trouble, try simply showing up. Don't worry if you don't have any advice. Don't be concerned if the words you try to say are bumbling and awkward. Just being there will probably be enough.

What a powerful lesson these three silent men have taught us.

For your next devotional reading, go to page 545.

²¹to those who long for death that does
    not come,
  who search for it more than for
    hidden treasure,
²²who are filled with gladness
  and rejoice when they reach the
    grave?
²³Why is life given to a man
  whose way is hidden,
  whom God has hedged in?
²⁴For sighing comes to me instead of
    food;
  my groans pour out like water.
²⁵What I feared has come upon me;
  what I dreaded has happened to me.
²⁶I have no peace, no quietness;
  I have no rest, but only turmoil."

Eliphaz

4 Then Eliphaz the Temanite replied:

²"If someone ventures a word with you,
    will you be impatient?
  But who can keep from speaking?
³Think how you have instructed many,
  how you have strengthened feeble
    hands.
⁴Your words have supported those who
    stumbled;
  you have strengthened faltering
    knees.
⁵But now trouble comes to you, and you
    are discouraged;
  it strikes you, and you are dismayed.
⁶Should not your piety be your
    confidence
  and your blameless ways your hope?

⁷"Consider now: Who, being innocent,
    has ever perished?
  Where were the upright ever
    destroyed?
⁸As I have observed, those who plow evil
  and those who sow trouble reap it.
⁹At the breath of God they are
    destroyed;
  at the blast of his anger they perish.
¹⁰The lions may roar and growl,
  yet the teeth of the great lions are
    broken.
¹¹The lion perishes for lack of prey,
  and the cubs of the lioness are
    scattered.

¹²"A word was secretly brought to me,
  my ears caught a whisper of it.
¹³Amid disquieting dreams in the night,
  when deep sleep falls on men,
¹⁴fear and trembling seized me
  and made all my bones shake.

¹⁵A spirit glided past my face,
  and the hair on my body stood on
    end.
¹⁶It stopped,
  but I could not tell what it was.
  A form stood before my eyes,
  and I heard a hushed voice:
¹⁷'Can a mortal be more righteous than
    God?
  Can a man be more pure than his
    Maker?
¹⁸If God places no trust in his servants,
  if he charges his angels with error,
¹⁹how much more those who live in
    houses of clay,
  whose foundations are in the dust,
  who are crushed more readily than a
    moth!
²⁰Between dawn and dusk they are
    broken to pieces;
  unnoticed, they perish forever.
²¹Are not the cords of their tent pulled
    up,
  so that they die without wisdom?'ᵃ

5 "Call if you will, but who will answer
    you?
  To which of the holy ones will you
    turn?
²Resentment kills a fool,
  and envy slays the simple.
³I myself have seen a fool taking root,
  but suddenly his house was cursed.
⁴His children are far from safety,
  crushed in court without a defender.
⁵The hungry consume his harvest,
  taking it even from among thorns,
  and the thirsty pant after his wealth.
⁶For hardship does not spring from the
    soil,
  nor does trouble sprout from the
    ground.
⁷Yet man is born to trouble
  as surely as sparks fly upward.

⁸"But if it were I, I would appeal to God;
  I would lay my cause before him.
⁹He performs wonders that cannot be
    fathomed,
  miracles that cannot be counted.
¹⁰He bestows rain on the earth;
  he sends water upon the countryside.
¹¹The lowly he sets on high,
  and those who mourn are lifted to
    safety.
¹²He thwarts the plans of the crafty,
  so that their hands achieve no
    success.

ᵃ21 Some interpreters end the quotation after
verse 17.

Choosing Good Friends

Key Verse: *"If someone ventures a word with you, will you be impatient? But who can keep from speaking?"* Job 4:2

Text: Job 4:1–6 *(Dad or child reads the text.)*

QUIET **TIMES** WITH **Dad**

DAD READS: Someone once said, "A good friend is a gift we give ourselves." When I look back over the past few years, I can tell you that good friends are exactly that: wonderful gifts.

Child reads: I am glad for the gift of good friends, too. I'm happy that they help me when I need them and I'm glad that they let me help them when they're in trouble. Good friends make every day better.

DAD READS: The story of Job is a story about friends. Terrible things had happened to Job and these friends tried to be helpful. The first time they came to visit Job, they sat quietly with him, letting him know that they loved him no matter what. I'm sure this made Job happy, just to know that he had friends who were willing to be with him.

Child reads: Job's friends decided to give him some advice. These men did their best to be truly helpful to their sad friend. But some of their words were valuable and some of their words were not.

DAD READS: What we need to learn about this story is that Job's friends did their best. I know this sounds unkind, but if Job had wanted more help than his friends could give him, he should have chosen better friends before these bad things happened.

Child reads: This is something you and I need to think about all the time. The people we choose as our friends need to be the kind of people who will know how to help us when we really need help. If we choose good friends, then we'll get good help.

DAD READS: I need to think about this lesson. I need to be sure that my friends are the kind of people who love God, people who want to please and obey him. Then when I need their help, I know that their words will be good words . . . God's words.

Child reads: I want you to have good friends. I want you to help me choose good friends, too.

DAD READS: Let me pray this prayer with you:

Our Father in heaven, thank you for friends. Thank you for the help our friends can bring us when we are sad or in trouble. Please help us to remember to choose our friends carefully. Help us to remember that some day you will use our friends to tell us what you want us to do. And thank you for your friendship and love. We love you. In Jesus' name, *Amen.*

For your next devotional reading, go to page 555.

¹³He catches the wise in their craftiness,
and the schemes of the wily are
swept away.
¹⁴Darkness comes upon them in the
daytime;
at noon they grope as in the night.
¹⁵He saves the needy from the sword in
their mouth;
he saves them from the clutches of
the powerful.
¹⁶So the poor have hope,
and injustice shuts its mouth.

¹⁷"Blessed is the man whom God
corrects;
so do not despise the discipline of
the Almighty.ᵃ
¹⁸For he wounds, but he also binds up;
he injures, but his hands also heal.
¹⁹From six calamities he will rescue you;
in seven no harm will befall you.
²⁰In famine he will ransom you from
death,
and in battle from the stroke of the
sword.
²¹You will be protected from the lash of
the tongue,
and need not fear when destruction
comes.
²²You will laugh at destruction and
famine,
and need not fear the beasts of the
earth.
²³For you will have a covenant with the
stones of the field,
and the wild animals will be at peace
with you.
²⁴You will know that your tent is secure;
you will take stock of your property
and find nothing missing.
²⁵You will know that your children will be
many,
and your descendants like the grass
of the earth.
²⁶You will come to the grave in full vigor,
like sheaves gathered in season.

²⁷"We have examined this, and it is true.
So hear it and apply it to yourself."

Job

6 Then Job replied:

²"If only my anguish could be weighed
and all my misery be placed on the
scales!
³It would surely outweigh the sand of
the seas—
no wonder my words have been
impetuous.

⁴The arrows of the Almighty are in me,
my spirit drinks in their poison;
God's terrors are marshaled against
me.
⁵Does a wild donkey bray when it has
grass,
or an ox bellow when it has fodder?
⁶Is tasteless food eaten without salt,
or is there flavor in the white of an
eggᵇ?
⁷I refuse to touch it;
such food makes me ill.

⁸"Oh, that I might have my request,
that God would grant what I hope
for,
⁹that God would be willing to crush me,
to let loose his hand and cut me off!
¹⁰Then I would still have this
consolation—
my joy in unrelenting pain—
that I had not denied the words of
the Holy One.

¹¹"What strength do I have, that I should
still hope?
What prospects, that I should be
patient?
¹²Do I have the strength of stone?
Is my flesh bronze?
¹³Do I have any power to help myself,
now that success has been driven
from me?

¹⁴"A despairing man should have the
devotion of his friends,
even though he forsakes the fear of
the Almighty.
¹⁵But my brothers are as undependable
as intermittent streams,
as the streams that overflow
¹⁶when darkened by thawing ice
and swollen with melting snow,
¹⁷but that cease to flow in the dry season,
and in the heat vanish from their
channels.
¹⁸Caravans turn aside from their routes;
they go up into the wasteland and
perish.
¹⁹The caravans of Tema look for water,
the traveling merchants of Sheba
look in hope.
²⁰They are distressed, because they had
been confident;
they arrive there, only to be
disappointed.
²¹Now you too have proved to be of no
help;

ᵃ17 Hebrew *Shaddai*; here and throughout Job
ᵇ6 The meaning of the Hebrew for this phrase is
uncertain.

you see something dreadful and are
    afraid.
²² Have I ever said, 'Give something on
        my behalf,
    pay a ransom for me from your
        wealth,
²³ deliver me from the hand of the enemy,
    ransom me from the clutches of the
        ruthless'?

²⁴ "Teach me, and I will be quiet;
    show me where I have been wrong.
²⁵ How painful are honest words!
    But what do your arguments prove?
²⁶ Do you mean to correct what I say,
    and treat the words of a despairing
        man as wind?
²⁷ You would even cast lots for the
        fatherless
    and barter away your friend.

²⁸ "But now be so kind as to look at me.
    Would I lie to your face?
²⁹ Relent, do not be unjust;
    reconsider, for my integrity is at
        stake.ᵃ
³⁰ Is there any wickedness on my lips?
    Can my mouth not discern malice?

7 "Does not man have hard service on
        earth?
    Are not his days like those of a hired
        man?
² Like a slave longing for the evening
        shadows,
    or a hired man waiting eagerly for his
        wages,
³ so I have been allotted months of
        futility,
    and nights of misery have been
        assigned to me.
⁴ When I lie down I think, 'How long
        before I get up?'
    The night drags on, and I toss till
        dawn.
⁵ My body is clothed with worms and
        scabs,
    my skin is broken and festering.

⁶ "My days are swifter than a weaver's
        shuttle,
    and they come to an end without
        hope.
⁷ Remember, O God, that my life is but a
        breath;
    my eyes will never see happiness
        again.
⁸ The eye that now sees me will see me
        no longer;
    you will look for me, but I will be no
        more.
⁹ As a cloud vanishes and is gone,

so he who goes down to the graveᵇ
    does not return.
¹⁰ He will never come to his house again;
    his place will know him no more.

¹¹ "Therefore I will not keep silent;
    I will speak out in the anguish of my
        spirit,
    I will complain in the bitterness of
        my soul.
¹² Am I the sea, or the monster of the
        deep,
    that you put me under guard?
¹³ When I think my bed will comfort me
    and my couch will ease my
        complaint,
¹⁴ even then you frighten me with dreams
    and terrify me with visions,
¹⁵ so that I prefer strangling and death,
    rather than this body of mine.
¹⁶ I despise my life; I would not live
        forever.
    Let me alone; my days have no
        meaning.

¹⁷ "What is man that you make so much
        of him,
    that you give him so much attention,
¹⁸ that you examine him every morning
    and test him every moment?
¹⁹ Will you never look away from me,
    or let me alone even for an instant?
²⁰ If I have sinned, what have I done to
        you,
    O watcher of men?
    Why have you made me your target?
    Have I become a burden to you?ᶜ
²¹ Why do you not pardon my offenses
    and forgive my sins?
    For I will soon lie down in the dust;
    you will search for me, but I will be
        no more."

Bildad

8 Then Bildad the Shuhite replied:

² "How long will you say such things?
    Your words are a blustering wind.
³ Does God pervert justice?
    Does the Almighty pervert what is
        right?
⁴ When your children sinned against
        him,
    he gave them over to the penalty of
        their sin.

ᵃ29 Or *my righteousness still stands*   ᵇ9 Hebrew
Sheol   ᶜ20 A few manuscripts of the Masoretic
Text, an ancient Hebrew scribal tradition and
Septuagint; most manuscripts of the Masoretic
Text *I have become a burden to myself.*

[5] But if you will look to God
and plead with the Almighty,
[6] if you are pure and upright,
even now he will rouse himself on
your behalf
and restore you to your rightful place.
[7] Your beginnings will seem humble,
so prosperous will your future be.

[8] "Ask the former generations
and find out what their fathers
learned,
[9] for we were born only yesterday and
know nothing,
and our days on earth are but a
shadow.
[10] Will they not instruct you and tell you?
Will they not bring forth words from
their understanding?
[11] Can papyrus grow tall where there is no
marsh?
Can reeds thrive without water?
[12] While still growing and uncut,
they wither more quickly than grass.
[13] Such is the destiny of all who forget
God;
so perishes the hope of the godless.
[14] What he trusts in is fragile[a];
what he relies on is a spider's web.
[15] He leans on his web, but it gives way;
he clings to it, but it does not hold.
[16] He is like a well-watered plant in the
sunshine,
spreading its shoots over the garden;
[17] it entwines its roots around a pile of
rocks
and looks for a place among the
stones.
[18] But when it is torn from its spot,
that place disowns it and says,
'I never saw you.'
[19] Surely its life withers away,
and[b] from the soil other plants grow.

[20] "Surely God does not reject a blameless
man
or strengthen the hands of evildoers.
[21] He will yet fill your mouth with
laughter
and your lips with shouts of joy.
[22] Your enemies will be clothed in shame,
and the tents of the wicked will be no
more."

Job

9 Then Job replied:

[2] "Indeed, I know that this is true.
But how can a mortal be righteous
before God?

[3] Though one wished to dispute with
him,
he could not answer him one time
out of a thousand.
[4] His wisdom is profound, his power is
vast.
Who has resisted him and come out
unscathed?
[5] He moves mountains without their
knowing it
and overturns them in his anger.
[6] He shakes the earth from its place
and makes its pillars tremble.
[7] He speaks to the sun and it does not
shine;
he seals off the light of the stars.
[8] He alone stretches out the heavens
and treads on the waves of the sea.
[9] He is the Maker of the Bear and Orion,
the Pleiades and the constellations
of the south.
[10] He performs wonders that cannot be
fathomed,
miracles that cannot be counted.
[11] When he passes me, I cannot see him;
when he goes by, I cannot perceive
him.
[12] If he snatches away, who can stop him?
Who can say to him, 'What are you
doing?'
[13] God does not restrain his anger;
even the cohorts of Rahab cowered
at his feet.

[14] "How then can I dispute with him?
How can I find words to argue with
him?
[15] Though I were innocent, I could not
answer him;
I could only plead with my Judge for
mercy.
[16] Even if I summoned him and he
responded,
I do not believe he would give me a
hearing.
[17] He would crush me with a storm
and multiply my wounds for no
reason.
[18] He would not let me regain my breath
but would overwhelm me with
misery.
[19] If it is a matter of strength, he is
mighty!
And if it is a matter of justice, who
will summon him[c]?
[20] Even if I were innocent, my mouth
would condemn me;

---

[a]14 The meaning of the Hebrew for this word is
uncertain.   [b]19 Or *Surely all the joy it has / is that*
[c]19 See Septuagint; Hebrew *me.*

if I were blameless, it would
pronounce me guilty.
²¹ "Although I am blameless,
I have no concern for myself;
I despise my own life.
²² It is all the same; that is why I say,
'He destroys both the blameless and
the wicked.'
²³ When a scourge brings sudden death,
he mocks the despair of the
innocent.
²⁴ When a land falls into the hands of the
wicked,
he blindfolds its judges.
If it is not he, then who is it?

²⁵ "My days are swifter than a runner;
they fly away without a glimpse of
joy.
²⁶ They skim past like boats of papyrus,
like eagles swooping down on their
prey.
²⁷ If I say, 'I will forget my complaint,
I will change my expression, and
smile,'
²⁸ I still dread all my sufferings,
for I know you will not hold me
innocent.
²⁹ Since I am already found guilty,
why should I struggle in vain?
³⁰ Even if I washed myself with soap ᵃ
and my hands with washing soda,
³¹ you would plunge me into a slime pit
so that even my clothes would detest
me.

³² "He is not a man like me that I might
answer him,
that we might confront each other in
court.
³³ If only there were someone to arbitrate
between us,
to lay his hand upon us both,
³⁴ someone to remove God's rod from me,
so that his terror would frighten me
no more.
³⁵ Then I would speak up without fear of
him,
but as it now stands with me, I
cannot.

10 "I loathe my very life;
therefore I will give free rein to
my complaint
and speak out in the bitterness of my
soul.
² I will say to God: Do not condemn me,
but tell me what charges you have
against me.
³ Does it please you to oppress me,
to spurn the work of your hands,

while you smile on the schemes of
the wicked?
⁴ Do you have eyes of flesh?
Do you see as a mortal sees?
⁵ Are your days like those of a mortal
or your years like those of a man,
⁶ that you must search out my faults
and probe after my sin—
⁷ though you know that I am not guilty
and that no one can rescue me from
your hand?

⁸ "Your hands shaped me and made me.
Will you now turn and destroy me?
⁹ Remember that you molded me like
clay.
Will you now turn me to dust
again?
¹⁰ Did you not pour me out like milk
and curdle me like cheese,
¹¹ clothe me with skin and flesh
and knit me together with bones and
sinews?
¹² You gave me life and showed me
kindness,
and in your providence watched over
my spirit.

¹³ "But this is what you concealed in your
heart,
and I know that this was in your
mind:
¹⁴ If I sinned, you would be watching me
and would not let my offense go
unpunished.
¹⁵ If I am guilty—woe to me!
Even if I am innocent, I cannot lift
my head,
for I am full of shame
and drowned in ᵇ my affliction.
¹⁶ If I hold my head high, you stalk me
like a lion
and again display your awesome
power against me.
¹⁷ You bring new witnesses against me
and increase your anger toward me;
your forces come against me wave
upon wave.

¹⁸ "Why then did you bring me out of the
womb?
I wish I had died before any eye saw
me.
¹⁹ If only I had never come into being,
or had been carried straight from the
womb to the grave!
²⁰ Are not my few days almost over?
Turn away from me so I can have a
moment's joy

ᵃ30 Or *snow*   ᵇ15 Or *and aware of*

²¹before I go to the place of no return,
to the land of gloom and deep
shadow,ᵃ
²²to the land of deepest night,
of deep shadow and disorder,
where even the light is like
darkness."

Zophar

11 Then Zophar the Naamathite replied:

²"Are all these words to go unanswered?
Is this talker to be vindicated?
³Will your idle talk reduce men to
silence?
Will no one rebuke you when you
mock?
⁴You say to God, 'My beliefs are flawless
and I am pure in your sight.'
⁵Oh, how I wish that God would speak,
that he would open his lips against
you
⁶and disclose to you the secrets of
wisdom,
for true wisdom has two sides.
Know this: God has even forgotten
some of your sin.

⁷"Can you fathom the mysteries of God?
Can you probe the limits of the
Almighty?
⁸They are higher than the heavens—
what can you do?
They are deeper than the depths of
the graveᵇ—what can you
know?
⁹Their measure is longer than the earth
and wider than the sea.

¹⁰"If he comes along and confines you in
prison
and convenes a court, who can
oppose him?
¹¹Surely he recognizes deceitful men;
and when he sees evil, does he not
take note?
¹²But a witless man can no more become
wise
than a wild donkey's colt can be born
a man.ᶜ

¹³"Yet if you devote your heart to him
and stretch out your hands to him,
¹⁴if you put away the sin that is in your
hand
and allow no evil to dwell in your
tent,
¹⁵then you will lift up your face without
shame;
you will stand firm and without fear.
¹⁶You will surely forget your trouble,
recalling it only as waters gone by.
¹⁷Life will be brighter than noonday,
and darkness will become like
morning.
¹⁸You will be secure, because there is
hope;
you will look about you and take
your rest in safety.
¹⁹You will lie down, with no one to make
you afraid,
and many will court your favor.
²⁰But the eyes of the wicked will fail,
and escape will elude them;
their hope will become a dying
gasp."

Job

12 Then Job replied:

²"Doubtless you are the people,
and wisdom will die with you!
³But I have a mind as well as you;
I am not inferior to you.
Who does not know all these things?

⁴"I have become a laughingstock to my
friends,
though I called upon God and he
answered—
a mere laughingstock, though
righteous and blameless!
⁵Men at ease have contempt for
misfortune
as the fate of those whose feet are
slipping.
⁶The tents of marauders are
undisturbed,
and those who provoke God are
secure—
those who carry their god in their
hands.ᵈ

⁷"But ask the animals, and they will
teach you,
or the birds of the air, and they will
tell you;
⁸or speak to the earth, and it will teach
you,
or let the fish of the sea inform you.
⁹Which of all these does not know
that the hand of the LORD has done
this?
¹⁰In his hand is the life of every creature
and the breath of all mankind.
¹¹Does not the ear test words
as the tongue tastes food?

ᵃ21 Or *and the shadow of death*; also in verse 22
ᵇ8 Hebrew *than Sheol*   ᶜ12 Or *wild donkey can be
born tame*   ᵈ6 Or *secure / in what God's hand
brings them*

¹²Is not wisdom found among the aged?
  Does not long life bring
    understanding?

¹³"To God belong wisdom and power;
  counsel and understanding are his.
¹⁴What he tears down cannot be rebuilt;
  the man he imprisons cannot be
    released.
¹⁵If he holds back the waters, there is
    drought;
  if he lets them loose, they devastate
    the land.
¹⁶To him belong strength and victory;
  both deceived and deceiver are his.
¹⁷He leads counselors away stripped
  and makes fools of judges.
¹⁸He takes off the shackles put on by
    kings
  and ties a loincloth*ᵃ* around their
    waist.
¹⁹He leads priests away stripped
  and overthrows men long
    established.
²⁰He silences the lips of trusted advisers
  and takes away the discernment of
    elders.
²¹He pours contempt on nobles
  and disarms the mighty.
²²He reveals the deep things of darkness
  and brings deep shadows into the
    light.
²³He makes nations great, and destroys
    them;
  he enlarges nations, and disperses
    them.
²⁴He deprives the leaders of the earth of
    their reason;
  he sends them wandering through a
    trackless waste.
²⁵They grope in darkness with no light;
  he makes them stagger like
    drunkards.

13 "My eyes have seen all this,
  my ears have heard and
    understood it.
²What you know, I also know;
  I am not inferior to you.
³But I desire to speak to the Almighty
  and to argue my case with God.
⁴You, however, smear me with lies;
  you are worthless physicians, all of
    you!
⁵If only you would be altogether silent!
  For you, that would be wisdom.
⁶Hear now my argument;
  listen to the plea of my lips.
⁷Will you speak wickedly on God's
    behalf?
  Will you speak deceitfully for him?

⁸Will you show him partiality?
  Will you argue the case for God?
⁹Would it turn out well if he examined
    you?
  Could you deceive him as you might
    deceive men?
¹⁰He would surely rebuke you
  if you secretly showed partiality.
¹¹Would not his splendor terrify you?
  Would not the dread of him fall on
    you?
¹²Your maxims are proverbs of ashes;
  your defenses are defenses of clay.

¹³"Keep silent and let me speak;
  then let come to me what may.
¹⁴Why do I put myself in jeopardy
  and take my life in my hands?
¹⁵Though he slay me, yet will I hope in
    him;
  I will surely*ᵇ* defend my ways to his
    face.
¹⁶Indeed, this will turn out for my
    deliverance,
  for no godless man would dare come
    before him!
¹⁷Listen carefully to my words;
  let your ears take in what I say.
¹⁸Now that I have prepared my case,
  I know I will be vindicated.
¹⁹Can anyone bring charges against me?
  If so, I will be silent and die.

²⁰"Only grant me these two things, O God,
  and then I will not hide from you:
²¹Withdraw your hand far from me,
  and stop frightening me with your
    terrors.
²²Then summon me and I will answer,
  or let me speak, and you reply.
²³How many wrongs and sins have I
    committed?
  Show me my offense and my sin.
²⁴Why do you hide your face
  and consider me your enemy?
²⁵Will you torment a windblown leaf?
  Will you chase after dry chaff?
²⁶For you write down bitter things
    against me
  and make me inherit the sins of my
    youth.
²⁷You fasten my feet in shackles;
  you keep close watch on all my paths
  by putting marks on the soles of my
    feet.

²⁸"So man wastes away like something
    rotten,
  like a garment eaten by moths.

ᵃ18 Or *shackles of kings / and ties a belt*   *ᵇ15* Or *He
will surely slay me; I have no hope — / yet I will*

14

"Man born of woman
is of few days and full of trouble.
² He springs up like a flower and withers away;
like a fleeting shadow, he does not endure.
³ Do you fix your eye on such a one?
Will you bring him[a] before you for judgment?
⁴ Who can bring what is pure from the impure?
No one!
⁵ Man's days are determined;
you have decreed the number of his months
and have set limits he cannot exceed.
⁶ So look away from him and let him alone,
till he has put in his time like a hired man.

⁷ "At least there is hope for a tree:
If it is cut down, it will sprout again,
and its new shoots will not fail.
⁸ Its roots may grow old in the ground
and its stump die in the soil,
⁹ yet at the scent of water it will bud
and put forth shoots like a plant.
¹⁰ But man dies and is laid low;
he breathes his last and is no more.
¹¹ As water disappears from the sea
or a riverbed becomes parched and dry,
¹² so man lies down and does not rise;
till the heavens are no more, men will not awake
or be roused from their sleep.

¹³ "If only you would hide me in the grave[b]
and conceal me till your anger has passed!
If only you would set me a time
and then remember me!
¹⁴ If a man dies, will he live again?
All the days of my hard service
I will wait for my renewal[c] to come.
¹⁵ You will call and I will answer you;
you will long for the creature your hands have made.
¹⁶ Surely then you will count my steps
but not keep track of my sin.
¹⁷ My offenses will be sealed up in a bag;
you will cover over my sin.

¹⁸ "But as a mountain erodes and crumbles
and as a rock is moved from its place,
¹⁹ as water wears away stones

and torrents wash away the soil,
so you destroy man's hope.
²⁰ You overpower him once for all, and he is gone;
you change his countenance and send him away.
²¹ If his sons are honored, he does not know it;
if they are brought low, he does not see it.
²² He feels but the pain of his own body
and mourns only for himself."

Eliphaz

15

Then Eliphaz the Temanite replied:

² "Would a wise man answer with empty notions
or fill his belly with the hot east wind?
³ Would he argue with useless words,
with speeches that have no value?
⁴ But you even undermine piety
and hinder devotion to God.
⁵ Your sin prompts your mouth;
you adopt the tongue of the crafty.
⁶ Your own mouth condemns you, not mine;
your own lips testify against you.

⁷ "Are you the first man ever born?
Were you brought forth before the hills?
⁸ Do you listen in on God's council?
Do you limit wisdom to yourself?
⁹ What do you know that we do not know?
What insights do you have that we do not have?
¹⁰ The gray-haired and the aged are on our side,
men even older than your father.
¹¹ Are God's consolations not enough for you,
words spoken gently to you?
¹² Why has your heart carried you away,
and why do your eyes flash,
¹³ so that you vent your rage against God
and pour out such words from your mouth?

¹⁴ "What is man, that he could be pure,
or one born of woman, that he could be righteous?
¹⁵ If God places no trust in his holy ones,
if even the heavens are not pure in his eyes,

a3 Septuagint, Vulgate and Syriac; Hebrew me
b13 Hebrew Sheol   c14 Or release

¹⁶how much less man, who is vile and
    corrupt,
    who drinks up evil like water!

¹⁷"Listen to me and I will explain to you;
    let me tell you what I have seen,
¹⁸what wise men have declared,
    hiding nothing received from their
    fathers
¹⁹(to whom alone the land was given
    when no alien passed among them):
²⁰All his days the wicked man suffers
    torment,
    the ruthless through all the years
    stored up for him.
²¹Terrifying sounds fill his ears;
    when all seems well, marauders
    attack him.
²²He despairs of escaping the darkness;
    he is marked for the sword.
²³He wanders about—food for vultures^a;
    he knows the day of darkness is at
    hand.
²⁴Distress and anguish fill him with terror;
    they overwhelm him, like a king
    poised to attack,
²⁵because he shakes his fist at God
    and vaunts himself against the
    Almighty,
²⁶defiantly charging against him
    with a thick, strong shield.

²⁷"Though his face is covered with fat
    and his waist bulges with flesh,
²⁸he will inhabit ruined towns
    and houses where no one lives,
    houses crumbling to rubble.
²⁹He will no longer be rich and his
    wealth will not endure,
    nor will his possessions spread over
    the land.
³⁰He will not escape the darkness;
    a flame will wither his shoots,
    and the breath of God's mouth will
    carry him away.
³¹Let him not deceive himself by trusting
    what is worthless,
    for he will get nothing in return.
³²Before his time he will be paid in full,
    and his branches will not flourish.
³³He will be like a vine stripped of its
    unripe grapes,
    like an olive tree shedding its
    blossoms.
³⁴For the company of the godless will be
    barren,
    and fire will consume the tents of
    those who love bribes.
³⁵They conceive trouble and give birth to
    evil;
    their womb fashions deceit."

Job

16 Then Job replied:

²"I have heard many things like these;
    miserable comforters are you all!
³Will your long-winded speeches never
    end?
    What ails you that you keep on
    arguing?
⁴I also could speak like you,
    if you were in my place;
    I could make fine speeches against you
    and shake my head at you.
⁵But my mouth would encourage you;
    comfort from my lips would bring
    you relief.

⁶"Yet if I speak, my pain is not relieved;
    and if I refrain, it does not go away.
⁷Surely, O God, you have worn me out;
    you have devastated my entire
    household.
⁸You have bound me—and it has
    become a witness;
    my gauntness rises up and testifies
    against me.
⁹God assails me and tears me in his
    anger
    and gnashes his teeth at me;
    my opponent fastens on me his
    piercing eyes.
¹⁰Men open their mouths to jeer at me;
    they strike my cheek in scorn
    and unite together against me.
¹¹God has turned me over to evil men
    and thrown me into the clutches of
    the wicked.
¹²All was well with me, but he shattered
    me;
    he seized me by the neck and
    crushed me.
    He has made me his target;
¹³   his archers surround me.
    Without pity, he pierces my kidneys
    and spills my gall on the ground.
¹⁴Again and again he bursts upon me;
    he rushes at me like a warrior.

¹⁵"I have sewed sackcloth over my skin
    and buried my brow in the dust.
¹⁶My face is red with weeping,
    deep shadows ring my eyes;
¹⁷yet my hands have been free of
    violence
    and my prayer is pure.

¹⁸"O earth, do not cover my blood;
    may my cry never be laid to rest!

^a23 Or *about, looking for food*

¹⁹Even now my witness is in heaven;
  my advocate is on high.
²⁰My intercessor is my friend^a
  as my eyes pour out tears to God;
²¹on behalf of a man he pleads with God
  as a man pleads for his friend.

²²"Only a few years will pass
  before I go on the journey of no
    return.

17 ¹My spirit is broken,
  my days are cut short,
  the grave awaits me.
²Surely mockers surround me;
  my eyes must dwell on their
    hostility.

³"Give me, O God, the pledge you
    demand.
  Who else will put up security for me?
⁴You have closed their minds to
    understanding;
  therefore you will not let them
    triumph.
⁵If a man denounces his friends for
    reward,
  the eyes of his children will fail.

⁶"God has made me a byword to
    everyone,
  a man in whose face people spit.
⁷My eyes have grown dim with grief;
  my whole frame is but a shadow.
⁸Upright men are appalled at this;
  the innocent are aroused against the
    ungodly.
⁹Nevertheless, the righteous will hold to
    their ways,
  and those with clean hands will grow
    stronger.

¹⁰"But come on, all of you, try again!
  I will not find a wise man among
    you.
¹¹My days have passed, my plans are
    shattered,
  and so are the desires of my heart.
¹²These men turn night into day;
  in the face of darkness they say,
    'Light is near.'
¹³If the only home I hope for is the
    grave,^b
  if I spread out my bed in darkness,
¹⁴if I say to corruption, 'You are my
    father,'
  and to the worm, 'My mother' or 'My
    sister,'
¹⁵where then is my hope?
  Who can see any hope for me?
¹⁶Will it go down to the gates of death^b?
  Will we descend together into the
    dust?"

Bildad

18 ¹Then Bildad the Shuhite replied:

²"When will you end these speeches?
  Be sensible, and then we can talk.
³Why are we regarded as cattle
  and considered stupid in your sight?
⁴You who tear yourself to pieces in your
    anger,
  is the earth to be abandoned for your
    sake?
  Or must the rocks be moved from
    their place?

⁵"The lamp of the wicked is snuffed out;
  the flame of his fire stops burning.
⁶The light in his tent becomes dark;
  the lamp beside him goes out.
⁷The vigor of his step is weakened;
  his own schemes throw him down.
⁸His feet thrust him into a net
  and he wanders into its mesh.
⁹A trap seizes him by the heel;
  a snare holds him fast.
¹⁰A noose is hidden for him on the
    ground;
  a trap lies in his path.
¹¹Terrors startle him on every side
  and dog his every step.
¹²Calamity is hungry for him;
  disaster is ready for him when he
    falls.
¹³It eats away parts of his skin;
  death's firstborn devours his limbs.
¹⁴He is torn from the security of his tent
  and marched off to the king of terrors.
¹⁵Fire resides^c in his tent;
  burning sulfur is scattered over his
    dwelling.
¹⁶His roots dry up below
  and his branches wither above.
¹⁷The memory of him perishes from the
    earth;
  he has no name in the land.
¹⁸He is driven from light into darkness
  and is banished from the world.
¹⁹He has no offspring or descendants
    among his people,
  no survivor where once he lived.
²⁰Men of the west are appalled at his fate;
  men of the east are seized with
    horror.
²¹Surely such is the dwelling of an evil
    man;
  such is the place of one who knows
    not God."

*^a20 Or My friends treat me with scorn
^b13, 16 Hebrew Sheol   ^c15 Or Nothing he had
remains*

Job

19 Then Job replied:

2 "How long will you torment me
and crush me with words?
3 Ten times now you have reproached me;
shamelessly you attack me.
4 If it is true that I have gone astray,
my error remains my concern alone.
5 If indeed you would exalt yourselves
above me
and use my humiliation against me,
6 then know that God has wronged me
and drawn his net around me.

7 "Though I cry, 'I've been wronged!' I
get no response;
though I call for help, there is no
justice.

8 He has blocked my way so I cannot
pass;
he has shrouded my paths in
darkness.
9 He has stripped me of my honor
and removed the crown from my
head.
10 He tears me down on every side till I
am gone;
he uproots my hope like a tree.
11 His anger burns against me;
he counts me among his enemies.
12 His troops advance in force;
they build a siege ramp against me
and encamp around my tent.

13 "He has alienated my brothers from
me;
my acquaintances are completely
estranged from me.

No Fair Piling On

DAILY INSIGHT

Only twice in my life have I tried my hand at organized football. The first time was in seventh grade when I, along with every other seventh grade boy, went out for the team. My other crack at the sport was as a freshman in college. I never dressed out for a game.

In my remarkably limited experience at this celebrated American sport, I have had the experience of knowing what "the pile" feels like. This happens when the ball carrier is tackled and those closest to him, whether teammates or opponents, pile themselves up like cordwood on this hapless player. By the time the game gets to the National Football League, these stacks of bodies weigh more than an Amtrak locomotive.

One consistent football rule from junior high to the big-time is this: When the play is over and the referee has blown his whistle, no additional players can join the pile. In other words, *no piling on*. The last thing the people at the bottom of this crush of humanity need is more humanity.

To my knowledge, Job never played organized football—not even as a junior high hopeful. But he clearly understood, from personal experience, the sensation of

MONDAY

Passage:
Job 19:21–27

Verse:
Job 19:25

having everyone jump on the pile. As you read the chapters leading up to today's text, you realize that nearly every single person who knew Job had joined the stack. At times he even thought he felt God's heft on the pile. Our suffering friend was about to perish under the sheer weight of it all.

Today's verse, "I know that my Redeemer lives," was written in the crush of this setting. Speaking through the unbearable pressure and pain, Job saw his rescuer—his Redeemer—doing something that he longed to do himself. He saw the Almighty *standing*.

Some days we can truly identify with Job under the pile. It even feels like the referee has turned his back and more people have unfairly joined the others who are against us.

Today's encouragement is a simple one. Regardless of the weight, the pain, the frustration, the inability to even breathe under the pressure, our God is still standing. No circumstances will ever take him down. No accusers will ever have their way with our Savior.

Take a deep breath. Look up from the mash and be glad. Your Redeemer has come.

For your next devotional reading, go to page 569.

¹⁴My kinsmen have gone away;
    my friends have forgotten me.
¹⁵My guests and my maidservants count
        me a stranger;
    they look upon me as an alien.
¹⁶I summon my servant, but he does not
        answer,
    though I beg him with my own
        mouth.
¹⁷My breath is offensive to my wife;
    I am loathsome to my own brothers.
¹⁸Even the little boys scorn me;
    when I appear, they ridicule me.
¹⁹All my intimate friends detest me;
    those I love have turned against me.
²⁰I am nothing but skin and bones;
    I have escaped with only the skin of
        my teeth.ᵃ

²¹"Have pity on me, my friends, have pity,
    for the hand of God has struck me.
²²Why do you pursue me as God does?
    Will you never get enough of my
        flesh?

²³"Oh, that my words were recorded,
    that they were written on a scroll,
²⁴that they were inscribed with an iron
        tool onᵇ lead,
    or engraved in rock forever!
²⁵I know that my Redeemerᶜ lives,
    and that in the end he will stand
        upon the earth.ᵈ
²⁶And after my skin has been destroyed,
    yetᵉ inᶠ my flesh I will see God;
²⁷I myself will see him
    with my own eyes—I, and not
        another.
    How my heart yearns within me!

²⁸"If you say, 'How we will hound him,
    since the root of the trouble lies in
        him,ᵍ'
²⁹you should fear the sword yourselves;
    for wrath will bring punishment by
        the sword,
    and then you will know that there is
        judgment.ʰ"

Zophar

20 Then Zophar the Naamathite re-
    plied:

²"My troubled thoughts prompt me to
        answer
    because I am greatly disturbed.
³I hear a rebuke that dishonors me,
    and my understanding inspires me
        to reply.

⁴"Surely you know how it has been from
        of old,

ever since manⁱ was placed on the
        earth,
⁵that the mirth of the wicked is brief,
    the joy of the godless lasts but a
        moment.
⁶Though his pride reaches to the
        heavens
    and his head touches the clouds,
⁷he will perish forever, like his own
        dung;
    those who have seen him will say,
        'Where is he?'
⁸Like a dream he flies away, no more to
        be found,
    banished like a vision of the night.
⁹The eye that saw him will not see him
        again;
    his place will look on him no more.
¹⁰His children must make amends to the
        poor;
    his own hands must give back his
        wealth.
¹¹The youthful vigor that fills his bones
    will lie with him in the dust.

¹²"Though evil is sweet in his mouth
    and he hides it under his tongue,
¹³though he cannot bear to let it go
    and keeps it in his mouth,
¹⁴yet his food will turn sour in his
        stomach;
    it will become the venom of serpents
        within him.
¹⁵He will spit out the riches he
        swallowed;
    God will make his stomach vomit
        them up.
¹⁶He will suck the poison of serpents;
    the fangs of an adder will kill him.
¹⁷He will not enjoy the streams,
    the rivers flowing with honey and
        cream.
¹⁸What he toiled for he must give back
        uneaten;
    he will not enjoy the profit from his
        trading.
¹⁹For he has oppressed the poor and left
        them destitute;
    he has seized houses he did not build.

²⁰"Surely he will have no respite from his
        craving;
    he cannot save himself by his
        treasure.

ᵃ20 Or only my gums   ᵇ24 Or and   ᶜ25 Or
defender   ᵈ25 Or upon my grave   ᵉ26 Or And after
I awake, / though this body, has been destroyed, /
then   ᶠ26 Or / apart from   ᵍ28 Many Hebrew
manuscripts, Septuagint and Vulgate; most
Hebrew manuscripts me   ʰ29 Or / that you may
come to know the Almighty   ⁱ4 Or Adam

²¹Nothing is left for him to devour;
his prosperity will not endure.
²²In the midst of his plenty, distress will
overtake him;
the full force of misery will come
upon him.
²³When he has filled his belly,
God will vent his burning anger
against him
and rain down his blows upon him.
²⁴Though he flees from an iron weapon,
a bronze-tipped arrow pierces him.
²⁵He pulls it out of his back,
the gleaming point out of his liver.
Terrors will come over him;
²⁶   total darkness lies in wait for his
treasures.
A fire unfanned will consume him
and devour what is left in his tent.
²⁷The heavens will expose his guilt;
the earth will rise up against him.
²⁸A flood will carry off his house,
rushing waters*a* on the day of God's
wrath.
²⁹Such is the fate God allots the wicked,
the heritage appointed for them by
God.”

Job

21

Then Job replied:

²“Listen carefully to my words;
let this be the consolation you give
me.
³Bear with me while I speak,
and after I have spoken, mock on.

⁴“Is my complaint directed to man?
Why should I not be impatient?
⁵Look at me and be astonished;
clap your hand over your mouth.
⁶When I think about this, I am terrified;
trembling seizes my body.
⁷Why do the wicked live on,
growing old and increasing in
power?
⁸They see their children established
around them,
their offspring before their eyes.
⁹Their homes are safe and free from fear;
the rod of God is not upon them.
¹⁰Their bulls never fail to breed;
their cows calve and do not miscarry.
¹¹They send forth their children as a
flock;
their little ones dance about.
¹²They sing to the music of tambourine
and harp;
they make merry to the sound of the
flute.

¹³They spend their years in prosperity
and go down to the grave*b* in peace.*c*
¹⁴Yet they say to God, ‘Leave us alone!
We have no desire to know your
ways.
¹⁵Who is the Almighty, that we should
serve him?
What would we gain by praying to
him?’
¹⁶But their prosperity is not in their own
hands,
so I stand aloof from the counsel of
the wicked.

¹⁷“Yet how often is the lamp of the
wicked snuffed out?
How often does calamity come upon
them,
the fate God allots in his anger?
¹⁸How often are they like straw before the
wind,
like chaff swept away by a gale?
¹⁹It is said, ‘God stores up a man's
punishment for his sons.’
Let him repay the man himself, so
that he will know it!
²⁰Let his own eyes see his destruction;
let him drink of the wrath of the
Almighty.*d*
²¹For what does he care about the family
he leaves behind
when his allotted months come to an
end?

²²“Can anyone teach knowledge to God,
since he judges even the highest?
²³One man dies in full vigor,
completely secure and at ease,
²⁴his body*e* well nourished,
his bones rich with marrow.
²⁵Another man dies in bitterness of soul,
never having enjoyed anything good.
²⁶Side by side they lie in the dust,
and worms cover them both.

²⁷“I know full well what you are thinking,
the schemes by which you would
wrong me.
²⁸You say, ‘Where now is the great man's
house,
the tents where wicked men lived?’
²⁹Have you never questioned those who
travel?
Have you paid no regard to their
accounts—

---

a28 Or *The possessions in his house will be carried
off, / washed away*   *b13* Hebrew *Sheol*   *c13* Or *in
an instant*   *d17-20* Verses 17 and 18 may be taken
as exclamations and 19 and 20 as declarations.
e24 The meaning of the Hebrew for this word is
uncertain.

30 that the evil man is spared from the
    day of calamity,
    that he is delivered from [a] the day of
    wrath?
31 Who denounces his conduct to his
    face?
    Who repays him for what he has
    done?
32 He is carried to the grave,
    and watch is kept over his tomb.
33 The soil in the valley is sweet to him;
    all men follow after him,
    and a countless throng goes [b] before
    him.
34 "So how can you console me with your
    nonsense?
    Nothing is left of your answers but
    falsehood!"

Eliphaz

22 Then Eliphaz the Temanite replied:

2 "Can a man be of benefit to God?
    Can even a wise man benefit him?
3 What pleasure would it give the
    Almighty if you were righteous?
    What would he gain if your ways
    were blameless?

4 "Is it for your piety that he rebukes you
    and brings charges against you?
5 Is not your wickedness great?
    Are not your sins endless?
6 You demanded security from your
    brothers for no reason;
    you stripped men of their clothing,
    leaving them naked.
7 You gave no water to the weary
    and you withheld food from the
    hungry,
8 though you were a powerful man,
    owning land—
    an honored man, living on it.
9 And you sent widows away
    empty-handed
    and broke the strength of the
    fatherless.
10 That is why snares are all around you,
    why sudden peril terrifies you,
11 why it is so dark you cannot see,
    and why a flood of water covers you.

12 "Is not God in the heights of heaven?
    And see how lofty are the highest
    stars!
13 Yet you say, 'What does God know?
    Does he judge through such
    darkness?
14 Thick clouds veil him, so he does not
    see us

as he goes about in the vaulted
    heavens.'
15 Will you keep to the old path
    that evil men have trod?
16 They were carried off before their time,
    their foundations washed away by a
    flood.
17 They said to God, 'Leave us alone!
    What can the Almighty do to us?'
18 Yet it was he who filled their houses
    with good things,
    so I stand aloof from the counsel of
    the wicked.

19 "The righteous see their ruin and rejoice;
    the innocent mock them, saying,
20 'Surely our foes are destroyed,
    and fire devours their wealth.'

21 "Submit to God and be at peace with
    him;
    in this way prosperity will come to
    you.
22 Accept instruction from his mouth
    and lay up his words in your heart.
23 If you return to the Almighty, you will
    be restored:
    If you remove wickedness far from
    your tent
24 and assign your nuggets to the dust,
    your gold of Ophir to the rocks in the
    ravines,
25 then the Almighty will be your gold,
    the choicest silver for you.
26 Surely then you will find delight in the
    Almighty
    and will lift up your face to God.
27 You will pray to him, and he will hear
    you,
    and you will fulfill your vows.
28 What you decide on will be done,
    and light will shine on your ways.
29 When men are brought low and you
    say, 'Lift them up!'
    then he will save the downcast.
30 He will deliver even one who is not
    innocent,
    who will be delivered through the
    cleanness of your hands."

Job

23 Then Job replied:

2 "Even today my complaint is bitter;
    his hand [c] is heavy in spite of [d] my
    groaning.

---

[a] 30 Or man is reserved for the day of calamity, / that
he is brought forth to   [b] 33 Or / as a countless
throng went   [c] 2 Septuagint and Syriac; Hebrew /
the hand on me   [d] 2 Or heavy on me in

³ If only I knew where to find him;
  if only I could go to his dwelling!
⁴ I would state my case before him
  and fill my mouth with arguments.
⁵ I would find out what he would answer
  me,
  and consider what he would say.
⁶ Would he oppose me with great
  power?
  No, he would not press charges
  against me.
⁷ There an upright man could present
  his case before him,
  and I would be delivered forever
  from my judge.

⁸ "But if I go to the east, he is not there;
  if I go to the west, I do not find him.
⁹ When he is at work in the north, I do
  not see him;
  when he turns to the south, I catch
  no glimpse of him.
¹⁰ But he knows the way that I take;
  when he has tested me, I will come
  forth as gold.
¹¹ My feet have closely followed his steps;
  I have kept to his way without
  turning aside.
¹² I have not departed from the
  commands of his lips;
  I have treasured the words of his
  mouth more than my daily
  bread.

¹³ "But he stands alone, and who can
  oppose him?
  He does whatever he pleases.
¹⁴ He carries out his decree against me,
  and many such plans he still has in
  store.
¹⁵ That is why I am terrified before him;
  when I think of all this, I fear him.
¹⁶ God has made my heart faint;
  the Almighty has terrified me.
¹⁷ Yet I am not silenced by the darkness,
  by the thick darkness that covers my
  face.

24 "Why does the Almighty not set
  times for judgment?
  Why must those who know him look
  in vain for such days?
² Men move boundary stones;
  they pasture flocks they have
  stolen.
³ They drive away the orphan's donkey
  and take the widow's ox in pledge.
⁴ They thrust the needy from the path
  and force all the poor of the land into
  hiding.
⁵ Like wild donkeys in the desert,

the poor go about their labor of
  foraging food;
  the wasteland provides food for their
  children.
⁶ They gather fodder in the fields
  and glean in the vineyards of the
  wicked.
⁷ Lacking clothes, they spend the night
  naked;
  they have nothing to cover
  themselves in the cold.
⁸ They are drenched by mountain rains
  and hug the rocks for lack of shelter.
⁹ The fatherless child is snatched from
  the breast;
  the infant of the poor is seized for a
  debt.
¹⁰ Lacking clothes, they go about naked;
  they carry the sheaves, but still go
  hungry.
¹¹ They crush olives among the terraces[a];
  they tread the winepresses, yet suffer
  thirst.
¹² The groans of the dying rise from the
  city,
  and the souls of the wounded cry out
  for help.
  But God charges no one with
  wrongdoing.

¹³ "There are those who rebel against the
  light,
  who do not know its ways
  or stay in its paths.
¹⁴ When daylight is gone, the murderer
  rises up
  and kills the poor and needy;
  in the night he steals forth like a
  thief.
¹⁵ The eye of the adulterer watches for
  dusk;
  he thinks, 'No eye will see me,'
  and he keeps his face concealed.
¹⁶ In the dark, men break into houses,
  but by day they shut themselves in;
  they want nothing to do with the
  light.
¹⁷ For all of them, deep darkness is their
  morning[b];
  they make friends with the terrors of
  darkness.[c]

¹⁸ "Yet they are foam on the surface of the
  water;
  their portion of the land is cursed,
  so that no one goes to the vineyards.

---

[a]11 Or *olives between the millstones*; the meaning
of the Hebrew for this word is uncertain.   [b]17 Or
them, their morning is like the shadow of death
[c]17 Or *of the shadow of death*

¹⁹As heat and drought snatch away the melted snow,
so the grave^a snatches away those who have sinned.
²⁰The womb forgets them,
the worm feasts on them;
evil men are no longer remembered
but are broken like a tree.
²¹They prey on the barren and childless woman,
and to the widow show no kindness.
²²But God drags away the mighty by his power;
though they become established,
they have no assurance of life.
²³He may let them rest in a feeling of security,
but his eyes are on their ways.
²⁴For a little while they are exalted, and then they are gone;
they are brought low and gathered up like all others;
they are cut off like heads of grain.

²⁵"If this is not so, who can prove me false
and reduce my words to nothing?"

Bildad

25 Then Bildad the Shuhite replied:

²"Dominion and awe belong to God;
he establishes order in the heights of heaven.
³Can his forces be numbered?
Upon whom does his light not rise?
⁴How then can a man be righteous before God?
How can one born of woman be pure?
⁵If even the moon is not bright
and the stars are not pure in his eyes,
⁶how much less man, who is but a maggot—
a son of man, who is only a worm!"

Job

26 Then Job replied:

²"How you have helped the powerless!
How you have saved the arm that is feeble!
³What advice you have offered to one without wisdom!
And what great insight you have displayed!
⁴Who has helped you utter these words?
And whose spirit spoke from your mouth?

⁵"The dead are in deep anguish,
those beneath the waters and all that live in them.
⁶Death^a is naked before God;
Destruction^b lies uncovered.
⁷He spreads out the northern skies over empty space;
he suspends the earth over nothing.
⁸He wraps up the waters in his clouds,
yet the clouds do not burst under their weight.
⁹He covers the face of the full moon,
spreading his clouds over it.
¹⁰He marks out the horizon on the face of the waters
for a boundary between light and darkness.
¹¹The pillars of the heavens quake,
aghast at his rebuke.
¹²By his power he churned up the sea;
by his wisdom he cut Rahab to pieces.
¹³By his breath the skies became fair;
his hand pierced the gliding serpent.
¹⁴And these are but the outer fringe of his works;
how faint the whisper we hear of him!
Who then can understand the thunder of his power?"

27 And Job continued his discourse:

²"As surely as God lives, who has denied me justice,
the Almighty, who has made me taste bitterness of soul,
³as long as I have life within me,
the breath of God in my nostrils,
⁴my lips will not speak wickedness,
and my tongue will utter no deceit.
⁵I will never admit you are in the right;
till I die, I will not deny my integrity.
⁶I will maintain my righteousness and never let go of it;
my conscience will not reproach me as long as I live.

⁷"May my enemies be like the wicked,
my adversaries like the unjust!
⁸For what hope has the godless when he is cut off,
when God takes away his life?
⁹Does God listen to his cry
when distress comes upon him?
¹⁰Will he find delight in the Almighty?
Will he call upon God at all times?

---

a19, 6 Hebrew Sheol   *b6 Hebrew* Abaddon

¹¹ "I will teach you about the power of
    God;
    the ways of the Almighty I will not
      conceal.
¹² You have all seen this yourselves.
    Why then this meaningless talk?

¹³ "Here is the fate God allots to the
    wicked,
    the heritage a ruthless man receives
      from the Almighty:
¹⁴ However many his children, their fate
    is the sword;
    his offspring will never have enough
      to eat.
¹⁵ The plague will bury those who survive
    him,
    and their widows will not weep for
      them.
¹⁶ Though he heaps up silver like dust
    and clothes like piles of clay,
¹⁷ what he lays up the righteous will wear,
    and the innocent will divide his
      silver.
¹⁸ The house he builds is like a moth's
    cocoon,
    like a hut made by a watchman.
¹⁹ He lies down wealthy, but will do so no
    more;
    when he opens his eyes, all is gone.
²⁰ Terrors overtake him like a flood;
    a tempest snatches him away in the
      night.
²¹ The east wind carries him off, and he is
    gone;
    it sweeps him out of his place.
²² It hurls itself against him without
    mercy
    as he flees headlong from its power.
²³ It claps its hands in derision
    and hisses him out of his place.

28 "There is a mine for silver
    and a place where gold is refined.
² Iron is taken from the earth,
    and copper is smelted from ore.
³ Man puts an end to the darkness;
    he searches the farthest recesses
    for ore in the blackest darkness.
⁴ Far from where people dwell he cuts a
    shaft,
    in places forgotten by the foot of
      man;
    far from men he dangles and sways.
⁵ The earth, from which food comes,
    is transformed below as by fire;
⁶ sapphires*ᵃ* come from its rocks,
    and its dust contains nuggets of
      gold.
⁷ No bird of prey knows that hidden
    path,

    no falcon's eye has seen it.
⁸ Proud beasts do not set foot on it,
    and no lion prowls there.
⁹ Man's hand assaults the flinty rock
    and lays bare the roots of the
      mountains.
¹⁰ He tunnels through the rock;
    his eyes see all its treasures.
¹¹ He searches*ᵇ* the sources of the rivers
    and brings hidden things to light.

¹² "But where can wisdom be found?
    Where does understanding dwell?
¹³ Man does not comprehend its worth;
    it cannot be found in the land of the
      living.
¹⁴ The deep says, 'It is not in me';
    the sea says, 'It is not with me.'
¹⁵ It cannot be bought with the finest
    gold,
    nor can its price be weighed in silver.
¹⁶ It cannot be bought with the gold of
    Ophir,
    with precious onyx or sapphires.
¹⁷ Neither gold nor crystal can compare
    with it,
    nor can it be had for jewels of gold.
¹⁸ Coral and jasper are not worthy of
    mention;
    the price of wisdom is beyond
      rubies.
¹⁹ The topaz of Cush cannot compare
    with it;
    it cannot be bought with pure gold.

²⁰ "Where then does wisdom come from?
    Where does understanding dwell?
²¹ It is hidden from the eyes of every
    living thing,
    concealed even from the birds of the
      air.
²² Destruction*ᶜ* and Death say,
    'Only a rumor of it has reached our
      ears.'
²³ God understands the way to it
    and he alone knows where it dwells,
²⁴ for he views the ends of the earth
    and sees everything under the
      heavens.
²⁵ When he established the force of the
    wind
    and measured out the waters,
²⁶ when he made a decree for the rain
    and a path for the thunderstorm,
²⁷ then he looked at wisdom and
    appraised it;
    he confirmed it and tested it.

ᵃ6 Or *lapis lazuli*; also in verse 16   *ᵇ11* Septuagint,
Aquila and Vulgate; Hebrew *He dams up*
ᶜ22 Hebrew *Abaddon*

²⁸And he said to man,
  'The fear of the Lord—that is
    wisdom,
  and to shun evil is understanding.' "

29

Job continued his discourse:

²"How I long for the months gone by,
  for the days when God watched over
    me,
³when his lamp shone upon my head
  and by his light I walked through
    darkness!
⁴Oh, for the days when I was in my
    prime,
  when God's intimate friendship
    blessed my house,
⁵when the Almighty was still with me
  and my children were around me,
⁶when my path was drenched with
    cream
  and the rock poured out for me
    streams of olive oil.

⁷"When I went to the gate of the city
  and took my seat in the public
    square,
⁸the young men saw me and stepped
    aside
  and the old men rose to their feet;
⁹the chief men refrained from speaking
  and covered their mouths with their
    hands;
¹⁰the voices of the nobles were hushed,
  and their tongues stuck to the roof of
    their mouths.
¹¹Whoever heard me spoke well of me,
  and those who saw me commended
    me,
¹²because I rescued the poor who cried
    for help,
  and the fatherless who had none to
    assist him.
¹³The man who was dying blessed me;
  I made the widow's heart sing.
¹⁴I put on righteousness as my clothing;
  justice was my robe and my turban.
¹⁵I was eyes to the blind
  and feet to the lame.
¹⁶I was a father to the needy;
  I took up the case of the stranger.
¹⁷I broke the fangs of the wicked
  and snatched the victims from their
    teeth.

¹⁸"I thought, 'I will die in my own house,
  my days as numerous as the grains
    of sand.
¹⁹My roots will reach to the water,
  and the dew will lie all night on my
    branches.

²⁰My glory will remain fresh in me,
  the bow ever new in my hand.'

²¹"Men listened to me expectantly,
  waiting in silence for my counsel.
²²After I had spoken, they spoke no
    more;
  my words fell gently on their ears.
²³They waited for me as for showers
  and drank in my words as the spring
    rain.
²⁴When I smiled at them, they scarcely
    believed it;
  the light of my face was precious to
    them.ᵃ
²⁵I chose the way for them and sat as
    their chief;
  I dwelt as a king among his troops;
  I was like one who comforts
    mourners.

30

"But now they mock me,
  men younger than I,
whose fathers I would have disdained
  to put with my sheep dogs.
²Of what use was the strength of their
    hands to me,
  since their vigor had gone from
    them?
³Haggard from want and hunger,
  they roamedᵇ the parched land
  in desolate wastelands at night.
⁴In the brush they gathered salt herbs,
  and their foodᶜ was the root of the
    broom tree.
⁵They were banished from their fellow
    men,
  shouted at as if they were thieves.
⁶They were forced to live in the dry
    stream beds,
  among the rocks and in holes in the
    ground.
⁷They brayed among the bushes
  and huddled in the undergrowth.
⁸A base and nameless brood,
  they were driven out of the land.

⁹"And now their sons mock me in song;
  I have become a byword among
    them.
¹⁰They detest me and keep their
    distance;
  they do not hesitate to spit in my
    face.
¹¹Now that God has unstrung my bow
    and afflicted me,
  they throw off restraint in my
    presence.

ᵃ24 The meaning of the Hebrew for this clause is
uncertain.   ᵇ3 Or *gnawed*   ᶜ4 Or *fuel*

¹²On my right the tribe*ᵃ* attacks;
  they lay snares for my feet,
  they build their siege ramps against
    me.
¹³They break up my road;
  they succeed in destroying me—
  without anyone's helping them.*ᵇ*
¹⁴They advance as through a gaping
    breach;
  amid the ruins they come rolling in.
¹⁵Terrors overwhelm me;
  my dignity is driven away as by the
    wind,
  my safety vanishes like a cloud.

¹⁶"And now my life ebbs away;
  days of suffering grip me.
¹⁷Night pierces my bones;
  my gnawing pains never rest.
¹⁸In his great power God becomes like
    clothing to me*ᶜ*;
  he binds me like the neck of my
    garment.
¹⁹He throws me into the mud,
  and I am reduced to dust and ashes.

²⁰"I cry out to you, O God, but you do not
    answer;
  I stand up, but you merely look at me.
²¹You turn on me ruthlessly;
  with the might of your hand you
    attack me.
²²You snatch me up and drive me before
    the wind;
  you toss me about in the storm.
²³I know you will bring me down to
    death,
  to the place appointed for all the
    living.

²⁴"Surely no one lays a hand on a broken
    man
  when he cries for help in his distress.
²⁵Have I not wept for those in trouble?
  Has not my soul grieved for the
    poor?
²⁶Yet when I hoped for good, evil came;
  when I looked for light, then came
    darkness.
²⁷The churning inside me never stops;
  days of suffering confront me.
²⁸I go about blackened, but not by the
    sun;
  I stand up in the assembly and cry
    for help.
²⁹I have become a brother of jackals,
  a companion of owls.
³⁰My skin grows black and peels;
  my body burns with fever.
³¹My harp is tuned to mourning,
  and my flute to the sound of wailing.

31 "I made a covenant with my eyes
  not to look lustfully at a girl.
²For what is man's lot from God above,
  his heritage from the Almighty on
    high?
³Is it not ruin for the wicked,
  disaster for those who do wrong?
⁴Does he not see my ways
  and count my every step?

⁵"If I have walked in falsehood
  or my foot has hurried after deceit—
⁶let God weigh me in honest scales
  and he will know that I am
    blameless—
⁷if my steps have turned from the path,
  if my heart has been led by my eyes,
  or if my hands have been defiled,
⁸then may others eat what I have sown,
  and may my crops be uprooted.

⁹"If my heart has been enticed by a
    woman,
  or if I have lurked at my neighbor's
    door,
¹⁰then may my wife grind another man's
    grain,
  and may other men sleep with her.
¹¹For that would have been shameful,
  a sin to be judged.
¹²It is a fire that burns to Destruction*ᵈ*;
  it would have uprooted my harvest.

¹³"If I have denied justice to my
    menservants and maidservants
  when they had a grievance against
    me,
¹⁴what will I do when God confronts me?
  What will I answer when called to
    account?
¹⁵Did not he who made me in the womb
    make them?
  Did not the same one form us both
    within our mothers?

¹⁶"If I have denied the desires of the poor
  or let the eyes of the widow grow
    weary,
¹⁷if I have kept my bread to myself,
  not sharing it with the fatherless—
¹⁸but from my youth I reared him as
    would a father,
  and from my birth I guided the
    widow—
¹⁹if I have seen anyone perishing for lack
    of clothing,
  or a needy man without a garment,

ᵃ12 The meaning of the Hebrew for this word is
uncertain. *ᵇ13* Or *me. / 'No one can help him,'*
⌊they say⌋. *ᶜ18* Hebrew; Septuagint *⌊God⌋ grasps
my clothing* *ᵈ12* Hebrew *Abaddon*

²⁰and his heart did not bless me
　　for warming him with the fleece
　　　from my sheep,
²¹if I have raised my hand against the
　　　fatherless,
　　knowing that I had influence in
　　　court,
²²then let my arm fall from the shoulder,
　　let it be broken off at the joint.
²³For I dreaded destruction from God,
　　and for fear of his splendor I could
　　　not do such things.

²⁴"If I have put my trust in gold
　　or said to pure gold, 'You are my
　　　security,'
²⁵if I have rejoiced over my great wealth,
　　the fortune my hands had gained,
²⁶if I have regarded the sun in its
　　　radiance
　　or the moon moving in splendor,
²⁷so that my heart was secretly enticed
　　and my hand offered them a kiss of
　　　homage,
²⁸then these also would be sins to be
　　　judged,
　　for I would have been unfaithful to
　　　God on high.

²⁹"If I have rejoiced at my enemy's
　　　misfortune
　　or gloated over the trouble that came
　　　to him—
³⁰I have not allowed my mouth to sin
　　by invoking a curse against his
　　　life—
³¹if the men of my household have never
　　　said,
　　'Who has not had his fill of Job's
　　　meat?'—
³²but no stranger had to spend the night
　　　in the street,
　　for my door was always open to the
　　　traveler—
³³if I have concealed my sin as men do,^a
　　by hiding my guilt in my heart
³⁴because I so feared the crowd
　　and so dreaded the contempt of the
　　　clans
　　that I kept silent and would not go
　　　outside

³⁵("Oh, that I had someone to hear me!
　　I sign now my defense—let the
　　　Almighty answer me;
　　let my accuser put his indictment in
　　　writing.
³⁶Surely I would wear it on my shoulder,
　　I would put it on like a crown.
³⁷I would give him an account of my
　　　every step;

like a prince I would approach
　　　him.)—
³⁸"if my land cries out against me
　　and all its furrows are wet with tears,
³⁹if I have devoured its yield without
　　　payment
　　or broken the spirit of its tenants,
⁴⁰then let briers come up instead of wheat
　　and weeds instead of barley."

The words of Job are ended.

Elihu

32 So these three men stopped answering Job, because he was righteous in his own eyes. ²But Elihu son of Barakel the Buzite, of the family of Ram, became very angry with Job for justifying himself rather than God. ³He was also angry with the three friends, because they had found no way to refute Job, and yet had condemned him.^b ⁴Now Elihu had waited before speaking to Job because they were older than he. ⁵But when he saw that the three men had nothing more to say, his anger was aroused.

⁶So Elihu son of Barakel the Buzite said:

"I am young in years,
　　and you are old;
that is why I was fearful,
　　not daring to tell you what I know.
⁷I thought, 'Age should speak;
　　advanced years should teach
　　　wisdom.'
⁸But it is the spirit^c in a man,
　　the breath of the Almighty, that gives
　　　him understanding.
⁹It is not only the old^d who are wise,
　　not only the aged who understand
　　　what is right.

¹⁰"Therefore I say: Listen to me;
　　I too will tell you what I know.
¹¹I waited while you spoke,
　　I listened to your reasoning;
　　while you were searching for words,
¹²　I gave you my full attention.
　　But not one of you has proved Job
　　　wrong;
　　none of you has answered his
　　　arguments.
¹³Do not say, 'We have found wisdom;
　　let God refute him, not man.'
¹⁴But Job has not marshaled his words
　　against me,

^a33 Or *as Adam did*　^b3 Masoretic Text; an ancient Hebrew scribal tradition *Job, and so had condemned God*　^c8 Or *Spirit*; also in verse 18　^d9 Or *many*; or *great*

and I will not answer him with your
arguments.

¹⁵ "They are dismayed and have no more
to say;
words have failed them.
¹⁶ Must I wait, now that they are silent,
now that they stand there with no
reply?
¹⁷ I too will have my say;
I too will tell what I know.
¹⁸ For I am full of words,
and the spirit within me compels
me;
¹⁹ inside I am like bottled-up wine,
like new wineskins ready to burst.
²⁰ I must speak and find relief;
I must open my lips and reply.
²¹ I will show partiality to no one,
nor will I flatter any man;
²² for if I were skilled in flattery,
my Maker would soon take me away.

33 "But now, Job, listen to my words;
pay attention to everything I say.
² I am about to open my mouth;
my words are on the tip of my
tongue.
³ My words come from an upright heart;
my lips sincerely speak what I know.
⁴ The Spirit of God has made me;
the breath of the Almighty gives me
life.
⁵ Answer me then, if you can;
prepare yourself and confront me.
⁶ I am just like you before God;
I too have been taken from clay.
⁷ No fear of me should alarm you,
nor should my hand be heavy upon
you.

⁸ "But you have said in my hearing—
I heard the very words—
⁹ 'I am pure and without sin;
I am clean and free from guilt.
¹⁰ Yet God has found fault with me;
he considers me his enemy.
¹¹ He fastens my feet in shackles;
he keeps close watch on all my
paths.'

¹² "But I tell you, in this you are not right,
for God is greater than man.
¹³ Why do you complain to him
that he answers none of man's
words^a?
¹⁴ For God does speak—now one way,
now another—
though man may not perceive it.
¹⁵ In a dream, in a vision of the night,
when deep sleep falls on men
as they slumber in their beds,

¹⁶ he may speak in their ears
and terrify them with warnings,
¹⁷ to turn man from wrongdoing
and keep him from pride,
¹⁸ to preserve his soul from the pit,^b
his life from perishing by the sword.^c
¹⁹ Or a man may be chastened on a bed of
pain
with constant distress in his bones,
²⁰ so that his very being finds food
repulsive
and his soul loathes the choicest
meal.
²¹ His flesh wastes away to nothing,
and his bones, once hidden, now
stick out.
²² His soul draws near to the pit,^d
and his life to the messengers of
death.^e

²³ "Yet if there is an angel on his side
as a mediator, one out of a thousand,
to tell a man what is right for him,
²⁴ to be gracious to him and say,
'Spare him from going down to the
pit;^f
I have found a ransom for him'—
²⁵ then his flesh is renewed like a child's;
it is restored as in the days of his
youth.
²⁶ He prays to God and finds favor with
him,
he sees God's face and shouts for joy;
he is restored by God to his righteous
state.
²⁷ Then he comes to men and says,
'I sinned, and perverted what was
right,
but I did not get what I deserved.
²⁸ He redeemed my soul from going down
to the pit,^g
and I will live to enjoy the light.'

²⁹ "God does all these things to a man—
twice, even three times—
³⁰ to turn back his soul from the pit,^h
that the light of life may shine on
him.

³¹ "Pay attention, Job, and listen to me;
be silent, and I will speak.
³² If you have anything to say, answer me;
speak up, for I want you to be
cleared.
³³ But if not, then listen to me;

---

^a13 Or *that he does not answer for any of his
actions* ^b18 Or *preserve him from the grave*
^c18 Or *from crossing the River* ^d22 Or *He draws
near to the grave* ^e22 Or *to the dead* ^f24 Or *grave*
^g28 Or *redeemed me from going down to the
grave* ^h30 Or *turn him back from the grave*

be silent, and I will teach you wisdom."

34 Then Elihu said:

2 "Hear my words, you wise men;
  listen to me, you men of learning.
3 For the ear tests words
  as the tongue tastes food.
4 Let us discern for ourselves what is right;
  let us learn together what is good.

5 "Job says, 'I am innocent,
  but God denies me justice.
6 Although I am right,
  I am considered a liar;
  although I am guiltless,
  his arrow inflicts an incurable wound.'
7 What man is like Job,
  who drinks scorn like water?
8 He keeps company with evildoers;
  he associates with wicked men.
9 For he says, 'It profits a man nothing
  when he tries to please God.'

10 "So listen to me, you men of understanding.
  Far be it from God to do evil,
  from the Almighty to do wrong.
11 He repays a man for what he has done;
  he brings upon him what his conduct deserves.
12 It is unthinkable that God would do wrong,
  that the Almighty would pervert justice.
13 Who appointed him over the earth?
  Who put him in charge of the whole world?
14 If it were his intention
  and he withdrew his spirit[a] and breath,
15 all mankind would perish together
  and man would return to the dust.

16 "If you have understanding, hear this;
  listen to what I say.
17 Can he who hates justice govern?
  Will you condemn the just and mighty One?
18 Is he not the One who says to kings,
  'You are worthless,'
  and to nobles, 'You are wicked,'
19 who shows no partiality to princes
  and does not favor the rich over the poor,
  for they are all the work of his hands?
20 They die in an instant, in the middle of the night;

the people are shaken and they pass away;
  the mighty are removed without human hand.

21 "His eyes are on the ways of men;
  he sees their every step.
22 There is no dark place, no deep shadow,
  where evildoers can hide.
23 God has no need to examine men further,
  that they should come before him for judgment.
24 Without inquiry he shatters the mighty
  and sets up others in their place.
25 Because he takes note of their deeds,
  he overthrows them in the night and they are crushed.
26 He punishes them for their wickedness
  where everyone can see them,
27 because they turned from following him
  and had no regard for any of his ways.
28 They caused the cry of the poor to come before him,
  so that he heard the cry of the needy.
29 But if he remains silent, who can condemn him?
  If he hides his face, who can see him?
  Yet he is over man and nation alike,
30   to keep a godless man from ruling,
  from laying snares for the people.

31 "Suppose a man says to God,
  'I am guilty but will offend no more.
32 Teach me what I cannot see;
  if I have done wrong, I will not do so again.'
33 Should God then reward you on your terms,
  when you refuse to repent?
  You must decide, not I;
  so tell me what you know.

34 "Men of understanding declare,
  wise men who hear me say to me,
35 'Job speaks without knowledge;
  his words lack insight.'
36 Oh, that Job might be tested to the utmost
  for answering like a wicked man!
37 To his sin he adds rebellion;
  scornfully he claps his hands among us
  and multiplies his words against God."

---

a14 Or Spirit

35

Then Elihu said:

2 "Do you think this is just?
  You say, 'I will be cleared by God.'[a]
3 Yet you ask him, 'What profit is it to
    me,[b]
  and what do I gain by not sinning?'

4 "I would like to reply to you
  and to your friends with you.
5 Look up at the heavens and see;
  gaze at the clouds so high above you.
6 If you sin, how does that affect him?
  If your sins are many, what does that
    do to him?
7 If you are righteous, what do you give
    to him,
  or what does he receive from your
    hand?
8 Your wickedness affects only a man like
    yourself,
  and your righteousness only the sons
    of men.

9 "Men cry out under a load of
    oppression;
  they plead for relief from the arm of
    the powerful.
10 But no one says, 'Where is God my
    Maker,
  who gives songs in the night,
11 who teaches more to us than to[c] the
    beasts of the earth
  and makes us wiser than[d] the birds
    of the air?'
12 He does not answer when men cry out
  because of the arrogance of the
    wicked.
13 Indeed, God does not listen to their
    empty plea;
  the Almighty pays no attention to it.
14 How much less, then, will he listen
  when you say that you do not see
    him,
  that your case is before him
  and you must wait for him,
15 and further, that his anger never
    punishes
  and he does not take the least notice
    of wickedness.[e]
16 So Job opens his mouth with empty
    talk;
  without knowledge he multiplies
    words."

36

Elihu continued:

2 "Bear with me a little longer and I will
    show you
  that there is more to be said in God's
    behalf.

3 I get my knowledge from afar;
  I will ascribe justice to my Maker.
4 Be assured that my words are not false;
  one perfect in knowledge is with you.

5 "God is mighty, but does not despise
    men;
  he is mighty, and firm in his purpose.
6 He does not keep the wicked alive
  but gives the afflicted their rights.
7 He does not take his eyes off the
    righteous;
  he enthrones them with kings
  and exalts them forever.
8 But if men are bound in chains,
  held fast by cords of affliction,
9 he tells them what they have done—
  that they have sinned arrogantly.
10 He makes them listen to correction
  and commands them to repent of
    their evil.
11 If they obey and serve him,
  they will spend the rest of their days
    in prosperity
  and their years in contentment.
12 But if they do not listen,
  they will perish by the sword[f]
  and die without knowledge.

13 "The godless in heart harbor
    resentment;
  even when he fetters them, they do
    not cry for help.
14 They die in their youth,
  among male prostitutes of the
    shrines.
15 But those who suffer he delivers in
    their suffering;
  he speaks to them in their affliction.

16 "He is wooing you from the jaws of
    distress
  to a spacious place free from
    restriction,
  to the comfort of your table laden
    with choice food.
17 But now you are laden with the
    judgment due the wicked;
  judgment and justice have taken
    hold of you.
18 Be careful that no one entices you by
    riches;
  do not let a large bribe turn you
    aside.
19 Would your wealth
  or even all your mighty efforts

a2 Or My righteousness is more than God's
b3 Or you   c11 Or teaches us by   d11 Or us wise by
e15 Symmachus, Theodotion and Vulgate; the
meaning of the Hebrew for this word is uncertain.
f12 Or will cross the River

sustain you so you would not be in
distress?
²⁰Do not long for the night,
to drag people away from their
homes.ᵃ
²¹Beware of turning to evil,
which you seem to prefer to affliction.

²²"God is exalted in his power.
Who is a teacher like him?
²³Who has prescribed his ways for him,
or said to him, 'You have done
wrong'?
²⁴Remember to extol his work,
which men have praised in song.
²⁵All mankind has seen it;
men gaze on it from afar.
²⁶How great is God—beyond our
understanding!
The number of his years is past
finding out.

²⁷"He draws up the drops of water,
which distill as rain to the streamsᵇ;
²⁸the clouds pour down their moisture
and abundant showers fall on
mankind.
²⁹Who can understand how he spreads
out the clouds,
how he thunders from his pavilion?
³⁰See how he scatters his lightning about
him,
bathing the depths of the sea.
³¹This is the way he governsᶜ the nations
and provides food in abundance.
³²He fills his hands with lightning
and commands it to strike its mark.
³³His thunder announces the coming
storm;
even the cattle make known its
approach.ᵈ

37 "At this my heart pounds
and leaps from its place.
²Listen! Listen to the roar of his voice,
to the rumbling that comes from his
mouth.
³He unleashes his lightning beneath the
whole heaven
and sends it to the ends of the earth.
⁴After that comes the sound of his roar;
he thunders with his majestic voice.
When his voice resounds,
he holds nothing back.
⁵God's voice thunders in marvelous
ways;
he does great things beyond our
understanding.
⁶He says to the snow, 'Fall on the earth,'
and to the rain shower, 'Be a mighty
downpour.'

⁷So that all men he has made may know
his work,
he stops every man from his labor.ᵉ
⁸The animals take cover;
they remain in their dens.
⁹The tempest comes out from its
chamber,
the cold from the driving winds.
¹⁰The breath of God produces ice,
and the broad waters become
frozen.
¹¹He loads the clouds with moisture;
he scatters his lightning through
them.
¹²At his direction they swirl around
over the face of the whole earth
to do whatever he commands them.
¹³He brings the clouds to punish men,
or to water his earthᶠ and show his
love.

¹⁴"Listen to this, Job;
stop and consider God's wonders.
¹⁵Do you know how God controls the
clouds
and makes his lightning flash?
¹⁶Do you know how the clouds hang
poised,
those wonders of him who is perfect
in knowledge?
¹⁷You who swelter in your clothes
when the land lies hushed under the
south wind,
¹⁸can you join him in spreading out the
skies,
hard as a mirror of cast bronze?

¹⁹"Tell us what we should say to him;
we cannot draw up our case because
of our darkness.
²⁰Should he be told that I want to speak?
Would any man ask to be swallowed
up?
²¹Now no one can look at the sun,
bright as it is in the skies
after the wind has swept them clean.
²²Out of the north he comes in golden
splendor;
God comes in awesome majesty.
²³The Almighty is beyond our reach and
exalted in power;
in his justice and great
righteousness, he does not
oppress.
²⁴Therefore, men revere him,

ᵃ20 The meaning of the Hebrew for verses 18-20 is
uncertain.   ᵇ27 Or *distill from the mist as rain*
ᶜ31 Or *nourishes*   ᵈ33 Or *announces his coming— /
the One zealous against evil*   ᵉ7 Or / *he fills all men
with fear by his power*   ᶠ13 Or *to favor them*

for does he not have regard for all the
wise in heart?ᵃ"

The LORD Speaks

38 Then the LORD answered Job out of
the storm. He said:

² "Who is this that darkens my counsel
with words without knowledge?
³ Brace yourself like a man;
I will question you,
and you shall answer me.

⁴ "Where were you when I laid the earth's
foundation?
Tell me, if you understand.

⁵ Who marked off its dimensions? Surely
you know!
Who stretched a measuring line
across it?
⁶ On what were its footings set,
or who laid its cornerstone—
⁷ while the morning stars sang together
and all the angelsᵇ shouted for joy?

⁸ "Who shut up the sea behind doors
when it burst forth from the womb,
⁹ when I made the clouds its garment
and wrapped it in thick darkness,
¹⁰ when I fixed limits for it

ᵃ24 Or *for he does not have regard for any who
think they are wise.*   ᵇ7 Hebrew *the sons of God*

Cashing Your Coupons

DAILY INSIGHT

TUESDAY

Passage:
Job 38:1–13

Verse:
Job 38:3

When our girls left home for college and other frontiers, my wife and I were left with what has become popularly known as an "empty nest." On one quiet, empty-nest Friday evening, Bobbie invited me to go grocery shopping with her. As was her custom, she brought along her accordion-like coupon organizer. It had separate sections to store coupons for cereal, soap, soups, condiments, and the like.

I had never been very interested in clipping coupons. As far as I was concerned, this promotional riffraff did nothing but gunk up my Sunday newspaper. But before we got halfway down the first aisle, I was hooked. Bobbie's efforts to carefully collect and organize these redemption slips were now going to be rewarded at the checkout counter. These simple printed vouchers would soon be transformed into cash money!

From the beginning of the account of Job and his trials, God collected Job's complaints like coupons. He even organized them into sections: Creator, Sustainer, Orchestrator of the universe. Then, in chapters 38 through 41, God visits the grocery store. Aisle by aisle, line by line, verse by verse, chapter by chapter, the Sovereign God gets ready to cash in his coupons at Job's checkout counter. Nowhere else in the Bible does God more

thoroughly defend himself.

Taking a step back, the thing that I find the most striking about this monologue is neither God's outburst nor the fact of his right to defend himself. To me, the most amazing thing is that *God chooses not to do this in other places in the Bible.* How many times in the Bible doesn't God cash in these "who-do-you-think-you-are" coupons? Instead of putting people in their rightful place when they deserve it, God more often than not is merciful and slow to anger. So God's power is not revealed in his speech to Job. Rather, it's revealed in his incredible restraint.

As a father, you probably have a stash of "I'm-the-dad-around-here" coupons. But every time you hold back from the lecture you think your family "deserves," you add more coupons to your accordion-like organizer. Now, take a lesson from God's actions in the Bible. Learn the power of mercy and restraint. Cash in these coupons only when the time comes to transform that withheld power into something truly important—and helpful—to your family.

Think about it. Do you need to reduce the frequency of your visits to the checkout counter?

For your next devotional reading, go to page 573.

and set its doors and bars in place,

¹¹when I said, 'This far you may come
and no farther;
here is where your proud waves
halt'?

¹²"Have you ever given orders to the
morning,
or shown the dawn its place,
¹³that it might take the earth by the
edges
and shake the wicked out of it?
¹⁴The earth takes shape like clay under a
seal;
its features stand out like those of a
garment.
¹⁵The wicked are denied their light,
and their upraised arm is broken.

¹⁶"Have you journeyed to the springs of
the sea
or walked in the recesses of the
deep?
¹⁷Have the gates of death been shown to
you?
Have you seen the gates of the
shadow of death*ᵃ*?
¹⁸Have you comprehended the vast
expanses of the earth?
Tell me, if you know all this.

¹⁹"What is the way to the abode of light?
And where does darkness reside?
²⁰Can you take them to their places?
Do you know the paths to their
dwellings?
²¹Surely you know, for you were already
born!
You have lived so many years!

²²"Have you entered the storehouses of
the snow
or seen the storehouses of the hail,
²³which I reserve for times of trouble,
for days of war and battle?
²⁴What is the way to the place where the
lightning is dispersed,
or the place where the east winds are
scattered over the earth?
²⁵Who cuts a channel for the torrents of
rain,
and a path for the thunderstorm,
²⁶to water a land where no man lives,
a desert with no one in it,
²⁷to satisfy a desolate wasteland
and make it sprout with grass?
²⁸Does the rain have a father?
Who fathers the drops of dew?
²⁹From whose womb comes the ice?
Who gives birth to the frost from the
heavens
³⁰when the waters become hard as stone,

when the surface of the deep is
frozen?

³¹"Can you bind the beautiful*ᵇ* Pleiades?
Can you loose the cords of Orion?
³²Can you bring forth the constellations
in their seasons*ᶜ*
or lead out the Bear*ᵈ* with its cubs?
³³Do you know the laws of the heavens?
Can you set up ˌGod's*ᵉ*ˌ dominion
over the earth?

³⁴"Can you raise your voice to the clouds
and cover yourself with a flood of
water?
³⁵Do you send the lightning bolts on
their way?
Do they report to you, 'Here we are'?
³⁶Who endowed the heart*ᶠ* with wisdom
or gave understanding to the mind*ᶠ*?
³⁷Who has the wisdom to count the
clouds?
Who can tip over the water jars of the
heavens
³⁸when the dust becomes hard
and the clods of earth stick together?

³⁹"Do you hunt the prey for the lioness
and satisfy the hunger of the lions
⁴⁰when they crouch in their dens
or lie in wait in a thicket?
⁴¹Who provides food for the raven
when its young cry out to God
and wander about for lack of food?

39 "Do you know when the mountain
goats give birth?
Do you watch when the doe bears
her fawn?
²Do you count the months till they bear?
Do you know the time they give birth?
³They crouch down and bring forth
their young;
their labor pains are ended.
⁴Their young thrive and grow strong in
the wilds;
they leave and do not return.

⁵"Who let the wild donkey go free?
Who untied his ropes?
⁶I gave him the wasteland as his home,
the salt flats as his habitat.
⁷He laughs at the commotion in the
town;
he does not hear a driver's shout.
⁸He ranges the hills for his pasture
and searches for any green thing.

ᵃ17 Or *gates of deep shadows*   *ᵇ31* Or *the twinkling;*
or *the chains of the*   *ᶜ32* Or *the morning star in its*
season   *ᵈ32* Or *out Leo*   *ᵉ33* Or *his;* or
their   *ᶠ36* The meaning of the Hebrew for this
word is uncertain.

⁹ "Will the wild ox consent to serve you?
Will he stay by your manger at night?
¹⁰ Can you hold him to the furrow with a
harness?
Will he till the valleys behind you?
¹¹ Will you rely on him for his great
strength?
Will you leave your heavy work to
him?
¹² Can you trust him to bring in your
grain
and gather it to your threshing floor?

¹³ "The wings of the ostrich flap joyfully,
but they cannot compare with the
pinions and feathers of the
stork.
¹⁴ She lays her eggs on the ground
and lets them warm in the sand,
¹⁵ unmindful that a foot may crush them,
that some wild animal may trample
them.
¹⁶ She treats her young harshly, as if they
were not hers;
she cares not that her labor was in
vain,
¹⁷ for God did not endow her with
wisdom
or give her a share of good sense.
¹⁸ Yet when she spreads her feathers to
run,
she laughs at horse and rider.

¹⁹ "Do you give the horse his strength
or clothe his neck with a flowing
mane?
²⁰ Do you make him leap like a locust,
striking terror with his proud
snorting?
²¹ He paws fiercely, rejoicing in his
strength,
and charges into the fray.
²² He laughs at fear, afraid of nothing;
he does not shy away from the
sword.
²³ The quiver rattles against his side,
along with the flashing spear and
lance.
²⁴ In frenzied excitement he eats up the
ground;
he cannot stand still when the
trumpet sounds.
²⁵ At the blast of the trumpet he snorts,
'Aha!'
He catches the scent of battle from
afar,
the shout of commanders and the
battle cry.

²⁶ "Does the hawk take flight by your
wisdom
and spread his wings toward the
south?
²⁷ Does the eagle soar at your command
and build his nest on high?
²⁸ He dwells on a cliff and stays there at
night;
a rocky crag is his stronghold.
²⁹ From there he seeks out his food;
his eyes detect it from afar.
³⁰ His young ones feast on blood,
and where the slain are, there is he."

40 The LORD said to Job:

² "Will the one who contends with the
Almighty correct him?
Let him who accuses God answer
him!"

³ Then Job answered the LORD:

⁴ "I am unworthy—how can I reply to
you?
I put my hand over my mouth.
⁵ I spoke once, but I have no answer—
twice, but I will say no more."

⁶ Then the LORD spoke to Job out of the
storm:

⁷ "Brace yourself like a man;
I will question you,
and you shall answer me.

⁸ "Would you discredit my justice?
Would you condemn me to justify
yourself?
⁹ Do you have an arm like God's,
and can your voice thunder like his?
¹⁰ Then adorn yourself with glory and
splendor,
and clothe yourself in honor and
majesty.
¹¹ Unleash the fury of your wrath,
look at every proud man and bring
him low,
¹² look at every proud man and humble
him,
crush the wicked where they stand.
¹³ Bury them all in the dust together;
shroud their faces in the grave.
¹⁴ Then I myself will admit to you
that your own right hand can save
you.

¹⁵ "Look at the behemoth,ᵃ
which I made along with you
and which feeds on grass like an ox.
¹⁶ What strength he has in his loins,
what power in the muscles of his
belly!

ᵃ15 Possibly the hippopotamus or the elephant

¹⁷His tail^a sways like a cedar;
   the sinews of his thighs are
      close-knit.
¹⁸His bones are tubes of bronze,
   his limbs like rods of iron.
¹⁹He ranks first among the works of God,
   yet his Maker can approach him with
      his sword.
²⁰The hills bring him their produce,
   and all the wild animals play nearby.
²¹Under the lotus plants he lies,
   hidden among the reeds in the
      marsh.
²²The lotuses conceal him in their
      shadow;
   the poplars by the stream surround
      him.
²³When the river rages, he is not
      alarmed;
   he is secure, though the Jordan
      should surge against his mouth.
²⁴Can anyone capture him by the eyes,^b
   or trap him and pierce his nose?

41 "Can you pull in the leviathan^c with a
      fishhook
   or tie down his tongue with a rope?
²Can you put a cord through his nose
   or pierce his jaw with a hook?
³Will he keep begging you for mercy?
   Will he speak to you with gentle
      words?
⁴Will he make an agreement with you
   for you to take him as your slave for
      life?
⁵Can you make a pet of him like a bird
   or put him on a leash for your girls?
⁶Will traders barter for him?
   Will they divide him up among the
      merchants?
⁷Can you fill his hide with harpoons
   or his head with fishing spears?
⁸If you lay a hand on him,
   you will remember the struggle and
      never do it again!
⁹Any hope of subduing him is false;
   the mere sight of him is
      overpowering.
¹⁰No one is fierce enough to rouse him.
   Who then is able to stand against
      me?
¹¹Who has a claim against me that I must
      pay?
   Everything under heaven belongs to
      me.
¹²"I will not fail to speak of his limbs,
   his strength and his graceful form.
¹³Who can strip off his outer coat?
   Who would approach him with a
      bridle?

¹⁴Who dares open the doors of his
      mouth,
   ringed about with his fearsome
      teeth?
¹⁵His back has^d rows of shields
   tightly sealed together;
¹⁶each is so close to the next
   that no air can pass between.
¹⁷They are joined fast to one another;
   they cling together and cannot be
      parted.
¹⁸His snorting throws out flashes of
      light;
   his eyes are like the rays of dawn.
¹⁹Firebrands stream from his mouth;
   sparks of fire shoot out.
²⁰Smoke pours from his nostrils
   as from a boiling pot over a fire of
      reeds.
²¹His breath sets coals ablaze,
   and flames dart from his mouth.
²²Strength resides in his neck;
   dismay goes before him.
²³The folds of his flesh are tightly joined;
   they are firm and immovable.
²⁴His chest is hard as rock,
   hard as a lower millstone.
²⁵When he rises up, the mighty are
      terrified;
   they retreat before his thrashing.
²⁶The sword that reaches him has no
      effect,
   nor does the spear or the dart or the
      javelin.
²⁷Iron he treats like straw
   and bronze like rotten wood.
²⁸Arrows do not make him flee;
   slingstones are like chaff to him.
²⁹A club seems to him but a piece of
      straw;
   he laughs at the rattling of the lance.
³⁰His undersides are jagged potsherds,
   leaving a trail in the mud like a
      threshing sledge.
³¹He makes the depths churn like a
      boiling caldron
   and stirs up the sea like a pot of
      ointment.
³²Behind him he leaves a glistening
      wake;
   one would think the deep had white
      hair.
³³Nothing on earth is his equal—
   a creature without fear.
³⁴He looks down on all that are
      haughty;
   he is king over all that are proud."

---

^a17 Possibly trunk   ^b24 Or *by a water hole*
^c1 Possibly the crocodile   ^d15 Or *His pride is his*

Job

42 Then Job replied to the LORD:

2 "I know that you can do all things;
 no plan of yours can be thwarted.
3 You asked, 'Who is this that obscures
 my counsel without
 knowledge?'
 Surely I spoke of things I did not
 understand,
 things too wonderful for me to know.

4 "You said, 'Listen now, and I will
 speak;
 I will question you,
 and you shall answer me.'

5 My ears had heard of you
 but now my eyes have seen you.
6 Therefore I despise myself
 and repent in dust and ashes."

Epilogue

7 After the LORD had said these things to Job, he said to Eliphaz the Temanite, "I am angry with you and your two friends, because you have not spoken of me what is right, as my servant Job has. 8 So now take seven bulls and seven rams and go to my servant Job and sacrifice a burnt offering for yourselves. My servant Job will pray for you, and I will accept his prayer and

Pay Me Now or Pay Me Later

Speeding down your favorite interstate, a sound begins to emanate from your trusty car. *What's that noise?* you wonder to yourself. *I don't remember hearing that before.* You turn the radio off to get a bearing on where it's coming from. Your amateur mechanic estimate? *Carbon build-up in the cylinders* (of course), so you check for state police and slam the accelerator to the floor. As the speedometer returns to your previous, nearly legal level, the offending sound returns. *Huh. Maybe it'll go away,* you actually muse. What a foolish thought.

Perhaps the most powerful advertisement ever conceived by the minds of Madison Avenue agents was the one they created for Fram filters. Perhaps you remember it. The story this television commercial told was of a situation like the imaginary one above. The point of the ad was summarized in the penetrating words spoken at the end by a guy displaying an eight-dollar oil filter in his hand: "You can pay me now or you can pay me later."

The message was crystal clear. Car problems don't go away. The sooner you deal with them, the better off you'll be.

Life's difficult problems don't go away either. We can mask them or deny them, but unless we deal with them head-on, they'll turn that eight-dollar oil filter into a

DAILY INSIGHT

WEDNESDAY

Passage:
Job 42:7–17

Verse:
Job 42:12a

two-thousand-dollar valve job.

Perhaps the most important lesson to be learned from Job's life is this one: *The sooner we deal with who God really is and who we are in contrast to him, the wiser and more satisfied we'll be.* If we want to learn this early in life, then the remainder of our lives we'll be rewarded … prosperous in God's almighty economy. If we wait until we're old men to make this discovery, we'll literally waste decades of potential usefulness and inner peace.

The second half of Job's life was more "blessed" than the first. The actual roll call of his family and the list of his possessions fill today's verses. But my suspicion is that if we were able to interview Job today, he would say that the greatest difference between the first half and the second half of his life was his personal experience with a holy God. In fact, he would probably admonish us to diligently pursue our heavenly Father as soon as we can, loving him and serving him with our whole beings.

Waiting to find answers to our nagging questions or waiting to fix our aching hearts will only cause our lives to break down. And, as Job would strongly attest, it's definitely not worth the delay.

For your next devotional reading, go to page 576.

not deal with you according to your folly. You have not spoken of me what is right, as my servant Job has." ⁹So Eliphaz the Temanite, Bildad the Shuhite and Zophar the Naamathite did what the LORD told them; and the LORD accepted Job's prayer.

¹⁰After Job had prayed for his friends, the LORD made him prosperous again and gave him twice as much as he had before. ¹¹All his brothers and sisters and everyone who had known him before came and ate with him in his house. They comforted and consoled him over all the trouble the LORD had brought upon him, and each one gave him a piece of silver^a and a gold ring.

¹²The LORD blessed the latter part of Job's life more than the first. He had four-teen thousand sheep, six thousand camels, a thousand yoke of oxen and a thousand donkeys. ¹³And he also had seven sons and three daughters. ¹⁴The first daughter he named Jemimah, the second Keziah and the third Keren-Happuch. ¹⁵Nowhere in all the land were there found women as beautiful as Job's daughters, and their father granted them an inheritance along with their brothers.

¹⁶After this, Job lived a hundred and forty years; he saw his children and their children to the fourth generation. ¹⁷And so he died, old and full of years.

^a11 Hebrew *him a kesitah*; a kesitah was a unit of money of unknown weight and value.

Inheritance that Need Not Be Divided

Job, the Rewarded Father

"The LORD blessed the latter part of Job's life more than the first" (42:12).

Text: Job 42

There may be no more horrific account of the bottom falling out of a man's life than the story of Job.

When we first met Job, he was living very well. "He had seven sons and three daughters, and he owned seven thousand sheep, three thousand camels, five hundred yoke of oxen and five hundred donkeys, and had a large number of servants. He was the greatest man among all the people of the East" (1:2–3). Life had been very, very good to Job. This happy family man had it all.

Then fire fell from heaven and killed his servants and livestock, enemies from neighboring lands turned hostile, and his children were wiped out in a natural disaster. After all this, disease wracked Job's body, and the friends who came to comfort him turned against him. Job's self-confidence evaporated as quickly as his net worth.

But because of Job's faithfulness and repentance, God restored everything he had lost. In fact, God *doubled* his faithful servant's net worth. He had so many material blessings that he side-stepped the status quo and "granted [his daughters] an inheritance along with their brothers" (42:15). Not only did his children receive many tangible things in their father's will, but they also received the legacy of his faithfulness when most people would have buckled under the pressure. In fact, the memory of Job's unbelievable willpower so impressed his children, and their children, that his story survives to this day. That, my friend, is a *legacy*.

Just in case you get tired of the work of living righteously and in obedience to your heavenly Father, remember Job's kids. They divided his wealth evenly, but each one inherited the example of their dad's godliness in full measure.

For a complete listing of Dads in the Bible, turn to page 1434.

Real men feel things deeply. Sometimes they find themselves in deep contemplation, considering life's most complex and troubling issues. Some men listen to classical music and enjoy occasional visits to art galleries and reading poetry. Some men even cry. Men who do these things have a great comrade in King David.

As the author of most of these psalms, David was a man's man. He had to make no apologies for his strength, his prowess, or his success in every visible area of life. But David was a man of profound depth. His transparency and vulnerability in this collection of songs opens a whole new landscape—an important dimension—for men. Tenderness, praise, sorrow for sin, joy, confession and singing at the top of his lungs—these things ought to be as much a part of a man's life as going to the office, undertaking physical labor and watching ESPN. As a man, it's perfectly all right for you to quietly read and meditate on the majesty and deep honesty of these psalms. You won't regret it.

Psalms

BOOK I
Psalms 1–41

Psalm 1

¹ Blessed is the man
    who does not walk in the counsel of
        the wicked
or stand in the way of sinners
    or sit in the seat of mockers.
² But his delight is in the law of the LORD,
    and on his law he meditates day and
        night.
³ He is like a tree planted by streams of
    water,

which yields its fruit in season
    and whose leaf does not wither.
    Whatever he does prospers.

⁴ Not so the wicked!
    They are like chaff
        that the wind blows away.
⁵ Therefore the wicked will not stand in
        the judgment,
    nor sinners in the assembly of the
        righteous.

⁶ For the LORD watches over the way of
        the righteous,
    but the way of the wicked will
        perish.

Psalm 2

[1] Why do the nations conspire[a]
    and the peoples plot in vain?
[2] The kings of the earth take their
    stand
    and the rulers gather together
    against the LORD
    and against his Anointed One.[b]
[3] "Let us break their chains," they say,
    "and throw off their fetters."

[4] The One enthroned in heaven laughs;
    the Lord scoffs at them.
[5] Then he rebukes them in his anger
    and terrifies them in his wrath,
    saying,
[6] "I have installed my King[c]
    on Zion, my holy hill."

[7] I will proclaim the decree of the LORD:

He said to me, "You are my Son[d];
today I have become your Father.[e]

[8] Ask of me,
    and I will make the nations your
    inheritance,
    the ends of the earth your
    possession.
[9] You will rule them with an iron
    scepter[f];
    you will dash them to pieces like
    pottery."

[10] Therefore, you kings, be wise;
    be warned, you rulers of the earth.
[11] Serve the LORD with fear
    and rejoice with trembling.
[12] Kiss the Son, lest he be angry
    and you be destroyed in your way,
    for his wrath can flare up in a
    moment.
    Blessed are all who take refuge in
    him.

[a]1 Hebrew; Septuagint *rage*   [b]2 Or *anointed one*
[c]6 Or *king*   [d]7 Or *son;* also in verse 12   [e]7 Or *have begotten you*   [f]9 Or *will break them with a rod of iron*

Handle with Care

DAILY INSIGHT

THURSDAY

Passage:
Psalm 1

Verse:
Psalm 1:1

Have you ever seen a head of state, a famous actor, or any world-renowned person traveling alone? I haven't either. It seems that whenever we catch a glimpse of these folks in an airport, on the late news, or in the newspaper, there are always several people quietly standing in the background. So who are these shadowed figures?

In the vernacular, these silent bystanders are called "handlers." And even though they seem to have nothing to say, they actually play an incredibly important role in the life of the person for whom they work. When the mini-cams turn away, the microphones are turned off, and the crowds dissipate, these handlers become counselors, sounding-boards to the stars. And more often than you and I would ever suspect, when an important person says or does something foolish, it's caused by one very simple thing: bad advice. He or she has chosen the wrong people as handlers.

The message of this very first psalm is

simple. Everyone, famous people and ordinary folk alike, has handlers. Choose yours carefully.

Truly happy is the man who doesn't seek advice from wicked people. Truly happy is the man who doesn't live—that is, voluntarily align himself—with sinners. And truly happy is the man who doesn't let cynics chart his life's course. The man who carefully selects his handlers because of their integrity, their obedience, and their faith will get the right input when he comes to them with the "what-do-you-think-I-should-do-here" questions. As it turns out, sound advice comes from people who have good handlers of their own.

Who stands in the shadows behind you? To whom do you go for input? Who are your advisors? Today, David gives us one of the secrets to being truly happy: Don't hang out with stupid counsel. Find good handlers, get good advice. You'll be glad you did.

For your next devotional reading, go to page 579.

Psalm 3

A psalm of David. When he fled
from his son Absalom.

[1] O LORD, how many are my foes!
How many rise up against me!
[2] Many are saying of me,
"God will not deliver him."   *Selah*[a]

[3] But you are a shield around me,
O LORD;
you bestow glory on me and lift[b] up
my head.
[4] To the LORD I cry aloud,
and he answers me from his holy
hill.   *Selah*

[5] I lie down and sleep;
I wake again, because the LORD
sustains me.
[6] I will not fear the tens of thousands
drawn up against me on every side.

[7] Arise, O LORD!
Deliver me, O my God!
Strike all my enemies on the jaw;
break the teeth of the wicked.

[8] From the LORD comes deliverance.
May your blessing be on your
people.   *Selah*

Psalm 4

For the director of music. With stringed
instruments. A psalm of David.

[1] Answer me when I call to you,
O my righteous God.
Give me relief from my distress;
be merciful to me and hear my
prayer.

[2] How long, O men, will you turn my
glory into shame[c]?
How long will you love delusions and
seek false gods[d]?   *Selah*
[3] Know that the LORD has set apart the
godly for himself;
the LORD will hear when I call to him.

[4] In your anger do not sin;
when you are on your beds,
search your hearts and be silent.
Selah
[5] Offer right sacrifices
and trust in the LORD.

[6] Many are asking, "Who can show us
any good?"
Let the light of your face shine upon
us, O LORD.

[7] You have filled my heart with greater
joy
than when their grain and new wine
abound.
[8] I will lie down and sleep in peace,
for you alone, O LORD,
make me dwell in safety.

Psalm 5

For the director of music. For flutes.
A psalm of David.

[1] Give ear to my words, O LORD,
consider my sighing.
[2] Listen to my cry for help,
my King and my God,
for to you I pray.
[3] In the morning, O LORD, you hear my
voice;
in the morning I lay my requests
before you
and wait in expectation.

[4] You are not a God who takes pleasure
in evil;
with you the wicked cannot dwell.
[5] The arrogant cannot stand in your
presence;
you hate all who do wrong.
[6] You destroy those who tell lies;
bloodthirsty and deceitful men
the LORD abhors.

[7] But I, by your great mercy,
will come into your house;
in reverence will I bow down
toward your holy temple.
[8] Lead me, O LORD, in your
righteousness
because of my enemies—
make straight your way before me.

[9] Not a word from their mouth can be
trusted;
their heart is filled with destruction.
Their throat is an open grave;
with their tongue they speak deceit.
[10] Declare them guilty, O God!
Let their intrigues be their downfall.
Banish them for their many sins,
for they have rebelled against you.

[11] But let all who take refuge in you be
glad;
let them ever sing for joy.
Spread your protection over them,

[a]2 A word of uncertain meaning, occurring
frequently in the Psalms; possibly a musical term
[b]3 Or LORD, / my Glorious One, who lifts   [c]2 Or you
dishonor my Glorious One   [d]2 Or seek lies

that those who love your name may
  rejoice in you.
¹²For surely, O LORD, you bless the
    righteous;
  you surround them with your favor
    as with a shield.

Psalm 6

For the director of music. With stringed
instruments. According to *sheminith.*[a]
A psalm of David.

¹O LORD, do not rebuke me in your
    anger
  or discipline me in your wrath.
²Be merciful to me, LORD, for I am faint;
  O LORD, heal me, for my bones are in
    agony.
³My soul is in anguish.
  How long, O LORD, how long?

⁴Turn, O LORD, and deliver me;
  save me because of your unfailing
    love.
⁵No one remembers you when he is
    dead.
  Who praises you from the grave[b]?

⁶I am worn out from groaning;
  all night long I flood my bed with
    weeping
  and drench my couch with tears.
⁷My eyes grow weak with sorrow;
  they fail because of all my foes.

⁸Away from me, all you who do evil,
  for the LORD has heard my weeping.
⁹The LORD has heard my cry for mercy;
  the LORD accepts my prayer.
¹⁰All my enemies will be ashamed and
    dismayed;
  they will turn back in sudden
    disgrace.

Psalm 7

A *shiggaion*[c] of David, which he sang to
the LORD concerning Cush, a Benjamite.

¹O LORD my God, I take refuge in you;
  save and deliver me from all who
    pursue me,
²or they will tear me like a lion
  and rip me to pieces with no one to
    rescue me.

³O LORD my God, if I have done this
  and there is guilt on my hands—

⁴if I have done evil to him who is at
    peace with me
  or without cause have robbed my
    foe—
⁵then let my enemy pursue and overtake
    me;
  let him trample my life to the
    ground
  and make me sleep in the dust.
                                Selah

⁶Arise, O LORD, in your anger;
  rise up against the rage of my
    enemies.
  Awake, my God; decree justice.
⁷Let the assembled peoples gather
    around you.
  Rule over them from on high;
⁸   let the LORD judge the peoples.
  Judge me, O LORD, according to my
    righteousness,
  according to my integrity, O Most
    High.
⁹O righteous God,
  who searches minds and hearts,
  bring to an end the violence of the
    wicked
  and make the righteous secure.

¹⁰My shield[d] is God Most High,
  who saves the upright in heart.
¹¹God is a righteous judge,
  a God who expresses his wrath every
    day.
¹²If he does not relent,
  he[e] will sharpen his sword;
  he will bend and string his bow.
¹³He has prepared his deadly weapons;
  he makes ready his flaming
    arrows.

¹⁴He who is pregnant with evil
  and conceives trouble gives birth to
    disillusionment.
¹⁵He who digs a hole and scoops it
    out
  falls into the pit he has made.
¹⁶The trouble he causes recoils on
    himself;
  his violence comes down on his own
    head.

¹⁷I will give thanks to the LORD because
    of his righteousness
  and will sing praise to the name of
    the LORD Most High.

---

*a*Title: Probably a musical term   *b*5 Hebrew
Sheol   *c*Title: Probably a literary or musical term
*d*10 Or *sovereign*   *e*12 Or *If a man does not
repent, / God*

Psalm 8

For the director of music. According to *gittith*.[a]
A psalm of David.

¹O LORD, our Lord,
   how majestic is your name in all the
      earth!

You have set your glory
   above the heavens.
²From the lips of children and infants

you have ordained praise[b]
   because of your enemies,
      to silence the foe and the avenger.

³When I consider your heavens,
   the work of your fingers,
the moon and the stars,
   which you have set in place,
⁴what is man that you are mindful of
      him,

[a]Title: Probably a musical term   [b]2 Or *strength*

Goosebumps

Not long ago, I was hustling through the airport toward an early morning flight. Since I was running a little late, my pace down the concourse was quick. Just then, I heard something that slowed me down—an unmistakable conversation between an astronaut and an air traffic controller. I glanced up at the CNN television monitor hanging from the ceiling, and witnessed the mighty space shuttle Columbia landing at the Kennedy Space Center. This eighty-five ton behemoth glided toward the runway as though it were a yellow maple leaf softly landing on my lawn.

I couldn't help myself. Late or not, I had to stop and watch. The touchdown was flawless. Puffs of white smoke burst from the tires as they greeted *terra firma*. A huge parachute was deployed, safely bringing the craft to a stop. The man in Houston gave a quick, monotone rundown: "Columbia has successfully completed her ten-day mission, encircling the earth 346 times and covering 6.4 million miles. Welcome home, Columbia."

Goosebumps covered my forearms. "What a miracle," I whispered.

Glancing around the waiting area, I saw a number of people—a businessman reading a fresh USA Today, a young family trying to keep their youngster close-by, a college student doing some last-minute digging through a textbook. Not one of them, not even the child, was paying the least bit of attention to the television. The incredible phenomenon of science, technol-

DAILY INSIGHT

FRIDAY
Passage:
Psalm 8
Verses:
Psalm 8:3–4

ogy and human ingenuity didn't even earn a lifted head or raised eye.

A trace of anger welled up inside me. "Unbelievable," I whispered.

Unfortunately, every time I read this psalm, it dawns on me that I'm as guilty as those people in the waiting area at Gate B-6. "O LORD, our Lord, how majestic is your name . . ." *Can you believe the Bulls lost again?* "When I consider your heavens . . ." *C'mon over here, honey, I don't want you to get lost in this airport.* "The moon and the stars which you have set in place . . ." *Let's see, the velocity of a falling object is its mass times the acceleration of gravity.*

I have grown so accustomed to God's miraculous handiwork that it no longer overwhelms me. In fact, sometimes I don't even bother to look up. But reading this psalm is like the familiar cadence of an astronaut checking in with Houston. I cannot help myself. I am almost forced to stop, look up, and when I see what's going on, those same chills cover my arms.

Are you tired of the headlines, the daily chores of fatherhood, and the rigors of study? Look up. Remember who this is you're worshiping. Recall what he's done. Rest in his love for you today and in his promise for tomorrow. How could you ever get accustomed to this?

Bring on those old goosebumps again.

For your next devotional reading, go to page 589.

the son of man that you care for him?
[5] You made him a little lower than the
heavenly beings[a]
and crowned him with glory and
honor.

[6] You made him ruler over the works of
your hands;
you put everything under his feet:
[7] all flocks and herds,
and the beasts of the field,
[8] the birds of the air,
and the fish of the sea,
all that swim the paths of the seas.

[9] O LORD, our Lord,
how majestic is your name in all the
earth!

Psalm 9[b]

For the director of music. To ₍the tune of₎
"The Death of the Son." A psalm of David.

[1] I will praise you, O LORD, with all my
heart;
I will tell of all your wonders.
[2] I will be glad and rejoice in you;
I will sing praise to your name,
O Most High.

[3] My enemies turn back;
they stumble and perish before
you.
[4] For you have upheld my right and my
cause;
you have sat on your throne, judging
righteously.
[5] You have rebuked the nations and
destroyed the wicked;
you have blotted out their name for
ever and ever.
[6] Endless ruin has overtaken the
enemy,
you have uprooted their cities;
even the memory of them has
perished.
[7] The LORD reigns forever;
he has established his throne for
judgment.
[8] He will judge the world in
righteousness;
he will govern the peoples with
justice.
[9] The LORD is a refuge for the
oppressed,
a stronghold in times of trouble.
[10] Those who know your name will trust
in you,
for you, LORD, have never forsaken
those who seek you.

[11] Sing praises to the LORD, enthroned in
Zion;
proclaim among the nations what he
has done.
[12] For he who avenges blood remembers;
he does not ignore the cry of the
afflicted.
[13] O LORD, see how my enemies persecute
me!
Have mercy and lift me up from the
gates of death,
[14] that I may declare your praises
in the gates of the Daughter of Zion
and there rejoice in your salvation.
[15] The nations have fallen into the pit
they have dug;
their feet are caught in the net they
have hidden.
[16] The LORD is known by his justice;
the wicked are ensnared by the work
of their hands.
Higgaion.[c] Selah
[17] The wicked return to the grave,[d]
all the nations that forget God.
[18] But the needy will not always be
forgotten,
nor the hope of the afflicted ever
perish.
[19] Arise, O LORD, let not man triumph;
let the nations be judged in your
presence.
[20] Strike them with terror, O LORD;
let the nations know they are but
men.
Selah

Psalm 10[b]

[1] Why, O LORD, do you stand far off?
Why do you hide yourself in times of
trouble?

[2] In his arrogance the wicked man hunts
down the weak,
who are caught in the schemes he
devises.
[3] He boasts of the cravings of his
heart;
he blesses the greedy and reviles the
LORD.
[4] In his pride the wicked does not seek
him;
in all his thoughts there is no room
for God.

[a]5 Or *than God*   [b]Psalms 9 and 10 may have been
originally a single acrostic poem, the stanzas of
which begin with the successive letters of the
Hebrew alphabet. In the Septuagint they constitute
one psalm.   [c]16 Or *Meditation*; possibly a musical
notation   [d]17 Hebrew *Sheol*

⁵His ways are always prosperous;
  he is haughty and your laws are far
    from him;
  he sneers at all his enemies.
⁶He says to himself, "Nothing will shake
    me;
  I'll always be happy and never have
    trouble."
⁷His mouth is full of curses and lies and
    threats;
  trouble and evil are under his
    tongue.
⁸He lies in wait near the villages;
  from ambush he murders the
    innocent,
  watching in secret for his victims.
⁹He lies in wait like a lion in cover;
  he lies in wait to catch the helpless;
  he catches the helpless and drags
    them off in his net.
¹⁰His victims are crushed, they collapse;
  they fall under his strength.
¹¹He says to himself, "God has
    forgotten;
  he covers his face and never sees."

¹²Arise, LORD! Lift up your hand, O God.
  Do not forget the helpless.
¹³Why does the wicked man revile God?
  Why does he say to himself,
  "He won't call me to account"?
¹⁴But you, O God, do see trouble and
    grief;
  you consider it to take it in hand.
  The victim commits himself to you;
  you are the helper of the fatherless.
¹⁵Break the arm of the wicked and evil
    man;
  call him to account for his
    wickedness
  that would not be found out.

¹⁶The LORD is King for ever and ever;
  the nations will perish from his land.
¹⁷You hear, O LORD, the desire of the
    afflicted;
  you encourage them, and you listen
    to their cry,
¹⁸defending the fatherless and the
    oppressed,
  in order that man, who is of the
    earth, may terrify no more.

Psalm 11

For the director of music. Of David.

¹In the LORD I take refuge.
  How then can you say to me:
  "Flee like a bird to your mountain.
²For look, the wicked bend their bows;

they set their arrows against the
    strings
  to shoot from the shadows
  at the upright in heart.
³When the foundations are being
    destroyed,
  what can the righteous do*a*?"

⁴The LORD is in his holy temple;
  the LORD is on his heavenly throne.
  He observes the sons of men;
  his eyes examine them.
⁵The LORD examines the righteous,
  but the wicked*b* and those who love
    violence
  his soul hates.
⁶On the wicked he will rain
  fiery coals and burning sulfur;
  a scorching wind will be their lot.

⁷For the LORD is righteous,
  he loves justice;
  upright men will see his face.

Psalm 12

For the director of music. According
to *sheminith.*c A psalm of David.

¹Help, LORD, for the godly are no more;
  the faithful have vanished from
    among men.
²Everyone lies to his neighbor;
  their flattering lips speak with
    deception.

³May the LORD cut off all flattering lips
  and every boastful tongue
⁴that says, "We will triumph with our
    tongues;
  we own our lips*d*—who is our
    master?"

⁵"Because of the oppression of the weak
  and the groaning of the needy,
  I will now arise," says the LORD.
  "I will protect them from those who
    malign them."
⁶And the words of the LORD are flawless,
  like silver refined in a furnace of clay,
  purified seven times.

⁷O LORD, you will keep us safe
  and protect us from such people
    forever.
⁸The wicked freely strut about
  when what is vile is honored among
    men.

*a*3 Or *what is the Righteous One doing* *b*5 Or *The
LORD, the Righteous One, examines the wicked,*
*c*Title: Probably a musical term *d*4 Or *l our lips
are our plowshares*

Psalm 13

For the director of music.
A psalm of David.

¹How long, O LORD? Will you forget me
forever?
How long will you hide your face
from me?
²How long must I wrestle with my
thoughts
and every day have sorrow in my
heart?
How long will my enemy triumph
over me?

³Look on me and answer, O LORD my
God.
Give light to my eyes, or I will sleep
in death;
⁴my enemy will say, "I have overcome
him,"
and my foes will rejoice when I fall.

⁵But I trust in your unfailing love;
my heart rejoices in your salvation.
⁶I will sing to the LORD,
for he has been good to me.

Psalm 14

For the director of music. Of David.

¹The fool[a] says in his heart,
"There is no God."
They are corrupt, their deeds are vile;
there is no one who does good.

²The LORD looks down from heaven
on the sons of men
to see if there are any who
understand,
any who seek God.
³All have turned aside,
they have together become corrupt;
there is no one who does good,
not even one.

⁴Will evildoers never learn—
those who devour my people as men
eat bread
and who do not call on the LORD?
⁵There they are, overwhelmed with
dread,
for God is present in the company of
the righteous.
⁶You evildoers frustrate the plans of the
poor,
but the LORD is their refuge.

⁷Oh, that salvation for Israel would
come out of Zion!

When the LORD restores the fortunes
of his people,
let Jacob rejoice and Israel be glad!

Psalm 15

A psalm of David.

¹LORD, who may dwell in your
sanctuary?
Who may live on your holy hill?

²He whose walk is blameless
and who does what is righteous,
who speaks the truth from his heart
³ and has no slander on his tongue,
who does his neighbor no wrong
and casts no slur on his fellowman,
⁴who despises a vile man
but honors those who fear the LORD,
who keeps his oath
even when it hurts,
⁵who lends his money without usury
and does not accept a bribe against
the innocent.

He who does these things
will never be shaken.

Psalm 16

A *miktam*[b] of David.

¹Keep me safe, O God,
for in you I take refuge.

²I said to the LORD, "You are my Lord;
apart from you I have no good
thing."
³As for the saints who are in the land,
they are the glorious ones in whom is
all my delight.[c]
⁴The sorrows of those will increase
who run after other gods.
I will not pour out their libations of
blood
or take up their names on my lips.

⁵LORD, you have assigned me my
portion and my cup;
you have made my lot secure.
⁶The boundary lines have fallen for me
in pleasant places;
surely I have a delightful inheritance.

⁷I will praise the LORD, who counsels
me;

a1 The Hebrew words rendered *fool* in Psalms
denote one who is morally deficient.   *b*Title:
Probably a literary or musical term   *c3* Or *As for
the pagan priests who are in the land / and the
nobles in whom all delight, I said:*

even at night my heart instructs
        me.
⁸I have set the LORD always before me.
    Because he is at my right hand,
    I will not be shaken.

⁹Therefore my heart is glad and my
        tongue rejoices;
    my body also will rest secure,
¹⁰because you will not abandon me to
        the grave,ᵃ
    nor will you let your Holy Oneᵇ see
        decay.
¹¹You have madeᶜ known to me the path
        of life;
    you will fill me with joy in your
        presence,
    with eternal pleasures at your right
        hand.

Psalm 17

A prayer of David.

¹Hear, O LORD, my righteous plea;
    listen to my cry.
Give ear to my prayer—
    it does not rise from deceitful lips.
²May my vindication come from you;
    may your eyes see what is right.

³Though you probe my heart and
        examine me at night,
    though you test me, you will find
        nothing;
    I have resolved that my mouth will
        not sin.
⁴As for the deeds of men—
    by the word of your lips
    I have kept myself
        from the ways of the violent.
⁵My steps have held to your paths;
    my feet have not slipped.

⁶I call on you, O God, for you will
        answer me;
    give ear to me and hear my prayer.
⁷Show the wonder of your great love,
    you who save by your right hand
    those who take refuge in you from
        their foes.
⁸Keep me as the apple of your eye;
    hide me in the shadow of your wings
⁹from the wicked who assail me,
    from my mortal enemies who
        surround me.
¹⁰They close up their callous hearts,
    and their mouths speak with
        arrogance.

*ᵃ10 Hebrew Sheol   ᵇ10 Or your faithful one   ᶜ11 Or
You will make*

HEY DAD
What is heaven like?

Text: Psalm 16:9–11

Our human minds aren't able to comprehend what heaven will be like. Even the
people who wrote the Bible weren't able to describe it! Ezekiel's description of
it is filled with phrases such as "what appeared to be" and "what looked like"
(Ezekiel 1:26–28). Even John's description of heaven in the book of Revelation
(see chapter 4), as majestic as it sounds, is limited. But David tells us, in Psalm
16:11, "You will fill me with joy in your presence, with eternal pleasures at your
right hand." So what we *do* know is that, in heaven, God will fill us with delight.
The joy we experience on earth is only a faint shadow of what we will experience there.

In her book *Heaven: Your Real Home*, Joni Eareckson Tada offers this thought: When we
see a road sign that says "Chicago: 50 miles," we don't think that the road sign is Chicago
itself. In the same way, when we see the road signs—or descriptions—that John, Ezekiel,
David, and others give us, we shouldn't mistake those signs for heaven itself (Tada, 21). The
Bible gives us the symbols, but we must use our faith to imagine conversing with the angels,
enjoying pleasures we've never known, and living in a place where God himself dwells.

Heaven must be incredible. After all, Jesus Christ was willing to die just so we could join
him there.

*Tada, Joni Eareckson. (1995). Heaven: Your Real Home. Grand Rapids, Michigan: Zondervan
Publishing House.*

For a complete listing of Questions Kids Ask, turn to page 1435.

¹¹They have tracked me down, they now
    surround me,
  with eyes alert, to throw me to the
    ground.
¹²They are like a lion hungry for prey,
  like a great lion crouching in cover.

¹³Rise up, O LORD, confront them, bring
    them down;
  rescue me from the wicked by your
    sword.
¹⁴O LORD, by your hand save me from
    such men,
  from men of this world whose
    reward is in this life.

  You still the hunger of those you
    cherish;
    their sons have plenty,
  and they store up wealth for their
    children.
¹⁵And I—in righteousness I will see your
    face;
  when I awake, I will be satisfied with
    seeing your likeness.

Psalm 18

For the director of music. Of David the
servant of the LORD. He sang to the LORD
the words of this song when the LORD
delivered him from the hand of all his enemies
and from the hand of Saul. He said:

¹I love you, O LORD, my strength.

²The LORD is my rock, my fortress and
    my deliverer;
  my God is my rock, in whom I take
    refuge.
  He is my shield and the horn[a] of my
    salvation, my stronghold.
³I call to the LORD, who is worthy of
    praise,
  and I am saved from my enemies.

⁴The cords of death entangled me;
  the torrents of destruction
    overwhelmed me.
⁵The cords of the grave[b] coiled around
    me;
  the snares of death confronted me.
⁶In my distress I called to the LORD;
  I cried to my God for help.
  From his temple he heard my voice;
    my cry came before him, into his
    ears.

⁷The earth trembled and quaked,
  and the foundations of the
    mountains shook;
  they trembled because he was angry.

⁸Smoke rose from his nostrils;
  consuming fire came from his
    mouth,
  burning coals blazed out of it.
⁹He parted the heavens and came down;
  dark clouds were under his feet.
¹⁰He mounted the cherubim and flew;
  he soared on the wings of the wind.
¹¹He made darkness his covering, his
    canopy around him—
  the dark rain clouds of the sky.
¹²Out of the brightness of his presence
    clouds advanced,
  with hailstones and bolts of
    lightning.
¹³The LORD thundered from heaven;
  the voice of the Most High
    resounded.[c]
¹⁴He shot his arrows and scattered the
    enemies,
  great bolts of lightning and routed
    them.
¹⁵The valleys of the sea were exposed
  and the foundations of the earth laid
    bare
  at your rebuke, O LORD,
  at the blast of breath from your
    nostrils.

¹⁶He reached down from on high and
    took hold of me;
  he drew me out of deep waters.
¹⁷He rescued me from my powerful
    enemy,
  from my foes, who were too strong
    for me.
¹⁸They confronted me in the day of my
    disaster,
  but the LORD was my support.
¹⁹He brought me out into a spacious
    place;
  he rescued me because he delighted
    in me.
²⁰The LORD has dealt with me according
    to my righteousness;
  according to the cleanness of my
    hands he has rewarded me.
²¹For I have kept the ways of the LORD;
  I have not done evil by turning from
    my God.
²²All his laws are before me;
  I have not turned away from his
    decrees.
²³I have been blameless before him
  and have kept myself from sin.

---

a2 Horn here symbolizes strength.   *b5* Hebrew
Sheol   *c13* Some Hebrew manuscripts and
Septuagint (see also 2 Samuel 22:14); most Hebrew
manuscripts *resounded, / amid hailstones and bolts
of lightning*

²⁴ The LORD has rewarded me according
to my righteousness,
according to the cleanness of my
hands in his sight.
²⁵ To the faithful you show yourself
faithful,
to the blameless you show yourself
blameless,
²⁶ to the pure you show yourself pure,
but to the crooked you show yourself
shrewd.
²⁷ You save the humble
but bring low those whose eyes are
haughty.
²⁸ You, O LORD, keep my lamp burning;
my God turns my darkness into light.
²⁹ With your help I can advance against a
troop*ᵃ*;
with my God I can scale a wall.

³⁰ As for God, his way is perfect;
the word of the LORD is flawless.
He is a shield
for all who take refuge in him.
³¹ For who is God besides the LORD?
And who is the Rock except our God?
³² It is God who arms me with strength
and makes my way perfect.
³³ He makes my feet like the feet of a
deer;
he enables me to stand on the
heights.
³⁴ He trains my hands for battle;
my arms can bend a bow of bronze.
³⁵ You give me your shield of victory,
and your right hand sustains me;
you stoop down to make me great.
³⁶ You broaden the path beneath me,
so that my ankles do not turn.

³⁷ I pursued my enemies and overtook
them;
I did not turn back till they were
destroyed.
³⁸ I crushed them so that they could not
rise;
they fell beneath my feet.
³⁹ You armed me with strength for battle;
you made my adversaries bow at my
feet.
⁴⁰ You made my enemies turn their backs
in flight,
and I destroyed my foes.
⁴¹ They cried for help, but there was no
one to save them—
to the LORD, but he did not answer.
⁴² I beat them as fine as dust borne on the
wind;
I poured them out like mud in the
streets.

⁴³ You have delivered me from the attacks
of the people;
you have made me the head of
nations;
people I did not know are subject to
me.
⁴⁴ As soon as they hear me, they obey me;
foreigners cringe before me.
⁴⁵ They all lose heart;
they come trembling from their
strongholds.

⁴⁶ The LORD lives! Praise be to my Rock!
Exalted be God my Savior!
⁴⁷ He is the God who avenges me,
who subdues nations under me,
⁴⁸ who saves me from my enemies.
You exalted me above my foes;
from violent men you rescued me.
⁴⁹ Therefore I will praise you among the
nations, O LORD;
I will sing praises to your name.
⁵⁰ He gives his king great victories;
he shows unfailing kindness to his
anointed,
to David and his descendants
forever.

Psalm 19

For the director of music.
A psalm of David.

¹ The heavens declare the glory of God;
the skies proclaim the work of his
hands.
² Day after day they pour forth speech;
night after night they display
knowledge.
³ There is no speech or language
where their voice is not heard.ᵇ
⁴ Their voiceᶜ goes out into all the earth,
their words to the ends of the world.

In the heavens he has pitched a tent for
the sun,
⁵ which is like a bridegroom coming
forth from his pavilion,
like a champion rejoicing to run his
course.
⁶ It rises at one end of the heavens
and makes its circuit to the other;
nothing is hidden from its heat.

⁷ The law of the LORD is perfect,
reviving the soul.

*ᵃ29 Or can run through a barricade   ᵇ3 Or They
have no speech, there are no words; / no sound is
heard from them   ᶜ4 Septuagint, Jerome and
Syriac; Hebrew line*

The statutes of the LORD are
    trustworthy,
  making wise the simple.
⁸ The precepts of the LORD are right,
    giving joy to the heart.
  The commands of the LORD are radiant,
    giving light to the eyes.
⁹ The fear of the LORD is pure,
    enduring forever.
  The ordinances of the LORD are sure
    and altogether righteous.
¹⁰ They are more precious than gold,
    than much pure gold;
  they are sweeter than honey,
    than honey from the comb.
¹¹ By them is your servant warned;
    in keeping them there is great
      reward.

¹² Who can discern his errors?
    Forgive my hidden faults.
¹³ Keep your servant also from willful
      sins;
    may they not rule over me.
  Then will I be blameless,
    innocent of great transgression.

¹⁴ May the words of my mouth and the
      meditation of my heart
    be pleasing in your sight,
  O LORD, my Rock and my Redeemer.

Psalm 20

For the director of music.
A psalm of David.

¹ May the LORD answer you when you
    are in distress;
  may the name of the God of Jacob
    protect you.
² May he send you help from the
      sanctuary
    and grant you support from Zion.
³ May he remember all your sacrifices
    and accept your burnt offerings.   Selah
⁴ May he give you the desire of your
      heart
    and make all your plans succeed.
⁵ We will shout for joy when you are
      victorious
    and will lift up our banners in the
      name of our God.
  May the LORD grant all your requests.

⁶ Now I know that the LORD saves his
      anointed;
    he answers him from his holy heaven
      with the saving power of his right
        hand.

⁷ Some trust in chariots and some in
      horses,
    but we trust in the name of the LORD
      our God.
⁸ They are brought to their knees and
      fall,
    but we rise up and stand firm.
⁹ O LORD, save the king!
    Answerᵃ us when we call!

Psalm 21

For the director of music.
A psalm of David.

¹ O LORD, the king rejoices in your
      strength.
    How great is his joy in the victories
      you give!
² You have granted him the desire of his
      heart
    and have not withheld the request of
      his lips.   Selah
³ You welcomed him with rich blessings
    and placed a crown of pure gold on
      his head.
⁴ He asked you for life, and you gave it to
      him—
    length of days, for ever and ever.
⁵ Through the victories you gave, his
      glory is great;
    you have bestowed on him splendor
      and majesty.
⁶ Surely you have granted him eternal
      blessings
    and made him glad with the joy of
      your presence.
⁷ For the king trusts in the LORD;
    through the unfailing love of the
      Most High
    he will not be shaken.

⁸ Your hand will lay hold on all your
      enemies;
    your right hand will seize your foes.
⁹ At the time of your appearing
    you will make them like a fiery
      furnace.
  In his wrath the LORD will swallow
      them up,
    and his fire will consume them.
¹⁰ You will destroy their descendants from
      the earth,
    their posterity from mankind.
¹¹ Though they plot evil against you
    and devise wicked schemes, they
      cannot succeed;
¹² for you will make them turn their backs

ᵃ9 Or save! / O King, answer

when you aim at them with drawn bow.

¹³ Be exalted, O LORD, in your strength;
we will sing and praise your might.

Psalm 22

For the director of music. To the tune of
"The Doe of the Morning."
A psalm of David.

¹ My God, my God, why have you forsaken me?
Why are you so far from saving me,
so far from the words of my groaning?
² O my God, I cry out by day, but you do not answer,
by night, and am not silent.

³ Yet you are enthroned as the Holy One;
you are the praise of Israel.ᵃ
⁴ In you our fathers put their trust;
they trusted and you delivered them.
⁵ They cried to you and were saved;
in you they trusted and were not disappointed.

⁶ But I am a worm and not a man,
scorned by men and despised by the people.
⁷ All who see me mock me;
they hurl insults, shaking their heads:
⁸ "He trusts in the LORD;
let the LORD rescue him.
Let him deliver him,
since he delights in him."

⁹ Yet you brought me out of the womb;
you made me trust in you
even at my mother's breast.
¹⁰ From birth I was cast upon you;
from my mother's womb you have been my God.
¹¹ Do not be far from me,
for trouble is near
and there is no one to help.

¹² Many bulls surround me;
strong bulls of Bashan encircle me.
¹³ Roaring lions tearing their prey
open their mouths wide against me.
¹⁴ I am poured out like water,

ᵃ3 Or *Yet you are holy, / enthroned on the praises of Israel*

HEY DAD

Why do I sometimes feel like God's not there?

QUESTIONS KIDS ASK

Text: Psalm 22:1–2

At different times we've all felt, as David did at the beginning of this psalm, like God just wasn't there. We knew he said he would never leave us, but it still felt like he was on vacation. Why? Why does God sometimes seem to forsake us?

In his famous book, *The Screwtape Letters*, C.S. Lewis offers great insight on this question. The narrator in this book is a senior demon who is counseling a junior demon on how to pull a Christian away from God's service. In this passage, the Christian is feeling that God has forsaken him, and old Screwtape has this to say:

> [God] wants [His children] to learn to walk and must therefore take away His hand; and if only the will to walk is really there He is pleased even with their stumbles. Do not be deceived … our cause is never more in danger than when a human, no longer desiring, but still intending, to do our Enemy's [God's] will, looks round upon a universe from which every trace of Him seems to have vanished, and asks why he has been forsaken, and still obeys (p. 39).

Remember, God's goal is not to force us to love him. He wants us to love him by *choice*. He's helping us grow up, and little by little, he's teaching us to walk with him. Just as a little child needs to "go it alone" before he or she can learn to walk, so also God needs to take away his hand so that we will learn to walk in his way no matter what the circumstances.

Lewis, C.S. (1961). The Screwtape Letters. New York: Collier Books.

For a complete listing of Questions Kids Ask, turn to page 1435.

and all my bones are out of joint.
My heart has turned to wax;
  it has melted away within me.
¹⁵ My strength is dried up like a potsherd,
  and my tongue sticks to the roof of
    my mouth;
  you lay me*a* in the dust of death.
¹⁶ Dogs have surrounded me;
  a band of evil men has encircled me,
  they have pierced*b* my hands and my
    feet.
¹⁷ I can count all my bones;
  people stare and gloat over me.
¹⁸ They divide my garments among them
  and cast lots for my clothing.

¹⁹ But you, O LORD, be not far off;
  O my Strength, come quickly to help
    me.
²⁰ Deliver my life from the sword,
  my precious life from the power of
    the dogs.
²¹ Rescue me from the mouth of the
    lions;
  save*c* me from the horns of the wild
    oxen.

²² I will declare your name to my
    brothers;
  in the congregation I will praise you.
²³ You who fear the LORD, praise him!
  All you descendants of Jacob, honor
    him!
  Revere him, all you descendants of
    Israel!
²⁴ For he has not despised or disdained
  the suffering of the afflicted one;
he has not hidden his face from him
  but has listened to his cry for help.

²⁵ From you comes the theme of my
    praise in the great assembly;
  before those who fear you*d* will I
    fulfill my vows.
²⁶ The poor will eat and be satisfied;
  they who seek the LORD will praise
    him—
  may your hearts live forever!
²⁷ All the ends of the earth
  will remember and turn to the LORD,
  and all the families of the nations
  will bow down before him,
²⁸ for dominion belongs to the LORD
  and he rules over the nations.

²⁹ All the rich of the earth will feast and
    worship;
  all who go down to the dust will
    kneel before him—
  those who cannot keep themselves
    alive.
³⁰ Posterity will serve him;

future generations will be told about
  the Lord.
³¹ They will proclaim his righteousness
  to a people yet unborn—
  for he has done it.

Psalm 23

A psalm of David.

¹ The LORD is my shepherd, I shall not be
  in want.
²   He makes me lie down in green
    pastures,
he leads me beside quiet waters,
³   he restores my soul.
He guides me in paths of righteousness
  for his name's sake.
⁴ Even though I walk
  through the valley of the shadow of
    death,*e*
I will fear no evil,
  for you are with me;
your rod and your staff,
  they comfort me.

⁵ You prepare a table before me
  in the presence of my enemies.
You anoint my head with oil;
  my cup overflows.
⁶ Surely goodness and love will follow
    me
  all the days of my life,
and I will dwell in the house of the LORD
  forever.

Psalm 24

Of David. A psalm.

¹ The earth is the LORD's, and everything
  in it,
  the world, and all who live in it;
² for he founded it upon the seas
  and established it upon the waters.

³ Who may ascend the hill of the LORD?
  Who may stand in his holy place?
⁴ He who has clean hands and a pure
    heart,
  who does not lift up his soul to an
    idol
  or swear by what is false.*f*
⁵ He will receive blessing from the LORD
  and vindication from God his Savior.

a15 Or / *I am laid*   *b16* Some Hebrew manuscripts,
Septuagint and Syriac; most Hebrew manuscripts /
like the lion,   *c21* Or / *you have heard*
d25 Hebrew *him*   *e4* Or *through the darkest valley*
f4 Or *swear falsely*

Our Good Shepherd

Key Verse: *"The LORD is my shepherd, I shall not be in want."* Psalm 23:1

Text: Psalm 23 *(Dad or child reads the text.)*

QUIET TIMES WITH Dad

DAD READS: Have you ever wakened in the middle of the night and felt afraid? It might be a strange sound that wakes you up and makes your heart beat fast. Unknown noises in the dark can frighten even the bravest person.

Child reads: Sometimes I am afraid at night … strange noises and darkness scare me, too. But knowing that you are close to me makes me feel safe. I know that when I'm really scared, I can call you and you will come.

DAD READS: The twenty-third Psalm tells a story about our heavenly Father—a Shepherd who tenderly cares for his sheep. It promises us that wherever we are and whatever we're afraid of, he will always be with us, even when our dads aren't there. He tells us that when it comes to the things we need, he will take care of everything.

Child reads: God's promise to you and me is wonderful. And it means that there is never a good reason to be afraid. He will always be with us, even when it's dark and we can't see him. I am so glad that I have a loving Shepherd like this.

DAD READS: Being afraid is not something that only children feel. There are times during my day when I also feel afraid. So, even though I'm a grown-up, I am glad to have a Shepherd who cares for me.

Child reads: I want to always be thankful to God for his love for me. I want to always remember that I don't need to be afraid. I also want my friends to know that Jesus wants to be their Shepherd, too.

DAD READS: Let me pray this prayer with you:

Our Father in heaven, thank you for being our loving Shepherd. Thank you for taking care of all our needs. Please forgive us for the times when we are afraid or when we act like we don't have enough. Help us to remember that you will give us everything we truly need. We love you. In Jesus' name, Amen.

For your next devotional reading, go to page 592.

⁶Such is the generation of those who
    seek him,
  who seek your face, O God of
    Jacob.ᵃ   *Selah*

⁷Lift up your heads, O you gates;
  be lifted up, you ancient doors,
  that the King of glory may come in.
⁸Who is this King of glory?
  The LORD strong and mighty,
  the LORD mighty in battle.
⁹Lift up your heads, O you gates;
  lift them up, you ancient doors,
  that the King of glory may come in.
¹⁰Who is he, this King of glory?
  The LORD Almighty—
  he is the King of glory.   *Selah*

Psalm 25ᵇ

Of David.

¹To you, O LORD, I lift up my soul;
² in you I trust, O my God.

Do not let me be put to shame,
  nor let my enemies triumph over me.
³No one whose hope is in you
  will ever be put to shame,
but they will be put to shame
  who are treacherous without excuse.

⁴Show me your ways, O LORD,
  teach me your paths;
⁵guide me in your truth and teach me,
  for you are God my Savior,
  and my hope is in you all day long.
⁶Remember, O LORD, your great mercy
    and love,
  for they are from of old.
⁷Remember not the sins of my youth
  and my rebellious ways;
  according to your love remember me,
  for you are good, O LORD.

ᵃ6 Two Hebrew manuscripts and Syriac (see also
Septuagint); most Hebrew manuscripts *face,
Jacob*   ᵇThis psalm is an acrostic poem, the verses
of which begin with the successive letters of the
Hebrew alphabet.

Children Who Love God, Too
The Dad Who Fears the Lord

DADS
IN THE
BIBLE

*"Who, then, is the man that fears the LORD? . . .
He will spend his days in prosperity, and
his descendants will inherit the land"* (25:12–13).

Text: Psalm 25

Some Sunday morning, without being too conspicuous, take a look at the dads in your congregation. How engaged are they in the service? Do they look like they're enthralled with God's holy presence, or do they look like they're watching someone change their car's oil down at the corner service station?

The next time you're at a big ball game, look around at the dads in the stands. Don't worry about being inconspicuous this time; no one really cares what you do at a ball game. How engaged are these men in what's going on?

Maybe the above isn't a fair comparison. But the point is, our children are watching what we do. If we get fired up reading about the stock market over breakfast, they'll get the idea that stocks are worth being interested in. If they see us "Ooooh" and "Ahhh" over someone's new sports car, they'll grow up knowing that their dad gets fired up about nice cars. But if they see us in the presence of a holy God, sleepily checking our watches or mumbling our way through the hymns, they'll decide that knowing God is about as exciting as watching a passing freight train.

Your children will inherit something from you. Chances are far better than not that they will take with them the same passions you demonstrated in their presence—your love for sports, your enthusiasm over the stock market, your affection for fine cars, and your passion for God.

"Who, then, is the man that fears the LORD?" (25:12). Where is the guy who loves being in God's presence, who literally can't *wait* to enjoy his heavenly Father's nearness? When you find him, look at his kids. They'll be easy to spot. They are the "descendants" who will inherit the land.

For a complete listing of Dads in the Bible, turn to page 1434.

⁸Good and upright is the LORD;
   therefore he instructs sinners in his
      ways.
⁹He guides the humble in what is right
   and teaches them his way.
¹⁰All the ways of the LORD are loving and
      faithful
   for those who keep the demands of
      his covenant.
¹¹For the sake of your name, O LORD,
   forgive my iniquity, though it is
      great.
¹²Who, then, is the man that fears the
      LORD?
   He will instruct him in the way
      chosen for him.
¹³He will spend his days in prosperity,
   and his descendants will inherit the
      land.
¹⁴The LORD confides in those who fear
      him;
   he makes his covenant known to
      them.
¹⁵My eyes are ever on the LORD,
   for only he will release my feet from
      the snare.

¹⁶Turn to me and be gracious to me,
   for I am lonely and afflicted.
¹⁷The troubles of my heart have
      multiplied;
   free me from my anguish.
¹⁸Look upon my affliction and my
      distress
   and take away all my sins.
¹⁹See how my enemies have increased
   and how fiercely they hate me!
²⁰Guard my life and rescue me;
   let me not be put to shame,
   for I take refuge in you.
²¹May integrity and uprightness protect
      me,
   because my hope is in you.

²²Redeem Israel, O God,
   from all their troubles!

Psalm 26

Of David.

¹Vindicate me, O LORD,
   for I have led a blameless life;
 I have trusted in the LORD
   without wavering.
²Test me, O LORD, and try me,
   examine my heart and my mind;
³for your love is ever before me,
   and I walk continually in your truth.
⁴I do not sit with deceitful men,
   nor do I consort with hypocrites;

⁵I abhor the assembly of evildoers
   and refuse to sit with the wicked.
⁶I wash my hands in innocence,
   and go about your altar, O LORD,
⁷proclaiming aloud your praise
   and telling of all your wonderful
      deeds.
⁸I love the house where you live, O LORD,
   the place where your glory dwells.

⁹Do not take away my soul along with
      sinners,
   my life with bloodthirsty men,
¹⁰in whose hands are wicked schemes,
   whose right hands are full of bribes.
¹¹But I lead a blameless life;
   redeem me and be merciful to me.

¹²My feet stand on level ground;
   in the great assembly I will praise the
      LORD.

Psalm 27

Of David.

¹The LORD is my light and my
      salvation—
   whom shall I fear?
 The LORD is the stronghold of my life—
   of whom shall I be afraid?
²When evil men advance against me
   to devour my flesh,[a]
 when my enemies and my foes attack
      me,
   they will stumble and fall.
³Though an army besiege me,
   my heart will not fear;
 though war break out against me,
   even then will I be confident.

⁴One thing I ask of the LORD,
   this is what I seek:
 that I may dwell in the house of the
      LORD
   all the days of my life,
 to gaze upon the beauty of the LORD
   and to seek him in his temple.
⁵For in the day of trouble
   he will keep me safe in his dwelling;
 he will hide me in the shelter of his
      tabernacle
   and set me high upon a rock.
⁶Then my head will be exalted
   above the enemies who surround
      me;
 at his tabernacle will I sacrifice with
      shouts of joy;
   I will sing and make music to the
      LORD.

[a]2 Or to slander me

⁷Hear my voice when I call, O Lᴏʀᴅ;
    be merciful to me and answer me.
⁸My heart says of you, "Seek his[a] face!"
    Your face, Lᴏʀᴅ, I will seek.
⁹Do not hide your face from me,
    do not turn your servant away in
        anger;
    you have been my helper.
    Do not reject me or forsake me,
        O God my Savior.
¹⁰Though my father and mother forsake
    me,
    the Lᴏʀᴅ will receive me.

¹¹Teach me your way, O Lᴏʀᴅ;
    lead me in a straight path
        because of my oppressors.
¹²Do not turn me over to the desire of my
        foes,
    for false witnesses rise up against
        me,
    breathing out violence.
¹³I am still confident of this:
    I will see the goodness of the Lᴏʀᴅ

a8 Or To you, O my heart, he has said, "Seek my

No Fear

MONDAY

Passage:
Psalm 27

Verse:
Psalm 27:1

In May of 1968, my college roommate, Steve Oldham, and I packed up our ten-speed Schwinn Super Sport bicycles, drove to Chicago and boarded a plane for San Francisco. There we met up with thirty-eight college classmates and set out to ride our bikes to New York City.

Our first day on the road started like some kind of party. The Golden Gate Bridge provided a spectacular backdrop as the press took photos of our group. As our police motorcycle escort whisked us through the cities of San Francisco and Oakland, we college men felt like Olympic marathoners, entering the stadium for the final two laps. But our trip was just beginning. We had four thousand miles to go.

Directly out of Oakland, we headed north on St. Mary's road. In just a few miles, we went from sea level to an altitude of almost two thousand feet. I kept checking to see if my tires were flat. *This must be what it's like to jog in waist-deep molasses,* I thought. As I powered up the hills, my legs and chest felt as though they were about to burst into flames. Have you ever had that feeling?

But then a sensation even more painful than my aching legs and burning lungs began to overwhelm me—sheer terror. The fact that I had signed up for this trip and had thirty-nine more days to go created the most intense sense of panic that I could ever describe to you. I deeply regretted ever

agreeing to do such a foolish thing and, frankly, wanted to go home to my parents in Chicago … immediately.

I finished the first day having had very little conversation with my riding colleagues. Over bowls of stew that night, some of the guys were jostling each other about being out of shape. Others were joking about their sore rear ends. I sat silently at the perimeter, on the edge of tears.

But in the middle of that first night, lying on my air mattress and trying to quiet my throbbing muscles, a verse came to my mind. It washed over me like a cool drink on a hot day: "The Lᴏʀᴅ is my light and my salvation—whom shall I fear? The Lᴏʀᴅ is the stronghold of my life—of whom shall I be afraid?" (27:1)

That's it, I whispered over the sound of my slumbering buddies. *The Lord … the stronghold … no fear.* That moment changed my life. That promise, seared into my heart like a ranchers brand, became my hope in the face of total desperation. *Thank you, heavenly Father,* I sighed.

Five weeks later a grown-up young man landed on the banks of the Hudson River. And more than three decades later, I still cling to these precious words as my life's verse.

Perhaps this promise fits today's overwhelming challenges for you: *The Lord … the stronghold … no fear.* Take them. They're all yours.

For your next devotional reading, go to page 595.

in the land of the living.
¹⁴ Wait for the LORD;
    be strong and take heart
    and wait for the LORD.

Psalm 28

Of David.

¹ To you I call, O LORD my Rock;
    do not turn a deaf ear to me.
For if you remain silent,
    I will be like those who have gone
        down to the pit.
² Hear my cry for mercy
    as I call to you for help,
as I lift up my hands
    toward your Most Holy Place.

³ Do not drag me away with the wicked,
    with those who do evil,
who speak cordially with their
        neighbors
    but harbor malice in their hearts.
⁴ Repay them for their deeds
    and for their evil work;
repay them for what their hands have
        done
    and bring back upon them what they
        deserve.
⁵ Since they show no regard for the
        works of the LORD
    and what his hands have done,
he will tear them down
    and never build them up again.

⁶ Praise be to the LORD,
    for he has heard my cry for mercy.
⁷ The LORD is my strength and my shield;
    my heart trusts in him, and I am
        helped.
My heart leaps for joy
    and I will give thanks to him in song.

⁸ The LORD is the strength of his people,
    a fortress of salvation for his
        anointed one.
⁹ Save your people and bless your
        inheritance;
    be their shepherd and carry them
        forever.

Psalm 29

A psalm of David.

¹ Ascribe to the LORD, O mighty ones,
    ascribe to the LORD glory and
        strength.
² Ascribe to the LORD the glory due his
        name;

worship the LORD in the splendor of
    hisᵃ holiness.
³ The voice of the LORD is over the
        waters;
    the God of glory thunders,
    the LORD thunders over the mighty
        waters.
⁴ The voice of the LORD is powerful;
    the voice of the LORD is majestic.
⁵ The voice of the LORD breaks the
        cedars;
    the LORD breaks in pieces the cedars
        of Lebanon.
⁶ He makes Lebanon skip like a calf,
    Sirionᵇ like a young wild ox.
⁷ The voice of the LORD strikes
    with flashes of lightning.
⁸ The voice of the LORD shakes the
        desert;
    the LORD shakes the Desert of
        Kadesh.
⁹ The voice of the LORD twists the oaksᶜ
    and strips the forests bare.
And in his temple all cry, "Glory!"

¹⁰ The LORD sitsᵈ enthroned over the flood;
    the LORD is enthroned as King
        forever.
¹¹ The LORD gives strength to his people;
    the LORD blesses his people with
        peace.

Psalm 30

*A psalm. A song. For the dedication
of the temple.ᵉ Of David.*

¹ I will exalt you, O LORD,
    for you lifted me out of the depths
    and did not let my enemies gloat
        over me.
² O LORD my God, I called to you for help
    and you healed me.
³ O LORD, you brought me up from the
        graveᶠ;
    you spared me from going down into
        the pit.

⁴ Sing to the LORD, you saints of his;
    praise his holy name.
⁵ For his anger lasts only a moment,
    but his favor lasts a lifetime;
weeping may remain for a night,
    but rejoicing comes in the morning.

⁶ When I felt secure, I said,
    "I will never be shaken."

ᵃ*2 Or* LORD *with the splendor of* ᵇ*6 That is, Mount
Hermon* ᶜ*9 Or* LORD *makes the deer give birth*
ᵈ*10 Or sat* ᵉ*Title: Or palace* ᶠ*3 Hebrew Sheol*

⁷O LORD, when you favored me,
    you made my mountain*a* stand
    firm;
but when you hid your face,
    I was dismayed.

⁸To you, O LORD, I called;
    to the Lord I cried for mercy:
⁹"What gain is there in my destruction,*b*
    in my going down into the pit?
Will the dust praise you?
    Will it proclaim your faithfulness?
¹⁰Hear, O LORD, and be merciful to me;
    O LORD, be my help."

¹¹You turned my wailing into dancing;
    you removed my sackcloth and
    clothed me with joy,
¹²that my heart may sing to you and not
    be silent.
O LORD my God, I will give you
    thanks forever.

Psalm 31

For the director of music.
A psalm of David.

¹In you, O LORD, I have taken refuge;
    let me never be put to shame;
    deliver me in your righteousness.
²Turn your ear to me,
    come quickly to my rescue;
be my rock of refuge,
    a strong fortress to save me.
³Since you are my rock and my fortress,
    for the sake of your name lead and
    guide me.
⁴Free me from the trap that is set for
    me,
    for you are my refuge.
⁵Into your hands I commit my spirit;
    redeem me, O LORD, the God of
    truth.

⁶I hate those who cling to worthless
    idols;
    I trust in the LORD.
⁷I will be glad and rejoice in your love,
    for you saw my affliction
    and knew the anguish of my soul.
⁸You have not handed me over to the
    enemy
    but have set my feet in a spacious
    place.

⁹Be merciful to me, O LORD, for I am in
    distress;
    my eyes grow weak with sorrow,
    my soul and my body with grief.
¹⁰My life is consumed by anguish
    and my years by groaning;

my strength fails because of my
    affliction,*c*
    and my bones grow weak.
¹¹Because of all my enemies,
    I am the utter contempt of my
    neighbors;
I am a dread to my friends—
    those who see me on the street flee
    from me.
¹²I am forgotten by them as though I
    were dead;
    I have become like broken
    pottery.
¹³For I hear the slander of many;
    there is terror on every side;
they conspire against me
    and plot to take my life.

¹⁴But I trust in you, O LORD;
    I say, "You are my God."
¹⁵My times are in your hands;
    deliver me from my enemies
    and from those who pursue me.
¹⁶Let your face shine on your servant;
    save me in your unfailing love.
¹⁷Let me not be put to shame, O LORD,
    for I have cried out to you;
but let the wicked be put to shame
    and lie silent in the grave.*d*
¹⁸Let their lying lips be silenced,
    for with pride and contempt
    they speak arrogantly against the
    righteous.

¹⁹How great is your goodness,
    which you have stored up for those
    who fear you,
which you bestow in the sight of men
    on those who take refuge in you.
²⁰In the shelter of your presence you hide
    them
    from the intrigues of men;
in your dwelling you keep them safe
    from accusing tongues.

²¹Praise be to the LORD,
    for he showed his wonderful love to
    me
    when I was in a besieged city.
²²In my alarm I said,
    "I am cut off from your sight!"
Yet you heard my cry for mercy
    when I called to you for help.

²³Love the LORD, all his saints!
    The LORD preserves the faithful,
    but the proud he pays back in full.
²⁴Be strong and take heart,
    all you who hope in the LORD.

---

a7 Or *hill country*   *b9* Or *there if I am silenced*
c10 Or *guilt*   *d17* Hebrew *Sheol*

Psalm 32

Of David. A *maskil.*[a]

1 Blessed is he
    whose transgressions are forgiven,
    whose sins are covered.
2 Blessed is the man
    whose sin the LORD does not count
        against him
    and in whose spirit is no deceit.

3 When I kept silent,
    my bones wasted away
    through my groaning all day long.
4 For day and night
    your hand was heavy upon me;
  my strength was sapped
    as in the heat of summer.   *Selah*

5 Then I acknowledged my sin to you
    and did not cover up my iniquity.
  I said, "I will confess
    my transgressions to the
        LORD"—
  and you forgave
    the guilt of my sin.   *Selah*

6 Therefore let everyone who is godly
        pray to you
    while you may be found;
  surely when the mighty waters rise,
    they will not reach him.
7 You are my hiding place;
    you will protect me from trouble
    and surround me with songs of
        deliverance.   *Selah*

[a] Title: Probably a literary or musical term

That Hateful Little Book

DAILY INSIGHT

TUESDAY

Passage:
Psalm 32

Verses:
Psalm 32:1–2

The word "hate" was rarely used around our house. Very early in their lives, our daughters learned that, unless they were talking about monsters or poisonous snakes, they couldn't use this word. "I hate you," for example, would have meant permanent and eternal exile to their bedrooms. (They'd probably still be in those rooms, even though we've moved a couple of times.)

However, notwithstanding this house rule that I personally enforced, there was an object I grew up hating as much as monsters and poisonous snakes—no, actually *more* than these. The object was a black-and-gray-speckled, spiral-bound, eight-by-ten book, and each of my teachers had one on their desks. Long before the days of computer record-keeping, teachers from grade school through high school used these books. Printed on the cover were the words, "Student Records."

Why did I feel so strongly? Because these record books contained inside information about me. They recorded every late paper, every failing grade, every citizenship *faux pas* ... everything I didn't want anyone to know. Perhaps the most memorable dimension of my hatred for the book was the way it kept me from truly appreciating my teachers ... especially those whose books contained lots of bad Robert Wolgemuth marks.

King David lived a life filled with tardiness, failure, and poor citizenship. And he knew what it was to have all of these marks indelibly inscribed on the public record. He also knew how this deficiency affected his relationship with his heavenly Father.

Because of his willingness to confess his sin, is it any wonder that David wrote the opening lines to this psalm? Can you blame him for referring to the forgiven person (in this case, himself) as "blessed," which can also be translated as "truly happy"? It's as though that despised record book found its way to the desk's precipice, fell into the trash can and was delivered to the city dump for burning.

Imagine the feeling ... sins forgiven ... sins forgotten. The best part of this truth is the transforming effect it can have between student and teacher, between sinner and Savior.

Confess your sins. Watch them burn. Then bask in the love and embrace of the Teacher.

For your next devotional reading, go to page 600.

Protection: Love Stands Guard

*"I will instruct you and teach you in the way you should go;
I will counsel you and watch over you."* Psalm 32:8

BUILDING YOUR CHILDREN

As a dad, the dangers from which you protect your children come in many forms. When they're very small, you may protect them from sharp knives or hot things in the kitchen. As they grow older you may need to protect them from the neighbor's snarling dog. But when they become teenagers, the scenario changes a bit.

Coming home from work one evening, I noticed a shiny European coupe parked in front of our house. "Nice," I remember whispering out loud. "Very nice."

Steven was a senior in high school. I had already suspected that he was interested in our daughter Julie because of his recent visits to our church. Julie was only a week short of her sixteenth birthday, and Steven knew the rules that Julie and I had agreed to: (1) No "single" dating until Julie turned sixteen, and (2) boys must be "interviewed" by me.

Steven was tall and handsome, a varsity basketball player with a physique to match. He followed me into my study where I invited him to sit in the chair across from my desk.

I asked Steven about the car out front. He told me that he had bought it last summer and had spent a lot of time fixing it up with his dad.

"Sounds like a special car," I said. "Now, Steven, what would you have said if I had come to your house last night, knocked on the door, and asked you if I could borrow your car for the evening?"

Steven took no time to respond. "I'd have said 'No way.' "

"Why?" I replied, acting as though his answer fascinated me.

"Well, because I don't know you. I don't know how you drive. I don't know how you'd treat my car. I'm not sure I can trust you. That car's important to me." Steven's narrowed eyes let me know he was very serious.

I leaned forward on my elbows, taking just a moment to make sure he was listening carefully. "That's interesting, Steven," I finally said. "I know exactly what you're saying. Tonight you've come to my house and asked to take our daughter out for the evening. And before I let you do that, I want to find out who you are." He understood.

We talked about what was important to him, his sports, his family, his favorite subjects in school, his plans for next year, and his faith. I told him a little about our family and assured him that he would always be welcome in our home. I told him that our daughter's friends were our friends. He seemed appreciative. When we finished our conversation, we both stood up and shook hands.

"You know, Mr. Wolgemuth, if I have a sixteen-year-old daughter of my own some day, I'll do what you did today."

The story of my interviewing Steven is an example of fairly thorough emotional protection. I was exercising my right to keep Julie from being hurt by this older boy. I wasn't angry; I didn't threaten him. But I did, without a doubt, put him on notice: "Be careful with this girl. She belongs to a family who dearly loves her."

"What if I have a son?" you might be asking. Good question. Although we didn't have a son, I have made the following suggestion to friends of mine who have boys. It has been met with rave reviews. Suggest that your son volunteer for an interview with his date's dad. He can lead the discussion as the suitor. The point is that once he is connected with the girl's family, he will be more apt to consider himself accountable to that family. This will protect both your son and his date.

Protecting your children is your right and your privilege, but there's no need to be overbearing about it. In fact, you can actually have fun with it. It's going to take some of your time, but that's okay. Your kids are worth it.

⁸I will instruct you and teach you in the
    way you should go;
  I will counsel you and watch over
    you.
⁹Do not be like the horse or the mule,
    which have no understanding
  but must be controlled by bit and
    bridle
  or they will not come to you.
¹⁰Many are the woes of the wicked,
    but the LORD's unfailing love
  surrounds the man who trusts in
    him.

¹¹Rejoice in the LORD and be glad, you
    righteous;
  sing, all you who are upright in heart!

Psalm 33

¹Sing joyfully to the LORD, you
    righteous;
  it is fitting for the upright to praise
    him.
²Praise the LORD with the harp;
  make music to him on the
    ten-stringed lyre.
³Sing to him a new song;
  play skillfully, and shout for joy.

⁴For the word of the LORD is right and
    true;
  he is faithful in all he does.
⁵The LORD loves righteousness and
    justice;
  the earth is full of his unfailing love.

⁶By the word of the LORD were the
    heavens made,
  their starry host by the breath of his
    mouth.
⁷He gathers the waters of the sea into
    jars*a*;
  he puts the deep into storehouses.
⁸Let all the earth fear the LORD;
  let all the people of the world revere
    him.
⁹For he spoke, and it came to be;
  he commanded, and it stood firm.
¹⁰The LORD foils the plans of the nations;
  he thwarts the purposes of the
    peoples.
¹¹But the plans of the LORD stand firm
    forever,
  the purposes of his heart through all
    generations.

¹²Blessed is the nation whose God is the
    LORD,
  the people he chose for his
    inheritance.
¹³From heaven the LORD looks down

and sees all mankind;
¹⁴from his dwelling place he watches
    all who live on earth—
¹⁵he who forms the hearts of all,
  who considers everything they do.
¹⁶No king is saved by the size of his army;
  no warrior escapes by his great
    strength.
¹⁷A horse is a vain hope for deliverance;
  despite all its great strength it cannot
    save.
¹⁸But the eyes of the LORD are on those
    who fear him,
  on those whose hope is in his
    unfailing love,
¹⁹to deliver them from death
  and keep them alive in famine.

²⁰We wait in hope for the LORD;
  he is our help and our shield.
²¹In him our hearts rejoice,
  for we trust in his holy name.
²²May your unfailing love rest upon us,
    O LORD,
  even as we put our hope in you.

Psalm 34*b*

Of David. When he pretended to be insane
    before Abimelech, who drove
    him away, and he left.

¹I will extol the LORD at all times;
  his praise will always be on my lips.
²My soul will boast in the LORD;
  let the afflicted hear and rejoice.
³Glorify the LORD with me;
  let us exalt his name together.

⁴I sought the LORD, and he answered
    me;
  he delivered me from all my fears.
⁵Those who look to him are radiant;
  their faces are never covered with
    shame.
⁶This poor man called, and the LORD
    heard him;
  he saved him out of all his troubles.
⁷The angel of the LORD encamps around
    those who fear him,
  and he delivers them.

⁸Taste and see that the LORD is good;
  blessed is the man who takes refuge
    in him.
⁹Fear the LORD, you his saints,
  for those who fear him lack nothing.
¹⁰The lions may grow weak and hungry,

*a7 Or sea as into a heap   *b*This psalm is an
acrostic poem, the verses of which begin with
the successive letters of the Hebrew alphabet.

but those who seek the LORD lack no
good thing.
[11] Come, my children, listen to me;
I will teach you the fear of the LORD.
[12] Whoever of you loves life
and desires to see many good days,
[13] keep your tongue from evil
and your lips from speaking lies.
[14] Turn from evil and do good;
seek peace and pursue it.

[15] The eyes of the LORD are on the
righteous
and his ears are attentive to their cry;
[16] the face of the LORD is against those
who do evil,
to cut off the memory of them from
the earth.

[17] The righteous cry out, and the LORD
hears them;
he delivers them from all their
troubles.
[18] The LORD is close to the brokenhearted
and saves those who are crushed in
spirit.

[19] A righteous man may have many
troubles,
but the LORD delivers him from them
all;
[20] he protects all his bones,
not one of them will be broken.

[21] Evil will slay the wicked;
the foes of the righteous will be
condemned.
[22] The LORD redeems his servants;
no one will be condemned who takes
refuge in him.

Psalm 35

Of David.

[1] Contend, O LORD, with those who
contend with me;
fight against those who fight against
me.
[2] Take up shield and buckler;
arise and come to my aid.
[3] Brandish spear and javelin[a]
against those who pursue me.
Say to my soul,
"I am your salvation."

[4] May those who seek my life
be disgraced and put to shame;
may those who plot my ruin
be turned back in dismay.
[5] May they be like chaff before the
wind,

with the angel of the LORD driving
them away;
[6] may their path be dark and slippery,
with the angel of the LORD pursuing
them.
[7] Since they hid their net for me without
cause
and without cause dug a pit for me,
[8] may ruin overtake them by surprise—
may the net they hid entangle them,
may they fall into the pit, to their
ruin.

[9] Then my soul will rejoice in the LORD
and delight in his salvation.
[10] My whole being will exclaim,
"Who is like you, O LORD?
You rescue the poor from those too
strong for them,
the poor and needy from those who
rob them."

[11] Ruthless witnesses come forward;
they question me on things I know
nothing about.
[12] They repay me evil for good
and leave my soul forlorn.
[13] Yet when they were ill, I put on
sackcloth
and humbled myself with fasting.
When my prayers returned to me
unanswered,
[14]   I went about mourning
as though for my friend or brother.
I bowed my head in grief
as though weeping for my mother.
[15] But when I stumbled, they gathered in
glee;
attackers gathered against me when I
was unaware.
They slandered me without ceasing.
[16] Like the ungodly they maliciously
mocked[b];
they gnashed their teeth at me.
[17] O Lord, how long will you look on?
Rescue my life from their ravages,
my precious life from these lions.
[18] I will give you thanks in the great
assembly;
among throngs of people I will praise
you.

[19] Let not those gloat over me
who are my enemies without cause;
let not those who hate me without
reason
maliciously wink the eye.
[20] They do not speak peaceably,
but devise false accusations

---

*a*3 Or *and block the way*   *b*16 Septuagint; Hebrew
may mean *ungodly circle of mockers.*

against those who live quietly in the
land.
²¹ They gape at me and say, "Aha! Aha!
With our own eyes we have seen it."

²² O LORD, you have seen this; be not
silent.
Do not be far from me, O Lord.
²³ Awake, and rise to my defense!
Contend for me, my God and Lord.
²⁴ Vindicate me in your righteousness,
O LORD my God;
do not let them gloat over me.
²⁵ Do not let them think, "Aha, just what
we wanted!"
or say, "We have swallowed him up."

²⁶ May all who gloat over my distress
be put to shame and confusion;
may all who exalt themselves over me
be clothed with shame and disgrace.
²⁷ May those who delight in my
vindication
shout for joy and gladness;
may they always say, "The LORD be
exalted,
who delights in the well-being of his
servant."
²⁸ My tongue will speak of your
righteousness
and of your praises all day long.

Psalm 36

For the director of music.
Of David the servant of the LORD.

¹ An oracle is within my heart
concerning the sinfulness of the
wicked:ᵃ
There is no fear of God
before his eyes.
² For in his own eyes he flatters himself
too much to detect or hate his sin.
³ The words of his mouth are wicked and
deceitful;
he has ceased to be wise and to do
good.
⁴ Even on his bed he plots evil;
he commits himself to a sinful
course
and does not reject what is wrong.

⁵ Your love, O LORD, reaches to the
heavens,
your faithfulness to the skies.
⁶ Your righteousness is like the mighty
mountains,
your justice like the great deep.
O LORD, you preserve both man and
beast.

⁷ How priceless is your unfailing love!
Both high and low among men
findᵇ refuge in the shadow of your
wings.
⁸ They feast on the abundance of your
house;
you give them drink from your river
of delights.
⁹ For with you is the fountain of life;
in your light we see light.

¹⁰ Continue your love to those who know
you,
your righteousness to the upright in
heart.
¹¹ May the foot of the proud not come
against me,
nor the hand of the wicked drive me
away.
¹² See how the evildoers lie fallen—
thrown down, not able to rise!

Psalm 37ᶜ

Of David.

¹ Do not fret because of evil men
or be envious of those who do
wrong;
² for like the grass they will soon wither,
like green plants they will soon die
away.

³ Trust in the LORD and do good;
dwell in the land and enjoy safe
pasture.
⁴ Delight yourself in the LORD
and he will give you the desires of
your heart.

⁵ Commit your way to the LORD;
trust in him and he will do this:
⁶ He will make your righteousness shine
like the dawn,
the justice of your cause like the
noonday sun.

⁷ Be still before the LORD and wait
patiently for him;
do not fret when men succeed in
their ways,
when they carry out their wicked
schemes.

⁸ Refrain from anger and turn from
wrath;
do not fret—it leads only to evil.

ᵃ1 Or heart: / Sin proceeds from the wicked.   ᵇ7 Or
love, O God! / Men find; or love! / Both heavenly
beings and men / find   ᶜThis psalm is an acrostic
poem, the stanzas of which begin with the
successive letters of the Hebrew alphabet.

⁹For evil men will be cut off,
   but those who hope in the Lord will
      inherit the land.
¹⁰A little while, and the wicked will be no
      more;
   though you look for them, they will
      not be found.
¹¹But the meek will inherit the land
   and enjoy great peace.

¹²The wicked plot against the righteous
   and gnash their teeth at them;
¹³but the Lord laughs at the wicked,
   for he knows their day is coming.

¹⁴The wicked draw the sword
   and bend the bow
   to bring down the poor and needy,
      to slay those whose ways are upright.
¹⁵But their swords will pierce their own
      hearts,
   and their bows will be broken.

¹⁶Better the little that the righteous have
   than the wealth of many wicked;
¹⁷for the power of the wicked will be
      broken,
   but the Lord upholds the righteous.
¹⁸The days of the blameless are known to
      the Lord,
   and their inheritance will endure
      forever.
¹⁹In times of disaster they will not
      wither;
   in days of famine they will enjoy
      plenty.
²⁰But the wicked will perish:
   The Lord's enemies will be like the
      beauty of the fields,
   they will vanish—vanish like smoke.
²¹The wicked borrow and do not
      repay,
   but the righteous give generously;

Fornication for Fun and Profit

DAILY INSIGHT

WEDNESDAY

Passage:
Psalm 37:1–9

Verse:
Psalm 37:4

I was channel surfing the other night and happened on one of those entertainment shows—kind of like a video version of "People Magazine." The image of a Hollywood star flashed on camera, and I stopped clicking. I've seen some of his pictures, and was interested in what he might have to say.

During the interview, the actor disclosed that, because he's so much in demand, he now makes $12 million per movie. Then, in response to a question about his personal life—which is the real reason for this show's existence—he talked about his girlfriend. And in a tone of voice filled with as much remorse as if he were giving directions to the closest bowling alley, he talked about waking up one morning, rolling over and asking her to marry him.

I surfed on. *Is this fair?* I mused as my thumb guided me to CNN's Headline News.

As far back as I can remember, I have been doing battle with sin. At times it has wrapped itself around me like a powerful snake, squeezing the very life out of me. Sometimes I am victorious, and sometimes I'm not. When righteousness wins, I celebrate. When sin wins, I pay. Now I come across a guy who doesn't seem to suffer at all in the face of unabashed immorality. And not only does he fail to pay for his fornication, it's almost as if he gets paid to engage in it. *No, it's not fair.*

The psalms are filled with quotable quotes, and today's verse is certainly one of them. It provides the right perspective on the conundrum you'll face if you watch one of those celebrity shows tonight. "Delight yourself in the Lord and he will give you the desires of your heart." That's a lot more than $12 million worth of peace and joy.

With this priority firmly in place, you'll probably never be interviewed by one of the reporters for "Hollywood's Best Trash Tonight" or "Sleeping Around for Fun and Profit." But that's okay. If you were interviewed, most people would surf on when it got to your segment anyway. Stories like yours and mine just don't make for great ratings.

For your next devotional reading, go to page 604.

²²those the LORD blesses will inherit the
land,
but those he curses will be cut off.
²³If the LORD delights in a man's way,
he makes his steps firm;
²⁴though he stumble, he will not fall,
for the LORD upholds him with his
hand.
²⁵I was young and now I am old,
yet I have never seen the righteous
forsaken
or their children begging bread.
²⁶They are always generous and lend
freely;
their children will be blessed.
²⁷Turn from evil and do good;
then you will dwell in the land
forever.
²⁸For the LORD loves the just
and will not forsake his faithful ones.

They will be protected forever,
but the offspring of the wicked will
be cut off;
²⁹the righteous will inherit the land
and dwell in it forever.
³⁰The mouth of the righteous man utters
wisdom,
and his tongue speaks what is just.
³¹The law of his God is in his heart;
his feet do not slip.

³²The wicked lie in wait for the
righteous,
seeking their very lives;
³³but the LORD will not leave them in
their power
or let them be condemned when
brought to trial.

³⁴Wait for the LORD
and keep his way.
He will exalt you to inherit the land;
when the wicked are cut off, you will
see it.

³⁵I have seen a wicked and ruthless man
flourishing like a green tree in its
native soil,
³⁶but he soon passed away and was no
more;
though I looked for him, he could
not be found.

³⁷Consider the blameless, observe the
upright;
there is a future*a* for the man of
peace.
³⁸But all sinners will be destroyed;
the future*b* of the wicked will be cut
off.

³⁹The salvation of the righteous comes
from the LORD;

a37 Or there will be posterity   b38 Or posterity

HEY DAD
Why do bad people seem to get away with things?

QUESTIONS KIDS ASK

Text: Psalm 37

Sometimes people who disobey God seem to be more successful than those who
serve him wholeheartedly. This doesn't make much sense. After all, doesn't God
promise to bless those who live righteously (Proverbs 10:6), and aren't the wages
of sin death (Romans 6:23)?

God knew this question would come up, so he gave us an answer: "Don't let this
apparent injustice discourage you. I am in control." Psalm 37 says, "Do not fret
because of evil men or be envious of those who do wrong; for like the grass they
will soon wither, like green plants they will soon die away. . . do not fret when men succeed
in their ways, when they carry out their wicked schemes" (vv. 1,7).

God promises that "those who hope in the LORD will inherit the land" (v. 9). He also says
that he upholds the righteous with his hand, that the children of the righteous will be
blessed, and that there is a future for those who live in peace (vv. 24, 26, 37).

Many of the promises God makes direct us to the future. He promises that our obedience
to him is not in vain, even if it seems at times that he doesn't notice. So obey God and live in
the hope of his promises. And remember, obedience to God includes loving our successful
neighbors—even those who carry out their wicked schemes against us (Romans 12:14).

For a complete listing of Questions Kids Ask, turn to page 1435.

he is their stronghold in time of
    trouble.
⁴⁰The LORD helps them and delivers
    them;
he delivers them from the wicked
    and saves them,
because they take refuge in him.

Psalm 38

A psalm of David. A petition.

¹O LORD, do not rebuke me in your
    anger
  or discipline me in your wrath.
²For your arrows have pierced me,
    and your hand has come down upon
    me.
³Because of your wrath there is no
    health in my body;
  my bones have no soundness
    because of my sin.
⁴My guilt has overwhelmed me
  like a burden too heavy to bear.

⁵My wounds fester and are loathsome
  because of my sinful folly.
⁶I am bowed down and brought very
    low;
  all day long I go about mourning.
⁷My back is filled with searing pain;
  there is no health in my body.
⁸I am feeble and utterly crushed;
  I groan in anguish of heart.

⁹All my longings lie open before you,
    O Lord;
  my sighing is not hidden from you.
¹⁰My heart pounds, my strength fails
    me;
  even the light has gone from my
    eyes.
¹¹My friends and companions avoid me
    because of my wounds;
  my neighbors stay far away.
¹²Those who seek my life set their traps,
    those who would harm me talk of my
    ruin;
  all day long they plot deception.

¹³I am like a deaf man, who cannot hear,
    like a mute, who cannot open his
    mouth;
¹⁴I have become like a man who does not
    hear,
  whose mouth can offer no reply.
¹⁵I wait for you, O LORD;
  you will answer, O Lord my God.
¹⁶For I said, "Do not let them gloat
    or exalt themselves over me when
    my foot slips."

¹⁷For I am about to fall,
  and my pain is ever with me.
¹⁸I confess my iniquity;
  I am troubled by my sin.
¹⁹Many are those who are my vigorous
    enemies;
  those who hate me without reason
    are numerous.
²⁰Those who repay my good with evil
    slander me when I pursue what is
    good.

²¹O LORD, do not forsake me;
  be not far from me, O my God.
²²Come quickly to help me,
  O Lord my Savior.

Psalm 39

*For the director of music. For Jeduthun.
A psalm of David.*

¹I said, "I will watch my ways
    and keep my tongue from sin;
  I will put a muzzle on my mouth
    as long as the wicked are in my
    presence."
²But when I was silent and still,
    not even saying anything good,
  my anguish increased.
³My heart grew hot within me,
    and as I meditated, the fire burned;
  then I spoke with my tongue:

⁴"Show me, O LORD, my life's end
    and the number of my days;
  let me know how fleeting is my life.
⁵You have made my days a mere
    handbreadth;
  the span of my years is as nothing
    before you.
  Each man's life is but a breath.   *Selah*
⁶Man is a mere phantom as he goes to
    and fro:
  He bustles about, but only in vain;
  he heaps up wealth, not knowing
    who will get it.

⁷"But now, Lord, what do I look for?
  My hope is in you.
⁸Save me from all my transgressions;
  do not make me the scorn of fools.
⁹I was silent; I would not open my
    mouth,
  for you are the one who has done
    this.
¹⁰Remove your scourge from me;
  I am overcome by the blow of your
    hand.
¹¹You rebuke and discipline men for
    their sin;

you consume their wealth like a
  moth—
  each man is but a breath.   *Selah*

[12] "Hear my prayer, O LORD,
  listen to my cry for help;
  be not deaf to my weeping.
For I dwell with you as an alien,
  a stranger, as all my fathers were.
[13] Look away from me, that I may rejoice
  again
  before I depart and am no more."

Psalm 40

For the director of music.
Of David. A psalm.

[1] I waited patiently for the LORD;
  he turned to me and heard my cry.
[2] He lifted me out of the slimy pit,
  out of the mud and mire;
he set my feet on a rock
  and gave me a firm place to stand.
[3] He put a new song in my mouth,
  a hymn of praise to our God.
Many will see and fear
  and put their trust in the LORD.

[4] Blessed is the man
  who makes the LORD his trust,
who does not look to the proud,
  to those who turn aside to false
    gods.[a]
[5] Many, O LORD my God,
  are the wonders you have done.
The things you planned for us
  no one can recount to you;
were I to speak and tell of them,
  they would be too many to declare.

[6] Sacrifice and offering you did not
    desire,
  but my ears you have pierced[b,c];
burnt offerings and sin offerings
  you did not require.
[7] Then I said, "Here I am, I have come—
  it is written about me in the scroll.[d]
[8] I desire to do your will, O my God;
  your law is within my heart."

[9] I proclaim righteousness in the great
    assembly;
  I do not seal my lips,
  as you know, O LORD.
[10] I do not hide your righteousness in my
    heart;
  I speak of your faithfulness and
    salvation.
I do not conceal your love and your
    truth
  from the great assembly.

[11] Do not withhold your mercy from me,
    O LORD;
  may your love and your truth always
    protect me.
[12] For troubles without number surround
    me;
  my sins have overtaken me, and I
    cannot see.
They are more than the hairs of my
    head,
  and my heart fails within me.

[13] Be pleased, O LORD, to save me;
  O LORD, come quickly to help me.
[14] May all who seek to take my life
  be put to shame and confusion;
may all who desire my ruin
  be turned back in disgrace.
[15] May those who say to me, "Aha! Aha!"
  be appalled at their own shame.
[16] But may all who seek you
  rejoice and be glad in you;
may those who love your salvation
  always say,
  "The LORD be exalted!"

[17] Yet I am poor and needy;
  may the Lord think of me.
You are my help and my deliverer;
  O my God, do not delay.

Psalm 41

For the director of music.
A psalm of David.

[1] Blessed is he who has regard for the
    weak;
  the LORD delivers him in times of
    trouble.
[2] The LORD will protect him and preserve
    his life;
  he will bless him in the land
  and not surrender him to the desire
    of his foes.
[3] The LORD will sustain him on his
    sickbed
  and restore him from his bed of
    illness.
[4] I said, "O LORD, have mercy on me;
  heal me, for I have sinned against
    you."
[5] My enemies say of me in malice,
  "When will he die and his name
    perish?"
[6] Whenever one comes to see me,

---

[a]4 Or *to falsehood*   [b]6 Hebrew; Septuagint *but a*
body you have prepared for me (see also
Symmachus and Theodotion)   [c]6 Or *opened*
[d]7 Or *come / with the scroll written for me*

he speaks falsely, while his heart
gathers slander;
then he goes out and spreads it
abroad.
⁷All my enemies whisper together
against me;
they imagine the worst for me,
saying,
⁸"A vile disease has beset him;
he will never get up from the place
where he lies."

⁹Even my close friend, whom I trusted,
he who shared my bread,
has lifted up his heel against me.
¹⁰But you, O LORD, have mercy on me;
raise me up, that I may repay them.
¹¹I know that you are pleased with me,
for my enemy does not triumph over
me.
¹²In my integrity you uphold me
and set me in your presence
forever.

Worth the Wait

DAILY INSIGHT

THURSDAY

Passage:
Psalm 42:1–6a

Verse:
Psalm 42:2

Mrs. Sands was my fourth grade teacher. A soft and lovely person with lots of teaching experience, she was my first teacher in a new school. I remember her being especially tender toward this frightened, nine-year-old boy. But the most vivid memories I have of fourth grade are not of Mrs. Sands or Whittier School. They are not of our classroom with squeaky wooden floors and lift-top desks to hold all our things. What I remember most about fourth grade is *waiting*.

For some reason, during that year of my life, three o'clock never came. Almost every day around one o'clock, I'd glance at the huge, round time piece on the wall above Mrs. Sands' desk. My heart would sink, knowing I had to sit there for two more hours … two very *long* hours. And there was absolutely nothing I could do about it … except wait.

Much of childhood is about not getting what you want when you want it. Surely you remember what it was like to be told, "You can't have that now. It'll spoil your dinner." "Not now. You have to wait for Christmas morning." "Sit quietly at your desks until the bell has rung."

Thankfully, most of our days of waiting are behind us. Being able, as adults, to control more of our lives is a blessing. Certainly, some things that we want we still can't have, but we have far more control of the events of our lives today than we did when we were nine. Correct?

Yes, but we miss something when we no longer have to wait. With waiting comes wonder … hope … the thrill of receiving what we've so desperately anticipated. Dinner tasted so much better because I was really hungry. Christmas morning was filled with awe and wonder because I didn't shake the packages. After school, my mother's open arms were exactly what this lonely nine-year-old boy desperately longed for.

The writer of today's psalm knew all about the breathless anticipation of waiting. He drew us a verbal picture of a thirsty deer, longing—even panting—for a cool stream to satisfy him. Then he told us that his soul, the deepest part of his life, couldn't *wait* for God's presence. The experience of God's tender presence was the only thing that would satisfy his deepest hunger.

Do you pride yourself in getting what you want when you want it? Have you lost the wonder of anticipation and longing?

If you have found yourself leaning toward the precipice of instant gratification, watch your child … no, in fact, *become* your child. Remember your wide eyes and pounding heart, knowing that the big day is right around the corner. Then fill your own heart with the kind of love for your heavenly Father that mysteriously draws you to want more—more of his love, more of his forgiveness, more of his guidance … more of him.

I'll bet you can hardly wait.

For your next devotional reading, go to page 610.

¹³Praise be to the LORD, the God of Israel,
   from everlasting to everlasting.
      Amen and Amen.

BOOK II
Psalms 42–72

Psalm 42 [a]

For the director of music.
A *maskil* [b] of the Sons of Korah.

¹As the deer pants for streams of water,
   so my soul pants for you, O God.
²My soul thirsts for God, for the living
      God.
   When can I go and meet with God?
³My tears have been my food
      day and night,
   while men say to me all day long,
      "Where is your God?"
⁴These things I remember
      as I pour out my soul:
   how I used to go with the multitude,
      leading the procession to the house
         of God,
   with shouts of joy and thanksgiving
      among the festive throng.

⁵Why are you downcast, O my soul?
   Why so disturbed within me?
Put your hope in God,
   for I will yet praise him,
      my Savior and ⁶my God.

My [c] soul is downcast within me;
   therefore I will remember you
from the land of the Jordan,
   the heights of Hermon—from Mount
      Mizar.
⁷Deep calls to deep
   in the roar of your waterfalls;
all your waves and breakers
   have swept over me.

⁸By day the LORD directs his love,
   at night his song is with me—
   a prayer to the God of my life.

⁹I say to God my Rock,
   "Why have you forgotten me?
Why must I go about mourning,
   oppressed by the enemy?"
¹⁰My bones suffer mortal agony
   as my foes taunt me,
saying to me all day long,
   "Where is your God?"

¹¹Why are you downcast, O my soul?
   Why so disturbed within me?

Put your hope in God,
   for I will yet praise him,
      my Savior and my God.

Psalm 43 [a]

¹Vindicate me, O God,
   and plead my cause against an
      ungodly nation;
   rescue me from deceitful and wicked
      men.
²You are God my stronghold.
   Why have you rejected me?
Why must I go about mourning,
   oppressed by the enemy?
³Send forth your light and your truth,
   let them guide me;
let them bring me to your holy
      mountain,
   to the place where you dwell.
⁴Then will I go to the altar of God,
   to God, my joy and my delight.
I will praise you with the harp,
   O God, my God.

⁵Why are you downcast, O my soul?
   Why so disturbed within me?
Put your hope in God,
   for I will yet praise him,
      my Savior and my God.

Psalm 44 [a]

For the director of music.
Of the Sons of Korah. A *maskil.* [d]

¹We have heard with our ears, O God;
   our fathers have told us
what you did in their days,
   in days long ago.
²With your hand you drove out the
      nations
   and planted our fathers;
you crushed the peoples
   and made our fathers flourish.
³It was not by their sword that they won
      the land,
   nor did their arm bring them
      victory;
it was your right hand, your arm,
   and the light of your face, for you
      loved them.

ᵃIn many Hebrew manuscripts Psalms 42 and 43
constitute one psalm.   ᵇTitle: Probably a literary
or musical term   ᶜ5,6 A few Hebrew manuscripts,
Septuagint and Syriac; most Hebrew manuscripts
praise him: for his saving help. / ⁶O my God, my
ᵈTitle: Probably a literary or musical term

⁴You are my King and my God,
  who decrees^a victories for Jacob.
⁵Through you we push back our
      enemies;
  through your name we trample our
      foes.
⁶I do not trust in my bow,
  my sword does not bring me
      victory;
⁷but you give us victory over our
      enemies,
  you put our adversaries to shame.
⁸In God we make our boast all day long,
  and we will praise your name
      forever.   *Selah*

⁹But now you have rejected and
      humbled us;
  you no longer go out with our
      armies.
¹⁰You made us retreat before the enemy,
  and our adversaries have plundered
      us.
¹¹You gave us up to be devoured like
      sheep
  and have scattered us among the
      nations.
¹²You sold your people for a pittance,
  gaining nothing from their sale.
¹³You have made us a reproach to our
      neighbors,
  the scorn and derision of those
      around us.
¹⁴You have made us a byword among the
      nations;
  the peoples shake their heads at us.
¹⁵My disgrace is before me all day long,
  and my face is covered with shame
¹⁶at the taunts of those who reproach
      and revile me,
  because of the enemy, who is bent
      on revenge.

¹⁷All this happened to us,
  though we had not forgotten you
  or been false to your covenant.
¹⁸Our hearts had not turned back;
  our feet had not strayed from your
      path.
¹⁹But you crushed us and made us a
      haunt for jackals
  and covered us over with deep
      darkness.

²⁰If we had forgotten the name of our
      God
  or spread out our hands to a foreign
      god,
²¹would not God have discovered it,
  since he knows the secrets of the
      heart?

²²Yet for your sake we face death all day
      long;
  we are considered as sheep to be
      slaughtered.
²³Awake, O Lord! Why do you sleep?
  Rouse yourself! Do not reject us
      forever.
²⁴Why do you hide your face
  and forget our misery and
      oppression?
²⁵We are brought down to the dust;
  our bodies cling to the ground.
²⁶Rise up and help us;
  redeem us because of your unfailing
      love.

Psalm 45

For the director of music. To the tune
of "Lilies." Of the Sons of Korah. A *maskil.*^b
A wedding song.

¹My heart is stirred by a noble theme
  as I recite my verses for the king;
  my tongue is the pen of a skillful
      writer.

²You are the most excellent of men
  and your lips have been anointed
      with grace,
  since God has blessed you forever.
³Gird your sword upon your side,
      O mighty one;
  clothe yourself with splendor and
      majesty.
⁴In your majesty ride forth victoriously
  in behalf of truth, humility and
      righteousness;
  let your right hand display awesome
      deeds.
⁵Let your sharp arrows pierce the hearts
      of the king's enemies;
  let the nations fall beneath your feet.
⁶Your throne, O God, will last for ever
      and ever;
  a scepter of justice will be the
      scepter of your kingdom.
⁷You love righteousness and hate
      wickedness;
  therefore God, your God, has set you
      above your companions
  by anointing you with the oil of joy.
⁸All your robes are fragrant with myrrh
      and aloes and cassia;
  from palaces adorned with ivory

<hr>

^a4 Septuagint, Aquila and Syriac; Hebrew *King,
O God; I command*   ^bTitle: Probably a literary or
musical term

the music of the strings makes you
    glad.
⁹ Daughters of kings are among your
    honored women;
    at your right hand is the royal bride
      in gold of Ophir.

¹⁰ Listen, O daughter, consider and give
    ear:
    Forget your people and your father's
      house.
¹¹ The king is enthralled by your beauty;
    honor him, for he is your lord.
¹² The Daughter of Tyre will come with a
    gift,ᵃ
    men of wealth will seek your favor.

¹³ All glorious is the princess within ʟher
    chamberʲ;
    her gown is interwoven with gold.
¹⁴ In embroidered garments she is led to
    the king;
    her virgin companions follow her
    and are brought to you.
¹⁵ They are led in with joy and
    gladness;
    they enter the palace of the king.

¹⁶ Your sons will take the place of your
    fathers;
    you will make them princes
      throughout the land.
¹⁷ I will perpetuate your memory through
    all generations;
    therefore the nations will praise you
      for ever and ever.

Psalm 46

For the director of music. Of the Sons
of Korah. According to *alamoth.*ᵇ A song.

¹ God is our refuge and strength,
    an ever-present help in trouble.
² Therefore we will not fear, though the
    earth give way
    and the mountains fall into the heart
      of the sea,
³ though its waters roar and foam
    and the mountains quake with their
      surging.   *Selah*

⁴ There is a river whose streams make
    glad the city of God,
    the holy place where the Most High
      dwells.
⁵ God is within her, she will not fall;
    God will help her at break of day.
⁶ Nations are in uproar, kingdoms fall;
    he lifts his voice, the earth melts.

⁷ The LORD Almighty is with us;

the God of Jacob is our
    fortress.   *Selah*

⁸ Come and see the works of the LORD,
    the desolations he has brought on
      the earth.
⁹ He makes wars cease to the ends of the
    earth;
    he breaks the bow and shatters the
      spear,
    he burns the shieldsᶜ with fire.
¹⁰ "Be still, and know that I am God;
    I will be exalted among the nations,
    I will be exalted in the earth."

¹¹ The LORD Almighty is with us;
    the God of Jacob is our fortress.
             Selah

Psalm 47

For the director of music.
Of the Sons of Korah. A psalm.

¹ Clap your hands, all you nations;
    shout to God with cries of joy.
² How awesome is the LORD Most High,
    the great King over all the earth!
³ He subdued nations under us,
    peoples under our feet.
⁴ He chose our inheritance for us,
    the pride of Jacob, whom he loved.
             Selah

⁵ God has ascended amid shouts of joy,
    the LORD amid the sounding of
      trumpets.
⁶ Sing praises to God, sing praises;
    sing praises to our King, sing praises.

⁷ For God is the King of all the earth;
    sing to him a psalmᵈ of praise.
⁸ God reigns over the nations;
    God is seated on his holy throne.
⁹ The nobles of the nations assemble
    as the people of the God of Abraham,
for the kingsᵉ of the earth belong to God;
    he is greatly exalted.

Psalm 48

A song. A psalm of the Sons of Korah.

¹ Great is the LORD, and most worthy of
    praise,
    in the city of our God, his holy
      mountain.

ᵃ12 Or *A Tyrian robe is among the gifts* ᵇTitle:
Probably a musical term ᶜ9 Or *chariots* ᵈ7 Or *a
maskil* (probably a literary or musical term)
ᵉ9 Or *shields*

²It is beautiful in its loftiness,
the joy of the whole earth.
Like the utmost heights of Zaphon*a* is
Mount Zion,
the*b* city of the Great King.
³God is in her citadels;
he has shown himself to be her
fortress.

⁴When the kings joined forces,
when they advanced together,
⁵they saw her, and were astounded;
they fled in terror.
⁶Trembling seized them there,
pain like that of a woman in labor.
⁷You destroyed them like ships of
Tarshish
shattered by an east wind.

⁸As we have heard,
so have we seen
in the city of the LORD Almighty,
in the city of our God:
God makes her secure forever. *Selah*

⁹Within your temple, O God,
we meditate on your unfailing love.
¹⁰Like your name, O God,
your praise reaches to the ends of
the earth;
your right hand is filled with
righteousness.
¹¹Mount Zion rejoices,
the villages of Judah are glad
because of your judgments.

¹²Walk about Zion, go around her,
count her towers,
¹³consider well her ramparts,
view her citadels,
that you may tell of them to the next
generation.
¹⁴For this God is our God for ever and
ever;
he will be our guide even to the end.

Psalm 49

For the director of music.
Of the Sons of Korah. A psalm.

¹Hear this, all you peoples;
listen, all who live in this world,
²both low and high,
rich and poor alike:
³My mouth will speak words of
wisdom;
the utterance from my heart will give
understanding.
⁴I will turn my ear to a proverb;
with the harp I will expound my
riddle:

⁵Why should I fear when evil days come,
when wicked deceivers surround
me—
⁶those who trust in their wealth
and boast of their great riches?
⁷No man can redeem the life of another
or give to God a ransom for him—
⁸the ransom for a life is costly,
no payment is ever enough—
⁹that he should live on forever
and not see decay.

¹⁰For all can see that wise men die;
the foolish and the senseless alike
perish
and leave their wealth to others.
¹¹Their tombs will remain their houses*c*
forever,
their dwellings for endless
generations,
though they had*d* named lands after
themselves.

¹²But man, despite his riches, does not
endure;
he is*e* like the beasts that perish.

¹³This is the fate of those who trust in
themselves,
and of their followers, who approve
their sayings. *Selah*
¹⁴Like sheep they are destined for the
grave,*f*
and death will feed on them.
The upright will rule over them in the
morning;
their forms will decay in the grave,*f*
far from their princely mansions.
¹⁵But God will redeem my life*g* from the
grave;
he will surely take me to himself.
Selah

¹⁶Do not be overawed when a man grows
rich,
when the splendor of his house
increases;
¹⁷for he will take nothing with him when
he dies,
his splendor will not descend with
him.
¹⁸Though while he lived he counted
himself blessed—
and men praise you when you
prosper—

---

a2 Zaphon can refer to a sacred mountain or the
direction north.   *b2* Or *earth, / Mount Zion, on the
northern side / of the*   *c11* Septuagint and Syriac;
Hebrew *In their thoughts their houses will remain*
d11 Or */ for they have*   *e12* Hebrew; Septuagint and
Syriac read verse 12 the same as verse 20.
f14 Hebrew *Sheol*; also in verse 15   *g15* Or *soul*

¹⁹he will join the generation of his
     fathers,
  who will never see the light ˌof lifeˌ.

²⁰A man who has riches without
     understanding
  is like the beasts that perish.

Psalm 50

A psalm of Asaph.

¹The Mighty One, God, the LORD,
  speaks and summons the earth
  from the rising of the sun to the
     place where it sets.
²From Zion, perfect in beauty,
  God shines forth.
³Our God comes and will not be silent;
  a fire devours before him,
  and around him a tempest rages.
⁴He summons the heavens above,
  and the earth, that he may judge his
     people:
⁵"Gather to me my consecrated ones,
  who made a covenant with me by
     sacrifice."
⁶And the heavens proclaim his
     righteousness,
  for God himself is judge.   *Selah*

⁷"Hear, O my people, and I will speak,
  O Israel, and I will testify against
     you:
  I am God, your God.
⁸I do not rebuke you for your sacrifices
  or your burnt offerings, which are
     ever before me.
⁹I have no need of a bull from your stall
  or of goats from your pens,
¹⁰for every animal of the forest is mine,
  and the cattle on a thousand hills.
¹¹I know every bird in the mountains,
  and the creatures of the field are
     mine.
¹²If I were hungry I would not tell you,
  for the world is mine, and all that is
     in it.
¹³Do I eat the flesh of bulls
  or drink the blood of goats?
¹⁴Sacrifice thank offerings to God,
  fulfill your vows to the Most High,
¹⁵and call upon me in the day of trouble;
  I will deliver you, and you will honor
     me."

¹⁶But to the wicked, God says:

"What right have you to recite my laws
  or take my covenant on your lips?
¹⁷You hate my instruction
  and cast my words behind you.

¹⁸When you see a thief, you join with
     him;
  you throw in your lot with adulterers.
¹⁹You use your mouth for evil
  and harness your tongue to deceit.
²⁰You speak continually against your
     brother
  and slander your own mother's son.
²¹These things you have done and I kept
     silent;
  you thought I was altogether*ᵃ* like
     you.
But I will rebuke you
  and accuse you to your face.

²²"Consider this, you who forget God,
  or I will tear you to pieces, with none
     to rescue:
²³He who sacrifices thank offerings
     honors me,
  and he prepares the way
  so that I may show him*ᵇ* the
     salvation of God."

Psalm 51

*For the director of music.
A psalm of David. When the prophet
Nathan came to him after David had
committed adultery with Bathsheba.*

¹Have mercy on me, O God,
  according to your unfailing love;
  according to your great compassion
  blot out my transgressions.
²Wash away all my iniquity
  and cleanse me from my sin.

³For I know my transgressions,
  and my sin is always before me.
⁴Against you, you only, have I sinned
  and done what is evil in your sight,
  so that you are proved right when you
     speak
  and justified when you judge.
⁵Surely I was sinful at birth,
  sinful from the time my mother
     conceived me.
⁶Surely you desire truth in the inner
     parts*ᶜ*;
  you teach*ᵈ* me wisdom in the inmost
     place.

⁷Cleanse me with hyssop, and I will be
     clean;
  wash me, and I will be whiter than
     snow.

*ᵃ21 Or thought the 'I ᴀᴍ' was   ᵇ23 Or and to him
who considers his way / I will show   ᶜ6 The
meaning of the Hebrew for this phrase is
uncertain.   ᵈ6 Or you desired . . . ; / you taught*

⁸Let me hear joy and gladness;
    let the bones you have crushed
      rejoice.
⁹Hide your face from my sins
    and blot out all my iniquity.
¹⁰Create in me a pure heart, O God,
    and renew a steadfast spirit within me.

¹¹Do not cast me from your presence
    or take your Holy Spirit from me.
¹²Restore to me the joy of your salvation
    and grant me a willing spirit, to
      sustain me.
¹³Then I will teach transgressors your
    ways,

Asking Forgiveness, Being Pardoned

DAILY INSIGHT

The story of Richard Nixon's presidency may be one of the saddest in American history.

After a failed bid for the presidency in 1960 against a young and charismatic John Kennedy, Nixon decided to enter the private sector. His parting words to the press were, "You won't have Richard Nixon to kick around any more." How pathetically untrue those words would become.

As happens so often in public life, you can take the man out of politics, but you can't take the politician out of the man. Richard Nixon returned to the campaign for the presidency in 1968, soundly defeating Minnesota's Hubert Humphrey. In 1972, he won a second term by an even greater margin of victory. Things were going well for this once-bitter man.

Unfortunately, during the 1972 campaign, Richard Nixon's associates broke the law. And, according to nearly every journalist and biographer since, Nixon knew all about it and tried to cover it up. A hearing followed that brought White House staffers and cabinet secretaries before senate committees. Ultimately, Richard Nixon resigned in shame. Several hours later, his successor issued him a pardon. With that incredibly unpopular pardon, Gerald Ford sealed his own political fate.

Richard Nixon may have been legally forgiven of his crime, but most of the American people weren't on board. When this former president, brilliant statesman and world class diplomat died almost twenty years later, newscasts recalled the disgrace of the Watergate scandal.

The world did not forgive Richard Nixon. Why? Because Richard Nixon never con-

FRIDAY
Passage:
Psalm 51:7–13
Verses:
Psalm 51:10–12

fessed his transgression. Never. Although his final two decades were filled with myriad opportunities to make his offense right, not *once* did this proud man face the public and apologize. So, because he didn't ask, we didn't forgive him.

King David's crime made Richard Nixon's offense look like a parking violation. This powerful king committed adultery and tried to cover it up with the murder of an innocent and loyal soldier. But the prophet Nathan, armed with all the evidence he needed, scheduled a meeting with David. In a dramatic moment, King David fell to his knees in confession and remorse.

This psalm is the result of that meeting. Miraculously, David was forgiven … first by his heavenly Father, then by his people. Imagine the incredible release this sinful man must have felt to be able to put this iniquity behind him.

What if, in the mid-seventies, Richard Nixon had asked you for advice? More than likely, you would have played Nathan to Nixon's David. You would have suggested—perhaps even begged—that he ask the world to forgive him. If he had, he would have been forgiven.

Now consider this: Is there a friend or family member who needs to have a meeting with *you*? Are you foolishly holding back from confessing something? Don't wait to ask for forgiveness. Don't suffer unnecessarily under the weight of what you've done. God will give you the strength to confess, and the absolute assurance of your pardon.

For your next devotional reading, go to page 615.

and sinners will turn back to you.
¹⁴ Save me from bloodguilt, O God,
    the God who saves me,
    and my tongue will sing of your
        righteousness.
¹⁵ O Lord, open my lips,
    and my mouth will declare your
        praise.
¹⁶ You do not delight in sacrifice, or I
        would bring it;
    you do not take pleasure in burnt
        offerings.
¹⁷ The sacrifices of God are*ᵃ* a broken
        spirit;
    a broken and contrite heart,
    O God, you will not despise.

¹⁸ In your good pleasure make Zion
        prosper;
    build up the walls of Jerusalem.
¹⁹ Then there will be righteous sacrifices,
    whole burnt offerings to delight
        you;
    then bulls will be offered on your
        altar.

Psalm 52

For the director of music. A *maskil*ᵇ of David.
When Doeg the Edomite had gone to Saul
  and told him: "David has gone
    to the house of Ahimelech."

¹ Why do you boast of evil, you mighty
        man?
    Why do you boast all day long,
    you who are a disgrace in the eyes of
        God?
² Your tongue plots destruction;
    it is like a sharpened razor,
    you who practice deceit.
³ You love evil rather than good,
    falsehood rather than speaking the
        truth.   *Selah*
⁴ You love every harmful word,
    O you deceitful tongue!

⁵ Surely God will bring you down to
        everlasting ruin:
    He will snatch you up and tear you
        from your tent;
    he will uproot you from the land of
        the living.   *Selah*
⁶ The righteous will see and fear;
    they will laugh at him, saying,
⁷ "Here now is the man
    who did not make God his
        stronghold
  but trusted in his great wealth
    and grew strong by destroying
        others!"

⁸ But I am like an olive tree
    flourishing in the house of God;
  I trust in God's unfailing love
    for ever and ever.
⁹ I will praise you forever for what you
        have done;
  in your name I will hope, for your
    name is good.
  I will praise you in the presence of
    your saints.

Psalm 53

For the director of music. According
  to *mahalath.*ᶜ A *maskil*ᵇ of David.

¹ The fool says in his heart,
    "There is no God."
They are corrupt, and their ways are
        vile;
    there is no one who does good.

² God looks down from heaven
    on the sons of men
to see if there are any who understand,
    any who seek God.
³ Everyone has turned away,
    they have together become corrupt;
there is no one who does good,
    not even one.

⁴ Will the evildoers never learn—
    those who devour my people as men
        eat bread
    and who do not call on God?
⁵ There they were, overwhelmed with
        dread,
    where there was nothing to dread.
God scattered the bones of those who
        attacked you;
  you put them to shame, for God
    despised them.

⁶ Oh, that salvation for Israel would
        come out of Zion!
  When God restores the fortunes of
    his people,
  let Jacob rejoice and Israel be glad!

Psalm 54

For the director of music. With stringed
  instruments. A *maskil*ᵇ of David.
When the Ziphites had gone to Saul
  and said, "Is not David hiding among us?"

¹ Save me, O God, by your name;
    vindicate me by your might.

a17 Or *My sacrifice, O God, is* ᵇTitle: Probably a
literary or musical term ᶜTitle: Probably a musical
term

²Hear my prayer, O God;
  listen to the words of my mouth.

³Strangers are attacking me;
  ruthless men seek my life—
  men without regard for God.   *Selah*

⁴Surely God is my help;
  the Lord is the one who sustains me.

⁵Let evil recoil on those who slander
    me;
  in your faithfulness destroy them.

⁶I will sacrifice a freewill offering to you;
  I will praise your name, O LORD,
  for it is good.
⁷For he has delivered me from all my
    troubles,
  and my eyes have looked in triumph
    on my foes.

Psalm 55

For the director of music. With stringed
instruments. A *maskil*ᵃ of David.

¹Listen to my prayer, O God,
  do not ignore my plea;
²   hear me and answer me.
  My thoughts trouble me and I am
    distraught
³   at the voice of the enemy,
    at the stares of the wicked;
  for they bring down suffering upon me
  and revile me in their anger.

⁴My heart is in anguish within me;
  the terrors of death assail me.
⁵Fear and trembling have beset me;
  horror has overwhelmed me.
⁶I said, "Oh, that I had the wings of a
    dove!
  I would fly away and be at rest—
⁷I would flee far away
  and stay in the desert;   *Selah*
⁸I would hurry to my place of shelter,
  far from the tempest and storm."

⁹Confuse the wicked, O Lord, confound
    their speech,
  for I see violence and strife in the
    city.
¹⁰Day and night they prowl about on its
    walls;
  malice and abuse are within it.
¹¹Destructive forces are at work in the
    city;
  threats and lies never leave its
    streets.

¹²If an enemy were insulting me,
  I could endure it;

if a foe were raising himself against me,
  I could hide from him.
¹³But it is you, a man like myself,
  my companion, my close friend,
¹⁴with whom I once enjoyed sweet
    fellowship
  as we walked with the throng at the
    house of God.

¹⁵Let death take my enemies by
    surprise;
  let them go down alive to the
    grave,ᵇ
  for evil finds lodging among them.

¹⁶But I call to God,
  and the LORD saves me.
¹⁷Evening, morning and noon
  I cry out in distress,
  and he hears my voice.
¹⁸He ransoms me unharmed
  from the battle waged against me,
  even though many oppose me.
¹⁹God, who is enthroned forever,
  will hear them and afflict them—
                                    Selah
men who never change their ways
  and have no fear of God.

²⁰My companion attacks his friends;
  he violates his covenant.
²¹His speech is smooth as butter,
  yet war is in his heart;
  his words are more soothing than oil,
  yet they are drawn swords.

²²Cast your cares on the LORD
  and he will sustain you;
  he will never let the righteous fall.
²³But you, O God, will bring down the
    wicked
  into the pit of corruption;
bloodthirsty and deceitful men
  will not live out half their days.

But as for me, I trust in you.

Psalm 56

For the director of music. To ⌊the tune of⌋
"A Dove on Distant Oaks." Of David.
A *miktam.*ᵃ When the Philistines
had seized him in Gath.

¹Be merciful to me, O God, for men
    hotly pursue me;
  all day long they press their attack.
²My slanderers pursue me all day long;
  many are attacking me in their pride.

ᵃTitle: Probably a literary or musical term
ᵇ15 Hebrew *Sheol*

³When I am afraid,
  I will trust in you.
⁴In God, whose word I praise,
  in God I trust; I will not be afraid.
  What can mortal man do to me?

⁵All day long they twist my words;
  they are always plotting to harm me.
⁶They conspire, they lurk,
  they watch my steps,
  eager to take my life.

⁷On no account let them escape;
  in your anger, O God, bring down the
    nations.
⁸Record my lament;
  list my tears on your scrollᵃ—
  are they not in your record?

⁹Then my enemies will turn back
  when I call for help.
  By this I will know that God is for
    me.

¹⁰In God, whose word I praise,
  in the LORD, whose word I praise—
¹¹in God I trust; I will not be afraid.
  What can man do to me?

¹²I am under vows to you, O God;
  I will present my thank offerings to
    you.
¹³For you have delivered meᵇ from death
  and my feet from stumbling,
  that I may walk before God
  in the light of life.ᶜ

Psalm 57

For the director of music. To the tune of
"Do Not Destroy." Of David. A *miktam.*ᵈ
When he had fled from Saul into the cave.

¹Have mercy on me, O God, have mercy
    on me,
  for in you my soul takes refuge.
  I will take refuge in the shadow of your
    wings
  until the disaster has passed.

²I cry out to God Most High,
  to God, who fulfills his purpose for
    me.
³He sends from heaven and saves me,
  rebuking those who hotly pursue
    me;   *Selah*
  God sends his love and his
    faithfulness.

⁴I am in the midst of lions;
  I lie among ravenous beasts—
  men whose teeth are spears and
    arrows,
  whose tongues are sharp swords.

⁵Be exalted, O God, above the heavens;
  let your glory be over all the earth.

⁶They spread a net for my feet—
  I was bowed down in distress.
  They dug a pit in my path—
  but they have fallen into it
    themselves.   *Selah*

⁷My heart is steadfast, O God,
  my heart is steadfast;
  I will sing and make music.
⁸Awake, my soul!
  Awake, harp and lyre!
  I will awaken the dawn.

⁹I will praise you, O Lord, among the
    nations;
  I will sing of you among the peoples.
¹⁰For great is your love, reaching to the
    heavens;
  your faithfulness reaches to the
    skies.

¹¹Be exalted, O God, above the heavens;
  let your glory be over all the earth.

Psalm 58

For the director of music. To the tune of
"Do Not Destroy." Of David. A *miktam.*ᵈ

¹Do you rulers indeed speak justly?
  Do you judge uprightly among men?
²No, in your heart you devise injustice,
  and your hands mete out violence on
    the earth.
³Even from birth the wicked go astray;
  from the womb they are wayward
    and speak lies.
⁴Their venom is like the venom of a
    snake,
  like that of a cobra that has stopped
    its ears,
⁵that will not heed the tune of the
    charmer,
  however skillful the enchanter may
    be.

⁶Break the teeth in their mouths, O God;
  tear out, O LORD, the fangs of the
    lions!
⁷Let them vanish like water that flows
    away;
  when they draw the bow, let their
    arrows be blunted.
⁸Like a slug melting away as it moves
    along,

ᵃ8 Or *I put my tears in your wineskin*   ᵇ13 Or *my
soul*   ᶜ13 Or *the land of the living*   ᵈTitle: Probably
a literary or musical term

like a stillborn child, may they not see
the sun.

⁹ Before your pots can feel ⌊the heat of⌋
the thorns—
whether they be green or dry—the
wicked will be swept away.ᵃ
¹⁰ The righteous will be glad when they
are avenged,
when they bathe their feet in the
blood of the wicked.
¹¹ Then men will say,
"Surely the righteous still are
rewarded;
surely there is a God who judges the
earth."

Psalm 59

For the director of music. ⌊To the tune of⌋
"Do Not Destroy." Of David. A *miktam*.ᵇ
When Saul had sent men to watch
David's house in order to kill him.

¹ Deliver me from my enemies, O God;
protect me from those who rise up
against me.
² Deliver me from evildoers
and save me from bloodthirsty men.

³ See how they lie in wait for me!
Fierce men conspire against me
for no offense or sin of mine, O LORD.
⁴ I have done no wrong, yet they are
ready to attack me.
Arise to help me; look on my plight!
⁵ O LORD God Almighty, the God of
Israel,
rouse yourself to punish all the
nations;
show no mercy to wicked traitors. *Selah*

⁶ They return at evening,
snarling like dogs,
and prowl about the city.
⁷ See what they spew from their
mouths—
they spew out swords from their lips,
and they say, "Who can hear us?"
⁸ But you, O LORD, laugh at them;
you scoff at all those nations.

⁹ O my Strength, I watch for you;
you, O God, are my fortress, ¹⁰my
loving God.

God will go before me
and will let me gloat over those who
slander me.
¹¹ But do not kill them, O Lord our
shield,ᶜ

or my people will forget.
In your might make them wander
about,
and bring them down.
¹² For the sins of their mouths,
for the words of their lips,
let them be caught in their pride.
For the curses and lies they utter,
¹³   consume them in wrath,
consume them till they are no more.
Then it will be known to the ends of the
earth
that God rules over Jacob. *Selah*

¹⁴ They return at evening,
snarling like dogs,
and prowl about the city.
¹⁵ They wander about for food
and howl if not satisfied.
¹⁶ But I will sing of your strength,
in the morning I will sing of your
love;
for you are my fortress,
my refuge in times of trouble.

¹⁷ O my Strength, I sing praise to you;
you, O God, are my fortress, my
loving God.

Psalm 60

For the director of music. To ⌊the tune of⌋
"The Lily of the Covenant." A *miktam*ᵇ of David.
For teaching. When he fought Aram
Naharaimᵈand Aram Zobah,ᵉ and when Joab
returned and struck down twelve thousand
Edomites in the Valley of Salt.

¹ You have rejected us, O God, and burst
forth upon us;
you have been angry—now restore us!
² You have shaken the land and torn it
open;
mend its fractures, for it is quaking.
³ You have shown your people desperate
times;
you have given us wine that makes
us stagger.
⁴ But for those who fear you, you have
raised a banner
to be unfurled against the bow. *Selah*

⁵ Save us and help us with your right
hand,

ᵃ9 The meaning of the Hebrew for this verse is
uncertain. ᵇTitle: Probably a literary or musical
term ᶜ11 Or *sovereign* ᵈTitle: That is, Arameans
of Northwest Mesopotamia ᵉTitle: That is,
Arameans of central Syria

People Who Would Rather Boo than Cheer

Key Verse: *"O my Strength, I watch for you; you, O God, are my fortress."* Psalm 59:9

Text: Psalm 59:1–10a *(Dad or child reads the text.)*

QUIET TIMES WITH Dad

DAD READS: Have you ever watched a game on television where the fans were booing the home team? I'm always surprised that people pay their money to go to these games, then they sit there moaning. They wail that the referees are blind and stupid, they hate the other team, or they just think the players aren't good enough. Whatever the reason, these people just seem to enjoy complaining and griping.

Child reads: How strange that some people have fun being grumpy. I feel sorry for people like this. And I'm glad I don't live in their houses!

DAD READS: Yes, it is sad that many people in the world would rather boo than cheer. These unhappy people are glad when bad things happen to others. Sometimes I come across such people—people who seem to want me to make mistakes, people who want me to fail.

Child reads: I know what this is like, because sometimes people enjoy pushing me around and making me feel bad even though I have not done anything to them. These people make me feel very sad.

DAD READS: David was going to be the next king of Israel, and many people were glad that good things were going to happen to him. But King Saul wasn't one of these people. He didn't want David to be the next king. He wanted David

to fail. So Saul sent men to hurt David. Can you imagine how David must have felt?

Child reads: David did the only thing he could do. He did what I need to do with the people who want bad things to happen to me. David asked God to take care of those people. Then David told God that his heavenly Father's protection was enough. No matter what unkind people did to David, he knew that he was safe.

DAD READS: You and I need to remember this when it seems as if unkind people are surrounding us. We need to remember this when we hear more boos than cheers.

Child reads: I'm glad that God is always with us, always cheering for us. I know that no matter what, he still loves and protects us. Let me pray this prayer with you:

Our Father in heaven, thank you for loving us. And thank you for cheering for us and protecting us. Please help us to forgive the people who seem to want us to fail. Help us to trust you to take care of those people. And help us to feel safe because of your love. We love you. In Jesus' name, **Amen.**

For your next devotional reading, go to page 619.

that those you love may be
delivered.
[6] God has spoken from his sanctuary:
"In triumph I will parcel out
Shechem
and measure off the Valley of
Succoth.
[7] Gilead is mine, and Manasseh is mine;
Ephraim is my helmet,
Judah my scepter.
[8] Moab is my washbasin,
upon Edom I toss my sandal;
over Philistia I shout in triumph."

[9] Who will bring me to the fortified
city?
Who will lead me to Edom?
[10] Is it not you, O God, you who have
rejected us
and no longer go out with our
armies?
[11] Give us aid against the enemy,
for the help of man is worthless.
[12] With God we will gain the victory,
and he will trample down our
enemies.

Psalm 61

For the director of music.
With stringed instruments. Of David.

[1] Hear my cry, O God;
listen to my prayer.

[2] From the ends of the earth I call to
you,
I call as my heart grows faint;
lead me to the rock that is higher
than I.
[3] For you have been my refuge,
a strong tower against the foe.

[4] I long to dwell in your tent forever
and take refuge in the shelter of your
wings.   *Selah*
[5] For you have heard my vows, O God;
you have given me the heritage of
those who fear your name.

[6] Increase the days of the king's life,
his years for many generations.
[7] May he be enthroned in God's presence
forever;
appoint your love and faithfulness to
protect him.

[8] Then will I ever sing praise to your
name
and fulfill my vows day after day.

Psalm 62

For the director of music.
For Jeduthun. A psalm of David.

[1] My soul finds rest in God alone;
my salvation comes from him.
[2] He alone is my rock and my salvation;
he is my fortress, I will never be
shaken.

[3] How long will you assault a man?
Would all of you throw him down—
this leaning wall, this tottering
fence?
[4] They fully intend to topple him
from his lofty place;
they take delight in lies.
With their mouths they bless,
but in their hearts they curse.   *Selah*

[5] Find rest, O my soul, in God alone;
my hope comes from him.
[6] He alone is my rock and my salvation;
he is my fortress, I will not be
shaken.
[7] My salvation and my honor depend on
God[a];
he is my mighty rock, my refuge.
[8] Trust in him at all times, O people;
pour out your hearts to him,
for God is our refuge.   *Selah*

[9] Lowborn men are but a breath,
the highborn are but a lie;
if weighed on a balance, they are
nothing;
together they are only a breath.
[10] Do not trust in extortion
or take pride in stolen goods;
though your riches increase,
do not set your heart on them.

[11] One thing God has spoken,
two things have I heard:
that you, O God, are strong,
[12]   and that you, O Lord, are loving.
Surely you will reward each person
according to what he has done.

Psalm 63

A psalm of David.
When he was in the Desert of Judah.

[1] O God, you are my God,
earnestly I seek you;

---
[a]7 Or / *God Most High is my salvation and
my honor*

my soul thirsts for you,
my body longs for you,
in a dry and weary land
where there is no water.

[2] I have seen you in the sanctuary
and beheld your power and your
glory.
[3] Because your love is better than life,
my lips will glorify you.
[4] I will praise you as long as I live,
and in your name I will lift up my
hands.
[5] My soul will be satisfied as with the
richest of foods;
with singing lips my mouth will
praise you.

[6] On my bed I remember you;
I think of you through the watches of
the night.
[7] Because you are my help,
I sing in the shadow of your wings.
[8] My soul clings to you;
your right hand upholds me.

[9] They who seek my life will be
destroyed;
they will go down to the depths of
the earth.
[10] They will be given over to the sword
and become food for jackals.
[11] But the king will rejoice in God;
all who swear by God's name will
praise him,
while the mouths of liars will be
silenced.

Psalm 64

For the director of music.
A psalm of David.

[1] Hear me, O God, as I voice my
complaint;
protect my life from the threat of the
enemy.
[2] Hide me from the conspiracy of the
wicked,
from that noisy crowd of evildoers.
[3] They sharpen their tongues like swords
and aim their words like deadly
arrows.
[4] They shoot from ambush at the
innocent man;
they shoot at him suddenly, without
fear.
[5] They encourage each other in evil
plans,
they talk about hiding their snares;

they say, "Who will see them[a]?"
[6] They plot injustice and say,
"We have devised a perfect plan!"
Surely the mind and heart of man are
cunning.

[7] But God will shoot them with arrows;
suddenly they will be struck down.
[8] He will turn their own tongues against
them
and bring them to ruin;
all who see them will shake their
heads in scorn.

[9] All mankind will fear;
they will proclaim the works of God
and ponder what he has done.
[10] Let the righteous rejoice in the LORD
and take refuge in him;
let all the upright in heart praise him!

Psalm 65

For the director of music.
A psalm of David. A song.

[1] Praise awaits[b] you, O God, in Zion;
to you our vows will be fulfilled.
[2] O you who hear prayer,
to you all men will come.
[3] When we were overwhelmed by sins,
you forgave[c] our transgressions.
[4] Blessed are those you choose
and bring near to live in your courts!
We are filled with the good things of
your house,
of your holy temple.

[5] You answer us with awesome deeds of
righteousness,
O God our Savior,
the hope of all the ends of the earth
and of the farthest seas,
[6] who formed the mountains by your
power,
having armed yourself with strength,
[7] who stilled the roaring of the seas,
the roaring of their waves,
and the turmoil of the nations.
[8] Those living far away fear your
wonders;
where morning dawns and evening
fades
you call forth songs of joy.

[9] You care for the land and water it;
you enrich it abundantly.
The streams of God are filled with water

---

[a]5 Or *us*   [b]1 Or *befits*; the meaning of the Hebrew
for this word is uncertain.   [c]3 Or *made
atonement for*

to provide the people with grain,
for so you have ordained it.[a]
¹⁰You drench its furrows
and level its ridges;
you soften it with showers
and bless its crops.
¹¹You crown the year with your bounty,
and your carts overflow with
abundance.
¹²The grasslands of the desert overflow;
the hills are clothed with gladness.
¹³The meadows are covered with flocks
and the valleys are mantled with
grain;
they shout for joy and sing.

Psalm 66

For the director of music.
A song. A psalm.

¹Shout with joy to God, all the earth!
² Sing the glory of his name;
make his praise glorious!
³Say to God, "How awesome are your
deeds!
So great is your power
that your enemies cringe before you.
⁴All the earth bows down to you;
they sing praise to you,
they sing praise to your name."
                                    Selah

⁵Come and see what God has done,
how awesome his works in man's
behalf!
⁶He turned the sea into dry land,
they passed through the waters on
foot—
come, let us rejoice in him.
⁷He rules forever by his power,
his eyes watch the nations—
let not the rebellious rise up against
him.   *Selah*

⁸Praise our God, O peoples,
let the sound of his praise be heard;
⁹he has preserved our lives
and kept our feet from slipping.
¹⁰For you, O God, tested us;
you refined us like silver.
¹¹You brought us into prison
and laid burdens on our backs.
¹²You let men ride over our heads;
we went through fire and water,
but you brought us to a place of
abundance.

¹³I will come to your temple with burnt
offerings
and fulfill my vows to you—

¹⁴vows my lips promised and my mouth
spoke
when I was in trouble.
¹⁵I will sacrifice fat animals to you
and an offering of rams;
I will offer bulls and goats.   *Selah*

¹⁶Come and listen, all you who fear God;
let me tell you what he has done for
me.
¹⁷I cried out to him with my mouth;
his praise was on my tongue.
¹⁸If I had cherished sin in my heart,
the Lord would not have listened;
¹⁹but God has surely listened
and heard my voice in prayer.
²⁰Praise be to God,
who has not rejected my prayer
or withheld his love from me!

Psalm 67

For the director of music. With stringed
instruments. A psalm. A song.

¹May God be gracious to us and bless us
and make his face shine upon us,
                                    Selah
²that your ways may be known on earth,
your salvation among all nations.

³May the peoples praise you, O God;
may all the peoples praise you.
⁴May the nations be glad and sing for
joy,
for you rule the peoples justly
and guide the nations of the earth.
                                    Selah
⁵May the peoples praise you, O God;
may all the peoples praise you.

⁶Then the land will yield its harvest,
and God, our God, will bless us.
⁷God will bless us,
and all the ends of the earth will fear
him.

Psalm 68

For the director of music. Of David.
A psalm. A song.

¹May God arise, may his enemies be
scattered;
may his foes flee before him.
²As smoke is blown away by the wind,
may you blow them away;
as wax melts before the fire,
may the wicked perish before God.

ª9 Or for that is how you prepare the land

³But may the righteous be glad
　　and rejoice before God;
　　may they be happy and joyful.

⁴Sing to God, sing praise to his name,
　　extol him who rides on the clouds*ᵃ*—
　　his name is the LORD—
　　and rejoice before him.

⁵A father to the fatherless, a defender of
　　widows,
　　is God in his holy dwelling.

⁶God sets the lonely in families,*ᵇ*
　　he leads forth the prisoners with
　　　singing;
　　but the rebellious live in a
　　　sun-scorched land.

⁷When you went out before your people,
　　O God,

*ᵃ4 Or / prepare the way for him who rides through
the deserts   ᵇ6 Or the desolate in a homeland*

Triples to Dead Center and God's Happy People

DAILY INSIGHT

MONDAY

Passage:
Psalm 67

Verse:
Psalm 67:3

In spring of 1989 my company published *Out of the Blue,* the story of Los Angeles pitching phenom Orel Hershiser. The previous fall he had almost single-handedly led the Dodgers through the World Series as they defeated the mighty Oakland Athletics. With the newly-released book just hitting the marketplace, I escorted Orel to television interviews and book signings all around the country. Going to games before or after the interviews was all part of the duty. Yes, it was a dirty job, but *someone* had to do it.

One perfect June afternoon, I found myself at Dodger Stadium. As was his custom, Orel had given me a great ticket for a seat in the second deck and right behind home plate—the section where players' families and friends sit. There I met Dave and Jan Hotchkin, good friends of the Hershisers. I introduced myself to them, and Dave and I chatted for a while. After we had covered the traditional introduction bases, we were ready for baseball.

Orel's first pitch was a slider that nipped the outside corner. Strike one. It was the beginning of what would turn into a classic pitcher's battle. By the bottom of the sixth inning, there was still no score. While this kind of game can be boring to some, it's not when the guy on the mound is your best friend.

Then Orel, a remarkably successful batter (for a pitcher), stepped to the plate. The first pitch was high and tight—a little telegram from the opposing hurler. Orel leaned back ever so slightly to avoid being grazed. Ball one.

The next pitch was the one he was looking for … a belt-high fastball. Wasting no time, Orel turned on the pitch and sent a screaming line drive to dead center field. The loyal Dodger fans erupted as the ball rocketed over the center fielder's head. Moments later, Orel slid into third base. *Safe!*

In that moment something very strange happened. Dave Hotchkin, whom I had known for approximately ninety minutes, became my closest friend. We embraced, stepped back to "high-five" a couple of times, then embraced again. All of this was followed by a solid minute of dancing, screaming, hooting and generally making an obnoxious racket. We were instant comrades. Jan excused herself to get some nachos.

Today's psalm challenges "all the people" to praise God. And if we do, it promises, "the land will yield its harvest." In other words, mutual celebration brings people together and helps us accomplish great things. If, after that sixth-inning blast, someone had given Dave and me a task to do together, our cooperation would have been flawless. The "harvest" would have been plentiful because we had joined each other in mutual celebration.

This is a snapshot of God's people. When we realize how worthy he is of our adoration, our relationships with each other will be sealed, and the work he asks us to do on his behalf will be accomplished. Worship him enthusiastically, and you'll find someone to "high-five" in the process.

For your next devotional reading, go to page 620.

when you marched through the
    wasteland,   *Selah*
⁸the earth shook,
    the heavens poured down rain,
  before God, the One of Sinai,
    before God, the God of Israel.
⁹You gave abundant showers, O God;
    you refreshed your weary
      inheritance.
¹⁰Your people settled in it,
    and from your bounty, O God, you
      provided for the poor.

¹¹The Lord announced the word,
    and great was the company of those
      who proclaimed it:
¹²"Kings and armies flee in haste;
    in the camps men divide the
      plunder.
¹³Even while you sleep among the
      campfires,ᵃ
    the wings of my dove are sheathed
      with silver,
    its feathers with shining gold."

ᵃ13 Or saddlebags

Great Advice from King David . . . and My Mother

DAILY INSIGHT

TUESDAY

Passage:
Psalm 69:6–16

Verse:
Psalm 69:6

It was going to be the biggest deal of my life. My business partner and I had orchestrated the purchase of a major corporation. We had done our due diligence, we had met with the executives of the for-sale company, we had prepared a business plan, we had raised all the money we would need to make an offer ... and several counter offers. We also had plenty of top-notch, meter-running lawyers and hard-charging brokers on the point.

The rush of this deal was like nothing I had ever experienced before. I thought about our transaction all the time. I can remember waking up in the morning, lying quietly for a split second, then having "the deal" scream into my mind like a siren. I strategized about it in the shower and talked about it over oatmeal. My wife was very patient. I thought about the deal while driving to the office, eating lunch, sitting in church, flying on airplanes, jogging ... you get the idea. Finally, on one mid-summer Tuesday afternoon, we tendered our opening offer.

The next morning, only a few hours after the company's board had met to "accept our proposal," I got a call from a broker. Somehow a very clever buyer—with a no-shop deal—had come to the table at the last moment. With no opportunity to let us counter-offer, the board accepted the other proposal. Our whole Wall Street transaction had slipped through our fingers. I was sick, broken, angry, embarrassed and confused. *How could this have happened?*

The first two words of today's psalm say it all: "Save me." King David must have just lost the deal of a lifetime. He was nearly delusional: "I'm drowning and my throat is parched." That's okay, David, I know just how you felt.

As a kid, my mother used to lean in on me when I was facing an unusually horrible youngster-type crisis. "Robert," she'd warn, "this is a test. How well you do will be an example ... for good or not-so-good." Her wise words came crashing back on my consciousness that July morning. *It's not what happens to me that matters*, I recalled from something I had read, *it's what happens to me that really counts.*

Did you read verse 6? "May those who hope in you not be disgraced because of me." The lesson is unmistakable. My friends are watching me when the deal goes bad, when my faith is shattered, when things don't turn out as I had planned. It's my chance to show them how my love for God and his love for me is absolutely enough. My reaction to failure delivers an opportunity—a test—to prove how adequate he is to meet my needs. It's *my* chance to make *him* look good.

Thanks for the reminder, David. Thanks, Mom.

For your next devotional reading, go to page 624.

14When the Almighty^a scattered the kings
in the land,
it was like snow fallen on Zalmon.

15The mountains of Bashan are majestic
mountains;
rugged are the mountains of Bashan.
16Why gaze in envy, O rugged
mountains,
at the mountain where God chooses
to reign,
where the LORD himself will dwell
forever?
17The chariots of God are tens of
thousands
and thousands of thousands;
the Lord has come from Sinai into
his sanctuary.
18When you ascended on high,
you led captives in your train;
you received gifts from men,
even from^b the rebellious—
that you,^c O LORD God, might dwell
there.

19Praise be to the Lord, to God our
Savior,
who daily bears our burdens.   *Selah*
20Our God is a God who saves;
from the Sovereign LORD comes
escape from death.

21Surely God will crush the heads of his
enemies,
the hairy crowns of those who go on
in their sins.
22The Lord says, "I will bring them from
Bashan;
I will bring them from the depths of
the sea,
23that you may plunge your feet in the
blood of your foes,
while the tongues of your dogs have
their share."

24Your procession has come into view,
O God,
the procession of my God and King
into the sanctuary.
25In front are the singers, after them the
musicians;
with them are the maidens playing
tambourines.
26Praise God in the great congregation;
praise the LORD in the assembly of
Israel.
27There is the little tribe of Benjamin,
leading them,
there the great throng of Judah's
princes,
and there the princes of Zebulun and
of Naphtali.

28Summon your power, O God^d;
show us your strength, O God, as you
have done before.
29Because of your temple at Jerusalem
kings will bring you gifts.
30Rebuke the beast among the reeds,
the herd of bulls among the calves of
the nations.
Humbled, may it bring bars of silver.
Scatter the nations who delight in
war.
31Envoys will come from Egypt;
Cush^e will submit herself to God.

32Sing to God, O kingdoms of the earth,
sing praise to the Lord,   *Selah*
33to him who rides the ancient skies
above,
who thunders with mighty voice.
34Proclaim the power of God,
whose majesty is over Israel,
whose power is in the skies.
35You are awesome, O God, in your
sanctuary;
the God of Israel gives power and
strength to his people.

Praise be to God!

Psalm 69

For the director of music.
To the tune of "Lilies." Of David.

1Save me, O God,
for the waters have come up to my
neck.
2I sink in the miry depths,
where there is no foothold.
I have come into the deep waters;
the floods engulf me.
3I am worn out calling for help;
my throat is parched.
My eyes fail,
looking for my God.
4Those who hate me without reason
outnumber the hairs of my head;
many are my enemies without cause,
those who seek to destroy me.
I am forced to restore
what I did not steal.

5You know my folly, O God;
my guilt is not hidden from you.

6May those who hope in you
not be disgraced because of me,

a14 Hebrew *Shaddai*   *b18* Or *gifts for men, / even*
c18 Or *they*   *d28* Many Hebrew manuscripts,
Septuagint and Syriac; most Hebrew manuscripts
Your God has summoned power for you   *e31* That
is, the upper Nile region

O Lord, the LORD Almighty;
may those who seek you
not be put to shame because of me,
O God of Israel.
⁷ For I endure scorn for your sake,
and shame covers my face.
⁸ I am a stranger to my brothers,
an alien to my own mother's sons;
⁹ for zeal for your house consumes me,
and the insults of those who insult
you fall on me.
¹⁰ When I weep and fast,
I must endure scorn;
¹¹ when I put on sackcloth,
people make sport of me.
¹² Those who sit at the gate mock me,
and I am the song of the drunkards.

¹³ But I pray to you, O LORD,
in the time of your favor;
in your great love, O God,
answer me with your sure
salvation.
¹⁴ Rescue me from the mire,
do not let me sink;
deliver me from those who hate me,
from the deep waters.
¹⁵ Do not let the floodwaters engulf me
or the depths swallow me up
or the pit close its mouth over me.
¹⁶ Answer me, O LORD, out of the
goodness of your love;
in your great mercy turn to me.
¹⁷ Do not hide your face from your
servant;
answer me quickly, for I am in
trouble.
¹⁸ Come near and rescue me;
redeem me because of my foes.

¹⁹ You know how I am scorned, disgraced
and shamed;
all my enemies are before you.
²⁰ Scorn has broken my heart
and has left me helpless;
I looked for sympathy, but there was
none,
for comforters, but I found none.
²¹ They put gall in my food
and gave me vinegar for my thirst.

²² May the table set before them become
a snare;
may it become retribution and*a* a
trap.
²³ May their eyes be darkened so they
cannot see,
and their backs be bent forever.
²⁴ Pour out your wrath on them;
let your fierce anger overtake them.
²⁵ May their place be deserted;

let there be no one to dwell in their
tents.
²⁶ For they persecute those you wound
and talk about the pain of those you
hurt.
²⁷ Charge them with crime upon crime;
do not let them share in your
salvation.
²⁸ May they be blotted out of the book of
life
and not be listed with the
righteous.

²⁹ I am in pain and distress;
may your salvation, O God, protect
me.
³⁰ I will praise God's name in song
and glorify him with thanksgiving.
³¹ This will please the LORD more than
an ox,
more than a bull with its horns and
hoofs.
³² The poor will see and be glad—
you who seek God, may your hearts
live!
³³ The LORD hears the needy
and does not despise his captive
people.

³⁴ Let heaven and earth praise him,
the seas and all that move in them,
³⁵ for God will save Zion
and rebuild the cities of Judah.
Then people will settle there and
possess it;
³⁶ the children of his servants will
inherit it,
and those who love his name will
dwell there.

Psalm 70

For the director of music.
Of David. A petition.

¹ Hasten, O God, to save me;
O LORD, come quickly to help me.
² May those who seek my life
be put to shame and confusion;
may all who desire my ruin
be turned back in disgrace.
³ May those who say to me, "Aha! Aha!"
turn back because of their shame.
⁴ But may all who seek you
rejoice and be glad in you;
may those who love your salvation
always say,
"Let God be exalted!"

a22 Or snare / and their fellowship become

⁵Yet I am poor and needy;
    come quickly to me, O God.
You are my help and my deliverer;
    O LORD, do not delay.

Psalm 71

¹In you, O LORD, I have taken refuge;
    let me never be put to shame.
²Rescue me and deliver me in your
        righteousness;
    turn your ear to me and save me.
³Be my rock of refuge,
    to which I can always go;
give the command to save me,
    for you are my rock and my fortress.
⁴Deliver me, O my God, from the hand
        of the wicked,
    from the grasp of evil and cruel men.

⁵For you have been my hope,
    O Sovereign LORD,
    my confidence since my youth.
⁶From birth I have relied on you;
    you brought me forth from my
        mother's womb.
    I will ever praise you.
⁷I have become like a portent to many,
    but you are my strong refuge.
⁸My mouth is filled with your praise,
    declaring your splendor all day long.

⁹Do not cast me away when I am old;
    do not forsake me when my strength
        is gone.
¹⁰For my enemies speak against me;
    those who wait to kill me conspire
        together.
¹¹They say, "God has forsaken him;
    pursue him and seize him,
    for no one will rescue him."
¹²Be not far from me, O God;
    come quickly, O my God, to help me.
¹³May my accusers perish in shame;
    may those who want to harm me
    be covered with scorn and disgrace.

¹⁴But as for me, I will always have hope;
    I will praise you more and more.
¹⁵My mouth will tell of your
        righteousness,
    of your salvation all day long,
    though I know not its measure.
¹⁶I will come and proclaim your mighty
        acts, O Sovereign LORD;
    I will proclaim your righteousness,
        yours alone.
¹⁷Since my youth, O God, you have
        taught me,
    and to this day I declare your
        marvelous deeds.

¹⁸Even when I am old and gray,
    do not forsake me, O God,
    till I declare your power to the next
        generation,
    your might to all who are to come.

¹⁹Your righteousness reaches to the skies,
        O God,
    you who have done great things.
    Who, O God, is like you?
²⁰Though you have made me see
        troubles, many and bitter,
    you will restore my life again;
from the depths of the earth
    you will again bring me up.
²¹You will increase my honor
    and comfort me once again.

²²I will praise you with the harp
    for your faithfulness, O my God;
I will sing praise to you with the lyre,
    O Holy One of Israel.
²³My lips will shout for joy
    when I sing praise to you—
    I, whom you have redeemed.
²⁴My tongue will tell of your righteous
        acts
    all day long,
for those who wanted to harm me
    have been put to shame and
        confusion.

Psalm 72

Of Solomon.

¹Endow the king with your justice,
        O God,
    the royal son with your
        righteousness.
²He will[a] judge your people in
        righteousness,
    your afflicted ones with justice.
³The mountains will bring prosperity to
        the people,
    the hills the fruit of righteousness.
⁴He will defend the afflicted among the
        people
    and save the children of the needy;
    he will crush the oppressor.

⁵He will endure[b] as long as the sun,
    as long as the moon, through all
        generations.
⁶He will be like rain falling on a mown
        field,
    like showers watering the earth.
⁷In his days the righteous will flourish;

---

[a]2 Or *May he*; similarly in verses 3-11 and 17
[b]5 Septuagint; Hebrew *You will be feared*

prosperity will abound till the moon is
no more.

8 He will rule from sea to sea
and from the River[a] to the ends of
the earth.[b]
9 The desert tribes will bow before him
and his enemies will lick the dust.
10 The kings of Tarshish and of distant
shores
will bring tribute to him;
the kings of Sheba and Seba
will present him gifts.
11 All kings will bow down to him
and all nations will serve him.

12 For he will deliver the needy who cry
out,
the afflicted who have no one to
help.
13 He will take pity on the weak and the
needy
and save the needy from death.
14 He will rescue them from oppression
and violence,
for precious is their blood in his
sight.

[a]8 That is, the Euphrates   [b]8 Or *the end of the land*

This Game Is History

DAILY INSIGHT

WEDNESDAY
Passage:
Psalm 73:23–28
Verse:
Psalm 73:26

Back in the early seventies, before the heyday of the VCR, Chicago's WGN replayed Chicago Bulls' games for the benefit of those fans who had missed the game earlier in the evening. Since Michael Jordan was only in the fourth grade at that time, this delayed broadcast gave us two chances to see our favorite team lose.

Through a mutual friend, I had met Pat Williams, the Bulls' General Manager. At a party, Pat told a story about how the night before he had been visiting with some college prospects. He had hoped to catch the game against Rick Barry and the Golden State Warriors, but because of a delayed flight he had missed the entire broadcast. Knowing, however, that WGN was going to broadcast the game again, he hurried home to catch the action.

In less than an hour, Pat was in his den watching the rebroadcast. And, because he had been careful to avoid anyone who would tell him the outcome, he paced back and forth, heart racing, watching the lead change hands. The game was down to two minutes on the clock—meaning that it could be at least forty minutes before it would actually be over. The score was tied. Pat's telephone rang and without thinking, he picked it up.

"Can you believe it?" shouted one of his colleagues. "What a great game!"

Pat slammed the phone down, angry that the suspense had been spoiled. But in a couple of minutes he found himself doing something he had been unable to do before the call—sitting in his favorite oversized chair, resting in the assurance of the outcome.

Now you may be wondering, *What does a guy sitting in his easy chair in Chicago have to do with this psalm?* Just look at the first twenty-two verses, and you'll see the similarities. This desperate man is pacing back and forth, overwhelmed with frustration over the prosperity and seemingly impenetrable power of wicked men. His rage is about to get the best of him when his brooding is interrupted with the truth: "God is the strength of my heart ... those who are far from you will perish."

Can't you picture the psalmist taking a deep breath, remembering God's victorious presence in his life and resting in this promise? Just like Pat Williams, this frustrated and anxiety ridden man was able to sit back and relax.

Do you see something of yourself in these two people? If you do, quit your pacing. Your God is in control. What you are seeing is not live action ... the game has been over since before the beginning of time.

For your next devotional reading, go to page 637.

¹⁵ Long may he live!
 May gold from Sheba be given him.
 May people ever pray for him
 and bless him all day long.
¹⁶ Let grain abound throughout the land;
 on the tops of the hills may it sway.
 Let its fruit flourish like Lebanon;
 let it thrive like the grass of the field.
¹⁷ May his name endure forever;
 may it continue as long as the sun.

 All nations will be blessed through him,
 and they will call him blessed.

¹⁸ Praise be to the LORD God, the God of
 Israel,
 who alone does marvelous deeds.
¹⁹ Praise be to his glorious name forever;
 may the whole earth be filled with
 his glory.
 Amen and Amen.

²⁰ This concludes the prayers of David
 son of Jesse.

BOOK III
Psalms 73–89

Psalm 73

A psalm of Asaph.

¹ Surely God is good to Israel,
 to those who are pure in heart.

² But as for me, my feet had almost
 slipped;
 I had nearly lost my foothold.
³ For I envied the arrogant
 when I saw the prosperity of the
 wicked.

⁴ They have no struggles;
 their bodies are healthy and strong.[a]
⁵ They are free from the burdens
 common to man;
 they are not plagued by human ills.
⁶ Therefore pride is their necklace;
 they clothe themselves with
 violence.
⁷ From their callous hearts comes
 iniquity[b];
 the evil conceits of their minds know
 no limits.
⁸ They scoff, and speak with malice;
 in their arrogance they threaten
 oppression.
⁹ Their mouths lay claim to heaven,
 and their tongues take possession of
 the earth.

¹⁰ Therefore their people turn to them
 and drink up waters in abundance.[c]
¹¹ They say, "How can God know?
 Does the Most High have
 knowledge?"

¹² This is what the wicked are like—
 always carefree, they increase in
 wealth.

¹³ Surely in vain have I kept my heart
 pure;
 in vain have I washed my hands in
 innocence.
¹⁴ All day long I have been plagued;
 I have been punished every
 morning.

¹⁵ If I had said, "I will speak thus,"
 I would have betrayed your children.
¹⁶ When I tried to understand all this,
 it was oppressive to me
¹⁷ till I entered the sanctuary of God;
 then I understood their final destiny.

¹⁸ Surely you place them on slippery
 ground;
 you cast them down to ruin.
¹⁹ How suddenly are they destroyed,
 completely swept away by terrors!
²⁰ As a dream when one awakes,
 so when you arise, O Lord,
 you will despise them as fantasies.

²¹ When my heart was grieved
 and my spirit embittered,
²² I was senseless and ignorant;
 I was a brute beast before you.

²³ Yet I am always with you;
 you hold me by my right hand.
²⁴ You guide me with your counsel,
 and afterward you will take me into
 glory.
²⁵ Whom have I in heaven but you?
 And earth has nothing I desire
 besides you.
²⁶ My flesh and my heart may fail,
 but God is the strength of my heart
 and my portion forever.

²⁷ Those who are far from you will perish;
 you destroy all who are unfaithful to
 you.
²⁸ But as for me, it is good to be near God.
 I have made the Sovereign LORD my
 refuge;
 I will tell of all your deeds.

---

a4 With a different word division of the Hebrew;
Masoretic Text *struggles at their death; / their
bodies are healthy* *b7* Syriac (see also Septuagint);
Hebrew *Their eyes bulge with fat* *c10* The meaning
of the Hebrew for this verse is uncertain.

Psalm 74

A maskil[a] of Asaph.

¹ Why have you rejected us forever,
O God?
Why does your anger smolder
against the sheep of your
pasture?
² Remember the people you purchased
of old,
the tribe of your inheritance, whom
you redeemed—
Mount Zion, where you dwelt.
³ Turn your steps toward these
everlasting ruins,
all this destruction the enemy has
brought on the sanctuary.

⁴ Your foes roared in the place where you
met with us;
they set up their standards as signs.
⁵ They behaved like men wielding axes
to cut through a thicket of trees.
⁶ They smashed all the carved paneling
with their axes and hatchets.
⁷ They burned your sanctuary to the
ground;
they defiled the dwelling place of
your Name.
⁸ They said in their hearts, "We will crush
them completely!"
They burned every place where God
was worshiped in the land.
⁹ We are given no miraculous signs;
no prophets are left,
and none of us knows how long this
will be.

¹⁰ How long will the enemy mock you,
O God?
Will the foe revile your name forever?
¹¹ Why do you hold back your hand, your
right hand?
Take it from the folds of your
garment and destroy them!

¹² But you, O God, are my king from of
old;
you bring salvation upon the earth.
¹³ It was you who split open the sea by
your power;
you broke the heads of the monster
in the waters.
¹⁴ It was you who crushed the heads of
Leviathan
and gave him as food to the
creatures of the desert.
¹⁵ It was you who opened up springs and
streams;
you dried up the ever flowing rivers.

¹⁶ The day is yours, and yours also the
night;
you established the sun and moon.
¹⁷ It was you who set all the boundaries of
the earth;
you made both summer and winter.
¹⁸ Remember how the enemy has mocked
you, O LORD,
how foolish people have reviled your
name.
¹⁹ Do not hand over the life of your dove
to wild beasts;
do not forget the lives of your
afflicted people forever.
²⁰ Have regard for your covenant,
because haunts of violence fill the
dark places of the land.
²¹ Do not let the oppressed retreat in
disgrace;
may the poor and needy praise your
name.
²² Rise up, O God, and defend your cause;
remember how fools mock you all
day long.
²³ Do not ignore the clamor of your
adversaries,
the uproar of your enemies, which
rises continually.

Psalm 75

*For the director of music.
To the tune of "Do Not Destroy."
A psalm of Asaph. A song.*

¹ We give thanks to you, O God,
we give thanks, for your Name is
near;
men tell of your wonderful deeds.

² You say, "I choose the appointed time;
it is I who judge uprightly.
³ When the earth and all its people
quake,
it is I who hold its pillars firm.   *Selah*
⁴ To the arrogant I say, 'Boast no more,'
and to the wicked, 'Do not lift up
your horns.
⁵ Do not lift your horns against heaven;
do not speak with outstretched
neck.' "

⁶ No one from the east or the west
or from the desert can exalt a man.
⁷ But it is God who judges:
He brings one down, he exalts
another.
⁸ In the hand of the LORD is a cup

---

*a*Title: Probably a literary or musical term

full of foaming wine mixed with
  spices;
he pours it out, and all the wicked of
  the earth
drink it down to its very dregs.

⁹As for me, I will declare this forever;
  I will sing praise to the God of Jacob.
¹⁰I will cut off the horns of all the wicked,
  but the horns of the righteous will be
  lifted up.

Psalm 76

For the director of music. With stringed
instruments. A psalm of Asaph. A song.

¹In Judah God is known;
  his name is great in Israel.
²His tent is in Salem,
  his dwelling place in Zion.
³There he broke the flashing arrows,
  the shields and the swords, the
  weapons of war.   *Selah*

⁴You are resplendent with light,
  more majestic than mountains rich
  with game.
⁵Valiant men lie plundered,
  they sleep their last sleep;
not one of the warriors
  can lift his hands.
⁶At your rebuke, O God of Jacob,
  both horse and chariot lie still.
⁷You alone are to be feared.
  Who can stand before you when you
  are angry?
⁸From heaven you pronounced
  judgment,
  and the land feared and was quiet—
⁹when you, O God, rose up to judge,
  to save all the afflicted of the land.
                        Selah
¹⁰Surely your wrath against men brings
  you praise,
  and the survivors of your wrath are
  restrained.ᵃ

¹¹Make vows to the Lᴏʀᴅ your God and
  fulfill them;
  let all the neighboring lands
  bring gifts to the One to be feared.
¹²He breaks the spirit of rulers;
  he is feared by the kings of the earth.

Psalm 77

For the director of music. For Jeduthun. Of Asaph.
A psalm.

¹I cried out to God for help;
  I cried out to God to hear me.

²When I was in distress, I sought the
  Lord;
  at night I stretched out untiring
  hands
  and my soul refused to be
  comforted.

³I remembered you, O God, and I
  groaned;
  I mused, and my spirit grew faint.
                        Selah
⁴You kept my eyes from closing;
  I was too troubled to speak.
⁵I thought about the former days,
  the years of long ago;
⁶I remembered my songs in the night.
  My heart mused and my spirit
  inquired:

⁷"Will the Lord reject forever?
  Will he never show his favor again?
⁸Has his unfailing love vanished forever?
  Has his promise failed for all time?
⁹Has God forgotten to be merciful?
  Has he in anger withheld his
  compassion?"   *Selah*

¹⁰Then I thought, "To this I will appeal:
  the years of the right hand of the
  Most High."
¹¹I will remember the deeds of the Lᴏʀᴅ;
  yes, I will remember your miracles of
  long ago.
¹²I will meditate on all your works
  and consider all your mighty deeds.

¹³Your ways, O God, are holy.
  What god is so great as our God?
¹⁴You are the God who performs
  miracles;
  you display your power among the
  peoples.
¹⁵With your mighty arm you redeemed
  your people,
  the descendants of Jacob and Joseph.
                        Selah

¹⁶The waters saw you, O God,
  the waters saw you and writhed;
  the very depths were convulsed.
¹⁷The clouds poured down water,
  the skies resounded with thunder;
  your arrows flashed back and forth.
¹⁸Your thunder was heard in the
  whirlwind,
  your lightning lit up the world;
  the earth trembled and quaked.
¹⁹Your path led through the sea,
  your way through the mighty waters,

ᵃ10 Or *Surely the wrath of men brings you praise, /
and with the remainder of wrath you arm
yourself*

though your footprints were not
seen.

20 You led your people like a flock
by the hand of Moses and Aaron.

Psalm 78

A *maskil*[a] of Asaph.

1 O my people, hear my teaching;
listen to the words of my mouth.
2 I will open my mouth in parables,
I will utter hidden things, things
from of old—
3 what we have heard and known,
what our fathers have told us.
4 We will not hide them from their
children;
we will tell the next generation
the praiseworthy deeds of the LORD,
his power, and the wonders he has
done.
5 He decreed statutes for Jacob
and established the law in Israel,
which he commanded our forefathers
to teach their children,
6 so the next generation would know
them,
even the children yet to be born,
and they in turn would tell their
children.
7 Then they would put their trust in God
and would not forget his deeds
but would keep his commands.
8 They would not be like their
forefathers—
a stubborn and rebellious
generation,
whose hearts were not loyal to God,
whose spirits were not faithful to
him.
9 The men of Ephraim, though armed
with bows,
turned back on the day of battle;
10 they did not keep God's covenant
and refused to live by his law.
11 They forgot what he had done,
the wonders he had shown them.
12 He did miracles in the sight of their
fathers
in the land of Egypt, in the region of
Zoan.
13 He divided the sea and led them
through;
he made the water stand firm like a
wall.
14 He guided them with the cloud by day
and with light from the fire all night.

15 He split the rocks in the desert
and gave them water as abundant as
the seas;
16 he brought streams out of a rocky crag
and made water flow down like
rivers.
17 But they continued to sin against him,
rebelling in the desert against the
Most High.
18 They willfully put God to the test
by demanding the food they craved.
19 They spoke against God, saying,
"Can God spread a table in the
desert?
20 When he struck the rock, water gushed
out,
and streams flowed abundantly.
But can he also give us food?
Can he supply meat for his people?"
21 When the LORD heard them, he was
very angry;
his fire broke out against Jacob,
and his wrath rose against Israel,
22 for they did not believe in God
or trust in his deliverance.
23 Yet he gave a command to the skies
above
and opened the doors of the
heavens;
24 he rained down manna for the people
to eat,
he gave them the grain of heaven.
25 Men ate the bread of angels;
he sent them all the food they could
eat.
26 He let loose the east wind from the
heavens
and led forth the south wind by his
power.
27 He rained meat down on them like
dust,
flying birds like sand on the
seashore.
28 He made them come down inside their
camp,
all around their tents.
29 They ate till they had more than
enough,
for he had given them what they
craved.
30 But before they turned from the food
they craved,
even while it was still in their
mouths,
31 God's anger rose against them;
he put to death the sturdiest among
them,

[a]Title: Probably a literary or musical term

cutting down the young men of
Israel.
32 In spite of all this, they kept on sinning;
in spite of his wonders, they did not
believe.
33 So he ended their days in futility
and their years in terror.
34 Whenever God slew them, they would
seek him;
they eagerly turned to him again.
35 They remembered that God was their
Rock,
that God Most High was their
Redeemer.
36 But then they would flatter him with
their mouths,
lying to him with their tongues;
37 their hearts were not loyal to him,
they were not faithful to his
covenant.
38 Yet he was merciful;
he forgave their iniquities
and did not destroy them.
Time after time he restrained his anger
and did not stir up his full wrath.
39 He remembered that they were but
flesh,
a passing breeze that does not
return.
40 How often they rebelled against him in
the desert
and grieved him in the wasteland!
41 Again and again they put God to the
test;
they vexed the Holy One of Israel.
42 They did not remember his power—
the day he redeemed them from the
oppressor,
43 the day he displayed his miraculous
signs in Egypt,
his wonders in the region of Zoan.
44 He turned their rivers to blood;
they could not drink from their
streams.
45 He sent swarms of flies that devoured
them,
and frogs that devastated them.
46 He gave their crops to the grasshopper,
their produce to the locust.
47 He destroyed their vines with hail
and their sycamore-figs with sleet.
48 He gave over their cattle to the hail,
their livestock to bolts of lightning.
49 He unleashed against them his hot
anger,
his wrath, indignation and
hostility—
a band of destroying angels.
50 He prepared a path for his anger;

he did not spare them from death
but gave them over to the plague.
51 He struck down all the firstborn of
Egypt,
the firstfruits of manhood in the
tents of Ham.
52 But he brought his people out like a
flock;
he led them like sheep through the
desert.
53 He guided them safely, so they were
unafraid;
but the sea engulfed their enemies.
54 Thus he brought them to the border of
his holy land,
to the hill country his right hand had
taken.
55 He drove out nations before them
and allotted their lands to them as
an inheritance;
he settled the tribes of Israel in their
homes.
56 But they put God to the test
and rebelled against the Most High;
they did not keep his statutes.
57 Like their fathers they were disloyal
and faithless,
as unreliable as a faulty bow.
58 They angered him with their high
places;
they aroused his jealousy with their
idols.
59 When God heard them, he was very
angry;
he rejected Israel completely.
60 He abandoned the tabernacle of
Shiloh,
the tent he had set up among men.
61 He sent the ark of his might into
captivity,
his splendor into the hands of the
enemy.
62 He gave his people over to the sword;
he was very angry with his
inheritance.
63 Fire consumed their young men,
and their maidens had no wedding
songs;
64 their priests were put to the sword,
and their widows could not weep.
65 Then the Lord awoke as from sleep,
as a man wakes from the stupor of
wine.
66 He beat back his enemies;
he put them to everlasting shame.
67 Then he rejected the tents of Joseph,
he did not choose the tribe of
Ephraim;
68 but he chose the tribe of Judah,

Mount Zion, which he loved.
⁶⁹ He built his sanctuary like the heights,
    like the earth that he established
        forever.
⁷⁰ He chose David his servant
    and took him from the sheep pens;
⁷¹ from tending the sheep he brought
        him
    to be the shepherd of his people
        Jacob,
    of Israel his inheritance.
⁷² And David shepherded them with
        integrity of heart;
    with skillful hands he led them.

Psalm 79

A psalm of Asaph.

¹ O God, the nations have invaded your
        inheritance;
    they have defiled your holy temple,
    they have reduced Jerusalem to
        rubble.
² They have given the dead bodies of
        your servants
    as food to the birds of the air,
    the flesh of your saints to the beasts
        of the earth.
³ They have poured out blood like water
    all around Jerusalem,
    and there is no one to bury the dead.
⁴ We are objects of reproach to our
        neighbors,
    of scorn and derision to those
        around us.

⁵ How long, O LORD? Will you be angry
        forever?
    How long will your jealousy burn like
        fire?
⁶ Pour out your wrath on the nations
    that do not acknowledge you,
    on the kingdoms
    that do not call on your name;
⁷ for they have devoured Jacob
    and destroyed his homeland.
⁸ Do not hold against us the sins of the
        fathers;
    may your mercy come quickly to
        meet us,
    for we are in desperate need.

⁹ Help us, O God our Savior,
    for the glory of your name;
    deliver us and forgive our sins
    for your name's sake.
¹⁰ Why should the nations say,
    "Where is their God?"

Before our eyes, make known among
        the nations
    that you avenge the outpoured blood
        of your servants.
¹¹ May the groans of the prisoners come
        before you;
    by the strength of your arm
    preserve those condemned to die.

¹² Pay back into the laps of our neighbors
        seven times
    the reproach they have hurled at
        you, O Lord.
¹³ Then we your people, the sheep of your
        pasture,
    will praise you forever;
    from generation to generation
    we will recount your praise.

Psalm 80

For the director of music.
To the tune of, "The Lilies of the Covenant."
Of Asaph. A psalm.

¹ Hear us, O Shepherd of Israel,
    you who lead Joseph like a flock;
    you who sit enthroned between the
        cherubim, shine forth
²   before Ephraim, Benjamin and
        Manasseh.
    Awaken your might;
    come and save us.

³ Restore us, O God;
    make your face shine upon us,
    that we may be saved.

⁴ O LORD God Almighty,
    how long will your anger smolder
    against the prayers of your people?
⁵ You have fed them with the bread of
        tears;
    you have made them drink tears by
        the bowlful.
⁶ You have made us a source of
        contention to our neighbors,
    and our enemies mock us.

⁷ Restore us, O God Almighty;
    make your face shine upon us,
    that we may be saved.

⁸ You brought a vine out of Egypt;
    you drove out the nations and
        planted it.
⁹ You cleared the ground for it,
    and it took root and filled the land.
¹⁰ The mountains were covered with its
        shade,
    the mighty cedars with its branches.

11 It sent out its boughs to the Sea,[a]
  its shoots as far as the River.[b]

12 Why have you broken down its walls
  so that all who pass by pick its
    grapes?
13 Boars from the forest ravage it
  and the creatures of the field feed on
    it.
14 Return to us, O God Almighty!
  Look down from heaven and see!
Watch over this vine,
15   the root your right hand has planted,
  the son[c] you have raised up for
    yourself.

16 Your vine is cut down, it is burned with
    fire;
  at your rebuke your people perish.
17 Let your hand rest on the man at your
    right hand,
  the son of man you have raised up
    for yourself.
18 Then we will not turn away from you;
  revive us, and we will call on your
    name.

19 Restore us, O LORD God Almighty;
  make your face shine upon us,
  that we may be saved.

Psalm 81

For the director of music.
According to *gittith*.[d] Of Asaph.

1 Sing for joy to God our strength;
  shout aloud to the God of Jacob!
2 Begin the music, strike the tambourine,
  play the melodious harp and lyre.

3 Sound the ram's horn at the New
    Moon,
  and when the moon is full, on the
    day of our Feast;
4 this is a decree for Israel,
  an ordinance of the God of Jacob.
5 He established it as a statute for Joseph
  when he went out against Egypt,
  where we heard a language we did
    not understand.[e]

6 He says, "I removed the burden from
    their shoulders;
  their hands were set free from the
    basket.
7 In your distress you called and I
    rescued you,
  I answered you out of a
    thundercloud;
  I tested you at the waters of
    Meribah.   *Selah*

8 "Hear, O my people, and I will warn
    you—
  if you would but listen to me,
    O Israel!
9 You shall have no foreign god among
    you;
  you shall not bow down to an alien
    god.
10 I am the LORD your God,
  who brought you up out of Egypt.
  Open wide your mouth and I will
    fill it.

11 "But my people would not listen to me;
  Israel would not submit to me.
12 So I gave them over to their stubborn
    hearts
  to follow their own devices.

13 "If my people would but listen to me,
  if Israel would follow my ways,
14 how quickly would I subdue their
    enemies
  and turn my hand against their foes!
15 Those who hate the LORD would cringe
    before him,
  and their punishment would last
    forever.
16 But you would be fed with the finest of
    wheat;
  with honey from the rock I would
    satisfy you."

Psalm 82

A psalm of Asaph.

1 God presides in the great assembly;
  he gives judgment among the
    "gods":

2 "How long will you[f] defend the unjust
  and show partiality to the wicked?
                    Selah
3 Defend the cause of the weak and
    fatherless;
  maintain the rights of the poor and
    oppressed.
4 Rescue the weak and needy;
  deliver them from the hand of the
    wicked.

5 "They know nothing, they understand
    nothing.
  They walk about in darkness;
  all the foundations of the earth are
    shaken.

---

[a]11 Probably the Mediterranean   [b]11 That is, the
Euphrates   [c]15 Or *branch*   [d]Title: Probably a
musical term   [e]5 Or *I and we heard a voice we had
not known*   [f]2 The Hebrew is plural.

6 "I said, 'You are "gods";
  you are all sons of the Most High.'
7 But you will die like mere men;
  you will fall like every other ruler."

8 Rise up, O God, judge the earth,
  for all the nations are your
    inheritance.

Psalm 83

A song. A psalm of Asaph.

1 O God, do not keep silent;
  be not quiet, O God, be not still.
2 See how your enemies are astir,
  how your foes rear their heads.
3 With cunning they conspire against
    your people;
  they plot against those you cherish.
4 "Come," they say, "let us destroy them
    as a nation,
  that the name of Israel be
    remembered no more."

5 With one mind they plot together;
  they form an alliance against you—
6 the tents of Edom and the
    Ishmaelites,
  of Moab and the Hagrites,
7 Gebal,a Ammon and Amalek,
  Philistia, with the people of Tyre.
8 Even Assyria has joined them
  to lend strength to the descendants
    of Lot.   Selah

9 Do to them as you did to Midian,
  as you did to Sisera and Jabin at the
    river Kishon,
10 who perished at Endor
  and became like refuse on the
    ground.
11 Make their nobles like Oreb and Zeeb,
  all their princes like Zebah and
    Zalmunna,
12 who said, "Let us take possession
  of the pasturelands of God."

13 Make them like tumbleweed, O my
    God,
  like chaff before the wind.
14 As fire consumes the forest
  or a flame sets the mountains
    ablaze,
15 so pursue them with your tempest
  and terrify them with your storm.
16 Cover their faces with shame
  so that men will seek your name,
    O LORD.

17 May they ever be ashamed and
    dismayed;

may they perish in disgrace.
18 Let them know that you, whose name is
    the LORD—
  that you alone are the Most High
    over all the earth.

Psalm 84

For the director of music. According to *gittith.*b
Of the Sons of Korah. A psalm.

1 How lovely is your dwelling place,
  O LORD Almighty!
2 My soul yearns, even faints,
  for the courts of the LORD;
my heart and my flesh cry out
  for the living God.

3 Even the sparrow has found a home,
  and the swallow a nest for herself,
  where she may have her young—
a place near your altar,
  O LORD Almighty, my King and my
    God.
4 Blessed are those who dwell in your
    house;
  they are ever praising you.   *Selah*

5 Blessed are those whose strength is in
    you,
  who have set their hearts on
    pilgrimage.
6 As they pass through the Valley of Baca,
  they make it a place of springs;
  the autumn rains also cover it with
    pools.c
7 They go from strength to strength,
  till each appears before God in
    Zion.

8 Hear my prayer, O LORD God Almighty;
  listen to me, O God of Jacob.   *Selah*
9 Look upon our shield,d O God;
  look with favor on your anointed
    one.

10 Better is one day in your courts
  than a thousand elsewhere;
I would rather be a doorkeeper in the
    house of my God
  than dwell in the tents of the
    wicked.
11 For the LORD God is a sun and shield;
  the LORD bestows favor and honor;
no good thing does he withhold
  from those whose walk is blameless.

12 O LORD Almighty,
  blessed is the man who trusts in you.

a7 That is, Byblos   bTitle: Probably a musical
term   c6 Or *blessings*   d9 Or *sovereign*

Psalm 85

For the director of music.
Of the Sons of Korah. A psalm.

[1] You showed favor to your land, O LORD;
  you restored the fortunes of Jacob.
[2] You forgave the iniquity of your people
  and covered all their sins.   *Selah*
[3] You set aside all your wrath
  and turned from your fierce anger.

[4] Restore us again, O God our Savior,
  and put away your displeasure
    toward us.
[5] Will you be angry with us forever?
  Will you prolong your anger through
    all generations?
[6] Will you not revive us again,
  that your people may rejoice in you?
[7] Show us your unfailing love, O LORD,
  and grant us your salvation.

[8] I will listen to what God the LORD will
    say;
  he promises peace to his people, his
    saints—
  but let them not return to folly.
[9] Surely his salvation is near those who
    fear him,
  that his glory may dwell in our land.

[10] Love and faithfulness meet together;
  righteousness and peace kiss each
    other.
[11] Faithfulness springs forth from the
    earth,
  and righteousness looks down from
    heaven.
[12] The LORD will indeed give what is good,
  and our land will yield its harvest.
[13] Righteousness goes before him
  and prepares the way for his steps.

Psalm 86

A prayer of David.

[1] Hear, O LORD, and answer me,
  for I am poor and needy.
[2] Guard my life, for I am devoted to you.
  You are my God; save your servant
  who trusts in you.
[3] Have mercy on me, O Lord,
  for I call to you all day long.
[4] Bring joy to your servant,
  for to you, O Lord,
  I lift up my soul.
[5] You are forgiving and good, O Lord,
  abounding in love to all who call to
    you.

[6] Hear my prayer, O LORD;
  listen to my cry for mercy.
[7] In the day of my trouble I will call to
    you,
  for you will answer me.

[8] Among the gods there is none like you,
    O Lord;
  no deeds can compare with yours.
[9] All the nations you have made
  will come and worship before you,
    O Lord;
  they will bring glory to your name.
[10] For you are great and do marvelous
    deeds;
  you alone are God.

[11] Teach me your way, O LORD,
  and I will walk in your truth;
  give me an undivided heart,
  that I may fear your name.
[12] I will praise you, O Lord my God, with
    all my heart;
  I will glorify your name forever.
[13] For great is your love toward me;
  you have delivered me from the
    depths of the grave.[a]

[14] The arrogant are attacking me, O God;
  a band of ruthless men seeks my
    life—
  men without regard for you.
[15] But you, O Lord, are a compassionate
    and gracious God,
  slow to anger, abounding in love and
    faithfulness.
[16] Turn to me and have mercy on me;
  grant your strength to your servant
  and save the son of your
    maidservant.[b]
[17] Give me a sign of your goodness,
  that my enemies may see it and be
    put to shame,
  for you, O LORD, have helped me and
    comforted me.

Psalm 87

Of the Sons of Korah. A psalm. A song.

[1] He has set his foundation on the holy
    mountain;
[2]   the LORD loves the gates of Zion
  more than all the dwellings of Jacob.
[3] Glorious things are said of you,
  O city of God: *Selah*
[4] "I will record Rahab[c] and Babylon
  among those who acknowledge me—

---

[a]13 Hebrew *Sheol*   [b]16 Or *save your faithful son*
[c]4 A poetic name for Egypt

Philistia too, and Tyre, along with
  Cush[a]—
and will say, 'This[b] one was born in
  Zion.' "

⁵ Indeed, of Zion it will be said,
  "This one and that one were born in
    her,
  and the Most High himself will
    establish her."
⁶ The LORD will write in the register of
    the peoples:
  "This one was born in Zion."   *Selah*
⁷ As they make music they will sing,
  "All my fountains are in you."

Psalm 88

A song. A psalm of the Sons of Korah.
For the director of music.
According to *mahalath leannoth.*[c]
A *maskil*[d] of Heman the Ezrahite.

¹ O LORD, the God who saves me,
  day and night I cry out before you.
² May my prayer come before you;
  turn your ear to my cry.

³ For my soul is full of trouble
  and my life draws near the grave.[e]
⁴ I am counted among those who go
    down to the pit;
  I am like a man without strength.
⁵ I am set apart with the dead,
  like the slain who lie in the grave,
whom you remember no more,
  who are cut off from your care.

⁶ You have put me in the lowest pit,
  in the darkest depths.
⁷ Your wrath lies heavily upon me;
  you have overwhelmed me with all
    your waves.   *Selah*
⁸ You have taken from me my closest
    friends
  and have made me repulsive to
    them.
I am confined and cannot escape;
⁹ my eyes are dim with grief.

I call to you, O LORD, every day;
  I spread out my hands to you.
¹⁰ Do you show your wonders to the dead?
  Do those who are dead rise up and
    praise you?   *Selah*
¹¹ Is your love declared in the grave,
  your faithfulness in Destruction[f]?
¹² Are your wonders known in the place
    of darkness,
  or your righteous deeds in the land
    of oblivion?

¹³ But I cry to you for help, O LORD;
  in the morning my prayer comes
    before you.
¹⁴ Why, O LORD, do you reject me
  and hide your face from me?
¹⁵ From my youth I have been afflicted
    and close to death;
  I have suffered your terrors and am
    in despair.
¹⁶ Your wrath has swept over me;
  your terrors have destroyed me.
¹⁷ All day long they surround me like a
    flood;
  they have completely engulfed me.
¹⁸ You have taken my companions and
    loved ones from me;
  the darkness is my closest friend.

Psalm 89

A *maskil*[d] of Ethan the Ezrahite.

¹ I will sing of the LORD's great love
    forever;
  with my mouth I will make your
    faithfulness known through all
    generations.
² I will declare that your love stands firm
    forever,
  that you established your
    faithfulness in heaven itself.

³ You said, "I have made a covenant with
    my chosen one,
  I have sworn to David my servant,
⁴ 'I will establish your line forever
  and make your throne firm through
    all generations.' "   *Selah*

⁵ The heavens praise your wonders,
    O LORD,
  your faithfulness too, in the
    assembly of the holy ones.
⁶ For who in the skies above can
    compare with the LORD?
  Who is like the LORD among the
    heavenly beings?
⁷ In the council of the holy ones God is
    greatly feared;
  he is more awesome than all who
    surround him.
⁸ O LORD God Almighty, who is like you?
  You are mighty, O LORD, and your
    faithfulness surrounds you.

*a4 That is, the upper Nile region   b4 Or "O Rahab
and Babylon, / Philistia, Tyre and Cush, / I will
record concerning those who acknowledge me: /
'This   cTitle: Possibly a tune, "The Suffering of
Affliction"   dTitle: Probably a literary or musical
term   e3 Hebrew Sheol   f11 Hebrew Abaddon*

⁹You rule over the surging sea;
   when its waves mount up, you still
      them.
¹⁰You crushed Rahab like one of the slain;
   with your strong arm you scattered
      your enemies.
¹¹The heavens are yours, and yours also
      the earth;
   you founded the world and all that is
      in it.
¹²You created the north and the south;
   Tabor and Hermon sing for joy at
      your name.
¹³Your arm is endued with power;
   your hand is strong, your right hand
      exalted.

¹⁴Righteousness and justice are the
      foundation of your throne;
   love and faithfulness go before you.
¹⁵Blessed are those who have learned to
      acclaim you,
   who walk in the light of your
      presence, O LORD.
¹⁶They rejoice in your name all day long;
   they exult in your righteousness.
¹⁷For you are their glory and strength,
   and by your favor you exalt our
      horn.ᵃ
¹⁸Indeed, our shieldᵇ belongs to the
      LORD,
   our king to the Holy One of Israel.

¹⁹Once you spoke in a vision,
   to your faithful people you said:
   "I have bestowed strength on a warrior;
   I have exalted a young man from
      among the people.
²⁰I have found David my servant;
   with my sacred oil I have anointed
      him.
²¹My hand will sustain him;
   surely my arm will strengthen him.
²²No enemy will subject him to tribute;
   no wicked man will oppress him.
²³I will crush his foes before him
   and strike down his adversaries.
²⁴My faithful love will be with him,
   and through my name his hornᶜ will
      be exalted.
²⁵I will set his hand over the sea,
   his right hand over the rivers.
²⁶He will call out to me, 'You are my
      Father,
   my God, the Rock my Savior.'
²⁷I will also appoint him my firstborn,
   the most exalted of the kings of the
      earth.
²⁸I will maintain my love to him forever,
   and my covenant with him will never
      fail.

²⁹I will establish his line forever,
   his throne as long as the heavens
      endure.

³⁰"If his sons forsake my law
   and do not follow my statutes,
³¹if they violate my decrees
   and fail to keep my commands,
³²I will punish their sin with the rod,
   their iniquity with flogging;
³³but I will not take my love from him,
   nor will I ever betray my faithfulness.
³⁴I will not violate my covenant
   or alter what my lips have uttered.
³⁵Once for all, I have sworn by my
      holiness—
   and I will not lie to David—
³⁶that his line will continue forever
   and his throne endure before me like
      the sun;
³⁷it will be established forever like the
      moon,
   the faithful witness in the sky." Selah

³⁸But you have rejected, you have
      spurned,
   you have been very angry with your
      anointed one.
³⁹You have renounced the covenant with
      your servant
   and have defiled his crown in the
      dust.
⁴⁰You have broken through all his walls
   and reduced his strongholds to
      ruins.
⁴¹All who pass by have plundered him;
   he has become the scorn of his
      neighbors.
⁴²You have exalted the right hand of his
      foes;
   you have made all his enemies
      rejoice.
⁴³You have turned back the edge of his
      sword
   and have not supported him in
      battle.
⁴⁴You have put an end to his splendor
   and cast his throne to the ground.
⁴⁵You have cut short the days of his
      youth;
   you have covered him with a mantle
      of shame.   Selah

⁴⁶How long, O LORD? Will you hide
      yourself forever?
   How long will your wrath burn like
      fire?
⁴⁷Remember how fleeting is my life.

ᵃ17 Horn here symbolizes strong one.   ᵇ18 Or
sovereign   ᶜ24 Horn here symbolizes strength.

For what futility you have created all
    men!
[48] What man can live and not see death,
    or save himself from the power of the
    grave[a]?   *Selah*
[49] O Lord, where is your former great love,
    which in your faithfulness you swore
    to David?
[50] Remember, Lord, how your servant
    has[b] been mocked,
    how I bear in my heart the taunts of
    all the nations,
[51] the taunts with which your enemies
    have mocked, O LORD,
    with which they have mocked every
    step of your anointed one.

[52] Praise be to the LORD forever!
    Amen and Amen.

BOOK IV

Psalms 90–106

Psalm 90

A prayer of Moses the man of God.

[1] Lord, you have been our dwelling place
    throughout all generations.
[2] Before the mountains were born
    or you brought forth the earth and
    the world,
    from everlasting to everlasting you
    are God.
[3] You turn men back to dust,
    saying, "Return to dust, O sons of
    men."
[4] For a thousand years in your sight
    are like a day that has just gone by,
    or like a watch in the night.
[5] You sweep men away in the sleep of
    death;
    they are like the new grass of the
    morning—
[6] though in the morning it springs up
    new,
    by evening it is dry and withered.
[7] We are consumed by your anger
    and terrified by your indignation.
[8] You have set our iniquities before you,
    our secret sins in the light of your
    presence.
[9] All our days pass away under your
    wrath;
    we finish our years with a moan.
[10] The length of our days is seventy
    years—
    or eighty, if we have the strength;

yet their span[c] is but trouble and
    sorrow,
    for they quickly pass, and we fly
    away.
[11] Who knows the power of your anger?
    For your wrath is as great as the fear
    that is due you.
[12] Teach us to number our days aright,
    that we may gain a heart of wisdom.
[13] Relent, O LORD! How long will it be?
    Have compassion on your servants.
[14] Satisfy us in the morning with your
    unfailing love,
    that we may sing for joy and be glad
    all our days.
[15] Make us glad for as many days as you
    have afflicted us,
    for as many years as we have seen
    trouble.
[16] May your deeds be shown to your
    servants,
    your splendor to their children.
[17] May the favor[d] of the Lord our God rest
    upon us;
    establish the work of our hands for
    us—
    yes, establish the work of our hands.

Psalm 91

[1] He who dwells in the shelter of the
    Most High
    will rest in the shadow of the
    Almighty.[e]
[2] I will say[f] of the LORD, "He is my refuge
    and my fortress,
    my God, in whom I trust."
[3] Surely he will save you from the
    fowler's snare
    and from the deadly pestilence.
[4] He will cover you with his feathers,
    and under his wings you will find
    refuge;
    his faithfulness will be your shield
    and rampart.
[5] You will not fear the terror of night,
    nor the arrow that flies by day,
[6] nor the pestilence that stalks in the
    darkness,
    nor the plague that destroys at
    midday.
[7] A thousand may fall at your side,
    ten thousand at your right hand,
    but it will not come near you.

---

*a48 Hebrew Sheol   b50 Or your servants have
c10 Or yet the best of them   d17 Or beauty
e1 Hebrew Shaddai   f2 Or He says*

8 You will only observe with your eyes
    and see the punishment of the
    wicked.
9 If you make the Most High your
    dwelling—
    even the LORD, who is my refuge—
10 then no harm will befall you,
    no disaster will come near your tent.
11 For he will command his angels
    concerning you
    to guard you in all your ways;
12 they will lift you up in their hands,
    so that you will not strike your foot
    against a stone.

13 You will tread upon the lion and the
    cobra;
    you will trample the great lion and
    the serpent.
14 "Because he loves me," says the LORD,
    "I will rescue him;
    I will protect him, for he
    acknowledges my name.
15 He will call upon me, and I will answer
    him;
    I will be with him in trouble,
    I will deliver him and honor him.
16 With long life will I satisfy him
    and show him my salvation."

Do You Have Something in a Three-Bedroom, Two-and-a-Half Bath?

DAILY INSIGHT

THURSDAY

Passage:
Psalm 91:9–16

Verses:
Psalm 91:9,10

As far as I'm concerned, the traditional wedding ceremony should give the bride and groom a chance to clear the air regarding vacation preferences. "Blanche, do you promise to love Harold, even though he only wants to sit on a beach and read a novel on vacation? And Harold, do you promise before God and these witnesses to walk through a flea market with Blanche when you're on vacation? And do you promise not to gripe, mumble, or shuffle your feet when you're doing it?"

For the first several years of our marriage, summer vacations were a definite sticking point. Because we hadn't discussed expectations, Bobbie and I would come home from a "week off" frustrated and angry. It took several years before I admitted to Bobbie that sightseeing was not high on my things-I-really-enjoy-doing-on-vacation list.

One such summer we were castle-hopping in Europe. Granted, these structures were unbelievable—for example, Mad King Ludwig's bedroom had draperies made out of weasel pelts—but once you've seen a castle, you've essentially seen a castle.

Standing in the courtyard of one particular palace and studying the intricate stonework, something dawned on me. These structures weren't just fancy homes,

they were *fortresses*, built to protect a king or nobleman's family and a few hundred of his closest friends in time of war. They were as important to these people as Fort Sumter was to General Lee. In dragging myself from tour bus to tour bus, I had completely overlooked the fact that these incredible buildings saved families during hostile times. The thick walls, towering turrets, and drawbridges were more than mere decoration.

You and I live in a war zone. The internal and external forces that seek to take us and our families hostage are as real today as the warriors who once tried to besiege those European castles. But God has built up our homes to be like fortresses; he protects them with his own foot soldiers.

When we overlook the fact that we are living in a war zone, our appreciation for God's loving protection diminishes in value. But when we truly pay attention to this fact, then our hearts should be filled with gratitude for his wings, his eyes, his hands, and his tireless angels standing guard.

You need a fortress. Without one, you and your family don't stand a chance. Your present dwelling will never do.

For your next devotional reading, go to page 645.

Psalm 92

A psalm. A song. For the Sabbath day.

[1] It is good to praise the LORD
and make music to your name,
O Most High,
[2] to proclaim your love in the morning
and your faithfulness at night,
[3] to the music of the ten-stringed lyre
and the melody of the harp.

[4] For you make me glad by your deeds,
O LORD;
I sing for joy at the works of your
hands.
[5] How great are your works, O LORD,
how profound your thoughts!
[6] The senseless man does not know,
fools do not understand,
[7] that though the wicked spring up like
grass
and all evildoers flourish,
they will be forever destroyed.

[8] But you, O LORD, are exalted forever.

[9] For surely your enemies, O LORD,
surely your enemies will perish;
all evildoers will be scattered.
[10] You have exalted my horn[a] like that of a
wild ox;
fine oils have been poured upon me.
[11] My eyes have seen the defeat of my
adversaries;
my ears have heard the rout of my
wicked foes.

[12] The righteous will flourish like a palm
tree,
they will grow like a cedar of
Lebanon;
[13] planted in the house of the LORD,
they will flourish in the courts of our
God.
[14] They will still bear fruit in old age,
they will stay fresh and green,
[15] proclaiming, "The LORD is upright;
he is my Rock, and there is no
wickedness in him."

Psalm 93

[1] The LORD reigns, he is robed in
majesty;
the LORD is robed in majesty
and is armed with strength.
The world is firmly established;
it cannot be moved.
[2] Your throne was established long ago;
you are from all eternity.

[3] The seas have lifted up, O LORD,
the seas have lifted up their voice;
the seas have lifted up their
pounding waves.
[4] Mightier than the thunder of the great
waters,
mightier than the breakers of the
sea—
the LORD on high is mighty.

[a] 10 Horn here symbolizes strength.

HEY DAD
Do I have a guardian angel?

Text: Psalm 91:11–12

Angels have many different job descriptions. We know that they rejoice when someone becomes a Christian (Luke 15:10), they make announcements for God (1 Thessalonians 4:16), and God uses them to serve us and to minister to us (Hebrews 1:14). And while the Bible doesn't tell us that every person has his or her own guardian angel, it *does* say that for those who make the Lord our refuge, "He will command his angels concerning you to guard you in all your ways; they will lift you up in their hands, so that you will not strike your foot against a stone" (Psalm 91:11–12).

The word "guard" in this verse is translated from the Hebrew word *shâmar*, which means "to protect, to attend to, and to hedge about as with thorns." Imagine that. God actually commands his angels to surround us like a hedge of thorns. Not only are these heavenly sentinels keeping us from running into danger, but, like a wall of thorns, they're also keeping danger from running into us!

For a complete listing of Questions Kids Ask, turn to page 1435.

⁵Your statutes stand firm;
  holiness adorns your house
  for endless days, O LORD.

Psalm 94

¹O LORD, the God who avenges,
  O God who avenges, shine forth.
²Rise up, O Judge of the earth;
  pay back to the proud what they
    deserve.
³How long will the wicked, O LORD,
  how long will the wicked be jubilant?

⁴They pour out arrogant words;
  all the evildoers are full of boasting.
⁵They crush your people, O LORD;
  they oppress your inheritance.
⁶They slay the widow and the alien;
  they murder the fatherless.
⁷They say, "The LORD does not see;
  the God of Jacob pays no heed."

⁸Take heed, you senseless ones among
    the people;
  you fools, when will you become
    wise?
⁹Does he who implanted the ear not
    hear?
  Does he who formed the eye not see?
¹⁰Does he who disciplines nations not
    punish?
  Does he who teaches man lack
    knowledge?
¹¹The LORD knows the thoughts of man;
  he knows that they are futile.

¹²Blessed is the man you discipline,
    O LORD,
  the man you teach from your law;
¹³you grant him relief from days of
    trouble,
  till a pit is dug for the wicked.
¹⁴For the LORD will not reject his people;
  he will never forsake his inheritance.
¹⁵Judgment will again be founded on
    righteousness,
  and all the upright in heart will
    follow it.

¹⁶Who will rise up for me against the
    wicked?
  Who will take a stand for me against
    evildoers?
¹⁷Unless the LORD had given me help,
  I would soon have dwelt in the
    silence of death.
¹⁸When I said, "My foot is slipping,"
  your love, O LORD, supported me.
¹⁹When anxiety was great within me,
  your consolation brought joy to my
    soul.

²⁰Can a corrupt throne be allied with
    you—
  one that brings on misery by its
    decrees?
²¹They band together against the
    righteous
  and condemn the innocent to death.
²²But the LORD has become my fortress,
  and my God the rock in whom I take
    refuge.
²³He will repay them for their sins
  and destroy them for their
    wickedness;
  the LORD our God will destroy them.

Psalm 95

¹Come, let us sing for joy to the LORD;
  let us shout aloud to the Rock of our
    salvation.
²Let us come before him with
    thanksgiving
  and extol him with music and song.

³For the LORD is the great God,
  the great King above all gods.
⁴In his hand are the depths of the earth,
  and the mountain peaks belong to
    him.
⁵The sea is his, for he made it,
  and his hands formed the dry land.

⁶Come, let us bow down in worship,
  let us kneel before the LORD our
    Maker;
⁷for he is our God
  and we are the people of his pasture,
  the flock under his care.

Today, if you hear his voice,
⁸ do not harden your hearts as you did
    at Meribah,ᵃ
  as you did that day at Massahᵇ in the
    desert,
⁹where your fathers tested and tried me,
  though they had seen what I did.
¹⁰For forty years I was angry with that
    generation;
  I said, "They are a people whose
    hearts go astray,
  and they have not known my ways."
¹¹So I declared on oath in my anger,
  "They shall never enter my rest."

Psalm 96

¹Sing to the LORD a new song;
  sing to the LORD, all the earth.

ᵃ8 Meribah means quarreling. ᵇ8 Massah means testing.

² Sing to the LORD, praise his name;
  proclaim his salvation day after day.
³ Declare his glory among the nations,
  his marvelous deeds among all
  peoples.

⁴ For great is the LORD and most worthy
  of praise;
  he is to be feared above all gods.
⁵ For all the gods of the nations are idols,
  but the LORD made the heavens.
⁶ Splendor and majesty are before him;
  strength and glory are in his
  sanctuary.

⁷ Ascribe to the LORD, O families of
  nations,
  ascribe to the LORD glory and
  strength.
⁸ Ascribe to the LORD the glory due his
  name;
  bring an offering and come into his
  courts.
⁹ Worship the LORD in the splendor of
  his*ª holiness;
  tremble before him, all the earth.

¹⁰ Say among the nations, "The LORD
  reigns."
  The world is firmly established, it
  cannot be moved;
  he will judge the peoples with equity.
¹¹ Let the heavens rejoice, let the earth be
  glad;
  let the sea resound, and all that is in
  it;
¹² let the fields be jubilant, and
  everything in them.
  Then all the trees of the forest will sing
  for joy;
¹³ they will sing before the LORD, for he
  comes,
  he comes to judge the earth.
  He will judge the world in
  righteousness
  and the peoples in his truth.

Psalm 97

¹ The LORD reigns, let the earth be glad;
  let the distant shores rejoice.
² Clouds and thick darkness surround
  him;
  righteousness and justice are the
  foundation of his throne.
³ Fire goes before him
  and consumes his foes on every side.
⁴ His lightning lights up the world;
  the earth sees and trembles.
⁵ The mountains melt like wax before
  the LORD,

before the Lord of all the earth.
⁶ The heavens proclaim his
  righteousness,
  and all the peoples see his glory.

⁷ All who worship images are put to
  shame,
  those who boast in idols—
  worship him, all you gods!

⁸ Zion hears and rejoices
  and the villages of Judah are glad
  because of your judgments, O LORD.
⁹ For you, O LORD, are the Most High
  over all the earth;
  you are exalted far above all gods.

¹⁰ Let those who love the LORD hate evil,
  for he guards the lives of his faithful
  ones
  and delivers them from the hand of
  the wicked.
¹¹ Light is shed upon the righteous
  and joy on the upright in heart.
¹² Rejoice in the LORD, you who are
  righteous,
  and praise his holy name.

Psalm 98

A psalm.

¹ Sing to the LORD a new song,
  for he has done marvelous things;
  his right hand and his holy arm
  have worked salvation for him.
² The LORD has made his salvation
  known
  and revealed his righteousness to the
  nations.
³ He has remembered his love
  and his faithfulness to the house of
  Israel;
  all the ends of the earth have seen
  the salvation of our God.

⁴ Shout for joy to the LORD, all the earth,
  burst into jubilant song with music;
⁵ make music to the LORD with the harp,
  with the harp and the sound of
  singing,
⁶ with trumpets and the blast of the
  ram's horn—
  shout for joy before the LORD, the
  King.

⁷ Let the sea resound, and everything in
  it,
  the world, and all who live in it.
⁸ Let the rivers clap their hands,

ª9 Or LORD with the splendor of

let the mountains sing together for
      joy;
⁹ let them sing before the LORD,
      for he comes to judge the earth.
   He will judge the world in
      righteousness
   and the peoples with equity.

Psalm 99

¹ The LORD reigns,
      let the nations tremble;
   he sits enthroned between the
      cherubim,

let the earth shake.
² Great is the LORD in Zion;
      he is exalted over all the nations.
³ Let them praise your great and
      awesome name—
      he is holy.

⁴ The King is mighty, he loves justice—
      you have established equity;
   in Jacob you have done
      what is just and right.
⁵ Exalt the LORD our God
      and worship at his footstool;
      he is holy.

Thank You

DAILY INSIGHT

FRIDAY

Passage:
Psalm 100

Verse:
Psalm 100:5

Over the next few minutes you and I are going to watch a short highlight video of your life. It won't take too long, and I promise it will be worth it.

From the moment you drew your first breath, someone took care of your every need. The nurse in the hospital brought you to your mother. Can you see her tenderly holding you while your eyes tried to focus on this loving person with the familiar voice? "I'll always love you," she probably said, and for the next dozen years or so, she proved it. She took care of your bumps, your fears and your broken heart. But because you were only a kid, you didn't say "thank you" as often as you should have. Now you're a grown man and it's time to get caught up. "Thank you, Mother."

Then you soon came to know a person with a lower voice, a man who loved you as much as your mother did. It felt different when he held you—sometimes awkward, sometimes a little rambunctious—but you knew his were loving arms, too. This man worked hard to provide for you. And, when he could, he'd take you to the back yard and throw you a ball. You really should have thanked him more, but you were busy getting tall and strong. Now you're a man and time's a-wasting. "Thank you, Dad."

Or perhaps teachers, coaches, ministers, neighbors, grandparents, uncles and aunts took time to care for you. They listened to your stories and dared to challenge you with what you could become. They were models of patience, discipline, fairness, courage and caring. You didn't thank them for their example that often, and now it's time to make that right. "Thanks, each one of you."

Today you have a family of your very own. You have children who want to make you proud. You're actually one of the luckiest men you know. But because you're awfully busy, you're a little behind in your expressions of gratitude. "Thank you, precious family."

Then there's your heavenly Father. He knew you and he loved you before there were galaxies, oceans, or trees. He was there when you were conceived, and he gave you what you needed to grow. He loved you as a boy—unlovely as you were. He gave you people to care for you, talents, strength and wisdom. And today, decades later, he still calls you his own. Are you current with your gratitude to him?

One day a man sat down and wrote the words to this profound psalm. Someone must have reminded him that he was overdue on his expressions of thanksgiving. So, in just a few verses, he made it right.

Are you a little behind on your "thank you's"? Today would be a great day to get caught up.

For your next devotional reading, go to page 645.

[6] Moses and Aaron were among his
     priests,
   Samuel was among those who called
     on his name;
   they called on the LORD
   and he answered them.
[7] He spoke to them from the pillar of
     cloud;
   they kept his statutes and the
     decrees he gave them.

[8] O LORD our God,
   you answered them;
   you were to Israel[a] a forgiving God,
     though you punished their
     misdeeds.[b]
[9] Exalt the LORD our God
   and worship at his holy mountain,
   for the LORD our God is holy.

Psalm 100

A psalm. For giving thanks.

[1] Shout for joy to the LORD, all the earth.
[2]   Worship the LORD with gladness;
   come before him with joyful songs.
[3] Know that the LORD is God.
   It is he who made us, and we are his[c];
   we are his people, the sheep of his
     pasture.

[4] Enter his gates with thanksgiving
   and his courts with praise;
   give thanks to him and praise his
     name.
[5] For the LORD is good and his love
     endures forever;
   his faithfulness continues through all
     generations.

Psalm 101

Of David. A psalm.

[1] I will sing of your love and justice;
   to you, O LORD, I will sing praise.
[2] I will be careful to lead a blameless
     life—
   when will you come to me?

   I will walk in my house
   with blameless heart.
[3] I will set before my eyes
   no vile thing.

   The deeds of faithless men I hate;
   they will not cling to me.
[4] Men of perverse heart shall be far from
     me;
   I will have nothing to do with evil.

[5] Whoever slanders his neighbor in
     secret,
   him will I put to silence;
   whoever has haughty eyes and a proud
     heart,
   him will I not endure.

[6] My eyes will be on the faithful in the
     land,
   that they may dwell with me;
   he whose walk is blameless
   will minister to me.

[7] No one who practices deceit
   will dwell in my house;
   no one who speaks falsely
   will stand in my presence.

[8] Every morning I will put to silence
   all the wicked in the land;
   I will cut off every evildoer
   from the city of the LORD.

Psalm 102

A prayer of an afflicted man.
When he is faint and pours out
his lament before the LORD.

[1] Hear my prayer, O LORD;
   let my cry for help come to you.
[2] Do not hide your face from me
   when I am in distress.
   Turn your ear to me;
   when I call, answer me quickly.

[3] For my days vanish like smoke;
   my bones burn like glowing
     embers.
[4] My heart is blighted and withered like
     grass;
   I forget to eat my food.
[5] Because of my loud groaning
   I am reduced to skin and bones.
[6] I am like a desert owl,
   like an owl among the ruins.
[7] I lie awake; I have become
   like a bird alone on a roof.
[8] All day long my enemies taunt me;
   those who rail against me use my
     name as a curse.
[9] For I eat ashes as my food
   and mingle my drink with tears
[10] because of your great wrath,
   for you have taken me up and
     thrown me aside.
[11] My days are like the evening shadow;
   I wither away like grass.

---

[a]8 Hebrew *them*   [b]8 Or / *an avenger of the wrongs
done to them*   [c]3 Or *and not we ourselves*

¹²But you, O Lord sit enthroned
forever;
your renown endures through all
generations.
¹³You will arise and have compassion on
Zion,
for it is time to show favor to her;
the appointed time has come.
¹⁴For her stones are dear to your
servants;
her very dust moves them to pity.
¹⁵The nations will fear the name of the
Lord,
all the kings of the earth will revere
your glory.
¹⁶For the Lord will rebuild Zion
and appear in his glory.
¹⁷He will respond to the prayer of the
destitute;
he will not despise their plea.

¹⁸Let this be written for a future
generation,
that a people not yet created may
praise the Lord:
¹⁹"The Lord looked down from his
sanctuary on high,
from heaven he viewed the earth,

²⁰to hear the groans of the prisoners
and release those condemned to
death."
²¹So the name of the Lord will be
declared in Zion
and his praise in Jerusalem
²²when the peoples and the kingdoms
assemble to worship the Lord.

²³In the course of my life*ᵃ* he broke my
strength;
he cut short my days.
²⁴So I said:
"Do not take me away, O my God, in
the midst of my days;
your years go on through all
generations.
²⁵In the beginning you laid the
foundations of the earth,
and the heavens are the work of your
hands.
²⁶They will perish, but you remain;
they will all wear out like a
garment.
Like clothing you will change them
and they will be discarded.

ᵃ23 Or By his power

Stopping and Stooping
God, the Compassionate Father

*"As a father has compassion on his children,
so the Lord has compassion on those
who fear him"* (103:13).

DADS
IN THE
BIBLE

Text: Psalm 103

Have you ever tried to sympathize with a child's trouble or soothe a scuffed knee without squatting down and stooping to his or her level? Of course, such a thing is impossible. Unless a child sees the understanding on your face, and unless he or she sees it down on his or her level, that child won't be able to accept your comfort.

The psalmist David saw that God demonstrated this kind of care for his children. In this psalm, David called it "compassion." God the Father takes moments from his busy schedule—keeping the stars and planets on their charted courses, growing food for a hungry world, or raising up and bringing down world leaders—to stoop to our level and have compassion on his bumped and bruised children.

Jesus reinforced David's observation in the New Testament: "Are not two sparrows sold for a penny? Yet not one of them will fall to the ground apart from the will of your Father . . . So don't be afraid; you are worth more than many sparrows" (Matthew 10:29, 31).

You're a busy man. You've got places to go, people to see, deals to get done. But our busy heavenly Father, the Creator of the universe, has compassion. He's never too busy to stop, never too proud to stoop. It's a good thing, too. How else could we ever see his face?

Look carefully; this Father's got lots of love. He stops, then he stoops. I guess if he can do it, so can we.

For a complete listing of Dads in the Bible, turn to page 1434.

²⁷But you remain the same,
   and your years will never end.
²⁸The children of your servants will live
      in your presence;
   their descendants will be established
      before you."

Psalm 103

Of David.

¹Praise the LORD, O my soul;
   all my inmost being, praise his holy
      name.
²Praise the LORD, O my soul,
   and forget not all his benefits—
³who forgives all your sins
   and heals all your diseases,
⁴who redeems your life from the pit
   and crowns you with love and
      compassion,
⁵who satisfies your desires with good
      things
   so that your youth is renewed like
      the eagle's.

⁶The LORD works righteousness
   and justice for all the oppressed.

⁷He made known his ways to Moses,
   his deeds to the people of Israel:
⁸The LORD is compassionate and
      gracious,
   slow to anger, abounding in love.
⁹He will not always accuse,
   nor will he harbor his anger forever;
¹⁰he does not treat us as our sins deserve
   or repay us according to our
      iniquities.
¹¹For as high as the heavens are above
      the earth,
   so great is his love for those who fear
      him;
¹²as far as the east is from the west,
   so far has he removed our
      transgressions from us.
¹³As a father has compassion on his
      children,
   so the LORD has compassion on
      those who fear him;
¹⁴for he knows how we are formed,
   he remembers that we are dust.
¹⁵As for man, his days are like grass,
   he flourishes like a flower of the field;
¹⁶the wind blows over it and it is gone,
   and its place remembers it no more.
¹⁷But from everlasting to everlasting
   the LORD's love is with those who fear
      him,
   and his righteousness with their
      children's children—

¹⁸with those who keep his covenant
   and remember to obey his precepts.

¹⁹The LORD has established his throne in
      heaven,
   and his kingdom rules over all.

²⁰Praise the LORD, you his angels,
   you mighty ones who do his
      bidding,
   who obey his word.
²¹Praise the LORD, all his heavenly hosts,
   you his servants who do his will.
²²Praise the LORD, all his works
   everywhere in his dominion.

Praise the LORD, O my soul.

Psalm 104

¹Praise the LORD, O my soul.

O LORD my God, you are very great;
   you are clothed with splendor and
      majesty.
²He wraps himself in light as with a
      garment;
   he stretches out the heavens like a
      tent
³   and lays the beams of his upper
      chambers on their waters.
He makes the clouds his chariot
   and rides on the wings of the wind.
⁴He makes winds his messengers,ᵃ
   flames of fire his servants.

⁵He set the earth on its foundations;
   it can never be moved.
⁶You covered it with the deep as with a
      garment;
   the waters stood above the
      mountains.
⁷But at your rebuke the waters fled,
   at the sound of your thunder they
      took to flight;
⁸they flowed over the mountains,
   they went down into the valleys,
   to the place you assigned for them.
⁹You set a boundary they cannot cross;
   never again will they cover the earth.

¹⁰He makes springs pour water into the
      ravines;
   it flows between the mountains.
¹¹They give water to all the beasts of the
      field;
   the wild donkeys quench their thirst.
¹²The birds of the air nest by the waters;
   they sing among the branches.
¹³He waters the mountains from his
      upper chambers;

ᵃ4 Or *angels*

God's Advertisements Are Everywhere

Key Verse: *"Praise the LORD, O my soul, and forget not all his benefits."* Psalm 103:2

Text: Psalm 103:1–19 *(Dad or child reads the text.)*

QUIET TIMES WITH Dad

DAD READS: When a company wants to sell what they make or do, their people sit down and make lists of the things their products will do for people. If they make cars, they may decide to sell them based on the fact that their cars will help people be safe. If they make medicine, they may decide to advertise that sick people who use their products will feel better. If they make mouthwash, they may decide to tell people that their mouthwash will help people make more friends. These things—safety, feeling better, making friends—are called "benefits."

Child reads: When I watch advertisements on television I can tell that companies really want us to know that we will be happy if we use the things they make. We'll run faster and score more points if we wear their shoes, or we'll be smarter if we use their computers.

DAD READS: Did you know that God has benefits, too? It's true. We just read about some of them. He wants us to know that following him and loving him brings us good things.

Child reads: Here are some of God's benefits: He forgives our sins, he heals us, he saves us, he rewards us, he satisfies us, he is tender, he waits to get angry, and he is filled with love for you and me.

DAD READS: When I stop and think about it, God has "advertisements" everywhere. When we feel forgiven after we confess our sins, when we enjoy his creation, or when we feel loved by our family, we are enjoying God's good things—his benefits.

Child reads: Some people think that being a Christian is like doing homework or running laps—a lot of hard work and not a lot of fun. But the things we have read today tell us that knowing and loving God fills us with wonderful things. I need to remember to tell my friends all about God's benefits.

DAD READS: I need to remember this, too. I want my friends to know about God's benefits. Let me pray this prayer with you:

Our Father in heaven, thank you for your generous benefits. Thank you for forgiving, healing, and loving us. Help us to never forget that you put these gifts all around us. And help us to be so excited about your benefits that we want to tell our friends about you. We love you. In Jesus' name, *Amen.*

For your next devotional reading, go to page 653.

the earth is satisfied by the fruit of
his work.
¹⁴He makes grass grow for the cattle,
and plants for man to cultivate—
bringing forth food from the earth:
¹⁵wine that gladdens the heart of man,
oil to make his face shine,
and bread that sustains his heart.
¹⁶The trees of the LORD are well watered,
the cedars of Lebanon that he
planted.
¹⁷There the birds make their nests;
the stork has its home in the pine
trees.
¹⁸The high mountains belong to the wild
goats;
the crags are a refuge for the coneys.ᵃ

¹⁹The moon marks off the seasons,
and the sun knows when to go down.
²⁰You bring darkness, it becomes night,
and all the beasts of the forest
prowl.
²¹The lions roar for their prey
and seek their food from God.
²²The sun rises, and they steal away;
they return and lie down in their
dens.
²³Then man goes out to his work,
to his labor until evening.

²⁴How many are your works, O LORD!
In wisdom you made them all;
the earth is full of your creatures.
²⁵There is the sea, vast and spacious,

teeming with creatures beyond
number—
living things both large and small.
²⁶There the ships go to and fro,
and the leviathan, which you formed
to frolic there.

²⁷These all look to you
to give them their food at the proper
time.
²⁸When you give it to them,
they gather it up;
when you open your hand,
they are satisfied with good things.
²⁹When you hide your face,
they are terrified;
when you take away their breath,
they die and return to the dust.
³⁰When you send your Spirit,
they are created,
and you renew the face of the earth.

³¹May the glory of the LORD endure
forever;
may the LORD rejoice in his works—
³²he who looks at the earth, and it
trembles,
who touches the mountains, and
they smoke.

³³I will sing to the LORD all my life;
I will sing praise to my God as long
as I live.

ᵃ18 That is, the hyrax or rock badger

HEY DAD

How strong is God?

Text: Psalm 104:1–9

QUESTIONS KIDS ASK

This psalm gives us a picturesque answer to this question. In reviewing God's acts of creating and sustaining the universe, this psalmist leaves us breathless.

Who else could "stretch out the heavens like a tent"? The heavens are so vast, even our biggest and best telescopes can't see the end of them. They're huge! And God is so strong that he can take them by one end and spread them out like we might spread out a sheet when we're making our bed.

Who else could "wrap himself in light" like you might put on a bathrobe? God's clothes glitter with the stars of the heavens.

Who else could "set the earth on its foundations"? Imagine picking up a marble and placing it on a golf tee. This is a crude comparison, but to God, the earth is like a marble—it's tiny and lightweight. Think of something too heavy for you to lift by yourself—a piano, a car engine, a Sumo wrestler. Now think once more about God lifting the earth and setting it on its foundation.

God is immeasurably big and incalculably strong. But, thankfully, he also loves us more than we will ever know.

For a complete listing of Questions Kids Ask, turn to page 1435.

[34] May my meditation be pleasing to him,
as I rejoice in the LORD.
[35] But may sinners vanish from the earth
and the wicked be no more.

Praise the LORD, O my soul.

Praise the LORD.[a]

Psalm 105

[1] Give thanks to the LORD, call on his
name;
make known among the nations
what he has done.
[2] Sing to him, sing praise to him;
tell of all his wonderful acts.
[3] Glory in his holy name;
let the hearts of those who seek the
LORD rejoice.
[4] Look to the LORD and his strength;
seek his face always.

[5] Remember the wonders he has done,
his miracles, and the judgments he
pronounced,
[6] O descendants of Abraham his servant,
O sons of Jacob, his chosen ones.
[7] He is the LORD our God;
his judgments are in all the earth.

[8] He remembers his covenant forever,
the word he commanded, for a
thousand generations,
[9] the covenant he made with Abraham,
the oath he swore to Isaac.
[10] He confirmed it to Jacob as a decree,
to Israel as an everlasting covenant:
[11] "To you I will give the land of Canaan
as the portion you will inherit."

[12] When they were but few in number,
few indeed, and strangers in it,
[13] they wandered from nation to nation,
from one kingdom to another.
[14] He allowed no one to oppress them;
for their sake he rebuked kings:
[15] "Do not touch my anointed ones;
do my prophets no harm."

[16] He called down famine on the land
and destroyed all their supplies of
food;
[17] and he sent a man before them—
Joseph, sold as a slave.
[18] They bruised his feet with shackles,
his neck was put in irons,
[19] till what he foretold came to pass,
till the word of the LORD proved him
true.
[20] The king sent and released him,
the ruler of peoples set him free.
[21] He made him master of his household,

ruler over all he possessed,
[22] to instruct his princes as he pleased
and teach his elders wisdom.

[23] Then Israel entered Egypt;
Jacob lived as an alien in the land of
Ham.
[24] The LORD made his people very fruitful;
he made them too numerous for
their foes,
[25] whose hearts he turned to hate his
people,
to conspire against his servants.
[26] He sent Moses his servant,
and Aaron, whom he had chosen.
[27] They performed his miraculous signs
among them,
his wonders in the land of Ham.
[28] He sent darkness and made the land
dark—
for had they not rebelled against his
words?
[29] He turned their waters into blood,
causing their fish to die.
[30] Their land teemed with frogs,
which went up into the bedrooms of
their rulers.
[31] He spoke, and there came swarms of
flies,
and gnats throughout their country.
[32] He turned their rain into hail,
with lightning throughout their land;
[33] he struck down their vines and fig
trees
and shattered the trees of their
country.
[34] He spoke, and the locusts came,
grasshoppers without number;
[35] they ate up every green thing in their
land,
ate up the produce of their soil.
[36] Then he struck down all the firstborn
in their land,
the firstfruits of all their manhood.
[37] He brought out Israel, laden with silver
and gold,
and from among their tribes no one
faltered.
[38] Egypt was glad when they left,
because dread of Israel had fallen on
them.
[39] He spread out a cloud as a covering,
and a fire to give light at night.
[40] They asked, and he brought them
quail
and satisfied them with the bread of
heaven.

---

[a]35 Hebrew *Hallelu Yah*; in the Septuagint this line
stands at the beginning of Psalm 105.

⁴¹He opened the rock, and water gushed
      out;
   like a river it flowed in the desert.

⁴²For he remembered his holy promise
   given to his servant Abraham.
⁴³He brought out his people with
      rejoicing,
   his chosen ones with shouts of joy;
⁴⁴he gave them the lands of the nations,
   and they fell heir to what others had
      toiled for—
⁴⁵that they might keep his precepts
   and observe his laws.

Praise the LORD.ᵃ

Psalm 106

¹Praise the LORD.ᵇ

Give thanks to the LORD, for he is good;
   his love endures forever.
²Who can proclaim the mighty acts of
      the LORD
   or fully declare his praise?
³Blessed are they who maintain justice,
   who constantly do what is right.
⁴Remember me, O LORD, when you
      show favor to your people,
   come to my aid when you save them,
⁵that I may enjoy the prosperity of your
      chosen ones,
   that I may share in the joy of your
      nation
   and join your inheritance in giving
      praise.

⁶We have sinned, even as our fathers
      did;
   we have done wrong and acted
      wickedly.
⁷When our fathers were in Egypt,
   they gave no thought to your
      miracles;
   they did not remember your many
      kindnesses,
   and they rebelled by the sea, the Red
      Sea.ᶜ
⁸Yet he saved them for his name's sake,
   to make his mighty power known.
⁹He rebuked the Red Sea, and it dried up;
   he led them through the depths as
      through a desert.
¹⁰He saved them from the hand of the
      foe;
   from the hand of the enemy he
      redeemed them.
¹¹The waters covered their adversaries;
   not one of them survived.
¹²Then they believed his promises
   and sang his praise.

¹³But they soon forgot what he had done
   and did not wait for his counsel.
¹⁴In the desert they gave in to their
      craving;
   in the wasteland they put God to the
      test.
¹⁵So he gave them what they asked for,
   but sent a wasting disease upon
      them.

¹⁶In the camp they grew envious of
      Moses
   and of Aaron, who was consecrated
      to the LORD.
¹⁷The earth opened up and swallowed
      Dathan;
   it buried the company of Abiram.
¹⁸Fire blazed among their followers;
   a flame consumed the wicked.
¹⁹At Horeb they made a calf
   and worshiped an idol cast from
      metal.
²⁰They exchanged their Glory
   for an image of a bull, which eats
      grass.
²¹They forgot the God who saved them,
   who had done great things in Egypt,
²²miracles in the land of Ham
   and awesome deeds by the Red Sea.
²³So he said he would destroy them—
   had not Moses, his chosen one,
   stood in the breach before him
   to keep his wrath from destroying
      them.

²⁴Then they despised the pleasant land;
   they did not believe his promise.
²⁵They grumbled in their tents
   and did not obey the LORD.
²⁶So he swore to them with uplifted hand
   that he would make them fall in the
      desert,
²⁷make their descendants fall among the
      nations
   and scatter them throughout the
      lands.

²⁸They yoked themselves to the Baal of
      Peor
   and ate sacrifices offered to lifeless
      gods;
²⁹they provoked the LORD to anger by
      their wicked deeds,
   and a plague broke out among them.
³⁰But Phinehas stood up and intervened,
   and the plague was checked.

ᵃ45 Hebrew *Hallelu Yah*   ᵇ1 Hebrew *Hallelu Yah*;
also in verse 48   ᶜ7 Hebrew *Yam Suph*; that is, Sea
of Reeds; also in verses 9 and 22

³¹ This was credited to him as
righteousness
for endless generations to come.

³² By the waters of Meribah they angered
the LORD,
and trouble came to Moses because
of them;
³³ for they rebelled against the Spirit of
God,
and rash words came from Moses'
lips.*ᵃ*

³⁴ They did not destroy the peoples
as the LORD had commanded them,
³⁵ but they mingled with the nations
and adopted their customs.
³⁶ They worshiped their idols,
which became a snare to them.
³⁷ They sacrificed their sons
and their daughters to demons.
³⁸ They shed innocent blood,
the blood of their sons and
daughters,
whom they sacrificed to the idols of
Canaan,
and the land was desecrated by their
blood.
³⁹ They defiled themselves by what they
did;
by their deeds they prostituted
themselves.

⁴⁰ Therefore the LORD was angry with his
people
and abhorred his inheritance.
⁴¹ He handed them over to the nations,
and their foes ruled over them.
⁴² Their enemies oppressed them
and subjected them to their power.
⁴³ Many times he delivered them,
but they were bent on rebellion
and they wasted away in their sin.

⁴⁴ But he took note of their distress
when he heard their cry;
⁴⁵ for their sake he remembered his
covenant
and out of his great love he relented.
⁴⁶ He caused them to be pitied
by all who held them captive.

⁴⁷ Save us, O LORD our God,
and gather us from the nations,
that we may give thanks to your holy
name
and glory in your praise.

⁴⁸ Praise be to the LORD, the God of Israel,
from everlasting to everlasting.
Let all the people say, "Amen!"

Praise the LORD.

BOOK V

Psalms 107–150

Psalm 107

¹ Give thanks to the LORD, for he is good;
his love endures forever.
² Let the redeemed of the LORD say
this—
those he redeemed from the hand of
the foe,
³ those he gathered from the lands,
from east and west, from north and
south.*ᵇ*

⁴ Some wandered in desert wastelands,
finding no way to a city where they
could settle.
⁵ They were hungry and thirsty,
and their lives ebbed away.
⁶ Then they cried out to the LORD in their
trouble,
and he delivered them from their
distress.
⁷ He led them by a straight way
to a city where they could settle.
⁸ Let them give thanks to the LORD for
his unfailing love
and his wonderful deeds for men,
⁹ for he satisfies the thirsty
and fills the hungry with good
things.

¹⁰ Some sat in darkness and the deepest
gloom,
prisoners suffering in iron chains,
¹¹ for they had rebelled against the words
of God
and despised the counsel of the Most
High.
¹² So he subjected them to bitter labor;
they stumbled, and there was no one
to help.
¹³ Then they cried to the LORD in their
trouble,
and he saved them from their
distress.
¹⁴ He brought them out of darkness and
the deepest gloom
and broke away their chains.
¹⁵ Let them give thanks to the LORD for
his unfailing love
and his wonderful deeds for men,
¹⁶ for he breaks down gates of bronze
and cuts through bars of iron.

¹⁷ Some became fools through their
rebellious ways

---

*ᵃ33 Or against his spirit, / and rash words came
from his lips   ᵇ3 Hebrew north and the sea*

and suffered affliction because of
their iniquities.
¹⁸ They loathed all food
and drew near the gates of death.
¹⁹ Then they cried to the LORD in their
trouble,
and he saved them from their
distress.
²⁰ He sent forth his word and healed
them;
he rescued them from the grave.
²¹ Let them give thanks to the LORD for
his unfailing love
and his wonderful deeds for men.
²² Let them sacrifice thank offerings
and tell of his works with songs of
joy.

²³ Others went out on the sea in ships;
they were merchants on the mighty
waters.
²⁴ They saw the works of the LORD,
his wonderful deeds in the deep.
²⁵ For he spoke and stirred up a tempest
that lifted high the waves.
²⁶ They mounted up to the heavens and
went down to the depths;
in their peril their courage melted
away.
²⁷ They reeled and staggered like drunken
men;
they were at their wits' end.
²⁸ Then they cried out to the LORD in their
trouble,
and he brought them out of their
distress.
²⁹ He stilled the storm to a whisper;
the waves of the sea were hushed.
³⁰ They were glad when it grew calm,
and he guided them to their desired
haven.
³¹ Let them give thanks to the LORD for
his unfailing love
and his wonderful deeds for men.
³² Let them exalt him in the assembly of
the people
and praise him in the council of the
elders.

³³ He turned rivers into a desert,
flowing springs into thirsty ground,
³⁴ and fruitful land into a salt waste,
because of the wickedness of those
who lived there.
³⁵ He turned the desert into pools of
water
and the parched ground into flowing
springs;
³⁶ there he brought the hungry to live,
and they founded a city where they
could settle.

³⁷ They sowed fields and planted
vineyards
that yielded a fruitful harvest;
³⁸ he blessed them, and their numbers
greatly increased,
and he did not let their herds
diminish.

³⁹ Then their numbers decreased, and
they were humbled
by oppression, calamity and sorrow;
⁴⁰ he who pours contempt on nobles
made them wander in a trackless
waste.
⁴¹ But he lifted the needy out of their
affliction
and increased their families like
flocks.
⁴² The upright see and rejoice,
but all the wicked shut their mouths.

⁴³ Whoever is wise, let him heed these
things
and consider the great love of the
LORD.

Psalm 108

A song. A psalm of David.

¹ My heart is steadfast, O God;
I will sing and make music with all
my soul.
² Awake, harp and lyre!
I will awaken the dawn.
³ I will praise you, O LORD, among the
nations;
I will sing of you among the peoples.
⁴ For great is your love, higher than the
heavens;
your faithfulness reaches to the
skies.
⁵ Be exalted, O God, above the heavens,
and let your glory be over all the
earth.

⁶ Save us and help us with your right
hand,
that those you love may be
delivered.
⁷ God has spoken from his sanctuary:
"In triumph I will parcel out
Shechem
and measure off the Valley of
Succoth.
⁸ Gilead is mine, Manasseh is mine;
Ephraim is my helmet,
Judah my scepter.
⁹ Moab is my washbasin,
upon Edom I toss my sandal;
over Philistia I shout in triumph."

[10] Who will bring me to the fortified city?
  Who will lead me to Edom?
[11] Is it not you, O God, you who have
      rejected us
  and no longer go out with our
      armies?
[12] Give us aid against the enemy,
  for the help of man is worthless.
[13] With God we will gain the victory,
  and he will trample down our
      enemies.

Psalm 109

For the director of music.
Of David. A psalm.

[1] O God, whom I praise,
  do not remain silent,
[2] for wicked and deceitful men
  have opened their mouths against
      me;
  they have spoken against me with
      lying tongues.
[3] With words of hatred they surround me;
  they attack me without cause.
[4] In return for my friendship they accuse
      me,
  but I am a man of prayer.
[5] They repay me evil for good,
  and hatred for my friendship.

[6] Appoint[a] an evil man[b] to oppose him;
  let an accuser[c] stand at his right
      hand.
[7] When he is tried, let him be found
      guilty,
  and may his prayers condemn him.
[8] May his days be few;
  may another take his place of
      leadership.
[9] May his children be fatherless
  and his wife a widow.
[10] May his children be wandering
      beggars;
  may they be driven[d] from their
      ruined homes.
[11] May a creditor seize all he has;
  may strangers plunder the fruits of
      his labor.
[12] May no one extend kindness to him
  or take pity on his fatherless
      children.
[13] May his descendants be cut off,
  their names blotted out from the
      next generation.
[14] May the iniquity of his fathers be
      remembered before the LORD;
  may the sin of his mother never be
      blotted out.

[15] May their sins always remain before
      the LORD,
  that he may cut off the memory of
      them from the earth.
[16] For he never thought of doing a
      kindness,
  but hounded to death the poor
  and the needy and the
      brokenhearted.
[17] He loved to pronounce a curse—
  may it[e] come on him;
  he found no pleasure in blessing—
  may it be[f] far from him.
[18] He wore cursing as his garment;
  it entered into his body like water,
  into his bones like oil.
[19] May it be like a cloak wrapped about
      him,
  like a belt tied forever around him.
[20] May this be the LORD's payment to my
      accusers,
  to those who speak evil of me.

[21] But you, O Sovereign LORD,
  deal well with me for your name's
      sake;
  out of the goodness of your love,
      deliver me.
[22] For I am poor and needy,
  and my heart is wounded within me.
[23] I fade away like an evening shadow;
  I am shaken off like a locust.
[24] My knees give way from fasting;
  my body is thin and gaunt.
[25] I am an object of scorn to my accusers;
  when they see me, they shake their
      heads.

[26] Help me, O LORD my God;
  save me in accordance with your
      love.
[27] Let them know that it is your hand,
  that you, O LORD, have done it.
[28] They may curse, but you will bless;
  when they attack they will be put to
      shame,
  but your servant will rejoice.
[29] My accusers will be clothed with
      disgrace
  and wrapped in shame as in a cloak.

[30] With my mouth I will greatly extol the
      LORD;
  in the great throng I will praise him.
[31] For he stands at the right hand of
      the needy one,

---

a6 Or They say: "Appoint (with quotation marks at
the end of verse 19)   *b6 Or the Evil One   c6 Or let
Satan   d10 Septuagint; Hebrew sought   e17 Or
curse, / and it has   f17 Or blessing, / and it is*

to save his life from those who
condemn him.

Psalm 110

Of David. A psalm.

¹ The LORD says to my Lord:
  "Sit at my right hand
until I make your enemies
  a footstool for your feet."

² The LORD will extend your mighty
    scepter from Zion;
  you will rule in the midst of your
    enemies.
³ Your troops will be willing
  on your day of battle.
Arrayed in holy majesty,
  from the womb of the dawn
  you will receive the dew of your
    youth.ᵃ

⁴ The LORD has sworn
  and will not change his mind:
"You are a priest forever,
  in the order of Melchizedek."

⁵ The Lord is at your right hand;
  he will crush kings on the day of his
    wrath.
⁶ He will judge the nations, heaping up
    the dead
  and crushing the rulers of the whole
    earth.
⁷ He will drink from a brook beside the
    wayᵇ;
  therefore he will lift up his head.

Psalm 111ᶜ

¹ Praise the LORD.ᵈ

I will extol the LORD with all my heart
  in the council of the upright and in
    the assembly.

² Great are the works of the LORD;
  they are pondered by all who delight
    in them.
³ Glorious and majestic are his deeds,
  and his righteousness endures
    forever.
⁴ He has caused his wonders to be
    remembered;
  the LORD is gracious and
    compassionate.
⁵ He provides food for those who fear
    him;
  he remembers his covenant forever.
⁶ He has shown his people the power of
    his works,

giving them the lands of other
    nations.
⁷ The works of his hands are faithful and
    just;
  all his precepts are trustworthy.
⁸ They are steadfast for ever and ever,
  done in faithfulness and
    uprightness.
⁹ He provided redemption for his people;
  he ordained his covenant forever—
  holy and awesome is his name.

¹⁰ The fear of the LORD is the beginning of
    wisdom;
  all who follow his precepts have
    good understanding.
To him belongs eternal praise.

Psalm 112ᶜ

¹ Praise the LORD.ᵈ

Blessed is the man who fears the
    LORD,
  who finds great delight in his
    commands.

² His children will be mighty in the
    land;
  the generation of the upright will be
    blessed.
³ Wealth and riches are in his house,
  and his righteousness endures
    forever.
⁴ Even in darkness light dawns for the
    upright,
  for the gracious and compassionate
    and righteous man.ᵉ
⁵ Good will come to him who is generous
    and lends freely,
  who conducts his affairs with justice.
⁶ Surely he will never be shaken;
  a righteous man will be remembered
    forever.
⁷ He will have no fear of bad news;
  his heart is steadfast, trusting in the
    LORD.
⁸ His heart is secure, he will have no fear;
  in the end he will look in triumph on
    his foes.
⁹ He has scattered abroad his gifts to the
    poor,
  his righteousness endures forever;
  his hornᶠ will be lifted high in honor.

ᵃ3 Or / *your young men will come to you like the
dew*   ᵇ7 Or / *The One who grants succession will
set him in authority*   ᶜThis psalm is an acrostic
poem, the lines of which begin with the successive
letters of the Hebrew alphabet.   ᵈ1 Hebrew
Hallelu Yah   ᵉ4 Or / *for the Lord is gracious and
compassionate and righteous*   ᶠ9 *Horn* here
symbolizes dignity.

¹⁰The wicked man will see and be vexed,
   he will gnash his teeth and waste
      away;
   the longings of the wicked will come
      to nothing.

Psalm 113

¹Praise the LORD.ᵃ

Praise, O servants of the LORD,
   praise the name of the LORD.

²Let the name of the LORD be praised,
   both now and forevermore.
³From the rising of the sun to the place
      where it sets,
   the name of the LORD is to be
      praised.

⁴The LORD is exalted over all the nations,
   his glory above the heavens.
⁵Who is like the LORD our God,

ᵃ1 Hebrew *Hallelu Yah*; also in verse 9

It's What You Stand For

DAILY INSIGHT

MONDAY

Passage:
Psalm 112:1–9

Verse:
Psalm 112:1

Every successful chief executive officer knows something very important about his or her company: It's not what the company builds or does that's truly important; it's what the company *stands for* that really counts.

For example, Wal-Mart doesn't just sell stuff at a discount, they want to "exceed their customers' expectations by offering the best prices on top-quality products in the most hospitable retail environment." Marriott doesn't just give you a clean place to sleep when you're on the road, they want to "provide a full range of lodging choices—from luxury accommodations to comfortable, economy hotels—for both the business and pleasure traveler." And in addition to vacuuming all the cash from your pockets when you step off the plane in Orlando, Disney wants "to make people happy as they experience the magic of Disney."

Because you know these companies and have used their products and services, these why-we-do-what-we-do statements come as no surprise to you. And if you actually worked for one of these companies, these statements would be indelibly seared into your consciousness.

You're a dad ... your family's CEO. Everyone knows what you did to get this title, and most people know what a man has to do to maintain his good standing as a dad: be faithful to his wife; provide food, shelter and clothing for his family; and be a person of exemplary character. But why do

you do these things? What motivates you? What should people expect from your family because of your leadership? How would they summarize your "family business?" And what would your own family say?

Today's psalm may be the most important one you will ever read. It opens with an incredibly succinct challenge to your heart and motivation as your family's CEO: "Blessed is the man who fears [that is, honors and obeys] the LORD, who finds great delight in his commands."

Then what follows is a wonderful list of promises to your family ... your children will be mighty, each generation will be truly happy, and in God's economy, they will be wealthy. There are even some assurances for you: light in the darkness as a reward for being gracious, compassionate and righteous; good things in return for generosity; a steadfast heart; security; honor. These are things that every man wants.

What the CEO's of Wal-Mart, Marriott, and Disney do every day flows directly from what they believe about themselves—from the "why" of their existence. Similarly, what happens in our families will be a direct result of the things we stand for.

Today's challenge to you cannot be forgotten: Honor and obey God and delight in his ways. Tell your family that this is what motivates you. Then watch how it impacts everything around your house.

For your next devotional reading, go to page 656.

the One who sits enthroned on high,
⁶who stoops down to look
on the heavens and the earth?

⁷He raises the poor from the dust
and lifts the needy from the ash heap;
⁸he seats them with princes,
with the princes of their people.
⁹He settles the barren woman in her
home
as a happy mother of children.

Praise the LORD.

Psalm 114

¹When Israel came out of Egypt,
the house of Jacob from a people of
foreign tongue,
²Judah became God's sanctuary,
Israel his dominion.

³The sea looked and fled,
the Jordan turned back;
⁴the mountains skipped like rams,
the hills like lambs.

⁵Why was it, O sea, that you fled,
O Jordan, that you turned back,
⁶you mountains, that you skipped like
rams,
you hills, like lambs?

⁷Tremble, O earth, at the presence of the
Lord,
at the presence of the God of Jacob,
⁸who turned the rock into a pool,
the hard rock into springs of water.

Psalm 115

¹Not to us, O LORD, not to us
but to your name be the glory,
because of your love and
faithfulness.

²Why do the nations say,
"Where is their God?"
³Our God is in heaven;
he does whatever pleases him.
⁴But their idols are silver and gold,
made by the hands of men.
⁵They have mouths, but cannot speak,
eyes, but they cannot see;
⁶they have ears, but cannot hear,
noses, but they cannot smell;
⁷they have hands, but cannot feel,
feet, but they cannot walk;
nor can they utter a sound with their
throats.
⁸Those who make them will be like
them,
and so will all who trust in them.

⁹O house of Israel, trust in the LORD—
he is their help and shield.
¹⁰O house of Aaron, trust in the LORD—
he is their help and shield.
¹¹You who fear him, trust in the LORD—
he is their help and shield.

¹²The LORD remembers us and will bless
us:
He will bless the house of Israel,
he will bless the house of Aaron,
¹³he will bless those who fear the LORD—
small and great alike.

¹⁴May the LORD make you increase,
both you and your children.
¹⁵May you be blessed by the LORD,
the Maker of heaven and earth.

¹⁶The highest heavens belong to the
LORD,
but the earth he has given to man.
¹⁷It is not the dead who praise the LORD,
those who go down to silence;
¹⁸it is we who extol the LORD,
both now and forevermore.

Praise the LORD.ᵃ

Psalm 116

¹I love the LORD, for he heard my voice;
he heard my cry for mercy.
²Because he turned his ear to me,
I will call on him as long as I live.

³The cords of death entangled me,
the anguish of the graveᵇ came upon
me;
I was overcome by trouble and
sorrow.
⁴Then I called on the name of the LORD:
"O LORD, save me!"

⁵The LORD is gracious and righteous;
our God is full of compassion.
⁶The LORD protects the simplehearted;
when I was in great need, he saved
me.

⁷Be at rest once more, O my soul,
for the LORD has been good to you.

⁸For you, O LORD, have delivered my
soul from death,
my eyes from tears,
my feet from stumbling,
⁹that I may walk before the LORD
in the land of the living.
¹⁰I believed; thereforeᶜ I said,
"I am greatly afflicted."

ᵃ18 Hebrew *Hallelu Yah*   ᵇ3 Hebrew *Sheol*   ᶜ10 Or
believed even when

¹¹ And in my dismay I said,
   "All men are liars."

¹² How can I repay the LORD
   for all his goodness to me?
¹³ I will lift up the cup of salvation
   and call on the name of the LORD.
¹⁴ I will fulfill my vows to the LORD
   in the presence of all his people.

¹⁵ Precious in the sight of the LORD
   is the death of his saints.
¹⁶ O LORD, truly I am your servant;
   I am your servant, the son of your
      maidservant^a;
   you have freed me from my chains.

¹⁷ I will sacrifice a thank offering to you
   and call on the name of the LORD.
¹⁸ I will fulfill my vows to the LORD
   in the presence of all his people,
¹⁹ in the courts of the house of the
      LORD—
   in your midst, O Jerusalem.

   Praise the LORD.^b

Psalm 117

¹ Praise the LORD, all you nations;
   extol him, all you peoples.
² For great is his love toward us,
   and the faithfulness of the LORD
      endures forever.

   Praise the LORD.^b

Psalm 118

¹ Give thanks to the LORD, for he is good;
   his love endures forever.

² Let Israel say:
   "His love endures forever."
³ Let the house of Aaron say:
   "His love endures forever."
⁴ Let those who fear the LORD say:
   "His love endures forever."

⁵ In my anguish I cried to the LORD,
   and he answered by setting me free.
⁶ The LORD is with me; I will not be
      afraid.
   What can man do to me?
⁷ The LORD is with me; he is my helper.
   I will look in triumph on my
      enemies.

⁸ It is better to take refuge in the LORD
   than to trust in man.
⁹ It is better to take refuge in the LORD
   than to trust in princes.

¹⁰ All the nations surrounded me,
   but in the name of the LORD I cut
      them off.
¹¹ They surrounded me on every side,
   but in the name of the LORD I cut
      them off.
¹² They swarmed around me like bees,
   but they died out as quickly as
      burning thorns;
   in the name of the LORD I cut them
      off.

¹³ I was pushed back and about to fall,
   but the LORD helped me.
¹⁴ The LORD is my strength and my song;
   he has become my salvation.

¹⁵ Shouts of joy and victory
   resound in the tents of the righteous:
   "The LORD's right hand has done
      mighty things!
¹⁶   The LORD's right hand is lifted high;
   the LORD's right hand has done
      mighty things!"

¹⁷ I will not die but live,
   and will proclaim what the LORD has
      done.
¹⁸ The LORD has chastened me severely,
   but he has not given me over to
      death.

¹⁹ Open for me the gates of
      righteousness;
   I will enter and give thanks to the
      LORD.
²⁰ This is the gate of the LORD
   through which the righteous may
      enter.
²¹ I will give you thanks, for you answered
      me;
   you have become my salvation.

²² The stone the builders rejected
   has become the capstone;
²³ the LORD has done this,
   and it is marvelous in our eyes.
²⁴ This is the day the LORD has made;
   let us rejoice and be glad in it.

²⁵ O LORD, save us;
   O LORD, grant us success.
²⁶ Blessed is he who comes in the name of
      the LORD.
   From the house of the LORD we bless
      you.^c
²⁷ The LORD is God,
   and he has made his light shine
      upon us.

^a16 Or *servant, your faithful son*   ^b19,2 Hebrew
Hallelu Yah   ^c26 The Hebrew is plural.

With boughs in hand, join in the festal
     procession
   up*a* to the horns of the altar.

28 You are my God, and I will give you
     thanks;
   you are my God, and I will exalt you.

29 Give thanks to the LORD, for he is good;
   his love endures forever.

Psalm 119*b*

א Aleph

1 Blessed are they whose ways are
     blameless,

who walk according to the law of the
     LORD.
2 Blessed are they who keep his statutes
   and seek him with all their heart.
3 They do nothing wrong;
   they walk in his ways.
4 You have laid down precepts
   that are to be fully obeyed.
5 Oh, that my ways were steadfast
   in obeying your decrees!
6 Then I would not be put to shame

*a27 Or Bind the festal sacrifice with ropes / and
take it   b This psalm is an acrostic poem; the verses
of each stanza begin with the same letter of the
Hebrew alphabet.*

Biology and Your Bible

Next to the dictionary, my high school biology text was the biggest book I had ever seen. I'll never forget the first time I sat down at the kitchen table and thumbed through it. The book's pages seemed so ominous. I remember being filled with dread at the thought of having to study the whole thing.

However, much to my surprise, over the next few days of sitting in Mr. Dusek's class, I began to enjoy the subject. In a couple of weeks, I found myself actually looking forward to fifth period—complete with the unmistakable smell of formaldehyde. By Halloween, I was in love with biology. I even announced to my parents that I might become a doctor.

Over the next several months, my once-intimidating biology book became my favorite text. Not only did I not *dread* it, I could hardly wait to pore over the information it contained. Why the transformation? The answer is simple. I had decided to make a life of the subject, and I couldn't afford to miss anything the book had for me.

In the same way, the Bible is a fairly ominous volume. Many men are filled with dread at the thought of having to read or—perish the thought—study its pages. But just as soon as these men decide to be Christ-followers, the Bible becomes their

DAILY INSIGHT

TUESDAY

Passage:
Psalm 119:9–11,
105,133
Verse:
Psalm 119:11

most beloved text. It contains the words they have chosen to live by. A deliberate decision to use the book as a guide for life changes everything.

The verses you read today ought to be all the motivation you need to turn this sizable and once-threatening volume into one of your favorites. If you have a sin problem—and we all do—God's Word is our greatest protection. Tucking the Scriptures into your heart keeps you from sin. If you have a problem seeing your everyday life from a spiritual vantage point, this book will give you a new perspective on everything. And if you need direction, God's Spirit promises to provide it for you.

The difference between this average and sometimes bored sophomore in high school and a tenacious student of the book was simply a conscious decision to become what the text taught. And my love for the subject continues to this day.

Do you want God's words to jump off these pages? Then make the same decision I made about biology sitting in Mr. Dusek's class. "God, I want to be your man. I want victory over sin. I want eyes to see where I am. And I want direction for tomorrow." This will change everything.

For your next devotional reading, go to page 663.

when I consider all your commands.
⁷I will praise you with an upright heart
  as I learn your righteous laws.
⁸I will obey your decrees;
  do not utterly forsake me.

ב Beth

⁹How can a young man keep his way
    pure?
  By living according to your word.
¹⁰I seek you with all my heart;
  do not let me stray from your
    commands.
¹¹I have hidden your word in my heart
  that I might not sin against you.
¹²Praise be to you, O LORD;
  teach me your decrees.
¹³With my lips I recount
  all the laws that come from your
    mouth.
¹⁴I rejoice in following your statutes
  as one rejoices in great riches.
¹⁵I meditate on your precepts
  and consider your ways.
¹⁶I delight in your decrees;
  I will not neglect your word.

ג Gimel

¹⁷Do good to your servant, and I will live;
  I will obey your word.
¹⁸Open my eyes that I may see
  wonderful things in your law.
¹⁹I am a stranger on earth;
  do not hide your commands from
    me.
²⁰My soul is consumed with longing
  for your laws at all times.
²¹You rebuke the arrogant, who are
    cursed
  and who stray from your commands.
²²Remove from me scorn and contempt,
  for I keep your statutes.
²³Though rulers sit together and slander
    me,
  your servant will meditate on your
    decrees.
²⁴Your statutes are my delight;
  they are my counselors.

ד Daleth

²⁵I am laid low in the dust;
  preserve my life according to your
    word.
²⁶I recounted my ways and you answered
    me;
  teach me your decrees.
²⁷Let me understand the teaching of your
    precepts;
  then I will meditate on your
    wonders.

²⁸My soul is weary with sorrow;
  strengthen me according to your
    word.
²⁹Keep me from deceitful ways;
  be gracious to me through your law.
³⁰I have chosen the way of truth;
  I have set my heart on your laws.
³¹I hold fast to your statutes, O LORD;
  do not let me be put to shame.
³²I run in the path of your commands,
  for you have set my heart free.

ה He

³³Teach me, O LORD, to follow your
    decrees;
  then I will keep them to the end.
³⁴Give me understanding, and I will keep
    your law
  and obey it with all my heart.
³⁵Direct me in the path of your
    commands,
  for there I find delight.
³⁶Turn my heart toward your statutes
  and not toward selfish gain.
³⁷Turn my eyes away from worthless
    things;
  preserve my life according to your
    word.ᵃ
³⁸Fulfill your promise to your servant,
  so that you may be feared.
³⁹Take away the disgrace I dread,
  for your laws are good.
⁴⁰How I long for your precepts!
  Preserve my life in your
    righteousness.

ו Waw

⁴¹May your unfailing love come to me,
    O LORD,
  your salvation according to your
    promise;
⁴²then I will answer the one who taunts
    me,
  for I trust in your word.
⁴³Do not snatch the word of truth from
    my mouth,
  for I have put my hope in your laws.
⁴⁴I will always obey your law,
  for ever and ever.
⁴⁵I will walk about in freedom,
  for I have sought out your precepts.
⁴⁶I will speak of your statutes before
    kings
  and will not be put to shame,
⁴⁷for I delight in your commands
  because I love them.

ᵃ37 Two manuscripts of the Masoretic Text and
Dead Sea Scrolls; most manuscripts of the
Masoretic Text *life in your way*

⁴⁸ I lift up my hands to^a your commands,
    which I love,
  and I meditate on your decrees.

ז   Zayin

⁴⁹ Remember your word to your servant,
    for you have given me hope.
⁵⁰ My comfort in my suffering is this:
    Your promise preserves my life.
⁵¹ The arrogant mock me without
    restraint,
  but I do not turn from your law.
⁵² I remember your ancient laws, O LORD,
    and I find comfort in them.
⁵³ Indignation grips me because of the
    wicked,
  who have forsaken your law.
⁵⁴ Your decrees are the theme of my song
    wherever I lodge.
⁵⁵ In the night I remember your name,
    O LORD,
  and I will keep your law.
⁵⁶ This has been my practice:
    I obey your precepts.

ח   Heth

⁵⁷ You are my portion, O LORD;
    I have promised to obey your words.
⁵⁸ I have sought your face with all my
    heart;
  be gracious to me according to your
    promise.
⁵⁹ I have considered my ways
    and have turned my steps to your
    statutes.
⁶⁰ I will hasten and not delay
    to obey your commands.
⁶¹ Though the wicked bind me with
    ropes,
  I will not forget your law.
⁶² At midnight I rise to give you thanks
    for your righteous laws.
⁶³ I am a friend to all who fear you,
    to all who follow your precepts.
⁶⁴ The earth is filled with your love,
    O LORD;
  teach me your decrees.

ט   Teth

⁶⁵ Do good to your servant
    according to your word, O LORD.
⁶⁶ Teach me knowledge and good
    judgment,
  for I believe in your commands.
⁶⁷ Before I was afflicted I went astray,
    but now I obey your word.
⁶⁸ You are good, and what you do is good;
    teach me your decrees.
⁶⁹ Though the arrogant have smeared me
    with lies,

  I keep your precepts with all my
    heart.
⁷⁰ Their hearts are callous and unfeeling,
    but I delight in your law.
⁷¹ It was good for me to be afflicted
    so that I might learn your decrees.
⁷² The law from your mouth is more
    precious to me
  than thousands of pieces of silver
    and gold.

י   Yodh

⁷³ Your hands made me and formed me;
    give me understanding to learn your
    commands.
⁷⁴ May those who fear you rejoice when
    they see me,
  for I have put my hope in your word.
⁷⁵ I know, O LORD, that your laws are
    righteous,
  and in faithfulness you have afflicted
    me.
⁷⁶ May your unfailing love be my comfort,
    according to your promise to your
    servant.
⁷⁷ Let your compassion come to me that I
    may live,
  for your law is my delight.
⁷⁸ May the arrogant be put to shame for
    wronging me without cause;
  but I will meditate on your precepts.
⁷⁹ May those who fear you turn to me,
    those who understand your statutes.
⁸⁰ May my heart be blameless toward
    your decrees,
  that I may not be put to shame.

כ   Kaph

⁸¹ My soul faints with longing for your
    salvation,
  but I have put my hope in your word.
⁸² My eyes fail, looking for your promise;
    I say, "When will you comfort me?"
⁸³ Though I am like a wineskin in the
    smoke,
  I do not forget your decrees.
⁸⁴ How long must your servant wait?
    When will you punish my
    persecutors?
⁸⁵ The arrogant dig pitfalls for me,
    contrary to your law.
⁸⁶ All your commands are trustworthy;
    help me, for men persecute me
    without cause.
⁸⁷ They almost wiped me from the earth,
    but I have not forsaken your
    precepts.
⁸⁸ Preserve my life according to your love,

---

^a48 Or *for*

and I will obey the statutes of your
   mouth.

ל   Lamedh

⁸⁹Your word, O LORD, is eternal;
   it stands firm in the heavens.
⁹⁰Your faithfulness continues through all
      generations;
   you established the earth, and it
      endures.
⁹¹Your laws endure to this day,
   for all things serve you.
⁹²If your law had not been my delight,
   I would have perished in my
      affliction.
⁹³I will never forget your precepts,
   for by them you have preserved my
      life.
⁹⁴Save me, for I am yours;
   I have sought out your precepts.
⁹⁵The wicked are waiting to destroy me,
   but I will ponder your statutes.
⁹⁶To all perfection I see a limit;
   but your commands are boundless.

מ   Mem

⁹⁷Oh, how I love your law!
   I meditate on it all day long.
⁹⁸Your commands make me wiser than
      my enemies,
   for they are ever with me.
⁹⁹I have more insight than all my
      teachers,
   for I meditate on your statutes.
¹⁰⁰I have more understanding than the
      elders,
   for I obey your precepts.
¹⁰¹I have kept my feet from every evil
      path
   so that I might obey your word.
¹⁰²I have not departed from your laws,
   for you yourself have taught me.
¹⁰³How sweet are your words to my taste,
   sweeter than honey to my mouth!
¹⁰⁴I gain understanding from your
      precepts;
   therefore I hate every wrong path.

נ   Nun

¹⁰⁵Your word is a lamp to my feet
   and a light for my path.
¹⁰⁶I have taken an oath and confirmed it,
   that I will follow your righteous laws.
¹⁰⁷I have suffered much;
   preserve my life, O LORD, according
      to your word.
¹⁰⁸Accept, O LORD, the willing praise of
      my mouth,
   and teach me your laws.

¹⁰⁹Though I constantly take my life in my
      hands,
   I will not forget your law.
¹¹⁰The wicked have set a snare for me,
   but I have not strayed from your
      precepts.
¹¹¹Your statutes are my heritage forever;
   they are the joy of my heart.
¹¹²My heart is set on keeping your
      decrees
   to the very end.

ס   Samekh

¹¹³I hate double-minded men,
   but I love your law.
¹¹⁴You are my refuge and my shield;
   I have put my hope in your word.
¹¹⁵Away from me, you evildoers,
   that I may keep the commands of my
      God!
¹¹⁶Sustain me according to your promise,
      and I will live;
   do not let my hopes be dashed.
¹¹⁷Uphold me, and I will be delivered;
   I will always have regard for your
      decrees.
¹¹⁸You reject all who stray from your
      decrees,
   for their deceitfulness is in vain.
¹¹⁹All the wicked of the earth you discard
      like dross;
   therefore I love your statutes.
¹²⁰My flesh trembles in fear of you;
   I stand in awe of your laws.

ע   Ayin

¹²¹I have done what is righteous and just;
   do not leave me to my oppressors.
¹²²Ensure your servant's well-being;
   let not the arrogant oppress me.
¹²³My eyes fail, looking for your salvation,
   looking for your righteous promise.
¹²⁴Deal with your servant according to
      your love
   and teach me your decrees.
¹²⁵I am your servant; give me
      discernment
   that I may understand your statutes.
¹²⁶It is time for you to act, O LORD;
   your law is being broken.
¹²⁷Because I love your commands
   more than gold, more than pure
      gold,
¹²⁸and because I consider all your
      precepts right,
   I hate every wrong path.

פ   Pe

¹²⁹Your statutes are wonderful;
   therefore I obey them.

¹³⁰The unfolding of your words gives
    light;
  it gives understanding to the simple.
¹³¹I open my mouth and pant,
  longing for your commands.
¹³²Turn to me and have mercy on me,
    as you always do to those who love
    your name.
¹³³Direct my footsteps according to your
    word;
  let no sin rule over me.
¹³⁴Redeem me from the oppression of
    men,
  that I may obey your precepts.
¹³⁵Make your face shine upon your
    servant
  and teach me your decrees.
¹³⁶Streams of tears flow from my eyes,
  for your law is not obeyed.

צ Tsadhe

¹³⁷Righteous are you, O LORD,
  and your laws are right.
¹³⁸The statutes you have laid down are
    righteous;
  they are fully trustworthy.
¹³⁹My zeal wears me out,
  for my enemies ignore your words.
¹⁴⁰Your promises have been thoroughly
    tested,
  and your servant loves them.
¹⁴¹Though I am lowly and despised,
  I do not forget your precepts.
¹⁴²Your righteousness is everlasting
  and your law is true.
¹⁴³Trouble and distress have come
    upon me,
  but your commands are my delight.
¹⁴⁴Your statutes are forever right;
  give me understanding that I may
    live.

ק Qoph

¹⁴⁵I call with all my heart; answer me,
    O LORD,
  and I will obey your decrees.
¹⁴⁶I call out to you; save me
  and I will keep your statutes.
¹⁴⁷I rise before dawn and cry for help;
  I have put my hope in your word.
¹⁴⁸My eyes stay open through the
    watches of the night,
  that I may meditate on your
    promises.
¹⁴⁹Hear my voice in accordance with
    your love;
  preserve my life, O LORD, according
    to your laws.
¹⁵⁰Those who devise wicked schemes are
    near,

but they are far from your law.
¹⁵¹Yet you are near, O LORD,
  and all your commands are true.
¹⁵²Long ago I learned from your statutes
  that you established them to last
    forever.

ר Resh

¹⁵³Look upon my suffering and
    deliver me,
  for I have not forgotten your law.
¹⁵⁴Defend my cause and redeem me;
  preserve my life according to your
    promise.
¹⁵⁵Salvation is far from the wicked,
  for they do not seek out your
    decrees.
¹⁵⁶Your compassion is great, O LORD;
  preserve my life according to your
    laws.
¹⁵⁷Many are the foes who persecute me,
  but I have not turned from your
    statutes.
¹⁵⁸I look on the faithless with loathing,
  for they do not obey your word.
¹⁵⁹See how I love your precepts;
  preserve my life, O LORD, according
    to your love.
¹⁶⁰All your words are true;
  all your righteous laws are eternal.

שׁ Sin and Shin

¹⁶¹Rulers persecute me without cause,
  but my heart trembles at your word.
¹⁶²I rejoice in your promise
  like one who finds great spoil.
¹⁶³I hate and abhor falsehood
  but I love your law.
¹⁶⁴Seven times a day I praise you
  for your righteous laws.
¹⁶⁵Great peace have they who love your
    law,
  and nothing can make them
    stumble.
¹⁶⁶I wait for your salvation, O LORD,
  and I follow your commands.
¹⁶⁷I obey your statutes,
  for I love them greatly.
¹⁶⁸I obey your precepts and your statutes,
  for all my ways are known to you.

ת Taw

¹⁶⁹May my cry come before you, O LORD;
  give me understanding according to
    your word.
¹⁷⁰May my supplication come before you;
  deliver me according to your
    promise.
¹⁷¹May my lips overflow with praise,
  for you teach me your decrees.

172May my tongue sing of your word,
    for all your commands are
        righteous.
173May your hand be ready to help me,
    for I have chosen your precepts.
174I long for your salvation, O LORD,
    and your law is my delight.
175Let me live that I may praise you,
    and may your laws sustain me.
176I have strayed like a lost sheep.
    Seek your servant,
    for I have not forgotten your
        commands.

Psalm 120

A song of ascents.

1 I call on the LORD in my distress,
    and he answers me.
2 Save me, O LORD, from lying lips
    and from deceitful tongues.

3 What will he do to you,
    and what more besides, O deceitful
        tongue?
4 He will punish you with a warrior's
        sharp arrows,
    with burning coals of the broom tree.

5 Woe to me that I dwell in Meshech,
    that I live among the tents of Kedar!

6 Too long have I lived
    among those who hate peace.
7 I am a man of peace;
    but when I speak, they are for war.

Psalm 121

A song of ascents.

1 I lift up my eyes to the hills—
    where does my help come from?
2 My help comes from the LORD,
    the Maker of heaven and earth.

3 He will not let your foot slip—
    he who watches over you will not
        slumber;
4 indeed, he who watches over Israel
    will neither slumber nor sleep.

5 The LORD watches over you—
    the LORD is your shade at your right
        hand;
6 the sun will not harm you by day,
    nor the moon by night.

7 The LORD will keep you from all
        harm—
    he will watch over your life;
8 the LORD will watch over your coming
        and going
    both now and forevermore.

HEY DAD
Does God have a night light in his bedroom?

Text: Psalm 121

No, God doesn't have a night light in his bedroom. How do we know this? First, because darkness and light are the same to God (Psalm 139:12). He created both, and he doesn't fear the darkness. Second, we know this because God never sleeps. But your child doesn't have to take your word for it; the Bible tells us clearly that God never slumbers.

Sometimes children are afraid to sleep in the dark, but they can learn to feel safe knowing that God is watching over them. This psalm says, "He who watches over you will not slumber; indeed, he who watches over Israel will neither slumber nor sleep … The LORD will keep you from all harm—he will watch over your life" (vv. 3–7). God himself is watching over us all the time!

This psalm holds great comfort for dads, too. When David wrote this, he probably wasn't afraid to sleep in the dark, but the many pressures of being a king weighed heavily on him. Instead of giving in to the pressure and stress of his responsibility and overwhelming workload, David recognized that he had a helper, one who was forever watchful—the Maker of heaven and earth.

What a great encouragement to turn our problems, worries and fears over to the One who never sleeps.

For a complete listing of Questions Kids Ask, turn to page 1435.

Psalm 122

A song of ascents. Of David.

[1] I rejoiced with those who said to me,
  "Let us go to the house of the LORD."
[2] Our feet are standing
  in your gates, O Jerusalem.

[3] Jerusalem is built like a city
  that is closely compacted together.
[4] That is where the tribes go up,
  the tribes of the LORD,
  to praise the name of the LORD
  according to the statute given to
  Israel.
[5] There the thrones for judgment stand,
  the thrones of the house of David.

[6] Pray for the peace of Jerusalem:
  "May those who love you be secure.
[7] May there be peace within your walls
  and security within your citadels."
[8] For the sake of my brothers and
  friends,
  I will say, "Peace be within you."
[9] For the sake of the house of the LORD
  our God,
  I will seek your prosperity.

Psalm 123

A song of ascents.

[1] I lift up my eyes to you,
  to you whose throne is in heaven.
[2] As the eyes of slaves look to the hand of
  their master,
  as the eyes of a maid look to the
  hand of her mistress,
  so our eyes look to the LORD our God,
  till he shows us his mercy.

[3] Have mercy on us, O LORD, have mercy
  on us,
  for we have endured much
  contempt.
[4] We have endured much ridicule from
  the proud,
  much contempt from the arrogant.

Psalm 124

A song of ascents. Of David.

[1] If the LORD had not been on our side—
  let Israel say—
[2] if the LORD had not been on our side
  when men attacked us,
[3] when their anger flared against us,
  they would have swallowed us alive;

[4] the flood would have engulfed us,
  the torrent would have swept over us,
[5] the raging waters
  would have swept us away.

[6] Praise be to the LORD,
  who has not let us be torn by their
  teeth.
[7] We have escaped like a bird
  out of the fowler's snare;
  the snare has been broken,
  and we have escaped.
[8] Our help is in the name of the LORD,
  the Maker of heaven and earth.

Psalm 125

A song of ascents.

[1] Those who trust in the LORD are like
  Mount Zion,
  which cannot be shaken but endures
  forever.
[2] As the mountains surround Jerusalem,
  so the LORD surrounds his people
  both now and forevermore.

[3] The scepter of the wicked will not
  remain
  over the land allotted to the
  righteous,
  for then the righteous might use
  their hands to do evil.

[4] Do good, O LORD, to those who are
  good,
  to those who are upright in heart.
[5] But those who turn to crooked ways
  the LORD will banish with the
  evildoers.

Peace be upon Israel.

Psalm 126

A song of ascents.

[1] When the LORD brought back the
  captives to[a] Zion,
  we were like men who dreamed.[b]
[2] Our mouths were filled with laughter,
  our tongues with songs of joy.
  Then it was said among the nations,
  "The LORD has done great things for
  them."
[3] The LORD has done great things for us,
  and we are filled with joy.

[4] Restore our fortunes,[c] O LORD,
  like streams in the Negev.

---

[a]1 Or LORD *restored the fortunes of*   [b]1 Or *men*
restored to health   [c]4 Or *Bring back our captives*

⁵Those who sow in tears
    will reap with songs of joy.
⁶He who goes out weeping,
    carrying seed to sow,
will return with songs of joy,
    carrying sheaves with him.

Psalm 127

A song of ascents. Of Solomon.

¹Unless the LORD builds the house,
    its builders labor in vain.
Unless the LORD watches over the city,
    the watchmen stand guard in vain.

²In vain you rise early
    and stay up late,
toiling for food to eat—
    for he grants sleep to*a* those he loves.

³Sons are a heritage from the LORD,
    children a reward from him.
⁴Like arrows in the hands of a warrior
    are sons born in one's youth.
⁵Blessed is the man
    whose quiver is full of them.
They will not be put to shame
    when they contend with their
        enemies in the gate.

a2 Or eat— / for while they sleep he provides for

Choosing the Right Builder

DAILY INSIGHT

WEDNESDAY

Passage:
Psalm 127

Verse:
Psalm 127:1a

We were about to build our dream house. Bobbie and I had discussed doing this for a long time. The basic floor plan had come from a house we had visited—and loved—when we lived in the Chicago area. We found a parcel of land in Tennessee that was just right, and we were ready to go. We had the house plan, the land and the dream. We only needed one more thing—the right builder.

Since this was the first house we had built, we thought it might be a good idea to do a little checking around. We discovered that some of our friends who had built their homes had had wonderful experiences and, of course, some had been through a nightmare. Some builders had been prompt and fair. Others had been undependable and crooked. Some disappeared when the house was completed and others hung in there, continuing to be available for those inevitable adjustments for months—or years—to come. We kept checking around. This process of choosing the right builder was even more important than we thought.

If selecting the right contractor to build your house is a big deal, how much more important is it to find just the right "Build-er" for what goes inside? Let me suggest that you first check references. If this Build-er is any good, then plenty of families will vouch for his dependability. Don't turn this responsibility over to anyone who doesn't have a lot of happy customers.

For centuries, in cities, suburbs and rural settings, the Lord has been in the home-building business. His happy customers are legion; your town is full of such families. If you have any questions about the reliability of this Contractor, check those references.

A house that the Lord builds is inhabited by a family who honors him. Prayers at meal-time and bedtime are auto-matic. Time alone with God finds its way into everyone's schedule. Family worship and church membership are predict-able activities. References to God's goodness, faithfulness, and grace mark ordinary conversations: "How good God was to give us such a pleasant day for our picnic." "I'm not sure what to do. Would you pray about it with me?"

Any attempt to assemble a family without this Builder is to set yourself up for the greatest of nightmares—far worse than leaky roofs or cracking foundations. The Lord has a great reputation. He builds a solid house and has a great plan for ongoing maintenance. His skill and avail-ability are legendary. When you ask the Lord to build your house, you simply can't go wrong.

For your next devotional reading, go to page 664.

Psalm 128

A song of ascents.

1 Blessed are all who fear the LORD,
who walk in his ways.
2 You will eat the fruit of your labor;
blessings and prosperity will be
yours.
3 Your wife will be like a fruitful vine
within your house;
your sons will be like olive shoots
around your table.
4 Thus is the man blessed
who fears the LORD.

5 May the LORD bless you from Zion
all the days of your life;
may you see the prosperity of
Jerusalem,
6 and may you live to see your
children's children.

Peace be upon Israel.

Psalm 129

A song of ascents.

1 They have greatly oppressed me from
my youth—
let Israel say—

Stop

DAILY INSIGHT

THURSDAY

Passage:
Psalm 131

Verse:
Psalm 131:2a

In 1982, I was slated to travel to Hawaii to participate in a book release—Ah, the suffering I had to do for the company! But during the months leading up to this trip, I had not been feeling well. It was nothing bad enough to send me to a hospital, to bed, or to even make me call my doctor; I had simply felt weak and lethargic and I had no appetite. Finally, at Bobbie's insistence, I went in for some tests a few days before flying from Dallas to Oahu.

Early the second morning of my stay in Hawaii, my hotel telephone rang. Glancing at the digital clock on the nightstand, I saw that it was only 3:30. The voice on the other end of the phone was Darlene Tate, my secretary. "Robert," she began, "I'm sorry to be calling you so early, but I have terrible news."

My heart froze. "What happened? What's wrong?" I responded, now as wide awake as I had ever been in my life. "The report came back from your doctor," she replied. "You have hepatitis. Pack your bags; you're on the next flight back to Dallas." I have never felt such a paradox of emotions. I was relieved that no one had been in an accident, but chagrined that I was sick and had to end this trip to paradise.

The next day I found myself sitting on the examining table in my doctor's office. "You're going to have to go to bed," he said,

his face telling me that this wasn't the opening line to a joke. "There is no medicine I can give you. No prescription except rest." After a dramatic pause, he spoke again. "Robert, you've been running too hard. Your liver will shut down if you keep up this pace. But if you come to a complete stop long enough, your body will actually fix itself. No other medication will be necessary."

I turned off the radio for the short drive home. *How can I afford to stop?* I wondered. *Who's going to take care of the business?* Still, for the next ten days, I did absolutely nothing but rest. I didn't even watch any quiz shows on television. I just slept. And incredibly … I got well. In a week and a half I felt like a brand-new person.

Today's psalm was written by a busy and frazzled king. Can you imagine the work of keeping a whole country in order? So David stopped. He set the "wonderful things," "great matters," and even his pride aside. And in the quiet, he felt God's arms, like those of a compassionate mother, literally healing his soul.

Wake up! This is a serious matter. Stop running, turn off the radio and sit quietly … let God touch your soul. No other medication will be necessary.

For your next devotional reading, go to page 667.

² they have greatly oppressed me from
my youth,
but they have not gained the victory
over me.
³ Plowmen have plowed my back
and made their furrows long.
⁴ But the LORD is righteous;
he has cut me free from the cords of
the wicked.

⁵ May all who hate Zion
be turned back in shame.
⁶ May they be like grass on the roof,
which withers before it can grow;
⁷ with it the reaper cannot fill his hands,
nor the one who gathers fill his arms.
⁸ May those who pass by not say,
"The blessing of the LORD be upon
you;
we bless you in the name of the
LORD."

Psalm 130

A song of ascents.

¹ Out of the depths I cry to you, O LORD;
²   O Lord, hear my voice.
Let your ears be attentive
to my cry for mercy.

³ If you, O LORD, kept a record of sins,
O Lord, who could stand?
⁴ But with you there is forgiveness;
therefore you are feared.

⁵ I wait for the LORD, my soul waits,
and in his word I put my hope.
⁶ My soul waits for the Lord
more than watchmen wait for the
morning,
more than watchmen wait for the
morning.

⁷ O Israel, put your hope in the LORD,
for with the LORD is unfailing love
and with him is full redemption.
⁸ He himself will redeem Israel
from all their sins.

Psalm 131

A song of ascents. Of David.

¹ My heart is not proud, O LORD,
my eyes are not haughty;
I do not concern myself with great
matters
or things too wonderful for me.
² But I have stilled and quieted my soul;
like a weaned child with its mother,

like a weaned child is my soul within
me.

³ O Israel, put your hope in the LORD
both now and forevermore.

Psalm 132

A song of ascents.

¹ O LORD, remember David
and all the hardships he endured.

² He swore an oath to the LORD
and made a vow to the Mighty One
of Jacob:
³ "I will not enter my house
or go to my bed—
⁴ I will allow no sleep to my eyes,
no slumber to my eyelids,
⁵ till I find a place for the LORD,
a dwelling for the Mighty One of
Jacob."

⁶ We heard it in Ephrathah,
we came upon it in the fields of
Jaar:[a][b]
⁷ "Let us go to his dwelling place;
let us worship at his footstool—
⁸ arise, O LORD, and come to your resting
place,
you and the ark of your might.
⁹ May your priests be clothed with
righteousness;
may your saints sing for joy."

¹⁰ For the sake of David your servant,
do not reject your anointed one.

¹¹ The LORD swore an oath to David,
a sure oath that he will not revoke:
"One of your own descendants
I will place on your throne—
¹² if your sons keep my covenant
and the statutes I teach them,
then their sons will sit
on your throne for ever and ever."

¹³ For the LORD has chosen Zion,
he has desired it for his dwelling:
¹⁴ "This is my resting place for ever and
ever;
here I will sit enthroned, for I have
desired it—
¹⁵ I will bless her with abundant
provisions;
her poor will I satisfy with food.
¹⁶ I will clothe her priests with salvation,
and her saints will ever sing for joy.

[a]6 That is, Kiriath Jearim   [b]6 Or *heard of it in
Ephrathah, / we found it in the fields of Jaar.* (And
no quotes around verses 7-9)

[17] "Here I will make a horn[a] grow for
David
and set up a lamp for my anointed
one.
[18] I will clothe his enemies with shame,
but the crown on his head will be
resplendent."

Psalm 133

A song of ascents. Of David.

[1] How good and pleasant it is
when brothers live together in unity!
[2] It is like precious oil poured on the
head,
running down on the beard,
running down on Aaron's beard,
down upon the collar of his robes.
[3] It is as if the dew of Hermon
were falling on Mount Zion.
For there the LORD bestows his
blessing,
even life forevermore.

Psalm 134

A song of ascents.

[1] Praise the LORD, all you servants of the
LORD
who minister by night in the house
of the LORD.
[2] Lift up your hands in the sanctuary
and praise the LORD.

[3] May the LORD, the Maker of heaven and
earth,
bless you from Zion.

Psalm 135

[1] Praise the LORD.[b]

Praise the name of the LORD;
praise him, you servants of the LORD,
[2] you who minister in the house of the
LORD,
in the courts of the house of our
God.

[3] Praise the LORD, for the LORD is good;
sing praise to his name, for that is
pleasant.
[4] For the LORD has chosen Jacob to be his
own,
Israel to be his treasured possession.

[5] I know that the LORD is great,
that our Lord is greater than all gods.
[6] The LORD does whatever pleases him,

in the heavens and on the earth,
in the seas and all their depths.
[7] He makes clouds rise from the ends of
the earth;
he sends lightning with the rain
and brings out the wind from his
storehouses.

[8] He struck down the firstborn of Egypt,
the firstborn of men and animals.
[9] He sent his signs and wonders into
your midst, O Egypt,
against Pharaoh and all his servants.
[10] He struck down many nations
and killed mighty kings—
[11] Sihon king of the Amorites,
Og king of Bashan
and all the kings of Canaan—
[12] and he gave their land as an
inheritance,
an inheritance to his people Israel.

[13] Your name, O LORD, endures forever,
your renown, O LORD, through all
generations.
[14] For the LORD will vindicate his people
and have compassion on his
servants.

[15] The idols of the nations are silver and
gold,
made by the hands of men.
[16] They have mouths, but cannot speak,
eyes, but they cannot see;
[17] they have ears, but cannot hear,
nor is there breath in their mouths.
[18] Those who make them will be like
them,
and so will all who trust in them.

[19] O house of Israel, praise the LORD;
O house of Aaron, praise the LORD;
[20] O house of Levi, praise the LORD;
you who fear him, praise the LORD.
[21] Praise be to the LORD from Zion,
to him who dwells in Jerusalem.

Praise the LORD.

Psalm 136

[1] Give thanks to the LORD, for he is good.
His love endures forever.
[2] Give thanks to the God of gods.
His love endures forever.
[3] Give thanks to the Lord of lords:
His love endures forever.

[4] to him who alone does great wonders,
His love endures forever.

---

[a]17 *Horn* here symbolizes strong one, that is, king.
[b]1 Hebrew *Hallelu Yah;* also in verses 3 and 21

⁵who by his understanding made the
   heavens,
       His love endures forever.
⁶who spread out the earth upon the
   waters,
       His love endures forever.
⁷who made the great lights—
       His love endures forever.
⁸the sun to govern the day,
       His love endures forever.
⁹the moon and stars to govern the night;
       His love endures forever.
¹⁰to him who struck down the firstborn
   of Egypt
       His love endures forever.

¹¹and brought Israel out from among
   them
       His love endures forever.
¹²with a mighty hand and outstretched
   arm;
       His love endures forever.
¹³to him who divided the Red Sea*a*
   asunder
       His love endures forever.
¹⁴and brought Israel through the midst
   of it,
       His love endures forever.

a13 Hebrew *Yam Suph*; that is, Sea of Reeds; also in
verse 15

Love Forever, Monroe

DAILY INSIGHT

FRIDAY

Passage:
Psalm 136

Verse:
Psalm 136:1

"Longer than always is a long, long time, but far beyond forever, you'll be mine." These lyrics are from a tune that was popular in the sixties entitled, "More." Because the verses went on and on about how much one person loved another, many couples adopted it as "their song."

Because the song takes me back to my high school days, I'm reminded of how often and how casually the words "always" and "forever" were used when it came to expressions of affection. In fact, thumbing through my high school yearbook reveals such closings as, "Love always, Cindy"; "Your forever friend, Dave"; "Always, Larry." I'm confident that I signed many of my friend's yearbooks the same way. Although we weren't intentionally lying, what my friends and I actually knew about "always" and "forever" at seventeen was about as much as we knew about life itself ... very little.

My grandfather, an artisan with words, wrote most of his love letters to Susie, his lifelong love, in the form of sonnets and poems. He signed these treasures with the words, "Love forever, Monroe."

My grandfather's "forever" turned into a sixty-five year romance with my grandmother, ending with her death in 1975. Before his own death at age ninety-nine, this love affair led to nine children, thirty-five grandchildren, and numerous great

grandchildren—including six great-great grandchildren. When my grandfather wrote "Love forever," he meant it.

Today's psalm includes one line that's repeated twenty-six times: "His love endures forever." This line follows a series of short statements that recount God's faithfulness to his people down through the centuries. And, of course, even though this was penned many years ago, it could also describe God's acts in history up through—and including—ten seconds ago. God's love lasts forever.

When you and I think of "always" and "forever" love, we cannot afford to let our minds wander back to high school where the words were forgotten before the ink was dry. We can't even afford to think of the great examples of lifelong love, like Monroe and Susie's. "Always" and "forever" are, well, *always* and *forever*. God's love hangs on literally through all past and future eternity. He loved us before time began and will continue to do so long after this world is gone and time is no more.

It's as though this psalm is a personal note to you and me:
Dear child, I love you.
Always,
God.
These are words we can count on.

For your next devotional reading, go to page 669.

¹⁵but swept Pharaoh and his army into
the Red Sea;
His love endures forever.
¹⁶to him who led his people through the
desert,
His love endures forever.
¹⁷who struck down great kings,
His love endures forever.
¹⁸and killed mighty kings—
His love endures forever.
¹⁹Sihon king of the Amorites
His love endures forever.
²⁰and Og king of Bashan—
His love endures forever.
²¹and gave their land as an inheritance,
His love endures forever.
²²an inheritance to his servant Israel;
His love endures forever.

²³to the One who remembered us in our
low estate
His love endures forever.
²⁴and freed us from our enemies,
His love endures forever.
²⁵and who gives food to every creature.
His love endures forever.
²⁶Give thanks to the God of heaven.
His love endures forever.

Psalm 137

¹By the rivers of Babylon we sat and
wept
when we remembered Zion.
²There on the poplars
we hung our harps,
³for there our captors asked us for
songs,
our tormentors demanded songs of
joy;
they said, "Sing us one of the songs
of Zion!"

⁴How can we sing the songs of the LORD
while in a foreign land?
⁵If I forget you, O Jerusalem,
may my right hand forget its skill.
⁶May my tongue cling to the roof of my
mouth
if I do not remember you,
if I do not consider Jerusalem
my highest joy.

⁷Remember, O LORD, what the Edomites
did
on the day Jerusalem fell.
"Tear it down," they cried,
"tear it down to its foundations!"

⁸O Daughter of Babylon, doomed to
destruction,

happy is he who repays you
for what you have done to us—
⁹he who seizes your infants
and dashes them against the rocks.

Psalm 138

Of David.

¹I will praise you, O LORD, with all my
heart;
before the "gods" I will sing your
praise.
²I will bow down toward your holy
temple
and will praise your name
for your love and your faithfulness,
for you have exalted above all things
your name and your word.
³When I called, you answered me;
you made me bold and stouthearted.

⁴May all the kings of the earth praise
you, O LORD,
when they hear the words of your
mouth.
⁵May they sing of the ways of the LORD,
for the glory of the LORD is great.

⁶Though the LORD is on high, he looks
upon the lowly,
but the proud he knows from afar.
⁷Though I walk in the midst of trouble,
you preserve my life;
you stretch out your hand against the
anger of my foes,
with your right hand you save me.
⁸The LORD will fulfill his purpose for
me;
your love, O LORD, endures
forever—
do not abandon the works of your
hands.

Psalm 139

For the director of music.
Of David. A psalm.

¹O LORD, you have searched me
and you know me.
²You know when I sit and when I rise;
you perceive my thoughts from afar.
³You discern my going out and my lying
down;
you are familiar with all my ways.
⁴Before a word is on my tongue
you know it completely, O LORD.

⁵You hem me in—behind and before;
you have laid your hand upon me.

God's Inside Miracles

Key Verse: *"You created my inmost being; you knit me together in my mother's womb. I praise you because I am fearfully and wonderfully made."* Psalm 139:13,14a

Text: Psalm 139:13–16, 23, 24 *(Dad or child reads the text.)*

QUIET **TIMES** WITH **Dad**

DAD READS: Every time a baby is born, it's a miracle. *(Take a moment to recall your child's birth.)*

Child reads: I have seen pictures of a baby forming inside its mother's body. I find it hard to believe that I was really inside of my mother. It's really hard for me to imagine that you were inside of your mother, too!

DAD READS: From the moment we were both conceived, God was there with us. Although it was dark and quiet, we were not alone. He was there, making every part of us. In only three weeks our little hearts were beating. In six weeks, we had fingers and toes—ten of each.

Child reads: Even though we don't remember anything about being inside our mothers, God does. He remembers every day when something new happened to our tiny bodies.

DAD READS: When David wrote these words, he had never seen any pictures of what a developing baby looks like. He didn't know anything about how long it took for hearts to start beating or for fingers and toes to grow. But when he thought about the miracle of birth he was filled with wonder, so he said to God, "I praise you because I am fearfully and wonderfully made; your works are wonderful."

Child reads: When I see things that are wonderful—like a fireworks show or an athlete diving off a high platform—sometimes I make a gasping sound: "Ahhhhh!" But when I think about how God made both of our bodies, how he quietly fit them together in the dark and in the quiet, it's so wonderful, I can hardly make a sound.

DAD READS: Just like God could see inside our mother's body when we were forming, he can see inside of us. He even knows what we're thinking.

Child reads: I want God to be happy when he sees inside of you and me. I want him to be excited because he sees good thoughts and kind thoughts and clean thoughts, just like I know he is excited when he sees a little baby forming inside his or her mother.

DAD READS: I want God to be pleased when he sees inside of us, too. I'm glad that, even when God sees things inside of us that shouldn't be there, he offers to forgive us and make us clean again if we tell him that we're sorry and ask for forgiveness. Let me pray this prayer with you:

Our Father in heaven, thank you for the miracle of babies. Thank you for being there when we were being formed inside of our mothers. And help us to also remember that you can see inside of us right now. Forgive our sins and help our thoughts to be good and kind and clean. Please help us to make you happy so that others can see how much we love you. In Jesus' name, Amen.

For your next devotional reading, go to page 678.

⁶Such knowledge is too wonderful for
    me,
  too lofty for me to attain.

⁷Where can I go from your Spirit?
  Where can I flee from your
    presence?
⁸If I go up to the heavens, you are there;
  if I make my bed in the depths,ᵃ you
    are there.
⁹If I rise on the wings of the dawn,
  if I settle on the far side of the sea,
¹⁰even there your hand will guide me,
  your right hand will hold me fast.

¹¹If I say, "Surely the darkness will hide
    me
  and the light become night around
    me,"
¹²even the darkness will not be dark to
    you;
  the night will shine like the day,
  for darkness is as light to you.

¹³For you created my inmost being;
  you knit me together in my mother's
    womb.
¹⁴I praise you because I am fearfully and
    wonderfully made;
  your works are wonderful,
  I know that full well.
¹⁵My frame was not hidden from you
  when I was made in the secret place.
  When I was woven together in the
    depths of the earth,
¹⁶   your eyes saw my unformed body.
  All the days ordained for me
    were written in your book
    before one of them came to be.

¹⁷How precious toᵇ me are your
    thoughts, O God!
  How vast is the sum of them!
¹⁸Were I to count them,
  they would outnumber the grains of
    sand.
  When I awake,
  I am still with you.

¹⁹If only you would slay the wicked,
    O God!
  Away from me, you bloodthirsty
    men!
²⁰They speak of you with evil intent;
  your adversaries misuse your name.
²¹Do I not hate those who hate you,
    O LORD,
  and abhor those who rise up against
    you?
²²I have nothing but hatred for them;
  I count them my enemies.

²³Search me, O God, and know my heart;
  test me and know my anxious
    thoughts.
²⁴See if there is any offensive way in me,
  and lead me in the way everlasting.

Psalm 140

For the director of music.
A psalm of David.

¹Rescue me, O LORD, from evil men;
  protect me from men of violence,
²who devise evil plans in their hearts
  and stir up war every day.
³They make their tongues as sharp as a
    serpent's;
  the poison of vipers is on their lips.
                                    Selah

⁴Keep me, O LORD, from the hands of
    the wicked;
  protect me from men of violence
  who plan to trip my feet.
⁵Proud men have hidden a snare for me;
  they have spread out the cords of
    their net
  and have set traps for me along my
    path.   *Selah*

⁶O LORD, I say to you, "You are my God."
  Hear, O LORD, my cry for mercy.
⁷O Sovereign LORD, my strong deliverer,
  who shields my head in the day of
    battle—
⁸do not grant the wicked their desires,
    O LORD;
  do not let their plans succeed,
  or they will become proud.   *Selah*

⁹Let the heads of those who surround
    me
  be covered with the trouble their lips
    have caused.
¹⁰Let burning coals fall upon them;
  may they be thrown into the fire,
  into miry pits, never to rise.
¹¹Let slanderers not be established in the
    land;
  may disaster hunt down men of
    violence.
¹²I know that the LORD secures justice for
    the poor
  and upholds the cause of the needy.
¹³Surely the righteous will praise your
    name
  and the upright will live before you.

ᵃ8 Hebrew *Sheol*   ᵇ17 Or *concerning*

Psalm 141

A psalm of David.

¹ O LORD, I call to you; come quickly to
 me.
  Hear my voice when I call to you.
² May my prayer be set before you like
 incense;
  may the lifting up of my hands be
  like the evening sacrifice.

³ Set a guard over my mouth, O LORD;
  keep watch over the door of my lips.
⁴ Let not my heart be drawn to what is
 evil,
  to take part in wicked deeds
 with men who are evildoers;
  let me not eat of their delicacies.

⁵ Let a righteous man*ᵃ* strike me—it is a
 kindness;
  let him rebuke me—it is oil on my
  head.
  My head will not refuse it.

 Yet my prayer is ever against the deeds
  of evildoers;
⁶   their rulers will be thrown down
   from the cliffs,
  and the wicked will learn that my
   words were well spoken.
⁷ They will say, "As one plows and
   breaks up the earth,
  so our bones have been scattered at
   the mouth of the grave.*ᵇ*"

⁸ But my eyes are fixed on you,
  O Sovereign LORD;
  in you I take refuge—do not give me
  over to death.
⁹ Keep me from the snares they have laid
 for me,
  from the traps set by evildoers.
¹⁰ Let the wicked fall into their own nets,
  while I pass by in safety.

Psalm 142

*A maskilᶜ of David.
When he was in the cave. A prayer.*

¹ I cry aloud to the LORD;
  I lift up my voice to the LORD for
  mercy.
² I pour out my complaint before him;
  before him I tell my trouble.

³ When my spirit grows faint within me,
  it is you who know my way.
 In the path where I walk
  men have hidden a snare for me.

⁴ Look to my right and see;
  no one is concerned for me.
 I have no refuge;
  no one cares for my life.

⁵ I cry to you, O LORD;
  I say, "You are my refuge,
  my portion in the land of the living."
⁶ Listen to my cry,
  for I am in desperate need;
 rescue me from those who pursue me,
  for they are too strong for me.
⁷ Set me free from my prison,
  that I may praise your name.

 Then the righteous will gather about
  me
  because of your goodness to me.

Psalm 143

A psalm of David.

¹ O LORD, hear my prayer,
  listen to my cry for mercy;
 in your faithfulness and righteousness
  come to my relief.
² Do not bring your servant into
  judgment,
  for no one living is righteous before
  you.

³ The enemy pursues me,
  he crushes me to the ground;
 he makes me dwell in darkness
  like those long dead.
⁴ So my spirit grows faint within me;
  my heart within me is dismayed.

⁵ I remember the days of long ago;
  I meditate on all your works
  and consider what your hands have
  done.
⁶ I spread out my hands to you;
  my soul thirsts for you like a parched
  land.   *Selah*

⁷ Answer me quickly, O LORD;
  my spirit fails.
 Do not hide your face from me
  or I will be like those who go down to
  the pit.
⁸ Let the morning bring me word of your
  unfailing love,
  for I have put my trust in you.
 Show me the way I should go,
  for to you I lift up my soul.
⁹ Rescue me from my enemies, O LORD,
  for I hide myself in you.

ᵃ5 Or *Let the Righteous One*   *ᵇ7* Hebrew *Sheol*
*ᶜ*Title: Probably a literary or musical term

¹⁰ Teach me to do your will,
  for you are my God;
may your good Spirit
  lead me on level ground.

¹¹ For your name's sake, O LORD, preserve
    my life;
  in your righteousness, bring me out
    of trouble.
¹² In your unfailing love, silence my
    enemies;
  destroy all my foes,
    for I am your servant.

Psalm 144

Of David.

¹ Praise be to the LORD my Rock,
  who trains my hands for war,
  my fingers for battle.
² He is my loving God and my fortress,
  my stronghold and my deliverer,
my shield, in whom I take refuge,
  who subdues peoples[a] under me.

³ O LORD, what is man that you care for
    him,
  the son of man that you think of
    him?
⁴ Man is like a breath;
  his days are like a fleeting shadow.

⁵ Part your heavens, O LORD, and come
    down;
  touch the mountains, so that they
    smoke.
⁶ Send forth lightning and scatter the
    enemies;
  shoot your arrows and rout them.
⁷ Reach down your hand from on high;
  deliver me and rescue me
 from the mighty waters,
  from the hands of foreigners
⁸ whose mouths are full of lies,
  whose right hands are deceitful.

⁹ I will sing a new song to you, O God;
  on the ten-stringed lyre I will make
    music to you,
¹⁰ to the One who gives victory to kings,
  who delivers his servant David from
    the deadly sword.

¹¹ Deliver me and rescue me
  from the hands of foreigners
whose mouths are full of lies,
  whose right hands are deceitful.

¹² Then our sons in their youth
  will be like well-nurtured plants,
 and our daughters will be like pillars
  carved to adorn a palace.

¹³ Our barns will be filled
  with every kind of provision.
Our sheep will increase by thousands,
  by tens of thousands in our fields;
¹⁴ our oxen will draw heavy loads.[b]
There will be no breaching of walls,
  no going into captivity,
  no cry of distress in our streets.

¹⁵ Blessed are the people of whom this is
    true;
  blessed are the people whose God is
    the LORD.

Psalm 145[c]

A psalm of praise. Of David.

¹ I will exalt you, my God the King;
  I will praise your name for ever and
    ever.
² Every day I will praise you
  and extol your name for ever and
    ever.
³ Great is the LORD and most worthy of
    praise;
  his greatness no one can fathom.
⁴ One generation will commend your
    works to another;
  they will tell of your mighty acts.
⁵ They will speak of the glorious
    splendor of your majesty,
  and I will meditate on your
    wonderful works.[d]
⁶ They will tell of the power of your
    awesome works,
  and I will proclaim your great deeds.
⁷ They will celebrate your abundant
    goodness
  and joyfully sing of your
    righteousness.

⁸ The LORD is gracious and
    compassionate,
  slow to anger and rich in love.
⁹ The LORD is good to all;
  he has compassion on all he has
    made.
¹⁰ All you have made will praise you,
    O LORD;

---

[a]2 Many manuscripts of the Masoretic Text, Dead
Sea Scrolls, Aquila, Jerome and Syriac; most
manuscripts of the Masoretic Text *subdues my
people*   [b]14 Or *our chieftains will be firmly
established*   [c]This psalm is an acrostic poem, the
verses of which (including verse 13b) begin with
the successive letters of the Hebrew alphabet.
[d]5 Dead Sea Scrolls and Syriac (see also
Septuagint); Masoretic Text *On the glorious
splendor of your majesty / and on your wonderful
works I will meditate*

your saints will extol you.
¹¹They will tell of the glory of your
    kingdom
    and speak of your might,
¹²so that all men may know of your
    mighty acts
    and the glorious splendor of your
    kingdom.
¹³Your kingdom is an everlasting
    kingdom,
    and your dominion endures through
    all generations.

The LORD is faithful to all his promises
    and loving toward all he has made.ᵃ
¹⁴The LORD upholds all those who fall
    and lifts up all who are bowed down.
¹⁵The eyes of all look to you,
    and you give them their food at the
    proper time.
¹⁶You open your hand
    and satisfy the desires of every living
    thing.

¹⁷The LORD is righteous in all his ways
    and loving toward all he has made.
¹⁸The LORD is near to all who call on
    him,
    to all who call on him in truth.
¹⁹He fulfills the desires of those who fear
    him;
    he hears their cry and saves them.
²⁰The LORD watches over all who love
    him,
    but all the wicked he will destroy.

²¹My mouth will speak in praise of the
    LORD.
    Let every creature praise his holy
    name
    for ever and ever.

Psalm 146

¹Praise the LORD.ᵇ

Praise the LORD, O my soul.
²   I will praise the LORD all my life;
    I will sing praise to my God as long
    as I live.

³Do not put your trust in princes,
    in mortal men, who cannot save.
⁴When their spirit departs, they return
    to the ground;
    on that very day their plans come to
    nothing.
⁵Blessed is he whose help is the God of
    Jacob,
    whose hope is in the LORD his God,
⁶the Maker of heaven and earth,
    the sea, and everything in them—

the LORD, who remains faithful
    forever.
⁷He upholds the cause of the oppressed
    and gives food to the hungry.
The LORD sets prisoners free,
⁸   the LORD gives sight to the blind,
    the LORD lifts up those who are bowed
    down,
    the LORD loves the righteous.
⁹The LORD watches over the alien
    and sustains the fatherless and the
    widow,
    but he frustrates the ways of the
    wicked.

¹⁰The LORD reigns forever,
    your God, O Zion, for all generations.

Praise the LORD.

Psalm 147

¹Praise the LORD.ᶜ

How good it is to sing praises to our
    God,
    how pleasant and fitting to praise
    him!

²The LORD builds up Jerusalem;
    he gathers the exiles of Israel.
³He heals the brokenhearted
    and binds up their wounds.
⁴He determines the number of the stars
    and calls them each by name.
⁵Great is our Lord and mighty in power;
    his understanding has no limit.
⁶The LORD sustains the humble
    but casts the wicked to the ground.

⁷Sing to the LORD with thanksgiving;
    make music to our God on the harp.
⁸He covers the sky with clouds;
    he supplies the earth with rain
    and makes grass grow on the hills.
⁹He provides food for the cattle
    and for the young ravens when they
    call.

¹⁰His pleasure is not in the strength of
    the horse,
    nor his delight in the legs of a man;
¹¹the LORD delights in those who fear
    him,
    who put their hope in his unfailing
    love.

ᵃ13 One manuscript of the Masoretic Text, Dead
Sea Scrolls and Syriac (see also Septuagint); most
manuscripts of the Masoretic Text do not have the
last two lines of verse 13.   ᵇ1 Hebrew *Hallelu Yah*;
also in verse 10   ᶜ1 Hebrew *Hallelu Yah*; also in
verse 20

¹²Extol the LORD, O Jerusalem;
  praise your God, O Zion,
¹³for he strengthens the bars of your
    gates
  and blesses your people within you.
¹⁴He grants peace to your borders
  and satisfies you with the finest of
    wheat.

¹⁵He sends his command to the earth;
  his word runs swiftly.
¹⁶He spreads the snow like wool
  and scatters the frost like ashes.
¹⁷He hurls down his hail like pebbles.
  Who can withstand his icy blast?
¹⁸He sends his word and melts them;
  he stirs up his breezes, and the
    waters flow.

¹⁹He has revealed his word to Jacob,
  his laws and decrees to Israel.
²⁰He has done this for no other nation;
  they do not know his laws.

  Praise the LORD.

Psalm 148

¹Praise the LORD.[a]

Praise the LORD from the heavens,
  praise him in the heights above.
²Praise him, all his angels,
  praise him, all his heavenly hosts.
³Praise him, sun and moon,
  praise him, all you shining stars.
⁴Praise him, you highest heavens
  and you waters above the skies.
⁵Let them praise the name of the
    LORD,
  for he commanded and they were
    created.
⁶He set them in place for ever and ever;
  he gave a decree that will never pass
    away.

⁷Praise the LORD from the earth,
  you great sea creatures and all ocean
    depths,
⁸lightning and hail, snow and clouds,
  stormy winds that do his bidding,
⁹you mountains and all hills,
  fruit trees and all cedars,
¹⁰wild animals and all cattle,
  small creatures and flying birds,
¹¹kings of the earth and all nations,
  you princes and all rulers on earth,
¹²young men and maidens,
  old men and children.

¹³Let them praise the name of the LORD,
  for his name alone is exalted;
  his splendor is above the earth and
    the heavens.
¹⁴He has raised up for his people a
    horn,[b]
  the praise of all his saints,
  of Israel, the people close to his
    heart.

  Praise the LORD.

Psalm 149

¹Praise the LORD.[c]

Sing to the LORD a new song,
  his praise in the assembly of the
    saints.

²Let Israel rejoice in their Maker;
  let the people of Zion be glad in their
    King.
³Let them praise his name with dancing
  and make music to him with
    tambourine and harp.
⁴For the LORD takes delight in his
    people;
  he crowns the humble with
    salvation.
⁵Let the saints rejoice in this honor
  and sing for joy on their beds.

⁶May the praise of God be in their
    mouths
  and a double-edged sword in their
    hands,
⁷to inflict vengeance on the nations
  and punishment on the peoples,
⁸to bind their kings with fetters,
  their nobles with shackles of iron,
⁹to carry out the sentence written
    against them.
  This is the glory of all his saints.

  Praise the LORD.

Psalm 150

¹Praise the LORD.[d]

Praise God in his sanctuary;
  praise him in his mighty heavens.

---

[a]1 Hebrew *Hallelu Yah*; also in verse 14   [b]14 *Horn* here symbolizes strong one, that is, king.
[c]1 Hebrew *Hallelu Yah*; also in verse 9   [d]1 Hebrew *Hallelu Yah*; also in verse 6

²Praise him for his acts of power;
  praise him for his surpassing
    greatness.
³Praise him with the sounding of the
    trumpet,
  praise him with the harp and lyre,
⁴praise him with tambourine and
    dancing,

praise him with the strings and
    flute,
⁵praise him with the clash of cymbals,
  praise him with resounding cymbals.

⁶Let everything that has breath praise
    the LORD.

Praise the LORD.

Solomon was a wise guy . . . but not in the way you and I used this phrase when we tussled with our neighborhood pals. Solomon was truly a wise man, and he was convinced that we should also be wise. His words of wisdom, collected in this book of Proverbs, may be the most complete and profound assembly of insight and common sense ever convened in one place. His perceptiveness on our need to be better listeners, his candor about the perils of lust, and his advice to us as husbands, sons and fathers stands as a powerful contrast to the shallow drivel we hear too often from "armchair experts."

Take some time to regularly soak in these Proverbs. Doing so will be like a daily regimen of taking vitamins: it'll keep your mind healthy and your character strong.

Proverbs

Prologue: Purpose and Theme

1 The proverbs of Solomon son of David, king of Israel:

² for attaining wisdom and discipline;
   for understanding words of insight;
³ for acquiring a disciplined and prudent life,
   doing what is right and just and fair;
⁴ for giving prudence to the simple,
   knowledge and discretion to the young—
⁵ let the wise listen and add to their learning,
   and let the discerning get guidance—
⁶ for understanding proverbs and parables,
   the sayings and riddles of the wise.

⁷ The fear of the LORD is the beginning of knowledge,
   but fools[a] despise wisdom and discipline.

Exhortations to Embrace Wisdom

Warning Against Enticement

⁸ Listen, my son, to your father's instruction
   and do not forsake your mother's teaching.
⁹ They will be a garland to grace your head
   and a chain to adorn your neck.

¹⁰ My son, if sinners entice you,
   do not give in to them.
¹¹ If they say, "Come along with us;
   let's lie in wait for someone's blood,
   let's waylay some harmless soul;
¹² let's swallow them alive, like the grave,[b]
   and whole, like those who go down to the pit;

a7 The Hebrew words rendered *fool* in Proverbs, and often elsewhere in the Old Testament, denote one who is morally deficient.   *b12* Hebrew *Sheol*

13 we will get all sorts of valuable things
  and fill our houses with plunder;
14 throw in your lot with us,
  and we will share a common
    purse"—
15 my son, do not go along with them,
  do not set foot on their paths;
16 for their feet rush into sin,
  they are swift to shed blood.
17 How useless to spread a net
  in full view of all the birds!
18 These men lie in wait for their own
    blood;
  they waylay only themselves!
19 Such is the end of all who go after
    ill-gotten gain;
  it takes away the lives of those who
    get it.

Warning Against Rejecting Wisdom

20 Wisdom calls aloud in the street,
  she raises her voice in the public
    squares;
21 at the head of the noisy streets*a* she
    cries out,
  in the gateways of the city she makes
    her speech:

22 "How long will you simple ones*b* love
    your simple ways?
  How long will mockers delight in
    mockery
  and fools hate knowledge?
23 If you had responded to my rebuke,
  I would have poured out my heart to
    you
  and made my thoughts known to
    you.
24 But since you rejected me when I
    called
  and no one gave heed when I
    stretched out my hand,
25 since you ignored all my advice
  and would not accept my rebuke,
26 I in turn will laugh at your disaster;
  I will mock when calamity overtakes
    you—
27 when calamity overtakes you like a
    storm,
  when disaster sweeps over you like a
    whirlwind,

a21 Hebrew; Septuagint / on the tops of the walls
b22 The Hebrew word rendered simple *in Proverbs
generally denotes one without moral direction and
inclined to evil.*

Like Father, Like Son
Solomon, the Wise Father

*"My son, if you accept my words and store up my
commands within you, turning your ear to wisdom
and applying your heart to understanding . . .
then you will understand the fear of the Lᴏʀᴅ and
find the knowledge of God" (2:1–2, 5).*

Text: Proverbs 1

Solomon will forever be remembered as Israel's wisest king. And, no doubt, he would have
bragged about how bright his children were as well. But wise old Solomon didn't leave
anything to chance; he didn't just figure that his children would pick up this wisdom on
their own.

The book of Proverbs is actually a love note to Solomon's children. Wise and wealthy as
he was, he saw the value of children who "attain[ed] wisdom and discipline . . . acquir[ed] a
disciplined and prudent life, [and did] what [was] right and just and fair" (1:2–3). Solomon
stopped and took the time to pour this wisdom into his children. As a result of his efforts,
men and women throughout history have basked in the glow of these wise words.

Do you wonder where Solomon got the idea to give this wisdom to his children himself?
How did he figure out that they probably wouldn't just pick it up on their own?

David told his son just before his own death, "Be strong, show yourself a man, and
observe what the Lᴏʀᴅ your God requires" (1 Kings 2:2–3). *What a good idea,* Solomon must
have thought to himself as he shuffled off to his bedroom. *When I have children of my own,
I think I'll do the same.*

Like father, like son.

For a complete listing of Dads in the Bible, turn to page 1434.

when distress and trouble
    overwhelm you.
28 "Then they will call to me but I will not
    answer;
they will look for me but will not
    find me.
29 Since they hated knowledge
    and did not choose to fear the LORD,
30 since they would not accept my advice
    and spurned my rebuke,

31 they will eat the fruit of their ways
    and be filled with the fruit of their
    schemes.
32 For the waywardness of the simple will
    kill them,
    and the complacency of fools will
    destroy them;
33 but whoever listens to me will live in
    safety
    and be at ease, without fear of
    harm."

You're One Smart Dad

For over ten years I worked with teenagers—first as a full-time minister and then as a volunteer after I went into business. During those years the kids often used me as a sounding-board for their problems, and the ones I heard about most often had to do with their parents: "My dad is too busy for me"; "My mother doesn't have a clue what's going on in the world"; "My parents hate my friends." After a few years, I figured I had just about heard it all.

But then there was Rick. Although he was only sixteen when I met him, I knew he was a little brighter than his peers. Not that Rick got better grades than his buddies, it just seemed that he had more sense about him than other guys his age. Talking to Rick was like talking to a friend.

One afternoon we were sitting at the Howard Johnson's on Sheridan Road, sipping cokes. "I don't ever want you to tell my parents I told you this," Rick said with a wry smile, "but most of the time they're *right*." I didn't need to say anything. As a teenager, I had silently thought the same thing. "In fact," Rick continued, "the older I get, the smarter my dad gets!"

Here's the bottom line: As a dad, you are smarter and wiser than your children. You have experienced more of life, and you can see things they cannot. So, how can you transfer your wisdom to the next generation? The first word of today's text says it all: *Listen*. Your children must learn how to "listen" to you.

DAILY INSIGHT

MONDAY

Passage:
Proverbs 1:8–19

Verse:
Proverbs 1:8

People who have hearing impairments have taught me how to listen with their eyes. They say that they can compensate for their hearing loss in this way, and our children must compensate for their own "hearing impairments" in the same way. *If they're not watching you, they're not listening.* And if your children are not listening, how will your experience and wisdom ever do any good in their lives?

You have heard this so many times, but perhaps this time it will make more sense than ever. If you aren't intentional about spending one-on-one, face-to-face time with your child, they may *never* listen to you. If your conversation with them is always on the run or in a crowded room, they will never pick it up.

"Listen, my son, to your father's instruction and do not forsake your mother's teaching." Can you imagine Solomon saying this to his son with his eyes focused on his dinner plate? Can you imagine him making this comment in an offhand way while reading a book? No. This statement is deeply weakened when spoken by a father who refuses to say these words while looking straight into his child's eyes.

You *are* smarter than your kids. You *do* have much wisdom to share. Take confidence in this truth, then find ways to communicate it, intentionally, lovingly, in a normal tone of voice, and without distractions.

Your kid is lucky to have a dad like you. Don't tell him; he already knows it.

For your next devotional reading, go to page 680.

Moral Benefits of Wisdom

2 My son, if you accept my words
and store up my commands within
you,
[2] turning your ear to wisdom
and applying your heart to
understanding,
[3] and if you call out for insight
and cry aloud for understanding,
[4] and if you look for it as for silver
and search for it as for hidden
treasure,
[5] then you will understand the fear of the
LORD
and find the knowledge of God.
[6] For the LORD gives wisdom,
and from his mouth come
knowledge and understanding.
[7] He holds victory in store for the
upright,
he is a shield to those whose walk is
blameless,
[8] for he guards the course of the just
and protects the way of his faithful
ones.
[9] Then you will understand what is right
and just
and fair—every good path.
[10] For wisdom will enter your heart,
and knowledge will be pleasant to
your soul.
[11] Discretion will protect you,
and understanding will guard you.
[12] Wisdom will save you from the ways of
wicked men,
from men whose words are perverse,
[13] who leave the straight paths
to walk in dark ways,
[14] who delight in doing wrong
and rejoice in the perverseness of
evil,
[15] whose paths are crooked
and who are devious in their ways.
[16] It will save you also from the
adulteress,
from the wayward wife with her
seductive words,
[17] who has left the partner of her youth
and ignored the covenant she made
before God.[a]
[18] For her house leads down to death
and her paths to the spirits of the
dead.
[19] None who go to her return
or attain the paths of life.
[20] Thus you will walk in the ways of good
men

and keep to the paths of the
righteous.
[21] For the upright will live in the land,
and the blameless will remain in it;
[22] but the wicked will be cut off from the
land,
and the unfaithful will be torn from it.

Further Benefits of Wisdom

3 My son, do not forget my teaching,
but keep my commands in your
heart,
[2] for they will prolong your life many
years
and bring you prosperity.

[3] Let love and faithfulness never leave
you;
bind them around your neck,
write them on the tablet of your
heart.
[4] Then you will win favor and a good
name
in the sight of God and man.

[5] Trust in the LORD with all your heart
and lean not on your own
understanding;
[6] in all your ways acknowledge him,
and he will make your paths
straight.[b]

[7] Do not be wise in your own eyes;
fear the LORD and shun evil.
[8] This will bring health to your body
and nourishment to your bones.

[9] Honor the LORD with your wealth,
with the firstfruits of all your crops;
[10] then your barns will be filled to
overflowing,
and your vats will brim over with
new wine.

[11] My son, do not despise the LORD's
discipline
and do not resent his rebuke,
[12] because the LORD disciplines those he
loves,
as a father[c] the son he delights in.

[13] Blessed is the man who finds wisdom,
the man who gains understanding,
[14] for she is more profitable than silver
and yields better returns than gold.
[15] She is more precious than rubies;
nothing you desire can compare with
her.
[16] Long life is in her right hand;
in her left hand are riches and honor.

---

[a]17 Or *covenant of her God*   [b]6 Or *will direct your*
paths   [c]12 Hebrew; Septuagint / *and he punishes*

¹⁷Her ways are pleasant ways,
    and all her paths are peace.
¹⁸She is a tree of life to those who
        embrace her;
    those who lay hold of her will be
        blessed.

¹⁹By wisdom the LORD laid the earth's
        foundations,
    by understanding he set the heavens
        in place;
²⁰by his knowledge the deeps were
        divided,
    and the clouds let drop the dew.

²¹My son, preserve sound judgment and
        discernment,
    do not let them out of your sight;
²²they will be life for you,
    an ornament to grace your neck.
²³Then you will go on your way in safety,
    and your foot will not stumble;
²⁴when you lie down, you will not be
        afraid;
    when you lie down, your sleep will
        be sweet.
²⁵Have no fear of sudden disaster
    or of the ruin that overtakes the
        wicked,

Full Barns and Lots of Wine

Can we talk about money?

Over twenty years ago I heard a sermon that had a profound effect on my thinking about wealth. Reverend Richard Freeman, our senior minister, explained that every day we carry around an actual written list of those things that are truly important to us—our priorities in black and white.

What could this be? I remember thinking. *What do I carry around that does this?*

As was his style, Reverend Freeman broke the suspense at just the perfect moment. "The register in your checkbook gives you all the information you need to understand what's most important to you." I remember sitting there in shock. What an insight!

The Bible has some very important things to say about money. Today's text tells us to "Honor the LORD with your wealth." Look carefully at the words. This does not say, "Give the Lord all your wealth." Some may lead you to believe that if you have money, you're not pleasing God. Nothing could be further from the truth.

However, if the way you spend your money doesn't honor God, then you are in the wrong. If you spend it only for your own pleasure and comfort and without a view toward the needs of your family or the needs of the world, the Bible calls this sin. If your money is what makes you who you are, then you're in love with your wealth. The Bible warns that, "the love of money is

DAILY INSIGHT

TUESDAY

Passage:
Proverbs 3:1–10

Verses:
Proverbs 3:9–10

a root of all kinds of evil" (1 Timothy 6:10). What's more, if having money in the bank makes you feel secure, be very careful. Money is not trustworthy. It will disappoint you. Only God can truly be trusted (3:5).

Sitting at the First United Methodist Church in Waco, Texas, that Sunday morning, I had a morbid and very frightening vision. In my mind's eye, I saw the contents of my checkbook register being projected onto a huge screen for everyone to see. Then I saw Reverend Freeman using a long wooden pointer—like the one my geography teacher used to locate Mozambique—showing everyone, expenditure by expenditure; how messed up my priorities were. I resolved to make certain that, in the future, my check register would be acceptable for public consumption.

What does your checkbook register look like? What do you use your money for? What does it mean to you? How much faith do you have in its power?

Honor the Lord with your money. Make every expenditure acceptable from his viewpoint. Once you do, your "barns" will be bursting at the seams and your "wine cellar" will be filled with lots of valuable grape juice.

Remember this the next time you whip out your checkbook.

For your next devotional reading, go to page 683.

Discipline: Love Must Be Painful

"The LORD disciplines those he loves."
Proverbs 3:12a

BUILDING YOUR CHILDREN

One of the great misunderstandings of the whole concept of "love" is that when you love someone, your job is to always make him or her happy; to make sure he or she is always pleased with you. This is not so.

Just below my left shoulder, at the top of my arm, is a dime-sized scar. A doctor gave me this scar when I was seven. All I remember about getting my smallpox vaccination was that the physician used *two needles* to inflict this terrible thing on me.

In the past few years, I have learned what a smallpox vaccination really is. It's literally . . . *smallpox*. Of course, it's administered safely, under sound medical conditions, but it's really small pox—a little dose of the real thing.

Over the years you have probably met people who were wonderfully gifted, but who had lived lives of pathetic failure. Why? Because they didn't have the inner discipline to take all those brain cells and line them up to accomplish something truly productive. The book of Proverbs is full of advice for such people.

Now, follow me on this one: Since living out an undisciplined life is an extremely unpleasant experience, then disciplining your children should be small doses of the real thing—painful inflictions under sound and loving family conditions.

And what constitutes "painful," effective discipline? For starters, it's *not* words.

Imagine speeding along your favorite lonesome road, oblivious to the speed limit. Suddenly, you see a person in the distance—he looks a lot like a police officer— standing on the shoulder of the road. As you fly past him, you see him in your rearview mirror, screaming at you. You can tell that he's really into it because he's jumping up and down, shaking his fists, and, although he's way back there by now, he looks really mad.

Do you slow down? Hardly.

Unfortunately—and this is from personal experience—this is not what really happens. Police officers understand the value of swift (do not try to outrun that plain-looking, black car) and painful (what *else* could you have done with that $150?) action as a direct result of your intentional (you saw the signs) disobedience.

For your son or daughter, painful discipline may be a spanking, or it may be taking away a privilege. But, in order to be effective, it must provide enough discomfort for them to say to themselves, *You know,* that *wasn't fun. I think I'll do whatever I can to avoid that in the future.* Mission accomplished.

But discipline must also be fair. The Old Testament calls this "eye for eye, tooth for tooth, hand for hand, foot for foot" (Exodus 21:24). Actually, this is a simple principle: Jewish law provided that if you stole a man's mule, you had to replace it. If you burned his barn down, you were responsible to rebuild it. If you took someone's life, you should pay for it with your own.

Fairness in discipline means that the punishment should match the "crime." If your child leaves a mess, make her clean it up. Don't spank her and clean it up yourself. If your child hurts his friend, walk him to his friend's house and make him ask for forgiveness. If your children blatantly disobey you, spank them. And always remember that when you're disciplining your child, it's intended to be a helpful lesson for him, not an opportunity to assuage your own anger. You are issuing a little dose of the real thing . . . under sound, safe, family conditions.

A spanking when your child is six is not nearly as painful as a lost job or a broken marriage when he's twenty-eight because you didn't teach him how to control himself. Your children may not understand this form of "love" when they're small, but some day they'll understand that it was one of the most precious gifts you gave them.

²⁶for the LORD will be your confidence
and will keep your foot from being
snared.

²⁷Do not withhold good from those who
deserve it,
when it is in your power to act.
²⁸Do not say to your neighbor,
"Come back later; I'll give it
tomorrow"—
when you now have it with you.

²⁹Do not plot harm against your
neighbor,
who lives trustfully near you.
³⁰Do not accuse a man for no reason—
when he has done you no harm.

³¹Do not envy a violent man
or choose any of his ways,
³²for the LORD detests a perverse man
but takes the upright into his
confidence.

³³The LORD's curse is on the house of the
wicked,
but he blesses the home of the
righteous.
³⁴He mocks proud mockers
but gives grace to the humble.
³⁵The wise inherit honor,
but fools he holds up to shame.

Wisdom Is Supreme

4 Listen, my sons, to a father's
instruction;
pay attention and gain
understanding.
²I give you sound learning,
so do not forsake my teaching.
³When I was a boy in my father's house,
still tender, and an only child of my
mother,
⁴he taught me and said,
"Lay hold of my words with all your
heart;
keep my commands and you will live.
⁵Get wisdom, get understanding;
do not forget my words or swerve
from them.
⁶Do not forsake wisdom, and she will
protect you;
love her, and she will watch over you.
⁷Wisdom is supreme; therefore get
wisdom.
Though it cost all you have,ᵃ get
understanding.
⁸Esteem her, and she will exalt you;
embrace her, and she will honor you.
⁹She will set a garland of grace on your
head

and present you with a crown of
splendor."

¹⁰Listen, my son, accept what I say,
and the years of your life will be
many.
¹¹I guide you in the way of wisdom
and lead you along straight paths.
¹²When you walk, your steps will not be
hampered;
when you run, you will not stumble.
¹³Hold on to instruction, do not let it go;
guard it well, for it is your life.
¹⁴Do not set foot on the path of the
wicked
or walk in the way of evil men.
¹⁵Avoid it, do not travel on it;
turn from it and go on your way.
¹⁶For they cannot sleep till they do evil;
they are robbed of slumber till they
make someone fall.
¹⁷They eat the bread of wickedness
and drink the wine of violence.

¹⁸The path of the righteous is like the
first gleam of dawn,
shining ever brighter till the full light
of day.
¹⁹But the way of the wicked is like deep
darkness;
they do not know what makes them
stumble.

²⁰My son, pay attention to what I say;
listen closely to my words.
²¹Do not let them out of your sight,
keep them within your heart;
²²for they are life to those who find them
and health to a man's whole body.
²³Above all else, guard your heart,
for it is the wellspring of life.
²⁴Put away perversity from your mouth;
keep corrupt talk far from your lips.
²⁵Let your eyes look straight ahead,
fix your gaze directly before you.
²⁶Make levelᵇ paths for your feet
and take only ways that are firm.
²⁷Do not swerve to the right or the left;
keep your foot from evil.

Warning Against Adultery

5 My son, pay attention to my wisdom,
listen well to my words of insight,
²that you may maintain discretion
and your lips may preserve
knowledge.
³For the lips of an adulteress drip honey,
and her speech is smoother than oil;
⁴but in the end she is bitter as gall,

ᵃ7 Or *Whatever else you get*   ᵇ26 Or *Consider the*

sharp as a double-edged sword.
⁵Her feet go down to death;
   her steps lead straight to the grave.ᵃ
⁶She gives no thought to the way of life;
   her paths are crooked, but she knows
      it not.
⁷Now then, my sons, listen to me;
   do not turn aside from what I say.
⁸Keep to a path far from her,
   do not go near the door of her house,
⁹lest you give your best strength to
      others

and your years to one who is cruel,
¹⁰lest strangers feast on your wealth
   and your toil enrich another man's
      house.
¹¹At the end of your life you will groan,
   when your flesh and body are spent.
¹²You will say, "How I hated discipline!
   How my heart spurned correction!
¹³I would not obey my teachers
   or listen to my instructors.

ᵃ5 Hebrew *Sheol*

Adultery - 1, Larry - 0

DAILY INSIGHT

WEDNESDAY

Passage:
Proverbs 5:1–10

Verses:
Proverbs 5:3–4

The other day while walking the thirteen-and-a-half miles between gate four and gate thirty-nine at the Dallas Fort Worth airport, I bumped into Larry. To tell the truth, I almost didn't recognize him. He looked twenty years older than the last time I had seen him, just a few short years ago. Although he was thirty pounds heavier, his face looked gaunt and drawn. We spoke only briefly; under the circumstances, we didn't have much to say to each other.

To put it bluntly, Larry was, at one point in his life, a wild-eyed, nostril-flaring, chop-licking sex maniac. His record of extramarital exploits had as many entries as the "Smith" listing in a telephone book—from babysitters to women in airplane bathrooms. Incredibly, his activities had been completely hidden from those of us who thought we knew him ... especially his wife and four children.

Late one night I had received a phone call from a mutual friend. He apologized for waking me up, then said, "I've just heard that Larry tried to seduce a woman in Phoenix. I think you should talk to him and see what's going on."

The next day I was on a plane to visit with Larry. Line-by-line I spelled out the accusations, and line-by-line he denied each one. One month later, after I had received more information, I made the trip again. Predictably, Larry classified the allegations as ugly rumors. Wanting with all my heart to believe my friend, I got back on the plane and flew home.

Two weeks later, Larry's wife called me. Suspicious of Larry's behavior, she had decided to do some investigating of her own. Tragically, her intelligence work uncovered decades of her husband's gross unfaithfulness. I paid Larry one more visit. This time, however, I was armed with a letter from his wife, chronicling the truth she had discovered—unexplainable phone bills, unfamiliar contraceptives in his office, and even confessions from some of Larry's victims. Because Larry still would not take any responsibility for his life, she ordered him out of the house. One year later their divorce was final.

The words in this proverb ought to burn their way into our conscious minds like a hissing branding iron. "The lips of an adulteress drip honey ... but in the end she is bitter as gall."

As I looked at my friend that day at DFW, I saw the truth of this verse. The inescapable consequence of Larry's lurid past had taken a predictable and visible toll. "Larry, I haven't seen you for so long. How are you?" was all I said. "Fine, just fine," was his steely-eyed reply. With no hint of repentance or remorse or regret, Larry had said all he was going to say. We stood there for a silent moment, then hustled off in opposite directions to meet our waiting airplanes.

Adultery - 1, Larry - 0.

For your next devotional reading, go to page 688.

¹⁴I have come to the brink of utter ruin
in the midst of the whole assembly."

¹⁵Drink water from your own cistern,
running water from your own well.
¹⁶Should your springs overflow in the
streets,
your streams of water in the public
squares?
¹⁷Let them be yours alone,
never to be shared with strangers.
¹⁸May your fountain be blessed,
and may you rejoice in the wife of
your youth.
¹⁹A loving doe, a graceful deer—
may her breasts satisfy you always,
may you ever be captivated by her
love.
²⁰Why be captivated, my son, by an
adulteress?
Why embrace the bosom of another
man's wife?
²¹For a man's ways are in full view of the
LORD,
and he examines all his paths.

²²The evil deeds of a wicked man
ensnare him;
the cords of his sin hold him fast.
²³He will die for lack of discipline,
led astray by his own great folly.

Warnings Against Folly

6 My son, if you have put up security for
your neighbor,
if you have struck hands in pledge
for another,
²if you have been trapped by what you
said,
ensnared by the words of your
mouth,
³then do this, my son, to free yourself,
since you have fallen into your
neighbor's hands:
Go and humble yourself;
press your plea with your neighbor!
⁴Allow no sleep to your eyes,
no slumber to your eyelids.
⁵Free yourself, like a gazelle from the
hand of the hunter,

HEY DAD
Does God hate anything?

Text: Proverbs 6:16–19

God doesn't hate any people, but the Bible says there are at least seven things that he detests. These seven things can be summed up with one little word: sin. As a perfect being, God abhors anything that rebels against his perfection, and this listing contains several types of rebellion.

- **Pride:** God hates "haughty eyes," because he knows just how ridiculous it is when any person thinks he or she is better than another person. In God's eyes, we are all of equal value.
- **Lying:** God is Truth, and he hates it when we tell big lies, "little" lies, or any lies.
- **Murder:** God hates "hands that shed innocent blood." We see a lot of this today—drive-by shootings, terrorist acts, bombings. God hates such senseless destruction of human life.
- **Conspiracy:** God hates a "heart that devises wicked schemes," or that plots and plans to do evil.
- **Willingness to do evil:** God hates "feet that are quick to rush into evil," feet that act out the wicked plans of the heart.
- **Betrayal:** God hates it when people lie so that other individuals will be hurt.
- **Dissension:** This sin could include gossiping, cheating, stealing, lying—anything that pits one person against another and takes their focus off their identity as God's children.

Here we have a very clear list of actions and activities that God hates or finds detestable. They all have to do with things that distance us from himself and from living peacefully with others. As we are careful to avoid doing the things on this list, we will find ourselves being drawn closer to God and to others.

For a complete listing of Questions Kids Ask, turn to page 1435.

like a bird from the snare of the
fowler.

⁶ Go to the ant, you sluggard;
   consider its ways and be wise!
⁷ It has no commander,
   no overseer or ruler,
⁸ yet it stores its provisions in summer
   and gathers its food at harvest.

⁹ How long will you lie there, you
   sluggard?
   When will you get up from your
   sleep?
¹⁰ A little sleep, a little slumber,
   a little folding of the hands to rest—
¹¹ and poverty will come on you like a
   bandit
   and scarcity like an armed man.ᵃ

¹² A scoundrel and villain,
   who goes about with a corrupt
   mouth,
¹³   who winks with his eye,
   signals with his feet
   and motions with his fingers,
¹⁴   who plots evil with deceit in his
   heart—
   he always stirs up dissension.
¹⁵ Therefore disaster will overtake him in
   an instant;
   he will suddenly be destroyed—
   without remedy.

¹⁶ There are six things the LORD hates,
   seven that are detestable to him:
¹⁷   haughty eyes,
   a lying tongue,
   hands that shed innocent blood,
¹⁸   a heart that devises wicked
   schemes,
   feet that are quick to rush into evil,
¹⁹   a false witness who pours out lies
   and a man who stirs up dissension
   among brothers.

Warning Against Adultery

²⁰ My son, keep your father's commands
   and do not forsake your mother's
   teaching.
²¹ Bind them upon your heart forever;
   fasten them around your neck.
²² When you walk, they will guide you;
   when you sleep, they will watch over
   you;
   when you awake, they will speak to
   you.
²³ For these commands are a lamp,
   this teaching is a light,
   and the corrections of discipline
   are the way to life,

²⁴ keeping you from the immoral woman,
   from the smooth tongue of the
   wayward wife.
²⁵ Do not lust in your heart after her
   beauty
   or let her captivate you with her eyes,
²⁶ for the prostitute reduces you to a loaf
   of bread,
   and the adulteress preys upon your
   very life.
²⁷ Can a man scoop fire into his lap
   without his clothes being burned?
²⁸ Can a man walk on hot coals
   without his feet being scorched?
²⁹ So is he who sleeps with another man's
   wife;
   no one who touches her will go
   unpunished.

³⁰ Men do not despise a thief if he steals
   to satisfy his hunger when he is
   starving.
³¹ Yet if he is caught, he must pay
   sevenfold,
   though it costs him all the wealth of
   his house.
³² But a man who commits adultery lacks
   judgment;
   whoever does so destroys himself.
³³ Blows and disgrace are his lot,
   and his shame will never be wiped
   away;
³⁴ for jealousy arouses a husband's fury,
   and he will show no mercy when he
   takes revenge.
³⁵ He will not accept any compensation;
   he will refuse the bribe, however
   great it is.

Warning Against the Adulteress

7 My son, keep my words
   and store up my commands within
   you.
² Keep my commands and you will live;
   guard my teachings as the apple of
   your eye.
³ Bind them on your fingers;
   write them on the tablet of your
   heart.
⁴ Say to wisdom, "You are my sister,"
   and call understanding your
   kinsman;
⁵ they will keep you from the adulteress,
   from the wayward wife with her
   seductive words.

⁶ At the window of my house
   I looked out through the lattice.

ᵃ11 Or *like a vagrant / and scarcity like a beggar*

⁷I saw among the simple,
  I noticed among the young men,
  a youth who lacked judgment.
⁸He was going down the street near her
    corner,
  walking along in the direction of her
    house
⁹at twilight, as the day was fading,
  as the dark of night set in.
¹⁰Then out came a woman to meet him,
  dressed like a prostitute and with
    crafty intent.
¹¹(She is loud and defiant,
  her feet never stay at home;
¹²now in the street, now in the squares,
  at every corner she lurks.)
¹³She took hold of him and kissed him
  and with a brazen face she said:
¹⁴"I have fellowship offerings*ᵃ* at home;
  today I fulfilled my vows.
¹⁵So I came out to meet you;
  I looked for you and have found you!
¹⁶I have covered my bed
  with colored linens from Egypt.
¹⁷I have perfumed my bed
  with myrrh, aloes and cinnamon.
¹⁸Come, let's drink deep of love till
    morning;
  let's enjoy ourselves with love!
¹⁹My husband is not at home;
  he has gone on a long journey.
²⁰He took his purse filled with money
  and will not be home till full moon."

²¹With persuasive words she led him
    astray;
  she seduced him with her smooth talk.
²²All at once he followed her
  like an ox going to the slaughter,
  like a deer*ᵇ* stepping into a noose*ᶜ*
²³ till an arrow pierces his liver,
  like a bird darting into a snare,
  little knowing it will cost him his life.

²⁴Now then, my sons, listen to me;
  pay attention to what I say.
²⁵Do not let your heart turn to her ways
  or stray into her paths.
²⁶Many are the victims she has brought
    down;
  her slain are a mighty throng.
²⁷Her house is a highway to the grave,*ᵈ*
  leading down to the chambers of
    death.

Wisdom's Call

8 Does not wisdom call out?
  Does not understanding raise her
    voice?

²On the heights along the way,
  where the paths meet, she takes her
    stand;
³beside the gates leading into the city,
  at the entrances, she cries aloud:
⁴"To you, O men, I call out;
  I raise my voice to all mankind.
⁵You who are simple, gain prudence;
  you who are foolish, gain
    understanding.
⁶Listen, for I have worthy things to say;
  I open my lips to speak what is right.
⁷My mouth speaks what is true,
  for my lips detest wickedness.
⁸All the words of my mouth are just;
  none of them is crooked or perverse.
⁹To the discerning all of them are right;
  they are faultless to those who have
    knowledge.
¹⁰Choose my instruction instead of
    silver,
  knowledge rather than choice gold,
¹¹for wisdom is more precious than
    rubies,
  and nothing you desire can compare
    with her.

¹²"I, wisdom, dwell together with
    prudence;
  I possess knowledge and discretion.
¹³To fear the LORD is to hate evil;
  I hate pride and arrogance,
  evil behavior and perverse speech.
¹⁴Counsel and sound judgment are mine;
  I have understanding and power.
¹⁵By me kings reign
  and rulers make laws that are just;
¹⁶by me princes govern,
  and all nobles who rule on earth.*ᵉ*
¹⁷I love those who love me,
  and those who seek me find me.
¹⁸With me are riches and honor,
  enduring wealth and prosperity.
¹⁹My fruit is better than fine gold;
  what I yield surpasses choice silver.
²⁰I walk in the way of righteousness,
  along the paths of justice,
²¹bestowing wealth on those who
    love me
  and making their treasuries full.

²²"The LORD brought me forth as the first
    of his works,*ᶠ,ᵍ*

ᵃ14 Traditionally *peace offerings*   *ᵇ22* Syriac (see
also Septuagint); Hebrew *fool*   *ᶜ22* The meaning of
the Hebrew for this line is uncertain.   *ᵈ27* Hebrew
Sheol   *ᵉ16* Many Hebrew manuscripts and
Septuagint; most Hebrew manuscripts *and
nobles—all righteous rulers*   *ᶠ22* Or *way*; or
dominion   *ᵍ22* Or *The LORD possessed me at the
beginning of his work*; or *The LORD brought me
forth at the beginning of his work*

before his deeds of old;

²³ I was appointed[a] from eternity,
    from the beginning, before the world
      began.

²⁴ When there were no oceans, I was
      given birth,
    when there were no springs
      abounding with water;

²⁵ before the mountains were settled in
      place,
    before the hills, I was given birth,

²⁶ before he made the earth or its fields
    or any of the dust of the world.

²⁷ I was there when he set the heavens in
      place,
    when he marked out the horizon on
      the face of the deep,

²⁸ when he established the clouds above
    and fixed securely the fountains of
      the deep,

²⁹ when he gave the sea its boundary
    so the waters would not overstep his
      command,
and when he marked out the
      foundations of the earth.

³⁰   Then I was the craftsman at his side.
I was filled with delight day after day,
    rejoicing always in his presence,

³¹ rejoicing in his whole world
    and delighting in mankind.

³² "Now then, my sons, listen to me;
    blessed are those who keep my ways.

³³ Listen to my instruction and be wise;
    do not ignore it.

³⁴ Blessed is the man who listens to me,
    watching daily at my doors,
    waiting at my doorway.

³⁵ For whoever finds me finds life
    and receives favor from the LORD.

³⁶ But whoever fails to find me harms
      himself;
    all who hate me love death."

Invitations of Wisdom and of Folly

9 Wisdom has built her house;
    she has hewn out its seven pillars.

² She has prepared her meat and mixed
      her wine;
    she has also set her table.

³ She has sent out her maids, and she
      calls
    from the highest point of the city.

⁴ "Let all who are simple come in here!"
    she says to those who lack judgment.

⁵ "Come, eat my food
    and drink the wine I have mixed.

⁶ Leave your simple ways and you will
      live;
    walk in the way of understanding.

⁷ "Whoever corrects a mocker invites
      insult;
    whoever rebukes a wicked man
      incurs abuse.

⁸ Do not rebuke a mocker or he will hate
      you;
    rebuke a wise man and he will love
      you.

⁹ Instruct a wise man and he will be
      wiser still;
    teach a righteous man and he will
      add to his learning.

¹⁰ "The fear of the LORD is the beginning
      of wisdom,
    and knowledge of the Holy One is
      understanding.

¹¹ For through me your days will be many,
    and years will be added to your life.

¹² If you are wise, your wisdom will
      reward you;
    if you are a mocker, you alone will
      suffer."

¹³ The woman Folly is loud;
    she is undisciplined and without
      knowledge.

¹⁴ She sits at the door of her house,
    on a seat at the highest point of the
      city,

¹⁵ calling out to those who pass by,
    who go straight on their way.

¹⁶ "Let all who are simple come in here!"
    she says to those who lack judgment.

¹⁷ "Stolen water is sweet;
    food eaten in secret is delicious!"

¹⁸ But little do they know that the dead
      are there,
    that her guests are in the depths of
      the grave.[b]

Proverbs of Solomon

10 The proverbs of Solomon:

A wise son brings joy to his father,
    but a foolish son grief to his mother.

² Ill-gotten treasures are of no value,
    but righteousness delivers from death.

³ The LORD does not let the righteous go
      hungry
    but he thwarts the craving of the
      wicked.

⁴ Lazy hands make a man poor,
    but diligent hands bring wealth.

⁵ He who gathers crops in summer is a
      wise son,

---

a23 Or fashioned   *b18 Hebrew Sheol*

but he who sleeps during harvest is a disgraceful son.

⁶Blessings crown the head of the righteous,
but violence overwhelms the mouth of the wicked.ᵃ

⁷The memory of the righteous will be a blessing,
but the name of the wicked will rot.

⁸The wise in heart accept commands,
but a chattering fool comes to ruin.

⁹The man of integrity walks securely,
but he who takes crooked paths will be found out.

¹⁰He who winks maliciously causes grief,
and a chattering fool comes to ruin.

ᵃ6 Or *but the mouth of the wicked conceals violence*; also in verse 11

And That's Not All!

DAILY INSIGHT

THURSDAY

Passage:
Proverbs 10:27–32

Verse:
Proverbs 10:27

I'll bet there isn't a television producer alive who hasn't said a little prayer of thanks for the advent of the infomercial. We've come a long way from the days of video test patterns on the screen all night, and there is plenty of air time to fill.

These all-night shows sell things from impenetrable car wax, to machines that promise perfectly shaped rear ends, to amazing and time-saving cooking appliances, to video tapes that guarantee to fix every relationship. One of the universal features of these high-pressure sales pitches—besides an overly enthusiastic "host" and obnoxious audience participation—is the bonus.

After you've heard all about the benefits of the product and you're well aware that not a single store in the solar system carries this thing, the sales person informs you that you'd better "call now." And then, if you weren't completely convinced, he or she offers the clinching line: "And that's not all!" This is the frosting on the cake, the gravy on the platter, the generous "freebie" that you get when you purchase the product—even if it's something as mismatched as a set of amazing Japanese knives to go with your "Hits of the Sixties" compact disc set.

Unless you possess the internal constitution of General George Patton, in your insomniac stupor you find yourself unconsciously dialing the toll-free number and giving a total stranger your credit card number, your Social Security number, and the name of your firstborn child.

The Proverbs, with all due respect to Solomon, are something like those infomercials. You and I are presented with a profound promise, followed with a second statement … a kind of "and that's not all!" kicker.

Usually these little couplets make a lot of sense. When you and I read them, we often find ourselves sighing with resolve over their truths. But today's Proverb (10:27) seems confusing. The last time I checked, plenty of godless folks were still having birthdays. This second promise seems as unrelated to reality as the stainless cutlery that's being shipped with my Beatles collection.

The text says that the "years of the wicked are cut short." It doesn't say that the unrighteous are the ones who will actually die first. But it does say that the later years of unrepentant people will be filled with trouble and discouragement—cut short in quality, not necessarily quantity.

A longer, happier life because one honors the Lord? Now that's something you and I can really use. There's no credit card number needed to get this product. And the additional reminder that those who choose to shake their fists in God's merciful face will pay a devastating personal price is a warning more valuable than the sharpest carving knife the Orient has to offer.

Honor God. Live obediently, wholly free from guilt and hopelessness. And that's not all. If you don't honor him, you may still have birthday parties, but they probably won't be a lot of fun.

For your next devotional reading, go to page 690.

¹¹The mouth of the righteous is a
  fountain of life,
    but violence overwhelms the mouth
    of the wicked.

¹²Hatred stirs up dissension,
    but love covers over all wrongs.

¹³Wisdom is found on the lips of the
  discerning,
    but a rod is for the back of him who
    lacks judgment.

¹⁴Wise men store up knowledge,
    but the mouth of a fool invites ruin.

¹⁵The wealth of the rich is their fortified
  city,
    but poverty is the ruin of the poor.

¹⁶The wages of the righteous bring them
  life,
    but the income of the wicked brings
    them punishment.

¹⁷He who heeds discipline shows the way
  to life,
    but whoever ignores correction leads
    others astray.

¹⁸He who conceals his hatred has lying
  lips,
    and whoever spreads slander is a
    fool.

¹⁹When words are many, sin is not
  absent,
    but he who holds his tongue is wise.

²⁰The tongue of the righteous is choice
  silver,
    but the heart of the wicked is of little
    value.

²¹The lips of the righteous nourish many,
    but fools die for lack of judgment.

²²The blessing of the LORD brings wealth,
    and he adds no trouble to it.

²³A fool finds pleasure in evil conduct,
    but a man of understanding delights
    in wisdom.

²⁴What the wicked dreads will overtake
  him;
    what the righteous desire will be
    granted.

²⁵When the storm has swept by, the
  wicked are gone,
    but the righteous stand firm forever.

²⁶As vinegar to the teeth and smoke to
  the eyes,
    so is a sluggard to those who send
    him.

²⁷The fear of the LORD adds length to life,
    but the years of the wicked are cut
    short.

²⁸The prospect of the righteous is joy,
    but the hopes of the wicked come to
    nothing.

²⁹The way of the LORD is a refuge for the
  righteous,
    but it is the ruin of those who do evil.

³⁰The righteous will never be uprooted,
    but the wicked will not remain in the
    land.

³¹The mouth of the righteous brings
  forth wisdom,
    but a perverse tongue will be cut out.

³²The lips of the righteous know what is
  fitting,
    but the mouth of the wicked only
    what is perverse.

11 The LORD abhors dishonest scales,
      but accurate weights are his delight.

²When pride comes, then comes
  disgrace,
    but with humility comes wisdom.

³The integrity of the upright guides
  them,
    but the unfaithful are destroyed by
    their duplicity.

⁴Wealth is worthless in the day of wrath,
    but righteousness delivers from
    death.

⁵The righteousness of the blameless
  makes a straight way for them,
    but the wicked are brought down by
    their own wickedness.

⁶The righteousness of the upright
  delivers them,
    but the unfaithful are trapped by evil
    desires.

⁷When a wicked man dies, his hope
  perishes;
    all he expected from his power
    comes to nothing.

⁸The righteous man is rescued from
  trouble,
    and it comes on the wicked instead.

⁹With his mouth the godless destroys
  his neighbor,
    but through knowledge the righteous
    escape.

¹⁰When the righteous prosper, the city
  rejoices;

when the wicked perish, there are
shouts of joy.
11 Through the blessing of the upright a
city is exalted,
but by the mouth of the wicked it is
destroyed.
12 A man who lacks judgment derides his
neighbor,
but a man of understanding holds
his tongue.
13 A gossip betrays a confidence,
but a trustworthy man keeps a secret.

14 For lack of guidance a nation falls,
but many advisers make victory
sure.
15 He who puts up security for another
will surely suffer,
but whoever refuses to strike hands
in pledge is safe.
16 A kindhearted woman gains respect,
but ruthless men gain only wealth.
17 A kind man benefits himself,
but a cruel man brings trouble on
himself.

That's Your Dad on Page 106

Who's the richest man in the world? Every year, various magazines publish lists of the "Top 100 (or 500 or 1,000) Richest Men in the World." I don't know about you, but I am always fascinated with these lists. As I look over the income figures, I calculate how much the top earners make in a month, a week, a day. Last time, I figured that one man actually made $30 million a day in interest. *$30 million a day*—imagine that!

You and I are going on a little trip to our local convenience store. C'mon, jump in my car. I'll be happy to drive.

We pull into the parking lot, nearly missing two kids on skateboards, ice drinks in hand. We head inside the store, walk past the hot dog rotisserie, donut display case, and racks of candy to the magazine rack. There, amidst the customary news, sports, bodybuilding and auto magazines, we spot the one we came to the store to buy. It's a financial periodical, and this issue's feature is "The Richest Man in the World."

We can't wait to read the article, so we sit down on the bench right in front of the store. You turn to page 105, and start reading out loud about how the magazine ascertained the winner of this year's distinction.

Page 106 has a full-page photograph of "The Richest Man in the World." As you turn to it, you gasp in disbelief. The look in

DAILY INSIGHT

FRIDAY
Passage:
Proverbs 11:24–29
Verse:
Proverbs 11:24

your eye is a strange mix of shock and exhilaration; I'm not sure if you're going to yell or faint. Right there, in this month's issue of World Finance, is a color photograph of ... *your dad*! In that moment you realize that, as one of his children, your inheritance will be so great that, try as you might, you will never be able to spend it all ... not in your entire lifetime.

Are you ready for this? Even though our story is completely make-believe, it's the absolute truth! Your heavenly Father is not only the richest man in the world, he's the richest being in the universe. Your inheritance is more vast than you will ever be able to comprehend.

With this inheritance comes responsibility. Today's verse gives us as sobering a thought as we have ever contemplated. Before your children have access to this inheritance, it's going to have to pass through your hands. It's your choice. You can take this inheritance, invest it wisely and pass it in full measure to your family. Or you can be a fool and squander the lavish wealth your Father has for you, sending little but empty promises to the next generation.

In a few decades, your children will visit the same convenience store and thumb through the special issue of World Finance. Whose picture will they find on page 106?

For your next devotional reading, go to page 694.

¹⁸The wicked man earns deceptive
wages,
but he who sows righteousness reaps
a sure reward.

¹⁹The truly righteous man attains life,
but he who pursues evil goes to his
death.

²⁰The LORD detests men of perverse heart
but he delights in those whose ways
are blameless.

²¹Be sure of this: The wicked will not go
unpunished,
but those who are righteous will go
free.

²²Like a gold ring in a pig's snout
is a beautiful woman who shows no
discretion.

²³The desire of the righteous ends only in
good,
but the hope of the wicked only in
wrath.

²⁴One man gives freely, yet gains even
more;
another withholds unduly, but
comes to poverty.

²⁵A generous man will prosper;
he who refreshes others will himself
be refreshed.

²⁶People curse the man who hoards
grain,
but blessing crowns him who is
willing to sell.

²⁷He who seeks good finds goodwill,
but evil comes to him who searches
for it.

²⁸Whoever trusts in his riches will fall,
but the righteous will thrive like a
green leaf.

²⁹He who brings trouble on his family
will inherit only wind,
and the fool will be servant to the
wise.

³⁰The fruit of the righteous is a tree of
life,
and he who wins souls is wise.

³¹If the righteous receive their due on
earth,
how much more the ungodly and the
sinner!

12 Whoever loves discipline loves
knowledge,
but he who hates correction is
stupid.

²A good man obtains favor from the
LORD,
but the LORD condemns a crafty man.

³A man cannot be established through
wickedness,
but the righteous cannot be
uprooted.

⁴A wife of noble character is her
husband's crown,
but a disgraceful wife is like decay in
his bones.

⁵The plans of the righteous are just,
but the advice of the wicked is
deceitful.

⁶The words of the wicked lie in wait for
blood,
but the speech of the upright rescues
them.

⁷Wicked men are overthrown and are no
more,
but the house of the righteous stands
firm.

⁸A man is praised according to his
wisdom,
but men with warped minds are
despised.

⁹Better to be a nobody and yet have a
servant
than pretend to be somebody and
have no food.

¹⁰A righteous man cares for the needs of
his animal,
but the kindest acts of the wicked are
cruel.

¹¹He who works his land will have
abundant food,
but he who chases fantasies lacks
judgment.

¹²The wicked desire the plunder of evil
men,
but the root of the righteous
flourishes.

¹³An evil man is trapped by his sinful talk,
but a righteous man escapes trouble.

¹⁴From the fruit of his lips a man is filled
with good things
as surely as the work of his hands
rewards him.

¹⁵The way of a fool seems right to him,
but a wise man listens to advice.

¹⁶A fool shows his annoyance at once,
but a prudent man overlooks an
insult.

¹⁷ A truthful witness gives honest
testimony,
but a false witness tells lies.

¹⁸ Reckless words pierce like a sword,
but the tongue of the wise brings
healing.

¹⁹ Truthful lips endure forever,
but a lying tongue lasts only a
moment.

²⁰ There is deceit in the hearts of those
who plot evil,
but joy for those who promote
peace.

²¹ No harm befalls the righteous,
but the wicked have their fill of
trouble.

²² The LORD detests lying lips,
but he delights in men who are
truthful.

²³ A prudent man keeps his knowledge to
himself,
but the heart of fools blurts out
folly.

²⁴ Diligent hands will rule,
but laziness ends in slave labor.

²⁵ An anxious heart weighs a man down,
but a kind word cheers him up.

²⁶ A righteous man is cautious in
friendship,ᵃ
but the way of the wicked leads them
astray.

²⁷ The lazy man does not roastᵇ his game,
but the diligent man prizes his
possessions.

²⁸ In the way of righteousness there is life;
along that path is immortality.

13 A wise son heeds his father's
instruction,
but a mocker does not listen to
rebuke.

² From the fruit of his lips a man enjoys
good things,
but the unfaithful have a craving for
violence.

³ He who guards his lips guards his life,
but he who speaks rashly will come
to ruin.

⁴ The sluggard craves and gets nothing,
but the desires of the diligent are
fully satisfied.

⁵ The righteous hate what is false,
but the wicked bring shame and
disgrace.

⁶ Righteousness guards the man of
integrity,
but wickedness overthrows the
sinner.

⁷ One man pretends to be rich, yet has
nothing;

ᵃ26 Or *man is a guide to his neighbor* ᵇ27 The
meaning of the Hebrew for this word is uncertain.

HEY DAD

If I'm supposed to love everybody, why shouldn't I be friends with everybody?

Text: Proverbs 13:20

Jesus tells us to love everyone, even our enemies (Luke 6:27, 35). But Proverbs 13:20 says that if we are to grow wise, we must walk with wise people. If we choose "fools" as companions, we'll suffer harm.

A "companion" is much more than an acquaintance; he or she is one who becomes a close friend, a "traveling buddy," even a mate. If we choose companions who don't love God or don't act according to his Word, we're told in no uncertain terms that we're walking straight into trouble.

As dads, our job is to protect our children from harm. Therefore, our job is to teach them to choose friends wisely. And this lesson is every bit as important for us as it is for our kids. Our companions are either making us wiser or leading us right into harm's way.

The Bible doesn't contradict itself at all on this issue. Love your neighbor. Love your enemy. But choose your friends with care.

For a complete listing of Questions Kids Ask, turn to page 1435.

another pretends to be poor, yet has
great wealth.

[8] A man's riches may ransom his life,
but a poor man hears no threat.

[9] The light of the righteous shines
brightly,
but the lamp of the wicked is snuffed
out.

[10] Pride only breeds quarrels,
but wisdom is found in those who
take advice.

[11] Dishonest money dwindles away,
but he who gathers money little by
little makes it grow.

[12] Hope deferred makes the heart sick,
but a longing fulfilled is a tree of life.

[13] He who scorns instruction will pay for
it,
but he who respects a command is
rewarded.

[14] The teaching of the wise is a fountain
of life,
turning a man from the snares of
death.

[15] Good understanding wins favor,
but the way of the unfaithful is
hard.[a]

[16] Every prudent man acts out of
knowledge,
but a fool exposes his folly.

[17] A wicked messenger falls into trouble,
but a trustworthy envoy brings
healing.

[18] He who ignores discipline comes to
poverty and shame,
but whoever heeds correction is
honored.

[19] A longing fulfilled is sweet to the soul,
but fools detest turning from evil.

[20] He who walks with the wise grows wise,
but a companion of fools suffers
harm.

[21] Misfortune pursues the sinner,
but prosperity is the reward of the
righteous.

[22] A good man leaves an inheritance for
his children's children,
but a sinner's wealth is stored up for
the righteous.

[23] A poor man's field may produce
abundant food,
but injustice sweeps it away.

[24] He who spares the rod hates his son,
but he who loves him is careful to
discipline him.

[25] The righteous eat to their hearts'
content,
but the stomach of the wicked goes
hungry.

14 The wise woman builds her house,
but with her own hands the foolish
one tears hers down.

[2] He whose walk is upright fears the LORD,
but he whose ways are devious
despises him.

[3] A fool's talk brings a rod to his back,
but the lips of the wise protect them.

[4] Where there are no oxen, the manger is
empty,
but from the strength of an ox comes
an abundant harvest.

[5] A truthful witness does not deceive,
but a false witness pours out lies.

[6] The mocker seeks wisdom and finds
none,
but knowledge comes easily to the
discerning.

[7] Stay away from a foolish man,
for you will not find knowledge on
his lips.

[8] The wisdom of the prudent is to give
thought to their ways,
but the folly of fools is deception.

[9] Fools mock at making amends for sin,
but goodwill is found among the
upright.

[10] Each heart knows its own bitterness,
and no one else can share its joy.

[11] The house of the wicked will be
destroyed,
but the tent of the upright will
flourish.

[12] There is a way that seems right to a man,
but in the end it leads to death.

[13] Even in laughter the heart may ache,
and joy may end in grief.

[14] The faithless will be fully repaid for
their ways,
and the good man rewarded for his.

[15] A simple man believes anything,
but a prudent man gives thought to
his steps.

[a] 15 Or *unfaithful does not endure*

Loving You, Correcting You

Key Verse: *"He who spares the rod hates his son, but he who loves him is careful to discipline him."* Proverbs 13:24

Text: Proverbs 13:20–25 *(Dad or child reads the text.)*

QUIET TIMES WITH Dad

DAD READS: One of my favorite things about watching sports on television is marveling at the physical skills of the athletes. It amazes me that these men and women can run so fast, jump so high and be so agile and strong.

Child reads: I also love to watch these people playing basketball, hockey, football, baseball, or rocketing down the slopes on skis. I wonder how they got to be so fast and powerful.

DAD READS: Every once in a while athletes will say that they were just born with special skills and abilities. But most of the time they will admit that their skill really comes from the hard work of practice. They have not simply been given these talents, they have developed and improved them through years of painful training and discipline. And most great athletes have great coaches who make this possible.

Child reads: If people had the choice of being given their athletic abilities or having to work hard to earn them, most of them would probably choose the easy way. Most of the time, discipline is not fun.

DAD READS: The words we read today from Proverbs talk about the hard work and pain of discipline. They remind dads that if they choose not to correct their children, they are actually being unkind and unloving to them! If I were to do what I really want to do, I would never make your life unpleasant. I would say "yes" to everything. But in doing so, I would actually be ruining your life. Like an undisciplined athlete, you would lose every race, and that would be very sad for both of us.

Child reads: I don't like discipline either. I would rather have everything my way and never be corrected by my dad. But I know that this would not be good for me. I'm glad that you have decided to love me so much that you are willing to discipline and correct me.

DAD READS: I know that God loves me so much that he also disciplines me when I disobey. I also know that the more I allow God to correct me when I'm wrong, the better dad I will be for you.

Child reads: Thank you for wanting to be obedient to God, and thank you for loving me so much that you are willing to shape me into the person God wants me to be, too. Let me pray this prayer with you:

Our Father in heaven, thank you for loving us so much that you are willing to discipline and correct us. Thank you for giving me a dad who wants to obey you, and help me to learn to be obedient, too. Please give my dad the wisdom to be a good coach for me and help me to be a willing learner. In Jesus' name, Amen.

For your next devotional reading, go to page 696.

¹⁶A wise man fears the LORD and shuns
evil,
but a fool is hotheaded and reckless.

¹⁷A quick-tempered man does foolish
things,
and a crafty man is hated.

¹⁸The simple inherit folly,
but the prudent are crowned with
knowledge.

¹⁹Evil men will bow down in the presence
of the good,
and the wicked at the gates of the
righteous.

²⁰The poor are shunned even by their
neighbors,
but the rich have many friends.

²¹He who despises his neighbor sins,
but blessed is he who is kind to the
needy.

²²Do not those who plot evil go astray?
But those who plan what is good
find^a love and faithfulness.

²³All hard work brings a profit,
but mere talk leads only to poverty.

²⁴The wealth of the wise is their crown,
but the folly of fools yields folly.

²⁵A truthful witness saves lives,
but a false witness is deceitful.

²⁶He who fears the LORD has a secure
fortress,
and for his children it will be a refuge.

²⁷The fear of the LORD is a fountain of
life,
turning a man from the snares of
death.

²⁸A large population is a king's glory,
but without subjects a prince is
ruined.

²⁹A patient man has great
understanding,
but a quick-tempered man displays
folly.

³⁰A heart at peace gives life to the body,
but envy rots the bones.

³¹He who oppresses the poor shows
contempt for their Maker,
but whoever is kind to the needy
honors God.

³²When calamity comes, the wicked are
brought down,
but even in death the righteous have
a refuge.

³³Wisdom reposes in the heart of the
discerning
and even among fools she lets herself
be known.^b

³⁴Righteousness exalts a nation,
but sin is a disgrace to any people.

³⁵A king delights in a wise servant,
but a shameful servant incurs his
wrath.

15

A gentle answer turns away wrath,
but a harsh word stirs up anger.

²The tongue of the wise commends
knowledge,
but the mouth of the fool gushes
folly.

³The eyes of the LORD are everywhere,
keeping watch on the wicked and the
good.

⁴The tongue that brings healing is a tree
of life,
but a deceitful tongue crushes the
spirit.

⁵A fool spurns his father's discipline,
but whoever heeds correction shows
prudence.

⁶The house of the righteous contains
great treasure,
but the income of the wicked brings
them trouble.

⁷The lips of the wise spread knowledge;
not so the hearts of fools.

⁸The LORD detests the sacrifice of the
wicked,
but the prayer of the upright pleases
him.

⁹The LORD detests the way of the wicked
but he loves those who pursue
righteousness.

¹⁰Stern discipline awaits him who leaves
the path;
he who hates correction will die.

¹¹Death and Destruction^c lie open before
the LORD—
how much more the hearts of men!

¹²A mocker resents correction;
he will not consult the wise.

¹³A happy heart makes the face cheerful,
but heartache crushes the spirit.

^a22 Or show   ^b33 Hebrew; Septuagint and Syriac /
but in the heart of fools she is not known
^c11 Hebrew Sheol and Abaddon

¹⁴The discerning heart seeks knowledge,
but the mouth of a fool feeds on folly.

¹⁵All the days of the oppressed are
wretched,
but the cheerful heart has a
continual feast.

¹⁶Better a little with the fear of the LORD
than great wealth with turmoil.

¹⁷Better a meal of vegetables where there
is love
than a fattened calf with hatred.

¹⁸A hot-tempered man stirs up dissension,
but a patient man calms a quarrel.

¹⁹The way of the sluggard is blocked with
thorns,
but the path of the upright is a
highway.

²⁰A wise son brings joy to his father,
but a foolish man despises his
mother.

²¹Folly delights a man who lacks
judgment,

Especially Gentle

DAILY INSIGHT

MONDAY

Passage:
Proverbs 15:1–9

Verse:
Proverbs 15:1

A long time ago I was in a far-away city on business. Though my next day promised to be busy, the unfamiliar bed I was sleeping in wasn't helping me prepare; I was experiencing a full night of competition-quality tossing and turning. Around two o'clock, I reached for the remote and flipped the television on. Completely unfamiliar with the sequence of channels on this cable network, I slowly clicked one channel at a time. *Thirty-five channels and nothing's on,* I thought to myself as I rolled over, burying my face in a pillow.

Still unable to sleep, I began to mentally recap what I had just seen. *What if an intergalactic space traveler had seen what I just saw?* I thought to myself. *And what would he think if he were looking for an answer to the question, "What is a man?"*

I went back to my review. Championship "wrestling," now *there's* a great place to start. Where do they get these guys? Can't you see the classified ad: "Wanted. Strong, fat, hairy man with plenty of strategically located tattoos. Must be willing to cover himself with Vaseline and throw other strong, fat, hairy men around a boxing ring. No experience necessary." Then I flashed back to a few old sitcoms I had seen featuring Jackie Gleason, Dick Van Dyke, Desi Arnaz—men who yell a lot, men who trip over things; men who don't have a clue. And what about the music videos? There I saw men with leather pants so tight they look like a coat of gloss black enamel,

gyrating and sweating to what some call music. Finally I remembered the political roundtables featuring men whose vigorous and rude interruptions included name-calling and bitter stereotyping. *What would that space traveler think?*

The next thing I knew it was morning. But as I got up to shave and shower, I couldn't shake the images I'd seen in the middle of the night. Over breakfast I thought about my wife and my children, and the indescribable gift God had given me to be their husband and daddy. I thought about God's call to be his man for them, in spite of the weird and confusing images of manhood that cycled through my brain. And I thought of a word … the very word that opens today's Proverb: Gentle.

I saw our girls in their fuzzy yellow sleepers, pattering down the stairs to bowls of Corn Pops© or oatmeal. I saw my precious wife, hustling to cover for me in my absence. I envisioned what it would be like to see them in two days. And I could feel their loving embrace.

Folks sitting around me in the hotel restaurant must have thought there was something wrong with my breakfast. I pushed my toast back, bowed my head, and with my eyes swimming in tears, I asked my heavenly Father to make me more tender. More loving. More forgiving. More gentle. Especially gentle.

Amen.

For your next devotional reading, go to page 704.

Laughter: Are You Fun to Live With?

"A happy heart makes the face cheerful, but heartache crushes the spirit." Proverbs 15:13

BUILDING YOUR CHILDREN

"C'mon, Dad, lighten up."

For most men, life is not a laughing matter. The job of keeping food on the family table and a roof over head is nothing to take lightly. Throw in the task of keeping your family safe from all kinds of danger, whether that be the visible kind (the neighbor's nasty dog) or the kind you can't see (a classmate's nasty mouth), and you realize that life is really serious business. Finally, you have your own relationships to keep under control, and let's not go into detail about the fact that your own body is slowly falling apart because you're getting older.

In the face of all this serious responsibility, you might need some help in lightening up.

When our daughters were quite small, someone challenged me with the question, "Are you fun to live with?" At first I became defensive. But after I took an honest look at myself, the right answer to the question was, "Probably not."

So I decided to get serious about being more fun to live with, about intentionally creating more laughter in our home. I went to a local bookstore and bought some riddle books. I kept these near me at dinner time, just to spice up the conversation. We learned to play hide and seek inside the house—Julie always hid in the hall closet. I made up some games of my own, like "monster on the landing." We discovered together that the laughter brought a wonderful balance to all the necessary, serious stuff.

A few years ago I also found some help in the book of Proverbs (15:12–15). Maybe the lessons I learned will be helpful to you, too.

First, *encourage laughter in your home, but not cynicism.* Mocking is like poison in your home. A cynical comment at the expense of someone, especially a youngster, is never funny. Don't allow this of yourself, and don't allow it of others. Even

non-verbal insults—rolled eyes and mock smiles—can be ugly and painful. Again, don't do this, and don't allow others to do it. Laugh *with,* not *at* your children. Find books filled with fun things so you can have your child read the jokes, then get the "credit" for the laughter. You'll be laughing with them, not at their often-sensitive spirits. If they do something awkward or childish, be sure that they are laughing at themselves before you join in. Do not start this laughter. If you do, you will break their hearts, and this is never a laughing matter.

Second, *laugh at yourself.* Although it is always a bad idea to laugh at your children, it's almost always a good idea to be the brunt of the joke yourself. Everyday circumstances will give you the unintentional opportunity to make your kids laugh. One morning you may put on two different-colored socks or spill your orange juice at breakfast. Put on a big smile and let your children know that it's okay for them to chuckle at your expense. You can start this with, "Can you believe how silly your dad is?" then rear back and laugh.

Another way for your children to laugh at their dad is for you to recall things you did as a boy. They love to hear stories of awkward and embarrassing moments when you were growing up. They'll laugh and they'll be relieved to know that their own awkward and embarrassing childhood moments aren't going to kill them.

And finally, *smile.* "A happy heart makes the face cheerful." What does your face look like when your brain is in neutral? To find this answer to this question, a mirror can be your best friend! It will show you what your family sees when you're not thinking about anything in particular. Do you look angry? Bored? Tired? Or is there a smile on your resting face? This proverb (15:13) tells us that our faces will reflect what's in our hearts. Fill your heart with good things.

but a man of understanding keeps a
straight course.

²²Plans fail for lack of counsel,
but with many advisers they succeed.

²³A man finds joy in giving an apt reply—
and how good is a timely word!

²⁴The path of life leads upward for the
wise
to keep him from going down to the
grave.ᵃ

²⁵The LORD tears down the proud man's
house
but he keeps the widow's boundaries
intact.

²⁶The LORD detests the thoughts of the
wicked,
but those of the pure are pleasing to
him.

²⁷A greedy man brings trouble to his
family,
but he who hates bribes will live.

²⁸The heart of the righteous weighs its
answers,
but the mouth of the wicked gushes
evil.

²⁹The LORD is far from the wicked
but he hears the prayer of the
righteous.

³⁰A cheerful look brings joy to the heart,
and good news gives health to the
bones.

³¹He who listens to a life-giving rebuke
will be at home among the wise.

³²He who ignores discipline despises
himself,
but whoever heeds correction gains
understanding.

³³The fear of the LORD teaches a man
wisdom,ᵇ
and humility comes before honor.

16 To man belong the plans of the
heart,
but from the LORD comes the reply of
the tongue.

²All a man's ways seem innocent to him,
but motives are weighed by the
LORD.

³Commit to the LORD whatever you do,
and your plans will succeed.

⁴The LORD works out everything for his
own ends—
even the wicked for a day of disaster.

⁵The LORD detests all the proud of heart.
Be sure of this: They will not go
unpunished.

⁶Through love and faithfulness sin is
atoned for;
through the fear of the LORD a man
avoids evil.

⁷When a man's ways are pleasing to the
LORD,
he makes even his enemies live at
peace with him.

⁸Better a little with righteousness
than much gain with injustice.

⁹In his heart a man plans his course,
but the LORD determines his steps.

¹⁰The lips of a king speak as an oracle,
and his mouth should not betray
justice.

¹¹Honest scales and balances are from
the LORD;
all the weights in the bag are of his
making.

¹²Kings detest wrongdoing,
for a throne is established through
righteousness.

¹³Kings take pleasure in honest lips;
they value a man who speaks the
truth.

¹⁴A king's wrath is a messenger of death,
but a wise man will appease it.

¹⁵When a king's face brightens, it means
life;
his favor is like a rain cloud in
spring.

¹⁶How much better to get wisdom than
gold,
to choose understanding rather than
silver!

¹⁷The highway of the upright avoids evil;
he who guards his way guards his
life.

¹⁸Pride goes before destruction,
a haughty spirit before a fall.

¹⁹Better to be lowly in spirit and among
the oppressed
than to share plunder with the
proud.

²⁰Whoever gives heed to instruction
prospers,

ᵃ24 Hebrew *Sheol*   ᵇ33 Or *Wisdom teaches the fear
of the LORD*

and blessed is he who trusts in the
LORD.

²¹ The wise in heart are called discerning,
and pleasant words promote
instruction.ᵃ

²² Understanding is a fountain of life to
those who have it,
but folly brings punishment to fools.

²³ A wise man's heart guides his mouth,
and his lips promote instruction.ᵇ

²⁴ Pleasant words are a honeycomb,
sweet to the soul and healing to the
bones.

²⁵ There is a way that seems right to a
man,
but in the end it leads to death.

²⁶ The laborer's appetite works for him;
his hunger drives him on.

²⁷ A scoundrel plots evil,
and his speech is like a scorching
fire.

²⁸ A perverse man stirs up dissension,
and a gossip separates close friends.

²⁹ A violent man entices his neighbor
and leads him down a path that is
not good.

³⁰ He who winks with his eye is plotting
perversity;
he who purses his lips is bent on evil.

³¹ Gray hair is a crown of splendor;
it is attained by a righteous life.

³² Better a patient man than a warrior,
a man who controls his temper than
one who takes a city.

³³ The lot is cast into the lap,
but its every decision is from the
LORD.

17 Better a dry crust with peace and
quiet
than a house full of feasting,ᶜ with
strife.

² A wise servant will rule over a
disgraceful son,
and will share the inheritance as one
of the brothers.

³ The crucible for silver and the furnace
for gold,
but the LORD tests the heart.

⁴ A wicked man listens to evil lips;
a liar pays attention to a malicious
tongue.

⁵ He who mocks the poor shows
contempt for their Maker;
whoever gloats over disaster will not
go unpunished.

⁶ Children's children are a crown to the
aged,
and parents are the pride of their
children.

⁷ Arrogantᵈ lips are unsuited to a fool—
how much worse lying lips to a ruler!

⁸ A bribe is a charm to the one who gives
it;
wherever he turns, he succeeds.

⁹ He who covers over an offense
promotes love,
but whoever repeats the matter
separates close friends.

¹⁰ A rebuke impresses a man of
discernment
more than a hundred lashes a fool.

¹¹ An evil man is bent only on rebellion;
a merciless official will be sent
against him.

¹² Better to meet a bear robbed of her
cubs
than a fool in his folly.

¹³ If a man pays back evil for good,
evil will never leave his house.

¹⁴ Starting a quarrel is like breaching a
dam;
so drop the matter before a dispute
breaks out.

¹⁵ Acquitting the guilty and condemning
the innocent—
the LORD detests them both.

¹⁶ Of what use is money in the hand of a
fool,
since he has no desire to get wisdom?

¹⁷ A friend loves at all times,
and a brother is born for adversity.

¹⁸ A man lacking in judgment strikes
hands in pledge
and puts up security for his
neighbor.

¹⁹ He who loves a quarrel loves sin;
he who builds a high gate invites
destruction.

²⁰ A man of perverse heart does not
prosper;

ᵃ21 Or *words make a man persuasive*   ᵇ23 Or
mouth / and makes his lips persuasive   ᶜ1 Hebrew
sacrifices   ᵈ7 Or *Eloquent*

he whose tongue is deceitful falls
into trouble.

²¹ To have a fool for a son brings grief;
there is no joy for the father of a fool.

²² A cheerful heart is good medicine,
but a crushed spirit dries up the
bones.

²³ A wicked man accepts a bribe in secret
to pervert the course of justice.

²⁴ A discerning man keeps wisdom in
view,
but a fool's eyes wander to the ends
of the earth.

²⁵ A foolish son brings grief to his father
and bitterness to the one who bore
him.

²⁶ It is not good to punish an innocent
man,
or to flog officials for their integrity.

²⁷ A man of knowledge uses words with
restraint,
and a man of understanding is even-
tempered.

²⁸ Even a fool is thought wise if he keeps
silent,
and discerning if he holds his
tongue.

18 An unfriendly man pursues selfish
ends;
he defies all sound judgment.

² A fool finds no pleasure in
understanding
but delights in airing his own
opinions.

³ When wickedness comes, so does
contempt,
and with shame comes disgrace.

⁴ The words of a man's mouth are deep
waters,
but the fountain of wisdom is a
bubbling brook.

⁵ It is not good to be partial to the
wicked
or to deprive the innocent of justice.

⁶ A fool's lips bring him strife,
and his mouth invites a beating.

⁷ A fool's mouth is his undoing,
and his lips are a snare to his soul.

⁸ The words of a gossip are like choice
morsels;
they go down to a man's inmost
parts.

⁹ One who is slack in his work
is brother to one who destroys.

¹⁰ The name of the LORD is a strong tower;
the righteous run to it and are safe.

¹¹ The wealth of the rich is their fortified
city;
they imagine it an unscalable wall.

¹² Before his downfall a man's heart is
proud,
but humility comes before honor.

¹³ He who answers before listening—
that is his folly and his shame.

¹⁴ A man's spirit sustains him in sickness,
but a crushed spirit who can bear?

¹⁵ The heart of the discerning acquires
knowledge;
the ears of the wise seek it out.

¹⁶ A gift opens the way for the giver
and ushers him into the presence of
the great.

¹⁷ The first to present his case seems
right,
till another comes forward and
questions him.

¹⁸ Casting the lot settles disputes
and keeps strong opponents apart.

¹⁹ An offended brother is more unyielding
than a fortified city,
and disputes are like the barred gates
of a citadel.

²⁰ From the fruit of his mouth a man's
stomach is filled;
with the harvest from his lips he is
satisfied.

²¹ The tongue has the power of life and
death,
and those who love it will eat its fruit.

²² He who finds a wife finds what is good
and receives favor from the LORD.

²³ A poor man pleads for mercy,
but a rich man answers harshly.

²⁴ A man of many companions may come
to ruin,
but there is a friend who sticks closer
than a brother.

19 Better a poor man whose walk is
blameless
than a fool whose lips are perverse.

² It is not good to have zeal without
knowledge,
nor to be hasty and miss the way.

³A man's own folly ruins his life,
  yet his heart rages against the LORD.

⁴Wealth brings many friends,
  but a poor man's friend deserts him.

⁵A false witness will not go unpunished,
  and he who pours out lies will not go
    free.

⁶Many curry favor with a ruler,
  and everyone is the friend of a man
    who gives gifts.

⁷A poor man is shunned by all his
    relatives—
  how much more do his friends avoid
    him!
  Though he pursues them with
    pleading,
  they are nowhere to be found.ᵃ

⁸He who gets wisdom loves his own
    soul;
  he who cherishes understanding
    prospers.

⁹A false witness will not go unpunished,
  and he who pours out lies will
    perish.

¹⁰It is not fitting for a fool to live in
    luxury—
  how much worse for a slave to rule
    over princes!

¹¹A man's wisdom gives him patience;
  it is to his glory to overlook an
    offense.

¹²A king's rage is like the roar of a lion,
  but his favor is like dew on the grass.

¹³A foolish son is his father's ruin,
  and a quarrelsome wife is like a
    constant dripping.

¹⁴Houses and wealth are inherited from
    parents,
  but a prudent wife is from the LORD.

¹⁵Laziness brings on deep sleep,
  and the shiftless man goes hungry.

¹⁶He who obeys instructions guards his
    life,
  but he who is contemptuous of his
    ways will die.

¹⁷He who is kind to the poor lends to the
    LORD,
  and he will reward him for what he
    has done.

¹⁸Discipline your son, for in that there is
    hope;
  do not be a willing party to his death.

¹⁹A hot-tempered man must pay the
    penalty;
  if you rescue him, you will have to do
    it again.

²⁰Listen to advice and accept instruction,
  and in the end you will be wise.

²¹Many are the plans in a man's heart,
  but it is the LORD's purpose that
    prevails.

²²What a man desires is unfailing loveᵇ;
  better to be poor than a liar.

²³The fear of the LORD leads to life:
  Then one rests content, untouched
    by trouble.

²⁴The sluggard buries his hand in the
    dish;
  he will not even bring it back to his
    mouth!

²⁵Flog a mocker, and the simple will
    learn prudence;
  rebuke a discerning man, and he will
    gain knowledge.

²⁶He who robs his father and drives out
    his mother
  is a son who brings shame and
    disgrace.

²⁷Stop listening to instruction, my son,
  and you will stray from the words of
    knowledge.

²⁸A corrupt witness mocks at justice,
  and the mouth of the wicked gulps
    down evil.

²⁹Penalties are prepared for mockers,
  and beatings for the backs of fools.

20 Wine is a mocker and beer a
    brawler;
  whoever is led astray by them is not
    wise.

²A king's wrath is like the roar of a lion;
  he who angers him forfeits his life.

³It is to a man's honor to avoid strife,
  but every fool is quick to quarrel.

⁴A sluggard does not plow in season;
  so at harvest time he looks but finds
    nothing.

⁵The purposes of a man's heart are deep
    waters,
  but a man of understanding draws
    them out.

ᵃ7 The meaning of the Hebrew for this sentence is
uncertain. ᵇ22 Or *A man's greed is his shame*

⁶ Many a man claims to have unfailing
    love,
    but a faithful man who can find?

⁷ The righteous man leads a blameless
    life;
    blessed are his children after him.

⁸ When a king sits on his throne to judge,
    he winnows out all evil with his eyes.

⁹ Who can say, "I have kept my heart
    pure;
    I am clean and without sin"?

¹⁰ Differing weights and differing
    measures—
    the LORD detests them both.

¹¹ Even a child is known by his actions,
    by whether his conduct is pure and
    right.

¹² Ears that hear and eyes that see—
    the LORD has made them both.

¹³ Do not love sleep or you will grow poor;
    stay awake and you will have food to
    spare.

¹⁴ "It's no good, it's no good!" says the
    buyer;
    then off he goes and boasts about his
    purchase.

¹⁵ Gold there is, and rubies in abundance,
    but lips that speak knowledge are a
    rare jewel.

¹⁶ Take the garment of one who puts up
    security for a stranger;
    hold it in pledge if he does it for a
    wayward woman.

¹⁷ Food gained by fraud tastes sweet to a
    man,
    but he ends up with a mouth full of
    gravel.

¹⁸ Make plans by seeking advice;
    if you wage war, obtain guidance.

¹⁹ A gossip betrays a confidence;
    so avoid a man who talks too much.

²⁰ If a man curses his father or mother,
    his lamp will be snuffed out in pitch
    darkness.

²¹ An inheritance quickly gained at the
    beginning
    will not be blessed at the end.

²² Do not say, "I'll pay you back for this
    wrong!"
    Wait for the LORD, and he will deliver
    you.

²³ The LORD detests differing weights,
    and dishonest scales do not please
    him.

²⁴ A man's steps are directed by the LORD.
    How then can anyone understand
    his own way?

²⁵ It is a trap for a man to dedicate
    something rashly
    and only later to consider his vows.

²⁶ A wise king winnows out the wicked;
    he drives the threshing wheel over
    them.

²⁷ The lamp of the LORD searches the
    spirit of a man[a];
    it searches out his inmost being.

²⁸ Love and faithfulness keep a king
    safe;
    through love his throne is made
    secure.

²⁹ The glory of young men is their
    strength,
    gray hair the splendor of the old.

³⁰ Blows and wounds cleanse away evil,
    and beatings purge the inmost
    being.

21 The king's heart is in the hand
    of the LORD;
    he directs it like a watercourse
    wherever he pleases.

² All a man's ways seem right to him,
    but the LORD weighs the heart.

³ To do what is right and just
    is more acceptable to the LORD than
    sacrifice.

⁴ Haughty eyes and a proud heart,
    the lamp of the wicked, are sin!

⁵ The plans of the diligent lead to
    profit
    as surely as haste leads to poverty.

⁶ A fortune made by a lying tongue
    is a fleeting vapor and a deadly
    snare.[b]

⁷ The violence of the wicked will drag
    them away,
    for they refuse to do what is right.

⁸ The way of the guilty is devious,
    but the conduct of the innocent is
    upright.

---

a27 Or *The spirit of man is the LORD's lamp*
b6 Some Hebrew manuscripts, Septuagint and
Vulgate; most Hebrew manuscripts *vapor for those
who seek death*

⁹Better to live on a corner of the roof
  than share a house with a
    quarrelsome wife.

¹⁰The wicked man craves evil;
  his neighbor gets no mercy from
    him.

¹¹When a mocker is punished, the simple
    gain wisdom;
  when a wise man is instructed, he
    gets knowledge.

¹²The Righteous One*ᵃ* takes note of the
    house of the wicked
  and brings the wicked to ruin.

¹³If a man shuts his ears to the cry of the
    poor,
  he too will cry out and not be
    answered.

¹⁴A gift given in secret soothes anger,
  and a bribe concealed in the cloak
    pacifies great wrath.

¹⁵When justice is done, it brings joy to
    the righteous
  but terror to evildoers.

¹⁶A man who strays from the path of
    understanding
  comes to rest in the company of the
    dead.

¹⁷He who loves pleasure will become
    poor;
  whoever loves wine and oil will never
    be rich.

¹⁸The wicked become a ransom for the
    righteous,
  and the unfaithful for the upright.

¹⁹Better to live in a desert
  than with a quarrelsome and
    ill-tempered wife.

²⁰In the house of the wise are stores of
    choice food and oil,
  but a foolish man devours all he has.

²¹He who pursues righteousness and love
  finds life, prosperity*ᵇ* and honor.

²²A wise man attacks the city of the
    mighty
  and pulls down the stronghold in
    which they trust.

²³He who guards his mouth and his
    tongue
  keeps himself from calamity.

²⁴The proud and arrogant man—
    "Mocker" is his name;
  he behaves with overweening pride.

²⁵The sluggard's craving will be the death
    of him,
  because his hands refuse to work.

²⁶All day long he craves for more,
  but the righteous give without
    sparing.

²⁷The sacrifice of the wicked is
    detestable—
  how much more so when brought
    with evil intent!

²⁸A false witness will perish,
  and whoever listens to him will be
    destroyed forever.*ᶜ*

²⁹A wicked man puts up a bold front,
  but an upright man gives thought to
    his ways.

³⁰There is no wisdom, no insight, no plan
  that can succeed against the LORD.

³¹The horse is made ready for the day of
    battle,
  but victory rests with the LORD.

22 A good name is more desirable than
      great riches;
  to be esteemed is better than silver
    or gold.

²Rich and poor have this in common:
  The LORD is the Maker of them all.

³A prudent man sees danger and takes
    refuge,
  but the simple keep going and suffer
    for it.

⁴Humility and the fear of the LORD
  bring wealth and honor and life.

⁵In the paths of the wicked lie thorns
    and snares,
  but he who guards his soul stays far
    from them.

⁶Train*ᵈ* a child in the way he should go,
  and when he is old he will not turn
    from it.

⁷The rich rule over the poor,
  and the borrower is servant to the
    lender.

⁸He who sows wickedness reaps trouble,
  and the rod of his fury will be
    destroyed.

⁹A generous man will himself be
    blessed,
  for he shares his food with the poor.

ᵃ12 Or The righteous man   ᵇ21 Or righteousness
ᶜ28 Or / but the words of an obedient man will
live on   ᵈ6 Or Start

¹⁰Drive out the mocker, and out goes
    strife;
  quarrels and insults are ended.

¹¹He who loves a pure heart and whose
    speech is gracious
  will have the king for his friend.

¹²The eyes of the LORD keep watch over
    knowledge,
  but he frustrates the words of the
    unfaithful.

¹³The sluggard says, "There is a lion
    outside!"

or, "I will be murdered in the
    streets!"

¹⁴The mouth of an adulteress is a deep
    pit;
  he who is under the LORD's wrath will
    fall into it.

¹⁵Folly is bound up in the heart of a
    child,
  but the rod of discipline will drive it
    far from him.

¹⁶He who oppresses the poor to increase
    his wealth

Don't Step Right Up

DAILY INSIGHT

The only truly significant frustration of my college career was trying to decide what I was going to be "when I grew up." I had some classmates who, the day they hit campus, knew beyond a shadow of a doubt. Jim Hall was going to be a doctor. Steve Oldham was going to be a coach. Dan Boyd was going to be a professional photographer. Herb Shaw was going to be a CPA. Danny Alley was going to eat pizza. But I had no idea.

Suspecting this career ambivalence, my college professors were like carnival hawkers … "Step right up! Be this. Be that." Dr. Heath thought I should research ancient languages. Dr. Harrison thought I'd make a decent doctor. Dr. Wilson thought parish ministry would be perfect for me.

As a dad, you sometimes find yourself tempted to encourage your children to "step right up" and try to sell them on your dreams. Sometimes they feel the pressure to become what you want them to become. Because you want the best for your kids, it's tough to avoid this temptation. But it's even tougher to grow up under it.

Today's verse speaks directly to this problem. It's one you should plant deeply into your conscious mind: "Train a child in the way he should go." Look at the words again. "Train"—we understand what it means to be an effective coach. "A child"—we've got one of those. "In the way"—all of life is directional. There's no such thing as

TUESDAY

Passage:
Proverbs 22:1–6

Verse:
Proverbs 22:6

sitting still. We know that. "He should go"—now *there's* the clincher.

Being an effective dad has nothing to do with creating a clone of yourself. This is not an exercise in aiming your child at *your* target. Rather, it means helping your child to go in the direction he or she should go. To follow his or her own calling and develop his or her own gifts and strengths. To listen to God's voice in his or her own life.

Let me illustrate. Several years ago, I was having lunch with one of my closest friends. Often when we get together we joke and laugh, making a public nuisance of ourselves. But this time the conversation was gravely serious. At one point in the conversation my friend said something I'll never forget. "I'm a grown man. I have two children, two cars, a career, and a mortgage of my own. And, I've just discovered that I have become *exactly* what my parents wanted me to become. I have no idea who *I* am."

Don't allow this to happen to your kids. Don't try to get them to follow your agenda. Your job is to expose them to every option imaginable, to encourage them to pursue their own dreams, then to do whatever you can to help them be successful.

Train your child in the way he or she should go. Someday he or she will thank you for this.

For your next devotional reading, go to page 707.

and he who gives gifts to the rich—
  both come to poverty.

Sayings of the Wise

¹⁷ Pay attention and listen to the sayings
    of the wise;
  apply your heart to what I teach,
¹⁸ for it is pleasing when you keep them
    in your heart
  and have all of them ready on your
    lips.
¹⁹ So that your trust may be in the LORD,
  I teach you today, even you.
²⁰ Have I not written thirty^a sayings for
    you,
  sayings of counsel and knowledge,
²¹ teaching you true and reliable words,
  so that you can give sound answers
    to him who sent you?

²² Do not exploit the poor because they
    are poor
  and do not crush the needy in court,
²³ for the LORD will take up their case
  and will plunder those who plunder
    them.

²⁴ Do not make friends with a
    hot-tempered man,
  do not associate with one easily
    angered,
²⁵ or you may learn his ways
  and get yourself ensnared.

²⁶ Do not be a man who strikes hands in
    pledge
  or puts up security for debts;
²⁷ if you lack the means to pay,
  your very bed will be snatched from
    under you.

²⁸ Do not move an ancient boundary
    stone
  set up by your forefathers.

²⁹ Do you see a man skilled in his work?
  He will serve before kings;
  he will not serve before obscure
    men.

23 When you sit to dine with a ruler,
  note well what^b is before you,
² and put a knife to your throat
  if you are given to gluttony.
³ Do not crave his delicacies,
  for that food is deceptive.

⁴ Do not wear yourself out to get rich;
  have the wisdom to show restraint.
⁵ Cast but a glance at riches, and they are
    gone,
  for they will surely sprout wings
  and fly off to the sky like an eagle.

⁶ Do not eat the food of a stingy man,
  do not crave his delicacies;
⁷ for he is the kind of man
  who is always thinking about the
    cost.^c
  "Eat and drink," he says to you,
  but his heart is not with you.
⁸ You will vomit up the little you have
    eaten
  and will have wasted your
    compliments.

⁹ Do not speak to a fool,
  for he will scorn the wisdom of your
    words.

¹⁰ Do not move an ancient boundary
    stone
  or encroach on the fields of the
    fatherless,
¹¹ for their Defender is strong;
  he will take up their case against
    you.

¹² Apply your heart to instruction
  and your ears to words of knowledge.

¹³ Do not withhold discipline from a
    child;
  if you punish him with the rod, he
    will not die.
¹⁴ Punish him with the rod
  and save his soul from death.^d

¹⁵ My son, if your heart is wise,
  then my heart will be glad;
¹⁶ my inmost being will rejoice
  when your lips speak what is right.

¹⁷ Do not let your heart envy sinners,
  but always be zealous for the fear of
    the LORD.
¹⁸ There is surely a future hope for you,
  and your hope will not be cut off.

¹⁹ Listen, my son, and be wise,
  and keep your heart on the right
    path.
²⁰ Do not join those who drink too much
    wine
  or gorge themselves on meat,
²¹ for drunkards and gluttons become
    poor,
  and drowsiness clothes them in rags.

²² Listen to your father, who gave you life,
  and do not despise your mother
    when she is old.
²³ Buy the truth and do not sell it;

---

^a20 Or *not formerly written*; or *not written excellent*
^b1 Or *who*   ^c7 Or *for as he thinks within himself,
/ so he is*; or *for as he puts on a feast, / so he is*
^d14 Hebrew *Sheol*

get wisdom, discipline and
understanding.
²⁴ The father of a righteous man has great
joy;
he who has a wise son delights in
him.
²⁵ May your father and mother be glad;
may she who gave you birth rejoice!

²⁶ My son, give me your heart
and let your eyes keep to my ways,
²⁷ for a prostitute is a deep pit
and a wayward wife is a narrow well.
²⁸ Like a bandit she lies in wait,
and multiplies the unfaithful among
men.

²⁹ Who has woe? Who has sorrow?
Who has strife? Who has complaints?
Who has needless bruises? Who has
bloodshot eyes?
³⁰ Those who linger over wine,
who go to sample bowls of mixed
wine.
³¹ Do not gaze at wine when it is red,
when it sparkles in the cup,
when it goes down smoothly!
³² In the end it bites like a snake
and poisons like a viper.
³³ Your eyes will see strange sights
and your mind imagine confusing
things.
³⁴ You will be like one sleeping on the
high seas,
lying on top of the rigging.
³⁵ "They hit me," you will say, "but I'm not
hurt!
They beat me, but I don't feel it!
When will I wake up
so I can find another drink?"

24 Do not envy wicked men,
do not desire their company;
² for their hearts plot violence,
and their lips talk about making
trouble.

³ By wisdom a house is built,
and through understanding it is
established;
⁴ through knowledge its rooms are filled
with rare and beautiful treasures.

⁵ A wise man has great power,
and a man of knowledge increases
strength;
⁶ for waging war you need guidance,
and for victory many advisers.

⁷ Wisdom is too high for a fool;
in the assembly at the gate he has
nothing to say.

⁸ He who plots evil
will be known as a schemer.
⁹ The schemes of folly are sin,
and men detest a mocker.

¹⁰ If you falter in times of trouble,
how small is your strength!
¹¹ Rescue those being led away to death;
hold back those staggering toward
slaughter.
¹² If you say, "But we knew nothing about
this,"
does not he who weighs the heart
perceive it?
Does not he who guards your life know
it?
Will he not repay each person
according to what he has done?

¹³ Eat honey, my son, for it is good;
honey from the comb is sweet to
your taste.
¹⁴ Know also that wisdom is sweet to your
soul;
if you find it, there is a future hope
for you,
and your hope will not be cut off.

¹⁵ Do not lie in wait like an outlaw against
a righteous man's house,
do not raid his dwelling place;
¹⁶ for though a righteous man falls seven
times, he rises again,
but the wicked are brought down by
calamity.

¹⁷ Do not gloat when your enemy falls;
when he stumbles, do not let your
heart rejoice,
¹⁸ or the LORD will see and disapprove
and turn his wrath away from him.

¹⁹ Do not fret because of evil men
or be envious of the wicked,
²⁰ for the evil man has no future hope,
and the lamp of the wicked will be
snuffed out.

²¹ Fear the LORD and the king, my son,
and do not join with the rebellious,
²² for those two will send sudden
destruction upon them,
and who knows what calamities they
can bring?

Further Sayings of the Wise

²³ These also are sayings of the wise:

To show partiality in judging is not
good:
²⁴ Whoever says to the guilty, "You are
innocent"—

peoples will curse him and nations
     denounce him.
[25] But it will go well with those who
     convict the guilty,
   and rich blessing will come upon
     them.

[26] An honest answer
   is like a kiss on the lips.

[27] Finish your outdoor work
   and get your fields ready;
   after that, build your house.

[28] Do not testify against your neighbor
     without cause,
   or use your lips to deceive.
[29] Do not say, "I'll do to him as he has
     done to me;

I'll pay that man back for what he
     did."

[30] I went past the field of the sluggard,
   past the vineyard of the man who
     lacks judgment;
[31] thorns had come up everywhere,
   the ground was covered with weeds,
   and the stone wall was in ruins.
[32] I applied my heart to what I observed
   and learned a lesson from what I saw:
[33] A little sleep, a little slumber,
   a little folding of the hands to rest—
[34] and poverty will come on you like a
     bandit
   and scarcity like an armed man.[a]

a34 Or like a vagrant / and scarcity like a beggar

The House You Are Building Is for You

DAILY INSIGHT

WEDNESDAY

Passage:
Proverbs 24:1–6

Verses:
Proverbs 24:3–4

Once upon a time, there was a rich and prominent man who wanted to build a house for his family. When the architect had finished drawing his house plan, this man searched high and low until he found just the right builder.

When he finally chose the builder, he said, "I'm going to give you access to a building fund. In that fund I've placed enough money to allow you to purchase the finest materials money can buy. I've also included enough to generously cover your expenses and fees. Now I'm going on a long journey, so build me this house as I know you can. I trust you."

The builder got an idea. *Even though the plans call for the highest quality materials,* he thought, *I can use cheap products for the places the owner cannot see. Think of the extra money I can make!*

The builder took his idea to his Saturday morning breakfast friends. They thought his idea was a good one. They laughed at the thought of the rich man never knowing what was going to be used inside his walls.

A year later, the rich man returned. The house was finished, and the crooked builder gave the man a grand tour of the place. The rich man was impressed, and he was grateful. "You have built me a beautiful house,"

he finally said. "I am so glad I chose you as my builder."

Then he did something the builder never dreamed he would do. He took the house keys the builder had just given to him and handed them back.

"Life has been good to me," said the man. "I have made more money than I ever thought possible. I have more things than I could ever use, more assets than I could ever spend. Because you have been so faithful in building this beautiful house for me, I would like to give it back to you."

The builder tried to be happy. He wanted the man to think that he was thankful. But he knew that now he had to live in a house built with second-rate things. A house not truly fit to live in. A house built by a fool.

"By wisdom a house is built ... its rooms are filled with rare and beautiful treasures. A wise man has great power ... for waging war you need guidance, and for victory many advisers."

How could he have known that the house he was building was for himself? How could his friends have known?

Sleep well, Mr. Builder. Sleep well, foolish man.

For your next devotional reading, go to page 710.

More Proverbs of Solomon

25 These are more proverbs of Solomon, copied by the men of Hezekiah king of Judah:

² It is the glory of God to conceal a matter;
  to search out a matter is the glory of kings.

³ As the heavens are high and the earth is deep,
  so the hearts of kings are unsearchable.

⁴ Remove the dross from the silver,
  and out comes material for*ᵃ* the silversmith;
⁵ remove the wicked from the king's presence,
  and his throne will be established through righteousness.

⁶ Do not exalt yourself in the king's presence,
  and do not claim a place among great men;
⁷ it is better for him to say to you, "Come up here,"
  than for him to humiliate you before a nobleman.

What you have seen with your eyes
⁸ do not bringᵇ hastily to court,
  for what will you do in the end
  if your neighbor puts you to shame?

⁹ If you argue your case with a neighbor,
  do not betray another man's confidence,
¹⁰ or he who hears it may shame you
  and you will never lose your bad reputation.

¹¹ A word aptly spoken
  is like apples of gold in settings of silver.

¹² Like an earring of gold or an ornament of fine gold
  is a wise man's rebuke to a listening ear.

¹³ Like the coolness of snow at harvest time
  is a trustworthy messenger to those who send him;
  he refreshes the spirit of his masters.

¹⁴ Like clouds and wind without rain
  is a man who boasts of gifts he does not give.

¹⁵ Through patience a ruler can be persuaded,

and a gentle tongue can break a bone.

¹⁶ If you find honey, eat just enough—
  too much of it, and you will vomit.

¹⁷ Seldom set foot in your neighbor's house—
  too much of you, and he will hate you.

¹⁸ Like a club or a sword or a sharp arrow
  is the man who gives false testimony against his neighbor.

¹⁹ Like a bad tooth or a lame foot
  is reliance on the unfaithful in times of trouble.

²⁰ Like one who takes away a garment on a cold day,
  or like vinegar poured on soda,
  is one who sings songs to a heavy heart.

²¹ If your enemy is hungry, give him food to eat;
  if he is thirsty, give him water to drink.
²² In doing this, you will heap burning coals on his head,
  and the LORD will reward you.

²³ As a north wind brings rain,
  so a sly tongue brings angry looks.

²⁴ Better to live on a corner of the roof
  than share a house with a quarrelsome wife.

²⁵ Like cold water to a weary soul
  is good news from a distant land.

²⁶ Like a muddied spring or a polluted well
  is a righteous man who gives way to the wicked.

²⁷ It is not good to eat too much honey,
  nor is it honorable to seek one's own honor.

²⁸ Like a city whose walls are broken down
  is a man who lacks self-control.

26 Like snow in summer or rain in harvest,
  honor is not fitting for a fool.

² Like a fluttering sparrow or a darting swallow,
  an undeserved curse does not come to rest.

ᵃ4 Or *comes a vessel from*   ᵇ7,8 Or *nobleman / on whom you had set your eyes.* / ⁸*Do not go*

³A whip for the horse, a halter for the
donkey,
and a rod for the backs of fools!

⁴Do not answer a fool according to his
folly,
or you will be like him yourself.

⁵Answer a fool according to his folly,
or he will be wise in his own eyes.

⁶Like cutting off one's feet or drinking
violence
is the sending of a message by the
hand of a fool.

⁷Like a lame man's legs that hang limp
is a proverb in the mouth of a fool.

⁸Like tying a stone in a sling
is the giving of honor to a fool.

⁹Like a thornbush in a drunkard's hand
is a proverb in the mouth of a fool.

¹⁰Like an archer who wounds at random
is he who hires a fool or any
passer-by.

¹¹As a dog returns to its vomit,
so a fool repeats his folly.

¹²Do you see a man wise in his own eyes?
There is more hope for a fool than
for him.

¹³The sluggard says, "There is a lion in
the road,
a fierce lion roaming the streets!"

¹⁴As a door turns on its hinges,
so a sluggard turns on his bed.

¹⁵The sluggard buries his hand in the
dish;
he is too lazy to bring it back to his
mouth.

¹⁶The sluggard is wiser in his own eyes
than seven men who answer
discreetly.

¹⁷Like one who seizes a dog by the ears
is a passer-by who meddles in a
quarrel not his own.

¹⁸Like a madman shooting
firebrands or deadly arrows
¹⁹is a man who deceives his neighbor
and says, "I was only joking!"

²⁰Without wood a fire goes out;
without gossip a quarrel dies down.

²¹As charcoal to embers and as wood to
fire,
so is a quarrelsome man for kindling
strife.

²²The words of a gossip are like choice
morsels;
they go down to a man's inmost parts.

²³Like a coating of glazeᵃ over
earthenware
are fervent lips with an evil heart.

²⁴A malicious man disguises himself with
his lips,
but in his heart he harbors deceit.

²⁵Though his speech is charming, do not
believe him,
for seven abominations fill his heart.

²⁶His malice may be concealed by
deception,
but his wickedness will be exposed
in the assembly.

²⁷If a man digs a pit, he will fall into it;
if a man rolls a stone, it will roll back
on him.

²⁸A lying tongue hates those it hurts,
and a flattering mouth works ruin.

27 Do not boast about tomorrow,
for you do not know what a day may
bring forth.

²Let another praise you, and not your
own mouth;
someone else, and not your own lips.

³Stone is heavy and sand a burden,
but provocation by a fool is heavier
than both.

⁴Anger is cruel and fury overwhelming,
but who can stand before jealousy?

⁵Better is open rebuke
than hidden love.

⁶Wounds from a friend can be trusted,
but an enemy multiplies kisses.

⁷He who is full loathes honey,
but to the hungry even what is bitter
tastes sweet.

⁸Like a bird that strays from its nest
is a man who strays from his home.

⁹Perfume and incense bring joy to the
heart,
and the pleasantness of one's friend
springs from his earnest
counsel.

¹⁰Do not forsake your friend and the
friend of your father,
and do not go to your brother's house
when disaster strikes you—

ᵃ23 With a different word division of the Hebrew;
Masoretic Text *of silver dross*

better a neighbor nearby than a
brother far away.

¹¹ Be wise, my son, and bring joy to my
heart;
then I can answer anyone who treats
me with contempt.

¹² The prudent see danger and take
refuge,
but the simple keep going and suffer
for it.

¹³ Take the garment of one who puts up
security for a stranger;
hold it in pledge if he does it for a
wayward woman.

¹⁴ If a man loudly blesses his neighbor
early in the morning,
it will be taken as a curse.

¹⁵ A quarrelsome wife is like
a constant dripping on a rainy day;
¹⁶ restraining her is like restraining the
wind
or grasping oil with the hand.

¹⁷ As iron sharpens iron,
so one man sharpens another.

¹⁸ He who tends a fig tree will eat its fruit,
and he who looks after his master
will be honored.

¹⁹ As water reflects a face,
so a man's heart reflects the man.

²⁰ Death and Destruction[a] are never
satisfied,
and neither are the eyes of man.

a20 Hebrew Sheol and Abaddon

Tomorrow and Other Presumptions

DAILY INSIGHT

"There is nothing quite as sobering as canceling appointments for a once-busy dead man."

Bobbie and I heard these words many years ago as we sat in the audience under the teaching of one of our favorite authors. The power of these words still grips me.

Most men I know carry some kind of calendar. The one I carry is huge. It includes places for my license and credit cards along with monthly and daily calendars. In fact, just yesterday I ordered twelve more months' worth of pages. This is sound planning, wouldn't you agree? Come to think of it, it's pretty presumptuous, too.

Several years ago, I attended a seminar designed to help people effectively use these organizers. One of the seminar leader's statements reminded me of the quote from our author friend. "Never use anything but a pencil when you're filling out your calendar," he advised. "You never know what will happen." Not bad for a traveling time-management salesman.

Although King Solomon never carried a planner or attended a time-management seminar, he certainly understood all of these things. "Do not boast about tomorrow, for you do not know what a day may

THURSDAY

Passage:
Proverbs 27:1–6

Verse:
Proverbs 27:1

bring forth," he wisely said, pencil in hand.

My grandmother took this exhortation seriously. She never talked about future plans without prefacing them with, "The Lord willing." "The Lord willing, we'll have roasted chicken for dinner." "The Lord willing, we'll go to the store tomorrow." "The Lord willing, we'll see you this summer." As a kid, this really irritated me. *The Lord willing, you'll stop saying, "The Lord willing,"* I used to mutter under my breath.

Little did I realize how appropriate and profound this phrase was. In fact, my wife and I now use it ourselves, many times a day. Grandmother would be proud.

Carrying a calendar is good. Planning is a wise use of your time. Knowing what's coming next week, next month, and next year makes a lot of sense. But be sure to write this stuff in pencil, and be careful about being too confident. The Lord willing, we'll even get to tomorrow.

By the way, is there anything you ought to take care of just in case someone else has to cancel all your appointments next week?

For your next devotional reading, go to page 712.

²¹ The crucible for silver and the furnace
for gold,
but man is tested by the praise he
receives.

²² Though you grind a fool in a mortar,
grinding him like grain with a pestle,
you will not remove his folly from
him.

²³ Be sure you know the condition of your
flocks,
give careful attention to your herds;
²⁴ for riches do not endure forever,
and a crown is not secure for all
generations.
²⁵ When the hay is removed and new
growth appears
and the grass from the hills is
gathered in,
²⁶ the lambs will provide you with
clothing,
and the goats with the price of a
field.
²⁷ You will have plenty of goats' milk
to feed you and your family
and to nourish your servant girls.

28 The wicked man flees though no one
pursues,
but the righteous are as bold as a
lion.

² When a country is rebellious, it has
many rulers,
but a man of understanding and
knowledge maintains order.

³ A ruler ᵃ who oppresses the poor
is like a driving rain that leaves no
crops.

⁴ Those who forsake the law praise the
wicked,
but those who keep the law resist
them.

⁵ Evil men do not understand justice,
but those who seek the LORD
understand it fully.

⁶ Better a poor man whose walk is
blameless
than a rich man whose ways are
perverse.

⁷ He who keeps the law is a discerning
son,
but a companion of gluttons
disgraces his father.

⁸ He who increases his wealth by
exorbitant interest
amasses it for another, who will be
kind to the poor.

⁹ If anyone turns a deaf ear to the law,
even his prayers are detestable.

¹⁰ He who leads the upright along an evil
path
will fall into his own trap,
but the blameless will receive a good
inheritance.

¹¹ A rich man may be wise in his own eyes,
but a poor man who has
discernment sees through him.

¹² When the righteous triumph, there is
great elation;
but when the wicked rise to power,
men go into hiding.

¹³ He who conceals his sins does not
prosper,
but whoever confesses and
renounces them finds mercy.

¹⁴ Blessed is the man who always fears
the LORD,
but he who hardens his heart falls
into trouble.

¹⁵ Like a roaring lion or a charging bear
is a wicked man ruling over a
helpless people.

¹⁶ A tyrannical ruler lacks judgment,
but he who hates ill-gotten gain will
enjoy a long life.

¹⁷ A man tormented by the guilt of murder
will be a fugitive till death;
let no one support him.

¹⁸ He whose walk is blameless is kept
safe,
but he whose ways are perverse will
suddenly fall.

¹⁹ He who works his land will have
abundant food,
but the one who chases fantasies will
have his fill of poverty.

²⁰ A faithful man will be richly blessed,
but one eager to get rich will not go
unpunished.

²¹ To show partiality is not good—
yet a man will do wrong for a piece
of bread.

²² A stingy man is eager to get rich
and is unaware that poverty awaits
him.

²³ He who rebukes a man will in the end
gain more favor
than he who has a flattering tongue.

ᵃ3 Or *A poor man*

²⁴He who robs his father or mother
   and says, "It's not wrong"—
he is partner to him who
   destroys.

²⁵A greedy man stirs up dissension,
   but he who trusts in the LORD will
      prosper.

²⁶He who trusts in himself is a fool,
   but he who walks in wisdom is kept
      safe.

²⁷He who gives to the poor will lack
      nothing,
   but he who closes his eyes to them
      receives many curses.

²⁸When the wicked rise to power, people
      go into hiding;

but when the wicked perish, the
   righteous thrive.

29 A man who remains stiff-necked
         after many rebukes
will suddenly be destroyed—without
   remedy.

²When the righteous thrive, the people
      rejoice;
   when the wicked rule, the people
      groan.

³A man who loves wisdom brings joy to
      his father,
   but a companion of prostitutes
      squanders his wealth.

⁴By justice a king gives a country
      stability,

A Visit to Solomon's Cafeteria

DAILY INSIGHT

Every once in a while over the years, our family has gone out to eat at a cafeteria. When our daughters were small, we made up the "Judging Game." As we stood in the winding line waiting to fill our trays, we gave people ahead of us grades based on their food selections. Whole wheat bread earned a person an "A." Brussels sprouts received an "A+," although we felt sorry for the guy who had to eat them. French silk pie got a "D." Two desserts and the customer had to go back one full grade.

We did this quietly, of course. No one besides us ever knew we were doing such a rude and judgmental thing!

Today's text is like sliding your tray down the stainless steel rails at Luby's (or Morrison's or whatever the cafeteria in your town is called) and looking over a bunch of choices. As you move down the line, decide which ones you'll place on your tray.

Priorities (28:1). Why do you push so hard? Is it because you really have that much to do, or are you just afraid to fail? Are you avoiding something? What ... or whom? Be a lion. Know who you are and let your work serve you ... not the other way around.

Leadership (28:2). You're the only dad in the house. If you don't be the dad, who will?

FRIDAY
Passage:
Proverbs 28:1–9
Verse:
Proverbs 28:1

It's your choice—either pay attention and lovingly take charge or allow your family to sink into complete chaos.

Tenderness (28:3). Don't forget the "little" people in your life—the waitress, the neighbor kid, the clerk, that child of yours who is so different from you. If you ignore them, they'll drown.

Consistency (28:4–7). If your children's obedience is important to you, perhaps you ought to double check the speedometer the next time they're riding with you. Since cleaning their rooms is one of your favorite whipping posts, let's take a little tour of your garage.

Fairness (28:5). The same measure you use to issue justice and grace in your home will be used to measure your performance. Jesus said, "Forgive us our debts as we forgive our debtors."

Stewardship (28:6–8). Although there's very little in the way of financial commission paid out for right living, earning a piece of anything dishonestly will eventually make you sick to your stomach.

Which of these is for you today? By the way, if you're giving out grades, these are all good for you. Give them "A+'s!"

For your next devotional reading, go to page 714.

but one who is greedy for bribes
  tears it down.

⁵ Whoever flatters his neighbor
  is spreading a net for his feet.

⁶ An evil man is snared by his own sin,
  but a righteous one can sing and be
    glad.

⁷ The righteous care about justice for the
    poor,
  but the wicked have no such concern.

⁸ Mockers stir up a city,
  but wise men turn away anger.

⁹ If a wise man goes to court with a fool,
  the fool rages and scoffs, and there is
    no peace.

¹⁰ Bloodthirsty men hate a man of
    integrity
  and seek to kill the upright.

¹¹ A fool gives full vent to his anger,
  but a wise man keeps himself under
    control.

¹² If a ruler listens to lies,
  all his officials become wicked.

¹³ The poor man and the oppressor have
    this in common:
  The LORD gives sight to the eyes of
    both.

¹⁴ If a king judges the poor with fairness,
  his throne will always be secure.

¹⁵ The rod of correction imparts wisdom,
  but a child left to himself disgraces
    his mother.

¹⁶ When the wicked thrive, so does sin,
  but the righteous will see their
    downfall.

¹⁷ Discipline your son, and he will give
    you peace;
  he will bring delight to your soul.

¹⁸ Where there is no revelation, the
    people cast off restraint;
  but blessed is he who keeps the law.

¹⁹ A servant cannot be corrected by mere
    words;
  though he understands, he will not
    respond.

²⁰ Do you see a man who speaks in haste?
  There is more hope for a fool than
    for him.

²¹ If a man pampers his servant from
    youth,
  he will bring grief[a] in the end.

²² An angry man stirs up dissension,
  and a hot-tempered one commits
    many sins.

²³ A man's pride brings him low,
  but a man of lowly spirit gains honor.

²⁴ The accomplice of a thief is his own
    enemy;
  he is put under oath and dare not
    testify.

²⁵ Fear of man will prove to be a snare,
  but whoever trusts in the LORD is
    kept safe.

²⁶ Many seek an audience with a ruler,
  but it is from the LORD that man gets
    justice.

²⁷ The righteous detest the dishonest;
  the wicked detest the upright.

Sayings of Agur

30 The sayings of Agur son of Jakeh—an
  oracle[b]:

This man declared to Ithiel,
  to Ithiel and to Ucal:[c]

² "I am the most ignorant of men;
  I do not have a man's understanding.
³ I have not learned wisdom,
  nor have I knowledge of the Holy
    One.
⁴ Who has gone up to heaven and come
    down?
  Who has gathered up the wind in the
    hollow of his hands?
Who has wrapped up the waters in his
    cloak?
  Who has established all the ends of
    the earth?
What is his name, and the name of his
    son?
  Tell me if you know!

⁵ "Every word of God is flawless;
  he is a shield to those who take
    refuge in him.
⁶ Do not add to his words,
  or he will rebuke you and prove you
    a liar.

⁷ "Two things I ask of you, O LORD;
  do not refuse me before I die:
⁸ Keep falsehood and lies far from me;
  give me neither poverty nor riches,

---

[a]21 The meaning of the Hebrew for this word is
uncertain.   [b]1 Or *Jakeh of Massa*   [c]1 Masoretic
Text; with a different word division of the Hebrew
declared, "I am weary, O God; / I am weary, O God,
and faint.

It's the Little Things

Key Verse: *"Four things on earth are small, yet they are extremely wise."* Proverbs 30:24

Text: Proverbs 30:24–28 *(Dad or child reads the text.)*

DAD READS: When a man falls in love with a woman and decides to ask her to marry him, he gives her something very precious and very small—a diamond ring. The tiny gem in this ring is very valuable, and it has a lot of power! In fact, when a woman receives a diamond from a man, her life will never be the same. And neither will his.

Child reads: Sometimes little things can be very important things. A whole engine can stop working when a little part breaks. A strong chain can break when one tiny link gives out. A grown person gets sick and goes to bed when a tiny germ enters his body. Little things can do big things.

DAD READS: The verses we read today are about little things that do great things. Tiny ants can carry around objects that are ten times their own weight. Little badgers can made homes out of solid rock. Locusts are small insects that can destroy a huge crop. And lizards, even though they're not that hard to catch, can slither anywhere . . . even where kings live!

Child reads: I'm a little person. Even though I'm growing, I'm not as big as I'll be some day. These verses tell me that even though I'm small, I can do great things. I can serve people, and because most people like children, I can be welcome almost anywhere.

DAD READS: These verses also remind us that children, without the loving correction of their parents, can also do bad things . . . destroying things and going places where they shouldn't.

Child reads: Another verse in the Bible also tells us about little things having great power. "Don't let anyone look down on you because you are young, but set an example . . . in speech, in life, in love, in faith and in purity" (1 Timothy 4:12). Jesus also told grown-ups that children should be their examples of faith in him.

DAD READS: You and I usually talk about dads being the teachers and children being the students. But I want you to know that I want to learn from you, too. I want you to show me how to live, how to love, how to believe, and how to keep myself pure.

Child reads: I want to do these things, too. I know that you are watching me, and this helps me to be a better person. Thank you for being willing to learn from me. Let me pray this prayer with you:

Our Father in heaven, thank you for telling us about little things that do great things. Help me to remember that even though I'm a child, I can do mighty things for you. Help me to live as you want me to live, to love with your love, to believe with my whole heart, and to be pure. In Jesus' name, Amen.

For your next devotional reading, go to page 718.

but give me only my daily bread.
⁹Otherwise, I may have too much and
disown you
and say, 'Who is the Lord?'
Or I may become poor and steal,
and so dishonor the name of my
God.

¹⁰"Do not slander a servant to his master,
or he will curse you, and you will pay
for it.

¹¹"There are those who curse their
fathers
and do not bless their mothers;
¹²those who are pure in their own eyes
and yet are not cleansed of their filth;
¹³those whose eyes are ever so haughty,
whose glances are so disdainful;
¹⁴those whose teeth are swords
and whose jaws are set with knives
to devour the poor from the earth,
the needy from among mankind.

¹⁵"The leech has two daughters.
'Give! Give!' they cry.

"There are three things that are never
satisfied,
four that never say, 'Enough!':
¹⁶the grave,ᵃ the barren womb,
land, which is never satisfied with
water,
and fire, which never says, 'Enough!'

¹⁷"The eye that mocks a father,
that scorns obedience to a mother,
will be pecked out by the ravens of the
valley,
will be eaten by the vultures.

¹⁸"There are three things that are too
amazing for me,
four that I do not understand:
¹⁹the way of an eagle in the sky,
the way of a snake on a rock,
the way of a ship on the high seas,
and the way of a man with a maiden.

²⁰"This is the way of an adulteress:
She eats and wipes her mouth
and says, 'I've done nothing wrong.'

²¹"Under three things the earth trembles,
under four it cannot bear up:
²²a servant who becomes king,
a fool who is full of food,
²³an unloved woman who is married,
and a maidservant who displaces her
mistress.

²⁴"Four things on earth are small,
yet they are extremely wise:
²⁵Ants are creatures of little strength,

yet they store up their food in the
summer;
²⁶coneysᵇ are creatures of little power,
yet they make their home in the
crags;
²⁷locusts have no king,
yet they advance together in ranks;
²⁸a lizard can be caught with the hand,
yet it is found in kings' palaces.

²⁹"There are three things that are stately
in their stride,
four that move with stately bearing:
³⁰a lion, mighty among beasts,
who retreats before nothing;
³¹a strutting rooster, a he-goat,
and a king with his army around
him.ᶜ

³²"If you have played the fool and exalted
yourself,
or if you have planned evil,
clap your hand over your mouth!
³³For as churning the milk produces
butter,
and as twisting the nose produces
blood,
so stirring up anger produces strife."

Sayings of King Lemuel

31 The sayings of King Lemuel—an
oracleᵈ his mother taught him:

²"O my son, O son of my womb,
O son of my vows,ᵉ
³do not spend your strength on
women,
your vigor on those who ruin kings.

⁴"It is not for kings, O Lemuel—
not for kings to drink wine,
not for rulers to crave beer,
⁵lest they drink and forget what the law
decrees,
and deprive all the oppressed of their
rights.
⁶Give beer to those who are perishing,
wine to those who are in anguish;
⁷let them drink and forget their poverty
and remember their misery no
more.

⁸"Speak up for those who cannot speak
for themselves,
for the rights of all who are destitute.
⁹Speak up and judge fairly;
defend the rights of the poor and
needy."

ᵃ16 Hebrew *Sheol*   ᵇ26 That is, the hyrax or rock
badger   ᶜ31 Or *king secure against revolt*   ᵈ1 Or *of
Lemuel king of Massa, which*   ᵉ2 Or / *the answer to
my prayers*

Epilogue: The Wife of Noble Character

[10a]"A wife of noble character who can find?
    She is worth far more than rubies.
[11]Her husband has full confidence in her
    and lacks nothing of value.
[12]She brings him good, not harm,
    all the days of her life.
[13]She selects wool and flax
    and works with eager hands.
[14]She is like the merchant ships,
    bringing her food from afar.
[15]She gets up while it is still dark;
    she provides food for her family
    and portions for her servant girls.
[16]She considers a field and buys it;
    out of her earnings she plants a
        vineyard.
[17]She sets about her work vigorously;
    her arms are strong for her tasks.
[18]She sees that her trading is profitable,
    and her lamp does not go out at
        night.
[19]In her hand she holds the distaff
    and grasps the spindle with her
        fingers.
[20]She opens her arms to the poor
    and extends her hands to the needy.
[21]When it snows, she has no fear for her
        household;
    for all of them are clothed in scarlet.
[22]She makes coverings for her bed;
    she is clothed in fine linen and
        purple.

[23]Her husband is respected at the city
        gate,
    where he takes his seat among the
        elders of the land.
[24]She makes linen garments and sells
        them,
    and supplies the merchants with
        sashes.
[25]She is clothed with strength and
        dignity;
    she can laugh at the days to come.
[26]She speaks with wisdom,
    and faithful instruction is on her
        tongue.
[27]She watches over the affairs of her
        household
    and does not eat the bread of
        idleness.
[28]Her children arise and call her blessed;
    her husband also, and he praises her:
[29]"Many women do noble things,
    but you surpass them all."
[30]Charm is deceptive, and beauty is
        fleeting;
    but a woman who fears the LORD is
        to be praised.
[31]Give her the reward she has earned,
    and let her works bring her praise at
        the city gate.

a10 Verses 10-31 are an acrostic, each verse
beginning with a successive letter of the Hebrew
alphabet.

The book of Ecclesiastes will probably never be required reading for the attendees of motivational rallies. Its words will doubtlessly be forever stricken from those little day-at-a-time inspirational flip-calendars. (Can't you see flipping to February 18 and finding, "The fool folds his hands and ruins himself"? Now *there's* something that'll get your day started with a smile.)

But consider these questions: Who was your favorite teacher or professor? Who was the coach you'll never forget? When was your dad most helpful to you? The answer to all of these questions is something you already know. These people were memorable when they were tough on you, when they may have said, "That may be good enough for some other kid, but it's not good enough for you. You can be a great one, and I love you too much to let you get away with cutting corners." This book is filled with tough, take-a-lap stuff, but it might be exactly what dads need. It could even become one of your favorites.

Ecclesiastes

Everything Is Meaningless

1 The words of the Teacher,[a] son of David, king in Jerusalem:

[2] "Meaningless! Meaningless!"
    says the Teacher.
"Utterly meaningless!
    Everything is meaningless."

[3] What does man gain from all his labor
    at which he toils under the sun?
[4] Generations come and generations go,
    but the earth remains forever.
[5] The sun rises and the sun sets,
    and hurries back to where it rises.
[6] The wind blows to the south
    and turns to the north;

round and round it goes,
    ever returning on its course.
[7] All streams flow into the sea,
    yet the sea is never full.
To the place the streams come from,
    there they return again.
[8] All things are wearisome,
    more than one can say.
The eye never has enough of seeing,
    nor the ear its fill of hearing.
[9] What has been will be again,
    what has been done will be done
      again;
there is nothing new under the sun.
[10] Is there anything of which one can say,

---

[a]1 Or *leader of the assembly*; also in verses 2 and 12

"Look! This is something new"?
It was here already, long ago;
it was here before our time.
[11] There is no remembrance of men of old,
and even those who are yet to come
will not be remembered
by those who follow.

Wisdom Is Meaningless

[12] I, the Teacher, was king over Israel in Jerusalem. [13] I devoted myself to study and to explore by wisdom all that is done under heaven. What a heavy burden God has laid on men! [14] I have seen all the things that are done under the sun; all of them are meaningless, a chasing after the wind.

[15] What is twisted cannot be
straightened;
what is lacking cannot be counted.

[16] I thought to myself, "Look, I have grown and increased in wisdom more than anyone who has ruled over Jerusa-

A Little Message from a Blitzing Safety

I've often wondered what it would be like to be a successful quarterback in the National Football League. How would it feel to throw a last-minute, game-winning touchdown pass or scramble out of the pocket and run for the first down? What if seventy thousand fans were screaming for me? What a rush that would be.

Not long ago, I was watching one of those do-or-die NFL games—the winners make the playoffs, the losers get the rest of the year off. The quarterback dropped back, setting up for a pass to the wide receiver on a post pattern. The opposing team had called a safety blitz, and as the unsuspecting quarterback was preparing to release the ball, a fleet-footed and hard-charging defenseman had him in his cross-hairs. He blindsided the quarterback and pummeled him to the unforgiving earth as the force of the blow sent the loose football skittering to the ground. Fortunately, an attentive offensive lineman smothered it.

For the fallen field commander, the lights were out. For several minutes the quarterback lay motionless. Then, thankfully, he moved his hands. His feet followed closely behind. No broken neck—this time. The sigh of relief from the crowd was audible.

In a few minutes, a golf-cart-turned-stretcher was wheeling the bruised athlete from the field. And in a few more minutes, his replacement was barking out signals of his own, and the hometown fans were

DAILY INSIGHT

MONDAY

Passage:
Ecclesiastes 1:1–9

Verses:
Ecclesiastes 1:3–4

now shouting for the new guy.

As I watched, I couldn't help but imagine what the injured quarterback felt as he lay on an examining table in the locker room. He could probably hear the cheers and chants of the crowd upstairs ... but their cheers were for someone else. *After all I've sacrificed*, he might have groaned, *they're hollering for someone else.*

Solomon writes today's text from a locker room examining table. He reminds us that sometimes our work brings nothing but frustration and futility. We gain nothing. We make no progress. Youngsters, new recruits, young bucks—generations of them—blindside and slam us mercilessly to the ground. And then we're forgotten.

During this writing, Solomon is no candidate for a motivational speech at one of those positive-thinking rallies. He sends all of us a strong reminder. "Be careful what you cling to," he seems to say. "Be careful what you love." "Be careful how you invest yourself and what you put your hand to."

If you and I think we're immortal ... or irreplaceable ... or inexhaustible ... we're in for a powerful message from a blitzing safety. What we thought was here to stay could be gone tomorrow.

Time is *not* on your side. Cling only to those things worthy of your love, your investment and your work. Anything less will be a complete waste of your time.

For your next devotional reading, go to page 721.

lem before me; I have experienced much of wisdom and knowledge." [17]Then I applied myself to the understanding of wisdom, and also of madness and folly, but I learned that this, too, is a chasing after the wind.

[18]For with much wisdom comes much
    sorrow;
  the more knowledge, the more grief.

Pleasures Are Meaningless

I thought in my heart, "Come now, I will test you with pleasure to find out what is good." But that also proved to be meaningless. [2]"Laughter," I said, "is foolish. And what does pleasure accomplish?" [3]I tried cheering myself with wine, and embracing folly—my mind still guiding me with wisdom. I wanted to see what was worthwhile for men to do under heaven during the few days of their lives. [4]I undertook great projects: I built houses for myself and planted vineyards. [5]I made gardens and parks and planted all kinds of fruit trees in them. [6]I made reservoirs to water groves of flourishing trees. [7]I bought male and female slaves and had other slaves who were born in my house. I also owned more herds and flocks than anyone in Jerusalem before me. [8]I amassed silver and gold for myself, and the treasure of kings and provinces. I acquired men and women singers, and a harem[a] as well—the delights of the heart of man. [9]I became greater by far than anyone in Jerusalem before me. In all this my wisdom stayed with me.

[10]I denied myself nothing my eyes
    desired;
  I refused my heart no pleasure.
My heart took delight in all my work,
    and this was the reward for all my
    labor.
[11]Yet when I surveyed all that my hands
    had done
  and what I had toiled to achieve,
everything was meaningless, a chasing
    after the wind;
  nothing was gained under the sun.

Wisdom and Folly Are Meaningless

[12]Then I turned my thoughts to consider
    wisdom,
  and also madness and folly.
What more can the king's successor do
  than what has already been done?
[13]I saw that wisdom is better than folly,
  just as light is better than darkness.

[14]The wise man has eyes in his head,
  while the fool walks in the darkness;
but I came to realize
  that the same fate overtakes them
    both.

[15]Then I thought in my heart,

"The fate of the fool will overtake me
    also.
  What then do I gain by being wise?"
I said in my heart,
  "This too is meaningless."
[16]For the wise man, like the fool, will not
    be long remembered;
  in days to come both will be forgotten.
Like the fool, the wise man too must die!

Toil Is Meaningless

[17]So I hated life, because the work that is done under the sun was grievous to me. All of it is meaningless, a chasing after the wind. [18]I hated all the things I had toiled for under the sun, because I must leave them to the one who comes after me. [19]And who knows whether he will be a wise man or a fool? Yet he will have control over all the work into which I have poured my effort and skill under the sun. This too is meaningless. [20]So my heart began to despair over all my toilsome labor under the sun. [21]For a man may do his work with wisdom, knowledge and skill, and then he must leave all he owns to someone who has not worked for it. This too is meaningless and a great misfortune. [22]What does a man get for all the toil and anxious striving with which he labors under the sun? [23]All his days his work is pain and grief; even at night his mind does not rest. This too is meaningless.

[24]A man can do nothing better than to eat and drink and find satisfaction in his work. This too, I see, is from the hand of God, [25]for without him, who can eat or find enjoyment? [26]To the man who pleases him, God gives wisdom, knowledge and happiness, but to the sinner he gives the task of gathering and storing up wealth to hand it over to the one who pleases God. This too is meaningless, a chasing after the wind.

A Time for Everything

There is a time for everything,
  and a season for every activity under
    heaven:

---

[a]8 The meaning of the Hebrew for this phrase is uncertain.

² a time to be born and a time to die,
  a time to plant and a time to uproot,
³ a time to kill and a time to heal,
  a time to tear down and a time to
    build,
⁴ a time to weep and a time to laugh,
  a time to mourn and a time to dance,
⁵ a time to scatter stones and a time to
    gather them,
  a time to embrace and a time to
    refrain,
⁶ a time to search and a time to give
    up,
  a time to keep and a time to throw
    away,
⁷ a time to tear and a time to mend,
  a time to be silent and a time to
    speak,
⁸ a time to love and a time to hate,
  a time for war and a time for peace.

⁹What does the worker gain from his toil? ¹⁰I have seen the burden God has laid on men. ¹¹He has made everything beautiful in its time. He has also set eternity in the hearts of men; yet they cannot fathom what God has done from beginning to end. ¹²I know that there is nothing better for men than to be happy and do good while they live. ¹³That everyone may eat and drink, and find satisfaction in all his toil—this is the gift of God. ¹⁴I know that everything God does will endure forever; nothing can be added to it and nothing

taken from it. God does it so that men will revere him.

¹⁵Whatever is has already been,
  and what will be has been before;
  and God will call the past to
    account.ᵃ

¹⁶And I saw something else under the sun:

In the place of judgment—wickedness
    was there,
  in the place of justice—wickedness
    was there.

¹⁷I thought in my heart,

"God will bring to judgment
  both the righteous and the wicked,
for there will be a time for every
    activity,
  a time for every deed."

¹⁸I also thought, "As for men, God tests them so that they may see that they are like the animals. ¹⁹Man's fate is like that of the animals; the same fate awaits them both: As one dies, so dies the other. All have the same breathᵇ; man has no advantage over the animal. Everything is meaningless. ²⁰All go to the same place; all come from dust, and to dust all return. ²¹Who knows if the spirit of man rises up-

ᵃ15 Or *God calls back the past*   ᵇ19 Or *spirit*

HEY DAD
Where did God come from?

Text: Ecclesiastes 3:11–14

"Where did God come from?" Easy to ask—impossible to answer. Most dads like to be able to provide answers to such questions, but take heart! We can tell our kids we don't know without losing face. The Bible says it's *impossible* for man to know where God came from and then tells us why.

Ecclesiastes 3:11 says God has "set eternity in the hearts of men; yet they cannot fathom what God has done from beginning to end." Think about this. Instinctively, we know that we aren't the highest power in the universe. From the time we're born, something inside of us points us to God. Once we recognize God, that same something leads us—and our children—to ask, "Where did God come from?" But even though God made us to live eternally, right now we can't even begin to comprehend eternity.

Why can't we answer this question? Verse 14 says that God doesn't let us know everything because he wants us to honor him and revere him by faith. So if we think we've totally figured God out, we're hopelessly deluded. There is no way that a sinful, finite mind can even begin to scratch the surface of comprehending an infinite and utterly perfect God.

"Where does God come from?" You don't know? Don't worry. God planned it that way.

For a complete listing of Questions Kids Ask, turn to page 1435.

ward and if the spirit of the animal[a] goes down into the earth?"

22 So I saw that there is nothing better for a man than to enjoy his work, because that is his lot. For who can bring him to see what will happen after him?

Oppression, Toil, Friendlessness

4 Again I looked and saw all the oppression that was taking place under the sun:

I saw the tears of the oppressed—
    and they have no comforter;

power was on the side of their
        oppressors—
    and they have no comforter.
2 And I declared that the dead,
    who had already died,
are happier than the living,
    who are still alive.
3 But better than both
    is he who has not yet been,
who has not seen the evil
    that is done under the sun.

[a]21 Or Who knows the spirit of man, which rises upward, or the spirit of the animal, which

Trading for What's Behind Door Number Two

DAILY INSIGHT

TUESDAY

Passage:
Ecclesiastes 3:9–14

Verse:
Ecclesiastes 3:13

"You have a choice. You can keep your thousand dollars or trade it for what's behind door number two where Carol is standing." If I close my eyes, I can still see the "Let's Make a Deal" set and hear Monty Hall's slick salesman's voice.

"Oh, Monty, Monty," the confused contestant would blubber. "I don't know what to do." This poor person knew that door number two could hide any number of things—from a brand-new ski boat to a broken-down pack mule, complete with his hillbilly hat from "Hee Haw."

Genesis records the account of a man who had the Garden of Eden safely in his grasp and traded it for a taste of the fruit behind door number two. A worn-out donkey would have been a delight compared to what Adam actually received in exchange. "By the sweat of your brow," God commanded, "you will eat your food" (Genesis 3:19).

Millennia have passed since God's curse on Adam's free time. Kingdoms have come and gone. Many have continued to grovel in their sin, but some of God's people have discovered the euphoria of forgiveness and hope through the blood of a perfect Lamb. So in today's text, King Solomon provides us with another employment choice. "You can trade the sweat and toil behind door number two for the box that Johnny is bringing down the aisle right now."

"I'll take the box," we say without think-

ing. "Purposeless work is not for me."

As Solomon lifts the top off the box we hear these words, "Every man may eat and drink, and find satisfaction in all his toil—this is a gift from God." Did you hear that? Work is a not a curse. Work is a blessing.

How is it with you? Do you look forward to another day of work or does the thought of it create a sinking feeling in the pit of your stomach? Are you Adam or are you Solomon? Will you choose meaningless sweat or purposeful accomplishment; God's gift or his curse?

You spend more of your waking hours engaged in work than in any other activity. Can you imagine that your gracious heavenly Father, the One who has given you life and who lovingly sustains it, would want you to dread the largest slice of your life? Not a chance.

This might be a day for you to carefully examine what you're doing with your work. Is the work of your hands satisfying to you? Do you feel God's blessing on your labor? If the answer is "yes" to these questions, you've got something to be thankful for. If it's "no," this may be a good time to take a careful look at what you're doing.

Monty Hall may have something for you in his pocket. If you want my advice, I'd trade for it. What do you have to lose?

For your next devotional reading, go to page 723.

⁴And I saw that all labor and all achievement spring from man's envy of his neighbor. This too is meaningless, a chasing after the wind.

⁵The fool folds his hands
   and ruins himself.
⁶Better one handful with tranquillity
   than two handfuls with toil
   and chasing after the wind.

⁷Again I saw something meaningless under the sun:

⁸There was a man all alone;
   he had neither son nor brother.
There was no end to his toil,
   yet his eyes were not content with
      his wealth.
"For whom am I toiling," he asked,
   "and why am I depriving myself of
      enjoyment?"
This too is meaningless—
   a miserable business!

⁹Two are better than one,
   because they have a good return for
      their work:
¹⁰If one falls down,
   his friend can help him up.
But pity the man who falls
   and has no one to help him up!
¹¹Also, if two lie down together, they will
      keep warm.
   But how can one keep warm
      alone?
¹²Though one may be overpowered,
   two can defend themselves.
A cord of three strands is not quickly
   broken.

Advancement Is Meaningless

¹³Better a poor but wise youth than an old but foolish king who no longer knows how to take warning. ¹⁴The youth may have come from prison to the kingship, or he may have been born in poverty within his kingdom. ¹⁵I saw that all who lived and walked under the sun followed the youth, the king's successor. ¹⁶There was no end to all the people who were before them. But those who came later were not pleased with the successor. This too is meaningless, a chasing after the wind.

Stand in Awe of God

5 Guard your steps when you go to the house of God. Go near to listen rather than to offer the sacrifice of fools, who do not know that they do wrong.

²Do not be quick with your mouth,
   do not be hasty in your heart
      to utter anything before God.
God is in heaven
   and you are on earth,
      so let your words be few.
³As a dream comes when there are
      many cares,
   so the speech of a fool when there
      are many words.

⁴When you make a vow to God, do not delay in fulfilling it. He has no pleasure in fools; fulfill your vow. ⁵It is better not to vow than to make a vow and not fulfill it. ⁶Do not let your mouth lead you into sin. And do not protest to the temple messenger, "My vow was a mistake." Why should God be angry at what you say and destroy the work of your hands? ⁷Much dreaming and many words are meaningless. Therefore stand in awe of God.

Riches Are Meaningless

⁸If you see the poor oppressed in a district, and justice and rights denied, do not be surprised at such things; for one official is eyed by a higher one, and over them both are others higher still. ⁹The increase from the land is taken by all; the king himself profits from the fields.

¹⁰Whoever loves money never has money
      enough;
   whoever loves wealth is never
      satisfied with his income.
This too is meaningless.

¹¹As goods increase,
   so do those who consume them.
And what benefit are they to the owner
   except to feast his eyes on them?

¹²The sleep of a laborer is sweet,
   whether he eats little or much,
but the abundance of a rich man
   permits him no sleep.

¹³I have seen a grievous evil under the sun:

   wealth hoarded to the harm of its
      owner,
¹⁴   or wealth lost through some
         misfortune,
   so that when he has a son
      there is nothing left for him.
¹⁵Naked a man comes from his mother's
      womb,
   and as he comes, so he departs.
He takes nothing from his labor
   that he can carry in his hand.

16This too is a grievous evil:

As a man comes, so he departs,
    and what does he gain,
    since he toils for the wind?
17All his days he eats in darkness,
    with great frustration, affliction and
    anger.

18Then I realized that it is good and proper for a man to eat and drink, and to find satisfaction in his toilsome labor un-der the sun during the few days of life God has given him—for this is his lot. **19**Moreover, when God gives any man wealth and possessions, and enables him to enjoy them, to accept his lot and be happy in his work—this is a gift of God. **20**He seldom reflects on the days of his life, because God keeps him occupied with gladness of heart.

6 I have seen another evil under the sun, and it weighs heavily on men: **2**God

Many Hands Make Light Work

DAILY INSIGHT

WEDNESDAY

Passage:
Ecclesiastes 4:9–12
Verse:
Ecclesiastes 4:9

When I was in high school, the churches in our town decided to reserve the big pavilion at the county fair grounds for a week-long youth conference. During one of the evening meetings, the power went out. Since no storm was racing through the city, we knew bad weather hadn't knocked it out.

The host of the event went to the center of the platform and called out, "Don't panic. We've lost power, but we think we can fix it." Then he asked all of us to raise our arms high into the air. "Do you believe in the wisdom of old Chinese prov-erbs?" the enthusiastic man shouted. We already had our hands in the air.

"Yes," we shouted, having no idea what was going on.

"Well, I want you to shake your hands." We obeyed. "Now really *shake* them." We really shook them.

In a moment, the lights were on. The microphone popped its return to life. Everyone shouted, happy to be able to see again, but we were still waiting for the Chinese proverb.

Our cheesy host went back to the microphone. "Confucius say, 'Many hands make light work.' "

Well-deserved groans and catcalls came from everywhere. But soon we were laughing at ourselves, having been caught in such a set-up. Decades later, not only do I remember this silly trick, but I am certain of its truth.

Families are a lot of work. Have you noticed? Around the house there is always something to pick up, clean up, fix up or put up. And most of us—especially dads—would rather be served than serve. Although we wouldn't actually call it laziness, between you and me, this is pretty much what it is.

Today, King Solomon is delivering a timely message to us. He's telling us to pitch in. He's challenging us to change a diaper, empty the dishwasher, or offer a Diet Coke to our wife. He's reminding us that this family thing involves a team effort; we're working together for each other. Helping out is one simple way of showing our wife and children that we really are thankful for them.

Several years ago, Patrick Morley decided to act on this truth. Right after dinner, he announced, "I'll do the dinner dishes." His wife and kids sat at the table, stunned at the offer. The next night, he did the same ... and the next night, and the next night. For two solid weeks, Patrick did the dinner dishes.

Early one morning, Patrick flipped on the bathroom light and saw something he had never seen before. There, right in the middle of his line of vision, taped to the mirror, was a note from his wife. "Thanks for being my best friend," was all it said.

Look around. You have plenty of little things to do. Rally the troops together. Lead the charge. Get busy. Many hands make light work, and you've got two of them.

For your next devotional reading, go to page 725.

gives a man wealth, possessions and honor, so that he lacks nothing his heart desires, but God does not enable him to enjoy them, and a stranger enjoys them instead. This is meaningless, a grievous evil.

³A man may have a hundred children and live many years; yet no matter how long he lives, if he cannot enjoy his prosperity and does not receive proper burial, I say that a stillborn child is better off than he. ⁴It comes without meaning, it departs in darkness, and in darkness its name is shrouded. ⁵Though it never saw the sun or knew anything, it has more rest than does that man— ⁶even if he lives a thousand years twice over but fails to enjoy his prosperity. Do not all go to the same place?

⁷All man's efforts are for his mouth,
  yet his appetite is never satisfied.
⁸What advantage has a wise man
  over a fool?
What does a poor man gain
  by knowing how to conduct himself
    before others?
⁹Better what the eye sees
  than the roving of the appetite.
This too is meaningless,
  a chasing after the wind.

¹⁰Whatever exists has already been
    named,
  and what man is has been known;
no man can contend
  with one who is stronger than he.
¹¹The more the words,
  the less the meaning,
  and how does that profit anyone?

¹²For who knows what is good for a man in life, during the few and meaningless days he passes through like a shadow? Who can tell him what will happen under the sun after he is gone?

Wisdom

7 A good name is better than fine
    perfume,
  and the day of death better than the
    day of birth.
²It is better to go to a house of mourning
  than to go to a house of feasting,
  for death is the destiny of every man;
    the living should take this to heart.
³Sorrow is better than laughter,
  because a sad face is good for the
    heart.
⁴The heart of the wise is in the house of
    mourning,

but the heart of fools is in the house
    of pleasure.
⁵It is better to heed a wise man's
    rebuke
  than to listen to the song of fools.
⁶Like the crackling of thorns under the
    pot,
  so is the laughter of fools.
  This too is meaningless.

⁷Extortion turns a wise man into a fool,
  and a bribe corrupts the heart.

⁸The end of a matter is better than its
    beginning,
  and patience is better than pride.
⁹Do not be quickly provoked in your
    spirit,
  for anger resides in the lap of fools.

¹⁰Do not say, "Why were the old days
    better than these?"
  For it is not wise to ask such
    questions.

¹¹Wisdom, like an inheritance, is a good
    thing
  and benefits those who see the sun.
¹²Wisdom is a shelter
  as money is a shelter,
  but the advantage of knowledge is this:
    that wisdom preserves the life of its
    possessor.

¹³Consider what God has done:

Who can straighten
  what he has made crooked?
¹⁴When times are good, be happy;
  but when times are bad, consider:
God has made the one
  as well as the other.
Therefore, a man cannot discover
  anything about his future.

¹⁵In this meaningless life of mine I have seen both of these:

a righteous man perishing in his
    righteousness,
  and a wicked man living long in his
    wickedness.
¹⁶Do not be overrighteous,
  neither be overwise—
  why destroy yourself?
¹⁷Do not be overwicked,
  and do not be a fool—
  why die before your time?
¹⁸It is good to grasp the one
  and not let go of the other.
  The man who fears God will avoid all
    ⸢extremes⸣.ᵃ

ᵃ18 Or *will follow them both*

19 Wisdom makes one wise man more
powerful
than ten rulers in a city.
20 There is not a righteous man on earth
who does what is right and never
sins.
21 Do not pay attention to every word
people say,
or you may hear your servant cursing
you—
22 for you know in your heart
that many times you yourself have
cursed others.

23 All this I tested by wisdom and I said,

"I am determined to be wise"—
but this was beyond me.
24 Whatever wisdom may be,
it is far off and most profound—
who can discover it?
25 So I turned my mind to understand,
to investigate and to search out
wisdom and the scheme of
things
and to understand the stupidity of
wickedness
and the madness of folly.

Wake Up and Smell . . . the Sediment

I'm a morning person. Ninety-five percent of the time, I'm the first one to the office. Some of this is sheer enthusiasm for the day and some of it is trying to keep up with the smart ones (if you were in the slow group in grade school too, you know what I mean).

Anyway, the first job of the day is making coffee. Over the years, I have become pretty adept at this challenging task. But there's something about making the coffee that makes me angry. If you've come across this, you'll know exactly what I mean.

Sometimes, when I get to the coffee maker, I discover that the last person out of the office the day before neglected to turn it off. And there, at the bottom of the glass carafe are six or eight cups of hot coffee reduced to a putrid, rock-hard sediment. (Shades of high school chemistry class.) The coffee room smells like a dirty sock.

Having come across this the other day, I started thinking about it in terms of human life. The day we were born, God filled us with fresh hot life and put us on a slow-heating burner. From that moment until the day we die, you and I are being reduced to sediment at the bottom of life's coffee carafe. At our funerals, people will pass by our caskets and view these remains. Someone will deliver a eulogy, and our entire lifetime will be reduced to a three-minute speech.

DAILY INSIGHT

THURSDAY

Passage:
Ecclesiastes 7:1–4

Verse:
Ecclesiastes 7:1

Is this fair? No. Is this the way it is? Yes.

And we can't say that we weren't warned. From our first report card to our last performance review, countless hours of tireless work are reduced to one single letter grade or one forgettable raise in pay. How could all this labor and effort be summarized so concisely, so briefly, so abruptly? But it is.

Although we don't know what inspired King Solomon to write today's text, it sounds a lot like he jotted these words down right after attending someone's funeral. Maybe the experience of listening to a man's eulogy made him take a hard look at what was important in life. "What am I doing that's a complete waste of time?" he might have mused. Or, "What should I do with my time that I've been completely avoiding?"

"Death is the destiny of every man; the living should take this to heart ... a sad face is good" (7:2b–3b), Solomon wrote, almost sounding happy about this experience of mourning. These are powerful thoughts.

Waking up and smelling the sediment has a way of pulling our lives back in line. Don't waste your time today on things that will vanish in the steam. Never forget this.

Oh, and if you're the last one out, please turn off the coffee maker. Thanks.

For your next devotional reading, go to page 728.

²⁶I find more bitter than death
   the woman who is a snare,
   whose heart is a trap
   and whose hands are chains.
The man who pleases God will escape
   her,
   but the sinner she will ensnare.

²⁷"Look," says the Teacher,ᵃ "this is what
I have discovered:

"Adding one thing to another to
   discover the scheme of things—
²⁸   while I was still searching
   but not finding—
I found one ⌞upright⌟ man among a
   thousand,
   but not one ⌞upright⌟ woman among
   them all.
²⁹This only have I found:
   God made mankind upright,
   but men have gone in search of
   many schemes."

8 Who is like the wise man?
   Who knows the explanation of things?
Wisdom brightens a man's face
   and changes its hard appearance.

Obey the King

²Obey the king's command, I say, because you took an oath before God. ³Do
not be in a hurry to leave the king's presence. Do not stand up for a bad cause, for
he will do whatever he pleases. ⁴Since a
king's word is supreme, who can say to
him, "What are you doing?"

⁵Whoever obeys his command will
   come to no harm,
   and the wise heart will know the
   proper time and procedure.
⁶For there is a proper time and
   procedure for every matter,
   though a man's misery weighs
   heavily upon him.

⁷Since no man knows the future,
   who can tell him what is to come?
⁸No man has power over the wind to
   contain itᵇ;
   so no one has power over the day of
   his death.
As no one is discharged in time of war,
   so wickedness will not release those
   who practice it.

⁹All this I saw, as I applied my mind to
everything done under the sun. There is
a time when a man lords it over others
to his ownᶜ hurt. ¹⁰Then too, I saw the
wicked buried—those who used to come

and go from the holy place and receive
praiseᵈ in the city where they did this.
This too is meaningless.

¹¹When the sentence for a crime is not
quickly carried out, the hearts of the
people are filled with schemes to do
wrong. ¹²Although a wicked man commits
a hundred crimes and still lives a long
time, I know that it will go better with
God-fearing men, who are reverent before God. ¹³Yet because the wicked do not
fear God, it will not go well with them, and
their days will not lengthen like a shadow.

¹⁴There is something else meaningless
that occurs on earth: righteous men who
get what the wicked deserve, and wicked
men who get what the righteous deserve.
This too, I say, is meaningless. ¹⁵So I commend the enjoyment of life, because
nothing is better for a man under the sun
than to eat and drink and be glad. Then
joy will accompany him in his work all the
days of the life God has given him under
the sun.

¹⁶When I applied my mind to know
wisdom and to observe man's labor on
earth—his eyes not seeing sleep day or
night— ¹⁷then I saw all that God has done.
No one can comprehend what goes on
under the sun. Despite all his efforts to
search it out, man cannot discover its
meaning. Even if a wise man claims he
knows, he cannot really comprehend it.

A Common Destiny for All

9 So I reflected on all this and concluded
   that the righteous and the wise and
what they do are in God's hands, but no
man knows whether love or hate awaits
him. ²All share a common destiny—the
righteous and the wicked, the good and
the bad,ᵉ the clean and the unclean, those
who offer sacrifices and those who do not.

As it is with the good man,
   so with the sinner;
as it is with those who take oaths,
   so with those who are afraid to take
   them.

³This is the evil in everything that happens under the sun: The same destiny
overtakes all. The hearts of men, moreover, are full of evil and there is madness

---

ᵃ27 Or *leader of the assembly*   ᵇ8 Or *over his spirit
to retain it*   ᶜ9 Or *to their*   ᵈ10 Some Hebrew
manuscripts and Septuagint (Aquila); most
Hebrew manuscripts *and are forgotten*
ᵉ2 Septuagint (Aquila), Vulgate and Syriac; Hebrew
does not have *and the bad.*

in their hearts while they live, and afterward they join the dead. [4]Anyone who is among the living has hope[a]—even a live dog is better off than a dead lion!

[5]For the living know that they will die,
  but the dead know nothing;
they have no further reward,
  and even the memory of them is
    forgotten.
[6]Their love, their hate
  and their jealousy have long since
    vanished;
never again will they have a part
  in anything that happens under the
    sun.

[7]Go, eat your food with gladness, and drink your wine with a joyful heart, for it is now that God favors what you do. [8]Always be clothed in white, and always anoint your head with oil. [9]Enjoy life with your wife, whom you love, all the days of this meaningless life that God has given you under the sun— all your meaningless days. For this is your lot in life and in your toilsome labor under the sun. [10]Whatever your hand finds to do, do it with all your might, for in the grave,[b] where you are going, there is neither working nor planning nor knowledge nor wisdom.

[11]I have seen something else under the sun:

The race is not to the swift
  or the battle to the strong,
nor does food come to the wise
  or wealth to the brilliant
  or favor to the learned;
but time and chance happen to them
  all.

[12]Moreover, no man knows when his hour will come:

As fish are caught in a cruel net,
  or birds are taken in a snare,
so men are trapped by evil times
  that fall unexpectedly upon them.

Wisdom Better Than Folly

[13]I also saw under the sun this example of wisdom that greatly impressed me: [14]There was once a small city with only a few people in it. And a powerful king came against it, surrounded it and built huge siegeworks against it. [15]Now there lived in that city a man poor but wise, and he saved the city by his wisdom. But nobody remembered that poor man. [16]So I said, "Wisdom is better than strength."

But the poor man's wisdom is despised, and his words are no longer heeded.

[17]The quiet words of the wise are more to
    be heeded
  than the shouts of a ruler of fools.
[18]Wisdom is better than weapons of war,
  but one sinner destroys much good.

10 As dead flies give perfume a bad
    smell,
  so a little folly outweighs wisdom
    and honor.
[2]The heart of the wise inclines to the
    right,
  but the heart of the fool to the left.
[3]Even as he walks along the road,
  the fool lacks sense
  and shows everyone how stupid he
    is.
[4]If a ruler's anger rises against you,
  do not leave your post;
  calmness can lay great errors to rest.

[5]There is an evil I have seen under the
    sun,
  the sort of error that arises from a
    ruler:
[6]Fools are put in many high positions,
  while the rich occupy the low ones.
[7]I have seen slaves on horseback,
  while princes go on foot like slaves.

[8]Whoever digs a pit may fall into it;
  whoever breaks through a wall may
    be bitten by a snake.
[9]Whoever quarries stones may be
    injured by them;
  whoever splits logs may be
    endangered by them.

[10]If the ax is dull
    and its edge unsharpened,
  more strength is needed
    but skill will bring success.

[11]If a snake bites before it is charmed,
  there is no profit for the charmer.

[12]Words from a wise man's mouth are
    gracious,
  but a fool is consumed by his own
    lips.
[13]At the beginning his words are folly;
    at the end they are wicked
      madness—
[14] and the fool multiplies words.

No one knows what is coming—
  who can tell him what will happen
    after him?

[a]4 Or *What then is to be chosen? With all who live,
there is hope*   [b]10 Hebrew *Sheol*

¹⁵A fool's work wearies him;
  he does not know the way to town.

¹⁶Woe to you, O land whose king was a
    servant[a]
  and whose princes feast in the
    morning.
¹⁷Blessed are you, O land whose king is
    of noble birth
  and whose princes eat at a proper
    time—
  for strength and not for
    drunkenness.

¹⁸If a man is lazy, the rafters sag;
  if his hands are idle, the house leaks.

¹⁹A feast is made for laughter,
  and wine makes life merry,
  but money is the answer for
    everything.

²⁰Do not revile the king even in your
    thoughts,
  or curse the rich in your bedroom,

  ͣ16 Or *king is a child*

When You Least Expect It

Our company had decided to produce a video series—four sessions with one of America's premier communicators addressing a large audience. As one of the individuals responsible for picking up the tab for this project, I had the privilege of sitting wherever I wanted during the shooting.

For the first session, my wife and I sat in the audience. In the second session, I sat backstage. The third session found me in the balcony, surveying the whole scene. But the fourth session was my favorite: I sat in the production truck, next to the director.

Right there in front of us were six small television screens. Three of these cameras were on the speaker, and three were on the audience. Gazing at these screens was like peeking through a keyhole. Because of the magic of hidden cameras and telephoto lenses, none of these folks had any idea that they were being watched.

For a solid hour I listened to the director call the shots, and for a solid hour I followed the cameras as they stealthily filmed people's faces. This was so much fun I didn't hear a word the speaker said! In that sixty minutes, I saw folks dozing off, chomping on gum (in spite of our request that they not chew it), whispering to their neighbors, and deftly picking their noses.

King Solomon must have had a bad day. Someone must have caught him, as Allen Funt on "Candid Camera" used to say, "in the act of being himself." He was angry and

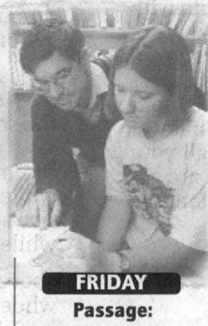

FRIDAY
Passage:
Ecclesiastes 9:11–18
Verse:
Ecclesiastes 9:17

embarrassed. "Time and chance happen," he moaned. "As fish in cruel nets or birds in a snare, men are trapped by evil times."

Although the Bible clearly states that in God's sovereignty there truly is no such thing as "random," we often feel as if time and chance take their toll on our lives. Hidden cameras take shots of us in compromising poses, projecting them on the big screen for all to see.

What is Solomon's advice? It's a profound thing. Did you catch it?

Once upon a time a vicious tyrant decided to send his troops to surprise an innocent city and lay it to ruin (9:14). But this tiny borough had a secret weapon—a quiet and wise man who understood the unexplainable power of anonymous obedience and right thinking day after day. Eventually, the deeds of this seemingly inconsequential man saved the city.

The solution to the hot lights of spontaneous public scrutiny is to commit yourself to quietly, diligently, and faithfully doing right. Yes, the hidden cameras will take an occasional bite out of your pride, but your determination to continue to do right will overshadow your embarrassment and your fear. And you'll keep doing right.

Commit yourself to obedience. Every time. And don't be afraid of the hidden cameras you cannot control. You'll be all right.

For your next devotional reading, go to page 730.

because a bird of the air may carry your
words,
and a bird on the wing may report
what you say.

Bread Upon the Waters

11 Cast your bread upon the waters,
for after many days you will find it
again.
[2] Give portions to seven, yes to eight,
for you do not know what disaster
may come upon the land.

[3] If clouds are full of water,
they pour rain upon the earth.
Whether a tree falls to the south or to
the north,
in the place where it falls, there will it
lie.
[4] Whoever watches the wind will not
plant;
whoever looks at the clouds will not
reap.

[5] As you do not know the path of the
wind,
or how the body is formed[a] in a
mother's womb,
so you cannot understand the work of
God,
the Maker of all things.

[6] Sow your seed in the morning,
and at evening let not your hands be
idle,
for you do not know which will
succeed,
whether this or that,
or whether both will do equally well.

Remember Your Creator While Young

[7] Light is sweet,
and it pleases the eyes to see the
sun.
[8] However many years a man may live,
let him enjoy them all.
But let him remember the days of
darkness,
for they will be many.
Everything to come is meaningless.

[9] Be happy, young man, while you are
young,
and let your heart give you joy in the
days of your youth.
Follow the ways of your heart
and whatever your eyes see,
but know that for all these things
God will bring you to judgment.
[10] So then, banish anxiety from your
heart

and cast off the troubles of your
body,
for youth and vigor are meaningless.

12 Remember your Creator
in the days of your youth,
before the days of trouble come
and the years approach when you
will say,
"I find no pleasure in them"—
[2] before the sun and the light
and the moon and the stars grow
dark,
and the clouds return after the rain;
[3] when the keepers of the house tremble,
and the strong men stoop,
when the grinders cease because they
are few,
and those looking through the
windows grow dim;
[4] when the doors to the street are closed
and the sound of grinding fades;
when men rise up at the sound of
birds,
but all their songs grow faint;
[5] when men are afraid of heights
and of dangers in the streets;
when the almond tree blossoms
and the grasshopper drags himself
along
and desire no longer is stirred.
Then man goes to his eternal home
and mourners go about the streets.

[6] Remember him—before the silver cord
is severed,
or the golden bowl is broken;
before the pitcher is shattered at the
spring,
or the wheel broken at the well,
[7] and the dust returns to the ground it
came from,
and the spirit returns to God who
gave it.

[8] "Meaningless! Meaningless!" says the
Teacher.[b]
"Everything is meaningless!"

The Conclusion of the Matter

[9] Not only was the Teacher wise, but also
he imparted knowledge to the people.
He pondered and searched out and set
in order many proverbs. [10] The Teacher
searched to find just the right words, and
what he wrote was upright and true.
[11] The words of the wise are like goads,

---

[a]5 Or *know how life* (or *the spirit*) / *enters the body
being formed*   [b]8 Or *the leader of the assembly*; also
in verses 9 and 10

Remembering God

Key Verse: *"Remember your Creator in the days of your youth."* Ecclesiastes 12:1a

Text: Ecclesiastes 12:1 *(Dad or child reads the text.)*

QUIET
TIMES
WITH Dad

DAD READS: Two things happen when people get old. The first one is that they begin to forget things. The second thing is . . . uh . . . I don't remember what the second thing is! Oh, I'm just kidding. But it is true that when people get older, sometimes their memories start to fade.

Child reads: Yes, it's sad that older people can sometimes lose their memories. One of the good things about being young is that I can remember. I'm glad that I am young.

DAD READS: The verse we read today is one of the most important verses in the Bible about remembering. The verse talks to young people, like you, and it tells you not to forget about God . . . especially while you are young. Actually, King Solomon, who wrote these words, wasn't worried that you would actually *forget* God. But, because of all the things that can distract a busy young person like you, he warns you to not let other things get in the way of remembering who God is and how much he loves you.

Child reads: Even though I always want to remember how much God loves me and even though I always want to love him, many things in my life could get in the way . . . school, friends, sports, music, and my family. These are good things, but they should never be more important to me than God.

DAD READS: Even though this Bible verse tells people who are young to remember God, I know that I must also

remember him. My busy life is also full of things that could get in the way of remembering how much God loves me and that I must love him. Work, reading, friends, sports and my family cannot get in the way of remembering God.

Child reads: Knowing and loving God is the most important thing in all the world. I know that his love for me and my love for him will make the biggest difference for the rest of my life. And I don't want anything to get in the way of this very important relationship. I want to learn about God in the Bible. I want to remember to pray about everything. And I want to spend time with my dad, talking about how good God is.

DAD READS: You and I will help each other to remember God. We will help each other to remember those things you just said . . . to read the Bible, pray, and talk to each other about him. Let me pray this prayer with you:

Our Father in heaven, we have talked about a very important thing today. We have said that there is nothing more important in all of life than remembering who you are. Thank you for telling us about this. Please don't let anything get in the way of our love for you. In Jesus' name, Amen.

For your next devotional reading, go to page 733.

their collected sayings like firmly embed-
ded nails—given by one Shepherd. [12]Be
warned, my son, of anything in addition
to them.

Of making many books there is no end,
and much study wearies the body.

[13]Now all has been heard;

here is the conclusion of the matter:
Fear God and keep his
commandments,
for this is the whole duty of man.
[14]For God will bring every deed into
judgment,
including every hidden thing,
whether it is good or evil.

What are you particularly good at? "Let's see," you might respond, "I'm good at driving a golf ball long and straight off the tee; making good investments; selling things I really believe in; waxing my car on a cool spring day." Okay, this is good. But the Song of Songs introduces us to something you may not be very good at . . . at least not as good as you are at reading a balance sheet or fixing a leaking pipe. This is a book about tenderness—the stuff that "speaks" to the heart of your wife and the soul of your child. The answer to "Who's picking up the kids from soccer?" is all part of keeping a family going. "Clean your room" is often a necessary command. But holding your baby—regardless of her age—and speaking delicate words of love binds families together like nothing else.

Solomon was an important man. "King" would look pretty good on anyone's business card. But he was a man who knew all about gentleness and kindhearted affection. This ought to be on your list of things you do well . . . right next to smoking a softball over the left-field fence.

Song of Songs

Solomon's Song of Songs.

Beloved[a]

2 Let him kiss me with the kisses of his mouth—
　　for your love is more delightful than wine.
3 Pleasing is the fragrance of your perfumes;
　　your name is like perfume poured out.
　　No wonder the maidens love you!
4 Take me away with you—let us hurry!
　　Let the king bring me into his chambers.

Friends

We rejoice and delight in you[b];
　　we will praise your love more than wine.

Beloved

How right they are to adore you!

5 Dark am I, yet lovely,
　　O daughters of Jerusalem,

---

[a]Primarily on the basis of the gender of the Hebrew pronouns used, male and female speakers are indicated in the margins by the captions *Lover* and *Beloved* respectively. The words of others are marked *Friends*. In some instances the divisions and their captions are debatable.　[b]4 The Hebrew is masculine singular.

dark like the tents of Kedar,
like the tent curtains of Solomon.[a]
[6] Do not stare at me because I am dark,
because I am darkened by the sun.
My mother's sons were angry with me
and made me take care of the
vineyards;
my own vineyard I have neglected.
[7] Tell me, you whom I love, where you
graze your flock

and where you rest your sheep at
midday.
Why should I be like a veiled woman
beside the flocks of your friends?

Friends

[8] If you do not know, most beautiful of
women,

[a]5 Or *Salma*

Wherefore Art Thou, Romeo?

I was in love. There was absolutely no doubt about it. Kathy Roan was a woman who represented everything I could have ever hoped for. She was beautiful and bright. She was articulate and tender. She was unusually successful, and her interactions with her associates brimmed with integrity. She was highly respected at work by her superiors.

I thought about her nearly every waking moment. Whether I was in meetings, researching projects, commuting to work, or dozing off to sleep at night, I longed to see Kathy. To be with her. To talk with her. There is nothing I wouldn't have done to win her love.

Actually, Kathy and I had never spoken about our relationship. Until now, our conversations had remained on the professional level. I had done my best to mask my infatuation with her. I had even restrained myself from discussing my feelings for her among my own colleagues, but I was running out of time. I knew that my heart would no longer hold back, that I would soon have to tell her how I felt.

One early spring afternoon, the opportunity presented itself. At last I was going to be able to tell her how much I longed to hold her and tell her that I loved her.

We were actually on a field assignment, having been appointed to the same task force. "I know you're busy, and I'm so sorry to interrupt you," I boldly said, stopping her in mid-sentence as she dialogued with one of our associates. "This is going to sound crazy, but I would love to have chance to get to know you. I don't want to be too

MONDAY
Passage:
Song of Songs 1:1–4,
15–16
Verses:
Song of Songs 1:15–16

bold, but would you be willing to see me this weekend?"

My words stunned her. We stood there, looking straight into each other's eyes for a nervous moment. And then, unexpectedly and without warning, the bell rang. Kathy Roan and I, along with all the other Whittier School fourth graders, started running back to the building from the soccer field so we wouldn't be late. Our teacher didn't like it when recess went too long.

Do you remember your first love? Do you remember how you "accidentally" let your hand brush against hers, hoping she would not resist? Every nerve ending in your body was inexplicably transported to your fingers. Do you remember collecting the courage to kiss a girl for the first time? And how about the excitement of pursuing the woman who would one day become your wife?

You've come a long way from the playground. Perhaps the brief dialogue we read today is here to remind you that your wife still longs for sensitive affection from the one who worked so hard to win her love. Although the tender words of love you used to speak have been eclipsed by discussions about schedules, car pools and trash in the kitchen, she still needs the romance of your first embrace.

Do something today that takes you back to those days of grade-school love. Be daring. Lavish her with something she doesn't expect. You never know when the bell will ring and this golden opportunity will end. Recess never lasts long enough.

For your next devotional reading, go to page 738.

follow the tracks of the sheep
and graze your young goats
by the tents of the shepherds.

Lover

⁹I liken you, my darling, to a mare
harnessed to one of the chariots of
Pharaoh.
¹⁰Your cheeks are beautiful with earrings,
your neck with strings of jewels.
¹¹We will make you earrings of gold,
studded with silver.

Beloved

¹²While the king was at his table,
my perfume spread its fragrance.
¹³My lover is to me a sachet of myrrh
resting between my breasts.
¹⁴My lover is to me a cluster of henna
blossoms
from the vineyards of En Gedi.

Lover

¹⁵How beautiful you are, my darling!
Oh, how beautiful!
Your eyes are doves.

Beloved

¹⁶How handsome you are, my lover!
Oh, how charming!
And our bed is verdant.

Lover

¹⁷The beams of our house are cedars;
our rafters are firs.

Beloved [a]

2 I am a rose[b] of Sharon,
a lily of the valleys.

Lover

²Like a lily among thorns
is my darling among the maidens.

Beloved

³Like an apple tree among the trees of
the forest
is my lover among the young men.
I delight to sit in his shade,
and his fruit is sweet to my taste.
⁴He has taken me to the banquet hall,
and his banner over me is love.
⁵Strengthen me with raisins,
refresh me with apples,
for I am faint with love.
⁶His left arm is under my head,
and his right arm embraces me.
⁷Daughters of Jerusalem, I charge you
by the gazelles and by the does of the
field:

Do not arouse or awaken love
until it so desires.

⁸Listen! My lover!
Look! Here he comes,
leaping across the mountains,
bounding over the hills.
⁹My lover is like a gazelle or a young
stag.
Look! There he stands behind our
wall,
gazing through the windows,
peering through the lattice.
¹⁰My lover spoke and said to me,
"Arise, my darling,
my beautiful one, and come with me.
¹¹See! The winter is past;
the rains are over and gone.
¹²Flowers appear on the earth;
the season of singing has come,
the cooing of doves
is heard in our land.
¹³The fig tree forms its early fruit;
the blossoming vines spread their
fragrance.
Arise, come, my darling;
my beautiful one, come with me."

Lover

¹⁴My dove in the clefts of the rock,
in the hiding places on the
mountainside,
show me your face,
let me hear your voice;
for your voice is sweet,
and your face is lovely.
¹⁵Catch for us the foxes,
the little foxes
that ruin the vineyards,
our vineyards that are in bloom.

Beloved

¹⁶My lover is mine and I am his;
he browses among the lilies.
¹⁷Until the day breaks
and the shadows flee,
turn, my lover,
and be like a gazelle
or like a young stag
on the rugged hills.[c]

3 All night long on my bed
I looked for the one my heart loves;
I looked for him but did not find
him.
²I will get up now and go about the city,
through its streets and squares;
I will search for the one my heart loves.

---

[a]1 Or *Lover*   [b]1 Possibly a member of the crocus
family   [c]17 Or *the hills of Bether*

So I looked for him but did not find
    him.
³The watchmen found me
    as they made their rounds in the city.
"Have you seen the one my heart
    loves?"
⁴Scarcely had I passed them
    when I found the one my heart loves.
I held him and would not let him go
    till I had brought him to my mother's
    house,
    to the room of the one who
    conceived me.
⁵Daughters of Jerusalem, I charge you
    by the gazelles and by the does of the
    field:
Do not arouse or awaken love
    until it so desires.

⁶Who is this coming up from the desert
    like a column of smoke,
perfumed with myrrh and incense
    made from all the spices of the
    merchant?
⁷Look! It is Solomon's carriage,
    escorted by sixty warriors,
    the noblest of Israel,
⁸all of them wearing the sword,
    all experienced in battle,
each with his sword at his side,
    prepared for the terrors of the night.
⁹King Solomon made for himself the
    carriage;
    he made it of wood from Lebanon.
¹⁰Its posts he made of silver,
    its base of gold.
Its seat was upholstered with purple,
    its interior lovingly inlaid
    by*a* the daughters of Jerusalem.
¹¹Come out, you daughters of Zion,
    and look at King Solomon wearing
    the crown,
    the crown with which his mother
    crowned him
on the day of his wedding,
    the day his heart rejoiced.

Lover

4 How beautiful you are, my darling!
    Oh, how beautiful!
    Your eyes behind your veil are doves.
Your hair is like a flock of goats
    descending from Mount Gilead.
²Your teeth are like a flock of sheep just
    shorn,
    coming up from the washing.
Each has its twin;
    not one of them is alone.
³Your lips are like a scarlet ribbon;
    your mouth is lovely.

Your temples behind your veil
    are like the halves of a pomegranate.
⁴Your neck is like the tower of David,
    built with elegance*b*;
on it hang a thousand shields,
    all of them shields of warriors.
⁵Your two breasts are like two fawns,
    like twin fawns of a gazelle
    that browse among the lilies.
⁶Until the day breaks
    and the shadows flee,
I will go to the mountain of myrrh
    and to the hill of incense.
⁷All beautiful you are, my darling;
    there is no flaw in you.

⁸Come with me from Lebanon, my bride,
    come with me from Lebanon.
Descend from the crest of Amana,
    from the top of Senir, the summit of
    Hermon,
from the lions' dens
    and the mountain haunts of the
    leopards.
⁹You have stolen my heart, my sister, my
    bride;
you have stolen my heart
with one glance of your eyes,
    with one jewel of your necklace.
¹⁰How delightful is your love, my sister,
    my bride!
How much more pleasing is your
    love than wine,
and the fragrance of your perfume
    than any spice!
¹¹Your lips drop sweetness as the
    honeycomb, my bride;
    milk and honey are under your
    tongue.
The fragrance of your garments is
    like that of Lebanon.
¹²You are a garden locked up, my sister,
    my bride;
    you are a spring enclosed, a sealed
    fountain.
¹³Your plants are an orchard of
    pomegranates
    with choice fruits,
    with henna and nard,
¹⁴   nard and saffron,
    calamus and cinnamon,
    with every kind of incense tree,
    with myrrh and aloes
    and all the finest spices.
¹⁵You are*c* a garden fountain,
    a well of flowing water
    streaming down from Lebanon.

a10 Or *its inlaid interior a gift of love / from*
b4 The meaning of the Hebrew for this word is
uncertain.   *c15* Or *I am* (spoken by the *Beloved*)

Beloved

¹⁶Awake, north wind,
    and come, south wind!
Blow on my garden,
    that its fragrance may spread abroad.
Let my lover come into his garden
    and taste its choice fruits.

Lover

5 I have come into my garden, my sister,
    my bride;
    I have gathered my myrrh with my
        spice.
    I have eaten my honeycomb and my
        honey;
    I have drunk my wine and my milk.

Friends

Eat, O friends, and drink;
    drink your fill, O lovers.

Beloved

²I slept but my heart was awake.
    Listen! My lover is knocking:
"Open to me, my sister, my darling,
    my dove, my flawless one.
My head is drenched with dew,
    my hair with the dampness of the
        night."
³I have taken off my robe—
    must I put it on again?
I have washed my feet—
    must I soil them again?
⁴My lover thrust his hand through the
        latch-opening;
    my heart began to pound for him.
⁵I arose to open for my lover,
    and my hands dripped with myrrh,
    my fingers with flowing myrrh,
    on the handles of the lock.
⁶I opened for my lover,
    but my lover had left; he was gone.
    My heart sank at his departure.ᵃ
I looked for him but did not find him.
    I called him but he did not answer.
⁷The watchmen found me
    as they made their rounds in the city.
They beat me, they bruised me;
    they took away my cloak,
    those watchmen of the walls!
⁸O daughters of Jerusalem, I charge
        you—
    if you find my lover,
    what will you tell him?
    Tell him I am faint with love.

Friends

⁹How is your beloved better than others,
    most beautiful of women?

How is your beloved better than others,
    that you charge us so?

Beloved

¹⁰My lover is radiant and ruddy,
    outstanding among ten thousand.
¹¹His head is purest gold;
    his hair is wavy
    and black as a raven.
¹²His eyes are like doves
    by the water streams,
    washed in milk,
    mounted like jewels.
¹³His cheeks are like beds of spice
    yielding perfume.
His lips are like lilies
    dripping with myrrh.
¹⁴His arms are rods of gold
    set with chrysolite.
His body is like polished ivory
    decorated with sapphires.ᵇ
¹⁵His legs are pillars of marble
    set on bases of pure gold.
His appearance is like Lebanon,
    choice as its cedars.
¹⁶His mouth is sweetness itself;
    he is altogether lovely.
This is my lover, this my friend,
    O daughters of Jerusalem.

Friends

6 Where has your lover gone,
    most beautiful of women?
Which way did your lover turn,
    that we may look for him with you?

Beloved

²My lover has gone down to his garden,
    to the beds of spices,
to browse in the gardens
    and to gather lilies.
³I am my lover's and my lover is mine;
    he browses among the lilies.

Lover

⁴You are beautiful, my darling, as Tirzah,
    lovely as Jerusalem,
    majestic as troops with banners.
⁵Turn your eyes from me;
    they overwhelm me.
Your hair is like a flock of goats
    descending from Gilead.
⁶Your teeth are like a flock of sheep
    coming up from the washing.
Each has its twin,
    not one of them is alone.
⁷Your temples behind your veil

ᵃ6 Or *heart had gone out to him when he spoke*
ᵇ14 Or *lapis lazuli*

are like the halves of a pomegranate.
8 Sixty queens there may be,
   and eighty concubines,
   and virgins beyond number;
9 but my dove, my perfect one, is unique,
   the only daughter of her mother,
   the favorite of the one who bore her.
The maidens saw her and called her
      blessed;
   the queens and concubines praised
      her.

Friends

10 Who is this that appears like the dawn,
   fair as the moon, bright as the sun,
   majestic as the stars in procession?

Lover

11 I went down to the grove of nut trees
   to look at the new growth in the
      valley,
to see if the vines had budded
   or the pomegranates were in bloom.
12 Before I realized it,
   my desire set me among the royal
      chariots of my people.[a]

Friends

13 Come back, come back, O Shulammite;
   come back, come back, that we may
      gaze on you!

Lover

Why would you gaze on the
      Shulammite
   as on the dance of Mahanaim?

7 How beautiful your sandaled feet,
   O prince's daughter!
Your graceful legs are like jewels,
   the work of a craftsman's hands.
2 Your navel is a rounded goblet
   that never lacks blended wine.
Your waist is a mound of wheat
   encircled by lilies.
3 Your breasts are like two fawns,
   twins of a gazelle.
4 Your neck is like an ivory tower.
Your eyes are the pools of Heshbon
   by the gate of Bath Rabbim.
Your nose is like the tower of Lebanon
   looking toward Damascus.
5 Your head crowns you like Mount
      Carmel.
   Your hair is like royal tapestry;
   the king is held captive by its tresses.
6 How beautiful you are and how
      pleasing,
   O love, with your delights!
7 Your stature is like that of the palm,

and your breasts like clusters of fruit.
8 I said, "I will climb the palm tree;
   I will take hold of its fruit."
May your breasts be like the clusters of
      the vine,
   the fragrance of your breath like
      apples,
9   and your mouth like the best wine.

Beloved

May the wine go straight to my lover,
   flowing gently over lips and teeth.[b]

10 I belong to my lover,
   and his desire is for me.
11 Come, my lover, let us go to the
      countryside,
   let us spend the night in the villages.[c]
12 Let us go early to the vineyards
   to see if the vines have budded,
if their blossoms have opened,
   and if the pomegranates are in
      bloom—
   there I will give you my love.
13 The mandrakes send out their
      fragrance,
   and at our door is every delicacy,
both new and old,
   that I have stored up for you, my
      lover.

8 If only you were to me like a brother,
   who was nursed at my mother's
      breasts!
Then, if I found you outside,
   I would kiss you,
   and no one would despise me.
2 I would lead you
   and bring you to my mother's house—
      she who has taught me.
I would give you spiced wine to drink,
   the nectar of my pomegranates.
3 His left arm is under my head
   and his right arm embraces me.
4 Daughters of Jerusalem, I charge you:
   Do not arouse or awaken love
   until it so desires.

Friends

5 Who is this coming up from the desert
   leaning on her lover?

Beloved

Under the apple tree I roused you;
   there your mother conceived you,
   there she who was in labor gave you
      birth.

[a]12 Or *among the chariots of Amminadab;* or
among the chariots of the people of the prince
[b]9 Septuagint, Aquila, Vulgate and Syriac; Hebrew
lips of sleepers   [c]11 Or *henna bushes*

⁶Place me like a seal over your heart,
　　like a seal on your arm;
for love is as strong as death,
　　its jealousy*a* unyielding as the grave.*b*
It burns like blazing fire,
　　like a mighty flame.*c*
⁷Many waters cannot quench love;
　　rivers cannot wash it away.
If one were to give

all the wealth of his house for love,
　　it*d* would be utterly scorned.

Friends

⁸We have a young sister,
　　and her breasts are not yet grown.

a6 Or ardor　*b6 Hebrew Sheol*　*c6 Or / like the very flame of the Lord*　*d7 Or he*

Your Family Loves You

DAILY INSIGHT

It was early evening—another crystal clear dusk under a big Texas sky. Bobbie and I were on the way to our Bible study, and though we had lived in Waco for only a year, this small group of friends was becoming very important to us. We looked forward to our time together every week.

As we were driving through our subdivision, a piercing sound rudely interrupted our conversation. I glanced into my rearview mirror and saw a huge hook and ladder truck bearing down on us. I pulled to the side of the road and the truck screamed past us, shaking our car with its velocity. We sat there for a moment, collecting our thoughts from this loud interruption. Then my curiosity overwhelmed my wife's need to make our Bible study on time, and I stomped on the accelerator. I had to find out where the truck was going.

In a few blocks, even before we actually reached the fire, we could see a huge glow in the early evening sky. And when we rounded the corner where the truck had now stopped, I saw something I had never seen before: a house on fire. This was not one of those little nuisance kitchen smoulderers, where all you see from the outside is smoke. No, this house was completely engulfed in flames.

Bobbie and I ran to the front yard of the across-the-street neighbors to watch. As the flames rocketed seventy-five feet in the air, we took a few steps back; the heat was literally too much to handle even though we stood hundreds of feet from the house. The popping and crackling of this inferno were almost deafening. The authority and

TUESDAY

Passage:
Song of Songs 8:6–7

Verse:
Song of Songs 8:6

absolute intensity of the flames left us with nothing to say. In what seemed like only a few minutes, the house was completely consumed.

Solomon talks about love in this context, likening it to a "blazing fire"—a mighty flame. Love is "as strong as death," King Solomon writes. Nothing can quench it or wash it away.

We will hear the word "love" spoken today. We may even speak it ourselves. But, lest we consign this word to a child's penny valentine or a whimpering teenager expressing himself in a love note, we cannot forget its unmistakable power.

The phrase "I love you" changed your life. Once a single man, free to move about at will, "I love you" inextricably bound you to one woman for the rest of your life. "I love you" gave you a child—a little person who relentlessly watches your every move, keeping you on the straight and narrow. "I love you" forced you to confront your closest friend with his dishonesty, his secret bout with adultery. "I love you" cost you that friendship.

"I love you" opened our heavenly Father's hand to welcome us—sinful as we were—to himself. "I love you" gave us Jesus, who endured the cross for those sins.

"I love you" is about the serious stuff of life. Its impact changes people. Its power moves them away from their complacency. It alters their plans. It renders them speechless.

You love your family. Your family loves you. Love changes everything.

For your next devotional reading, go to page 741.

What shall we do for our sister
for the day she is spoken for?
[9] If she is a wall,
we will build towers of silver on her.
If she is a door,
we will enclose her with panels of
cedar.

Beloved

[10] I am a wall,
and my breasts are like towers.
Thus I have become in his eyes
like one bringing contentment.
[11] Solomon had a vineyard in Baal
Hamon;
he let out his vineyard to tenants.
Each was to bring for its fruit
a thousand shekels[a] of silver.
[12] But my own vineyard is mine to give;

the thousand shekels are for you,
O Solomon,
and two hundred[b] are for those who
tend its fruit.

Lover

[13] You who dwell in the gardens
with friends in attendance,
let me hear your voice!

Beloved

[14] Come away, my lover,
and be like a gazelle
or like a young stag
on the spice-laden mountains.

[a]11 That is, about 25 pounds (about 11.5
kilograms); also in verse 12   [b]12 That is, about
5 pounds (about 2.3 kilograms)

Being an ambassador would be fun. Think of it—you'd live in a really terrific place, like France, and speak on behalf of the United States of America, the world's most super superpower. You'd be invited to all the parties, you'd cut ribbons at building dedications, and you'd kiss babies everywhere. But what if you were the ambassador of Mozambique and your assignment was Burma? "Hmmm," you might say, "let me think about that for a minute or two."

Isaiah's ambassadorial appointment should have been as fun as being an American in Paris, but it was worse than hanging out in Burma. Of course, Isaiah was "representing" the Sovereign God of the universe, and it doesn't get any better than that. But he first had to pass God's personal inspection, then he had to tell his own people—his family and his closest friends—how fallen and sinful they were.

How would you feel about *that* assignment? "Hey, about that opening in Burma . . ."

Isaiah

1 The vision concerning Judah and Jerusalem that Isaiah son of Amoz saw during the reigns of Uzziah, Jotham, Ahaz and Hezekiah, kings of Judah.

A Rebellious Nation

²Hear, O heavens! Listen, O earth!
  For the LORD has spoken:
"I reared children and brought them
    up,
  but they have rebelled against me.
³The ox knows his master,
    the donkey his owner's manger,
  but Israel does not know,
    my people do not understand."

⁴Ah, sinful nation,
  a people loaded with guilt,
a brood of evildoers,
  children given to corruption!
They have forsaken the LORD;
  they have spurned the Holy One of
    Israel
  and turned their backs on him.

⁵Why should you be beaten anymore?
  Why do you persist in rebellion?
Your whole head is injured,
  your whole heart afflicted.
⁶From the sole of your foot to the top of
    your head
  there is no soundness—
only wounds and welts
  and open sores,
not cleansed or bandaged
  or soothed with oil.

⁷Your country is desolate,
    your cities burned with fire;
your fields are being stripped by
        foreigners
    right before you,
        laid waste as when overthrown by
            strangers.
⁸The Daughter of Zion is left
    like a shelter in a vineyard,
like a hut in a field of melons,
    like a city under siege.
⁹Unless the LORD Almighty
    had left us some survivors,
we would have become like Sodom,
    we would have been like Gomorrah.

¹⁰Hear the word of the LORD,
    you rulers of Sodom;
listen to the law of our God,
    you people of Gomorrah!
¹¹"The multitude of your sacrifices—
    what are they to me?" says the LORD.
"I have more than enough of burnt
        offerings,
    of rams and the fat of fattened
        animals;
I have no pleasure
    in the blood of bulls and lambs and
        goats.
¹²When you come to appear before me,
    who has asked this of you,

Kids and Other Failed Investments

The candy machine was just down the hall from my college room. The proximity of this electronic goody store posed three specific problems. The first was the way the loose change in my pocket, complete- ly on its own, exchanged itself for milk chocolate. The second problem was the racket that the machine made every time it delivered a treat, easily within earshot of our room. Worst of all, however, was the noise we heard when the vending ma- chine failed to deliver what the hungry student had expected.

You know the frustration of not getting what you've paid for. You slip your hard-earned money into the slot believing that you'll be rewarded, but you get noth- ing. The stock market, the man who comes to fix your leaking pipes, or the Snickers™ bar you can actually see through the glass ... sometimes faithful investments produce disappointing returns.

There may be no investment more sizable than the investment we make in our children. From the moment they arrive in the world, our lives become a circular sequence of self-denial on their behalf. We sacrifice time, energy and money for these little ones. And frankly, because of this investment, we have expectations. Why shouldn't we? We've scrimped and scraped. We've said "no" to ourselves so we could say "yes" to our children. We've put the money

DAILY INSIGHT

WEDNESDAY

Passage:
Isaiah 1:2–7

Verse:
Isaiah 1:2

into the slot, heard it drop through the mechanism, and pushed the buttons ... except for one thing. Our children cannot be bought. They're not Milky Way™ bars or hot stock opportunities. No amount of investment we pour into our children will guarantee that they won't rebel against us. This can be frustrating, but it's true.

Today's passage tells us we're in excellent company as frustrated dads: even God had children who shook their fists in his face. The opening words to the book of Isaiah chronicle Israel's rebellion: they were "[a] sinful nation ... people loaded with guilt ... children given to corruption." And do you know what God did with his wayward children? No, he didn't squash them under his thumb. Instead, he warned them of the natural consequences of their foolishness (1:7), he appealed to their sensibilities (1:18), and he promised to love and forgive them (1:18).

Do you have a rebellious child? Do you have a friend who is suffering under the ominous weight of this indescribable pain? Let these words bring you encouragement and hope. Warn your child, appeal to your child, love and forgive your child. Then wait. This is exactly what God did, and it's what he expects of you.

For your next devotional reading, go to page 747.

this trampling of my courts?
¹³ Stop bringing meaningless offerings!
  Your incense is detestable to me.
New Moons, Sabbaths and
      convocations—
  I cannot bear your evil assemblies.
¹⁴ Your New Moon festivals and your
      appointed feasts
  my soul hates.
They have become a burden to me;
  I am weary of bearing them.
¹⁵ When you spread out your hands in
      prayer,
  I will hide my eyes from you;
even if you offer many prayers,
  I will not listen.
Your hands are full of blood;
¹⁶   wash and make yourselves clean.
Take your evil deeds
  out of my sight!
Stop doing wrong,
¹⁷   learn to do right!
Seek justice,
  encourage the oppressed.ᵃ
Defend the cause of the fatherless,
  plead the case of the widow.

¹⁸ "Come now, let us reason together,"
  says the LORD.
"Though your sins are like scarlet,
  they shall be as white as snow;
though they are red as crimson,
  they shall be like wool.
¹⁹ If you are willing and obedient,
  you will eat the best from the land;
²⁰ but if you resist and rebel,
  you will be devoured by the sword."
          For the mouth of the LORD
              has spoken.

²¹ See how the faithful city
  has become a harlot!
She once was full of justice;
  righteousness used to dwell in her—
  but now murderers!
²² Your silver has become dross,
  your choice wine is diluted with
      water.
²³ Your rulers are rebels,
  companions of thieves;
they all love bribes
  and chase after gifts.
They do not defend the cause of the
      fatherless;
  the widow's case does not come
      before them.
²⁴ Therefore the Lord, the LORD Almighty,
  the Mighty One of Israel, declares:
"Ah, I will get relief from my foes
  and avenge myself on my enemies.
²⁵ I will turn my hand against you;

I will thoroughly purge away your
      dross
  and remove all your impurities.
²⁶ I will restore your judges as in days of
      old,
  your counselors as at the beginning.
Afterward you will be called
  the City of Righteousness,
  the Faithful City."

²⁷ Zion will be redeemed with justice,
  her penitent ones with
      righteousness.
²⁸ But rebels and sinners will both be
      broken,
  and those who forsake the LORD will
      perish.

²⁹ "You will be ashamed because of the
      sacred oaks
  in which you have delighted;
you will be disgraced because of the
      gardens
  that you have chosen.
³⁰ You will be like an oak with fading
      leaves,
  like a garden without water.
³¹ The mighty man will become tinder
  and his work a spark;
both will burn together,
  with no one to quench the fire."

The Mountain of the LORD

2 This is what Isaiah son of Amoz saw
concerning Judah and Jerusalem:

² In the last days

the mountain of the LORD's temple will
      be established
  as chief among the mountains;
it will be raised above the hills,
  and all nations will stream to it.

³ Many peoples will come and say,

"Come, let us go up to the mountain of
      the LORD,
  to the house of the God of Jacob.
He will teach us his ways,
  so that we may walk in his paths."
The law will go out from Zion,
  the word of the LORD from
      Jerusalem.
⁴ He will judge between the nations
  and will settle disputes for many
      peoples.
They will beat their swords into
      plowshares
  and their spears into pruning hooks.

ᵃ17 Or / rebuke the oppressor

Nation will not take up sword against
nation,
nor will they train for war anymore.

⁵Come, O house of Jacob,
let us walk in the light of the LORD.

The Day of the LORD

⁶You have abandoned your people,
the house of Jacob.
They are full of superstitions from the
East;
they practice divination like the
Philistines
and clasp hands with pagans.
⁷Their land is full of silver and gold;
there is no end to their treasures.
Their land is full of horses;
there is no end to their chariots.
⁸Their land is full of idols;
they bow down to the work of their
hands,
to what their fingers have made.
⁹So man will be brought low
and mankind humbled—
do not forgive them.ᵃ

¹⁰Go into the rocks,
hide in the ground
from dread of the LORD
and the splendor of his majesty!
¹¹The eyes of the arrogant man will be
humbled
and the pride of men brought low;
the LORD alone will be exalted in that
day.

¹²The LORD Almighty has a day in store
for all the proud and lofty,
for all that is exalted
(and they will be humbled),
¹³for all the cedars of Lebanon, tall and
lofty,
and all the oaks of Bashan,
¹⁴for all the towering mountains
and all the high hills,
¹⁵for every lofty tower
and every fortified wall,
¹⁶for every trading shipᵇ
and every stately vessel.
¹⁷The arrogance of man will be brought
low
and the pride of men humbled;
the LORD alone will be exalted in that
day,
¹⁸   and the idols will totally disappear.

¹⁹Men will flee to caves in the rocks
and to holes in the ground
from dread of the LORD
and the splendor of his majesty,

when he rises to shake the earth.
²⁰In that day men will throw away
to the rodents and bats
their idols of silver and idols of gold,
which they made to worship.
²¹They will flee to caverns in the rocks
and to the overhanging crags
from dread of the LORD
and the splendor of his majesty,
when he rises to shake the earth.

²²Stop trusting in man,
who has but a breath in his nostrils.
Of what account is he?

Judgment on Jerusalem and Judah

3 See now, the Lord,
the LORD Almighty,
is about to take from Jerusalem and
Judah
both supply and support:
all supplies of food and all supplies of
water,
²   the hero and warrior,
the judge and prophet,
the soothsayer and elder,
³the captain of fifty and man of rank,
the counselor, skilled craftsman and
clever enchanter.

⁴I will make boys their officials;
mere children will govern them.
⁵People will oppress each other—
man against man, neighbor against
neighbor.
The young will rise up against the old,
the base against the honorable.

⁶A man will seize one of his brothers
at his father's home, and say,
"You have a cloak, you be our leader;
take charge of this heap of ruins!"
⁷But in that day he will cry out,
"I have no remedy.
I have no food or clothing in my
house;
do not make me the leader of the
people."

⁸Jerusalem staggers,
Judah is falling;
their words and deeds are against the
LORD,
defying his glorious presence.
⁹The look on their faces testifies against
them;
they parade their sin like Sodom;
they do not hide it.
Woe to them!

ᵃ9 Or *not raise them up*   ᵇ16 Hebrew *every ship of*
Tarshish

They have brought disaster upon
   themselves.

[10] Tell the righteous it will be well with
   them,
      for they will enjoy the fruit of their
         deeds.
[11] Woe to the wicked! Disaster is upon
   them!
They will be paid back for what their
   hands have done.

[12] Youths oppress my people,
   women rule over them.
O my people, your guides lead you
   astray;
   they turn you from the path.

[13] The LORD takes his place in court;
   he rises to judge the people.
[14] The LORD enters into judgment
   against the elders and leaders of his
      people:
"It is you who have ruined my
   vineyard;
   the plunder from the poor is in your
      houses.
[15] What do you mean by crushing my
   people
   and grinding the faces of the poor?"
                  declares the Lord,
                  the LORD Almighty.

[16] The LORD says,
   "The women of Zion are haughty,
walking along with outstretched necks,
   flirting with their eyes,
tripping along with mincing steps,
   with ornaments jingling on their
      ankles.
[17] Therefore the Lord will bring sores on
      the heads of the women of
         Zion;
      the LORD will make their scalps bald."

[18] In that day the Lord will snatch away
their finery: the bangles and headbands
and crescent necklaces, [19] the earrings and
bracelets and veils, [20] the headdresses and
ankle chains and sashes, the perfume
bottles and charms, [21] the signet rings and
nose rings, [22] the fine robes and the capes
and cloaks, the purses [23] and mirrors, and
the linen garments and tiaras and shawls.

[24] Instead of fragrance there will be a
      stench;
   instead of a sash, a rope;
instead of well-dressed hair, baldness;
   instead of fine clothing, sackcloth;
   instead of beauty, branding.
[25] Your men will fall by the sword,
   your warriors in battle.

[26] The gates of Zion will lament and
      mourn;
   destitute, she will sit on the ground.
4 In that day seven women
   will take hold of one man
and say, "We will eat our own food
   and provide our own clothes;
only let us be called by your name.
   Take away our disgrace!"

The Branch of the LORD

[2] In that day the Branch of the LORD will
be beautiful and glorious, and the fruit of
the land will be the pride and glory of the
survivors in Israel. [3] Those who are left in
Zion, who remain in Jerusalem, will be
called holy, all who are recorded among
the living in Jerusalem. [4] The Lord will
wash away the filth of the women of Zion;
he will cleanse the bloodstains from
Jerusalem by a spirit[a] of judgment and a
spirit[a] of fire. [5] Then the LORD will create
over all of Mount Zion and over those who
assemble there a cloud of smoke by day
and a glow of flaming fire by night; over all
the glory will be a canopy. [6] It will be a
shelter and shade from the heat of the
day, and a refuge and hiding place from
the storm and rain.

The Song of the Vineyard

5 I will sing for the one I love
   a song about his vineyard:
My loved one had a vineyard
   on a fertile hillside.
[2] He dug it up and cleared it of stones
   and planted it with the choicest
      vines.
He built a watchtower in it
   and cut out a winepress as well.
Then he looked for a crop of good
   grapes,
   but it yielded only bad fruit.

[3] "Now you dwellers in Jerusalem and
      men of Judah,
   judge between me and my vineyard.
[4] What more could have been done for
      my vineyard
   than I have done for it?
When I looked for good grapes,
   why did it yield only bad?
[5] Now I will tell you
   what I am going to do to my
      vineyard:
I will take away its hedge,
   and it will be destroyed;
I will break down its wall,

a4 Or the Spirit

and it will be trampled.
⁶ I will make it a wasteland,
　neither pruned nor cultivated,
　and briers and thorns will grow
　　there.
I will command the clouds
　not to rain on it."

⁷ The vineyard of the LORD Almighty
　is the house of Israel,
and the men of Judah
　are the garden of his delight.
And he looked for justice, but saw
　　bloodshed;
　for righteousness, but heard cries of
　　distress.

Woes and Judgments

⁸ Woe to you who add house to house
　and join field to field
till no space is left
　and you live alone in the land.

⁹ The LORD Almighty has declared in my
hearing:

"Surely the great houses will become
　　desolate,
　the fine mansions left without
　　occupants.
¹⁰ A ten-acre*a* vineyard will produce only
　a bath*b* of wine,
　a homer*c* of seed only an ephah*d* of
　　grain."

¹¹ Woe to those who rise early in the
　　morning
　to run after their drinks,
who stay up late at night
　till they are inflamed with wine.
¹² They have harps and lyres at their
　　banquets,
　tambourines and flutes and wine,
but they have no regard for the deeds
　　of the LORD,
　no respect for the work of his
　　hands.
¹³ Therefore my people will go into exile
　for lack of understanding;
their men of rank will die of hunger
　and their masses will be parched
　　with thirst.
¹⁴ Therefore the grave*e* enlarges its
　　appetite
　and opens its mouth without limit;
into it will descend their nobles and
　　masses
　with all their brawlers and revelers.
¹⁵ So man will be brought low
　and mankind humbled,
　the eyes of the arrogant humbled.

¹⁶ But the LORD Almighty will be exalted
　by his justice,
and the holy God will show himself
　holy by his righteousness.
¹⁷ Then sheep will graze as in their own
　　pasture;
　lambs will feed*f* among the ruins of
　　the rich.

¹⁸ Woe to those who draw sin along with
　cords of deceit,
and wickedness as with cart ropes,
¹⁹ to those who say, "Let God hurry,
　let him hasten his work
　so we may see it.
Let it approach,
　let the plan of the Holy One of Israel
　　come,
　so we may know it."

²⁰ Woe to those who call evil good
　and good evil,
who put darkness for light
　and light for darkness,
who put bitter for sweet
　and sweet for bitter.

²¹ Woe to those who are wise in their own
　　eyes
　and clever in their own sight.

²² Woe to those who are heroes at
　　drinking wine
　and champions at mixing drinks,
²³ who acquit the guilty for a bribe,
　but deny justice to the innocent.
²⁴ Therefore, as tongues of fire lick up straw
　and as dry grass sinks down in the
　　flames,
so their roots will decay
　and their flowers blow away like dust;
for they have rejected the law of the
　LORD Almighty
　and spurned the word of the Holy
　One of Israel.
²⁵ Therefore the LORD's anger burns
　against his people;
　his hand is raised and he strikes
　them down.
The mountains shake,
　and the dead bodies are like refuse in
　the streets.

Yet for all this, his anger is not turned
　　away,
　his hand is still upraised.

a10 Hebrew *ten-yoke,* that is, the land plowed by 10
yoke of oxen in one day　*b10* That is, probably
about 6 gallons (about 22 liters)　*c10* That is,
probably about 6 bushels (about 220 liters)
d10 That is, probably about 3/5 bushel (about 22
liters)　*e14* Hebrew *Sheol*　*f17* Septuagint; Hebrew
/ *strangers will eat*

²⁶He lifts up a banner for the distant
    nations,
  he whistles for those at the ends of
    the earth.
Here they come,
  swiftly and speedily!
²⁷Not one of them grows tired or
    stumbles,
  not one slumbers or sleeps;
not a belt is loosened at the waist,
  not a sandal thong is broken.
²⁸Their arrows are sharp,
  all their bows are strung;
their horses' hoofs seem like flint,
  their chariot wheels like a whirlwind.
²⁹Their roar is like that of the lion,
  they roar like young lions;
they growl as they seize their prey
  and carry it off with no one to rescue.
³⁰In that day they will roar over it
  like the roaring of the sea.
And if one looks at the land,
  he will see darkness and distress;
  even the light will be darkened by
    the clouds.

Isaiah's Commission

6 In the year that King Uzziah died, I saw
the Lord seated on a throne, high and
exalted, and the train of his robe filled the
temple. ²Above him were seraphs, each
with six wings: With two wings they covered their faces, with two they covered
their feet, and with two they were flying.
³And they were calling to one another:

"Holy, holy, holy is the LORD Almighty;
  the whole earth is full of his glory."

⁴At the sound of their voices the doorposts and thresholds shook and the temple was filled with smoke.

⁵"Woe to me!" I cried. "I am ruined! For
I am a man of unclean lips, and I live
among a people of unclean lips, and my
eyes have seen the King, the LORD Almighty."

⁶Then one of the seraphs flew to me
with a live coal in his hand, which he had
taken with tongs from the altar. ⁷With it he
touched my mouth and said, "See, this
has touched your lips; your guilt is taken
away and your sin atoned for."

⁸Then I heard the voice of the Lord saying, "Whom shall I send? And who will go
for us?"

And I said, "Here am I. Send me!"

⁹He said, "Go and tell this people:

" 'Be ever hearing, but never
    understanding;
  be ever seeing, but never perceiving.'

HEY DAD

Why doesn't God just let everyone know he is real?

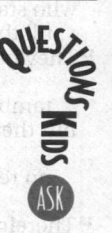

Text: Isaiah 6:1–5

Make no mistake about it: God *could* prove to the world that he's real. He could
blaze into the sky with a mighty army proclaiming his majesty. But if God showed
himself to the world this way, it would rob us of our choice to love him.

  Picture it: With a blinding light and with thousands of angels by his side, God,
who is holy and awesome beyond our understanding, appears. He announces,
"I am the great I AM—Jehovah himself! You, O sinner, should die for your sin. But
because I love you, I'll spare your life and make you my child. All you have to do is
accept this gift."

  In the face of this awesome display, can you imagine anyone mulling it over and saying,
"Naaah. That's okay. I appreciate the offer, but no thanks." What an absurd thought! If God
appeared like this, we would fall on our faces like Isaiah. We would come undone. We would
be so painfully aware of his holiness and of our filthiness that we might even want to die
just to escape that stark truth.

  Here's the great part. God *does* appear to us, and he *does* make us this very offer. But he
usually does it without the drama. He wants us to love him by choice. He doesn't want to
impress us or entertain us. He doesn't need the special effects. He simply wants to make us
what he originally had in mind: people who bear his image and choose to love him out of
gratitude for what he's done for us.

For a complete listing of Questions Kids Ask, turn to page 1435.

¹⁰Make the heart of this people
　　calloused;
　make their ears dull
　　and close their eyes.ᵃ
Otherwise they might see with their
　　eyes,
　hear with their ears,
　　understand with their hearts,
and turn and be healed."

¹¹Then I said, "For how long, O Lord?"
And he answered:

"Until the cities lie ruined
　　and without inhabitant,
until the houses are left deserted
　　and the fields ruined and ravaged,

¹²until the LORD has sent everyone far
　　away
　and the land is utterly forsaken.
¹³And though a tenth remains in the
　　land,
　it will again be laid waste.
But as the terebinth and oak
　leave stumps when they are cut
　　down,
　so the holy seed will be the stump in
　　the land."

ᵃ9,10 Hebrew; Septuagint *'You will be ever hearing,
but never understanding; / you will be ever seeing,
but never perceiving.' / ¹⁰This people's heart has
become calloused; / they hardly hear with their ears,
/ and they have closed their eyes*

Be Very Careful

**DAILY
INSIGHT**

THURSDAY

Passage:
Isaiah 6:1–8

Verses:
Isaiah 6:5

My wife, Bobbie, has no affection whatsoever for the Fourth of July. Of course, I'm not referring to our nation's celebration of independence from the tyranny of eighteenth century British rule. I'm referring to fireworks.

Neither of us grew up in states where private citizens could buy or detonate fireworks. So, after we married and moved to a state where such activity was legal, I loaded up. I told my wife that I bought and shot off fireworks so our girls would have a special experience of celebrating our nation's freedom. She wasn't listening.

One of the more interesting moments during the Wolgemuth family fireworks show was when one of these Chinese delights didn't go off. I had lit the fuse, seen the sparks, heard the unmistakable hissing sound, run like crazy … but nothing had happened. In a few minutes, the girls had uncovered their ears and had declared that one a "dud."

Unfortunately, it was my job to go back to the misfired device to see what had happened. If you have ever done this, you know exactly what I'm describing. The last thing you'd ever do is boldly walk up to the firecracker, pick it up and look it over. No, actually, what you do is carefully tiptoe toward the fizzled waste of money, senses on full alert. Your heart is pounding in your temples. Your children are cheering you on. Your wife is in the house, dialing 9-1-1. You're literally shaking at the thought that it still might blow up. This is not funny.

Now think about this: Have you ever approached your church sanctuary in this same way? The Bible—and especially the Old Testament—warns us about entering God's presence casually or glibly. It cautions us never to forget his awesomeness, his power, his restraint in light of our sinfulness.

To this point in the story, Isaiah has been reminding folks of their sinfulness. Suddenly he's reminded of his own. This account is in the Scripture to help us remember that our God is an exalted God. Coming into his presence should make our hearts race. It should make our feet tread lightly, our hands tremble. We are standing before pure dynamite.

With this image firmly in our minds, isn't it incredible that this same God loves us and tenderly calls himself our Father? Let the contrast of these two incredible truths bury themselves deeply in our hearts today.

By the way, I gave up on the fireworks. Bobbie was right. Several years ago a dad in our town said "so long" to his right hand on Independence Day. I'm pretty sure this isn't what the founding fathers had in mind.

For your next devotional reading, go to page 750.

The Sign of Immanuel

7 When Ahaz son of Jotham, the son of Uzziah, was king of Judah, King Rezin of Aram and Pekah son of Remaliah king of Israel marched up to fight against Jerusalem, but they could not overpower it.

2Now the house of David was told, "Aram has allied itself with*ª* Ephraim"; so the hearts of Ahaz and his people were shaken, as the trees of the forest are shaken by the wind.

3Then the LORD said to Isaiah, "Go out, you and your son Shear-Jashub,*ᵇ* to meet Ahaz at the end of the aqueduct of the Upper Pool, on the road to the Washerman's Field. **4**Say to him, 'Be careful, keep calm and don't be afraid. Do not lose heart because of these two smoldering stubs of firewood—because of the fierce anger of Rezin and Aram and of the son of Remaliah. **5**Aram, Ephraim and Remaliah's son have plotted your ruin, saying, **6**"Let us invade Judah; let us tear it apart and divide it among ourselves, and make the son of Tabeel king over it." **7**Yet this is what the Sovereign LORD says:

" 'It will not take place,
   it will not happen,
8for the head of Aram is Damascus,
   and the head of Damascus is only
      Rezin.
  Within sixty-five years
   Ephraim will be too shattered to be a
      people.
9The head of Ephraim is Samaria,
   and the head of Samaria is only
      Remaliah's son.
  If you do not stand firm in your faith,
   you will not stand at all.' "

10Again the LORD spoke to Ahaz, **11**"Ask the LORD your God for a sign, whether in the deepest depths or in the highest heights."

12But Ahaz said, "I will not ask; I will not put the LORD to the test."

13Then Isaiah said, "Hear now, you house of David! Is it not enough to try the patience of men? Will you try the patience of my God also? **14**Therefore the Lord himself will give you*ᶜ* a sign: The virgin will be with child and will give birth to a son, and*ᵈ* will call him Immanuel.*ᵉ* **15**He will eat curds and honey when he knows enough to reject the wrong and choose the right. **16**But before the boy knows enough to reject the wrong and choose the right, the land of the two kings you dread will be laid waste. **17**The LORD will bring on you

and on your people and on the house of your father a time unlike any since Ephraim broke away from Judah—he will bring the king of Assyria."

18In that day the LORD will whistle for flies from the distant streams of Egypt and for bees from the land of Assyria. **19**They will all come and settle in the steep ravines and in the crevices in the rocks, on all the thornbushes and at all the water holes. **20**In that day the Lord will use a razor hired from beyond the River*ᶠ*—the king of Assyria—to shave your head and the hair of your legs, and to take off your beards also. **21**In that day, a man will keep alive a young cow and two goats. **22**And because of the abundance of the milk they give, he will have curds to eat. All who remain in the land will eat curds and honey. **23**In that day, in every place where there were a thousand vines worth a thousand silver shekels,*ᵍ* there will be only briers and thorns. **24**Men will go there with bow and arrow, for the land will be covered with briers and thorns. **25**As for all the hills once cultivated by the hoe, you will no longer go there for fear of the briers and thorns; they will become places where cattle are turned loose and where sheep run.

Assyria, the LORD's Instrument

8 The LORD said to me, "Take a large scroll and write on it with an ordinary pen: Maher-Shalal-Hash-Baz.*ʰ* **2**And I will call in Uriah the priest and Zechariah son of Jeberekiah as reliable witnesses for me."

3Then I went to the prophetess, and she conceived and gave birth to a son. And the LORD said to me, "Name him Maher-Shalal-Hash-Baz. **4**Before the boy knows how to say 'My father' or 'My mother,' the wealth of Damascus and the plunder of Samaria will be carried off by the king of Assyria."

5The LORD spoke to me again:

6"Because this people has rejected
   the gently flowing waters of Shiloah
  and rejoices over Rezin
   and the son of Remaliah,

ª2 Or *has set up camp in* *ᵇ3 Shear-Jashub* means *a remnant will return.* *ᶜ14* The Hebrew is plural. *ᵈ14* Masoretic Text; Dead Sea Scrolls *and he* or *and they* *ᵉ14 Immanuel* means *God with us.* *ᶠ20* That is, the Euphrates *ᵍ23* That is, about 25 pounds (about 11.5 kilograms) *ʰ1 Maher-Shalal-Hash-Baz* means *quick to the plunder, swift to the spoil;* also in verse 3.

⁷therefore the Lord is about to bring
  against them
 the mighty floodwaters of the
   River*a*—
 the king of Assyria with all his pomp.
It will overflow all its channels,
  run over all its banks
⁸and sweep on into Judah, swirling over
  it,
 passing through it and reaching up
   to the neck.
 Its outspread wings will cover the
   breadth of your land,
 O Immanuel*b*!"

⁹Raise the war cry,*c* you nations, and be
  shattered!
 Listen, all you distant lands.
 Prepare for battle, and be shattered!
 Prepare for battle, and be shattered!
¹⁰Devise your strategy, but it will be
  thwarted;
 propose your plan, but it will not
   stand,
 for God is with us.*d*

Fear God

¹¹The LORD spoke to me with his strong
hand upon me, warning me not to follow
the way of this people. He said:

¹²"Do not call conspiracy
  everything that these people call
   conspiracy*e*;
 do not fear what they fear,
  and do not dread it.
¹³The LORD Almighty is the one you are
   to regard as holy,
 he is the one you are to fear,
 he is the one you are to dread,
¹⁴and he will be a sanctuary;
  but for both houses of Israel he will be
 a stone that causes men to stumble
  and a rock that makes them fall.
 And for the people of Jerusalem he will
   be
 a trap and a snare.
¹⁵Many of them will stumble;
 they will fall and be broken,
 they will be snared and captured."

¹⁶Bind up the testimony
 and seal up the law among my
   disciples.
¹⁷I will wait for the LORD,
 who is hiding his face from the
   house of Jacob.
 I will put my trust in him.

¹⁸Here am I, and the children the LORD
has given me. We are signs and symbols in

Israel from the LORD Almighty, who dwells
on Mount Zion.
¹⁹When men tell you to consult mediums and spiritists, who whisper and mutter, should not a people inquire of their
God? Why consult the dead on behalf of
the living? ²⁰To the law and to the testimony! If they do not speak according to
this word, they have no light of dawn.
²¹Distressed and hungry, they will roam
through the land; when they are famished, they will become enraged and,
looking upward, will curse their king and
their God. ²²Then they will look toward
the earth and see only distress and darkness and fearful gloom, and they will be
thrust into utter darkness.

To Us a Child Is Born

9 Nevertheless, there will be no more
  gloom for those who were in distress.
In the past he humbled the land of Zebulun and the land of Naphtali, but in the future he will honor Galilee of the Gentiles,
by the way of the sea, along the Jordan—

²The people walking in darkness
  have seen a great light;
 on those living in the land of the
   shadow of death*f*
 a light has dawned.
³You have enlarged the nation
  and increased their joy;
 they rejoice before you
  as people rejoice at the harvest,
 as men rejoice
  when dividing the plunder.
⁴For as in the day of Midian's defeat,
  you have shattered
 the yoke that burdens them,
  the bar across their shoulders,
  the rod of their oppressor.
⁵Every warrior's boot used in battle
  and every garment rolled in blood
 will be destined for burning,
  will be fuel for the fire.
⁶For to us a child is born,
  to us a son is given,
  and the government will be on his
   shoulders.
 And he will be called
  Wonderful Counselor,*g* Mighty God,
  Everlasting Father, Prince of Peace.
⁷Of the increase of his government and
   peace

*a7 That is, the Euphrates   b8 Immanuel means
God with us.   c9 Or Do your worst   d10 Hebrew
Immanuel   e12 Or Do not call for a treaty / every
time these people call for a treaty   f2 Or land of
darkness   g6 Or Wonderful, Counselor*

there will be no end.
He will reign on David's throne
  and over his kingdom,
establishing and upholding it
  with justice and righteousness
  from that time on and forever.
The zeal of the LORD Almighty
  will accomplish this.

The LORD's Anger Against Israel

⁸ The Lord has sent a message against
    Jacob;
  it will fall on Israel.
⁹ All the people will know it—
    Ephraim and the inhabitants of
      Samaria—

It's a War out There

DAILY INSIGHT

FRIDAY

Passage:
Isaiah 9:6–7

Verse:
Isaiah 9:6

When was the last time you felt an overwhelming sense of gratitude for your freedom? If you're anything like me, it's been a while.

When I turned eighteen, I drove to the Army recruiting office in the basement of our local Post Office and registered for the draft. Because America was deeply involved in the Vietnam War, registration was mandatory. The following year the first draft lottery was held, and because my number was 285, Uncle Sam looked the other way.

However, because the conflict in Southeast Asia happened during my lifetime, I have been drawn to the stories of battle, especially the horrific accounts of prisoners of war. I have read stories of men who made up entire code languages for undetected communication with their fellow prisoners. I have read of men who played imaginary golf matches, only to come home and find their handicap improved by ten strokes. I have read about men for whom the promised embrace of their families and the smell of fresh, clean air literally drove them to survive the torture. For these men, only one thing could have possibly kept them alive: *hope*.

Sometimes the hope-filled verses that we read today get lost in the Christmas celebration: "For to us a child is born, to us a son is given." In the frantic hustle of wrapping paper, tree trimming and travel, we forget the setting in which these words were first spoken. The Jews were in a living nightmare. Centuries of hostile external forces and internal corruption had laid their precious nation to ruin. They had

nothing left except for the hope to which they had clung for centuries: hope for a Savior, hope for a rescuer, hope for a loving and forgiving Father.

So God sent his son, the incarnation of himself; a conqueror who could set all captives free. This Messiah would redeem Israel and all mankind—past, present, and future.

I'll admit that, in my lifetime, I've never wanted anything as badly as the POW's wanted their freedom or the Israelites longed for a King. I haven't been surrounded by hostile forces, and I haven't lived as disobediently as the Jews.

Or have I? Come to think of it, I'll bet that if I could see the forces swirling around me that seek to destroy me (Ephesians 6:12), I would long for escape. And if I could see, in the cold light of day, the abject sinfulness of my own life, my heart would be filled with shame. Isaiah's message to his suffering people is a message for us today. We are prisoners of a war between principalities and powers. We are in desperate need of someone to save us from our cold hearts of rebellion.

The freedoms we enjoy in this country abound. Thousands have fought and died to preserve this freedom. The freedom we have in Jesus Christ came through the sacrifice of God's Son on the cross. We've heard before that "the price of freedom is eternal vigilance"; in this world, that may be true. But the price of freedom in Jesus Christ is eternal *thankfulness*. Take a moment today to thank God for the freedom he's given you—in this world and the next.

For your next devotional reading, go to page 754.

who say with pride
and arrogance of heart,
¹⁰"The bricks have fallen down,
but we will rebuild with dressed
stone;
the fig trees have been felled,
but we will replace them with
cedars."
¹¹But the LORD has strengthened Rezin's
foes against them
and has spurred their enemies on.
¹²Arameans from the east and Philistines
from the west
have devoured Israel with open
mouth.

Yet for all this, his anger is not turned
away,
his hand is still upraised.

¹³But the people have not returned to
him who struck them,
nor have they sought the LORD
Almighty.
¹⁴So the LORD will cut off from Israel both
head and tail,
both palm branch and reed in a
single day;
¹⁵the elders and prominent men are the
head,
the prophets who teach lies are the
tail.
¹⁶Those who guide this people mislead
them,
and those who are guided are led
astray.
¹⁷Therefore the Lord will take no
pleasure in the young men,
nor will he pity the fatherless and
widows,
for everyone is ungodly and wicked,
every mouth speaks vileness.

Yet for all this, his anger is not turned
away,
his hand is still upraised.

¹⁸Surely wickedness burns like a fire;
it consumes briers and thorns,
it sets the forest thickets ablaze,
so that it rolls upward in a column of
smoke.
¹⁹By the wrath of the LORD Almighty
the land will be scorched
and the people will be fuel for the fire;
no one will spare his brother.
²⁰On the right they will devour,
but still be hungry;
on the left they will eat,
but not be satisfied.
Each will feed on the flesh of his own
offspring[a]:

²¹ Manasseh will feed on Ephraim, and
Ephraim on Manasseh;
together they will turn against Judah.

Yet for all this, his anger is not turned
away,
his hand is still upraised.

10 Woe to those who make unjust laws,
to those who issue oppressive
decrees,
²to deprive the poor of their rights
and withhold justice from the
oppressed of my people,
making widows their prey
and robbing the fatherless.
³What will you do on the day of
reckoning,
when disaster comes from afar?
To whom will you run for help?
Where will you leave your riches?
⁴Nothing will remain but to cringe
among the captives
or fall among the slain.

Yet for all this, his anger is not turned
away,
his hand is still upraised.

God's Judgment on Assyria

⁵"Woe to the Assyrian, the rod of my
anger,
in whose hand is the club of my
wrath!
⁶I send him against a godless nation,
I dispatch him against a people who
anger me,
to seize loot and snatch plunder,
and to trample them down like mud
in the streets.
⁷But this is not what he intends,
this is not what he has in mind;
his purpose is to destroy,
to put an end to many nations.
⁸'Are not my commanders all kings?' he
says.
⁹ 'Has not Calno fared like
Carchemish?
Is not Hamath like Arpad,
and Samaria like Damascus?
¹⁰As my hand seized the kingdoms of the
idols,
kingdoms whose images excelled
those of Jerusalem and
Samaria—
¹¹shall I not deal with Jerusalem and her
images
as I dealt with Samaria and her
idols?' "

a20 Or *arm*

¹²When the Lord has finished all his work against Mount Zion and Jerusalem, he will say, "I will punish the king of Assyria for the willful pride of his heart and the haughty look in his eyes. ¹³For he says:

" 'By the strength of my hand I have done this,
    and by my wisdom, because I have understanding.
I removed the boundaries of nations,
    I plundered their treasures;
    like a mighty one I subdued*ᵃ* their kings.
¹⁴As one reaches into a nest,
    so my hand reached for the wealth of the nations;
as men gather abandoned eggs,
    so I gathered all the countries;
not one flapped a wing,
    or opened its mouth to chirp.' "

¹⁵Does the ax raise itself above him who swings it,
    or the saw boast against him who uses it?
As if a rod were to wield him who lifts it up,
    or a club brandish him who is not wood!
¹⁶Therefore, the Lord, the LORD Almighty, will send a wasting disease upon his sturdy warriors;
under his pomp a fire will be kindled like a blazing flame.
¹⁷The Light of Israel will become a fire, their Holy One a flame;
in a single day it will burn and consume
    his thorns and his briers.
¹⁸The splendor of his forests and fertile fields
    it will completely destroy,
    as when a sick man wastes away.
¹⁹And the remaining trees of his forests will be so few
    that a child could write them down.

The Remnant of Israel

²⁰In that day the remnant of Israel,
    the survivors of the house of Jacob,
will no longer rely on him
    who struck them down
but will truly rely on the LORD,
    the Holy One of Israel.
²¹A remnant will return,*ᵇ* a remnant of Jacob
    will return to the Mighty God.
²²Though your people, O Israel, be like the sand by the sea,

only a remnant will return.
Destruction has been decreed,
    overwhelming and righteous.
²³The Lord, the LORD Almighty, will carry out
    the destruction decreed upon the whole land.

²⁴Therefore, this is what the Lord, the LORD Almighty, says:

"O my people who live in Zion,
    do not be afraid of the Assyrians,
who beat you with a rod
    and lift up a club against you, as Egypt did.
²⁵Very soon my anger against you will end
    and my wrath will be directed to their destruction."

²⁶The LORD Almighty will lash them with a whip,
    as when he struck down Midian at the rock of Oreb;
and he will raise his staff over the waters,
    as he did in Egypt.
²⁷In that day their burden will be lifted from your shoulders,
    their yoke from your neck;
the yoke will be broken
    because you have grown so fat.*ᶜ*

²⁸They enter Aiath;
    they pass through Migron;
    they store supplies at Micmash.
²⁹They go over the pass, and say,
    "We will camp overnight at Geba."
Ramah trembles;
    Gibeah of Saul flees.
³⁰Cry out, O Daughter of Gallim!
    Listen, O Laishah!
    Poor Anathoth!
³¹Madmenah is in flight;
    the people of Gebim take cover.
³²This day they will halt at Nob;
    they will shake their fist
at the mount of the Daughter of Zion,
    at the hill of Jerusalem.

³³See, the Lord, the LORD Almighty,
    will lop off the boughs with great power.
The lofty trees will be felled,
    the tall ones will be brought low.
³⁴He will cut down the forest thickets with an ax;
    Lebanon will fall before the Mighty One.

ᵃ13 Or / I subdued the mighty,   ᵇ21 Hebrew shear-jashub; also in verse 22   ᶜ27 Hebrew; Septuagint broken / from your shoulders

The Branch From Jesse

11 A shoot will come up from the stump
of Jesse;
from his roots a Branch will bear
fruit.
[2] The Spirit of the LORD will rest on
him—
the Spirit of wisdom and of
understanding,
the Spirit of counsel and of power,
the Spirit of knowledge and of the
fear of the LORD—
[3] and he will delight in the fear of the
LORD.

He will not judge by what he sees with
his eyes,
or decide by what he hears with his
ears;
[4] but with righteousness he will judge
the needy,
with justice he will give decisions for
the poor of the earth.
He will strike the earth with the rod of
his mouth;
with the breath of his lips he will slay
the wicked.
[5] Righteousness will be his belt
and faithfulness the sash around his
waist.

[6] The wolf will live with the lamb,
the leopard will lie down with the
goat,
the calf and the lion and the yearling[a]
together;
and a little child will lead them.
[7] The cow will feed with the bear,
their young will lie down together,
and the lion will eat straw like the ox.
[8] The infant will play near the hole of the
cobra,
and the young child put his hand
into the viper's nest.
[9] They will neither harm nor destroy
on all my holy mountain,
for the earth will be full of the
knowledge of the LORD
as the waters cover the sea.

[10] In that day the Root of Jesse will stand
as a banner for the peoples; the nations
will rally to him, and his place of rest will
be glorious. [11] In that day the Lord will
reach out his hand a second time to re-
claim the remnant that is left of his people
from Assyria, from Lower Egypt, from Upper Egypt,[b] from Cush,[c] from Elam, from
Babylonia,[d] from Hamath and from the islands of the sea.

[12] He will raise a banner for the nations
and gather the exiles of Israel;
he will assemble the scattered people
of Judah
from the four quarters of the earth.
[13] Ephraim's jealousy will vanish,
and Judah's enemies[e] will be cut off;
Ephraim will not be jealous of Judah,
nor Judah hostile toward Ephraim.
[14] They will swoop down on the slopes of
Philistia to the west;
together they will plunder the people
to the east.
They will lay hands on Edom and
Moab,
and the Ammonites will be subject to
them.
[15] The LORD will dry up
the gulf of the Egyptian sea;
with a scorching wind he will sweep his
hand
over the Euphrates River.[f]
He will break it up into seven streams
so that men can cross over in
sandals.
[16] There will be a highway for the
remnant of his people
that is left from Assyria,
as there was for Israel
when they came up from Egypt.

Songs of Praise

12 In that day you will say:

"I will praise you, O LORD.
Although you were angry with me,
your anger has turned away
and you have comforted me.
[2] Surely God is my salvation;
I will trust and not be afraid.
The LORD, the LORD, is my strength and
my song;
he has become my salvation."
[3] With joy you will draw water
from the wells of salvation.

[4] In that day you will say:

"Give thanks to the LORD, call on his
name;
make known among the nations
what he has done,
and proclaim that his name is
exalted.
[5] Sing to the LORD, for he has done
glorious things;

---

[a]6 Hebrew; Septuagint *lion will feed*   [b]11 Hebrew
from Pathros   [c]11 That is, the upper Nile region
[d]11 Hebrew *Shinar*   [e]13 Or *hostility*   [f]15 Hebrew
the River

They will make captives of their
    captors
  and rule over their oppressors.

³On the day the LORD gives you relief
from suffering and turmoil and cruel
bondage, ⁴you will take up this taunt
against the king of Babylon:

How the oppressor has come to an end!
  How his fury*a* has ended!
⁵The LORD has broken the rod of the
    wicked,
  the scepter of the rulers,
⁶which in anger struck down peoples

with unceasing blows,
  and in fury subdued nations
  with relentless aggression.
⁷All the lands are at rest and at peace;
  they break into singing.
⁸Even the pine trees and the cedars of
    Lebanon
  exult over you and say,
"Now that you have been laid low,
  no woodsman comes to cut us
    down."

a4 Dead Sea Scrolls, Septuagint and Syriac; the
meaning of the word in the Masoretic Text is
uncertain.

A Lesson from a Fuzzy Man

DAILY INSIGHT

MONDAY

Passage:
Isaiah 14:1–7

Verse:
Isaiah 14:7

I come from a long line of hairy men. Like Esau, my grandfather, my dad, my brothers and I were given a hefty crop of dark body fur on our faces, arms, chests, and legs. I had to shave every day long before I graduated from high school.

Soon after this, something very painful started to happen. Little whiskers growing out of my face and neck would sometimes get to the surface of my skin, then take a U-turn. Instead of continuing to grow out into fresh air, these nasty little shafts of protein would bury themselves back into my body. No razor in the world could dig these rebels out. So, armed with a needle and tweezers, I have been forced over the years to dig these ingrown hairs out, groaning all the while. This is not a pretty picture.

Anger and frustration are like the hairs growing from your face. If they are free to emerge from the surface of your consciousness, they can be dealt with—eliminated by the razor sharpness of confession and forgiveness. If not extracted, pent-up hostility can have a mercilessly crippling effect.

Isaiah paints a hopeful picture for his people in these verses, one of release from conflict and from the anger that has buried their nation in hopeless bondage. "The LORD will … settle them" (14:1). Picture these families, who had been festering under their sin and unresolved internal conflict, finding fresh air in their homeland.

Imagine the release they would experience from open confession and forgiveness from each other—everything would be settled at last. Furthermore, Isaiah announces the painful invasions of "the oppressor has come to an end" (14:4). Not only can the people be released from the desperate erosion of ingrown hatred, but their enemies would no longer invade their nation's tender flesh. "The day of the LORD" would bring all of this to an end.

How is it with you? Have you denied the healing that could be yours with your parents or your siblings by avoiding the issue and burying your feelings? Is your relationship with your wife crippled by unresolved conflict? Are there colleagues and associates who need your forgiveness? Or are these things burying their way into your soul where they cannot be reached … or removed … or healed?

Isaiah's promise today is for Israel's serenity—an end to the bitterness and conflict. Perhaps you look at the "face" of your closest relationships and see no ugly U-turns. Everything is in the open. All wrongs have been confessed and forgiven. Or perhaps it's time to experience the temporary discomfort of giving this conflict and bitterness some fresh air and confession, pulling this shameful thing out by its root. You don't have to keep living with this kind of ongoing pain.

For your next devotional reading, go to page 763.

⁹The grave*a* below is all astir
   to meet you at your coming;
it rouses the spirits of the departed to
      greet you—
   all those who were leaders in the
      world;
it makes them rise from their
      thrones—
   all those who were kings over the
      nations.
¹⁰They will all respond,
   they will say to you,
"You also have become weak, as we are;
   you have become like us."
¹¹All your pomp has been brought down
      to the grave,
   along with the noise of your harps;
maggots are spread out beneath you
   and worms cover you.

¹²How you have fallen from heaven,
   O morning star, son of the dawn!
You have been cast down to the earth,
   you who once laid low the nations!
¹³You said in your heart,
   "I will ascend to heaven;
I will raise my throne
   above the stars of God;
I will sit enthroned on the mount of
      assembly,
   on the utmost heights of the sacred
      mountain.*b*
¹⁴I will ascend above the tops of the
      clouds;
   I will make myself like the Most
      High."
¹⁵But you are brought down to the
      grave,
   to the depths of the pit.

¹⁶Those who see you stare at you,
   they ponder your fate:
"Is this the man who shook the earth
   and made kingdoms tremble,
¹⁷the man who made the world a desert,
   who overthrew its cities
   and would not let his captives go
      home?"

¹⁸All the kings of the nations lie in state,
   each in his own tomb.
¹⁹But you are cast out of your tomb
   like a rejected branch;
you are covered with the slain,
   with those pierced by the sword,
   those who descend to the stones of
      the pit.
Like a corpse trampled underfoot,
²⁰   you will not join them in burial,
for you have destroyed your land
   and killed your people.

The offspring of the wicked
   will never be mentioned again.
²¹Prepare a place to slaughter his sons
   for the sins of their forefathers;
they are not to rise to inherit the land
   and cover the earth with their cities.

²²"I will rise up against them,"
   declares the LORD Almighty.
"I will cut off from Babylon her name
   and survivors,
her offspring and descendants,"
   declares the LORD.
²³"I will turn her into a place for owls
   and into swampland;
I will sweep her with the broom of
      destruction,"
declares the LORD Almighty.

A Prophecy Against Assyria

²⁴The LORD Almighty has sworn,

"Surely, as I have planned, so it will be,
   and as I have purposed, so it will
      stand.
²⁵I will crush the Assyrian in my land;
   on my mountains I will trample him
      down.
His yoke will be taken from my people,
   and his burden removed from their
      shoulders."
²⁶This is the plan determined for the
      whole world;
   this is the hand stretched out over all
      nations.
²⁷For the LORD Almighty has purposed,
   and who can thwart him?
His hand is stretched out, and who
   can turn it back?

A Prophecy Against the Philistines

²⁸This oracle came in the year King
Ahaz died:

²⁹Do not rejoice, all you Philistines,
   that the rod that struck you is broken;
from the root of that snake will spring
      up a viper,
   its fruit will be a darting, venomous
      serpent.
³⁰The poorest of the poor will find
      pasture,
   and the needy will lie down in safety.
But your root I will destroy by famine;
   it will slay your survivors.

³¹Wail, O gate! Howl, O city!
   Melt away, all you Philistines!

a9 Hebrew *Sheol*; also in verses 11 and 15
b13 Or *the north*; Hebrew *Zaphon*

and the flower becomes a ripening
    grape,
he will cut off the shoots with pruning
    knives,
and cut down and take away the
    spreading branches.
[6] They will all be left to the mountain
    birds of prey
and to the wild animals;
the birds will feed on them all
    summer,
    the wild animals all winter.

[7] At that time gifts will be brought to the
LORD Almighty

from a people tall and
    smooth-skinned,
    from a people feared far and wide,
an aggressive nation of strange speech,
    whose land is divided by rivers—

the gifts will be brought to Mount Zion,
the place of the Name of the LORD Almighty.

A Prophecy About Egypt

19 An oracle concerning Egypt:

See, the LORD rides on a swift cloud
    and is coming to Egypt.
The idols of Egypt tremble before him,
    and the hearts of the Egyptians melt
    within them.
[2] "I will stir up Egyptian against
    Egyptian—
brother will fight against brother,
    neighbor against neighbor,
    city against city,
    kingdom against kingdom.
[3] The Egyptians will lose heart,
    and I will bring their plans to
    nothing;
they will consult the idols and the
    spirits of the dead,
    the mediums and the spiritists.
[4] I will hand the Egyptians over
    to the power of a cruel master,
and a fierce king will rule over them,"
    declares the Lord, the LORD Almighty.

[5] The waters of the river will dry up,
    and the riverbed will be parched and
    dry.
[6] The canals will stink;
    the streams of Egypt will dwindle
    and dry up.
The reeds and rushes will wither,
[7]   also the plants along the Nile,
    at the mouth of the river.
Every sown field along the Nile

will become parched, will blow away
    and be no more.
[8] The fishermen will groan and lament,
    all who cast hooks into the Nile;
those who throw nets on the water
    will pine away.
[9] Those who work with combed flax will
    despair,
    the weavers of fine linen will lose
    hope.
[10] The workers in cloth will be dejected,
    and all the wage earners will be sick
    at heart.
[11] The officials of Zoan are nothing but
    fools;
    the wise counselors of Pharaoh give
    senseless advice.
How can you say to Pharaoh,
    "I am one of the wise men,
    a disciple of the ancient kings"?
[12] Where are your wise men now?
    Let them show you and make known
    what the LORD Almighty
    has planned against Egypt.
[13] The officials of Zoan have become
    fools,
    the leaders of Memphis[a] are
    deceived;
the cornerstones of her peoples
    have led Egypt astray.
[14] The LORD has poured into them
    a spirit of dizziness;
they make Egypt stagger in all that she
    does,
    as a drunkard staggers around in his
    vomit.
[15] There is nothing Egypt can do—
    head or tail, palm branch or reed.

[16] In that day the Egyptians will be like
women. They will shudder with fear at the
uplifted hand that the LORD Almighty
raises against them. [17] And the land of Judah will bring terror to the Egyptians;
everyone to whom Judah is mentioned
will be terrified, because of what the LORD
Almighty is planning against them.

[18] In that day five cities in Egypt will
speak the language of Canaan and swear
allegiance to the LORD Almighty. One of
them will be called the City of Destruction.[b]

[19] In that day there will be an altar to the
LORD in the heart of Egypt, and a monument to the LORD at its border. [20] It will be a

---

[a]13 Hebrew *Noph*   [b]18 Most manuscripts of the
Masoretic Text; some manuscripts of the Masoretic
Text, Dead Sea Scrolls and Vulgate *City of the Sun*
(that is, Heliopolis)

sign and witness to the LORD Almighty in the land of Egypt. When they cry out to the LORD because of their oppressors, he will send them a savior and defender, and he will rescue them. ²¹So the LORD will make himself known to the Egyptians, and in that day they will acknowledge the LORD. They will worship with sacrifices and grain offerings; they will make vows to the LORD and keep them. ²²The LORD will strike Egypt with a plague; he will strike them and heal them. They will turn to the LORD, and he will respond to their pleas and heal them.

²³In that day there will be a highway from Egypt to Assyria. The Assyrians will go to Egypt and the Egyptians to Assyria. The Egyptians and Assyrians will worship together. ²⁴In that day Israel will be the third, along with Egypt and Assyria, a blessing on the earth. ²⁵The LORD Almighty will bless them, saying, "Blessed be Egypt my people, Assyria my handiwork, and Israel my inheritance."

A Prophecy Against Egypt and Cush

20 In the year that the supreme commander, sent by Sargon king of Assyria, came to Ashdod and attacked and captured it— ²at that time the LORD spoke through Isaiah son of Amoz. He said to him, "Take off the sackcloth from your body and the sandals from your feet." And he did so, going around stripped and barefoot.

³Then the LORD said, "Just as my servant Isaiah has gone stripped and barefoot for three years, as a sign and portent against Egypt and Cush,ᵃ ⁴so the king of Assyria will lead away stripped and barefoot the Egyptian captives and Cushite exiles, young and old, with buttocks bared—to Egypt's shame. ⁵Those who trusted in Cush and boasted in Egypt will be afraid and put to shame. ⁶In that day the people who live on this coast will say, 'See what has happened to those we relied on, those we fled to for help and deliverance from the king of Assyria! How then can we escape?'"

A Prophecy Against Babylon

21 An oracle concerning the Desert by the Sea:

Like whirlwinds sweeping through the
    southland,
an invader comes from the desert,
    from a land of terror.

²A dire vision has been shown to me:
    The traitor betrays, the looter takes
        loot.
Elam, attack! Media, lay siege!
    I will bring to an end all the groaning
        she caused.

³At this my body is racked with pain,
    pangs seize me, like those of a
        woman in labor;
I am staggered by what I hear,
    I am bewildered by what I see.
⁴My heart falters,
    fear makes me tremble;
the twilight I longed for
    has become a horror to me.

⁵They set the tables,
    they spread the rugs,
    they eat, they drink!
Get up, you officers,
    oil the shields!

⁶This is what the Lord says to me:

"Go, post a lookout
    and have him report what he sees.
⁷When he sees chariots
    with teams of horses,
riders on donkeys
    or riders on camels,
let him be alert,
    fully alert."

⁸And the lookoutᵇ shouted,

"Day after day, my lord, I stand on the
        watchtower;
    every night I stay at my post.
⁹Look, here comes a man in a chariot
    with a team of horses.
And he gives back the answer:
    'Babylon has fallen, has fallen!
All the images of its gods
    lie shattered on the ground!'"

¹⁰O my people, crushed on the threshing
        floor,
    I tell you what I have heard
from the LORD Almighty,
    from the God of Israel.

A Prophecy Against Edom

¹¹An oracle concerning Dumahᶜ:

Someone calls to me from Seir,
    "Watchman, what is left of the night?
    Watchman, what is left of the night?"
¹²The watchman replies,

ᵃ3 That is, the upper Nile region; also in verse 5
ᵇ8 Dead Sea Scrolls and Syriac; Masoretic Text
A lion   ᶜ11 Dumah means silence or stillness, a
wordplay on Edom.

"Morning is coming, but also the
night.
If you would ask, then ask;
and come back yet again."

A Prophecy Against Arabia

¹³An oracle concerning Arabia:

You caravans of Dedanites,
who camp in the thickets of Arabia,
¹⁴ bring water for the thirsty;
you who live in Tema,
bring food for the fugitives.
¹⁵They flee from the sword,
from the drawn sword,
from the bent bow
and from the heat of battle.

¹⁶This is what the Lord says to me:
"Within one year, as a servant bound by
contract would count it, all the pomp of
Kedar will come to an end. ¹⁷The survivors
of the bowmen, the warriors of Kedar, will
be few." The LORD, the God of Israel, has
spoken.

A Prophecy About Jerusalem

22 An oracle concerning the Valley of
Vision:

What troubles you now,
that you have all gone up on the roofs,
²O town full of commotion,
O city of tumult and revelry?
Your slain were not killed by the sword,
nor did they die in battle.
³All your leaders have fled together;
they have been captured without
using the bow.
All you who were caught were taken
prisoner together,
having fled while the enemy was still
far away.
⁴Therefore I said, "Turn away from me;
let me weep bitterly.
Do not try to console me
over the destruction of my people."

⁵The Lord, the LORD Almighty, has a day
of tumult and trampling and terror
in the Valley of Vision,
a day of battering down walls
and of crying out to the mountains.
⁶Elam takes up the quiver,
with her charioteers and horses;
Kir uncovers the shield.
⁷Your choicest valleys are full of chariots,
and horsemen are posted at the city
gates;
⁸ the defenses of Judah are stripped
away.

And you looked in that day
to the weapons in the Palace of the
Forest;
⁹you saw that the City of David
had many breaches in its defenses;
you stored up water
in the Lower Pool.
¹⁰You counted the buildings in
Jerusalem
and tore down houses to strengthen
the wall.
¹¹You built a reservoir between the two
walls
for the water of the Old Pool,
but you did not look to the One who
made it,
or have regard for the One who
planned it long ago.

¹²The Lord, the LORD Almighty,
called you on that day
to weep and to wail,
to tear out your hair and put on
sackcloth.
¹³But see, there is joy and revelry,
slaughtering of cattle and killing of
sheep,
eating of meat and drinking of wine!
"Let us eat and drink," you say,
"for tomorrow we die!"

¹⁴The LORD Almighty has revealed this
in my hearing: "Till your dying day this sin
will not be atoned for," says the Lord, the
LORD Almighty.

¹⁵This is what the Lord, the LORD Almighty, says:

"Go, say to this steward,
to Shebna, who is in charge of the
palace:
¹⁶What are you doing here and who gave
you permission
to cut out a grave for yourself here,
hewing your grave on the height
and chiseling your resting place in
the rock?

¹⁷"Beware, the LORD is about to take firm
hold of you
and hurl you away, O you mighty
man.
¹⁸He will roll you up tightly like a ball
and throw you into a large country.
There you will die
and there your splendid chariots will
remain—
you disgrace to your master's house!
¹⁹I will depose you from your office,
and you will be ousted from your
position.

²⁰"In that day I will summon my servant, Eliakim son of Hilkiah. ²¹I will clothe him with your robe and fasten your sash around him and hand your authority over to him. He will be a father to those who live in Jerusalem and to the house of Judah. ²²I will place on his shoulder the key to the house of David; what he opens no one can shut, and what he shuts no one can open. ²³I will drive him like a peg into a firm place; he will be a seat*ᵃ* of honor for the house of his father. ²⁴All the glory of his family will hang on him: its offspring and offshoots—all its lesser vessels, from the bowls to all the jars.

²⁵"In that day," declares the LORD Almighty, "the peg driven into the firm place will give way; it will be sheared off and will fall, and the load hanging on it will be cut down." The LORD has spoken.

A Prophecy About Tyre

23 An oracle concerning Tyre:

Wail, O ships of Tarshish!
    For Tyre is destroyed
    and left without house or harbor.
From the land of Cyprus*ᵇ*
    word has come to them.

² Be silent, you people of the island
    and you merchants of Sidon,
    whom the seafarers have enriched.
³ On the great waters
    came the grain of the Shihor;
the harvest of the Nile*ᶜ* was the revenue
    of Tyre,

ᵃ23 Or *throne*   *ᵇ1* Hebrew *Kittim*   *ᶜ2,3* Masoretic Text; one Dead Sea Scroll *Sidon, / who cross over the sea; / your envoys ³are on the great waters. / The grain of the Shihor, / the harvest of the Nile,*

You Hold Firm. They'll Hold Firm, Too

DAILY INSIGHT

TUESDAY

Passage:
Isaiah 22:20–25

Verse:
Isaiah 22:23

Have you ever had this experience? You open the bathroom door and find that something is impeding the door's progress. So you wedge your head between the door and the jamb, and behind the door you see a pile of robes and pajamas covered with a thin layer of drywall dust. The hook you thought you had firmly installed has given way, and the result is a big mess. Time to get the Dust Buster™, some patching compound, and a better anchor bolt.

This image parallels the image we read about in today's story. Eliakim was the second in command in Judah, sort of a prime minister directly under the king. Among other things, he was responsible for screening visitors and ushering people into the presence of the king. The text gives us a terrific word picture to understand Eliakim's role and what kind of person he was … at least initially: "I will drive him like a peg into a firm place … his family will hang on him."

The king was like a firm wall. Eliakim was a "peg," tightly fastened to this wall just inside the back door. And the people—Eliakim's family—were like the clothes safely hanging on this peg. Do you have this picture in mind? The peg counted on the firmness of the wall and the clothes counted on the dependability of the peg. As long as the peg held, they were safe.

Unfortunately, Eliakim couldn't handle the load. And because of his failure, his family fell as well. Eliakim's family counted on him not to lose his grip. They knew that if he failed, their fall would be certain.

This is an incredible picture of our role as fathers. Our hearts are firmly grounded in the covenant promises of the King of Kings, and our families depend on this security. As long as we hold firm, they are safe. When we fail, the impact on them is sure. What's more, as fathers, we have the responsibility to pass on the assurance and grounding we have in God to our families. They are counting on our love and discipline.

Eliakim couldn't handle the load. Even though the king stood firm, he failed. Too bad for Eliakim, and too bad for his family.

For your next devotional reading, go to page 766.

and she became the marketplace of
the nations.
4 Be ashamed, O Sidon, and you,
O fortress of the sea,
for the sea has spoken:
"I have neither been in labor nor given
birth;
I have neither reared sons nor
brought up daughters."
5 When word comes to Egypt,
they will be in anguish at the report
from Tyre.

6 Cross over to Tarshish;
wail, you people of the island.
7 Is this your city of revelry,
the old, old city,
whose feet have taken her
to settle in far-off lands?
8 Who planned this against Tyre,
the bestower of crowns,
whose merchants are princes,
whose traders are renowned in the
earth?
9 The LORD Almighty planned it,
to bring low the pride of all glory
and to humble all who are renowned
on the earth.

10 Till^a your land as along the Nile,
O Daughter of Tarshish,
for you no longer have a harbor.
11 The LORD has stretched out his hand
over the sea
and made its kingdoms tremble.
He has given an order concerning
Phoenicia^b
that her fortresses be destroyed.
12 He said, "No more of your reveling,
O Virgin Daughter of Sidon, now
crushed!

"Up, cross over to Cyprus^c;
even there you will find no rest."
13 Look at the land of the
Babylonians,^{d}
this people that is now of no
account!
The Assyrians have made it
a place for desert creatures;
they raised up their siege towers,
they stripped its fortresses bare
and turned it into a ruin.

14 Wail, you ships of Tarshish;
your fortress is destroyed!

15 At that time Tyre will be forgotten for
seventy years, the span of a king's life. But
at the end of these seventy years, it will
happen to Tyre as in the song of the prostitute:

16 "Take up a harp, walk through the city,
O prostitute forgotten;
play the harp well, sing many a song,
so that you will be remembered."

17 At the end of seventy years, the LORD
will deal with Tyre. She will return to her
hire as a prostitute and will ply her trade
with all the kingdoms on the face of the
earth. **18** Yet her profit and her earnings
will be set apart for the LORD; they will not
be stored up or hoarded. Her profits will
go to those who live before the LORD, for
abundant food and fine clothes.

The LORD's Devastation of the Earth

24 See, the LORD is going to lay waste the
earth
and devastate it;
he will ruin its face
and scatter its inhabitants—
2 it will be the same
for priest as for people,
for master as for servant,
for mistress as for maid,
for seller as for buyer,
for borrower as for lender,
for debtor as for creditor.
3 The earth will be completely laid waste
and totally plundered.
The LORD has spoken this word.

4 The earth dries up and withers,
the world languishes and withers,
the exalted of the earth languish.
5 The earth is defiled by its people;
they have disobeyed the laws,
violated the statutes
and broken the everlasting covenant.
6 Therefore a curse consumes the earth;
its people must bear their guilt.
Therefore earth's inhabitants are
burned up,
and very few are left.
7 The new wine dries up and the vine
withers;
all the merrymakers groan.
8 The gaiety of the tambourines is stilled,
the noise of the revelers has stopped,
the joyful harp is silent.
9 No longer do they drink wine with a
song;
the beer is bitter to its drinkers.
10 The ruined city lies desolate;
the entrance to every house is
barred.

^{a}10 Dead Sea Scrolls and some Septuagint
manuscripts; Masoretic Text *Go through*
^{b}11 Hebrew *Canaan* ^{c}12 Hebrew *Kittim* ^{d}13 Or
Chaldeans

¹¹ In the streets they cry out for wine;
     all joy turns to gloom,
     all gaiety is banished from the
          earth.
¹² The city is left in ruins,
     its gate is battered to pieces.
¹³ So will it be on the earth
     and among the nations,
     as when an olive tree is beaten,
     or as when gleanings are left after the
          grape harvest.

¹⁴ They raise their voices, they shout for
          joy;
     from the west they acclaim the
          LORD's majesty.
¹⁵ Therefore in the east give glory to the
          LORD;
     exalt the name of the LORD, the God
          of Israel,
     in the islands of the sea.
¹⁶ From the ends of the earth we hear
          singing:
     "Glory to the Righteous One."

But I said, "I waste away, I waste
          away!
     Woe to me!
The treacherous betray!
     With treachery the treacherous
          betray!"
¹⁷ Terror and pit and snare await you,
     O people of the earth.
¹⁸ Whoever flees at the sound of terror
     will fall into a pit;
whoever climbs out of the pit
     will be caught in a snare.

The floodgates of the heavens are
          opened,
     the foundations of the earth shake.
¹⁹ The earth is broken up,
     the earth is split asunder,
     the earth is thoroughly shaken.
²⁰ The earth reels like a drunkard,
     it sways like a hut in the wind;
so heavy upon it is the guilt of its
          rebellion
     that it falls—never to rise again.

²¹ In that day the LORD will punish
     the powers in the heavens above
     and the kings on the earth below.
²² They will be herded together
     like prisoners bound in a dungeon;
they will be shut up in prison
     and be punished[a] after many days.
²³ The moon will be abashed, the sun
          ashamed;
     for the LORD Almighty will reign
on Mount Zion and in Jerusalem,
     and before its elders, gloriously.

Praise to the LORD

25 O LORD, you are my God;
     I will exalt you and praise your
          name,
for in perfect faithfulness
     you have done marvelous things,
     things planned long ago.
² You have made the city a heap of
          rubble,
     the fortified town a ruin,
the foreigners' stronghold a city no
          more;
     it will never be rebuilt.
³ Therefore strong peoples will honor
          you;
     cities of ruthless nations will revere
          you.
⁴ You have been a refuge for the poor,
     a refuge for the needy in his distress,
a shelter from the storm
     and a shade from the heat.
For the breath of the ruthless
     is like a storm driving against a wall
⁵   and like the heat of the desert.
You silence the uproar of foreigners;
     as heat is reduced by the shadow of a
          cloud,
so the song of the ruthless is stilled.

⁶ On this mountain the LORD Almighty
          will prepare
     a feast of rich food for all peoples,
a banquet of aged wine—
     the best of meats and the finest of
          wines.
⁷ On this mountain he will destroy
     the shroud that enfolds all peoples,
the sheet that covers all nations;
⁸   he will swallow up death forever.
The Sovereign LORD will wipe away the
          tears
     from all faces;
he will remove the disgrace of his
          people
     from all the earth.
                    The LORD has spoken.

⁹ In that day they will say,

"Surely this is our God;
     we trusted in him, and he saved us.
This is the LORD, we trusted in him;
     let us rejoice and be glad in his
          salvation."

¹⁰ The hand of the LORD will rest on this
          mountain;
     but Moab will be trampled under
          him

a22 Or *released*

as straw is trampled down in the
manure.
[11] They will spread out their hands in it,
as a swimmer spreads out his hands
to swim.
God will bring down their pride
despite the cleverness[a] of their
hands.

[12] He will bring down your high fortified
walls
and lay them low;
he will bring them down to the ground,
to the very dust.

[a]11 The meaning of the Hebrew for this word is
uncertain.

Bear

DAILY INSIGHT

WEDNESDAY

Passage:
Isaiah 26:1–4

Verse:
Isaiah 26:3

Have I told you about my little dog? I haven't? Well, it's about time I bring you up to speed on some inside family stuff.

In 1993, when our nest was about to empty out for good, my wife, Bobbie, announced that she wanted a "lap dog." We already had a mid-sized Sheltie named Abbey, but she was way too big to hold. Another dog—not to mention a *little* dog—was not something I thought we needed. But Bobbie had "that look" in her eye. I acquiesced.

After conducting some research, we selected a silver Yorkshire Terrier—adult weight, six pounds. And in order for her to have a chance with the Jamisons' gigantic black Labrador across the street, we named her "Bear."

When Bear was ten weeks old, Bobbie flew to Pennsylvania to spend a few days with her parents. Left alone with our puppy, I found myself reluctantly paying special attention to her. By week's end we were inseparable. She curled up on my neck when I watched television. She sat on my lap when I read the newspaper. By the time Bobbie returned from her trip, Bear was all mine.

Over the years, I've been amazed at the way this little dog works so hard to please me. (I know that this may be nauseating to you, but please stay with me for a few more minutes. Thanks.) Bear's favorite place in the house is wherever I am. When I'm sitting at my computer, she wants to be on my lap. When I step outside to get the mail, she shows me her teeth to welcome me back from my forty second trip. When I come home from a real business trip, she is completely crazed with joy; she jumps up on her hind legs and dances my welcome home.

Can you believe that I'm talking about a *dog*? A dog who can't go hunting with me or do *anything* useful? I can't either.

Now imagine a conversation between the omnipotent God of the galaxies and his angels. Our heavenly Father has just told his associates about me. His fondness for me has clearly come through in his description. His emissaries look at him, just like you're looking at me right now, and they say, "Your Honor, do you know who you're talking about? You're talking about a mortal here. Wolgemuth is only a man—a human filled with sinfulness and pride. Aren't you going a little overboard?"

My heavenly Father is almost humored at their lack of understanding. "You should see," he finally says, "how much he wants to please me, in spite of himself." Does the Creator of the universe have more important things to do than to be concerned about my peace? Does he have bigger assignments than loving me? Yes, absolutely. But still he remains undistracted.

"God will keep Robert in perfect peace, when Robert's mind is steadfast, because Robert has absolute trust in God." I want to be steadfast—loyal, unwavering, dependable, resolute—in my love for God. I want to know his presence and experience the luxury of never leaving his sight. In my innermost soul, I want to feel safe, secure, at home in his arms. Don't you?

By the way, I haven't told many people about Bear. Actually, it's a little embarrassing. Thanks for keeping this a secret.

For your next devotional reading, go to page 773.

A Song of Praise

26 In that day this song will be sung in the land of Judah:

We have a strong city;
    God makes salvation
    its walls and ramparts.
2 Open the gates
    that the righteous nation may enter,
    the nation that keeps faith.
3 You will keep in perfect peace
    him whose mind is steadfast,
    because he trusts in you.
4 Trust in the LORD forever,
    for the LORD, the LORD, is the Rock
    eternal.
5 He humbles those who dwell on high,
    he lays the lofty city low;
he levels it to the ground
    and casts it down to the dust.
6 Feet trample it down—
    the feet of the oppressed,
    the footsteps of the poor.

7 The path of the righteous is level;
    O upright One, you make the way of
    the righteous smooth.
8 Yes, LORD, walking in the way of your
    laws,*a*
    we wait for you;
your name and renown
    are the desire of our hearts.
9 My soul yearns for you in the night;
    in the morning my spirit longs for
    you.
When your judgments come upon the
    earth,

the people of the world learn
    righteousness.
10 Though grace is shown to the wicked,
    they do not learn righteousness;
even in a land of uprightness they go
    on doing evil
    and regard not the majesty of the
    LORD.
11 O LORD, your hand is lifted high,
    but they do not see it.
Let them see your zeal for your people
    and be put to shame;
    let the fire reserved for your enemies
    consume them.

12 LORD, you establish peace for us;
    all that we have accomplished you
    have done for us.
13 O LORD, our God, other lords besides
    you have ruled over us,
    but your name alone do we honor.
14 They are now dead, they live no more;
    those departed spirits do not rise.
You punished them and brought them
    to ruin;
    you wiped out all memory of them.
15 You have enlarged the nation,
    O LORD;
    you have enlarged the nation.
You have gained glory for yourself;
    you have extended all the borders of
    the land.

16 LORD, they came to you in their
    distress;
    when you disciplined them,

a8 Or judgments

HEY DAD
What is "grace"?

Text: Isaiah 26:10

Simply put, grace is a good thing that comes to us, not by our own efforts, but as a gift—even an undeserved gift—from another. We cannot earn grace, because, by its very definition, it is "unearnable."

    Grace is Jesus Christ offering the thief on the cross an eternity of paradise for a moment of belief (Luke 23:43). Grace is an employer paying a full day's wages to an employee who has done an hour's work (Matthew 20:1–16). Grace is a father killing the fattened calf for the disobedient and wayward son who only returned home when he ran out of money (Luke 15:22–24). And the greatest example of grace is the salvation Christ offers us (Ephesians 2:8).

    No matter how good we are, trying to *earn* God's favor would be like trying to jump to the top of a cliff from the bottom of the Grand Canyon. But God's grace catches us at the top of our own leap and carries us all the way to the peak of the cliff. Isn't that amazing?

QUESTIONS KIDS ASK

For a complete listing of Questions Kids Ask, turn to page 1435.

they could barely whisper a prayer.*ᵃ*
¹⁷As a woman with child and about to
  give birth
  writhes and cries out in her pain,
  so were we in your presence,
  O LORD.
¹⁸We were with child, we writhed in pain,
  but we gave birth to wind.
We have not brought salvation to the
  earth;
  we have not given birth to people of
  the world.

¹⁹But your dead will live;
  their bodies will rise.
You who dwell in the dust,
  wake up and shout for joy.
Your dew is like the dew of the
  morning;
  the earth will give birth to her dead.

²⁰Go, my people, enter your rooms
  and shut the doors behind you;
hide yourselves for a little while
  until his wrath has passed by.
²¹See, the LORD is coming out of his
  dwelling
  to punish the people of the earth for
  their sins.
The earth will disclose the blood shed
  upon her;
  she will conceal her slain no longer.

Deliverance of Israel

27 In that day,

  the LORD will punish with his sword,
  his fierce, great and powerful sword,
Leviathan the gliding serpent,
  Leviathan the coiling serpent;
he will slay the monster of the sea.

²In that day—

"Sing about a fruitful vineyard:
³ I, the LORD, watch over it;
  I water it continually.
I guard it day and night
  so that no one may harm it.
⁴ I am not angry.
If only there were briers and thorns
  confronting me!
  I would march against them in
  battle;
  I would set them all on fire.
⁵Or else let them come to me for refuge;
  let them make peace with me,
  yes, let them make peace with me."

⁶In days to come Jacob will take root,
  Israel will bud and blossom
  and fill all the world with fruit.

⁷Has ˎthe LORDˎ struck her
  as he struck down those who struck
  her?
Has she been killed
  as those were killed who killed her?
⁸By warfare*ᵇ* and exile you contend with
  her—
  with his fierce blast he drives her
  out,
  as on a day the east wind blows.
⁹By this, then, will Jacob's guilt be
  atoned for,
  and this will be the full fruitage of
  the removal of his sin:
When he makes all the altar stones
  to be like chalk stones crushed to
  pieces,
  no Asherah poles*ᶜ* or incense altars
  will be left standing.
¹⁰The fortified city stands desolate,
  an abandoned settlement, forsaken
  like the desert;
there the calves graze,
  there they lie down;
  they strip its branches bare.
¹¹When its twigs are dry, they are broken
  off
  and women come and make fires
  with them.
For this is a people without
  understanding;
  so their Maker has no compassion
  on them,
  and their Creator shows them no
  favor.

¹²In that day the LORD will thresh from
the flowing Euphrates*ᵈ* to the Wadi of
Egypt, and you, O Israelites, will be gathered up one by one. ¹³And in that day a
great trumpet will sound. Those who were
perishing in Assyria and those who were
exiled in Egypt will come and worship the
LORD on the holy mountain in Jerusalem.

Woe to Ephraim

28 Woe to that wreath, the pride of
  Ephraim's drunkards,
  to the fading flower, his glorious
  beauty,
set on the head of a fertile valley—
  to that city, the pride of those laid
  low by wine!
²See, the Lord has one who is powerful
  and strong.

ᵃ16 The meaning of the Hebrew for this clause is
uncertain.   *ᵇ8* See Septuagint; the meaning of the
Hebrew for this word is uncertain.   *ᶜ9* That is,
symbols of the goddess Asherah   *ᵈ12* Hebrew
River

Like a hailstorm and a destructive
    wind,
like a driving rain and a flooding
    downpour,
  he will throw it forcefully to the
    ground.
³That wreath, the pride of Ephraim's
    drunkards,
  will be trampled underfoot.
⁴That fading flower, his glorious beauty,
  set on the head of a fertile valley,
will be like a fig ripe before harvest—
  as soon as someone sees it and takes
    it in his hand,
  he swallows it.

⁵In that day the LORD Almighty
  will be a glorious crown,
a beautiful wreath
  for the remnant of his people.
⁶He will be a spirit of justice
  to him who sits in judgment,
a source of strength
  to those who turn back the battle at
    the gate.

⁷And these also stagger from wine
  and reel from beer:
Priests and prophets stagger from beer
  and are befuddled with wine;
they reel from beer,
  they stagger when seeing visions,
  they stumble when rendering
    decisions.
⁸All the tables are covered with vomit
  and there is not a spot without filth.

⁹"Who is it he is trying to teach?
  To whom is he explaining his
    message?
To children weaned from their milk,
  to those just taken from the breast?
¹⁰For it is:
  Do and do, do and do,
  rule on rule, rule on rule*a*;
  a little here, a little there."

¹¹Very well then, with foreign lips and
    strange tongues
  God will speak to this people,
¹²to whom he said,
  "This is the resting place, let the
    weary rest";
and, "This is the place of repose"—
  but they would not listen.
¹³So then, the word of the LORD to them
    will become:
  Do and do, do and do,
  rule on rule, rule on rule;
  a little here, a little there—
so that they will go and fall backward,
  be injured and snared and captured.

¹⁴Therefore hear the word of the LORD,
    you scoffers
  who rule this people in Jerusalem.
¹⁵You boast, "We have entered into a
    covenant with death,
  with the grave*b* we have made an
    agreement.
When an overwhelming scourge
    sweeps by,
  it cannot touch us,
for we have made a lie our refuge
  and falsehood*c* our hiding place."

¹⁶So this is what the Sovereign LORD
says:

"See, I lay a stone in Zion,
  a tested stone,
a precious cornerstone for a sure
    foundation;
  the one who trusts will never be
    dismayed.
¹⁷I will make justice the measuring line
  and righteousness the plumb line;
hail will sweep away your refuge, the
    lie,
  and water will overflow your hiding
    place.
¹⁸Your covenant with death will be
    annulled;
  your agreement with the grave will
    not stand.
When the overwhelming scourge
    sweeps by,
  you will be beaten down by it.
¹⁹As often as it comes it will carry you
    away;
  morning after morning, by day and
    by night,
  it will sweep through."

The understanding of this message
  will bring sheer terror.
²⁰The bed is too short to stretch out on,
  the blanket too narrow to wrap
    around you.
²¹The LORD will rise up as he did at
    Mount Perazim,
  he will rouse himself as in the Valley
    of Gibeon—
to do his work, his strange work,
  and perform his task, his alien task.
²²Now stop your mocking,
  or your chains will become heavier;
the Lord, the LORD Almighty, has told
    me

*a10 Hebrew / sav lasav sav lasav / kav lakav kav
lakav (possibly meaningless sounds; perhaps
a mimicking of the prophet's words); also in
verse 13   b15 Hebrew Sheol; also in verse 18
c15 Or false gods*

of the destruction decreed against
the whole land.

²³Listen and hear my voice;
pay attention and hear what I say.
²⁴When a farmer plows for planting, does
he plow continually?
Does he keep on breaking up and
harrowing the soil?
²⁵When he has leveled the surface,
does he not sow caraway and scatter
cummin?
Does he not plant wheat in its place,ᵃ
barley in its plot,ᵃ
and spelt in its field?
²⁶His God instructs him
and teaches him the right way.

²⁷Caraway is not threshed with a sledge,
nor is a cartwheel rolled over
cummin;
caraway is beaten out with a rod,
and cummin with a stick.
²⁸Grain must be ground to make bread;
so one does not go on threshing it
forever.
Though he drives the wheels of his
threshing cart over it,
his horses do not grind it.
²⁹All this also comes from the LORD
Almighty,
wonderful in counsel and
magnificent in wisdom.

Woe to David's City

29 Woe to you, Ariel, Ariel,
the city where David settled!
Add year to year
and let your cycle of festivals go on.
²Yet I will besiege Ariel;
she will mourn and lament,
she will be to me like an altar
hearth.ᵇ
³I will encamp against you all around;
I will encircle you with towers
and set up my siege works against
you.
⁴Brought low, you will speak from the
ground;
your speech will mumble out of the
dust.
Your voice will come ghostlike from the
earth;
out of the dust your speech will
whisper.

⁵But your many enemies will become
like fine dust,
the ruthless hordes like blown chaff.
Suddenly, in an instant,
⁶   the LORD Almighty will come

with thunder and earthquake and great
noise,
with windstorm and tempest and
flames of a devouring fire.
⁷Then the hordes of all the nations that
fight against Ariel,
that attack her and her fortress and
besiege her,
will be as it is with a dream,
with a vision in the night—
⁸as when a hungry man dreams that he
is eating,
but he awakens, and his hunger
remains;
as when a thirsty man dreams that he is
drinking,
but he awakens faint, with his thirst
unquenched.
So will it be with the hordes of all the
nations
that fight against Mount Zion.

⁹Be stunned and amazed,
blind yourselves and be sightless;
be drunk, but not from wine,
stagger, but not from beer.
¹⁰The LORD has brought over you a deep
sleep:
He has sealed your eyes (the
prophets);
he has covered your heads (the
seers).

¹¹For you this whole vision is nothing
but words sealed in a scroll. And if you
give the scroll to someone who can read,
and say to him, "Read this, please," he will
answer, "I can't; it is sealed." ¹²Or if you
give the scroll to someone who cannot
read, and say, "Read this, please," he will
answer, "I don't know how to read."

¹³The Lord says:

"These people come near to me with
their mouth
and honor me with their lips,
but their hearts are far from me.
Their worship of me
is made up only of rules taught by
men.ᶜ
¹⁴Therefore once more I will astound
these people
with wonder upon wonder;
the wisdom of the wise will perish,
the intelligence of the intelligent will
vanish."

ᵃ25 The meaning of the Hebrew for this word is
uncertain.   ᵇ2 The Hebrew for *altar hearth*
sounds like the Hebrew for *Ariel.*   ᶜ13 Hebrew;
Septuagint *They worship me in vain; / their
teachings are but rules taught by men*

¹⁵Woe to those who go to great depths
    to hide their plans from the LORD,
who do their work in darkness and
        think,
    "Who sees us? Who will know?"
¹⁶You turn things upside down,
    as if the potter were thought to be
        like the clay!
Shall what is formed say to him who
        formed it,
    "He did not make me"?
Can the pot say of the potter,
    "He knows nothing"?

¹⁷In a very short time, will not Lebanon
        be turned into a fertile field
    and the fertile field seem like a forest?
¹⁸In that day the deaf will hear the words
        of the scroll,
    and out of gloom and darkness
        the eyes of the blind will see.
¹⁹Once more the humble will rejoice in
        the LORD;
    the needy will rejoice in the Holy
        One of Israel.
²⁰The ruthless will vanish,
    the mockers will disappear,
    and all who have an eye for evil will
        be cut down—
²¹those who with a word make a man out
        to be guilty,
    who ensnare the defender in court
    and with false testimony deprive the
        innocent of justice.

²²Therefore this is what the LORD, who
redeemed Abraham, says to the house of
Jacob:

    "No longer will Jacob be ashamed;
        no longer will their faces grow pale.
²³When they see among them their
        children,
    the work of my hands,
    they will keep my name holy;
    they will acknowledge the holiness of
        the Holy One of Jacob,
    and will stand in awe of the God of
        Israel.
²⁴Those who are wayward in spirit will
        gain understanding;
    those who complain will accept
        instruction."

Woe to the Obstinate Nation

30 "Woe to the obstinate children,"
    declares the LORD,
"to those who carry out plans that are
        not mine,
    forming an alliance, but not by my
        Spirit,

heaping sin upon sin;
²who go down to Egypt
    without consulting me;
who look for help to Pharaoh's
        protection,
    to Egypt's shade for refuge.
³But Pharaoh's protection will be to your
        shame,
    Egypt's shade will bring you disgrace.
⁴Though they have officials in Zoan
    and their envoys have arrived in
        Hanes,
⁵everyone will be put to shame
    because of a people useless to them,
who bring neither help nor advantage,
    but only shame and disgrace."

⁶An oracle concerning the animals of
the Negev:

Through a land of hardship and
        distress,
    of lions and lionesses,
    of adders and darting snakes,
the envoys carry their riches on
        donkeys' backs,
    their treasures on the humps of
        camels,
to that unprofitable nation,
⁷   to Egypt, whose help is utterly
        useless.
Therefore I call her
    Rahab the Do-Nothing.

⁸Go now, write it on a tablet for them,
    inscribe it on a scroll,
that for the days to come
    it may be an everlasting witness.
⁹These are rebellious people, deceitful
        children,
    children unwilling to listen to the
        LORD's instruction.
¹⁰They say to the seers,
    "See no more visions!"
and to the prophets,
    "Give us no more visions of what is
        right!
Tell us pleasant things,
    prophesy illusions.
¹¹Leave this way,
    get off this path,
and stop confronting us
    with the Holy One of Israel!"

¹²Therefore, this is what the Holy One of
Israel says:

    "Because you have rejected this
        message,
    relied on oppression
    and depended on deceit,
¹³this sin will become for you

like a high wall, cracked and bulging,
  that collapses suddenly, in an instant.
[14] It will break in pieces like pottery,
    shattered so mercilessly
  that among its pieces not a fragment
      will be found
    for taking coals from a hearth
    or scooping water out of a cistern."

[15] This is what the Sovereign LORD, the
Holy One of Israel, says:

  "In repentance and rest is your
      salvation,
    in quietness and trust is your
      strength,
    but you would have none of it.
[16] You said, 'No, we will flee on horses.'
    Therefore you will flee!
  You said, 'We will ride off on swift
      horses.'
    Therefore your pursuers will be swift!
[17] A thousand will flee
    at the threat of one;
  at the threat of five
    you will all flee away,
  till you are left
    like a flagstaff on a mountaintop,
    like a banner on a hill."

[18] Yet the LORD longs to be gracious to
      you;
  he rises to show you compassion.
  For the LORD is a God of justice.
    Blessed are all who wait for him!

[19] O people of Zion, who live in Jerusalem, you will weep no more. How gracious
he will be when you cry for help! As soon
as he hears, he will answer you. [20] Although the Lord gives you the bread of
adversity and the water of affliction, your
teachers will be hidden no more; with
your own eyes you will see them.
[21] Whether you turn to the right or to the
left, your ears will hear a voice behind
you, saying, "This is the way; walk in it."
[22] Then you will defile your idols overlaid
with silver and your images covered with
gold; you will throw them away like a
menstrual cloth and say to them, "Away
with you!"

[23] He will also send you rain for the seed
you sow in the ground, and the food that
comes from the land will be rich and
plentiful. In that day your cattle will graze
in broad meadows. [24] The oxen and donkeys that work the soil will eat fodder and
mash, spread out with fork and shovel.
[25] In the day of great slaughter, when the
towers fall, streams of water will flow on
every high mountain and every lofty hill.
[26] The moon will shine like the sun, and
the sunlight will be seven times brighter,
like the light of seven full days, when the
LORD binds up the bruises of his people
and heals the wounds he inflicted.

[27] See, the Name of the LORD comes from
      afar,
    with burning anger and dense
      clouds of smoke;
  his lips are full of wrath,
    and his tongue is a consuming fire.
[28] His breath is like a rushing torrent,
    rising up to the neck.
  He shakes the nations in the sieve of
      destruction;
    he places in the jaws of the peoples
    a bit that leads them astray.
[29] And you will sing
    as on the night you celebrate a holy
      festival;
  your hearts will rejoice
    as when people go up with flutes
  to the mountain of the LORD,
    to the Rock of Israel.
[30] The LORD will cause men to hear his
      majestic voice
    and will make them see his arm
      coming down
  with raging anger and consuming fire,
    with cloudburst, thunderstorm and
      hail.
[31] The voice of the LORD will shatter
      Assyria;
    with his scepter he will strike them
      down.
[32] Every stroke the LORD lays on them
    with his punishing rod
  will be to the music of tambourines
      and harps,
    as he fights them in battle with the
      blows of his arm.
[33] Topheth has long been prepared;
    it has been made ready for the king.
  Its fire pit has been made deep and
      wide,
    with an abundance of fire and wood;
  the breath of the LORD,
    like a stream of burning sulfur,
    sets it ablaze.

Woe to Those Who Rely on Egypt

31 Woe to those who go down to Egypt
      for help,
    who rely on horses,
  who trust in the multitude of their
      chariots
    and in the great strength of their
      horsemen,

but do not look to the Holy One of
  Israel,
  or seek help from the LORD.
² Yet he too is wise and can bring
  disaster;
  he does not take back his words.
He will rise up against the house of the
  wicked,
  against those who help evildoers.
³ But the Egyptians are men and not
  God;
  their horses are flesh and not spirit.
When the LORD stretches out his hand,
  he who helps will stumble,
  he who is helped will fall;
  both will perish together.

⁴ This is what the LORD says to me:

"As a lion growls,
  a great lion over his prey—
and though a whole band of shepherds
  is called together against him,
he is not frightened by their shouts
  or disturbed by their clamor—
so the LORD Almighty will come down
  to do battle on Mount Zion and on
  its heights.
⁵ Like birds hovering overhead,
  the LORD Almighty will shield
  Jerusalem;
he will shield it and deliver it,
  he will 'pass over' it and will rescue it."

Terra Not So *Firma*

DAILY INSIGHT

THURSDAY

Passage:
Isaiah 31:1–3

Verse:
Isaiah 31:1

In January of 1993 our family had flown to southern California to spend the week with some of our closest friends. On Sunday night, my friend Lenny and I drove to Palm Springs for a Monday of golf. Our families stayed back in Pasadena.

At exactly 3:30 the next morning, I woke to something I had never heard before. It was a cracking sound, reminiscent of lifting a sticking window sash. And then, incredibly, our hotel room began to roll. Lenny sat up. "We're having an earthquake!" he choked out. I flipped on the light. "It's a big one," Lenny said after about twenty seconds of indescribable waves. Fifteen seconds later it was over.

We dialed our families back in Pasadena. They were hysterical. We found that what we had experienced in the desert was nothing compared to what had happened a hundred miles to the west. When we saw the news the next morning, we saw freeways—the very ones we had traveled only hours before—twisted and broken.

Over the next few days, it dawned on me why earthquakes are so awful. As I watched the local news shows and listened to the trembling voices of the victims, I learned that the lack of warning and property damage are not the worst parts of living through these natural disasters. No,

the greatest ruin an earthquake delivers is in the hearts of people who can no longer count on the dependability of solid ground. *Terra firma* has lost its *firma*.

Today's text was a blazing reminder from the prophet Isaiah to his people. "Woe to those who ... rely on horses ... [or] chariots ... [or the] strength of their horsemen," he declared. "The Egyptians are men and not God."

The Israelites were filled with insecurity. "We're tired of trusting a God we cannot see," they must have said. "Give us those strong and dependable Egyptians. They're like solid ground. We can count on them. They'll protect us." But Isaiah responded, "When the LORD stretches out his hand ... [you] will perish."

What can you count on ... your job, your car, your Maytag™? How about your stock portfolio? Your relationships? Your health?

Isaiah reminds us that none of these things are worthy of our absolute trust. Incredible as it may sound, they will all let us down. But trusting in God will never bring disappointment. He is enough. His reliability is legendary. His faithfulness is completely sure ... absolutely *firma*.

For your next devotional reading, go to page 777.

[6]Return to him you have so greatly revolted against, O Israelites. [7]For in that day every one of you will reject the idols of silver and gold your sinful hands have made.

[8]"Assyria will fall by a sword that is not
    of man;
    a sword, not of mortals, will devour
        them.
They will flee before the sword
    and their young men will be put to
        forced labor.
[9]Their stronghold will fall because of
        terror;
    at sight of the battle standard their
        commanders will panic,"
declares the LORD,
    whose fire is in Zion,
    whose furnace is in Jerusalem.

The Kingdom of Righteousness

32 See, a king will reign in righteousness
    and rulers will rule with justice.
[2]Each man will be like a shelter from the
        wind
    and a refuge from the storm,
like streams of water in the desert
    and the shadow of a great rock in a
        thirsty land.
[3]Then the eyes of those who see will no
        longer be closed,
    and the ears of those who hear will
        listen.
[4]The mind of the rash will know and
        understand,
    and the stammering tongue will be
        fluent and clear.
[5]No longer will the fool be called noble
    nor the scoundrel be highly respected.
[6]For the fool speaks folly,
    his mind is busy with evil:
He practices ungodliness
    and spreads error concerning the
        LORD;
the hungry he leaves empty
    and from the thirsty he withholds
        water.
[7]The scoundrel's methods are wicked,
    he makes up evil schemes
to destroy the poor with lies,
    even when the plea of the needy is
        just.
[8]But the noble man makes noble plans,
    and by noble deeds he stands.

The Women of Jerusalem

[9]You women who are so complacent,
    rise up and listen to me;
you daughters who feel secure,
    hear what I have to say!
[10]In little more than a year
    you who feel secure will tremble;
the grape harvest will fail,
    and the harvest of fruit will not come.
[11]Tremble, you complacent women;
    shudder, you daughters who feel
        secure!
Strip off your clothes,
    put sackcloth around your waists.
[12]Beat your breasts for the pleasant
        fields,
    for the fruitful vines
[13]and for the land of my people,
    a land overgrown with thorns and
        briers—
yes, mourn for all houses of merriment
    and for this city of revelry.
[14]The fortress will be abandoned,
    the noisy city deserted;
citadel and watchtower will become a
        wasteland forever,
    the delight of donkeys, a pasture for
        flocks,
[15]till the Spirit is poured upon us from on
        high,
    and the desert becomes a fertile
        field,
    and the fertile field seems like a
        forest.
[16]Justice will dwell in the desert
    and righteousness live in the fertile
        field.
[17]The fruit of righteousness will be
        peace;
    the effect of righteousness will be
        quietness and confidence
        forever.
[18]My people will live in peaceful dwelling
        places,
    in secure homes,
    in undisturbed places of rest.
[19]Though hail flattens the forest
    and the city is leveled completely,
[20]how blessed you will be,
    sowing your seed by every stream,
    and letting your cattle and donkeys
        range free.

Distress and Help

33 Woe to you, O destroyer,
    you who have not been destroyed!
Woe to you, O traitor,
    you who have not been betrayed!
When you stop destroying,
    you will be destroyed;
when you stop betraying,
    you will be betrayed.

² O LORD, be gracious to us;
　　we long for you.
　Be our strength every morning,
　　our salvation in time of distress.
³ At the thunder of your voice, the
　　peoples flee;
　　when you rise up, the nations scatter.
⁴ Your plunder, O nations, is harvested as
　　by young locusts;
　　like a swarm of locusts men pounce
　　　on it.

⁵ The LORD is exalted, for he dwells on
　　high;
　　he will fill Zion with justice and
　　　righteousness.
⁶ He will be the sure foundation for your
　　times,
　　a rich store of salvation and wisdom
　　　and knowledge;
　　the fear of the LORD is the key to this
　　　treasure.ᵃ

⁷ Look, their brave men cry aloud in the
　　streets;
　　the envoys of peace weep bitterly.
⁸ The highways are deserted,
　　no travelers are on the roads.
　The treaty is broken,
　　its witnessesᵇ are despised,
　　no one is respected.
⁹ The land mournsᶜ and wastes away,
　　Lebanon is ashamed and withers;
　Sharon is like the Arabah,
　　and Bashan and Carmel drop their
　　　leaves.

¹⁰ "Now will I arise," says the LORD.
　　"Now will I be exalted;
　　now will I be lifted up.
¹¹ You conceive chaff,
　　you give birth to straw;
　　your breath is a fire that consumes
　　　you.
¹² The peoples will be burned as if to
　　lime;
　　like cut thornbushes they will be set
　　　ablaze."

¹³ You who are far away, hear what I have
　　done;
　　you who are near, acknowledge my
　　　power!
¹⁴ The sinners in Zion are terrified;
　　trembling grips the godless:
　"Who of us can dwell with the
　　　consuming fire?
　Who of us can dwell with everlasting
　　　burning?"
¹⁵ He who walks righteously
　　and speaks what is right,
　who rejects gain from extortion
　　and keeps his hand from accepting
　　　bribes,
　who stops his ears against plots of
　　　murder
　　and shuts his eyes against
　　　contemplating evil—
¹⁶ this is the man who will dwell on the
　　heights,
　　whose refuge will be the mountain
　　　fortress.
　His bread will be supplied,
　　and water will not fail him.

¹⁷ Your eyes will see the king in his beauty
　　and view a land that stretches afar.
¹⁸ In your thoughts you will ponder the
　　former terror:
　"Where is that chief officer?
　Where is the one who took the
　　　revenue?
　Where is the officer in charge of the
　　　towers?"
¹⁹ You will see those arrogant people no
　　more,
　　those people of an obscure speech,
　　with their strange, incomprehensible
　　　tongue.

²⁰ Look upon Zion, the city of our festivals;
　　your eyes will see Jerusalem,
　　a peaceful abode, a tent that will not
　　　be moved;
　its stakes will never be pulled up,
　　nor any of its ropes broken.
²¹ There the LORD will be our Mighty One.
　　It will be like a place of broad rivers
　　　and streams.
　No galley with oars will ride them,
　　no mighty ship will sail them.
²² For the LORD is our judge,
　　the LORD is our lawgiver,
　　the LORD is our king;
　　it is he who will save us.

²³ Your rigging hangs loose:
　　The mast is not held secure,
　　the sail is not spread.
　Then an abundance of spoils will be
　　　divided
　　and even the lame will carry off
　　　plunder.
²⁴ No one living in Zion will say, "I am ill";
　　and the sins of those who dwell there
　　　will be forgiven.

Judgment Against the Nations

34 Come near, you nations, and listen;
　　pay attention, you peoples!

ᵃ6 Or *is a treasure from him*　ᵇ8 Dead Sea Scrolls;
Masoretic Text / *the cities*　ᶜ9 Or *dries up*

Let the earth hear, and all that is in it,
  the world, and all that comes out of
  it!
²The LORD is angry with all nations;
  his wrath is upon all their armies.
He will totally destroy*a* them,
  he will give them over to slaughter.
³Their slain will be thrown out,
  their dead bodies will send up a
    stench;
  the mountains will be soaked with
    their blood.
⁴All the stars of the heavens will be
    dissolved
  and the sky rolled up like a scroll;
all the starry host will fall
  like withered leaves from the vine,
  like shriveled figs from the fig tree.

⁵My sword has drunk its fill in the
    heavens;
  see, it descends in judgment on Edom,
  the people I have totally destroyed.
⁶The sword of the LORD is bathed in
    blood,
  it is covered with fat—
  the blood of lambs and goats,
  fat from the kidneys of rams.
For the LORD has a sacrifice in Bozrah
  and a great slaughter in Edom.
⁷And the wild oxen will fall with them,
  the bull calves and the great bulls.
Their land will be drenched with blood,
  and the dust will be soaked with fat.

⁸For the LORD has a day of vengeance,
  a year of retribution, to uphold Zion's
    cause.
⁹Edom's streams will be turned into
    pitch,
  her dust into burning sulfur;
  her land will become blazing pitch!
¹⁰It will not be quenched night and day;
  its smoke will rise forever.
From generation to generation it will
    lie desolate;
  no one will ever pass through it
    again.
¹¹The desert owl*b* and screech owl*b* will
    possess it;
  the great owl*b* and the raven will nest
    there.
God will stretch out over Edom
  the measuring line of chaos
  and the plumb line of desolation.
¹²Her nobles will have nothing there to
    be called a kingdom,
  all her princes will vanish away.
¹³Thorns will overrun her citadels,
  nettles and brambles her
    strongholds.

She will become a haunt for jackals,
  a home for owls.
¹⁴Desert creatures will meet with hyenas,
  and wild goats will bleat to each
    other;
there the night creatures will also
    repose
  and find for themselves places of
    rest.
¹⁵The owl will nest there and lay eggs,
  she will hatch them, and care for her
    young under the shadow of her
    wings;
there also the falcons will gather,
  each with its mate.

¹⁶Look in the scroll of the LORD and
read:

None of these will be missing,
  not one will lack her mate.
For it is his mouth that has given the
    order,
  and his Spirit will gather them
    together.
¹⁷He allots their portions;
  his hand distributes them by
    measure.
They will possess it forever
  and dwell there from generation to
    generation.

Joy of the Redeemed

35 The desert and the parched land will
    be glad;
  the wilderness will rejoice and
    blossom.
Like the crocus, ²it will burst into
    bloom;
  it will rejoice greatly and shout for
    joy.
The glory of Lebanon will be given to it,
  the splendor of Carmel and Sharon;
they will see the glory of the LORD,
  the splendor of our God.

³Strengthen the feeble hands,
  steady the knees that give way;
⁴say to those with fearful hearts,
  "Be strong, do not fear;
your God will come,
  he will come with vengeance;
with divine retribution
  he will come to save you."

⁵Then will the eyes of the blind be
    opened

---

a2 The Hebrew term refers to the irrevocable giving
over of things or persons to the LORD, often by
totally destroying them; also in verse 5.   *b11* The
precise identification of these birds is uncertain.

and the ears of the deaf unstopped.
[6] Then will the lame leap like a deer,
    and the mute tongue shout for joy.
Water will gush forth in the wilderness
    and streams in the desert.
[7] The burning sand will become a pool,
    the thirsty ground bubbling springs.
In the haunts where jackals once lay,
    grass and reeds and papyrus will
    grow.

[8] And a highway will be there;
    it will be called the Way of Holiness.
The unclean will not journey on it;

it will be for those who walk in that
    Way;
    wicked fools will not go about on it.[a]
[9] No lion will be there,
    nor will any ferocious beast get up
    on it;
    they will not be found there.
But only the redeemed will walk
    there,
[10]   and the ransomed of the LORD will
    return.

[a]8 Or / the simple will not stray from it

You're Not Afraid? Good for You.

DAILY INSIGHT

For centuries people have been captivated with the idea of creatures from other planets visiting Earth. Cave wall scratchings, mysterious stone formations, box office receipts and last week's tabloids chronicle our fascination with the possibility of extra-terrestrial life. Surfing through our television channels tonight, we might even come across a black-and-white movie from the forties, featuring bright lights from heaven and dazed people standing helplessly in a corn-field, staring skyward.

It's almost as though we *want* to be visited from outer space, but we're frightened at the thought that these crea-tures might actually show up!

The Bible records several visitations from heavenly beings, and Isaiah predicts one in today's passage. One of the words the Bible commonly uses to describe the light that celestial visitations throw off is "glory," and the people who see this light typically react in fear. But the visitors' response to these trembling people is consistent. The angels said it to the shep-herds on the night of Jesus' birth (Luke 2:10). Jesus said it to John in Revelation 1:17. And, as we read today, Isaiah said it to the Jews. "Be strong, do not fear" (35:4a).

But Isaiah draws a distinction in the middle of this verse. "Your God will come, he will come with vengeance; with divine retribution he will come to save you"

FRIDAY
Passage:
Isaiah 35:1–7
Verse:
Isaiah 35:1

(35:4b). In other words, those who are ready, who are living for his call, should not be wor-ried. Those whom God has already pardoned need not be concerned about his vengeance or his retribution. If this de-scribes you, he has no score to settle with you. Since you have already "seen" him, his coming will not be frighten-ing news.

If, on the other hand, you haven't met him, if you only know *about* him, but do not *know* him, this would be a good day to personally connect with the Almighty.

"Father in heaven," you could pray. "I'm not ready for your visit, because I'm not living for you. I need to experience and embrace the forgiveness of my sin through the gift of your Son, Jesus. I confess my sin and welcome your grace. Now, please help me to live in the light of your presence, to know you and to live a life that honors you. Thank you. Amen."

If you prayed this prayer, you need not fear bright lights in the sky or open corn-fields again. No checkout tabloid will make your heart beat faster. The fact is that *our planet has already been visited*. You know this for sure because you just talked to the Visitor, and he told you not to be afraid. You did what you were told, and he literally saved your life.

Good for you.

For your next devotional reading, go to page 782.

and how you rage against me.
²⁹Because you rage against me
    and because your insolence has
        reached my ears,
I will put my hook in your nose
    and my bit in your mouth,
and I will make you return
    by the way you came.

³⁰"This will be the sign for you, O Hezekiah:

"This year you will eat what grows by
    itself,
and the second year what springs
    from that.
But in the third year sow and reap,
    plant vineyards and eat their fruit.
³¹Once more a remnant of the house of
    Judah
    will take root below and bear fruit
        above.
³²For out of Jerusalem will come a
    remnant,
    and out of Mount Zion a band of
        survivors.
The zeal of the LORD Almighty
    will accomplish this.

³³"Therefore this is what the LORD says concerning the king of Assyria:

"He will not enter this city
    or shoot an arrow here.
He will not come before it with shield
    or build a siege ramp against it.
³⁴By the way that he came he will return;
    he will not enter this city,"
                  declares the LORD.
³⁵"I will defend this city and save it,
    for my sake and for the sake of David
    my servant!"

³⁶Then the angel of the LORD went out and put to death a hundred and eighty-five thousand men in the Assyrian camp. When the people got up the next morning—there were all the dead bodies! ³⁷So Sennacherib king of Assyria broke camp and withdrew. He returned to Nineveh and stayed there.

³⁸One day, while he was worshiping in the temple of his god Nisroch, his sons Adrammelech and Sharezer cut him down with the sword, and they escaped to the land of Ararat. And Esarhaddon his son succeeded him as king.

Hezekiah's Illness

38 In those days Hezekiah became ill and was at the point of death. The prophet Isaiah son of Amoz went to him

and said, "This is what the LORD says: Put your house in order, because you are going to die; you will not recover."

²Hezekiah turned his face to the wall and prayed to the LORD, ³"Remember, O LORD, how I have walked before you faithfully and with wholehearted devotion and have done what is good in your eyes." And Hezekiah wept bitterly.

⁴Then the word of the LORD came to Isaiah: ⁵"Go and tell Hezekiah, 'This is what the LORD, the God of your father David, says: I have heard your prayer and seen your tears; I will add fifteen years to your life. ⁶And I will deliver you and this city from the hand of the king of Assyria. I will defend this city.

⁷"'This is the LORD's sign to you that the LORD will do what he has promised: ⁸I will make the shadow cast by the sun go back the ten steps it has gone down on the stairway of Ahaz.'" So the sunlight went back the ten steps it had gone down.

⁹A writing of Hezekiah king of Judah after his illness and recovery:

¹⁰I said, "In the prime of my life
    must I go through the gates of death[a]
    and be robbed of the rest of my
        years?"
¹¹I said, "I will not again see the LORD,
    the LORD, in the land of the living;
no longer will I look on mankind,
    or be with those who now dwell in
        this world.[b]
¹²Like a shepherd's tent my house
    has been pulled down and taken
        from me.
Like a weaver I have rolled up my life,
    and he has cut me off from the loom;
    day and night you made an end of
        me.
¹³I waited patiently till dawn,
    but like a lion he broke all my bones;
    day and night you made an end of
        me.
¹⁴I cried like a swift or thrush,
    I moaned like a mourning dove.
My eyes grew weak as I looked to the
    heavens.
I am troubled; O Lord, come to my
    aid!"

¹⁵But what can I say?
    He has spoken to me, and he himself
        has done this.
I will walk humbly all my years
    because of this anguish of my soul.

a10 Hebrew *Sheol*   *b11* A few Hebrew manuscripts; most Hebrew manuscripts *in the place of cessation*

¹⁶Lord, by such things men live;
    and my spirit finds life in them too.
You restored me to health
    and let me live.
¹⁷Surely it was for my benefit
    that I suffered such anguish.
In your love you kept me
    from the pit of destruction;
you have put all my sins
    behind your back.
¹⁸For the grave*ᵃ* cannot praise you,
    death cannot sing your praise;
those who go down to the pit
    cannot hope for your faithfulness.
¹⁹The living, the living—they praise you,
    as I am doing today;
fathers tell their children
    about your faithfulness.

²⁰The LORD will save me,
    and we will sing with stringed
        instruments
all the days of our lives
    in the temple of the LORD.

²¹Isaiah had said, "Prepare a poultice of figs and apply it to the boil, and he will recover."

²²Hezekiah had asked, "What will be the sign that I will go up to the temple of the LORD?"

Envoys From Babylon

39 At that time Merodach-Baladan son of Baladan king of Babylon sent Hezekiah letters and a gift, because he had heard of his illness and recovery. ²Hezekiah received the envoys gladly and showed them what was in his storehouses—the silver, the gold, the spices, the fine oil, his entire armory and everything found among his treasures. There was nothing in his palace or in all his kingdom that Hezekiah did not show them.

³Then Isaiah the prophet went to King Hezekiah and asked, "What did those men say, and where did they come from?"

"From a distant land," Hezekiah replied. "They came to me from Babylon."

⁴The prophet asked, "What did they see in your palace?"

"They saw everything in my palace," Hezekiah said. "There is nothing among my treasures that I did not show them."

⁵Then Isaiah said to Hezekiah, "Hear the word of the LORD Almighty: ⁶The time will surely come when everything in your palace, and all that your fathers have stored up until this day, will be carried off to Babylon. Nothing will be left, says the LORD. ⁷And some of your descendants, your own flesh and blood who will be born to you, will be taken away, and they will become eunuchs in the palace of the king of Babylon."

⁸"The word of the LORD you have spoken is good," Hezekiah replied. For he thought, "There will be peace and security in my lifetime."

Comfort for God's People

40 Comfort, comfort my people,
    says your God.
²Speak tenderly to Jerusalem,
    and proclaim to her
that her hard service has been
        completed,
    that her sin has been paid for,
that she has received from the LORD's
        hand
    double for all her sins.

³A voice of one calling:
"In the desert prepare
    the way for the LORD*ᵇ*;
make straight in the wilderness
    a highway for our God.*ᶜ*
⁴Every valley shall be raised up,
    every mountain and hill made low;
the rough ground shall become level,
    the rugged places a plain.
⁵And the glory of the LORD will be
        revealed,
    and all mankind together will see it.
        For the mouth of the LORD
            has spoken."

⁶A voice says, "Cry out."
    And I said, "What shall I cry?"

"All men are like grass,
    and all their glory is like the flowers
        of the field.
⁷The grass withers and the flowers fall,
    because the breath of the LORD blows
        on them.
    Surely the people are grass.
⁸The grass withers and the flowers fall,
    but the word of our God stands
        forever."

⁹You who bring good tidings to Zion,
    go up on a high mountain.
You who bring good tidings to
        Jerusalem,*ᵈ*

ᵃ18 Hebrew Sheol   ᵇ3 Or A voice of one calling in the desert: / "Prepare the way for the LORD   ᶜ3 Hebrew; Septuagint make straight the paths of our God   ᵈ9 Or O Zion, bringer of good tidings, / go up on a high mountain. / O Jerusalem, bringer of good tidings

Jesus Is Coming! Jesus Is Coming!

Key Verse: *"A voice of one calling: 'In the desert prepare the way for the LORD; make straight in the wilderness a highway for our God.'"* Isaiah 40:3

Text: Isaiah 40:1–5 *(Dad or child reads the text.)*

DAD READS: Late at night, on April 18, 1775, a forty-year-old man named Paul Revere jumped on his horse to deliver an urgent message to the sleeping residents of Lexington and Concord. Because there were no telephones for him to use or radios to broadcast the news, this brave man rode from house to house shouting, "The British are coming! The British are coming!"

QUIET TIMES WITH Dad

Child reads: The people whom Paul Revere woke up that night must have wondered why this man was making all the racket. "Why can't this wait until morning?" they must have said. "What is so important about getting this news right now?"

DAD READS: They couldn't actually ask Paul Revere these questions, because he was in a hurry and didn't have time to stop and talk. But later the people understood what he had done, and they were very happy that he had wakened them from their sleep.

Child reads: The people were very glad that Paul Revere had told them to get ready. If he hadn't done this, they would have all been surprised and unprepared.

DAD READS: That's right. A long, long time ago another brave man did the same thing that Paul Revere did. He didn't have a horse, but he went from village to village with a message for the people. "Jesus is coming. Jesus is coming," he told them. His name was John the Baptist, and because he wasn't in as much of a hurry as Paul Revere was, he stopped to tell the people that someone was coming who could forgive their sins. He told the people to get ready for Jesus.

Child reads: The people must have been very surprised to learn that Jesus could forgive their sins. They knew that God could do this, but John the Baptist had said that Jesus was a man. What the people found out later was that Jesus was not just a man. He was also God and he had the power to love these people and to forgive their sins.

DAD READS: Today, you and I are just like Paul Revere and John the Baptist. When we go to school or to work we can tell people how wonderful Jesus is. We can say that Jesus loves everyone and he wants them to love him, too. Some people will thank us for this good news, and some will tell us to mind our own business. We will know just how Paul Revere and John the Baptist felt!

Child reads: I am glad that someone told you about Jesus. And I'm glad that someone told me about him, too. Telling others about how wonderful Jesus is ought to be something we get excited about doing. I want them to hear this good news. Let me pray this prayer with you:

Our Father in heaven, we love you. Thank you for people who tell others about you. Thank you for people who know about your love and your forgiveness. Help us to be so excited about you that we want to tell our friends at school and at work, too. And please help us to be so loving and kind to others that people will know that you are with us. We love you. In Jesus' name, Amen.

For your next devotional reading, go to page 784.

lift up your voice with a shout,
lift it up, do not be afraid;
  say to the towns of Judah,
    "Here is your God!"
[10] See, the Sovereign LORD comes with
    power,
  and his arm rules for him.
See, his reward is with him,
  and his recompense accompanies
    him.
[11] He tends his flock like a shepherd:
  He gathers the lambs in his arms
and carries them close to his heart;
  he gently leads those that have
    young.

[12] Who has measured the waters in the
    hollow of his hand,
  or with the breadth of his hand
    marked off the heavens?
Who has held the dust of the earth in a
    basket,
  or weighed the mountains on the
    scales
  and the hills in a balance?
[13] Who has understood the mind[a] of the
    LORD,
  or instructed him as his
    counselor?
[14] Whom did the LORD consult to
    enlighten him,
  and who taught him the right way?
Who was it that taught him knowledge
  or showed him the path of
    understanding?

[15] Surely the nations are like a drop in a
    bucket;
  they are regarded as dust on the
    scales;
  he weighs the islands as though they
    were fine dust.
[16] Lebanon is not sufficient for altar fires,
  nor its animals enough for burnt
    offerings.
[17] Before him all the nations are as nothing;
  they are regarded by him as worthless
    and less than nothing.

[18] To whom, then, will you compare God?
  What image will you compare him to?
[19] As for an idol, a craftsman casts it,
  and a goldsmith overlays it with gold
  and fashions silver chains for it.
[20] A man too poor to present such an
    offering
  selects wood that will not rot.
He looks for a skilled craftsman
  to set up an idol that will not topple.

[21] Do you not know?
  Have you not heard?

Has it not been told you from the
    beginning?
Have you not understood since the
    earth was founded?
[22] He sits enthroned above the circle of
    the earth,
  and its people are like grasshoppers.
He stretches out the heavens like a
    canopy,
  and spreads them out like a tent to
    live in.
[23] He brings princes to naught
  and reduces the rulers of this world
    to nothing.
[24] No sooner are they planted,
  no sooner are they sown,
  no sooner do they take root in the
    ground,
than he blows on them and they wither,
  and a whirlwind sweeps them away
    like chaff.

[25] "To whom will you compare me?
  Or who is my equal?" says the Holy
    One.
[26] Lift your eyes and look to the heavens:
  Who created all these?
He who brings out the starry host one
    by one,
  and calls them each by name.
Because of his great power and mighty
    strength,
  not one of them is missing.

[27] Why do you say, O Jacob,
  and complain, O Israel,
"My way is hidden from the LORD;
  my cause is disregarded by my God"?
[28] Do you not know?
  Have you not heard?
The LORD is the everlasting God,
  the Creator of the ends of the earth.
He will not grow tired or weary,
  and his understanding no one can
    fathom.
[29] He gives strength to the weary
  and increases the power of the weak.
[30] Even youths grow tired and weary,
  and young men stumble and fall;
[31] but those who hope in the LORD
  will renew their strength.
They will soar on wings like eagles;
  they will run and not grow weary,
  they will walk and not be faint.

The Helper of Israel

41 "Be silent before me, you islands!
  Let the nations renew their strength!

---

[a]13 Or *Spirit;* or *spirit*

Let them come forward and speak;
   let us meet together at the place of
     judgment.

2 "Who has stirred up one from the east,
   calling him in righteousness to his
     service[a]?
He hands nations over to him
   and subdues kings before him.
He turns them to dust with his sword,
   to windblown chaff with his bow.
3 He pursues them and moves on
    unscathed,
   by a path his feet have not traveled
    before.

4 Who has done this and carried it
    through,
   calling forth the generations from
    the beginning?
I, the LORD—with the first of them
   and with the last—I am he."

5 The islands have seen it and fear;
   the ends of the earth tremble.
They approach and come forward;
6   each helps the other
   and says to his brother, "Be strong!"
7 The craftsman encourages the
    goldsmith,

a2 Or / whom victory meets at every step

First Prize Won't Be Good Enough

DAILY INSIGHT

MONDAY
Passage:
Isaiah 40:18–25
Verse:
Isaiah 40:25

In the seven years that my wife and I worked with teenagers, one game emerged as a perennial favorite. It was called, "The Bigger and Better Scavenger Hunt." This game involved dividing the kids into teams, giving each team a shiny penny, and instructing them to go from door to door exchanging what they had for something that was bigger and better.

On one particular night the teams returned within the appointed hour with an amazing bounty. The first team was carrying an old ping-pong table. Another group was rolling a lawn mower. The winning team came back to home base, literally pushing an old car down the street! In one hour, these clever and persuasive kids had eventually transformed one cent into an automobile. Incredible.

When you and I were born, God blessed us with gifts and talents. And to one degree or another, our parents, our teachers, our coaches, our supervisors, and our friends have challenged us to take these abilities and trade them up. "You've got a lifetime to take these things and exchange them, one at a time, for bigger and better things." So we took our shiny pennies and dashed into life, hoping to win the prize for the biggest and the best.

The problem with this game is that we are forever limited in what we can achieve because it is always just one step up from something we have in our hands. And contrary to what any self-empowerment guru has to say, such trading up will never bring lasting happiness. We can move through life, trading raw talent into wood, then into silver, and finally to gold, but these accomplishments will someday vanish like the sawdust on our garage floor—here today, gone with a sudden puff of air.

Isaiah never played "The Bigger and Better" game, but his understanding of the principle was flawless. "If you want the peace that comes from knowing God," he says to us in this context, "you're not going to be able to trade up for it. He is thoroughly incomparable to anything this world can offer."

Submitting our lives to our faithful heavenly Father brings more pleasure than anything we could ever trade for. Acknowledging our inability to ever reach his presence by our own efforts, but inviting him in nonetheless, brings incredible wholeness and purpose to life.

Turning a shiny penny into an automobile in sixty minutes is no small task. But God's presence and peace cannot be achieved by human effort. He will never be traded for. Nothing you have is good enough . . . except your faith to believe in him.

For your next devotional reading, go to page 785.

and he who smooths with the
hammer
spurs on him who strikes the anvil.
He says of the welding, "It is good."
He nails down the idol so it will not
topple.

⁸"But you, O Israel, my servant,
Jacob, whom I have chosen,
you descendants of Abraham my
friend,

⁹I took you from the ends of the earth,
from its farthest corners I called you.
I said, 'You are my servant';
I have chosen you and have not
rejected you.
¹⁰So do not fear, for I am with you;
do not be dismayed, for I am your
God.
I will strengthen you and help you;
I will uphold you with my righteous
right hand.

Walk, Run, Soar

DAILY INSIGHT

TUESDAY

Passage:
Isaiah 40:28–31

Verse:
Isaiah 40:31

When I was in eighth grade, I joined the track team. I had always been an enthusiastic spectator of the Summer Olympics, and figured that if I was ever going to win one of those gold medals, I'd better get started. On the first day of practice I surveyed the possible events and measured each one against the reality of my five-foot, two-inch, one-hundred-pound frame. I chose the 880-yard run.

Although our distance coach was a fine person, his entire coaching repertoire consisted of one thing. We'd assemble on the street in front of our school, and this clever coach would say, "Okay, boys, let's run." (Of course, he never actually ran with us, he'd just say "let's" because that's what teachers and coaches always say.) So we ran.

Ten years later, Jim Fixx wrote a book called *Running*. My friend, John Clarkson, and I read the book and decided that running was a good idea. So we went out and bought expensive running shoes. Then we ran.

In the decades since, I have tried to continue to exercise, opting several years ago for machines that issued less impact on my knees than jogging. But I have not abandoned my interest in running. In fact, not long ago, I watched the entire running of the New York City Marathon on television. And, because I know how incredibly challenging this sport can be, I wasn't bored for even a moment. The sight of anyone clicking off four-and-a-half-minute miles for two solid hours captivates and overwhelms me. This is completely beyond my comprehension.

Today's text reminds us that, like it or not, we're all in a race. In the New Testament, the apostle Paul underscores this truth as well (1 Corinthians 9:24–27). And just as we get fatigued running in a real race, the rigors of life can be completely exhausting. Isaiah knew that there would be times when God's people—including us—would grow "tired and weary" in this race, so he wrote these words to give people hope—encouragement for our worn out legs and oxygen-deprived lungs.

Although running is typically a solitary sport, sometimes runners *do* get help. Every once in a while, back in eighth grade, one of our mothers would drive by in her wood-sided station wagon as we wound our way through the neighborhood. Overwhelmed with compassion, she would slow down as if to invite us to get in—a tempting proposal. And as I recently watched that marathon, I noticed crowds cheering, bands playing, and aid stations that offered help and encouragement to both the world-class and the third-class runners.

Now, picture your heavenly Father. He's not actually offering you a ride to lift you from the challenge of the race, but he *is* promising renewed courage and strength for the race—power when your legs are aching and confidence when you don't think you can go on.

Hope in the Lord. His dependability is legendary. Walk ... run ... *soar* down this road.

For your next devotional reading, go to page 790.

¹¹ "All who rage against you
   will surely be ashamed and
      disgraced;
   those who oppose you
      will be as nothing and perish.
¹² Though you search for your enemies,
      you will not find them.
   Those who wage war against you
      will be as nothing at all.
¹³ For I am the LORD, your God,
   who takes hold of your right hand
   and says to you, Do not fear;
      I will help you.
¹⁴ Do not be afraid, O worm Jacob,
      O little Israel,
   for I myself will help you," declares the
      LORD,
      your Redeemer, the Holy One of
         Israel.
¹⁵ "See, I will make you into a threshing
      sledge,
   new and sharp, with many teeth.
   You will thresh the mountains and
      crush them,
      and reduce the hills to chaff.
¹⁶ You will winnow them, the wind will
      pick them up,
      and a gale will blow them away.
   But you will rejoice in the LORD
      and glory in the Holy One of Israel.

¹⁷ "The poor and needy search for water,
      but there is none;
   their tongues are parched with thirst.
   But I the LORD will answer them;
      I, the God of Israel, will not forsake
         them.
¹⁸ I will make rivers flow on barren
      heights,
      and springs within the valleys.
   I will turn the desert into pools of
      water,
      and the parched ground into springs.
¹⁹ I will put in the desert
      the cedar and the acacia, the myrtle
         and the olive.
   I will set pines in the wasteland,
      the fir and the cypress together,
²⁰ so that people may see and know,
      may consider and understand,
   that the hand of the LORD has done this,
      that the Holy One of Israel has
         created it.

²¹ "Present your case," says the LORD.
      "Set forth your arguments," says
         Jacob's King.
²² "Bring in ⌊your idols⌋ to tell us
      what is going to happen.
   Tell us what the former things were,
      so that we may consider them

and know their final outcome.
   Or declare to us the things to come,
²³   tell us what the future holds,
      so we may know that you are gods.
   Do something, whether good or bad,
      so that we will be dismayed and
         filled with fear.
²⁴ But you are less than nothing
      and your works are utterly worthless;
      he who chooses you is detestable.

²⁵ "I have stirred up one from the north,
      and he comes—
      one from the rising sun who calls on
         my name.
   He treads on rulers as if they were
      mortar,
      as if he were a potter treading the
         clay.
²⁶ Who told of this from the beginning, so
      we could know,
      or beforehand, so we could say, 'He
         was right'?
   No one told of this,
      no one foretold it,
      no one heard any words from you.
²⁷ I was the first to tell Zion, 'Look, here
      they are!'
   I gave to Jerusalem a messenger of
      good tidings.
²⁸ I look but there is no one—
      no one among them to give counsel,
      no one to give answer when I ask
         them.
²⁹ See, they are all false!
      Their deeds amount to nothing;
      their images are but wind and
         confusion.

The Servant of the LORD

42 "Here is my servant, whom I uphold,
   my chosen one in whom I delight;
   I will put my Spirit on him
      and he will bring justice to the
         nations.
² He will not shout or cry out,
      or raise his voice in the streets.
³ A bruised reed he will not break,
      and a smoldering wick he will not
         snuff out.
   In faithfulness he will bring forth
      justice;
⁴   he will not falter or be discouraged
   till he establishes justice on earth.
      In his law the islands will put their
         hope."

⁵ This is what God the LORD says—
   he who created the heavens and
      stretched them out,

who spread out the earth and all that
comes out of it,
who gives breath to its people,
and life to those who walk on it:
⁶ "I, the LORD, have called you in
righteousness;
I will take hold of your hand.
I will keep you and will make you
to be a covenant for the people
and a light for the Gentiles,
⁷ to open eyes that are blind,
to free captives from prison
and to release from the dungeon
those who sit in darkness.

⁸ "I am the LORD; that is my name!
I will not give my glory to another
or my praise to idols.
⁹ See, the former things have taken
place,
and new things I declare;
before they spring into being
I announce them to you."

Song of Praise to the LORD

¹⁰ Sing to the LORD a new song,
his praise from the ends of the earth,
you who go down to the sea, and all
that is in it,
you islands, and all who live in them.
¹¹ Let the desert and its towns raise their
voices;
let the settlements where Kedar lives
rejoice.
Let the people of Sela sing for joy;
let them shout from the
mountaintops.
¹² Let them give glory to the LORD
and proclaim his praise in the islands.
¹³ The LORD will march out like a mighty
man,
like a warrior he will stir up his zeal;
with a shout he will raise the battle cry
and will triumph over his enemies.

¹⁴ "For a long time I have kept silent,
I have been quiet and held myself
back.
But now, like a woman in childbirth,
I cry out, I gasp and pant.
¹⁵ I will lay waste the mountains and hills
and dry up all their vegetation;
I will turn rivers into islands
and dry up the pools.
¹⁶ I will lead the blind by ways they have
not known,
along unfamiliar paths I will guide
them;
I will turn the darkness into light before
them

and make the rough places smooth.
These are the things I will do;
I will not forsake them.
¹⁷ But those who trust in idols,
who say to images, 'You are our
gods,'
will be turned back in utter shame.

Israel Blind and Deaf

¹⁸ "Hear, you deaf;
look, you blind, and see!
¹⁹ Who is blind but my servant,
and deaf like the messenger I send?
Who is blind like the one committed to
me,
blind like the servant of the LORD?
²⁰ You have seen many things, but have
paid no attention;
your ears are open, but you hear
nothing."
²¹ It pleased the LORD
for the sake of his righteousness
to make his law great and glorious.
²² But this is a people plundered and
looted,
all of them trapped in pits
or hidden away in prisons.
They have become plunder,
with no one to rescue them;
they have been made loot,
with no one to say, "Send them
back."

²³ Which of you will listen to this
or pay close attention in time to
come?
²⁴ Who handed Jacob over to become
loot,
and Israel to the plunderers?
Was it not the LORD,
against whom we have sinned?
For they would not follow his ways;
they did not obey his law.
²⁵ So he poured out on them his burning
anger,
the violence of war.
It enveloped them in flames, yet they
did not understand;
it consumed them, but they did not
take it to heart.

Israel's Only Savior

43 But now, this is what the LORD says—
he who created you, O Jacob,
he who formed you, O Israel:
"Fear not, for I have redeemed you;
I have summoned you by name; you
are mine.
² When you pass through the waters,

I will be with you;
and when you pass through the rivers,
    they will not sweep over you.
When you walk through the fire,
    you will not be burned;
    the flames will not set you ablaze.
³For I am the LORD, your God,
    the Holy One of Israel, your Savior;
I give Egypt for your ransom,
    Cush[a] and Seba in your stead.
⁴Since you are precious and honored in
        my sight,
    and because I love you,
I will give men in exchange for you,
    and people in exchange for your life.
⁵Do not be afraid, for I am with you;
    I will bring your children from the
        east
    and gather you from the west.
⁶I will say to the north, 'Give them up!'
    and to the south, 'Do not hold them
        back.'
Bring my sons from afar
    and my daughters from the ends of
        the earth—
⁷everyone who is called by my name,
    whom I created for my glory,
    whom I formed and made."

⁸Lead out those who have eyes but are
        blind,
    who have ears but are deaf.
⁹All the nations gather together
    and the peoples assemble.
Which of them foretold this
    and proclaimed to us the former
        things?
Let them bring in their witnesses to
        prove they were right,
    so that others may hear and say, "It is
        true."
¹⁰"You are my witnesses," declares the
        LORD,
    "and my servant whom I have
        chosen,
so that you may know and believe me
    and understand that I am he.
Before me no god was formed,
    nor will there be one after me.
¹¹I, even I, am the LORD,
    and apart from me there is no savior.
¹²I have revealed and saved and
        proclaimed—
    I, and not some foreign god among
        you.
You are my witnesses," declares the
        LORD, "that I am God.
¹³   Yes, and from ancient days I am he.
No one can deliver out of my hand.
    When I act, who can reverse it?"

God's Mercy and Israel's Unfaithfulness

¹⁴This is what the LORD says—
    your Redeemer, the Holy One of
        Israel:
    "For your sake I will send to Babylon
        and bring down as fugitives all the
            Babylonians,[b]
    in the ships in which they took pride.
¹⁵I am the LORD, your Holy One,
    Israel's Creator, your King."

¹⁶This is what the LORD says—
    he who made a way through the sea,
    a path through the mighty waters,
¹⁷who drew out the chariots and horses,
    the army and reinforcements
        together,
    and they lay there, never to rise again,
    extinguished, snuffed out like a wick:
¹⁸"Forget the former things;
    do not dwell on the past.
¹⁹See, I am doing a new thing!
    Now it springs up; do you not
        perceive it?
I am making a way in the desert
    and streams in the wasteland.
²⁰The wild animals honor me,
    the jackals and the owls,
because I provide water in the desert
    and streams in the wasteland,
to give drink to my people, my chosen,
²¹   the people I formed for myself
    that they may proclaim my praise.

²²"Yet you have not called upon me,
        O Jacob,
    you have not wearied yourselves for
        me, O Israel.
²³You have not brought me sheep for
        burnt offerings,
    nor honored me with your sacrifices.
I have not burdened you with grain
        offerings
    nor wearied you with demands for
        incense.
²⁴You have not bought any fragrant
        calamus for me,
    or lavished on me the fat of your
        sacrifices.
But you have burdened me with your
        sins
    and wearied me with your offenses.

²⁵"I, even I, am he who blots out
    your transgressions, for my own
        sake,
    and remembers your sins no more.
²⁶Review the past for me,

---

a3 That is, the upper Nile region   *b14* Or
Chaldeans

let us argue the matter together;
state the case for your innocence.
²⁷ Your first father sinned;
your spokesmen rebelled against
me.
²⁸ So I will disgrace the dignitaries of your
temple,
and I will consign Jacob to
destruction*a*
and Israel to scorn.

Israel the Chosen

44 "But now listen, O Jacob, my
servant,
Israel, whom I have chosen.
² This is what the LORD says—
he who made you, who formed you
in the womb,
and who will help you:
Do not be afraid, O Jacob, my servant,
Jeshurun, whom I have chosen.
³ For I will pour water on the thirsty
land,
and streams on the dry ground;
I will pour out my Spirit on your
offspring,
and my blessing on your
descendants.
⁴ They will spring up like grass in a
meadow,
like poplar trees by flowing streams.
⁵ One will say, 'I belong to the LORD';
another will call himself by the name
of Jacob;
still another will write on his hand,
'The LORD's,'
and will take the name Israel.

The LORD, Not Idols

⁶ "This is what the LORD says—
Israel's King and Redeemer, the LORD
Almighty:
I am the first and I am the last;
apart from me there is no God.
⁷ Who then is like me? Let him proclaim
it.
Let him declare and lay out before
me
what has happened since I established
my ancient people,
and what is yet to come—
yes, let him foretell what will come.
⁸ Do not tremble, do not be afraid.
Did I not proclaim this and foretell it
long ago?
You are my witnesses. Is there any God
besides me?
No, there is no other Rock; I know
not one."

⁹ All who make idols are nothing,
and the things they treasure are
worthless.
Those who would speak up for them
are blind;
they are ignorant, to their own
shame.
¹⁰ Who shapes a god and casts an idol,
which can profit him nothing?
¹¹ He and his kind will be put to shame;
craftsmen are nothing but men.
Let them all come together and take
their stand;
they will be brought down to terror
and infamy.
¹² The blacksmith takes a tool
and works with it in the coals;
he shapes an idol with hammers,
he forges it with the might of his
arm.
He gets hungry and loses his strength;
he drinks no water and grows faint.
¹³ The carpenter measures with a line
and makes an outline with a marker;
he roughs it out with chisels
and marks it with compasses.
He shapes it in the form of man,
of man in all his glory,
that it may dwell in a shrine.
¹⁴ He cut down cedars,
or perhaps took a cypress or oak.
He let it grow among the trees of the
forest,
or planted a pine, and the rain made
it grow.
¹⁵ It is man's fuel for burning;
some of it he takes and warms
himself,
he kindles a fire and bakes bread.
But he also fashions a god and
worships it;
he makes an idol and bows down to
it.
¹⁶ Half of the wood he burns in the fire;
over it he prepares his meal,
he roasts his meat and eats his fill.
He also warms himself and says,
"Ah! I am warm; I see the fire."
¹⁷ From the rest he makes a god, his idol;
he bows down to it and worships.
He prays to it and says,
"Save me; you are my god."
¹⁸ They know nothing, they understand
nothing;
their eyes are plastered over so they
cannot see,

*a*28 The Hebrew term refers to the irrevocable
giving over of things or persons to the LORD, often
by totally destroying them.

and their minds closed so they
    cannot understand.
¹⁹ No one stops to think,
    no one has the knowledge or
       understanding to say,
"Half of it I used for fuel;
    I even baked bread over its coals,

I roasted meat and I ate.
    Shall I make a detestable thing from
       what is left?
    Shall I bow down to a block of
       wood?"
²⁰ He feeds on ashes, a deluded heart
    misleads him;

The Woodsman

DAILY INSIGHT

WEDNESDAY

Passage:
Isaiah 44:13–22

Verse:
Isaiah 44:22

Once upon a time there was a man who chose to move his wife and children to the solitude of a beautiful woods, far away from the rigors of duty and the dread of obligation. Learning to "live off the land" was quite a challenge for this adventurous dad. But soon he found a resourcefulness he had never known before. Instead of adjusting the thermostat, he brought in more wood. Instead of slipping a snack into the microwave, he learned to cook hearty meals over an open fire. Content in their self-sufficiency, soon both the man and his family forgot the "conveniences" of the city.

Because his home was surrounded by thousands of towering trees—hardwoods and softwoods alike—the man discovered the many wonderful uses of wood. Oak provided many hours of slow-burning warmth. Maple, cherry and walnut provided excellent material for making furniture. Pine and cedar were wonderful for building and, because they were soft and malleable, also gave him hours of enjoyment as he discovered the pleasure of carving and whittling. He had no idea that he could create such beautiful things with his own hands. Even his wife and children were impressed with the beauty of his work.

As the years passed, the struggles of raising a family took their toll on the intimacy that the man and his wife had once enjoyed. Open conversation gave way to a cool exchange of facts. Tenderness was replaced with utility. One by one, the man's children grew, leaving their forest home to seek their own fortunes. Were it not for the man's visits to his work shed, now full of statues and sculptures, he would have

found himself completely alone. Somehow the grace with which he had fashioned each piece now provided a solace that he hadn't thought possible.

Late one night, a spring thunderstorm raged through the woods. The man woke to the sound of huge tree limbs, moaning under the weight of their sodden leaves. Lightning filled the sky with such repetition that it seemed like midday.

Suddenly the unmistakable explosion of lightning hitting earth made the man leap from his bed. Through his window, the man saw his shed burning with such an intensity that he could actually hear the crackling roar over the storm's clamor. He ran from his house, still wearing his night clothes, out to the small barn that raged with fire. The man stood helplessly by as the things he had so tenderly created burned into a pile of black, smoldering ashes.

The only thing darker than this lingering residue was the heart of this lonely man. For when his affection for his wife had chilled, he had lost part of his heart. And when his children had left their home, another portion of his soul had been stilled. And now, all that he had left to love was gone forever.

The downpour subsided as the morning light slowly broke on the horizon. The man, soaked and sad, shuffled through the mud back to his cabin, feeling more empty and alone than he had ever felt in his life. Everything was gone.

"Return to me," says the Lord. "For I have redeemed you."

For your next devotional reading, go to page 792.

he cannot save himself, or say,
"Is not this thing in my right hand a
lie?"

²¹ "Remember these things, O Jacob,
for you are my servant, O Israel.
I have made you, you are my servant;
O Israel, I will not forget you.
²² I have swept away your offenses like a
cloud,
your sins like the morning mist.
Return to me,
for I have redeemed you."

²³ Sing for joy, O heavens, for the LORD
has done this;
shout aloud, O earth beneath.
Burst into song, you mountains,
you forests and all your trees,
for the LORD has redeemed Jacob,
he displays his glory in Israel.

Jerusalem to Be Inhabited

²⁴ "This is what the LORD says—
your Redeemer, who formed you in
the womb:

I am the LORD,
who has made all things,
who alone stretched out the heavens,
who spread out the earth by myself,
²⁵ who foils the signs of false prophets
and makes fools of diviners,
who overthrows the learning of the
wise
and turns it into nonsense,
²⁶ who carries out the words of his
servants
and fulfills the predictions of his
messengers,

who says of Jerusalem, 'It shall be
inhabited,'
of the towns of Judah, 'They shall be
built,'
and of their ruins, 'I will restore
them,'
²⁷ who says to the watery deep, 'Be dry,
and I will dry up your streams,'
²⁸ who says of Cyrus, 'He is my shepherd
and will accomplish all that I please;
he will say of Jerusalem, "Let it be
rebuilt,"
and of the temple, "Let its
foundations be laid." '

45 "This is what the LORD says to his
anointed,
to Cyrus, whose right hand I take
hold of
to subdue nations before him

and to strip kings of their armor,
to open doors before him
so that gates will not be shut:
² I will go before you
and will level the mountains^a;
I will break down gates of bronze
and cut through bars of iron.
³ I will give you the treasures of darkness,
riches stored in secret places,
so that you may know that I am the
LORD,
the God of Israel, who summons you
by name.
⁴ For the sake of Jacob my servant,
of Israel my chosen,
I summon you by name
and bestow on you a title of honor,
though you do not acknowledge me.
⁵ I am the LORD, and there is no other;
apart from me there is no God.
I will strengthen you,
though you have not acknowledged
me,
⁶ so that from the rising of the sun
to the place of its setting
men may know there is none besides
me.
I am the LORD, and there is no other.
⁷ I form the light and create darkness,
I bring prosperity and create
disaster;
I, the LORD, do all these things.

⁸ "You heavens above, rain down
righteousness;
let the clouds shower it down.
Let the earth open wide,
let salvation spring up,
let righteousness grow with it;
I, the LORD, have created it.

⁹ "Woe to him who quarrels with his
Maker,
to him who is but a potsherd among
the potsherds on the ground.
Does the clay say to the potter,
'What are you making?'
Does your work say,
'He has no hands'?
¹⁰ Woe to him who says to his father,
'What have you begotten?'
or to his mother,
'What have you brought to birth?'

¹¹ "This is what the LORD says—
the Holy One of Israel, and its Maker:
Concerning things to come,
do you question me about my
children,

^{a}2 Dead Sea Scrolls and Septuagint; the meaning of
the word in the Masoretic Text is uncertain.

or give me orders about the work of
my hands?
¹²It is I who made the earth
and created mankind upon it.
My own hands stretched out the
heavens;
I marshaled their starry hosts.
¹³I will raise up Cyrus*a* in my
righteousness:
I will make all his ways straight.
He will rebuild my city

and set my exiles free,
but not for a price or reward,
says the LORD Almighty."

¹⁴This is what the LORD says:

"The products of Egypt and the
merchandise of Cush,*b*
and those tall Sabeans—

a13 Hebrew *him*   *b14* That is, the upper Nile
region

Underwear on the Floor and the Sovereignty of God

As a teenager I attended a
number of large, Christian
rallies. To this day, I still remember what one of the more persuasive communicators said:
"God cannot change your high
school unless he does it through
you!" he thundered. "You must
be his representative on
campus because he can *only*
do his work if *you* let him."
I remember being troubled by
these words even as an impres-
sionable sixteen-year-old. Did
I *really* control God's work in
the world?

The thought of this troubled
me because I grew up in a home
where the father was … well …
he was the *father*. He wasn't
cruel or overbearing; in fact, we
knew without a doubt that he loved us.
It's just that when my dad spoke, we listened. When he told us to do something, we
did it … or at least we made it *look* like
we were doing it! A hard-working and
focused man of German descent, not many
people messed with Dad … especially his
children.

If my dad wanted to communicate a
message to me, he would find a way to do
so. If I had, for example, a nasty habit of
leaving my underwear on my bedroom
floor, my dad would never have wrung his
hands and said to my mother, "You know,
dear, Robert refuses to pick up his underwear, and there's nothing I can do about it.
I'm so frustrated." That statement is so
preposterous that it makes me smile.

Because he was the dad, he would have
found a way to get to me. This is why the
speaker's words at the youth rally were so

DAILY INSIGHT

THURSDAY

Passage:
Isaiah 45:1–7
Verse:
Isaiah 45:6

troublesome. *If my dad takes
steps to get my attention, even
when I continue to disobey,*
I remember thinking, *then why
wouldn't God also stay on my
case until I really heard his
voice?* Not bad for a kid who
had just gotten his driver's
license.

Today's text is a case in
point. Here God used an uncon-
ventional means—the unbe-
lieving King Cyrus of Persia—to
communicate to his people. In
fact, God called Cyrus "his
anointed." How could this be?
The answer is very simple and
very, very profound. Please do
not miss this.

God will use whomever he
chooses to accomplish exactly
what he wants. One person's refusal to
show up for God doesn't hamper his work in
the world. If God had wanted to show up at
my high school, he could have used me, or
the janitor, or the president of the student
council.

Now apply this to your own life. Is God
calling you to send a message to another
person? And, on the flipside, is God working
through another person in your life—your
boss, your child, your wife, your neighbor—
to speak to you?

If my dad would have stopped at nothing to let me know how he felt about my
underwear on the floor, the Sovereign and
Almighty God will not stand around wringing his hands, hoping that his children will
somehow let him be God. It's a preposterous concept, don't you think?

For your next devotional reading, go to page 796.

they will come over to you
  and will be yours;
they will trudge behind you,
  coming over to you in chains.
They will bow down before you
  and plead with you, saying,
'Surely God is with you, and there is no
    other;
  there is no other god.' "

¹⁵ Truly you are a God who hides himself,
  O God and Savior of Israel.
¹⁶ All the makers of idols will be put to
    shame and disgraced;
  they will go off into disgrace
    together.
¹⁷ But Israel will be saved by the LORD
  with an everlasting salvation;
you will never be put to shame or
    disgraced,
  to ages everlasting.

¹⁸ For this is what the LORD says—
he who created the heavens,
  he is God;
he who fashioned and made the earth,
  he founded it;
he did not create it to be empty,
  but formed it to be inhabited—
he says:
"I am the LORD,
  and there is no other.
¹⁹ I have not spoken in secret,
  from somewhere in a land of
    darkness;
I have not said to Jacob's descendants,
  'Seek me in vain.'
I, the LORD, speak the truth;
  I declare what is right.

²⁰ "Gather together and come;
  assemble, you fugitives from the
    nations.
Ignorant are those who carry about
    idols of wood,
  who pray to gods that cannot save.
²¹ Declare what is to be, present it—
  let them take counsel together.
Who foretold this long ago,
  who declared it from the distant
    past?
Was it not I, the LORD?
  And there is no God apart from me,
a righteous God and a Savior;
  there is none but me.

²² "Turn to me and be saved,
  all you ends of the earth;
  for I am God, and there is no other.
²³ By myself I have sworn,
  my mouth has uttered in all integrity
  a word that will not be revoked:

Before me every knee will bow;
  by me every tongue will swear.
²⁴ They will say of me, 'In the LORD alone
  are righteousness and strength.' "
All who have raged against him
  will come to him and be put to
    shame.
²⁵ But in the LORD all the descendants of
    Israel
  will be found righteous and will
    exult.

Gods of Babylon

46 Bel bows down, Nebo stoops low;
    their idols are borne by beasts of
      burden.ᵃ
The images that are carried about are
    burdensome,
  a burden for the weary.
² They stoop and bow down together;
  unable to rescue the burden,
  they themselves go off into captivity.

³ "Listen to me, O house of Jacob,
  all you who remain of the house of
    Israel,
you whom I have upheld since you
    were conceived,
  and have carried since your birth.
⁴ Even to your old age and gray hairs
  I am he, I am he who will sustain
    you.
I have made you and I will carry you;
  I will sustain you and I will rescue
    you.

⁵ "To whom will you compare me or
    count me equal?
  To whom will you liken me that we
    may be compared?
⁶ Some pour out gold from their bags
  and weigh out silver on the scales;
they hire a goldsmith to make it into a
    god,
  and they bow down and worship it.
⁷ They lift it to their shoulders and carry
    it;
  they set it up in its place, and there it
    stands.
From that spot it cannot move.
  Though one cries out to it, it does not
    answer;
  it cannot save him from his troubles.

⁸ "Remember this, fix it in mind,
  take it to heart, you rebels.
⁹ Remember the former things, those of
    long ago;
  I am God, and there is no other;

ᵃ1 Or *are but beasts and cattle*

I am God, and there is none like me.
¹⁰I make known the end from the
    beginning,
  from ancient times, what is still to
    come.
I say: My purpose will stand,
  and I will do all that I please.
¹¹From the east I summon a bird of prey;
  from a far-off land, a man to fulfill
    my purpose.
What I have said, that will I bring
    about;
  what I have planned, that will I do.
¹²Listen to me, you stubborn-hearted,
  you who are far from righteousness.
¹³I am bringing my righteousness near,
  it is not far away;
  and my salvation will not be delayed.
I will grant salvation to Zion,
  my splendor to Israel.

The Fall of Babylon

47 "Go down, sit in the dust,
  Virgin Daughter of Babylon;
sit on the ground without a throne,
  Daughter of the Babylonians.ᵃ
No more will you be called
  tender or delicate.
²Take millstones and grind flour;
  take off your veil.
Lift up your skirts, bare your legs,
  and wade through the streams.
³Your nakedness will be exposed
  and your shame uncovered.
I will take vengeance;
  I will spare no one."

⁴Our Redeemer—the LORD Almighty is
    his name—
  is the Holy One of Israel.

⁵"Sit in silence, go into darkness,
  Daughter of the Babylonians;
no more will you be called
  queen of kingdoms.
⁶I was angry with my people
  and desecrated my inheritance;
I gave them into your hand,
  and you showed them no mercy.
Even on the aged
  you laid a very heavy yoke.
⁷You said, 'I will continue forever—
  the eternal queen!'
But you did not consider these things
  or reflect on what might happen.

⁸"Now then, listen, you wanton creature,
  lounging in your security
and saying to yourself,
  'I am, and there is none besides me.

I will never be a widow
  or suffer the loss of children.'
⁹Both of these will overtake you
  in a moment, on a single day:
  loss of children and widowhood.
They will come upon you in full
    measure,
  in spite of your many sorceries
  and all your potent spells.
¹⁰You have trusted in your wickedness
  and have said, 'No one sees me.'
Your wisdom and knowledge mislead
    you
  when you say to yourself,
  'I am, and there is none besides me.'
¹¹Disaster will come upon you,
  and you will not know how to
    conjure it away.
A calamity will fall upon you
  that you cannot ward off with a
    ransom;
  a catastrophe you cannot foresee
  will suddenly come upon you.

¹²"Keep on, then, with your magic spells
  and with your many sorceries,
  which you have labored at since
    childhood.
Perhaps you will succeed,
  perhaps you will cause terror.
¹³All the counsel you have received has
    only worn you out!
Let your astrologers come forward,
  those stargazers who make predictions
    month by month,
  let them save you from what is
    coming upon you.
¹⁴Surely they are like stubble;
  the fire will burn them up.
They cannot even save themselves
  from the power of the flame.
Here are no coals to warm anyone;
  here is no fire to sit by.
¹⁵That is all they can do for you—
  these you have labored with
  and trafficked with since childhood.
Each of them goes on in his error;
  there is not one that can save you.

Stubborn Israel

48 "Listen to this, O house of Jacob,
  you who are called by the name of
    Israel
  and come from the line of Judah,
you who take oaths in the name of the
    LORD
  and invoke the God of Israel—
  but not in truth or righteousness—

ᵃ1 Or *Chaldeans*; also in verse 5

²you who call yourselves citizens of the
holy city
and rely on the God of Israel—
the LORD Almighty is his name:
³I foretold the former things long ago,
my mouth announced them and I
made them known;
then suddenly I acted, and they
came to pass.
⁴For I knew how stubborn you were;
the sinews of your neck were iron,
your forehead was bronze.
⁵Therefore I told you these things long
ago;
before they happened I announced
them to you
so that you could not say,
'My idols did them;
my wooden image and metal god
ordained them.'
⁶You have heard these things; look at
them all.
Will you not admit them?

"From now on I will tell you of new
things,
of hidden things unknown to you.
⁷They are created now, and not long ago;
you have not heard of them before
today.
So you cannot say,
'Yes, I knew of them.'
⁸You have neither heard nor
understood;
from of old your ear has not been
open.
Well do I know how treacherous you are;
you were called a rebel from birth.
⁹For my own name's sake I delay my
wrath;
for the sake of my praise I hold it
back from you,
so as not to cut you off.
¹⁰See, I have refined you, though not as
silver;
I have tested you in the furnace of
affliction.
¹¹For my own sake, for my own sake, I do
this.
How can I let myself be defamed?
I will not yield my glory to another.

Israel Freed

¹²"Listen to me, O Jacob,
Israel, whom I have called:
I am he;
I am the first and I am the last.
¹³My own hand laid the foundations of
the earth,

and my right hand spread out the
heavens;
when I summon them,
they all stand up together.

¹⁴"Come together, all of you, and listen:
Which of the idols has foretold these
things?
The LORD's chosen ally
will carry out his purpose against
Babylon;
his arm will be against the
Babylonians.^a
¹⁵I, even I, have spoken;
yes, I have called him.
I will bring him,
and he will succeed in his mission.

¹⁶"Come near me and listen to this:

"From the first announcement I have
not spoken in secret;
at the time it happens, I am there."

And now the Sovereign LORD has sent
me,
with his Spirit.

¹⁷This is what the LORD says—
your Redeemer, the Holy One of
Israel:
"I am the LORD your God,
who teaches you what is best for you,
who directs you in the way you
should go.
¹⁸If only you had paid attention to my
commands,
your peace would have been like a
river,
your righteousness like the waves of
the sea.
¹⁹Your descendants would have been like
the sand,
your children like its numberless
grains;
their name would never be cut off
nor destroyed from before me."

²⁰Leave Babylon,
flee from the Babylonians!
Announce this with shouts of joy
and proclaim it.
Send it out to the ends of the earth;
say, "The LORD has redeemed his
servant Jacob."
²¹They did not thirst when he led them
through the deserts;
he made water flow for them from
the rock;
he split the rock
and water gushed out.

^a14 Or *Chaldeans*; also in verse 20

²² "There is no peace," says the LORD, "for the wicked."

The Servant of the LORD

49 Listen to me, you islands;
hear this, you distant nations:
Before I was born the LORD called me;
from my birth he has made mention
of my name.
² He made my mouth like a sharpened
sword,
in the shadow of his hand he hid me;
he made me into a polished arrow

and concealed me in his quiver.
³ He said to me, "You are my servant,
Israel, in whom I will display my
splendor."
⁴ But I said, "I have labored to no
purpose;
I have spent my strength in vain and
for nothing.
Yet what is due me is in the LORD's hand,
and my reward is with my God."

⁵ And now the LORD says—
he who formed me in the womb to
be his servant

Ride on, Tenderfoot

Have you ever ridden a horse? Two hundred years ago, this would have been a silly question. But since we no longer need to mount our steeds to get to the general store, most of the folks you and I know would say "no" to this question. Or if they have ridden a horse, it was probably at a summer camp, riding on a glue-factory-bound swayback, lazily trudging along a prescribed trail—not exactly the kind of experience that qualifies as actually riding.

Don't be defensive. I'm with you. Summer camp horseback riding is all I have ever done, too. I was and will always be a riding amateur—in cowboy parlance, a "tenderfoot." And although many years have passed since I've ridden, there's still something I can't figure out about this experience. In fact, I have watched old western movies and the Kentucky Derby in an attempt to shed light on the subject. As I recall, when my horse picked up its tortoise-like pace, my easy ride turned into a jolting experience. Strangely, it seemed like when the saddle was going down, I was going up. And when the saddle was going up, I was headed south. The jarring hurt from my tailbone to the fillings in my teeth.

But as I have studied the way professionals ride, the opposite occurs. The rider and the horse travel on parallel tracks, painlessly gliding up and down together … the horse goes up, the rider goes up. The horse descends, the rider effortlessly

DAILY INSIGHT

FRIDAY
Passage:
Isaiah 48:17–19
Verse:
Isaiah 48:17

follows. This is a beautiful sight.

Today's text tells us about God's faithful intervention in the lives of the Israelites. Isaiah is also talking straight to us when he says that God "teaches you what is best for you" and that he "directs you in the way you should go." God's ways are like a horse, and we're the riders.

We have a choice. We can learn obedience and flow seamlessly along with God's best for our lives, or we can be disobedient and experience teeth-jarring impact with each of his steps.

All of this begs these questions: Why would we ever want to experience anything but the joy of submission? Why would we choose to bounce painfully through life, fighting God's admonitions to us and resisting his best for our lives? I don't know the answers to these questions. Strangely, however, the temptation to resist God's voice remains powerful.

As the experienced teacher at summer camp, "Ranger Isaiah" gathers us together and tells us to listen. "If you [pay] attention … your peace [will be] like a river, your righteousness like the waves of the sea." Your ride down the trail of life will be smooth and seamless; you'll ride like a pro.

Have you had enough bone-jarring living? Trust God's voice. Rest in his Word. Ride on, Tenderfoot.

For your next devotional reading, go to page 802.

to bring Jacob back to him
   and gather Israel to himself,
for I am honored in the eyes of the
      LORD
   and my God has been my strength—
⁶he says:
"It is too small a thing for you to be my
      servant
   to restore the tribes of Jacob
   and bring back those of Israel I have
      kept.
I will also make you a light for the
      Gentiles,
   that you may bring my salvation to
      the ends of the earth."

⁷This is what the LORD says—
   the Redeemer and Holy One of
      Israel—
to him who was despised and abhorred
      by the nation,
   to the servant of rulers:
"Kings will see you and rise up,
   princes will see and bow down,
because of the LORD, who is faithful,
   the Holy One of Israel, who has
      chosen you."

Restoration of Israel

⁸This is what the LORD says:

"In the time of my favor I will answer
      you,
   and in the day of salvation I will help
      you;
I will keep you and will make you
   to be a covenant for the people,
to restore the land
   and to reassign its desolate
      inheritances,
⁹to say to the captives, 'Come out,'
   and to those in darkness, 'Be free!'

"They will feed beside the roads
   and find pasture on every barren hill.
¹⁰They will neither hunger nor thirst,
   nor will the desert heat or the sun
      beat upon them.
He who has compassion on them will
      guide them
   and lead them beside springs of
      water.
¹¹I will turn all my mountains into roads,
   and my highways will be raised up.
¹²See, they will come from afar—
   some from the north, some from the
      west,
   some from the region of Aswan.ᵃ"

¹³Shout for joy, O heavens;
   rejoice, O earth;

burst into song, O mountains!
For the LORD comforts his people
   and will have compassion on his
      afflicted ones.

¹⁴But Zion said, "The LORD has forsaken
      me,
   the Lord has forgotten me."

¹⁵"Can a mother forget the baby at her
      breast
   and have no compassion on the
      child she has borne?
Though she may forget,
   I will not forget you!
¹⁶See, I have engraved you on the palms
      of my hands;
   your walls are ever before me.
¹⁷Your sons hasten back,
   and those who laid you waste depart
      from you.
¹⁸Lift up your eyes and look around;
   all your sons gather and come to
      you.
As surely as I live," declares the LORD,
   "you will wear them all as
      ornaments;
   you will put them on, like a bride.

¹⁹"Though you were ruined and made
      desolate
   and your land laid waste,
now you will be too small for your
      people,
   and those who devoured you will be
      far away.
²⁰The children born during your
      bereavement
   will yet say in your hearing,
'This place is too small for us;
   give us more space to live in.'
²¹Then you will say in your heart,
   'Who bore me these?
I was bereaved and barren;
   I was exiled and rejected.
Who brought these up?
I was left all alone,
   but these—where have they come
      from?' "

²²This is what the Sovereign LORD says:

"See, I will beckon to the Gentiles,
   I will lift up my banner to the peoples;
they will bring your sons in their arms
   and carry your daughters on their
      shoulders.
²³Kings will be your foster fathers,
   and their queens your nursing
      mothers.

ᵃ12 Dead Sea Scrolls; Masoretic Text *Sinim*

They will bow down before you with
    their faces to the ground;
they will lick the dust at your feet.
Then you will know that I am the LORD;
    those who hope in me will not be
    disappointed."

24 Can plunder be taken from warriors,
    or captives rescued from the fierce*?

25 But this is what the LORD says:

"Yes, captives will be taken from
    warriors,
    and plunder retrieved from the
    fierce;
I will contend with those who contend
    with you,
    and your children I will save.
26 I will make your oppressors eat their
    own flesh;
    they will be drunk on their own
    blood, as with wine.
Then all mankind will know
    that I, the LORD, am your Savior,
    your Redeemer, the Mighty One of
    Jacob."

Israel's Sin and the Servant's Obedience

50 This is what the LORD says:

"Where is your mother's certificate of
    divorce
    with which I sent her away?
Or to which of my creditors
    did I sell you?
Because of your sins you were sold;
    because of your transgressions your
    mother was sent away.
2 When I came, why was there no one?
    When I called, why was there no one
    to answer?
Was my arm too short to ransom you?
    Do I lack the strength to rescue you?
By a mere rebuke I dry up the sea,
    I turn rivers into a desert;
    their fish rot for lack of water
    and die of thirst.
3 I clothe the sky with darkness
    and make sackcloth its covering."

4 The Sovereign LORD has given me an
    instructed tongue,
    to know the word that sustains the
    weary.
He wakens me morning by morning,
    wakens my ear to listen like one
    being taught.
5 The Sovereign LORD has opened my
    ears,
    and I have not been rebellious;

I have not drawn back.
6 I offered my back to those who beat
    me,
    my cheeks to those who pulled out
    my beard;
I did not hide my face
    from mocking and spitting.
7 Because the Sovereign LORD helps me,
    I will not be disgraced.
Therefore have I set my face like flint,
    and I know I will not be put to
    shame.
8 He who vindicates me is near.
    Who then will bring charges against
    me?
Let us face each other!
Who is my accuser?
    Let him confront me!
9 It is the Sovereign LORD who helps me.
    Who is he that will condemn me?
They will all wear out like a garment;
    the moths will eat them up.

10 Who among you fears the LORD
    and obeys the word of his servant?
Let him who walks in the dark,
    who has no light,
trust in the name of the LORD
    and rely on his God.
11 But now, all you who light fires
    and provide yourselves with flaming
    torches,
go, walk in the light of your fires
    and of the torches you have set
    ablaze.
This is what you shall receive from my
    hand:
    You will lie down in torment.

Everlasting Salvation for Zion

51 "Listen to me, you who pursue
    righteousness
    and who seek the LORD:
Look to the rock from which you were
    cut
    and to the quarry from which you
    were hewn;
2 look to Abraham, your father,
    and to Sarah, who gave you birth.
When I called him he was but one,
    and I blessed him and made him
    many.
3 The LORD will surely comfort Zion
    and will look with compassion on all
    her ruins;
he will make her deserts like Eden,

*a24 Dead Sea Scrolls, Vulgate and Syriac (see also
Septuagint and verse 25); Masoretic Text
righteous*

her wastelands like the garden of the
LORD.
Joy and gladness will be found in her,
thanksgiving and the sound of
singing.

⁴"Listen to me, my people;
hear me, my nation:
The law will go out from me;
my justice will become a light to the
nations.
⁵My righteousness draws near speedily,
my salvation is on the way,
and my arm will bring justice to the
nations.
The islands will look to me
and wait in hope for my arm.
⁶Lift up your eyes to the heavens,
look at the earth beneath;
the heavens will vanish like smoke,
the earth will wear out like a garment
and its inhabitants die like flies.
But my salvation will last forever,
my righteousness will never fail.

⁷"Hear me, you who know what is right,
you people who have my law in your
hearts:
Do not fear the reproach of men
or be terrified by their insults.
⁸For the moth will eat them up like a
garment;
the worm will devour them like wool.
But my righteousness will last forever,
my salvation through all
generations."

⁹Awake, awake! Clothe yourself with
strength,
O arm of the LORD;
awake, as in days gone by,
as in generations of old.
Was it not you who cut Rahab to pieces,
who pierced that monster through?
¹⁰Was it not you who dried up the sea,
the waters of the great deep,
who made a road in the depths of the
sea
so that the redeemed might cross
over?
¹¹The ransomed of the LORD will return.
They will enter Zion with singing;
everlasting joy will crown their
heads.
Gladness and joy will overtake them,
and sorrow and sighing will flee
away.

¹²"I, even I, am he who comforts you.
Who are you that you fear mortal
men,
the sons of men, who are but grass,

¹³that you forget the LORD your Maker,
who stretched out the heavens
and laid the foundations of the
earth,
that you live in constant terror every
day
because of the wrath of the
oppressor,
who is bent on destruction?
For where is the wrath of the
oppressor?
¹⁴   The cowering prisoners will soon be
set free;
they will not die in their dungeon,
nor will they lack bread.
¹⁵For I am the LORD your God,
who churns up the sea so that its
waves roar—
the LORD Almighty is his name.
¹⁶I have put my words in your mouth
and covered you with the shadow of
my hand—
I who set the heavens in place,
who laid the foundations of the
earth,
and who say to Zion, 'You are my
people.' "

The Cup of the LORD's Wrath

¹⁷Awake, awake!
Rise up, O Jerusalem,
you who have drunk from the hand of
the LORD
the cup of his wrath,
you who have drained to its dregs
the goblet that makes men stagger.
¹⁸Of all the sons she bore
there was none to guide her;
of all the sons she reared
there was none to take her by the
hand.
¹⁹These double calamities have come
upon you—
who can comfort you?—
ruin and destruction, famine and
sword—
who canᵃ console you?
²⁰Your sons have fainted;
they lie at the head of every street,
like antelope caught in a net.
They are filled with the wrath of the
LORD
and the rebuke of your God.

²¹Therefore hear this, you afflicted one,
made drunk, but not with wine.
²²This is what your Sovereign LORD says,

ᵃ19 Dead Sea Scrolls, Septuagint, Vulgate and
Syriac; Masoretic Text / how can I

your God, who defends his people:
"See, I have taken out of your hand
  the cup that made you stagger;
from that cup, the goblet of my wrath,
  you will never drink again.
²³I will put it into the hands of your
    tormentors,
  who said to you,
  'Fall prostrate that we may walk over
    you.'
And you made your back like the ground,
  like a street to be walked over."

52 Awake, awake, O Zion,
   clothe yourself with strength.
Put on your garments of splendor,
  O Jerusalem, the holy city.
The uncircumcised and defiled
  will not enter you again.
²Shake off your dust;
  rise up, sit enthroned, O Jerusalem.
Free yourself from the chains on your
    neck,
  O captive Daughter of Zion.

³For this is what the LORD says:

"You were sold for nothing,
  and without money you will be
    redeemed."

⁴For this is what the Sovereign LORD
says:

"At first my people went down to Egypt
    to live;
  lately, Assyria has oppressed them.

⁵"And now what do I have here?" declares the LORD.

"For my people have been taken away
    for nothing,
  and those who rule them mock,ᵃ"
                    declares the LORD.
"And all day long
  my name is constantly blasphemed.
⁶Therefore my people will know my
    name;
  therefore in that day they will know
that it is I who foretold it.
  Yes, it is I."

⁷How beautiful on the mountains
  are the feet of those who bring good
    news,
who proclaim peace,
  who bring good tidings,
  who proclaim salvation,
who say to Zion,
  "Your God reigns!"
⁸Listen! Your watchmen lift up their
    voices;

together they shout for joy.
When the LORD returns to Zion,
  they will see it with their own eyes.
⁹Burst into songs of joy together,
  you ruins of Jerusalem,
for the LORD has comforted his people,
  he has redeemed Jerusalem.
¹⁰The LORD will lay bare his holy arm
  in the sight of all the nations,
and all the ends of the earth will see
  the salvation of our God.

¹¹Depart, depart, go out from there!
  Touch no unclean thing!
Come out from it and be pure,
  you who carry the vessels of the
    LORD.
¹²But you will not leave in haste
  or go in flight;
for the LORD will go before you,
  the God of Israel will be your rear
    guard.

The Suffering and Glory of the Servant

¹³See, my servant will act wiselyᵇ;
  he will be raised and lifted up and
    highly exalted.
¹⁴Just as there were many who were
    appalled at himᶜ—
  his appearance was so disfigured
    beyond that of any man
and his form marred beyond human
    likeness—
¹⁵so will he sprinkle many nations,ᵈ
  and kings will shut their mouths
    because of him.
For what they were not told, they will
    see,
  and what they have not heard, they
    will understand.

53 Who has believed our message
   and to whom has the arm of the
     LORD been revealed?
²He grew up before him like a tender
    shoot,
  and like a root out of dry ground.
He had no beauty or majesty to attract
    us to him,
  nothing in his appearance that we
    should desire him.
³He was despised and rejected by men,
  a man of sorrows, and familiar with
    suffering.
Like one from whom men hide their
    faces

ᵃ5 Dead Sea Scrolls and Vulgate; Masoretic Text
wail   ᵇ13 Or will prosper   ᶜ14 Hebrew you
ᵈ15 Hebrew; Septuagint so will many nations
marvel at him

he was despised, and we esteemed
   him not.

⁴Surely he took up our infirmities
   and carried our sorrows,
yet we considered him stricken by God,
   smitten by him, and afflicted.
⁵But he was pierced for our
      transgressions,
   he was crushed for our iniquities;
the punishment that brought us peace
      was upon him,
   and by his wounds we are healed.
⁶We all, like sheep, have gone astray,
   each of us has turned to his own
      way;
and the LORD has laid on him
   the iniquity of us all.

⁷He was oppressed and afflicted,
   yet he did not open his mouth;
he was led like a lamb to the
      slaughter,
   and as a sheep before her shearers is
      silent,
   so he did not open his mouth.
⁸By oppression*a* and judgment he was
      taken away.
   And who can speak of his
      descendants?
For he was cut off from the land of the
      living;
   for the transgression of my people he
      was stricken.*b*
⁹He was assigned a grave with the
      wicked,
   and with the rich in his death,

though he had done no violence,
   nor was any deceit in his mouth.

¹⁰Yet it was the LORD's will to crush him
      and cause him to suffer,
   and though the LORD makes*c* his life
      a guilt offering,
he will see his offspring and prolong
      his days,
   and the will of the LORD will prosper
      in his hand.
¹¹After the suffering of his soul,
   he will see the light of life,*d* and be
      satisfied*e*;
by his knowledge*f* my righteous servant
   will justify many,
   and he will bear their iniquities.
¹²Therefore I will give him a portion
      among the great,*g*
   and he will divide the spoils with the
      strong,*h*
because he poured out his life unto
      death,
   and was numbered with the
      transgressors.
For he bore the sin of many,
   and made intercession for the
      transgressors.

a8 Or *From arrest*   *b8* Or *away. / Yet who of his
generation considered / that he was cut off from the
land of the living / for the transgression of my
people, / to whom the blow was due?*   *c10* Hebrew
though you make   *d11* Dead Sea Scrolls (see also
Septuagint); Masoretic Text does not have *the light
of life.*   *e11* Or (with Masoretic Text) *¹¹He will see
the result of the suffering of his soul / and be satisfied*
f11 Or *by knowledge of him*   *g12* Or *many*   *h12* Or
numerous

HEY DAD
What did Jesus look like?

Text: Isaiah 53:2

We do not know exactly what Jesus looked like. God told the Israelites not to make statues or images of any kind, because those images would resemble the false gods of Israel's neighbors. So none of the Jews who actually saw Jesus painted or sculpted his likeness. We can assume, though, that Jesus looked like other Nazarenes of his day. He was probably bearded, had dark hair and skin, and wore a tunic and sandals.

If Jesus had wanted us to know what he looked like, he would have preserved an image of his appearance. The fact that he did not do so tells us that he wanted to be remembered for something *other* than the way he looked. He was the Word of God made into flesh. He wanted us to esteem his *actions* and his *words*.

This is good news for us. No matter what we look like on the outside, we can still look like Jesus in the ways that really count!

QUESTIONS KIDS ASK

For a complete listing of Questions Kids Ask, turn to page 1435.

Where Are You?

Key Verse: *"We all, like sheep, have gone astray, each of us has turned to his own way; and the LORD has laid on him the iniquity of us all."* Isaiah 53:6

Text: Isaiah 53:4–6 *(Dad or child reads the text.)*

QUIET TIMES with Dad

DAD READS: Have you ever been lost? When a child gets lost, both the parents and the child are frightened. I have seen parents at the shopping mall, calling out the name of their son or daughter. "They were here just a minute ago," these frightened dads and moms say. "Then they just disappeared."

Child reads: The Bible tells us that, as God's children, we are like sheep. And one of the things that sheep do is wander away from the shepherd. They nibble a little grass here and nibble a little grass there. Then they look around and can't find the other sheep. And they can't find their shepherd. This makes sheep scared. It frightens the shepherd, too.

DAD READS: The verses we read today were written by a man named Isaiah. And even though he wrote these words a long, long time before Jesus was born in Bethlehem, he was telling his friends that a Savior was going to be born. He reminded the people that they were like sheep because they were lost. Then he told them that Jesus, the Good Shepherd, would give his life to save his sheep.

Child reads: Sometimes, at Christmas, we forget that the baby Jesus came to give his life for us. We forget that a long time before he was born, people like Isaiah were telling God's people that a Savior was coming to find lost people and to save them from their sins.

DAD READS: I am so glad that saving us was God's plan. I'm glad that when we feel lost, we do not need to be afraid. We can call to our heavenly Father—our Shepherd—and he will find us. He will love us and he will save us, just like the parents at the shopping mall who find their child and scoop her up in their arms.

Child reads: Many people are afraid. They feel lost and they are scared. You and I can tell them that Jesus has found us, and we can show them that he loves us. Let me pray this prayer with you:

Our Father in heaven, we love you. Thank you for giving your life to find me and to save me. Thank you that we never need to be afraid again … that you, our loving Good Shepherd have given your life to lift us up into your arms and save us. Please help us to remember this. And please help us to tell our friends about our Savior who gave his life to save us. We love you. In Jesus' name, Amen.

For your next devotional reading, go to page 816.

The Future Glory of Zion

54 "Sing, O barren woman,
    you who never bore a child;
burst into song, shout for joy,
    you who were never in labor;
because more are the children of the
        desolate woman
    than of her who has a husband,"
                        says the LORD.
2 "Enlarge the place of your tent,
    stretch your tent curtains wide,
        do not hold back;
lengthen your cords,
    strengthen your stakes.
3 For you will spread out to the right and
        to the left;
    your descendants will dispossess
        nations
    and settle in their desolate cities.

4 "Do not be afraid; you will not suffer
        shame.
    Do not fear disgrace; you will not be
        humiliated.
You will forget the shame of your youth
    and remember no more the reproach
        of your widowhood.
5 For your Maker is your husband—
    the LORD Almighty is his name—
the Holy One of Israel is your
        Redeemer;
    he is called the God of all the earth.
6 The LORD will call you back
    as if you were a wife deserted and
        distressed in spirit—
a wife who married young,
    only to be rejected," says your God.
7 "For a brief moment I abandoned you,
    but with deep compassion I will
        bring you back.
8 In a surge of anger
    I hid my face from you for a
        moment,
but with everlasting kindness
    I will have compassion on you,"
    says the LORD your Redeemer.

9 "To me this is like the days of Noah,
    when I swore that the waters of Noah
        would never again cover the
        earth.
So now I have sworn not to be angry
        with you,
    never to rebuke you again.
10 Though the mountains be shaken
    and the hills be removed,
yet my unfailing love for you will not be
        shaken
    nor my covenant of peace be
        removed,"
says the LORD, who has compassion
    on you.

11 "O afflicted city, lashed by storms and
        not comforted,
    I will build you with stones of
        turquoise,[a]
    your foundations with sapphires.[b]
12 I will make your battlements of rubies,
    your gates of sparkling jewels,
    and all your walls of precious stones.
13 All your sons will be taught by the
        LORD,
    and great will be your children's
        peace.
14 In righteousness you will be
        established:
Tyranny will be far from you;
    you will have nothing to fear.
Terror will be far removed;
    it will not come near you.
15 If anyone does attack you, it will not be
        my doing;
    whoever attacks you will surrender
        to you.

16 "See, it is I who created the blacksmith
    who fans the coals into flame
    and forges a weapon fit for its work.
And it is I who have created the
        destroyer to work havoc;
17   no weapon forged against you will
        prevail,
    and you will refute every tongue that
        accuses you.
This is the heritage of the servants of
        the LORD,
    and this is their vindication from
        me,"
                    declares the LORD.

Invitation to the Thirsty

55 "Come, all you who are thirsty,
    come to the waters;
and you who have no money,
    come, buy and eat!
Come, buy wine and milk
    without money and without cost.
2 Why spend money on what is not
        bread,
    and your labor on what does not
        satisfy?
Listen, listen to me, and eat what is
        good,
    and your soul will delight in the
        richest of fare.
3 Give ear and come to me;
    hear me, that your soul may live.

---

[a]11 The meaning of the Hebrew for this word is
uncertain.   [b]11 Or *lapis lazuli*

I will make an everlasting covenant
    with you,
  my faithful love promised to David.
⁴ See, I have made him a witness to the
    peoples,
  a leader and commander of the
    peoples.
⁵ Surely you will summon nations you
    know not,
  and nations that do not know you
    will hasten to you,
because of the LORD your God,
  the Holy One of Israel,
  for he has endowed you with
    splendor."

⁶ Seek the LORD while he may be found;
  call on him while he is near.
⁷ Let the wicked forsake his way
  and the evil man his thoughts.
Let him turn to the LORD, and he will
    have mercy on him,
  and to our God, for he will freely
    pardon.

⁸ "For my thoughts are not your
    thoughts,
  neither are your ways my ways,"
            declares the LORD.
⁹ "As the heavens are higher than the
    earth,
  so are my ways higher than your
    ways
  and my thoughts than your
    thoughts.
¹⁰ As the rain and the snow
  come down from heaven,
and do not return to it
  without watering the earth
and making it bud and flourish,
  so that it yields seed for the sower
    and bread for the eater,
¹¹ so is my word that goes out from my
    mouth:
  It will not return to me empty,
but will accomplish what I desire
  and achieve the purpose for which I
    sent it.
¹² You will go out in joy
  and be led forth in peace;
the mountains and hills
  will burst into song before you,
and all the trees of the field
  will clap their hands.
¹³ Instead of the thornbush will grow the
    pine tree,
  and instead of briers the myrtle will
    grow.
This will be for the LORD's renown,
  for an everlasting sign,
  which will not be destroyed."

Salvation for Others

56 This is what the LORD says:

"Maintain justice
  and do what is right,
for my salvation is close at hand
  and my righteousness will soon be
    revealed.
² Blessed is the man who does this,
  the man who holds it fast,
who keeps the Sabbath without
    desecrating it,
  and keeps his hand from doing any
    evil."

³ Let no foreigner who has bound
    himself to the LORD say,
  "The LORD will surely exclude me
    from his people."
And let not any eunuch complain,
  "I am only a dry tree."

⁴ For this is what the LORD says:

"To the eunuchs who keep my
    Sabbaths,
  who choose what pleases me
  and hold fast to my covenant—
⁵ to them I will give within my temple
    and its walls
  a memorial and a name
  better than sons and daughters;
I will give them an everlasting name
  that will not be cut off.
⁶ And foreigners who bind themselves to
    the LORD
  to serve him,
to love the name of the LORD,
  and to worship him,
all who keep the Sabbath without
    desecrating it
  and who hold fast to my covenant—
⁷ these I will bring to my holy mountain
  and give them joy in my house of
    prayer.
Their burnt offerings and sacrifices
  will be accepted on my altar;
for my house will be called
  a house of prayer for all nations."
⁸ The Sovereign LORD declares—
  he who gathers the exiles of Israel:
"I will gather still others to them
  besides those already gathered."

God's Accusation Against the Wicked

⁹ Come, all you beasts of the field,
  come and devour, all you beasts of
    the forest!
¹⁰ Israel's watchmen are blind,
  they all lack knowledge;

they are all mute dogs,
  they cannot bark;
they lie around and dream,
  they love to sleep.
¹¹They are dogs with mighty appetites;
  they never have enough.
They are shepherds who lack
    understanding;
  they all turn to their own way,
  each seeks his own gain.
¹²"Come," each one cries, "let me get
    wine!
  Let us drink our fill of beer!
And tomorrow will be like today,
  or even far better."

57 The righteous perish,
  and no one ponders it in his heart;
devout men are taken away,
  and no one understands
that the righteous are taken away
  to be spared from evil.
²Those who walk uprightly
  enter into peace;
  they find rest as they lie in death.

³"But you—come here, you sons of a
    sorceress,
  you offspring of adulterers and
    prostitutes!
⁴Whom are you mocking?
  At whom do you sneer
  and stick out your tongue?
Are you not a brood of rebels,
  the offspring of liars?
⁵You burn with lust among the oaks
  and under every spreading tree;
you sacrifice your children in the
    ravines
  and under the overhanging crags.
⁶The idols among the smooth stones of
    the ravines are your portion;
  they, they are your lot.
Yes, to them you have poured out drink
    offerings
  and offered grain offerings.
  In the light of these things, should I
    relent?
⁷You have made your bed on a high and
    lofty hill;
  there you went up to offer your
    sacrifices.
⁸Behind your doors and your doorposts
  you have put your pagan symbols.
Forsaking me, you uncovered your bed,
  you climbed into it and opened it
    wide;
you made a pact with those whose
    beds you love,
  and you looked on their nakedness.

⁹You went to Molech[a] with olive oil
  and increased your perfumes.
You sent your ambassadors[b] far away;
  you descended to the grave[c] itself!
¹⁰You were wearied by all your ways,
  but you would not say, 'It is
    hopeless.'
You found renewal of your strength,
  and so you did not faint.

¹¹"Whom have you so dreaded and
    feared
  that you have been false to me,
and have neither remembered me
  nor pondered this in your hearts?
Is it not because I have long been silent
  that you do not fear me?
¹²I will expose your righteousness and
    your works,
  and they will not benefit you.
¹³When you cry out for help,
  let your collection of idols save you!
The wind will carry all of them off,
  a mere breath will blow them away.
But the man who makes me his refuge
  will inherit the land
  and possess my holy mountain."

Comfort for the Contrite

¹⁴And it will be said:

"Build up, build up, prepare the road!
  Remove the obstacles out of the way
    of my people."
¹⁵For this is what the high and lofty One
    says—
  he who lives forever, whose name is
    holy:
"I live in a high and holy place,
  but also with him who is contrite
    and lowly in spirit,
to revive the spirit of the lowly
  and to revive the heart of the
    contrite.
¹⁶I will not accuse forever,
  nor will I always be angry,
for then the spirit of man would grow
    faint before me—
  the breath of man that I have created.
¹⁷I was enraged by his sinful greed;
  I punished him, and hid my face in
    anger,
  yet he kept on in his willful ways.
¹⁸I have seen his ways, but I will heal
    him;
  I will guide him and restore comfort
    to him,
¹⁹   creating praise on the lips of the
    mourners in Israel.

_ª9 Or_ to the king   _ᵇ9 Or_ idols   _ᶜ9 Hebrew_ Sheol

Peace, peace, to those far and near,"
  says the LORD. "And I will heal them."
20 But the wicked are like the tossing sea,
  which cannot rest,
  whose waves cast up mire and mud.
21 "There is no peace," says my God, "for
  the wicked."

True Fasting

58 "Shout it aloud, do not hold back.
Raise your voice like a trumpet.
Declare to my people their rebellion
  and to the house of Jacob their sins.
2 For day after day they seek me out;
  they seem eager to know my ways,
as if they were a nation that does what
  is right
  and has not forsaken the commands
  of its God.
They ask me for just decisions
  and seem eager for God to come
  near them.
3 'Why have we fasted,' they say,
  'and you have not seen it?
Why have we humbled ourselves,
  and you have not noticed?'

"Yet on the day of your fasting, you do
  as you please
  and exploit all your workers.
4 Your fasting ends in quarreling and
  strife,
  and in striking each other with
  wicked fists.
You cannot fast as you do today
  and expect your voice to be heard on
  high.
5 Is this the kind of fast I have chosen,
  only a day for a man to humble
  himself?
Is it only for bowing one's head like a
  reed
  and for lying on sackcloth and ashes?
Is that what you call a fast,
  a day acceptable to the LORD?

6 "Is not this the kind of fasting I have
  chosen:
to loose the chains of injustice
  and untie the cords of the yoke,
to set the oppressed free
  and break every yoke?
7 Is it not to share your food with the
  hungry
  and to provide the poor wanderer
  with shelter—
when you see the naked, to clothe
  him,
  and not to turn away from your own
  flesh and blood?

8 Then your light will break forth like the
  dawn,
  and your healing will quickly appear;
then your righteousness[a] will go before
  you,
  and the glory of the LORD will be
  your rear guard.
9 Then you will call, and the LORD will
  answer;
  you will cry for help, and he will say:
  Here am I.

"If you do away with the yoke of
  oppression,
  with the pointing finger and
  malicious talk,
10 and if you spend yourselves in behalf of
  the hungry
  and satisfy the needs of the
  oppressed,
then your light will rise in the darkness,
  and your night will become like the
  noonday.
11 The LORD will guide you always;
  he will satisfy your needs in a
  sun-scorched land
  and will strengthen your frame.
You will be like a well-watered garden,
  like a spring whose waters never fail.
12 Your people will rebuild the ancient
  ruins
  and will raise up the age-old
  foundations;
you will be called Repairer of Broken
  Walls,
  Restorer of Streets with Dwellings.

13 "If you keep your feet from breaking
  the Sabbath
  and from doing as you please on my
  holy day,
if you call the Sabbath a delight
  and the LORD's holy day honorable,
and if you honor it by not going your
  own way
  and not doing as you please or
  speaking idle words,
14 then you will find your joy in the LORD,
  and I will cause you to ride on the
  heights of the land
  and to feast on the inheritance of
  your father Jacob."
         The mouth of the LORD
         has spoken.

Sin, Confession and Redemption

59 Surely the arm of the LORD is not too
  short to save,
  nor his ear too dull to hear.

---

a 8 Or *your righteous One*

² But your iniquities have separated
    you from your God;
your sins have hidden his face from you,
    so that he will not hear.
³ For your hands are stained with blood,
    your fingers with guilt.
Your lips have spoken lies,
    and your tongue mutters wicked
        things.
⁴ No one calls for justice;
    no one pleads his case with integrity.
They rely on empty arguments and
        speak lies;
    they conceive trouble and give birth
        to evil.
⁵ They hatch the eggs of vipers
    and spin a spider's web.
Whoever eats their eggs will die,
    and when one is broken, an adder is
        hatched.
⁶ Their cobwebs are useless for clothing;
    they cannot cover themselves with
        what they make.
Their deeds are evil deeds,
    and acts of violence are in their hands.
⁷ Their feet rush into sin;
    they are swift to shed innocent
        blood.
Their thoughts are evil thoughts;
    ruin and destruction mark their
        ways.
⁸ The way of peace they do not know;
    there is no justice in their paths.
They have turned them into crooked
        roads;
    no one who walks in them will know
        peace.

⁹ So justice is far from us,
    and righteousness does not reach us.
We look for light, but all is darkness;
    for brightness, but we walk in deep
        shadows.
¹⁰ Like the blind we grope along the wall,
    feeling our way like men without
        eyes.
At midday we stumble as if it were
        twilight;
    among the strong, we are like the
        dead.
¹¹ We all growl like bears;
    we moan mournfully like doves.
We look for justice, but find none;
    for deliverance, but it is far away.

¹² For our offenses are many in your sight,
    and our sins testify against us.
Our offenses are ever with us,
    and we acknowledge our iniquities:
¹³ rebellion and treachery against the
        LORD,
turning our backs on our God,
fomenting oppression and revolt,
    uttering lies our hearts have
        conceived.
¹⁴ So justice is driven back,
    and righteousness stands at a
        distance;
truth has stumbled in the streets,
    honesty cannot enter.
¹⁵ Truth is nowhere to be found,
    and whoever shuns evil becomes a
        prey.

The LORD looked and was displeased
    that there was no justice.
¹⁶ He saw that there was no one,
    he was appalled that there was no
        one to intervene;
so his own arm worked salvation for
        him,
    and his own righteousness sustained
        him.
¹⁷ He put on righteousness as his
        breastplate,
    and the helmet of salvation on his
        head;
he put on the garments of vengeance
    and wrapped himself in zeal as in a
        cloak.
¹⁸ According to what they have done,
    so will he repay
wrath to his enemies
    and retribution to his foes;
    he will repay the islands their due.
¹⁹ From the west, men will fear the name
        of the LORD,
    and from the rising of the sun, they
        will revere his glory.
For he will come like a pent-up flood
    that the breath of the LORD drives
        along.ᵃ

²⁰ "The Redeemer will come to Zion,
    to those in Jacob who repent of their
        sins,"
                    declares the LORD.

²¹ "As for me, this is my covenant with
them," says the LORD. "My Spirit, who is on
you, and my words that I have put in your
mouth will not depart from your mouth, or
from the mouths of your children, or from
the mouths of their descendants from this
time on and forever," says the LORD.

The Glory of Zion

60 "Arise, shine, for your light has
        come,

ᵃ19 Or *When the enemy comes in like a flood, / the
Spirit of the LORD will put him to flight*

and the glory of the LORD rises upon
   you.
² See, darkness covers the earth
   and thick darkness is over the
      peoples,
but the LORD rises upon you
   and his glory appears over you.
³ Nations will come to your light,
   and kings to the brightness of your
      dawn.

⁴ "Lift up your eyes and look about you:
   All assemble and come to you;
your sons come from afar,
   and your daughters are carried on
      the arm.
⁵ Then you will look and be radiant,
   your heart will throb and swell with
      joy;
the wealth on the seas will be brought
      to you,
   to you the riches of the nations will
      come.
⁶ Herds of camels will cover your land,
   young camels of Midian and Ephah.
And all from Sheba will come,
   bearing gold and incense
   and proclaiming the praise of the
      LORD.
⁷ All Kedar's flocks will be gathered to
      you,
   the rams of Nebaioth will serve you;
they will be accepted as offerings on
      my altar,
   and I will adorn my glorious temple.

⁸ "Who are these that fly along like
      clouds,
   like doves to their nests?
⁹ Surely the islands look to me;
   in the lead are the ships of Tarshish,ᵃ
bringing your sons from afar,
   with their silver and gold,
to the honor of the LORD your God,
   the Holy One of Israel,
   for he has endowed you with
      splendor.

¹⁰ "Foreigners will rebuild your walls,
   and their kings will serve you.
Though in anger I struck you,
   in favor I will show you compassion.
¹¹ Your gates will always stand open,
   they will never be shut, day or night,
so that men may bring you the wealth
      of the nations—
   their kings led in triumphal
      procession.
¹² For the nation or kingdom that will not
      serve you will perish;
   it will be utterly ruined.

¹³ "The glory of Lebanon will come to
      you,
   the pine, the fir and the cypress
      together,
to adorn the place of my sanctuary;
   and I will glorify the place of my feet.
¹⁴ The sons of your oppressors will come
      bowing before you;
   all who despise you will bow down at
      your feet
and will call you the City of the LORD,
   Zion of the Holy One of Israel.

¹⁵ "Although you have been forsaken and
      hated,
   with no one traveling through,
I will make you the everlasting pride
   and the joy of all generations.
¹⁶ You will drink the milk of nations
   and be nursed at royal breasts.
Then you will know that I, the LORD, am
      your Savior,
   your Redeemer, the Mighty One of
      Jacob.
¹⁷ Instead of bronze I will bring you gold,
   and silver in place of iron.
Instead of wood I will bring you
      bronze,
   and iron in place of stones.
I will make peace your governor
   and righteousness your ruler.
¹⁸ No longer will violence be heard in
      your land,
   nor ruin or destruction within your
      borders,
but you will call your walls Salvation
   and your gates Praise.
¹⁹ The sun will no more be your light by
      day,
   nor will the brightness of the moon
      shine on you,
for the LORD will be your everlasting
      light,
   and your God will be your glory.
²⁰ Your sun will never set again,
   and your moon will wane no more;
the LORD will be your everlasting light,
   and your days of sorrow will end.
²¹ Then will all your people be righteous
   and they will possess the land
      forever.
They are the shoot I have planted,
   the work of my hands,
   for the display of my splendor.
²² The least of you will become a
      thousand,
   the smallest a mighty nation.
I am the LORD;
   in its time I will do this swiftly."

ᵃ9 Or *the trading ships*

The Year of the Lord's Favor

61 The Spirit of the Sovereign LORD is
on me,
because the LORD has anointed me
to preach good news to the poor.
He has sent me to bind up the
brokenhearted,
to proclaim freedom for the captives
and release from darkness for the
prisoners,[a]
² to proclaim the year of the LORD's favor
and the day of vengeance of our God,
to comfort all who mourn,
³   and provide for those who grieve in
Zion—
to bestow on them a crown of beauty
instead of ashes,
the oil of gladness
instead of mourning,
and a garment of praise
instead of a spirit of despair.
They will be called oaks of
righteousness,
a planting of the LORD
for the display of his splendor.

⁴ They will rebuild the ancient ruins
and restore the places long
devastated;
they will renew the ruined cities
that have been devastated for
generations.
⁵ Aliens will shepherd your flocks;
foreigners will work your fields and
vineyards.
⁶ And you will be called priests of the
LORD,
you will be named ministers of our
God.
You will feed on the wealth of nations,
and in their riches you will boast.

⁷ Instead of their shame
my people will receive a double
portion,
and instead of disgrace
they will rejoice in their inheritance;
and so they will inherit a double
portion in their land,
and everlasting joy will be theirs.

⁸ "For I, the LORD, love justice;
I hate robbery and iniquity.
In my faithfulness I will reward them
and make an everlasting covenant
with them.
⁹ Their descendants will be known
among the nations
and their offspring among the
peoples.

All who see them will acknowledge
that they are a people the LORD has
blessed."

¹⁰ I delight greatly in the LORD;
my soul rejoices in my God.
For he has clothed me with garments of
salvation
and arrayed me in a robe of
righteousness,
as a bridegroom adorns his head like a
priest,
and as a bride adorns herself with
her jewels.
¹¹ For as the soil makes the sprout come up
and a garden causes seeds to grow,
so the Sovereign LORD will make
righteousness and praise
spring up before all nations.

Zion's New Name

62 For Zion's sake I will not keep silent,
for Jerusalem's sake I will not remain
quiet,
till her righteousness shines out like
the dawn,
her salvation like a blazing torch.
² The nations will see your
righteousness,
and all kings your glory;
you will be called by a new name
that the mouth of the LORD will
bestow.
³ You will be a crown of splendor in the
LORD's hand,
a royal diadem in the hand of your
God.
⁴ No longer will they call you Deserted,
or name your land Desolate.
But you will be called Hephzibah,[b]
and your land Beulah[c];
for the LORD will take delight in you,
and your land will be married.
⁵ As a young man marries a maiden,
so will your sons[d] marry you;
as a bridegroom rejoices over his bride,
so will your God rejoice over you.

⁶ I have posted watchmen on your walls,
O Jerusalem;
they will never be silent day or night.
You who call on the LORD,
give yourselves no rest,
⁷ and give him no rest till he establishes
Jerusalem
and makes her the praise of the
earth.

---

[a]1 Hebrew; Septuagint *the blind*   [b]4 *Hephzibah*
means *my delight is in her.*   [c]4 *Beulah* means
married.   [d]5 Or *Builder*

⁸The LORD has sworn by his right hand
   and by his mighty arm:
"Never again will I give your grain
   as food for your enemies,
and never again will foreigners drink
   the new wine
   for which you have toiled;
⁹but those who harvest it will eat it
   and praise the LORD,
and those who gather the grapes will
   drink it
   in the courts of my sanctuary."

¹⁰Pass through, pass through the gates!
   Prepare the way for the people.
Build up, build up the highway!
   Remove the stones.
Raise a banner for the nations.

¹¹The LORD has made proclamation
   to the ends of the earth:
"Say to the Daughter of Zion,
   'See, your Savior comes!
See, his reward is with him,
   and his recompense accompanies
   him.'"
¹²They will be called the Holy People,
   the Redeemed of the LORD;
and you will be called Sought After,
   the City No Longer Deserted.

God's Day of Vengeance and Redemption

63 Who is this coming from Edom,
   from Bozrah, with his garments
      stained crimson?
Who is this, robed in splendor,
   striding forward in the greatness of
      his strength?

"It is I, speaking in righteousness,
   mighty to save."

²Why are your garments red,
   like those of one treading the
      winepress?

³"I have trodden the winepress alone;
   from the nations no one was with
      me.
I trampled them in my anger
   and trod them down in my wrath;
their blood spattered my garments,
   and I stained all my clothing.
⁴For the day of vengeance was in my
      heart,
   and the year of my redemption has
      come.
⁵I looked, but there was no one to help,
   I was appalled that no one gave
      support;
so my own arm worked salvation for
      me,

and my own wrath sustained me.
⁶I trampled the nations in my anger;
   in my wrath I made them drunk
   and poured their blood on the
      ground."

Praise and Prayer

⁷I will tell of the kindnesses of the LORD,
   the deeds for which he is to be
      praised,
   according to all the LORD has done
      for us—
yes, the many good things he has done
   for the house of Israel,
   according to his compassion and
      many kindnesses.
⁸He said, "Surely they are my people,
   sons who will not be false to me";
   and so he became their Savior.
⁹In all their distress he too was
      distressed,
   and the angel of his presence saved
      them.
In his love and mercy he redeemed
      them;
   he lifted them up and carried them
   all the days of old.
¹⁰Yet they rebelled
   and grieved his Holy Spirit.
So he turned and became their enemy
   and he himself fought against them.

¹¹Then his people recalled[a] the days of
      old,
   the days of Moses and his people—
where is he who brought them through
      the sea,
   with the shepherd of his flock?
Where is he who set
   his Holy Spirit among them,
¹²who sent his glorious arm of power
   to be at Moses' right hand,
who divided the waters before them,
   to gain for himself everlasting
      renown,
¹³who led them through the depths?
Like a horse in open country,
   they did not stumble;
¹⁴like cattle that go down to the plain,
   they were given rest by the Spirit of
      the LORD.
This is how you guided your people
   to make for yourself a glorious name.

¹⁵Look down from heaven and see
   from your lofty throne, holy and
      glorious.
Where are your zeal and your might?

ᵃ11 Or *But may he recall*

Your tenderness and compassion are
  withheld from us.
¹⁶ But you are our Father,
    though Abraham does not know us
    or Israel acknowledge us;
  you, O LORD, are our Father,
    our Redeemer from of old is your
      name.
¹⁷ Why, O LORD, do you make us wander
      from your ways
    and harden our hearts so we do not
      revere you?
  Return for the sake of your servants,
    the tribes that are your
      inheritance.
¹⁸ For a little while your people possessed
      your holy place,
    but now our enemies have trampled
      down your sanctuary.
¹⁹ We are yours from of old;
    but you have not ruled over them,
    they have not been called by your
      name.ᵃ

64 Oh, that you would rend the
    heavens and come down,
  that the mountains would tremble
    before you!
² As when fire sets twigs ablaze
    and causes water to boil,
  come down to make your name known
    to your enemies
    and cause the nations to quake
      before you!
³ For when you did awesome things that
      we did not expect,
    you came down, and the mountains
      trembled before you.
⁴ Since ancient times no one has heard,
    no ear has perceived,
  no eye has seen any God besides you,
    who acts on behalf of those who wait
      for him.
⁵ You come to the help of those who
      gladly do right,
    who remember your ways.
  But when we continued to sin against
      them,
    you were angry.
    How then can we be saved?
⁶ All of us have become like one who is
      unclean,
    and all our righteous acts are like
      filthy rags;
  we all shrivel up like a leaf,
    and like the wind our sins sweep us
      away.
⁷ No one calls on your name
    or strives to lay hold of you;
  for you have hidden your face from us

and made us waste away because of
  our sins.
⁸ Yet, O LORD, you are our Father.
    We are the clay, you are the potter;
    we are all the work of your hand.
⁹ Do not be angry beyond measure,
      O LORD;
    do not remember our sins forever.
  Oh, look upon us, we pray,
    for we are all your people.
¹⁰ Your sacred cities have become a
      desert;
    even Zion is a desert, Jerusalem a
      desolation.
¹¹ Our holy and glorious temple, where
      our fathers praised you,
    has been burned with fire,
    and all that we treasured lies in
      ruins.
¹² After all this, O LORD, will you hold
      yourself back?
    Will you keep silent and punish us
      beyond measure?

Judgment and Salvation

65 "I revealed myself to those who did
    not ask for me;
  I was found by those who did not
    seek me.
  To a nation that did not call on my
      name,
    I said, 'Here am I, here am I.'
² All day long I have held out my hands
    to an obstinate people,
  who walk in ways not good,
    pursuing their own imaginations—
³ a people who continually provoke me
      to my very face,
  offering sacrifices in gardens
    and burning incense on altars of
      brick;
⁴ who sit among the graves
    and spend their nights keeping
      secret vigil;
  who eat the flesh of pigs,
    and whose pots hold broth of
      unclean meat;
⁵ who say, 'Keep away; don't come near
      me,
    for I am too sacred for you!'
  Such people are smoke in my nostrils,
    a fire that keeps burning all day.

⁶ "See, it stands written before me:
    I will not keep silent but will pay
      back in full;
    I will pay it back into their laps—

ᵃ19 Or We are like those you have never ruled, / like
those never called by your name

7 both your sins and the sins of your
fathers,"
   says the LORD.
"Because they burned sacrifices on the
   mountains
   and defied me on the hills,
I will measure into their laps
   the full payment for their former
   deeds."

8 This is what the LORD says:

"As when juice is still found in a cluster
   of grapes
   and men say, 'Don't destroy it,
   there is yet some good in it,'
so will I do in behalf of my servants;
   I will not destroy them all.
9 I will bring forth descendants from
   Jacob,
   and from Judah those who will
   possess my mountains;
my chosen people will inherit them,
   and there will my servants live.
10 Sharon will become a pasture for flocks,
   and the Valley of Achor a resting
   place for herds,
   for my people who seek me.

11 "But as for you who forsake the LORD
   and forget my holy mountain,
who spread a table for Fortune
   and fill bowls of mixed wine for
   Destiny,
12 I will destine you for the sword,
   and you will all bend down for the
   slaughter;
for I called but you did not answer,
   I spoke but you did not listen.
You did evil in my sight
   and chose what displeases me."

13 Therefore this is what the Sovereign
LORD says:

"My servants will eat,
   but you will go hungry;
my servants will drink,
   but you will go thirsty;
my servants will rejoice,
   but you will be put to shame.
14 My servants will sing
   out of the joy of their hearts,
but you will cry out
   from anguish of heart
   and wail in brokenness of spirit.
15 You will leave your name
   to my chosen ones as a curse;
the Sovereign LORD will put you to
   death,
   but to his servants he will give
   another name.

16 Whoever invokes a blessing in the land
   will do so by the God of truth;
he who takes an oath in the land
   will swear by the God of truth.
For the past troubles will be forgotten
   and hidden from my eyes.

New Heavens and a New Earth

17 "Behold, I will create
   new heavens and a new earth.
The former things will not be
   remembered,
   nor will they come to mind.
18 But be glad and rejoice forever
   in what I will create,
for I will create Jerusalem to be a delight
   and its people a joy.
19 I will rejoice over Jerusalem
   and take delight in my people;
the sound of weeping and of crying
   will be heard in it no more.

20 "Never again will there be in it
   an infant who lives but a few days,
   or an old man who does not live out
   his years;
he who dies at a hundred
   will be thought a mere youth;
he who fails to reacha a hundred
   will be considered accursed.
21 They will build houses and dwell in
   them;
   they will plant vineyards and eat
   their fruit.
22 No longer will they build houses and
   others live in them,
   or plant and others eat.
For as the days of a tree,
   so will be the days of my people;
my chosen ones will long enjoy
   the works of their hands.
23 They will not toil in vain
   or bear children doomed to
   misfortune;
for they will be a people blessed by the
   LORD,
   they and their descendants with
   them.
24 Before they call I will answer;
   while they are still speaking I will
   hear.
25 The wolf and the lamb will feed
   together,
   and the lion will eat straw like the ox,
   but dust will be the serpent's food.
They will neither harm nor destroy
   on all my holy mountain,"
                    says the LORD.

a20 Or / the sinner who reaches

Judgment and Hope

66 This is what the Lord says:

"Heaven is my throne,
    and the earth is my footstool.
Where is the house you will build for
        me?
    Where will my resting place be?
² Has not my hand made all these things,
    and so they came into being?"
                            declares the LORD.

"This is the one I esteem:
    he who is humble and contrite in
        spirit,
    and trembles at my word.
³ But whoever sacrifices a bull
    is like one who kills a man,
and whoever offers a lamb,
    like one who breaks a dog's neck;
whoever makes a grain offering
    is like one who presents pig's blood,
and whoever burns memorial incense,
    like one who worships an idol.
They have chosen their own ways,
    and their souls delight in their
        abominations;
⁴ so I also will choose harsh treatment
        for them
    and will bring upon them what they
        dread.
For when I called, no one answered,
    when I spoke, no one listened.
They did evil in my sight
    and chose what displeases me."

⁵ Hear the word of the LORD,
    you who tremble at his word:
"Your brothers who hate you,
    and exclude you because of my
        name, have said,
'Let the LORD be glorified,
    that we may see your joy!'
    Yet they will be put to shame.
⁶ Hear that uproar from the city,
    hear that noise from the temple!
It is the sound of the LORD
    repaying his enemies all they
        deserve.

⁷ "Before she goes into labor,
    she gives birth;
before the pains come upon her,
    she delivers a son.
⁸ Who has ever heard of such a thing?
    Who has ever seen such things?
Can a country be born in a day
    or a nation be brought forth in a
        moment?
Yet no sooner is Zion in labor

than she gives birth to her children.
⁹ Do I bring to the moment of birth
    and not give delivery?" says the
        LORD.
"Do I close up the womb
    when I bring to delivery?" says your
        God.
¹⁰ "Rejoice with Jerusalem and be glad for
        her,
    all you who love her;
rejoice greatly with her,
    all you who mourn over her.
¹¹ For you will nurse and be satisfied
    at her comforting breasts;
you will drink deeply
    and delight in her overflowing
        abundance."

¹² For this is what the LORD says:

"I will extend peace to her like a river,
    and the wealth of nations like a
        flooding stream;
you will nurse and be carried on her
        arm
    and dandled on her knees.
¹³ As a mother comforts her child,
    so will I comfort you;
and you will be comforted over
        Jerusalem."

¹⁴ When you see this, your heart will
        rejoice
    and you will flourish like grass;
the hand of the LORD will be made
        known to his servants,
    but his fury will be shown to his foes.
¹⁵ See, the LORD is coming with fire,
    and his chariots are like a whirlwind;
he will bring down his anger with fury,
    and his rebuke with flames of fire.
¹⁶ For with fire and with his sword
    the LORD will execute judgment
        upon all men,
    and many will be those slain by the
        LORD.

¹⁷ "Those who consecrate and purify themselves to go into the gardens, following the one in the midst of[a] those who eat the flesh of pigs and rats and other abominable things—they will meet their end together," declares the LORD.

¹⁸ "And I, because of their actions and their imaginations, am about to come[b] and gather all nations and tongues, and they will come and see my glory.

¹⁹ "I will set a sign among them, and I will send some of those who survive to the

---

[a]17 Or gardens behind one of your temples, and
[b]18 The meaning of the Hebrew for this clause is uncertain.

nations—to Tarshish, to the Libyans[a] and Lydians (famous as archers), to Tubal and Greece, and to the distant islands that have not heard of my fame or seen my glory. They will proclaim my glory among the nations. **20**And they will bring all your brothers, from all the nations, to my holy mountain in Jerusalem as an offering to the LORD—on horses, in chariots and wagons, and on mules and camels," says the LORD. "They will bring them, as the Israelites bring their grain offerings, to the temple of the LORD in ceremonially clean vessels. **21**And I will select some of them also to be priests and Levites," says the LORD.

22"As the new heavens and the new earth that I make will endure before me," declares the LORD, "so will your name and descendants endure. **23**From one New Moon to another and from one Sabbath to another, all mankind will come and bow down before me," says the LORD. **24**"And they will go out and look upon the dead bodies of those who rebelled against me; their worm will not die, nor will their fire be quenched, and they will be loathsome to all mankind."

[a]19 Some Septuagint manuscripts *Put* (Libyans); Hebrew *Pul*

You have been called. God has an assignment for you that literally has your name—and no one else's name—on it. Your life is not accidental. Your vocation is holy. Your family is God's gift to you and you alone.

The book of Jeremiah opens with the affirmation that what is true about you and your special calling was also true for Jeremiah. God told this ordinary man, "Before I formed you in the womb I knew you, before you were born I set you apart" (1:5). I'm certain Jeremiah was aghast at the news. But as incredible as this was for the prophet to hear, this was not a one-time event. The Sovereign God says the same to you. You are called. Your assignments have been planned since before there were oceans. Listen carefully to Jeremiah when he speaks. Actually, he sounds like a man who had been told that he was "the man for the job"—the one who could do it best.

How are you doing with your charge?

Jeremiah

1 The words of Jeremiah son of Hilkiah, one of the priests at Anathoth in the territory of Benjamin. ²The word of the LORD came to him in the thirteenth year of the reign of Josiah son of Amon king of Judah, ³and through the reign of Jehoiakim son of Josiah king of Judah, down to the fifth month of the eleventh year of Zedekiah son of Josiah king of Judah, when the people of Jerusalem went into exile.

The Call of Jeremiah

⁴The word of the LORD came to me, saying,

⁵ "Before I formed you in the womb I
    knew*a* you,
  before you were born I set you apart;

I appointed you as a prophet to the
    nations."

⁶"Ah, Sovereign LORD," I said, "I do not know how to speak; I am only a child."

⁷But the LORD said to me, "Do not say, 'I am only a child.' You must go to everyone I send you to and say whatever I command you. ⁸Do not be afraid of them, for I am with you and will rescue you," declares the LORD.

⁹Then the LORD reached out his hand and touched my mouth and said to me, "Now, I have put my words in your mouth. ¹⁰See, today I appoint you over nations and kingdoms to uproot and tear down, to destroy and overthrow, to build and to plant."

a5 Or chose

¹¹The word of the LORD came to me: "What do you see, Jeremiah?"

"I see the branch of an almond tree," I replied.

¹²The LORD said to me, "You have seen correctly, for I am watching*a* to see that my word is fulfilled."

¹³The word of the LORD came to me again: "What do you see?"

"I see a boiling pot, tilting away from the north," I answered.

¹⁴The LORD said to me, "From the north disaster will be poured out on all who live in the land. ¹⁵I am about to summon all the peoples of the northern kingdoms," declares the LORD.

"Their kings will come and set up their thrones
in the entrance of the gates of
Jerusalem;
they will come against all her
surrounding walls
and against all the towns of Judah.
¹⁶I will pronounce my judgments on my
people
because of their wickedness in
forsaking me,
in burning incense to other gods
and in worshiping what their hands
have made.

¹⁷"Get yourself ready! Stand up and say to them whatever I command you. Do not be terrified by them, or I will terrify you

a 12 The Hebrew for watching sounds like the Hebrew for almond tree.

It's Not How You Play the Game

DAILY INSIGHT

MONDAY

Passage:
Jeremiah 1:4–9

Verse:
Jeremiah 1:5

"Life is a sport," asserts one of the most popular sport drinks in the marketplace. "Drink it up."

It should come as no surprise to you that one of the most powerful forces in our world is competition. And I admit, from the time I was a small boy, I've been a staunch competitor in this game of life. When my mother would ask me to ride my bike to the store for her, I'd ask her to time me so I could challenge my personal-best grocery run. When playing touch football in the backyard with my brothers, the only thing that mattered was who won or lost, not how we played the game. My wife will admit that her husband throws himself around the room when his favorite team loses a big game. And my children will attest to the countless made-up games we played, such as guessing the number of passing railroad cars while we waited at the signal.

Competition helps me to be my best. It keeps me from slowing down, even when I'm tired. It drives me to excel in every area. Life can be a great big game to be won.

But there is one area of my life—and yours—in which there is no need for competition. This truth comes through clearly in the words of Jeremiah's call: "Before you were born I set you apart" (1:5). In other words, God was saying to this prophet,

"You're a one of a kind, Jeremiah. I have no templates, no stencils. You can look around all you want, but you're the only man who is just like you."

Please do not miss this spellbinding truth: There is no competition in God's plan for you and me. His calling is as individualized as each person's fingerprint; it belongs to no one else.

Does this mean that before my parents had ever met, God had a specific work for me to accomplish? Yes, it does. And does this mean that I should celebrate when I see someone doing something special for God? Yes, it does. And does this mean that when people try to coerce me into walking a certain way because that's what someone else did, I should graciously challenge them? Yes, it does. And does this mean that if I want to discover the greatest joy in living, I need to take my focus away from others and tenaciously seek God's singular direction for me? Again, the answer is in the affirmative.

Jeremiah's appointment was to be a prophet. If he had stooped to be a mighty king, he would have lived with deep regret. What has God called you to? Whatever it is, it's all yours. There's no winning or losing in this game ... there's only obedience.

For your next devotional reading, go to page 817.

before them. [18]Today I have made you a fortified city, an iron pillar and a bronze wall to stand against the whole land— against the kings of Judah, its officials, its priests and the people of the land. [19]They will fight against you but will not overcome you, for I am with you and will rescue you," declares the LORD.

Israel Forsakes God

2 The word of the LORD came to me: [2]"Go and proclaim in the hearing of Jerusalem:

" 'I remember the devotion of your
        youth,
    how as a bride you loved me
and followed me through the desert,
    through a land not sown.
[3]Israel was holy to the LORD,
    the firstfruits of his harvest;
all who devoured her were held guilty,
    and disaster overtook them,' "
                    declares the LORD.

[4]Hear the word of the LORD, O house of
        Jacob,
    all you clans of the house of Israel.

Absolutely Stupid Diplomacy

DAILY INSIGHT

TUESDAY

Passage:
Jeremiah 2:4–9

Verse:
Jeremiah 2:9

The battle is heating up. What had begun as an inconsequential skirmish is quickly becoming the pivotal confrontation of the entire war. The commanding officer calls his faithful forces together. "Troops," he says in a gentle voice, "I want you to know that I really appreciate you. I also want you to know that all I expect from you now is a good solid effort. If you get tired of fighting, just lay back, put your combat boots up and take a little siesta. You deserve it."

It's fourth and goal in the last quarter of the championship game. It has been a mighty defensive battle to this point, and the crowd is at a fever pitch. Now the head coach has called for his final time-out. Although not his usual style, the coach strides onto the field and calls his team together for one last huddle. "Guys," the coach says, "you've all worked very hard this afternoon, and I think that's great. We're in a tight spot, but you can do whatever you want on this last play. Who wants to make a suggestion?"

Your child is about to ride into life-threatening danger. The street-ward slope of your driveway has drawn her little tricycle toward the path of a car speeding down the road in her direction. As you watch from your front porch, you call out, "Yoo hoo, Honey. How many times does Daddy need to tell you? Please turn yourself around right now. Don't make me come out there and get you."

Israel's brazen disobedience had grown to unthinkable dimensions. So God called Jeremiah to confront the people, to tell them that their sinfulness would lead to certain peril. "Okay, you guys," Jeremiah began, "I know that it's Monday and some of you have had a tough weekend, but ..."

Of course, Jeremiah did no such thing. He examined God's words, took a deep breath, and told his wayward people the unvarnished truth. "You came and defiled my land and made my inheritance detestable .... I bring charges against you ... and ... against your children's children." Jeremiah didn't mince his words. How could he? This was no time for diplomacy.

Would any commanding officer, head football coach, or father react as portrayed in the above scenarios? Hardly. Neither could Jeremiah afford to be courteous. "I understand," you might be saying. "Drastic times call for drastic measures." And, of course, you'd be right.

As a dad, you know that some situations call for kindness, gentleness and tact, while others call for loving but unwavering confrontation. Sometimes your love for your family calls you to courtesy, and sometimes it calls you radical action. Carefully assess each situation. Ask God for wisdom. Then do what's appropriate. It could save someone's life.

For your next devotional reading, go to page 820.

⁵This is what the LORD says:

"What fault did your fathers find in me,
    that they strayed so far from me?
They followed worthless idols
    and became worthless themselves.
⁶They did not ask, 'Where is the LORD,
    who brought us up out of Egypt
and led us through the barren
        wilderness,
    through a land of deserts and rifts,
a land of drought and darkness,ᵃ
    a land where no one travels and no
        one lives?'
⁷I brought you into a fertile land
    to eat its fruit and rich produce.
But you came and defiled my land
    and made my inheritance detestable.
⁸The priests did not ask,
    'Where is the LORD?'
Those who deal with the law did not
        know me;
    the leaders rebelled against me.
The prophets prophesied by Baal,
    following worthless idols.

⁹"Therefore I bring charges against you
        again,"
                declares the LORD.
    "And I will bring charges against your
        children's children.
¹⁰Cross over to the coasts of Kittimᵇ and
        look,
    send to Kedarᶜ and observe closely;
    see if there has ever been anything
        like this:
¹¹Has a nation ever changed its gods?
    (Yet they are not gods at all.)
But my people have exchanged theirᵈ
        Glory
    for worthless idols.
¹²Be appalled at this, O heavens,
    and shudder with great horror,"
                declares the LORD.
¹³"My people have committed two sins:
They have forsaken me,
    the spring of living water,
and have dug their own cisterns,
    broken cisterns that cannot hold
        water.
¹⁴Is Israel a servant, a slave by birth?
    Why then has he become plunder?
¹⁵Lions have roared;
    they have growled at him.
They have laid waste his land;
    his towns are burned and deserted.
¹⁶Also, the men of Memphisᵉ and
        Tahpanhes
    have shaved the crown of your head.ᶠ
¹⁷Have you not brought this on
        yourselves

by forsaking the LORD your God
    when he led you in the way?
¹⁸Now why go to Egypt
    to drink water from the Shihorᵍ?
And why go to Assyria
    to drink water from the Riverʰ?
¹⁹Your wickedness will punish you;
    your backsliding will rebuke you.
Consider then and realize
    how evil and bitter it is for you
when you forsake the LORD your God
    and have no awe of me,"
                declares the Lord,
                the LORD Almighty.

²⁰"Long ago you broke off your yoke
    and tore off your bonds;
    you said, 'I will not serve you!'
Indeed, on every high hill
    and under every spreading tree
    you lay down as a prostitute.
²¹I had planted you like a choice vine
    of sound and reliable stock.
How then did you turn against me
    into a corrupt, wild vine?
²²Although you wash yourself with soda
    and use an abundance of soap,
    the stain of your guilt is still before
        me,"
                declares the Sovereign LORD.
²³"How can you say, 'I am not defiled;
    I have not run after the Baals'?
See how you behaved in the valley;
    consider what you have done.
You are a swift she-camel
    running here and there,
²⁴a wild donkey accustomed to the
        desert,
    sniffing the wind in her craving—
    in her heat who can restrain her?
Any males that pursue her need not tire
        themselves;
    at mating time they will find her.
²⁵Do not run until your feet are bare
    and your throat is dry.
But you said, 'It's no use!
    I love foreign gods,
    and I must go after them.'

²⁶"As a thief is disgraced when he is
        caught,
    so the house of Israel is disgraced—
they, their kings and their officials,
    their priests and their prophets.

ᵃ6 Or *and the shadow of death*   ᵇ10 That is, Cyprus
and western coastlands   ᶜ10 The home of Bedouin
tribes in the Syro-Arabian desert   ᵈ11 Masoretic
Text; an ancient Hebrew scribal tradition *my*
ᵉ16 Hebrew *Noph*   ᶠ16 Or *have cracked your skull*
ᵍ18 That is, a branch of the Nile   ʰ18 That is, the
Euphrates

²⁷They say to wood, 'You are my father,'
and to stone, 'You gave me birth.'
They have turned their backs to me
and not their faces;
yet when they are in trouble, they say,
'Come and save us!'
²⁸Where then are the gods you made for
yourselves?
Let them come if they can save you
when you are in trouble!
For you have as many gods
as you have towns, O Judah.

²⁹"Why do you bring charges against me?
You have all rebelled against me,"
declares the LORD.
³⁰"In vain I punished your people;
they did not respond to correction.
Your sword has devoured your prophets
like a ravening lion.

³¹"You of this generation, consider the
word of the LORD:

"Have I been a desert to Israel
or a land of great darkness?
Why do my people say, 'We are free to
roam;
we will come to you no more'?
³²Does a maiden forget her jewelry,
a bride her wedding ornaments?
Yet my people have forgotten me,
days without number.
³³How skilled you are at pursuing love!
Even the worst of women can learn
from your ways.
³⁴On your clothes men find
the lifeblood of the innocent poor,
though you did not catch them
breaking in.
Yet in spite of all this
³⁵ you say, 'I am innocent;
he is not angry with me.'
But I will pass judgment on you
because you say, 'I have not sinned.'
³⁶Why do you go about so much,
changing your ways?
You will be disappointed by Egypt
as you were by Assyria.
³⁷You will also leave that place
with your hands on your head,
for the LORD has rejected those you
trust;
you will not be helped by them.

3 "If a man divorces his wife
and she leaves him and marries
another man,
should he return to her again?
Would not the land be completely
defiled?

But you have lived as a prostitute with
many lovers—
would you now return to me?"
declares the LORD.
²"Look up to the barren heights and see.
Is there any place where you have
not been ravished?
By the roadside you sat waiting for
lovers,
sat like a nomad^a in the desert.
You have defiled the land
with your prostitution and
wickedness.
³Therefore the showers have been
withheld,
and no spring rains have fallen.
Yet you have the brazen look of a
prostitute;
you refuse to blush with shame.
⁴Have you not just called to me:
'My Father, my friend from my youth,
⁵will you always be angry?
Will your wrath continue forever?'
This is how you talk,
but you do all the evil you can."

Unfaithful Israel

⁶During the reign of King Josiah, the
LORD said to me, "Have you seen what
faithless Israel has done? She has gone
up on every high hill and under every
spreading tree and has committed adul-
tery there. ⁷I thought that after she had
done all this she would return to me but
she did not, and her unfaithful sister
Judah saw it. ⁸I gave faithless Israel her
certificate of divorce and sent her away
because of all her adulteries. Yet I saw that
her unfaithful sister Judah had no fear;
she also went out and committed adultery. ⁹Because Israel's immorality mattered so little to her, she defiled the land
and committed adultery with stone and
wood. ¹⁰In spite of all this, her unfaithful
sister Judah did not return to me with all
her heart, but only in pretense," declares
the LORD.

¹¹The LORD said to me, "Faithless Israel
is more righteous than unfaithful Judah.
¹²Go, proclaim this message toward the
north:

" 'Return, faithless Israel,' declares the
LORD,
'I will frown on you no longer,
for I am merciful,' declares the LORD,
'I will not be angry forever.
¹³Only acknowledge your guilt—

^a2 Or *an Arab*

you have rebelled against the LORD
    your God,
you have scattered your favors to
    foreign gods
    under every spreading tree,
    and have not obeyed me,' "
                    declares the LORD.

14"Return, faithless people," declares the LORD, "for I am your husband. I will choose you—one from a town and two from a clan—and bring you to Zion. **15**Then I will give you shepherds after my own heart, who will lead you with knowledge and understanding. **16**In those days,

The Talk

DAILY INSIGHT

WEDNESDAY

Passage:
Jeremiah 3:19–22

Verse:
Jeremiah 3:19

I had grown up in a no-nonsense Christian home. My parents had drilled into me the importance of honesty, godliness and clean living. I had been more protected from the storms of foolishness and rebellion than most of my friends. I had lived to this point on someone else's discipline. Someone else's conduct. Someone else's faith. Now, it was show time.

With a handful of my college friends as willing accomplices, I began to slip from the moorings of my earlier life. Lying about attending honor classes, cheating on tests and driving to Ohio to drink 3.2 percent beer were only outward symptoms of the U-turn my spirit was making. The weekly calls to my parents vanished into silence.

To this day, I do not know how my dad found out about his son's rebellion. But his radar had picked up something on the screen, and he was troubled. The Friday after Thanksgiving in 1967, as our family was enjoying the day together, my dad asked me to come to his bedroom. The sobriety and resolve in his voice and on his face were undeniable. As a small boy, a request like this would have meant a certain spanking. But as a nineteen-year-old, I towered over my father. A spanking wasn't in the cards.

In the corner of my parents' room sat a small desk on which my dad wrote checks and kept the family financials. He walked straight to his desk and sat down. I felt awkward, standing in front of my dad as he sat in his chair, appearing much shorter now than before.

"Robert," he started. "I've heard that you're living on the edge at school." I didn't speak. I didn't move. "You know," he contin-

ued, "I've been doing some thinking. I spent an awful lot of time on the road as you were growing up. I should have spent more time with you than I did. I realize that now and am very sorry about it."

I could not have predicted what was coming next, but it was a moment that indelibly burned its way into my heart, a moment I will never forget.

"Son," my dad finally said after another spell of pregnant silence, "if you'd like to come home after this semester, you can enroll in a local college. I'll quit my job, and we can catch up on some of that lost time together."

My dad was the president of a worldwide ministry. His travels took him to strategic meetings with dignitaries around the globe. But as he sat there, looking into the face of this insubordinate boy, this man loved me enough to permanently interrupt his own success. I was stunned.

Jeremiah records God's pleading with his children. "I am your Father," he seemed to be saying, "and you are my child. There isn't anything I wouldn't do for you."

My father's words that November afternoon began to melt my heart. *How can I disappoint a man who loves me like this?* I recall thinking as I trudged down the stairs to my room. *How can I voluntarily crush his soul?*

In spite of God's tender plea, Israel did not change. Tragically, their separation from their heavenly Father cost them everything. I wasn't nearly as successful in resisting my dad's love. And for that, I will be eternally grateful.

For your next devotional reading, go to page 832.

when your numbers have increased greatly in the land," declares the LORD, "men will no longer say, 'The ark of the covenant of the LORD.' It will never enter their minds or be remembered; it will not be missed, nor will another one be made. [17]At that time they will call Jerusalem The Throne of the LORD, and all nations will gather in Jerusalem to honor the name of the LORD. No longer will they follow the stubbornness of their evil hearts. [18]In those days the house of Judah will join the house of Israel, and together they will come from a northern land to the land I gave your forefathers as an inheritance.

[19]"I myself said,

" 'How gladly would I treat you like
    sons
  and give you a desirable land,
  the most beautiful inheritance of any
    nation.'
I thought you would call me 'Father'
  and not turn away from following
    me.
[20]But like a woman unfaithful to her
    husband,
  so you have been unfaithful to me,
    O house of Israel,"
                  declares the LORD.

[21]A cry is heard on the barren heights,
  the weeping and pleading of the
    people of Israel,
because they have perverted their
    ways
  and have forgotten the LORD their
    God.

[22]"Return, faithless people;
  I will cure you of backsliding."

"Yes, we will come to you,
  for you are the LORD our God.
[23]Surely the idolatrous commotion on
    the hills
  and mountains is a deception;
surely in the LORD our God
  is the salvation of Israel.
[24]From our youth shameful gods have
    consumed
  the fruits of our fathers' labor—
  their flocks and herds,
  their sons and daughters.
[25]Let us lie down in our shame,
  and let our disgrace cover us.
We have sinned against the LORD our
    God,
  both we and our fathers;
from our youth till this day
  we have not obeyed the LORD our
    God."

4 "If you will return, O Israel,
  return to me,"
                  declares the LORD.
"If you put your detestable idols out of
    my sight
  and no longer go astray,
[2]and if in a truthful, just and righteous
    way
  you swear, 'As surely as the LORD
    lives,'
then the nations will be blessed by him
  and in him they will glory."

[3]This is what the LORD says to the men of Judah and to Jerusalem:

"Break up your unplowed ground
  and do not sow among thorns.
[4]Circumcise yourselves to the LORD,
  circumcise your hearts,
  you men of Judah and people of
    Jerusalem,
or my wrath will break out and burn
    like fire
  because of the evil you have done—
  burn with no one to quench it.

Disaster From the North

[5]"Announce in Judah and proclaim in
    Jerusalem and say:
  'Sound the trumpet throughout the
    land!'
Cry aloud and say:
  'Gather together!
  Let us flee to the fortified cities!'
[6]Raise the signal to go to Zion!
  Flee for safety without delay!
For I am bringing disaster from the
    north,
  even terrible destruction."

[7]A lion has come out of his lair;
  a destroyer of nations has set out.
He has left his place
  to lay waste your land.
Your towns will lie in ruins
  without inhabitant.
[8]So put on sackcloth,
  lament and wail,
for the fierce anger of the LORD
  has not turned away from us.

[9]"In that day," declares the LORD,
  "the king and the officials will lose
    heart,
the priests will be horrified,
  and the prophets will be appalled."

[10]Then I said, "Ah, Sovereign LORD, how completely you have deceived this people and Jerusalem by saying, 'You will have peace,' when the sword is at our throats."

¹¹At that time this people and Jerusalem will be told, "A scorching wind from the barren heights in the desert blows toward my people, but not to winnow or cleanse; ¹²a wind too strong for that comes from me.ᵃ Now I pronounce my judgments against them."

¹³Look! He advances like the clouds,
    his chariots come like a whirlwind,
his horses are swifter than eagles.
    Woe to us! We are ruined!
¹⁴O Jerusalem, wash the evil from your
        heart and be saved.
    How long will you harbor wicked
        thoughts?
¹⁵A voice is announcing from Dan,
    proclaiming disaster from the hills of
        Ephraim.
¹⁶"Tell this to the nations,
    proclaim it to Jerusalem:
'A besieging army is coming from a
        distant land,
    raising a war cry against the cities of
        Judah.
¹⁷They surround her like men guarding a
        field,
    because she has rebelled against
        me,' "
                    declares the LORD.
¹⁸"Your own conduct and actions
    have brought this upon you.
This is your punishment.
    How bitter it is!
    How it pierces to the heart!"

¹⁹Oh, my anguish, my anguish!
    I writhe in pain.
Oh, the agony of my heart!
    My heart pounds within me,
    I cannot keep silent.
For I have heard the sound of the
        trumpet;
    I have heard the battle cry.
²⁰Disaster follows disaster;
    the whole land lies in ruins.
In an instant my tents are destroyed,
    my shelter in a moment.
²¹How long must I see the battle
        standard
    and hear the sound of the trumpet?

²²"My people are fools;
    they do not know me.
They are senseless children;
    they have no understanding.
They are skilled in doing evil;
    they know not how to do good."

²³I looked at the earth,
    and it was formless and empty;
and at the heavens,
    and their light was gone.
²⁴I looked at the mountains,
    and they were quaking;
    all the hills were swaying.
²⁵I looked, and there were no people;
    every bird in the sky had flown away.
²⁶I looked, and the fruitful land was a
        desert;
    all its towns lay in ruins
    before the LORD, before his fierce
        anger.

²⁷This is what the LORD says:

"The whole land will be ruined,
    though I will not destroy it
        completely.
²⁸Therefore the earth will mourn
    and the heavens above grow dark,
because I have spoken and will not
        relent,
    I have decided and will not turn
        back."

²⁹At the sound of horsemen and archers
    every town takes to flight.
Some go into the thickets;
    some climb up among the rocks.
All the towns are deserted;
    no one lives in them.

³⁰What are you doing, O devastated one?
    Why dress yourself in scarlet
    and put on jewels of gold?
Why shade your eyes with paint?
    You adorn yourself in vain.
Your lovers despise you;
    they seek your life.

³¹I hear a cry as of a woman in labor,
    a groan as of one bearing her first
        child—
the cry of the Daughter of Zion gasping
        for breath,
    stretching out her hands and saying,
"Alas! I am fainting;
    my life is given over to murderers."

Not One Is Upright

5 "Go up and down the streets of
        Jerusalem,
    look around and consider,
    search through her squares.
If you can find but one person
    who deals honestly and seeks the
        truth,
    I will forgive this city.
²Although they say, 'As surely as the
        LORD lives,'
    still they are swearing falsely."

ᵃ12 Or comes at my command

³O LORD, do not your eyes look for truth?
    You struck them, but they felt no
        pain;
    you crushed them, but they refused
        correction.
They made their faces harder than
        stone
    and refused to repent.
⁴I thought, "These are only the poor;
    they are foolish,
for they do not know the way of the
        LORD,
    the requirements of their God.
⁵So I will go to the leaders
    and speak to them;
surely they know the way of the LORD,
    the requirements of their God."
But with one accord they too had
        broken off the yoke
    and torn off the bonds.
⁶Therefore a lion from the forest will
        attack them,
    a wolf from the desert will ravage
        them,
a leopard will lie in wait near their
        towns
    to tear to pieces any who venture
        out,
for their rebellion is great
    and their backslidings many.

⁷"Why should I forgive you?
    Your children have forsaken me
    and sworn by gods that are not gods.
I supplied all their needs,
    yet they committed adultery
    and thronged to the houses of
        prostitutes.
⁸They are well-fed, lusty stallions,
    each neighing for another man's
        wife.
⁹Should I not punish them for this?"
    declares the LORD.
"Should I not avenge myself
    on such a nation as this?

¹⁰"Go through her vineyards and ravage
        them,
    but do not destroy them completely.
Strip off her branches,
    for these people do not belong to the
        LORD.
¹¹The house of Israel and the house of
        Judah
    have been utterly unfaithful to me,"
                    declares the LORD.

¹²They have lied about the LORD;
    they said, "He will do nothing!
No harm will come to us;
    we will never see sword or famine.
¹³The prophets are but wind
    and the word is not in them;
    so let what they say be done to
        them."

¹⁴Therefore this is what the LORD God
Almighty says:

"Because the people have spoken these
        words,
    I will make my words in your mouth
        a fire
    and these people the wood it
        consumes.
¹⁵O house of Israel," declares the LORD,
    "I am bringing a distant nation
        against you—
an ancient and enduring nation,
    a people whose language you do not
        know,
    whose speech you do not
        understand.
¹⁶Their quivers are like an open grave;
    all of them are mighty warriors.
¹⁷They will devour your harvests and
        food,
    devour your sons and daughters;
    they will devour your flocks and herds,
        devour your vines and fig trees.
With the sword they will destroy
    the fortified cities in which you trust.

¹⁸"Yet even in those days," declares the
LORD, "I will not destroy you completely.
¹⁹And when the people ask, 'Why has the
LORD our God done all this to us?' you will
tell them, 'As you have forsaken me and
served foreign gods in your own land, so
now you will serve foreigners in a land not
your own.'

²⁰"Announce this to the house of Jacob
    and proclaim it in Judah:
²¹Hear this, you foolish and senseless
        people,
    who have eyes but do not see,
    who have ears but do not hear:
²²Should you not fear me?" declares the
        LORD.
"Should you not tremble in my
        presence?
I made the sand a boundary for the sea,
    an everlasting barrier it cannot cross.
The waves may roll, but they cannot
        prevail;
    they may roar, but they cannot cross
        it.
²³But these people have stubborn and
        rebellious hearts;
    they have turned aside and gone
        away.
²⁴They do not say to themselves,

'Let us fear the LORD our God,
who gives autumn and spring rains in
  season,
who assures us of the regular weeks
  of harvest.'
[25] Your wrongdoings have kept these
  away;
your sins have deprived you of good.

[26] "Among my people are wicked men
who lie in wait like men who snare
  birds
and like those who set traps to catch
  men.
[27] Like cages full of birds,
their houses are full of deceit;
they have become rich and powerful
[28]   and have grown fat and sleek.
Their evil deeds have no limit;
they do not plead the case of the
  fatherless to win it,
they do not defend the rights of the
  poor.
[29] Should I not punish them for this?"
  declares the LORD.
"Should I not avenge myself
on such a nation as this?

[30] "A horrible and shocking thing
has happened in the land:
[31] The prophets prophesy lies,
the priests rule by their own authority,
and my people love it this way.
But what will you do in the end?

Jerusalem Under Siege

6 "Flee for safety, people of Benjamin!
  Flee from Jerusalem!
Sound the trumpet in Tekoa!
  Raise the signal over Beth Hakkerem!
For disaster looms out of the north,
  even terrible destruction.
[2] I will destroy the Daughter of Zion,
  so beautiful and delicate.
[3] Shepherds with their flocks will come
  against her;
they will pitch their tents around her,
  each tending his own portion."

[4] "Prepare for battle against her!
  Arise, let us attack at noon!
But, alas, the daylight is fading,
  and the shadows of evening grow
  long.
[5] So arise, let us attack at night
  and destroy her fortresses!"

[6] This is what the LORD Almighty says:

"Cut down the trees
  and build siege ramps against
  Jerusalem.

This city must be punished;
  it is filled with oppression.
[7] As a well pours out its water,
  so she pours out her wickedness.
Violence and destruction resound in
  her;
her sickness and wounds are ever
  before me.
[8] Take warning, O Jerusalem,
  or I will turn away from you
and make your land desolate
  so no one can live in it."

[9] This is what the LORD Almighty says:

"Let them glean the remnant of Israel
  as thoroughly as a vine;
pass your hand over the branches
  again,
like one gathering grapes."

[10] To whom can I speak and give
  warning?
Who will listen to me?
Their ears are closed[a]
  so they cannot hear.
The word of the LORD is offensive to
  them;
they find no pleasure in it.
[11] But I am full of the wrath of the LORD,
  and I cannot hold it in.

"Pour it out on the children in the
  street
and on the young men gathered
  together;
both husband and wife will be caught
  in it,
and the old, those weighed down
  with years.
[12] Their houses will be turned over to
  others,
together with their fields and their
  wives,
when I stretch out my hand
  against those who live in the land,"
                            declares the LORD.
[13] "From the least to the greatest,
  all are greedy for gain;
prophets and priests alike,
  all practice deceit.
[14] They dress the wound of my people
  as though it were not serious.
'Peace, peace,' they say,
  when there is no peace.
[15] Are they ashamed of their loathsome
  conduct?
No, they have no shame at all;
  they do not even know how to blush.
So they will fall among the fallen;

---

[a] 10 Hebrew *uncircumcised*

they will be brought down when I
    punish them,"
                                    says the LORD.

¹⁶ This is what the LORD says:

"Stand at the crossroads and look;
    ask for the ancient paths,
ask where the good way is, and walk in
        it,
    and you will find rest for your souls.
    But you said, 'We will not walk in it.'
¹⁷ I appointed watchmen over you and
        said,
    'Listen to the sound of the trumpet!'
    But you said, 'We will not listen.'
¹⁸ Therefore hear, O nations;
    observe, O witnesses,
    what will happen to them.
¹⁹ Hear, O earth:
I am bringing disaster on this people,
    the fruit of their schemes,
because they have not listened to my
        words
    and have rejected my law.
²⁰ What do I care about incense from
        Sheba
    or sweet calamus from a distant
        land?
Your burnt offerings are not
        acceptable;
    your sacrifices do not please me."

²¹ Therefore this is what the LORD says:

"I will put obstacles before this people.
Fathers and sons alike will stumble
        over them;
    neighbors and friends will perish."

²² This is what the LORD says:

"Look, an army is coming
    from the land of the north;
a great nation is being stirred up
    from the ends of the earth.
²³ They are armed with bow and spear;
    they are cruel and show no mercy.
They sound like the roaring sea
    as they ride on their horses;
they come like men in battle formation
    to attack you, O Daughter of Zion."

²⁴ We have heard reports about them,
    and our hands hang limp.
Anguish has gripped us,
    pain like that of a woman in labor.
²⁵ Do not go out to the fields
    or walk on the roads,
for the enemy has a sword,
    and there is terror on every side.
²⁶ O my people, put on sackcloth
    and roll in ashes;

mourn with bitter wailing
    as for an only son,
for suddenly the destroyer
    will come upon us.

²⁷ "I have made you a tester of metals
    and my people the ore,
that you may observe
    and test their ways.
²⁸ They are all hardened rebels,
    going about to slander.
They are bronze and iron;
    they all act corruptly.
²⁹ The bellows blow fiercely
    to burn away the lead with fire,
but the refining goes on in vain;
    the wicked are not purged out.
³⁰ They are called rejected silver,
    because the LORD has rejected
        them."

False Religion Worthless

7 This is the word that came to Jeremiah
from the LORD: ²"Stand at the gate of
the LORD's house and there proclaim this
message:

" 'Hear the word of the LORD, all you
people of Judah who come through these
gates to worship the LORD. ³This is what
the LORD Almighty, the God of Israel, says:
Reform your ways and your actions, and
I will let you live in this place. ⁴Do not
trust in deceptive words and say, "This is
the temple of the LORD, the temple of the
LORD, the temple of the LORD!" ⁵If you
really change your ways and your actions
and deal with each other justly, ⁶if you do
not oppress the alien, the fatherless or the
widow and do not shed innocent blood in
this place, and if you do not follow other
gods to your own harm, ⁷then I will let you
live in this place, in the land I gave your
forefathers for ever and ever. ⁸But look,
you are trusting in deceptive words that
are worthless.

⁹" 'Will you steal and murder, commit
adultery and perjury,^a burn incense to
Baal and follow other gods you have not
known, ¹⁰and then come and stand before
me in this house, which bears my Name,
and say, "We are safe"—safe to do all these
detestable things? ¹¹Has this house, which
bears my Name, become a den of robbers
to you? But I have been watching! declares the LORD.

¹²" 'Go now to the place in Shiloh where
I first made a dwelling for my Name,
and see what I did to it because of the

^a9 Or *and swear by false gods*

wickedness of my people Israel. ¹³While you were doing all these things, declares the LORD, I spoke to you again and again, but you did not listen; I called you, but you did not answer. ¹⁴Therefore, what I did to Shiloh I will now do to the house that bears my Name, the temple you trust in, the place I gave to you and your fathers. ¹⁵I will thrust you from my presence, just as I did all your brothers, the people of Ephraim.'

¹⁶"So do not pray for this people nor offer any plea or petition for them; do not plead with me, for I will not listen to you. ¹⁷Do you not see what they are doing in the towns of Judah and in the streets of Jerusalem? ¹⁸The children gather wood, the fathers light the fire, and the women knead the dough and make cakes of bread for the Queen of Heaven. They pour out drink offerings to other gods to provoke me to anger. ¹⁹But am I the one they are provoking? declares the LORD. Are they not rather harming themselves, to their own shame?

²⁰"'Therefore this is what the Sovereign LORD says: My anger and my wrath will be poured out on this place, on man and beast, on the trees of the field and on the fruit of the ground, and it will burn and not be quenched.'

²¹"'This is what the LORD Almighty, the God of Israel, says: Go ahead, add your burnt offerings to your other sacrifices and eat the meat yourselves! ²²For when I brought your forefathers out of Egypt and spoke to them, I did not just give them commands about burnt offerings and sacrifices, ²³but I gave them this command: Obey me, and I will be your God and you will be my people. Walk in all the ways I command you, that it may go well with you. ²⁴But they did not listen or pay attention; instead, they followed the stubborn inclinations of their evil hearts. They went backward and not forward. ²⁵From the time your forefathers left Egypt until now, day after day, again and again I sent you my servants the prophets. ²⁶But they did not listen to me or pay attention. They were stiff-necked and did more evil than their forefathers.'

²⁷"When you tell them all this, they will not listen to you; when you call to them, they will not answer. ²⁸Therefore say to them, 'This is the nation that has not obeyed the LORD its God or responded to correction. Truth has perished; it has vanished from their lips. ²⁹Cut off your hair and throw it away; take up a lament on the barren heights, for the LORD has re-

jected and abandoned this generation that is under his wrath.

The Valley of Slaughter

³⁰"'The people of Judah have done evil in my eyes, declares the LORD. They have set up their detestable idols in the house that bears my Name and have defiled it. ³¹They have built the high places of Topheth in the Valley of Ben Hinnom to burn their sons and daughters in the fire—something I did not command, nor did it enter my mind. ³²So beware, the days are coming, declares the LORD, when people will no longer call it Topheth or the Valley of Ben Hinnom, but the Valley of Slaughter, for they will bury the dead in Topheth until there is no more room. ³³Then the carcasses of this people will become food for the birds of the air and the beasts of the earth, and there will be no one to frighten them away. ³⁴I will bring an end to the sounds of joy and gladness and to the voices of bride and bridegroom in the towns of Judah and the streets of Jerusalem, for the land will become desolate.

8 "'At that time, declares the LORD, the bones of the kings and officials of Judah, the bones of the priests and prophets, and the bones of the people of Jerusalem will be removed from their graves. ²They will be exposed to the sun and the moon and all the stars of the heavens, which they have loved and served and which they have followed and consulted and worshiped. They will not be gathered up or buried, but will be like refuse lying on the ground. ³Wherever I banish them, all the survivors of this evil nation will prefer death to life, declares the LORD Almighty.'

Sin and Punishment

⁴"Say to them, 'This is what the LORD says:

" 'When men fall down, do they not get
     up?
  When a man turns away, does he not
     return?
⁵ Why then have these people turned
     away?
  Why does Jerusalem always turn
     away?
They cling to deceit;
  they refuse to return.
⁶ I have listened attentively,
  but they do not say what is right.

No one repents of his wickedness,
    saying, "What have I done?"
Each pursues his own course
    like a horse charging into battle.
[7] Even the stork in the sky
    knows her appointed seasons,
and the dove, the swift and the thrush
    observe the time of their migration.
But my people do not know
    the requirements of the LORD.

[8] " 'How can you say, "We are wise,
    for we have the law of the LORD,"
when actually the lying pen of the
       scribes
    has handled it falsely?
[9] The wise will be put to shame;
    they will be dismayed and trapped.
Since they have rejected the word of
       the LORD,
    what kind of wisdom do they have?
[10] Therefore I will give their wives to
       other men
    and their fields to new owners.
From the least to the greatest,
    all are greedy for gain;
prophets and priests alike,
    all practice deceit.
[11] They dress the wound of my people
    as though it were not serious.
"Peace, peace," they say,
    when there is no peace.
[12] Are they ashamed of their loathsome
       conduct?
    No, they have no shame at all;
    they do not even know how to blush.
So they will fall among the fallen;
    they will be brought down when they
       are punished,
          says the LORD.

[13] " 'I will take away their harvest,
          declares the LORD.
    There will be no grapes on the vine.
There will be no figs on the tree,
    and their leaves will wither.
What I have given them
    will be taken from them.[a]' "

[14] "Why are we sitting here?
    Gather together!
Let us flee to the fortified cities
    and perish there!
For the LORD our God has doomed us
       to perish
    and given us poisoned water to
       drink,
    because we have sinned against him.
[15] We hoped for peace
    but no good has come,
for a time of healing
    but there was only terror.
[16] The snorting of the enemy's horses
    is heard from Dan;
at the neighing of their stallions
    the whole land trembles.
They have come to devour
    the land and everything in it,
    the city and all who live there."

[17] "See, I will send venomous snakes
       among you,
    vipers that cannot be charmed,
    and they will bite you,"
          declares the LORD.

[18] O my Comforter[b] in sorrow,
    my heart is faint within me.
[19] Listen to the cry of my people
    from a land far away:
"Is the LORD not in Zion?
    Is her King no longer there?"

"Why have they provoked me to anger
       with their images,
    with their worthless foreign idols?"

[20] "The harvest is past,
    the summer has ended,
    and we are not saved."

[21] Since my people are crushed, I am
       crushed;
    I mourn, and horror grips me.
[22] Is there no balm in Gilead?
    Is there no physician there?
Why then is there no healing
    for the wound of my people?

9 [1] Oh, that my head were a spring of
       water
    and my eyes a fountain of tears!
I would weep day and night
    for the slain of my people.
[2] Oh, that I had in the desert
    a lodging place for travelers,
so that I might leave my people
    and go away from them;
for they are all adulterers,
    a crowd of unfaithful people.

[3] "They make ready their tongue
    like a bow, to shoot lies;
it is not by truth
    that they triumph[c] in the land.
They go from one sin to another;
    they do not acknowledge me,"
          declares the LORD.
[4] "Beware of your friends;
    do not trust your brothers.
For every brother is a deceiver,[d]

---

[a]13 The meaning of the Hebrew for this sentence is
uncertain.   [b]18 The meaning of the Hebrew for
this word is uncertain.   [c]3 Or lies; / they are not
valiant for truth   [d]4 Or a deceiving Jacob

and every friend a slanderer.
⁵Friend deceives friend,
     and no one speaks the truth.
They have taught their tongues to lie;
     they weary themselves with sinning.
⁶You[a] live in the midst of deception;
     in their deceit they refuse to
          acknowledge me,"
                              declares the LORD.

⁷Therefore this is what the LORD Almighty says:

"See, I will refine and test them,
     for what else can I do
because of the sin of my people?
⁸Their tongue is a deadly arrow;
     it speaks with deceit.
With his mouth each speaks cordially
          to his neighbor,
     but in his heart he sets a trap for
          him.
⁹Should I not punish them for this?"
          declares the LORD.
"Should I not avenge myself
     on such a nation as this?"

¹⁰I will weep and wail for the mountains
          and take up a lament concerning the
               desert pastures.
They are desolate and untraveled,
     and the lowing of cattle is not
          heard.
The birds of the air have fled
     and the animals are gone.

¹¹"I will make Jerusalem a heap of
          ruins,
     a haunt of jackals;
and I will lay waste the towns of Judah
     so no one can live there."

¹²What man is wise enough to understand this? Who has been instructed by the LORD and can explain it? Why has the land been ruined and laid waste like a desert that no one can cross?

¹³The LORD said, "It is because they have forsaken my law, which I set before them; they have not obeyed me or followed my law. ¹⁴Instead, they have followed the stubbornness of their hearts; they have followed the Baals, as their fathers taught them." ¹⁵Therefore, this is what the LORD Almighty, the God of Israel, says: "See, I will make this people eat bitter food and drink poisoned water. ¹⁶I will scatter them among nations that neither they nor their fathers have known, and I will pursue them with the sword until I have destroyed them."

¹⁷This is what the LORD Almighty says:

"Consider now! Call for the wailing
          women to come;
     send for the most skillful of them.
¹⁸Let them come quickly
     and wail over us
till our eyes overflow with tears
     and water streams from our
          eyelids.
¹⁹The sound of wailing is heard from
          Zion;
     'How ruined we are!
     How great is our shame!
We must leave our land
     because our houses are in ruins.' "

²⁰Now, O women, hear the word of the
          LORD;
     open your ears to the words of his
          mouth.
Teach your daughters how to wail;
     teach one another a lament.
²¹Death has climbed in through our
          windows
     and has entered our fortresses;
it has cut off the children from the
          streets
     and the young men from the public
          squares.

²²Say, "This is what the LORD declares:

" 'The dead bodies of men will lie
     like refuse on the open field,
like cut grain behind the reaper,
     with no one to gather them.' "

²³This is what the LORD says:

"Let not the wise man boast of his
          wisdom
     or the strong man boast of his
          strength
     or the rich man boast of his riches,
²⁴but let him who boasts boast about
          this:
     that he understands and knows me,
that I am the LORD, who exercises
          kindness,
     justice and righteousness on earth,
     for in these I delight,"
                              declares the LORD.

²⁵"The days are coming," declares the LORD, "when I will punish all who are circumcised only in the flesh— ²⁶Egypt, Judah, Edom, Ammon, Moab and all who live in the desert in distant places.[b] For all these nations are really uncircumcised, and even the whole house of Israel is uncircumcised in heart."

---

[a]6 That is, Jeremiah (the Hebrew is singular)
[b]26 Or *desert and who clip the hair by their foreheads*

God and Idols

10 Hear what the LORD says to you, O house of Israel. ²This is what the LORD says:

"Do not learn the ways of the nations
    or be terrified by signs in the sky,
    though the nations are terrified by
        them.
³For the customs of the peoples are
        worthless;
    they cut a tree out of the forest,
    and a craftsman shapes it with his
        chisel.
⁴They adorn it with silver and gold;
    they fasten it with hammer and nails
    so it will not totter.
⁵Like a scarecrow in a melon patch,
    their idols cannot speak;
they must be carried
    because they cannot walk.
Do not fear them;
    they can do no harm
    nor can they do any good."

⁶No one is like you, O LORD;
    you are great,
    and your name is mighty in power.
⁷Who should not revere you,
    O King of the nations?
    This is your due.
Among all the wise men of the nations
    and in all their kingdoms,
    there is no one like you.
⁸They are all senseless and foolish;
    they are taught by worthless wooden
        idols.
⁹Hammered silver is brought from
        Tarshish
    and gold from Uphaz.
What the craftsman and goldsmith
        have made
    is then dressed in blue and purple—
    all made by skilled workers.
¹⁰But the LORD is the true God;
    he is the living God, the eternal
        King.
When he is angry, the earth trembles;
    the nations cannot endure his wrath.

¹¹"Tell them this: 'These gods, who did not make the heavens and the earth, will perish from the earth and from under the heavens.'"[a]

¹²But God made the earth by his power;
    he founded the world by his wisdom
    and stretched out the heavens by his
        understanding.
¹³When he thunders, the waters in the
        heavens roar;

he makes clouds rise from the ends of
        the earth.
He sends lightning with the rain
    and brings out the wind from his
        storehouses.

¹⁴Everyone is senseless and without
        knowledge;
    every goldsmith is shamed by his
        idols.
His images are a fraud;
    they have no breath in them.
¹⁵They are worthless, the objects of
        mockery;
    when their judgment comes, they
        will perish.
¹⁶He who is the Portion of Jacob is not
        like these,
    for he is the Maker of all things,
including Israel, the tribe of his
        inheritance—
    the LORD Almighty is his name.

Coming Destruction

¹⁷Gather up your belongings to leave the
        land,
    you who live under siege.
¹⁸For this is what the LORD says:
    "At this time I will hurl out
        those who live in this land;
    I will bring distress on them
        so that they may be captured."

¹⁹Woe to me because of my injury!
    My wound is incurable!
Yet I said to myself,
    "This is my sickness, and I must
        endure it."
²⁰My tent is destroyed;
    all its ropes are snapped.
My sons are gone from me and are no
        more;
    no one is left now to pitch my tent
    or to set up my shelter.
²¹The shepherds are senseless
    and do not inquire of the LORD;
so they do not prosper
    and all their flock is scattered.
²²Listen! The report is coming—
    a great commotion from the land of
        the north!
It will make the towns of Judah
        desolate,
    a haunt of jackals.

Jeremiah's Prayer

²³I know, O LORD, that a man's life is not
        his own;

---

a11 The text of this verse is in Aramaic.

it is not for man to direct his steps.
²⁴ Correct me, LORD, but only with
     justice—
not in your anger,
     lest you reduce me to nothing.
²⁵ Pour out your wrath on the nations
     that do not acknowledge you,
     on the peoples who do not call on
          your name.
For they have devoured Jacob;
     they have devoured him completely
     and destroyed his homeland.

The Covenant Is Broken

11 This is the word that came to Jeremiah
from the LORD: ²"Listen to the terms of
this covenant and tell them to the people
of Judah and to those who live in Jerusalem. ³Tell them that this is what the LORD,
the God of Israel, says: 'Cursed is the man
who does not obey the terms of this covenant— ⁴the terms I commanded your
forefathers when I brought them out of
Egypt, out of the iron-smelting furnace.' I
said, 'Obey me and do everything I command you, and you will be my people, and
I will be your God. ⁵Then I will fulfill the
oath I swore to your forefathers, to give
them a land flowing with milk and
honey'—the land you possess today."
     I answered, "Amen, LORD."
     ⁶The LORD said to me, "Proclaim all
these words in the towns of Judah and in
the streets of Jerusalem: 'Listen to the
terms of this covenant and follow them.
⁷From the time I brought your forefathers
up from Egypt until today, I warned them
again and again, saying, "Obey me." ⁸But
they did not listen or pay attention; instead, they followed the stubbornness of
their evil hearts. So I brought on them all
the curses of the covenant I had commanded them to follow but that they did
not keep.' "
     ⁹Then the LORD said to me, "There is a
conspiracy among the people of Judah
and those who live in Jerusalem. ¹⁰They
have returned to the sins of their forefathers, who refused to listen to my words.
They have followed other gods to serve
them. Both the house of Israel and the
house of Judah have broken the covenant
I made with their forefathers. ¹¹Therefore
this is what the LORD says: 'I will bring on
them a disaster they cannot escape. Although they cry out to me, I will not listen
to them. ¹²The towns of Judah and the
people of Jerusalem will go and cry out to
the gods to whom they burn incense, but

they will not help them at all when disaster strikes. ¹³You have as many gods as you
have towns, O Judah; and the altars you
have set up to burn incense to that
shameful god Baal are as many as the
streets of Jerusalem.'
     ¹⁴"Do not pray for this people nor offer
any plea or petition for them, because I
will not listen when they call to me in the
time of their distress.

¹⁵ "What is my beloved doing in my
          temple
     as she works out her evil schemes
          with many?
     Can consecrated meat avert your
          punishment?
When you engage in your wickedness,
     then you rejoice.ᵃ"

¹⁶ The LORD called you a thriving olive
          tree
     with fruit beautiful in form.
But with the roar of a mighty storm
     he will set it on fire,
     and its branches will be broken.

¹⁷The LORD Almighty, who planted you,
has decreed disaster for you, because the
house of Israel and the house of Judah
have done evil and provoked me to anger
by burning incense to Baal.

Plot Against Jeremiah

     ¹⁸Because the LORD revealed their plot
to me, I knew it, for at that time he showed
me what they were doing. ¹⁹I had been
like a gentle lamb led to the slaughter; I
did not realize that they had plotted
against me, saying,

"Let us destroy the tree and its fruit;
     let us cut him off from the land of the
          living,
     that his name be remembered no
          more."
²⁰ But, O LORD Almighty, you who judge
          righteously
     and test the heart and mind,
let me see your vengeance upon them,
     for to you I have committed my
          cause.

     ²¹"Therefore this is what the LORD says
about the men of Anathoth who are seeking your life and saying, 'Do not prophesy
in the name of the LORD or you will die by
our hands'— ²²therefore this is what the
LORD Almighty says: 'I will punish them.

ᵃ15 Or *Could consecrated meat avert your
punishment? / Then you would rejoice*

Their young men will die by the sword, their sons and daughters by famine. ²³Not even a remnant will be left to them, because I will bring disaster on the men of Anathoth in the year of their punishment.' "

Jeremiah's Complaint

12 You are always righteous, O LORD,
when I bring a case before you.
Yet I would speak with you about your
justice:
Why does the way of the wicked
prosper?
Why do all the faithless live at ease?
²You have planted them, and they have
taken root;
they grow and bear fruit.
You are always on their lips
but far from their hearts.
³Yet you know me, O LORD;
you see me and test my thoughts
about you.
Drag them off like sheep to be
butchered!
Set them apart for the day of
slaughter!
⁴How long will the land lie parched[a]
and the grass in every field be
withered?
Because those who live in it are wicked,
the animals and birds have perished.
Moreover, the people are saying,
"He will not see what happens to us."

God's Answer

⁵"If you have raced with men on foot
and they have worn you out,
how can you compete with horses?
If you stumble in safe country,[b]
how will you manage in the thickets
by[c] the Jordan?
⁶Your brothers, your own family—
even they have betrayed you;
they have raised a loud cry against
you.
Do not trust them,
though they speak well of you.

⁷"I will forsake my house,
abandon my inheritance;
I will give the one I love
into the hands of her enemies.
⁸My inheritance has become to me
like a lion in the forest.
She roars at me;
therefore I hate her.
⁹Has not my inheritance become to me
like a speckled bird of prey
that other birds of prey surround and

attack?
Go and gather all the wild beasts;
bring them to devour.
¹⁰Many shepherds will ruin my vineyard
and trample down my field;
they will turn my pleasant field
into a desolate wasteland.
¹¹It will be made a wasteland,
parched and desolate before me;
the whole land will be laid waste
because there is no one who cares.
¹²Over all the barren heights in the desert
destroyers will swarm,
for the sword of the LORD will devour
from one end of the land to the
other;
no one will be safe.
¹³They will sow wheat but reap thorns;
they will wear themselves out but
gain nothing.
So bear the shame of your harvest
because of the LORD's fierce anger."

¹⁴This is what the LORD says: "As for all my wicked neighbors who seize the inheritance I gave my people Israel, I will uproot them from their lands and I will uproot the house of Judah from among them. ¹⁵But after I uproot them, I will again have compassion and will bring each of them back to his own inheritance and his own country. ¹⁶And if they learn well the ways of my people and swear by my name, saying, 'As surely as the LORD lives'—even as they once taught my people to swear by Baal—then they will be established among my people. ¹⁷But if any nation does not listen, I will completely uproot and destroy it," declares the LORD.

A Linen Belt

13 This is what the LORD said to me: "Go and buy a linen belt and put it around your waist, but do not let it touch water." ²So I bought a belt, as the LORD directed, and put it around my waist.

³Then the word of the LORD came to me a second time: ⁴"Take the belt you bought and are wearing around your waist, and go now to Perath[d] and hide it there in a crevice in the rocks." ⁵So I went and hid it at Perath, as the LORD told me.

⁶Many days later the LORD said to me, "Go now to Perath and get the belt I told you to hide there." ⁷So I went to Perath and

---

^a4 Or *land mourn*   ^b5 Or *If you put your trust in a land of safety*   ^c5 Or *the flooding of*   ^d4 Or possibly *the Euphrates*; also in verses 5-7

dug up the belt and took it from the place where I had hidden it, but now it was ruined and completely useless.

⁸Then the word of the LORD came to me: ⁹"This is what the LORD says: 'In the same way I will ruin the pride of Judah and the great pride of Jerusalem. ¹⁰These wicked people, who refuse to listen to my words, who follow the stubbornness of their hearts and go after other gods to serve and worship them, will be like this belt— completely useless! ¹¹For as a belt is bound around a man's waist, so I bound the whole house of Israel and the whole house of Judah to me,' declares the LORD, 'to be my people for my renown and praise and honor. But they have not listened.'

Wineskins

¹²"Say to them: 'This is what the LORD, the God of Israel, says: Every wineskin should be filled with wine.' And if they say to you, 'Don't we know that every wineskin should be filled with wine?' ¹³then tell them, 'This is what the LORD says: I am go-

Make His Family Proud

Life can be interesting when you have a funny last name.

For starters, mine is difficult to spell. And even when people spell it correctly, the name is difficult to pronounce. As a youngster on the first day of school, I can remember teachers gazing at my last name as listed on the role, hoping to get close when they said it out loud.

The enjoyable side of having a unique last name are the rare moments when I meet another "Wolgemuth." Several years ago, as visitors were identifying themselves in our Sunday School class, a woman stood to say her name. "I'm Nancy Wolgemuth," she said. And, of course, I cut a trail to her after class to get more information on where she was from. Our mutual name gave us an immediate camaraderie.

Do you know that your name is precious? Your identification with your parents and their parents is a powerful thing. And as a dad, you are passing this name on to another generation who will continue to carry it forward when you're gone.

The Israelites also had a family name— they were known as "God's people." Over the centuries there had been times when those who bore this name made God proud. This wasn't one of those times. So God instructed Jeremiah to illustrate what the people had done with God's name.

Jeremiah followed God's instructions as outlined in today's passage, then dug up his sash and showed it to the people. "You

DAILY INSIGHT

THURSDAY

Passage:
Jeremiah 13:1–11

Verse:
Jeremiah 13:10

wicked people," Jeremiah said as he held up the disgusting piece of linen. "You refused to listen to God's words, you followed your own stubbornness, and you followed false gods. You should be something God is proud to wear, but you are completely useless!" (13:10)

How embarrassed God's people must have been as they were reminded of what they had done to God's name. How graphic Jeremiah's illustration was to them. As an ornament, they were to enhance God's beauty; as a practical piece of clothing, they were to serve faithfully. The people failed miserably on both counts. They were useless.

You and I share a common name. We are called "Christians." This name immediately connects us with people everywhere who believe in the name of Jesus Christ. Some of us received this name from our parents, some from other caring adults. Either way, we are now wearing this name and will pass it on to our children when we die.

What if God asked your family to graphically illustrate your effectiveness in showing the world God's name? Would you go completely unrecognized, useless as one who bears God's name? Or would you hear, "Hey, you look familiar. I think I know your Father. You're a Christian, aren't you?"

Now go and make his family proud.

For your next devotional reading, go to page 837.

ing to fill with drunkenness all who live in this land, including the kings who sit on David's throne, the priests, the prophets and all those living in Jerusalem. **14**I will smash them one against the other, fathers and sons alike, declares the LORD. I will allow no pity or mercy or compassion to keep me from destroying them.' "

Threat of Captivity

15Hear and pay attention,
  do not be arrogant,
  for the LORD has spoken.
16Give glory to the LORD your God
  before he brings the darkness,
before your feet stumble
  on the darkening hills.
You hope for light,
  but he will turn it to thick darkness
  and change it to deep gloom.
17But if you do not listen,
  I will weep in secret
  because of your pride;
my eyes will weep bitterly,
  overflowing with tears,
because the LORD's flock will be
    taken captive.

18Say to the king and to the queen
    mother,
  "Come down from your thrones,
for your glorious crowns
  will fall from your heads."
19The cities in the Negev will be shut up,
  and there will be no one to open
    them.
All Judah will be carried into exile,
  carried completely away.

20Lift up your eyes and see
  those who are coming from the
    north.
Where is the flock that was entrusted to
    you,
  the sheep of which you boasted?
21What will you say when ⌊the LORD⌋ sets
    over you
  those you cultivated as your special
    allies?
Will not pain grip you
  like that of a woman in labor?
22And if you ask yourself,
  "Why has this happened to me?"—
it is because of your many sins
  that your skirts have been torn off
  and your body mistreated.
23Can the Ethiopian*ᵃ* change his skin
  or the leopard its spots?
Neither can you do good
  who are accustomed to doing evil.

24"I will scatter you like chaff
  driven by the desert wind.
25This is your lot,
  the portion I have decreed for you,"
                  declares the LORD,
  "because you have forgotten me
  and trusted in false gods.
26I will pull up your skirts over your face
  that your shame may be seen—
27your adulteries and lustful neighings,
  your shameless prostitution!
I have seen your detestable acts
  on the hills and in the fields.
Woe to you, O Jerusalem!
  How long will you be unclean?"

Drought, Famine, Sword

14 This is the word of the LORD to
Jeremiah concerning the drought:

2"Judah mourns,
  her cities languish;
they wail for the land,
  and a cry goes up from Jerusalem.
3The nobles send their servants for
    water;
  they go to the cisterns
  but find no water.
They return with their jars unfilled;
  dismayed and despairing,
  they cover their heads.
4The ground is cracked
  because there is no rain in the land;
the farmers are dismayed
  and cover their heads.
5Even the doe in the field
  deserts her newborn fawn
  because there is no grass.
6Wild donkeys stand on the barren
    heights
  and pant like jackals;
their eyesight fails
  for lack of pasture."

7Although our sins testify against us,
  O LORD, do something for the sake of
    your name.
For our backsliding is great;
  we have sinned against you.
8O Hope of Israel,
  its Savior in times of distress,
why are you like a stranger in the land,
  like a traveler who stays only a night?
9Why are you like a man taken by
    surprise,
  like a warrior powerless to save?
You are among us, O LORD,

---

*ᵃ*23 Hebrew *Cushite* (probably a person from the upper Nile region)

and we bear your name;
do not forsake us!

[10]This is what the LORD says about this people:

"They greatly love to wander;
they do not restrain their feet.
So the LORD does not accept them;
he will now remember their
wickedness
and punish them for their sins."

[11]Then the LORD said to me, "Do not pray for the well-being of this people. [12]Although they fast, I will not listen to their cry; though they offer burnt offerings and grain offerings, I will not accept them. Instead, I will destroy them with the sword, famine and plague."

[13]But I said, "Ah, Sovereign LORD, the prophets keep telling them, 'You will not see the sword or suffer famine. Indeed, I will give you lasting peace in this place.' "

[14]Then the LORD said to me, "The prophets are prophesying lies in my name. I have not sent them or appointed them or spoken to them. They are prophesying to you false visions, divinations, idolatries[a] and the delusions of their own minds. [15]Therefore, this is what the LORD says about the prophets who are prophesying in my name: I did not send them, yet they are saying, 'No sword or famine will touch this land.' Those same prophets will perish by sword and famine. [16]And the people they are prophesying to will be thrown out into the streets of Jerusalem because of the famine and sword. There will be no one to bury them or their wives, their sons or their daughters. I will pour out on them the calamity they deserve.

[17]"Speak this word to them:

" 'Let my eyes overflow with tears
night and day without ceasing;
for my virgin daughter—my people—
has suffered a grievous wound,
a crushing blow.
[18]If I go into the country,
I see those slain by the sword;
if I go into the city,
I see the ravages of famine.
Both prophet and priest
have gone to a land they know not.' "

[19]Have you rejected Judah completely?
Do you despise Zion?
Why have you afflicted us
so that we cannot be healed?
We hoped for peace
but no good has come,

for a time of healing
but there is only terror.
[20]O LORD, we acknowledge our
wickedness
and the guilt of our fathers;
we have indeed sinned against you.
[21]For the sake of your name do not
despise us;
do not dishonor your glorious
throne.
Remember your covenant with us
and do not break it.
[22]Do any of the worthless idols of the
nations bring rain?
Do the skies themselves send down
showers?
No, it is you, O LORD our God.
Therefore our hope is in you,
for you are the one who does all this.

15 Then the LORD said to me: "Even if Moses and Samuel were to stand before me, my heart would not go out to this people. Send them away from my presence! Let them go! [2]And if they ask you, 'Where shall we go?' tell them, 'This is what the LORD says:

" 'Those destined for death, to death;
those for the sword, to the sword;
those for starvation, to starvation;
those for captivity, to captivity.'

[3]"I will send four kinds of destroyers against them," declares the LORD, "the sword to kill and the dogs to drag away and the birds of the air and the beasts of the earth to devour and destroy. [4]I will make them abhorrent to all the kingdoms of the earth because of what Manasseh son of Hezekiah king of Judah did in Jerusalem.

[5]"Who will have pity on you,
O Jerusalem?
Who will mourn for you?
Who will stop to ask how you are?
[6]You have rejected me," declares the
LORD.
"You keep on backsliding.
So I will lay hands on you and destroy
you;
I can no longer show compassion.
[7]I will winnow them with a winnowing
fork
at the city gates of the land.
I will bring bereavement and
destruction on my people,
for they have not changed their ways.
[8]I will make their widows more numerous

a14 Or *visions, worthless divinations*

than the sand of the sea.
At midday I will bring a destroyer
    against the mothers of their young
        men;
suddenly I will bring down on them
    anguish and terror.
⁹The mother of seven will grow faint
    and breathe her last.
Her sun will set while it is still day;
    she will be disgraced and
        humiliated.
I will put the survivors to the sword
    before their enemies,"
                    declares the LORD.

¹⁰Alas, my mother, that you gave me
        birth,
    a man with whom the whole land
        strives and contends!
I have neither lent nor borrowed,
    yet everyone curses me.

¹¹The LORD said,

"Surely I will deliver you for a good
        purpose;
    surely I will make your enemies
        plead with you
    in times of disaster and times of
        distress.

¹²"Can a man break iron—
    iron from the north—or bronze?
¹³Your wealth and your treasures
    I will give as plunder, without
        charge,
because of all your sins
    throughout your country.
¹⁴I will enslave you to your enemies
    inᵃ a land you do not know,
for my anger will kindle a fire
    that will burn against you."

¹⁵You understand, O LORD;
    remember me and care for me.
    Avenge me on my persecutors.
You are long-suffering—do not take me
        away;
    think of how I suffer reproach for
        your sake.
¹⁶When your words came, I ate them;
    they were my joy and my heart's
        delight,
for I bear your name,
    O LORD God Almighty.
¹⁷I never sat in the company of revelers,
    never made merry with them;
I sat alone because your hand was on
        me
    and you had filled me with
        indignation.
¹⁸Why is my pain unending

and my wound grievous and
        incurable?
Will you be to me like a deceptive
        brook,
    like a spring that fails?

¹⁹Therefore this is what the LORD says:

"If you repent, I will restore you
    that you may serve me;
if you utter worthy, not worthless, words,
    you will be my spokesman.
Let this people turn to you,
    but you must not turn to them.
²⁰I will make you a wall to this people,
    a fortified wall of bronze;
they will fight against you
    but will not overcome you,
for I am with you
    to rescue and save you,"
                    declares the LORD.
²¹"I will save you from the hands of the
        wicked
    and redeem you from the grasp of
        the cruel."

Day of Disaster

16 Then the word of the LORD came to
me: ²"You must not marry and have
sons or daughters in this place." ³For this
is what the LORD says about the sons and
daughters born in this land and about
the women who are their mothers and
the men who are their fathers: ⁴"They will
die of deadly diseases. They will not be
mourned or buried but will be like refuse
lying on the ground. They will perish by
sword and famine, and their dead bodies
will become food for the birds of the air
and the beasts of the earth."

⁵For this is what the LORD says: "Do not
enter a house where there is a funeral
meal; do not go to mourn or show sympathy, because I have withdrawn my
blessing, my love and my pity from this
people," declares the LORD. ⁶"Both high
and low will die in this land. They will not
be buried or mourned, and no one will
cut himself or shave his head for them.
⁷No one will offer food to comfort those
who mourn for the dead—not even for a
father or a mother—nor will anyone give
them a drink to console them.

⁸"And do not enter a house where there is
feasting and sit down to eat and drink. ⁹For
this is what the LORD Almighty, the God of

ᵃ14 Some Hebrew manuscripts, Septuagint and
Syriac (see also Jer. 17:4); most Hebrew
manuscripts *I will cause your enemies to bring
you / into*

Israel, says: Before your eyes and in your days I will bring an end to the sounds of joy and gladness and to the voices of bride and bridegroom in this place.

¹⁰"When you tell these people all this and they ask you, 'Why has the LORD decreed such a great disaster against us? What wrong have we done? What sin have we committed against the LORD our God?' ¹¹then say to them, 'It is because your fathers forsook me,' declares the LORD, 'and followed other gods and served and worshiped them. They forsook me and did not keep my law. ¹²But you have behaved more wickedly than your fathers. See how each of you is following the stubbornness of his evil heart instead of obeying me. ¹³So I will throw you out of this land into a land neither you nor your fathers have known, and there you will serve other gods day and night, for I will show you no favor.'

¹⁴"However, the days are coming," declares the LORD, "when men will no longer say, 'As surely as the LORD lives, who brought the Israelites up out of Egypt,' ¹⁵but they will say, 'As surely as the LORD lives, who brought the Israelites up out of the land of the north and out of all the countries where he had banished them.' For I will restore them to the land I gave their forefathers.

¹⁶"But now I will send for many fishermen," declares the LORD, "and they will catch them. After that I will send for many hunters, and they will hunt them down on every mountain and hill and from the crevices of the rocks. ¹⁷My eyes are on all their ways; they are not hidden from me, nor is their sin concealed from my eyes. ¹⁸I will repay them double for their wickedness and their sin, because they have defiled my land with the lifeless forms of their vile images and have filled my inheritance with their detestable idols."

¹⁹O LORD, my strength and my fortress,
    my refuge in time of distress,
to you the nations will come
    from the ends of the earth and say,
"Our fathers possessed nothing but
        false gods,
    worthless idols that did them no
        good.
²⁰Do men make their own gods?
    Yes, but they are not gods!"

²¹"Therefore I will teach them—
    this time I will teach them
    my power and might.

Then they will know
    that my name is the LORD.

17 "Judah's sin is engraved with an iron
        tool,
    inscribed with a flint point,
on the tablets of their hearts
    and on the horns of their altars.
²Even their children remember
    their altars and Asherah poles*ᵃ*
beside the spreading trees
    and on the high hills.
³My mountain in the land
    and your*ᵇ* wealth and all your
        treasures
I will give away as plunder,
    together with your high places,
    because of sin throughout your
        country.
⁴Through your own fault you will lose
    the inheritance I gave you.
I will enslave you to your enemies
    in a land you do not know,
for you have kindled my anger,
    and it will burn forever."

⁵This is what the LORD says:

"Cursed is the one who trusts in man,
    who depends on flesh for his
        strength
    and whose heart turns away from the
        LORD.
⁶He will be like a bush in the
        wastelands;
    he will not see prosperity when it
        comes.
He will dwell in the parched places of
        the desert,
    in a salt land where no one lives.

⁷"But blessed is the man who trusts in
        the LORD,
    whose confidence is in him.
⁸He will be like a tree planted by the
        water
    that sends out its roots by the
        stream.
It does not fear when heat comes;
    its leaves are always green.
It has no worries in a year of drought
    and never fails to bear fruit."

⁹The heart is deceitful above all things
    and beyond cure.
    Who can understand it?

¹⁰"I the LORD search the heart
    and examine the mind,
to reward a man according to his

*ᵃ2 That is, symbols of the goddess Asherah
ᵇ2,3 Or hills / ³and the mountains of the
land. / Your*

conduct,
according to what his deeds deserve."

[11] Like a partridge that hatches eggs it did not lay
is the man who gains riches by unjust means.
When his life is half gone, they will desert him,
and in the end he will prove to be a fool.

[12] A glorious throne, exalted from the beginning,
is the place of our sanctuary.
[13] O LORD, the hope of Israel,
all who forsake you will be put to shame.
Those who turn away from you will be written in the dust
because they have forsaken the LORD, the spring of living water.

[14] Heal me, O LORD, and I will be healed;
save me and I will be saved,
for you are the one I praise.
[15] They keep saying to me,
"Where is the word of the LORD?
Let it now be fulfilled!"
[16] I have not run away from being your shepherd;
you know I have not desired the day of despair.
What passes my lips is open before

Those Nasty Ruts

The lane to my grandfather's farm wasn't paved until I was an adult. So as a child, I remember hearing the crunch of the gravel under the tires of my dad's car that last mile before arriving at the family homestead.

Every few months, my uncle Allon would take the front scoop of his tractor and drag it down the surface of the lane. The deep ruts that had been created by constant traffic needed to be leveled off.

As a grown man, I have thought a lot about those deep grooves in my grandfather's lane. Why? Because they remind me of my propensity to sin. I'm sure this sounds a little abstract, but stay with me for just a moment.

In the text we read today, Jeremiah tells us something about our hearts—the place where our drives and desires are born. He refers to our hearts as "deceitful" and "desperately wicked." Then he adds "who can figure them out?"

My heart is drawn to the deep ruts of rebellion. Try as I might to stay out of these grooves, my tires slip helplessly into them. I make resolutions. I confess my transgressions. I try and try to live a life pleasing to the Lord, but my heart is drawn toward the ruts of sin. It's inevitable that the pull of these ditches will win out over my efforts to avoid them.

DAILY INSIGHT

FRIDAY

Passage:
Jeremiah 17:9–12

Verse:
Jeremiah 17:9

Why is sin so compelling? Because sin is comfortable. Sin is enjoyable. Sin often feels better than obedience. Its rewards are immediate. Its payoff is instantaneous. Its magnetism is powerful.

For centuries, many people have resisted the truth of the ruts in my grandfather's lane. "Man is essentially good," these people have said. "If you want to find wholeness and happiness and righteousness, look inside. It's already there. Just reach down and you'll find salvation." Don't believe this. It's a lie. My heart is deceitful. Yours is wicked. No one can figure us out. So what should we do?

God spoke through Jeremiah and gave us the answer. "Let me search your heart and examine your mind," the Lord said. "I will reward a man according to his conduct, according to what his deeds deserve."

As a disobedient man, I must recognize my sinfulness, ask God to search me and then be satisfied with his benefits. And although his dividends may not seem like the most satisfying right now, they ultimately lead to eternal life. The ruts lead to death. The right choice seems fairly obvious, doesn't it?

For your next devotional reading, go to page 839.

you.
¹⁷Do not be a terror to me;
   you are my refuge in the day of
      disaster.
¹⁸Let my persecutors be put to shame,
   but keep me from shame;
let them be terrified,
   but keep me from terror.
Bring on them the day of disaster;
   destroy them with double
      destruction.

Keeping the Sabbath Holy

¹⁹This is what the LORD said to me: "Go
and stand at the gate of the people,
through which the kings of Judah go in
and out; stand also at all the other gates of
Jerusalem. ²⁰Say to them, 'Hear the word
of the LORD, O kings of Judah and all
people of Judah and everyone living in
Jerusalem who come through these gates.
²¹This is what the LORD says: Be careful
not to carry a load on the Sabbath day or
bring it through the gates of Jerusalem.
²²Do not bring a load out of your houses
or do any work on the Sabbath, but keep
the Sabbath day holy, as I commanded
your forefathers. ²³Yet they did not listen
or pay attention; they were stiff-necked
and would not listen or respond to discipline. ²⁴But if you are careful to obey me,
declares the LORD, and bring no load
through the gates of this city on the Sabbath, but keep the Sabbath day holy by
not doing any work on it, ²⁵then kings
who sit on David's throne will come
through the gates of this city with their officials. They and their officials will come
riding in chariots and on horses, accompanied by the men of Judah and those
living in Jerusalem, and this city will be
inhabited forever. ²⁶People will come
from the towns of Judah and the villages
around Jerusalem, from the territory of
Benjamin and the western foothills, from
the hill country and the Negev, bringing
burnt offerings and sacrifices, grain
offerings, incense and thank offerings
to the house of the LORD. ²⁷But if you
do not obey me to keep the Sabbath
day holy by not carrying any load as
you come through the gates of Jerusalem on the Sabbath day, then I will
kindle an unquenchable fire in the gates
of Jerusalem that will consume her fortresses.' "

At the Potter's House

18 This is the word that came to
Jeremiah from the LORD: ²"Go down
to the potter's house, and there I will give
you my message." ³So I went down to the
potter's house, and I saw him working at
the wheel. ⁴But the pot he was shaping
from the clay was marred in his hands; so
the potter formed it into another pot,
shaping it as seemed best to him.

⁵Then the word of the LORD came to me:
⁶"O house of Israel, can I not do with you
as this potter does?" declares the LORD.
"Like clay in the hand of the potter, so are
you in my hand, O house of Israel. ⁷If at
any time I announce that a nation or
kingdom is to be uprooted, torn down
and destroyed, ⁸and if that nation I
warned repents of its evil, then I will relent and not inflict on it the disaster I had
planned. ⁹And if at another time I announce that a nation or kingdom is to be
built up and planted, ¹⁰and if it does evil
in my sight and does not obey me, then I
will reconsider the good I had intended to
do for it.

¹¹"Now therefore say to the people of
Judah and those living in Jerusalem, 'This
is what the LORD says: Look! I am preparing a disaster for you and devising a plan
against you. So turn from your evil ways,
each one of you, and reform your ways
and your actions.' ¹²But they will reply, 'It's
no use. We will continue with our own
plans; each of us will follow the stubbornness of his evil heart.' "

¹³Therefore this is what the LORD says:

"Inquire among the nations:
   Who has ever heard anything like
      this?
A most horrible thing has been done
   by Virgin Israel.
¹⁴Does the snow of Lebanon
   ever vanish from its rocky slopes?
Do its cool waters from distant sources
   ever cease to flow?ᵃ
¹⁵Yet my people have forgotten me;
   they burn incense to worthless idols,
   which made them stumble in their
      ways
   and in the ancient paths.
They made them walk in bypaths
   and on roads not built up.
¹⁶Their land will be laid waste,
   an object of lasting scorn;

ᵃ14 The meaning of the Hebrew for this sentence is
uncertain.

The Potter

Key Verse: *"O house of Israel, can I not do with you as this potter does? ... Like clay in the hand ... so are you in my hand."* Jeremiah 18:6

Text: Jeremiah 18:1–6 *(Dad or child reads the text.)*

QUIET TIMES WITH Dad

DAD READS: Have you ever seen a potter? He sits down in front of a flat, spinning wheel. He takes a lump of soft clay and puts it on the wheel, then he gently puts his hands around the spinning clay. The squeezing and shaping movement of his hands turns the clay into something the potter wants to make ... something useful, something beautiful.

Child reads: The Bible tells us that God wants us to be like soft clay on a spinning wheel. He wants to shape us into something he can use. He wants us to become beautiful for him.

DAD READS: I know this sounds funny, but sometimes you and I act like we would rather shape ourselves than to have our heavenly Father be the potter. How silly it would be to think the soft clay could become something useful and beautiful without the potter's skillful hands.

Child reads: Just like the clay could never make something of itself without the potter, you and I cannot be who God wants us to be without letting him love us and form us into his people. We should tell God that we want him to be the potter.

DAD READS: But what if the clay on the wheel isn't soft? What if it's hard and cold? The potter won't be able to shape it very easily, will he?

Child reads: No, he will probably use another piece of clay if this one isn't soft. I must be willing to listen to God's voice. I must pray. I must confess my sins and thank him for his forgiveness. I must be thankful. When I do these things, my heart will be soft enough for him to shape me into the person he wants me to be.

DAD READS: I am thankful for God the potter. I want to always be willing to let my heart be soft so he will make me into the kind of man who pleases him. I know you want the same for your heart, too. Let me pray this prayer with you:

Our Father in heaven, we love you. Thank you for the story of the potter. Thank you for wanting to love me and shape me into someone you can use—someone who is truly beautiful in your eyes. Please fill me with your love and your grace so my heart is soft enough for the potter. We love you. In Jesus' name, *Amen.*

For your next devotional reading, go to page 851.

all who pass by will be appalled
and will shake their heads.
¹⁷Like a wind from the east,
    I will scatter them before their
        enemies;
I will show them my back and not my
        face
    in the day of their disaster."

¹⁸They said, "Come, let's make plans against Jeremiah; for the teaching of the law by the priest will not be lost, nor will counsel from the wise, nor the word from the prophets. So come, let's attack him with our tongues and pay no attention to anything he says."

¹⁹Listen to me, O LORD;
    hear what my accusers are saying!
²⁰Should good be repaid with evil?
    Yet they have dug a pit for me.
Remember that I stood before you
    and spoke in their behalf
    to turn your wrath away from them.
²¹So give their children over to famine;
    hand them over to the power of the
        sword.
Let their wives be made childless and
        widows;
    let their men be put to death,
    their young men slain by the sword
        in battle.
²²Let a cry be heard from their houses
    when you suddenly bring invaders
        against them,
for they have dug a pit to capture me
    and have hidden snares for my feet.
²³But you know, O LORD,
    all their plots to kill me.
Do not forgive their crimes
    or blot out their sins from your sight.
Let them be overthrown before you;
    deal with them in the time of your
        anger.

19 This is what the LORD says: "Go and buy a clay jar from a potter. Take along some of the elders of the people and of the priests ²and go out to the Valley of Ben Hinnom, near the entrance of the Potsherd Gate. There proclaim the words I tell you, ³and say, 'Hear the word of the LORD, O kings of Judah and people of Jerusalem. This is what the LORD Almighty, the God of Israel, says: Listen! I am going to bring a disaster on this place that will make the ears of everyone who hears of it tingle. ⁴For they have forsaken me and made this a place of foreign gods; they have burned sacrifices in it to gods that neither they nor their fathers nor the

kings of Judah ever knew, and they have filled this place with the blood of the innocent. ⁵They have built the high places of Baal to burn their sons in the fire as offerings to Baal—something I did not command or mention, nor did it enter my mind. ⁶So beware, the days are coming, declares the LORD, when people will no longer call this place Topheth or the Valley of Ben Hinnom, but the Valley of Slaughter.

⁷" 'In this place I will ruin*a* the plans of Judah and Jerusalem. I will make them fall by the sword before their enemies, at the hands of those who seek their lives, and I will give their carcasses as food to the birds of the air and the beasts of the earth. ⁸I will devastate this city and make it an object of scorn; all who pass by will be appalled and will scoff because of all its wounds. ⁹I will make them eat the flesh of their sons and daughters, and they will eat one another's flesh during the stress of the siege imposed on them by the enemies who seek their lives.'

¹⁰"Then break the jar while those who go with you are watching, ¹¹and say to them, 'This is what the LORD Almighty says: I will smash this nation and this city just as this potter's jar is smashed and cannot be repaired. They will bury the dead in Topheth until there is no more room. ¹²This is what I will do to this place and to those who live here, declares the LORD. I will make this city like Topheth. ¹³The houses in Jerusalem and those of the kings of Judah will be defiled like this place, Topheth—all the houses where they burned incense on the roofs to all the starry hosts and poured out drink offerings to other gods.' "

¹⁴Jeremiah then returned from Topheth, where the LORD had sent him to prophesy, and stood in the court of the LORD's temple and said to all the people, ¹⁵"This is what the LORD Almighty, the God of Israel, says: 'Listen! I am going to bring on this city and the villages around it every disaster I pronounced against them, because they were stiff-necked and would not listen to my words.' "

Jeremiah and Pashhur

20 When the priest Pashhur son of Immer, the chief officer in the temple of the LORD, heard Jeremiah prophesying these things, ²he had Jeremiah the proph-

a7 The Hebrew for ruin sounds like the Hebrew for jar (see verses 1 and 10).

et beaten and put in the stocks at the Upper Gate of Benjamin at the LORD's temple. ³The next day, when Pashhur released him from the stocks, Jeremiah said to him, "The LORD's name for you is not Pashhur, but Magor-Missabib.ᵃ ⁴For this is what the LORD says: 'I will make you a terror to yourself and to all your friends; with your own eyes you will see them fall by the sword of their enemies. I will hand all Judah over to the king of Babylon, who will carry them away to Babylon or put them to the sword. ⁵I will hand over to their enemies all the wealth of this city—all its products, all its valuables and all the treasures of the kings of Judah. They will take it away as plunder and carry it off to Babylon. ⁶And you, Pashhur, and all who live in your house will go into exile to Babylon. There you will die and be buried, you and all your friends to whom you have prophesied lies.'"

Jeremiah's Complaint

⁷O LORD, you deceivedᵇ me, and I was
    deceivedᵇ;
  you overpowered me and prevailed.
I am ridiculed all day long;
    everyone mocks me.
⁸Whenever I speak, I cry out
  proclaiming violence and
    destruction.
So the word of the LORD has brought
    me
  insult and reproach all day long.
⁹But if I say, "I will not mention him
  or speak any more in his name,"
his word is in my heart like a fire,
  a fire shut up in my bones.
I am weary of holding it in;
  indeed, I cannot.
¹⁰I hear many whispering,
  "Terror on every side!
  Report him! Let's report him!"
All my friends
  are waiting for me to slip, saying,
"Perhaps he will be deceived;
  then we will prevail over him
  and take our revenge on him."

¹¹But the LORD is with me like a mighty
    warrior;
  so my persecutors will stumble and
    not prevail.
They will fail and be thoroughly
    disgraced;
  their dishonor will never be
    forgotten.
¹²O LORD Almighty, you who examine the
    righteous

and probe the heart and mind,
  let me see your vengeance upon them,
  for to you I have committed my
    cause.

¹³Sing to the LORD!
  Give praise to the LORD!
He rescues the life of the needy
  from the hands of the wicked.

¹⁴Cursed be the day I was born!
  May the day my mother bore me not
    be blessed!
¹⁵Cursed be the man who brought my
    father the news,
  who made him very glad, saying,
  "A child is born to you—a son!"
¹⁶May that man be like the towns
  the LORD overthrew without pity.
May he hear wailing in the morning,
  a battle cry at noon.
¹⁷For he did not kill me in the womb,
  with my mother as my grave,
  her womb enlarged forever.
¹⁸Why did I ever come out of the womb
  to see trouble and sorrow
  and to end my days in shame?

God Rejects Zedekiah's Request

21 The word came to Jeremiah from the LORD when King Zedekiah sent to him Pashhur son of Malkijah and the priest Zephaniah son of Maaseiah. They said: ²"Inquire now of the LORD for us because Nebuchadnezzarᶜ king of Babylon is attacking us. Perhaps the LORD will perform wonders for us as in times past so that he will withdraw from us."

³But Jeremiah answered them, "Tell Zedekiah, ⁴'This is what the LORD, the God of Israel, says: I am about to turn against you the weapons of war that are in your hands, which you are using to fight the king of Babylon and the Babyloniansᵈ who are outside the wall besieging you. And I will gather them inside this city. ⁵I myself will fight against you with an outstretched hand and a mighty arm in anger and fury and great wrath. ⁶I will strike down those who live in this city—both men and animals—and they will die of a terrible plague. ⁷After that, declares the LORD, I will hand over Zedekiah king of Judah, his officials and the people in this city who survive the plague, sword

---

ᵃ3 *Magor-Missabib* means *terror on every side.*
ᵇ7 Or *persuaded*   ᶜ2 Hebrew *Nebuchadrezzar,* of which *Nebuchadnezzar* is a variant; here and often in Jeremiah and Ezekiel   ᵈ4 Or *Chaldeans*; also in verse 9

and famine, to Nebuchadnezzar king of Babylon and to their enemies who seek their lives. He will put them to the sword; he will show them no mercy or pity or compassion.'

⁸"Furthermore, tell the people, 'This is what the LORD says: See, I am setting before you the way of life and the way of death. ⁹Whoever stays in this city will die by the sword, famine or plague. But whoever goes out and surrenders to the Babylonians who are besieging you will live; he will escape with his life. ¹⁰I have determined to do this city harm and not good, declares the LORD. It will be given into the hands of the king of Babylon, and he will destroy it with fire.'

¹¹"Moreover, say to the royal house of Judah, 'Hear the word of the LORD; ¹²O house of David, this is what the LORD says:

" 'Administer justice every morning;
    rescue from the hand of his
        oppressor
    the one who has been robbed,
or my wrath will break out and burn
        like fire
    because of the evil you have done—
    burn with no one to quench it.
¹³I am against you, ⌊Jerusalem,⌋
    you who live above this valley
    on the rocky plateau,
                    declares the LORD—
    you who say, "Who can come against us?
    Who can enter our refuge?"
¹⁴I will punish you as your deeds
        deserve,
                    declares the LORD.
    I will kindle a fire in your forests
        that will consume everything around
        you.' "

Judgment Against Evil Kings

22 This is what the LORD says: "Go down to the palace of the king of Judah and proclaim this message there: ²'Hear the word of the LORD, O king of Judah, you who sit on David's throne—you, your officials and your people who come through these gates. ³This is what the LORD says: Do what is just and right. Rescue from the hand of his oppressor the one who has been robbed. Do no wrong or violence to the alien, the fatherless or the widow, and do not shed innocent blood in this place. ⁴For if you are careful to carry out these commands, then kings who sit on David's throne will come through the gates of this palace, riding in chariots and on horses, accompanied by their officials and their

people. ⁵But if you do not obey these commands, declares the LORD, I swear by myself that this palace will become a ruin.' "

⁶For this is what the LORD says about the palace of the king of Judah:

"Though you are like Gilead to me,
    like the summit of Lebanon,
I will surely make you like a desert,
    like towns not inhabited.
⁷I will send destroyers against you,
    each man with his weapons,
and they will cut up your fine cedar
        beams
    and throw them into the fire.

⁸"People from many nations will pass by this city and will ask one another, 'Why has the LORD done such a thing to this great city?' ⁹And the answer will be: 'Because they have forsaken the covenant of the LORD their God and have worshiped and served other gods.' "

¹⁰Do not weep for the dead ⌊king⌋ or
    mourn his loss;
rather, weep bitterly for him who is
        exiled,
    because he will never return
    nor see his native land again.

¹¹For this is what the LORD says about Shallum[a] son of Josiah, who succeeded his father as king of Judah but has gone from this place: "He will never return. ¹²He will die in the place where they have led him captive; he will not see this land again."

¹³"Woe to him who builds his palace by
        unrighteousness,
    his upper rooms by injustice,
making his countrymen work for
        nothing,
    not paying them for their labor.
¹⁴He says, 'I will build myself a great
        palace
    with spacious upper rooms.'
So he makes large windows in it,
    panels it with cedar
    and decorates it in red.

¹⁵"Does it make you a king
    to have more and more cedar?
Did not your father have food and
        drink?
    He did what was right and just,
    so all went well with him.
¹⁶He defended the cause of the poor and
        needy,

a11 Also called Jehoahaz

and so all went well.
Is that not what it means to know me?"
declares the LORD.
¹⁷ "But your eyes and your heart
    are set only on dishonest gain,
on shedding innocent blood
    and on oppression and extortion."

¹⁸Therefore this is what the LORD says
about Jehoiakim son of Josiah king of Judah:

"They will not mourn for him:
    'Alas, my brother! Alas, my sister!'
They will not mourn for him:
    'Alas, my master! Alas, his splendor!'
¹⁹He will have the burial of a donkey—
    dragged away and thrown
    outside the gates of Jerusalem."

²⁰ "Go up to Lebanon and cry out,
    let your voice be heard in Bashan,
cry out from Abarim,
    for all your allies are crushed.
²¹ I warned you when you felt secure,
    but you said, 'I will not listen!'
This has been your way from your
        youth;
    you have not obeyed me.
²²The wind will drive all your shepherds
        away,
    and your allies will go into exile.
Then you will be ashamed and
        disgraced
    because of all your wickedness.
²³You who live in 'Lebanon,ᵃ'
    who are nestled in cedar buildings,
how you will groan when pangs come
        upon you,
    pain like that of a woman in labor!

²⁴ "As surely as I live," declares the LORD,
"even if you, Jehoiachinᵇ son of Jehoiakim
king of Judah, were a signet ring on my
right hand, I would still pull you off. ²⁵I
will hand you over to those who seek your
life, those you fear—to Nebuchadnezzar
king of Babylon and to the Babylonians.ᶜ
²⁶I will hurl you and the mother who gave
you birth into another country, where
neither of you was born, and there you
both will die. ²⁷You will never come back
to the land you long to return to."

²⁸ Is this man Jehoiachin a despised,
        broken pot,
    an object no one wants?
Why will he and his children be hurled
        out,
    cast into a land they do not know?
²⁹O land, land, land,
    hear the word of the LORD!

³⁰This is what the LORD says:
"Record this man as if childless,
    a man who will not prosper in his
        lifetime,
for none of his offspring will prosper,
    none will sit on the throne of David
    or rule anymore in Judah."

The Righteous Branch

23 "Woe to the shepherds who are destroying and scattering the sheep of
my pasture!" declares the LORD. ²There-
fore this is what the LORD, the God of Israel, says to the shepherds who tend my
people: "Because you have scattered my
flock and driven them away and have not
bestowed care on them, I will bestow
punishment on you for the evil you have
done," declares the LORD. ³"I myself will
gather the remnant of my flock out of all
the countries where I have driven them
and will bring them back to their pasture,
where they will be fruitful and increase in
number. ⁴I will place shepherds over them
who will tend them, and they will no
longer be afraid or terrified, nor will any
be missing," declares the LORD.

⁵ "The days are coming," declares the
        LORD,
    "when I will raise up to Davidᵈ a
        righteous Branch,
a King who will reign wisely
    and do what is just and right in the
        land.
⁶ In his days Judah will be saved
    and Israel will live in safety.
This is the name by which he will be
        called:
    The LORD Our Righteousness.

⁷"So then, the days are coming," declares
the LORD, "when people will no longer say,
'As surely as the LORD lives, who brought
the Israelites up out of Egypt,' ⁸but they
will say, 'As surely as the LORD lives, who
brought the descendants of Israel up out
of the land of the north and out of all the
countries where he had banished them.'
Then they will live in their own land."

Lying Prophets

⁹Concerning the prophets:

My heart is broken within me;
    all my bones tremble.

ᵃ23 That is, the palace in Jerusalem (see
1 Kings 7:2)   ᵇ24 Hebrew *Coniah*, a variant of
Jehoiachin; also in verse 28   ᶜ25 Or *Chaldeans*
ᵈ5 Or *up from David's line*

I am like a drunken man,
  like a man overcome by wine,
because of the LORD
  and his holy words.
¹⁰The land is full of adulterers;
  because of the curse*a* the land lies
    parched*b*
  and the pastures in the desert are
    withered.
The ˌprophets¸ follow an evil course
  and use their power unjustly.
¹¹"Both prophet and priest are godless;
  even in my temple I find their
    wickedness,"
                  declares the LORD.
¹²"Therefore their path will become
    slippery;
  they will be banished to darkness
    and there they will fall.
I will bring disaster on them
  in the year they are punished,"
                  declares the LORD.

¹³"Among the prophets of Samaria
  I saw this repulsive thing:
They prophesied by Baal
  and led my people Israel astray.
¹⁴And among the prophets of Jerusalem
  I have seen something horrible:
They commit adultery and live a lie.
They strengthen the hands of evildoers,
  so that no one turns from his
    wickedness.
They are all like Sodom to me;
  the people of Jerusalem are like
    Gomorrah."

¹⁵Therefore, this is what the LORD Almighty says concerning the prophets:

"I will make them eat bitter food
  and drink poisoned water,
because from the prophets of Jerusalem
  ungodliness has spread throughout
    the land."

¹⁶This is what the LORD Almighty says:

"Do not listen to what the prophets are
    prophesying to you;
  they fill you with false hopes.
They speak visions from their own
    minds,
  not from the mouth of the LORD.
¹⁷They keep saying to those who despise
    me,
  'The LORD says: You will have peace.'
And to all who follow the stubbornness
    of their hearts
  they say, 'No harm will come to you.'
¹⁸But which of them has stood in the
    council of the LORD

to see or to hear his word?
Who has listened and heard his
    word?
¹⁹See, the storm of the LORD
  will burst out in wrath,
a whirlwind swirling down
  on the heads of the wicked.
²⁰The anger of the LORD will not turn
    back
  until he fully accomplishes
  the purposes of his heart.
In days to come
  you will understand it clearly.
²¹I did not send these prophets,
  yet they have run with their message;
I did not speak to them,
  yet they have prophesied.
²²But if they had stood in my council,
  they would have proclaimed my
    words to my people
and would have turned them from
    their evil ways
  and from their evil deeds.

²³"Am I only a God nearby,"
                  declares the LORD,
  "and not a God far away?
²⁴Can anyone hide in secret places
  so that I cannot see him?"
                  declares the LORD.
  "Do not I fill heaven and earth?"
                  declares the LORD.

²⁵"I have heard what the prophets say who prophesy lies in my name. They say, 'I had a dream! I had a dream!' ²⁶How long will this continue in the hearts of these lying prophets, who prophesy the delusions of their own minds? ²⁷They think the dreams they tell one another will make my people forget my name, just as their fathers forgot my name through Baal worship. ²⁸Let the prophet who has a dream tell his dream, but let the one who has my word speak it faithfully. For what has straw to do with grain?" declares the LORD. ²⁹"Is not my word like fire," declares the LORD, "and like a hammer that breaks a rock in pieces?

³⁰"Therefore," declares the LORD, "I am against the prophets who steal from one another words supposedly from me. ³¹Yes," declares the LORD, "I am against the prophets who wag their own tongues and yet declare, 'The LORD declares.' ³²Indeed, I am against those who prophesy false dreams," declares the LORD. "They tell them and lead my people astray with their reckless lies, yet I did not send or ap-

*a*10 Or *because of these things*   *b*10 Or *land mourns* point them. They do not benefit these people in the least," declares the LORD.

False Oracles and False Prophets

[33]"When these people, or a prophet or a priest, ask you, 'What is the oracle[a] of the LORD?' say to them, 'What oracle?[b] I will forsake you, declares the LORD.' [34]If a prophet or a priest or anyone else claims, 'This is the oracle of the LORD,' I will punish that man and his household. [35]This is what each of you keeps on saying to his friend or relative: 'What is the LORD's answer?' or 'What has the LORD spoken?' [36]But you must not mention 'the oracle of the LORD' again, because every man's own word becomes his oracle and so you distort the words of the living God, the LORD Almighty, our God. [37]This is what you keep saying to a prophet: 'What is the LORD's answer to you?' or 'What has the LORD spoken?' [38]Although you claim, 'This is the oracle of the LORD,' this is what the LORD says: You used the words 'This is the oracle of the LORD,' even though I told you that you must not claim, 'This is the oracle of the LORD.' [39]Therefore, I will surely forget you and cast you out of my presence along with the city I gave to you and your fathers. [40]I will bring upon you everlasting disgrace—everlasting shame that will not be forgotten."

Two Baskets of Figs

24 After Jehoiachin[c] son of Jehoiakim king of Judah and the officials, the craftsmen and the artisans of Judah were carried into exile from Jerusalem to Babylon by Nebuchadnezzar king of Babylon, the LORD showed me two baskets of figs placed in front of the temple of the LORD. [2]One basket had very good figs, like those that ripen early; the other basket had very poor figs, so bad they could not be eaten. [3]Then the LORD asked me, "What do you see, Jeremiah?"

"Figs," I answered. "The good ones are very good, but the poor ones are so bad they cannot be eaten."

[4]Then the word of the LORD came to me: [5]"This is what the LORD, the God of Israel, says: 'Like these good figs, I regard as good the exiles from Judah, whom I sent away from this place to the land of the Babylonians.[d] [6]My eyes will watch over them for their good, and I will bring them back to this land. I will build them up and not tear them down; I will plant them and not uproot them. [7]I will give them a heart

to know me, that I am the LORD. They will be my people, and I will be their God, for they will return to me with all their heart. [8]"'But like the poor figs, which are so bad they cannot be eaten,' says the LORD, 'so will I deal with Zedekiah king of Judah, his officials and the survivors from Jerusalem, whether they remain in this land or live in Egypt. [9]I will make them abhorrent and an offense to all the kingdoms of the earth, a reproach and a byword, an object of ridicule and cursing, wherever I banish them. [10]I will send the sword, famine and plague against them until they are destroyed from the land I gave to them and their fathers.'"

Seventy Years of Captivity

25 The word came to Jeremiah concerning all the people of Judah in the fourth year of Jehoiakim son of Josiah king of Judah, which was the first year of Nebuchadnezzar king of Babylon. [2]So Jeremiah the prophet said to all the people of Judah and to all those living in Jerusalem: [3]For twenty-three years—from the thirteenth year of Josiah son of Amon king of Judah until this very day—the word of the LORD has come to me and I have spoken to you again and again, but you have not listened.

[4]And though the LORD has sent all his servants the prophets to you again and again, you have not listened or paid any attention. [5]They said, "Turn now, each of you, from your evil ways and your evil practices, and you can stay in the land the LORD gave to you and your fathers for ever and ever. [6]Do not follow other gods to serve and worship them; do not provoke me to anger with what your hands have made. Then I will not harm you."

[7]"But you did not listen to me," declares the LORD, "and you have provoked me with what your hands have made, and you have brought harm to yourselves."

[8]Therefore the LORD Almighty says this: "Because you have not listened to my words, [9]I will summon all the peoples of the north and my servant Nebuchadnezzar king of Babylon," declares the LORD, "and I will bring them against this land and its inhabitants and against all the surrounding nations. I will completely

[a]33 Or *burden* (see Septuagint and Vulgate) [b]33 Hebrew; Septuagint and Vulgate *'You are the burden.* (The Hebrew for *oracle* and *burden* is the same.) [c]1 Hebrew *Jeconiah,* a variant of *Jehoiachin* [d]5 Or *Chaldeans*

Judah to Serve Nebuchadnezzar

27 Early in the reign of Zedekiah[a] son of Josiah king of Judah, this word came to Jeremiah from the LORD: [2]This is what the LORD said to me: "Make a yoke out of straps and crossbars and put it on your neck. [3]Then send word to the kings of Edom, Moab, Ammon, Tyre and Sidon through the envoys who have come to Jerusalem to Zedekiah king of Judah. [4]Give them a message for their masters and say, 'This is what the LORD Almighty, the God of Israel, says: "Tell this to your masters: [5]With my great power and outstretched arm I made the earth and its people and the animals that are on it, and I give it to anyone I please. [6]Now I will hand all your countries over to my servant Nebuchadnezzar king of Babylon; I will make even the wild animals subject to him. [7]All nations will serve him and his son and his grandson until the time for his land comes; then many nations and great kings will subjugate him.

[8]" ' "If, however, any nation or kingdom will not serve Nebuchadnezzar king of Babylon or bow its neck under his yoke, I will punish that nation with the sword, famine and plague, declares the LORD, until I destroy it by his hand. [9]So do not listen to your prophets, your diviners, your interpreters of dreams, your mediums or your sorcerers who tell you, 'You will not serve the king of Babylon.' [10]They prophesy lies to you that will only serve to remove you far from your lands; I will banish you and you will perish. [11]But if any nation will bow its neck under the yoke of the king of Babylon and serve him, I will let that nation remain in its own land to till it and to live there, declares the LORD." ' "

[12]I gave the same message to Zedekiah king of Judah. I said, "Bow your neck under the yoke of the king of Babylon; serve him and his people, and you will live. [13]Why will you and your people die by the sword, famine and plague with which the LORD has threatened any nation that will not serve the king of Babylon? [14]Do not listen to the words of the prophets who say to you, 'You will not serve the king of Babylon,' for they are prophesying lies to you. [15]'I have not sent them,' declares the LORD. 'They are prophesying lies in my name. Therefore, I will banish you and you will perish, both you and the prophets who prophesy to you.' "

[16]Then I said to the priests and all these people, "This is what the LORD says: Do not listen to the prophets who say, 'Very soon now the articles from the LORD's house will be brought back from Babylon.' They are prophesying lies to you. [17]Do not listen to them. Serve the king of Babylon, and you will live. Why should this city become a ruin? [18]If they are prophets and have the word of the LORD, let them plead with the LORD Almighty that the furnishings remaining in the house of the LORD and in the palace of the king of Judah and in Jerusalem not be taken to Babylon. [19]For this is what the LORD Almighty says about the pillars, the Sea, the movable stands and the other furnishings that are left in this city, [20]which Nebuchadnezzar king of Babylon did not take away when he carried Jehoiachin[b] son of Jehoiakim king of Judah into exile from Jerusalem to Babylon, along with all the nobles of Judah and Jerusalem— [21]yes, this is what the LORD Almighty, the God of Israel, says about the things that are left in the house of the LORD and in the palace of the king of Judah and in Jerusalem: [22]'They will be taken to Babylon and there they will remain until the day I come for them,' declares the LORD. 'Then I will bring them back and restore them to this place.' "

The False Prophet Hananiah

28 In the fifth month of that same year, the fourth year, early in the reign of Zedekiah king of Judah, the prophet Hananiah son of Azzur, who was from Gibeon, said to me in the house of the LORD in the presence of the priests and all the people: [2]"This is what the LORD Almighty, the God of Israel, says: 'I will break the yoke of the king of Babylon. [3]Within two years I will bring back to this place all the articles of the LORD's house that Nebuchadnezzar king of Babylon removed from here and took to Babylon. [4]I will also bring back to this place Jehoiachin[b] son of Jehoiakim king of Judah and all the other exiles from Judah who went to Babylon,' declares the LORD, 'for I will break the yoke of the king of Babylon.' "

[5]Then the prophet Jeremiah replied to the prophet Hananiah before the priests and all the people who were standing in

---

[a]1 A few Hebrew manuscripts and Syriac (see also Jer. 27:3, 12 and 28:1); most Hebrew manuscripts *Jehoiakim* (Most Septuagint manuscripts do not have this verse.)   [b]20,4 Hebrew *Jeconiah,* a variant of *Jehoiachin*

the house of the LORD. [6]He said, "Amen! May the LORD do so! May the LORD fulfill the words you have prophesied by bringing the articles of the LORD's house and all the exiles back to this place from Babylon. [7]Nevertheless, listen to what I have to say in your hearing and in the hearing of all the people: [8]From early times the prophets who preceded you and me have prophesied war, disaster and plague against many countries and great kingdoms. [9]But the prophet who prophesies peace will be recognized as one truly sent by the LORD only if his prediction comes true."

[10]Then the prophet Hananiah took the yoke off the neck of the prophet Jeremiah and broke it, [11]and he said before all the people, "This is what the LORD says: 'In the same way will I break the yoke of Nebuchadnezzar king of Babylon off the neck of all the nations within two years.' " At this, the prophet Jeremiah went on his way.

[12]Shortly after the prophet Hananiah had broken the yoke off the neck of the prophet Jeremiah, the word of the LORD came to Jeremiah: [13]"Go and tell Hananiah, 'This is what the LORD says: You have broken a wooden yoke, but in its place you will get a yoke of iron. [14]This is what the LORD Almighty, the God of Israel, says: I will put an iron yoke on the necks of all these nations to make them serve Nebuchadnezzar king of Babylon, and they will serve him. I will even give him control over the wild animals.' "

[15]Then the prophet Jeremiah said to Hananiah the prophet, "Listen, Hananiah! The LORD has not sent you, yet you have persuaded this nation to trust in lies. [16]Therefore, this is what the LORD says: 'I am about to remove you from the face of the earth. This very year you are going to die, because you have preached rebellion against the LORD.' "

[17]In the seventh month of that same year, Hananiah the prophet died.

A Letter to the Exiles

29 This is the text of the letter that the prophet Jeremiah sent from Jerusalem to the surviving elders among the exiles and to the priests, the prophets and all the other people Nebuchadnezzar had carried into exile from Jerusalem to Babylon. [2](This was after King Jehoiachin[a] and the queen mother, the court officials and the leaders of Judah and Jerusalem,

the craftsmen and the artisans had gone into exile from Jerusalem.) [3]He entrusted the letter to Elasah son of Shaphan and to Gemariah son of Hilkiah, whom Zedekiah king of Judah sent to King Nebuchadnezzar in Babylon. It said:

[4]This is what the LORD Almighty, the God of Israel, says to all those I carried into exile from Jerusalem to Babylon: [5]"Build houses and settle down; plant gardens and eat what they produce. [6]Marry and have sons and daughters; find wives for your sons and give your daughters in marriage, so that they too may have sons and daughters. Increase in number there; do not decrease. [7]Also, seek the peace and prosperity of the city to which I have carried you into exile. Pray to the LORD for it, because if it prospers, you too will prosper." [8]Yes, this is what the LORD Almighty, the God of Israel, says: "Do not let the prophets and diviners among you deceive you. Do not listen to the dreams you encourage them to have. [9]They are prophesying lies to you in my name. I have not sent them," declares the LORD.

[10]This is what the LORD says: "When seventy years are completed for Babylon, I will come to you and fulfill my gracious promise to bring you back to this place. [11]For I know the plans I have for you," declares the LORD, "plans to prosper you and not to harm you, plans to give you hope and a future. [12]Then you will call upon me and come and pray to me, and I will listen to you. [13]You will seek me and find me when you seek me with all your heart. [14]I will be found by you," declares the LORD, "and will bring you back from captivity.[b] I will gather you from all the nations and places where I have banished you," declares the LORD, "and will bring you back to the place from which I carried you into exile."

[15]You may say, "The LORD has raised up prophets for us in Babylon," [16]but this is what the LORD says about the king who sits on David's throne and all the people who remain in this city, your countrymen who did not go with you into exile— [17]yes, this is what the LORD Almighty

[a]2 Hebrew *Jeconiah*, a variant of *Jehoiachin*
[b]14 Or *will restore your fortunes*

says: "I will send the sword, famine and plague against them and I will make them like poor figs that are so bad they cannot be eaten. [18]I will pursue them with the sword, famine and plague and will make them abhorrent to all the kingdoms of the earth and an object of cursing and horror, of scorn and reproach, among all the nations where I drive them. [19]For they have not listened to my words," declares the LORD, "words that I sent to them again and again by my servants the prophets. And you exiles have not listened either," declares the LORD.

[20]Therefore, hear the word of the LORD, all you exiles whom I have sent away from Jerusalem to Babylon. [21]This is what the LORD Almighty, the God of Israel, says about Ahab son of Kolaiah and Zedekiah son of Maaseiah, who are prophesying lies to you in my name: "I will hand them over to Nebuchadnezzar king of Babylon, and he will put them to death before your very eyes. [22]Because of them, all the exiles from Judah who are in Babylon will use this curse: 'The LORD treat you like Zedekiah and Ahab, whom the king of Babylon burned in the fire.' [23]For they have done outrageous things in Israel; they have committed adultery with their neighbors' wives and in my name have spoken lies, which I did not tell them to do. I know it and am a witness to it," declares the LORD.

Message to Shemaiah

[24]Tell Shemaiah the Nehelamite, [25]"This is what the LORD Almighty, the God of Israel, says: You sent letters in your own name to all the people in Jerusalem, to Zephaniah son of Maaseiah the priest, and to all the other priests. You said to Zephaniah, [26]'The LORD has appointed you priest in place of Jehoiada to be in charge of the house of the LORD; you should put any madman who acts like a prophet into the stocks and neck-irons. [27]So why have you not reprimanded Jeremiah from Anathoth, who poses as a prophet among you? [28]He has sent this message to us in Babylon: It will be a long time. Therefore build houses and settle down; plant gardens and eat what they produce.' "

[29]Zephaniah the priest, however, read

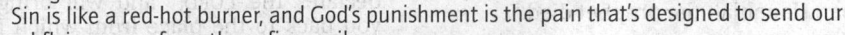

HEY DAD
Why does God have to punish us?

Text: Jeremiah 29:10–13

God doesn't have to punish us, but he punishes us because he loves us.

How does this work? Well, imagine what your life would be like if you couldn't feel physical pain. That sounds great at first, but what would happen if you grabbed onto a red hot stove burner? That burner would begin melting its way into the soft flesh of your hand. By the time the stench of burning flesh reached your nose, telling you that something was wrong, your hand would be permanently damaged. Fortunately, God gave us the gift of physical pain to warn us of danger.

Sin is like a red-hot burner, and God's punishment is the pain that's designed to send our hand flying away from those fiery coils.

Throughout the Old Testament, we see God punishing the Israelites again and again—not because he enjoyed it, but because he wanted them to pull back from the pain and come back to him. God sent the Israelites into Babylonian exile for seventy years, an action that was intended to help them see that they'd been holding on to red-hot burners for too long. This painful experience was all part of God's ultimate plan for his children: "For I know the plans I have for you … plans to prosper you and not to harm you, plans to give you hope and a future. Then you will call upon me and come and pray to me, and I will listen to you" (v. 11).

God punishes us because he loves us and wants the very best for us. Pretty simple, isn't it?

For a complete listing of Questions Kids Ask, turn to page 1435.

the letter to Jeremiah the prophet. ³⁰Then the word of the LORD came to Jeremiah: ³¹"Send this message to all the exiles: 'This is what the LORD says about Shemaiah the Nehelamite: Because Shemaiah has prophesied to you, even though I did not send him, and has led you to believe a lie, ³²this is what the LORD says: I will surely punish Shemaiah the Nehelamite and his descendants. He will have no one left among this people, nor will he see the good things I will do for my people, declares the LORD, because he has preached rebellion against me.' "

Restoration of Israel

30 This is the word that came to Jeremiah from the LORD: ²"This is what the LORD, the God of Israel, says: 'Write in a book all the words I have spoken to you. ³The days are coming,' declares the LORD, 'when I will bring my people Israel and Judah back from captivity*a* and restore them to the land I gave their forefathers to possess,' says the LORD."

a3 Or will restore the fortunes of my people Israel and Judah

What Do You Mean, "Welcome to Detroit"?

A folder sat on my desk, bulging with information, itineraries and airline tickets. My new job as a sales rep would have me visiting customers from Seattle to Miami, San Diego to Rhode Island. So my secretary and I had mapped out my first sales trip, and I was ready to go.

However, before leaving for this trip, I had my weekly appointment with my boss, Bill Slemp. A man at the opposite end of his career, Bill had been an extremely successful executive with several major corporations. When I walked into his office for our meeting, I found him doing something that fascinated me.

Spread out on his small conference table were a bunch of airline tickets, his personal calendar, and a typed itinerary. A veteran of hundreds of sales trips, Bill was going through these arrangements, meticulously checking the accuracy of every single plane ticket, every single rental car and hotel reservation. *How needless,* I remember thinking, *to go over all that stuff so carefully. Doesn't he trust his travel agent? Doesn't he think his secretary can get it right?*

Over twenty years and hundreds of business trips later, my business associates will tell you that I *never* leave for a trip without spreading out my tickets, my itinerary, and my calendar and making certain that every single item is correct. From

DAILY INSIGHT

MONDAY

Passage:
Jeremiah 29:10–14

Verse:
Jeremiah 29:11

personal experience, Bill Slemp knew the incredible frustration of getting messed up a thousand miles from home and wanted to do everything he possibly could to avoid it. I have since learned the same lesson, and learned it well: "I'm sorry, sir, I have no reservation in that name." "Well then, what do you mean, 'Welcome to Detroit?'" Ugh.

Now, take another look at today's text. It tells us that God's itinerary for his people was—and is—a good plan. The Israelites' seventy year exile was not designed to harm them. God's painstaking, event-by-event strategy *did* include his punishment for their waywardness. However, it also included a hope and a future.

Sometimes life seems more like a computer error than God's plan—as if you have a seven minute layover in Los Angeles to get from American to Delta. But there are no errors. God has the events of your life spread out like the airline tickets and itineraries on Bill's table. He is reviewing every detail of your tomorrows. And his "gracious promise" is that his plans are for your good.

God, through Jeremiah, tells us to "call upon me and come and pray to me, and I will listen to you." I'd encourage you to do this right now. There isn't a more flawless travel agent in the heavens. Trust him.

For your next devotional reading, go to page 857.

⁴These are the words the LORD spoke concerning Israel and Judah: ⁵"This is what the LORD says:

" 'Cries of fear are heard—
    terror, not peace.
⁶Ask and see:
    Can a man bear children?
Then why do I see every strong man
    with his hands on his stomach like a
        woman in labor,
    every face turned deathly pale?
⁷How awful that day will be!
    None will be like it.
It will be a time of trouble for Jacob,
    but he will be saved out of it.

⁸" 'In that day,' declares the LORD
        Almighty,
    'I will break the yoke off their necks
and will tear off their bonds;
    no longer will foreigners enslave
        them.
⁹Instead, they will serve the LORD their
        God
    and David their king,
    whom I will raise up for them.

¹⁰" 'So do not fear, O Jacob my servant;
    do not be dismayed, O Israel,'
                    declares the LORD.
'I will surely save you out of a distant
        place,
    your descendants from the land of
        their exile.
Jacob will again have peace and
        security,
    and no one will make him afraid.
¹¹I am with you and will save you,'
    declares the LORD.
'Though I completely destroy all the
        nations
    among which I scatter you,
    I will not completely destroy you.
I will discipline you but only with
        justice;
    I will not let you go entirely
        unpunished.'

¹²"This is what the LORD says:

" 'Your wound is incurable,
    your injury beyond healing.
¹³There is no one to plead your cause,
    no remedy for your sore,
    no healing for you.
¹⁴All your allies have forgotten you;
    they care nothing for you.
I have struck you as an enemy would
    and punished you as would the
        cruel,
because your guilt is so great

and your sins so many.
¹⁵Why do you cry out over your wound,
    your pain that has no cure?
Because of your great guilt and many
        sins
    I have done these things to you.

¹⁶" 'But all who devour you will be
        devoured;
    all your enemies will go into exile.
Those who plunder you will be
        plundered;
    all who make spoil of you I will
        despoil.
¹⁷But I will restore you to health
    and heal your wounds,'
                    declares the LORD,
'because you are called an outcast,
    Zion for whom no one cares.'

¹⁸"This is what the LORD says:

" 'I will restore the fortunes of Jacob's
        tents
    and have compassion on his
        dwellings;
the city will be rebuilt on her ruins,
    and the palace will stand in its
        proper place.
¹⁹From them will come songs of
        thanksgiving
    and the sound of rejoicing.
I will add to their numbers,
    and they will not be decreased;
I will bring them honor,
    and they will not be disdained.
²⁰Their children will be as in days of
        old,
    and their community will be
        established before me;
    I will punish all who oppress them.
²¹Their leader will be one of their own;
    their ruler will arise from among
        them.
I will bring him near and he will come
        close to me,
    for who is he who will devote himself
        to be close to me?'
                    declares the LORD.
²²" 'So you will be my people,
    and I will be your God.' "

²³See, the storm of the LORD
    will burst out in wrath,
a driving wind swirling down
    on the heads of the wicked.
²⁴The fierce anger of the LORD will not
        turn back
    until he fully accomplishes
    the purposes of his heart.
In days to come
    you will understand this.

31 "At that time," declares the LORD, "I will be the God of all the clans of Israel, and they will be my people."
²This is what the LORD says:

"The people who survive the sword
  will find favor in the desert;
  I will come to give rest to Israel."

³The LORD appeared to us in the past,ᵃ saying:

"I have loved you with an everlasting
    love;
  I have drawn you with
    loving-kindness.
⁴I will build you up again
  and you will be rebuilt, O Virgin
    Israel.
Again you will take up your
    tambourines
  and go out to dance with the joyful.
⁵Again you will plant vineyards
  on the hills of Samaria;
the farmers will plant them
  and enjoy their fruit.
⁶There will be a day when watchmen cry
    out
  on the hills of Ephraim,
'Come, let us go up to Zion,
  to the LORD our God.' "

⁷This is what the LORD says:

"Sing with joy for Jacob;
  shout for the foremost of the nations.
Make your praises heard, and say,
  'O LORD, save your people,
  the remnant of Israel.'
⁸See, I will bring them from the land of
    the north
  and gather them from the ends of
    the earth.
Among them will be the blind and the
    lame,
  expectant mothers and women in
    labor;
  a great throng will return.
⁹They will come with weeping;
  they will pray as I bring them back.
I will lead them beside streams of water
  on a level path where they will not
    stumble,
because I am Israel's father,
  and Ephraim is my firstborn son.

¹⁰"Hear the word of the LORD, O nations;
  proclaim it in distant coastlands:
'He who scattered Israel will gather
    them
  and will watch over his flock like a
    shepherd.'
¹¹For the LORD will ransom Jacob

and redeem them from the hand of
  those stronger than they.
¹²They will come and shout for joy on the
    heights of Zion;
  they will rejoice in the bounty of the
    LORD—
the grain, the new wine and the oil,
  the young of the flocks and herds.
They will be like a well-watered garden,
  and they will sorrow no more.
¹³Then maidens will dance and be glad,
  young men and old as well.
I will turn their mourning into
    gladness;
  I will give them comfort and joy
    instead of sorrow.
¹⁴I will satisfy the priests with
    abundance,
  and my people will be filled with my
    bounty,"
                    declares the LORD.

¹⁵This is what the LORD says:

"A voice is heard in Ramah,
  mourning and great weeping,
Rachel weeping for her children
  and refusing to be comforted,
  because her children are no more."

¹⁶This is what the LORD says:

"Restrain your voice from weeping
  and your eyes from tears,
for your work will be rewarded,"
                    declares the LORD.
  "They will return from the land of
    the enemy.
¹⁷So there is hope for your future,"
                    declares the LORD.
  "Your children will return to their
    own land.

¹⁸"I have surely heard Ephraim's
    moaning:
'You disciplined me like an unruly
    calf,
  and I have been disciplined.
Restore me, and I will return,
  because you are the LORD my God.
¹⁹After I strayed,
  I repented;
after I came to understand,
  I beat my breast.
I was ashamed and humiliated
  because I bore the disgrace of my
    youth.'
²⁰Is not Ephraim my dear son,
  the child in whom I delight?
Though I often speak against him,

ᵃ3 Or LORD has appeared to us from afar

I still remember him.
Therefore my heart yearns for him;
   I have great compassion for him,"
                       declares the LORD.

21 "Set up road signs;
      put up guideposts.
   Take note of the highway,
      the road that you take.
   Return, O Virgin Israel,
      return to your towns.
22 How long will you wander,
      O unfaithful daughter?
   The LORD will create a new thing on
         earth—
      a woman will surround^a a man."

23This is what the LORD Almighty, the God of Israel, says: "When I bring them back from captivity,^{b} the people in the land of Judah and in its towns will once again use these words: 'The LORD bless you, O righteous dwelling, O sacred mountain.' 24People will live together in Judah and all its towns—farmers and those who move about with their flocks. 25I will refresh the weary and satisfy the faint."

26At this I awoke and looked around. My sleep had been pleasant to me.

27"The days are coming," declares the LORD, "when I will plant the house of Israel and the house of Judah with the offspring of men and of animals. 28Just as I watched over them to uproot and tear down, and to overthrow, destroy and bring disaster, so I will watch over them to build and to plant," declares the LORD. 29"In those days people will no longer say,

   'The fathers have eaten sour grapes,
      and the children's teeth are set on
         edge.'

30Instead, everyone will die for his own sin; whoever eats sour grapes—his own teeth will be set on edge.

31 "The time is coming," declares the
         LORD,
      "when I will make a new covenant
   with the house of Israel
      and with the house of Judah.
32 It will not be like the covenant
      I made with their forefathers
   when I took them by the hand
      to lead them out of Egypt,
   because they broke my covenant,
      though I was a husband to^c them,^{d}"
                       declares the LORD.
33 "This is the covenant I will make with
      the house of Israel

after that time," declares the LORD.
"I will put my law in their minds
   and write it on their hearts.
I will be their God,
   and they will be my people.
34 No longer will a man teach his
         neighbor,
   or a man his brother, saying, 'Know
      the LORD,'
because they will all know me,
   from the least of them to the
         greatest,"
                       declares the LORD.
"For I will forgive their wickedness
   and will remember their sins no
      more."

35This is what the LORD says,

he who appoints the sun
   to shine by day,
who decrees the moon and stars
   to shine by night,
who stirs up the sea
   so that its waves roar—
   the LORD Almighty is his name:
36 "Only if these decrees vanish from my
         sight,"
      declares the LORD,
"will the descendants of Israel ever
         cease
   to be a nation before me."

37This is what the LORD says:

"Only if the heavens above can be
         measured
   and the foundations of the earth
      below be searched out
will I reject all the descendants of Israel
   because of all they have done,"
                       declares the LORD.

38"The days are coming," declares the LORD, "when this city will be rebuilt for me from the Tower of Hananel to the Corner Gate. 39The measuring line will stretch from there straight to the hill of Gareb and then turn to Goah. 40The whole valley where dead bodies and ashes are thrown, and all the terraces out to the Kidron Valley on the east as far as the corner of the Horse Gate, will be holy to the LORD. The city will never again be uprooted or demolished."

Jeremiah Buys a Field

32 This is the word that came to Jeremiah from the LORD in the tenth

^{a}22 Or *will go about seeking*; or *will protect*
^{b}23 Or *I restore their fortunes* ^{c}32 Hebrew; Septuagint and Syriac / *and I turned away from*
^{d}32 Or *was their master*

year of Zedekiah king of Judah, which was the eighteenth year of Nebuchadnezzar. [2]The army of the king of Babylon was then besieging Jerusalem, and Jeremiah the prophet was confined in the courtyard of the guard in the royal palace of Judah.

[3]Now Zedekiah king of Judah had imprisoned him there, saying, "Why do you prophesy as you do? You say, 'This is what the LORD says: I am about to hand this city over to the king of Babylon, and he will capture it. [4]Zedekiah king of Judah will not escape out of the hands of the Babylonians[a] but will certainly be handed over to the king of Babylon, and will speak with him face to face and see him with his own eyes. [5]He will take Zedekiah to Babylon, where he will remain until I deal with him, declares the LORD. If you fight against the Babylonians, you will not succeed.' "

[6]Jeremiah said, "The word of the LORD came to me: [7]Hanamel son of Shallum your uncle is going to come to you and say, 'Buy my field at Anathoth, because as nearest relative it is your right and duty to buy it.'

[8]"Then, just as the LORD had said, my cousin Hanamel came to me in the courtyard of the guard and said, 'Buy my field at Anathoth in the territory of Benjamin. Since it is your right to redeem it and possess it, buy it for yourself.'

"I knew that this was the word of the LORD; [9]so I bought the field at Anathoth from my cousin Hanamel and weighed out for him seventeen shekels[b] of silver. [10]I signed and sealed the deed, had it witnessed, and weighed out the silver on the scales. [11]I took the deed of purchase—the sealed copy containing the terms and conditions, as well as the unsealed copy— [12]and I gave this deed to Baruch son of Neriah, the son of Mahseiah, in the presence of my cousin Hanamel and of the witnesses who had signed the deed and of all the Jews sitting in the courtyard of the guard.

[13]"In their presence I gave Baruch these instructions: [14]'This is what the LORD Almighty, the God of Israel, says: Take these documents, both the sealed and unsealed copies of the deed of purchase, and put them in a clay jar so they will last a long time. [15]For this is what the LORD Almighty, the God of Israel, says: Houses, fields and vineyards will again be bought in this land.'

[16]"After I had given the deed of purchase to Baruch son of Neriah, I prayed to the LORD:

[17]"Ah, Sovereign LORD, you have made the heavens and the earth by your great power and outstretched arm. Nothing is too hard for you. [18]You show love to thousands but bring the punishment for the fathers' sins into the laps of their children after them. O great and powerful God, whose name is the LORD Almighty, [19]great are your purposes and mighty are your deeds. Your eyes are open to all the ways of men; you reward everyone according to his conduct and as his deeds deserve. [20]You performed miraculous signs and wonders in Egypt and have continued them to this day, both in Israel and among all mankind, and have gained the renown that is still yours. [21]You brought your people Israel out of Egypt with signs and wonders, by a mighty hand and an outstretched arm and with great terror. [22]You gave them this land you had sworn to give their forefathers, a land flowing with milk and honey. [23]They came in and took possession of it, but they did not obey you or follow your law; they did not do what you commanded them to do. So you brought all this disaster upon them.

[24]"See how the siege ramps are built up to take the city. Because of the sword, famine and plague, the city will be handed over to the Babylonians who are attacking it. What you said has happened, as you now see. [25]And though the city will be handed over to the Babylonians, you, O Sovereign LORD, say to me, 'Buy the field with silver and have the transaction witnessed.' "

[26]Then the word of the LORD came to Jeremiah: [27]"I am the LORD, the God of all mankind. Is anything too hard for me? [28]Therefore, this is what the LORD says: I am about to hand this city over to the Babylonians and to Nebuchadnezzar king of Babylon, who will capture it. [29]The Babylonians who are attacking this city will come in and set it on fire; they will burn it down, along with the houses where the people provoked me to anger by burning incense on the roofs to Baal and by pouring out drink offerings to other gods. [30]"The people of Israel and Judah have

---

[a]4 Or *Chaldeans*; also in verses 5, 24, 25, 28, 29 and 43   [b]9 That is, about 7 ounces (about 200 grams)

done nothing but evil in my sight from their youth; indeed, the people of Israel have done nothing but provoke me with what their hands have made, declares the LORD. ³¹From the day it was built until now, this city has so aroused my anger and wrath that I must remove it from my sight. ³²The people of Israel and Judah have provoked me by all the evil they have done—they, their kings and officials, their priests and prophets, the men of Judah and the people of Jerusalem. ³³They turned their backs to me and not their faces; though I taught them again and again, they would not listen or respond to discipline. ³⁴They set up their abominable idols in the house that bears my Name and defiled it. ³⁵They built high places for Baal in the Valley of Ben Hinnom to sacrifice their sons and daughtersᵃ to Molech, though I never commanded, nor did it enter my mind, that they should do such a detestable thing and so make Judah sin.

³⁶"You are saying about this city, 'By the sword, famine and plague it will be handed over to the king of Babylon'; but this is what the LORD, the God of Israel, says: ³⁷I will surely gather them from all the lands where I banish them in my furious anger and great wrath; I will bring them back to this place and let them live in safety. ³⁸They will be my people, and I will be their God. ³⁹I will give them singleness of heart and action, so that they will always fear me for their own good and the good of their children after them. ⁴⁰I will make an everlasting covenant with them: I will never stop doing good to them, and I will inspire them to fear me, so that they will never turn away from me. ⁴¹I will rejoice in doing them good and will assuredly plant them in this land with all my heart and soul.

⁴²"This is what the LORD says: As I have brought all this great calamity on this people, so I will give them all the prosperity I have promised them. ⁴³Once more fields will be bought in this land of which you say, 'It is a desolate waste, without men or animals, for it has been handed over to the Babylonians.' ⁴⁴Fields will be bought for silver, and deeds will be signed, sealed and witnessed in the territory of Benjamin, in the villages around Jerusalem, in the towns of Judah and in the towns of the hill country, of the western foothills and of the Negev, because I will restore their fortunes,ᵇ declares the LORD."

Promise of Restoration

33 While Jeremiah was still confined in the courtyard of the guard, the word of the LORD came to him a second time: ²"This is what the LORD says, he who made the earth, the LORD who formed it and established it—the LORD is his name: ³'Call to me and I will answer you and tell you great and unsearchable things you do not know.' ⁴For this is what the LORD, the God of Israel, says about the houses in this city and the royal palaces of Judah that have been torn down to be used against the siege ramps and the swordᶜ ⁵in the fight with the Babylonians: 'They will be filled with the dead bodies of the men I will slay in my anger and wrath. I will hide my face from this city because of all its wickedness.

⁶" 'Nevertheless, I will bring health and healing to it; I will heal my people and will let them enjoy abundant peace and security. ⁷I will bring Judah and Israel back from captivityᵈ and will rebuild them as they were before. ⁸I will cleanse them from all the sin they have committed against me and will forgive all their sins of rebellion against me. ⁹Then this city will bring me renown, joy, praise and honor before all nations on earth that hear of all the good things I do for it; and they will be in awe and will tremble at the abundant prosperity and peace I provide for it.'

¹⁰"This is what the LORD says: 'You say about this place, "It is a desolate waste, without men or animals." Yet in the towns of Judah and the streets of Jerusalem that are deserted, inhabited by neither men nor animals, there will be heard once more ¹¹the sounds of joy and gladness, the voices of bride and bridegroom, and the voices of those who bring thank offerings to the house of the LORD, saying,

"Give thanks to the LORD Almighty,
   for the LORD is good;
   his love endures forever."

For I will restore the fortunes of the land as they were before,' says the LORD. ¹²"This is what the LORD Almighty says: 'In this place, desolate and without men or animals—in all its towns there will again be pastures for shepherds to rest their flocks. ¹³In the towns of the hill country, of the western foothills and of

ᵃ35 Or *to make their sons and daughters pass through the fire*   ᵇ44 Or *will bring them back from captivity*   ᶜ5 Or *Chaldeans*   ᵈ7 Or *will restore the fortunes of Judah and Israel*

the Negev, in the territory of Benjamin, in the villages around Jerusalem and in the towns of Judah, flocks will again pass under the hand of the one who counts them,' says the LORD.

¹⁴" 'The days are coming,' declares the LORD, 'when I will fulfill the gracious promise I made to the house of Israel and to the house of Judah.

¹⁵" 'In those days and at that time
I will make a righteous Branch
    sprout from David's line;
he will do what is just and right in
    the land.

¹⁶In those days Judah will be saved
and Jerusalem will live in safety.
This is the name by which it[a] will be
    called:
    The LORD Our Righteousness.'

¹⁷For this is what the LORD says: 'David will never fail to have a man to sit on the throne of the house of Israel, ¹⁸nor will the priests, who are Levites, ever fail to have a man to stand before me continually to offer burnt offerings, to burn grain offerings and to present sacrifices.' "

[a] 16 Or he

God, Star One

DAILY INSIGHT

TUESDAY

Passage:
Jeremiah 33:1–5

Verse:
Jeremiah 33:3

Fastened to my belt, straight down from my left arm, is a little electronic device. It's a pager, and I cannot tell you how much I resisted getting this little plastic ball-and-chain. I explained to my clients and business associates that sometimes I was simply unavailable. I apologized when they protested. But when my *family* told me that they'd like to be able to reach me anytime, I immediately clipped on the electronic handcuffs.

When you call my toll-free pager number you hear a recording of my voice. I instruct you to "Key in your phone number so I can return your call." Then I add a little postscript. "If this is urgent and you want me to drop whatever I'm doing right now and call you immediately, please add 'star one' to your telephone number."

I always do my best to return all my pages as soon as I can, but when I get a "star one," I search for a phone like a man possessed. I have yanked my car off the freeway in my quest for a pay phone. I've mooched cell phones from my friends at lunch. I've even used one of those airplane telephones, it's blurry connection making me sound like Neil Armstrong: *"That's one small step for man, one giant leap for mankind."* Anyway, in spite of myself, I truly am grateful for my little pager. Being a simple phone call away from my family has brought us closer together, and my business

associates would also testify that it has helped me respond better to their requests.

Jeremiah and many other Israelites were in Babylonian prisons, far away from Israel's main communication uplink with God—the temple in Jerusalem. Because of their disobedience, God had allowed Nebuchadnezzar and his mighty army to have their way with the Israelites. Now, as they sat in exile, God's people felt isolated and afraid—hopelessly out of range of the temple and its twenty-four-hour priests.

So God told Jeremiah to tell the people something extremely important. "Call to me and I will answer," he said. "Even though you're hundreds of miles from your homes and feeling completely alienated from me, I am reliably available. Call me. You won't even need a telephone. I'll assume that it's a star one, and I'll instantly return your page."

Here's the message for you and me: God is never out of range. His ear is always tuned to our call. He is always listening.

The next time you see a pager fastened to someone's belt, remember something very important. The sovereign God of the universe is never out of range. Wherever you may find yourself, God is just a simple call away.

For your next devotional reading, go to page 873.

[19]The word of the LORD came to Jeremiah: [20]"This is what the LORD says: 'If you can break my covenant with the day and my covenant with the night, so that day and night no longer come at their appointed time, [21]then my covenant with David my servant—and my covenant with the Levites who are priests ministering before me—can be broken and David will no longer have a descendant to reign on his throne. [22]I will make the descendants of David my servant and the Levites who minister before me as countless as the stars of the sky and as measureless as the sand on the seashore.' "

[23]The word of the LORD came to Jeremiah: [24]"Have you not noticed that these people are saying, 'The LORD has rejected the two kingdoms[a] he chose'? So they despise my people and no longer regard them as a nation. [25]This is what the LORD says: 'If I have not established my covenant with day and night and the fixed laws of heaven and earth, [26]then I will reject the descendants of Jacob and David my servant and will not choose one of his sons to rule over the descendants of Abraham, Isaac and Jacob. For I will restore their fortunes[b] and have compassion on them.' "

Warning to Zedekiah

34 While Nebuchadnezzar king of Babylon and all his army and all the kingdoms and peoples in the empire he ruled were fighting against Jerusalem and all its surrounding towns, this word came to Jeremiah from the LORD: [2]"This is what the LORD, the God of Israel, says: Go to Zedekiah king of Judah and tell him, 'This is what the LORD says: I am about to hand this city over to the king of Babylon, and he will burn it down. [3]You will not escape from his grasp but will surely be captured and handed over to him. You will see the king of Babylon with your own eyes, and he will speak with you face to face. And you will go to Babylon.

[4]" 'Yet hear the promise of the LORD, O Zedekiah king of Judah. This is what the LORD says concerning you: You will not die by the sword; [5]you will die peacefully. As people made a funeral fire in honor of your fathers, the former kings who preceded you, so they will make a fire in your honor and lament, "Alas, O master!" I myself make this promise, declares the LORD.' "

[6]Then Jeremiah the prophet told all this to Zedekiah king of Judah, in Jerusalem, [7]while the army of the king of Babylon was fighting against Jerusalem and the other cities of Judah that were still holding out—Lachish and Azekah. These were the only fortified cities left in Judah.

Freedom for Slaves

[8]The word came to Jeremiah from the LORD after King Zedekiah had made a covenant with all the people in Jerusalem to proclaim freedom for the slaves. [9]Everyone was to free his Hebrew slaves, both male and female; no one was to hold a fellow Jew in bondage. [10]So all the officials and people who entered into this covenant agreed that they would free their male and female slaves and no longer hold them in bondage. They agreed, and set them free. [11]But afterward they changed their minds and took back the slaves they had freed and enslaved them again.

[12]Then the word of the LORD came to Jeremiah: [13]"This is what the LORD, the God of Israel, says: I made a covenant with your forefathers when I brought them out of Egypt, out of the land of slavery. I said, [14]'Every seventh year each of you must free any fellow Hebrew who has sold himself to you. After he has served you six years, you must let him go free.'[c] Your fathers, however, did not listen to me or pay attention to me. [15]Recently you repented and did what is right in my sight: Each of you proclaimed freedom to his countrymen. You even made a covenant before me in the house that bears my Name. [16]But now you have turned around and profaned my name; each of you has taken back the male and female slaves you had set free to go where they wished. You have forced them to become your slaves again.

[17]"Therefore, this is what the LORD says: You have not obeyed me; you have not proclaimed freedom for your fellow countrymen. So I now proclaim 'freedom' for you, declares the LORD—'freedom' to fall by the sword, plague and famine. I will make you abhorrent to all the kingdoms of the earth. [18]The men who have violated my covenant and have not fulfilled the terms of the covenant they made before me, I will treat like the calf they cut in two and then walked between its pieces. [19]The

a24 Or *families*   b26 Or *will bring them back from captivity*   c14 Deut. 15:12

leaders of Judah and Jerusalem, the court officials, the priests and all the people of the land who walked between the pieces of the calf, **20**I will hand over to their enemies who seek their lives. Their dead bodies will become food for the birds of the air and the beasts of the earth.

21"I will hand Zedekiah king of Judah and his officials over to their enemies who seek their lives, to the army of the king of Babylon, which has withdrawn from you. **22**I am going to give the order, declares the LORD, and I will bring them back to this city. They will fight against it, take it and burn it down. And I will lay waste the towns of Judah so no one can live there."

The Recabites

35 This is the word that came to Jeremiah from the LORD during the reign of Jehoiakim son of Josiah king of Judah: **2**"Go to the Recabite family and invite them to come to one of the side rooms of the house of the LORD and give them wine to drink."

3So I went to get Jaazaniah son of Jeremiah, the son of Habazziniah, and his brothers and all his sons—the whole family of the Recabites. **4**I brought them into the house of the LORD, into the room of the sons of Hanan son of Igdaliah the man of God. It was next to the room of the officials, which was over that of Maaseiah son of Shallum the doorkeeper. **5**Then I set bowls full of wine and some cups before the men of the Recabite family and said to them, "Drink some wine."

6But they replied, "We do not drink wine, because our forefather Jonadab son of Recab gave us this command: 'Neither you nor your descendants must ever drink wine. **7**Also you must never build houses, sow seed or plant vineyards; you must never have any of these things, but must always live in tents. Then you will live a long time in the land where you are nomads.' **8**We have obeyed everything our forefather Jonadab son of Recab commanded us. Neither we nor our wives nor our sons and daughters have ever drunk wine **9**or built houses to live in or had vineyards, fields or crops. **10**We have lived in tents and have fully obeyed everything our forefather Jonadab commanded us. **11**But when Nebuchadnezzar king of Babylon invaded this land, we said, 'Come, we must go to Jerusalem to escape the Babylonian*a* and Aramean armies.' So we have remained in Jerusalem."

12Then the word of the LORD came to Jeremiah, saying: **13**"This is what the LORD Almighty, the God of Israel, says: Go and tell the men of Judah and the people of Jerusalem, 'Will you not learn a lesson and obey my words?' declares the LORD. **14**'Jonadab son of Recab ordered his sons not to drink wine and this command has been kept. To this day they do not drink wine, because they obey their forefather's command. But I have spoken to you again and again, yet you have not obeyed me. **15**Again and again I sent all my servants the prophets to you. They said, "Each of you must turn from your wicked ways and reform your actions; do not follow other gods to serve them. Then you will live in the land I have given to you and your fathers." But you have not paid attention or listened to me. **16**The descendants of Jonadab son of Recab have carried out the command their forefather gave them, but these people have not obeyed me.'

17"Therefore, this is what the LORD God Almighty, the God of Israel, says: 'Listen! I am going to bring on Judah and on everyone living in Jerusalem every disaster I pronounced against them. I spoke to them, but they did not listen; I called to them, but they did not answer.' "

18Then Jeremiah said to the family of the Recabites, "This is what the LORD Almighty, the God of Israel, says: 'You have obeyed the command of your forefather Jonadab and have followed all his instructions and have done everything he ordered.' **19**Therefore, this is what the LORD Almighty, the God of Israel, says: 'Jonadab son of Recab will never fail to have a man to serve me.' "

Jehoiakim Burns Jeremiah's Scroll

36 In the fourth year of Jehoiakim son of Josiah king of Judah, this word came to Jeremiah from the LORD: **2**"Take a scroll and write on it all the words I have spoken to you concerning Israel, Judah and all the other nations from the time I began speaking to you in the reign of Josiah till now. **3**Perhaps when the people of Judah hear about every disaster I plan to inflict on them, each of them will turn from his wicked way; then I will forgive their wickedness and their sin."

4So Jeremiah called Baruch son of Neriah, and while Jeremiah dictated all the words the LORD had spoken to him, Baruch wrote them on the scroll. **5**Then

a11 Or Chaldean

Jeremiah told Baruch, "I am restricted; I cannot go to the LORD's temple. ⁶So you go to the house of the LORD on a day of fasting and read to the people from the scroll the words of the LORD that you wrote as I dictated. Read them to all the people of Judah who come in from their towns. ⁷Perhaps they will bring their petition before the LORD, and each will turn from his wicked ways, for the anger and wrath pronounced against this people by the LORD are great."

⁸Baruch son of Neriah did everything Jeremiah the prophet told him to do; at the LORD's temple he read the words of the LORD from the scroll. ⁹In the ninth month of the fifth year of Jehoiakim son of Josiah king of Judah, a time of fasting before the LORD was proclaimed for all the people in Jerusalem and those who had come from the towns of Judah. ¹⁰From the room of Gemariah son of Shaphan the secretary, which was in the upper courtyard at the entrance of the New Gate of the temple, Baruch read to all the people at the LORD's temple the words of Jeremiah from the scroll.

¹¹When Micaiah son of Gemariah, the son of Shaphan, heard all the words of the LORD from the scroll, ¹²he went down to the secretary's room in the royal palace, where all the officials were sitting: Elishama the secretary, Delaiah son of Shemaiah, Elnathan son of Acbor, Gemariah son of Shaphan, Zedekiah son of Hananiah, and all the other officials. ¹³After Micaiah told them everything he had heard Baruch read to the people from the scroll, ¹⁴all the officials sent Jehudi son of Nethaniah, the son of Shelemiah, the son of Cushi, to say to Baruch, "Bring the scroll from which you have read to the people and come." So Baruch son of Neriah went to them with the scroll in his hand. ¹⁵They said to him, "Sit down, please, and read it to us."

So Baruch read it to them. ¹⁶When they heard all these words, they looked at each other in fear and said to Baruch, "We must report all these words to the king." ¹⁷Then they asked Baruch, "Tell us, how did you come to write all this? Did Jeremiah dictate it?"

¹⁸"Yes," Baruch replied, "he dictated all these words to me, and I wrote them in ink on the scroll."

¹⁹Then the officials said to Baruch, "You and Jeremiah, go and hide. Don't let anyone know where you are."

²⁰After they put the scroll in the room of Elishama the secretary, they went to the king in the courtyard and reported everything to him. ²¹The king sent Jehudi to get the scroll, and Jehudi brought it from the room of Elishama the secretary and read it to the king and all the officials standing beside him. ²²It was the ninth month and the king was sitting in the winter apartment, with a fire burning in the firepot in front of him. ²³Whenever Jehudi had read three or four columns of the scroll, the king cut them off with a scribe's knife and threw them into the firepot, until the entire scroll was burned in the fire. ²⁴The king and all his attendants who heard all these words showed no fear, nor did they tear their clothes. ²⁵Even though Elnathan, Delaiah and Gemariah urged the king not to burn the scroll, he would not listen to them. ²⁶Instead, the king commanded Jerahmeel, a son of the king, Seraiah son of Azriel and Shelemiah son of Abdeel to arrest Baruch the scribe and Jeremiah the prophet. But the LORD had hidden them.

²⁷After the king burned the scroll containing the words that Baruch had written at Jeremiah's dictation, the word of the LORD came to Jeremiah: ²⁸"Take another scroll and write on it all the words that were on the first scroll, which Jehoiakim king of Judah burned up. ²⁹Also tell Jehoiakim king of Judah, 'This is what the LORD says: You burned that scroll and said, "Why did you write on it that the king of Babylon would certainly come and destroy this land and cut off both men and animals from it?" ³⁰Therefore, this is what the LORD says about Jehoiakim king of Judah: He will have no one to sit on the throne of David; his body will be thrown out and exposed to the heat by day and the frost by night. ³¹I will punish him and his children and his attendants for their wickedness; I will bring on them and those living in Jerusalem and the people of Judah every disaster I pronounced against them, because they have not listened.' "

³²So Jeremiah took another scroll and gave it to the scribe Baruch son of Neriah, and as Jeremiah dictated, Baruch wrote on it all the words of the scroll that Jehoiakim king of Judah had burned in the fire. And many similar words were added to them.

Jeremiah in Prison

37 Zedekiah son of Josiah was made king of Judah by Nebuchadnezzar king

of Babylon; he reigned in place of Jehoi-achin[a] son of Jehoiakim. [2]Neither he nor his attendants nor the people of the land paid any attention to the words the LORD had spoken through Jeremiah the prophet.

[3]King Zedekiah, however, sent Jehucal son of Shelemiah with the priest Zephaniah son of Maaseiah to Jeremiah the prophet with this message: "Please pray to the LORD our God for us."

[4]Now Jeremiah was free to come and go among the people, for he had not yet been put in prison. [5]Pharaoh's army had marched out of Egypt, and when the Babylonians[b] who were besieging Jerusalem heard the report about them, they withdrew from Jerusalem.

[6]Then the word of the LORD came to Jeremiah the prophet: [7]"This is what the LORD, the God of Israel, says: Tell the king of Judah, who sent you to inquire of me, 'Pharaoh's army, which has marched out to support you, will go back to its own land, to Egypt. [8]Then the Babylonians will return and attack this city; they will capture it and burn it down.' [9]This is what the LORD says: Do not deceive yourselves, thinking, 'The Babylonians will surely leave us.' They will not! [10]Even if you were to defeat the entire Babylonian[c] army that is attacking you and only wounded men were left in their tents, they would come out and burn this city down."

[11]After the Babylonian army had withdrawn from Jerusalem because of Pharaoh's army, [12]Jeremiah started to leave the city to go to the territory of Benjamin to get his share of the property among the people there. [13]But when he reached the Benjamin Gate, the captain of the guard, whose name was Irijah son of Shelemiah, the son of Hananiah, arrested him and said, "You are deserting to the Babylonians!"

[14]"That's not true!" Jeremiah said. "I am not deserting to the Babylonians." But Irijah would not listen to him; instead, he arrested Jeremiah and brought him to the officials. [15]They were angry with Jeremiah and had him beaten and imprisoned in the house of Jonathan the secretary, which they had made into a prison.

[16]Jeremiah was put into a vaulted cell in a dungeon, where he remained a long time. [17]Then King Zedekiah sent for him and had him brought to the palace, where he asked him privately, "Is there any word from the LORD?"

"Yes," Jeremiah replied, "you will be handed over to the king of Babylon."

[18]Then Jeremiah said to King Zedekiah, "What crime have I committed against you or your officials or this people, that you have put me in prison? [19]Where are your prophets who prophesied to you, 'The king of Babylon will not attack you or this land'? [20]But now, my lord the king, please listen. Let me bring my petition before you: Do not send me back to the house of Jonathan the secretary, or I will die there."

[21]King Zedekiah then gave orders for Jeremiah to be placed in the courtyard of the guard and given bread from the street of the bakers each day until all the bread in the city was gone. So Jeremiah remained in the courtyard of the guard.

Jeremiah Thrown Into a Cistern

38 Shephatiah son of Mattan, Gedaliah son of Pashhur, Jehucal[d] son of Shelemiah, and Pashhur son of Malkijah heard what Jeremiah was telling all the people when he said, [2]"This is what the LORD says: 'Whoever stays in this city will die by the sword, famine or plague, but whoever goes over to the Babylonians[e] will live. He will escape with his life; he will live.' [3]And this is what the LORD says: 'This city will certainly be handed over to the army of the king of Babylon, who will capture it.' "

[4]Then the officials said to the king, "This man should be put to death. He is discouraging the soldiers who are left in this city, as well as all the people, by the things he is saying to them. This man is not seeking the good of these people but their ruin."

[5]"He is in your hands," King Zedekiah answered. "The king can do nothing to oppose you."

[6]So they took Jeremiah and put him into the cistern of Malkijah, the king's son, which was in the courtyard of the guard. They lowered Jeremiah by ropes into the cistern; it had no water in it, only mud, and Jeremiah sank down into the mud.

[7]But Ebed-Melech, a Cushite,[f] an official[g] in the royal palace, heard that they had put Jeremiah into the cistern. While the king was sitting in the Benjamin Gate,

---

[a]1 Hebrew *Coniah*, a variant of *Jehoiachin*
[b]5 Or *Chaldeans*; also in verses 8, 9, 13 and 14
[c]10 Or *Chaldean*; also in verse 11   [d]1 Hebrew *Jucal*, a variant of *Jehucal*   [e]2 Or *Chaldeans*; also in verses 18, 19 and 23   [f]7 Probably from the upper Nile region   [g]7 Or *a eunuch*

[8]Ebed-Melech went out of the palace and said to him, [9]"My lord the king, these men have acted wickedly in all they have done to Jeremiah the prophet. They have thrown him into a cistern, where he will starve to death when there is no longer any bread in the city."

[10]Then the king commanded Ebed-Melech the Cushite, "Take thirty men from here with you and lift Jeremiah the prophet out of the cistern before he dies."

[11]So Ebed-Melech took the men with him and went to a room under the treasury in the palace. He took some old rags and worn-out clothes from there and let them down with ropes to Jeremiah in the cistern. [12]Ebed-Melech the Cushite said to Jeremiah, "Put these old rags and worn-out clothes under your arms to pad the ropes." Jeremiah did so, [13]and they pulled him up with the ropes and lifted him out of the cistern. And Jeremiah remained in the courtyard of the guard.

Zedekiah Questions Jeremiah Again

[14]Then King Zedekiah sent for Jeremiah the prophet and had him brought to the third entrance to the temple of the LORD. "I am going to ask you something," the king said to Jeremiah. "Do not hide anything from me."

[15]Jeremiah said to Zedekiah, "If I give you an answer, will you not kill me? Even if I did give you counsel, you would not listen to me."

[16]But King Zedekiah swore this oath secretly to Jeremiah: "As surely as the LORD lives, who has given us breath, I will neither kill you nor hand you over to those who are seeking your life."

[17]Then Jeremiah said to Zedekiah, "This is what the LORD God Almighty, the God of Israel, says: 'If you surrender to the officers of the king of Babylon, your life will be spared and this city will not be burned down; you and your family will live. [18]But if you will not surrender to the officers of the king of Babylon, this city will be handed over to the Babylonians and they will burn it down; you yourself will not escape from their hands.' "

[19]King Zedekiah said to Jeremiah, "I am afraid of the Jews who have gone over to the Babylonians, for the Babylonians may hand me over to them and they will mistreat me."

[20]"They will not hand you over," Jeremiah replied. "Obey the LORD by doing what I tell you. Then it will go well with you, and your life will be spared. [21]But if you refuse to surrender, this is what the LORD has revealed to me: [22]All the women left in the palace of the king of Judah will be brought out to the officials of the king of Babylon. Those women will say to you:

" 'They misled you and overcame
        you—
    those trusted friends of yours.
Your feet are sunk in the mud;
    your friends have deserted you.'

[23]"All your wives and children will be brought out to the Babylonians. You yourself will not escape from their hands but will be captured by the king of Babylon; and this city will[a] be burned down."

[24]Then Zedekiah said to Jeremiah, "Do not let anyone know about this conversation, or you may die. [25]If the officials hear that I talked with you, and they come to you and say, 'Tell us what you said to the king and what the king said to you; do not hide it from us or we will kill you,' [26]then tell them, 'I was pleading with the king not to send me back to Jonathan's house to die there.' "

[27]All the officials did come to Jeremiah and question him, and he told them everything the king had ordered him to say. So they said no more to him, for no one had heard his conversation with the king.

[28]And Jeremiah remained in the courtyard of the guard until the day Jerusalem was captured.

The Fall of Jerusalem

39 This is how Jerusalem was taken: [1]In the ninth year of Zedekiah king of Judah, in the tenth month, Nebuchadnezzar king of Babylon marched against Jerusalem with his whole army and laid siege to it. [2]And on the ninth day of the fourth month of Zedekiah's eleventh year, the city wall was broken through. [3]Then all the officials of the king of Babylon came and took seats in the Middle Gate: Nergal-Sharezer of Samgar, Nebo-Sarsekim[b] a chief officer, Nergal-Sharezer a high official and all the other officials of the king of Babylon. [4]When Zedekiah king of Judah and all the soldiers saw them, they fled; they left the city at night by way of the king's garden, through the gate between the two walls, and headed toward the Arabah.[c]

a23 Or *and you will cause this city to*   b3 Or *Nergal-Sharezer, Samgar-Nebo, Sarsekim*   c4 Or *the Jordan Valley*

⁵But the Babylonianᵃ army pursued them and overtook Zedekiah in the plains of Jericho. They captured him and took him to Nebuchadnezzar king of Babylon at Riblah in the land of Hamath, where he pronounced sentence on him. ⁶There at Riblah the king of Babylon slaughtered the sons of Zedekiah before his eyes and also killed all the nobles of Judah. ⁷Then he put out Zedekiah's eyes and bound him with bronze shackles to take him to Babylon.

⁸The Babyloniansᵇ set fire to the royal palace and the houses of the people and broke down the walls of Jerusalem. ⁹Nebuzaradan commander of the imperial guard carried into exile to Babylon the people who remained in the city, along with those who had gone over to him, and the rest of the people. ¹⁰But Nebuzaradan the commander of the guard left behind in the land of Judah some of the poor people, who owned nothing; and at that time he gave them vineyards and fields.

¹¹Now Nebuchadnezzar king of Babylon had given these orders about Jeremiah through Nebuzaradan commander of the imperial guard: ¹²"Take him and look after him; don't harm him but do for him whatever he asks." ¹³So Nebuzaradan the commander of the guard, Nebushazban a chief officer, Nergal-Sharezer a high official and all the other officers of the king of Babylon ¹⁴sent and had Jeremiah taken out of the courtyard of the guard. They turned him over to Gedaliah son of Ahikam, the son of Shaphan, to take him back to his home. So he remained among his own people.

¹⁵While Jeremiah had been confined in the courtyard of the guard, the word of the LORD came to him: ¹⁶"Go and tell Ebed-Melech the Cushite, 'This is what the LORD Almighty, the God of Israel, says: I am about to fulfill my words against this city through disaster, not prosperity. At that time they will be fulfilled before your eyes. ¹⁷But I will rescue you on that day, declares the LORD; you will not be handed over to those you fear. ¹⁸I will save you; you will not fall by the sword but will escape with your life, because you trust in me, declares the LORD.'"

Jeremiah Freed

40 The word came to Jeremiah from the LORD after Nebuzaradan commander of the imperial guard had released him at Ramah. He had found

Jeremiah bound in chains among all the captives from Jerusalem and Judah who were being carried into exile to Babylon. ²When the commander of the guard found Jeremiah, he said to him, "The LORD your God decreed this disaster for this place. ³And now the LORD has brought it about; he has done just as he said he would. All this happened because you people sinned against the LORD and did not obey him. ⁴But today I am freeing you from the chains on your wrists. Come with me to Babylon, if you like, and I will look after you; but if you do not want to, then don't come. Look, the whole country lies before you; go wherever you please." ⁵However, before Jeremiah turned to go,ᶜ Nebuzaradan added, "Go back to Gedaliah son of Ahikam, the son of Shaphan, whom the king of Babylon has appointed over the towns of Judah, and live with him among the people, or go anywhere else you please."

Then the commander gave him provisions and a present and let him go. ⁶So Jeremiah went to Gedaliah son of Ahikam at Mizpah and stayed with him among the people who were left behind in the land.

Gedaliah Assassinated

⁷When all the army officers and their men who were still in the open country heard that the king of Babylon had appointed Gedaliah son of Ahikam as governor over the land and had put him in charge of the men, women and children who were the poorest in the land and who had not been carried into exile to Babylon, ⁸they came to Gedaliah at Mizpah—Ishmael son of Nethaniah, Johanan and Jonathan the sons of Kareah, Seraiah son of Tanhumeth, the sons of Ephai the Netophathite, and Jaazaniahᵈ the son of the Maacathite, and their men. ⁹Gedaliah son of Ahikam, the son of Shaphan, took an oath to reassure them and their men. "Do not be afraid to serve the Babylonians,ᵉ" he said. "Settle down in the land and serve the king of Babylon, and it will go well with you. ¹⁰I myself will stay at Mizpah to represent you before the Babylonians who come to us, but you are to harvest the wine, summer fruit and oil, and put them in your storage jars, and live in the towns you have taken over."

¹¹When all the Jews in Moab, Ammon,

ᵃ5 Or *Chaldean*   ᵇ8 Or *Chaldeans*   ᶜ5 Or *Jeremiah answered*   ᵈ8 Hebrew *Jezaniah*, a variant of *Jaazaniah*   ᵉ9 Or *Chaldeans*; also in verse 10

Edom and all the other countries heard that the king of Babylon had left a remnant in Judah and had appointed Gedaliah son of Ahikam, the son of Shaphan, as governor over them, [12]they all came back to the land of Judah, to Gedaliah at Mizpah, from all the countries where they had been scattered. And they harvested an abundance of wine and summer fruit.

[13]Johanan son of Kareah and all the army officers still in the open country came to Gedaliah at Mizpah [14]and said to him, "Don't you know that Baalis king of the Ammonites has sent Ishmael son of Nethaniah to take your life?" But Gedaliah son of Ahikam did not believe them.

[15]Then Johanan son of Kareah said privately to Gedaliah in Mizpah, "Let me go and kill Ishmael son of Nethaniah, and no one will know it. Why should he take your life and cause all the Jews who are gathered around you to be scattered and the remnant of Judah to perish?"

[16]But Gedaliah son of Ahikam said to Johanan son of Kareah, "Don't do such a thing! What you are saying about Ishmael is not true."

41 In the seventh month Ishmael son of Nethaniah, the son of Elishama, who was of royal blood and had been one of the king's officers, came with ten men to Gedaliah son of Ahikam at Mizpah. While they were eating together there, [2]Ishmael son of Nethaniah and the ten men who were with him got up and struck down Gedaliah son of Ahikam, the son of Shaphan, with the sword, killing the one whom the king of Babylon had appointed as governor over the land. [3]Ishmael also killed all the Jews who were with Gedaliah at Mizpah, as well as the Babylonian[a] soldiers who were there.

[4]The day after Gedaliah's assassination, before anyone knew about it, [5]eighty men who had shaved off their beards, torn their clothes and cut themselves came from Shechem, Shiloh and Samaria, bringing grain offerings and incense with them to the house of the LORD. [6]Ishmael son of Nethaniah went out from Mizpah to meet them, weeping as he went. When he met them, he said, "Come to Gedaliah son of Ahikam." [7]When they went into the city, Ishmael son of Nethaniah and the men who were with him slaughtered them and threw them into a cistern. [8]But ten of them said to Ishmael, "Don't kill us! We have wheat and barley, oil and honey, hidden in a field." So he let them alone and did not kill them with the others.

[9]Now the cistern where he threw all the bodies of the men he had killed along with Gedaliah was the one King Asa had made as part of his defense against Baasha king of Israel. Ishmael son of Nethaniah filled it with the dead.

[10]Ishmael made captives of all the rest of the people who were in Mizpah—the king's daughters along with all the others who were left there, over whom Nebuzaradan commander of the imperial guard had appointed Gedaliah son of Ahikam. Ishmael son of Nethaniah took them captive and set out to cross over to the Ammonites.

[11]When Johanan son of Kareah and all the army officers who were with him heard about all the crimes Ishmael son of Nethaniah had committed, [12]they took all their men and went to fight Ishmael son of Nethaniah. They caught up with him near the great pool in Gibeon. [13]When all the people Ishmael had with him saw Johanan son of Kareah and the army officers who were with him, they were glad. [14]All the people Ishmael had taken captive at Mizpah turned and went over to Johanan son of Kareah. [15]But Ishmael son of Nethaniah and eight of his men escaped from Johanan and fled to the Ammonites

Flight to Egypt

[16]Then Johanan son of Kareah and all the army officers who were with him led away all the survivors from Mizpah whom he had recovered from Ishmael son of Nethaniah after he had assassinated Gedaliah son of Ahikam: the soldiers, women, children and court officials he had brought from Gibeon. [17]And they went on, stopping at Geruth Kimham near Bethlehem on their way to Egypt [18]to escape the Babylonians.[b] They were afraid of them because Ishmael son of Nethaniah had killed Gedaliah son of Ahikam, whom the king of Babylon had appointed as governor over the land.

42 Then all the army officers, including Johanan son of Kareah and Jezaniah[c] son of Hoshaiah, and all the people from the least to the greatest approached [2]Jeremiah the prophet and said to him, "Please hear our petition and pray to the LORD your God for this entire remnant. For as you now see, though we were once many, now only a few are left. [3]Pray that the LORD your God will tell us where we should go and what we should do."

⁴"I have heard you," replied Jeremiah the prophet. "I will certainly pray to the LORD your God as you have requested; I will tell you everything the LORD says and will keep nothing back from you." ⁵Then they said to Jeremiah, "May the LORD be a true and faithful witness against us if we do not act in accordance with everything the LORD your God sends you to tell us. ⁶Whether it is favorable or unfavorable, we will obey the LORD our God, to whom we are sending you, so that it will go well with us, for we will obey the LORD our God."

⁷Ten days later the word of the LORD came to Jeremiah. ⁸So he called together Johanan son of Kareah and all the army officers who were with him and all the people from the least to the greatest. ⁹He said to them, "This is what the LORD, the God of Israel, to whom you sent me to present your petition, says: ¹⁰'If you stay in this land, I will build you up and not tear you down; I will plant you and not uproot you, for I am grieved over the disaster I have inflicted on you. ¹¹Do not be afraid of the king of Babylon, whom you now fear. Do not be afraid of him, declares the LORD, for I am with you and will save you and deliver you from his hands. ¹²I will show you compassion so that he will have compassion on you and restore you to your land.'

¹³"However, if you say, 'We will not stay in this land,' and so disobey the LORD your God, ¹⁴and if you say, 'No, we will go and live in Egypt, where we will not see war or hear the trumpet or be hungry for bread,' ¹⁵then hear the word of the LORD, O remnant of Judah. This is what the LORD Almighty, the God of Israel, says: 'If you are determined to go to Egypt and you do go to settle there, ¹⁶then the sword you fear will overtake you there, and the famine you dread will follow you into Egypt, and there you will die. ¹⁷Indeed, all who are determined to go to Egypt to settle there will die by the sword, famine and plague; not one of them will survive or escape the disaster I will bring on them.' ¹⁸This is what the LORD Almighty, the God of Israel, says: 'As my anger and wrath have been poured out on those who lived in Jerusalem, so will my wrath be poured out on you when you go to Egypt. You will be an object of cursing and horror, of condemnation and reproach; you will never see this place again.'

¹⁹"O remnant of Judah, the LORD has told you, 'Do not go to Egypt.' Be sure of this: I warn you today ²⁰that you made a fatal mistakeᵃ when you sent me to the LORD your God and said, 'Pray to the LORD our God for us; tell us everything he says and we will do it.' ²¹I have told you today, but you still have not obeyed the LORD your God in all he sent me to tell you. ²²So now, be sure of this: You will die by the sword, famine and plague in the place where you want to go to settle."

43 When Jeremiah finished telling the people all the words of the LORD their God—everything the LORD had sent him to tell them— ²Azariah son of Hoshaiah and Johanan son of Kareah and all the arrogant men said to Jeremiah, "You are lying! The LORD our God has not sent you to say, 'You must not go to Egypt to settle there.' ³But Baruch son of Neriah is inciting you against us to hand us over to the Babylonians,ᵇ so they may kill us or carry us into exile to Babylon."

⁴So Johanan son of Kareah and all the army officers and all the people disobeyed the LORD's command to stay in the land of Judah. ⁵Instead, Johanan son of Kareah and all the army officers led away all the remnant of Judah who had come back to live in the land of Judah from all the nations where they had been scattered. ⁶They also led away all the men, women and children and the king's daughters whom Nebuzaradan commander of the imperial guard had left with Gedaliah son of Ahikam, the son of Shaphan, and Jeremiah the prophet and Baruch son of Neriah. ⁷So they entered Egypt in disobedience to the LORD and went as far as Tahpanhes.

⁸In Tahpanhes the word of the LORD came to Jeremiah: ⁹"While the Jews are watching, take some large stones with you and bury them in clay in the brick pavement at the entrance to Pharaoh's palace in Tahpanhes. ¹⁰Then say to them, 'This is what the LORD Almighty, the God of Israel, says: I will send for my servant Nebuchadnezzar king of Babylon, and I will set his throne over these stones I have buried here; he will spread his royal canopy above them. ¹¹He will come and attack Egypt, bringing death to those destined for death, captivity to those destined for captivity, and the sword to those destined for the sword. ¹²Heᶜ will set fire

ᵃ20 Or you erred in your hearts ᵇ3 Or Chaldeans
ᶜ12 Or I

to the temples of the gods of Egypt; he will burn their temples and take their gods captive. As a shepherd wraps his garment around him, so will he wrap Egypt around himself and depart from there unscathed. [13]There in the temple of the sun[a] in Egypt he will demolish the sacred pillars and will burn down the temples of the gods of Egypt.' "

Disaster Because of Idolatry

44 This word came to Jeremiah concerning all the Jews living in Lower Egypt—in Migdol, Tahpanhes and Memphis[b]—and in Upper Egypt[c]: [2]"This is what the LORD Almighty, the God of Israel, says: You saw the great disaster I brought on Jerusalem and on all the towns of Judah. Today they lie deserted and in ruins [3]because of the evil they have done. They provoked me to anger by burning incense and by worshiping other gods that neither they nor you nor your fathers ever knew. [4]Again and again I sent my servants the prophets, who said, 'Do not do this detestable thing that I hate!' [5]But they did not listen or pay attention; they did not turn from their wickedness or stop burning incense to other gods. [6]Therefore, my fierce anger was poured out; it raged against the towns of Judah and the streets of Jerusalem and made them the desolate ruins they are today.

[7]"Now this is what the LORD God Almighty, the God of Israel, says: Why bring such great disaster on yourselves by cutting off from Judah the men and women, the children and infants, and so leave yourselves without a remnant? [8]Why provoke me to anger with what your hands have made, burning incense to other gods in Egypt, where you have come to live? You will destroy yourselves and make yourselves an object of cursing and reproach among all the nations on earth. [9]Have you forgotten the wickedness committed by your fathers and by the kings and queens of Judah and the wickedness committed by you and your wives in the land of Judah and the streets of Jerusalem? [10]To this day they have not humbled themselves or shown reverence, nor have they followed my law and the decrees I set before you and your fathers.

[11]"Therefore, this is what the LORD Almighty, the God of Israel, says: I am determined to bring disaster on you and to destroy all Judah. [12]I will take away the remnant of Judah who were determined to go to Egypt to settle there. They will all perish in Egypt; they will fall by the sword or die from famine. From the least to the greatest, they will die by sword or famine. They will become an object of cursing and horror, of condemnation and reproach. [13]I will punish those who live in Egypt with the sword, famine and plague, as I punished Jerusalem. [14]None of the remnant of Judah who have gone to live in Egypt will escape or survive to return to the land of Judah, to which they long to return and live; none will return except a few fugitives."

[15]Then all the men who knew that their wives were burning incense to other gods, along with all the women who were present—a large assembly—and all the people living in Lower and Upper Egypt,[d] said to Jeremiah, [16]"We will not listen to the message you have spoken to us in the name of the LORD! [17]We will certainly do everything we said we would: We will burn incense to the Queen of Heaven and will pour out drink offerings to her just as we and our fathers, our kings and our officials did in the towns of Judah and in the streets of Jerusalem. At that time we had plenty of food and were well off and suffered no harm. [18]But ever since we stopped burning incense to the Queen of Heaven and pouring out drink offerings to her, we have had nothing and have been perishing by sword and famine."

[19]The women added, "When we burned incense to the Queen of Heaven and poured out drink offerings to her, did not our husbands know that we were making cakes like her image and pouring out drink offerings to her?"

[20]Then Jeremiah said to all the people, both men and women, who were answering him, [21]"Did not the LORD remember and think about the incense burned in the towns of Judah and the streets of Jerusalem by you and your fathers, your kings and your officials and the people of the land? [22]When the LORD could no longer endure your wicked actions and the detestable things you did, your land became an object of cursing and a desolate waste without inhabitants, as it is today. [23]Because you have burned incense and have sinned against the LORD and have not obeyed him or followed his law or his decrees or his stipulations, this

---

[a]13 Or *in Heliopolis*   [b]1 Hebrew *Noph*
[c]1 Hebrew *in Pathros*   [d]15 Hebrew *in Egypt and Pathros*

disaster has come upon you, as you now see."

²⁴Then Jeremiah said to all the people, including the women, "Hear the word of the LORD, all you people of Judah in Egypt. ²⁵This is what the LORD Almighty, the God of Israel, says: You and your wives have shown by your actions what you promised when you said, 'We will certainly carry out the vows we made to burn incense and pour out drink offerings to the Queen of Heaven.'

"Go ahead then, do what you promised! Keep your vows! ²⁶But hear the word of the LORD, all Jews living in Egypt: 'I swear by my great name,' says the LORD, 'that no one from Judah living anywhere in Egypt will ever again invoke my name or swear, "As surely as the Sovereign LORD lives." ²⁷For I am watching over them for harm, not for good; the Jews in Egypt will perish by sword and famine until they are all destroyed. ²⁸Those who escape the sword and return to the land of Judah from Egypt will be very few. Then the whole remnant of Judah who came to live in Egypt will know whose word will stand— mine or theirs.

²⁹" 'This will be the sign to you that I will punish you in this place,' declares the LORD, 'so that you will know that my threats of harm against you will surely stand.' ³⁰This is what the LORD says: 'I am going to hand Pharaoh Hophra king of Egypt over to his enemies who seek his life, just as I handed Zedekiah king of Judah over to Nebuchadnezzar king of Babylon, the enemy who was seeking his life.' "

A Message to Baruch

45 This is what Jeremiah the prophet told Baruch son of Neriah in the fourth year of Jehoiakim son of Josiah king of Judah, after Baruch had written on a scroll the words Jeremiah was then dictating: ²"This is what the LORD, the God of Israel, says to you, Baruch: ³You said, 'Woe to me! The LORD has added sorrow to my pain; I am worn out with groaning and find no rest.' "

⁴⌊The LORD said,⌋ "Say this to him: 'This is what the LORD says: I will overthrow what I have built and uproot what I have planted, throughout the land. ⁵Should you then seek great things for yourself? Seek them not. For I will bring disaster on all people, declares the LORD, but wherever you go I will let you escape with your life.' "

A Message About Egypt

46 This is the word of the LORD that came to Jeremiah the prophet concerning the nations:

²Concerning Egypt:

This is the message against the army of Pharaoh Neco king of Egypt, which was defeated at Carchemish on the Euphrates River by Nebuchadnezzar king of Babylon in the fourth year of Jehoiakim son of Josiah king of Judah:

³ "Prepare your shields, both large and
　　small,
　　and march out for battle!
⁴ Harness the horses,
　　mount the steeds!
Take your positions
　　with helmets on!
Polish your spears,
　　put on your armor!
⁵ What do I see?
　　They are terrified,
they are retreating,
　　their warriors are defeated.
They flee in haste
　　without looking back,
　　and there is terror on every side,"
　　　　　　　　　　declares the LORD.
⁶ "The swift cannot flee
　　nor the strong escape.
In the north by the River Euphrates
　　they stumble and fall.
⁷ "Who is this that rises like the Nile,
　　like rivers of surging waters?
⁸ Egypt rises like the Nile,
　　like rivers of surging waters.
She says, 'I will rise and cover the earth;
　　I will destroy cities and their people.'
⁹ Charge, O horses!
　　Drive furiously, O charioteers!
March on, O warriors—
　　men of Cushᵃ and Put who carry
　　shields,
　　men of Lydia who draw the bow.
¹⁰ But that day belongs to the Lord, the
　　LORD Almighty—
　　a day of vengeance, for vengeance on
　　his foes.
The sword will devour till it is satisfied,
　　till it has quenched its thirst with
　　blood.
For the Lord, the LORD Almighty, will
　　offer sacrifice
　　in the land of the north by the River
　　Euphrates.

ᵃ9 That is, the upper Nile region

¹¹ "Go up to Gilead and get balm,
  O Virgin Daughter of Egypt.
But you multiply remedies in vain;
  there is no healing for you.
¹² The nations will hear of your shame;
  your cries will fill the earth.
One warrior will stumble over another;
  both will fall down together."

¹³ This is the message the LORD spoke to Jeremiah the prophet about the coming of Nebuchadnezzar king of Babylon to attack Egypt:

¹⁴ "Announce this in Egypt, and proclaim
    it in Migdol;
  proclaim it also in Memphis ᵃ and
    Tahpanhes:
'Take your positions and get ready,
  for the sword devours those around
    you.'
¹⁵ Why will your warriors be laid low?
  They cannot stand, for the LORD will
    push them down.
¹⁶ They will stumble repeatedly;
  they will fall over each other.
They will say, 'Get up, let us go back
  to our own people and our native
    lands,
away from the sword of the
    oppressor.'
¹⁷ There they will exclaim,
  'Pharaoh king of Egypt is only a loud
    noise;
he has missed his opportunity.'

¹⁸ "As surely as I live," declares the King,
  whose name is the LORD Almighty,
"one will come who is like Tabor
    among the mountains,
  like Carmel by the sea.
¹⁹ Pack your belongings for exile,
  you who live in Egypt,
for Memphis will be laid waste
  and lie in ruins without inhabitant.

²⁰ "Egypt is a beautiful heifer,
  but a gadfly is coming
    against her from the north.
²¹ The mercenaries in her ranks
  are like fattened calves.
They too will turn and flee together,
  they will not stand their ground,
for the day of disaster is coming upon
    them,
  the time for them to be punished.
²² Egypt will hiss like a fleeing serpent
  as the enemy advances in force;
they will come against her with axes,
  like men who cut down trees.
²³ They will chop down her forest,"
                    declares the LORD,

"dense though it be.
They are more numerous than locusts,
  they cannot be counted.
²⁴ The Daughter of Egypt will be put to
    shame,
  handed over to the people of the
    north."

²⁵ The LORD Almighty, the God of Israel, says: "I am about to bring punishment on Amon god of Thebes, ᵇ on Pharaoh, on Egypt and her gods and her kings, and on those who rely on Pharaoh. ²⁶ I will hand them over to those who seek their lives, to Nebuchadnezzar king of Babylon and his officers. Later, however, Egypt will be inhabited as in times past," declares the LORD.

²⁷ "Do not fear, O Jacob my servant;
  do not be dismayed, O Israel.
I will surely save you out of a distant
    place,
  your descendants from the land of
    their exile.
Jacob will again have peace and
    security,
  and no one will make him afraid.
²⁸ Do not fear, O Jacob my servant,
  for I am with you," declares the LORD.
"Though I completely destroy all the
    nations
  among which I scatter you,
  I will not completely destroy you.
I will discipline you but only with
    justice;
  I will not let you go entirely
    unpunished."

A Message About the Philistines

47 This is the word of the LORD that came to Jeremiah the prophet concerning the Philistines before Pharaoh attacked Gaza:

²This is what the LORD says:

"See how the waters are rising in the
    north;
  they will become an overflowing
    torrent.
They will overflow the land and
    everything in it,
  the towns and those who live in
    them.
The people will cry out;
  all who dwell in the land will wail
³ at the sound of the hoofs of galloping
    steeds,

ᵃ14 Hebrew *Noph*; also in verse 19   ᵇ25 Hebrew *No*

at the noise of enemy chariots
and the rumble of their wheels.
Fathers will not turn to help their
children;
their hands will hang limp.
⁴For the day has come
to destroy all the Philistines
and to cut off all survivors
who could help Tyre and Sidon.
The LORD is about to destroy the
Philistines,
the remnant from the coasts of
Caphtor.ᵃ
⁵Gaza will shave her head in mourning;
Ashkelon will be silenced.
O remnant on the plain,
how long will you cut yourselves?

⁶" 'Ah, sword of the LORD,' you cry,
'how long till you rest?
Return to your scabbard;
cease and be still.'
⁷But how can it rest
when the LORD has commanded it,
when he has ordered it
to attack Ashkelon and the coast?"

A Message About Moab

48 Concerning Moab:

This is what the LORD Almighty, the God
of Israel, says:

"Woe to Nebo, for it will be ruined.
Kiriathaim will be disgraced and
captured;
the strongholdᵇ will be disgraced and
shattered.
²Moab will be praised no more;
in Heshbonᶜ men will plot her
downfall:
'Come, let us put an end to that
nation.'
You too, O Madmen,ᵈ will be silenced;
the sword will pursue you.
³Listen to the cries from Horonaim,
cries of great havoc and destruction.
⁴Moab will be broken;
her little ones will cry out.ᵉ
⁵They go up the way to Luhith,
weeping bitterly as they go;
on the road down to Horonaim
anguished cries over the destruction
are heard.
⁶Flee! Run for your lives;
become like a bushᶠ in the desert.
⁷Since you trust in your deeds and
riches,
you too will be taken captive,
and Chemosh will go into exile,

together with his priests and
officials.
⁸The destroyer will come against every
town,
and not a town will escape.
The valley will be ruined
and the plateau destroyed,
because the LORD has spoken.
⁹Put salt on Moab,
for she will be laid wasteᵍ;
her towns will become desolate,
with no one to live in them.

¹⁰"A curse on him who is lax in doing the
LORD's work!
A curse on him who keeps his sword
from bloodshed!

¹¹"Moab has been at rest from youth,
like wine left on its dregs,
not poured from one jar to another—
she has not gone into exile.
So she tastes as she did,
and her aroma is unchanged.
¹²But days are coming,"
declares the LORD,
"when I will send men who pour from
jars,
and they will pour her out;
they will empty her jars
and smash her jugs.
¹³Then Moab will be ashamed of
Chemosh,
as the house of Israel was ashamed
when they trusted in Bethel.

¹⁴"How can you say, 'We are warriors,
men valiant in battle'?
¹⁵Moab will be destroyed and her towns
invaded;
her finest young men will go down in
the slaughter,"
declares the King, whose name is the
LORD Almighty.
¹⁶"The fall of Moab is at hand;
her calamity will come quickly.
¹⁷Mourn for her, all who live around her,
all who know her fame;
say, 'How broken is the mighty scepter,
how broken the glorious staff!'

¹⁸"Come down from your glory
and sit on the parched ground,
O inhabitants of the Daughter of
Dibon,
for he who destroys Moab

ᵃ4 That is, Crete   ᵇ1 Or / Misgab   ᶜ2 The Hebrew
for Heshbon sounds like the Hebrew for plot.
ᵈ2 The name of the Moabite town Madmen sounds
like the Hebrew for be silenced.   ᵉ4 Hebrew;
Septuagint / proclaim it to Zoar   ᶠ6 Or like Aroer
ᵍ9 Or Give wings to Moab, / for she will fly away

will come up against you
and ruin your fortified cities.
¹⁹ Stand by the road and watch,
you who live in Aroer.
Ask the man fleeing and the woman
escaping,
ask them, 'What has happened?'
²⁰ Moab is disgraced, for she is shattered.
Wail and cry out!
Announce by the Arnon
that Moab is destroyed.
²¹ Judgment has come to the plateau—
to Holon, Jahzah and Mephaath,
²² to Dibon, Nebo and Beth
Diblathaim,
²³ to Kiriathaim, Beth Gamul and Beth
Meon,
²⁴ to Kerioth and Bozrah—
to all the towns of Moab, far and
near.
²⁵ Moab's horn[a] is cut off;
her arm is broken,"
declares the LORD.

²⁶ "Make her drunk,
for she has defied the LORD.
Let Moab wallow in her vomit;
let her be an object of ridicule.
²⁷ Was not Israel the object of your
ridicule?
Was she caught among thieves,
that you shake your head in scorn
whenever you speak of her?
²⁸ Abandon your towns and dwell among
the rocks,
you who live in Moab.
Be like a dove that makes its nest
at the mouth of a cave.

²⁹ "We have heard of Moab's pride—
her overweening pride and conceit,
her pride and arrogance
and the haughtiness of her heart.
³⁰ I know her insolence but it is futile,"
declares the LORD,
"and her boasts accomplish nothing.
³¹ Therefore I wail over Moab,
for all Moab I cry out,
I moan for the men of Kir Hareseth.
³² I weep for you, as Jazer weeps,
O vines of Sibmah.
Your branches spread as far as the sea;
they reached as far as the sea of
Jazer.
The destroyer has fallen
on your ripened fruit and grapes.
³³ Joy and gladness are gone
from the orchards and fields of
Moab.
I have stopped the flow of wine from
the presses;

no one treads them with shouts of
joy.
Although there are shouts,
they are not shouts of joy.

³⁴ "The sound of their cry rises
from Heshbon to Elealeh and Jahaz,
from Zoar as far as Horonaim and
Eglath Shelishiyah,
for even the waters of Nimrim are
dried up.
³⁵ In Moab I will put an end
to those who make offerings on the
high places
and burn incense to their gods,"
declares the LORD.
³⁶ "So my heart laments for Moab like a
flute;
it laments like a flute for the men of
Kir Hareseth.
The wealth they acquired is gone.
³⁷ Every head is shaved
and every beard cut off;
every hand is slashed
and every waist is covered with
sackcloth.
³⁸ On all the roofs in Moab
and in the public squares
there is nothing but mourning,
for I have broken Moab
like a jar that no one wants,"
declares the LORD.
³⁹ "How shattered she is! How they wail!
How Moab turns her back in shame!
Moab has become an object of
ridicule,
an object of horror to all those
around her."

⁴⁰ This is what the LORD says:

"Look! An eagle is swooping down,
spreading its wings over Moab.
⁴¹ Kerioth[b] will be captured
and the strongholds taken.
In that day the hearts of Moab's
warriors
will be like the heart of a woman in
labor.
⁴² Moab will be destroyed as a nation
because she defied the LORD.
⁴³ Terror and pit and snare await you,
O people of Moab,"
declares the LORD.
⁴⁴ "Whoever flees from the terror
will fall into a pit,
whoever climbs out of the pit
will be caught in a snare;
for I will bring upon Moab

---

a25 Horn here symbolizes strength.   *b41* Or *The cities*

the year of her punishment,"
                                    declares the LORD.

45 "In the shadow of Heshbon
       the fugitives stand helpless,
for a fire has gone out from Heshbon,
       a blaze from the midst of Sihon;
it burns the foreheads of Moab,
       the skulls of the noisy boasters.
46 Woe to you, O Moab!
       The people of Chemosh are
          destroyed;
your sons are taken into exile
       and your daughters into captivity.

47 "Yet I will restore the fortunes of Moab
       in days to come,"
                                    declares the LORD.

Here ends the judgment on Moab.

A Message About Ammon

49 Concerning the Ammonites:

This is what the LORD says:

"Has Israel no sons?
       Has she no heirs?
Why then has Molech[a] taken
          possession of Gad?
       Why do his people live in its towns?
2 But the days are coming,"
                                    declares the LORD,
"when I will sound the battle cry
       against Rabbah of the Ammonites;
it will become a mound of ruins
       and its surrounding villages will be
          set on fire.
Then Israel will drive out
       those who drove her out,"
                                    says the LORD.
3 "Wail, O Heshbon, for Ai is destroyed!
       Cry out, O inhabitants of Rabbah!
Put on sackcloth and mourn;
       rush here and there inside the walls,
for Molech will go into exile,
       together with his priests and officials.
4 Why do you boast of your valleys,
       boast of your valleys so fruitful?
O unfaithful daughter,
       you trust in your riches and say,
'Who will attack me?'
5 I will bring terror on you
       from all those around you,"
                                    declares the Lord,
                                    the LORD Almighty.
"Every one of you will be driven away,
       and no one will gather the fugitives.

6 "Yet afterward, I will restore the
       fortunes of the Ammonites,"
                                    declares the LORD.

A Message About Edom

7 Concerning Edom:

This is what the LORD Almighty says:

"Is there no longer wisdom in Teman?
       Has counsel perished from the
          prudent?
       Has their wisdom decayed?
8 Turn and flee, hide in deep caves,
       you who live in Dedan,
for I will bring disaster on Esau
       at the time I punish him.
9 If grape pickers came to you,
       would they not leave a few grapes?
If thieves came during the night,
       would they not steal only as much as
          they wanted?
10 But I will strip Esau bare;
       I will uncover his hiding places,
       so that he cannot conceal himself.
His children, relatives and neighbors
          will perish,
       and he will be no more.
11 Leave your orphans; I will protect their
          lives.
       Your widows too can trust in me."

12 This is what the LORD says: "If those
who do not deserve to drink the cup must
drink it, why should you go unpunished?
You will not go unpunished, but must
drink it. **13** I swear by myself," declares the
LORD, "that Bozrah will become a ruin and
an object of horror, of reproach and of
cursing; and all its towns will be in ruins
forever."

14 I have heard a message from the LORD:
       An envoy was sent to the nations to
          say,
"Assemble yourselves to attack it!
       Rise up for battle!"
15 "Now I will make you small among the
          nations,
       despised among men.
16 The terror you inspire
       and the pride of your heart have
          deceived you,
you who live in the clefts of the rocks,
       who occupy the heights of the hill.
Though you build your nest as high as
          the eagle's,
       from there I will bring you down,"
                                    declares the LORD.
17 "Edom will become an object of horror;
       all who pass by will be appalled and
          will scoff

a1 Or *their king*; Hebrew *malcam*; also in verse 3

because of all its wounds.
[18] As Sodom and Gomorrah were
overthrown,
along with their neighboring towns,"
says the LORD,
"so no one will live there;
no man will dwell in it.

[19] "Like a lion coming up from Jordan's
thickets
to a rich pastureland,
I will chase Edom from its land in an
instant.
Who is the chosen one I will appoint
for this?
Who is like me and who can challenge
me?
And what shepherd can stand
against me?"
[20] Therefore, hear what the LORD has
planned against Edom,
what he has purposed against those
who live in Teman:
The young of the flock will be dragged
away;
he will completely destroy their
pasture because of them.
[21] At the sound of their fall the earth will
tremble;
their cry will resound to the Red Sea.[a]
[22] Look! An eagle will soar and swoop
down,
spreading its wings over Bozrah.
In that day the hearts of Edom's warriors
will be like the heart of a woman in
labor.

A Message About Damascus

[23] Concerning Damascus:

"Hamath and Arpad are dismayed,
for they have heard bad news.
They are disheartened,
troubled like[b] the restless sea.
[24] Damascus has become feeble,
she has turned to flee
and panic has gripped her;
anguish and pain have seized her,
pain like that of a woman in labor.
[25] Why has the city of renown not been
abandoned,
the town in which I delight?
[26] Surely, her young men will fall in the
streets;
all her soldiers will be silenced in
that day,"
declares the LORD Almighty.
[27] "I will set fire to the walls of Damascus;
it will consume the fortresses of Ben-
Hadad."

A Message About Kedar and Hazor

[28] Concerning Kedar and the kingdoms
of Hazor, which Nebuchadnezzar king of
Babylon attacked:

This is what the LORD says:

"Arise, and attack Kedar
and destroy the people of the East.
[29] Their tents and their flocks will be
taken;
their shelters will be carried off
with all their goods and camels.
Men will shout to them,
'Terror on every side!'
[30] "Flee quickly away!
Stay in deep caves, you who live in
Hazor,"
declares the LORD.
"Nebuchadnezzar king of Babylon has
plotted against you;
he has devised a plan against you.
[31] "Arise and attack a nation at ease,
which lives in confidence,"
declares the LORD,
"a nation that has neither gates nor
bars;
its people live alone.
[32] Their camels will become plunder,
and their large herds will be booty.
I will scatter to the winds those who are
in distant places[c]
and will bring disaster on them from
every side,"
declares the LORD.
[33] "Hazor will become a haunt of jackals,
a desolate place forever.
No one will live there;
no man will dwell in it."

A Message About Elam

[34] This is the word of the LORD that came
to Jeremiah the prophet concerning
Elam, early in the reign of Zedekiah king
of Judah:

[35] This is what the LORD Almighty says:

"See, I will break the bow of Elam,
the mainstay of their might.
[36] I will bring against Elam the four winds
from the four quarters of the
heavens;
I will scatter them to the four winds,
and there will not be a nation
where Elam's exiles do not go.

[a]21 Hebrew *Yam Suph*; that is, Sea of Reeds
[b]23 Hebrew *on* or *by*   [c]32 Or *who clip the hair by
their foreheads*

³⁷ I will shatter Elam before their foes,
  before those who seek their lives;
I will bring disaster upon them,
  even my fierce anger,"
                            declares the LORD.
  "I will pursue them with the sword
    until I have made an end of them.
³⁸ I will set my throne in Elam
  and destroy her king and officials,"
                            declares the LORD.
³⁹ "Yet I will restore the fortunes of Elam
  in days to come,"
                            declares the LORD.

A Message About Babylon

50 This is the word the LORD spoke
     through Jeremiah the prophet concerning Babylon and the land of the Babylonians[a]:

² "Announce and proclaim among the
     nations,
  lift up a banner and proclaim it;
  keep nothing back, but say,
  'Babylon will be captured;

[a]1 Or *Chaldeans*; also in verses 8, 25, 35 and 45

Excuse Me, Aren't You Forgetting Something?

DAILY INSIGHT

WEDNESDAY

Passage:
Jeremiah 50:1–5

Verse:
Jeremiah 50:1

Please don't tell anyone about this, but there's a chair in my office that speaks to me. For several years its upholstered voice has been perfectly clear.

I have always known that time alone with God—private prayer—is a critical part of a man's life. Some of my earliest recollections of my own dad are seeing him on his knees in the darkness of the early morning. But getting into a routine of prayer was a difficult habit for me to develop.

Several years ago, while I was building some closet shelves, it dawned on me that if I needed a place for organizing things for storage, I probably ought to have a place for prayer. So I chose a particular chair across from my office desk. It seemed like just the right venue for conversations with God. When I pray, I kneel at this chair.

Over the next few years, even though I had made the promise to pray at this chair every day, sometimes I'd plop down in my desk chair in the early morning hours and dive into my to-do list. *Let's see, I've got to return so-and-so's call. I need to finish this proposal and do some fine-tuning on that contract.* And when I'd look up from my work and gaze across the desk, I'd see the chair. "Uh, excuse me," it would say to me in a gentle but very direct tone of voice, "aren't you overlooking something? Haven't you forgotten to pray?"

"You're right," I'd respond. "I let the stack of work get in the way again. I didn't pray today."

I would get up, walk around my desk, and kneel down for my daily talk with my heavenly Father. Then, before returning to my place, I'd whisper a "thank you" to my faithful chair for the reminder.

Either Jeremiah was one of the world's most disciplined "prayer warriors," or he had a chair like mine. In either case, this was a man who was in touch with God. In fact, most of his writing includes the words, "This is what the LORD Almighty says." Jeremiah's walk with God was so intimate and so predictable that he could actually repeat the words he had heard from heaven.

Can you imagine a higher goal than to have this kind of connection with the sovereign Creator of the universe? Can you imagine the thrill of being led every day by his almighty hand? If this sounds good to you, give it a shot yourself. Make contact with your heavenly Father a part of your daily routine.

Now, you may be able to do this just by deciding to do it. That's great. However, for those of us from the slow group who never received our diplomas, you may need a talking chair. And, if I can give you a little piece of advice … you probably ought to keep this a secret. Some folks just won't believe it.

For your next devotional reading, go to page 885.

Bel will be put to shame,
    Marduk filled with terror.
Her images will be put to shame
    and her idols filled with terror.'
³A nation from the north will attack her
    and lay waste her land.
No one will live in it;
    both men and animals will flee away.

⁴"In those days, at that time,"
    declares the LORD,
"the people of Israel and the people of
        Judah together
    will go in tears to seek the LORD their
        God.
⁵They will ask the way to Zion
    and turn their faces toward it.
They will come and bind themselves to
        the LORD
    in an everlasting covenant
    that will not be forgotten.

⁶"My people have been lost sheep;
    their shepherds have led them astray
    and caused them to roam on the
        mountains.
They wandered over mountain and hill
    and forgot their own resting place.
⁷Whoever found them devoured them;
    their enemies said, 'We are not guilty,
for they sinned against the LORD, their
        true pasture,
    the LORD, the hope of their fathers.'

⁸"Flee out of Babylon;
    leave the land of the Babylonians,
    and be like the goats that lead the
        flock.
⁹For I will stir up and bring against
        Babylon
    an alliance of great nations from the
        land of the north.
They will take up their positions
        against her,
    and from the north she will be
        captured.
Their arrows will be like skilled warriors
    who do not return empty-handed.
¹⁰So Babylonia*ᵃ* will be plundered;
    all who plunder her will have their
        fill,"
            declares the LORD.

¹¹"Because you rejoice and are glad,
    you who pillage my inheritance,
because you frolic like a heifer
        threshing grain
    and neigh like stallions,
¹²your mother will be greatly ashamed;
    she who gave you birth will be
        disgraced.
She will be the least of the nations—

a wilderness, a dry land, a desert.
¹³Because of the LORD's anger she will
        not be inhabited
    but will be completely desolate.
All who pass Babylon will be horrified
        and scoff
    because of all her wounds.

¹⁴"Take up your positions around Babylon,
    all you who draw the bow.
Shoot at her! Spare no arrows,
    for she has sinned against the LORD.
¹⁵Shout against her on every side!
    She surrenders, her towers fall,
    her walls are torn down.
Since this is the vengeance of the LORD,
    take vengeance on her;
    do to her as she has done to others.
¹⁶Cut off from Babylon the sower,
    and the reaper with his sickle at
        harvest.
Because of the sword of the oppressor
    let everyone return to his own people,
    let everyone flee to his own land.

¹⁷"Israel is a scattered flock
    that lions have chased away.
The first to devour him
    was the king of Assyria;
the last to crush his bones
    was Nebuchadnezzar king of
        Babylon."

¹⁸Therefore this is what the LORD Almighty, the God of Israel, says:

"I will punish the king of Babylon and
        his land
    as I punished the king of Assyria.
¹⁹But I will bring Israel back to his own
        pasture
    and he will graze on Carmel and
        Bashan;
his appetite will be satisfied
    on the hills of Ephraim and Gilead.
²⁰In those days, at that time,"
    declares the LORD,
"search will be made for Israel's guilt,
    but there will be none,
and for the sins of Judah,
    but none will be found,
    for I will forgive the remnant I spare.

²¹"Attack the land of Merathaim
    and those who live in Pekod.
Pursue, kill and completely destroy*ᵇ*
        them,"
            declares the LORD.

*ᵃ10 Or Chaldea ᵇ21 The Hebrew term refers to the
irrevocable giving over of things or persons to the
LORD, often by totally destroying them; also in
verse 26.*

"Do everything I have commanded
you.
²²The noise of battle is in the land,
the noise of great destruction!
²³How broken and shattered
is the hammer of the whole earth!
How desolate is Babylon
among the nations!
²⁴I set a trap for you, O Babylon,
and you were caught before you
knew it;
you were found and captured
because you opposed the LORD.
²⁵The LORD has opened his arsenal
and brought out the weapons of his
wrath,
for the Sovereign LORD Almighty has
work to do
in the land of the Babylonians.
²⁶Come against her from afar.
Break open her granaries;
pile her up like heaps of grain.
Completely destroy her
and leave her no remnant.
²⁷Kill all her young bulls;
let them go down to the slaughter!
Woe to them! For their day has come,
the time for them to be punished.
²⁸Listen to the fugitives and refugees
from Babylon
declaring in Zion
how the LORD our God has taken
vengeance,
vengeance for his temple.

²⁹"Summon archers against Babylon,
all those who draw the bow.
Encamp all around her;
let no one escape.
Repay her for her deeds;
do to her as she has done.
For she has defied the LORD,
the Holy One of Israel.
³⁰Therefore, her young men will fall in
the streets;
all her soldiers will be silenced in
that day,"
declares the LORD.
³¹"See, I am against you, O arrogant
one,"
declares the Lord, the LORD
Almighty,
"for your day has come,
the time for you to be punished.
³²The arrogant one will stumble and fall
and no one will help her up;
I will kindle a fire in her towns
that will consume all who are around
her."

³³This is what the LORD Almighty says:

"The people of Israel are oppressed,
and the people of Judah as well.
All their captors hold them fast,
refusing to let them go.
³⁴Yet their Redeemer is strong;
the LORD Almighty is his name.
He will vigorously defend their cause
so that he may bring rest to their
land,
but unrest to those who live in
Babylon.

³⁵"A sword against the Babylonians!"
declares the LORD—
"against those who live in Babylon
and against her officials and wise
men!
³⁶A sword against her false prophets!
They will become fools.
A sword against her warriors!
They will be filled with terror.
³⁷A sword against her horses and
chariots
and all the foreigners in her ranks!
They will become women.
A sword against her treasures!
They will be plundered.
³⁸A drought onᵃ her waters!
They will dry up.
For it is a land of idols,
idols that will go mad with terror.

³⁹"So desert creatures and hyenas will
live there,
and there the owl will dwell.
It will never again be inhabited
or lived in from generation to
generation.
⁴⁰As God overthrew Sodom and
Gomorrah
along with their neighboring towns,"
declares the LORD,
"so no one will live there;
no man will dwell in it.

⁴¹"Look! An army is coming from the
north;
a great nation and many kings
are being stirred up from the ends of
the earth.
⁴²They are armed with bows and spears;
they are cruel and without mercy.
They sound like the roaring sea
as they ride on their horses;
they come like men in battle formation
to attack you, O Daughter of
Babylon.
⁴³The king of Babylon has heard reports
about them,
and his hands hang limp.

ᵃ38 Or A sword against

Anguish has gripped him,
  pain like that of a woman in labor.
[44] Like a lion coming up from Jordan's
    thickets
  to a rich pastureland,
I will chase Babylon from its land in an
    instant.
  Who is the chosen one I will appoint
    for this?
Who is like me and who can challenge
    me?
  And what shepherd can stand
    against me?"
[45] Therefore, hear what the LORD has
    planned against Babylon,
  what he has purposed against the
    land of the Babylonians:
The young of the flock will be dragged
    away;
  he will completely destroy their
    pasture because of them.
[46] At the sound of Babylon's capture the
    earth will tremble;
  its cry will resound among the
    nations.

51 This is what the LORD says:

"See, I will stir up the spirit of a
    destroyer
  against Babylon and the people of
    Leb Kamai.[a]
[2] I will send foreigners to Babylon
  to winnow her and to devastate her
    land;
they will oppose her on every side
  in the day of her disaster.
[3] Let not the archer string his bow,
  nor let him put on his armor.
Do not spare her young men;
  completely destroy[b] her army.
[4] They will fall down slain in Babylon,[c]
  fatally wounded in her streets.
[5] For Israel and Judah have not been
    forsaken
  by their God, the LORD Almighty,
though their land[d] is full of guilt
  before the Holy One of Israel.

[6] "Flee from Babylon!
  Run for your lives!
  Do not be destroyed because of her
    sins.
It is time for the LORD's vengeance;
  he will pay her what she deserves.
[7] Babylon was a gold cup in the LORD's
    hand;
  she made the whole earth drunk.
The nations drank her wine;
  therefore they have now gone mad.

[8] Babylon will suddenly fall and be
    broken.
  Wail over her!
Get balm for her pain;
  perhaps she can be healed.

[9] " 'We would have healed Babylon,
  but she cannot be healed;
let us leave her and each go to his own
    land,
  for her judgment reaches to the
    skies,
  it rises as high as the clouds.'

[10] " 'The LORD has vindicated us;
  come, let us tell in Zion
  what the LORD our God has done.'

[11] "Sharpen the arrows,
  take up the shields!
The LORD has stirred up the kings of the
    Medes,
  because his purpose is to destroy
    Babylon.
The LORD will take vengeance,
  vengeance for his temple.
[12] Lift up a banner against the walls of
    Babylon!
  Reinforce the guard,
station the watchmen,
  prepare an ambush!
The LORD will carry out his purpose,
  his decree against the people of
    Babylon.
[13] You who live by many waters
  and are rich in treasures,
your end has come,
  the time for you to be cut off.
[14] The LORD Almighty has sworn by
    himself:
  I will surely fill you with men, as with
    a swarm of locusts,
  and they will shout in triumph over
    you.

[15] "He made the earth by his power;
  he founded the world by his wisdom
  and stretched out the heavens by his
    understanding.
[16] When he thunders, the waters in the
    heavens roar;
  he makes clouds rise from the ends
    of the earth.
He sends lightning with the rain
  and brings out the wind from his
    storehouses.

---

[a]1 *Leb Kamai* is a cryptogram for Chaldea, that is,
Babylonia.   [b]3 The Hebrew term refers to the
irrevocable giving over of things or persons to
the LORD, often by totally destroying them.
[c]4 Or *Chaldea*   [d]5 Or *I and the land of the
Babylonians*

¹⁷ "Every man is senseless and without
    knowledge;
  every goldsmith is shamed by his
    idols.
  His images are a fraud;
    they have no breath in them.
¹⁸ They are worthless, the objects of
    mockery;
  when their judgment comes, they
    will perish.
¹⁹ He who is the Portion of Jacob is not
    like these,
  for he is the Maker of all things,
  including the tribe of his inheritance—
    the LORD Almighty is his name.

²⁰ "You are my war club,
    my weapon for battle—
  with you I shatter nations,
    with you I destroy kingdoms,
²¹ with you I shatter horse and rider,
    with you I shatter chariot and driver,
²² with you I shatter man and woman,
    with you I shatter old man and
    youth,
  with you I shatter young man and
    maiden,
²³ with you I shatter shepherd and flock,
    with you I shatter farmer and oxen,
    with you I shatter governors and
    officials.

²⁴ "Before your eyes I will repay Babylon
and all who live in Babylonia*a* for all the
wrong they have done in Zion," declares
the LORD.

²⁵ "I am against you, O destroying
    mountain,
  you who destroy the whole earth,"
                    declares the LORD.
  "I will stretch out my hand against you,
    roll you off the cliffs,
    and make you a burned-out
    mountain.
²⁶ No rock will be taken from you for a
    cornerstone,
  nor any stone for a foundation,
    for you will be desolate forever,"
                    declares the LORD.
²⁷ "Lift up a banner in the land!
  Blow the trumpet among the
    nations!
  Prepare the nations for battle against
    her;
  summon against her these
    kingdoms:
    Ararat, Minni and Ashkenaz.
  Appoint a commander against her;
    send up horses like a swarm of
    locusts.

²⁸ Prepare the nations for battle against
    her—
  the kings of the Medes,
    their governors and all their officials,
    and all the countries they rule.
²⁹ The land trembles and writhes,
  for the LORD's purposes against
    Babylon stand—
  to lay waste the land of Babylon
    so that no one will live there.
³⁰ Babylon's warriors have stopped
    fighting;
    they remain in their strongholds.
  Their strength is exhausted;
    they have become like women.
  Her dwellings are set on fire;
    the bars of her gates are broken.
³¹ One courier follows another
    and messenger follows messenger
  to announce to the king of Babylon
    that his entire city is captured,
³² the river crossings seized,
    the marshes set on fire,
    and the soldiers terrified."

³³ This is what the LORD Almighty, the God
of Israel, says:

  "The Daughter of Babylon is like a
    threshing floor
  at the time it is trampled;
    the time to harvest her will soon
    come."

³⁴ "Nebuchadnezzar king of Babylon has
    devoured us,
  he has thrown us into confusion,
    he has made us an empty jar.
  Like a serpent he has swallowed us
    and filled his stomach with our
    delicacies,
    and then has spewed us out.
³⁵ May the violence done to our flesh*b* be
    upon Babylon,"
    say the inhabitants of Zion.
  "May our blood be on those who live in
    Babylonia,"
    says Jerusalem.

³⁶ Therefore, this is what the LORD says:

  "See, I will defend your cause
    and avenge you;
  I will dry up her sea
    and make her springs dry.
³⁷ Babylon will be a heap of ruins,
    a haunt of jackals,
  an object of horror and scorn,
    a place where no one lives.
³⁸ Her people all roar like young lions,

---
a24 Or *Chaldea;* also in verse 35 *b35* Or *done to us
and to our children*

they growl like lion cubs.
³⁹But while they are aroused,
    I will set out a feast for them
    and make them drunk,
so that they shout with laughter—
    then sleep forever and not awake,"
                        declares the LORD.
⁴⁰"I will bring them down
    like lambs to the slaughter,
    like rams and goats.

⁴¹"How Sheshach^a will be captured,
    the boast of the whole earth seized!
What a horror Babylon will be
    among the nations!
⁴²The sea will rise over Babylon;
    its roaring waves will cover her.
⁴³Her towns will be desolate,
    a dry and desert land,
a land where no one lives,
    through which no man travels.
⁴⁴I will punish Bel in Babylon
    and make him spew out what he has
        swallowed.
The nations will no longer stream to
        him.
    And the wall of Babylon will fall.

⁴⁵"Come out of her, my people!
    Run for your lives!
    Run from the fierce anger of the
        LORD.
⁴⁶Do not lose heart or be afraid
    when rumors are heard in the land;
one rumor comes this year, another the
        next,
    rumors of violence in the land
    and of ruler against ruler.
⁴⁷For the time will surely come
    when I will punish the idols of
        Babylon;
her whole land will be disgraced
    and her slain will all lie fallen within
        her.
⁴⁸Then heaven and earth and all that is
        in them
    will shout for joy over Babylon,
for out of the north
    destroyers will attack her,"
                        declares the LORD.

⁴⁹"Babylon must fall because of Israel's
        slain,
    just as the slain in all the earth
    have fallen because of Babylon.
⁵⁰You who have escaped the sword,
    leave and do not linger!
Remember the LORD in a distant land,
    and think on Jerusalem."

⁵¹"We are disgraced,
    for we have been insulted

and shame covers our faces,
    because foreigners have entered
    the holy places of the LORD's
        house."

⁵²"But days are coming," declares the
        LORD,
    "when I will punish her idols,
and throughout her land
    the wounded will groan.
⁵³Even if Babylon reaches the sky
    and fortifies her lofty stronghold,
    I will send destroyers against her,"
                        declares the LORD.

⁵⁴"The sound of a cry comes from
        Babylon,
    the sound of great destruction
    from the land of the Babylonians.^b
⁵⁵The LORD will destroy Babylon;
    he will silence her noisy din.
Waves of enemies will rage like great
        waters;
    the roar of their voices will resound.
⁵⁶A destroyer will come against
        Babylon;
    her warriors will be captured,
    and their bows will be broken.
For the LORD is a God of retribution;
    he will repay in full.
⁵⁷I will make her officials and wise men
        drunk,
    her governors, officers and warriors
        as well;
they will sleep forever and not awake,"
    declares the King, whose name is the
        LORD Almighty.

⁵⁸This is what the LORD Almighty says:

"Babylon's thick wall will be leveled
    and her high gates set on fire;
the peoples exhaust themselves for
        nothing,
    the nations' labor is only fuel for the
        flames."

⁵⁹This is the message Jeremiah gave to
the staff officer Seraiah son of Neriah, the
son of Mahseiah, when he went to Babylon with Zedekiah king of Judah in the
fourth year of his reign. ⁶⁰Jeremiah had
written on a scroll about all the disasters
that would come upon Babylon—all that
had been recorded concerning Babylon.
⁶¹He said to Seraiah, "When you get to
Babylon, see that you read all these words
aloud. ⁶²Then say, 'O LORD, you have said
you will destroy this place, so that neither

---

^a41 *Sheshach* is a cryptogram for Babylon.
^b54 Or *Chaldeans*

man nor animal will live in it; it will be desolate forever.' ⁶³When you finish reading this scroll, tie a stone to it and throw it into the Euphrates. ⁶⁴Then say, 'So will Babylon sink to rise no more because of the disaster I will bring upon her. And her people will fall.' "

The words of Jeremiah end here.

The Fall of Jerusalem

52 Zedekiah was twenty-one years old when he became king, and he reigned in Jerusalem eleven years. His mother's name was Hamutal daughter of Jeremiah; she was from Libnah. ²He did evil in the eyes of the LORD, just as Jehoiakim had done. ³It was because of the LORD's anger that all this happened to Jerusalem and Judah, and in the end he thrust them from his presence.

Now Zedekiah rebelled against the king of Babylon.

⁴So in the ninth year of Zedekiah's reign, on the tenth day of the tenth month, Nebuchadnezzar king of Babylon marched against Jerusalem with his whole army. They camped outside the city and built siege works all around it. ⁵The city was kept under siege until the eleventh year of King Zedekiah.

⁶By the ninth day of the fourth month the famine in the city had become so severe that there was no food for the people to eat. ⁷Then the city wall was broken through, and the whole army fled. They left the city at night through the gate between the two walls near the king's garden, though the Babylonians^a were surrounding the city. They fled toward the Arabah,^b ⁸but the Babylonian^c army pursued King Zedekiah and overtook him in the plains of Jericho. All his soldiers were separated from him and scattered, ⁹and he was captured.

He was taken to the king of Babylon at Riblah in the land of Hamath, where he pronounced sentence on him. ¹⁰There at Riblah the king of Babylon slaughtered the sons of Zedekiah before his eyes; he also killed all the officials of Judah. ¹¹Then he put out Zedekiah's eyes, bound him with bronze shackles and took him to Babylon, where he put him in prison till the day of his death.

¹²On the tenth day of the fifth month, in the nineteenth year of Nebuchadnezzar king of Babylon, Nebuzaradan commander of the imperial guard, who served the king of Babylon, came to Jerusalem.

¹³He set fire to the temple of the LORD, the royal palace and all the houses of Jerusalem. Every important building he burned down. ¹⁴The whole Babylonian army under the commander of the imperial guard broke down all the walls around Jerusalem. ¹⁵Nebuzaradan the commander of the guard carried into exile some of the poorest people and those who remained in the city, along with the rest of the craftsmen^d and those who had gone over to the king of Babylon. ¹⁶But Nebuzaradan left behind the rest of the poorest people of the land to work the vineyards and fields.

¹⁷The Babylonians broke up the bronze pillars, the movable stands and the bronze Sea that were at the temple of the LORD and they carried all the bronze to Babylon. ¹⁸They also took away the pots, shovels, wick trimmers, sprinkling bowls, dishes and all the bronze articles used in the temple service. ¹⁹The commander of the imperial guard took away the basins, censers, sprinkling bowls, pots, lampstands, dishes and bowls used for drink offerings—all that were made of pure gold or silver.

²⁰The bronze from the two pillars, the Sea and the twelve bronze bulls under it, and the movable stands, which King Solomon had made for the temple of the LORD, was more than could be weighed. ²¹Each of the pillars was eighteen cubits high and twelve cubits in circumference^e; each was four fingers thick, and hollow. ²²The bronze capital on top of the one pillar was five cubits^f high and was decorated with a network and pomegranates of bronze all around. The other pillar, with its pomegranates, was similar. ²³There were ninety-six pomegranates on the sides; the total number of pomegranates above the surrounding network was a hundred.

²⁴The commander of the guard took as prisoners Seraiah the chief priest, Zephaniah the priest next in rank and the three doorkeepers. ²⁵Of those still in the city, he took the officer in charge of the fighting men, and seven royal advisers. He also took the secretary who was chief officer in charge of conscripting the people of the land and sixty of his men who were found

^a7 Or *Chaldeans*; also in verse 17 ^b7 Or *the Jordan Valley* ^c8 Or *Chaldean*; also in verse 14 ^d15 Or *populace* ^e21 That is, about 27 feet (about 8.1 meters) high and 18 feet (about 5.4 meters) in circumference ^f22 That is, about 7 1/2 feet (about 2.3 meters)

in the city. [26]Nebuzaradan the commander took them all and brought them to the king of Babylon at Riblah. [27]There at Riblah, in the land of Hamath, the king had them executed.

So Judah went into captivity, away from her land. [28]This is the number of the people Nebuchadnezzar carried into exile:

in the seventh year, 3,023 Jews;
[29]in Nebuchadnezzar's eighteenth year, 832 people from Jerusalem;
[30]in his twenty-third year,
745 Jews taken into exile by Nebuzaradan the commander of the imperial guard.
There were 4,600 people in all.

Jehoiachin Released

[31]In the thirty-seventh year of the exile of Jehoiachin king of Judah, in the year Evil-Merodach[a] became king of Babylon, he released Jehoiachin king of Judah and freed him from prison on the twenty-fifth day of the twelfth month. [32]He spoke kindly to him and gave him a seat of honor higher than those of the other kings who were with him in Babylon. [33]So Jehoiachin put aside his prison clothes and for the rest of his life ate regularly at the king's table. [34]Day by day the king of Babylon gave Jehoiachin a regular allowance as long as he lived, till the day of his death.

[a]31 Also called Amel-Marduk

Beloved Christian author, artist and speaker Joni Eareckson Tada has been a quadriplegic for over thirty years. It has been that long since she's had any sensation or movement in her hands or her feet. Imagine the despair of knowing that the rest of your life would hold confinement to a wheelchair and complete dependence on others . . . for *everything*.

In January of 1993, a pre-dawn earthquake rocked the Tadas' house. Joni's precious husband literally threw himself on top of his motionless wife to protect her from falling plaster. Moments later, Joni was sitting in her wheelchair on the back deck of her home. As she looked over the devastation, she began singing. At first her notes were quiet and subdued, but soon they swelled to top-of-the-lungs decibels. "Our God is an awesome God," Joni sang, "He reigns from heaven above with wisdom, power, and love. Our God is an awesome God."

The prophet Jeremiah, who authored this book of Lamentations, and Joni would have been soul mates. Right in the middle of the most awful devastation he had ever seen, Jeremiah wrote the words, "Great is [God's] faithfulness" (3:23). Isn't that incredible? As you read through this short book, reflect on how our great God has shown his faithfulness to you.

Lamentations

1 *a* How deserted lies the city,
   once so full of people!
How like a widow is she,
   who once was great among the
      nations!
She who was queen among the
      provinces
   has now become a slave.

2 Bitterly she weeps at night,
   tears are upon her cheeks.
Among all her lovers
   there is none to comfort her.

All her friends have betrayed her;
   they have become her enemies.

3 After affliction and harsh labor,
   Judah has gone into exile.
She dwells among the nations;
   she finds no resting place.
All who pursue her have overtaken her
   in the midst of her distress.

*a*This chapter is an acrostic poem, the verses of which begin with the successive letters of the Hebrew alphabet.

⁴The roads to Zion mourn,
for no one comes to her appointed
feasts.
All her gateways are desolate,
her priests groan,
her maidens grieve,
and she is in bitter anguish.

⁵Her foes have become her masters;
her enemies are at ease.
The LORD has brought her grief
because of her many sins.
Her children have gone into exile,
captive before the foe.

⁶All the splendor has departed
from the Daughter of Zion.
Her princes are like deer
that find no pasture;
in weakness they have fled
before the pursuer.

⁷In the days of her affliction and
wandering
Jerusalem remembers all the
treasures
that were hers in days of old.
When her people fell into enemy
hands,
there was no one to help her.
Her enemies looked at her
and laughed at her destruction.

⁸Jerusalem has sinned greatly
and so has become unclean.
All who honored her despise her,
for they have seen her nakedness;
she herself groans
and turns away.

⁹Her filthiness clung to her skirts;
she did not consider her future.
Her fall was astounding;
there was none to comfort her.
"Look, O LORD, on my affliction,
for the enemy has triumphed."

¹⁰The enemy laid hands
on all her treasures;
she saw pagan nations
enter her sanctuary—
those you had forbidden
to enter your assembly.

¹¹All her people groan
as they search for bread;
they barter their treasures for food
to keep themselves alive.
"Look, O LORD, and consider,
for I am despised."

¹²"Is it nothing to you, all you who pass
by?
Look around and see.

Is any suffering like my suffering
that was inflicted on me,
that the LORD brought on me
in the day of his fierce anger?

¹³"From on high he sent fire,
sent it down into my bones.
He spread a net for my feet
and turned me back.
He made me desolate,
faint all the day long.

¹⁴"My sins have been bound into a
yoke*a*;
by his hands they were woven
together.
They have come upon my neck
and the Lord has sapped my
strength.
He has handed me over
to those I cannot withstand.

¹⁵"The Lord has rejected
all the warriors in my midst;
he has summoned an army against me
to*b* crush my young men.
In his winepress the Lord has trampled
the Virgin Daughter of Judah.

¹⁶"This is why I weep
and my eyes overflow with tears.
No one is near to comfort me,
no one to restore my spirit.
My children are destitute
because the enemy has prevailed."

¹⁷Zion stretches out her hands,
but there is no one to comfort her.
The LORD has decreed for Jacob
that his neighbors become his foes;
Jerusalem has become
an unclean thing among them.

¹⁸"The LORD is righteous,
yet I rebelled against his command.
Listen, all you peoples;
look upon my suffering.
My young men and maidens
have gone into exile.

¹⁹"I called to my allies
but they betrayed me.
My priests and my elders
perished in the city
while they searched for food
to keep themselves alive.

²⁰"See, O LORD, how distressed I am!
I am in torment within,
and in my heart I am disturbed,

---

a14 Most Hebrew manuscripts; Septuagint *He kept
watch over my sins   b15* Or *has set a time for me /
when he will*

for I have been most rebellious.
Outside, the sword bereaves;
  inside, there is only death.

²¹ "People have heard my groaning,
  but there is no one to comfort me.
All my enemies have heard of my
    distress;
  they rejoice at what you have done.
May you bring the day you have
    announced
  so they may become like me.

²² "Let all their wickedness come before
    you;
  deal with them
as you have dealt with me
  because of all my sins.
My groans are many
  and my heart is faint."

2 ᵃ How the Lord has covered the
    Daughter of Zion
  with the cloud of his anger ᵇ!
He has hurled down the splendor of
    Israel
  from heaven to earth;
he has not remembered his footstool
  in the day of his anger.

² Without pity the Lord has swallowed
    up
  all the dwellings of Jacob;
in his wrath he has torn down
  the strongholds of the Daughter of
    Judah.
He has brought her kingdom and its
    princes
  down to the ground in dishonor.

³ In fierce anger he has cut off
  every horn ᶜ of Israel.
He has withdrawn his right hand
  at the approach of the enemy.
He has burned in Jacob like a flaming
    fire
  that consumes everything around it.

⁴ Like an enemy he has strung his bow;
  his right hand is ready.
Like a foe he has slain
  all who were pleasing to the eye;
he has poured out his wrath like fire
  on the tent of the Daughter of
    Zion.

⁵ The Lord is like an enemy;
  he has swallowed up Israel.
He has swallowed up all her palaces
  and destroyed her strongholds.
He has multiplied mourning and
    lamentation
  for the Daughter of Judah.

⁶ He has laid waste his dwelling like a
    garden;
  he has destroyed his place of
    meeting.
The LORD has made Zion forget
  her appointed feasts and her
    Sabbaths;
in his fierce anger he has spurned
  both king and priest.

⁷ The Lord has rejected his altar
  and abandoned his sanctuary.
He has handed over to the enemy
  the walls of her palaces;
they have raised a shout in the house of
    the LORD
  as on the day of an appointed feast.

⁸ The LORD determined to tear down
  the wall around the Daughter of
    Zion.
He stretched out a measuring line
  and did not withhold his hand from
    destroying.
He made ramparts and walls lament;
  together they wasted away.

⁹ Her gates have sunk into the ground;
  their bars he has broken and
    destroyed.
Her king and her princes are exiled
  among the nations,
  the law is no more,
and her prophets no longer find
  visions from the LORD.

¹⁰ The elders of the Daughter of Zion
  sit on the ground in silence;
they have sprinkled dust on their heads
  and put on sackcloth.
The young women of Jerusalem
  have bowed their heads to the
    ground.

¹¹ My eyes fail from weeping,
  I am in torment within,
my heart is poured out on the ground
  because my people are destroyed,
because children and infants faint
  in the streets of the city.

¹² They say to their mothers,
  "Where is bread and wine?"
as they faint like wounded men
  in the streets of the city,
as their lives ebb away
  in their mothers' arms.

ᵃThis chapter is an acrostic poem, the verses of
which begin with the successive letters of the
Hebrew alphabet.   ᵇ1 Or How the Lord in his anger
/ has treated the Daughter of Zion with contempt
ᶜ3 Or / all the strength; or every king; horn here
symbolizes strength.

¹³ What can I say for you?
   With what can I compare you,
   O Daughter of Jerusalem?
To what can I liken you,
   that I may comfort you,
   O Virgin Daughter of Zion?
Your wound is as deep as the sea.
   Who can heal you?

¹⁴ The visions of your prophets
   were false and worthless;
they did not expose your sin
   to ward off your captivity.
The oracles they gave you
   were false and misleading.

¹⁵ All who pass your way
   clap their hands at you;
they scoff and shake their heads
   at the Daughter of Jerusalem:
"Is this the city that was called
   the perfection of beauty,
   the joy of the whole earth?"

¹⁶ All your enemies open their mouths
   wide against you;
they scoff and gnash their teeth
   and say, "We have swallowed her up.
This is the day we have waited for;
   we have lived to see it."

¹⁷ The LORD has done what he planned;
   he has fulfilled his word,
   which he decreed long ago.
He has overthrown you without pity,
   he has let the enemy gloat over you,
   he has exalted the horn*ᵃ* of your foes.

¹⁸ The hearts of the people
   cry out to the Lord.
O wall of the Daughter of Zion,
   let your tears flow like a river
   day and night;
give yourself no relief,
   your eyes no rest.

¹⁹ Arise, cry out in the night,
   as the watches of the night begin;
pour out your heart like water
   in the presence of the Lord.
Lift up your hands to him
   for the lives of your children,
who faint from hunger
   at the head of every street.

²⁰ "Look, O LORD, and consider:
   Whom have you ever treated like this?
Should women eat their offspring,
   the children they have cared for?
Should priest and prophet be killed
   in the sanctuary of the Lord?

²¹ "Young and old lie together
   in the dust of the streets;

my young men and maidens
   have fallen by the sword.
You have slain them in the day of your
      anger;
   you have slaughtered them without
      pity.

²² "As you summon to a feast day,
   so you summoned against me terrors
      on every side.
In the day of the LORD's anger
   no one escaped or survived;
those I cared for and reared,
   my enemy has destroyed."

3 *ᵇ* I am the man who has seen affliction
   by the rod of his wrath.
² He has driven me away and made me
      walk
   in darkness rather than light;
³ indeed, he has turned his hand against
      me
   again and again, all day long.

⁴ He has made my skin and my flesh
      grow old
   and has broken my bones.
⁵ He has besieged me and surrounded
      me
   with bitterness and hardship.
⁶ He has made me dwell in darkness
   like those long dead.

⁷ He has walled me in so I cannot
      escape;
   he has weighed me down with
      chains.
⁸ Even when I call out or cry for help,
   he shuts out my prayer.
⁹ He has barred my way with blocks of
      stone;
   he has made my paths crooked.

¹⁰ Like a bear lying in wait,
   like a lion in hiding,
¹¹ he dragged me from the path and
      mangled me
   and left me without help.
¹² He drew his bow
   and made me the target for his
      arrows.

¹³ He pierced my heart
   with arrows from his quiver.
¹⁴ I became the laughingstock of all my
      people;
   they mock me in song all day long.

ᵃ17 Horn here symbolizes strength.   *ᵇ* This chapter
is an acrostic poem; the verses of each stanza
begin with the successive letters of the Hebrew
alphabet, and the verses within each stanza begin
with the same letter.

¹⁵He has filled me with bitter herbs
  and sated me with gall.

¹⁶He has broken my teeth with gravel;
  he has trampled me in the dust.
¹⁷I have been deprived of peace;
  I have forgotten what prosperity is.
¹⁸So I say, "My splendor is gone
  and all that I had hoped from the
  LORD."

¹⁹I remember my affliction and my
  wandering,
  the bitterness and the gall.
²⁰I well remember them,

and my soul is downcast within me.
²¹Yet this I call to mind
  and therefore I have hope:

²²Because of the LORD's great love we are
  not consumed,
  for his compassions never fail.
²³They are new every morning;
  great is your faithfulness.
²⁴I say to myself, "The LORD is my
  portion;
  therefore I will wait for him."

²⁵The LORD is good to those whose hope
  is in him,

This Entrepreneur's Lesson

DAILY INSIGHT

THURSDAY
Passage:
Lamentations 3:1–9,
22–24
Verses:
Lamentations 3:22–23

On my forty-fourth birthday, I received the phone call every entrepreneur dreads. The voice on the other end of the line was a very familiar one. The man had, for thirteen years, been one of my closest friends.

"Robert," he began, "We have to call the note on your business loan. I know what this means, and I'm sorry. I'm your friend, but I'm also a man under authority. I have to do what I have to do."

I hung up the phone and sat there stunned. My five-year-old dream had come to an end. I walked into my business partner's office, closed the door behind me, and gave him the awful news. Our eyes welled up with tears as we began to realize the impact of what had just happened.

A few minutes later we pulled our whole staff together; they had no idea what they were about to hear. My partner and I had done our best to protect them from the rough seas our business had encountered, but now we had to tell them they were out of work and should start looking for other jobs.

I went back to my office and called Bobbie. When I heard her voice, I broke down, sobbing uncontrollably. Once I gathered my composure, I told her what had happened. "We've lost everything, Honey," I said. "I can't believe it."

Over the next few days I made dozens of phone calls. One of the first was to a man to whom our business owed tens of thousands of dollars. I told him that the purpose of my call was to let him know that I was closing the doors to my business; he was never going to see his money. There was a moment of silence. I braced myself.

"I know you've done your best, Robert," Patrick began. "God has been faithful to both of us in the past, and he'll be faithful in the future. He will provide."

I was overwhelmed by Patrick's response. I thanked him for his understanding and promised that if there was anything I could ever do to make this up to him, I would. He thanked me, offered a short prayer over the phone, and we said good-bye. I'll never forget this man's wise words.

Jeremiah couldn't have said it better. In fact, Jeremiah did say the same thing. "God has made me walk in the darkness ... he has weighed me down with chains ... he has barred my way with blocks of stones ... however, because of his great love, we are not consumed. Great is God's faithfulness."

This was true for Jeremiah in his distress. It was true for me when our business folded. And it's true for you today. No unexpected phone call will ever take that away.

For your next devotional reading, go to page 890.
For your next devotional reading, go to page 890.

to the one who seeks him;
²⁶ it is good to wait quietly
for the salvation of the LORD.
²⁷ It is good for a man to bear the yoke
while he is young.

²⁸ Let him sit alone in silence,
for the LORD has laid it on him.
²⁹ Let him bury his face in the dust—
there may yet be hope.
³⁰ Let him offer his cheek to one who
would strike him,
and let him be filled with disgrace.

³¹ For men are not cast off
by the Lord forever.
³² Though he brings grief, he will show
compassion,
so great is his unfailing love.
³³ For he does not willingly bring
affliction
or grief to the children of men.

³⁴ To crush underfoot
all prisoners in the land,
³⁵ to deny a man his rights
before the Most High,
³⁶ to deprive a man of justice—
would not the Lord see such things?

³⁷ Who can speak and have it happen
if the Lord has not decreed it?
³⁸ Is it not from the mouth of the Most
High
that both calamities and good things
come?
³⁹ Why should any living man complain
when punished for his sins?

⁴⁰ Let us examine our ways and test them,
and let us return to the LORD.
⁴¹ Let us lift up our hearts and our hands
to God in heaven, and say:
⁴² "We have sinned and rebelled
and you have not forgiven.

⁴³ "You have covered yourself with anger
and pursued us;
you have slain without pity.
⁴⁴ You have covered yourself with a cloud
so that no prayer can get through.
⁴⁵ You have made us scum and refuse
among the nations.

⁴⁶ "All our enemies have opened their
mouths
wide against us.
⁴⁷ We have suffered terror and pitfalls,
ruin and destruction."
⁴⁸ Streams of tears flow from my eyes
because my people are destroyed.

⁴⁹ My eyes will flow unceasingly,
without relief,

⁵⁰ until the LORD looks down
from heaven and sees.
⁵¹ What I see brings grief to my soul
because of all the women of my city.

⁵² Those who were my enemies without
cause
hunted me like a bird.
⁵³ They tried to end my life in a pit
and threw stones at me;
⁵⁴ the waters closed over my head,
and I thought I was about to be cut
off.

⁵⁵ I called on your name, O LORD,
from the depths of the pit.
⁵⁶ You heard my plea: "Do not close your
ears
to my cry for relief."
⁵⁷ You came near when I called you,
and you said, "Do not fear."

⁵⁸ O Lord, you took up my case;
you redeemed my life.
⁵⁹ You have seen, O LORD, the wrong done
to me.
Uphold my cause!
⁶⁰ You have seen the depth of their
vengeance,
all their plots against me.

⁶¹ O LORD, you have heard their insults,
all their plots against me—
⁶² what my enemies whisper and mutter
against me all day long.
⁶³ Look at them! Sitting or standing,
they mock me in their songs.

⁶⁴ Pay them back what they deserve,
O LORD,
for what their hands have done.
⁶⁵ Put a veil over their hearts,
and may your curse be on them!
⁶⁶ Pursue them in anger and destroy them
from under the heavens of the LORD.

4 ᵃ How the gold has lost its luster,
the fine gold become dull!
The sacred gems are scattered
at the head of every street.

² How the precious sons of Zion,
once worth their weight in gold,
are now considered as pots of clay,
the work of a potter's hands!

³ Even jackals offer their breasts
to nurse their young,
but my people have become heartless
like ostriches in the desert.

ᵃThis chapter is an acrostic poem, the verses of
which begin with the successive letters of the
Hebrew alphabet.

⁴ Because of thirst the infant's tongue
    sticks to the roof of its mouth;
the children beg for bread,
    but no one gives it to them.

⁵ Those who once ate delicacies
    are destitute in the streets.
Those nurtured in purple
    now lie on ash heaps.

⁶ The punishment of my people
    is greater than that of Sodom,
which was overthrown in a moment
    without a hand turned to help her.

⁷ Their princes were brighter than snow
    and whiter than milk,
their bodies more ruddy than rubies,
    their appearance like sapphires.ᵃ

⁸ But now they are blacker than soot;
    they are not recognized in the
        streets.
Their skin has shriveled on their bones;
    it has become as dry as a stick.

⁹ Those killed by the sword are better off
    than those who die of famine;
racked with hunger, they waste away
    for lack of food from the field.

¹⁰ With their own hands compassionate
        women
    have cooked their own children,
who became their food
    when my people were destroyed.

¹¹ The LORD has given full vent to his
        wrath;
    he has poured out his fierce anger.
He kindled a fire in Zion
    that consumed her foundations.

¹² The kings of the earth did not believe,
    nor did any of the world's people,
that enemies and foes could enter
    the gates of Jerusalem.

¹³ But it happened because of the sins of
        her prophets
    and the iniquities of her priests,
who shed within her
    the blood of the righteous.

¹⁴ Now they grope through the streets
    like men who are blind.
They are so defiled with blood
    that no one dares to touch their
        garments.

¹⁵ "Go away! You are unclean!" men cry to
        them.
    "Away! Away! Don't touch us!"
When they flee and wander about,
    people among the nations say,
    "They can stay here no longer."

¹⁶ The LORD himself has scattered them;
    he no longer watches over them.
The priests are shown no honor,
    the elders no favor.

ᵃ7 Or *lapis lazuli*

HEY DAD
What happens when God gets mad?

Text: Lamentations 4:6–16

God's anger is more fierce than we can even begin to imagine. Very few people have ever seen anything even close to a full measure of God's wrath, but the Israelites who lived in Jerusalem in 586 BC saw the "full vent" of God's anger.

Israel had become so corrupt that even the prophets and priests were guilty of shedding innocent blood. The very ones who were supposed to intercede for sinful people were murderers themselves! Though God had warned the people time and time again, they continued to rebel. Pushed past the point of mercy, God poured his wrath down on all of Jerusalem. The Babylonian army blazed into the city, demolished it, and carried most of the Israelites away as slaves.

The once-arrogant Israelites were devastated. Those who were left in the city scraped for food and water. And Jeremiah tells us that the priests were left groping through the streets like blind men, their clothes so blood soaked that people wouldn't go near them but would run and cry out, "Go away! You are unclean!" (v. 15).

Can you imagine such a scene? God is loving and merciful, but he's also just and holy. He will not tolerate blatant rebellion, and we never … ever … want to see him angry!

QUESTIONS KIDS ASK

For a complete listing of Questions Kids Ask, turn to page 1435.

17 Moreover, our eyes failed,
    looking in vain for help;
from our towers we watched
    for a nation that could not save us.

18 Men stalked us at every step,
    so we could not walk in our streets.
Our end was near, our days were
        numbered,
    for our end had come.

19 Our pursuers were swifter
    than eagles in the sky;
they chased us over the mountains
    and lay in wait for us in the desert.

20 The LORD's anointed, our very life
        breath,
    was caught in their traps.
We thought that under his shadow
    we would live among the nations.

21 Rejoice and be glad, O Daughter of
        Edom,
    you who live in the land of Uz.
But to you also the cup will be
        passed;
    you will be drunk and stripped
        naked.

22 O Daughter of Zion, your punishment
        will end;
    he will not prolong your exile.
But, O Daughter of Edom, he will
    punish your sin
    and expose your wickedness.

5 Remember, O LORD, what has
        happened to us;
    look, and see our disgrace.
2 Our inheritance has been turned over
        to aliens,
    our homes to foreigners.
3 We have become orphans and
        fatherless,
    our mothers like widows.
4 We must buy the water we drink;

    our wood can be had only at a price.
5 Those who pursue us are at our heels;
    we are weary and find no rest.
6 We submitted to Egypt and Assyria
    to get enough bread.
7 Our fathers sinned and are no more,
    and we bear their punishment.
8 Slaves rule over us,
    and there is none to free us from
        their hands.
9 We get our bread at the risk of our lives
    because of the sword in the desert.
10 Our skin is hot as an oven,
    feverish from hunger.
11 Women have been ravished in Zion,
    and virgins in the towns of Judah.
12 Princes have been hung up by their
        hands;
    elders are shown no respect.
13 Young men toil at the millstones;
    boys stagger under loads of wood.
14 The elders are gone from the city gate;
    the young men have stopped their
        music.
15 Joy is gone from our hearts;
    our dancing has turned to mourning.
16 The crown has fallen from our head.
    Woe to us, for we have sinned!
17 Because of this our hearts are faint,
    because of these things our eyes
        grow dim
18 for Mount Zion, which lies desolate,
    with jackals prowling over it.

19 You, O LORD, reign forever;
    your throne endures from generation
        to generation.
20 Why do you always forget us?
    Why do you forsake us so long?
21 Restore us to yourself, O LORD, that we
        may return;
    renew our days as of old
22 unless you have utterly rejected us
    and are angry with us beyond
        measure.

Which of these sounds better to you: "He's a visionary?" or "He's a creamer?" Yes, most men would prefer being called "visionaries" versus being dubbed "dreamers." They want people to know them for their down-to-earth abilities to contribute; they don't want to be known as guys with their heads in the clouds. Although some of his contemporaries must have thought Ezekiel was a dreamer, he truly was a visionary. The things he saw and reported were God's way of helping Ezekiel's fellow captives in Babylon to see the truth in a new way.

One of the great challenges in being a dad is seeing ahead, planning, being ready for tomorrow. Reading the book of Ezekiel helps us to understand the important difference between wildly forecasting what's around the corner on the one hand, and on the other hand seeking God's guidance to "see" what only he can see, then getting ready for it.

Ezekiel

The Living Creatures and the Glory of the LORD

1 In the[a] thirtieth year, in the fourth month on the fifth day, while I was among the exiles by the Kebar River, the heavens were opened and I saw visions of God.

[2] On the fifth of the month—it was the fifth year of the exile of King Jehoiachin— [3] the word of the LORD came to Ezekiel the priest, the son of Buzi,[b] by the Kebar River in the land of the Babylonians.[c] There the hand of the LORD was upon him.

[4] I looked, and I saw a windstorm coming out of the north—an immense cloud with flashing lightning and surrounded by brilliant light. The center of the fire looked like glowing metal, [5] and in the fire was what looked like four living creatures. In appearance their form was that of a

man, [6] but each of them had four faces and four wings. [7] Their legs were straight; their feet were like those of a calf and gleamed like burnished bronze. [8] Under their wings on their four sides they had the hands of a man. All four of them had faces and wings, [9] and their wings touched one another. Each one went straight ahead; they did not turn as they moved.

[10] Their faces looked like this: Each of the four had the face of a man, and on the right side each had the face of a lion, and on the left the face of an ox; each also had the face of an eagle. [11] Such were their faces. Their wings were spread out upward; each had two wings, one touching the wing of another creature on either

---

[a]1 Or my   [b]3 Or Ezekiel son of Buzi the priest
[c]3 Or Chaldeans

side, and two wings covering its body. [12]Each one went straight ahead. Wherever the spirit would go, they would go, without turning as they went. [13]The appearance of the living creatures was like burning coals of fire or like torches. Fire moved back and forth among the creatures; it was bright, and lightning flashed out of it. [14]The creatures sped back and forth like flashes of lightning.

[15]As I looked at the living creatures, I saw a wheel on the ground beside each creature with its four faces. [16]This was the appearance and structure of the wheels:

They sparkled like chrysolite, and all four looked alike. Each appeared to be made like a wheel intersecting a wheel. [17]As they moved, they would go in any one of the four directions the creatures faced; the wheels did not turn about[a] as the creatures went. [18]Their rims were high and awesome, and all four rims were full of eyes all around.

[19]When the living creatures moved, the wheels beside them moved; and when the living creatures rose from the ground,

[a]17 Or *aside*

Ah, Saturday Morning

Don't you love Saturday mornings? You go to bed late Friday night, knowing you can sleep in as long as you want. But one particular Saturday morning, something's gone wrong. You're lying in bed wide awake, and there's no going back to sleep.

The dawning sun is barely squeezing through the blinds. You glance at the clock on your night stand: 6:12! *Why is it so tough to wake up on a weekday when I* have *to get up,* you think, *but now that I can sleep as late as I want to, I'm lying here wide awake?*

The answer is simple. You've got a project. You've been looking forward to starting it for a long time. Sitting on your driveway is a stack of pressure-treated wood, which was delivered this week. You've been to The Home Depot and loaded up. You've got your galvanized nails and bolts, a new drill bit and several bags of premixed concrete. You can hardly wait to get started. Because your wife doesn't have a project this morning, you quietly pull on a pair of old jeans and slip out your bedroom door, down the stairs, and into the garage.

There's something powerful about being called to a task—even one that's going to require a lot of blood, sweat and tears. Ezekiel knew all about this kind of call. But his didn't come from an alarm clock or from the anticipation of a building project; Ezekiel's call came directly from

DAILY INSIGHT

FRIDAY

Passage:
Ezekiel 2:1–9

Verse:
Ezekiel 2:2

God. "Stand up on your feet, and I will speak to you," the Almighty commanded the prophet.

And then God gave Ezekiel his orders. "I'm sending you to the Israelites, to a rebellious nation. They and their fathers have lived in revolt against me. Whether they listen or not, they will know that a prophet has been among them. Do not be afraid of them or their words. You must speak my words to them."

Can you imagine an assignment like this? God told this man to be salt in his tasteless world, light in the darkness all around him. But can't you also imagine the adrenaline coursing through Ezekiel's body? *Sure this is a difficult assignment,* he must have thought, *but God has called me. He's promised to go with me. And he has told me not to be afraid. Let me at those rebellious Israelites.*

Guess what? That voice you hear is God calling you. He has given you unique talents and a sphere of influence: husband, father, co-worker, neighbor, friend. And he has commanded you to be a prophet—a man who speaks a language bursting with God's holiness and grace.

Get up. You've got work to do. But aren't you excited? I'll bet you can hardly wait to get busy. It isn't every day that a man hears directly from heaven!

For your next devotional reading, go to page 898.

the wheels also rose. [20]Wherever the spirit would go, they would go, and the wheels would rise along with them, because the spirit of the living creatures was in the wheels. [21]When the creatures moved, they also moved; when the creatures stood still, they also stood still; and when the creatures rose from the ground, the wheels rose along with them, because the spirit of the living creatures was in the wheels.

[22]Spread out above the heads of the living creatures was what looked like an expanse, sparkling like ice, and awesome. [23]Under the expanse their wings were stretched out one toward the other, and each had two wings covering its body. [24]When the creatures moved, I heard the sound of their wings, like the roar of rushing waters, like the voice of the Almighty,[a] like the tumult of an army. When they stood still, they lowered their wings.

[25]Then there came a voice from above the expanse over their heads as they stood with lowered wings. [26]Above the expanse over their heads was what looked like a throne of sapphire,[b] and high above on the throne was a figure like that of a man. [27]I saw that from what appeared to be his

waist up he looked like glowing metal, as if full of fire, and that from there down he looked like fire; and brilliant light surrounded him. [28]Like the appearance of a rainbow in the clouds on a rainy day, so was the radiance around him.

This was the appearance of the likeness of the glory of the LORD. When I saw it, I fell facedown, and I heard the voice of one speaking.

Ezekiel's Call

2 He said to me, "Son of man, stand up on your feet and I will speak to you." [2]As he spoke, the Spirit came into me and raised me to my feet, and I heard him speaking to me.

[3]He said: "Son of man, I am sending you to the Israelites, to a rebellious nation that has rebelled against me; they and their fathers have been in revolt against me to this very day. [4]The people to whom I am sending you are obstinate and stubborn. Say to them, 'This is what the Sovereign LORD says.' [5]And whether they listen or

[a]24 Hebrew *Shaddai*   [b]26 Or *lapis lazuli*

HEY DAD
What's a prophet?

Text: Ezekiel 2:3–5

A prophet is one who carries a message from God to the people. Priests or teachers don't raise up or appoint prophets; only God can commission them, as he did Ezekiel in this passage. In the Old Testament, prophets were often met by angry kings or scornful crowds, so in order to be successful, they couldn't be intimidated by their audience (Lockyer, 878).

Sometimes at God's direction, prophets acted out their messages. According to Ezekiel 4, Ezekiel had to lie on his left side for three hundred and ninety days and on his right side for forty more in an elaborate display symbolizing Israel's sinfulness. Isaiah 20 tells us that Isaiah went barefoot for three years as a visible prophecy to Egypt, Cush and the King of Assyria. Take a moment to read these amazing accounts!

What kind of people did God choose to be prophets? Many different kinds of people. Sometimes God even used people who didn't worship him to deliver his message. Numbers 22:4–24:25 tells us the story of Balaam, a man who cursed and blessed people for money. God wanted to bless the Israelites, and he used Balaam to do it even though Balaam didn't worship him.

Though the Old Testament prophets came from many walks of life—farmers (Amos), princes (Moses), and priests (Ezekiel) among them—they all had one thing in common. They all delivered "a faithful proclamation of God's word, not their own" (Lockyer, 878).

Lockyer, H. (Ed.). (1986). Nelson's Illustrated Bible Dictionary. *Nashville, Tennessee: Thomas Nelson Publishers.*

For a complete listing of Questions Kids Ask, turn to page 1435.

fail to listen—for they are a rebellious house—they will know that a prophet has been among them. **6**And you, son of man, do not be afraid of them or their words. Do not be afraid, though briers and thorns are all around you and you live among scorpions. Do not be afraid of what they say or terrified by them, though they are a rebellious house. **7**You must speak my words to them, whether they listen or fail to listen, for they are rebellious. **8**But you, son of man, listen to what I say to you. Do not rebel like that rebellious house; open your mouth and eat what I give you."

9Then I looked, and I saw a hand stretched out to me. In it was a scroll, **10**which he unrolled before me. On both sides of it were written words of lament and mourning and woe.

3 And he said to me, "Son of man, eat what is before you, eat this scroll; then go and speak to the house of Israel." **2**So I opened my mouth, and he gave me the scroll to eat.

3Then he said to me, "Son of man, eat this scroll I am giving you and fill your stomach with it." So I ate it, and it tasted as sweet as honey in my mouth.

4He then said to me: "Son of man, go now to the house of Israel and speak my words to them. **5**You are not being sent to a people of obscure speech and difficult language, but to the house of Israel— **6**not to many peoples of obscure speech and difficult language, whose words you cannot understand. Surely if I had sent you to them, they would have listened to you. **7**But the house of Israel is not willing to listen to you because they are not willing to listen to me, for the whole house of Israel is hardened and obstinate. **8**But I will make you as unyielding and hardened as they are. **9**I will make your forehead like the hardest stone, harder than flint. Do not be afraid of them or terrified by them, though they are a rebellious house."

10And he said to me, "Son of man, listen carefully and take to heart all the words I speak to you. **11**Go now to your countrymen in exile and speak to them. Say to them, 'This is what the Sovereign LORD says,' whether they listen or fail to listen." **12**Then the Spirit lifted me up, and I heard behind me a loud rumbling sound—May the glory of the LORD be praised in his dwelling place!— **13**the sound of the wings of the living creatures brushing against each other and the sound of the wheels beside them, a loud rumbling sound. **14**The Spirit then lifted me up and took me away, and I went in bitterness and in the anger of my spirit, with the strong hand of the LORD upon me. **15**I came to the exiles who lived at Tel Abib near the Kebar River. And there, where they were living, I sat among them for seven days—overwhelmed.

Warning to Israel

16At the end of seven days the word of the LORD came to me: **17**"Son of man, I have made you a watchman for the house of Israel; so hear the word I speak and give them warning from me. **18**When I say to a wicked man, 'You will surely die,' and you do not warn him or speak out to dissuade him from his evil ways in order to save his life, that wicked man will die for*a* his sin, and I will hold you accountable for his blood. **19**But if you do warn the wicked man and he does not turn from his wickedness or from his evil ways, he will die for his sin; but you will have saved yourself.

20"Again, when a righteous man turns from his righteousness and does evil, and I put a stumbling block before him, he will die. Since you did not warn him, he will die for his sin. The righteous things he did will not be remembered, and I will hold you accountable for his blood. **21**But if you do warn the righteous man not to sin and he does not sin, he will surely live because he took warning, and you will have saved yourself."

22The hand of the LORD was upon me there, and he said to me, "Get up and go out to the plain, and there I will speak to you." **23**So I got up and went out to the plain. And the glory of the LORD was standing there, like the glory I had seen by the Kebar River, and I fell facedown. **24**Then the Spirit came into me and raised me to my feet. He spoke to me and said: "Go, shut yourself inside your house. **25**And you, son of man, they will tie with ropes; you will be bound so that you cannot go out among the people. **26**I will make your tongue stick to the roof of your mouth so that you will be silent and unable to rebuke them, though they are a rebellious house. **27**But when I speak to you, I will open your mouth and you shall say to them, 'This is what the Sovereign LORD says.' Whoever will listen let him listen, and whoever will refuse let him refuse; for they are a rebellious house.

---

a18 Or in; also in verses 19 and 20

Siege of Jerusalem Symbolized

4 "Now, son of man, take a clay tablet, put it in front of you and draw the city of Jerusalem on it. [2]Then lay siege to it: Erect siege works against it, build a ramp up to it, set up camps against it and put battering rams around it. [3]Then take an iron pan, place it as an iron wall between you and the city and turn your face toward it. It will be under siege, and you shall besiege it. This will be a sign to the house of Israel.

[4]"Then lie on your left side and put the sin of the house of Israel upon yourself.[a] You are to bear their sin for the number of days you lie on your side. [5]I have assigned you the same number of days as the years of their sin. So for 390 days you will bear the sin of the house of Israel.

[6]"After you have finished this, lie down again, this time on your right side, and bear the sin of the house of Judah. I have assigned you 40 days, a day for each year. [7]Turn your face toward the siege of Jerusalem and with bared arm prophesy against her. [8]I will tie you up with ropes so that you cannot turn from one side to the other until you have finished the days of your siege.

[9]"Take wheat and barley, beans and lentils, millet and spelt; put them in a storage jar and use them to make bread for yourself. You are to eat it during the 390 days you lie on your side. [10]Weigh out twenty shekels[b] of food to eat each day and eat it at set times. [11]Also measure out a sixth of a hin[c] of water and drink it at set times. [12]Eat the food as you would a barley cake; bake it in the sight of the people, using human excrement for fuel." [13]The LORD said, "In this way the people of Israel will eat defiled food among the nations where I will drive them."

[14]Then I said, "Not so, Sovereign LORD! I have never defiled myself. From my youth until now I have never eaten anything found dead or torn by wild animals. No unclean meat has ever entered my mouth."

[15]"Very well," he said, "I will let you bake your bread over cow manure instead of human excrement."

[16]He then said to me: "Son of man, I will cut off the supply of food in Jerusalem. The people will eat rationed food in anxiety and drink rationed water in despair, [17]for food and water will be scarce. They will be appalled at the sight of each other and will waste away because of[d] their sin.

5 "Now, son of man, take a sharp sword and use it as a barber's razor to shave your head and your beard. Then take a set of scales and divide up the hair. [2]When the days of your siege come to an end, burn a third of the hair with fire inside the city. Take a third and strike it with the sword all around the city. And scatter a third to the wind. For I will pursue them with drawn sword. [3]But take a few strands of hair and tuck them away in the folds of your garment. [4]Again, take a few of these and throw them into the fire and burn them up. A fire will spread from there to the whole house of Israel.

[5]"This is what the Sovereign LORD says: This is Jerusalem, which I have set in the center of the nations, with countries all around her. [6]Yet in her wickedness she has rebelled against my laws and decrees more than the nations and countries around her. She has rejected my laws and has not followed my decrees.

[7]"Therefore this is what the Sovereign LORD says: You have been more unruly than the nations around you and have not followed my decrees or kept my laws. You have not even[e] conformed to the standards of the nations around you.

[8]"Therefore this is what the Sovereign LORD says: I myself am against you, Jerusalem, and I will inflict punishment on you in the sight of the nations. [9]Because of all your detestable idols, I will do to you what I have never done before and will never do again. [10]Therefore in your midst fathers will eat their children, and children will eat their fathers. I will inflict punishment on you and will scatter all your survivors to the winds. [11]Therefore as surely as I live, declares the Sovereign LORD, because you have defiled my sanctuary with all your vile images and detestable practices, I myself will withdraw my favor; I will not look on you with pity or spare you. [12]A third of your people will die of the plague or perish by famine inside you; a third will fall by the sword outside your walls; and a third I will scatter to the winds and pursue with drawn sword.

[13]"Then my anger will cease and my wrath against them will subside, and I will be avenged. And when I have spent my wrath upon them, they will know that I the LORD have spoken in my zeal.

[a]4 Or your side   [b]10 That is, about 8 ounces (about 0.2 kilogram)   [c]11 That is, about 2/3 quart (about 0.6 liter)   [d]17 Or away in   [e]7 Most Hebrew manuscripts; some Hebrew manuscripts and Syriac You have

¹⁴"I will make you a ruin and a reproach among the nations around you, in the sight of all who pass by. ¹⁵You will be a reproach and a taunt, a warning and an object of horror to the nations around you when I inflict punishment on you in anger and in wrath and with stinging rebuke. I the LORD have spoken. ¹⁶When I shoot at you with my deadly and destructive arrows of famine, I will shoot to destroy you. I will bring more and more famine upon you and cut off your supply of food. ¹⁷I will send famine and wild beasts against you, and they will leave you childless. Plague and bloodshed will sweep through you, and I will bring the sword against you. I the LORD have spoken."

A Prophecy Against the Mountains of Israel

6 The word of the LORD came to me: ²"Son of man, set your face against the mountains of Israel; prophesy against them ³and say: 'O mountains of Israel, hear the word of the Sovereign LORD. This is what the Sovereign LORD says to the mountains and hills, to the ravines and valleys: I am about to bring a sword against you, and I will destroy your high places. ⁴Your altars will be demolished and your incense altars will be smashed; and I will slay your people in front of your idols. ⁵I will lay the dead bodies of the Israelites in front of their idols, and I will scatter your bones around your altars. ⁶Wherever you live, the towns will be laid waste and the high places demolished, so that your altars will be laid waste and devastated, your idols smashed and ruined, your incense altars broken down, and what you have made wiped out. ⁷Your people will fall slain among you, and you will know that I am the LORD.

⁸" 'But I will spare some, for some of you will escape the sword when you are scattered among the lands and nations. ⁹Then in the nations where they have been carried captive, those who escape will remember me—how I have been grieved by their adulterous hearts, which have turned away from me, and by their eyes, which have lusted after their idols. They will loathe themselves for the evil they have done and for all their detestable practices. ¹⁰And they will know that I am the LORD; I did not threaten in vain to bring this calamity on them.

¹¹" 'This is what the Sovereign LORD says: Strike your hands together and stamp your feet and cry out "Alas!" because of all the wicked and detestable practices of the house of Israel, for they will fall by the sword, famine and plague. ¹²He that is far away will die of the plague, and he that is near will fall by the sword, and he that survives and is spared will die of famine. So will I spend my wrath upon them. ¹³And they will know that I am the LORD, when their people lie slain among their idols around their altars, on every high hill and on all the mountaintops, under every spreading tree and every leafy oak—places where they offered fragrant incense to all their idols. ¹⁴And I will stretch out my hand against them and make the land a desolate waste from the desert to Diblah*ᵃ*—wherever they live. Then they will know that I am the LORD.' "

The End Has Come

7 The word of the LORD came to me: ²"Son of man, this is what the Sovereign LORD says to the land of Israel: The end! The end has come upon the four corners of the land. ³The end is now upon you and I will unleash my anger against you. I will judge you according to your conduct and repay you for all your detestable practices. ⁴I will not look on you with pity or spare you; I will surely repay you for your conduct and the detestable practices among you. Then you will know that I am the LORD.

⁵"This is what the Sovereign LORD says: Disaster! An unheard-of*ᵇ* disaster is coming. ⁶The end has come! The end has come! It has roused itself against you. It has come! ⁷Doom has come upon you—you who dwell in the land. The time has come, the day is near; there is panic, not joy, upon the mountains. ⁸I am about to pour out my wrath on you and spend my anger against you; I will judge you according to your conduct and repay you for all your detestable practices. ⁹I will not look on you with pity or spare you; I will repay you in accordance with your conduct and the detestable practices among you. Then you will know that it is I the LORD who strikes the blow.

¹⁰"The day is here! It has come! Doom has burst forth, the rod has budded, arrogance has blossomed! ¹¹Violence has grown into*ᶜ* a rod to punish wickedness;

ᵃ14 Most Hebrew manuscripts; a few Hebrew manuscripts *Riblah*   *ᵇ5* Most Hebrew manuscripts; some Hebrew manuscripts and Syriac *Disaster after*   *ᶜ11* Or *The violent one has become*

none of the people will be left, none of that crowd—no wealth, nothing of value. ¹²The time has come, the day has arrived. Let not the buyer rejoice nor the seller grieve, for wrath is upon the whole crowd. ¹³The seller will not recover the land he has sold as long as both of them live, for the vision concerning the whole crowd will not be reversed. Because of their sins, not one of them will preserve his life. ¹⁴Though they blow the trumpet and get everything ready, no one will go into battle, for my wrath is upon the whole crowd.

¹⁵"Outside is the sword, inside are plague and famine; those in the country will die by the sword, and those in the city will be devoured by famine and plague. ¹⁶All who survive and escape will be in the mountains, moaning like doves of the valleys, each because of his sins. ¹⁷Every hand will go limp, and every knee will become as weak as water. ¹⁸They will put on sackcloth and be clothed with terror. Their faces will be covered with shame and their heads will be shaved. ¹⁹They will throw their silver into the streets, and their gold will be an unclean thing. Their silver and gold will not be able to save them in the day of the LORD's wrath. They will not satisfy their hunger or fill their stomachs with it, for it has made them stumble into sin. ²⁰They were proud of their beautiful jewelry and used it to make their detestable idols and vile images. Therefore I will turn these into an unclean thing for them. ²¹I will hand it all over as plunder to foreigners and as loot to the wicked of the earth, and they will defile it. ²²I will turn my face away from them, and they will desecrate my treasured place; robbers will enter it and desecrate it.

²³"Prepare chains, because the land is full of bloodshed and the city is full of violence. ²⁴I will bring the most wicked of the nations to take possession of their houses; I will put an end to the pride of the mighty, and their sanctuaries will be desecrated. ²⁵When terror comes, they will seek peace, but there will be none. ²⁶Calamity upon calamity will come, and rumor upon rumor. They will try to get a vision from the prophet; the teaching of the law by the priest will be lost, as will the counsel of the elders. ²⁷The king will mourn, the prince will be clothed with despair, and the hands of the people of the land will tremble. I will deal with them according to their conduct, and by their own standards I will judge them. Then they will know that I am the LORD."

Idolatry in the Temple

8 In the sixth year, in the sixth month on the fifth day, while I was sitting in my house and the elders of Judah were sitting before me, the hand of the Sovereign LORD came upon me there. ²I looked, and I saw a figure like that of a man.ᵃ From what appeared to be his waist down he was like fire, and from there up his appearance was as bright as glowing metal. ³He stretched out what looked like a hand and took me by the hair of my head. The Spirit lifted me up between earth and heaven and in visions of God he took me to Jerusalem, to the entrance to the north gate of the inner court, where the idol that provokes to jealousy stood. ⁴And there before me was the glory of the God of Israel, as in the vision I had seen in the plain.

⁵Then he said to me, "Son of man, look toward the north." So I looked, and in the entrance north of the gate of the altar I saw this idol of jealousy.

⁶And he said to me, "Son of man, do you see what they are doing—the utterly detestable things the house of Israel is doing here, things that will drive me far from my sanctuary? But you will see things that are even more detestable."

⁷Then he brought me to the entrance to the court. I looked, and I saw a hole in the wall. ⁸He said to me, "Son of man, now dig into the wall." So I dug into the wall and saw a doorway there.

⁹And he said to me, "Go in and see the wicked and detestable things they are doing here." ¹⁰So I went in and looked, and I saw portrayed all over the walls all kinds of crawling things and detestable animals and all the idols of the house of Israel. ¹¹In front of them stood seventy elders of the house of Israel, and Jaazaniah son of Shaphan was standing among them. Each had a censer in his hand, and a fragrant cloud of incense was rising.

¹²He said to me, "Son of man, have you seen what the elders of the house of Israel are doing in the darkness, each at the shrine of his own idol? They say, 'The LORD does not see us; the LORD has forsaken the land.' " ¹³Again, he said, "You will see them doing things that are even more detestable."

¹⁴Then he brought me to the entrance

ᵃ2 Or *saw a fiery figure*

to the north gate of the house of the LORD, and I saw women sitting there, mourning for Tammuz. ¹⁵He said to me, "Do you see this, son of man? You will see things that are even more detestable than this."

¹⁶He then brought me into the inner court of the house of the LORD, and there at the entrance to the temple, between the portico and the altar, were about twenty-five men. With their backs toward the temple of the LORD and their faces toward the east, they were bowing down to the sun in the east.

¹⁷He said to me, "Have you seen this, son of man? Is it a trivial matter for the house of Judah to do the detestable things they are doing here? Must they also fill the land with violence and continually provoke me to anger? Look at them putting the branch to their nose! ¹⁸Therefore I will deal with them in anger; I will not look on them with pity or spare them. Although they shout in my ears, I will not listen to them."

Idolaters Killed

9 Then I heard him call out in a loud voice, "Bring the guards of the city here, each with a weapon in his hand." ²And I saw six men coming from the direction of the upper gate, which faces north, each with a deadly weapon in his hand. With them was a man clothed in linen who had a writing kit at his side. They came in and stood beside the bronze altar.

³Now the glory of the God of Israel went up from above the cherubim, where it had been, and moved to the threshold of the temple. Then the LORD called to the man clothed in linen who had the writing kit at his side ⁴and said to him, "Go throughout the city of Jerusalem and put a mark on the foreheads of those who grieve and lament over all the detestable things that are done in it."

⁵As I listened, he said to the others, "Follow him through the city and kill, without showing pity or compassion. ⁶Slaughter old men, young men and maidens, women and children, but do not touch anyone who has the mark. Begin at my sanctuary." So they began with the elders who were in front of the temple.

⁷Then he said to them, "Defile the temple and fill the courts with the slain. Go!" So they went out and began killing throughout the city. ⁸While they were killing and I was left alone, I fell facedown,

crying out, "Ah, Sovereign LORD! Are you going to destroy the entire remnant of Israel in this outpouring of your wrath on Jerusalem?"

⁹He answered me, "The sin of the house of Israel and Judah is exceedingly great; the land is full of bloodshed and the city is full of injustice. They say, 'The LORD has forsaken the land; the LORD does not see.' ¹⁰So I will not look on them with pity or spare them, but I will bring down on their own heads what they have done."

¹¹Then the man in linen with the writing kit at his side brought back word, saying, "I have done as you commanded."

The Glory Departs From the Temple

10 I looked, and I saw the likeness of a throne of sapphire[a] above the expanse that was over the heads of the cherubim. ²The LORD said to the man clothed in linen, "Go in among the wheels beneath the cherubim. Fill your hands with burning coals from among the cherubim and scatter them over the city." And as I watched, he went in.

³Now the cherubim were standing on the south side of the temple when the man went in, and a cloud filled the inner court. ⁴Then the glory of the LORD rose from above the cherubim and moved to the threshold of the temple. The cloud filled the temple, and the court was full of the radiance of the glory of the LORD. ⁵The sound of the wings of the cherubim could be heard as far away as the outer court, like the voice of God Almighty[b] when he speaks.

⁶When the LORD commanded the man in linen, "Take fire from among the wheels, from among the cherubim," the man went in and stood beside a wheel. ⁷Then one of the cherubim reached out his hand to the fire that was among them. He took up some of it and put it into the hands of the man in linen, who took it and went out. ⁸(Under the wings of the cherubim could be seen what looked like the hands of a man.)

⁹I looked, and I saw beside the cherubim four wheels, one beside each of the cherubim; the wheels sparkled like chrysolite. ¹⁰As for their appearance, the four of them looked alike; each was like a wheel intersecting a wheel. ¹¹As they moved, they would go in any one of the four directions the cherubim faced; the wheels did

a1 Or *lapis lazuli*   *b5* Hebrew *El-Shaddai*

not turn about[a] as the cherubim went. The cherubim went in whatever direction the head faced, without turning as they went. [12]Their entire bodies, including their backs, their hands and their wings, were completely full of eyes, as were their four wheels. [13]I heard the wheels being called "the whirling wheels." [14]Each of the cherubim had four faces: One face was that of a cherub, the second the face of a man, the third the face of a lion, and the fourth the face of an eagle.

[15]Then the cherubim rose upward. These were the living creatures I had seen by the Kebar River. [16]When the cherubim moved, the wheels beside them moved; and when the cherubim spread their wings to rise from the ground, the wheels did not leave their side. [17]When the cherubim stood still, they also stood still; and when the cherubim rose, they rose with them, because the spirit of the living creatures was in them.

[18]Then the glory of the LORD departed from over the threshold of the temple and stopped above the cherubim. [19]While I watched, the cherubim spread their wings and rose from the ground, and as they went, the wheels went with them. They stopped at the entrance to the east gate of the LORD's house, and the glory of the God of Israel was above them. [20]These were the living creatures I had seen beneath the God of Israel by the Kebar River, and I realized that they were cherubim. [21]Each had four faces and four wings, and under their wings was what looked like the hands of a man. [22]Their faces had the same appearance as those I had seen by the Kebar River. Each one went straight ahead.

Judgment on Israel's Leaders

11 Then the Spirit lifted me up and brought me to the gate of the house of the LORD that faces east. There at the entrance to the gate were twenty-five men, and I saw among them Jaazaniah son of Azzur and Pelatiah son of Benaiah, leaders of the people. [2]The LORD said to me, "Son of man, these are the men who are plotting evil and giving wicked advice in this city. [3]They say, 'Will it not soon be time to build houses?[b] This city is a cooking pot, and we are the meat.' [4]Therefore prophesy against them; prophesy, son of man."

[5]Then the Spirit of the LORD came upon me, and he told me to say: "This is what

the LORD says: That is what you are saying, O house of Israel, but I know what is going through your mind. [6]You have killed many people in this city and filled its streets with the dead.

[7]"Therefore this is what the Sovereign LORD says: The bodies you have thrown there are the meat and this city is the pot, but I will drive you out of it. [8]You fear the sword, and the sword is what I will bring against you, declares the Sovereign LORD. [9]I will drive you out of the city and hand you over to foreigners and inflict punishment on you. [10]You will fall by the sword, and I will execute judgment on you at the borders of Israel. Then you will know that I am the LORD. [11]This city will not be a pot for you, nor will you be the meat in it; I will execute judgment on you at the borders of Israel. [12]And you will know that I am the LORD, for you have not followed my decrees or kept my laws but have conformed to the standards of the nations around you."

[13]Now as I was prophesying, Pelatiah son of Benaiah died. Then I fell facedown and cried out in a loud voice, "Ah, Sovereign LORD! Will you completely destroy the remnant of Israel?"

[14]The word of the LORD came to me: [15]"Son of man, your brothers—your brothers who are your blood relatives[c] and the whole house of Israel—are those of whom the people of Jerusalem have said, 'They are[d] far away from the LORD; this land was given to us as our possession.'

Promised Return of Israel

[16]"Therefore say: 'This is what the Sovereign LORD says: Although I sent them far away among the nations and scattered them among the countries, yet for a little while I have been a sanctuary for them in the countries where they have gone.'

[17]"Therefore say: 'This is what the Sovereign LORD says: I will gather you from the nations and bring you back from the countries where you have been scattered, and I will give you back the land of Israel again.'

[18]"They will return to it and remove all its vile images and detestable idols. [19]I will give them an undivided heart and put a new spirit in them; I will remove from

[a]11 Or aside   [b]3 Or This is not the time to build houses.   [c]15 Or are in exile with you (see Septuagint and Syriac)   [d]15 Or those to whom the people of Jerusalem have said, 'Stay

Thanks For the Punishment

Key Verse: *"This is what the Sovereign LORD says: I will gather you from the nations and bring you back from the countries where you have been scattered, and I will give you back the land of Israel again."* Ezekiel 11:17

Text: Ezekiel 11:17–20 *(Dad or child reads the text.)*

QUIET
TIMES
WITH **Dad**

DAD READS: No one likes to be punished. When I was a young boy, I hated being spanked or having privileges taken from me. But now I know that punishment was good for me.

Child reads: I don't like to be punished either. I would rather have you just look the other way when I disobey or do something that I know I shouldn't. But I also know that punishment is good for me. I know that it helps me to grow into the person God wants me to be.

DAD READS: I know this may be hard for you to believe, but sometimes adults get punished. We may not get spanked or sent to our rooms, but when grownups do foolish things, we are punished, too. Sometimes adults who do terrible things are sent to prison. Sometimes they lose their jobs because they were dishonest. Punishment is always painful, but it's usually good for us.

Child reads: When I am punished by someone who truly loves me, I feel better when it's over, even though the punishment hurts. I'm glad that someone wants me to grow up to be obedient, to be someone who knows how to control myself. This is why punishment is important.

DAD READS: The Bible verses we read today tell us how God feels about us. Even though he punishes us when we sin, he puts his arms around us like a loving Father after the punishment is over and tells us how much he loves us. He tells us that he wants us to be obedient and to follow him so we will not need to be punished again.

Child reads: I want to grow up to be a strong and obedient person. I know that to be this person, sometimes I will need you to correct me or punish me. I'm glad that I have a dad who loves me so much that he is willing to help me to do good and right things, just like God does with all of us.

DAD READS: Although I'm grown up, I still have a lot to learn. God teaches me new things each day, and sometimes he teaches me through punishing me. I know that God loves me, and that is why he does this. I want to be a dad who listens to God just like I want you to be a person who listens to me. Let me pray this prayer with you:

Our Father in heaven, we love you. Thank you for loving us so much that you are willing to correct us and punish us. I want to be a dad who lives in such a way that you are pleased with me. Please help me to be this kind of loving dad to _____. Thank you for your discipline and your love. We love you. In Jesus' name, **Amen.**

For your next devotional reading, go to page 926.

them their heart of stone and give them a heart of flesh. ²⁰Then they will follow my decrees and be careful to keep my laws. They will be my people, and I will be their God. ²¹But as for those whose hearts are devoted to their vile images and detestable idols, I will bring down on their own heads what they have done, declares the Sovereign LORD."

²²Then the cherubim, with the wheels beside them, spread their wings, and the glory of the God of Israel was above them. ²³The glory of the LORD went up from within the city and stopped above the mountain east of it. ²⁴The Spirit lifted me up and brought me to the exiles in Babylonia*a* in the vision given by the Spirit of God.

Then the vision I had seen went up from me, ²⁵and I told the exiles everything the LORD had shown me.

The Exile Symbolized

12 The word of the LORD came to me: ²"Son of man, you are living among a rebellious people. They have eyes to see but do not see and ears to hear but do not hear, for they are a rebellious people.

³"Therefore, son of man, pack your belongings for exile and in the daytime, as they watch, set out and go from where you are to another place. Perhaps they will understand, though they are a rebellious house. ⁴During the daytime, while they watch, bring out your belongings packed for exile. Then in the evening, while they are watching, go out like those who go into exile. ⁵While they watch, dig through the wall and take your belongings out through it. ⁶Put them on your shoulder as they are watching and carry them out at dusk. Cover your face so that you cannot see the land, for I have made you a sign to the house of Israel."

⁷So I did as I was commanded. During the day I brought out my things packed for exile. Then in the evening I dug through the wall with my hands. I took my belongings out at dusk, carrying them on my shoulders while they watched.

⁸In the morning the word of the LORD came to me: ⁹"Son of man, did not that rebellious house of Israel ask you, 'What are you doing?'

¹⁰"Say to them, 'This is what the Sovereign LORD says: This oracle concerns the prince in Jerusalem and the whole house of Israel who are there.' ¹¹Say to them, 'I am a sign to you.'

"As I have done, so it will be done to them. They will go into exile as captives.

¹²"The prince among them will put his things on his shoulder at dusk and leave, and a hole will be dug in the wall for him to go through. He will cover his face so that he cannot see the land. ¹³I will spread my net for him, and he will be caught in my snare; I will bring him to Babylonia, the land of the Chaldeans, but he will not see it, and there he will die. ¹⁴I will scatter to the winds all those around him—his staff and all his troops—and I will pursue them with drawn sword.

¹⁵"They will know that I am the LORD, when I disperse them among the nations and scatter them through the countries. ¹⁶But I will spare a few of them from the sword, famine and plague, so that in the nations where they go they may acknowledge all their detestable practices. Then they will know that I am the LORD."

¹⁷The word of the LORD came to me: ¹⁸"Son of man, tremble as you eat your food, and shudder in fear as you drink your water. ¹⁹Say to the people of the land: 'This is what the Sovereign LORD says about those living in Jerusalem and in the land of Israel: They will eat their food in anxiety and drink their water in despair, for their land will be stripped of everything in it because of the violence of all who live there. ²⁰The inhabited towns will be laid waste and the land will be desolate. Then you will know that I am the LORD.' "

²¹The word of the LORD came to me: ²²"Son of man, what is this proverb you have in the land of Israel: 'The days go by and every vision comes to nothing'? ²³Say to them, 'This is what the Sovereign LORD says: I am going to put an end to this proverb, and they will no longer quote it in Israel.' Say to them, 'The days are near when every vision will be fulfilled. ²⁴For there will be no more false visions or flattering divinations among the people of Israel. ²⁵But I the LORD will speak what I will, and it shall be fulfilled without delay. For in your days, you rebellious house, I will fulfill whatever I say, declares the Sovereign LORD.' "

²⁶The word of the LORD came to me: ²⁷"Son of man, the house of Israel is saying, 'The vision he sees is for many years from now, and he prophesies about the distant future.'

²⁸"Therefore say to them, 'This is what

^a24 Or *Chaldea*

the Sovereign LORD says: None of my words will be delayed any longer; whatever I say will be fulfilled, declares the Sovereign LORD.' "

False Prophets Condemned

13 The word of the LORD came to me: ²"Son of man, prophesy against the prophets of Israel who are now prophesying. Say to those who prophesy out of their own imagination: 'Hear the word of the LORD! ³This is what the Sovereign LORD says: Woe to the foolish*a* prophets who follow their own spirit and have seen nothing! ⁴Your prophets, O Israel, are like jackals among ruins. ⁵You have not gone up to the breaks in the wall to repair it for the house of Israel so that it will stand firm in the battle on the day of the LORD. ⁶Their visions are false and their divinations a lie. They say, "The LORD declares," when the LORD has not sent them; yet they expect their words to be fulfilled. ⁷Have you not seen false visions and uttered lying divinations when you say, "The LORD declares," though I have not spoken?

⁸" 'Therefore this is what the Sovereign LORD says: Because of your false words and lying visions, I am against you, declares the Sovereign LORD. ⁹My hand will be against the prophets who see false visions and utter lying divinations. They will not belong to the council of my people or be listed in the records of the house of Israel, nor will they enter the land of Israel. Then you will know that I am the Sovereign LORD.

¹⁰" 'Because they lead my people astray, saying, "Peace," when there is no peace, and because, when a flimsy wall is built, they cover it with whitewash, ¹¹therefore tell those who cover it with whitewash that it is going to fall. Rain will come in torrents, and I will send hailstones hurtling down, and violent winds will burst forth. ¹²When the wall collapses, will people not ask you, "Where is the whitewash you covered it with?"

¹³" 'Therefore this is what the Sovereign LORD says: In my wrath I will unleash a violent wind, and in my anger hailstones and torrents of rain will fall with destructive fury. ¹⁴I will tear down the wall you have covered with whitewash and will level it to the ground so that its foundation will be laid bare. When it*b* falls, you will be destroyed in it; and you will know that I am the LORD. ¹⁵So I will spend my wrath against the wall and against those who covered it with whitewash. I will say to you, "The wall is gone and so are those who whitewashed it, ¹⁶those prophets of Israel who prophesied to Jerusalem and saw visions of peace for her when there was no peace, declares the Sovereign LORD." '

¹⁷"Now, son of man, set your face against the daughters of your people who prophesy out of their own imagination. Prophesy against them ¹⁸and say, 'This is what the Sovereign LORD says: Woe to the women who sew magic charms on all their wrists and make veils of various lengths for their heads in order to ensnare people. Will you ensnare the lives of my people but preserve your own? ¹⁹You have profaned me among my people for a few handfuls of barley and scraps of bread. By lying to my people, who listen to lies, you have killed those who should not have died and have spared those who should not live.

²⁰" 'Therefore this is what the Sovereign LORD says: I am against your magic charms with which you ensnare people like birds and I will tear them from your arms; I will set free the people that you ensnare like birds. ²¹I will tear off your veils and save my people from your hands, and they will no longer fall prey to your power. Then you will know that I am the LORD. ²²Because you disheartened the righteous with your lies, when I had brought them no grief, and because you encouraged the wicked not to turn from their evil ways and so save their lives, ²³therefore you will no longer see false visions or practice divination. I will save my people from your hands. And then you will know that I am the LORD.' "

Idolaters Condemned

14 Some of the elders of Israel came to me and sat down in front of me. ²Then the word of the LORD came to me: ³"Son of man, these men have set up idols in their hearts and put wicked stumbling blocks before their faces. Should I let them inquire of me at all? ⁴Therefore speak to them and tell them, 'This is what the Sovereign LORD says: When any Israelite sets up idols in his heart and puts a wicked stumbling block before his face and then goes to a prophet, I the LORD will answer him myself in keeping with his great idolatry. ⁵I will do this to recapture the

---

a3 Or *wicked*   *b14* Or *the city*

hearts of the people of Israel, who have all deserted me for their idols.'

⁶"Therefore say to the house of Israel, 'This is what the Sovereign LORD says: Repent! Turn from your idols and renounce all your detestable practices!

⁷" 'When any Israelite or any alien living in Israel separates himself from me and sets up idols in his heart and puts a wicked stumbling block before his face and then goes to a prophet to inquire of me, I the LORD will answer him myself. ⁸I will set my face against that man and make him an example and a byword. I will cut him off from my people. Then you will know that I am the LORD.

⁹" 'And if the prophet is enticed to utter a prophecy, I the LORD have enticed that prophet, and I will stretch out my hand against him and destroy him from among my people Israel. ¹⁰They will bear their guilt—the prophet will be as guilty as the one who consults him. ¹¹Then the people of Israel will no longer stray from me, nor will they defile themselves anymore with all their sins. They will be my people, and I will be their God, declares the Sovereign LORD.' "

Judgment Inescapable

¹²The word of the LORD came to me: ¹³"Son of man, if a country sins against me by being unfaithful and I stretch out my hand against it to cut off its food supply and send famine upon it and kill its men and their animals, ¹⁴even if these three men—Noah, Daniel[a] and Job—were in it, they could save only themselves by their righteousness, declares the Sovereign LORD.

¹⁵"Or if I send wild beasts through that country and they leave it childless and it becomes desolate so that no one can pass through it because of the beasts, ¹⁶as surely as I live, declares the Sovereign LORD, even if these three men were in it, they could not save their own sons or daughters. They alone would be saved, but the land would be desolate.

¹⁷"Or if I bring a sword against that country and say, 'Let the sword pass throughout the land,' and I kill its men and their animals, ¹⁸as surely as I live, declares the Sovereign LORD, even if these three men were in it, they could not save their own sons or daughters. They alone would be saved.

¹⁹"Or if I send a plague into that land and pour out my wrath upon it through bloodshed, killing its men and their animals, ²⁰as surely as I live, declares the Sovereign LORD, even if Noah, Daniel and Job were in it, they could save neither son nor daughter. They would save only themselves by their righteousness.

²¹"For this is what the Sovereign LORD says: How much worse will it be when I send against Jerusalem my four dreadful judgments—sword and famine and wild beasts and plague—to kill its men and their animals! ²²Yet there will be some survivors—sons and daughters who will be brought out of it. They will come to you, and when you see their conduct and their actions, you will be consoled regarding the disaster I have brought upon Jerusalem—every disaster I have brought upon it. ²³You will be consoled when you see their conduct and their actions, for you will know that I have done nothing in it without cause, declares the Sovereign LORD."

Jerusalem, A Useless Vine

15 The word of the LORD came to me: ²"Son of man, how is the wood of a vine better than that of a branch on any of the trees in the forest? ³Is wood ever taken from it to make anything useful? Do they make pegs from it to hang things on? ⁴And after it is thrown on the fire as fuel and the fire burns both ends and chars the middle, is it then useful for anything? ⁵If it was not useful for anything when it was whole, how much less can it be made into something useful when the fire has burned it and it is charred?

⁶"Therefore this is what the Sovereign LORD says: As I have given the wood of the vine among the trees of the forest as fuel for the fire, so will I treat the people living in Jerusalem. ⁷I will set my face against them. Although they have come out of the fire, the fire will yet consume them. And when I set my face against them, you will know that I am the LORD. ⁸I will make the land desolate because they have been unfaithful, declares the Sovereign LORD."

An Allegory of Unfaithful Jerusalem

16 The word of the LORD came to me: ²"Son of man, confront Jerusalem with her detestable practices ³and say, 'This is what the Sovereign LORD says to

---

a14 Or Danel; the Hebrew spelling may suggest a person other than the prophet Daniel; also in verse 20.

Jerusalem: Your ancestry and birth were in the land of the Canaanites; your father was an Amorite and your mother a Hittite. ⁴On the day you were born your cord was not cut, nor were you washed with water to make you clean, nor were you rubbed with salt or wrapped in cloths. ⁵No one looked on you with pity or had compassion enough to do any of these things for you. Rather, you were thrown out into the open field, for on the day you were born you were despised.

⁶" 'Then I passed by and saw you kicking about in your blood, and as you lay there in your blood I said to you, "Live!"ᵃ ⁷I made you grow like a plant of the field. You grew up and developed and became the most beautiful of jewels.ᵇ Your breasts were formed and your hair grew, you who were naked and bare.

⁸" 'Later I passed by, and when I looked at you and saw that you were old enough for love, I spread the corner of my garment over you and covered your nakedness. I gave you my solemn oath and entered into a covenant with you, declares the Sovereign LORD, and you became mine.

⁹" 'I bathedᶜ you with water and washed the blood from you and put ointments on you. ¹⁰I clothed you with an embroidered dress and put leather sandals on you. I dressed you in fine linen and covered you with costly garments. ¹¹I adorned you with jewelry: I put bracelets on your arms and a necklace around your neck, ¹²and I put a ring on your nose, earrings on your ears and a beautiful crown on your head. ¹³So you were adorned with gold and silver; your clothes were of fine linen and costly fabric and embroidered cloth. Your food was fine flour, honey and olive oil. You became very beautiful and rose to be a queen. ¹⁴And your fame spread among the nations on account of your beauty, because the splendor I had given you made your beauty perfect, declares the Sovereign LORD.

¹⁵" 'But you trusted in your beauty and used your fame to become a prostitute. You lavished your favors on anyone who passed by and your beauty became his.ᵈ ¹⁶You took some of your garments to make gaudy high places, where you carried on your prostitution. Such things should not happen, nor should they ever occur. ¹⁷You also took the fine jewelry I gave you, the jewelry made of my gold and silver, and you made for yourself male idols and engaged in prostitution

with them. ¹⁸And you took your embroidered clothes to put on them, and you offered my oil and incense before them. ¹⁹Also the food I provided for you—the fine flour, olive oil and honey I gave you to eat—you offered as fragrant incense before them. That is what happened, declares the Sovereign LORD.

²⁰" 'And you took your sons and daughters whom you bore to me and sacrificed them as food to the idols. Was your prostitution not enough? ²¹You slaughtered my children and sacrificed themᵉ to the idols. ²²In all your detestable practices and your prostitution you did not remember the days of your youth, when you were naked and bare, kicking about in your blood.

²³" 'Woe! Woe to you, declares the Sovereign LORD. In addition to all your other wickedness, ²⁴you built a mound for yourself and made a lofty shrine in every public square. ²⁵At the head of every street you built your lofty shrines and degraded your beauty, offering your body with increasing promiscuity to anyone who passed by. ²⁶You engaged in prostitution with the Egyptians, your lustful neighbors, and provoked me to anger with your increasing promiscuity. ²⁷So I stretched out my hand against you and reduced your territory; I gave you over to the greed of your enemies, the daughters of the Philistines, who were shocked by your lewd conduct. ²⁸You engaged in prostitution with the Assyrians too, because you were insatiable; and even after that, you still were not satisfied. ²⁹Then you increased your promiscuity to include Babylonia,ᶠ a land of merchants, but even with this you were not satisfied.

³⁰" 'How weak-willed you are, declares the Sovereign LORD, when you do all these things, acting like a brazen prostitute! ³¹When you built your mounds at the head of every street and made your lofty shrines in every public square, you were unlike a prostitute, because you scorned payment.

³²" 'You adulterous wife! You prefer strangers to your own husband! ³³Every prostitute receives a fee, but you give gifts to all your lovers, bribing them to come to

ᵃ6 A few Hebrew manuscripts, Septuagint and Syriac; most Hebrew manuscripts *"Live!" And as you lay there in your blood I said to you, "Live!"* ᵇ7 Or *became mature* ᶜ9 Or *I had bathed* ᵈ15 Most Hebrew manuscripts; one Hebrew manuscript (see some Septuagint manuscripts) *by. Such a thing should not happen* ᵉ21 Or *and made them pass through the fire* ᶠ29 Or *Chaldea*

you from everywhere for your illicit favors. ³⁴So in your prostitution you are the opposite of others; no one runs after you for your favors. You are the very opposite, for you give payment and none is given to you.

³⁵" 'Therefore, you prostitute, hear the word of the LORD! ³⁶This is what the Sovereign LORD says: Because you poured out your wealth*a* and exposed your nakedness in your promiscuity with your lovers, and because of all your detestable idols, and because you gave them your children's blood, ³⁷therefore I am going to gather all your lovers, with whom you found pleasure, those you loved as well as those you hated. I will gather them against you from all around and will strip you in front of them, and they will see all your nakedness. ³⁸I will sentence you to the punishment of women who commit adultery and who shed blood; I will bring upon you the blood vengeance of my wrath and jealous anger. ³⁹Then I will hand you over to your lovers, and they will tear down your mounds and destroy your lofty shrines. They will strip you of your clothes and take your fine jewelry and leave you naked and bare. ⁴⁰They will bring a mob against you, who will stone you and hack you to pieces with their swords. ⁴¹They will burn down your houses and inflict punishment on you in the sight of many women. I will put a stop to your prostitution, and you will no longer pay your lovers. ⁴²Then my wrath against you will subside and my jealous anger will turn away from you; I will be calm and no longer angry.

⁴³" 'Because you did not remember the days of your youth but enraged me with all these things, I will surely bring down on your head what you have done, declares the Sovereign LORD. Did you not add lewdness to all your other detestable practices?

⁴⁴" 'Everyone who quotes proverbs will quote this proverb about you: "Like mother, like daughter." ⁴⁵You are a true daughter of your mother, who despised her husband and her children; and you are a true sister of your sisters, who despised their husbands and their children. Your mother was a Hittite and your father an Amorite. ⁴⁶Your older sister was Samaria, who lived to the north of you with her daughters; and your younger sister, who lived to the south of you with her daughters, was Sodom. ⁴⁷You not only walked in their ways and copied their detestable

practices, but in all your ways you soon became more depraved than they. ⁴⁸As surely as I live, declares the Sovereign LORD, your sister Sodom and her daughters never did what you and your daughters have done.

⁴⁹" 'Now this was the sin of your sister Sodom: She and her daughters were arrogant, overfed and unconcerned; they did not help the poor and needy. ⁵⁰They were haughty and did detestable things before me. Therefore I did away with them as you have seen. ⁵¹Samaria did not commit half the sins you did. You have done more detestable things than they, and have made your sisters seem righteous by all these things you have done. ⁵²Bear your disgrace, for you have furnished some justification for your sisters. Because your sins were more vile than theirs, they appear more righteous than you. So then, be ashamed and bear your disgrace, for you have made your sisters appear righteous.

⁵³" 'However, I will restore the fortunes of Sodom and her daughters and of Samaria and her daughters, and your fortunes along with them, ⁵⁴so that you may bear your disgrace and be ashamed of all you have done in giving them comfort. ⁵⁵And your sisters, Sodom with her daughters and Samaria with her daughters, will return to what they were before; and you and your daughters will return to what you were before. ⁵⁶You would not even mention your sister Sodom in the day of your pride, ⁵⁷before your wickedness was uncovered. Even so, you are now scorned by the daughters of Edom*b* and all her neighbors and the daughters of the Philistines—all those around you who despise you. ⁵⁸You will bear the consequences of your lewdness and your detestable practices, declares the LORD.

⁵⁹" 'This is what the Sovereign LORD says: I will deal with you as you deserve, because you have despised my oath by breaking the covenant. ⁶⁰Yet I will remember the covenant I made with you in the days of your youth, and I will establish an everlasting covenant with you. ⁶¹Then you will remember your ways and be ashamed when you receive your sisters, both those who are older than you and those who are younger. I will give them to you as daughters, but not on the basis of my covenant with you. ⁶²So I will establish

a36 Or *lust*   *b57* Many Hebrew manuscripts and Syriac; most Hebrew manuscripts, Septuagint and Vulgate *Aram*

my covenant with you, and you will know that I am the LORD. [63]Then, when I make atonement for you for all you have done, you will remember and be ashamed and never again open your mouth because of your humiliation, declares the Sovereign LORD.' "

Two Eagles and a Vine

17 The word of the LORD came to me: [2]"Son of man, set forth an allegory and tell the house of Israel a parable. [3]Say to them, 'This is what the Sovereign LORD says: A great eagle with powerful wings, long feathers and full plumage of varied colors came to Lebanon. Taking hold of the top of a cedar, [4]he broke off its topmost shoot and carried it away to a land of merchants, where he planted it in a city of traders.

[5]" 'He took some of the seed of your land and put it in fertile soil. He planted it like a willow by abundant water, [6]and it sprouted and became a low, spreading vine. Its branches turned toward him, but its roots remained under it. So it became a vine and produced branches and put out leafy boughs.

[7]" 'But there was another great eagle with powerful wings and full plumage. The vine now sent out its roots toward him from the plot where it was planted and stretched out its branches to him for water. [8]It had been planted in good soil by abundant water so that it would produce branches, bear fruit and become a splendid vine.'

[9]"Say to them, 'This is what the Sovereign LORD says: Will it thrive? Will it not be uprooted and stripped of its fruit so that it withers? All its new growth will wither. It will not take a strong arm or many people to pull it up by the roots. [10]Even if it is transplanted, will it thrive? Will it not wither completely when the east wind strikes it—wither away in the plot where it grew?' "

[11]Then the word of the LORD came to me: [12]"Say to this rebellious house, 'Do you not know what these things mean?' Say to them: 'The king of Babylon went to Jerusalem and carried off her king and her nobles, bringing them back with him to Babylon. [13]Then he took a member of the royal family and made a treaty with him, putting him under oath. He also carried away the leading men of the land, [14]so that the kingdom would be brought low, unable to rise again, surviving only by

keeping his treaty. [15]But the king rebelled against him by sending his envoys to Egypt to get horses and a large army. Will he succeed? Will he who does such things escape? Will he break the treaty and yet escape?

[16]" 'As surely as I live, declares the Sovereign LORD, he shall die in Babylon, in the land of the king who put him on the throne, whose oath he despised and whose treaty he broke. [17]Pharaoh with his mighty army and great horde will be of no help to him in war, when ramps are built and siege works erected to destroy many lives. [18]He despised the oath by breaking the covenant. Because he had given his hand in pledge and yet did all these things, he shall not escape.

[19]" 'Therefore this is what the Sovereign LORD says: As surely as I live, I will bring down on his head my oath that he despised and my covenant that he broke. [20]I will spread my net for him, and he will be caught in my snare. I will bring him to Babylon and execute judgment upon him there because he was unfaithful to me. [21]All his fleeing troops will fall by the sword, and the survivors will be scattered to the winds. Then you will know that I the LORD have spoken.

[22]" 'This is what the Sovereign LORD says: I myself will take a shoot from the very top of a cedar and plant it; I will break off a tender sprig from its topmost shoots and plant it on a high and lofty mountain. [23]On the mountain heights of Israel I will plant it; it will produce branches and bear fruit and become a splendid cedar. Birds of every kind will nest in it; they will find shelter in the shade of its branches. [24]All the trees of the field will know that I the LORD bring down the tall tree and make the low tree grow tall. I dry up the green tree and make the dry tree flourish.

" 'I the LORD have spoken, and I will do it.' "

The Soul Who Sins Will Die

18 The word of the LORD came to me: [2]"What do you people mean by quoting this proverb about the land of Israel:

" 'The fathers eat sour grapes,
    and the children's teeth are set on
        edge'?

[3]"As surely as I live, declares the Sovereign LORD, you will no longer quote this proverb in Israel. [4]For every living soul belongs to me, the father as well as the son—

both alike belong to me. The soul who sins is the one who will die.

5 "Suppose there is a righteous man
   who does what is just and right.
6 He does not eat at the mountain
     shrines
   or look to the idols of the house of
     Israel.
He does not defile his neighbor's wife
   or lie with a woman during her
     period.
7 He does not oppress anyone,
   but returns what he took in pledge
     for a loan.
He does not commit robbery
   but gives his food to the hungry
   and provides clothing for the naked.
8 He does not lend at usury
   or take excessive interest.ᵃ
He withholds his hand from doing
     wrong
   and judges fairly between man and
     man.
9 He follows my decrees
   and faithfully keeps my laws.
That man is righteous;
   he will surely live,
               declares the Sovereign LORD.

10 "Suppose he has a violent son, who sheds blood or does any of these other thingsᵇ 11(though the father has done none of them):

"He eats at the mountain shrines.
He defiles his neighbor's wife.
12 He oppresses the poor and needy.
He commits robbery.
He does not return what he took in
     pledge.
He looks to the idols.
He does detestable things.
13 He lends at usury and takes excessive
     interest.

Will such a man live? He will not! Because he has done all these detestable things, he will surely be put to death and his blood will be on his own head.

14 "But suppose this son has a son who sees all the sins his father commits, and though he sees them, he does not do such things:

15 "He does not eat at the mountain
     shrines
   or look to the idols of the house of
     Israel.
He does not defile his neighbor's wife.
16 He does not oppress anyone
   or require a pledge for a loan.

He does not commit robbery
   but gives his food to the hungry
   and provides clothing for the naked.
17 He withholds his hand from sinᶜ
   and takes no usury or excessive
     interest.
He keeps my laws and follows my
     decrees.

He will not die for his father's sin; he will surely live. 18But his father will die for his own sin, because he practiced extortion, robbed his brother and did what was wrong among his people.

19 "Yet you ask, 'Why does the son not share the guilt of his father?' Since the son has done what is just and right and has been careful to keep all my decrees, he will surely live. 20The soul who sins is the one who will die. The son will not share the guilt of the father, nor will the father share the guilt of the son. The righteousness of the righteous man will be credited to him, and the wickedness of the wicked will be charged against him.

21 "But if a wicked man turns away from all the sins he has committed and keeps all my decrees and does what is just and right, he will surely live; he will not die. 22None of the offenses he has committed will be remembered against him. Because of the righteous things he has done, he will live. 23Do I take any pleasure in the death of the wicked? declares the Sovereign LORD. Rather, am I not pleased when they turn from their ways and live?

24 "But if a righteous man turns from his righteousness and commits sin and does the same detestable things the wicked man does, will he live? None of the righteous things he has done will be remembered. Because of the unfaithfulness he is guilty of and because of the sins he has committed, he will die.

25 "Yet you say, 'The way of the Lord is not just.' Hear, O house of Israel: Is my way unjust? Is it not your ways that are unjust? 26If a righteous man turns from his righteousness and commits sin, he will die for it; because of the sin he has committed he will die. 27But if a wicked man turns away from the wickedness he has committed and does what is just and right, he will save his life. 28Because he considers all the offenses he has committed and turns away from them, he will surely live; he will not die. 29Yet the house

---

ᵃ8 Or take interest; similarly in verses 13 and 17   ᵇ10 Or things to a brother   ᶜ17 Septuagint (see also verse 8); Hebrew from the poor

of Israel says, 'The way of the Lord is not just.' Are my ways unjust, O house of Israel? Is it not your ways that are unjust?

³⁰"Therefore, O house of Israel, I will judge you, each one according to his ways, declares the Sovereign LORD. Repent! Turn away from all your offenses; then sin will not be your downfall. ³¹Rid yourselves of all the offenses you have committed, and get a new heart and a new spirit. Why will you die, O house of Israel? ³²For I take no pleasure in the death of anyone, declares the Sovereign LORD. Repent and live!

A Lament for Israel's Princes

19 "Take up a lament concerning the princes of Israel ²and say:

" 'What a lioness was your mother
    among the lions!
She lay down among the young lions
    and reared her cubs.
³She brought up one of her cubs,
    and he became a strong lion.
He learned to tear the prey
    and he devoured men.
⁴The nations heard about him,
    and he was trapped in their pit.
They led him with hooks
    to the land of Egypt.

⁵" 'When she saw her hope unfulfilled,
    her expectation gone,
she took another of her cubs
    and made him a strong lion.
⁶He prowled among the lions,
    for he was now a strong lion.
He learned to tear the prey
    and he devoured men.
⁷He broke down^a their strongholds
    and devastated their towns.
The land and all who were in it
    were terrified by his roaring.
⁸Then the nations came against him,
    those from regions round about.
They spread their net for him,
    and he was trapped in their pit.
⁹With hooks they pulled him into a cage
    and brought him to the king of
        Babylon.
They put him in prison,
    so his roar was heard no longer
        on the mountains of Israel.

¹⁰" 'Your mother was like a vine in your
        vineyard^b
    planted by the water;
it was fruitful and full of branches
    because of abundant water.
¹¹Its branches were strong,

fit for a ruler's scepter.
It towered high
    above the thick foliage,
conspicuous for its height
    and for its many branches.
¹²But it was uprooted in fury
    and thrown to the ground.
The east wind made it shrivel,
    it was stripped of its fruit;
its strong branches withered
    and fire consumed them.
¹³Now it is planted in the desert,
    in a dry and thirsty land.
¹⁴Fire spread from one of its main^c
        branches
    and consumed its fruit.
No strong branch is left on it
    fit for a ruler's scepter.'

This is a lament and is to be used as a lament."

Rebellious Israel

20 In the seventh year, in the fifth month on the tenth day, some of the elders of Israel came to inquire of the LORD, and they sat down in front of me.

²Then the word of the LORD came to me: ³"Son of man, speak to the elders of Israel and say to them, 'This is what the Sovereign LORD says: Have you come to inquire of me? As surely as I live, I will not let you inquire of me, declares the Sovereign LORD.'

⁴"Will you judge them? Will you judge them, son of man? Then confront them with the detestable practices of their fathers ⁵and say to them: 'This is what the Sovereign LORD says: On the day I chose Israel, I swore with uplifted hand to the descendants of the house of Jacob and revealed myself to them in Egypt. With uplifted hand I said to them, "I am the LORD your God." ⁶On that day I swore to them that I would bring them out of Egypt into a land I had searched out for them, a land flowing with milk and honey, the most beautiful of all lands. ⁷And I said to them, "Each of you, get rid of the vile images you have set your eyes on, and do not defile yourselves with the idols of Egypt. I am the LORD your God."

⁸" 'But they rebelled against me and would not listen to me; they did not get rid of the vile images they had set their eyes on, nor did they forsake the idols of

^a7 Targum (see Septuagint); Hebrew *He knew* ^b10 Two Hebrew manuscripts; most Hebrew manuscripts *your blood* ^c14 Or *from under its*

Egypt. So I said I would pour out my wrath on them and spend my anger against them in Egypt. ⁹But for the sake of my name I did what would keep it from being profaned in the eyes of the nations they lived among and in whose sight I had revealed myself to the Israelites by bringing them out of Egypt. ¹⁰Therefore I led them out of Egypt and brought them into the desert. ¹¹I gave them my decrees and made known to them my laws, for the man who obeys them will live by them. ¹²Also I gave them my Sabbaths as a sign between us, so they would know that I the LORD made them holy.

¹³" 'Yet the people of Israel rebelled against me in the desert. They did not follow my decrees but rejected my laws—although the man who obeys them will live by them—and they utterly desecrated my Sabbaths. So I said I would pour out my wrath on them and destroy them in the desert. ¹⁴But for the sake of my name I did what would keep it from being profaned in the eyes of the nations in whose sight I had brought them out. ¹⁵Also with uplifted hand I swore to them in the desert that I would not bring them into the land I had given them—a land flowing with milk and honey, most beautiful of all lands— ¹⁶because they rejected my laws and did not follow my decrees and desecrated my Sabbaths. For their hearts were devoted to their idols. ¹⁷Yet I looked on them with pity and did not destroy them or put an end to them in the desert. ¹⁸I said to their children in the desert, "Do not follow the statutes of your fathers or keep their laws or defile yourselves with their idols. ¹⁹I am the LORD your God; follow my decrees and be careful to keep my laws. ²⁰Keep my Sabbaths holy, that they may be a sign between us. Then you will know that I am the LORD your God."

²¹" 'But the children rebelled against me: They did not follow my decrees, they were not careful to keep my laws—although the man who obeys them will live by them—and they desecrated my Sabbaths. So I said I would pour out my wrath on them and spend my anger against them in the desert. ²²But I withheld my hand, and for the sake of my name I did what would keep it from being profaned in the eyes of the nations in whose sight I had brought them out. ²³Also with uplifted hand I swore to them in the desert that I would disperse them among the nations and scatter them through the countries, ²⁴because they had not obeyed my

laws but had rejected my decrees and desecrated my Sabbaths, and their eyes lusted after their fathers' idols. ²⁵I also gave them over to statutes that were not good and laws they could not live by; ²⁶I let them become defiled through their gifts—the sacrifice of every firstborn*—that I might fill them with horror so they would know that I am the LORD.'

²⁷"Therefore, son of man, speak to the people of Israel and say to them, 'This is what the Sovereign LORD says: In this also your fathers blasphemed me by forsaking me: ²⁸When I brought them into the land I had sworn to give them and they saw any high hill or any leafy tree, there they offered their sacrifices, made offerings that provoked me to anger, presented their fragrant incense and poured out their drink offerings. ²⁹Then I said to them: What is this high place you go to?' " (It is called Bamah* to this day.)

Judgment and Restoration

³⁰"Therefore say to the house of Israel: 'This is what the Sovereign LORD says: Will you defile yourselves the way your fathers did and lust after their vile images? ³¹When you offer your gifts—the sacrifice of your sons in* the fire—you continue to defile yourselves with all your idols to this day. Am I to let you inquire of me, O house of Israel? As surely as I live, declares the Sovereign LORD, I will not let you inquire of me.

³²" 'You say, "We want to be like the nations, like the peoples of the world, who serve wood and stone." But what you have in mind will never happen. ³³As surely as I live, declares the Sovereign LORD, I will rule over you with a mighty hand and an outstretched arm and with outpoured wrath. ³⁴I will bring you from the nations and gather you from the countries where you have been scattered—with a mighty hand and an outstretched arm and with outpoured wrath. ³⁵I will bring you into the desert of the nations and there, face to face, I will execute judgment upon you. ³⁶As I judged your fathers in the desert of the land of Egypt, so I will judge you, declares the Sovereign LORD. ³⁷I will take note of you as you pass under my rod, and I will bring you into the bond of the covenant. ³⁸I will purge you of those who revolt and rebel against me. Although I will

---

a26 Or —*making every firstborn pass through the fire*   *b29* Bamah means *high place.*   *c31* Or — *making your sons pass through*

bring them out of the land where they are living, yet they will not enter the land of Israel. Then you will know that I am the LORD.

³⁹" 'As for you, O house of Israel, this is what the Sovereign LORD says: Go and serve your idols, every one of you! But afterward you will surely listen to me and no longer profane my holy name with your gifts and idols. ⁴⁰For on my holy mountain, the high mountain of Israel, declares the Sovereign LORD, there in the land the entire house of Israel will serve me, and there I will accept them. There I will require your offerings and your choice gifts,ᵃ along with all your holy sacrifices. ⁴¹I will accept you as fragrant incense when I bring you out from the nations and gather you from the countries where you have been scattered, and I will show myself holy among you in the sight of the nations. ⁴²Then you will know that I am the LORD, when I bring you into the land of Israel, the land I had sworn with uplifted hand to give to your fathers. ⁴³There you will remember your conduct and all the actions by which you have defiled yourselves, and you will loathe yourselves for all the evil you have done. ⁴⁴You will know that I am the LORD, when I deal with you for my name's sake and not according to your evil ways and your corrupt practices, O house of Israel, declares the Sovereign LORD.' "

Prophecy Against the South

⁴⁵The word of the LORD came to me: ⁴⁶"Son of man, set your face toward the south; preach against the south and prophesy against the forest of the southland. ⁴⁷Say to the southern forest: 'Hear the word of the LORD. This is what the Sovereign LORD says: I am about to set fire to you, and it will consume all your trees, both green and dry. The blazing flame will not be quenched, and every face from south to north will be scorched by it. ⁴⁸Everyone will see that I the LORD have kindled it; it will not be quenched.' "

⁴⁹Then I said, "Ah, Sovereign LORD! They are saying of me, 'Isn't he just telling parables?' "

Babylon, God's Sword of Judgment

21 The word of the LORD came to me: ²"Son of man, set your face against Jerusalem and preach against the sanctuary. Prophesy against the land of Israel

³and say to her: 'This is what the LORD says: I am against you. I will draw my sword from its scabbard and cut off from you both the righteous and the wicked. ⁴Because I am going to cut off the righteous and the wicked, my sword will be unsheathed against everyone from south to north. ⁵Then all people will know that I the LORD have drawn my sword from its scabbard; it will not return again.'

⁶"Therefore groan, son of man! Groan before them with broken heart and bitter grief. ⁷And when they ask you, 'Why are you groaning?' you shall say, 'Because of the news that is coming. Every heart will melt and every hand go limp; every spirit will become faint and every knee become as weak as water.' It is coming! It will surely take place, declares the Sovereign LORD."

⁸The word of the LORD came to me: ⁹"Son of man, prophesy and say, 'This is what the Lord says:

" 'A sword, a sword,
    sharpened and polished—
¹⁰sharpened for the slaughter,
    polished to flash like lightning!

" 'Shall we rejoice in the scepter of my son Judah? The sword despises every such stick.

¹¹" 'The sword is appointed to be
        polished,
    to be grasped with the hand;
it is sharpened and polished,
    made ready for the hand of the
        slayer.
¹²Cry out and wail, son of man,
    for it is against my people;
    it is against all the princes of Israel.
They are thrown to the sword
    along with my people.
Therefore beat your breast.

¹³" 'Testing will surely come. And what if the scepter of Judah, which the sword despises, does not continue? declares the Sovereign LORD.'

¹⁴"So then, son of man, prophesy
    and strike your hands together.
Let the sword strike twice,
    even three times.
It is a sword for slaughter—
    a sword for great slaughter,
    closing in on them from every side.
¹⁵So that hearts may melt
    and the fallen be many,

ᵃ40 Or and the gifts of your firstfruits

I have stationed the sword for
        slaughter^a
    at all their gates.
Oh! It is made to flash like lightning,
    it is grasped for slaughter.
¹⁶O sword, slash to the right,
    then to the left,
    wherever your blade is turned.
¹⁷I too will strike my hands together,
    and my wrath will subside.
I the LORD have spoken."

¹⁸The word of the LORD came to me:
¹⁹"Son of man, mark out two roads for the
sword of the king of Babylon to take, both
starting from the same country. Make a
signpost where the road branches off to
the city. ²⁰Mark out one road for the sword
to come against Rabbah of the Ammon-
ites and another against Judah and fortified Jerusalem. ²¹For the king of Babylon
will stop at the fork in the road, at the
junction of the two roads, to seek an
omen: He will cast lots with arrows, he
will consult his idols, he will examine the
liver. ²²Into his right hand will come the
lot for Jerusalem, where he is to set up
battering rams, to give the command to
slaughter, to sound the battle cry, to set
battering rams against the gates, to build
a ramp and to erect siege works. ²³It will
seem like a false omen to those who have
sworn allegiance to him, but he will remind them of their guilt and take them
captive.
²⁴"Therefore this is what the Sovereign
LORD says: 'Because you people have
brought to mind your guilt by your open
rebellion, revealing your sins in all that
you do—because you have done this, you
will be taken captive.
²⁵" 'O profane and wicked prince of Is-
rael, whose day has come, whose time of
punishment has reached its climax, ²⁶this
is what the Sovereign LORD says: Take off
the turban, remove the crown. It will not
be as it was: The lowly will be exalted and
the exalted will be brought low. ²⁷A ruin! A
ruin! I will make it a ruin! It will not be restored until he comes to whom it right-
fully belongs; to him I will give it.'
²⁸"And you, son of man, prophesy and
say, 'This is what the Sovereign LORD says
about the Ammonites and their insults:

" 'A sword, a sword,
    drawn for the slaughter,
    polished to consume
    and to flash like lightning!
²⁹Despite false visions concerning you
    and lying divinations about you,

it will be laid on the necks
    of the wicked who are to be slain,
whose day has come,
    whose time of punishment has
        reached its climax.
³⁰Return the sword to its scabbard.
    In the place where you were
        created,
    in the land of your ancestry,
        I will judge you.
³¹I will pour out my wrath upon you
    and breathe out my fiery anger
        against you;
I will hand you over to brutal men,
    men skilled in destruction.
³²You will be fuel for the fire,
    your blood will be shed in your land,
you will be remembered no more;
    for I the LORD have spoken.' "

Jerusalem's Sins

22 The word of the LORD came to me:
²"Son of man, will you judge her? Will
you judge this city of bloodshed? Then
confront her with all her detestable practices ³and say: 'This is what the Sovereign
LORD says: O city that brings on herself
doom by shedding blood in her midst and
defiles herself by making idols, ⁴you have
become guilty because of the blood you
have shed and have become defiled by
the idols you have made. You have
brought your days to a close, and the end
of your years has come. Therefore I will
make you an object of scorn to the nations and a laughingstock to all the countries. ⁵Those who are near and those who
are far away will mock you, O infamous
city, full of turmoil.
⁶" 'See how each of the princes of Israel
who are in you uses his power to shed
blood. ⁷In you they have treated father
and mother with contempt; in you they
have oppressed the alien and mistreated
the fatherless and the widow. ⁸You have
despised my holy things and desecrated
my Sabbaths. ⁹In you are slanderous men
bent on shedding blood; in you are those
who eat at the mountain shrines and
commit lewd acts. ¹⁰In you are those who
dishonor their fathers' bed; in you are
those who violate women during their
period, when they are ceremonially unclean. ¹¹In you one man commits a detestable offense with his neighbor's wife,
another shamefully defiles his daughter-
in-law, and another violates his sister, his

^a15 Septuagint; the meaning of the Hebrew for this
word is uncertain.

own father's daughter. ¹²In you men accept bribes to shed blood; you take usury and excessive interest*a* and make unjust gain from your neighbors by extortion. And you have forgotten me, declares the Sovereign LORD.

¹³" 'I will surely strike my hands together at the unjust gain you have made and at the blood you have shed in your midst. ¹⁴Will your courage endure or your hands be strong in the day I deal with you? I the LORD have spoken, and I will do it. ¹⁵I will disperse you among the nations and scatter you through the countries; and I will put an end to your uncleanness. ¹⁶When you have been defiled*b* in the eyes of the nations, you will know that I am the LORD.' "

¹⁷Then the word of the LORD came to me: ¹⁸"Son of man, the house of Israel has become dross to me; all of them are the copper, tin, iron and lead left inside a furnace. They are but the dross of silver. ¹⁹Therefore this is what the Sovereign LORD says: 'Because you have all become dross, I will gather you into Jerusalem. ²⁰As men gather silver, copper, iron, lead and tin into a furnace to melt it with a fiery blast, so will I gather you in my anger and my wrath and put you inside the city and melt you. ²¹I will gather you and I will blow on you with my fiery wrath, and you will be melted inside her. ²²As silver is melted in a furnace, so you will be melted inside her, and you will know that I the LORD have poured out my wrath upon you.' "

²³Again the word of the LORD came to me: ²⁴"Son of man, say to the land, 'You are a land that has had no rain or showers*c* in the day of wrath.' ²⁵There is a conspiracy of her princes*d* within her like a roaring lion tearing its prey; they devour people, take treasures and precious things and make many widows within her. ²⁶Her priests do violence to my law and profane my holy things; they do not distinguish between the holy and the common; they teach that there is no difference between the unclean and the clean; and they shut their eyes to the keeping of my Sabbaths, so that I am profaned among them. ²⁷Her officials within her are like wolves tearing their prey; they shed blood and kill people to make unjust gain. ²⁸Her prophets whitewash these deeds for them by false visions and lying divinations. They say, 'This is what the Sovereign LORD says'—when the LORD has not spoken. ²⁹The people of the land practice extor-

tion and commit robbery; they oppress the poor and needy and mistreat the alien, denying them justice.

³⁰"I looked for a man among them who would build up the wall and stand before me in the gap on behalf of the land so I would not have to destroy it, but I found none. ³¹So I will pour out my wrath on them and consume them with my fiery anger, bringing down on their own heads all they have done, declares the Sovereign LORD."

Two Adulterous Sisters

23 The word of the LORD came to me: ²"Son of man, there were two women, daughters of the same mother. ³They became prostitutes in Egypt, engaging in prostitution from their youth. In that land their breasts were fondled and their virgin bosoms caressed. ⁴The older was named Oholah, and her sister was Oholibah. They were mine and gave birth to sons and daughters. Oholah is Samaria, and Oholibah is Jerusalem.

⁵"Oholah engaged in prostitution while she was still mine; and she lusted after her lovers, the Assyrians—warriors ⁶clothed in blue, governors and commanders, all of them handsome young men, and mounted horsemen. ⁷She gave herself as a prostitute to all the elite of the Assyrians and defiled herself with all the idols of everyone she lusted after. ⁸She did not give up the prostitution she began in Egypt, when during her youth men slept with her, caressed her virgin bosom and poured out their lust upon her.

⁹"Therefore I handed her over to her lovers, the Assyrians, for whom she lusted. ¹⁰They stripped her naked, took away her sons and daughters and killed her with the sword. She became a byword among women, and punishment was inflicted on her.

¹¹"Her sister Oholibah saw this, yet in her lust and prostitution she was more depraved than her sister. ¹²She too lusted after the Assyrians—governors and commanders, warriors in full dress, mounted horsemen, all handsome young men. ¹³I saw that she too defiled herself; both of them went the same way.

¹⁴"But she carried her prostitution still further. She saw men portrayed on a wall,

---

*a*12 Or *usury and interest*   *b*16 Or *When I have allotted you your inheritance*   *c*24 Septuagint; Hebrew *has not been cleansed or rained on*   *d*25 Septuagint; Hebrew *prophets*

figures of Chaldeans*a* portrayed in red, ¹⁵with belts around their waists and flowing turbans on their heads; all of them looked like Babylonian chariot officers, natives of Chaldea.*b* ¹⁶As soon as she saw them, she lusted after them and sent messengers to them in Chaldea. ¹⁷Then the Babylonians came to her, to the bed of love, and in their lust they defiled her. After she had been defiled by them, she turned away from them in disgust. ¹⁸When she carried on her prostitution openly and exposed her nakedness, I turned away from her in disgust, just as I had turned away from her sister. ¹⁹Yet she became more and more promiscuous as she recalled the days of her youth, when she was a prostitute in Egypt. ²⁰There she lusted after her lovers, whose genitals were like those of donkeys and whose emission was like that of horses. ²¹So you longed for the lewdness of your youth, when in Egypt your bosom was caressed and your young breasts fondled.*c*

²²"Therefore, Oholibah, this is what the Sovereign LORD says: I will stir up your lovers against you, those you turned away from in disgust, and I will bring them against you from every side— ²³the Babylonians and all the Chaldeans, the men of Pekod and Shoa and Koa, and all the Assyrians with them, handsome young men, all of them governors and commanders, chariot officers and men of high rank, all mounted on horses. ²⁴They will come against you with weapons,*d* chariots and wagons and with a throng of people; they will take up positions against you on every side with large and small shields and with helmets. I will turn you over to them for punishment, and they will punish you according to their standards. ²⁵I will direct my jealous anger against you, and they will deal with you in fury. They will cut off your noses and your ears, and those of you who are left will fall by the sword. They will take away your sons and daughters, and those of you who are left will be consumed by fire. ²⁶They will also strip you of your clothes and take your fine jewelry. ²⁷So I will put a stop to the lewdness and prostitution you began in Egypt. You will not look on these things with longing or remember Egypt anymore.

²⁸"For this is what the Sovereign LORD says: I am about to hand you over to those you hate, to those you turned away from in disgust. ²⁹They will deal with you in hatred and take away everything you have

worked for. They will leave you naked and bare, and the shame of your prostitution will be exposed. Your lewdness and promiscuity ³⁰have brought this upon you, because you lusted after the nations and defiled yourself with their idols. ³¹You have gone the way of your sister; so I will put her cup into your hand.

³²"This is what the Sovereign LORD says:

"You will drink your sister's cup,
    a cup large and deep;
it will bring scorn and derision,
    for it holds so much.
³³ You will be filled with drunkenness and
        sorrow,
    the cup of ruin and desolation,
    the cup of your sister Samaria.
³⁴ You will drink it and drain it dry;
    you will dash it to pieces
    and tear your breasts.

I have spoken, declares the Sovereign LORD.

³⁵"Therefore this is what the Sovereign LORD says: Since you have forgotten me and thrust me behind your back, you must bear the consequences of your lewdness and prostitution."

³⁶The LORD said to me: "Son of man, will you judge Oholah and Oholibah? Then confront them with their detestable practices, ³⁷for they have committed adultery and blood is on their hands. They committed adultery with their idols; they even sacrificed their children, whom they bore to me,*e* as food for them. ³⁸They have also done this to me: At that same time they defiled my sanctuary and desecrated my Sabbaths. ³⁹On the very day they sacrificed their children to their idols, they entered my sanctuary and desecrated it. That is what they did in my house.

⁴⁰"They even sent messengers for men who came from far away, and when they arrived you bathed yourself for them, painted your eyes and put on your jewelry. ⁴¹You sat on an elegant couch, with a table spread before it on which you had placed the incense and oil that belonged to me.

⁴²"The noise of a carefree crowd was around her; Sabeans*f* were brought from the desert along with men from the

---

a14 Or Babylonians   b15 Or Babylonia; also in verse 16   c21 Syriac (see also verse 3); Hebrew caressed because of your young breasts   d24 The meaning of the Hebrew for this word is uncertain. e37 Or even made the children they bore to me pass through the fire   f42 Or drunkards rabble, and they put bracelets on the arms of the woman and her sister and beautiful crowns on their heads. ⁴³Then I said about the one worn out by adultery, 'Now let them use her as a prostitute, for that is all she is.' ⁴⁴And they slept with her. As men sleep with a prostitute, so they slept with those lewd women, Oholah and Oholibah. ⁴⁵But righteous men will sentence them to the punishment of women who commit adultery and shed blood, because they are adulterous and blood is on their hands.

⁴⁶"This is what the Sovereign LORD says: Bring a mob against them and give them over to terror and plunder. ⁴⁷The mob will stone them and cut them down with their swords; they will kill their sons and daughters and burn down their houses.

⁴⁸"So I will put an end to lewdness in the land, that all women may take warning and not imitate you. ⁴⁹You will suffer the penalty for your lewdness and bear the consequences of your sins of idolatry. Then you will know that I am the Sovereign LORD."

The Cooking Pot

24 In the ninth year, in the tenth month on the tenth day, the word of the LORD came to me: ²"Son of man, record this date, this very date, because the king of Babylon has laid siege to Jerusalem this very day. ³Tell this rebellious house a parable and say to them: 'This is what the Sovereign LORD says:

" 'Put on the cooking pot; put it on
    and pour water into it.
⁴Put into it the pieces of meat,
    all the choice pieces—the leg and the
        shoulder.
Fill it with the best of these bones;
⁵   take the pick of the flock.
Pile wood beneath it for the bones;
    bring it to a boil
    and cook the bones in it.

⁶" 'For this is what the Sovereign LORD says:

" 'Woe to the city of bloodshed,
    to the pot now encrusted,
    whose deposit will not go away!
Empty it piece by piece
    without casting lots for them.

⁷" 'For the blood she shed is in her
        midst:
    She poured it on the bare rock;
    she did not pour it on the ground,

where the dust would cover it.
⁸To stir up wrath and take revenge
    I put her blood on the bare rock,
    so that it would not be covered.

⁹" 'Therefore this is what the Sovereign LORD says:

" 'Woe to the city of bloodshed!
    I, too, will pile the wood high.
¹⁰So heap on the wood
    and kindle the fire.
Cook the meat well,
    mixing in the spices;
    and let the bones be charred.
¹¹Then set the empty pot on the coals
    till it becomes hot and its copper
        glows
so its impurities may be melted
    and its deposit burned away.
¹²It has frustrated all efforts;
    its heavy deposit has not been
        removed,
    not even by fire.

¹³" 'Now your impurity is lewdness. Because I tried to cleanse you but you would not be cleansed from your impurity, you will not be clean again until my wrath against you has subsided.

¹⁴" 'I the LORD have spoken. The time has come for me to act. I will not hold back; I will not have pity, nor will I relent. You will be judged according to your conduct and your actions, declares the Sovereign LORD.' "

Ezekiel's Wife Dies

¹⁵The word of the LORD came to me: ¹⁶"Son of man, with one blow I am about to take away from you the delight of your eyes. Yet do not lament or weep or shed any tears. ¹⁷Groan quietly; do not mourn for the dead. Keep your turban fastened and your sandals on your feet; do not cover the lower part of your face or eat the customary food of mourners."

¹⁸So I spoke to the people in the morning, and in the evening my wife died. The next morning I did as I had been commanded.

¹⁹Then the people asked me, "Won't you tell us what these things have to do with us?"

²⁰So I said to them, "The word of the LORD came to me: ²¹Say to the house of Israel, 'This is what the Sovereign LORD says: I am about to desecrate my sanctuary—the stronghold in which you take pride, the delight of your eyes, the object

of your affection. The sons and daughters you left behind will fall by the sword. ²²And you will do as I have done. You will not cover the lower part of your face or eat the customary food of mourners. ²³You will keep your turbans on your heads and your sandals on your feet. You will not mourn or weep but will waste away because of[a] your sins and groan among yourselves. ²⁴Ezekiel will be a sign to you; you will do just as he has done. When this happens, you will know that I am the Sovereign LORD.'

²⁵"And you, son of man, on the day I take away their stronghold, their joy and glory, the delight of their eyes, their heart's desire, and their sons and daughters as well— ²⁶on that day a fugitive will come to tell you the news. ²⁷At that time your mouth will be opened; you will speak with him and will no longer be silent. So you will be a sign to them, and they will know that I am the LORD."

A Prophecy Against Ammon

25 The word of the LORD came to me: ²"Son of man, set your face against the Ammonites and prophesy against them. ³Say to them, 'Hear the word of the Sovereign LORD. This is what the Sovereign LORD says: Because you said "Aha!" over my sanctuary when it was desecrated and over the land of Israel when it was laid waste and over the people of Judah when they went into exile, ⁴therefore I am going to give you to the people of the East as a possession. They will set up their camps and pitch their tents among you; they will eat your fruit and drink your milk. ⁵I will turn Rabbah into a pasture for camels and Ammon into a resting place for sheep. Then you will know that I am the LORD. ⁶For this is what the Sovereign LORD says: Because you have clapped your hands and stamped your feet, rejoicing with all the malice of your heart against the land of Israel, ⁷therefore I will stretch out my hand against you and give you as plunder to the nations. I will cut you off from the nations and exterminate you from the countries. I will destroy you, and you will know that I am the LORD.' "

A Prophecy Against Moab

⁸"This is what the Sovereign LORD says: 'Because Moab and Seir said, "Look, the house of Judah has become like all the other nations," ⁹therefore I will expose the flank of Moab, beginning at its fron-

tier towns—Beth Jeshimoth, Baal Meon and Kiriathaim—the glory of that land. ¹⁰I will give Moab along with the Ammonites to the people of the East as a possession, so that the Ammonites will not be remembered among the nations; ¹¹and I will inflict punishment on Moab. Then they will know that I am the LORD.' "

A Prophecy Against Edom

¹²"This is what the Sovereign LORD says: 'Because Edom took revenge on the house of Judah and became very guilty by doing so, ¹³therefore this is what the Sovereign LORD says: I will stretch out my hand against Edom and kill its men and their animals. I will lay it waste, and from Teman to Dedan they will fall by the sword. ¹⁴I will take vengeance on Edom by the hand of my people Israel, and they will deal with Edom in accordance with my anger and my wrath; they will know my vengeance, declares the Sovereign LORD.' "

A Prophecy Against Philistia

¹⁵"This is what the Sovereign LORD says: 'Because the Philistines acted in vengeance and took revenge with malice in their hearts, and with ancient hostility sought to destroy Judah, ¹⁶therefore this is what the Sovereign LORD says: I am about to stretch out my hand against the Philistines, and I will cut off the Kerethites and destroy those remaining along the coast. ¹⁷I will carry out great vengeance on them and punish them in my wrath. Then they will know that I am the LORD, when I take vengeance on them.' "

A Prophecy Against Tyre

26 In the eleventh year, on the first day of the month, the word of the LORD came to me: ²"Son of man, because Tyre has said of Jerusalem, 'Aha! The gate to the nations is broken, and its doors have swung open to me; now that she lies in ruins I will prosper,' ³therefore this is what the Sovereign LORD says: I am against you, O Tyre, and I will bring many nations against you, like the sea casting up its waves. ⁴They will destroy the walls of Tyre and pull down her towers; I will scrape away her rubble and make her a bare rock. ⁵Out in the sea she will become a place to spread fishnets, for I have spoken, declares the Sovereign LORD. She will

a23 Or away in

become plunder for the nations, ⁶and her settlements on the mainland will be ravaged by the sword. Then they will know that I am the LORD.

⁷"For this is what the Sovereign LORD says: From the north I am going to bring against Tyre Nebuchadnezzarᵃ king of Babylon, king of kings, with horses and chariots, with horsemen and a great army. ⁸He will ravage your settlements on the mainland with the sword; he will set up siege works against you, build a ramp up to your walls and raise his shields against you. ⁹He will direct the blows of his battering rams against your walls and demolish your towers with his weapons. ¹⁰His horses will be so many that they will cover you with dust. Your walls will tremble at the noise of the war horses, wagons and chariots when he enters your gates as men enter a city whose walls have been broken through. ¹¹The hoofs of his horses will trample all your streets; he will kill your people with the sword, and your strong pillars will fall to the ground. ¹²They will plunder your wealth and loot your merchandise; they will break down your walls and demolish your fine houses and throw your stones, timber and rubble into the sea. ¹³I will put an end to your noisy songs, and the music of your harps will be heard no more. ¹⁴I will make you a bare rock, and you will become a place to spread fishnets. You will never be rebuilt, for I the LORD have spoken, declares the Sovereign LORD.

¹⁵"This is what the Sovereign LORD says to Tyre: Will not the coastlands tremble at the sound of your fall, when the wounded groan and the slaughter takes place in you? ¹⁶Then all the princes of the coast will step down from their thrones and lay aside their robes and take off their embroidered garments. Clothed with terror, they will sit on the ground, trembling every moment, appalled at you. ¹⁷Then they will take up a lament concerning you and say to you:

" 'How you are destroyed, O city of
    renown,
  peopled by men of the sea!
You were a power on the seas,
    you and your citizens;
you put your terror
    on all who lived there.
¹⁸Now the coastlands tremble
    on the day of your fall;
  the islands in the sea
    are terrified at your collapse.'

¹⁹"This is what the Sovereign LORD says: When I make you a desolate city, like cities no longer inhabited, and when I bring the ocean depths over you and its vast waters cover you, ²⁰then I will bring you down with those who go down to the pit, to the people of long ago. I will make you dwell in the earth below, as in ancient ruins, with those who go down to the pit, and you will not return or take your placeᵇ in the land of the living. ²¹I will bring you to a horrible end and you will be no more. You will be sought, but you will never again be found, declares the Sovereign LORD."

A Lament for Tyre

27 The word of the LORD came to me: ²"Son of man, take up a lament concerning Tyre. ³Say to Tyre, situated at the gateway to the sea, merchant of peoples on many coasts, 'This is what the Sovereign LORD says:

" 'You say, O Tyre,
  "I am perfect in beauty."
⁴Your domain was on the high seas;
  your builders brought your beauty to
    perfection.
⁵They made all your timbers
  of pine trees from Senirᶜ;
they took a cedar from Lebanon
  to make a mast for you.
⁶Of oaks from Bashan
  they made your oars;
of cypress woodᵈ from the coasts of
    Cyprusᵉ
  they made your deck, inlaid with
    ivory.
⁷Fine embroidered linen from Egypt
    was your sail
  and served as your banner;
your awnings were of blue and purple
  from the coasts of Elishah.
⁸Men of Sidon and Arvad were your
    oarsmen;
  your skilled men, O Tyre, were
    aboard as your seamen.
⁹Veteran craftsmen of Gebalᶠ were on
    board
  as shipwrights to caulk your seams.
All the ships of the sea and their
    sailors

came alongside to trade for your wares.

¹⁰ " 'Men of Persia, Lydia and Put
    served as soldiers in your army.
They hung their shields and helmets on
    your walls,
    bringing you splendor.
¹¹ Men of Arvad and Helech
    manned your walls on every side;
    men of Gammad
    were in your towers.
They hung their shields around your
    walls;
    they brought your beauty to
        perfection.

¹² " 'Tarshish did business with you because of your great wealth of goods; they exchanged silver, iron, tin and lead for your merchandise.

¹³ " 'Greece, Tubal and Meshech traded with you; they exchanged slaves and articles of bronze for your wares.

¹⁴ " 'Men of Beth Togarmah exchanged work horses, war horses and mules for your merchandise.

¹⁵ " 'The men of Rhodes*a* traded with you, and many coastlands were your customers; they paid you with ivory tusks and ebony.

¹⁶ " 'Aram*b* did business with you because of your many products; they exchanged turquoise, purple fabric, embroidered work, fine linen, coral and rubies for your merchandise.

¹⁷ " 'Judah and Israel traded with you; they exchanged wheat from Minnith and confections,*c* honey, oil and balm for your wares.

¹⁸ " 'Damascus, because of your many products and great wealth of goods, did business with you in wine from Helbon and wool from Zahar.

¹⁹ " 'Danites and Greeks from Uzal bought your merchandise; they exchanged wrought iron, cassia and calamus for your wares.

²⁰ " 'Dedan traded in saddle blankets with you.

²¹ " 'Arabia and all the princes of Kedar were your customers; they did business with you in lambs, rams and goats.

²² " 'The merchants of Sheba and Raamah traded with you; for your merchandise they exchanged the finest of all kinds of spices and precious stones, and gold.

²³ " 'Haran, Canneh and Eden and merchants of Sheba, Asshur and Kilmad traded with you. ²⁴ In your marketplace they traded with you beautiful garments, blue fabric, embroidered work and multicolored rugs with cords twisted and tightly knotted.

²⁵ " 'The ships of Tarshish serve
    as carriers for your wares.
You are filled with heavy cargo
    in the heart of the sea.
²⁶ Your oarsmen take you
    out to the high seas.
But the east wind will break you to
        pieces
    in the heart of the sea.
²⁷ Your wealth, merchandise and wares,
    your mariners, seamen and
        shipwrights,
    your merchants and all your soldiers,
        and everyone else on board
will sink into the heart of the sea
    on the day of your shipwreck.
²⁸ The shorelands will quake
    when your seamen cry out.
²⁹ All who handle the oars
    will abandon their ships;
the mariners and all the seamen
    will stand on the shore.
³⁰ They will raise their voice
    and cry bitterly over you;
they will sprinkle dust on their heads
    and roll in ashes.
³¹ They will shave their heads because of
        you
    and will put on sackcloth.
They will weep over you with anguish
        of soul
    and with bitter mourning.
³² As they wail and mourn over you,
    they will take up a lament
        concerning you:
"Who was ever silenced like Tyre,
    surrounded by the sea?"
³³ When your merchandise went out on
        the seas,
    you satisfied many nations;
with your great wealth and your wares
    you enriched the kings of the earth.
³⁴ Now you are shattered by the sea
    in the depths of the waters;
your wares and all your company
    have gone down with you.
³⁵ All who live in the coastlands
    are appalled at you;
their kings shudder with horror
    and their faces are distorted with fear.
³⁶ The merchants among the nations hiss
        at you;

*a*15 Septuagint; Hebrew *Dedan*   *b*16 Most Hebrew manuscripts; some Hebrew manuscripts and Syriac *Edom*   *c*17 The meaning of the Hebrew for this word is uncertain.

you have come to a horrible end
and will be no more.' "

A Prophecy Against the King of Tyre

28 The word of the LORD came to me: [2]"Son of man, say to the ruler of Tyre, 'This is what the Sovereign LORD says:

" 'In the pride of your heart
    you say, "I am a god;
I sit on the throne of a god
    in the heart of the seas."
But you are a man and not a god,
    though you think you are as wise as a
        god.
[3]Are you wiser than Daniel[a]?
    Is no secret hidden from you?
[4]By your wisdom and understanding
    you have gained wealth for yourself
and amassed gold and silver
    in your treasuries.
[5]By your great skill in trading
    you have increased your wealth,
and because of your wealth
    your heart has grown proud.

[6]" 'Therefore this is what the Sovereign
LORD says:

" 'Because you think you are wise,
    as wise as a god,
[7]I am going to bring foreigners against
    you,
    the most ruthless of nations;
they will draw their swords against
        your beauty and wisdom
    and pierce your shining splendor.
[8]They will bring you down to the pit,
    and you will die a violent death
    in the heart of the seas.
[9]Will you then say, "I am a god,"
    in the presence of those who kill
        you?
You will be but a man, not a god,
    in the hands of those who slay you.
[10]You will die the death of the
        uncircumcised
    at the hands of foreigners.

I have spoken, declares the Sovereign
LORD.' "

[11]The word of the LORD came to me: [12]"Son of man, take up a lament concerning the king of Tyre and say to him: 'This is what the Sovereign LORD says:

" 'You were the model of perfection,
    full of wisdom and perfect in beauty.
[13]You were in Eden,
    the garden of God;
every precious stone adorned you:

ruby, topaz and emerald,
    chrysolite, onyx and jasper,
    sapphire,[b] turquoise and beryl.[c]
Your settings and mountings[d] were
        made of gold;
    on the day you were created they
        were prepared.
[14]You were anointed as a guardian
        cherub,
    for so I ordained you.
You were on the holy mount of God;
    you walked among the fiery stones.
[15]You were blameless in your ways
    from the day you were created
    till wickedness was found in you.
[16]Through your widespread trade
    you were filled with violence,
    and you sinned.
So I drove you in disgrace from the
        mount of God,
    and I expelled you, O guardian
        cherub,
    from among the fiery stones.
[17]Your heart became proud
    on account of your beauty,
and you corrupted your wisdom
    because of your splendor.
So I threw you to the earth;
    I made a spectacle of you before
        kings.
[18]By your many sins and dishonest trade
    you have desecrated your
        sanctuaries.
So I made a fire come out from you,
    and it consumed you,
and I reduced you to ashes on the
        ground
    in the sight of all who were watching.
[19]All the nations who knew you
    are appalled at you;
you have come to a horrible end
    and will be no more.' "

A Prophecy Against Sidon

[20]The word of the LORD came to me: [21]"Son of man, set your face against Sidon; prophesy against her [22]and say: 'This is what the Sovereign LORD says:

" 'I am against you, O Sidon,
    and I will gain glory within you.
They will know that I am the LORD,
    when I inflict punishment on her
    and show myself holy within her.

---

[a]*3 Or *Danel*; the Hebrew spelling may suggest a person other than the prophet Daniel.   [b]*13 Or *lapis lazuli*   [c]*13 The precise identification of some of these precious stones is uncertain.   [d]*13 The meaning of the Hebrew for this phrase is uncertain.

23 I will send a plague upon her
    and make blood flow in her streets.
The slain will fall within her,
    with the sword against her on every
        side.
Then they will know that I am the
        LORD.

24 " 'No longer will the people of Israel
have malicious neighbors who are painful
briers and sharp thorns. Then they will
know that I am the Sovereign LORD.
25 " 'This is what the Sovereign LORD
says: When I gather the people of Israel
from the nations where they have been
scattered, I will show myself holy among
them in the sight of the nations. Then they
will live in their own land, which I gave to
my servant Jacob. 26 They will live there in
safety and will build houses and plant
vineyards; they will live in safety when I
inflict punishment on all their neighbors
who maligned them. Then they will know
that I am the LORD their God.' "

A Prophecy Against Egypt

29 In the tenth year, in the tenth month
    on the twelfth day, the word of the
LORD came to me: 2 "Son of man, set your
face against Pharaoh king of Egypt and
prophesy against him and against all
Egypt. 3 Speak to him and say: 'This is
what the Sovereign LORD says:

" 'I am against you, Pharaoh king of
        Egypt,
    you great monster lying among your
        streams.
You say, "The Nile is mine;
    I made it for myself."
4 But I will put hooks in your jaws
    and make the fish of your streams
        stick to your scales.
I will pull you out from among your
        streams,
    with all the fish sticking to your
        scales.
5 I will leave you in the desert,
    you and all the fish of your streams.
You will fall on the open field
    and not be gathered or picked up.
I will give you as food
    to the beasts of the earth and the
        birds of the air.
6 Then all who live in Egypt will know that I
am the LORD.

" 'You have been a staff of reed for the
house of Israel. 7 When they grasped you
with their hands, you splintered and you

tore open their shoulders; when they
leaned on you, you broke and their backs
were wrenched.[a]
8 " 'Therefore this is what the Sovereign
LORD says: I will bring a sword against you
and kill your men and their animals.
9 Egypt will become a desolate wasteland.
Then they will know that I am the LORD.

" 'Because you said, "The Nile is mine; I
made it," 10 therefore I am against you and
against your streams, and I will make the
land of Egypt a ruin and a desolate waste
from Migdol to Aswan, as far as the border
of Cush.[b] 11 No foot of man or animal will
pass through it; no one will live there for
forty years. 12 I will make the land of Egypt
desolate among devastated lands, and
her cities will lie desolate forty years
among ruined cities. And I will disperse
the Egyptians among the nations and
scatter them through the countries.

13 " 'Yet this is what the Sovereign LORD
says: At the end of forty years I will gather
the Egyptians from the nations where
they were scattered. 14 I will bring them
back from captivity and return them to
Upper Egypt,[c] the land of their ancestry.
There they will be a lowly kingdom. 15 It
will be the lowliest of kingdoms and will
never again exalt itself above the other
nations. I will make it so weak that it will
never again rule over the nations. 16 Egypt
will no longer be a source of confidence
for the people of Israel but will be a reminder of their sin in turning to her for
help. Then they will know that I am the
Sovereign LORD.' "

17 In the twenty-seventh year, in the first
month on the first day, the word of the
LORD came to me: 18 "Son of man, Nebuchadnezzar king of Babylon drove his
army in a hard campaign against Tyre; every head was rubbed bare and every
shoulder made raw. Yet he and his army
got no reward from the campaign he led
against Tyre. 19 Therefore this is what the
Sovereign LORD says: I am going to give
Egypt to Nebuchadnezzar king of Babylon, and he will carry off its wealth. He
will loot and plunder the land as pay for
his army. 20 I have given him Egypt as a reward for his efforts because he and his
army did it for me, declares the Sovereign
LORD.
21 "On that day I will make a horn[d] grow

a7 Syriac (see also Septuagint and Vulgate); Hebrew
and you caused their backs to stand   b10 That is,
the upper Nile region   c14 Hebrew to Pathros
d21 Horn here symbolizes strength.

for the house of Israel, and I will open your mouth among them. Then they will know that I am the LORD."

A Lament for Egypt

30 The word of the LORD came to me: [2]"Son of man, prophesy and say: 'This is what the Sovereign LORD says:

" 'Wail and say,
"Alas for that day!"
[3] For the day is near,
the day of the LORD is near—
a day of clouds,
a time of doom for the nations.
[4] A sword will come against Egypt,
and anguish will come upon Cush.[a]
When the slain fall in Egypt,
her wealth will be carried away
and her foundations torn down.

[5] Cush and Put, Lydia and all Arabia, Libya[b] and the people of the covenant land will fall by the sword along with Egypt.

[6]" 'This is what the LORD says:

" 'The allies of Egypt will fall
and her proud strength will fail.
From Migdol to Aswan
they will fall by the sword within her,
declares the Sovereign LORD.
[7]" 'They will be desolate
among desolate lands,
and their cities will lie
among ruined cities.
[8] Then they will know that I am the
LORD,
when I set fire to Egypt
and all her helpers are crushed.

[9]" 'On that day messengers will go out from me in ships to frighten Cush out of her complacency. Anguish will take hold of them on the day of Egypt's doom, for it is sure to come.

[10]" 'This is what the Sovereign LORD says:

" 'I will put an end to the hordes of
Egypt
by the hand of Nebuchadnezzar king
of Babylon.
[11] He and his army—the most ruthless of
nations—
will be brought in to destroy the
land.
They will draw their swords against
Egypt
and fill the land with the slain.
[12] I will dry up the streams of the Nile

and sell the land to evil men;
by the hand of foreigners
I will lay waste the land and
everything in it.

I the LORD have spoken.

[13]" 'This is what the Sovereign LORD says:

" 'I will destroy the idols
and put an end to the images in
Memphis.[c]
No longer will there be a prince in
Egypt,
and I will spread fear throughout the
land.
[14] I will lay waste Upper Egypt,[d]
set fire to Zoan
and inflict punishment on Thebes.[e]
[15] I will pour out my wrath on Pelusium,[f]
the stronghold of Egypt,
and cut off the hordes of Thebes.
[16] I will set fire to Egypt;
Pelusium will writhe in agony.
Thebes will be taken by storm;
Memphis will be in constant distress.
[17] The young men of Heliopolis[g] and
Bubastis[h]
will fall by the sword,
and the cities themselves will go into
captivity.
[18] Dark will be the day at Tahpanhes
when I break the yoke of Egypt;
there her proud strength will come
to an end.
She will be covered with clouds,
and her villages will go into captivity.
[19] So I will inflict punishment on Egypt,
and they will know that I am the
LORD.' "

[20] In the eleventh year, in the first month on the seventh day, the word of the LORD came to me: [21]"Son of man, I have broken the arm of Pharaoh king of Egypt. It has not been bound up for healing or put in a splint so as to become strong enough to hold a sword. [22] Therefore this is what the Sovereign LORD says: I am against Pharaoh king of Egypt. I will break both his arms, the good arm as well as the broken one, and make the sword fall from his hand. [23] I will disperse the Egyptians among the nations and scatter them through the countries. [24] I will strengthen

---

[a]4 That is, the upper Nile region; also in verses 5 and 9   [b]5 Hebrew *Cub*   [c]13 Hebrew *Noph*; also in verse 16   [d]14 Hebrew *waste Pathros*   [e]14 Hebrew *No*; also in verses 15 and 16   [f]15 Hebrew *Sin*; also in verse 16   [g]17 Hebrew *Awen* (or *On*)   [h]17 Hebrew *Pi Beseth*

the arms of the king of Babylon and put my sword in his hand, but I will break the arms of Pharaoh, and he will groan before him like a mortally wounded man. **25**I will strengthen the arms of the king of Babylon, but the arms of Pharaoh will fall limp. Then they will know that I am the LORD, when I put my sword into the hand of the king of Babylon and he brandishes it against Egypt. **26**I will disperse the Egyptians among the nations and scatter them through the countries. Then they will know that I am the LORD."

A Cedar in Lebanon

31 In the eleventh year, in the third month on the first day, the word of the LORD came to me: **2**"Son of man, say to Pharaoh king of Egypt and to his hordes:

" 'Who can be compared with you in
    majesty?
3Consider Assyria, once a cedar in
    Lebanon,
  with beautiful branches
    overshadowing the forest;
it towered on high,
  its top above the thick foliage.
4The waters nourished it,
  deep springs made it grow tall;
their streams flowed
  all around its base
and sent their channels
  to all the trees of the field.
5So it towered higher
  than all the trees of the field;
its boughs increased
  and its branches grew long,
spreading because of abundant
    waters.
6All the birds of the air
  nested in its boughs,
all the beasts of the field
  gave birth under its branches;
all the great nations
  lived in its shade.
7It was majestic in beauty,
  with its spreading boughs,
for its roots went down
  to abundant waters.
8The cedars in the garden of God
  could not rival it,
nor could the pine trees
  equal its boughs,
nor could the plane trees
  compare with its branches—
no tree in the garden of God
  could match its beauty.
9I made it beautiful
  with abundant branches,

the envy of all the trees of Eden
  in the garden of God.

10" 'Therefore this is what the Sovereign LORD says: Because it towered on high, lifting its top above the thick foliage, and because it was proud of its height, **11**I handed it over to the ruler of the nations, for him to deal with according to its wickedness. I cast it aside, **12**and the most ruthless of foreign nations cut it down and left it. Its boughs fell on the mountains and in all the valleys; its branches lay broken in all the ravines of the land. All the nations of the earth came out from under its shade and left it. **13**All the birds of the air settled on the fallen tree, and all the beasts of the field were among its branches. **14**Therefore no other trees by the waters are ever to tower proudly on high, lifting their tops above the thick foliage. No other trees so well-watered are ever to reach such a height; they are all destined for death, for the earth below, among mortal men, with those who go down to the pit.

15" 'This is what the Sovereign LORD says: On the day it was brought down to the grave[a] I covered the deep springs with mourning for it; I held back its streams, and its abundant waters were restrained. Because of it I clothed Lebanon with gloom, and all the trees of the field withered away. **16**I made the nations tremble at the sound of its fall when I brought it down to the grave with those who go down to the pit. Then all the trees of Eden, the choicest and best of Lebanon, all the trees that were well-watered, were consoled in the earth below. **17**Those who lived in its shade, its allies among the nations, had also gone down to the grave with it, joining those killed by the sword.

18" 'Which of the trees of Eden can be compared with you in splendor and majesty? Yet you, too, will be brought down with the trees of Eden to the earth below; you will lie among the uncircumcised, with those killed by the sword.

" 'This is Pharaoh and all his hordes, declares the Sovereign LORD.' "

A Lament for Pharaoh

32 In the twelfth year, in the twelfth month on the first day, the word of the LORD came to me: **2**"Son of man, take up a lament concerning Pharaoh king of Egypt and say to him:

---

*a*15 Hebrew *Sheol*; also in verses 16 and 17

" 'You are like a lion among the
　　nations;
you are like a monster in the seas
thrashing about in your streams,
　　churning the water with your feet
　　and muddying the streams.
3" 'This is what the Sovereign LORD
says:

" 'With a great throng of people
　　I will cast my net over you,
　　and they will haul you up in my
　　　net.
4I will throw you on the land
　　and hurl you on the open field.
I will let all the birds of the air settle on
　　　you
　　and all the beasts of the earth gorge
　　　themselves on you.
5I will spread your flesh on the
　　　mountains
　　and fill the valleys with your
　　　remains.
6I will drench the land with your flowing
　　　blood
　　all the way to the mountains,
　　and the ravines will be filled with
　　　your flesh.
7When I snuff you out, I will cover the
　　　heavens
　　and darken their stars;
　I will cover the sun with a cloud,
　　and the moon will not give its light.
8All the shining lights in the heavens
　　I will darken over you;
　I will bring darkness over your land,
　　　declares the Sovereign LORD.
9I will trouble the hearts of many
　　　peoples
　　when I bring about your destruction
　　　among the nations,
　　among*a* lands you have not known.
10I will cause many peoples to be
　　　appalled at you,
　　and their kings will shudder with
　　　horror because of you
　　when I brandish my sword before
　　　them.
On the day of your downfall
　　each of them will tremble
　　every moment for his life.

11" 'For this is what the Sovereign LORD
says:

" 'The sword of the king of Babylon
　　will come against you.
12I will cause your hordes to fall
　　by the swords of mighty men—
　　the most ruthless of all nations.
They will shatter the pride of Egypt,

and all her hordes will be
　　overthrown.
13I will destroy all her cattle
　　from beside abundant waters
no longer to be stirred by the foot of
　　man
　　or muddied by the hoofs of cattle.
14Then I will let her waters settle
　　and make her streams flow like oil,
　　　declares the Sovereign LORD.
15When I make Egypt desolate
　　and strip the land of everything in it,
when I strike down all who live there,
　　then they will know that I am the
　　　LORD.'

16"This is the lament they will chant for
her. The daughters of the nations will
chant it; for Egypt and all her hordes they
will chant it, declares the Sovereign
LORD."

17In the twelfth year, on the fifteenth
day of the month, the word of the LORD
came to me: **18**"Son of man, wail for the
hordes of Egypt and consign to the earth
below both her and the daughters of
mighty nations, with those who go down
to the pit. **19**Say to them, 'Are you more favored than others? Go down and be laid
among the uncircumcised.' **20**They will
fall among those killed by the sword. The
sword is drawn; let her be dragged off
with all her hordes. **21**From within the
grave*b* the mighty leaders will say of Egypt
and her allies, 'They have come down and
they lie with the uncircumcised, with
those killed by the sword.'

22"Assyria is there with her whole army;
she is surrounded by the graves of all her
slain, all who have fallen by the sword.
23Their graves are in the depths of the pit
and her army lies around her grave. All
who had spread terror in the land of the
living are slain, fallen by the sword.

24"Elam is there, with all her hordes
around her grave. All of them are slain,
fallen by the sword. All who had spread
terror in the land of the living went
down uncircumcised to the earth below.
They bear their shame with those who go
down to the pit. **25**A bed is made for her
among the slain, with all her hordes
around her grave. All of them are uncircumcised, killed by the sword. Because
their terror had spread in the land of the
living, they bear their shame with those

*a9 Hebrew; Septuagint bring you into captivity
among the nations, / to   b21 Hebrew Sheol; also in
verse 27*

who go down to the pit; they are laid among the slain. ²⁶"Meshech and Tubal are there, with all their hordes around their graves. All of them are uncircumcised, killed by the sword because they spread their terror in the land of the living. ²⁷Do they not lie with the other uncircumcised warriors who have fallen, who went down to the grave with their weapons of war, whose swords were placed under their heads? The punishment for their sins rested on their bones, though the terror of these warriors had stalked through the land of the living. ²⁸"You too, O Pharaoh, will be broken and will lie among the uncircumcised, with those killed by the sword. ²⁹"Edom is there, her kings and all her princes; despite their power, they are laid with those killed by the sword. They lie with the uncircumcised, with those who go down to the pit. ³⁰"All the princes of the north and all the Sidonians are there; they went down with the slain in disgrace despite the terror caused by their power. They lie uncircumcised with those killed by the sword and bear their shame with those who go down to the pit. ³¹"Pharaoh—he and all his army—will see them and he will be consoled for all his hordes that were killed by the sword, declares the Sovereign LORD. ³²Although I had him spread terror in the land of the living, Pharaoh and all his hordes will be laid among the uncircumcised, with those killed by the sword, declares the Sovereign LORD."

Ezekiel a Watchman

33 The word of the LORD came to me: ²"Son of man, speak to your countrymen and say to them: 'When I bring the sword against a land, and the people of the land choose one of their men and make him their watchman, ³and he sees the sword coming against the land and blows the trumpet to warn the people, ⁴then if anyone hears the trumpet but does not take warning and the sword comes and takes his life, his blood will be on his own head. ⁵Since he heard the sound of the trumpet but did not take warning, his blood will be on his own head. If he had taken warning, he would have saved himself. ⁶But if the watchman sees the sword coming and does not blow the trumpet to warn the people and the

sword comes and takes the life of one of them, that man will be taken away because of his sin, but I will hold the watchman accountable for his blood.'

⁷"Son of man, I have made you a watchman for the house of Israel; so hear the word I speak and give them warning from me. ⁸When I say to the wicked, 'O wicked man, you will surely die,' and you do not speak out to dissuade him from his ways, that wicked man will die for*ª* his sin, and I will hold you accountable for his blood. ⁹But if you do warn the wicked man to turn from his ways and he does not do so, he will die for his sin, but you will have saved yourself.

¹⁰"Son of man, say to the house of Israel, 'This is what you are saying: "Our offenses and sins weigh us down, and we are wasting away because of*ᵇ* them. How then can we live?" ' ¹¹Say to them, 'As surely as I live, declares the Sovereign LORD, I take no pleasure in the death of the wicked, but rather that they turn from their ways and live. Turn! Turn from your evil ways! Why will you die, O house of Israel?'

¹²"Therefore, son of man, say to your countrymen, 'The righteousness of the righteous man will not save him when he disobeys, and the wickedness of the wicked man will not cause him to fall when he turns from it. The righteous man, if he sins, will not be allowed to live because of his former righteousness.' ¹³If I tell the righteous man that he will surely live, but then he trusts in his righteousness and does evil, none of the righteous things he has done will be remembered; he will die for the evil he has done. ¹⁴And if I say to the wicked man, 'You will surely die,' but he then turns away from his sin and does what is just and right— ¹⁵if he gives back what he took in pledge for a loan, returns what he has stolen, follows the decrees that give life, and does no evil, he will surely live; he will not die. ¹⁶None of the sins he has committed will be remembered against him. He has done what is just and right; he will surely live.

¹⁷"Yet your countrymen say, 'The way of the Lord is not just.' But it is their way that is not just. ¹⁸If a righteous man turns from his righteousness and does evil, he will die for it. ¹⁹And if a wicked man turns away from his wickedness and does what is just and right, he will live by doing so. ²⁰Yet, O house of Israel, you say, 'The way

ᵃ8 Or in; also in verse 9   ᵇ10 Or away in

of the Lord is not just.' But I will judge each of you according to his own ways."

Jerusalem's Fall Explained

²¹In the twelfth year of our exile, in the tenth month on the fifth day, a man who had escaped from Jerusalem came to me and said, "The city has fallen!" ²²Now the evening before the man arrived, the hand of the LORD was upon me, and he opened my mouth before the man came to me in the morning. So my mouth was opened and I was no longer silent.

²³Then the word of the LORD came to me: ²⁴"Son of man, the people living in those ruins in the land of Israel are saying, 'Abraham was only one man, yet he possessed the land. But we are many; surely the land has been given to us as our possession.' ²⁵Therefore say to them, 'This is what the Sovereign LORD says: Since you eat meat with the blood still in it and look to your idols and shed blood, should you then possess the land? ²⁶You rely on your sword, you do detestable things, and each of you defiles his neighbor's wife. Should you then possess the land?'

²⁷"Say this to them: 'This is what the Sovereign LORD says: As surely as I live, those who are left in the ruins will fall by the sword, those out in the country I will give to the wild animals to be devoured, and those in strongholds and caves will die of a plague. ²⁸I will make the land a desolate waste, and her proud strength will come to an end, and the mountains of Israel will become desolate so that no one will cross them. ²⁹Then they will know that I am the LORD, when I have made the land a desolate waste because of all the detestable things they have done.'

³⁰"As for you, son of man, your countrymen are talking together about you by the walls and at the doors of the houses, saying to each other, 'Come and hear the message that has come from the LORD.' ³¹My people come to you, as they usually do, and sit before you to listen to your words, but they do not put them into practice. With their mouths they express devotion, but their hearts are greedy for unjust gain. ³²Indeed, to them you are nothing more than one who sings love songs with a beautiful voice and plays an instrument well, for they hear your words but do not put them into practice.

³³"When all this comes true—and it surely will—then they will know that a prophet has been among them."

Shepherds and Sheep

34 The word of the LORD came to me: ²"Son of man, prophesy against the shepherds of Israel; prophesy and say to them: 'This is what the Sovereign LORD says: Woe to the shepherds of Israel who only take care of themselves! Should not shepherds take care of the flock? ³You eat the curds, clothe yourselves with the wool and slaughter the choice animals, but you do not take care of the flock. ⁴You have not strengthened the weak or healed the sick or bound up the injured. You have not brought back the strays or searched for the lost. You have ruled them harshly and brutally. ⁵So they were scattered because there was no shepherd, and when they were scattered they became food for all the wild animals. ⁶My sheep wandered over all the mountains and on every high hill. They were scattered over the whole earth, and no one searched or looked for them.

⁷" 'Therefore, you shepherds, hear the word of the LORD: ⁸As surely as I live, declares the Sovereign LORD, because my flock lacks a shepherd and so has been plundered and has become food for all the wild animals, and because my shepherds did not search for my flock but cared for themselves rather than for my flock, ⁹therefore, O shepherds, hear the word of the LORD: ¹⁰This is what the Sovereign LORD says: I am against the shepherds and will hold them accountable for my flock. I will remove them from tending the flock so that the shepherds can no longer feed themselves. I will rescue my flock from their mouths, and it will no longer be food for them.

¹¹" 'For this is what the Sovereign LORD says: I myself will search for my sheep and look after them. ¹²As a shepherd looks after his scattered flock when he is with them, so will I look after my sheep. I will rescue them from all the places where they were scattered on a day of clouds and darkness. ¹³I will bring them out from the nations and gather them from the countries, and I will bring them into their own land. I will pasture them on the mountains of Israel, in the ravines and in all the settlements in the land. ¹⁴I will tend them in a good pasture, and the mountain heights of Israel will be their grazing land. There they will lie down in good grazing land, and there they will feed in a rich pasture on the mountains of Israel. ¹⁵I myself will tend my sheep and have them

lie down, declares the Sovereign LORD. ¹⁶I will search for the lost and bring back the strays. I will bind up the injured and strengthen the weak, but the sleek and the strong I will destroy. I will shepherd the flock with justice.

¹⁷ 'As for you, my flock, this is what the Sovereign LORD says: I will judge between one sheep and another, and between rams and goats. ¹⁸Is it not enough for you to feed on the good pasture? Must you also trample the rest of your pasture with your feet? Is it not enough for you to drink clear water? Must you also muddy the rest with your feet? ¹⁹Must my flock feed on what you have trampled and drink what you have muddied with your feet?

²⁰ 'Therefore this is what the Sovereign LORD says to them: See, I myself will judge between the fat sheep and the lean sheep. ²¹Because you shove with flank and shoulder, butting all the weak sheep with your horns until you have driven them away, ²²I will save my flock, and they will no longer be plundered. I will judge between one sheep and another. ²³I will place over them one shepherd, my servant David, and he will tend them; he will tend them and be their shepherd. ²⁴I the LORD will be their God, and my servant David will be prince among them. I the LORD have spoken.

²⁵ 'I will make a covenant of peace with them and rid the land of wild beasts so that they may live in the desert and sleep in the forests in safety. ²⁶I will bless them and the places surrounding my hill.ᶜ I will send down showers in season; there will be showers of blessing. ²⁷The trees of the field will yield their fruit and the ground will yield its crops; the people will be secure in their land. They will know that I am the LORD, when I break the bars of their yoke and rescue them from the hands of those who enslaved them. ²⁸They will no longer be plundered by the nations, nor will wild animals devour them. They will live in safety, and no one will make them afraid. ²⁹I will provide for them a land renowned for its crops, and they will no longer be victims of famine in the land or bear the scorn of the nations. ³⁰Then they will know that I, the LORD their God, am with them and that they, the house of Israel, are my people, declares the Sovereign LORD. ³¹You my sheep, the sheep of my pasture, are people, and I am your God, declares the Sovereign LORD.' "

A Prophecy Against Edom

35 The word of the LORD came to me: ²"Son of man, set your face against Mount Seir; prophesy against it ³and say: 'This is what the Sovereign LORD says: I am against you, Mount Seir, and I will stretch out my hand against you and make you a desolate waste. ⁴I will turn your towns into ruins and you will be desolate. Then you will know that I am the LORD.

⁵ 'Because you harbored an ancient hostility and delivered the Israelites over to the sword at the time of their calamity, the time their punishment reached its climax, ⁶therefore as surely as I live, declares the Sovereign LORD, I will give you over to bloodshed and it will pursue you. Since you did not hate bloodshed, bloodshed will pursue you. ⁷I will make Mount Seir a desolate waste and cut off from it all who come and go. ⁸I will fill your mountains with the slain; those killed by the sword will fall on your hills and in your valleys and in all your ravines. ⁹I will make you desolate forever; your towns will not be inhabited. Then you will know that I am the LORD.

¹⁰ 'Because you have said, "These two nations and countries will be ours and we will take possession of them," even though I the LORD was there, ¹¹therefore as surely as I live, declares the Sovereign LORD, I will treat you in accordance with the anger and jealousy you showed in your hatred of them and I will make myself known among them when I judge you. ¹²Then you will know that I the LORD have heard all the contemptible things you have said against the mountains of Israel. You said, "They have been laid waste and have been given over to us to devour." ¹³You boasted against me and spoke against me without restraint, and I heard it. ¹⁴This is what the Sovereign LORD says: While the whole earth rejoices, I will make you desolate. ¹⁵Because you rejoiced when the inheritance of the house of Israel became desolate, that is how I will treat you. You will be desolate, O Mount Seir, you and all of Edom. Then they will know that I am the LORD.' "

A Prophecy to the Mountains of Israel

36 "Son of man, prophesy to the mountains of Israel and say, 'O mountains

ᵃ26 Or *I will make them and the places surrounding my hill a blessing*

of Israel, hear the word of the LORD. ²This is what the Sovereign LORD says: The enemy said of you, "Aha! The ancient heights have become our possession." ' ³Therefore prophesy and say, 'This is what the Sovereign LORD says: Because they ravaged and hounded you from every side so that you became the possession of the rest of the nations and the object of people's malicious talk and slander, ⁴therefore, O mountains of Israel, hear the word of the Sovereign LORD: This is what the Sovereign LORD says to the mountains and hills, to the ravines and valleys, to the desolate ruins and the deserted towns that have been plundered and ridiculed by the rest of the nations around you— ⁵this is what the Sovereign LORD says: In my burning zeal I have spoken against the rest of the nations, and against all Edom, for with glee and with malice in their hearts they made my land their own possession so that they might plunder its pastureland.' ⁶Therefore prophesy concerning the land of Israel and say to the mountains and hills, to the ravines and valleys: 'This is what the Sovereign LORD says: I speak in my jealous wrath because you have suffered the scorn of the nations. ⁷Therefore this is what the Sovereign LORD says: I swear with uplifted hand that the nations around you will also suffer scorn.

⁸" 'But you, O mountains of Israel, will produce branches and fruit for my people Israel, for they will soon come home. ⁹I am concerned for you and will look on you with favor; you will be plowed and sown, ¹⁰and I will multiply the number of people upon you, even the whole house of Israel. The towns will be inhabited and the ruins rebuilt. ¹¹I will increase the number of men and animals upon you, and they will be fruitful and become numerous. I will settle people on you as in the past and will make you prosper more than before. Then you will know that I am the LORD. ¹²I will cause people, my people Israel, to walk upon you. They will possess you, and you will be their inheritance; you will never again deprive them of their children.

¹³" 'This is what the Sovereign LORD says: Because people say to you, "You devour men and deprive your nation of its children," ¹⁴therefore you will no longer devour men or make your nation childless, declares the Sovereign LORD. ¹⁵No longer will I make you hear the taunts of the nations, and no longer will you suffer the scorn of the peoples or cause your nation to fall, declares the Sovereign LORD.' "

¹⁶Again the word of the LORD came to me: ¹⁷"Son of man, when the people of Israel were living in their own land, they defiled it by their conduct and their actions. Their conduct was like a woman's monthly uncleanness in my sight. ¹⁸So I poured out my wrath on them because they had shed blood in the land and because they had defiled it with their idols. ¹⁹I dispersed them among the nations, and they were scattered through the countries; I judged them according to their conduct and their actions. ²⁰And wherever they went among the nations they profaned my holy name, for it was said of them, 'These are the LORD's people, and yet they had to leave his land.' ²¹I had concern for my holy name, which the house of Israel profaned among the nations where they had gone.

²²"Therefore say to the house of Israel, 'This is what the Sovereign LORD says: It is not for your sake, O house of Israel, that I am going to do these things, but for the sake of my holy name, which you have profaned among the nations where you have gone. ²³I will show the holiness of my great name, which has been profaned among the nations, the name you have profaned among them. Then the nations will know that I am the LORD, declares the Sovereign LORD, when I show myself holy through you before their eyes.

²⁴" 'For I will take you out of the nations; I will gather you from all the countries and bring you back into your own land. ²⁵I will sprinkle clean water on you, and you will be clean; I will cleanse you from all your impurities and from all your idols. ²⁶I will give you a new heart and put a new spirit in you; I will remove from you your heart of stone and give you a heart of flesh. ²⁷And I will put my Spirit in you and move you to follow my decrees and be careful to keep my laws. ²⁸You will live in the land I gave your forefathers; you will be my people, and I will be your God. ²⁹I will save you from all your uncleanness. I will call for the grain and make it plentiful and will not bring famine upon you. ³⁰I will increase the fruit of the trees and the crops of the field, so that you will no longer suffer disgrace among the nations because of famine. ³¹Then you will remember your evil ways and wicked deeds, and you will loathe yourselves for your sins and detestable practices. ³²I want you to know that I am not doing this for your

sake, declares the Sovereign LORD. Be ashamed and disgraced for your conduct, O house of Israel!

33" 'This is what the Sovereign LORD says: On the day I cleanse you from all your sins, I will resettle your towns, and the ruins will be rebuilt. **34**The desolate land will be cultivated instead of lying desolate in the sight of all who pass through it. **35**They will say, "This land that was laid waste has become like the garden of Eden; the cities that were lying in ruins, desolate and destroyed, are now fortified and inhabited." **36**Then the nations around you that remain will know that I the LORD have rebuilt what was destroyed and have replanted what was desolate. I the LORD have spoken, and I will do it.'

37"This is what the Sovereign LORD says: Once again I will yield to the plea of the house of Israel and do this for them: I will make their people as numerous as sheep, **38**as numerous as the flocks for offerings at Jerusalem during her appointed feasts. So will the ruined cities be filled with flocks of people. Then they will know that I am the LORD."

The Valley of Dry Bones

37 The hand of the LORD was upon me, and he brought me out by the Spirit of the LORD and set me in the middle of a valley; it was full of bones. **2**He led me back and forth among them, and I saw a great many bones on the floor of the valley, bones that were very dry. **3**He asked me, "Son of man, can these bones live?"

I said, "O Sovereign LORD, you alone know."

4Then he said to me, "Prophesy to these bones and say to them, 'Dry bones, hear the word of the LORD! **5**This is what the Sovereign LORD says to these bones: I will make breath*a* enter you, and you will come to life. **6**I will attach tendons to you and make flesh come upon you and cover you with skin; I will put breath in you, and you will come to life. Then you will know that I am the LORD.' "

7So I prophesied as I was commanded. And as I was prophesying, there was a noise, a rattling sound, and the bones came together, bone to bone. **8**I looked, and tendons and flesh appeared on them and skin covered them, but there was no breath in them.

9Then he said to me, "Prophesy to the breath; prophesy, son of man, and say to it, 'This is what the Sovereign LORD says:

Come from the four winds, O breath, and breathe into these slain, that they may live.' " **10**So I prophesied as he commanded me, and breath entered them; they came to life and stood up on their feet—a vast army.

11Then he said to me: "Son of man, these bones are the whole house of Israel. They say, 'Our bones are dried up and our hope is gone; we are cut off.' **12**Therefore prophesy and say to them: 'This is what the Sovereign LORD says: O my people, I am going to open your graves and bring you up from them; I will bring you back to the land of Israel. **13**Then you, my people, will know that I am the LORD, when I open your graves and bring you up from them. **14**I will put my Spirit in you and you will live, and I will settle you in your own land. Then you will know that I the LORD have spoken, and I have done it, declares the LORD.' "

One Nation Under One King

15The word of the LORD came to me: **16**"Son of man, take a stick of wood and write on it, 'Belonging to Judah and the Israelites associated with him.' Then take another stick of wood, and write on it, 'Ephraim's stick, belonging to Joseph and all the house of Israel associated with him.' **17**Join them together into one stick so that they will become one in your hand.

18"When your countrymen ask you, 'Won't you tell us what you mean by this?' **19**say to them, 'This is what the Sovereign LORD says: I am going to take the stick of Joseph—which is in Ephraim's hand—and of the Israelite tribes associated with him, and join it to Judah's stick, making them a single stick of wood, and they will become one in my hand.' **20**Hold before their eyes the sticks you have written on **21**and say to them, 'This is what the Sovereign LORD says: I will take the Israelites out of the nations where they have gone. I will gather them from all around and bring them back into their own land. **22**I will make them one nation in the land, on the mountains of Israel. There will be one king over all of them and they will never again be two nations or be divided into two kingdoms. **23**They will no longer defile themselves with their idols and vile images or with any of their offenses, for I will save them from all their sinful

*a5 The Hebrew for this word can also mean *wind* or *spirit* (see verses 6-14).

backsliding,^{a} and I will cleanse them. They will be my people, and I will be their God.

^{24}" 'My servant David will be king over them, and they will all have one shepherd. They will follow my laws and be careful to keep my decrees. ^{25}They will live in the land I gave to my servant Jacob, the land where your fathers lived. They and their children and their children's children will live there forever, and David my servant will be their prince forever. ^{26}I will make a covenant of peace with them; it will be an everlasting covenant. I will establish them and increase their numbers, and I will put

my sanctuary among them forever. ^{27}My dwelling place will be with them; I will be their God, and they will be my people. ^{28}Then the nations will know that I the LORD make Israel holy, when my sanctuary is among them forever.' "

A Prophecy Against Gog

38 The word of the LORD came to me: ^{2}"Son of man, set your face against

^{a}23 Many Hebrew manuscripts (see also Septuagint); most Hebrew manuscripts *all their dwelling places where they sinned*

Them Bones

DAILY INSIGHT

MONDAY

Passage:
Ezekiel 37:1–10

Verse:
Ezekiel 37:10

Like millions of Americans, I remember it like it was yesterday. On November 22, 1963, at eleven o'clock in the morning, I was standing in my high school library, waiting for our librarian to fill out a hall pass for me to return to study hall. Our principal broke in on the loudspeaker. "President Kennedy has just been shot while riding in a motorcade in Dallas," he announced. "We do not know how seriously he has been injured, but I will give you more information as soon as it is available."

In a few minutes, I was back in my study hall. The rest of my classmates and I sat in stunned silence. In less than an hour, the principle was back on the intercom. His words resonated in my ears: "President Kennedy is dead." We gasped in disbelief. Some of us cried.

And then the principle said something very interesting. "Mrs. Kennedy and the President's body will soon be flown back to Washington." I remember thinking, *Hey, wait a minute. Why didn't he say, "President Kennedy" was being flown back to Washington? Why did he say "the President's body"?*

You and I are men. We are dads. We are more than just bodies, more than an assembly of water and chemicals. But why? What makes us who we are, in addition to simply the sum total of our bones, blood, organs and skin? Today's passage sheds an interesting light on these questions.

Ezekiel had a vision. In this dream, God brought Ezekiel to the rim of a valley. As he looked across its wide expanse, he saw that the floor of the canyon was covered with bones. What a gruesome sight this must have been.

Then, as if it were a great puzzle, God began to assemble these bones, connecting them with tendons and flesh. But they were still only bodies until God gave these bodies breath, as he did to Adam's body way back in the book of Genesis (2:7). At that moment these bones "came to life."

When Jesus appeared to his disciples following his resurrection (John 20:22), he did something even more incredible than making men out of lifeless bodies. Jesus gathered his disciples together and he *breathed* on them. "Be filled with the Holy Spirit," he said. It was as though Jesus was saying, "Until now you have only been men, as pathetic as the bones in Ezekiel's valley. Now take a deep breath—be filled with my Spirit."

Take a deep breath … hold it … now let it out. When you were born, the doctor slapped your backside and you took that first mouthful of air. Over the years your frail, naked body changed, and you became a man. Now it's time to take another gulp of air, to let God's Spirit fill you. Once you do, you'll begin a growth process unlike anything you've ever experienced before. You'll never be the same.

For your next devotional reading, go to page 940.

Gog, of the land of Magog, the chief prince of[a] Meshech and Tubal; prophesy against him ³and say: 'This is what the Sovereign LORD says: I am against you, O Gog, chief prince of[b] Meshech and Tubal. ⁴I will turn you around, put hooks in your jaws and bring you out with your whole army—your horses, your horsemen fully armed, and a great horde with large and small shields, all of them brandishing their swords. ⁵Persia, Cush[c] and Put will be with them, all with shields and helmets, ⁶also Gomer with all its troops, and Beth Togarmah from the far north with all its troops—the many nations with you.

⁷" 'Get ready; be prepared, you and all the hordes gathered about you, and take command of them. ⁸After many days you will be called to arms. In future years you will invade a land that has recovered from war, whose people were gathered from many nations to the mountains of Israel, which had long been desolate. They had been brought out from the nations, and now all of them live in safety. ⁹You and all your troops and the many nations with you will go up, advancing like a storm; you will be like a cloud covering the land.

¹⁰" 'This is what the Sovereign LORD says: On that day thoughts will come into your mind and you will devise an evil scheme. ¹¹You will say, "I will invade a land of unwalled villages; I will attack a peaceful and unsuspecting people—all of them living without walls and without gates and bars. ¹²I will plunder and loot and turn my hand against the resettled ruins and the people gathered from the nations, rich in livestock and goods, living at the center of the land." ¹³Sheba and Dedan and the merchants of Tarshish and all her villages[d] will say to you, "Have you come to plunder? Have you gathered your hordes to loot, to carry off silver and gold, to take away livestock and goods and to seize much plunder?" '

¹⁴"Therefore, son of man, prophesy and say to Gog: 'This is what the Sovereign LORD says: In that day, when my people Israel are living in safety, will you not take notice of it? ¹⁵You will come from your place in the far north, you and many nations with you, all of them riding on horses, a great horde, a mighty army. ¹⁶You will advance against my people Israel like a cloud that covers the land. In days to come, O Gog, I will bring you against my land, so that the nations may know me when I show myself holy through you before their eyes.

¹⁷" 'This is what the Sovereign LORD says: Are you not the one I spoke of in former days by my servants the prophets of Israel? At that time they prophesied for years that I would bring you against them. ¹⁸This is what will happen in that day: When Gog attacks the land of Israel, my hot anger will be aroused, declares the Sovereign LORD. ¹⁹In my zeal and fiery wrath I declare that at that time there shall be a great earthquake in the land of Israel. ²⁰The fish of the sea, the birds of the air, the beasts of the field, every creature that moves along the ground, and all the people on the face of the earth will tremble at my presence. The mountains will be overturned, the cliffs will crumble and every wall will fall to the ground. ²¹I will summon a sword against Gog on all my mountains, declares the Sovereign LORD. Every man's sword will be against his brother. ²²I will execute judgment upon him with plague and bloodshed; I will pour down torrents of rain, hailstones and burning sulfur on him and on his troops and on the many nations with him. ²³And so I will show my greatness and my holiness, and I will make myself known in the sight of many nations. Then they will know that I am the LORD.'

39 "Son of man, prophesy against Gog and say: 'This is what the Sovereign LORD says: I am against you, O Gog, chief prince of[b] Meshech and Tubal. ²I will turn you around and drag you along. I will bring you from the far north and send you against the mountains of Israel. ³Then I will strike your bow from your left hand and make your arrows drop from your right hand. ⁴On the mountains of Israel you will fall, you and all your troops and the nations with you. I will give you as food to all kinds of carrion birds and to the wild animals. ⁵You will fall in the open field, for I have spoken, declares the Sovereign LORD. ⁶I will send fire on Magog and on those who live in safety in the coastlands, and they will know that I am the LORD.

⁷" 'I will make known my holy name among my people Israel. I will no longer let my holy name be profaned, and the nations will know that I the LORD am the Holy One in Israel. ⁸It is coming! It will

---

[a]2 Or *the prince of Rosh.*   [b]3,1 Or *Gog, prince of Rosh.*   [c]5 That is, the upper Nile region   [d]13 Or *her strong lions*

surely take place, declares the Sovereign LORD. This is the day I have spoken of.

⁹" 'Then those who live in the towns of Israel will go out and use the weapons for fuel and burn them up—the small and large shields, the bows and arrows, the war clubs and spears. For seven years they will use them for fuel. ¹⁰They will not need to gather wood from the fields or cut it from the forests, because they will use the weapons for fuel. And they will plunder those who plundered them and loot those who looted them, declares the Sovereign LORD.

¹¹" 'On that day I will give Gog a burial place in Israel, in the valley of those who travel east toward*a* the Sea.*b* It will block the way of travelers, because Gog and all his hordes will be buried there. So it will be called the Valley of Hamon Gog.*c*

¹²" 'For seven months the house of Israel will be burying them in order to cleanse the land. ¹³All the people of the land will bury them, and the day I am glorified will be a memorable day for them, declares the Sovereign LORD.

¹⁴" 'Men will be regularly employed to cleanse the land. Some will go throughout the land and, in addition to them, others will bury those that remain on the ground. At the end of the seven months they will begin their search. ¹⁵As they go through the land and one of them sees a human bone, he will set up a marker beside it until the gravediggers have buried it in the Valley of Hamon Gog. ¹⁶(Also a town called Hamonah*d* will be there.) And so they will cleanse the land.'

¹⁷"Son of man, this is what the Sovereign LORD says: Call out to every kind of bird and all the wild animals: 'Assemble and come together from all around to the sacrifice I am preparing for you, the great sacrifice on the mountains of Israel. There you will eat flesh and drink blood. ¹⁸You will eat the flesh of mighty men and drink the blood of the princes of the earth as if they were rams and lambs, goats and bulls—all of them fattened animals from Bashan. ¹⁹At the sacrifice I am preparing for you, you will eat fat till you are glutted and drink blood till you are drunk. ²⁰At my table you will eat your fill of horses and riders, mighty men and soldiers of every kind,' declares the Sovereign LORD.

²¹"I will display my glory among the nations, and all the nations will see the punishment I inflict and the hand I lay upon them. ²²From that day forward the house of Israel will know that I am the LORD their

God. ²³And the nations will know that the people of Israel went into exile for their sin, because they were unfaithful to me. So I hid my face from them and handed them over to their enemies, and they all fell by the sword. ²⁴I dealt with them according to their uncleanness and their offenses, and I hid my face from them.

²⁵"Therefore this is what the Sovereign LORD says: I will now bring Jacob back from captivity*e* and will have compassion on all the people of Israel, and I will be zealous for my holy name. ²⁶They will forget their shame and all the unfaithfulness they showed toward me when they lived in safety in their land with no one to make them afraid. ²⁷When I have brought them back from the nations and have gathered them from the countries of their enemies, I will show myself holy through them in the sight of many nations. ²⁸Then they will know that I am the LORD their God, for though I sent them into exile among the nations, I will gather them to their own land, not leaving any behind. ²⁹I will no longer hide my face from them, for I will pour out my Spirit on the house of Israel, declares the Sovereign LORD."

The New Temple Area

40 In the twenty-fifth year of our exile, at the beginning of the year, on the tenth of the month, in the fourteenth year after the fall of the city—on that very day the hand of the LORD was upon me and he took me there. ²In visions of God he took me to the land of Israel and set me on a very high mountain, on whose south side were some buildings that looked like a city. ³He took me there, and I saw a man whose appearance was like bronze; he was standing in the gateway with a linen cord and a measuring rod in his hand. ⁴The man said to me, "Son of man, look with your eyes and hear with your ears and pay attention to everything I am going to show you, for that is why you have been brought here. Tell the house of Israel everything you see."

The East Gate to the Outer Court

⁵I saw a wall completely surrounding the temple area. The length of the mea-

---

a11 Or *of*   *b11* That is, the Dead Sea   *c11 Hamon Gog* means *hordes of Gog.*   *d16 Hamonah* means *horde.*   *e25* Or *now restore the fortunes of Jacob*

suring rod in the man's hand was six long cubits, each of which was a cubit[a] and a handbreadth.[b] He measured the wall; it was one measuring rod thick and one rod high. [6]Then he went to the gate facing east. He climbed its steps and measured the threshold of the gate; it was one rod deep.[c] [7]The alcoves for the guards were one rod long and one rod wide, and the projecting walls between the alcoves were five cubits thick. And the threshold of the gate next to the portico facing the temple was one rod deep. [8]Then he measured the portico of the gateway; [9]it[d] was eight cubits deep and its jambs were two cubits thick. The portico of the gateway faced the temple.

[10]Inside the east gate were three alcoves on each side; the three had the same measurements, and the faces of the projecting walls on each side had the same measurements. [11]Then he measured the width of the entrance to the gateway; it was ten cubits and its length was thirteen cubits. [12]In front of each alcove was a wall one cubit high, and the alcoves were six cubits square. [13]Then he measured the gateway from the top of the rear wall of one alcove to the top of the opposite one; the distance was twenty-five cubits from one parapet opening to the opposite one. [14]He measured along the faces of the projecting walls all around the inside of the gateway—sixty cubits. The measurement was up to the portico[e] facing the courtyard.[f] [15]The distance from the entrance of the gateway to the far end of its portico was fifty cubits. [16]The alcoves and the projecting walls inside the gateway were surmounted by narrow parapet openings all around, as was the portico; the openings all around faced inward. The faces of the projecting walls were decorated with palm trees.

The Outer Court

[17]Then he brought me into the outer court. There I saw some rooms and a pavement that had been constructed all around the court; there were thirty rooms along the pavement. [18]It abutted the sides of the gateways and was as wide as they were long; this was the lower pavement. [19]Then he measured the distance from the inside of the lower gateway to the outside of the inner court; it was a hundred cubits on the east side as well as on the north.

The North Gate

[20]Then he measured the length and width of the gate facing north, leading into the outer court. [21]Its alcoves—three on each side—its projecting walls and its portico had the same measurements as those of the first gateway. It was fifty cubits long and twenty-five cubits wide. [22]Its openings, its portico and its palm tree decorations had the same measurements as those of the gate facing east. Seven steps led up to it, with its portico opposite them. [23]There was a gate to the inner court facing the north gate, just as there was on the east. He measured from one gate to the opposite one; it was a hundred cubits.

The South Gate

[24]Then he led me to the south side and I saw a gate facing south. He measured its jambs and its portico, and they had the same measurements as the others. [25]The gateway and its portico had narrow openings all around, like the openings of the others. It was fifty cubits long and twenty-five cubits wide. [26]Seven steps led up to it, with its portico opposite them; it had palm tree decorations on the faces of the projecting walls on each side. [27]The inner court also had a gate facing south, and he measured from this gate to the outer gate on the south side; it was a hundred cubits.

Gates to the Inner Court

[28]Then he brought me into the inner court through the south gate, and he measured the south gate; it had the same measurements as the others. [29]Its alcoves, its projecting walls and its portico had the same measurements as the others. The gateway and its portico had openings all around. It was fifty cubits long and twenty-five cubits wide. [30](The porticoes of the gateways around the inner court were twenty-five cubits wide and five cubits deep.) [31]Its portico faced the outer court; palm trees decorated its jambs, and eight steps led up to it.

[a]5 The common cubit was about 1 1/2 feet (about 0.5 meter).   [b]5 That is, about 3 inches (about 8 centimeters)   [c]6 Septuagint; Hebrew *deep, the first threshold, one rod deep*   [d]8,9 Many Hebrew manuscripts, Septuagint, Vulgate and Syriac; most Hebrew manuscripts *gateway facing the temple; it was one rod deep.* [9]*Then he measured the portico of the gateway; it*   [e]14 Septuagint; Hebrew *projecting wall*   [f]14 The meaning of the Hebrew for this verse is uncertain.

³²Then he brought me to the inner court on the east side, and he measured the gateway; it had the same measurements as the others. ³³Its alcoves, its projecting walls and its portico had the same measurements as the others. The gateway and its portico had openings all around. It was fifty cubits long and twenty-five cubits wide. ³⁴Its portico faced the outer court; palm trees decorated the jambs on either side, and eight steps led up to it.

³⁵Then he brought me to the north gate and measured it. It had the same measurements as the others, ³⁶as did its alcoves, its projecting walls and its portico, and it had openings all around. It was fifty cubits long and twenty-five cubits wide. ³⁷Its portico*a* faced the outer court; palm trees decorated the jambs on either side, and eight steps led up to it.

The Rooms for Preparing Sacrifices

³⁸A room with a doorway was by the portico in each of the inner gateways, where the burnt offerings were washed. ³⁹In the portico of the gateway were two tables on each side, on which the burnt offerings, sin offerings and guilt offerings were slaughtered. ⁴⁰By the outside wall of the portico of the gateway, near the steps at the entrance to the north gateway were two tables, and on the other side of the steps were two tables. ⁴¹So there were four tables on one side of the gateway and four on the other—eight tables in all—on which the sacrifices were slaughtered. ⁴²There were also four tables of dressed stone for the burnt offerings, each a cubit and a half long, a cubit and a half wide and a cubit high. On them were placed the utensils for slaughtering the burnt offerings and the other sacrifices. ⁴³And double-pronged hooks, each a handbreadth long, were attached to the wall all around. The tables were for the flesh of the offerings.

Rooms for the Priests

⁴⁴Outside the inner gate, within the inner court, were two rooms, one*b* at the side of the north gate and facing south, and another at the side of the south*c* gate and facing north. ⁴⁵He said to me, "The room facing south is for the priests who have charge of the temple, ⁴⁶and the room facing north is for the priests who have charge of the altar. These are the sons of Zadok, who are the only Levites who may draw near to the LORD to minister before him."

⁴⁷Then he measured the court: It was square—a hundred cubits long and a hundred cubits wide. And the altar was in front of the temple.

The Temple

⁴⁸He brought me to the portico of the temple and measured the jambs of the portico; they were five cubits wide on either side. The width of the entrance was fourteen cubits and its projecting walls were*d* three cubits wide on either side. ⁴⁹The portico was twenty cubits wide, and twelve*e* cubits from front to back. It was reached by a flight of stairs,*f* and there were pillars on each side of the jambs.

41 Then the man brought me to the outer sanctuary and measured the jambs; the width of the jambs was six cubits*g* on each side.*h* ²The entrance was ten cubits wide, and the projecting walls on each side of it were five cubits wide. He also measured the outer sanctuary; it was forty cubits long and twenty cubits wide.

³Then he went into the inner sanctuary and measured the jambs of the entrance; each was two cubits wide. The entrance was six cubits wide, and the projecting walls on each side of it were seven cubits wide. ⁴And he measured the length of the inner sanctuary; it was twenty cubits, and its width was twenty cubits across the end of the outer sanctuary. He said to me, "This is the Most Holy Place."

⁵Then he measured the wall of the temple; it was six cubits thick, and each side room around the temple was four cubits wide. ⁶The side rooms were on three levels, one above another, thirty on each level. There were ledges all around the wall of the temple to serve as supports for the side rooms, so that the supports were not inserted into the wall of the temple. ⁷The side rooms all around the temple were wider at each successive level. The structure surrounding the temple was built in ascending stages, so that the rooms widened as one went upward. A stairway went up from the lowest floor to the top floor through the middle floor.

---

a 37 Septuagint (see also verses 31 and 34); Hebrew *jambs*   *b* 44 Septuagint; Hebrew *were rooms for singers, which were*   *c* 44 Septuagint; Hebrew *east*   *d* 48 Septuagint; Hebrew *entrance was*   *e* 49 Septuagint; Hebrew *eleven*;   *f* 49 Hebrew; Septuagint *Ten steps led up to it*   *g* 1 The common cubit was about 1 1/2 feet (about 0.5 meter).   *h* 1 One Hebrew manuscript and Septuagint; most Hebrew manuscripts *side, the width of the tent*

8I saw that the temple had a raised base all around it, forming the foundation of the side rooms. It was the length of the rod, six long cubits. **9**The outer wall of the side rooms was five cubits thick. The open area between the side rooms of the temple **10**and the priests' rooms was twenty cubits wide all around the temple. **11**There were entrances to the side rooms from the open area, one on the north and another on the south; and the base adjoining the open area was five cubits wide all around.

12The building facing the temple courtyard on the west side was seventy cubits wide. The wall of the building was five cubits thick all around, and its length was ninety cubits.

13Then he measured the temple; it was a hundred cubits long, and the temple courtyard and the building with its walls were also a hundred cubits long. **14**The width of the temple courtyard on the east, including the front of the temple, was a hundred cubits.

15Then he measured the length of the building facing the courtyard at the rear of the temple, including its galleries on each side; it was a hundred cubits.

The outer sanctuary, the inner sanctuary and the portico facing the court, **16**as well as the thresholds and the narrow windows and galleries around the three of them—everything beyond and including the threshold was covered with wood. The floor, the wall up to the windows, and the windows were covered. **17**In the space above the outside of the entrance to the inner sanctuary and on the walls at regular intervals all around the inner and outer sanctuary **18**were carved cherubim and palm trees. Palm trees alternated with cherubim. Each cherub had two faces: **19**the face of a man toward the palm tree on one side and the face of a lion toward the palm tree on the other. They were carved all around the whole temple. **20**From the floor to the area above the entrance, cherubim and palm trees were carved on the wall of the outer sanctuary.

21The outer sanctuary had a rectangular doorframe, and the one at the front of the Most Holy Place was similar. **22**There was a wooden altar three cubits high and two cubits square*a*; its corners, its base*b* and its sides were of wood. The man said to me, "This is the table that is before the LORD." **23**Both the outer sanctuary and the Most Holy Place had double doors. **24**Each door had two leaves—two hinged leaves for each door. **25**And on the doors of the outer sanctuary were carved cherubim and palm trees like those carved on the walls, and there was a wooden overhang on the front of the portico. **26**On the sidewalls of the portico were narrow windows with palm trees carved on each side. The side rooms of the temple also had overhangs.

Rooms for the Priests

42 Then the man led me northward into the outer court and brought me to the rooms opposite the temple courtyard and opposite the outer wall on the north side. **2**The building whose door faced north was a hundred cubits*c* long and fifty cubits wide. **3**Both in the section twenty cubits from the inner court and in the section opposite the pavement of the outer court, gallery faced gallery at the three levels. **4**In front of the rooms was an inner passageway ten cubits wide and a hundred cubits*d* long. Their doors were on the north. **5**Now the upper rooms were narrower, for the galleries took more space from them than from the rooms on the lower and middle floors of the building. **6**The rooms on the third floor had no pillars, as the courts had; so they were smaller in floor space than those on the lower and middle floors. **7**There was an outer wall parallel to the rooms and the outer court; it extended in front of the rooms for fifty cubits. **8**While the row of rooms on the side next to the outer court was fifty cubits long, the row on the side nearest the sanctuary was a hundred cubits long. **9**The lower rooms had an entrance on the east side as one enters them from the outer court.

10On the south side*e* along the length of the wall of the outer court, adjoining the temple courtyard and opposite the outer wall, were rooms **11**with a passageway in front of them. These were like the rooms on the north; they had the same length and width, with similar exits and dimensions. Similar to the doorways on the north **12**were the doorways of the rooms on the south. There was a doorway at the beginning of the passageway that was parallel to the corresponding wall extending eastward, by which one enters the rooms.

a22 Septuagint; Hebrew *long*   *b22* Septuagint; Hebrew *length*   *c2* The common cubit was about 1 1/2 feet (about 0.5 meter).   *d4* Septuagint and Syriac; Hebrew *and one cubit*   *e10* Septuagint; Hebrew *Eastward*

¹³Then he said to me, "The north and south rooms facing the temple courtyard are the priests' rooms, where the priests who approach the LORD will eat the most holy offerings. There they will put the most holy offerings—the grain offerings, the sin offerings and the guilt offerings—for the place is holy. ¹⁴Once the priests enter the holy precincts, they are not to go into the outer court until they leave behind the garments in which they minister, for these are holy. They are to put on other clothes before they go near the places that are for the people."

¹⁵When he had finished measuring what was inside the temple area, he led me out by the east gate and measured the area all around: ¹⁶He measured the east side with the measuring rod; it was five hundred cubits.[a] ¹⁷He measured the north side; it was five hundred cubits[b] by the measuring rod. ¹⁸He measured the south side; it was five hundred cubits by the measuring rod. ¹⁹Then he turned to the west side and measured; it was five hundred cubits by the measuring rod. ²⁰So he measured the area on all four sides. It had a wall around it, five hundred cubits long and five hundred cubits wide, to separate the holy from the common.

The Glory Returns to the Temple

43 Then the man brought me to the gate facing east, ²and I saw the glory of the God of Israel coming from the east. His voice was like the roar of rushing waters, and the land was radiant with his glory. ³The vision I saw was like the vision I had seen when he[c] came to destroy the city and like the visions I had seen by the Kebar River, and I fell facedown. ⁴The glory of the LORD entered the temple through the gate facing east. ⁵Then the Spirit lifted me up and brought me into the inner court, and the glory of the LORD filled the temple.

⁶While the man was standing beside me, I heard someone speaking to me from inside the temple. ⁷He said: "Son of man, this is the place of my throne and the place for the soles of my feet. This is where I will live among the Israelites forever. The house of Israel will never again defile my holy name—neither they nor their kings—by their prostitution[d] and the lifeless idols[e] of their kings at their high places. ⁸When they placed their threshold next to my threshold and their doorposts beside my doorposts, with only a wall be-

tween me and them, they defiled my holy name by their detestable practices. So I destroyed them in my anger. ⁹Now let them put away from me their prostitution and the lifeless idols of their kings, and I will live among them forever.

¹⁰"Son of man, describe the temple to the people of Israel, that they may be ashamed of their sins. Let them consider the plan, ¹¹and if they are ashamed of all they have done, make known to them the design of the temple—its arrangement, its exits and entrances—its whole design and all its regulations[f] and laws. Write these down before them so that they may be faithful to its design and follow all its regulations.

¹²"This is the law of the temple: All the surrounding area on top of the mountain will be most holy. Such is the law of the temple.

The Altar

¹³"These are the measurements of the altar in long cubits, that cubit being a cubit[g] and a handbreadth[h]: Its gutter is a cubit deep and a cubit wide, with a rim of one span[i] around the edge. And this is the height of the altar: ¹⁴From the gutter on the ground up to the lower ledge it is two cubits high and a cubit wide, and from the smaller ledge up to the larger ledge it is four cubits high and a cubit wide. ¹⁵The altar hearth is four cubits high, and four horns project upward from the hearth. ¹⁶The altar hearth is square, twelve cubits long and twelve cubits wide. ¹⁷The upper ledge also is square, fourteen cubits long and fourteen cubits wide, with a rim of half a cubit and a gutter of a cubit all around. The steps of the altar face east."

¹⁸Then he said to me, "Son of man, this is what the Sovereign LORD says: These will be the regulations for sacrificing burnt offerings and sprinkling blood upon the altar when it is built: ¹⁹You are to give a young bull as a sin offering to the priests, who are Levites, of the family of Zadok, who come near to minister before

---

a16 See Septuagint of verse 17; Hebrew *rods*; also in verses 18 and 19.   *b17* Septuagint; Hebrew *rods* *c3* Some Hebrew manuscripts and Vulgate; most Hebrew manuscripts *I*   *d7* Or *their spiritual adultery*; also in verse 9   *e7* Or *the corpses*; also in verse 9   *f11* Some Hebrew manuscripts and Septuagint; most Hebrew manuscripts *regulations and its whole design*   *g13* The common cubit was about 1 1/2 feet (about 0.5 meter).   *h13* That is, about 3 inches (about 8 centimeters)   *i13* That is, about 9 inches (about 22 centimeters)

me, declares the Sovereign LORD. ²⁰You are to take some of its blood and put it on the four horns of the altar and on the four corners of the upper ledge and all around the rim, and so purify the altar and make atonement for it. ²¹You are to take the bull for the sin offering and burn it in the designated part of the temple area outside the sanctuary.

²²"On the second day you are to offer a male goat without defect for a sin offering, and the altar is to be purified as it was purified with the bull. ²³When you have finished purifying it, you are to offer a young bull and a ram from the flock, both without defect. ²⁴You are to offer them before the LORD, and the priests are to sprinkle salt on them and sacrifice them as a burnt offering to the LORD.

²⁵"For seven days you are to provide a male goat daily for a sin offering; you are also to provide a young bull and a ram from the flock, both without defect. ²⁶For seven days they are to make atonement for the altar and cleanse it; thus they will dedicate it. ²⁷At the end of these days, from the eighth day on, the priests are to present your burnt offerings and fellowship offerings*a* on the altar. Then I will accept you, declares the Sovereign LORD."

The Prince, the Levites, the Priests

44 Then the man brought me back to the outer gate of the sanctuary, the one facing east, and it was shut. ²The LORD said to me, "This gate is to remain shut. It must not be opened; no one may enter through it. It is to remain shut because the LORD, the God of Israel, has entered through it. ³The prince himself is the only one who may sit inside the gateway to eat in the presence of the LORD. He is to enter by way of the portico of the gateway and go out the same way."

⁴Then the man brought me by way of the north gate to the front of the temple. I looked and saw the glory of the LORD filling the temple of the LORD, and I fell facedown.

⁵The LORD said to me, "Son of man, look carefully, listen closely and give attention to everything I tell you concerning all the regulations regarding the temple of the LORD. Give attention to the entrance of the temple and all the exits of the sanctuary. ⁶Say to the rebellious house of Israel, 'This is what the Sovereign LORD says: Enough of your detestable practices,

O house of Israel! ⁷In addition to all your other detestable practices, you brought foreigners uncircumcised in heart and flesh into my sanctuary, desecrating my temple while you offered me food, fat and blood, and you broke my covenant. ⁸Instead of carrying out your duty in regard to my holy things, you put others in charge of my sanctuary. ⁹This is what the Sovereign LORD says: No foreigner uncircumcised in heart and flesh is to enter my sanctuary, not even the foreigners who live among the Israelites.

¹⁰" 'The Levites who went far from me when Israel went astray and who wandered from me after their idols must bear the consequences of their sin. ¹¹They may serve in my sanctuary, having charge of the gates of the temple and serving in it; they may slaughter the burnt offerings and sacrifices for the people and stand before the people and serve them. ¹²But because they served them in the presence of their idols and made the house of Israel fall into sin, therefore I have sworn with uplifted hand that they must bear the consequences of their sin, declares the Sovereign LORD. ¹³They are not to come near to serve me as priests or come near any of my holy things or my most holy offerings; they must bear the shame of their detestable practices. ¹⁴Yet I will put them in charge of the duties of the temple and all the work that is to be done in it.

¹⁵" 'But the priests, who are Levites and descendants of Zadok and who faithfully carried out the duties of my sanctuary when the Israelites went astray from me, are to come near to minister before me; they are to stand before me to offer sacrifices of fat and blood, declares the Sovereign LORD. ¹⁶They alone are to enter my sanctuary; they alone are to come near my table to minister before me and perform my service.

¹⁷" 'When they enter the gates of the inner court, they are to wear linen clothes; they must not wear any woolen garment while ministering at the gates of the inner court or inside the temple. ¹⁸They are to wear linen turbans on their heads and linen undergarments around their waists. They must not wear anything that makes them perspire. ¹⁹When they go out into the outer court where the people are, they are to take off the clothes they have been ministering in and are to leave them in the sacred rooms, and put on other

a27 Traditionally peace offerings

clothes, so that they do not consecrate the people by means of their garments. [20] 'They must not shave their heads or let their hair grow long, but they are to keep the hair of their heads trimmed. [21]No priest is to drink wine when he enters the inner court. [22]They must not marry widows or divorced women; they may marry only virgins of Israelite descent or widows of priests. [23]They are to teach my people the difference between the holy and the common and show them how to distinguish between the unclean and the clean.

[24] 'In any dispute, the priests are to serve as judges and decide it according to my ordinances. They are to keep my laws and my decrees for all my appointed feasts, and they are to keep my Sabbaths holy.

[25] 'A priest must not defile himself by going near a dead person; however, if the dead person was his father or mother, son or daughter, brother or unmarried sister, then he may defile himself. [26]After he is cleansed, he must wait seven days. [27]On the day he goes into the inner court of the sanctuary to minister in the sanctuary, he is to offer a sin offering for himself, declares the Sovereign LORD.

[28] 'I am to be the only inheritance the priests have. You are to give them no possession in Israel; I will be their possession. [29]They will eat the grain offerings, the sin offerings and the guilt offerings; and everything in Israel devoted[a] to the LORD will belong to them. [30]The best of all the firstfruits and of all your special gifts will belong to the priests. You are to give them the first portion of your ground meal so that a blessing may rest on your household. [31]The priests must not eat anything, bird or animal, found dead or torn by wild animals.

Division of the Land

45 " 'When you allot the land as an inheritance, you are to present to the LORD a portion of the land as a sacred district, 25,000 cubits long and 20,000[b] cubits wide; the entire area will be holy. [2]Of this, a section 500 cubits square is to be for the sanctuary, with 50 cubits around it for open land. [3]In the sacred district, measure off a section 25,000 cubits[c] long and 10,000 cubits[d] wide. In it will be the sanctuary, the Most Holy Place. [4]It will be the sacred portion of the land for the priests, who minister in the sanctuary and who draw near to minister before the LORD. It

will be a place for their houses as well as a holy place for the sanctuary. [5]An area 25,000 cubits long and 10,000 cubits wide will belong to the Levites, who serve in the temple, as their possession for towns to live in.[e]

[6] 'You are to give the city as its property an area 5,000 cubits wide and 25,000 cubits long, adjoining the sacred portion; it will belong to the whole house of Israel.

[7] 'The prince will have the land bordering each side of the area formed by the sacred district and the property of the city. It will extend westward from the west side and eastward from the east side, running lengthwise from the western to the eastern border parallel to one of the tribal portions. [8]This land will be his possession in Israel. And my princes will no longer oppress my people but will allow the house of Israel to possess the land according to their tribes.

[9] 'This is what the Sovereign LORD says: You have gone far enough, O princes of Israel! Give up your violence and oppression and do what is just and right. Stop dispossessing my people, declares the Sovereign LORD. [10]You are to use accurate scales, an accurate ephah[f] and an accurate bath.[g] [11]The ephah and the bath are to be the same size, the bath containing a tenth of a homer[h] and the ephah a tenth of a homer; the homer is to be the standard measure for both. [12]The shekel[i] is to consist of twenty gerahs. Twenty shekels plus twenty-five shekels plus fifteen shekels equal one mina.[j]

Offerings and Holy Days

[13] 'This is the special gift you are to offer: a sixth of an ephah from each homer of wheat and a sixth of an ephah from each homer of barley. [14]The prescribed portion of oil, measured by the bath, is a tenth of a bath from each cor (which consists of ten baths or one homer, for ten baths are equivalent to a homer). [15]Also one sheep is to be taken from every flock of two hundred from the well-watered

---

a29 The Hebrew term refers to the irrevocable giving over of things or persons to the LORD.   b1 Septuagint (see also verses 3 and 5 and 48:9); Hebrew 10,000   c3 That is, about 7 miles (about 12 kilometers)   d3 That is, about 3 miles (about 5 kilometers)   e5 Septuagint; Hebrew temple; they will have as their possession 20 rooms   f10 An ephah was a dry measure.   g10 A bath was a liquid measure.   h11 A homer was a dry measure.   i12 A shekel weighed about 2/5 ounce (about 11.5 grams).   j12 That is, 60 shekels; the common mina was 50 shekels.

pastures of Israel. These will be used for the grain offerings, burnt offerings and fellowship offerings[a] to make atonement for the people, declares the Sovereign LORD. [16]All the people of the land will participate in this special gift for the use of the prince in Israel. [17]It will be the duty of the prince to provide the burnt offerings, grain offerings and drink offerings at the festivals, the New Moons and the Sabbaths—at all the appointed feasts of the house of Israel. He will provide the sin offerings, grain offerings, burnt offerings and fellowship offerings to make atonement for the house of Israel.

[18]" 'This is what the Sovereign LORD says: In the first month on the first day you are to take a young bull without defect and purify the sanctuary. [19]The priest is to take some of the blood of the sin offering and put it on the doorposts of the temple, on the four corners of the upper ledge of the altar and on the gateposts of the inner court. [20]You are to do the same on the seventh day of the month for anyone who sins unintentionally or through ignorance; so you are to make atonement for the temple.

[21]" 'In the first month on the fourteenth day you are to observe the Passover, a feast lasting seven days, during which you shall eat bread made without yeast. [22]On that day the prince is to provide a bull as a sin offering for himself and for all the people of the land. [23]Every day during the seven days of the Feast he is to provide seven bulls and seven rams without defect as a burnt offering to the LORD, and a male goat for a sin offering. [24]He is to provide as a grain offering an ephah for each bull and an ephah for each ram, along with a hin[b] of oil for each ephah.

[25]" 'During the seven days of the Feast, which begins in the seventh month on the fifteenth day, he is to make the same provision for sin offerings, burnt offerings, grain offerings and oil.'

46 " 'This is what the Sovereign LORD says: The gate of the inner court facing east is to be shut on the six working days, but on the Sabbath day and on the day of the New Moon it is to be opened. [2]The prince is to enter from the outside through the portico of the gateway and stand by the gatepost. The priests are to sacrifice his burnt offering and his fellowship offerings.[c] He is to worship at the threshold of the gateway and then go out, but the gate will not be shut until evening. [3]On the Sabbaths and New Moons the

people of the land are to worship in the presence of the LORD at the entrance to that gateway. [4]The burnt offering the prince brings to the LORD on the Sabbath day is to be six male lambs and a ram, all without defect. [5]The grain offering given with the ram is to be an ephah,[d] and the grain offering with the lambs is to be as much as he pleases, along with a hin[e] of oil for each ephah. [6]On the day of the New Moon he is to offer a young bull, six lambs and a ram, all without defect. [7]He is to provide as a grain offering one ephah with the bull, one ephah with the ram, and with the lambs as much as he wants to give, along with a hin of oil with each ephah. [8]When the prince enters, he is to go in through the portico of the gateway, and he is to come out the same way.

[9]" 'When the people of the land come before the LORD at the appointed feasts, whoever enters by the north gate to worship is to go out the south gate; and whoever enters by the south gate is to go out the north gate. No one is to return through the gate by which he entered, but each is to go out the opposite gate. [10]The prince is to be among them, going in when they go in and going out when they go out.

[11]" 'At the festivals and the appointed feasts, the grain offering is to be an ephah with a bull, an ephah with a ram, and with the lambs as much as one pleases, along with a hin of oil for each ephah. [12]When the prince provides a freewill offering to the LORD—whether a burnt offering or fellowship offerings—the gate facing east is to be opened for him. He shall offer his burnt offering or his fellowship offerings as he does on the Sabbath day. Then he shall go out, and after he has gone out, the gate will be shut.

[13]" 'Every day you are to provide a year-old lamb without defect for a burnt offering to the LORD; morning by morning you shall provide it. [14]You are also to provide with it morning by morning a grain offering, consisting of a sixth of an ephah with a third of a hin of oil to moisten the flour. The presenting of this grain offering to the LORD is a lasting ordinance. [15]So the lamb and the grain offering and the oil shall be provided morning by morning for a regular burnt offering.

---

[a]15 Traditionally *peace offerings*; also in verse 17   [b]24 That is, probably about 4 quarts (about 4 liters)   [c]2 Traditionally *peace offerings*; also in verse 12   [d]5 That is, probably about 3/5 bushel (about 22 liters)   [e]5 That is, probably about 4 quarts (about 4 liters)

[16]" 'This is what the Sovereign LORD says: If the prince makes a gift from his inheritance to one of his sons, it will also belong to his descendants; it is to be their property by inheritance. [17]If, however, he makes a gift from his inheritance to one of his servants, the servant may keep it until the year of freedom; then it will revert to the prince. His inheritance belongs to his sons only; it is theirs. [18]The prince must not take any of the inheritance of the people, driving them off their property. He is to give his sons their inheritance out of his own property, so that none of my people will be separated from his property.' "

[19]Then the man brought me through the entrance at the side of the gate to the sacred rooms facing north, which belonged to the priests, and showed me a place at the western end. [20]He said to me, "This is the place where the priests will cook the guilt offering and the sin offering and bake the grain offering, to avoid bringing them into the outer court and consecrating the people."

[21]He then brought me to the outer court and led me around to its four corners, and I saw in each corner another court. [22]In the four corners of the outer court were enclosed[a] courts, forty cubits long and thirty cubits wide; each of the courts in the four corners was the same size. [23]Around the inside of each of the four courts was a ledge of stone, with places for fire built all around under the ledge. [24]He said to me, "These are the kitchens where those who minister at the temple will cook the sacrifices of the people."

The River From the Temple

47 The man brought me back to the entrance of the temple, and I saw water coming out from under the threshold of the temple toward the east (for the temple faced east). The water was coming down from under the south side of the temple, south of the altar. [2]He then brought me out through the north gate and led me around the outside to the outer gate facing east, and the water was flowing from the south side.

[3]As the man went eastward with a measuring line in his hand, he measured off a thousand cubits[b] and then led me through water that was ankle-deep. [4]He measured off another thousand cubits and led me through water that was knee-deep. He measured off another thousand

and led me through water that was up to the waist. [5]He measured off another thousand, but now it was a river that I could not cross, because the water had risen and was deep enough to swim in—a river that no one could cross. [6]He asked me, "Son of man, do you see this?"

Then he led me back to the bank of the river. [7]When I arrived there, I saw a great number of trees on each side of the river. [8]He said to me, "This water flows toward the eastern region and goes down into the Arabah,[c] where it enters the Sea.[d] When it empties into the Sea,[d] the water there becomes fresh. [9]Swarms of living creatures will live wherever the river flows. There will be large numbers of fish, because this water flows there and makes the salt water fresh; so where the river flows everything will live. [10]Fishermen will stand along the shore; from En Gedi to En Eglaim there will be places for spreading nets. The fish will be of many kinds—like the fish of the Great Sea.[e] [11]But the swamps and marshes will not become fresh; they will be left for salt. [12]Fruit trees of all kinds will grow on both banks of the river. Their leaves will not wither, nor will their fruit fail. Every month they will bear, because the water from the sanctuary flows to them. Their fruit will serve for food and their leaves for healing."

The Boundaries of the Land

[13]This is what the Sovereign LORD says: "These are the boundaries by which you are to divide the land for an inheritance among the twelve tribes of Israel, with two portions for Joseph. [14]You are to divide it equally among them. Because I swore with uplifted hand to give it to your forefathers, this land will become your inheritance.

[15]"This is to be the boundary of the land:

"On the north side it will run from the Great Sea by the Hethlon road past Lebo[f] Hamath to Zedad, [16]Berothah[g] and Sibraim (which lies on the border between Damascus and Hamath), as far as Hazer Hatticon, which is on the border of Hauran.

[a]22 The meaning of the Hebrew for this word is uncertain.   [b]3 That is, about 1,500 feet (about 450 meters)   [c]8 Or the Jordan Valley   [d]8 That is, the Dead Sea   [e]10 That is, the Mediterranean; also in verses 15, 19 and 20   [f]15 Or past the entrance to   [g]15,16 See Septuagint and Ezekiel 48:1; Hebrew road to go into Zedad, [16]Hamath, Berothah

¹⁷The boundary will extend from the sea to Hazar Enan,ᵃ along the northern border of Damascus, with the border of Hamath to the north. This will be the north boundary. ¹⁸On the east side the boundary will run between Hauran and Damascus, along the Jordan between Gilead and the land of Israel, to the eastern sea and as far as Tamar.ᵇ This will be the east boundary. ¹⁹"On the south side it will run from Tamar as far as the waters of Meribah Kadesh, then along the Wadi of Egypt to the Great Sea. This will be the south boundary. ²⁰"On the west side, the Great Sea will be the boundary to a point opposite Leboᶜ Hamath. This will be the west boundary.

²¹"You are to distribute this land among yourselves according to the tribes of Israel. ²²You are to allot it as an inheritance for yourselves and for the aliens who have settled among you and who have children. You are to consider them as native-born Israelites; along with you they are to be allotted an inheritance among the tribes of Israel. ²³In whatever tribe the alien settles, there you are to give him his inheritance," declares the Sovereign LORD.

The Division of the Land

48 "These are the tribes, listed by name: At the northern frontier, Dan will have one portion; it will follow the Hethlon road to Leboᵈ Hamath; Hazar Enan and the northern border of Damascus next to Hamath will be part of its border from the east side to the west side.

²"Asher will have one portion; it will border the territory of Dan from east to west.

³"Naphtali will have one portion; it will border the territory of Asher from east to west.

⁴"Manasseh will have one portion; it will border the territory of Naphtali from east to west.

⁵"Ephraim will have one portion; it will border the territory of Manasseh from east to west.

⁶"Reuben will have one portion; it will border the territory of Ephraim from east to west.

⁷"Judah will have one portion; it will border the territory of Reuben from east to west.

⁸"Bordering the territory of Judah from east to west will be the portion you are to present as a special gift. It will be 25,000 cubitsᵉ wide, and its length from east to west will equal one of the tribal portions; the sanctuary will be in the center of it.

⁹"The special portion you are to offer to the LORD will be 25,000 cubits long and 10,000 cubitsᶠ wide. ¹⁰This will be the sacred portion for the priests. It will be 25,000 cubits long on the north side, 10,000 cubits wide on the west side, 10,000 cubits wide on the east side and 25,000 cubits long on the south side. In the center of it will be the sanctuary of the LORD. ¹¹This will be for the consecrated priests, the Zadokites, who were faithful in serving me and did not go astray as the Levites did when the Israelites went astray. ¹²It will be a special gift to them from the sacred portion of the land, a most holy portion, bordering the territory of the Levites.

¹³"Alongside the territory of the priests, the Levites will have an allotment 25,000 cubits long and 10,000 cubits wide. Its total length will be 25,000 cubits and its width 10,000 cubits. ¹⁴They must not sell or exchange any of it. This is the best of the land and must not pass into other hands, because it is holy to the LORD.

¹⁵"The remaining area, 5,000 cubits wide and 25,000 cubits long, will be for the common use of the city, for houses and for pastureland. The city will be in the center of it ¹⁶and will have these measurements: the north side 4,500 cubits, the south side 4,500 cubits, the east side 4,500 cubits, and the west side 4,500 cubits. ¹⁷The pastureland for the city will be 250 cubits on the north, 250 cubits on the south, 250 cubits on the east, and 250 cubits on the west. ¹⁸What remains of the area, bordering on the sacred portion and running the length of it, will be 10,000 cubits on the east side and 10,000 cubits on the west side. Its produce will supply food for the workers of the city. ¹⁹The workers from the city who farm it will come from all the tribes of Israel. ²⁰The entire portion will be a square, 25,000 cubits on each side. As a special gift you will set aside the sacred portion, along with the property of the city.

ᵃ17 Hebrew *Enon,* a variant of *Enan*
ᵇ18 Septuagint and Syriac; Hebrew *Israel. You will measure to the eastern sea*   ᶜ20 Or *opposite the entrance to*   ᵈ1 Or *to the entrance to*   ᵉ8 That is, about 7 miles (about 12 kilometers)   ᶠ9 That is, about 3 miles (about 5 kilometers)

²¹"What remains on both sides of the area formed by the sacred portion and the city property will belong to the prince. It will extend eastward from the 25,000 cubits of the sacred portion to the eastern border, and westward from the 25,000 cubits to the western border. Both these areas running the length of the tribal portions will belong to the prince, and the sacred portion with the temple sanctuary will be in the center of them. ²²So the property of the Levites and the property of the city will lie in the center of the area that belongs to the prince. The area belonging to the prince will lie between the border of Judah and the border of Benjamin.

²³"As for the rest of the tribes: Benjamin will have one portion; it will extend from the east side to the west side.

²⁴"Simeon will have one portion; it will border the territory of Benjamin from east to west.

²⁵"Issachar will have one portion; it will border the territory of Simeon from east to west.

²⁶"Zebulun will have one portion; it will border the territory of Issachar from east to west.

²⁷"Gad will have one portion; it will border the territory of Zebulun from east to west.

²⁸"The southern boundary of Gad will run south from Tamar to the waters of Meribah Kadesh, then along the Wadi of Egypt to the Great Sea.ᵃ

²⁹"This is the land you are to allot as an inheritance to the tribes of Israel, and these will be their portions," declares the Sovereign LORD.

The Gates of the City

³⁰"These will be the exits of the city: Beginning on the north side, which is 4,500 cubits long, ³¹the gates of the city will be named after the tribes of Israel. The three gates on the north side will be the gate of Reuben, the gate of Judah and the gate of Levi.

³²"On the east side, which is 4,500 cubits long, will be three gates: the gate of Joseph, the gate of Benjamin and the gate of Dan.

³³"On the south side, which measures 4,500 cubits, will be three gates: the gate of Simeon, the gate of Issachar and the gate of Zebulun.

³⁴"On the west side, which is 4,500 cubits long, will be three gates: the gate of Gad, the gate of Asher and the gate of Naphtali.

³⁵"The distance all around will be 18,000 cubits.

"And the name of the city from that time on will be:

THE LORD IS THERE."

ᵃ28 That is, the Mediterranean

"Come on, be brave." You've heard these words from a parent when a kid is about to get his tetanus booster. There he stands, trembling, in full view of the nurse who's preparing to plunge a needle the size of Utah into his arm. "Be brave." Maybe you've even heard yourself say this to your own child with a scraped knee or a broken heart.

The book of Daniel tells the story of men who took the encouragement to "be brave" to a whole new level. These men weren't staring at an ominous hypodermic syringe or trying to tough out a scuff on the knee; they were standing literally face-to-face with their own deaths. "Give up this silly faith of yours," they were told, "or you'll burn. Stop praying to your God or face the lions." But they stood firm.

Holding out for what one believes in the face of perilous consequences is no easy assignment. In fact, bailing out just to avoid a little embarrassment happens all too often. Who can blame us for not wanting to unnecessarily attract attention? "Live and let live," we think to ourselves.

But then there's Daniel.

Daniel

Daniel's Training in Babylon

1 In the third year of the reign of Jehoiakim king of Judah, Nebuchadnezzar king of Babylon came to Jerusalem and besieged it. ²And the Lord delivered Jehoiakim king of Judah into his hand, along with some of the articles from the temple of God. These he carried off to the temple of his god in Babylonia*ᵃ* and put in the treasure house of his god.

³Then the king ordered Ashpenaz, chief of his court officials, to bring in some of the Israelites from the royal family and the nobility— ⁴young men without any physical defect, handsome, showing aptitude for every kind of learning, well informed, quick to understand, and qualified to serve in the king's palace. He was to teach them the language and literature of the Babylonians.*ᵇ* ⁵The king assigned them a daily amount of food and wine from the king's table. They were to be trained for three years, and after that they were to enter the king's service.

⁶Among these were some from Judah: Daniel, Hananiah, Mishael and Azariah. ⁷The chief official gave them new names:

ᵃ2 Hebrew *Shinar*   *ᵇ4* Or *Chaldeans*

to Daniel, the name Belteshazzar; to Hananiah, Shadrach; to Mishael, Meshach; and to Azariah, Abednego.

⁸But Daniel resolved not to defile himself with the royal food and wine, and he asked the chief official for permission not to defile himself this way. ⁹Now God had caused the official to show favor and sympathy to Daniel, ¹⁰but the official told Daniel, "I am afraid of my lord the king, who has assigned your *a* food and drink. Why should he see you looking worse than the other young men your age? The king would then have my head because of you."

¹¹Daniel then said to the guard whom the chief official had appointed over Daniel, Hananiah, Mishael and Azariah, ¹²"Please test your servants for ten days: Give us nothing but vegetables to eat and water to drink. ¹³Then compare our appearance with that of the young men who eat the royal food, and treat your servants in accordance with what you see." ¹⁴So he agreed to this and tested them for ten days.

¹⁵At the end of the ten days they looked

a10 The Hebrew for *your* and *you* in this verse is plural.

Please Pass the Broccoli

How much do you care about your car? For most men, the answer to this question will range from, "I take care of my car ... scheduled maintenance on the engine and regular washings when it's dirty," to "I love my car. I rub it with a diaper whenever I get the chance. It gets parked at the far end of a shopping mall so no one can come close to it. A door ding would be the end of me. And my best friend is the service guy at the dealership."

Most men feel that their car or truck is more than just transportation. Even if it isn't the latest model, they take a certain level of pride in what they drive. And they know that there will always be a direct relationship between what happens to the car's internal workings and the car's long-term reliability. You may not be the kind of guy who spends two hours polishing every nook and cranny on your chrome wheel covers, but you'd never think of putting anything in the tank but good stuff.

You know where I'm going with this, don't you?

After they were captured, Daniel and his friends were selected for service in the king's court. But when these four men got to the training table and saw what the King's chefs were going to be feeding them, they signaled for the maitre d' and asked for a different menu. You've read the story about

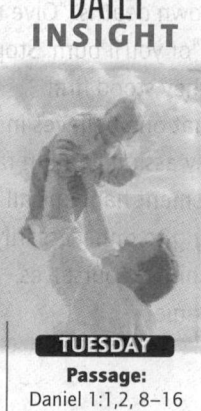

DAILY INSIGHT

TUESDAY

Passage:
Daniel 1:1,2, 8–16

Verse:
Daniel 1:15

the test that Daniel proposed after the steward refused to grant Daniel and his friends their wish. Ten days after the test began, after eating vegetables instead of Twinkies™ and chips like the rest of the troops, Daniel and his three friends were taken before King Nebuchadnezzar himself for their check-ups. "The king talked with them, and he found none equal to Daniel, Hananiah, Mishael, and Azariah" (1:19). They had passed the test.

Let's go back to your car for a minute. What would you say if someone offered to pour a soft drink into your gas tank? What if they suggested putting bacon grease into your transmission? We both know what you'd do. Why? Because your car's performance has everything to do with what you put into it.

At the risk of sounding like your mother, what makes you think that your body is any different than your car?

Of course, the message of the story about Daniel and his three friends has as much to do with the men's loyalty toward their God as it does their selection of food. But since the subject has come up, this may be a good time to reassess your own diet. What are your putting into your body that you ought to cut back on? And what's missing from *your* training table?

For your next devotional reading, go to page 943.

healthier and better nourished than any of the young men who ate the royal food. [16]So the guard took away their choice food and the wine they were to drink and gave them vegetables instead.

[17]To these four young men God gave knowledge and understanding of all kinds of literature and learning. And Daniel could understand visions and dreams of all kinds.

[18]At the end of the time set by the king to bring them in, the chief official presented them to Nebuchadnezzar. [19]The king talked with them, and he found none equal to Daniel, Hananiah, Mishael and Azariah; so they entered the king's service. [20]In every matter of wisdom and understanding about which the king questioned them, he found them ten times better than all the magicians and enchanters in his whole kingdom. [21]And Daniel remained there until the first year of King Cyrus.

Nebuchadnezzar's Dream

2 In the second year of his reign, Nebuchadnezzar had dreams; his mind was troubled and he could not sleep. [2]So the king summoned the magicians, enchanters, sorcerers and astrologers[a] to tell him what he had dreamed. When they came in and stood before the king, [3]he said to them, "I have had a dream that troubles me and I want to know what it means.[b]"

[4]Then the astrologers answered the king in Aramaic,[c] "O king, live forever! Tell your servants the dream, and we will interpret it."

[5]The king replied to the astrologers, "This is what I have firmly decided: If you do not tell me what my dream was and interpret it, I will have you cut into pieces and your houses turned into piles of rubble. [6]But if you tell me the dream and explain it, you will receive from me gifts and rewards and great honor. So tell me the dream and interpret it for me."

[7]Once more they replied, "Let the king tell his servants the dream, and we will interpret it."

[8]Then the king answered, "I am certain that you are trying to gain time, because you realize that this is what I have firmly decided: [9]If you do not tell me the dream, there is just one penalty for you. You have conspired to tell me misleading and wicked things, hoping the situation will change. So then, tell me the dream, and I will know that you can interpret it for me."

[10]The astrologers answered the king, "There is not a man on earth who can do what the king asks! No king, however great and mighty, has ever asked such a thing of any magician or enchanter or astrologer. [11]What the king asks is too difficult. No one can reveal it to the king except the gods, and they do not live among men."

[12]This made the king so angry and furious that he ordered the execution of all the wise men of Babylon. [13]So the decree was issued to put the wise men to death, and men were sent to look for Daniel and his friends to put them to death.

[14]When Arioch, the commander of the king's guard, had gone out to put to death the wise men of Babylon, Daniel spoke to him with wisdom and tact. [15]He asked the king's officer, "Why did the king issue such a harsh decree?" Arioch then explained the matter to Daniel. [16]At this, Daniel went in to the king and asked for time, so that he might interpret the dream for him.

[17]Then Daniel returned to his house and explained the matter to his friends Hananiah, Mishael and Azariah. [18]He urged them to plead for mercy from the God of heaven concerning this mystery, so that he and his friends might not be executed with the rest of the wise men of Babylon. [19]During the night the mystery was revealed to Daniel in a vision. Then Daniel praised the God of heaven [20]and said:

"Praise be to the name of God for ever and ever;
    wisdom and power are his.
[21]He changes times and seasons;
    he sets up kings and deposes them.
He gives wisdom to the wise
    and knowledge to the discerning.
[22]He reveals deep and hidden things;
    he knows what lies in darkness,
    and light dwells with him.
[23]I thank and praise you, O God of my fathers:
    You have given me wisdom and power,
you have made known to me what we asked of you,
    you have made known to us the dream of the king."

*a*2 Or *Chaldeans*; also in verses 4, 5 and 10
*b*3 Or *was* *c*4 The text from here through chapter 7 is in Aramaic.

Daniel Interprets the Dream

24Then Daniel went to Arioch, whom the king had appointed to execute the wise men of Babylon, and said to him, "Do not execute the wise men of Babylon. Take me to the king, and I will interpret his dream for him."

25Arioch took Daniel to the king at once and said, "I have found a man among the exiles from Judah who can tell the king what his dream means."

26The king asked Daniel (also called Belteshazzar), "Are you able to tell me what I saw in my dream and interpret it?"

27Daniel replied, "No wise man, enchanter, magician or diviner can explain to the king the mystery he has asked about, **28**but there is a God in heaven who reveals mysteries. He has shown King Nebuchadnezzar what will happen in days to come. Your dream and the visions that passed through your mind as you lay on your bed are these:

29"As you were lying there, O king, your mind turned to things to come, and the revealer of mysteries showed you what is going to happen. **30**As for me, this mystery has been revealed to me, not because I have greater wisdom than other living men, but so that you, O king, may know the interpretation and that you may understand what went through your mind.

31"You looked, O king, and there before you stood a large statue—an enormous, dazzling statue, awesome in appearance. **32**The head of the statue was made of pure gold, its chest and arms of silver, its belly and thighs of bronze, **33**its legs of iron, its feet partly of iron and partly of baked clay. **34**While you were watching, a rock was cut out, but not by human hands. It struck the statue on its feet of iron and clay and smashed them. **35**Then the iron, the clay, the bronze, the silver and the gold were broken to pieces at the same time and became like chaff on a threshing floor in the summer. The wind swept them away without leaving a trace. But the rock that struck the statue became a huge mountain and filled the whole earth.

36"This was the dream, and now we will interpret it to the king. **37**You, O king, are the king of kings. The God of heaven has given you dominion and power and might and glory; **38**in your hands he has placed mankind and the beasts of the field and the birds of the air. Wherever they live, he has made you ruler over them all. You are that head of gold.

39"After you, another kingdom will rise, inferior to yours. Next, a third kingdom, one of bronze, will rule over the whole earth. **40**Finally, there will be a fourth kingdom, strong as iron—for iron breaks and smashes everything—and as iron breaks things to pieces, so it will crush and break all the others. **41**Just as you saw that the feet and toes were partly of baked clay and partly of iron, so this will be a divided kingdom; yet it will have some of the strength of iron in it, even as you saw iron mixed with clay. **42**As the toes were partly iron and partly clay, so this kingdom will be partly strong and partly brittle. **43**And just as you saw the iron mixed with baked clay, so the people will be a mixture and will not remain united, any more than iron mixes with clay.

44"In the time of those kings, the God of heaven will set up a kingdom that will never be destroyed, nor will it be left to another people. It will crush all those kingdoms and bring them to an end, but it will itself endure forever. **45**This is the meaning of the vision of the rock cut out of a mountain, but not by human hands—a rock that broke the iron, the bronze, the clay, the silver and the gold to pieces.

"The great God has shown the king what will take place in the future. The dream is true and the interpretation is trustworthy."

46Then King Nebuchadnezzar fell prostrate before Daniel and paid him honor and ordered that an offering and incense be presented to him. **47**The king said to Daniel, "Surely your God is the God of gods and the Lord of kings and a revealer of mysteries, for you were able to reveal this mystery."

48Then the king placed Daniel in a high position and lavished many gifts on him. He made him ruler over the entire province of Babylon and placed him in charge of all its wise men. **49**Moreover, at Daniel's request the king appointed Shadrach, Meshach and Abednego administrators over the province of Babylon, while Daniel himself remained at the royal court.

The Image of Gold and the Fiery Furnace

3 King Nebuchadnezzar made an image of gold, ninety feet high and nine feet*a* wide, and set it up on the plain of Dura in the province of Babylon. **2**He then sum-

*a*1 Aramaic *sixty cubits high and six cubits wide* (about 27 meters high and 2.7 meters wide) moned the satraps, prefects, governors, advisers, treasurers, judges, magistrates and all the other provincial officials to come to the dedication of the image he had set up. ³So the satraps, prefects, governors, advisers, treasurers, judges, magistrates and all the other provincial officials assembled for the dedication of the image that King Nebuchadnezzar had set up, and they stood before it.

⁴Then the herald loudly proclaimed, "This is what you are commanded to do, O peoples, nations and men of every language: ⁵As soon as you hear the sound of the horn, flute, zither, lyre, harp, pipes and all kinds of music, you must fall down and worship the image of gold that King Nebuchadnezzar has set up. ⁶Whoever does not fall down and worship will immediately be thrown into a blazing furnace."

⁷Therefore, as soon as they heard the

It's a Little Hot in Here

I hope this isn't going to insult you, but political conventions seem like a total waste of time to me. Spending millions of dollars on my own birthday party would be horrendous, but it would look like a sound investment compared to these four-day party-line hullabaloos.

Despite these feelings, I found myself actually watching the proceedings at the 1992 Republican Convention The line-up for the presidential nomination included a man who had gone public with his personal faith in Christ. Several political commentators had been lured into one of the network broadcast booths, and their "insights" on religion were remarkably sobering.

"All of these candidates are religious men," one man observed. "But this particular candidate has, in my opinion, gone too far. He has allowed his faith to get in the way of what he says and what he thinks." The others in the booth chuckled. Imagine anything so outrageous as a man actually being *affected* by what he believes!

The story of the three Jewish men's singular obedience to their heavenly Father is pretty remarkable. In an attempt to bring some semblance of unity to his kingdom, Nebuchadnezzar created a one-size-fits-all god—a huge idol made of solid gold. And he fully expected everyone, even the Israelites whom his army had captured, to bow down. Unfortunately, King Nebuchadnezzar and his associates misjudged the commitment of Shadrach, Meshach, and Abednego.

DAILY INSIGHT

WEDNESDAY

Passage: Daniel 3:1–12

Verse: Daniel 3:12

Exactly like the presidential candidate who "let his religion get in the way," these men made the tactical "error" of standing up to the incredible pressure of the godless culture that surrounded them. An enraged King Nebuchadnezzar sentenced them to die.

Just for the fun of it, look through the third chapter of Daniel. Try to find the names of *any* of the captive Jews who bowed down. I can save you a few minutes if you'd rather not take the time. You'll not find the name of one Israelite who collapsed under the pressure of his culture, even though there were probably thousands to choose from.

You probably remember the end of the story of Shadrach, Meshach, and Abednego. The angry Babylonians tossed them into a furnace. But God provided an angel to join these men in the midst of the fire, and their lives were spared.

To be known as "forgettable" is probably not your goal in life. "He who made no waves" would be a shameful thing to have chiseled on your tombstone. Do you want to make a name for yourself, to be known as one of God's own? Then dare to stand up for what you believe. Don't be afraid to let God's love and grace affect your thinking, your lifestyle and your decisions. Sure, it might get a little hot in there, but God has plenty of angels to dispatch. He even has a few who are particularly skilled at protecting obedient men from the flames.

For your next devotional reading, go to page 946.

sound of the horn, flute, zither, lyre, harp and all kinds of music, all the peoples, nations and men of every language fell down and worshiped the image of gold that King Nebuchadnezzar had set up.

⁸At this time some astrologers*a* came forward and denounced the Jews. ⁹They said to King Nebuchadnezzar, "O king, live forever! ¹⁰You have issued a decree, O king, that everyone who hears the sound of the horn, flute, zither, lyre, harp, pipes and all kinds of music must fall down and worship the image of gold, ¹¹and that whoever does not fall down and worship will be thrown into a blazing furnace. ¹²But there are some Jews whom you have set over the affairs of the province of Babylon—Shadrach, Meshach and Abednego—who pay no attention to you, O king. They neither serve your gods nor worship the image of gold you have set up."

¹³Furious with rage, Nebuchadnezzar summoned Shadrach, Meshach and Abednego. So these men were brought before the king, ¹⁴and Nebuchadnezzar said to them, "Is it true, Shadrach, Meshach and Abednego, that you do not serve my gods or worship the image of gold I have set up? ¹⁵Now when you hear the sound of the horn, flute, zither, lyre, harp, pipes and all kinds of music, if you are ready to fall down and worship the image I made, very good. But if you do not worship it, you will be thrown immediately into a blazing furnace. Then what god will be able to rescue you from my hand?"

¹⁶Shadrach, Meshach and Abednego replied to the king, "O Nebuchadnezzar, we do not need to defend ourselves before you in this matter. ¹⁷If we are thrown into the blazing furnace, the God we serve is able to save us from it, and he will rescue us from your hand, O king. ¹⁸But even if he does not, we want you to know, O king, that we will not serve your gods or worship the image of gold you have set up."

¹⁹Then Nebuchadnezzar was furious with Shadrach, Meshach and Abednego, and his attitude toward them changed. He ordered the furnace heated seven times hotter than usual ²⁰and commanded some of the strongest soldiers in his army to tie up Shadrach, Meshach and Abednego and throw them into the blazing furnace. ²¹So these men, wearing their robes, trousers, turbans and other clothes, were bound and thrown into the blazing furnace. ²²The king's command was so ur-

gent and the furnace so hot that the flames of the fire killed the soldiers who took up Shadrach, Meshach and Abednego, ²³and these three men, firmly tied, fell into the blazing furnace.

²⁴Then King Nebuchadnezzar leaped to his feet in amazement and asked his advisers, "Weren't there three men that we tied up and threw into the fire?"

They replied, "Certainly, O king."

²⁵He said, "Look! I see four men walking around in the fire, unbound and unharmed, and the fourth looks like a son of the gods."

²⁶Nebuchadnezzar then approached the opening of the blazing furnace and shouted, "Shadrach, Meshach and Abednego, servants of the Most High God, come out! Come here!"

So Shadrach, Meshach and Abednego came out of the fire, ²⁷and the satraps, prefects, governors and royal advisers crowded around them. They saw that the fire had not harmed their bodies, nor was a hair of their heads singed; their robes were not scorched, and there was no smell of fire on them.

²⁸Then Nebuchadnezzar said, "Praise be to the God of Shadrach, Meshach and Abednego, who has sent his angel and rescued his servants! They trusted in him and defied the king's command and were willing to give up their lives rather than serve or worship any god except their own God. ²⁹Therefore I decree that the people of any nation or language who say anything against the God of Shadrach, Meshach and Abednego be cut into pieces and their houses be turned into piles of rubble, for no other god can save in this way."

³⁰Then the king promoted Shadrach, Meshach and Abednego in the province of Babylon.

Nebuchadnezzar's Dream of a Tree

4 King Nebuchadnezzar,

To the peoples, nations and men of every language, who live in all the world:

May you prosper greatly!

²It is my pleasure to tell you about the miraculous signs and wonders that the Most High God has performed for me.

---

a8 Or Chaldeans

³ How great are his signs,
    how mighty his wonders!
His kingdom is an eternal
    kingdom;
    his dominion endures from
        generation to generation.

⁴I, Nebuchadnezzar, was at home in my palace, contented and prosperous. ⁵I had a dream that made me afraid. As I was lying in my bed, the images and visions that passed through my mind terrified me. ⁶So I commanded that all the wise men of Babylon be brought before me to interpret the dream for me. ⁷When the magicians, enchanters, astrologers*a* and diviners came, I told them the dream, but they could not interpret it for me. ⁸Finally, Daniel came into my presence and I told him the dream. (He is called Belteshazzar, after the name of my god, and the spirit of the holy gods is in him.)

⁹I said, "Belteshazzar, chief of the magicians, I know that the spirit of the holy gods is in you, and no mystery is too difficult for you. Here is my dream; interpret it for me. ¹⁰These are the visions I saw while lying in my bed: I looked, and there before me stood a tree in the middle of the land. Its height was enormous. ¹¹The tree grew large and strong and its top touched the sky; it was visible to the ends of the earth. ¹²Its leaves were beautiful, its fruit abundant, and on it was food for all. Under it the beasts of the field found shelter, and the birds of the air lived in its branches; from it every creature was fed.

¹³"In the visions I saw while lying in my bed, I looked, and there before me was a messenger,*b* a holy one, coming down from heaven. ¹⁴He called in a loud voice: 'Cut down the tree and trim off its branches; strip off its leaves and scatter its fruit. Let the animals flee from under it and the birds from its branches. ¹⁵But let the stump and its roots, bound with iron and bronze, remain in the ground, in the grass of the field.

" 'Let him be drenched with the dew of heaven, and let him live with the animals among the plants of the earth. ¹⁶Let his mind be changed from that of a man and let him be given the mind of an animal, till seven times*c* pass by for him.

¹⁷" 'The decision is announced by messengers, the holy ones declare the verdict, so that the living may know that the Most High is sovereign over the kingdoms of men and gives them to anyone he wishes and sets over them the lowliest of men.'

¹⁸"This is the dream that I, King Nebuchadnezzar, had. Now, Belteshazzar, tell me what it means, for none of the wise men in my kingdom can interpret it for me. But you can, because the spirit of the holy gods is in you."

Daniel Interprets the Dream

¹⁹Then Daniel (also called Belteshazzar) was greatly perplexed for a time, and his thoughts terrified him. So the king said, "Belteshazzar, do not let the dream or its meaning alarm you."

Belteshazzar answered, "My lord, if only the dream applied to your enemies and its meaning to your adversaries! ²⁰The tree you saw, which grew large and strong, with its top touching the sky, visible to the whole earth, ²¹with beautiful leaves and abundant fruit, providing food for all, giving shelter to the beasts of the field, and having nesting places in its branches for the birds of the air— ²²you, O king, are that tree! You have become great and strong; your greatness has grown until it reaches the sky, and your dominion extends to distant parts of the earth.

²³"You, O king, saw a messenger, a holy one, coming down from heaven and saying, 'Cut down the tree and destroy it, but leave the stump, bound with iron and bronze, in the grass of the field, while its roots remain in the ground. Let him be drenched with the dew of heaven; let him live like the wild animals, until seven times pass by for him.'

²⁴"This is the interpretation, O king, and this is the decree the Most High has issued against my lord the king: ²⁵You will be driven away from people and will live with the wild animals; you will eat grass like cattle and be drenched with the dew of heaven. Seven times will pass by

a7 Or Chaldeans   b13 Or watchman; also in verses 17 and 23   c16 Or years; also in verses 23, 25 and 32

for you until you acknowledge that the Most High is sovereign over the kingdoms of men and gives them to anyone he wishes. ²⁶The command to leave the stump of the tree with its roots means that your kingdom will be restored to you when you acknowledge that Heaven rules. ²⁷Therefore, O king, be pleased to accept my advice: Renounce your sins by doing what is right, and your wickedness by being kind to the oppressed. It may be that then your prosperity will continue."

The Dream Is Fulfilled

²⁸All this happened to King Nebuchadnezzar. ²⁹Twelve months later, as the king was walking on the roof of the royal palace of Babylon, ³⁰he said, "Is not this the great Babylon I have built as the royal residence, by my mighty power and for the glory of my majesty?"

³¹The words were still on his lips when a voice came from heaven, "This is what is decreed for you, King Nebuchadnezzar: Your royal author-

Babylon, Rome and the '69 Mets

DAILY INSIGHT

THURSDAY

Passage:
Daniel 4:28–34

Verse:
Daniel 4:31

The New York Yankees of the fifties. The UCLA Bruins under John Wooden. The Miami Dolphins of the sixties. The Edmonton Oilers of the eighties. The Chicago Bulls of the nineties. These are some of history's most outstanding sports dynasties.

During the "reigns" of these teams, it almost seemed as if they would never be unseated. The legacy of raw talent seemed to create an impenetrable shield against future defeat. But in every case, the mantle passed. The dynasty melted into standings in the cellar. Highlight reels were filed in the archives, and trophies began collecting dust. It's a shame, isn't it?

Several years ago, I had the privilege of meeting a top executive at the pinnacle of his success. His prowess in the boardroom was almost legendary, but infidelity in the dark was his secret stock and trade. But when his dual life was discovered, the man was transformed from a confident, respected and successful manager to a pathetic, sniveling creature, hiding out in a one-bedroom flat. It's a shame, isn't it?

King Nebuchadnezzar was a powerful man. The chronicles of his successful military campaigns were legion. His wealth ranked him among the most affluent in the known world. One day, as the king was taking a stroll on the roof of his new palace, he condensed this great accomplishment;

"I have built ... the royal residence, by my mighty power and for the glory of my majesty," he gloated like a fool. But the Sovereign God had other plans. In a matter of moments, this strident king was "driven away from people and ate grass like cattle. His body was drenched with the dew of heaven until his hair grew like the feathers of an eagle and his nails like the claws of a bird." It's a shame, isn't it?

There's a message in these stories for every man whom you and I know. Solomon summarized it this way, "Pride goes before destruction, a haughty spirit before a fall" (Proverbs 16:18).

Nebuchadnezzar came back to power after his humiliating stint on his knees. When he did, he "raised [his eyes] toward heaven ... praised the Most High ... and glorified him who lives forever" (4:34). That's good theology for a pagan king; sound perspective from a man who had thought that *he* was a dynasty.

History will continue to recall for us the tragic accounts of those who assumed that what they had would never be taken away ... Babylon, Rome and the '69 Mets. The big trophies will pass from city to city, from veteran to rookie, from player to player. The mighty will fall. But our God's reign, his dynasty alone, will never fall.

For your next devotional reading, go to page 948.

ity has been taken from you. ³²You will be driven away from people and will live with the wild animals; you will eat grass like cattle. Seven times will pass by for you until you acknowledge that the Most High is sovereign over the kingdoms of men and gives them to anyone he wishes."

³³Immediately what had been said about Nebuchadnezzar was fulfilled. He was driven away from people and ate grass like cattle. His body was drenched with the dew of heaven until his hair grew like the feathers of an eagle and his nails like the claws of a bird.

³⁴At the end of that time, I, Nebuchadnezzar, raised my eyes toward heaven, and my sanity was restored. Then I praised the Most High; I honored and glorified him who lives forever.

His dominion is an eternal dominion;
    his kingdom endures from
        generation to generation.
³⁵All the peoples of the earth
    are regarded as nothing.
He does as he pleases
    with the powers of heaven
    and the peoples of the earth.
No one can hold back his hand
    or say to him: "What have you
        done?"

³⁶At the same time that my sanity was restored, my honor and splendor were returned to me for the glory of my kingdom. My advisers and nobles sought me out, and I was restored to my throne and became even greater than before. ³⁷Now I, Nebuchadnezzar, praise and exalt and glorify the King of heaven, because everything he does is right and all his ways are just. And those who walk in pride he is able to humble.

The Writing on the Wall

5 King Belshazzar gave a great banquet for a thousand of his nobles and drank wine with them. ²While Belshazzar was drinking his wine, he gave orders to bring in the gold and silver goblets that Nebuchadnezzar his father*ᵃ* had taken from the temple in Jerusalem, so that the king and his nobles, his wives and his concubines might drink from them. ³So they brought in the gold goblets that had been taken from the temple of God in Jerusalem, and

the king and his nobles, his wives and his concubines drank from them. ⁴As they drank the wine, they praised the gods of gold and silver, of bronze, iron, wood and stone.

⁵Suddenly the fingers of a human hand appeared and wrote on the plaster of the wall, near the lampstand in the royal palace. The king watched the hand as it wrote. ⁶His face turned pale and he was so frightened that his knees knocked together and his legs gave way.

⁷The king called out for the enchanters, astrologers*ᵇ* and diviners to be brought and said to these wise men of Babylon, "Whoever reads this writing and tells me what it means will be clothed in purple and have a gold chain placed around his neck, and he will be made the third highest ruler in the kingdom."

⁸Then all the king's wise men came in, but they could not read the writing or tell the king what it meant. ⁹So King Belshazzar became even more terrified and his face grew more pale. His nobles were baffled.

¹⁰The queen,*ᶜ* hearing the voices of the king and his nobles, came into the banquet hall. "O king, live forever!" she said. "Don't be alarmed! Don't look so pale! ¹¹There is a man in your kingdom who has the spirit of the holy gods in him. In the time of your father he was found to have insight and intelligence and wisdom like that of the gods. King Nebuchadnezzar your father—your father the king, I say—appointed him chief of the magicians, enchanters, astrologers and diviners. ¹²This man Daniel, whom the king called Belteshazzar, was found to have a keen mind and knowledge and understanding, and also the ability to interpret dreams, explain riddles and solve difficult problems. Call for Daniel, and he will tell you what the writing means."

¹³So Daniel was brought before the king, and the king said to him, "Are you Daniel, one of the exiles my father the king brought from Judah? ¹⁴I have heard that the spirit of the gods is in you and that you have insight, intelligence and outstanding wisdom. ¹⁵The wise men and enchanters were brought before me to read this writing and tell me what it means, but they could not explain it. ¹⁶Now I have heard that you are able to

ᵃ2 Or *ancestor;* or *predecessor;* also in verses 11, 13 and 18   *ᵇ7* Or *Chaldeans;* also in verse 11   *ᶜ10* Or *queen mother*

give interpretations and to solve difficult problems. If you can read this writing and tell me what it means, you will be clothed in purple and have a gold chain placed around your neck, and you will be made the third highest ruler in the kingdom."

¹⁷Then Daniel answered the king, "You may keep your gifts for yourself and give your rewards to someone else. Nevertheless, I will read the writing for the king and tell him what it means.

¹⁸"O king, the Most High God gave your father Nebuchadnezzar sovereignty and greatness and glory and splendor. ¹⁹Because of the high position he gave him, all the peoples and nations and men of every language dreaded and feared him. Those the king wanted to put to death, he put to death; those he wanted to spare, he spared; those he wanted to promote, he promoted; and those he wanted to humble, he humbled. ²⁰But when his heart became arrogant and hardened with pride, he was deposed from his royal throne

Handwriting on the Wall

The offer was a generous one, a prestigious opportunity at a respected corporation. I had to decide if this was God's provision or a test. Ten days later, after a lot of soul-searching, I turned the offer down.

My life hasn't turned out like I thought it would. After having spent several years in career ministry—working with high school students and their families—I took a job in the corporate world. At that moment, I figured that I would probably spend the rest of my life in business, receiving a for-he's-a-jolly-good-fellow party and gold watch at the other end.

But following the closing of my publishing company, I moved my office into our home. Starched white shirts and dark suits gave way to golf shirts and jeans. Business lunches with colleagues over linen tablecloths were replaced by peanut butter and jelly on whole wheat bread. I loved this, but, as I said, it's not exactly what I expected.

How did I make the decision not to accept the lucrative offer to return to corporate life? Well, I took the advice of a seasoned veteran of the faith. His counsel was straightforward. "If you want to know what God's will is for tomorrow, look where he's blessed in the past, then just keep doing that for the future." In other words, this decision ought to be as clear as hand-writing on the wall.

King Belshazzar didn't have to do much soul searching to know God's will. In fact,

FRIDAY

Passage:
Daniel 5:1–9, 13–17

Verse:
Daniel 5:17

he wasn't even looking for it. But, right in the middle of a raucous party, a "human hand appeared and wrote on the plaster of the wall" (5:5). Can't you see the king trying to shake the cobwebs out of his inebriated head as he watched? "His face turned pale and he was so frightened that his knees knocked together and his legs gave way" (5:6). Truthfully, all of this was Belshazzar's associates' fault. Friends don't let friends see visions from God while drunk. Still, through the haze of alcohol, Belshazzar knew that something miraculous had happened to him. God's visible interventions in human history tend to be more than a little overwhelming.

Looking back over your life, there should be absolutely no question in your mind that God has had a plan for a long time. You can chronicle those places where his blessing has been apparent and those places where he seemed to have blessed the other person. This should tell you something.

Use these historical events in your life like stepping stones to the future. Make tomorrow's decisions based on what you experienced yesterday. God's plan for your life will always contain some measure of pure faith, but his past activity in your life ought to send you off in the right direction. You may not see God's handwriting on the wall, but his plan should be as clear to you as if he were.

For your next devotional reading, go to page 951.

and stripped of his glory. ²¹He was driven away from people and given the mind of an animal; he lived with the wild donkeys and ate grass like cattle; and his body was drenched with the dew of heaven, until he acknowledged that the Most High God is sovereign over the kingdoms of men and sets over them anyone he wishes.

²²"But you his son,ᵃ O Belshazzar, have not humbled yourself, though you knew all this. ²³Instead, you have set yourself up against the Lord of heaven. You had the goblets from his temple brought to you, and you and your nobles, your wives and your concubines drank wine from them. You praised the gods of silver and gold, of bronze, iron, wood and stone, which cannot see or hear or understand. But you did not honor the God who holds in his hand your life and all your ways. ²⁴Therefore he sent the hand that wrote the inscription.

²⁵"This is the inscription that was written:

MENE, MENE, TEKEL, PARSINᵇ

²⁶"This is what these words mean:

*Mene*ᶜ: God has numbered the days of your reign and brought it to an end.

²⁷*Tekel*ᵈ: You have been weighed on the scales and found wanting.

²⁸*Peres*ᵉ: Your kingdom is divided and given to the Medes and Persians."

²⁹Then at Belshazzar's command, Daniel was clothed in purple, a gold chain was placed around his neck, and he was proclaimed the third highest ruler in the kingdom.

³⁰That very night Belshazzar, king of the Babylonians,ᶠ was slain, ³¹and Darius the Mede took over the kingdom, at the age of sixty-two.

Daniel in the Den of Lions

6 It pleased Darius to appoint 120 satraps to rule throughout the kingdom, ²with three administrators over them, one of whom was Daniel. The satraps were made accountable to them so that the king might not suffer loss. ³Now Daniel so distinguished himself among the administrators and the satraps by his exceptional qualities that the king planned to set him over the whole kingdom. ⁴At this, the administrators and the satraps tried to find grounds for charges against Daniel in his conduct of government affairs, but they were unable to do so. They could find no corruption in him, because he was trustworthy and neither corrupt nor negligent. ⁵Finally these men said, "We will never find any basis for charges against this man Daniel unless it has something to do with the law of his God."

⁶So the administrators and the satraps went as a group to the king and said: "O King Darius, live forever! ⁷The royal administrators, prefects, satraps, advisers and governors have all agreed that the king should issue an edict and enforce the decree that anyone who prays to any god or man during the next thirty days, except to you, O king, shall be thrown into the lions' den. ⁸Now, O king, issue the decree and put it in writing so that it cannot be altered—in accordance with the laws of the Medes and Persians, which cannot be repealed." ⁹So King Darius put the decree in writing.

¹⁰Now when Daniel learned that the decree had been published, he went home to his upstairs room where the windows opened toward Jerusalem. Three times a day he got down on his knees and prayed, giving thanks to his God, just as he had done before. ¹¹Then these men went as a group and found Daniel praying and asking God for help. ¹²So they went to the king and spoke to him about his royal decree: "Did you not publish a decree that during the next thirty days anyone who prays to any god or man except to you, O king, would be thrown into the lions' den?"

The king answered, "The decree stands—in accordance with the laws of the Medes and Persians, which cannot be repealed."

¹³Then they said to the king, "Daniel, who is one of the exiles from Judah, pays no attention to you, O king, or to the decree you put in writing. He still prays three times a day." ¹⁴When the king heard this, he was greatly distressed; he was determined to rescue Daniel and made every effort until sundown to save him.

¹⁵Then the men went as a group to the king and said to him, "Remember, O king, that according to the law of the Medes

---

ᵃ22 Or *descendant*; or *successor*   ᵇ25 Aramaic *UPARSIN* (that is, *AND PARSIN*)   ᶜ26 *Mene* can mean *numbered* or *mina* (a unit of money).   ᵈ27 *Tekel* can mean *weighed* or *shekel*.   ᵉ28 *Peres* (the singular of *Parsin*) can mean *divided* or *Persia* or *a half mina* or *a half shekel*.   ᶠ30 Or *Chaldeans*

and Persians no decree or edict that the king issues can be changed."

16So the king gave the order, and they brought Daniel and threw him into the lions' den. The king said to Daniel, "May your God, whom you serve continually, rescue you!"

17A stone was brought and placed over the mouth of the den, and the king sealed it with his own signet ring and with the rings of his nobles, so that Daniel's situation might not be changed. **18**Then the king returned to his palace and spent the night without eating and without any entertainment being brought to him. And he could not sleep.

19At the first light of dawn, the king got up and hurried to the lions' den. **20**When he came near the den, he called to Daniel in an anguished voice, "Daniel, servant of the living God, has your God, whom you serve continually, been able to rescue you from the lions?"

21Daniel answered, "O king, live forever! **22**My God sent his angel, and he shut the mouths of the lions. They have not hurt me, because I was found innocent in his sight. Nor have I ever done any wrong before you, O king."

23The king was overjoyed and gave orders to lift Daniel out of the den. And when Daniel was lifted from the den, no wound was found on him, because he had trusted in his God.

24At the king's command, the men who had falsely accused Daniel were brought in and thrown into the lions' den, along with their wives and children. And before they reached the floor of the den, the lions overpowered them and crushed all their bones.

25Then King Darius wrote to all the peoples, nations and men of every language throughout the land:

"May you prosper greatly!

26"I issue a decree that in every part of my kingdom people must fear and reverence the God of Daniel.

"For he is the living God
  and he endures forever;
his kingdom will not be destroyed,
  his dominion will never end.
27He rescues and he saves;
  he performs signs and wonders
  in the heavens and on the earth.
He has rescued Daniel
  from the power of the lions."

28So Daniel prospered during the reign of Darius and the reign of Cyrus[a] the Persian.

Daniel's Dream of Four Beasts

7 In the first year of Belshazzar king of Babylon, Daniel had a dream, and visions passed through his mind as he was lying on his bed. He wrote down the substance of his dream.

[a]28 Or *Darius, that is, the reign of Cyrus*

HEY DAD
Do I have to close my eyes when I pray?

Text: Daniel 6:10

We don't necessarily have to close our eyes and kneel every time we pray. Sometimes we might want to talk to God in a place where kneeling or closing our eyes would not be appropriate (driving a car, for example). And because the Bible tells us to pray without ceasing—that is, whenever we want and very often—we know that we don't have to wait until we're by our bedside to talk to God.

But it's also important to remember that our bodily position does affect our prayers. C.S. Lewis says, "For [we] constantly forget what [we] must always remember, that [we] are animals and that whatever [our] bodies do affects [our] souls" (p. 20).

So, kneeling to show reverence puts us in the right position to be humble, and closing our eyes helps us to focus on God and block out distractions. That's what Daniel did when he went to his upstairs room and got on his knees to pray three times every day. So while we don't *have* to kneel and close our eyes when we pray, doing so is a good thing to practice.

Lewis, C.S. (1961). The Screwtape Letters. New York: Collier Books.

For a complete listing of Questions Kids Ask, turn to page 1435.

Hungry Lions and a Good Night's Sleep

Key Verse: *"My God sent his angel, and he shut the mouths of the lions."* Daniel 6:22a

Text: Daniel 6:6–8, 19–22 *(Dad or child reads the text.)*

QUIET TIMES with Dad

DAD READS: When do you get really hungry? Maybe you get hungry at school when it's almost lunch time, or maybe you're hungry when you come home from school, and you can hardly wait until dinner.

Child reads: Yes, I get hungry at those times. When do you get really hungry, Dad? Maybe you miss lunch because you get busy and by dinnertime, you can't wait to eat.

DAD READS: When wild animals are hungry, they don't have to wait to eat. They go find something to eat right away. Their mothers never worry about them "spoiling their dinner."

Child reads: The Bible story about Daniel is a wonderful one. The verses we read today told us that, even though King Darius said that no one could pray, Daniel loved God so much that he prayed anyway. When the king's helpers caught Daniel praying, they told the king about it, and he threw Daniel into a cave filled with hungry lions.

DAD READS: Amazingly, even though hungry lions never have to wait to eat, these hungry lions didn't hurt Daniel. He prayed, asking his heavenly Father to protect him. And God closed the lions' mouths. Can't you see Daniel, sleeping next to the lions like they were great big stuffed animals? In the New Testament, a man named Peter calls the devil a "roaring lion" (1 Peter 5:8). He tells us that this lion walks around looking for dinner

Child reads: But just like God kept Daniel safe from real lions, he can also keep you and me safe from the Devil. After he had spent the night sleeping with the lions, Daniel told King Darius, "My God sent his angels."

DAD READS: Did you know that those very same angels will protect you and me from the Devil? Even though he is hungry and would like to hurt you and me, God promises that he will close Satan's mouth, just like he kept the lions from hurting Daniel.

Child reads: Daniel loved God and always wanted to obey him. I want to love God, too. I'm glad that he will protect me from hungry lions. Let me pray this prayer with you:

Our Father in heaven, we love you. Thank you for Daniel. Thank you for your protection from the devil. He is a roaring lion, and he would like to hurt my dad and me. But you have promised to keep us safe if we love you, if we obey you, and if we ask you to keep the lion's mouth shut. Thank you because when you are with us we never have to be afraid. We love you. In Jesus' name, Amen.

For your next devotional reading, go to page 960.

²Daniel said: "In my vision at night I looked, and there before me were the four winds of heaven churning up the great sea. ³Four great beasts, each different from the others, came up out of the sea.

⁴"The first was like a lion, and it had the wings of an eagle. I watched until its wings were torn off and it was lifted from the ground so that it stood on two feet like a man, and the heart of a man was given to it.

⁵"And there before me was a second beast, which looked like a bear. It was raised up on one of its sides, and it had three ribs in its mouth between its teeth. It was told, 'Get up and eat your fill of flesh!'

⁶"After that, I looked, and there before me was another beast, one that looked like a leopard. And on its back it had four wings like those of a bird. This beast had four heads, and it was given authority to rule.

⁷"After that, in my vision at night I looked, and there before me was a fourth beast—terrifying and frightening and very powerful. It had large iron teeth; it crushed and devoured its victims and trampled underfoot whatever was left. It was different from all the former beasts, and it had ten horns.

⁸"While I was thinking about the horns, there before me was another horn, a little one, which came up among them; and three of the first horns were uprooted before it. This horn had eyes like the eyes of a man and a mouth that spoke boastfully.

⁹"As I looked,

"thrones were set in place,
    and the Ancient of Days took his
        seat.
His clothing was as white as snow;
    the hair of his head was white like
        wool.
His throne was flaming with fire,
    and its wheels were all ablaze.
¹⁰A river of fire was flowing,
    coming out from before him.
Thousands upon thousands attended
        him;
    ten thousand times ten thousand
        stood before him.
The court was seated,
    and the books were opened.

¹¹"Then I continued to watch because of the boastful words the horn was speaking. I kept looking until the beast was slain and its body destroyed and thrown into the blazing fire. ¹²(The other beasts had been stripped of their authority,

HEY DAD

Was Daniel scared when he was in the lions' den?

Text: Daniel 6:16–23

The Bible doesn't say that Daniel wasn't scared, and chances are, he probably *was* afraid. Daniel wasn't a hero because he could laugh in the face of those hungry, drooling lions—not many people could. Daniel was a hero because he loved God so much that he chose to face death rather than to disobey him.

How could Daniel have been so brave? He was courageous because he had been obedient to God all along—both in the small things and in the big things. If he hadn't trained himself to obey God every day by always telling the truth, doing his job well, and treating others with kindness, he probably would have buckled when he heard the king's decree not to worship anyone but him. He probably would have thought, "God will understand if I don't pray to him just this time. It's only for thirty days. He wouldn't want me to die!"

But Daniel refused to dishonor God. And he knew that, whatever God's plan was for his life, that plan would be best. After all, he had seen God rescue Shadrach, Meshach and Abednego from the fiery furnace. Daniel knew that God cared about him, and he knew that God takes care of his children. So he faced what could have been his death with courage. And how did God repay him? He sent an angel to close those lions' mouths.

How's that for a reminder of why we can trust God? The same God who protected Daniel from the lions is working in our lives today. So when trouble strikes, do what Daniel did (see v. 10).

For a complete listing of Questions Kids Ask, turn to page 1435.

but were allowed to live for a period of time.)

[13]"In my vision at night I looked, and there before me was one like a son of man, coming with the clouds of heaven. He approached the Ancient of Days and was led into his presence. [14]He was given authority, glory and sovereign power; all peoples, nations and men of every language worshiped him. His dominion is an everlasting dominion that will not pass away, and his kingdom is one that will never be destroyed.

The Interpretation of the Dream

[15]"I, Daniel, was troubled in spirit, and the visions that passed through my mind disturbed me. [16]I approached one of those standing there and asked him the true meaning of all this.

"So he told me and gave me the interpretation of these things: [17]'The four great beasts are four kingdoms that will rise from the earth. [18]But the saints of the Most High will receive the kingdom and will possess it forever—yes, for ever and ever.'

[19]"Then I wanted to know the true meaning of the fourth beast, which was different from all the others and most terrifying, with its iron teeth and bronze claws—the beast that crushed and devoured its victims and trampled underfoot whatever was left. [20]I also wanted to know about the ten horns on its head and about the other horn that came up, before which three of them fell—the horn that looked more imposing than the others and that had eyes and a mouth that spoke boastfully. [21]As I watched, this horn was waging war against the saints and defeating them, [22]until the Ancient of Days came and pronounced judgment in favor of the saints of the Most High, and the time came when they possessed the kingdom.

[23]"He gave me this explanation: 'The fourth beast is a fourth kingdom that will appear on earth. It will be different from all the other kingdoms and will devour the whole earth, trampling it down and crushing it. [24]The ten horns are ten kings who will come from this kingdom. After them another king will arise, different from the earlier ones; he will subdue three kings. [25]He will speak against the Most High and oppress his saints and try to change the set times and the laws. The saints will be handed over to him for a time, times and half a time.[a]

[26]"'But the court will sit, and his power will be taken away and completely destroyed forever. [27]Then the sovereignty, power and greatness of the kingdoms under the whole heaven will be handed over to the saints, the people of the Most High. His kingdom will be an everlasting kingdom, and all rulers will worship and obey him.'

[28]"This is the end of the matter. I, Daniel, was deeply troubled by my thoughts, and my face turned pale, but I kept the matter to myself."

Daniel's Vision of a Ram and a Goat

8 In the third year of King Belshazzar's reign, I, Daniel, had a vision, after the one that had already appeared to me. [2]In my vision I saw myself in the citadel of Susa in the province of Elam; in the vision I was beside the Ulai Canal. [3]I looked up, and there before me was a ram with two horns, standing beside the canal, and the horns were long. One of the horns was longer than the other but grew up later. [4]I watched the ram as he charged toward the west and the north and the south. No animal could stand against him, and none could rescue from his power. He did as he pleased and became great.

[5]As I was thinking about this, suddenly a goat with a prominent horn between his eyes came from the west, crossing the whole earth without touching the ground. [6]He came toward the two-horned ram I had seen standing beside the canal and charged at him in great rage. [7]I saw him attack the ram furiously, striking the ram and shattering his two horns. The ram was powerless to stand against him; the goat knocked him to the ground and trampled on him, and none could rescue the ram from his power. [8]The goat became very great, but at the height of his power his large horn was broken off, and in its place four prominent horns grew up toward the four winds of heaven.

[9]Out of one of them came another horn, which started small but grew in power to the south and to the east and toward the Beautiful Land. [10]It grew until it reached the host of the heavens, and it threw some of the starry host down to the earth and trampled on them. [11]It set itself up to be as great as the Prince of the host; it took away the daily sacrifice from him, and the place of his sanctuary was

[a]25 Or *for a year, two years and half a year*

the ruler, comes, there will be seven 'sevens,' and sixty-two 'sevens.' It will be rebuilt with streets and a trench, but in times of trouble. [26]After the sixty-two 'sevens,' the Anointed One will be cut off and will have nothing.[a] The people of the ruler who will come will destroy the city and the sanctuary. The end will come like a flood: War will continue until the end, and desolations have been decreed. [27]He will confirm a covenant with many for one 'seven.'[b] In the middle of the 'seven'[b] he will put an end to sacrifice and offering. And on a wing of the temple he will set up an abomination that causes desolation, until the end that is decreed is poured out on him.[c][d]

Daniel's Vision of a Man

10 In the third year of Cyrus king of Persia, a revelation was given to Daniel (who was called Belteshazzar). Its message was true and it concerned a great war.[e] The understanding of the message came to him in a vision.

[2]At that time I, Daniel, mourned for three weeks. [3]I ate no choice food; no meat or wine touched my lips; and I used no lotions at all until the three weeks were over.

[4]On the twenty-fourth day of the first month, as I was standing on the bank of the great river, the Tigris, [5]I looked up and there before me was a man dressed in linen, with a belt of the finest gold around his waist. [6]His body was like chrysolite, his face like lightning, his eyes like flaming torches, his arms and legs like the gleam of burnished bronze, and his voice like the sound of a multitude.

[7]I, Daniel, was the only one who saw the vision; the men with me did not see it, but such terror overwhelmed them that they fled and hid themselves. [8]So I was left alone, gazing at this great vision; I had no strength left, my face turned deathly pale and I was helpless. [9]Then I heard him speaking, and as I listened to him, I fell into a deep sleep, my face to the ground.

[10]A hand touched me and set me trembling on my hands and knees. [11]He said, "Daniel, you who are highly esteemed, consider carefully the words I am about to speak to you, and stand up, for I have now been sent to you." And when he said this to me, I stood up trembling.

[12]Then he continued, "Do not be afraid, Daniel. Since the first day that you set your mind to gain understanding and to humble yourself before your God, your

words were heard, and I have come in response to them. [13]But the prince of the Persian kingdom resisted me twenty-one days. Then Michael, one of the chief princes, came to help me, because I was detained there with the king of Persia. [14]Now I have come to explain to you what will happen to your people in the future, for the vision concerns a time yet to come."

[15]While he was saying this to me, I bowed with my face toward the ground and was speechless. [16]Then one who looked like a man[f] touched my lips, and I opened my mouth and began to speak. I said to the one standing before me, "I am overcome with anguish because of the vision, my lord, and I am helpless. [17]How can I, your servant, talk with you, my lord? My strength is gone and I can hardly breathe."

[18]Again the one who looked like a man touched me and gave me strength. [19]"Do not be afraid, O man highly esteemed," he said. "Peace! Be strong now; be strong."

When he spoke to me, I was strengthened and said, "Speak, my lord, since you have given me strength."

[20]So he said, "Do you know why I have come to you? Soon I will return to fight against the prince of Persia, and when I go, the prince of Greece will come; [21]but first I will tell you what is written in the Book of Truth. (No one supports me against them except Michael, your prince.

11 [1]And in the first year of Darius the Mede, I took my stand to support and protect him.)

The Kings of the South and the North

[2]"Now then, I tell you the truth: Three more kings will appear in Persia, and then a fourth, who will be far richer than all the others. When he has gained power by his wealth, he will stir up everyone against the kingdom of Greece. [3]Then a mighty king will appear, who will rule with great power and do as he pleases. [4]After he has appeared, his empire will be broken up and parceled out toward the four winds of heaven. It will not go to his descendants, nor will it have the power he exercised,

---

[a]26 Or *off and will have no one;* or *off, but not for himself*   [b]27 Or *'week'*   [c]27 Or *it*   [d]27 Or *And one who causes desolation will come upon the pinnacle of the abominable ⌊temple⌋, until the end that is decreed is poured out on the desolated ⌊city⌋*   [e]1 Or *true and burdensome*   [f]16 Most manuscripts of the Masoretic Text; one manuscript of the Masoretic Text, Dead Sea Scrolls and Septuagint *Then something that looked like a man's hand*

because his empire will be uprooted and given to others.

⁵"The king of the South will become strong, but one of his commanders will become even stronger than he and will rule his own kingdom with great power. ⁶After some years, they will become allies. The daughter of the king of the South will go to the king of the North to make an alliance, but she will not retain her power, and he and his power*a* will not last. In those days she will be handed over, together with her royal escort and her father*b* and the one who supported her.

⁷"One from her family line will arise to take her place. He will attack the forces of the king of the North and enter his fortress; he will fight against them and be victorious. ⁸He will also seize their gods, their metal images and their valuable articles of silver and gold and carry them off to Egypt. For some years he will leave the king of the North alone. ⁹Then the king of the North will invade the realm of the king of the South but will retreat to his own country. ¹⁰His sons will prepare for war and assemble a great army, which will sweep on like an irresistible flood and carry the battle as far as his fortress.

¹¹"Then the king of the South will march out in a rage and fight against the king of the North, who will raise a large army, but it will be defeated. ¹²When the army is carried off, the king of the South will be filled with pride and will slaughter many thousands, yet he will not remain triumphant. ¹³For the king of the North will muster another army, larger than the first; and after several years, he will advance with a huge army fully equipped.

¹⁴"In those times many will rise against the king of the South. The violent men among your own people will rebel in fulfillment of the vision, but without success. ¹⁵Then the king of the North will come and build up siege ramps and will capture a fortified city. The forces of the South will be powerless to resist; even their best troops will not have the strength to stand. ¹⁶The invader will do as he pleases; no one will be able to stand against him. He will establish himself in the Beautiful Land and will have the power to destroy it. ¹⁷He will determine to come with the might of his entire kingdom and will make an alliance with the king of the South. And he will give him a daughter in marriage in order to overthrow the kingdom, but his plans*c* will not succeed or help him. ¹⁸Then he will turn

his attention to the coastlands and will take many of them, but a commander will put an end to his insolence and will turn his insolence back upon him. ¹⁹After this, he will turn back toward the fortresses of his own country but will stumble and fall, to be seen no more.

²⁰"His successor will send out a tax collector to maintain the royal splendor. In a few years, however, he will be destroyed, yet not in anger or in battle.

²¹"He will be succeeded by a contemptible person who has not been given the honor of royalty. He will invade the kingdom when its people feel secure, and he will seize it through intrigue. ²²Then an overwhelming army will be swept away before him; both it and a prince of the covenant will be destroyed. ²³After coming to an agreement with him, he will act deceitfully, and with only a few people he will rise to power. ²⁴When the richest provinces feel secure, he will invade them and will achieve what neither his fathers nor his forefathers did. He will distribute plunder, loot and wealth among his followers. He will plot the overthrow of fortresses—but only for a time.

²⁵"With a large army he will stir up his strength and courage against the king of the South. The king of the South will wage war with a large and very powerful army, but he will not be able to stand because of the plots devised against him. ²⁶Those who eat from the king's provisions will try to destroy him; his army will be swept away, and many will fall in battle. ²⁷The two kings, with their hearts bent on evil, will sit at the same table and lie to each other, but to no avail, because an end will still come at the appointed time. ²⁸The king of the North will return to his own country with great wealth, but his heart will be set against the holy covenant. He will take action against it and then return to his own country.

²⁹"At the appointed time he will invade the South again, but this time the outcome will be different from what it was before. ³⁰Ships of the western coastlands*d* will oppose him, and he will lose heart. Then he will turn back and vent his fury against the holy covenant. He will return and show favor to those who forsake the holy covenant.

³¹"His armed forces will rise up to desecrate the temple fortress and will abolish

---

a6 Or *offspring*   *b6* Or *child* (see Vulgate and Syriac)   *c17* Or *but she*   *d30* Hebrew *of Kittim*

said, "Call him Lo-Ammi,^{a} for you are not my people, and I am not your God.

^{10}"Yet the Israelites will be like the sand on the seashore, which cannot be measured or counted. In the place where it was said to them, 'You are not my people,' they will be called 'sons of the living God.' ^{11}The people of Judah and the people of Israel will be reunited, and they will appoint one leader and will come up out of the land, for great will be the day of Jezreel.

2 "Say of your brothers, 'My people,' and of your sisters, 'My loved one.'

Israel Punished and Restored

^{2}"Rebuke your mother, rebuke her, for she is not my wife, and I am not her husband. Let her remove the adulterous look from her face

^{a}9 *Lo-Ammi* means *not my people.*

The Bride Wore Black

Don't you just love new things? I do, too. There's something special about peeling that clear, plastic stuff off CD's, batteries, or even toothbrushes and being the first person to enjoy whatever it is.

In today's reading we encounter something that doesn't exactly appeal to those of us who gravitate toward "new" things. Hosea was a man whom God had called as a prophet. As he was preparing for his ministry to the Israelites, God visited him with a message: "Go, take to yourself an adulterous wife." Assuming that Hosea was like you and me, he must have been stunned with this directive. Certainly Hosea had hoped to find a nice Jewish girl—a virgin from a good home—to be his lifelong companion. How Hosea must have been crushed with this assignment. But, in obedience to God, Hosea asked a prostitute named Gomer to become his bride.

Can you imagine how difficult it must have been for Hosea on their wedding night? *This should be the celebration of a lifetime,* he must have thought, *but instead, I'm wondering what she's thinking … I wonder how I compare to the other men she has known?*

Doesn't your heart go out to Hosea? Don't you think that this faithful young minister deserved better than this? Don't you wish he could have married his high-school sweetheart, a young woman who would have been ecstatic about spending her first night with her precious, innocent

DAILY INSIGHT

MONDAY

Passage:
Hosea 1:1–11

Verse:
Hosea 1:11

husband? Instead, Hosea married a woman who had been used, a hardened woman for whom the thrill was gone from life. Our hearts ache for Hosea, don't they?

Now we know how God felt. The people whom he had loved and protected had "slept around." In worshiping other gods, they had flaunted their unfaithfulness to him, literally bringing their false gods into the holiest of places and shamelessly brandishing their infidelity.

God was furious that his people had been so foolish, so calloused, so arrogant. But mostly, God's heart was broken. What could have been a holy union between himself and his beloved people had become the subject of laughter and ridicule. So God told Hosea that it wasn't good enough for him to know about this spiritual adultery; he wanted Hosea to *feel* it … to literally *live* with the heartbreak of loving a rugged harlot instead of a cherished and virtuous bride. What an incredible lesson.

Now, just in case you and I are tempted to get carried away with how despicable Gomer was and how loving Hosea was to tenderly take her into his home, consider that this is another illustration of exactly what it's like for God to love *us.* Even though we callously and arrogantly sinned against him, he loved us more that we could ever know; more than we deserved; even more than we loved our childhood sweetheart. Isn't this awesome?

For your next devotional reading, go to page 962.

and the unfaithfulness from between
her breasts.
³Otherwise I will strip her naked
and make her as bare as on the day
she was born;
I will make her like a desert,
turn her into a parched land,
and slay her with thirst.
⁴I will not show my love to her children,
because they are the children of
adultery.
⁵Their mother has been unfaithful
and has conceived them in
disgrace.
She said, 'I will go after my lovers,
who give me my food and my water,
my wool and my linen, my oil and
my drink.'
⁶Therefore I will block her path with
thornbushes;
I will wall her in so that she cannot
find her way.
⁷She will chase after her lovers but not
catch them;
she will look for them but not find
them.
Then she will say,
'I will go back to my husband as at
first,
for then I was better off than now.'
⁸She has not acknowledged that I was
the one
who gave her the grain, the new wine
and oil,
who lavished on her the silver and
gold—
which they used for Baal.

⁹"Therefore I will take away my grain
when it ripens,
and my new wine when it is ready.
I will take back my wool and my linen,
intended to cover her nakedness.
¹⁰So now I will expose her lewdness
before the eyes of her lovers;
no one will take her out of my hands.
¹¹I will stop all her celebrations:
her yearly festivals, her New Moons,
her Sabbath days—all her appointed
feasts.
¹²I will ruin her vines and her fig trees,
which she said were her pay from her
lovers;
I will make them a thicket,
and wild animals will devour them.
¹³I will punish her for the days
she burned incense to the Baals;
she decked herself with rings and
jewelry,
and went after her lovers,

but me she forgot,"
declares the LORD.

¹⁴"Therefore I am now going to allure
her;
I will lead her into the desert
and speak tenderly to her.
¹⁵There I will give her back her vineyards,
and will make the Valley of Achor ᵃ a
door of hope.
There she will sing ᵇ as in the days of
her youth,
as in the day she came up out of
Egypt.

¹⁶"In that day," declares the LORD,
"you will call me 'my husband';
you will no longer call me 'my
master.' ᶜ'
¹⁷I will remove the names of the Baals
from her lips;
no longer will their names be
invoked.
¹⁸In that day I will make a covenant for
them
with the beasts of the field and the
birds of the air
and the creatures that move along
the ground.
Bow and sword and battle
I will abolish from the land,
so that all may lie down in safety.
¹⁹I will betroth you to me forever;
I will betroth you in ᵈ righteousness
and justice,
in ᵉ love and compassion.
²⁰I will betroth you in faithfulness,
and you will acknowledge the LORD.

²¹"In that day I will respond,"
declares the LORD—
"I will respond to the skies,
and they will respond to the earth;
²²and the earth will respond to the grain,
the new wine and oil,
and they will respond to Jezreel. ᶠ
²³I will plant her for myself in the land;
I will show my love to the one I called
'Not my loved one.' ᵍ
I will say to those called 'Not my
people,' ʰ 'You are my people';
and they will say, 'You are my God.' "

Hosea's Reconciliation With His Wife

3 The LORD said to me, "Go, show your
love to your wife again, though she is

ᵃ15 Achor means trouble.   ᵇ15 Or respond
ᶜ16 Hebrew baal   ᵈ19 Or with; also in verse 20
ᵉ19 Or with   ᶠ22 Jezreel means God plants.
ᵍ23 Hebrew Lo-Ruhamah   ʰ23 Hebrew Lo-Ammi

loved by another and is an adulteress. Love her as the LORD loves the Israelites, though they turn to other gods and love the sacred raisin cakes."

²So I bought her for fifteen shekels[a] of silver and about a homer and a lethek[b] of barley. ³Then I told her, "You are to live with[c] me many days; you must not be a prostitute or be intimate with any man, and I will live with[c] you."

⁴For the Israelites will live many days without king or prince, without sacrifice

a2 That is, about 6 ounces (about 170 grams)
b2 That is, probably about 10 bushels (about 330 liters)   c3 Or *wait for*

Forgive . . . One More Time

DAILY INSIGHT

TUESDAY

Passage:
Hosea 3:1–5

Verse:
Hosea 3:5

For what seems like decades, cartoonist Charles Schultz has inaugurated the football season with a variation on the same Peanuts comic strip. Charlie Brown, ever the trusting innocent, sets up to place kick a football held by Lucy. As he's been the victim of her trickery in the past, at first he flatly refuses to set himself up again. Somehow Lucy convinces him that this time, she's had a change of heart. As Charlie storms across the field preparing to put his leg into it, Lucy's change of heart has a change of heart. She yanks the ball back and poor old Charlie winds up on his backside, once again.

Lucy's annual antics are trivial compared to what Gomer pulled on Hosea, but the end result was pretty much the same.

One can only imagine the conversations that Hosea must have had with his wife, a former prostitute. "I'm aware of the life you've lived," Hosea must have said to Gomer. "But if you're going to be my wife and bear my children, you're going to have to give up that life. No more walking the streets. No more satisfying lines of lust-filled suitors. I forgive you for the past, but from now on, I'm your only lover. Deal? Deal."

But like Lucy and the football, Gomer couldn't resist. In spite of Hosea's pleadings, the seduction of her former life pulled her back on to the street. "Where's Mom?" Hosea's children must have asked. Where's Mom, indeed. Hosea had had enough of this. "I'm tired of being the laughing stock of my neighbors," he must have told God.

But, as God has a tendency to do, Hosea's heavenly Father had other plans.

"Go, show your love to your wife again," the Almighty told this broken man.

"Forgive her ... again?" Hosea must have argued. "Yes," was God's response. "And, not only do I want you to forgive her, I want you to bring your hard-earned money to the sidewalk where she's selling herself, and I want you to buy her back."

Can you feel Hosea's heart pounding in his chest? The outrageous notion that this treacherous prostitute was to receive his loving tenderness once again was almost more than he could bear. But Hosea fulfilled his unbelievable assignment. He went to the marketplace, found his wayward wife, bought her back and promised, "I will live with you."

Simon Peter, in his inimitable fashion, asked Jesus the following question, "Lord, how many times shall I forgive my brother when he sins against me?" Then as an afterthought, thinking that he'd pick a nice big number, he added, "Up to seven times?" Jesus answered Peter, "I tell you, not seven times, but seventy-seven times" (Matthew 18:21–22). "But, Jesus," Peter must have muttered under his breath, "What if they don't deserve it?" Have you heard the story about Hosea and Gomer, Peter? It's pretty unbelievable.

Who needs your forgiveness? "But," you may say, "I've forgiven him before. I've given him one more chance, and he has wronged me again." Have you heard the story about God and his sinful people? It's pretty unbelievable.

For your next devotional reading, go to page 972.

or sacred stones, without ephod or idol. ⁵Afterward the Israelites will return and seek the LORD their God and David their king. They will come trembling to the LORD and to his blessings in the last days.

The Charge Against Israel

4 Hear the word of the LORD, you
Israelites,
because the LORD has a charge to
bring
against you who live in the land:
"There is no faithfulness, no love,
no acknowledgment of God in the
land.
²There is only cursing,ᵃ lying and
murder,
stealing and adultery;
they break all bounds,
and bloodshed follows bloodshed.
³Because of this the land mourns,ᵇ
and all who live in it waste away;
the beasts of the field and the birds of
the air
and the fish of the sea are dying.

⁴"But let no man bring a charge,
let no man accuse another,
for your people are like those
who bring charges against a priest.
⁵You stumble day and night,
and the prophets stumble with you.
So I will destroy your mother—
⁶ my people are destroyed from lack of
knowledge.

"Because you have rejected knowledge,
I also reject you as my priests;
because you have ignored the law of
your God,
I also will ignore your children.
⁷The more the priests increased,
the more they sinned against me;
they exchangedᶜ theirᵈ Glory for
something disgraceful.
⁸They feed on the sins of my people
and relish their wickedness.
⁹And it will be: Like people, like priests.
I will punish both of them for their
ways
and repay them for their deeds.

¹⁰"They will eat but not have enough;
they will engage in prostitution but
not increase,
because they have deserted the LORD
to give themselves ¹¹to prostitution,
to old wine and new,
which take away the understanding
¹²of my people.
They consult a wooden idol

and are answered by a stick of wood.
A spirit of prostitution leads them
astray;
they are unfaithful to their God.
¹³They sacrifice on the mountaintops
and burn offerings on the hills,
under oak, poplar and terebinth,
where the shade is pleasant.
Therefore your daughters turn to
prostitution
and your daughters-in-law to
adultery.

¹⁴"I will not punish your daughters
when they turn to prostitution,
nor your daughters-in-law
when they commit adultery,
because the men themselves consort
with harlots
and sacrifice with shrine
prostitutes—
a people without understanding will
come to ruin!

¹⁵"Though you commit adultery,
O Israel,
let not Judah become guilty.

"Do not go to Gilgal;
do not go up to Beth Aven.ᵉ
And do not swear, 'As surely as the
LORD lives!'
¹⁶The Israelites are stubborn,
like a stubborn heifer.
How then can the LORD pasture them
like lambs in a meadow?
¹⁷Ephraim is joined to idols;
leave him alone!
¹⁸Even when their drinks are gone,
they continue their prostitution;
their rulers dearly love shameful
ways.
¹⁹A whirlwind will sweep them away,
and their sacrifices will bring them
shame.

Judgment Against Israel

5 "Hear this, you priests!
Pay attention, you Israelites!
Listen, O royal house!
This judgment is against you:
You have been a snare at Mizpah,
a net spread out on Tabor.
²The rebels are deep in slaughter.

ᵃ2 That is, to pronounce a curse upon   ᵇ3 Or
dries up   ᶜ7 Syriac and an ancient Hebrew scribal
tradition; Masoretic Text I will exchange
ᵈ7 Masoretic Text; an ancient Hebrew scribal
tradition my   ᵉ15 Beth Aven means house of
wickedness (a name for Bethel, which means
house of God).

I will discipline all of them.
³I know all about Ephraim;
    Israel is not hidden from me.
Ephraim, you have now turned to
        prostitution;
    Israel is corrupt.

⁴"Their deeds do not permit them
    to return to their God.
A spirit of prostitution is in their heart;
    they do not acknowledge the LORD.
⁵Israel's arrogance testifies against
        them;
    the Israelites, even Ephraim, stumble
        in their sin;
    Judah also stumbles with them.
⁶When they go with their flocks and
        herds
    to seek the LORD,
they will not find him;
    he has withdrawn himself from them.
⁷They are unfaithful to the LORD;
    they give birth to illegitimate
        children.
Now their New Moon festivals
    will devour them and their fields.

⁸"Sound the trumpet in Gibeah,
    the horn in Ramah.
Raise the battle cry in Beth Aven*a*;
    lead on, O Benjamin.
⁹Ephraim will be laid waste
    on the day of reckoning.
Among the tribes of Israel
    I proclaim what is certain.
¹⁰Judah's leaders are like those
    who move boundary stones.
I will pour out my wrath on them
    like a flood of water.
¹¹Ephraim is oppressed,
    trampled in judgment,
    intent on pursuing idols.*b*
¹²I am like a moth to Ephraim,
    like rot to the people of Judah.

¹³"When Ephraim saw his sickness,
    and Judah his sores,
then Ephraim turned to Assyria,
    and sent to the great king for help.
But he is not able to cure you,
    not able to heal your sores.
¹⁴For I will be like a lion to Ephraim,
    like a great lion to Judah.
I will tear them to pieces and go away;
    I will carry them off, with no one to
        rescue them.
¹⁵Then I will go back to my place
    until they admit their guilt.
And they will seek my face;
    in their misery they will earnestly
        seek me."

Israel Unrepentant

6 "Come, let us return to the LORD.
    He has torn us to pieces
    but he will heal us;
he has injured us
    but he will bind up our wounds.
²After two days he will revive us;
    on the third day he will restore us,
    that we may live in his presence.
³Let us acknowledge the LORD;
    let us press on to acknowledge him.
As surely as the sun rises,
    he will appear;
he will come to us like the winter rains,
    like the spring rains that water the
        earth."

⁴"What can I do with you, Ephraim?
    What can I do with you, Judah?
Your love is like the morning mist,
    like the early dew that disappears.
⁵Therefore I cut you in pieces with my
        prophets,
    I killed you with the words of my
        mouth;
    my judgments flashed like lightning
        upon you.
⁶For I desire mercy, not sacrifice,
    and acknowledgment of God rather
        than burnt offerings.
⁷Like Adam,*c* they have broken the
        covenant—
    they were unfaithful to me there.
⁸Gilead is a city of wicked men,
    stained with footprints of blood.
⁹As marauders lie in ambush for a man,
    so do bands of priests;
they murder on the road to Shechem,
    committing shameful crimes.
¹⁰I have seen a horrible thing
    in the house of Israel.
There Ephraim is given to prostitution
    and Israel is defiled.

¹¹"Also for you, Judah,
    a harvest is appointed.

"Whenever I would restore the fortunes
        of my people,
7 ¹ whenever I would heal Israel,
    the sins of Ephraim are exposed
    and the crimes of Samaria revealed.
They practice deceit,
    thieves break into houses,
    bandits rob in the streets;
²but they do not realize

---

*a*8 *Beth Aven* means *house of wickedness* (a name
for Bethel, which means *house of God*).   *b*11 The
meaning of the Hebrew for this word is uncertain.
*c*7 Or *As at Adam;* or *Like men*

that I remember all their evil deeds.
Their sins engulf them;
they are always before me.

³ "They delight the king with their
wickedness,
the princes with their lies.
⁴ They are all adulterers,
burning like an oven
whose fire the baker need not stir
from the kneading of the dough till it
rises.
⁵ On the day of the festival of our king
the princes become inflamed with
wine,
and he joins hands with the
mockers.
⁶ Their hearts are like an oven;
they approach him with intrigue.
Their passion smolders all night;
in the morning it blazes like a
flaming fire.
⁷ All of them are hot as an oven;
they devour their rulers.
All their kings fall,
and none of them calls on me.

⁸ "Ephraim mixes with the nations;
Ephraim is a flat cake not turned
over.
⁹ Foreigners sap his strength,
but he does not realize it.
His hair is sprinkled with gray,
but he does not notice.
¹⁰ Israel's arrogance testifies against him,
but despite all this
he does not return to the LORD his God
or search for him.

¹¹ "Ephraim is like a dove,
easily deceived and senseless—
now calling to Egypt,
now turning to Assyria.
¹² When they go, I will throw my net over
them;
I will pull them down like birds of the
air.
When I hear them flocking together,
I will catch them.
¹³ Woe to them,
because they have strayed from me!
Destruction to them,
because they have rebelled against
me!
I long to redeem them
but they speak lies against me.
¹⁴ They do not cry out to me from their
hearts
but wail upon their beds.
They gather together*a* for grain and
new wine

but turn away from me.
¹⁵ I trained them and strengthened them,
but they plot evil against me.
¹⁶ They do not turn to the Most High;
they are like a faulty bow.
Their leaders will fall by the sword
because of their insolent words.
For this they will be ridiculed
in the land of Egypt.

Israel to Reap the Whirlwind

8 "Put the trumpet to your lips!
An eagle is over the house of the LORD
because the people have broken my
covenant
and rebelled against my law.
² Israel cries out to me,
'O our God, we acknowledge you!'
³ But Israel has rejected what is good;
an enemy will pursue him.
⁴ They set up kings without my consent;
they choose princes without my
approval.
With their silver and gold
they make idols for themselves
to their own destruction.
⁵ Throw out your calf-idol, O Samaria!
My anger burns against them.
How long will they be incapable of
purity?
⁶ They are from Israel!
This calf—a craftsman has made it;
it is not God.
It will be broken in pieces,
that calf of Samaria.

⁷ "They sow the wind
and reap the whirlwind.
The stalk has no head;
it will produce no flour.
Were it to yield grain,
foreigners would swallow it up.
⁸ Israel is swallowed up;
now she is among the nations
like a worthless thing.
⁹ For they have gone up to Assyria
like a wild donkey wandering alone.
Ephraim has sold herself to lovers.
¹⁰ Although they have sold themselves
among the nations,
I will now gather them together.
They will begin to waste away
under the oppression of the mighty
king.

¹¹ "Though Ephraim built many altars for
sin offerings,

*a14 Most Hebrew manuscripts; some Hebrew
manuscripts and Septuagint They slash themselves*

these have become altars for sinning.
¹²I wrote for them the many things of my
    law,
  but they regarded them as
      something alien.
¹³They offer sacrifices given to me
  and they eat the meat,
  but the LORD is not pleased with
      them.
Now he will remember their
      wickedness
  and punish their sins:
  They will return to Egypt.
¹⁴Israel has forgotten his Maker
  and built palaces;
  Judah has fortified many towns.
But I will send fire upon their cities
  that will consume their fortresses."

Punishment for Israel

9 Do not rejoice, O Israel;
  do not be jubilant like the other
      nations.
For you have been unfaithful to your
      God;
  you love the wages of a prostitute
  at every threshing floor.
²Threshing floors and winepresses will
      not feed the people;
  the new wine will fail them.
³They will not remain in the LORD's land;
  Ephraim will return to Egypt
  and eat unclean*ᵃ* food in Assyria.
⁴They will not pour out wine offerings
      to the LORD,
  nor will their sacrifices please him.
Such sacrifices will be to them like the
      bread of mourners;
  all who eat them will be unclean.
This food will be for themselves;
  it will not come into the temple of
      the LORD.

⁵What will you do on the day of your
      appointed feasts,
  on the festival days of the LORD?
⁶Even if they escape from destruction,
  Egypt will gather them,
  and Memphis will bury them.
Their treasures of silver will be taken
      over by briers,
  and thorns will overrun their tents.
⁷The days of punishment are coming,
  the days of reckoning are at hand.
  Let Israel know this.
Because your sins are so many
  and your hostility so great,
the prophet is considered a fool,
  the inspired man a maniac.
⁸The prophet, along with my God,

is the watchman over Ephraim,*ᵇ*
  yet snares await him on all his paths,
  and hostility in the house of his God.
⁹They have sunk deep into corruption,
  as in the days of Gibeah.
God will remember their wickedness
  and punish them for their sins.

¹⁰"When I found Israel,
  it was like finding grapes in the
      desert;
when I saw your fathers,
  it was like seeing the early fruit on
      the fig tree.
But when they came to Baal Peor,
  they consecrated themselves to that
      shameful idol
  and became as vile as the thing they
      loved.
¹¹Ephraim's glory will fly away like a
      bird—
  no birth, no pregnancy, no
      conception.
¹²Even if they rear children,
  I will bereave them of every one.
Woe to them
  when I turn away from them!
¹³I have seen Ephraim, like Tyre,
  planted in a pleasant place.
But Ephraim will bring out
  their children to the slayer."

¹⁴Give them, O LORD—
  what will you give them?
Give them wombs that miscarry
  and breasts that are dry.

¹⁵"Because of all their wickedness in
      Gilgal,
  I hated them there.
Because of their sinful deeds,
  I will drive them out of my house.
I will no longer love them;
  all their leaders are rebellious.
¹⁶Ephraim is blighted,
  their root is withered,
  they yield no fruit.
Even if they bear children,
  I will slay their cherished offspring."

¹⁷My God will reject them
  because they have not obeyed him;
  they will be wanderers among the
      nations.

10 Israel was a spreading vine;
  he brought forth fruit for himself.
As his fruit increased,
  he built more altars;

ᵃ3 That is, ceremonially unclean   *ᵇ8* Or *The
prophet is the watchman over Ephraim, / the people
of my God*

as his land prospered,
he adorned his sacred stones.
² Their heart is deceitful,
and now they must bear their guilt.
The LORD will demolish their altars
and destroy their sacred stones.

³ Then they will say, "We have no king
because we did not revere the LORD.
But even if we had a king,
what could he do for us?"
⁴ They make many promises,
take false oaths
and make agreements;
therefore lawsuits spring up
like poisonous weeds in a plowed
field.
⁵ The people who live in Samaria fear
for the calf-idol of Beth Aven.ᵃ
Its people will mourn over it,
and so will its idolatrous priests,
those who had rejoiced over its
splendor,
because it is taken from them into
exile.
⁶ It will be carried to Assyria
as tribute for the great king.
Ephraim will be disgraced;
Israel will be ashamed of its wooden
idols.ᵇ
⁷ Samaria and its king will float away
like a twig on the surface of the
waters.
⁸ The high places of wickednessᶜ will be
destroyed—
it is the sin of Israel.
Thorns and thistles will grow up
and cover their altars.
Then they will say to the mountains,
"Cover us!"
and to the hills, "Fall on us!"

⁹ "Since the days of Gibeah, you have
sinned, O Israel,
and there you have remained.ᵈ
Did not war overtake
the evildoers in Gibeah?
¹⁰ When I please, I will punish them;
nations will be gathered against
them
to put them in bonds for their
double sin.
¹¹ Ephraim is a trained heifer
that loves to thresh;
so I will put a yoke
on her fair neck.
I will drive Ephraim,
Judah must plow,
and Jacob must break up the ground.
¹² Sow for yourselves righteousness,
reap the fruit of unfailing love,

and break up your unplowed ground;
for it is time to seek the LORD,
until he comes
and showers righteousness on you.
¹³ But you have planted wickedness,
you have reaped evil,
you have eaten the fruit of
deception.
Because you have depended on your
own strength
and on your many warriors,
¹⁴ the roar of battle will rise against your
people,
so that all your fortresses will be
devastated—
as Shalman devastated Beth Arbel on
the day of battle,
when mothers were dashed to the
ground with their children.
¹⁵ Thus will it happen to you, O Bethel,
because your wickedness is great.
When that day dawns,
the king of Israel will be completely
destroyed.

God's Love for Israel

11 "When Israel was a child, I loved
him,
and out of Egypt I called my son.
² But the more Iᵉ called Israel,
the further they went from me.ᶠ
They sacrificed to the Baals
and they burned incense to images.
³ It was I who taught Ephraim to walk,
taking them by the arms;
but they did not realize
it was I who healed them.
⁴ I led them with cords of human
kindness,
with ties of love;
I lifted the yoke from their neck
and bent down to feed them.

⁵ "Will they not return to Egypt
and will not Assyria rule over them
because they refuse to repent?
⁶ Swords will flash in their cities,
will destroy the bars of their gates
and put an end to their plans.
⁷ My people are determined to turn from
me.
Even if they call to the Most High,
he will by no means exalt them.

ᵃ5 *Beth Aven* means *house of wickedness* (a name
for Bethel, which means *house of God*).   ᵇ6 Or *its
counsel*   ᶜ8 Hebrew *aven,* a reference to Beth Aven
(a derogatory name for Bethel)   ᵈ9 Or *there a
stand was taken*   ᵉ2 Some Septuagint
manuscripts; Hebrew *they*   ᶠ2 Septuagint;
Hebrew *them*

8 "How can I give you up, Ephraim?
  How can I hand you over, Israel?
How can I treat you like Admah?
  How can I make you like Zeboiim?
My heart is changed within me;
  all my compassion is aroused.
9 I will not carry out my fierce anger,
  nor will I turn and devastate
    Ephraim.
For I am God, and not man—
  the Holy One among you.
I will not come in wrath.ᵃ
10 They will follow the LORD;
  he will roar like a lion.
When he roars,
  his children will come trembling
    from the west.
11 They will come trembling
  like birds from Egypt,
  like doves from Assyria.
I will settle them in their homes,"
  declares the LORD.

Israel's Sin

12 Ephraim has surrounded me with lies,
  the house of Israel with deceit.
And Judah is unruly against God,
  even against the faithful Holy One.

12 ¹Ephraim feeds on the wind;
  he pursues the east wind all day
  and multiplies lies and violence.
He makes a treaty with Assyria
  and sends olive oil to Egypt.
² The LORD has a charge to bring against
    Judah;
  he will punish Jacobᵇ according to
    his ways
  and repay him according to his deeds.
³ In the womb he grasped his brother's
    heel;
  as a man he struggled with God.
⁴ He struggled with the angel and
    overcame him;
  he wept and begged for his favor.
He found him at Bethel
  and talked with him there—
⁵ the LORD God Almighty,
  the LORD is his name of renown!
⁶ But you must return to your God;
  maintain love and justice,
  and wait for your God always.

⁷ The merchant uses dishonest scales;
  he loves to defraud.
⁸ Ephraim boasts,
  "I am very rich; I have become
    wealthy.
With all my wealth they will not find
    in me
  any iniquity or sin."

⁹ "I am the LORD your God,
  ⌞who brought you⌟ out ofᶜ Egypt;
I will make you live in tents again,
  as in the days of your appointed
    feasts.
10 I spoke to the prophets,
  gave them many visions
  and told parables through them."

11 Is Gilead wicked?
  Its people are worthless!
Do they sacrifice bulls in Gilgal?
  Their altars will be like piles of
    stones
  on a plowed field.
12 Jacob fled to the country of Aramᵈ;
  Israel served to get a wife,
  and to pay for her he tended sheep.
13 The LORD used a prophet to bring Israel
    up from Egypt,
  by a prophet he cared for him.
14 But Ephraim has bitterly provoked him
    to anger;
  his Lord will leave upon him the guilt
    of his bloodshed
  and will repay him for his contempt.

The LORD's Anger Against Israel

13 When Ephraim spoke, men trembled;
  he was exalted in Israel.
But he became guilty of Baal worship
    and died.
² Now they sin more and more;
  they make idols for themselves from
    their silver,
cleverly fashioned images,
  all of them the work of craftsmen.
It is said of these people,
  "They offer human sacrifice
  and kissᵉ the calf-idols."
³ Therefore they will be like the morning
    mist,
  like the early dew that disappears,
  like chaff swirling from a threshing
    floor,
  like smoke escaping through a
    window.

⁴ "But I am the LORD your God,
  ⌞who brought you⌟ out ofᶜ Egypt.
You shall acknowledge no God but me,
  no Savior except me.
⁵ I cared for you in the desert,
  in the land of burning heat.
⁶ When I fed them, they were satisfied;

ᵃ9 Or come against any city   ᵇ2 Jacob means he
grasps the heel (figuratively, he deceives).   ᶜ9,4 Or
God / ever since you were in   ᵈ12 That is,
Northwest Mesopotamia   ᵉ2 Or "Men who
sacrifice / kiss

when they were satisfied, they
  became proud;
then they forgot me.
⁷ So I will come upon them like a lion,
  like a leopard I will lurk by the path.
⁸ Like a bear robbed of her cubs,
  I will attack them and rip them open.
Like a lion I will devour them;
  a wild animal will tear them apart.

⁹ "You are destroyed, O Israel,
  because you are against me, against
    your helper.
¹⁰ Where is your king, that he may save
    you?
  Where are your rulers in all your
    towns,
of whom you said,
  'Give me a king and princes'?
¹¹ So in my anger I gave you a king,
  and in my wrath I took him away.
¹² The guilt of Ephraim is stored up,
  his sins are kept on record.
¹³ Pains as of a woman in childbirth come
    to him,
  but he is a child without wisdom;
when the time arrives,
  he does not come to the opening of
    the womb.

¹⁴ "I will ransom them from the power of
    the graveᵃ;
  I will redeem them from death.
Where, O death, are your plagues?
  Where, O grave,ᵃ is your destruction?

  "I will have no compassion,
¹⁵   even though he thrives among his
        brothers.
An east wind from the LORD will come,
  blowing in from the desert;
his spring will fail
  and his well dry up.
His storehouse will be plundered
  of all its treasures.
¹⁶ The people of Samaria must bear their
    guilt,
  because they have rebelled against
    their God.
They will fall by the sword;
  their little ones will be dashed to the
    ground,
  their pregnant women ripped open."

Repentance to Bring Blessing

14 Return, O Israel, to the LORD your
      God.
  Your sins have been your downfall!
² Take words with you
  and return to the LORD.
Say to him:
  "Forgive all our sins
and receive us graciously,
  that we may offer the fruit of our
    lips.ᵇ
³ Assyria cannot save us;
  we will not mount war-horses.
We will never again say 'Our gods'
  to what our own hands have made,
  for in you the fatherless find
    compassion."

⁴ "I will heal their waywardness
  and love them freely,
  for my anger has turned away from
    them.
⁵ I will be like the dew to Israel;
  he will blossom like a lily.
Like a cedar of Lebanon
  he will send down his roots;
⁶   his young shoots will grow.
His splendor will be like an olive
    tree,
  his fragrance like a cedar of
    Lebanon.
⁷ Men will dwell again in his shade.
  He will flourish like the grain.
He will blossom like a vine,
  and his fame will be like the wine
    from Lebanon.
⁸ O Ephraim, what more have Iᶜ to do
    with idols?
  I will answer him and care for him.
I am like a green pine tree;
  your fruitfulness comes from me."

⁹ Who is wise? He will realize these
    things.
  Who is discerning? He will
    understand them.
The ways of the LORD are right;
  the righteous walk in them,
  but the rebellious stumble in them.

ᵃ14 Hebrew *Sheol*   ᵇ2 Or *offer our lips as sacrifices
of bulls*   ᶜ8 Or *What more has Ephraim*

Life is a team sport, more like basketball or soccer than like golf or tennis. Now this may be hard for most men to fully appreciate. Too entrepreneurial to be dependent on others, they've learned—the hard way—that if they want something done correctly, they usually have to do it themselves.

Not so with the prophet Joel. He was a team player. He understood how God uses the gifts and abilities of each team member—sons, daughters, young men, old men, servants, women—to accomplish his work and deliver his message of discipline and grace.

You are not the Lone Ranger. You have not been given the task of living out your faith in a vacuum. God has given you a team—neighbors, extended family, friends from church, colleagues at work, your own family and others—to be his emissaries; they are the catalysts of his faithfulness, his goodness and his love.

Joel

1 The word of the LORD that came to Joel son of Pethuel.

An Invasion of Locusts

2 Hear this, you elders;
  listen, all who live in the land.
Has anything like this ever happened
  in your days
  or in the days of your forefathers?
3 Tell it to your children,
  and let your children tell it to their
    children,
  and their children to the next
    generation.
4 What the locust swarm has left
  the great locusts have eaten;
what the great locusts have left
  the young locusts have eaten;
what the young locusts have left
  other locusts*a* have eaten.

5 Wake up, you drunkards, and weep!
  Wail, all you drinkers of wine;
wail because of the new wine,
  for it has been snatched from your
    lips.
6 A nation has invaded my land,
  powerful and without number;
it has the teeth of a lion,
  the fangs of a lioness.
7 It has laid waste my vines
  and ruined my fig trees.

---

*a4 The precise meaning of the four Hebrew words used here for locusts is uncertain.

It has stripped off their bark
    and thrown it away,
    leaving their branches white.

⁸Mourn like a virgin*a* in sackcloth
    grieving for the husband*b* of her
        youth.
⁹Grain offerings and drink offerings
    are cut off from the house of the
        LORD.
The priests are in mourning,
    those who minister before the LORD.
¹⁰The fields are ruined,
    the ground is dried up*c*;
    the grain is destroyed,
    the new wine is dried up,
    the oil fails.
¹¹Despair, you farmers,
    wail, you vine growers;
grieve for the wheat and the barley,
    because the harvest of the field is
        destroyed.
¹²The vine is dried up
    and the fig tree is withered;
the pomegranate, the palm and the
        apple tree—
    all the trees of the field—are dried up.
Surely the joy of mankind
    is withered away.

A Call to Repentance

¹³Put on sackcloth, O priests, and mourn;
    wail, you who minister before the
        altar.
Come, spend the night in sackcloth,
    you who minister before my God;
for the grain offerings and drink
        offerings
    are withheld from the house of your
        God.
¹⁴Declare a holy fast;
    call a sacred assembly.
Summon the elders
    and all who live in the land
to the house of the LORD your God,
    and cry out to the LORD.

¹⁵Alas for that day!
    For the day of the LORD is near;
    it will come like destruction from the
        Almighty.*d*
¹⁶Has not the food been cut off
    before our very eyes—
joy and gladness
    from the house of our God?
¹⁷The seeds are shriveled
    beneath the clods.*e*
The storehouses are in ruins,
    the granaries have been broken
        down,

for the grain has dried up.
¹⁸How the cattle moan!
    The herds mill about
because they have no pasture;
    even the flocks of sheep are
        suffering.

¹⁹To you, O LORD, I call,
    for fire has devoured the open
        pastures
    and flames have burned up all the
        trees of the field.
²⁰Even the wild animals pant for you;
    the streams of water have dried up
    and fire has devoured the open
        pastures.

An Army of Locusts

2 Blow the trumpet in Zion;
    sound the alarm on my holy hill.
Let all who live in the land tremble,
    for the day of the LORD is coming.
It is close at hand—
²   a day of darkness and gloom,
    a day of clouds and blackness.
Like dawn spreading across the
        mountains
    a large and mighty army comes,
such as never was of old
    nor ever will be in ages to come.

³Before them fire devours,
    behind them a flame blazes.
Before them the land is like the garden
        of Eden,
    behind them, a desert waste—
    nothing escapes them.
⁴They have the appearance of horses;
    they gallop along like cavalry.
⁵With a noise like that of chariots
    they leap over the mountaintops,
like a crackling fire consuming stubble,
    like a mighty army drawn up for
        battle.

⁶At the sight of them, nations are in
        anguish;
    every face turns pale.
⁷They charge like warriors;
    they scale walls like soldiers.
They all march in line,
    not swerving from their course.
⁸They do not jostle each other;
    each marches straight ahead.
They plunge through defenses
    without breaking ranks.
⁹They rush upon the city;

*a8 Or young woman   b8 Or betrothed
c10 Or ground mourns   d15 Hebrew Shaddai
e17 The meaning of the Hebrew for this word is
uncertain.*

they run along the wall.
They climb into the houses;
　like thieves they enter through the
　　windows.

¹⁰Before them the earth shakes,
　the sky trembles,
the sun and moon are darkened,
　and the stars no longer shine.
¹¹The LORD thunders
　at the head of his army;
his forces are beyond number,

and mighty are those who obey his
　　command.
The day of the LORD is great;
　it is dreadful.
Who can endure it?

Rend Your Heart

¹²"Even now," declares the LORD,
　"return to me with all your heart,
　with fasting and weeping and
　　mourning."

Starting at Quarterback . . .

The reporters crowded into the locker room, moving from player to player. On this particular Super Bowl Sunday, the coach allowed media representatives in, provided they didn't prove to be too much of a distraction. He had, however, drawn the line: All media representatives had to leave the locker room two hours before game time.

One by one, each player gave the typical pre-game drivel, "Our opponents are very good, but we're ready. We've got a great organization behind us, and our team is really focused." But then, to the surprise of the media, each player included the following: "I'm so pumped to play today that, even though I've spent all season playing free safety (or offensive tackle, or tight end), I've decided to start at quarterback." Unbeknownst to the coach, each player had decided that *he* was going to be the one throwing the passes, handing the ball to the running back, running the huddle and calling the audibles.

As the reporters gathered outside the locker room, they scratched their heads in disbelief. Although they didn't typically share notes, they talked quietly amongst themselves. "These guys are crazy," they said. "They don't have a chance out there today. How can a powerful offensive tackle expect to play a finesse position like quarterback?"

Can't you hear the sports agents and the players' union representatives screaming? Not to mention the coach!

While this story is pure fiction, it carries

DAILY INSIGHT

WEDNESDAY

Passage:
Joel 2:25–28

Verse:
Joel 2:28

a valuable lesson for dads today. God has put your family together for good reasons. His wonderful plan is that each family member will play a unique role, a role that builds toward the good of the whole family.

The prophet Joel reminds us of something critically important: When God decides to "pour out [his] Spirit on all people," he's going to call all players to take their positions on the field. He's going to use the mouths of your children to speak his voice. He's going to invite life's veterans—your aged grandparents, parents, uncles, aunts—to see what you can't see. And God promises to give you the unique ability to have a vision, to set the goals and standards high for your team.

You're a dad. You've got seriously important work to do. At times, you may think that everyone and everything depends on you. Not so. When God's Spirit visits your family—and he does on a regular basis—he's going to use each person … your children, your wife, your parents, and you, to bring his love and healing to each other and to your neighborhood.

Celebrate the gifts of each person in your family. Be glad that, in his marvelous plan, he made running backs, pulling guards, middle linebackers, and quarterbacks. By the way, today may be a good day to encourage your whole team. They're working just as hard as you, but they rarely get as much of the credit.

For your next devotional reading, go to page 977.

¹³ Rend your heart
  and not your garments.
Return to the LORD your God,
  for he is gracious and
    compassionate,
slow to anger and abounding in love,
  and he relents from sending
    calamity.
¹⁴ Who knows? He may turn and have pity
  and leave behind a blessing—
grain offerings and drink offerings
  for the LORD your God.

¹⁵ Blow the trumpet in Zion,
  declare a holy fast,
  call a sacred assembly.
¹⁶ Gather the people,
  consecrate the assembly;
bring together the elders,
  gather the children,
  those nursing at the breast.
Let the bridegroom leave his room
  and the bride her chamber.
¹⁷ Let the priests, who minister before the
    LORD,
  weep between the temple porch and
    the altar.
Let them say, "Spare your people,
    O LORD.
  Do not make your inheritance an
    object of scorn,
  a byword among the nations.
Why should they say among the
    peoples,
  'Where is their God?' "

The LORD's Answer

¹⁸ Then the LORD will be jealous for his
    land
  and take pity on his people.
  ¹⁹ The LORD will reply[a] to them:

"I am sending you grain, new wine and
    oil,
  enough to satisfy you fully;
never again will I make you
  an object of scorn to the nations.

²⁰ "I will drive the northern army far from
    you,
  pushing it into a parched and barren
    land,
with its front columns going into the
    eastern sea[b]
  and those in the rear into the
    western sea.[c]
And its stench will go up;
  its smell will rise."

Surely he has done great things.[d]
²¹   Be not afraid, O land;

be glad and rejoice.
Surely the LORD has done great things.
²²   Be not afraid, O wild animals,
  for the open pastures are becoming
    green.
The trees are bearing their fruit;
  the fig tree and the vine yield their
    riches.
²³ Be glad, O people of Zion,
  rejoice in the LORD your God,
for he has given you
  the autumn rains in righteousness.[e]
He sends you abundant showers,
  both autumn and spring rains, as
    before.
²⁴ The threshing floors will be filled with
    grain;
  the vats will overflow with new wine
    and oil.

²⁵ "I will repay you for the years the
    locusts have eaten—
  the great locust and the young
    locust,
  the other locusts and the locust
    swarm[f]—
my great army that I sent among you.
²⁶ You will have plenty to eat, until you
    are full,
  and you will praise the name of the
    LORD your God,
  who has worked wonders for you;
never again will my people be shamed.
²⁷ Then you will know that I am in Israel,
  that I am the LORD your God,
  and that there is no other;
never again will my people be shamed.

The Day of the LORD

²⁸ "And afterward,
  I will pour out my Spirit on all
    people.
Your sons and daughters will prophesy,
  your old men will dream dreams,
  your young men will see visions.
²⁹ Even on my servants, both men and
    women,
  I will pour out my Spirit in those
    days.
³⁰ I will show wonders in the heavens
  and on the earth,
  blood and fire and billows of smoke.
³¹ The sun will be turned to darkness

ᵃ18,19 Or LORD was jealous . . . / and took pity . . . /
¹⁹The LORD replied   ᵇ20 That is, the Dead Sea
ᶜ20 That is, the Mediterranean   ᵈ20 Or rise. / Surely
it has done great things."   ᵉ23 Or / the teacher for
righteousness: ᶠ25 The precise meaning of the
four Hebrew words used here for locusts is
uncertain.

and the moon to blood
before the coming of the great and
dreadful day of the LORD.
³²And everyone who calls
on the name of the LORD will be
saved;
for on Mount Zion and in Jerusalem
there will be deliverance,
as the LORD has said,
among the survivors
whom the LORD calls.

The Nations Judged

3 "In those days and at that time,
when I restore the fortunes of Judah
and Jerusalem,
²I will gather all nations
and bring them down to the Valley of
Jehoshaphat.*
There I will enter into judgment
against them
concerning my inheritance, my
people Israel,
for they scattered my people among
the nations
and divided up my land.
³They cast lots for my people
and traded boys for prostitutes;
they sold girls for wine
that they might drink.

⁴"Now what have you against me,
O Tyre and Sidon and all you regions of
Philistia? Are you repaying me for something I have done? If you are paying me
back, I will swiftly and speedily return
on your own heads what you have done.
⁵For you took my silver and my gold and
carried off my finest treasures to your
temples. ⁶You sold the people of Judah
and Jerusalem to the Greeks, that you
might send them far from their homeland.
⁷"See, I am going to rouse them out of
the places to which you sold them, and I
will return on your own heads what you
have done. ⁸I will sell your sons and
daughters to the people of Judah, and they
will sell them to the Sabeans, a nation far
away." The LORD has spoken.

⁹Proclaim this among the nations:
Prepare for war!
Rouse the warriors!
Let all the fighting men draw near
and attack.
¹⁰Beat your plowshares into swords
and your pruning hooks into spears.
Let the weakling say,
"I am strong!"

¹¹Come quickly, all you nations from
every side,
and assemble there.

Bring down your warriors, O LORD!

¹²"Let the nations be roused;
let them advance into the Valley of
Jehoshaphat,
for there I will sit
to judge all the nations on every side.
¹³Swing the sickle,
for the harvest is ripe.
Come, trample the grapes,
for the winepress is full
and the vats overflow—
so great is their wickedness!"

¹⁴Multitudes, multitudes
in the valley of decision!
For the day of the LORD is near
in the valley of decision.
¹⁵The sun and moon will be darkened,
and the stars no longer shine.
¹⁶The LORD will roar from Zion
and thunder from Jerusalem;
the earth and the sky will tremble.
But the LORD will be a refuge for his
people,
a stronghold for the people of Israel.

Blessings for God's People

¹⁷"Then you will know that I, the LORD
your God,
dwell in Zion, my holy hill.
Jerusalem will be holy;
never again will foreigners invade her.

¹⁸"In that day the mountains will drip
new wine,
and the hills will flow with milk;
all the ravines of Judah will run with
water.
A fountain will flow out of the LORD's
house
and will water the valley of acacias.*
¹⁹But Egypt will be desolate,
Edom a desert waste,
because of violence done to the people
of Judah,
in whose land they shed innocent
blood.
²⁰Judah will be inhabited forever
and Jerusalem through all generations.
²¹Their bloodguilt, which I have not
pardoned,
I will pardon."

The LORD dwells in Zion!

ª2 Jehoshaphat means *the LORD judges;* also in
verse 12.   *ᵇ18* Or *Valley of Shittim*

If you would like to know one of the great secrets of the Bible, the book of Amos reveals it. Truth be told, it's not a secret at all: *The main things are the plain things*. For centuries, scholars have argued over religion's minutia. But the great challenge of our faith is listening, understanding and obeying the things we fully understand.

Amos must have known all about this. He proved it by delivering a knockout punch to the bickering and wayward Jews. "The Sovereign LORD does nothing without revealing his plan" (3:7). Can you believe how mightily profound that is? How much that statement reveals about our heavenly Father? That kind of straightforward wisdom tells us a lot about Amos. As you read his message, you'll find out that Amos was a straight shooter.

Amos

1 The words of Amos, one of the shepherds of Tekoa—what he saw concerning Israel two years before the earthquake, when Uzziah was king of Judah and Jeroboam son of Jehoash[a] was king of Israel.

²He said:

"The LORD roars from Zion
  and thunders from Jerusalem;
the pastures of the shepherds dry up,[b]
  and the top of Carmel withers."

Judgment on Israel's Neighbors

³This is what the LORD says:

"For three sins of Damascus,
  even for four, I will not turn back my
    wrath.
Because she threshed Gilead
  with sledges having iron teeth,
⁴I will send fire upon the house of
    Hazael

that will consume the fortresses of
    Ben-Hadad.
⁵I will break down the gate of
    Damascus;
  I will destroy the king who is in[c] the
    Valley of Aven[d]
and the one who holds the scepter in
    Beth Eden.
The people of Aram will go into exile
    to Kir,"

                              says the LORD.

⁶This is what the LORD says:

"For three sins of Gaza,
  even for four, I will not turn back my
    wrath.
Because she took captive whole
    communities
  and sold them to Edom,

---

a1 Hebrew *Joash,* a variant of *Jehoash*   *b2* Or *shepherds mourn*   *c5* Or *the inhabitants of*   *d5* Aven means *wickedness.*

7 I will send fire upon the walls of Gaza
    that will consume her fortresses.
8 I will destroy the king*a* of Ashdod
    and the one who holds the scepter in
        Ashkelon.
I will turn my hand against Ekron,
    till the last of the Philistines is dead,"
            says the Sovereign LORD.

9 This is what the LORD says:

"For three sins of Tyre,
    even for four, I will not turn back ˌmy
        wrathˌ.
Because she sold whole communities
        of captives to Edom,
    disregarding a treaty of brotherhood,
10 I will send fire upon the walls of Tyre
    that will consume her fortresses."

11 This is what the LORD says:

"For three sins of Edom,
    even for four, I will not turn back ˌmy
        wrathˌ.
Because he pursued his brother with a
        sword,
    stifling all compassion,*b*
because his anger raged continually
    and his fury flamed unchecked,
12 I will send fire upon Teman
    that will consume the fortresses of
        Bozrah."

13 This is what the LORD says:

"For three sins of Ammon,
    even for four, I will not turn back ˌmy
        wrathˌ.
Because he ripped open the pregnant
        women of Gilead
    in order to extend his borders,
14 I will set fire to the walls of Rabbah
    that will consume her fortresses
amid war cries on the day of battle,
    amid violent winds on a stormy day.
15 Her king*c* will go into exile,
    he and his officials together,"
            says the LORD.

2 This is what the LORD says:

"For three sins of Moab,
    even for four, I will not turn back ˌmy
        wrathˌ
Because he burned, as if to lime,
    the bones of Edom's king,
2 I will send fire upon Moab
    that will consume the fortresses of
        Kerioth.*d*
Moab will go down in great tumult
    amid war cries and the blast of the
        trumpet.

3 I will destroy her ruler
    and kill all her officials with him,"
            says the LORD.

4 This is what the LORD says:

"For three sins of Judah,
    even for four, I will not turn back ˌmy
        wrathˌ.
Because they have rejected the law of
        the LORD
    and have not kept his decrees,
because they have been led astray by
        false gods,*e*
    the gods*f* their ancestors followed,
5 I will send fire upon Judah
    that will consume the fortresses of
        Jerusalem."

Judgment on Israel

6 This is what the LORD says:

"For three sins of Israel,
    even for four, I will not turn back ˌmy
        wrathˌ.
They sell the righteous for silver,
    and the needy for a pair of sandals.
7 They trample on the heads of the poor
    as upon the dust of the ground
    and deny justice to the oppressed.
Father and son use the same girl
    and so profane my holy name.
8 They lie down beside every altar
    on garments taken in pledge.
In the house of their god
    they drink wine taken as fines.

9 "I destroyed the Amorite before them,
    though he was tall as the cedars
    and strong as the oaks.
I destroyed his fruit above
    and his roots below.
10 "I brought you up out of Egypt,
    and I led you forty years in the desert
    to give you the land of the Amorites.
11 I also raised up prophets from among
        your sons
    and Nazirites from among your
        young men.
Is this not true, people of Israel?"
            declares the LORD.
12 "But you made the Nazirites drink wine
    and commanded the prophets not to
        prophesy.

13 "Now then, I will crush you
    as a cart crushes when loaded with
        grain.

a8 Or *inhabitants*   *b11* Or *sword / and destroyed his
allies*   *c15* Or */ Molech*; Hebrew *malcam*   *d2* Or *of
her cities*   *e4* Or *by lies*   *f4* Or *lies*

¹⁴The swift will not escape,
   the strong will not muster their
      strength,
   and the warrior will not save his
      life.
¹⁵The archer will not stand his ground,
   the fleet-footed soldier will not get
      away,
   and the horseman will not save his
      life.
¹⁶Even the bravest warriors
   will flee naked on that day,"
                  declares the LORD.

Witnesses Summoned Against Israel

3 Hear this word the LORD has spoken
   against you, O people of Israel—
against the whole family I brought up out
of Egypt:

² "You only have I chosen
   of all the families of the earth;
   therefore I will punish you
      for all your sins."

³ Do two walk together
   unless they have agreed to do so?

Duh

DAILY INSIGHT

THURSDAY

Passage:
Amos 3:1–7

Verse:
Amos 3:7

When our girls were in grade school, the little expression, "Duh!" made its way into our family vocabulary. We used this word when someone commented about something that should have been obvious to everyone. Here's a sample: "It's raining outside." "Where else would it be raining, Dad? How 'bout the family room? Duh."

At first, I tried to stop it because it felt cynical—and more than a little cruel. But once we established that this expression would only be used in fun and that people's feelings could not be trampled on, I found myself using it, too. Sometimes no other word said as much.

Not too long ago, I was looking for my reading glasses. I was sure that I had seen them just a few minutes before, but they were nowhere to be found. I searched everywhere—no glasses. Finally, in complete frustration, I asked one of my colleagues if she had seen my reading glasses. "Do you mean the glasses you have propped up in your hair?" "Uh, yes, there they are," I sheepishly responded. "Duh." We both laughed.

As he spoke to the people of Israel, Amos made statements that should have been obvious to everyone. As with the voice of the Almighty One, he said to the disobedient people, "You only have I chosen … therefore I will punish you for your sins." After centuries of God's visible faithfulness, this should have been perfectly clear. They already knew that they were God's chosen people. They already knew that he did not wink at their sin. And they already knew that their heavenly Father never did anything unintentionally. Duh.

But just in case the people missed it, Amos gave the people a series of obvious scenarios … Old Testament "duhs," if you will. "Do two walk together unless they have agreed to do so?" Of course they don't. "Does a lion roar in the thicket when he has no prey?" Why would he do that? "Does a bird fall into a trap on the ground where no snare has been set?" What a silly question. Duh.

Once the people had been lulled into the pattern of absurd questions with obvious answers, Amos addressed their complacency. "The Sovereign LORD does nothing without revealing his plan."

As with the Israelites, God has called us to be his children. He has also given us children to lead in calling us to be fathers, and he requires our faithfulness. He will not tolerate our willful disobedience, and he knows exactly what he's doing in the world and in our lives.

Okay, so this is something we already knew? Are we sure we didn't need a reminder? Are we positive? Then why do we have such a hard time living it?

Duh.

For your next devotional reading, go to page 985.

⁴Does a lion roar in the thicket
   when he has no prey?
Does he growl in his den
   when he has caught nothing?
⁵Does a bird fall into a trap on the
   ground
   where no snare has been set?
Does a trap spring up from the earth
   when there is nothing to catch?
⁶When a trumpet sounds in a city,
   do not the people tremble?
When disaster comes to a city,
   has not the LORD caused it?

⁷Surely the Sovereign LORD does nothing
   without revealing his plan
   to his servants the prophets.

⁸The lion has roared—
   who will not fear?
The Sovereign LORD has spoken—
   who can but prophesy?

⁹Proclaim to the fortresses of Ashdod
   and to the fortresses of Egypt:
"Assemble yourselves on the
     mountains of Samaria;
see the great unrest within her
   and the oppression among her
     people."

¹⁰"They do not know how to do right,"
   declares the LORD,
"who hoard plunder and loot in their
     fortresses."

¹¹Therefore this is what the Sovereign
LORD says:

"An enemy will overrun the land;
   he will pull down your strongholds
   and plunder your fortresses."

¹²This is what the LORD says:

"As a shepherd saves from the lion's
    mouth
   only two leg bones or a piece of an
     ear,
so will the Israelites be saved,
those who sit in Samaria
   on the edge of their beds
   and in Damascus on their
     couches.ᵃ"

¹³"Hear this and testify against the
house of Jacob," declares the Lord, the
LORD God Almighty.

¹⁴"On the day I punish Israel for her sins,
   I will destroy the altars of Bethel;
the horns of the altar will be cut off
   and fall to the ground.
¹⁵I will tear down the winter house
   along with the summer house;

the houses adorned with ivory will be
   destroyed
and the mansions will be
   demolished,"
                   declares the LORD.

Israel Has Not Returned to God

4 Hear this word, you cows of Bashan
   on Mount Samaria,
you women who oppress the poor
   and crush the needy
and say to your husbands, "Bring us
    some drinks!"
²The Sovereign LORD has sworn by his
   holiness:
"The time will surely come
when you will be taken away with
    hooks,
   the last of you with fishhooks.
³You will each go straight out
   through breaks in the wall,
and you will be cast out toward
    Harmon,ᵇ"
                   declares the LORD.
⁴"Go to Bethel and sin;
   go to Gilgal and sin yet more.
Bring your sacrifices every morning,
   your tithes every three years.ᶜ
⁵Burn leavened bread as a thank offering
   and brag about your freewill
    offerings—
boast about them, you Israelites,
   for this is what you love to do,"
          declares the Sovereign LORD.

⁶"I gave you empty stomachsᵈ in every
    city
and lack of bread in every town,
   yet you have not returned to me,"
                 declares the LORD.

⁷"I also withheld rain from you
   when the harvest was still three
    months away.
I sent rain on one town,
   but withheld it from another.
One field had rain;
   another had none and dried up.
⁸People staggered from town to town for
    water
   but did not get enough to drink,
   yet you have not returned to me,"
                 declares the LORD.

⁹"Many times I struck your gardens and
   vineyards,

ᵃ12 The meaning of the Hebrew for this line is
uncertain.   ᵇ3 Masoretic Text; with a different
word division of the Hebrew (see Septuagint) *out,
O mountain of oppression*   ᶜ4 Or *tithes on the third
day*   ᵈ6 Hebrew *you cleanness of teeth*

I struck them with blight and
　　mildew.
Locusts devoured your fig and olive
　　trees,
　yet you have not returned to me,"
　　　　　　　　declares the LORD.

¹⁰"I sent plagues among you
　　as I did to Egypt.
I killed your young men with the
　　sword,
　along with your captured horses.
I filled your nostrils with the stench of
　　your camps,
　yet you have not returned to me,"
　　　　　　　　declares the LORD.

¹¹"I overthrew some of you
　　as I*ᵃ* overthrew Sodom and
　　Gomorrah.
You were like a burning stick snatched
　　from the fire,
　yet you have not returned to me,"
　　　　　　　　declares the LORD.

¹²"Therefore this is what I will do to you,
　　Israel,
　and because I will do this to you,
　　prepare to meet your God, O Israel."

¹³He who forms the mountains,
　　creates the wind,
　and reveals his thoughts to man,
he who turns dawn to darkness,
　　and treads the high places of the
　　　earth—
　the LORD God Almighty is his name.

A Lament and Call to Repentance

5 Hear this word, O house of Israel, this
lament I take up concerning you:

²"Fallen is Virgin Israel,
　　never to rise again,
deserted in her own land,
　　with no one to lift her up."

³This is what the Sovereign LORD says:

"The city that marches out a thousand
　　strong for Israel
　will have only a hundred left;
the town that marches out a hundred
　　strong
　will have only ten left."

⁴This is what the LORD says to the house
of Israel:

"Seek me and live;
⁵　do not seek Bethel,
do not go to Gilgal,
　do not journey to Beersheba.
For Gilgal will surely go into exile,

and Bethel will be reduced to
　　nothing.*ᵇ*"
⁶Seek the LORD and live,
　　or he will sweep through the house
　　　of Joseph like a fire;
　it will devour,
　　and Bethel will have no one to
　　　quench it.

⁷You who turn justice into bitterness
　　and cast righteousness to the ground
⁸(he who made the Pleiades and Orion,
　　who turns blackness into dawn
　　and darkens day into night,
　who calls for the waters of the sea
　　and pours them out over the face of
　　　the land—
　　the LORD is his name—
⁹he flashes destruction on the
　　stronghold
　　and brings the fortified city to ruin),
¹⁰you hate the one who reproves in court
　　and despise him who tells the truth.

¹¹You trample on the poor
　　and force him to give you grain.
Therefore, though you have built stone
　　mansions,
　you will not live in them;
though you have planted lush vineyards,
　you will not drink their wine.
¹²For I know how many are your offenses
　　and how great your sins.

You oppress the righteous and take
　　bribes
　and you deprive the poor of justice
　　in the courts.
¹³Therefore the prudent man keeps quiet
　　in such times,
　for the times are evil.

¹⁴Seek good, not evil,
　　that you may live.
Then the LORD God Almighty will be
　　with you,
　just as you say he is.
¹⁵Hate evil, love good;
　　maintain justice in the courts.
Perhaps the LORD God Almighty will
　　have mercy
　on the remnant of Joseph.

¹⁶Therefore this is what the Lord, the
LORD God Almighty, says:

"There will be wailing in all the streets
　　and cries of anguish in every public
　　　square.

---

*ᵃ*11 Hebrew *God*　*ᵇ*5 Or *grief*; or *wickedness*;
Hebrew *aven*, a reference to Beth Aven (a
derogatory name for Bethel)

The farmers will be summoned to
weep
and the mourners to wail.
¹⁷There will be wailing in all the
vineyards,
for I will pass through your midst,"
says the LORD.

The Day of the LORD

¹⁸Woe to you who long
for the day of the LORD!
Why do you long for the day of the
LORD?
That day will be darkness, not light.
¹⁹It will be as though a man fled from a
lion
only to meet a bear,
as though he entered his house
and rested his hand on the wall
only to have a snake bite him.
²⁰Will not the day of the LORD be
darkness, not light—
pitch-dark, without a ray of
brightness?

²¹"I hate, I despise your religious
feasts;
I cannot stand your assemblies.
²²Even though you bring me burnt
offerings and grain offerings,
I will not accept them.
Though you bring choice fellowship
offerings,ᵃ
I will have no regard for them.
²³Away with the noise of your songs!
I will not listen to the music of your
harps.
²⁴But let justice roll on like a river,
righteousness like a never-failing
stream!

²⁵"Did you bring me sacrifices and
offerings
forty years in the desert, O house of
Israel?
²⁶You have lifted up the shrine of your
king,
the pedestal of your idols,
the star of your godᵇ—
which you made for yourselves.
²⁷Therefore I will send you into exile
beyond Damascus,"
says the LORD, whose name is God
Almighty.

Woe to the Complacent

6 Woe to you who are complacent in
Zion,
and to you who feel secure on Mount
Samaria,

you notable men of the foremost
nation,
to whom the people of Israel come!
²Go to Calneh and look at it;
go from there to great Hamath,
and then go down to Gath in Philistia.
Are they better off than your two
kingdoms?
Is their land larger than yours?
³You put off the evil day
and bring near a reign of terror.
⁴You lie on beds inlaid with ivory
and lounge on your couches.
You dine on choice lambs
and fattened calves.
⁵You strum away on your harps like
David
and improvise on musical
instruments.
⁶You drink wine by the bowlful
and use the finest lotions,
but you do not grieve over the ruin of
Joseph.
⁷Therefore you will be among the first to
go into exile;
your feasting and lounging will end.

The LORD Abhors the Pride of Israel

⁸The Sovereign LORD has sworn by himself—the LORD God Almighty declares:

"I abhor the pride of Jacob
and detest his fortresses;
I will deliver up the city
and everything in it."

⁹If ten men are left in one house, they
too will die. ¹⁰And if a relative who is to
burn the bodies comes to carry them out
of the house and asks anyone still hiding
there, "Is anyone with you?" and he says,
"No," then he will say, "Hush! We must not
mention the name of the LORD."

¹¹For the LORD has given the command,
and he will smash the great house
into pieces
and the small house into bits.

¹²Do horses run on the rocky crags?
Does one plow there with oxen?
But you have turned justice into poison
and the fruit of righteousness into
bitterness—
¹³you who rejoice in the conquest of Lo
Debarᶜ

ᵃ22 Traditionally *peace offerings*   ᵇ26 Or *lifted up*
*Sakkuth your king / and Kaiwan your idols, / your
star-gods*; Septuagint *lifted up the shrine of Molech
/ and the star of your god Rephan, / their idols*
ᶜ13 *Lo Debar* means *nothing*.

and say, "Did we not take Karnaim*a* by our own strength?"

14 For the LORD God Almighty declares,
"I will stir up a nation against you,
  O house of Israel,
that will oppress you all the way
  from Lebo*b* Hamath to the valley of
  the Arabah."

Locusts, Fire and a Plumb Line

7 This is what the Sovereign LORD showed me: He was preparing swarms of locusts after the king's share had been harvested and just as the second crop was coming up. **2** When they had stripped the land clean, I cried out, "Sovereign LORD, forgive! How can Jacob survive? He is so small!"

3 So the LORD relented.
"This will not happen," the LORD said.
4 This is what the Sovereign LORD showed me: The Sovereign LORD was calling for judgment by fire; it dried up the great deep and devoured the land. **5** Then I cried out, "Sovereign LORD, I beg you, stop! How can Jacob survive? He is so small!"

6 So the LORD relented.
"This will not happen either," the Sovereign LORD said.

7 This is what he showed me: The Lord was standing by a wall that had been built true to plumb, with a plumb line in his hand. **8** And the LORD asked me, "What do you see, Amos?"

"A plumb line," I replied.

Then the Lord said, "Look, I am setting a plumb line among my people Israel; I will spare them no longer.

9 "The high places of Isaac will be
    destroyed
  and the sanctuaries of Israel will be
    ruined;
  with my sword I will rise against the
    house of Jeroboam."

Amos and Amaziah

10 Then Amaziah the priest of Bethel sent a message to Jeroboam king of Israel: "Amos is raising a conspiracy against you in the very heart of Israel. The land cannot bear all his words. **11** For this is what Amos is saying:

" 'Jeroboam will die by the sword,
    and Israel will surely go into exile,
    away from their native land.' "

12 Then Amaziah said to Amos, "Get out, you seer! Go back to the land of Judah. Earn your bread there and do your prophesying there. **13** Don't prophesy anymore at Bethel, because this is the king's sanctuary and the temple of the kingdom."

14 Amos answered Amaziah, "I was neither a prophet nor a prophet's son, but I was a shepherd, and I also took care of sycamore-fig trees. **15** But the LORD took me from tending the flock and said to me, 'Go, prophesy to my people Israel.' **16** Now then, hear the word of the LORD. You say,

" 'Do not prophesy against Israel,
    and stop preaching against the
      house of Isaac.'

17 "Therefore this is what the LORD says:

" 'Your wife will become a prostitute in
    the city,
  and your sons and daughters will fall
    by the sword.
Your land will be measured and
    divided up,
  and you yourself will die in a pagan*c*
    country.
And Israel will certainly go into exile,
    away from their native land.' "

A Basket of Ripe Fruit

8 This is what the Sovereign LORD showed me: a basket of ripe fruit. **2** "What do you see, Amos?" he asked.

"A basket of ripe fruit," I answered.

Then the LORD said to me, "The time is ripe for my people Israel; I will spare them no longer.

3 "In that day," declares the Sovereign LORD, "the songs in the temple will turn to wailing.*d* Many, many bodies—flung everywhere! Silence!"

4 Hear this, you who trample the needy
  and do away with the poor of the
    land,

5 saying,

"When will the New Moon be over
    that we may sell grain,
and the Sabbath be ended
    that we may market wheat?"—
skimping the measure,
  boosting the price
  and cheating with dishonest scales,
6 buying the poor with silver

---

a13 Karnaim means *horns; horn* here symbolizes strength.   *b14* Or *from the entrance to*   *c17* Hebrew *an unclean*   *d3* Or *"the temple singers will wail*

and the needy for a pair of sandals,
  selling even the sweepings with the
    wheat.

⁷The LORD has sworn by the Pride of Jacob: "I will never forget anything they have done.

⁸"Will not the land tremble for this,
  and all who live in it mourn?
The whole land will rise like the Nile;
  it will be stirred up and then sink
    like the river of Egypt.

⁹"In that day," declares the Sovereign LORD,

"I will make the sun go down at
    noon
  and darken the earth in broad
    daylight.
¹⁰I will turn your religious feasts into
    mourning
  and all your singing into weeping.
I will make all of you wear sackcloth
  and shave your heads.
I will make that time like mourning for
    an only son
  and the end of it like a bitter day.

¹¹"The days are coming," declares the
    Sovereign LORD,
  "when I will send a famine through
    the land—
not a famine of food or a thirst for
    water,
  but a famine of hearing the words of
    the LORD.
¹²Men will stagger from sea to sea
  and wander from north to east,
searching for the word of the LORD,
  but they will not find it.

¹³"In that day

"the lovely young women and strong
    young men
  will faint because of thirst.
¹⁴They who swear by the shame[a] of
    Samaria,
  or say, 'As surely as your god lives,
    O Dan,'
or, 'As surely as the god[b] of Beersheba
    lives'—
they will fall,
  never to rise again."

Israel to Be Destroyed

9 I saw the Lord standing by the altar, and he said:

"Strike the tops of the pillars
  so that the thresholds shake.

Bring them down on the heads of all
    the people;
  those who are left I will kill with the
    sword.
Not one will get away,
  none will escape.
²Though they dig down to the depths of
    the grave,[c]
  from there my hand will take them.
Though they climb up to the heavens,
  from there I will bring them down.
³Though they hide themselves on the
    top of Carmel,
  there I will hunt them down and
    seize them.
Though they hide from me at the
    bottom of the sea,
  there I will command the serpent to
    bite them.
⁴Though they are driven into exile by
    their enemies,
  there I will command the sword to
    slay them.
I will fix my eyes upon them
  for evil and not for good."

⁵The Lord, the LORD Almighty,
  he who touches the earth and it
    melts,
  and all who live in it mourn—
the whole land rises like the Nile,
  then sinks like the river of Egypt—
⁶he who builds his lofty palace[d] in the
    heavens
  and sets its foundation[e] on the earth,
who calls for the waters of the sea
  and pours them out over the face of
    the land—
  the LORD is his name.

⁷"Are not you Israelites
  the same to me as the Cushites[f]?"
            declares the LORD.
"Did I not bring Israel up from Egypt,
  the Philistines from Caphtor[g]
  and the Arameans from Kir?

⁸"Surely the eyes of the Sovereign LORD
  are on the sinful kingdom.
I will destroy it
  from the face of the earth—
yet I will not totally destroy
  the house of Jacob,"
            declares the LORD.
⁹"For I will give the command,

---

[a]14 Or by Ashima; or by the idol   [b]14 Or power
[c]2 Hebrew to Sheol   [d]6 The meaning of the Hebrew
for this phrase is uncertain.   [e]6 The meaning of
the Hebrew for this word is uncertain.   [f]7 That is,
people from the upper Nile region   [g]7 That is,
Crete

and I will shake the house of Israel
among all the nations
as grain is shaken in a sieve,
and not a pebble will reach the
ground.
[10] All the sinners among my people
will die by the sword,
all those who say,
'Disaster will not overtake or meet us.'

Israel's Restoration

[11] "In that day I will restore
David's fallen tent.
I will repair its broken places,
restore its ruins,
and build it as it used to be,
[12] so that they may possess the remnant
of Edom
and all the nations that bear my
name,[a]"
declares the LORD,
who will do these things.

[13] "The days are coming," declares the
LORD,

"when the reaper will be overtaken by
the plowman
and the planter by the one treading
grapes.
New wine will drip from the
mountains
and flow from all the hills.
[14] I will bring back my exiled[b] people
Israel;
they will rebuild the ruined cities
and live in them.
They will plant vineyards and drink
their wine;
they will make gardens and eat their
fruit.
[15] I will plant Israel in their own land,
never again to be uprooted
from the land I have given them,"

says the LORD your God.

[a]12 Hebrew; Septuagint *so that the remnant of
men / and all the nations that bear my name
may seek the Lord*   [b]14 Or *will restore the
fortunes of my*

Haughtiness is a disease—one that afflicts everyone who doesn't have it! Proud people are so often blind to their own arrogance that they make everyone else sick. The book of Obadiah is only twenty-one verses long, but it contains a solid reminder of this truth.

Imagine that you are an Edomite soldier who is about to swoop down on the floundering Israelites. One morning you unfold the newspaper and read these headlines: "Though you soar like the eagle and make your nest among the stars, from there I will bring you down" (v. 4). How would you feel?

Obadiah's searing message to Edom wasn't just for them. The Bible is laced with this truth: If you're proud, you'll fall. God wants you to boast only in *his* power and might. Then his love will give you a quiet confidence and the humility to be the man he wants you to be—a husband, a father, a friend. Obadiah knew all about this.

Obadiah

¹The vision of Obadiah.

This is what the Sovereign LORD says about Edom—

We have heard a message from the
LORD:
    An envoy was sent to the nations to
        say,
"Rise, and let us go against her for
        battle"—

²"See, I will make you small among the
        nations;
    you will be utterly despised.
³The pride of your heart has deceived
        you,
    you who live in the clefts of the
        rocks*a*
    and make your home on the heights,
you who say to yourself,

    'Who can bring me down to the
        ground?'
⁴Though you soar like the eagle
    and make your nest among the stars,
    from there I will bring you down,"
                    declares the LORD.
⁵"If thieves came to you,
    if robbers in the night—
Oh, what a disaster awaits you—
    would they not steal only as much as
        they wanted?
If grape pickers came to you,
    would they not leave a few
        grapes?
⁶But how Esau will be ransacked,
    his hidden treasures pillaged!
⁷All your allies will force you to the
        border;

a3 Or of Sela

your friends will deceive and
  overpower you;
those who eat your bread will set a trap
  for you,[a]
but you will not detect it.

[8] "In that day," declares the LORD,
  "will I not destroy the wise men of
  Edom,
  men of understanding in the
  mountains of Esau?
[9] Your warriors, O Teman, will be
  terrified,
  and everyone in Esau's mountains

will be cut down in the slaughter.
[10] Because of the violence against your
  brother Jacob,
  you will be covered with shame;
  you will be destroyed forever.
[11] On the day you stood aloof
  while strangers carried off his wealth
  and foreigners entered his gates
  and cast lots for Jerusalem,
  you were like one of them.

---

[a]7 The meaning of the Hebrew for this clause is
uncertain.

I'm Going to Bring You Down

DAILY INSIGHT

FRIDAY
Passage:
Obadiah 1–4
Verse:
Obadiah 4

In his prime, Muhammad Ali was, according to many experts, the best boxer ever to step into the ring. He was also very good for the sport, assuming that lots of publicity for such a brutal sport could be called "good."

As a teenager, I can recall watching this brash young fighter, wagging his finger at an opponent. His verbal taunts were as relentless as his left jab. "I'm going to bring you down," he told Floyd Patterson, the reigning heavyweight champion of the world, in 1965. And Ali took him down. In the years to follow, Muhammad Ali directed his pointed finger and audacious claims in the faces of the likes of the behemoth Sonny Liston and the mighty Joe Frazier. In those days, there wasn't a boxer alive who didn't fear the great Ali. No boxer could stand under his pitiless attack.

One of the most often repeated themes in the Bible is this: When our hearts become proud, God will, in his own way, level us out. "Though you soar like an eagle and make your nest among the stars, from there I will bring you down," God told his contemptuous people through the prophet Obadiah.

In time, even the stupendous Muhammad Ali went down ... his age and his own poor health became the supreme victors.

"Pride goes before destruction, a haughty spirit before a fall" (Proverbs 16:18), Solomon warned. "A man's pride brings him low, but a man of lowly spirit gains honor"

(29:23). "The meek shall inherit the earth," Jesus would tell his followers centuries later.

There are two important principles at work here. First, God will use whatever and whomever he chooses to humble his people. Muhammad Ali wasn't exactly a modest character himself, yet God may use someone just like this in your life to bring you to a place of submission before him. While we may question his tactics, God's goal is to create a contrite heart in us, and he'll use whatever it takes to get us there (see also Romans 9:17).

Second, humility—a servant's heart and a gentle tongue—is the natural consequence of a grateful spirit. Yet humility is one of those elusive goals that you must *forget* in order to achieve! The more you try to not think about yourself, the more difficult it will be for you to be humble.

Humility is the by-product of something else. It's the result of understanding one's own sinfulness and God's holiness. It's the consequence of one's daily commitment to pursue his righteousness. Humility comes when one discovers who one is in Christ, accepts one's place before him, then forgets all of that and obediently pursues him.

Our God is a mighty God. He has called us to be his followers. He is the One who deserves all the glory. Kind of makes you proud just thinking about it, doesn't it?

For your next devotional reading, go to page 988.

¹²You should not look down on your
    brother
  in the day of his misfortune,
nor rejoice over the people of Judah
  in the day of their destruction,
nor boast so much
  in the day of their trouble.
¹³You should not march through the
    gates of my people
  in the day of their disaster,
nor look down on them in their
    calamity
  in the day of their disaster,
nor seize their wealth
  in the day of their disaster.
¹⁴You should not wait at the crossroads
  to cut down their fugitives,
nor hand over their survivors
  in the day of their trouble.

¹⁵ "The day of the LORD is near
  for all nations.
As you have done, it will be done to
    you;
  your deeds will return upon your
    own head.
¹⁶Just as you drank on my holy hill,
  so all the nations will drink
    continually;
they will drink and drink
  and be as if they had never been.
¹⁷But on Mount Zion will be
    deliverance;

it will be holy,
  and the house of Jacob
  will possess its inheritance.
¹⁸The house of Jacob will be a fire
  and the house of Joseph a flame;
the house of Esau will be stubble,
  and they will set it on fire and
    consume it.
There will be no survivors
  from the house of Esau."
              The LORD has spoken.

¹⁹People from the Negev will occupy
  the mountains of Esau,
and people from the foothills will
    possess
  the land of the Philistines.
They will occupy the fields of Ephraim
  and Samaria,
  and Benjamin will possess Gilead.
²⁰This company of Israelite exiles who
    are in Canaan
  will possess the land as far as
    Zarephath;
the exiles from Jerusalem who are in
    Sepharad
  will possess the towns of the Negev.
²¹Deliverers will go up onᵃ Mount
    Zion
  to govern the mountains of Esau.
  And the kingdom will be the LORD's.

ᵃ21 Or *from*

HEY DAD

Is being proud good or bad?

Text: Obadiah 3–4

Pride can be a good thing, and pride can be a bad thing.

  When someone "takes pride" in his work, it is generally considered a good thing. We value those who have a high standard and who do quality work. We also hear people say "be proud of who you are" or "be proud of your name." Again, these are good things. These statements tell us that we shouldn't feel embarrassed about the way we look or think or about our work or family.

  But sinful pride doesn't only enjoy having something, it enjoys having *more* of it than the next person. This kind of pride makes us happy that we have more money or a better job or better toys than someone else. It's in the *comparison* that we become proud.

  Sinful pride is a very dangerous thing. For to know God is to understand that we have no reason to boast. It was this kind of pride that turned an angel into Satan himself (Luke 10:18, Revelation 12:3–9). Everything we have has been given to us by our heavenly Father.

  So, take pleasure in a job well done or in pleasing someone important to you. Take pleasure in your son's or daughter's or father's or mother's achievements. But beware of thinking yourself better than those around you (see Philippians 2:3).

For a complete listing of Questions Kids Ask, turn to page 1435.

"Hide and seek" is a favorite childhood game. It seems as if young children never tire of it. One of the things that small children learn early on is that if they select just the right little space to tuck themselves into, they become literally "unfindable." Searching for such a child is usually in vain, until Dad gets to know the best hiding places.

Although he should have known better, Jonah thought he could hide from God by slipping himself into the belly of a ship headed for Spain. Sure enough, the book of Jonah is filled with adventure, suspense, and intrigue. But don't be misled. The message of this story is not about a boat going west, a storm tearing the craft apart, or even a big fish. The story of Jonah reminds us that wherever we are, however we're acting, whatever we're thinking, we cannot hide from the living God. He's well aware of the trickiest hiding places—be they physical, mental or emotional—and he cannot be given the slip. What's more, God can and does choose to use us to accomplish his purposes, whatever those may be.

Jonah

Jonah Flees From the LORD

1 The word of the LORD came to Jonah son of Amittai: ²"Go to the great city of Nineveh and preach against it, because its wickedness has come up before me."

³But Jonah ran away from the LORD and headed for Tarshish. He went down to Joppa, where he found a ship bound for that port. After paying the fare, he went aboard and sailed for Tarshish to flee from the LORD.

⁴Then the LORD sent a great wind on the sea, and such a violent storm arose that the ship threatened to break up. ⁵All the sailors were afraid and each cried out to his own god. And they threw the cargo into the sea to lighten the ship.

But Jonah had gone below deck, where he lay down and fell into a deep sleep. ⁶The captain went to him and said, "How can you sleep? Get up and call on your god! Maybe he will take notice of us, and we will not perish."

⁷Then the sailors said to each other, "Come, let us cast lots to find out who is responsible for this calamity." They cast lots and the lot fell on Jonah.

⁸So they asked him, "Tell us, who is responsible for making all this trouble for

You Can't Do That!

Key Verse: *"But Jonah ran away from the Lord and headed for Tarshish . . . to flee from the Lord."* Jonah 1:3

Text: Jonah 1:1–17 *(Dad or child reads the text.)*

QUIET TIMES WITH Dad

DAD READS: What would happen if a basketball player decided to run with the ball instead of dribbling it? What would happen if a hockey player picked up the puck and threw it into the goal with his hand? What would happen if a baseball player decided to run to third base from home plate instead of first base?

Child reads: If I was watching a game on television and saw the athletes doing these things, I'd probably say right out loud, "Hey, you can't do that!" All of these sports have rules, and when a player decides to break a rule, one of the referees will stop him. Players have to obey the rules or else they can't play.

DAD READS: Jonah was something like one of those athletes. He knew God, and he knew the rules. One of those rules was that he should never disobey God. But when God gave him an assignment, Jonah decided to break the rules and go his own way. When Jonah did this, God turned everything upside down.

Child reads: Yes, Jonah should have known better. He was foolish to try to run away from God. He should have known that God would punish him if he disobeyed. And God did punish Jonah by allowing him to spend three days inside of a great fish.

DAD READS: The story of Jonah is a very important story for you and me. It tells us that if we don't listen to God and if we try to run away, we will not be happy. We will feel like Jonah did in the middle of the storm.

Child reads: When we tell God that we are sorry for disobeying him, we will feel calm, just like the men on the boat did after the storm. God will let us know that he has forgiven us by helping us to feel peaceful and clean.

DAD READS: Then God will give us another chance to obey him, just like he gave Jonah a second chance. When God told Jonah what to do after the fish brought him back to the beach, Jonah obeyed God. He knew better than to disobey God again.

Child reads: Sometimes you and I disobey. Although we know the rules, we disobey anyway. But we should know better.

DAD READS: I want to follow God's rules. I want to be honest and truthful. I want to be kind to others. I know you do, too. Let me pray this prayer with you:

Our Father in heaven, we love you.

Thank you for the story of Jonah.

We don't want to make you unhappy.

And we don't want to have to go

through storms like Jonah did.

Please help us to always remember

to obey you. And thank you for

forgiving us when we don't. We love

you. In Jesus' name, **Amen.**

For your next devotional reading, go to page 992.

us? What do you do? Where do you come from? What is your country? From what people are you?"

⁹He answered, "I am a Hebrew and I worship the LORD, the God of heaven, who made the sea and the land."

¹⁰This terrified them and they asked, "What have you done?" (They knew he was running away from the LORD, because he had already told them so.)

¹¹The sea was getting rougher and rougher. So they asked him, "What should we do to you to make the sea calm down for us?"

¹²"Pick me up and throw me into the sea," he replied, "and it will become calm. I know that it is my fault that this great storm has come upon you."

¹³Instead, the men did their best to row back to land. But they could not, for the sea grew even wilder than before. ¹⁴Then they cried to the LORD, "O LORD, please do not let us die for taking this man's life. Do not hold us accountable for killing an innocent man, for you, O LORD, have done as you pleased." ¹⁵Then they took Jonah and threw him overboard, and the raging sea grew calm. ¹⁶At this the men greatly feared the LORD, and they offered a

sacrifice to the LORD and made vows to him.

¹⁷But the LORD provided a great fish to swallow Jonah, and Jonah was inside the fish three days and three nights.

Jonah's Prayer

2 From inside the fish Jonah prayed to the LORD his God. ²He said:

"In my distress I called to the LORD,
  and he answered me.
From the depths of the grave*a* I called
    for help,
  and you listened to my cry.
³You hurled me into the deep,
  into the very heart of the seas,
  and the currents swirled about me;
all your waves and breakers
  swept over me.
⁴I said, 'I have been banished
  from your sight;
yet I will look again
  toward your holy temple.'
⁵The engulfing waters threatened
  me,*b*
  the deep surrounded me;

---

*a*2 Hebrew *Sheol*   *b*5 Or *waters were at my throat*

HEY DAD

Can a man really live inside a fish for three days?

Text: Jonah 1:17

Amazingly, besides the Biblical story of Jonah, other historical accounts document people surviving inside a fish for several days.

One such story recounts an incident that happened off the coast of Maine in the early 1900's. Several fishermen out on a small boat were trying to land a huge fish. They had been successful in bringing the fish close to the boat and were trying to kill it with their harpoons and spears. Unexpectedly, the fish gave a violent flip of its tail, knocking one of the fishermen into the water. The fish turned, swallowed the man, and swam away.

Three days later, the fishermen hooked this same fish again and were able to drag it to shore. Cutting open its belly, they found their friend inside, still alive. His skin was bleached white from the fish's stomach acid, and he was seriously disoriented. But within a few weeks, he was completely well.

In the New Testament, Jesus refers to Jonah and the big fish as a historical event. He says, "For as Jonah was for three days and three nights in the belly of a huge fish ..." (Matthew 12:40). It's just like we would say, "As Abraham Lincoln was the president of the United States ..." or "As Aunt Peggy had us over for dinner last Thanksgiving ..."

Remember that God created Jonah, and he created the big fish, too. God created the air that Jonah breathed inside the fish's belly and whatever Jonah ate or drank during his voyage. (Don't spend too much time thinking about this one.) The story of Jonah is no fairy tale. It actually happened.

For a complete listing of Questions Kids Ask, turn to page 1435.

QUESTIONS KIDS ASK

seaweed was wrapped around my
head.
⁶To the roots of the mountains I sank
down;
the earth beneath barred me in
forever.
But you brought my life up from the pit,
O LORD my God.

⁷"When my life was ebbing away,
I remembered you, LORD,
and my prayer rose to you,
to your holy temple.

⁸"Those who cling to worthless idols
forfeit the grace that could be theirs.
⁹But I, with a song of thanksgiving,
will sacrifice to you.
What I have vowed I will make good.
Salvation comes from the LORD."

¹⁰And the LORD commanded the fish,
and it vomited Jonah onto dry land.

Jonah Goes to Nineveh

3 Then the word of the LORD came to
Jonah a second time: ²"Go to the great
city of Nineveh and proclaim to it the
message I give you."
³Jonah obeyed the word of the LORD
and went to Nineveh. Now Nineveh was a
very important city—a visit required
three days. ⁴On the first day, Jonah started
into the city. He proclaimed: "Forty more
days and Nineveh will be overturned."
⁵The Ninevites believed God. They declared a fast, and all of them, from the
greatest to the least, put on sackcloth.
⁶When the news reached the king of
Nineveh, he rose from his throne, took off
his royal robes, covered himself with
sackcloth and sat down in the dust. ⁷Then
he issued a proclamation in Nineveh:

"By the decree of the king and his
nobles:

Do not let any man or beast, herd
or flock, taste anything; do not let
them eat or drink. ⁸But let man and
beast be covered with sackcloth. Let
everyone call urgently on God. Let
them give up their evil ways and their
violence. ⁹Who knows? God may yet
relent and with compassion turn
from his fierce anger so that we will
not perish."

¹⁰When God saw what they did and how
they turned from their evil ways, he had
compassion and did not bring upon them
the destruction he had threatened.

Jonah's Anger at the LORD's Compassion

4 But Jonah was greatly displeased and
became angry. ²He prayed to the LORD,
"O LORD, is this not what I said when I was
still at home? That is why I was so quick to
flee to Tarshish. I knew that you are a gracious and compassionate God, slow to
anger and abounding in love, a God who
relents from sending calamity. ³Now,
O LORD, take away my life, for it is better
for me to die than to live."
⁴But the LORD replied, "Have you any
right to be angry?"
⁵Jonah went out and sat down at a place
east of the city. There he made himself a
shelter, sat in its shade and waited to see
what would happen to the city. ⁶Then the
LORD God provided a vine and made it
grow up over Jonah to give shade for his
head to ease his discomfort, and Jonah
was very happy about the vine. ⁷But at
dawn the next day God provided a worm,
which chewed the vine so that it withered.
⁸When the sun rose, God provided a
scorching east wind, and the sun blazed
on Jonah's head so that he grew faint. He
wanted to die, and said, "It would be better for me to die than to live."
⁹But God said to Jonah, "Do you have a
right to be angry about the vine?"
"I do," he said. "I am angry enough to
die."
¹⁰But the LORD said, "You have been
concerned about this vine, though you
did not tend it or make it grow. It sprang
up overnight and died overnight. ¹¹But
Nineveh has more than a hundred and
twenty thousand people who cannot tell
their right hand from their left, and many
cattle as well. Should I not be concerned
about that great city?"

"It's no big deal" may be an appropriate response from a man to his wife when their airplane hits a little turbulence. And if he says these words with enough confidence and surety, she's usually satisfied. But if that airplane was doing a spinning nose-dive straight down and was about to bury itself into some craggy mountainside, "It's no big deal" wouldn't do very much to allay *anyone's* anxiety.

The residents of Judah in Micah's time must have been sauntering around town, assuring each other that, in spite of their awful sin, God's judgment would be "no big deal." Then Micah came along and completely spoiled these haughty people's day. When your heavenly Father returns, Micah said, "the mountains [will] melt beneath him, and the valleys split apart, like wax before the fire, like water rushing down a slope" (1:4). No big deal? Hardly. As you read this short book, soak up this imagery and realize that God does not make light of sin.

Micah

1 The word of the LORD that came to Micah of Moresheth during the reigns of Jotham, Ahaz and Hezekiah, kings of Judah—the vision he saw concerning Samaria and Jerusalem.

² Hear, O peoples, all of you,
  listen, O earth and all who are in it,
that the Sovereign LORD may witness
    against you,
  the Lord from his holy temple.

Judgment Against Samaria and Jerusalem

³ Look! The LORD is coming from his
    dwelling place;
  he comes down and treads the high
    places of the earth.
⁴ The mountains melt beneath him
  and the valleys split apart,

like wax before the fire,
  like water rushing down a slope.
⁵ All this is because of Jacob's
    transgression,
  because of the sins of the house of
    Israel.
What is Jacob's transgression?
  Is it not Samaria?
What is Judah's high place?
  Is it not Jerusalem?

⁶ "Therefore I will make Samaria a heap
    of rubble,
  a place for planting vineyards.
I will pour her stones into the valley
  and lay bare her foundations.
⁷ All her idols will be broken to pieces;
  all her temple gifts will be burned
    with fire;
  I will destroy all her images.

Since she gathered her gifts from the
wages of prostitutes,
as the wages of prostitutes they will
again be used."

Weeping and Mourning

[8] Because of this I will weep and wail;
I will go about barefoot and naked.
I will howl like a jackal
and moan like an owl.
[9] For her wound is incurable;
it has come to Judah.
It[a] has reached the very gate of my
people,
even to Jerusalem itself.
[10] Tell it not in Gath[b];
weep not at all.[c]

In Beth Ophrah[d]
roll in the dust.
[11] Pass on in nakedness and shame,
you who live in Shaphir.[e]
Those who live in Zaanan[f]
will not come out.
Beth Ezel is in mourning;
its protection is taken from you.
[12] Those who live in Maroth[g] writhe in
pain,

[a]9 Or He   [b]10 Gath sounds like the Hebrew for tell.
[c]10 Hebrew; Septuagint may suggest not in Acco.
The Hebrew for in Acco sounds like the Hebrew for
weep.   [d]10 Beth Ophrah means house of dust.
[e]11 Shaphir means pleasant.   [f]11 Zaanan sounds
like the Hebrew for come out.   [g]12 Maroth sounds
like the Hebrew for bitter.

Just Wait until Your Father Comes Home

DAILY INSIGHT

MONDAY

Passage:
Micah 1:1–7

Verse:
Micah 1:3

Although she didn't take me up on this too many times, I made a deal with my wife when our children were young. If ever there were a "situation" that needed a dad's attention discipline-wise, I was willing to drop everything, jump in the car, and drive home from the office to deal with it.

If the situation wasn't that urgent, but still called for Dad's "heft," Bobbie would tell the girls that I'd deal with it later. "Just wait until Daddy gets home," she would say. This usually got their attention.

Gratefully, as I said, this didn't happen very often in our house. Frankly, coming home to shackled prisoners wasn't as fun as being able to celebrate my arrival with hugs and laughter. But sometimes the dad needs to be the dad.

In the passage for today, the prophet Micah does something along these lines. He was fed up with the shameless sin and disobedience he saw among the people of Israel. He was at the end of his prophetic rope, so he said to the people, "You just wait until your Father gets home. He'll deal with this." And then, just in case they thought that God was coming back for a birthday party, he reminded the people that when he comes, "the mountains melt beneath him and the valleys split apart, like

wax before the fire, like water rushing down a slope."

"Now what are we going to do?" the people must have said to each other. "We're in serious trouble."

If you and I had been among the crowd that day, we might have said, "Why don't we clean up our act right now? Then, when our heavenly Father comes to judge us, he won't be too harsh."

For centuries, people have been predicting Christ's return to earth. The sermon title, "Jesus Is Coming Soon," has appeared in church bulletins the world over. Best-selling books have been written. Songs have been sung. Bumper stickers have been slapped on the backs of cars. And, yes, Jesus is coming back in a visible body someday. This truth ought to shape our activity. As we would've suggested to the Jews in Micah's day, this ought to help us "clean up our act."

But guess what? God's "return" to his people, through his Spirit, is a daily occurrence. The fact that "our heavenly Father is going to deal with this," ought to make a difference in our conduct. And unless we favor melting mountains and splitting valleys, avoiding his heavy hand might be a good idea.

For your next devotional reading, go to page 1000.

waiting for relief,
because disaster has come from the
    LORD,
    even to the gate of Jerusalem.
¹³ You who live in Lachish,ᵃ
    harness the team to the chariot.
You were the beginning of sin
    to the Daughter of Zion,
for the transgressions of Israel
    were found in you.
¹⁴ Therefore you will give parting gifts
    to Moresheth Gath.
The town of Aczibᵇ will prove deceptive
    to the kings of Israel.
¹⁵ I will bring a conqueror against you
    who live in Mareshah.ᶜ
He who is the glory of Israel
    will come to Adullam.
¹⁶ Shave your heads in mourning
    for the children in whom you
        delight;
    make yourselves as bald as the vulture,
    for they will go from you into exile.

Man's Plans and God's

2 Woe to those who plan iniquity,
    to those who plot evil on their beds!
At morning's light they carry it out
    because it is in their power to do it.
² They covet fields and seize them,
    and houses, and take them.
They defraud a man of his home,
    a fellowman of his inheritance.

³ Therefore, the LORD says:

"I am planning disaster against this
        people,
    from which you cannot save
        yourselves.
You will no longer walk proudly,
    for it will be a time of calamity.
⁴ In that day men will ridicule you;
    they will taunt you with this
        mournful song:
'We are utterly ruined;
    my people's possession is divided up.
He takes it from me!
    He assigns our fields to traitors.' "

⁵ Therefore you will have no one in the
        assembly of the LORD
    to divide the land by lot.

False Prophets

⁶ "Do not prophesy," their prophets say.
    "Do not prophesy about these
        things;
    disgrace will not overtake us."
⁷ Should it be said, O house of Jacob:

"Is the Spirit of the LORD angry?
    Does he do such things?"

"Do not my words do good
    to him whose ways are upright?
⁸ Lately my people have risen up
    like an enemy.
You strip off the rich robe
    from those who pass by without a
        care,
    like men returning from battle.
⁹ You drive the women of my people
    from their pleasant homes.
You take away my blessing
    from their children forever.
¹⁰ Get up, go away!
    For this is not your resting place,
because it is defiled,
    it is ruined, beyond all remedy.
¹¹ If a liar and deceiver comes and says,
    'I will prophesy for you plenty of
        wine and beer,'
    he would be just the prophet for this
        people!

Deliverance Promised

¹² "I will surely gather all of you, O Jacob;
    I will surely bring together the
        remnant of Israel.
I will bring them together like sheep in
        a pen,
    like a flock in its pasture;
    the place will throng with people.
¹³ One who breaks open the way will go
        up before them;
    they will break through the gate and
        go out.
Their king will pass through before
        them,
    the LORD at their head."

Leaders and Prophets Rebuked

3 Then I said,

"Listen, you leaders of Jacob,
    you rulers of the house of Israel.
Should you not know justice,
²   you who hate good and love evil;
who tear the skin from my people
    and the flesh from their bones;
³ who eat my people's flesh,
    strip off their skin
    and break their bones in pieces;
who chop them up like meat for the
        pan,
    like flesh for the pot?"

ᵃ13 Lachish sounds like the Hebrew for team.
ᵇ14 Aczib means deception.   ᶜ15 Mareshah sounds
like the Hebrew for conqueror.

[4] Then they will cry out to the LORD,
   but he will not answer them.
At that time he will hide his face from
      them
   because of the evil they have done.

[5] This is what the LORD says:

"As for the prophets
   who lead my people astray,
if one feeds them,
   they proclaim 'peace';
if he does not,
   they prepare to wage war against him.
[6] Therefore night will come over you,
      without visions,
   and darkness, without divination.
The sun will set for the prophets,
   and the day will go dark for them.
[7] The seers will be ashamed
   and the diviners disgraced.
They will all cover their faces
   because there is no answer from
      God."

[8] But as for me, I am filled with power,
   with the Spirit of the LORD,
   and with justice and might,
to declare to Jacob his transgression,
   to Israel his sin.
[9] Hear this, you leaders of the house of
      Jacob,
   you rulers of the house of Israel,
who despise justice
   and distort all that is right;
[10] who build Zion with bloodshed,
   and Jerusalem with wickedness.
[11] Her leaders judge for a bribe,
   her priests teach for a price,
   and her prophets tell fortunes for
      money.
Yet they lean upon the LORD and say,
   "Is not the LORD among us?
   No disaster will come upon us."
[12] Therefore because of you,
   Zion will be plowed like a field,
Jerusalem will become a heap of
      rubble,
   the temple hill a mound overgrown
      with thickets.

The Mountain of the LORD

4 In the last days

the mountain of the LORD's temple will
   be established

HEY DAD

Why didn't the Israelites believe God's prophets?

Text: Micah 3:12

Many times in the Old and New Testaments, writers state that the Israelites refused to listen to the prophets whom God sent to proclaim his messages. Why didn't these people just listen to the prophets, repent and avoid God's anger?

   To begin with, some of the people thought the prophets were crazy. God often called his messengers to lead unusual lives. Ezekiel is a classic example of God calling a prophet to erratic behavior to get his point across (see Ezekiel 4, for example). And God told Hosea to marry an adulterous woman, because God wanted to show how he loved the "adulterous" Israelites who had turned to false gods. The Israelites probably thought Hosea was out of his mind.

   And although the prophets' predictions were true, often many years passed before God fulfilled these prophecies. Micah told the leaders of Israel that because of their corruption, God would reduce Israel to a heap of rubble. And God did just that—almost a hundred and twenty years later. The people didn't see imminent danger, so they didn't respond to Micah's message.

   But before we become quick to judge this attitude, we need to look at our own attitudes. The Israelites didn't believe the prophets for the same reasons we also don't believe the truth. We don't *want* to believe it. We don't want to believe that we are so evil that God could reduce our lives to a heap of rubble. We want to see the loving side of God without seeing the holy and just side.

   But we can learn from the Israelites' mistakes. Search out the truth, and ask God to help you hear—and respond to—his voice.

QUESTIONS KIDS ASK

For a complete listing of Questions Kids Ask, turn to page 1435.

as chief among the mountains;
it will be raised above the hills,
  and peoples will stream to it.

² Many nations will come and say,

"Come, let us go up to the mountain of
    the LORD,
  to the house of the God of Jacob.
He will teach us his ways,
  so that we may walk in his paths."
The law will go out from Zion,
  the word of the LORD from
    Jerusalem.
³ He will judge between many peoples
  and will settle disputes for strong
    nations far and wide.
They will beat their swords into
    plowshares
  and their spears into pruning hooks.
Nation will not take up sword against
    nation,
  nor will they train for war anymore.
⁴ Every man will sit under his own vine
  and under his own fig tree,
and no one will make them afraid,
  for the LORD Almighty has spoken.
⁵ All the nations may walk
  in the name of their gods;
we will walk in the name of the LORD
  our God for ever and ever.

The LORD's Plan

⁶ "In that day," declares the LORD,

"I will gather the lame;
  I will assemble the exiles
  and those I have brought to grief.
⁷ I will make the lame a remnant,
  those driven away a strong nation.
The LORD will rule over them in Mount
    Zion
  from that day and forever.
⁸ As for you, O watchtower of the flock,
  O stronghold*a* of the Daughter of
    Zion,
the former dominion will be restored to
    you;
  kingship will come to the Daughter
    of Jerusalem."

⁹ Why do you now cry aloud—
  have you no king?
Has your counselor perished,
  that pain seizes you like that of a
    woman in labor?
¹⁰ Writhe in agony, O Daughter of Zion,
  like a woman in labor,
for now you must leave the city
  to camp in the open field.
You will go to Babylon;

there you will be rescued.
There the LORD will redeem you
  out of the hand of your enemies.

¹¹ But now many nations
  are gathered against you.
They say, "Let her be defiled,
  let our eyes gloat over Zion!"
¹² But they do not know
  the thoughts of the LORD;
they do not understand his plan,
  he who gathers them like sheaves to
    the threshing floor.
¹³ "Rise and thresh, O Daughter of
    Zion,
  for I will give you horns of iron;
I will give you hoofs of bronze
  and you will break to pieces many
    nations."

You will devote their ill-gotten gains to
    the LORD,
  their wealth to the Lord of all the
    earth.

A Promised Ruler From Bethlehem

5 Marshal your troops, O city of troops,*b*
  for a siege is laid against us.
They will strike Israel's ruler
  on the cheek with a rod.

² "But you, Bethlehem Ephrathah,
  though you are small among the
    clans*c* of Judah,
out of you will come for me
  one who will be ruler over Israel,
whose origins*d* are from of old,
  from ancient times.*e*"

³ Therefore Israel will be abandoned
  until the time when she who is in
    labor gives birth
and the rest of his brothers return
  to join the Israelites.

⁴ He will stand and shepherd his flock
  in the strength of the LORD,
  in the majesty of the name of the
    LORD his God.
And they will live securely, for then his
    greatness
  will reach to the ends of the earth.
⁵   And he will be their peace.

Deliverance and Destruction

When the Assyrian invades our land
  and marches through our fortresses,

---

*a8 Or hill   b1 Or Strengthen your walls, O walled
city   c2 Or rulers   d2 Hebrew goings out   e2 Or
from days of eternity*

we will raise against him seven
  shepherds,
    even eight leaders of men.
[6] They will rule[a] the land of Assyria with
    the sword,
  the land of Nimrod with drawn
    sword.[b]
He will deliver us from the Assyrian
  when he invades our land
  and marches into our borders.

[7] The remnant of Jacob will be
  in the midst of many peoples
like dew from the LORD,
  like showers on the grass,
which do not wait for man
  or linger for mankind.
[8] The remnant of Jacob will be among
    the nations,
  in the midst of many peoples,
like a lion among the beasts of the
    forest,
  like a young lion among flocks of
    sheep,
which mauls and mangles as it goes,
  and no one can rescue.
[9] Your hand will be lifted up in triumph
    over your enemies,
  and all your foes will be destroyed.

[10] "In that day," declares the LORD,

"I will destroy your horses from among
    you
  and demolish your chariots.
[11] I will destroy the cities of your land
  and tear down all your strongholds.
[12] I will destroy your witchcraft
  and you will no longer cast spells.
[13] I will destroy your carved images
  and your sacred stones from among
    you;
you will no longer bow down
  to the work of your hands.
[14] I will uproot from among you your
    Asherah poles[c]
  and demolish your cities.
[15] I will take vengeance in anger and
    wrath
  upon the nations that have not
    obeyed me."

The LORD's Case Against Israel

6 Listen to what the LORD says:

"Stand up, plead your case before the
    mountains;
  let the hills hear what you have to
    say.
[2] Hear, O mountains, the LORD's
    accusation;

listen, you everlasting foundations of
    the earth.
For the LORD has a case against his
    people;
  he is lodging a charge against Israel.

[3] "My people, what have I done to you?
  How have I burdened you? Answer
    me.
[4] I brought you up out of Egypt
  and redeemed you from the land of
    slavery.
I sent Moses to lead you,
  also Aaron and Miriam.
[5] My people, remember
  what Balak king of Moab counseled
  and what Balaam son of Beor
    answered.
Remember your journey from Shittim
    to Gilgal,
  that you may know the righteous
    acts of the LORD."

[6] With what shall I come before the LORD
  and bow down before the exalted
    God?
Shall I come before him with burnt
    offerings,
  with calves a year old?
[7] Will the LORD be pleased with
    thousands of rams,
  with ten thousand rivers of oil?
Shall I offer my firstborn for my
    transgression,
  the fruit of my body for the sin of my
    soul?
[8] He has showed you, O man, what is
    good.
  And what does the LORD require of
    you?
To act justly and to love mercy
  and to walk humbly with your God.

Israel's Guilt and Punishment

[9] Listen! The LORD is calling to the city—
  and to fear your name is wisdom—
  "Heed the rod and the One who
    appointed it.[d]
[10] Am I still to forget, O wicked house,
  your ill-gotten treasures
  and the short ephah,[e] which is
    accursed?
[11] Shall I acquit a man with dishonest
    scales,
  with a bag of false weights?
[12] Her rich men are violent;

---

[a]6 Or crush   [b]6 Or Nimrod in its gates
[c]14 That is, symbols of the goddess Asherah
[d]9 The meaning of the Hebrew for this line is
uncertain.   [e]10 An ephah was a dry measure.

her people are liars
and their tongues speak deceitfully.
¹³Therefore, I have begun to destroy you,
to ruin you because of your sins.
¹⁴You will eat but not be satisfied;
your stomach will still be empty.ᵃ
You will store up but save nothing,
because what you save I will give to
the sword.
¹⁵You will plant but not harvest;
you will press olives but not use the
oil on yourselves,
you will crush grapes but not drink
the wine.
¹⁶You have observed the statutes of Omri
and all the practices of Ahab's house,
and you have followed their
traditions.
Therefore I will give you over to ruin
and your people to derision;
you will bear the scorn of the
nations.ᵇ"

Israel's Misery

7 What misery is mine!
I am like one who gathers summer fruit
at the gleaning of the vineyard;
there is no cluster of grapes to eat,
none of the early figs that I crave.
²The godly have been swept from the
land;
not one upright man remains.
All men lie in wait to shed blood;
each hunts his brother with a net.
³Both hands are skilled in doing evil;
the ruler demands gifts,
the judge accepts bribes,
the powerful dictate what they
desire—
they all conspire together.
⁴The best of them is like a brier,
the most upright worse than a thorn
hedge.
The day of your watchmen has come,
the day God visits you.
Now is the time of their confusion.
⁵Do not trust a neighbor;
put no confidence in a friend.
Even with her who lies in your embrace
be careful of your words.
⁶For a son dishonors his father,
a daughter rises up against her
mother,
a daughter-in-law against her mother-
in-law—
a man's enemies are the members of
his own household.

⁷But as for me, I watch in hope for the
LORD,

I wait for God my Savior;
my God will hear me.

Israel Will Rise

⁸Do not gloat over me, my enemy!
Though I have fallen, I will rise.
Though I sit in darkness,
the LORD will be my light.
⁹Because I have sinned against him,
I will bear the LORD's wrath,
until he pleads my case
and establishes my right.
He will bring me out into the light;
I will see his righteousness.
¹⁰Then my enemy will see it
and will be covered with shame,
she who said to me,
"Where is the LORD your God?"
My eyes will see her downfall;
even now she will be trampled
underfoot
like mire in the streets.

¹¹The day for building your walls will
come,
the day for extending your
boundaries.
¹²In that day people will come to you
from Assyria and the cities of
Egypt,
even from Egypt to the Euphrates
and from sea to sea
and from mountain to mountain.
¹³The earth will become desolate
because of its inhabitants,
as the result of their deeds.

Prayer and Praise

¹⁴Shepherd your people with your staff,
the flock of your inheritance,
which lives by itself in a forest,
in fertile pasturelands.ᶜ
Let them feed in Bashan and Gilead
as in days long ago.

¹⁵"As in the days when you came out of
Egypt,
I will show them my wonders."

¹⁶Nations will see and be ashamed,
deprived of all their power.
They will lay their hands on their
mouths
and their ears will become deaf.
¹⁷They will lick dust like a snake,
like creatures that crawl on the
ground.

ᵃ14 The meaning of the Hebrew for this word is
uncertain.   ᵇ16 Septuagint; Hebrew *scorn due my
people*   ᶜ14 Or *in the middle of Carmel*

They will come trembling out of their
    dens;
  they will turn in fear to the LORD our
    God
  and will be afraid of you.
¹⁸Who is a God like you,
  who pardons sin and forgives the
    transgression
  of the remnant of his inheritance?
You do not stay angry forever

but delight to show mercy.
¹⁹You will again have compassion
    on us;
  you will tread our sins underfoot
  and hurl all our iniquities into the
    depths of the sea.
²⁰You will be true to Jacob,
  and show mercy to Abraham,
  as you pledged on oath to our fathers
    in days long ago.

There's nothing quite as satisfying as being part of a family . . . and nothing quite as lonely as having no one who really loves you living close by. Ask the single person who lives hundreds of miles away from any relatives. How hard it can be to live day after day without feeling the warmth of loving hugs and the sound of familiar voices.

Although Nahum certainly had many hard things to say to the enemies of the Jews, his underlying message was to God's people: "The LORD is good, a refuge in times of trouble" (1:7). When you belong to God, you've got a home—a refuge where people care, where they love you as part of the team regardless of what you've done. This place is God's family. For the Israelites, Nahum was like an angry coach, nose to nose with a blind umpire, arguing his own player's case. As you read this book, imagine how the Israelites must have embraced this family, how they must have relished being on this team. And imagine how much they must have loved Nahum.

Nahum

An oracle concerning Nineveh. The book of the vision of Nahum the Elkoshite.

The LORD's Anger Against Nineveh

² The LORD is a jealous and avenging God;
the LORD takes vengeance and is filled with wrath.
The LORD takes vengeance on his foes
and maintains his wrath against his enemies.
³ The LORD is slow to anger and great in power;
the LORD will not leave the guilty unpunished.

His way is in the whirlwind and the storm,
and clouds are the dust of his feet.
⁴ He rebukes the sea and dries it up;
he makes all the rivers run dry.
Bashan and Carmel wither
and the blossoms of Lebanon fade.
⁵ The mountains quake before him
and the hills melt away.
The earth trembles at his presence,
the world and all who live in it.
⁶ Who can withstand his indignation?
Who can endure his fierce anger?
His wrath is poured out like fire;
the rocks are shattered before him.

⁷ The LORD is good,
a refuge in times of trouble.

He cares for those who trust in him,
⁸ but with an overwhelming flood
he will make an end of ˌNinevehˌ;
he will pursue his foes into darkness.

⁹Whatever they plot against the LORD
heᵃ will bring to an end;
trouble will not come a second time.
¹⁰They will be entangled among thorns
and drunk from their wine;
they will be consumed like dry
stubble.ᵇ
¹¹From you, ˌO Ninevehˌ has one come
forth

who plots evil against the LORD
and counsels wickedness.

¹²This is what the LORD says:

"Although they have allies and are
numerous,
they will be cut off and pass away.
Although I have afflicted you, ˌO Judah,ˌ
I will afflict you no more.

ᵃ9 Or *What do you foes plot against the LORD?* / He
ᵇ10 The meaning of the Hebrew for this verse is
uncertain.

Go Black. Go White. Go Believers, Whoever You Are.

Living life as a Chicago Bears fan has not been easy. Except when they won the Super Bowl in 1985, I have watched them, year after year, enter each season with high hopes and finish the regular schedule with excuses. As I said, it's not been easy, but I am still a hopelessly devoted Bears fan.

One Sunday afternoon last year I checked out the NFL fare. To my delight, the Bears' game was being televised in Tennessee, something that rarely happens. But, only a few minutes into the game, I discovered that I didn't recognize most of the players on the team. Sure, the uniforms were exactly the same ... the familiar black and white with orange trim. But despite my best efforts to be an informed fan, I knew virtually nothing about the players themselves.

How interesting, I remember thinking to myself. *Being a fan essentially means cheering for uniforms! Go black. Go white. Go orange. Go Bears, whoever you are.*

The first six verses of Nahum tell us what it's like to be wearing the wrong uniform—to be God's opponent. "The LORD takes vengeance on his foes ... the mountains quake before him ... His wrath is poured out like fire; the rocks are shattered before him." This sounds like a linebacker I'd prefer to avoid.

And then Nahum gives us a sense of what it feels like to be the home team. "The LORD is good, a refuge in times of trouble.

DAILY INSIGHT

TUESDAY

Passage:
Nahum 1:1–8

Verse:
Nahum 1:7

He cares for those who trust in him."

Many things that you and I do identify as God's children—players on his squad, if you will. Certainly, our membership in a church is an important one. This is a must. Join a fellowship close to your home and get involved.

What you say also gives people a glimpse of your "uniform." Players who love their team and their coach speak well of them, even when they're not prompted. Loyal players even look forward to practice because they know that their performance on the field is enhanced by the self-discipline of practice.

The Bible calls God's team, "the body of Christ." In sports terms, it means that those of us who call God our Father are automatically issued a new appreciation for God's ongoing grace, a new set of values, rearranged priorities, a heightened sensitivity to our own sinfulness, and a desire for right living. This "uniform" marks us as his people.

Wear this uniform today. Wear it humbly but with confidence, just like the Bears wore theirs in 1985. And by the way, your family can also be identified with your heavenly Father. Make sure each of your children has an outfit of their very own. These uniforms come in all sizes.

For your next devotional reading, go to page 1005.

¹³Now I will break their yoke from your
neck
    and tear your shackles away."

¹⁴The LORD has given a command
concerning you, ˌNinevehˌ:
    "You will have no descendants to
    bear your name.
I will destroy the carved images and
    cast idols
    that are in the temple of your gods.
I will prepare your grave,
    for you are vile."

¹⁵Look, there on the mountains,
    the feet of one who brings good
    news,
    who proclaims peace!
Celebrate your festivals, O Judah,
    and fulfill your vows.
No more will the wicked invade you;
    they will be completely destroyed.

Nineveh to Fall

2 An attacker advances against you,
    ˌNinevehˌ.
    Guard the fortress,
    watch the road,
    brace yourselves,
    marshal all your strength!

²The LORD will restore the splendor of
    Jacob
    like the splendor of Israel,
though destroyers have laid them
    waste
    and have ruined their vines.

³The shields of his soldiers are red;
    the warriors are clad in scarlet.
The metal on the chariots flashes
    on the day they are made ready;
    the spears of pine are brandished.ᵃ

⁴The chariots storm through the streets,
    rushing back and forth through the
    squares.
They look like flaming torches;
    they dart about like lightning.

⁵He summons his picked troops,
    yet they stumble on their way.
They dash to the city wall;
    the protective shield is put in place.
⁶The river gates are thrown open
    and the palace collapses.
⁷It is decreedᵇ that ˌthe cityˌ
    be exiled and carried away.
Its slave girls moan like doves
    and beat upon their breasts.
⁸Nineveh is like a pool,
    and its water is draining away.
"Stop! Stop!" they cry,

but no one turns back.
⁹Plunder the silver!
    Plunder the gold!
The supply is endless,
    the wealth from all its treasures!
¹⁰She is pillaged, plundered, stripped!
    Hearts melt, knees give way,
    bodies tremble, every face grows
    pale.

¹¹Where now is the lions' den,
    the place where they fed their young,
where the lion and lioness went,
    and the cubs, with nothing to fear?
¹²The lion killed enough for his cubs
    and strangled the prey for his mate,
filling his lairs with the kill
    and his dens with the prey.

¹³"I am against you,"
    declares the LORD Almighty.
"I will burn up your chariots in smoke,
    and the sword will devour your
    young lions.
I will leave you no prey on the earth.
The voices of your messengers
    will no longer be heard."

Woe to Nineveh

3 Woe to the city of blood,
    full of lies,
full of plunder,
    never without victims!
²The crack of whips,
    the clatter of wheels,
galloping horses
    and jolting chariots!
³Charging cavalry,
    flashing swords
    and glittering spears!
Many casualties,
    piles of dead,
bodies without number,
    people stumbling over the corpses—
⁴all because of the wanton lust of a
    harlot,
    alluring, the mistress of sorceries,
who enslaved nations by her
    prostitution
    and peoples by her witchcraft.

⁵"I am against you," declares the LORD
    Almighty.
    "I will lift your skirts over your face.
I will show the nations your nakedness
    and the kingdoms your shame.
⁶I will pelt you with filth,

ᵃ3 Hebrew; Septuagint and Syriac / the horsemen
rush to and fro   ᵇ7 The meaning of the Hebrew for
this word is uncertain.

I will treat you with contempt
and make you a spectacle.
[7] All who see you will flee from you and
say,
'Nineveh is in ruins—who will
mourn for her?'
Where can I find anyone to comfort
you?"

[8] Are you better than Thebes,[a]
situated on the Nile,
with water around her?
The river was her defense,
the waters her wall.
[9] Cush[b] and Egypt were her boundless
strength;
Put and Libya were among her allies.
[10] Yet she was taken captive
and went into exile.
Her infants were dashed to pieces
at the head of every street.
Lots were cast for her nobles,
and all her great men were put in
chains.
[11] You too will become drunk;
you will go into hiding
and seek refuge from the enemy.

[12] All your fortresses are like fig trees
with their first ripe fruit;
when they are shaken,
the figs fall into the mouth of the eater.
[13] Look at your troops—
they are all women!
The gates of your land
are wide open to your enemies;
fire has consumed their bars.

[14] Draw water for the siege,
strengthen your defenses!

Work the clay,
tread the mortar,
repair the brickwork!
[15] There the fire will devour you;
the sword will cut you down
and, like grasshoppers, consume
you.
Multiply like grasshoppers,
multiply like locusts!
[16] You have increased the number of your
merchants
till they are more than the stars of
the sky,
but like locusts they strip the land
and then fly away.
[17] Your guards are like locusts,
your officials like swarms of locusts
that settle in the walls on a cold
day—
but when the sun appears they fly
away,
and no one knows where.

[18] O king of Assyria, your shepherds[c]
slumber;
your nobles lie down to rest.
Your people are scattered on the
mountains
with no one to gather them.
[19] Nothing can heal your wound;
your injury is fatal.
Everyone who hears the news about
you
claps his hands at your fall,
for who has not felt
your endless cruelty?

---

[a]8 Hebrew *No Amon*   [b]9 That is, the upper Nile
region   [c]18 Or *rulers*

"Lord give me patience . . . and give it to me right now!" Maybe you've seen these words artfully laid out on a plaque in someone's office. Every time I see this little slogan, it makes me smile. But for the prophet Habakkuk, waiting was no laughing matter. This brave man spent his days warning the Jews who lived in Judah that their sin was going to bring spiritual and physical ruin, and that the hostile Babylonians were breathing down their necks. But Habakkuk had to be patient.

Like a Dad expecting his daughter's boyfriend to bring her home from a date, Habakkuk waited for God to act: "In our time make [your deeds] known," he pleaded (3:2). Habakkuk is all about honest questions, delayed gratification, and satisfaction in the meantime. If you hurry, you can read it in just a few minutes.

Habakkuk

1 The oracle that Habakkuk the prophet received.

Habakkuk's Complaint

² How long, O LORD, must I call for help,
    but you do not listen?
Or cry out to you, "Violence!"
    but you do not save?
³ Why do you make me look at injustice?
    Why do you tolerate wrong?
Destruction and violence are before me;
    there is strife, and conflict abounds.
⁴ Therefore the law is paralyzed,
    and justice never prevails.
The wicked hem in the righteous,
    so that justice is perverted.

The LORD's Answer

⁵ "Look at the nations and watch—
    and be utterly amazed.

For I am going to do something in your days
    that you would not believe,
    even if you were told.
⁶ I am raising up the Babylonians,ᵃ
    that ruthless and impetuous people,
who sweep across the whole earth
    to seize dwelling places not their own.
⁷ They are a feared and dreaded people;
    they are a law to themselves
    and promote their own honor.
⁸ Their horses are swifter than leopards,
    fiercer than wolves at dusk.
Their cavalry gallops headlong;
    their horsemen come from afar.
They fly like a vulture swooping to devour;
⁹   they all come bent on violence.

ᵃ6 Or *Chaldeans*

Their hordes[a] advance like a desert
    wind
  and gather prisoners like sand.
[10]They deride kings
  and scoff at rulers.
They laugh at all fortified cities;
  they build earthen ramps and
    capture them.
[11]Then they sweep past like the wind and
    go on—
  guilty men, whose own strength is
    their god."

Habakkuk's Second Complaint

[12]O LORD, are you not from everlasting?
  My God, my Holy One, we will not
    die.
O LORD, you have appointed them to
    execute judgment;
  O Rock, you have ordained them to
    punish.
[13]Your eyes are too pure to look on evil;
  you cannot tolerate wrong.
Why then do you tolerate the
    treacherous?
  Why are you silent while the wicked
    swallow up those more righteous
    than themselves?
[14]You have made men like fish in the
    sea,
  like sea creatures that have no ruler.
[15]The wicked foe pulls all of them up
    with hooks,
  he catches them in his net,
  he gathers them up in his dragnet;
  and so he rejoices and is glad.
[16]Therefore he sacrifices to his net
  and burns incense to his dragnet,
for by his net he lives in luxury
  and enjoys the choicest food.
[17]Is he to keep on emptying his net,
  destroying nations without mercy?

2 I will stand at my watch
  and station myself on the ramparts;
I will look to see what he will say to me,
  and what answer I am to give to this
    complaint.[b]

The LORD's Answer

[2]Then the LORD replied:

"Write down the revelation
  and make it plain on tablets
  so that a herald[c] may run with it.
[3]For the revelation awaits an appointed
    time;
  it speaks of the end
    and will not prove false.
Though it linger, wait for it;

it[d] will certainly come and will not
    delay.

[4]"See, he is puffed up;
  his desires are not upright—
  but the righteous will live by his
    faith[e]—
[5]indeed, wine betrays him;
  he is arrogant and never at rest.
Because he is as greedy as the grave[f]
  and like death is never satisfied,
he gathers to himself all the nations
  and takes captive all the peoples.

[6]"Will not all of them taunt him with
ridicule and scorn, saying,

" 'Woe to him who piles up stolen goods
  and makes himself wealthy by
    extortion!
How long must this go on?'
[7]Will not your debtors[g] suddenly arise?
  Will they not wake up and make you
    tremble?
  Then you will become their victim.
[8]Because you have plundered many
    nations,
  the peoples who are left will plunder
    you.
For you have shed man's blood;
  you have destroyed lands and cities
    and everyone in them.

[9]"Woe to him who builds his realm by
    unjust gain
  to set his nest on high,
  to escape the clutches of ruin!
[10]You have plotted the ruin of many
    peoples,
  shaming your own house and
    forfeiting your life.
[11]The stones of the wall will cry out,
  and the beams of the woodwork will
    echo it.

[12]"Woe to him who builds a city with
    bloodshed
  and establishes a town by crime!
[13]Has not the LORD Almighty determined
  that the people's labor is only fuel for
    the fire,
  that the nations exhaust themselves
    for nothing?
[14]For the earth will be filled with the
    knowledge of the glory of the
    LORD,
  as the waters cover the sea.

---

[a]9 The meaning of the Hebrew for this word is
uncertain. [b]1 Or *and what to answer when I am
rebuked* [c]2 Or *so that whoever reads it* [d]3 Or
Though he linger, wait for him; / he [e]4 Or
faithfulness [f]5 Hebrew *Sheol* [g]7 Or *creditors*

¹⁵ "Woe to him who gives drink to his
      neighbors,
      pouring it from the wineskin till they
      are drunk,
      so that he can gaze on their naked
      bodies.
¹⁶ You will be filled with shame instead of
      glory.
      Now it is your turn! Drink and be
      exposed[a]!

The cup from the LORD's right hand is
      coming around to you,
      and disgrace will cover your glory.
¹⁷ The violence you have done to
      Lebanon will overwhelm you,
      and your destruction of animals will
      terrify you.

a16 Masoretic Text; Dead Sea Scrolls, Aquila, Vulgate
and Syriac (see also Septuagint) and stagger

Time Is on Your Side

DAILY INSIGHT

WEDNESDAY

Passage:
Habakkuk 3:1–3, 16–19

Verse:
Habakkuk 3:19

"Time is money."

The first time I heard this phrase—probably in my first Introduction to Business class in college—I had no earthly idea what it meant. And, even though I'm sure that I learned from my textbook and my professor what "time is money" meant, I have certainly become more familiar, in these intervening years, with what it really means.

During the years that I owned a publishing business, my partner and I entertained the possibility of being purchased by larger companies on several occasions. On one of these occasions, I had disclosed my financial statements and was waiting for a response. I desperately needed the cash that this acquisition would represent and the buyer knew it. So he took his time, and I sweated it out. The more I sweated, the more he could negotiate on price. Time was money.

The prophet Habakkuk, like most of the Old Testament prophets, was running out of emotional capital ... patience. Habakkuk's task must have been overwhelming ... warning people, day after day, of the certain results of their sinfulness. Habakkuk needed a "loan." He frantically longed for some good news. So he did the only thing he could do. He entered into the Lord's presence, stood in awe of God's faithfulness, and asked for more funds: "Renew [your deeds] in our day," Habakkuk pleaded, "in our time make them known; in wrath remember mercy" (3:2).

In the midst of his oppression, Habak-

kuk cried out to God, "My heart pounded, my lips quivered ... decay crept into my bones, and my legs trembled" (3:16). Sounds like a visit to Habakkuk's banker for sure. It's almost as if the prophet was saying, "The note is coming due, heavenly Father. My creditors are circling above me."

"He owns the cattle on a thousand hills, the wealth in every mine.
He owns the rivers and the rocks and rills, the sun and stars that shine.
Wonderful riches more than tongue can tell.
He is my Father, so they're mine as well."

Although I don't think this little song had been written when Habakkuk was having his financial crisis, I do wish I could have sung it for him. Actually, as I read along, Habakkuk could have sung it to me.

"I will wait patiently ... though the fig tree does not bud and there are no grapes on the vines, though the olive crop fails and the fields produce no food, though there are no sheep in the pen and no cattle in the stalls, yet I will rejoice in the LORD" (3:16b–18).

Do you have any notes coming due? Are you fretting because someone else has all the money—and all the power? Well, get up and face your creditors. Do what you can, but do not be afraid. Since time is money and your Father has all the capital you'll ever need, you can wait this one out. Time is on *your* side.

For your next devotional reading, go to page 1008.

For you have shed man's blood;
  you have destroyed lands and cities
    and everyone in them.

¹⁸ "Of what value is an idol, since a man
      has carved it?
  Or an image that teaches lies?
For he who makes it trusts in his own
      creation;
  he makes idols that cannot speak.
¹⁹ Woe to him who says to wood, 'Come
      to life!'
  Or to lifeless stone, 'Wake up!'
Can it give guidance?
  It is covered with gold and silver;
    there is no breath in it.
²⁰ But the LORD is in his holy temple;
  let all the earth be silent before him.' "

Habakkuk's Prayer

3 A prayer of Habakkuk the prophet. On
  shigionoth.[a]

² LORD, I have heard of your fame;
  I stand in awe of your deeds, O LORD.
Renew them in our day,
  in our time make them known;
    in wrath remember mercy.

³ God came from Teman,
  the Holy One from Mount Paran.
                              Selah[b]
His glory covered the heavens
  and his praise filled the earth.
⁴ His splendor was like the sunrise;
  rays flashed from his hand,
    where his power was hidden.
⁵ Plague went before him;
  pestilence followed his steps.
⁶ He stood, and shook the earth;
  he looked, and made the nations
    tremble.
The ancient mountains crumbled
  and the age-old hills collapsed.
His ways are eternal.
⁷ I saw the tents of Cushan in distress,
  the dwellings of Midian in anguish.

⁸ Were you angry with the rivers,
    O LORD?
  Was your wrath against the streams?
Did you rage against the sea
  when you rode with your horses
    and your victorious chariots?
⁹ You uncovered your bow,
  you called for many arrows.   *Selah*

You split the earth with rivers;
¹⁰ the mountains saw you and
      writhed.
Torrents of water swept by;
  the deep roared
    and lifted its waves on high.

¹¹ Sun and moon stood still in the
      heavens
  at the glint of your flying arrows,
    at the lightning of your flashing
      spear.
¹² In wrath you strode through the earth
  and in anger you threshed the
    nations.
¹³ You came out to deliver your people,
  to save your anointed one.
You crushed the leader of the land of
    wickedness,
  you stripped him from head to foot.
                              Selah
¹⁴ With his own spear you pierced his
      head
  when his warriors stormed out to
    scatter us,
gloating as though about to devour
  the wretched who were in hiding.
¹⁵ You trampled the sea with your horses,
  churning the great waters.

¹⁶ I heard and my heart pounded,
  my lips quivered at the sound;
decay crept into my bones,
  and my legs trembled.
Yet I will wait patiently for the day of
    calamity
  to come on the nation invading us.
¹⁷ Though the fig tree does not bud
  and there are no grapes on the vines,
though the olive crop fails
  and the fields produce no food,
though there are no sheep in the pen
  and no cattle in the stalls,
¹⁸ yet I will rejoice in the LORD,
  I will be joyful in God my Savior.

¹⁹ The Sovereign LORD is my strength;
  he makes my feet like the feet of a
    deer,
  he enables me to go on the heights.

For the director of music. On my
    stringed instruments.

---

a1 Probably a literary or musical term   *b3* A word
of uncertain meaning; possibly a musical term;
also in verses 9 and 13

Have you ever said of someone, "That guy lives (or drives or eats or drinks or works) like there's no tomorrow?" What you're saying is that this person is acting like today is all he's got. He pushes himself as though no consequences will result from what he does. What a foolish man this is. Why? Because there will always be a "tomorrow." It may actually be the next day on the calendar or it may be standing in the presence of God and giving an account, but there's *going* to be a tomorrow. What you do today will mean something, somewhere in the future.

Zephaniah tried to teach this lesson to the Israelites who lived during King Josiah's reign. He proclaimed that God's silence in the face of Israel's self-destruction was a demonstration of his mercy, not of his frailty. Much of what is recorded in this book is written in the future tense. "There's going to be a tomorrow," Zephaniah was saying. "It will not be pleasant. Make no mistake about it."

Think about what you're going to do today. Then think about Zephaniah's urgent message.

Zephaniah

1 The word of the LORD that came to Zephaniah son of Cushi, the son of Gedaliah, the son of Amariah, the son of Hezekiah, during the reign of Josiah son of Amon king of Judah:

Warning of Coming Destruction

2 "I will sweep away everything
     from the face of the earth,"
                         declares the LORD.
3 "I will sweep away both men and
     animals;
   I will sweep away the birds of the air
     and the fish of the sea.

The wicked will have only heaps of
     rubble[a]
   when I cut off man from the face of
     the earth,"
                         declares the LORD.

Against Judah

4 "I will stretch out my hand against
     Judah
   and against all who live in
     Jerusalem.

[a]3 The meaning of the Hebrew for this line is uncertain.

I will cut off from this place every
　　remnant of Baal,
　the names of the pagan and the
　　idolatrous priests—
[5] those who bow down on the roofs
　　to worship the starry host,
　those who bow down and swear by the
　　LORD
　and who also swear by Molech,[a]
[6] those who turn back from following the
　　LORD
　and neither seek the LORD nor
　　inquire of him.

[7] Be silent before the Sovereign LORD,
　　for the day of the LORD is near.
　The LORD has prepared a sacrifice;
　　he has consecrated those he has
　　　invited.
[8] On the day of the LORD's sacrifice
　　I will punish the princes
　　and the king's sons
　and all those clad
　　in foreign clothes.
[9] On that day I will punish

[a]5 Hebrew *Malcam*, that is, Milcom

The Power of Unused Power

DAILY INSIGHT

THURSDAY

Passage:
Zephaniah 1:2–7a

Verse:
Zephaniah 1:7a

How fast will your car go? You don't know? Well, how high do the numbers on your speedometer go—one hundred thirty ... one forty ... one fifty? And you've probably never even approached one hundred. Right? Wow, just think of all that raw, unused power! It's enough to make your heart pound, isn't it?

If you're mechanically inclined enough to understand what's really going on under your hood, you know something about this power. You know that if you actually drove at those speeds very often, you could cause serious damage to your finely-tuned engine ... not to mention the damage you could do to your stellar driving record.

Sometimes power is more powerful when it's not used.

That principle is highlighted in today's reading. Did you notice that Zephaniah's prophecies are all written in future tense? He was telling the people of the terrible things that would happen to them if they continued in their disobedience and sinfulness. He was reminding them of something they had known all along—when God chooses to unleash his power, the results can be devastating. "Do whatever you can," Zephaniah seemed to be saying, "to avoid the Sovereign Lord's wrath and power."

In your job as a dad, you have a high-powered disciplinary engine with its own imaginary speedometer. This instrument registers numbers much higher than posted and safe speed limits. Do you have the right to push your accelerator to the floor and demonstrate some of that power? Of course you do, and sometimes that's all you can do.

But most experts agree that if you spend too much time at those high speeds, you'll do damage to yourself, not to mention those around you. So sometimes that power is more powerful when it's not used. When your children see you voluntarily holding back, they'll be impressed with—and thankful for—your restraint. They may even be willing to get in line without you having to squeeze the accelerator.

Sometimes dads are called on to use their power. Their families need the strong voice, the demonstration of authority, or the painful discipline. It's not enjoyable, but it is necessary. Yet even when you could use that power, it's usually better to hold back, leaving some of that brute force unused.

God's restraint—his mercy and his grace—is what makes him so awesome. Does he have the power to do whatever he wants? Of course he does. But most of the time it's his tenderness and patience that melts our defiance and realigns our wayward hearts.

Perhaps you need to discover the power of unused power. Your family will be grateful.

For your next devotional reading, go to page 1013.

all who avoid stepping on the
 threshold,[a]
who fill the temple of their gods
 with violence and deceit.

[10] "On that day," declares the LORD,
 "a cry will go up from the Fish Gate,
 wailing from the New Quarter,
 and a loud crash from the hills.
[11] Wail, you who live in the market
 district[b];
 all your merchants will be wiped out,
 all who trade with[c] silver will be
 ruined.
[12] At that time I will search Jerusalem
 with lamps
 and punish those who are
 complacent,
 who are like wine left on its dregs,
who think, 'The LORD will do nothing,
 either good or bad.'
[13] Their wealth will be plundered,
 their houses demolished.
They will build houses
 but not live in them;
they will plant vineyards
 but not drink the wine.

The Great Day of the LORD

[14] "The great day of the LORD is near—
 near and coming quickly.
Listen! The cry on the day of the LORD
 will be bitter,
 the shouting of the warrior there.
[15] That day will be a day of wrath,
 a day of distress and anguish,
 a day of trouble and ruin,
 a day of darkness and gloom,
 a day of clouds and blackness,
[16] a day of trumpet and battle cry
 against the fortified cities
 and against the corner towers.
[17] I will bring distress on the people
 and they will walk like blind men,
 because they have sinned against the
 LORD.
Their blood will be poured out like dust
 and their entrails like filth.
[18] Neither their silver nor their gold
 will be able to save them
 on the day of the LORD's wrath.
In the fire of his jealousy
 the whole world will be consumed,
for he will make a sudden end
 of all who live in the earth."

2 Gather together, gather together,
 O shameful nation,
[2] before the appointed time arrives
 and that day sweeps on like chaff,

before the fierce anger of the LORD
 comes upon you,
 before the day of the LORD's wrath
 comes upon you.
[3] Seek the LORD, all you humble of the
 land,
 you who do what he commands.
Seek righteousness, seek humility;
 perhaps you will be sheltered
 on the day of the LORD's anger.

Against Philistia

[4] Gaza will be abandoned
 and Ashkelon left in ruins.
At midday Ashdod will be emptied
 and Ekron uprooted.
[5] Woe to you who live by the sea,
 O Kerethite people;
the word of the LORD is against you,
 O Canaan, land of the Philistines.

"I will destroy you,
 and none will be left."

[6] The land by the sea, where the
 Kerethites[d] dwell,
will be a place for shepherds and
 sheep pens.
[7] It will belong to the remnant of the
 house of Judah;
 there they will find pasture.
In the evening they will lie down
 in the houses of Ashkelon.
The LORD their God will care for them;
 he will restore their fortunes.[e]

Against Moab and Ammon

[8] "I have heard the insults of Moab
 and the taunts of the Ammonites,
who insulted my people
 and made threats against their land.
[9] Therefore, as surely as I live,"
 declares the LORD Almighty, the God
 of Israel,
"surely Moab will become like Sodom,
 the Ammonites like Gomorrah—
a place of weeds and salt pits,
 a wasteland forever.
The remnant of my people will plunder
 them;
 the survivors of my nation will
 inherit their land."
[10] This is what they will get in return for
 their pride,
 for insulting and mocking the people
 of the LORD Almighty.

[a]9 See 1 Samuel 5:5.   [b]11 Or *the Mortar*   [c]11 Or *in*
[d]6 The meaning of the Hebrew for this word is
uncertain.   [e]7 Or *will bring back their captives*

[11] The LORD will be awesome to them
  when he destroys all the gods of the
    land.
The nations on every shore will
    worship him,
  every one in its own land.

Against Cush

[12] "You too, O Cushites,[a]
  will be slain by my sword."

Against Assyria

[13] He will stretch out his hand against the
    north
  and destroy Assyria,
leaving Nineveh utterly desolate
  and dry as the desert.
[14] Flocks and herds will lie down there,
  creatures of every kind.
The desert owl and the screech owl
  will roost on her columns.
Their calls will echo through the
    windows,
  rubble will be in the doorways,
  the beams of cedar will be exposed.
[15] This is the carefree city
  that lived in safety.
She said to herself,
  "I am, and there is none besides me."
What a ruin she has become,
  a lair for wild beasts!
All who pass by her scoff
  and shake their fists.

The Future of Jerusalem

3 Woe to the city of oppressors,
  rebellious and defiled!
[2] She obeys no one,
  she accepts no correction.
She does not trust in the LORD,
  she does not draw near to her God.
[3] Her officials are roaring lions,
  her rulers are evening wolves,
  who leave nothing for the morning.
[4] Her prophets are arrogant;
  they are treacherous men.
Her priests profane the sanctuary
  and do violence to the law.
[5] The LORD within her is righteous;
  he does no wrong.
Morning by morning he dispenses his
    justice,
  and every new day he does not fail,
  yet the unrighteous know no shame.

[6] "I have cut off nations;
  their strongholds are demolished.
I have left their streets deserted,
  with no one passing through.

Their cities are destroyed;
  no one will be left—no one at all.
[7] I said to the city,
  'Surely you will fear me
  and accept correction!'
Then her dwelling would not be cut off,
  nor all my punishments come upon
    her.
But they were still eager
  to act corruptly in all they did.
[8] Therefore wait for me," declares the
    LORD,
  "for the day I will stand up to testify.[b]
I have decided to assemble the nations,
  to gather the kingdoms
and to pour out my wrath on them—
  all my fierce anger.
The whole world will be consumed
  by the fire of my jealous anger.

[9] "Then will I purify the lips of the
    peoples,
  that all of them may call on the name
    of the LORD
  and serve him shoulder to shoulder.
[10] From beyond the rivers of Cush[c]
  my worshipers, my scattered people,
  will bring me offerings.
[11] On that day you will not be put to
    shame
  for all the wrongs you have done to
    me,
because I will remove from this city
  those who rejoice in their pride.
Never again will you be haughty
  on my holy hill.
[12] But I will leave within you
  the meek and humble,
  who trust in the name of the LORD.
[13] The remnant of Israel will do no wrong;
  they will speak no lies,
  nor will deceit be found in their
    mouths.
They will eat and lie down
  and no one will make them afraid."

[14] Sing, O Daughter of Zion;
  shout aloud, O Israel!
Be glad and rejoice with all your heart,
  O Daughter of Jerusalem!
[15] The LORD has taken away your
    punishment,
  he has turned back your enemy.
The LORD, the King of Israel, is with
    you;
  never again will you fear any harm.
[16] On that day they will say to Jerusalem,

---

[a]12 That is, people from the upper Nile region
[b]8 Septuagint and Syriac; Hebrew *will rise up to
plunder*   [c]10 That is, the upper Nile region

"Do not fear, O Zion;
do not let your hands hang limp.
[17] The LORD your God is with you,
he is mighty to save.
He will take great delight in you,
he will quiet you with his love,
he will rejoice over you with
singing."

[18] "The sorrows for the appointed feasts
I will remove from you;
they are a burden and a reproach to
you.[a]
[19] At that time I will deal
with all who oppressed you;
I will rescue the lame

and gather those who have been
scattered.
I will give them praise and honor
in every land where they were put to
shame.
[20] At that time I will gather you;
at that time I will bring you home.
I will give you honor and praise
among all the peoples of the earth
when I restore your fortunes[b]
before your very eyes,"

says the LORD.

[a]18 Or *"I will gather you who mourn for the
appointed feasts; / your reproach is a burden to
you*   [b]20 Or *I bring back your captives*

We hear a lot of talk these days about priorities, and such talk is warranted. After all, whether we realize it or not, every daily activity we engage in reflects our priorities like a mirror. Some companies even set up workshops on this issue and pay their employees to attend.

Well, if Haggai had led one such workshop, he would have had a lesson prepared about priorities. Listen to what he said to the people coming back from years in captivity: "Don't take care of your own house," he warned. "Rebuild God's house first." Now, Haggai wasn't just talking about physical structures here. His references didn't only relate to bricks and mortar. He was telling the people—and especially the men—to never put their personal desires, goals, aspirations, or even their *families*, ahead of God.

What does your day planner look like? Listen for God's word to you, through Haggai, about your priorities.

Haggai

A Call to Build the House of the LORD

1 In the second year of King Darius, on the first day of the sixth month, the word of the LORD came through the prophet Haggai to Zerubbabel son of Shealtiel, governor of Judah, and to Joshua[a] son of Jehozadak, the high priest:

²This is what the LORD Almighty says: "These people say, 'The time has not yet come for the LORD's house to be built.'"

³Then the word of the LORD came through the prophet Haggai: ⁴"Is it a time for you yourselves to be living in your paneled houses, while this house remains a ruin?"

⁵Now this is what the LORD Almighty says: "Give careful thought to your ways. ⁶You have planted much, but have harvested little. You eat, but never have enough. You drink, but never have your fill. You put on clothes, but are not warm. You earn wages, only to put them in a purse with holes in it."

⁷This is what the LORD Almighty says: "Give careful thought to your ways. ⁸Go up into the mountains and bring down timber and build the house, so that I may take pleasure in it and be honored," says the LORD. ⁹"You expected much, but see, it turned out to be little. What you brought home, I blew away. Why?" declares the LORD Almighty. "Because of my house, which remains a ruin, while each of you is busy with his own house. ¹⁰Therefore, because of you the heavens have withheld their dew and the earth its crops. ¹¹I called

---

a1 A variant of *Jeshua*; here and elsewhere in Haggai

for a drought on the fields and the mountains, on the grain, the new wine, the oil and whatever the ground produces, on men and cattle, and on the labor of your hands."

¹²Then Zerubbabel son of Shealtiel, Joshua son of Jehozadak, the high priest, and the whole remnant of the people obeyed the voice of the LORD their God and the message of the prophet Haggai, because the LORD their God had sent him. And the people feared the LORD.

¹³Then Haggai, the LORD's messenger, gave this message of the LORD to the people: "I am with you," declares the LORD. ¹⁴So the LORD stirred up the spirit of Zerubbabel son of Shealtiel, governor of Judah, and the spirit of Joshua son of Jehozadak, the high priest, and the spirit

Little Churches Everywhere

One of the most incredible facts about your body is that every single cell contains the entire formula for you. Every blood cell, every skin cell, even cells from your hair (what's left of it) tell the complete story of everything that makes you who you are.

The invention of the scientific instruments and technology that give us this information has literally transformed medicine, criminology … and the church. Let me explain.

Because they can use this technology to diagnose illnesses or learn about your tendency toward certain medical malfunctions, a physician's ability to be accurate in his diagnosis has greatly enhanced his effectiveness. And investigators who are looking for the perpetrator of a crime can use anything—hair, blood, anything—to track down the ones responsible and put them behind bars (unless, of course, those perpetrators have expensive lawyers).

"Okay," you're probably saying, "but what does this have to do with the church?"

In the time of the Old Testament, the people who worshiped at the temple lived in "paneled" homes. In these lovely homes, the father had the responsibility of leading his family into the presence of the Sovereign God every day. So these families were supposed to be the cells that made up the temple, each one containing the complete picture of what the whole church looked like.

Unfortunately, many of the dads of Haggai's time were not doing what the law required. They were neglecting their re-

DAILY INSIGHT

FRIDAY
Passage:
Haggai 1:1–8
Verses:
Haggai 1:7–8

sponsibility as the spiritual heads of their homes. What's worse, even though God's people were living in real homes, God's house was in ruin. So, through the prophet Haggai, God told the people to gather materials and build a temple to honor him.

"You have planted much, but have harvested little. You eat, but never have enough. You drink, but never have your fill. You put on clothes, but are not warm. You earn wages, only to put them in a purse with holes in it" (1:6). A quick reading of verses 7–11 reveals why this was happening. God reminded them that their poverty was not the result of *their* homelessness, but of *his*! Until a public place was built that honored God using their private homes as a model, they could expect to continue to live in spiritual squalor.

Our homes are miniature churches. They ought to reveal the complete formula of what it looks like when our heavenly Father is celebrated; where his people are respected and tenderly protected; where leadership and humility look exactly like Dad.

Our homes ought to be places where we are as comfortable talking about God's goodness and grace as we are about "What's for dinner?" or "Whose socks are these?" You are the parish minister of your family. Your neighbors are living right next door to a sanctuary. Do they know it? Show them … although I wouldn't suggest buying a steeple for your garage.

For your next devotional reading, go to page 1025.

of the whole remnant of the people. They came and began to work on the house of the LORD Almighty, their God, ¹⁵on the twenty-fourth day of the sixth month in the second year of King Darius.

The Promised Glory of the New House

2 On the twenty-first day of the seventh month, the word of the LORD came through the prophet Haggai: ²"Speak to Zerubbabel son of Shealtiel, governor of Judah, to Joshua son of Jehozadak, the high priest, and to the remnant of the people. Ask them, ³'Who of you is left who saw this house in its former glory? How does it look to you now? Does it not seem to you like nothing? ⁴But now be strong, O Zerubbabel,' declares the LORD. 'Be strong, O Joshua son of Jehozadak, the high priest. Be strong, all you people of the land,' declares the LORD, 'and work. For I am with you,' declares the LORD Almighty. ⁵'This is what I covenanted with you when you came out of Egypt. And my Spirit remains among you. Do not fear.'

⁶"This is what the LORD Almighty says: 'In a little while I will once more shake the heavens and the earth, the sea and the dry land. ⁷I will shake all nations, and the desired of all nations will come, and I will fill this house with glory,' says the LORD Almighty. ⁸'The silver is mine and the gold is mine,' declares the LORD Almighty. ⁹'The glory of this present house will be greater than the glory of the former house,' says the LORD Almighty. 'And in this place I will grant peace,' declares the LORD Almighty."

Blessings for a Defiled People

¹⁰On the twenty-fourth day of the ninth month, in the second year of Darius, the word of the LORD came to the prophet Haggai: ¹¹"This is what the LORD Almighty says: 'Ask the priests what the law says: ¹²If a person carries consecrated meat in the fold of his garment, and that fold touches some bread or stew, some wine, oil or other food, does it become consecrated?'"

The priests answered, "No."

¹³Then Haggai said, "If a person defiled by contact with a dead body touches one of these things, does it become defiled?"

"Yes," the priests replied, "it becomes defiled."

¹⁴Then Haggai said, " 'So it is with this people and this nation in my sight,' declares the LORD. 'Whatever they do and whatever they offer there is defiled.

¹⁵" 'Now give careful thought to this from this day onᵃ—consider how things were before one stone was laid on another in the LORD's temple. ¹⁶When anyone came to a heap of twenty measures, there were only ten. When anyone went to a wine vat to draw fifty measures, there were only twenty. ¹⁷I struck all the work of your hands with blight, mildew and hail, yet you did not turn to me,' declares the LORD. ¹⁸'From this day on, from this twenty-fourth day of the ninth month, give careful thought to the day when the foundation of the LORD's temple was laid. Give careful thought: ¹⁹Is there yet any seed left in the barn? Until now, the vine and the fig tree, the pomegranate and the olive tree have not borne fruit.

" 'From this day on I will bless you.' "

Zerubbabel the LORD's Signet Ring

²⁰The word of the LORD came to Haggai a second time on the twenty-fourth day of the month: ²¹"Tell Zerubbabel governor of Judah that I will shake the heavens and the earth. ²²I will overturn royal thrones and shatter the power of the foreign kingdoms. I will overthrow chariots and their drivers; horses and their riders will fall, each by the sword of his brother.

²³" 'On that day,' declares the LORD Almighty, 'I will take you, my servant Zerubbabel son of Shealtiel,' declares the LORD, 'and I will make you like my signet ring, for I have chosen you,' declares the LORD Almighty."

ᵃ15 Or *to the days past*

What kind of mileage does your car or truck get? A few decades ago when gas prices were low, we didn't worry about these kinds of things. Massive cars were marketed based on raw power and cubic inches, not on miles per gallon.

The prophet Zechariah introduces us to a fuel source that has great potential to go a long way. While it may not power an internal combustion engine, it *will* provide power and comfort to human beings. The fuel? Encouragement. The Jews to whom Zechariah spoke were devastated. They had been living in exile, and as they returned to their beloved city they saw its destruction. Their precious homes were lying in ruin. But Zechariah knew that a little encouragement goes a long way: "[The LORD] will return," he said, "and dwell in Jerusalem … The city streets will be filled with boys and girls playing there" (8:3, 5).

Even though Zechariah knew nothing about miles per gallon, he fully understood that a drop of reassurance was worth hours of hard work. Unlike black gold, encouragement is a limitless resource. It's abundant, and it's free. Help yourself.

Zechariah

A Call to Return to the LORD

1 In the eighth month of the second year of Darius, the word of the LORD came to the prophet Zechariah son of Berekiah, the son of Iddo:

²"The LORD was very angry with your forefathers. ³Therefore tell the people: This is what the LORD Almighty says: 'Return to me,' declares the LORD Almighty, 'and I will return to you,' says the LORD Almighty. ⁴Do not be like your forefathers, to whom the earlier prophets proclaimed: This is what the LORD Almighty says: 'Turn from your evil ways and your evil practices.' But they would not listen or pay attention to me, declares the LORD. ⁵Where

are your forefathers now? And the prophets, do they live forever? ⁶But did not my words and my decrees, which I commanded my servants the prophets, overtake your forefathers?

"Then they repented and said, 'The LORD Almighty has done to us what our ways and practices deserve, just as he determined to do.' "

The Man Among the Myrtle Trees

⁷On the twenty-fourth day of the eleventh month, the month of Shebat, in the second year of Darius, the word of the LORD came to the prophet Zechariah son of Berekiah, the son of Iddo.

[8]During the night I had a vision—and there before me was a man riding a red horse! He was standing among the myrtle trees in a ravine. Behind him were red, brown and white horses.

[9]I asked, "What are these, my lord?"

The angel who was talking with me answered, "I will show you what they are."

[10]Then the man standing among the myrtle trees explained, "They are the ones the LORD has sent to go throughout the earth."

[11]And they reported to the angel of the LORD, who was standing among the myrtle trees, "We have gone throughout the earth and found the whole world at rest and in peace."

[12]Then the angel of the LORD said, "LORD Almighty, how long will you withhold mercy from Jerusalem and from the towns of Judah, which you have been angry with these seventy years?" [13]So the LORD spoke kind and comforting words to the angel who talked with me.

[14]Then the angel who was speaking to me said, "Proclaim this word: This is what the LORD Almighty says: 'I am very jealous for Jerusalem and Zion, [15]but I am very angry with the nations that feel secure. I was only a little angry, but they added to the calamity.'

[16]"Therefore, this is what the LORD says: 'I will return to Jerusalem with mercy, and there my house will be rebuilt. And the measuring line will be stretched out over Jerusalem,' declares the LORD Almighty.

[17]"Proclaim further: This is what the LORD Almighty says: 'My towns will again overflow with prosperity, and the LORD will again comfort Zion and choose Jerusalem.' "

Four Horns and Four Craftsmen

[18]Then I looked up—and there before me were four horns! [19]I asked the angel who was speaking to me, "What are these?"

He answered me, "These are the horns that scattered Judah, Israel and Jerusalem."

[20]Then the LORD showed me four craftsmen. [21]I asked, "What are these coming to do?"

He answered, "These are the horns that scattered Judah so that no one could raise his head, but the craftsmen have come to terrify them and throw down these horns of the nations who lifted up their horns

against the land of Judah to scatter its people."

A Man With a Measuring Line

2 Then I looked up—and there before me was a man with a measuring line in his hand! [2]I asked, "Where are you going?"

He answered me, "To measure Jerusalem, to find out how wide and how long it is."

[3]Then the angel who was speaking to me left, and another angel came to meet him [4]and said to him: "Run, tell that young man, 'Jerusalem will be a city without walls because of the great number of men and livestock in it. [5]And I myself will be a wall of fire around it,' declares the LORD, 'and I will be its glory within.'

[6]"Come! Come! Flee from the land of the north," declares the LORD, "for I have scattered you to the four winds of heaven," declares the LORD.

[7]"Come, O Zion! Escape, you who live in the Daughter of Babylon!" [8]For this is what the LORD Almighty says: "After he has honored me and has sent me against the nations that have plundered you—for whoever touches you touches the apple of his eye— [9]I will surely raise my hand against them so that their slaves will plunder them.[a] Then you will know that the LORD Almighty has sent me.

[10]"Shout and be glad, O Daughter of Zion. For I am coming, and I will live among you," declares the LORD. [11]"Many nations will be joined with the LORD in that day and will become my people. I will live among you and you will know that the LORD Almighty has sent me to you. [12]The LORD will inherit Judah as his portion in the holy land and will again choose Jerusalem. [13]Be still before the LORD, all mankind, because he has roused himself from his holy dwelling."

Clean Garments for the High Priest

3 Then he showed me Joshua[b] the high priest standing before the angel of the LORD, and Satan[c] standing at his right side to accuse him. [2]The LORD said to Satan, "The LORD rebuke you, Satan! The LORD, who has chosen Jerusalem, rebuke you! Is not this man a burning stick snatched from the fire?"

[3]Now Joshua was dressed in filthy

---

[a]8,9 Or says after . . . eye: [9]"I . . . plunder them."   [b]1 A variant of Jeshua; here and elsewhere in Zechariah   [c]1 Satan means accuser.

clothes as he stood before the angel. ⁴The angel said to those who were standing before him, "Take off his filthy clothes."

Then he said to Joshua, "See, I have taken away your sin, and I will put rich garments on you."

⁵Then I said, "Put a clean turban on his head." So they put a clean turban on his head and clothed him, while the angel of the LORD stood by.

⁶The angel of the LORD gave this charge to Joshua: ⁷"This is what the LORD Almighty says: 'If you will walk in my ways and keep my requirements, then you will govern my house and have charge of my courts, and I will give you a place among these standing here.

⁸"'Listen, O high priest Joshua and your associates seated before you, who are men symbolic of things to come: I am going to bring my servant, the Branch. ⁹See, the stone I have set in front of Joshua! There are seven eyes*ᵃ* on that one stone, and I will engrave an inscription on it,' says the LORD Almighty, 'and I will remove the sin of this land in a single day.

¹⁰"'In that day each of you will invite his neighbor to sit under his vine and fig tree,' declares the LORD Almighty."

The Gold Lampstand and the Two Olive Trees

4 Then the angel who talked with me returned and wakened me, as a man is wakened from his sleep. ²He asked me, "What do you see?"

I answered, "I see a solid gold lampstand with a bowl at the top and seven lights on it, with seven channels to the lights. ³Also there are two olive trees by it, one on the right of the bowl and the other on its left."

⁴I asked the angel who talked with me, "What are these, my lord?"

⁵He answered, "Do you not know what these are?"

"No, my lord," I replied.

⁶So he said to me, "This is the word of the LORD to Zerubbabel: 'Not by might nor by power, but by my Spirit,' says the LORD Almighty.

⁷"What*ᵇ* are you, O mighty mountain? Before Zerubbabel you will become level ground. Then he will bring out the capstone to shouts of 'God bless it! God bless it!' "

⁸Then the word of the LORD came to me: ⁹"The hands of Zerubbabel have laid the foundation of this temple; his hands will

also complete it. Then you will know that the LORD Almighty has sent me to you.

¹⁰"Who despises the day of small things? Men will rejoice when they see the plumb line in the hand of Zerubbabel.

"(These seven are the eyes of the LORD, which range throughout the earth.)"

¹¹Then I asked the angel, "What are these two olive trees on the right and the left of the lampstand?"

¹²Again I asked him, "What are these two olive branches beside the two gold pipes that pour out golden oil?"

¹³He replied, "Do you not know what these are?"

"No, my lord," I said.

¹⁴So he said, "These are the two who are anointed to*ᶜ* serve the Lord of all the earth."

The Flying Scroll

5 I looked again—and there before me was a flying scroll!

²He asked me, "What do you see?"

I answered, "I see a flying scroll, thirty feet long and fifteen feet wide.*ᵈ*"

³And he said to me, "This is the curse that is going out over the whole land; for according to what it says on one side, every thief will be banished, and according to what it says on the other, everyone who swears falsely will be banished. ⁴The LORD Almighty declares, 'I will send it out, and it will enter the house of the thief and the house of him who swears falsely by my name. It will remain in his house and destroy it, both its timbers and its stones.' "

The Woman in a Basket

⁵Then the angel who was speaking to me came forward and said to me, "Look up and see what this is that is appearing."

⁶I asked, "What is it?"

He replied, "It is a measuring basket.*ᵉ*" And he added, "This is the iniquity*ᶠ* of the people throughout the land."

⁷Then the cover of lead was raised, and there in the basket sat a woman! ⁸He said, "This is wickedness," and he pushed her back into the basket and pushed the lead cover down over its mouth.

⁹Then I looked up—and there before me were two women, with the wind in their wings! They had wings like those of a

*ᵃ*9 Or *facets* *ᵇ*7 Or *Who* *ᶜ*14 Or *two who bring oil and* *ᵈ*2 Hebrew *twenty cubits long and ten cubits wide* (about 9 meters long and 4.5 meters wide) *ᵉ*6 Hebrew *an ephah*; also in verses 7-11 *ᶠ*6 Or *appearance*

stork, and they lifted up the basket between heaven and earth.

¹⁰"Where are they taking the basket?" I asked the angel who was speaking to me.

¹¹He replied, "To the country of Babylonia*ᵃ* to build a house for it. When it is ready, the basket will be set there in its place."

Four Chariots

6 I looked up again—and there before me were four chariots coming out from between two mountains—mountains of bronze! ²The first chariot had red horses, the second black, ³the third white, and the fourth dappled—all of them powerful. ⁴I asked the angel who was speaking to me, "What are these, my lord?"

⁵The angel answered me, "These are the four spirits*ᵇ* of heaven, going out from standing in the presence of the Lord of the whole world. ⁶The one with the black horses is going toward the north country, the one with the white horses toward the west,*ᶜ* and the one with the dappled horses toward the south."

⁷When the powerful horses went out, they were straining to go throughout the earth. And he said, "Go throughout the earth!" So they went throughout the earth.

⁸Then he called to me, "Look, those going toward the north country have given my Spirit*ᵈ* rest in the land of the north."

A Crown for Joshua

⁹The word of the Lord came to me: ¹⁰"Take ⸢silver and gold⸣ from the exiles Heldai, Tobijah and Jedaiah, who have arrived from Babylon. Go the same day to the house of Josiah son of Zephaniah. ¹¹Take the silver and gold and make a crown, and set it on the head of the high priest, Joshua son of Jehozadak. ¹²Tell him this is what the Lord Almighty says: 'Here is the man whose name is the Branch, and he will branch out from his place and build the temple of the Lord. ¹³It is he who will build the temple of the Lord, and he will be clothed with majesty and will sit and rule on his throne. And he will be a priest on his throne. And there will be harmony between the two.' ¹⁴The crown will be given to Heldai,*ᵉ* Tobijah, Jedaiah and Hen*ᶠ* son of Zephaniah as a memorial in the temple of the Lord. ¹⁵Those who are far away will come and help to build the temple of the Lord, and you will know that the Lord Almighty has sent me to

you. This will happen if you diligently obey the Lord your God."

Justice and Mercy, Not Fasting

7 In the fourth year of King Darius, the word of the Lord came to Zechariah on the fourth day of the ninth month, the month of Kislev. ²The people of Bethel had sent Sharezer and Regem-Melech, together with their men, to entreat the Lord ³by asking the priests of the house of the Lord Almighty and the prophets, "Should I mourn and fast in the fifth month, as I have done for so many years?"

⁴Then the word of the Lord Almighty came to me: ⁵"Ask all the people of the land and the priests, 'When you fasted and mourned in the fifth and seventh months for the past seventy years, was it really for me that you fasted? ⁶And when you were eating and drinking, were you not just feasting for yourselves? ⁷Are these not the words the Lord proclaimed through the earlier prophets when Jerusalem and its surrounding towns were at rest and prosperous, and the Negev and the western foothills were settled?' "

⁸And the word of the Lord came again to Zechariah: ⁹"This is what the Lord Almighty says: 'Administer true justice; show mercy and compassion to one another. ¹⁰Do not oppress the widow or the fatherless, the alien or the poor. In your hearts do not think evil of each other.'

¹¹"But they refused to pay attention; stubbornly they turned their backs and stopped up their ears. ¹²They made their hearts as hard as flint and would not listen to the law or to the words that the Lord Almighty had sent by his Spirit through the earlier prophets. So the Lord Almighty was very angry.

¹³" 'When I called, they did not listen; so when they called, I would not listen,' says the Lord Almighty. ¹⁴'I scattered them with a whirlwind among all the nations, where they were strangers. The land was left so desolate behind them that no one could come or go. This is how they made the pleasant land desolate.' "

The Lord Promises to Bless Jerusalem

8 Again the word of the Lord Almighty came to me. ²This is what the Lord Almighty says: "I am very jealous for Zion; I am burning with jealousy for her."

ᵃ11 Hebrew Shinar   ᵇ5 Or winds   ᶜ6 Or horses after them   ᵈ8 Or spirit   ᵉ14 Syriac; Hebrew Helem   ᶠ14 Or and the gracious one, the

³This is what the LORD says: "I will return to Zion and dwell in Jerusalem. Then Jerusalem will be called the City of Truth, and the mountain of the LORD Almighty will be called the Holy Mountain."

⁴This is what the LORD Almighty says: "Once again men and women of ripe old age will sit in the streets of Jerusalem, each with cane in hand because of his age. ⁵The city streets will be filled with boys and girls playing there."

⁶This is what the LORD Almighty says: "It may seem marvelous to the remnant of this people at that time, but will it seem marvelous to me?" declares the LORD Almighty.

⁷This is what the LORD Almighty says: "I will save my people from the countries of the east and the west. ⁸I will bring them back to live in Jerusalem; they will be my people, and I will be faithful and righteous to them as their God."

⁹This is what the LORD Almighty says: "You who now hear these words spoken by the prophets who were there when the foundation was laid for the house of the LORD Almighty, let your hands be strong so that the temple may be built. ¹⁰Before that time there were no wages for man or beast. No one could go about his business safely because of his enemy, for I had turned every man against his neighbor. ¹¹But now I will not deal with the remnant of this people as I did in the past," declares the LORD Almighty.

¹²"The seed will grow well, the vine will yield its fruit, the ground will produce its crops, and the heavens will drop their dew. I will give all these things as an inheritance to the remnant of this people. ¹³As you have been an object of cursing among the nations, O Judah and Israel, so will I save you, and you will be a blessing. Do not be afraid, but let your hands be strong."

¹⁴This is what the LORD Almighty says: "Just as I had determined to bring disaster upon you and showed no pity when your fathers angered me," says the LORD Almighty, ¹⁵"so now I have determined to do good again to Jerusalem and Judah. Do not be afraid. ¹⁶These are the things you are to do: Speak the truth to each other, and render true and sound judgment in your courts; ¹⁷do not plot evil against your neighbor, and do not love to swear falsely. I hate all this," declares the LORD.

¹⁸Again the word of the LORD Almighty came to me. ¹⁹This is what the LORD Almighty says: "The fasts of the fourth, fifth, seventh and tenth months will become joyful and glad occasions and happy festivals for Judah. Therefore love truth and peace."

²⁰This is what the LORD Almighty says: "Many peoples and the inhabitants of many cities will yet come, ²¹and the inhabitants of one city will go to another and say, 'Let us go at once to entreat the LORD and seek the LORD Almighty. I myself am going.' ²²And many peoples and powerful nations will come to Jerusalem to seek the LORD Almighty and to entreat him."

²³This is what the LORD Almighty says: "In those days ten men from all languages and nations will take firm hold of one Jew by the hem of his robe and say, 'Let us go with you, because we have heard that God is with you.' "

Judgment on Israel's Enemies

An Oracle

9 The word of the LORD is against the land of Hadrach
    and will rest upon Damascus—
for the eyes of men and all the tribes of Israel
    are on the LORD—ᵃ
² and upon Hamath too, which borders on it,
    and upon Tyre and Sidon, though they are very skillful.
³ Tyre has built herself a stronghold;
    she has heaped up silver like dust,
    and gold like the dirt of the streets.
⁴ But the Lord will take away her possessions
    and destroy her power on the sea,
    and she will be consumed by fire.
⁵ Ashkelon will see it and fear;
    Gaza will writhe in agony,
    and Ekron too, for her hope will wither.
Gaza will lose her king
    and Ashkelon will be deserted.
⁶ Foreigners will occupy Ashdod,
    and I will cut off the pride of the Philistines.
⁷ I will take the blood from their mouths,
    the forbidden food from between their teeth.
Those who are left will belong to our God
    and become leaders in Judah,
    and Ekron will be like the Jebusites.

ᵃ1 Or *Damascus. / For the eye of the LORD is on all mankind, / as well as on the tribes of Israel,*

⁸ But I will defend my house
  against marauding forces.
Never again will an oppressor overrun
  my people,
  for now I am keeping watch.

The Coming of Zion's King

⁹ Rejoice greatly, O Daughter of Zion!
  Shout, Daughter of Jerusalem!
See, your king[a] comes to you,
  righteous and having salvation,
  gentle and riding on a donkey,
  on a colt, the foal of a donkey.
¹⁰ I will take away the chariots from
    Ephraim
  and the war-horses from Jerusalem,
  and the battle bow will be broken.
He will proclaim peace to the
    nations.
  His rule will extend from sea to sea
  and from the River[b] to the ends of
    the earth.[c]
¹¹ As for you, because of the blood of my
    covenant with you,
  I will free your prisoners from the
    waterless pit.
¹² Return to your fortress, O prisoners of
    hope;
  even now I announce that I will
    restore twice as much to you.
¹³ I will bend Judah as I bend my bow
  and fill it with Ephraim.
I will rouse your sons, O Zion,
  against your sons, O Greece,
  and make you like a warrior's sword.

The LORD Will Appear

¹⁴ Then the LORD will appear over
    them;
  his arrow will flash like lightning.
The Sovereign LORD will sound the
    trumpet;
  he will march in the storms of the
    south,
¹⁵   and the LORD Almighty will shield
    them.
They will destroy
  and overcome with slingstones.
They will drink and roar as with wine;
  they will be full like a bowl
  used for sprinkling[d] the corners of
    the altar.
¹⁶ The LORD their God will save them on
    that day
  as the flock of his people.
They will sparkle in his land
  like jewels in a crown.
¹⁷ How attractive and beautiful they will
    be!

Grain will make the young men
    thrive,
  and new wine the young women.

The LORD Will Care for Judah

10 Ask the LORD for rain in the
    springtime;
  it is the LORD who makes the storm
    clouds.
He gives showers of rain to men,
  and plants of the field to everyone.
² The idols speak deceit,
  diviners see visions that lie;
they tell dreams that are false,
  they give comfort in vain.
Therefore the people wander like sheep
  oppressed for lack of a shepherd.

³ "My anger burns against the
    shepherds,
  and I will punish the leaders;
for the LORD Almighty will care
  for his flock, the house of Judah,
  and make them like a proud horse in
    battle.
⁴ From Judah will come the cornerstone,
  from him the tent peg,
  from him the battle bow,
  from him every ruler.
⁵ Together they[e] will be like mighty men
  trampling the muddy streets in
    battle.
Because the LORD is with them,
  they will fight and overthrow the
    horsemen.

⁶ "I will strengthen the house of Judah
  and save the house of Joseph.
I will restore them
  because I have compassion on them.
They will be as though
  I had not rejected them,
for I am the LORD their God
  and I will answer them.
⁷ The Ephraimites will become like
    mighty men,
  and their hearts will be glad as with
    wine.
Their children will see it and be
    joyful;
  their hearts will rejoice in the LORD.
⁸ I will signal for them
  and gather them in.
Surely I will redeem them;
  they will be as numerous as before.
⁹ Though I scatter them among the
    peoples,

*a9 Or King   b10 That is, the Euphrates   c10 Or the
end of the land   d15 Or bowl, / like   e4,5 Or ruler,
all of them together. / 5They*

yet in distant lands they will
　　remember me.
They and their children will survive,
　　and they will return.
¹⁰I will bring them back from Egypt
　　and gather them from Assyria.
I will bring them to Gilead and
　　Lebanon,
　　and there will not be room enough
　　　for them.
¹¹They will pass through the sea of
　　trouble;
　　the surging sea will be subdued
　　and all the depths of the Nile will dry
　　　up.
Assyria's pride will be brought down
　　and Egypt's scepter will pass away.
¹²I will strengthen them in the LORD
　　and in his name they will walk,"
　　　　　　declares the LORD.

11 Open your doors, O Lebanon,
　　so that fire may devour your cedars!
²Wail, O pine tree, for the cedar has
　　fallen;
　　the stately trees are ruined!
Wail, oaks of Bashan;
　　the dense forest has been cut down!
³Listen to the wail of the shepherds;
　　their rich pastures are destroyed!
Listen to the roar of the lions;
　　the lush thicket of the Jordan is
　　　ruined!

Two Shepherds

⁴This is what the LORD my God says:
"Pasture the flock marked for slaughter.
⁵Their buyers slaughter them and go unpunished. Those who sell them say,
'Praise the LORD, I am rich!' Their own
shepherds do not spare them. ⁶For I will
no longer have pity on the people of the
land," declares the LORD. "I will hand
everyone over to his neighbor and his
king. They will oppress the land, and I will
not rescue them from their hands."

⁷So I pastured the flock marked for
slaughter, particularly the oppressed of
the flock. Then I took two staffs and called
one Favor and the other Union, and I pastured the flock. ⁸In one month I got rid of
the three shepherds.

The flock detested me, and I grew weary of them ⁹and said, "I will not be your
shepherd. Let the dying die, and the perishing perish. Let those who are left eat
one another's flesh."

¹⁰Then I took my staff called Favor and
broke it, revoking the covenant I had
made with all the nations. ¹¹It was re-

voked on that day, and so the afflicted of
the flock who were watching me knew it
was the word of the LORD.

¹²I told them, "If you think it best, give
me my pay; but if not, keep it." So they
paid me thirty pieces of silver.

¹³And the LORD said to me, "Throw it to
the potter"—the handsome price at
which they priced me! So I took the thirty
pieces of silver and threw them into the
house of the LORD to the potter.

¹⁴Then I broke my second staff called
Union, breaking the brotherhood between Judah and Israel.

¹⁵Then the LORD said to me, "Take again
the equipment of a foolish shepherd.
¹⁶For I am going to raise up a shepherd
over the land who will not care for the lost,
or seek the young, or heal the injured, or
feed the healthy, but will eat the meat of
the choice sheep, tearing off their hoofs.

¹⁷"Woe to the worthless shepherd,
　　who deserts the flock!
May the sword strike his arm and his
　　right eye!
May his arm be completely withered,
　　his right eye totally blinded!"

Jerusalem's Enemies to Be Destroyed

An Oracle

12 This is the word of the LORD concerning Israel. The LORD, who stretches
out the heavens, who lays the foundation
of the earth, and who forms the spirit of
man within him, declares: ²"I am going to
make Jerusalem a cup that sends all the
surrounding peoples reeling. Judah will
be besieged as well as Jerusalem. ³On that
day, when all the nations of the earth are
gathered against her, I will make Jerusalem an immovable rock for all the nations.
All who try to move it will injure themselves. ⁴On that day I will strike every horse
with panic and its rider with madness," declares the LORD. "I will keep a watchful eye
over the house of Judah, but I will blind all
the horses of the nations. ⁵Then the leaders of Judah will say in their hearts, 'The
people of Jerusalem are strong, because
the LORD Almighty is their God.'

⁶"On that day I will make the leaders of
Judah like a firepot in a woodpile, like a
flaming torch among sheaves. They will
consume right and left all the surrounding peoples, but Jerusalem will remain intact in her place.

⁷"The LORD will save the dwellings of
Judah first, so that the honor of the house

of David and of Jerusalem's inhabitants may not be greater than that of Judah. **⁸**On that day the LORD will shield those who live in Jerusalem, so that the feeblest among them will be like David, and the house of David will be like God, like the Angel of the LORD going before them. **⁹**On that day I will set out to destroy all the nations that attack Jerusalem.

Mourning for the One They Pierced

¹⁰"And I will pour out on the house of David and the inhabitants of Jerusalem a spirit*ᵃ* of grace and supplication. They will look on*ᵇ* me, the one they have pierced, and they will mourn for him as one mourns for an only child, and grieve bitterly for him as one grieves for a first-born son. **¹¹**On that day the weeping in Jerusalem will be great, like the weeping of Hadad Rimmon in the plain of Megiddo. **¹²**The land will mourn, each clan by itself, with their wives by themselves: the clan of the house of David and their wives, the clan of the house of Nathan and their wives, **¹³**the clan of the house of Levi and their wives, the clan of Shimei and their wives, **¹⁴**and all the rest of the clans and their wives.

Cleansing From Sin

13 "On that day a fountain will be opened to the house of David and the inhabitants of Jerusalem, to cleanse them from sin and impurity.

²"On that day, I will banish the names of the idols from the land, and they will be remembered no more," declares the LORD Almighty. "I will remove both the prophets and the spirit of impurity from the land. **³**And if anyone still prophesies, his father and mother, to whom he was born, will say to him, 'You must die, because you have told lies in the LORD's name.' When he prophesies, his own parents will stab him.

⁴"On that day every prophet will be ashamed of his prophetic vision. He will not put on a prophet's garment of hair in order to deceive. **⁵**He will say, 'I am not a prophet. I am a farmer; the land has been my livelihood since my youth.*ᶜ*' **⁶**If someone asks him, 'What are these wounds on your body*ᵈ*?' he will answer, 'The wounds I was given at the house of my friends.'

The Shepherd Struck, the Sheep Scattered

⁷ "Awake, O sword, against my shepherd,
    against the man who is close to me!"

declares the LORD Almighty.
"Strike the shepherd,
    and the sheep will be scattered,
    and I will turn my hand against the
      little ones.
⁸ In the whole land," declares the LORD,
    "two-thirds will be struck down and
      perish;
    yet one-third will be left in it.
⁹ This third I will bring into the fire;
    I will refine them like silver
    and test them like gold.
They will call on my name
    and I will answer them;
I will say, 'They are my people,'
    and they will say, 'The LORD is our
      God.'"

The LORD Comes and Reigns

14 A day of the LORD is coming when your plunder will be divided among you.

²I will gather all the nations to Jerusalem to fight against it; the city will be captured, the houses ransacked, and the women raped. Half of the city will go into exile, but the rest of the people will not be taken from the city. **³**Then the LORD will go out and fight against those nations, as he fights in the day of battle. **⁴**On that day his feet will stand on the Mount of Olives, east of Jerusalem, and the Mount of Olives will be split in two from east to west, forming a great valley, with half of the mountain moving north and half moving south. **⁵**You will flee by my mountain valley, for it will extend to Azel. You will flee as you fled from the earthquake*ᵉ* in the days of Uzziah king of Judah. Then the LORD my God will come, and all the holy ones with him. **⁶**On that day there will be no light, no cold or frost. **⁷**It will be a unique day, without daytime or nighttime—a day known to the LORD. When evening comes, there will be light.

⁸On that day living water will flow out from Jerusalem, half to the eastern sea*ᶠ* and half to the western sea,*ᵍ* in summer and in winter. **⁹**The LORD will be king over the whole earth. On that day there will be one LORD, and his name the only name. **¹⁰**The whole land, from Geba to Rim-

---

ᵃ10 Or the Spirit   *ᵇ10 Or to*   *ᶜ5 Or farmer; a man sold me in my youth*   *ᵈ6 Or wounds between your hands*   *ᵉ5 Or ⁵My mountain valley will be blocked and will extend to Azel. It will be blocked as it was blocked because of the earthquake*   *ᶠ8 That is, the Dead Sea*   *ᵍ8 That is, the Mediterranean*

mon, south of Jerusalem, will become like the Arabah. But Jerusalem will be raised up and remain in its place, from the Benjamin Gate to the site of the First Gate, to the Corner Gate, and from the Tower of Hananel to the royal winepresses. ¹¹It will be inhabited; never again will it be destroyed. Jerusalem will be secure.

¹²This is the plague with which the LORD will strike all the nations that fought against Jerusalem: Their flesh will rot while they are still standing on their feet, their eyes will rot in their sockets, and their tongues will rot in their mouths. ¹³On that day men will be stricken by the LORD with great panic. Each man will seize the hand of another, and they will attack each other. ¹⁴Judah too will fight at Jerusalem. The wealth of all the surrounding nations will be collected—great quantities of gold and silver and clothing. ¹⁵A similar plague will strike the horses and mules, the camels and donkeys, and all the animals in those camps.

¹⁶Then the survivors from all the nations that have attacked Jerusalem will go up year after year to worship the King, the LORD Almighty, and to celebrate the Feast of Tabernacles. ¹⁷If any of the peoples of the earth do not go up to Jerusalem to worship the King, the LORD Almighty, they will have no rain. ¹⁸If the Egyptian people do not go up and take part, they will have no rain. The LORDᵃ will bring on them the plague he inflicts on the nations that do not go up to celebrate the Feast of Tabernacles. ¹⁹This will be the punishment of Egypt and the punishment of all the nations that do not go up to celebrate the Feast of Tabernacles.

²⁰On that day HOLY TO THE LORD will be inscribed on the bells of the horses, and the cooking pots in the LORD's house will be like the sacred bowls in front of the altar. ²¹Every pot in Jerusalem and Judah will be holy to the LORD Almighty, and all who come to sacrifice will take some of the pots and cook in them. And on that day there will no longer be a Canaaniteᵇ in the house of the LORD Almighty.

ᵃ18 Or part, then the LORD   ᵇ21 Or merchant

Statistics reveal the brutal truth: the tragedy of broken marriages is rampant in our culture. Some surveys tell us that for most people, the sting of going through a divorce and of being rejected by their spouses is more painful than experiencing that spouse's death. If you have gone through this painful separation, you know. But Malachi heard God say something that may surprise you. It's tucked away here in the Old Testament, yet it's as up-to-date as the latest university research on this issue. God announced, "I hate divorce" (2:16), and although he was talking about the chaos of broken families, he was also giving us a chance to experience what it felt like to be the Sovereign Creator of the universe, only to be rejected by the crown of his creation . . . his bride.

What a picture! But isn't it amazing that the book of Malachi sits on the threshold of the story of the Messiah—God in human form? And since divorce hurts more than a loved one's death, Jesus came and died so we could be reconciled, healed from the pain of "separation" from our heavenly Father. How amazing!

Malachi

1 An oracle: The word of the LORD to Israel through Malachi.ᵃ

Jacob Loved, Esau Hated

²"I have loved you," says the LORD.
"But you ask, 'How have you loved us?'
"Was not Esau Jacob's brother?" the LORD says. "Yet I have loved Jacob, ³but Esau I have hated, and I have turned his mountains into a wasteland and left his inheritance to the desert jackals."
⁴Edom may say, "Though we have been crushed, we will rebuild the ruins."
But this is what the LORD Almighty says:

"They may build, but I will demolish. They will be called the Wicked Land, a people always under the wrath of the LORD. ⁵You will see it with your own eyes and say, 'Great is the LORD—even beyond the borders of Israel!'

Blemished Sacrifices

⁶"A son honors his father, and a servant his master. If I am a father, where is the honor due me? If I am a master, where is the respect due me?" says the LORD

ᵃ1 *Malachi* means *my messenger.*

You Should Know Better

Key Verse: *"A son honors his father, and a servant [honors] his master."* Malachi 1:6a

Text: Malachi 1:6–9 *(Dad or child reads the text.)*

QUIET
TIMES
WITH **Dad**

DAD READS: Sometimes when I do foolish things, I whisper these words to myself: *Why did I do that? I should know better.* Sometimes people say these words when they do silly things like hitting their golf ball into the lake. And sometimes people say these words when they do more serious things, like saying unkind or thoughtless words to people whom they love.

Child reads: One of the reasons why I am going to school is to learn about things I should do and things I should not do. I learn about certain laws that I should not break. Because of gravity, I'll hurt myself if I jump off a high tower. I should be careful around certain reptiles, because they are poisonous. Learning about these things helps me to "know better."

DAD READS: In the Old Testament certain men became priests. Just like the minister at our church, their job was to help the people to know God and to love him with their whole hearts. And, in the same way that there are schools today for people who want to be ministers, men who wanted to be priests had to go through special training to learn how to be priests.

Child reads: Malachi was a prophet. That means he had the job of telling people news from God. Today we read one of those important messages. God told the priests that they were being disobedient and that they should know better.

DAD READS: God told the priests something he wanted them to remind the people about. God said, "A son honors his father, and a servant [honors] his master." Then God added something very important. He said that fathers and masters need to be respected. I guess that the priests had forgotten to tell the people this. They should have known better.

Child reads: I know that you want me to respect you. I know that when I say or do things that hurt your feelings, I am not honoring you. I am not respecting you. And, although I am not a priest and haven't been to a special school, I should know better than to forget this.

DAD READS: Malachi's words are very true. Dads want to be respected. Malachi also wanted us to know that God, our heavenly Father, wants our respect, too. We can be respectful of our fathers by always telling them the truth, always saying kind things about them, and never disobeying them.

Child reads: I want to treat both of my fathers—my heavenly Father and you—with kindness and respect. And even though I ought to know better than to forget these things, I want you to remind me of this when I do forget. Let me pray this prayer with you:

Our Father in heaven, we love you. Thank you for all the things we know. Thank you that I know better than to be disrespectful of you or my dad. Help my dad and me to always love and honor you and each other. And thank you for forgiving us when we don't. In Jesus' name, **Amen.**

For your next devotional reading, go to page 1032.

Almighty. "It is you, O priests, who show contempt for my name.

"But you ask, 'How have we shown contempt for your name?'

[7]"You place defiled food on my altar.

"But you ask, 'How have we defiled you?'

"By saying that the LORD's table is contemptible. [8]When you bring blind animals for sacrifice, is that not wrong? When you sacrifice crippled or diseased animals, is that not wrong? Try offering them to your governor! Would he be pleased with you? Would he accept you?" says the LORD Almighty.

[9]"Now implore God to be gracious to us. With such offerings from your hands, will he accept you?"—says the LORD Almighty.

[10]"Oh, that one of you would shut the temple doors, so that you would not light useless fires on my altar! I am not pleased with you," says the LORD Almighty, "and I will accept no offering from your hands. [11]My name will be great among the nations, from the rising to the setting of the sun. In every place incense and pure offerings will be brought to my name, because my name will be great among the nations," says the LORD Almighty. [12]"But you profane it by saying of the Lord's table, 'It is defiled,' and of its food, 'It is contemptible.' [13]And you say, 'What a burden!' and you sniff at it contemptuously," says the LORD Almighty.

"When you bring injured, crippled or diseased animals and offer them as sacrifices, should I accept them from your hands?" says the LORD. [14]"Cursed is the cheat who has an acceptable male in his flock and vows to give it, but then sacrifices a blemished animal to the Lord. For I am a great king," says the LORD Almighty, "and my name is to be feared among the nations.

Admonition for the Priests

2 "And now this admonition is for you, O priests. [2]If you do not listen, and if you do not set your heart to honor my name," says the LORD Almighty, "I will send a curse upon you, and I will curse your blessings. Yes, I have already cursed them, because you have not set your heart to honor me.

[3]"Because of you I will rebuke[a] your descendants[b]; I will spread on your faces the offal from your festival sacrifices, and you will be carried off with it. [4]And you

will know that I have sent you this admonition so that my covenant with Levi may continue," says the LORD Almighty. [5]"My covenant was with him, a covenant of life and peace, and I gave them to him; this called for reverence and he revered me and stood in awe of my name. [6]True instruction was in his mouth and nothing false was found on his lips. He walked with me in peace and uprightness, and turned many from sin.

[7]"For the lips of a priest ought to preserve knowledge, and from his mouth men should seek instruction—because he is the messenger of the LORD Almighty. [8]But you have turned from the way and by your teaching have caused many to stumble; you have violated the covenant with Levi," says the LORD Almighty. [9]"So I have caused you to be despised and humiliated before all the people, because you have not followed my ways but have shown partiality in matters of the law."

Judah Unfaithful

[10]Have we not all one Father[c]? Did not one God create us? Why do we profane the covenant of our fathers by breaking faith with one another?

[11]Judah has broken faith. A detestable thing has been committed in Israel and in Jerusalem: Judah has desecrated the sanctuary the LORD loves, by marrying the daughter of a foreign god. [12]As for the man who does this, whoever he may be, may the LORD cut him off from the tents of Jacob[d]—even though he brings offerings to the LORD Almighty.

[13]Another thing you do: You flood the LORD's altar with tears. You weep and wail because he no longer pays attention to your offerings or accepts them with pleasure from your hands. [14]You ask, "Why?" It is because the LORD is acting as the witness between you and the wife of your youth, because you have broken faith with her, though she is your partner, the wife of your marriage covenant.

[15]Has not the LORD made them one? In flesh and spirit they are his. And why one? Because he was seeking godly offspring.[e]

---

[a]3 Or *cut off* (see Septuagint)   [b]3 Or *will blight your grain*   [c]10 Or *father*   [d]12 Or [12]May the LORD cut off from the tents of Jacob anyone who gives testimony in behalf of the man who does this   [e]15 Or [15]But the one who is our father did not do this, not as long as life remained in him. And what was he seeking? An offspring from God

So guard yourself in your spirit, and do not break faith with the wife of your youth.

¹⁶"I hate divorce," says the LORD God of Israel, "and I hate a man's covering himself*a* with violence as well as with his garment," says the LORD Almighty.

So guard yourself in your spirit, and do not break faith.

The Day of Judgment

¹⁷You have wearied the LORD with your words.

"How have we wearied him?" you ask.

By saying, "All who do evil are good in the eyes of the LORD, and he is pleased with them" or "Where is the God of justice?"

3 "See, I will send my messenger, who will prepare the way before me. Then suddenly the Lord you are seeking will come to his temple; the messenger of the covenant, whom you desire, will come," says the LORD Almighty.

²But who can endure the day of his coming? Who can stand when he appears? For he will be like a refiner's fire or a launderer's soap. ³He will sit as a refiner and purifier of silver; he will purify the Levites and refine them like gold and silver. Then the LORD will have men who will bring offerings in righteousness, ⁴and the offerings of Judah and Jerusalem will be acceptable to the LORD, as in days gone by, as in former years.

⁵"So I will come near to you for judgment. I will be quick to testify against sorcerers, adulterers and perjurers, against those who defraud laborers of their wages, who oppress the widows and the fatherless, and deprive aliens of justice, but do not fear me," says the LORD Almighty.

Robbing God

⁶"I the LORD do not change. So you, O descendants of Jacob, are not destroyed. ⁷Ever since the time of your forefathers you have turned away from my decrees and have not kept them. Return to me, and I will return to you," says the LORD Almighty.

"But you ask, 'How are we to return?'

⁸"Will a man rob God? Yet you rob me.

"But you ask, 'How do we rob you?'

"In tithes and offerings. ⁹You are under a curse—the whole nation of you—because you are robbing me. ¹⁰Bring the whole tithe into the storehouse, that there may be food in my house. Test me in this," says the LORD Almighty, "and see if I will not throw open the floodgates of heaven and pour out so much blessing that you will not have room enough for it. ¹¹I will prevent pests from devouring your crops, and the vines in your fields will not cast their fruit," says the LORD Almighty. ¹²"Then all the nations will call you

a16 Or his wife

HEY DAD
What is tithing?

Text: Malachi 3:9–10

"Tithing" is a word that means giving ten percent of our income to further God's work in the world. By tithing, we show God that we are thankful for the blessings he's given us. When we tithe, we also acknowledge that God owns everything we have anyway, and that we want to honor him by giving some of that back to him.

Tithing is a part of God's plan to keep his church in order. Our tithes go to pay the staff's salary, cover the bills for the church, and help others who are needy. It's important to God that we honor him with our finances. Through the prophet Malachi, the Lord told the Israelites to tithe faithfully. "Test me in this," he said, "and see if I will not throw open the floodgates of heaven and pour out so much blessing that you will not have room enough for it" (v. 10).

And one more thing ... we don't honor God so that he will honor us. We honor him because he's God, and he deserves it. Look at how he's already blessed you, then consider how much of what you own comes from God's hand.

QUESTIONS Kids ASK

For a complete listing of Questions Kids Ask, turn to page 1435.

blessed, for yours will be a delightful land," says the LORD Almighty.

[13]"You have said harsh things against me," says the LORD.

"Yet you ask, 'What have we said against you?'

[14]"You have said, 'It is futile to serve God. What did we gain by carrying out his requirements and going about like mourners before the LORD Almighty? [15]But now we call the arrogant blessed. Certainly the evildoers prosper, and even those who challenge God escape.' "

[16]Then those who feared the LORD talked with each other, and the LORD listened and heard. A scroll of remembrance was written in his presence concerning those who feared the LORD and honored his name.

[17]"They will be mine," says the LORD Almighty, "in the day when I make up my treasured possession.[a] I will spare them, just as in compassion a man spares his son who serves him. [18]And you will again see the distinction between the righteous and the wicked, between those who serve God and those who do not.

The Day of the LORD

[4] "Surely the day is coming; it will burn like a furnace. All the arrogant and every evildoer will be stubble, and that day that is coming will set them on fire," says the LORD Almighty. "Not a root or a branch will be left to them. [2]But for you who revere my name, the sun of righteousness will rise with healing in its wings. And you will go out and leap like calves released from the stall. [3]Then you will trample down the wicked; they will be ashes under the soles of your feet on the day when I do these things," says the LORD Almighty.

[4]"Remember the law of my servant Moses, the decrees and laws I gave him at Horeb for all Israel.

[5]"See, I will send you the prophet Elijah before that great and dreadful day of the LORD comes. [6]He will turn the hearts of the fathers to their children, and the hearts of the children to their fathers; or else I will come and strike the land with a curse."

[a]17 Or Almighty, "my treasured possession, in the day when I act

New
TESTAMENT

Matthew was a tax collector. Ordinarily, such a profession would keep an individual off of most people's Christmas card lists. But Matthew suffered far more than the occasional holiday snub; his job was to collect taxes from his own people, then turn the funds over to a foreign government. How did Matthew get involved in this profession? He literally bid for the right to secure this extremely lucrative position. He "sold" the Roman-held government on his ability to be thorough. Then once he secured the job, Matthew had to "sell" the Jews on their responsibility to pay their fair share to the Romans.

Any sales rep will tell you that his or her greatest ally in closing the deal is information—irrefutable evidence that the "product" is sound. Is it any wonder that Matthew's story is filled with more verifying documentation—Old Testament confirmation that Jesus Christ is really the Son of God—than the other accounts of Jesus' life? It's no wonder if you're a salesman.

Matthew

The Genealogy of Jesus

1 A record of the genealogy of Jesus Christ the son of David, the son of Abraham:

²Abraham was the father of Isaac,
  Isaac the father of Jacob,
  Jacob the father of Judah and his brothers,
  ³Judah the father of Perez and Ze-rah, whose mother was Tamar,
  Perez the father of Hezron,
  Hezron the father of Ram,
  ⁴Ram the father of Amminadab,
  Amminadab the father of Nah-shon,
  Nahshon the father of Salmon,
  ⁵Salmon the father of Boaz, whose mother was Rahab,

Boaz the father of Obed, whose mother was Ruth,
  Obed the father of Jesse,
  ⁶and Jesse the father of King David.

David was the father of Solomon, whose mother had been Uriah's wife,
  ⁷Solomon the father of Rehoboam,
  Rehoboam the father of Abijah,
  Abijah the father of Asa,
  ⁸Asa the father of Jehoshaphat,
  Jehoshaphat the father of Jehoram,
  Jehoram the father of Uzziah,
  ⁹Uzziah the father of Jotham,
  Jotham the father of Ahaz,
  Ahaz the father of Hezekiah,
  ¹⁰Hezekiah the father of Manasseh,

Manasseh the father of Amon,
Amon the father of Josiah,
¹¹and Josiah the father of Jeconiah[a]
and his brothers at the time of
the exile to Babylon.

¹²After the exile to Babylon:
Jeconiah was the father of Shealtiel,
Shealtiel the father of Zerubbabel,
¹³Zerubbabel the father of Abiud,

Abiud the father of Eliakim,
Eliakim the father of Azor,
¹⁴Azor the father of Zadok,
Zadok the father of Akim,
Akim the father of Eliud,
¹⁵Eliud the father of Eleazar,
Eleazar the father of Matthan,

ᵃ11 That is, Jehoiachin; also in verse 12

Are You in Here?

DAILY INSIGHT

MONDAY

Passage:
Matthew 1:1,2,16,17

Verse:
Matthew 1:1

When I was in high school, I fell into the unmistakable classification of "late bloomer." Because I was the youngest person in my class and was smaller than most of my male peers, life wasn't easy for me. However, something in my hereditary constitution did not allow me to simply give up. I repeatedly tried out for various sports, hoping that a strong will and a little extra hustle would count for something.

Although I never made a varsity squad in high school, I did finish my pre-college career with some of my dignity intact. I had made many wonderful friends, had performed in the school's talent show and participated in several other clubs and activities. *At least,* I remember thinking, *I'll have a good list of activities next to my name in my senior yearbook.*

I'll never forget the day we received our yearbooks. I was standing in the foyer, just outside the school's auditorium, and had just been handed the *1965 Wheaton Community High School Ilium.* I quickly scanned the senior pages. And there, right between the pictures of Dennis Wiss and Ann Woodward, the place where I had found myself lined up in every study hall for four years, was . . .

Nothing.

I looked again, quickly turning the adjacent pages to see if, perhaps, I had been listed out of sequence. Again I found nothing.

Filled with terror, I turned to find someone to tell. Standing two feet from me was my friend Meredith Poe, the yearbook editor. "I'm not in here," I said to Meredith. "You completely missed me." Quickly thumbing through her own copy, she confirmed my assertion. "I'm so sorry," she finally said to me, here face turning ashen, "Oh, no . . . uh . . . I'm so . . . so sorry." She turned and walked away.

The genealogies in Matthew are about as spell-binding as reading the names of students in a yearbook. Unless you're looking for your own name, in which case it's an adventure to search for and a victory to find (present company excluded, of course).

Matthew's list of the Messiah's ancestors starts with Abraham and stops with Jesus' name. What we now know is that this list actually continues after the birth of Jesus. Of course, this genealogy is not found in the Bible. It is, however, listed in what the apostle John calls "the Lamb's book of life" (Revelation 21:27).

This "yearbook" we hear about in the book of Revelation has nothing to do with ancestral lineage or bloodline. The names recorded in the "Lamb's book," the most important yearbook in the history of humankind, are there because of a different kind of "bloodline": the sacrificial blood of Jesus. Those who show up in this book are adopted into God's family, heirs to an eternal spiritual reward.

Matthew and the other Gospel writers tell the story of how to get your name in this book. If you miss this one, it won't be Meredith Poe's fault.

For your next devotional reading, go to page 1034.

Matthan the father of Jacob, **16**and Jacob the father of Joseph, the husband of Mary, of whom was born Jesus, who is called Christ.

17Thus there were fourteen generations in all from Abraham to David, fourteen from David to the exile to Babylon, and fourteen from the exile to the Christ.*a*

The Birth of Jesus Christ

18This is how the birth of Jesus Christ came about: His mother Mary was pledged to be married to Joseph, but before they came together, she was found to be with child through the Holy Spirit. **19**Because Joseph her husband was a righteous man and did not want to expose her to public disgrace, he had in mind to divorce her quietly. **20**But after he had considered this, an angel of the Lord appeared to him in a dream and said, "Joseph son of David, do not be afraid to take Mary home as your wife, because what is conceived in her is from the Holy Spirit. **21**She will give birth to a son, and you are to give him the name Jesus,*b* because he will save his people from their sins."

22All this took place to fulfill what the Lord had said through the prophet: **23**"The virgin will be with child and will give birth to a son, and they will call him Immanuel"*c*—which means, "God with us."

24When Joseph woke up, he did what the angel of the Lord had commanded him and took Mary home as his wife. **25**But he had no union with her until she gave birth to a son. And he gave him the name Jesus.

a17 Or Messiah. "The Christ" (Greek) and "the Messiah" (Hebrew) both mean "the Anointed One." *b21 Jesus* is the Greek form of *Joshua,* which means *the LORD saves.* *c23* Isaiah 7:14

Not Exactly What This Dad Had in Mind
Joseph, the Trusting Father

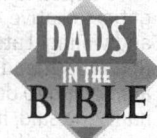
DADS
IN THE
BIBLE

"When Joseph woke up, he did what the angel of the Lord had commanded him" (1:24).

Text: Matthew 1:18–25

"I'm pregnant." No man ever wants to hear these words coming from the lips of his fiancée—especially no man who is known to his friends as "righteous."

Joseph had kept his end of the bargain. He had remained faithful to the vow of chastity he had made to Mary at their engagement. But, evidently, Mary had been unfaithful, and this was devastating news. *I will take care of this quietly,* he resolved. *There's no need to make a spectacle of her.*

Joseph seemed so on top of it. So in charge. So confident. But don't you wonder how he felt inside the first night he crawled into bed, having heard that his bride-to-be had been unfaithful and, as if that weren't bad enough, that she had lied about the circumstances of her conception? How awful for this man.

But, as he slept, God spoke to Joseph through an angel, "Do not be afraid to take Mary home as your wife, because what is conceived in her is from the Holy Spirit. She will give birth to a son, and you are to give him the name Jesus, because he will save his people from their sins" (1:20–21). Talk about a paradigm shift!

Even though this isn't exactly what he had in mind for his first experience as a dad, Joseph obeyed. Did Joseph, at times, doubt? He must have. But did he push through that doubt and continue to move forward by faith? The record is here for all to see.

The Bible includes very little information about Jesus' earthly father. We know he lived in Nazareth. We know he was a carpenter. We know he was a devout Jew, but the thing we will always remember about this dad was his obedience.

"When Joseph woke up, he did what the angel of the Lord had commanded him." Enough said.

For a complete listing of Dads in the Bible, turn to page 1434.

The Visit of the Magi

2 After Jesus was born in Bethlehem in Judea, during the time of King Herod, Magi[a] from the east came to Jerusalem ²and asked, "Where is the one who has been born king of the Jews? We saw his star in the east [b] and have come to worship him."

³When King Herod heard this he was disturbed, and all Jerusalem with him. ⁴When he had called together all the people's chief priests and teachers of the law, he asked them where the Christ[c] was to be born. ⁵"In Bethlehem in Judea," they replied, "for this is what the prophet has written:

⁶ " 'But you, Bethlehem, in the land of Judah,
are by no means least among the rulers of Judah;

[a]1 Traditionally *Wise Men*   [b]2 Or *star when it rose*   [c]4 Or *Messiah*

Redford, Joseph, and God's Son

DAILY INSIGHT

TUESDAY

Passage: Matthew 1:18–25

Verse: Matthew 1:24

I'll never forget Redford, partly because his was such an unusual first name, but mostly because of his story.

One of Redford's closest friends, in the small North Dakota town where he grew up, fell in love with the cutest girl in school. Emily was everything a red-blooded teenage boy could have hoped for: happy, energetic, talkative, beautiful ... and willing. Late one night, Redford's friend called. "What am I going to do? She's pregnant," he said, his voice bursting through the phone lines. "She wants to go away, have the baby, put it up for adoption, and then come back. She's not putting any pressure on me to marry her, so I think this is a good plan." Redford just listened.

Emily quietly disappeared. Life in rural North Dakota returned to normal, quite unimpeded by the predictable whispers.

Several years later, an afternoon Greyhound brought Emily home. The locals were shocked to see her, especially with three children in tow. A five-year-old boy held one of her hands, his blonde hair and blue eyes recognizable gifts from his well-known daddy. A strikingly beautiful, dark-skinned girl held her other hand. She looked to be about three. And strapped to her chest in one of those canvas slings, was a newborn. The town's cheerleader-turned-woman-of-the-world had come home.

When Redford heard the news, he immediately looked for Emily. He found her in her parents' house, feeding the infant. Kneeling on the floor beside Emily, Redford tenderly put his arms around his old friend. "I'm so glad to see you," he said, embracing both the girl and her tiny baby. "Welcome home."

In the weeks that followed, Redford renewed his friendship with Emily, offering to help in whatever way he could. In what seemed like no time at all, they were desperately in love. In six months they were married, and today, Redford, Emily, and their little eclectic family live in a frame house, just inside the city limits of the same North Dakota town.

Joseph was faced with the dilemma of a lifetime. Mary, his fiancée, was pregnant. Incredibly and completely out of character, she had lied to him, claiming to still be a virgin. *A virgin?* he must have muttered to himself, *I wasn't born yesterday.* But in a dream, God told Joseph to take Mary as his wife. "This child is from the Holy Spirit," God told him, "and this baby's going to save his people from their sins." So, in a quiet ceremony, Joseph married Mary, tenderly taking her into his home.

Two thousand years later, Jesus Christ is faced with a dilemma. You and I, his wayward and unfaithful boys, need a home. God's loving embrace is the best news we could ever receive.

Thanks, Redford, for your mercy. Thanks, Joseph, for your faithfulness. Thank you, heavenly Father, for your grace.

For your next devotional reading, go to page 1040.

for out of you will come a ruler
    who will be the shepherd of my
        people Israel.'*a*"

[7]Then Herod called the Magi secretly
and found out from them the exact time
the star had appeared. [8]He sent them to
Bethlehem and said, "Go and make a
careful search for the child. As soon as you
find him, report to me, so that I too may
go and worship him."
[9]After they had heard the king, they
went on their way, and the star they had
seen in the east*b* went ahead of them until
it stopped over the place where the child
was. [10]When they saw the star, they were
overjoyed. [11]On coming to the house, they
saw the child with his mother Mary, and
they bowed down and worshiped him.
Then they opened their treasures and
presented him with gifts of gold and of incense and of myrrh. [12]And having been
warned in a dream not to go back to Herod, they returned to their country by another route.

The Escape to Egypt

[13]When they had gone, an angel of the
Lord appeared to Joseph in a dream. "Get
up," he said, "take the child and his
mother and escape to Egypt. Stay there

until I tell you, for Herod is going to
search for the child to kill him."
[14]So he got up, took the child and his
mother during the night and left for
Egypt, [15]where he stayed until the death
of Herod. And so was fulfilled what the
Lord had said through the prophet: "Out
of Egypt I called my son."*c*
[16]When Herod realized that he had
been outwitted by the Magi, he was furious, and he gave orders to kill all the boys
in Bethlehem and its vicinity who were
two years old and under, in accordance
with the time he had learned from the
Magi. [17]Then what was said through the
prophet Jeremiah was fulfilled:

[18]"A voice is heard in Ramah,
    weeping and great mourning,
Rachel weeping for her children
    and refusing to be comforted,
because they are no more."*d*

The Return to Nazareth

[19]After Herod died, an angel of the Lord
appeared in a dream to Joseph in Egypt
[20]and said, "Get up, take the child and his
mother and go to the land of Israel, for

*a*6 Micah 5:2   *b*9 Or *seen when it rose*   *c*15 Hosea
11:1   *d*18 Jer. 31:15

HEY DAD
Was Jesus really born on December 25th?

Text: Matthew 1:18–25

Actually, Jesus probably was not born on December the 25th or even in winter.
Luke tells us that shepherds were watching their sheep out in the field at night
(Luke 2:8). But during the winter in Bethlehem, sheep had to be kept under cover
due to cold weather, rain and sparse pasture. The shepherds visited by angels
were probably out in the fields because the weather was warm.
    So, why do we celebrate Christmas in the winter? "December 25th was chosen
by early Christian leaders for both practical and symbolic reasons" (Ward, 24). The
Romans began their most popular annual feast, the Saturnalia, on December 25th.
On this date each year, the sun began to turn from a "winter sun" to a "summer sun."
To the Romans, this astronomical change represented the death of winter and the return of
the life-giving seasons of spring and summer. This feast was already a part of the early
Christians' lives and seemed an appropriate time to celebrate the birth of Jesus, as well.
To Christians the nativity means that spiritual rebirth is now possible and that life has been
renewed for all of humankind.

Ward, K. (Ed.). (1987). Jesus and His Times. *Pleasantville, New York: The Reader's Digest Association.*

For a complete listing of Questions Kids Ask, turn to page 1435.

those who were trying to take the child's life are dead."

²¹So he got up, took the child and his mother and went to the land of Israel. ²²But when he heard that Archelaus was reigning in Judea in place of his father Herod, he was afraid to go there. Having been warned in a dream, he withdrew to the district of Galilee, ²³and he went and lived in a town called Nazareth. So was fulfilled what was said through the prophets: "He will be called a Nazarene."

John the Baptist Prepares the Way

3 In those days John the Baptist came, preaching in the Desert of Judea ²and saying, "Repent, for the kingdom of heaven is near." ³This is he who was spoken of through the prophet Isaiah:

"A voice of one calling in the desert,
'Prepare the way for the Lord,
    make straight paths for him.' "ᵃ

⁴John's clothes were made of camel's hair, and he had a leather belt around his waist. His food was locusts and wild honey. ⁵People went out to him from Jerusalem and all Judea and the whole region of the Jordan. ⁶Confessing their sins, they were baptized by him in the Jordan River. ⁷But when he saw many of the Pharisees and Sadducees coming to where he

was baptizing, he said to them: "You brood of vipers! Who warned you to flee from the coming wrath? ⁸Produce fruit in keeping with repentance. ⁹And do not think you can say to yourselves, 'We have Abraham as our father.' I tell you that out of these stones God can raise up children for Abraham. ¹⁰The ax is already at the root of the trees, and every tree that does not produce good fruit will be cut down and thrown into the fire.

¹¹"I baptize you withᵇ water for repentance. But after me will come one who is more powerful than I, whose sandals I am not fit to carry. He will baptize you with the Holy Spirit and with fire. ¹²His winnowing fork is in his hand, and he will clear his threshing floor, gathering his wheat into the barn and burning up the chaff with unquenchable fire."

The Baptism of Jesus

¹³Then Jesus came from Galilee to the Jordan to be baptized by John. ¹⁴But John tried to deter him, saying, "I need to be baptized by you, and do you come to me?"

¹⁵Jesus replied, "Let it be so now; it is proper for us to do this to fulfill all righteousness." Then John consented.

ᵃ3 Isaiah 40:3   ᵇ11 Or *in*

HEY DAD
How did the wise men know Bethlehem's star meant Jesus had been born?

Text: Matthew 2:1–2

The Magi or "wise men" probably came from Persia or Babylon—civilizations that were unaware of prophecies foretelling Jesus' birth. According to many scholars, "the Magi were experts in astrology and magic" (Ward, 29).

Most likely Zoroastrians, these men regularly scanned the heavens for unusual phenomena. "Throughout the Mediterranean world at that time astrology was highly regarded as a science ... It was only natural to them that deeply significant news would be announced by a rare and startling celestial phenomenon" (Ward, 29).

It may seem strange that astrologers or magicians who were not even Jews were among the first to know of Jesus' birth. But God spoke to them because they were *listening*. God wants everyone to know about his Son and his plan for salvation. He can speak to us in any way he chooses—even in the stars.

Ward, K. (Ed.). (1987). Jesus and His Times. Pleasantville, New York: The Reader's Digest Association.

For a complete listing of Questions Kids Ask, turn to page 1435.

16As soon as Jesus was baptized, he went up out of the water. At that moment heaven was opened, and he saw the Spirit of God descending like a dove and lighting on him. **17**And a voice from heaven said, "This is my Son, whom I love; with him I am well pleased."

The Temptation of Jesus

4 Then Jesus was led by the Spirit into the desert to be tempted by the devil. **2**After fasting forty days and forty nights, he was hungry. **3**The tempter came to him and said, "If you are the Son of God, tell these stones to become bread."

4Jesus answered, "It is written: 'Man does not live on bread alone, but on every word that comes from the mouth of God.'*a*"

5Then the devil took him to the holy city and had him stand on the highest point of the temple. **6**"If you are the Son of God," he said, "throw yourself down. For it is written:

" 'He will command his angels
        concerning you,
    and they will lift you up in their
        hands,
so that you will not strike your foot
        against a stone.'*b*"

7Jesus answered him, "It is also written: 'Do not put the Lord your God to the test.'*c*"

8Again, the devil took him to a very high mountain and showed him all the kingdoms of the world and their splendor. **9**"All this I will give you," he said, "if you will bow down and worship me."

10Jesus said to him, "Away from me, Satan! For it is written: 'Worship the Lord your God, and serve him only.'*d*"

11Then the devil left him, and angels came and attended him.

Jesus Begins to Preach

12When Jesus heard that John had been put in prison, he returned to Galilee. **13**Leaving Nazareth, he went and lived in Capernaum, which was by the lake in the area of Zebulun and Naphtali— **14**to fulfill what was said through the prophet Isaiah:

15"Land of Zebulun and land of Naphtali,
        the way to the sea, along the Jordan,
        Galilee of the Gentiles—
16the people living in darkness
        have seen a great light;
on those living in the land of the
        shadow of death
    a light has dawned."*e*

17From that time on Jesus began to preach, "Repent, for the kingdom of heaven is near."

a4 Deut. 8:3   *b6* Psalm 91:11,12   *c7* Deut. 6:16
d10 Deut. 6:13   *e16* Isaiah 9:1,2

HEY DAD
Is Santa Claus real?

Text: Matthew 2:11

Whether or not you teach your child about Santa Claus, at some point this question is bound to arise.

Why not tell your children about the real Saint Nicholas and his life's goal to serve Jesus by serving others? Nicholas was born in Patara, Licia, around 300 AD. When he was a teenager, Nicholas learned that a certain honorable man in his town had no money to pay the dowries for his three daughters. This meant that they would not be able to get married, which would bring shame on the whole family.

Moved by their situation, Nicholas tossed a sack of dowry money into an open window late one night. Barely making it through the window, the money landed in a stocking that had been hung there to dry. Nicholas continued his anonymous giving until all three girls had married.

Later becoming a priest, Nicholas was well known for his servant heart. Our gift giving today stems from the tradition he began over 1,600 years ago.

For a complete listing of Questions Kids Ask, turn to page 1435.

The Calling of the First Disciples

18As Jesus was walking beside the Sea of Galilee, he saw two brothers, Simon called Peter and his brother Andrew. They were casting a net into the lake, for they were fishermen. **19**"Come, follow me," Jesus said, "and I will make you fishers of men." **20**At once they left their nets and followed him.

21Going on from there, he saw two other brothers, James son of Zebedee and his brother John. They were in a boat with their father Zebedee, preparing their nets. Jesus called them, **22**and immediately they left the boat and their father and followed him.

Jesus Heals the Sick

23Jesus went throughout Galilee, teaching in their synagogues, preaching the good news of the kingdom, and healing every disease and sickness among the people. **24**News about him spread all over Syria, and people brought to him all who were ill with various diseases, those suffering severe pain, the demon-possessed, those having seizures, and the paralyzed, and he healed them. **25**Large crowds from Galilee, the Decapolis,*a* Jerusalem, Judea and the region across the Jordan followed him.

The Beatitudes

5 Now when he saw the crowds, he went up on a mountainside and sat down. His disciples came to him, **2**and he began to teach them, saying:

3"Blessed are the poor in spirit,
    for theirs is the kingdom of heaven.
4Blessed are those who mourn,
    for they will be comforted.
5Blessed are the meek,
    for they will inherit the earth.
6Blessed are those who hunger and
        thirst for righteousness,
    for they will be filled.
7Blessed are the merciful,
    for they will be shown mercy.
8Blessed are the pure in heart,
    for they will see God.
9Blessed are the peacemakers,
    for they will be called sons of God.
10Blessed are those who are persecuted
        because of righteousness,
    for theirs is the kingdom of heaven.

11"Blessed are you when people insult you, persecute you and falsely say all kinds of evil against you because of me. **12**Rejoice and be glad, because great is your reward in heaven, for in the same

a25 That is, the Ten Cities

HEY DAD
How many years ago was Jesus born?

Text: Matthew 2:19–21

Jesus was born a little over two thousand years ago. Since our calendar is based from the year of Christ's birth, we call the years before Christ was born "BC" (Before Christ) and the years after his birth "AD" (*Anno Domine*, which is Latin for "In the Year of Our Lord"). Most people logically conclude Christ was born in the year 1 AD. We now know, however, that Christ was actually born a few years earlier.

Historical records prove that Jesus was born during the reign of King Herod the Great, but this king died four years before 1 AD. Therefore, most scholars think Christ was born in what we would now call 6 BC or 7 BC. Dionysius Exiguus, the monk who calculated the year of the nativity that is used as our calendar baseline, lacked some information critical to determining its exact date. The current calendar system was already in widespread use when his error was discovered, so it remains to this day.

Ward, K. (Ed.). (1987). Jesus and His Times. Pleasantville, New York: The Reader's Digest Association.

For a complete listing of Questions Kids Ask, turn to page 1435.

way they persecuted the prophets who were before you.

Salt and Light

¹³"You are the salt of the earth. But if the salt loses its saltiness, how can it be made salty again? It is no longer good for anything, except to be thrown out and trampled by men.

¹⁴"You are the light of the world. A city on a hill cannot be hidden. ¹⁵Neither do people light a lamp and put it under a bowl. Instead they put it on its stand, and it gives light to everyone in the house. ¹⁶In the same way, let your light shine before men, that they may see your good deeds and praise your Father in heaven.

The Fulfillment of the Law

¹⁷"Do not think that I have come to abolish the Law or the Prophets; I have not come to abolish them but to fulfill them. ¹⁸I tell you the truth, until heaven and earth disappear, not the smallest letter, not the least stroke of a pen, will by any means disappear from the Law until everything is accomplished. ¹⁹Anyone who breaks one of the least of these commandments and teaches others to do the same will be called least in the kingdom of heaven, but whoever practices and teaches these commands will be called great in the kingdom of heaven. ²⁰For I tell you that unless your righteousness surpasses that of the Pharisees and the teachers of the law, you will certainly not enter the kingdom of heaven.

Murder

²¹"You have heard that it was said to the people long ago, 'Do not murder,ᵃ and anyone who murders will be subject to judgment.' ²²But I tell you that anyone who is angry with his brotherᵇ will be subject to judgment. Again, anyone who says to his brother, 'Raca,ᶜ' is answerable to the Sanhedrin. But anyone who says, 'You fool!' will be in danger of the fire of hell.

²³"Therefore, if you are offering your gift at the altar and there remember that your brother has something against you, ²⁴leave your gift there in front of the altar. First go and be reconciled to your brother; then come and offer your gift.

²⁵"Settle matters quickly with your adversary who is taking you to court. Do it while you are still with him on the way, or he may hand you over to the judge, and the judge may hand you over to the of-

ficer, and you may be thrown into prison. ²⁶I tell you the truth, you will not get out until you have paid the last penny.ᵈ

Adultery

²⁷"You have heard that it was said, 'Do not commit adultery.'ᵉ ²⁸But I tell you that anyone who looks at a woman lustfully has already committed adultery with her in his heart. ²⁹If your right eye causes you to sin, gouge it out and throw it away. It is better for you to lose one part of your body than for your whole body to be thrown into hell. ³⁰And if your right hand causes you to sin, cut it off and throw it away. It is better for you to lose one part of your body than for your whole body to go into hell.

Divorce

³¹"It has been said, 'Anyone who divorces his wife must give her a certificate of divorce.'ᶠ ³²But I tell you that anyone who divorces his wife, except for marital unfaithfulness, causes her to become an adulteress, and anyone who marries the divorced woman commits adultery.

Oaths

³³"Again, you have heard that it was said to the people long ago, 'Do not break your oath, but keep the oaths you have made to the Lord.' ³⁴But I tell you, Do not swear at all: either by heaven, for it is God's throne; ³⁵or by the earth, for it is his footstool; or by Jerusalem, for it is the city of the Great King. ³⁶And do not swear by your head, for you cannot make even one hair white or black. ³⁷Simply let your 'Yes' be 'Yes,' and your 'No,' 'No'; anything beyond this comes from the evil one.

An Eye for an Eye

³⁸"You have heard that it was said, 'Eye for eye, and tooth for tooth.'ᵍ ³⁹But I tell you, Do not resist an evil person. If someone strikes you on the right cheek, turn to him the other also. ⁴⁰And if someone wants to sue you and take your tunic, let him have your cloak as well. ⁴¹If someone forces you to go one mile, go with him two miles. ⁴²Give to the one who asks you, and do not turn away from the one who wants to borrow from you.

ᵃ21 Exodus 20:13   ᵇ22 Some manuscripts *brother without cause*   ᶜ22 An Aramaic term of contempt   ᵈ26 Greek *kodrantes*   ᵉ27 Exodus 20:14   ᶠ31 Deut. 24:1   ᵍ38 Exodus 21:24; Lev. 24:20; Deut. 19:21

Love for Enemies

43"You have heard that it was said, 'Love your neighbor*a* and hate your enemy.' **44**But I tell you: Love your enemies*b* and pray for those who persecute you, **45**that you may be sons of your Father in heaven. He causes his sun to rise on the evil and the good, and sends rain on the righteous and the unrighteous. **46**If you love those who love you, what reward will you get? Are not even the tax collectors doing that? **47**And if you greet only your brothers, what are you doing more than others? Do not even pagans do that? **48**Be perfect, therefore, as your heavenly Father is perfect.

a43 Lev. 19:18   *b44* Some late manuscripts *enemies, bless those who curse you, do good to those who hate you*

Ready, Aim, Speak

DAILY INSIGHT

WEDNESDAY

Passage:
Matthew 5:21–25, 33–37

Verse:
Matthew 5:37

Taylor University, my college alma mater, had a dinnertime custom for many years. Every weekday evening, at exactly 6:00, the doors of the dining hall would open, but only for the women. The ladies would stream in, filling every other seat at the round, eight-person tables.

Once the dining hall was exactly half-filled, the men were released, set free to prowl the tables, looking for a select seat. Other students waited on tables, family style. I'm sure a family atmosphere with pleasant conversation is what the well-intentioned founders of the tradition had intended to create, although the consistently empty seats at some women's tables spoke more harshly and hurtfully than words ever could.

I remember one dinner in the spring of my freshman year. I was sitting with seven of my classmates—three men and four women. We were engaged in the usual college chatter when someone mentioned the breakup of one of Taylor's "fixture" couples. He was a sophomore; she was a freshman—one of our own.

All side conversations at the table stopped. Everyone wanted to hear about the couple's break-up. One of the girls reported that Carla had decided to break off the relationship. "Irreconcilable differences," she said. "Carla loved Stephen, but there was just no future in it."

I, however, had been privy to other information. "That's not what I heard," I glibly announced. "I heard that Stephen really let her have it. He really hadn't liked her all that much and just told her so. He broke her heart, but ... oh, well, these things happen." My story continued; I was a veritable fountain of gossip that evening, and everyone listened.

When I finished my thorough report, I took a breath and looked up into the faces of my classmates. They were ashen, gazing at me in disbelief. As I looked more closely, I discovered that they weren't actually looking at me. They were looking just *above* me at—you guessed it, our student waitress. It was Carla.

I will remember that moment for the rest of my life— what it felt like to be sitting there, trapped in the crossfire of my friend's pain and the disbelieving stares of my tablemates. I don't recall ever feeling such embarrassment, such shame.

Words have *unbelievable* power. Clustered together well, they can restore and renew your family. They can lift your children's hearts and heal their spirits. Words can refresh a child's self-esteem, but words can also cause incredible pain. And, once spoken, they can never be unsaid.

In his Sermon on the Mount, Jesus reminded followers of the remarkable power of spoken words. He reminds us that mouths can be like loaded guns, and that words can be like the deadly bullets that fly from them.

Protect your children from sniper fire— from each other and from you. The life you save may be your own.

For your next devotional reading, go to page 1041.

Giving to the Needy

6 "Be careful not to do your 'acts of righteousness' before men, to be seen by them. If you do, you will have no reward from your Father in heaven.

²"So when you give to the needy, do not announce it with trumpets, as the hypocrites do in the synagogues and on the streets, to be honored by men. I tell you the truth, they have received their reward in full. ³But when you give to the needy, do not let your left hand know what your right hand is doing, ⁴so that your giving may be in secret. Then your Father, who sees what is done in secret, will reward you.

Prayer

⁵"And when you pray, do not be like the hypocrites, for they love to pray standing in the synagogues and on the street corners to be seen by men. I tell you the

---

Show Us How to Pray

DAILY INSIGHT

THURSDAY

Passage:
Matthew 6:5–13

Verses:
Matthew 6:7–8

Several years ago, our older daughter was teaching fifth grade at a Christian school in North Carolina. She began each day with open prayer time.

One morning, a boy began praying for his dog. "Dear God," he began, "please bless Rascal today." Missy held her breath. "Please help him to be obedient to my mom while I'm here at school. And please help him not to run out into the busy street in front of our house." Unfortunately, he wasn't quite finished. "And Lord, please help Rascal to get rid of his nasty ringworm."

Missy silently gasped ... but none of the children laughed. No one even made a sound. *Of course,* the children were silently saying, *praying for Rascal's ringworm seems perfectly reasonable to us.*

It's good that children are so comfortable taking their most important concerns boldly to God. But when it comes to prayer—either on their own or with their children—many dads are stymied. "I can do all right with asking God to bless the food," they tell me. "But beyond that, I'm kind of lost."

In the Lord's Prayer, Jesus gave us a wonderful pattern to follow when we pray, either alone or with our kids.

Praise and Thank You's. When you pray, always begin by thanking God for his goodness. If your child is young when you start this, you're going to hear your heavenly Father get thanked for a whole lot of interesting things: birds, bicycles, Grandma, a new box of Cap'n Crunch® cereal. That's

okay, let it roll. You're helping your children to remember that everything they have—including life itself—is a precious gift from God's hand.

Please Forgive Me's. You probably won't have too much difficulty with this, since most children have a great deal of sensitivity about their own shortcomings. But it's still important that you help them identify specifics. Having your daughter pray, "Forgive me for not sharing my toys with Jennifer," when she's three will translate to seeking God's grace when life gets a lot more complex and dangerous later on.

Requests. As with their lists of "thank you's," this might be a long one: "Bless Uncle Fred and Aunt Blanche, bless my trucks (or my dolls), bless my mom and my dad (Amen), help Stephanie get over the flu, please give us a sunny day for the picnic tomorrow ... ." Again, let this roll. Your child is learning that the Sovereign Lord of the universe is a God of blessing—of good and perfect gifts.

Finally, close the prayer with one more expression of gratitude.

There you have it—a bird's eye view of the Lord's Prayer. Use this pattern consistently, and you'll find that your family will soon get the hang of it. Think of it. You are ushering your family into the presence of a holy God. You're teaching them how to speak to him, knowing he's eager to listen. This is a very good thing.

For your next devotional reading, go to page 1042.

truth, they have received their reward in full. ⁶But when you pray, go into your room, close the door and pray to your Father, who is unseen. Then your Father, who sees what is done in secret, will reward you. ⁷And when you pray, do not keep on babbling like pagans, for they think they will be heard because of their many words. ⁸Do not be like them, for your Father knows what you need before you ask him.

⁹"This, then, is how you should pray:

" 'Our Father in heaven,
hallowed be your name,

¹⁰your kingdom come,
your will be done
on earth as it is in heaven.
¹¹Give us today our daily bread.
¹²Forgive us our debts,
as we also have forgiven our debtors.
¹³And lead us not into temptation,
but deliver us from the evil one.ᵃ'

¹⁴For if you forgive men when they sin against you, your heavenly Father will

ᵃ13 Or *from evil*; some late manuscripts *one, / for yours is the kingdom and the power and the glory forever. Amen.*

We Invest in Our Children

DAILY INSIGHT

FRIDAY

Passage:
Matthew 6:25–33

Verse:
Matthew 6:33

Under normal circumstances, panel discussions are about as spell-binding to me as watching my bran flakes soak up skim milk. But this one was an exception.

Bobbie and I were attending a Christian conference sponsored by one of our favorite ministries. The experts at the bench were advising us about how to invest our capital in such a way as to allow for tax-sheltered security, provide for retirement, and make funds available for charitable work when we're gone.

One of the men on the panel had lived his whole life under communist domination in Eastern Europe. I figured that Peter and his family had never been challenged with questions about 401K's and IRA's. He sat silently at his microphone for the first thirty minutes of the discussion, until the moderator asked, "So, Peter, what do you think about all of this?"

Peter cleared his throat, nervously sat up straight, and slid the microphone closer. "Well," he said in his deep accent. "We don't have retirement plans where I come from."

We froze in our seats. No one even blinked. After a pause, Peter continued, "We don't have investment plans; we have *families*."

Although the session continued for another half-hour, I didn't hear another word. I made no additional notes on my yellow legal pad.

Long before there were stockbrokers and no-load mutual funds, centuries prior to retirement plans and investment counselors, men and women had children. They raised these children with lavish love and unwavering discipline. The children grew up and their parents grew old. When Dad and Mom got so feeble that they could no longer support themselves, the family simply took over.

"I wonder what would happen to families everywhere," I said to my wife later that day, "if parents knew that in their old age they would be completely dependent on their children. How differently would we raise our children if we knew that they'd use these learned skills to care for us when we were unable to care for ourselves?"

I came home from the conference a different dad. Of course, I didn't fire my financial adviser or cash in my portfolio, but I did look differently at the investment I was making in my children. *What if,* I remember thinking, *my personal long-term security was only a dividend of my investment in my family now? What if I had no other collateral than this?*

I still have no idea why the conference planner put Peter on the stand that day—unless God did it to literally change my life. Yes, maybe that was the reason.

For your next devotional reading, go to page 1044.

also forgive you. **15**But if you do not forgive men their sins, your Father will not forgive your sins.

Fasting

16"When you fast, do not look somber as the hypocrites do, for they disfigure their faces to show men they are fasting. I tell you the truth, they have received their reward in full. **17**But when you fast, put oil on your head and wash your face, **18**so that it will not be obvious to men that you are fasting, but only to your Father, who is unseen; and your Father, who sees what is done in secret, will reward you.

Treasures in Heaven

19"Do not store up for yourselves treasures on earth, where moth and rust destroy, and where thieves break in and steal. **20**But store up for yourselves treasures in heaven, where moth and rust do not destroy, and where thieves do not break in and steal. **21**For where your treasure is, there your heart will be also.

22"The eye is the lamp of the body. If your eyes are good, your whole body will be full of light. **23**But if your eyes are bad, your whole body will be full of darkness. If then the light within you is darkness, how great is that darkness!

24"No one can serve two masters. Either he will hate the one and love the other, or he will be devoted to the one and despise the other. You cannot serve both God and Money.

Do Not Worry

25"Therefore I tell you, do not worry about your life, what you will eat or drink; or about your body, what you will wear. Is not life more important than food, and the body more important than clothes? **26**Look at the birds of the air; they do not sow or reap or store away in barns, and yet your heavenly Father feeds them. Are you not much more valuable than they? **27**Who of you by worrying can add a single hour to his life*a*? **28**"And why do you worry about clothes? See how the lilies of the field grow. They do not labor or spin. **29**Yet I tell you that not even Solomon in all his splendor was dressed like one of these. **30**If that is how God clothes the grass of the field, which is here today and tomorrow is thrown into the fire, will he not much more clothe you, O you of little faith? **31**So do not worry,

saying, 'What shall we eat?' or 'What shall we drink?' or 'What shall we wear?' **32**For the pagans run after all these things, and your heavenly Father knows that you need them. **33**But seek first his kingdom and his righteousness, and all these things will be given to you as well. **34**Therefore do not worry about tomorrow, for tomorrow will worry about itself. Each day has enough trouble of its own.

Judging Others

7 "Do not judge, or you too will be judged. **2**For in the same way you judge others, you will be judged, and with the measure you use, it will be measured to you.

3"Why do you look at the speck of sawdust in your brother's eye and pay no attention to the plank in your own eye? **4**How can you say to your brother, 'Let me take the speck out of your eye,' when all the time there is a plank in your own eye? **5**You hypocrite, first take the plank out of your own eye, and then you will see clearly to remove the speck from your brother's eye.

6"Do not give dogs what is sacred; do not throw your pearls to pigs. If you do, they may trample them under their feet, and then turn and tear you to pieces.

Ask, Seek, Knock

7"Ask and it will be given to you; seek and you will find; knock and the door will be opened to you. **8**For everyone who asks receives; he who seeks finds; and to him who knocks, the door will be opened.

9"Which of you, if his son asks for bread, will give him a stone? **10**Or if he asks for a fish, will give him a snake? **11**If you, then, though you are evil, know how to give good gifts to your children, how much more will your Father in heaven give good gifts to those who ask him! **12**So in everything, do to others what you would have them do to you, for this sums up the Law and the Prophets.

The Narrow and Wide Gates

13"Enter through the narrow gate. For wide is the gate and broad is the road that leads to destruction, and many enter through it. **14**But small is the gate and narrow the road that leads to life, and only a few find it.

a27 Or single cubit to his height

Rock Solid Lives

Key Verse: *"Everyone who hears these words of mine and puts them into practice is like a wise man who built his house on the rock."* Matthew 7:24

Text: Matthew 7:24–28 *(Dad or child reads the text.)*

DAD READS: When contractors build tall buildings, they spend a lot of time and money making sure that they have dug a hole deep enough for the foundation. Then they make sure that they have poured enough concrete into the ground so that the building will be solid. They know that strong foundations make strong buildings.

Child reads: Sometimes buildings face difficult challenges. Terrible winds blow against them, rain pours down on them, and sometimes even earthquakes shake them. But if their builders have made sure that their foundations are strong, the buildings will not be hurt by these things.

DAD READS: When Jesus was a little boy, he worked with his dad in a carpenter's shop. And even though they didn't build skyscrapers, Joseph must have taught his son how to build solid houses. He must have taught Jesus that it was important to make sure all kinds of buildings had good foundations.

Child reads: When Jesus told his followers about houses that were built on a rock and houses that were built on sand, he was helping them to see how important it was for them to listen to his words and obey them. He was telling them that when we live God's way, our lives will be solid—like the house on the rock.

DAD READS: That's right. And Jesus was also saying that when people only hear his words, but then just go on living the way they did before, their lives are going to fall apart when difficult things come their way.

QUIET **TIMES** WITH **Dad**

Child reads: These difficult things are all around us. Because of what I hear at school or see on television, I am tempted to disobey God's laws every day. You are tempted to do bad things, too. Sometimes it is very hard to keep these things from ruining our lives.

DAD READS: Jesus was telling the people that they didn't have the strength to resist temptation all by themselves. They needed the solid foundation that came from listening to him and obeying his words. We can never forget this. God does something for us that we cannot do for ourselves. He helps us to stand, even when the winds are strong, when the rains are really pouring down, and when the earth shakes under our feet.

Child reads: I am so glad that we have a God who helps us to stand strong. Let me pray this prayer with you:

Our Father in heaven, we love you. Thank you for being strong enough to hold us, even when we are tempted to disobey. Thank you that we do not have to fight the wind and the rain and the earthquakes all alone. Please help my dad and me to always listen carefully to your voice, then help us to obey so that our lives can stand strong. We love you. In Jesus' name, **Amen.**

For your next devotional reading, go to page 1047.

A Tree and Its Fruit

15"Watch out for false prophets. They come to you in sheep's clothing, but inwardly they are ferocious wolves. **16**By their fruit you will recognize them. Do people pick grapes from thornbushes, or figs from thistles? **17**Likewise every good tree bears good fruit, but a bad tree bears bad fruit. **18**A good tree cannot bear bad fruit, and a bad tree cannot bear good fruit. **19**Every tree that does not bear good fruit is cut down and thrown into the fire. **20**Thus, by their fruit you will recognize them.

21"Not everyone who says to me, 'Lord, Lord,' will enter the kingdom of heaven, but only he who does the will of my Father who is in heaven. **22**Many will say to me on that day, 'Lord, Lord, did we not prophesy in your name, and in your name drive out demons and perform many miracles?' **23**Then I will tell them plainly, 'I never knew you. Away from me, you evildoers!'

The Wise and Foolish Builders

24"Therefore everyone who hears these words of mine and puts them into practice is like a wise man who built his house on the rock. **25**The rain came down, the streams rose, and the winds blew and beat against that house; yet it did not fall, because it had its foundation on the rock. **26**But everyone who hears these words of mine and does not put them into practice is like a foolish man who built his house on sand. **27**The rain came down, the streams rose, and the winds blew and beat against that house, and it fell with a great crash."

28When Jesus had finished saying these things, the crowds were amazed at his teaching, **29**because he taught as one who had authority, and not as their teachers of the law.

The Man With Leprosy

8 When he came down from the mountainside, large crowds followed him. **2**A man with leprosy[a] came and knelt before him and said, "Lord, if you are willing, you can make me clean."

3Jesus reached out his hand and touched the man. "I am willing," he said. "Be clean!" Immediately he was cured[b] of his leprosy. **4**Then Jesus said to him, "See that you don't tell anyone. But go, show yourself to the priest and offer the gift Moses commanded, as a testimony to them."

The Faith of the Centurion

5When Jesus had entered Capernaum, a centurion came to him, asking for help. **6**"Lord," he said, "my servant lies at home paralyzed and in terrible suffering."

7Jesus said to him, "I will go and heal him."

8The centurion replied, "Lord, I do not deserve to have you come under my roof. But just say the word, and my servant will be healed. **9**For I myself am a man under authority, with soldiers under me. I tell this one, 'Go,' and he goes; and that one, 'Come,' and he comes. I say to my servant, 'Do this,' and he does it."

10When Jesus heard this, he was astonished and said to those following him, "I tell you the truth, I have not found anyone in Israel with such great faith. **11**I say to you that many will come from the east and the west, and will take their places at the feast with Abraham, Isaac and Jacob in the kingdom of heaven. **12**But the subjects of the kingdom will be thrown outside, into the darkness, where there will be weeping and gnashing of teeth."

13Then Jesus said to the centurion, "Go! It will be done just as you believed it would." And his servant was healed at that very hour.

Jesus Heals Many

14When Jesus came into Peter's house, he saw Peter's mother-in-law lying in bed with a fever. **15**He touched her hand and the fever left her, and she got up and began to wait on him.

16When evening came, many who were demon-possessed were brought to him, and he drove out the spirits with a word and healed all the sick. **17**This was to fulfill what was spoken through the prophet Isaiah:

"He took up our infirmities
    and carried our diseases."[c]

The Cost of Following Jesus

18When Jesus saw the crowd around him, he gave orders to cross to the other side of the lake. **19**Then a teacher of the

---

a2 The Greek word was used for various diseases affecting the skin—not necessarily leprosy.
b3 Greek *made clean*   *c17* Isaiah 53:4

law came to him and said, "Teacher, I will follow you wherever you go."

²⁰Jesus replied, "Foxes have holes and birds of the air have nests, but the Son of Man has no place to lay his head."

²¹Another disciple said to him, "Lord, first let me go and bury my father."

²²But Jesus told him, "Follow me, and let the dead bury their own dead."

Jesus Calms the Storm

²³Then he got into the boat and his disciples followed him. ²⁴Without warning, a furious storm came up on the lake, so that the waves swept over the boat. But Jesus was sleeping. ²⁵The disciples went and woke him, saying, "Lord, save us! We're going to drown!"

²⁶He replied, "You of little faith, why are you so afraid?" Then he got up and rebuked the winds and the waves, and it was completely calm.

²⁷The men were amazed and asked, "What kind of man is this? Even the winds and the waves obey him!"

The Healing of Two Demon-possessed Men

²⁸When he arrived at the other side in the region of the Gadarenes,ᵃ two demon-possessed men coming from the tombs met him. They were so violent that no one could pass that way. ²⁹"What do you want with us, Son of God?" they shouted. "Have you come here to torture us before the appointed time?"

³⁰Some distance from them a large herd of pigs was feeding. ³¹The demons begged Jesus, "If you drive us out, send us into the herd of pigs."

³²He said to them, "Go!" So they came out and went into the pigs, and the whole herd rushed down the steep bank into the lake and died in the water. ³³Those tending the pigs ran off, went into the town and reported all this, including what had happened to the demon-possessed men. ³⁴Then the whole town went out to meet Jesus. And when they saw him, they pleaded with him to leave their region.

Jesus Heals a Paralytic

9 Jesus stepped into a boat, crossed over and came to his own town. ²Some men brought to him a paralytic, lying on a mat. When Jesus saw their faith, he said to the paralytic, "Take heart, son; your sins are forgiven."

³At this, some of the teachers of the law said to themselves, "This fellow is blaspheming!"

⁴Knowing their thoughts, Jesus said, "Why do you entertain evil thoughts in your hearts? ⁵Which is easier: to say, 'Your sins are forgiven,' or to say, 'Get up and walk'? ⁶But so that you may know that the Son of Man has authority on earth to forgive sins . . ." Then he said to the paralytic, "Get up, take your mat and go home." ⁷And the man got up and went home. ⁸When the crowd saw this, they were filled with awe; and they praised God, who had given such authority to men.

The Calling of Matthew

⁹As Jesus went on from there, he saw a man named Matthew sitting at the tax collector's booth. "Follow me," he told him, and Matthew got up and followed him.

¹⁰While Jesus was having dinner at Matthew's house, many tax collectors and "sinners" came and ate with him and his disciples. ¹¹When the Pharisees saw this, they asked his disciples, "Why does your teacher eat with tax collectors and 'sinners'?"

¹²On hearing this, Jesus said, "It is not the healthy who need a doctor, but the sick. ¹³But go and learn what this means: 'I desire mercy, not sacrifice.'ᵇ For I have not come to call the righteous, but sinners."

Jesus Questioned About Fasting

¹⁴Then John's disciples came and asked him, "How is it that we and the Pharisees fast, but your disciples do not fast?"

¹⁵Jesus answered, "How can the guests of the bridegroom mourn while he is with them? The time will come when the bridegroom will be taken from them; then they will fast.

¹⁶"No one sews a patch of unshrunk cloth on an old garment, for the patch will pull away from the garment, making the tear worse. ¹⁷Neither do men pour new wine into old wineskins. If they do, the skins will burst, the wine will run out and the wineskins will be ruined. No, they pour new wine into new wineskins, and both are preserved."

A Dead Girl and a Sick Woman

¹⁸While he was saying this, a ruler came and knelt before him and said, "My

---

ᵃ28 Some manuscripts *Gergesenes*; others *Gerasenes*   ᵇ13 Hosea 6:6

daughter has just died. But come and put your hand on her, and she will live." **19**Jesus got up and went with him, and so did his disciples.

20Just then a woman who had been subject to bleeding for twelve years came up behind him and touched the edge of his cloak. **21**She said to herself, "If I only touch his cloak, I will be healed."

22Jesus turned and saw her. "Take heart, daughter," he said, "your faith has healed you." And the woman was healed from that moment.

23When Jesus entered the ruler's house and saw the flute players and the noisy crowd, **24**he said, "Go away. The girl is not dead but asleep." But they laughed at him. **25**After the crowd had been put outside, he went in and took the girl by the hand, and she got up. **26**News of this spread through all that region.

Jesus Heals the Blind and Mute

27As Jesus went on from there, two blind men followed him, calling out, "Have mercy on us, Son of David!"

28When he had gone indoors, the blind

Life-changing Lessons from Unexpected Places

In the early nineties, when we moved into a little subdivision tucked into a few Tennessee foothills, I found a wonderful, winding, five-and-a-half-mile course for running. It provided just enough terrain and scenery to make for an interesting workout, but it wasn't so difficult that I'd become discouraged.

The only thing I didn't like about this run was the dog living between miles three and four. He was a Husky, gray with black eyes, and he was *mean*. Sometimes he'd stand on the road where I could see him as I approached. At other times he'd hide behind a tree or a barn, just waiting to scare me. When I got to a certain spot on the road, he'd charge—barking, and snarling as if I were some specially flavored dog chow.

I hated this dog. I plotted his demise. I thought of driving up the road late some night and shooting his lights out. Then I decided to buy a can of Mace. *I'll teach him who's boss around these hills.*

But before I had a chance to buy the Mace, I bumped into the guy who lived at the end of our street. I knew he was a runner, too, so I asked if he knew about "my" five-and-a-half-mile course. He said he did. I asked him if he had seen the Husky. He said he had. I asked if the dog had frightened him the way he frightened me.

"At first he did," my neighbor said.

"At first?" I returned.

"Yes, until one day I decided to stop

DAILY INSIGHT

MONDAY

Passage:
Matthew 8:5–13

Verse:
Matthew 8:13

running for a moment," he replied. "I squatted down in the middle of the road and petted him. The dog rolled over on his back, begging me to scratch his tummy. Now I actually look forward to seeing him when I run."

I felt so stupid—so ashamed of myself. My neighbor, without even knowing it, had taught me a powerful lesson in kindness.

Just as I learned a lesson that day, the Jews who followed Jesus were about to learn something about faith from a very unlikely person—a Roman military officer. This "pagan" soldier came to Jesus and asked the Savior to heal his ailing servant. Jesus agreed to come to the military man's home immediately, but the centurion refused. "Just say the word," the man told the Messiah, "and my servant will be healed" (v. 8).

Jesus was astonished by this Gentile's faith, and said, "I have not found anyone in Israel with such great faith." The Israelites must have been mortified.

God has a lot to teach us. Some of it will come by way of traditional means—by reading his Word, listening to our ministers teach, spending time in prayer. But some of the lessons are going to come from unexpected places. Listen carefully. Pay attention. God's truth will show up in all kinds of unusual forms.

For your next devotional reading, go to page 1050.

men came to him, and he asked them, "Do you believe that I am able to do this?" "Yes, Lord," they replied.

²⁹Then he touched their eyes and said, "According to your faith will it be done to you"; ³⁰and their sight was restored. Jesus warned them sternly, "See that no one knows about this." ³¹But they went out and spread the news about him all over that region.

³²While they were going out, a man who was demon-possessed and could not talk was brought to Jesus. ³³And when the demon was driven out, the man who had been mute spoke. The crowd was amazed and said, "Nothing like this has ever been seen in Israel."

³⁴But the Pharisees said, "It is by the prince of demons that he drives out demons."

The Workers Are Few

³⁵Jesus went through all the towns and villages, teaching in their synagogues, preaching the good news of the kingdom and healing every disease and sickness. ³⁶When he saw the crowds, he had compassion on them, because they were harassed and helpless, like sheep without a shepherd. ³⁷Then he said to his disciples, "The harvest is plentiful but the workers are few. ³⁸Ask the Lord of the harvest, therefore, to send out workers into his harvest field."

Jesus Sends Out the Twelve

10 He called his twelve disciples to him and gave them authority to drive out evil*a* spirits and to heal every disease and sickness.

²These are the names of the twelve apostles: first, Simon (who is called Peter) and his brother Andrew; James son of Zebedee, and his brother John; ³Philip and Bartholomew; Thomas and Matthew the tax collector; James son of Alphaeus, and Thaddaeus; ⁴Simon the Zealot and Judas Iscariot, who betrayed him.

⁵These twelve Jesus sent out with the following instructions: "Do not go among the Gentiles or enter any town of the Samaritans. ⁶Go rather to the lost sheep of Israel. ⁷As you go, preach this message: 'The kingdom of heaven is near.' ⁸Heal the sick, raise the dead, cleanse those who have leprosy,*b* drive out demons. Freely you have received, freely give. ⁹Do not take along any gold or silver or copper in your belts; ¹⁰take no bag for the journey,

or extra tunic, or sandals or a staff; for the worker is worth his keep.

¹¹"Whatever town or village you enter, search for some worthy person there and stay at his house until you leave. ¹²As you enter the home, give it your greeting. ¹³If the home is deserving, let your peace rest on it; if it is not, let your peace return to you. ¹⁴If anyone will not welcome you or listen to your words, shake the dust off your feet when you leave that home or town. ¹⁵I tell you the truth, it will be more bearable for Sodom and Gomorrah on the day of judgment than for that town. ¹⁶I am sending you out like sheep among wolves. Therefore be as shrewd as snakes and as innocent as doves.

¹⁷"Be on your guard against men; they will hand you over to the local councils and flog you in their synagogues. ¹⁸On my account you will be brought before governors and kings as witnesses to them and to the Gentiles. ¹⁹But when they arrest you, do not worry about what to say or how to say it. At that time you will be given what to say, ²⁰for it will not be you speaking, but the Spirit of your Father speaking through you.

²¹"Brother will betray brother to death, and a father his child; children will rebel against their parents and have them put to death. ²²All men will hate you because of me, but he who stands firm to the end will be saved. ²³When you are persecuted in one place, flee to another. I tell you the truth, you will not finish going through the cities of Israel before the Son of Man comes.

²⁴"A student is not above his teacher, nor a servant above his master. ²⁵It is enough for the student to be like his teacher, and the servant like his master. If the head of the house has been called Beelzebub,*c* how much more the members of his household!

²⁶"So do not be afraid of them. There is nothing concealed that will not be disclosed, or hidden that will not be made known. ²⁷What I tell you in the dark, speak in the daylight; what is whispered in your ear, proclaim from the roofs. ²⁸Do not be afraid of those who kill the body but cannot kill the soul. Rather, be afraid of the One who can destroy both soul and body in hell. ²⁹Are not two sparrows sold for a

---

*a*1 Greek *unclean*   *b*8 The Greek word was used for various diseases affecting the skin—not necessarily leprosy.   *c*25 Greek *Beezeboul* or *Beelzeboul*

penny[a]? Yet not one of them will fall to the ground apart from the will of your Father. [30]And even the very hairs of your head are all numbered. [31]So don't be afraid; you are worth more than many sparrows.

[32]"Whoever acknowledges me before men, I will also acknowledge him before my Father in heaven. [33]But whoever disowns me before men, I will disown him before my Father in heaven.

[34]"Do not suppose that I have come to bring peace to the earth. I did not come to bring peace, but a sword. [35]For I have come to turn

" 'a man against his father,
    a daughter against her mother,
  a daughter-in-law against her mother-
      in-law—
[36]   a man's enemies will be the members
      of his own household.'[b]

[37]"Anyone who loves his father or mother more than me is not worthy of me; anyone who loves his son or daughter more than me is not worthy of me; [38]and anyone who does not take his cross and follow me is not worthy of me. [39]Whoever finds his life will lose it, and whoever loses his life for my sake will find it.

[40]"He who receives you receives me, and he who receives me receives the one who sent me. [41]Anyone who receives a prophet because he is a prophet will receive a prophet's reward, and anyone who receives a righteous man because he is a righteous man will receive a righteous man's reward. [42]And if anyone gives even a cup of cold water to one of these little ones because he is my disciple, I tell you the truth, he will certainly not lose his reward."

Jesus and John the Baptist

After Jesus had finished instructing his twelve disciples, he went on from there to teach and preach in the towns of Galilee.[c]

[2]When John heard in prison what Christ was doing, he sent his disciples [3]to ask him, "Are you the one who was to come, or should we expect someone else?"

[4]Jesus replied, "Go back and report to John what you hear and see: [5]The blind receive sight, the lame walk, those who have leprosy[d] are cured, the deaf hear, the dead are raised, and the good news is preached to the poor. [6]Blessed is the man who does not fall away on account of me."

[7]As John's disciples were leaving, Jesus began to speak to the crowd about John: "What did you go out into the desert to see? A reed swayed by the wind? [8]If not, what did you go out to see? A man dressed in fine clothes? No, those who wear fine clothes are in kings' palaces. [9]Then what did you go out to see? A prophet? Yes, I tell you, and more than a prophet. [10]This is the one about whom it is written:

" 'I will send my messenger ahead of
      you,
    who will prepare your way before
      you.'[e]

[11]I tell you the truth: Among those born of women there has not risen anyone greater than John the Baptist; yet he who is least in the kingdom of heaven is greater than he. [12]From the days of John the Baptist until now, the kingdom of heaven has been forcefully advancing, and forceful men lay hold of it. [13]For all the Prophets and the Law prophesied until John. [14]And if you are willing to accept it, he is the Elijah who was to come. [15]He who has ears, let him hear.

[16]"To what can I compare this generation? They are like children sitting in the marketplaces and calling out to others:

[17]" 'We played the flute for you,
      and you did not dance;
  we sang a dirge,
      and you did not mourn.'

[18]For John came neither eating nor drinking, and they say, 'He has a demon.' [19]The Son of Man came eating and drinking, and they say, 'Here is a glutton and a drunkard, a friend of tax collectors and "sinners." ' But wisdom is proved right by her actions."

Woe on Unrepentant Cities

[20]Then Jesus began to denounce the cities in which most of his miracles had been performed, because they did not repent. [21]"Woe to you, Korazin! Woe to you, Bethsaida! If the miracles that were performed in you had been performed in Tyre and Sidon, they would have repented long ago in sackcloth and ashes. [22]But I tell you, it will be more bearable for Tyre and Sidon on the day of judgment than for you. [23]And you, Capernaum, will you

---

[a]29 Greek an assarion   [b]36 Micah 7:6   [c]1 Greek in their towns   [d]5 The Greek word was used for various diseases affecting the skin—not necessarily leprosy.   [e]10 Mal. 3:1

be lifted up to the skies? No, you will go down to the depths.*a* If the miracles that were performed in you had been performed in Sodom, it would have remained to this day. [24]But I tell you that it will be more bearable for Sodom on the day of judgment than for you."

Rest for the Weary

[25]At that time Jesus said, "I praise you, Father, Lord of heaven and earth, because you have hidden these things from the wise and learned, and revealed them to little children. [26]Yes, Father, for this was your good pleasure.

[27]"All things have been committed to me by my Father. No one knows the Son except the Father, and no one knows the Father except the Son and those to whom the Son chooses to reveal him.

[28]"Come to me, all you who are weary and burdened, and I will give you rest. [29]Take my yoke upon you and learn from me, for I am gentle and humble in heart, and you will find rest for your souls. [30]For my yoke is easy and my burden is light."

a23 Greek *Hades*

The Rogers Boys: Roy and Fred

DAILY INSIGHT

TUESDAY

Passage:
Matthew 11:25–30

Verse:
Matthew 11:30

When our girls were barely old enough to walk, they were introduced to the program, "Mr. Rogers' Neighborhood." And, even though I actually had the chance to meet Fred Rogers in person, I must admit that I couldn't stand his television show. He acted so meek ... so wimpy ... so absolutely benign. I preferred the Roy Rogers (no relation to Fred) of my youth. Give me Trigger and six-shooters. Forget the cardigan sweaters, the songs and the puppet displays.

In spite of my own biases, however, I noticed that our children were completely taken with Fred Rogers. His gentleness won their hearts. His lessons made an indelible impression on their minds. His approachability melted their souls.

As men, our lives are filled with the rush of competition. Our nostrils flare at the thrill of the deal—daring, winning and profiting. In our experience, weaklings finish last. But in the text we read today, Jesus dropped a bomb on his followers—especially those men who, like me, would have strongly preferred cowboys to soft-spoken puppeteers. "Little children have the answers," he said to them. He went on to say, "I am gentle and humble in heart, and you will find rest for your souls."

As men, this truth must make its way into our minds. God's power will rarely be revealed to us in the noise and the fury. Instead, his voice will usually penetrate our experiences in a whisper—a gentle tug in our hearts, a quiet nudge.

As fathers, our heavenly Father tells us that if we are to love our children in a way they will understand, we must be willing to stop, to listen and to be tender and gentle. Our personal style may make us more comfortable shouting orders from the sidelines, like some anxious high-school football coach. But God calls us to shed the cleats and don the soft sneakers, to delicately win our children by our compassion and care.

As a grown up, you're probably like me—more a Roy Rogers than a Fred Rogers kind of guy. Don't apologize for that. It's perfectly understandable. But Jesus reminds us today that his life-changing truth usually comes to us in gentle, unobtrusive ways. And he tells us that only through our tenderness will our children's lives be touched.

Of course, they need the sideline coaching, the course-altering directives from their dad that adjust their performance. But your children must have your tenderness, or you'll miss their hearts. So, go ahead and enjoy Roy, but Fred's going to win this one.

For your next devotional reading, go to page 1053.

Lord of the Sabbath

12 At that time Jesus went through the grainfields on the Sabbath. His disciples were hungry and began to pick some heads of grain and eat them. ²When the Pharisees saw this, they said to him, "Look! Your disciples are doing what is unlawful on the Sabbath."

³He answered, "Haven't you read what David did when he and his companions were hungry? ⁴He entered the house of God, and he and his companions ate the consecrated bread—which was not lawful for them to do, but only for the priests. ⁵Or haven't you read in the Law that on the Sabbath the priests in the temple desecrate the day and yet are innocent? ⁶I tell you that one*ᵃ* greater than the temple is here. ⁷If you had known what these words mean, 'I desire mercy, not sacrifice,'*ᵇ* you would not have condemned the innocent. ⁸For the Son of Man is Lord of the Sabbath."

⁹Going on from that place, he went into their synagogue, ¹⁰and a man with a shriveled hand was there. Looking for a reason to accuse Jesus, they asked him, "Is it lawful to heal on the Sabbath?"

¹¹He said to them, "If any of you has a sheep and it falls into a pit on the Sabbath, will you not take hold of it and lift it out? ¹²How much more valuable is a man than a sheep! Therefore it is lawful to do good on the Sabbath."

¹³Then he said to the man, "Stretch out your hand." So he stretched it out and it was completely restored, just as sound as the other. ¹⁴But the Pharisees went out and plotted how they might kill Jesus.

God's Chosen Servant

¹⁵Aware of this, Jesus withdrew from that place. Many followed him, and he healed all their sick, ¹⁶warning them not to tell who he was. ¹⁷This was to fulfill what was spoken through the prophet Isaiah:

¹⁸ "Here is my servant whom I have chosen,
     the one I love, in whom I delight;
  I will put my Spirit on him,
     and he will proclaim justice to the nations.
¹⁹ He will not quarrel or cry out;
     no one will hear his voice in the streets.
²⁰ A bruised reed he will not break,

and a smoldering wick he will not snuff out,
  till he leads justice to victory.
²¹   In his name the nations will put their hope."*ᶜ*

Jesus and Beelzebub

²²Then they brought him a demon-possessed man who was blind and mute, and Jesus healed him, so that he could both talk and see. ²³All the people were astonished and said, "Could this be the Son of David?"

²⁴But when the Pharisees heard this, they said, "It is only by Beelzebub,*ᵈ* the prince of demons, that this fellow drives out demons."

²⁵Jesus knew their thoughts and said to them, "Every kingdom divided against itself will be ruined, and every city or household divided against itself will not stand. ²⁶If Satan drives out Satan, he is divided against himself. How then can his kingdom stand? ²⁷And if I drive out demons by Beelzebub, by whom do your people drive them out? So then, they will be your judges. ²⁸But if I drive out demons by the Spirit of God, then the kingdom of God has come upon you.

²⁹ "Or again, how can anyone enter a strong man's house and carry off his possessions unless he first ties up the strong man? Then he can rob his house.

³⁰ "He who is not with me is against me, and he who does not gather with me scatters. ³¹And so I tell you, every sin and blasphemy will be forgiven men, but the blasphemy against the Spirit will not be forgiven. ³²Anyone who speaks a word against the Son of Man will be forgiven, but anyone who speaks against the Holy Spirit will not be forgiven, either in this age or in the age to come.

³³ "Make a tree good and its fruit will be good, or make a tree bad and its fruit will be bad, for a tree is recognized by its fruit. ³⁴You brood of vipers, how can you who are evil say anything good? For out of the overflow of the heart the mouth speaks. ³⁵The good man brings good things out of the good stored up in him, and the evil man brings evil things out of the evil stored up in him. ³⁶But I tell you that men will have to give account on the day of judgment for every careless word they have spoken. ³⁷For by your words you will

---

ᵃ6 Or *something*; also in verses 41 and 42
ᵇ7 Hosea 6:6   *ᶜ21* Isaiah 42:1-4   *ᵈ24* Greek *Beezeboul* or *Beelzeboul*; also in verse 27

be acquitted, and by your words you will be condemned."

The Sign of Jonah

38Then some of the Pharisees and teachers of the law said to him, "Teacher, we want to see a miraculous sign from you."

39He answered, "A wicked and adulterous generation asks for a miraculous sign! But none will be given it except the sign of the prophet Jonah. **40**For as Jonah was three days and three nights in the belly of a huge fish, so the Son of Man will be three days and three nights in the heart of the earth. **41**The men of Nineveh will stand up at the judgment with this generation and condemn it; for they repented at the preaching of Jonah, and now one*a* greater than Jonah is here. **42**The Queen of the South will rise at the judgment with this generation and condemn it; for she came from the ends of the earth to listen to Solomon's wisdom, and now one greater than Solomon is here.

43"When an evil*b* spirit comes out of a man, it goes through arid places seeking rest and does not find it. **44**Then it says, 'I will return to the house I left.' When it arrives, it finds the house unoccupied, swept clean and put in order. **45**Then it goes and takes with it seven other spirits more wicked than itself, and they go in and live there. And the final condition of that man is worse than the first. That is how it will be with this wicked generation."

Jesus' Mother and Brothers

46While Jesus was still talking to the crowd, his mother and brothers stood outside, wanting to speak to him. **47**Someone told him, "Your mother and brothers are standing outside, wanting to speak to you."*c*

48He replied to him, "Who is my mother, and who are my brothers?" **49**Pointing to his disciples, he said, "Here are my mother and my brothers. **50**For whoever does the will of my Father in heaven is my brother and sister and mother."

The Parable of the Sower

13 That same day Jesus went out of the house and sat by the lake. **2**Such large crowds gathered around him that he got into a boat and sat in it, while all the people stood on the shore. **3**Then he told them many things in parables, saying: "A

farmer went out to sow his seed. **4**As he was scattering the seed, some fell along the path, and the birds came and ate it up. **5**Some fell on rocky places, where it did not have much soil. It sprang up quickly, because the soil was shallow. **6**But when the sun came up, the plants were scorched, and they withered because they had no root. **7**Other seed fell among thorns, which grew up and choked the plants. **8**Still other seed fell on good soil, where it produced a crop—a hundred, sixty or thirty times what was sown. **9**He who has ears, let him hear."

10The disciples came to him and asked, "Why do you speak to the people in parables?"

11He replied, "The knowledge of the secrets of the kingdom of heaven has been given to you, but not to them. **12**Whoever has will be given more, and he will have an abundance. Whoever does not have, even what he has will be taken from him. **13**This is why I speak to them in parables:

"Though seeing, they do not see;
  though hearing, they do not hear or
    understand.

14In them is fulfilled the prophecy of Isaiah:

" 'You will be ever hearing but never
      understanding;
  you will be ever seeing but never
      perceiving.
15For this people's heart has become
      calloused;
  they hardly hear with their ears,
  and they have closed their eyes.
Otherwise they might see with their
      eyes,
  hear with their ears,
  understand with their hearts
and turn, and I would heal them.'*d*

16But blessed are your eyes because they see, and your ears because they hear. **17**For I tell you the truth, many prophets and righteous men longed to see what you see but did not see it, and to hear what you hear but did not hear it.

18"Listen then to what the parable of the sower means: **19**When anyone hears the message about the kingdom and does not understand it, the evil one comes and snatches away what was sown in his heart. This is the seed sown along the path. **20**The one who received the seed

a41 Or something; also in verse 42   *b43* Greek *unclean.*   *c47* Some manuscripts do not have verse 47.   *d15* Isaiah 6:9,10

that fell on rocky places is the man who hears the word and at once receives it with joy. ²¹But since he has no root, he lasts only a short time. When trouble or persecution comes because of the word, he quickly falls away. ²²The one who received the seed that fell among the thorns is the man who hears the word, but the worries of this life and the deceitfulness of wealth choke it, making it unfruitful. ²³But the one who received the seed that fell on good soil is the man who hears the word and understands it. He produces a crop, yielding a hundred, sixty or thirty times what was sown."

The Parable of the Weeds

²⁴Jesus told them another parable: "The kingdom of heaven is like a man who sowed good seed in his field. ²⁵But while everyone was sleeping, his enemy came and sowed weeds among the wheat, and went away. ²⁶When the wheat sprouted and formed heads, then the weeds also appeared.

Are You Listening to Me?

DAILY INSIGHT

WEDNESDAY

Passage:
Matthew 13:1–9

Verse:
Matthew 13:9

Our little Missy had many special skills. She was our first child, so of course we knew she was a one-in-a-million kid, but some things about her seemed quite unusual. One of those things was Missy's ability to pay attention. With an unbelievable level of intensity, she noticed everything that went on around her.

One afternoon as I shuffled into the house after a tough day at work, Missy decided that it was time for a talk with Daddy. I sat down and she sat on my lap, facing me, and began her recitation of the day's goings-on. At first, I was interested. But, frankly, as the monologue wore on, I got distracted and started looking around the room. Okay, I'll admit I was a little bored. After all, I had had my own busy day.

Missy stopped talking. She knew I wasn't listening. So she reached up with her hands, gripped my cheeks in her fists, and turned my face toward hers. In the no-nonsense, I'm-not-kidding-at-all voice that we had come to expect from her, Missy said, "Daddy, *look at me* when I'm talking to you."

Jesus had something to say to a large crowd of people, and he wanted them to listen. He told them about a farmer who was spreading seed, using this familiar frame of reference to tell them about the words he had been speaking—words he scattered like seeds. The four places these powerful little seeds landed represented the different kinds of people who heard Jesus' words.

Just for a moment, let's pretend that Jesus is scattering these words on you and me.

"Some of my words are landing on deaf ears," he might say to us. "You're so self-sufficient, so sure of yourself. You're like the hard path. These words don't have a chance to take root in your hard heart.

"Some of my words you receive enthusiastically," he might continue. "You're excited. You're motivated. But you receive *everything* enthusiastically ... you get all fired up about the new Corvette and the Cubs' two-game winning streak. My words are no different to you than these temporary and frivolous things.

"Some of you hear my words, and you even obey them," Jesus might say to some of us. "But you're covered over with heavy responsibilities and relentless distractions. You sincerely intend to be a follower, a real disciple, but, frankly, your calendar doesn't have room for me.

"Some of you let my words sink in," He might finally say. "You've experienced the benefits of living God's way, and your lives and your families will never be the same."

Had a busy day? Getting distracted? Jesus would do what he did with the crowd after this story: verbally take your cheeks in his hands, turn your face toward his, and say, "He who has ears, let him hear."

Missy would be proud.

For your next devotional reading, go to page 1054.

²⁷"The owner's servants came to him and said, 'Sir, didn't you sow good seed in your field? Where then did the weeds come from?'

²⁸" 'An enemy did this,' he replied.

"The servants asked him, 'Do you want us to go and pull them up?'

²⁹" 'No,' he answered, 'because while you are pulling the weeds, you may root up the wheat with them. ³⁰Let both grow together until the harvest. At that time I will tell the harvesters: First collect the weeds and tie them in bundles to be burned; then gather the wheat and bring it into my barn.' "

The Parables of the Mustard Seed and the Yeast

³¹He told them another parable: "The kingdom of heaven is like a mustard seed, which a man took and planted in his field. ³²Though it is the smallest of all your seeds, yet when it grows, it is the largest of garden plants and becomes a tree, so that

One-carat Diamonds and Other Great Investments

Having been a hopeless entrepreneur all my life, I have always looked for ways to stay busy—and to make a little money with my activity, too. In college, I decided not to take a traditional job and looked for other ways to generate a dependable revenue stream. If you had been a Taylor University male student in the late sixties, you would have been able to visit room 215 in Wengatz Hall and buy custom-made, pinpoint Oxford dress shirts; flowers for your dates; or a diamond ring if you were at that stage in the dating relationship. My roommate was extremely patient with all of this merchandising.

One of the interesting things I noticed about selling these things from my college room was the spending habits of my customers. When a student went to buy a shirt for himself, he was fairly careful about how much he would spend. And when he was shopping for a corsage, he usually held back on being too exorbitant.

But when the same young man had decided on a lifelong companion and was going to slap a diamond on her hand, he went crazy. He lost all sense of what would be reasonable to spend given his current net worth. He should have known better, but he didn't ... which, of course, pleased the diamond merchant in room 215. Love is a wonderful thing.

The Gospels are filled with stories about people who, when confronted with the truth of the Savior, did what no one expected them to do. Some left their careers to

DAILY
INSIGHT

THURSDAY

Passage:
Matthew 13:44–46

Verses:
Matthew 13:45–46

follow Jesus. Some faced the ridicule of their friends. And some even gave their lives. Jesus' parables in the short reading for today reflect that type of radical commitment, one that goes way beyond a penniless college senior going for the one-carat brilliant round-cut.

The words that fill the pages of this book may threaten your security. If you invest your life in these words and principles, they could even shake the solidarity of your plans for the future. These words may have serious implications regarding your job, your habits, your friends, or your net worth. God's Word has that effect on people.

But there's one thing I forgot to mention. Perhaps the happiest moments I can remember from my college career—not counting midnight trips to the Pizza King in Hartford City—were the faces of the men when I delivered their flawless diamonds to them. They had cashed it in for these marvelous little crystalline rocks; it would take them years to pay the bill, and they were absolutely delighted with the wisdom of their investment.

Jesus calls us to embark on the same dangerous adventure—to be irrevocably captivated with following him. The payoff is a sure thing. What other explanation could there possibly be for the countless faithful people who have gone before us?

God's love is a more wonderful thing.

For your next devotional reading, go to page 1056.

the birds of the air come and perch in its branches."

³³He told them still another parable: "The kingdom of heaven is like yeast that a woman took and mixed into a large amount^a of flour until it worked all through the dough."

³⁴Jesus spoke all these things to the crowd in parables; he did not say anything to them without using a parable. ³⁵So was fulfilled what was spoken through the prophet:

"I will open my mouth in parables,
    I will utter things hidden since the
        creation of the world."^b

The Parable of the Weeds Explained

³⁶Then he left the crowd and went into the house. His disciples came to him and said, "Explain to us the parable of the weeds in the field."

³⁷He answered, "The one who sowed the good seed is the Son of Man. ³⁸The field is the world, and the good seed stands for the sons of the kingdom. The weeds are the sons of the evil one, ³⁹and the enemy who sows them is the devil. The harvest is the end of the age, and the harvesters are angels.

⁴⁰"As the weeds are pulled up and burned in the fire, so it will be at the end of the age. ⁴¹The Son of Man will send out his angels, and they will weed out of his kingdom everything that causes sin and all who do evil. ⁴²They will throw them into the fiery furnace, where there will be weeping and gnashing of teeth. ⁴³Then the righteous will shine like the sun in the kingdom of their Father. He who has ears, let him hear.

The Parables of the Hidden Treasure and the Pearl

⁴⁴"The kingdom of heaven is like treasure hidden in a field. When a man found it, he hid it again, and then in his joy went and sold all he had and bought that field.

⁴⁵"Again, the kingdom of heaven is like a merchant looking for fine pearls. ⁴⁶When he found one of great value, he went away and sold everything he had and bought it.

The Parable of the Net

⁴⁷"Once again, the kingdom of heaven is like a net that was let down into the lake and caught all kinds of fish. ⁴⁸When it was full, the fishermen pulled it up on the shore. Then they sat down and collected the good fish in baskets, but threw the bad away. ⁴⁹This is how it will be at the end of the age. The angels will come and separate the wicked from the righteous ⁵⁰and throw them into the fiery furnace, where there will be weeping and gnashing of teeth.

⁵¹"Have you understood all these things?" Jesus asked.

"Yes," they replied.

⁵²He said to them, "Therefore every teacher of the law who has been instructed about the kingdom of heaven is like the owner of a house who brings out of his storeroom new treasures as well as old."

A Prophet Without Honor

⁵³When Jesus had finished these parables, he moved on from there. ⁵⁴Coming to his hometown, he began teaching the people in their synagogue, and they were amazed. "Where did this man get this wisdom and these miraculous powers?" they asked. ⁵⁵"Isn't this the carpenter's son? Isn't his mother's name Mary, and aren't his brothers James, Joseph, Simon and Judas? ⁵⁶Aren't all his sisters with us? Where then did this man get all these things?" ⁵⁷And they took offense at him.

But Jesus said to them, "Only in his hometown and in his own house is a prophet without honor."

⁵⁸And he did not do many miracles there because of their lack of faith.

John the Baptist Beheaded

14 At that time Herod the tetrarch heard the reports about Jesus, ²and he said to his attendants, "This is John the Baptist; he has risen from the dead! That is why miraculous powers are at work in him."

³Now Herod had arrested John and bound him and put him in prison because of Herodias, his brother Philip's wife, ⁴for John had been saying to him: "It is not lawful for you to have her." ⁵Herod wanted to kill John, but he was afraid of the people, because they considered him a prophet.

⁶On Herod's birthday the daughter of Herodias danced for them and pleased Herod so much ⁷that he promised with an oath to give her whatever she asked. ⁸Prompted by her mother, she said, "Give me here on a platter the head of John the Baptist." ⁹The king was distressed, but

^a33 Greek three satas (probably about 1/2 bushel or 22 liters)   ^b35 Psalm 78:2

because of his oaths and his dinner guests, he ordered that her request be granted [10]and had John beheaded in the prison. [11]His head was brought in on a platter and given to the girl, who carried it to her mother. [12]John's disciples came and took his body and buried it. Then they went and told Jesus.

Jesus Feeds the Five Thousand

[13]When Jesus heard what had happened, he withdrew by boat privately to a solitary place. Hearing of this, the crowds followed him on foot from the towns. [14]When Jesus landed and saw a large crowd, he had compassion on them and healed their sick.

[15]As evening approached, the disciples came to him and said, "This is a remote place, and it's already getting late. Send the crowds away, so they can go to the villages and buy themselves some food."

[16]Jesus replied, "They do not need to go away. You give them something to eat."

Lions and Tigers and Bears, Oh My!

For some reason, my boss had decided to hold our sales conference at a remote camp facility. On the first night, following our first sales presentation, the camp director paid us a visit. He seemed very confident and professional. He had outlined several "features" of this special place, including being "over a hundred miles from the nearest hospital." Nice feature. But he assured us that we were "safe out here." I seem to remember reading the same quote from the steward's log on the Titanic.

Anyway, our meeting was dismissed, and I had to walk the hundred yards or so back to my cabin. When I stepped outside I was gripped by the darkness. I was faced with deep woods, no lights, and a soft rain falling. *I've watched too much television for this to be any fun at all,* I silently mused.

I gingerly started walking down the path, one careful step after another. Suddenly I realized that I wasn't alone. I don't remember what led me to believe this; I just knew. I stood silently, frozen by the thought of the perilous possibilities. Then, ever so slowly, I reached my hand forward trying to determine if the hair on my neck was standing straight up for any particular reason.

My cold, trembling hand met a warm, wet coat of fur. Thank goodness for a change of clothes back in the cabin. That's when I heard, much to my relief, the unmistakable snort of a horse. One of the

DAILY INSIGHT

FRIDAY

Passage:
Matthew 14:22–32

Verse:
Matthew 14:31

"features" the camp director had left out was a riding stable, complete with lots of friendly, sway-backed nags who roamed the grounds. My fear subsided as I side-stepped the huge animal and went on toward my cabin, muttering, "Thanks for the warning, Mr. Camp Director."

Fear can be a horrible and debilitating thing. It can create self-doubt and dread. It can actually rob us of any of life's pleasures. Fear can literally freeze us in our tracks. Just ask Jesus' disciples.

The disciples were in a small boat, miles from shore. The wind was blowing at gale-force velocity, and even though these men were seasoned fishermen, they were scared. Apparently Jesus' previous assurances of his faithful presence with them wasn't enough.

So Jesus made the trip out to them, walking on the sea and saying, "Take courage! It is I. Don't be afraid." As soon as he stepped into their boat, the winds subsided along with the disciples' fear.

Are you afraid? Has the reality of the things you know that you have to do, surrounded by the ominous dark of the unknown future, gotten the best of you? Jesus' message to us is pretty clear. "Of *course* you can't see. Of *course* you don't know what lies ahead. But you have my promise. Reach out. Take courage. Don't be afraid. It's me."

Finally, a Camp Director we can trust.

For your next devotional reading, go to page 1061.

[17]"We have here only five loaves of bread and two fish," they answered. [18]"Bring them here to me," he said. [19]And he directed the people to sit down on the grass. Taking the five loaves and the two fish and looking up to heaven, he gave thanks and broke the loaves. Then he gave them to the disciples, and the disciples gave them to the people. [20]They all ate and were satisfied, and the disciples picked up twelve basketfuls of broken pieces that were left over. [21]The number of those who ate was about five thousand men, besides women and children.

Jesus Walks on the Water

[22]Immediately Jesus made the disciples get into the boat and go on ahead of him to the other side, while he dismissed the crowd. [23]After he had dismissed them, he went up on a mountainside by himself to pray. When evening came, he was there alone, [24]but the boat was already a considerable distance[a] from land, buffeted by the waves because the wind was against it.

[25]During the fourth watch of the night Jesus went out to them, walking on the lake. [26]When the disciples saw him walking on the lake, they were terrified. "It's a ghost," they said, and cried out in fear.

[27]But Jesus immediately said to them: "Take courage! It is I. Don't be afraid."

[28]"Lord, if it's you," Peter replied, "tell me to come to you on the water."

[29]"Come," he said.

Then Peter got down out of the boat, walked on the water and came toward Jesus. [30]But when he saw the wind, he was afraid and, beginning to sink, cried out, "Lord, save me!"

[31]Immediately Jesus reached out his hand and caught him. "You of little faith," he said, "why did you doubt?"

[32]And when they climbed into the boat, the wind died down. [33]Then those who were in the boat worshiped him, saying, "Truly you are the Son of God."

[34]When they had crossed over, they landed at Gennesaret. [35]And when the men of that place recognized Jesus, they sent word to all the surrounding country. People brought all their sick to him [36]and begged him to let the sick just touch the edge of his cloak, and all who touched him were healed.

Clean and Unclean

15 Then some Pharisees and teachers of the law came to Jesus from Jerusalem and asked, [2]"Why do your disciples break the tradition of the elders? They don't wash their hands before they eat!"

[3]Jesus replied, "And why do you break the command of God for the sake of your tradition? [4]For God said, 'Honor your father and mother'[b] and 'Anyone who curses his father or mother must be put to death.'[c] [5]But you say that if a man says to his father or mother, 'Whatever help you might otherwise have received from me is a gift devoted to God,' [6]he is not to 'honor his father[d]' with it. Thus you nullify the word of God for the sake of your tradition. [7]You hypocrites! Isaiah was right when he prophesied about you:

[8]" 'These people honor me with their
     lips,
   but their hearts are far from me.
[9]They worship me in vain;
   their teachings are but rules taught
     by men.'[e]"

[10]Jesus called the crowd to him and said, "Listen and understand. [11]What goes into a man's mouth does not make him 'unclean,' but what comes out of his mouth, that is what makes him 'unclean.' "

[12]Then the disciples came to him and asked, "Do you know that the Pharisees were offended when they heard this?"

[13]He replied, "Every plant that my heavenly Father has not planted will be pulled up by the roots. [14]Leave them; they are blind guides.[f] If a blind man leads a blind man, both will fall into a pit."

[15]Peter said, "Explain the parable to us."

[16]"Are you still so dull?" Jesus asked them. [17]"Don't you see that whatever enters the mouth goes into the stomach and then out of the body? [18]But the things that come out of the mouth come from the heart, and these make a man 'unclean.' [19]For out of the heart come evil thoughts, murder, adultery, sexual immorality, theft, false testimony, slander. [20]These are what make a man 'unclean'; but eating with unwashed hands does not make him 'unclean.' "

The Faith of the Canaanite Woman

[21]Leaving that place, Jesus withdrew to the region of Tyre and Sidon. [22]A Canaanite woman from that vicinity came to him, crying out, "Lord, Son of David, have

---

[a]24 Greek *many stadia*   [b]4 Exodus 20:12; Deut. 5:16   [c]4 Exodus 21:17; Lev. 20:9   [d]6 Some manuscripts *father or his mother*   [e]9 Isaiah 29:13   [f]14 Some manuscripts *guides of the blind*

mercy on me! My daughter is suffering terribly from demon-possession."

²³Jesus did not answer a word. So his disciples came to him and urged him, "Send her away, for she keeps crying out after us."

²⁴He answered, "I was sent only to the lost sheep of Israel."

²⁵The woman came and knelt before him. "Lord, help me!" she said.

²⁶He replied, "It is not right to take the children's bread and toss it to their dogs."

²⁷"Yes, Lord," she said, "but even the dogs eat the crumbs that fall from their masters' table."

²⁸Then Jesus answered, "Woman, you have great faith! Your request is granted." And her daughter was healed from that very hour.

Jesus Feeds the Four Thousand

²⁹Jesus left there and went along the Sea of Galilee. Then he went up on a mountainside and sat down. ³⁰Great crowds came to him, bringing the lame, the blind, the crippled, the mute and many others, and laid them at his feet; and he healed them. ³¹The people were amazed when they saw the mute speaking, the crippled made well, the lame walking and the blind seeing. And they praised the God of Israel.

³²Jesus called his disciples to him and said, "I have compassion for these people; they have already been with me three days and have nothing to eat. I do not want to send them away hungry, or they may collapse on the way."

³³His disciples answered, "Where could we get enough bread in this remote place to feed such a crowd?"

³⁴"How many loaves do you have?" Jesus asked.

"Seven," they replied, "and a few small fish."

³⁵He told the crowd to sit down on the ground. ³⁶Then he took the seven loaves and the fish, and when he had given thanks, he broke them and gave them to the disciples, and they in turn to the people. ³⁷They all ate and were satisfied. Afterward the disciples picked up seven basketfuls of broken pieces that were left over. ³⁸The number of those who ate was four thousand, besides women and children. ³⁹After Jesus had sent the crowd away, he got into the boat and went to the vicinity of Magadan.

The Demand for a Sign

16 The Pharisees and Sadducees came to Jesus and tested him by asking him to show them a sign from heaven.

²He replied,ᵃ "When evening comes, you say, 'It will be fair weather, for the sky is red,' ³and in the morning, 'Today it will be stormy, for the sky is red and overcast.' You know how to interpret the appearance of the sky, but you cannot interpret the signs of the times. ⁴A wicked and adulterous generation looks for a miraculous sign, but none will be given it except the sign of Jonah." Jesus then left them and went away.

The Yeast of the Pharisees and Sadducees

⁵When they went across the lake, the disciples forgot to take bread. ⁶"Be careful," Jesus said to them. "Be on your guard against the yeast of the Pharisees and Sadducees."

⁷They discussed this among themselves and said, "It is because we didn't bring any bread."

⁸Aware of their discussion, Jesus asked, "You of little faith, why are you talking among yourselves about having no bread? ⁹Do you still not understand? Don't you remember the five loaves for the five thousand, and how many basketfuls you gathered? ¹⁰Or the seven loaves for the four thousand, and how many basketfuls you gathered? ¹¹How is it you don't understand that I was not talking to you about bread? But be on your guard against the yeast of the Pharisees and Sadducees." ¹²Then they understood that he was not telling them to guard against the yeast used in bread, but against the teaching of the Pharisees and Sadducees.

Peter's Confession of Christ

¹³When Jesus came to the region of Caesarea Philippi, he asked his disciples, "Who do people say the Son of Man is?"

¹⁴They replied, "Some say John the Baptist; others say Elijah; and still others, Jeremiah or one of the prophets."

¹⁵"But what about you?" he asked. "Who do you say I am?"

¹⁶Simon Peter answered, "You are the Christ,ᵇ the Son of the living God."

¹⁷Jesus replied, "Blessed are you, Simon

ᵃ2 Some early manuscripts do not have the rest of verse 2 and all of verse 3. ᵇ16 Or *Messiah*; also in verse 20

son of Jonah, for this was not revealed to you by man, but by my Father in heaven. [18]And I tell you that you are Peter,[a] and on this rock I will build my church, and the gates of Hades[b] will not overcome it.[c] [19]I will give you the keys of the kingdom of heaven; whatever you bind on earth will be[d] bound in heaven, and whatever you loose on earth will be[d] loosed in heaven." [20]Then he warned his disciples not to tell anyone that he was the Christ.

Jesus Predicts His Death

[21]From that time on Jesus began to explain to his disciples that he must go to Jerusalem and suffer many things at the hands of the elders, chief priests and teachers of the law, and that he must be killed and on the third day be raised to life. [22]Peter took him aside and began to rebuke him. "Never, Lord!" he said. "This shall never happen to you!"

[23]Jesus turned and said to Peter, "Get behind me, Satan! You are a stumbling block to me; you do not have in mind the things of God, but the things of men."

[24]Then Jesus said to his disciples, "If anyone would come after me, he must deny himself and take up his cross and follow me. [25]For whoever wants to save his life[e] will lose it, but whoever loses his life for me will find it. [26]What good will it be for a man if he gains the whole world, yet forfeits his soul? Or what can a man give in exchange for his soul? [27]For the Son of Man is going to come in his Father's glory with his angels, and then he will reward each person according to what he has done. [28]I tell you the truth, some who are standing here will not taste death before they see the Son of Man coming in his kingdom."

The Transfiguration

17 After six days Jesus took with him Peter, James and John the brother of James, and led them up a high mountain by themselves. [2]There he was transfigured before them. His face shone like the sun, and his clothes became as white as the light. [3]Just then there appeared before them Moses and Elijah, talking with Jesus.

[4]Peter said to Jesus, "Lord, it is good for us to be here. If you wish, I will put up three shelters—one for you, one for Moses and one for Elijah."

[5]While he was still speaking, a bright cloud enveloped them, and a voice from the cloud said, "This is my Son, whom I love; with him I am well pleased. Listen to him!"

[6]When the disciples heard this, they fell facedown to the ground, terrified. [7]But Jesus came and touched them. "Get up," he said. "Don't be afraid." [8]When they looked up, they saw no one except Jesus.

[9]As they were coming down the mountain, Jesus instructed them, "Don't tell anyone what you have seen, until the Son of Man has been raised from the dead."

[10]The disciples asked him, "Why then do the teachers of the law say that Elijah must come first?"

[11]Jesus replied, "To be sure, Elijah comes and will restore all things. [12]But I tell you, Elijah has already come, and they did not recognize him, but have done to him everything they wished. In the same way the Son of Man is going to suffer at their hands." [13]Then the disciples understood that he was talking to them about John the Baptist.

The Healing of a Boy With a Demon

[14]When they came to the crowd, a man approached Jesus and knelt before him. [15]"Lord, have mercy on my son," he said. "He has seizures and is suffering greatly. He often falls into the fire or into the water. [16]I brought him to your disciples, but they could not heal him."

[17]"O unbelieving and perverse generation," Jesus replied, "how long shall I stay with you? How long shall I put up with you? Bring the boy here to me." [18]Jesus rebuked the demon, and it came out of the boy, and he was healed from that moment.

[19]Then the disciples came to Jesus in private and asked, "Why couldn't we drive it out?"

[20]He replied, "Because you have so little faith. I tell you the truth, if you have faith as small as a mustard seed, you can say to this mountain, 'Move from here to there' and it will move. Nothing will be impossible for you.[f]"

[22]When they came together in Galilee, he said to them, "The Son of Man is going to be betrayed into the hands of men. [23]They will kill him, and on the third day he will be raised to life." And the disciples were filled with grief.

---

[a]18 Peter means rock.   [b]18 Or hell   [c]18 Or not prove stronger than it   [d]19 Or have been   [e]25 The Greek word means either life or soul; also in verse 26.   [f]20 Some manuscripts you. [21]But this kind does not go out except by prayer and fasting.

The Temple Tax

24After Jesus and his disciples arrived in Capernaum, the collectors of the two-drachma tax came to Peter and asked, "Doesn't your teacher pay the temple tax*a*?"

25"Yes, he does," he replied.

When Peter came into the house, Jesus was the first to speak. "What do you think, Simon?" he asked. "From whom do the kings of the earth collect duty and taxes—from their own sons or from others?"

26"From others," Peter answered.

"Then the sons are exempt," Jesus said to him. **27**"But so that we may not offend them, go to the lake and throw out your line. Take the first fish you catch; open its mouth and you will find a four-drachma coin. Take it and give it to them for my tax and yours."

The Greatest in the Kingdom of Heaven

18 At that time the disciples came to Jesus and asked, "Who is the greatest in the kingdom of heaven?"

2He called a little child and had him stand among them. **3**And he said: "I tell you the truth, unless you change and become like little children, you will never enter the kingdom of heaven. **4**Therefore, whoever humbles himself like this child is the greatest in the kingdom of heaven.

5"And whoever welcomes a little child like this in my name welcomes me. **6**But if anyone causes one of these little ones who believe in me to sin, it would be better for him to have a large millstone hung around his neck and to be drowned in the depths of the sea.

7"Woe to the world because of the things that cause people to sin! Such things must come, but woe to the man through whom they come! **8**If your hand or your foot causes you to sin, cut it off and throw it away. It is better for you to enter life maimed or crippled than to have two hands or two feet and be thrown into eternal fire. **9**And if your eye causes you to sin, gouge it out and throw it away. It is better for you to enter life with one eye than to have two eyes and be thrown into the fire of hell.

The Parable of the Lost Sheep

10"See that you do not look down on one of these little ones. For I tell you that their angels in heaven always see the face of my Father in heaven.*b*

12"What do you think? If a man owns a hundred sheep, and one of them wanders away, will he not leave the ninety-nine on the hills and go to look for the one that wandered off? **13**And if he finds it, I tell you the truth, he is happier about that one sheep than about the ninety-nine that did not wander off. **14**In the same way your Father in heaven is not willing that any of these little ones should be lost.

A Brother Who Sins Against You

15"If your brother sins against you,*c* go and show him his fault, just between the two of you. If he listens to you, you have won your brother over. **16**But if he will not listen, take one or two others along, so that 'every matter may be established by the testimony of two or three witnesses.'*d* **17**If he refuses to listen to them, tell it to the church; and if he refuses to listen even to the church, treat him as you would a pagan or a tax collector.

18"I tell you the truth, whatever you bind on earth will be*e* bound in heaven, and whatever you loose on earth will be*e* loosed in heaven.

19"Again, I tell you that if two of you on earth agree about anything you ask for, it will be done for you by my Father in heaven. **20**For where two or three come together in my name, there am I with them."

The Parable of the Unmerciful Servant

21Then Peter came to Jesus and asked, "Lord, how many times shall I forgive my brother when he sins against me? Up to seven times?"

22Jesus answered, "I tell you, not seven times, but seventy-seven times.*f*

23"Therefore, the kingdom of heaven is like a king who wanted to settle accounts with his servants. **24**As he began the settlement, a man who owed him ten thousand talents*g* was brought to him. **25**Since he was not able to pay, the master ordered that he and his wife and his children and all that he had be sold to repay the debt.

26"The servant fell on his knees before him. 'Be patient with me,' he begged, 'and I will pay back everything.' **27**The servant's master took pity on him, canceled the debt and let him go.

---

*a*24 Greek *the two drachmas*   *b*10 Some manuscripts *heaven.* 11 *The Son of Man came to save what was lost.*   *c*15 Some manuscripts do not have *against you.*   *d*16 Deut. 19:15   *e*18 Or *have been*   *f*22 Or *seventy times seven*   *g*24 That is, millions of dollars

Are Those New Glasses?

Key Verse: *"The servant's master took pity on him, canceled the debt and let him go."* Matthew 18:27

Text: Matthew 18:21–35 *(Dad or child reads the text.)*

DAD READS: Many people wear eyeglasses to help them see more clearly. Without eyeglasses, these folks would have a hard time seeing a chalkboard, reading the newspaper or driving a car. Glasses help eyes that need help. They assist people in seeing what they couldn't see very well without them.

QUIET **TIMES** WITH **Dad**

Child reads: The master in today's story was using something like glasses when he forgave his servant. These "forgiveness glasses" helped him to see past the debt. When he looked at this man who could not pay, he had compassion on him and forgave him his debt. Sadly, the servant wasn't wearing the same kind of glasses when he went to another man who owed him money.

DAD READS: God is a lot like the master in this story. When we come to him asking for forgiveness for our sins, he looks at us through the lenses of Christ's death for us, and he forgives us. When someone has done something bad to us and we forgive him or her, it is as if we have borrowed God's "forgiveness glasses." Without God's example of forgiveness, we would have a hard time forgiving others.

Child reads: But if we are like the servant in today's story and refuse to forgive others, then Jesus says that God finds it more difficult to forgive us. God's example of forgiveness, his "glasses," should help us to forgive others. But if those glasses haven't helped us to see others in a loving and forgiving way, God will not forgive us when he looks at us either.

DAD READS: We can't survive without God's forgiveness. Without

his mercy, our lives would be miserable. So we must forgive others, even if we think they don't deserve our forgiveness. We must put on God's "forgiveness glasses" to see these people who have done something against us in a new way. We want God to see us in this same way, forgiving us because we have forgiven others.

Child reads: I want to be a forgiving person. I want God to be happy with the way I treat others. I want him to forgive me, too. How sad it would be if God would not forgive me because I had not forgiven others.

DAD READS: We must forgive those who do bad things to us. This is important to God. Just like you do, I also want to be a forgiving person. I also want God to be happy with the way I treat others—including you. I want to know God's forgiveness, too. Let me pray this prayer with you:

Our Father in heaven, we love you. Thank you for this important lesson. Through this story, you have reminded us that when we are forgiving, we will be forgiven. Please help us to remember this in our family. Please don't let us miss your forgiveness because we have not forgiven each other. We love you, and we thank you for your love. In Jesus' name, **Amen.**

For your next devotional reading, go to page 1064.

²⁸"But when that servant went out, he found one of his fellow servants who owed him a hundred denarii.ᵃ He grabbed him and began to choke him. 'Pay back what you owe me!' he demanded.

²⁹"His fellow servant fell to his knees and begged him, 'Be patient with me, and I will pay you back.'

³⁰"But he refused. Instead, he went off and had the man thrown into prison until he could pay the debt. ³¹When the other servants saw what had happened, they were greatly distressed and went and told their master everything that had happened.

³²"Then the master called the servant in. 'You wicked servant,' he said, 'I canceled all that debt of yours because you begged me to. ³³Shouldn't you have had mercy on your fellow servant just as I had on you?' ³⁴In anger his master turned him over to the jailers to be tortured, until he should pay back all he owed.

³⁵"This is how my heavenly Father will treat each of you unless you forgive your brother from your heart."

Divorce

19 When Jesus had finished saying these things, he left Galilee and went into the region of Judea to the other side of the Jordan. ²Large crowds followed him, and he healed them there.

³Some Pharisees came to him to test him. They asked, "Is it lawful for a man to divorce his wife for any and every reason?"

⁴"Haven't you read," he replied, "that at the beginning the Creator 'made them male and female,'ᵇ ⁵and said, 'For this reason a man will leave his father and mother and be united to his wife, and the two will become one flesh'ᶜ? ⁶So they are no longer two, but one. Therefore what God has joined together, let man not separate."

⁷"Why then," they asked, "did Moses command that a man give his wife a certificate of divorce and send her away?"

⁸Jesus replied, "Moses permitted you to divorce your wives because your hearts were hard. But it was not this way from the beginning. ⁹I tell you that anyone who divorces his wife, except for marital unfaithfulness, and marries another woman commits adultery."

¹⁰The disciples said to him, "If this is the situation between a husband and wife, it is better not to marry."

¹¹Jesus replied, "Not everyone can accept this word, but only those to whom it has been given. ¹²For some are eunuchs because they were born that way; others were made that way by men; and others have renounced marriageᵈ because of the kingdom of heaven. The one who can accept this should accept it."

The Little Children and Jesus

¹³Then little children were brought to Jesus for him to place his hands on them and pray for them. But the disciples rebuked those who brought them.

ᵃ28 That is, a few dollars   ᵇ4 Gen. 1:27
ᶜ5 Gen. 2:24   ᵈ12 Or *have made themselves eunuchs*

HEY DAD
Why do we have to forgive people who hurt us?

Text: Matthew 18:21–35

Peter wondered about this very issue, and he asked Jesus how many times he had to forgive someone. "Seventy-seven times," Jesus replied, meaning that forgiveness must be unlimited.

Jesus taught that we must forgive others because God has forgiven us. The parable of the unmerciful servant illustrates his point. The master in this parable canceled a servant's huge debt. When he discovered that his servant did not extend the same forgiveness to another, the master became furious. He reinstated the debt and threw his servant in jail until he could repay what he owed. Jesus warns us that, in the same way, God will not forgive us unless we in turn forgive others.

The choice is simple. We do not have to forgive others—unless we want God to forgive *us*.

QUESTIONS KIDS ASK

For a complete listing of Questions Kids Ask, turn to page 1435.

¹⁴Jesus said, "Let the little children come to me, and do not hinder them, for the kingdom of heaven belongs to such as these." ¹⁵When he had placed his hands on them, he went on from there.

The Rich Young Man

¹⁶Now a man came up to Jesus and asked, "Teacher, what good thing must I do to get eternal life?"

¹⁷"Why do you ask me about what is good?" Jesus replied. "There is only One who is good. If you want to enter life, obey the commandments."

¹⁸"Which ones?" the man inquired.

Jesus replied, " 'Do not murder, do not commit adultery, do not steal, do not give false testimony, ¹⁹honor your father and mother,'ᵃ and 'love your neighbor as yourself.'ᵇ"

²⁰"All these I have kept," the young man said. "What do I still lack?"

²¹Jesus answered, "If you want to be perfect, go, sell your possessions and give to the poor, and you will have treasure in heaven. Then come, follow me."

²²When the young man heard this, he went away sad, because he had great wealth.

²³Then Jesus said to his disciples, "I tell you the truth, it is hard for a rich man to enter the kingdom of heaven. ²⁴Again I tell you, it is easier for a camel to go through the eye of a needle than for a rich man to enter the kingdom of God."

²⁵When the disciples heard this, they were greatly astonished and asked, "Who then can be saved?"

²⁶Jesus looked at them and said, "With man this is impossible, but with God all things are possible."

²⁷Peter answered him, "We have left everything to follow you! What then will there be for us?"

²⁸Jesus said to them, "I tell you the truth, at the renewal of all things, when the Son of Man sits on his glorious throne, you who have followed me will also sit on twelve thrones, judging the twelve tribes of Israel. ²⁹And everyone who has left houses or brothers or sisters or father or motherᶜ or children or fields for my sake will receive a hundred times as much and will inherit eternal life. ³⁰But many who are first will be last, and many who are last will be first.

The Parable of the Workers in the Vineyard

20 "For the kingdom of heaven is like a landowner who went out early in the morning to hire men to work in his vineyard. ²He agreed to pay them a denarius for the day and sent them into his vineyard.

³"About the third hour he went out and saw others standing in the marketplace doing nothing. ⁴He told them, 'You also go and work in my vineyard, and I will pay you whatever is right.' ⁵So they went.

ᵃ19 Exodus 20:12-16; Deut. 5:16-20   ᵇ19 Lev. 19:18
ᶜ29 Some manuscripts *mother or wife*

HEY DAD
How do I love someone I don't even like?

Text: Matthew 19:19

The Bible tells us to love our neighbors as ourselves. So, how do we love ourselves? Sometimes we don't *like* ourselves very much, and sometimes we even hate our own actions. However, we love ourselves by giving ourselves the benefit of the doubt when we make mistakes. We believe that we are on our way to becoming better people and always hope for our own well being. We believe that God loves us. In the same way, we do not need always to be *fond* of our neighbors or approve of everything they do to *love* them.

So how *do* we love people we do not like? First, we don't waste time trying to create phony feelings of affection for them. That is not the point. Instead, we give them the benefit of the doubt and wish them the best, even if they have hurt us. We treat them with respect and preserve their dignity. We recognize that God loves them as much as he loves us. When we decide to treat others this way, we might just start to like them, after all!

QUESTIONS KIDS ASK

For a complete listing of Questions Kids Ask, turn to page 1435.

"He went out again about the sixth hour and the ninth hour and did the same thing. ⁶About the eleventh hour he went out and found still others standing around. He asked them, 'Why have you been standing here all day long doing nothing?'

⁷" 'Because no one has hired us,' they answered.

"He said to them, 'You also go and work in my vineyard.'

⁸"When evening came, the owner of the vineyard said to his foreman, 'Call the workers and pay them their wages, beginning with the last ones hired and going on to the first.'

⁹"The workers who were hired about the eleventh hour came and each received a denarius. ¹⁰So when those came who were hired first, they expected to receive more. But each one of them also received a denarius. ¹¹When they received it, they began to grumble against the landowner. ¹²"These men who were hired last worked only one hour,' they said, 'and you have made them equal to us who

This Isn't Fair

The voice on the other end of the telephone was a familiar one, but I had never heard her so distressed. "What's the matter, Paula?" I asked. "Are you okay?"

"Have you seen the news on CNN today?" Paula asked. When I told her that I hadn't had a chance, Paula proceeded to tell me that one of history's most heinous criminals, a serial killer and mass murderer sitting it out on death row, had just asked Christ into his life. My friend was livid. "Tell me that this horrible man will not go to heaven when he's executed," Paula pled. "Please tell me this."

I stood silent, holding the cordless telephone in the kitchen. I said nothing, but my mind was spinning. "We have no way of knowing exactly what has happened to this man," I finally said. "But, if this is true, and if he has asked God to pardon him for his sins, he's going to heaven for sure."

Now it was Paula's turn to be silent.

"To be perfectly honest," I said after a few moments, almost thinking out loud, "I don't like it either."

Why should this man, months before his scheduled and well-deserved execution, have the same right to glory as missionaries who have given fifty years, nurses who have tenderly ministered to the sick and dying, or parents who have faithfully sacrificed so their children would walk in the Truth? How could this be?

DAILY INSIGHT

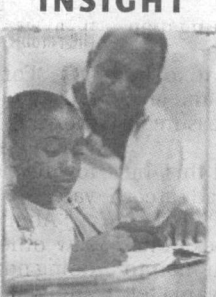

MONDAY

Passage:
Matthew 20:1–16

Verse:
Matthew 20:16

The story of the landowner is perhaps the most troubling of all the parables, especially to those of us who live by the merit system. Paying someone a full day's wages after only one hour of work just seems unfair ... it *is* unfair. Pity the poor sucker who's been at it for twelve hours and gets the same wage as one who just clocked in an hour ago. How could the landowner be so inequitable ... so heartless?

Here's the grim truth. The repentant serial killer and the devout parson will both receive God's blessing, his pardon, and a share of his eternal glory forever ... in equal measure. Why? Because neither the sinner nor the saint actually *deserves* the Sovereign Lord's favor. Even though the activities of these people have been worlds apart, their hearts are equally deceitful, equally wicked, and equally in need of redemption.

God's favor cannot be earned. And it cannot be denied. It is ours because God has decided to give it to us—period. And difficult thought this may be for me, I have only one choice ... to be thankful that he will "pay" me what he promised at the end of my "work day."

This is no time to compare my performance with someone else's effort. There is no competition for God's favor, only gratitude for what he has done and will do for all those who accept his forgiveness.

For your next devotional reading, go to page 1072.

have borne the burden of the work and the heat of the day.'

¹³"But he answered one of them, 'Friend, I am not being unfair to you. Didn't you agree to work for a denarius? ¹⁴Take your pay and go. I want to give the man who was hired last the same as I gave you. ¹⁵Don't I have the right to do what I want with my own money? Or are you envious because I am generous?'

¹⁶"So the last will be first, and the first will be last."

Jesus Again Predicts His Death

¹⁷Now as Jesus was going up to Jerusalem, he took the twelve disciples aside and said to them, ¹⁸"We are going up to Jerusalem, and the Son of Man will be betrayed to the chief priests and the teachers of the law. They will condemn him to death ¹⁹and will turn him over to the Gentiles to be mocked and flogged and crucified. On the third day he will be raised to life!"

A Mother's Request

²⁰Then the mother of Zebedee's sons came to Jesus with her sons and, kneeling down, asked a favor of him.

²¹"What is it you want?" he asked.

She said, "Grant that one of these two sons of mine may sit at your right and the other at your left in your kingdom."

²²"You don't know what you are asking," Jesus said to them. "Can you drink the cup I am going to drink?"

"We can," they answered.

²³Jesus said to them, "You will indeed drink from my cup, but to sit at my right or left is not for me to grant. These places belong to those for whom they have been prepared by my Father."

²⁴When the ten heard about this, they were indignant with the two brothers. ²⁵Jesus called them together and said, "You know that the rulers of the Gentiles lord it over them, and their high officials exercise authority over them. ²⁶Not so with you. Instead, whoever wants to become great among you must be your servant, ²⁷and whoever wants to be first must be your slave— ²⁸just as the Son of Man did not come to be served, but to serve, and to give his life as a ransom for many."

Two Blind Men Receive Sight

²⁹As Jesus and his disciples were leaving Jericho, a large crowd followed him. ³⁰Two blind men were sitting by the roadside, and when they heard that Jesus was going by, they shouted, "Lord, Son of David, have mercy on us!"

HEY DAD
Did Jesus speak English?

Text: Matthew 21:11

Although Jesus' words in the Bible have been translated into English, Jesus didn't speak English. He grew up in Israel, in a village called Nazareth, fifteen miles from the Sea of Galilee. On today's maps, this city is in the northern part of Israel, surrounded by Lebanon, Syria and Jordan. The language the people spoke in Nazareth was Aramaic. More specifically, Jesus spoke Galilean Aramaic.

Jews who had been educated in Greek considered this Galilean dialect crude and uncultured. People from Jerusalem looked down upon the Galileans as unsophisticated and rustic. And the "stern religious leaders of Jerusalem distrusted the Jews from Galilee, suspecting them of being less than strict in their observance of the law" (Ward, 92).

Jesus came to bring us freedom from the law. And he came as a man from Nazareth. How fitting that the humble Son of God spoke a language thought to be lowly and unsophisticated. Everything about him, including the language he spoke, shows us how important are "the least of these" (Matthew 25:40).

Ward, K. (Ed.). (1987). Jesus and His Times. Pleasantville, New York: The Reader's Digest Association.

For a complete listing of Questions Kids Ask, turn to page 1435.

³¹The crowd rebuked them and told them to be quiet, but they shouted all the louder, "Lord, Son of David, have mercy on us!"

³²Jesus stopped and called them. "What do you want me to do for you?" he asked.

³³"Lord," they answered, "we want our sight."

³⁴Jesus had compassion on them and touched their eyes. Immediately they received their sight and followed him.

The Triumphal Entry

21 As they approached Jerusalem and came to Bethphage on the Mount of Olives, Jesus sent two disciples, ²saying to them, "Go to the village ahead of you, and at once you will find a donkey tied there, with her colt by her. Untie them and bring them to me. ³If anyone says anything to you, tell him that the Lord needs them, and he will send them right away."

⁴This took place to fulfill what was spoken through the prophet:

⁵"Say to the Daughter of Zion,
  'See, your king comes to you,
gentle and riding on a donkey,
  on a colt, the foal of a donkey.' "^a

⁶The disciples went and did as Jesus had instructed them. ⁷They brought the donkey and the colt, placed their cloaks on them, and Jesus sat on them. ⁸A very large crowd spread their cloaks on the road, while others cut branches from the trees and spread them on the road. ⁹The crowds that went ahead of him and those that followed shouted,

"Hosanna^b to the Son of David!"

"Blessed is he who comes in the name of the Lord!"^c

"Hosanna^b in the highest!"

¹⁰When Jesus entered Jerusalem, the whole city was stirred and asked, "Who is this?"

¹¹The crowds answered, "This is Jesus, the prophet from Nazareth in Galilee."

Jesus at the Temple

¹²Jesus entered the temple area and drove out all who were buying and selling there. He overturned the tables of the money changers and the benches of those selling doves. ¹³"It is written," he said to them, " 'My house will be called a house of prayer,'^d but you are making it a 'den of robbers.'^e "

¹⁴The blind and the lame came to him at the temple, and he healed them. ¹⁵But when the chief priests and the teachers of the law saw the wonderful things he did and the children shouting in the temple area, "Hosanna to the Son of David," they were indignant.

¹⁶"Do you hear what these children are saying?" they asked him.

"Yes," replied Jesus, "have you never read,

" 'From the lips of children and infants you have ordained praise'^f?"

¹⁷And he left them and went out of the city to Bethany, where he spent the night.

The Fig Tree Withers

¹⁸Early in the morning, as he was on his way back to the city, he was hungry. ¹⁹Seeing a fig tree by the road, he went up to it but found nothing on it except leaves. Then he said to it, "May you never bear fruit again!" Immediately the tree withered.

²⁰When the disciples saw this, they were amazed. "How did the fig tree wither so quickly?" they asked.

²¹Jesus replied, "I tell you the truth, if you have faith and do not doubt, not only can you do what was done to the fig tree, but also you can say to this mountain, 'Go, throw yourself into the sea,' and it will be done. ²²If you believe, you will receive whatever you ask for in prayer."

The Authority of Jesus Questioned

²³Jesus entered the temple courts, and, while he was teaching, the chief priests and the elders of the people came to him. "By what authority are you doing these things?" they asked. "And who gave you this authority?"

²⁴Jesus replied, "I will also ask you one question. If you answer me, I will tell you by what authority I am doing these things. ²⁵John's baptism—where did it come from? Was it from heaven, or from men?"

They discussed it among themselves and said, "If we say, 'From heaven,' he will ask, 'Then why didn't you believe him?' ²⁶But if we say, 'From men'—we are afraid of the people, for they all hold that John was a prophet."

a5 Zech. 9:9   *b9* A Hebrew expression meaning "Save!" which became an exclamation of praise; also in verse 15   *c9* Psalm 118:26   *d13* Isaiah 56:7   *e13* Jer. 7:11   *f16* Psalm 8:2

²⁷So they answered Jesus, "We don't know."

Then he said, "Neither will I tell you by what authority I am doing these things.

The Parable of the Two Sons

²⁸"What do you think? There was a man who had two sons. He went to the first and said, 'Son, go and work today in the vineyard.'

²⁹" 'I will not,' he answered, but later he changed his mind and went.

³⁰"Then the father went to the other son and said the same thing. He answered, 'I will, sir,' but he did not go.

³¹"Which of the two did what his father wanted?"

"The first," they answered.

Jesus said to them, "I tell you the truth, the tax collectors and the prostitutes are entering the kingdom of God ahead of you. ³²For John came to you to show you the way of righteousness, and you did not believe him, but the tax collectors and the prostitutes did. And even after you saw this, you did not repent and believe him.

The Parable of the Tenants

³³"Listen to another parable: There was a landowner who planted a vineyard. He put a wall around it, dug a winepress in it and built a watchtower. Then he rented the vineyard to some farmers and went away on a journey. ³⁴When the harvest time approached, he sent his servants to the tenants to collect his fruit.

³⁵"The tenants seized his servants; they beat one, killed another, and stoned a third. ³⁶Then he sent other servants to them, more than the first time, and the tenants treated them the same way. ³⁷Last of all, he sent his son to them. 'They will respect my son,' he said.

³⁸"But when the tenants saw the son, they said to each other, 'This is the heir. Come, let's kill him and take his inheritance.' ³⁹So they took him and threw him out of the vineyard and killed him.

⁴⁰"Therefore, when the owner of the vineyard comes, what will he do to those tenants?"

⁴¹"He will bring those wretches to a wretched end," they replied, "and he will rent the vineyard to other tenants, who will give him his share of the crop at harvest time."

⁴²Jesus said to them, "Have you never read in the Scriptures:

" 'The stone the builders rejected
    has become the capstone^a;
the Lord has done this,
    and it is marvelous in our eyes'^b?

⁴³"Therefore I tell you that the kingdom of God will be taken away from you and given to a people who will produce its fruit. ⁴⁴He who falls on this stone will be broken to pieces, but he on whom it falls will be crushed."^c

⁴⁵When the chief priests and the Pharisees heard Jesus' parables, they knew he was talking about them. ⁴⁶They looked for a way to arrest him, but they were afraid of the crowd because the people held that he was a prophet.

The Parable of the Wedding Banquet

22 Jesus spoke to them again in parables, saying: ²"The kingdom of heaven is like a king who prepared a wedding banquet for his son. ³He sent his servants to those who had been invited to the banquet to tell them to come, but they refused to come.

⁴"Then he sent some more servants and said, 'Tell those who have been invited that I have prepared my dinner: My oxen and fattened cattle have been butchered, and everything is ready. Come to the wedding banquet.'

⁵"But they paid no attention and went off—one to his field, another to his business. ⁶The rest seized his servants, mistreated them and killed them. ⁷The king was enraged. He sent his army and destroyed those murderers and burned their city.

⁸"Then he said to his servants, 'The wedding banquet is ready, but those I invited did not deserve to come. ⁹Go to the street corners and invite to the banquet anyone you find.' ¹⁰So the servants went out into the streets and gathered all the people they could find, both good and bad, and the wedding hall was filled with guests.

¹¹"But when the king came in to see the guests, he noticed a man there who was not wearing wedding clothes. ¹²'Friend,' he asked, 'how did you get in here without wedding clothes?' The man was speechless.

¹³"Then the king told the attendants, 'Tie him hand and foot, and throw him outside, into the darkness, where there will be weeping and gnashing of teeth.'

^a42 Or *cornerstone*   ^b42 Psalm 118:22,23
^c44 Some manuscripts do not have verse 44.

¹⁴"For many are invited, but few are chosen."

Paying Taxes to Caesar

¹⁵Then the Pharisees went out and laid plans to trap him in his words. ¹⁶They sent their disciples to him along with the Herodians. "Teacher," they said, "we know you are a man of integrity and that you teach the way of God in accordance with the truth. You aren't swayed by men, because you pay no attention to who they are. ¹⁷Tell us then, what is your opinion? Is it right to pay taxes to Caesar or not?"

¹⁸But Jesus, knowing their evil intent, said, "You hypocrites, why are you trying to trap me? ¹⁹Show me the coin used for paying the tax." They brought him a denarius, ²⁰and he asked them, "Whose portrait is this? And whose inscription?"

²¹"Caesar's," they replied.

Then he said to them, "Give to Caesar what is Caesar's, and to God what is God's."

²²When they heard this, they were amazed. So they left him and went away.

Marriage at the Resurrection

²³That same day the Sadducees, who say there is no resurrection, came to him with a question. ²⁴"Teacher," they said, "Moses told us that if a man dies without having children, his brother must marry the widow and have children for him. ²⁵Now there were seven brothers among us. The first one married and died, and since he had no children, he left his wife to his brother. ²⁶The same thing happened to the second and third brother, right on down to the seventh. ²⁷Finally, the woman died. ²⁸Now then, at the resurrection, whose wife will she be of the seven, since all of them were married to her?"

²⁹Jesus replied, "You are in error because you do not know the Scriptures or the power of God. ³⁰At the resurrection people will neither marry nor be given in marriage; they will be like the angels in heaven. ³¹But about the resurrection of the dead—have you not read what God said to you, ³²'I am the God of Abraham, the God of Isaac, and the God of Jacob'ᵃ? He is not the God of the dead but of the living."

³³When the crowds heard this, they were astonished at his teaching.

The Greatest Commandment

³⁴Hearing that Jesus had silenced the Sadducees, the Pharisees got together. ³⁵One of them, an expert in the law, tested him with this question: ³⁶"Teacher, which is the greatest commandment in the Law?"

³⁷Jesus replied: " 'Love the Lord your God with all your heart and with all your soul and with all your mind.'ᵇ ³⁸This is the first and greatest commandment. ³⁹And the second is like it: 'Love your neighbor as yourself.'ᶜ ⁴⁰All the Law and the Prophets hang on these two commandments."

Whose Son Is the Christ?

⁴¹While the Pharisees were gathered together, Jesus asked them, ⁴²"What do you think about the Christᵈ? Whose son is he?"

"The son of David," they replied.

⁴³He said to them, "How is it then that David, speaking by the Spirit, calls him 'Lord'? For he says,

⁴⁴ " 'The Lord said to my Lord:
    "Sit at my right hand
  until I put your enemies
    under your feet." 'ᵉ

⁴⁵If then David calls him 'Lord,' how can he be his son?" ⁴⁶No one could say a word in reply, and from that day on no one dared to ask him any more questions.

Seven Woes

23 Then Jesus said to the crowds and to his disciples: ²"The teachers of the law and the Pharisees sit in Moses' seat. ³So you must obey them and do everything they tell you. But do not do what they do, for they do not practice what they preach. ⁴They tie up heavy loads and put them on men's shoulders, but they themselves are not willing to lift a finger to move them.

⁵"Everything they do is done for men to see: They make their phylacteriesᶠ wide and the tassels on their garments long; ⁶they love the place of honor at banquets and the most important seats in the synagogues; ⁷they love to be greeted in the marketplaces and to have men call them 'Rabbi.'

⁸"But you are not to be called 'Rabbi,' for you have only one Master and you are

---

ᵃ32 Exodus 3:6   ᵇ37 Deut. 6:5   ᶜ39 Lev. 9:18
ᵈ42 Or *Messiah*   ᵉ44 Psalm 110:1   ᶠ5 That is, boxes
containing Scripture verses, worn on forehead
and arm

all brothers. ⁹And do not call anyone on earth 'father,' for you have one Father, and he is in heaven. ¹⁰Nor are you to be called 'teacher,' for you have one Teacher, the Christ.ᵃ ¹¹The greatest among you will be your servant. ¹²For whoever exalts himself will be humbled, and whoever humbles himself will be exalted.

¹³"Woe to you, teachers of the law and Pharisees, you hypocrites! You shut the kingdom of heaven in men's faces. You yourselves do not enter, nor will you let those enter who are trying to.ᵇ

¹⁵"Woe to you, teachers of the law and Pharisees, you hypocrites! You travel over land and sea to win a single convert, and when he becomes one, you make him twice as much a son of hell as you are.

¹⁶"Woe to you, blind guides! You say, 'If anyone swears by the temple, it means nothing; but if anyone swears by the gold of the temple, he is bound by his oath.' ¹⁷You blind fools! Which is greater: the gold, or the temple that makes the gold sacred? ¹⁸You also say, 'If anyone swears by the altar, it means nothing; but if anyone swears by the gift on it, he is bound by his oath.' ¹⁹You blind men! Which is greater: the gift, or the altar that makes the gift sacred? ²⁰Therefore, he who swears by the altar swears by it and by everything on it. ²¹And he who swears by the temple swears by it and by the one who dwells in it. ²²And he who swears by heaven swears by God's throne and by the one who sits on it.

²³"Woe to you, teachers of the law and Pharisees, you hypocrites! You give a tenth of your spices—mint, dill and cummin. But you have neglected the more important matters of the law—justice, mercy and faithfulness. You should have practiced the latter, without neglecting the former. ²⁴You blind guides! You strain out a gnat but swallow a camel.

²⁵"Woe to you, teachers of the law and Pharisees, you hypocrites! You clean the outside of the cup and dish, but inside they are full of greed and self-indulgence. ²⁶Blind Pharisee! First clean the inside of the cup and dish, and then the outside also will be clean.

²⁷"Woe to you, teachers of the law and Pharisees, you hypocrites! You are like whitewashed tombs, which look beautiful on the outside but on the inside are full of dead men's bones and everything unclean. ²⁸In the same way, on the outside you appear to people as righteous but on the inside you are full of hypocrisy and wickedness.

²⁹"Woe to you, teachers of the law and Pharisees, you hypocrites! You build tombs for the prophets and decorate the graves of the righteous. ³⁰And you say, 'If we had lived in the days of our forefathers, we would not have taken part with them in shedding the blood of the prophets.' ³¹So you testify against yourselves that you are the descendants of those who murdered the prophets. ³²Fill up, then, the measure of the sin of your forefathers!

³³"You snakes! You brood of vipers! How will you escape being condemned to hell? ³⁴Therefore I am sending you prophets and wise men and teachers. Some of them you will kill and crucify; others you will flog in your synagogues and pursue from town to town. ³⁵And so upon you will come all the righteous blood that has been shed on earth, from the blood of righteous Abel to the blood of Zechariah son of Berekiah, whom you murdered between the temple and the altar. ³⁶I tell you the truth, all this will come upon this generation.

³⁷"O Jerusalem, Jerusalem, you who kill the prophets and stone those sent to you, how often I have longed to gather your children together, as a hen gathers her chicks under her wings, but you were not willing. ³⁸Look, your house is left to you desolate. ³⁹For I tell you, you will not see me again until you say, 'Blessed is he who comes in the name of the Lord.'ᶜ"

Signs of the End of the Age

24 Jesus left the temple and was walking away when his disciples came up to him to call his attention to its buildings. ²"Do you see all these things?" he asked. "I tell you the truth, not one stone here will be left on another; every one will be thrown down."

³As Jesus was sitting on the Mount of Olives, the disciples came to him privately. "Tell us," they said, "when will this happen, and what will be the sign of your coming and of the end of the age?"

⁴Jesus answered: "Watch out that no one deceives you. ⁵For many will come in my name, claiming, 'I am the Christ,'ᵈ and will deceive many. ⁶You will hear of wars and rumors of wars, but see to it that you

are not alarmed. Such things must happen, but the end is still to come. [7]Nation will rise against nation, and kingdom against kingdom. There will be famines and earthquakes in various places. [8]All these are the beginning of birth pains.

[9]"Then you will be handed over to be persecuted and put to death, and you will be hated by all nations because of me. [10]At that time many will turn away from the faith and will betray and hate each other, [11]and many false prophets will appear and deceive many people. [12]Because of the increase of wickedness, the love of most will grow cold, [13]but he who stands firm to the end will be saved. [14]And this gospel of the kingdom will be preached in the whole world as a testimony to all nations, and then the end will come.

[15]"So when you see standing in the holy place 'the abomination that causes desolation,'[a] spoken of through the prophet Daniel—let the reader understand—[16]then let those who are in Judea flee to the mountains. [17]Let no one on the roof of his house go down to take anything out of the house. [18]Let no one in the field go back to get his cloak. [19]How dreadful it will be in those days for pregnant women and nursing mothers! [20]Pray that your flight will not take place in winter or on the Sabbath. [21]For then there will be great distress, unequaled from the beginning of the world until now—and never to be equaled again. [22]If those days had not been cut short, no one would survive, but for the sake of the elect those days will be shortened. [23]At that time if anyone says to you, 'Look, here is the Christ!' or, 'There he is!' do not believe it. [24]For false Christs and false prophets will appear and perform great signs and miracles to deceive even the elect—if that were possible. [25]See, I have told you ahead of time.

[26]"So if anyone tells you, 'There he is, out in the desert,' do not go out; or, 'Here he is, in the inner rooms,' do not believe it. [27]For as lightning that comes from the east is visible even in the west, so will be the coming of the Son of Man. [28]Wherever there is a carcass, there the vultures will gather.

[29]"Immediately after the distress of those days

" 'the sun will be darkened,
    and the moon will not give its light;
the stars will fall from the sky,
    and the heavenly bodies will be shaken.'[b]

[30]"At that time the sign of the Son of Man will appear in the sky, and all the nations of the earth will mourn. They will see the Son of Man coming on the clouds of the sky, with power and great glory. [31]And he will send his angels with a loud trumpet call, and they will gather his elect from the four winds, from one end of the heavens to the other.

[32]"Now learn this lesson from the fig tree: As soon as its twigs get tender and its leaves come out, you know that summer is near. [33]Even so, when you see all these things, you know that it[c] is near, right at the door. [34]I tell you the truth, this generation[d] will certainly not pass away until all these things have happened. [35]Heaven and earth will pass away, but my words will never pass away.

The Day and Hour Unknown

[36]"No one knows about that day or hour, not even the angels in heaven, nor the Son,[e] but only the Father. [37]As it was in the days of Noah, so it will be at the coming of the Son of Man. [38]For in the days before the flood, people were eating and drinking, marrying and giving in marriage, up to the day Noah entered the ark; [39]and they knew nothing about what would happen until the flood came and took them all away. That is how it will be at the coming of the Son of Man. [40]Two men will be in the field; one will be taken and the other left. [41]Two women will be grinding with a hand mill; one will be taken and the other left.

[42]"Therefore keep watch, because you do not know on what day your Lord will come. [43]But understand this: If the owner of the house had known at what time of night the thief was coming, he would have kept watch and would not have let his house be broken into. [44]So you also must be ready, because the Son of Man will come at an hour when you do not expect him.

[45]"Who then is the faithful and wise servant, whom the master has put in charge of the servants in his household to give them their food at the proper time? [46]It will be good for that servant whose master finds him doing so when he returns. [47]I tell you the truth, he will put him in charge of all his possessions. [48]But suppose that servant is wicked and says to

[a]15 Daniel 9:27; 11:31; 12:11   [b]29 Isaiah 13:10; 34:4
[c]33 Or *he*   [d]34 Or *race*   [e]36 Some manuscripts do not have *nor the Son*.

himself, 'My master is staying away a long time,' ⁴⁹and he then begins to beat his fellow servants and to eat and drink with drunkards. ⁵⁰The master of that servant will come on a day when he does not expect him and at an hour he is not aware of. ⁵¹He will cut him to pieces and assign him a place with the hypocrites, where there will be weeping and gnashing of teeth.

The Parable of the Ten Virgins

25 "At that time the kingdom of heaven will be like ten virgins who took their lamps and went out to meet the bridegroom. ²Five of them were foolish and five were wise. ³The foolish ones took their lamps but did not take any oil with them. ⁴The wise, however, took oil in jars along with their lamps. ⁵The bridegroom was a long time in coming, and they all became drowsy and fell asleep.

⁶"At midnight the cry rang out: 'Here's the bridegroom! Come out to meet him!'

⁷"Then all the virgins woke up and trimmed their lamps. ⁸The foolish ones said to the wise, 'Give us some of your oil; our lamps are going out.'

⁹" 'No,' they replied, 'there may not be enough for both us and you. Instead, go to those who sell oil and buy some for yourselves.'

¹⁰"But while they were on their way to buy the oil, the bridegroom arrived. The virgins who were ready went in with him to the wedding banquet. And the door was shut.

¹¹"Later the others also came. 'Sir! Sir!' they said. 'Open the door for us!'

¹²"But he replied, 'I tell you the truth, I don't know you.'

¹³"Therefore keep watch, because you do not know the day or the hour.

The Parable of the Talents

¹⁴"Again, it will be like a man going on a journey, who called his servants and entrusted his property to them. ¹⁵To one he gave five talents[a] of money, to another two talents, and to another one talent, each according to his ability. Then he went on his journey. ¹⁶The man who had received the five talents went at once and put his money to work and gained five more. ¹⁷So also, the one with the two talents gained two more. ¹⁸But the man who had received the one talent went off, dug a hole in the ground and hid his master's money.

¹⁹"After a long time the master of those servants returned and settled accounts with them. ²⁰The man who had received the five talents brought the other five. 'Master,' he said, 'you entrusted me with five talents. See, I have gained five more.'

²¹"His master replied, 'Well done, good and faithful servant! You have been faithful with a few things; I will put you in charge of many things. Come and share your master's happiness!'

²²"The man with the two talents also came. 'Master,' he said, 'you entrusted me with two talents; see, I have gained two more.'

²³"His master replied, 'Well done, good and faithful servant! You have been faithful with a few things; I will put you in charge of many things. Come and share your master's happiness!'

²⁴"Then the man who had received the one talent came. 'Master,' he said, 'I knew that you are a hard man, harvesting where you have not sown and gathering where you have not scattered seed. ²⁵So I was afraid and went out and hid your talent in the ground. See, here is what belongs to you.'

²⁶"His master replied, 'You wicked, lazy servant! So you knew that I harvest where I have not sown and gather where I have not scattered seed? ²⁷Well then, you should have put my money on deposit with the bankers, so that when I returned I would have received it back with interest.

²⁸" 'Take the talent from him and give it to the one who has the ten talents. ²⁹For everyone who has will be given more, and he will have an abundance. Whoever does not have, even what he has will be taken from him. ³⁰And throw that worthless servant outside, into the darkness, where there will be weeping and gnashing of teeth.'

The Sheep and the Goats

³¹"When the Son of Man comes in his glory, and all the angels with him, he will sit on his throne in heavenly glory. ³²All the nations will be gathered before him, and he will separate the people one from another as a shepherd separates the sheep from the goats. ³³He will put the sheep on his right and the goats on his left.

³⁴"Then the King will say to those on his right, 'Come, you who are blessed by my Father; take your inheritance, the kingdom

---

[a]15 A talent was worth more than a thousand dollars.

prepared for you since the creation of the world. ³⁵For I was hungry and you gave me something to eat, I was thirsty and you gave me something to drink, I was a stranger and you invited me in, ³⁶I needed clothes and you clothed me, I was sick and you looked after me, I was in prison and you came to visit me.'

³⁷"Then the righteous will answer him, 'Lord, when did we see you hungry and feed you, or thirsty and give you something to drink? ³⁸When did we see you a stranger and invite you in, or needing clothes and clothe you? ³⁹When did we

see you sick or in prison and go to visit you?'

⁴⁰"The King will reply, 'I tell you the truth, whatever you did for one of the least of these brothers of mine, you did for me.'

⁴¹"Then he will say to those on his left, 'Depart from me, you who are cursed, into the eternal fire prepared for the devil and his angels. ⁴²For I was hungry and you gave me nothing to eat, I was thirsty and you gave me nothing to drink, ⁴³I was a stranger and you did not invite me in, I needed clothes and you did not clothe

Protect Your Life and Lose It

DAILY INSIGHT

Imagine going for a walk on your favorite beach. Can you feel the warm sand, the cool breeze, see the sunshine, hear the sound of the water? Good. Now bend down, grab a handful of sand, and look at it.

This sand is yours. You must protect it using only the hand that holds the sand. What will you do to ensure that the largest amount of sand stays in your hand?

For those of you who chose to close the sand in your grip, what happened? If you say that most of it fell to the beach, you're correct. What had been yours to hold has now fallen out of your grasp. If you had wanted to take perfect care of what was yours, you should have held it with an open hand. Now relate that image to the parable in Matthew 25.

The story of the talents in the hands of the three servants is often confusing. Some have accused Jesus of mocking the poor who have not been "given" as much as others. "Jesus says that 'everyone who has will be given more ... whoever does not have, even what he has will be taken from him' (v. 29). This is not fair." But this analysis of the story seriously misses the point.

You have been given a measure of God's goodness—talents from the Master. You and I probably know people who have more talents than we do, and we probably know people who have been given less. That would make us members of the "Two Talent

TUESDAY

Passage:
Matthew 25:14–30

Verse:
Matthew 25:21

Club." Now, what are we doing with our talents? Are we holding them with an open hand, using them, investing them, risking them, sharing them? Are we afraid that, in our clumsiness, we might lose them? Or worse, are we gripping the talents we have, hoping, for goodness' sake, that someone doesn't steal them?

The message of the story that Jesus told is crystal clear: It's not how much you have that matters. It's *what you do* with what you have that is important. If you try to protect your gifts and possessions or even hide them, the return of the Master will be a mighty embarrassing experience.

What is it that you could be doing—should be doing—for God? What talents do you have in that clenched fist? When someone at church asks for volunteers to deliver meals to shut-ins or to give up a Saturday to repair a house, do you stare at the floor? When your child asks you to help chaperone the school's field trip to the museum, do you quickly find a conflict in your schedule?

Give your talents away. Clamping down on them will only diminish them. Holding onto them will not bring you any pleasure or any joy whatsoever. Open your hand. Give yourself away. Serve the Master with a grateful and courageous heart.

For your next devotional reading, go to page 1075.

me, I was sick and in prison and you did not look after me.'

[44]"They also will answer, 'Lord, when did we see you hungry or thirsty or a stranger or needing clothes or sick or in prison, and did not help you?'

[45]"He will reply, 'I tell you the truth, whatever you did not do for one of the least of these, you did not do for me.'

[46]"Then they will go away to eternal punishment, but the righteous to eternal life."

The Plot Against Jesus

26 When Jesus had finished saying all these things, he said to his disciples, [2]"As you know, the Passover is two days away—and the Son of Man will be handed over to be crucified."

[3]Then the chief priests and the elders of the people assembled in the palace of the high priest, whose name was Caiaphas, [4]and they plotted to arrest Jesus in some sly way and kill him. [5]"But not during the Feast," they said, "or there may be a riot among the people."

Jesus Anointed at Bethany

[6]While Jesus was in Bethany in the home of a man known as Simon the Leper, [7]a woman came to him with an alabaster jar of very expensive perfume, which she poured on his head as he was reclining at the table.

[8]When the disciples saw this, they were indignant. "Why this waste?" they asked. [9]"This perfume could have been sold at a high price and the money given to the poor."

[10]Aware of this, Jesus said to them, "Why are you bothering this woman? She has done a beautiful thing to me. [11]The poor you will always have with you, but you will not always have me. [12]When she poured this perfume on my body, she did it to prepare me for burial. [13]I tell you the truth, wherever this gospel is preached throughout the world, what she has done will also be told, in memory of her."

Judas Agrees to Betray Jesus

[14]Then one of the Twelve—the one called Judas Iscariot—went to the chief priests [15]and asked, "What are you willing to give me if I hand him over to you?" So they counted out for him thirty silver coins. [16]From then on Judas watched for an opportunity to hand him over.

The Lord's Supper

[17]On the first day of the Feast of Unleavened Bread, the disciples came to Jesus and asked, "Where do you want us to make preparations for you to eat the Passover?"

[18]He replied, "Go into the city to a certain man and tell him, 'The Teacher says: My appointed time is near. I am going to celebrate the Passover with my disciples at your house.' " [19]So the disciples did as Jesus had directed them and prepared the Passover.

[20]When evening came, Jesus was reclining at the table with the Twelve. [21]And while they were eating, he said, "I tell you the truth, one of you will betray me."

[22]They were very sad and began to say to him one after the other, "Surely not I, Lord?"

[23]Jesus replied, "The one who has dipped his hand into the bowl with me will betray me. [24]The Son of Man will go just as it is written about him. But woe to that man who betrays the Son of Man! It would be better for him if he had not been born."

[25]Then Judas, the one who would betray him, said, "Surely not I, Rabbi?"

Jesus answered, "Yes, it is you."[a]

[26]While they were eating, Jesus took bread, gave thanks and broke it, and gave it to his disciples, saying, "Take and eat; this is my body."

[27]Then he took the cup, gave thanks and offered it to them, saying, "Drink from it, all of you. [28]This is my blood of the[b] covenant, which is poured out for many for the forgiveness of sins. [29]I tell you, I will not drink of this fruit of the vine from now on until that day when I drink it anew with you in my Father's kingdom."

[30]When they had sung a hymn, they went out to the Mount of Olives.

Jesus Predicts Peter's Denial

[31]Then Jesus told them, "This very night you will all fall away on account of me, for it is written:

" 'I will strike the shepherd,
    and the sheep of the flock will be
       scattered.'[c]

[32]But after I have risen, I will go ahead of you into Galilee."

[a]25 Or "You yourself have said it"   [b]28 Some manuscripts the new   [c]31 Zech. 13:7

[33]Peter replied, "Even if all fall away on account of you, I never will."

[34]"I tell you the truth," Jesus answered, "this very night, before the rooster crows, you will disown me three times."

[35]But Peter declared, "Even if I have to die with you, I will never disown you." And all the other disciples said the same.

Gethsemane

[36]Then Jesus went with his disciples to a place called Gethsemane, and he said to them, "Sit here while I go over there and pray." [37]He took Peter and the two sons of Zebedee along with him, and he began to be sorrowful and troubled. [38]Then he said to them, "My soul is overwhelmed with sorrow to the point of death. Stay here and keep watch with me."

[39]Going a little farther, he fell with his face to the ground and prayed, "My Father, if it is possible, may this cup be taken from me. Yet not as I will, but as you will."

[40]Then he returned to his disciples and found them sleeping. "Could you men not keep watch with me for one hour?" he asked Peter. [41]"Watch and pray so that you will not fall into temptation. The spirit is willing, but the body is weak."

[42]He went away a second time and prayed, "My Father, if it is not possible for this cup to be taken away unless I drink it, may your will be done."

[43]When he came back, he again found them sleeping, because their eyes were heavy. [44]So he left them and went away once more and prayed the third time, saying the same thing.

[45]Then he returned to the disciples and said to them, "Are you still sleeping and resting? Look, the hour is near, and the Son of Man is betrayed into the hands of sinners. [46]Rise, let us go! Here comes my betrayer!"

Jesus Arrested

[47]While he was still speaking, Judas, one of the Twelve, arrived. With him was a large crowd armed with swords and clubs, sent from the chief priests and the elders of the people. [48]Now the betrayer had arranged a signal with them: "The one I kiss is the man; arrest him." [49]Going at once to Jesus, Judas said, "Greetings, Rabbi!" and kissed him.

[50]Jesus replied, "Friend, do what you came for."[a]

Then the men stepped forward, seized Jesus and arrested him. [51]With that, one of Jesus' companions reached for his sword, drew it out and struck the servant of the high priest, cutting off his ear.

[52]"Put your sword back in its place," Jesus said to him, "for all who draw the sword will die by the sword. [53]Do you think I cannot call on my Father, and he will at once put at my disposal more than twelve legions of angels? [54]But how then would the Scriptures be fulfilled that say it must happen in this way?"

[55]At that time Jesus said to the crowd, "Am I leading a rebellion, that you have come out with swords and clubs to capture me? Every day I sat in the temple courts teaching, and you did not arrest me. [56]But this has all taken place that the writings of the prophets might be fulfilled." Then all the disciples deserted him and fled.

Before the Sanhedrin

[57]Those who had arrested Jesus took him to Caiaphas, the high priest, where the teachers of the law and the elders had assembled. [58]But Peter followed him at a distance, right up to the courtyard of the high priest. He entered and sat down with the guards to see the outcome.

[59]The chief priests and the whole Sanhedrin were looking for false evidence against Jesus so that they could put him to death. [60]But they did not find any, though many false witnesses came forward.

Finally two came forward [61]and declared, "This fellow said, 'I am able to destroy the temple of God and rebuild it in three days.' "

[62]Then the high priest stood up and said to Jesus, "Are you not going to answer? What is this testimony that these men are bringing against you?" [63]But Jesus remained silent.

The high priest said to him, "I charge you under oath by the living God: Tell us if you are the Christ,[b] the Son of God."

[64]"Yes, it is as you say," Jesus replied. "But I say to all of you: In the future you will see the Son of Man sitting at the right hand of the Mighty One and coming on the clouds of heaven."

[65]Then the high priest tore his clothes and said, "He has spoken blasphemy! Why do we need any more witnesses? Look, now you have heard the blasphemy. [66]What do you think?"

"He is worthy of death," they answered.

---

[a]50 Or *"Friend, why have you come?"*   [b]63 Or *Messiah*; also in verse 68

67Then they spit in his face and struck him with their fists. Others slapped him **68**and said, "Prophesy to us, Christ. Who hit you?"

Peter Disowns Jesus

69Now Peter was sitting out in the courtyard, and a servant girl came to him. "You also were with Jesus of Galilee," she said.

70But he denied it before them all. "I don't know what you're talking about," he said.

71Then he went out to the gateway, where another girl saw him and said to the people there, "This fellow was with Jesus of Nazareth."

72He denied it again, with an oath: "I don't know the man!"

73After a little while, those standing there went up to Peter and said, "Surely you are one of them, for your accent gives you away."

74Then he began to call down curses on himself and he swore to them, "I don't know the man!"

Immediately a rooster crowed. **75**Then Peter remembered the word Jesus had

---

Take It ... or Live It

DAILY INSIGHT

WEDNESDAY
Passage:
Matthew 26:47–49,
69–75; 27:5
Verse:
Matthew 26:75

Words have always fascinated me. Although, as a kid, I didn't aspire to spend the bulk of my career in publishing—the business of packaging words—I'm really not surprised that this is where I wound up.

For several years I worked for a man for whom English was a second language. Although he did very well, at times certain words would stump him, and he'd call me for help.

On one such occasion when I walked into Dan's office, his expression indicated that he was faced with some kind of conundrum. "What's the difference between 'unpredictable' and 'undependable'?" He asked in his familiar Middle-Eastern roll.

"'Unpredictable' would describe a mysterious person, someone whose next move was usually a surprise," I explained. "An unpredictable person would keep others guessing about his intentions. An undependable person," I continued, "would make a promise, then ignore it, hanging people out to dry." Dan understood.

Then, looking him square in the eye, I finished with a short postscript. "I wouldn't work for someone who was undependable ... but I *do* work for someone who's unpredictable!" A knowing smile graced Dan's face. He thanked me for the help, and I returned to my office.

Now, I have two words for *you*: remorse and repentance. What's the difference between these two words?

With today's verses in mind, we can actually give names to these two powerful words: Judas and Peter. On the night Jesus was arrested and tried, both of these men betrayed him. Judas did it with a kiss in the garden, Peter with an oath in the courtyard. Both of them had heard Jesus predict their disobedient acts, and both were crushed at their own sin.

But Judas, unwilling to face his guilt, went out and hanged himself. This pathetic turncoat took his own life. Peter, on the other hand, shattered by his transgression, broke down and wept like a child. Through those tears, Peter opened himself to confession, forgiveness, and resolve. In the years that followed, Judas became an embarrassing memory to those who had known him. Peter changed the world. Remorse and repentance: two similar words with incredibly potent differences.

It's a great temptation, when we're caught red-handed in a sin, to throw ourselves to the ground, groveling in remorse. But the message of these two unforgettable men is that while remorse ends a life, repentance starts one all over again.

Jesus Christ has already died for your sin. He paid the price on the cross. Recognize your failure, receive your pardon, and get on with it. Quit groveling and start celebrating. What a great plan.

For your next devotional reading, go to page 1078.

spoken: "Before the rooster crows, you will disown me three times." And he went outside and wept bitterly.

Judas Hangs Himself

27 Early in the morning, all the chief priests and the elders of the people came to the decision to put Jesus to death. [2]They bound him, led him away and handed him over to Pilate, the governor.

[3]When Judas, who had betrayed him, saw that Jesus was condemned, he was seized with remorse and returned the thirty silver coins to the chief priests and the elders. [4]"I have sinned," he said, "for I have betrayed innocent blood."

"What is that to us?" they replied. "That's your responsibility."

[5]So Judas threw the money into the temple and left. Then he went away and hanged himself.

[6]The chief priests picked up the coins and said, "It is against the law to put this into the treasury, since it is blood money." [7]So they decided to use the money to buy the potter's field as a burial place for foreigners. [8]That is why it has been called the Field of Blood to this day. [9]Then what was spoken by Jeremiah the prophet was fulfilled: "They took the thirty silver coins, the price set on him by the people of Israel, [10]and they used them to buy the potter's field, as the Lord commanded me."[a]

Jesus Before Pilate

[11]Meanwhile Jesus stood before the governor, and the governor asked him, "Are you the king of the Jews?"

"Yes, it is as you say," Jesus replied.

[12]When he was accused by the chief priests and the elders, he gave no answer. [13]Then Pilate asked him, "Don't you hear the testimony they are bringing against you?" [14]But Jesus made no reply, not even to a single charge—to the great amazement of the governor.

[15]Now it was the governor's custom at the Feast to release a prisoner chosen by the crowd. [16]At that time they had a notorious prisoner, called Barabbas. [17]So when the crowd had gathered, Pilate asked them, "Which one do you want me to release to you: Barabbas, or Jesus who is called Christ?" [18]For he knew it was out of envy that they had handed Jesus over to him.

[19]While Pilate was sitting on the judge's seat, his wife sent him this message: "Don't have anything to do with that innocent man, for I have suffered a great deal today in a dream because of him."

[20]But the chief priests and the elders persuaded the crowd to ask for Barabbas and to have Jesus executed.

[21]"Which of the two do you want me to release to you?" asked the governor.

"Barabbas," they answered.

[22]"What shall I do, then, with Jesus who is called Christ?" Pilate asked.

They all answered, "Crucify him!"

[23]"Why? What crime has he committed?" asked Pilate.

But they shouted all the louder, "Crucify him!"

[24]When Pilate saw that he was getting nowhere, but that instead an uproar was starting, he took water and washed his hands in front of the crowd. "I am innocent of this man's blood," he said. "It is your responsibility!"

[25]All the people answered, "Let his blood be on us and on our children!"

[26]Then he released Barabbas to them. But he had Jesus flogged, and handed him over to be crucified.

The Soldiers Mock Jesus

[27]Then the governor's soldiers took Jesus into the Praetorium and gathered the whole company of soldiers around him. [28]They stripped him and put a scarlet robe on him, [29]and then twisted together a crown of thorns and set it on his head. They put a staff in his right hand and knelt in front of him and mocked him. "Hail, king of the Jews!" they said. [30]They spit on him, and took the staff and struck him on the head again and again. [31]After they had mocked him, they took off the robe and put his own clothes on him. Then they led him away to crucify him.

The Crucifixion

[32]As they were going out, they met a man from Cyrene, named Simon, and they forced him to carry the cross. [33]They came to a place called Golgotha (which means The Place of the Skull). [34]There they offered Jesus wine to drink, mixed with gall; but after tasting it, he refused to drink it. [35]When they had crucified him, they divided up his clothes by casting lots.[b] [36]And sitting down, they kept watch

[a]10 See Zech. 11:12,13; Jer. 19:1-13; 32:6-9.
[b]35 A few late manuscripts *lots that the word spoken by the prophet might be fulfilled: "They divided my garments among themselves and cast lots for my clothing"* (Psalm 22:18)

over him there. **37**Above his head they placed the written charge against him: THIS IS JESUS, THE KING OF THE JEWS. **38**Two robbers were crucified with him, one on his right and one on his left. **39**Those who passed by hurled insults at him, shaking their heads **40**and saying, "You who are going to destroy the temple and build it in three days, save yourself! Come down from the cross, if you are the Son of God!" **41**In the same way the chief priests, the teachers of the law and the elders mocked him. **42**"He saved others," they said, "but he can't save himself! He's the King of Israel! Let him come down now from the cross, and we will believe in him. **43**He trusts in God. Let God rescue him now if he wants him, for he said, 'I am the Son of God.'" **44**In the same way the robbers who were crucified with him also heaped insults on him.

The Death of Jesus

45From the sixth hour until the ninth hour darkness came over all the land. **46**About the ninth hour Jesus cried out in a loud voice, *"Eloi, Eloi,*[a] *lama sabachthani?"*—which means, "My God, my God, why have you forsaken me?"[b] **47**When some of those standing there heard this, they said, "He's calling Elijah." **48**Immediately one of them ran and got a sponge. He filled it with wine vinegar, put it on a stick, and offered it to Jesus to drink. **49**The rest said, "Now leave him alone. Let's see if Elijah comes to save him."

50And when Jesus had cried out again in a loud voice, he gave up his spirit. **51**At that moment the curtain of the temple was torn in two from top to bottom. The earth shook and the rocks split. **52**The tombs broke open and the bodies of many holy people who had died were raised to life. **53**They came out of the tombs, and after Jesus' resurrection they went into the holy city and appeared to many people.

54When the centurion and those with him who were guarding Jesus saw the earthquake and all that had happened, they were terrified, and exclaimed, "Surely he was the Son[c] of God!"

55Many women were there, watching from a distance. They had followed Jesus from Galilee to care for his needs. **56**Among them were Mary Magdalene, Mary the mother of James and Joses, and the mother of Zebedee's sons.

The Burial of Jesus

57As evening approached, there came a rich man from Arimathea, named Joseph, who had himself become a disciple of Jesus. **58**Going to Pilate, he asked for Jesus' body, and Pilate ordered that it be given to him. **59**Joseph took the body, wrapped it in a clean linen cloth, **60**and placed it in his own new tomb that he had cut out of the rock. He rolled a big stone in front of the entrance to the tomb and went away. **61**Mary Magdalene and the other Mary were sitting there opposite the tomb.

The Guard at the Tomb

62The next day, the one after Preparation Day, the chief priests and the Pharisees went to Pilate. **63**"Sir," they said, "we remember that while he was still alive that deceiver said, 'After three days I will rise again.' **64**So give the order for the tomb to be made secure until the third day. Otherwise, his disciples may come and steal the body and tell the people that he has been raised from the dead. This last deception will be worse than the first."

65"Take a guard," Pilate answered. "Go, make the tomb as secure as you know how." **66**So they went and made the tomb secure by putting a seal on the stone and posting the guard.

The Resurrection

28 After the Sabbath, at dawn on the first day of the week, Mary Magdalene and the other Mary went to look at the tomb.

2There was a violent earthquake, for an angel of the Lord came down from heaven and, going to the tomb, rolled back the stone and sat on it. **3**His appearance was like lightning, and his clothes were white as snow. **4**The guards were so afraid of him that they shook and became like dead men.

5The angel said to the women, "Do not be afraid, for I know that you are looking for Jesus, who was crucified. **6**He is not here; he has risen, just as he said. Come and see the place where he lay. **7**Then go quickly and tell his disciples: 'He has risen from the dead and is going ahead of you into Galilee. There you will see him.' Now I have told you."

8So the women hurried away from the

a46 Some manuscripts *Eli, Eli*   *b46* Psalm 22:1
c54 Or *a son*

tomb, afraid yet filled with joy, and ran to tell his disciples. [9]Suddenly Jesus met them. "Greetings," he said. They came to him, clasped his feet and worshiped him. [10]Then Jesus said to them, "Do not be afraid. Go and tell my brothers to go to Galilee; there they will see me."

The Guards' Report

[11]While the women were on their way, some of the guards went into the city and reported to the chief priests everything that had happened. [12]When the chief priests had met with the elders and devised a plan, they gave the soldiers a large sum of money, [13]telling them, "You are to say, 'His disciples came during the night and stole him away while we were asleep.' [14]If this report gets to the governor, we will satisfy him and keep you out of trouble." [15]So the soldiers took the money and did as they were instructed. And this story has been widely circulated among the Jews to this very day.

The Great Commission

[16]Then the eleven disciples went to Galilee, to the mountain where Jesus had told them to go. [17]When they saw him, they worshiped him; but some doubted. [18]Then Jesus came to them and said, "All authority in heaven and on earth has been given to me. [19]Therefore go and make disciples of all nations, baptizing them in[a] the name of the Father and of the Son and of the Holy Spirit, [20]and teaching them to obey everything I have commanded you. And surely I am with you always, to the very end of the age."

[a]19 Or *into*; see Acts 8:16; 19:5; Romans 6:3; 1 Cor. 1:13; 10:2 and Gal. 3:27.

Don't Drop That Baton

DAILY
INSIGHT

THURSDAY

Passage:
Matthew 28:16–20

Verse:
Matthew 28:20

There is no event more thrilling in track and field than the relay race. It's the one running event that features teamwork, strategy and inevitable drama. Actually, the relay race is not about running at all. It's about the flight of the baton, handed from one tired athlete to a fresh athlete who's ready to dash down the track on his particular leg of the race.

Jesus' final words in Matthew's Gospel are all about passing the baton. "All authority in heaven and on earth has been given to me," Jesus said. The baton was in his hand. "Go and make disciples of all nations," he commanded them. Can't you hear the baton slapping into the hands of the disciples?

As dads, we also carry the baton. We received it from our heavenly Father, and now we find ourselves huffing and puffing down the backstretch. Our children are standing in the exchange area on the home stretch in front of the stands, watching us run and waiting to receive the baton when we've finished our lap.

The charge to dads is undeniably straightforward. Run well, and don't drop the baton when you hand it off to your children. They are counting on you to be faithful in both of these tasks.

When Jesus handed the baton to his disciples, he was entrusting his ministry to them. He knew that they would be representing him as "Christians"—"Christ followers." Our children represent *us*. "You must be Robert's daughter," a stranger might say to my Missy and Julie. Our job as dads is to run our race with endurance. Our faithfulness and visible experience of God's grace will give our children something to watch—a pattern worth emulating when they carry the baton on their own.

Actually, this is a three-man event. Jesus carries the baton first. He hands it to us, and his life and power give us a pattern and the power to run the next leg with authority. Then, when we come to the end of our story, our children carry it on.

I told you the relay was exciting!

For your next devotional reading, go to page 1081.

Mark was a young man—perhaps a teenager—when Jesus Christ walked planet Earth. Tradition tells us that he learned most of what he recorded from the apostle Peter's preaching. But when it came time for him to put pen to parchment, he didn't even mention the Messiah's birth. Most teenage boys couldn't care less about the details of babies or lineage. "What's the point?" they might say. "Forget this stuff; give me news I can use." So Mark's account is filled with the overwhelming emotion of a young man—observations from a person who was not an insider but whose life was radically changed by this man from Nazareth. Nearly half of Mark's book covers the final, incredible week before the Savior's crucifixion and resurrection.

Mark's writing ends after he records how Jesus revealed himself to his disciples, telling them to go and tell the world what had happened. Having heard Peter's stories and seen Jesus' power to transform lives, he was probably packing his own bags to tell everyone what he knew, regardless of the consequences. Young men are like that.

Mark

John the Baptist Prepares the Way

1 The beginning of the gospel about Jesus Christ, the Son of God.[a]

[2] It is written in Isaiah the prophet:

"I will send my messenger ahead of you,
    who will prepare your way"[b]—
[3] "a voice of one calling in the desert,
'Prepare the way for the Lord,
    make straight paths for him.' "[c]

[4] And so John came, baptizing in the desert region and preaching a baptism of repentance for the forgiveness of sins.

[5] The whole Judean countryside and all the people of Jerusalem went out to him. Confessing their sins, they were baptized by him in the Jordan River. [6] John wore clothing made of camel's hair, with a leather belt around his waist, and he ate locusts and wild honey. [7] And this was his message: "After me will come one more powerful than I, the thongs of whose sandals I am not worthy to stoop down and untie. [8] I baptize you with[d] water, but he will baptize you with the Holy Spirit."

[a]1 Some manuscripts do not have *the Son of God.*
[b]2 Mal. 3:1   [c]3 Isaiah 40:3   [d]8 Or *in*

The Baptism and Temptation of Jesus

[9]At that time Jesus came from Nazareth in Galilee and was baptized by John in the Jordan. [10]As Jesus was coming up out of the water, he saw heaven being torn open and the Spirit descending on him like a dove. [11]And a voice came from heaven: "You are my Son, whom I love; with you I am well pleased."

[12]At once the Spirit sent him out into the desert, [13]and he was in the desert forty days, being tempted by Satan. He was with the wild animals, and angels attended him.

The Calling of the First Disciples

[14]After John was put in prison, Jesus went into Galilee, proclaiming the good news of God. [15]"The time has come," he said. "The kingdom of God is near. Repent and believe the good news!"

[16]As Jesus walked beside the Sea of Galilee, he saw Simon and his brother Andrew casting a net into the lake, for they were fishermen. [17]"Come, follow me," Jesus said, "and I will make you fishers of men." [18]At once they left their nets and followed him.

[19]When he had gone a little farther, he saw James son of Zebedee and his brother John in a boat, preparing their nets. [20]Without delay he called them, and they left their father Zebedee in the boat with the hired men and followed him.

Jesus Drives Out an Evil Spirit

[21]They went to Capernaum, and when the Sabbath came, Jesus went into the synagogue and began to teach. [22]The people were amazed at his teaching, because he taught them as one who had authority, not as the teachers of the law. [23]Just then a man in their synagogue who was possessed by an evil[a] spirit cried out, [24]"What do you want with us, Jesus of Nazareth? Have you come to destroy us? I know who you are—the Holy One of God!"

[25]"Be quiet!" said Jesus sternly. "Come out of him!" [26]The evil spirit shook the man violently and came out of him with a shriek.

[27]The people were all so amazed that they asked each other, "What is this? A new teaching—and with authority! He even gives orders to evil spirits and they obey him." [28]News about him spread quickly over the whole region of Galilee.

Jesus Heals Many

[29]As soon as they left the synagogue, they went with James and John to the home of Simon and Andrew. [30]Simon's mother-in-law was in bed with a fever, and they told Jesus about her. [31]So he went to her, took her hand and helped her up. The fever left her and she began to wait on them.

[32]That evening after sunset the people brought to Jesus all the sick and demon-possessed. [33]The whole town gathered at the door, [34]and Jesus healed many who had various diseases. He also drove out many demons, but he would not let the demons speak because they knew who he was.

Jesus Prays in a Solitary Place

[35]Very early in the morning, while it was still dark, Jesus got up, left the house and went off to a solitary place, where he prayed. [36]Simon and his companions went to look for him, [37]and when they found him, they exclaimed: "Everyone is looking for you!"

[38]Jesus replied, "Let us go somewhere else—to the nearby villages—so I can preach there also. That is why I have come." [39]So he traveled throughout Galilee, preaching in their synagogues and driving out demons.

A Man With Leprosy

[40]A man with leprosy[b] came to him and begged him on his knees, "If you are willing, you can make me clean."

[41]Filled with compassion, Jesus reached out his hand and touched the man. "I am willing," he said. "Be clean!" [42]Immediately the leprosy left him and he was cured.

[43]Jesus sent him away at once with a strong warning: [44]"See that you don't tell this to anyone. But go, show yourself to the priest and offer the sacrifices that Moses commanded for your cleansing, as a testimony to them." [45]Instead he went out and began to talk freely, spreading the news. As a result, Jesus could no longer enter a town openly but stayed outside in lonely places. Yet the people still came to him from everywhere.

---

[a]23 Greek *unclean*; also in verses 26 and 27
[b]40 The Greek word was used for various diseases affecting the skin—not necessarily leprosy.

Jesus Heals a Paralytic

2 A few days later, when Jesus again en-tered Capernaum, the people heard that he had come home. [2]So many gathered that there was no room left, not even outside the door, and he preached the word to them. [3]Some men came, bringing to him a paralytic, carried by four of them. [4]Since they could not get him to Jesus because of the crowd, they made an opening in the roof above Jesus and, after digging through it, lowered the mat the paralyzed man was lying on. [5]When Jesus saw their faith, he said to the paralytic, "Son, your sins are forgiven."

[6]Now some teachers of the law were sitting there, thinking to themselves, [7]"Why does this fellow talk like that? He's blaspheming! Who can forgive sins but God alone?"

[8]Immediately Jesus knew in his spirit that this was what they were thinking in their hearts, and he said to them, "Why are you thinking these things? [9]Which is easier: to say to the paralytic, 'Your sins are forgiven,' or to say, 'Get up, take your mat and walk'? [10]But that you may know that the Son of Man has authority on earth to forgive sins . . ." He said to the paralytic, [11]"I tell you, get up, take your mat and go home." [12]He got up, took his mat and walked out in full view of them all. This amazed everyone and they praised God, saying, "We have never seen anything like this!"

Ouch!

DAILY INSIGHT

FRIDAY

Passage:
Mark 1:40–45

Verse:
Mark 1:42

Leprosy is a disease that, among its other physiological effects, deadens the nerves. A person with this condition would not notice, say, that the cup of coffee he was holding in his hand was too hot. He would walk out of the local beanery with his mind on other thoughts as his hand burned. Insensitivity is a dangerous thing.

A man with leprosy—the disease of unfeeling—came to Jesus and pleaded his case, "If you are willing," the man begged, "you can make me clean" (1:40).

Jesus was "filled with compassion"; he was struck with the man's desperation and faith. And then Jesus did something he was accustomed to doing. He "reached out his hand and touched the man" (1:41). Take a second to think about this. For the first time, perhaps in years, the man felt something. And incredibly, that "something"—God's very own hand—was also delivering his healing. What a life-changing moment.

As men, you and I are susceptible to emotional leprosy. We can contract this disease without even knowing it. For some of us, the cares, pressures and sheer pace of our lives have desensitized our hearts. We think. We do. But we do not feel. We have stopped touching, and we have stopped feeling the hand of others. The Bible would call this problem a disease that is no less perilous and life threatening than leprosy. And Jesus is in the business of healing this affliction.

God has blessed you with a family. In your mind's eye, take a moment and see each one. You're the luckiest man alive. What a gift each of these people is to you.

And now here's the question of the day. Do these people need your touch? Do you need to feel their tenderness? Do you need to be healed of your leprosy?

The man with leprosy was desperate. His desire to be healed was far more powerful than his interest in displaying good manners that day. He didn't care what it took. He wanted the Savior to know that he was tired of living a life of separation and isolation, so he went to his knees, right there in front of everyone. And he was healed.

Is your life devoid of tenderness? Are your children missing out on your touch? Go to your knees, and ask your Father for a more loving and compassionate heart. He will heal you.

For your next devotional reading, go to page 1085.

The Calling of Levi

¹³Once again Jesus went out beside the lake. A large crowd came to him, and he began to teach them. ¹⁴As he walked along, he saw Levi son of Alphaeus sitting at the tax collector's booth. "Follow me," Jesus told him, and Levi got up and followed him.

¹⁵While Jesus was having dinner at Levi's house, many tax collectors and "sinners" were eating with him and his disciples, for there were many who followed him. ¹⁶When the teachers of the law who were Pharisees saw him eating with the "sinners" and tax collectors, they asked his disciples: "Why does he eat with tax collectors and 'sinners'?"

¹⁷On hearing this, Jesus said to them, "It is not the healthy who need a doctor, but the sick. I have not come to call the righteous, but sinners."

Jesus Questioned About Fasting

¹⁸Now John's disciples and the Pharisees were fasting. Some people came and asked Jesus, "How is it that John's disciples and the disciples of the Pharisees are fasting, but yours are not?"

¹⁹Jesus answered, "How can the guests of the bridegroom fast while he is with them? They cannot, so long as they have him with them. ²⁰But the time will come when the bridegroom will be taken from them, and on that day they will fast.

²¹"No one sews a patch of unshrunk cloth on an old garment. If he does, the new piece will pull away from the old, making the tear worse. ²²And no one pours new wine into old wineskins. If he does, the wine will burst the skins, and both the wine and the wineskins will be ruined. No, he pours new wine into new wineskins."

Lord of the Sabbath

²³One Sabbath Jesus was going through the grainfields, and as his disciples walked along, they began to pick some heads of grain. ²⁴The Pharisees said to him, "Look, why are they doing what is unlawful on the Sabbath?"

²⁵He answered, "Have you never read what David did when he and his companions were hungry and in need? ²⁶In the days of Abiathar the high priest, he entered the house of God and ate the consecrated bread, which is lawful only for priests to eat. And he also gave some to his companions."

²⁷Then he said to them, "The Sabbath was made for man, not man for the Sabbath. ²⁸So the Son of Man is Lord even of the Sabbath."

3 Another time he went into the synagogue, and a man with a shriveled

HEY DAD

What is an apostle? Is it the same thing as a disciple?

Text: Mark 3:14–15

The Greek word *apostolos* means "an ambassador of the Gospel" or "an official commissioner of Christ." Jesus appointed twelve apostles "that they might be with him and that he might send them out to preach and to have authority to drive out demons."

Although the word "apostle" is occasionally used in the Bible as a general term meaning "messenger," it usually refers to people "who saw the risen Christ and were specially commissioned by him" (Lockyer, 78). Paul, not one of the twelve original disciples, refers to himself as an apostle because on the road to Damascus, he actually saw Jesus and heard his voice (Acts 9:3–6).

The apostles were also called Jesus' disciples, but the two terms differ greatly. "Disciple" comes from the Greek word *mathetes,* which means "a learner or pupil." These men were disciples because they learned under Jesus' instruction. While there were only a few apostles, Jesus has many disciples even today … people like you and me.

Lockyer, H. (Ed.). (1986). Nelson's Illustrated Bible Dictionary. *Nashville, Tennessee: Thomas Nelson Publishers.*

For a complete listing of Questions Kids Ask, turn to page 1435.

hand was there. ²Some of them were looking for a reason to accuse Jesus, so they watched him closely to see if he would heal him on the Sabbath. ³Jesus said to the man with the shriveled hand, "Stand up in front of everyone."

⁴Then Jesus asked them, "Which is lawful on the Sabbath: to do good or to do evil, to save life or to kill?" But they remained silent.

⁵He looked around at them in anger and, deeply distressed at their stubborn hearts, said to the man, "Stretch out your hand." He stretched it out, and his hand was completely restored. ⁶Then the Pharisees went out and began to plot with the Herodians how they might kill Jesus.

Crowds Follow Jesus

⁷Jesus withdrew with his disciples to the lake, and a large crowd from Galilee followed. ⁸When they heard all he was doing, many people came to him from Judea, Jerusalem, Idumea, and the regions across the Jordan and around Tyre and Sidon. ⁹Because of the crowd he told his disciples to have a small boat ready for him, to keep the people from crowding him. ¹⁰For he had healed many, so that those with diseases were pushing forward to touch him. ¹¹Whenever the evil* spirits saw him, they fell down before him and cried out, "You are the Son of God." ¹²But

he gave them strict orders not to tell who he was.

The Appointing of the Twelve Apostles

¹³Jesus went up on a mountainside and called to him those he wanted, and they came to him. ¹⁴He appointed twelve—designating them apostles*—that they might be with him and that he might send them out to preach ¹⁵and to have authority to drive out demons. ¹⁶These are the twelve he appointed: Simon (to whom he gave the name Peter); ¹⁷James son of Zebedee and his brother John (to them he gave the name Boanerges, which means Sons of Thunder); ¹⁸Andrew, Philip, Bartholomew, Matthew, Thomas, James son of Alphaeus, Thaddaeus, Simon the Zealot ¹⁹and Judas Iscariot, who betrayed him.

Jesus and Beelzebub

²⁰Then Jesus entered a house, and again a crowd gathered, so that he and his disciples were not even able to eat. ²¹When his family heard about this, they went to take charge of him, for they said, "He is out of his mind."

²²And the teachers of the law who came down from Jerusalem said, "He is

*11 Greek *unclean*; also in verse 30   *14 Some manuscripts do not have *designating them apostles.*

HEY DAD
What are parables? Why did Jesus use them?

Text: Mark 3:23

A parable is a story that has two meanings—a literal one and a figurative one. Parables were a common teaching tool used in Jewish schools to help students grasp the deeper meanings of Scripture. The word "parable" comes from the Greek word *parabole*, which means "a comparison."

But why didn't Jesus just say things in "plain Aramaic"? Because language is limited. We have all had feelings—love, joy, or grief—that were so deep that words could not express them. Using parables, Jesus could communicate profound truths more effectively through word pictures or metaphors.

Probably another reason Jesus used parables is that this type of teaching helped distinguish between those with calloused hearts and those who sought the truth. Parables blinded some and enlightened others. For true followers of Jesus, these parables became revelations that drew them to examine their understanding of God and themselves (Ward, 237). These "hidden" lessons have the same effect among Jesus' followers today.

Ward, K. (Ed.). (1987). Jesus and His Times. Pleasantville, New York: The Reader's Digest Association.

For a complete listing of Questions Kids Ask, turn to page 1435.

possessed by Beelzebub[a]! By the prince of demons he is driving out demons."

[23]So Jesus called them and spoke to them in parables: "How can Satan drive out Satan? [24]If a kingdom is divided against itself, that kingdom cannot stand. [25]If a house is divided against itself, that house cannot stand. [26]And if Satan opposes himself and is divided, he cannot stand; his end has come. [27]In fact, no one can enter a strong man's house and carry off his possessions unless he first ties up the strong man. Then he can rob his house. [28]I tell you the truth, all the sins and blasphemies of men will be forgiven them. [29]But whoever blasphemes against the Holy Spirit will never be forgiven; he is guilty of an eternal sin."

[30]He said this because they were saying, "He has an evil spirit."

Jesus' Mother and Brothers

[31]Then Jesus' mother and brothers arrived. Standing outside, they sent someone in to call him. [32]A crowd was sitting around him, and they told him, "Your mother and brothers are outside looking for you."

[33]"Who are my mother and my brothers?" he asked.

[34]Then he looked at those seated in a circle around him and said, "Here are my mother and my brothers! [35]Whoever does God's will is my brother and sister and mother."

The Parable of the Sower

4 Again Jesus began to teach by the lake. The crowd that gathered around him was so large that he got into a boat and sat in it out on the lake, while all the people were along the shore at the water's edge. [2]He taught them many things by parables, and in his teaching said: [3]"Listen! A farmer went out to sow his seed. [4]As he was scattering the seed, some fell along the path, and the birds came and ate it up. [5]Some fell on rocky places, where it did not have much soil. It sprang up quickly, because the soil was shallow. [6]But when the sun came up, the plants were scorched, and they withered because they had no root. [7]Other seed fell among thorns, which grew up and choked the plants, so that they did not bear grain. [8]Still other seed fell on good soil. It came up, grew and produced a crop, multiplying thirty, sixty, or even a hundred times."

[9]Then Jesus said, "He who has ears to hear, let him hear."

[10]When he was alone, the Twelve and the others around him asked him about the parables. [11]He told them, "The secret of the kingdom of God has been given to you. But to those on the outside everything is said in parables [12]so that,

" 'they may be ever seeing but never
        perceiving,
    and ever hearing but never
        understanding;
    otherwise they might turn and be
        forgiven!'[b]"

[13]Then Jesus said to them, "Don't you understand this parable? How then will you understand any parable? [14]The farmer sows the word. [15]Some people are like seed along the path, where the word is sown. As soon as they hear it, Satan comes and takes away the word that was sown in them. [16]Others, like seed sown on rocky places, hear the word and at once receive it with joy. [17]But since they have no root, they last only a short time. When trouble or persecution comes because of the word, they quickly fall away. [18]Still others, like seed sown among thorns, hear the word; [19]but the worries of this life, the deceitfulness of wealth and the desires for other things come in and choke the word, making it unfruitful. [20]Others, like seed sown on good soil, hear the word, accept it, and produce a crop—thirty, sixty or even a hundred times what was sown."

A Lamp on a Stand

[21]He said to them, "Do you bring in a lamp to put it under a bowl or a bed? Instead, don't you put it on its stand? [22]For whatever is hidden is meant to be disclosed, and whatever is concealed is meant to be brought out into the open. [23]If anyone has ears to hear, let him hear."

[24]"Consider carefully what you hear," he continued. "With the measure you use, it will be measured to you—and even more. [25]Whoever has will be given more; whoever does not have, even what he has will be taken from him."

The Parable of the Growing Seed

[26]He also said, "This is what the kingdom of God is like. A man scatters seed on the ground. [27]Night and day, whether he

---

[a]22 Greek Beezeboul or Beelzeboul
[b]12 Isaiah 6:9,10

Pick Me, Pick Me!

Key Verse: *"Jesus went up on a mountainside and called to him those he wanted, and they came to him."* Mark 3:13

Text: Mark 3:13–19 *(Dad or child reads the text.)*

QUIET TIMES WITH Dad

DAD READS: What if, some summer afternoon, the kids in our neighborhood decided to play a game of baseball? All of you gathered at a local school, and two "captains" began to pick the players they wanted on their teams. Back and forth they went until all the kids were on a team. The very last one picked was the little kid who kept shouting, "Pick me, pick me." Poor kid.

Child reads: When captains pick teams, I always like to be one of the first kids picked. It's not very fun to be one of the last kids to be chosen. When this happens, the captain is really saying that he doesn't think that I will help the team very much. This makes me feel bad.

DAD READS: Jesus had decided to pick a team—we call his team the "disciples." The verses we read today give us the names of the men he chose. Can you imagine how excited these people were when Jesus called their names? "Of all the people in the whole world whom I could select to be my disciple," Jesus was saying. "I think I'll choose ... you!" These men, who were very different from each other, must have been ecstatic.

Child reads: Even though Jesus picked the twelve disciples a long, long time ago, he is still looking for people to be in his family. When he chooses the members of this family, he calls the people he has picked "Christians." These people love him and promise to follow him.

DAD READS: That's right. And the wonderful truth about this is that Jesus—our heavenly Captain—has chosen you and me to be his followers. He has called our names and told us that we can carry his name. It's just like we wear a team uniform that says, "I belong to Jesus." And even though we don't really have a uniform, he wants us to let others know that he has chosen us.

Child reads: I want Jesus to be happy that he chose me. And I want others to know that they can be members of God's family, too. I am glad that Jesus picked disciples who were very different from each other. And I'm glad that he still chooses all kinds of different people to be his followers. Let me pray this prayer with you:

Our Father in heaven, we love you. Thank you for the story about picking your disciples a long time ago, and thank you for choosing my dad and me today. Forgive us when we forget that we are wearing your uniform. Please help us to invite our friends to join your family. We love you and we thank you for your love. In Jesus' name, Amen.

For your next devotional reading, go to page 1088.

sleeps or gets up, the seed sprouts and grows, though he does not know how. [28]All by itself the soil produces grain—first the stalk, then the head, then the full kernel in the head. [29]As soon as the grain is ripe, he puts the sickle to it, because the harvest has come."

The Parable of the Mustard Seed

[30]Again he said, "What shall we say the kingdom of God is like, or what parable shall we use to describe it? [31]It is like a mustard seed, which is the smallest seed you plant in the ground. [32]Yet when planted, it grows and becomes the largest of all garden plants, with such big branches that the birds of the air can perch in its shade."

[33]With many similar parables Jesus spoke the word to them, as much as they could understand. [34]He did not say anything to them without using a parable. But when he was alone with his own disciples, he explained everything.

Jesus Calms the Storm

[35]That day when evening came, he said to his disciples, "Let us go over to the other side." [36]Leaving the crowd behind, they took him along, just as he was, in the boat. There were also other boats with him. [37]A furious squall came up, and the waves broke over the boat, so that it was nearly swamped. [38]Jesus was in the stern, sleeping on a cushion. The disciples woke him and said to him, "Teacher, don't you care if we drown?"

[39]He got up, rebuked the wind and said to the waves, "Quiet! Be still!" Then the wind died down and it was completely calm.

[40]He said to his disciples, "Why are you so afraid? Do you still have no faith?"

[41]They were terrified and asked each other, "Who is this? Even the wind and the waves obey him!"

The Healing of a Demon-possessed Man

5 They went across the lake to the region of the Gerasenes.[a] [2]When Jesus got out of the boat, a man with an evil[b] spirit came from the tombs to meet him. [3]This man lived in the tombs, and no one could bind him any more, not even with a chain. [4]For he had often been chained hand and foot, but he tore the chains apart and broke the irons on his feet. No one was strong enough to subdue him. [5]Night and day among the tombs and in the hills he would cry out and cut himself with stones.

[6]When he saw Jesus from a distance, he ran and fell on his knees in front of him. [7]He shouted at the top of his voice, "What do you want with me, Jesus, Son of the Most High God? Swear to God that you won't torture me!" [8]For Jesus had said to him, "Come out of this man, you evil spirit!"

[9]Then Jesus asked him, "What is your name?"

"My name is Legion," he replied, "for we are many." [10]And he begged Jesus again and again not to send them out of the area.

[11]A large herd of pigs was feeding on the nearby hillside. [12]The demons begged Jesus, "Send us among the pigs; allow us to go into them." [13]He gave them permission, and the evil spirits came out and went into the pigs. The herd, about two thousand in number, rushed down the steep bank into the lake and were drowned.

[14]Those tending the pigs ran off and reported this in the town and countryside, and the people went out to see what had happened. [15]When they came to Jesus, they saw the man who had been possessed by the legion of demons, sitting there, dressed and in his right mind; and they were afraid. [16]Those who had seen it told the people what had happened to the demon-possessed man—and told about the pigs as well. [17]Then the people began to plead with Jesus to leave their region.

[18]As Jesus was getting into the boat, the man who had been demon-possessed begged to go with him. [19]Jesus did not let him, but said, "Go home to your family and tell them how much the Lord has done for you, and how he has had mercy on you." [20]So the man went away and began to tell in the Decapolis[c] how much Jesus had done for him. And all the people were amazed.

A Dead Girl and a Sick Woman

[21]When Jesus had again crossed over by boat to the other side of the lake, a large crowd gathered around him while he was by the lake. [22]Then one of the synagogue rulers, named Jairus, came there. Seeing Jesus, he fell at his feet [23]and pleaded ear-

---

[a]1 Some manuscripts *Gadarenes*; other manuscripts *Gergesenes*   [b]2 Greek *unclean*; also in verses 8 and 13   [c]20 That is, the Ten Cities

nestly with him, "My little daughter is dying. Please come and put your hands on her so that she will be healed and live." ^{24}So Jesus went with him.

A large crowd followed and pressed around him. ^{25}And a woman was there who had been subject to bleeding for twelve years. ^{26}She had suffered a great deal under the care of many doctors and had spent all she had, yet instead of getting better she grew worse. ^{27}When she heard about Jesus, she came up behind him in the crowd and touched his cloak, ^{28}because she thought, "If I just touch his clothes, I will be healed." ^{29}Immediately her bleeding stopped and she felt in her body that she was freed from her suffering.

^{30}At once Jesus realized that power had gone out from him. He turned around in the crowd and asked, "Who touched my clothes?"

^{31}"You see the people crowding against you," his disciples answered, "and yet you can ask, 'Who touched me?' "

^{32}But Jesus kept looking around to see who had done it. ^{33}Then the woman, knowing what had happened to her, came and fell at his feet and, trembling with fear, told him the whole truth. ^{34}He said to her, "Daughter, your faith has healed you. Go in peace and be freed from your suffering."

^{35}While Jesus was still speaking, some men came from the house of Jairus, the synagogue ruler. "Your daughter is dead," they said. "Why bother the teacher any more?"

^{36}Ignoring what they said, Jesus told the synagogue ruler, "Don't be afraid; just believe."

^{37}He did not let anyone follow him except Peter, James and John the brother of James. ^{38}When they came to the home of the synagogue ruler, Jesus saw a commotion, with people crying and wailing

Help Me Please, My Daughter Is Dying
Jairus, the Bold Father

DADS
IN THE
BIBLE

"My little daughter is dying. Please come and put your hands on her so that she will be healed and live" (5:23).

Text: Mark 5:21–42

In this chapter, we read that a little girl was dying. Her daddy, a Jewish leader who probably shouldn't have been doing this in public, "fell at [Jesus'] feet and pleaded earnestly with him, 'My little daughter is dying. Please come and put your hands on her so that she will be healed and live' " (5:22–23).

Jairus certainly would have been conscious of the staring crowd. "Isn't this Jairus?" they must have whispered. "We thought synagogue hot shots didn't believe in this Messiah," they doubtlessly hissed. Jairus must have felt the scorn, but he didn't care. His little girl was deathly ill. Any pretense would have to wait for the next debate down at the temple.

When children are in danger, dads go for it. Have you noticed? They'll dash into the street after a wayward toddler or whisk them into their arms in the face of a snarling dog. With no concern for their own safety or pride, dads' adrenaline will kick in at full power. The desperate Jairus must have felt that same rush as he pleaded with this Jesus, rumored to be a miracle worker.

Jesus followed Jairus and answered his plea with the words, "Little girl, I say to you, get up" (v. 41). "Immediately the girl stood up and walked around … at this they were completely astonished" (v. 42). Can you imagine how happy Jairus must have been? How grateful he must have been that he had dared to be bold?

If you think about it, our children *are* in danger. Evil tempts their souls and physical perils lurk around every corner. Once we acknowledge the reality of these hazards, we'll do away with our pride, seek out the Savior and throw ourselves at his feet. While you can't protect your child 24 hours a day, there is One who can and will. Jairus learned this. What a great example to follow.

For a complete listing of Dads in the Bible, turn to page 1434.

loudly. **39**He went in and said to them, "Why all this commotion and wailing? The child is not dead but asleep." **40**But they laughed at him.

After he put them all out, he took the child's father and mother and the disciples who were with him, and went in where the child was. **41**He took her by the hand and said to her, *"Talitha koum!"* (which means, "Little girl, I say to you, get up!"). **42**Immediately the girl stood up and walked around (she was twelve years old). At this they were completely astonished. **43**He gave strict orders not to let anyone know about this, and told them to give her something to eat.

A Prophet Without Honor

6 Jesus left there and went to his hometown, accompanied by his disciples. **2**When the Sabbath came, he began to teach in the synagogue, and many who heard him were amazed.

"Where did this man get these things?" they asked. "What's this wisdom that has been given him, that he even does miracles! **3**Isn't this the carpenter? Isn't this Mary's son and the brother of James, Joseph,*a* Judas and Simon? Aren't his sisters here with us?" And they took offense at him.

a3 Greek *Joses*, a variant of *Joseph*

A Father's Desperation

DAILY INSIGHT

MONDAY

Passage:
Mark 5:35–42

Verses:
Mark 5:41–42

It was October, 1974. Our second child was about to be born. My wife, Bobbie's, pregnancy seemed similar to her first. Many folks had assured her that the second pregnancy and delivery would actually be easier than the first. Do not buy used cars from these people.

Not only was Julie over two weeks late coming into this world, but the first few years of her life were a literal avalanche of specialists looking for the diagnosis and prognosis for her physical complications. Visits to neurologists, orthopedic specialists and pediatricians filled our young family's calendar.

In all our calls to these medical experts, we were looking for one thing: hope. We desperately wanted someone to tell us that Julie would walk and that her mind would be sound. Actually, Bobbie faced all of this much better than I did. This twenty-something father spent many hours staring into the darkness during midnight visits to the living room ... and countless hours weeping. Maybe it would have been the same with an ailing infant son, but for a little girl's daddy, this was the toughest challenge I had ever faced. I didn't know what was going to happen to my daughter, and I was desperately afraid.

To our amazement and gratitude, Julie walked on schedule. And each of her mental facilities was perfectly normal. But I have never forgotten the feeling of a dad's heartache over the pain of his little girl.

Today's story is about another father, Jairus, who grieved over his daughter's pain and pleaded with Jesus to heal her. Jesus was momentarily distracted after this request, and in the meantime several men came to Jairus with terrible news for him. Far more incredible than my personal struggle with our daughter's physical complications, this Daddy's girl was dead. Jairus was numb with grief.

Notice, however, Jesus' response. He didn't say anything about the dead girl. His first words were not a reassurance that the child was going to be all right. No, instead Jesus looked at this father and offered him the most incredible advice known to mankind: "Don't be afraid; just believe" (v. 36). Because you have read the whole story, you know that it has a happy—and absolutely miraculous—ending.

Jesus has some very sound advice for us hand-wringing fathers. He offers a bit of solace as we contemplate the need to care for and protect our children. "Don't be afraid; just believe."

Thank you, heavenly Father. I really needed that today.

For your next devotional reading, go to page 1094.

⁴Jesus said to them, "Only in his hometown, among his relatives and in his own house is a prophet without honor." ⁵He could not do any miracles there, except lay his hands on a few sick people and heal them. ⁶And he was amazed at their lack of faith.

Jesus Sends Out the Twelve

Then Jesus went around teaching from village to village. ⁷Calling the Twelve to him, he sent them out two by two and gave them authority over evil*a* spirits.

⁸These were his instructions: "Take nothing for the journey except a staff—no bread, no bag, no money in your belts. ⁹Wear sandals but not an extra tunic. ¹⁰Whenever you enter a house, stay there until you leave that town. ¹¹And if any place will not welcome you or listen to you, shake the dust off your feet when you leave, as a testimony against them."

¹²They went out and preached that people should repent. ¹³They drove out many demons and anointed many sick people with oil and healed them.

John the Baptist Beheaded

¹⁴King Herod heard about this, for Jesus' name had become well known. Some were saying,*b* "John the Baptist has been raised from the dead, and that is why miraculous powers are at work in him."

¹⁵Others said, "He is Elijah."

And still others claimed, "He is a prophet, like one of the prophets of long ago."

¹⁶But when Herod heard this, he said, "John, the man I beheaded, has been raised from the dead!"

¹⁷For Herod himself had given orders to have John arrested, and he had him bound and put in prison. He did this because of Herodias, his brother Philip's wife, whom he had married. ¹⁸For John had been saying to Herod, "It is not lawful for you to have your brother's wife." ¹⁹So Herodias nursed a grudge against John and wanted to kill him. But she was not

a7 Greek unclean   b14 Some early manuscripts He was saying

Shame on This Dad
Herod, the Spineless Father

"Because of his oaths and his dinner guests, he did not want to refuse her" (6:26).

Text: Mark 6:14–29

You've seen them in the grocery store. You've seen them at the shopping mall. You've even seen them in church.

I'm talking about dads who have decided to let their children be in charge. You can easily spot these fathers because they have this pathetic, pleading look on their faces. Their child has defied them, and they are begging this little person to turn from their wicked ways and obey their dad. Kids in charge . . . this is not a pretty sight.

Herod was a powerful man. His absolute authority extended in every direction, further than a person could run in a day. But in the midst of his birthday banquet, Herod got carried away. He forgot that he was in charge. In a weak moment of ecstasy and abject stupidity, he promised his stepdaughter anything she wanted (v. 22). And because Herod was married to a woman who wasn't afraid to be in charge, this promise cost this foolish man the life of John the Baptist—a man whom Herod might have secretly wanted to follow (see vv. 20,26).

You're in charge . . . not by brute force or by verbal demands, but by God's gracious decree. Your children want a dad who knows what he wants, a dad who doesn't pathetically beseech his children to "Please, please obey Daddy." Be that kind of a dad for your children, and they'll thank you for it in the long run.

Herod—and his friend John the Baptist—paid a dear price for his cowardice. He looked like a powerful man. He ran the affairs of an entire nation, but he seemed afraid to be a father. Shame on you, Herod. Shame on this dad.

For a complete listing of Dads in the Bible, turn to page 1434.

able to, [20]because Herod feared John and protected him, knowing him to be a righteous and holy man. When Herod heard John, he was greatly puzzled[a]; yet he liked to listen to him.

[21]Finally the opportune time came. On his birthday Herod gave a banquet for his high officials and military commanders and the leading men of Galilee. [22]When the daughter of Herodias came in and danced, she pleased Herod and his dinner guests.

The king said to the girl, "Ask me for anything you want, and I'll give it to you." [23]And he promised her with an oath, "Whatever you ask I will give you, up to half my kingdom."

[24]She went out and said to her mother, "What shall I ask for?"

"The head of John the Baptist," she answered.

[25]At once the girl hurried in to the king with the request: "I want you to give me right now the head of John the Baptist on a platter."

[26]The king was greatly distressed, but because of his oaths and his dinner guests, he did not want to refuse her. [27]So he immediately sent an executioner with orders to bring John's head. The man went, beheaded John in the prison, [28]and brought back his head on a platter. He presented it to the girl, and she gave it to her mother. [29]On hearing of this, John's disciples came and took his body and laid it in a tomb.

Jesus Feeds the Five Thousand

[30]The apostles gathered around Jesus and reported to him all they had done and taught. [31]Then, because so many people were coming and going that they did not even have a chance to eat, he said to them, "Come with me by yourselves to a quiet place and get some rest."

[32]So they went away by themselves in a boat to a solitary place. [33]But many who saw them leaving recognized them and ran on foot from all the towns and got there ahead of them. [34]When Jesus landed and saw a large crowd, he had compassion on them, because they were like sheep without a shepherd. So he began teaching them many things.

[35]By this time it was late in the day, so his disciples came to him. "This is a remote place," they said, "and it's already very late. [36]Send the people away so they can go to the surrounding countryside and villages and buy themselves something to eat."

[37]But he answered, "You give them something to eat."

They said to him, "That would take eight months of a man's wages[b]! Are we to go and spend that much on bread and give it to them to eat?"

[38]"How many loaves do you have?" he asked. "Go and see."

When they found out, they said, "Five—and two fish."

[39]Then Jesus directed them to have all the people sit down in groups on the green grass. [40]So they sat down in groups of hundreds and fifties. [41]Taking the five loaves and the two fish and looking up to heaven, he gave thanks and broke the loaves. Then he gave them to his disciples to set before the people. He also divided the two fish among them all. [42]They all ate and were satisfied, [43]and the disciples picked up twelve basketfuls of broken pieces of bread and fish. [44]The number of the men who had eaten was five thousand.

Jesus Walks on the Water

[45]Immediately Jesus made his disciples get into the boat and go on ahead of him to Bethsaida, while he dismissed the crowd. [46]After leaving them, he went up on a mountainside to pray.

[47]When evening came, the boat was in the middle of the lake, and he was alone on land. [48]He saw the disciples straining at the oars, because the wind was against them. About the fourth watch of the night he went out to them, walking on the lake. He was about to pass by them, [49]but when they saw him walking on the lake, they thought he was a ghost. They cried out, [50]because they all saw him and were terrified.

Immediately he spoke to them and said, "Take courage! It is I. Don't be afraid." [51]Then he climbed into the boat with them, and the wind died down. They were completely amazed, [52]for they had not understood about the loaves; their hearts were hardened.

[53]When they had crossed over, they landed at Gennesaret and anchored there. [54]As soon as they got out of the boat, people recognized Jesus. [55]They ran throughout that whole region and carried the sick on mats to wherever they heard

[a]20 Some early manuscripts *he did many things*
[b]37 Greek *take two hundred denarii*

he was. **56**And wherever he went—into villages, towns or countryside—they placed the sick in the marketplaces. They begged him to let them touch even the edge of his cloak, and all who touched him were healed.

Clean and Unclean

7 The Pharisees and some of the teachers of the law who had come from Jerusalem gathered around Jesus and **2**saw some of his disciples eating food with hands that were "unclean," that is, unwashed. **3**(The Pharisees and all the Jews do not eat unless they give their hands a ceremonial washing, holding to the tradition of the elders. **4**When they come from the marketplace they do not eat unless they wash. And they observe many other traditions, such as the washing of cups, pitchers and kettles.*a*)

5So the Pharisees and teachers of the law asked Jesus, "Why don't your disciples live according to the tradition of the elders instead of eating their food with 'unclean' hands?"

6He replied, "Isaiah was right when he prophesied about you hypocrites; as it is written:

" 'These people honor me with their
        lips,
    but their hearts are far from me.
7They worship me in vain;
    their teachings are but rules taught
        by men.'*b*

8You have let go of the commands of God and are holding on to the traditions of men."

9And he said to them: "You have a fine way of setting aside the commands of God in order to observe*c* your own traditions! **10**For Moses said, 'Honor your father and your mother,'*d* and, 'Anyone who curses his father or mother must be put to death.'*e* **11**But you say that if a man says to his father or mother: 'Whatever help you might otherwise have received from me is Corban' (that is, a gift devoted to God), **12**then you no longer let him do anything for his father or mother. **13**Thus you nullify the word of God by your tradition that you have handed down. And you do many things like that."

14Again Jesus called the crowd to him and said, "Listen to me, everyone, and understand this. **15**Nothing outside a man can make him 'unclean' by going into

him. Rather, it is what comes out of a man that makes him 'unclean.'*f*"

17After he had left the crowd and entered the house, his disciples asked him about this parable. **18**"Are you so dull?" he asked. "Don't you see that nothing that enters a man from the outside can make him 'unclean'? **19**For it doesn't go into his heart but into his stomach, and then out of his body." (In saying this, Jesus declared all foods "clean.")

20He went on: "What comes out of a man is what makes him 'unclean.' **21**For from within, out of men's hearts, come evil thoughts, sexual immorality, theft, murder, adultery, **22**greed, malice, deceit, lewdness, envy, slander, arrogance and folly. **23**All these evils come from inside and make a man 'unclean.' "

The Faith of a Syrophoenician Woman

24Jesus left that place and went to the vicinity of Tyre.*g* He entered a house and did not want anyone to know it; yet he could not keep his presence secret. **25**In fact, as soon as she heard about him, a woman whose little daughter was possessed by an evil*h* spirit came and fell at his feet. **26**The woman was a Greek, born in Syrian Phoenicia. She begged Jesus to drive the demon out of her daughter.

27"First let the children eat all they want," he told her, "for it is not right to take the children's bread and toss it to their dogs."

28"Yes, Lord," she replied, "but even the dogs under the table eat the children's crumbs."

29Then he told her, "For such a reply, you may go; the demon has left your daughter."

30She went home and found her child lying on the bed, and the demon gone.

The Healing of a Deaf and Mute Man

31Then Jesus left the vicinity of Tyre and went through Sidon, down to the Sea of Galilee and into the region of the Decapolis.*i* **32**There some people brought to him

---

*a*4 Some early manuscripts *pitchers, kettles and dining couches*   *b*6,7 Isaiah 29:13   *c*9 Some manuscripts *set up*   *d*10 Exodus 20:12; Deut. 5:16   *e*10 Exodus 21:17; Lev. 20:9   *f*15 Some early manuscripts *'unclean.'* *16If anyone has ears to hear, let him hear.*   *g*24 Many early manuscripts *Tyre and Sidon*   *h*25 Greek *unclean*   *i*31 That is, the Ten Cities

a man who was deaf and could hardly talk, and they begged him to place his hand on the man. ³³After he took him aside, away from the crowd, Jesus put his fingers into the man's ears. Then he spit and touched the man's tongue. ³⁴He looked up to heaven and with a deep sigh said to him, *"Eph-phatha!"* (which means, "Be opened!"). ³⁵At this, the man's ears were opened, his tongue was loosened and he began to speak plainly.

³⁶Jesus commanded them not to tell anyone. But the more he did so, the more they kept talking about it. ³⁷People were overwhelmed with amazement. "He has done everything well," they said. "He even makes the deaf hear and the mute speak."

Jesus Feeds the Four Thousand

8 During those days another large crowd gathered. Since they had nothing to eat, Jesus called his disciples to him and said, ²"I have compassion for these people; they have already been with me three days and have nothing to eat. ³If I send them home hungry, they will collapse on the way, because some of them have come a long distance."

⁴His disciples answered, "But where in this remote place can anyone get enough bread to feed them?"

⁵"How many loaves do you have?" Jesus asked.

"Seven," they replied.

⁶He told the crowd to sit down on the ground. When he had taken the seven loaves and given thanks, he broke them and gave them to his disciples to set before the people, and they did so. ⁷They had a few small fish as well; he gave thanks for them also and told the disciples to distribute them. ⁸The people ate and were satisfied. Afterward the disciples picked up seven basketfuls of broken pieces that were left over. ⁹About four thousand men were present. And having sent them away, ¹⁰he got into the boat with his disciples and went to the region of Dalmanutha.

¹¹The Pharisees came and began to question Jesus. To test him, they asked him for a sign from heaven. ¹²He sighed deeply and said, "Why does this generation ask for a miraculous sign? I tell you the truth, no sign will be given to it." ¹³Then he left them, got back into the boat and crossed to the other side.

The Yeast of the Pharisees and Herod

¹⁴The disciples had forgotten to bring bread, except for one loaf they had with them in the boat. ¹⁵"Be careful," Jesus warned them. "Watch out for the yeast of the Pharisees and that of Herod."

¹⁶They discussed this with one another and said, "It is because we have no bread."

¹⁷Aware of their discussion, Jesus asked them: "Why are you talking about having no bread? Do you still not see or understand? Are your hearts hardened? ¹⁸Do you have eyes but fail to see, and ears but fail to hear? And don't you remember? ¹⁹When I broke the five loaves for the five thousand, how many basketfuls of pieces did you pick up?"

"Twelve," they replied.

²⁰"And when I broke the seven loaves for the four thousand, how many basketfuls of pieces did you pick up?"

They answered, "Seven."

²¹He said to them, "Do you still not understand?"

The Healing of a Blind Man at Bethsaida

²²They came to Bethsaida, and some people brought a blind man and begged Jesus to touch him. ²³He took the blind man by the hand and led him outside the village. When he had spit on the man's eyes and put his hands on him, Jesus asked, "Do you see anything?"

²⁴He looked up and said, "I see people; they look like trees walking around."

²⁵Once more Jesus put his hands on the man's eyes. Then his eyes were opened, his sight was restored, and he saw everything clearly. ²⁶Jesus sent him home, saying, "Don't go into the village.ᵃ"

Peter's Confession of Christ

²⁷Jesus and his disciples went on to the villages around Caesarea Philippi. On the way he asked them, "Who do people say I am?"

²⁸They replied, "Some say John the Baptist; others say Elijah; and still others, one of the prophets."

²⁹"But what about you?" he asked. "Who do you say I am?"

Peter answered, "You are the Christ.ᵇ"

³⁰Jesus warned them not to tell anyone about him.

ᵃ26 Some manuscripts *Don't go and tell anyone in the village*   ᵇ29 Or *Messiah.* "The Christ" (Greek) and "the Messiah" (Hebrew) both mean "the Anointed One."

Jesus Predicts His Death

31He then began to teach them that the Son of Man must suffer many things and be rejected by the elders, chief priests and teachers of the law, and that he must be killed and after three days rise again. **32**He spoke plainly about this, and Peter took him aside and began to rebuke him.

33But when Jesus turned and looked at his disciples, he rebuked Peter. "Get behind me, Satan!" he said. "You do not have in mind the things of God, but the things of men."

34Then he called the crowd to him along with his disciples and said: "If anyone would come after me, he must deny himself and take up his cross and follow me. **35**For whoever wants to save his life*a* will lose it, but whoever loses his life for me and for the gospel will save it. **36**What good is it for a man to gain the whole world, yet forfeit his soul? **37**Or what can a man give in exchange for his soul? **38**If anyone is ashamed of me and my words in this adulterous and sinful generation, the Son of Man will be ashamed of him when he comes in his Father's glory with the holy angels."

9 And he said to them, "I tell you the truth, some who are standing here will not taste death before they see the kingdom of God come with power."

The Transfiguration

2After six days Jesus took Peter, James and John with him and led them up a high mountain, where they were all alone. There he was transfigured before them. **3**His clothes became dazzling white, whiter than anyone in the world could bleach them. **4**And there appeared before them Elijah and Moses, who were talking with Jesus.

5Peter said to Jesus, "Rabbi, it is good for us to be here. Let us put up three shelters—one for you, one for Moses and one for Elijah." **6**(He did not know what to say, they were so frightened.)

a35 The Greek word means either life or soul; also in verse 36.

The Gap Between Belief and Unbelief
The Persevering Father

"I do believe; help me overcome my unbelief!" (9:24).

DADS
IN THE
BIBLE

Text: Mark 9:14–27

For many years, the father with the demon-possessed son had dealt with his son's malady. Imagine the incredible distress and confusion for a dad whose son was demon possessed. Give him a broken arm, a bad case of the flu, but please, not *this*! Still, the more he attempted to help his son, the more futile the attempt seemed.

This father lived in the space between unbelief and belief. He wasn't a cynic. He *knew* his boy could be healed. But he had done everything he knew to do. Still, he wanted to believe. So, for what it was worth, he gathered up his courage one more time and brought his child to someone he hoped could help. "I asked your disciples to drive out the spirit, but they could not," he reported to the Savior (v. 18). One more failed attempt. Can't you just hear the agony in the voice of this desperate, frustrated father?

Suspecting the father's hesitancy, Jesus asked him to give a witness to his faith. "I do believe," the dad responded. Then he added something that every honest man would surely add, "Help me overcome my unbelief!" (v. 24).

Hey, Dad, how badly do you want your child to be healed? What's it worth to you to have him or her walk in the truth? What are you willing to do to have them follow God?

"I want it badly," you respond. "I'm willing to pay the price. I want to believe that I can help guide my child in the right way." Then, as an afterthought, you add, "But I'm still afraid. I'm afraid I don't really have enough faith. So, Father in heaven, please help my unbelief."

What did Jesus do in the face of this request? "Jesus took [the boy] by the hand and lifted him to his feet" (v. 27). No doubt, the persevering father's faith stood to its feet as well.

For a complete listing of Dads in the Bible, turn to page 1434.

⁷Then a cloud appeared and enveloped them, and a voice came from the cloud: "This is my Son, whom I love. Listen to him!"

⁸Suddenly, when they looked around, they no longer saw anyone with them except Jesus.

⁹As they were coming down the mountain, Jesus gave them orders not to tell anyone what they had seen until the Son of Man had risen from the dead. ¹⁰They kept the matter to themselves, discussing what "rising from the dead" meant.

¹¹And they asked him, "Why do the teachers of the law say that Elijah must come first?"

¹²Jesus replied, "To be sure, Elijah does come first, and restores all things. Why then is it written that the Son of Man must suffer much and be rejected? ¹³But I tell

Way Beyond "Groovy" and "Cool"

DAILY INSIGHT

TUESDAY

Passage:
Mark 9:2–8

Verse:
Mark 9:7

Every generation adopts a certain word that becomes their knee-jerk verbal response to something wonderful. When I was in college, "groovy" was our word. It was all that needed to be said when no other word would do. Simon and Garfunkel, the altitudinally mismatched duo, even recorded a song to capitalize on the popularity of our word. "Feelin' groovy" became standard conversational fare.

Over the decades, these knee-jerk words have come and gone. "Wow," "cool," and "awesome" have had their share of glory along with "groovy." Depending on our age, you and I have used one of these when no other words would do.

Peter, James and John, the disciples' executive committee, evidently had no such words to describe the vision they saw.

Today's passage gives no clue as to why these three had been summoned by their Master. All they knew was that Jesus led them to a high mountain. Suddenly, Jesus' body exploded in light. His clothes, doubtlessly soiled by road dust, instantly became blazingly pure, "whiter than anyone in the world could bleach them."

These rough-hewn fisherman had seen many amazing things in their day—fishnets overflowing with a midnight catch and thunderstorms instantly sweeping across their favorite lake—but this topped them all. The Scripture tells us that they "didn't know what to say" at this incredible sight. They didn't have a "word"—no "groovy," "wow," "cool," or "awesome" to draw from. But God knew what to say (v. 7).

If you and I could have been sitting with Peter, James and John as old men during their final days, there is little doubt that they would have vivid memories of this experience. They had glimpsed the glory of God and seen the supernatural character of his Son. I can imagine that, for years to come, when these men were tempted to treat God casually or to glibly enter his presence, they would have whispered to each other, "Remember the high mountain."

This morning, when I said my prayers for the day, I must admit that I wasn't thinking of Jesus on the high mountain. I spent very little time kneeling there in awe, terrorized by his indescribable presence. I foolishly and haphazardly dove into my "list."

If I had been kneeling there with Peter, James or John, my guess is that they would have encouraged me to take a second look at the One to whom I was talking. "Remember the high mountain," they would have said very softly.

I would have taken a second look, and been rendered speechless—mute in the presence of a spectacular and holy God. And even though I've got a personal backlog of knee-jerk words, none of them would have been adequate … nothing could have come close to being appropriate.

No wonder the disciples were silent.

For your next devotional reading, go to page 1095.

you, Elijah has come, and they have done to him everything they wished, just as it is written about him."

The Healing of a Boy With an Evil Spirit

¹⁴When they came to the other disciples, they saw a large crowd around them and the teachers of the law arguing with them. ¹⁵As soon as all the people saw Jesus, they were overwhelmed with wonder and ran to greet him.

¹⁶"What are you arguing with them about?" he asked.

¹⁷A man in the crowd answered, "Teacher, I brought you my son, who is possessed by a spirit that has robbed him of speech. ¹⁸Whenever it seizes him, it throws him to the ground. He foams at the mouth, gnashes his teeth and becomes rigid. I asked your disciples to drive out the spirit, but they could not."

¹⁹"O unbelieving generation," Jesus replied, "how long shall I stay with you?

Help My Unbelief

DAILY INSIGHT

WEDNESDAY

Passage:
Mark 9:17–24

Verse:
Mark 9:24

The night I spent in Wabash, Indiana may have been the most memorable night of my life.

It began as a lazy college Sunday afternoon in the spring of 1967. I was in my college dorm room "working" on an assignment when I heard someone knocking on a door down the hall. The knocking sounded formal … intentional … unfamiliar. When I looked down the hallway, to my surprise, I saw an Indiana State Trooper in full uniform. He turned and, seeing me gawking at him, said in a very sober tone of voice, "I'm looking for Mr. Scott Hawkins."

"I think he's out with his girlfriend, Jenny," I said, obviously eager to please this intimidating man. "Uh … why are you looking for Scott?" I courageously stammered . "Scott and I are good friends. We grew up in the same town and have known each other since grade school." The trooper seemed satisfied that I could be trusted with the news.

"Mr. Hawkins' family has been in an automobile accident near Wabash, and he needs to get to the Wabash General Hospital as soon as he possibly can," the trooper reported. His solemn face filled in the details.

"I'll take care of it," I volunteered, and took off to find Scott. My homework assignment would have to wait.

After I found Scott, he jumped in my car and we sped off to Wabash. There was very little conversation between us over the next sixty minutes, but the next twelve hours would forever be seared in my memory.

When we arrived at the hospital, we hurried to Scott's mother's room. The moment she saw us, she began weeping. Between heaving sobs, she told us what had happened. "The doctors have told me that Tim will be all right, but I know that Shelly is very seriously injured. I believe God will take care of her … but I'm very frightened," Mrs. Hawkins confessed about her daughter.

Scott and I quietly walked the halls of the hospital that night. Neither of us slept while his little sister held on. I don't remember being tired at all. There were more important things to do than sleep.

Three days later, Shelly died.

Several decades have passed since that night at Wabash General. I have gotten married and become a dad. And I have experienced the emotions of this terrified parent, desperately teetering between faith and un-faith, belief and unbelief, confidence and fear. "I trust you, Heavenly Father," I pray. "But I'm still afraid."

Can you identify with the dad in today's story? Can you hear his remarks to the Savior begin with, "I do believe"? And can you add, "Help me overcome my unbelief"? Have you ever felt like this too? That's okay, Dad. Jesus understands your fear. He is with you; I promise. Feel his presence; it's for real. That will have to be enough for now.

For your next devotional reading, go to page 1097.

How long shall I put up with you? Bring the boy to me."

20So they brought him. When the spirit saw Jesus, it immediately threw the boy into a convulsion. He fell to the ground and rolled around, foaming at the mouth.

21Jesus asked the boy's father, "How long has he been like this?"

"From childhood," he answered. **22**"It has often thrown him into fire or water to kill him. But if you can do anything, take pity on us and help us."

23" 'If you can'?" said Jesus. "Everything is possible for him who believes."

24Immediately the boy's father exclaimed, "I do believe; help me overcome my unbelief!"

25When Jesus saw that a crowd was running to the scene, he rebuked the evil*a* spirit. "You deaf and mute spirit," he said, "I command you, come out of him and never enter him again."

26The spirit shrieked, convulsed him violently and came out. The boy looked so much like a corpse that many said, "He's dead." **27**But Jesus took him by the hand and lifted him to his feet, and he stood up.

28After Jesus had gone indoors, his disciples asked him privately, "Why couldn't we drive it out?"

29He replied, "This kind can come out only by prayer.*b*"

30They left that place and passed through Galilee. Jesus did not want anyone to know where they were, **31**because he was teaching his disciples. He said to them, "The Son of Man is going to be betrayed into the hands of men. They will kill him, and after three days he will rise." **32**But they did not understand what he meant and were afraid to ask him about it.

Who Is the Greatest?

33They came to Capernaum. When he was in the house, he asked them, "What were you arguing about on the road?" **34**But they kept quiet because on the way they had argued about who was the greatest.

35Sitting down, Jesus called the Twelve and said, "If anyone wants to be first, he must be the very last, and the servant of all."

36He took a little child and had him stand among them. Taking him in his arms, he said to them, **37**"Whoever welcomes one of these little children in my name welcomes me; and whoever wel-

comes me does not welcome me but the one who sent me."

Whoever Is Not Against Us Is for Us

38"Teacher," said John, "we saw a man driving out demons in your name and we told him to stop, because he was not one of us."

39"Do not stop him," Jesus said. "No one who does a miracle in my name can in the next moment say anything bad about me, **40**for whoever is not against us is for us. **41**I tell you the truth, anyone who gives you a cup of water in my name because you belong to Christ will certainly not lose his reward.

Causing to Sin

42"And if anyone causes one of these little ones who believe in me to sin, it would be better for him to be thrown into the sea with a large millstone tied around his neck. **43**If your hand causes you to sin, cut it off. It is better for you to enter life maimed than with two hands to go into hell, where the fire never goes out.*c* **45**And if your foot causes you to sin, cut it off. It is better for you to enter life crippled than to have two feet and be thrown into hell.*d* **47**And if your eye causes you to sin, pluck it out. It is better for you to enter the kingdom of God with one eye than to have two eyes and be thrown into hell, **48**where

" 'their worm does not die,
    and the fire is not quenched.'*e*

49Everyone will be salted with fire.

50"Salt is good, but if it loses its saltiness, how can you make it salty again? Have salt in yourselves, and be at peace with each other."

Divorce

10 Jesus then left that place and went into the region of Judea and across the Jordan. Again crowds of people came to him, and as was his custom, he taught them.

2Some Pharisees came and tested him by asking, "Is it lawful for a man to divorce his wife?"

---

a25 Greek *unclean*   *b29* Some manuscripts *prayer and fasting*   *c43* Some manuscripts *out,* *44where /* " *'their worm does not die, / and the fire is not quenched.'*   *d45* Some manuscripts *hell,* *46where /* " *'their worm does not die, / and the fire is not quenched.'*   *e48* Isaiah 66:24

³"What did Moses command you?" he replied.

⁴They said, "Moses permitted a man to write a certificate of divorce and send her away."

⁵"It was because your hearts were hard that Moses wrote you this law," Jesus replied. ⁶"But at the beginning of creation God 'made them male and female.'ᵃ ⁷'For this reason a man will leave his father and mother and be united to his wife,ᵇ ⁸and the two will become one flesh.'ᶜ So they are no longer two, but one. ⁹Therefore what God has joined together, let man not separate."

¹⁰When they were in the house again, the disciples asked Jesus about this. ¹¹He

ᵃ6 Gen. 1:27   ᵇ7 Some early manuscripts do not have *and be united to his wife*.   ᶜ8 Gen. 2:24

Who's Going to Get Rid of Those Kids?

DAILY INSIGHT

THURSDAY

Passage:
Mark 10:13–16

Verse:
Mark 10:15

I was sitting in the front row, scanning my notes in preparation for the keynote address at a large church's annual family conference. This wasn't the first time I had given this particular talk, but a swarm of butterflies was having its way in my stomach.

The order of service was proceeding on schedule. The congregation was in fine voice as they sang their worship songs. Everybody seemed to be relaxed, enjoying themselves ... everyone, that is, except me. The front of the church, between the first row of seats and the platform, was literally *swarming* with kids. A few were sitting on the floor, dutifully singing along with the grownups. But most were tussling with their friends or trying their new tumbling routines.

Those kids had better not be here when I give my talk, I thought to myself. Of course, my countenance did not betray me. Anyone watching would have thought that I was delighted with this noisy collection of restless ankle-biters. *Who would have made such an outrageous arrangement?* I wondered, still looking piously engaged by the lovely worship music. *I won't speak with those noisy kids crawling around.*

When the pastor strode to the microphone to introduce me, he announced that all the children were to leave now and go to their "special service." *Whew,* I sighed, almost audibly.

The following morning, I picked up my Bible and read the verses you read today. Ouch. "What would Jesus have done last night?" I whispered out loud, already knowing the answer to my question, full well.

My life is way too formal, too traditional ... too much heavy starch. I loathe disorder and disruptions. Give me decorum, order, hands folded on the desks, and no pushing and shoving in line. Give me "inside," not "playground," voice levels from children.

But Jesus lived at the opposite end of this Germanic obsession of mine. He not only tolerated the children, he *welcomed* them. He not only welcomed them, he threw his disciples a fastball, a quarter of an inch from their pompous, pointed chins. "Anyone who will not receive the kingdom of God like a child will never enter it," the Master fired at his pontifical followers.

Our lives as fathers are filled with formality and structure. We carry detailed calendars, address books, and endless lists of things to do. We wear watches, start meetings on time, and abhor late-comers. We like having agendas and itineraries. We don't allow raucous activity in our homes and command our children to keep their living spaces orderly.

There is, of course, a time for demeanor and manners, for discipline and order. But sometimes we need to set aside our penchant for structure over spontaneity and throw caution to the wind. Besides, Jesus didn't simply think that this was a good idea; he told his followers that if they didn't loosen up, they'd miss out on knowing him. How's that for an incentive?

For your next devotional reading, go to page 1103.

answered, "Anyone who divorces his wife and marries another woman commits adultery against her. [12]And if she divorces her husband and marries another man, she commits adultery."

The Little Children and Jesus

[13]People were bringing little children to Jesus to have him touch them, but the disciples rebuked them. [14]When Jesus saw this, he was indignant. He said to them, "Let the little children come to me, and do not hinder them, for the kingdom of God belongs to such as these. [15]I tell you the truth, anyone who will not receive the kingdom of God like a little child will never enter it." [16]And he took the children in his arms, put his hands on them and blessed them.

The Rich Young Man

[17]As Jesus started on his way, a man ran up to him and fell on his knees before him. "Good teacher," he asked, "what must I do to inherit eternal life?"

[18]"Why do you call me good?" Jesus answered. "No one is good—except God alone. [19]You know the commandments: 'Do not murder, do not commit adultery, do not steal, do not give false testimony, do not defraud, honor your father and mother.'[a]"

[20]"Teacher," he declared, "all these I have kept since I was a boy."

[21]Jesus looked at him and loved him. "One thing you lack," he said. "Go, sell everything you have and give to the poor, and you will have treasure in heaven. Then come, follow me."

[22]At this the man's face fell. He went away sad, because he had great wealth.

[23]Jesus looked around and said to his disciples, "How hard it is for the rich to enter the kingdom of God!"

[24]The disciples were amazed at his words. But Jesus said again, "Children, how hard it is[b] to enter the kingdom of God! [25]It is easier for a camel to go through the eye of a needle than for a rich man to enter the kingdom of God."

[26]The disciples were even more amazed, and said to each other, "Who then can be saved?"

[27]Jesus looked at them and said, "With man this is impossible, but not with God; all things are possible with God."

[28]Peter said to him, "We have left everything to follow you!"

[29]"I tell you the truth," Jesus replied, "no one who has left home or brothers or sisters or mother or father or children or fields for me and the gospel [30]will fail to receive a hundred times as much in this present age (homes, brothers, sisters, mothers, children and fields—and with them, persecutions) and in the age to come, eternal life. [31]But many who are first will be last, and the last first."

Jesus Again Predicts His Death

[32]They were on their way up to Jerusalem, with Jesus leading the way, and the disciples were astonished, while those who followed were afraid. Again he took the Twelve aside and told them what was going to happen to him. [33]"We are going up to Jerusalem," he said, "and the Son of Man will be betrayed to the chief priests and teachers of the law. They will condemn him to death and will hand him over to the Gentiles, [34]who will mock him and spit on him, flog him and kill him. Three days later he will rise."

The Request of James and John

[35]Then James and John, the sons of Zebedee, came to him. "Teacher," they said, "we want you to do for us whatever we ask."

[36]"What do you want me to do for you?" he asked.

[37]They replied, "Let one of us sit at your right and the other at your left in your glory."

[38]"You don't know what you are asking," Jesus said. "Can you drink the cup I drink or be baptized with the baptism I am baptized with?"

[39]"We can," they answered.

Jesus said to them, "You will drink the cup I drink and be baptized with the baptism I am baptized with, [40]but to sit at my right or left is not for me to grant. These places belong to those for whom they have been prepared."

[41]When the ten heard about this, they became indignant with James and John. [42]Jesus called them together and said, "You know that those who are regarded as rulers of the Gentiles lord it over them, and their high officials exercise authority over them. [43]Not so with you. Instead, whoever wants to become great among you must be your servant, [44]and whoever wants to be first must be slave of all. [45]For

a19 Exodus 20:12-16; Deut. 5:16-20   *b24* Some manuscripts *is for those who trust in riches*

Affection: The Power of Touch

"[Jesus] took the children in his arms, put his hands on them and blessed them." Mark 10:16

If I could sit down with you right now and look into your eyes, I'd tell you not to miss this. No, I'd *beg* you not to miss this.

Part of the greatest privilege you have as a dad is the opportunity to communicate your affection to your children. One of the most important ways this is expressed is through touch. Hold your children when they're tiny, and stroke their faces with your hand. Hold their hands when they learn to walk. Visit their rooms just before they go to sleep, scratch their backs and kiss them goodnight. Hug them with your whole arms—wrap them up like they're in a blanket. Let their hearts know that they are absolutely secure in their dad's arms.

All of this takes some extra time. Meaningful touching like this doesn't happen on the fly. You have to slow down to make it count.

Let me illustrate this principle. Both of my maternal grandparents and my paternal grandmother lived their final years in a retirement center in South Central Pennsylvania. The first time my family visited, the director took us on a tour of the property. We were impressed with the tasteful decor and the good-natured, professional staff.

But I'll never forget one large room that we walked into. This room was literally *filled* with rocking chairs. The director explained to us that the facility hosted a day-care center for preschoolers, right in the middle of the home. The day care playground was located in the atrium, which was surrounded by the patron's rooms. Throughout the day, children's voices wafted through the complex.

Each day, right after lunch, the kids had "quiet time." They would toddle into this large, rocking-chair-filled room, looking for their special friend. Crawling up on this adopted lap, they would experience the touch—and, therefore, the love—of an elderly person with lots of it to give.

"Visiting this room during quiet time is an awesome thing," the director explained. "The room is intentionally darkened and the shadowed back-and-forth squeak of the rockers and soft sounds of talking or humming make it feel like a holy place. It's like walking into the hushed narthex of a great European cathedral."

The Nobel Prize for good ideas goes to the person who came up with this one.

Were you to eavesdrop on this scene, you would probably turn up very little in the way of lectures about life. Instead, you would see the power of touch wrapping itself into the souls of those little children, assuring them that they were worthy of someone's love, that life need not be frightening, that good was stronger than evil.

Hug your son. Pull your daughter onto your lap for a warm embrace. Stop running; take a minute, and touch your children.

My mother taught us something that her mother had taught her—kind of a "squeeze language." This is the way it works: Take your child's hand—church is a great place for this—and tenderly squeeze it four times in a row. The child responds with three squeezes. You return the three with two of your own, and your child ends this silent "conversation" with one final strong squeeze of your hand.

The interpretation of this squeezing conversation is, "Do you love me?" Four words, four squeezes. Her answer is, "Yes, I do." Three words, three squeezes. Get it? Your two-squeeze response is, "How much?" And her final answer comes in a strong squeeze (no interpretation necessary).

You might be thinking, *Aw, come on. Isn't this a little silly—holding, patting, squeezing? "Talking" in squeeze language? Couldn't I just go to the store and buy my kid something?*

No, it's not only not silly. In fact, it may be one of the most precious things you'll ever have between you and your child. It will be something you'll never outgrow. These may become the only "words" you'll be able to speak at awkward or painful moments. And the older you get, the more love you'll feel in touches coming from your child to you.

Of course, they will have learned this from you.

BUILDING YOUR CHILDREN

even the Son of Man did not come to be served, but to serve, and to give his life as a ransom for many."

Blind Bartimaeus Receives His Sight

[46]Then they came to Jericho. As Jesus and his disciples, together with a large crowd, were leaving the city, a blind man, Bartimaeus (that is, the Son of Timaeus), was sitting by the roadside begging. [47]When he heard that it was Jesus of Nazareth, he began to shout, "Jesus, Son of David, have mercy on me!"

[48]Many rebuked him and told him to be quiet, but he shouted all the more, "Son of David, have mercy on me!"

[49]Jesus stopped and said, "Call him."

So they called to the blind man, "Cheer up! On your feet! He's calling you." [50]Throwing his cloak aside, he jumped to his feet and came to Jesus.

[51]"What do you want me to do for you?" Jesus asked him.

The blind man said, "Rabbi, I want to see."

[52]"Go," said Jesus, "your faith has healed you." Immediately he received his sight and followed Jesus along the road.

The Triumphal Entry

11 As they approached Jerusalem and came to Bethphage and Bethany at the Mount of Olives, Jesus sent two of his disciples, [2]saying to them, "Go to the village ahead of you, and just as you enter it, you will find a colt tied there, which no one has ever ridden. Untie it and bring it here. [3]If anyone asks you, 'Why are you doing this?' tell him, 'The Lord needs it and will send it back here shortly.' "

[4]They went and found a colt outside in the street, tied at a doorway. As they untied it, [5]some people standing there asked, "What are you doing, untying that colt?" [6]They answered as Jesus had told them to, and the people let them go. [7]When they brought the colt to Jesus and threw their cloaks over it, he sat on it. [8]Many people spread their cloaks on the road, while others spread branches they had cut in the fields. [9]Those who went ahead and those who followed shouted,

"Hosanna![a]"

"Blessed is he who comes in the name of the Lord!"[b]

[10]"Blessed is the coming kingdom of our father David!"

"Hosanna in the highest!"

[11]Jesus entered Jerusalem and went to the temple. He looked around at everything, but since it was already late, he went out to Bethany with the Twelve.

Jesus Clears the Temple

[12]The next day as they were leaving Bethany, Jesus was hungry. [13]Seeing in the distance a fig tree in leaf, he went to find out if it had any fruit. When he reached it, he found nothing but leaves, because it was not the season for figs. [14]Then he said to the tree, "May no one ever eat fruit from you again." And his disciples heard him say it.

[15]On reaching Jerusalem, Jesus entered the temple area and began driving out those who were buying and selling there. He overturned the tables of the money changers and the benches of those selling doves, [16]and would not allow anyone to carry merchandise through the temple courts. [17]And as he taught them, he said, "Is it not written:

" 'My house will be called
    a house of prayer for all nations'[c]?

But you have made it 'a den of robbers.'[d]"

[18]The chief priests and the teachers of the law heard this and began looking for a way to kill him, for they feared him, because the whole crowd was amazed at his teaching.

[19]When evening came, they[e] went out of the city.

The Withered Fig Tree

[20]In the morning, as they went along, they saw the fig tree withered from the roots. [21]Peter remembered and said to Jesus, "Rabbi, look! The fig tree you cursed has withered!"

[22]"Have[f] faith in God," Jesus answered. [23]"I tell you the truth, if anyone says to this mountain, 'Go, throw yourself into the sea,' and does not doubt in his heart but believes that what he says will happen, it will be done for him. [24]Therefore I tell you, whatever you ask for in prayer, believe that you have received it, and it will be

[a]9 A Hebrew expression meaning "Save!" which became an exclamation of praise; also in verse 10   [b]9 Psalm 118:25,26   [c]17 Isaiah 56:7   [d]17 Jer. 7:11   [e]19 Some early manuscripts he   [f]22 Some early manuscripts If you have

yours. ²⁵And when you stand praying, if you hold anything against anyone, forgive him, so that your Father in heaven may forgive you your sins.ᵃ"

The Authority of Jesus Questioned

²⁷They arrived again in Jerusalem, and while Jesus was walking in the temple courts, the chief priests, the teachers of the law and the elders came to him. ²⁸"By what authority are you doing these things?" they asked. "And who gave you authority to do this?"

²⁹Jesus replied, "I will ask you one question. Answer me, and I will tell you by what authority I am doing these things. ³⁰John's baptism—was it from heaven, or from men? Tell me!"

³¹They discussed it among themselves and said, "If we say, 'From heaven,' he will ask, 'Then why didn't you believe him?' ³²But if we say, 'From men'..." (They feared the people, for everyone held that John really was a prophet.)

³³So they answered Jesus, "We don't know."

Jesus said, "Neither will I tell you by what authority I am doing these things."

The Parable of the Tenants

12 He then began to speak to them in parables: "A man planted a vineyard. He put a wall around it, dug a pit for the winepress and built a watchtower. Then he rented the vineyard to some farmers and went away on a journey. ²At harvest time he sent a servant to the tenants to collect from them some of the fruit of the vineyard. ³But they seized him, beat him and sent him away empty-handed. ⁴Then he sent another servant to them; they struck this man on the head and treated him shamefully. ⁵He sent still another, and that one they killed. He sent many others; some of them they beat, others they killed.

⁶"He had one left to send, a son, whom he loved. He sent him last of all, saying, 'They will respect my son.'

⁷"But the tenants said to one another, 'This is the heir. Come, let's kill him, and the inheritance will be ours.' ⁸So they took him and killed him, and threw him out of the vineyard.

⁹"What then will the owner of the vineyard do? He will come and kill those tenants and give the vineyard to others. ¹⁰Haven't you read this scripture:

" 'The stone the builders rejected
　　has become the capstoneᵇ;
¹¹the Lord has done this,
　　and it is marvelous in our eyes'ᶜ?"

¹²Then they looked for a way to arrest him because they knew he had spoken the parable against them. But they were afraid of the crowd; so they left him and went away.

Paying Taxes to Caesar

¹³Later they sent some of the Pharisees and Herodians to Jesus to catch him in his words. ¹⁴They came to him and said, "Teacher, we know you are a man of integrity. You aren't swayed by men, because you pay no attention to who they are; but you teach the way of God in accordance with the truth. Is it right to pay taxes to Caesar or not? ¹⁵Should we pay or shouldn't we?"

But Jesus knew their hypocrisy. "Why are you trying to trap me?" he asked. "Bring me a denarius and let me look at it." ¹⁶They brought the coin, and he asked them, "Whose portrait is this? And whose inscription?"

"Caesar's," they replied.

¹⁷Then Jesus said to them, "Give to Caesar what is Caesar's and to God what is God's."

And they were amazed at him.

Marriage at the Resurrection

¹⁸Then the Sadducees, who say there is no resurrection, came to him with a question. ¹⁹"Teacher," they said, "Moses wrote for us that if a man's brother dies and leaves a wife but no children, the man must marry the widow and have children for his brother. ²⁰Now there were seven brothers. The first one married and died without leaving any children. ²¹The second one married the widow, but he also died, leaving no child. It was the same with the third. ²²In fact, none of the seven left any children. Last of all, the woman died too. ²³At the resurrectionᵈ whose wife will she be, since the seven were married to her?"

²⁴Jesus replied, "Are you not in error because you do not know the Scriptures or the power of God? ²⁵When the dead rise,

ᵃ25 Some manuscripts *sins.* ²⁶*But if you do not forgive, neither will your Father who is in heaven forgive your sins.*　ᵇ10 Or *cornerstone*　ᶜ11 Psalm 118:22,23　ᵈ23 Some manuscripts *resurrection, when men rise from the dead,*

they will neither marry nor be given in marriage; they will be like the angels in heaven. [26]Now about the dead rising— have you not read in the book of Moses, in the account of the bush, how God said to him, 'I am the God of Abraham, the God of Isaac, and the God of Jacob'[a]? [27]He is not the God of the dead, but of the living. You are badly mistaken!"

The Greatest Commandment

[28]One of the teachers of the law came and heard them debating. Noticing that Jesus had given them a good answer, he asked him, "Of all the commandments, which is the most important?"

[29]"The most important one," answered Jesus, "is this: 'Hear, O Israel, the Lord our God, the Lord is one.[b] [30]Love the Lord your God with all your heart and with all your soul and with all your mind and with all your strength.'[c] [31]The second is this: 'Love your neighbor as yourself.'[d] There is no commandment greater than these."

[32]"Well said, teacher," the man replied. "You are right in saying that God is one and there is no other but him. [33]To love him with all your heart, with all your understanding and with all your strength, and to love your neighbor as yourself is more important than all burnt offerings and sacrifices."

[34]When Jesus saw that he had answered wisely, he said to him, "You are not far from the kingdom of God." And from then on no one dared ask him any more questions.

Whose Son Is the Christ?

[35]While Jesus was teaching in the temple courts, he asked, "How is it that the teachers of the law say that the Christ[e] is the son of David? [36]David himself, speaking by the Holy Spirit, declared:

" 'The Lord said to my Lord:
    "Sit at my right hand
until I put your enemies
    under your feet." '[f]

[37]David himself calls him 'Lord.' How then can he be his son?"

The large crowd listened to him with delight.

[38]As he taught, Jesus said, "Watch out for the teachers of the law. They like to walk around in flowing robes and be greeted in the marketplaces, [39]and have the most important seats in the synagogues and the places of honor at banquets. [40]They devour widows' houses and for a show make lengthy prayers. Such men will be punished most severely."

The Widow's Offering

[41]Jesus sat down opposite the place where the offerings were put and watched the crowd putting their money into the temple treasury. Many rich people threw in large amounts. [42]But a poor widow came and put in two very small copper coins,[g] worth only a fraction of a penny.[h]

[43]Calling his disciples to him, Jesus said, "I tell you the truth, this poor widow has put more into the treasury than all the others. [44]They all gave out of their wealth; but she, out of her poverty, put in everything—all she had to live on."

Signs of the End of the Age

13 As he was leaving the temple, one of his disciples said to him, "Look, Teacher! What massive stones! What magnificent buildings!"

[2]"Do you see all these great buildings?" replied Jesus. "Not one stone here will be left on another; every one will be thrown down."

[3]As Jesus was sitting on the Mount of Olives opposite the temple, Peter, James, John and Andrew asked him privately, [4]"Tell us, when will these things happen? And what will be the sign that they are all about to be fulfilled?"

[5]Jesus said to them: "Watch out that no one deceives you. [6]Many will come in my name, claiming, 'I am he,' and will deceive many. [7]When you hear of wars and rumors of wars, do not be alarmed. Such things must happen, but the end is still to come. [8]Nation will rise against nation, and kingdom against kingdom. There will be earthquakes in various places, and famines. These are the beginning of birth pains.

[9]"You must be on your guard. You will be handed over to the local councils and flogged in the synagogues. On account of me you will stand before governors and kings as witnesses to them. [10]And the gospel must first be preached to all nations. [11]Whenever you are arrested and brought to trial, do not worry beforehand about what to say. Just say whatever is given you

---

a26 Exodus 3:6   b29 Or the Lord our God is one Lord   c30 Deut. 6:4,5   d31 Lev. 19:18   e35 Or Messiah   f36 Psalm 110:1   g42 Greek two lepta   h42 Greek kodrantes

at the time, for it is not you speaking, but the Holy Spirit.

[12]"Brother will betray brother to death, and a father his child. Children will rebel against their parents and have them put to death. [13]All men will hate you because of me, but he who stands firm to the end will be saved.

[14]"When you see 'the abomination that causes desolation'[a] standing where it[b] does not belong—let the reader understand—then let those who are in Judea flee to the mountains. [15]Let no one on the roof of his house go down or enter the house to take anything out. [16]Let no one in the field go back to get his cloak. [17]How dreadful it will be in those days for pregnant women and nursing mothers! [18]Pray that this will not take place in winter, [19]because those will be days of distress unequaled from the beginning, when God

[a]14 Daniel 9:27; 11:31; 12:11   [b]14 Or he; also in verse 29

Lot Line Love

Two men and their families were being transferred from different cities to the same town. The moving vans had been carefully loaded, and both clans, kids and all, were packed up in their respective station wagons.

The first family stopped at the little convenience store just outside of their new hometown to buy a few things. "We're new in town," the dad informed the lady behind the counter. "What's it like to live here?" he asked. "Are the people friendly?"

The clerk, a long-time resident, responded with a question of her own. "What was it like in the town you just left?"

"Oh, it was terrific," the man quickly responded with a smile. "We had lots and lots of friends. We're really going to miss them; we loved that place."

The clerk replied, "Well, you're in luck. This is a great town. The people here are the finest folks you'll find anywhere. You'll make many new friends right away." The man and his family drove off, glad they had chosen such a delightful place to live.

In a few minutes, the second family arrived at the same convenience store to pick up a few things. "We're new in town," said the dad. "What's it like to live here? Are the people friendly?"

The insightful clerk responded with the same question she had asked before.

"Oh, it was terrible," the man snarled. "We're so glad to get out of that place. The people were all selfish gossips. We had no

DAILY INSIGHT

FRIDAY

Passage:
Mark 12:28–34

Verses:
Mark 12:30–31

friends because we didn't trust any of them," he added.

"Boy, I am sorry to hear that," replied the clerk. "You're in for a real shock. You thought the last town was bad, why, this place is a veritable cesspool of meddlers and snitches. I'd be surprised if you find a single friend in this place," she added.

If you want to have good neighbors, the cashier thought to herself as the second family pulled out of the parking lot, *you have to be good neighbors.*

Jesus had some straight words for the way we treat the folks next door. In fact, he drew three parallel lines, telling us that there is a direct relationship between what we believe about our heavenly Father, what we believe about ourselves, and how we handle the folks just on the other side of our lot lines or apartment walls.

Exactly what kind of a neighbor are you? How well does your love for others match your love for God? Would your neighbors be surprised to know that you worship and follow Christ, or would this knowledge fit perfectly with what they've seen in your life?

Keep your house in good repair, keep your dandelions under control, and promptly return the tools you've borrowed from the guy next door. Amazing as this might sound, these things may be as persuasive in introducing him to Jesus Christ as any Bible verse you could ever read to him.

For your next devotional reading, go to page 1112.

created the world, until now—and never to be equaled again. ²⁰If the Lord had not cut short those days, no one would survive. But for the sake of the elect, whom he has chosen, he has shortened them. ²¹At that time if anyone says to you, 'Look, here is the Christ*ᵃ*!' or, 'Look, there he is!' do not believe it. ²²For false Christs and false prophets will appear and perform signs and miracles to deceive the elect—if that were possible. ²³So be on your guard; I have told you everything ahead of time.

²⁴"But in those days, following that distress,

" 'the sun will be darkened,
    and the moon will not give its light;
²⁵the stars will fall from the sky,
    and the heavenly bodies will be
        shaken.'ᵇ

²⁶"At that time men will see the Son of Man coming in clouds with great power and glory. ²⁷And he will send his angels and gather his elect from the four winds, from the ends of the earth to the ends of the heavens.

²⁸"Now learn this lesson from the fig tree: As soon as its twigs get tender and its leaves come out, you know that summer is near. ²⁹Even so, when you see these things happening, you know that it is near, right at the door. ³⁰I tell you the truth, this generationᶜ will certainly not pass away until all these things have happened. ³¹Heaven and earth will pass away, but my words will never pass away.

The Day and Hour Unknown

³²"No one knows about that day or hour, not even the angels in heaven, nor the Son, but only the Father. ³³Be on guard! Be alertᵈ! You do not know when that time will come. ³⁴It's like a man going away: He leaves his house and puts his servants in charge, each with his assigned task, and tells the one at the door to keep watch.

³⁵"Therefore keep watch because you do not know when the owner of the house will come back—whether in the evening, or at midnight, or when the rooster crows, or at dawn. ³⁶If he comes suddenly, do not let him find you sleeping. ³⁷What I say to you, I say to everyone: 'Watch!' "

Jesus Anointed at Bethany

14 Now the Passover and the Feast of Unleavened Bread were only two days away, and the chief priests and the teach-

ers of the law were looking for some sly way to arrest Jesus and kill him. ²"But not during the Feast," they said, "or the people may riot."

³While he was in Bethany, reclining at the table in the home of a man known as Simon the Leper, a woman came with an alabaster jar of very expensive perfume, made of pure nard. She broke the jar and poured the perfume on his head.

⁴Some of those present were saying indignantly to one another, "Why this waste of perfume? ⁵It could have been sold for more than a year's wagesᵉ and the money given to the poor." And they rebuked her harshly.

⁶"Leave her alone," said Jesus. "Why are you bothering her? She has done a beautiful thing to me. ⁷The poor you will always have with you, and you can help them any time you want. But you will not always have me. ⁸She did what she could. She poured perfume on my body beforehand to prepare for my burial. ⁹I tell you the truth, wherever the gospel is preached throughout the world, what she has done will also be told, in memory of her."

¹⁰Then Judas Iscariot, one of the Twelve, went to the chief priests to betray Jesus to them. ¹¹They were delighted to hear this and promised to give him money. So he watched for an opportunity to hand him over.

The Lord's Supper

¹²On the first day of the Feast of Unleavened Bread, when it was customary to sacrifice the Passover lamb, Jesus' disciples asked him, "Where do you want us to go and make preparations for you to eat the Passover?"

¹³So he sent two of his disciples, telling them, "Go into the city, and a man carrying a jar of water will meet you. Follow him. ¹⁴Say to the owner of the house he enters, 'The Teacher asks: Where is my guest room, where I may eat the Passover with my disciples?' ¹⁵He will show you a large upper room, furnished and ready. Make preparations for us there."

¹⁶The disciples left, went into the city and found things just as Jesus had told them. So they prepared the Passover.

¹⁷When evening came, Jesus arrived with the Twelve. ¹⁸While they were reclining at the table eating, he said, "I tell you

---

ᵃ21 Or *Messiah*   ᵇ25 Isaiah 13:10; 34:4
ᶜ30 Or *race*   ᵈ33 Some manuscripts *alert and pray*   ᵉ5 Greek *than three hundred denarii*

the truth, one of you will betray me—one who is eating with me."

¹⁹They were saddened, and one by one they said to him, "Surely not I?"

²⁰"It is one of the Twelve," he replied, "one who dips bread into the bowl with me. ²¹The Son of Man will go just as it is written about him. But woe to that man who betrays the Son of Man! It would be better for him if he had not been born."

²²While they were eating, Jesus took bread, gave thanks and broke it, and gave it to his disciples, saying, "Take it; this is my body."

²³Then he took the cup, gave thanks and offered it to them, and they all drank from it.

²⁴"This is my blood of the*a* covenant, which is poured out for many," he said to them. ²⁵"I tell you the truth, I will not drink again of the fruit of the vine until that day when I drink it anew in the kingdom of God."

²⁶When they had sung a hymn, they went out to the Mount of Olives.

Jesus Predicts Peter's Denial

²⁷"You will all fall away," Jesus told them, "for it is written:

" 'I will strike the shepherd,
    and the sheep will be scattered.'*b*

²⁸But after I have risen, I will go ahead of you into Galilee."

²⁹Peter declared, "Even if all fall away, I will not."

³⁰"I tell you the truth," Jesus answered, "today—yes, tonight—before the rooster crows twice*c* you yourself will disown me three times."

³¹But Peter insisted emphatically, "Even if I have to die with you, I will never disown you." And all the others said the same.

Gethsemane

³²They went to a place called Gethsemane, and Jesus said to his disciples, "Sit here while I pray." ³³He took Peter, James and John along with him, and he began to be deeply distressed and troubled. ³⁴"My soul is overwhelmed with sorrow to the point of death," he said to them. "Stay here and keep watch."

³⁵Going a little farther, he fell to the ground and prayed that if possible the hour might pass from him. ³⁶"Abba,*d* Father," he said, "everything is possible for you. Take this cup from me. Yet not what I will, but what you will."

³⁷Then he returned to his disciples and found them sleeping. "Simon," he said to Peter, "are you asleep? Could you not keep watch for one hour? ³⁸Watch and pray so that you will not fall into temptation. The spirit is willing, but the body is weak."

³⁹Once more he went away and prayed the same thing. ⁴⁰When he came back, he again found them sleeping, because their eyes were heavy. They did not know what to say to him.

⁴¹Returning the third time, he said to them, "Are you still sleeping and resting? Enough! The hour has come. Look, the Son of Man is betrayed into the hands of sinners. ⁴²Rise! Let us go! Here comes my betrayer!"

Jesus Arrested

⁴³Just as he was speaking, Judas, one of the Twelve, appeared. With him was a crowd armed with swords and clubs, sent from the chief priests, the teachers of the law, and the elders.

⁴⁴Now the betrayer had arranged a signal with them: "The one I kiss is the man; arrest him and lead him away under guard." ⁴⁵Going at once to Jesus, Judas said, "Rabbi!" and kissed him. ⁴⁶The men seized Jesus and arrested him. ⁴⁷Then one of those standing near drew his sword and struck the servant of the high priest, cutting off his ear.

⁴⁸"Am I leading a rebellion," said Jesus, "that you have come out with swords and clubs to capture me? ⁴⁹Every day I was with you, teaching in the temple courts, and you did not arrest me. But the Scriptures must be fulfilled." ⁵⁰Then everyone deserted him and fled.

⁵¹A young man, wearing nothing but a linen garment, was following Jesus. When they seized him, ⁵²he fled naked, leaving his garment behind.

Before the Sanhedrin

⁵³They took Jesus to the high priest, and all the chief priests, elders and teachers of the law came together. ⁵⁴Peter followed him at a distance, right into the courtyard of the high priest. There he sat with the guards and warmed himself at the fire. ⁵⁵The chief priests and the whole

---

a24 Some manuscripts *the new*   *b27* Zech. 13:7
c30 Some early manuscripts do not have *twice*.
d36 Aramaic for *Father*

Sanhedrin were looking for evidence against Jesus so that they could put him to death, but they did not find any. [56]Many testified falsely against him, but their statements did not agree.

[57]Then some stood up and gave this false testimony against him: [58]"We heard him say, 'I will destroy this man-made temple and in three days will build another, not made by man.'" [59]Yet even then their testimony did not agree.

[60]Then the high priest stood up before them and asked Jesus, "Are you not going to answer? What is this testimony that these men are bringing against you?" [61]But Jesus remained silent and gave no answer.

Again the high priest asked him, "Are you the Christ,[a] the Son of the Blessed One?"

[62]"I am," said Jesus. "And you will see the Son of Man sitting at the right hand of the Mighty One and coming on the clouds of heaven."

[63]The high priest tore his clothes. "Why do we need any more witnesses?" he asked. [64]"You have heard the blasphemy. What do you think?"

They all condemned him as worthy of death. [65]Then some began to spit at him; they blindfolded him, struck him with their fists, and said, "Prophesy!" And the guards took him and beat him.

Peter Disowns Jesus

[66]While Peter was below in the courtyard, one of the servant girls of the high priest came by. [67]When she saw Peter warming himself, she looked closely at him.

"You also were with that Nazarene, Jesus," she said.

[68]But he denied it. "I don't know or understand what you're talking about," he said, and went out into the entryway.[b]

[69]When the servant girl saw him there, she said again to those standing around, "This fellow is one of them." [70]Again he denied it.

After a little while, those standing near said to Peter, "Surely you are one of them, for you are a Galilean."

[71]He began to call down curses on himself, and he swore to them, "I don't know this man you're talking about."

[72]Immediately the rooster crowed the second time.[c] Then Peter remembered the word Jesus had spoken to him: "Before the rooster crows twice[d] you will disown me three times." And he broke down and wept.

Jesus Before Pilate

15 Very early in the morning, the chief priests, with the elders, the teachers of the law and the whole Sanhedrin, reached a decision. They bound Jesus, led him away and handed him over to Pilate.

[2]"Are you the king of the Jews?" asked Pilate.

"Yes, it is as you say," Jesus replied.

[3]The chief priests accused him of many things. [4]So again Pilate asked him, "Aren't you going to answer? See how many things they are accusing you of."

[5]But Jesus still made no reply, and Pilate was amazed.

[6]Now it was the custom at the Feast to release a prisoner whom the people requested. [7]A man called Barabbas was in prison with the insurrectionists who had committed murder in the uprising. [8]The crowd came up and asked Pilate to do for them what he usually did.

[9]"Do you want me to release to you the king of the Jews?" asked Pilate, [10]knowing it was out of envy that the chief priests had handed Jesus over to him. [11]But the chief priests stirred up the crowd to have Pilate release Barabbas instead.

[12]"What shall I do, then, with the one you call the king of the Jews?" Pilate asked them.

[13]"Crucify him!" they shouted.

[14]"Why? What crime has he committed?" asked Pilate.

But they shouted all the louder, "Crucify him!"

[15]Wanting to satisfy the crowd, Pilate released Barabbas to them. He had Jesus flogged, and handed him over to be crucified.

The Soldiers Mock Jesus

[16]The soldiers led Jesus away into the palace (that is, the Praetorium) and called together the whole company of soldiers. [17]They put a purple robe on him, then twisted together a crown of thorns and set it on him. [18]And they began to call out to him, "Hail, king of the Jews!" [19]Again and again they struck him on the head with a staff and spit on him. Falling on their knees, they paid homage to him. [20]And

when they had mocked him, they took off the purple robe and put his own clothes on him. Then they led him out to crucify him.

The Crucifixion

²¹A certain man from Cyrene, Simon, the father of Alexander and Rufus, was passing by on his way in from the country, and they forced him to carry the cross. ²²They brought Jesus to the place called Golgotha (which means The Place of the Skull). ²³Then they offered him wine mixed with myrrh, but he did not take it. ²⁴And they crucified him. Dividing up his clothes, they cast lots to see what each would get.

²⁵It was the third hour when they crucified him. ²⁶The written notice of the charge against him read: THE KING OF THE JEWS. ²⁷They crucified two robbers with him, one on his right and one on his left.ª ²⁹Those who passed by hurled insults at him, shaking their heads and saying, "So! You who are going to destroy the temple and build it in three days, ³⁰come down from the cross and save yourself!"

³¹In the same way the chief priests and the teachers of the law mocked him among themselves. "He saved others," they said, "but he can't save himself! ³²Let this Christ,ᵇ this King of Israel, come down now from the cross, that we may see and believe." Those crucified with him also heaped insults on him.

The Death of Jesus

³³At the sixth hour darkness came over the whole land until the ninth hour. ³⁴And at the ninth hour Jesus cried out in a loud voice, *"Eloi, Eloi, lama sabachthani?"*—which means, "My God, my God, why have you forsaken me?"ᶜ

³⁵When some of those standing near heard this, they said, "Listen, he's calling Elijah."

³⁶One man ran, filled a sponge with wine vinegar, put it on a stick, and offered it to Jesus to drink. "Now leave him alone. Let's see if Elijah comes to take him down," he said.

³⁷With a loud cry, Jesus breathed his last.

³⁸The curtain of the temple was torn in two from top to bottom. ³⁹And when the centurion, who stood there in front of Jesus, heard his cry andᵈ saw how he died, he said, "Surely this man was the Sonᵉ of God!"

⁴⁰Some women were watching from a distance. Among them were Mary Magdalene, Mary the mother of James the younger and of Joses, and Salome. ⁴¹In Galilee these women had followed him and cared for his needs. Many other

ª27 Some manuscripts *left, ²⁸and the scripture was fulfilled which says, "He was counted with the lawless ones"* (Isaiah 53:12)   ᵇ32 Or *Messiah*   ᶜ34 Psalm 22:1   ᵈ39 Some manuscripts do not have *heard his cry and*   ᵉ39 Or *a son*

HEY DAD
Did Jesus' mom have a career?

QUESTIONS KIDS ASK

Text: Mark 15:40–41

During Jesus' time, most women's primary job was caring for their home and family. Some women worked in the fields or made frequent trips to the well to water the gardens. They also took care of the children. And, while the boys attended school, mothers taught their daughters all the strict dietary rules of the Jewish people. Mary, Jesus' mother, probably lived a life very much like other women in her village.

Women prepared meals twice a day. This involved grinding grain for flour, milking the goats, making cheese, and other labor-intensive preparations. (A typical dinner included onions, cucumbers, melons, eggs, nuts and fish or poultry.) Women also made clothes for their families.

King Solomon declared a virtuous wife a treasure, saying, "She watches over the affairs of her household and does not eat the bread of idleness" (Proverbs 31:27). How's *that* for a job description?

For a complete listing of Questions Kids Ask, turn to page 1435.

women who had come up with him to Jerusalem were also there.

The Burial of Jesus

⁴²It was Preparation Day (that is, the day before the Sabbath). So as evening approached, ⁴³Joseph of Arimathea, a prominent member of the Council, who was himself waiting for the kingdom of God, went boldly to Pilate and asked for Jesus' body. ⁴⁴Pilate was surprised to hear that he was already dead. Summoning the centurion, he asked him if Jesus had already died. ⁴⁵When he learned from the centurion that it was so, he gave the body to Joseph. ⁴⁶So Joseph bought some linen cloth, took down the body, wrapped it in the linen, and placed it in a tomb cut out of rock. Then he rolled a stone against the entrance of the tomb. ⁴⁷Mary Magdalene and Mary the mother of Joses saw where he was laid.

The Resurrection

16 When the Sabbath was over, Mary Magdalene, Mary the mother of James, and Salome bought spices so that they might go to anoint Jesus' body. ²Very early on the first day of the week, just after sunrise, they were on their way to the tomb ³and they asked each other, "Who will roll the stone away from the entrance of the tomb?"

⁴But when they looked up, they saw that the stone, which was very large, had been rolled away. ⁵As they entered the tomb, they saw a young man dressed in a white robe sitting on the right side, and they were alarmed.

⁶"Don't be alarmed," he said. "You are looking for Jesus the Nazarene, who was crucified. He has risen! He is not here. See the place where they laid him. ⁷But go, tell his disciples and Peter, 'He is going ahead of you into Galilee. There you will see him, just as he told you.' "

⁸Trembling and bewildered, the women went out and fled from the tomb. They said nothing to anyone, because they were afraid.

[The earliest manuscripts and some other ancient witnesses do not have Mark 16:9-20.]

⁹When Jesus rose early on the first day of the week, he appeared first to Mary Magdalene, out of whom he had driven seven demons. ¹⁰She went and told those who had been with him and who were mourning and weeping. ¹¹When they heard that Jesus was alive and that she had seen him, they did not believe it.

¹²Afterward Jesus appeared in a different form to two of them while they were walking in the country. ¹³These returned and reported it to the rest; but they did not believe them either.

¹⁴Later Jesus appeared to the Eleven as they were eating; he rebuked them for their lack of faith and their stubborn refusal to believe those who had seen him after he had risen.

¹⁵He said to them, "Go into all the world and preach the good news to all creation. ¹⁶Whoever believes and is baptized will be saved, but whoever does not believe will be condemned. ¹⁷And these signs will accompany those who believe: In my name they will drive out demons; they will speak in new tongues; ¹⁸they will pick up snakes with their hands; and when they drink deadly poison, it will not hurt them at all; they will place their hands on sick people, and they will get well."

¹⁹After the Lord Jesus had spoken to them, he was taken up into heaven and he sat at the right hand of God. ²⁰Then the disciples went out and preached everywhere, and the Lord worked with them and confirmed his word by the signs that accompanied it.

One would fully expect a physician to tell the story of Jesus with compassion and with a gentle bedside manner that reveals the true heart of the Savior. Luke begins his story with the birth of John the Baptist, then provides us with the Bible's most thorough account of the conception and nativity of Jesus . . . exactly what you'd expect from a gifted doctor. And no Gospel account gives us more information about the women whose lives affected Jesus, women whose lives were transformed by the Savior. These things set the Gospel of Luke apart from the other three accounts of Jesus' life.

This story shows us what happened when the loving Messiah touched real people—people who were homeless, downtrodden, scorned, hurting. Luke knew the power of tenderness; his message is filled with the compassion of a man who spent his days surrounded by the needy and the sick. As you read on, you'll see for yourself what happened when the Great Physician reached out to touch people.

Luke

Introduction

1 Many have undertaken to draw up an account of the things that have been fulfilled[a] among us, ²just as they were handed down to us by those who from the first were eyewitnesses and servants of the word. ³Therefore, since I myself have carefully investigated everything from the beginning, it seemed good also to me to write an orderly account for you, most excellent Theophilus, ⁴so that you may know the certainty of the things you have been taught.

The Birth of John the Baptist Foretold

⁵In the time of Herod king of Judea there was a priest named Zechariah, who belonged to the priestly division of Abijah; his wife Elizabeth was also a descendant of Aaron. ⁶Both of them were upright in the sight of God, observing all the Lord's commandments and regulations blamelessly. ⁷But they had no children, because Elizabeth was barren; and they were both well along in years.

⁸Once when Zechariah's division was on duty and he was serving as priest before God, ⁹he was chosen by lot, according to the custom of the priesthood, to go into the temple of the Lord and burn incense. ¹⁰And when the time for the burning of incense came, all the assembled worshipers were praying outside.

a1 Or been surely believed

¹¹Then an angel of the Lord appeared to him, standing at the right side of the altar of incense. ¹²When Zechariah saw him, he was startled and was gripped with fear. ¹³But the angel said to him: "Do not be afraid, Zechariah; your prayer has been heard. Your wife Elizabeth will bear you a son, and you are to give him the name John. ¹⁴He will be a joy and delight to you, and many will rejoice because of his birth, ¹⁵for he will be great in the sight of the Lord. He is never to take wine or other fermented drink, and he will be filled with the Holy Spirit even from birth.ᵃ ¹⁶Many of the people of Israel will he bring back to the Lord their God. ¹⁷And he will go on before the Lord, in the spirit and power of Elijah, to turn the hearts of the fathers to their children and the disobedient to the wisdom of the righteous—to make ready a people prepared for the Lord."

¹⁸Zechariah asked the angel, "How can I be sure of this? I am an old man and my wife is well along in years."

¹⁹The angel answered, "I am Gabriel. I stand in the presence of God, and I have been sent to speak to you and to tell you this good news. ²⁰And now you will be silent and not able to speak until the day this happens, because you did not believe my words, which will come true at their proper time."

²¹Meanwhile, the people were waiting for Zechariah and wondering why he stayed so long in the temple. ²²When he came out, he could not speak to them. They realized he had seen a vision in the temple, for he kept making signs to them but remained unable to speak.

²³When his time of service was completed, he returned home. ²⁴After this his wife Elizabeth became pregnant and for five months remained in seclusion. ²⁵"The Lord has done this for me," she said. "In these days he has shown his favor and taken away my disgrace among the people."

ᵃ15 Or *from his mother's womb*

Isn't This Great?
Zechariah, the Doubting Father

DADS
IN THE
BIBLE

"Zechariah asked the angel,
'How can I be sure of this?' " (1:18).

Text: Luke 1:5–25

People who live in Missouri pride themselves on living lives of doubt. They even have "The Show Me State" stamped on their license plates.

But when it comes to divine revelation, God isn't humored by this attitude. While Zechariah the priest dutifully performed the ceremony of refreshing the incense of the Most Holy Place, he was visited by an angel. This was not a dream. This angel was real and was telling him that his prayers for an heir had finally been answered.

"How can I be sure of this?" a skeptical Zechariah asked (v. 18).

"Zechariah, how could you *doubt* such a thing?" we might respond.

Here was a high priest, an ordained man of God, whose business it was to lead others to faith. Here was a man who, along with his wife, had prayed for an heir. Now this man stood face to face with an emissary from God himself. And all Zechariah could say was, "You're kidding, aren't you?"

To prove that he wasn't pleased with Zechariah's remark, God closed his mouth. When this pious man emerged from the Most Holy Place, he could not speak. The people were filled with wonder at what they were seeing.

If they had known that Zechariah's silence had resulted from his questioning of God's answer to his prayer, they may have been angry, as well. "Why doesn't the priest believe what he tells us to believe?" they could have said to each other.

It's time we replace our "I don't believe it" with "Isn't this great!" You may have never actually seen an angel show up with good news, but God's answers to your prayers are all around you. Believe it. He is answering. He is showing you. His handiwork is everywhere.

For a complete listing of Dads in the Bible, turn to page 1434.

The Birth of Jesus Foretold

26In the sixth month, God sent the angel Gabriel to Nazareth, a town in Galilee, **27**to a virgin pledged to be married to a man named Joseph, a descendant of David. The virgin's name was Mary. **28**The angel went to her and said, "Greetings, you who are highly favored! The Lord is with you."

29Mary was greatly troubled at his words and wondered what kind of greeting this might be. **30**But the angel said to her, "Do not be afraid, Mary, you have found favor with God. **31**You will be with child and give birth to a son, and you are to give him the name Jesus. **32**He will be great and will be called the Son of the Most High. The Lord God will give him the throne of his father David, **33**and he will reign over the house of Jacob forever; his kingdom will never end."

34"How will this be," Mary asked the angel, "since I am a virgin?"

35The angel answered, "The Holy Spirit will come upon you, and the power of the Most High will overshadow you. So the holy one to be born will be called[a] the Son of God. **36**Even Elizabeth your relative is going to have a child in her old age, and she who was said to be barren is in her sixth month. **37**For nothing is impossible with God."

38"I am the Lord's servant," Mary answered. "May it be to me as you have said." Then the angel left her.

Mary Visits Elizabeth

39At that time Mary got ready and hurried to a town in the hill country of Judea, **40**where she entered Zechariah's home and greeted Elizabeth. **41**When Elizabeth heard Mary's greeting, the baby leaped in her womb, and Elizabeth was filled with the Holy Spirit. **42**In a loud voice she exclaimed: "Blessed are you among women, and blessed is the child you will bear! **43**But why am I so favored, that the mother of my Lord should come to me? **44**As soon as the sound of your greeting reached my ears, the baby in my womb leaped for joy. **45**Blessed is she who has believed that what the Lord has said to her will be accomplished!"

Mary's Song

46And Mary said:

"My soul glorifies the Lord

47 and my spirit rejoices in God my
    Savior,
48for he has been mindful
    of the humble state of his servant.
From now on all generations will call
    me blessed,
49 for the Mighty One has done great
    things for me—
    holy is his name.
50His mercy extends to those who fear
    him,
    from generation to generation.
51He has performed mighty deeds with
    his arm;
    he has scattered those who are proud
    in their inmost thoughts.
52He has brought down rulers from their
    thrones
    but has lifted up the humble.
53He has filled the hungry with good
    things
    but has sent the rich away empty.
54He has helped his servant Israel,
    remembering to be merciful
55to Abraham and his descendants
    forever,
    even as he said to our fathers."

56Mary stayed with Elizabeth for about three months and then returned home.

The Birth of John the Baptist

57When it was time for Elizabeth to have her baby, she gave birth to a son. **58**Her neighbors and relatives heard that the Lord had shown her great mercy, and they shared her joy.

59On the eighth day they came to circumcise the child, and they were going to name him after his father Zechariah, **60**but his mother spoke up and said, "No! He is to be called John."

61They said to her, "There is no one among your relatives who has that name."

62Then they made signs to his father, to find out what he would like to name the child. **63**He asked for a writing tablet, and to everyone's astonishment he wrote, "His name is John." **64**Immediately his mouth was opened and his tongue was loosed, and he began to speak, praising God. **65**The neighbors were all filled with awe, and throughout the hill country of Judea people were talking about all these things. **66**Everyone who heard this wondered about it, asking, "What then is this child going to be?" For the Lord's hand was with him.

[a]35 Or *So the child to be born will becalled holy,*

Don't Be Afraid

Key Verse: *"Do not be afraid. I bring you good news of great joy that will be for all the people."* Luke 2:10

Text: Luke 2:8-14 *(Dad or child reads the text.)*

DAD READS: Sometimes, at night, we get frightened. Strange sounds in the house or tree branches raking the windows scare us. Being afraid at night is something we have both experienced, haven't we?

Child reads: When I'm scared at night, sometimes I call for you. Because you're my dad, I know that you will know what to do. You tell me that everything is okay. You make me feel better so I can go back to sleep. I'm glad I have a dad who helps me when I'm afraid.

DAD READS: A long time ago, a group of men sat on a hillside taking care of their sheep. These men were shepherds, and their job was to keep their sheep safe from wild animals or anything that would hurt them—just like fathers do with their children. Then something happened that was very scary . . . more frightening than hearing noises in the house at night.

Child reads: All at once, in the middle of the night, an angel stood before them. Then a bright light shone in the shepherds' faces, and many angels appeared. If this would have happened to me, I would have been very frightened!

DAD READS: Well, the shepherds were afraid too. They had never seen anything like this, even in the daytime. But then the angel said something to the shepherds. He said the very same thing that I say to you at night when you are awakened by a noise or a bad dream. The angel said to the shepherds, "Do not be afraid." Then the angel said, "I bring you good

QUIET
TIMES
WITH Dad

news of great joy ... a Savior has been born to you; he is Christ the Lord." This was very, very good news for these shepherds. They needed a Savior. They were living at a time when they were almost like slaves to a foreign government. "Maybe this Savior," they may have said to each other, "will set us free from the Romans."

Child reads: Jesus Christ was born that night. But he did not come to save the shepherds from the Romans; he came to save them from their sins. The angel knew that some day the shepherds would understand that being free from their sins was much more important than being free from anything else.

DAD READS: Yes, Jesus came to earth to forgive us for our sins. And the angels knew that when the shepherds understood that, they would never need to be afraid again. Let me pray this prayer with you:

Our Father in heaven, we love you. Thank you for coming to earth to save us from our sins. Thank you for telling the shepherds not to be afraid. We confess our sins to you and thank you for your forgiveness. Because of you, we never need to be afraid. We love you and we thank you for your love. In Jesus' name, Amen.

For your next devotional reading, go to page 1114.

Zechariah's Song

[67]His father Zechariah was filled with the Holy Spirit and prophesied:

[68]"Praise be to the Lord, the God of
    Israel,
  because he has come and has
    redeemed his people.
[69]He has raised up a horn[a] of salvation
    for us
  in the house of his servant David
[70](as he said through his holy prophets of
    long ago),
[71]salvation from our enemies
  and from the hand of all who
    hate us—
[72]to show mercy to our fathers
  and to remember his holy covenant,
[73]   the oath he swore to our father
    Abraham:
[74]to rescue us from the hand of our
    enemies,
  and to enable us to serve him
    without fear
[75]   in holiness and righteousness before
    him all our days.

[76]And you, my child, will be called a
    prophet of the Most High;
  for you will go on before the Lord to
    prepare the way for him,
[77]to give his people the knowledge of
    salvation
  through the forgiveness of their sins,
[78]because of the tender mercy of our
    God,
  by which the rising sun will come to
    us from heaven
[79]to shine on those living in darkness
  and in the shadow of death,
  to guide our feet into the path of
    peace."

[80]And the child grew and became strong in spirit; and he lived in the desert until he appeared publicly to Israel.

The Birth of Jesus

2 In those days Caesar Augustus issued a decree that a census should be taken of the entire Roman world. [2](This was the first census that took place while Quirinius was governor of Syria.) [3]And everyone went to his own town to register.

[4]So Joseph also went up from the town of Nazareth in Galilee to Judea, to Bethlehem the town of David, because he belonged to the house and line of David. [5]He went there to register with Mary, who was pledged to be married to him and was expecting a child. [6]While they were there, the time came for the baby to be born, [7]and she gave birth to her firstborn, a son. She wrapped him in cloths and placed him in a manger, because there was no room for them in the inn.

The Shepherds and the Angels

[8]And there were shepherds living out in the fields nearby, keeping watch over their flocks at night. [9]An angel of the Lord appeared to them, and the glory of the Lord shone around them, and they were terrified. [10]But the angel said to them, "Do not be afraid. I bring you good news of great joy that will be for all the people. [11]Today in the town of David a Savior has been born to you; he is Christ[b] the Lord. [12]This will be a sign to you: You will find a baby wrapped in cloths and lying in a manger."

[13]Suddenly a great company of the heavenly host appeared with the angel, praising God and saying,

[14]"Glory to God in the highest,
  and on earth peace to men on whom
    his favor rests."

[15]When the angels had left them and gone into heaven, the shepherds said to one another, "Let's go to Bethlehem and see this thing that has happened, which the Lord has told us about."

[16]So they hurried off and found Mary and Joseph, and the baby, who was lying in the manger. [17]When they had seen him, they spread the word concerning what had been told them about this child, [18]and all who heard it were amazed at what the shepherds said to them. [19]But Mary treasured up all these things and pondered them in her heart. [20]The shepherds returned, glorifying and praising God for all the things they had heard and seen, which were just as they had been told.

Jesus Presented in the Temple

[21]On the eighth day, when it was time to circumcise him, he was named Jesus, the name the angel had given him before he had been conceived.

[22]When the time of their purification according to the Law of Moses had been

---

[a]69 Horn here symbolizes strength.   [b]11 Or Messiah. "The Christ" (Greek) and "the Messiah" (Hebrew) both mean "the Anointed One"; also in verse 26.

completed, Joseph and Mary took him to Jerusalem to present him to the Lord [23](as it is written in the Law of the Lord, "Every firstborn male is to be consecrated to the Lord"[a]), [24]and to offer a sacrifice in keeping with what is said in the Law of the Lord: "a pair of doves or two young pigeons."[b]

[25]Now there was a man in Jerusalem called Simeon, who was righteous and devout. He was waiting for the consolation of Israel, and the Holy Spirit was upon him. [26]It had been revealed to him by the Holy Spirit that he would not die before he had seen the Lord's Christ. [27]Moved by the Spirit, he went into the temple courts. When the parents brought in the child Jesus to do for him what the custom of the Law required, [28]Simeon took him in his arms and praised God, saying:

[a]23 Exodus 13:2,12   [b]24 Lev. 12:8

What Will Become of You?

DAILY INSIGHT

MONDAY

Passage:
Luke 2:25–35

Verses:
Luke 2:34–35

A few days after our first child was born, we realized that we were about to go through the adjustment of our lives. But there was no turning back. Try as we might to return to full nights of sleep and lazy, selfishly designed evenings, they were gone forever.

Soon after Missy came home to live with us, I helplessly discovered that this little person was capturing my heart. I couldn't wait to get home from work to look at her and hold her.

Late one afternoon I was lying on the carpeted floor of our living room, cuddled next to her. She was on her tummy, a clean cloth diaper under her head, with her face turned toward me. I studied her tiny features—her velvety skin, little turned-up nose, and rosebud mouth.

We talked.

"Do you know who you are, little girl?" I asked. "You're Missy, and I'm your daddy. Do you know how glad I am that you came to live at our house? Do you know how much I love you?"

Occasionally her eyes would seem to focus.

I raised up enough to lean over and kiss her soft cheek. My hand rested on her back, softly patting. Drool trickled out of the corner of her mouth. As though it were yesterday, I can remember the breathtaking feeling in my soul, not unlike the moment a roller coaster begins its descent.

"This little girl is *my* responsibility," I breathed out loud. "I'm her daddy—the only one she'll ever have."

What will become of your children? Where will they go to college? Will they get married … and, if so, to whom? Where will they live? What will they do with their lives?

God preserved the life of a devout man named Simeon so he could give Jesus' parents a glimpse into their child's future. The words he spoke left no room for doubt that Mary and Joseph's boy would make an indelible mark on his people. "This child is destined to cause the falling and rising of many in Israel … and a sword will pierce your own soul too," the old man prophesied.

Jesus Christ's birth was the fulfillment of centuries of prophecy, and his call was, ultimately, to be the sacrifice for our sins on the cross. The Sovereign Lord had a specific plan and purpose for the baby Jesus.

And guess what? God also has a singular plan for your child. Although you probably have not bumped into any Simeons lately, God wants you to be ready for the task at hand. Your children are completely unique. They're not going to be normal, average, or simply run-of-the-mill kids. They're each one-of-a-kind.

The Creator of the universe has a marvelous blueprint for your children. And he has blessed you with the responsibility of shaping them to fit that design to perfection.

What an incredible privilege this is.

For your next devotional reading, go to page 1116.

29 "Sovereign Lord, as you have
      promised,
   you now dismiss*^a* your servant in
      peace.
30 For my eyes have seen your salvation,
31   which you have prepared in the sight
         of all people,
32 a light for revelation to the Gentiles
      and for glory to your people Israel."

33 The child's father and mother marveled at what was said about him. 34 Then Simeon blessed them and said to Mary, his mother: "This child is destined to cause the falling and rising of many in Israel, and to be a sign that will be spoken against, 35 so that the thoughts of many hearts will be revealed. And a sword will pierce your own soul too."

36 There was also a prophetess, Anna, the daughter of Phanuel, of the tribe of Asher. She was very old; she had lived with her husband seven years after her marriage, 37 and then was a widow until she was eighty-four.*^b* She never left the temple but worshiped night and day, fasting and praying. 38 Coming up to them at that very moment, she gave thanks to God and spoke about the child to all who were looking forward to the redemption of Jerusalem.

39 When Joseph and Mary had done everything required by the Law of the Lord, they returned to Galilee to their own town of Nazareth. 40 And the child grew and became strong; he was filled with wisdom, and the grace of God was upon him.

The Boy Jesus at the Temple

41 Every year his parents went to Jerusalem for the Feast of the Passover. 42 When he was twelve years old, they went up to the Feast, according to the custom. 43 After the Feast was over, while his parents were returning home, the boy Jesus stayed behind in Jerusalem, but they were unaware of it. 44 Thinking he was in their company, they traveled on for a day. Then they began looking for him among their relatives and friends. 45 When they did not find him, they went back to Jerusalem to look for him. 46 After three days they found him in the temple courts, sitting among the teachers, listening to them and asking them questions. 47 Everyone who heard him was amazed at his understanding and his answers. 48 When his parents saw him, they were astonished. His mother said to him, "Son, why have you treated us like this? Your father and I have been anxiously searching for you."

*^a29 Or promised, / now dismiss   ^b37 Or widow for
eighty-four years*

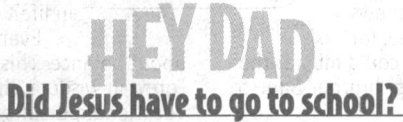

Did Jesus have to go to school?

Text: Luke 2:43–47

Jesus went to school like all other Jewish boys, beginning at the age of five. The school day lasted half a day, six days a week. Usually, a young boy spent the other half of his day learning a trade. Jesus probably learned carpentry from Joseph.

In class, boys learned Hebrew, which was of utmost importance since Moses' law was written in Hebrew. The boys then memorized passages of the law—only priests and teachers were allowed to actually write down these sacred words. Memorization also made it impossible for foreign powers to take away the Jews' religion. While an invading army could destroy books, they could not take God's law out of the Jews' hearts and minds.

At age ten, boys went on to the *bet Talmud* or the "house of learning" (Ward, 152). There they learned to argue, reason and interpret the law. Girls were not formally schooled, but their mothers taught them the practical applications of the same law the boys studied, especially dietary laws and traditions (Ward, 155).

Ward, K. (Ed.). (1987). Jesus and His Times. Pleasantville, New York: The Reader's Digest Association.

For a complete listing of Questions Kids Ask, turn to page 1435.

QUESTIONS Kids ASK

⁴⁹"Why were you searching for me?" he asked. "Didn't you know I had to be in my Father's house?" ⁵⁰But they did not understand what he was saying to them.

⁵¹Then he went down to Nazareth with them and was obedient to them. But his mother treasured all these things in her heart. ⁵²And Jesus grew in wisdom and stature, and in favor with God and men.

John the Baptist Prepares the Way

3 In the fifteenth year of the reign of Tiberius Caesar—when Pontius Pilate was governor of Judea, Herod tetrarch of Galilee, his brother Philip tetrarch of Iturea and Traconitis, and Lysanias tetrarch of Abilene— ²during the high priesthood of Annas and Caiaphas, the word of God came to John son of Zechariah in the

Please Help Me up Here, I'm Stuck

DAILY INSIGHT

TUESDAY

Passage:
Luke 2:41–52

Verse:
Luke 2:52

I am a card-carrying acrophobic; I'm desperately afraid of heights. I discovered this about myself when I was nine. Right next to my grandparents' farm house stood a windmill that, decades before, had been used to draw water from the well directly beneath it. One afternoon, I foolishly decided to climb the narrow steel ladder welded to the side of the tower.

But just as I was about to reach the pinnacle, I was suddenly and unexplainably gripped with fear. I felt abject terror as I had never felt it before. My knuckles were white. My throat was powder dry. I couldn't breathe or swallow. I stood there, immobilized, for several minutes before I could muster the breath to call for my older brother, Sam, to save me.

Thirty-five years later, I was building a house with my Sunday school class. Since I'm fairly adept at driving nails, I had volunteered to climb up to the top of the first floor framed walls to secure them.

When I had completed one section, I stood to walk across the three-and-a-half-inch wide "walkway" to the other side of the house. Suddenly, my legs froze. I could feel the pounding of my heart from my fingertips to my baseball cap. I was on the windmill again. This was not funny. I thought of calling for Sam, but he was in California.

Without looking up or down, I slowly reached my arms straight out from my sides and began to walk ... one treacherous step at a time. Halfway across the wall, I realized that my outstretched arms were providing the perfect antidote for my fear—they were giving me balance.

In much the same way, today's verse is the perfect antidote for the anxiety you may be feeling at this moment. Being successful at work, effectively fathering your kids, keeping your exercise and diet routine intact, spending enough time with your wife, being disciplined in your spiritual life, keeping your garage in order ... all of this can create such anxiety that you feel frozen to the windmill, unable to walk across the high wall. How does one achieve balance in life?

Even as a boy, Jesus knew about balance. This passage tells us that he "grew in wisdom," his intellectual and vocational pursuits, "stature," his physical conditioning, "in favor with God," his spiritual development, "and man," his relational challenges. Throughout his life, he kept his priorities in order. He refused to allow the stress and pressure of any one of these things to overshadow the others.

Then, one dark Friday afternoon, our Savior spread out his arms and gave his life for you and me. His provision of grace provided us with the luxury of living our lives in perfect balance—free from the fear of the past or the future, unencumbered by the relentless pressures of life, and free from threats or jeers from anyone or anything ... even our most crippling fears ... even our fear of heights.

Isn't this incredible?

For your next devotional reading, go to page 1119.

desert. ³He went into all the country around the Jordan, preaching a baptism of repentance for the forgiveness of sins. ⁴As is written in the book of the words of Isaiah the prophet:

"A voice of one calling in the desert,
'Prepare the way for the Lord,
    make straight paths for him.
⁵ Every valley shall be filled in,
    every mountain and hill made low.
The crooked roads shall become
    straight,
    the rough ways smooth.
⁶ And all mankind will see God's
    salvation.' "ᵃ

⁷John said to the crowds coming out to be baptized by him, "You brood of vipers! Who warned you to flee from the coming wrath? ⁸Produce fruit in keeping with repentance. And do not begin to say to yourselves, 'We have Abraham as our father.' For I tell you that out of these stones God can raise up children for Abraham. ⁹The ax is already at the root of the trees, and every tree that does not produce good fruit will be cut down and thrown into the fire."

¹⁰"What should we do then?" the crowd asked.

¹¹John answered, "The man with two tunics should share with him who has none, and the one who has food should do the same."

¹²Tax collectors also came to be baptized. "Teacher," they asked, "what should we do?"

¹³"Don't collect any more than you are required to," he told them.

¹⁴Then some soldiers asked him, "And what should we do?"

He replied, "Don't extort money and don't accuse people falsely—be content with your pay."

¹⁵The people were waiting expectantly and were all wondering in their hearts if John might possibly be the Christ.ᵇ ¹⁶John answered them all, "I baptize you withᶜ water. But one more powerful than I will come, the thongs of whose sandals I am not worthy to untie. He will baptize you with the Holy Spirit and with fire. ¹⁷His winnowing fork is in his hand to clear his threshing floor and to gather the wheat into his barn, but he will burn up the chaff with unquenchable fire." ¹⁸And with many other words John exhorted the people and preached the good news to them.

¹⁹But when John rebuked Herod the te-

trarch because of Herodias, his brother's wife, and all the other evil things he had done, ²⁰Herod added this to them all: He locked John up in prison.

The Baptism and Genealogy of Jesus

²¹When all the people were being baptized, Jesus was baptized too. And as he was praying, heaven was opened ²²and the Holy Spirit descended on him in bodily form like a dove. And a voice came from heaven: "You are my Son, whom I love; with you I am well pleased."

²³Now Jesus himself was about thirty years old when he began his ministry. He was the son, so it was thought, of Joseph,

the son of Heli, ²⁴the son of Matthat,
the son of Levi, the son of Melki,
the son of Jannai, the son of Joseph,
²⁵the son of Mattathias, the son of
    Amos,
the son of Nahum, the son of Esli,
the son of Naggai, ²⁶the son of Maath,
the son of Mattathias, the son of
    Semein,
the son of Josech, the son of Joda,
²⁷the son of Joanan, the son of Rhesa,
the son of Zerubbabel, the son of
    Shealtiel,
the son of Neri, ²⁸the son of Melki,
the son of Addi, the son of Cosam,
the son of Elmadam, the son of Er,
²⁹the son of Joshua, the son of Eliezer,
the son of Jorim, the son of Matthat,
the son of Levi, ³⁰the son of Simeon,
the son of Judah, the son of Joseph,
the son of Jonam, the son of Eliakim,
³¹the son of Melea, the son of Menna,
the son of Mattatha, the son of Na-
    than,
the son of David, ³²the son of Jesse,
the son of Obed, the son of Boaz,
the son of Salmon,ᵈ the son of Nah-
    shon,
³³the son of Amminadab, the son of
    Ram,ᵉ
the son of Hezron, the son of Perez,
the son of Judah, ³⁴the son of Jacob,
the son of Isaac, the son of Abraham,
the son of Terah, the son of Nahor,
³⁵the son of Serug, the son of Reu,
the son of Peleg, the son of Eber,
the son of Shelah, ³⁶the son of
    Cainan,

ᵃ6 Isaiah 40:3-5   ᵇ15 Or Messiah   ᶜ16 Or in
ᵈ32 Some early manuscripts Sala   ᵉ33 Some
manuscripts Amminadab, the son of Admin, the
son of Arni; other manuscripts vary widely.

the son of Arphaxad, the son of
  Shem,
the son of Noah, the son of Lamech,
37the son of Methuselah, the son of
  Enoch,
the son of Jared, the son of Mahalalel,
the son of Kenan, **38**the son of Enosh,
the son of Seth, the son of Adam,
the son of God.

The Temptation of Jesus

Jesus, full of the Holy Spirit, returned
from the Jordan and was led by the
Spirit in the desert, **2**where for forty days
he was tempted by the devil. He ate nothing during those days, and at the end of
them he was hungry.

3The devil said to him, "If you are the
Son of God, tell this stone to become
bread."

4Jesus answered, "It is written: 'Man
does not live on bread alone.'*a*"

5The devil led him up to a high place
and showed him in an instant all the kingdoms of the world. **6**And he said to him, "I
will give you all their authority and splendor, for it has been given to me, and I can
give it to anyone I want to. **7**So if you worship me, it will all be yours."

8Jesus answered, "It is written: 'Worship
the Lord your God and serve him only.'*b*"

9The devil led him to Jerusalem and had
him stand on the highest point of the
temple. "If you are the Son of God," he
said, "throw yourself down from here.
10For it is written:

" 'He will command his angels
    concerning you
  to guard you carefully;
11they will lift you up in their hands,
  so that you will not strike your foot
    against a stone.'*c*"

12Jesus answered, "It says: 'Do not put
the Lord your God to the test.'*d*"

13When the devil had finished all this
tempting, he left him until an opportune
time.

Jesus Rejected at Nazareth

14Jesus returned to Galilee in the power
of the Spirit, and news about him spread
through the whole countryside. **15**He
taught in their synagogues, and everyone
praised him.

16He went to Nazareth, where he had
been brought up, and on the Sabbath day
he went into the synagogue, as was his
custom. And he stood up to read. **17**The
scroll of the prophet Isaiah was handed to
him. Unrolling it, he found the place
where it is written:

18"The Spirit of the Lord is on me,
    because he has anointed me
  to preach good news to the poor.
He has sent me to proclaim freedom
    for the prisoners
  and recovery of sight for the blind,
to release the oppressed,

a4 Deut. 8:3   *b8* Deut. 6:13   *c11* Psalm 91:11,12
d12 Deut. 6:16

HEY DAD
Did Jesus ever want to do bad things?

Text: Luke 4:9–13

While it is hard to imagine that God could actually be tempted to sin, the Bible
says that Jesus *was* tempted. In fact, Jesus knew the strength of temptation better
than any other man who has ever lived. Why? Because he was the only one to
resist temptation completely. He knew its strength because he fought against it
so fiercely.

C.S. Lewis talks about this in *Mere Christianity.* He says that only when we walk
against the force of the wind do we really knows its strength. The soldier who
fights on the front line truly understands the horrors of war; the one who surrenders before
the battle begins knows little about the dangers of combat.

No matter how great the temptation you face, Jesus has proven that you can conquer it
(1 Corinthians 10:13). He has walked against the same wind, he has fought the same
battle—and won (Hebrews 2:18).

For a complete listing of Questions Kids Ask, turn to page 1435.

[19] to proclaim the year of the Lord's favor."[a]

[20]Then he rolled up the scroll, gave it back to the attendant and sat down. The eyes of everyone in the synagogue were fastened on him, [21]and he began by saying to them, "Today this scripture is fulfilled in your hearing."

[22]All spoke well of him and were amazed at the gracious words that came from his lips. "Isn't this Joseph's son?" they asked.

[23]Jesus said to them, "Surely you will quote this proverb to me: 'Physician, heal yourself! Do here in your hometown what we have heard that you did in Capernaum.'"

[24]"I tell you the truth," he continued, "no prophet is accepted in his hometown. [25]I assure you that there were many widows in Israel in Elijah's time, when the sky was shut for three and a half years and

[a]19 Isaiah 61:1,2

Do I Look Like a Terrorist?

DAILY INSIGHT

WEDNESDAY

Passage:
Luke 4:1–12

Verse:
Luke 4:8

As the doors slid open to the terminal, I felt great. My spirits were high; I had just prayed with my wife, who had dropped me off at the airport. And that nice kiss hadn't hurt my attitude either. I was ready for this business trip, whatever surprises it threw my way. I felt great … bulletproof.

In less than sixty seconds, I was standing at the x-ray machines and metal detectors. Only one of the three stations was working, and I reluctantly took my place in line behind the rest of the disgruntled would-be travelers. *Oh great,* I muttered to myself, *all these lines are closed. What a stupid waste of time.*

After a few minutes, I loaded my small suitcase and briefcase onto the conveyor belt. Once they had disappeared into the x-ray machine, I stepped through the electronic trellis.

BEEEEEEEP!

I stepped back. The x-ray police lady glared at me coldly. "You carrying a pager?" she snapped. "Yes ma'am," I responded, thoroughly ticked off at this interruption. "Can you make it beep?" she asked. Of course, I had no idea how to make it beep. Instead I scrolled through my last dozen pages on the little digital screen. She was satisfied.

As I turned to pick up my suitcase and briefcase, another x-ray police person stopped me. "You got a computer in there?" he asked. "Uh, yes I do," I responded, trying to keep my composure. "Turn it on for me," he ordered.

Standing there, waiting for my laptop to boot up, I felt myself filling with an uncanny sense of rage. I got mad at the terrorists who forced us into all this airport security; I got mad at the x-ray police; I got mad at the my computer manufacturer for making a laptop that booted up so slowly.

By the time the security checks were complete and I was off toward my gate, I was furious. The peace and confidence I had felt when I had entered the airport, just a few short minutes before, was a distant memory. I was looking for something to kick.

In today's passage Jesus Christ, God's Son, was preparing himself for a life of ministry. He had just been baptized. He had just heard God's voice (3:21–22) He must have been riding high.

But the next incident that Luke records shows Jesus coming face to face with a brutal barrage of temptations that make my airport debacle look like a day in heaven. Any one of these could have knocked Jesus off track. And what did he do? He repeated things he had learned from the Scriptures. And he spoke what he knew for sure, "Worship … God and serve him only" (v. 8).

The next time you get derailed—it may be a few minutes from right now—take confidence in the good stuff you've just put into your soul today. God's holy presence is yours. He will calm you down. I promise.

For your next devotional reading, go to page 1121.

there was a severe famine throughout the land. [26]Yet Elijah was not sent to any of them, but to a widow in Zarephath in the region of Sidon. [27]And there were many in Israel with leprosy[a] in the time of Elisha the prophet, yet not one of them was cleansed—only Naaman the Syrian."

[28]All the people in the synagogue were furious when they heard this. [29]They got up, drove him out of the town, and took him to the brow of the hill on which the town was built, in order to throw him down the cliff. [30]But he walked right through the crowd and went on his way.

Jesus Drives Out an Evil Spirit

[31]Then he went down to Capernaum, a town in Galilee, and on the Sabbath began to teach the people. [32]They were amazed at his teaching, because his message had authority.

[33]In the synagogue there was a man possessed by a demon, an evil[b] spirit. He cried out at the top of his voice, [34]"Ha! What do you want with us, Jesus of Nazareth? Have you come to destroy us? I know who you are—the Holy One of God!"

[35]"Be quiet!" Jesus said sternly. "Come out of him!" Then the demon threw the man down before them all and came out without injuring him.

[36]All the people were amazed and said to each other, "What is this teaching? With authority and power he gives orders to evil spirits and they come out!" [37]And the news about him spread throughout the surrounding area.

Jesus Heals Many

[38]Jesus left the synagogue and went to the home of Simon. Now Simon's mother-in-law was suffering from a high fever, and they asked Jesus to help her. [39]So he bent over her and rebuked the fever, and it left her. She got up at once and began to wait on them.

[40]When the sun was setting, the people brought to Jesus all who had various kinds of sickness, and laying his hands on each one, he healed them. [41]Moreover, demons came out of many people, shouting, "You are the Son of God!" But he rebuked them and would not allow them to speak, because they knew he was the Christ.[c]

[42]At daybreak Jesus went out to a solitary place. The people were looking for him and when they came to where he was, they tried to keep him from leaving them.

[43]But he said, "I must preach the good news of the kingdom of God to the other towns also, because that is why I was sent." [44]And he kept on preaching in the synagogues of Judea.[d]

The Calling of the First Disciples

5 One day as Jesus was standing by the Lake of Gennesaret,[e] with the people crowding around him and listening to the word of God, [2]he saw at the water's edge two boats, left there by the fishermen, who were washing their nets. [3]He got into one of the boats, the one belonging to Simon, and asked him to put out a little from shore. Then he sat down and taught the people from the boat.

[4]When he had finished speaking, he said to Simon, "Put out into deep water, and let down[f] the nets for a catch."

[5]Simon answered, "Master, we've worked hard all night and haven't caught anything. But because you say so, I will let down the nets."

[6]When they had done so, they caught such a large number of fish that their nets began to break. [7]So they signaled their partners in the other boat to come and help them, and they came and filled both boats so full that they began to sink.

[8]When Simon Peter saw this, he fell at Jesus' knees and said, "Go away from me, Lord; I am a sinful man!" [9]For he and all his companions were astonished at the catch of fish they had taken, [10]and so were James and John, the sons of Zebedee, Simon's partners.

Then Jesus said to Simon, "Don't be afraid; from now on you will catch men." [11]So they pulled their boats up on shore, left everything and followed him.

The Man With Leprosy

[12]While Jesus was in one of the towns, a man came along who was covered with leprosy.[g] When he saw Jesus, he fell with his face to the ground and begged him, "Lord, if you are willing, you can make me clean."

[13]Jesus reached out his hand and

---

[a]27 The Greek word was used for various diseases affecting the skin—not necessarily leprosy.
[b]33 Greek unclean; also in verse 36   [c]41 Or Messiah   [d]44 Or the land of the Jews; some manuscripts Galilee   [e]1 That is, Sea of Galilee   [f]4 The Greek verb is plural.   [g]12 The Greek word was used for various diseases affecting the skin—not necessarily leprosy.

touched the man. "I am willing," he said. "Be clean!" And immediately the leprosy left him.

[14]Then Jesus ordered him, "Don't tell anyone, but go, show yourself to the priest and offer the sacrifices that Moses commanded for your cleansing, as a testimony to them."

[15]Yet the news about him spread all the more, so that crowds of people came to hear him and to be healed of their sick-nesses. [16]But Jesus often withdrew to lonely places and prayed.

Jesus Heals a Paralytic

[17]One day as he was teaching, Pharisees and teachers of the law, who had come from every village of Galilee and from Judea and Jerusalem, were sitting there. And the power of the Lord was present for him to heal the sick. [18]Some men came

Empathize . . . and Be Satisfied

Here's a classic riddle from the days when my daughter was about five: **Q.** How do you catch a rabbit? **A.** Crawl into the bushes and make a sound like a carrot.

Now I have one for you. How do you "catch" your youngsters? Give up? Crawl into their world and try to understand what it's really like to be your kids. Try to see things the way they see them. Try to feel what they feel. The word is "empathy."

If the truth were known, we spend an awful lot of time isolated from what is going on with the other members of our family. After all, we have needs and pressures of our own, and sometimes we can barely keep up with the demands. Even though we know we should, we don't often take the time to understand what they're going through. And so, we don't "capture" them. We lead separate lives.

With the first parable in this passage, Jesus gave his disciples a graphic word picture to describe this principle. As you read it, think of your favorite pair of old cotton pants. If you patched a tear in them with fabric that had fewer miles on it, what would happen the first time your trusty old trousers went through the wash cycle? That's right, the new material in the patch would shrink, pull away from its rightful place, and ruin your precious pants. A patch that doesn't match the age of the fabric it's sewn to, ruins everything.

How much do you truly understand about what your children live with every day? When was the last time you visited

DAILY INSIGHT

THURSDAY

Passage:
Luke 5:36–39

Verse:
Luke 5:36

their school and walked the halls? How well do you know their friends? When was the last time you asked about their needs and their frustrations? Have you ever asked your child to describe what it's like to be your kid? When you do these things, you are literally matching your "patch" to the "fabric" of their lives.

Jesus' second parable, combined with the first, demonstrates these two unforgettable lessons. Please don't miss them. (1) *Work hard to understand what it's like to be your kids.* Take time to listen, to visit their world, and to empathize with their unique plight as your children. (2) *Do not try to become your kids.* Find happiness in being who you are … an adult. Don't give your son or daughter the impression that growing up is the penalty you're paying for staying alive. Give them something to look forward to, something to anticipate. Show them that they can have their youthful grape juice, but for you, there's nothing quite as satisfying as a sip of fine, aged wine (v. 39).

Do you want to be an award-winning dad? In these verses, Jesus tells you how: Compassionately empathize with the needs of each member in your family, and be completely satisfied to be who you are. In these two principles you have a great formula for successful fathering. Can you believe how incredibly helpful your Bible is?

For your next devotional reading, go to page 1123.

carrying a paralytic on a mat and tried to take him into the house to lay him before Jesus. ¹⁹When they could not find a way to do this because of the crowd, they went up on the roof and lowered him on his mat through the tiles into the middle of the crowd, right in front of Jesus.

²⁰When Jesus saw their faith, he said, "Friend, your sins are forgiven." ²¹The Pharisees and the teachers of the law began thinking to themselves, "Who is this fellow who speaks blasphemy? Who can forgive sins but God alone?"

²²Jesus knew what they were thinking and asked, "Why are you thinking these things in your hearts? ²³Which is easier: to say, 'Your sins are forgiven,' or to say, 'Get up and walk'? ²⁴But that you may know that the Son of Man has authority on earth to forgive sins . . ." He said to the paralyzed man, "I tell you, get up, take your mat and go home." ²⁵Immediately he stood up in front of them, took what he had been lying on and went home praising God. ²⁶Everyone was amazed and gave praise to God. They were filled with awe and said, "We have seen remarkable things today."

The Calling of Levi

²⁷After this, Jesus went out and saw a tax collector by the name of Levi sitting at his tax booth. "Follow me," Jesus said to him, ²⁸and Levi got up, left everything and followed him.

²⁹Then Levi held a great banquet for Jesus at his house, and a large crowd of tax collectors and others were eating with them. ³⁰But the Pharisees and the teachers of the law who belonged to their sect complained to his disciples, "Why do you eat and drink with tax collectors and 'sinners'?"

³¹Jesus answered them, "It is not the healthy who need a doctor, but the sick. ³²I have not come to call the righteous, but sinners to repentance."

Jesus Questioned About Fasting

³³They said to him, "John's disciples often fast and pray, and so do the disciples of the Pharisees, but yours go on eating and drinking."

³⁴Jesus answered, "Can you make the guests of the bridegroom fast while he is with them? ³⁵But the time will come when the bridegroom will be taken from them; in those days they will fast."

³⁶He told them this parable: "No one tears a patch from a new garment and sews it on an old one. If he does, he will have torn the new garment, and the patch from the new will not match the old. ³⁷And no one pours new wine into old wineskins. If he does, the new wine will burst the skins, the wine will run out and the wineskins will be ruined. ³⁸No, new wine must be poured into new wineskins. ³⁹And no one after drinking old wine wants the new, for he says, 'The old is better.'"

Lord of the Sabbath

6 One Sabbath Jesus was going through the grainfields, and his disciples began to pick some heads of grain, rub them in their hands and eat the kernels. ²Some of the Pharisees asked, "Why are you doing what is unlawful on the Sabbath?"

³Jesus answered them, "Have you never read what David did when he and his companions were hungry? ⁴He entered the house of God, and taking the consecrated bread, he ate what is lawful only for priests to eat. And he also gave some to his companions." ⁵Then Jesus said to them, "The Son of Man is Lord of the Sabbath."

⁶On another Sabbath he went into the synagogue and was teaching, and a man was there whose right hand was shriveled. ⁷The Pharisees and the teachers of the law were looking for a reason to accuse Jesus, so they watched him closely to see if he would heal on the Sabbath. ⁸But Jesus knew what they were thinking and said to the man with the shriveled hand, "Get up and stand in front of everyone." So he got up and stood there.

⁹Then Jesus said to them, "I ask you, which is lawful on the Sabbath: to do good or to do evil, to save life or to destroy it?"

¹⁰He looked around at them all, and then said to the man, "Stretch out your hand." He did so, and his hand was completely restored. ¹¹But they were furious and began to discuss with one another what they might do to Jesus.

The Twelve Apostles

¹²One of those days Jesus went out to a mountainside to pray, and spent the night praying to God. ¹³When morning came, he called his disciples to him and chose twelve of them, whom he also designated apostles: ¹⁴Simon (whom he named

Peter), his brother Andrew, James, John, Philip, Bartholomew, 15Matthew, Thomas, James son of Alphaeus, Simon who was called the Zealot, 16Judas son of James, and Judas Iscariot, who became a traitor.

Blessings and Woes

17He went down with them and stood on a level place. A large crowd of his disci-

ples was there and a great number of people from all over Judea, from Jerusalem, and from the coast of Tyre and Sidon, 18who had come to hear him and to be healed of their diseases. Those troubled by evil*a* spirits were cured, 19and the people all tried to touch him, because power was coming from him and healing them all.

a18 Greek *unclean*

Trade in that German Import for a Life

DAILY INSIGHT

FRIDAY

Passage:
Luke 6:12–16, 20–23

Verse:
Luke 6:23

My lunch appointment with Chuck was set for 11:30, and he arrived on time. Although I had never actually met Chuck, he had called for this meeting; he sounded pretty desperate, and he was buying.

The quick trip to the restaurant was enjoyable. Why wouldn't it be, since I was riding in his brand-new, hunter-green Porsche with tan leather seats? *I wonder what this is about?* I couldn't help but think as we made small talk about the weather. When we arrived, our hostess found us a good spot in the far corner of the local hangout.

"My wife and I have been coming to your church school class for a couple of months," Chuck began, wasting no more time with more small talk. "We haven't gone to church for years, but our sons are beginning to ask me questions about life and stuff, so I thought church might be a good idea." My new friend hesitated for just a few moments, almost as though he was catching his breath. "Robert," he finally blurted out, "I'm lost."

The previous Sunday, I had talked about how men and women who aren't following Christ as the Master of their lives are lost. Chuck was referring to that kind of lostness. Until he finished his club sandwich and I took care of my cobb salad, we discussed what it meant to follow Christ. Two days later, he called my office to tell me that he had decided to follow Jesus and asked him to forgive his sins. Ten years later, Chuck and his wife decided he should attend seminary and go into full-time vocational

ministry. The Porsche was one of the first "victims" of Chuck's lifestyle change—a sacrifice Chuck gladly made.

Jesus called twelve men to follow him. Very little is said about what these men left behind, but they probably left behind one or two of the first-century equivalents of Chuck's hunter-green Porsche. Interestingly, although Jesus was speaking to a large crowd in today's passage, he was actually "looking at his disciples" (v. 20). Here were a dozen men who must have wondered about their sanity ... leaving everything that was comfortable, familiar and safe to follow Jesus. But with laser-beam clarity, the Master had taken aim at their wondering souls.

Choosing to be God's man in your home, in your town, or in your workplace may not earn you any immediate or visible commissions. You may experience rejection, alienation and loneliness because of this decision. There will be times when you wonder if you've done the right thing. But Jesus' promise to you and me is certain: *What we see today isn't all there is.*

Someday, because of this partnership with our Savior, we will "rejoice ... and leap for joy." Many people have gone before us; they experienced this same uncertainty, and because they are with their heavenly Father today, their satisfaction is complete ... hot cars and free lunches for all of eternity.

For your next devotional reading, go to page 1125.

²⁰Looking at his disciples, he said:

"Blessed are you who are poor,
    for yours is the kingdom of God.
²¹Blessed are you who hunger now,
    for you will be satisfied.
Blessed are you who weep now,
    for you will laugh.
²²Blessed are you when men hate you,
    when they exclude you and insult
        you
    and reject your name as evil,
        because of the Son of Man.

²³"Rejoice in that day and leap for joy, because great is your reward in heaven. For that is how their fathers treated the prophets.

²⁴"But woe to you who are rich,
    for you have already received your
        comfort.
²⁵Woe to you who are well fed now,
    for you will go hungry.
Woe to you who laugh now,
    for you will mourn and weep.
²⁶Woe to you when all men speak well of
        you,
    for that is how their fathers treated
        the false prophets.

Love for Enemies

²⁷"But I tell you who hear me: Love your enemies, do good to those who hate you, ²⁸bless those who curse you, pray for those who mistreat you. ²⁹If someone strikes you on one cheek, turn to him the other also. If someone takes your cloak, do not stop him from taking your tunic. ³⁰Give to everyone who asks you, and if anyone takes what belongs to you, do not demand it back. ³¹Do to others as you would have them do to you.

³²"If you love those who love you, what credit is that to you? Even 'sinners' love those who love them. ³³And if you do good to those who are good to you, what credit is that to you? Even 'sinners' do that. ³⁴And if you lend to those from whom you expect repayment, what credit is that to you? Even 'sinners' lend to 'sinners,' expecting to be repaid in full. ³⁵But love your enemies, do good to them, and lend to them without expecting to get anything back. Then your reward will be great, and you will be sons of the Most High, because he is kind to the ungrateful and wicked. ³⁶Be merciful, just as your Father is merciful.

Judging Others

³⁷"Do not judge, and you will not be judged. Do not condemn, and you will not be condemned. Forgive, and you will be forgiven. ³⁸Give, and it will be given to you. A good measure, pressed down, shaken together and running over, will be poured into your lap. For with the measure you use, it will be measured to you."

³⁹He also told them this parable: "Can a blind man lead a blind man? Will they not both fall into a pit? ⁴⁰A student is not above his teacher, but everyone who is fully trained will be like his teacher.

⁴¹"Why do you look at the speck of sawdust in your brother's eye and pay no attention to the plank in your own eye? ⁴²How can you say to your brother, 'Brother, let me take the speck out of your eye,' when you yourself fail to see the plank in your own eye? You hypocrite, first take the plank out of your eye, and then you will see clearly to remove the speck from your brother's eye.

A Tree and Its Fruit

⁴³"No good tree bears bad fruit, nor does a bad tree bear good fruit. ⁴⁴Each tree is recognized by its own fruit. People do not pick figs from thornbushes, or grapes from briers. ⁴⁵The good man brings good things out of the good stored up in his heart, and the evil man brings evil things out of the evil stored up in his heart. For out of the overflow of his heart his mouth speaks.

The Wise and Foolish Builders

⁴⁶"Why do you call me, 'Lord, Lord,' and do not do what I say? ⁴⁷I will show you what he is like who comes to me and hears my words and puts them into practice. ⁴⁸He is like a man building a house, who dug down deep and laid the foundation on rock. When a flood came, the torrent struck that house but could not shake it, because it was well built. ⁴⁹But the one who hears my words and does not put them into practice is like a man who built a house on the ground without a foundation. The moment the torrent struck that house, it collapsed and its destruction was complete."

The Faith of the Centurion

7 When Jesus had finished saying all this in the hearing of the people, he entered

Nice Two-by-Four, Dad

Key Verse: *"First take the plank out of your eye, and then you will see clearly to remove the speck from your brother's eye."* Luke 6:42

Text: Luke 6:41–42 *(Dad or child reads the text.)*

DAD READS: Let's say that one day I went to my favorite Italian restaurant for lunch, and let's say that the chef decided to put a lot of garlic in my spaghetti sauce—a whole lot of garlic.

Child reads: Let's say that same day, I have a cheeseburger for lunch, and let's say that there were a few onions sprinkled on my sandwich—just a few onions.

QUIET **TIMES** WITH **Dad**

DAD READS: And let's say that I pick you up from school that day. When you get in our car, I reach over and give you a little hug. "Wow," I say to you, "what did you have for lunch today? You sure smell like onions."

Child reads: When you reach over and hug me, all I can smell is garlic. It's very, very strong, and it smells terrible. I can hardly breathe. *Wow, Dad, you smell awful,* I think to myself, but I decide not to say anything because I don't want you to feel bad. But I'm very surprised when you say something about my onions.

DAD READS: While this story is a little silly, it reminds me of the verses we read today. Jesus was saying that some people were so concerned about what was wrong with other people that they completely overlooked the things that might be wrong with them. It's just like my saying something about the few onions on your breath when my own reeks with garlic.

Child reads: This is a very important thing for both of us to remember. It's easy to say bad things about other people and forget we may be missing things about ourselves that

are worse. Jesus said that sometimes we see the tiny piece of sawdust in someone else's eye but don't notice that there is a great big board in our own eye. This is a funny picture, but it's a very serious thing to think about.

DAD READS: Yes it is a serious thing ... for both you and me. Jesus really knew how to help people to understand this important truth. He was reminding us to be tough on ourselves and to be gentle with others ... not the other way around.

Child reads: I'm thankful for this lesson. I am going to try to always correct myself first so I'm not looking for little pieces of sawdust in other people's eye while I have a big ol' two-by-four in my own eye.

DAD READS: What an important thing this is for us to remember together. Let me pray this prayer with you:

Our Father in heaven, we love you. Thank you for reminding us today about the foolishness of judging others before we judge ourselves. Please help us work on our own lives before we try to work on others' lives. Thank you for this very important lesson today. We love you, and we thank you for your love. In Jesus' name, **Amen.**

For your next devotional reading, go to page 1132.

Capernaum. ²There a centurion's servant, whom his master valued highly, was sick and about to die. ³The centurion heard of Jesus and sent some elders of the Jews to him, asking him to come and heal his servant. ⁴When they came to Jesus, they pleaded earnestly with him, "This man deserves to have you do this, ⁵because he loves our nation and has built our synagogue." ⁶So Jesus went with them.

He was not far from the house when the centurion sent friends to say to him: "Lord, don't trouble yourself, for I do not deserve to have you come under my roof. ⁷That is why I did not even consider myself worthy to come to you. But say the word, and my servant will be healed. ⁸For I myself am a man under authority, with soldiers under me. I tell this one, 'Go,' and he goes; and that one, 'Come,' and he comes. I say to my servant, 'Do this,' and he does it."

⁹When Jesus heard this, he was amazed at him, and turning to the crowd following him, he said, "I tell you, I have not found such great faith even in Israel." ¹⁰Then the men who had been sent returned to the house and found the servant well.

Jesus Raises a Widow's Son

¹¹Soon afterward, Jesus went to a town called Nain, and his disciples and a large crowd went along with him. ¹²As he approached the town gate, a dead person was being carried out—the only son of his mother, and she was a widow. And a large crowd from the town was with her. ¹³When the Lord saw her, his heart went out to her and he said, "Don't cry."

¹⁴Then he went up and touched the coffin, and those carrying it stood still. He said, "Young man, I say to you, get up!" ¹⁵The dead man sat up and began to talk, and Jesus gave him back to his mother.

¹⁶They were all filled with awe and praised God. "A great prophet has appeared among us," they said. "God has come to help his people." ¹⁷This news about Jesus spread throughout Judea[a] and the surrounding country.

Jesus and John the Baptist

¹⁸John's disciples told him about all these things. Calling two of them, ¹⁹he sent them to the Lord to ask, "Are you the one who was to come, or should we expect someone else?"

²⁰When the men came to Jesus, they said, "John the Baptist sent us to you to ask, 'Are you the one who was to come, or should we expect someone else?' "

²¹At that very time Jesus cured many who had diseases, sicknesses and evil spirits, and gave sight to many who were blind. ²²So he replied to the messengers, "Go back and report to John what you have seen and heard: The blind receive sight, the lame walk, those who have leprosy[b] are cured, the deaf hear, the dead are raised, and the good news is preached to the poor. ²³Blessed is the man who does not fall away on account of me."

²⁴After John's messengers left, Jesus began to speak to the crowd about John: "What did you go out into the desert to see? A reed swayed by the wind? ²⁵If not, what did you go out to see? A man dressed in fine clothes? No, those who wear expensive clothes and indulge in luxury are in palaces. ²⁶But what did you go out to see? A prophet? Yes, I tell you, and more than a prophet. ²⁷This is the one about whom it is written:

> " 'I will send my messenger ahead of
> you,
> who will prepare your way before
> you.'[c]

²⁸I tell you, among those born of women there is no one greater than John; yet the one who is least in the kingdom of God is greater than he."

²⁹(All the people, even the tax collectors, when they heard Jesus' words, acknowledged that God's way was right, because they had been baptized by John. ³⁰But the Pharisees and experts in the law rejected God's purpose for themselves, because they had not been baptized by John.)

³¹"To what, then, can I compare the people of this generation? What are they like? ³²They are like children sitting in the marketplace and calling out to each other:

> " 'We played the flute for you,
> and you did not dance;
> we sang a dirge,
> and you did not cry.'

³³For John the Baptist came neither eating bread nor drinking wine, and you say, 'He has a demon.' ³⁴The Son of Man came eating and drinking, and you say, 'Here is a

---

a17 Or *the land of the Jews*   *b22* The Greek word was used for various diseases affecting the skin— not necessarily leprosy.   *c27* Mal. 3:1

glutton and a drunkard, a friend of tax collectors and "sinners." ' ³⁵But wisdom is proved right by all her children."

Jesus Anointed by a Sinful Woman

³⁶Now one of the Pharisees invited Jesus to have dinner with him, so he went to the Pharisee's house and reclined at the table. ³⁷When a woman who had lived a sinful life in that town learned that Jesus was eating at the Pharisee's house, she brought an alabaster jar of perfume, ³⁸and as she stood behind him at his feet weeping, she began to wet his feet with her tears. Then she wiped them with her hair, kissed them and poured perfume on them.

³⁹When the Pharisee who had invited him saw this, he said to himself, "If this man were a prophet, he would know who is touching him and what kind of woman she is—that she is a sinner."

⁴⁰Jesus answered him, "Simon, I have something to tell you."

"Tell me, teacher," he said.

⁴¹"Two men owed money to a certain moneylender. One owed him five hundred denarii,ᵃ and the other fifty. ⁴²Neither of them had the money to pay him back, so he canceled the debts of both. Now which of them will love him more?"

⁴³Simon replied, "I suppose the one who had the bigger debt canceled."

"You have judged correctly," Jesus said.

⁴⁴Then he turned toward the woman and said to Simon, "Do you see this woman? I came into your house. You did not give me any water for my feet, but she wet my feet with her tears and wiped them with her hair. ⁴⁵You did not give me a kiss, but this woman, from the time I entered, has not stopped kissing my feet. ⁴⁶You did not put oil on my head, but she has poured perfume on my feet. ⁴⁷Therefore, I tell you, her many sins have been forgiven—for she loved much. But he who has been forgiven little loves little."

⁴⁸Then Jesus said to her, "Your sins are forgiven."

⁴⁹The other guests began to say among themselves, "Who is this who even forgives sins?"

⁵⁰Jesus said to the woman, "Your faith has saved you; go in peace."

The Parable of the Sower

8 After this, Jesus traveled about from one town and village to another, proclaiming the good news of the kingdom of God. The Twelve were with him, ²and also some women who had been cured of evil spirits and diseases: Mary (called Magdalene) from whom seven demons had come out; ³Joanna the wife of Cuza, the manager of Herod's household; Susanna; and many others. These women were helping to support them out of their own means.

⁴While a large crowd was gathering and people were coming to Jesus from town after town, he told this parable: ⁵"A farmer went out to sow his seed. As he was scattering the seed, some fell along the path; it was trampled on, and the birds of the air ate it up. ⁶Some fell on rock, and when it came up, the plants withered because they had no moisture. ⁷Other seed fell among thorns, which grew up with it and choked the plants. ⁸Still other seed fell on good soil. It came up and yielded a crop, a hundred times more than was sown."

When he said this, he called out, "He who has ears to hear, let him hear."

⁹His disciples asked him what this parable meant. ¹⁰He said, "The knowledge of the secrets of the kingdom of God has been given to you, but to others I speak in parables, so that,

" 'though seeing, they may not see;
   though hearing, they may not
      understand.'ᵇ

¹¹"This is the meaning of the parable: The seed is the word of God. ¹²Those along the path are the ones who hear, and then the devil comes and takes away the word from their hearts, so that they may not believe and be saved. ¹³Those on the rock are the ones who receive the word with joy when they hear it, but they have no root. They believe for a while, but in the time of testing they fall away. ¹⁴The seed that fell among thorns stands for those who hear, but as they go on their way they are choked by life's worries, riches and pleasures, and they do not mature. ¹⁵But the seed on good soil stands for those with a noble and good heart, who hear the word, retain it, and by persevering produce a crop.

A Lamp on a Stand

¹⁶"No one lights a lamp and hides it in a jar or puts it under a bed. Instead, he puts it on a stand, so that those who come in

---

ᵃ41 A denarius was a coin worth about a day's wages.   ᵇ10 Isaiah 6:9

can see the light. [17]For there is nothing hidden that will not be disclosed, and nothing concealed that will not be known or brought out into the open. [18]Therefore consider carefully how you listen. Whoever has will be given more; whoever does not have, even what he thinks he has will be taken from him."

Jesus' Mother and Brothers

[19]Now Jesus' mother and brothers came to see him, but they were not able to get near him because of the crowd. [20]Someone told him, "Your mother and brothers are standing outside, wanting to see you."

[21]He replied, "My mother and brothers are those who hear God's word and put it into practice."

Jesus Calms the Storm

[22]One day Jesus said to his disciples, "Let's go over to the other side of the lake." So they got into a boat and set out. [23]As they sailed, he fell asleep. A squall came down on the lake, so that the boat was being swamped, and they were in great danger.

[24]The disciples went and woke him, saying, "Master, Master, we're going to drown!"

He got up and rebuked the wind and the raging waters; the storm subsided, and all was calm. [25]"Where is your faith?" he asked his disciples.

In fear and amazement they asked one another, "Who is this? He commands even the winds and the water, and they obey him."

The Healing of a Demon-possessed Man

[26]They sailed to the region of the Gerasenes,[a] which is across the lake from Galilee. [27]When Jesus stepped ashore, he was met by a demon-possessed man from the town. For a long time this man had not worn clothes or lived in a house, but had lived in the tombs. [28]When he saw Jesus, he cried out and fell at his feet, shouting at the top of his voice, "What do you want with me, Jesus, Son of the Most High God? I beg you, don't torture me!" [29]For Jesus had commanded the evil[b] spirit to come out of the man. Many times it had seized him, and though he was chained hand and foot and kept under guard, he had broken his chains and had been driven by the demon into solitary places.

[30]Jesus asked him, "What is your name?"

"Legion," he replied, because many demons had gone into him. [31]And they begged him repeatedly not to order them to go into the Abyss.

[32]A large herd of pigs was feeding there on the hillside. The demons begged Jesus to let them go into them, and he gave them permission. [33]When the demons came out of the man, they went into the pigs, and the herd rushed down the steep bank into the lake and was drowned.

[34]When those tending the pigs saw what had happened, they ran off and reported this in the town and countryside, [35]and the people went out to see what had happened. When they came to Jesus, they found the man from whom the demons had gone out, sitting at Jesus' feet, dressed and in his right mind; and they were afraid. [36]Those who had seen it told the people how the demon-possessed man had been cured. [37]Then all the people of the region of the Gerasenes asked Jesus to leave them, because they were overcome with fear. So he got into the boat and left.

[38]The man from whom the demons had gone out begged to go with him, but Jesus sent him away, saying, [39]"Return home and tell how much God has done for you." So the man went away and told all over town how much Jesus had done for him.

A Dead Girl and a Sick Woman

[40]Now when Jesus returned, a crowd welcomed him, for they were all expecting him. [41]Then a man named Jairus, a ruler of the synagogue, came and fell at Jesus' feet, pleading with him to come to his house [42]because his only daughter, a girl of about twelve, was dying.

As Jesus was on his way, the crowds almost crushed him. [43]And a woman was there who had been subject to bleeding for twelve years,[c] but no one could heal her. [44]She came up behind him and touched the edge of his cloak, and immediately her bleeding stopped.

[45]"Who touched me?" Jesus asked.

When they all denied it, Peter said, "Master, the people are crowding and pressing against you."

[46]But Jesus said, "Someone touched

[a]26 Some manuscripts *Gadarenes*; other manuscripts *Gergesenes*; also in verse 37   [b]29 Greek *unclean*   [c]43 Many manuscripts *years, and she had spent all she had on doctors*

me; I know that power has gone out from me."

⁴⁷Then the woman, seeing that she could not go unnoticed, came trembling and fell at his feet. In the presence of all the people, she told why she had touched him and how she had been instantly healed. ⁴⁸Then he said to her, "Daughter, your faith has healed you. Go in peace."

⁴⁹While Jesus was still speaking, someone came from the house of Jairus, the synagogue ruler. "Your daughter is dead," he said. "Don't bother the teacher any more."

⁵⁰Hearing this, Jesus said to Jairus, "Don't be afraid; just believe, and she will be healed."

⁵¹When he arrived at the house of Jairus, he did not let anyone go in with him except Peter, John and James, and the child's father and mother. ⁵²Meanwhile, all the people were wailing and mourning for her. "Stop wailing," Jesus said. "She is not dead but asleep."

⁵³They laughed at him, knowing that she was dead. ⁵⁴But he took her by the hand and said, "My child, get up!" ⁵⁵Her spirit returned, and at once she stood up. Then Jesus told them to give her something to eat. ⁵⁶Her parents were astonished, but he ordered them not to tell anyone what had happened.

Jesus Sends Out the Twelve

9 When Jesus had called the Twelve together, he gave them power and authority to drive out all demons and to cure diseases, ²and he sent them out to preach the kingdom of God and to heal the sick. ³He told them: "Take nothing for the journey—no staff, no bag, no bread, no money, no extra tunic. ⁴Whatever house you enter, stay there until you leave that town. ⁵If people do not welcome you, shake the dust off your feet when you leave their town, as a testimony against them." ⁶So they set out and went from village to village, preaching the gospel and healing people everywhere.

⁷Now Herod the tetrarch heard about all that was going on. And he was perplexed, because some were saying that John had been raised from the dead, ⁸others that Elijah had appeared, and still others that one of the prophets of long ago had come back to life. ⁹But Herod said, "I beheaded John. Who, then, is this I hear such things about?" And he tried to see him.

Jesus Feeds the Five Thousand

¹⁰When the apostles returned, they reported to Jesus what they had done. Then he took them with him and they withdrew by themselves to a town called Bethsaida, ¹¹but the crowds learned about it and followed him. He welcomed them and spoke to them about the kingdom of God, and healed those who needed healing.

¹²Late in the afternoon the Twelve came to him and said, "Send the crowd away so they can go to the surrounding villages and countryside and find food and lodging, because we are in a remote place here."

¹³He replied, "You give them something to eat."

They answered, "We have only five loaves of bread and two fish—unless we go and buy food for all this crowd." ¹⁴(About five thousand men were there.)

But he said to his disciples, "Have them sit down in groups of about fifty each." ¹⁵The disciples did so, and everybody sat down. ¹⁶Taking the five loaves and the two fish and looking up to heaven, he gave thanks and broke them. Then he gave them to the disciples to set before the people. ¹⁷They all ate and were satisfied, and the disciples picked up twelve basketfuls of broken pieces that were left over.

Peter's Confession of Christ

¹⁸Once when Jesus was praying in private and his disciples were with him, he asked them, "Who do the crowds say I am?"

¹⁹They replied, "Some say John the Baptist; others say Elijah; and still others, that one of the prophets of long ago has come back to life."

²⁰"But what about you?" he asked. "Who do you say I am?"

Peter answered, "The Christ*ᵃ* of God."

²¹Jesus strictly warned them not to tell this to anyone. ²²And he said, "The Son of Man must suffer many things and be rejected by the elders, chief priests and teachers of the law, and he must be killed and on the third day be raised to life."

²³Then he said to them all: "If anyone would come after me, he must deny himself and take up his cross daily and follow me. ²⁴For whoever wants to save his life will lose it, but whoever loses his life for

---

ᵃ20 Or *Messiah*

me will save it. [25]What good is it for a man to gain the whole world, and yet lose or forfeit his very self? [26]If anyone is ashamed of me and my words, the Son of Man will be ashamed of him when he comes in his glory and in the glory of the Father and of the holy angels. [27]I tell you the truth, some who are standing here will not taste death before they see the kingdom of God."

The Transfiguration

[28]About eight days after Jesus said this, he took Peter, John and James with him and went up onto a mountain to pray. [29]As he was praying, the appearance of his face changed, and his clothes became as bright as a flash of lightning. [30]Two men, Moses and Elijah, [31]appeared in glorious splendor, talking with Jesus. They spoke about his departure, which he was about to bring to fulfillment at Jerusalem. [32]Peter and his companions were very sleepy, but when they became fully awake, they saw his glory and the two men standing with him. [33]As the men were leaving Jesus, Peter said to him, "Master, it is good for us to be here. Let us put up three shelters—one for you, one for Moses and one for Elijah." (He did not know what he was saying.)
[34]While he was speaking, a cloud appeared and enveloped them, and they were afraid as they entered the cloud. [35]A voice came from the cloud, saying, "This is my Son, whom I have chosen; listen to him." [36]When the voice had spoken, they found that Jesus was alone. The disciples kept this to themselves, and told no one at that time what they had seen.

The Healing of a Boy With an Evil Spirit

[37]The next day, when they came down from the mountain, a large crowd met him. [38]A man in the crowd called out, "Teacher, I beg you to look at my son, for he is my only child. [39]A spirit seizes him and he suddenly screams; it throws him into convulsions so that he foams at the mouth. It scarcely ever leaves him and is destroying him. [40]I begged your disciples to drive it out, but they could not."
[41]"O unbelieving and perverse generation," Jesus replied, "how long shall I stay with you and put up with you? Bring your son here."
[42]Even while the boy was coming, the demon threw him to the ground in a convulsion. But Jesus rebuked the evil[a] spirit,

healed the boy and gave him back to his father. [43]And they were all amazed at the greatness of God.
While everyone was marveling at all that Jesus did, he said to his disciples, [44]"Listen carefully to what I am about to tell you: The Son of Man is going to be betrayed into the hands of men." [45]But they did not understand what this meant. It was hidden from them, so that they did not grasp it, and they were afraid to ask him about it.

Who Will Be the Greatest?

[46]An argument started among the disciples as to which of them would be the greatest. [47]Jesus, knowing their thoughts, took a little child and had him stand beside him. [48]Then he said to them, "Whoever welcomes this little child in my name welcomes me; and whoever welcomes me welcomes the one who sent me. For he who is least among you all—he is the greatest."
[49]"Master," said John, "we saw a man driving out demons in your name and we tried to stop him, because he is not one of us."
[50]"Do not stop him," Jesus said, "for whoever is not against you is for you."

Samaritan Opposition

[51]As the time approached for him to be taken up to heaven, Jesus resolutely set out for Jerusalem. [52]And he sent messengers on ahead, who went into a Samaritan village to get things ready for him; [53]but the people there did not welcome him, because he was heading for Jerusalem. [54]When the disciples James and John saw this, they asked, "Lord, do you want us to call fire down from heaven to destroy them[b]?" [55]But Jesus turned and rebuked them, [56]and[c] they went to another village.

The Cost of Following Jesus

[57]As they were walking along the road, a man said to him, "I will follow you wherever you go."
[58]Jesus replied, "Foxes have holes and birds of the air have nests, but the Son of Man has no place to lay his head."
[59]He said to another man, "Follow me."

---

[a]42 Greek unclean   [b]54 Some manuscripts them, even as Elijah did   [c]55,56 Some manuscripts them. And he said, "You do not know what kind of spirit you are of, for the Son of Man did not come to destroy men's lives, but to save them." [56]And

But the man replied, "Lord, first let me go and bury my father."

⁶⁰Jesus said to him, "Let the dead bury their own dead, but you go and proclaim the kingdom of God."

⁶¹Still another said, "I will follow you, Lord; but first let me go back and say good-by to my family."

⁶²Jesus replied, "No one who puts his hand to the plow and looks back is fit for service in the kingdom of God."

Jesus Sends Out the Seventy-two

10 After this the Lord appointed seventy-two[a] others and sent them two by two ahead of him to every town and place where he was about to go. ²He told them, "The harvest is plentiful, but the workers are few. Ask the Lord of the harvest, therefore, to send out workers into his harvest field. ³Go! I am sending you out like lambs among wolves. ⁴Do not take a purse or bag or sandals; and do not greet anyone on the road.

⁵"When you enter a house, first say, 'Peace to this house.' ⁶If a man of peace is there, your peace will rest on him; if not, it will return to you. ⁷Stay in that house, eating and drinking whatever they give you, for the worker deserves his wages. Do not move around from house to house.

⁸"When you enter a town and are welcomed, eat what is set before you. ⁹Heal the sick who are there and tell them, 'The kingdom of God is near you.' ¹⁰But when you enter a town and are not welcomed, go into its streets and say, ¹¹'Even the dust of your town that sticks to our feet we wipe off against you. Yet be sure of this: The kingdom of God is near.' ¹²I tell you, it will be more bearable on that day for Sodom than for that town.

¹³"Woe to you, Korazin! Woe to you, Bethsaida! For if the miracles that were performed in you had been performed in Tyre and Sidon, they would have repented long ago, sitting in sackcloth and ashes. ¹⁴But it will be more bearable for Tyre and Sidon at the judgment than for you. ¹⁵And you, Capernaum, will you be lifted up to the skies? No, you will go down to the depths.[b]

¹⁶"He who listens to you listens to me; he who rejects you rejects me; but he who rejects me rejects him who sent me."

¹⁷The seventy-two returned with joy and said, "Lord, even the demons submit to us in your name."

¹⁸He replied, "I saw Satan fall like lightning from heaven. ¹⁹I have given you

---

[a]1 Some manuscripts *seventy*; also in verse 17
[b]15 Greek *Hades*

HEY DAD

In the parable of the Good Samaritan, why didn't the priest or Levite help the wounded man?

Text: Luke 10:25–37

It seems like priests and Levites would be the *first* people to help someone in need. Was Jesus saying that these men had hard hearts and did not care about hurting people? While that might have been the case, Jesus was probably making a different point.

According to Jewish law, a person who touched a dead person was considered ceremonially unclean for seven days (Numbers 19:11). During that period, a priest or Levite could not serve in the temple. So, if either man had reached out to help this victim and he was dead or died while in his care, the priest or Levite would have had to stay out of work for a whole week. Perhaps these men thought God would be more pleased if they performed their temple duties than if they helped this man. They were wrong.

The *letter* of the law told the priest and the Levite that they had temple duties to perform. But the *greatest* law commanded them to love their neighbor (v. 27). In this case, a Samaritan—someone whom the Jews considered lawless and unbelieving—actually pleased God the most.

Ward, K. (Ed.). (1987). Jesus and His Times. Pleasantville, New York: The Reader's Digest Association.

For a complete listing of Questions Kids Ask, turn to page 1435.

authority to trample on snakes and scorpions and to overcome all the power of the enemy; nothing will harm you. [20]However, do not rejoice that the spirits submit to you, but rejoice that your names are written in heaven."

[21]At that time Jesus, full of joy through the Holy Spirit, said, "I praise you, Father, Lord of heaven and earth, because you have hidden these things from the wise and learned, and revealed them to little children. Yes, Father, for this was your good pleasure.

[22]"All things have been committed to me by my Father. No one knows who the Son is except the Father, and no one knows who the Father is except the Son and those to whom the Son chooses to reveal him."

[23]Then he turned to his disciples and said privately, "Blessed are the eyes that see what you see. [24]For I tell you that

Stop Stepping over Your Family

The woman at the other end of the phone was furious. Her husband had, for many years, handled the family's finances foolishly, and she had just discovered a whole bunch of needless expenditures. "We're broke again," she wailed. "I've had it with Sid!"

Over the next several months I met with Sid. As we talked, I discovered that the money thing was only a symptom of a much bigger problem. Sid was driven. He would see something he wanted to accomplish, focus on this goal, and ignore everything else ... his wife, his family, his household responsibilities and his friends. He was on a mission and could not be distracted!

"Do you know what my problem is?" Sid finally admitted one day over cheese enchiladas. "I have a problem seeing."

"I didn't know you needed glasses," I replied, not having any idea where Sid was going.

"No, not a problem with my eyesight," he said. "I have a problem paying attention to anyone else but myself. I'm so focused on my tasks and goals that I'm literally stepping over the people who love me most."

This is exactly the message of the Good Samaritan. The Levite and the priest were each focused on what they had to do: take care of the temple and lead the people in worship, two extremely worthwhile assignments. So when they saw the injured man on the roadside, they didn't really *see* him. They saw themselves and their own tasks

DAILY INSIGHT

MONDAY

Passage:
Luke 10:30–37

Verse:
Luke 10:37

first, and since these jobs were so important, they looked past the person in need.

This story is about American dads. It's about you and me. It's a story that contains truth that simply cannot be ignored. We are focused—*really* focused. We're on a mission, and we'll not have our attention diverted. We are, after all, winners in the game of life, and we intend to keep winning.

Except for one thing. All of this focus on our tasks is actually focus on *ourselves. Oh, yeah?* we might rationalize, *we're really doing this for our families!* Are we saying that we've decided that it's actually good for the ones we love to lie there in the ditch, bleeding, while we hustle to town to close one more deal? Nice try.

Jesus was telling his disciples—and this includes you and me—that even God-jobs are no excuse for missing those who are lying at our feet ... those who need us even more than the parishioners needed religious help from the priest and the Levite. Wow, what a lesson.

By the way, Sid and his wife worked it out. They actually separated for several months, but Sid's wife allowed him to come back to his house for dinner every day. His assignment was to do the dishes. In no time, Sid's wife fell madly in love with her man, standing with a dishrag in his hand. She fell in love again with a man who had stopped stepping over her.

For your next devotional reading, go to page 1134.

many prophets and kings wanted to see what you see but did not see it, and to hear what you hear but did not hear it."

The Parable of the Good Samaritan

25On one occasion an expert in the law stood up to test Jesus. "Teacher," he asked, "what must I do to inherit eternal life?"

26"What is written in the Law?" he replied. "How do you read it?"

27He answered: " 'Love the Lord your God with all your heart and with all your soul and with all your strength and with all your mind'*a*; and, 'Love your neighbor as yourself.'*b*"

28"You have answered correctly," Jesus replied. "Do this and you will live."

29But he wanted to justify himself, so he asked Jesus, "And who is my neighbor?"

30In reply Jesus said: "A man was going down from Jerusalem to Jericho, when he fell into the hands of robbers. They stripped him of his clothes, beat him and went away, leaving him half dead. **31**A priest happened to be going down the same road, and when he saw the man, he passed by on the other side. **32**So too, a Levite, when he came to the place and saw him, passed by on the other side. **33**But a Samaritan, as he traveled, came where the man was; and when he saw him, he took pity on him. **34**He went to him and bandaged his wounds, pouring on oil and wine. Then he put the man on his own donkey, took him to an inn and took care of him. **35**The next day he took out two silver coins*c* and gave them to the innkeeper. 'Look after him,' he said, 'and when I return, I will reimburse you for any extra expense you may have.'

36"Which of these three do you think was a neighbor to the man who fell into the hands of robbers?"

37The expert in the law replied, "The one who had mercy on him."
Jesus told him, "Go and do likewise."

At the Home of Martha and Mary

38As Jesus and his disciples were on their way, he came to a village where a woman named Martha opened her home to him. **39**She had a sister called Mary, who sat at the Lord's feet listening to what he said. **40**But Martha was distracted by all the preparations that had to be made. She came to him and asked, "Lord, don't you care that my sister has left me to do the work by myself? Tell her to help me!"

41"Martha, Martha," the Lord answered, "you are worried and upset about many things, **42**but only one thing is needed.*d* Mary has chosen what is better, and it will not be taken away from her."

Jesus' Teaching on Prayer

11 One day Jesus was praying in a certain place. When he finished, one of his disciples said to him, "Lord, teach us to pray, just as John taught his disciples."

2He said to them, "When you pray, say:

" 'Father,*e*
hallowed be your name,
your kingdom come.*f*
3Give us each day our daily bread.
4Forgive us our sins,
    for we also forgive everyone who sins against us.*g*
And lead us not into temptation.*h* ' "

5Then he said to them, "Suppose one of you has a friend, and he goes to him at midnight and says, 'Friend, lend me three loaves of bread, **6**because a friend of mine on a journey has come to me, and I have nothing to set before him.'

7"Then the one inside answers, 'Don't bother me. The door is already locked, and my children are with me in bed. I can't get up and give you anything.' **8**I tell you, though he will not get up and give him the bread because he is his friend, yet because of the man's boldness*i* he will get up and give him as much as he needs.

9"So I say to you: Ask and it will be given to you; seek and you will find; knock and the door will be opened to you. **10**For everyone who asks receives; he who seeks finds; and to him who knocks, the door will be opened.

11"Which of you fathers, if your son asks for*j* a fish, will give him a snake instead? **12**Or if he asks for an egg, will give him a scorpion? **13**If you then, though you are evil, know how to give good gifts to your children, how much more will your Father in heaven give the Holy Spirit to those who ask him!"

*a*27 Deut. 6:5   *b*27 Lev. 19:18   *c*35 Greek *two denarii*   *d*42 Some manuscripts *but few things are needed—or only one*   *e*2 Some manuscripts *Our Father in heaven*   *f*2 Some manuscripts *come. May your will be done on earth as it is in heaven.*   *g*4 Greek *everyone who is indebted to us*   *h*4 Some manuscripts *temptation but deliver us from the evil one*   *i*8 Or *persistence*   *j*11 Some manuscripts *for bread, will give him a stone; or if he asks for*

Jesus and Beelzebub

14Jesus was driving out a demon that was mute. When the demon left, the man who had been mute spoke, and the crowd was amazed. **15**But some of them said, "By Beelzebub,*a* the prince of demons, he is driving out demons." **16**Others tested him by asking for a sign from heaven.

17Jesus knew their thoughts and said to them: "Any kingdom divided against itself will be ruined, and a house divided against itself will fall. **18**If Satan is divided against himself, how can his kingdom stand? I say this because you claim that I drive out demons by Beelzebub. **19**Now if I drive out demons by Beelzebub, by whom do your followers drive them out? So then, they will be your judges. **20**But if I drive out demons by the finger of God, then the kingdom of God has come to you.

21"When a strong man, fully armed, guards his own house, his possessions are safe. **22**But when someone stronger attacks and overpowers him, he takes away the armor in which the man trusted and divides up the spoils.

a15 Greek *Beezeboul* or *Beelzeboul*; also in verses 18 and 19

Oh, Honey, You Really Shouldn't Have!

DAILY INSIGHT

How are you at gift giving? Now, I didn't say, "How are you at spending adequate—perhaps even excessive—amounts of money on gifts."

My first lesson about this art form started with our first Christmas morning as husband and wife. Although we had exchanged a few small gifts the night before, I had saved my "big gift" for this occasion.

It was a big box. In fact, I had wrapped it all by myself. (What a guy.) "Tear into it," I announced, unable to delay the glory I would experience, basking in the glow of my wife's delight. But when Bobbie saw what it was, her eyes began to well up with tears. In a moment, the tears turned into an actual, bona fide cry.

Since that moment, I have learned two very important things about gift-giving. First, a gift to a woman that has a power cord is not a gift … I repeat, *if it must be plugged in to work, it will not count*. Second, in order for a gift to truly be recognized as one that says, "I love you so much," the recipient's personality and actual heartfelt needs must be carefully studied. This takes time.

Today's text speaks exactly to this issue. Jesus said that because God is our loving Father, he knows precisely who we are and what we need. So he's a superior gift-giver. His blessings are always wow-you-

TUESDAY

Passage: Luke 11:11–13

Verse: Luke 11:11

shouldn't-have perfect. "If your son wants a fish," Jesus challenged his followers, " you wouldn't make the mistake of giving him a snake." How well do you know your wife? How well do you know your children? When it's time for Christmas or a birthday or an anniversary or Valentine's Day (and *please* don't overlook Valentine's Day), do you dash out and grab the first thing you see? The line, "Hey, at least I remembered," may work for stand-up comics, but it isn't going to get any rave reviews in your house.

Be a great gift giver. Keep your ears and eyes open. When your wife makes a comment about someone's beautiful scarf, take note of the colors and style and write it down. When you see your son staring at his friend's new baseball glove, make a note of it. When your daughter sighs at the sight of something special, jot it in your day planner.

Before you know it, you'll hear, "Oh, Honey, you shouldn't have!" and "Dad, how did you know?" You'll win the Gift-giver of the Year Award every time. Best of all, you'll actually experience the truth of the phrase, "it's better to give than to receive."

Ignore this lesson at your own peril, my friend. Please trust me on this one.

For your next devotional reading, go to page 1137.

23"He who is not with me is against me, and he who does not gather with me, scatters.

24"When an evil[a] spirit comes out of a man, it goes through arid places seeking rest and does not find it. Then it says, 'I will return to the house I left.' 25When it arrives, it finds the house swept clean and put in order. 26Then it goes and takes seven other spirits more wicked than itself, and they go in and live there. And the final condition of that man is worse than the first."

27As Jesus was saying these things, a woman in the crowd called out, "Blessed is the mother who gave you birth and nursed you."

28He replied, "Blessed rather are those who hear the word of God and obey it."

The Sign of Jonah

29As the crowds increased, Jesus said, "This is a wicked generation. It asks for a miraculous sign, but none will be given it except the sign of Jonah. 30For as Jonah was a sign to the Ninevites, so also will the Son of Man be to this generation. 31The Queen of the South will rise at the judgment with the men of this generation and condemn them; for she came from the ends of the earth to listen to Solomon's wisdom, and now one[b] greater than Solomon is here. 32The men of Nineveh will stand up at the judgment with this generation and condemn it; for they repented at the preaching of Jonah, and now one greater than Jonah is here.

The Lamp of the Body

33"No one lights a lamp and puts it in a place where it will be hidden, or under a bowl. Instead he puts it on its stand, so that those who come in may see the light. 34Your eye is the lamp of your body. When your eyes are good, your whole body also is full of light. But when they are bad, your body also is full of darkness. 35See to it, then, that the light within you is not darkness. 36Therefore, if your whole body is

---

[a]24 Greek *unclean* [b]31 Or *something*; also in verse 32

The Master of the Open Hand
Generous fathers

"If you then, though you are evil, know how to give good gifts to your children, how much more will your Father in heaven give the Holy Spirit to those who ask him!" (11:13).

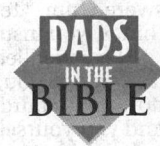

DADS IN THE BIBLE

Text: Luke 11:5–13

"How much do you love your child?" someone may ask you. "There isn't anything I wouldn't do for my son or my daughter. I'd give my life for them," you would spontaneously respond.

That's why this passage might initially strike you as odd. Jesus is teaching his disciples about prayer—about coming to God and laying their requests at his feet. To illustrate his point, he tells two stories. The first one demonstrates the need for persistence in prayer. The second one strikes at the heart of every father. "Which of you fathers, if your son asks for a fish, will give him a snake instead? Or if he asks for an egg, will give him a scorpion?" (v. 11).

Well, those are odd questions, you might say to yourself. *Of course, no father alive would do such awful things.* This is probably the same response the disciples had in response to Jesus' rhetorical query.

Then Jesus delivered the clincher. "If you then, though you are evil, know how to give good gifts to your children, how much more will your Father in heaven give the Holy Spirit to those who ask him!" (11:13).

The message to the people standing there should have been clear. Jesus was telling them to hold their possessions lightly. Children need to receive good gifts from their fallible dads. Then they can count on receiving even better gifts from their perfect Father—the Master of the open hand.

For a complete listing of Dads in the Bible, turn to page 1434.

full of light, and no part of it dark, it will be completely lighted, as when the light of a lamp shines on you."

Six Woes

37When Jesus had finished speaking, a Pharisee invited him to eat with him; so he went in and reclined at the table. **38**But the Pharisee, noticing that Jesus did not first wash before the meal, was surprised.

39Then the Lord said to him, "Now then, you Pharisees clean the outside of the cup and dish, but inside you are full of greed and wickedness. **40**You foolish people! Did not the one who made the outside make the inside also? **41**But give what is inside the dish,^{a} to the poor, and everything will be clean for you.

42"Woe to you Pharisees, because you give God a tenth of your mint, rue and all other kinds of garden herbs, but you neglect justice and the love of God. You should have practiced the latter without leaving the former undone.

43"Woe to you Pharisees, because you love the most important seats in the synagogues and greetings in the marketplaces.

44"Woe to you, because you are like unmarked graves, which men walk over without knowing it."

45One of the experts in the law answered him, "Teacher, when you say these things, you insult us also."

46Jesus replied, "And you experts in the law, woe to you, because you load people down with burdens they can hardly carry, and you yourselves will not lift one finger to help them.

47"Woe to you, because you build tombs for the prophets, and it was your forefathers who killed them. **48**So you testify that you approve of what your forefathers did; they killed the prophets, and you build their tombs. **49**Because of this, God in his wisdom said, 'I will send them prophets and apostles, some of whom they will kill and others they will persecute.' **50**Therefore this generation will be held responsible for the blood of all the prophets that has been shed since the beginning of the world, **51**from the blood of Abel to the blood of Zechariah, who was killed between the altar and the sanctuary. Yes, I tell you, this generation will be held responsible for it all.

52"Woe to you experts in the law, because you have taken away the key to knowledge. You yourselves have not entered, and you have hindered those who were entering."

53When Jesus left there, the Pharisees and the teachers of the law began to oppose him fiercely and to besiege him with questions, **54**waiting to catch him in something he might say.

Warnings and Encouragements

12 Meanwhile, when a crowd of many thousands had gathered, so that they were trampling on one another, Jesus began to speak first to his disciples, saying: "Be on your guard against the yeast of the Pharisees, which is hypocrisy. **2**There is nothing concealed that will not be dis-

^{a}41 Or *what you have*

HEY DAD
Does God really know me?

Text: Luke 12:7

God knows each of us in every detail. He knows what we like to eat, what kind of music we like, and our favorite color. Jesus said that God cares so much about each one of us that he has even numbered every hair on our heads!

Think about someone you know very well. You may know what time this person wakes up every day, what makes him or her laugh, and even whether or not he or she likes tomatoes. But do you know how many hairs are on this person's head?

The average person has about 125,000 hairs on his or her head. Every day when you brush your hair, you probably lose about fifty to seventy-five hairs (most of which grow back!). So every single day, the number of hairs on your head changes. But God still knows how many are there!

Jesus gave us this example so that we would understand just how personally God knows us. We're extremely important to him. Nobody knows us better!

QUESTIONS KIDS ASK

For a complete listing of Questions Kids Ask, turn to page 1435.

closed, or hidden that will not be made known. ³What you have said in the dark will be heard in the daylight, and what you have whispered in the ear in the inner rooms will be proclaimed from the roofs.

⁴"I tell you, my friends, do not be afraid of those who kill the body and after that can do no more. ⁵But I will show you whom you should fear: Fear him who, after the killing of the body, has power to throw you into hell. Yes, I tell you, fear him. ⁶Are not five sparrows sold for two pennies*? Yet not one of them is forgotten by God. ⁷Indeed, the very hairs of your head are all numbered. Don't be afraid; you are worth more than many sparrows.

⁸"I tell you, whoever acknowledges me before men, the Son of Man will also acknowledge him before the angels of God. ⁹But he who disowns me before men will be disowned before the angels of God. ¹⁰And everyone who speaks a word

*6 Greek *two assaria*

Of Bubble Gum and Full Barns

DAILY INSIGHT

WEDNESDAY

Passage:
Luke 12:13–21

Verse:
Luke 12:21

When I was a little kid, bubble gum was a big deal. Bazooka Joe® was as important to us as any political leader or sports hero.

Maybe one of the things that made bubble gum so appealing was that we were strongly discouraged from chewing it ... "strongly" as in, the federal government "strongly" warns you not to ignore those notices you get from the Internal Revenue Service. My mother told us that when she saw a kid blowing bubbles, "it looked like their insides were coming out." And since she didn't want her own children publicly displaying their entrails, she told us not to chew it.

One day my brother Ken happened onto a bunch of money. He lost his good sense, and plotted a walk to the corner market. His plan was to spend all his money on gum, then "chew it all on his walk back home." He knew that he had to return to the house with no remaining evidence.

After making his unauthorized purchase, Ken began slowly walking back home. One by one, he carefully unwrapped the pieces of gum, perusing so many Bazooka Joe® comics that he could have turned this in as summer reading. Ken was in heaven—reading, chewing and blowing bubbles.

As he walked, it dawned on him that all of this gum in his mouth was making his jaw sore. The horrendous glob was even beginning to gag him. This excursion into shameless and lavish spending wasn't as much fun as he had hoped it would be. Nonetheless, he tried to push through these contrary feelings and continued his homeward trek.

And then, one block from home, it happened. Just as he was blowing another bubble, our mother drove by. Imagine the terror of this moment. Ken should have known better: parents always show up.

When is enough, enough? When will we actually be satisfied with what we have, content to simply enjoy it and not continue pushing for more? I know this sounds fairly un-American, but why am I so driven to dissatisfaction with something when its only flaw is that there is a newer model on the market?

Jesus took aim at a lesson from a businessman who had had a superior year. Not content with a full barn, he tore it down to build a bigger barn ... more room for the glut. In the process, this successful man became self-sufficient. "I don't need anything or anyone," he must have told his adoring friends. "I don't even need God."

Just then the Sovereign Lord of the universe drove by. The foolish man met his Maker. The barn and its contents were sold at auction, and everyone forgot this great man. Somehow he had forgotten that when he got home, his pockets would be empty anyway. He should have known better: God always shows up.

For your next devotional reading, go to page 1141.

against the Son of Man will be forgiven, but anyone who blasphemes against the Holy Spirit will not be forgiven. [11]"When you are brought before synagogues, rulers and authorities, do not worry about how you will defend yourselves or what you will say, [12]for the Holy Spirit will teach you at that time what you should say."

The Parable of the Rich Fool

[13]Someone in the crowd said to him, "Teacher, tell my brother to divide the inheritance with me."

[14]Jesus replied, "Man, who appointed me a judge or an arbiter between you?" [15]Then he said to them, "Watch out! Be on your guard against all kinds of greed; a man's life does not consist in the abundance of his possessions."

[16]And he told them this parable: "The ground of a certain rich man produced a good crop. [17]He thought to himself, 'What shall I do? I have no place to store my crops.'

[18]"Then he said, 'This is what I'll do. I will tear down my barns and build bigger ones, and there I will store all my grain and my goods. [19]And I'll say to myself, "You have plenty of good things laid up for many years. Take life easy; eat, drink and be merry." '

[20]"But God said to him, 'You fool! This very night your life will be demanded from you. Then who will get what you have prepared for yourself?'

[21]"This is how it will be with anyone who stores up things for himself but is not rich toward God."

Do Not Worry

[22]Then Jesus said to his disciples: "Therefore I tell you, do not worry about your life, what you will eat; or about your body, what you will wear. [23]Life is more than food, and the body more than clothes. [24]Consider the ravens: They do not sow or reap, they have no storeroom or barn; yet God feeds them. And how much more valuable you are than birds! [25]Who of you by worrying can add a single hour to his life[a]? [26]Since you cannot do this very little thing, why do you worry about the rest?

[27]"Consider how the lilies grow. They do not labor or spin. Yet I tell you, not even Solomon in all his splendor was dressed like one of these. [28]If that is how God clothes the grass of the field, which is here today, and tomorrow is thrown into the fire, how much more will he clothe you, O you of little faith! [29]And do not set your heart on what you will eat or drink; do not worry about it. [30]For the pagan world runs after all such things, and your Father knows that you need them. [31]But seek his kingdom, and these things will be given to you as well.

[32]"Do not be afraid, little flock, for your Father has been pleased to give you the kingdom. [33]Sell your possessions and give to the poor. Provide purses for yourselves that will not wear out, a treasure in heaven that will not be exhausted, where no thief comes near and no moth destroys. [34]For where your treasure is, there your heart will be also.

Watchfulness

[35]"Be dressed ready for service and keep your lamps burning, [36]like men waiting for their master to return from a wedding banquet, so that when he comes and knocks they can immediately open the door for him. [37]It will be good for those servants whose master finds them watching when he comes. I tell you the truth, he will dress himself to serve, will have them recline at the table and will come and wait on them. [38]It will be good for those servants whose master finds them ready, even if he comes in the second or third watch of the night. [39]But understand this: If the owner of the house had known at what hour the thief was coming, he would not have let his house be broken into. [40]You also must be ready, because the Son of Man will come at an hour when you do not expect him."

[41]Peter asked, "Lord, are you telling this parable to us, or to everyone?"

[42]The Lord answered, "Who then is the faithful and wise manager, whom the master puts in charge of his servants to give them their food allowance at the proper time? [43]It will be good for that servant whom the master finds doing so when he returns. [44]I tell you the truth, he will put him in charge of all his possessions. [45]But suppose the servant says to himself, 'My master is taking a long time in coming,' and he then begins to beat the menservants and maidservants and to eat and drink and get drunk. [46]The master of that servant will come on a day when he does not expect him and at an hour he

[a]25 Or single cubit to his height

is not aware of. He will cut him to pieces and assign him a place with the unbelievers.

47"That servant who knows his master's will and does not get ready or does not do what his master wants will be beaten with many blows. **48**But the one who does not know and does things deserving punishment will be beaten with few blows. From everyone who has been given much, much will be demanded; and from the one who has been entrusted with much, much more will be asked.

Not Peace but Division

49"I have come to bring fire on the earth, and how I wish it were already kindled! **50**But I have a baptism to undergo, and how distressed I am until it is completed! **51**Do you think I came to bring peace on earth? No, I tell you, but division. **52**From now on there will be five in one family divided against each other, three against two and two against three. **53**They will be divided, father against son and son against father, mother against daughter and daughter against mother, mother-in-law against daughter-in-law and daughter-in-law against mother-in-law."

Interpreting the Times

54He said to the crowd: "When you see a cloud rising in the west, immediately you say, 'It's going to rain,' and it does. **55**And when the south wind blows, you say, 'It's going to be hot,' and it is. **56**Hypocrites! You know how to interpret the appearance of the earth and the sky. How is it that you don't know how to interpret this present time?

57"Why don't you judge for yourselves what is right? **58**As you are going with your adversary to the magistrate, try hard to be reconciled to him on the way, or he may drag you off to the judge, and the judge turn you over to the officer, and the officer throw you into prison. **59**I tell you, you will not get out until you have paid the last penny.*a*"

Repent or Perish

13 Now there were some present at that time who told Jesus about the Galileans whose blood Pilate had mixed with their sacrifices. **2**Jesus answered, "Do you think that these Galileans were worse sinners than all the other Galileans because

they suffered this way? **3**I tell you, no! But unless you repent, you too will all perish. **4**Or those eighteen who died when the tower in Siloam fell on them—do you think they were more guilty than all the others living in Jerusalem? **5**I tell you, no! But unless you repent, you too will all perish."

6Then he told this parable: "A man had a fig tree, planted in his vineyard, and he went to look for fruit on it, but did not find any. **7**So he said to the man who took care of the vineyard, 'For three years now I've been coming to look for fruit on this fig tree and haven't found any. Cut it down! Why should it use up the soil?'

8" 'Sir,' the man replied, 'leave it alone for one more year, and I'll dig around it and fertilize it. **9**If it bears fruit next year, fine! If not, then cut it down.'"

A Crippled Woman Healed on the Sabbath

10On a Sabbath Jesus was teaching in one of the synagogues, **11**and a woman was there who had been crippled by a spirit for eighteen years. She was bent over and could not straighten up at all. **12**When Jesus saw her, he called her forward and said to her, "Woman, you are set free from your infirmity." **13**Then he put his hands on her, and immediately she straightened up and praised God.

14Indignant because Jesus had healed on the Sabbath, the synagogue ruler said to the people, "There are six days for work. So come and be healed on those days, not on the Sabbath."

15The Lord answered him, "You hypocrites! Doesn't each of you on the Sabbath untie his ox or donkey from the stall and lead it out to give it water? **16**Then should not this woman, a daughter of Abraham, whom Satan has kept bound for eighteen long years, be set free on the Sabbath day from what bound her?"

17When he said this, all his opponents were humiliated, but the people were delighted with all the wonderful things he was doing.

The Parables of the Mustard Seed and the Yeast

18Then Jesus asked, "What is the kingdom of God like? What shall I compare it to? **19**It is like a mustard seed, which a man took and planted in his garden. It grew and became a tree, and the birds of the air perched in its branches."

a59 Greek *lepton*

20Again he asked, "What shall I compare the kingdom of God to? **21**It is like yeast that a woman took and mixed into a large amount*a* of flour until it worked all through the dough."

The Narrow Door

22Then Jesus went through the towns and villages, teaching as he made his way to Jerusalem. **23**Someone asked him, "Lord, are only a few people going to be saved?"

He said to them, **24**"Make every effort to enter through the narrow door, because many, I tell you, will try to enter and will not be able to. **25**Once the owner of the house gets up and closes the door, you will stand outside knocking and pleading, 'Sir, open the door for us.'

"But he will answer, 'I don't know you or where you come from.'

26"Then you will say, 'We ate and drank with you, and you taught in our streets.'

27"But he will reply, 'I don't know you or where you come from. Away from me, all you evildoers!'

28"There will be weeping there, and gnashing of teeth, when you see Abraham, Isaac and Jacob and all the prophets in the kingdom of God, but you yourselves thrown out. **29**People will come from east and west and north and south, and will take their places at the feast in the kingdom of God. **30**Indeed there are those who are last who will be first, and first who will be last."

Jesus' Sorrow for Jerusalem

31At that time some Pharisees came to Jesus and said to him, "Leave this place and go somewhere else. Herod wants to kill you."

32He replied, "Go tell that fox, 'I will drive out demons and heal people today and tomorrow, and on the third day I will reach my goal.' **33**In any case, I must keep going today and tomorrow and the next day—for surely no prophet can die outside Jerusalem!

34"O Jerusalem, Jerusalem, you who kill the prophets and stone those sent to you, how often I have longed to gather your children together, as a hen gathers her chicks under her wings, but you were not willing! **35**Look, your house is left to you desolate. I tell you, you will not see me again until you say, 'Blessed is he who comes in the name of the Lord.'*b*"

Jesus at a Pharisee's House

14 One Sabbath, when Jesus went to eat in the house of a prominent Pharisee, he was being carefully watched. **2**There in front of him was a man suffering from dropsy. **3**Jesus asked the Pharisees and experts in the law, "Is it lawful to heal on the Sabbath or not?" **4**But they remained silent. So taking hold of the man, he healed him and sent him away.

5Then he asked them, "If one of you has a son*c* or an ox that falls into a well on the Sabbath day, will you not immediately pull him out?" **6**And they had nothing to say.

7When he noticed how the guests picked the places of honor at the table, he told them this parable: **8**"When someone invites you to a wedding feast, do not take the place of honor, for a person more distinguished than you may have been invited. **9**If so, the host who invited both of you will come and say to you, 'Give this man your seat.' Then, humiliated, you will have to take the least important place. **10**But when you are invited, take the lowest place, so that when your host comes, he will say to you, 'Friend, move up to a better place.' Then you will be honored in the presence of all your fellow guests. **11**For everyone who exalts himself will be humbled, and he who humbles himself will be exalted."

12Then Jesus said to his host, "When you give a luncheon or dinner, do not invite your friends, your brothers or relatives, or your rich neighbors; if you do, they may invite you back and so you will be repaid. **13**But when you give a banquet, invite the poor, the crippled, the lame, the blind, **14**and you will be blessed. Although they cannot repay you, you will be repaid at the resurrection of the righteous."

The Parable of the Great Banquet

15When one of those at the table with him heard this, he said to Jesus, "Blessed is the man who will eat at the feast in the kingdom of God."

16Jesus replied: "A certain man was preparing a great banquet and invited many guests. **17**At the time of the banquet he sent his servant to tell those who had been invited, 'Come, for everything is now ready.'

a21 Greek *three satas* (probably about 1/2 bushel or 22 liters)   *b35* Psalm 118:26   *c5* Some manuscripts *donkey*

18"But they all alike began to make excuses. The first said, 'I have just bought a field, and I must go and see it. Please excuse me.'

19"Another said, 'I have just bought five yoke of oxen, and I'm on my way to try them out. Please excuse me.'

20"Still another said, 'I just got married, so I can't come.'

21"The servant came back and reported this to his master. Then the owner of the house became angry and ordered his servant, 'Go out quickly into the streets and alleys of the town and bring in the poor, the crippled, the blind and the lame.'

22" 'Sir,' the servant said, 'what you ordered has been done, but there is still room.'

23"Then the master told his servant, 'Go out to the roads and country lanes and make them come in, so that my house will be full. **24**I tell you, not one of those men

DAILY INSIGHT

THURSDAY

Passage:
Luke 14:15–24

Verse:
Luke 14:24

RSVP

This is going to sound presumptuous, but even though I have no official training in space exploration, I am confident that I could successfully orchestrate a mission. You see, I have planned a wedding.

My wife and I had been to dozens of these nuptial affairs, so when our daughter announced her engagement, I was confident that we could pull it off, on budget—no sweat. (Don't forget, you're hearing this from a lifelong Cubs fan.)

One of the more enlightening things we learned was a result of the process of assembling guest lists from both families and mailing invitations. Some people responded immediately to the "RSVP" printed on the engraved solicitations, and some completely ignored it. The wedding happened years ago, and we still haven't heard if some folks are coming.

We can't say we weren't warned. Experts—"wedding planners" who learn everything they know about price structures from trial lawyers—told us to expect a "significant" number of people who would never respond … never. They were right. We got an invoice for that helpful advice.

How incredible it is that people don't respond to an invitation to a party, complete with plenty of fun and free food! But this is nothing new. It's been going on for a long time.

Jesus was sitting at the dinner table of a prominent religious leader. He and those around him were discussing this very issue: Why do some people ignore RSVP's? I can just imagine the people sitting there, intrigued with Jesus' interest in discussing matters of dinner-party etiquette. "Boy," they must have said to each other, "this guy knows something about *everything.*"

Sitting here, a couple of millennia later, I wonder when it occurred to these dinner guests that Jesus was talking about his kingdom. In the story, when the man sent his servant to "tell those who had been invited, 'Come, for everything is now ready,' " he was not actually talking about people ignoring invitations to lavish dinner soirees. He was talking about our response to his invitation to feast at the table of his boundless grace. When the formal invitees decided that they had better things to do, the party host told his servants to look for people who were hungry and homeless—people for whom this feast represented survival, not simply another obligation on their social calendar.

And here's the message for us. This feast is worth canceling everything to attend. No other distraction should get in the way of our experience at God's table. Today, let's thank him for inviting us, not because we look good on his invitation list, but because without this meal, you and I would starve.

The invitation has arrived, and there's an RSVP printed in the corner. The table is set. Don't miss this celebration.

For your next devotional reading, go to page 1142.

who were invited will get a taste of my banquet.' "

The Cost of Being a Disciple

²⁵Large crowds were traveling with Jesus, and turning to them he said: ²⁶"If anyone comes to me and does not hate his father and mother, his wife and children, his brothers and sisters—yes, even his own life—he cannot be my disciple. ²⁷And anyone who does not carry his cross and follow me cannot be my disciple.

²⁸"Suppose one of you wants to build a tower. Will he not first sit down and estimate the cost to see if he has enough money to complete it? ²⁹For if he lays the foundation and is not able to finish it, everyone who sees it will ridicule him, ³⁰saying, 'This fellow began to build and was not able to finish.'

³¹"Or suppose a king is about to go to war against another king. Will he not first

Loving Down by Loving Up

DAILY INSIGHT

FRIDAY

Passage:
Luke 14:25–35

Verse:
Luke 14:27

I have a close friend who, after thirteen years of marriage, was facing a painful divorce. His days were filled with lawyer meetings and the inevitable hassle of deciding what stuff was whose. Right in the middle of this turmoil, his six-year-old daughter began to have wetting-her-pants accidents. They started at night, but eventually, they happened at all times of the day.

My frustrated friend challenged his child's "unacceptable" behavior. He read books, consulted experts, and tried punishment and rewards with his daughter—but to no avail.

Finally, after he had had enough of this foolishness, he picked up his little girl, walked to an overstuffed chair in the living room, and sat down. With all he was going through, a defiant child was the last thing he needed. He held her in his arms for a few quiet minutes, then broke the silence with a question. "Do you know how frustrated I am with you, Carrie? You're six years old. It's been a long time since you learned how to use the bathroom." Carrie's dad's anger and disappointment were clearly showing through his words. "You're a big girl. Big girls don't wet their pants. Babies wet their pants."

Carrie sat there, cuddled in her father's arms. She finally spoke to her father without looking at him. "Yes, and daddies hold their babies, don't they?"

Her words found my friend's heart like a smart bomb. The break-up of this marriage had deeply affected his child.

If you want to love "down," you have to be successful at loving "up."

Many years ago, during a particularly challenging time of dealing with the medical problems facing our newborn baby, I received a card from a close friend, several years my senior. After a few encouraging words, he wrote something I'll never forget: "Don't forget that the most important thing you can do to be the dad Julie is going to need is to never stop loving her mother."

The words hit me like a straight left. Somehow in the middle of all this uncertainty and pain, I had forgotten to keep my love for Bobbie on the front burner. If I wanted to be effective in loving Julie, I had to first love her mother … loving "down" by loving "up."

The words from today's text seem harsh—even brutal. "If anyone comes to me and does not hate his father and mother, his wife and children, his brothers and sisters—yes, even his own life—he cannot be my disciple" (v. 25). Actually, these words make a great deal of sense.

The best way—the only way—to love "down," is to first love "up." Love your children by loving your wife. Love your wife by loving yourself. Love yourself by loving your Creator. Jesus' words are logical and right. They are perfectly reasonable.

Ask Carrie. Ask Julie.

For your next devotional reading, go to page 1145.

sit down and consider whether he is able with ten thousand men to oppose the one coming against him with twenty thousand? ³²If he is not able, he will send a delegation while the other is still a long way off and will ask for terms of peace. ³³In the same way, any of you who does not give up everything he has cannot be my disciple.

³⁴"Salt is good, but if it loses its saltiness, how can it be made salty again? ³⁵It is fit neither for the soil nor for the manure pile; it is thrown out.

"He who has ears to hear, let him hear."

The Parable of the Lost Sheep

15 Now the tax collectors and "sinners" were all gathering around to hear him. ²But the Pharisees and the teachers

---

All Lostness Is Not Created Equal
The Prodigal's Father

"But while he was still a long way off, his father saw him and was filled with compassion for him; he ran to his son, threw his arms around him and kissed him" (15:20).

DADS
IN THE
BIBLE

Text: Luke 15:1–32

Here is one of the most famous of all Bible stories about a dad. Actually, this chapter contains not one but three very important stories. And in fact, all three contain critical truth for dads—especially dads with wayward children.

The first story is about innocently wandering off. A sheep, attempting to find better grass to nibble, moves from spot to spot. This activity eventually leads him so far from the rest of the flock that he loses his way. In this account, Jesus says that the shepherd searches for the wayward critter until he finds him.

The second story is about being misplaced. The coin in Jesus' story has no ability to get lost on its own. Its being lost is someone else's fault. The careless woman sets the hapless coin somewhere and then promptly forgets where. Or the coin slips out of her pocket or her purse. In either case, the coin's lostness certainly isn't because of anything the coin has done wrong. Recognizing that she has lost this coin, she turns her house upside-down until she finds it.

The third story is about open rebellion. A boy, second in his father's inheritance queue, tells his dad that he's had enough and wants his share of the money now. Unfortunately, with probably little education and even less common sense, the kid lives hard and fast, and quickly runs out of cash. Scripture tells us that once the thrill was gone, the lad "came to his senses," returning to his waiting father on his own.

As a dad, what might these stories say that would be helpful to me? What does each one seem to say about the treatment of lost things? Several years ago it hit me.

When children "innocently" wander off through a sequence of small, foolish decisions that lead to big problems, it's okay to go get them and encourage them back into the fold. And when children, because of the carelessness of others—an abusive or thoughtless acquaintance, coach or teacher—find themselves frustrated and angry, it's also appropriate to lovingly pursue them with hope and encouragement. But when children shake their rebellious fists at authority, daring anyone to stop them from pursuing their selfish aspirations, dads have little choice but to quietly wait, praying for these rebels to "come to their senses" and return.

Different kinds of "lostness;" different remedies.

As fathers guiding our children on this journey of faith, it's inevitable that our children will occasionally get lost. Jesus gives us some extremely helpful advice. He reminds us that sometimes it's acceptable to go after our kids—the gentle knock on the bedroom door or the scheduled breakfast to talk it over. And sometimes the only thing we can do is wait. And pray. And leave our hearts and our arms open for the day when those prayers are answered.

For a complete listing of Dads in the Bible, turn to page 1434.

of the law muttered, "This man welcomes sinners and eats with them."

[3] Then Jesus told them this parable: [4] "Suppose one of you has a hundred sheep and loses one of them. Does he not leave the ninety-nine in the open country and go after the lost sheep until he finds it? [5] And when he finds it, he joyfully puts it on his shoulders [6] and goes home. Then he calls his friends and neighbors together and says, 'Rejoice with me; I have found my lost sheep.' [7] I tell you that in the same way there will be more rejoicing in heaven over one sinner who repents than over ninety-nine righteous persons who do not need to repent.

The Parable of the Lost Coin

[8] "Or suppose a woman has ten silver coins[a] and loses one. Does she not light a lamp, sweep the house and search carefully until she finds it? [9] And when she finds it, she calls her friends and neighbors together and says, 'Rejoice with me; I have found my lost coin.' [10] In the same way, I tell you, there is rejoicing in the presence of the angels of God over one sinner who repents."

The Parable of the Lost Son

[11] Jesus continued: "There was a man who had two sons. [12] The younger one said to his father, 'Father, give me my share of the estate.' So he divided his property between them.

[13] "Not long after that, the younger son got together all he had, set off for a distant country and there squandered his wealth in wild living. [14] After he had spent everything, there was a severe famine in that whole country, and he began to be in need. [15] So he went and hired himself out to a citizen of that country, who sent him to his fields to feed pigs. [16] He longed to fill his stomach with the pods that the pigs were eating, but no one gave him anything.

[17] "When he came to his senses, he said, 'How many of my father's hired men have food to spare, and here I am starving to death! [18] I will set out and go back to my father and say to him: Father, I have sinned against heaven and against you. [19] I am no longer worthy to be called your son; make me like one of your hired men.' [20] So he got up and went to his father.

"But while he was still a long way off, his father saw him and was filled with compassion for him; he ran to his son, threw his arms around him and kissed him.

[21] "The son said to him, 'Father, I have sinned against heaven and against you. I am no longer worthy to be called your son.[b] [22] "But the father said to his servants, 'Quick! Bring the best robe and put it on him. Put a ring on his finger and sandals on his feet. [23] Bring the fattened calf and kill it. Let's have a feast and celebrate. [24] For this son of mine was dead and is alive again; he was lost and is found.' So they began to celebrate.

[25] "Meanwhile, the older son was in the field. When he came near the house, he heard music and dancing. [26] So he called one of the servants and asked him what was going on. [27] 'Your brother has come,' he replied, 'and your father has killed the fattened calf because he has him back safe and sound.'

[28] "The older brother became angry and refused to go in. So his father went out and pleaded with him. [29] But he answered his father, 'Look! All these years I've been slaving for you and never disobeyed your orders. Yet you never gave me even a young goat so I could celebrate with my friends. [30] But when this son of yours who has squandered your property with prostitutes comes home, you kill the fattened calf for him!'

[31] " 'My son,' the father said, 'you are always with me, and everything I have is yours. [32] But we had to celebrate and be glad, because this brother of yours was dead and is alive again; he was lost and is found.' "

The Parable of the Shrewd Manager

16 Jesus told his disciples: "There was a rich man whose manager was accused of wasting his possessions. [2] So he called him in and asked him, 'What is this I hear about you? Give an account of your management, because you cannot be manager any longer.'

[3] "The manager said to himself, 'What shall I do now? My master is taking away my job. I'm not strong enough to dig, and I'm ashamed to beg— [4] I know what I'll do so that, when I lose my job here, people will welcome me into their houses.'

[5] "So he called in each one of his

---

[a]8 Greek *ten drachmas,* each worth about a day's wages   [b]21 Some early manuscripts *son. Make me like one of your hired men.*

Home, Where We Belong

Key Verse: *"'For this son of mine was dead and is alive again; he was lost and is found.' So they began to celebrate."* Luke 15:24
Text: Luke 15:11–24 *(Dad or child reads the text.)*

QUIET
TIMES
WITH Dad

DAD READS: Every day, all over the world, children run away from home. They run away for different reasons. Some are afraid of their parents so, out of fear, they leave. Some run away because they have been influenced by friends who have challenged them to break away from traditions. Some young people run away from home just because they want to start their own lives, and they're not willing to stay home and finish growing up.

Child reads: How scary it must be for parents who discover that their child has run away. Many parents are frantic, so they try everything they can to find their son or daughter and to bring the runaway home. I have seen pictures of these runaways. Printed above the pictures are the words, "Have you seen this child?" The story that we read today talks about one such runaway. He asked his dad for the share of the money that he would get when his dad died, and he took off. How terribly sad this dad must have been to have such a rebellious son.

DAD READS: This story is amazing because, even though we believe that the dad loved his son very much, he did not run after his boy. He did not try to find him. As far as we know, he did absolutely nothing … except wait for his son to return. The father had tried to love his son when he was home, so even though he couldn't see or speak to the young man, the dad decided to keep loving him, hoping his love would draw the boy back home.

Child reads: At first, the son had a great time. He had money in his pocket and everything was looking good. But soon the money ran out. And because the boy didn't have an education or the skills to get a good job, he took a job feeding pigs. Pretty soon, the young man realized how foolish he had been. The Bible says that he "came to his senses."

DAD READS: How happy the dad was when his son decided to come home. The Bible tells us that he was so happy that the father "ran to his son, threw his arms around him, and kissed him." Can you imagine how surprised the young man must have been? He probably thought that he was going to be punished, but instead his father welcomed him home.

Child reads: Jesus told this story to make sure we understand how much our heavenly Father loves us, even when we don't deserve this love. The dad in this story gives us a perfect picture of God's love and grace. When we come to him and ask him for forgiveness, he throws his arms around us and celebrates our return to him.

DAD READS: I'm so glad that we have a loving heavenly Father like this. Let me pray this prayer with you:

Our Father in heaven, thank you that even when we run away from you, your love draws us back home. Please help us to "come to our senses" like the boy in the story. Help us to always remember to seek your forgiveness, and thank you that your love is always there to forgive us. We love you, and we thank you for this lesson. In Jesus' name, **Amen.**

For your next devotional reading, go to page 1148.

master's debtors. He asked the first, 'How much do you owe my master?'

6" 'Eight hundred gallons[a] of olive oil,' he replied.

"The manager told him, 'Take your bill, sit down quickly, and make it four hundred.'

7"Then he asked the second, 'And how much do you owe?'

" 'A thousand bushels[b] of wheat,' he replied.

"He told him, 'Take your bill and make it eight hundred.'

8"The master commended the dishonest manager because he had acted shrewdly. For the people of this world are more shrewd in dealing with their own kind than are the people of the light. 9I tell you, use worldly wealth to gain friends for yourselves, so that when it is gone, you will be welcomed into eternal dwellings.

10"Whoever can be trusted with very little can also be trusted with much, and whoever is dishonest with very little will also be dishonest with much. 11So if you have not been trustworthy in handling worldly wealth, who will trust you with true riches? 12And if you have not been trustworthy with someone else's property, who will give you property of your own?

13"No servant can serve two masters. Either he will hate the one and love the other, or he will be devoted to the one and despise the other. You cannot serve both God and Money."

14The Pharisees, who loved money, heard all this and were sneering at Jesus. 15He said to them, "You are the ones who justify yourselves in the eyes of men, but God knows your hearts. What is highly valued among men is detestable in God's sight.

Additional Teachings

16"The Law and the Prophets were proclaimed until John. Since that time, the good news of the kingdom of God is being preached, and everyone is forcing his way into it. 17It is easier for heaven and earth to disappear than for the least stroke of a pen to drop out of the Law.

18"Anyone who divorces his wife and marries another woman commits adultery, and the man who marries a divorced woman commits adultery.

The Rich Man and Lazarus

19"There was a rich man who was dressed in purple and fine linen and lived in luxury every day. 20At his gate was laid a beggar named Lazarus, covered with sores 21and longing to eat what fell from the rich man's table. Even the dogs came and licked his sores.

22"The time came when the beggar died and the angels carried him to Abraham's side. The rich man also died and was buried. 23In hell,[c] where he was in torment, he looked up and saw Abraham far away, with Lazarus by his side. 24So he called to him, 'Father Abraham, have pity on me and send Lazarus to dip the tip of his finger in water and cool my tongue, because I am in agony in this fire.'

25"But Abraham replied, 'Son, remember that in your lifetime you received your good things, while Lazarus received bad things, but now he is comforted here and you are in agony. 26And besides all this, between us and you a great chasm has been fixed, so that those who want to go from here to you cannot, nor can anyone cross over from there to us.'

27"He answered, 'Then I beg you, father, send Lazarus to my father's house, 28for I have five brothers. Let him warn them, so that they will not also come to this place of torment.'

29"Abraham replied, 'They have Moses and the Prophets; let them listen to them.'

30" 'No, father Abraham,' he said, 'but if someone from the dead goes to them, they will repent.'

31"He said to him, 'If they do not listen to Moses and the Prophets, they will not be convinced even if someone rises from the dead.' "

Sin, Faith, Duty

17 Jesus said to his disciples: "Things that cause people to sin are bound to come, but woe to that person through whom they come. 2It would be better for him to be thrown into the sea with a millstone tied around his neck than for him to cause one of these little ones to sin. 3So watch yourselves.

"If your brother sins, rebuke him, and if he repents, forgive him. 4If he sins against you seven times in a day, and seven times comes back to you and says, 'I repent,' forgive him."

5The apostles said to the Lord, "Increase our faith!"

6He replied, "If you have faith as small

a6 Greek one hundred batous (probably about 3 kiloliters)   b7 Greek one hundred korous (probably about 35 kiloliters)   c23 Greek Hades

as a mustard seed, you can say to this mulberry tree, 'Be uprooted and planted in the sea,' and it will obey you.

[7]"Suppose one of you had a servant plowing or looking after the sheep. Would he say to the servant when he comes in from the field, 'Come along now and sit down to eat'? [8]Would he not rather say, 'Prepare my supper, get yourself ready and wait on me while I eat and drink; after that you may eat and drink'? [9]Would he thank the servant because he did what he was told to do? [10]So you also, when you have done everything you were told to do, should say, 'We are unworthy servants; we have only done our duty.' "

Ten Healed of Leprosy

[11]Now on his way to Jerusalem, Jesus traveled along the border between Samaria and Galilee. [12]As he was going into a village, ten men who had leprosy[a] met him. They stood at a distance [13]and called out in a loud voice, "Jesus, Master, have pity on us!"

[14]When he saw them, he said, "Go, show yourselves to the priests." And as they went, they were cleansed.

[15]One of them, when he saw he was healed, came back, praising God in a loud voice. [16]He threw himself at Jesus' feet and thanked him—and he was a Samaritan.

[17]Jesus asked, "Were not all ten cleansed? Where are the other nine? [18]Was no one found to return and give praise to God except this foreigner?" [19]Then he said to him, "Rise and go; your faith has made you well."

The Coming of the Kingdom of God

[20]Once, having been asked by the Pharisees when the kingdom of God would come, Jesus replied, "The kingdom of God does not come with your careful observation, [21]nor will people say, 'Here it is,' or 'There it is,' because the kingdom of God is within[b] you."

[22]Then he said to his disciples, "The time is coming when you will long to see one of the days of the Son of Man, but you will not see it. [23]Men will tell you, 'There he is!' or 'Here he is!' Do not go running off after them. [24]For the Son of Man in his day[c] will be like the lightning, which flashes and lights up the sky from one end to the other. [25]But first he must suffer many things and be rejected by this generation.

[26]"Just as it was in the days of Noah, so also will it be in the days of the Son of Man. [27]People were eating, drinking, marrying and being given in marriage up to the day Noah entered the ark. Then the flood came and destroyed them all.

[28]"It was the same in the days of Lot. People were eating and drinking, buying and selling, planting and building. [29]But the day Lot left Sodom, fire and sulfur rained down from heaven and destroyed them all.

[30]"It will be just like this on the day the Son of Man is revealed. [31]On that day no one who is on the roof of his house, with his goods inside, should go down to get them. Likewise, no one in the field should go back for anything. [32]Remember Lot's wife! [33]Whoever tries to keep his life will lose it, and whoever loses his life will preserve it. [34]I tell you, on that night two people will be in one bed; one will be taken and the other left. [35]Two women will be grinding grain together; one will be taken and the other left.[d]"

[37]"Where, Lord?" they asked.

He replied, "Where there is a dead body, there the vultures will gather."

The Parable of the Persistent Widow

18 Then Jesus told his disciples a parable to show them that they should always pray and not give up. [2]He said: "In a certain town there was a judge who neither feared God nor cared about men. [3]And there was a widow in that town who kept coming to him with the plea, 'Grant me justice against my adversary.'

[4]"For some time he refused. But finally he said to himself, 'Even though I don't fear God or care about men, [5]yet because this widow keeps bothering me, I will see that she gets justice, so that she won't eventually wear me out with her coming!' "

[6]And the Lord said, "Listen to what the unjust judge says. [7]And will not God bring about justice for his chosen ones, who cry out to him day and night? Will he keep putting them off? [8]I tell you, he will see that they get justice, and quickly. However, when the Son of Man comes, will he find faith on the earth?"

---

[a]12 The Greek word was used for various diseases affecting the skin—not necessarily leprosy.   [b]21 Or *among*   [c]24 Some manuscripts do not have *in his day*.   [d]35 Some manuscripts *left.* [36]*Two men will be in the field; one will be taken and the other left.*

The Parable of the Pharisee and the Tax Collector

⁹To some who were confident of their own righteousness and looked down on everybody else, Jesus told this parable: ¹⁰"Two men went up to the temple to pray, one a Pharisee and the other a tax collector. ¹¹The Pharisee stood up and prayed about[a] himself: 'God, I thank you that I am not like other men—robbers, evildoers, adulterers—or even like this tax collector. ¹²I fast twice a week and give a tenth of all I get.'

¹³"But the tax collector stood at a distance. He would not even look up to heaven, but beat his breast and said, 'God, have mercy on me, a sinner.'

¹⁴"I tell you that this man, rather than the other, went home justified before God. For everyone who exalts himself will be humbled, and he who humbles himself will be exalted."

a11 Or to

How's Your Heart?

DAILY INSIGHT

MONDAY

Passage:
Luke 18:18–25

Verse:
Luke 18:22

"Do you see that man over there?" the man at the church retreat said to me. "That's Ron, and by all rights, he should be dead."

This guy had my attention. Why should Ron be dead?

Over the next few minutes I was told how Ron had a life-threatening heart problem. The vessels that supplied blood to his ticker were slowly deteriorating. His father and his grandfather had both died of heart failure when they were much younger than Ron was today. I excused myself and walked straight to Ron. After introducing myself, I told him of the news I had just heard, asking him to fill me in on the details. He willingly obliged.

As Ron and I talked, I heard what it was like to know that, at any minute and with no warning, a man's heart could shut down completely. I learned of a wonder drug developed by researchers at Stanford University that was keeping Ron alive.

"What's it like to have a heart like this?" I finally asked.

"For one thing," Ron answered, "I don't buy green bananas." We laughed. "For another thing, this condition helps me to keep short accounts. I never know if I'll have a second chance with any of my relationships, especially my relationship with God." I was almost entranced by this display of wit and wisdom. "Most of all," Ron concluded with a twinkle in his eye, "I'm thankful that I know I have a weak heart. I have completely changed my lifestyle—my exercise regimen, my rest and my diet. When you have a bad heart, nothing short of a radical transformation will do."

The "certain ruler" who came to Jesus in the passage also had a bad heart. Jesus had given the diagnosis: "Where your treasure is, there your heart will be also" (Matthew 6:21). Because of his dependence on his fiscal portfolio and his love for things, Jesus pronounced the man dead on arrival. Jesus, said to this astonished man, in effect, "Your heart has followed your bank account. So because of this heart problem, you're going have to do something radical. Take your net worth to zero, then you'll have enough room in your heart for me."

"When [the man] heard this, he became very sad, because he was a man of great wealth" (v. 23).

There is nothing wrong with having things. There is nothing evil about money. However, if you fasten your heart to it, if you fall in love with it, you're going to have an unpleasant conversation the next time you see Jesus.

You and I—regardless of our personal balance sheets—are unwittingly drawn to financial gain. We're lured by money's promise of security and satisfaction. This is a tough predicament. You see, we have a heart problem. Now that we know, we can join Ron and do something about it. This news could save our lives.

For your next devotional reading, go to page 1150.

The Little Children and Jesus

¹⁵People were also bringing babies to Jesus to have him touch them. When the disciples saw this, they rebuked them. ¹⁶But Jesus called the children to him and said, "Let the little children come to me, and do not hinder them, for the kingdom of God belongs to such as these. ¹⁷I tell you the truth, anyone who will not receive the kingdom of God like a little child will never enter it."

The Rich Ruler

¹⁸A certain ruler asked him, "Good teacher, what must I do to inherit eternal life?"

¹⁹"Why do you call me good?" Jesus answered. "No one is good—except God alone. ²⁰You know the commandments: 'Do not commit adultery, do not murder, do not steal, do not give false testimony, honor your father and mother.' ᵃ"

²¹"All these I have kept since I was a boy," he said.

²²When Jesus heard this, he said to him, "You still lack one thing. Sell everything you have and give to the poor, and you will have treasure in heaven. Then come, follow me."

²³When he heard this, he became very sad, because he was a man of great wealth. ²⁴Jesus looked at him and said, "How hard it is for the rich to enter the kingdom of God! ²⁵Indeed, it is easier for a camel to go through the eye of a needle than for a rich man to enter the kingdom of God."

²⁶Those who heard this asked, "Who then can be saved?"

²⁷Jesus replied, "What is impossible with men is possible with God."

²⁸Peter said to him, "We have left all we had to follow you!"

²⁹"I tell you the truth," Jesus said to them, "no one who has left home or wife or brothers or parents or children for the sake of the kingdom of God ³⁰will fail to receive many times as much in this age and, in the age to come, eternal life."

Jesus Again Predicts His Death

³¹Jesus took the Twelve aside and told them, "We are going up to Jerusalem, and everything that is written by the prophets about the Son of Man will be fulfilled. ³²He will be handed over to the Gentiles. They will mock him, insult him, spit on

him, flog him and kill him. ³³On the third day he will rise again."

³⁴The disciples did not understand any of this. Its meaning was hidden from them, and they did not know what he was talking about.

A Blind Beggar Receives His Sight

³⁵As Jesus approached Jericho, a blind man was sitting by the roadside begging. ³⁶When he heard the crowd going by, he asked what was happening. ³⁷They told him, "Jesus of Nazareth is passing by."

³⁸He called out, "Jesus, Son of David, have mercy on me!"

³⁹Those who led the way rebuked him and told him to be quiet, but he shouted all the more, "Son of David, have mercy on me!"

⁴⁰Jesus stopped and ordered the man to be brought to him. When he came near, Jesus asked him, ⁴¹"What do you want me to do for you?"

"Lord, I want to see," he replied.

⁴²Jesus said to him, "Receive your sight; your faith has healed you." ⁴³Immediately he received his sight and followed Jesus, praising God. When all the people saw it, they also praised God.

Zacchaeus the Tax Collector

19 Jesus entered Jericho and was passing through. ²A man was there by the name of Zacchaeus; he was a chief tax collector and was wealthy. ³He wanted to see who Jesus was, but being a short man he could not, because of the crowd. ⁴So he ran ahead and climbed a sycamore-fig tree to see him, since Jesus was coming that way.

⁵When Jesus reached the spot, he looked up and said to him, "Zacchaeus, come down immediately. I must stay at your house today." ⁶So he came down at once and welcomed him gladly.

⁷All the people saw this and began to mutter, "He has gone to be the guest of a 'sinner.'"

⁸But Zacchaeus stood up and said to the Lord, "Look, Lord! Here and now I give half of my possessions to the poor, and if I have cheated anybody out of anything, I will pay back four times the amount."

⁹Jesus said to him, "Today salvation has come to this house, because this man, too, is a son of Abraham. ¹⁰For the Son of Man came to seek and to save what was lost."

ᵃ20 Exodus 20:12-16; Deut. 5:16-20

The Parable of the Ten Minas

11While they were listening to this, he went on to tell them a parable, because he was near Jerusalem and the people thought that the kingdom of God was going to appear at once. **12**He said: "A man of noble birth went to a distant country to have himself appointed king and then to return. **13**So he called ten of his servants and gave them ten minas.*a* 'Put this money to work,' he said, 'until I come back.'

14"But his subjects hated him and sent a delegation after him to say, 'We don't want this man to be our king.'

15"He was made king, however, and re-turned home. Then he sent for the servants to whom he had given the money, in order to find out what they had gained with it.

16"The first one came and said, 'Sir, your mina has earned ten more.'

17" 'Well done, my good servant!' his master replied. 'Because you have been trustworthy in a very small matter, take charge of ten cities.'

18"The second came and said, 'Sir, your mina has earned five more.'

19"His master answered, 'You take charge of five cities.'

20"Then another servant came and

a13 A mina was about three months' wages.

Dad's on the Point

DAILY INSIGHT

TUESDAY

Passage:
Luke 19:1–10

Verse:
Luke 19:9

"Whose turn is it to be on the point?" my cycling friends called out at the end of our rest break. "Who's the first man for the next few miles?"

You have probably seen packs of serious bicyclists—six to eight riders—gliding down a road near your home. Because I spent thirty-nine consecutive days in 1968 riding from San Francisco to New York with my college buddies, I know a little about the dynamics. The guy out front, the one leading the group and facing the headwind, provides a literal envelope of free air behind him. After almost seven uninterrupted weeks of pedaling, our group became very adept at following the lead of the first rider—slip-streaming in his wake.

Zacchaeus knew something about this, too. When Jesus came to visit, this wealthy, resourceful tax collector invited Jesus to his home. That day, Zacchaeus' children learned about the power of the slip-stream—the tangible benefits of having a dad who was willing to get on the point and create an envelope of grace for them.

The text today tells the story of a man whose simple faith led him to seek out the Savior and whose childlike enthusiasm to see Jesus culminated in an actual encounter. It's safe to say that Zacchaeus was never the same again after this incident.

This rendezvous with the Savior opened his eyes to the needs of the unfortunate and disenfranchised: "Here and now I give half of my possessions to the poor." The meeting also became a boon to those whom Zacchaeus had swindled: "If I have cheated anybody out of anything, I will pay back four times the amount" (v. 8).

But the change that must have been the most satisfying for this little giant was what it did for his family. The notorious tax collector's courageous faith brought salvation, health and deliverance to his loved ones (vv. 9–10).

Does this mean that his wife and each of his children suddenly became God's children because of the profession of their husband and dad? No. But what we see in this story is a man who got on the point and provided his loved ones with an unfettered opportunity to know the Savior for themselves.

As dads, you and I have the same privilege of getting on the point for our families. Of course, riding up front is more exhausting than coasting behind. But the next time you get a chance to look into the faces of the precious people you call your own, you'll realize just how much they're worth it.

Now it's your turn up front.

For your next devotional reading, go to page 1158.

said, 'Sir, here is your mina; I have kept it laid away in a piece of cloth. ²¹I was afraid of you, because you are a hard man. You take out what you did not put in and reap what you did not sow.'

²²"His master replied, 'I will judge you by your own words, you wicked servant! You knew, did you, that I am a hard man, taking out what I did not put in, and reaping what I did not sow? ²³Why then didn't you put my money on deposit, so that when I came back, I could have collected it with interest?'

²⁴"Then he said to those standing by, 'Take his mina away from him and give it to the one who has ten minas.'

²⁵" 'Sir,' they said, 'he already has ten!'

²⁶"He replied, 'I tell you that to everyone who has, more will be given, but as for the one who has nothing, even what he has will be taken away. ²⁷But those enemies of mine who did not want me to be king over them—bring them here and kill them in front of me.' "

The Triumphal Entry

²⁸After Jesus had said this, he went on ahead, going up to Jerusalem. ²⁹As he approached Bethphage and Bethany at the hill called the Mount of Olives, he sent two of his disciples, saying to them, ³⁰"Go to the village ahead of you, and as you enter it, you will find a colt tied there, which no one has ever ridden. Untie it and bring it here. ³¹If anyone asks you, 'Why are you untying it?' tell him, 'The Lord needs it.' "

³²Those who were sent ahead went and found it just as he had told them. ³³As they were untying the colt, its owners asked them, "Why are you untying the colt?"

³⁴They replied, "The Lord needs it."

³⁵They brought it to Jesus, threw their cloaks on the colt and put Jesus on it. ³⁶As he went along, people spread their cloaks on the road.

³⁷When he came near the place where the road goes down the Mount of Olives, the whole crowd of disciples began joyfully to praise God in loud voices for all the miracles they had seen:

³⁸"Blessed is the king who comes in the name of the Lord!"ᵃ

"Peace in heaven and glory in the highest!"

³⁹Some of the Pharisees in the crowd said to Jesus, "Teacher, rebuke your disciples!"

⁴⁰"I tell you," he replied, "if they keep quiet, the stones will cry out."

⁴¹As he approached Jerusalem and saw the city, he wept over it ⁴²and said, "If you, even you, had only known on this day what would bring you peace—but now it is hidden from your eyes. ⁴³The days will come upon you when your enemies will build an embankment against you and encircle you and hem you in on every side. ⁴⁴They will dash you to the ground, you and the children within your walls. They will not leave one stone on another, because you did not recognize the time of God's coming to you."

Jesus at the Temple

⁴⁵Then he entered the temple area and began driving out those who were selling. ⁴⁶"It is written," he said to them, " 'My house will be a house of prayer'ᵇ; but you have made it 'a den of robbers.'ᶜ"

⁴⁷Every day he was teaching at the temple. But the chief priests, the teachers of the law and the leaders among the people were trying to kill him. ⁴⁸Yet they could not find any way to do it, because all the people hung on his words.

The Authority of Jesus Questioned

20 One day as he was teaching the people in the temple courts and preaching the gospel, the chief priests and the teachers of the law, together with the elders, came up to him. ²"Tell us by what authority you are doing these things," they said. "Who gave you this authority?"

³He replied, "I will also ask you a question. Tell me, ⁴John's baptism—was it from heaven, or from men?"

⁵They discussed it among themselves and said, "If we say, 'From heaven,' he will ask, 'Why didn't you believe him?' ⁶But if we say, 'From men,' all the people will stone us, because they are persuaded that John was a prophet."

⁷So they answered, "We don't know where it was from."

⁸Jesus said, "Neither will I tell you by what authority I am doing these things."

The Parable of the Tenants

⁹He went on to tell the people this parable: "A man planted a vineyard, rented it to some farmers and went away for a long

ᵃ38 Psalm 118:26   ᵇ46 Isaiah 56:7   ᶜ46 Jer. 7:11

time. [10]At harvest time he sent a servant to the tenants so they would give him some of the fruit of the vineyard. But the tenants beat him and sent him away empty-handed. [11]He sent another servant, but that one also they beat and treated shamefully and sent away empty-handed. [12]He sent still a third, and they wounded him and threw him out.

[13]"Then the owner of the vineyard said, 'What shall I do? I will send my son, whom I love; perhaps they will respect him.'

[14]"But when the tenants saw him, they talked the matter over. 'This is the heir,' they said. 'Let's kill him, and the inheritance will be ours.' [15]So they threw him out of the vineyard and killed him.

"What then will the owner of the vineyard do to them? [16]He will come and kill those tenants and give the vineyard to others."

When the people heard this, they said, "May this never be!"

[17]Jesus looked directly at them and asked, "Then what is the meaning of that which is written:

" 'The stone the builders rejected
    has become the capstone[a][b]?

[18]Everyone who falls on that stone will be broken to pieces, but he on whom it falls will be crushed."

[19]The teachers of the law and the chief priests looked for a way to arrest him immediately, because they knew he had spoken this parable against them. But they were afraid of the people.

Paying Taxes to Caesar

[20]Keeping a close watch on him, they sent spies, who pretended to be honest. They hoped to catch Jesus in something he said so that they might hand him over to the power and authority of the governor. [21]So the spies questioned him: "Teacher, we know that you speak and teach what is right, and that you do not show partiality but teach the way of God in accordance with the truth. [22]Is it right for us to pay taxes to Caesar or not?"

[23]He saw through their duplicity and said to them, [24]"Show me a denarius. Whose portrait and inscription are on it?"

[25]"Caesar's," they replied.

He said to them, "Then give to Caesar what is Caesar's, and to God what is God's."

[26]They were unable to trap him in what he had said there in public. And astonished by his answer, they became silent.

The Resurrection and Marriage

[27]Some of the Sadducees, who say there is no resurrection, came to Jesus with a question. [28]"Teacher," they said, "Moses wrote for us that if a man's brother dies and leaves a wife but no children, the man must marry the widow and have children for his brother. [29]Now there were seven brothers. The first one married a woman and died childless. [30]The second [31]and then the third married her, and in the same way the seven died, leaving no children. [32]Finally, the woman died too. [33]Now then, at the resurrection whose wife will she be, since the seven were married to her?"

[34]Jesus replied, "The people of this age marry and are given in marriage. [35]But those who are considered worthy of taking part in that age and in the resurrection from the dead will neither marry nor be given in marriage, [36]and they can no longer die; for they are like the angels. They are God's children, since they are children of the resurrection. [37]But in the account of the bush, even Moses showed that the dead rise, for he calls the Lord 'the God of Abraham, and the God of Isaac, and the God of Jacob.'[c] [38]He is not the God of the dead, but of the living, for to him all are alive."

[39]Some of the teachers of the law responded, "Well said, teacher!" [40]And no one dared to ask him any more questions.

Whose Son Is the Christ?

[41]Then Jesus said to them, "How is it that they say the Christ[d] is the Son of David? [42]David himself declares in the Book of Psalms:

" 'The Lord said to my Lord:
    "Sit at my right hand
[43]until I make your enemies
    a footstool for your feet." '[e]

[44]David calls him 'Lord.' How then can he be his son?"

[45]While all the people were listening, Jesus said to his disciples, [46]"Beware of the teachers of the law. They like to walk around in flowing robes and love to be greeted in the marketplaces and have the most important seats in the synagogues and the places of honor at banquets. [47]They devour widows' houses and for a

---

[a]17 Or *cornerstone*   [b]17 Psalm 118:22
[c]37 Exodus 3:6   [d]41 Or *Messiah*   [e]43 Psalm 110:1

show make lengthy prayers. Such men will be punished most severely."

The Widow's Offering

21 As he looked up, Jesus saw the rich putting their gifts into the temple treasury. ²He also saw a poor widow put in two very small copper coins.ᵃ ³"I tell you the truth," he said, "this poor widow has put in more than all the others. ⁴All these people gave their gifts out of their wealth; but she out of her poverty put in all she had to live on."

Signs of the End of the Age

⁵Some of his disciples were remarking about how the temple was adorned with beautiful stones and with gifts dedicated to God. But Jesus said, ⁶"As for what you see here, the time will come when not one stone will be left on another; every one of them will be thrown down."

⁷"Teacher," they asked, "when will these things happen? And what will be the sign that they are about to take place?"

⁸He replied: "Watch out that you are not deceived. For many will come in my name, claiming, 'I am he,' and, 'The time is near.' Do not follow them. ⁹When you hear of wars and revolutions, do not be frightened. These things must happen first, but the end will not come right away."

¹⁰Then he said to them: "Nation will rise against nation, and kingdom against kingdom. ¹¹There will be great earthquakes, famines and pestilences in various places, and fearful events and great signs from heaven.

¹²"But before all this, they will lay hands on you and persecute you. They will deliver you to synagogues and prisons, and you will be brought before kings and governors, and all on account of my name. ¹³This will result in your being witnesses to them. ¹⁴But make up your mind not to worry beforehand how you will defend yourselves. ¹⁵For I will give you words and wisdom that none of your adversaries will be able to resist or contradict. ¹⁶You will be betrayed even by parents, brothers, relatives and friends, and they will put some of you to death. ¹⁷All men will hate you because of me. ¹⁸But not a hair of your head will perish. ¹⁹By standing firm you will gain life.

²⁰"When you see Jerusalem being surrounded by armies, you will know that its desolation is near. ²¹Then let those who are in Judea flee to the mountains, let those in the city get out, and let those in the country not enter the city. ²²For this is the time of punishment in fulfillment of all that has been written. ²³How dreadful it will be in those days for pregnant women and nursing mothers! There will be great distress in the land and wrath against this people. ²⁴They will fall by the sword and will be taken as prisoners to all the nations. Jerusalem will be trampled on by the Gentiles until the times of the Gentiles are fulfilled.

²⁵"There will be signs in the sun, moon and stars. On the earth, nations will be in anguish and perplexity at the roaring and tossing of the sea. ²⁶Men will faint from terror, apprehensive of what is coming on the world, for the heavenly bodies will be shaken. ²⁷At that time they will see the Son of Man coming in a cloud with power and great glory. ²⁸When these things begin to take place, stand up and lift up your heads, because your redemption is drawing near."

²⁹He told them this parable: "Look at the fig tree and all the trees. ³⁰When they sprout leaves, you can see for yourselves and know that summer is near. ³¹Even so, when you see these things happening, you know that the kingdom of God is near.

³²"I tell you the truth, this generationᵇ will certainly not pass away until all these things have happened. ³³Heaven and earth will pass away, but my words will never pass away.

³⁴"Be careful, or your hearts will be weighed down with dissipation, drunkenness and the anxieties of life, and that day will close on you unexpectedly like a trap. ³⁵For it will come upon all those who live on the face of the whole earth. ³⁶Be always on the watch, and pray that you may be able to escape all that is about to happen, and that you may be able to stand before the Son of Man."

³⁷Each day Jesus was teaching at the temple, and each evening he went out to spend the night on the hill called the Mount of Olives, ³⁸and all the people came early in the morning to hear him at the temple.

Judas Agrees to Betray Jesus

22 Now the Feast of Unleavened Bread, called the Passover, was approaching, ²and the chief priests and the teachers of the law were looking for some way to get

ᵃ2 Greek *two lepta*   ᵇ32 Or *race*

rid of Jesus, for they were afraid of the people. ³Then Satan entered Judas, called Iscariot, one of the Twelve. ⁴And Judas went to the chief priests and the officers of the temple guard and discussed with them how he might betray Jesus. ⁵They were delighted and agreed to give him money. ⁶He consented, and watched for an opportunity to hand Jesus over to them when no crowd was present.

The Last Supper

⁷Then came the day of Unleavened Bread on which the Passover lamb had to be sacrificed. ⁸Jesus sent Peter and John, saying, "Go and make preparations for us to eat the Passover."

⁹"Where do you want us to prepare for it?" they asked.

¹⁰He replied, "As you enter the city, a man carrying a jar of water will meet you. Follow him to the house that he enters, ¹¹and say to the owner of the house, 'The Teacher asks: Where is the guest room, where I may eat the Passover with my disciples?' ¹²He will show you a large upper room, all furnished. Make preparations there."

¹³They left and found things just as Jesus had told them. So they prepared the Passover.

¹⁴When the hour came, Jesus and his apostles reclined at the table. ¹⁵And he said to them, "I have eagerly desired to eat this Passover with you before I suffer. ¹⁶For I tell you, I will not eat it again until it finds fulfillment in the kingdom of God."

¹⁷After taking the cup, he gave thanks and said, "Take this and divide it among you. ¹⁸For I tell you I will not drink again of the fruit of the vine until the kingdom of God comes."

¹⁹And he took bread, gave thanks and broke it, and gave it to them, saying, "This is my body given for you; do this in remembrance of me."

²⁰In the same way, after the supper he took the cup, saying, "This cup is the new covenant in my blood, which is poured out for you. ²¹But the hand of him who is going to betray me is with mine on the table. ²²The Son of Man will go as it has been decreed, but woe to that man who betrays him." ²³They began to question among themselves which of them it might be who would do this.

²⁴Also a dispute arose among them as to which of them was considered to be greatest. ²⁵Jesus said to them, "The kings of the Gentiles lord it over them; and those who exercise authority over them call themselves Benefactors. ²⁶But you are not to be like that. Instead, the greatest among you should be like the youngest, and the one who rules like the one who serves. ²⁷For who is greater, the one who is at the table or the one who serves? Is it not the one who is at the table? But I am among you as one who serves. ²⁸You are those who have stood by me in my trials. ²⁹And I confer on you a kingdom, just as my Father conferred one on me, ³⁰so that you may eat and drink at my table in my kingdom and sit on thrones, judging the twelve tribes of Israel.

³¹"Simon, Simon, Satan has asked to sift you[a] as wheat. ³²But I have prayed for you, Simon, that your faith may not fail. And when you have turned back, strengthen your brothers."

³³But he replied, "Lord, I am ready to go with you to prison and to death."

³⁴Jesus answered, "I tell you, Peter, before the rooster crows today, you will deny three times that you know me."

³⁵Then Jesus asked them, "When I sent you without purse, bag or sandals, did you lack anything?"

"Nothing," they answered.

³⁶He said to them, "But now if you have a purse, take it, and also a bag; and if you don't have a sword, sell your cloak and buy one. ³⁷It is written: 'And he was numbered with the transgressors'[b]; and I tell you that this must be fulfilled in me. Yes, what is written about me is reaching its fulfillment."

³⁸The disciples said, "See, Lord, here are two swords."

"That is enough," he replied.

Jesus Prays on the Mount of Olives

³⁹Jesus went out as usual to the Mount of Olives, and his disciples followed him. ⁴⁰On reaching the place, he said to them, "Pray that you will not fall into temptation." ⁴¹He withdrew about a stone's throw beyond them, knelt down and prayed, ⁴²"Father, if you are willing, take this cup from me; yet not my will, but yours be done." ⁴³An angel from heaven appeared to him and strengthened him. ⁴⁴And being in anguish, he prayed more earnestly, and his sweat was like drops of blood falling to the ground.[c]

a31 The Greek is plural. b37 Isaiah 53:12
c44 Some early manuscripts do not have verses 43 and 44.

45When he rose from prayer and went back to the disciples, he found them asleep, exhausted from sorrow. **46**"Why are you sleeping?" he asked them. "Get up and pray so that you will not fall into temptation."

Jesus Arrested

47While he was still speaking a crowd came up, and the man who was called Judas, one of the Twelve, was leading them. He approached Jesus to kiss him, **48**but Jesus asked him, "Judas, are you betraying the Son of Man with a kiss?"

49When Jesus' followers saw what was going to happen, they said, "Lord, should we strike with our swords?" **50**And one of them struck the servant of the high priest, cutting off his right ear.

51But Jesus answered, "No more of this!" And he touched the man's ear and healed him.

52Then Jesus said to the chief priests, the officers of the temple guard, and the elders, who had come for him, "Am I leading a rebellion, that you have come with swords and clubs? **53**Every day I was with you in the temple courts, and you did not lay a hand on me. But this is your hour—when darkness reigns."

Peter Disowns Jesus

54Then seizing him, they led him away and took him into the house of the high priest. Peter followed at a distance. **55**But when they had kindled a fire in the middle of the courtyard and had sat down together, Peter sat down with them. **56**A servant girl saw him seated there in the firelight. She looked closely at him and said, "This man was with him."

57But he denied it. "Woman, I don't know him," he said.

58A little later someone else saw him and said, "You also are one of them."

"Man, I am not!" Peter replied.

59About an hour later another asserted, "Certainly this fellow was with him, for he is a Galilean."

60Peter replied, "Man, I don't know what you're talking about!" Just as he was speaking, the rooster crowed. **61**The Lord turned and looked straight at Peter. Then Peter remembered the word the Lord had spoken to him: "Before the rooster crows today, you will disown me three times." **62**And he went outside and wept bitterly.

The Guards Mock Jesus

63The men who were guarding Jesus began mocking and beating him. **64**They blindfolded him and demanded, "Prophesy! Who hit you?" **65**And they said many other insulting things to him.

Jesus Before Pilate and Herod

66At daybreak the council of the elders of the people, both the chief priests and teachers of the law, met together, and Jesus was led before them. **67**"If you are the Christ,*a*" they said, "tell us."

Jesus answered, "If I tell you, you will not believe me, **68**and if I asked you, you would not answer. **69**But from now on, the Son of Man will be seated at the right hand of the mighty God."

70They all asked, "Are you then the Son of God?"

He replied, "You are right in saying I am."

71Then they said, "Why do we need any more testimony? We have heard it from his own lips."

23 Then the whole assembly rose and led him off to Pilate. **2**And they began to accuse him, saying, "We have found this man subverting our nation. He opposes payment of taxes to Caesar and claims to be Christ,*b* a king."

3So Pilate asked Jesus, "Are you the king of the Jews?"

"Yes, it is as you say," Jesus replied.

4Then Pilate announced to the chief priests and the crowd, "I find no basis for a charge against this man."

5But they insisted, "He stirs up the people all over Judea*c* by his teaching. He started in Galilee and has come all the way here."

6On hearing this, Pilate asked if the man was a Galilean. **7**When he learned that Jesus was under Herod's jurisdiction, he sent him to Herod, who was also in Jerusalem at that time.

8When Herod saw Jesus, he was greatly pleased, because for a long time he had been wanting to see him. From what he had heard about him, he hoped to see him perform some miracle. **9**He plied him with many questions, but Jesus gave him no answer. **10**The chief priests and the teachers of the law were standing there, vehemently accusing him. **11**Then Herod and his soldiers ridiculed and mocked

*a*67 Or *Messiah*   *b*2 Or *Messiah*; also in verses 35 and 39   *c*5 Or *over the land of the Jews*

him. Dressing him in an elegant robe, they sent him back to Pilate. [12]That day Herod and Pilate became friends—before this they had been enemies.

[13]Pilate called together the chief priests, the rulers and the people, [14]and said to them, "You brought me this man as one who was inciting the people to rebellion. I have examined him in your presence and have found no basis for your charges against him. [15]Neither has Herod, for he sent him back to us; as you can see, he has done nothing to deserve death. [16]Therefore, I will punish him and then release him.[a]"

[18]With one voice they cried out, "Away with this man! Release Barabbas to us!" [19](Barabbas had been thrown into prison for an insurrection in the city, and for murder.)

[20]Wanting to release Jesus, Pilate appealed to them again. [21]But they kept shouting, "Crucify him! Crucify him!"

[22]For the third time he spoke to them: "Why? What crime has this man committed? I have found in him no grounds for the death penalty. Therefore I will have him punished and then release him."

[23]But with loud shouts they insistently demanded that he be crucified, and their shouts prevailed. [24]So Pilate decided to grant their demand. [25]He released the man who had been thrown into prison for insurrection and murder, the one they asked for, and surrendered Jesus to their will.

The Crucifixion

[26]As they led him away, they seized Simon from Cyrene, who was on his way in from the country, and put the cross on him and made him carry it behind Jesus. [27]A large number of people followed him, including women who mourned and wailed for him. [28]Jesus turned and said to them, "Daughters of Jerusalem, do not weep for me; weep for yourselves and for your children. [29]For the time will come when you will say, 'Blessed are the barren women, the wombs that never bore and the breasts that never nursed!' [30]Then

> " 'they will say to the mountains, "Fall
> on us!"
> and to the hills, "Cover us!" ' [b]

[31]For if men do these things when the tree is green, what will happen when it is dry?"

[32]Two other men, both criminals, were also led out with him to be executed.

[33]When they came to the place called the Skull, there they crucified him, along with the criminals—one on his right, the other on his left. [34]Jesus said, "Father, forgive them, for they do not know what they are doing."[c] And they divided up his clothes by casting lots.

[35]The people stood watching, and the rulers even sneered at him. They said, "He saved others; let him save himself if he is the Christ of God, the Chosen One."

[36]The soldiers also came up and mocked him. They offered him wine vinegar [37]and said, "If you are the king of the Jews, save yourself."

[38]There was a written notice above him, which read: THIS IS THE KING OF THE JEWS.

[39]One of the criminals who hung there hurled insults at him: "Aren't you the Christ? Save yourself and us!"

[40]But the other criminal rebuked him. "Don't you fear God," he said, "since you are under the same sentence? [41]We are punished justly, for we are getting what our deeds deserve. But this man has done nothing wrong."

[42]Then he said, "Jesus, remember me when you come into your kingdom.[d]"

[43]Jesus answered him, "I tell you the truth, today you will be with me in paradise."

Jesus' Death

[44]It was now about the sixth hour, and darkness came over the whole land until the ninth hour, [45]for the sun stopped shining. And the curtain of the temple was torn in two. [46]Jesus called out with a loud voice, "Father, into your hands I commit my spirit." When he had said this, he breathed his last.

[47]The centurion, seeing what had happened, praised God and said, "Surely this was a righteous man." [48]When all the people who had gathered to witness this sight saw what took place, they beat their breasts and went away. [49]But all those who knew him, including the women who had followed him from Galilee, stood at a distance, watching these things.

Jesus' Burial

[50]Now there was a man named Joseph, a member of the Council, a good and up-

---

[a]16 Some manuscripts him." [17]Now he was obliged to release one man to them at the Feast.   [b]30 Hosea 10:8   [c]34 Some early manuscripts do not have this sentence.   [d]42 Some manuscripts come with your kingly power

right man, [51]who had not consented to their decision and action. He came from the Judean town of Arimathea and he was waiting for the kingdom of God. [52]Going to Pilate, he asked for Jesus' body. [53]Then he took it down, wrapped it in linen cloth and placed it in a tomb cut in the rock, one in which no one had yet been laid. [54]It was Preparation Day, and the Sabbath was about to begin.

[55]The women who had come with Jesus from Galilee followed Joseph and saw the tomb and how his body was laid in it. [56]Then they went home and prepared spices and perfumes. But they rested on the Sabbath in obedience to the commandment.

The Resurrection

24 On the first day of the week, very early in the morning, the women took the spices they had prepared and went to the tomb. [2]They found the stone rolled away from the tomb, [3]but when they entered, they did not find the body of the Lord Jesus. [4]While they were wondering about this, suddenly two men in clothes that gleamed like lightning stood beside them. [5]In their fright the women bowed down with their faces to the ground, but the men said to them, "Why do you look for the living among the dead? [6]He is not here; he has risen! Remember how he told you, while he was still with you in Galilee: [7]'The Son of Man must be delivered into the hands of sinful men, be crucified and on the third day be raised again.' " [8]Then they remembered his words.

[9]When they came back from the tomb, they told all these things to the Eleven and to all the others. [10]It was Mary Magdalene, Joanna, Mary the mother of James, and the others with them who told this to the apostles. [11]But they did not believe the women, because their words seemed to them like nonsense. [12]Peter, however, got up and ran to the tomb. Bending over, he saw the strips of linen lying by themselves, and he went away, wondering to himself what had happened.

On the Road to Emmaus

[13]Now that same day two of them were going to a village called Emmaus, about seven miles[a] from Jerusalem. [14]They were talking with each other about everything that had happened. [15]As they talked and discussed these things with each other, Jesus himself came up and walked along with them; [16]but they were kept from recognizing him.

[17]He asked them, "What are you discussing together as you walk along?"

They stood still, their faces downcast. [18]One of them, named Cleopas, asked him, "Are you only a visitor to Jerusalem and do not know the things that have happened there in these days?"

[19]"What things?" he asked.

"About Jesus of Nazareth," they replied. "He was a prophet, powerful in word and deed before God and all the people. [20]The chief priests and our rulers handed him over to be sentenced to death, and they crucified him; [21]but we had hoped that he was the one who was going to redeem Israel. And what is more, it is the third day since all this took place. [22]In addition, some of our women amazed us. They went to the tomb early this morning [23]but didn't find his body. They came and told us that they had seen a vision of angels, who said he was alive. [24]Then some of our companions went to the tomb and found it just as the women had said, but him they did not see."

[25]He said to them, "How foolish you are, and how slow of heart to believe all that the prophets have spoken! [26]Did not the Christ[b] have to suffer these things and then enter his glory?" [27]And beginning with Moses and all the Prophets, he explained to them what was said in all the Scriptures concerning himself.

[28]As they approached the village to which they were going, Jesus acted as if he were going farther. [29]But they urged him strongly, "Stay with us, for it is nearly evening; the day is almost over." So he went in to stay with them.

[30]When he was at the table with them, he took bread, gave thanks, broke it and began to give it to them. [31]Then their eyes were opened and they recognized him, and he disappeared from their sight. [32]They asked each other, "Were not our hearts burning within us while he talked with us on the road and opened the Scriptures to us?"

[33]They got up and returned at once to Jerusalem. There they found the Eleven and those with them, assembled together [34]and saying, "It is true! The Lord has risen and has appeared to Simon." [35]Then the

---

[a]13 Greek *sixty stadia* (about 11 kilometers)
[b]26 Or *Messiah*; also in verse 46

two told what had happened on the way, and how Jesus was recognized by them when he broke the bread.

Jesus Appears to the Disciples

36While they were still talking about this, Jesus himself stood among them and said to them, "Peace be with you."

37They were startled and frightened, thinking they saw a ghost. **38**He said to them, "Why are you troubled, and why do doubts rise in your minds? **39**Look at my hands and my feet. It is I myself! Touch me and see; a ghost does not have flesh and bones, as you see I have."

40When he had said this, he showed them his hands and feet. **41**And while they still did not believe it because of joy and amazement, he asked them, "Do you have anything here to eat?" **42**They gave him a piece of broiled fish, **43**and he took it and ate it in their presence.

44He said to them, "This is what I told you while I was still with you: Everything

You Just Gotta Believe

DAILY INSIGHT

WEDNESDAY

Passage:
Luke 24:13–32

Verses:
Luke 24:31–32

It's the state finals, and your local high school basketball team is down by two points. The game is already in overtime, and the clock shows only seven seconds left. So the coach calls a time out and puts together a screen play that will get the ball to his best three-point shooter, just outside the arc.

When he finishes with the assignments, he stretches out his hand, which is instantly surrounded by the hands of five exhausted players. He looks at each man, one by one, eye to eye. Then the coach says, "Well men, this is it. You've got the play. Now, you just gotta believe."

The next seven seconds go down as the most important in the school's athletic history. As time runs out, the three-point shot swishes in— *nothin' but net!* The gymnasium explodes with the kind of euphoria that only this kind of moment can create. These young men—and the coach, and the crowd, and the radio audience—know what it means to bridge the gap between faith and belief.

If I went to a flip chart and drew a horizontal line, labeling one end of the line "faith" and the other end, "no faith," you and I would likely fall somewhere between those two extremes. We're in pretty good shape with the facts. We can visualize the play. But this belief thing can be a real challenge sometimes.

Today's passage illustrates this challenge. Two men were on a seven-mile walk from Jerusalem to Emmaus on the first Sunday after Jesus' death. These two men had known Jesus and had seen his conviction and crucifixion. And because they hadn't spoken to anyone who had seen the risen Christ, they were still living with that news.

When these men described Jesus (ironically, to Jesus himself) in verse 19, they called him "a prophet." But, because of the recent events, they stopped short of calling him the Messiah. These men, too, were somewhere on the continuum between "faith" and "no faith." Later, when "their eyes were opened," they hustled back to Jerusalem to find out what had happened. They took action and moved toward faith. Read verses 33 through 35, and you can almost hear that three pointer "swish."

Do you, like these two men, sometimes have a hard time with faith? Do you tend to look at overwhelming circumstances and conclude that the odds are stacked against you? Are you sometimes too tired to hang in there?

Just a few short years after the two men finished their walk to Emmaus, the apostle Paul wrote these words: "[Faith is] not from yourselves, it is the gift of God" (Ephesians 2:8). This story about faith is true. Like God's grace, it's a gift.

Go ahead, Dad. Take your best shot. You just gotta believe.

For your next devotional reading, go to page 1161.

must be fulfilled that is written about me in the Law of Moses, the Prophets and the Psalms."

⁴⁵Then he opened their minds so they could understand the Scriptures. ⁴⁶He told them, "This is what is written: The Christ will suffer and rise from the dead on the third day, ⁴⁷and repentance and forgiveness of sins will be preached in his name to all nations, beginning at Jerusalem. ⁴⁸You are witnesses of these things. ⁴⁹I am going to send you what my Father has promised; but stay in the city until you have been clothed with power from on high."

The Ascension

⁵⁰When he had led them out to the vicinity of Bethany, he lifted up his hands and blessed them. ⁵¹While he was blessing them, he left them and was taken up into heaven. ⁵²Then they worshiped him and returned to Jerusalem with great joy. ⁵³And they stayed continually at the temple, praising God.

What was it actually like to live with Jesus—to walk with him, to hear his words, to witness his emotions, to enjoy his companionship, to feel his love? As "The disciple whom Jesus loved" (13:23), John knew the answer to these questions. Given John's close friendship with the Savior, it's not surprising that this account gives us the most thorough chronology of the events of Jesus' life. And John lets the story tell the message. Somehow he knew that if he would simply let us in on what really happened during the years of Jesus' earthly ministry, our lives would never be the same.

It's little wonder that the book of John is the best-selling and most-often-reprinted portion of the Bible, the best-selling book of all time. Do you want to know who Jesus was and what it was really like to be face-to-face with the Creator of the universe? Read on.

John

The Word Became Flesh

1 In the beginning was the Word, and the Word was with God, and the Word was God. ²He was with God in the beginning. ³Through him all things were made; without him nothing was made that has been made. ⁴In him was life, and that life was the light of men. ⁵The light shines in the darkness, but the darkness has not understood*ᵃ* it.

⁶There came a man who was sent from God; his name was John. ⁷He came as a witness to testify concerning that light, so that through him all men might believe. ⁸He himself was not the light; he came only as a witness to the light. ⁹The true light that gives light to every man was coming into the world.*ᵇ*

¹⁰He was in the world, and though the world was made through him, the world did not recognize him. ¹¹He came to that which was his own, but his own did not receive him. ¹²Yet to all who received him, to those who believed in his name, he gave the right to become children of God— ¹³children born not of natural descent,*ᶜ* nor of human decision or a husband's will, but born of God.

¹⁴The Word became flesh and made his dwelling among us. We have seen his glory, the glory of the One and Only,*ᵈ* who came from the Father, full of grace and truth.

ᵃ5 Or darkness, and the darkness has not overcome
ᵇ9 Or This was the true light that gives light to every man who comes into the world   *ᶜ13 Greek of bloods*   *ᵈ14 Or the Only Begotten*

¹⁵John testifies concerning him. He cries out, saying, "This was he of whom I said, 'He who comes after me has surpassed me because he was before me.' " ¹⁶From the fullness of his grace we have all received one blessing after another. ¹⁷For the law was given through Moses; grace and truth came through Jesus Christ. ¹⁸No one has ever seen God, but God the One and Only,*ᵃ,ᵇ* who is at the Father's side, has made him known.

John the Baptist Denies Being the Christ

¹⁹Now this was John's testimony when the Jews of Jerusalem sent priests and Levites to ask him who he was. ²⁰He did not fail to confess, but confessed freely, "I am not the Christ.*ᶜ*"

ᵃ18 Or *the Only Begotten*   ᵇ18 Some manuscripts *but the only* (or *only begotten*) *Son*   ᶜ20 Or *Messiah*. "The Christ" (Greek) and "the Messiah" (Hebrew) both mean "the Anointed One"; also in verse 25.

Get Out of the Way

DAILY INSIGHT

THURSDAY

Passage:
John 1:6–9

Verse:
John 1:8

My first assignment in publishing was to escort Harold Hughes, the former Iowa Senator and truck-driver-alcoholic-turned-believer, on a portion of his book tour. My charge was Chicago. My task was to do everything in my power to deliver the Senator to the right place at the right time.

When we first met, I knew that this rough-hewn man wasn't impressed with me. He had known life's brutal underside, and he saw me as a naïve, clear-skinned youngster, raised in a safe, white middle-class family, completely unfamiliar with the real stuff of life. Unfortunately, I had work to do and couldn't concern myself with the Senator's contempt. My job was to serve him, maximizing his energy and attention to the interviews and appearances on the itinerary. I worked like crazy to make this happen.

At the end of our third day together—the final day of the tour—Harold and I talked turkey over dinner. "You know," he said to me, "you're the kind of person I used to despise." Now *there's* an opening line to enhance your digestion. "But," the Senator continued, "I've watched how hard you have worked on my behalf, and I sincerely appreciate your serving attitude. I'm truly grateful for your efforts. Thank you."

I felt as though I had just received an Academy Award™. Although I didn't overdo my "thank you," his kind words had meant a lot.

John the Baptist's assignment was

something like mine. He was, if you will, the designated front man for the Messiah. He challenged people to confess their waywardness, told people about the coming Savior, and then bowed out. One of my friends said it this way, "John the Baptist prepared the way, declared the way, then got out of the way."

Actually, you and I have something in common with John. We are Christ's front men, his emissaries on earth. Our job, whether at work or in the home, is to lovingly confront and courageously challenge, then be invisible and allow God to do what only he can do.

Look at it this way. If I had decided that Senator Hughes needed some help behind the microphones, shaking hands or signing books, his visit to Chicago would have been a disaster. I would have, by my foolishness, confirmed his initial impressions of me.

Similarly, Jesus has not asked us to set policy, stand before the microphones, or even try through our own wisdom and creativity to convince people of their need for a Savior. His charge is simple: We are to tenderly challenge people to live righteously, be ready to tell others about Christ's amazing grace, then let God do the work.

Prepare the way, declare the way, then get out of the way. God is very good at what he does.

For your next devotional reading, go to page 1164.

²¹They asked him, "Then who are you? Are you Elijah?"

He said, "I am not."

"Are you the Prophet?"

He answered, "No."

²²Finally they said, "Who are you? Give us an answer to take back to those who sent us. What do you say about yourself?"

²³John replied in the words of Isaiah the prophet, "I am the voice of one calling in the desert, 'Make straight the way for the Lord.' "ᵃ

²⁴Now some Pharisees who had been sent ²⁵questioned him, "Why then do you baptize if you are not the Christ, nor Elijah, nor the Prophet?"

²⁶"I baptize withᵇ water," John replied, "but among you stands one you do not know. ²⁷He is the one who comes after me, the thongs of whose sandals I am not worthy to untie."

²⁸This all happened at Bethany on the other side of the Jordan, where John was baptizing.

Jesus the Lamb of God

²⁹The next day John saw Jesus coming toward him and said, "Look, the Lamb of God, who takes away the sin of the world! ³⁰This is the one I meant when I said, 'A man who comes after me has surpassed me because he was before me.' ³¹I myself did not know him, but the reason I came baptizing with water was that he might be revealed to Israel."

³²Then John gave this testimony: "I saw the Spirit come down from heaven as a dove and remain on him. ³³I would not have known him, except that the one who sent me to baptize with water told me, 'The man on whom you see the Spirit come down and remain is he who will baptize with the Holy Spirit.' ³⁴I have seen and I testify that this is the Son of God."

Jesus' First Disciples

³⁵The next day John was there again with two of his disciples. ³⁶When he saw Jesus passing by, he said, "Look, the Lamb of God!"

³⁷When the two disciples heard him say this, they followed Jesus. ³⁸Turning around, Jesus saw them following and asked, "What do you want?"

They said, "Rabbi" (which means Teacher), "where are you staying?"

³⁹"Come," he replied, "and you will see."

So they went and saw where he was staying, and spent that day with him. It was about the tenth hour.

⁴⁰Andrew, Simon Peter's brother, was one of the two who heard what John had said and who had followed Jesus. ⁴¹The first thing Andrew did was to find his brother Simon and tell him, "We have found the Messiah" (that is, the Christ). ⁴²And he brought him to Jesus.

Jesus looked at him and said, "You are Simon son of John. You will be called

ᵃ23 Isaiah 40:3   ᵇ26 Or in; also in verses 31 and 33

HEY DAD
How did we get the New Testament?

Text: John 1:1

We believe that God decided which books should go into the New Testament and that he guided people to put them together. The early Christian church recognized their need for one group of authoritative writings they could refer to again and again. This would also protect future generations from a watered-down version of the truth. So, the church officials established a canon (collection of writings) that included all the beliefs of the Christian church.

The standard they set for the canon required a book to be written by one of the apostles or someone very close to the apostles. They agreed to include the Gospels of Matthew, Mark, Luke and John; Paul's thirteen letters; and the letters of other apostles and their close companions. They did not include any letters written after the deaths of the apostles.

Thanks to the Holy Spirit working through these early church leaders, we know that the teachings we have in the New Testament today are trustworthy.

For a complete listing of Questions Kids Ask, turn to page 1435.

Cephas" (which, when translated, is Peter[a]).

Jesus Calls Philip and Nathanael

[43]The next day Jesus decided to leave for Galilee. Finding Philip, he said to him, "Follow me."

[44]Philip, like Andrew and Peter, was from the town of Bethsaida. [45]Philip found Nathanael and told him, "We have found the one Moses wrote about in the Law, and about whom the prophets also wrote—Jesus of Nazareth, the son of Joseph."

[46]"Nazareth! Can anything good come from there?" Nathanael asked.

"Come and see," said Philip.

[47]When Jesus saw Nathanael approaching, he said of him, "Here is a true Israelite, in whom there is nothing false."

[48]"How do you know me?" Nathanael asked.

Jesus answered, "I saw you while you were still under the fig tree before Philip called you."

[49]Then Nathanael declared, "Rabbi, you are the Son of God; you are the King of Israel."

[50]Jesus said, "You believe[b] because I told you I saw you under the fig tree. You shall see greater things than that." [51]He then added, "I tell you[c] the truth, you[c] shall see heaven open, and the angels of God ascending and descending on the Son of Man."

Jesus Changes Water to Wine

2 On the third day a wedding took place at Cana in Galilee. Jesus' mother was there, [2]and Jesus and his disciples had also been invited to the wedding. [3]When the wine was gone, Jesus' mother said to him, "They have no more wine."

[4]"Dear woman, why do you involve me?" Jesus replied. "My time has not yet come."

[5]His mother said to the servants, "Do whatever he tells you."

[6]Nearby stood six stone water jars, the kind used by the Jews for ceremonial washing, each holding from twenty to thirty gallons.[d]

[7]Jesus said to the servants, "Fill the jars with water"; so they filled them to the brim.

[8]Then he told them, "Now draw some out and take it to the master of the banquet."

They did so, [9]and the master of the banquet tasted the water that had been turned into wine. He did not realize where it had come from, though the servants who had drawn the water knew. Then he called the bridegroom aside [10]and said, "Everyone brings out the choice wine first and then the cheaper wine after the guests have had too much to drink; but you have saved the best till now."

[11]This, the first of his miraculous signs, Jesus performed at Cana in Galilee. He thus revealed his glory, and his disciples put their faith in him.

Jesus Clears the Temple

[12]After this he went down to Capernaum with his mother and brothers and his disciples. There they stayed for a few days. [13]When it was almost time for the Jewish Passover, Jesus went up to Jerusalem. [14]In the temple courts he found men selling cattle, sheep and doves, and others sitting at tables exchanging money. [15]So he made a whip out of cords, and drove all from the temple area, both sheep and cattle; he scattered the coins of the money changers and overturned their tables. [16]To those who sold doves he said, "Get these out of here! How dare you turn my Father's house into a market!"

[17]His disciples remembered that it is written: "Zeal for your house will consume me."[e]

[18]Then the Jews demanded of him, "What miraculous sign can you show us to prove your authority to do all this?"

[19]Jesus answered them, "Destroy this temple, and I will raise it again in three days."

[20]The Jews replied, "It has taken forty-six years to build this temple, and you are going to raise it in three days?" [21]But the temple he had spoken of was his body. [22]After he was raised from the dead, his disciples recalled what he had said. Then they believed the Scripture and the words that Jesus had spoken.

[23]Now while he was in Jerusalem at the Passover Feast, many people saw the miraculous signs he was doing and believed in his name.[f] [24]But Jesus would not entrust himself to them, for he knew all men. [25]He did not need man's testimony

[a]42 Both *Cephas* (Aramaic) and *Peter* (Greek) mean *rock*. [b]50 Or *Do you believe . . . ?* [c]51 The Greek is plural. [d]6 Greek *two to three metretes* (probably about 75 to 115 liters) [e]17 Psalm 69:9 [f]23 Or *and believed in him*

about man, for he knew what was in a man.

Jesus Teaches Nicodemus

3 Now there was a man of the Pharisees named Nicodemus, a member of the Jewish ruling council. ²He came to Jesus at night and said, "Rabbi, we know you are a teacher who has come from God. For no one could perform the miraculous signs you are doing if God were not with him."

³In reply Jesus declared, "I tell you the truth, no one can see the kingdom of God unless he is born again.*ᵃ*"

⁴"How can a man be born when he is old?" Nicodemus asked. "Surely he cannot enter a second time into his mother's womb to be born!"

⁵Jesus answered, "I tell you the truth, no one can enter the kingdom of God unless he is born of water and the Spirit. ⁶Flesh gives birth to flesh, but the Spirit*ᵇ* gives

ᵃ3 Or born from above; also in verse 7   ᵇ6 Or but spirit

No FHB on Grace

DAILY INSIGHT

FRIDAY

Passage:
John 2:1–11

Verse:
John 2:11

The front door of my childhood home was permanently open, allowing a constant stream of dinner guests. Because my parents had been missionaries and were involved in Christian ministry, most of these visitors were in the same vocation. In any case, there were lots of them. As children, my five siblings and I had the opportunity to meet many wonderful people—saints in the truest sense of the word.

Because we had so many dinner guests so often, my mother developed a secret code. If she was running short of something—green beans, for example—she would whisper in a voice only detectable by her direct offspring: "FHB the green beans," meaning, "family hold back" on the green beans. No one visiting our home knew about this code, only us. And because we wanted to avoid the embarrassment of running out of something, we'd pass on the green beans.

Jesus' first miracle was at a wedding reception. His mother may have had something to do with hosting the party because she was one of the first to know that the wine had run out, a *faux pas* of sizable proportions. It was too late to FHB on the wine; the stuff was gone. Mary came to Jesus with the news; "They have no more wine."

At first glance, Jesus' response sounds abrupt, even a little rude. His mother knew of his special calling and so she tried to

gently coerce him into fixing the problem. And, seeing the potential embarrassment of the party's host and the unavoidable disappointment of the guests, Jesus created some more wine. Not only did he create good wine, he created *great* wine. And not only did he create great wine, he created *one hundred and eighty gallons* of great wine, more than the party guests could have possibly consumed. No more FHB on the wine.

Over the next three years of ministry, Jesus performed many incredible miracles. He cast out demons. He healed sick people. He even breathed life into dead people. In the face of these Major-league miracles, some may consider this wedding-reception miracle to be rather inconsequential. Not so.

At certain times in our lives we call on God for healing. At other times disaster strikes and we call on our heavenly Father for supernatural intervention. But not a single day passes when we don't need his grace … the fine wine of his love and forgiveness.

So he gives this grace to us—not just enough, but more than we could ever drink … more than we could consume in a lifetime. God's grace is abundant and precious. It is poured out on us in lavish measure. There's no FHB on this. Drink up, my friend.

For your next devotional reading, go to page 1165.

Key Verse: *"For God so loved the world that he gave his one and only Son, that whoever believes in him shall not perish but have eternal life."* John 3:16
Text: John 3:16–21 *(Dad or child reads the text.)*

DAD READS: Only doctors used to wear pagers clipped to their belts, but now thousands of people from all walks of life use pagers every day. There is a dad named Dan Wolgemuth who lives in Kansas City. Dan wears a pager, and his three children do a very special thing with this pager. When they want to tell their dad that they love him, wherever he is—and he travels all over the world—they send him a message like this: 143-12.

QUIET
TIMES
WITH **Dad**

Child reads: That sounds neat, but what does it mean?

DAD READS: Dan's daughter, Alli, is twelve years old. The "12" means that this message is from her. The "143" means "I love you": one letter in "I," four letters in "love," and three letters in "you." If Andrew is sending the message, he puts a "17" after "143." If Erik sends the message, he puts "15" after "143." Even Dan's wife, Mary, sends "143's" to Dan. At first, no one else but Dan and his children understood this special code.

Child reads: What a fun and wonderful idea for this family!

DAD READS: One day, a long time ago, God decided to send a special message to us. God sent Jesus. He came in a little package called a baby. Many people did not understand who Jesus was. Many did not believe that he was God's only Son. Some people even wanted to kill him. But God sent him to earth to teach us how to love one another, and to die for our sins on the cross.

Child reads: I see! Jesus was God's "I love you" to the whole world. Through Jesus, his "143-GOD" is on everyone's pager. And when we believe this, we become his very own children.

DAD READS: This is the most important truth in the whole Bible. I'm so glad that God sent Jesus as a message of love. God's love for you and me gives us purpose and wholeness when we're frightened, confused, or lonely. His forgiveness and grace give us the freedom to love others—even people who are not easy to love.

Sometimes when Dan is with someone and one of his children sends a "143" message, Dan tells them about his family's secret code. People always like to hear about this special way that Andrew, Alli, and Erik "talk" to their dad.

Child reads: Every time we get a chance, we should tell people about Jesus, God's "143" to you and me. His love is something that everyone needs to hear about. Let me pray this prayer with you:

Our Father in heaven, we love you. Thank you for Jesus, your special "I love you" to the whole world. Thank you for coming to earth to forgive our sins. Please help us to always remember that your message is good news for everyone. We love you and we thank you for your love. In Jesus' name, **Amen.**

For your next devotional reading, go to page 1168.

birth to spirit. [7]You should not be surprised at my saying, 'You[a] must be born again.' [8]The wind blows wherever it pleases. You hear its sound, but you cannot tell where it comes from or where it is going. So it is with everyone born of the Spirit."

[9]"How can this be?" Nicodemus asked.

[10]"You are Israel's teacher," said Jesus, "and do you not understand these things? [11]I tell you the truth, we speak of what we know, and we testify to what we have seen, but still you people do not accept our testimony. [12]I have spoken to you of earthly things and you do not believe; how then will you believe if I speak of heavenly things? [13]No one has ever gone into heaven except the one who came from heaven—the Son of Man.[b] [14]Just as Moses lifted up the snake in the desert, so the Son of Man must be lifted up, [15]that everyone who believes in him may have eternal life.[c]

[16]"For God so loved the world that he gave his one and only Son,[d] that whoever believes in him shall not perish but have eternal life. [17]For God did not send his Son into the world to condemn the world, but to save the world through him. [18]Whoever believes in him is not condemned, but whoever does not believe stands condemned already because he has not believed in the name of God's one and only Son.[e] [19]This is the verdict: Light has come into the world, but men loved darkness instead of light because their deeds were evil. [20]Everyone who does evil hates the light, and will not come into the light for fear that his deeds will be exposed. [21]But whoever lives by the truth comes into the light, so that it may be seen plainly that what he has done has been done through God."[f]

John the Baptist's Testimony About Jesus

[22]After this, Jesus and his disciples went out into the Judean countryside, where he spent some time with them, and baptized. [23]Now John also was baptizing at Aenon near Salim, because there was plenty of water, and people were constantly coming to be baptized. [24](This was before John was put in prison.) [25]An argument developed between some of John's disciples and a certain Jew[g] over the matter of ceremonial washing. [26]They came to John and said to him, "Rabbi, that man who was with you on the other side of the Jordan—the one you testified about—

well, he is baptizing, and everyone is going to him."

[27]To this John replied, "A man can receive only what is given him from heaven. [28]You yourselves can testify that I said, 'I am not the Christ[h] but am sent ahead of him.' [29]The bride belongs to the bridegroom. The friend who attends the bridegroom waits and listens for him, and is full of joy when he hears the bridegroom's voice. That joy is mine, and it is now complete. [30]He must become greater; I must become less.

[31]"The one who comes from above is above all; the one who is from the earth belongs to the earth, and speaks as one from the earth. The one who comes from heaven is above all. [32]He testifies to what he has seen and heard, but no one accepts his testimony. [33]The man who has accepted it has certified that God is truthful. [34]For the one whom God has sent speaks the words of God, for God[i] gives the Spirit without limit. [35]The Father loves the Son and has placed everything in his hands. [36]Whoever believes in the Son has eternal life, but whoever rejects the Son will not see life, for God's wrath remains on him."[j]

Jesus Talks With a Samaritan Woman

4 The Pharisees heard that Jesus was gaining and baptizing more disciples than John, [2]although in fact it was not Jesus who baptized, but his disciples. [3]When the Lord learned of this, he left Judea and went back once more to Galilee. [4]Now he had to go through Samaria. [5]So he came to a town in Samaria called Sychar, near the plot of ground Jacob had given to his son Joseph. [6]Jacob's well was there, and Jesus, tired as he was from the journey, sat down by the well. It was about the sixth hour.

[7]When a Samaritan woman came to draw water, Jesus said to her, "Will you give me a drink?" [8](His disciples had gone into the town to buy food.)

[9]The Samaritan woman said to him, "You are a Jew and I am a Samaritan woman. How can you ask me for a drink?" (For Jews do not associate with Samaritans.[k])

---

a7 The Greek is plural. *b13* Some manuscripts *Man, who is in heaven* *c15* Or *believes may have eternal life in him* *d16* Or *his only begotten Son* *e18* Or *God's only begotten Son* *f21* Some interpreters end the quotation after verse 15. *g25* Some manuscripts *and certain Jews* *h28* Or *Messiah* *i34* Greek *he* *j36* Some interpreters end the quotation after verse 30. *k9* Or *do not use dishes Samaritans have used*

Faith: Jesus Loves Me, this I Know

"For God did not send his Son into the world to condemn the world, but to save the world through him." John 3:17

BUILDING YOUR CHILDREN

In the mid-seventies, I took my family to tour the Houston Astrodome. Walking into a building that size was unbelievable. Indoor baseball—wow! I remember gazing at the superstructure in amazement and asking the guide if pop flies wouldn't just bounce off that ceiling. "Don't they go higher than that?" She assured me that they very rarely do.

As part of the tour, the guide led our group into a small theater for a multimedia slide show. We saw how the Astrodome was built—my favorite part–and how many different kinds of activities it could hold. We saw great action shots of rodeos, baseball games, tractor pulls (this was Texas, remember), football games and rock concerts. The music behind these slides was exciting, loud, and raucous. We got the idea that this building holds many thrilling events.

Then the music faded into what sounded like an old hymn, played by the minister's lovely wife on a cheap, manual pump organ in some clapboard country church. Over this nice, unobtrusive and flat music, the announcer told us that the Astrodome is so versatile that it's even used for "religious" services.

I remember feeling sick. *Why,* I thought, *isn't our faith seen as just a normal part of life?*

Driving away from the Astrodome that day, Bobbie and I made a simple resolution: We will make our faith an everyday normal thing. Our children will see us treat our love for God as part of our daily routine—not as some clumsy diversion from real life. So that's what we did. And this is something you can do, too.

When riding in the car and talking with your son or daughter, include God in the conversation. For example, as you're driving along and you see a beautiful tree, say, "Wow, look at the beautiful tree. Isn't God wonderful to have created something like that for us to enjoy?" Your child will probably say, "Yeah, Dad." And that'll be all.

Do not add anything to it. Please do not say, "You know, it's like Reverend Smith said on Sunday morning at the 8:30 worship service and again at 11:00 . . . ." That's not normal. Just follow your statement with something ordinary, such as, "Honey, would you please tie your shoelaces so you don't trip over them when we get to the store? Thanks." Talk about God as though knowing him is a simple fact, not something mysterious or puzzling. Refer to him just as you would another dear friend. This is normal.

And think about this: When you and your child are talking to or about God, you are literally referring to the eternal Creator of the universe. So even though your conversation about your faith is "normal," make sure it still has plenty of awe in it.

Remind your child of God's majesty by occasionally reminding her of his creative genius. Let her know that when you pray, sometimes you kneel down because you are so honored to be in God's presence. Every once in a while, let her join you on your knees. She'll get the picture.

Finally, if your child is young, begin praying that God will send him other Christian adults who will love him for "free." These are other adults whose relationship with God is as much a part of their daily lives as yours is. These are people who, like you, love God, but they're not teachers ("Did you finish your homework?"); coaches ("Take another lap!"); extended family (When your Dad was little . . ."); or parents ("Clean your room"). These "free" adults will do almost as much to shape your child's life and thinking as you will. There are lots of good places to find folks like this, and your church is the best place to start.

You have the wonderful privilege of introducing your child to God. Have fun with this one.

¹⁰Jesus answered her, "If you knew the gift of God and who it is that asks you for a drink, you would have asked him and he would have given you living water."

¹¹"Sir," the woman said, "you have nothing to draw with and the well is deep. Where can you get this living water? ¹²Are you greater than our father Jacob, who gave us the well and drank from it himself, as did also his sons and his flocks and herds?"

¹³Jesus answered, "Everyone who drinks this water will be thirsty again, ¹⁴but whoever drinks the water I give him will never thirst. Indeed, the water I give him will become in him a spring of water welling up to eternal life."

¹⁵The woman said to him, "Sir, give me this water so that I won't get thirsty and have to keep coming here to draw water."

¹⁶He told her, "Go, call your husband and come back."

¹⁷"I have no husband," she replied.

Jesus said to her, "You are right when you say you have no husband. ¹⁸The fact is, you have had five husbands, and the man you now have is not your husband. What you have just said is quite true."

Custom-made Salvation

DAILY INSIGHT

I have always been a hopeless tinkerer—a true weekend warrior. So, since they were very young, our daughters have had the opportunity of being my helpers. Early on, I tried to impress on them that helping me was not to be taken as work, but as a privilege. (To this day, I still can't figure out why they never fully accepted that concept.) In any case, my girls were my helpers. And over the years, they became very good at it.

If you were to ask them about this today, they'd probably tell you about their long and illustrious careers as "go-for's"—"gophers," in the vernacular. As I was up on a high ladder or neatly tucked under the bathroom sink, they would stand by, ready to retrieve just the right tool for me. Early in their lives, they learned how to identify a pipe wrench, a caulking gun, a framing square, a chalk line or a cat's paw. Through this experience they learned that, even though you *can* use a hammer to drive a screw, it's always best to use a screwdriver. Always use the right tool for the job.

Jesus did the same thing with words, tailoring his conversation to meet people where they most needed to be challenged or at their point of deepest need.

Today's passage recounts a conversation Jesus had with a Samaritan woman. In the dry, dusty climate they were living in, water was a precious commodity. So when Jesus decided to challenge this woman's lifestyle

MONDAY
Passage:
John 4:4–15
Verses:
John 4:13–14

choices and offer her hope in a way she could easily understand, he offered "living water" to permanently quench her thirst. He used just the right words, the right understanding … the right "tool" for the job.

Jesus did this with others, as well. In the previous chapter we read that Jesus engaged in a late-night conversation with a Pharisee named Nicodemus. Here was a man who was proud of his chosen lineage—he was vain by virtue of his heritage. Recognizing this, Jesus told this man that he needed to be "born again" (3:7). And when a rich man came to Jesus looking for another arrow for his bulging quiver, Jesus told him to sell everything and follow him (Luke 18:18–25). Jesus custom-fit his recommendations to each man's particular compulsion.

If Jesus were to join you for lunch today and custom-make his presentation of hope to you, what would he say? Would he propose friendship for your loneliness, hope for your sagging heart, equity for your portfolio, rest for your exhaustion, order for the chaos in your life, or comfort for your fear?

Whatever your needs, God is ready to make you an offer. He knows exactly what you needed yesterday … what you need today … and what you'll need tomorrow.

God always uses just the right tool for the job. His salvation is custom-made.

For your next devotional reading, go to page 1170.

¹⁹"Sir," the woman said, "I can see that you are a prophet. ²⁰Our fathers worshiped on this mountain, but you Jews claim that the place where we must worship is in Jerusalem." ²¹Jesus declared, "Believe me, woman, a time is coming when you will worship the Father neither on this mountain nor in Jerusalem. ²²You Samaritans worship what you do not know; we worship what we do know, for salvation is from the Jews. ²³Yet a time is coming and has now come when the true worshipers will worship the Father in spirit and truth, for they are the kind of worshipers the Father seeks. ²⁴God is spirit, and his worshipers must worship in spirit and in truth."

²⁵The woman said, "I know that Messiah" (called Christ) "is coming. When he comes, he will explain everything to us."

²⁶Then Jesus declared, "I who speak to you am he."

The Disciples Rejoin Jesus

²⁷Just then his disciples returned and were surprised to find him talking with a woman. But no one asked, "What do you want?" or "Why are you talking with her?" ²⁸Then, leaving her water jar, the woman went back to the town and said to the people, ²⁹"Come, see a man who told me everything I ever did. Could this be the Christ[a]?" ³⁰They came out of the town and made their way toward him.

³¹Meanwhile his disciples urged him, "Rabbi, eat something." ³²But he said to them, "I have food to eat that you know nothing about." ³³Then his disciples said to each other, "Could someone have brought him food?" ³⁴"My food," said Jesus, "is to do the will of him who sent me and to finish his work. ³⁵Do you not say, 'Four months more and then the harvest'? I tell you, open your eyes and look at the fields! They are ripe for harvest. ³⁶Even now the reaper draws his wages, even now he harvests the crop for eternal life, so that the sower and the reaper may be glad together. ³⁷Thus the saying 'One sows and another reaps' is true. ³⁸I sent you to reap what you have not worked for. Others have done the hard work, and you have reaped the benefits of their labor."

Many Samaritans Believe

³⁹Many of the Samaritans from that town believed in him because of the woman's testimony, "He told me everything I ever did." ⁴⁰So when the Samaritans came to him, they urged him to stay with them, and he stayed two days. ⁴¹And because of his words many more became believers.

⁴²They said to the woman, "We no longer believe just because of what you said; now we have heard for ourselves, and we know that this man really is the Savior of the world."

Jesus Heals the Official's Son

⁴³After the two days he left for Galilee. ⁴⁴(Now Jesus himself had pointed out that a prophet has no honor in his own country.) ⁴⁵When he arrived in Galilee, the Galileans welcomed him. They had seen all that he had done in Jerusalem at the Passover Feast, for they also had been there.

⁴⁶Once more he visited Cana in Galilee, where he had turned the water into wine. And there was a certain royal official whose son lay sick at Capernaum. ⁴⁷When this man heard that Jesus had arrived in Galilee from Judea, he went to him and begged him to come and heal his son, who was close to death.

⁴⁸"Unless you people see miraculous signs and wonders," Jesus told him, "you will never believe."

⁴⁹The royal official said, "Sir, come down before my child dies."

⁵⁰Jesus replied, "You may go. Your son will live."

The man took Jesus at his word and departed. ⁵¹While he was still on the way, his servants met him with the news that his boy was living. ⁵²When he inquired as to the time when his son got better, they said to him, "The fever left him yesterday at the seventh hour."

⁵³Then the father realized that this was the exact time at which Jesus had said to him, "Your son will live." So he and all his household believed.

⁵⁴This was the second miraculous sign that Jesus performed, having come from Judea to Galilee.

The Healing at the Pool

5 Some time later, Jesus went up to Jerusalem for a feast of the Jews. ²Now there is in Jerusalem near the Sheep Gate a pool, which in Aramaic is called Bethesda[b] and which is surrounded by

[a]29 Or *Messiah* [b]2 Some manuscripts *Bethzatha*; other manuscripts *Bethsaida*

five covered colonnades. **³**Here a great number of disabled people used to lie— the blind, the lame, the paralyzed.*a* **⁵**One who was there had been an invalid for thirty-eight years. **⁶**When Jesus saw him lying there and learned that he had been in this condition for a long time, he asked him, "Do you want to get well?"

⁷"Sir," the invalid replied, "I have no one to help me into the pool when the water is stirred. While I am trying to get in, someone else goes down ahead of me."

⁸Then Jesus said to him, "Get up! Pick up your mat and walk." **⁹**At once the man was cured; he picked up his mat and walked.

The day on which this took place was a Sabbath, **¹⁰**and so the Jews said to the man who had been healed, "It is the Sabbath; the law forbids you to carry your mat."

¹¹But he replied, "The man who made me well said to me, 'Pick up your mat and walk.' "

¹²So they asked him, "Who is this fellow who told you to pick it up and walk?"

a3 Some less important manuscripts paralyzed— and they waited for the moving of the waters. 4From time to time an angel of the Lord would come down and stir up the waters. The first one into the pool after each such disturbance would be cured of whatever disease he had.

A Special Kind of Kindness

DAILY INSIGHT

Many dads struggle with life. Sometimes this struggle is visible to the naked eye and sometimes it's not. Some men face the demons of an unhappy childhood. Others deal with unresolved conflicts or unconfessed sin.

These things from their past can literally disable men. In some cases, these awful circumstances have become the reason why they have given up on life ... or have tragically failed.

Jesus was on his way to the temple feast when he passed a pool called *Bethesda*—the word means a "place of kindness." Tradition had it that when the water in this pool began to stir, the first person to touch it would be healed. There Jesus encountered a disabled man. As he did so often in working miracles of healing, Jesus changed this man's perspective, *then* he healed him ... heaping kindness upon kindness.

This man had been unable to walk for thirty-eight years. No doubt he had become a fixture in the area. He survived from the charity of passers-by; it wasn't much, but it was a living. When Jesus spoke to the man, he asked what must have sounded like a dreadfully inappropriate question: "Do you want to get well?" Jesus said to the poor man, whose gnarled and lifeless legs were tucked under his body.

"How rude. How thoughtless. Do I *want*

TUESDAY

Passage:
John 5:1–9

Verse:
John 5:6

to get well? Don't be ridiculous," the man could have said. "Of *course*, I want to be healed. I thought this place was called 'kindness.'"

But when we stop to think about it, this was the perfect— and ultimately kind—question. In his love, Jesus may have been saying to the man, "Do you have faith to believe that I can really heal you? Can you find the will to live independently?"

Notice that after Jesus asked the question, the man didn't respond with, "Yes, sir, of *course* I want to be healed." Instead he reminded Jesus that he had no one to help him get to the water when it stirred. This had been his story for thirty-eight years, and he was sticking to it.

But Jesus reached down and healed the man. Jesus told him to "Get up! Pick up your mat and walk." It was kindness upon kindness.

Have you been "disabled" by some past event in your life? Have you allowed this event to darken your past, hamper your present, and cast doubt on your future? Did someone wrong you, hurt you, or rob you? If so, are you ready for Jesus' brand of kindness? Allow him to give you the will to heal your yesterday, and lavish you with wholeness for tomorrow.

For your next devotional reading, go to page 1172.

[13]The man who was healed had no idea who it was, for Jesus had slipped away into the crowd that was there.

[14]Later Jesus found him at the temple and said to him, "See, you are well again. Stop sinning or something worse may happen to you." [15]The man went away and told the Jews that it was Jesus who had made him well.

Life Through the Son

[16]So, because Jesus was doing these things on the Sabbath, the Jews persecuted him. [17]Jesus said to them, "My Father is always at his work to this very day, and I, too, am working." [18]For this reason the Jews tried all the harder to kill him; not only was he breaking the Sabbath, but he was even calling God his own Father, making himself equal with God.

[19]Jesus gave them this answer: "I tell you the truth, the Son can do nothing by himself; he can do only what he sees his Father doing, because whatever the Father does the Son also does. [20]For the Father loves the Son and shows him all he does. Yes, to your amazement he will show him even greater things than these. [21]For just as the Father raises the dead and gives them life, even so the Son gives life to whom he is pleased to give it. [22]Moreover, the Father judges no one, but has entrusted all judgment to the Son, [23]that all may honor the Son just as they honor the Father. He who does not honor the Son does not honor the Father, who sent him.

[24]"I tell you the truth, whoever hears my word and believes him who sent me has eternal life and will not be condemned; he has crossed over from death to life. [25]I tell you the truth, a time is coming and has now come when the dead will hear the voice of the Son of God and those who hear will live. [26]For as the Father has life in himself, so he has granted the Son to have life in himself. [27]And he has given him authority to judge because he is the Son of Man.

[28]"Do not be amazed at this, for a time is coming when all who are in their graves will hear his voice [29]and come out—those who have done good will rise to live, and those who have done evil will rise to be condemned. [30]By myself I can do nothing; I judge only as I hear, and my judgment is just, for I seek not to please myself but him who sent me.

Testimonies About Jesus

[31]"If I testify about myself, my testimony is not valid. [32]There is another who testifies in my favor, and I know that his testimony about me is valid.

[33]"You have sent to John and he has testified to the truth. [34]Not that I accept human testimony; but I mention it that you may be saved. [35]John was a lamp that burned and gave light, and you chose for a time to enjoy his light.

[36]"I have testimony weightier than that of John. For the very work that the Father has given me to finish, and which I am doing, testifies that the Father has sent me. [37]And the Father who sent me has himself testified concerning me. You have never heard his voice nor seen his form, [38]nor does his word dwell in you, for you do not believe the one he sent. [39]You diligently study[a] the Scriptures because you think that by them you possess eternal life. These are the Scriptures that testify about me, [40]yet you refuse to come to me to have life.

[41]"I do not accept praise from men, [42]but I know you. I know that you do not have the love of God in your hearts. [43]I have come in my Father's name, and you do not accept me; but if someone else comes in his own name, you will accept him. [44]How can you believe if you accept praise from one another, yet make no effort to obtain the praise that comes from the only God[b]?

[45]"But do not think I will accuse you before the Father. Your accuser is Moses, on whom your hopes are set. [46]If you believed Moses, you would believe me, for he wrote about me. [47]But since you do not believe what he wrote, how are you going to believe what I say?"

Jesus Feeds the Five Thousand

6 Some time after this, Jesus crossed to the far shore of the Sea of Galilee (that is, the Sea of Tiberias), [2]and a great crowd of people followed him because they saw the miraculous signs he had performed on the sick. [3]Then Jesus went up on a mountainside and sat down with his disciples. [4]The Jewish Passover Feast was near.

[5]When Jesus looked up and saw a great crowd coming toward him, he said to Philip, "Where shall we buy bread for

a39 Or *Study diligently* (the imperative)   *b44* Some early manuscripts *the Only One*

these people to eat?" ⁶He asked this only to test him, for he already had in mind what he was going to do.

⁷Philip answered him, "Eight months' wages[a] would not buy enough bread for each one to have a bite!"

⁸Another of his disciples, Andrew, Simon Peter's brother, spoke up, ⁹"Here is a boy with five small barley loaves and two small fish, but how far will they go among so many?"

¹⁰Jesus said, "Have the people sit down." There was plenty of grass in that place, and the men sat down, about five thousand of them. ¹¹Jesus then took the loaves, gave thanks, and distributed to those who were seated as much as they wanted. He did the same with the fish.

¹²When they had all had enough to eat, he said to his disciples, "Gather the pieces that are left over. Let nothing be wasted." ¹³So they gathered them and filled twelve baskets with the pieces of the five barley loaves left over by those who had eaten.

¹⁴After the people saw the miraculous sign that Jesus did, they began to say, "Surely this is the Prophet who is to come into the world." ¹⁵Jesus, knowing that they

a7 Greek two hundred denarii

Pack Your Own Lunch

DAILY INSIGHT

WEDNESDAY

Passage:
John 6:5–13

Verse:
John 6:13

There were two kinds of kids in my high school: the cool kids and all the others … including me. Our school's unique line of demarcation was revealed every day at lunch. If you brought your lunch in a brown bag or—perish the thought—a lunch box, you were not cool. If you bought your lunch at the school cafeteria, you were cool. If you occasionally bought an ice cream sandwich, you were *very* cool. And so it went.

Since high school, I have successfully triumphed over living with the un-cool, brown-bag stigma. In fact, now that I have spent time carefully thinking through the brilliance of lunch packing and the life lessons it teaches, I am now *proud* of having carried my lunch. Check out this Brown Bagger's Clinic, taught by the boy in today's story who thought enough to take his lunch along when he went to see the Savior.

1. Be prepared. If you want to be able to eat later, you have to pack something before you're hungry, even though the smell of fish before 8:00 a.m. can be pretty nauseating. The Boy Scouts have touted this lesson since their founding. Business consultants would call this "thinking strategically." In all areas of life, project yourself into the future and ask yourself what you and your family will need to survive.

2. Get ready to work. Making a lunch takes time and effort. This morning routine will have you slamming doors and making a mess, but the end result will be worth it. While it may be easier to cruise through the drive-through windows of life whenever the urge presents itself, doing so is rarely good for you in the long run. Things that are worth doing are worth doing well, and doing things well requires effort.

3. Take responsibility. When you carry your lunch, *you* get to decide what you eat. And when you're happy with that, you'll never be tempted by another person's lunch bag. Realize that life offers a series of choices and that you, through the power of the Spirit, have the ability to choose the right things.

4. Look for miracles. Remember that, in simply packing a lunch, this boy contributed to one of the Bible's greatest miracles. Jesus can take what you have and use it for his glory if only you'll offer it up to him. You can't even begin to imagine what Jesus can do with a willing heart.

Wouldn't you know it, these incredible truths are brought to us by a kid who probably wasn't old enough to shave. A brown-bagging kid who will be, for all eternity, an example for all humankind. Isn't that just like Jesus?

For your next devotional reading, go to page 1176.

intended to come and make him king by force, withdrew again to a mountain by himself.

Jesus Walks on the Water

[16]When evening came, his disciples went down to the lake, [17]where they got into a boat and set off across the lake for Capernaum. By now it was dark, and Jesus had not yet joined them. [18]A strong wind was blowing and the waters grew rough. [19]When they had rowed three or three and a half miles,[a] they saw Jesus approaching the boat, walking on the water; and they were terrified. [20]But he said to them, "It is I; don't be afraid." [21]Then they were willing to take him into the boat, and immediately the boat reached the shore where they were heading.

[22]The next day the crowd that had stayed on the opposite shore of the lake realized that only one boat had been there, and that Jesus had not entered it with his disciples, but that they had gone away alone. [23]Then some boats from Tiberias landed near the place where the people had eaten the bread after the Lord had given thanks. [24]Once the crowd realized that neither Jesus nor his disciples were there, they got into the boats and went to Capernaum in search of Jesus.

Jesus the Bread of Life

[25]When they found him on the other side of the lake, they asked him, "Rabbi, when did you get here?"

[26]Jesus answered, "I tell you the truth, you are looking for me, not because you saw miraculous signs but because you ate the loaves and had your fill. [27]Do not work for food that spoils, but for food that endures to eternal life, which the Son of Man will give you. On him God the Father has placed his seal of approval."

[28]Then they asked him, "What must we do to do the works God requires?"

[29]Jesus answered, "The work of God is this: to believe in the one he has sent."

[30]So they asked him, "What miraculous sign then will you give that we may see it and believe you? What will you do? [31]Our forefathers ate the manna in the desert; as it is written: 'He gave them bread from heaven to eat.'[b]"

[32]Jesus said to them, "I tell you the truth, it is not Moses who has given you the bread from heaven, but it is my Father who gives you the true bread from heaven. [33]For the bread of God is he who comes down from heaven and gives life to the world."

[34]"Sir," they said, "from now on give us this bread."

[35]Then Jesus declared, "I am the bread of life. He who comes to me will never go hungry, and he who believes in me will never be thirsty. [36]But as I told you, you have seen me and still you do not believe. [37]All that the Father gives me will come to me, and whoever comes to me I will never drive away. [38]For I have come down from heaven not to do my will but to do the will of him who sent me. [39]And this is the will of him who sent me, that I shall lose none of all that he has given me, but raise them up at the last day. [40]For my Father's will is that everyone who looks to the Son and believes in him shall have eternal life, and I will raise him up at the last day."

[41]At this the Jews began to grumble about him because he said, "I am the bread that came down from heaven." [42]They said, "Is this not Jesus, the son of Joseph, whose father and mother we know? How can he now say, 'I came down from heaven'?"

[43]"Stop grumbling among yourselves," Jesus answered. [44]"No one can come to me unless the Father who sent me draws him, and I will raise him up at the last day. [45]It is written in the Prophets: 'They will all be taught by God.'[c] Everyone who listens to the Father and learns from him comes to me. [46]No one has seen the Father except the one who is from God; only he has seen the Father. [47]I tell you the truth, he who believes has everlasting life. [48]I am the bread of life. [49]Your forefathers ate the manna in the desert, yet they died. [50]But here is the bread that comes down from heaven, which a man may eat and not die. [51]I am the living bread that came down from heaven. If anyone eats of this bread, he will live forever. This bread is my flesh, which I will give for the life of the world."

[52]Then the Jews began to argue sharply among themselves, "How can this man give us his flesh to eat?"

[53]Jesus said to them, "I tell you the truth, unless you eat the flesh of the Son of Man and drink his blood, you have no life in you. [54]Whoever eats my flesh and drinks my blood has eternal life, and I will raise him up at the last day. [55]For my flesh is real food and my blood is real drink.

---

[a]19 Greek *rowed twenty-five or thirty stadia* (about 5 or 6 kilometers)   [b]31 Exodus 16:4; Neh. 9:15; Psalm 78:24,25   [c]45 Isaiah 54:13

[56]Whoever eats my flesh and drinks my blood remains in me, and I in him. [57]Just as the living Father sent me and I live because of the Father, so the one who feeds on me will live because of me. [58]This is the bread that came down from heaven. Your forefathers ate manna and died, but he who feeds on this bread will live forever." [59]He said this while teaching in the synagogue in Capernaum.

Many Disciples Desert Jesus

[60]On hearing it, many of his disciples said, "This is a hard teaching. Who can accept it?"

[61]Aware that his disciples were grumbling about this, Jesus said to them, "Does this offend you? [62]What if you see the Son of Man ascend to where he was before! [63]The Spirit gives life; the flesh counts for nothing. The words I have spoken to you are spirit[a] and they are life. [64]Yet there are some of you who do not believe." For Jesus had known from the beginning which of them did not believe and who would betray him. [65]He went on to say, "This is why I told you that no one can come to me unless the Father has enabled him."

[66]From this time many of his disciples turned back and no longer followed him.

[67]"You do not want to leave too, do you?" Jesus asked the Twelve.

[68]Simon Peter answered him, "Lord, to whom shall we go? You have the words of eternal life. [69]We believe and know that you are the Holy One of God."

[70]Then Jesus replied, "Have I not chosen you, the Twelve? Yet one of you is a devil!" [71](He meant Judas, the son of Simon Iscariot, who, though one of the Twelve, was later to betray him.)

Jesus Goes to the Feast of Tabernacles

7 After this, Jesus went around in Galilee, purposely staying away from Judea because the Jews there were waiting to take his life. [2]But when the Jewish Feast of Tabernacles was near, [3]Jesus' brothers said to him, "You ought to leave here and go to Judea, so that your disciples may see the miracles you do. [4]No one who wants to become a public figure acts in secret. Since you are doing these things, show yourself to the world." [5]For even his own brothers did not believe in him.

[6]Therefore Jesus told them, "The right time for me has not yet come; for you any time is right. [7]The world cannot hate

you, but it hates me because I testify that what it does is evil. [8]You go to the Feast. I am not yet[b] going up to this Feast, because for me the right time has not yet come." [9]Having said this, he stayed in Galilee.

[10]However, after his brothers had left for the Feast, he went also, not publicly, but in secret. [11]Now at the Feast the Jews were watching for him and asking, "Where is that man?"

[12]Among the crowds there was widespread whispering about him. Some said, "He is a good man."

Others replied, "No, he deceives the people." [13]But no one would say anything publicly about him for fear of the Jews.

Jesus Teaches at the Feast

[14]Not until halfway through the Feast did Jesus go up to the temple courts and begin to teach. [15]The Jews were amazed and asked, "How did this man get such learning without having studied?"

[16]Jesus answered, "My teaching is not my own. It comes from him who sent me. [17]If anyone chooses to do God's will, he will find out whether my teaching comes from God or whether I speak on my own. [18]He who speaks on his own does so to gain honor for himself, but he who works for the honor of the one who sent him is a man of truth; there is nothing false about him. [19]Has not Moses given you the law? Yet not one of you keeps the law. Why are you trying to kill me?"

[20]"You are demon-possessed," the crowd answered. "Who is trying to kill you?"

[21]Jesus said to them, "I did one miracle, and you are all astonished. [22]Yet, because Moses gave you circumcision (though actually it did not come from Moses, but from the patriarchs), you circumcise a child on the Sabbath. [23]Now if a child can be circumcised on the Sabbath so that the law of Moses may not be broken, why are you angry with me for healing the whole man on the Sabbath? [24]Stop judging by mere appearances, and make a right judgment."

Is Jesus the Christ?

[25]At that point some of the people of Jerusalem began to ask, "Isn't this the man

---

[a]63 Or *Spirit*   [b]8 Some early manuscripts do not have *yet*.

they are trying to kill? **26**Here he is, speaking publicly, and they are not saying a word to him. Have the authorities really concluded that he is the Christ*a*? **27**But we know where this man is from; when the Christ comes, no one will know where he is from."

28Then Jesus, still teaching in the temple courts, cried out, "Yes, you know me, and you know where I am from. I am not here on my own, but he who sent me is true. You do not know him, **29**but I know him because I am from him and he sent me."

30At this they tried to seize him, but no one laid a hand on him, because his time had not yet come. **31**Still, many in the crowd put their faith in him. They said, "When the Christ comes, will he do more miraculous signs than this man?"

32The Pharisees heard the crowd whispering such things about him. Then the chief priests and the Pharisees sent temple guards to arrest him.

33Jesus said, "I am with you for only a short time, and then I go to the one who sent me. **34**You will look for me, but you will not find me; and where I am, you cannot come."

35The Jews said to one another, "Where does this man intend to go that we cannot find him? Will he go where our people live scattered among the Greeks, and teach the Greeks? **36**What did he mean when he said, 'You will look for me, but you will not find me,' and 'Where I am, you cannot come'?"

37On the last and greatest day of the Feast, Jesus stood and said in a loud voice, "If anyone is thirsty, let him come to me and drink. **38**Whoever believes in me, as*b* the Scripture has said, streams of living water will flow from within him." **39**By this he meant the Spirit, whom those who believed in him were later to receive. Up to that time the Spirit had not been given, since Jesus had not yet been glorified.

40On hearing his words, some of the people said, "Surely this man is the Prophet."

41Others said, "He is the Christ."

Still others asked, "How can the Christ come from Galilee? **42**Does not the Scripture say that the Christ will come from David's family*c* and from Bethlehem, the town where David lived?" **43**Thus the people were divided because of Jesus. **44**Some wanted to seize him, but no one laid a hand on him.

Unbelief of the Jewish Leaders

45Finally the temple guards went back to the chief priests and Pharisees, who asked them, "Why didn't you bring him in?"

46"No one ever spoke the way this man does," the guards declared.

47"You mean he has deceived you also?" the Pharisees retorted. **48**"Has any of the rulers or of the Pharisees believed in him? **49**No! But this mob that knows nothing of the law—there is a curse on them."

50Nicodemus, who had gone to Jesus earlier and who was one of their own number, asked, **51**"Does our law condemn anyone without first hearing him to find out what he is doing?"

52They replied, "Are you from Galilee, too? Look into it, and you will find that a prophet*d* does not come out of Galilee."

[The earliest manuscripts and many other ancient witnesses do not have John 7:53-8:11.]

53Then each went to his own home.

8 But Jesus went to the Mount of Olives. **2**At dawn he appeared again in the temple courts, where all the people gathered around him, and he sat down to teach them. **3**The teachers of the law and the Pharisees brought in a woman caught in adultery. They made her stand before the group **4**and said to Jesus, "Teacher, this woman was caught in the act of adultery. **5**In the Law Moses commanded us to stone such women. Now what do you say?" **6**They were using this question as a trap, in order to have a basis for accusing him.

But Jesus bent down and started to write on the ground with his finger. **7**When they kept on questioning him, he straightened up and said to them, "If any one of you is without sin, let him be the first to throw a stone at her." **8**Again he stooped down and wrote on the ground.

9At this, those who heard began to go away one at a time, the older ones first, until only Jesus was left, with the woman still standing there. **10**Jesus straightened up and asked her, "Woman, where are they? Has no one condemned you?"

11"No one, sir," she said.

a26 Or Messiah; also in verses 27, 31, 41 and 42
b37,38 Or / If anyone is thirsty, let him come to me. / And let him drink, 38who believes in me. / As
c42 Greek seed d52 Two early manuscripts the Prophet

"Then neither do I condemn you," Jesus declared. "Go now and leave your life of sin."

The Validity of Jesus' Testimony

[12]When Jesus spoke again to the people, he said, "I am the light of the world. Who-ever follows me will never walk in darkness, but will have the light of life."

[13]The Pharisees challenged him, "Here you are, appearing as your own witness; your testimony is not valid."

[14]Jesus answered, "Even if I testify on my own behalf, my testimony is valid, for I know where I came from and where I am going. But you have no idea where I come from or where I am going. [15]You judge by

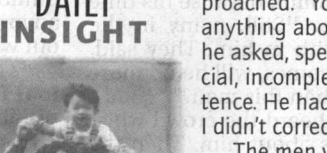

Red-handed

I have no idea where the expression "red-handed" came from. Nonetheless, you and I know what "red-handed" means. We also know it's more fun to use this phrase than to have it used on you. Following is a case in point.

As a boy, every summer I looked forward to hanging out with a kid from Tulsa named J.R. Whitby. Our families camped together at a family conference center every year. In addition to liking J.R. as a friend, I always looked forward to the array of fireworks he'd bring along. These were legal in Oklahoma, but they were not legal in Indiana. Unfortunately, the family camp was located in the Hoosier State.

One day J.R. and I decided to slide to the edge of firecracker safety. "What would happen if we lit a cherry bomb, put a big tin can over it, then stood on the can?" I wondered out loud. J.R. thought it was a terrific idea. He lit the cherry bomb, quickly set a can on top, and I stood on the can. The exploding firecracker sent a shock wave from the soles of my tennis shoes to the top of my baseball cap.

Thankfully, but not fittingly, I survived without a scratch. The juice can, however, wasn't so fortunate. The impact of the explosion literally turned it inside out. J.R. and I exulted at the success of our adventure. Boys.

Moments later, we were walking across the campground. However, not having had the presence of mind to throw away the evidence, I was carrying the shrapnel in my hand. Presently, a city police officer ap-

DAILY INSIGHT

THURSDAY

Passage:
John 8:1–11

Verse:
John 8:7

proached. "You boys know anything about the fireworks?" he asked, speaking in an official, incomplete police sentence. He had us red-handed. I didn't correct his English.

The men we read about in today's passage thought they had caught an adulterous woman red-handed. Hearing that Jesus was building a soft-on-crime reputation, these self-righteous men brought her to Jesus to see if he would break the law himself through leniency toward the woman. "Now, what do you say?" they challenged.

Of course, this woman had done a despicable thing, and Jesus did not wink at this crime. He knew that adultery broke hearts and created chaos. Yet, as if to ignore the accusers, Jesus stooped down and made a few marks in the dirt with his finger. They continued their sanctimonious charges. So Jesus "straightened up" and said, "If any one of you is without sin, let him be the first to throw a stone at her." I love this picture.

Jesus had delivered a knock-out punch. These men gathered around the woman each held the graphic evidence of their own sinfulness—as visible as the torn up tin can in my thirteen-year-old hand. There they were, red-handed, cold-busted sinners, just like the woman ... just like us. But Jesus forgave them all, starting with the adulterous lady standing there, continuing with each of the men in the circle, and finishing with you and me. Isn't this incredible?

For your next devotional reading, go to page 1179.

human standards; I pass judgment on no one. **16**But if I do judge, my decisions are right, because I am not alone. I stand with the Father, who sent me. **17**In your own Law it is written that the testimony of two men is valid. **18**I am one who testifies for myself; my other witness is the Father, who sent me."

19Then they asked him, "Where is your father?"

"You do not know me or my Father," Jesus replied. "If you knew me, you would know my Father also." **20**He spoke these words while teaching in the temple area near the place where the offerings were put. Yet no one seized him, because his time had not yet come.

21Once more Jesus said to them, "I am going away, and you will look for me, and you will die in your sin. Where I go, you cannot come."

22This made the Jews ask, "Will he kill himself? Is that why he says, 'Where I go, you cannot come'?"

23But he continued, "You are from below; I am from above. You are of this world; I am not of this world. **24**I told you that you would die in your sins; if you do not believe that I am ˌthe one I claim to be,ᵃ you will indeed die in your sins."

25"Who are you?" they asked.

"Just what I have been claiming all along," Jesus replied. **26**"I have much to say in judgment of you. But he who sent me is reliable, and what I have heard from him I tell the world."

27They did not understand that he was telling them about his Father. **28**So Jesus said, "When you have lifted up the Son of Man, then you will know that I am ˌthe one I claim to be, and that I do nothing on my own but speak just what the Father has taught me. **29**The one who sent me is with me; he has not left me alone, for I always do what pleases him." **30**Even as he spoke, many put their faith in him.

The Children of Abraham

31To the Jews who had believed him, Jesus said, "If you hold to my teaching, you are really my disciples. **32**Then you will know the truth, and the truth will set you free."

33They answered him, "We are Abraham's descendantsᵇ and have never been slaves of anyone. How can you say that we shall be set free?"

34Jesus replied, "I tell you the truth, everyone who sins is a slave to sin. **35**Now

a slave has no permanent place in the family, but a son belongs to it forever. **36**So if the Son sets you free, you will be free indeed. **37**I know you are Abraham's descendants. Yet you are ready to kill me, because you have no room for my word. **38**I am telling you what I have seen in the Father's presence, and you do what you have heard from your father.ᶜ

39"Abraham is our father," they answered.

"If you were Abraham's children," said Jesus, "then you wouldᵈ do the things Abraham did. **40**As it is, you are determined to kill me, a man who has told you the truth that I heard from God. Abraham did not do such things. **41**You are doing the things your own father does."

"We are not illegitimate children," they protested. "The only Father we have is God himself."

The Children of the Devil

42Jesus said to them, "If God were your Father, you would love me, for I came from God and now am here. I have not come on my own; but he sent me. **43**Why is my language not clear to you? Because you are unable to hear what I say. **44**You belong to your father, the devil, and you want to carry out your father's desire. He was a murderer from the beginning, not holding to the truth, for there is no truth in him. When he lies, he speaks his native language, for he is a liar and the father of lies. **45**Yet because I tell the truth, you do not believe me! **46**Can any of you prove me guilty of sin? If I am telling the truth, why don't you believe me? **47**He who belongs to God hears what God says. The reason you do not hear is that you do not belong to God."

The Claims of Jesus About Himself

48The Jews answered him, "Aren't we right in saying that you are a Samaritan and demon-possessed?"

49"I am not possessed by a demon," said Jesus, "but I honor my Father and you dishonor me. **50**I am not seeking glory for myself; but there is one who seeks it, and he is the judge. **51**I tell you the truth, if anyone keeps my word, he will never see death."

ᵃ24 Or *I am he*; also in verse 28   ᵇ33 Greek *seed*; also in verse 37   ᶜ38 Or *presence. Therefore do what you have heard from the Father.*   ᵈ39 Some early manuscripts *"If you are Abraham's children," said Jesus, "then*

⁵²At this the Jews exclaimed, "Now we know that you are demon-possessed! Abraham died and so did the prophets, yet you say that if anyone keeps your word, he will never taste death. ⁵³Are you greater than our father Abraham? He died, and so did the prophets. Who do you think you are?"

⁵⁴Jesus replied, "If I glorify myself, my glory means nothing. My Father, whom you claim as your God, is the one who glorifies me. ⁵⁵Though you do not know him, I know him. If I said I did not, I would be a liar like you, but I do know him and keep his word. ⁵⁶Your father Abraham rejoiced at the thought of seeing my day; he saw it and was glad."

⁵⁷"You are not yet fifty years old," the Jews said to him, "and you have seen Abraham!"

⁵⁸"I tell you the truth," Jesus answered, "before Abraham was born, I am!" ⁵⁹At this, they picked up stones to stone him, but Jesus hid himself, slipping away from the temple grounds.

Jesus Heals a Man Born Blind

9 As he went along, he saw a man blind from birth. ²His disciples asked him, "Rabbi, who sinned, this man or his parents, that he was born blind?"

³"Neither this man nor his parents sinned," said Jesus, "but this happened so that the work of God might be displayed in his life. ⁴As long as it is day, we must do the work of him who sent me. Night is coming, when no one can work. ⁵While I am in the world, I am the light of the world."

⁶Having said this, he spit on the ground, made some mud with the saliva, and put it on the man's eyes. ⁷"Go," he told him, "wash in the Pool of Siloam" (this word means Sent). So the man went and washed, and came home seeing.

⁸His neighbors and those who had formerly seen him begging asked, "Isn't this the same man who used to sit and beg?" ⁹Some claimed that he was.

Others said, "No, he only looks like him."

But he himself insisted, "I am the man."

Be God's Son
Satan, the Lying Father

"[The devil] was a murderer from the beginning, not holding to the truth, for there is no truth in him . . . he is a liar and the father of lies" (8:44).

DADS
IN THE
BIBLE

Text: John 8:42–47

It's hard to imagine this, but there are men out there who are evil. They're irresponsible, lazy and hateful. Worst of all, they refuse to tell the truth. Their father is Satan himself.

Unfortunately, sometimes these awful men impregnate women, becoming biological dads. In doing this, these men sometimes begin a new generation of irresponsible, lazy, hateful, liars—a horrible thing to consider.

The lamentable thing we know about evil men is that, many times, like their own children, they too are the descendants of equally corrupt men who are also Satan's hopeless children. What a horrendous cycle. What a dreadful thing this is.

But how can this awful succession be stopped? How can evil men be replaced by a generation of faithful children? Jesus provides us with a very straightforward solution. "He who belongs to God hears what God says" (v. 47).

If you know men whose fathers were murderers or thieves, or if your own father was a liar, you can help to break this cycle . . . or you can break it in your own life. Get close to God's Word. Surround yourself with men who know him. Put yourself in places where his truth is being taught. Listen to God.

The God of Abraham, Isaac, and Jacob wants to be your heavenly Father. He wants to adopt you into his family so you can learn from a Father who cares for you—a Dad who lovingly tells you the truth.

The children of a man who decides to listen to a new Father will be the beneficiaries of the inheritance of such a faithful man. God is speaking to you. Listen to his voice. Be his child.

For a complete listing of Dads in the Bible, turn to page 1434.

¹⁰"How then were your eyes opened?" they demanded.

¹¹He replied, "The man they call Jesus made some mud and put it on my eyes. He told me to go to Siloam and wash. So I went and washed, and then I could see."

¹²"Where is this man?" they asked him.

"I don't know," he said.

The Pharisees Investigate the Healing

¹³They brought to the Pharisees the man who had been blind. ¹⁴Now the day on which Jesus had made the mud and opened the man's eyes was a Sabbath. ¹⁵Therefore the Pharisees also asked him how he had received his sight. "He put mud on my eyes," the man replied, "and I washed, and now I see."

¹⁶Some of the Pharisees said, "This man is not from God, for he does not keep the Sabbath."

But others asked, "How can a sinner do such miraculous signs?" So they were divided.

¹⁷Finally they turned again to the blind

Through the Eyes of Pain

DAILY INSIGHT

FRIDAY

Passage:
John 9:1–12

Verse:
John 9:3

In 1978, a young, athletic girl named Joni Eareckson dove into the Chesapeake Bay. Her head struck a submerged rock, breaking her neck. In preparing to dive, this seventeen-year-old swimmer had stood on her feet for the last time in her life.

Thirty years later, I was on the phone with Joni. Our mutual interests in publishing had brought us together as colleagues ... and dear friends. In the process of this conversation, Joni told me that she's looking forward to heaven. *Of course,* I remember thinking, *you'll be able to get back on those legs and dance up a storm.* But Joni had something else in mind.

"I can't wait to meet Jesus," she told me. "I'm going to present him with one of my old Everest & Jennings wheelchairs, and I'm going to thank him for the privilege he gave me to live my life as a quadriplegic."

I was stunned. Speechlessness is a common evidence of being in the presence of a saint. "Are you serious?" I returned.

"I sure am," Joni answered in a lilting voice I have come to love. "This chair has allowed me to see God and to share in his suffering. If it weren't for my disability, I wouldn't know him or love him as I do."

Joni's words were ringing in my ears as I read the story of the disciples challenging Jesus with a tough question about a blind man. "Who sinned, this man or his parents?" Even today, this issue haunts many people, believers and skeptics alike.

Because the Sovereign God of the universe is not bound by time or space, he had already met Joni when his disciples asked this question. He had also met countless saints who had, because of their suffering, brought unmistakable glory to him. So Jesus answered the disciples with plenty of evidence to support his thesis. "This happened so that the work of God might be displayed in his life."

You and I may never experience the spectacular peril of a severed spinal cord. We may live our lives with our eyesight intact. But we're going to experience pain, loss, doubt and grief. We will find ourselves questioning God's judgment in allowing us to be so severely set back. During those times, we need to remember that God's purposes are always the same. He acts, he moves, he decides our futures based on our circumstances' ability to deliver praise to his holy name.

Jesus healed the blind man. He did not heal Joni. He may heal us or restore our net worth ... or not. But, regardless, our task is—and will always be—to rest in his grace. Our charge is to take comfort that, though we may be in the midst of darkness, he is the light of the world (v. 5).

Thank God for the pain. It provides for us the privilege of seeing ... and glorifying him.

For your next devotional reading, go to page 1181.

man, "What have you to say about him? It was your eyes he opened."

The man replied, "He is a prophet."

18The Jews still did not believe that he had been blind and had received his sight until they sent for the man's parents. **19**"Is this your son?" they asked. "Is this the one you say was born blind? How is it that now he can see?"

20"We know he is our son," the parents answered, "and we know he was born blind. **21**But how he can see now, or who opened his eyes, we don't know. Ask him. He is of age; he will speak for himself." **22**His parents said this because they were afraid of the Jews, for already the Jews had decided that anyone who acknowledged that Jesus was the Christ*a* would be put out of the synagogue. **23**That was why his parents said, "He is of age; ask him."

24A second time they summoned the man who had been blind. "Give glory to God,*b*" they said. "We know this man is a sinner."

25He replied, "Whether he is a sinner or not, I don't know. One thing I do know. I was blind but now I see!"

26Then they asked him, "What did he do to you? How did he open your eyes?"

27He answered, "I have told you already and you did not listen. Why do you want to hear it again? Do you want to become his disciples, too?"

28Then they hurled insults at him and said, "You are this fellow's disciple! We are disciples of Moses! **29**We know that God spoke to Moses, but as for this fellow, we don't even know where he comes from."

30The man answered, "Now that is remarkable! You don't know where he comes from, yet he opened my eyes. **31**We know that God does not listen to sinners. He listens to the godly man who does his will. **32**Nobody has ever heard of opening the eyes of a man born blind. **33**If this man were not from God, he could do nothing."

34To this they replied, "You were steeped in sin at birth; how dare you lecture us!" And they threw him out.

Spiritual Blindness

35Jesus heard that they had thrown him out, and when he found him, he said, "Do you believe in the Son of Man?"

36"Who is he, sir?" the man asked. "Tell me so that I may believe in him."

37Jesus said, "You have now seen him; in fact, he is the one speaking with you."

38Then the man said, "Lord, I believe," and he worshiped him.

39Jesus said, "For judgment I have come into this world, so that the blind will see and those who see will become blind."

40Some Pharisees who were with him heard him say this and asked, "What? Are we blind too?"

41Jesus said, "If you were blind, you would not be guilty of sin; but now that you claim you can see, your guilt remains.

The Shepherd and His Flock

10 "I tell you the truth, the man who does not enter the sheep pen by the gate, but climbs in by some other way, is a thief and a robber. **2**The man who enters by the gate is the shepherd of his sheep. **3**The watchman opens the gate for him, and the sheep listen to his voice. He calls his own sheep by name and leads them out. **4**When he has brought out all his own, he goes on ahead of them, and his sheep follow him because they know his voice. **5**But they will never follow a stranger; in fact, they will run away from him because they do not recognize a stranger's voice." **6**Jesus used this figure of speech, but they did not understand what he was telling them.

7Therefore Jesus said again, "I tell you the truth, I am the gate for the sheep. **8**All who ever came before me were thieves and robbers, but the sheep did not listen to them. **9**I am the gate; whoever enters through me will be saved.*c* He will come in and go out, and find pasture. **10**The thief comes only to steal and kill and destroy; I have come that they may have life, and have it to the full.

11"I am the good shepherd. The good shepherd lays down his life for the sheep. **12**The hired hand is not the shepherd who owns the sheep. So when he sees the wolf coming, he abandons the sheep and runs away. Then the wolf attacks the flock and scatters it. **13**The man runs away because he is a hired hand and cares nothing for the sheep.

14"I am the good shepherd; I know my sheep and my sheep know me— **15**just as the Father knows me and I know the Father—and I lay down my life for the sheep. **16**I have other sheep that are not of this sheep pen. I must bring them also. They too will listen to my voice, and there shall

---

a22 Or *Messiah*   *b24* A solemn charge to tell the truth (see Joshua 7:19)   *c9* Or *kept safe*

Our Shepherd

Key Verse: *"He calls his own sheep by name and leads them out . . . and his sheep follow him because they know his voice."* John 10:3, 4
Text: John 10:1–21 *(Dad or child reads the text.)*

QUIET TIMES WITH Dad

DAD READS: I love your name. I remember the day your mother and I decided what to call you. We had many names to choose from, but we chose *your* name on purpose, just like my parents picked my name on purpose. And now that you're much older than you were when we gave you your name, this name is even more precious than it was when we gave it to you.

Child reads: Most everyone loves the sound of his or her own name. When I'm in a crowd at school and I hear one of my friends call my name, it makes me feel good. When I hear my name, I know that someone really knows me and wants to be with me.

DAD READS: One day Jesus was telling his followers about a shepherd who knew each one of his sheep by name. When the shepherd called his sheep by name, they stopped being afraid and even followed him away from the safety of their fenced-in yard. Of course, this meant that they could get lost or hurt, but because the shepherd knew their names, they trusted him. The sheep knew and trusted their shepherd's voice even when they couldn't see him.

Child reads: Jesus was telling the people about himself. As our good shepherd, Jesus loves us and knows each one of our names. In fact, the Bible tells us that Jesus even knows how many hairs there are on our heads (Matthew 10:30)! I guess he knows us pretty well.

DAD READS: Sometimes I feel lonely. Even as a grownup, there are times when I feel alone. The verses we read today promise me that God knows my name. If I listen carefully, he will call me and tell me that he loves me. And because I love him, I recognize his voice. This gives me the hope and confidence I need to follow my shepherd.

Child reads: I know that when you follow Jesus, the good shepherd, he will teach you how to be our family's shepherd, too. I'm glad that I have a dad who loves Jesus and wants to take care of his family. This makes me feel happy, knowing that my dad is listening to God's voice.

DAD READS: If we didn't have a shepherd, we would be lost. I'm glad that we have a loving shepherd, and I'm glad that we can trust and follow him. Let me pray this prayer with you:

Our Father in heaven, thank you for being a shepherd who knows us, who loves us, and who even knows our names. Please forgive us for the times when we wander away. Help us to always listen carefully to your voice and to follow you. We love you, and we thank you for your love. In Jesus' name, Amen.

For your next devotional reading, go to page 1184.

be one flock and one shepherd. [17]The reason my Father loves me is that I lay down my life—only to take it up again. [18]No one takes it from me, but I lay it down of my own accord. I have authority to lay it down and authority to take it up again. This command I received from my Father."

[19]At these words the Jews were again divided. [20]Many of them said, "He is demon-possessed and raving mad. Why listen to him?"

[21]But others said, "These are not the sayings of a man possessed by a demon. Can a demon open the eyes of the blind?"

The Unbelief of the Jews

[22]Then came the Feast of Dedication[a] at Jerusalem. It was winter, [23]and Jesus was in the temple area walking in Solomon's Colonnade. [24]The Jews gathered around him, saying, "How long will you keep us in suspense? If you are the Christ,[b] tell us plainly."

[25]Jesus answered, "I did tell you, but you do not believe. The miracles I do in my Father's name speak for me, [26]but you do not believe because you are not my sheep. [27]My sheep listen to my voice; I know them, and they follow me. [28]I give them eternal life, and they shall never perish; no one can snatch them out of my hand. [29]My Father, who has given them to me, is greater than all[c]; no one can snatch them out of my Father's hand. [30]I and the Father are one."

[31]Again the Jews picked up stones to stone him, [32]but Jesus said to them, "I have shown you many great miracles from the Father. For which of these do you stone me?"

[33]"We are not stoning you for any of these," replied the Jews, "but for blasphemy, because you, a mere man, claim to be God."

[34]Jesus answered them, "Is it not written in your Law, 'I have said you are gods'[d]? [35]If he called them 'gods,' to whom the word of God came—and the Scripture cannot be broken— [36]what about the one whom the Father set apart as his very own and sent into the world? Why then do you accuse me of blasphemy because I said, 'I am God's Son'? [37]Do not believe me unless I do what my Father does. [38]But if I do it, even though you do not believe me, believe the miracles, that you may know and understand that the Father is in me, and I in the Father." [39]Again they tried to seize him, but he escaped their grasp.

[40]Then Jesus went back across the Jordan to the place where John had been baptizing in the early days. Here he stayed [41]and many people came to him. They said, "Though John never performed a miraculous sign, all that John said about this man was true." [42]And in that place many believed in Jesus.

The Death of Lazarus

11 Now a man named Lazarus was sick. He was from Bethany, the village of Mary and her sister Martha. [2]This Mary, whose brother Lazarus now lay sick, was the same one who poured perfume on the Lord and wiped his feet with her hair. [3]So the sisters sent word to Jesus, "Lord, the one you love is sick."

[4]When he heard this, Jesus said, "This sickness will not end in death. No, it is for God's glory so that God's Son may be glorified through it." [5]Jesus loved Martha and her sister and Lazarus. [6]Yet when he heard that Lazarus was sick, he stayed where he was two more days.

[7]Then he said to his disciples, "Let us go back to Judea."

[8]"But Rabbi," they said, "a short while ago the Jews tried to stone you, and yet you are going back there?"

[9]Jesus answered, "Are there not twelve hours of daylight? A man who walks by day will not stumble, for he sees by this world's light. [10]It is when he walks by night that he stumbles, for he has no light."

[11]After he had said this, he went on to tell them, "Our friend Lazarus has fallen asleep; but I am going there to wake him up."

[12]His disciples replied, "Lord, if he sleeps, he will get better." [13]Jesus had been speaking of his death, but his disciples thought he meant natural sleep.

[14]So then he told them plainly, "Lazarus is dead, [15]and for your sake I am glad I was not there, so that you may believe. But let us go to him."

[16]Then Thomas (called Didymus) said to the rest of the disciples, "Let us also go, that we may die with him."

Jesus Comforts the Sisters

[17]On his arrival, Jesus found that Lazarus had already been in the tomb for four days. [18]Bethany was less than two miles[e]

---

[a]22 That is, Hanukkah   [b]24 Or *Messiah*   [c]29 Many early manuscripts *What my Father has given me is greater than all*   [d]34 Psalm 82:6   [e]18 Greek *fifteen stadia* (about 3 kilometers)

from Jerusalem, [19]and many Jews had come to Martha and Mary to comfort them in the loss of their brother. [20]When Martha heard that Jesus was coming, she went out to meet him, but Mary stayed at home.

[21]"Lord," Martha said to Jesus, "if you had been here, my brother would not have died. [22]But I know that even now God will give you whatever you ask."

[23]Jesus said to her, "Your brother will rise again."

[24]Martha answered, "I know he will rise again in the resurrection at the last day."

[25]Jesus said to her, "I am the resurrection and the life. He who believes in me will live, even though he dies; [26]and whoever lives and believes in me will never die. Do you believe this?"

[27]"Yes, Lord," she told him, "I believe that you are the Christ,[a] the Son of God, who was to come into the world."

[28]And after she had said this, she went back and called her sister Mary aside. "The Teacher is here," she said, "and is asking for you." [29]When Mary heard this, she got up quickly and went to him. [30]Now Jesus had not yet entered the village, but was still at the place where Martha had met him. [31]When the Jews who had been with Mary in the house, comforting her, noticed how quickly she got up and went out, they followed her, supposing she was going to the tomb to mourn there.

[32]When Mary reached the place where Jesus was and saw him, she fell at his feet and said, "Lord, if you had been here, my brother would not have died."

[33]When Jesus saw her weeping, and the Jews who had come along with her also weeping, he was deeply moved in spirit and troubled. [34]"Where have you laid him?" he asked.

"Come and see, Lord," they replied.

[35]Jesus wept.

[36]Then the Jews said, "See how he loved him!"

[37]But some of them said, "Could not he who opened the eyes of the blind man have kept this man from dying?"

Jesus Raises Lazarus From the Dead

[38]Jesus, once more deeply moved, came to the tomb. It was a cave with a stone laid across the entrance. [39]"Take away the stone," he said.

"But, Lord," said Martha, the sister of the dead man, "by this time there is a bad odor, for he has been there four days."

[40]Then Jesus said, "Did I not tell you that if you believed, you would see the glory of God?"

[41]So they took away the stone. Then Jesus looked up and said, "Father, I thank you that you have heard me. [42]I knew that you always hear me, but I said this for the benefit of the people standing here, that they may believe that you sent me."

[43]When he had said this, Jesus called in a loud voice, "Lazarus, come out!" [44]The dead man came out, his hands and feet wrapped with strips of linen, and a cloth around his face.

Jesus said to them, "Take off the grave clothes and let him go."

The Plot to Kill Jesus

[45]Therefore many of the Jews who had come to visit Mary, and had seen what Jesus did, put their faith in him. [46]But some of them went to the Pharisees and told them what Jesus had done. [47]Then the chief priests and the Pharisees called a meeting of the Sanhedrin.

"What are we accomplishing?" they asked. "Here is this man performing many miraculous signs. [48]If we let him go on like this, everyone will believe in him, and then the Romans will come and take away both our place[b] and our nation."

[49]Then one of them, named Caiaphas, who was high priest that year, spoke up, "You know nothing at all! [50]You do not realize that it is better for you that one man die for the people than that the whole nation perish."

[51]He did not say this on his own, but as high priest that year he prophesied that Jesus would die for the Jewish nation, [52]and not only for that nation but also for the scattered children of God, to bring them together and make them one. [53]So from that day on they plotted to take his life.

[54]Therefore Jesus no longer moved about publicly among the Jews. Instead he withdrew to a region near the desert, to a village called Ephraim, where he stayed with his disciples.

[55]When it was almost time for the Jewish Passover, many went up from the country to Jerusalem for their ceremonial cleansing before the Passover. [56]They kept looking for Jesus, and as they stood in the temple area they asked one another, "What do you think? Isn't he coming to

[a]27 Or *Messiah*   [b]48 Or *temple*

the Feast at all?" [57]But the chief priests and Pharisees had given orders that if anyone found out where Jesus was, he should report it so that they might arrest him.

Jesus Anointed at Bethany

12 Six days before the Passover, Jesus arrived at Bethany, where Lazarus lived, whom Jesus had raised from the dead. [2]Here a dinner was given in Jesus' honor. Martha served, while Lazarus was among those reclining at the table with him.

[3]Then Mary took about a pint[a] of pure nard, an expensive perfume; she poured it on Jesus' feet and wiped his feet with her hair. And the house was filled with the fragrance of the perfume.

[4]But one of his disciples, Judas Iscariot, who was later to betray him, objected, [5]"Why wasn't this perfume sold and the money given to the poor? It was worth a year's wages.[b]" [6]He did not say this because he cared about the poor but because he was a thief; as keeper of the

[a]3 Greek *a litra* (probably about 0.5 liter)   [b]5 Greek *three hundred denarii*

Words

DAILY INSIGHT

"I love you." "Will you marry me?" "I now pronounce you man and wife." "It's a girl." "Daddy, I love you." "Daddy, I love him." "Who gives this woman to be married to this man?" "I love you, Granddaddy."

These are just words. But in every case, when I spoke them or heard them, these words literally changed my life. And they continue to change my life.

Down through recorded history people have spoken words that have never been forgotten. "Give me liberty or give me death." "Never give up … never, never give up … never, never, never give up." "That's one small step for man, one giant leap for mankind." But from the beginning of time, perhaps no more important words were ever spoken than the ones Jesus uttered at the grave of his friend.

A flurry of activity had led the Savior to the town of Bethany. Mary and Martha had first sent word to Jesus, "Lord, the one you love is sick." Soon this was followed by Jesus' own diagnosis; "Lazarus is dead."

So Jesus went to see Mary and Martha. Filled with grief, they met him as he was entering their town. "If you had been here," they pled with him, "[our] brother would not have died." Struck with grief over his friend's death and the people's lack of faith, Jesus wept.

The people led the Master to the cemetery where Lazarus had been buried. "Take

MONDAY

Passage:
John 11:38–44

Verse:
John 11:43

away the stone," Jesus ordered. And then the Messiah spoke the words that will forever be remembered by men and women everywhere. "Lazarus," Jesus said, "come out!"

The Sovereign God of the universe—the one who had brought everything into existence with that same voice—had spoken. Jesus called his friend by name. If he hadn't, *every* grave would have emptied at the sound of his holy voice.

At the sound of Jesus' command, warm blood coursed through Lazarus' cold veins. His chest rose, and fresh air swept into his collapsed lungs. Brain waves exploded inside his darkened head. Underneath his grave clothes, his eyes fluttered and his pupils constricted. Jesus had spoken, and Lazarus was alive.

Once Lazarus was back in the warm sunshine but wrapped from head to toe with strips of cloth, Jesus gave one more command. It was a call to the people standing there, gawking at the living mummy before them. "Take off the grave clothes and let him go."

God's words give life. His admonition for us to tenderly "unwrap" the lives of those who have just been made alive, is also clear. These are not just words. They're powerful words—life-giving and life-altering words.

Listen to these words. Let them change your life.

For your next devotional reading, go to page 1186.

money bag, he used to help himself to what was put into it.

[7]"Leave her alone," Jesus replied. "It was intended that she should save this perfume for the day of my burial. [8]You will always have the poor among you, but you will not always have me."

[9]Meanwhile a large crowd of Jews found out that Jesus was there and came, not only because of him but also to see Lazarus, whom he had raised from the dead. [10]So the chief priests made plans to kill Lazarus as well, [11]for on account of him many of the Jews were going over to Jesus and putting their faith in him.

The Triumphal Entry

[12]The next day the great crowd that had come for the Feast heard that Jesus was on his way to Jerusalem. [13]They took palm branches and went out to meet him, shouting,

"Hosanna![a]"

"Blessed is he who comes in the name of the Lord!"[b]

"Blessed is the King of Israel!"

[14]Jesus found a young donkey and sat upon it, as it is written,

[15]"Do not be afraid, O Daughter of Zion;
    see, your king is coming,
    seated on a donkey's colt."[c]

[16]At first his disciples did not understand all this. Only after Jesus was glorified did they realize that these things had been written about him and that they had done these things to him.

[17]Now the crowd that was with him when he called Lazarus from the tomb and raised him from the dead continued to spread the word. [18]Many people, because they had heard that he had given this miraculous sign, went out to meet him. [19]So the Pharisees said to one another, "See, this is getting us nowhere. Look how the whole world has gone after him!"

Jesus Predicts His Death

[20]Now there were some Greeks among those who went up to worship at the Feast. [21]They came to Philip, who was from Bethsaida in Galilee, with a request. "Sir," they said, "we would like to see Jesus." [22]Philip went to tell Andrew; Andrew and Philip in turn told Jesus.

[23]Jesus replied, "The hour has come for the Son of Man to be glorified. [24]I tell you

the truth, unless a kernel of wheat falls to the ground and dies, it remains only a single seed. But if it dies, it produces many seeds. [25]The man who loves his life will lose it, while the man who hates his life in this world will keep it for eternal life. [26]Whoever serves me must follow me; and where I am, my servant also will be. My Father will honor the one who serves me.

[27]"Now my heart is troubled, and what shall I say? 'Father, save me from this hour'? No, it was for this very reason I came to this hour. [28]Father, glorify your name!"

Then a voice came from heaven, "I have glorified it, and will glorify it again." [29]The crowd that was there and heard it said it had thundered; others said an angel had spoken to him.

[30]Jesus said, "This voice was for your benefit, not mine. [31]Now is the time for judgment on this world; now the prince of this world will be driven out. [32]But I, when I am lifted up from the earth, will draw all men to myself." [33]He said this to show the kind of death he was going to die.

[34]The crowd spoke up, "We have heard from the Law that the Christ[d] will remain forever, so how can you say, 'The Son of Man must be lifted up'? Who is this 'Son of Man'?"

[35]Then Jesus told them, "You are going to have the light just a little while longer. Walk while you have the light, before darkness overtakes you. The man who walks in the dark does not know where he is going. [36]Put your trust in the light while you have it, so that you may become sons of light." When he had finished speaking, Jesus left and hid himself from them.

The Jews Continue in Their Unbelief

[37]Even after Jesus had done all these miraculous signs in their presence, they still would not believe in him. [38]This was to fulfill the word of Isaiah the prophet:

"Lord, who has believed our message
    and to whom has the arm of the Lord
        been revealed?"[e]

[39]For this reason they could not believe, because, as Isaiah says elsewhere:

[40]"He has blinded their eyes
    and deadened their hearts,

---

[a]13 A Hebrew expression meaning "Save!" which became an exclamation of praise   [b]13 Psalm 118:25,26   [c]15 Zech. 9:9   [d]34 Or Messiah   [e]38 Isaiah 53:1

so they can neither see with their eyes,
nor understand with their hearts,
nor turn—and I would heal them."[a]

⁴¹Isaiah said this because he saw Jesus' glory and spoke about him. ⁴²Yet at the same time many even among the leaders believed in him. But because of the Pharisees they would not confess their faith for fear they would be put out of the synagogue; ⁴³for they loved praise from men more than praise from God.

⁴⁴Then Jesus cried out, "When a man believes in me, he does not believe in me only, but in the one who sent me. ⁴⁵When he looks at me, he sees the one who sent me. ⁴⁶I have come into the world as a light, so that no one who believes in me should stay in darkness.

⁴⁷"As for the person who hears my words but does not keep them, I do not judge him. For I did not come to judge the world, but to save it. ⁴⁸There is a judge for

a40 Isaiah 6:10

Seeds, Self-Sacrifice, and Your Baby

DAILY INSIGHT

TUESDAY

Passage:
John 12:23–26

Verse:
John 12:24

Did you adopt your child? That's great. What a perfect picture this is of our entrance into God's family by his invitation. If your wife had your child the other way, I'd like to have a few minutes of your time. Can we talk about pregnancy?

For the first few months of my wife's pregnancies, mornings were the worst. I remember feeling so bad to see her sick at the start of nearly every day. *I'm responsible for this,* I would think to myself. Once the morning sickness ended, my wife's body began to inflate like a beach ball. Awestruck, I tried to imagine what this must've felt like—to give myself so completely to something in such a tangible way. I wondered if I would be willing to do such a thing to have a child. I changed the subject.

Both of our babies were born in the early fall, which meant that Bobbie spent two very hot summers standing directly in front of our window-mounted air conditioner, set on its highest output. She was a good sport, but I knew she was miserable. *I'm responsible for this,* I would think to myself.

When we went to the hospital for the birth of our first child, my wife faced what could be described as sheer panic. Extracting this kid from her body was a brutal experience. Three years later, the second delivery was even worse. I will never forget what my wife went through to have our children. I will always be thankful for her longsuffering ... and grateful that I'm a man.

When Jesus issued the illustration you read today, he was describing the price he was about to pay with his own death. His sacrifice provided the way for us to experience life. This is another inconceivable thing. Jesus went to the cross alone. If he hadn't, where would we be? This principle—sacrifice producing life—is also a picture of what our wives went through to have our children.

For nine full months—and for years afterward—this woman who loves you "died" to herself. She set aside her pride to share her body with someone who would, during those nine months, upset her stomach and keep her awake at night with all that tumbling and kicking inside. Finally, this little someone would deliver terrorizing pain at its birth. Think of the price your wife paid so that you could have the privilege of being someone's father.

Isn't this a powerful picture of what it looks like when a "kernel of wheat falls to the ground and dies ... [so] it produces many seeds?" Does your wife know how grateful you are that she went through this treacherous experience of self-denial and pain for your child ... and for you?

Today would be a perfect day to make sure that she knows, for sure, that you love her and are grateful for what she did. What do you think, Dad? You are responsible for this.

For your next devotional reading, go to page 1187.

the one who rejects me and does not accept my words; that very word which I spoke will condemn him at the last day. [49]For I did not speak of my own accord, but the Father who sent me commanded me what to say and how to say it. [50]I know that his command leads to eternal life. So whatever I say is just what the Father has told me to say."

Jesus Washes His Disciples' Feet

13 It was just before the Passover Feast. Jesus knew that the time had come for him to leave this world and go to the Fa-

ther. Having loved his own who were in the world, he now showed them the full extent of his love.[a]

[2]The evening meal was being served, and the devil had already prompted Judas Iscariot, son of Simon, to betray Jesus. [3]Jesus knew that the Father had put all things under his power, and that he had come from God and was returning to God; [4]so he got up from the meal, took off his outer clothing, and wrapped a towel around his waist. [5]After that, he poured water into a basin and began to wash his

[a]1 Or he loved them to the last

Some Kind of Power

I have a very special picture tucked away in my memory that I'd like to show you. It's a photograph of my friend, Orel Hershiser, pitching.

If you follow the sport, you may be saying, "Big deal. Pitching is what Orel does for a living. What's so special about a picture of him throwing a baseball?" Good question.

Well, in this particular photo, Orel is not wearing a baseball uniform. He's not in a baseball stadium or even throwing from a pitcher's mound. He's standing on a broken concrete slab right next to a grade school in Guatemala. Gathered around him are a dozen aspiring baseball players, not believing what they're seeing. This Cy-Young-Award-winning athlete is teaching them how to pitch.

If you're going to learn how to throw a baseball, you might as well learn from one of the best, right? Yet these young children from Central America never in their wildest dreams expected to receive free lessons from a Major-League-World-Series-winner kind of best! Orel wanted to show these kids that he loved them, so he showed them by serving them.

Jesus' disciples knew what this felt like. The setting of the Last Supper was very informal, contrary to the many artists' renditions of the scene. These men were celebrating the Passover in the traditional

WEDNESDAY

Passage:
John 13:1–8

Verse:
John 13:5

way, reclining on the floor.

Suddenly, Jesus stood up, took off his outer robe, tied a towel around his waist, poured water into a basin, and began washing his disciples' filthy feet. Here was the Sovereign Creator of the universe, the long-hoped-for Messiah, the Savior of mankind on his knees, rinsing road dirt. *Where's the house boy?* they must have thought to themselves. *Jesus shouldn't be doing this!* Peter's recorded protest is surely the same as all the other disciples' outrage. What was happening was unthinkable.

So what *was* Jesus doing? What was he "saying" in this moment of subservient humility? Actually, he was saying the same thing my friend Orel was saying to these precious Guatemalan boys: Love requires humility—power demands service.

Do we want respect at home? Of course, we do. Do we want to own up to our responsibility as the "head of our homes"? Absolutely. Then we have to trade in our professional uniform for a work shirt, our crown for a basin, our robe for a towel. We're going to have to get off our high horse, and get on our knees. Confessing. Washing. Forgiving. Serving. Jesus' example on this unforgettable night ought to be enough.

For your next devotional reading, go to page 1190.

disciples' feet, drying them with the towel that was wrapped around him.

6He came to Simon Peter, who said to him, "Lord, are you going to wash my feet?"

7Jesus replied, "You do not realize now what I am doing, but later you will understand."

8"No," said Peter, "you shall never wash my feet."

Jesus answered, "Unless I wash you, you have no part with me."

9"Then, Lord," Simon Peter replied, "not just my feet but my hands and my head as well!"

10Jesus answered, "A person who has had a bath needs only to wash his feet; his whole body is clean. And you are clean, though not every one of you." **11**For he knew who was going to betray him, and that was why he said not every one was clean.

12When he had finished washing their feet, he put on his clothes and returned to his place. "Do you understand what I have done for you?" he asked them. **13**"You call me 'Teacher' and 'Lord,' and rightly so, for that is what I am. **14**Now that I, your Lord and Teacher, have washed your feet, you also should wash one another's feet. **15**I have set you an example that you should do as I have done for you. **16**I tell you the truth, no servant is greater than his master, nor is a messenger greater than the one who sent him. **17**Now that you know these things, you will be blessed if you do them.

Jesus Predicts His Betrayal

18"I am not referring to all of you; I know those I have chosen. But this is to fulfill the scripture: 'He who shares my bread has lifted up his heel against me.'*a*

19"I am telling you now before it happens, so that when it does happen you will believe that I am He. **20**I tell you the truth, whoever accepts anyone I send accepts me; and whoever accepts me accepts the one who sent me."

21After he had said this, Jesus was troubled in spirit and testified, "I tell you the truth, one of you is going to betray me."

22His disciples stared at one another, at a loss to know which of them he meant. **23**One of them, the disciple whom Jesus loved, was reclining next to him. **24**Simon Peter motioned to this disciple and said, "Ask him which one he means."

25Leaning back against Jesus, he asked him, "Lord, who is it?"

26Jesus answered, "It is the one to whom I will give this piece of bread when I have dipped it in the dish." Then, dipping the piece of bread, he gave it to Judas Iscariot, son of Simon. **27**As soon as Judas took the bread, Satan entered into him.

"What you are about to do, do quickly," Jesus told him, **28**but no one at the meal understood why Jesus said this to him. **29**Since Judas had charge of the money, some thought Jesus was telling him to buy what was needed for the Feast, or to give something to the poor. **30**As soon as Judas had taken the bread, he went out. And it was night.

Jesus Predicts Peter's Denial

31When he was gone, Jesus said, "Now is the Son of Man glorified and God is glorified in him. **32**If God is glorified in him,*b* God will glorify the Son in himself, and will glorify him at once.

33"My children, I will be with you only a little longer. You will look for me, and just as I told the Jews, so I tell you now: Where I am going, you cannot come.

34"A new command I give you: Love one another. As I have loved you, so you must love one another. **35**By this all men will know that you are my disciples, if you love one another."

36Simon Peter asked him, "Lord, where are you going?"

Jesus replied, "Where I am going, you cannot follow now, but you will follow later."

37Peter asked, "Lord, why can't I follow you now? I will lay down my life for you."

38Then Jesus answered, "Will you really lay down your life for me? I tell you the truth, before the rooster crows, you will disown me three times!

Jesus Comforts His Disciples

14 "Do not let your hearts be troubled. Trust in God*c*; trust also in me. **2**In my Father's house are many rooms; if it were not so, I would have told you. I am going there to prepare a place for you. **3**And if I go and prepare a place for you, I will come back and take you to be with me that you also may be where I am. **4**You know the way to the place where I am going."

a18 Psalm 41:9   *b32* Many early manuscripts do not have *If God is glorified in him.*   *c1* Or *You trust in God*

Jesus the Way to the Father

5Thomas said to him, "Lord, we don't know where you are going, so how can we know the way?"

6Jesus answered, "I am the way and the truth and the life. No one comes to the Father except through me. **7**If you really knew me, you would know[a] my Father as well. From now on, you do know him and have seen him."

8Philip said, "Lord, show us the Father and that will be enough for us."

9Jesus answered: "Don't you know me, Philip, even after I have been among you such a long time? Anyone who has seen me has seen the Father. How can you say, 'Show us the Father'? **10**Don't you believe that I am in the Father, and that the Father is in me? The words I say to you are not just my own. Rather, it is the Father, living in me, who is doing his work. **11**Believe me when I say that I am in the Father and the Father is in me; or at least believe on the evidence of the miracles themselves. **12**I tell you the truth, anyone who has faith in me will do what I have been doing. He will do even greater things than these, because I am going to the Father. **13**And I will do whatever you ask in my name, so that the Son may bring glory to the Father. **14**You may ask me for anything in my name, and I will do it.

Jesus Promises the Holy Spirit

15"If you love me, you will obey what I command. **16**And I will ask the Father, and he will give you another Counselor to be with you forever— **17**the Spirit of truth. The world cannot accept him, because it neither sees him nor knows him. But you know him, for he lives with you and will be[b] in you. **18**I will not leave you as orphans; I will come to you. **19**Before long, the world will not see me anymore, but you will see me. Because I live, you also will live. **20**On that day you will realize that I am in my Father, and you are in me, and I am in you. **21**Whoever has my commands and obeys them, he is the one who loves me. He who loves me will be loved by my Father, and I too will love him and show myself to him."

22Then Judas (not Judas Iscariot) said, "But, Lord, why do you intend to show yourself to us and not to the world?"

23Jesus replied, "If anyone loves me, he will obey my teaching. My Father will love him, and we will come to him and make our home with him. **24**He who does not love me will not obey my teaching. These words you hear are not my own; they belong to the Father who sent me.

25"All this I have spoken while still with you. **26**But the Counselor, the Holy Spirit, whom the Father will send in my name, will teach you all things and will remind you of everything I have said to you. **27**Peace I leave with you; my peace I give you. I do not give to you as the world gives. Do not let your hearts be troubled and do not be afraid.

28"You heard me say, 'I am going away and I am coming back to you.' If you loved me, you would be glad that I am going to the Father, for the Father is greater than I. **29**I have told you now before it happens, so that when it does happen you will believe. **30**I will not speak with you much longer, for the prince of this world is coming. He has no hold on me, **31**but the world must learn that I love the Father and that I do exactly what my Father has commanded me.

"Come now; let us leave.

The Vine and the Branches

15 "I am the true vine, and my Father is the gardener. **2**He cuts off every branch in me that bears no fruit, while every branch that does bear fruit he prunes[c] so that it will be even more fruitful. **3**You are already clean because of the word I have spoken to you. **4**Remain in me, and I will remain in you. No branch can bear fruit by itself; it must remain in the vine. Neither can you bear fruit unless you remain in me.

5"I am the vine; you are the branches. If a man remains in me and I in him, he will bear much fruit; apart from me you can do nothing. **6**If anyone does not remain in me, he is like a branch that is thrown away and withers; such branches are picked up, thrown into the fire and burned. **7**If you remain in me and my words remain in you, ask whatever you wish, and it will be given you. **8**This is to my Father's glory, that you bear much fruit, showing yourselves to be my disciples.

9"As the Father has loved me, so have I loved you. Now remain in my love. **10**If you obey my commands, you will remain in my love, just as I have obeyed my Father's

---

[a]7 Some early manuscripts *If you really have known me, you will know* [b]17 Some early manuscripts *and is* [c]2 The Greek for *prunes* also means *cleans.*

commands and remain in his love. [11]I have told you this so that my joy may be in you and that your joy may be complete. [12]My command is this: Love each other as I have loved you. [13]Greater love has no one than this, that he lay down his life for his friends. [14]You are my friends if you do what I command. [15]I no longer call you servants, because a servant does not know his master's business. Instead, I have called you friends, for everything that I learned from my Father I have made known to you. [16]You did not choose me, but I chose you and appointed you to go and bear fruit—fruit that will last. Then the Father will give you whatever you ask in my name. [17]This is my command: Love each other.

The World Hates the Disciples

[18]"If the world hates you, keep in mind that it hated me first. [19]If you belonged to the world, it would love you as its own. As it is, you do not belong to the world, but I have chosen you out of the world. That is

What's He Doing in this Movie?

DAILY INSIGHT

THURSDAY

Passage:
John 15:1–8

Verse:
John 15:5

At one time in my eclectic past, I did a one-day stint as a wedding photographer. I think I charged two hundred dollars for my services. Had the mother of the bride known how little I knew about what I was doing, she would have expired on the spot. Fortunately for me, faking it was an ability I received in full measure at birth. The bride's mother had no idea.

Three decades later, as the father of the bride, I was on the other end of this transaction. Suffice it to say, two hundred dollars barely covered the cost of the photographer's private limousine. Probably out of guilt, the photographer threw in a free video. His wife walked around the whole time the wedding was going on, a high-quality video camera resting on her shoulder. My wife and I are crazy about this video; in fact, I'd say we like it more than the still photographs we bought, if we hadn't paid so much for them.

Several years ago, this precious video found its way into the box of a video we had rented, and the rented video found its way into our memorabilia drawer! Three days later we got a call from a very nice couple who had curled up for the evening to watch one of their favorite shoot-em-up, nail-biting adventure flicks. This couple expected to see Stallone in fatigues in Southeast Asia, but they got me in a tuxedo at First Presbyterian Church.

Here's the principle: If you want to see the right movie, you've got to be sure you're plugging the correct videotape into your VCR. This works in the reverse, too. You can't play a videotape in a compact disc player. If you want a certain result, you're going to have to be plugged into the right *source*.

Jesus used an illustration from a more agrarian time to prove his point, comparing this truth to a vine and its branches: "No branch can bear fruit by itself; it must remain in the vine. Neither can you bear fruit unless you remain in me" (v. 4). Being a man who lives in such a way that your friends and your family are actually blessed because of your life is a very, very tall order. In fact, Jesus was quick to say that if we're not connected to him, our "fruit" will be worthless and our "branch" will die. And dead branches are only good for bonfires.

This principle isn't very deep. We all know that if we're not connecting ourselves to the right stuff, our disobedient lives will show it. We can't expect to fill our lives with sin and have others see purity and righteousness. As computer programmers sometimes say, "Garbage in, garbage out."

If, in the quietness of your own heart, you know that you've got a problem that others can … or could … or *will* see, check which source you're connected to. "Apart from me, you can do nothing," Jesus said.

For your next devotional reading, go to page 1197.

why the world hates you. [20]Remember the words I spoke to you: 'No servant is greater than his master.'[a] If they persecuted me, they will persecute you also. If they obeyed my teaching, they will obey yours also. [21]They will treat you this way because of my name, for they do not know the One who sent me. [22]If I had not come and spoken to them, they would not be guilty of sin. Now, however, they have no excuse for their sin. [23]He who hates me hates my Father as well. [24]If I had not done among them what no one else did, they would not be guilty of sin. But now they have seen these miracles, and yet they have hated both me and my Father. [25]But this is to fulfill what is written in their Law: 'They hated me without reason.'[b]

[26]"When the Counselor comes, whom I will send to you from the Father, the Spirit of truth who goes out from the Father, he will testify about me. [27]And you also must testify, for you have been with me from the beginning.

16 "All this I have told you so that you will not go astray. [2]They will put you out of the synagogue; in fact, a time is coming when anyone who kills you will think he is offering a service to God. [3]They will do such things because they have not known the Father or me. [4]I have told you this, so that when the time comes you will remember that I warned you. I did not tell you this at first because I was with you.

The Work of the Holy Spirit

[5]"Now I am going to him who sent me, yet none of you asks me, 'Where are you going?' [6]Because I have said these things, you are filled with grief. [7]But I tell you the truth: It is for your good that I am going away. Unless I go away, the Counselor will not come to you; but if I go, I will send him to you. [8]When he comes, he will convict the world of guilt[c] in regard to sin and righteousness and judgment: [9]in regard to sin, because men do not believe in me; [10]in regard to righteousness, because I am going to the Father, where you can see me no longer; [11]and in regard to judgment, because the prince of this world now stands condemned.

[12]"I have much more to say to you, more than you can now bear. [13]But when he, the Spirit of truth, comes, he will guide you into all truth. He will not speak on his own; he will speak only what he hears, and he will tell you what is yet to come. [14]He will bring glory to me by taking from

what is mine and making it known to you. [15]All that belongs to the Father is mine. That is why I said the Spirit will take from what is mine and make it known to you.

[16]"In a little while you will see me no more, and then after a little while you will see me."

The Disciples' Grief Will Turn to Joy

[17]Some of his disciples said to one another, "What does he mean by saying, 'In a little while you will see me no more, and then after a little while you will see me,' and 'Because I am going to the Father'?" [18]They kept asking, "What does he mean by 'a little while'? We don't understand what he is saying."

[19]Jesus saw that they wanted to ask him about this, so he said to them, "Are you asking one another what I meant when I said, 'In a little while you will see me no more, and then after a little while you will see me'? [20]I tell you the truth, you will weep and mourn while the world rejoices. You will grieve, but your grief will turn to joy. [21]A woman giving birth to a child has pain because her time has come; but when her baby is born she forgets the anguish because of her joy that a child is born into the world. [22]So with you: Now is your time of grief, but I will see you again and you will rejoice, and no one will take away your joy. [23]In that day you will no longer ask me anything. I tell you the truth, my Father will give you whatever you ask in my name. [24]Until now you have not asked for anything in my name. Ask and you will receive, and your joy will be complete.

[25]"Though I have been speaking figuratively, a time is coming when I will no longer use this kind of language but will tell you plainly about my Father. [26]In that day you will ask in my name. I am not saying that I will ask the Father on your behalf. [27]No, the Father himself loves you because you have loved me and have believed that I came from God. [28]I came from the Father and entered the world; now I am leaving the world and going back to the Father."

[29]Then Jesus' disciples said, "Now you are speaking clearly and without figures of speech. [30]Now we can see that you know all things and that you do not even need to have anyone ask you questions.

[a]20 John 13:16   [b]25 Psalms 35:19; 69:4   [c]8 Or *will expose the guilt of the world*

This makes us believe that you came from God."

[31]"You believe at last!"[a] Jesus answered. [32]"But a time is coming, and has come, when you will be scattered, each to his own home. You will leave me all alone. Yet I am not alone, for my Father is with me.

[33]"I have told you these things, so that in me you may have peace. In this world you will have trouble. But take heart! I have overcome the world."

Jesus Prays for Himself

17 After Jesus said this, he looked toward heaven and prayed:

"Father, the time has come. Glorify your Son, that your Son may glorify you. [2]For you granted him authority over all people that he might give eternal life to all those you have given him. [3]Now this is eternal life: that they may know you, the only true God, and Jesus Christ, whom you have sent. [4]I have brought you glory on earth by completing the work you gave me to do. [5]And now, Father, glorify me in your presence with the glory I had with you before the world began.

Jesus Prays for His Disciples

[6]"I have revealed you[b] to those whom you gave me out of the world. They were yours; you gave them to me and they have obeyed your word. [7]Now they know that everything you have given me comes from you. [8]For I gave them the words you gave me and they accepted them. They knew

with certainty that I came from you, and they believed that you sent me. [9]I pray for them. I am not praying for the world, but for those you have given me, for they are yours. [10]All I have is yours, and all you have is mine. And glory has come to me through them. [11]I will remain in the world no longer, but they are still in the world, and I am coming to you. Holy Father, protect them by the power of your name—the name you gave me—so that they may be one as we are one. [12]While I was with them, I protected them and kept them safe by that name you gave me. None has been lost except the one doomed to destruction so that Scripture would be fulfilled.

[13]"I am coming to you now, but I say these things while I am still in the world, so that they may have the full measure of my joy within them. [14]I have given them your word and the world has hated them, for they are not of the world any more than I am of the world. [15]My prayer is not that you take them out of the world but that you protect them from the evil one. [16]They are not of the world, even as I am not of it. [17]Sanctify[c] them by the truth; your word is truth. [18]As you sent me into the world, I have sent them into the world. [19]For them I sanctify myself, that they too may be truly sanctified.

[a]31 Or "Do you now believe?" [b]6 Greek your name; also in verse 26 [c]17 Greek hagiazo (set apart for sacred use or make holy); also in verse 19

HEY DAD
Does Jesus pray to God for me?

Text: John 16:26–28

Jesus definitely talks to God on our behalf. Hebrews 4:14–16 tells us that we can approach God's throne of grace boldly because Jesus is our great high priest. He pleads our case. In fact, Jesus is the only way to God the Father (John 14:6).

But do we have to pray to Jesus so that he can pray to God for us? No. Jesus told his disciples that one day they would ask for things in his name. But he stressed that the Father loved them as much as Jesus did. So, they did not have to pray to Jesus; they could pray directly to the Father.

Jesus' words are for us, too. Sometimes we may think of God the Father as judgmental. Jesus dispels that idea. God *is* just; he will judge the wicked. But he is also merciful and loving. That same perfect, almighty, holy God will care for us—because we are his own.

For a complete listing of Questions Kids Ask, turn to page 1435.

QUESTIONS KIDS ASK

Jesus Prays for All Believers

20"My prayer is not for them alone. I pray also for those who will believe in me through their message, **21**that all of them may be one, Father, just as you are in me and I am in you. May they also be in us so that the world may believe that you have sent me. **22**I have given them the glory that you gave me, that they may be one as we are one: **23**I in them and you in me. May they be brought to complete unity to let the world know that you sent me and have loved them even as you have loved me.

24"Father, I want those you have given me to be with me where I am, and to see my glory, the glory you have given me because you loved me before the creation of the world.

25"Righteous Father, though the world does not know you, I know you, and they know that you have sent me. **26**I have made you known to them, and will continue to make you known in order that the love you have for me may be in them and that I myself may be in them."

Jesus Arrested

18 When he had finished praying, Jesus left with his disciples and crossed the Kidron Valley. On the other side there was an olive grove, and he and his disciples went into it.

2Now Judas, who betrayed him, knew the place, because Jesus had often met there with his disciples. **3**So Judas came to the grove, guiding a detachment of soldiers and some officials from the chief priests and Pharisees. They were carrying torches, lanterns and weapons.

4Jesus, knowing all that was going to happen to him, went out and asked them, "Who is it you want?"

5"Jesus of Nazareth," they replied.

"I am he," Jesus said. (And Judas the traitor was standing there with them.) **6**When Jesus said, "I am he," they drew back and fell to the ground.

7Again he asked them, "Who is it you want?"

And they said, "Jesus of Nazareth."

8"I told you that I am he," Jesus answered. "If you are looking for me, then let these men go." **9**This happened so that the words he had spoken would be fulfilled: "I have not lost one of those you gave me."[a]

10Then Simon Peter, who had a sword, drew it and struck the high priest's servant, cutting off his right ear. (The servant's name was Malchus.)

11Jesus commanded Peter, "Put your sword away! Shall I not drink the cup the Father has given me?"

Jesus Taken to Annas

12Then the detachment of soldiers with its commander and the Jewish officials arrested Jesus. They bound him **13**and brought him first to Annas, who was the father-in-law of Caiaphas, the high priest that year. **14**Caiaphas was the one who had advised the Jews that it would be good if one man died for the people.

Peter's First Denial

15Simon Peter and another disciple were following Jesus. Because this disciple was known to the high priest, he went with Jesus into the high priest's courtyard, **16**but Peter had to wait outside at the door. The other disciple, who was known to the high priest, came back, spoke to the girl on duty there and brought Peter in.

17"You are not one of his disciples, are you?" the girl at the door asked Peter.

He replied, "I am not."

18It was cold, and the servants and officials stood around a fire they had made to keep warm. Peter also was standing with them, warming himself.

The High Priest Questions Jesus

19Meanwhile, the high priest questioned Jesus about his disciples and his teaching.

20"I have spoken openly to the world," Jesus replied. "I always taught in synagogues or at the temple, where all the Jews come together. I said nothing in secret. **21**Why question me? Ask those who heard me. Surely they know what I said."

22When Jesus said this, one of the officials nearby struck him in the face. "Is this the way you answer the high priest?" he demanded.

23"If I said something wrong," Jesus replied, "testify as to what is wrong. But if I spoke the truth, why did you strike me?" **24**Then Annas sent him, still bound, to Caiaphas the high priest.[b]

*a*9 John 6:39   *b*24 Or (Now Annas had sent him, still bound, to Caiaphas the high priest.)

Peter's Second and Third Denials

25As Simon Peter stood warming himself, he was asked, "You are not one of his disciples, are you?"

He denied it, saying, "I am not."

26One of the high priest's servants, a relative of the man whose ear Peter had cut off, challenged him, "Didn't I see you with him in the olive grove?" **27**Again Peter denied it, and at that moment a rooster began to crow.

Jesus Before Pilate

28Then the Jews led Jesus from Caiaphas to the palace of the Roman governor. By now it was early morning, and to avoid ceremonial uncleanness the Jews did not enter the palace; they wanted to be able to eat the Passover. **29**So Pilate came out to them and asked, "What charges are you bringing against this man?"

30"If he were not a criminal," they replied, "we would not have handed him over to you."

31Pilate said, "Take him yourselves and judge him by your own law."

"But we have no right to execute anyone," the Jews objected. **32**This happened so that the words Jesus had spoken indicating the kind of death he was going to die would be fulfilled.

33Pilate then went back inside the palace, summoned Jesus and asked him, "Are you the king of the Jews?"

34"Is that your own idea," Jesus asked, "or did others talk to you about me?"

35"Am I a Jew?" Pilate replied. "It was your people and your chief priests who handed you over to me. What is it you have done?"

36Jesus said, "My kingdom is not of this world. If it were, my servants would fight to prevent my arrest by the Jews. But now my kingdom is from another place."

37"You are a king, then!" said Pilate.

Jesus answered, "You are right in saying I am a king. In fact, for this reason I was born, and for this I came into the world, to testify to the truth. Everyone on the side of truth listens to me."

38"What is truth?" Pilate asked. With this he went out again to the Jews and said, "I find no basis for a charge against him. **39**But it is your custom for me to release to you one prisoner at the time of the Passover. Do you want me to release 'the king of the Jews'?"

40They shouted back, "No, not him! Give us Barabbas!" Now Barabbas had taken part in a rebellion.

Jesus Sentenced to Be Crucified

19 Then Pilate took Jesus and had him flogged. **2**The soldiers twisted together a crown of thorns and put it on his head. They clothed him in a purple robe **3**and went up to him again and again, saying, "Hail, king of the Jews!" And they struck him in the face.

4Once more Pilate came out and said to the Jews, "Look, I am bringing him out to you to let you know that I find no basis for a charge against him." **5**When Jesus came out wearing the crown of thorns and the purple robe, Pilate said to them, "Here is the man!"

6As soon as the chief priests and their officials saw him, they shouted, "Crucify! Crucify!"

But Pilate answered, "You take him and crucify him. As for me, I find no basis for a charge against him."

7The Jews insisted, "We have a law, and according to that law he must die, because he claimed to be the Son of God."

8When Pilate heard this, he was even more afraid, **9**and he went back inside the palace. "Where do you come from?" he asked Jesus, but Jesus gave him no answer. **10**"Do you refuse to speak to me?" Pilate said. "Don't you realize I have power either to free you or to crucify you?"

11Jesus answered, "You would have no power over me if it were not given to you from above. Therefore the one who handed me over to you is guilty of a greater sin."

12From then on, Pilate tried to set Jesus free, but the Jews kept shouting, "If you let this man go, you are no friend of Caesar. Anyone who claims to be a king opposes Caesar."

13When Pilate heard this, he brought Jesus out and sat down on the judge's seat at a place known as the Stone Pavement (which in Aramaic is Gabbatha). **14**It was the day of Preparation of Passover Week, about the sixth hour.

"Here is your king," Pilate said to the Jews.

15But they shouted, "Take him away! Take him away! Crucify him!"

"Shall I crucify your king?" Pilate asked.

"We have no king but Caesar," the chief priests answered.

16Finally Pilate handed him over to them to be crucified.

The Crucifixion

So the soldiers took charge of Jesus. [17]Carrying his own cross, he went out to the place of the Skull (which in Aramaic is called Golgotha). [18]Here they crucified him, and with him two others—one on each side and Jesus in the middle.

[19]Pilate had a notice prepared and fastened to the cross. It read: JESUS OF NAZARETH, THE KING OF THE JEWS. [20]Many of the Jews read this sign, for the place where Jesus was crucified was near the city, and the sign was written in Aramaic, Latin and Greek. [21]The chief priests of the Jews protested to Pilate, "Do not write 'The King of the Jews,' but that this man claimed to be king of the Jews."

[22]Pilate answered, "What I have written, I have written."

[23]When the soldiers crucified Jesus, they took his clothes, dividing them into four shares, one for each of them, with the undergarment remaining. This garment was seamless, woven in one piece from top to bottom. [24]"Let's not tear it," they said to one another. "Let's decide by lot who will get it."

This happened that the scripture might be fulfilled which said,

"They divided my garments among
        them
    and cast lots for my clothing."[a]

So this is what the soldiers did. [25]Near the cross of Jesus stood his mother, his mother's sister, Mary the wife of Clopas, and Mary Magdalene. [26]When Jesus saw his mother there, and the disciple whom he loved standing nearby, he said to his mother, "Dear woman, here is your son," [27]and to the disciple, "Here is your mother." From that time on, this disciple took her into his home.

The Death of Jesus

[28]Later, knowing that all was now completed, and so that the Scripture would be fulfilled, Jesus said, "I am thirsty." [29]A jar of wine vinegar was there, so they soaked a sponge in it, put the sponge on a stalk of the hyssop plant, and lifted it to Jesus' lips. [30]When he had received the drink, Jesus said, "It is finished." With that, he bowed his head and gave up his spirit.

[31]Now it was the day of Preparation, and the next day was to be a special Sabbath. Because the Jews did not want the bodies left on the crosses during the Sab-

bath, they asked Pilate to have the legs broken and the bodies taken down. [32]The soldiers therefore came and broke the legs of the first man who had been crucified with Jesus, and then those of the other. [33]But when they came to Jesus and found that he was already dead, they did not break his legs. [34]Instead, one of the soldiers pierced Jesus' side with a spear, bringing a sudden flow of blood and water. [35]The man who saw it has given testimony, and his testimony is true. He knows that he tells the truth, and he testifies so that you also may believe. [36]These things happened so that the scripture would be fulfilled: "Not one of his bones will be broken,"[b] [37]and, as another scripture says, "They will look on the one they have pierced."[c]

The Burial of Jesus

[38]Later, Joseph of Arimathea asked Pilate for the body of Jesus. Now Joseph was a disciple of Jesus, but secretly because he feared the Jews. With Pilate's permission, he came and took the body away. [39]He was accompanied by Nicodemus, the man who earlier had visited Jesus at night. Nicodemus brought a mixture of myrrh and aloes, about seventy-five pounds.[d] [40]Taking Jesus' body, the two of them wrapped it, with the spices, in strips of linen. This was in accordance with Jewish burial customs. [41]At the place where Jesus was crucified, there was a garden, and in the garden a new tomb, in which no one had ever been laid. [42]Because it was the Jewish day of Preparation and since the tomb was nearby, they laid Jesus there.

The Empty Tomb

20 Early on the first day of the week, while it was still dark, Mary Magdalene went to the tomb and saw that the stone had been removed from the entrance. [2]So she came running to Simon Peter and the other disciple, the one Jesus loved, and said, "They have taken the Lord out of the tomb, and we don't know where they have put him!"

[3]So Peter and the other disciple started for the tomb. [4]Both were running, but the other disciple outran Peter and reached the tomb first. [5]He bent over and looked

---

[a]24 Psalm 22:18   [b]36 Exodus 12:46; Num. 9:12; Psalm 34:20   [c]37 Zech. 12:10   [d]39 Greek a hundred litrai (about 34 kilograms)

in at the strips of linen lying there but did not go in. ⁶Then Simon Peter, who was behind him, arrived and went into the tomb. He saw the strips of linen lying there, ⁷as well as the burial cloth that had been around Jesus' head. The cloth was folded up by itself, separate from the linen. ⁸Finally the other disciple, who had reached the tomb first, also went inside. He saw and believed. ⁹(They still did not understand from Scripture that Jesus had to rise from the dead.)

Jesus Appears to Mary Magdalene

¹⁰Then the disciples went back to their homes, ¹¹but Mary stood outside the tomb crying. As she wept, she bent over to look into the tomb ¹²and saw two angels in white, seated where Jesus' body had been, one at the head and the other at the foot.

¹³They asked her, "Woman, why are you crying?"

"They have taken my Lord away," she said, "and I don't know where they have put him." ¹⁴At this, she turned around and saw Jesus standing there, but she did not realize that it was Jesus.

¹⁵"Woman," he said, "why are you crying? Who is it you are looking for?"

Thinking he was the gardener, she said, "Sir, if you have carried him away, tell me where you have put him, and I will get him."

¹⁶Jesus said to her, "Mary."

She turned toward him and cried out in Aramaic, "Rabboni!" (which means Teacher).

¹⁷Jesus said, "Do not hold on to me, for I have not yet returned to the Father. Go instead to my brothers and tell them, 'I am returning to my Father and your Father, to my God and your God.'"

¹⁸Mary Magdalene went to the disciples with the news: "I have seen the Lord!" And she told them that he had said these things to her.

Jesus Appears to His Disciples

¹⁹On the evening of that first day of the week, when the disciples were together, with the doors locked for fear of the Jews, Jesus came and stood among them and said, "Peace be with you!" ²⁰After he said this, he showed them his hands and side. The disciples were overjoyed when they saw the Lord.

²¹Again Jesus said, "Peace be with you! As the Father has sent me, I am sending

you." ²²And with that he breathed on them and said, "Receive the Holy Spirit. ²³If you forgive anyone his sins, they are forgiven; if you do not forgive them, they are not forgiven."

Jesus Appears to Thomas

²⁴Now Thomas (called Didymus), one of the Twelve, was not with the disciples when Jesus came. ²⁵So the other disciples told him, "We have seen the Lord!"

But he said to them, "Unless I see the nail marks in his hands and put my finger where the nails were, and put my hand into his side, I will not believe it."

²⁶A week later his disciples were in the house again, and Thomas was with them. Though the doors were locked, Jesus came and stood among them and said, "Peace be with you!" ²⁷Then he said to Thomas, "Put your finger here; see my hands. Reach out your hand and put it into my side. Stop doubting and believe."

²⁸Thomas said to him, "My Lord and my God!"

²⁹Then Jesus told him, "Because you have seen me, you have believed; blessed are those who have not seen and yet have believed."

³⁰Jesus did many other miraculous signs in the presence of his disciples, which are not recorded in this book. ³¹But these are written that you may*ᵃ* believe that Jesus is the Christ, the Son of God, and that by believing you may have life in his name.

Jesus and the Miraculous Catch of Fish

21 Afterward Jesus appeared again to his disciples, by the Sea of Tiberias.*ᵇ* It happened this way: ²Simon Peter, Thomas (called Didymus), Nathanael from Cana in Galilee, the sons of Zebedee, and two other disciples were together. ³"I'm going out to fish," Simon Peter told them, and they said, "We'll go with you." So they went out and got into the boat, but that night they caught nothing.

⁴Early in the morning, Jesus stood on the shore, but the disciples did not realize that it was Jesus.

⁵He called out to them, "Friends, haven't you any fish?"

"No," they answered.

⁶He said, "Throw your net on the right side of the boat and you will find some."

---

*ᵃ*31 Some manuscripts *may continue to*   *ᵇ*1 That is, Sea of Galilee

When they did, they were unable to haul the net in because of the large number of fish.

⁷Then the disciple whom Jesus loved said to Peter, "It is the Lord!" As soon as Simon Peter heard him say, "It is the Lord," he wrapped his outer garment around him (for he had taken it off) and jumped into the water. ⁸The other disciples followed in the boat, towing the net full of fish, for they were not far from shore, about a hundred yards.ᵃ ⁹When they landed, they saw a fire of burning coals there with fish on it, and some bread.

¹⁰Jesus said to them, "Bring some of the fish you have just caught."

¹¹Simon Peter climbed aboard and dragged the net ashore. It was full of large fish, 153, but even with so many the net was not torn. ¹²Jesus said to them, "Come and have breakfast." None of the disciples dared ask him, "Who are you?" They knew

ᵃ8 Greek *about two hundred cubits* (about 90 meters)

Taking Good Care of God's Kids

DAILY INSIGHT

FRIDAY
Passage:
John 21:15–17
Verse:
John 21:15

I may be the luckiest man alive. John Crawford, one of the ministers in our church, owns a great big Chevy diesel pickup truck, and because he's a man of the cloth and can hardly say "no" to one of his faithful parishioners, he lets me borrow it whenever I want. How terrific is this?

Last year, when I was doing a little remodeling work in our daughter's house, I asked John if I could borrow "Big Blue." Now, if you've ever borrowed a car or truck from one of your friends, you know that this can be a little tricky.

On a scale from one to ten, carelessness to fastidiousness, renting a car from Hertz™ is a one. Driving your own car is a seven. But using a car or truck that belongs to one of your friends is a nine. If the owner is your minister, it's a ten. The last thing you want is for something bad to happen to the Reverend's vehicle while it's under your care.

Now let's take a minute to relate this principle to kids. Who "owns" your kids? Well, given the above scale, if they were the property of some corporate conglomerate and you had them only for a few years, you'd probably take care of them a certain way. If you determined that they were yours to do with as you thought best, then you'd take care of them another way. But what if your children belonged to God? What if, out of the kindness and generosity of his heart, he loaned them to you? Then how would you take care of those kids?

The passage we read today shows the risen Christ having a heart-to-heart with Simon Peter. This was a difficult encounter because both of them knew that Peter had compromised his loyalty to the Savior several nights before. Three times Jesus asked Peter if he loved him—an exact match to the number of times Peter had verbally denied his Lord. And when Peter reaffirmed his love for Jesus, he heard the following: "Feed my lambs . . . Take care of my sheep . . . Feed my sheep."

For a moment, put yourself in Peter's place. You have just heard Jesus Christ ask if you love him. "Sure," you answer, "of course, I do." If he asked you three times or thirty times, you'd say the same thing, right? Right.

Then, in response to your affirmation of your love for him, the Master tells you the same thing he told Peter. "Take care of my children." If your kids were leased to you, that would be one thing. Even if they were your own personal property, that would be another. But God has given your precious family to you to care for, nurture and lovingly lead into faith.

Take even better care of them than I took care of John Crawford's "Big Blue." Your children are on loan to you from your heavenly Father, and you know how *he* takes care of his things.

For your next devotional reading, go to page 1200.

it was the Lord. ¹³Jesus came, took the bread and gave it to them, and did the same with the fish. ¹⁴This was now the third time Jesus appeared to his disciples after he was raised from the dead.

Jesus Reinstates Peter

¹⁵When they had finished eating, Jesus said to Simon Peter, "Simon son of John, do you truly love me more than these?"

"Yes, Lord," he said, "you know that I love you."

Jesus said, "Feed my lambs."

¹⁶Again Jesus said, "Simon son of John, do you truly love me?"

He answered, "Yes, Lord, you know that I love you."

Jesus said, "Take care of my sheep."

¹⁷The third time he said to him, "Simon son of John, do you love me?"

Peter was hurt because Jesus asked him the third time, "Do you love me?" He said, "Lord, you know all things; you know that I love you."

Jesus said, "Feed my sheep. ¹⁸I tell you the truth, when you were younger you dressed yourself and went where you wanted; but when you are old you will stretch out your hands, and someone else will dress you and lead you where you do not want to go." ¹⁹Jesus said this to indicate the kind of death by which Peter would glorify God. Then he said to him, "Follow me!"

²⁰Peter turned and saw that the disciple whom Jesus loved was following them. (This was the one who had leaned back against Jesus at the supper and had said, "Lord, who is going to betray you?") ²¹When Peter saw him, he asked, "Lord, what about him?"

²²Jesus answered, "If I want him to remain alive until I return, what is that to you? You must follow me." ²³Because of this, the rumor spread among the brothers that this disciple would not die. But Jesus did not say that he would not die; he only said, "If I want him to remain alive until I return, what is that to you?"

²⁴This is the disciple who testifies to these things and who wrote them down. We know that his testimony is true.

²⁵Jesus did many other things as well. If every one of them were written down, I suppose that even the whole world would not have room for the books that would be written.

HEY DAD

Why are there four Gospels? Don't they all say the same thing?

Text: John 21:25

Taken together, Matthew, Mark, Luke and John give us a fuller account of Jesus' life than one Gospel could. Each Gospel is also written for a slightly different audience.

Matthew wrote mainly to the Jews by including Jesus' detailed genealogy and evidence that Jesus is the Messiah, the fulfillment of ancient prophecy (Matthew 13:13–16). Mark's Gospel is filled with stories about Jesus' miracles and teachings. It focuses on the events of Christ's life on earth.

Luke's Gospel appealed to the Gentiles by demonstrating Jesus' compassion for people who were poor, or sick, or outcasts (Luke 17:11–17). And John, who had a special friendship with the Good Shepherd, used a direct approach in his Gospel to reveal that Jesus is the Son of God and that he came to save us (John 1:14 and 3:16).

All four Gospels have a unique perspective and purpose. And each tells us something different about Jesus—the Messiah, the miracle worker, the compassionate one, the Savior.

For a complete listing of Questions Kids Ask, turn to page 1435.

QUESTIONS KIDS ASK

Jesus' final words to his disciples (1:8) challenged them to remember what they had seen, then to go and tell everyone. The book of Acts takes us on a journey that begins with the risen Savior's commission and continues through the building of the early church. In this story you'll meet Stephen, whose spilled blood fueled the fires of passion for those who would follow in his footsteps. You'll meet a young Jewish zealot named Saul, whose hatred for these brave believers was transformed after the Messiah invaded his life on a quiet Damascus-bound road. You'll also watch as Jesus' disciples became Spirit-filled apostles who powerfully delivered the Gospel message.

This is the story of spreading a simple message of faith and grace. Beginning in Jerusalem, the power of this message changed the world forever. And its impact is still changing the world, all the way to your home and your heart. The best part of this story is that Jesus graciously promised his followers that, as they set out to tell others of his salvation, they would not go alone. What was true then is still true today. This same Holy Spirit still empowers you right now.

Acts

Jesus Taken Up Into Heaven

1 In my former book, Theophilus, I wrote about all that Jesus began to do and to teach [2]until the day he was taken up to heaven, after giving instructions through the Holy Spirit to the apostles he had chosen. [3]After his suffering, he showed himself to these men and gave many convincing proofs that he was alive. He appeared to them over a period of forty days and spoke about the kingdom of God. [4]On one occasion, while he was eating with them, he gave them this command: "Do not leave Jerusalem, but wait for the gift my Father promised, which you have heard me speak about. [5]For John baptized with[a] water, but in a few days you will be baptized with the Holy Spirit."

[6]So when they met together, they asked him, "Lord, are you at this time going to restore the kingdom to Israel?"

[7]He said to them: "It is not for you to know the times or dates the Father has set by his own authority. [8]But you will receive power when the Holy Spirit comes on you;

[a]5 Or *in*

Basketball, Tennis, Golf and Living Like Jesus

Key Verse: *"You will receive power when the Holy Spirit comes on you; and you will be my witnesses in Jerusalem, and in all Judea and Samaria, and to the ends of the earth."* Acts 1:8
Text: Acts 1:3–9 *(Dad or child reads the text.)*

DAD READS: One of the most amazing things about modern medicine is the transplant procedure. A doctor can take a heart from one person and put it in another person. He can take a kidney or a liver and move it from one body to another. This is a wonderful thing.

Child reads: What if a doctor could transplant other things besides hearts, kidneys, or livers to help you do certain things better than you can right now? What if a doctor could give you Michael Jordan's legs for jumping, or Michael Chang's arm for serving a tennis ball, or Tiger Woods' body for swinging a golf club? Wouldn't that be fun?

DAD READS: Yes that would be great. Can you imagine how surprised my friends would be the first time I played a game of basketball, or a tennis match, or a round of golf with the help of Jordan's legs, Chang's arm, or Tiger's swing? Boy, would they be surprised!

Child reads: One day Jesus was visiting with his disciples. He was telling them that he had to leave . . . to go back to heaven. They were sad until Jesus told them that, even though his body was going to be gone, he was going to leave his Spirit— the Holy Spirit—with them. He said that this Holy Spirit would be with them wherever they would go. It was going to be just like having God transplanted into their lives!

DAD READS: Can you imagine how wonderful that must have sounded to Jesus' disciples? They had been with Jesus for three years. They had listened to the words he had spoken, they had seen the incredible miracles he had performed, and they had seen how much he loved people. They must have been so excited to know that now they would have his Spirit inside of them to help them speak the same words, heal just like Jesus did, and love others, too.

Child reads: The most wonderful thing about this is that the very same Holy Spirit can be inside of us. When we invite him to come into our lives, God's Holy Spirit helps us to be just like Jesus. And he wants us to tell our friends about how he is living inside of us. Of course, we couldn't do any of this without a transplant.

DAD READS: I am so glad that Jesus promised to give the disciples his Holy Spirit. I'm also happy that he promises to give you and me the same thing. Imagine how different our lives will be with God living inside. Let me pray this prayer with you:

Our Father in heaven, we love you. Thank you for your Holy Spirit. Thank you for promising that you would live inside of your disciples. And thank you for living inside of us, too. This means that, wherever we go and whatever we do, you will be our strength. We love you, and we thank you for your love. In Jesus' name, **Amen.**

For your next devotional reading, go to page 1202.

and you will be my witnesses in Jerusalem, and in all Judea and Samaria, and to the ends of the earth."

[9]After he said this, he was taken up before their very eyes, and a cloud hid him from their sight.

[10]They were looking intently up into the sky as he was going, when suddenly two men dressed in white stood beside them. [11]"Men of Galilee," they said, "why do you stand here looking into the sky? This same Jesus, who has been taken from you into heaven, will come back in the same way you have seen him go into heaven."

Matthias Chosen to Replace Judas

[12]Then they returned to Jerusalem from the hill called the Mount of Olives, a Sabbath day's walk[a] from the city. [13]When they arrived, they went upstairs to the room where they were staying. Those present were Peter, John, James and Andrew; Philip and Thomas, Bartholomew and Matthew; James son of Alphaeus and Simon the Zealot, and Judas son of James. [14]They all joined together constantly in prayer, along with the women and Mary the mother of Jesus, and with his brothers.

[15]In those days Peter stood up among the believers[b] (a group numbering about a hundred and twenty) [16]and said, "Brothers, the Scripture had to be fulfilled which the Holy Spirit spoke long ago through the mouth of David concerning Judas, who served as guide for those who arrested Jesus— [17]he was one of our number and shared in this ministry."

[18](With the reward he got for his wickedness, Judas bought a field; there he fell headlong, his body burst open and all his intestines spilled out. [19]Everyone in Jerusalem heard about this, so they called that field in their language Akeldama, that is, Field of Blood.)

[20]"For," said Peter, "it is written in the book of Psalms,

" 'May his place be deserted;
    let there be no one to dwell in it,'[c]

and,

" 'May another take his place of
    leadership.'[d]

[21]Therefore it is necessary to choose one of the men who have been with us the whole time the Lord Jesus went in and out among us, [22]beginning from John's baptism to the time when Jesus was taken up from us. For one of these must become a witness with us of his resurrection."

[23]So they proposed two men: Joseph called Barsabbas (also known as Justus) and Matthias. [24]Then they prayed, "Lord, you know everyone's heart. Show us which of these two you have chosen [25]to take over this apostolic ministry, which Judas left to go where he belongs." [26]Then they cast lots, and the lot fell to Matthias; so he was added to the eleven apostles.

The Holy Spirit Comes at Pentecost

2 When the day of Pentecost came, they were all together in one place. [2]Suddenly a sound like the blowing of a violent wind came from heaven and filled the whole house where they were sitting. [3]They saw what seemed to be tongues of fire that separated and came to rest on each of them. [4]All of them were filled with the Holy Spirit and began to speak in other tongues[e] as the Spirit enabled them.

[5]Now there were staying in Jerusalem God-fearing Jews from every nation under heaven. [6]When they heard this sound, a crowd came together in bewilderment, because each one heard them speaking in his own language. [7]Utterly amazed, they asked: "Are not all these men who are speaking Galileans? [8]Then how is it that each of us hears them in his own native language? [9]Parthians, Medes and Elamites; residents of Mesopotamia, Judea and Cappadocia, Pontus and Asia, [10]Phrygia and Pamphylia, Egypt and the parts of Libya near Cyrene; visitors from Rome [11](both Jews and converts to Judaism); Cretans and Arabs—we hear them declaring the wonders of God in our own tongues!" [12]Amazed and perplexed, they asked one another, "What does this mean?"

[13]Some, however, made fun of them and said, "They have had too much wine.[f]"

Peter Addresses the Crowd

[14]Then Peter stood up with the Eleven, raised his voice and addressed the crowd: "Fellow Jews and all of you who live in Jerusalem, let me explain this to you; listen carefully to what I say. [15]These men are not drunk, as you suppose. It's only nine

---

[a]12 That is, about 3/4 mile (about 1,100 meters)
[b]15 Greek *brothers*   [c]20 Psalm 69:25   [d]20 Psalm 109:8   [e]4 Or *languages*; also in verse 11   [f]13 Or *sweet wine*

in the morning! **16**No, this is what was spoken by the prophet Joel:

17 " 'In the last days, God says,
I will pour out my Spirit on all
people.
Your sons and daughters will prophesy,
your young men will see visions,
your old men will dream dreams.
18Even on my servants, both men and
women,
I will pour out my Spirit in those
days,
and they will prophesy.
19I will show wonders in the heaven
above

and signs on the earth below,
blood and fire and billows of
smoke.
20The sun will be turned to darkness
and the moon to blood
before the coming of the great and
glorious day of the Lord.
21And everyone who calls
on the name of the Lord will be
saved.'*a*

22"Men of Israel, listen to this: Jesus of Nazareth was a man accredited by God to you by miracles, wonders and signs,

a21 Joel 2:28-32

God's Windbag

DAILY INSIGHT

MONDAY

Passage:
Acts 2:1–13

Verse:
Acts 2:2

On an unseasonably warm Saturday, the day before Easter, 1988, I was in my office catching up on some correspondence. The view from my window confirmed the report of a big storm moving in. The trees in front of our building bent low under the force of the heavy winds and rain. And then, as suddenly as the storm had started, it came to an incredibly abrupt end. The trees stood straight and motionless. This stillness seemed strange—almost eerie. A few hours later I found out that, in those moments, a tornado was ripping through our town only a few short miles from where I was sitting.

Did you know that no one has ever seen a tornado? "What?" you're saying. "I have seen plenty of them in photographs and on television. I've even seen depictions of tornadoes in the movies." You're right. I have seen them, too.

But what you and I have actually seen has been the *effects* of tornadoes—the dirt and debris and moisture that the funnel cloud has picked up along the way. Because a tornado is nothing but swiftly moving wind, you and I have never actually *seen* a tornado. But, as my wife and I found out later that afternoon as we drove through the devastated area, the effects of those howling winds are obvious to everyone.

On the day of Pentecost, exactly fifty days after Passover, God's Holy Spirit paid a visit to the disciples. His calling card was the "sound like the blowing of a violent wind ... from heaven" (2:2). The effect of this miraculous visitation was visible in tongues of fire and audible as the men began speaking in languages they had never studied. But the wind itself was not visible.

God the Father and God the Holy Spirit are like the wind. "No one has ever seen God," the apostle John wrote, "but if we love one another, God lives in us and his love is made complete in us" (1 John 4:12). In the same way, no one will ever actually *see* God living in you, but the effects of his presence ought to be a complete sensory experience for everyone around you.

Sometimes as a dad, God's presence in your life is going to look like a strong wind, rearranging things that are out of order. At other times, his appearance will resemble a tropical breeze, comforting and reassuring you and everyone at your house.

God's power is invisible, but unmistakable. And his plan is to stretch you over this invisible force—to give it a voice, a pair of hands and a life that demonstrates that power. Let God fill you with his Spirit today. The strength of this wind could be life-changing for everyone you know.

For your next devotional reading, go to page 1204.

which God did among you through him, as you yourselves know. ²³This man was handed over to you by God's set purpose and foreknowledge; and you, with the help of wicked men,ᵃ put him to death by nailing him to the cross. ²⁴But God raised him from the dead, freeing him from the agony of death, because it was impossible for death to keep its hold on him. ²⁵David said about him:

" 'I saw the Lord always before me.
 Because he is at my right hand,
 I will not be shaken.
²⁶Therefore my heart is glad and my
    tongue rejoices;
 my body also will live in hope,
²⁷because you will not abandon me to
    the grave,
 nor will you let your Holy One see
    decay.
²⁸You have made known to me the paths
    of life;
 you will fill me with joy in your
    presence.'ᵇ

²⁹"Brothers, I can tell you confidently that the patriarch David died and was buried, and his tomb is here to this day. ³⁰But he was a prophet and knew that God had promised him on oath that he would place one of his descendants on his throne. ³¹Seeing what was ahead, he spoke of the resurrection of the Christ,ᶜ that he was not abandoned to the grave, nor did his body see decay. ³²God has raised this Jesus to life, and we are all witnesses of the fact. ³³Exalted to the right hand of God, he has received from the Father the promised Holy Spirit and has poured out what you now see and hear. ³⁴For David did not ascend to heaven, and yet he said,

" 'The Lord said to my Lord:
  "Sit at my right hand
³⁵until I make your enemies
  a footstool for your feet." 'ᵈ

³⁶"Therefore let all Israel be assured of this: God has made this Jesus, whom you crucified, both Lord and Christ."

³⁷When the people heard this, they were cut to the heart and said to Peter and the other apostles, "Brothers, what shall we do?"

³⁸Peter replied, "Repent and be baptized, every one of you, in the name of Jesus Christ for the forgiveness of your sins. And you will receive the gift of the Holy Spirit. ³⁹The promise is for you and your children and for all who are far off— for all whom the Lord our God will call."

⁴⁰With many other words he warned them; and he pleaded with them, "Save yourselves from this corrupt generation." ⁴¹Those who accepted his message were baptized, and about three thousand were added to their number that day.

The Fellowship of the Believers

⁴²They devoted themselves to the apostles' teaching and to the fellowship, to the breaking of bread and to prayer. ⁴³Everyone was filled with awe, and many wonders and miraculous signs were done by the apostles. ⁴⁴All the believers were together and had everything in common. ⁴⁵Selling their possessions and goods, they gave to anyone as he had need. ⁴⁶Every day they continued to meet together in the temple courts. They broke bread in their homes and ate together with glad and sincere hearts, ⁴⁷praising God and enjoying the favor of all the people. And the Lord added to their number daily those who were being saved.

Peter Heals the Crippled Beggar

3 One day Peter and John were going up to the temple at the time of prayer—at three in the afternoon. ²Now a man crippled from birth was being carried to the temple gate called Beautiful, where he was put every day to beg from those going into the temple courts. ³When he saw Peter and John about to enter, he asked them for money. ⁴Peter looked straight at him, as did John. Then Peter said, "Look at us!" ⁵So the man gave them his attention, expecting to get something from them.

⁶Then Peter said, "Silver or gold I do not have, but what I have I give you. In the name of Jesus Christ of Nazareth, walk." ⁷Taking him by the right hand, he helped him up, and instantly the man's feet and ankles became strong. ⁸He jumped to his feet and began to walk. Then he went with them into the temple courts, walking and jumping, and praising God. ⁹When all the people saw him walking and praising God, ¹⁰they recognized him as the same man who used to sit begging at the temple gate called Beautiful, and they were filled with wonder and amazement at what had happened to him.

ᵃ23 Or of those not having the law (that is, Gentiles)
ᵇ28 Psalm 16:8-11   ᶜ31 Or Messiah. "The Christ" (Greek) and "the Messiah" (Hebrew) both mean "the Anointed One"; also in verse 36.
ᵈ35 Psalm 110:1

Peter Speaks to the Onlookers

[11]While the beggar held on to Peter and John, all the people were astonished and came running to them in the place called Solomon's Colonnade. [12]When Peter saw this, he said to them: "Men of Israel, why does this surprise you? Why do you stare at us as if by our own power or godliness we had made this man walk? [13]The God of Abraham, Isaac and Jacob, the God of our fathers, has glorified his servant Jesus. You handed him over to be killed, and you disowned him before Pilate, though he had decided to let him go. [14]You disowned the Holy and Righteous One and asked that a murderer be released to you. [15]You killed the author of life, but God raised him from the dead. We are witnesses of this. [16]By faith in the name of Jesus, this man whom you see and know was made strong. It is Jesus' name and the faith that comes through him that has given this complete healing to him, as you can all see.

The Perfect Gift

DAILY INSIGHT

TUESDAY

Passage:
Acts 2:36–41

Verse:
Acts 2:39

Christmas can be such a terrific time of the year. It can also be an overwhelming hassle. Don't you agree? Decorating the house, doing the Christmas card thing and finding gifts for everyone on "the list" (what do you buy your twelve-year-old nephew?) are only a few of the "duties" that come along with this season. By the time the actual day arrives, you're exhausted.

However, regardless of the trauma it cost you to get to Christmas morning, there's something so magical about this day that you completely forget the trouble it was to get here. This is especially true if you've got little ones around.

Our daughters had grown up. The older one was married and had a family, and our younger daughter had her own adult life. It had been a long time since Christmas morning had included someone in a fuzzy sleeper with sewn-on feet and a drop seat.

Christmas, 1997, changed all that. Everyone was home, and the magic was back. Abby, our granddaughter, came sliding down the stairs on her tummy, feet first, the way all one-year-olds do. And when she saw what Nanny had prepared for this moment, she didn't know what to do. She froze. Her eyes scanned the room. Soon her stare rested on the little white hand-painted table and chairs. Sitting in one of the chairs was a beautiful doll, in the other chair, a big brown teddy bear, fuzzier than she was. Her eyes had found something she really wanted.

Abby looked at her parents. She looked at Nanny and Granddaddy. We all had huge—and I'm pretty sure, goofy—smiles on our faces. And then Aunt Julie said the words that a child loves to hear on Christmas morning. "It's for you, Abby. It's for you."

No words can adequately describe the face of a child when she realizes that something she really would like to have … is hers. It's an awesome thing.

In the passage we read for today, the apostle Peter was preaching the sermon of his life. Jesus had gone back to heaven and had passed the baton to the disciples. Like a brother who had just sent his older sibling off to college, Peter was stepping up. Looking at the huge crowd that had gathered, Peter spoke these words: "Receive the gift of the Holy Spirit … for you and your children" (vv. 38–39). In effect, Peter was saying, "It's for you, my friends. It's for you."

That day three thousand people received the gift. It was a moment that none of them would ever forget. When did you receive the gift? And how many of your friends and colleagues need to hear the words, "It's for you, my friend. It's for you." God's Holy Spirit is the perfect present for you, for your children, and for everyone on your list … on Christmas or any other morning.

For your next devotional reading, go to page 1206.

[17]"Now, brothers, I know that you acted in ignorance, as did your leaders. [18]But this is how God fulfilled what he had foretold through all the prophets, saying that his Christ[a] would suffer. [19]Repent, then, and turn to God, so that your sins may be wiped out, that times of refreshing may come from the Lord, [20]and that he may send the Christ, who has been appointed for you—even Jesus. [21]He must remain in heaven until the time comes for God to restore everything, as he promised long ago through his holy prophets. [22]For Moses said, 'The Lord your God will raise up for you a prophet like me from among your own people; you must listen to everything he tells you. [23]Anyone who does not listen to him will be completely cut off from among his people.'[b]

[24]"Indeed, all the prophets from Samuel on, as many as have spoken, have foretold these days. [25]And you are heirs of the prophets and of the covenant God made with your fathers. He said to Abraham, 'Through your offspring all peoples on earth will be blessed.'[c] [26]When God raised up his servant, he sent him first to you to bless you by turning each of you from your wicked ways."

Peter and John Before the Sanhedrin

4 The priests and the captain of the temple guard and the Sadducees came up to Peter and John while they were speaking to the people. [2]They were greatly disturbed because the apostles were teaching the people and proclaiming in Jesus the resurrection of the dead. [3]They seized Peter and John, and because it was evening, they put them in jail until the next day. [4]But many who heard the message believed, and the number of men grew to about five thousand.

[5]The next day the rulers, elders and teachers of the law met in Jerusalem. [6]Annas the high priest was there, and so were Caiaphas, John, Alexander and the other men of the high priest's family. [7]They had Peter and John brought before them and began to question them: "By what power or what name did you do this?"

[8]Then Peter, filled with the Holy Spirit, said to them: "Rulers and elders of the people! [9]If we are being called to account today for an act of kindness shown to a cripple and are asked how he was healed, [10]then know this, you and all the people of Israel: It is by the name of Jesus Christ of Nazareth, whom you crucified but whom God raised from the dead, that this man stands before you healed. [11]He is

" 'the stone you builders rejected,
    which has become the capstone.[d,e]

[12]Salvation is found in no one else, for there is no other name under heaven given to men by which we must be saved."

[13]When they saw the courage of Peter and John and realized that they were unschooled, ordinary men, they were astonished and they took note that these men had been with Jesus. [14]But since they could see the man who had been healed standing there with them, there was nothing they could say. [15]So they ordered them to withdraw from the Sanhedrin and then conferred together. [16]"What are we going to do with these men?" they asked. "Everybody living in Jerusalem knows they have done an outstanding miracle, and we cannot deny it. [17]But to stop this thing from spreading any further among the people, we must warn these men to speak no longer to anyone in this name."

[18]Then they called them in again and commanded them not to speak or teach at all in the name of Jesus. [19]But Peter and John replied, "Judge for yourselves whether it is right in God's sight to obey you rather than God. [20]For we cannot help speaking about what we have seen and heard."

[21]After further threats they let them go. They could not decide how to punish them, because all the people were praising God for what had happened. [22]For the man who was miraculously healed was over forty years old.

The Believers' Prayer

[23]On their release, Peter and John went back to their own people and reported all that the chief priests and elders had said to them. [24]When they heard this, they raised their voices together in prayer to God. "Sovereign Lord," they said, "you made the heaven and the earth and the sea, and everything in them. [25]You spoke by the Holy Spirit through the mouth of your servant, our father David:

" 'Why do the nations rage
    and the peoples plot in vain?

a18 Or *Messiah*; also in verse 20   *b23* Deut. 18:15,18,19   *c25* Gen. 22:18; 26:4   *d11* Or *cornerstone*   *e11* Psalm 118:22

26The kings of the earth take their stand
and the rulers gather together
against the Lord
and against his Anointed One.*a'b*

27Indeed Herod and Pontius Pilate met together with the Gentiles and the people*c*
of Israel in this city to conspire against
your holy servant Jesus, whom you
anointed. 28They did what your power
and will had decided beforehand should
happen. 29Now, Lord, consider their
threats and enable your servants to speak
your word with great boldness. 30Stretch

out your hand to heal and perform miraculous signs and wonders through the
name of your holy servant Jesus."

31After they prayed, the place where
they were meeting was shaken. And they
were all filled with the Holy Spirit and
spoke the word of God boldly.

The Believers Share Their Possessions

32All the believers were one in heart and
mind. No one claimed that any of his pos-

*a26 That is, Christ or Messiah   b26 Psalm 2:1,2
c27 The Greek is plural.*

Help Yourself to Everything

Giving money away has always
been very easy for me.

Now, before you get upset
at the stridency of this statement, let me quickly assure you
that I didn't pick this up on my
own. I learned it from my dad …
who learned it from his dad …
who probably learned it from his
dad. Dads have a profound
effect on their children's attitudes toward giving.

For instance, as incredible as
this sounds, my grandfather
never locked the doors of his
home. "If someone comes to
our house in need, they're
welcome to anything we have
here," he told me. As a child, I
never saw my dad handle an
offering plate without putting
something into it—even on vacation. No
doubt, he also wanted his children to witness the satisfaction of giving. Mission
accomplished, Dad.

Because I had seen this modeled and
truly didn't know any other way to act, our
girls will tell you that, thanks to his dad and
his grandfather, their dad does the same
thing. The best part of this is that I have
learned that there is joy in the simple act of
giving. In other words, stewardship is its
own reward. Another way of saying this
might be that a man is measured not by
how much he has, but by how much he
gives away.

The members of the early church knew
about this. They "shared everything they
had … [so] there were no needy persons
among them" (vv. 32–34). Those who had

DAILY INSIGHT

WEDNESDAY

Passage:
Acts 4:32–37

Verse:
Acts 4:32

been blessed with possessions
turned their attention away
from their own success and
lavished their good fortune
on others.

Whenever I read this story
I'm reminded of a lunch I
had with a man named Ted
Sherman in 1971. My wife and
I were in career youth ministry,
and dependent upon the kindness of God's faithful servants
to survive. While we were
waiting for lunch to arrive, Ted
told me that he was going to
invest in our ministry.

Before I even had a chance
to say, "Thank you," Ted said
something I'll never forget: "I
have a teenage son, and I hope
he gets involved in your work,"
Ted said, "but I want you to know that my
gift is not a bribe. If my kid decides not to
come to your meetings, that's okay. I'll still
give." He paused for a moment and then
continued, "And by the way, please never
feel obligated to thank me for my giving.
This money doesn't belong to me in the first
place. Giving is something that brings me a
great deal of pleasure all by itself. A 'thank
you' note from you will not make it worthwhile."

Although I never asked Ted Sherman
about his dad, I'll bet he was a generous
man, too. Ted learned this from someone,
and dads can be the best teachers on the
subject of giving.

How generous will your children be?

For your next devotional reading, go to page 1210.

sessions was his own, but they shared everything they had. [33]With great power the apostles continued to testify to the resurrection of the Lord Jesus, and much grace was upon them all. [34]There were no needy persons among them. For from time to time those who owned lands or houses sold them, brought the money from the sales [35]and put it at the apostles' feet, and it was distributed to anyone as he had need.

[36]Joseph, a Levite from Cyprus, whom the apostles called Barnabas (which means Son of Encouragement), [37]sold a field he owned and brought the money and put it at the apostles' feet.

Ananias and Sapphira

[5] Now a man named Ananias, together with his wife Sapphira, also sold a piece of property. [2]With his wife's full knowledge he kept back part of the money for himself, but brought the rest and put it at the apostles' feet.

[3]Then Peter said, "Ananias, how is it that Satan has so filled your heart that you have lied to the Holy Spirit and have kept for yourself some of the money you received for the land? [4]Didn't it belong to you before it was sold? And after it was sold, wasn't the money at your disposal? What made you think of doing such a thing? You have not lied to men but to God."

[5]When Ananias heard this, he fell down and died. And great fear seized all who heard what had happened. [6]Then the young men came forward, wrapped up his body, and carried him out and buried him.

[7]About three hours later his wife came in, not knowing what had happened. [8]Peter asked her, "Tell me, is this the price you and Ananias got for the land?"

"Yes," she said, "that is the price."

[9]Peter said to her, "How could you agree to test the Spirit of the Lord? Look! The feet of the men who buried your husband are at the door, and they will carry you out also."

[10]At that moment she fell down at his feet and died. Then the young men came in and, finding her dead, carried her out and buried her beside her husband. [11]Great fear seized the whole church and all who heard about these events.

The Apostles Heal Many

[12]The apostles performed many miraculous signs and wonders among the people. And all the believers used to meet together in Solomon's Colonnade. [13]No one else dared join them, even though they were highly regarded by the people. [14]Nevertheless, more and more men and women believed in the Lord and were added to their number. [15]As a result, people brought the sick into the streets and laid them on beds and mats so that at least Peter's shadow might fall on some of them as he passed by. [16]Crowds gathered also from the towns around Jerusalem, bringing their sick and those tormented by evil[a] spirits, and all of them were healed.

The Apostles Persecuted

[17]Then the high priest and all his associates, who were members of the party of the Sadducees, were filled with jealousy. [18]They arrested the apostles and put them in the public jail. [19]But during the night an angel of the Lord opened the doors of the jail and brought them out. [20]"Go, stand in the temple courts," he said, "and tell the people the full message of this new life."

[21]At daybreak they entered the temple courts, as they had been told, and began to teach the people.

When the high priest and his associates arrived, they called together the Sanhedrin—the full assembly of the elders of Israel—and sent to the jail for the apostles. [22]But on arriving at the jail, the officers did not find them there. So they went back and reported, [23]"We found the jail securely locked, with the guards standing at the doors; but when we opened them, we found no one inside." [24]On hearing this report, the captain of the temple guard and the chief priests were puzzled, wondering what would come of this.

[25]Then someone came and said, "Look! The men you put in jail are standing in the temple courts teaching the people." [26]At that, the captain went with his officers and brought the apostles. They did not use force, because they feared that the people would stone them.

[27]Having brought the apostles, they made them appear before the Sanhedrin to be questioned by the high priest. [28]"We gave you strict orders not to teach in this name," he said. "Yet you have filled Jerusalem with your teaching and are determined to make us guilty of this man's blood."

[a]16 Greek unclean

²⁹Peter and the other apostles replied: "We must obey God rather than men! ³⁰The God of our fathers raised Jesus from the dead—whom you had killed by hanging him on a tree. ³¹God exalted him to his own right hand as Prince and Savior that he might give repentance and forgiveness of sins to Israel. ³²We are witnesses of these things, and so is the Holy Spirit, whom God has given to those who obey him."

³³When they heard this, they were furious and wanted to put them to death. ³⁴But a Pharisee named Gamaliel, a teacher of the law, who was honored by all the people, stood up in the Sanhedrin and ordered that the men be put outside for a little while. ³⁵Then he addressed them: "Men of Israel, consider carefully what you intend to do to these men. ³⁶Some time ago Theudas appeared, claiming to be somebody, and about four hundred men rallied to him. He was killed, all his followers were dispersed, and it all came to nothing. ³⁷After him, Judas the Galilean appeared in the days of the census and led a band of people in revolt. He too was killed, and all his followers were scattered. ³⁸Therefore, in the present case I advise you: Leave these men alone! Let them go! For if their purpose or activity is of human origin, it will fail. ³⁹But if it is from God, you will not be able to stop these men; you will only find yourselves fighting against God."

⁴⁰His speech persuaded them. They called the apostles in and had them flogged. Then they ordered them not to speak in the name of Jesus, and let them go.

⁴¹The apostles left the Sanhedrin, rejoicing because they had been counted worthy of suffering disgrace for the Name. ⁴²Day after day, in the temple courts and from house to house, they never stopped teaching and proclaiming the good news that Jesus is the Christ.ᵃ

The Choosing of the Seven

6 In those days when the number of disciples was increasing, the Grecian Jews among them complained against the Hebraic Jews because their widows were being overlooked in the daily distribution of food. ²So the Twelve gathered all the disciples together and said, "It would not be right for us to neglect the ministry of the word of God in order to wait on tables. ³Brothers, choose seven men from among you who are known to be full of the Spirit and wisdom. We will turn this responsibility over to them ⁴and will give our attention to prayer and the ministry of the word."

⁵This proposal pleased the whole group. They chose Stephen, a man full of faith and of the Holy Spirit; also Philip, Procorus, Nicanor, Timon, Parmenas, and Nicolas from Antioch, a convert to Juda-

ᵃ42 Or *Messiah*

HEY DAD
Did the disciples get into trouble for following Jesus?

Text: Acts 5:27–42

Jesus' apostles faced rejection and even punishment for following him. Acts 5 records one incident. The Sanhedrin—the highest court of Jewish law—had issued a strict order: No one was to teach of Jesus' life, his death or his resurrection; nor was anyone to teach in his name. The apostles disregarded that order, and now had to answer for their disobedience.

Facing an angry hearing, the apostles said, "We must obey God rather than men!" (v. 29). This answer enraged the Sanhedrin even more, because it implied that the court opposed God's direction. But a well-respected Pharisee named Gamaliel addressed the council and warned them, "If their purpose or activity is of human origin, it will fail. But if it is from God, you will not be able to stop these men" (vv. 38–39). Wise words, Gamaliel.

The apostles were beaten, reprimanded and released. Yet, beatings and threats did not discourage these faithful men—even though, ultimately, their obedience to God's call cost them their lives.

QUESTIONS KIDS ASK

For a complete listing of Questions Kids Ask, turn to page 1435.

ism. [6]They presented these men to the apostles, who prayed and laid their hands on them.

[7]So the word of God spread. The number of disciples in Jerusalem increased rapidly, and a large number of priests became obedient to the faith.

Stephen Seized

[8]Now Stephen, a man full of God's grace and power, did great wonders and miraculous signs among the people. [9]Opposition arose, however, from members of the Synagogue of the Freedmen (as it was called)—Jews of Cyrene and Alexandria as well as the provinces of Cilicia and Asia. These men began to argue with Stephen, [10]but they could not stand up against his wisdom or the Spirit by whom he spoke. [11]Then they secretly persuaded some men to say, "We have heard Stephen speak words of blasphemy against Moses and against God."

[12]So they stirred up the people and the elders and the teachers of the law. They seized Stephen and brought him before the Sanhedrin. [13]They produced false witnesses, who testified, "This fellow never stops speaking against this holy place and against the law. [14]For we have heard him say that this Jesus of Nazareth will destroy this place and change the customs Moses handed down to us."

[15]All who were sitting in the Sanhedrin looked intently at Stephen, and they saw that his face was like the face of an angel.

Stephen's Speech to the Sanhedrin

7 Then the high priest asked him, "Are these charges true?"

[2]To this he replied: "Brothers and fathers, listen to me! The God of glory appeared to our father Abraham while he was still in Mesopotamia, before he lived in Haran. [3]'Leave your country and your people,' God said, 'and go to the land I will show you.'[a]

[4]"So he left the land of the Chaldeans and settled in Haran. After the death of his father, God sent him to this land where you are now living. [5]He gave him no inheritance here, not even a foot of ground. But God promised him that he and his descendants after him would possess the land, even though at that time Abraham had no child. [6]God spoke to him in this way: 'Your descendants will be strangers in a country not their own, and they will be enslaved and mistreated four hundred

years. [7]But I will punish the nation they serve as slaves,' God said, 'and afterward they will come out of that country and worship me in this place.'[b] [8]Then he gave Abraham the covenant of circumcision. And Abraham became the father of Isaac and circumcised him eight days after his birth. Later Isaac became the father of Jacob, and Jacob became the father of the twelve patriarchs.

[9]"Because the patriarchs were jealous of Joseph, they sold him as a slave into Egypt. But God was with him [10]and rescued him from all his troubles. He gave Joseph wisdom and enabled him to gain the goodwill of Pharaoh king of Egypt; so he made him ruler over Egypt and all his palace.

[11]"Then a famine struck all Egypt and Canaan, bringing great suffering, and our fathers could not find food. [12]When Jacob heard that there was grain in Egypt, he sent our fathers on their first visit. [13]On their second visit, Joseph told his brothers who he was, and Pharaoh learned about Joseph's family. [14]After this, Joseph sent for his father Jacob and his whole family, seventy-five in all. [15]Then Jacob went down to Egypt, where he and our fathers died. [16]Their bodies were brought back to Shechem and placed in the tomb that Abraham had bought from the sons of Hamor at Shechem for a certain sum of money.

[17]"As the time drew near for God to fulfill his promise to Abraham, the number of our people in Egypt greatly increased. [18]Then another king, who knew nothing about Joseph, became ruler of Egypt. [19]He dealt treacherously with our people and oppressed our forefathers by forcing them to throw out their newborn babies so that they would die.

[20]"At that time Moses was born, and he was no ordinary child.[c] For three months he was cared for in his father's house. [21]When he was placed outside, Pharaoh's daughter took him and brought him up as her own son. [22]Moses was educated in all the wisdom of the Egyptians and was powerful in speech and action.

[23]"When Moses was forty years old, he decided to visit his fellow Israelites. [24]He saw one of them being mistreated by an Egyptian, so he went to his defense and avenged him by killing the Egyptian. [25]Moses thought that his own people would realize that God was using him to

[a]3 Gen. 12:1   [b]7 Gen. 15:13,14   [c]20 Or *was fair in the sight of God*

rescue them, but they did not. [26]The next day Moses came upon two Israelites who were fighting. He tried to reconcile them by saying, 'Men, you are brothers; why do you want to hurt each other?'

[27]"But the man who was mistreating the other pushed Moses aside and said, 'Who made you ruler and judge over us? [28]Do you want to kill me as you killed the Egyptian yesterday?'[a] [29]When Moses heard this, he fled to Midian, where he settled as a foreigner and had two sons.

[30]"After forty years had passed, an angel appeared to Moses in the flames of a burning bush in the desert near Mount Sinai. [31]When he saw this, he was amazed at the sight. As he went over to look more closely, he heard the Lord's voice: [32]'I am the God of your fathers, the God of Abraham, Isaac and Jacob.'[b] Moses trembled with fear and did not dare to look.

[33]"Then the Lord said to him, 'Take off

[a]28 Exodus 2:14   [b]32 Exodus 3:6

Mr. Quid Pro Quo

DAILY INSIGHT

THURSDAY

Passage:
Acts 7:54—8:1

Verses:
Acts 7:59–60

A tiny nation's borders are threatened. An enemy is aggressively bearing down on her sovereignty. A neighboring nation comes to the rescue and squashes the threat. The next time the neighboring nation needs a favor, she calls on the tiny nation whose life she saved. This is called *quid pro quo*. When someone does something kind for you, it's only natural that you return the favor. A dinner party at Mike and Gail's means that the next time we're having a dinner party at our house, Mike and Gail are on the list. This is a happy *quid pro quo*.

But what if someone gives his *life* for you?

A small bookcase stood behind the overstuffed chair in the corner of my parent's living room. One of the volumes in that case was a huge book titled *Foxes Book of Martyrs*. The tome was filled with actual accounts of individuals who, because of their love for Jesus Christ, were willing to die for him. I can vividly remember sitting on the floor behind that chair. Slowly I would turn the pages, my eyes fixed on the graphic drawings of how these incredibly courageous men and women gladly endured the most grisly torture imaginable instead of denying their loyalty and love for their Savior.

My eyes would well up with tears as I read about these people facing their own death with complete peace. Apparently the "reward" of having made the right choice far outweighed the ultimate "penalty" of taking the easy way out.

The passage you read today is also soaked in the blood of a martyr: Stephen. Perhaps one of the bravest men in the Bible, Stephen stood tall in the face of the Sanhedrin, the highest Jewish court of the day. These self-righteous men accused Stephen of blasphemy and challenged his love and loyalty to Jesus. With a few simple words Stephen would have saved himself from execution that day. Had he renounced his love for Jesus, the story would have been much different. Stephen's words cost him his life.

Although worldwide persecution of Christians continues today, it's safe to say that our defense of our Savior will probably never be as severe as these. But we are—and will be constantly—challenged to com-promise what's right. Even today we may find ourselves looking at tempting circumstances and intimidating accusers in the eye. And although our loyalty to Jesus Christ may cost us, it will always be rewarding.

Jesus said, "Greater love has no one than this, than he lay down his life for his friends." (John 15:13)

I love to envision Stephen and Jesus meeting in heaven. "Thank you," Jesus must have said to his loyal friend. "You're welcome," Stephen may have replied, "but you did it for me." *Quid pro quo.*

For your next devotional reading, go to page 1213.

your sandals; the place where you are standing is holy ground. ³⁴I have indeed seen the oppression of my people in Egypt. I have heard their groaning and have come down to set them free. Now come, I will send you back to Egypt.'ᵃ

³⁵"This is the same Moses whom they had rejected with the words, 'Who made you ruler and judge?' He was sent to be their ruler and deliverer by God himself, through the angel who appeared to him in the bush. ³⁶He led them out of Egypt and did wonders and miraculous signs in Egypt, at the Red Seaᵇ and for forty years in the desert.

³⁷"This is that Moses who told the Israelites, 'God will send you a prophet like me from your own people.'ᶜ ³⁸He was in the assembly in the desert, with the angel who spoke to him on Mount Sinai, and with our fathers; and he received living words to pass on to us.

³⁹"But our fathers refused to obey him. Instead, they rejected him and in their hearts turned back to Egypt. ⁴⁰They told Aaron, 'Make us gods who will go before us. As for this fellow Moses who led us out of Egypt—we don't know what has happened to him!'ᵈ ⁴¹That was the time they made an idol in the form of a calf. They brought sacrifices to it and held a celebration in honor of what their hands had made. ⁴²But God turned away and gave them over to the worship of the heavenly bodies. This agrees with what is written in the book of the prophets:

" 'Did you bring me sacrifices and
        offerings
    forty years in the desert, O house of
        Israel?
⁴³You have lifted up the shrine of Molech
        and the star of your god Rephan,
    the idols you made to worship.
Therefore I will send you into exile'ᵉ
        beyond Babylon.

⁴⁴"Our forefathers had the tabernacle of the Testimony with them in the desert. It had been made as God directed Moses, according to the pattern he had seen. ⁴⁵Having received the tabernacle, our fathers under Joshua brought it with them when they took the land from the nations God drove out before them. It remained in the land until the time of David, ⁴⁶who enjoyed God's favor and asked that he might provide a dwelling place for the God of Jacob.ᶠ ⁴⁷But it was Solomon who built the house for him.

⁴⁸"However, the Most High does not live in houses made by men. As the prophet says:

⁴⁹" 'Heaven is my throne,
        and the earth is my footstool.
    What kind of house will you build
        for me?
                    says the Lord.
    Or where will my resting place be?
⁵⁰Has not my hand made all these things?'ᵍ

⁵¹"You stiff-necked people, with uncircumcised hearts and ears! You are just like your fathers: You always resist the Holy Spirit! ⁵²Was there ever a prophet your fathers did not persecute? They even killed those who predicted the coming of the Righteous One. And now you have betrayed and murdered him— ⁵³you who have received the law that was put into effect through angels but have not obeyed it."

The Stoning of Stephen

⁵⁴When they heard this, they were furious and gnashed their teeth at him. ⁵⁵But Stephen, full of the Holy Spirit, looked up to heaven and saw the glory of God, and Jesus standing at the right hand of God. ⁵⁶"Look," he said, "I see heaven open and the Son of Man standing at the right hand of God."

⁵⁷At this they covered their ears and, yelling at the top of their voices, they all rushed at him, ⁵⁸dragged him out of the city and began to stone him. Meanwhile, the witnesses laid their clothes at the feet of a young man named Saul.

⁵⁹While they were stoning him, Stephen prayed, "Lord Jesus, receive my spirit." ⁶⁰Then he fell on his knees and cried out, "Lord, do not hold this sin against them." When he had said this, he fell asleep.

8 And Saul was there, giving approval to his death.

The Church Persecuted and Scattered

On that day a great persecution broke out against the church at Jerusalem, and all except the apostles were scattered throughout Judea and Samaria. ²Godly men buried Stephen and mourned deeply for him. ³But Saul began to destroy the church. Going from house to house, he dragged off men and women and put them in prison.

ᵃ34 Exodus 3:5,7,8,10   ᵇ36 That is, Sea of Reeds
ᶜ37 Deut. 18:15   ᵈ40 Exodus 32:1   ᵉ43 Amos 5:25-27
ᶠ46 Some early manuscripts *the house of Jacob*
ᵍ50 Isaiah 66:1,2

Philip in Samaria

⁴Those who had been scattered preached the word wherever they went. ⁵Philip went down to a city in Samaria and proclaimed the Christ[a] there. ⁶When the crowds heard Philip and saw the miraculous signs he did, they all paid close attention to what he said. ⁷With shrieks, evil[b] spirits came out of many, and many paralytics and cripples were healed. ⁸So there was great joy in that city.

Simon the Sorcerer

⁹Now for some time a man named Simon had practiced sorcery in the city and amazed all the people of Samaria. He boasted that he was someone great, ¹⁰and all the people, both high and low, gave him their attention and exclaimed, "This man is the divine power known as the Great Power." ¹¹They followed him because he had amazed them for a long time with his magic. ¹²But when they believed Philip as he preached the good news of the kingdom of God and the name of Jesus Christ, they were baptized, both men and women. ¹³Simon himself believed and was baptized. And he followed Philip everywhere, astonished by the great signs and miracles he saw.

¹⁴When the apostles in Jerusalem heard that Samaria had accepted the word of God, they sent Peter and John to them. ¹⁵When they arrived, they prayed for them that they might receive the Holy Spirit, ¹⁶because the Holy Spirit had not yet come upon any of them; they had simply been baptized into[c] the name of the Lord Jesus. ¹⁷Then Peter and John placed their hands on them, and they received the Holy Spirit.

¹⁸When Simon saw that the Spirit was given at the laying on of the apostles' hands, he offered them money ¹⁹and said, "Give me also this ability so that everyone on whom I lay my hands may receive the Holy Spirit."

²⁰Peter answered: "May your money perish with you, because you thought you could buy the gift of God with money! ²¹You have no part or share in this ministry, because your heart is not right before God. ²²Repent of this wickedness and pray to the Lord. Perhaps he will forgive you for having such a thought in your heart. ²³For I see that you are full of bitterness and captive to sin."

²⁴Then Simon answered, "Pray to the Lord for me so that nothing you have said may happen to me."

²⁵When they had testified and proclaimed the word of the Lord, Peter and John returned to Jerusalem, preaching the gospel in many Samaritan villages.

Philip and the Ethiopian

²⁶Now an angel of the Lord said to Philip, "Go south to the road—the desert road—that goes down from Jerusalem to Gaza." ²⁷So he started out, and on his way he met an Ethiopian[d] eunuch, an important official in charge of all the treasury of Candace, queen of the Ethiopians. This man had gone to Jerusalem to worship, ²⁸and on his way home was sitting in his chariot reading the book of Isaiah the prophet. ²⁹The Spirit told Philip, "Go to that chariot and stay near it."

³⁰Then Philip ran up to the chariot and heard the man reading Isaiah the prophet. "Do you understand what you are reading?" Philip asked.

³¹"How can I," he said, "unless someone explains it to me?" So he invited Philip to come up and sit with him.

³²The eunuch was reading this passage of Scripture:

> "He was led like a sheep to the
>   slaughter,
>   and as a lamb before the shearer is
>   silent,
>   so he did not open his mouth.
> ³³In his humiliation he was deprived of
>   justice.
>   Who can speak of his descendants?
>   For his life was taken from the
>   earth."[e]

³⁴The eunuch asked Philip, "Tell me, please, who is the prophet talking about, himself or someone else?" ³⁵Then Philip began with that very passage of Scripture and told him the good news about Jesus.

³⁶As they traveled along the road, they came to some water and the eunuch said, "Look, here is water. Why shouldn't I be baptized?"[f] ³⁸And he gave orders to stop the chariot. Then both Philip and the eunuch went down into the water and Philip baptized him. ³⁹When they came up out of the water, the Spirit of the Lord sud-

---

a5 Or *Messiah*   b7 Greek *unclean*   c16 Or *in*
d27 That is, from the upper Nile region   e33 Isaiah 53:7,8   f36 Some late manuscripts *baptized?"*
37*Philip said, "If you believe with all your heart, you may." The eunuch answered, "I believe that Jesus Christ is the Son of God."*

denly took Philip away, and the eunuch did not see him again, but went on his way rejoicing. ⁴⁰Philip, however, appeared at Azotus and traveled about, preaching the gospel in all the towns until he reached Caesarea.

Saul's Conversion

9 Meanwhile, Saul was still breathing out murderous threats against the Lord's disciples. He went to the high priest ²and asked him for letters to the synagogues in Damascus, so that if he found any there who belonged to the Way, whether men or women, he might take them as prisoners to Jerusalem. ³As he neared Damascus on his journey, suddenly a light from heaven flashed around him. ⁴He fell to the ground and heard a voice say to him, "Saul, Saul, why do you persecute me?"

⁵"Who are you, Lord?" Saul asked.

"I am Jesus, whom you are persecuting," he replied. ⁶"Now get up and go into the city, and you will be told what you must do."

⁷The men traveling with Saul stood

Showtime

DAILY INSIGHT

FRIDAY

Passage: Acts 8:26–35

Verse: Acts 8:35

When I was in college, someone invited me to take part in an off-Broadway play, *The Fantastiks*, which was to be performed and directed by students. I reluctantly agreed. In a week, to my complete amazement, I had the part of El Gallo. In a few weeks, I went from reluctance to enthusiasm. The more we practiced, the more comfortable I became with my lines and the more I thoroughly enjoyed this experience.

The first and only performance was on a Saturday night. I'll never forget the last ten minutes before the scheduled start of the play when I was to walk to center stage and sing the classic, "Try to Remember." I stood quietly, alone in the shadows. I reviewed what I had learned, what I had memorized, and remembered the countless rehearsals. Of course, I was nervous, but I was also ready. My heart began to race with excitement and anticipation. It was showtime.

Philip must have known this feeling. One day, an angel of the Lord appeared to Philip and asked him to take a trip from home toward the city of Gaza. Philip had no idea why God had asked him to go on this journey. He just obeyed.

Not far from home, Philip passed a man in a chariot who was reading a passage from Isaiah. "Do you understand what are you reading?" Philip asked. "How can I," the man replied, "unless someone explains it to me?" (vv. 30–31).

As one of Jesus' disciples, Philip had rehearsed and had been waiting for this moment. This was what he had prayed for when Jesus had challenged his disciples to be his "witnesses in Jerusalem, and in all Judea and Samaria, and to the ends of the earth" (1:8). For Philip, the curtain was about to go up. It was showtime.

So, taking all that he had learned, coupled with the power that Jesus had promised, Philip told the man about his Savior. The man listened intently to Philip's words, was convicted of his own sin, and received God's grace right there on the spot.

This story provides a perfect backdrop for God's gracious call on our lives. He wants us to prepare ourselves—to read, study and pray—for the moments in our lives when the curtain goes up and we are called on to "give an account of [ourselves] to God" (Romans 14:12).

My favorite part of the story of Philip and the man from Ethiopia is that during the years while Philip was training for this moment, God was also preparing *this man's* heart to hear Philip's words. I wonder, who in your world is God preparing to hear your words? Keep reading, keep studying, and keep praying. The curtain is about to go up. Soon it will be showtime for you, too.

For your next devotional reading, go to page 1214.

Surprise!

Key Verse: *"As [Saul] neared Damascus on his journey, suddenly a light from heaven flashed around him. He fell to the ground and heard a voice say to him, 'Saul, Saul, why do you persecute me?' "* Acts 9:3–4

Text: Acts 9:1–8 *(Dad or child reads the text.)*

QUIET TIMES WITH Dad

DAD READS: Sometimes birthday parties are planned—the person who is celebrating one more candle on his or her cake knows all about the celebration. But sometimes birthday parties are a complete surprise. The birthday person walks into the room and everyone shouts, "Surprise!" This is a wonderful kind of surprise.

Child reads: But not all surprises are good surprises. Sometimes a car pulls right out in front of our car and we go plowing into it. This is not a good surprise. Sometimes we trip over a step we didn't see. This is not a good surprise. And sometimes one of our friends says something unkind to us. This is also not a good surprise.

DAD READS: We have all had good and bad surprises in our lives. Today we read about a man whose name was Saul. He didn't know it, but as he was walking down the road one day, he got a big surprise. A bright light from the sky—brighter than the sun—flashed in Saul's face.

Child reads: This light surprised and scared Saul just like it would have surprised and scared you or me. Then Saul heard a voice coming from the sky. Saul realized that the voice was God's voice, and Saul knew that he had been doing terrible things to God's people. This would have *really* surprised and scared us!

DAD READS: You're right. Being surprised by God would not be a good thing if we were disobeying him and

doing terrible things like Saul had been doing. That day, Saul could have done two different things. He could have been angry that God had caught him being disobedient or he could have surrendered to his heavenly Father, choosing to follow him instead of defying him. I'm glad that Saul chose to follow God and obey him.

Child reads: If God wanted to, he could make a bright light flash in our eyes and speak to us in a big voice from heaven. His light will most likely come to us through other kinds of surprises and his voice will most likely come through other people's voices.

DAD READS: But no matter how he is going to come to us, God wants to surprise us. And he wants us to be obedient to him, day after day, so that when we see his "light" and hear his "voice," our surprise will be a good surprise and not a bad one.

Child reads: I want to be ready for God's surprises. Let me pray this prayer with you:

Our Father in heaven, we love you. Thank you for surprises. My dad and I know that you could come to us anytime, even when we don't expect it. Please help us to always be ready for you. Help my dad and me to be obedient so that your light and your voice is a good surprise. We love you and we thank you for your love. In Jesus' name, **Amen.**

For your next devotional reading, go to page 1217.

there speechless; they heard the sound but did not see anyone. [8]Saul got up from the ground, but when he opened his eyes he could see nothing. So they led him by the hand into Damascus. [9]For three days he was blind, and did not eat or drink anything.

[10]In Damascus there was a disciple named Ananias. The Lord called to him in a vision, "Ananias!"

"Yes, Lord," he answered.

[11]The Lord told him, "Go to the house of Judas on Straight Street and ask for a man from Tarsus named Saul, for he is praying. [12]In a vision he has seen a man named Ananias come and place his hands on him to restore his sight."

[13]"Lord," Ananias answered, "I have heard many reports about this man and all the harm he has done to your saints in Jerusalem. [14]And he has come here with authority from the chief priests to arrest all who call on your name."

[15]But the Lord said to Ananias, "Go! This man is my chosen instrument to carry my name before the Gentiles and their kings and before the people of Israel. [16]I will show him how much he must suffer for my name."

[17]Then Ananias went to the house and entered it. Placing his hands on Saul, he said, "Brother Saul, the Lord—Jesus, who appeared to you on the road as you were coming here—has sent me so that you may see again and be filled with the Holy Spirit." [18]Immediately, something like scales fell from Saul's eyes, and he could see again. He got up and was baptized, [19]and after taking some food, he regained his strength.

Saul in Damascus and Jerusalem

Saul spent several days with the disciples in Damascus. [20]At once he began to preach in the synagogues that Jesus is the Son of God. [21]All those who heard him were astonished and asked, "Isn't he the man who raised havoc in Jerusalem among those who call on this name? And hasn't he come here to take them as prisoners to the chief priests?" [22]Yet Saul grew more and more powerful and baffled the Jews living in Damascus by proving that Jesus is the Christ.[a]

[23]After many days had gone by, the Jews conspired to kill him, [24]but Saul learned of their plan. Day and night they kept close watch on the city gates in order to kill him. [25]But his followers took him by night

and lowered him in a basket through an opening in the wall.

[26]When he came to Jerusalem, he tried to join the disciples, but they were all afraid of him, not believing that he really was a disciple. [27]But Barnabas took him and brought him to the apostles. He told them how Saul on his journey had seen the Lord and that the Lord had spoken to him, and how in Damascus he had preached fearlessly in the name of Jesus. [28]So Saul stayed with them and moved about freely in Jerusalem, speaking boldly in the name of the Lord. [29]He talked and debated with the Grecian Jews, but they tried to kill him. [30]When the brothers learned of this, they took him down to Caesarea and sent him off to Tarsus.

[31]Then the church throughout Judea, Galilee and Samaria enjoyed a time of peace. It was strengthened; and encouraged by the Holy Spirit, it grew in numbers, living in the fear of the Lord.

Aeneas and Dorcas

[32]As Peter traveled about the country, he went to visit the saints in Lydda. [33]There he found a man named Aeneas, a paralytic who had been bedridden for eight years. [34]"Aeneas," Peter said to him, "Jesus Christ heals you. Get up and take care of your mat." Immediately Aeneas got up. [35]All those who lived in Lydda and Sharon saw him and turned to the Lord.

[36]In Joppa there was a disciple named Tabitha (which, when translated, is Dorcas[b]), who was always doing good and helping the poor. [37]About that time she became sick and died, and her body was washed and placed in an upstairs room. [38]Lydda was near Joppa; so when the disciples heard that Peter was in Lydda, they sent two men to him and urged him, "Please come at once!"

[39]Peter went with them, and when he arrived he was taken upstairs to the room. All the widows stood around him, crying and showing him the robes and other clothing that Dorcas had made while she was still with them.

[40]Peter sent them all out of the room; then he got down on his knees and prayed. Turning toward the dead woman, he said, "Tabitha, get up." She opened her eyes, and seeing Peter she sat up. [41]He took her by the hand and helped her to

---

[a]22 Or Messiah   [b]36 Both Tabitha (Aramaic) and Dorcas (Greek) mean gazelle.

her feet. Then he called the believers and the widows and presented her to them alive. ⁴²This became known all over Joppa, and many people believed in the Lord. ⁴³Peter stayed in Joppa for some time with a tanner named Simon.

Cornelius Calls for Peter

10 At Caesarea there was a man named Cornelius, a centurion in what was known as the Italian Regiment. ²He and all his family were devout and God-fearing; he gave generously to those in need and prayed to God regularly. ³One day at about three in the afternoon he had a vision. He distinctly saw an angel of God, who came to him and said, "Cornelius!"

⁴Cornelius stared at him in fear. "What is it, Lord?" he asked.

The angel answered, "Your prayers and gifts to the poor have come up as a memorial offering before God. ⁵Now send men to Joppa to bring back a man named Simon who is called Peter. ⁶He is staying with Simon the tanner, whose house is by the sea."

⁷When the angel who spoke to him had gone, Cornelius called two of his servants and a devout soldier who was one of his attendants. ⁸He told them everything that had happened and sent them to Joppa.

Peter's Vision

⁹About noon the following day as they were on their journey and approaching the city, Peter went up on the roof to pray. ¹⁰He became hungry and wanted something to eat, and while the meal was being prepared, he fell into a trance. ¹¹He saw heaven opened and something like a large sheet being let down to earth by its four corners. ¹²It contained all kinds of four-footed animals, as well as reptiles of the earth and birds of the air. ¹³Then a voice told him, "Get up, Peter. Kill and eat."

¹⁴"Surely not, Lord!" Peter replied. "I have never eaten anything impure or unclean."

¹⁵The voice spoke to him a second time, "Do not call anything impure that God has made clean."

¹⁶This happened three times, and immediately the sheet was taken back to heaven.

¹⁷While Peter was wondering about the meaning of the vision, the men sent by Cornelius found out where Simon's house was and stopped at the gate. ¹⁸They called out, asking if Simon who was known as Peter was staying there.

¹⁹While Peter was still thinking about the vision, the Spirit said to him, "Simon, three*a* men are looking for you. ²⁰So get up and go downstairs. Do not hesitate to go with them, for I have sent them."

²¹Peter went down and said to the men, "I'm the one you're looking for. Why have you come?"

²²The men replied, "We have come from Cornelius the centurion. He is a righteous and God-fearing man, who is respected by all the Jewish people. A holy angel told him to have you come to his house so that he could hear what you have to say." ²³Then Peter invited the men into the house to be his guests.

Peter at Cornelius's House

The next day Peter started out with them, and some of the brothers from Joppa went along. ²⁴The following day he arrived in Caesarea. Cornelius was expecting them and had called together his relatives and close friends. ²⁵As Peter entered the house, Cornelius met him and fell at his feet in reverence. ²⁶But Peter made him get up. "Stand up," he said, "I am only a man myself."

²⁷Talking with him, Peter went inside and found a large gathering of people. ²⁸He said to them: "You are well aware that it is against our law for a Jew to associate with a Gentile or visit him. But God has shown me that I should not call any man impure or unclean. ²⁹So when I was sent for, I came without raising any objection. May I ask why you sent for me?"

³⁰Cornelius answered: "Four days ago I was in my house praying at this hour, at three in the afternoon. Suddenly a man in shining clothes stood before me ³¹and said, 'Cornelius, God has heard your prayer and remembered your gifts to the poor. ³²Send to Joppa for Simon who is called Peter. He is a guest in the home of Simon the tanner, who lives by the sea.' ³³So I sent for you immediately, and it was good of you to come. Now we are all here in the presence of God to listen to everything the Lord has commanded you to tell us."

³⁴Then Peter began to speak: "I now realize how true it is that God does not show favoritism ³⁵but accepts men from every nation who fear him and do what is right.

a19 One early manuscript *two;* other manuscripts do not have the number.

³⁶You know the message God sent to the people of Israel, telling the good news of peace through Jesus Christ, who is Lord of all. ³⁷You know what has happened throughout Judea, beginning in Galilee after the baptism that John preached— ³⁸how God anointed Jesus of Nazareth with the Holy Spirit and power, and how he went around doing good and healing all who were under the power of the devil, because God was with him.

³⁹"We are witnesses of everything he did in the country of the Jews and in Jerusalem. They killed him by hanging him on a tree, ⁴⁰but God raised him from the dead on the third day and caused him to be seen. ⁴¹He was not seen by all the people, but by witnesses whom God had already chosen—by us who ate and drank with him after he rose from the dead. ⁴²He commanded us to preach to the people and to testify that he is the one whom God

Throw Away Those Crutches

DAILY INSIGHT

MONDAY

Passage:
Acts 10:9–16

Verse:
Acts 10:15

Mitch Rienick was one of my best friends in high school. A strong and agile young man, Mitch was also a linebacker on the football team. One fall Friday night, in a close game against our school's biggest rival, Mitch broke his leg. On Sunday afternoon, I went to see him. He seemed to be in good humor despite the reality of this season-ending situation.

After talking and joking for a few minutes, Mitch asked if I would be willing to carry his books for the next six weeks. "Since we're in all the same classes and since I'm on crutches, I'll need help." Of course, I gladly agreed.

For the next six weeks, Mitch and I became quite the pair. I didn't mind the extra weight of his books, and Mitch quickly learned how to maneuver through the crowds, his athleticism unmistakably showing through.

I'll never forget the day Mitch was to get his cast removed. We should have been excited that Mitch was going to be back on his own wheels. Instead, a dark cloud of melancholy hung over us. "I'm going to miss the crutches," Mitch finally confessed. "I've gotten so good at using them, I can move faster with them than without them." I agreed, but we both knew that it was time for Mitch to put them aside.

Although he didn't yet know it, Peter was also reluctant to give up a crutch. God opened the apostle's eyes through the vision we read today, telling him to "Kill and eat."

Peter was traumatized by the order. Why? Because among these creatures were animals that Peter, according to his Jewish traditions, had been told not to eat. "Surely not, Lord," he protested. "I have never eaten anything impure or unclean." The Lord responded, "Do not call anything impure that God has made clean" (v. 15).

It was as though God was saying to Peter, "These laws and customs were good. They used to be necessary. But, Peter, they were crutches. Now, through Jesus, your life has been changed. You're free, my friend, to live without those crutches." This vision was also a parable, a way of preparing Peter to bring the Good News of the Gospel to a non-Jewish man, the Roman centurion spoken of in the rest of this chapter.

You may be still clinging to some old useless crutches. These crutches may represent certain ways your father or your grandfather acted or spoke. Your predecessors may never have thought of lifting a finger to help around the house or to bathe their children. Expressions of love and affection may have been completely foreign to them.

But if you find yourself hanging on to these "manly" ways, then it's time you free yourself from the past. These are not sacred rites, these are crutches. Throw them away. It's time to start some of your own customs. Enjoy the freedom that new ways of acting and speaking—your own legs— will bring.

For your next devotional reading, go to page 1223.

appointed as judge of the living and the dead. **⁴³**All the prophets testify about him that everyone who believes in him receives forgiveness of sins through his name."

⁴⁴While Peter was still speaking these words, the Holy Spirit came on all who heard the message. **⁴⁵**The circumcised believers who had come with Peter were astonished that the gift of the Holy Spirit had been poured out even on the Gentiles. **⁴⁶**For they heard them speaking in tongues*ᵃ* and praising God.

Then Peter said, **⁴⁷**"Can anyone keep these people from being baptized with water? They have received the Holy Spirit just as we have." **⁴⁸**So he ordered that they be baptized in the name of Jesus Christ. Then they asked Peter to stay with them for a few days.

Peter Explains His Actions

11 The apostles and the brothers throughout Judea heard that the Gentiles also had received the word of God. **²**So when Peter went up to Jerusalem, the circumcised believers criticized him **³**and said, "You went into the house of uncircumcised men and ate with them."

⁴Peter began and explained everything to them precisely as it had happened: **⁵**"I was in the city of Joppa praying, and

in a trance I saw a vision. I saw something like a large sheet being let down from heaven by its four corners, and it came down to where I was. **⁶**I looked into it and saw four-footed animals of the earth, wild beasts, reptiles, and birds of the air. **⁷**Then I heard a voice telling me, 'Get up, Peter. Kill and eat.'

⁸"I replied, 'Surely not, Lord! Nothing impure or unclean has ever entered my mouth.'

⁹"The voice spoke from heaven a second time, 'Do not call anything impure that God has made clean.' **¹⁰**This happened three times, and then it was all pulled up to heaven again.

¹¹"Right then three men who had been sent to me from Caesarea stopped at the house where I was staying. **¹²**The Spirit told me to have no hesitation about going with them. These six brothers also went with me, and we entered the man's house. **¹³**He told us how he had seen an angel appear in his house and say, 'Send to Joppa for Simon who is called Peter. **¹⁴**He will bring you a message through which you and all your household will be saved.'

¹⁵"As I began to speak, the Holy Spirit came on them as he had come on us at the beginning. **¹⁶**Then I remembered what

ᵃ46 Or other languages

HEY DAD
If Jesus taught peace,
why did the Romans hate Christians and kill them?

Text: Acts 11:19–21

The Romans were very suspicious of this new religious group. They thought Christians were cannibals—didn't they claim to eat flesh and drink blood? And rumors suggested that Christians practiced incest—weren't "brothers" and "sisters" known to meet secretly? Of course, these were horrible distortions of what Christians believed and practiced. Most of all, Romans hated Christians because they refused to worship Roman gods.

The most rampant persecution of Christians occurred while Nero was emperor of Rome. Nero was popular at first, but eventually developed a reputation for self-indulgence and an obsession for shaping Rome to fit his own tastes. When a raging fire destroyed the entire city in AD 64, the people accused Nero of burning Rome himself.

Nero needed a scapegoat, and he needed one fast, so he chose the Christians. Quickly, the Romans turned their anger from Nero to the Christians, and they made execution of Christians a spectator sport.

Most of the time, Christians lived peaceably with their neighbors. But sometimes they were asked a question: Life or Christ? Which would you choose?

For a complete listing of Questions Kids Ask, turn to page 1435.

the Lord had said: 'John baptized with[a] water, but you will be baptized with the Holy Spirit.' [17]So if God gave them the same gift as he gave us, who believed in the Lord Jesus Christ, who was I to think that I could oppose God?"

[18]When they heard this, they had no further objections and praised God, saying, "So then, God has granted even the Gentiles repentance unto life."

The Church in Antioch

[19]Now those who had been scattered by the persecution in connection with Stephen traveled as far as Phoenicia, Cyprus and Antioch, telling the message only to Jews. [20]Some of them, however, men from Cyprus and Cyrene, went to Antioch and began to speak to Greeks also, telling them the good news about the Lord Jesus. [21]The Lord's hand was with them, and a great number of people believed and turned to the Lord.

[22]News of this reached the ears of the church at Jerusalem, and they sent Barnabas to Antioch. [23]When he arrived and saw the evidence of the grace of God, he was glad and encouraged them all to remain true to the Lord with all their hearts. [24]He was a good man, full of the Holy Spirit and faith, and a great number of people were brought to the Lord.

[25]Then Barnabas went to Tarsus to look for Saul, [26]and when he found him, he brought him to Antioch. So for a whole year Barnabas and Saul met with the church and taught great numbers of people. The disciples were called Christians first at Antioch.

[27]During this time some prophets came down from Jerusalem to Antioch. [28]One of them, named Agabus, stood up and through the Spirit predicted that a severe famine would spread over the entire Roman world. (This happened during the reign of Claudius.) [29]The disciples, each according to his ability, decided to provide help for the brothers living in Judea. [30]This they did, sending their gift to the elders by Barnabas and Saul.

Peter's Miraculous Escape From Prison

12 It was about this time that King Herod arrested some who belonged to the church, intending to persecute them. [2]He had James, the brother of John, put to death with the sword. [3]When he saw that this pleased the Jews, he proceeded to seize Peter also. This happened during the

Feast of Unleavened Bread. [4]After arresting him, he put him in prison, handing him over to be guarded by four squads of four soldiers each. Herod intended to bring him out for public trial after the Passover.

[5]So Peter was kept in prison, but the church was earnestly praying to God for him.

[6]The night before Herod was to bring him to trial, Peter was sleeping between two soldiers, bound with two chains, and sentries stood guard at the entrance. [7]Suddenly an angel of the Lord appeared and a light shone in the cell. He struck Peter on the side and woke him up. "Quick, get up!" he said, and the chains fell off Peter's wrists.

[8]Then the angel said to him, "Put on your clothes and sandals." And Peter did so. "Wrap your cloak around you and follow me," the angel told him. [9]Peter followed him out of the prison, but he had no idea that what the angel was doing was really happening; he thought he was seeing a vision. [10]They passed the first and second guards and came to the iron gate leading to the city. It opened for them by itself, and they went through it. When they had walked the length of one street, suddenly the angel left him.

[11]Then Peter came to himself and said, "Now I know without a doubt that the Lord sent his angel and rescued me from Herod's clutches and from everything the Jewish people were anticipating."

[12]When this had dawned on him, he went to the house of Mary the mother of John, also called Mark, where many people had gathered and were praying. [13]Peter knocked at the outer entrance, and a servant girl named Rhoda came to answer the door. [14]When she recognized Peter's voice, she was so overjoyed she ran back without opening it and exclaimed, "Peter is at the door!"

[15]"You're out of your mind," they told her. When she kept insisting that it was so, they said, "It must be his angel."

[16]But Peter kept on knocking, and when they opened the door and saw him, they were astonished. [17]Peter motioned with his hand for them to be quiet and described how the Lord had brought him out of prison. "Tell James and the brothers about this," he said, and then he left for another place.

[18]In the morning, there was no small

[a]16 Or in

commotion among the soldiers as to what had become of Peter. [19]After Herod had a thorough search made for him and did not find him, he cross-examined the guards and ordered that they be executed.

Herod's Death

Then Herod went from Judea to Caesarea and stayed there a while. [20]He had been quarreling with the people of Tyre and Sidon; they now joined together and sought an audience with him. Having secured the support of Blastus, a trusted personal servant of the king, they asked for peace, because they depended on the king's country for their food supply.

[21]On the appointed day Herod, wearing his royal robes, sat on his throne and delivered a public address to the people. [22]They shouted, "This is the voice of a god, not of a man." [23]Immediately, because Herod did not give praise to God, an angel of the Lord struck him down, and he was eaten by worms and died.

[24]But the word of God continued to increase and spread.

[25]When Barnabas and Saul had finished their mission, they returned from[a] Jerusalem, taking with them John, also called Mark.

Barnabas and Saul Sent Off

13 In the church at Antioch there were prophets and teachers: Barnabas, Simeon called Niger, Lucius of Cyrene, Manaen (who had been brought up with Herod the tetrarch) and Saul. [2]While they were worshiping the Lord and fasting, the Holy Spirit said, "Set apart for me Barnabas and Saul for the work to which I have called them." [3]So after they had fasted and prayed, they placed their hands on them and sent them off.

On Cyprus

[4]The two of them, sent on their way by the Holy Spirit, went down to Seleucia and sailed from there to Cyprus. [5]When they arrived at Salamis, they proclaimed the word of God in the Jewish synagogues. John was with them as their helper.

[6]They traveled through the whole island until they came to Paphos. There they met a Jewish sorcerer and false prophet named Bar-Jesus, [7]who was an attendant of the proconsul, Sergius Paulus. The proconsul, an intelligent man, sent for Barnabas and Saul because he

wanted to hear the word of God. [8]But Elymas the sorcerer (for that is what his name means) opposed them and tried to turn the proconsul from the faith. [9]Then Saul, who was also called Paul, filled with the Holy Spirit, looked straight at Elymas and said, [10]"You are a child of the devil and an enemy of everything that is right! You are full of all kinds of deceit and trickery. Will you never stop perverting the right ways of the Lord? [11]Now the hand of the Lord is against you. You are going to be blind, and for a time you will be unable to see the light of the sun."

Immediately mist and darkness came over him, and he groped about, seeking someone to lead him by the hand. [12]When the proconsul saw what had happened, he believed, for he was amazed at the teaching about the Lord.

In Pisidian Antioch

[13]From Paphos, Paul and his companions sailed to Perga in Pamphylia, where John left them to return to Jerusalem. [14]From Perga they went on to Pisidian Antioch. On the Sabbath they entered the synagogue and sat down. [15]After the reading from the Law and the Prophets, the synagogue rulers sent word to them, saying, "Brothers, if you have a message of encouragement for the people, please speak."

[16]Standing up, Paul motioned with his hand and said: "Men of Israel and you Gentiles who worship God, listen to me! [17]The God of the people of Israel chose our fathers; he made the people prosper during their stay in Egypt, with mighty power he led them out of that country, [18]he endured their conduct[b] for about forty years in the desert, [19]he overthrew seven nations in Canaan and gave their land to his people as their inheritance. [20]All this took about 450 years.

"After this, God gave them judges until the time of Samuel the prophet. [21]Then the people asked for a king, and he gave them Saul son of Kish, of the tribe of Benjamin, who ruled forty years. [22]After removing Saul, he made David their king. He testified concerning him: 'I have found David son of Jesse a man after my own heart; he will do everything I want him to do.'

[23]"From this man's descendants God has brought to Israel the Savior Jesus,

as he promised. ²⁴Before the coming of Jesus, John preached repentance and baptism to all the people of Israel. ²⁵As John was completing his work, he said: 'Who do you think I am? I am not that one. No, but he is coming after me, whose sandals I am not worthy to untie.'

²⁶"Brothers, children of Abraham, and you God-fearing Gentiles, it is to us that this message of salvation has been sent. ²⁷The people of Jerusalem and their rulers did not recognize Jesus, yet in condemning him they fulfilled the words of the prophets that are read every Sabbath. ²⁸Though they found no proper ground for a death sentence, they asked Pilate to have him executed. ²⁹When they had carried out all that was written about him, they took him down from the tree and laid him in a tomb. ³⁰But God raised him from the dead, ³¹and for many days he was seen by those who had traveled with him from Galilee to Jerusalem. They are now his witnesses to our people.

³²"We tell you the good news: What God promised our fathers ³³he has fulfilled for us, their children, by raising up Jesus. As it is written in the second Psalm:

" 'You are my Son;
    today I have become your Father.'^{a'b}

³⁴The fact that God raised him from the dead, never to decay, is stated in these words:

" 'I will give you the holy and sure
    blessings promised to David.'^c

³⁵So it is stated elsewhere:

" 'You will not let your Holy One see
    decay.'^d

³⁶"For when David had served God's purpose in his own generation, he fell asleep; he was buried with his fathers and his body decayed. ³⁷But the one whom God raised from the dead did not see decay.

³⁸"Therefore, my brothers, I want you to know that through Jesus the forgiveness of sins is proclaimed to you. ³⁹Through him everyone who believes is justified from everything you could not be justified from by the law of Moses. ⁴⁰Take care that what the prophets have said does not happen to you:

⁴¹" 'Look, you scoffers,
    wonder and perish,
for I am going to do something in your
    days

that you would never believe,
    even if someone told you.'^e"

⁴²As Paul and Barnabas were leaving the synagogue, the people invited them to speak further about these things on the next Sabbath. ⁴³When the congregation was dismissed, many of the Jews and devout converts to Judaism followed Paul and Barnabas, who talked with them and urged them to continue in the grace of God.

⁴⁴On the next Sabbath almost the whole city gathered to hear the word of the Lord. ⁴⁵When the Jews saw the crowds, they were filled with jealousy and talked abusively against what Paul was saying.

⁴⁶Then Paul and Barnabas answered them boldly: "We had to speak the word of God to you first. Since you reject it and do not consider yourselves worthy of eternal life, we now turn to the Gentiles. ⁴⁷For this is what the Lord has commanded us:

" 'I have made you^f a light for the
    Gentiles,
    that you^f may bring salvation to the
    ends of the earth.'^g"

⁴⁸When the Gentiles heard this, they were glad and honored the word of the Lord; and all who were appointed for eternal life believed.

⁴⁹The word of the Lord spread through the whole region. ⁵⁰But the Jews incited the God-fearing women of high standing and the leading men of the city. They stirred up persecution against Paul and Barnabas, and expelled them from their region. ⁵¹So they shook the dust from their feet in protest against them and went to Iconium. ⁵²And the disciples were filled with joy and with the Holy Spirit.

In Iconium

14 At Iconium Paul and Barnabas went as usual into the Jewish synagogue. There they spoke so effectively that a great number of Jews and Gentiles believed. ²But the Jews who refused to believe stirred up the Gentiles and poisoned their minds against the brothers. ³So Paul and Barnabas spent considerable time there, speaking boldly for the Lord, who confirmed the message of his grace by enabling them to do miraculous signs and wonders. ⁴The people of the city were

---

^a33 Or *have begotten you*   ^b33 Psalm 2:7
^c34 Isaiah 55:3   ^d35 Psalm 16:10   ^e41 Hab. 1:5
^f47 The Greek is singular.   ^g47 Isaiah 49:6

divided; some sided with the Jews, others with the apostles. **⁵**There was a plot afoot among the Gentiles and Jews, together with their leaders, to mistreat them and stone them. **⁶**But they found out about it and fled to the Lycaonian cities of Lystra and Derbe and to the surrounding country, **⁷**where they continued to preach the good news.

In Lystra and Derbe

⁸In Lystra there sat a man crippled in his feet, who was lame from birth and had never walked. **⁹**He listened to Paul as he was speaking. Paul looked directly at him, saw that he had faith to be healed **¹⁰**and called out, "Stand up on your feet!" At that, the man jumped up and began to walk.

¹¹When the crowd saw what Paul had done, they shouted in the Lycaonian language, "The gods have come down to us in human form!" **¹²**Barnabas they called Zeus, and Paul they called Hermes because he was the chief speaker. **¹³**The priest of Zeus, whose temple was just outside the city, brought bulls and wreaths to the city gates because he and the crowd wanted to offer sacrifices to them.

¹⁴But when the apostles Barnabas and Paul heard of this, they tore their clothes and rushed out into the crowd, shouting: **¹⁵**"Men, why are you doing this? We too are only men, human like you. We are bringing you good news, telling you to turn from these worthless things to the living God, who made heaven and earth and sea and everything in them. **¹⁶**In the past, he let all nations go their own way. **¹⁷**Yet he has not left himself without testimony: He has shown kindness by giving you rain from heaven and crops in their seasons; he provides you with plenty of food and fills your hearts with joy." **¹⁸**Even with these words, they had difficulty keeping the crowd from sacrificing to them.

¹⁹Then some Jews came from Antioch and Iconium and won the crowd over. They stoned Paul and dragged him outside the city, thinking he was dead. **²⁰**But after the disciples had gathered around him, he got up and went back into the city. The next day he and Barnabas left for Derbe.

The Return to Antioch in Syria

²¹They preached the good news in that city and won a large number of disciples.

Then they returned to Lystra, Iconium and Antioch, **²²**strengthening the disciples and encouraging them to remain true to the faith. "We must go through many hardships to enter the kingdom of God," they said. **²³**Paul and Barnabas appointed elders*ᵃ* for them in each church and, with prayer and fasting, committed them to the Lord, in whom they had put their trust. **²⁴**After going through Pisidia, they came into Pamphylia, **²⁵**and when they had preached the word in Perga, they went down to Attalia.

²⁶From Attalia they sailed back to Antioch, where they had been committed to the grace of God for the work they had now completed. **²⁷**On arriving there, they gathered the church together and reported all that God had done through them and how he had opened the door of faith to the Gentiles. **²⁸**And they stayed there a long time with the disciples.

The Council at Jerusalem

15 Some men came down from Judea to Antioch and were teaching the brothers: "Unless you are circumcised, according to the custom taught by Moses, you cannot be saved." **²**This brought Paul and Barnabas into sharp dispute and debate with them. So Paul and Barnabas were appointed, along with some other believers, to go up to Jerusalem to see the apostles and elders about this question. **³**The church sent them on their way, and as they traveled through Phoenicia and Samaria, they told how the Gentiles had been converted. This news made all the brothers very glad. **⁴**When they came to Jerusalem, they were welcomed by the church and the apostles and elders, to whom they reported everything God had done through them.

⁵Then some of the believers who belonged to the party of the Pharisees stood up and said, "The Gentiles must be circumcised and required to obey the law of Moses."

⁶The apostles and elders met to consider this question. **⁷**After much discussion, Peter got up and addressed them: "Brothers, you know that some time ago God made a choice among you that the Gentiles might hear from my lips the message of the gospel and believe. **⁸**God, who knows the heart, showed that he accepted

---

ᵃ23 Or Barnabas ordained elders; or Barnabas had elders elected

them by giving the Holy Spirit to them, just as he did to us. [9]He made no distinction between us and them, for he purified their hearts by faith. [10]Now then, why do you try to test God by putting on the necks of the disciples a yoke that neither we nor our fathers have been able to bear? [11]No! We believe it is through the grace of our Lord Jesus that we are saved, just as they are."

[12]The whole assembly became silent as they listened to Barnabas and Paul telling about the miraculous signs and wonders God had done among the Gentiles through them. [13]When they finished, James spoke up: "Brothers, listen to me. [14]Simon[a] has described to us how God at first showed his concern by taking from the Gentiles a people for himself. [15]The words of the prophets are in agreement with this, as it is written:

[a]14 Greek *Simeon*, a variant of *Simon*; that is, Peter

The Buddy System

DAILY INSIGHT

TUESDAY

Passage:
Acts 15:1–5

Verse:
Acts 15:4

In 1986, my friend Mike Hyatt and I sat down to talk about the future. We had worked together for five years in two different companies located in two different states. We had enjoyed the mutual respect our collegial relationship had forged, so we decided to start a business together.

Over the next few years, Mike and I built a successful company that some said was one of the leading enterprises in our industry. The bottom line of our venture was undeniable: Mike and I could not have done this without each other. The skills, abilities, financial resources and experiences that we each enjoyed were brought to the table and used in full measure. We built our company on the buddy system—I helped, supported and encouraged Mike as he made his contribution, and he did the same with me. It was great.

Paul and Barnabas were colleagues, and even though they didn't see things exactly the same way, they were committed to working together, and they were successful. Their efforts "made all the brothers very glad ... [because of] everything God had done through them" (vv. 3–4). What Paul and Barnabas had done as a team, they couldn't have done separately. Their relationship was a New Testament version of the buddy system in action.

After sixteen years of working together, Mike and I, just like Paul and Barnabas, went our separate ways. We had been called to new things—things that no longer included working with each other. Like Paul and Barnabas, we parted as friends, colleagues who had been glad that God had allowed us to multiply our efforts by working as a team.

Several years ago, I had the privilege of spending a few hours with Dr. Neil Clark Warren, a very successful Christian psychologist. He told me that when he meets with new clients, he always asks the same question to open their conversation: "Tell me about your three closest friends."

Dr. Warren said that most women quickly jump into their answers. "Let's see ... well, there's Donna and Cindy and Julie, and I have to say Betty ... and oh, you said three. Only three? I can't limit it to just three." Most men, on the other hand, sit there staring for a few moments. "What exactly do you mean, 'closest friends?' " they stammer.

You and I are incredibly busy. Our lives are filled to the brim with obligations and tasks. Finding and keeping close friends—men who really know who we are and who love us enough to tell us the truth about ourselves—are a rarity. This is a shame ... but it's true.

Outside of the support of your family, God does not desire that you live your life solo. He does not want you to face your vocation and your future by yourself. The task of making it successfully through life is a whole different thing. Don't do this thing alone. Be Paul and find a Barnabas. This buddy system is terrific.

For your next devotional reading, go to page 1226.

16 " 'After this I will return
    and rebuild David's fallen tent.
  Its ruins I will rebuild,
    and I will restore it,
17 that the remnant of men may seek the
      Lord,
    and all the Gentiles who bear my
      name,
  says the Lord, who does these things'[a]
18   that have been known for ages.[b]

19"It is my judgment, therefore, that we
should not make it difficult for the Gentiles who are turning to God. 20Instead we
should write to them, telling them to abstain from food polluted by idols, from
sexual immorality, from the meat of
strangled animals and from blood. 21For
Moses has been preached in every city
from the earliest times and is read in the
synagogues on every Sabbath."

The Council's Letter to Gentile Believers

22Then the apostles and elders, with the
whole church, decided to choose some
of their own men and send them to Antioch with Paul and Barnabas. They chose
Judas (called Barsabbas) and Silas, two
men who were leaders among the brothers. 23With them they sent the following
letter:

  The apostles and elders, your brothers,

  To the Gentile believers in Antioch,
  Syria and Cilicia:

  Greetings.

  24We have heard that some went
  out from us without our authoriza-
  tion and disturbed you, troubling
  your minds by what they said. 25So
  we all agreed to choose some men
  and send them to you with our dear
  friends Barnabas and Paul— 26men
  who have risked their lives for the
  name of our Lord Jesus Christ.
  27Therefore we are sending Judas and
  Silas to confirm by word of mouth
  what we are writing. 28It seemed
  good to the Holy Spirit and to us not
  to burden you with anything beyond
  the following requirements: 29You are
  to abstain from food sacrificed to
  idols, from blood, from the meat of
  strangled animals and from sexual
  immorality. You will do well to avoid
  these things.

  Farewell.

30The men were sent off and went down
to Antioch, where they gathered the
church together and delivered the letter.
31The people read it and were glad for
its encouraging message. 32Judas and Silas, who themselves were prophets, said
much to encourage and strengthen the
brothers. 33After spending some time
there, they were sent off by the brothers
with the blessing of peace to return to
those who had sent them.[c] 35But Paul and
Barnabas remained in Antioch, where
they and many others taught and
preached the word of the Lord.

Disagreement Between Paul and Barnabas

36Some time later Paul said to Barnabas, "Let us go back and visit the brothers
in all the towns where we preached the
word of the Lord and see how they are doing." 37Barnabas wanted to take John, also
called Mark, with them, 38but Paul did not
think it wise to take him, because he had
deserted them in Pamphylia and had not
continued with them in the work. 39They
had such a sharp disagreement that they
parted company. Barnabas took Mark and
sailed for Cyprus, 40but Paul chose Silas
and left, commended by the brothers to
the grace of the Lord. 41He went through
Syria and Cilicia, strengthening the
churches.

Timothy Joins Paul and Silas

16 He came to Derbe and then to Lystra,
    where a disciple named Timothy
lived, whose mother was a Jewess and a
believer, but whose father was a Greek.
2The brothers at Lystra and Iconium
spoke well of him. 3Paul wanted to take
him along on the journey, so he circumcised him because of the Jews who lived
in that area, for they all knew that his father was a Greek. 4As they traveled from
town to town, they delivered the decisions
reached by the apostles and elders in
Jerusalem for the people to obey. 5So the
churches were strengthened in the faith
and grew daily in numbers.

Paul's Vision of the Man of Macedonia

6Paul and his companions traveled
throughout the region of Phrygia and Galatia, having been kept by the Holy Spirit

a17 Amos 9:11,12   b17,18 Some manuscripts
things'— / 18known to the Lord for ages is his work
c33 Some manuscripts them, 34but Silas decided to
remain there

from preaching the word in the province of Asia. [7]When they came to the border of Mysia, they tried to enter Bithynia, but the Spirit of Jesus would not allow them to. [8]So they passed by Mysia and went down to Troas. [9]During the night Paul had a vision of a man of Macedonia standing and begging him, "Come over to Macedonia and help us." [10]After Paul had seen the vision, we got ready at once to leave for Macedonia, concluding that God had called us to preach the gospel to them.

Lydia's Conversion in Philippi

[11]From Troas we put out to sea and sailed straight for Samothrace, and the next day on to Neapolis. [12]From there we traveled to Philippi, a Roman colony and the leading city of that district of Macedonia. And we stayed there several days.

[13]On the Sabbath we went outside the city gate to the river, where we expected to find a place of prayer. We sat down and began to speak to the women who had gathered there. [14]One of those listening was a woman named Lydia, a dealer in purple cloth from the city of Thyatira, who was a worshiper of God. The Lord opened her heart to respond to Paul's message. [15]When she and the members of her household were baptized, she invited us to her home. "If you consider me a believer in the Lord," she said, "come and stay at my house." And she persuaded us.

Paul and Silas in Prison

[16]Once when we were going to the place of prayer, we were met by a slave girl who had a spirit by which she predicted the future. She earned a great deal of money for her owners by fortune-telling. [17]This girl followed Paul and the rest of us, shouting, "These men are servants of the Most High God, who are telling you the way to be saved." [18]She kept this up for many days. Finally Paul became so troubled that he turned around and said to the spirit, "In the name of Jesus Christ I command you to come out of her!" At that moment the spirit left her.

[19]When the owners of the slave girl realized that their hope of making money was gone, they seized Paul and Silas and dragged them into the marketplace to face the authorities. [20]They brought them before the magistrates and said, "These men are Jews, and are throwing our city into an uproar [21]by advocating customs unlawful for us Romans to accept or practice."

[22]The crowd joined in the attack against Paul and Silas, and the magistrates ordered them to be stripped and beaten. [23]After they had been severely flogged, they were thrown into prison, and the jailer was commanded to guard them carefully. [24]Upon receiving such orders, he put them in the inner cell and fastened their feet in the stocks.

[25]About midnight Paul and Silas were praying and singing hymns to God, and the other prisoners were listening to them. [26]Suddenly there was such a violent earthquake that the foundations of the prison were shaken. At once all the prison doors flew open, and everybody's chains came loose. [27]The jailer woke up, and when he saw the prison doors open, he drew his sword and was about to kill himself because he thought the prisoners had escaped. [28]But Paul shouted, "Don't harm yourself! We are all here!"

[29]The jailer called for lights, rushed in and fell trembling before Paul and Silas. [30]He then brought them out and asked, "Sirs, what must I do to be saved?"

[31]They replied, "Believe in the Lord Jesus, and you will be saved—you and your household." [32]Then they spoke the word of the Lord to him and to all the others in his house. [33]At that hour of the night the jailer took them and washed their wounds; then immediately he and all his family were baptized. [34]The jailer brought them into his house and set a meal before them; he was filled with joy because he had come to believe in God—he and his whole family.

[35]When it was daylight, the magistrates sent their officers to the jailer with the order: "Release those men." [36]The jailer told Paul, "The magistrates have ordered that you and Silas be released. Now you can leave. Go in peace."

[37]But Paul said to the officers: "They beat us publicly without a trial, even though we are Roman citizens, and threw us into prison. And now do they want to get rid of us quietly? No! Let them come themselves and escort us out."

[38]The officers reported this to the magistrates, and when they heard that Paul and Silas were Roman citizens, they were alarmed. [39]They came to appease them and escorted them from the prison, requesting them to leave the city. [40]After Paul and Silas came out of the prison, they went to Lydia's house, where they met

with the brothers and encouraged them. Then they left.

In Thessalonica

17 When they had passed through Amphipolis and Apollonia, they came to Thessalonica, where there was a Jewish synagogue. **2**As his custom was, Paul went into the synagogue, and on three Sabbath days he reasoned with them from the Scriptures, **3**explaining and proving that the Christ*a* had to suffer and rise from the dead. "This Jesus I am proclaiming to you is the Christ,*a*" he said. **4**Some of the Jews were persuaded and joined Paul and Silas, as did a large number of God-fearing Greeks and not a few prominent women.

5But the Jews were jealous; so they rounded up some bad characters from the marketplace, formed a mob and started a riot in the city. They rushed to Jason's

a3 Or Messiah

A Dad's Faith, His Family's Joy

DAILY INSIGHT

WEDNESDAY

Passage:
Acts 16:25–34

Verse:
Acts 16:34

Teaching a large Sunday school class for many years has made me somewhat visible in a town the size of Nashville. Usually I don't mind this, except when bumping into me at the hardware store makes someone feel bad because they have missed a few Sundays. At these moments, I know exactly what it's like to feel like a policeman with a radar gun. And I don't like it.

One such chance meeting was at the concession window during a concert intermission. Steve and Amy were lovely people, and my wife and I had enjoyed the company of their family in the past. When we bumped in to them, we realized that we hadn't seen them for a long time.

Unlike some others, Steve and Amy spoke with boldness and confidence. "We haven't been to Sunday school or church for several months," Amy said after greeting me. "And we'll probably never come back." "We're tired of being told we're sinners." Steve chimed in. "We don't need that negative stuff in our lives. And we certainly don't want our children to be exposed to such pessimistic input."

"I'm sorry," was all I could say before the lights flickered, informing us that the second half of the concert was about to begin. We said our "good-byes" and our friends disappeared into the darkening auditorium.

The story of the Philippian jailer is one of the Bible's most remarkable stories of how God's grace can affect a father. Here was a man faced with the trauma of failure on the job. Jailers not only got fired when prisoners escaped, they often lost their lives as well. Following a midnight earthquake that turned the prison to rubble, the jailer was preparing to take his life. Paul and Silas shouted at the jailer who was about to impale himself on his sword, "We are all here!" (v. 28). Completely overwhelmed by this act of mercy, the jailer fell to his knees before his gracious captives. "Sirs," he cried. "What must I do to be saved?" (v. 30).

That night, not only was the jailer brought into a relationship with God, but he also invited Paul and Silas to his home. As a result, the jailer "was filled with joy because he had come to believe in God—he and his whole family" (v. 34).

My wife and I were saddened that our friends had decided not to recognize their sinfulness and their need for a Savior. We were sorry that we would not be able to enjoy the fun of worshiping with them again at church. But mostly, we were disconsolate that the joy that only comes with the experience of God's mercy would never grace their home with joy. Our prayer for this family is that, like the Philippian jailer, they will eventually find the truth and freedom that comes with an intimate knowledge of who God is and who they are.

Confess your sinfulness, enjoy his grace, then let your experience with Christ infect your family. Let it bring joy to your home.

For your next devotional reading, go to page 1230.

house in search of Paul and Silas in order to bring them out to the crowd.ᵃ ⁶But when they did not find them, they dragged Jason and some other brothers before the city officials, shouting: "These men who have caused trouble all over the world have now come here, ⁷and Jason has welcomed them into his house. They are all defying Caesar's decrees, saying that there is another king, one called Jesus." ⁸When they heard this, the crowd and the city officials were thrown into turmoil. ⁹Then they made Jason and the others post bond and let them go.

In Berea

¹⁰As soon as it was night, the brothers sent Paul and Silas away to Berea. On arriving there, they went to the Jewish synagogue. ¹¹Now the Bereans were of more noble character than the Thessalonians, for they received the message with great eagerness and examined the Scriptures every day to see if what Paul said was true. ¹²Many of the Jews believed, as did also a number of prominent Greek women and many Greek men. ¹³When the Jews in Thessalonica learned that Paul was preaching the word of God at Berea, they went there too, agitating the crowds and stirring them up. ¹⁴The brothers immediately sent Paul to the coast, but Silas and Timothy stayed at Berea. ¹⁵The men who escorted Paul brought him to Athens and then left with instructions for Silas and Timothy to join him as soon as possible.

In Athens

¹⁶While Paul was waiting for them in Athens, he was greatly distressed to see that the city was full of idols. ¹⁷So he reasoned in the synagogue with the Jews and the God-fearing Greeks, as well as in the marketplace day by day with those who happened to be there. ¹⁸A group of Epicurean and Stoic philosophers began to dispute with him. Some of them asked, "What is this babbler trying to say?" Others remarked, "He seems to be advocating foreign gods." They said this because Paul was preaching the good news about Jesus and the resurrection. ¹⁹Then they took him and brought him to a meeting of the Areopagus, where they said to him, "May we know what this new teaching is that you are presenting? ²⁰You are bringing some strange ideas to our ears, and we want to know what they mean." ²¹(All the Athenians and the foreigners who lived there spent their time doing nothing but talking about and listening to the latest ideas.)

²²Paul then stood up in the meeting of the Areopagus and said: "Men of Athens! I see that in every way you are very religious. ²³For as I walked around and looked carefully at your objects of worship, I even found an altar with this inscription: TO AN UNKNOWN GOD. Now what you worship as something unknown I am going to proclaim to you.

²⁴"The God who made the world and everything in it is the Lord of heaven and earth and does not live in temples built by hands. ²⁵And he is not served by human hands, as if he needed anything, because he himself gives all men life and breath and everything else. ²⁶From one man he made every nation of men, that they should inhabit the whole earth; and he determined the times set for them and the exact places where they should live. ²⁷God did this so that men would seek him and perhaps reach out for him and find him, though he is not far from each one of us. ²⁸'For in him we live and move and have our being.' As some of your own poets have said, 'We are his offspring.'

²⁹"Therefore since we are God's offspring, we should not think that the divine being is like gold or silver or stone—an image made by man's design and skill. ³⁰In the past God overlooked such ignorance, but now he commands all people everywhere to repent. ³¹For he has set a day when he will judge the world with justice by the man he has appointed. He has given proof of this to all men by raising him from the dead."

³²When they heard about the resurrection of the dead, some of them sneered, but others said, "We want to hear you again on this subject." ³³At that, Paul left the Council. ³⁴A few men became followers of Paul and believed. Among them was Dionysius, a member of the Areopagus, also a woman named Damaris, and a number of others.

In Corinth

18 After this, Paul left Athens and went to Corinth. ²There he met a Jew named Aquila, a native of Pontus, who had recently come from Italy with his wife Priscilla, because Claudius had ordered all the Jews to leave Rome. Paul went to

---

ᵃ5 Or *the assembly of the people*

see them, [3]and because he was a tentmaker as they were, he stayed and worked with them. [4]Every Sabbath he reasoned in the synagogue, trying to persuade Jews and Greeks.

[5]When Silas and Timothy came from Macedonia, Paul devoted himself exclusively to preaching, testifying to the Jews that Jesus was the Christ.[a] [6]But when the Jews opposed Paul and became abusive, he shook out his clothes in protest and said to them, "Your blood be on your own heads! I am clear of my responsibility. From now on I will go to the Gentiles."

[7]Then Paul left the synagogue and went next door to the house of Titius Justus, a worshiper of God. [8]Crispus, the synagogue ruler, and his entire household believed in the Lord; and many of the Corinthians who heard him believed and were baptized.

[9]One night the Lord spoke to Paul in a vision: "Do not be afraid; keep on speaking, do not be silent. [10]For I am with you, and no one is going to attack and harm you, because I have many people in this city." [11]So Paul stayed for a year and a half, teaching them the word of God.

[12]While Gallio was proconsul of Achaia, the Jews made a united attack on Paul and brought him into court. [13]"This man," they charged, "is persuading the people to worship God in ways contrary to the law."

[14]Just as Paul was about to speak, Gallio said to the Jews, "If you Jews were making a complaint about some misdemeanor or serious crime, it would be reasonable for me to listen to you. [15]But since it involves questions about words and names and your own law—settle the matter yourselves. I will not be a judge of such things." [16]So he had them ejected from the court. [17]Then they all turned on Sosthenes the synagogue ruler and beat him in front of the court. But Gallio showed no concern whatever.

Priscilla, Aquila and Apollos

[18]Paul stayed on in Corinth for some time. Then he left the brothers and sailed for Syria, accompanied by Priscilla and Aquila. Before he sailed, he had his hair cut off at Cenchrea because of a vow he had taken. [19]They arrived at Ephesus, where Paul left Priscilla and Aquila. He himself went into the synagogue and reasoned with the Jews. [20]When they asked him to spend more time with them, he declined. [21]But as he left, he promised, "I will come back if it is God's will." Then he set sail from Ephesus. [22]When he landed at Caesarea, he went up and greeted the church and then went down to Antioch.

[23]After spending some time in Antioch, Paul set out from there and traveled from place to place throughout the region of Galatia and Phrygia, strengthening all the disciples.

[24]Meanwhile a Jew named Apollos, a native of Alexandria, came to Ephesus. He was a learned man, with a thorough knowledge of the Scriptures. [25]He had been instructed in the way of the Lord, and he spoke with great fervor[b] and taught about Jesus accurately, though he knew only the baptism of John. [26]He began to speak boldly in the synagogue. When Priscilla and Aquila heard him, they invited him to their home and explained to him the way of God more adequately.

[27]When Apollos wanted to go to Achaia, the brothers encouraged him and wrote to the disciples there to welcome him. On arriving, he was a great help to those who by grace had believed. [28]For he vigorously refuted the Jews in public debate, proving from the Scriptures that Jesus was the Christ.

Paul in Ephesus

19 While Apollos was at Corinth, Paul took the road through the interior and arrived at Ephesus. There he found some disciples [2]and asked them, "Did you receive the Holy Spirit when[c] you believed?"

They answered, "No, we have not even heard that there is a Holy Spirit."

[3]So Paul asked, "Then what baptism did you receive?"

"John's baptism," they replied.

[4]Paul said, "John's baptism was a baptism of repentance. He told the people to believe in the one coming after him, that is, in Jesus." [5]On hearing this, they were baptized into[d] the name of the Lord Jesus. [6]When Paul placed his hands on them, the Holy Spirit came on them, and they spoke in tongues[e] and prophesied. [7]There were about twelve men in all.

[8]Paul entered the synagogue and spoke boldly there for three months, arguing persuasively about the kingdom of God. [9]But some of them became obstinate; they refused to believe and publicly ma-

ligned the Way. So Paul left them. He took the disciples with him and had discussions daily in the lecture hall of Tyrannus. ¹⁰This went on for two years, so that all the Jews and Greeks who lived in the province of Asia heard the word of the Lord.

¹¹God did extraordinary miracles through Paul, ¹²so that even handkerchiefs and aprons that had touched him were taken to the sick, and their illnesses were cured and the evil spirits left them.

¹³Some Jews who went around driving out evil spirits tried to invoke the name of the Lord Jesus over those who were demon-possessed. They would say, "In the name of Jesus, whom Paul preaches, I command you to come out." ¹⁴Seven sons of Sceva, a Jewish chief priest, were doing this. ¹⁵One day the evil spirit answered them, "Jesus I know, and I know about Paul, but who are you?" ¹⁶Then the man who had the evil spirit jumped on them and overpowered them all. He gave them such a beating that they ran out of the house naked and bleeding.

¹⁷When this became known to the Jews and Greeks living in Ephesus, they were all seized with fear, and the name of the Lord Jesus was held in high honor. ¹⁸Many of those who believed now came and openly confessed their evil deeds. ¹⁹A number who had practiced sorcery brought their scrolls together and burned them publicly. When they calculated the value of the scrolls, the total came to fifty thousand drachmas.ᵃ ²⁰In this way the word of the Lord spread widely and grew in power.

²¹After all this had happened, Paul decided to go to Jerusalem, passing through Macedonia and Achaia. "After I have been there," he said, "I must visit Rome also." ²²He sent two of his helpers, Timothy and Erastus, to Macedonia, while he stayed in the province of Asia a little longer.

The Riot in Ephesus

²³About that time there arose a great disturbance about the Way. ²⁴A silversmith named Demetrius, who made silver shrines of Artemis, brought in no little business for the craftsmen. ²⁵He called them together, along with the workmen in related trades, and said: "Men, you know we receive a good income from this business. ²⁶And you see and hear how this fellow Paul has convinced and led astray large numbers of people here in Ephesus and in practically the whole province of Asia. He says that man-made gods are no gods at all. ²⁷There is danger not only that our trade will lose its good name, but also that the temple of the great goddess Artemis will be discredited, and the goddess herself, who is worshiped throughout the province of Asia and the world, will be robbed of her divine majesty."

²⁸When they heard this, they were furious and began shouting: "Great is Artemis of the Ephesians!" ²⁹Soon the whole city was in an uproar. The people seized Gaius and Aristarchus, Paul's traveling companions from Macedonia, and rushed as one man into the theater. ³⁰Paul wanted to appear before the crowd, but the disciples would not let him. ³¹Even some of the officials of the province, friends of Paul, sent him a message begging him not to venture into the theater.

³²The assembly was in confusion: Some were shouting one thing, some another. Most of the people did not even know why they were there. ³³The Jews pushed Alexander to the front, and some of the crowd shouted instructions to him. He motioned for silence in order to make a defense before the people. ³⁴But when they realized he was a Jew, they all shouted in unison for about two hours: "Great is Artemis of the Ephesians!"

³⁵The city clerk quieted the crowd and said: "Men of Ephesus, doesn't all the world know that the city of Ephesus is the guardian of the temple of the great Artemis and of her image, which fell from heaven? ³⁶Therefore, since these facts are undeniable, you ought to be quiet and not do anything rash. ³⁷You have brought these men here, though they have neither robbed temples nor blasphemed our goddess. ³⁸If, then, Demetrius and his fellow craftsmen have a grievance against anybody, the courts are open and there are proconsuls. They can press charges. ³⁹If there is anything further you want to bring up, it must be settled in a legal assembly. ⁴⁰As it is, we are in danger of being charged with rioting because of today's events. In that case we would not be able to account for this commotion, since there is no reason for it." ⁴¹After he had said this, he dismissed the assembly.

Through Macedonia and Greece

20 When the uproar had ended, Paul sent for the disciples and, after en-

---

ᵃ19 A drachma was a silver coin worth about a day's wages.

couraging them, said good-by and set out for Macedonia. ²He traveled through that area, speaking many words of encouragement to the people, and finally arrived in Greece, ³where he stayed three months. Because the Jews made a plot against him just as he was about to sail for Syria, he decided to go back through Macedonia. ⁴He was accompanied by Sopater son of Pyrrhus from Berea, Aristarchus and Secundus from Thessalonica, Gaius from Derbe, Timothy also, and Tychicus and Trophimus from the province of Asia. ⁵These men went on ahead and waited for us at Troas. ⁶But we sailed from Philippi after the Feast of Unleavened Bread, and five days later joined the others at Troas, where we stayed seven days.

Sleeping Through the Brilliance

DAILY INSIGHT

THURSDAY

Passage:
Acts 20:7–12

Verse:
Acts 20:10

Dr. Meredith Haines was a wise historian and a great professor. His lectures were filled with a wealth of information of eras gone by. I had the privilege of taking a class with Dr. Haines in college. Unfortunately, the class was held at 7:30 in the morning—not exactly a college student's most lucid time of the day. Falling asleep in Dr. Haines' class was a rite of passage for college freshmen at Taylor University.

One of the traditions of this class was the daily opening prayer. Some students were more traumatized by the potential of being called on for this prayer than they were by Dr. Haines' legendary exams. School folklore had it that the year before I took this course, one student (we'll call him Larry) had walked into Dr. Haines' class, slumped into his chair, and immediately fallen asleep.

Twenty minutes into the lecture, one of Larry's "friends" jarred his arm. "Dr. Haines wants you to pray," is all Larry heard. Shooting to his feet, just as the class was getting the lowdown on the Peloponisian Wars, a tragically unaware Larry abruptly ushered the entire class to the throne of grace. Three sentences into the prayer, everyone figured out what had just happened and exploded into uproarious laughter. Gratefully—especially for the horrified Larry—Dr. Haines also had a sense of humor.

A young man named Eutychus had Larry's problem. The teacher was the apostle Paul who, at least for one listener, was competing head-to-head with the sandman. On and on Paul spoke. And unfortunately for Eutychus, the sandman won. The young man fell asleep sitting on a windowsill and fell three stories to a tragic death. At this point, the situation lost its sense of humor. Imagine how terrible Paul must have felt.

Fortunately, the story had a good ending. Paul quickly ran to the street level, literally throwing his body on top of the young man's corpse. In an instant, Eutychus was alive again. What an incredible testimony to the power of Paul's message that night!

There are times as dads that we, like Paul, get a little carried away in our passion to drive our lessons home to our children. Instead of having empathy for our listeners and their needs, we're on a mission to make our points … at all costs.

At those times, whose needs are you trying to meet—yours or your kids'? Is finishing a lecture with a stunning climax more important than making certain your child truly understands? Are you just making a speech, or are you really trying to communicate?

Maybe you're great at communicating with your children. If you're not sure, slow down, back away from the microphone, and listen. If you do this, you'll be more successful making those profound points. Lighten up, and listen to what you're saying. Quit preaching, and get in touch. There's no doubt that your children will be delighted with this approach.

By the way, were those Peloponesian Wars in the third or fourth centuries? I got to bed a little late last night.

For your next devotional reading, go to page 1236.

Eutychus Raised From the Dead at Troas

⁷On the first day of the week we came together to break bread. Paul spoke to the people and, because he intended to leave the next day, kept on talking until midnight. **⁸**There were many lamps in the upstairs room where we were meeting. **⁹**Seated in a window was a young man named Eutychus, who was sinking into a deep sleep as Paul talked on and on. When he was sound asleep, he fell to the ground from the third story and was picked up dead. **¹⁰**Paul went down, threw himself on the young man and put his arms around him. "Don't be alarmed," he said. "He's alive!" **¹¹**Then he went upstairs again and broke bread and ate. After talking until daylight, he left. **¹²**The people took the young man home alive and were greatly comforted.

Paul's Farewell to the Ephesian Elders

¹³We went on ahead to the ship and sailed for Assos, where we were going to take Paul aboard. He had made this arrangement because he was going there on foot. **¹⁴**When he met us at Assos, we took him aboard and went on to Mitylene. **¹⁵**The next day we set sail from there and arrived off Kios. The day after that we crossed over to Samos, and on the following day arrived at Miletus. **¹⁶**Paul had decided to sail past Ephesus to avoid spending time in the province of Asia, for he was in a hurry to reach Jerusalem, if possible, by the day of Pentecost.

¹⁷From Miletus, Paul sent to Ephesus for the elders of the church. **¹⁸**When they arrived, he said to them: "You know how I lived the whole time I was with you, from the first day I came into the province of Asia. **¹⁹**I served the Lord with great humility and with tears, although I was severely tested by the plots of the Jews. **²⁰**You know that I have not hesitated to preach anything that would be helpful to you but have taught you publicly and from house to house. **²¹**I have declared to both Jews and Greeks that they must turn to God in repentance and have faith in our Lord Jesus.

²²"And now, compelled by the Spirit, I am going to Jerusalem, not knowing what will happen to me there. **²³**I only know that in every city the Holy Spirit warns me that prison and hardships are facing me. **²⁴**However, I consider my life worth nothing to me, if only I may finish the race and complete the task the Lord Jesus has given me—the task of testifying to the gospel of God's grace.

²⁵"Now I know that none of you among whom I have gone about preaching the kingdom will ever see me again. **²⁶**Therefore, I declare to you today that I am innocent of the blood of all men. **²⁷**For I have not hesitated to proclaim to you the whole will of God. **²⁸**Keep watch over yourselves and all the flock of which the Holy Spirit has made you overseers.ᵃ Be shepherds of the church of God,ᵇ which he bought with his own blood. **²⁹**I know that after I leave, savage wolves will come in among you and will not spare the flock. **³⁰**Even from your own number men will arise and distort the truth in order to draw away disciples after them. **³¹**So be on your guard! Remember that for three years I never stopped warning each of you night and day with tears.

³²"Now I commit you to God and to the word of his grace, which can build you up and give you an inheritance among all those who are sanctified. **³³**I have not coveted anyone's silver or gold or clothing. **³⁴**You yourselves know that these hands of mine have supplied my own needs and the needs of my companions. **³⁵**In everything I did, I showed you that by this kind of hard work we must help the weak, remembering the words the Lord Jesus himself said: 'It is more blessed to give than to receive.' "

³⁶When he had said this, he knelt down with all of them and prayed. **³⁷**They all wept as they embraced him and kissed him. **³⁸**What grieved them most was his statement that they would never see his face again. Then they accompanied him to the ship.

On to Jerusalem

21 After we had torn ourselves away from them, we put out to sea and sailed straight to Cos. The next day we went to Rhodes and from there to Patara. **²**We found a ship crossing over to Phoenicia, went on board and set sail. **³**After sighting Cyprus and passing to the south of it, we sailed on to Syria. We landed at Tyre, where our ship was to unload its cargo. **⁴**Finding the disciples there, we stayed with them seven days. Through the Spirit they urged Paul not to go on to Jerusalem. **⁵**But when our time was up, we left and

---

ᵃ28 Traditionally *bishops*   ᵇ28 Many manuscripts *of the Lord*

continued on our way. All the disciples and their wives and children accompanied us out of the city, and there on the beach we knelt to pray. [6]After saying good-by to each other, we went aboard the ship, and they returned home.

[7]We continued our voyage from Tyre and landed at Ptolemais, where we greeted the brothers and stayed with them for a day. [8]Leaving the next day, we reached Caesarea and stayed at the house of Philip the evangelist, one of the Seven. [9]He had four unmarried daughters who prophesied.

[10]After we had been there a number of days, a prophet named Agabus came down from Judea. [11]Coming over to us, he took Paul's belt, tied his own hands and feet with it and said, "The Holy Spirit says, 'In this way the Jews of Jerusalem will bind the owner of this belt and will hand him over to the Gentiles.'"

[12]When we heard this, we and the people there pleaded with Paul not to go up to Jerusalem. [13]Then Paul answered, "Why are you weeping and breaking my heart? I am ready not only to be bound, but also to die in Jerusalem for the name of the Lord Jesus." [14]When he would not be dissuaded, we gave up and said, "The Lord's will be done."

[15]After this, we got ready and went up to Jerusalem. [16]Some of the disciples from Caesarea accompanied us and brought us to the home of Mnason, where we were to stay. He was a man from Cyprus and one of the early disciples.

Paul's Arrival at Jerusalem

[17]When we arrived at Jerusalem, the brothers received us warmly. [18]The next day Paul and the rest of us went to see James, and all the elders were present. [19]Paul greeted them and reported in detail what God had done among the Gentiles through his ministry.

[20]When they heard this, they praised God. Then they said to Paul: "You see, brother, how many thousands of Jews have believed, and all of them are zealous for the law. [21]They have been informed that you teach all the Jews who live among the Gentiles to turn away from Moses, telling them not to circumcise their children or live according to our customs. [22]What shall we do? They will certainly hear that you have come, [23]so do what we tell you. There are four men with us who have made a vow. [24]Take these men, join in their purification rites and pay their expenses, so that they can have their heads shaved. Then everybody will know there is no truth in these reports about you, but that you yourself are living in obedience to the law. [25]As for the Gentile believers, we have written to them our decision that they should abstain from food sacrificed to idols, from blood, from the meat of strangled animals and from sexual immorality."

[26]The next day Paul took the men and purified himself along with them. Then he went to the temple to give notice of the date when the days of purification would end and the offering would be made for each of them.

Paul Arrested

[27]When the seven days were nearly over, some Jews from the province of Asia saw Paul at the temple. They stirred up the whole crowd and seized him, [28]shouting, "Men of Israel, help us! This is the man who teaches all men everywhere against our people and our law and this place. And besides, he has brought Greeks into the temple area and defiled this holy place." [29](They had previously seen Trophimus the Ephesian in the city with Paul and assumed that Paul had brought him into the temple area.)

[30]The whole city was aroused, and the people came running from all directions. Seizing Paul, they dragged him from the temple, and immediately the gates were shut. [31]While they were trying to kill him, news reached the commander of the Roman troops that the whole city of Jerusalem was in an uproar. [32]He at once took some officers and soldiers and ran down to the crowd. When the rioters saw the commander and his soldiers, they stopped beating Paul.

[33]The commander came up and arrested him and ordered him to be bound with two chains. Then he asked who he was and what he had done. [34]Some in the crowd shouted one thing and some another, and since the commander could not get at the truth because of the uproar, he ordered that Paul be taken into the barracks. [35]When Paul reached the steps, the violence of the mob was so great he had to be carried by the soldiers. [36]The crowd that followed kept shouting, "Away with him!"

Paul Speaks to the Crowd

[37]As the soldiers were about to take Paul into the barracks, he asked the

commander, "May I say something to you?"

"Do you speak Greek?" he replied. [38]"Aren't you the Egyptian who started a revolt and led four thousand terrorists out into the desert some time ago?"

[39]Paul answered, "I am a Jew, from Tarsus in Cilicia, a citizen of no ordinary city. Please let me speak to the people."

[40]Having received the commander's permission, Paul stood on the steps and motioned to the crowd. When they were all silent, he said to them in Aramaic[a]:

22

[1]"Brothers and fathers, listen now to my defense."

[2]When they heard him speak to them in Aramaic, they became very quiet.

Then Paul said: [3]"I am a Jew, born in Tarsus of Cilicia, but brought up in this city. Under Gamaliel I was thoroughly trained in the law of our fathers and was just as zealous for God as any of you are today. [4]I persecuted the followers of this Way to their death, arresting both men and women and throwing them into prison, [5]as also the high priest and all the Council can testify. I even obtained letters from them to their brothers in Damascus, and went there to bring these people as prisoners to Jerusalem to be punished.

[6]"About noon as I came near Damascus, suddenly a bright light from heaven flashed around me. [7]I fell to the ground and heard a voice say to me, 'Saul! Saul! Why do you persecute me?'

[8]" 'Who are you, Lord?' I asked.

" 'I am Jesus of Nazareth, whom you are persecuting,' he replied. [9]My companions saw the light, but they did not understand the voice of him who was speaking to me.

[10]" 'What shall I do, Lord?' I asked.

" 'Get up,' the Lord said, 'and go into Damascus. There you will be told all that you have been assigned to do.' [11]My companions led me by the hand into Damascus, because the brilliance of the light had blinded me.

[12]"A man named Ananias came to see me. He was a devout observer of the law and highly respected by all the Jews living there. [13]He stood beside me and said, 'Brother Saul, receive your sight!' And at that very moment I was able to see him.

[14]"Then he said: 'The God of our fathers has chosen you to know his will and to see the Righteous One and to hear words from his mouth. [15]You will be his witness to all men of what you have seen and heard. [16]And now what are you waiting for? Get up, be baptized and wash your sins away, calling on his name.'

[17]"When I returned to Jerusalem and was praying at the temple, I fell into a trance [18]and saw the Lord speaking. 'Quick!' he said to me. 'Leave Jerusalem immediately, because they will not accept your testimony about me.'

[19]" 'Lord,' I replied, 'these men know that I went from one synagogue to another to imprison and beat those who believe in you. [20]And when the blood of your martyr[b] Stephen was shed, I stood there giving my approval and guarding the clothes of those who were killing him.'

[21]"Then the Lord said to me, 'Go; I will send you far away to the Gentiles.' "

Paul the Roman Citizen

[22]The crowd listened to Paul until he said this. Then they raised their voices and shouted, "Rid the earth of him! He's not fit to live!"

[23]As they were shouting and throwing off their cloaks and flinging dust into the air, [24]the commander ordered Paul to be taken into the barracks. He directed that he be flogged and questioned in order to find out why the people were shouting at him like this. [25]As they stretched him out to flog him, Paul said to the centurion standing there, "Is it legal for you to flog a Roman citizen who hasn't even been found guilty?"

[26]When the centurion heard this, he went to the commander and reported it. "What are you going to do?" he asked. "This man is a Roman citizen."

[27]The commander went to Paul and asked, "Tell me, are you a Roman citizen?"

"Yes, I am," he answered.

[28]Then the commander said, "I had to pay a big price for my citizenship."

"But I was born a citizen," Paul replied.

[29]Those who were about to question him withdrew immediately. The commander himself was alarmed when he realized that he had put Paul, a Roman citizen, in chains.

Before the Sanhedrin

[30]The next day, since the commander wanted to find out exactly why Paul was being accused by the Jews, he released him and ordered the chief priests and all the Sanhedrin to assemble. Then he

[a]40 Or possibly Hebrew; also in 22:2   [b]20 Or witness

brought Paul and had him stand before them.

23 Paul looked straight at the Sanhedrin and said, "My brothers, I have fulfilled my duty to God in all good conscience to this day." ²At this the high priest Ananias ordered those standing near Paul to strike him on the mouth. ³Then Paul said to him, "God will strike you, you whitewashed wall! You sit there to judge me according to the law, yet you yourself violate the law by commanding that I be struck!"

⁴Those who were standing near Paul said, "You dare to insult God's high priest?"

⁵Paul replied, "Brothers, I did not realize that he was the high priest; for it is written: 'Do not speak evil about the ruler of your people.'ᵃ"

⁶Then Paul, knowing that some of them were Sadducees and the others Pharisees, called out in the Sanhedrin, "My brothers, I am a Pharisee, the son of a Pharisee. I stand on trial because of my hope in the resurrection of the dead." ⁷When he said this, a dispute broke out between the Pharisees and the Sadducees, and the assembly was divided. ⁸(The Sadducees say that there is no resurrection, and that there are neither angels nor spirits, but the Pharisees acknowledge them all.)

⁹There was a great uproar, and some of the teachers of the law who were Pharisees stood up and argued vigorously. "We find nothing wrong with this man," they said. "What if a spirit or an angel has spoken to him?" ¹⁰The dispute became so violent that the commander was afraid Paul would be torn to pieces by them. He ordered the troops to go down and take him away from them by force and bring him into the barracks.

¹¹The following night the Lord stood near Paul and said, "Take courage! As you have testified about me in Jerusalem, so you must also testify in Rome."

The Plot to Kill Paul

¹²The next morning the Jews formed a conspiracy and bound themselves with an oath not to eat or drink until they had killed Paul. ¹³More than forty men were involved in this plot. ¹⁴They went to the chief priests and elders and said, "We have taken a solemn oath not to eat anything until we have killed Paul. ¹⁵Now then, you and the Sanhedrin petition the commander to bring him before you on the pretext of wanting more accurate information about his case. We are ready to kill him before he gets here."

¹⁶But when the son of Paul's sister heard of this plot, he went into the barracks and told Paul.

¹⁷Then Paul called one of the centurions and said, "Take this young man to the commander; he has something to tell him." ¹⁸So he took him to the commander.

The centurion said, "Paul, the prisoner, sent for me and asked me to bring this young man to you because he has something to tell you."

¹⁹The commander took the young man by the hand, drew him aside and asked, "What is it you want to tell me?"

²⁰He said: "The Jews have agreed to ask you to bring Paul before the Sanhedrin tomorrow on the pretext of wanting more accurate information about him. ²¹Don't give in to them, because more than forty of them are waiting in ambush for him. They have taken an oath not to eat or drink until they have killed him. They are ready now, waiting for your consent to their request."

²²The commander dismissed the young man and cautioned him, "Don't tell anyone that you have reported this to me."

Paul Transferred to Caesarea

²³Then he called two of his centurions and ordered them, "Get ready a detachment of two hundred soldiers, seventy horsemen and two hundred spearmenᵇ to go to Caesarea at nine tonight. ²⁴Provide mounts for Paul so that he may be taken safely to Governor Felix."

²⁵He wrote a letter as follows:

²⁶Claudius Lysias,

To His Excellency, Governor Felix:

Greetings.

²⁷This man was seized by the Jews and they were about to kill him, but I came with my troops and rescued him, for I had learned that he is a Roman citizen. ²⁸I wanted to know why they were accusing him, so I brought him to their Sanhedrin. ²⁹I found that the accusation had to do with questions about their law, but there was no charge against him that deserved death or imprisonment. ³⁰When I

ᵃ5 Exodus 22:28   ᵇ23 The meaning of the Greek for this word is uncertain.

was informed of a plot to be carried out against the man, I sent him to you at once. I also ordered his accusers to present to you their case against him.

31So the soldiers, carrying out their orders, took Paul with them during the night and brought him as far as Antipatris. 32The next day they let the cavalry go on with him, while they returned to the barracks. 33When the cavalry arrived in Caesarea, they delivered the letter to the governor and handed Paul over to him. 34The governor read the letter and asked what province he was from. 35he said, "I will hear your case when your accusers get here." Then he ordered that Paul be kept under guard in Herod's palace.

The Trial Before Felix

24 Five days later the high priest Ananias went down to Caesarea with some of the elders and a lawyer named Tertullus, and they brought their charges against Paul before the governor. 2When Paul was called in, Tertullus presented his case before Felix: "We have enjoyed a long period of peace under you, and your foresight has brought about reforms in this nation. 3Everywhere and in every way, most excellent Felix, we acknowledge this with profound gratitude. 4But in order not to weary you further, I would request that you be kind enough to hear us briefly.

5"We have found this man to be a troublemaker, stirring up riots among the Jews all over the world. He is a ringleader of the Nazarene sect 6and even tried to desecrate the temple; so we seized him. 8Bya examining him yourself you will be able to learn the truth about all these charges we are bringing against him."

9The Jews joined in the accusation, asserting that these things were true.

10When the governor motioned for him to speak, Paul replied: "I know that for a number of years you have been a judge over this nation; so I gladly make my defense. 11You can easily verify that no more than twelve days ago I went up to Jerusalem to worship. 12My accusers did not find me arguing with anyone at the temple, or stirring up a crowd in the synagogues or anywhere else in the city. 13And they cannot prove to you the charges they are now making against me. 14However, I admit that I worship the God of our fathers as a

follower of the Way, which they call a sect. I believe everything that agrees with the Law and that is written in the Prophets, 15and I have the same hope in God as these men, that there will be a resurrection of both the righteous and the wicked. 16So I strive always to keep my conscience clear before God and man.

17"After an absence of several years, I came to Jerusalem to bring my people gifts for the poor and to present offerings. 18I was ceremonially clean when they found me in the temple courts doing this. There was no crowd with me, nor was I involved in any disturbance. 19But there are some Jews from the province of Asia, who ought to be here before you and bring charges if they have anything against me. 20Or these who are here should state what crime they found in me when I stood before the Sanhedrin— 21unless it was this one thing I shouted as I stood in their presence: 'It is concerning the resurrection of the dead that I am on trial before you today.' "

22Then Felix, who was well acquainted with the Way, adjourned the proceedings. "When Lysias the commander comes," he said, "I will decide your case." 23He ordered the centurion to keep Paul under guard but to give him some freedom and permit his friends to take care of his needs.

24Several days later Felix came with his wife Drusilla, who was a Jewess. He sent for Paul and listened to him as he spoke about faith in Christ Jesus. 25As Paul discoursed on righteousness, self-control and the judgment to come, Felix was afraid and said, "That's enough for now! You may leave. When I find it convenient, I will send for you." 26At the same time he was hoping that Paul would offer him a bribe, so he sent for him frequently and talked with him.

27When two years had passed, Felix was succeeded by Porcius Festus, but because Felix wanted to grant a favor to the Jews, he left Paul in prison.

The Trial Before Festus

25 Three days after arriving in the province, Festus went up from Caesarea to Jerusalem, 2where the chief priests and

---

a6-8 Some manuscripts him and wanted to judge him according to our law. 7But the commander, Lysias, came and with the use of much force snatched him from our hands 8and ordered his accusers to come before you. By

Jewish leaders appeared before him and presented the charges against Paul. ³They urgently requested Festus, as a favor to them, to have Paul transferred to Jerusalem, for they were preparing an ambush to kill him along the way. ⁴Festus answered, "Paul is being held at Caesarea, and I myself am going there soon. ⁵Let some of your leaders come with me and press charges against the man there, if he has done anything wrong."

⁶After spending eight or ten days with them, he went down to Caesarea, and the next day he convened the court and or-

dered that Paul be brought before him. ⁷When Paul appeared, the Jews who had come down from Jerusalem stood around him, bringing many serious charges against him, which they could not prove.

⁸Then Paul made his defense: "I have done nothing wrong against the law of the Jews or against the temple or against Caesar."

⁹Festus, wishing to do the Jews a favor, said to Paul, "Are you willing to go up to Jerusalem and stand trial before me there on these charges?"

¹⁰Paul answered: "I am now standing

The Luxury of a Clear Conscience

"All I can do is all I can do," I said, making a sincere and valiant attempt not to be disrespectful. "You know how hard I work—how committed I am to my very best efforts here." I took a deep breath, thinking it might be my last gulp of clean air in this particular job. "And all I can do ought to be enough for you."

Did I mention that this speech was presented to my boss, the Executive Vice President of the corporation? Over the years, I haven't done this kind of thing very often. But because he was a man who encouraged candor among his direct reports, and because he believed in me, he didn't tell me to clean out my desk or spruce up my résumé! I kept my job that day.

"I strive always to keep my conscience clear before God and man," the apostle Paul declared in an extremely volatile setting (v. 16). Imagine the courage, confidence and self-assurance it took to say such a thing in the face of one's accusers. But regardless of the possible consequences, this is exactly what he said.

What does it mean to have a clear conscience? It means that you can say with a straight face, "I have done everything I can do. There are no sins to confess. No stones left to turn. Look wherever you want, but there will be no surprises."

We are living in a time when men are quietly scrambling to hide from their pasts.

DAILY INSIGHT

FRIDAY

Passage:
Acts 24:10–16

Verse:
Acts 24:16

Senate committee hearings and disclosures from "sources close to the situation" bring us predictable fare. Every day we hear of yet another man whose treacherous history is brought into the light of day; the evening news is filled with alibis and meticulously worded responses.

Where are the Pauls? Where are the leaders who have truly lived and worked with integrity? Where are the men—anywhere, in any walk of life—who live with clear consciences?

And how is it with you and me? Have we told and confessed all? Do we live our lives just one small step ahead of the truth of our past, or do we rest because we've withheld no secrets?

The implications of this message could be incredibly important. It may mean that before the sun has set on this day, you must hold a meeting or place a phone call. You may have some confessions to submit ... a record to clear up. And because of these disclosures, there could be consequences. But my guess is that Paul would promise us that a soul vindicated from full disclosure is well worth any price we may have to pay.

All you can do is all you can do. All you can say is all you can say. Just be certain that you've done and said everything you *can* do and say. Regardless of the cost, it'll be worth it.

For your next devotional reading, go to page 1239.

before Caesar's court, where I ought to be tried. I have not done any wrong to the Jews, as you yourself know very well. ¹¹If, however, I am guilty of doing anything deserving death, I do not refuse to die. But if the charges brought against me by these Jews are not true, no one has the right to hand me over to them. I appeal to Caesar!"

¹²After Festus had conferred with his council, he declared: "You have appealed to Caesar. To Caesar you will go!"

Festus Consults King Agrippa

¹³A few days later King Agrippa and Bernice arrived at Caesarea to pay their respects to Festus. ¹⁴Since they were spending many days there, Festus discussed Paul's case with the king. He said: "There is a man here whom Felix left as a prisoner. ¹⁵When I went to Jerusalem, the chief priests and elders of the Jews brought charges against him and asked that he be condemned.

¹⁶"I told them that it is not the Roman custom to hand over any man before he has faced his accusers and has had an opportunity to defend himself against their charges. ¹⁷When they came here with me, I did not delay the case, but convened the court the next day and ordered the man to be brought in. ¹⁸When his accusers got up to speak, they did not charge him with any of the crimes I had expected. ¹⁹Instead, they had some points of dispute with him about their own religion and about a dead man named Jesus who Paul claimed was alive. ²⁰I was at a loss how to investigate such matters; so I asked if he would be willing to go to Jerusalem and stand trial there on these charges. ²¹When Paul made his appeal to be held over for the Emperor's decision, I ordered him held until I could send him to Caesar."

²²Then Agrippa said to Festus, "I would like to hear this man myself."

He replied, "Tomorrow you will hear him."

Paul Before Agrippa

²³The next day Agrippa and Bernice came with great pomp and entered the audience room with the high ranking officers and the leading men of the city. At the command of Festus, Paul was brought in. ²⁴Festus said: "King Agrippa, and all who are present with us, you see this man! The whole Jewish community has peti-tioned me about him in Jerusalem and here in Caesarea, shouting that he ought not to live any longer. ²⁵I found he had done nothing deserving of death, but because he made his appeal to the Emperor I decided to send him to Rome. ²⁶But I have nothing definite to write to His Majesty about him. Therefore I have brought him before all of you, and especially before you, King Agrippa, so that as a result of this investigation I may have something to write. ²⁷For I think it is unreasonable to send on a prisoner without specifying the charges against him."

26 Then Agrippa said to Paul, "You have permission to speak for yourself."

So Paul motioned with his hand and began his defense: ²"King Agrippa, I consider myself fortunate to stand before you today as I make my defense against all the accusations of the Jews, ³and especially so because you are well acquainted with all the Jewish customs and controversies. Therefore, I beg you to listen to me patiently.

⁴"The Jews all know the way I have lived ever since I was a child, from the beginning of my life in my own country, and also in Jerusalem. ⁵They have known me for a long time and can testify, if they are willing, that according to the strictest sect of our religion, I lived as a Pharisee. ⁶And now it is because of my hope in what God has promised our fathers that I am on trial today. ⁷This is the promise our twelve tribes are hoping to see fulfilled as they earnestly serve God day and night. O king, it is because of this hope that the Jews are accusing me. ⁸Why should any of you consider it incredible that God raises the dead?

⁹"I too was convinced that I ought to do all that was possible to oppose the name of Jesus of Nazareth. ¹⁰And that is just what I did in Jerusalem. On the authority of the chief priests I put many of the saints in prison, and when they were put to death, I cast my vote against them. ¹¹Many a time I went from one synagogue to another to have them punished, and I tried to force them to blaspheme. In my obsession against them, I even went to foreign cities to persecute them.

¹²"On one of these journeys I was going to Damascus with the authority and commission of the chief priests. ¹³About noon, O king, as I was on the road, I saw a light from heaven, brighter than the sun, blazing around me and my companions. ¹⁴We all fell to the ground, and I heard a voice

saying to me in Aramaic,[a] 'Saul, Saul, why do you persecute me? It is hard for you to kick against the goads.'

[15]"Then I asked, 'Who are you, Lord?'

" 'I am Jesus, whom you are persecuting,' the Lord replied. [16]'Now get up and stand on your feet. I have appeared to you to appoint you as a servant and as a witness of what you have seen of me and what I will show you. [17]I will rescue you from your own people and from the Gentiles. I am sending you to them [18]to open their eyes and turn them from darkness to light, and from the power of Satan to God, so that they may receive forgiveness of sins and a place among those who are sanctified by faith in me.'

[19]"So then, King Agrippa, I was not disobedient to the vision from heaven. [20]First to those in Damascus, then to those in Jerusalem and in all Judea, and to the Gentiles also, I preached that they should repent and turn to God and prove their repentance by their deeds. [21]That is why the Jews seized me in the temple courts and tried to kill me. [22]But I have had God's help to this very day, and so I stand here and testify to small and great alike. I am saying nothing beyond what the prophets and Moses said would happen— [23]that the Christ[b] would suffer and, as the first to rise from the dead, would proclaim light to his own people and to the Gentiles."

[24]At this point Festus interrupted Paul's defense. "You are out of your mind, Paul!" he shouted. "Your great learning is driving you insane."

[25]"I am not insane, most excellent Festus," Paul replied. "What I am saying is true and reasonable. [26]The king is familiar with these things, and I can speak freely to him. I am convinced that none of this has escaped his notice, because it was not done in a corner. [27]King Agrippa, do you believe the prophets? I know you do."

[28]Then Agrippa said to Paul, "Do you think that in such a short time you can persuade me to be a Christian?"

[29]Paul replied, "Short time or long—I pray God that not only you but all who are listening to me today may become what I am, except for these chains."

[30]The king rose, and with him the governor and Bernice and those sitting with them. [31]They left the room, and while talking with one another, they said, "This man is not doing anything that deserves death or imprisonment."

[32]Agrippa said to Festus, "This man could have been set free if he had not appealed to Caesar."

Paul Sails for Rome

27 When it was decided that we would sail for Italy, Paul and some other prisoners were handed over to a centurion named Julius, who belonged to the Imperial Regiment. [2]We boarded a ship from Adramyttium about to sail for ports along the coast of the province of Asia, and we put out to sea. Aristarchus, a Macedonian from Thessalonica, was with us.

[3]The next day we landed at Sidon; and Julius, in kindness to Paul, allowed him to go to his friends so they might provide for his needs. [4]From there we put out to sea again and passed to the lee of Cyprus because the winds were against us. [5]When we had sailed across the open sea off the coast of Cilicia and Pamphylia, we landed at Myra in Lycia. [6]There the centurion found an Alexandrian ship sailing for Italy and put us on board. [7]We made slow headway for many days and had difficulty arriving off Cnidus. When the wind did not allow us to hold our course, we sailed to the lee of Crete, opposite Salmone. [8]We moved along the coast with difficulty and came to a place called Fair Havens, near the town of Lasea.

[9]Much time had been lost, and sailing had already become dangerous because by now it was after the Fast.[c] So Paul warned them, [10]"Men, I can see that our voyage is going to be disastrous and bring great loss to ship and cargo, and to our own lives also." [11]But the centurion, instead of listening to what Paul said, followed the advice of the pilot and of the owner of the ship. [12]Since the harbor was unsuitable to winter in, the majority decided that we should sail on, hoping to reach Phoenix and winter there. This was a harbor in Crete, facing both southwest and northwest.

The Storm

[13]When a gentle south wind began to blow, they thought they had obtained what they wanted; so they weighed anchor and sailed along the shore of Crete. [14]Before very long, a wind of hurricane force, called the "northeaster," swept down from the island. [15]The ship was caught by the storm and could not head

[a]14 Or *Hebrew*   [b]23 Or *Messiah*   [c]9 That is, the Day of Atonement (Yom Kippur)

Paul and Dad, God's Trusty Messengers

Key Verse: *"So keep up your courage . . . for I have faith in God that it will happen just as he told me."* Acts 27:25
Text: Acts 27:13–25 *(Dad or child reads the text.)*

DAD READS: Most people know about Jonah and the great fish; most also know about Noah and the flood. But lots of people don't know much about this other exciting sea story from the Bible. It's the story about how the apostle Paul almost lost his life when a ship he was on ran into a storm.

Child reads: You're right, I don't know much about this story either. But we can learn some important lessons from what we read about Paul and his experience on a boat. Maybe the most wonderful thing we learn from this story is how God saved 276 people's lives, even though they were on this broken boat for over two weeks after the terrible storm.

DAD READS: What a miracle that no one was drowned in the accident! They all made it to shore safely. But this did not come as a surprise to Paul. Today's key verse tells us that God's angel had spoken to Paul and commanded him saying, "Do not be afraid." Sometimes God speaks to a group (like a family) by speaking to one person (like a dad or a mom), and asking that person to tell the others.

Child reads: Because you are the dad in our family and because we trust you to listen to God speak and obey his voice, sometimes our family counts on you in the same way that these frightened people counted on Paul. I know that being God's messenger can be a lonely job, but sometimes our family needs you to be our "Paul."

DAD READS: Sometimes when families are facing the future and

QUIET **TIMES** WITH **Dad**

they don't know what is going to happen, they feel afraid. A dad must be a good listener. He needs to know how his family is feeling so he will know how to comfort and reassure them.

Child reads: Thank you for listening to God's voice. Thank you, too, for listening to the things our family needs. And thanks for being a dad who is willing to encourage and direct our family.

DAD READS: You're welcome. But this job would be impossible if I had to do it without God's direction. So I'm thankful to God for his direction in my life first. Paul and the others on the ship were in serious trouble, and they were very afraid. This moment called for someone to be the leader, and God chose Paul. When I hear God's voice and I know that he has a message for our family, I will be obedient, just like Paul.

Child reads: I am so glad that I have a dad like you. Let me pray this prayer with you:

Our Father in heaven, we love you. Thank you for my dad. Thank you that he wants to listen to your voice and that he wants to obey you. Help my dad to be brave, and help me to be brave, too. We love you, and we thank you for your love. In Jesus' name, **Amen.**

For your next devotional reading, go to page 1243.

into the wind; so we gave way to it and were driven along. ¹⁶As we passed to the lee of a small island called Cauda, we were hardly able to make the lifeboat secure. ¹⁷When the men had hoisted it aboard, they passed ropes under the ship itself to hold it together. Fearing that they would run aground on the sandbars of Syrtis, they lowered the sea anchor and let the ship be driven along. ¹⁸We took such a violent battering from the storm that the next day they began to throw the cargo overboard. ¹⁹On the third day, they threw the ship's tackle overboard with their own hands. ²⁰When neither sun nor stars appeared for many days and the storm continued raging, we finally gave up all hope of being saved.

²¹After the men had gone a long time without food, Paul stood up before them and said: "Men, you should have taken my advice not to sail from Crete; then you would have spared yourselves this damage and loss. ²²But now I urge you to keep up your courage, because not one of you will be lost; only the ship will be destroyed. ²³Last night an angel of the God whose I am and whom I serve stood beside me ²⁴and said, 'Do not be afraid, Paul. You must stand trial before Caesar; and God has graciously given you the lives of all who sail with you.' ²⁵So keep up your courage, men, for I have faith in God that it will happen just as he told me. ²⁶Nevertheless, we must run aground on some island."

The Shipwreck

²⁷On the fourteenth night we were still being driven across the Adriatic[a] Sea, when about midnight the sailors sensed they were approaching land. ²⁸They took soundings and found that the water was a hundred and twenty feet[b] deep. A short time later they took soundings again and found it was ninety feet[c] deep. ²⁹Fearing that we would be dashed against the rocks, they dropped four anchors from the stern and prayed for daylight. ³⁰In an attempt to escape from the ship, the sailors let the lifeboat down into the sea, pretending they were going to lower some anchors from the bow. ³¹Then Paul said to the centurion and the soldiers, "Unless these men stay with the ship, you cannot be saved." ³²So the soldiers cut the ropes that held the lifeboat and let it fall away.

³³Just before dawn Paul urged them all to eat. "For the last fourteen days," he said, "you have been in constant suspense and have gone without food—you haven't eaten anything. ³⁴Now I urge you to take some food. You need it to survive. Not one of you will lose a single hair from his head." ³⁵After he said this, he took some bread and gave thanks to God in front of them all. Then he broke it and began to eat. ³⁶They were all encouraged and ate some food themselves. ³⁷Altogether there were 276 of us on board. ³⁸When they had eaten as much as they wanted, they lightened the ship by throwing the grain into the sea.

³⁹When daylight came, they did not recognize the land, but they saw a bay with a sandy beach, where they decided to run the ship aground if they could. ⁴⁰Cutting loose the anchors, they left them in the sea and at the same time untied the ropes that held the rudders. Then they hoisted the foresail to the wind and made for the beach. ⁴¹But the ship struck a sandbar and ran aground. The bow stuck fast and would not move, and the stern was broken to pieces by the pounding of the surf.

⁴²The soldiers planned to kill the prisoners to prevent any of them from swimming away and escaping. ⁴³But the centurion wanted to spare Paul's life and kept them from carrying out their plan. He ordered those who could swim to jump overboard first and get to land. ⁴⁴The rest were to get there on planks or on pieces of the ship. In this way everyone reached land in safety.

Ashore on Malta

28 Once safely on shore, we found out that the island was called Malta. ²The islanders showed us unusual kindness. They built a fire and welcomed us all because it was raining and cold. ³Paul gathered a pile of brushwood and, as he put it on the fire, a viper, driven out by the heat, fastened itself on his hand. ⁴When the islanders saw the snake hanging from his hand, they said to each other, "This man must be a murderer; for though he escaped from the sea, Justice has not allowed him to live." ⁵But Paul shook the snake off into the fire and suffered no ill effects. ⁶The people expected him to swell up or suddenly fall dead, but after waiting a long time and seeing nothing unusual

---

[a]27 In ancient times the name referred to an area extending well south of Italy.   [b]28 Greek *twenty orguias* (about 37 meters)   [c]28 Greek *fifteen orguias* (about 27 meters)

happen to him, they changed their minds and said he was a god.

⁷There was an estate nearby that belonged to Publius, the chief official of the island. He welcomed us to his home and for three days entertained us hospitably. ⁸His father was sick in bed, suffering from fever and dysentery. Paul went in to see him and, after prayer, placed his hands on him and healed him. ⁹When this had happened, the rest of the sick on the island came and were cured. ¹⁰They honored us in many ways and when we were ready to sail, they furnished us with the supplies we needed.

Arrival at Rome

¹¹After three months we put out to sea in a ship that had wintered in the island. It was an Alexandrian ship with the figurehead of the twin gods Castor and Pollux. ¹²We put in at Syracuse and stayed there three days. ¹³From there we set sail and arrived at Rhegium. The next day the south wind came up, and on the following day we reached Puteoli. ¹⁴There we found some brothers who invited us to spend a week with them. And so we came to Rome. ¹⁵The brothers there had heard that we were coming, and they traveled as far as the Forum of Appius and the Three Taverns to meet us. At the sight of these men Paul thanked God and was encouraged. ¹⁶When we got to Rome, Paul was allowed to live by himself, with a soldier to guard him.

Paul Preaches at Rome Under Guard

¹⁷Three days later he called together the leaders of the Jews. When they had assembled, Paul said to them: "My brothers, although I have done nothing against our people or against the customs of our ancestors, I was arrested in Jerusalem and handed over to the Romans. ¹⁸They examined me and wanted to release me, because I was not guilty of any crime deserving death. ¹⁹But when the Jews objected, I was compelled to appeal to Caesar—not that I had any charge to bring against my own people. ²⁰For this reason I have asked to see you and talk with you. It is because of the hope of Israel that I am bound with this chain."

²¹They replied, "We have not received any letters from Judea concerning you, and none of the brothers who have come from there has reported or said anything bad about you. ²²But we want to hear what your views are, for we know that people everywhere are talking against this sect."

²³They arranged to meet Paul on a certain day, and came in even larger numbers to the place where he was staying. From morning till evening he explained and declared to them the kingdom of God and tried to convince them about Jesus from the Law of Moses and from the Prophets. ²⁴Some were convinced by what he said, but others would not believe. ²⁵They disagreed among themselves and began to leave after Paul had made this final statement: "The Holy Spirit spoke the truth to your forefathers when he said through Isaiah the prophet:

²⁶ " 'Go to this people and say,
  "You will be ever hearing but never
        understanding;
    you will be ever seeing but never
        perceiving."
²⁷ For this people's heart has become
        calloused;
    they hardly hear with their ears,
    and they have closed their eyes.
  Otherwise they might see with their
        eyes,
    hear with their ears,
    understand with their hearts
  and turn, and I would heal them.'ᵃ

²⁸"Therefore I want you to know that God's salvation has been sent to the Gentiles, and they will listen!"ᵇ

³⁰For two whole years Paul stayed there in his own rented house and welcomed all who came to see him. ³¹Boldly and without hindrance he preached the kingdom of God and taught about the Lord Jesus Christ.

ᵃ27 Isaiah 6:9,10   ᵇ28 Some manuscripts listen!"
²⁹After he said this, the Jews left, arguing vigorously among themselves.

When you buy a new car, the salesperson at the dealership sits down with you to review the manual of operation. He or she thumbs through it, showing you each section: engine maintenance, options packages, safety tips, and more. Then he or she encourages you to take the book home and read it from cover to cover. Some automobile manufacturers even require buyers to sign a statement warranting that the salesperson "has shown them the manual and has encouraged them to read it thoroughly." These folks are serious. Of course, most men sign the statement, then slide the manual into the glove compartment and never, ever look at it again.

But what if, instead of the owner's manual being compiled by the manufacturer, it was written by a user . . . someone who would talk about what it was actually like to own and use this car? The book of Romans is a user's guide to the Christian faith that was inspired by the Manufacturer, but written by a user. Whatever you do, don't let this one stay in the glove box.

Romans

1 Paul, a servant of Christ Jesus, called to be an apostle and set apart for the gospel of God— [2]the gospel he promised beforehand through his prophets in the Holy Scriptures [3]regarding his Son, who as to his human nature was a descendant of David, [4]and who through the Spirit[a] of holiness was declared with power to be the Son of God[b] by his resurrection from the dead: Jesus Christ our Lord. [5]Through him and for his name's sake, we received grace and apostleship to call people from among all the Gentiles to the obedience that comes from faith. [6]And you also are among those who are called to belong to Jesus Christ.

[7]To all in Rome who are loved by God and called to be saints:

Grace and peace to you from God our Father and from the Lord Jesus Christ.

Paul's Longing to Visit Rome

[8]First, I thank my God through Jesus Christ for all of you, because your faith is being reported all over the world. [9]God, whom I serve with my whole heart in preaching the gospel of his Son, is my witness how constantly I remember you [10]in my prayers at all times; and I pray that now at last by God's will the way may be opened for me to come to you.

[11]I long to see you so that I may impart to you some spiritual gift to make you

[a]4 Or *who as to his spirit* [b]4 Or *was appointed to be the Son of God with power*

strong— [12]that is, that you and I may be mutually encouraged by each other's faith. [13]I do not want you to be unaware, brothers, that I planned many times to come to you (but have been prevented from doing so until now) in order that I might have a harvest among you, just as I have had among the other Gentiles.

[14]I am obligated both to Greeks and non-Greeks, both to the wise and the foolish. [15]That is why I am so eager to preach the gospel also to you who are at Rome.

[16]I am not ashamed of the gospel, because it is the power of God for the salvation of everyone who believes: first for the Jew, then for the Gentile. [17]For in the gospel a righteousness from God is revealed, a righteousness that is by faith from first to last,[a] just as it is written: "The righteous will live by faith."[b]

[a]17 Or *is from faith to faith*   [b]17 Hab. 2:4

Hang On, Bill. Please Don't Let Go.

DAILY INSIGHT

MONDAY

Passage:
Romans 1:18–24

Verse:
Romans 1:18

Whitewater rafting wasn't something I had ever wanted to do. As wimpy as this may sound to you, it looked very dangerous. But, in the spring of 1974, twenty high-schoolers and four adults (and I use that term loosely in this case) set out for the Green River, Utah's most notorious killer.

Once we got to the river and I saw the size of the two rafts, I felt a little better. The big raft was twenty-eight feet long and carried all the gear as well as most of the riders. The second raft was sixteen feet long and was clearly for the more daring of the company. I rode on the big one—cowards prefer either large or extra large.

By the time we were into our third day, I was gaining confidence. So on this day, I agreed to ride in the smaller raft. *What could possibly go wrong?* I mused. Unbeknownst to me, this was the day for "Dead Man's Curve."

By mid-morning, the river was swift and restless; it almost seemed angry. My heart was racing right along with the current when I asked, "Does anyone know the bus schedule out here?" No one responded. Paddling for your life has a way of keeping you focused.

When our raft hit the first "hole" created by the combination of the rushing water and large rocks beneath the surface, I started to holler. It was like being on a roller coaster without the track. When we hit the second hole, Bill Jackson—a tough, all-state linebacker—got flicked off the front of the raft like a fly. He traveled the length of the raft in the air, then crashed into the whitewater directly behind the boat where I was having my devotions.

I reached out as far as I could and, miraculously, grabbed Bill's hand. For two or three more raging minutes, we did business with "Dead Man's Curve." And during every second, I screamed at the top of my lungs, "Hang on! Hang on! Please hang on, Bill. Don't let go!"

For centuries, people have painted, written and preached about what God's wrath might actually look like. Many believe that God's way of dealing with mankind's rebellion is to do something drastic—sending fire from heaven or some other disaster. But the apostle Paul gives us an absolutely spell-binding look at the truth. When God is finally fed up with man's defiant rebellion, he does the most painful and vicious thing he can do.

He lets go.

Paul says that God "gives [us] over." And when he does, we find ourselves tumbling through the rapids, completely unprotected by the safety of our vessel. This horrific solo voyage spells certain death.

The prayer we should have memorized when we were kids, right along with "Now I lay me down to sleep," was this one: "Dear God, don't let go. Don't let go. Please God, don't let go."

Bill didn't let go and, happily, we both survived "Dead Man's Curve." So much for male bonding.

For your next devotional reading, go to page 1246.

God's Wrath Against Mankind

[18]The wrath of God is being revealed from heaven against all the godlessness and wickedness of men who suppress the truth by their wickedness, [19]since what may be known about God is plain to them, because God has made it plain to them. [20]For since the creation of the world God's invisible qualities—his eternal power and divine nature—have been clearly seen, being understood from what has been made, so that men are without excuse.

[21]For although they knew God, they neither glorified him as God nor gave thanks to him, but their thinking became futile and their foolish hearts were darkened. [22]Although they claimed to be wise, they became fools [23]and exchanged the glory of the immortal God for images made to look like mortal man and birds and animals and reptiles.

[24]Therefore God gave them over in the sinful desires of their hearts to sexual impurity for the degrading of their bodies with one another. [25]They exchanged the truth of God for a lie, and worshiped and served created things rather than the Creator—who is forever praised. Amen.

[26]Because of this, God gave them over to shameful lusts. Even their women exchanged natural relations for unnatural ones. [27]In the same way the men also abandoned natural relations with women and were inflamed with lust for one another. Men committed indecent acts with other men, and received in themselves the due penalty for their perversion.

[28]Furthermore, since they did not think it worthwhile to retain the knowledge of God, he gave them over to a depraved mind, to do what ought not to be done. [29]They have become filled with every kind of wickedness, evil, greed and depravity. They are full of envy, murder, strife, deceit and malice. They are gossips, [30]slanderers, God-haters, insolent, arrogant and boastful; they invent ways of doing evil; they disobey their parents; [31]they are senseless, faithless, heartless, ruthless. [32]Although they know God's righteous decree that those who do such things deserve death, they not only continue to do these very things but also approve of those who practice them.

God's Righteous Judgment

2 You, therefore, have no excuse, you who pass judgment on someone else, for at whatever point you judge the other, you are condemning yourself, because you who pass judgment do the same things. [2]Now we know that God's judgment against those who do such things is based on truth. [3]So when you, a mere man, pass judgment on them and yet do the same things, do you think you will escape God's judgment? [4]Or do you show contempt for the riches of his kindness, tolerance and patience, not realizing that God's kindness leads you toward repentance?

[5]But because of your stubbornness and your unrepentant heart, you are storing up wrath against yourself for the day of God's wrath, when his righteous judgment will be revealed. [6]God "will give to each person according to what he has done."[a] [7]To those who by persistence in doing good seek glory, honor and immortality, he will give eternal life. [8]But for those who are self-seeking and who reject the truth and follow evil, there will be wrath and anger. [9]There will be trouble and distress for every human being who does evil: first for the Jew, then for the Gentile; [10]but glory, honor and peace for everyone who does good: first for the Jew, then for the Gentile. [11]For God does not show favoritism.

[12]All who sin apart from the law will also perish apart from the law, and all who sin under the law will be judged by the law. [13]For it is not those who hear the law who are righteous in God's sight, but it is those who obey the law who will be declared righteous. [14](Indeed, when Gentiles, who do not have the law, do by nature things required by the law, they are a law for themselves, even though they do not have the law, [15]since they show that the requirements of the law are written on their hearts, their consciences also bearing witness, and their thoughts now accusing, now even defending them.) [16]This will take place on the day when God will judge men's secrets through Jesus Christ, as my gospel declares.

The Jews and the Law

[17]Now you, if you call yourself a Jew; if you rely on the law and brag about your relationship to God; [18]if you know his will and approve of what is superior because you are instructed by the law; [19]if you are convinced that you are a guide for the

[a]6 Psalm 62:12; Prov. 24:12

blind, a light for those who are in the dark, [20]an instructor of the foolish, a teacher of infants, because you have in the law the embodiment of knowledge and truth— [21]you, then, who teach others, do you not teach yourself? You who preach against stealing, do you steal? [22]You who say that people should not commit adultery, do you commit adultery? You who abhor idols, do you rob temples? [23]You who brag about the law, do you dishonor God by breaking the law? [24]As it is written: "God's name is blasphemed among the Gentiles because of you."[a]

[25]Circumcision has value if you observe the law, but if you break the law, you have become as though you had not been circumcised. [26]If those who are not circumcised keep the law's requirements, will they not be regarded as though they were circumcised? [27]The one who is not circumcised physically and yet obeys the law will condemn you who, even though you have the[b] written code and circumcision, are a lawbreaker.

[28]A man is not a Jew if he is only one outwardly, nor is circumcision merely outward and physical. [29]No, a man is a Jew if he is one inwardly; and circumcision is circumcision of the heart, by the Spirit, not by the written code. Such a man's praise is not from men, but from God.

God's Faithfulness

3 What advantage, then, is there in being a Jew, or what value is there in circumcision? [2]Much in every way! First of all, they have been entrusted with the very words of God.

[3]What if some did not have faith? Will their lack of faith nullify God's faithfulness? [4]Not at all! Let God be true, and every man a liar. As it is written:

"So that you may be proved right when you speak
and prevail when you judge."[c]

[5]But if our unrighteousness brings out God's righteousness more clearly, what shall we say? That God is unjust in bringing his wrath on us? (I am using a human argument.) [6]Certainly not! If that were so, how could God judge the world? [7]Someone might argue, "If my falsehood enhances God's truthfulness and so increases his glory, why am I still condemned as a sinner?" [8]Why not say—as we are being slanderously reported as saying and as some claim that we say—

"Let us do evil that good may result"? Their condemnation is deserved.

No One Is Righteous

[9]What shall we conclude then? Are we any better[d]? Not at all! We have already made the charge that Jews and Gentiles alike are all under sin. [10]As it is written:

"There is no one righteous, not even one;
[11] there is no one who understands,
   no one who seeks God.
[12]All have turned away,
   they have together become worthless;
there is no one who does good,
   not even one."[e]
[13]"Their throats are open graves;
   their tongues practice deceit."[f]
"The poison of vipers is on their lips."[g]
[14] "Their mouths are full of cursing and
   bitterness."[h]
[15]"Their feet are swift to shed blood;
[16] ruin and misery mark their ways,
[17]and the way of peace they do not
   know."[i]
[18] "There is no fear of God before their
   eyes."[j]

[19]Now we know that whatever the law says, it says to those who are under the law, so that every mouth may be silenced and the whole world held accountable to God. [20]Therefore no one will be declared righteous in his sight by observing the law; rather, through the law we become conscious of sin.

Righteousness Through Faith

[21]But now a righteousness from God, apart from law, has been made known, to which the Law and the Prophets testify. [22]This righteousness from God comes through faith in Jesus Christ to all who believe. There is no difference, [23]for all have sinned and fall short of the glory of God, [24]and are justified freely by his grace through the redemption that came by Christ Jesus. [25]God presented him as a sacrifice of atonement,[k] through faith in his blood. He did this to demonstrate his justice, because in his forbearance he had left the sins committed beforehand unpunished— [26]he did it to demonstrate his

---

a24 Isaiah 52:5; Ezek. 36:22   b27 Or who, by means of a   c4 Psalm 51:4   d9 Or worse e12 Psalms 14:1-3;53:1-3; Eccles. 7:20 f13 Psalm 5:9   g13 Psalm 140:3   h14 Psalm 10:7 i17 Isaiah 59:7,8   j18 Psalm 36:1   k25 Or as the one who would turn aside his wrath, taking away sin

justice at the present time, so as to be just and the one who justifies those who have faith in Jesus.

²⁷Where, then, is boasting? It is excluded. On what principle? On that of observing the law? No, but on that of faith. ²⁸For we maintain that a man is justified by faith apart from observing the law. ²⁹Is God the God of Jews only? Is he not the God of Gentiles too? Yes, of Gentiles too, ³⁰since there is only one God, who will justify the circumcised by faith and the uncircumcised through that same faith. ³¹Do we, then, nullify the law by this faith? Not at all! Rather, we uphold the law.

Abraham Justified by Faith

4 What then shall we say that Abraham, our forefather, discovered in this matter? ²If, in fact, Abraham was justified by works, he had something to boast about—but not before God. ³What does the Scripture say? "Abraham believed God, and it was credited to him as righteousness."ᵃ

⁴Now when a man works, his wages are not credited to him as a gift, but as an obligation. ⁵However, to the man who does not work but trusts God who justifies the wicked, his faith is credited as righteousness. ⁶David says the same thing when he speaks of the blessedness of the man to whom God credits righteousness apart from works:

⁷ "Blessed are they
   whose transgressions are forgiven,

ᵃ3 Gen. 15:6; also in verse 22

Tell the Whole Story, Dad

Bill Glass was one of my heroes. Not only was number eighty with the Cleveland Browns a totally dominant force on the gridiron, but he was also a deeply committed Christian man. When Bill retired from the game, he started a prison ministry. Who better than a powerful football player—a true man's man—to challenge inmates to confess their sins and receive God's gift of grace?

For many years, during his talks to prisoners inside the impenetrable walls and twisted barbed wire, Bill would ask, "How many of you sitting here heard your fathers tell you that some day you'd wind up in a place like this?" The overwhelming majority would raise their hands. "Yes," they would be saying, "Based on what my dad told me, I fully expected to spend my life paying for my crimes."

The words that Paul wrote to the church in Rome should grip us as though our dads are telling us that someday we'll be thrown in prison. "All have sinned," he pronounced, "and fall short of the glory of God" (v. 23). As sinners, Paul was saying, we don't have a chance. Thankfully, this was not the end of Paul's report. When he had the people's undivided attention, he added this: But you

DAILY INSIGHT

TUESDAY

Passage:
Romans 3:21–24

Verses:
Romans 3:23–24

"are justified freely by his grace through the redemption that came by Christ Jesus" (v. 24).

Dads who only tell one of these two truths to their children are making a monumental error. If all they talk about is "falling short," their kids, like those prisoners, will live with the guilty assurance that they are sinners. Their conduct may even come to match this self-image. But dads who only talk about grace eliminate their chances to bring discipline and structure to their children. Although children with permissive fathers may not wind up in jail, their lives will, in fact, be a sentence. No discipline equals no joy.

The message for you and me is crystal clear. We have a two-fold responsibility as dads. It's imperative that our children understand that they are sinners—sinful enough, perhaps, to land them in prison. This ought to be fairly effortless; after all, they got most of this sinfulness from us. But, as Paul did, we need to also let them know the part about being justified—that they're innocent because of God's loving grace. Take this truth with you today.

For your next devotional reading, go to page 1248.

whose sins are covered.
[8] Blessed is the man
   whose sin the Lord will never count
      against him."[a]

[9] Is this blessedness only for the circumcised, or also for the uncircumcised? We have been saying that Abraham's faith was credited to him as righteousness. [10] Under what circumstances was it credited? Was it after he was circumcised, or before? It was not after, but before! [11] And he received the sign of circumcision, a seal of the righteousness that he had by faith while he was still uncircumcised. So then, he is the father of all who believe but have not been circumcised, in order that righteousness might be credited to them. [12] And he is also the father of the circumcised who not only are circumcised but who also walk in the footsteps of the faith that our father Abraham had before he was circumcised.

[13] It was not through law that Abraham and his offspring received the promise that he would be heir of the world, but through the righteousness that comes by faith. [14] For if those who live by law are heirs, faith has no value and the promise is worthless, [15] because law brings wrath. And where there is no law there is no transgression.

[16] Therefore, the promise comes by faith, so that it may be by grace and may be guaranteed to all Abraham's offspring—not only to those who are of the law but also to those who are of the faith of Abraham. He is the father of us all. [17] As it is written: "I have made you a father of many nations."[b] He is our father in the sight of God, in whom he believed—the God who gives life to the dead and calls things that are not as though they were.

[18] Against all hope, Abraham in hope believed and so became the father of many nations, just as it had been said to him, "So shall your offspring be."[c] [19] Without weakening in his faith, he faced the fact that his body was as good as dead—since he was about a hundred years old—and that Sarah's womb was also dead. [20] Yet he did not waver through unbelief regarding the promise of God, but was strengthened in his faith and gave glory to God, [21] being fully persuaded that God had power to do what he had promised. [22] This is why "it was credited to him as righteousness." [23] The words "it was credited to him" were written not for him alone, [24] but also for us, to whom God will

credit righteousness—for us who believe in him who raised Jesus our Lord from the dead. [25] He was delivered over to death for our sins and was raised to life for our justification.

Peace and Joy

5 Therefore, since we have been justified through faith, we[d] have peace with God through our Lord Jesus Christ, [2] through whom we have gained access by faith into this grace in which we now stand. And we[d] rejoice in the hope of the glory of God. [3] Not only so, but we[d] also rejoice in our sufferings, because we know that suffering produces perseverance; [4] perseverance, character; and character, hope. [5] And hope does not disappoint us, because God has poured out his love into our hearts by the Holy Spirit, whom he has given us.

[6] You see, at just the right time, when we were still powerless, Christ died for the ungodly. [7] Very rarely will anyone die for a righteous man, though for a good man someone might possibly dare to die. [8] But God demonstrates his own love for us in this: While we were still sinners, Christ died for us.

[9] Since we have now been justified by his blood, how much more shall we be saved from God's wrath through him! [10] For if, when we were God's enemies, we were reconciled to him through the death of his Son, how much more, having been reconciled, shall we be saved through his life! [11] Not only is this so, but we also rejoice in God through our Lord Jesus Christ, through whom we have now received reconciliation.

Death Through Adam, Life Through Christ

[12] Therefore, just as sin entered the world through one man, and death through sin, and in this way death came to all men, because all sinned— [13] for before the law was given, sin was in the world. But sin is not taken into account when there is no law. [14] Nevertheless, death reigned from the time of Adam to the time of Moses, even over those who did not sin by breaking a command, as did Adam, who was a pattern of the one to come.

[15] But the gift is not like the trespass. For if the many died by the trespass of the one man, how much more did God's grace and

---

[a]8 Psalm 32:1,2   [b]17 Gen. 17:5   [c]18 Gen. 15:5
[d]1,2,3 Or let us

the gift that came by the grace of the one man, Jesus Christ, overflow to the many! [16]Again, the gift of God is not like the result of the one man's sin: The judgment followed one sin and brought condemnation, but the gift followed many trespasses and brought justification. [17]For if, by the trespass of the one man, death reigned through that one man, how much more will those who receive God's abundant provision of grace and of the gift of righteousness reign in life through the one man, Jesus Christ.

[18]Consequently, just as the result of one trespass was condemnation for all men, so also the result of one act of righteousness was justification that brings life for all men. [19]For just as through the disobedience of the one man the many were made sinners, so also through the obedience of the one man the many will be made righteous.

[20]The law was added so that the trespass might increase. But where sin increased, grace increased all the more, [21]so that, just as sin reigned in death, so also

Duh Word ub duh Lord

DAILY INSIGHT

WEDNESDAY

Passage:
Romans 5:1–8

Verses:
Romans 5:3–4

"Dem bones, dem bones, dem dry bones," we used to sing in biology class, as Mr. Dusek wheeled the actual human skeleton named "Charlie" to the front of the classroom. "Duh foot bone's connected to duh ankle bone; duh ankle bone's connected to duh shin bone; duh shin bone's connected to duh knee bone," and so on and so forth the lyrics went. The song ends with, "now hear duh word ub duh Lord." With apologies to the apostle, when I read Paul's wonderful sequence in these verses, it always reminds me of Charlie.

I know that you and I want to experience the incredible peace that only God can provide. We want to be able to "gain access by faith into his grace." And we want to run like Charlie used to run. So here's the sequence ... right from "duh word ub duh Lord:"

You and I have experienced suffering. This may have been our own physical pain, the traumatic loss of a job, or the anguish that comes with walking through these struggles with a family member or a close friend. Suffering is a fact of life, but Paul gives us good news. Suffering is connected to perseverance.

Perseverance is that quality that keeps us from quitting. It's the stuff of the final lap. Perseverance is that discipline that helps us tenaciously hang in there when we don't feel like it—when discouragement and frustration loom over us like a dark cloud. Perseverance is like the raw material of life, and Paul has more good news. Perseverance is connected to character.

Character is who we are when no one's looking. It's the structure of our lives that includes many non-negotiables: truth-telling, faith, fidelity, kindness, transparency, tenderness. And this is built through learning perseverance, which is perfected through suffering. Finally, Paul gives us one more piece of good news. Character is connected to hope.

Hope gets us out of bed in the morning. Hope is the reason why we can look forward to today ... and tomorrow ... and next week. God is fashioning us to be his men. But he wants this to also be what we dream about ... what we hope for. "For it is God who works in you to will and to act according to his good purposes" (Philippians 2:13). God gives us a future, and then he plants hope in our hearts to trust in his presence until we eventually get there. And this trust brings peace.

So there we have it ... the full circle: peace, suffering, perseverance, character, hope, and back to peace again. Although I can't imagine the tune being quite as catchy as "Dry Bones," maybe someone will come up with a song to help us remember this wonderful truth. Until they come up with the ditty, Romans 5 will have to do.

Now you can run, Charlie. You can run.

For your next devotional reading, go to page 1251.

grace might reign through righteousness to bring eternal life through Jesus Christ our Lord.

Dead to Sin, Alive in Christ

6 What shall we say, then? Shall we go on sinning so that grace may increase? **2**By no means! We died to sin; how can we live in it any longer? **3**Or don't you know that all of us who were baptized into Christ Jesus were baptized into his death? **4**We were therefore buried with him through baptism into death in order that, just as Christ was raised from the dead through the glory of the Father, we too may live a new life.

5If we have been united with him like this in his death, we will certainly also be united with him in his resurrection. **6**For we know that our old self was crucified with him so that the body of sin might be done away with,[a] that we should no longer be slaves to sin— **7**because anyone who has died has been freed from sin.

8Now if we died with Christ, we believe that we will also live with him. **9**For we know that since Christ was raised from the dead, he cannot die again; death no longer has mastery over him. **10**The death he died, he died to sin once for all; but the life he lives, he lives to God.

11In the same way, count yourselves dead to sin but alive to God in Christ Jesus. **12**Therefore do not let sin reign in your mortal body so that you obey its evil desires. **13**Do not offer the parts of your body to sin, as instruments of wickedness, but rather offer yourselves to God, as those who have been brought from death to life; and offer the parts of your body to him as instruments of righteousness. **14**For sin shall not be your master, because you are not under law, but under grace.

Slaves to Righteousness

15What then? Shall we sin because we are not under law but under grace? By no means! **16**Don't you know that when you offer yourselves to someone to obey him as slaves, you are slaves to the one whom you obey—whether you are slaves to sin, which leads to death, or to obedience, which leads to righteousness? **17**But thanks be to God that, though you used to be slaves to sin, you wholeheartedly obeyed the form of teaching to which you were entrusted. **18**You have been set free from sin and have become slaves to righteousness.

19I put this in human terms because you are weak in your natural selves. Just as you used to offer the parts of your body in slavery to impurity and to ever-increasing wickedness, so now offer them in slavery to righteousness leading to holiness. **20**When you were slaves to sin, you were free from the control of righteousness. **21**What benefit did you reap at that time from the things you are now ashamed of? Those things result in death! **22**But now that you have been set free from sin and have become slaves to God, the benefit you reap leads to holiness, and the result is eternal life. **23**For the wages of sin is death, but the gift of God is eternal life in[b] Christ Jesus our Lord.

An Illustration From Marriage

7 Do you not know, brothers—for I am speaking to men who know the law—that the law has authority over a man only as long as he lives? **2**For example, by law a married woman is bound to her husband as long as he is alive, but if her husband dies, she is released from the law of marriage. **3**So then, if she marries another man while her husband is still alive, she is called an adulteress. But if her husband dies, she is released from that law and is not an adulteress, even though she marries another man.

4So, my brothers, you also died to the law through the body of Christ, that you might belong to another, to him who was raised from the dead, in order that we might bear fruit to God. **5**For when we were controlled by the sinful nature,[c] the sinful passions aroused by the law were at work in our bodies, so that we bore fruit for death. **6**But now, by dying to what once bound us, we have been released from the law so that we serve in the new way of the Spirit, and not in the old way of the written code.

Struggling With Sin

7What shall we say, then? Is the law sin? Certainly not! Indeed I would not have known what sin was except through the law. For I would not have known what coveting really was if the law had not said, "Do not covet."[d] **8**But sin, seizing the opportunity afforded by the commandment, produced in me every kind of

---

[a]6 Or *be rendered powerless*   [b]23 Or *through*
[c]5 Or *the flesh*; also in verse 25   [d]7 Exodus 20:17;
Deut. 5:21

Conduct: Loving Well, Living Right

"For sin shall not be your master, because you are not under law, but under grace . . . Shall we sin because we are not under law but under grace? By no means!"
Romans 6:14–15

BUILDING YOUR CHILDREN

Let's say that you call me tomorrow to tell me that you'll be in the area this weekend. You ask if I might be free on Saturday to for a driving tour of the county. I say, "No problem, sounds great." We set a time, I give you directions to the house, and we hang up.

The following Saturday, at the appointed time, you ring my doorbell. We exchange greetings and walk back down the sidewalk toward your car. But when we get there, I mention that I'd prefer to ride in the back seat. Thinking it's a strange suggestion, you try to talk me out of it. But I insist, and as we back out of the driveway, you get the feeling that you're a cab driver in your own car. *This really feels weird,* you think to yourself.

As we turn out of the driveway, I ask if you've ever driven around my town before. You say that you haven't. I tell you that I'll be happy to show you around. But when we come to the stop sign leading into our subdivision, I sit there in silence.

"Which way should I turn?" you ask.

"Oh, you just go ahead," I reply.

"But I don't know where I'm going," you counter.

"That's okay," I say from the back seat, "I'll let you know."

You take a moment, then turn left. But the moment the car clears the intersection, I lean forward from the back seat and slap your face with my open hand. The impact of the blow sends your sunglasses flying. You're so shocked that it takes a minute for you to say anything, but you gather your composure and glance over your shoulder.

What was *that?*" you exclaim.

"Wrong turn," I shoot back.

More than a little bewildered, you look for an opportunity to make a safe U-turn and head back down the road in the correct direction. For the next several hours as we tour my county, I never tell you where we're going or which way to turn at intersections. I only let you know, with my open hand, if you've made the wrong choice. Not surprisingly, this is the last time we go on any driving tours together.

This scenario is obviously ridiculous. Who would ever do such a thoughtless and contemptuous thing to a friend? How could I have ever expected you to do any better unless I had told you, in advance, where we were going and the best way to get there?

Tragically, many children live in this kind of environment every day. The only real directions they get from their parents are those painful physical or verbal "slaps" when they've made a wrong choice. And although you and I would never be guilty of actually being as brutal and unfair as I was in our story, I can assure you that what I've described is a perfect snapshot of what it sometimes feels like to be a kid. For your child, life can be a confusing sequence of figuring out what *you* want. This should never be the case.

Love your children with all your heart. Pour affection on them, discipline them and fill your home with laughter. Talk to your children and let them know, in advance, what is expected of them. Commit yourself to being a godly example to them, ushering them into the presence of a holy God as often as you can. When you do these things, the "rules" will rarely be unclear. There will never be a time when your child feels like he or she is being "slapped" into obedience.

As you integrate this principle into your life, reflect on your relationship to God as the perfect example. You try to avoid displeasing him because of his love and grace, not because you're afraid he'll slap you. And just in case you need wisdom in leading your child into proper conduct, God's power is always available.

covetous desire. For apart from law, sin is dead. [9]Once I was alive apart from law; but when the commandment came, sin sprang to life and I died. [10]I found that the very commandment that was intended to bring life actually brought death. [11]For sin, seizing the opportunity afforded by the commandment, deceived me, and through the commandment put me to death. [12]So then, the law is holy, and the commandment is holy, righteous and good.

[13]Did that which is good, then, become death to me? By no means! But in order that sin might be recognized as sin, it pro-

duced death in me through what was good, so that through the commandment sin might become utterly sinful.

[14]We know that the law is spiritual; but I am unspiritual, sold as a slave to sin. [15]I do not understand what I do. For what I want to do I do not do, but what I hate I do. [16]And if I do what I do not want to do, I agree that the law is good. [17]As it is, it is no longer I myself who do it, but it is sin living in me. [18]I know that nothing good lives in me, that is, in my sinful nature.[a]

[a]18 Or *my flesh*

God's Unretractable Rules

What is the most important tool in your tool box? What's the one thing that, if not faithfully used, will render every one of your projects a total disaster? Give up? It's your tape measure.

I'm actually not sure why this is true, but I have quite a collection of tape measures. I've got one in my desk drawer at the office, one permanently in my tool belt, one in the kitchen catch-all drawer, and one lying loose in my work shop. The tape measures I'm referring to are the ones that usually come in a palm-size chrome case with a big yellow tape-retraction button on the edge and a clip for your belt.

The reason that the tape measure is the most important tool in your workshop is that it represents the standard by which everything else is gauged. The little inch marks on this tool are unarguable. These marks are the law. Debate this fact at your own peril.

Sometimes when I am cutting a large number of boards that are to be trimmed to the same length, I create a "pattern board." I take a piece of wood and use my tape measure, making absolutely certain that it is cut exactly to the desired length. Then I use that "pattern board" to measure each of the other boards to be cut.

A good friend of mine was cutting rafters for the first house he ever built. Instead of using a pattern board, he cut one board and used it to mark the next one. After he cut

DAILY INSIGHT

THURSDAY

Passage:
Romans 7:7–12

Verse:
Romans 7:12

that board, he used it to measure the next one. By the time he had cut all of his rafters—about thirty of them—his last board was almost a full *three inches* longer than the first.

If you want to be a good carpenter, you've got to have a standard. The same is true if you're a dad.

The Bible is, for us, a standard. Starting with the Law—the Ten Commandments—of the Old Testament and continuing through every chapter, the Scripture is our tape measure. It provides for all mankind a trustworthy image of what is right and wrong. In fact, the apostle Paul wrote, "I would not have known what sin was except through the law" (v. 7). God's law is the unchanging standard that shows us how far from the mark we have fallen. It also gives us a picture of the best way to get back on track.

When a man's children are small, before they personally experience the truth and the discipline of God's law, they have something they can count on—a pattern board. This is a man, cut to exact measurements, who shows his family what God's tape measure has shown him—the value of personal confession, trusting faith and the Father's grace.

When you use God's standards, building a lovely house is well within your reach.

For your next devotional reading, go to page 1253.

For I have the desire to do what is good, but I cannot carry it out. [19]For what I do is not the good I want to do; no, the evil I do not want to do—this I keep on doing. [20]Now if I do what I do not want to do, it is no longer I who do it, but it is sin living in me that does it.

[21]So I find this law at work: When I want to do good, evil is right there with me. [22]For in my inner being I delight in God's law; [23]but I see another law at work in the members of my body, waging war against the law of my mind and making me a prisoner of the law of sin at work within my members. [24]What a wretched man I am! Who will rescue me from this body of death? [25]Thanks be to God—through Jesus Christ our Lord!

So then, I myself in my mind am a slave to God's law, but in the sinful nature a slave to the law of sin.

Life Through the Spirit

8 Therefore, there is now no condemnation for those who are in Christ Jesus,[a] [2]because through Christ Jesus the law of the Spirit of life set me free from the law of sin and death. [3]For what the law was powerless to do in that it was weakened by the sinful nature,[b] God did by sending his own Son in the likeness of sinful man to be a sin offering.[c] And so he condemned sin in sinful man,[d] [4]in order that the righteous requirements of the law might be fully met in us, who do not live according to the sinful nature but according to the Spirit.

[5]Those who live according to the sinful nature have their minds set on what that nature desires; but those who live in accordance with the Spirit have their minds set on what the Spirit desires. [6]The mind of sinful man[e] is death, but the mind controlled by the Spirit is life and peace; [7]the sinful mind[f] is hostile to God. It does not submit to God's law, nor can it do so. [8]Those controlled by the sinful nature cannot please God.

[9]You, however, are controlled not by the sinful nature but by the Spirit, if the Spirit of God lives in you. And if anyone does not have the Spirit of Christ, he does not belong to Christ. [10]But if Christ is in you, your body is dead because of sin, yet your spirit is alive because of righteousness. [11]And if the Spirit of him who raised Jesus from the dead is living in you, he who raised Christ from the dead will also give life to your mortal bodies through his Spirit, who lives in you.

[12]Therefore, brothers, we have an obligation—but it is not to the sinful nature, to live according to it. [13]For if you live according to the sinful nature, you will die; but if by the Spirit you put to death the misdeeds of the body, you will live, [14]because those who are led by the Spirit of God are sons of God. [15]For you did not re-

[a]1 Some later manuscripts *Jesus, who do not live according to the sinful nature but according to the Spirit,*   [b]3 Or *the flesh*; also in verses 4, 5, 8, 9, 12 and 13   [c]3 Or *man, for sin*   [d]3 Or *in the flesh*   [e]6 Or *mind set on the flesh*   [f]7 Or *the mind set on the flesh*

HEY DAD
Why do Christians still do bad things?

Text: Romans 7:19–25

When we become Christians, we receive a new nature—a nature that loves God's law and hates sin. But we still struggle to be obedient because sin continues to live in us (v. 20).

Does this mean we are not responsible for our actions because we cannot help ourselves? Absolutely not! Paul says, "You, however, are controlled not by the sinful nature but by the Spirit, if the Spirit of God lives in you" (8:9). With the Spirit's help, we still must *choose* to do the right thing.

We learn two important lessons from this truth. First, we should not assume that others are *not* Christians simply because they struggle with sin or sometimes do bad things. Second, we should not be discouraged by the war within us to be obedient. Knowing that we are no longer *controlled* by our sinful nature, we can be even more determined to win the battle!

For a complete listing of Questions Kids Ask, turn to page 1435..

ceive a spirit that makes you a slave again to fear, but you received the Spirit of sonship.[a] And by him we cry, "*Abba*,[b] Father." [16]The Spirit himself testifies with our spirit that we are God's children. [17]Now if we are children, then we are heirs—heirs of God and co-heirs with Christ, if indeed we share in his sufferings in order that we may also share in his glory.

Future Glory

[18]I consider that our present sufferings are not worth comparing with the glory that will be revealed in us. [19]The creation waits in eager expectation for the sons of God to be revealed. [20]For the creation was subjected to frustration, not by its own choice, but by the will of the one who subjected it, in hope [21]that[c] the creation itself will be liberated from its bondage to decay and brought into the glorious freedom of the children of God.

[22]We know that the whole creation has been groaning as in the pains of childbirth

---

a15 Or *adoption*   *b15* Aramaic for *Father*
c20,21 Or *subjected it in hope.* *21For*

Captain John K. Mitchell

I knew Captain John K. Mitchell for two hours and fifty-five minutes, exactly the time it took to fly from Nashville to Phoenix. John was sitting in the window seat, and I was on the aisle. Mercifully, the center seat was unoccupied. Thank goodness for elbowroom.

As soon as I had slipped my briefcase under the seat in front of me, I turned and greeted my seatmate. John was a naval officer, transferring to another plane in Phoenix, then continuing on to San Diego. John's eyes twinkled when he told me that he was going to be able to spend some time with friends on the West Coast. "Where's your wife?" I asked, having seen his wedding band. "Oh, I lost Florence four years ago," he responded, his eyes telling me that the pain was still fresh.

"I'm so sorry," I apologized. "That's okay," John quickly responded. "During the time God gave us together, we lived by the verse, 'And we know that in all things God works for the good of those who love him.' God was so good to me to give me the years I did have with Florence."

What courage, I thought to myself. *What faith.* The story of John and Florence Mitchell goes back to the day when this young bride and groom committed love and loyalty to each other, "in sickness and in health." And even though John had been called on to care for his wife like he had never quite expected, that twinkle in his eye let me know that if he had it to do

DAILY INSIGHT

FRIDAY

Passage:
Romans 8:28, 31–39

Verse:
Romans 8:28

over, he wouldn't change a thing.

Even though I was at thirty thousand feet, scooting away from my own wife at over six hundred knots, my heart was drawn back to her. "In sickness and in health, Honey," I breathed. "I promise to love you regardless of the way 'all things' work for us, too." This courageous navy captain had inspired me.

The apostle Paul's promise is good. If we love God, we will be called in line with his perfect purposes. And this high calling will give us the courage to face life's challenges, even its tragedies.

John knew about this truth. "I'm the luckiest man alive to have been married to Florence," he finally said. "She was the most wonderful girl in the world." You see, John and Florence Mitchell had been married for sixty-six years. A full thirty years before her death, a stroke had mercilessly stricken her, rendering her an invalid. "I took care of her every single day," Captain Mitchell told me. "I wouldn't have had it any other way. It was my honor."

God may not work "all things" exactly according to our plans. But if we walk with our heavenly Father, if we obey his call, we will, like Captain John K. Mitchell, be able to look back when we're ninety-three and declare all things "good."

Thank you, John. Thanks for your courage, your loyalty and your faithfulness.

For your next devotional reading, go to page 1255.

right up to the present time. ²³Not only so, but we ourselves, who have the firstfruits of the Spirit, groan inwardly as we wait eagerly for our adoption as sons, the redemption of our bodies. ²⁴For in this hope we were saved. But hope that is seen is no hope at all. Who hopes for what he already has? ²⁵But if we hope for what we do not yet have, we wait for it patiently.

²⁶In the same way, the Spirit helps us in our weakness. We do not know what we ought to pray for, but the Spirit himself intercedes for us with groans that words cannot express. ²⁷And he who searches our hearts knows the mind of the Spirit, because the Spirit intercedes for the saints in accordance with God's will.

More Than Conquerors

²⁸And we know that in all things God works for the good of those who love him,[a] who[b] have been called according to his purpose. ²⁹For those God foreknew he also predestined to be conformed to the likeness of his Son, that he might be the firstborn among many brothers. ³⁰And those he predestined, he also called; those he called, he also justified; those he justified, he also glorified.

³¹What, then, shall we say in response to this? If God is for us, who can be against us? ³²He who did not spare his own Son, but gave him up for us all—how will he not also, along with him, graciously give us all things? ³³Who will bring any charge against those whom God has chosen? It is God who justifies. ³⁴Who is he that condemns? Christ Jesus, who died—more than that, who was raised to life—is at the right hand of God and is also interceding for us. ³⁵Who shall separate us from the love of Christ? Shall trouble or hardship or persecution or famine or nakedness or danger or sword? ³⁶As it is written:

> "For your sake we face death all day long;
> we are considered as sheep to be slaughtered."[c]

³⁷No, in all these things we are more than conquerors through him who loved us. ³⁸For I am convinced that neither death nor life, neither angels nor demons,[d] neither the present nor the future, nor any powers, ³⁹neither height nor depth, nor anything else in all creation, will be able to separate us from the love of God that is in Christ Jesus our Lord.

God's Sovereign Choice

9 I speak the truth in Christ—I am not lying, my conscience confirms it in the Holy Spirit— ²I have great sorrow and unceasing anguish in my heart. ³For I could wish that I myself were cursed and cut off from Christ for the sake of my brothers, those of my own race, ⁴the people of Israel. Theirs is the adoption as sons; theirs the divine glory, the covenants, the receiving of the law, the temple worship and the promises. ⁵Theirs are the patriarchs, and from them is traced the human

---

a28 Some manuscripts *And we know that all things work together for good to those who love God*   *b28* Or *works together with those who love him to bring about what is good—with those who* *c36* Psalm 44:22   *d38* Or *nor heavenly rulers*

HEY DAD

Could I ever do anything that would make God stop loving me?

Text: Romans 8:35–39

The Bible makes it very clear: Nothing that we can do will make God stop loving us. There is nothing high enough, low enough, or wide enough to keep Christ's love from us. Death itself cannot keep God from loving us!

But that doesn't mean we can do anything we want and God will still approve. Romans 6:19 says, "Just as you used to offer the parts of your body in slavery to impurity and to ever-increasing wickedness, so now offer them in slavery to righteousness leading to holiness." Paul does not say that God will *bless* us no matter what, but he says God will *love* us no matter what.

What a great comfort this is—the holy and perfect God loves us, even when we're the most unlovable.

QUESTIONS KIDS ASK

For a complete listing of Questions Kids Ask, turn to page 1435.

Don't Leave Me Now

Key Verse: *"For I am convinced that [nothing] will be able to separate us from the love of God that is in Christ Jesus our Lord."* Romans 8:38–39

Text: Romans 8:37–39 *(Dad or child reads the text.)*

QUIET
TIMES
WITH Dad

DAD READS: If you have ever read about whales, you know that baby whales stay close to their mothers for many months after they're born. This is also true of tigers, kangaroos and many other animals. These baby animals feel safe and secure right next to their mothers, but eventually, they grow up and have to go into a nasty and sometimes dangerous world all alone.

Child reads: Sometimes in church, I can hear little kids crying at the top of their lungs because they don't want their parents to leave them in the nursery. When I was a little kid, I didn't like to be apart from my parents either. Being right next to my dad and my mom makes me feel protected and safe. But someday I'll grow up and be separated from my parents, just like those animals.

DAD READS: Being separated from the people we really love can be a scary thing. But the verses we read today talk about something that will never, ever happen to us. We will never be separated from our heavenly Father. Nothing can ever come between us. There could never be a time or a place where he is not there. While we may find ourselves far away from everyone we love, God will always be there.

Child reads: As I grow up, short times away from my dad and my mom will be good for me. But whether my trip away from home is a very short one or a very long one, God will always be there ... always. Being away from him would never be a good thing.

DAD READS: Knowing that you will never be separated from a heavenly Father who loves you will always make my separation from you less frightening for both you and me. This means that there will never be a place dark enough that God cannot see you and me, no land too far away for him to visit, no danger so scary that he is too frightened to come along. God is everywhere ... all the time ... no matter what. This is wonderful news for us.

Child reads: What we have talked about today is true right now. God is here with us at this very minute. Let's talk to him:

Our Father in heaven, we love you. Thank you for always being with us. Please forgive my dad and me for the times when we have acted like you weren't there. Help us always to be thankful and always to live like you are right there with us. We love you, and we thank you for your love. In Jesus' name, **Amen.**

For your next devotional reading, go to page 1259.

ancestry of Christ, who is God over all, forever praised![a] Amen.

[6]It is not as though God's word had failed. For not all who are descended from Israel are Israel. [7]Nor because they are his descendants are they all Abraham's children. On the contrary, "It is through Isaac that your offspring will be reckoned."[b] [8]In other words, it is not the natural children who are God's children, but it is the children of the promise who are regarded as Abraham's offspring. [9]For this was how the promise was stated: "At the appointed time I will return, and Sarah will have a son."[c]

[10]Not only that, but Rebekah's children had one and the same father, our father Isaac. [11]Yet, before the twins were born or had done anything good or bad—in order that God's purpose in election might stand: [12]not by works but by him who calls—she was told, "The older will serve the younger."[d] [13]Just as it is written: "Jacob I loved, but Esau I hated."[e]

[14]What then shall we say? Is God unjust? Not at all! [15]For he says to Moses,

"I will have mercy on whom I have
    mercy,
and I will have compassion on whom
    I have compassion."[f]

[16]It does not, therefore, depend on man's desire or effort, but on God's mercy. [17]For the Scripture says to Pharaoh: "I raised you up for this very purpose, that I might display my power in you and that my name might be proclaimed in all the earth."[g] [18]Therefore God has mercy on whom he wants to have mercy, and he hardens whom he wants to harden.

[19]One of you will say to me: "Then why does God still blame us? For who resists his will?" [20]But who are you, O man, to talk back to God? "Shall what is formed say to him who formed it, 'Why did you make me like this?'"[h] [21]Does not the potter have the right to make out of the same lump of clay some pottery for noble purposes and some for common use?

[22]What if God, choosing to show his wrath and make his power known, bore with great patience the objects of his wrath—prepared for destruction? [23]What if he did this to make the riches of his glory known to the objects of his mercy, whom he prepared in advance for glory— [24]even us, whom he also called, not only from the Jews but also from the Gentiles? [25]As he says in Hosea:

"I will call them 'my people' who are
    not my people;
and I will call her 'my loved one' who
    is not my loved one,"[i]

[26]and,

"It will happen that in the very place
    where it was said to them,
'You are not my people,'
they will be called 'sons of the living
    God.' "[j]

[27]Isaiah cries out concerning Israel:

"Though the number of the Israelites
    be like the sand by the sea,
    only the remnant will be saved.
[28]For the Lord will carry out
    his sentence on earth with speed and
    finality."[k]

[29]It is just as Isaiah said previously:

"Unless the Lord Almighty
    had left us descendants,
we would have become like Sodom,
    we would have been like
    Gomorrah."[l]

Israel's Unbelief

[30]What then shall we say? That the Gentiles, who did not pursue righteousness, have obtained it, a righteousness that is by faith; [31]but Israel, who pursued a law of righteousness, has not attained it. [32]Why not? Because they pursued it not by faith but as if it were by works. They stumbled over the "stumbling stone." [33]As it is written:

"See, I lay in Zion a stone that causes
    men to stumble
and a rock that makes them fall,
and the one who trusts in him will
    never be put to shame."[m]

10 Brothers, my heart's desire and prayer to God for the Israelites is that they may be saved. [2]For I can testify about them that they are zealous for God, but their zeal is not based on knowledge. [3]Since they did not know the righteousness that comes from God and sought to establish their own, they did not submit to God's righteousness. [4]Christ is the end

---

[a]5 Or *Christ, who is over all. God be forever praised!* Or *Christ. God who is over all be forever praised!*
[b]7 Gen. 21:12   [c]9 Gen. 18:10,14   [d]12 Gen. 25:23
[e]13 Mal. 1:2,3   [f]15 Exodus 33:19   [g]17 Exodus 9:16
[h]20 Isaiah 29:16; 45:9   [i]25 Hosea 2:23
[j]26 Hosea 1:10   [k]28 Isaiah 10:22,23   [l]29 Isaiah 1:9
[m]33 Isaiah 8:14;

of the law so that there may be righteousness for everyone who believes.

[5]Moses describes in this way the righteousness that is by the law: "The man who does these things will live by them."[a] [6]But the righteousness that is by faith says: "Do not say in your heart, 'Who will ascend into heaven?'[b]" (that is, to bring Christ down) [7]"or 'Who will descend into the deep?'[c]" (that is, to bring Christ up from the dead). [8]But what does it say? "The word is near you; it is in your mouth and in your heart,"[d] that is, the word of faith we are proclaiming: [9]That if you confess with your mouth, "Jesus is Lord," and believe in your heart that God raised him from the dead, you will be saved. [10]For it is with your heart that you believe and are justified, and it is with your mouth that you confess and are saved. [11]As the Scripture says, "Anyone who trusts in him will never be put to shame."[e] [12]For there is no difference between Jew and Gentile—the same Lord is Lord of all and richly blesses all who call on him, [13]for, "Everyone who calls on the name of the Lord will be saved."[f]

[14]How, then, can they call on the one they have not believed in? And how can they believe in the one of whom they have not heard? And how can they hear without someone preaching to them? [15]And how can they preach unless they are sent? As it is written, "How beautiful are the feet of those who bring good news!"[g]

[16]But not all the Israelites accepted the good news. For Isaiah says, "Lord, who has believed our message?"[h] [17]Consequently, faith comes from hearing the message, and the message is heard through the word of Christ. [18]But I ask: Did they not hear? Of course they did:

"Their voice has gone out into all the
    earth,
  their words to the ends of the
    world."[i]

[19]Again I ask: Did Israel not understand? First, Moses says,

"I will make you envious by those who
    are not a nation;

28:16
*a*5 Lev. 18:5   *b*6 Deut. 30:12   *c*7 Deut. 30:13
*d*8 Deut. 30:14   *e*11 Isaiah 28:16   *f*13 Joel 2:32

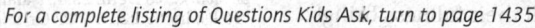

HEY DAD
Does God love Jews more than he loves others?

Text: Romans 10:11–21

In Exodus 4:22, God called Israel his "firstborn son." God did not say that Israel was his only "son" among the nations, but this firstborn status is a special designation.

What distinguishes a firstborn son? Looking all the way back to Moses' time, perhaps the most important distinction was that the firstborn son was set aside as the Lord's property. In fact, Hebrew parents presented their one-month-old, firstborn son to a priest and actually had to "redeem" him, or buy him back, from the priest.

When a firstborn son's father died, this special child inherited twice as much of the family's wealth as his siblings, and he assumed the leadership role in his family. He cared for his mother and acted as a father to his unmarried sisters. He also assumed the role of the priest of the home.

Now for the big question: Do we have to be Jewish by descent to be recipients of God's covenant promises? The Bible says no. Romans 10:12–13 makes clear that, "there is no difference between Jew and Gentile—the same Lord is Lord of all and richly blesses all who call on him, for, "Everyone who calls on the name of the Lord will be saved."

For centuries, God *did* give a special blessing to the Israelites, but today this blessing is given to everyone who loves him in equal and lavish portions.

Lockyer, H. (Ed.). (1986). Nelson's Illustrated Bible Dictionary. Nashville, Tennessee: Thomas Nelson Publishers.

For a complete listing of Questions Kids Ask, turn to page 1435.

I will make you angry by a nation
    that has no understanding."[a]

[20]And Isaiah boldly says,

"I was found by those who did not seek
    me;
I revealed myself to those who did
    not ask for me."[b]

[21]But concerning Israel he says,

"All day long I have held out my hands
    to a disobedient and obstinate
    people."[c]

The Remnant of Israel

I ask then: Did God reject his people?
By no means! I am an Israelite myself,
a descendant of Abraham, from the tribe
of Benjamin. [2]God did not reject his people, whom he foreknew. Don't you know
what the Scripture says in the passage
about Elijah—how he appealed to God
against Israel: [3]"Lord, they have killed
your prophets and torn down your altars;
I am the only one left, and they are trying
to kill me"[d]? [4]And what was God's answer
to him? "I have reserved for myself seven
thousand who have not bowed the knee
to Baal."[e] [5]So too, at the present time there
is a remnant chosen by grace. [6]And if by
grace, then it is no longer by works; if it
were, grace would no longer be grace.[f]

[7]What then? What Israel sought so earnestly it did not obtain, but the elect did.
The others were hardened, [8]as it is written:

"God gave them a spirit of stupor,
    eyes so that they could not see
    and ears so that they could not hear,
to this very day."[g]

[9]And David says:

"May their table become a snare and a
    trap,
    a stumbling block and a retribution
    for them.
[10]May their eyes be darkened so they
    cannot see,
    and their backs be bent forever."[h]

Ingrafted Branches

[11]Again I ask: Did they stumble so as to
fall beyond recovery? Not at all! Rather,
because of their transgression, salvation
has come to the Gentiles to make Israel
envious. [12]But if their transgression
means riches for the world, and their loss
means riches for the Gentiles, how much
greater riches will their fullness bring!

[13]I am talking to you Gentiles. Inas-
much as I am the apostle to the Gentiles, I
make much of my ministry [14]in the hope
that I may somehow arouse my own
people to envy and save some of them.
[15]For if their rejection is the reconciliation
of the world, what will their acceptance
be but life from the dead? [16]If the part of
the dough offered as firstfruits is holy,
then the whole batch is holy; if the root is
holy, so are the branches.

[17]If some of the branches have been
broken off, and you, though a wild olive
shoot, have been grafted in among the
others and now share in the nourishing
sap from the olive root, [18]do not boast
over those branches. If you do, consider
this: You do not support the root, but the
root supports you. [19]You will say then,
"Branches were broken off so that I could
be grafted in." [20]Granted. But they were
broken off because of unbelief, and you
stand by faith. Do not be arrogant, but
be afraid. [21]For if God did not spare the
natural branches, he will not spare you
either.

[22]Consider therefore the kindness and
sternness of God: sternness to those who
fell, but kindness to you, provided that
you continue in his kindness. Otherwise,
you also will be cut off. [23]And if they do
not persist in unbelief, they will be grafted
in, for God is able to graft them in again.
[24]After all, if you were cut out of an olive
tree that is wild by nature, and contrary to
nature were grafted into a cultivated olive
tree, how much more readily will these,
the natural branches, be grafted into their
own olive tree!

All Israel Will Be Saved

[25]I do not want you to be ignorant of
this mystery, brothers, so that you may
not be conceited: Israel has experienced a
hardening in part until the full number of
the Gentiles has come in. [26]And so all Israel will be saved, as it is written:

"The deliverer will come from Zion;
    he will turn godlessness away from
      Jacob.
[27]And this is[i] my covenant with them
    when I take away their sins."[j]

---

g15 Isaiah 52:7   *h16* Isaiah 53:1   *i18* Psalm 19:4
a19 Deut. 32:21   *b20* Isaiah 65:1   *c21* Isaiah 65:2
d3 1 Kings 19:10,14   *e4* 1 Kings 19:18   *f6* Some
manuscripts *by grace. But if by works, then it is
no longer grace; if it were, work would no longer
be work.*   *g8* Deut. 29:4; Isaiah 29:10
h10 Psalm 69:22,23   *i27* Or *will be*

[28]As far as the gospel is concerned, they are enemies on your account; but as far as election is concerned, they are loved on account of the patriarchs, [29]for God's gifts and his call are irrevocable. [30]Just as you who were at one time disobedient to God have now received mercy as a result of their disobedience, [31]so they too have now become disobedient in order that they too may now[a] receive mercy as a result of God's mercy to you. [32]For God has bound all men over to disobedience so that he may have mercy on them all.

Doxology

[33]Oh, the depth of the riches of the
    wisdom and[b] knowledge
    of God!
How unsearchable his judgments,
    and his paths beyond tracing out!
[34]"Who has known the mind of the Lord?
    Or who has been his counselor?"[c]
[35]"Who has ever given to God,

j27 Isaiah 59:20, 21; 27:9; Jer. 31:33,34
a31 Some manuscripts do not have *now.* *b33* Or

Plastic Slugs and Mayonnaise Jugs

DAILY INSIGHT

MONDAY

Passage:
Romans 12:1–8

Verse:
Romans 12:2

You haven't really lived until you've toured a mayonnaise factory. My friend Mike Rose owned such a plant, and because I had told him that I love machinery, he invited me to visit.

When I drove up to the building, I noticed a huge silo standing next to the building. It reminded me of the tall steel cylinders next to my grandfathers' and my uncles' barns. I made a mental note to be sure to ask what was inside that silo.

The receptionist was gracious. "I'll tell Mr. Rose that you're here," she said, acting as though she were expecting me. In a couple of minutes, Mike came out to greet me. "Let's do the tour first," he suggested. Naturally, I was delighted with this idea.

For the next hour, Mike introduced me to the mayo manufacturing process as he walked me through the cleanest factory I had ever seen. I saw mayonnaise belching out of a three-inch pipe at break-neck speed—quite a spectacle. The silo outside, I learned, was filled with egg yolks. "Egg yolks?" I exclaimed. Not wanting to think about those little yellow slime balls squishing together by the ton, I quickly changed the subject.

But to me, the most interesting piece of equipment at the factory was the machine that made the white plastic mayonnaise jugs, the kind you might see on the shelf in a restaurant kitchen. These jugs were made from plastic plugs about the size of small Tootsie Rolls®. Mike had these little white things shipped to his company by freight car loads, and this machine melted them into a thick, milky liquid that got literally sucked into a mold. In the twinkling of an eye, these little pellets became plastic jugs. Mike had to drag me away from this machine. Fascinating.

The apostle Paul's words for today might be restated, "Don't let the world suck you into its mold." Wow … shades of making plastic jugs at Mike's factory. And what a powerful word picture this is of what it's really like to live in our world. Like those plastic slugs, we can become something we had no intention of becoming with almost no effort.

So what's a man to do? Thankfully, Paul helps us out. He challenges us to avoid being "conformed"—sucked into someone's mold, and instead to "be transformed"—allowing the raw material of our lives to be shaped into God's image.

And how do we go through this metamorphosis? Again, Paul tells us directly: "By the renewing of [our] minds." What we read, what we watch, what we listen to, who we follow … all of these things affect what rests in the crevices of our minds.

The power of the Holy Spirit working in your heart will work to accomplish this transformation. You don't need to be afraid, but do be very careful. The sucking sound you hear is just around the corner.

For your next devotional reading, go to page 1261.

that God should repay him?"ᵃ
³⁶ For from him and through him and to
him are all things.
To him be the glory forever! Amen.

Living Sacrifices

12 Therefore, I urge you, brothers, in
view of God's mercy, to offer your bodies as living sacrifices, holy and pleasing
to God—this is your spiritualᵇ act of worship. **²** Do not conform any longer to the
pattern of this world, but be transformed
by the renewing of your mind. Then you
will be able to test and approve what
God's will is—his good, pleasing and perfect will.

³ For by the grace given me I say to every
one of you: Do not think of yourself more
highly than you ought, but rather think of
yourself with sober judgment, in accordance with the measure of faith God has
given you. **⁴** Just as each of us has one body
with many members, and these members
do not all have the same function, **⁵** so in
Christ we who are many form one body,
and each member belongs to all the others. **⁶** We have different gifts, according to
the grace given us. If a man's gift is prophesying, let him use it in proportion to hisᶜ
faith. **⁷** If it is serving, let him serve; if it is
teaching, let him teach; **⁸** if it is encouraging, let him encourage; if it is contributing
to the needs of others, let him give generously; if it is leadership, let him govern
diligently; if it is showing mercy, let him
do it cheerfully.

Love

⁹ Love must be sincere. Hate what is evil;
cling to what is good. **¹⁰** Be devoted to one
another in brotherly love. Honor one another above yourselves. **¹¹** Never be lacking in zeal, but keep your spiritual fervor,
serving the Lord. **¹²** Be joyful in hope,
patient in affliction, faithful in prayer.
¹³ Share with God's people who are in
need. Practice hospitality.

¹⁴ Bless those who persecute you; bless
and do not curse. **¹⁵** Rejoice with those
who rejoice; mourn with those who
mourn. **¹⁶** Live in harmony with one another. Do not be proud, but be willing to
associate with people of low position.ᵈ Do
not be conceited.

¹⁷ Do not repay anyone evil for evil. Be
careful to do what is right in the eyes of
everybody. **¹⁸** If it is possible, as far as it depends on you, live at peace with everyone.
¹⁹ Do not take revenge, my friends, but
leave room for God's wrath, for it is written: "It is mine to avenge; I will repay,"ᵉ
says the Lord. **²⁰** On the contrary:

"If your enemy is hungry, feed him;
if he is thirsty, give him something to
drink.
In doing this, you will heap burning
coals on his head."ᶠ

²¹ Do not be overcome by evil, but overcome evil with good.

riches and the wisdom and the   ᶜ*34 Isaiah 40:13*
ᵃ*35 Job 41:11*   ᵇ*1 Or reasonable*   ᶜ*6 Or in
agreement with the*   ᵈ*16 Or willing to do menial*

HEY DAD
If someone hurts me, why can't I hurt that person back?

Text: Romans 12:17–21

The Bible says that if someone hurts us, we should still treat that person with
kindness. This might seem unfair at first. Why should someone be able to hurt us
and get away with it? Well, that person will not *really* get away with it.

God will repay those who do evil. How he repays them is up to him, but we are
not supposed to take matters into our own hands. We can follow Christ's example
and trust God.

We cannot control a person's actions, but we *can* treat that person with love in
spite of those actions. This is what Paul meant when he said, "as far as it depends on you,
live at peace with everyone" (v. 18). God instructs us to feed our enemy if he is hungry and
to give him something to drink if he is thirsty. When we're kind to our enemies, we overcome
evil with good.

QUESTIONS Kids ASK

For a complete listing of Questions Kids Ask, turn to page 1435.

Submission to the Authorities

13 Everyone must submit himself to the governing authorities, for there is no authority except that which God has established. The authorities that exist have been established by God. ²Consequently, he who rebels against the authority is rebelling against what God has instituted, and those who do so will bring judgment on themselves. ³For rulers hold no terror for those who do right, but for those who do wrong. Do you want to be free from fear of the one in authority? Then do what is right and he will commend you. ⁴For he is God's servant to do you good. But if you do wrong, be afraid, for he does not bear the sword for nothing. He is God's servant, an agent of wrath to bring punishment on the wrongdoer. ⁵Therefore, it is necessary to submit to the authorities, not only because of possible punishment but also because of conscience.

⁶This is also why you pay taxes, for the

Go Ahead, Give Your Kids a Fine

DAILY INSIGHT

Some of the more innovative high-school civics classes include a visit to an actual courtroom. This involves taking kids down to the local traffic court and allowing them to see, first-hand, the justice system in action. For most of these soon-to-be drivers, this experience also provides a supplement to their driver's education courses that ranks right up there with that ever-popular film, the sentimental favorite of every driver's ed instructor, "Blood on the Highway."

The very first thing these students learn in this situation is that the judge is in control—make no mistake about who is in charge in the courtroom. And regardless of the convoluted (and sometimes downright ridiculous) tales these traffic offenders may tell in their defense, the judge has the last word.

Why can the judge do this? Because he or she has the *authority* to do this. And who gave the judge permission to do so? *We did* when we decided to live in this country and pay taxes. In fact, we probably voted for him or her in the last election.

The words we read today may be the most important you ever read as a father. "There is no authority except that which God has established" (v. 1). The apostle Paul reminds us that under God and with his blessing, there is a chain of command, a sequence of authorities and subordinates. And depending on the situation, you're either an authority or a subordinate.

If you have any actual personal memories of the courtroom scene above (either as

TUESDAY

Passage:
Romans 13:1–5

Verse:
Romans 13:5

a spectator or a defendant), you understand being a subordinate. If you have a boss—a foreman or the board of directors—you understand being a subordinate. If you have a wife ... I'm just kidding. In any case, being a subordinate is something you have felt all your life. But how about the other end of the spectrum? Do you know about being an authority figure?

Please listen carefully. These words are not coming from me. They are yours to examine straight from God's Word. You have authority in your home. You are a boss, a commanding officer and a principal for your children. Of course, your discipline must be thoughtful and fair, but you do not need to get their permission to exercise it. As clearly as that judge has the right to cut your story short and slap you with a fine, you have the absolute right and privilege to take responsibility for your family.

And how can you and I learn the secrets of being a great superior, a fair judge, a helpful coach? We get our clues by being loyal to the authority over us. As we learn what a faithful subject looks like and what fair leadership feels like, we become a better example to our children, our subordinates, of how they are to act—both with us and in society.

Take this authority; it's yours. Be very careful with this authority. And continue to be a faithful subordinate. It's a great combination.

For your next devotional reading, go to page 1266.

authorities are God's servants, who give their full time to governing. [7]Give everyone what you owe him: If you owe taxes, pay taxes; if revenue, then revenue; if respect, then respect; if honor, then honor.

Love, for the Day Is Near

[8]Let no debt remain outstanding, except the continuing debt to love one another, for he who loves his fellowman has fulfilled the law. [9]The commandments, "Do not commit adultery," "Do not murder," "Do not steal," "Do not covet,"[a] and whatever other commandment there may be, are summed up in this one rule: "Love your neighbor as yourself."[b] [10]Love does no harm to its neighbor. Therefore love is the fulfillment of the law.

[11]And do this, understanding the present time. The hour has come for you to wake up from your slumber, because our salvation is nearer now than when we first believed. [12]The night is nearly over; the day is almost here. So let us put aside the deeds of darkness and put on the armor of light. [13]Let us behave decently, as in the daytime, not in orgies and drunkenness, not in sexual immorality and debauchery, not in dissension and jealousy. [14]Rather, clothe yourselves with the Lord Jesus Christ, and do not think about how to gratify the desires of the sinful nature.[c]

The Weak and the Strong

14 Accept him whose faith is weak, without passing judgment on disputable matters. [2]One man's faith allows him to eat everything, but another man, whose faith is weak, eats only vegetables. [3]The man who eats everything must not look down on him who does not, and the man who does not eat everything must not condemn the man who does, for God has accepted him. [4]Who are you to judge someone else's servant? To his own master he stands or falls. And he will stand, for the Lord is able to make him stand.

[5]One man considers one day more sacred than another; another man considers every day alike. Each one should be fully convinced in his own mind. [6]He who regards one day as special, does so to the Lord. He who eats meat, eats to the Lord, for he gives thanks to God; and he who abstains, does so to the Lord and gives thanks to God. [7]For none of us lives to himself alone and none of us dies to himself alone. [8]If we live, we live to the Lord; and if we die, we die to the Lord. So,

whether we live or die, we belong to the Lord.

[9]For this very reason, Christ died and returned to life so that he might be the Lord of both the dead and the living. [10]You, then, why do you judge your brother? Or why do you look down on your brother? For we will all stand before God's judgment seat. [11]It is written:

" 'As surely as I live,' says the Lord,
'every knee will bow before me;
    every tongue will confess to God.' "[d]

[12]So then, each of us will give an account of himself to God.

[13]Therefore let us stop passing judgment on one another. Instead, make up your mind not to put any stumbling block or obstacle in your brother's way. [14]As one who is in the Lord Jesus, I am fully convinced that no food[e] is unclean in itself. But if anyone regards something as unclean, then for him it is unclean. [15]If your brother is distressed because of what you eat, you are no longer acting in love. Do not by your eating destroy your brother for whom Christ died. [16]Do not allow what you consider good to be spoken of as evil. [17]For the kingdom of God is not a matter of eating and drinking, but of righteousness, peace and joy in the Holy Spirit, [18]because anyone who serves Christ in this way is pleasing to God and approved by men.

[19]Let us therefore make every effort to do what leads to peace and to mutual edification. [20]Do not destroy the work of God for the sake of food. All food is clean, but it is wrong for a man to eat anything that causes someone else to stumble. [21]It is better not to eat meat or drink wine or to do anything else that will cause your brother to fall.

[22]So whatever you believe about these things keep between yourself and God. Blessed is the man who does not condemn himself by what he approves. [23]But the man who has doubts is condemned if he eats, because his eating is not from faith; and everything that does not come from faith is sin.

15 We who are strong ought to bear with the failings of the weak and not to please ourselves. [2]Each of us should please his neighbor for his good, to build him up. [3]For even Christ did not please

---

work [e]19 Deut. 32:35 [f]20 Prov. 25:21,22
[a]9 Exodus 20:13-15,17; Deut. 5:17-19,21
[b]9 Lev. 19:18 [c]14 Or *the flesh* [d]11 Isaiah 45:23

himself but, as it is written: "The insults of those who insult you have fallen on me."[a] [4]For everything that was written in the past was written to teach us, so that through endurance and the encouragement of the Scriptures we might have hope.

[5]May the God who gives endurance and encouragement give you a spirit of unity among yourselves as you follow Christ Jesus, [6]so that with one heart and mouth you may glorify the God and Father of our Lord Jesus Christ.

[7]Accept one another, then, just as Christ accepted you, in order to bring praise to God. [8]For I tell you that Christ has become a servant of the Jews[b] on behalf of God's truth, to confirm the promises made to the patriarchs [9]so that the Gentiles may glorify God for his mercy, as it is written:

"Therefore I will praise you among the Gentiles;
  I will sing hymns to your name."[c]

[10]Again, it says,

"Rejoice, O Gentiles, with his people."[d]

[11]And again,

"Praise the Lord, all you Gentiles,
  and sing praises to him, all you peoples."[e]

[12]And again, Isaiah says,

"The Root of Jesse will spring up,
  one who will arise to rule over the nations;
the Gentiles will hope in him."[f]

[13]May the God of hope fill you with all joy and peace as you trust in him, so that you may overflow with hope by the power of the Holy Spirit.

Paul the Minister to the Gentiles

[14]I myself am convinced, my brothers, that you yourselves are full of goodness, complete in knowledge and competent to instruct one another. [15]I have written you quite boldly on some points, as if to remind you of them again, because of the grace God gave me [16]to be a minister of Christ Jesus to the Gentiles with the priestly duty of proclaiming the gospel of God, so that the Gentiles might become an offering acceptable to God, sanctified by the Holy Spirit. [17]Therefore I glory in Christ Jesus in my

service to God. [18]I will not venture to speak of anything except what Christ has accomplished through me in leading the Gentiles to obey God by what I have said and done— [19]by the power of signs and miracles, through the power of the Spirit. So from Jerusalem all the way around to Illyricum, I have fully proclaimed the gospel of Christ. [20]It has always been my ambition to preach the gospel where Christ was not known, so that I would not be building on someone else's foundation. [21]Rather, as it is written:

"Those who were not told about him will see,
  and those who have not heard will understand."[g]

[22]This is why I have often been hindered from coming to you.

Paul's Plan to Visit Rome

[23]But now that there is no more place for me to work in these regions, and since I have been longing for many years to see you, [24]I plan to do so when I go to Spain. I hope to visit you while passing through and to have you assist me on my journey there, after I have enjoyed your company for a while. [25]Now, however, I am on my way to Jerusalem in the service of the saints there. [26]For Macedonia and Achaia were pleased to make a contribution for the poor among the saints in Jerusalem. [27]They were pleased to do it, and indeed they owe it to them. For if the Gentiles have shared in the Jews' spiritual blessings, they owe it to the Jews to share with them their material blessings. [28]So after I have completed this task and have made sure that they have received this fruit, I will go to Spain and visit you on the way. [29]I know that when I come to you, I will come in the full measure of the blessing of Christ.

[30]I urge you, brothers, by our Lord Jesus Christ and by the love of the Spirit, to join me in my struggle by praying to God for me. [31]Pray that I may be rescued from the unbelievers in Judea and that my service in Jerusalem may be acceptable to the saints there, [32]so that by God's will I may come to you with joy and together with you be refreshed. [33]The God of peace be with you all. Amen.

---

[e]14 Or *that nothing*   [a]3 Psalm 69:9   [b]8 Greek *circumcision*
[c]9 2 Samuel 22:50; Psalm 18:49   [d]10 Deut. 32:43

Personal Greetings

16 I commend to you our sister Phoebe, a servant[a] of the church in Cenchrea. [2]I ask you to receive her in the Lord in a way worthy of the saints and to give her any help she may need from you, for she has been a great help to many people, including me.

[3]Greet Priscilla[b] and Aquila, my fellow workers in Christ Jesus. [4]They risked their lives for me. Not only I but all the churches of the Gentiles are grateful to them.

[5]Greet also the church that meets at their house.

Greet my dear friend Epenetus, who was the first convert to Christ in the province of Asia.

[6]Greet Mary, who worked very hard for you.

[7]Greet Andronicus and Junias, my relatives who have been in prison with me. They are outstanding among the apostles, and they were in Christ before I was.

[8]Greet Ampliatus, whom I love in the Lord.

[9]Greet Urbanus, our fellow worker in Christ, and my dear friend Stachys.

[10]Greet Apelles, tested and approved in Christ.

Greet those who belong to the household of Aristobulus.

[11]Greet Herodion, my relative.

Greet those in the household of Narcissus who are in the Lord.

[12]Greet Tryphena and Tryphosa, those women who work hard in the Lord.

Greet my dear friend Persis, another woman who has worked very hard in the Lord.

[13]Greet Rufus, chosen in the Lord, and his mother, who has been a mother to me, too.

[14]Greet Asyncritus, Phlegon, Hermes, Patrobas, Hermas and the brothers with them.

[15]Greet Philologus, Julia, Nereus and his sister, and Olympas and all the saints with them.

[16]Greet one another with a holy kiss.

All the churches of Christ send greetings.

[17]I urge you, brothers, to watch out for those who cause divisions and put obstacles in your way that are contrary to the teaching you have learned. Keep away from them. [18]For such people are not serving our Lord Christ, but their own appetites. By smooth talk and flattery they deceive the minds of naive people. [19]Everyone has heard about your obedience, so I am full of joy over you; but I want you to be wise about what is good, and innocent about what is evil.

[20]The God of peace will soon crush Satan under your feet.

The grace of our Lord Jesus be with you.

[21]Timothy, my fellow worker, sends his greetings to you, as do Lucius, Jason and Sosipater, my relatives.

[22]I, Tertius, who wrote down this letter, greet you in the Lord.

[23]Gaius, whose hospitality I and the whole church here enjoy, sends you his greetings.

Erastus, who is the city's director of public works, and our brother Quartus send you their greetings.[c]

[25]Now to him who is able to establish you by my gospel and the proclamation of Jesus Christ, according to the revelation of the mystery hidden for long ages past, [26]but now revealed and made known through the prophetic writings by the command of the eternal God, so that all nations might believe and obey him— [27]to the only wise God be glory forever through Jesus Christ! Amen.

---

e11 Psalm 117:1   *f12* Isaiah 11:10   *g21* Isaiah 52:15
a1 Or *deaconess*   *b3* Greek *Prisca*, a variant of *Priscilla*   *c23* Some manuscripts *their greetings.*
24May the grace of our Lord Jesus Christ be with all of you. Amen.

Where do you live? Whether your home is in a rural area where the closest neighbor is a mile away, or whether you live in an apartment complex, four-and-a-half inches from the person next door, you live in a community. Your place of residence comes with a kitchen, a bathroom, and a community of people that learns to get along, to live together, and to actually enjoy each other.

As a dad, however, you don't have to go outside to find a "community." You've got one right where you live, wherever that may be. That community is, of course, your family. The book of 1 Corinthians gives readers a glimpse of what it means to live with neighbors. The principles we read here also help us to know what to do at home—how to be the dad, how to lead and how to serve. And since you've decided to have a family (and since there's no turning back), what follows ought to be a big help.

1 Corinthians

1 Paul, called to be an apostle of Christ Jesus by the will of God, and our brother Sosthenes,

²To the church of God in Corinth, to those sanctified in Christ Jesus and called to be holy, together with all those everywhere who call on the name of our Lord Jesus Christ—their Lord and ours:

³Grace and peace to you from God our Father and the Lord Jesus Christ.

Thanksgiving

⁴I always thank God for you because of his grace given you in Christ Jesus. ⁵For in him you have been enriched in every way—in all your speaking and in all your knowledge— ⁶because our testimony about Christ was confirmed in you.

⁷Therefore you do not lack any spiritual gift as you eagerly wait for our Lord Jesus Christ to be revealed. ⁸He will keep you strong to the end, so that you will be blameless on the day of our Lord Jesus Christ. ⁹God, who has called you into fellowship with his Son Jesus Christ our Lord, is faithful.

Divisions in the Church

¹⁰I appeal to you, brothers, in the name of our Lord Jesus Christ, that all of you agree with one another so that there may be no divisions among you and that you may be perfectly united in mind and thought. ¹¹My brothers, some from Chloe's household have informed me that there are quarrels among you. ¹²What I mean is this: One of you says, "I follow

Paul"; another, "I follow Apollos"; another, "I follow Cephas[a]"; still another, "I follow Christ."

[13] Is Christ divided? Was Paul crucified for you? Were you baptized into[b] the name of Paul? [14] I am thankful that I did not baptize any of you except Crispus and Gaius, [15] so no one can say that you were baptized into my name. [16] (Yes, I also baptized the household of Stephanas; beyond that, I don't remember if I baptized anyone else.) [17] For Christ did not send me to baptize, but to preach the gospel—not with words of human wisdom, lest the cross of Christ be emptied of its power.

Christ the Wisdom and Power of God

[18] For the message of the cross is foolishness to those who are perishing, but to us who are being saved it is the power of God. [19] For it is written:

a12 That is, Peter   b13 Or in; also in verse 15

Such a Nice Ring to It

DAILY INSIGHT

WEDNESDAY

Passage:
1 Corinthians 1:4–10

Verse:
1 Corinthians 1:10

Many years ago, I noticed an announcement in the church bulletin: "The bell ringers will practice on Wednesday evening at 6:30 in the choir room annex." *Bell ringers?* I pondered, sitting there between the "prelude" and the "call to worship." *Who—or what—are bell ringers? I wonder if these folks all show up looking like Santa Claus? Or maybe they work local boxing matches. When they die, are they eulogized as dead ringers?* Instead of quietly meditating before the upcoming service, I was sitting there imagining myself a stand-up comedian. Shameful.

Not too long after that, the bell ringers performed in a worship service. They walked to several long tables covered with brass bells that ranged in size from a tiny tinker bell to a couple of bells that looked big enough to hang in a church tower. And when these bell ringers started doing their thing, I was completely taken with this glorious music. Every note, every chord was flawlessly played as these white-glove-and-robe-clad volunteers snapped their wrists in perfect sequence. The notes lifted my spirits. The performance was angelic ... awesome. I was sorry that I had been so cynical. Shame on me.

Several years later, sitting in our church during another glorious bell-ringing prelude, it hit me. *What a great illustration of a family this is, God's family and my family.* The idea grew.

Bells come in all sizes. Each one makes a different sound. Bell ringers also come in all shapes and sizes. Fortunately, most music directors don't ask the big guys to tinkle the tiny ones or ask the petite women to be Quasimodo. But what if, during an anthem, one ringer decided to ignore the music in front of her? Not only would he sound terrible, but the whole piece of music would be destroyed. If one person didn't cooperate, every ringer would suffer.

Today's verses remind me of the bell ringers. "You do not lack any spiritual gift as you eagerly wait for our Lord Jesus Christ to be revealed," Paul reports to the Corinthians (1:7). "I appeal to you ... that all of you agree with one another so that there may be no divisions among you and that you may be perfectly united in mind and thought" (1:10). Notice that Paul did not say, "You must be perfectly the same ... looking exactly alike and playing the same bells." No, he challenged the people to show up to practice, to pull together, to encourage each other, to play their own parts ... to be unified.

As the dad in your home, you will be called on to direct a little bell-ringing band. If you need to, take them to hear a bell choir, then tell them about "perfect unity." They'll get the picture. "Perfect unity" is something every family could use. Hey, dad, that sound has a nice ring to it, don't you think?

For your next devotional reading, go to page 1268.

"I will destroy the wisdom of the wise;
the intelligence of the intelligent I
will frustrate."[a]

[20]Where is the wise man? Where is the scholar? Where is the philosopher of this age? Has not God made foolish the wisdom of the world? [21]For since in the wisdom of God the world through its wisdom did not know him, God was pleased through the foolishness of what was preached to save those who believe. [22]Jews demand miraculous signs and Greeks look for wisdom, [23]but we preach Christ crucified: a stumbling block to Jews and foolishness to Gentiles, [24]but to those whom God has called, both Jews and Greeks, Christ the power of God and the wisdom of God. [25]For the foolishness of God is wiser than man's wisdom, and the weakness of God is stronger than man's strength.

[26]Brothers, think of what you were when you were called. Not many of you were wise by human standards; not many were influential; not many were of noble birth. [27]But God chose the foolish things of the world to shame the wise; God chose the weak things of the world to shame the strong. [28]He chose the lowly things of this world and the despised things—and the things that are not—to nullify the things that are, [29]so that no one may boast before him. [30]It is because of him that you are in Christ Jesus, who has become for us wisdom from God—that is, our righteousness, holiness and redemption. [31]Therefore, as it is written: "Let him who boasts boast in the Lord."[b]

2

When I came to you, brothers, I did not come with eloquence or superior wisdom as I proclaimed to you the testimony about God.[c] [2]For I resolved to know nothing while I was with you except Jesus Christ and him crucified. [3]I came to you in weakness and fear, and with much trembling. [4]My message and my preaching were not with wise and persuasive words, but with a demonstration of the Spirit's power, [5]so that your faith might not rest on men's wisdom, but on God's power.

Wisdom From the Spirit

[6]We do, however, speak a message of wisdom among the mature, but not the wisdom of this age or of the rulers of this age, who are coming to nothing. [7]No, we speak of God's secret wisdom, a wisdom that has been hidden and that God destined for our glory before time began. [8]None of the rulers of this age understood it, for if they had, they would not have crucified the Lord of glory. [9]However, as it is written:

"No eye has seen,
no ear has heard,
no mind has conceived
what God has prepared for those
who love him"[d]—

[10]but God has revealed it to us by his Spirit.

[a]19 Isaiah 29:14   [b]31 Jer. 9:24   [c]1 Some manuscripts as I proclaimed to you God's mystery   [d]9 Isaiah 64:4

HEY DAD
Is the Holy Spirit scary?

Text: 1 Corinthians 2:10–11

The Holy Spirit is not scary at all. He is not like the ghosts you might have seen in a scary movie. Like God the Father and Jesus, he is holy, merciful, compassionate and loving. And if you're a Christian, he lives inside of you!

The Holy Spirit is the Comforter and Counselor that Jesus promised to send us when he went to be with the Father (John 14:16–17). Whenever you feel a tugging to do the right thing or you understand something about God that you did not understand before, that's the work of the Holy Spirit. When you find yourself growing as a Christian, that's the work of the Holy Spirit. When you feel the peace and hope of God in the middle of a seemingly hopeless situation, that's the work of—you guessed it—the Holy Spirit.

In fact, the Holy Spirit living inside us gives us freedom from fear. Scary? No way!

QUESTIONS Kids ASK

For a complete listing of Questions Kids Ask, turn to page 1435.

The Spirit searches all things, even the deep things of God. ¹¹For who among men knows the thoughts of a man except the man's spirit within him? In the same way no one knows the thoughts of God except the Spirit of God. ¹²We have not received the spirit of the world but the Spirit who is from God, that we may understand what God has freely given us. ¹³This is what we speak, not in words taught us by human wisdom but in words taught by the Spirit, expressing spiritual truths in spiritual words.ᵃ ¹⁴The man without the Spirit does not accept the things that come from the Spirit of God, for they are foolishness to him, and he cannot under-

stand them, because they are spiritually discerned. ¹⁵The spiritual man makes judgments about all things, but he himself is not subject to any man's judgment:

¹⁶ "For who has known the mind of the
Lord
that he may instruct him?"ᵇ

But we have the mind of Christ.

On Divisions in the Church

3 Brothers, I could not address you as spiritual but as worldly—mere infants

---

ᵃ13 Or *Spirit, interpreting spiritual truths to spiritual men*   ᵇ16 Isaiah 40:13

God's Sovereign Voice, Your Family and Your Radio

The next time you're in your car, take a look at the radio there on the dash. You'll see that it has two separate frequency bands: AM and FM. Look at all the choices you have on both of these bands. In fact, just for the fun of it, turn the radio on and tune it from left to right, one click at a time. Okay, now turn your radio off again.

I have a very important question for you. Even though your radio is in the "off" position, are all those stations still transmitting? Yes. Even though you cannot hear a thing, are they still sending out their words and music on the airwaves? Yes. And does the fact that you have your radio off have any affect whatsoever on the signal? Absolutely not. It's still out there, you're just not receiving it.

The profound message of the words we read today is as real as a radio station faithfully sending out a signal filled with informative voices and pleasant music, but falling on "deaf" radios. The apostle Paul is telling us that, because we are men, we know our own thoughts (v. 11). Our radios are tuned in to the "man" station. But if we want to hear *God's* words, we're going to have to make a conscious decision, a deliberate adjustment, to our souls' receivers.

Paul confidently informed his readers, "We speak, not in words taught us by human wisdom but in words taught by the

DAILY INSIGHT

THURSDAY

Passage:
1 Corinthians 2:10–14

Verse:
1 Corinthians 2:11

Spirit, expressing spiritual truths in spiritual words" (v. 13). If we want to hear God's Spirit, if we want him to lead, inform and encourage us, we'd better tune our radio to his frequency.

This is a profound and powerful thing. If we miss this, our life of faith will only be religion. There will be no passion, no fulfillment, no joy, no purpose, no direction, no hope … basically, no anything.

Not surprisingly, this truth doesn't only relate to our relationship with our heavenly Father; it's also a perfect illustration of our ability to effectively communicate with our children. Picture your family sitting around the dinner table. Do you see engaging conversation? Do you hear spontaneous laughter? Do you sense love and empathy, or do your kids look like a bunch of radios in the "off" position— with plenty of waves being transmitted, but no receivers in the correct position?

Take another look at your radio. Instead of seeing the numbers on the AM and FM bands, see the Holy Spirit. See your children. See your extended family. See your friends. See your colleagues at work. See those in your world who are in need.

Go ahead. Turn it on. Tune it in. Enjoy each of these wonderful stations. They're waiting for you.

For your next devotional reading, go to page 1271.

in Christ. [2]I gave you milk, not solid food, for you were not yet ready for it. Indeed, you are still not ready. [3]You are still worldly. For since there is jealousy and quarreling among you, are you not worldly? Are you not acting like mere men? [4]For when one says, "I follow Paul," and another, "I follow Apollos," are you not mere men?

[5]What, after all, is Apollos? And what is Paul? Only servants, through whom you came to believe—as the Lord has assigned to each his task. [6]I planted the seed, Apollos watered it, but God made it grow. [7]So neither he who plants nor he who waters is anything, but only God, who makes things grow. [8]The man who plants and the man who waters have one purpose, and each will be rewarded according to his own labor. [9]For we are God's fellow workers; you are God's field, God's building.

[10]By the grace God has given me, I laid a foundation as an expert builder, and someone else is building on it. But each one should be careful how he builds. [11]For no one can lay any foundation other than the one already laid, which is Jesus Christ. [12]If any man builds on this foundation using gold, silver, costly stones, wood, hay or straw, [13]his work will be shown for what it is, because the Day will bring it to light. It will be revealed with fire, and the fire will test the quality of each man's work. [14]If what he has built survives, he will receive his reward. [15]If it is burned up, he will suffer loss; he himself will be saved, but only as one escaping through the flames.

[16]Don't you know that you yourselves are God's temple and that God's Spirit lives in you? [17]If anyone destroys God's temple, God will destroy him; for God's temple is sacred, and you are that temple.

[18]Do not deceive yourselves. If any one of you thinks he is wise by the standards of this age, he should become a "fool" so that he may become wise. [19]For the wisdom of this world is foolishness in God's sight. As it is written: "He catches the wise in their craftiness"[a]; [20]and again, "The Lord knows that the thoughts of the wise are futile."[b] [21]So then, no more boasting about men! All things are yours, [22]whether Paul or Apollos or Cephas[c] or the world or life or death or the present or the future—all are yours, [23]and you are of Christ, and Christ is of God.

Apostles of Christ

4 So then, men ought to regard us as servants of Christ and as those entrusted with the secret things of God. [2]Now it is required that those who have been given a trust must prove faithful. [3]I care very little if I am judged by you or by any human court; indeed, I do not even judge myself. [4]My conscience is clear, but that does not make me innocent. It is the Lord who judges me. [5]Therefore judge nothing before the appointed time; wait till the Lord comes. He will bring to light what is hidden in darkness and will expose the motives of men's hearts. At that time each will receive his praise from God.

[6]Now, brothers, I have applied these things to myself and Apollos for your benefit, so that you may learn from us the meaning of the saying, "Do not go beyond what is written." Then you will not take pride in one man over against another. [7]For who makes you different from anyone else? What do you have that you did not receive? And if you did receive it, why do you boast as though you did not?

[8]Already you have all you want! Already you have become rich! You have become kings—and that without us! How I wish that you really had become kings so that we might be kings with you! [9]For it seems to me that God has put us apostles on display at the end of the procession, like men condemned to die in the arena. We have been made a spectacle to the whole universe, to angels as well as to men. [10]We are fools for Christ, but you are so wise in Christ! We are weak, but you are strong! You are honored, we are dishonored! [11]To this very hour we go hungry and thirsty, we are in rags, we are brutally treated, we are homeless. [12]We work hard with our own hands. When we are cursed, we bless; when we are persecuted, we endure it; [13]when we are slandered, we answer kindly. Up to this moment we have become the scum of the earth, the refuse of the world.

[14]I am not writing this to shame you, but to warn you, as my dear children. [15]Even though you have ten thousand guardians in Christ, you do not have many fathers, for in Christ Jesus I became your father through the gospel. [16]Therefore I urge you to imitate me. [17]For this reason I am sending to you Timothy, my son whom I love, who is faithful in the Lord. He will remind you of my way of life in Christ Jesus, which agrees with what I teach everywhere in every church.

[a]19 Job 5:13   [b]20 Psalm 94:11   [c]22 That is, Peter

[18]Some of you have become arrogant, as if I were not coming to you. [19]But I will come to you very soon, if the Lord is willing, and then I will find out not only how these arrogant people are talking, but what power they have. [20]For the kingdom of God is not a matter of talk but of power. [21]What do you prefer? Shall I come to you with a whip, or in love and with a gentle spirit?

Expel the Immoral Brother!

5 It is actually reported that there is sexual immorality among you, and of a kind that does not occur even among pagans: A man has his father's wife. [2]And you are proud! Shouldn't you rather have been filled with grief and have put out of your fellowship the man who did this? [3]Even though I am not physically present, I am with you in spirit. And I have already passed judgment on the one who did this, just as if I were present. [4]When you are assembled in the name of our Lord Jesus and I am with you in spirit, and the power of our Lord Jesus is present, [5]hand this man over to Satan, so that the sinful nature[a] may be destroyed and his spirit saved on the day of the Lord.

[6]Your boasting is not good. Don't you know that a little yeast works through the whole batch of dough? [7]Get rid of the old yeast that you may be a new batch without yeast—as you really are. For Christ, our Passover lamb, has been sacrificed. [8]Therefore let us keep the Festival, not with the old yeast, the yeast of malice and wickedness, but with bread without yeast, the bread of sincerity and truth.

[9]I have written you in my letter not to associate with sexually immoral people— [10]not at all meaning the people of this world who are immoral, or the greedy and swindlers, or idolaters. In that case you would have to leave this world. [11]But now I am writing you that you must not associate with anyone who calls himself a brother but is sexually immoral or greedy, an idolater or a slanderer, a drunkard or a swindler. With such a man do not even eat.

[12]What business is it of mine to judge those outside the church? Are you not to judge those inside? [13]God will judge those outside. "Expel the wicked man from among you."[b]

Lawsuits Among Believers

6 If any of you has a dispute with another, dare he take it before the ungodly for judgment instead of before the saints? [2]Do you not know that the saints will judge the world? And if you are to judge the world, are you not competent to judge trivial cases? [3]Do you not know that we will judge angels? How much more the things of this life! [4]Therefore, if you have disputes about such matters, appoint as judges even men of little account in the church![c] [5]I say this to shame you. Is it possible that there is nobody among you wise enough to judge a dispute between believers? [6]But instead, one brother goes to law against another—and this in front of unbelievers!

[7]The very fact that you have lawsuits among you means you have been completely defeated already. Why not rather be wronged? Why not rather be cheated? [8]Instead, you yourselves cheat and do wrong, and you do this to your brothers.

[9]Do you not know that the wicked will not inherit the kingdom of God? Do not be deceived: Neither the sexually immoral nor idolaters nor adulterers nor male prostitutes nor homosexual offenders [10]nor thieves nor the greedy nor drunkards nor slanderers nor swindlers will inherit the kingdom of God. [11]And that is what some of you were. But you were washed, you were sanctified, you were justified in the name of the Lord Jesus Christ and by the Spirit of our God.

Sexual Immorality

[12]"Everything is permissible for me"— but not everything is beneficial. "Everything is permissible for me"—but I will not be mastered by anything. [13]"Food for the stomach and the stomach for food"— but God will destroy them both. The body is not meant for sexual immorality, but for the Lord, and the Lord for the body. [14]By his power God raised the Lord from the dead, and he will raise us also. [15]Do you not know that your bodies are members of Christ himself? Shall I then take the members of Christ and unite them with a prostitute? Never! [16]Do you not know that he who unites himself with a prostitute is one with her in body? For it is said, "The two will become one flesh."[d] [17]But he who unites himself with the Lord is one with him in spirit.

---

[a]5 Or *that his body*; or *that the flesh*   [b]13 Deut. 17:7; 19:19; 21:21; 22:21,24; 24:7   [c]4 Or *matters, do you appoint as judges men of little account in the church?*   [d]16 Gen. 2:24

¹⁸Flee from sexual immorality. All other sins a man commits are outside his body, but he who sins sexually sins against his own body. ¹⁹Do you not know that your body is a temple of the Holy Spirit, who is in you, whom you have received from God? You are not your own; ²⁰you were bought at a price. Therefore honor God with your body.

Marriage

7 Now for the matters you wrote about: It is good for a man not to marry.ᵃ ²But since there is so much immorality, each man should have his own wife, and each

ᵃ1 Or "It is good for a man not to have sexual relations with a woman."

Friends Fly Free

DAILY INSIGHT

FRIDAY
Passage:
1 Corinthians 6:12–20
Verses:
1 Corinthians 6:19–20

My first experience with business travel was in 1976. I was in space advertising sales for a very, very small magazine—so small that I was the entire sales force. I had customers from coast to coast.

One of the things I noticed about being a married man on the road was how much I thought about sex out there. The moment I stepped into O'Hare International Airport, my pulse picked up ten or twelve beats. When I stopped to buy a newspaper, my eyes were drawn from the Chicago Tribune to the rack of magazines above me. Because this was before shrink-wrapping, I sometimes picked up one of these four-color slicks and quickly thumbed through it—good articles, I had heard. The ten to twelve pulse beats became forty-five or fifty. I was fully aerobic.

That was a long time ago. And now all of this stuff gets delivered to our homes via telephone wires and coaxial cables. And the "prime time" airwaves are not much cleaner. Promiscuity, infidelity, aberrant behavior, fornication and adultery are no longer whispered in hushed tones; they're fully celebrated in sitcoms and reported in graphic detail on the nightly news.

My guess is that you're right with me. You know about being aerobic. You know about this sexual stuff. You hate it ... and you love it. It repulses you ... and you're mysteriously drawn to it.

Can we talk? This is just between you and me, okay? There are two reasons why you and I must stay away from this poi-son— two solid reasons that must plant themselves deeply in our minds before our pounding hearts take over for our brain cells.

First, the apostle Paul summed it up this way: "You are not your own; you were bought at a price." If you're a married man, listen up: Your wife has picked up the tab for you. When she married you, she invested everything she had—body, mind and spirit—to buy you. And whether you're married or not, Jesus Christ also paid for you. Your body is his temple. And because you and I are actually the personal property of our Savior, we literally have no rights on the open market. Even our thoughts are "captives" (2 Corinthians 10:5).

The second reason to stay pure is a fairly obvious one, and it's true every time: *Immorality creates chaos.* Even if it's not acted out, it keeps our hearts restless and off-balance. It denies us focus. And if it is acted out, it rips our lives apart and crushes those whom we love. Impurity is pure hell—every single time. Remember this the next time you're on a business trip, or surfing the internet, or sitting with your thumb on the TV remote.

One of the things I've learned about business trips is that, if I'm not traveling alone, all of this temptation is much less overwhelming—much easier to flee. Now that I think about it, I do have a Savior who can go along. Plus, I have plenty of mileage, and friends fly free.

For your next devotional reading, go to page 1274.

woman her own husband. ³The husband should fulfill his marital duty to his wife, and likewise the wife to her husband. ⁴The wife's body does not belong to her alone but also to her husband. In the same way, the husband's body does not belong to him alone but also to his wife. ⁵Do not deprive each other except by mutual consent and for a time, so that you may devote yourselves to prayer. Then come together again so that Satan will not tempt you because of your lack of self-control. ⁶I say this as a concession, not as a command. ⁷I wish that all men were as I am. But each man has his own gift from God; one has this gift, another has that.

⁸Now to the unmarried and the widows I say: It is good for them to stay unmarried, as I am. ⁹But if they cannot control themselves, they should marry, for it is better to marry than to burn with passion.

¹⁰To the married I give this command (not I, but the Lord): A wife must not separate from her husband. ¹¹But if she does, she must remain unmarried or else be reconciled to her husband. And a husband must not divorce his wife.

¹²To the rest I say this (I, not the Lord): If any brother has a wife who is not a believer and she is willing to live with him, he must not divorce her. ¹³And if a woman has a husband who is not a believer and he is willing to live with her, she must not divorce him. ¹⁴For the unbelieving husband has been sanctified through his wife, and the unbelieving wife has been sanctified through her believing husband. Otherwise your children would be unclean, but as it is, they are holy.

¹⁵But if the unbeliever leaves, let him do so. A believing man or woman is not bound in such circumstances; God has called us to live in peace. ¹⁶How do you know, wife, whether you will save your husband? Or, how do you know, husband, whether you will save your wife?

¹⁷Nevertheless, each one should retain the place in life that the Lord assigned to him and to which God has called him. This is the rule I lay down in all the churches. ¹⁸Was a man already circumcised when he was called? He should not become uncircumcised. Was a man uncircumcised when he was called? He should not be circumcised. ¹⁹Circumcision is nothing and uncircumcision is nothing. Keeping God's commands is what counts. ²⁰Each one should remain in the situation which he was in when God called him. ²¹Were you a slave when you were called? Don't let it trouble you—although if you can gain your freedom, do so. ²²For he who was a slave when he was called by the Lord is the Lord's freedman; similarly, he who was a free man when he was called is Christ's slave. ²³You were bought at a price; do not become slaves of men. ²⁴Brothers, each man, as responsible to God, should remain in the situation God called him to.

²⁵Now about virgins: I have no command from the Lord, but I give a judgment as one who by the Lord's mercy is trustworthy. ²⁶Because of the present crisis, I think that it is good for you to remain as you are. ²⁷Are you married? Do not seek a divorce. Are you unmarried? Do not look for a wife. ²⁸But if you do marry, you have not sinned; and if a virgin marries, she has not sinned. But those who marry will face many troubles in this life, and I want to spare you this.

²⁹What I mean, brothers, is that the time is short. From now on those who have wives should live as if they had none; ³⁰those who mourn, as if they did not; those who are happy, as if they were not; those who buy something, as if it were not theirs to keep; ³¹those who use the things of the world, as if not engrossed in them. For this world in its present form is passing away.

³²I would like you to be free from concern. An unmarried man is concerned about the Lord's affairs—how he can please the Lord. ³³But a married man is concerned about the affairs of this world—how he can please his wife—³⁴and his interests are divided. An unmarried woman or virgin is concerned about the Lord's affairs: Her aim is to be devoted to the Lord in both body and spirit. But a married woman is concerned about the affairs of this world—how she can please her husband. ³⁵I am saying this for your own good, not to restrict you, but that you may live in a right way in undivided devotion to the Lord.

³⁶If anyone thinks he is acting improperly toward the virgin he is engaged to, and if she is getting along in years and he feels he ought to marry, he should do as he wants. He is not sinning. They should get married. ³⁷But the man who has settled the matter in his own mind, who is under no compulsion but has control over his own will, and who has made up his mind not to marry the virgin—this man also does the right thing. ³⁸So then, he who marries the virgin does right, but

he who does not marry her does even better.[a]

39A woman is bound to her husband as long as he lives. But if her husband dies, she is free to marry anyone she wishes, but he must belong to the Lord. **40**In my judgment, she is happier if she stays as she is—and I think that I too have the Spirit of God.

Food Sacrificed to Idols

8 Now about food sacrificed to idols: We know that we all possess knowledge.[b] Knowledge puffs up, but love builds up. **2**The man who thinks he knows something does not yet know as he ought to know. **3**But the man who loves God is known by God.

4So then, about eating food sacrificed to idols: We know that an idol is nothing at all in the world and that there is no God but one. **5**For even if there are so-called gods, whether in heaven or on earth (as indeed there are many "gods" and many "lords"), **6**yet for us there is but one God, the Father, from whom all things came and for whom we live; and there is but one Lord, Jesus Christ, through whom all things came and through whom we live.

7But not everyone knows this. Some people are still so accustomed to idols that when they eat such food they think of it as having been sacrificed to an idol, and since their conscience is weak, it is defiled. **8**But food does not bring us near to God; we are no worse if we do not eat, and no better if we do.

9Be careful, however, that the exercise of your freedom does not become a stumbling block to the weak. **10**For if anyone with a weak conscience sees you who have this knowledge eating in an idol's temple, won't he be emboldened to eat what has been sacrificed to idols? **11**So this weak brother, for whom Christ died, is destroyed by your knowledge. **12**When you sin against your brothers in this way and wound their weak conscience, you sin against Christ. **13**Therefore, if what I eat causes my brother to fall into sin, I will never eat meat again, so that I will not cause him to fall.

The Rights of an Apostle

9 Am I not free? Am I not an apostle? Have I not seen Jesus our Lord? Are you not the result of my work in the Lord? **2**Even though I may not be an apostle to others, surely I am to you! For you are the seal of my apostleship in the Lord.

3This is my defense to those who sit in judgment on me. **4**Don't we have the right to food and drink? **5**Don't we have the right to take a believing wife along with us, as do the other apostles and the Lord's brothers and Cephas[c]? **6**Or is it only I and Barnabas who must work for a living?

7Who serves as a soldier at his own expense? Who plants a vineyard and does not eat of its grapes? Who tends a flock and does not drink of the milk? **8**Do I say this merely from a human point of view? Doesn't the Law say the same thing? **9**For it is written in the Law of Moses: "Do not muzzle an ox while it is treading out the grain."[d] Is it about oxen that God is concerned? **10**Surely he says this for us, doesn't he? Yes, this was written for us, because when the plowman plows and the thresher threshes, they ought to do so in the hope of sharing in the harvest. **11**If we have sown spiritual seed among you, is it too much if we reap a material harvest from you? **12**If others have this right of support from you, shouldn't we have it all the more?

But we did not use this right. On the contrary, we put up with anything rather than hinder the gospel of Christ. **13**Don't you know that those who work in the temple get their food from the temple, and those who serve at the altar share in what is offered on the altar? **14**In the same way, the Lord has commanded that those who preach the gospel should receive their living from the gospel.

15But I have not used any of these rights. And I am not writing this in the hope that you will do such things for me. I would rather die than have anyone deprive me of this boast. **16**Yet when I preach the gospel, I cannot boast, for I am compelled to preach. Woe to me if I do not preach the gospel! **17**If I preach voluntarily, I have a reward; if not voluntarily, I am simply discharging the trust committed

---

a36-38 Or 36If anyone thinks he is not treating his daughter properly, and if she is getting along in years, and he feels she ought to marry, he should do as he wants. He is not sinning. He should let her get married. 37But the man who has settled the matter in his own mind, who is under no compulsion but has control over his own will, and who has made up his mind to keep the virgin unmarried—this man also does the right thing. 38So then, he who gives his virgin in marriage does right, but he who does not give her in marriage does even better.   b1 Or "We all possess knowledge," as you say   c5 That is, Peter   d9 Deut. 25:4

Key Verse: *"Do you know that in a race all the runners run, but only one gets the prize? Run in such a way as to get the prize."* 1 Corinthians 9:24
Text: 1 Corinthians 9:24–27 *(Dad or child reads the text.)*

QUIET TIMES WITH Dad

DAD READS: Once upon a time there was an nineteen-year-old boy named Ralph Foote. Ralph went to a small Christian college in Indiana, and he loved to run. Ralph dreamed that he would be the best runner in the history of that school, so he practiced—a lot.

Child reads: Life is like a race. The verses we read today tell us that. And if we are going to have any chance for winning this race, we are going to have to work very hard. We will have to practice and train so we can do our best.

DAD READS: At the end of his sophomore year, Ralph competed in the two-mile run at the conference track meet. When the gun sounded, the runners took off. But by the time the runners had finished the first mile, the lead pack was down to three ... two men from other schools and Ralph Foote.

Child reads: Life is like a race. Practice and training are a lot of hard work. Running laps, doing my homework, and helping around the house are things I'd rather not do. But if I ever want to win life's race, I will have to learn how to practice and train, even if doing so isn't a lot of fun.

DAD READS: On the final lap, a single runner exploded from the pack of three men. Everyone in the stadium stood and cheered. This lead runner had been practicing and training for this moment. When he crossed the finish line, his teammates surrounded him in celebra-

tion. Not only had Ralph won the race, he had beat the school record by eleven seconds and the conference record by more than ten seconds!

Child reads: Because my life is like a race, I want to be the best "runner" I can be, just like Ralph was. I want to be the best son/daughter I can be, the best brother/sister I can be, the best student I can be, and the best friend I can be.

DAD READS: God is pleased when we take the gifts and abilities he has given us and use them in the very best way we can. Let's run our race looking to Jesus, and let's begin by praying together:

Our Father in heaven, we love you. Thank you for stories that inspire us to be our best. Please forgive us for not wanting to practice and train like we should. Help us to run our race to please you. We love you and we thank you for your love. In Jesus' name, **Amen.**

For your next devotional reading, go to page 1276.

to me. [18]What then is my reward? Just this: that in preaching the gospel I may offer it free of charge, and so not make use of my rights in preaching it.

[19]Though I am free and belong to no man, I make myself a slave to everyone, to win as many as possible. [20]To the Jews I became like a Jew, to win the Jews. To those under the law I became like one under the law (though I myself am not under the law), so as to win those under the law. [21]To those not having the law I became like one not having the law (though I am not free from God's law but am under Christ's law), so as to win those not having the law. [22]To the weak I became weak, to win the weak. I have become all things to all men so that by all possible means I might save some. [23]I do all this for the sake of the gospel, that I may share in its blessings.

[24]Do you not know that in a race all the runners run, but only one gets the prize? Run in such a way as to get the prize. [25]Everyone who competes in the games goes into strict training. They do it to get a crown that will not last; but we do it to get a crown that will last forever. [26]Therefore I do not run like a man running aimlessly; I do not fight like a man beating the air. [27]No, I beat my body and make it my slave so that after I have preached to others, I myself will not be disqualified for the prize.

Warnings From Israel's History

10 For I do not want you to be ignorant of the fact, brothers, that our forefathers were all under the cloud and that they all passed through the sea. [2]They were all baptized into Moses in the cloud and in the sea. [3]They all ate the same spiritual food [4]and drank the same spiritual drink; for they drank from the spiritual rock that accompanied them, and that rock was Christ. [5]Nevertheless, God was not pleased with most of them; their bodies were scattered over the desert.

[6]Now these things occurred as examples[a] to keep us from setting our hearts on evil things as they did. [7]Do not be idolaters, as some of them were; as it is written: "The people sat down to eat and drink and got up to indulge in pagan revelry."[b] [8]We should not commit sexual immorality, as some of them did—and in one day twenty-three thousand of them died. [9]We should not test the Lord, as some of them did—and were killed by snakes. [10]And do

not grumble, as some of them did—and were killed by the destroying angel.

[11]These things happened to them as examples and were written down as warnings for us, on whom the fulfillment of the ages has come. [12]So, if you think you are standing firm, be careful that you don't fall! [13]No temptation has seized you except what is common to man. And God is faithful; he will not let you be tempted beyond what you can bear. But when you are tempted, he will also provide a way out so that you can stand up under it.

Idol Feasts and the Lord's Supper

[14]Therefore, my dear friends, flee from idolatry. [15]I speak to sensible people; judge for yourselves what I say. [16]Is not the cup of thanksgiving for which we give thanks a participation in the blood of Christ? And is not the bread that we break a participation in the body of Christ? [17]Because there is one loaf, we, who are many, are one body, for we all partake of the one loaf.

[18]Consider the people of Israel: Do not those who eat the sacrifices participate in the altar? [19]Do I mean then that a sacrifice offered to an idol is anything, or that an idol is anything? [20]No, but the sacrifices of pagans are offered to demons, not to God, and I do not want you to be participants with demons. [21]You cannot drink the cup of the Lord and the cup of demons too; you cannot have a part in both the Lord's table and the table of demons. [22]Are we trying to arouse the Lord's jealousy? Are we stronger than he?

The Believer's Freedom

[23]"Everything is permissible"—but not everything is beneficial. "Everything is permissible"—but not everything is constructive. [24]Nobody should seek his own good, but the good of others.

[25]Eat anything sold in the meat market without raising questions of conscience, [26]for, "The earth is the Lord's, and everything in it."[c]

[27]If some unbeliever invites you to a meal and you want to go, eat whatever is put before you without raising questions of conscience. [28]But if anyone says to you, "This has been offered in sacrifice," then do not eat it, both for the sake of the man who told you and for conscience' sake[d]—

[a]6 Or *types*; also in verse 11   [b]7 Exodus 32:6
[c]26 Psalm 24:1   [d]28 Some manuscripts *conscience' sake, for "the earth is the Lord's and everything in it"*

²⁹the other man's conscience, I mean, not yours. For why should my freedom be judged by another's conscience? ³⁰If I take part in the meal with thankfulness, why am I denounced because of something I thank God for?

³¹So whether you eat or drink or whatever you do, do it all for the glory of God. ³²Do not cause anyone to stumble, whether Jews, Greeks or the church of God— ³³even as I try to please everybody in every way. For I am not seeking my own good but the good of many, so that they may be saved. ¹Follow my example, as I follow the example of Christ.

Propriety in Worship

²I praise you for remembering me in everything and for holding to the teachings,ᵃ just as I passed them on to you.

ᵃ2 Or *traditions*

Cool Springs Boulevard, not Bell Road

DAILY INSIGHT

Bell Road stretches east from our town and runs through several miles of rolling hills. When our family moved to the area, Bell Road was a lazy country road. But in the past fifteen years, the sides of this road have literally erupted with shopping centers, movie theaters, offices, churches and apartment buildings.

Ten years into this explosive development, the state decided to go ahead and widen Bell Road. Three full years of construction only made this problem worse. Every time I drive on this packed highway, I'm reminded that, as handsome as it is, it was built too late.

When Cool Springs Boulevard was built, I was actually a little surprised. Here, in the middle of nowhere, was a beautiful four-lane highway complete with turning lanes, medians and traffic lights. *Perfect in case some farmer needs to herd his cows on smooth pavement,* I mused. Today, with several huge office buildings, apartment complexes, and one of the largest shopping malls in the cosmos directly adjacent to Cool Springs Boulevard, those traffic lights and turning lanes are being put to excellent use. I wonder if the folks who built Cool Springs Boulevard learned something from those who remodeled Bell Road.

Preparing for the discipline of living righteously is like building a wide road before it is actually necessary—before the weight of heavy traffic brings everything to a pathetic standstill. The lessons of living

MONDAY
Passage:
1 Corinthians
10:1–5,11–13
Verse:
1 Corinthians 10:13

righteously are often learned by watching what happens in the lives of people who decide not to do so.

Way back in the Old Testament, the Israelites lived for the moment. If they felt like building an idol, they built an idol. If they felt like satisfying their passions with debauchery, they went ahead without delay … or remorse. "God was not pleased with most of them; their bodies were scattered over the desert," the apostle Paul writes (v. 5).

So why did God preserve the record of his people's folly? For the same reason the Cool Springs guys watched the Bell Road guys. "These things … were written down as warnings for us," Paul says (v. 11). So before we deliberately walk the way these folks walked, we can see the devastating results. All of this precedes Paul's often-quoted promise (v. 13).

Sometimes people live without knowledge of the past or a plan for the future. Then, when they get hopelessly snarled in a traffic jam, they call on God to save them. God does provide for a "way out," but his way also provides plenty of notice before it's too late.

Build your life in such a way that you're ready for trouble *before* it comes, and learn from those who have gone before you. God's faithfulness includes his help in the discipline of preparation as well as in salvation from disaster … Cool Springs Boulevard, not Bell Road.

For your next devotional reading, go to page 1278.

[3]Now I want you to realize that the head of every man is Christ, and the head of the woman is man, and the head of Christ is God. [4]Every man who prays or prophesies with his head covered dishonors his head. [5]And every woman who prays or prophesies with her head uncovered dishonors her head—it is just as though her head were shaved. [6]If a woman does not cover her head, she should have her hair cut off; and if it is a disgrace for a woman to have her hair cut or shaved off, she should cover her head. [7]A man ought not to cover his head,[a] since he is the image and glory of God; but the woman is the glory of man. [8]For man did not come from woman, but woman from man; [9]neither was man created for woman, but woman for man. [10]For this reason, and because of the angels, the woman ought to have a sign of authority on her head. [11]In the Lord, however, woman is not independent of man, nor is man independent of woman. [12]For as woman came from man, so also man is born of woman. But everything comes from God. [13]Judge for yourselves: Is it proper for a woman to pray to God with her head uncovered? [14]Does not the very nature of things teach you that if a man has long hair, it is a disgrace to him, [15]but that if a woman has long hair, it is her glory? For long hair is given to her as a covering. [16]If anyone wants to be contentious about this, we have no other practice—nor do the churches of God.

The Lord's Supper

[17]In the following directives I have no praise for you, for your meetings do more harm than good. [18]In the first place, I hear that when you come together as a church, there are divisions among you, and to some extent I believe it. [19]No doubt there have to be differences among you to show which of you have God's approval. [20]When you come together, it is not the Lord's Supper you eat, [21]for as you eat, each of you goes ahead without waiting for anybody else. One remains hungry, another gets drunk. [22]Don't you have homes to eat and drink in? Or do you despise the church of God and humiliate those who have nothing? What shall I say to you? Shall I praise you for this? Certainly not!

[23]For I received from the Lord what I also passed on to you: The Lord Jesus, on the night he was betrayed, took bread, [24]and when he had given thanks, he broke

it and said, "This is my body, which is for you; do this in remembrance of me." [25]In the same way, after supper he took the cup, saying, "This cup is the new covenant in my blood; do this, whenever you drink it, in remembrance of me." [26]For whenever you eat this bread and drink this cup, you proclaim the Lord's death until he comes.

[27]Therefore, whoever eats the bread or drinks the cup of the Lord in an unworthy manner will be guilty of sinning against the body and blood of the Lord. [28]A man ought to examine himself before he eats of the bread and drinks of the cup. [29]For anyone who eats and drinks without recognizing the body of the Lord eats and drinks judgment on himself. [30]That is why many among you are weak and sick, and a number of you have fallen asleep. [31]But if we judged ourselves, we would not come under judgment. [32]When we are judged by the Lord, we are being disciplined so that we will not be condemned with the world. [33]So then, my brothers, when you come together to eat, wait for each other. [34]If anyone is hungry, he should eat at home, so that when you meet together it may not result in judgment.

And when I come I will give further directions.

Spiritual Gifts

12 Now about spiritual gifts, brothers, I do not want you to be ignorant. [2]You know that when you were pagans, somehow or other you were influenced and led astray to mute idols. [3]Therefore I tell you that no one who is speaking by the Spirit of God says, "Jesus be cursed," and no one can say, "Jesus is Lord," except by the Holy Spirit.

[4]There are different kinds of gifts, but the same Spirit. [5]There are different kinds of service, but the same Lord. [6]There are different kinds of working, but the same God works all of them in all men.

[7]Now to each one the manifestation of the Spirit is given for the common good. [8]To one there is given through the Spirit

a4-7 Or [4]Every man who prays or prophesies with long hair dishonors his head. [5]And every woman who prays or prophesies with no covering of hair on her head dishonors her head—she is just like one of the "shorn women." [6]If a woman has no covering, let her be for now with short hair, but since it is a disgrace for a woman to have her hair shorn or shaved, she should grow it again. [7]A man ought not to have long hair

the message of wisdom, to another the message of knowledge by means of the same Spirit, [9]to another faith by the same Spirit, to another gifts of healing by that one Spirit, [10]to another miraculous powers, to another prophecy, to another distinguishing between spirits, to another speaking in different kinds of tongues,[a] and to still another the interpretation of tongues.[a] [11]All these are the work of one and the same Spirit, and he gives them to each one, just as he determines.

One Body, Many Parts

[12]The body is a unit, though it is made up of many parts; and though all its parts are many, they form one body. So it is with Christ. [13]For we were all baptized by[b] one Spirit into one body—whether Jews or Greeks, slave or free—and we were all given the one Spirit to drink.

[a]10 Or languages; also in verse 28   [b]13 Or with; or in

Sadie, Sadie, Faithful Lady

DAILY INSIGHT

TUESDAY

Passage:
1 Corinthians 12:21–27

Verse:
1 Corinthians 12:27

Because of my love for dogs, I frequently stop surfing the television channels when I see anything that has to do with canines. Several years ago, I spotted an amazing program about a dog named Sadie. For sixty minutes, I didn't move. Sadie was a little black and white Border Collie. The setting was the pristine hills of Scotland. Her master, Lucien O'Grady, was a fifth-generation sheepherder. Sadie was a working dog.

O'Grady described how he communicated with Sadie with some audible signals and some simple hand motions. But in every case, Sadie was impeccably dutiful. To demonstrate, O'Grady showed us how Sadie could move the flock from one hillside to another.

You should have seen this incredible animal doing what she had been carefully trained to do. The sheep, munching on little tufts of grass, weren't too interested in moving from this lovely spot to any other. So when the Border Collie began to bark, the sheep looked thoroughly annoyed. They began to complain and bleat. "Go away. Leave us alone," they seemed to be saying in pathetic-sounding sheep language.

But Sadie was not to be dissuaded. Once she had the flock's attention, she began to move them toward the new hillside according to O'Grady's direction. Most of the sheep moved in the right direction, but a few refused to budge. And some—either in defiance or stupidity—trotted off in the opposite direction. But Sadie knew exactly what to do in each of these situations. Sometimes she'd bark. Sometimes she'd nip at a sheep's bony legs. One time she just stood there, studying the face of a particularly rebellious sheep. "I will win this," she might as well have been saying. "You can go to the next hill peacefully or you can go against your will, but you will go. I promise you that." In a few moments, the sheep acquiesced.

Eventually, the flock was in its new home and Sadie, the Border Collie, came running—it seemed impossible that she'd have any energy left—back to Lucien O'Grady. He lovingly patted her nose with a "Good girl, Sadie. Good girl." The dog lay down next to her master, waiting for her next assignment.

This is a perfect picture of what the apostle Paul was talking about in this passage. There are big sheep and little sheep ... compliant sheep and defiant sheep ... slothful sheep and industrious sheep, but every single one is an important member of the flock.

And, although he never saw the show about Sadie, I'm sure Paul would have agreed that she was the perfect image of a dad, armed with instructions from the Master, skillfully and successfully moving each of these lambs to the next hill, knowing precisely what to do with each one. Don't you just love shows about dogs?

For your next devotional reading, go to page 1280.

[14]Now the body is not made up of one part but of many. [15]If the foot should say, "Because I am not a hand, I do not belong to the body," it would not for that reason cease to be part of the body. [16]And if the ear should say, "Because I am not an eye, I do not belong to the body," it would not for that reason cease to be part of the body. [17]If the whole body were an eye, where would the sense of hearing be? If the whole body were an ear, where would the sense of smell be? [18]But in fact God has arranged the parts in the body, every one of them, just as he wanted them to be. [19]If they were all one part, where would the body be? [20]As it is, there are many parts, but one body.

[21]The eye cannot say to the hand, "I don't need you!" And the head cannot say to the feet, "I don't need you!" [22]On the contrary, those parts of the body that seem to be weaker are indispensable, [23]and the parts that we think are less honorable we treat with special honor. And the parts that are unpresentable are treated with special modesty, [24]while our presentable parts need no special treatment. But God has combined the members of the body and has given greater honor to the parts that lacked it, [25]so that there should be no division in the body, but that its parts should have equal concern for each other. [26]If one part suffers, every part suffers with it; if one part is honored, every part rejoices with it.

[27]Now you are the body of Christ, and each one of you is a part of it. [28]And in the church God has appointed first of all apostles, second prophets, third teachers, then workers of miracles, also those having gifts of healing, those able to help others, those with gifts of administration, and those speaking in different kinds of tongues. [29]Are all apostles? Are all prophets? Are all teachers? Do all work miracles? [30]Do all have gifts of healing? Do all speak in tongues[a]? Do all interpret? [31]But eagerly desire[b] the greater gifts.

Love

And now I will show you the most excellent way.

13 If I speak in the tongues[c] of men and of angels, but have not love, I am only a resounding gong or a clanging cymbal. [2]If I have the gift of prophecy and can fathom all mysteries and all knowledge, and if I have a faith that can move mountains, but have not love, I am nothing. [3]If I

give all I possess to the poor and surrender my body to the flames,[d] but have not love, I gain nothing.

[4]Love is patient, love is kind. It does not envy, it does not boast, it is not proud. [5]It is not rude, it is not self-seeking, it is not easily angered, it keeps no record of wrongs. [6]Love does not delight in evil but rejoices with the truth. [7]It always protects, always trusts, always hopes, always perseveres.

[8]Love never fails. But where there are prophecies, they will cease; where there are tongues, they will be stilled; where there is knowledge, it will pass away. [9]For we know in part and we prophesy in part, [10]but when perfection comes, the imperfect disappears. [11]When I was a child, I talked like a child, I thought like a child, I reasoned like a child. When I became a man, I put childish ways behind me. [12]Now we see but a poor reflection as in a mirror; then we shall see face to face. Now I know in part; then I shall know fully, even as I am fully known.

[13]And now these three remain: faith, hope and love. But the greatest of these is love.

Gifts of Prophecy and Tongues

14 Follow the way of love and eagerly desire spiritual gifts, especially the gift of prophecy. [2]For anyone who speaks in a tongue[e] does not speak to men but to God. Indeed, no one understands him; he utters mysteries with his spirit.[f] [3]But everyone who prophesies speaks to men for their strengthening, encouragement and comfort. [4]He who speaks in a tongue edifies himself, but he who prophesies edifies the church. [5]I would like every one of you to speak in tongues,[g] but I would rather have you prophesy. He who prophesies is greater than one who speaks in tongues,[g] unless he interprets, so that the church may be edified.

[6]Now, brothers, if I come to you and speak in tongues, what good will I be to you, unless I bring you some revelation or knowledge or prophecy or word of instruction? [7]Even in the case of lifeless things that make sounds, such as the flute or harp, how will anyone know what tune

---

[a]30 Or *other languages*   [b]31 Or *But you are eagerly desiring*   [c]1 Or *languages*   [d]3 Some early manuscripts *body that I may boast*   [e]2 Or *another language*; also in verses 4, 13, 14, 19, 26 and 27   [f]2 Or *by the Spirit*   [g]5 Or *other languages*; also in verses 6, 18, 22, 23 and 39

is being played unless there is a distinction in the notes? **⁸**Again, if the trumpet does not sound a clear call, who will get ready for battle? **⁹**So it is with you. Unless you speak intelligible words with your tongue, how will anyone know what you are saying? You will just be speaking into the air. **¹⁰**Undoubtedly there are all sorts of languages in the world, yet none of them is without meaning. **¹¹**If then I do not grasp the meaning of what someone is saying, I am a foreigner to the speaker, and he is a foreigner to me. **¹²**So it is with you. Since you are eager to have spiritual gifts, try to excel in gifts that build up the church.

¹³For this reason anyone who speaks in a tongue should pray that he may interpret what he says. **¹⁴**For if I pray in a tongue, my spirit prays, but my mind is unfruitful. **¹⁵**So what shall I do? I will pray with my spirit, but I will also pray with my

"How Do I Love Thee? Let Me Count the Ways."

DAILY INSIGHT

WEDNESDAY

Passage:
1 Corinthians 13:1–13

Verse:
1 Corinthians 13:1

"How do I love thee? Let me count the ways." The words of Elisabeth Barrett Browning's classic poem return to me over the years. I can clearly remember saying them in front of the church, waiting for my fiancée to come down the aisle with her father. As I look back on this experience, what really amazes me about my standing there is not that I narrated the poem. What stuns me is how little I knew, as a twenty-two-year-old youngster, about love.

Of course, I knew it was important to love God, to love Bobbie, and to love our children some day, but I really didn't have a clue. The apostle Paul summarized what I'm saying when he wrote this passage. Listen to this: If I have the gift of prophecy, if I can fathom all mysteries, if I have all knowledge, if I have faith, if I give all I possess to the poor, even if I actually sacrifice my body for right causes, but do not love others, "I am nothing" (13:2).

For me, love was important in every relationship—as important as many other qualities like intelligence, financial security and faith. But Paul's declaration is that none of these things count for anything unless I first *love*.

Marriage is love's graduate school; those of us who are married have earned the equivalent of a master's degree. After the wedding I soon found that love means giving when you're exhausted from a busy day or worried about tomorrow. Loving my new wife was an exercise in patience, humility, transparency, self-denial, service and tenderness. Now *there* were a few things I could count.

But if marriage is the master's degree, children are the Ph.D.

In the spring of 1986, our daughter, Julie, was admitted to Vanderbilt Hospital for corrective surgery on her foot. Standing in the hallway next to Julie's gurney, just outside the huge double doors leading into the operating room, Bobbie and I prayed with her. We prayed for wisdom for Dr. Green and courage for Julie. And right after the "Amen" we watched the orderly wheel her through those doors and out of sight. "I love you, Julie," I called out. The doors swung shut with a thud.

At that moment I was gripped with an overwhelming sense of fear. Tears welled up in my eyes. My precious little girl was going under the surgeon's knife and there was absolutely nothing I could do. Helplessness is not my favorite emotion. Bobbie and I stood there silently, frozen in an embrace.

"Lord, please give me wisdom. Please give me understanding. Please give me patience. Please give me the resources to provide for this little girl. But most of all, Father in heaven, give me love … *your* kind of love for my daughter and her mom. And then help me to learn how to love you. Teach me to adore my family as you do.

"And how should I love them? Heavenly Father, please help me count the ways. Amen."

For your next devotional reading, go to page 1282.

mind; I will sing with my spirit, but I will also sing with my mind. [16]If you are praising God with your spirit, how can one who finds himself among those who do not understand[a] say "Amen" to your thanksgiving, since he does not know what you are saying? [17]You may be giving thanks well enough, but the other man is not edified.

[18]I thank God that I speak in tongues more than all of you. [19]But in the church I would rather speak five intelligible words to instruct others than ten thousand words in a tongue.

[20]Brothers, stop thinking like children. In regard to evil be infants, but in your thinking be adults. [21]In the Law it is written:

"Through men of strange tongues
    and through the lips of foreigners
I will speak to this people,
    but even then they will not listen to
        me,"[b]

says the Lord.

[22]Tongues, then, are a sign, not for believers but for unbelievers; prophecy, however, is for believers, not for unbelievers. [23]So if the whole church comes together and everyone speaks in tongues, and some who do not understand[c] or some unbelievers come in, will they not say that you are out of your mind? [24]But if an unbeliever or someone who does not understand[d] comes in while everybody is prophesying, he will be convinced by all that he is a sinner and will be judged by all, [25]and the secrets of his heart will be laid bare. So he will fall down and worship God, exclaiming, "God is really among you!"

Orderly Worship

[26]What then shall we say, brothers? When you come together, everyone has a hymn, or a word of instruction, a revelation, a tongue or an interpretation. All of these must be done for the strengthening of the church. [27]If anyone speaks in a tongue, two—or at the most three—should speak, one at a time, and someone must interpret. [28]If there is no interpreter, the speaker should keep quiet in the church and speak to himself and God.

[29]Two or three prophets should speak, and the others should weigh carefully what is said. [30]And if a revelation comes to someone who is sitting down, the first speaker should stop. [31]For you can all prophesy in turn so that everyone may be instructed and encouraged. [32]The spirits of prophets are subject to the control of prophets. [33]For God is not a God of disorder but of peace.

As in all the congregations of the saints, [34]women should remain silent in the churches. They are not allowed to speak, but must be in submission, as the Law says. [35]If they want to inquire about something, they should ask their own husbands at home; for it is disgraceful for a woman to speak in the church.

[36]Did the word of God originate with you? Or are you the only people it has reached? [37]If anybody thinks he is a prophet or spiritually gifted, let him acknowledge that what I am writing to you is the Lord's command. [38]If he ignores this, he himself will be ignored.[e]

[39]Therefore, my brothers, be eager to prophesy, and do not forbid speaking in tongues. [40]But everything should be done in a fitting and orderly way.

The Resurrection of Christ

15 Now, brothers, I want to remind you of the gospel I preached to you, which you received and on which you have taken your stand. [2]By this gospel you are saved, if you hold firmly to the word I preached to you. Otherwise, you have believed in vain.

[3]For what I received I passed on to you as of first importance[f]: that Christ died for our sins according to the Scriptures, [4]that he was buried, that he was raised on the third day according to the Scriptures, [5]and that he appeared to Peter,[g] and then to the Twelve. [6]After that, he appeared to more than five hundred of the brothers at the same time, most of whom are still living, though some have fallen asleep. [7]Then he appeared to James, then to all the apostles, [8]and last of all he appeared to me also, as to one abnormally born.

[9]For I am the least of the apostles and do not even deserve to be called an apostle, because I persecuted the church of God. [10]But by the grace of God I am what I am, and his grace to me was not without effect. No, I worked harder than all of them—yet not I, but the grace of God that was with me. [11]Whether, then, it was I or

---

*a16 Or among the inquirers   b21 Isaiah 28:11,12
c23 Or some inquirers   d24 Or or some inquirer
e38 Some manuscripts If he is ignorant of this, let
him be ignorant   f3 Or you at the first   g5 Greek
Cephas*

they, this is what we preach, and this is what you believed.

The Resurrection of the Dead

¹²But if it is preached that Christ has been raised from the dead, how can some of you say that there is no resurrection of the dead? ¹³If there is no resurrection of the dead, then not even Christ has been raised. ¹⁴And if Christ has not been raised,

our preaching is useless and so is your faith. ¹⁵More than that, we are then found to be false witnesses about God, for we have testified about God that he raised Christ from the dead. But he did not raise him if in fact the dead are not raised. ¹⁶For if the dead are not raised, then Christ has not been raised either. ¹⁷And if Christ has not been raised, your faith is futile; you are still in your sins. ¹⁸Then those also who have fallen asleep in Christ are lost.

Bad Company, Big Results

DAILY INSIGHT

"I'm not affected by outside forces," I heard a man boast while waiting in line at a plumbing supply company in Waco, Texas. "Nobody tells me what to do. I know who I am and what I want. I'm a self-made man."

Well, I silently mused, *you certainly are the exception. Most of the people I know are deeply influenced by their surroundings … including me.*

A few years in the advertising business helped me to more fully understand this truth—people are *profoundly* affected by outside forces. But don't take my word for it; just think of the untold millions of dollars spent on television advertising during the Super Bowl. Companies *invest*—they do not spend—all this money to capture our attention for a few brief seconds. For them, this is a wise investment because they know how easily influenced we can be. The audience—educated, self-motivated, and bright though we may be—is profoundly influenced by these ads.

Now, if external persuasion makes an impact on grown men and women, then how much more true is this for our children? You already know the answer to this question, don't you?

The apostle Paul summed it up in just a few words. "Bad company corrupts good character." For you and me, the implications of this are simple. If we surround ourselves with people who aren't like what we want to be, we're looking for trouble. If thirty seconds of our attention is worth a million

THURSDAY
Passage:
1 Corinthians 15:33–34
Verse:
1 Corinthians 15:33

dollars, what are years and years of bad company worth?

And what about our children? What do we do when they bring home questionable friends—"bad company"? If it hasn't already happened, you can be relatively certain it will. The natural temptation of parents in this situation is to distance themselves from this friend and, in the process, from their own child. Don't do this.

You'll probably hear your daughter or son complain, "You don't even know who my friend really is." So do your very best to get to know your child's friend. In your child's presence, ask the friend questions about things he/she enjoys doing. Ask about significant past accomplishments and dreams for the future. Try to pick up clues about this person's motives and character. As much as you are able, do not interrogate! Ask questions just as you would of someone your own age.

This process will begin to give your child a snapshot of this person's character, clues as to who this friend really is. One-on-one questions with your child after the friend leaves are appropriate. Slamming the door on the friendship probably won't be.

You and I and our children are deeply affected by outside influences. The guy in the plumbing supply store could have been a one of a kind, but he probably just wasn't thinking clearly that day. No one is really self-made. Today, examine the company *you* keep. What will you find?

For your next devotional reading, go to page 1288.

¹⁹If only for this life we have hope in Christ, we are to be pitied more than all men.

²⁰But Christ has indeed been raised from the dead, the firstfruits of those who have fallen asleep. **²¹**For since death came through a man, the resurrection of the dead comes also through a man. **²²**For as in Adam all die, so in Christ all will be made alive. **²³**But each in his own turn: Christ, the firstfruits; then, when he comes, those who belong to him. **²⁴**Then the end will come, when he hands over the kingdom to God the Father after he has destroyed all dominion, authority and power. **²⁵**For he must reign until he has put all his enemies under his feet. **²⁶**The last enemy to be destroyed is death. **²⁷**For he "has put everything under his feet."*ᵃ* Now when it says that "everything" has been put under him, it is clear that this does not include God himself, who put everything under Christ. **²⁸**When he has done this, then the Son himself will be made subject to him who put everything under him, so that God may be all in all.

²⁹Now if there is no resurrection, what will those do who are baptized for the dead? If the dead are not raised at all, why are people baptized for them? **³⁰**And as for us, why do we endanger ourselves every hour? **³¹**I die every day—I mean that, brothers—just as surely as I glory over you in Christ Jesus our Lord. **³²**If I fought wild beasts in Ephesus for merely human reasons, what have I gained? If the dead are not raised,

> "Let us eat and drink,
>   for tomorrow we die."*ᵇ*

³³Do not be misled: "Bad company corrupts good character." **³⁴**Come back to your senses as you ought, and stop sinning; for there are some who are ignorant of God—I say this to your shame.

The Resurrection Body

³⁵But someone may ask, "How are the dead raised? With what kind of body will they come?" **³⁶**How foolish! What you sow does not come to life unless it dies. **³⁷**When you sow, you do not plant the body that will be, but just a seed, perhaps of wheat or of something else. **³⁸**But God gives it a body as he has determined, and to each kind of seed he gives its own body. **³⁹**All flesh is not the same: Men have one kind of flesh, animals have another, birds another and fish another. **⁴⁰**There are also heavenly bodies and there are earthly bodies; but the splendor of the heavenly bodies is one kind, and the splendor of the earthly bodies is another. **⁴¹**The sun has one kind of splendor, the moon

ᵃ27 Psalm 8:6   *ᵇ32* Isaiah 22:13

HEY DAD
What happens when we die?

Text: 1 Corinthians 15:20

Dying may seem unlike anything we have ever experienced, but Paul simply calls it "falling asleep." In fact, going to heaven will probably be the most familiar experience we could possibly have. After all, it's what we were created for! We were *made* to worship God and to enjoy his company without any hindrance of sin. When we are in heaven, we will finally know what this feels like. And we will at last see the Savior whom we already know and love!

Sometimes on car trips, children fall asleep in the back seat. When they get home, their moms or dads pick them up and take them to their own beds. Then when they wake up, the children realize that they are not in the car any more. They are at home.

Imagine falling asleep and then waking up in a place where you feel warm, safe, relieved, joyful, and—most of all—loved! How do *you* think it will it feel to wake up in heaven, Jesus' wonderful house?

For a complete listing of Questions Kids Ask, turn to page 1435.

another and the stars another; and star differs from star in splendor.

[42]So will it be with the resurrection of the dead. The body that is sown is perishable, it is raised imperishable; [43]it is sown in dishonor, it is raised in glory; it is sown in weakness, it is raised in power; [44]it is sown a natural body, it is raised a spiritual body.

If there is a natural body, there is also a spiritual body. [45]So it is written: "The first man Adam became a living being"[a]; the last Adam, a life-giving spirit. [46]The spiritual did not come first, but the natural, and after that the spiritual. [47]The first man was of the dust of the earth, the second man from heaven. [48]As was the earthly man, so are those who are of the earth; and as is the man from heaven, so also are those who are of heaven. [49]And just as we have borne the likeness of the earthly man, so shall we[b] bear the likeness of the man from heaven.

[50]I declare to you, brothers, that flesh and blood cannot inherit the kingdom of God, nor does the perishable inherit the imperishable. [51]Listen, I tell you a mystery: We will not all sleep, but we will all be changed— [52]in a flash, in the twinkling of an eye, at the last trumpet. For the trumpet will sound, the dead will be raised imperishable, and we will be changed. [53]For the perishable must clothe itself with the imperishable, and the mortal with immortality. [54]When the perishable has been clothed with the imperishable, and the mortal with immortality, then the saying that is written will come true: "Death has been swallowed up in victory."[c]

[55]"Where, O death, is your victory?
    Where, O death, is your sting?"[d]

[56]The sting of death is sin, and the power of sin is the law. [57]But thanks be to God! He gives us the victory through our Lord Jesus Christ.

[58]Therefore, my dear brothers, stand firm. Let nothing move you. Always give yourselves fully to the work of the Lord, because you know that your labor in the Lord is not in vain.

The Collection for God's People

16 Now about the collection for God's people: Do what I told the Galatian churches to do. [2]On the first day of every week, each one of you should set aside a sum of money in keeping with his income, saving it up, so that when I come no collections will have to be made. [3]Then, when I arrive, I will give letters of introduction to the men you approve and send them with your gift to Jerusalem. [4]If it seems advisable for me to go also, they will accompany me.

Personal Requests

[5]After I go through Macedonia, I will come to you—for I will be going through Macedonia. [6]Perhaps I will stay with you awhile, or even spend the winter, so that you can help me on my journey, wherever I go. [7]I do not want to see you now and make only a passing visit; I hope to spend some time with you, if the Lord permits. [8]But I will stay on at Ephesus until Pentecost, [9]because a great door for effective work has opened to me, and there are many who oppose me.

[10]If Timothy comes, see to it that he has nothing to fear while he is with you, for he is carrying on the work of the Lord, just as I am. [11]No one, then, should refuse to accept him. Send him on his way in peace so that he may return to me. I am expecting him along with the brothers.

[12]Now about our brother Apollos: I strongly urged him to go to you with the brothers. He was quite unwilling to go now, but he will go when he has the opportunity.

[13]Be on your guard; stand firm in the faith; be men of courage; be strong. [14]Do everything in love.

[15]You know that the household of Stephanas were the first converts in Achaia, and they have devoted themselves to the service of the saints. I urge you, brothers, [16]to submit to such as these and to everyone who joins in the work, and labors at it. [17]I was glad when Stephanas, Fortunatus and Achaicus arrived, because they have supplied what was lacking from you. [18]For they refreshed my spirit and yours also. Such men deserve recognition.

Final Greetings

[19]The churches in the province of Asia send you greetings. Aquila and Priscilla[e]

[a]45 Gen. 2:7   [b]49 Some early manuscripts *so let us*
[c]54 Isaiah 25:8   [d]55 Hosea 13:14   [e]19 Greek *Prisca*, a variant of *Priscilla*

greet you warmly in the Lord, and so does the church that meets at their house. [20]All the brothers here send you greetings. Greet one another with a holy kiss.

[21]I, Paul, write this greeting in my own hand.

[22]If anyone does not love the Lord—a curse be on him. Come, O Lord[a]!

[23]The grace of the Lord Jesus be with you.

[24]My love to all of you in Christ Jesus. Amen.[b]

[a]22 In Aramaic the expression *Come, O Lord* is *Marana tha.*   [b]24 Some manuscripts do not have *Amen.*

Living in obedience to Jesus Christ is hard work, and no one knew that better than the apostle Paul. This second letter to the Corinthians was written from the road. You may think you know what that's like, but musty hotel rooms and defective rental cars would have looked like pure luxury to Paul. Missionary life was tough—including "hardships," "despair," even the "sentence of death." But this treacherous road became even more difficult when Paul and his traveling companions were criticized by people who should have known better . . . fellow believers who should have been lavishing gratitude and encouragement on these ambassadors of grace.

At certain times in our lives, people will celebrate our commitment to Christ and cheer our unfailing desire to be men of God. At times our friends will tell us how much they admire our love for our children, our desire to spend time with them, our commitment to consistently and fairly love and discipline them. And then there are other times. When such times come, let the eternal truths Paul presents in this letter encourage and sustain you.

2 Corinthians

1 Paul, an apostle of Christ Jesus by the will of God, and Timothy our brother,

To the church of God in Corinth, together with all the saints throughout Achaia:

²Grace and peace to you from God our Father and the Lord Jesus Christ.

The God of All Comfort

³Praise be to the God and Father of our Lord Jesus Christ, the Father of compassion and the God of all comfort, ⁴who comforts us in all our troubles, so that we can comfort those in any trouble with the comfort we ourselves have received from God. ⁵For just as the sufferings of Christ flow over into our lives, so also through Christ our comfort overflows. ⁶If we are distressed, it is for your comfort and salvation; if we are comforted, it is for your comfort, which produces in you patient endurance of the same sufferings we suffer. ⁷And our hope for you is firm, because we know that just as you share in our sufferings, so also you share in our comfort.

⁸We do not want you to be uninformed, brothers, about the hardships we suffered in the province of Asia. We were under

great pressure, far beyond our ability to endure, so that we despaired even of life. [9]Indeed, in our hearts we felt the sentence of death. But this happened that we might not rely on ourselves but on God, who raises the dead. [10]He has delivered us from such a deadly peril, and he will deliver us. On him we have set our hope that he will continue to deliver us, [11]as you help us by your prayers. Then many will give thanks on our[a] behalf for the gracious favor granted us in answer to the prayers of many.

Paul's Change of Plans

[12]Now this is our boast: Our conscience testifies that we have conducted ourselves in the world, and especially in our relations with you, in the holiness and sincerity that are from God. We have done so not according to worldly wisdom but according to God's grace. [13]For we do not write you anything you cannot read or understand. And I hope that, [14]as you have understood us in part, you will come to understand fully that you can boast of us just as we will boast of you in the day of the Lord Jesus.

[15]Because I was confident of this, I planned to visit you first so that you might benefit twice. [16]I planned to visit you on my way to Macedonia and to come back to you from Macedonia, and then to have you send me on my way to Judea. [17]When I planned this, did I do it lightly? Or do I make my plans in a worldly manner so that in the same breath I say, "Yes, yes" and "No, no"?

[18]But as surely as God is faithful, our message to you is not "Yes" and "No." [19]For the Son of God, Jesus Christ, who was preached among you by me and Silas[b] and Timothy, was not "Yes" and "No," but in him it has always been "Yes." [20]For no matter how many promises God has made, they are "Yes" in Christ. And so through him the "Amen" is spoken by us to the glory of God. [21]Now it is God who makes both us and you stand firm in Christ. He anointed us, [22]set his seal of ownership on us, and put his Spirit in our hearts as a deposit, guaranteeing what is to come.

[23]I call God as my witness that it was in order to spare you that I did not return to Corinth. [24]Not that we lord it over your faith, but we work with you for your joy, because it is by faith you stand firm. [1]So I made up my mind that I would not make another painful visit to you. [2]For if I grieve you, who is left to make me glad but you whom I have grieved? [3]I wrote as I did so that when I came I should not be distressed by those who ought to make me rejoice. I had confidence in all of you, that you would all share my joy. [4]For I wrote you out of great distress and anguish of heart and with many tears, not to grieve you but to let you know the depth of my love for you.

Forgiveness for the Sinner

[5]If anyone has caused grief, he has not so much grieved me as he has grieved all of you, to some extent—not to put it too severely. [6]The punishment inflicted on him by the majority is sufficient for him. [7]Now instead, you ought to forgive and comfort him, so that he will not be overwhelmed by excessive sorrow. [8]I urge you, therefore, to reaffirm your love for him. [9]The reason I wrote you was to see if you would stand the test and be obedient in everything. [10]If you forgive anyone, I also forgive him. And what I have forgiven—if there was anything to forgive—I have forgiven in the sight of Christ for your sake, [11]in order that Satan might not outwit us. For we are not unaware of his schemes.

Ministers of the New Covenant

[12]Now when I went to Troas to preach the gospel of Christ and found that the Lord had opened a door for me, [13]I still had no peace of mind, because I did not find my brother Titus there. So I said good-by to them and went on to Macedonia.

[14]But thanks be to God, who always leads us in triumphal procession in Christ and through us spreads everywhere the fragrance of the knowledge of him. [15]For we are to God the aroma of Christ among those who are being saved and those who are perishing. [16]To the one we are the smell of death; to the other, the fragrance of life. And who is equal to such a task? [17]Unlike so many, we do not peddle the word of God for profit. On the contrary, in Christ we speak before God with sincerity, like men sent from God.

3 Are we beginning to commend ourselves again? Or do we need, like some people, letters of recommendation to you

---

[a]11 Many manuscripts *your*   [b]19 Greek *Silvanus*, a variant of *Silas*

or from you? **2**You yourselves are our letter, written on our hearts, known and read by everybody. **3**You show that you are a letter from Christ, the result of our ministry, written not with ink but with the Spirit of the living God, not on tablets of stone but on tablets of human hearts.

4Such confidence as this is ours through Christ before God. **5**Not that we are competent in ourselves to claim anything for ourselves, but our competence comes from God. **6**He has made us competent as ministers of a new covenant—not of the letter but of the Spirit; for the letter kills, but the Spirit gives life.

The Glory of the New Covenant

7Now if the ministry that brought death, which was engraved in letters on stone, came with glory, so that the Israelites could not look steadily at the face of Moses because of its glory, fading though it was, **8**will not the ministry of the Spirit be even more glorious? **9**If the ministry that condemns men is glorious, how much more glorious is the ministry that brings righteousness! **10**For what was glorious has no glory now in comparison with the surpassing glory. **11**And if what was fading away came with glory, how

Great Letters of Recommendation

DAILY INSIGHT

FRIDAY

Passage:
2 Corinthians 2:14—3:3

Verse:
2 Corinthians 3:2

Over the several decades I have spent in business, I have had numerous opportunities to interview applicants for various jobs I have posted. After carefully reviewing résumés and holding extended conversations with these prospective employees, I have usually had a good idea of their fit … or their nonfit. But I've rarely hired them without first calling a few of their references. "What are this person's work habits?" I'll ask. "How well does this person get along with colleagues, superiors and subordinates? Would you hire this person for this position?" This input has been very, very helpful.

Endorsements and recommendations are powerful tools in understanding the person that you're thinking of hiring. If you've read today's verses, you know exactly where all of this is going, don't you? If you haven't, then you might want to fasten your seat belt. "You are a letter from Christ," the apostle Paul wrote to the Corinthian Christians, "written not with ink but with the Spirit of the living God, not on tablets of stone but on tablets of human hearts" (3:3).

Go ahead and take a moment to let this sink in. As powerful and influential as endorsements and letters of recommendation are to employers and applicants, you and I are literally *notarized documents* for the living God. If people want to know who

God is, then watching and listening to us ought to give them an accurate snapshot.

Actually, as a dad, there's another interesting dimension of this truth. Growing up as preacher's kids, my cousin Ray and I became accustomed to going to summer camps where our dads were the ones standing behind the microphone. If we had a dollar for every time someone asked us our names and said, "You must be Sam and Eber's boys," I'd be driving a German import today. (Wait a minute, Ray *does* drive a German import! Hmmm.)

Ray and I became "letters of endorsement" for our preacher dads. While this may not have sat well during our adolescent years, today we're proud to be known as our godly fathers' sons. And your children are your letters of endorsement, just as you are for your heavenly Father. This means that as you obey him and then teach your children to obey you, your children become a confirming postscript on your letter. Isn't this great?

If you want my advice, never hire a person without first checking references. And, if I was a seeker who was one of your friends, I'd read your letter before I considered belief in God. I might even take a look at that postscript.

For your next devotional reading, go to page 1290.

much greater is the glory of that which lasts! [12]Therefore, since we have such a hope, we are very bold. [13]We are not like Moses, who would put a veil over his face to keep the Israelites from gazing at it while the radiance was fading away. [14]But their minds were made dull, for to this day the same veil remains when the old covenant is read. It has not been removed, because only in Christ is it taken away. [15]Even to this day when Moses is read, a veil covers their hearts. [16]But whenever anyone turns to the Lord, the veil is taken away. [17]Now the Lord is the Spirit, and where the Spirit of the Lord is, there is freedom. [18]And we, who with unveiled faces all reflect[a] the Lord's glory, are being transformed into his likeness with ever-increasing glory, which comes from the Lord, who is the Spirit.

Treasures in Jars of Clay

4 Therefore, since through God's mercy we have this ministry, we do not lose heart. [2]Rather, we have renounced secret and shameful ways; we do not use deception, nor do we distort the word of God. On the contrary, by setting forth the truth plainly we commend ourselves to every man's conscience in the sight of God. [3]And even if our gospel is veiled, it is veiled to those who are perishing. [4]The god of this age has blinded the minds of unbelievers, so that they cannot see the light of the gospel of the glory of Christ, who is the image of God. [5]For we do not preach ourselves, but Jesus Christ as Lord, and ourselves as your servants for Jesus' sake. [6]For God, who said, "Let light shine out of darkness,"[b] made his light shine in our hearts to give us the light of the knowledge of the glory of God in the face of Christ.

[7]But we have this treasure in jars of clay to show that this all-surpassing power is from God and not from us. [8]We are hard pressed on every side, but not crushed; perplexed, but not in despair; [9]persecuted, but not abandoned; struck down, but not destroyed. [10]We always carry around in our body the death of Jesus, so that the life of Jesus may also be revealed in our body. [11]For we who are alive are always being given over to death for Jesus' sake, so that his life may be revealed in our mortal body. [12]So then, death is at work in us, but life is at work in you.

[13]It is written: "I believed; therefore I

have spoken."[c] With that same spirit of faith we also believe and therefore speak, [14]because we know that the one who raised the Lord Jesus from the dead will also raise us with Jesus and present us with you in his presence. [15]All this is for your benefit, so that the grace that is reaching more and more people may cause thanksgiving to overflow to the glory of God.

[16]Therefore we do not lose heart. Though outwardly we are wasting away, yet inwardly we are being renewed day by day. [17]For our light and momentary troubles are achieving for us an eternal glory that far outweighs them all. [18]So we fix our eyes not on what is seen, but on what is unseen. For what is seen is temporary, but what is unseen is eternal.

Our Heavenly Dwelling

5 Now we know that if the earthly tent we live in is destroyed, we have a building from God, an eternal house in heaven, not built by human hands. [2]Meanwhile we groan, longing to be clothed with our heavenly dwelling, [3]because when we are clothed, we will not be found naked. [4]For while we are in this tent, we groan and are burdened, because we do not wish to be unclothed but to be clothed with our heavenly dwelling, so that what is mortal may be swallowed up by life. [5]Now it is God who has made us for this very purpose and has given us the Spirit as a deposit, guaranteeing what is to come.

[6]Therefore we are always confident and know that as long as we are at home in the body we are away from the Lord. [7]We live by faith, not by sight. [8]We are confident, I say, and would prefer to be away from the body and at home with the Lord. [9]So we make it our goal to please him, whether we are at home in the body or away from it. [10]For we must all appear before the judgment seat of Christ, that each one may receive what is due him for the things done while in the body, whether good or bad.

The Ministry of Reconciliation

[11]Since, then, we know what it is to fear the Lord, we try to persuade men. What we are is plain to God, and I hope it is also plain to your conscience. [12]We are not trying to commend ourselves to you again,

a18 Or *contemplate*   *b6* Gen. 1:3
c13 Psalm 116:10

Settling Our Account at God's Bank

Key Verse: *"If anyone is in Christ, he is a new creation; the old has gone, the new has come!"* 2 Corinthians 5:17
Text: 2 Corinthians 5:17–21 *(Dad or child reads the text.)*

QUIET TIMES WITH **Dad**

DAD READS: Sometimes when I want to buy something, I write a check to pay for it. When I give someone a check with something written on it, I am giving that person permission to ask our bank to send them money that we have there. Then, at the end of every month, our bank sends us an envelope. Inside this envelope are all the checks I wrote over the past thirty days. The envelope also includes a letter that tells us how much money we have left in the bank.

Child reads: Banks do a lot more than hold people's money in those great big vaults. Helping us with checks, like you have just told me, is another one of those things that banks do.

DAD READS: When I get the envelope at the end of the month, I try to match the amount of money the bank tells me that I have with what I think I have in the bank. This process is called "reconciliation." What this means is that I am settling my relationship with the bank. This is a very important thing when we deal with banks. It is also an important thing when we think about God's love for us.

Child reads: The verses we read today use this same word, "reconciliation" (v. 18). They tell us that God has settled our account with him. Before Jesus was born, the Israelites performed detailed, costly rituals to reconcile themselves to God. But, because of God's love for us and because of what Jesus did for us on the cross, we don't owe him anything more. Just like you try to do every month with our bank, what God thinks we owe him and what we think we owe him matches. That amount is nothing but our love and thanks for what he has done for us.

DAD READS: One of the wonderful things about being reconciled to God is that I am now free to settle my "accounts" with other people. Getting everything right with God comes first, but then I can tell others that I love and forgive them, too.

Child reads: The first verse we read today tells us that everyone can be "new," even people who have done terrible things. When we accept God's forgiveness of our sin, our friendship with him is perfect. This is something I want. This must be a very important theme in the Bible.

DAD READS: Yes it is. In fact, this verse explains exactly why God sent Jesus. It tells us that he doesn't want us to live our lives in debt to his "bank." He loves us, he forgives us, and then he gives us a very good reason to be thankful. Because of Jesus, all accounts are settled; we are completely free. Let me pray this prayer with you:

Our Father in heaven, we love you. Thank you for graciously forgiving our sin. We want to be reconciled with you, and we want to be reconciled with each other. Help us to always remember that this is why Jesus came—to pay the price for our sin. We love you and we thank you for your love. In Jesus' name, **Amen.**

For your next devotional reading, go to page 1294.

but are giving you an opportunity to take pride in us, so that you can answer those who take pride in what is seen rather than in what is in the heart. [13]If we are out of our mind, it is for the sake of God; if we are in our right mind, it is for you. [14]For Christ's love compels us, because we are convinced that one died for all, and therefore all died. [15]And he died for all, that those who live should no longer live for themselves but for him who died for them and was raised again.

[16]So from now on we regard no one from a worldly point of view. Though we once regarded Christ in this way, we do so no longer. [17]Therefore, if anyone is in Christ, he is a new creation; the old has gone, the new has come! [18]All this is from God, who reconciled us to himself through Christ and gave us the ministry of reconciliation: [19]that God was reconciling the world to himself in Christ, not counting men's sins against them. And he has committed to us the message of reconciliation. [20]We are therefore Christ's ambassadors, as though God were making his appeal through us. We implore you on Christ's behalf: Be reconciled to God. [21]God made him who had no sin to be sin[a] for us, so that in him we might become the righteousness of God.

6 As God's fellow workers we urge you not to receive God's grace in vain. [2]For he says,

"In the time of my favor I heard you,
    and in the day of salvation I helped
        you."[b]

I tell you, now is the time of God's favor, now is the day of salvation.

Paul's Hardships

[3]We put no stumbling block in anyone's path, so that our ministry will not be discredited. [4]Rather, as servants of God we commend ourselves in every way: in great endurance; in troubles, hardships and distresses; [5]in beatings, imprisonments and riots; in hard work, sleepless nights and hunger; [6]in purity, understanding, patience and kindness; in the Holy Spirit and in sincere love; [7]in truthful speech and in the power of God; with weapons of righteousness in the right hand and in the left; [8]through glory and dishonor, bad report and good report; genuine, yet regarded as impostors; [9]known, yet regarded as unknown; dying, and yet we live on; beaten, and yet not killed; [10]sorrowful, yet always rejoicing; poor, yet making many rich; having nothing, and yet possessing everything.

[11]We have spoken freely to you, Corinthians, and opened wide our hearts to you. [12]We are not withholding our affection from you, but you are withholding yours from us. [13]As a fair exchange—I speak as to my children—open wide your hearts also.

Do Not Be Yoked With Unbelievers

[14]Do not be yoked together with unbelievers. For what do righteousness and wickedness have in common? Or what fellowship can light have with darkness? [15]What harmony is there between Christ and Belial[c]? What does a believer have in common with an unbeliever? [16]What agreement is there between the temple of God and idols? For we are the temple of the living God. As God has said: "I will live with them and walk among them, and I will be their God, and they will be my people."[d]

[17]"Therefore come out from them
    and be separate,
                    says the Lord.
Touch no unclean thing,
    and I will receive you."[e]
[18]"I will be a Father to you,
    and you will be my sons and
        daughters,
            says the Lord Almighty."[f]

7 Since we have these promises, dear friends, let us purify ourselves from everything that contaminates body and spirit, perfecting holiness out of reverence for God.

Paul's Joy

[2]Make room for us in your hearts. We have wronged no one, we have corrupted no one, we have exploited no one. [3]I do not say this to condemn you; I have said before that you have such a place in our hearts that we would live or die with you. [4]I have great confidence in you; I take great pride in you. I am greatly encouraged; in all our troubles my joy knows no bounds.

[5]For when we came into Macedonia, this body of ours had no rest, but we were

---

[a]21 Or *be a sin offering*   [b]2 Isaiah 49:8   [c]15 Greek *Beliar*, a variant of *Belial*   [d]16 Lev. 26:12; Jer. 32:38; Ezek. 37:27   [e]17 Isaiah 52:11; Ezek. 20:34,41   [f]18 2 Samuel 7:14; 7:8

harassed at every turn—conflicts on the outside, fears within. [6]But God, who comforts the downcast, comforted us by the coming of Titus, [7]and not only by his coming but also by the comfort you had given him. He told us about your longing for me, your deep sorrow, your ardent concern for me, so that my joy was greater than ever.

[8]Even if I caused you sorrow by my letter, I do not regret it. Though I did regret it—I see that my letter hurt you, but only for a little while— [9]yet now I am happy, not because you were made sorry, but because your sorrow led you to repentance. For you became sorrowful as God intended and so were not harmed in any way by us. [10]Godly sorrow brings repentance that leads to salvation and leaves no regret, but worldly sorrow brings death. [11]See what this godly sorrow has produced in you: what earnestness, what eagerness to clear yourselves, what indignation, what alarm, what longing, what concern, what readiness to see justice done. At every point you have proved yourselves to be innocent in this matter. [12]So even though I wrote to you, it was not on account of the one who did the wrong or of the injured party, but rather that before God you could see for yourselves how devoted to us you are. [13]By all this we are encouraged.

In addition to our own encouragement, we were especially delighted to see how happy Titus was, because his spirit has been refreshed by all of you. [14]I had boasted to him about you, and you have not embarrassed me. But just as every-

thing we said to you was true, so our boasting about you to Titus has proved to be true as well. [15]And his affection for you is all the greater when he remembers that you were all obedient, receiving him with fear and trembling. [16]I am glad I can have complete confidence in you.

Generosity Encouraged

8 And now, brothers, we want you to know about the grace that God has given the Macedonian churches. [2]Out of the most severe trial, their overflowing joy and their extreme poverty welled up in rich generosity. [3]For I testify that they gave as much as they were able, and even beyond their ability. Entirely on their own, [4]they urgently pleaded with us for the privilege of sharing in this service to the saints. [5]And they did not do as we expected, but they gave themselves first to the Lord and then to us in keeping with God's will. [6]So we urged Titus, since he had earlier made a beginning, to bring also to completion this act of grace on your part. [7]But just as you excel in everything—in faith, in speech, in knowledge, in complete earnestness and in your love for us[a]—see that you also excel in this grace of giving.

[8]I am not commanding you, but I want to test the sincerity of your love by comparing it with the earnestness of others. [9]For you know the grace of our Lord Jesus Christ, that though he was rich, yet for your sakes he became poor, so that you

[a]7 Some manuscripts in our love for you

HEY DAD
Is saying "I'm sorry" the same as repenting?

Text: 2 Corinthians 7:8–11

Repenting is very different than just saying we're sorry. When we say we're sorry, we admit we were wrong and that we feel bad about what we did. When we repent, we not only admit we are wrong, but we also fix what we have broken. We stop, turn around and start walking in the other direction.

Now, which is better, feeling guilty or repenting? Paul says repentance leads to salvation and leaves no regret. But he doesn't stop there. He goes on to say that worldly sorrow brings *death*. We're not dealing with two degrees of good, here. We're dealing with two paths: repentance leading to salvation, and worldly sorrow—just saying "I'm sorry" with no intention of changing our behavior—leading to death.

Can you think of an offense you have committed? Confess it, fix it and then reverse it.

QUESTIONS KIDS ASK

For a complete listing of Questions Kids Ask, turn to page 1435.

through his poverty might become rich. ¹⁰And here is my advice about what is best for you in this matter: Last year you were the first not only to give but also to have the desire to do so. ¹¹Now finish the work, so that your eager willingness to do it may be matched by your completion of it, according to your means. ¹²For if the willingness is there, the gift is acceptable according to what one has, not according to what he does not have.

¹³Our desire is not that others might be relieved while you are hard pressed, but that there might be equality. ¹⁴At the present time your plenty will supply what they need, so that in turn their plenty will supply what you need. Then there will be equality, ¹⁵as it is written: "He who gathered much did not have too much, and he who gathered little did not have too little."ᵃ

Titus Sent to Corinth

¹⁶I thank God, who put into the heart of Titus the same concern I have for you. ¹⁷For Titus not only welcomed our appeal, but he is coming to you with much enthusiasm and on his own initiative. ¹⁸And we are sending along with him the brother who is praised by all the churches for his service to the gospel. ¹⁹What is more, he was chosen by the churches to accompany us as we carry the offering, which we administer in order to honor the Lord himself and to show our eagerness to help. ²⁰We want to avoid any criticism of the way we administer this liberal gift. ²¹For we are taking pains to do what is right, not only in the eyes of the Lord but also in the eyes of men.

²²In addition, we are sending with them our brother who has often proved to us in many ways that he is zealous, and now even more so because of his great confidence in you. ²³As for Titus, he is my partner and fellow worker among you; as for our brothers, they are representatives of the churches and an honor to Christ. ²⁴Therefore show these men the proof of your love and the reason for our pride in you, so that the churches can see it.

9 There is no need for me to write to you about this service to the saints. ²For I know your eagerness to help, and I have been boasting about it to the Macedonians, telling them that since last year you in Achaia were ready to give; and your enthusiasm has stirred most of them to action. ³But I am sending the brothers in

order that our boasting about you in this matter should not prove hollow, but that you may be ready, as I said you would be. ⁴For if any Macedonians come with me and find you unprepared, we—not to say anything about you—would be ashamed of having been so confident. ⁵So I thought it necessary to urge the brothers to visit you in advance and finish the arrangements for the generous gift you had promised. Then it will be ready as a generous gift, not as one grudgingly given.

Sowing Generously

⁶Remember this: Whoever sows sparingly will also reap sparingly, and whoever sows generously will also reap generously. ⁷Each man should give what he has decided in his heart to give, not reluctantly or under compulsion, for God loves a cheerful giver. ⁸And God is able to make all grace abound to you, so that in all things at all times, having all that you need, you will abound in every good work. ⁹As it is written:

"He has scattered abroad his gifts to the poor;
  his righteousness endures forever."ᵇ

¹⁰Now he who supplies seed to the sower and bread for food will also supply and increase your store of seed and will enlarge the harvest of your righteousness. ¹¹You will be made rich in every way so that you can be generous on every occasion, and through us your generosity will result in thanksgiving to God.

¹²This service that you perform is not only supplying the needs of God's people but is also overflowing in many expressions of thanks to God. ¹³Because of the service by which you have proved yourselves, men will praise God for the obedience that accompanies your confession of the gospel of Christ, and for your generosity in sharing with them and with everyone else. ¹⁴And in their prayers for you their hearts will go out to you, because of the surpassing grace God has given you. ¹⁵Thanks be to God for his indescribable gift!

Paul's Defense of His Ministry

10 By the meekness and gentleness of Christ, I appeal to you—I, Paul, who am "timid" when face to face with you, but "bold" when away! ²I beg you that

ᵃ15 Exodus 16:18   ᵇ9 Psalm 112:9

when I come I may not have to be as bold as I expect to be toward some people who think that we live by the standards of this world. ³For though we live in the world, we do not wage war as the world does. ⁴The weapons we fight with are not the weapons of the world. On the contrary, they have divine power to demolish strongholds. ⁵We demolish arguments and every pretension that sets itself up against the knowledge of God, and we take captive every thought to make it obedient to Christ. ⁶And we will be ready to punish every act of disobedience, once your obedience is complete.

⁷You are looking only on the surface of things.ᵃ If anyone is confident that he belongs to Christ, he should consider again

ᵃ7 Or *Look at the obvious facts*

Terri Loves Her Daddy

DAILY INSIGHT

MONDAY

Passage:
2 Corinthians 9:6–11

Verse:
2 Corinthians 9:7

My good friend Warren arrived home early one morning after taking the "red eye" from the West Coast into Chicago. He sneaked in the door and tiptoed to his room, finally laying his weary bones in bed just as the alarm clocks started to ring in his children's bedrooms. What was bedtime for him on that night was wake-up time for his family.

Warren's wife, Cheryl, did the best she could to keep their three children quiet as they dressed for school and ate breakfast together. Although Warren was not awake, he wasn't asleep either. He continued to lie there in never-never land, his eyes closed but his ears hearing everything. After Cheryl hustled the two older kids out the front door and off to school, Warren determined that he could now catch some quality sack time.

Just at that moment, he heard his bedroom doorknob slowly turning. The door squeaked open, and Warren squeezed a peek through his resting eyelids. It was Terri, their not-quite-ready-for-kindergarten four-year-old.

What's she up to? Warren wondered. *Didn't Cheryl tell the children to not disturb me?*

Gently closing the door behind her, Terri tiptoed toward her dad. She carefully walked up to the edge of the bed, and through his closed eyes Warren could sense his young daughter's face only inches from his. After standing there for a few moments, Terri leaned over and tenderly gave her daddy a kiss on the cheek.

Despite his appearance of slumber, Warren was wide awake. Terri turned and walked to the corner of the room. Taking hold of a chair, she slowly dragged it back to Warren's bedside. Once it was in place, Terri climbed onto the chair. She crossed her legs, folded her hands on her lap, and stared at the sleeping man she loved.

Until her older brother and sister came home for lunch, three hours later, the only time Terri moved was to lean over and gently kiss Warren on the cheek again. This she did every fifteen or twenty minutes without prompting or reward. Warren did not sleep.

When he told me this story, Warren's eyes filled with tears of overwhelming love and gratitude for this unforgettable morning. Terri had given her daddy the most precious thing an adoring daughter could have given—a free gift of love and affection with no expectation of any remuneration. No accolades. No pressure from anyone. No awareness that her daddy even knew what was going on. A very free gift.

"Each man should give what he has decided in his heart to give, not reluctantly or under compulsion, for God loves a cheerful giver," Paul tells us in today's passage. Without a doubt, Warren's story would have made the apostle smile.

Early one morning many years ago, just outside of Chicago, a four-year-old girl gave her grown-up daddy a lesson in cheerful giving that he would never forget. And now this story is yours to enjoy.

Go kiss someone who's sound asleep.

For your next devotional reading, go to page 1301.

that we belong to Christ just as much as he. [8]For even if I boast somewhat freely about the authority the Lord gave us for building you up rather than pulling you down, I will not be ashamed of it. [9]I do not want to seem to be trying to frighten you with my letters. [10]For some say, "His letters are weighty and forceful, but in person he is unimpressive and his speaking amounts to nothing." [11]Such people should realize that what we are in our letters when we are absent, we will be in our actions when we are present.

[12]We do not dare to classify or compare ourselves with some who commend themselves. When they measure themselves by themselves and compare themselves with themselves, they are not wise. [13]We, however, will not boast beyond proper limits, but will confine our boasting to the field God has assigned to us, a field that reaches even to you. [14]We are not going too far in our boasting, as would be the case if we had not come to you, for we did get as far as you with the gospel of Christ. [15]Neither do we go beyond our limits by boasting of work done by others.[a] Our hope is that, as your faith continues to grow, our area of activity among you will greatly expand, [16]so that we can preach the gospel in the regions beyond you. For we do not want to boast about work already done in another man's territory. [17]But, "Let him who boasts boast in the Lord."[b] [18]For it is not the one who commends himself who is approved, but the one whom the Lord commends.

Paul and the False Apostles

11 I hope you will put up with a little of my foolishness; but you are already doing that. [2]I am jealous for you with a godly jealousy. I promised you to one husband, to Christ, so that I might present you as a pure virgin to him. [3]But I am afraid that just as Eve was deceived by the serpent's cunning, your minds may somehow be led astray from your sincere and pure devotion to Christ. [4]For if someone comes to you and preaches a Jesus other than the Jesus we preached, or if you receive a different spirit from the one you received, or a different gospel from the one you accepted, you put up with it easily enough. [5]But I do not think I am in the least inferior to those "super-apostles." [6]I may not be a trained speaker, but I do have knowledge. We have made this perfectly clear to you in every way.

[7]Was it a sin for me to lower myself in order to elevate you by preaching the gospel of God to you free of charge? [8]I robbed other churches by receiving support from them so as to serve you. [9]And when I was with you and needed something, I was not a burden to anyone, for the brothers who came from Macedonia supplied what I needed. I have kept myself from being a burden to you in any way, and will continue to do so. [10]As surely as the truth of Christ is in me, nobody in the regions of Achaia will stop this boasting of mine. [11]Why? Because I do not love you? God knows I do! [12]And I will keep on doing what I am doing in order to cut the ground from under those who want an opportunity to be considered equal with us in the things they boast about.

[13]For such men are false apostles, deceitful workmen, masquerading as apostles of Christ. [14]And no wonder, for Satan himself masquerades as an angel of light. [15]It is not surprising, then, if his servants masquerade as servants of righteousness. Their end will be what their actions deserve.

Paul Boasts About His Sufferings

[16]I repeat: Let no one take me for a fool. But if you do, then receive me just as you would a fool, so that I may do a little boasting. [17]In this self-confident boasting I am not talking as the Lord would, but as a fool. [18]Since many are boasting in the way the world does, I too will boast. [19]You gladly put up with fools since you are so wise! [20]In fact, you even put up with anyone who enslaves you or exploits you or takes advantage of you or pushes himself forward or slaps you in the face. [21]To my shame I admit that we were too weak for that!

What anyone else dares to boast about—I am speaking as a fool—I also dare to boast about. [22]Are they Hebrews? So am I. Are they Israelites? So am I. Are they Abraham's descendants? So am I. [23]Are they servants of Christ? (I am out of my mind to talk like this.) I am more. I have worked much harder, been in prison more frequently, been flogged more

---

[a]13-15 Or [13]We, however, will not boast about things that cannot be measured, but we will boast according to the standard of measurement that the God of measure has assigned us—a measurement that relates even to you. [14] . . . [15]Neither do we boast about things that cannot be measured in regard to the work done by others.   [b]17 Jer. 9:24

severely, and been exposed to death again and again. [24]Five times I received from the Jews the forty lashes minus one. [25]Three times I was beaten with rods, once I was stoned, three times I was shipwrecked, I spent a night and a day in the open sea, [26]I have been constantly on the move. I have been in danger from rivers, in danger from bandits, in danger from my own countrymen, in danger from Gentiles; in danger in the city, in danger in the country, in danger at sea; and in danger from false brothers. [27]I have labored and toiled and have often gone without sleep; I have known hunger and thirst and have often gone without food; I have been cold and naked. [28]Besides everything else, I face daily the pressure of my concern for all the churches. [29]Who is weak, and I do not feel weak? Who is led into sin, and I do not inwardly burn?

[30]If I must boast, I will boast of the things that show my weakness. [31]The God and Father of the Lord Jesus, who is to be praised forever, knows that I am not lying. [32]In Damascus the governor under King Aretas had the city of the Damascenes guarded in order to arrest me. [33]But I was lowered in a basket from a window in the wall and slipped through his hands.

Paul's Vision and His Thorn

12 I must go on boasting. Although there is nothing to be gained, I will go on to visions and revelations from the Lord. [2]I know a man in Christ who fourteen years ago was caught up to the third heaven. Whether it was in the body or out of the body I do not know—God knows. [3]And I know that this man—whether in the body or apart from the body I do not know, but God knows— [4]was caught up to paradise. He heard inexpressible things, things that man is not permitted to tell. [5]I will boast about a man like that, but I will not boast about myself, except about my weaknesses. [6]Even if I should choose to boast, I would not be a fool, because I would be speaking the truth. But I refrain, so no one will think more of me than is warranted by what I do or say.

[7]To keep me from becoming conceited because of these surpassingly great revelations, there was given me a thorn in my flesh, a messenger of Satan, to torment me. [8]Three times I pleaded with the Lord to take it away from me. [9]But he said to me, "My grace is sufficient for you, for my power is made perfect in weakness."

Therefore I will boast all the more gladly about my weaknesses, so that Christ's power may rest on me. [10]That is why, for Christ's sake, I delight in weaknesses, in insults, in hardships, in persecutions, in difficulties. For when I am weak, then I am strong.

Paul's Concern for the Corinthians

[11]I have made a fool of myself, but you drove me to it. I ought to have been commended by you, for I am not in the least inferior to the "super-apostles," even though I am nothing. [12]The things that mark an apostle—signs, wonders and miracles—were done among you with great perseverance. [13]How were you inferior to the other churches, except that I was never a burden to you? Forgive me this wrong!

[14]Now I am ready to visit you for the third time, and I will not be a burden to you, because what I want is not your possessions but you. After all, children should not have to save up for their parents, but parents for their children. [15]So I will very gladly spend for you everything I have and expend myself as well. If I love you more, will you love me less? [16]Be that as it may, I have not been a burden to you. Yet, crafty fellow that I am, I caught you by trickery! [17]Did I exploit you through any of the men I sent you? [18]I urged Titus to go to you and I sent our brother with him. Titus did not exploit you, did he? Did we not act in the same spirit and follow the same course?

[19]Have you been thinking all along that we have been defending ourselves to you? We have been speaking in the sight of God as those in Christ; and everything we do, dear friends, is for your strengthening. [20]For I am afraid that when I come I may not find you as I want you to be, and you may not find me as you want me to be. I fear that there may be quarreling, jealousy, outbursts of anger, factions, slander, gossip, arrogance and disorder. [21]I am afraid that when I come again my God will humble me before you, and I will be grieved over many who have sinned earlier and have not repented of the impurity, sexual sin and debauchery in which they have indulged.

Final Warnings

13 This will be my third visit to you. "Every matter must be established by

the testimony of two or three witnesses."[a] [2]I already gave you a warning when I was with you the second time. I now repeat it while absent: On my return I will not spare those who sinned earlier or any of the others, [3]since you are demanding proof that Christ is speaking through me. He is not weak in dealing with you, but is powerful among you. [4]For to be sure, he was crucified in weakness, yet he lives by God's power. Likewise, we are weak in him, yet by God's power we will live with him to serve you.

[5]Examine yourselves to see whether you are in the faith; test yourselves. Do you not realize that Christ Jesus is in you—unless, of course, you fail the test? [6]And I trust that you will discover that we have not failed the test. [7]Now we pray to God that you will not do anything wrong. Not that people will see that we have stood the test but that you will do what is right even though we may seem to have failed. [8]For we cannot do anything against the truth, but only for the truth. [9]We are glad whenever we are weak but you are strong; and our prayer is for your perfection. [10]This is why I write these things when I am absent, that when I come I may not have to be harsh in my use of authority—the authority the Lord gave me for building you up, not for tearing you down.

Final Greetings

[11]Finally, brothers, good-by. Aim for perfection, listen to my appeal, be of one mind, live in peace. And the God of love and peace will be with you.

[12]Greet one another with a holy kiss. [13]All the saints send their greetings.

[14]May the grace of the Lord Jesus Christ, and the love of God, and the fellowship of the Holy Spirit be with you all.

[a]1 Deut. 19:15

What if someone told you that this little collection of chapters—the book of Galatians—contained the unequivocal secret to living a successful, victorious, awe-inspiring Christian life? Well, these pages *do* contain the heretofore classified mystery of how to please your heavenly Father, how to lead others to faith, and how set an example for your wife and children as a man of God.

In fact, let's cut to the chase and discover this enigmatic truth right now. Ready? Here it is. *You cannot, under any circumstances whatsoever, do any of the above.* The secret to living a prosperous Christian life is coming to the full understanding that it is *impossible* to live a prosperous Christian life. God's Holy Spirit—his power released inside a man—does all this through us. Our challenge is not to plumb the depths of our abilities, to fine-tune our skills, or to try harder. Our task is to admit our need for God's filling and to submit to his control.

Paul lived a stellar Christian life because he discovered that he couldn't.

Galatians

Paul, an apostle—sent not from men nor by man, but by Jesus Christ and God the Father, who raised him from the dead— ²and all the brothers with me,

To the churches in Galatia:

³Grace and peace to you from God our Father and the Lord Jesus Christ, ⁴who gave himself for our sins to rescue us from the present evil age, according to the will of our God and Father, ⁵to whom be glory for ever and ever. Amen.

No Other Gospel

⁶I am astonished that you are so quickly deserting the one who called you by the grace of Christ and are turning to a different gospel— ⁷which is really no gospel at all. Evidently some people are throwing you into confusion and are trying to pervert the gospel of Christ. ⁸But even if we or an angel from heaven should preach a gospel other than the one we preached to you, let him be eternally condemned! ⁹As we have already said, so now I say again: If anybody is preaching to you a gospel other than what you accepted, let him be eternally condemned!

¹⁰Am I now trying to win the approval of men, or of God? Or am I trying to please men? If I were still trying to please men, I would not be a servant of Christ.

Paul Called by God

[11]I want you to know, brothers, that the gospel I preached is not something that man made up. [12]I did not receive it from any man, nor was I taught it; rather, I received it by revelation from Jesus Christ.

[13]For you have heard of my previous way of life in Judaism, how intensely I persecuted the church of God and tried to destroy it. [14]I was advancing in Judaism beyond many Jews of my own age and was extremely zealous for the traditions of my fathers. [15]But when God, who set me apart from birth[a] and called me by his grace, was pleased [16]to reveal his Son in me so that I might preach him among the Gentiles, I did not consult any man, [17]nor did I go up to Jerusalem to see those who were apostles before I was, but I went immediately into Arabia and later returned to Damascus.

[18]Then after three years, I went up to Jerusalem to get acquainted with Peter[b] and stayed with him fifteen days. [19]I saw none of the other apostles—only James, the Lord's brother. [20]I assure you before God that what I am writing you is no lie. [21]Later I went to Syria and Cilicia. [22]I was personally unknown to the churches of Judea that are in Christ. [23]They only heard the report: "The man who formerly persecuted us is now preaching the faith he once tried to destroy." [24]And they praised God because of me.

Paul Accepted by the Apostles

2 Fourteen years later I went up again to Jerusalem, this time with Barnabas. I took Titus along also. [2]I went in response to a revelation and set before them the gospel that I preach among the Gentiles. But I did this privately to those who seemed to be leaders, for fear that I was running or had run my race in vain. [3]Yet not even Titus, who was with me, was compelled to be circumcised, even though he was a Greek. [4]This matter arose, because some false brothers had infiltrated our ranks to spy on the freedom we have in Christ Jesus and to make us slaves. [5]We did not give in to them for a moment, so that the truth of the gospel might remain with you.

[6]As for those who seemed to be important—whatever they were makes no difference to me; God does not judge by external appearance—those men added nothing to my message. [7]On the contrary, they saw that I had been entrusted with the task of preaching the gospel to the Gentiles,[c] just as Peter had been to the Jews.[d] [8]For God, who was at work in the ministry of Peter as an apostle to the Jews, was also at work in my ministry as an apostle to the Gentiles. [9]James, Peter[e] and John, those reputed to be pillars, gave me and Barnabas the right hand of fellowship when they recognized the grace given to me. They agreed that we should go to the Gentiles, and they to the Jews. [10]All they asked was that we should continue to remember the poor, the very thing I was eager to do.

[a]15 Or *from my mother's womb*   [b]18 Greek *Cephas*
[c]7 Greek *uncircumcised*   [d]7 Greek *circumcised*;
also in verses 8 and 9   [e]9 Greek *Cephas*; also in
verses 11 and 14

HEY DAD
Is anybody too bad for God to save?

Text: Galatians 1:13

No one is "so bad" that God cannot save that person. Let's compare two people. One is in prison for stealing some money to *feed* his family. The other one is in prison for *killing* his family. Which one would be easier for God to save? Are you ready for this? The answer is: They are both the same.

God does not need us to be good before he can save us. He is much bigger than that. From a Christian's point of view, no one was more terrible than Saul of Tarsus, who made it his life's work to hunt down Jesus' followers and throw them in prison. Saul, later called Paul, said this of himself: "You [Galatians] have heard of my previous way of life in Judaism, how intensely I persecuted the church of God and tried to destroy it." This man was guilty of persecuting God's family. And God did not just save him, he also used Paul to take the news of salvation to the world!

For a complete listing of Questions Kids Ask, turn to page 1435.

Paul Opposes Peter

11When Peter came to Antioch, I opposed him to his face, because he was clearly in the wrong. **12**Before certain men came from James, he used to eat with the Gentiles. But when they arrived, he began to draw back and separate himself from the Gentiles because he was afraid of those who belonged to the circumcision group. **13**The other Jews joined him in his hypocrisy, so that by their hypocrisy even Barnabas was led astray.

14When I saw that they were not acting in line with the truth of the gospel, I said to Peter in front of them all, "You are a Jew, yet you live like a Gentile and not like a Jew. How is it, then, that you force Gentiles to follow Jewish customs?

15"We who are Jews by birth and not 'Gentile sinners' **16**know that a man is not justified by observing the law, but by faith in Jesus Christ. So we, too, have put our faith in Christ Jesus that we may be justified by faith in Christ and not by observing the law, because by observing the law no one will be justified.

17"If, while we seek to be justified in Christ, it becomes evident that we ourselves are sinners, does that mean that Christ promotes sin? Absolutely not! **18**If I rebuild what I destroyed, I prove that I am a lawbreaker. **19**For through the law I died to the law so that I might live for God. **20**I have been crucified with Christ and I no longer live, but Christ lives in me. The life I live in the body, I live by faith in the Son of God, who loved me and gave himself for me. **21**I do not set aside the grace of God, for if righteousness could be gained through the law, Christ died for nothing!"[a]

Faith or Observance of the Law

3 You foolish Galatians! Who has bewitched you? Before your very eyes Jesus Christ was clearly portrayed as crucified. **2**I would like to learn just one thing from you: Did you receive the Spirit by observing the law, or by believing what you heard? **3**Are you so foolish? After beginning with the Spirit, are you now trying to attain your goal by human effort? **4**Have you suffered so much for nothing—if it really was for nothing? **5**Does God give you his Spirit and work miracles among you because you observe the law, or because you believe what you heard?

6Consider Abraham: "He believed God, and it was credited to him as righteousness."[b] **7**Understand, then, that those who believe are children of Abraham. **8**The Scripture foresaw that God would justify the Gentiles by faith, and announced the gospel in advance to Abraham: "All nations will be blessed through you."[c] **9**So those who have faith are blessed along with Abraham, the man of faith.

10All who rely on observing the law are under a curse, for it is written: "Cursed is everyone who does not continue to do everything written in the Book of the Law."[d]

a21 Some interpreters end the quotation after verse 14. *b6* Gen. 15:6 *c8* Gen. 12:3; 18:18; 22:18 *d10* Deut. 27:26

HEY DAD
If I'm really good, will God love me more?

Text: Galatians 3:1–6

God's love does not depend on our actions. That's a good thing, because we could *never* be good enough to earn or deserve God's love.

The believers in Galatia struggled with this very question. We become Christians by believing in Jesus as our Savior, not by being good. Yet, even though they were Christians, these church members had returned to their old patterns of trying to earn God's favor by following Old Testament law.

But Paul reminded the church that "[Abraham] believed God, and it was credited to him as righteousness" (v. 6). God gave the law to Moses some 430 years after Abraham's death. So, Abraham could not have earned God's love by following God's written laws.

The Bible unquestionably teaches us to obey, love and serve God. But we are to do this not to make God love *us*, but because we love *him*! What an important difference.

For a complete listing of Questions Kids Ask, turn to page 1435.

For a complete listing of Questions Kids Ask, turn to page 1435.

[11] Clearly no one is justified before God by the law, because, "The righteous will live by faith."[a] [12] The law is not based on faith; on the contrary, "The man who does these things will live by them."[b] [13] Christ redeemed us from the curse of the law by becoming a curse for us, for it is written: "Cursed is everyone who is hung on a tree."[c] [14] He redeemed us in order that the blessing given to Abraham might come to the Gentiles through Christ Jesus, so that by faith we might receive the promise of the Spirit.

[a]11 Hab. 2:4   [b]12 Lev. 18:5   [c]13 Deut. 21:23

You Have to Be This Tall to Ride

DAILY INSIGHT

Until that summer day in 1970, I had no idea how truly incompatible my wife and I were. Young love has a way of shielding such issues.

I had just picked Bobbie up from work, and we were headed back to our apartment when I spotted a carnival in the parking lot of a shopping mall. "Hey," I said in a tone that let my wife know a brilliant idea was on its way. "Let's go play at that carnival over there." Although she was tired from a full day's work as a dental assistant, Bobbie responded brightly, "Sure ... let's do it!"

I found a nice wide parking spot—door dings in parking lots infuriate me—and we headed off for the ticket window. While waiting for my change, I noticed a plywood cut-out of a child, plainly printed on which were the words, "You must be taller than me to enjoy any of the rides." *No problem here*, I thought to myself.

We walked to the first ride, the Spinning Tea Cup. "Oh *boy!*" Bobbie exclaimed, her voice reminiscent of a kid at her birthday party. "Ugh," I groaned. Spinning makes me nauseated. I threw up in second grade on the merry-go-round. "Okay," Bobbie's voice trailed off, making no attempt to hide her disappointment. Right across the way was the Roller Demon, a high-speed roller coaster. "Let's do the Demon!" I blurted out. "Yuk," Bobbie responded. "I hate fast rides." We kept walking.

We paused a moment at one of the arcade booths. "Hooray," my wife shouted. "Let's see if you can win a teddy bear for me." I sneered, "Those things are so rigged, I wouldn't waste my time." She was crestfallen. "Then can we please go do the Ferris wheel?" Bobbie asked. My heart sank. "Do you have any idea how acrophobic I am?" I confessed. "Heights freak me out. I'd rather die than get on that thing."

We continued to trudge through the carnival, unable to find one we both would enjoy. In a few minutes we gave up. On the way out, we gave our tickets to a kid standing in front of the Tilt-a-Whirl. I couldn't even look at it. *The plywood cut-out at the ticket window should have said something about spousal incompatibility,* I silently grumbled.

For centuries, God's chosen people wandered through life, living under the law while longing for the Messiah. "But when the time had fully come, God sent his Son," the apostle Paul wrote (4:4). These Hebrews were heirs, but they were like children, not quite tall enough to enjoy the rides. So they sat on the sidelines, incompatible with God's free grace, waiting and hoping for the promised Redeemer.

So God sent Jesus who welcomed them and us as his sons, making us tall enough to ride. Then he sent his Spirit, binding us to our brothers and sisters, conquering the agony of irreconcilable differences.

You're standing today at life's ticket window, waiting for your tickets to ride. The plywood sign standing right there is in the shape of a cross. "You must be redeemed in order to enjoy any of these rides," it clearly reads. "And you need God's grace to love those you're traveling with."

Don't miss the joy. Don't miss the friendship. Enjoy the ride.

TUESDAY

Passage:
Galatians 3:26—4:7

Verses:
Galatians 3:28–29

For your next devotional reading, go to page 1304.

The Law and the Promise

[15]Brothers, let me take an example from everyday life. Just as no one can set aside or add to a human covenant that has been duly established, so it is in this case. [16]The promises were spoken to Abraham and to his seed. The Scripture does not say "and to seeds," meaning many people, but "and to your seed,"[a] meaning one person, who is Christ. [17]What I mean is this: The law, introduced 430 years later, does not set aside the covenant previously established by God and thus do away with the promise. [18]For if the inheritance depends on the law, then it no longer depends on a promise; but God in his grace gave it to Abraham through a promise.

[19]What, then, was the purpose of the law? It was added because of transgressions until the Seed to whom the promise referred had come. The law was put into effect through angels by a mediator. [20]A mediator, however, does not represent just one party; but God is one.

[21]Is the law, therefore, opposed to the promises of God? Absolutely not! For if a law had been given that could impart life, then righteousness would certainly have come by the law. [22]But the Scripture declares that the whole world is a prisoner of sin, so that what was promised, being given through faith in Jesus Christ, might be given to those who believe.

[23]Before this faith came, we were held prisoners by the law, locked up until faith should be revealed. [24]So the law was put in charge to lead us to Christ[b] that we might be justified by faith. [25]Now that faith has come, we are no longer under the supervision of the law.

Sons of God

[26]You are all sons of God through faith in Christ Jesus, [27]for all of you who were baptized into Christ have clothed yourselves with Christ. [28]There is neither Jew nor Greek, slave nor free, male nor female, for you are all one in Christ Jesus. [29]If you belong to Christ, then you are Abraham's seed, and heirs according to the promise.

4 What I am saying is that as long as the heir is a child, he is no different from a slave, although he owns the whole estate. [2]He is subject to guardians and trustees until the time set by his father. [3]So also, when we were children, we were in slavery under the basic principles of the world. [4]But when the time had fully come, God sent his Son, born of a woman, born under law, [5]to redeem those under law, that we might receive the full rights of sons. [6]Because you are sons, God sent the Spirit of his Son into our hearts, the Spirit who calls out, "Abba,[c] Father." [7]So you are no longer a slave, but a son; and since you are a son, God has made you also an heir.

Paul's Concern for the Galatians

[8]Formerly, when you did not know God, you were slaves to those who by nature

[a]16 Gen. 12:7; 13:15; 24:7   [b]24 Or charge until Christ came   [c]6 Aramaic for Father

HEY DAD
What is God's opinion of racism?

Text: Galatians 3:26–29

We probably all have prejudices against people we consider strange or who think differently than we do. In Jesus' day, the Jews and the Samaritans despised each other. In America, we see racism among Asians, African Americans, Caucasians, Hispanics and many other groups. Sometimes people learn prejudice from their parents. Sometimes they base their feelings on one or two bad experiences with a member of a different race.

Regardless of the reasons for it, racism is wrong. "There is neither Jew nor Greek, slave nor free, male nor female, for you are all one in Christ Jesus" (v. 28). Christ loves all people equally, and so should we.

We must train ourselves to see others as Christ sees them. This is especially true if they are Christians. All Christians are part of our family. While we are looking down on others, we cannot possibly be looking up at God. Which focus do you think is the better choice?

For a complete listing of Questions Kids Ask, turn to page 1435.

are not gods. ⁹But now that you know
God—or rather are known by God—how
is it that you are turning back to those
weak and miserable principles? Do you
wish to be enslaved by them all over
again? ¹⁰You are observing special days
and months and seasons and years! ¹¹I
fear for you, that somehow I have wasted
my efforts on you.

¹²I plead with you, brothers, become
like me, for I became like you. You have
done me no wrong. ¹³As you know, it was
because of an illness that I first preached
the gospel to you. ¹⁴Even though my illness was a trial to you, you did not treat
me with contempt or scorn. Instead, you
welcomed me as if I were an angel of God,
as if I were Christ Jesus himself. ¹⁵What
has happened to all your joy? I can testify
that, if you could have done so, you would
have torn out your eyes and given them to
me. ¹⁶Have I now become your enemy by
telling you the truth?

¹⁷Those people are zealous to win you
over, but for no good. What they want is
to alienate you ₍from us₎, so that you may
be zealous for them. ¹⁸It is fine to be zealous, provided the purpose is good, and
to be so always and not just when I
am with you. ¹⁹My dear children, for
whom I am again in the pains of childbirth until Christ is formed in you, ²⁰how
I wish I could be with you now and
change my tone, because I am perplexed
about you!

Hagar and Sarah

²¹Tell me, you who want to be under the
law, are you not aware of what the law
says? ²²For it is written that Abraham had
two sons, one by the slave woman and the
other by the free woman. ²³His son by the
slave woman was born in the ordinary
way; but his son by the free woman was
born as the result of a promise.

²⁴These things may be taken figuratively, for the women represent two covenants. One covenant is from Mount Sinai
and bears children who are to be slaves:
This is Hagar. ²⁵Now Hagar stands for
Mount Sinai in Arabia and corresponds to
the present city of Jerusalem, because she
is in slavery with her children. ²⁶But the
Jerusalem that is above is free, and she is
our mother. ²⁷For it is written:

"Be glad, O barren woman,
    who bears no children;
break forth and cry aloud,
    you who have no labor pains;

because more are the children of the
    desolate woman
than of her who has a husband."ᵃ

²⁸Now you, brothers, like Isaac, are children of promise. ²⁹At that time the son
born in the ordinary way persecuted the
son born by the power of the Spirit. It is
the same now. ³⁰But what does the Scripture say? "Get rid of the slave woman and
her son, for the slave woman's son will
never share in the inheritance with the
free woman's son."ᵇ ³¹Therefore, brothers,
we are not children of the slave woman,
but of the free woman.

Freedom in Christ

5 It is for freedom that Christ has set us
free. Stand firm, then, and do not let
yourselves be burdened again by a yoke of
slavery.

²Mark my words! I, Paul, tell you that if
you let yourselves be circumcised, Christ
will be of no value to you at all. ³Again I
declare to every man who lets himself be
circumcised that he is obligated to obey
the whole law. ⁴You who are trying to be
justified by law have been alienated from
Christ; you have fallen away from grace.
⁵But by faith we eagerly await through the
Spirit the righteousness for which we
hope. ⁶For in Christ Jesus neither circumcision nor uncircumcision has any value.
The only thing that counts is faith expressing itself through love.

⁷You were running a good race. Who cut
in on you and kept you from obeying the
truth? ⁸That kind of persuasion does not
come from the one who calls you. ⁹"A little
yeast works through the whole batch of
dough." ¹⁰I am confident in the Lord that
you will take no other view. The one who
is throwing you into confusion will pay
the penalty, whoever he may be. ¹¹Broth-
ers, if I am still preaching circumcision,
why am I still being persecuted? In that
case the offense of the cross has been
abolished. ¹²As for those agitators, I wish
they would go the whole way and emas-
culate themselves!

¹³You, my brothers, were called to be
free. But do not use your freedom to indulge the sinful natureᶜ; rather, serve one
another in love. ¹⁴The entire law is
summed up in a single command: "Love
your neighbor as yourself."ᵈ ¹⁵If you keep
on biting and devouring each other,

ᵃ27 Isaiah 54:1   ᵇ30 Gen. 21:10   ᶜ13 Or the flesh;
also in verses 16, 17, 19 and 24   ᵈ14 Lev. 19:18

watch out or you will be destroyed by each other.

Life by the Spirit

[16]So I say, live by the Spirit, and you will not gratify the desires of the sinful nature.

[17]For the sinful nature desires what is contrary to the Spirit, and the Spirit what is contrary to the sinful nature. They are in conflict with each other, so that you do not do what you want. [18]But if you are led by the Spirit, you are not under law. [19]The acts of the sinful nature are obvi-

Frozen Up and Fruitless

DAILY INSIGHT

Have you ever been completely frozen? I'm not talking about the kind of frozen that happens when a sub-zero wind chill cuts through your warmest winter clothing, or the kind of frozen that happens when your engine oil reservoir runs dry. I'm talking about the frozen that comes when stress and pressure bring you to the breaking point.

Several months before I froze up, I had moved my family to a new city. The career decision seemed right. Running a growing division of an aggressive, publicly-traded company sounded like the perfect next step. But the day our plane touched down in our new hometown, the company's stock price began to drop. Although I knew I couldn't have been responsible, I also knew that I'd have to deal with the fallout. Several months later, sales began to slide. Other divisions began bleeding red ink. Serious personnel problems loomed ominously on the horizon. The pressure was overwhelming.

Late one afternoon, I returned to my office emotionally exhausted from a particularly brutal meeting with senior management. I slumped into my chair, looking at the pink, call-back slips that covered my desk. Several had "Urgent" written on them in big letters.

That's when I froze. I simply *couldn't move*.

Just then, an idea flashed into my brain. I literally felt a quick burst of energy. "I'm going to call Doc," I said, talking as though there was someone else in my office. I still knew his direct number by heart. The phone on the other end only rang once. "Hello," my former boss said in his familiar South Carolina drawl, "Doc," I said, choking

WEDNESDAY
Passage:
Galatians 5:22–26
Verse:
Galatians 5:22

back the tears, "it's me."

"Hello, Robert," my old friend responded. "How you doin'?" Words failed me as I began sobbing uncontrollably. After I regained my composure, I told Doc what was going on and how poorly I was handling the pressure. "How can I help you, my friend?" he finally asked, his voice filled with genuine compassion. "Tell me what you'd do if you were me," was my immediate response.

Over the next thirty minutes, my former boss, a seasoned veteran of stress and pressure, poured himself into me, filling me with assurance and wisdom I had never known before. Here I was, working for my former company's toughest competitor, still soaking in the kindness of an old friend—a man who should have celebrated the opposition's misfortune. The experience was life-changing.

Sometimes the circumstances of life stop us cold. Sometimes family pressures and work stress leave us frozen in our tracks, completely unable to move. But when we have completely run out of answers, when our solutions are woefully inadequate, when our energy and our desire to go on have vanished, God's Holy Spirit picks up the phone on the first ring. "Love, joy, peace, patience, kindness, goodness, faithfulness, gentleness and self-control" are then ours for the asking.

Let the Sovereign God of the universe thaw your cold heart. Let his grace free your aching soul. Be filled with his Spirit … he'll deliver you. I promise.

Thank you Father in heaven. Thank you, Doc.

For your next devotional reading, go to page 1305.

ous: sexual immorality, impurity and debauchery; [20]idolatry and witchcraft; hatred, discord, jealousy, fits of rage, selfish ambition, dissensions, factions [21]and envy; drunkenness, orgies, and the like. I warn you, as I did before, that those who live like this will not inherit the kingdom of God.

[22]But the fruit of the Spirit is love, joy, peace, patience, kindness, goodness, faithfulness, [23]gentleness and self-control. Against such things there is no law.

You Sow; You Reap. Ask God.

DAILY INSIGHT

THURSDAY

Passage:
Galatians 6:7–10

Verse:
Galatians 6:7

Hollywood is rarely a friend to the Christian faith. The violence, the gratuitous sex, the foul language, the celebration of illicit relationships, the unfortunate images of fathers and the distortion of Biblical truths fight against who we are and what we believe.

There have been exceptions. No one but Hollywood could have brought us such Biblically based epics as The Ten Commandments and Ben Hur. And Hollywood has also produced films such as Chariots of Fire that have strong, faith-building themes. Animators have even given us a block buster on the life of Moses. So there have been a few wonderful exceptions.

Although my wife and I haven't been voracious movie-goers, we have taken in a number of shows in the decades we've been together. Invariably, our favorite films are the ones that present healing redemption in the lives of their characters, or the ones that undeniably reinforce Biblical truth.

One such movie we saw many years ago did the latter exceptionally well. This film featured Michael Douglas as a young, happily married marketing executive who sent his wife, played by Annette Benning, and their child off to visit the grandparents for the weekend. On Saturday morning he hosted a special meeting at his office, attended by several of his associates and a female consultant played by Glenn Close.

The movie skillfully led viewers into the beginnings of what would become, for these two characters, a weekend filled with passion. Given Hollywood's propensity to treat this subject with gratuity, these scenes were graphically depicted—something my wife and I didn't appreciate. Then, in the pre-dawn hours of Monday morning,

Michael Douglas's character said good-bye and drove home. A few hours later, Annette Benning's character and their daughter returned from their happy weekend.

More often than not, these furious trysts are treated with a wink and an "adults will be adults" grin. Not this time. Glenn Close, revealing her character's deeply psychotic nature, pursued her lover. It was subtle at first, but as he tried to brush off her advances, her anger at his rejection exploded into vicious rage. What had begun as a weekend of hot-blooded consent became the nightmare of Douglas's life.

As we were driving away from the movie theater that night, I said to my wife, "A man reaps what he sows" (6:7b). She agreed that this movie had strikingly depicted that truth.

Ironically, this movie may have actually discouraged more weekend rendezvous than any sermon ever preached. The message was clear: sleep with a partner other than your spouse, and you'll pay the price. What the movie missed was the rationale behind this truth, which had nothing to do with the emotional health of either party. "Commit adultery and pay" is true because *God says* it's true. "Do not be deceived: God cannot be mocked" (6:7a). Sin has consequences—every single time.

God's laws are like that. Obey them, and you'll ultimately enjoy life as it was truly meant to be enjoyed. Break these laws, and you'll pay a desperate price. Sometimes, even though we know better, Biblical truth feels confining, restrictive and unfairly binding. This Biblical truth feels like a breath of fresh air.

For your next devotional reading, go to page 1308.

[24]Those who belong to Christ Jesus have crucified the sinful nature with its passions and desires. [25]Since we live by the Spirit, let us keep in step with the Spirit. [26]Let us not become conceited, provoking and envying each other.

Doing Good to All

6 Brothers, if someone is caught in a sin, you who are spiritual should restore him gently. But watch yourself, or you also may be tempted. [2]Carry each other's burdens, and in this way you will fulfill the law of Christ. [3]If anyone thinks he is something when he is nothing, he deceives himself. [4]Each one should test his own actions. Then he can take pride in himself, without comparing himself to somebody else, [5]for each one should carry his own load.

[6]Anyone who receives instruction in the word must share all good things with his instructor.

[7]Do not be deceived: God cannot be mocked. A man reaps what he sows. [8]The one who sows to please his sinful nature, from that nature[a] will reap destruction; the one who sows to please the Spirit, from the Spirit will reap eternal life. [9]Let us not become weary in doing good, for at the proper time we will reap a harvest if we do not give up. [10]Therefore, as we have opportunity, let us do good to all people, especially to those who belong to the family of believers.

Not Circumcision but a New Creation

[11]See what large letters I use as I write to you with my own hand!

[12]Those who want to make a good impression outwardly are trying to compel you to be circumcised. The only reason they do this is to avoid being persecuted for the cross of Christ. [13]Not even those who are circumcised obey the law, yet they want you to be circumcised that they may boast about your flesh. [14]May I never boast except in the cross of our Lord Jesus Christ, through which[b] the world has been crucified to me, and I to the world. [15]Neither circumcision nor uncircumcision means anything; what counts is a new creation. [16]Peace and mercy to all who follow this rule, even to the Israel of God.

[17]Finally, let no one cause me trouble, for I bear on my body the marks of Jesus.

[18]The grace of our Lord Jesus Christ be with your spirit, brothers. Amen.

[a]8 Or *his flesh, from the flesh*   [b]14 Or *whom*

Sometimes obedience to Christ seems abstract, theoretical, difficult to grasp. What does it look like for a man to get along with fellow believers? How does he live out his Christianity at work? How can he maximize his relationship with his wife? What is the best way to effectively parent his children and motivate them to follow Christ? How can he face and defeat the temptations that constantly swirl around him?

Someone must have asked these very same questions of the apostle Paul, because the book of Ephesians is filled with very practical answers to every one of these questions. The next time someone challenges you with the unrealistic and ethereal expectations of your faith, show them this book. By the way, if you're feeling a little overwhelmed by the task of being God's man in your home, you've come to the right place.

Ephesians

Paul, an apostle of Christ Jesus by the will of God,

To the saints in Ephesus,[a] the faithful[b] in Christ Jesus:

[2]Grace and peace to you from God our Father and the Lord Jesus Christ.

Spiritual Blessings in Christ

[3]Praise be to the God and Father of our Lord Jesus Christ, who has blessed us in the heavenly realms with every spiritual blessing in Christ. [4]For he chose us in him before the creation of the world to be holy and blameless in his sight. In love [5]he[c] predestined us to be adopted as his sons through Jesus Christ, in accordance with his pleasure and will— [6]to the praise of his glorious grace, which he has freely given us in the One he loves. [7]In him we have redemption through his blood, the forgiveness of sins, in accordance with the riches of God's grace [8]that he lavished on us with

all wisdom and understanding. [9]And he[d] made known to us the mystery of his will according to his good pleasure, which he purposed in Christ, [10]to be put into effect when the times will have reached their fulfillment—to bring all things in heaven and on earth together under one head, even Christ.

[11]In him we were also chosen,[e] having been predestined according to the plan of him who works out everything in conformity with the purpose of his will, [12]in order that we, who were the first to hope in Christ, might be for the praise of his glory. [13]And you also were included in Christ when you heard the word of truth, the gospel of your salvation. Having believed, you were marked in him with a seal, the promised Holy Spirit, [14]who is a deposit

---

[a]1 Some early manuscripts do not have *in Ephesus*.
[b]1 Or *believers who are* [c]4,5 Or *sight in love.* [5]*He*
[d]8,9 Or *us. With all wisdom and understanding,* [9]*he*
[e]11 Or *were made heirs*

guaranteeing our inheritance until the redemption of those who are God's possession—to the praise of his glory.

Thanksgiving and Prayer

15For this reason, ever since I heard about your faith in the Lord Jesus and your love for all the saints, **16**I have not stopped giving thanks for you, remembering you in my prayers. **17**I keep asking that the God of our Lord Jesus Christ, the glorious Father, may give you the Spirit[a] of wisdom and revelation, so that you may know him better. **18**I pray also that the eyes of your heart may be enlightened in order that you may know the hope to which he has called you, the riches of his glorious inheritance in the saints, **19**and his incomparably great power for us who believe. That power is like the working of his mighty strength, **20**which he exerted in Christ when he raised him from the dead and seated him at his right hand in the heavenly realms, **21**far above all rule and authority, power and dominion, and ev-

[a]17 Or *a spirit*

God's Building Materials

DAILY INSIGHT

FRIDAY

Passage:
Ephesians 2:11–22

Verses:
Ephesians 2:19–20

When I was a young man, I took a job with a contractor to help pay my college tuition. I had always been fascinated with construction, and this was my chance to get in on the ground floor, so to speak.

My very first day on the job, in early June of 1965, we were pouring footings for a house in Glen Ellyn, Illinois. By the time I found the job site, a cement-mixer was already there discharging concrete into the forms. My boss and his assistant were helping to direct the heavy gray stuff into the right places. Thinking this was going to be fun, I grabbed a hoe. This was my first experience of working with concrete. By the end of the day, I discovered why all cement workers are big and strong. My muscles felt like pasta.

Over the next several summers, I learned what I had discovered earlier in my mother's kitchen during an ill-fated attempt to bake a chocolate cake. Every worthwhile thing consists of a mix of strange ingredients, and if you follow someone who is experienced in working with these things, you're going to get what you're looking for.

Building a beautiful and sturdy house takes concrete, steel, lumber, wire, copper pipe, brick—set with a mixture of cement and lime—heavy lumber, window sashes, plywood, tile, grout, and so forth. And in order for all of these things to come together in a way that creates a livable and lovely dwelling, it's best to have experienced folks as the teachers.

The apostle Paul calls the ingredients that make up God's house, "foreigners and aliens." These elements are the gravel, plaster board, and asphalt shingles of his house. However, in God's miraculous fashion, he takes these unlikely ingredients—just look at us!—and, out of them, creates a "household" ... a "holy temple." Wow.

As we have discovered throughout the Scriptures, this is a perfect image of our own homes. We start with unlikely components, individuals who truly want to live together but who are as different as concrete and insulation, as opposite as reinforcing rods and glass. But God calls dads—unlikely general contractors like you and me—to take these components and build a wonderful family, a strong and safe home.

Doing this successfully takes a lot of work. It takes a great deal of patience. Most of all, building this house takes confidence in the One with all the experience. Trust God with the integrity of the elements and the experience of using an unlikely mix of ingredients to produce a wonderful outcome. After all, he's done this plenty of times before.

For your next devotional reading, go to page 1312.

ery title that can be given, not only in the present age but also in the one to come. ²²And God placed all things under his feet and appointed him to be head over everything for the church, ²³which is his body, the fullness of him who fills everything in every way.

Made Alive in Christ

2 As for you, you were dead in your transgressions and sins, ²in which you used to live when you followed the ways of this world and of the ruler of the kingdom of the air, the spirit who is now at work in those who are disobedient. ³All of us also lived among them at one time, gratifying the cravings of our sinful nature[a] and following its desires and thoughts. Like the rest, we were by nature objects of wrath. ⁴But because of his great love for us, God, who is rich in mercy, ⁵made us alive with Christ even when we were dead in transgressions—it is by grace you have been saved. ⁶And God raised us up with Christ and seated us with him in the heavenly realms in Christ Jesus, ⁷in order that in the coming ages he might show the incomparable riches of his grace, expressed in his kindness to us in Christ Jesus. ⁸For it is by grace you have been saved, through faith—and this not from yourselves, it is the gift of God— ⁹not by works, so that no one can boast. ¹⁰For we are God's workmanship, created in Christ Jesus to do good works, which God prepared in advance for us to do.

One in Christ

¹¹Therefore, remember that formerly you who are Gentiles by birth and called "uncircumcised" by those who call themselves "the circumcision" (that done in the body by the hands of men)— ¹²remember that at that time you were separate from Christ, excluded from citizenship in Israel and foreigners to the covenants of the promise, without hope and without God in the world. ¹³But now in Christ Jesus you who once were far away have been brought near through the blood of Christ.

¹⁴For he himself is our peace, who has made the two one and has destroyed the barrier, the dividing wall of hostility, ¹⁵by abolishing in his flesh the law with its commandments and regulations. His purpose was to create in himself one new man out of the two, thus making peace, ¹⁶and in this one body to reconcile both of them to God through the cross, by which he put to death their hostility. ¹⁷He came and preached peace to you who were far away and peace to those who were near. ¹⁸For through him we both have access to the Father by one Spirit.

¹⁹Consequently, you are no longer foreigners and aliens, but fellow citizens with God's people and members of God's household, ²⁰built on the foundation of the apostles and prophets, with Christ Jesus himself as the chief cornerstone. ²¹In him the whole building is joined together and rises to become a holy temple in the Lord. ²²And in him you too are being built together to become a dwelling in which God lives by his Spirit.

Paul the Preacher to the Gentiles

3 For this reason I, Paul, the prisoner of Christ Jesus for the sake of you Gentiles—

²Surely you have heard about the administration of God's grace that was given to me for you, ³that is, the mystery made known to me by revelation, as I have already written briefly. ⁴In reading this, then, you will be able to understand my insight into the mystery of Christ, ⁵which was not made known to men in other generations as it has now been revealed by the Spirit to God's holy apostles and prophets. ⁶This mystery is that through the gospel the Gentiles are heirs together with Israel, members together of one body, and sharers together in the promise in Christ Jesus.

⁷I became a servant of this gospel by the gift of God's grace given me through the working of his power. ⁸Although I am less than the least of all God's people, this grace was given me: to preach to the Gentiles the unsearchable riches of Christ, ⁹and to make plain to everyone the administration of this mystery, which for ages past was kept hidden in God, who created all things. ¹⁰His intent was that now, through the church, the manifold wisdom of God should be made known to the rulers and authorities in the heavenly realms, ¹¹according to his eternal purpose which he accomplished in Christ Jesus our Lord. ¹²In him and through faith in him we may approach God with freedom and confidence. ¹³I ask you, therefore, not to be discouraged because of my sufferings for you, which are your glory.

[a]3 Or *our flesh*

A Prayer for the Ephesians

14For this reason I kneel before the Father, **15**from whom his whole family*a* in heaven and on earth derives its name. **16**I pray that out of his glorious riches he may strengthen you with power through his Spirit in your inner being, **17**so that Christ may dwell in your hearts through faith. And I pray that you, being rooted and established in love, **18**may have power, together with all the saints, to grasp how wide and long and high and deep is the love of Christ, **19**and to know this love that surpasses knowledge—that you may be filled to the measure of all the fullness of God.

20Now to him who is able to do immeasurably more than all we ask or imagine, according to his power that is at work within us, **21**to him be glory in the church and in Christ Jesus throughout all generations, for ever and ever! Amen.

Unity in the Body of Christ

4 As a prisoner for the Lord, then, I urge you to live a life worthy of the calling you have received. **2**Be completely humble and gentle; be patient, bearing with one another in love. **3**Make every effort to keep the unity of the Spirit through the bond of peace. **4**There is one body and one Spirit— just as you were called to one hope when you were called— **5**one Lord, one faith, one baptism; **6**one God and Fa-

ther of all, who is over all and through all and in all.

7But to each one of us grace has been given as Christ apportioned it. **8**This is why it*b* says:

"When he ascended on high,
  he led captives in his train
  and gave gifts to men."*c*

9(What does "he ascended" mean except that he also descended to the lower, earthly regions*d*? **10**He who descended is the very one who ascended higher than all the heavens, in order to fill the whole universe.) **11**It was he who gave some to be apostles, some to be prophets, some to be evangelists, and some to be pastors and teachers, **12**to prepare God's people for works of service, so that the body of Christ may be built up **13**until we all reach unity in the faith and in the knowledge of the Son of God and become mature, attaining to the whole measure of the fullness of Christ.

14Then we will no longer be infants, tossed back and forth by the waves, and blown here and there by every wind of teaching and by the cunning and craftiness of men in their deceitful scheming. **15**Instead, speaking the truth in love, we will in all things grow up into him who is the Head, that is, Christ. **16**From him the

*a*15 Or *whom all fatherhood*   *b*8 Or *God*
*c*8 Psalm 68:18   *d*9 Or *the depths of the earth*

HEY DAD

Should I tell the truth, even if it hurts someone's feelings?

Text: Ephesians 4:25

While telling the truth is important, being tactful and kind is also important. So, it is not okay to constantly blurt out hurtful opinions in the name of truth. On the other hand, we must not temper our beliefs just to avoid hurt feelings.

Paul instructed the Ephesians to "put off falsehood and speak truthfully to [their] neighbor[s]." This is especially true in the church. Because we are members of the same body, we are to treat others as if they were a part of ourselves. We must lovingly confront wrong behavior because it damages the church, the body of Jesus Christ. Imagine breaking your arm but trying to convince your brain that your arm was not broken. It sounds absurd, doesn't it? You would *want* your brain to know so you could get that arm into a cast as quickly as possible!

It is not fun to tell a friend that his or her "arm is broken," but we need to tell that friend the truth so he or she can avoid greater pain later. Wouldn't you want someone to do the same for you?

QUESTIONS KIDS ASK

For a complete listing of Questions Kids Ask, turn to page 1435.

whole body, joined and held together by every supporting ligament, grows and builds itself up in love, as each part does its work.

Living as Children of Light

17So I tell you this, and insist on it in the Lord, that you must no longer live as the Gentiles do, in the futility of their thinking. **18**They are darkened in their understanding and separated from the life of God because of the ignorance that is in them due to the hardening of their hearts. **19**Having lost all sensitivity, they have given themselves over to sensuality so as to indulge in every kind of impurity, with a continual lust for more.

20You, however, did not come to know Christ that way. **21**Surely you heard of him and were taught in him in accordance with the truth that is in Jesus. **22**You were taught, with regard to your former way of life, to put off your old self, which is being corrupted by its deceitful desires; **23**to be made new in the attitude of your minds; **24**and to put on the new self, created to be like God in true righteousness and holiness.

25Therefore each of you must put off falsehood and speak truthfully to his neighbor, for we are all members of one body. **26**"In your anger do not sin"*a*: Do not let the sun go down while you are still angry, **27**and do not give the devil a foothold. **28**He who has been stealing must steal no longer, but must work, doing something useful with his own hands, that he may have something to share with those in need.

29Do not let any unwholesome talk come out of your mouths, but only what is helpful for building others up according to their needs, that it may benefit those who listen. **30**And do not grieve the Holy Spirit of God, with whom you were sealed for the day of redemption. **31**Get rid of all bitterness, rage and anger, brawling and slander, along with every form of malice. **32**Be kind and compassionate to one another, forgiving each other, just as in Christ God forgave you.

5 Be imitators of God, therefore, as dearly loved children **2**and live a life of love, just as Christ loved us and gave himself up for us as a fragrant offering and sacrifice to God.

3But among you there must not be even a hint of sexual immorality, or of any kind of impurity, or of greed, because these are improper for God's holy people. **4**Nor should there be obscenity, foolish talk or coarse joking, which are out of place, but rather thanksgiving. **5**For of this you can be sure: No immoral, impure or greedy person—such a man is an idolater—has any inheritance in the kingdom of Christ and of God.*b* **6**Let no one deceive you with empty words, for because of such things God's wrath comes on those who are disobedient. **7**Therefore do not be partners with them.

a26 Psalm 4:4   *b5* Or *kingdom of the Christ and God*

Does God ever get sad?

Text: Ephesians 4:30—5:1

God *does* get sad. He is sad when we do things that are wrong. Ephesians 4:30 says we should not "grieve" the Holy Spirit. And the original Greek word for "grieve" means to distress, to be sad, to cause grief, to be in heaviness, to make sorry.

When we are filled with bitterness, rage, anger, gossip and hatred, we make God sad. We make his heart heavy. So the Bible tells us to be "imitators of God" (5:1).

Just as we can make God sad, we can also make him happy. Imagine that. When we choose to do the right things, to love and speak encouraging words to others, to tell the truth, to honor our parents and to forgive others, we please God.

Our choices are important to God. Good ones please him. Bad ones make him sad. So, it is important that we make the right choices!

For a complete listing of Questions Kids Ask, turn to page 1435.

Our Three-legged Family

Key Verse: *"Be kind and compassionate to one another, forgiving each other, just as in Christ God forgave you."* Ephesians 4:32
Text: Ephesians 4:29–32 *(Dad or child reads the text.)*

QUIET TIMES WITH Dad

DAD READS: Have you ever seen a three-legged stool? Years ago, farmers would sit on these when they milked their cows.

Child reads: Yes, and I have also seen photographers using three-legged stands called "tripods" to hold their cameras steady. These tripods have three legs instead of four because three-legged things never wobble.

DAD READS: Today's verse could be our family's three-legged milking stool ... our very own family tripod. The three legs are kindness, compassion or tenderness, and forgiveness. Practicing these three things in our home will help us to hold everything steady.

Child reads: Kindness is doing nice things for each other, especially when we're not asked to do them. Surprising you by doing a chore that you didn't ask me to do would be a kind thing. Doing kind things for each other keeps families from wobbling.

DAD READS: Compassion, or tenderness, is listening to each other when we have something to say. Compassion not only helps me to know what you're going through, it also helps me to feel what you are feeling. The Bible tells us to "Rejoice with those who rejoice; mourn with those who mourn" (Romans 12:15). This is compassion. Being tender at our home keeps our family from wobbling.

Child reads: The third leg is forgiveness. This is asking other people to pardon us for unkind things

we do and say. Forgiveness also means that I forgive others when they do unkind things to me. When Jesus was dying on the cross, he asked his Father to "forgive" the horrible things that these people had done to him. If he can forgive, I can, too. Forgiving each other will keep our family from wobbling.

DAD READS: There they are, the three legs on our family milking stool ... the three legs on our own tripod: kindness, compassion, and forgiveness. If we use these three legs every day, our family will be strong. If we are kind to each other, listen carefully, and are quick to forgive each other, our home will not wobble or fall. Let me pray this prayer with you:

Our Father in heaven, we love you. Thank you for kindness, compassion, and forgiveness—the three things that will keep our family from shaking or falling. Thank you that Jesus modeled these three things during his life on earth; help us to model them for others. We love you and we thank you for your love. In Jesus' name, **Amen.**

For your next devotional reading, go to page 1313.

[8]For you were once darkness, but now you are light in the Lord. Live as children of light [9](for the fruit of the light consists in all goodness, righteousness and truth) [10]and find out what pleases the Lord. [11]Have nothing to do with the fruitless deeds of darkness, but rather expose them. [12]For it is shameful even to mention what the disobedient do in secret. [13]But everything exposed by the light becomes visible, [14]for it is light that makes everything visible. This is why it is said:

"Wake up, O sleeper,
   rise from the dead,
and Christ will shine on you."

[15]Be very careful, then, how you live—not as unwise but as wise, [16]making the most of every opportunity, because the days are evil. [17]Therefore do not be foolish, but understand what the Lord's will is. [18]Do not get drunk on wine, which leads to debauchery. Instead, be filled with the Spirit. [19]Speak to one another with psalms, hymns and spiritual songs. Sing and make music in your heart to the Lord, [20]always giving thanks to God the Father for everything, in the name of our Lord Jesus Christ.
[21]Submit to one another out of reverence for Christ.

Volleyball, Anyone?

DAILY INSIGHT

MONDAY

Passage:
Ephesians 5:21–28

Verse:
Ephesians 5:21

Volleyball has always been one of my favorite sports. I have many happy memories of playing the game at summer camp and at family reunions. I like volleyball because it is truly a team sport, an activity where people actually help each other win the game. When the ball comes to me, I can hit it to someone else who then hits it to another person for the winning spike.

I also enjoy tennis. But when the ball comes to me, I'm the only one who can smash it back. Even doubles tennis doesn't allow for any sharing. Doubles players can't lob the little yellow ball to their partners for the winning smash; all they can do is cover different parts of the same court.

Paul writes about the marriage team in this famous passage, "Submit to one another out of reverence for Christ" (5:21). If he had had access to the two sports, this athletics-minded apostle might have said it this way: "Marriage is not like singles tennis. It's not even like doubles tennis. Marriage is more like volleyball, and you and your family are on the same team."

Isn't this a great picture? Challenges, circumstances, or opportunities come flying across the net. Someone takes the initial hit. This may come at some level of personal sacrifice, especially if the ball came over the net as a result of the opponent's vicious spike. Diving on the ground to save the ball or taking the shot in the face are not unusual in this game.

But good volleyball players save the ball to someone on their own team; they rarely hit it right back where it came from. The second team member is the most important person in this play. He or she takes the save from the first player and directs it to the best person to win the point.

Over the centuries, many people—insecure men especially—have taken five singly-selected words from today's text, "Wives, submit to your husbands," and have used them to beat their own inflated chests. This is neither a pretty sight nor is it Biblical. Men who have done this have perpetuated a vicious lie.

Of course, every working team has individuals who are willing to assume strategic roles. Some have rocket serves, some dive to the floor for saves, and others specialize in spikes. God's plan is for dads to keep an eye on the entire family, making certain that each player is thoroughly trained, coached and motivated. But his job is to serve, to share, to participate and to give his life for the whole team.

Good dads do not have tennis racquets in their hands; they are playing a different game. Get ready, here comes a volleyball right now. It's really moving, and it's headed right for you. You can do this.

For your next devotional reading, go to page 1314.

Wives and Husbands

²²Wives, submit to your husbands as to the Lord. ²³For the husband is the head of the wife as Christ is the head of the church, his body, of which he is the Savior. ²⁴Now as the church submits to Christ, so also wives should submit to their husbands in everything.

²⁵Husbands, love your wives, just as Christ loved the church and gave himself up for her ²⁶to make her holy, cleansing*ᵃ* her by the washing with water through the word, ²⁷and to present her to himself as a radiant church, without stain or wrinkle or any other blemish, but holy and blameless. ²⁸In this same way, husbands ought to love their wives as their own bodies. He who loves his wife loves himself. ²⁹After all, no one ever hated his own body, but he feeds and cares for it, just as Christ does the church— ³⁰for we are members of his body. ³¹"For this reason a man will leave his father and mother and be united to his wife, and the two will become one flesh."*ᵇ* ³²This is a

ᵃ26 Or *having cleansed*   *ᵇ31* Gen. 2:24

Training—This Time You Go First

DAILY INSIGHT

From 1965 to 1968, during the summers between my college years, I worked for Richard Whitmer & Son, a small-time building contractor. The "& Son" on his truck was technically true, but his son, my good friend, had opted for something a little less sweaty. Jim was a photographer.

During the years I worked for him, Dick Whitmer had one full-time employee: me. And I loved it. I watched this wonderfully skilled craftsman line up the forms for a foundation, cut and fit wood with flawless precision, lay brick "straight and true" (his favorite expression), safely wire a house for electricity, and much more.

After several years of doing the menial tasks, my boss invited me to begin trying the skilled work myself. I loved the challenge, but it was a great comfort to begin learning these trades with the seasoned craftsman close by. As I would take a shot at connecting two wires or setting a brick in place, Dick was right there to make certain it was done correctly. I don't recall him ever sneering an answer to a stupid question or snatching something out of my hand because I was doing it improperly.

The apostle Paul tells us about a similar situation in which the craftsman is a dad, and the building project is his children. The words "Bring them up in the training and instruction of the Lord" reminds us to instruct our kids—our understudies and

TUESDAY

Passage:
Ephesians 6:1–9

Verse:
Ephesians 6:4

apprentices—as God would have us train them (6:4). When they are older, they will learn their own lessons from the Master.

What happens if we fail to be the hands-on trainer? What do we do when we try to tell our kids what to do without providing them with a live demonstration? The text says it best ... we "exasperate" them. What a powerful word!

In the dozens of years since my college days, I have tackled many building projects on my own. Some of these have included things I watched my boss, the craftsman, do himself. And some have pushed me way beyond my level of experience or training. I boldly assumed that I'd be able to figure it out on my own ... and I was usually wrong.

Have you been there? Do you know how it feels to literally be stuck with no one to help you? Your hands actually feel weak. You're defeated. Angry. "How can I go on without anyone to show me what to do?" you mumble to yourself. Pretty miserable, isn't it?

This Scripture challenges us to do our best to keep our children from experiencing this feeling. We must make sure that they don't have to go through the frustration of being told what to do without the luxury of first watching us do it ourselves.

Don't exasperate your kids. You go first.

For your next devotional reading, go to page 1315.

profound mystery—but I am talking about Christ and the church. [33]However, each one of you also must love his wife as he loves himself, and the wife must respect her husband.

Children and Parents

6 Children, obey your parents in the Lord, for this is right. [2]"Honor your father and mother"—which is the first commandment with a promise— [3]"that it may go well with you and that you may enjoy long life on the earth."[a]

[4]Fathers, do not exasperate your children; instead, bring them up in the training and instruction of the Lord.

Slaves and Masters

[5]Slaves, obey your earthly masters with respect and fear, and with sincerity of

[a]3 Deut. 5:16

The Right Stuff

DAILY INSIGHT

WEDNESDAY

Passage:
Ephesians 6:10–18

Verses:
Ephesians 6:10–11

The very first time you buy sports equipment for your son or daughter, you're amazed— not so much at the price, but at how incredibly flimsy this "equipment" is. If you slipped one of those cheap helmets onto a player in the National Football League, you'd have shards of plastic everywhere after just one collision ... and probably pieces of the player's head, too. A child's hockey stick would look like a handful of Popsickle™ sticks the moment it tried to stop a real puck.

All of this, of course, is no surprise to the manufacturers of this children's equipment. "This helmet is not to be used to protect a child's head," you'll read somewhere on the helmet. "This hockey stick is only a child's toy."

As your son or daughter begins to excel in a particular sport, the equipment begins to get more and more substantial ... right along with the price. But you're happy to pay more for equipment that does the job. After all, that's your posterity out there, and you want his or her head securely protected.

The more ambitious the opposition, the more sound the protective equipment must be. So, what if the competition is "the powers of this dark world and ... the spiritual forces of evil in the heavenly realms" (6:12)? Then you and I need the best equipment available.

The apostle Paul called this protective gear, "the full armor of God." Truth, righteousness, peace, faith, and salvation are necessary if we are going to survive the onslaughts of the wicked one. Look back over the list. These are accouterments money can't buy.

But wait a minute. First, Paul tells us to be strong; then he tells us to suit up because we don't have a chance to be strong. Is Paul telling us to do two opposite things here?

Admittedly, most of us don't like this. We feel like we're tough enough to take on the opposition alone. We don't mind the rigors of a challenge, even one that seems monumental. But let's not fool ourselves. Our opponent is Satan himself, the Prince of Darkness. If our intention is to take him on without a belt, one breastplate short, barefooted, having left our shield in the locker room and our helmet on the sidelines, we're dead. We have no chance at all.

The greater the opponent, the more sober the necessary protection. If we're going to be serious about being God's man in our home—and who among us doesn't want to be—then we're going to have to admit to our heavenly Father that we're incapable of doing this without him.

"Father in heaven, please give me the discipline to follow you. Forgive me for ever thinking that I could do this on my own. I need your truth. I need your righteousness. I need your peace. I need faith. I need your grace."

You're in the big leagues now. You'd better be ready with the right stuff.

For your next devotional reading, go to page 1318.

heart, just as you would obey Christ. [6]Obey them not only to win their favor when their eye is on you, but like slaves of Christ, doing the will of God from your heart. [7]Serve wholeheartedly, as if you were serving the Lord, not men, [8]because you know that the Lord will reward everyone for whatever good he does, whether he is slave or free.

[9]And masters, treat your slaves in the same way. Do not threaten them, since you know that he who is both their Master and yours is in heaven, and there is no favoritism with him.

The Armor of God

[10]Finally, be strong in the Lord and in his mighty power. [11]Put on the full armor of God so that you can take your stand against the devil's schemes. [12]For our struggle is not against flesh and blood, but against the rulers, against the authorities, against the powers of this dark world and against the spiritual forces of evil in the heavenly realms. [13]Therefore put on the full armor of God, so that when the day of evil comes, you may be able to stand your ground, and after you have done everything, to stand. [14]Stand firm then, with the belt of truth buckled around your waist, with the breastplate of

righteousness in place, [15]and with your feet fitted with the readiness that comes from the gospel of peace. [16]In addition to all this, take up the shield of faith, with which you can extinguish all the flaming arrows of the evil one. [17]Take the helmet of salvation and the sword of the Spirit, which is the word of God. [18]And pray in the Spirit on all occasions with all kinds of prayers and requests. With this in mind, be alert and always keep on praying for all the saints.

[19]Pray also for me, that whenever I open my mouth, words may be given me so that I will fearlessly make known the mystery of the gospel, [20]for which I am an ambassador in chains. Pray that I may declare it fearlessly, as I should.

Final Greetings

[21]Tychicus, the dear brother and faithful servant in the Lord, will tell you everything, so that you also may know how I am and what I am doing. [22]I am sending him to you for this very purpose, that you may know how we are, and that he may encourage you.

[23]Peace to the brothers, and love with faith from God the Father and the Lord Jesus Christ. [24]Grace to all who love our Lord Jesus Christ with an undying love.

It's not what happens to you that matters, it's what *happens* when something happens to you that truly counts. We can't necessarily control our circumstances, but we can usually control our reactions when circumstances change. The great challenge is not to try to adjust to inevitable changes and tough times, because we can't. Our challenge is to learn how to live peaceably with them, as did the apostle Paul.

Paul wrote the book of Philippians from a prison cell. This was probably not Paul's preferred ministry base, and it certainly wasn't a pleasant place. But when you read this book, you'll find that it's written from a healthy perspective that reveals Paul's thanksgiving and deep joy. Paul understood that change was inevitable and that times would be tough. So he took the raw materials of his circumstances and built something incredibly encouraging out of them. And if Paul can do this sitting in a jail cell, we can do it no matter what our circumstances.

Philippians

Paul and Timothy, servants of Christ Jesus,

To all the saints in Christ Jesus at Philippi, together with the overseers[a] and deacons:

²Grace and peace to you from God our Father and the Lord Jesus Christ.

Thanksgiving and Prayer

³I thank my God every time I remember you. ⁴In all my prayers for all of you, I always pray with joy ⁵because of your partnership in the gospel from the first day until now, ⁶being confident of this, that he who began a good work in you will carry it on to completion until the day of Christ Jesus.

⁷It is right for me to feel this way about all of you, since I have you in my heart; for whether I am in chains or defending and confirming the gospel, all of you share in God's grace with me. ⁸God can testify how I long for all of you with the affection of Christ Jesus.

⁹And this is my prayer: that your love may abound more and more in knowledge and depth of insight, ¹⁰so that you may be able to discern what is best and may be pure and blameless until the day of Christ, ¹¹filled with the fruit of righteousness that comes through Jesus Christ—to the glory and praise of God.

Paul's Chains Advance the Gospel

¹²Now I want you to know, brothers, that what has happened to me has really served to advance the gospel. ¹³As a result,

---

a1 Traditionally bishops

it has become clear throughout the whole palace guard[a] and to everyone else that I am in chains for Christ. [14]Because of my chains, most of the brothers in the Lord have been encouraged to speak the word of God more courageously and fearlessly.

[15]It is true that some preach Christ out of envy and rivalry, but others out of goodwill. [16]The latter do so in love, knowing that I am put here for the defense of the gospel. [17]The former preach Christ out of selfish ambition, not sincerely, supposing that they can stir up trouble for me while I am in chains.[b] [18]But what does it matter? The important thing is that in every way, whether from false motives or true, Christ is preached. And because of this I rejoice.

Yes, and I will continue to rejoice, [19]for I know that through your prayers and the help given by the Spirit of Jesus Christ, what has happened to me will turn out for

[a]13 Or whole palace   [b]16,17 Some late manuscripts have verses 16 and 17 in reverse order.

Be a Thank-you-note Man

DAILY INSIGHT

THURSDAY

Passage:
Philippians 1:1–11

Verse:
Philippians 1:3

I have had some wonderful friends over the years, but there has always been something very unusual about Billy Webb. It took me a while to figure out what was so special about this particular friend.

You see, Billy Webb has a terrific sense of humor. His stories, mostly about himself, are legendary. I love to be with Billy, partly because he makes me laugh. But it's more than that; I have lots of other friends who also make me laugh.

Billy Webb loves God and truly wants to be a husband and father who honors him. We've talked many times about this dimension of our lives, and he is as earnest about being God's man as anyone I know. But I am fortunate to have a number of friends who also want to be God's man.

Billy Webb is an extraordinarily successful businessman. His record of victories has put him in the kind of fiscal position that many men could only hope for. But quite a number of my friends have also found success in the marketplace.

Then one day, it hit me. Billy is a handwritten thank-you-note man. From the very first time we met for lunch until our most recent outing, I've received a note in the mail a few days later from him. These notes are not long and drawn out; in fact, they usually fit on one side of a four-by-six card. But even when he has picked up the tab for lunch, Billy thanks me for my time and for my friendship.

After receiving a few of these, I went out and bought my own "thank you" cards so I could be a "Billy Webb" in the lives of other men, just like Billy had been in mine.

The apostle Paul was a "Billy Webb" kind of friend. He opened nearly every one of his thirteen New Testament letters with a "thank you." This letter to the church in Philippi is especially strong. "I thank my God every time I remember you. In all my prayers for all of you, I always pray with joy because of your partnership in the gospel," he wrote (vv. 3–5).

Paul was important in the hearts of these Christians because he consistently demonstrated his thankfulness for his friends. Did this mean that Paul was a push-over? Not hardly. In his letters, Paul often took folks on with a vengeance. He called them to account for their deeds, gave them clear instructions on how to conduct themselves, and warned them of the direction in which they were headed. But, somehow, they were able to hear what he had to say. Why? Because Paul was a man who always started with "thank you."

Are you a "Billy Webb" kind of thank-you-note man in the lives of your children, family and friends? Being such a man only takes a moment, but the dividends are astonishing. Try it. You'll see.

For your next devotional reading, go to page 1320.

my deliverance.[a] **20**I eagerly expect and hope that I will in no way be ashamed, but will have sufficient courage so that now as always Christ will be exalted in my body, whether by life or by death. **21**For to me, to live is Christ and to die is gain. **22**If I am to go on living in the body, this will mean fruitful labor for me. Yet what shall I choose? I do not know! **23**I am torn between the two: I desire to depart and be with Christ, which is better by far; **24**but it is more necessary for you that I remain in the body. **25**Convinced of this, I know that I will remain, and I will continue with all of you for your progress and joy in the faith, **26**so that through my being with you again your joy in Christ Jesus will overflow on account of me.

27Whatever happens, conduct yourselves in a manner worthy of the gospel of Christ. Then, whether I come and see you or only hear about you in my absence, I will know that you stand firm in one spirit, contending as one man for the faith of the gospel **28**without being frightened in any way by those who oppose you. This is a sign to them that they will be destroyed, but that you will be saved—and that by God. **29**For it has been granted to you on behalf of Christ not only to believe on him, but also to suffer for him, **30**since you are going through the same struggle you saw I had, and now hear that I still have.

Imitating Christ's Humility

2 If you have any encouragement from being united with Christ, if any comfort from his love, if any fellowship with the Spirit, if any tenderness and compassion, **2**then make my joy complete by being like-minded, having the same love, being one in spirit and purpose. **3**Do nothing out of selfish ambition or vain conceit, but in humility consider others better than yourselves. **4**Each of you should look not only to your own interests, but also to the interests of others.

5Your attitude should be the same as that of Christ Jesus:

6Who, being in very nature[b] God,
did not consider equality with God
something to be grasped,
7but made himself nothing,
taking the very nature[c] of a servant,
being made in human likeness.
8And being found in appearance as a man,
he humbled himself
and became obedient to death—
even death on a cross!
9Therefore God exalted him to the highest place
and gave him the name that is above every name,
10that at the name of Jesus every knee should bow,
in heaven and on earth and under the earth,
11and every tongue confess that Jesus Christ is Lord,
to the glory of God the Father.

---

[a]19 Or *salvation*   [b]6 Or *in the form of*   [c]7 Or *the form*

HEY DAD

Why aren't we supposed to complain? It doesn't really hurt anyone.

Text: Philippians 2:14–15

Paul tells us to "do everything without complaining or arguing." As Christians, we are to have a cheerful spirit so that we will become blameless and pure—without fault. In that way, we will stand out among those who are not Christians, and they will recognize that we are "children of God."

If we have joyful hearts and do not complain or argue, people around us will begin to think, "I wonder why he is so cheerful all the time," or "How can she live with that without complaining?" or "Why doesn't he ever say anything bad about anyone?" Soon, they may want to find that same joy and strength we have found in Jesus Christ.

By mastering this one area, we will become like stars shining on a dark generation. So, do you want to be a star? Here is an authentic way to become one!

Questions Kids ASK

For a complete listing of Questions Kids Ask, turn to page 1435.

Shining as Stars

[12]Therefore, my dear friends, as you have always obeyed—not only in my presence, but now much more in my absence—continue to work out your salvation with fear and trembling, [13]for it is God who works in you to will and to act according to his good purpose.

[14]Do everything without complaining or arguing, [15]so that you may become blameless and pure, children of God without fault in a crooked and depraved generation, in which you shine like stars in the universe [16]as you hold out[a] the word of life—in order that I may boast on the day of Christ that I did not run or labor for nothing. [17]But even if I am being poured out like a drink offering on the sacrifice and service coming from your faith, I am glad and rejoice with all of you. [18]So you too should be glad and rejoice with me.

[a]16 Or hold on to

Three Field Trips to a Place Called "Humility"

DAILY INSIGHT

FRIDAY

Passage:
Philippians 2:3–11

Verse:
Philippians 2:3

Let's go on a field trip to find evidence of true humility in your community.

First, we'll head to your state's penitentiary. The purpose of our visit will be to see if the tragic experience of incarceration has humbled any of these men. If being locked in a nine-by-twelve and staring at a concrete wall for a few decades doesn't bring contrition, then what possibly could?

Imagine our consternation as we meet with one inmate after another. Not only do we find very little humility, we have never met so many *innocent* men who are the pathetic victims of capricious parents, unfair circumstances or an unjust system.

Our second stop is a little monastery, tucked away in an unobtrusive little village not far from your home. With all the winding roads and unmarked intersections, this place isn't easy to find, but eventually we arrive at what appears to be a large, stone church. A man who knows about our visit greets us as we enter through large, carved-wood doors.

We thought we were coming to visit with a handful of men, but to our amazement and delight, our afternoon is like a visit with angels. Humility oozes out of the windows of this place. In answer to our questions these men say, "Yes, we are sinners, ashamed as we can be. Thank God for his grace. What would we do without it?"

We have time for one more short field trip. For this one, we open our Bibles and read the following words: "Do nothing out of selfish ambition or vain conceit, but in humility consider others better than yourselves ... your attitude should be the same as that of Christ Jesus: Who, being in very nature God, did not consider equality with God something to be grasped, but made himself nothing ... he humbled himself" (2:3,5–8a).

And then it hits us. No matter how hard we try to be humble, our circumstances will never create humility. The inmates proved that even public humiliation doesn't do the job. But then we discovered men who had decided to humble *themselves* by seeking God's holy presence, his grace and pardon. In doing this, they discovered how desperately sinful they were.

Finally, there was Jesus. Here was the Creator of the universe, one who had every right to strut his stuff through life and show off his awesome power. Instead, he laid it aside and became "a servant ... obedient to death—even death on a cross!" (2:7–8) Because of Jesus' humility, God exalted him to the highest place.

It doesn't take a rocket scientist to find a lesson in this passage for all of us. Nothing will ever make us humble ... except a visit to the presence of God and a conscious decision to consider others better than ourselves.

For your next devotional reading, go to page 1322.

Timothy and Epaphroditus

[19]I hope in the Lord Jesus to send Timothy to you soon, that I also may be cheered when I receive news about you. [20]I have no one else like him, who takes a genuine interest in your welfare. [21]For everyone looks out for his own interests, not those of Jesus Christ. [22]But you know that Timothy has proved himself, because as a son with his father he has served with me in the work of the gospel. [23]I hope, therefore, to send him as soon as I see how things go with me. [24]And I am confident in the Lord that I myself will come soon.

[25]But I think it is necessary to send back to you Epaphroditus, my brother, fellow worker and fellow soldier, who is also your messenger, whom you sent to take care of my needs. [26]For he longs for all of you and is distressed because you heard he was ill. [27]Indeed he was ill, and almost died. But God had mercy on him, and not on him only but also on me, to spare me sorrow upon sorrow. [28]Therefore I am all the more eager to send him, so that when you see him again you may be glad and I may have less anxiety. [29]Welcome him in the Lord with great joy, and honor men like him, [30]because he almost died for the work of Christ, risking his life to make up for the help you could not give me.

No Confidence in the Flesh

3 Finally, my brothers, rejoice in the Lord! It is no trouble for me to write the same things to you again, and it is a safeguard for you.

[2]Watch out for those dogs, those men who do evil, those mutilators of the flesh. [3]For it is we who are the circumcision, we who worship by the Spirit of God, who glory in Christ Jesus, and who put no confidence in the flesh— [4]though I myself have reasons for such confidence.

If anyone else thinks he has reasons to put confidence in the flesh, I have more: [5]circumcised on the eighth day, of the people of Israel, of the tribe of Benjamin, a Hebrew of Hebrews; in regard to the law, a Pharisee; [6]as for zeal, persecuting the church; as for legalistic righteousness, faultless.

[7]But whatever was to my profit I now consider loss for the sake of Christ. [8]What is more, I consider everything a loss compared to the surpassing greatness of knowing Christ Jesus my Lord, for whose sake I have lost all things. I consider them

rubbish, that I may gain Christ [9]and be found in him, not having a righteousness of my own that comes from the law, but that which is through faith in Christ—the righteousness that comes from God and is by faith. [10]I want to know Christ and the power of his resurrection and the fellowship of sharing in his sufferings, becoming like him in his death, [11]and so, somehow, to attain to the resurrection from the dead.

Pressing on Toward the Goal

[12]Not that I have already obtained all this, or have already been made perfect, but I press on to take hold of that for which Christ Jesus took hold of me. [13]Brothers, I do not consider myself yet to have taken hold of it. But one thing I do: Forgetting what is behind and straining toward what is ahead, [14]I press on toward the goal to win the prize for which God has called me heavenward in Christ Jesus.

[15]All of us who are mature should take such a view of things. And if on some point you think differently, that too God will make clear to you. [16]Only let us live up to what we have already attained.

[17]Join with others in following my example, brothers, and take note of those who live according to the pattern we gave you. [18]For, as I have often told you before and now say again even with tears, many live as enemies of the cross of Christ. [19]Their destiny is destruction, their god is their stomach, and their glory is in their shame. Their mind is on earthly things. [20]But our citizenship is in heaven. And we eagerly await a Savior from there, the Lord Jesus Christ, [21]who, by the power that enables him to bring everything under his control, will transform our lowly bodies so that they will be like his glorious body.

4 Therefore, my brothers, you whom I love and long for, my joy and crown, that is how you should stand firm in the Lord, dear friends!

Exhortations

[2]I plead with Euodia and I plead with Syntyche to agree with each other in the Lord. [3]Yes, and I ask you, loyal yokefellow,[a] help these women who have contended at my side in the cause of the gospel, along with Clement and the rest of my fellow workers, whose names are in the book of life.

[a]3 Or loyal Syzygus

A Good Kind of Anxious

Key Verse: *"Do not be anxious about anything, but in everything, by prayer and petition, with thanksgiving, present your requests to God."* Philippians 4:6
Text: Philippians 4:4–8 *(Dad or child reads the text.)*

QUIET
TIMES
WITH Dad

Child reads: Sometimes being "anxious" is a good thing. I love it when Christmas is right around the corner. I get anxious to see if you like what I bought for you. And I can't wait for our family vacations. I get anxious for the fun of being together and going to special places. This is a good kind of "anxious."

DAD READS: But there is a bad kind of "anxious," the kind that makes us nervous. Sometimes it even makes us sick to our stomachs. This is the kind of "anxious" that makes me worry about whether or not we will have enough money to pay for Christmas or be safe on our vacation. Sometimes this kind of "anxious" keeps us from enjoying anything. We can be so tense that all the happiness is taken out of our lives.

Child reads: Today's key verse says, "Do not be anxious about anything" (4:6). This does not mean that we shouldn't look forward to Christmas or family vacations, but it does mean that we shouldn't have any of the "bad anxious" in our lives. We should never worry about things that we can't do anything about.

DAD READS: That's right. The apostle Paul tells us not to be anxious. But he also tells us how to keep from being anxious: by telling God about our needs and by being truly thankful for everything he has done for our family. When we do this, he will give us a special kind of peace that will replace our worry.

Child reads: We also read about a list of things that will keep us from being "bad anxious." If we keep these important things in our minds, we will not feel troubled or afraid.

DAD READS: Here are some things we need to put in our minds: fair things, honest things, clean things, beautiful things, and repeatable things. When we hold these things in our minds, then they push out worry and fear ... the bad kind of "anxious."

Child reads: I want to be able to look forward to fun and happy events. I want to have the good kind of "anxious." But I don't want to worry. I don't want to be afraid. I want to stay away from the bad kind of "anxious." The things we just read will help you and me to have hearts and minds like Jesus. Let me pray this prayer with you:

Our Father in heaven, we love you. Thank you for promising us that we don't have to worry and be afraid. Please help us to put fair things, honest things, clean things, beautiful things, and repeatable things into our minds. We are anxious to be like Jesus, and that's a good kind of anxious. We love you and we thank you for your love. In Jesus' name, Amen.

For your next devotional reading, go to page 1325.

[4] Rejoice in the Lord always. I will say it again: Rejoice! [5] Let your gentleness be evident to all. The Lord is near. [6] Do not be anxious about anything, but in everything, by prayer and petition, with thanksgiving, present your requests to God. [7] And the peace of God, which transcends all understanding, will guard your hearts and your minds in Christ Jesus.

[8] Finally, brothers, whatever is true, whatever is noble, whatever is right, whatever is pure, whatever is lovely, whatever is admirable—if anything is excellent or praiseworthy—think about such things. [9] Whatever you have learned or received or heard from me, or seen in me—put it into practice. And the God of peace will be with you.

Thanks for Their Gifts

[10] I rejoice greatly in the Lord that at last you have renewed your concern for me. Indeed, you have been concerned, but you had no opportunity to show it. [11] I am not saying this because I am in need, for I have learned to be content whatever the circumstances. [12] I know what it is to be in need, and I know what it is to have plenty. I have learned the secret of being content in any and every situation, whether well fed or hungry, whether living in plenty or in want. [13] I can do everything through him who gives me strength.

[14] Yet it was good of you to share in my troubles. [15] Moreover, as you Philippians know, in the early days of your acquaintance with the gospel, when I set out from Macedonia, not one church shared with me in the matter of giving and receiving, except you only; [16] for even when I was in Thessalonica, you sent me aid again and again when I was in need. [17] Not that I am looking for a gift, but I am looking for what may be credited to your account. [18] I have received full payment and even more; I am amply supplied, now that I have received from Epaphroditus the gifts you sent. They are a fragrant offering, an acceptable sacrifice, pleasing to God. [19] And my God will meet all your needs according to his glorious riches in Christ Jesus.

[20] To our God and Father be glory for ever and ever. Amen.

Final Greetings

[21] Greet all the saints in Christ Jesus. The brothers who are with me send greetings. [22] All the saints send you greetings, especially those who belong to Caesar's household.

[23] The grace of the Lord Jesus Christ be with your spirit. Amen.[a]

[a]23 Some manuscripts do not have *Amen*.

Whose photographs do you carry in your wallet? You've probably got one of your wife in there. No doubt you have some shots of your children, too. Have you considered why you carry these pictures around with you? The first reason is pretty obvious. A dad never knows when someone might ask if he or she can see the family. This rarely happens, so most dads whip out the snapshots of their kids completely unprompted and uninvited. "Would you like to see them?" he might say after telling someone about his children. "Uh, sure," the person might say, knowing that regardless of his reaction, those pictures are coming out.

But the other reason why a dad carries pictures is to have this reminder of his family—these people whom he desperately loves—close by, no matter where he goes. In the book of Colossians, the apostle Paul included a few verbal "photographs" of Jesus Christ. They're incredible shots. He placed them there to show people, but there's no doubt that he tucked these in there so that neither he nor his readers would ever forget who loved him and whom he was serving. What a nice idea.

Colossians

1 Paul, an apostle of Christ Jesus by the will of God, and Timothy our brother,

[2] To the holy and faithful[a] brothers in Christ at Colosse:

Grace and peace to you from God our Father.[b]

Thanksgiving and Prayer

[3] We always thank God, the Father of our Lord Jesus Christ, when we pray for you, [4] because we have heard of your faith in Christ Jesus and of the love you have for all the saints— [5] the faith and love that spring from the hope that is stored up for you in heaven and that you have already heard about in the word of truth, the gospel [6] that has come to you. All over the world this gospel is bearing fruit and growing, just as it has been doing among you since the day you heard it and understood God's grace in all its truth. [7] You learned it from Epaphras, our dear fellow servant, who is a faithful minister of

[a]2 Or *believing* [b]2 Some manuscripts *Father and the Lord Jesus Christ*

Christ on our[a] behalf, [8]and who also told us of your love in the Spirit.

[9]For this reason, since the day we heard about you, we have not stopped praying for you and asking God to fill you with the knowledge of his will through all spiritual wisdom and understanding. [10]And we pray this in order that you may live a life worthy of the Lord and may please him in every way: bearing fruit in every good work, growing in the knowledge of God, [11]being strengthened with all power according to his glorious might so that you may have great endurance and patience, and joyfully [12]giving thanks to the Father,

who has qualified you[b] to share in the inheritance of the saints in the kingdom of light. [13]For he has rescued us from the dominion of darkness and brought us into the kingdom of the Son he loves, [14]in whom we have redemption,[c] the forgiveness of sins.

The Supremacy of Christ

[15]He is the image of the invisible God, the firstborn over all creation. [16]For by

[a]7 Some manuscripts *your*   *[b]12* Some manuscripts *us*   *[c]14* A few late manuscripts *redemption through his blood*

That's My Daughter. That's My Son.

DAILY INSIGHT

MONDAY

Passage:
Colossians 1:15–20

Verse:
Colossians 1:19

Is there anything in all the world more wonderful than being a dad? I don't think so. In fact, God knows just how we feel.

In January of 1985, our daughter Missy was in the eighth grade. We had moved to Nashville less than a year before, and we were having a hard time finding a school where Missy was comfortable. Missy asked to transfer mid-year, and although I desperately wanted my daughter to learn the virtue of sticking to it, I decided that this probably wasn't the time to teach that lesson. I acquiesced.

Missy and her mom walked into her new school on the day of spring play tryouts. And even though she had never been in a production in her life, Missy knew that this would be a great way to meet new friends. Pushing through her fear and apprehension, she tried out for the play, securing a spot in the chorus. When I heard about this accomplishment, I couldn't have been more proud. Being a dad is something very special.

Three years later, our second daughter decided to try out for the junior high cheerleading squad. Because of some serious problems with her leg at birth, we had been warned by some nervous doctors that she would have some life-long limitations. Now, like those apprehensive physicians, Bobbie and I were warning Julie that some of those kicks and dance steps would

be next to impossible to execute. True to form and not to be dissuaded from her dreams, Julie tried out. She was a cheerleader for the next five years and, once again, I discovered that being a dad is something very special.

We know the challenge of filling this role of "dad" in our children's lives. We know how much work it is to be a good dad, and they know the rigors of being good kids. But above all of these important tasks, we know full well the spectacular joy that comes along with just being a dad ... of having a child of our very, very own. This is a truly awesome thing.

God understands this feeling. He was proud of his Son. And the passage we read for today tells us why in vivid detail. Jesus is the firstborn, Creator, the eternally existent glue who holds all things together, the master of every believer—including you and me, the one who conquered death, and the great reconciler of all men.

So the heavenly Father "was pleased to have all his fullness dwell in [Jesus]" (1:19). God's supreme and exquisite Son received his father's full blessing. As dads we understand just a tiny bit of what God the Father must have felt.

There is nothing more wonderful than being a dad. And God knows just how we feel.

For your next devotional reading, go to page 1328.

him all things were created: things in heaven and on earth, visible and invisible, whether thrones or powers or rulers or authorities; all things were created by him and for him. ¹⁷He is before all things, and in him all things hold together. ¹⁸And he is the head of the body, the church; he is the beginning and the firstborn from among the dead, so that in everything he might have the supremacy. ¹⁹For God was pleased to have all his fullness dwell in him, ²⁰and through him to reconcile to himself all things, whether things on earth or things in heaven, by making peace through his blood, shed on the cross.

²¹Once you were alienated from God and were enemies in your minds because of[a] your evil behavior. ²²But now he has reconciled you by Christ's physical body through death to present you holy in his sight, without blemish and free from accusation— ²³if you continue in your faith, established and firm, not moved from the hope held out in the gospel. This is the gospel that you heard and that has been proclaimed to every creature under heaven, and of which I, Paul, have become a servant.

Paul's Labor for the Church

²⁴Now I rejoice in what was suffered for you, and I fill up in my flesh what is still lacking in regard to Christ's afflictions, for the sake of his body, which is the church. ²⁵I have become its servant by the commission God gave me to present to you the word of God in its fullness— ²⁶the mystery that has been kept hidden for ages and generations, but is now disclosed to the saints. ²⁷To them God has chosen to make known among the Gentiles the glorious riches of this mystery, which is Christ in you, the hope of glory.

²⁸We proclaim him, admonishing and teaching everyone with all wisdom, so that we may present everyone perfect in Christ. ²⁹To this end I labor, struggling with all his energy, which so powerfully works in me.

2 I want you to know how much I am struggling for you and for those at Laodicea, and for all who have not met me personally. ²My purpose is that they may be encouraged in heart and united in love, so that they may have the full riches of complete understanding, in order that they may know the mystery of God, namely, Christ, ³in whom are hidden all the treasures of wisdom and knowledge. ⁴I tell you this so that no one may deceive you by fine-sounding arguments. ⁵For though I am absent from you in body, I am present with you in spirit and delight to see how orderly you are and how firm your faith in Christ is.

[a]21 Or minds, as shown by

HEY DAD
Why are all other religions wrong?

Text: Colossians 2:13–15, 23

It is very hard to understand that, of all the religions in the world, Christianity is the only one that is true. After all, don't other religions encourage people to be loving, to be wise and to become better people? Some of them even worship one God. Couldn't that be the same God we worship?

One word separates Christianity from all other religions: *grace*. Only Christianity teaches that humans are totally incapable of being good enough to reach heaven. Paul says that *God* makes us alive with Christ; we do not do so ourselves. By taking our sins with him to the cross, Jesus extended God's grace to us and became the way—the *only* way—to heaven and peace with God (John 14:6).

Though other religions may "have an appearance of wisdom" (v. 23), they really are foolish. We can never be good enough to have fellowship with God. We *need* grace. And so do the people who do not know it, yet.

Now it is *our* turn to be messengers of grace.

QUESTIONS KIDS ASK

For a complete listing of Questions Kids Ask, turn to page 1435.

Freedom From Human Regulations Through Life With Christ

6So then, just as you received Christ Jesus as Lord, continue to live in him, **7**rooted and built up in him, strengthened in the faith as you were taught, and overflowing with thankfulness.

8See to it that no one takes you captive through hollow and deceptive philosophy, which depends on human tradition and the basic principles of this world rather than on Christ.

9For in Christ all the fullness of the Deity lives in bodily form, **10**and you have been given fullness in Christ, who is the head over every power and authority. **11**In him you were also circumcised, in the putting off of the sinful nature,*a* not with a circumcision done by the hands of men but with the circumcision done by Christ, **12**having been buried with him in baptism and raised with him through your faith in the power of God, who raised him from the dead.

13When you were dead in your sins and in the uncircumcision of your sinful nature,*b* God made you*c* alive with Christ. He forgave us all our sins, **14**having canceled the written code, with its regulations, that was against us and that stood opposed to us; he took it away, nailing it to the cross. **15**And having disarmed the powers and authorities, he made a public spectacle of them, triumphing over them by the cross.*d*

16Therefore do not let anyone judge you by what you eat or drink, or with regard to a religious festival, a New Moon celebration or a Sabbath day. **17**These are a shadow of the things that were to come; the reality, however, is found in Christ. **18**Do not let anyone who delights in false humility and the worship of angels disqualify you for the prize. Such a person goes into great detail about what he has seen, and his unspiritual mind puffs him up with idle notions. **19**He has lost connection with the Head, from whom the whole body, supported and held together by its ligaments and sinews, grows as God causes it to grow.

20Since you died with Christ to the basic principles of this world, why, as though you still belonged to it, do you submit to its rules: **21**"Do not handle! Do not taste! Do not touch!"? **22**These are all destined to perish with use, because they are based on human commands and teachings.

23Such regulations indeed have an appearance of wisdom, with their self-imposed worship, their false humility and their harsh treatment of the body, but they lack any value in restraining sensual indulgence.

Rules for Holy Living

3 Since, then, you have been raised with Christ, set your hearts on things above, where Christ is seated at the right hand of God. **2**Set your minds on things above, not on earthly things. **3**For you died, and your life is now hidden with Christ in God. **4**When Christ, who is your*e* life, appears, then you also will appear with him in glory.

5Put to death, therefore, whatever belongs to your earthly nature: sexual immorality, impurity, lust, evil desires and greed, which is idolatry. **6**Because of these, the wrath of God is coming.*f* **7**You used to walk in these ways, in the life you once lived. **8**But now you must rid yourselves of all such things as these: anger, rage, malice, slander, and filthy language from your lips. **9**Do not lie to each other, since you have taken off your old self with its practices **10**and have put on the new self, which is being renewed in knowledge in the image of its Creator. **11**Here there is no Greek or Jew, circumcised or uncircumcised, barbarian, Scythian, slave or free, but Christ is all, and is in all.

12Therefore, as God's chosen people, holy and dearly loved, clothe yourselves with compassion, kindness, humility, gentleness and patience. **13**Bear with each other and forgive whatever grievances you may have against one another. Forgive as the Lord forgave you. **14**And over all these virtues put on love, which binds them all together in perfect unity.

15Let the peace of Christ rule in your hearts, since as members of one body you were called to peace. And be thankful. **16**Let the word of Christ dwell in you richly as you teach and admonish one another with all wisdom, and as you sing psalms, hymns and spiritual songs with gratitude in your hearts to God. **17**And whatever you do, whether in word or deed, do it all in the name of the Lord Jesus, giving thanks to God the Father through him.

a11 Or *the flesh*   *b13* Or *your flesh*   *c13* Some manuscripts *us*   *d15* Or *them in him*   *e4* Some manuscripts *our*   *f6* Some early manuscripts *coming on those who are disobedient*

Rules for Christian Households

[18]Wives, submit to your husbands, as is fitting in the Lord.

[19]Husbands, love your wives and do not be harsh with them.

[20]Children, obey your parents in everything, for this pleases the Lord.

[21]Fathers, do not embitter your children, or they will become discouraged.

[22]Slaves, obey your earthly masters in everything; and do it, not only when their eye is on you and to win their favor, but with sincerity of heart and reverence for the Lord. [23]Whatever you do, work at it with all your heart, as working for the Lord, not for men, [24]since you know that you will receive an inheritance from the Lord as a reward. It is the Lord Christ you are serving. [25]Anyone who does wrong will be repaid for his wrong, and there is no favoritism.

Singing for Fun and Profit

DAILY INSIGHT

TUESDAY

Passage:
Colossians 3:15–17

Verse:
Colossians 3:17

Music has always played an important role in the life of my family. My guess is that this is true for you, too.

When my dad was a very young man, his mother sent him off to a voice teacher. My grandmother did not want her only child growing up without knowing the joy of music. My mother's family needed no such lessons. If you had lived in Lancaster County, Pennsylvania in the twenties and thirties, you would have known of the singing Monroe Dourte family. My dad and mother didn't miss a beat in passing their singing tradition on to their children. From the time we were very small, my five siblings and I sang along with our mother at churches and missions.

In the summer of 1967, I was sitting at the National Youth for Christ Annual Conference when a young man and woman from Washington D.C. stepped to the microphone to sing a duet. Sitting there, I couldn't help but notice how beautiful the girl was. I figured she was probably "taken" by the boy she was singing with. I was wrong. Two and a half years later, I married Bobbie Gardner, the pretty singer from our nation's capital.

With all of this musical heritage, our children were destined to be surrounded by music, and they have been. Our family has enjoyed all kinds of music together. From the time they were very small, we taught our children little tunes. On family vacations, we brought along all kinds of children's music tapes, and they played them over and over (and over) again.

Now there's a dimension to all of this music memorabilia I haven't mentioned. It's something the apostle Paul told the church in Colosse many centuries ago. "Let the word of Christ dwell in you richly as you teach and admonish one another with all wisdom, and as you sing psalms, hymns and spiritual songs with gratitude in your hearts to God" (3:16). Beginning with my parents' parents, and cascading down through my own parents and my wife, I have learned about God through music.

Most of this learning has been seared into my heart by way of classic hymns such as "A Mighty Fortress Is Our God," "O Worship the King," and "Great Is Thy Faithfulness." Because my parents made it a priority, these great hymns have poured sound theology into my soul. Bobbie and I have passed it on to our own children, and they are now doing the same.

Your voice doesn't have to be worthy of a recording contract to give your children the gift of music. Getting those tapes and encouraging your child to learn about your heavenly Father through this powerful medium will be an investment that will last forever. The last time we sang hymns with my dad's mother, she was one hundred and one. She remembered all the words.

Don't miss this chance to let your heart and your home be God's forever dwelling place.

For your next devotional reading, go to page 1329.

4 Masters, provide your slaves with what is right and fair, because you know that you also have a Master in heaven.

Further Instructions

²Devote yourselves to prayer, being watchful and thankful. ³And pray for us, too, that God may open a door for our message, so that we may proclaim the mystery of Christ, for which I am in chains.

⁴Pray that I may proclaim it clearly, as I should. ⁵Be wise in the way you act toward outsiders; make the most of every opportunity. ⁶Let your conversation be always full of grace, seasoned with salt, so that you may know how to answer everyone.

Final Greetings

⁷Tychicus will tell you all the news about me. He is a dear brother, a faithful

The Secret of Success

In the early 1950's, a young man named Bill Slemp got a job with Frigidaire™. He was fresh out of the army, but without a college education, Bill was forced to start at the bottom. His first assignment was to run the machine that wound copper wire around armatures, the center mechanism in electric motors. Knowing that this task was beneath the intelligence of most people, but grateful that he had a job, Bill made a decision. *If all I ever do for this company is wind copper wire,* he silently resolved, *then I'm going to be the best armature-winder this company has ever had.*

Bill's supervisors couldn't help but notice this young man's tenacity. His attitude, even though he was doing unskilled work, seemed out of place. So they decided to put Bill Slemp to the ultimate test. One by one they began promoting Bill's colleagues—young men who didn't have the drive, work ethic or attitude that Bill exhibited. Of course, Bill noticed. But he reviewed his resolve ... *the best armature-winder this company has ever had.* There's no mention here of promotions or fairness.

After eighteen months of seamless commitment, a senior executive approached Bill Slemp's workstation. "Hello, Bill. I wonder if you would follow me," the man said. "Several of my colleagues would like to meet with you."

As he walked to the meeting, Bill Slemp's head was spinning. *What have I done?* he wondered. He was led into a room filled with more supervisors, managers and vice-presidents than he had ever seen before.

DAILY INSIGHT

WEDNESDAY

Passage:
Colossians 3:18–24

Verses:
Colossians 3:23–24

"Bill," one of the men began, "we've all been watching you. In fact, soon after you came to work for this company, we couldn't help but notice your diligence and superior attitude." The man paused. "We thought you looked like something special, but we wanted to be sure. So we started promoting men around you who weren't working as hard as you were—men who were slackers and loafers. Amazingly, none of this discouraged you. Your work never suffered; your attitude remained consistent and strong." Then he spoke words my friend Bill Slemp never forgot. "Bill, you have just wound copper wire on your last armature."

Twenty years later, Bill Slemp left Frigidaire™ as one of the most successful Senior Vice Presidents that company had ever known. And a few years after that, I went to work for this amazing man.

In today's passage, the apostle Paul gives us a list of things we must do every day in order to "receive an inheritance from the Lord." He does not promise instant recognition or immediate success; he only gives us the list. Wives, respect your husbands; husbands, love your wives; children, obey your parents; dads, don't embitter your children; workers, obey your supervisors.

Make these things a priority. Be the best wife, husband, kid, dad or employee you've ever known. Don't be motivated by success; rather, be driven by faithfulness. The reward will come when you least expect it.

For your next devotional reading, go to page 1332.

minister and fellow servant in the Lord. [8]I am sending him to you for the express purpose that you may know about our[a] circumstances and that he may encourage your hearts. [9]He is coming with Onesimus, our faithful and dear brother, who is one of you. They will tell you everything that is happening here.

[10]My fellow prisoner Aristarchus sends you his greetings, as does Mark, the cousin of Barnabas. (You have received instructions about him; if he comes to you, welcome him.) [11]Jesus, who is called Justus, also sends greetings. These are the only Jews among my fellow workers for the kingdom of God, and they have proved a comfort to me. [12]Epaphras, who is one of you and a servant of Christ Jesus, sends greetings. He is always wrestling in prayer for you, that you may stand firm in all the will of God, mature and fully assured. [13]I vouch for him that he is working hard for you and for those at Laodicea and Hierapolis. [14]Our dear friend Luke, the doctor, and Demas send greetings. [15]Give my greetings to the brothers at Laodicea, and to Nympha and the church in her house.

[16]After this letter has been read to you, see that it is also read in the church of the Laodiceans and that you in turn read the letter from Laodicea.

[17]Tell Archippus: "See to it that you complete the work you have received in the Lord."

[18]I, Paul, write this greeting in my own hand. Remember my chains. Grace be with you.

[a]8 Some manuscripts *that he may know about your*

As a dad, you're crazy about your family. And even though everyone in your house is substantially imperfect—including (especially?!) yourself—you wouldn't trade them in for anything. Well, did you know that this isn't your only family? And I'm not talking about your extended family. I'm talking about your "Sunday morning family". . . the family whom you "adopted" when you joined your church.

The book of 1 Thessalonians was written by the apostle Paul to his "family." In fact, over and over again he calls his church cronies "brothers." Sounds like a family, doesn't it? Now, you may say to yourself, "We attend a local church, but I wouldn't exactly call the other men who attend, my 'brothers.' They're nice guys, but my plate is pretty full. I hardly have time for one family, let alone two!" Most men understand this dilemma. But bypassing this second family means missing out on powerful, perhaps even life-changing, relationships. This book tells us about the benefits of fostering those family relationships.

1 Thessalonians

Paul, Silas[a] and Timothy,

To the church of the Thessalonians in God the Father and the Lord Jesus Christ:

Grace and peace to you.[b]

Thanksgiving for the Thessalonians' Faith

[2]We always thank God for all of you, mentioning you in our prayers. [3]We continually remember before our God and Father your work produced by faith, your labor prompted by love, and your endurance inspired by hope in our Lord Jesus Christ.

[4]For we know, brothers loved by God, that he has chosen you, [5]because our gos-pel came to you not simply with words, but also with power, with the Holy Spirit and with deep conviction. You know how we lived among you for your sake. [6]You became imitators of us and of the Lord; in spite of severe suffering, you welcomed the message with the joy given by the Holy Spirit. [7]And so you became a model to all the believers in Macedonia and Achaia. [8]The Lord's message rang out from you not only in Macedonia and Achaia—your faith in God has become known everywhere. Therefore we do not need to say

[a]1 Greek *Silvanus*, a variant of *Silas*   [b]1 Some early manuscripts *you from God our Father and the Lord Jesus Christ*

anything about it, ⁹for they themselves report what kind of reception you gave us. They tell how you turned to God from idols to serve the living and true God, ¹⁰and to wait for his Son from heaven, whom he raised from the dead—Jesus, who rescues us from the coming wrath.

Paul's Ministry in Thessalonica

2 You know, brothers, that our visit to you was not a failure. ²We had previ-

ously suffered and been insulted in Philippi, as you know, but with the help of our God we dared to tell you his gospel in spite of strong opposition. ³For the appeal we make does not spring from error or impure motives, nor are we trying to trick you. ⁴On the contrary, we speak as men approved by God to be entrusted with the gospel. We are not trying to please men but God, who tests our hearts. ⁵You know we never used flattery, nor did we put on a mask to cover up greed—God is our wit-

Tuck Up Those Little Wheels and Fly

Several years ago, when I was unable to get a non-stop flight from the West Coast to Nashville, I was forced to take a direct flight. This meant that I had the delightful experience of visiting Memphis on the way to Nashville. Unusually tired from a week of work in California, I decided to stay on the plane while we refueled and got a fresh load of passengers.

I sat there in my window seat, gazing at the other planes on the tarmac. Soon I was mesmerized by something I had never noticed before. In fact, tired and punchy as I was, this thing became so humorous to me that I began to laugh—not, however, loud enough for my fellow passengers to be concerned for their own safety.

What I saw was the contrast between the gargantuan size of these huge aircraft, compared to the tiny wheels that transported them from place to place. The dissimilarity was actually laughable.

Once airborne again, I laid my head back on the seat and deliberated on what I had just seen. *Of course,* I remember thinking, *airplane wheels look funny beneath these lumbering giants. These wheels are only necessary when the planes are on the ground for refueling. Planes aren't designed to cruise around airports, they're built to fly. And when they do, those minuscule wheels are completely invisible.*

Paul, Silas, and Timothy were writing a letter—a thank-you note—to their friends in Thessalonica. The text we read today

DAILY INSIGHT

THURSDAY

Passage:
1 Thessalonians 1:2–8

Verse:
1 Thessalonians 1:4

celebrates that these messengers had successfully carried God's message to the people of that town. Verses 4–6 outline the details of the amazing things these believers received.

But, as good as these things are, they are essentially "airport things." If the believers had only received this great stuff from these three faithful teachers so they could lumber around the church on their tiny wheels, it would have been a terrible shame.

But this didn't happen. These believers took the inspiration they had received from Paul's "maintenance crew," shot out to the active runway, and then soared: "And so you became a model to all the believers in Macedonia and Achaia ... your faith in God has become known everywhere" (vv. 7–8). When the time came for them to tuck in their wheels and streak into the sky, they took what they had learned and did what God had prepared them to do.

These days, Christians have more information available to them than in any previous era—books, study Bibles, audio tapes, video tapes, brilliant teachers of the Word, and conferences where they can hear these teachers speak. And there has never been a time when Christians have been less effective in changing their culture.

The reason ought to be clear. This is good stuff, but it's airport stuff. God calls us to fly.

For your next devotional reading, go to page 1334.

ness. ⁶We were not looking for praise from men, not from you or anyone else.

As apostles of Christ we could have been a burden to you, ⁷but we were gentle among you, like a mother caring for her little children. ⁸We loved you so much that we were delighted to share with you not only the gospel of God but our lives as well, because you had become so dear to us. ⁹Surely you remember, brothers, our toil and hardship; we worked night and day in order not to be a burden to anyone while we preached the gospel of God to you.

¹⁰You are witnesses, and so is God, of how holy, righteous and blameless we were among you who believed. ¹¹For you know that we dealt with each of you as a father deals with his own children, ¹²encouraging, comforting and urging you to live lives worthy of God, who calls you into his kingdom and glory.

¹³And we also thank God continually because, when you received the word of God, which you heard from us, you accepted it not as the word of men, but as it actually is, the word of God, which is at work in you who believe. ¹⁴For you, brothers, became imitators of God's churches in Judea, which are in Christ Jesus: You suffered from your own countrymen the same things those churches suffered from the Jews, ¹⁵who killed the Lord Jesus and the prophets and also drove us out. They displease God and are hostile to all men ¹⁶in their effort to keep us from speaking to the Gentiles so that they may be saved. In this way they always heap up their sins to the limit. The wrath of God has come upon them at last.^a

Paul's Longing to See the Thessalonians

¹⁷But, brothers, when we were torn away from you for a short time (in person, not in thought), out of our intense longing we made every effort to see you. ¹⁸For we wanted to come to you—certainly I, Paul, did, again and again—but Satan stopped us. ¹⁹For what is our hope, our joy, or the crown in which we will glory in the presence of our Lord Jesus when he comes? Is it not you? ²⁰Indeed, you are our glory and joy.

3 So when we could stand it no longer, we thought it best to be left by ourselves in Athens. ²We sent Timothy, who is our brother and God's fellow worker^b in spreading the gospel of Christ, to strengthen and encourage you in your faith, ³so that no one would be unsettled by these trials. You know quite well that we were destined for them. ⁴In fact, when we were with you, we kept telling you that we would be persecuted. And it turned out that way, as you well know. ⁵For this reason, when I could stand it no longer, I sent to find out about your faith. I was afraid that in some way the tempter might have tempted you and our efforts might have been useless.

Timothy's Encouraging Report

⁶But Timothy has just now come to us from you and has brought good news about your faith and love. He has told us that you always have pleasant memories of us and that you long to see us, just as we also long to see you. ⁷Therefore, brothers, in all our distress and persecution we were encouraged about you because of your faith. ⁸For now we really live, since you are standing firm in the Lord. ⁹How can we thank God enough for you in return for all the joy we have in the presence of our God because of you? ¹⁰Night and day we pray most earnestly that we may see you again and supply what is lacking in your faith.

¹¹Now may our God and Father himself and our Lord Jesus clear the way for us to come to you. ¹²May the Lord make your love increase and overflow for each other and for everyone else, just as ours does for you. ¹³May he strengthen your hearts so that you will be blameless and holy in the presence of our God and Father when our Lord Jesus comes with all his holy ones.

Living to Please God

4 Finally, brothers, we instructed you how to live in order to please God, as in fact you are living. Now we ask you and urge you in the Lord Jesus to do this more and more. ²For you know what instructions we gave you by the authority of the Lord Jesus.

³It is God's will that you should be sanctified: that you should avoid sexual immorality; ⁴that each of you should learn to control his own body^c in a way that is holy and honorable, ⁵not in passionate lust like the heathen, who do not know God;

---

^a16 Or *them fully* ^b2 Some manuscripts *brother and fellow worker;* other manuscripts *brother and God's servant* ^c4 Or *learn to live with his own wife;* or *learn to acquire a wife*

⁶and that in this matter no one should wrong his brother or take advantage of him. The Lord will punish men for all such sins, as we have already told you and warned you. ⁷For God did not call us to be impure, but to live a holy life. ⁸Therefore, he who rejects this instruction does not reject man but God, who gives you his Holy Spirit.

⁹Now about brotherly love we do not need to write to you, for you yourselves have been taught by God to love each other. ¹⁰And in fact, you do love all the brothers throughout Macedonia. Yet we

I Still Miss You, Jerry

DAILY INSIGHT

FRIDAY

Passage:
1 Thessalonians 4:1–8

Verse:
1 Thessalonians 4:7

For me, one of the great benefits of working in career youth ministry was having the chance to be a partner with other men in youth work around the world. In the winter of 1975, I traveled to South America on a teaching mission for youth leaders in Buenos Aires. My partner on this trip was one of the most important youth professionals in the United States. Jerry had worked for Youth for Christ since the early fifties and was one of the most prominent experts anywhere.

We flew to Buenos Aires where, for the next week, we led sessions on effective youth ministry for several dozen young South American ministers. Even though I taught a few sessions, Jerry was the expert. I was honored to just be there. It was a great experience.

Over the next ten years, Jerry and I stayed in touch. There weren't many contacts, but when one of us would call the other, it was one of those pick-up-right-where-we-left-off deals. I'm sure you have some of those, too.

And then I got a telephone call I will never forget. Several months earlier, while working on a youth event, Jerry had collapsed. "I guess I'm not a youngster anymore," he had quipped to some of the young leaders. The caller gave me the doctor's report. " Jerry has been suffering from full-blown AIDS." I remember gasping in disbelief. "This is impossible," I heard myself saying out loud.

Jerry had married a colleague of mine from Chicago. They had two beautiful children. But Jerry had led a double life. He had lived as a straight man with a wife, children, and youth ministry while also living a secret life of hard-core promiscuity and sin. When I heard about this, I wept.

The prognosis was clear: Jerry only had a very short time to live. I jumped on an airplane and went to see him in Southern California, only to find that by this time he was an unrecognizable shell. I sat next to his bed and held his hand. We talked and laughed as we remembered our time in South America. We cried openly as he talked about this life I knew nothing about.

A few months later, we talked on the phone one last time. He told me that he loved me, and I said the same. He told me he was sorry that his life was ending this way and he told me that he was thankful for God's grace and forgiveness. I told him I was, too. Then we said good-bye. The next day, Jerry died.

The apostle Paul did not tell the recipients of this courageous letter to "avoid sexual immorality" because God is some cosmic spoil-sport, straight out of Victorian England. He told these men to live this way because if they didn't, their hearts would be shattered by their careless disobedience. Their families would be standing, as Jerry's wife and the kids did, in front of a portrait of Jerry at the memorial service, faces ashen from indescribable grief.

Sexual purity is not God's great practical joke on men who have testosterone mercilessly coursing through their veins. Purity is his blessing. It's his promise. Cross this line and you will die.

I still miss you, Jerry.

For your next devotional reading, go to page 1336.

urge you, brothers, to do so more and more.

[11]Make it your ambition to lead a quiet life, to mind your own business and to work with your hands, just as we told you, [12]so that your daily life may win the respect of outsiders and so that you will not be dependent on anybody.

The Coming of the Lord

[13]Brothers, we do not want you to be ignorant about those who fall asleep, or to grieve like the rest of men, who have no hope. [14]We believe that Jesus died and rose again and so we believe that God will bring with Jesus those who have fallen asleep in him. [15]According to the Lord's own word, we tell you that we who are still alive, who are left till the coming of the Lord, will certainly not precede those who have fallen asleep. [16]For the Lord himself will come down from heaven, with a loud command, with the voice of the archangel and with the trumpet call of God, and the dead in Christ will rise first. [17]After that, we who are still alive and are left will be caught up together with them in the clouds to meet the Lord in the air. And so we will be with the Lord forever. [18]Therefore encourage each other with these words.

5 Now, brothers, about times and dates we do not need to write to you, [2]for you know very well that the day of the Lord will come like a thief in the night. [3]While people are saying, "Peace and safety," destruction will come on them suddenly, as labor pains on a pregnant woman, and they will not escape.

[4]But you, brothers, are not in darkness so that this day should surprise you like a thief. [5]You are all sons of the light and sons of the day. We do not belong to the night or to the darkness. [6]So then, let us not be like others, who are asleep, but let us be alert and self-controlled. [7]For those who sleep, sleep at night, and those who get drunk, get drunk at night. [8]But since we belong to the day, let us be self-controlled, putting on faith and love as a breastplate, and the hope of salvation as a helmet. [9]For God did not appoint us to suffer wrath but to receive salvation through our Lord Jesus Christ. [10]He died for us so that, whether we are awake or asleep, we may live together with him. [11]Therefore encourage one another and build each other up, just as in fact you are doing.

Final Instructions

[12]Now we ask you, brothers, to respect those who work hard among you, who are over you in the Lord and who admonish you. [13]Hold them in the highest regard in love because of their work. Live in peace with each other. [14]And we urge you, brothers, warn those who are idle, encourage the timid, help the weak, be patient with everyone. [15]Make sure that nobody pays back wrong for wrong, but always try to be kind to each other and to everyone else.

HEY DAD
If Jesus was perfect, why did some people hate him?

Text: 1 Thessalonians 4:1–2

Some people hated Jesus *because* he was perfect! The Pharisees, for example, looked foolish and petty in comparison to Jesus, and he publicly rebuked them for being arrogant and sinful (Matthew 23:27–28). He was perfect; they were imperfect, and they hated him.

Furthermore, Jesus always spoke the truth. That meant he inevitably stepped on some toes. Four hundred years before Jesus was born, Socrates, the philosopher from Athens, said that a truly righteous person would be so foreign and unacceptable to human society that he would be beaten, humiliated and crucified.

We can learn an incredibly important lesson here: We should strive to please God, not people (v. 1). We can't please everyone. In fact, the more we try to please God, the more some people will dislike us. But how wonderful it would be to hear these words, "This is my Son . . . with him I am well pleased" (2 Peter 1:17).

For a complete listing of Questions Kids Ask, turn to page 1435.

QUIET TIMES WITH Dad

DAD READS: When we watch a game on television, one of the things we don't think about very much is how important the rules of the game are. When a baseball lands outside the white line, it's always a foul ball. When a football is kicked through the goal posts on fourth down, it's always three points. When a hockey player leaves his feet to check another player, it's always a penalty. And when a golfer hits his ball out of bounds, it's always a one-stroke penalty.

Child reads: Sometimes I don't like rules. Sometimes I think that my life would be so much easier if I could just do what I want to do and never have to worry about being told that I can't act that way. But like in sports, life rules help everything to be better. Rules help our family to have more fun.

DAD READS: This is right. While we sometimes think that rules exist to keep us from enjoying ourselves, in reality the opposite is true. Can you imagine how confusing sports would be without rules and referees to make sure the rules are followed? It would be terrible. It wouldn't be any fun to play. Rules are a good thing.

Child reads: The verses we read today are like rules for our family. There are fourteen things we must do to be a happy family. Here are the rules: 1. Respect authority; 2. Live in peace with each other; 3. Work hard; 4. Help each other; 5. Have patience;

6. Be kind to others, even when you've been wronged.

DAD READS: 7. Be joyful always; 8. Pray all the time; 9. Be thankful for everything; 10. Listen carefully to God's Spirit when he speaks to us; 11. Listen to teachers of God's Word; 12. Live to please God; 13. Be happy when good things happen; 14. Stay away from evil. Families, just like all sports, have rules. These rules not only keep the game in order, they help make the game more fun. When our family does these things, we will not only have a family that is in good order, we will have a lot more fun, too.

Child reads: I want us to have a happy family. I want all of us to follow the rules. Let me pray this prayer with you:

Our Father in heaven, we love you. Thank you for rules that help keep our family in order, and that help us to be happier. Please forgive us when we break these rules. Help us to remind each other of your rules for happy families. We love you, and we thank you for your love. In Jesus' name, **Amen.**

For your next devotional reading, go to page 1339.

[16]Be joyful always; [17]pray continually; [18]give thanks in all circumstances, for this is God's will for you in Christ Jesus.

[19]Do not put out the Spirit's fire; [20]do not treat prophecies with contempt. [21]Test everything. Hold on to the good. [22]Avoid every kind of evil.

[23]May God himself, the God of peace, sanctify you through and through. May your whole spirit, soul and body be kept blameless at the coming of our Lord Jesus Christ. [24]The one who calls you is faithful and he will do it.

[25]Brothers, pray for us. [26]Greet all the brothers with a holy kiss. [27]I charge you before the Lord to have this letter read to all the brothers.

[28]The grace of our Lord Jesus Christ be with you.

HEY DAD

Do the words, "pray continually" mean that we shouldn't stop praying, even for a minute?

Text: 1 Thessalonians 5:16–18

When Paul told the Thessalonians that they were to "pray continually" (v. 17), he probably did not mean every minute of the day. Rather, he encouraged these believers to have an enduring relationship with God and to talk to him often. The Thessalonian church was facing adversity. Paul did not want these new Christians to try to handle hard times on their own or to turn away from God in the face of persecution. That's why he told them not to give up, but to pray often.

We also need to maintain our relationship with God, no matter what our circumstances. When we face difficult times or tough decisions, or when things could not be better, we're told exactly what to do: Be joyful, pray continually, and give thanks. Why? Because "this is God's will for [us] in Christ Jesus" (v. 18).

For a complete listing of Questions Kids Ask, turn to page 1435.

Your faith in Jesus Christ is a hot marketplace commodity. It's as up to date as today's issue of *The Wall Street Journal*. It's as contemporary as the latest matrix management idea. It's as helpful as the new office computer network. It's as useful as the most innovative tools in the shop. Your faith works.

The apostle Paul explains why faith is a living, growing entity in this second letter to the Thessalonians. He celebrates the fact that our love for Christ is increasing: "Your faith is growing" (1:3). As we discover more of God's love and grace, we come closer to the Savior. This is good. Paul also challenges us to stay busy, reminding us that our faith *works*. "Never tire of doing what is right," he encourages us (3:13). This is also good.

Let your faith in Christ translate into diligence and productivity. Let those around you be happy that you're on their team because your heart is right and your hands are fruitful. That's a terrific combination.

2 Thessalonians

1 Paul, Silas[a] and Timothy,

To the church of the Thessalonians in God our Father and the Lord Jesus Christ:

²Grace and peace to you from God the Father and the Lord Jesus Christ.

Thanksgiving and Prayer

³We ought always to thank God for you, brothers, and rightly so, because your faith is growing more and more, and the love every one of you has for each other is increasing. ⁴Therefore, among God's churches we boast about your perseverance and faith in all the persecutions and trials you are enduring.

⁵All this is evidence that God's judgment is right, and as a result you will be counted worthy of the kingdom of God, for which you are suffering. ⁶God is just: He will pay back trouble to those who trouble you ⁷and give relief to you who are troubled, and to us as well. This will happen when the Lord Jesus is revealed from heaven in blazing fire with his powerful angels. ⁸He will punish those who do not know God and do not obey the gospel of

a1 Greek *Silvanus*, a variant of *Silas*

our Lord Jesus. [9]They will be punished with everlasting destruction and shut out from the presence of the Lord and from the majesty of his power [10]on the day he comes to be glorified in his holy people and to be marveled at among all those who have believed. This includes you, because you believed our testimony to you.

[11]With this in mind, we constantly pray for you, that our God may count you worthy of his calling, and that by his power he may fulfill every good purpose of yours and every act prompted by your faith. [12]We pray this so that the name of our Lord Jesus may be glorified in you, and you in him, according to the grace of our God and the Lord Jesus Christ.[a]

The Man of Lawlessness

2 Concerning the coming of our Lord Jesus Christ and our being gathered to him, we ask you, brothers, [2]not to become easily unsettled or alarmed by some prophecy, report or letter supposed to have come from us, saying that the day of the Lord has already come. [3]Don't let anyone deceive you in any way, for ˌthat day

[a]12 Or God and Lord, Jesus Christ

The Natives Are Very Confused

DAILY INSIGHT

MONDAY
Passage:
2 Thessalonians 3:6–13
Verse:
2 Thessalonians 3:13

In his classic novel, *Hawaii*, James Michener tells of the first missionary voyage to the Pacific Islands. Even though these missionaries meant well, instead of converting Hawaiians, they turned the people and their culture upside down. The natives were very confused.

After reading this tale, I wondered what would have happened if these missionaries had touched the Hawaiian people as Christ would have done. Then I applied this question to *my* place of business.

What would it look like, I wondered, *if Christ showed up where I work? What would he do? How would he act? How would he treat his unbelieving colleagues?* As Christian men in the workplace, these questions should drive us all.

Unless you are independently wealthy and, therefore, answer to no one, you have a boss. You have been entrusted to oversee things that don't belong to you—time, resources, equipment, or subordinates. How do you deal with all these things as a Christian?

There must have also been some Christian businessmen at the church in Thessalonica. And Paul must have felt challenged to show them what it actually looked like to be a "missionary" to the marketplace. Paul summed up his advice very simply. "Keep away from every brother who is idle ... if a man will not work, he shall not eat ... never tire of doing what is right" (vv. 6,10,13).

Does this mean that the only thing you need to do to demonstrate your faith at work is to be diligent? Does this mean that if you are a faithful steward of the corporate funds that other men will automatically confess their sins and follow Christ? Not necessarily.

But what Paul is telling us is that if we are foolish with the assets that have been entrusted to us, if we shave the truth on our expense reports, if we are careless with our spending and our time, and if we are thoughtless of subordinates and disrespectful of our superiors, then any witness we might give of our Christian faith will be ruined. The Bible on our bookshelf, the prayer we whisper at lunch, the gospel song we hum, and the witness we give will be a side-splitting joke.

Hard work is Christian. Careful spending of corporate assets is Christian. Personal integrity at every level is Christian. Honest confrontation of the facts with your boss and empathy with your employees is Christian.

If you are not doing these things and have decided not to, please take the Bible off your shelf, stop bowing for grace, and quit making all those Christian noises. The natives are very confused.

For your next devotional reading, go to page 1344.

will not come, until the rebellion occurs and the man of lawlessness[a] is revealed, the man doomed to destruction. [4]He will oppose and will exalt himself over everything that is called God or is worshiped, so that he sets himself up in God's temple, proclaiming himself to be God.

[5]Don't you remember that when I was with you I used to tell you these things? [6]And now you know what is holding him back, so that he may be revealed at the proper time. [7]For the secret power of lawlessness is already at work; but the one who now holds it back will continue to do so till he is taken out of the way. [8]And then the lawless one will be revealed, whom the Lord Jesus will overthrow with the breath of his mouth and destroy by the splendor of his coming. [9]The coming of the lawless one will be in accordance with the work of Satan displayed in all kinds of counterfeit miracles, signs and wonders, [10]and in every sort of evil that deceives those who are perishing. They perish because they refused to love the truth and so be saved. [11]For this reason God sends them a powerful delusion so that they will believe the lie [12]and so that all will be condemned who have not believed the truth but have delighted in wickedness.

Stand Firm

[13]But we ought always to thank God for you, brothers loved by the Lord, because from the beginning God chose you[b] to be saved through the sanctifying work of the Spirit and through belief in the truth. [14]He called you to this through our gospel, that you might share in the glory of our Lord Jesus Christ. [15]So then, brothers, stand firm and hold to the teachings[c] we passed on to you, whether by word of mouth or by letter.

[16]May our Lord Jesus Christ himself and God our Father, who loved us and by his grace gave us eternal encouragement and good hope, [17]encourage your hearts and strengthen you in every good deed and word.

Request for Prayer

3 Finally, brothers, pray for us that the message of the Lord may spread rapidly and be honored, just as it was with you. [2]And pray that we may be delivered from wicked and evil men, for not everyone has faith. [3]But the Lord is faithful, and he will strengthen and protect you from the evil one. [4]We have confidence in the Lord that you are doing and will continue to do the things we command. [5]May the Lord direct your hearts into God's love and Christ's perseverance.

Warning Against Idleness

[6]In the name of the Lord Jesus Christ, we command you, brothers, to keep away from every brother who is idle and does not live according to the teaching[d] you received from us. [7]For you yourselves know how you ought to follow our example. We were not idle when we were with you, [8]nor did we eat anyone's food without paying for it. On the contrary, we worked night and day, laboring and toiling so that we would not be a burden to any of you. [9]We did this, not because we do not have the right to such help, but in order to make ourselves a model for you to follow. [10]For even when we were with you, we gave you this rule: "If a man will not work, he shall not eat."

[11]We hear that some among you are idle. They are not busy; they are busybodies. [12]Such people we command and urge in the Lord Jesus Christ to settle down and earn the bread they eat. [13]And as for you, brothers, never tire of doing what is right.

[14]If anyone does not obey our instruction in this letter, take special note of him. Do not associate with him, in order that he may feel ashamed. [15]Yet do not regard him as an enemy, but warn him as a brother.

Final Greetings

[16]Now may the Lord of peace himself give you peace at all times and in every way. The Lord be with all of you.

[17]I, Paul, write this greeting in my own hand, which is the distinguishing mark in all my letters. This is how I write.

[18]The grace of our Lord Jesus Christ be with you all.

---

[a]3 Some manuscripts *sin*   [b]13 Some manuscripts *because God chose you as his firstfruits*   [c]15 Or *traditions*   [d]6 Or *tradition*

The book of 1 Timothy was written to the apostle Paul's young protégé. Do you have an apprentice—someone who works by your side and learns from your knowledge, skill and experience? "Can't say as I do," you may be saying to yourself. "So what does this book have in it for me?"

Consider the following statement: Even if you're a work-all-by-yourself entrepreneur, even if you never plan to teach anyone what you do day to day, you *do* have an apprentice. You're a dad, and that means you've got a young set of eyes watching you like the hidden camera down at the corner convenience store. Since you're the master craftsman, even if it's just with your own child, Paul gives you some very interesting advice about this role: It requires personal vulnerability (1:16), and an ability to learn from your student (4:12).

As you read Paul's instruction to Timothy, think about how you'll pass on your legacy to your own child. For dads, this letter to Timothy is a God-send. Literally.

1 Timothy

1 Paul, an apostle of Christ Jesus by the command of God our Savior and of Christ Jesus our hope,

[2] To Timothy my true son in the faith:

Grace, mercy and peace from God the Father and Christ Jesus our Lord.

Warning Against False Teachers of the Law

[3] As I urged you when I went into Macedonia, stay there in Ephesus so that you may command certain men not to teach false doctrines any longer [4] nor to devote themselves to myths and endless genealogies. These promote controversies rather than God's work—which is by faith. [5] The goal of this command is love, which

comes from a pure heart and a good conscience and a sincere faith. [6] Some have wandered away from these and turned to meaningless talk. [7] They want to be teachers of the law, but they do not know what they are talking about or what they so confidently affirm.

[8] We know that the law is good if one uses it properly. [9] We also know that law[a] is made not for the righteous but for lawbreakers and rebels, the ungodly and sinful, the unholy and irreligious; for those who kill their fathers or mothers, for murderers, [10] for adulterers and perverts, for slave traders and liars and perjurers—

[a]9 Or *that the law*

and for whatever else is contrary to the sound doctrine [11]that conforms to the glorious gospel of the blessed God, which he entrusted to me.

The Lord's Grace to Paul

[12]I thank Christ Jesus our Lord, who has given me strength, that he considered me faithful, appointing me to his service. [13]Even though I was once a blasphemer and a persecutor and a violent man, I was shown mercy because I acted in ignorance and unbelief. [14]The grace of our Lord was poured out on me abundantly, along with the faith and love that are in Christ Jesus.

[15]Here is a trustworthy saying that deserves full acceptance: Christ Jesus came into the world to save sinners—of whom I am the worst. [16]But for that very reason I was shown mercy so that in me, the worst of sinners, Christ Jesus might display his unlimited patience as an example for those who would believe on him and receive eternal life. [17]Now to the King eternal, immortal, invisible, the only God, be honor and glory for ever and ever. Amen.

[18]Timothy, my son, I give you this instruction in keeping with the prophecies once made about you, so that by following them you may fight the good fight, [19]holding on to faith and a good conscience. Some have rejected these and so have shipwrecked their faith. [20]Among them are Hymenaeus and Alexander, whom I have handed over to Satan to be taught not to blaspheme.

Instructions on Worship

2 I urge, then, first of all, that requests, prayers, intercession and thanksgiving be made for everyone— [2]for kings and all those in authority, that we may live peaceful and quiet lives in all godliness and holiness. [3]This is good, and pleases God our Savior, [4]who wants all men to be saved and to come to a knowledge of the truth. [5]For there is one God and one mediator between God and men, the man Christ Jesus, [6]who gave himself as a ransom for all men—the testimony given in its proper time. [7]And for this purpose I was appointed a herald and an apostle—I am telling the truth, I am not lying—and a teacher of the true faith to the Gentiles.

[8]I want men everywhere to lift up holy hands in prayer, without anger or disputing.

[9]I also want women to dress modestly, with decency and propriety, not with braided hair or gold or pearls or expensive clothes, [10]but with good deeds, appropriate for women who profess to worship God.

[11]A woman should learn in quietness and full submission. [12]I do not permit a woman to teach or to have authority over a man; she must be silent. [13]For Adam was formed first, then Eve. [14]And Adam was not the one deceived; it was the woman who was deceived and became a sinner. [15]But women[a] will be saved[b] through childbearing—if they continue in faith, love and holiness with propriety.

Overseers and Deacons

3 Here is a trustworthy saying: If anyone sets his heart on being an overseer,[c] he desires a noble task. [2]Now the overseer must be above reproach, the husband of but one wife, temperate, self-controlled, respectable, hospitable, able to teach, [3]not given to drunkenness, not violent but gentle, not quarrelsome, not a lover of money. [4]He must manage his own family well and see that his children obey him with proper respect. [5](If anyone does not know how to manage his own family, how can he take care of God's church?) [6]He must not be a recent convert, or he may become conceited and fall under the same judgment as the devil. [7]He must also have a good reputation with outsiders, so that he will not fall into disgrace and into the devil's trap.

[8]Deacons, likewise, are to be men worthy of respect, sincere, not indulging in much wine, and not pursuing dishonest gain. [9]They must keep hold of the deep truths of the faith with a clear conscience. [10]They must first be tested; and then if there is nothing against them, let them serve as deacons.

[11]In the same way, their wives[d] are to be women worthy of respect, not malicious talkers but temperate and trustworthy in everything.

[12]A deacon must be the husband of but one wife and must manage his children and his household well. [13]Those who have served well gain an excellent standing and great assurance in their faith in Christ Jesus.

[14]Although I hope to come to you soon, I am writing you these instructions so

---

[a]15 Greek *she*   [b]15 Or *restored*   [c]1 Traditionally *bishop*; also in verse 2   [d]11 Or *way, deaconesses*

that, [15]if I am delayed, you will know how people ought to conduct themselves in God's household, which is the church of the living God, the pillar and foundation of the truth. [16]Beyond all question, the mystery of godliness is great:

He[a] appeared in a body,[b]
was vindicated by the Spirit,
was seen by angels,
was preached among the nations,
was believed on in the world,
was taken up in glory.

Instructions to Timothy

4 The Spirit clearly says that in later times some will abandon the faith and follow deceiving spirits and things taught by demons. [2]Such teachings come through hypocritical liars, whose consciences have been seared as with a hot iron. [3]They forbid people to marry and order them to abstain from certain foods, which God created to be received with thanksgiving by those who believe and who know the truth. [4]For everything God created is good, and nothing is to be rejected if it is received with thanksgiving, [5]because it is consecrated by the word of God and prayer.

[6]If you point these things out to the brothers, you will be a good minister of Christ Jesus, brought up in the truths of the faith and of the good teaching that you have followed. [7]Have nothing to do with godless myths and old wives' tales; rather, train yourself to be godly. [8]For

physical training is of some value, but godliness has value for all things, holding promise for both the present life and the life to come. [9]This is a trustworthy saying that deserves full acceptance [10](and for this we labor and strive), that we have put our hope in the living God, who is the Savior of all men, and especially of those who believe. [11]Command and teach these things. [12]Don't let anyone look down on you because you are young, but set an example for the believers in speech, in life, in love, in faith and in purity. [13]Until I come, devote yourself to the public reading of Scripture, to preaching and to teaching. [14]Do not neglect your gift, which was given you through a prophetic message when the body of elders laid their hands on you.

[15]Be diligent in these matters; give yourself wholly to them, so that everyone may see your progress. [16]Watch your life and doctrine closely. Persevere in them, because if you do, you will save both yourself and your hearers.

Advice About Widows, Elders and Slaves

5 Do not rebuke an older man harshly, but exhort him as if he were your father. Treat younger men as brothers, [2]older women as mothers, and younger women as sisters, with absolute purity.

[3]Give proper recognition to those

[a]16 Some manuscripts *God*   [b]16 Or *in the flesh*

HEY DAD
Am I too young for God to use?

Text: 1 Timothy 4:12

No one is too young for God to use! Timothy was just a young man when Paul told him to set an example for other Christians in his "speech, in life, in love, in faith and in purity." No matter what your age, you can certainly take this passage as your own.

Sometimes adults can overlook children because they have not yet experienced the real stuff of life. But to discount children is to miss their fresh innocence and the wonder in their eyes when they discover something for the first time.

God treasures childlike qualities. When the disciples tried to keep children from Jesus, he became indignant (Mark 10:13–16). He said that unless the disciples received the kingdom of God like little children, they would never be able to enter it.

Jesus consistently reminded his followers that, in many ways, children are examples to us all.

QUESTIONS KIDS ASK

For a complete listing of Questions Kids Ask, turn to page 1435.

widows who are really in need. **4**But if a widow has children or grandchildren, these should learn first of all to put their religion into practice by caring for their own family and so repaying their parents and grandparents, for this is pleasing to God. **5**The widow who is really in need and left all alone puts her hope in God and continues night and day to pray and to ask God for help. **6**But the widow who lives for pleasure is dead even while she lives. **7**Give the people these instructions, too, so that no one may be open to blame. **8**If anyone does not provide for his relatives, and especially for his immediate family, he has denied the faith and is worse than an unbeliever.

9No widow may be put on the list of widows unless she is over sixty, has been faithful to her husband,*a* **10**and is well known for her good deeds, such as bringing up children, showing hospitality,

a9 Or has had but one husband

Children Are the Best Teachers

DAILY INSIGHT

One dry and windy summer day when I was young, my little brother and I walked out into the field behind our house. I was pulling my trusty red Radio Flyer™, on top of which was a large box that contained all of the week's burnable household trash. Disposing of this waste was one of my regular household chores.

Once the fire was blazing, I had one of those "brilliant" boyhood ideas. Without saying anything, I picked up a burning torch and laid it down in the dry grass. In what seemed like a moment, the wind caught the flame and sent the fire racing through the dry grass. I panicked, vainly attempting to stamp out the spreading fire.

At that moment, my mother looked out from the kitchen window and saw what looked like her two sons standing inside a blazing inferno. She grabbed a bucket, filled it with water, and raced to save our lives. Although she spilled the bucket's contents on the way, she swept us up into her arms and pulled us from the center of the blaze. A few minutes after the fire department arrived, everything was under control.

That night, my dad asked for a full report. "The breeze must have picked up a burning piece of paper and started the field on fire," I said, lying to my father's face.

"Well, Dan, is this the way it happened?" my father asked my younger accomplice.

I stood there, silently pleading with my little brother to go with me on this one. He looked at our father, glanced at me, then said, "No, sir. Robert started the fire himself. I saw him do it."

Although I tried to convince my dad that Dan was lying, he knew better. Maybe it was because Dan didn't have any reason to lie … and I did. Or maybe it was because of the innocence of youth—the full-faced honesty that so often characterizes youngsters, as yet untainted by the pride and cynicism that often comes with growing up.

The words you read today speak directly to this truth. In fact, as a dad, this text is a blazing reminder (no pun intended) that you have lots to learn from your children. Their straightforward integrity and innocence can actually be a guide. "Don't let anyone look down on you because you are young, but set an example for the believers in speech, in life, in love, in faith and in purity" (4:12).

Having raised two children, I can recall many times when their openness and sincerity instructed me … when their honesty and faith challenged my cunning and fear. The next time you're with your family, think of yourself in a classroom. You are the student, and your children are the instructors. This is the way it's supposed to be. To be sure, my little brother walked to the front of the classroom and taught his big brother a lesson that day. Children can be the best teachers.

TUESDAY

Passage:
1 Timothy 4:9–16
Verse:
1 Timothy 4:12

For your next devotional reading, go to page 1345.

washing the feet of the saints, helping those in trouble and devoting herself to all kinds of good deeds.

[11]As for younger widows, do not put them on such a list. For when their sensual desires overcome their dedication to Christ, they want to marry. [12]Thus they bring judgment on themselves, because they have broken their first pledge. [13]Besides, they get into the habit of being idle and going about from house to house. And not only do they become idlers, but also gossips and busybodies, saying things they ought not to. [14]So I counsel younger widows to marry, to have children, to manage their homes and to give the enemy no opportunity for slander. [15]Some have in fact already turned away to follow Satan.

[16]If any woman who is a believer has widows in her family, she should help them and not let the church be burdened with them, so that the church can help those widows who are really in need.

You Are Here

DAILY INSIGHT

WEDNESDAY

Passage:
1 Timothy 5:1–8

Verse:
1 Timothy 5:8

Visiting huge shopping malls while traveling on business has always been a favorite pastime of mine. Perhaps the hustle and bustle of shoppers helps me overcome some of the loneliness. Perhaps seeing happy families together draws me to my own clan, far away. Or maybe it's because I just like to buy stuff!

Not long ago I was in Phoenix, and decided to go on another adventure through a big shopping mall. After a few wrong turns, I found the big, lighted directory. I stood there for a few minutes, surveying the way the mall was laid out—anchor department stores, specialty stores, food courts.

Just as I selected the bookstore I wanted to visit, I discovered a problem—a very serious problem. Some practical joker had pulled the "You are here" sticker off the directory. "How can I possibly get to where I want to go from where I am, unless I know where I am?" I said out loud, as though I was ordering a burger at a drive-in window. No one answered.

The text you read today describes the landscape of our relationships as clearly as the directory at that Phoenix mall. "Do not rebuke an older man harshly ... treat younger men as brothers, older women as mothers, and younger women as sisters, with absolute purity. Give proper recognition to those widows who are really in need ... if anyone does not provide for his relatives, and especially for his immediate family, he has denied the faith and is worse than an unbeliever" (5:1–3, 8).

But these instructions are a hopeless waste of space unless you and I step back and take an honest look at where we are in relation to them. If we simply blow by them without pausing to consider the names and faces that fit these instructions from our own experience, we'll be as lost as I was that day in Phoenix.

Life is a lot of hard work, and many different people count on us to pull through. They watch us to see how we speak, how we react under pressure, and how we honor others and them. We can never go on vacation from these responsibilities. But if we haven't taken a sober look at where we are in these relationships—if we have looked the other way rather than dealing honestly with our propensity for selfishness, dishonor and laziness, these relationships will never be healed.

"Father in heaven," we may need to pray. "I am impatient with my elders, patronizing to young people, unaware of people in need, and insensitive to my family. But your presence helps me to admit my lostness, your grace forgives me of these failings, and your wisdom gives me the direction I need. Help me to wake up to your calling to be an example of your love to those whom I deal with on a daily basis. Thank you. Amen."

For your next devotional reading, go to page 1346.

[17]The elders who direct the affairs of the church well are worthy of double honor, especially those whose work is preaching and teaching. [18]For the Scripture says, "Do not muzzle the ox while it is treading out the grain,"[a] and "The worker deserves his wages."[b] [19]Do not entertain an accusation against an elder unless it is brought

[a]18 Deut. 25:4   [b]18 Luke 10:7

The Nasty Heartbreaker

DAILY INSIGHT

THURSDAY

Passage:
1 Timothy 6:3–11

Verse:
1 Timothy 6:10

"It has come to my attention that you have started a chain letter on campus, Mr. Wolgemuth." Sam Delcamp, the Dean of Students at Taylor University, spoke in a tone that told me he was something less than thrilled with my latest entrepreneurial venture.

What had begun with an innocent Thanksgiving-break meeting with a friend's father had turned into a nightmare. The man who had made the initial chain-letter pitch to me was a CPA, so I figured it must be legitimate. The plan carried an investment of $75, but promised astronomical returns if everything went according to plan. I loved the sound of that.

Rationalizing that I would give twenty percent of my earnings to mission work, I turned the letter loose on my campus. I found two willing classmates, explained the scheme to them, and had them racing to their rooms for the money. Selling has always been very, very good to me.

The letter exploded on our campus. Three days later, I received the fateful phone call.

"At last count, Mr. Wolgemuth, there are three hundred Taylor University men involved in this letter," Dr. Delcamp said soberly. "This letter must stop. *Right now*."

Less than twenty-four hours later, the Dean called me in to his office. "Yesterday, I asked that this letter be stopped. Not only has it *not* stopped," he continued, "but the letter has spread to every university within a fifty mile radius of our campus. I have spoken with most of the college deans in the state already today." He paused. I braced myself. "Mr. Wolgemuth, if I hear of just one more letter exchanging hands, you will be sent home immediately."

If the Dean hadn't asked me to leave his office, I might still be sitting there, wondering what I was going to do. I walked back to my room, picked up a spiral notebook, and walked to room 101. If the guys had bought into the chain-letter scheme, I wrote their names down, asked if they were out any money, and wrote the amount down next to their names. I told them that the Dean had ordered that no more letters be sold, and that I would do what I could do to cover their losses. Then I moved to room 102. When I finished with Wengatz Hall, I trudged across campus to Morris Hall, then to Swallow Robin Hall.

By the time I got back to my room, close to midnight, I collapsed on the bed in sheer frustration. But my efforts paid off; I got to finish the semester. At the end of the next summer, I went through the list I had made and wrote dozens of checks, settling accounts with each man. My lesson cost me $2,200. But looking back, it was really worth a lot more.

The apostle Paul wrote to his young friend, Timothy, "People who want to get rich fall into temptation and a trap and into many foolish and harmful desires that plunge men into ruin and destruction. For the love of money is a root of all kinds of evil." I had learned this lesson firsthand. Paul then urged Timothy to "pursue righteousness, godliness, faith, love, endurance and gentleness" (6:11).

What incredible wisdom this is for a young man to hear.

I am grateful for the investment Dr. Delcamp "encouraged" me to make as a nineteen-year-old boy. I fell in love with money, and she stood me up, the nasty heartbreaker.

For your next devotional reading, go to page 1349.

by two or three witnesses. ²⁰Those who sin are to be rebuked publicly, so that the others may take warning.

²¹I charge you, in the sight of God and Christ Jesus and the elect angels, to keep these instructions without partiality, and to do nothing out of favoritism.

²²Do not be hasty in the laying on of hands, and do not share in the sins of others. Keep yourself pure.

²³Stop drinking only water, and use a little wine because of your stomach and your frequent illnesses.

²⁴The sins of some men are obvious, reaching the place of judgment ahead of them; the sins of others trail behind them. ²⁵In the same way, good deeds are obvious, and even those that are not cannot be hidden.

6 All who are under the yoke of slavery should consider their masters worthy of full respect, so that God's name and our teaching may not be slandered. ²Those who have believing masters are not to show less respect for them because they are brothers. Instead, they are to serve them even better, because those who benefit from their service are believers, and dear to them. These are the things you are to teach and urge on them.

Love of Money

³If anyone teaches false doctrines and does not agree to the sound instruction of our Lord Jesus Christ and to godly teaching, ⁴he is conceited and understands nothing. He has an unhealthy interest in controversies and quarrels about words that result in envy, strife, malicious talk, evil suspicions ⁵and constant friction between men of corrupt mind, who have been robbed of the truth and who think that godliness is a means to financial gain.

⁶But godliness with contentment is great gain. ⁷For we brought nothing into the world, and we can take nothing out of it. ⁸But if we have food and clothing, we will be content with that. ⁹People who

want to get rich fall into temptation and a trap and into many foolish and harmful desires that plunge men into ruin and destruction. ¹⁰For the love of money is a root of all kinds of evil. Some people, eager for money, have wandered from the faith and pierced themselves with many griefs.

Paul's Charge to Timothy

¹¹But you, man of God, flee from all this, and pursue righteousness, godliness, faith, love, endurance and gentleness. ¹²Fight the good fight of the faith. Take hold of the eternal life to which you were called when you made your good confession in the presence of many witnesses. ¹³In the sight of God, who gives life to everything, and of Christ Jesus, who while testifying before Pontius Pilate made the good confession, I charge you ¹⁴to keep this command without spot or blame until the appearing of our Lord Jesus Christ, ¹⁵which God will bring about in his own time—God, the blessed and only Ruler, the King of kings and Lord of lords, ¹⁶who alone is immortal and who lives in unapproachable light, whom no one has seen or can see. To him be honor and might forever. Amen.

¹⁷Command those who are rich in this present world not to be arrogant nor to put their hope in wealth, which is so uncertain, but to put their hope in God, who richly provides us with everything for our enjoyment. ¹⁸Command them to do good, to be rich in good deeds, and to be generous and willing to share. ¹⁹In this way they will lay up treasure for themselves as a firm foundation for the coming age, so that they may take hold of the life that is truly life.

²⁰Timothy, guard what has been entrusted to your care. Turn away from godless chatter and the opposing ideas of what is falsely called knowledge, ²¹which some have professed and in so doing have wandered from the faith.

Grace be with you.

Moments before his death, Thomas Hobbes (1588-1679), the great British philosopher, said, "I am about to take my last voyage, a great leap into the dark." And moments before drawing his last breath, circus magnate P.T. Barnum (1810–1891) asked, "How were the receipts today in Madison Square Garden?"

It's interesting, isn't it, how people see things at the end of their lives? As the apostle Paul approached the close of his own life and ministry, he summarized what he wanted Timothy to remember: "Be strong in the grace that is in Christ Jesus . . . entrust [this grace] to reliable men who will also be qualified to teach others. Endure hardship with us like a good soldier . . . the Lord will give you insight into all this" (2:1-7).

Paul was ready to die because his heavenly Father had taught him how to *live*. The book of 2 Timothy gives us a glimpse into Paul's life, and sets up a model for us to follow as we consider encouraging and passing our faith on to our children.

2 Timothy

1 Paul, an apostle of Christ Jesus by the will of God, according to the promise of life that is in Christ Jesus,

²To Timothy, my dear son:

Grace, mercy and peace from God the Father and Christ Jesus our Lord.

Encouragement to Be Faithful

³I thank God, whom I serve, as my forefathers did, with a clear conscience, as night and day I constantly remember you in my prayers. ⁴Recalling your tears, I long to see you, so that I may be filled with joy. ⁵I have been reminded of your sincere faith, which first lived in your grandmother Lois and in your mother Eunice and, I am persuaded, now lives in you also. ⁶For this reason I remind you to fan into flame the gift of God, which is in you through the laying on of my hands. ⁷For God did not give us a spirit of timidity, but a spirit of power, of love and of self-discipline.

⁸So do not be ashamed to testify about our Lord, or ashamed of me his prisoner. But join with me in suffering for the gospel, by the power of God, ⁹who has saved us and called us to a holy life—not because of anything we have done but because of his own purpose and grace. This grace was given us in Christ Jesus before the beginning of time, ¹⁰but it has now

been revealed through the appearing of our Savior, Christ Jesus, who has destroyed death and has brought life and immortality to light through the gospel. [11]And of this gospel I was appointed a herald and an apostle and a teacher. [12]That is why I am suffering as I am. Yet I am not ashamed, because I know whom I have believed, and am convinced that he is able to guard what I have entrusted to him for that day. [13]What you heard from me, keep as the

pattern of sound teaching, with faith and love in Christ Jesus. [14]Guard the good deposit that was entrusted to you—guard it with the help of the Holy Spirit who lives in us.

[15]You know that everyone in the province of Asia has deserted me, including Phygelus and Hermogenes. [16]May the Lord show mercy to the household of Onesiphorus, because he often refreshed me and was not ashamed of my chains. [17]On the contrary, when he

How a Family Works

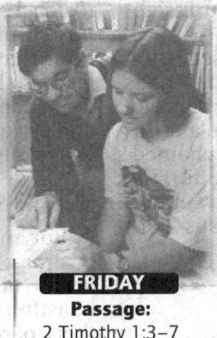

DAILY INSIGHT

FRIDAY

Passage:
2 Timothy 1:3–7

Verse:
2 Timothy 1:7

I think I've figured out how families are supposed to work. I haven't checked with any psychologists or therapists, but I really don't think I need to. I'm sure of this one.

While I was actively promoting my first book, *She Calls Me Daddy,* I found myself on many radio and television talk shows. I really enjoyed the spontaneity of this live call-in format. But after a dozen shows, something hit me. I had written a book for dads raising daughters, so it would stand to reason that most of my callers would have been men. Right?

Wrong. With only a few exceptions, every caller had been a grown woman. These women thanked me for writing this book, and told me that their relationship to their dad—good or bad—continued to be the most important relationship in their lives ... even though many were now married and had kids of their own.

So I looked back on my own life. *Who spoke to my soul?* I asked myself. *Who helped me to believe in myself?* Easy questions to answer ... my mother did all of these things. My dad taught me a lot of the "how" of life, but my mother poured on the encouragement. "You can do it," I can still hear her say. "I know you can."

Did you read what the apostle Paul wrote to Timothy? "I have been reminded of your sincere faith" (1:5). And where did Timothy get this "faith?" From his "grandmother Lois and ... [his] mother Eunice." Timothy, the man whom the great apostle

called, "my dear son," got his convictions from the women in his life. This confirms my theory.

Because of the way God made us, we are naturally drawn, even at a very early age, to the affection and advocacy of the parent of the opposite sex. We counted on our moms, and so do our sons. Our wives looked to their fathers for tenderness and assurance. Our daughters look to us.

If you had a terrific mother, you're hanging right in there with me. If your wife had a great dad, you're really on board. But what about the men who didn't have such a mother? And what about the women who didn't have that kind of father? Believe it or not, Paul has something to say to us about this. "For God did not give us a spirit of timidity, but a spirit of power, of love and of self-discipline" (1:7).

Paul says that we have God-given power. Through the Spirit, we can use that power to reverse the affects of negative relationships in our lives. If your wife didn't have a daddy who loved her, then you love your wife and be willing to give your life for her (Ephesians 5). If you didn't have a mother who poured affirmation on you, then you dig down and find the self-discipline to be tender to your daughter.

So there you have it ... a strategy for making your family work, specific instructions on how to do it, and the power to pull it off. Isn't this awesome?

For your next devotional reading, go to page 1351.

was in Rome, he searched hard for me until he found me. [18]May the Lord grant that he will find mercy from the Lord on that day! You know very well in how many ways he helped me in Ephesus.

2 You then, my son, be strong in the grace that is in Christ Jesus. [2]And the things you have heard me say in the presence of many witnesses entrust to reliable men who will also be qualified to teach others. [3]Endure hardship with us like a good soldier of Christ Jesus. [4]No one serving as a soldier gets involved in civilian affairs—he wants to please his commanding officer. [5]Similarly, if anyone competes as an athlete, he does not receive the victor's crown unless he competes according to the rules. [6]The hardworking farmer should be the first to receive a share of the crops. [7]Reflect on what I am saying, for the Lord will give you insight into all this.

[8]Remember Jesus Christ, raised from the dead, descended from David. This is my gospel, [9]for which I am suffering even to the point of being chained like a criminal. But God's word is not chained. [10]Therefore I endure everything for the sake of the elect, that they too may obtain the salvation that is in Christ Jesus, with eternal glory.

[11]Here is a trustworthy saying:

If we died with him,
   we will also live with him;
[12]if we endure,
   we will also reign with him.
If we disown him,
   he will also disown us;
[13]if we are faithless,
   he will remain faithful,
   for he cannot disown himself.

A Workman Approved by God

[14]Keep reminding them of these things. Warn them before God against quarreling about words; it is of no value, and only ruins those who listen. [15]Do your best to present yourself to God as one approved, a workman who does not need to be ashamed and who correctly handles the word of truth. [16]Avoid godless chatter, because those who indulge in it will become more and more ungodly. [17]Their teaching will spread like gangrene. Among them are Hymenaeus and Philetus, [18]who have wandered away from the truth. They say that the resurrection has already taken place, and they destroy the faith of some. [19]Nevertheless, God's solid foundation stands firm, sealed with this inscription: "The Lord knows those who are his,"[a] and, "Everyone who confesses the name of the Lord must turn away from wickedness."

[20]In a large house there are articles not only of gold and silver, but also of wood and clay; some are for noble purposes and some for ignoble. [21]If a man cleanses himself from the latter, he will be an instrument for noble purposes, made holy, useful to the Master and prepared to do any good work.

[22]Flee the evil desires of youth, and pursue righteousness, faith, love and peace, along with those who call on the Lord out of a pure heart. [23]Don't have anything to do with foolish and stupid arguments, because you know they produce quarrels. [24]And the Lord's servant must not quarrel; instead, he must be kind to everyone, able to teach, not resentful. [25]Those who oppose him he must gently instruct, in the hope that God will grant them repentance leading them to a knowledge of the truth, [26]and that they will come to their senses and escape from the trap of the devil, who has taken them captive to do his will.

Godlessness in the Last Days

3 But mark this: There will be terrible times in the last days. [2]People will be lovers of themselves, lovers of money, boastful, proud, abusive, disobedient to their parents, ungrateful, unholy, [3]without love, unforgiving, slanderous, without self-control, brutal, not lovers of the good, [4]treacherous, rash, conceited, lovers of pleasure rather than lovers of God— [5]having a form of godliness but denying its power. Have nothing to do with them.

[6]They are the kind who worm their way into homes and gain control over weak-willed women, who are loaded down with sins and are swayed by all kinds of evil desires, [7]always learning but never able to acknowledge the truth. [8]Just as Jannes and Jambres opposed Moses, so also these men oppose the truth—men of depraved minds, who, as far as the faith is concerned, are rejected. [9]But they will not get very far because, as in the case of those men, their folly will be clear to everyone.

Paul's Charge to Timothy

[10]You, however, know all about my teaching, my way of life, my purpose, faith, patience, love, endurance, [11]persecutions,

[a]19 Num. 16:5 (see Septuagint)

Daddy's Home

Key Verse: *"Do your best to present yourself to God as one approved, a workman who does not need to be ashamed and who correctly handles the word of truth."* 2 Timothy 2:15

Text: 2 Timothy 2:14–16 *(Dad or child reads the text.)*

DAD READS: "Daddy's home!" These are two words every dad loves to hear because they usually mean that the workday is over and that someone is glad to see him. I love to hear these words, too. It's an awesome thing to hear a happy little person say, "Daddy's home."

Child reads: When a daddy comes home and everyone is glad to see him, it means that this is a family who loves each other. This family is glad when everyone is together. What a happy thing it is when families love each other that way and when they are excited to see each other.

DAD READS: Yes, this is a wonderful thing. But sometimes children don't look forward to their daddy coming home. Sometimes this is because their daddy is mean and unkind. But sometimes children don't yell, "Daddy's home," because they aren't ready to see him. Maybe they have been disobedient, or maybe they didn't finish their chores, or maybe they did something unkind to their little brother and they don't want their daddy to find out. When daddies come home and children aren't ready for him, they hide.

Child reads: The Bible tells us that we need to be ready for God's visits. It says, "present yourself to God as one approved" (2:15). It's like God has come to our house and we are supposed to come out of our rooms and stand in front of him. The Bible tells us that we shouldn't be ashamed when this happens, because we will not have done anything that would make him sad.

QUIET
TIMES
WITH Dad

DAD READS: This isn't just for little children. Just as kids don't want to have to hide when God visits, dads don't want to be embarrassed either when their heavenly Father comes home. And today we read about two things that we can do that will please him. The first is what we're doing right now … reading the Bible. God promises to speak to us when we read his Word. This will help us to be obedient and to not be ashamed.

Child reads: We also need to be careful about how we talk to each other. The words we read today tell us to "avoid godless chatter." This means that the things that come out of our mouths should make our heavenly Father happy. They must be words that don't make us ashamed when God hears us speak.

DAD READS: "Daddy's home" are two words God also loves to hear. He knows that when we're happy to see him, it is because we have studied his Word and we have been very careful about the words we have said. Let me pray this prayer with you:

Our Father in heaven, we love you. Thank you for this very important lesson. We want to be happy when you come to our house. Thank you for the chance you have given us to read the Bible and listen to your voice. And please help us to speak words that make you happy. We love you, and we thank you for your love. In Jesus' name, Amen.

For your next devotional reading, go to page 1355.

sufferings—what kinds of things happened to me in Antioch, Iconium and Lystra, the persecutions I endured. Yet the Lord rescued me from all of them. [12]In fact, everyone who wants to live a godly life in Christ Jesus will be persecuted, [13]while evil men and impostors will go from bad to worse, deceiving and being deceived. [14]But as for you, continue in what you have learned and have become convinced of, because you know those from whom you learned it, [15]and how from infancy you have known the holy Scriptures, which are able to make you wise for salvation through faith in Christ Jesus. [16]All Scripture is God-breathed and is useful for teaching, rebuking, correcting and training in righteousness, [17]so that the man of God may be thoroughly equipped for every good work.

4 In the presence of God and of Christ Jesus, who will judge the living and the dead, and in view of his appearing and his kingdom, I give you this charge: [2]Preach the Word; be prepared in season and out of season; correct, rebuke and encourage—with great patience and careful instruction. [3]For the time will come when men will not put up with sound doctrine. Instead, to suit their own desires, they will gather around them a great number of teachers to say what their itching ears want to hear. [4]They will turn their ears away from the truth and turn aside to myths. [5]But you, keep your head in all situations, endure hardship, do the work of an evangelist, discharge all the duties of your ministry.

[6]For I am already being poured out like a drink offering, and the time has come for my departure. [7]I have fought the good fight, I have finished the race, I have kept the faith. [8]Now there is in store for me the crown of righteousness, which the Lord, the righteous Judge, will award to me on that day—and not only to me, but also to all who have longed for his appearing.

Personal Remarks

[9]Do your best to come to me quickly, [10]for Demas, because he loved this world, has deserted me and has gone to Thessalonica. Crescens has gone to Galatia, and Titus to Dalmatia. [11]Only Luke is with me. Get Mark and bring him with you, because he is helpful to me in my ministry. [12]I sent Tychicus to Ephesus. [13]When you come, bring the cloak that I left with Carpus at Troas, and my scrolls, especially the parchments.

[14]Alexander the metalworker did me a great deal of harm. The Lord will repay him for what he has done. [15]You too should be on your guard against him, because he strongly opposed our message.

[16]At my first defense, no one came to my support, but everyone deserted me. May it not be held against them. [17]But the Lord stood at my side and gave me strength, so that through me the message might be fully proclaimed and all the Gentiles might hear it. And I was delivered from the lion's mouth. [18]The Lord will rescue me from every evil attack and will bring me safely to his heavenly kingdom. To him be glory for ever and ever. Amen.

HEY DAD
How does the Bible really help us?

Text: 2 Timothy 3:14–17

In this passage Paul describes the Bible in very practical terms: It is an instruction book for right living. As God's Word, the Bible is the ultimate authority on what is right and what is wrong. It helps us to live in line with God's will for our lives. It is the one tool that will help make us "wise for salvation through faith in Christ Jesus" (v. 15).

Scripture is also useful for "training in righteousness, so that the man of God may be thoroughly equipped for every good work" (vv. 16–17). Reading, studying and memorizing the Scripture helps us become more like Christ so that when temptation or the opportunity for a good work arises, we will be well prepared. We'll know what to do and have all the tools necessary to do the job well.

For a complete listing of Questions Kids Ask, turn to page 1435.

Final Greetings

[19]Greet Priscilla[a] and Aquila and the household of Onesiphorus. [20]Erastus stayed in Corinth, and I left Trophimus sick in Miletus. [21]Do your best to get here before winter. Eubulus greets you, and so do Pudens, Linus, Claudia and all the brothers.

[22]The Lord be with your spirit. Grace be with you.

---

[a]19 Greek *Prisca*, a variant of *Priscilla*

If you've ever visited a law office, you've probably seen an extensive library. Row after row of books—mostly case histories—line the walls of this room, and computers glow with large amounts of on-line information that's well organized and safely stored for easy retrieval. Why do lawyers have all these resources, and why does one often find them poring over these volumes? The answer is simple. They're professionals, and they want to be ready. People are counting on them to know their stuff and to know it well.

Titus was a minister who was called to serve a church in Crete, an island off the coast of Greece. His charge was a difficult one, and it's likely that Titus didn't have access to much information to help him in his calling. Can't you see this young pastor poring over each word of this letter from Paul? After all, Titus was a professional, and like a lawyer, he wanted to be prepared.

You're a Christian. You're also a dad. Because your family looks to you to know your stuff, this small book is just one of 66 that you need to study. God's Word is your library. Are you prepared?

Titus

1 Paul, a servant of God and an apostle of Jesus Christ for the faith of God's elect and the knowledge of the truth that leads to godliness— 2a faith and knowledge resting on the hope of eternal life, which God, who does not lie, promised before the beginning of time, 3and at his appointed season he brought his word to light through the preaching entrusted to me by the command of God our Savior,

4To Titus, my true son in our common faith:

Grace and peace from God the Father and Christ Jesus our Savior.

Titus's Task on Crete

5The reason I left you in Crete was that you might straighten out what was left unfinished and appoint*a* elders in every town, as I directed you. 6An elder must be blameless, the husband of but one wife, a man whose children believe and are not

*a*5 Or *ordain*

open to the charge of being wild and disobedient. [7]Since an overseer[a] is entrusted with God's work, he must be blameless— not overbearing, not quick-tempered, not given to drunkenness, not violent, not pursuing dishonest gain. [8]Rather he must be hospitable, one who loves what is good, who is self-controlled, upright, holy and disciplined. [9]He must hold firmly to the trustworthy message as it has been taught, so that he can encourage others by sound doctrine and refute those who oppose it.

[10]For there are many rebellious people,

[a]7 Traditionally *bishop*

The Rotten Potatoes Always Win

DAILY
INSIGHT

MONDAY

Passage:
Titus 1:10–11,15–16

Verse:
Titus 1:15

My grandparents' home in Lancaster County, Pennsylvania, featured a fruit cellar. Many times, as the kid who had been assigned to kitchen duty, I was sent down there to retrieve something.

Now, just in case you don't know what a fruit cellar is, I'll be happy to tell you. Off of that basement of my grandparents' home was a small room, three or four additional steps deeper than the foundation of the house. This was the fruit cellar, a room that had been carved out of the dirt and lined with large rocks. Shelves in this room were stocked with my grandmother's canned peaches and tomatoes, and bushel baskets of potatoes, carrots and apples. Because they were dug deep in the earth, these cellars stayed cool year-round and kept fruit and vegetables from deteriorating too quickly.

I remember going to this little room as though it were yesterday. Grabbing a jar of peaches wasn't too scary, but reaching into a bushel basket of potatoes always made my stomach tighten up. I well remember the gripping fear that I'd meet some furry, nasty critter in there—who was also retrieving something for *its* grandmother, no doubt.

While this fear was never realized, I do remember bringing a potato to my grandmother one time that made her snap to attention as though someone had just dropped an ice cube down her back. She ran down the basement steps, and came back up carrying the whole basket of potatoes. Dumping the potatoes onto the kitchen table, she picked up each one and meticulously examined it from top to bottom. "One of the potatoes you brought up was rotten," she explained. "If I don't destroy the rotten ones, they'll all be ruined."

The apostle Paul reminds us that there are, in fact, some rotten potatoes out there: "rebellious people, mere talkers and deceivers, [people who are] ruining whole households by teaching things they ought not to teach ... their minds and consciences are corrupted ... [they are] detestable, disobedient and unfit for doing anything good" (1:10,11, 15–16). And the instructions the apostle gives his friend, Titus, reflect exactly what my grandmother did to those foul potatoes from the fruit cellar. "They must be silenced," he orders (1:11). Throw the rotten ones out. Why? Because Paul knew what my grandmother knew: contemptible potatoes are contagious. Unless these potatoes are rooted out and separated from the others, the whole basket can be spoiled in no time.

I don't know about you, but I tend to be a live-and-let-live kind of guy. Given a choice between confronting a Christian friend caught in sin and hoping he figures it out for himself, I usually prefer the latter. *Who do I think I am?* I may say. *After all, I've got a few rotten spots myself.*

Paul knew Titus well enough to know that they both were flawed men. Nonetheless, his instructions were crisp and straightforward. "Save the whole basket," Paul was telling his protégé. "If you don't, the rotten potatoes will win."

For your next devotional reading, go to page 1361.

mere talkers and deceivers, especially those of the circumcision group. [11]They must be silenced, because they are ruining whole households by teaching things they ought not to teach—and that for the sake of dishonest gain. [12]Even one of their own prophets has said, "Cretans are always liars, evil brutes, lazy gluttons." [13]This testimony is true. Therefore, rebuke them sharply, so that they will be sound in the faith [14]and will pay no attention to Jewish myths or to the commands of those who reject the truth. [15]To the pure, all things are pure, but to those who are corrupted and do not believe, nothing is pure. In fact, both their minds and consciences are corrupted. [16]They claim to know God, but by their actions they deny him. They are detestable, disobedient and unfit for doing anything good.

What Must Be Taught to Various Groups

2 You must teach what is in accord with sound doctrine. [2]Teach the older men to be temperate, worthy of respect, self-controlled, and sound in faith, in love and in endurance.

[3]Likewise, teach the older women to be reverent in the way they live, not to be slanderers or addicted to much wine, but to teach what is good. [4]Then they can train the younger women to love their husbands and children, [5]to be self-controlled and pure, to be busy at home, to be kind, and to be subject to their husbands, so that no one will malign the word of God.

[6]Similarly, encourage the young men to be self-controlled. [7]In everything set them an example by doing what is good. In your teaching show integrity, seriousness [8]and soundness of speech that cannot be condemned, so that those who oppose you may be ashamed because they have nothing bad to say about us.

[9]Teach slaves to be subject to their masters in everything, to try to please them, not to talk back to them, [10]and not to steal from them, but to show that they can be fully trusted, so that in every way they will make the teaching about God our Savior attractive.

[11]For the grace of God that brings salvation has appeared to all men. [12]It teaches us to say "No" to ungodliness and worldly passions, and to live self-controlled, upright and godly lives in this present age, [13]while we wait for the blessed hope—the glorious appearing of our great God and Savior, Jesus Christ, [14]who gave himself for us to redeem us from all wickedness and to purify for himself a people that are his very own, eager to do what is good.

[15]These, then, are the things you should teach. Encourage and rebuke with all authority. Do not let anyone despise you.

Doing What Is Good

3 Remind the people to be subject to rulers and authorities, to be obedient, to

HEY DAD

Do I have to obey my teacher, even if he or she is mean?

Text: Titus 3:1–2

In almost all cases, the answer to this question is "yes." If our government does not honor God, or if our rulers—bosses, teachers, Presidents—do things we do not agree with, we are still supposed to obey them.

Even Jesus obeyed the ruling authorities. During Jesus' time, the Romans ruled Israel. They worshiped pagan gods and practiced rituals that God detested. But when asked whether or not the Jews should pay taxes to this evil empire, Jesus said they should give to Caesar what was Caesar's—taxes—and give to God what was God's (Matthew 22:21).

So, you do not like the President? Or your teacher? Or your boss? Guess what. That is not an excuse to break the law or to undermine that person's authority. You may only disobey if he or she commands you to break one of God's laws. Remember Daniel? He refused to pray to King Darius, even though the law required it (Daniel 6:10). This was the right decision, and a good model for us to follow.

Taxes? Give them to Caesar. Glory and honor? Give that to God.

For a complete listing of Questions Kids Ask, turn to page 1435.

QUESTIONS KIDS ASK

be ready to do whatever is good, **²**to slander no one, to be peaceable and considerate, and to show true humility toward all men.

³At one time we too were foolish, disobedient, deceived and enslaved by all kinds of passions and pleasures. We lived in malice and envy, being hated and hating one another. **⁴**But when the kindness and love of God our Savior appeared, **⁵**he saved us, not because of righteous things we had done, but because of his mercy. He saved us through the washing of rebirth and renewal by the Holy Spirit, **⁶**whom he poured out on us generously through Jesus Christ our Savior, **⁷**so that, having been justified by his grace, we might become heirs having the hope of eternal life. **⁸**This is a trustworthy saying. And I want you to stress these things, so that those who have trusted in God may be careful to devote themselves to doing what is good. These things are excellent and profitable for everyone.

⁹But avoid foolish controversies and genealogies and arguments and quarrels about the law, because these are unprofitable and useless. **¹⁰**Warn a divisive person once, and then warn him a second time. After that, have nothing to do with him. **¹¹**You may be sure that such a man is warped and sinful; he is self-condemned.

Final Remarks

¹²As soon as I send Artemas or Tychicus to you, do your best to come to me at Nicopolis, because I have decided to winter there. **¹³**Do everything you can to help Zenas the lawyer and Apollos on their way and see that they have everything they need. **¹⁴**Our people must learn to devote themselves to doing what is good, in order that they may provide for daily necessities and not live unproductive lives.

¹⁵Everyone with me sends you greetings. Greet those who love us in the faith.

Grace be with you all.

"I'm sorry, I was wrong. Will you please forgive me?" These words reveal a man's repentant heart, expose his own judgment on what he has just done or said, and solicit a charitable response from the one he has offended. These can be difficult words for a man to say to his wife, his child, his coworker, or his friend. But these simple words can have an enormous effect—from soothing a child's hurt feelings to saving a decades-long marriage.

This tiny letter from the apostle Paul to a man named Philemon carries a similarly significant message of repentance and a request for reconciliation. How interesting that we never hear what Philemon did when he received this letter from Paul. Did he, like the father awaiting the lost son, welcome his former slave back home? The fact that this letter found its way into the Bible gives us some indication that he did. It's likely that Philemon found, as many people have, that the only thing more gratifying than being pardoned is being the person who is doing the pardoning.

Philemon

¹Paul, a prisoner of Christ Jesus, and Timothy our brother,

To Philemon our dear friend and fellow worker, ²to Apphia our sister, to Archippus our fellow soldier and to the church that meets in your home:

³Grace to you and peace from God our Father and the Lord Jesus Christ.

Thanksgiving and Prayer

⁴I always thank my God as I remember you in my prayers, ⁵because I hear about your faith in the Lord Jesus and your love for all the saints. ⁶I pray that you may be active in sharing your faith, so that you will have a full understanding of every good thing we have in Christ. ⁷Your love has given me great joy and encouragement, because you, brother, have refreshed the hearts of the saints.

Paul's Plea for Onesimus

⁸Therefore, although in Christ I could be bold and order you to do what you ought to do, ⁹yet I appeal to you on the basis of love. I then, as Paul—an old man and now also a prisoner of Christ Jesus— ¹⁰I appeal to you for my son Onesimus,ᵃ who became my son while I was in chains. ¹¹For-

ᵃ10 Onesimus means *useful*.

merly he was useless to you, but now he has become useful both to you and to me. [12]I am sending him—who is my very heart—back to you. [13]I would have liked to keep him with me so that he could take your place in helping me while I am in chains for the gospel. [14]But I did not want to do anything without your consent, so that any favor you do will be spontaneous and not forced. [15]Perhaps the reason he was separated from you for a little while was that you might have him back for good— [16]no longer as a slave, but better than a slave, as a dear brother. He is very dear to me but even dearer to you, both as a man and as a brother in the Lord.

[17]So if you consider me a partner, welcome him as you would welcome me. [18]If he has done you any wrong or owes you anything, charge it to me. [19]I, Paul, am writing this with my own hand. I will pay it back—not to mention that you owe me your very self. [20]I do wish, brother, that I may have some benefit from you in the Lord; refresh my heart in Christ. [21]Confident of your obedience, I write to you, knowing that you will do even more than I ask.

[22]And one thing more: Prepare a guest room for me, because I hope to be restored to you in answer to your prayers.

[23]Epaphras, my fellow prisoner in Christ Jesus, sends you greetings. [24]And so do Mark, Aristarchus, Demas and Luke, my fellow workers.

[25]The grace of the Lord Jesus Christ be with your spirit.

What do Cooperstown, New York; Springfield, Massachusetts and Canton, Ohio have in common? Any guy worth the salt on his potato chips knows that these three cities boast the National Baseball Hall of Fame, the Basketball Hall of Fame and the Pro Football Hall of Fame, respectively. Each year thousands of tourists flock to these places to relive the glorious careers of their favorite sports heroes.

But did you know that the Bible has a Hall of Fame as well? Hebrews chapter 11 boasts a Hall of Faith, a verbal newsreel of many faithful Old Testament men and women who sacrificed everything to follow God. The writer of this book tells us that *we too* can be inductees into this wonderful Hall of Faith—members of the "great cloud of witnesses" (12:1), cheering others on in the faith.

Although the writer of this book decided to remain anonymous, we can surely consider him an unnamed inductee. This book provides us with many shining examples of the way God would have all Christians live until, at the end of our lives, our induction into eternal life is complete.

Hebrews

The Son Superior to Angels

1 In the past God spoke to our forefathers through the prophets at many times and in various ways, ²but in these last days he has spoken to us by his Son, whom he appointed heir of all things, and through whom he made the universe. ³The Son is the radiance of God's glory and the exact representation of his being, sustaining all things by his powerful word. After he had provided purification for sins, he sat down at the right hand of the Majesty in heaven. ⁴So he became as much superior to the angels as the name he has inherited is superior to theirs.

⁵For to which of the angels did God ever say,

"You are my Son;
  today I have become your Father[a]"[b]?

Or again,

"I will be his Father,
  and he will be my Son"[c]?

⁶And again, when God brings his firstborn into the world, he says,

"Let all God's angels worship him."[d]

[a]5 Or *have begotten you*   [b]5 Psalm 2:7
[c]5 2 Samuel 7:14; 1 Chron. 17:13   [d]6 Deut. 32:43
(see Dead Sea Scrolls and Septuagint)

[7]In speaking of the angels he says,

"He makes his angels winds,
    his servants flames of fire."[a]

[8]But about the Son he says,

"Your throne, O God, will last for ever
    and ever,
and righteousness will be the scepter
    of your kingdom.
[9]You have loved righteousness and
    hated wickedness;

therefore God, your God, has set you
    above your companions
by anointing you with the oil of joy."[b]

[10]He also says,

"In the beginning, O Lord, you laid the
    foundations of the earth,
and the heavens are the work of your
    hands.

[a]7 Psalm 104:4   [b]9 Psalm 45:6,7

Our Fathers' Dominant Genes

DAILY INSIGHT

TUESDAY

Passage:
Hebrews 1:1–4

Verse:
Hebrews 1:3

Medicine has always fascinated me. In fact, until I changed my college major to Biblical Literature, I was on a track preparing for medical school. I loved those pre-med courses. Human anatomy was great, and comparative anatomy was even more fun—I had never seen a better-looking cat. But my favorite was genetics.

If you've taken genetics, you know that it is the study of dominant and recessive traits that are either passed on to offspring or wait in the wings for another recessive partner. It's also the study of probabilities. For me it was the blending of two of my favorite subjects: science and math. Each day in genetics was like a great adventure for me.

Every time a baby is born, its extended family members become accomplished geneticists. "Oh, look, she has her daddy's nose." "If that isn't his mother's chin, I don't know what is." But did you know that when we believe in Christ, when we come to faith in him, when we experience his grace through the forgiveness of our sins ... we become newborns? We literally take on our ancestors' characteristics as though through the miracle of genetics.

The writer to the Hebrews explains it this way. "In the past God spoke to our forefathers through the prophets ... but in these last days he has spoken to us by his Son, whom he appointed heir of all things" (1:1–2). God's gift of wholeness and grace came cascading down through the patriarchs and the prophets, was embodied in

God's only begotten Son, and then came to us, his very own sons.

Every person whom God's gift touched was changed. Once they had come in contact with the sovereign Creator of the universe, they were born again. Others may have said of them, "He has his mother's faith." "Oh, can't you see how she teaches just like her dad?" "He's got that encouraging touch, just like his grandfather."

In another genetics-related statement, the writer of Hebrews tells us, "The Son is the radiance of God's glory and the exact representation of his being." My uncle would have said that Jesus was the "spitting image of his daddy" (where that expression came from, I have no idea).

As Christians, we have a spectacular heritage. You and I have Abraham's daring, Isaac's faith, Jacob's tenacity, Joseph's moral courage, Daniel's consistency, Jeremiah's transparency, Jonah's contrition and Hosea's obedience. Most importantly, however, through the salvation that is ours in Christ, God's Son, we have Jesus' holiness.

And given God's power to face each day with the assurance of who we are, God gives us gifts that have the potential of literally overcoming evil. My genetics professor, Dr. Elizabeth Poe, would have correctly called these, "Our Father's dominant genes."

For your next devotional reading, go to page 1364.

¹¹They will perish, but you remain;
 they will all wear out like a garment.
¹²You will roll them up like a robe;
 like a garment they will be changed.
But you remain the same,
 and your years will never end."ᵃ

¹³To which of the angels did God ever say,

"Sit at my right hand
until I make your enemies
 a footstool for your feet"ᵇ?

¹⁴Are not all angels ministering spirits sent to serve those who will inherit salvation?

Warning to Pay Attention

2 We must pay more careful attention, therefore, to what we have heard, so that we do not drift away. ²For if the message spoken by angels was binding, and every violation and disobedience received its just punishment, ³how shall we escape if we ignore such a great salvation? This salvation, which was first announced by the Lord, was confirmed to us by those who heard him. ⁴God also testified to it by signs, wonders and various miracles, and gifts of the Holy Spirit distributed according to his will.

Jesus Made Like His Brothers

⁵It is not to angels that he has subjected the world to come, about which we are speaking. ⁶But there is a place where someone has testified:

"What is man that you are mindful of
 him,
 the son of man that you care for him?
⁷You made him a littleᶜ lower than the
 angels;
 you crowned him with glory and
 honor
⁸ and put everything under his feet."ᵈ

In putting everything under him, God left nothing that is not subject to him. Yet at present we do not see everything subject to him. ⁹But we see Jesus, who was made a little lower than the angels, now crowned with glory and honor because he suffered death, so that by the grace of God he might taste death for everyone. ¹⁰In bringing many sons to glory, it was fitting that God, for whom and through whom everything exists, should make the author of their salvation perfect through suffering. ¹¹Both the one who makes men holy and those who are made holy are of

the same family. So Jesus is not ashamed to call them brothers. ¹²He says,

"I will declare your name to my
 brothers;
 in the presence of the congregation I
 will sing your praises."ᵉ

¹³And again,

"I will put my trust in him."ᶠ

And again he says,

"Here am I, and the children God has
 given me."ᵍ

¹⁴Since the children have flesh and blood, he too shared in their humanity so that by his death he might destroy him who holds the power of death—that is, the devil— ¹⁵and free those who all their lives were held in slavery by their fear of death. ¹⁶For surely it is not angels he helps, but Abraham's descendants. ¹⁷For this reason he had to be made like his brothers in every way, in order that he might become a merciful and faithful high priest in service to God, and that he might make atonement forʰ the sins of the people. ¹⁸Because he himself suffered when he was tempted, he is able to help those who are being tempted.

Jesus Greater Than Moses

3 Therefore, holy brothers, who share in the heavenly calling, fix your thoughts on Jesus, the apostle and high priest whom we confess. ²He was faithful to the one who appointed him, just as Moses was faithful in all God's house. ³Jesus has been found worthy of greater honor than Moses, just as the builder of a house has greater honor than the house itself. ⁴For every house is built by someone, but God is the builder of everything. ⁵Moses was faithful as a servant in all God's house, testifying to what would be said in the future. ⁶But Christ is faithful as a son over God's house. And we are his house, if we hold on to our courage and the hope of which we boast.

Warning Against Unbelief

⁷So, as the Holy Spirit says:

"Today, if you hear his voice,
⁸ do not harden your hearts

ᵃ12 Psalm 102:25-27   ᵇ13 Psalm 110:1   ᶜ7 Or him for a little while; also in verse 9   ᵈ8 Psalm 8:4-6   ᵉ12 Psalm 22:22   ᶠ13 Isaiah 8:17   ᵍ13 Isaiah 8:18   ʰ17 Or and that he might turn aside God's wrath, taking away

as you did in the rebellion,
    during the time of testing in the
        desert,
[9]where your fathers tested and tried me
    and for forty years saw what I did.
[10]That is why I was angry with that
        generation,
    and I said, 'Their hearts are always
        going astray,
    and they have not known my ways.'
[11]So I declared on oath in my anger,
    'They shall never enter my rest.' "[a]

[12]See to it, brothers, that none of you has a sinful, unbelieving heart that turns away from the living God. [13]But encourage one another daily, as long as it is called Today, so that none of you may be hardened by sin's deceitfulness. [14]We have come to share in Christ if we hold firmly till the end the confidence we had at first. [15]As has just been said:

"Today, if you hear his voice,
    do not harden your hearts
    as you did in the rebellion."[b]

[16]Who were they who heard and rebelled? Were they not all those Moses led out of Egypt? [17]And with whom was he angry for forty years? Was it not with those who sinned, whose bodies fell in the desert? [18]And to whom did God swear that they would never enter his rest if not to those who disobeyed[c]? [19]So we see that they were not able to enter, because of their unbelief.

A Sabbath-Rest for the People of God

4 Therefore, since the promise of entering his rest still stands, let us be careful that none of you be found to have fallen short of it. [2]For we also have had the gospel preached to us, just as they did; but the message they heard was of no value to them, because those who heard did not combine it with faith.[d] [3]Now we who have believed enter that rest, just as God has said,

"So I declared on oath in my anger,
    'They shall never enter my rest.' "[e]

And yet his work has been finished since the creation of the world. [4]For somewhere he has spoken about the seventh day in these words: "And on the seventh day God rested from all his work."[f] [5]And again in the passage above he says, "They shall never enter my rest."

[6]It still remains that some will enter that rest, and those who formerly had the gospel preached to them did not go in, because of their disobedience. [7]Therefore God again set a certain day, calling it Today, when a long time later he spoke through David, as was said before:

"Today, if you hear his voice,
    do not harden your hearts."[b]

[8]For if Joshua had given them rest, God would not have spoken later about another day. [9]There remains, then, a Sabbath-rest for the people of God; [10]for anyone who enters God's rest also rests from his own work, just as God did from his. [11]Let us, therefore, make every effort to enter that rest, so that no one will fall by following their example of disobedience.

[12]For the word of God is living and active. Sharper than any double-edged sword, it penetrates even to dividing soul and spirit, joints and marrow; it judges the thoughts and attitudes of the heart. [13]Nothing in all creation is hidden from God's sight. Everything is uncovered and laid bare before the eyes of him to whom we must give account.

Jesus the Great High Priest

[14]Therefore, since we have a great high priest who has gone through the heavens,[g] Jesus the Son of God, let us hold firmly to the faith we profess. [15]For we do not have a high priest who is unable to sympathize with our weaknesses, but we have one who has been tempted in every way, just as we are—yet was without sin. [16]Let us then approach the throne of grace with confidence, so that we may receive mercy and find grace to help us in our time of need.

5 Every high priest is selected from among men and is appointed to represent them in matters related to God, to offer gifts and sacrifices for sins. [2]He is able to deal gently with those who are ignorant and are going astray, since he himself is subject to weakness. [3]This is why he has to offer sacrifices for his own sins, as well as for the sins of the people.

[4]No one takes this honor upon himself; he must be called by God, just as Aaron was. [5]So Christ also did not take upon himself the glory of becoming a high priest. But God said to him,

---

[a]11 Psalm 95:7-11   [b]15,7 Psalm 95:7,8   [c]18 Or
disbelieved   [d]2 Many manuscripts because they
did not share in the faith of those who obeyed
[e]3 Psalm 95:11; also in verse 5   [f]4 Gen. 2:2   [g]14 Or
gone into heaven

"You are my Son;
today I have become your Father."*b

⁶And he says in another place,

"You are a priest forever,
in the order of Melchizedek."c

⁷During the days of Jesus' life on earth,
he offered up prayers and petitions with
loud cries and tears to the one who could
save him from death, and he was heard
because of his reverent submission. ⁸Although he was a son, he learned obedience from what he suffered ⁹and, once
made perfect, he became the source of

*5 Or *have begotten you* b5 Psalm 2:7
c6 Psalm 110:4

You Know What to Do

DAILY INSIGHT

WEDNESDAY

Passage:
Hebrews 5:1–5

Verse:
Hebrews 5:4

What an awesome honor it must have been for a man to be selected high priest. Here was a mortal given the privilege to represent his people to the face of the Almighty. However, before the high priest was allowed to proceed with his spellbinding duties, he had "to offer sacrifices for his own sins" (5:3).

As a dad, you are the high priest of your family. This is a big challenge. And, I must confess, I was at times a pretty sloppy father, not deserving of any honor at all.

On one award-winning spring Saturday morning, my wife Bobbie left for a few hours and asked me to watch the girls, who were four and a half and one and a half at the time. Over the years, I've discovered that many dads think that "keeping an eye on the kids" is roughly the same assignment as "keeping an eye on the smoke alarm." If it's not wailing at plaster-cracking decibels, it must be okay. That Saturday morning, I was one of those dads.

I was in the garage, sharpening the blade on my lawn mower. The girls and their friend, Laura Green, had begun playing in the front yard, but soon got bored. When Missy came into the garage to retrieve the stroller, I wisely said, "Be careful," without even looking up from my blade-sharpening. For the next several minutes, Missy and Laura took turns pushing Julie back and forth on the sidewalk in front of our house.

Then they decided to make up a new game. This game was called the "Let's-take-the-stroller-to-the-top-of-our-steep-drive-way-and-see-how-fast-we-can-get-this-thing-going game"—with Julie still on board, of course. My lawn mower blade was looking good. *This thing will take out small trees,* I proudly admired, oblivious to what was going on in the driveway.

After a few breakneck voyages down the hill, Julie tried to stop the stroller herself, jamming her sneakers down onto the asphalt. The stroller flipped forward, end over end, until it came to rest at the bottom of the driveway. The "smoke alarms" began to wail. By the time I reached the girls, they were both out of control. Laura Green was nowhere to be found.

Julie was lying on her side, her nose and lips bleeding. I knelt next to her, sheer panic sweeping over me. I tried to comfort and reassure her as I gently opened her bleeding mouth and surveyed the shocking damage. *I'm a dead man,* I thought. *How will I ever explain this to Bobbie?* The truth is, I had failed. When Bobbie got home, she let me have it. I told her I was sorry, but she was too busy tending to Julie. I felt awful.

Even the highest-ranking priest was a sinner. And before he was able to assume his appointed role, he had to confess his own failure and lack of qualification to do this job.

You've got a huge job ahead of you as the high priest of your home. As ready as you might think you are to lead this family, you've got some of your own failure to confess.

You know what to do.

For your next devotional reading, go to page 1366.

eternal salvation for all who obey him [10]and was designated by God to be high priest in the order of Melchizedek.

Warning Against Falling Away

[11]We have much to say about this, but it is hard to explain because you are slow to learn. [12]In fact, though by this time you ought to be teachers, you need someone to teach you the elementary truths of God's word all over again. You need milk, not solid food! [13]Anyone who lives on milk, being still an infant, is not acquainted with the teaching about righteousness. [14]But solid food is for the mature, who by constant use have trained themselves to distinguish good from evil.

6 Therefore let us leave the elementary teachings about Christ and go on to maturity, not laying again the foundation of repentance from acts that lead to death,[a] and of faith in God, [2]instruction about baptisms, the laying on of hands, the resurrection of the dead, and eternal judgment. [3]And God permitting, we will do so.

[4]It is impossible for those who have once been enlightened, who have tasted the heavenly gift, who have shared in the Holy Spirit, [5]who have tasted the goodness of the word of God and the powers of the coming age, [6]if they fall away, to be brought back to repentance, because[b] to their loss they are crucifying the Son of God all over again and subjecting him to public disgrace.

[7]Land that drinks in the rain often falling on it and that produces a crop useful to those for whom it is farmed receives the blessing of God. [8]But land that produces thorns and thistles is worthless and is in danger of being cursed. In the end it will be burned.

[9]Even though we speak like this, dear friends, we are confident of better things in your case—things that accompany salvation. [10]God is not unjust; he will not forget your work and the love you have shown him as you have helped his people and continue to help them. [11]We want each of you to show this same diligence to the very end, in order to make your hope sure. [12]We do not want you to become lazy, but to imitate those who through faith and patience inherit what has been promised.

The Certainty of God's Promise

[13]When God made his promise to Abraham, since there was no one greater for

him to swear by, he swore by himself, [14]saying, "I will surely bless you and give you many descendants."[c] [15]And so after waiting patiently, Abraham received what was promised.

[16]Men swear by someone greater than themselves, and the oath confirms what is said and puts an end to all argument. [17]Because God wanted to make the unchanging nature of his purpose very clear to the heirs of what was promised, he confirmed it with an oath. [18]God did this so that, by two unchangeable things in which it is impossible for God to lie, we who have fled to take hold of the hope offered to us may be greatly encouraged. [19]We have this hope as an anchor for the soul, firm and secure. It enters the inner sanctuary behind the curtain, [20]where Jesus, who went before us, has entered on our behalf. He has become a high priest forever, in the order of Melchizedek.

Melchizedek the Priest

7 This Melchizedek was king of Salem and priest of God Most High. He met Abraham returning from the defeat of the kings and blessed him, [2]and Abraham gave him a tenth of everything. First, his name means "king of righteousness"; then also, "king of Salem" means "king of peace." [3]Without father or mother, without genealogy, without beginning of days or end of life, like the Son of God he remains a priest forever.

[4]Just think how great he was: Even the patriarch Abraham gave him a tenth of the plunder! [5]Now the law requires the descendants of Levi who become priests to collect a tenth from the people—that is, their brothers—even though their brothers are descended from Abraham. [6]This man, however, did not trace his descent from Levi, yet he collected a tenth from Abraham and blessed him who had the promises. [7]And without doubt the lesser person is blessed by the greater. [8]In the one case, the tenth is collected by men who die; but in the other case, by him who is declared to be living. [9]One might even say that Levi, who collects the tenth, paid the tenth through Abraham, [10]because when Melchizedek met Abraham, Levi was still in the body of his ancestor.

---

[a]1 Or from useless rituals   [b]6 Or repentance while   [c]14 Gen. 22:17

Jesus Like Melchizedek

[11]If perfection could have been attained through the Levitical priesthood (for on the basis of it the law was given to the people), why was there still need for another priest to come—one in the order of Melchizedek, not in the order of Aaron? [12]For when there is a change of the priesthood, there must also be a change of the law. [13]He of whom these things are said belonged to a different tribe, and no one from that tribe has ever served at the altar. [14]For it is clear that our Lord descended from Judah, and in regard to that tribe Moses said nothing about priests. [15]And what we have said is even more clear if another priest like Melchizedek appears, [16]one who has become a priest not on the basis of a regulation as to his ancestry but on the basis of the power of an indestructible life. [17]For it is declared:

"You are a priest forever,
    in the order of Melchizedek."[a]

[a]17 Psalm 110:4

The Employee of the Month, That's Who

DAILY INSIGHT

THURSDAY

Passage:
Hebrews 6:7–12

Verse:
Hebrews 6:10

Not long ago, I was looking for a parking spot in the pouring rain. I had dropped my family off at the front door of the restaurant and was desperately searching for a place close enough to avoid getting soaked. As you well know, finding a good parking spot is a big deal. Sometimes it's a treat to find one at all. And then I spotted it—the closest space to the front door, not counting handicapped spaces. "I must be livin' right," I whispered as I whipped the steering wheel to the left.

And then I saw it, a sign that said, "This space reserved for the Employee of the Month." I sat there in silence. The only noise was that of my wipers, sloshing the water on my windshield. *Employee of the Month,* I seethed. *Who gives a rip?*

I'm going to interrupt this gripping tale for a question. It is, in fact, a very good question: Who cares about the Employee of the Month? *The Employee of the Month, that's who.* Recognition for a job well done is an incredibly powerful thing.

One of the greatest frustrations among men is the feeling that we're not truly appreciated. We faithfully trudge off to work every day, "bringing home the bacon" so our families can survive. And one of the greatest frustrations among wives and mothers is that they, too, feel unappreciated. Most women in the world have two jobs—one in and one outside of the home. To them, their work is usually met with outbreaks of overt thanklessness. And how

about your children? Frankly, you have expectations for them to act like adults—so, because they're kids, they usually feel like they're failing to meet up to your standards. Most of the time they are doing their best, and they, too, can feel unappreciated—unrewarded for their genuine efforts.

"God is not unjust," the writer to the Hebrews tells us. "He will not forget your work." (6:10a). "He rewards those who earnestly seek him" (11:6). These are comforting words in the face of the frustration that most family members feel.

I have good news. Just now, you got your recognition. You heard that God hasn't overlooked your hard work and your faithfulness. Because he's watching, he knows that you really *do* want to be his man in your home. And, in spite of your failings, he knows that you're doing pretty well. "Congratulations," God is saying to you and me. "I have seen what you've done, and I'm grateful. Good work, dad." Now it's time for you to pass this news on to those other unappreciated members of your clan. It's time for you to post an "Employee of the Month" sign.

I sat through lunch with my family at the restaurant that day, completely drenched—including my shoes and socks. *I hope that Employee of the Month appreciates this,* I silently shivered.

You know, I'll bet he or she did.

For your next devotional reading, go to page 1369.

[18]The former regulation is set aside because it was weak and useless [19](for the law made nothing perfect), and a better hope is introduced, by which we draw near to God.

[20]And it was not without an oath! Others became priests without any oath, [21]but he became a priest with an oath when God said to him:

"The Lord has sworn
  and will not change his mind:
'You are a priest forever.' "[a]

[22]Because of this oath, Jesus has become the guarantee of a better covenant.

[23]Now there have been many of those priests, since death prevented them from continuing in office; [24]but because Jesus lives forever, he has a permanent priesthood. [25]Therefore he is able to save completely[b] those who come to God through him, because he always lives to intercede for them.

[26]Such a high priest meets our need—one who is holy, blameless, pure, set apart from sinners, exalted above the heavens. [27]Unlike the other high priests, he does not need to offer sacrifices day after day, first for his own sins, and then for the sins of the people. He sacrificed for their sins once for all when he offered himself. [28]For the law appoints as high priests men who are weak; but the oath, which came after the law, appointed the Son, who has been made perfect forever.

The High Priest of a New Covenant

8 The point of what we are saying is this: We do have such a high priest, who sat down at the right hand of the throne of the Majesty in heaven, [2]and who serves in the sanctuary, the true tabernacle set up by the Lord, not by man.

[3]Every high priest is appointed to offer both gifts and sacrifices, and so it was necessary for this one also to have something to offer. [4]If he were on earth, he would not be a priest, for there are already men who offer the gifts prescribed by the law. [5]They serve at a sanctuary that is a copy and shadow of what is in heaven. This is why Moses was warned when he was about to build the tabernacle: "See to it that you make everything according to the pattern shown you on the mountain."[c] [6]But the ministry Jesus has received is as superior to theirs as the covenant of which he is mediator is superior to the old one, and it is founded on better promises.

[7]For if there had been nothing wrong with that first covenant, no place would have been sought for another. [8]But God found fault with the people and said[d]:

"The time is coming, declares the Lord,
  when I will make a new covenant
with the house of Israel
  and with the house of Judah.
[9]It will not be like the covenant
  I made with their forefathers
when I took them by the hand
  to lead them out of Egypt,
because they did not remain faithful to
    my covenant,
  and I turned away from them,
        declares the Lord.
[10]This is the covenant I will make with
  the house of Israel
    after that time, declares the Lord.
I will put my laws in their minds
  and write them on their hearts.
I will be their God,
  and they will be my people.
[11]No longer will a man teach his
    neighbor,
  or a man his brother, saying, 'Know
    the Lord,'
because they will all know me,
  from the least of them to the
    greatest.
[12]For I will forgive their wickedness
  and will remember their sins no
    more."[e]

[13]By calling this covenant "new," he has made the first one obsolete; and what is obsolete and aging will soon disappear.

Worship in the Earthly Tabernacle

9 Now the first covenant had regulations for worship and also an earthly sanctuary. [2]A tabernacle was set up. In its first room were the lampstand, the table and the consecrated bread; this was called the Holy Place. [3]Behind the second curtain was a room called the Most Holy Place, [4]which had the golden altar of incense and the gold-covered ark of the covenant. This ark contained the gold jar of manna, Aaron's staff that had budded, and the stone tablets of the covenant. [5]Above the ark were the cherubim of the Glory, overshadowing the atonement cover.[f] But we cannot discuss these things in detail now.

[6]When everything had been arranged

---

[a]21 Psalm 110:4   [b]25 Or *forever*   [c]5 Exodus 25:40
[d]8 Some manuscripts may be translated *fault and said to the people.*   [e]12 Jer. 31:31-34
[f]5 Traditionally *the mercy seat*

like this, the priests entered regularly into the outer room to carry on their ministry. [7]But only the high priest entered the inner room, and that only once a year, and never without blood, which he offered for himself and for the sins the people had committed in ignorance. [8]The Holy Spirit was showing by this that the way into the Most Holy Place had not yet been disclosed as long as the first tabernacle was still standing. [9]This is an illustration for the present time, indicating that the gifts and sacrifices being offered were not able to clear the conscience of the worshiper. [10]They are only a matter of food and drink and various ceremonial washings—external regulations applying until the time of the new order.

The Blood of Christ

[11]When Christ came as high priest of the good things that are already here,[a] he went through the greater and more perfect tabernacle that is not man-made, that is to say, not a part of this creation. [12]He did not enter by means of the blood of goats and calves; but he entered the Most Holy Place once for all by his own blood, having obtained eternal redemption. [13]The blood of goats and bulls and the ashes of a heifer sprinkled on those who are ceremonially unclean sanctify them so that they are outwardly clean. [14]How much more, then, will the blood of Christ, who through the eternal Spirit offered himself unblemished to God, cleanse our consciences from acts that lead to death,[b] so that we may serve the living God!

[15]For this reason Christ is the mediator of a new covenant, that those who are called may receive the promised eternal inheritance—now that he has died as a ransom to set them free from the sins committed under the first covenant.

[16]In the case of a will,[c] it is necessary to prove the death of the one who made it, [17]because a will is in force only when somebody has died; it never takes effect while the one who made it is living. [18]This is why even the first covenant was not put into effect without blood. [19]When Moses had proclaimed every commandment of the law to all the people, he took the blood of calves, together with water, scarlet wool and branches of hyssop, and sprinkled the scroll and all the people. [20]He said, "This is the blood of the covenant, which God has commanded you to

keep."[d] [21]In the same way, he sprinkled with the blood both the tabernacle and everything used in its ceremonies. [22]In fact, the law requires that nearly everything be cleansed with blood, and without the shedding of blood there is no forgiveness.

[23]It was necessary, then, for the copies of the heavenly things to be purified with these sacrifices, but the heavenly things themselves with better sacrifices than these. [24]For Christ did not enter a man-made sanctuary that was only a copy of the true one; he entered heaven itself, now to appear for us in God's presence. [25]Nor did he enter heaven to offer himself again and again, the way the high priest enters the Most Holy Place every year with blood that is not his own. [26]Then Christ would have had to suffer many times since the creation of the world. But now he has appeared once for all at the end of the ages to do away with sin by the sacrifice of himself. [27]Just as man is destined to die once, and after that to face judgment, [28]so Christ was sacrificed once to take away the sins of many people; and he will appear a second time, not to bear sin, but to bring salvation to those who are waiting for him.

Christ's Sacrifice Once for All

10 The law is only a shadow of the good things that are coming—not the realities themselves. For this reason it can never, by the same sacrifices repeated endlessly year after year, make perfect those who draw near to worship. [2]If it could, would they not have stopped being offered? For the worshipers would have been cleansed once for all, and would no longer have felt guilty for their sins. [3]But those sacrifices are an annual reminder of sins, [4]because it is impossible for the blood of bulls and goats to take away sins.

[5]Therefore, when Christ came into the world, he said:

"Sacrifice and offering you did not desire,
    but a body you prepared for me;
[6]with burnt offerings and sin offerings
    you were not pleased.
[7]Then I said, 'Here I am—it is written about me in the scroll—

---

[a]11 Some early manuscripts *are to come*   [b]14 Or *from useless rituals*   [c]16 Same Greek word as *covenant*; also in verse 17   [d]20 Exodus 24:8

I have come to do your will,
O God.' "[a]

8First he said, "Sacrifices and offerings, burnt offerings and sin offerings you did not desire, nor were you pleased with them" (although the law required them to be made). **9**Then he said, "Here I am, I have come to do your will." He sets aside the first to establish the second. **10**And by that will, we have been made holy through the sacrifice of the body of Jesus Christ once for all.

11Day after day every priest stands and performs his religious duties; again and again he offers the same sacrifices, which can never take away sins. **12**But when this priest had offered for all time one sacrifice for sins, he sat down at the right hand of God. **13**Since that time he waits for his

*a*7 Psalm 40:6-8 (see Septuagint)

A Clean Conscience

"Jim is gone." The woman's voice on the other end of the telephone was desperate. "I came home from work, and his closet was empty. I have no idea where he is." My friend began weeping uncontrollably.

Jim and Suzanne were members of our Sunday school class in Texas. Although we didn't see each other socially, my wife and I felt like we knew them pretty well. They seemed like a fairly normal, all-American couple—a nice dog, two jobs, three kids, and a station wagon with imitation wood sides.

As the weeks unfolded, we discovered that Jim had had a "friend" in Dallas for years. Apparently, he had thought that he could sustain the hypocrisy—and for a long, long time he had been successful. But eventually he folded. I guess his conscience got the best of him. Very few men can survive a dirty conscience.

Back in the Old Testament, men suffering from the malady of a dirty conscience went to the temple carrying an unblemished animal from their own flock. The priest killed the animal and sprinkled the blood on the altar and on them, and the men were declared "forgiven."

"They [were] outwardly clean," the writer to the Hebrews tells us in verse 13. "How much more, then, will the blood of Christ, who through the eternal Spirit offered himself unblemished to God, cleanse our consciences from acts that lead to death, so that we may serve the living God!" (v. 14). Now, because of the blood of

DAILY INSIGHT

FRIDAY
Passage:
Hebrews 9:11–14
Verse:
Hebrews 9:10

Christ, we are forgiven through something we experience—something we literally can feel—something that changes us forever: a clean conscience.

I never saw Jim again. He literally disappeared to start a new life, free from the obligations of his family, free from accountability.

"We're not Jim," you and I might be saying. "We're still here. We're hanging in there. We're toughing it out."

Ah, but we *are* Jim. You and I struggle every moment with the disparity between who we are and who we know we ought to be. We wrestle with past failure and sin, desperately agonizing over a conscience that is, more often than not, dirty. This struggle is a quiet one, invisible to our wives, our children and our friends, but we know it's there.

We must not let this day pass without letting this message be seared deeply into our hearts. Through Jesus Christ and his sacrificial blood for our sins, we can know forgiveness. We can feel his presence. Our past, regardless of its circumstances and its outcomes, is covered. We can be clean through and through—no need to suffer in silence any more … no need to hide. This is the best news we could have heard. It may have literally saved our lives.

You see, you and I know this is true. We've seen it for ourselves. We're no exception to the rule. Very few men can survive a dirty conscience.

For your next devotional reading, go to page 1371.

enemies to be made his footstool, [14]because by one sacrifice he has made perfect forever those who are being made holy.

[15]The Holy Spirit also testifies to us about this. First he says:

[16] "This is the covenant I will make with them
    after that time, says the Lord.
I will put my laws in their hearts,
    and I will write them on their
        minds."[a]

[17]Then he adds:

"Their sins and lawless acts
    I will remember no more."[b]

[18]And where these have been forgiven, there is no longer any sacrifice for sin.

A Call to Persevere

[19]Therefore, brothers, since we have confidence to enter the Most Holy Place by the blood of Jesus, [20]by a new and living way opened for us through the curtain, that is, his body, [21]and since we have a great priest over the house of God, [22]let us draw near to God with a sincere heart in full assurance of faith, having our hearts sprinkled to cleanse us from a guilty conscience and having our bodies washed with pure water. [23]Let us hold unswervingly to the hope we profess, for he who promised is faithful. [24]And let us consider how we may spur one another on toward love and good deeds. [25]Let us not give up meeting together, as some are in the habit of doing, but let us encourage one another—and all the more as you see the Day approaching.

[26]If we deliberately keep on sinning after we have received the knowledge of the truth, no sacrifice for sins is left, [27]but only a fearful expectation of judgment and of raging fire that will consume the enemies of God. [28]Anyone who rejected the law of Moses died without mercy on the testimony of two or three witnesses. [29]How much more severely do you think a man deserves to be punished who has trampled the Son of God under foot, who has treated as an unholy thing the blood of the covenant that sanctified him, and who has insulted the Spirit of grace? [30]For we know him who said, "It is mine to avenge; I will repay,"[c] and again, "The Lord will judge his people."[d] [31]It is a dreadful thing to fall into the hands of the living God.

[32]Remember those earlier days after you had received the light, when you stood your ground in a great contest in the face of suffering. [33]Sometimes you were publicly exposed to insult and persecution; at other times you stood side by side with those who were so treated. [34]You sympathized with those in prison and joyfully accepted the confiscation of your property, because you knew that you yourselves had better and lasting possessions.

[35]So do not throw away your confidence; it will be richly rewarded. [36]You need to persevere so that when you have done the will of God, you will receive what he has promised. [37]For in just a very little while,

"He who is coming will come and will
    not delay.
[38]   But my righteous one[e] will live by
        faith.
And if he shrinks back,
    I will not be pleased with him."[f]

[39]But we are not of those who shrink back and are destroyed, but of those who believe and are saved.

By Faith

11 Now faith is being sure of what we hope for and certain of what we do not see. [2]This is what the ancients were commended for.

[3]By faith we understand that the universe was formed at God's command, so that what is seen was not made out of what was visible.

[4]By faith Abel offered God a better sacrifice than Cain did. By faith he was commended as a righteous man, when God spoke well of his offerings. And by faith he still speaks, even though he is dead.

[5]By faith Enoch was taken from this life, so that he did not experience death; he could not be found, because God had taken him away. For before he was taken, he was commended as one who pleased God. [6]And without faith it is impossible to please God, because anyone who comes to him must believe that he exists and that he rewards those who earnestly seek him.

[7]By faith Noah, when warned about things not yet seen, in holy fear built an ark to save his family. By his faith he condemned the world and became heir of the righteousness that comes by faith.

[a]16 Jer. 31:33   [b]17 Jer. 31:34   [c]30 Deut. 32:35
[d]30 Deut. 32:36; Psalm 135:14   [e]38 One early
manuscript *But the righteous*   [f]38 Hab. 2:3,4

The Hall of Faith

Key Verse: *"Now faith is being sure of what we hope for and certain of what we do not see."* Hebrews 11:1

Text: Hebrews 11:1–3, 13–16 *(Dad or child reads the text.)*

QUIET
TIMES
WITH Dad

DAD READS: Whether an athlete is playing pee wee soccer or pitching in the World Series, he or she dreams of one thing—a goal that is achieved by only very few people. This dream is to be good enough to be inducted into the Hall of Fame.

Child reads: When people are inducted into a Hall of Fame, they know they have arrived. They are the very best of the very best in their sport. Their names will live on and on because very few were as good as they were. This must be a great honor to be put into the Hall of Fame.

DAD READS: Yes, this is a great honor for all athletes who make it to this level. But did you know that there is a place where special people have their names listed who have loved God and have continued to trust in him? Some people have called this the great "Hall of Faith." In this passage we read about Abel, Enoch, Noah, Abraham, Sarah, Isaac, Jacob, Joseph, Moses and Rahab. We also read about people who made it to the Hall of Faith, but whose names are known only to God.

Child reads: There is no honor more wonderful than being listed in God's Hall of Faith. Wouldn't it be awesome if people thought of you and me when they wanted an example of someone who truly followed Jesus?

DAD READS: Many people don't think that making God's Hall of Faith is a very exciting goal. But you and I know better. We know that loving, trusting, and serving is what God wants us to do.

Child reads: The athletes whose names are in the Hall of Fame worked very hard to get there. Along the way, their friends must have said, "Hey, you don't have to work that hard. Take a break. Lighten up." But these people didn't stop working. They knew what they wanted to achieve and they didn't let anyone talk them out of it.

DAD READS: I want to be a person who doesn't get discouraged from my faith. I want to love, trust and serve God with my whole heart. I want to work as hard as an athlete who wants to have his name in the Hall of Fame. I want God to be able to say to me, "Well done, friend. You're going to be inducted into my 'Hall of Faith.' "

Child reads: I want this, too. I want God to be happy with how well I have followed him. Let me pray this prayer with you:

Our Father in heaven, we love you. Thank you for the Hall of Faith. Thank you for so many people who have lived to please you. We want you to be happy with us, too. Please help us, every day, to remember the Hall of Faith and those people whose biggest dream was to be faithful. We love you, and we thank you for your love. In Jesus' name, Amen.

For your next devotional reading, go to page 1372.

[8]By faith Abraham, when called to go to a place he would later receive as his inheritance, obeyed and went, even though he did not know where he was going. [9]By faith he made his home in the promised land like a stranger in a foreign country; he lived in tents, as did Isaac and Jacob, who were heirs with him of the same promise. [10]For he was looking forward to the city with foundations, whose architect and builder is God.

[11]By faith Abraham, even though he was past age—and Sarah herself was barren—was enabled to become a father because he[a] considered him faithful who had made the promise. [12]And so from this one man, and he as good as dead, came descendants as numerous as the stars in the sky and as countless as the sand on the seashore.

[13]All these people were still living by faith when they died. They did not receive the things promised; they only saw them

[a]11 Or By faith even Sarah, who was past age, was enabled to bear children because she

Get in Shape and Follow Jesus

Life is a distance race. It is not a sprint. My good friend, Bill Butterworth, found this out firsthand.

In school, Bill was a field-events man specializing in the shot put and the discus. At one particular track meet, Bill sat dejectedly in the stands after competing unsuccessfully in his two events. Just then, his friends approached him with some great news. "Well, Bill, this must be your lucky day," they announced. "It looks like you're gonna get another chance!"

One of the athletes entered in the quarter-mile race had pulled a muscle running the 220. Having only competed in two events, Bill was allowed one more. As he was whisked off to the starting line for the running of the event, Bill asked himself, *How am I supposed to run this thing?* His daze was rudely interrupted by the crack of the gun. Bill was off and running.

After the first turn, "Mr. Field Events" was feeling pretty strong. He picked up his pace. By the back straightaway, he was in the lead. *This is unbelievable!* This hefty adolescent was thinking to himself. *All these years, slaving away over at the shot put and discus circle, when the truth is, I'm a runner!* By the time he got to the third turn, something unexpected happened. Thinking this was a sprint and not a distance run, Bill hadn't laid out a plan to finish this race. He was exhausted and collapsed in a writhing heap in the shadow of the visitors' goal post.

DAILY INSIGHT

MONDAY

Passage:
Hebrews 12:1–3

Verse:
Hebrews 12:3

The writer to the Hebrews gives us a perfect snapshot of life's race as it is meant to be run (12:1). Did you catch the two great challenges of successfully running this distance race? The first challenge involves those things over which we have control. These are the habits that keep us out of shape and the willful disobedience against God's laws that critically obstruct our running.

The second challenge is "the race marked out for us." Life is not run on an oval track. We can't see the twists and turns of our course. We make our plans, but someone else marks where we do most of our running, and surprises are a sure thing.

So what is a runner to do? The directions are clearly described here: Get in shape and follow Jesus. Running this race will be far less painful if you're not stopping every few yards, desperately sucking in more air because you're encumbered by foolish habits and debilitating sin. And running this race will be far less confusing if you determine to faithfully read God's Word, spend time in meaningful conversation with him, and resolve to obey him. If you do these things, the rigors of the stress and the confusion of this uncharted course will be far less overwhelming … and far more successful.

Life is a distance race, not a sprint. Get in shape and trust Jesus. You can do this.

For your next devotional reading, go to page 1377.

and welcomed them from a distance. And they admitted that they were aliens and strangers on earth. [14]People who say such things show that they are looking for a country of their own. [15]If they had been thinking of the country they had left, they would have had opportunity to return. [16]Instead, they were longing for a better country—a heavenly one. Therefore God is not ashamed to be called their God, for he has prepared a city for them.

[17]By faith Abraham, when God tested him, offered Isaac as a sacrifice. He who had received the promises was about to sacrifice his one and only son, [18]even though God had said to him, "It is through Isaac that your offspring[a] will be reckoned."[b] [19]Abraham reasoned that God could raise the dead, and figuratively speaking, he did receive Isaac back from death.

[20]By faith Isaac blessed Jacob and Esau in regard to their future.

[21]By faith Jacob, when he was dying, blessed each of Joseph's sons, and worshiped as he leaned on the top of his staff.

[22]By faith Joseph, when his end was near, spoke about the exodus of the Israelites from Egypt and gave instructions about his bones.

[23]By faith Moses' parents hid him for three months after he was born, because they saw he was no ordinary child, and they were not afraid of the king's edict.

[24]By faith Moses, when he had grown up, refused to be known as the son of Pharaoh's daughter. [25]He chose to be mistreated along with the people of God rather than to enjoy the pleasures of sin for a short time. [26]He regarded disgrace for the sake of Christ as of greater value than the treasures of Egypt, because he was looking ahead to his reward. [27]By faith he left Egypt, not fearing the king's anger; he persevered because he saw him who is invisible. [28]By faith he kept the Passover and the sprinkling of blood, so that the destroyer of the firstborn would not touch the firstborn of Israel.

[29]By faith the people passed through the Red Sea[c] as on dry land; but when the Egyptians tried to do so, they were drowned.

[30]By faith the walls of Jericho fell, after the people had marched around them for seven days.

[31]By faith the prostitute Rahab, because she welcomed the spies, was not killed with those who were disobedient.[d]

[32]And what more shall I say? I do not have time to tell about Gideon, Barak, Samson, Jephthah, David, Samuel and the prophets, [33]who through faith conquered kingdoms, administered justice, and gained what was promised; who shut the mouths of lions, [34]quenched the fury of the flames, and escaped the edge of the sword; whose weakness was turned to strength; and who became powerful in battle and routed foreign armies. [35]Women received back their dead, raised to life again. Others were tortured and refused to be released, so that they might gain a better resurrection. [36]Some faced jeers and flogging, while still others were chained and put in prison. [37]They were stoned[e]; they were sawed in two; they were put to death by the sword. They went about in sheepskins and goatskins, destitute, persecuted and mistreated— [38]the world was not worthy of them. They wandered in deserts and mountains, and in caves and holes in the ground.

[39]These were all commended for their faith, yet none of them received what had been promised. [40]God had planned something better for us so that only together with us would they be made perfect.

God Disciplines His Sons

12 Therefore, since we are surrounded by such a great cloud of witnesses, let us throw off everything that hinders and the sin that so easily entangles, and let us run with perseverance the race marked out for us. [2]Let us fix our eyes on Jesus, the author and perfecter of our faith, who for the joy set before him endured the cross, scorning its shame, and sat down at the right hand of the throne of God. [3]Consider him who endured such opposition from sinful men, so that you will not grow weary and lose heart.

[4]In your struggle against sin, you have not yet resisted to the point of shedding your blood. [5]And you have forgotten that word of encouragement that addresses you as sons:

"My son, do not make light of the
        Lord's discipline,
    and do not lose heart when he
        rebukes you,
[6]because the Lord disciplines those he
        loves,

[a]18 Greek *seed*   [b]18 Gen. 21:12   [c]29 That is, Sea of Reeds   [d]31 Or *unbelieving*   [e]37 Some early manuscripts *stoned; they were put to the test;*

and he punishes everyone he accepts as a son."[a]

[7]Endure hardship as discipline; God is treating you as sons. For what son is not disciplined by his father? [8]If you are not disciplined (and everyone undergoes discipline), then you are illegitimate children and not true sons. [9]Moreover, we have all had human fathers who disciplined us and we respected them for it. How much more should we submit to the Father of our spirits and live! [10]Our fathers disciplined us for a little while as they thought best; but God disciplines us for our good, that we may share in his holiness. [11]No discipline seems pleasant at the time, but painful. Later on, however, it produces a harvest of righteousness and peace for those who have been trained by it.

[12]Therefore, strengthen your feeble arms and weak knees. [13]"Make level paths for your feet,"[b] so that the lame may not be disabled, but rather healed.

Warning Against Refusing God

[14]Make every effort to live in peace with all men and to be holy; without holiness no one will see the Lord. [15]See to it that no one misses the grace of God and that no bitter root grows up to cause trouble and defile many. [16]See that no one is sexually immoral, or is godless like Esau, who for a single meal sold his inheritance rights as the oldest son. [17]Afterward, as you know, when he wanted to inherit this blessing, he was rejected. He could bring about no change of mind, though he sought the blessing with tears.

[18]You have not come to a mountain that can be touched and that is burning with fire; to darkness, gloom and storm; [19]to a trumpet blast or to such a voice speaking words that those who heard it begged that no further word be spoken to them, [20]because they could not bear what was commanded: "If even an animal touches the mountain, it must be stoned."[c] [21]The sight was so terrifying that Moses said, "I am trembling with fear."[d]

[22]But you have come to Mount Zion, to the heavenly Jerusalem, the city of the living God. You have come to thousands upon thousands of angels in joyful assembly, [23]to the church of the firstborn, whose names are written in heaven. You have come to God, the judge of all men, to the spirits of righteous men made perfect, [24]to Jesus the mediator of a new covenant, and to the sprinkled blood that speaks a better word than the blood of Abel. [25]See to it that you do not refuse him who speaks. If they did not escape when they refused him who warned them on earth, how much less will we, if we turn away from him who warns us from heaven? [26]At that time his voice shook the earth, but now he has promised, "Once more I will shake not only the earth but also the heavens."[e] [27]The words "once more" indicate the removing of what can be shaken—that is, created things—so that what cannot be shaken may remain.

[28]Therefore, since we are receiving a kingdom that cannot be shaken, let us be thankful, and so worship God acceptably with reverence and awe, [29]for our "God is a consuming fire."[f]

Concluding Exhortations

13 Keep on loving each other as brothers. [2]Do not forget to entertain strangers, for by so doing some people have entertained angels without knowing it. [3]Remember those in prison as if you were their fellow prisoners, and those who are mistreated as if you yourselves were suffering.

[4]Marriage should be honored by all, and the marriage bed kept pure, for God will judge the adulterer and all the sexually immoral. [5]Keep your lives free from the love of money and be content with what you have, because God has said,

"Never will I leave you;
    never will I forsake you."[g]

[6]So we say with confidence,

"The Lord is my helper; I will not be
    afraid.
    What can man do to me?"[h]

[7]Remember your leaders, who spoke the word of God to you. Consider the outcome of their way of life and imitate their faith. [8]Jesus Christ is the same yesterday and today and forever.

[9]Do not be carried away by all kinds of strange teachings. It is good for our hearts to be strengthened by grace, not by ceremonial foods, which are of no value to those who eat them. [10]We have an altar from which those who minister at the tabernacle have no right to eat.

[11]The high priest carries the blood of animals into the Most Holy Place as a sin

---

a6 Prov. 3:11,12   *b13* Prov. 4:26   *c20* Exodus 19:12,13
d21 Deut. 9:19   *e26* Haggai 2:6   *f29* Deut. 4:24
g5 Deut. 31:6   *h6* Psalm 118:6,7

offering, but the bodies are burned outside the camp. [12]And so Jesus also suffered outside the city gate to make the people holy through his own blood. [13]Let us, then, go to him outside the camp, bearing the disgrace he bore. [14]For here we do not have an enduring city, but we are looking for the city that is to come. [15]Through Jesus, therefore, let us continually offer to God a sacrifice of praise—the fruit of lips that confess his name. [16]And do not forget to do good and to share with others, for with such sacrifices God is pleased.

[17]Obey your leaders and submit to their authority. They keep watch over you as men who must give an account. Obey them so that their work will be a joy, not a burden, for that would be of no advantage to you.

[18]Pray for us. We are sure that we have a clear conscience and desire to live honorably in every way. [19]I particularly urge you to pray so that I may be restored to you soon.

[20]May the God of peace, who through the blood of the eternal covenant brought back from the dead our Lord Jesus, that great Shepherd of the sheep, [21]equip you with everything good for doing his will, and may he work in us what is pleasing to him, through Jesus Christ, to whom be glory for ever and ever. Amen.

[22]Brothers, I urge you to bear with my word of exhortation, for I have written you only a short letter.

[23]I want you to know that our brother Timothy has been released. If he arrives soon, I will come with him to see you.

[24]Greet all your leaders and all God's people. Those from Italy send you their greetings.

[25]Grace be with you all.

James is the kind of guy you'd like to meet for breakfast every Wednesday morning at your local "greasy spoon." In the early church, James had a reputation for being the one to approach for counsel and encouragement. He had that rare combination of compassion and take-no-prisoners candor. He had a practical, godly wisdom that people recognized and appreciated.

There's a good reason why James had this reputation. As Jesus' half-brother, James spent his early years living in the same house as the Savior. So what did James learn? The answer to this question comes out in his writing. Living day-to-day with Jesus taught James what faith was like in the nitty-gritty everyday details of life. He tells us how to face trials, how to resist temptation, how to deal with anger, and how to "walk what we talk." He also shows us how to confess our sins to others and how to pray for each other. That's advice every dad can use.

Spend some time with James today. His short book makes a great breakfast companion.

James

James, a servant of God and of the Lord Jesus Christ,

To the twelve tribes scattered among the nations:

Greetings.

Trials and Temptations

²Consider it pure joy, my brothers, whenever you face trials of many kinds, ³because you know that the testing of your faith develops perseverance. ⁴Perseverance must finish its work so that you may be mature and complete, not lacking anything. ⁵If any of you lacks wisdom, he should ask God, who gives generously to all without finding fault, and it will be given to him. ⁶But when he asks, he must believe and not doubt, because he who doubts is like a wave of the sea, blown and tossed by the wind. ⁷That man should not think he will receive anything from the Lord; ⁸he is a double-minded man, unstable in all he does.

⁹The brother in humble circumstances ought to take pride in his high position. ¹⁰But the one who is rich should take pride in his low position, because he will pass away like a wild flower. ¹¹For the sun

rises with scorching heat and withers the plant; its blossom falls and its beauty is destroyed. In the same way, the rich man will fade away even while he goes about his business.

¹²Blessed is the man who perseveres under trial, because when he has stood the test, he will receive the crown of life that God has promised to those who love him.

¹³When tempted, no one should say, "God is tempting me." For God cannot be tempted by evil, nor does he tempt anyone; ¹⁴but each one is tempted when, by his own evil desire, he is dragged away and enticed. ¹⁵Then, after desire has conceived, it gives birth to sin; and sin, when it is full-grown, gives birth to death. ¹⁶Don't be deceived, my dear brothers. ¹⁷Every good and perfect gift is from above, coming down from the Father of the heavenly lights, who does not change

Straight Talk

DAILY INSIGHT

TUESDAY

Passage:
James 1:2–8

Verses:
James 1:2–4

Having framed many walls during my years of construction work, I have always made certain that I have my sixteen-pound sledgehammer close by, as well as my level. I lay the two-by-fours down on the deck, making sure that they're relatively straight. I look down the edge of each one to make sure the crowns are all going in the same direction—almost every milled piece of lumber has an arc running from top to bottom. Then I nail the wall together.

Once I stand the framed wall in place, I do my very best to make sure that it's square with the other walls and perfectly vertical—the bubble on the level has to be *exactly* in the middle. I bring my sledgehammer along because, at moments like these, it's the best thing available to encourage the walls to be exact. In fact, my children will tell you that I actually call my sledgehammer, "The Encourager."

Unfortunately, this process takes a long time, and the equipment is very noisy to use. Given a choice, I'd rather work quickly and have a Chopin concerto playing in the background than have all that banging and racket going on. But because I enjoy hanging wallpaper on straight walls, time-consuming and noisy though it might be to get those walls perfect, I'd prefer disruptive and straight to serene and crooked.

I am confident that James would agree with this conversation about hard work, sledgehammers and precise walls. The goal, he would have said, is to be "mature and complete, not lacking anything" (v. 4). The way to achieve this lofty goal is to pay the price of perseverance—taking the time to lay your motives out before you act, making sure they're straight from beginning to end; squaring your actions with God's revealed will; living life with steadfast determination and resolve, persistence and tenacity. And the way to earn all of these admirable qualities is to "face trials of many kinds"—the sledgehammers of failure, frustration and defeat.

Have you ever seen an "artist's rendering" of a building that's not been built? Sometimes you see them hanging in the lobbies of large corporations. "Our Company's Dream for the Future" might be written under the rendering. As the work begins on the building project, the smart general contractor will have copies made of that artist's rendering posted around the construction site. "Work with this goal in mind," he might tell his crew. "All this thankless toil might be a little more meaningful if we have a picture of what we're building for you to clearly see."

Experiencing "pure joy" while "facing trials of many kinds" is only possible with an artist's rendering of "mature and complete" close by. The sledgehammer isn't quite as annoying and intrusive if you keep that great-looking building in mind.

This brings a whole new meaning to the phrase "straight talk," doesn't it?

For your next devotional reading, go to page 1378.

like shifting shadows. [18]He chose to give us birth through the word of truth, that we might be a kind of firstfruits of all he created.

Listening and Doing

[19]My dear brothers, take note of this: Everyone should be quick to listen, slow to speak and slow to become angry, [20]for man's anger does not bring about the righteous life that God desires. [21]Therefore, get rid of all moral filth and the evil that is so prevalent and humbly accept the word planted in you, which can save you.

[22]Do not merely listen to the word, and so deceive yourselves. Do what it says. [23]Anyone who listens to the word but does not do what it says is like a man who looks

Huh?

DAILY INSIGHT

WEDNESDAY

Passage:
James 1:19–25

Verses:
James 1:19–20

"Hi, I'm Leonard and I live in the two-story frame house on the corner." "Huh? Uh huh," you grunt, scanning the room for someone you actually care about. "My wife, June, and I just moved from Cheboygan; we have three kids, Monica, Bruce and Ashley. I'm in the insurance business, and I actually prefer the Bears over the Packers, even though I was born in Green Bay."

"Hmm, that's nice," you softly throw back. *Where is Steve?* you wonder, continuing to scan the crowd. Suddenly your wife walks up. She puts out her hand and says to Leonard, "Hi, there." There is a momentary pause, as both Leonard and your wife look to you to make the introduction. You're completely caught off guard. Even though your new neighbor has given you his complete resume, you didn't hear a single word he said.

People who have hearing impairments have taught me a lot about listening. If you've ever had a conversation with a skilled lip-reader, you know what I'm talking about. These people have taught me that, if I'm going to hear, I'm going to have to watch.

Listening is something you do with your eyes, not just with your ears. You didn't hear Leonard because you were looking for Steve.

Now consider this scenario. Your son is desperate to talk to someone—anyone who will listen. The struggle with the incredible pressure of temptation—cheating, drugs, sex—is about all he can stand. He's about to explode with the conflict of what he wants to do and what he knows that he

ought to do. *Should I talk to my dad?* he wonders. *Will he really listen to me, or will he lay one more of his brilliant speeches on me? Will he pay attention to how I'm feeling or will he be checking his watch for his next appointment?*

If you were your child, would *you* pour your heart out to you? Would you have any confidence that your words were truly heard—that you'd receive focused attention and empathy? Or would you take all of this stuff to your buddies at school?

So many dads are angry about what's happening to their kids. They blame the culture. They curse the school district. They lambaste their children's friends. Do you ever wonder if these dads are angry because they weren't "quick to listen and slow to speak"? While their children would have preferred to bring their deepest questions to their fathers, these dads were somewhere else making a name for themselves. And even when they *were* there, they *weren't* there.

You and I have ears; they come as standard equipment. We have no choice but to use them. But how can we get the most out of our ears? By also using our eyes. And what do we get for all this? Less embarrassment and anger, a better rapport with our friends and family members, and more peace.

Quit scanning the room. Stop checking your watch. Someone's got something to say to you. Don't miss it.

For your next devotional reading, go to page 1379.

at his face in a mirror **24**and, after looking at himself, goes away and immediately forgets what he looks like. **25**But the man who looks intently into the perfect law that gives freedom, and continues to do this, not forgetting what he has heard, but doing it—he will be blessed in what he does.

26If anyone considers himself religious and yet does not keep a tight rein on his tongue, he deceives himself and his reli-

gion is worthless. **27**Religion that God our Father accepts as pure and faultless is this: to look after orphans and widows in their distress and to keep oneself from being polluted by the world.

Favoritism Forbidden

2 My brothers, as believers in our glorious Lord Jesus Christ, don't show favoritism. **2**Suppose a man comes into your

---

Show and Tell

INSIGHT

THURSDAY

Passage:
James 2:14–26

Verse:
James 2:24

At the end of a long day, you walk out to the parking lot. As you approach your car, you see that some considerate soul has left a nice, paint-chipping ding in the passenger's side door of your newly financed sedan. As you slump into the driver's seat, absolutely furious, you notice one of your co-worker's business cards stuck in the windshield wiper. Scrawled on the backside of the card is this message: "Swung my door too wide. Come see me and I'll give you a $20 for your trouble."

Will you be inclined to take the twenty and forgive this unrepentant—and obviously deluded—individual? Probably not. Why not? Because this person hasn't proven that he or she is sorry for what he or she did. In fact, the offer of twenty dollars, which won't even pay for the body shop laborer's first coffee break, is a pathetic attempt at reconciliation.

In the passage we read for today, James has a similar message for us. Here he brings up the delicate balance between faith and works in relation to our salvation. We can't buy our way into God's grace. We don't gain entrance to the Holy One by being good enough. Why? Because "There is no one righteous, not even one" (Romans 3:10). Only our simple confession of repentance and faith in him will give us the full measure of his grace.

"But wait a minute," you might be saying. "What if someone takes this truth to the extreme? What if someone says, 'faith by itself' is good enough?" James calls that

person "dead" (2:17–24). If you say that you believe, you'd better be ready to back it up with what you *do*. You know, "put your money where your mouth is."

The lesson here may be the most important you've ever heard. What you say had better be backed up by what you do. If it's not, quit talking. "If anyone considers himself religious and yet does not keep a tight rein on his tongue, he deceives himself and his religion is worthless" (1:26). "What good is it, my brothers, if a man claims to have faith but has no deeds?" (2:14). "As the body without the spirit is dead, so faith without deeds is dead" (2:26).

Think of it this way. That's *your* business card stuck under the windshield wiper.

What will you do to make the situation right again? First, you'll ask for the person's forgiveness. Then you'll call your insurance agent to see if your policy will cover damage inflicted on another vehicle. You'll back up your words with your actions.

Dads are good "doers." They faithfully work to provide for their families. But if a dad hates his work and resents his family, what good is it? Dads are also good talkers. Many dads are fairly open about how much they love God and others. But kind words are only that—kind words—unless they're backed up with actions.

James has the answer: Work *and* faith ... do *and* believe ... show *and* tell.

For your next devotional reading, go to page 1381.

meeting wearing a gold ring and fine clothes, and a poor man in shabby clothes also comes in. ³If you show special attention to the man wearing fine clothes and say, "Here's a good seat for you," but say to the poor man, "You stand there" or "Sit on the floor by my feet," ⁴have you not discriminated among yourselves and become judges with evil thoughts?

⁵Listen, my dear brothers: Has not God chosen those who are poor in the eyes of the world to be rich in faith and to inherit the kingdom he promised those who love him? ⁶But you have insulted the poor. Is it not the rich who are exploiting you? Are they not the ones who are dragging you into court? ⁷Are they not the ones who are slandering the noble name of him to whom you belong?

⁸If you really keep the royal law found in Scripture, "Love your neighbor as yourself,"[a] you are doing right. ⁹But if you show favoritism, you sin and are convicted by the law as lawbreakers. ¹⁰For whoever keeps the whole law and yet stumbles at just one point is guilty of breaking all of it. ¹¹For he who said, "Do not commit adultery,"[b] also said, "Do not murder."[c] If you do not commit adultery but do commit murder, you have become a lawbreaker.

¹²Speak and act as those who are going to be judged by the law that gives freedom, ¹³because judgment without mercy will be shown to anyone who has not been merciful. Mercy triumphs over judgment!

Faith and Deeds

¹⁴What good is it, my brothers, if a man claims to have faith but has no deeds? Can such faith save him? ¹⁵Suppose a brother or sister is without clothes and daily food. ¹⁶If one of you says to him, "Go, I wish you well; keep warm and well fed," but does nothing about his physical needs, what good is it? ¹⁷In the same way, faith by itself, if it is not accompanied by action, is dead.

¹⁸But someone will say, "You have faith; I have deeds."

Show me your faith without deeds, and I will show you my faith by what I do. ¹⁹You believe that there is one God. Good! Even the demons believe that—and shudder.

²⁰You foolish man, do you want evidence that faith without deeds is useless[d]? ²¹Was not our ancestor Abraham considered righteous for what he did when he offered his son Isaac on the altar? ²²You see that his faith and his actions were working together, and his faith was made complete by what he did. ²³And the scripture was fulfilled that says, "Abraham believed God, and it was credited to him as righteousness,"[e] and he was called God's friend. ²⁴You see that a person is justified by what he does and not by faith alone.

[a]8 Lev. 19:18   [b]11 Exodus 20:14; Deut. 5:18
[c]11 Exodus 20:13; Deut. 5:17   [d]20 Some early manuscripts *dead*   [e]23 Gen. 15:6

HEY DAD
Can something be right at some times and wrong at other times?

Text: James 1:5

Some guidelines are absolute. The Ten Commandments, for example, never change. It is never right to commit adultery, murder someone or love anything more than you love God. But other things are more like keys on a piano. The notes are not right or wrong by themselves; it depends on how they're played within a song.

For example, fighting seems like a *bad* thing. But, throughout the Bible God allows fighting to protect one's family or one's country. Compassion is considered a *good* thing, yet at times we must put our feelings aside to see that justice is not ignored.

With God's wisdom and good counsel from godly people, we can learn to do the right thing when the line between right and wrong is not clear. Solomon said, "Wisdom is supreme; therefore get wisdom. Though it cost all you have, get understanding" (Proverbs 4:7). This is the kind of wisdom that only comes from God.

QUESTIONS KIDS ASK

For a complete listing of Questions Kids Ask, turn to page 1435.

²⁵In the same way, was not even Rahab the prostitute considered righteous for what she did when she gave lodging to the spies and sent them off in a different direction? ²⁶As the body without the spirit is dead, so faith without deeds is dead.

Taming the Tongue

3 Not many of you should presume to be teachers, my brothers, because you know that we who teach will be judged more strictly. ²We all stumble in many ways. If anyone is never at fault in what he says, he is a perfect man, able to keep his whole body in check. ³When we put bits into the mouths of horses to make them obey us, we can turn the whole animal. ⁴Or take ships as an example. Although they are so large and are driven by strong winds, they are steered by a very small rudder wherever the pilot wants to go. ⁵Likewise the tongue is a small part of the body, but it makes great boasts. Consider what a great forest is set on fire by a small spark. ⁶The tongue also

Poof, Now You're Gone . . . Surprise!

I love surprising, but I hate surprises.

As a kid, cutting the grass was always my job. If I could cut the grass before my dad asked me to do it, then he'd be surprised when he came home from work. I loved surprising him, so I was motivated to get the lawn done. On the other hand, if my dad said, "Please cut the grass today" before he left for the office, the joy was completely gone. I love surprising.

Let me give you another example. Normally, planning parties isn't my thing. I don't know why, but I'd rather drive a nail or sink a long putt than set up a punch bowl or stretch streamers across a room. But as my wife and I approached our twenty-fifth wedding anniversary, I got an idea. *I'll surprise Bobbie with a party,* I decided. *I'll fly the kids in and have it a few weeks before the actual date. She'll never know.* I had never been so motivated in my life. I loved planning this party. I couldn't wait to get my hands on the punchbowl and stretch those crinkled streamers around the room. I love surprising.

Over the years, I have had many surprises come my way. Some of these were supposed to be good—for example, a surprise birthday party when I turned thirty. Some weren't so good—for example, the phone call I received on my forty-fourth birthday that announced the demise of my business. In both of these cases, I didn't like the surprise at all.

DAILY INSIGHT

FRIDAY

Passage:
James 4:13–17

Verse:
James 4:14

My family and my business associates have heard me say this many times: "If you think you see something coming, tell me about it. Don't surprise me." I'm quite serious about this. I love surprising, but I hate surprises.

Not long ago, I asked the people in our Sunday school class, "How many of you, at this stage of life, are exactly where you thought you'd be when you were growing up?" Of the two hundred people sitting there, not one hand went up. Life is full of surprises for all of us.

The apostle James has something to report to us. "Now listen, you who say, 'Today or tomorrow we will go to this or that city, spend a year there, carry on business and make money ... What is your life? You are a mist that appears for a little while and then vanishes" (vv. 13–14). Now you're here. Now you're gone ... poof ... surprise! (See Luke chapter 12 for one of the Bible's most poignant illustrations of this text.)

Before you and I go to bed tonight, we ought to do something. We ought to brace ourselves like we do when a balloon is about to pop. We may have a tomorrow, or we may not. We may have another birthday, or we may not. Our life has been filled with surprises, and there are more just around the corner. We'd better get ready. And we should start by praying the prayer in verse 15.

For your next devotional reading, go to page 1383.

is a fire, a world of evil among the parts of the body. It corrupts the whole person, sets the whole course of his life on fire, and is itself set on fire by hell.

[7] All kinds of animals, birds, reptiles and creatures of the sea are being tamed and have been tamed by man, [8] but no man can tame the tongue. It is a restless evil, full of deadly poison.

[9] With the tongue we praise our Lord and Father, and with it we curse men, who have been made in God's likeness. [10] Out of the same mouth come praise and cursing. My brothers, this should not be. [11] Can both fresh water and salt[a] water flow from the same spring? [12] My brothers, can a fig tree bear olives, or a grapevine bear figs? Neither can a salt spring produce fresh water.

Two Kinds of Wisdom

[13] Who is wise and understanding among you? Let him show it by his good life, by deeds done in the humility that comes from wisdom. [14] But if you harbor bitter envy and selfish ambition in your hearts, do not boast about it or deny the truth. [15] Such "wisdom" does not come down from heaven but is earthly, unspiri-

tual, of the devil. [16] For where you have envy and selfish ambition, there you find disorder and every evil practice.

[17] But the wisdom that comes from heaven is first of all pure; then peace-loving, considerate, submissive, full of mercy and good fruit, impartial and sincere. [18] Peacemakers who sow in peace raise a harvest of righteousness.

Submit Yourselves to God

4 What causes fights and quarrels among you? Don't they come from your desires that battle within you? [2] You want something but don't get it. You kill and covet, but you cannot have what you want. You quarrel and fight. You do not have, because you do not ask God. [3] When you ask, you do not receive, because you ask with wrong motives, that you may spend what you get on your pleasures.

[4] You adulterous people, don't you know that friendship with the world is hatred toward God? Anyone who chooses to be a friend of the world becomes an enemy of God. [5] Or do you think Scripture says without reason that the spirit he caused to live

a11 Greek bitter (see also verse 14)

HEY DAD

If prayer really works, why don't doctors prescribe it?

Text: James 5:14–16

While you won't find it at a pharmacy, some doctors may already be prescribing prayer! In 1992, a group of researchers established the National Institute of Healthcare Research (NIHR) to study what they call "the forgotten factor"—the effects of faith and prayer on health. Their findings are no surprise to Christians.

Numerous studies show that churchgoers have lower rates of anxiety-related illnesses and depression. One study showed that if elderly patients had an active prayer life or found solace in their faith, they were *fourteen times* more likely to survive surgery.

One cardiologist at the San Francisco General Medical Center conducted a study on intercessory prayer. He assigned half of his serious heart patients to Christians outside the hospital that agreed to pray for them over a ten-month period.

At the end of that time, the patients receiving prayer needed less medicine and mechanical assistance than the others did. "These data suggest that intercessory prayer to the Judeo-Christian God has a beneficial therapeutic effect in patients admitted to a CCU [cardiac care unit]" (Byrd, 829).

So today's doctors and researchers are now finding out what James 5:15 has told us all along: Prayer works.

Byrd, Randoph C. Southern Medical Journal. July, 1988; 81(7): 826–9.

For a complete listing of Questions Kids Ask, turn to page 1435.

Talking to God

Key Verse: *"Confess your sins to each other and pray for each other so that you may be healed. The prayer of a righteous man is powerful and effective."* James 5:16

Text: James 5:13–16 *(Dad or child reads the text.)*

QUIET
TIMES
WITH **Dad**

DAD READS: I love to talk with you. I know that it is one of the most important things we can do. Talking to each other helps us to understand each other. Talking helps us to celebrate when good things happen and to cry together when awful things happen. If we couldn't talk to each other, we would hardly know each other. I'm so glad that we can be together and talk.

Child reads: I know that some kids can't talk to their dads. Some kids are afraid of their fathers. Some kids don't think their dads care about them. But I have a dad who wants to know all about me—a dad who does care. I'm so glad that I have a dad like this.

DAD READS: Did you know that what we have been talking about is exactly what needs to happen between us and our heavenly Father? We can learn to know him by talking to him through prayer. We can tell him about our cares and our fears and our joys.

Child reads: The Bible verses we read today say something very important about talking to God. They tell us that we should pray when we're happy, we should pray when we're in trouble, and we should pray when we're sick. When we pray, God listens carefully to us.

DAD READS: The very same God who created everything in the universe wants to hear us talk to him. He wants us to get to know who he his and he wants us to tell him who we are. He wants to hear everything about us. He wants to celebrate with us when we're happy, cry with us when we're sad and heal us when we're sick.

Child reads: The time that we spend together like this helps us to understand each other. Spending time together also helps me to remember how much I love you and how much you love me.

DAD READS: We should be thankful that we love each other so much that we want to spend time together and talk. And we should be so thankful that our heavenly Father loves us and wants to spend time with us, too. I want to be a dad who prays.

Child reads: I want to be someone who prays, too. I want God to know that I will always try to tell him everything so he can laugh with me, cry with me, and heal me. Let me pray this prayer with you:

Our Father in heaven, we love you. Thank you for wanting to talk to us, and thank you for promising to listen to us when we talk to you. Please forgive my dad and me for not praying as much as we should. Help us to remember how important it is to talk to each other, and help us to always remember to talk to you, too. We love you and we thank you for your love. In Jesus' name, **Amen.**

For your next devotional reading, go to page 1387.

in us envies intensely?[a] [6]But he gives us more grace. That is why Scripture says:

"God opposes the proud
   but gives grace to the humble."[b]

[7]Submit yourselves, then, to God. Resist the devil, and he will flee from you. [8]Come near to God and he will come near to you. Wash your hands, you sinners, and purify your hearts, you double-minded. [9]Grieve, mourn and wail. Change your laughter to mourning and your joy to gloom. [10]Humble yourselves before the Lord, and he will lift you up.

[11]Brothers, do not slander one another. Anyone who speaks against his brother or judges him speaks against the law and judges it. When you judge the law, you are not keeping it, but sitting in judgment on it. [12]There is only one Lawgiver and Judge, the one who is able to save and destroy. But you—who are you to judge your neighbor?

Boasting About Tomorrow

[13]Now listen, you who say, "Today or tomorrow we will go to this or that city, spend a year there, carry on business and make money." [14]Why, you do not even know what will happen tomorrow. What is your life? You are a mist that appears for a little while and then vanishes. [15]Instead, you ought to say, "If it is the Lord's will, we will live and do this or that." [16]As it is, you boast and brag. All such boasting is evil. [17]Anyone, then, who knows the good he ought to do and doesn't do it, sins.

Warning to Rich Oppressors

5 Now listen, you rich people, weep and wail because of the misery that is coming upon you. [2]Your wealth has rotted, and moths have eaten your clothes. [3]Your gold and silver are corroded. Their corrosion will testify against you and eat your flesh like fire. You have hoarded wealth in the last days. [4]Look! The wages you failed to pay the workmen who mowed your fields are crying out against you. The cries of the harvesters have reached the ears of the Lord Almighty. [5]You have lived on earth in luxury and self-indulgence. You have fattened yourselves in the day of slaughter.[c] [6]You have condemned and murdered innocent men, who were not opposing you.

Patience in Suffering

[7]Be patient, then, brothers, until the Lord's coming. See how the farmer waits for the land to yield its valuable crop and how patient he is for the autumn and spring rains. [8]You too, be patient and stand firm, because the Lord's coming is near. [9]Don't grumble against each other, brothers, or you will be judged. The Judge is standing at the door!

[10]Brothers, as an example of patience in the face of suffering, take the prophets who spoke in the name of the Lord. [11]As you know, we consider blessed those who have persevered. You have heard of Job's perseverance and have seen what the Lord finally brought about. The Lord is full of compassion and mercy.

[12]Above all, my brothers, do not swear—not by heaven or by earth or by anything else. Let your "Yes" be yes, and your "No," no, or you will be condemned.

The Prayer of Faith

[13]Is any one of you in trouble? He should pray. Is anyone happy? Let him sing songs of praise. [14]Is any one of you sick? He should call the elders of the church to pray over him and anoint him with oil in the name of the Lord. [15]And the prayer offered in faith will make the sick person well; the Lord will raise him up. If he has sinned, he will be forgiven. [16]Therefore confess your sins to each other and pray for each other so that you may be healed. The prayer of a righteous man is powerful and effective.

[17]Elijah was a man just like us. He prayed earnestly that it would not rain, and it did not rain on the land for three and a half years. [18]Again he prayed, and the heavens gave rain, and the earth produced its crops.

[19]My brothers, if one of you should wander from the truth and someone should bring him back, [20]remember this: Whoever turns a sinner from the error of his way will save him from death and cover over a multitude of sins.

---

[a]5 Or that God jealously longs for the spirit that he made to live in us; or that the Spirit he caused to live in us longs jealously   [b]6 Prov. 3:34   [c]5 Or yourselves as in a day of feasting

As a young man, Peter probably wouldn't have been caught dead saying, "Grace and peace be yours in abundance" (1:2). He was a man's man, an outspoken blue-collar worker, a tough guy. He probably paid attention only to men just like himself. But, right in the middle of his career, Peter's brother Andrew dragged him into the presence of a man who would unalterably change his life.

Jesus gave Peter an example of tenderness and compassion he had never known before. Through the power of the Spirit Peter took that gift, mixed it with the vitality and force that had marked his life to that point, and turned the combination into something that changed the world. This short book shows us both the new Peter: "Like newborn babies, crave pure spiritual milk" (2:2) and the old Peter "Therefore, since Christ suffered in his body, arm yourselves also with the same attitude" (4:1).

Peter lived his faith intentionally. Read this book, and you'll see for yourself.

1 Peter

Peter, an apostle of Jesus Christ,

To God's elect, strangers in the world, scattered throughout Pontus, Galatia, Cappadocia, Asia and Bithynia, ²who have been chosen according to the foreknowledge of God the Father, through the sanctifying work of the Spirit, for obedience to Jesus Christ and sprinkling by his blood:

Grace and peace be yours in abundance.

Praise to God for a Living Hope

³Praise be to the God and Father of our Lord Jesus Christ! In his great mercy he has given us new birth into a living hope through the resurrection of Jesus Christ from the dead, ⁴and into an inheritance that can never perish, spoil or fade—kept in heaven for you, ⁵who through faith are shielded by God's power until the coming of the salvation that is ready to be revealed in the last time. ⁶In this you greatly rejoice, though now for a little while you may have had to suffer grief in all kinds of trials. ⁷These have come so that your faith—of greater worth than gold, which perishes even though refined by fire—may be proved genuine and may result in praise, glory and honor when Jesus Christ is revealed. ⁸Though you have not seen him, you love him; and even though you do not see him now, you believe in him and are filled with an inexpressible and glorious joy, ⁹for you are receiving the

goal of your faith, the salvation of your souls.

¹⁰Concerning this salvation, the prophets, who spoke of the grace that was to come to you, searched intently and with the greatest care, ¹¹trying to find out the time and circumstances to which the Spirit of Christ in them was pointing when he predicted the sufferings of Christ and the glories that would follow. ¹²It was revealed to them that they were not serving themselves but you, when they spoke of the things that have now been told you by those who have preached the gospel to you by the Holy Spirit sent from heaven. Even angels long to look into these things.

Be Holy

¹³Therefore, prepare your minds for action; be self-controlled; set your hope fully on the grace to be given you when Jesus Christ is revealed. ¹⁴As obedient children, do not conform to the evil desires you had when you lived in ignorance. ¹⁵But just as he who called you is holy, so be holy in all you do; ¹⁶for it is written: "Be holy, because I am holy."ᵃ

¹⁷Since you call on a Father who judges each man's work impartially, live your lives as strangers here in reverent fear. ¹⁸For you know that it was not with per-

ᵃ16 Lev. 11:44,45; 19:2; 20:7

HEY DAD

How can God be one person and three persons at the same time?

Text: 1 Peter 1:1–2

The Bible teaches us, from the very beginning of Genesis, that our one God has three entities. In Genesis 1:1–3 we see the three parts of the Trinity represented: God the Father (creating), God the Spirit (hovering), and God the Son (speaking, as explained by John 1:1–5). At Jesus' baptism the Father speaks, the Son is present, and the Holy Spirit descends upon him "like a dove" (Matthew 3:16–17). And Jesus himself testifies to this reality when he commands his disciples to "go and make disciples of all nations, baptizing them in the name of the Father and of the Son and of the Holy Spirit" (Matthew 28:19). Finally, in the verses cited above, the apostle Peter also testifies to the reality of the Trinity.

The fact that these three entities are, at the same time, also wholly and completely one God is beyond human comprehension. While some theologians have tried to define it in human terms (such as, one human person has a mind, a body and a will), each illustration falls far short of the true reality of what our Triune God is and does. This doctrine is something we simply have to accept in faith.

One theologian, however, has summed up how Christians can "know" about the work of the Triune God in their own lives. Cornelius Plantinga, Jr. writes, "In some profound and mysterious way, believers feel and experience the operations of the Trinity. The first of these operations is creation ... when we now see the works of God's hand, when we marvel at the intricacy of a new, well-born child, we experience the creative work of God. This is the chief work of the Father.

"Again ... when we consciously feel that we have been saved from ruining ourselves and redeemed from selling ourselves to the highest bidder—then we experience the redeeming work of his Son.

"Finally ... as we grow in grace and knowledge of God—then we experience the sanctifying work of the Holy Spirit ... The same Trinity of persons which creates us also redeems us and sanctifies us" (Plantinga, 59).

While this doctrine may puzzle us now, we look forward to a time when we will fully understand this wonder. "Now we see but a poor reflection as in a mirror; then we shall see face to face. Now I know in part; then I shall know fully, even as I am fully known" (1 Corinthians 13:12).

Plantinga Jr., Cornelius. (1979). A Place to Stand. Grand Rapids, Michigan: CRC Publications, 1979.

For a complete listing of Questions Kids Ask, turn to page 1435.

ishable things such as silver or gold that you were redeemed from the empty way of life handed down to you from your forefathers, [19]but with the precious blood of Christ, a lamb without blemish or defect. [20]He was chosen before the creation of the world, but was revealed in these last times for your sake. [21]Through him you believe in God, who raised him from the dead and glorified him, and so your faith and hope are in God.

[22]Now that you have purified your-selves by obeying the truth so that you have sincere love for your brothers, love one another deeply, from the heart.[a] [23]For you have been born again, not of perishable seed, but of imperishable, through the living and enduring word of God. [24]For,

"All men are like grass,
    and all their glory is like the flowers
        of the field;

[a]22 Some early manuscripts from a pure heart

Your Family's Very Own Priest

DAILY INSIGHT

MONDAY

Passage:
1 Peter 2:4–10

Verse:
1 Peter 2:9

When was the last time you took a good look at your Yellow Pages®? In there you'll find that there are more specialists walking around the streets of your town than you can imagine. From small animal veterinarians to explosives technicians, people have found very specialized, precise occupations in the interest of keeping groceries in the pantry.

My father was a minister. For the first five years of my life, he pastored the Fairview Avenue Brethren in Christ Church. It was a plain and simple place with very few adornments. There were no tapestries, no hand-painted icons, no gold-leaf trim. We didn't even have an organ or a piano.

In the years since then, I have had the privilege of experiencing many different forms of worship—from formal Orthodox and Roman Catholic services to spontaneous Pentecostal and Holiness celebrations. But regardless of the worship style, I have always been drawn to the role of the person conducting the service. I have met somber clerics whose faces were reminiscent of Mount Rushmore. I have also met ministers who could have been successful stand-up comedians on the side.

In this world of specialists, isn't it nice to know that some are called to be ministers, to bring their flock into the presence of God? Aren't you glad that you and I can go ahead and specialize in something else? Not so fast, dad. Read verses 4–5, and you'll find out that in God's Yellow Pages®,

every Christian dad in your town is listed under "Priest," including you and me.

Years ago, I met a Jesuit priest who told me of a time when he was preparing to enter the sanctuary to conduct mass. Father John Powell stopped in his tracks, catching his own reflected image in the full-length mirror that stood by the entrance to the chancel. He paused to drink in his own striking appearance, outfitted as he was in his stunning vestments.

At that moment, he caught a glimpse of a crucifix hanging in the corner of the room. "I fell to my knees," Father Powell told me. "Who did I think I was? I was on my way to be the priest for this congregation, and I needed God's grace more than any of them." Pouring his heart out to his heavenly Father, this contrite man confessed his unworthiness. In a few moments, Father Powell stood to his feet ... ready to be the priest once more.

This is a snapshot of what God requires of us. We are to know his Word and listen to his voice so we can say to our family, "This is what God is saying to us." Then we must be the ones who stand in the presence of a holy God and plead our families' case. And we must begin this prayer by confessing our own inadequacy and sin.

You're a card-carrying priest. Your family is your congregation, and your home is your sanctuary. And now you know exactly what to do.

For your next devotional reading, go to page 1388.

the grass withers and the flowers fall,
²⁵ but the word of the Lord stands
   forever."[a]

And this is the word that was preached to you.

2 Therefore, rid yourselves of all malice and all deceit, hypocrisy, envy, and slander of every kind. ²Like newborn babies, crave pure spiritual milk, so that by it you may grow up in your salvation, ³now that you have tasted that the Lord is good.

The Living Stone and a Chosen People

⁴As you come to him, the living Stone—rejected by men but chosen by God and precious to him— ⁵you also, like living

I've Had Some Kind of "Weak"

DAILY INSIGHT

TUESDAY

Passage:
1 Peter 3:8–12

Verse:
1 Peter 3:7

For some reason, I have spent my life surrounded by women. In addition to my mother—the most significant woman in my early life—I had a sister eight years older than me. Then when I was eight, I got a little sister. When I got married, another woman became a wonderful addition to my life. We had two children ... both girls. In 1996 our first grandchild was born ... a little girl. In fact, over the years I've had five dogs, and even *they* were "women"!

The apostle Peter's words in verse 7 are tailor-made for me, and for all of us who live with women. Some foolish men have taken these words to mean that they have a right to lord it over the women in their lives—elbowing them out of the way as if they were walking the aisles of a crowded hardware store. But this notion is dead wrong. Living with women—at least the ones in my life—requires much more finesse. It's more like walking through a gift shop filled with delicate things, beautiful things, and breakable things.

When the apostle uses the word "weaker," he places it in the context of a woman's need for more respect, more honor and more consideration. But I can tell you from personal experience, "weaker" certainly doesn't mean "weaker."

When my older sister, Ruth, was eleven years old, our parents took a short-term missionary assignment to Japan. Unfortunately, the only American school was seventy-five miles away. My sister was in charge of three younger brothers ages nine, seven and five as we made the trek: a one-mile walk, a bus ride, a long train ride that included a transfer in a viciously crowded station, and another two-mile walk ... each way ... every day. But Ruth was tough and smart, and nobody messed with us.

Twelve years later, Ruth married Stan and raised three children. When her children went off to school, she went back to school and got her broker's license, eventually building her own business and handling the personal wealth of dozens of clients. She's not exactly "weak," if you know what I mean.

Then there's my little sister, Debbie. During my years of adolescent rebellion, she loved me and cheered for me, even when I didn't deserve it. As a grown woman, she has home-schooled her four gifted children, taught English to Polish immigrants, started several successful businesses, performed as a soloist for countless church services and weddings, stood fearlessly as a political activist, and has been a faithful wife to Randal. She's not exactly "weak," if you know what I mean.

I could go on and on about my mother, my wife, and my daughters. And you could tell me your stories of the important women in your life. But the apostle gave us a summary of these incredible women—delicate, tender, valuable and beautiful—and he commanded us to honor and respect them because of their beauty, courage and stamina.

Women are ... well, they're incredible, aren't they?

For your next devotional reading, go to page 1392.

stones, are being built into a spiritual house to be a holy priesthood, offering spiritual sacrifices acceptable to God through Jesus Christ. **6**For in Scripture it says:

"See, I lay a stone in Zion,
a chosen and precious cornerstone,
and the one who trusts in him
will never be put to shame."[a]

7Now to you who believe, this stone is precious. But to those who do not believe,

"The stone the builders rejected
has become the capstone,[b]"[c]

8and,

"A stone that causes men to stumble
and a rock that makes them fall."[d]

They stumble because they disobey the message—which is also what they were destined for.

9But you are a chosen people, a royal priesthood, a holy nation, a people belonging to God, that you may declare the praises of him who called you out of darkness into his wonderful light. **10**Once you were not a people, but now you are the people of God; once you had not received mercy, but now you have received mercy. **11**Dear friends, I urge you, as aliens and strangers in the world, to abstain from sinful desires, which war against your soul. **12**Live such good lives among the pagans that, though they accuse you of doing wrong, they may see your good deeds and glorify God on the day he visits us.

Submission to Rulers and Masters

13Submit yourselves for the Lord's sake to every authority instituted among men: whether to the king, as the supreme authority, **14**or to governors, who are sent by him to punish those who do wrong and to commend those who do right. **15**For it is God's will that by doing good you should silence the ignorant talk of foolish men. **16**Live as free men, but do not use your freedom as a cover-up for evil; live as servants of God. **17**Show proper respect to everyone: Love the brotherhood of believers, fear God, honor the king.

18Slaves, submit yourselves to your masters with all respect, not only to those who are good and considerate, but also to those who are harsh. **19**For it is commendable if a man bears up under the pain of unjust suffering because he is conscious of God. **20**But how is it to your credit if you

receive a beating for doing wrong and endure it? But if you suffer for doing good and you endure it, this is commendable before God. **21**To this you were called, because Christ suffered for you, leaving you an example, that you should follow in his steps.

22"He committed no sin,
and no deceit was found in his
mouth."[e]

23When they hurled their insults at him, he did not retaliate; when he suffered, he made no threats. Instead, he entrusted himself to him who judges justly. **24**He himself bore our sins in his body on the tree, so that we might die to sins and live for righteousness; by his wounds you have been healed. **25**For you were like sheep going astray, but now you have returned to the Shepherd and Overseer of your souls.

Wives and Husbands

3 Wives, in the same way be submissive to your husbands so that, if any of them do not believe the word, they may be won over without words by the behavior of their wives, **2**when they see the purity and reverence of your lives. **3**Your beauty should not come from outward adornment, such as braided hair and the wearing of gold jewelry and fine clothes. **4**Instead, it should be that of your inner self, the unfading beauty of a gentle and quiet spirit, which is of great worth in God's sight. **5**For this is the way the holy women of the past who put their hope in God used to make themselves beautiful. They were submissive to their own husbands, **6**like Sarah, who obeyed Abraham and called him her master. You are her daughters if you do what is right and do not give way to fear.

7Husbands, in the same way be considerate as you live with your wives, and treat them with respect as the weaker partner and as heirs with you of the gracious gift of life, so that nothing will hinder your prayers.

Suffering for Doing Good

8Finally, all of you, live in harmony with one another; be sympathetic, love as brothers, be compassionate and humble. **9**Do not repay evil with evil or insult with

---

[a]6 Isaiah 28:16   [b]7 Or cornerstone   [c]7 Psalm 118:22
[d]8 Isaiah 8:14   [e]22 Isaiah 53:9

insult, but with blessing, because to this you were called so that you may inherit a blessing. [10]For,

"Whoever would love life
    and see good days
must keep his tongue from evil
    and his lips from deceitful speech.
[11]He must turn from evil and do good;
    he must seek peace and pursue it.
[12]For the eyes of the Lord are on the
        righteous
    and his ears are attentive to their
        prayer,
but the face of the Lord is against those
    who do evil."[a]

[13]Who is going to harm you if you are eager to do good? [14]But even if you should suffer for what is right, you are blessed. "Do not fear what they fear[b]; do not be frightened."[c] [15]But in your hearts set apart Christ as Lord. Always be prepared to give an answer to everyone who asks you to give the reason for the hope that you have. But do this with gentleness and respect, [16]keeping a clear conscience, so that those who speak maliciously against your good behavior in Christ may be ashamed of their slander. [17]It is better, if it is God's will, to suffer for doing good than for doing evil. [18]For Christ died for sins once for all, the righteous for the unrighteous, to bring you to God. He was put to death in the body but made alive by the Spirit, [19]through whom[d] also he went and preached to the spirits in prison [20]who disobeyed long ago when God waited patiently in the days of Noah while the ark

was being built. In it only a few people, eight in all, were saved through water, [21]and this water symbolizes baptism that now saves you also—not the removal of dirt from the body but the pledge[e] of a good conscience toward God. It saves you by the resurrection of Jesus Christ, [22]who has gone into heaven and is at God's right hand—with angels, authorities and powers in submission to him.

Living for God

4 Therefore, since Christ suffered in his body, arm yourselves also with the same attitude, because he who has suffered in his body is done with sin. [2]As a result, he does not live the rest of his earthly life for evil human desires, but rather for the will of God. [3]For you have spent enough time in the past doing what pagans choose to do—living in debauchery, lust, drunkenness, orgies, carousing and detestable idolatry. [4]They think it strange that you do not plunge with them into the same flood of dissipation, and they heap abuse on you. [5]But they will have to give account to him who is ready to judge the living and the dead. [6]For this is the reason the gospel was preached even to those who are now dead, so that they might be judged according to men in regard to the body, but live according to God in regard to the spirit.

[7]The end of all things is near. Therefore

[a]12 Psalm 34:12-16   [b]14 Or *not fear their threats*
[c]14 Isaiah 8:12   [d]18,19 Or *alive in the spirit,*
[19]*through which*   [e]21 Or *response*

HEY DAD
What is the fish symbol on the back of that car?

Text: 1 Peter 4:12–17

This symbol held special significance for early Christians. The sign of the fish (*ichthys* in Greek) helped them identify each other during times of severe persecution. To the followers of Christ, the *ichthys* represented baptism and reminded them that Christ had called them to be fishers of men and women.

Ichthys also forms an acronym in Greek for "Jesus Christ, God's Son, Savior," which summarizes the entire salvation message. Jesus was the Messiah Israel had been expecting. He is the Son of God, and salvation comes through him.

The fish you see on cars serves much the same purpose today that it did almost two thousand years ago. It helps Christians recognize each other, and it reminds us of the one we serve—Jesus Christ, God's Son, the Savior.

Ward, K.(Ed.). (1987). Jesus and His Times. Pleasantville, New York: The Reader's Digest Association.

For a complete listing of Questions Kids Ask, turn to page 1435.

QUESTIONS KIDS ASK

be clear minded and self-controlled so that you can pray. **8**Above all, love each other deeply, because love covers over a multitude of sins. **9**Offer hospitality to one another without grumbling. **10**Each one should use whatever gift he has received to serve others, faithfully administering God's grace in its various forms. **11**If anyone speaks, he should do it as one speaking the very words of God. If anyone serves, he should do it with the strength God provides, so that in all things God may be praised through Jesus Christ. To him be the glory and the power for ever and ever. Amen.

Suffering for Being a Christian

12Dear friends, do not be surprised at the painful trial you are suffering, as though something strange were happening to you. **13**But rejoice that you participate in the sufferings of Christ, so that you may be overjoyed when his glory is revealed. **14**If you are insulted because of the name of Christ, you are blessed, for the Spirit of glory and of God rests on you. **15**If you suffer, it should not be as a murderer or thief or any other kind of criminal, or even as a meddler. **16**However, if you suffer as a Christian, do not be ashamed, but praise God that you bear that name. **17**For it is time for judgment to begin with the family of God; and if it begins with us, what will the outcome be for those who do not obey the gospel of God? **18**And,

"If it is hard for the righteous to be
    saved,
  what will become of the ungodly and
    the sinner?"[a]

19So then, those who suffer according to God's will should commit themselves to their faithful Creator and continue to do good.

To Elders and Young Men

5 To the elders among you, I appeal as a fellow elder, a witness of Christ's sufferings and one who also will share in the glory to be revealed: **2**Be shepherds of God's flock that is under your care, serving as overseers—not because you must, but because you are willing, as God wants you to be; not greedy for money, but eager to serve; **3**not lording it over those entrusted to you, but being examples to the flock. **4**And when the Chief Shepherd appears, you will receive the crown of glory that will never fade away.

5Young men, in the same way be submissive to those who are older. All of you, clothe yourselves with humility toward one another, because,

"God opposes the proud
  but gives grace to the humble."[b]

6Humble yourselves, therefore, under God's mighty hand, that he may lift you

[a]18 Prov. 11:31 [b]5 Prov. 3:34

HEY DAD
What does the devil look like?

Text: 1 Peter 5:8–9

Often when we hear someone mention "the devil," we picture a little red imp with horns and a pointed tail, toting a pitchfork. But the Bible says that Satan is a fallen angel, and that angels are spirits. This means they do not have bodies like people do. Unless an angel takes on bodily form, we are not able to see it. So, technically speaking, the devil does not "look like" anything at all.

Still, the devil is very real. Peter describes him as our "enemy," and portrays him as a lion who wants to attack and kill us. He is God's enemy as well, and will stop at nothing to tempt us to disobey God. This may sound scary, but as Christians we have power over him. God's Spirit lives within us, and that Spirit is infinitely more powerful than the devil. James advises, "Resist the devil, and he will flee from you" (James 4:7).

If we're expecting to see the devil in a red suit, we will never recognize him. But the more we read God's Word and understand what God wants us to do, the more easily we will be able to "resist him, standing firm in the faith" (v. 9).

For a complete listing of Questions Kids Ask, turn to page 1435.

up in due time. ⁷Cast all your anxiety on him because he cares for you.

⁸Be self-controlled and alert. Your enemy the devil prowls around like a roaring lion looking for someone to devour. ⁹Resist him, standing firm in the faith, because you know that your brothers throughout the world are undergoing the same kind of sufferings.

¹⁰And the God of all grace, who called you to his eternal glory in Christ, after you

have suffered a little while, will himself restore you and make you strong, firm and steadfast. ¹¹To him be the power for ever and ever. Amen.

Final Greetings

¹²With the help of Silas,ᵃ whom I regard as a faithful brother, I have written to you

ᵃ12 Greek *Silvanus*, a variant of *Silas*

Not-so-nice Kitty

DAILY INSIGHT

WEDNESDAY

Passage:
1 Peter 5:6–11

Verse:
1 Peter 5:8

"What's so great about this?" I whispered to my brother as we looked into a fenced area containing about two hundred alligators. "They look dead."

My brother and I had begged my father to stop at this alligator farm as we traveled from Chicago to Boca Raton, Florida. We'd seen the billboards a full hundred miles before the farm and hadn't let up since then. But these alligators, most of which were the size of station wagons, looked like logs floating in a river waiting for the paper mill—completely benign and harmless. Not exactly a stem-winding experience for a twelve-year-old boy.

Just as we were about to leave, the farm's keeper showed up to serve lunch. When the alligators saw him move to the edge of the fence, they began to shuffle around. "They *are* alive," I whispered to my brother.

The man reached into the huge bucket he had brought with him. He pulled out a half chicken, and tossed it into the alligators' pen. At that moment, these sleepy giants literally exploded from their lethargy. The still water turned to foam, and the gargantuan reptiles leapt into the air, rolling and snapping their jaws with absolute fury. We stood there aghast at this awesome sight.

Whenever I read this passage, I think of those alligators. Peter uses the image of a lion as he describes our enemy, the devil, but the connection to these huge reptiles is easy to make. We've all been to the zoo and seen the lions sunning themselves, looking

tame and sluggish. But throw something delectable in their direction, and they, too, will erupt in a frenzy.

Peter knew exactly what he was talking about. He had come too close to this dozing lion. "Nice kitty," Peter had whispered when he boastfully announced that he would never betray his Savior (Matthew 26:35). "Nice kitty," he said as he warmed himself by the fire on the night before Jesus' crucifixion (Mark 14:54–71). But this was feeding time. The lion pounced, devouring his vulnerable prey.

Our lives are filled with lazy alligators and sleeping lions that wait for us to get close enough so they can consume us. What can we do? Thankfully, Peter tells us. "Humble [yourself];" recognize that you're up against a vicious foe. Trust God; "cast all your anxiety on him," because worrying makes you more vulnerable. "Be self-controlled and alert"— no further explanation needed. When we do these things, God will "restore [us] and make [us] strong, firm and steadfast" (vv. 6–10).

And be encouraged. You're not alone in this battle. Remember that there are many others—men like Peter—who are "your brothers throughout the world [and] are undergoing the same kind of sufferings" (v. 9). They're protected, too.

Just remember, Satan may seem harmless, lying there with his eyes closed. He may look safe, peaceable and approachable. He's not.

For your next devotional reading, go to page 1397.

briefly, encouraging you and testifying that this is the true grace of God. Stand fast in it.

¹³She who is in Babylon, chosen togeth-er with you, sends you her greetings, and so does my son Mark. ¹⁴Greet one another with a kiss of love.

Peace to all of you who are in Christ.

Junk mail is a fact of life. Every day your letter carrier delivers one more "once in a lifetime" opportunity or the ever popular, "You have already won!" If you were to sit down with the direct marketing experts who write these letters (don't call it "junk mail" to them), they'd reveal that if you want the reader to really pay attention to a bit of information, put it in the postscript—the PS at the end of the letter.

Peter knew something about this fact, because he packed this little book—his own PS—with information he didn't want his readers to miss. "Make every effort to add to your faith goodness; and to goodness, knowledge; and to knowledge, self-control; and to self-control, perseverance; and to perseverance, godliness; and to godliness, brotherly kindness; and to brotherly kindness, love" (1:5-7). Peter was writing to people who were being challenged by heresy and temptation, much the same as we are today. He said, in effect, "Don't cut corners. Don't miss the basics. Hang in there." Reading 2 Peter gives us the truth in concentrated form.

2 Peter

1 Simon Peter, a servant and apostle of Jesus Christ,

To those who through the righteousness of our God and Savior Jesus Christ have received a faith as precious as ours:

²Grace and peace be yours in abundance through the knowledge of God and of Jesus our Lord.

Making One's Calling and Election Sure

³His divine power has given us everything we need for life and godliness through our knowledge of him who called us by his own glory and goodness. ⁴Through these he has given us his very great and precious promises, so that through them you may participate in the divine nature and escape the corruption in the world caused by evil desires.

⁵For this very reason, make every effort to add to your faith goodness; and to goodness, knowledge; ⁶and to knowledge, self-control; and to self-control, perseverance; and to perseverance, godliness; ⁷and to godliness, brotherly kindness; and to brotherly kindness, love. ⁸For if you possess these qualities in increasing measure, they will keep you from being ineffective and unproductive in your knowledge of our Lord Jesus Christ. ⁹But if

anyone does not have them, he is near-sighted and blind, and has forgotten that he has been cleansed from his past sins. [10]Therefore, my brothers, be all the more eager to make your calling and election sure. For if you do these things, you will never fall, [11]and you will receive a rich welcome into the eternal kingdom of our Lord and Savior Jesus Christ.

Prophecy of Scripture

[12]So I will always remind you of these things, even though you know them and are firmly established in the truth you now have. [13]I think it is right to refresh your memory as long as I live in the tent of this body, [14]because I know that I will soon put it aside, as our Lord Jesus Christ has made clear to me. [15]And I will make every effort to see that after my departure you will always be able to remember these things.

[16]We did not follow cleverly invented stories when we told you about the power and coming of our Lord Jesus Christ, but we were eyewitnesses of his majesty. [17]For he received honor and glory from God the Father when the voice came to him from the Majestic Glory, saying, "This is my Son, whom I love; with him I am well pleased."[a] [18]We ourselves heard this voice that came from heaven when we were with him on the sacred mountain.

[19]And we have the word of the prophets made more certain, and you will do well to pay attention to it, as to a light shining in a dark place, until the day dawns and the morning star rises in your hearts. [20]Above all, you must understand that no prophecy of Scripture came about by the prophet's own interpretation. [21]For prophecy never had its origin in the will of man, but men spoke from God as they were carried along by the Holy Spirit.

False Teachers and Their Destruction

2 But there were also false prophets among the people, just as there will be false teachers among you. They will secretly introduce destructive heresies, even denying the sovereign Lord who bought them—bringing swift destruction on themselves. [2]Many will follow their shameful ways and will bring the way of truth into disrepute. [3]In their greed these teachers will exploit you with stories they have made up. Their condemnation has long been hanging over them, and their destruction has not been sleeping.

[4]For if God did not spare angels when they sinned, but sent them to hell,[b] putting them into gloomy dungeons[c] to be held for judgment; [5]if he did not spare the ancient world when he brought the flood

[a]17 Matt. 17:5; Mark 9:7; Luke 9:35   [b]4 Greek *Tartarus*   [c]4 Some manuscripts *into chains of darkness*

HEY DAD
How did the people who wrote the Bible know what to write?

Text: 2 Peter 1:20–21

Good question. Did the Bible's writers have a heavenly dictation machine? Did they close their eyes and let God move the pen? Well, nothing indicates that it worked that way. The Bible says that the Holy Spirit "inspired" the writers or "carried them along." He guided the writers by giving them wisdom and a message, but they expressed it in their own words.

Each portion of the Bible reveals something about the person who wrote it. David, for example, wrote the Psalms in a very vulnerable and passionate way. We know he was sensitive and open hearted by the words he chose. Paul's letters are very forthright and calculated. From this we know that Paul was a logical thinker, one who knew how to argue, explain and persuade. God can—and does—use different kinds of people to do his will!

Though the Bible is complete, the Holy Spirit continues to enlighten us in much the same way. He teaches each of us in a way that makes sense to us. As we follow God and listen carefully to his voice, we begin to discover God's plan for our own lives.

QUESTIONS KIDS ASK

For a complete listing of Questions Kids Ask, turn to page 1435.

on its ungodly people, but protected Noah, a preacher of righteousness, and seven others; ⁶if he condemned the cities of Sodom and Gomorrah by burning them to ashes, and made them an example of what is going to happen to the ungodly; ⁷and if he rescued Lot, a righteous man, who was distressed by the filthy lives of lawless men ⁸(for that righteous man, living among them day after day, was tormented in his righteous soul by the lawless deeds he saw and heard)— ⁹if this is so, then the Lord knows how to rescue godly men from trials and to hold the unrighteous for the day of judgment, while continuing their punishment.ᵃ ¹⁰This is especially true of those who follow the corrupt desire of the sinful natureᵇ and despise authority.

Bold and arrogant, these men are not afraid to slander celestial beings; ¹¹yet even angels, although they are stronger and more powerful, do not bring slanderous accusations against such beings in the presence of the Lord. ¹²But these men blaspheme in matters they do not understand. They are like brute beasts, creatures of instinct, born only to be caught and destroyed, and like beasts they too will perish.

¹³They will be paid back with harm for the harm they have done. Their idea of pleasure is to carouse in broad daylight. They are blots and blemishes, reveling in their pleasures while they feast with you.ᶜ ¹⁴With eyes full of adultery, they never stop sinning; they seduce the unstable; they are experts in greed—an accursed brood! ¹⁵They have left the straight way and wandered off to follow the way of Balaam son of Beor, who loved the wages of wickedness. ¹⁶But he was rebuked for his wrongdoing by a donkey—a beast without speech—who spoke with a man's voice and restrained the prophet's madness.

¹⁷These men are springs without water and mists driven by a storm. Blackest darkness is reserved for them. ¹⁸For they mouth empty, boastful words and, by appealing to the lustful desires of sinful human nature, they entice people who are just escaping from those who live in error. ¹⁹They promise them freedom, while they themselves are slaves of depravity—for a man is a slave to whatever has mastered him. ²⁰If they have escaped the corruption of the world by knowing our Lord and Savior Jesus Christ and are again entangled in it and overcome, they are worse off at the end than they were at the beginning. ²¹It would have been better for them not to have known the way of righteousness, than to have known it and then to turn their backs on the sacred command that was passed on to them. ²²Of them the proverbs are true: "A dog returns to its vomit,"ᵈ and, "A sow that is washed goes back to her wallowing in the mud."

The Day of the Lord

3 Dear friends, this is now my second letter to you. I have written both of them as reminders to stimulate you to wholesome thinking. ²I want you to recall the words spoken in the past by the holy prophets and the command given by our Lord and Savior through your apostles.

³First of all, you must understand that in the last days scoffers will come, scoffing and following their own evil desires. ⁴They will say, "Where is this 'coming' he promised? Ever since our fathers died, everything goes on as it has since the beginning of creation." ⁵But they deliberately forget that long ago by God's word the heavens existed and the earth was formed out of water and by water. ⁶By these waters also the world of that time was deluged and destroyed. ⁷By the same word the present heavens and earth are reserved for fire, being kept for the day of judgment and destruction of ungodly men.

⁸But do not forget this one thing, dear friends: With the Lord a day is like a thousand years, and a thousand years are like a day. ⁹The Lord is not slow in keeping his promise, as some understand slowness. He is patient with you, not wanting anyone to perish, but everyone to come to repentance.

¹⁰But the day of the Lord will come like a thief. The heavens will disappear with a roar; the elements will be destroyed by fire, and the earth and everything in it will be laid bare.ᵉ ¹¹Since everything will be destroyed in this way, what kind of people ought you to be? You ought to live holy and godly lives ¹²as you look forward to the day of God and speed its coming.ᶠ That day will bring about the destruction of the heavens by fire, and the elements will melt in the

---

ᵃ9 Or *unrighteous for punishment until the day of judgment*   ᵇ10 Or *the flesh*   ᶜ13 Some manuscripts *in their love feasts*   ᵈ22 Prov. 26:11   ᵉ10 Some manuscripts *be burned up*   ᶠ12 Or *as you wait eagerly for the day of God to come*

heat. [13]But in keeping with his promise we are looking forward to a new heaven and a new earth, the home of righteousness.

[14]So then, dear friends, since you are looking forward to this, make every effort to be found spotless, blameless and at peace with him. [15]Bear in mind that our Lord's patience means salvation, just as our dear brother Paul also wrote you with the wisdom that God gave him. [16]He writes the same way in all his letters, speaking in them of these matters. His let-ters contain some things that are hard to understand, which ignorant and unstable people distort, as they do the other Scrip-tures, to their own destruction.

[17]Therefore, dear friends, since you al-ready know this, be on your guard so that you may not be carried away by the error of lawless men and fall from your secure position. [18]But grow in the grace and knowledge of our Lord and Savior Jesus Christ. To him be glory both now and for-ever! Amen.

Don't Force It

DAILY INSIGHT

THURSDAY

Passage:
2 Peter 3:8–9

Verse:
2 Peter 3:9

I had carefully spread all the pieces to my P-51 Mustang out on the newspaper. The instruc-tions were right in front of me, and I was meticulously putting each piece of this model togeth-er in the proper order. But, for some reason, two pieces weren't fitting together properly. I double-checked the instructions. I was sure these were the right parts; why wouldn't they fit?

At that moment, my dad walked through the kitchen and saw me straining to get these two plastic pieces to fit. He stopped to watch as the veins in my neck bulged and my eyes nearly popped out of their sockets. "Hey, Son, don't force it," my dad said calmly. "If it doesn't fit, don't force it." Then this wise man turned and walked away, never realiz-ing the profound influence these words would have on nearly every dimension of my life since.

I am a hard-driving, entrepreneurial, task-oriented, and focused man. I have made a life of taking on more responsibility than I've had time to fulfill, saying "yes" when I should have said "no," and feeling guilty because I didn't sign up for every-thing. I have lived on the fast-track, hustling when I lacked skill and talking when I had nothing to say. I have prided myself at being a perfectionist, and I wake up every morning on time without an alarm clock.

I needed to hear my dad's prophetic words when I was building that plastic model on the kitchen table, and I need to hear them now. "Hey, Son, don't force it. If it doesn't fit, don't force it."

Did you know that God is not in a hurry? He knows exact-ly who he is and what he's doing. He has not written checks he cannot cash. Frenzy and chaos are not his compan-ions. Peter tells us that he is patient with us, and that he keeps his promises (v. 9).

This concept runs counter to my chemistry. "Think of how I can help God if I'm living at high speed," I rationalize. "After all, isn't God better served by industrious husbands and dads who race through life with the accelerator glued to the floorboard?"

No, actually, he isn't. God isn't frantically looking for volunteers to do his work. He's not wringing his hands, hoping I do what he cannot do without me. My task as his disciple is a fairly simple one: "Make every effort to be found spotless, blameless and at peace with him" (v. 14). I need to stop racing and take time to rest.

I know you've got lots to do. So do I. But look at us—the veins in our necks are bulging and our eyes are bugging out. Slow down. God is better served by a man who isn't moving so fast that he can't afford the time to rest and listen. "Hey, Son," our precious and patient heavenly Father is saying to us. "Don't force it."

For your next devotional reading, go to page 1399.

set our hearts at rest in his presence [20]whenever our hearts condemn us. For God is greater than our hearts, and he knows everything. [21]Dear friends, if our hearts do not condemn us, we have confidence before God [22]and receive from him anything we ask, because we obey his commands and do what pleases him. [23]And this is his command: to believe in the name of his Son, Jesus Christ, and to love one another as he commanded us. [24]Those who obey his commands live in him, and he in them. And this is how we know that he lives in us: We know it by the Spirit he gave us.

Test the Spirits

[4] Dear friends, do not believe every spirit, but test the spirits to see whether they are from God, because many false prophets have gone out into the world. [2]This is how you can recognize the Spirit of God: Every spirit that acknowledges that Jesus Christ has come in the flesh is from God, [3]but every spirit that does not acknowledge Jesus is not from God. This is the spirit of the antichrist, which you have heard is coming and even now is already in the world. [4]You, dear children, are from God and have overcome them, because the one who is in you is greater than the one who is in the world. [5]They are from the world and therefore speak from the viewpoint of the world, and the world listens to them. [6]We are from God, and whoever knows God listens to us; but whoever is not from God does not listen to us. This is how we recognize the Spirit[a] of truth and the spirit of falsehood.

God's Love and Ours

[7]Dear friends, let us love one another, for love comes from God. Everyone who loves has been born of God and knows God. [8]Whoever does not love does not know God, because God is love. [9]This is how God showed his love among us: He sent his one and only Son[b] into the world that we might live through him. [10]This is love: not that we loved God, but that he loved us and sent his Son as an atoning sacrifice for[c] our sins. [11]Dear friends, since God so loved us, we also ought to love one another. [12]No one has ever seen God; but if we love one another, God lives in us and his love is made complete in us.

[13]We know that we live in him and he in us, because he has given us of his Spirit.

[14]And we have seen and testify that the Father has sent his Son to be the Savior of the world. [15]If anyone acknowledges that Jesus is the Son of God, God lives in him and he in God. [16]And so we know and rely on the love God has for us.

God is love. Whoever lives in love lives in God, and God in him. [17]In this way, love is made complete among us so that we will have confidence on the day of judgment, because in this world we are like him. [18]There is no fear in love. But perfect love drives out fear, because fear has to do with punishment. The one who fears is not made perfect in love.

[19]We love because he first loved us. [20]If anyone says, "I love God," yet hates his brother, he is a liar. For anyone who does not love his brother, whom he has seen, cannot love God, whom he has not seen. [21]And he has given us this command: Whoever loves God must also love his brother.

Faith in the Son of God

[5] Everyone who believes that Jesus is the Christ is born of God, and everyone who loves the father loves his child as well. [2]This is how we know that we love the children of God: by loving God and carrying out his commands. [3]This is love for God: to obey his commands. And his commands are not burdensome, [4]for everyone born of God overcomes the world. This is the victory that has overcome the world, even our faith. [5]Who is it that overcomes the world? Only he who believes that Jesus is the Son of God.

[6]This is the one who came by water and blood—Jesus Christ. He did not come by water only, but by water and blood. And it is the Spirit who testifies, because the Spirit is the truth. [7]For there are three that testify: [8]the[d] Spirit, the water and the blood; and the three are in agreement. [9]We accept man's testimony, but God's testimony is greater because it is the testimony of God, which he has given about his Son. [10]Anyone who believes in the Son of God has this testimony in his heart. Anyone who does not believe God has made him out to be a liar, because he has

[a]6 Or *spirit* [b]9 Or *his only begotten Son* [c]10 Or *as the one who would turn aside his wrath, taking away* [d]7,8 Late manuscripts of the Vulgate *testify in heaven: the Father, the Word and the Holy Spirit, and these three are one. 8And there are three that testify on earth: the* (not found in any Greek manuscript before the sixteenth century)

not believed the testimony God has given about his Son. [11]And this is the testimony: God has given us eternal life, and this life is in his Son. [12]He who has the Son has life; he who does not have the Son of God does not have life.

Concluding Remarks

[13]I write these things to you who believe in the name of the Son of God so that you may know that you have eternal life. [14]This is the confidence we have in approaching God: that if we ask anything according to his will, he hears us. [15]And if we know that he hears us—whatever we ask—we know that we have what we asked of him.

[16]If anyone sees his brother commit a sin that does not lead to death, he should pray and God will give him life. I refer to those whose sin does not lead to death. There is a sin that leads to death. I am not saying that he should pray about that. [17]All wrongdoing is sin, and there is sin that does not lead to death.

[18]We know that anyone born of God does not continue to sin; the one who was born of God keeps him safe, and the evil one cannot harm him. [19]We know that we are children of God, and that the whole world is under the control of the evil one. [20]We know also that the Son of God has come and has given us understanding, so that we may know him who is true. And we are in him who is true—even in his Son Jesus Christ. He is the true God and eternal life.

[21]Dear children, keep yourselves from idols.

does what is evil has not seen God. [12]Demetrius is well spoken of by everyone—and even by the truth itself. We also speak well of him, and you know that our testimony is true.

[13]I have much to write you, but I do not want to do so with pen and ink. [14]I hope to see you soon, and we will talk face to face.

Peace to you. The friends here send their greetings. Greet the friends there by name.

Your Vegetable Garden's Water Boy

DAILY INSIGHT

TUESDAY

Passage:
3 John 2–4

Verse:
3 John 4

In the early seventies, the company I was working for moved into a new office building. Because ours was the first new building in the development, and because we had quite a bit of open space around us, some of us asked the developer if we could use that empty land to plant our own vegetable gardens.

He saw no problem with this; however, he warned us that if the land should sell before harvest time, we'd have to understand. Bean plants don't hold up very well under a bulldozer's scoop.

I took advantage of this opportunity right away. It was great. I rented a tiller, got the dirt all nice and loose, and bought seeds. I watched with pride as the shoots emerged a few weeks later, and as the shoots bloomed into leaves. Having my own vegetable garden was so much fun.

But it wasn't easy. This garden was a few hundred yards away from any water source, and I had to take the water to my growing and thirsty plants by hand. And as the hot summer wore on, my plants didn't look as good as they had in the spring.

Imagine if, in the face of this disappointing foliage, I had walked out to my garden and said, "You're a disgrace. Just look at you. You're getting all ugly and brown. Some of your leaves are wilting. Some of them are completely falling off. A few of you almost look dead. You ought to be ashamed." What a ridiculous monologue that would have been. How could I accuse my plants of drying out if I hadn't done my part to carry the water out to them?

You probably know where I'm going with this one, don't you?

A dad is accountable, even on a hot July day after he's put in a full day of work, to care for and nurture his family. As a parent, he's responsible to help "carry the water"—physically, emotionally and spiritually—and to be available for his kids, his tender plants. Sometimes a dad surveys his family and says, "Just look at you. You're out of control. You're an embarrassment to me. Why don't you just shape up?" But a dad who stands in judgment without having first done his part has no basis for criticism.

John knew about the importance of cultivation and nurture. Speaking to believers who were under his spiritual guidance, he said, "I have no greater joy than to hear that my children are walking in the truth." That's quite a statement. Why is having faithful children such a great joy? Because it's such hard work. As my dad used to say, "Nothing worthwhile comes easily."

You and your wife decided to plant this "vegetable garden," and your plants need water. Yes, you may have to walk a few hundred yards in the hot sun to quench their thirst, but there's no way you're going to let anyone bulldoze your beans. Get ready to work hard, holding firm to the promise of a productive harvest.

For your next devotional reading, go to page 1410.

Imagine that you're a kid again, sitting around the dinner table with your family. Right after your big brother takes a mouthful of potatoes, he holds his spoon high, flips up the bill of his baseball cap, and announces to your family that he is the Grand Poobah of the household. You laugh. You think the poor boy is delusional. You suggest that he seek medical help.

For Jude, this was no joke. His brother, Jesus Christ, was the longed-for Messiah, the Creator of the universe, the very Son of the Living God. And, just as we would have done if our sibling had made such an outrageous claim, "even [Jesus'] own brothers did not believe in him" (John 7:5). But, either during Jesus' ministry or after his ascension, Jude eventually got on board: "They all joined together constantly in prayer . . . with his brothers" (Acts 1:14).

So enthusiastic was Jude's support of his big Brother that he wrote this short letter, warning Christians that "certain men . . . have secretly slipped in among you" to corrupt the pure teaching of the Gospel (v. 4). Jude was Jesus' kid brother, so we don't have to wonder how Jude was so adept at spotting cynics and unbelievers, do we?

Jude

¹Jude, a servant of Jesus Christ and a brother of James,

To those who have been called, who are loved by God the Father and kept by[a] Jesus Christ:

²Mercy, peace and love be yours in abundance.

The Sin and Doom of Godless Men

³Dear friends, although I was very eager to write to you about the salvation we share, I felt I had to write and urge you to contend for the faith that was once for all entrusted to the saints. ⁴For certain men whose condemnation was written about[b] long ago have secretly slipped in among you. They are godless men, who change the grace of our God into a license for immorality and deny Jesus Christ our only Sovereign and Lord.

⁵Though you already know all this, I want to remind you that the Lord[c] delivered his people out of Egypt, but later destroyed those who did not believe. ⁶And

---

*a*1 Or *for*; or *in*   *b*4 Or *men who were marked out for condemnation*   *c*5 Some early manuscripts *Jesus*

Every spring, high school auditoriums and college stadiums around the world hold ceremonies to honor young men and women who have successfully completed their course work. Most of these graduates don robes and funny little square hats with tassels to receive their diplomas, verifying this significant accomplishment. Incredibly, this finishing observance is called *commencement*, which means "initiation" or "beginning." These ceremonies signal not so much the end of one era as the beginning of another. The graduates are starting a new life.

Because it comes at the end of the Bible, some consider the book of Revelation to be the finish line—the end of the story. We know better, don't we? Our lives on this earth are just the course work. We've only spent a few years sitting in the library, listening to lectures and enduring the tests. But Revelation is our commencement. We're getting ready to live forever.

Live today in the light of that eternal perspective.

Revelation

Prologue

1 The revelation of Jesus Christ, which God gave him to show his servants what must soon take place. He made it known by sending his angel to his servant John, **2** who testifies to everything he saw—that is, the word of God and the testimony of Jesus Christ. **3** Blessed is the one who reads the words of this prophecy, and blessed are those who hear it and take to heart what is written in it, because the time is near.

Greetings and Doxology

4 John,

To the seven churches in the province of Asia:

Grace and peace to you from him who is, and who was, and who is to come, and from the seven spirits*a* before his throne, **5** and from Jesus Christ, who is the faithful witness, the firstborn from the dead, and the ruler of the kings of the earth.

To him who loves us and has freed us from our sins by his blood, **6** and has made us to be a kingdom and priests to serve his God and Father—to him be glory and power for ever and ever! Amen.

7 Look, he is coming with the clouds,
    and every eye will see him,
    even those who pierced him;

a4 Or the sevenfold Spirit

and all the peoples of the earth will mourn because of him.
So shall it be! Amen.

[8]"I am the Alpha and the Omega," says the Lord God, "who is, and who was, and who is to come, the Almighty."

One Like a Son of Man

[9]I, John, your brother and companion in the suffering and kingdom and patient endurance that are ours in Jesus, was on the island of Patmos because of the word of God and the testimony of Jesus. [10]On the Lord's Day I was in the Spirit, and I heard behind me a loud voice like a trumpet, [11]which said: "Write on a scroll what you see and send it to the seven churches: to Ephesus, Smyrna, Pergamum, Thyatira, Sardis, Philadelphia and Laodicea."

[12]I turned around to see the voice that was speaking to me. And when I turned I saw seven golden lampstands, [13]and among the lampstands was someone "like a son of man,"[a] dressed in a robe reaching down to his feet and with a golden sash around his chest. [14]His head and hair were white like wool, as white as snow, and his eyes were like blazing fire. [15]His feet were like bronze glowing in a furnace, and his voice was like the sound of rushing waters. [16]In his right hand he held seven stars, and out of his mouth came a sharp double-edged sword. His face was like the sun shining in all its brilliance.

[17]When I saw him, I fell at his feet as though dead. Then he placed his right hand on me and said: "Do not be afraid. I am the First and the Last. [18]I am the Living One; I was dead, and behold I am alive for ever and ever! And I hold the keys of death and Hades.

[19]"Write, therefore, what you have seen, what is now and what will take place later. [20]The mystery of the seven stars that you saw in my right hand and of the seven golden lampstands is this: The seven stars are the angels[b] of the seven churches, and the seven lampstands are the seven churches.

To the Church in Ephesus

2 "To the angel[c] of the church in Ephesus write:

These are the words of him who holds the seven stars in his right hand and walks among the seven golden lampstands: [2]I know your deeds, your hard work and your perseverance. I know that you cannot tolerate wicked men, that you have tested those who claim to be apostles but are not, and have found them false. [3]You have persevered and have endured hardships for my name, and have not grown weary.

[4]Yet I hold this against you: You have forsaken your first love. [5]Remember the height from which you have fallen! Repent and do the things you did at first. If you do not repent, I will come to you and remove your lampstand from its place. [6]But you have this in your favor: You hate the practices of the Nicolaitans, which I also hate.

[a]13 Daniel 7:13   [b]20 Or messengers   [c]1 Or messenger; also in verses 8, 12 and 18

HEY DAD
Why is church on Sunday?

Text: Revelation 1:10

Believers in the early church named Sunday the "Lord's Day." Some of the very people who had walked and talked with Jesus gathered together on Sundays to worship him—much like we do today.

The Lord's Day is different from the Sabbath, the Jewish day of rest. The Sabbath, which is observed on Saturday, commemorates the day that God rested after he created the universe. The Lord's Day commemorates Christ's resurrection.

We can worship God on any—and every—day of the week, but Christians set Sundays apart to rejoice because that's when Jesus had risen from the dead. What better reason is there to celebrate?

For a complete listing of Questions Kids Ask, turn to page 1435.

[7]He who has an ear, let him hear what the Spirit says to the churches. To him who overcomes, I will give the right to eat from the tree of life, which is in the paradise of God.

To the Church in Smyrna

[8]"To the angel of the church in Smyrna write:

These are the words of him who is the First and the Last, who died and came to life again. [9]I know your afflictions and your poverty—yet you are rich! I know the slander of those who say they are Jews and are not, but are a synagogue of Satan. [10]Do not be afraid of what you are about to suffer. I tell you, the devil will put some of you in prison to test you, and you will suffer persecution for ten days. Be faithful, even to the point of

Thank You, Sweet Alice

One particular Sunday morning, a day that I will never forget, our Sunday school class sang our opening chorus, "This is the Day that the Lord has Made." As I scanned the class that day, I saw my friend Alice Rogers. For many years—probably eight or nine—my friend Alice Rogers, now eighty-seven years old, had been my unofficial helper.

To make finding Scripture references easier, our class had purchased identical Bibles a few years before. Since I didn't have one of these at home, I'd had to scramble to find the page numbers before each class. Had to, that is, until I realized that Alice did this before every class session as well. Since she always sat in the same seat in the second row, I developed a habit of checking her Bible for the page numbers of the day's passages.

On this day, in typical fashion, I looked at Alice and smiled. She handed her Bible to me, returning my smile. After I got the page numbers, I said, "Thank you, sweet Alice."

We were cutting through a seven-part series on the basics of our faith. This Sunday was session number four: "Jesus Christ Is God." I dove into the lesson. "Jesus is perfect," I said, giving several Scriptural references to underscore this truth. "Jesus is the Creator of the universe," I continued, again following this up with a few confirming verses from our Bibles.

I closed the lesson with my final point, "Jesus Christ is glorified." I read from Mark 9, where Jesus took three of his disciples to a high mountain and showed them

DAILY INSIGHT

THURSDAY

Passage:
Revelation 1:12–18

Verse:
Revelation 1:17

his glorified body. Then I took the class to the detailed account of the transfigured Savior we have recorded here in Revelation, chapter one. "When we see Jesus," I concluded, "we will not see a sandal-clad, middle-eastern peasant carpenter. We will fall on our faces at the sight of this exalted Lord."

Class was dismissed with a prayer, and everyone who hadn't attended the early worship service, including Alice Rogers, headed toward the sanctuary. She sat in her favorite second-row spot— just as she did in Sunday school. Then, during the organ prelude, Alice gently laid her head on her daughter's shoulder and fell asleep.

In less than ten minutes, Alice Rogers was in the presence of her magnificent Savior.

How could any of us have known that this precious woman, who had only moments before been listening to a description of her glorified Lord, was soon to be ushered into his incredible presence? "We were just talking about you," she may have said, her voice trembling with wonder.

Had I known, I would have surely stopped Alice Rogers on her way to the sanctuary. "Please say 'hello' to Jesus for me," I'd have asked her. "Tell him 'thank you' for being so glorious. Oh, and tell him 'thank you' for loving me."

"I'll see you again soon," I would have said with a hug. "Thank you, sweet Alice."

For your next devotional reading, go to page 1416.

death, and I will give you the crown of life.

¹¹He who has an ear, let him hear what the Spirit says to the churches. He who overcomes will not be hurt at all by the second death.

To the Church in Pergamum

¹²"To the angel of the church in Pergamum write:

These are the words of him who has the sharp, double-edged sword. ¹³I know where you live—where Satan has his throne. Yet you remain true to my name. You did not renounce your faith in me, even in the days of Antipas, my faithful witness, who was put to death in your city—where Satan lives.

¹⁴Nevertheless, I have a few things against you: You have people there who hold to the teaching of Balaam, who taught Balak to entice the Israelites to sin by eating food sacrificed to idols and by committing sexual immorality. ¹⁵Likewise you also have those who hold to the teaching of the Nicolaitans. ¹⁶Repent therefore! Otherwise, I will soon come to you and will fight against them with the sword of my mouth.

¹⁷He who has an ear, let him hear what the Spirit says to the churches. To him who overcomes, I will give some of the hidden manna. I will also give him a white stone with a new name written on it, known only to him who receives it.

To the Church in Thyatira

¹⁸"To the angel of the church in Thyatira write:

These are the words of the Son of God, whose eyes are like blazing fire and whose feet are like burnished bronze. ¹⁹I know your deeds, your love and faith, your service and perseverance, and that you are now doing more than you did at first.

²⁰Nevertheless, I have this against you: You tolerate that woman Jezebel, who calls herself a prophetess. By her teaching she misleads my servants into sexual immorality and the eating of food sacrificed to idols. ²¹I have given her time to repent of her immorality, but she is unwilling. ²²So I will cast her on a bed of suffering,

and I will make those who commit adultery with her suffer intensely, unless they repent of her ways. ²³I will strike her children dead. Then all the churches will know that I am he who searches hearts and minds, and I will repay each of you according to your deeds. ²⁴Now I say to the rest of you in Thyatira, to you who do not hold to her teaching and have not learned Satan's so-called deep secrets (I will not impose any other burden on you): ²⁵Only hold on to what you have until I come.

²⁶To him who overcomes and does my will to the end, I will give authority over the nations—

²⁷'He will rule them with an iron
    scepter;
  he will dash them to pieces like
    pottery'ᵃ—

just as I have received authority from my Father. ²⁸I will also give him the morning star. ²⁹He who has an ear, let him hear what the Spirit says to the churches.

To the Church in Sardis

3 "To the angel*ᵇ* of the church in Sardis write:

These are the words of him who holds the seven spiritsᶜ of God and the seven stars. I know your deeds; you have a reputation of being alive, but you are dead. ²Wake up! Strengthen what remains and is about to die, for I have not found your deeds complete in the sight of my God. ³Remember, therefore, what you have received and heard; obey it, and repent. But if you do not wake up, I will come like a thief, and you will not know at what time I will come to you.

⁴Yet you have a few people in Sardis who have not soiled their clothes. They will walk with me, dressed in white, for they are worthy. ⁵He who overcomes will, like them, be dressed in white. I will never blot out his name from the book of life, but will acknowledge his name before my Father and his angels. ⁶He who has an ear, let him hear what the Spirit says to the churches.

ᵃ27 Psalm 2:9 ᵇ1 Or *messenger*; also in verses 7 and 14 ᶜ1 Or *the sevenfold Spirit*

To the Church in Philadelphia

7 "To the angel of the church in Philadelphia write:

These are the words of him who is holy and true, who holds the key of David. What he opens no one can shut, and what he shuts no one can open. 8 I know your deeds. See, I have placed before you an open door that no one can shut. I know that you have little strength, yet you have kept my word and have not denied my name. 9 I will make those who are of the synagogue of Satan, who claim to be Jews though they are not, but are liars—I will make them come and fall down at your feet and acknowledge that I have loved you. 10 Since you have kept my command to endure patiently, I will also keep you from the hour of trial that is going to come

My Dad's Special Kind of Love

"This hurts me more than it hurts you."

Help me understand the logic of this, I used to wonder as my dad's strong hand made its way to my tender rear end. *This hurts you more than it hurts me? I don't think so.*

This was the most important of all the things I promised I would never say to my own children. And I truly don't recall ever saying those words to my children. But the older I've gotten, the smarter my dad has become, and I have come to learn exactly what he meant by this phrase.

When it comes to distributing consistent discipline, every dad faces a difficult and, at times, painful challenge. Why? Because most of us cherish peace and quiet, especially in our homes. We'd rather look the other way when our children step out of line, hoping that, on their own, they'll eventually figure out what they did wrong and how they should go about fixing it.

I will be eternally thankful that my dad never adhered to this philosophy. This Pennsylvania farmer, turned preacher, turned missionary, turned corporate executive was unequivocally tough on me. There were times when my dad knew how unhappy I was with him. He knew that I would be far more likely to celebrate his fathering techniques if he'd back off.

But my dad was relentless. Whether I slacked off on a chore, told a lie, or dishonored another person, he jumped on me like a crow on a June bug. It was as though he was saying, "Taking short cuts might be

DAILY INSIGHT

FRIDAY

Passage:
Revelation 3:19–22

Verse:
Revelation 3:19

acceptable for other boys, but you, Robert, aren't 'other boys.' You're my boy, and I'll not let you get away with this."

Now that I'm many years older than my dad was when he disciplined me, I can clearly see this discipline for what it was. Now, grateful as I am for every single moment of his correction, I can say the words: My dad loved me.

"Those whom I love I rebuke and discipline" (3:19). My dad's punishments and strict demands on me must have been painful. Although he did many kind things for me, those times must have seemed to him overshadowed by the difficult times. And, frankly, he was right. Going to a ball game with my dad was great fun, but his discipline made all the happiness vanish from my face. He knew this, but he didn't seem to mind the pain. My dad knew that he was the only dad I'd ever have. He was willing to pay the price to be the best dad I could have needed. Now, old and wise as I am, I know why he never slacked off. He loved me too much.

Oh, and there's one more thing. Again, this didn't mean that much to me as a young, strong-willed boy, but every morning of my life, until I left for college, I woke and heard the barely audible sound of my dad praying in our dark basement. I know that some of these prayers were for me.

Thanks, Dad. I will be forever grateful for your love … your special kind of love.

For your next devotional reading, go to page 1420.

upon the whole world to test those who live on the earth. [11]I am coming soon. Hold on to what you have, so that no one will take your crown. [12]Him who overcomes I will make a pillar in the temple of my God. Never again will he leave it. I will write on him the name of my God and the name of the city of my God, the new Jerusalem, which is coming down out of heaven from my God; and I will also write on him my new name. [13]He who has an ear, let him hear what the Spirit says to the churches.

To the Church in Laodicea

[14]"To the angel of the church in Laodicea write:

These are the words of the Amen, the faithful and true witness, the ruler of God's creation. [15]I know your deeds, that you are neither cold nor hot. I wish you were either one or the other! [16]So, because you are lukewarm—neither hot nor cold—I am about to spit you out of my mouth. [17]You say, 'I am rich; I have acquired wealth and do not need a thing.' But you do not realize that you are wretched, pitiful, poor, blind and naked. [18]I counsel you to buy from me gold refined in the fire, so you can become rich; and white clothes to wear, so you can cover your shameful nakedness; and salve to put on your eyes, so you can see.

[19]Those whom I love I rebuke and discipline. So be earnest, and repent. [20]Here I am! I stand at the door and knock. If anyone hears my voice and opens the door, I will come in and eat with him, and he with me.

[21]To him who overcomes, I will give the right to sit with me on my throne, just as I overcame and sat down with my Father on his throne. [22]He who has an ear, let him hear what the Spirit says to the churches."

The Throne in Heaven

4 After this I looked, and there before me was a door standing open in heaven. And the voice I had first heard speaking to me like a trumpet said, "Come up here, and I will show you what must take place after this." [2]At once I was in the Spirit, and there before me was a throne in heaven with someone sitting on it. [3]And the one who sat there had the appearance of jasper and carnelian. A rainbow, resembling an emerald, encircled the throne. [4]Surrounding the throne were twenty-four other thrones, and seated on them were twenty-four elders. They were dressed in white and had crowns of gold on their heads. [5]From the throne came flashes of lightning, rumblings and peals of thunder. Before the throne, seven lamps were blazing. These are the seven spirits[a] of God. [6]Also before the throne there was

[a]5 Or *the sevenfold Spirit*

What time is it in heaven?

Text: Revelation 4:1–11

Heaven, God's home, does not have a time zone, because God is eternal. That means that right now, while you and I are in the present, God is also in every moment that has ever been and that ever will be!

Think about it another way. Right now, you and I are taking up one tiny space on the earth. We cannot be every place in the world at the same time. We're not big enough! But the sky touches every single spot in the world at the very same time. The sky encompasses the earth; it wraps all the way around it.

That is the way God encompasses time. And he has "set eternity in [our] hearts" (Ecclesiastes 3:11). One day, when we go to heaven, we will know how it feels to live in eternity with God. This sounds exciting, doesn't it?

Don't worry about bringing a watch to heaven. You won't need it.

For a complete listing of Questions Kids Ask, turn to page 1435.

what looked like a sea of glass, clear as crystal.

In the center, around the throne, were four living creatures, and they were covered with eyes, in front and in back. [7]The first living creature was like a lion, the second was like an ox, the third had a face like a man, the fourth was like a flying eagle. [8]Each of the four living creatures had six wings and was covered with eyes all around, even under his wings. Day and night they never stop saying:

"Holy, holy, holy
is the Lord God Almighty,
who was, and is, and is to come."

[9]Whenever the living creatures give glory, honor and thanks to him who sits on the throne and who lives for ever and ever, [10]the twenty-four elders fall down before him who sits on the throne, and worship him who lives for ever and ever. They lay their crowns before the throne and say:

[11]"You are worthy, our Lord and God,
    to receive glory and honor and
        power,
    for you created all things,
        and by your will they were created
        and have their being."

The Scroll and the Lamb

5 Then I saw in the right hand of him who sat on the throne a scroll with writing on both sides and sealed with seven seals. [2]And I saw a mighty angel proclaiming in a loud voice, "Who is worthy to break the seals and open the scroll?" [3]But no one in heaven or on earth or under the earth could open the scroll or even look inside it. [4]I wept and wept because no one was found who was worthy to open the scroll or look inside. [5]Then one of the elders said to me, "Do not weep! See, the Lion of the tribe of Judah, the Root of David, has triumphed. He is able to open the scroll and its seven seals."

[6]Then I saw a Lamb, looking as if it had been slain, standing in the center of the throne, encircled by the four living creatures and the elders. He had seven horns and seven eyes, which are the seven spirits[a] of God sent out into all the earth. [7]He came and took the scroll from the right hand of him who sat on the throne. [8]And when he had taken it, the four living creatures and the twenty-four elders fell down before the Lamb. Each one had a harp and they were holding golden bowls full of incense, which are the prayers of the saints. [9]And they sang a new song:

"You are worthy to take the scroll
    and to open its seals,
because you were slain,
    and with your blood you purchased
        men for God
    from every tribe and language and
        people and nation.
[10]You have made them to be a kingdom
        and priests to serve our God,
    and they will reign on the earth."

[11]Then I looked and heard the voice of many angels, numbering thousands upon thousands, and ten thousand times ten thousand. They encircled the throne and the living creatures and the elders. [12]In a loud voice they sang:

"Worthy is the Lamb, who was slain,
to receive power and wealth and
        wisdom and strength
and honor and glory and praise!"

[13]Then I heard every creature in heaven and on earth and under the earth and on the sea, and all that is in them, singing:

"To him who sits on the throne and to
        the Lamb
be praise and honor and glory and
        power,
            for ever and ever!"

[14]The four living creatures said, "Amen," and the elders fell down and worshiped.

The Seals

6 I watched as the Lamb opened the first of the seven seals. Then I heard one of the four living creatures say in a voice like thunder, "Come!" [2]I looked, and there before me was a white horse! Its rider held a bow, and he was given a crown, and he rode out as a conqueror bent on conquest.

[3]When the Lamb opened the second seal, I heard the second living creature say, "Come!" [4]Then another horse came out, a fiery red one. Its rider was given power to take peace from the earth and to make men slay each other. To him was given a large sword.

[5]When the Lamb opened the third seal, I heard the third living creature say, "Come!" I looked, and there before me was a black horse! Its rider was holding a

a6 Or the sevenfold Spirit

pair of scales in his hand. **6**Then I heard what sounded like a voice among the four living creatures, saying, "A quart*a* of wheat for a day's wages,*b* and three quarts of barley for a day's wages,*b* and do not damage the oil and the wine!"

7When the Lamb opened the fourth seal, I heard the voice of the fourth living creature say, "Come!" **8**I looked, and there before me was a pale horse! Its rider was named Death, and Hades was following close behind him. They were given power over a fourth of the earth to kill by sword, famine and plague, and by the wild beasts of the earth.

9When he opened the fifth seal, I saw under the altar the souls of those who had been slain because of the word of God and the testimony they had maintained. **10**They called out in a loud voice, "How long, Sovereign Lord, holy and true, until you judge the inhabitants of the earth and avenge our blood?" **11**Then each of them was given a white robe, and they were told to wait a little longer, until the number of their fellow servants and brothers who were to be killed as they had been was completed.

12I watched as he opened the sixth seal. There was a great earthquake. The sun turned black like sackcloth made of goat hair, the whole moon turned blood red, **13**and the stars in the sky fell to earth, as late figs drop from a fig tree when shaken by a strong wind. **14**The sky receded like a scroll, rolling up, and every mountain and island was removed from its place.

15Then the kings of the earth, the princes, the generals, the rich, the mighty, and every slave and every free man hid in caves and among the rocks of the mountains. **16**They called to the mountains and the rocks, "Fall on us and hide us from the face of him who sits on the throne and from the wrath of the Lamb! **17**For the great day of their wrath has come, and who can stand?"

144,000 Sealed

7 After this I saw four angels standing at the four corners of the earth, holding back the four winds of the earth to prevent any wind from blowing on the land or on the sea or on any tree. **2**Then I saw another angel coming up from the east, having the seal of the living God. He called out in a loud voice to the four angels who had been given power to harm the land and the sea: **3**"Do not harm the land or the sea or the trees until we put a seal on the foreheads of the servants of our God." **4**Then I heard the number of those who were sealed: 144,000 from all the tribes of Israel.

5 From the tribe of Judah 12,000 were sealed,
  from the tribe of Reuben 12,000,
  from the tribe of Gad 12,000,
6 from the tribe of Asher 12,000,
  from the tribe of Naphtali 12,000,
  from the tribe of Manasseh 12,000,
7 from the tribe of Simeon 12,000,
  from the tribe of Levi 12,000,
  from the tribe of Issachar 12,000,
8 from the tribe of Zebulun 12,000,
  from the tribe of Joseph 12,000,
  from the tribe of Benjamin 12,000.

The Great Multitude in White Robes

9After this I looked and there before me was a great multitude that no one could count, from every nation, tribe, people and language, standing before the throne and in front of the Lamb. They were wearing white robes and were holding palm branches in their hands. **10**And they cried out in a loud voice:

  "Salvation belongs to our God,
  who sits on the throne,
  and to the Lamb."

11All the angels were standing around the throne and around the elders and the four living creatures. They fell down on their faces before the throne and worshiped God, **12**saying:

  "Amen!
  Praise and glory
  and wisdom and thanks and honor
  and power and strength
  be to our God for ever and ever.
  Amen!"

13Then one of the elders asked me, "These in white robes—who are they, and where did they come from?"

14I answered, "Sir, you know."

And he said, "These are they who have come out of the great tribulation; they have washed their robes and made them white in the blood of the Lamb. **15**Therefore,

  "they are before the throne of God
  and serve him day and night in his
    temple;

a6 Greek *a choinix* (probably about a liter)
b6 Greek *a denarius*

It's Going to Be an Awesome Thing

QUIET
TIMES
WITH **Dad**

DAD READS: What is the most awesome thing you have ever seen? Some people say that half-time at the Super Bowl is wonderful. I have heard that the opening and closing celebrations at the Olympics are spectacular, too. Someday I'd like to see the Fourth of July fireworks show in Washington.

Child reads: There are other awesome things to see in this world, too. The Grand Canyon, beautiful mountains, or a perfect sunset . . . these are wonderful things, too. Although these things are amazing, the passage we read for today tells us of an even more awesome celebration.

DAD READS: This celebration will be unlike any celebration anyone has ever seen. God's people will come from every land, and young and old, black and white, rich and poor, powerful and frail will see Jesus. Standing around him will be thousands of angels. It will be an absolutely glorious sight! You and I will be there, too.

Child reads: The Bible says that when we all see Jesus, we will fall down and put our faces on the ground. It will be so unbelievable and so amazing that we won't know what else to do.

DAD READS: Sometimes when we pray, we forget that we are actually speaking to this One whom we will someday see. We get so accustomed to talking to him that we forget that he is the God who made the heavens and the earth. He is the One who led the people in the Bible in all the stories we have read together. He is the

One who loved us so much that he was willing to die so that we could be forgiven of our sins. And when we see him, he will be so grand that we will not know what to do. He will be like no one we have ever seen before.

Child reads: I am so glad the God who made the sun, the moon, and the stars loves me enough to stop and talk with me. In fact, he calls me his very own child. This is so wonderful that it's hard to imagine.

DAD READS: But it's true. Someday you and I, our family, and all God's children will see Jesus. We will be standing with millions of people. We will sing and we will shout. It will be an awesome thing. I am looking forward to that day. You and I will really be with Jesus! Let me pray this prayer with you:

Our Father in heaven, we love you. Thank you for your greatness. Forgive us when we forget who you are. Heavenly Father, we look forward to the day when our family will see you. Thank you for forgiving our sin. Thank you for helping us to live for you. Now, please help us to be joyful because of that awesome day of celebration that is coming. We love you, and we thank you for your love. In Jesus' name, **Amen.**

For your next devotional reading go to page 3.

and he who sits on the throne will
    spread his tent over them.
[16] Never again will they hunger;
    never again will they thirst.
The sun will not beat upon them,
    nor any scorching heat.
[17] For the Lamb at the center of the
    throne will be their shepherd;
he will lead them to springs of living
    water.
And God will wipe away every tear
    from their eyes."

The Seventh Seal and the Golden Censer

8 When he opened the seventh seal,
there was silence in heaven for about
half an hour.
[2] And I saw the seven angels who stand
before God, and to them were given seven
trumpets.
[3] Another angel, who had a golden censer, came and stood at the altar. He was
given much incense to offer, with the
prayers of all the saints, on the golden
altar before the throne. [4] The smoke of
the incense, together with the prayers of
the saints, went up before God from the
angel's hand. [5] Then the angel took the
censer, filled it with fire from the altar,
and hurled it on the earth; and there came
peals of thunder, rumblings, flashes of
lightning and an earthquake.

The Trumpets

[6] Then the seven angels who had the
seven trumpets prepared to sound them.
[7] The first angel sounded his trumpet,
and there came hail and fire mixed with
blood, and it was hurled down upon the
earth. A third of the earth was burned up,
a third of the trees were burned up, and all
the green grass was burned up.
[8] The second angel sounded his trumpet, and something like a huge mountain,
all ablaze, was thrown into the sea. A third
of the sea turned into blood, [9] a third of the
living creatures in the sea died, and a
third of the ships were destroyed.
[10] The third angel sounded his trumpet,
and a great star, blazing like a torch, fell
from the sky on a third of the rivers and on
the springs of water— [11] the name of the
star is Wormwood.[a] A third of the waters
turned bitter, and many people died from
the waters that had become bitter.
[12] The fourth angel sounded his trumpet, and a third of the sun was struck, a
third of the moon, and a third of the stars,
so that a third of them turned dark. A third
of the day was without light, and also a
third of the night.

[13] As I watched, I heard an eagle that
was flying in midair call out in a loud
voice: "Woe! Woe! Woe to the inhabitants
of the earth, because of the trumpet blasts
about to be sounded by the other three
angels!"

9 The fifth angel sounded his trumpet,
and I saw a star that had fallen from
the sky to the earth. The star was given the
key to the shaft of the Abyss. [2] When he
opened the Abyss, smoke rose from it
like the smoke from a gigantic furnace.
The sun and sky were darkened by the
smoke from the Abyss. [3] And out of the
smoke locusts came down upon the earth
and were given power like that of scorpions of the earth. [4] They were told not to
harm the grass of the earth or any plant or
tree, but only those people who did not
have the seal of God on their foreheads.
[5] They were not given power to kill them,
but only to torture them for five months.
And the agony they suffered was like that
of the sting of a scorpion when it strikes a
man. [6] During those days men will seek
death, but will not find it; they will long to
die, but death will elude them.
[7] The locusts looked like horses prepared for battle. On their heads they wore
something like crowns of gold, and their
faces resembled human faces. [8] Their hair
was like women's hair, and their teeth
were like lions' teeth. [9] They had breastplates like breastplates of iron, and the
sound of their wings was like the thunder-
ing of many horses and chariots rushing
into battle. [10] They had tails and stings like
scorpions, and in their tails they had
power to torment people for five months.
[11] They had as king over them the angel of
the Abyss, whose name in Hebrew is
Abaddon, and in Greek, Apollyon.[b]
[12] The first woe is past; two other woes
are yet to come.
[13] The sixth angel sounded his trumpet,
and I heard a voice coming from the
horns[c] of the golden altar that is before
God. [14] It said to the sixth angel who had
the trumpet, "Release the four angels who
are bound at the great river Euphrates."
[15] And the four angels who had been kept
ready for this very hour and day and
month and year were released to kill a
third of mankind. [16] The number of the

---

[a]11 That is, Bitterness   [b]11 Abaddon and Apollyon
mean Destroyer.   [c]13 That is, projections

mounted troops was two hundred million. I heard their number. [17]The horses and riders I saw in my vision looked like this: Their breastplates were fiery red, dark blue, and yellow as sulfur. The heads of the horses resembled the heads of lions, and out of their mouths came fire, smoke and sulfur. [18]A third of mankind was killed by the three plagues of fire, smoke and sulfur that came out of their mouths. [19]The power of the horses was in their mouths and in their tails; for their tails were like snakes, having heads with which they inflict injury.

[20]The rest of mankind that were not killed by these plagues still did not repent of the work of their hands; they did not stop worshiping demons, and idols of gold, silver, bronze, stone and wood—idols that cannot see or hear or walk. [21]Nor did they repent of their murders, their magic arts, their sexual immorality or their thefts.

The Angel and the Little Scroll

10 Then I saw another mighty angel coming down from heaven. He was robed in a cloud, with a rainbow above his head; his face was like the sun, and his legs were like fiery pillars. [2]He was holding a little scroll, which lay open in his hand. He planted his right foot on the sea and his left foot on the land, [3]and he gave a loud shout like the roar of a lion. When he shouted, the voices of the seven thunders spoke. [4]And when the seven thunders spoke, I was about to write; but I heard a voice from heaven say, "Seal up what the seven thunders have said and do not write it down."

[5]Then the angel I had seen standing on the sea and on the land raised his right hand to heaven. [6]And he swore by him who lives for ever and ever, who created the heavens and all that is in them, the earth and all that is in it, and the sea and all that is in it, and said, "There will be no more delay! [7]But in the days when the seventh angel is about to sound his trumpet, the mystery of God will be accomplished, just as he announced to his servants the prophets."

[8]Then the voice that I had heard from heaven spoke to me once more: "Go, take the scroll that lies open in the hand of the angel who is standing on the sea and on the land."

[9]So I went to the angel and asked him to give me the little scroll. He said to me, "Take it and eat it. It will turn your stomach sour, but in your mouth it will be as sweet as honey." [10]I took the little scroll from the angel's hand and ate it. It tasted as sweet as honey in my mouth, but when I had eaten it, my stomach turned sour. [11]Then I was told, "You must prophesy again about many peoples, nations, languages and kings."

The Two Witnesses

11 I was given a reed like a measuring rod and was told, "Go and measure the temple of God and the altar, and count the worshipers there. [2]But exclude the outer court; do not measure it, because it has been given to the Gentiles. They will trample on the holy city for 42 months. [3]And I will give power to my two witnesses, and they will prophesy for 1,260 days, clothed in sackcloth." [4]These are the two olive trees and the two lampstands that stand before the Lord of the earth. [5]If anyone tries to harm them, fire comes from their mouths and devours their enemies. This is how anyone who wants to harm them must die. [6]These men have power to shut up the sky so that it will not rain during the time they are prophesying; and they have power to turn the waters into blood and to strike the earth with every kind of plague as often as they want.

[7]Now when they have finished their testimony, the beast that comes up from the Abyss will attack them, and overpower and kill them. [8]Their bodies will lie in the street of the great city, which is figuratively called Sodom and Egypt, where also their Lord was crucified. [9]For three and a half days men from every people, tribe, language and nation will gaze on their bodies and refuse them burial. [10]The inhabitants of the earth will gloat over them and will celebrate by sending each other gifts, because these two prophets had tormented those who live on the earth.

[11]But after the three and a half days a breath of life from God entered them, and they stood on their feet, and terror struck those who saw them. [12]Then they heard a loud voice from heaven saying to them, "Come up here." And they went up to heaven in a cloud, while their enemies looked on.

[13]At that very hour there was a severe earthquake and a tenth of the city collapsed. Seven thousand people were killed in the earthquake, and the survivors

were terrified and gave glory to the God of heaven.

[14]The second woe has passed; the third woe is coming soon.

The Seventh Trumpet

[15]The seventh angel sounded his trumpet, and there were loud voices in heaven, which said:

"The kingdom of the world has become
    the kingdom of our Lord and of
    his Christ,
  and he will reign for ever and ever."

[16]And the twenty-four elders, who were seated on their thrones before God, fell on their faces and worshiped God, [17]saying:

"We give thanks to you, Lord God
    Almighty,
  the One who is and who was,
because you have taken your great
    power
  and have begun to reign.
[18]The nations were angry;
  and your wrath has come.
The time has come for judging the dead,
  and for rewarding your servants the
    prophets
and your saints and those who
    reverence your name,
  both small and great—
and for destroying those who destroy
    the earth."

[19]Then God's temple in heaven was opened, and within his temple was seen the ark of his covenant. And there came flashes of lightning, rumblings, peals of thunder, an earthquake and a great hailstorm.

The Woman and the Dragon

12 A great and wondrous sign appeared in heaven: a woman clothed with the sun, with the moon under her feet and a crown of twelve stars on her head. [2]She was pregnant and cried out in pain as she was about to give birth. [3]Then another sign appeared in heaven: an enormous red dragon with seven heads and ten horns and seven crowns on his heads. [4]His tail swept a third of the stars out of the sky and flung them to the earth. The dragon stood in front of the woman who was about to give birth, so that he might devour her child the moment it was born. [5]She gave birth to a son, a male child, who will rule all the nations with an iron scepter. And her child was snatched up to God

and to his throne. [6]The woman fled into the desert to a place prepared for her by God, where she might be taken care of for 1,260 days.

[7]And there was war in heaven. Michael and his angels fought against the dragon, and the dragon and his angels fought back. [8]But he was not strong enough, and they lost their place in heaven. [9]The great dragon was hurled down—that ancient serpent called the devil, or Satan, who leads the whole world astray. He was hurled to the earth, and his angels with him.

[10]Then I heard a loud voice in heaven say:

"Now have come the salvation and the
    power and the kingdom of our
    God,
  and the authority of his Christ.
For the accuser of our brothers,
  who accuses them before our God
    day and night,
  has been hurled down.
[11]They overcame him
  by the blood of the Lamb
  and by the word of their testimony;
they did not love their lives so much
  as to shrink from death.
[12]Therefore rejoice, you heavens
  and you who dwell in them!
But woe to the earth and the sea,
  because the devil has gone down to
    you!
He is filled with fury,
  because he knows that his time is
    short."

[13]When the dragon saw that he had been hurled to the earth, he pursued the woman who had given birth to the male child. [14]The woman was given the two wings of a great eagle, so that she might fly to the place prepared for her in the desert, where she would be taken care of for a time, times and half a time, out of the serpent's reach. [15]Then from his mouth the serpent spewed water like a river, to overtake the woman and sweep her away with the torrent. [16]But the earth helped the woman by opening its mouth and swallowing the river that the dragon had spewed out of his mouth. [17]Then the dragon was enraged at the woman and went off to make war against the rest of her offspring—those who obey God's commandments and hold to the testimony of Jesus. [1]And the dragon[a] stood on the shore of the sea.

13

[a]1 Some late manuscripts *And I*

The Beast out of the Sea

And I saw a beast coming out of the sea. He had ten horns and seven heads, with ten crowns on his horns, and on each head a blasphemous name. [2]The beast I saw resembled a leopard, but had feet like those of a bear and a mouth like that of a lion. The dragon gave the beast his power and his throne and great authority. [3]One of the heads of the beast seemed to have had a fatal wound, but the fatal wound had been healed. The whole world was astonished and followed the beast. [4]Men worshiped the dragon because he had given authority to the beast, and they also worshiped the beast and asked, "Who is like the beast? Who can make war against him?"

[5]The beast was given a mouth to utter proud words and blasphemies and to exercise his authority for forty-two months. [6]He opened his mouth to blaspheme God, and to slander his name and his dwelling place and those who live in heaven. [7]He was given power to make war against the saints and to conquer them. And he was given authority over every tribe, people, language and nation. [8]All inhabitants of the earth will worship the beast—all whose names have not been written in the book of life belonging to the Lamb that was slain from the creation of the world.[a]

[9]He who has an ear, let him hear.

[10]If anyone is to go into captivity,
   into captivity he will go.
If anyone is to be killed[b] with the
      sword,
   with the sword he will be killed.

This calls for patient endurance and faithfulness on the part of the saints.

The Beast out of the Earth

[11]Then I saw another beast, coming out of the earth. He had two horns like a lamb, but he spoke like a dragon. [12]He exercised all the authority of the first beast on his behalf, and made the earth and its inhabitants worship the first beast, whose fatal wound had been healed. [13]And he performed great and miraculous signs, even causing fire to come down from heaven to earth in full view of men. [14]Because of the signs he was given power to do on behalf of the first beast, he deceived the inhabitants of the earth. He ordered them to set up an image in honor of the beast who was wounded by the sword and yet lived. [15]He was given power to give breath to the image of the first beast, so that it could speak and cause all who refused to worship the image to be killed. [16]He also forced everyone, small and great, rich and poor, free and slave, to receive a mark on his right hand or on his forehead, [17]so that no one could buy or sell unless he had the mark, which is the name of the beast or the number of his name.

[18]This calls for wisdom. If anyone has insight, let him calculate the number of the beast, for it is man's number. His number is 666.

The Lamb and the 144,000

14 Then I looked, and there before me was the Lamb, standing on Mount Zion, and with him 144,000 who had his name and his Father's name written on their foreheads. [2]And I heard a sound from heaven like the roar of rushing waters and like a loud peal of thunder. The sound I heard was like that of harpists playing their harps. [3]And they sang a new song before the throne and before the four living creatures and the elders. No one could learn the song except the 144,000 who had been redeemed from the earth. [4]These are those who did not defile themselves with women, for they kept themselves pure. They follow the Lamb wherever he goes. They were purchased from among men and offered as firstfruits to God and the Lamb. [5]No lie was found in their mouths; they are blameless.

The Three Angels

[6]Then I saw another angel flying in midair, and he had the eternal gospel to proclaim to those who live on the earth—to every nation, tribe, language and people. [7]He said in a loud voice, "Fear God and give him glory, because the hour of his judgment has come. Worship him who made the heavens, the earth, the sea and the springs of water."

[8]A second angel followed and said, "Fallen! Fallen is Babylon the Great, which made all the nations drink the maddening wine of her adulteries."

[9]A third angel followed them and said in a loud voice: "If anyone worships the beast and his image and receives his mark

---

[a]8 Or *written from the creation of the world in the book of life belonging to the Lamb that was slain*   [b]10 Some manuscripts *anyone kills*

on the forehead or on the hand, [10]he, too, will drink of the wine of God's fury, which has been poured full strength into the cup of his wrath. He will be tormented with burning sulfur in the presence of the holy angels and of the Lamb. [11]And the smoke of their torment rises for ever and ever. There is no rest day or night for those who worship the beast and his image, or for anyone who receives the mark of his name." [12]This calls for patient endurance on the part of the saints who obey God's commandments and remain faithful to Jesus.

[13]Then I heard a voice from heaven say, "Write: Blessed are the dead who die in the Lord from now on."

"Yes," says the Spirit, "they will rest from their labor, for their deeds will follow them."

The Harvest of the Earth

[14]I looked, and there before me was a white cloud, and seated on the cloud was one "like a son of man"[a] with a crown of gold on his head and a sharp sickle in his hand. [15]Then another angel came out of the temple and called in a loud voice to him who was sitting on the cloud, "Take your sickle and reap, because the time to reap has come, for the harvest of the earth is ripe." [16]So he who was seated on the cloud swung his sickle over the earth, and the earth was harvested.

[17]Another angel came out of the temple in heaven, and he too had a sharp sickle. [18]Still another angel, who had charge of the fire, came from the altar and called in a loud voice to him who had the sharp sickle, "Take your sharp sickle and gather the clusters of grapes from the earth's vine, because its grapes are ripe." [19]The angel swung his sickle on the earth, gathered its grapes and threw them into the great winepress of God's wrath. [20]They were trampled in the winepress outside the city, and blood flowed out of the press, rising as high as the horses' bridles for a distance of 1,600 stadia.[b]

Seven Angels With Seven Plagues

15 I saw in heaven another great and marvelous sign: seven angels with the seven last plagues—last, because with them God's wrath is completed. [2]And I saw what looked like a sea of glass mixed with fire and, standing beside the sea, those who had been victorious over the beast and his image and over the number of his name. They held harps given them by God [3]and sang the song of Moses the servant of God and the song of the Lamb:

"Great and marvelous are your deeds,
    Lord God Almighty.
Just and true are your ways,
    King of the ages.
[4]Who will not fear you, O Lord,
    and bring glory to your name?
For you alone are holy.
All nations will come
    and worship before you,
for your righteous acts have been
    revealed."

[5]After this I looked and in heaven the temple, that is, the tabernacle of the Testimony, was opened. [6]Out of the temple came the seven angels with the seven plagues. They were dressed in clean, shining linen and wore golden sashes around their chests. [7]Then one of the four living creatures gave to the seven angels seven golden bowls filled with the wrath of God, who lives for ever and ever. [8]And the temple was filled with smoke from the glory of God and from his power, and no one could enter the temple until the seven plagues of the seven angels were completed.

The Seven Bowls of God's Wrath

16 Then I heard a loud voice from the temple saying to the seven angels, "Go, pour out the seven bowls of God's wrath on the earth."

[2]The first angel went and poured out his bowl on the land, and ugly and painful sores broke out on the people who had the mark of the beast and worshiped his image.

[3]The second angel poured out his bowl on the sea, and it turned into blood like that of a dead man, and every living thing in the sea died.

[4]The third angel poured out his bowl on the rivers and springs of water, and they became blood. [5]Then I heard the angel in charge of the waters say:

"You are just in these judgments,
    you who are and who were, the Holy
        One,
    because you have so judged;
[6]for they have shed the blood of your
        saints and prophets,

[a]14 Daniel 7:13   [b]20 That is, about 180 miles
(about 300 kilometers)

and you have given them blood to drink as they deserve."

[7]And I heard the altar respond:

"Yes, Lord God Almighty,
    true and just are your judgments."

[8]The fourth angel poured out his bowl on the sun, and the sun was given power to scorch people with fire. [9]They were seared by the intense heat and they cursed the name of God, who had control over these plagues, but they refused to repent and glorify him.

[10]The fifth angel poured out his bowl on the throne of the beast, and his kingdom was plunged into darkness. Men gnawed their tongues in agony [11]and cursed the God of heaven because of their pains and their sores, but they refused to repent of what they had done.

[12]The sixth angel poured out his bowl on the great river Euphrates, and its water was dried up to prepare the way for the kings from the East. [13]Then I saw three evil[a] spirits that looked like frogs; they came out of the mouth of the dragon, out of the mouth of the beast and out of the mouth of the false prophet. [14]They are spirits of demons performing miraculous signs, and they go out to the kings of the whole world, to gather them for the battle on the great day of God Almighty.

[15]"Behold, I come like a thief! Blessed is he who stays awake and keeps his clothes with him, so that he may not go naked and be shamefully exposed."

[16]Then they gathered the kings together to the place that in Hebrew is called Armageddon.

[17]The seventh angel poured out his bowl into the air, and out of the temple came a loud voice from the throne, saying, "It is done!" [18]Then there came flashes of lightning, rumblings, peals of thunder and a severe earthquake. No earthquake like it has ever occurred since man has been on earth, so tremendous was the quake. [19]The great city split into three parts, and the cities of the nations collapsed. God remembered Babylon the Great and gave her the cup filled with the wine of the fury of his wrath. [20]Every island fled away and the mountains could not be found. [21]From the sky huge hailstones of about a hundred pounds each fell upon men. And they cursed God on account of the plague of hail, because the plague was so terrible.

The Woman on the Beast

17 One of the seven angels who had the seven bowls came and said to me, "Come, I will show you the punishment of the great prostitute, who sits on many waters. [2]With her the kings of the earth committed adultery and the inhabitants of the earth were intoxicated with the wine of her adulteries."

[3]Then the angel carried me away in the Spirit into a desert. There I saw a woman sitting on a scarlet beast that was covered with blasphemous names and had seven heads and ten horns. [4]The woman was dressed in purple and scarlet, and was glittering with gold, precious stones and pearls. She held a golden cup in her hand, filled with abominable things and the filth of her adulteries. [5]This title was written on her forehead:

MYSTERY
BABYLON THE GREAT
THE MOTHER OF PROSTITUTES
AND OF THE ABOMINATIONS OF THE EARTH.

[6]I saw that the woman was drunk with the blood of the saints, the blood of those who bore testimony to Jesus.

When I saw her, I was greatly astonished. [7]Then the angel said to me: "Why are you astonished? I will explain to you the mystery of the woman and of the beast she rides, which has the seven heads and ten horns. [8]The beast, which you saw, once was, now is not, and will come up out of the Abyss and go to his destruction. The inhabitants of the earth whose names have not been written in the book of life from the creation of the world will be astonished when they see the beast, because he once was, now is not, and yet will come.

[9]"This calls for a mind with wisdom. The seven heads are seven hills on which the woman sits. [10]They are also seven kings. Five have fallen, one is, the other has not yet come; but when he does come, he must remain for a little while. [11]The beast who once was, and now is not, is an eighth king. He belongs to the seven and is going to his destruction.

[12]"The ten horns you saw are ten kings who have not yet received a kingdom, but who for one hour will receive authority as kings along with the beast. [13]They have one purpose and will give their power and authority to the beast. [14]They will make

a13 Greek *unclean*

war against the Lamb, but the Lamb will overcome them because he is Lord of lords and King of kings—and with him will be his called, chosen and faithful followers."

¹⁵Then the angel said to me, "The waters you saw, where the prostitute sits, are peoples, multitudes, nations and languages. ¹⁶The beast and the ten horns you saw will hate the prostitute. They will bring her to ruin and leave her naked; they will eat her flesh and burn her with fire. ¹⁷For God has put it into their hearts to accomplish his purpose by agreeing to give the beast their power to rule, until God's words are fulfilled. ¹⁸The woman you saw is the great city that rules over the kings of the earth."

The Fall of Babylon

18 After this I saw another angel coming down from heaven. He had great authority, and the earth was illuminated by his splendor. ²With a mighty voice he shouted:

"Fallen! Fallen is Babylon the Great!
    She has become a home for demons
and a haunt for every evilᵃ spirit,
    a haunt for every unclean and
        detestable bird.
³For all the nations have drunk
    the maddening wine of her
        adulteries.
The kings of the earth committed
        adultery with her,
    and the merchants of the earth grew
        rich from her excessive
        luxuries."

⁴Then I heard another voice from heaven say:

"Come out of her, my people,
    so that you will not share in her sins,
    so that you will not receive any of her
        plagues;
⁵for her sins are piled up to heaven,
    and God has remembered her
        crimes.
⁶Give back to her as she has given;
    pay her back double for what she has
        done.
Mix her a double portion from her
        own cup.
⁷Give her as much torture and grief
    as the glory and luxury she gave
        herself.
In her heart she boasts,
    'I sit as queen; I am not a widow,
    and I will never mourn.'

⁸Therefore in one day her plagues will
        overtake her:
    death, mourning and famine.
She will be consumed by fire,
    for mighty is the Lord God who
        judges her.

⁹"When the kings of the earth who committed adultery with her and shared her luxury see the smoke of her burning, they will weep and mourn over her. ¹⁰Terrified at her torment, they will stand far off and cry:

" 'Woe! Woe, O great city,
    O Babylon, city of power!
In one hour your doom has come!'

¹¹"The merchants of the earth will weep and mourn over her because no one buys their cargoes any more— ¹²cargoes of gold, silver, precious stones and pearls; fine linen, purple, silk and scarlet cloth; every sort of citron wood, and articles of every kind made of ivory, costly wood, bronze, iron and marble; ¹³cargoes of cinnamon and spice, of incense, myrrh and frankincense, of wine and olive oil, of fine flour and wheat; cattle and sheep; horses and carriages; and bodies and souls of men.

¹⁴"They will say, 'The fruit you longed for is gone from you. All your riches and splendor have vanished, never to be recovered.' ¹⁵The merchants who sold these things and gained their wealth from her will stand far off, terrified at her torment. They will weep and mourn ¹⁶and cry out:

" 'Woe! Woe, O great city,
    dressed in fine linen, purple and
        scarlet,
    and glittering with gold, precious
        stones and pearls!
¹⁷In one hour such great wealth has been
        brought to ruin!'

"Every sea captain, and all who travel by ship, the sailors, and all who earn their living from the sea, will stand far off. ¹⁸When they see the smoke of her burning, they will exclaim, 'Was there ever a city like this great city?' ¹⁹They will throw dust on their heads, and with weeping and mourning cry out:

" 'Woe! Woe, O great city,
    where all who had ships on the sea
        became rich through her wealth!
In one hour she has been brought to
        ruin!

ᵃ2 Greek *unclean*

²⁰Rejoice over her, O heaven!
  Rejoice, saints and apostles and
      prophets!
  God has judged her for the way she
      treated you.' "

²¹Then a mighty angel picked up a boulder the size of a large millstone and threw it into the sea, and said:

"With such violence
  the great city of Babylon will be
      thrown down,
  never to be found again.
²²The music of harpists and musicians,
      flute players and trumpeters,
  will never be heard in you again.
No workman of any trade
  will ever be found in you again.
The sound of a millstone
  will never be heard in you again.
²³The light of a lamp
  will never shine in you again.
The voice of bridegroom and bride
  will never be heard in you again.
Your merchants were the world's great
      men.
  By your magic spell all the nations
      were led astray.
²⁴In her was found the blood of prophets
      and of the saints,
  and of all who have been killed on
      the earth."

Hallelujah!

19 After this I heard what sounded like the roar of a great multitude in heaven shouting:

"Hallelujah!
Salvation and glory and power belong
      to our God,
² for true and just are his judgments.
He has condemned the great prostitute
  who corrupted the earth by her
      adulteries.
He has avenged on her the blood of his
      servants."

³And again they shouted:

"Hallelujah!
The smoke from her goes up for ever
      and ever."

⁴The twenty-four elders and the four living creatures fell down and worshiped God, who was seated on the throne. And they cried:

"Amen, Hallelujah!"

⁵Then a voice came from the throne, saying:

"Praise our God,
  all you his servants,
you who fear him,
  both small and great!"

⁶Then I heard what sounded like a great multitude, like the roar of rushing waters and like loud peals of thunder, shouting:

"Hallelujah!
  For our Lord God Almighty reigns.
⁷Let us rejoice and be glad
  and give him glory!
For the wedding of the Lamb has come,
  and his bride has made herself ready."

HEY DAD

Does the Bible say we shouldn't do drugs?

Text: Revelation 18:23; 22:15

While you won't find "say no to drugs" in the Bible, Scripture says more about this issue than you may think.

Revelation 18:23 says, "By your [Babylon's] magic spell all the nations were led astray." And Revelation 22:15 says, "Outside are the dogs, those who practice magic arts, the sexually immoral, the murderers, the idolaters and everyone who loves and practices falsehood."

The word "magic" here comes from the Greek word *pharmakeia*. We get the English word "pharmaceutical" from that same Greek word. It refers to those who use drugs to induce trances or to bring about supernatural powers. (This same word is also used in Revelation 9:21 and 21:8.)

There is no room for doubt; these magicians or drug users were sinning. They were grouped with murderers, idolaters and the sexually immoral. If you need a Biblical perspective on illegal drugs, Revelation is a great place to start.

QUESTIONS KIDS ASK

For a complete listing of Questions Kids Ask, turn to page 1435.

[8]Fine linen, bright and clean,
    was given her to wear."
(Fine linen stands for the righteous acts of
the saints.)

[9]Then the angel said to me, "Write:
'Blessed are those who are invited to the
wedding supper of the Lamb!' " And he
added, "These are the true words of God."
[10]At this I fell at his feet to worship him.
But he said to me, "Do not do it! I am a fellow servant with you and with your brothers who hold to the testimony of Jesus.
Worship God! For the testimony of Jesus is
the spirit of prophecy."

The Rider on the White Horse

[11]I saw heaven standing open and there
before me was a white horse, whose rider
is called Faithful and True. With justice he
judges and makes war. [12]His eyes are like
blazing fire, and on his head are many
crowns. He has a name written on him
that no one knows but he himself. [13]He is
dressed in a robe dipped in blood, and his
name is the Word of God. [14]The armies of
heaven were following him, riding on
white horses and dressed in fine linen,
white and clean. [15]Out of his mouth
comes a sharp sword with which to strike
down the nations. "He will rule them with
an iron scepter."[a] He treads the winepress
of the fury of the wrath of God Almighty.
[16]On his robe and on his thigh he has this
name written:

    KING OF KINGS AND LORD OF LORDS.

[17]And I saw an angel standing in the
sun, who cried in a loud voice to all the
birds flying in midair, "Come, gather together for the great supper of God, [18]so
that you may eat the flesh of kings, generals, and mighty men, of horses and their
riders, and the flesh of all people, free and
slave, small and great."

[19]Then I saw the beast and the kings of
the earth and their armies gathered together to make war against the rider on
the horse and his army. [20]But the beast
was captured, and with him the false
prophet who had performed the miraculous signs on his behalf. With these signs
he had deluded those who had received
the mark of the beast and worshiped his
image. The two of them were thrown alive
into the fiery lake of burning sulfur. [21]The
rest of them were killed with the sword
that came out of the mouth of the rider on

the horse, and all the birds gorged themselves on their flesh.

The Thousand Years

20 And I saw an angel coming down out
of heaven, having the key to the
Abyss and holding in his hand a great
chain. [2]He seized the dragon, that ancient
serpent, who is the devil, or Satan, and
bound him for a thousand years. [3]He
threw him into the Abyss, and locked and
sealed it over him, to keep him from deceiving the nations anymore until the
thousand years were ended. After that, he
must be set free for a short time.

[4]I saw thrones on which were seated
those who had been given authority to
judge. And I saw the souls of those who
had been beheaded because of their testimony for Jesus and because of the word of
God. They had not worshiped the beast or
his image and had not received his mark
on their foreheads or their hands. They
came to life and reigned with Christ a
thousand years. [5](The rest of the dead did
not come to life until the thousand years
were ended.) This is the first resurrection.
[6]Blessed and holy are those who have part
in the first resurrection. The second death
has no power over them, but they will be
priests of God and of Christ and will reign
with him for a thousand years.

Satan's Doom

[7]When the thousand years are over, Satan will be released from his prison [8]and
will go out to deceive the nations in the
four corners of the earth—Gog and Magog—to gather them for battle. In number
they are like the sand on the seashore.
[9]They marched across the breadth of the
earth and surrounded the camp of God's
people, the city he loves. But fire came
down from heaven and devoured them.
[10]And the devil, who deceived them, was
thrown into the lake of burning sulfur,
where the beast and the false prophet had
been thrown. They will be tormented day
and night for ever and ever.

The Dead Are Judged

[11]Then I saw a great white throne and
him who was seated on it. Earth and sky
fled from his presence, and there was no
place for them. [12]And I saw the dead, great
and small, standing before the throne,

[a]15 Psalm 2:9

and books were opened. Another book was opened, which is the book of life. The dead were judged according to what they had done as recorded in the books. ¹³The sea gave up the dead that were in it, and death and Hades gave up the dead that were in them, and each person was judged according to what he had done. ¹⁴Then death and Hades were thrown into the lake of fire. The lake of fire is the second death. ¹⁵If anyone's name was not found written in the book of life, he was thrown into the lake of fire.

The New Jerusalem

21 Then I saw a new heaven and a new earth, for the first heaven and the first earth had passed away, and there was no longer any sea. ²I saw the Holy City, the new Jerusalem, coming down out of heaven from God, prepared as a bride beautifully dressed for her husband. ³And I heard a loud voice from the throne saying, "Now the dwelling of God is with men, and he will live with them. They will be his people, and God himself will be with them and be their God. ⁴He will wipe every tear from their eyes. There will be no more death or mourning or crying or pain, for the old order of things has passed away."

⁵He who was seated on the throne said, "I am making everything new!" Then he said, "Write this down, for these words are trustworthy and true."

⁶He said to me: "It is done. I am the Alpha and the Omega, the Beginning and the End. To him who is thirsty I will give to drink without cost from the spring of the water of life. ⁷He who overcomes will inherit all this, and I will be his God and he will be my son. ⁸But the cowardly, the unbelieving, the vile, the murderers, the sexually immoral, those who practice magic arts, the idolaters and all liars—their place will be in the fiery lake of burning sulfur. This is the second death."

⁹One of the seven angels who had the seven bowls full of the seven last plagues came and said to me, "Come, I will show you the bride, the wife of the Lamb." ¹⁰And he carried me away in the Spirit to a mountain great and high, and showed me the Holy City, Jerusalem, coming down out of heaven from God. ¹¹It shone with the glory of God, and its brilliance was like that of a very precious jewel, like a jasper, clear as crystal. ¹²It had a great, high wall with twelve gates, and with twelve

angels at the gates. On the gates were written the names of the twelve tribes of Israel. ¹³There were three gates on the east, three on the north, three on the south and three on the west. ¹⁴The wall of the city had twelve foundations, and on them were the names of the twelve apostles of the Lamb.

¹⁵The angel who talked with me had a measuring rod of gold to measure the city, its gates and its walls. ¹⁶The city was laid out like a square, as long as it was wide. He measured the city with the rod and found it to be 12,000 stadia[a] in length, and as wide and high as it is long. ¹⁷He measured its wall and it was 144 cubits[b] thick,[c] by man's measurement, which the angel was using. ¹⁸The wall was made of jasper, and the city of pure gold, as pure as glass. ¹⁹The foundations of the city walls were decorated with every kind of precious stone. The first foundation was jasper, the second sapphire, the third chalcedony, the fourth emerald, ²⁰the fifth sardonyx, the sixth carnelian, the seventh chrysolite, the eighth beryl, the ninth topaz, the tenth chrysoprase, the eleventh jacinth, and the twelfth amethyst.[d] ²¹The twelve gates were twelve pearls, each gate made of a single pearl. The great street of the city was of pure gold, like transparent glass.

²²I did not see a temple in the city, because the Lord God Almighty and the Lamb are its temple. ²³The city does not need the sun or the moon to shine on it, for the glory of God gives it light, and the Lamb is its lamp. ²⁴The nations will walk by its light, and the kings of the earth will bring their splendor into it. ²⁵On no day will its gates ever be shut, for there will be no night there. ²⁶The glory and honor of the nations will be brought into it. ²⁷Nothing impure will ever enter it, nor will anyone who does what is shameful or deceitful, but only those whose names are written in the Lamb's book of life.

The River of Life

22 Then the angel showed me the river of the water of life, as clear as crystal, flowing from the throne of God and of the Lamb ²down the middle of the great street of the city. On each side of the river stood

---

a16 That is, about 1,400 miles (about 2,200 kilometers)   *b17* That is, about 200 feet (about 65 meters)   *c17* Or *high*   *d20* The precise identification of some of these precious stones is uncertain.

the tree of life, bearing twelve crops of fruit, yielding its fruit every month. And the leaves of the tree are for the healing of the nations. ³No longer will there be any curse. The throne of God and of the Lamb will be in the city, and his servants will serve him. ⁴They will see his face, and his name will be on their foreheads. ⁵There will be no more night. They will not need the light of a lamp or the light of the sun, for the Lord God will give them light. And they will reign for ever and ever.

⁶The angel said to me, "These words are trustworthy and true. The Lord, the God of the spirits of the prophets, sent his angel to show his servants the things that must soon take place."

Jesus Is Coming

⁷"Behold, I am coming soon! Blessed is he who keeps the words of the prophecy in this book."

⁸I, John, am the one who heard and saw these things. And when I had heard and seen them, I fell down to worship at the feet of the angel who had been showing them to me. ⁹But he said to me, "Do not do it! I am a fellow servant with you and with your brothers the prophets and of all who keep the words of this book. Worship God!"

¹⁰Then he told me, "Do not seal up the words of the prophecy of this book, because the time is near. ¹¹Let him who does wrong continue to do wrong; let him who is vile continue to be vile; let him who does right continue to do right; and let him who is holy continue to be holy."

¹²"Behold, I am coming soon! My reward is with me, and I will give to everyone according to what he has done. ¹³I am the Alpha and the Omega, the First and the Last, the Beginning and the End.

¹⁴"Blessed are those who wash their robes, that they may have the right to the tree of life and may go through the gates into the city. ¹⁵Outside are the dogs, those who practice magic arts, the sexually immoral, the murderers, the idolaters and everyone who loves and practices falsehood.

¹⁶"I, Jesus, have sent my angel to give you^a this testimony for the churches. I am the Root and the Offspring of David, and the bright Morning Star."

¹⁷The Spirit and the bride say, "Come!" And let him who hears say, "Come!" Whoever is thirsty, let him come; and whoever wishes, let him take the free gift of the water of life.

¹⁸I warn everyone who hears the words of the prophecy of this book: If anyone adds anything to them, God will add to him the plagues described in this book. ¹⁹And if anyone takes words away from this book of prophecy, God will take away from him his share in the tree of life and in the holy city, which are described in this book.

²⁰He who testifies to these things says, "Yes, I am coming soon."

Amen. Come, Lord Jesus.

²¹The grace of the Lord Jesus be with God's people. Amen.

^{a}16 The Greek is plural.

Weights and Measures

	Biblical Unit		Approximate American Equivalent	Approximate Metric Equivalent
WEIGHTS	talent	(60 minas)	75 pounds	34 kilograms
	mina	(50 shekels)	1¼ pounds	0.6 kilogram
	shekel	(2 bekas)	$^2/_5$ ounce	11.5 grams
	pim	($^2/_3$ shekel)	$^1/_3$ ounce	7.6 grams
	beka	(10 gerahs)	$^1/_5$ ounce	5.5 grams
	gerah		$^1/_{50}$ ounce	0.6 gram
LENGTH	cubit		18 inches	0.5 meter
	span		9 inches	23 centimeters
	handbreadth		3 inches	8 centimeters
CAPACITY				
Dry Measure	cor [homer]	(10 ephahs)	6 bushels	220 liters
	lethek	(5 ephahs)	3 bushels	110 liters
	ephah	(10 omers)	$^3/_5$ bushel	22 liters
	seah	($^1/_3$ ephah)	7 quarts	7.3 liters
	omer	($^1/_{10}$ ephah)	2 quarts	2 liters
	cab	($^1/_{18}$ ephah)	1 quart	1 liter
Liquid Measure	bath	(1 ephah)	6 gallons	22 liters
	hin	($^1/_6$ bath)	4 quarts	4 liters
	log	($^1/_{72}$ bath)	$^1/_3$ quart	0.3 liter

The figures of the table are calculated on the basis of a shekel equaling 11.5 grams, a cubit equaling 18 inches and an ephah equaling 22 liters. The quart referred to is either a dry quart (slightly larger than a liter) or a liquid quart (slightly smaller than a liter), whichever is applicable. The ton referred to in the footnotes is the American ton of 2,000 pounds.

This table is based upon the best available information, but it is not intended to be mathematically precise; like the measurement equivalents in the footnotes, it merely gives approximate amounts and distances. Weights and measures differed somewhat at various times and places in the ancient world. There is uncertainty particularly about the ephah and the bath; further discoveries may shed more light on these units of capacity.

Dads in the Bible Index

This index lists, in Biblical order, each of the 30 *Dads in the Bible* character profiles found within the text of *The Devotional Bible for Dads*.

Questions Kids Ask Index

This index lists, in alphabetical order according to key word, each of the 100 *Questions Kids Ask* features found within the text of *The Devotional Bible for Dads*.

Fruit of the Spirit Topical Index

But the fruit of the Spirit is love, joy, peace, patience, kindness,
goodness, faithfulness, gentleness and self-control.
GALATIANS 5:22–23

This index has been provided with the intent of helping you tailor your study around the fruit of the Spirit as outlined in the passage above. The index includes a complete listing of all of the Daily Insights and Quiet Times with Dad that are included in *The Devotional Bible for Dads*. Each one has been categorized as reflecting one of the nine fruits of the Spirit. This listing is arranged in Biblical order to further facilitate your study.

Fruit of the Spirit	Text	Page	Title	Topic
Love	Genesis 28:1, 10–17	38	Your Child's Marriage Partner	Jacob chooses a wife; your child will choose a partner
Love	Exodus 13:1–10	86	Reverend Dad	Dad as the priest of the home
Love	Leviticus 24:17–22	145	Be Fairly Tough	Eye for an eye: fair punishment
Love	Deuteronomy 5:6–29	203	First Things First	Ten Commandments
Love	Deuteronomy 21:18–21	219	Tender and Very Tough	Handling incorrigible kids
Love	Joshua 18:1–7	255	A Special Place for Everyone	Setting boundaries for your kids
Love	Ruth 1:1–18	290	No Trouble with the In-laws	Dealing with your in-laws
Love	1 Samuel 8:1–3	303	Balloons—the Soaring and the Popping Kind	Samuel and his sons
Love	1 Samuel 14:24–28	310	Plenty of Speed Limit Signs	Household rules: the importance of fairness and clarity
Love	2 Samuel 7:5–29	337	The Impossible Dream	God's promise to Solomon, and to you
Love	2 Samuel 18:1–17, 25–33	351	Love for a Lifetime	David mourns Absalom
Love	2 Kings 2:1–6	398	Hey, Brother	The importance of friendships
Love	Esther 2:1–7	531	Just a Little, Unfortunate Kid	Adoption
Love	Job 2:1–13	543	Articulate Silence	Silent support for suffering friends
Love	Psalm 23	589	Our Good Shepherd	Everything we need, he supplies
Love	Psalm 136	667	Love Forever, Monroe	God's love endures forever
Love	Proverbs 13:20–25	694	Loving You, Correcting You	Spare the rod. . .
Love	Proverbs 22:1–6	704	Don't Step Right Up	Training a child in the way he or she should go

Fruit of the Spirit	Text	Page	Title	Topic
Joy	2 Corinthians 5:17–21	1290	Settling Our Account at God's Bank	Jesus settles all our accounts
Joy	Galatians 5:22–26	1304	Frozen Up and Fruitless	The fruit of the Spirit
Joy	Revelation 1:12–18	1414	Thank You, Sweet Alice	Being ready to see Jesus
Joy	Revelation 7:9–12	1420	It's Going to Be an Awesome Thing	Seeing Jesus, the Lamb, in heaven
Peace	Genesis 12:1–8	18	The New Kids on the Block	Following God's call
Peace	Genesis 45:1–15	62	A Relationship Fixer-upper	Repairing relationships
Peace	Exodus 17:8–16	92	No Lone Rangers Here	Dads can't lead alone
Peace	1 Chronicles 21:8–17	453	Choosing Your Poison	David chooses God's wrath, not people's wrath
Peace	2 Chronicles 12:1–8	476	Can Someone Give Me a Hand with this Thing?	Rehoboam and Jeroboam: the importance of brotherhood
Peace	Psalm 27	592	No Fear	The Lord is our stronghold
Peace	Psalm 91:9–16	637	Do You Have Something in a Three-bedroom, Two-and-a-half Bath?	Numbering our days: perspective
Peace	Proverbs 27:1–6	710	Tomorrow and Other Presumptions	Planning with God in mind
Peace	Ecclesiastes 1:1–9	718	A Little Message from a Blitzing Safety	Priorities in the face of unpredictability
Peace	Ecclesiastes 3:9–14	721	Trading for What's Behind Door Number Two	The blessing of work
Peace	Isaiah 11:6–9	754	No More Fighting	Understanding God, loving others
Peace	Isaiah 14:1–7	756	A Lesson from a Fuzzy Man	Family unity
Peace	Isaiah 26:1–4	766	Bear	Trust equals peace
Peace	Isaiah 35:1–7	777	You're not Afraid? Good for You.	Living a life that honors God
Peace	Isaiah 44:13–22	790	The Woodsman	God has redeemed us
Peace	Jeremiah 29:10–14	851	What Do You Mean, "Welcome to Detroit"?	God's good plan for our lives
Peace	Ezekiel 37:1–10	926	Them Bones	God's life-giving breath
Peace	Amos 3:1–7	977	Duh	God knows what he's doing

Fruit of the Spirit	Text	Page	Title	Topic
Self-control	Exodus 32:19–25	108	Don't Make Me Laugh	Be the dad. Seriously.
Self-control	Deuteronomy 4:25–31	200	Listen Up, Boys	Covenant rewards for following God
Self-control	Judges 16:4–20	282	Samson's Expensive Haircut	Samson: strength isn't everything
Self-control	2 Samuel 11:1–17	341	Great Game, Dad	David and Bathsheba: learning to say "no"
Self-control	1 Kings 12:1–15	380	Headlines from Hell	From whom do you seek advice?
Self-control	2 Kings 22:3–7	424	Could I Please Have a Receipt on That?	Living with integrity
Self-control	2 Chronicles 7:11–22	471	Are You for Real?	Representing God with integrity
Self-control	Job 38:1–13	569	Cashing Your Coupons	God's restraint—and ours
Self-control	Isaiah 6:1–8	747	Be Very Careful	Healthy respect for God's position
Self-control	Isaiah 45:1–7	792	Underwear on the Floor and the Sovereignty of God	God's tasks will be accomplished
Self-control	Jeremiah 13:1–11	832	Make His Family Proud	Wearing your Christianity on your sleeve
Self-control	Jeremiah 17:9–12	837	Those Nasty Ruts	Inescapable sinfulness
Self-control	Lamentations 3:1–9, 22–24	885	This Entrepreneur's Lesson	Trusting God's faithfulness
Self-control	Daniel 1:1,2,8–16	940	Please Pass the Broccoli	The importance of what goes in the "tank"
Self-control	Daniel 4:28–34	946	Babylon, Rome and the '69 Mets	The mighty will fall, but not God
Self-control	Obadiah 1–4	985	I'm Going to Bring you Down	Our pride and God's glory
Self-control	Jonah1:1–17	988	You Can't Do That!	The prophet's foolish disobedience
Self-control	Zephaniah 1:2–7a	1008	The Power of Unused Power	Mirroring God's restraint
Self-control	Matthew 5:21–25, 33–37	1040	Ready, Aim, Speak	The power of words
Self-control	Matthew 14:22–32	1056	Lions and Tigers and Bears, Oh My!	Trusting in Jesus when the water is rough
Self-control	Mark 9:2–8	1094	Way Beyond "Groovy" and "Cool"	Jesus' transfiguration

<u>Notes</u>

Notes

Notes

The Devotional Bible for Dads

Notes written by Robert Wolgemuth

Editorial management by Jennifer Case Cortez

Zondervan project management and editorial
by Michael Vander Klipp

Zondervan production management
by Jean Entingh

Zondervan art direction by Cindy Davis

Interior design by Sharon Wright, Belmont, MI

Cover design by Chris Tobias, Grand Rapids, MI

Interior proofreading by Peachtree Editorial
and Proofreading Service, Peachtree City, GA

Interior typesetting
by The Livingstone Corporation, Carol Stream, IL

Printing and binding
by R.R. Donnelley, Crawfordsville, IN

Guarantee

Care